W9-BBG-676

SUPPLEMENTAL READING AND WRITING HELP

VirtuaLit Interactive Tutorials

Available on the *LiterActive* CD-ROM and at the book's companion site, these tutorials offer close readings, coverage of literary elements, cultural contexts, and critical approaches for

- Kate Chopin's "The Story of an Hour"
- Nathaniel Hawthorne's "Young Goodman Brown"
- Jamaica Kincaid's "Girl"
- Elizabeth Bishop's "The Fish"
- Theodore Roethke's "My Papa's Waltz"
- Andrew Marvell's "To His Coy Mistress"

LiterActive CD-ROM

This student-friendly resource provides

- *VirtuaLit Interactive Tutorials* (see above)
- *A Multimedia & Documents Library:* hundreds of images, audio and video clips, and contextual documents supporting 43 authors
- *A Research & Documentation Guide:* advice for working with sources—how to find, evaluate, summarize, interpret, and document them
- *LitLinks:* a wealth of biographical information on the authors in the anthology

Book Companion Site

See the inside back cover for resources available at the anthology's Web site,

bedfordstmartins.com/meyercompact.

EIGHTH EDITION

THE COMPACT BEDFORD INTRODUCTION TO LITERATURE

Reading · Thinking · Writing

Michael Meyer

University of Connecticut

BEDFORD/ST. MARTIN'S   Boston ◆ New York

For Bedford/St. Martin's

Senior Developmental Editor: Ellen Thibault
Production Editor: Jessica Skrocki
Production Supervisor: Andrew Ensor
Marketing Manager: Adrienne Petsick
Editorial Assistant: Stephanie Naudin
Copy Editor: Edward Cone
Art Director: Lucy Krikorian
Text Design: Claire Seng-Niemoeller/Linda M. Robertson
Cover Design: Donna Lee Dennison
Cover Art: "On the Phone" by Patti Mollica. © 2007. Represented by Morgan Gaynin, Inc.
Composition: TexTech International
Printing and Binding: Quebecor World Taunton

President: Joan E. Feinberg
Editorial Director: Denise B. Wydra
Editor in Chief: Karen S. Henry
Director of Marketing: Karen Melton Soeltz
Director of Editing, Design, and Production: Marcia Cohen
Managing Editor: Shuli Traub

Library of Congress Control Number: 2007934706

For information, write: Bedford/St. Martin's, 75 Arlington Street, Boston, MA 02116
(617-399-4000)

ISBN-10: 0-312-46959-4
ISBN-13: 978-0-312-46959-7
ISBN-10: 0-312-47411-3 (high school edition)
ISBN-13: 978-0-312-47411-9

Acknowledgments

FICTION

Fleur Adcock. "The Video" from *Poems 1960–2000* by Fleur Adcock (Bloodaxe Books, 2000). Copyright © 2000 by Fleur Adcock. Reprinted by permission of Bloodaxe Books Ltd.

Martin Amis. "The Last Days of Muhammad Atta," *The New Yorker,* April 24, 2006. Copyright © 2006 by Martin Amis. Reprinted by permission of the Wylie Agency.

Acknowledgments and copyrights are continued at the back of the book on pages 1644–1652, which constitute an extension of the copyright page. It is a violation of the law to reproduce these selections by any means whatsoever without the written permission of the copyright holder.

For My Wife
Regina Barreca

About Michael Meyer

Michael Meyer has taught writing and literature courses for more than thirty years — since 1981 at the University of Connecticut and before that at the University of North Carolina at Charlotte and the College of William and Mary. In addition to being an experienced teacher, Meyer is a highly regarded literary scholar. His scholarly articles have appeared in distinguished journals such as *American Literature, Studies in the American Renaissance,* and *Virginia Quarterly Review.* An internationally recognized authority on Henry David Thoreau, Meyer is a former president of the Thoreau Society and coauthor (with Walter Harding) of *The New Thoreau Handbook,* a standard reference source. His first book, *Several More Lives to Live: Thoreau's Political Reputation in America,* was awarded the Ralph Henry Gabriel Prize by the American Studies Association. He is also the editor of *Frederick Douglass: The Narrative and Selected Writings* and the author of *The Little, Brown Guide to Writing Research Papers,* Third Edition. His other books for Bedford/St. Martin's include *The Bedford Introduction to Literature,* Eighth Edition; *Poetry: An Introduction,* Fifth Edition; and *Thinking and Writing about Literature,* Second Edition.

Preface for Instructors

Like its predecessors, the eighth edition of *The Compact Bedford Introduction to Literature* assumes that reading and understanding literature offers a valuable means of apprehending life in its richness and diversity. This book also reflects the hope that its selections will inspire students to become lifelong readers of imaginative literature, as well as more thoughtful and skillful writers.

As before, the text is flexibly organized into four parts focusing on fiction, poetry, drama, and critical thinking and writing. The first three parts explain the literary elements of each genre and how to write about them. These three parts also explore several additional approaches to reading literature and conclude with an anthology of literary works. The fourth part provides detailed instruction on thinking, reading, and writing about literature that can be assigned selectively throughout the course. Sample student papers and more than 2,000 assignments appear in the text, offering students the support they need to read and write about literature.

Class-tested in thousands of literature courses, *The Compact Bedford Introduction to Literature* accommodates many different teaching styles. The eighth edition features more sample close readings and student papers, a new one-of-a-kind chapter created with author Julia Alvarez, and three new case studies on humor and satire.

FEATURES OF *THE COMPACT BEDFORD INTRODUCTION TO LITERATURE*, EIGHTH EDITION

A description of the features and content that have long made *The Compact Bedford Introduction to Literature* a favorite of students and teachers follows. What is new to this edition is described on pages ix–xi.

A wide and well-balanced selection of literature

Forty-six stories, 350 poems, and 17 plays represent a variety of periods, nationalities, cultures, styles, and voices — from the serious to the humorous, and from the traditional to the contemporary. Each selection has been chosen for its appeal to students and for its effectiveness in demonstrating the elements, significance, and pleasures of literature. As in previous editions, canonical works by Ernest Hemingway, John Keats, Langston Hughes, Susan Glaspell, and many others are generously represented. In addition, there are many contemporary selections from writers such as Lee Smith, Julia Alvarez, Martín Espada, Billy Collins, and David Henry Hwang.

Many options for teaching and learning about literature

Over eight editions, in its continuing effort to make literature come to life for students, and the course a pleasure to teach for instructors, *The Compact Bedford Introduction to Literature* has developed and refined these innovative features:

PERSPECTIVES ON LITERATURE   More than one hundred intriguing documents—including personal journals, letters, critical essays, interviews, and contextual images—appear throughout the book to stimulate class discussion and writing.

CONNECTIONS BETWEEN "POPULAR" AND "LITERARY" CULTURE   The fiction, poetry, and drama introductions incorporate examples from popular culture, effectively introducing students to the literary elements of a given genre through what they already know. For example, students are introduced to the elements of fiction through excerpts from a romance novel and from *Tarzan of the Apes;* to the elements of poetry through greeting card verse and song lyrics by Bruce Springsteen; and to elements of drama through television scripts from *Seinfeld* and *Will & Grace.* A unique visual portfolio, Encountering Poetry, presents images that demonstrate how literature is woven into the fabric of popular culture and art. These images, including advertisements, posters, cartoons, and Web screens, help students recognize the imprint of literature on their everyday lives.

From "Encountering Poetry."

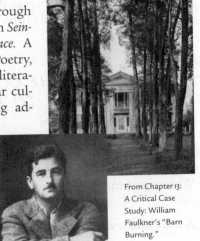

From Chapter 13: A Critical Case Study: William Faulkner's "Barn Burning."

CASE STUDIES THAT TREAT AUTHORS IN DEPTH   Each genre section includes chapters that focus closely on two or more major figures. There are three stories each by Nathaniel Hawthorne and Flannery O'Connor; an extensive selection of poems by Emily Dickinson, Robert Frost, and Langston Hughes; and a play each by Sophocles and Shakespeare with a generous amount of background material. Complementing the literature in these chapters are biographical introductions (with author photographs); critical perspectives (including complementary critical readings where writers argue for different interpretations of the same texts); cultural documents (such as letters and draft manuscript pages); and a generous collection of images that serve to contextualize the works. A variety of critical thinking and writing questions follow the selections to stimulate student responses. All of these supplementary materials help students engage more fully with the writers and their works.

CRITICAL AND THEMATIC CASE STUDIES   Each *Critical Case Study* gathers four or more critical analyses of a single work—for example, Henrik Ibsen's *A Doll House*—to illustrate a variety of contemporary critical approaches. Each *Thematic Case Study* invites students to explore literature through a particular topic, such as "Love and Longing" and "Teaching and Learning" in poetry. Two generously illustrated *Thematic Case Studies* explore intercultural themes and the influence of the South on literature. "Border Crossings," a unique full-color unit, pairs seven poems with visual texts on the theme of crossing racial, class-based, and geographical borders. Chapter 14: "The Literature of the South" reprints major

From "Border Crossings."

statements about southern literature and a collection of images—including paintings, an etching, and documentary photographs—that offer contexts for the many works by southern writers included in the anthology.

ACCESSIBLE COVERAGE OF LITERARY THEORY   For instructors who wish to incorporate literary theory into their courses, Chapter 46: "Critical Strategies for Reading" introduces students to a variety of critical strategies, ranging from formalism to cultural criticism. In brief examples the approaches are applied in analyzing Kate Chopin's "The Story of an Hour" as well as other works, so that students will develop a sense of how to use these strategies in their own reading and writing.

Unsurpassed help with reading, writing, and research

CRITICAL READING   To encourage the critical reading and thinking that are essential to writing about literature, advice on how to read literature appears at the beginning of each genre section. Throughout the book,

A Sample Close Reading

The title could point to the brevity of the story—only 23 short paragraphs—or to the decisive nature of what happens in a very short period of time. Or both.

KATE CHOPIN (1851–1904)
The Story of an Hour   1894

Mrs. Mallard's first name, (Louise) is not given until paragraph 17, yet her sister Josephine is named immediately. This emphasizes Mrs. Mallard's married identity.

Given the nature of the cause of Mrs. Mallard death at the story's end, it's worth noting the ambiguous description that she "was afflicted with a heart trouble." Is this one of Chopin's

Knowing that Mrs. Mallard was afflicted with a heart trouble, great care was taken to break to her as gently as possible the news of her husband's death.

It was her sister Josephine who told her, in broken sentences, veiled hints that revealed in half concealing. Her husband's friend Richards was there, too, near her. It was he who had been in the newspaper office when intelligence of the railroad disaster was received, with Brently Mallard's name leading the list of "killed." He had only taken the time to assure himself of its truth by a second telegram, and had hastened to forestall any less careful, less tender friend in bearing the sad message.

annotated selections model close, critical reading. Sample Close Readings of selections including Kate Chopin's "Story of an Hour" (Fiction), William Hathaway's "Oh, Oh" (Poetry), and Susan Glaspell's *Trifles* (Drama) provide analyses of the language, images, and other literary elements at work in these selections. Interpretive annotations clearly show students the process of close reading and provide examples of the kind of critical thinking that leads to strong academic writing.

Later in the book, Chapter 47: "Reading and Writing" describes how to read a work closely, annotate a text, take notes, keep a reading journal, and develop a topic into a thesis; it also includes a section on arguing persuasively about literature. An Index of Terms appears at the back of the book, and a glossary provides thorough explanations of more than two hundred terms central to the study of literature.

THE WRITING AND RESEARCH PROCESS Seven chapters (2, 10, 19, 28, 39, 47, 48) cover every step of the writing process—from generating topics to documenting sources—while 30 sample student papers model the results.

Of these chapters, three—"Writing about Fiction" (2), "Writing about Poetry" (19), and "Writing about Drama" (39)—focus on genre-specific writing assignments. Another, "Reading and Writing" (47), offers models of the types of papers most frequently assigned in the introductory course, including explication, analysis, and comparison-contrast. Students will also find a useful chapter (49) on developing strategies for taking essay examinations.

Integrated throughout the book are "Questions for Writing" units that guide students through particular writing tasks. These units cover reading and writing responsively; developing a topic into a revised thesis; incorporating secondary sources; applying a critical approach to a work; and writing about multiple works by an author.

Two unique chapters, "Combining the Elements of Fiction: A Writing Process" (10) and "Combining the Elements of Poetry: A Writing Process" (28), help students understand how literary elements work together to contribute to the overall effect and meaning of a work, and how to write papers that do justice to this complex interplay of elements. For fiction, the emphasis is on how to develop a thesis and write an analysis paper, and for poetry, the focus is on writing an explication of a poem.

Chapter 48, "The Literary Research Paper," offers detailed advice for finding, evaluating, and incorporating print as well as online sources in a paper. It also includes the most current MLA documentation guidelines. A sample student research paper models the chapter's main points.

A helpful reference chart on the book's inside front cover outlines all of the book's resources for reading and writing about literature to help students find the writing advice they need.

QUESTIONS AND ASSIGNMENTS FOR CRITICAL READING AND WRITING More than two thousand questions and assignments—"Considerations for Critical Thinking and Writing," "Connections to Other Selections," "First Response" prompts, "Critical Strategies" questions, and "Creative Response" assignments—spark students' interest, sharpen their thinking, and improve their reading, discussion, and writing skills.

NEW TO THIS EDITION

103 fresh selections

TWELVE STORIES, 84 POEMS, AND 7 PLAYS representing canonical, multicultural, contemporary, and popular literature are new to this edition. Complementing the addition of several classic literary works that have long made classroom discussion come alive are numerous stories, poems, and plays that appear for the first time in an introduction to literature anthology. These new works include stories by Martin Amis, Achy Obejas, and Ha Jin; poems by Sharon Olds and Cathy Song; and plays by David Ives and Woody Allen.

Ha Jin, author of the story "Love in the Air."

Achy Obejas, author of the story "We Came All the Way from Cuba So You Could Dress Like This?"

More reading help — models that are practical and visual

FOUR NEW SAMPLE CLOSE READINGS offer critical, annotated versions of William Faulkner's "A Rose for Emily," Ralph Ellison's "Battle Royal," Elizabeth Bishop's "Manners," and John Donne's "Death Be Not Proud." This popular feature, new to the previous edition of the book, is designed to help students approach literature with open minds and pencils in hand.

More writing help — student samples that offer analysis and documentation

SIXTEEN NEW PIECES OF SAMPLE STUDENT WRITING model for students how to analyze and argue about literature and how to support their ideas by citing examples. The papers, located in the Elements chapters of Fiction and Poetry, include a new full-length paper in Chapter 10, and 15 brief essays—

about 2 paragraphs each — that include parenthetical citations and Works Cited lists. Brief and complete enough to help students, but not to overwhelm, these papers enrich the book's already robust collection of student writing, which is now 30 samples strong.

Enriching new case study chapters that deepen students' understanding of literature

- **A ONE-OF-A-KIND CHAPTER ON JULIA ALVAREZ** Developed in collaboration with the poet herself — and exclusive to Michael Meyer's anthologies — this exciting new chapter presents five of Alvarez's favorite poems. In brief introductions to each piece, this acclaimed author and writing teacher shares her personal take on each poem, offering students insights they can get in no other anthology. A generous collection of images offers personal, cultural, and historical contexts for Alvarez's work and includes multiple drafts of a sonnet that illustrate her remarkable creative process.

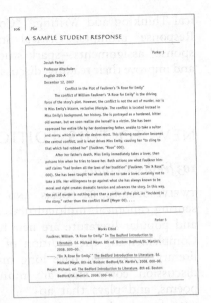

106 | Plot

A SAMPLE STUDENT RESPONSE

Parker 1

Josiah Parker
Professor Altschuler
English 200-A
December 12, 2007

Conflict in the Plot of Faulkner's "A Rose for Emily"

The conflict of William Faulkner's "A Rose for Emily" is the driving force of the story's plot. However, the conflict is not the act of murder, nor is it Miss Emily's bizarre, reclusive lifestyle. The conflict is located instead in Miss Emily's background, her history. She is portrayed as a hardened, bitter old woman, but we soon realize she herself is a victim. She has been oppressed her entire life by her domineering father, unable to take a suitor — the central conflict, and is what drives Miss Emily, causing her "to cling to that which had robbed her" (Faulkner, "Rose" 000).

After her father's death, Miss Emily immediately takes a lover, then poisons him when he tries to leave her. Both actions are what Faulkner himself claims "had broken all the laws of her tradition" (Faulkner, "On 'A Rose'" 000). She has been taught her whole life not to take a lover, certainly not to take a life. Her willingness to go against what she has always known to be moral and right creates dramatic tension and advances the story. In this way, the act of murder is nothing more than a portion of the plot, an "incident in the story," rather than the conflict itself (Meyer 00). . . .

Parker 5

Works Cited

Faulkner, William. "A Rose for Emily." In *The Bedford Introduction to Literature*. Ed. Michael Meyer. 8th ed. Boston: Bedford/St. Martin's, 2008. 000–00.

———. "On 'A Rose for Emily.'" *The Bedford Introduction to Literature*. Ed. Michael Meyer. 8th ed. Boston: Bedford/St. Martin's, 2008. 000–00.

Meyer, Michael, ed. *The Bedford Introduction to Literature*. 8th ed. Boston: Bedford/St. Martin's, 2008. 000–00.

A new sample student paper on William Faulkner's "A Rose for Emily" makes an argument about the story and includes parenthetical citations and a Works Cited page.

- **THREE NEW CASE STUDY CHAPTERS ON HUMOR AND SATIRE** Because serious literature doesn't always keep a straight face, three new thematic chapters present literary works with a humorous side. The **fiction** chapter collects reader favorites such as T. C. Boyle's "Carnal Knowledge" (on love, animal rights, and some angry turkeys) and a new story by southern writer Lee Smith, "The Happy Memories Club" (on the "wild, unbridled yearnings of the heart" that transcend age, told by a narrator who would have done Flannery O'Connor proud). The **poetry** chapter includes such new gems as Peter Schmitt's "Friends with Numbers" (about math, love, and loneliness) and Thomas Lux's "Commercial Leech Farming Today" (on the intersection of vanity, capital-

Julia Alvarez, poet, novelist, essayist, writing instructor.

Woody Allen, author of the play *Old Saybrook.*

ism, and a humble bloodsucking parasite). The **drama** chapter features David Ives's *Moby-Dude* (think Jeff Spicoli of *Fast Times at Ridgemont High* explicating the great American novel) and Woody Allen's *Old Saybrook* (in which a playwright's characters spin wildly out of control).

ANCILLARIES

Print resources

- **SPIRAL-BOUND INSTRUCTOR'S MANUAL:** *Resources for Teaching* THE COMPACT BEDFORD INTRODUCTION TO LITERATURE, Eighth Edition. ISBN-10: 0-312-47409-1; ISBN-13: 978-0-312-47409-6. The most comprehensive resource of its kind, this manual supports every selection, offering abundant resources for new and experienced instructors. The manual now includes a comprehensive thematic table of contents. An online version is available at *bedfordstmartins.com/meyercompact*.

- **LITERARY REPRINTS** Titles in the Case Studies in Contemporary Criticism series, Bedford Cultural Editions series, and the Bedford Shakespeare Series can be shrink-wrapped with *The Compact Bedford Introduction to Literature* for instructors who want to teach longer works in conjunction with the anthology. To learn more, visit bedfordstmartins .com/literaryreprints.

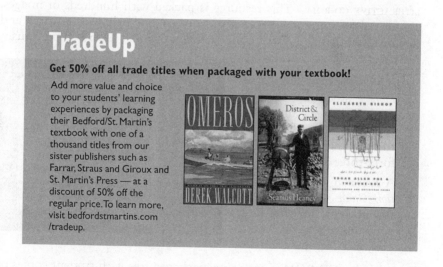

TradeUp

Get 50% off all trade titles when packaged with your textbook!

Add more value and choice to your students' learning experiences by packaging their Bedford/St. Martin's textbook with one of a thousand titles from our sister publishers such as Farrar, Straus and Giroux and St. Martin's Press — at a discount of 50% off the regular price. To learn more, visit bedfordstmartins.com /tradeup.

New media resources

BOOK COMPANION SITE AT BEDFORDSTMARTINS.COM/MEYERCOMPACT Cross-referenced throughout the anthology, the companion site offers unsurpassed resources to help students explore and write about literature, including:

- The *VirtuaLit Interactive and Fiction Tutorials*, offering in-depth readings with coverage of literary elements, cultural contexts, and critical approaches for:

  Elizabeth Bishop's "The Fish"
  Theodore Roethke's "My Papa's Waltz"
  Andrew Marvell's "To His Coy Mistress"
  Kate Chopin's "The Story of an Hour"
  Nathaniel Hawthorne's "Young Goodman Brown"
  Jamaica Kincaid's "Girl"

- *Annotated LitLinks* that offer biographical information on the writers in the anthology and provide students with a starting point for their research

- *LitQuizzes* on the stories, the elements of poetry, and the plays in the book, with a gradebook for instructors

- *LitGloss*, a glossary that offers quick access to hundreds of literary terms

- A PDF version of the Instructor's Manual: *Resources for Teaching THE COMPACT BEDFORD INTRODUCTION TO LITERATURE.*

COURSE MANAGEMENT CONTENT   A variety of student and instructor resources developed for *The Compact Bedford Introduction to Literature* is ready for use in course management systems such as WebCT and Blackboard. For more information, visit bedfordstmartins.com/cms.

LITERACTIVE CD-ROM   This resource is packed with hundreds of images, contextual documents, audio and video clips, and help with research and documentation. In addition to the VirtuaLit tutorials described previously, LiterActive offers:

- A *Multimedia and Documents Library* stocked with hundreds of images, audio and video clips, and contextual documents supporting forty-three authors

- A *Research and Documentation Guide* with advice for students on how to find, evaluate, summarize, interpret, and document sources

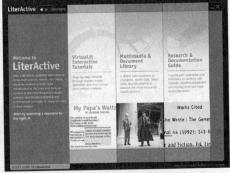

LiterActive CD-ROM.

To order this CD-ROM, a $10 value, packaged free with student copies of the book, use package ISBN-10: 0-312-47818-6; ISBN-13: 978-0-312-47818-6. For more information, visit bedfordstmartins.com/literactive.

I-SERIES CD-ROMS   This helpful and imaginative series of tutorials and exercises helps your students work with visual texts, form and support arguments, and research and document their writing through practice with real-life sources. To order an i•series CD-ROM, each a $10 value, packaged free with the anthology, use the corresponding package ISBN listed below.

ix visual exercises
See bedfordstmartins.com/ix
Package ISBN-10: 0-312-48677-4; ISBN-13: 978-0-312-48677-8

i•claim visualizing argument
See bedfordstmartins.com/iclaim
Package ISBN-10: 0-312-48678-2; ISBN-13: 978-0-312-48678-5

i•cite visualizing sources
See bedfordstmartins.com/icite
Package ISBN-10: 0-312-47817-8; ISBN-13: 978-0-312-47817-9

LITERATURE ALOUD, TWO-CD SET ISBN-10: 0-312-43011-6; ISBN-13: 978-0-312-43011-5. These audio recordings feature celebrated writers and actors reading stories, poems, and selected scenes from *The Compact Bedford Introduction to Literature*.

VIDEO AND DVD LIBRARY Selected videos and DVDs of plays and stories included in the text are available from Bedford/St. Martin's video library to qualified adopters.

ACKNOWLEDGMENTS

This book has benefited from the ideas, suggestions, and corrections of scores of careful readers who helped transform various stages of an evolving manuscript into a finished book and into subsequent editions. I remain grateful to those I have thanked in previous prefaces, particularly the late Robert Wallace of Case Western Reserve University. In addition, many instructors who used the seventh edition of *The Compact Bedford Introduction to Literature* responded to a questionnaire for the book. For their valuable comments and advice I am grateful to Judith Allen-Leventhal, College of Southern Maryland; Jean M. Crockett, Cleveland State Community College; Eileen Donovan-Kranz, Boston College; Patrick M. Ellingham, Broward Community College; Dwedor Ford, Clayton State University; Rebecca Gorman, State College of Denver; Erich Hintze, College of Southern Maryland; Mark H. Leichliter, University of Northern Colorado; Rich Miller, Suffolk University; Candace Nadon, University of Denver; Diana Nystedt, Palo Alto College; Karen Lee Osborne, Columbia College Chicago; Michael Suwak, College of Southern Maryland; and Donna Winchell, Clemson University. I am also grateful to our advisory group of reviewers from Northern Kentucky University: Deborah F. Allan, Paige Byam, Tiffany N. Hinton, Kerry Holleran, Tonya Krouse, and Mari H. York.

I would also like to give special thanks to the following instructors who contributed teaching tips to *Resources for Teaching* THE COMPACT BEDFORD INTRODUCTION TO LITERATURE: Sandra Adickes, Winona State University; Helen J. Aling, Northwestern College; Sr. Anne Denise Brenann, College of Mt. St. Vincent; Robin Calitri, Merced College; James H. Clemmer, Austin Peay State University; Robert Croft, Gainesville College; Thomas Edwards, Westbrook College; Elizabeth Kleinfeld, Red Rocks Community College; Olga Lyles, University of Nevada; Timothy Peters, Boston University, Catherine Rusco, Muskegon Community College; Robert M. St. John, DePaul University; Richard Stoner, Broome Community College; Nancy Veiga, Modesto Junior College; Karla Walters, University of New Mexico; and Joseph Zeppetello, Ulster Community College.

I am also indebted to those who cheerfully answered questions and generously provided miscellaneous bits of information. What might have seemed to them like inconsequential conversations turned out to be important leads. Among these friends and colleagues are Raymond Anselment, Barbara Campbell, Ann Charters, Karen Chow, John Christie, Eleni Coundouriotis, Irving Cummings, William Curtin, Patrick Hogan, Lee Jacobus, Thomas Jambeck, Bonnie Januszewski-Ytuarte, Greta Little, George Monteiro, Brenda Murphy, Joel Myerson, Thomas Recchio, William Sheidley, Stephanie Smith, Milton Stern, Kenneth Wilson, and the dedicated reference librarians at the Homer Babbidge Library, University of Connecticut.

I continue to be grateful for what I have learned from teaching my students and for the many student papers I have received over the years that I have used in various forms to serve as good and accessible models of student writing. I am also indebted to Stefanie Wortman for her extensive work on the eighth edition of *Resources for Teaching* THE COMPACT BEDFORD INTRODUCTION TO LITERATURE and for her work on the LitQuizzes available at the book's companion Web site.

At Bedford/St. Martin's, my debts once again require more time to acknowledge than the deadline allows. Charles H. Christensen and Joan E. Feinberg initiated this project and launched it with their intelligence, energy, and sound advice. This book has also benefited from the savvy insights of Denise Wydra and Steve Scipione. Karen Henry, Kathy Retan, Alanya Harter, and Aron Keesbury tirelessly steered earlier editions through rough as well as becalmed moments; their work was as first rate as it was essential. As developmental editor for the eighth edition, Ellen Thibault navigated the book swiftly, smoothly, and (so it seemed) effortlessly to its happy conclusion; her valuable contributions richly remind me of how fortunate I am to be a Bedford/St. Martin's author. Christina Gerogiannis skillfully developed the book's teacher's manual for AP instructors. Stephanie Naudin developed the book's instructor's manual and handled a variety of tasks, including researching and preparing the indexes. Permissions were deftly arranged by Arthur Johnson and Jason Reblando. The difficult tasks of production were skillfully managed by Jessica Skrocki and supervised by Shuli Traub. Their attention to details and deadlines were essential to the completion of this project. Edward Cone provided careful copyediting, and Daniel Wein did meticulous proofreading. I thank all of the people at Bedford/St. Martin's — including Donna Dennison who designed the cover, and Adrienne Petsick, the marketing manager — who helped to make this formidable project a manageable one.

Finally, I am grateful to my sons Timothy and Matthew for all kinds of help, but mostly I'm just grateful they're my sons. And for making all the difference, I thank my wife, Regina Barreca.

Brief Contents

CRITICAL THINKING AND WRITING   1531

Contents

To seek the source, the impulse of a story is like tearing a flower to pieces for wantonness.
— KATE CHOPIN

Writing permits me to experience life as any number of strange creations.
— ALICE WALKER

I put a group of characters in some sort of predicament, and then watch them try to work themselves free.
— STEPHEN KING

It is not neces-
sary to portray
many characters.
The center of
gravity should be
in two persons:
him and her.

— ANTON
CHEKHOV

I think a little
menace is fine to
have in a story.
— RAYMOND
CARVER

Approaches to Fiction 317

My book, if you
would see
anything in it,
requires to be
read in the
clear, brown,
twilight atmo-
sphere in
which it was
written . . .
— NATHANIEL
HAWTHORNE

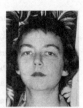

Every time a story of mine appears in a Freshman anthology, I have a vision of it, with its little organs laid open, like a frog in a bottle.
— FLANNERY O'CONNOR

It is the writer's privilege to help man endure by lifting his heart.
— WILLIAM FAULKNER

15. A Thematic Case Study: Humor and Satire   463

A Collection of Stories   499

16. An Album of Contemporary Stories   501

17. Stories for Further Reading   532

Writers lie. So do tape recorders and video cameras. So does memory. As a fiction writer this doesn't bother me at all.

—AMY BLOOM

POETRY 565

The Elements of Poetry 567

A poet has a duty to words . . . words can do wonderful things.

—GWENDOLYN BROOKS

Between my
finger and my
thumb / The
squat pen rests. /
I'll dig with it.
— SEAMUS HEANEY

22. Figures of Speech   681

Simile and Metaphor   683

Other Figures   686

Poems for Further Study   690

I would define, in brief, the Poetry of words as the Rhythmical Creation of Beauty. Its sole arbiter is Taste.

—EDGAR ALLAN POE

A short poem
need not be
small.

—MARVIN BELL

In poetry you have a form looking for a subject and a subject looking for a form. When they come together successfully you have a poem.

—W. H. AUDEN

Approaches to Poetry   829

My business is circumference.

— EMILY DICKINSON

A cartoon from a letter from Emily Dickinson to William Cowper Dickinson.

30. A Study of Robert Frost   *874*

A poem . . . begins as a lump in the throat, a sense of wrong, a homesickness, a love-sickness. . . .

— ROBERT FROST

A manuscript page from "Neither Out Far nor In Deep."

I believe that poetry should be direct, comprehensible, and the epitome of simplicity.
—LANGSTON HUGHES

I really believe being a reader turns you into a writer.
— JULIA ALVAREZ

For a man to become a poet . . . he must be in love or miserable.
— LORD BYRON

An Anthology of Poems   997

37. A Collection of Poems   1011

If there were no
poetry on any
day in the world,
poetry would be
invented that
day. For there
would be an
intolerable
hunger.

— MURIEL
  RUKEYSER

— LUCILLE
  CLIFTON

—WILLIAM
WORDSWORTH

DRAMA 1041

The Study of Drama 1043

I depict men
as they ought
to be . . .
—SOPHOCLES

A scene from
Othello.

[O]ne man in his
time plays many
parts . . .
— WILLIAM
SHAKESPEARE

The catastrophe
approaches,
inexorably,
inevitably. De-
spair, conflict,
and destruction.
— HENRIK IBSEN

A Collection of Plays 1359

All my work in some sense confronts the issue of fluidity of identity.
— DAVID HENRY HWANG

Critical Thinking and Writing 1531

My plays are about love, honor, duty, betrayal — things humans have written about since the beginning of time.
— AUGUST WILSON

The answers you get from literature depend upon the questions you pose.
— MARGARET ATWOOD

I can't write five words but that I change seven.
— DOROTHY PARKER

Strategies for Writing Essay Exams   1616

| QUESTIONS FOR WRITING
| *A Checklist for Essay Exams*   1617

THE
COMPACT
BEDFORD
INTRODUCTION TO
LITERATURE

Reading · Thinking · Writing

INTRODUCTION

Reading Imaginative Literature

© Jerry Bauer.

> Literature has been the salvation of the damned; literature has inspired and guided lovers, routed despair, and can perhaps . . . save the world.
> —JOHN CHEEVER

THE NATURE OF LITERATURE

Literature does not lend itself to a single tidy definition because the making of it over the centuries has been as complex, unwieldy, and natural as life itself. Is literature everything that has been written, from ancient prayers to graffiti? Does it include songs and stories that were not written down until many years after they were recited? Does literature include the television scripts from *Will & Grace* as well as Shakespeare's *King Lear*? Is literature only writing that has permanent value and continues to move us? Must literature be true or beautiful or moral? Should it be socially useful?

Although these kinds of questions are not conclusively answered in this book, they are implicitly raised by the stories, poems, and plays included here. No definition of literature, particularly a brief one, is likely to satisfy everyone because definitions tend to weaken and require qualification when

I

confronted by the uniqueness of individual works. In this context it is worth recalling Herman Melville's humorous use of a definition of a whale in *Moby-Dick* (1851). In the course of the novel Melville presents his imaginative and symbolic whale as inscrutable, but he begins with a quotation from Georges Cuvier, a French naturalist who defines a whale this way in his nineteenth-century study *The Animal Kingdom*: "The whale is a mammiferous animal without hind feet." Cuvier's description is technically correct, of course, but there is little wisdom in it. Melville understood that the reality of the whale (which he describes as the "ungraspable phantom of life") cannot be caught by isolated facts. If the full meaning of the whale is to be understood, it must be sought on the open sea of experience, where the whale itself is, rather than in exclusionary definitions. Facts and definitions are helpful; however, they do not always reveal the whole truth.

Despite Melville's reminder that a definition can be too limiting and even comical, it is useful for our purposes to describe literature as a fiction consisting of carefully arranged words designed to stir the imagination. Stories, poems, and plays are fictional. They are made up — imagined — even when based on actual historic events. Such imaginative writing differs from other kinds of writing because its purpose is not primarily to transmit facts or ideas. Imaginative literature is a source more of pleasure than of information, and we read it for basically the same reasons we listen to music or view a dance: enjoyment, delight, and satisfaction. Like other art forms, imaginative literature offers pleasure and usually attempts to convey a perspective, mood, feeling, or experience. Writers transform the facts the world provides — people, places, and objects — into experiences that suggest meanings.

Consider, for example, the difference between the following factual description of a snake and a poem on the same subject. Here is *Webster's Eleventh New Collegiate Dictionary*'s definition:

> any of numerous limbless scaled reptiles (suborder Serpentes syn. Ophidia) with a long tapering body and with salivary glands often modified to produce venom which is injected through grooved or tubular fangs.

Contrast this matter-of-fact definition with Emily Dickinson's poetic evocation of a snake in "A narrow Fellow in the Grass":

A narrow Fellow in the Grass
Occasionally rides —
You may have met Him — did you not
His notice sudden is —

The Grass divides as with a Comb —
A spotted shaft is seen —
And then it closes at your feet
And opens further on —

5

He likes a Boggy Acre
A floor too cool for Corn —
Yet when a Boy, and Barefoot —
I more than once at Noon

Have passed, I thought, a Whip lash
Unbraiding in the Sun
When stooping to secure it
It wrinkled, and was gone —

Several of Nature's People
I know, and they know me —
I feel for them a transport
Of cordiality —

But never met this Fellow
Attended, or alone
Without a tighter breathing
And Zero at the Bone —

10

15

20

The dictionary provides a succinct, anatomical description of what a snake is, while Dickinson's poem suggests what a snake can mean. The definition offers facts; the poem offers an experience. The dictionary would probably allow someone who had never seen a snake to sketch one with reasonable accuracy. The poem also provides some vivid subjective descriptions — for example, the snake dividing the grass "as with a Comb" — yet it offers more than a picture of serpentine movements. The poem conveys the ambivalence many people have about snakes — the kind of feeling, for example, so evident on the faces of visitors viewing the snakes at a zoo. In the poem there is both a fascination with and a horror of what might be called snakehood; this combination of feelings has been coiled in most of us since Adam and Eve.

That "narrow Fellow" so cordially introduced by way of a riddle (the word *snake* is never used in the poem) is, by the final stanza, revealed as a snake in the grass. In between, Dickinson uses language expressively to convey her meaning. For instance, in the line "His notice sudden is," listen to the *s* sound in each word and note how the verb *is* unexpectedly appears at the end, making the snake's hissing presence all the more "sudden." And anyone who has ever been surprised by a snake knows the "tighter breathing / And Zero at the Bone" that Dickinson evokes so successfully by the rhythm of her word choices and line breaks. Perhaps even more significant, Dickinson's poem allows those who have never encountered a snake to imagine such an experience.

A good deal more could be said about the numbing fear that undercuts the affection for nature at the beginning of this poem, but the point here is that imaginative literature gives us not so much the full, factual proportions of the world as some of its experiences and meanings. Instead of defining the world, literature encourages us to try it out in our imaginations.

THE VALUE OF LITERATURE

Mark Twain once shrewdly observed that a person who chooses not to read has no advantage over a person who is unable to read. In industrialized societies today, however, the question is not who reads, because nearly everyone can and does, but what is read. Why should anyone spend precious time with literature when there is so much reading material available that provides useful information about everything from the daily news to personal computers? Why should a literary artist's imagination compete for attention that could be spent on the firm realities that constitute everyday life? In fact, national best seller lists much less often include collections of stories, poems, or plays than they do cookbooks and, not surprisingly, diet books. Although such fare may be filling, it doesn't stay with us. Most people have other appetites too.

Certainly one of the most important values of literature is that it nourishes our emotional lives. An effective literary work may seem to speak directly to us, especially if we are ripe for it. The inner life that good writers reveal in their characters often gives us glimpses of some portion of ourselves. We can be moved to laugh, cry, tremble, dream, ponder, shriek, or rage with a character by simply turning a page instead of turning our lives upside down. Although the experience itself is imagined, the emotion is real. That's why the final chapters of a good adventure novel can make a reader's heart race as much as a 100-yard dash or why the repressed love of Hester Prynne in *The Scarlet Letter* by Nathaniel Hawthorne is painful to a sympathetic reader. Human emotions speak a universal language regardless of when or where a work was written.

In addition to appealing to our emotions, literature broadens our perspectives on the world. Most of the people we meet are pretty much like ourselves, and what we can see of the world even in a lifetime is astonishingly limited. Literature allows us to move beyond the inevitable boundaries of our own lives and culture because it introduces us to people different from ourselves, places remote from our neighborhoods, and times other than our own. Reading makes us more aware of life's possibilities as well as its subtleties and ambiguities. Put simply, people who read literature experience more life and have a keener sense of a common human identity than those who do not. It is true, of course, that many people go through life without reading imaginative literature, but that is a loss rather than a gain. They may find themselves troubled by the same kinds of questions that reveal Daisy Buchanan's restless, vague discontent in F. Scott Fitzgerald's *The Great Gatsby:* "What'll we do with ourselves this afternoon?" cried Daisy, "and the day after that, and the next thirty years?"

Sometimes students mistakenly associate literature more with school than with life. Accustomed to reading it in order to write a paper or pass an examination, students may perceive such reading as a chore instead of a pleasurable opportunity, something considerably less important than studying for the "practical" courses that prepare them for a career. The study of literature, however, is also practical because it engages you in the kinds of problem solving important in a variety of fields, from philosophy to science and technology. The interpretation of literary texts requires you to deal with uncertainties, value judgments, and emotions; these are unavoidable aspects of life.

People who make the most significant contributions to their professions — whether in business, engineering, teaching, or some other area — tend to be challenged rather than threatened by multiple possibilities. Instead of retreating to the way things have always been done, they bring freshness and creativity to their work. F. Scott Fitzgerald once astutely described the "test of a first-rate intelligence" as "the ability to hold two opposed ideas in the mind at the same time, and still retain the ability to function." People with such intelligence know how to read situations, shape questions, interpret details, and evaluate competing points of view. Equipped with a healthy respect for facts, they also understand the value of pursuing hunches and exercising their imaginations. Reading literature encourages a suppleness of mind that is helpful in any discipline or work.

Once you complete the requirements for your degree, what ultimately matters are not the courses listed on your transcript but the sensibilities and habits of mind that you bring to your work, friends, family, and, indeed, the rest of your life. A healthy economy changes and grows with the times; people do too if they are prepared for more than simply filling a job description. The range and variety of life that literature affords can help you to interpret your own experiences and the world in which you live.

To discover the insights that literature reveals requires careful reading and sensitivity. One of the purposes of a college introduction to literature class is to cultivate the analytic skills necessary for reading well. Class discussions often help establish a dialogue with a work that perhaps otherwise would not speak to you. Analytic skills can also be developed by writing about what you read. Writing is an effective means of clarifying your responses and ideas because it requires you to account for the author's use of language as well as your own. This book is based on two premises: that reading literature is pleasurable and that reading and understanding a work sensitively by thinking, talking, or writing about it increases the pleasure of experiencing it.

Understanding its basic elements — such as point of view, symbol, theme, tone, irony, and so on — is a prerequisite to an informed appreciation of literature. This kind of understanding allows you to perceive more in a literary work in much the same way that a spectator at a tennis match sees more if he or she understands the rules and conventions of the game. But literature is not simply a spectator sport. The analytic skills that open up literature also have their uses when you watch a television program or film and, more important, when you attempt to sort out the significance of the people, places, and events that constitute your own life. Literature enhances and sharpens your perceptions. What could be more lastingly practical as well as satisfying?

THE CHANGING LITERARY CANON

Perhaps the best reading creates some kind of change in us: we see more clearly; we're alert to nuances; we ask questions that previously didn't occur to us. Henry David Thoreau had that sort of reading in mind when he remarked in *Walden* that the books he valued most were those that caused him to date "a new era in his life from the reading." Readers are sometimes changed by literature, but it is also worth noting that the life of a literary work can also be affected by its readers. Melville's *Moby-Dick,* for example, was not valued as a classic until the 1920s, when critics rescued the novel from the obscurity of being cataloged in many libraries (including Yale's) not under fiction but under cetology, the study of whales. Indeed, many writers contemporary to Melville who were important and popular in the nineteenth century — William Cullen Bryant, Henry Wadsworth Longfellow, and James Russell Lowell, to name a few — are now mostly unread; their names appear more often on elementary schools built early in this century than in anthologies. Clearly, literary reputations and what is valued as great literature change over time and in the eyes of readers.

Such changes have accelerated during the past thirty years as the literary ***canon*** — those works considered by scholars, critics, and teachers to be the most important to read and study — has undergone a significant series of shifts. Writers who previously were overlooked, undervalued, neglected, or studiously ignored have been brought into focus in an effort to create a more diverse literary canon, one that recognizes the contributions of the many cultures that make up American society. Since the 1960s, for example, some critics have reassessed writings by women who had been left out of the standard literary traditions dominated by male writers. Many more female writers are now read alongside the male writers who traditionally populated literary history. Hence, a reader of Mark Twain and Stephen Crane is now just as likely to encounter Kate Chopin in a literary anthology. Until fairly recently Chopin was mostly regarded as a minor local colorist of Louisiana life. In the 1960s, however, the feminist movement helped to establish her present reputation as a significant voice in American literature owing to the feminist concerns so compellingly articulated by her female characters. This kind of enlargement of the canon also resulted from another reform movement of the 1960s. The civil rights movement sensitized literary critics to the political, moral, and aesthetic necessity of rediscovering African American literature, and more recently Asian and Hispanic writers have been making their way into the canon. Moreover, on a broader scale the canon is being revised and enlarged to include the works of writers from parts of the world other than the West, a development that reflects the changing values, concerns, and complexities of recent decades, when literary landscapes have shifted as dramatically as the political boundaries of Eastern Europe and the former Soviet Union.

No semester's reading list — or anthology — can adequately or accurately echo all the new voices competing to be heard as part of the mainstream literary canon, but recent efforts to open up the canon attempt to sensitize readers to the voices of women, minorities, and writers from all over the world. This development has not occurred without its urgent advocates or passionate dissenters. It's no surprise that issues about race, gender, and class often get people off the fence and on their feet (these controversies are discussed further in Chapter 46, "Critical Strategies for Reading"). Although what we regard as literature — whether it's called great, classic, or canonical — continues to generate debate, there is no question that such controversy will continue to reflect readers' values as well as the writers they admire.

FICTION

The Elements of Fiction

1

Reading Fiction

The short story makes a modest appeal for attention . . . it slips up on your blind side and wrassles you to the mat before you know what's grabbed you.
—TONI CADE BAMBARA

To seek the source, the impulse of a story is like tearing a flower to pieces for wantonness.
— KATE CHOPIN

READING FICTION RESPONSIVELY

Reading a literary work responsively can be an intensely demanding activity. Henry David Thoreau — about as intense and demanding a reader and writer as they come — insists that "books must be read as deliberately and reservedly as they were written." Thoreau is right about the necessity for a conscious, sustained involvement with a literary work. Imaginative literature does demand more from us than, say, browsing through *People* magazine in a dentist's waiting room, but Thoreau makes the process sound a little more daunting than it really is. For when we respond to the demands of responsive reading, our efforts are usually rewarded with pleasure as well as understanding. Careful, deliberate reading — the kind that engages a reader's imagination as it calls forth the writer's — is a means of exploration that can take a reader outside whatever circumstance or experience previously defined his or her world. Just as we respond moment by moment to people and situations in our lives, we also respond to literary works as we read them, though we may not be fully aware of how we are affected at each point along the way. The more conscious we are of how and why we respond to works in particular ways, the more likely we are to be imaginatively engaged in our reading.

In a very real sense both the reader and the author create the literary work. How a reader responds to a story, poem, or play will help to determine its meaning. The author arranges the various elements that constitute his or her craft — elements such as plot, character, setting, point of view, symbolism, theme, and style, which we will be examining in subsequent chapters and which are defined in the Glossary of Literary Terms (p. 1619) — but the author cannot completely control the reader's response any more than a person can absolutely predict how a remark or action will be received by a stranger, a friend, or even a family member. Few authors *tell* readers how to respond. Our sympathy, anger, confusion, laughter, sadness, or whatever the feeling might be is left up to us to experience. Writers may have the talent to evoke such feelings, but they don't have the power and authority to enforce them. Because of the range of possible responses produced by imaginative literature, there is no single, correct, definitive response or interpretation. Readings can be wrongheaded or foolish, and some readings are better than others — that is, more responsive to a work's details and more persuasive — but that doesn't mean there is only one possible reading of a work (see Chapter 2, "Writing about Fiction").

Experience tells us that different people respond differently to the same work. Consider, for example, how often we've heard Melville's *Moby-Dick* described as one of the greatest American novels. This, however, is how a reviewer in *New Monthly Magazine* described the book when it was published in 1851: it is "a huge dose of hyperbolical slang, maudlin sentimentalism and tragic-comic bubble and squeak." Melville surely did not intend or desire this response; but there it is, and it was not a singular, isolated reaction. This reading — like any reading — was influenced by the values, assumptions, and expectations that the readers brought to the novel from both previous readings and life experiences. The reviewer's refusal to take the book seriously may have caused him to miss the boat from the perspective of many other readers of *Moby-Dick,* but it indicates that even "classics" (perhaps especially those kinds of works) can generate disparate readings.

Consider the following brief story by Kate Chopin, a writer whose fiction (like Melville's) sometimes met with indifference or hostility in her own time. As you read, keep track of your responses to the central character, Mrs. Mallard. Write down your feelings about her in a substantial paragraph when you finish the story. Think, for example, about how you respond to the emotions she expresses concerning news of her husband's death. What do you think of her feelings

Web Explore contexts for Kate Chopin and approaches to this story on *LiterActive* or at bedfordstmartins.com/ meyercompact.

about marriage? Do you think you would react the way she does under similar circumstances?

KATE CHOPIN (1851–1904)

The Story of an Hour   *1894*

Knowing that Mrs. Mallard was afflicted with a heart trouble, great care was taken to break to her as gently as possible the news of her husband's death.

It was her sister Josephine who told her, in broken sentences; veiled hints that revealed in half concealing. Her husband's friend Richards was there, too, near her. It was he who had been in the newspaper office when intelligence of the railroad disaster was received, with Brently Mallard's name leading the list of "killed." He had only taken the time to assure himself of its truth by a second telegram, and had hastened to forestall any less careful, less tender friend in bearing the sad message.

She did not hear the story as many women have heard the same, with a paralyzed inability to accept its significance. She wept at once, with sudden, wild abandonment, in her sister's arms. When the storm of grief had spent itself she went away to her room alone. She would have no one follow her.

There stood, facing the open window, a comfortable, roomy armchair. Into this she sank, pressed down by a physical exhaustion that haunted her body and seemed to reach into her soul.

She could see in the open square before her house the tops of trees that ₅ were all aquiver with the new spring life. The delicious breath of rain was in the air. In the street below a peddler was crying his wares. The notes of a distant song which some one was singing reached her faintly, and countless sparrows were twittering in the eaves.

There were patches of blue sky showing here and there through the clouds that had met and piled one above the other in the west facing her window.

She sat with her head thrown back upon the cushion of the chair, quite motionless, except when a sob came up into her throat and shook her, as a child who has cried itself to sleep continues to sob in its dreams.

She was young, with a fair, calm face, whose lines bespoke repression and even a certain strength. But now there was a dull stare in her eyes, whose gaze was fixed away off yonder on one of those patches of blue sky. It was not a glance of reflection, but rather indicated a suspension of intelligent thought.

There was something coming to her and she was waiting for it, fearfully. What was it? She did not know; it was too subtle and elusive to name. But she felt it, creeping out of the sky, reaching toward her through the sounds, the scents, the color that filled the air.

Now her bosom rose and fell tumultuously. She was beginning to recog- ₁₀ nize this thing that was approaching to possess her, and she was striving to beat it back with her will — as powerless as her two white slender hands would have been.

When she abandoned herself a little whispered word escaped her slightly parted lips. She said it over and over under her breath: "free, free, free!" The vacant stare and the look of terror that had followed it went from her eyes.

They stayed keen and bright. Her pulses beat fast, and the coursing blood warmed and relaxed every inch of her body.

She did not stop to ask if it were or were not a monstrous joy that held her. A clear and exalted perception enabled her to dismiss the suggestion as trivial.

She knew that she would weep again when she saw the kind, tender hands folded in death; the face that had never looked save with love upon her, fixed and gray and dead. But she saw beyond that bitter moment a long procession of years to come that would belong to her absolutely. And she opened and spread her arms out to them in welcome.

There would be no one to live for her during those coming years; she would live for herself. There would be no powerful will bending hers in that blind persistence with which men and women believe they have a right to impose a private will upon a fellow-creature. A kind intention or a cruel intention made the act seem no less a crime as she looked upon it in that brief moment of illumination.

And yet she had loved him — sometimes. Often she had not. What did it 15 matter! What could love, the unsolved mystery, count for in face of this possession of self-assertion which she suddenly recognized as the strongest impulse of her being!

"Free! Body and soul free!" she kept whispering.

Josephine was kneeling before the closed door with her lips to the keyhole, imploring for admission. "Louise, open the door! I beg; open the door — you will make yourself ill. What are you doing, Louise? For heaven's sake open the door."

"Go away. I am not making myself ill." No; she was drinking in a very elixir of life through that open window.

Her fancy was running riot along those days ahead of her. Spring days, and summer days, and all sorts of days that would be her own. She breathed a quick prayer that life might be long. It was only yesterday she had thought with a shudder that life might be long.

She arose at length and opened the door to her sister's importunities. 20 There was a feverish triumph in her eyes, and she carried herself unwittingly like a goddess of Victory. She clasped her sister's waist, and together they descended the stairs. Richards stood waiting for them at the bottom.

Some one was opening the front door with a latchkey. It was Brently Mallard who entered, a little travel-stained, composedly carrying his gripsack and umbrella. He had been far from the scene of accident, and did not even know there had been one. He stood amazed at Josephine's piercing cry; at Richards' quick motion to screen him from the view of his wife.

But Richards was too late.

When the doctors came they said she had died of heart disease — of joy that kills.

A SAMPLE CLOSE READING

An Annotated Section of Kate Chopin's "The Story of an Hour"

Even as you read a story for the first time, you can highlight passages, circle or underline words, and write responses in the margins. Subsequent readings will yield more insights once you begin to understand how various elements such as plot, characterization, and wording build toward the conclusion and what you perceive to be the story's central ideas. The following annotations for the first eleven paragraphs of "The Story of an Hour" provide a perspective written by someone who had read the work several times. Your own approach might, of course, be quite different—as the sample paper that follows the annotated passage amply demonstrates.

KATE CHOPIN (1851–1904)

The Story of an Hour   1894

Knowing that Mrs. Mallard was afflicted with a heart trouble, great care was taken to break to her as gently as possible the news of her husband's death.

It was her sister Josephine who told her, in broken sentences; veiled hints that revealed in half concealing. Her husband's friend Richards was there, too, near her. It was he who had been in the newspaper office when intelligence of the railroad disaster was received, with Brently Mallard's name leading the list of "killed." He had only taken the time to assure himself of its truth by a second telegram, and had hastened to forestall any less careful, less tender friend in bearing the sad message.

She did not hear the story as many women have heard the same, with a paralyzed inability to accept its significance. She wept at once, with sudden, wild abandonment, in her sister's arms. When the storm of grief had spent itself she went away to her room alone. She would have no one follow her.

There stood, facing the open window, a comfortable, roomy armchair. Into this she sank, pressed down by a physical exhaustion that haunted her body and seemed to reach into her soul.

She could see in the open square before her house the 5 tops of trees that were all aquiver with the new spring life. The delicious breath of rain was in the air. In the street below a peddler was crying his wares. The notes of a distant song which some one was singing reached her faintly, and countless sparrows were twittering in the eaves.

There were patches of blue sky showing here and there through the clouds that had met and piled one above the other in the west facing her window.

She sat with her head thrown back upon the cushion of the chair, quite motionless, except when a sob came up into her throat and shook her, as a child who has cried itself to sleep continues to sob in its dreams.

She was young, with a fair, calm face, whose lines bespoke repression and even a certain strength. But now there was a dull stare in her eyes, whose gaze was fixed away off yonder on

---

The title could point to the brevity of the story—only 23 short paragraphs—or to the decisive nature of what happens in a very short period of time. Or both.

Mrs. Mallard's first name (Louise) is not given until paragraph 17, yet her sister Josephine is named immediately. This emphasizes Mrs. Mallard's married identity.

Given the nature of the cause of Mrs. Mallard's death at the story's end, it's worth noting the ambiguous description that she "was afflicted with a heart trouble." Is this one of Chopin's (rather than Josephine's) "veiled hints"?

When Mrs. Mallard weeps with "wild abandonment," the reader is again confronted with an ambiguous phrase: she grieves in an overwhelming manner yet seems to express relief at being abandoned by Brently's death.

These 3 paragraphs create an increasingly "open" atmosphere that leads to the "delicious" outside where there are inviting sounds and "patches of blue sky." There's a definite tension between the inside and outside worlds.

Though still stunned by grief, Mrs. Mallard begins to feel a change come over her owing to her growing awareness of a world outside her room.

What that change
is remains "too
subtle and elusive
to name."

Mrs. Mallard's
conflicted struggle
is described in pas-
sionate, physical
terms as if she is
"possess[ed]" by a
lover she is "power-
less" to resist.

Once she has "aban-
doned" herself (see
the "abandonment"
in paragraph three),
the reader realizes
that her love is to
be "free, free, free."
Her recognition
is evident in the
"coursing blood
[that] warmed and
relaxed every inch
of her body."

one of those patches of blue sky. It was not a glance of reflection, but rather indicated a suspension of intelligent
thought.

There was something coming to her and she was waiting
for it, fearfully. What was it? She did not know; it was too
subtle and elusive to name. But she felt it, creeping out of the
sky, reaching toward her through the sounds, the scents, the
color that filled the air.

Now her bosom rose and fell tumultuously. She was   10
beginning to recognize this thing that was approaching to
possess her, and she was striving to beat it back with her
will — as powerless as her two white slender hands would have
been.

When she abandoned herself a little whispered word
escaped her slightly parted lips. She said it over and over
under her breath: "free, free, free!" The vacant stare and the
look of terror that had followed it went from her eyes. They
stayed keen and bright. Her pulses beat fast, and the coursing
blood warmed and relaxed every inch of her body. . . .

Did you find Mrs. Mallard a sympathetic character? Some readers think
that she is callous, selfish, and unnatural — even monstrous — because she
ecstatically revels in her newly discovered sense of freedom so soon after
learning of her husband's presumed death. Others read her as a victim of
her inability to control her own life in a repressive, male-dominated society.
Is it possible to hold both views simultaneously, or are they mutually exclusive? Are your views in any way influenced by your being male or female?
Does your age affect your perception? What about your social and economic background? Does your nationality, race, or religion in any way
shape your attitudes? Do you have particular views about the institution of
marriage that inform your assessment of Mrs. Mallard's character? Have
other reading experiences — perhaps a familiarity with some of Chopin's
other stories — predisposed you one way or another to Mrs. Mallard?

Understanding potential influences might be useful in determining
whether a particular response to Mrs. Mallard is based primarily on the
story's details and their arrangement or on an overt or subtle bias that is
brought to the story. If you unconsciously project your beliefs and assumptions onto a literary work, you run the risk of distorting it to accommodate your prejudice. Your feelings can be a reliable guide to interpretation,
but you should be aware of what those feelings are based on.

Often specific questions about literary works cannot be answered
definitively. For example, Chopin does not explain why Mrs. Mallard suffers a heart attack at the end of this story. Is the shock of seeing her "dead"
husband simply too much for this woman "afflicted with a heart trouble"?
Does she die of what the doctors call a "joy that kills" because she is so glad
to see her husband? Is she so profoundly guilty about feeling "free" at her
husband's expense that she has a heart attack? Is her death a kind of willed
suicide in reaction to her loss of freedom? Your answers to these questions

will depend on which details you emphasize in your interpretation of the story and the kinds of perspectives and values you bring to it. If, for example, you read the story from a feminist perspective, you would be likely to pay close attention to Chopin's comments about marriage in paragraph 14. Or if you read the story as an oblique attack on the insensitivity of physicians of the period, you might want to find out whether Chopin wrote elsewhere about doctors (she did) and compare her comments with historic sources. (A number of critical strategies for reading, including feminist and historical approaches, appear in Chapter 51.)

Reading responsively makes you an active participant in the process of creating meaning in a literary work. The experience that you and the author create will most likely not be identical to another reader's encounter with the same work, but then that's true of nearly any experience you'll have, and it is part of the pleasure of reading. Indeed, talking and writing about literature is a way of sharing responses so that they can be enriched and deepened.

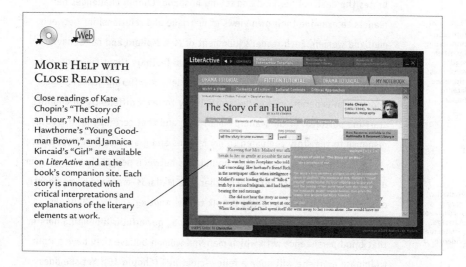

MORE HELP WITH CLOSE READING

Close readings of Kate Chopin's "The Story of an Hour," Nathaniel Hawthorne's "Young Goodman Brown," and Jamaica Kincaid's "Girl" are available on *LiterActive* and at the book's companion site. Each story is annotated with critical interpretations and explanations of the literary elements at work.

A SAMPLE PAPER

Differences in Responses to Kate Chopin's "The Story of an Hour"

The following paper was written in response to an assignment that called for a three- to four-page discussion of how different readers might interpret Mrs. Mallard's character. The paper is based on the story as well as on the discussion of reader-response criticism (pp. 1552–54) in Chapter 46, "Critical Strategies for Reading." As that discussion indicates, reader-response criticism is a critical approach that focuses on the reader rather than on the work itself in order to describe how the reader creates meaning from the text.

Wally Villa

Professor Bryant

English 210

March 12, 2008

Differences in Responses to

Kate Chopin's "The Story of an Hour"

Thesis providing writer's interpretation of story's purpose

Kate Chopin's "The Story of an Hour" appears merely to explore a woman's unpredictable reaction to her husband's assumed death and re-appearance, but actually Chopin offers Mrs. Mallard's bizarre story to reveal problems that are inherent in the institution of marriage. By offering this depiction of a marriage that stifles the woman to the point that she celebrates the death of her kind and loving husband, Chopin challenges her readers to examine their own views of marriage and relationships between

Introduction setting up other reader responses discussed later in paper

men and women. Each reader's judgment of Mrs. Mallard and her behavior inevitably stems from his or her own personal feelings about marriage and the influences of societal expectations. Readers of differing genders, ages, and marital experiences are, therefore, likely to react differently to Chopin's startling portrayal of the Mallards' marriage, and that certainly is true of my response to the story compared to my father's and grandmother's responses.

Analysis of story's portrayal of marriage, with textual evidence

Marriage often establishes boundaries between people that make them unable to communicate with each other. The Mallards' marriage was evidently crippled by both their inability to talk to one another and Mrs. Mallard's conviction that her marriage was defined by a "powerful will bending hers in that blind persistence with which men and women believe they have a right to impose a private will upon a fellow-creature" (Chopin 16). Yet she does not recognize that it is not just men who impose their will upon women and that the problems inherent in marriage affect men and women equally. To me,

Analysis of character and plot, connecting with story's purpose

Mrs. Mallard is a somewhat sympathetic character, and I appreciate her longing to live out the "years to come that would belong to her absolutely" (16). However, I also believe that she could have tried to improve her own situation somehow, either by reaching out to her husband or by abandoning the marriage altogether. Chopin uses Mrs. Mallard's tragedy to illuminate aspects of marriage that are harmful and, in this case, even deadly. Perhaps the

Mallards' relationship should be taken as a warning to others: sacrificing one's own happiness in order to satisfy societal expectations can poison one's life and even destroy entire families.

When my father read "The Story of an Hour," his reaction to Mrs. Mallard was more antagonistic than my own. He sees Chopin's story as a timeless "battle of the sexes," serving as further proof that men will never really be able to understand what it is that women want. Mrs. Mallard endures an obviously unsatisfying marriage without ever explaining to her husband that she feels trapped and unfulfilled. Mrs. Mallard dismisses the question of whether or not she is experiencing a "monstrous joy" (16) as trivial, but my father does not think that this is a trivial question. He believes Mrs. Mallard is guilty of a monstrous joy because she selfishly celebrates the death of her husband without ever having allowed him the opportunity to understand her feelings. He believes that, above all, Brently Mallard should be seen as the most victimized character in the story. Mr. Mallard is a good, kind man, with friends who care about him and a marriage that he thinks he can depend on. He "never looked save with love" (16) upon his wife, his only "crime" (16) was his presence in the house, and yet he is the one who is bereaved at the end of the story, for reasons he will never understand. Mrs. Mallard's passion for her newly discovered freedom is perhaps understandable, but according to my father, Mr. Mallard is the character most deserving of sympathy.

Maybe not surprisingly, my grandmother's interpretation of "The Story of an Hour" was radically different from both mine and my father's. My grandmother was married in 1936 and widowed in 1959 and therefore can identify with Chopin's characters, who live at the turn of the century. Her first reaction, aside from her unwavering support for Mrs. Mallard and her predicament, was that this story demonstrates the differences between the ways men and women related to each other a century ago and the way they relate today. Unlike my father, who thinks Mrs. Mallard is too passive, my grandmother believes that Mrs. Mallard doesn't even know that she is feeling repressed until after she is told that Brently is dead. In 1894, divorce was so scandalous and stigmatized that it simply wouldn't have been an option for Mrs. Mallard, and so her only way out of the marriage would have been one

Contrasting summary and analysis of another reader's response

Contrasting summary and analysis of another reader's response

Cultural and historical background providing context for response and story itself

of their deaths. Being relatively young, Mrs. Mallard probably considered herself doomed to a long life in an unhappy marriage. My grandmother also feels that, in spite of all we know of Mrs. Mallard's feelings about her husband and her marriage, she still manages to live up to everyone's expectations of her as a woman both in life and in death. She is a dutiful wife to Brently, as she is expected to be. She weeps "with sudden, wild abandonment" when she hears the news of his death; she locks herself in her room to cope with her new situation, and she has a fatal heart attack upon seeing her husband arrive home. Naturally the male doctors would think that she died of the "joy that kills" (16)--nobody could have guessed that she was unhappy with her life, and she would never have wanted them to know.

Interpretations of "The Story of an Hour" seem to vary according to the gender, age, and experience of the reader. While both male and female readers can certainly sympathize with Mrs. Mallard's plight, female readers-- as was evident in our class discussions--seem to relate more easily to her predicament and are quicker to exonerate her of any responsibility for her unhappy situation. Conversely, male readers are more likely to feel compassion for Mr. Mallard, who loses his wife for reasons that will always remain entirely unknown to him. Older readers probably understand more readily the strength of social forces and the difficulty of trying to deny societal expectations concerning gender roles in general and marriage in particular. Younger readers seem to feel that Mrs. Mallard is too passive and that she could have improved her domestic life immeasurably if she had taken the initiative to either improve or end her relationship with her husband. Ultimately, how each individual reader responds to Mrs. Mallard's story reveals his or her own ideas about marriage, society, and how men and women communicate with each other.

Work Cited

Chopin, Kate. "The Story of an Hour." The Compact Bedford Introduction to Literature. Ed. Michael Meyer. 8th ed. Boston: Bedford/St. Martin's, 2009. 15–16.

Margin notes:

Analysis supported with textual evidence

Conclusion summarizing reader responses explored in the paper

Before beginning your own writing assignment on fiction, you should review Chapter 2, "Writing about Fiction," as well as Chapter 47, "Reading and Writing," which provides a step-by-step explanation of how to choose a topic, develop a thesis, and organize various types of writing assignments. If you use outside sources, you should also be familiar with the conventional documentation procedures described in Chapter 48, "The Literary Research Paper."

EXPLORATIONS AND FORMULAS

Each time we pick up a work of fiction, go to the theater, or turn on the television, we have a trace of the same magical expectation that can be heard in the voice of a child who begs, "Tell me a story." Human beings have enjoyed stories ever since they learned to speak. Whatever the motive for creating stories—even if simply to delight or instruct—the basic human impulse to tell and hear stories existed long before the development of written language. Myths about the origins of the world and legends about the heroic exploits of demigods were among the earliest forms of storytelling to develop into oral traditions, which were eventually written down. These narratives are the ancestors of the stories we read on the printed page today. Unlike the early listeners to ancient myths and legends, we read our stories silently, but the pleasure derived from the mysterious power of someone else's artfully arranged words remains largely the same. Every one of us likes a good story.

The stories that appear in anthologies for college students are generally chosen for their high literary quality. Such stories can affect us at the deepest emotional level, reveal new insights into ourselves or the world, and stretch us by exercising our imaginations. They warrant careful reading and close study to appreciate the art that has gone into creating them. The following chapters on plot, character, setting, and other elements of literature are designed to provide the terms and concepts that can help us understand how a work of fiction achieves its effects and meanings. It is worth acknowledging, however, that many people buy and read fiction that is quite different from the stories usually anthologized in college texts. What about all those paperbacks with exciting, colorful covers near the cash registers in shopping malls and corner drugstores?

These books, known as *formula fiction,* are the adventure, western, detective, science fiction, and romance novels that entertain millions of readers annually. What makes them so popular? What do their characters, plots, and themes offer readers that accounts for the tremendous sales of stories with titles like *Caves of Doom, Silent Scream, Colt .45,* and *Forbidden Ecstasy?* Many of the writers included in this book have enjoyed wide popularity and written best sellers, but there are more readers of formula fiction than there are readers of Hemingway, Faulkner, or Oates, to name only a few. Formula novels do, of course, provide entertainment, but that makes them no different from serious stories, if entertainment means pleasure. Any of the stories in this or any other anthology can be read for pleasure.

Formula fiction, though, is usually characterized as escape literature. There are sensible reasons for this description. Adventure stories about soldiers of fortune are eagerly read by men who live pretty average lives doing ordinary jobs. Romance novels about attractive young women falling in love with tall, dark, handsome men are read mostly by women who dream themselves out of their familiar existences. The excitement, violence, and passion that such stories provide are a kind of reprieve from everyday experience.

And yet readers of serious fiction may also use it as a refuge, a liberation from monotony and boredom. Mark Twain's humorous stories have, for example, given countless hours of pleasurable relief to readers who would rather spend time in Twain's light and funny world than in their own. Others might prefer the terror of Edgar Allan Poe's fiction or the painful predicament of two lovers in a Joyce Carol Oates story.

Thus, to get at some of the differences between formula fiction and serious literature, it is necessary to go beyond the motives of the reader to the motives of the writer and the qualities of the work itself.

Unlike serious fiction, the books displayed next to the cash registers (and their short story equivalents on the magazine racks) are written with only one object: to be sold. They are aimed at specific consumer markets that can be counted on to buy them. This does not mean that all serious writers must live in cold garrets writing for audiences who have not yet discovered their work. No one writes to make a career of poverty. It does mean, however, that if a writer's primary purpose is to anticipate readers' generic expectations about when the next torrid love scene, bloody gunfight, or thrilling chase is due, there is little room to be original or to have something significant to say. There is little if any chance to explore seriously a character, idea, or incident if the major focus is not on the integrity of the work itself.

Although the specific elements of formula fiction differ depending on the type of story, some basic ingredients go into all westerns, mysteries, adventures, science fiction, and romances. From the very start, a reader can anticipate a happy ending for the central character, with whom he or she will identify. There may be suspense, but no matter what or how many the obstacles, complications, or near defeats, the hero or heroine succeeds and reaffirms the values and attitudes the reader brings to the story. Virtue triumphs, love conquers all, honesty is the best policy, and hard work guarantees success. Hence, the villains are corralled, the wedding vows are exchanged, the butler confesses, and gold is discovered at the last moment. The visual equivalents of such formula stories are readily available at movie theaters and in television series. Some are better than others, but all are relatively limited by the writer's goal of giving an audience what will sell.

Although formula fiction may not offer many surprises, it provides pleasure to a wide variety of readers. College professors, for example, are just as likely to be charmed by formula stories as anyone else. Readers of serious fiction who revel in exploring more challenging imaginative worlds can also enjoy formulaic stories, which offer little more than an image of the world as a simple place in which our assumptions and desires are confirmed. The familiarity of a given formula is emotionally satisfying because we are secure in our expectations of it. We know at the start of a Sherlock Holmes story that the mystery will be solved by that famous detective's relentless scientific analysis of the clues, but we take pleasure in seeing how Holmes unravels the mystery before us. Similarly, we know that James Bond's wit, grace, charm, courage, and skill will ultimately prevail over the diabolic schemes of eccentric villains, but we volunteer for the mission anyway.

Perhaps that happens for the same reason that we climb aboard a roller coaster: no matter how steep and sharp the curves, we stay on a track that is both exciting and safe. Although excitement, adventure, mystery, and romance are major routes to escape in formula fiction, most of us make that trip only temporarily, for a little relaxation and fun. Momentary relief from our everyday concerns is as healthy and desirable as an occasional daydream or fantasy. Such reading is a form of play because we — like spectators of or participants in a game — experience a formula of excitement, tension, and then release that can fascinate us regardless of how many times the game is played.

Many publishers of formula fiction — such as romance, adventure, or detective stories — issue a set number of new novels each month. Readers can buy them in stores or subscribe to them through the mail or online. These same publishers send "tip sheets" on request to authors who want to write for a particular series. The details of the formula differ from one series to another, but each tip sheet covers the basic elements that go into a story.

There are many kinds of formulaic romance novels; some include psychological terrors, some use historical settings, and some even incorporate time travel so that the hero or heroine can travel back in time and fall in love, and still others create mystery and suspense. Several publishers have recently released romances that reflect contemporary social concerns and issues; multicultural couples and gay and lesbian relationships as well as more explicit descriptions of sexual activities are now sometimes featured in these books. In general, however, the majority of romance novels are written to appeal to a readership that embraces more traditional societal expectations and values.

The following composite tip sheet summarizes the typical advice offered by publishers of romance novels. These are among the most popular titles published in the United States; it has been estimated that four out of every ten paperbacks sold are romance novels. The categories and the tone of the language in this composite tip sheet are derived from a number of publishers and provide a glimpse of how formula fiction is written and what the readers of romance novels are looking for in their escape literature.

A Composite of a Romance Tip Sheet

Plot

The story focuses on the growing relationship between the heroine and hero. After a number of complications, they discover lasting love and make a permanent commitment to each other in marriage. The plot should move quickly. Background information about the heroine should be kept to a minimum. The hero should appear as early as possible (preferably in the first chapter and no later than the second), so that the hero's and heroine's feelings about each other are in the foreground as they cope with misperceptions that keep them apart until the final pages of the story. The more tension created by their uncertainty about each other's love, the greater the excitement and anticipation for the reader.

Love is the major interest. Do not inject murder, extortion, international intrigue, hijacking, horror, or supernatural elements into the plot. Controversial social issues and politics, if mentioned at all, should never be allowed a significant role. Once the heroine and hero meet, they should clearly be interested in each other, but that interest should be complicated by some kind of misunderstanding. He, for example, might find her too ambitious, an opportunist, cold, or flirtatious; or he might assume that she is attached to someone else. She might think he is haughty, snobbish, power hungry, indifferent, or contemptuous of her. The reader knows what they do not: that eventually these obstacles will be overcome. Interest is sustained by keeping the lovers apart until very near the end so that the reader will stay with the plot to see how they get together.

Heroine

The heroine is a modern American woman between the ages of nineteen and twenty-eight who reflects today's concerns. The story is told in the third person from her point of view. She is attractive and nicely dressed but not glamorous; glitter and sophistication should be reserved for the other woman (the heroine's rival for the hero), whose flashiness will compare unfavorably with the heroine's modesty. When the heroine does dress up, however, her beauty should be stunningly apparent. Her trim figure is appealing but not abundant; a petite healthy appearance is desirable. Both her looks and her clothes should be generously detailed.

Her personality is spirited and independent without being pushy or stubborn because she knows when to give in. Although sensitive, she doesn't cry every time she is confronted with a problem (though she might cry in private moments). A sense of humor is helpful. Because she is on her own, away from parents (usually deceased) or other protective relationships, she is self-reliant as well as vulnerable. The story may begin with her on the verge of an important decision about her life. She is clearly competent but not entirely certain of her own qualities. She does not take her attractiveness for granted or realize how much the hero is drawn to her.

Common careers for the heroine include executive secretary, nurse, teacher, 5
interior designer, assistant manager, department store buyer, travel agent, or

struggling photographer (no menial work). She can also be a doctor, lawyer, or other professional. Her job can be described in some detail and made exciting, but it must not dominate her life. Although she is smart, she is not extremely intellectual or defined by her work. Often she meets the hero through work, but her major concerns center on love, marriage, home, and family. White wine is okay, but she never drinks alone — or uses drugs. She may be troubled, frustrated, threatened, and momentarily thwarted in the course of the story, but she never totally gives in to despair or desperation. She has strengths that the hero recognizes and admires.

Hero

The hero should be about ten years older than the heroine and can be foreign or American. He needn't be handsome in a traditional sense, but he must be strongly masculine. Always tall and well built (not brawny or thick) and usually dark, he looks as terrific in a three-piece suit as he does in sports clothes. His clothes reflect good taste and an affluent life-style. Very successful professionally and financially, he is a man in charge of whatever work he's engaged in (financier, doctor, publisher, architect, business executive, airline pilot, artist, etc.). His wealth is manifested in his sophistication and experience.

His past may be slightly mysterious or shrouded by some painful moment (perhaps with a woman) that he doesn't want to discuss. Whatever the circumstance — his wife's death or divorce are common — it was not his fault. Avoid chronic problems such as alcoholism, drug addiction, or sexual dysfunctions. To others he may appear moody, angry, unpredictable, and explosively passionate, but the heroine eventually comes to realize his warm, tender side. He should be attractive not only as a lover but also as a potential husband and father.

Secondary Characters

Because the major interest is in how the heroine will eventually get together with the hero, the other characters are used to advance the action. There are three major types:

(1) *The Other Woman:* Her vices serve to accent the virtues of the heroine; immediately beneath her glamorous sophistication is a deceptive, selfish, mean-spirited, rapacious predator. She may seem to have the hero in her clutches, but she never wins him in the end.

(2) *The Other Man:* He usually falls into two types: (a) the decent sort who is there when the hero isn't around and (b) the selfish sort who schemes rather than loves. Neither is a match for the hero.   10

(3) *Other Characters:* Like furniture, they fill in the background and are useful for positioning the hero and heroine. These characters are familiar types such as the hero's snobbish aunt, the heroine's troubled younger siblings, the loyal friend, or the office gossip. They should be realistic, but they must not be allowed to obscure the emphasis on the lovers. The hero may have children from a previous marriage, but they should rarely be seen or heard. It's usually simpler and better not to include them.

Setting

The setting is usually contemporary. Romantic, exciting places are best: New York City, London, Paris, Rio, the mountains, the ocean—wherever it is exotic and love's possibilities are the greatest. Marriage may take the heroine and hero to a pretty suburb or small town.

Love Scenes

The hero and heroine may make love before marriage. The choice will depend largely on the heroine's sensibilities and circumstances. She should reflect modern attitudes. If the lovers do engage in premarital sex, it should be made clear that neither is promiscuous, especially the heroine. Even if their relationship is consummated before marriage, their lovemaking should not occur until late in the story. There should be at least several passionate scenes, but complications, misunderstandings, and interruptions should keep the couple from actually making love until they have made a firm commitment to each other. Descrip-

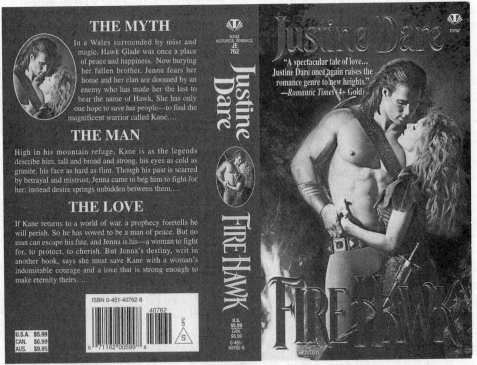

Romance novel. The cover for *FireHawk* (Penguin, 1997) illustrates another convention of romance formula fiction: its packaging demands an image of a man clasping a passionate beauty to his manly chest. As the back-cover copy suggests, this Topaz novel is a historical romance—a subcategory of the romance formula—and so a few of the guidelines on the tip sheet are modified (the setting is medieval Wales rather than contemporary America, for example). But most of the guidelines apply: Kane is strong and so is Jenna's powerful love.
By Richard Newton, from *FireHawk* by Justine Dare, © 1997 Janice Davis Smith.

tions should appeal to the senses; however, detailed, graphic close-ups are unacceptable. Passion can be presented sensually but not clinically; the lovemaking should be seen through a soft romantic lens. Violence and any out-of-the-way sexual acts should not even be hinted at. No coarse language.

Writing

Avoid extremely complex sentences, very long paragraphs, and lengthy descriptions. Use concise, vivid details to create the heroine's world. Be sure to include full descriptions of the hero's and heroine's physical features and clothes. Allow the reader to experience the romantic mood surrounding the lovers. Show how the heroine feels; do not simply report her feelings. Dialogue should sound like ordinary conversation, and the overall writing should be contemporary English without slang, difficult foreign expressions, strange dialects, racial epithets, or obscenities (*hell, damn,* and a few other mild swears are all right).

Length

About 55,000 to 65,000 words in ten to twelve chapters.   15

CONSIDERATIONS FOR CRITICAL THINKING AND WRITING

1. **FIRST RESPONSE.** Given the expectations implied by the tip sheet, what generalizations can you make about those likely to write formula fiction? Does the tip sheet change the way you think about romantic fiction or other kinds of formula fiction?

2. Who is the intended audience for this type of romance? Try to describe the audience in detail: How does a romance novel provide escape for these readers?

3. Why is it best that the heroine be "attractive and nicely dressed but not glamorous"? Why do you think publishers advise writers to include detailed descriptions of her clothes? Do you find the heroine appealing? Why or why not?

4. Why should the hero be "about ten years older than the heroine"? If he is divorced, why is it significant that "it was not his fault"?

5. Why do you think the hero and heroine are kept apart by complications until the end of the story? Does the outline of the plot sound familiar to you or remind you of any other stories?

6. Why do you think restrictions are placed on the love scenes?

7. Why are "extremely complex sentences, very long paragraphs, and lengthy descriptions" discouraged?

8. To what extent does the tip sheet describe the strategies used in popular television soap operas? How do you account for the appeal of these shows?

9. Explain how the tip sheet confirms traditional views of male and female roles in society. Does it accommodate any broken traditions?

10. Carefully examine the Topaz Historical Romance cover. How do the cover's images and copy reinforce what readers can expect from a romance novel?

11. Included in the marketing material that accompanies the Topaz Historical Romance is this notation: "Topaz is an Official Sponsor of the Mrs. America Pageant." Why do you suppose the publishers support this contest?

12. Write a tip sheet for another kind of popular formula story, such as a western or a detective story, that you have observed in a novel, television show, or film. How is the plot patterned? How are the characters made familiar? How is the setting related to the story? What are the obligatory scenes? How is the overall style consistent? To get started, you might consider an Agatha Christie novel, an episode from a police series on television, or a James Bond film.

13. Try writing a scene for a formula romance, or read the excerpt from Edgar Rice Burroughs's *Tarzan of the Apes* (p. 72) and try an adventure scene.

A COMPARISON OF TWO STORIES

Each of the following contemporary pieces of fiction is about a woman who experiences deep sorrow. The first, from *A Secret Sorrow* by Karen van der Zee, is an excerpt from a romance by Harlequin Books, a major publisher of formula fiction that has sold well over a billion copies of its romance titles — enough for about 20 percent of the world's population. The second piece, Gail Godwin's "A Sorrowful Woman," is a complete short story that originally appeared in *Esquire;* it is not a formula story. Unlike *A Secret Sorrow,* Godwin's story does not have a standard plot pattern employing familiar character types that appear in a series of separate but similar works.

Read each selection carefully and look for evidence of formulaic writing in the chapters from *A Secret Sorrow.* Pay particular attention to the advice on plotting and characterization offered in the composite tip sheet. As you read Godwin's short story, think about how it is different from van der Zee's excerpt; note also any similarities. The questions that follow the stories should help you consider how the experiences of reading the two are different.

KAREN VAN DER ZEE (B. 1947)

Born and raised in Holland, Karen van der Zee lives in the United States, where she has become a successful romance writer, contributing more than fifteen novels to the popular Harlequin series. This excerpt consists of the final two chapters of *A Secret Sorrow.* This is what has happened so far: The central character, Faye, is recuperating from

By permission of the author.

the psychological effects of a serious car accident in which she received a permanent internal injury. After the accident, she quits her job and breaks her engagement to Greg. She moves into her brother Chuck's house and falls in love with Kai, a visiting Texan and good friend of her brother. At the end of Chapter 10, Kai insists on knowing why she will not marry him and asks, "Who is Doctor Jaworski?"

From A Secret Sorrow   *1981*

Chapter Eleven

Faye could feel the blood drain from her face and for one horrifying moment she thought she was going to faint right in Kai's arms. The room tilted and everything swirled around in a wild madman's dance. She clutched at him for support, fighting for control, trying to focus at some point beyond his shoulder. Slowly, everything steadied.

"I . . . I don't know him," she murmured at last. "I. . . ."

He reached in the breast pocket of his shirt, took out a slip of paper, and held it out for her to see. One glance and Faye recognized it as the note from Doctor Martin with Doctor Jaworski's name scrawled on it, thickly underlined.

"How did you get that?" Her voice was a terrified whisper. She was still holding on, afraid she would fall if she let go.

"I found it on the floor in my bedroom. It must have fallen out of your 5 wallet along with everything else on Saturday morning."

Yes — oh God! Her legs were shaking so badly, she knew it was only his arms that kept her from falling.

"Who is Doctor Jaworski, Faye?" His voice was patiently persistent.

"I . . . he. . . ." Her voice broke. "Let me go, please let me go." She felt as if she were suffocating in his embrace and she struggled against him, feebly, but it was no use.

"He's a psychiatrist, isn't he?" His voice was gentle, very gentle, and she looked up at him in stunned surprise.

He knew, oh God, he knew. She closed her eyes, a helpless sense of in- 10 evitability engulfing her.

"You know," she whispered. "How do you know?"

"Simple. Two minutes on the phone to Chicago." He paused. "Doctor Martin — was he one of the doctors who treated you at the hospital?"

"Yes."

"Why did he give you Doctor Jaworski's name? Did he want you to make an appointment with him?"

"Yes." Despondency overtook her. There was no going back now. No es- 15 cape from the truth. No escape from his arms. Resistance faded and she felt numbed and lifeless. It didn't matter any more. Nothing mattered.

"Did you?" Kai repeated.

"Did I what?"

"See him — Doctor Jaworski."

"No."

"Why did Doctor Martin want you to see a psychiatrist?" 20

"I. . . ." Faye swallowed miserably. "It's . . . it's therapy for grieving . . . mourning." She made a helpless gesture with her hand. "When people lose a . . . a wife, or husband for instance, they go through a more or less predictable pattern of emotions. . . ." She gave him a quick glance, then looked away. "Like denial, anger. . . ."

". . . depression, mourning, acceptance," Kai finished for her, and she looked back at him in surprise.

"Yes."

His mouth twisted in a little smile. "I'm not totally ignorant about subjects other than agronomy." There was a momentary pause as he scrutinized her face. "Why did you need that kind of therapy, Faye?"

And then it was back again, the resistance, the revolt against his probing 25
questions. She stiffened in defense — her whole body growing rigid with instinctive rebellion.

"It's none of your business!"

"Oh, yes, it is. We're talking about our life together. Your life and mine."

She strained against him, hands pushing against his chest. "Let me go! Please let me go!" Panic changed into tears. She couldn't take his nearness any more, the feel of his hard body touching hers, the strength of him.

"No, Faye, no. You're going to tell me. Now. I'm not letting you go until you've told me everything. Everything, you hear?"

"I can't!" she sobbed. "I can't!" 30

"Faye," he said slowly, "you'll *have* to. You told me you love me, but you don't want to marry me. You have given me no satisfactory reasons, and I'll be damned if I'm going to accept your lack of explanations."

"You have no right to demand an explanation!"

"Oh, yes, I have. You're part of me, Faye. Part of my life."

"You talk as if you own me!" She was trembling, struggling to get away from him. She couldn't stand there, so close to him with all the pent-up despair inside her, the anger, the fear of what she knew not how to tell him.

His hands were warm and strong on her back, holding her steady. Then, 35
with one hand, he tilted back her head and made her look at him. "You gave me your love — I own that," he said softly. "True loving involves commitment, vulnerability, trust. Don't you trust me, Faye?"

New tears ran silently down her cheeks. "If I told you," she blurted out, "you wouldn't . . . you wouldn't. . . ."

"I wouldn't *what?*"

"You wouldn't want me any more!" The words were wrenched from her in blind, agonizing grief. "You wouldn't *want* me any more!"

He shook his head incredulously. "What makes you think you can make that decision for me? Do you have so little trust in my love for you?"

Faye didn't answer, couldn't answer. Through a mist of tears he was noth- 40
ing but a blur in front of her eyes.

"What is so terrible that you can't tell me?"

She shrank inwardly, as if shriveling away in pain. "Let me go," she whispered. "Please let me go and I'll tell you."

After a moment's hesitation Kai released her. Faye backed away from him, feeling like a terrified animal. She stood with her back against the wall, glad for the support, her whole body shaking. She took a deep breath and wiped her face dry with her hand.

"I'm afraid . . . afraid to marry you."

"Afraid?" He looked perplexed. "Afraid of what? Of me? Of marriage?"   45

Faye closed her eyes, taking another deep breath. "I can't be what you want me to be. We can't have the kind of life you want." She looked at him, standing only a few feet away, anguish tearing through her. "I'm so afraid . . . you'll be disappointed," she whispered.

"Oh God, Faye," he groaned, "I love you." He came toward her and panic surged through her as he held her against the wall, his hands reaching up to catch her face between them.

"Don't," she whispered. "Please, don't touch me." But it was no use. His mouth came down on hers and he kissed her with a hard, desperate passion.

"I love you," he said huskily. "I love you."

Faye wrenched her face free from his hands. "Don't touch me! Please don't   50
touch me!" She was sobbing now, her words barely audible. Her knees gave way and her back slid down along the wall until she crumpled on to the floor, face in her hands.

Kai took a step backward and pulled her up. "Stand up, Faye. For God's sake stand up!" He held her against the wall and she looked at him, seeing every line in his dark face, the intense blue of his eyes, and knew that this was the moment, that there was no more waiting.

And Kai knew it too. His eyes held hers locked in unrelenting demand. "Why should I be disappointed, Faye? *Why?*"

Her heart was thundering in her ears and it seemed as if she couldn't breathe, as if she were going to drown.

"Because . . . because I can't give you children! Because I can't get pregnant! I can't have babies! That's why!" Her voice was an agonized cry, torn from the depths of her misery. She yanked down his arms that held her locked against the wall and moved away from him. And then she saw his face.

It was ashen, gray under his tan. He stared at her as if he had never seen   55
her before.

"Oh my God, Faye. . . ." His voice was low and hoarse. "Why didn't you tell me, why. . . ."

Faye heard no more. She ran out the door, snatching her bag off the chair as she went by. The only thought in her mind was to get away — away from Kai and what was in his eyes.

She reached for Kai's spare set of car keys in her bag, doing it instinctively, knowing she couldn't walk home alone in the dark. How she managed to get the keys in the door lock and in the ignition she never knew. Somehow, she made it home.

The phone rang as Faye opened the front door and she heard Chuck answer it in the kitchen.

"She's just got in," he said into the mouthpiece, smiling at Faye as she   60
came into view. He listened for a moment, nodded. "Okay, fine with me."

Faye turned and walked up the stairs, taking deep breaths to calm her shattered nerves. Kai hadn't wasted any time checking up on her. She didn't care what he was telling Chuck, but she wasn't going to stand there listening to a one-sided conversation. But only a second later Chuck was behind her on the stairs.

"Kai wanted to know whether you'd arrived safely."

"I did, thank you," she said levelly, her voice surprisingly steady.

"I take it you ran out and took off with his car?"

"Did he say that?"

"No. He was *worried* about you. He wanted to make sure you went home." He sounded impatient, and she couldn't blame him. She was making life unbearable for everyone around her. Everybody worried about her. Everybody loved her. Everything should be right. Only it wasn't.

"Well, I'm home now, and I'm going to bed. Good night."

"Good night, Faye."

Faye lay in bed without any hope of sleep. Mechanically she started to sort through her thoughts and emotions, preparing mentally for the next confrontation. There would be one, she didn't doubt it for a moment. But she needed time — time to clear her head, time to look at everything in a reasonable, unemotional way.

It was a temptation to run — get in the car and keep driving, but it would be a stupid thing to do. There was no place for her to go, and Kai would find her, no matter what. If there was one thing she knew about Kai it was his stubbornness and his persistence. She had to stick it out, right here, get it over with, deal with it. Only she didn't know how.

She lay listening to the stillness, just a few sounds here and there — the house creaking, a car somewhere in the distance, a dog barking. She had to think, but her mind refused to cooperate. She *had* to think, decide what to say to Kai the next time she saw him, but she couldn't think, she *couldn't think.*

And then, as she heard the door open in the silence, the quiet footsteps coming up the stairs, she knew it was too late, that time had run out.

Without even knocking he came into her room and walked over to the bed. She could feel the mattress sag as his weight came down on it. Her heart was pounding like a sledgehammer, and then his arms came around her and he drew her against him.

"Faye," he said quietly, "please marry me."

"No," she said thickly. "No." She could feel him stiffen against her and she released herself from his arms and slid off the bed. She switched on the light and stood near the window, far from the bed, far from Kai. "I don't expect you to play the gentleman, I don't expect you to throw out a life of dreams just for the sake of chivalry. You don't have to marry me, Kai." She barely recognized her own voice. It was like the cool calm sound of a stranger, unemotional, cold. "You don't have to marry me," she repeated levelly, giving him a steady look.

Her words were underlined by the silence that followed, a silence loaded with a strange, vibrating energy, a force in itself, filling the room.

Kai rose to his feet, slowly, and the face that looked at her was like that of a stranger, a dangerous, angry stranger. Never before had she seen him so angry, so full of hot, fuming fury.

"Shut up," he said in a low, tight voice. "Shut up and stop playing the martyr!"

The sound of his voice and the words he said shocked Faye into silence. She stared at him open-mouthed, and then a slow, burning anger arose inside her.

"How dare you! How. . . ."

He strode toward her and took her upper arms and shook her. "Shut up and listen to me! What the hell are you thinking? What the hell did you expect

me to do when you told me? You throw me a bomb and then walk out on me!
What did you expect my reaction to be? Was I supposed to stay cool and calm
and tell you it didn't matter? Would you have married me then? Well, let me
tell you something! It matters! It matters to me! I am not apologizing for my
reaction!" He paused, breathing hard. "You know I always wanted children,
but what in God's name makes you think you're the only one who has the
right to feel bad about it? I have that right too, you hear! I love you, dammit,
and I want to marry you, and if we can't have children I have all the right in the
world to feel bad about it!"

He stopped talking. He was still breathing hard and he looked at her with
stormy blue eyes. Faye felt paralyzed by his tirade and she stared at him, incapable of speech. She couldn't move, she couldn't think.

"Why do you think I want you for my wife?" he continued on a calmer
note. "Because you're some kind of baby factory? What kind of man do you
think I am? I love *you,* not your procreating ability. So we have a problem. Well,
we'll learn to deal with it, one way or another."

There was another silence, and still Faye didn't speak, and she realized she
was crying, soundlessly, tears slowly dripping down her cheeks. She was staring at his chest, blindly, not knowing what to think, not thinking at all.

He lifted her chin, gently. "Look at me, Faye."   85
She did, but his face was only a blur.

"Faye, we're in this together—you and I. Don't you see that? It's not just
your problem, it's *ours.*"

"No," she whispered. "No!" She shook her head wildly. "You have a choice,
don't you see that? You don't have to marry me. You could marry someone else
and have children of your own."

"Oh, God, Faye," he groaned, "you're wrong. Don't you know? Don't you
see? I *don't* have a choice. I never did have a choice, or a chance. Not since I met
you and fell in love with you. I don't *want* anybody else, don't you understand
that? I want you, only you."

She wanted to believe it, give in to him. Never before had she wanted any-   90
thing more desperately than she wanted to give in to him now. But she couldn't,
she couldn't. . . . She closed her eyes, briefly, fighting for reason, common sense.

"Kai, I . . . I can't live all my life with your regret and your disappointment.
Every time we see some pregnant woman, every time we're with somebody
else's children I'll feel I've failed you! I. . . ." Her voice broke and new sobs came
unchecked.

He held her very tightly until she calmed down and then he put her from
him a little and gave her a dark, compelling look.

"It's not *my* regret, or *my* disappointment," he said with quiet emphasis.
"It's *ours.* We're not talking about *you* or *me.* We're talking about *us.* I love you,
and you love me, and that's the starting point, that comes first. From then on
we're in it together."

Faye moved out of his arms, away from him, but her legs wouldn't carry
her and she sank into a chair. She covered her face with her hands and tried
desperately to stop the crying, to stop the tears from coming and coming as if
they would never end.

"How . . . how can I ever believe it?"   95
"Because I'm asking you to," he said quietly. He knelt in front of her, took
her hands away from her wet face. "Look at me, Faye. No other woman can give

me what you can — yourself, your love, your warmth, your sense of humor. All the facets of your personality that make up the final you. I've known other women, Faye, but none of them have ever stirred in me any feelings that come close to what I feel for you. You're an original, remember? There's no replacement for an original. There are only copies, and I don't want a copy. To me you're special, and you'll have to believe it, take it on faith. That's what love is all about."

He was holding her hands in his, strong brown hands, and she was looking down on them, fighting with herself, fighting with everything inside her to believe what he was saying, to accept it, to give in to it.

Leaning forward, Kai kissed her gently on the mouth and smiled. "It's all been too much too soon for you, hasn't it? You never really got a chance to get over the shock, and when I fell in love with you it only made things worse." He smiled ruefully and Faye was surprised at his insight.

"Yes," she said. "It all happened too fast."

"Bad timing. If only we could have met later, after you'd sorted it all out in 100 your mind, then it would never have been such a crisis."

She looked at him doubtfully. "It wouldn't have changed the facts."

"No, but it might have changed your perspective."

Would it have? she wondered. Could she ever feel confident and secure in her worth as a woman? Or was she at this moment too emotionally bruised to accept that possibility?

"I don't understand," he said, "why I never guessed what was wrong. Now that I know, it all seems so obvious." He looked at her thoughtfully. "Faye," he said gently, "I want you to tell me exactly what happened to you, what Doctor Martin told you."

She stared at him, surprised a little. A thought stirred in the back of her 105 mind. Greg. He had never even asked. The why and the what had not interested him. But Kai, he wanted to know. She swallowed nervously and began the story, slowly, word for word, everything Doctor Martin had said. And he listened, quietly, not interrupting. "So you see," she said at last, "we don't have to hope for any miracles either."

"We'll make our own miracles," he said, and smiled. "Come here," he said then, "kiss me."

She did, shyly almost, until he took over and lifted her up and carried her to the bed. He looked down on her, eyes thoughtful. "I won't pretend I understand your feelings about this, the feelings you have about yourself as a woman, but I'll try." He paused for a moment. "Faye," he said then, speaking with slow emphasis, "don't *ever*, not for a single moment, think that you're not good enough for me. You're the best there is, Faye, the very best."

His mouth sought hers and he kissed her with gentle reassurance at first, then with rising ardor. His hands moved over her body, touching her with sensual, intimate caresses.

"You're my woman, Faye, you're mine. . . ."

Her senses reeled. She could never love anyone like she loved him. No one 110 had ever evoked in her this depth of emotion. This was real, this was forever. Kai wanted her as much as ever. No chivalry, this, no game of pretense, she was very sure of that. And when he lifted his face and looked at her, it was all there in his eyes and the wonder of it filled her with joy.

"Do you believe me now?" he whispered huskily. "Do you believe I love you and want you and need you?"

She nodded wordlessly, incapable of uttering a sound.

"And do you love me?"

Again she nodded, her eyes in his.

"Okay, then." In one smooth flowing movement he got to his feet. He crossed to the closet, opened it, and took out her suitcases. He put one on the end of the bed and began to pile her clothes in it, taking armfuls out of the closet.

Faye watched incredulously. "What are you doing?" she managed at last.

Kai kept on moving around, opening drawers, taking out her things, filling the suitcase until it could hold no more. "Get dressed. We're going home."

"Home . . . ?"

For a moment he stopped and he looked at her with a deep blue glitter in his eyes. "Yes, *home* — where you belong. With me, in my house, in my bed, in my arms."

"Oh, Kai," she said tremulously, smiling suddenly. "It's midnight!"

His eyes were very dark. "I've waited long enough, I'm not waiting any more. You're coming with me, now. And I'm not letting you out of my sight until we're safely married. I don't want you getting any crazy ideas about running off to save me from myself, or some such notion."

Her throat was dry. "Please, let's not rush into it! Let's think about it first!"

Calmly he zipped up the full suitcase, swung it off the bed, and put it near the door. "I'm not rushing into anything," he said levelly. "I've wanted to marry you for quite a while, remember?"

He crossed to the bed, sat down next to her, and put his arm around her. "Faye, I wish you wouldn't worry so. I'm not going to change my mind. And I haven't shelved my hopes for a family, either." There was a brief silence. "When we're ready to have kids, we'll have them. We'll adopt them. There are orphanages the world over, full of children in need of love and care. We'll do whatever it takes. We'll get them, one way or another."

Faye searched his face, faint hope flickering deep inside her.

"Would you want that?"

"Why not?"

"I don't know, really. I thought you . . . it isn't the same."

"No," he said levelly, "it isn't. Adoption is a different process from pregnancy and birth, but the kids will be ours just the same and we'll love them no less."

"Yes," she said, "yes." And suddenly it seemed as if a light had been turned on inside her, as if suddenly she could see again, a future with Kai, a future with children.

A bronzed hand lifted her face. "Look, Faye, I'll always be sorry. I'll always be sorry not to see you pregnant, not to see you with a big stomach knowing you're carrying my child, but I'll live."

Faye lowered her eyes and tears threatened again. With both his hands he cupped her face.

"Look at me, Faye. I want you to stop thinking of yourself as a machine with a defect. You're not a damaged piece of merchandise, you hear? You're a living, breathing human being, a warm-blooded female, and I love you."

Through a haze of tears she looked at him, giving a weak smile. "I love you too." She put her arms around him and he heaved an unsteady breath.

"Faye," he said huskily, "you're my first and only choice."   135

Chapter Twelve

Kai and Faye had their family, two girls and a boy. They came to them one at a time, from faraway places, with small faces and large dark eyes full of fear. In their faces Faye could read the tragedies of war and death and poverty. They were hungry for love, hungry for nourishment and care. At night they woke in terror, screaming, their memories alive in sleep.

Time passed, and in the low white ranch house under the blue skies of Texas they flourished like the crops in the fields. They grew tall and straight and healthy and the fear in their dark eyes faded. Like their father they wore jeans and boots and large-brimmed hats, and they rode horses and played the guitar. They learned to speak English with a Southern twang.

One day Kai and Faye watched them as they played in the garden, and joy and gratitude overflowed in Faye's heart. Life was good and filled with love.

"They're all ours," she said. Even now after all these years she sometimes still couldn't believe it was really so.

Kai smiled at her. His eyes, still very blue, crinkled at the corners. "Yes, and 140 you're all mine."

"They don't even look like us," she said. "Not even a tiny little bit." No blondes, no redheads.

Taking her in his arms, Kai kissed her. "They're true originals, like their mother. I wouldn't want it any other way."

There was love in his embrace and love in his words and in her heart there was no room now for doubt, no room for sorrow.

Sometimes in the night he would reach for her and she would wake to his touch, his hands on her breast, her stomach, searching. In the warm darkness of their bed she would come to him and they would hold each other close and she knew he had been dreaming.

She knew the dream. She was walking away from him, calling out that she 145 couldn't marry him, the words echoing all around. *"I can't marry you! I can't marry you!"* And Kai was standing there watching her go, terrified, unable to move, his legs frozen to the ground. He wanted to follow her, keep her from leaving, but his legs wouldn't move.

Kai had told her of the dream, of the panic that clutched at him as he watched her walk out of his life. And always he would wake and search for her in the big bed, and she knew of only one way to reassure him. And in the warm afterglow of lovemaking, their bodies close together, she knew that to him she was everything, to him she was the only woman, beautiful, complete, whole.

GAIL GODWIN (B. 1937)

Born in Birmingham, Alabama, Gail Godwin was educated at the University of North
Carolina and the University of Iowa, where
she earned a Ph.D. in English in 1971. She is
a full-time writer who has won grants from
the National Endowment for the Arts, the
Guggenheim Foundation, and the American
Institute for the Arts and Letters. Among
her novels are *Glass People* (1971), *A Mother
and Two Daughters* (1981), *The Finishing School*
(1985), *Evensong* (1999), and *Queen of the Underworld* (2006). Her short stories have been
collected in several volumes including *Dream
Children* (1976) and *Mr. Bedford and the Muses*
(1983).

© Jerry Bauer.

A Sorrowful Woman   1971

Once upon a time there was a wife and mother one too many times

One winter evening she looked at them: the husband durable, receptive, gentle;
the child a tender golden three. The sight of them made her so sad and sick she
did not want to see them ever again.

She told the husband these thoughts. He was attuned to her; he understood such things. He said he understood. What would she like him to do? "If
you could put the boy to bed and read him the story about the monkey who
ate too many bananas, I would be grateful." "Of course," he said. "Why, that's a
pleasure." And he sent her off to bed.

The next night it happened again. Putting the warm dishes away in the
cupboard, she turned and saw the child's gray eyes approving her movements.
In the next room was the man, his chin sunk in the open collar of his favorite
wool shirt. He was dozing after her good supper. The shirt was the gray of the
child's trusting gaze. She began yelping without tears, retching in between.
The man woke in alarm and carried her in his arms to bed. The boy followed
them up the stairs, saying, "It's all right, Mommy," but this made her scream.
"Mommy is sick," the father said, "go wait for me in your room."

The husband undressed her, abandoning her only long enough to root
beneath the eiderdown for her flannel gown. She stood naked except for her
bra, which hung by one strap down the side of her body; she had not the impetus to shrug it off. She looked down at the right nipple, shriveled with chill,
and thought, How absurd, a vertical bra. "If only there were instant sleep," she
said, hiccuping, and the husband bundled her into the gown and went out and

came back with a sleeping draught guaranteed swift. She was to drink a little glass of cognac followed by a big glass of dark liquid and afterwards there was just time to say Thank you and could you get him a clean pair of pajamas out of the laundry, it came back today.

The next day was Sunday and the husband brought her breakfast in bed 5 and let her sleep until it grew dark again. He took the child for a walk, and when they returned, red-cheeked and boisterous, the father made supper. She heard them laughing in the kitchen. He brought her up a tray of buttered toast, celery sticks, and black bean soup. "I am the luckiest woman," she said, crying real tears. "Nonsense," he said. "You need a rest from us," and went to prepare the sleeping draught, find the child's pajamas, select the story for the night.

She got up on Monday and moved about the house till noon. The boy, delighted to have her back, pretended he was a vicious tiger and followed her from room to room, growling and scratching. Whenever she came close, he would growl and scratch at her. One of his sharp little claws ripped her flesh, just above the wrist, and together they paused to watch a thin red line materialize on the inside of her pale arm and spill over in little beads. "Go away," she said. She got herself upstairs and locked the door. She called the husband's office and said, "I've locked myself away from him. I'm afraid." The husband told her in his richest voice to lie down, take it easy, and he was already on the phone to call one of the baby-sitters they often employed. Shortly after, she heard the girl let herself in, heard the girl coaxing the frightened child to come and play.

After supper several nights later, she hit the child. She had known she was going to do it when the father would see. "I'm sorry," she said, collapsing on the floor. The weeping child had run to hide. "What has happened to me, I'm not myself anymore." The man picked her tenderly from the floor and looked at her with much concern. "Would it help if we got, you know, a girl in? We could fix the room downstairs. I want you to feel freer," he said, understanding these things. "We have the money for a girl. I want you to think about it."

And now the sleeping draught was a nightly thing, she did not have to ask. He went down to the kitchen to mix it, he set it nightly beside her bed. The little glass and the big one, amber and deep rich brown, the flannel gown and the eiderdown.

The man put out the word and found the perfect girl. She was young, dynamic, and not pretty. "Don't bother with the room, I'll fix it up myself." Laughing, she employed her thousand energies. She painted the room white, fed the child lunch, read edifying books, raced the boy to the mailbox, hung her own watercolors on the fresh-painted walls, made spinach soufflé, cleaned a spot from the mother's coat, made them all laugh, danced in stocking feet to music in the white room after reading the child to sleep. She knitted dresses for herself and played chess with the husband. She washed and set the mother's soft ash-blonde hair and gave her neck rubs, offered to.

The woman now spent her winter afternoons in the big bedroom. She 10 made a fire in the hearth and put on slacks and an old sweater she had loved at school, and sat in the big chair and stared out the window at snow-ridden branches, or went away into long novels about other people moving through other winters.

The girl brought the child in twice a day, once in the later afternoon when he would tell of his day, all of it tumbling out quickly because there was not much time, and before he went to bed. Often now, the man took his wife to dinner. He made a courtship ceremony of it, inviting her beforehand so she could get used to the idea. They dressed and were beautiful together again and went out into the frosty night. Over candlelight he would say, "I think you are better, you know." "Perhaps I am," she would murmur. "You look . . . like a cloistered queen," he said once, his voice breaking curiously.

One afternoon the girl brought the child into the bedroom. "We've been out playing in the park. He found something he wants to give you, a surprise." The little boy approached her, smiling mysteriously. He placed his cupped hands in hers and left a live dry thing that spat brown juice in her palm and leapt away. She screamed and wrung her hands to be rid of the brown juice. "Oh, it was only a grasshopper," said the girl. Nimbly she crept to the edge of the curtain, did a quick knee bend, and reclaimed the creature, led the boy competently from the room.

"The girl upsets me," said the woman to her husband. He sat frowning on the side of the bed he had not entered for so long. "I'm sorry, but there it is." The husband stroked his creased brow and said he was sorry too. He really did not know what they would do without that treasure of a girl. "Why don't you stay here with me in bed," the woman said.

Next morning she fired the girl who cried and said, "I loved the little boy, what will become of him now?" But the mother turned away her face and the girl took down the watercolors from the walls, sheathed the records she had danced to, and went away.

"I don't know what we'll do. It's all my fault, I know. I'm such a burden, I know that."   15

"Let me think. I'll think of something." (Still understanding these things.)

"I know you will. You always do," she said.

With great care he rearranged his life. He got up hours early, did the shopping, cooked the breakfast, took the boy to nursery school. "We will manage," he said, "until you're better, however long that is." He did his work, collected the boy from the school, came home and made the supper, washed the dishes, got the child to bed. He managed everything. One evening, just as she was on the verge of swallowing her draught, there was a timid knock on her door. The little boy came in wearing his pajamas. "Daddy has fallen asleep on my bed and I can't get in. There's not room."

Very sedately she left her bed and went to the child's room. Things were much changed. Books were rearranged, toys. He'd done some new drawings. She came as a visitor to her son's room, wakened the father and helped him to bed. "Ah, he shouldn't have bothered you," said the man, leaning on his wife. "I've told him not to." He dropped into his own bed and fell asleep with a moan. Meticulously she undressed him. She folded and hung his clothes. She covered his body with the bedclothes. She flicked off the light that shone in his face.

The next day she moved her things into the girl's white room. She put her   20 hairbrush on the dresser; she put a note pad and pen beside the bed. She stocked the little room with cigarettes, books, bread, and cheese. She didn't need much.

At first the husband was dismayed. But he was receptive to her needs. He understood these things. "Perhaps the best thing is for you to follow it through," he said. "I want to be big enough to contain whatever you must do."

All day long she stayed in the white room. She was a young queen, a virgin in a tower; she was the previous inhabitant, the girl with all the energies. She tried these personalities on like costumes, then discarded them. The room had a new view of streets she'd never seen that way before. The sun hit the room in late afternoon and she took to brushing her hair in the sun. One day she decided to write a poem. "Perhaps a sonnet." She took up her pen and pad and began working from words that had lately lain in her mind. She had choices for the sonnet, ABAB or ABBA for a start. She pondered these possibilities until she tottered into a larger choice: she did not have to write a sonnet. Her poem could be six, eight, ten, thirteen lines, it could be any number of lines, and it did not even have to rhyme.

She put down the pen on top of the pad.

In the evenings, very briefly, she saw the two of them. They knocked on her door, a big knock and a little, and she would call Come in, and the husband would smile though he looked a bit tired, yet somehow this tiredness suited him. He would put her sleeping draught on the bedside table and say, "The boy and I have done all right today," and the child would kiss her. One night she tasted for the first time the power of his baby spit.

"I don't think I can see him anymore," she whispered sadly to the man. And 25 the husband turned away, but recovered admirably and said, "Of course, I see."

So the husband came alone. "I have explained to the boy," he said. "And we are doing fine. We are managing." He squeezed his wife's pale arm and put the two glasses on her table. After he had gone, she sat looking at the arm.

"I'm afraid it's come to that," she said. "Just push the notes under the door; I'll read them. And don't forget to leave the draught outside."

The man sat for a long time with his head in his hands. Then he rose and went away from her. She heard him in the kitchen where he mixed the draught in batches now to last a week at a time, storing it in a corner of the cupboard. She heard him come back, leave the big glass and the little one outside on the floor.

Outside her window the snow was melting from the branches, there were more people on the streets. She brushed her hair a lot and seldom read anymore. She sat in her window and brushed her hair for hours, and saw a boy fall off his new bicycle again and again, a dog chasing a squirrel, an old woman peek slyly over her shoulder and then extract a parcel from a garbage can.

In the evening she read the notes they slipped under her door. The child 30 could not write, so he drew and sometimes painted his. The notes were painstaking at first; the man and boy offering the final strength of their day to her. But sometimes, when they seemed to have had a bad day, there were only hurried scrawls.

One night, when the husband's note had been extremely short, loving but short, and there had been nothing from the boy, she stole out of her room as she often did to get more supplies, but crept upstairs instead and stood outside their doors, listening to the regular breathing of the man and boy asleep. She hurried back to her room and drank the draught.

She woke earlier now. It was spring, there were birds. She listened for sounds of the man and the boy eating breakfast; she listened for the roar of the motor when they drove away. One beautiful noon, she went out to look at her kitchen in the daylight. Things were changed. He had bought some new dish towels. Had the old ones worn out? The canisters seemed closer to the sink. She got out flour, baking powder, salt, milk (he bought a different brand of butter), and baked a loaf of bread and left it cooling on the table.

The force of the two joyful notes slipped under her door that evening pressed her into the corner of the little room; she had hardly space to breathe. As soon as possible, she drank the draught.

Now the days were too short. She was always busy. She woke with the first bird. Worked till the sun set. No time for hair brushing. Her fingers raced the hours.

Finally, in the nick of time, it was finished one late afternoon. Her veins 35 pumped and her forehead sparkled. She went to the cupboard, took what was hers, closed herself into the little white room and brushed her hair for a while.

The man and boy came home and found: five loaves of warm bread, a roast stuffed turkey, a glazed ham, three pies of different fillings, eight molds of the boy's favorite custard, two weeks' supply of fresh-laundered sheets and shirts and towels, two hand-knitted sweaters (both of the same gray color), a sheath of marvelous watercolor beasts accompanied by mad and fanciful stories nobody could ever make up again, and a tablet full of love sonnets addressed to the man. The house smelled redolently of renewal and spring. The man ran to the little room, could not contain himself to knock, flung back the door.

"Look, Mommy is sleeping," said the boy. "She's tired from doing all our things again." He dawdled in a stream of the last sun for that day and watched his father roll tenderly back her eyelids, lay his ear softly to her breast, test the delicate bones of her wrist. The father put down his face into her fresh-washed hair.

"Can we eat the turkey for supper?" the boy asked.

CONSIDERATIONS FOR CRITICAL THINKING AND WRITING

1. **FIRST RESPONSE.** How did you respond to the excerpt from *A Secret Sorrow* and to "A Sorrowful Woman"? Do you like one more than the other? Is one of the women — Faye or Godwin's unnamed wife — more likable than the other? Why do you think you respond the way you do to the characters and the stories — is your response intellectual, emotional, a result of authorial intent, a mix of these, or something else entirely?

2. Describe what you found appealing in each story. Can you point to passages in both that strike you as especially well written or interesting? Was there anything in either story that did not appeal to you? Why?

3. How do the two women's attitudes toward family life differ? How does that difference constitute the problem in each story?

4. How is the woman's problem in "A Sorrowful Woman" made more complex than Faye's in *A Secret Sorrow*? What is the purpose of the husband and child in Godwin's story?

5. How would you describe the theme — the central point and meaning — in each story?

6. To what extent might "A Sorrowful Woman" be regarded as an unromantic sequel to *A Secret Sorrow*?

7. Can both stories be read a second or third time and still be interesting? Why or why not?

8. Explain how you think a romance formula writer would end "A Sorrowful Woman," or write the ending yourself.

9. Contrast what marriage means in the two stories.

10. Discuss your feelings about the woman in "A Sorrowful Woman." How does she remain a sympathetic character in spite of her refusal to be a traditional wife and mother? (It may take more than one reading of the story to see that Godwin does sympathize with her.)

11. The happy ending of *A Secret Sorrow* may seem like that of a fairy tale, but it is realistically presented because there is nothing strange, mysterious, or fabulous that strains our ability to believe it could happen. In contrast, "A Sorrowful Woman" begins with an epigraph (*"Once upon a time…"*) that causes us to expect a fairy-tale ending, but that story is clearly a fairy tale gone wrong. Consider the two stories as fairy tales. How might "A Sorrowful Woman" be read as a dark version of "Sleeping Beauty"?

12. CRITICAL STRATEGIES. Read the section on feminist criticism in Chapter 46, "Critical Strategies for Reading." Based on that discussion, what do you think a feminist critic might have to say about these two stories?

Perspectives

KAY MUSSELL (B. 1943)

Are Feminism and Romance Novels Mutually Exclusive?   *1997*

If feminism and romance are mutually exclusive, a lot of romance writers and readers haven't heard the news yet. In my experience, the only people who think they are mutually exclusive are people who don't know much about romances — or about women, or dare I add about feminism? That last point may be provocative and subject to real debate.

Twenty years ago, when romance novels were getting a lot of attention in the media, I thought that their increased popularity and changing content had something to do with the challenge mounted by feminism to more traditional women. I saw romances back then as a kind of backlash against the more aggressive and controversial aspects of feminism — something that reaffirmed traditional values and made women who hadn't bought into the feminist critique feel validated about their own choices. I also expected romances to fade away as more and more women entered the labor force and became practical feminists if not theoretical or political feminists.

Was I ever wrong! Instead of quietly going the way of the Western (which is much less popular now than it was a few decades ago), romances have become one of the hottest areas of publishing. One reason, of course, is that romances have changed with the times. The newer romances incorporate feminist themes while still reaffirming more traditional notions about love and family. Moreover, many romance writers have openly claimed feminist values and, in the process, rejected easy stereotypes about themselves and their work. For example, see the essays by romance writers collected in Jayne Ann Krentz's *Dangerous Men & Adventurous Women.*

More difficult to illustrate, but I think equally important, is change in feminist thinking itself. Twenty or so years ago, when academic feminists first became interested in the romance genre, there was wider agreement among feminists themselves on what the feminist agenda should be — and conventional romantic relationships, widely assumed to be discriminatory toward women, were not part of it. Thus romances were seen as threatening to female autonomy. But as feminism has matured — and as feminist scholars have come to recognize a broader range of female experience — some scholars have challenged those earlier notions in productive ways.

I don't know how you can read many romances today as anything but feminist. To take just one issue: Heroes and heroines meet each other on a much more equal playing field. Heroes don't always dominate and heroines are frequently right. Heroines have expertise and aren't afraid to show it. Heroes aren't the fount of all wisdom and they actually have things to learn from heroines. This is true of both contemporary and historical romances. I'm not trying to argue that all romances before the 1990s featured unequal relationships or that all romances today are based on equality. That's clearly not the case. But in general heroines today have a lot more independence and authority than their counterparts did in earlier romances. I think that's clear evidence of the influence of feminism on romances and of the ability of romance novels to address contemporary concerns that women share.

From "All About Romance: The Back-Fence for Lovers of Romance Novels" accessed at *<likesbooks.com/mussell.html>.*

CONSIDERATIONS FOR CRITICAL THINKING AND WRITING

1. How might the excerpt from *A Secret Sorrow* be read "as a kind of backlash against the more aggressive and controversial aspects of feminism"?

2. Examine some recent romance novel covers and back-cover copy in a bookstore. What evidence is there to support or refute Mussell's claim that "newer romances incorporate feminist themes while still reaffirming more traditional notions about love and family"?

3. Write an essay in which you consider a book, film, or television program that seems to appeal to male fantasies, and explore some of the similarities and differences between male and female tastes in popular fiction.

THOMAS JEFFERSON (1743–1826)

On the Dangers of Reading Fiction 1818

A great obstacle to good education is the inordinate passion prevalent for novels, and the time lost in that reading which should be instructively employed. When this poison infects the mind, it destroys its tone and revolts it against wholesome reading. Reason and fact, plain and unadorned, are rejected. Nothing can engage attention unless dressed in all the figments of fancy, and nothing so bedecked comes amiss. The result is a bloated imagination, sickly judgment, and disgust towards all the real businesses of life. This mass of trash, however, is not without some distinction; some few modeling their narratives, although fictitious, on the incidents of real life, have been able to make them interesting and useful vehicles of a sound morality. . . . For a like reason, too, much poetry should not be indulged. Some is useful for forming style and taste. Pope, Dryden, Thompson, Shakespeare, and of the French, Molière, Racine, the Corneilles, may be read with pleasure and improvement.

Letter to Nathaniel Burwell, March 14, 1818,
in *The Writings of Thomas Jefferson*

CONSIDERATIONS FOR CRITICAL THINKING AND WRITING

1. Jefferson voices several common objections to fiction. What, according to him, are the changes associated with reading fiction? Are these concerns still expressed today? Why or why not? To what extent are Jefferson's arguments similar to twentieth-century objections to watching television?

2. Explain why you agree or disagree that works of fiction should serve as "useful vehicles of a sound morality."

3. How do you think Jefferson would regard Harlequin romances?

2

Writing about Fiction

Writing permits me to experience life as
any number of strange creations.
— ALICE WALKER

FROM READING TO WRITING

There's no question about it: writing about fiction is a different experience
from reading it. The novelist William Styron amply concedes that writing
to him is not so much about pleasure as it is about work: "Let's face it, writing is hell." Although Styron's lament concerns his own feelings about
writing prose fiction, he no doubt speaks for many other writers, including
essayists. Writing is, of course, work, but it is also a pleasure when it goes
well — when ideas feel solid and the writing is fluid. You can experience
that pleasure as well, if you approach writing as an intellectual and emotional opportunity rather than merely a sentence.

Just as reading fiction requires an imaginative, conscious response, so
does writing about fiction. Composing an essay is not just recording your

interpretive response to a work because the act of writing can change your response as you explore, clarify, and discover relationships you hadn't previously considered or recognized. Most writers discover new ideas and connections as they move through the process of rereading and annotating the text, taking notes, generating ideas, developing a thesis, and organizing an argumentative essay (these matters are detailed in Chapter 47, "Reading and Writing"). To become more conscious of the writing process, first study the following questions specifically aimed at sharpening your response to reading and writing about fiction. Then examine the case study of a student's paper in progress that takes you through writing a first response to reading, brainstorming for a paper topic, writing a first draft, revising, and writing the final paper.

Questions for Responsive Reading and Writing

The following questions can help you consider important elements of fiction that reveal your responses to a story's effects and meanings. The questions are general, so they will not always be relevant to a particular story. Many of them, however, should prove useful for thinking, talking, and writing about a work of fiction. If you are uncertain about the meaning of a term used in a question, consult the Glossary of Literary Terms beginning on page 1619 of this book. You should also find useful the discussion of various critical approaches to literature in Chapter 46, "Critical Strategies for Reading."

PLOT

1. Does the plot conform to a formula? Is it like those of any other stories you have read? Did you find it predictable?

2. What is the source and nature of the conflict for the protagonist? Was your major interest in the story based on what happens next or on some other concern? What does the title reveal now that you've finished the story?

3. Is the story told chronologically? If not, in what order are its events told, and what is the effect of that order on your response to the action?

4. What does the exposition reveal? Are flashbacks used? Did you see any foreshadowings? Where is the climax?

5. Is the conflict resolved at the end? Would you characterize the ending as happy, unhappy, or somewhere in between?

6. Is the plot unified? Is each incident somehow related to some other element in the story?

CHARACTER

7. Do you identify with the protagonist? Who (or what) is the antagonist?

8. Did your response to any characters change as you read? What do you think caused the change? Do any characters change and develop in the course of the story? How?

Questions for Responsive Reading and Writing

9. Are round, flat, or stock characters used? Is their behavior motivated and plausible?

10. How does the author reveal characters? Are they directly described or indirectly presented? Are the characters' names used to convey something about them?

11. What is the purpose of the minor characters? Are they individualized, or do they primarily represent ideas or attitudes?

SETTING

12. Is the setting important in shaping your response? If it were changed, would your response to the story's action and meaning be significantly different?

13. Is the setting used symbolically? Are the time, place, and atmosphere related to the theme?

14. Is the setting used as an antagonist?

POINT OF VIEW

15. Who tells the story? Is it a first-person or third-person narrator? Is it a major or minor character or one who does not participate in the action at all? How much does the narrator know? Does the point of view change at all in the course of the story?

16. Is the narrator reliable and objective? Does the narrator appear too innocent, emotional, or self-deluded to be trusted?

17. Does the author directly comment on the action?

18. If it were told from a different point of view, how would your response to the story change? Would anything be lost?

SYMBOLISM

19. Did you notice any symbols in the story? Are they actions, characters, settings, objects, or words?

20. How do the symbols contribute to your understanding of the story?

THEME

21. Did you find a theme? If so, what is it?

22. Is the theme stated directly, or is it developed implicitly through the plot, characters, or some other element?

23. Is the theme a confirmation of your values, or does it challenge them?

STYLE, TONE, AND IRONY

24. Do you think the style is consistent and appropriate throughout the story? Do all the characters use the same kind of language, or did you hear different voices?

25. Would you describe the level of diction as formal or informal? Are the sentences short and simple, long and complex, or some combination?

continued

Questions for Responsive Reading and Writing

26. How does the author's use of language contribute to the tone of the story? Did it seem, for example, intense, relaxed, sentimental, nostalgic, humorous, angry, sad, or remote?

27. Do you think the story is worth reading more than once? Does the author's use of language bear close scrutiny so that you feel and experience more with each reading?

CRITICAL STRATEGIES

28. Is there a particular critical approach that seems especially appropriate for this story? (See the discussion of critical strategies for reading beginning on p. 1533.)

29. How might biographical information about the author help you to determine the central concerns of the story?

30. How might historical information about the story provide a useful context for interpretation?

31. What kinds of evidence from the story are you focusing on to support your interpretation? Does your interpretation leave out any important elements that might undercut or qualify your interpretation?

32. To what extent do your own experiences, values, beliefs, and assumptions inform your interpretation?

33. Given that there are a variety of ways to interpret the story, which one seems the most useful to you?

A SAMPLE PAPER IN PROGRESS

The following student paper was written in response to an assignment that asked for a comparison and contrast of the treatment of marriage in the excerpt from Karen van der Zee's novel *A Secret Sorrow* (p. 31) and in Gail Godwin's short story "A Sorrowful Woman" (p. 39). The final draft of the paper is preceded by four distinct phases of composition: (1) an initial response, (2) a brainstorming exercise, (3) a preliminary draft of the paper, and (4) an annotated version of the preliminary draft that shows how the student thought about revising the paper. Maya Leigh's First Response is an informal paper based on questions supplied by the instructor: "How did you respond to each story? Do you like one more than the other? Is one of the women more likable than the other? Why do you think you respond the way you do? Is your response to the characters and the stories primarily intellectual, emotional, a result of authorial intention, a mix of these, or something else entirely?" (Spelling and grammatical errors in Maya's preliminary drafts have been silently corrected so as not to distract from her developing argument.)

A First Response to A Secret Sorrow *and* "*A Sorrowful Woman*"

Leigh 1

Maya Leigh

Professor Herlin

English 104

September 15, 2008

A First Response

Reading the excerpt from the Harlequin I was irritated by the seeming help-lessness of Faye; in the first chapter she is constantly on the edge of hysteria and can hardly stand up. I could do without all of the fainting, gasping, and general theatrics. I've read Harlequins before, and I usually skim through that stuff to get to the good romantic parts and the happy ending. What I like about these kinds of romance novels is the happy ending. Even though the ending is kind of clichéd with the white fence and blue skies, there is still something satisfying about having everything work out okay.

The Godwin story, of course, does not have a happy ending. It is a much more powerful story, and it is one that I could read several times, unlike the Harlequin. The Godwin woman bothers me too, because I can't really see what she has to complain about. Her husband is perfectly accom-modating and understanding. It seems that if she were unhappy with her life as a wife and mother and wanted to work or do something else, he wouldn't have a problem with it. She seems to throw away her life and hurt her family for nothing.

I enjoyed reading the Godwin story more just because it is well written and more complex, but I liked the ending of the Harlequin more. I think on an emotional level I liked the Harlequin better, and on an intellectual level I liked the Godwin story more. It is more satisfying emotionally to see a romance develop and end happily than it is to see the deterioration of a marriage and the suicide of a depressed woman. I don't really find either character particularly likable; toward the end when the Godwin woman comes out of her room and starts doing things again I begin to feel sympathy for her--I can understand her having a period of depression, but I want her to pull herself out of it, and when she doesn't, I am disappointed. Even though

Leigh 2

Faye is annoying in the beginning, because everything ends happily I am almost willing to forgive and forget my previous annoyance with her. If the Godwin woman hadn't killed herself and had returned to her family life, I would have liked her better, but because she doesn't I leave the story feeling discouraged.

Brainstorming

By listing these parallel but alternate treatments of marriage in each story, Maya begins to assemble an inventory of relevant topics related to the assignment. What becomes clear to her is that her approach will emphasize the differences in each story's portrayal of marriage.

A Sample Brainstorming List

Maya Leigh
Professor Herlin
English 104
September 17, 2008

A Brainstorm List

Marriage

Godwin	Harlequin
marriage as end of life — confining, weighty	marriage as end, goal — dreamlike, idyllic
husband — durable, receptive, understanding	husband — understanding, manly
p. 39 sight of family makes her sad and sick	p. 38 watching kids she feels that life is good + filled with love
house in winter — girl paints room white	white house in Texas under blue skies
the power of his baby spit and looking at arm p. 42	in husband's embrace no room for doubt or sorrow p. 38
family makes her sad	family makes her happy
weight pressing on her	weight lifted off her
impersonal — the husband, the child emphasis on roles	Kai, Faye, our children
dead in the end	beautiful, whole, complete in the end
crisis due to fear of always having husband and kid	crisis due to fear of never having husband and kids
feels incomplete and depressed as only wife and mother	feels incomplete and depressed not being wife and mother

Revising: First and Second Drafts

Maya's first draft of the paper pursues and develops many of the topics she noted while brainstorming. She explores in detail the differences between each story's treatment of marriage by examining each protagonist's role as wife and mother, her husband's response, the role played by her children, and the ending of each story. The second draft's annotations indicate that Maya has been able to distance herself enough from her first draft to critique its weak moments. In the annotations she recognizes, for example, that she needs a clearer thesis, some stronger transitions between paragraphs, some crisper and more detailed sentences to clarify points, and a more convincing conclusion as well as a more pointed title.

A Sample First Draft: Separate Sorrows

Maya Leigh

Professor Herlin

English 104

September 29, 2008

Separate Sorrows (Draft 1)

In both the excerpt from A Secret Sorrow and "A Sorrowful Woman," by Gail Godwin, the story is centered around ideas of marriage and family. However, marriage and family are presented in very different lights in the two stories. Karen van der Zee presents marriage with children as perfect and somewhat dream-like; it is what Faye, the heroine of A Secret Sorrow, wants, and what is necessary for her happiness. For Godwin's heroine, marriage and family are almost the antithesis of happiness; her home life seems to suffocate her and eventually leads her to commit suicide.

Both of the female protagonists in the two stories experience a crisis of sorts. In A Secret Sorrow Faye's crisis comes before marriage. She is distraught and upset because she cannot have children and fears that this will prevent her from marrying the man she loves. Both she and her beloved, Kai, have always wanted a marriage with children, and it is assumed that only under these circumstances will they truly be happy. Faye feels that her inability to have children is a fatal flaw. "Every time we see some pregnant woman, every time we're with somebody else's children I'll feel I've failed you!" (35). In "A Sorrowful Woman," however, the crisis comes after the marriage, when the woman has already procured her husband and child. Faye would be ecstatic in this woman's situation. The protagonist of the Godwin story, however, is not. Her husband and son bring her such sorrow that eventually she is unable to see them at all, and communicates only through notes stuck under her bedroom door. Faye's anxiety and fear is based on the thought of losing her man and never having children. In contrast, Godwin's character has a loving husband and child and is still filled with grief. In a Harlequin such as A Secret Sorrow, this is unimaginable; it goes against every formula of romance writing, where books always end with a wedding, and happiness after that is just assumed.

In A Secret Sorrow, marriage is portrayed as the end, as the goal of the story. It is what the heroine wants. The author works to let the reader know that only in this way will Faye be fulfilled and happy; it is what the entire story, with all the plot twists and romantic interludes, has been working toward. In "A Sorrowful Woman," marriage is the end, but is not the goal--it is quite literally the end of the woman's life. Though we don't see what her life was like before her emotional crisis, there are hints of it. When she moves into the new room she mentions seeing the streets from a whole new perspective, suggesting the previous monotony of her daily life. In addition, in the final paragraphs of the story when the character bakes pies and bread and washes and folds the laundry, her son says, "she's tired from doing all our things again," (Godwin 43) giving us an idea of what "our things" were, and what the woman did with her time before becoming ill.

In A Secret Sorrow Faye's inability to have children does not end Kai's love for her, and the two go on to get married and adopt children. Faye's married life is described in a very idyllic way--she raises her son and two daughters in a "white ranch house under the blue skies of Texas" (van der Zee 38). In other words, once she is married and has children there is no more anxiety, nothing more to fear. The author leads us to the conclusion that marriage solves all problems and is a source of unending happiness for all. This is a great difference from the Godwin tale, which takes place in the winter and maintains a sense of cold throughout the whole thing. Whenever Godwin describes the family it is not in the light, glowing terms of van der Zee, but always with a sense of weight or guilt or failure about it. The child's trusting gaze makes the protagonist begin "yelping without tears" (Godwin 39). Any sign of life or love increases her sorrow and makes her want to be rid of it. For example, when the hired girl brings her son to visit her with a grasshopper he's found--something both alive and from the outside world--she gets very upset and forces her husband to fire her. The girl is too much of an infringement on her space, and too much of a reminder of what she can no longer be.

Never is the difference between the two authors' portrayals of marriage more apparent than when both the women are viewing their families. Faye, sitting with her husband and watching her children play, felt that "life was good and filled with love" (van der Zee 38). Godwin's protagonist, on the other hand, says, "The sight of them made her so sad and sick she did not want to see them ever again" (39). When Kai, now her husband, embraces Faye, she feels that, "There was love in his embrace and love in his words and in her heart there was no room now for doubt, no room for sorrow" (van der Zee 38). When Godwin's heroine feels the loving touch of her husband's arm and the kiss of her child she cannot bear it and cuts off all direct contact with them. The situation of her marriage pushes her into a self-imposed imprisonment and lethargy. She feels unbearably sad because she can no longer be who they want and need her to be. She avoids them not because she does not love them, but rather because she loves them so much that it is too painful to see them and feel her failure.

When Faye's fears of losing Kai are assuaged, and she is happily married, it is as though a great weight has been lifted off of her. Godwin's character, on the other hand, feels her marriage as a great weight pressing in on her. The love of her husband and child weighs on her and immobilizes her. When she leaves her room for a day and leaves out freshly baked bread for her husband and son, they express their happiness in the notes they write to her that night, and "the force of the two joyful notes . . . pressed her into the corner of the little room; she had hardly space to breathe" (Godwin 43). Faye can be a traditional wife and mother, so her family is a source of joy. Godwin's character can no longer do this, and so her family is a representation of her failure, and the guilt presses her further and further into herself, until she can retreat no further and ends her life.

The endings of the two stories are powerful illustrations of the differences between them. In the end of A Secret Sorrow the author shows us Faye feeling "beautiful, complete, whole" (38) in her role as wife and mother. Godwin, on the other hand, shows us her heroine dead on her bed. Godwin first gives the reader hope, by showing all that the woman has done, and saying that "the house smelled redolently of renewal and spring" (43). This makes the blow even harder when we then discover, along with the husband and child, the woman's suicide.

Karen van der Zee creates a story full of emotional highs and lows, but one that leads up to--and ends with--marriage. After the marriage all plot twists and traumas come to a halt. Faye is brought to new life by her marriage and children; in it she finds completion of herself and total happiness. Godwin's tale, on the other hand, is full of anguish and emotion, but it all takes place after the marriage. The character she creates is stifled and killed by her marriage. There is no portrayal of unending happiness in her tale, but rather unending woe.

A Sample Second Draft: Separate Sorrows

Maya Leigh

Professor Herlin

English 104

October 3, 2008

Leigh 1

→ title works for Godwin—but does it for van der Zee?

Separate Sorrows (Draft 2))

Karen van der Zee's novel   *Gail Godwin's short story*

In both the excerpt from A Secret Sorrow and "A Sorrowful Woman," ~~by~~

plot   s

~~Gail Godwin,~~ the ~~story is~~ centered around ideas of marriage and family. How-

ever, marriage and family are presented in very different lights in the two

stories. Karen van der Zee presents marriage with children as perfect and

totally fulfilling   *protagonist*

~~somewhat dream-like;~~ it is what Faye, the ~~heroine~~ of A Secret Sorrow, wants ∕

unnamed protagonist

does she? or is she con- sumed by her role?

and what is necessary for her happiness. For Godwin's ~~heroine,~~ marriage and

family are almost the antithesis of happiness; her home life seems to suffo-

cate her and eventually leads her to commit suicide.

need a clear thesis here— is it that SS endorses marriage while SW problem- atizes it?

Both of the female protagonists in the two stories experience a crisis

~~of sorts.~~ In A Secret Sorrow Faye's crisis comes before marriage. She is dis-

traught and upset because she cannot have children and fears that this will

prevent her from marrying the man she loves. Both she and her beloved, Kai,

unclear referent

have always wanted a marriage with children, and (it) is assumed that only

under these circumstances will they truly be happy. Faye feels that her inabil-

that cuts her off from Kai's love

ity to have children is a fatal flaw. "Every time we see some pregnant woman,

every time we're with somebody else's children I'll feel I've failed you!" (35).

In "A Sorrowful Woman," however, the crisis comes after the marriage, when

secured   *Unlike who*

the woman has already ~~procured~~ her husband and child. Faye would be ec-

static in this woman's situation, ∕The protagonist of ~~the~~ Godwin's story ∕ ~~how-~~

Inexplicably,

~~ever,~~ is not. Her husband and son bring her such sorrow that eventually she is

~~ting~~

unable to see them at all, ~~and~~ communicates only through notes stuck under

her bedroom door. Faye's anxiety and fear is based on the thought of losing

her man and never having children. ~~In contrast,~~ Godwin's character has a loving husband and child ~~and is still~~ *yet she* filled with grief. ~~In a Harlequin such as~~ (in a Harlequin romance because)

~~A Secret Sorrow,~~ this ~~is~~ unimaginable ~~it goes against~~ every formula ~~of~~ *one of the most popular* — *sense of defeat would be*

romance writing~~;~~ ~~where books~~ *the plot* always end with a wedding, ~~and happiness~~ ~~after that is just assumed.~~ *with the assumption that the rest is happily ever after.*

In A Secret Sorrow, marriage is portrayed as ~~the end, as in~~ the goal. *Van der Zee*

~~It is what the heroine wants. The author~~ works to let the reader know that

only in this way will Faye be fulfilled and happy; it is what the entire story,

with all the plot twists and romantic interludes, ~~has been~~ working toward. (In)

"A Sorrowful Woman," (marriage is the end) *also* but not as in the goal--it is quite | *I like this!*

literally the end of the woman's life. Though we don't see what her life was

like before her emotional crisis, there are hints of it. When she moves into

need p. ref

the new room she mentions seeing the streets from a whole new perspective,

suggesting the previous monotony of her daily life. In addition, in the final

paragraphs of the story when the character bakes pies and bread and washes

and folds the laundry, her son says, "she's tired from doing all our things

again" (Godwin 43), giving us an idea of what "our things" were, and | *is she really ill? or just withdrawing from her life?*

the woman did with her time before becoming ill.

need transition | In A Secret Sorrow Faye's inability to have children does not end Kai's

love for her, and the two go on to get married and adopt children. Faye's mar-

ried life is described in a very idyllic way--she raises her son and two daugh-

ters in a "white ranch house under the blue skies of Texas" (van der Zee 38).

~~In other words,~~ once she is married and has children there is no more anxiety,

because the plot
~~nothing more to fear. The author~~ leads us to the conclusion that marriage

solves all problems and is a source of unending happiness ~~for all.~~ This ~~is a~~

ly
great differen~~ce~~ from ~~the~~ Godwin~~'s~~ tale, which takes place in the winter and

maintains a sense of cold ~~throughout the whole thing.~~ Whenever Godwin

that suggest
describes the family it is ~~not in~~ the ~~light, glowing~~ terms of van der Zee, but

~~always with a sense of~~ weight, or guilt, or failure ~~about it.~~ The child's trusting
gaze makes the protagonist begin "yelping without tears" (Godwin 39). *while* ~~A~~ny
sign of life or love increases her sorrow and makes her want to be rid of (it.) *unclear referent*
For example, when the hired girl brings her son to visit her with a grasshopper he's found — something both alive and from the outside world — she
gets very upset and forces her husband to fire ~~her.~~ *the girl* *Apparently,* ~~T~~he girl is too much of an
infringement on her space, and too much of a reminder of what she can no
longer be.

Never is the difference between the two authors' portrayals of marriage
more apparent than when both the women are viewing their families. Faye,
sitting with her husband and watching her children play, felt that "life was
good and filled with love" (van der Zee 38). Godwin's protagonist, on the
other hand, says, "The sight of them made her so sad and sick she did not
want to see them ever again" (39). When Kai, now her husband, embraces
Faye, she feels that, "There was love in his embrace and love in his words
and in her heart there was no room now for doubt, no room for sorrow" (van
der Zee 38). When Godwin's heroine feels the loving touch of her husband's
arm and the kiss of her child, she cannot bear it and cuts off all direct contact
with them. The situation of her marriage pushes her into a self-imposed
imprisonment and lethargy. She feels unbearably sad because she can no
longer be who they want and need her to be. She avoids them not because
she does not love them, but rather because she loves them so much that it
is too painful to see them and feel her failure.

should I use epigram here? or work into the thesis?

need → When Faye's fears of losing Kai are assuaged, and she is happily mar-
transition
ried, it is as though a great weight has been lifted off of her. Godwin's character, on the other hand, feels her marriage as a great weight pressing in on
and *~ing*
her. ~~The love of her husband and child weighs on her and~~ immobilizes her.

                                          puts
When she leaves her room for a day and ~~leaves~~ out freshly baked bread for

her husband and son, they express their happiness in the notes they write

to her that night, and "the force of the two joyful notes . . . pressed her into

the corner of the little room; she had hardly space to breathe" (Godwin 43).

        the
Faye can be a traditional wife and mother, so her family is a source

of joy. Godwin's character can no longer do this, and so her family ~~is a~~ repre-
       ⌐*s*   *own*
~~sent-ation of~~ her failure, and the guilt presses her further and further into

herself/ until she can retreat no further and ends her life.

The endings of the two stories are powerful illustrations of the differ-

ences between them. In the end of <u>A Secret Sorrow</u> the author shows us Faye

feeling "beautiful, complete, whole" (38) in her role as wife and mother.
                                 protagonist
Godwin, on the other hand, shows us her ~~heroine~~ dead on her bed. Godwin
seems to
~~first~~ gives the reader hope/ by showing all that the woman has done/ and

same
idyllic   saying that "the house smelled redolently of renewal and spring" (43). This
surround-
ings as   makes the blow even harder when we then discover, along with the husband
VDZ's   *death*
blue skies? and child, the woman's ~~suicide~~.

Karen van der Zee creates a story full of emotional highs and lows/ but

one that leads up to--and ends with--marriage. After the marriage all plot

twists and traumas come to a halt. Faye is brought to new life by her mar-
                                       fulfillment
riage and children; ~~in it~~ she finds ~~completion of herself~~ and total happiness.
                 story, however,   *confusion (?) that*
need   Godwin's ~~tale, on the other hand,~~ is full of anguish and ~~emotion, but it~~ all
some
very   takes place after the marriage. The character she creates is stifled and killed
brief
quotes   by her marriage. There is no portrayal of unending happiness in her tale, but
to make
conclusion rather unending (woe.) *is this the*
stronger?   *right word,*
                                     since she
                                     dies?

Need to add Works Cited!

Final Paper

The changes noted in Maya's annotations on her second draft are put to good use in the following final draft. By not insisting that Godwin's protagonist actually commits suicide, Maya shifts her attention away from this indeterminable death to the causes and effects of it. This shift leads her to a stronger thesis — that Godwin raises questions about the efficacy of marriage rather than endorsing it as a certain recipe for happiness the way van der Zee does. Maya also incorporates additional revisions, such as transitions (see, for example, the revision between paragraphs 3 and 4), clarifying sentences, and a fuller and more persuasive concluding paragraph.

Final Paper: Fulfillment or Failure?
Marriage in A Secret Sorrow *and "A Sorrowful Woman"*

Maya Leigh

Professor Herlin

English 104

October 10, 2008

Fulfillment or Failure?

Marriage in A Secret Sorrow and "A Sorrowful Woman"

Introduction comparing plots of both stories

Thesis contrasting treatment of marriage in both stories

Discussion of crisis in A Secret Sorrow with textual evidence

Discussion of crisis in "A Sorrowful Woman"

      In both the excerpt from Karen van der Zee's novel A Secret Sorrow and in Gail Godwin's short story "A Sorrowful Woman," the plots center around ideas of marriage and family. However, marriage and family are presented in very different lights in the two stories. Karen van der Zee presents marriage with children as perfect and totally fulfilling; it is what Faye, the protagonist of A Secret Sorrow, wants and what is necessary for her happiness. For Godwin's unnamed protagonist, marriage and family are almost the antithesis of happiness; her home life seems to suffocate her and eventually leads to her death. A Secret Sorrow directly endorses and encourages marriage, whereas "A Sorrowful Woman" indirectly questions and discourages it.

      Both of the female protagonists in the two stories experience a crisis. In A Secret Sorrow Faye's crisis comes before the marriage. She is distraught and upset because she cannot have children and fears that this will prevent her from marrying the man she loves. Both she and her beloved, Kai, desire marriage with children, and van der Zee suggests that only with these things will they truly be happy. Faye feels that her inability to have children is a fatal flaw that cuts her off from Kai's love. "Every time we see some pregnant woman, every time we're with somebody else's children I'll feel I've failed you!" (35). Faye's anxiety and fear are based on the thought of losing her man and never having children. In "A Sorrowful Woman," however, the crisis comes after the marriage, when the woman has already secured her husband and child. Unlike Faye, who would be ecstatic in this woman's situation, the protagonist of Godwin's story is not. Inexplicably, her husband and son bring her such sorrow that eventually she is unable to see them at all, communicating only through notes stuck under her bedroom door. Godwin's character has a loving husband and child, yet she is still filled with grief. This sense of defeat would be unimaginable in a Harlequin romance because it goes against one of the most popular formulas of romance writing: the plot always ends with a wedding, with the assumption that the rest is happily ever after.

> Statements contrasting crises in the plots of the two stories

In A Secret Sorrow, marriage is portrayed as the goal. Van der Zee works to let the reader know that only in this way will Faye be fulfilled and happy; it is what the entire story, with all the plot twists and romantic interludes, works toward. Marriage is also the end in "A Sorrowful Woman" but not as in the goal: it is quite literally the end of the woman's life. Though we don't see what her life was like before her emotional crisis, there are hints of it. When she moves into a new bedroom--away from her husband--she mentions seeing the streets from a whole new perspective (Godwin 42), suggesting the previous monotony of her daily life. In addition, in the final paragraphs of the story--when the character bakes pies and bread and washes and folds the laundry--her son says, "She's tired from doing all our things again" (43), giving us an idea of what "our things" were and what the woman did with her time before her crisis.

> Discussion contrasting function of marriage in both stories

> Textual evidence supporting analysis of "A Sorrowful Woman"

This monotony of marriage is absent in A Secret Sorrow. Faye's inability to have children does not end Kai's love for her, and the two go on to marry and adopt children. Faye's married life is described in a very idyllic way: she raises her son and two daughters in a "white ranch house under the blue skies of Texas" (van der Zee 38). Once she is married and has children, there is no more anxiety because the plot leads us to the conclusion that marriage solves all problems and is a source of unending happiness. This greatly differs from Godwin's tale, which takes place in winter and maintains a sense of cold. Whenever Godwin describes the family, it is in terms that suggest weight, guilt, or failure. The child's trusting gaze makes the protagonist begin "yelping without tears" (Godwin 39), and any sign of life or love increases her sorrow and makes her want to be alone. For example, when the hired girl brings her son to visit her with a grasshopper he's found

> Discussion contrasting married life and family in both stories, with textual evidence

(41)--something both alive and from the outside world--she gets very upset
and forces her husband to fire the girl. Apparently, the girl is too much of
an infringement on her space, too much of a reminder of what she can no
longer be.

Never is the difference between the two authors' portrayals of marriage
more apparent than when both women are viewing their families. Faye, sitting with her husband and watching her children play, feels that "life was
good and filled with love" (van der Zee 38). Godwin's protagonist, on the
other hand, says, "The sight of them made her so sad and sick she did not
want to see them ever again" (39). When Kai, now her husband, embraces
Faye, she feels, "There was love in his embrace and love in his words and
in her heart there was no room now for doubt, no room for sorrow" (van der
Zee 38). When Godwin's heroine feels the loving touch of her husband's arm
and the kiss of her child, she cannot bear it and cuts off all direct contact
with them. The situation of her marriage pushes her into a self-imposed imprisonment and lethargy. She feels unbearably sad because she can no longer
be who they want and need her to be. She avoids them not because she does
not love them but rather because she loves them so much that it is too painful to see them and feel her failure. The epigram to Godwin's story tells us
that "Once upon a time there was a wife and a mother one too many times"
(39). The addition of "one too many times" to this traditional story opening
forces the idea of repetition and monotony: it suggests that it is not that
state of being a wife and mother that is inherently bad but rather the fact
that that is all Godwin's character is. Day in and day out, too many times
over, the woman is just a wife and a mother, and it isn't enough for her.

In van der Zee's story there could be no such thing as too much
motherhood or too much of being a wife. When Faye's fears of losing Kai are
assuaged, and she is happily married, it is as though a great weight has been
lifted off her. Godwin's character, on the other hand, feels her marriage as a
great weight pressing on her and immobilizing her. When she leaves her room
for a day and puts out freshly baked bread for her husband and son, they
express their happiness in the notes they write to her that night, and "the
force of the two joyful notes . . . pressed her into the corner of the little

Analysis
contrasting
emotions
of protago-
nists in both
stories, with
textual
evidence

Analysis
contrasting
protagonists'
experience of
traditional
roles, with
textual
evidence

room; she had hardly space to breathe" (Godwin 43). Faye can be a traditional wife and mother, so her family is a source of joy. Godwin's character
can no longer be the traditional wife and mother, and so her family represents her own failure, and the guilt presses her further and further into herself until she can retreat no further and ends her life.

The endings of the two stories are powerful illustrations of the differences between them. In the end of A Secret Sorrow the author shows us Faye
feeling "beautiful, complete, whole" (38) in her role as wife and mother.
Godwin, on the other hand, shows us her protagonist dead on her bed. Godwin seems to give the reader hope by showing all that the woman has done
and saying that "the house smelled redolently of renewal and spring" (43).
This makes the blow even harder when we then discover, along with the
husband and child, the woman's death. The ambiguous way the death of
Godwin's unnamed protagonist is dealt with reinforces the author's negative
portrayal of marriage. It isn't explicitly written as a suicide, and Godwin
seems to encourage her readers to see it as the inevitable consequence of
her marriage.

Analysis contrasting conclusions of the two stories

Van der Zee creates a story full of emotional highs and lows, but one
that leads up to and ends with marriage. After the marriage all of the plot
twists and traumas come to a halt, replaced with peace and happiness. Faye
is brought to new life by her marriage and children; she finds fulfillment
of all of her desires in them. Godwin's story, however, is full of postmarital
anguish and confusion. The character she creates is stifled and most definitely unfulfilled by her marriage. A burst of creative energy right before
her death produces, among other things, "a sheath of marvelous watercolor
beasts accompanied by mad and fanciful stories nobody could ever make up
again, and a tablet full of love sonnets addressed to the man" (Godwin 43).
It is clear that the woman had talents and desires not met by the routine
duties of her marital life. For Faye, the protagonist of A Secret Sorrow, marriage is the happily-ever-after ending she has wanted all of her life; for
Godwin's protagonist, on the other hand, marriage is just a monotonous
and interminable ever after.

Conclusion summarizing paper's analyses

Leigh 5

Works Cited

Godwin, Gail. "A Sorrowful Woman." The Compact Bedford Introduction to
     Literature. Ed. Michael Meyer. 8th ed. Boston: Bedford/St. Martin's,
     2009. 39–43.

Van der Zee, Karen. From A Secret Sorrow. The Compact Bedford Introduction
     to Literature. Ed. Michael Meyer. 8th ed. Boston: Bedford/St. Martin's,
     2009. 31–38.

3

Plot

I put a group of characters in some sort of predicament, and then watch them try to work themselves free. My job isn't to help them work their way free, or manipulate them to safety — those are jobs which require the noisy jackhammer of plot — but to watch what happens and then write it down.

— STEPHEN KING

Never mistake motion for action.

— ERNEST HEMINGWAY

Created by a writer's imagination, a work of fiction need not be factual or historically accurate. Although actual people, places, and events may be included in fiction, facts are not as important as is the writer's use of them. We can learn much about Russian life in the early part of the nineteenth century from Leo Tolstoy's *War and Peace,* but that historical information is incidental to Tolstoy's exploration of human nature. Tolstoy, like most successful writers, makes us accept as real the world in his novel no matter how foreign it may be to our own reality. One of the ways a writer achieves this acceptance and engagement — and one of

Explore the literary element in this chapter on *LiterActive* or at bedfordstmartins.com/meyercompact.

a writer's few obligations — is to interest us in what is happening in the story. We are carried into the writer's fictional world by the plot.

Plot is the author's arrangement of incidents in a story. It is the organizing principle that controls the order of events. This structure is, in a sense, what remains after a writer deletes what is irrelevant to the story being told. We don't need to know, for example, what happens to Rip Van Winkle's faithful dog, Wolf, during his amiable master's twenty-year nap in the Catskill Mountains in order to be enchanted by Washington Irving's story of a henpecked husband. Instead, what is told takes on meaning as it is brought into focus by a skillful writer who selects and orders the events that constitute the story's plot.

Events can be presented in a variety of orders. A chronological arrangement begins with what happens first, then second, and so on, until the last incident is related. That is how "Rip Van Winkle" is told. The events in William Faulkner's "A Rose for Emily," however, are not arranged in chronological order because that would give away the story's surprise ending; instead, Faulkner moves back and forth between the past and present to provide information that leads up to the final startling moment (which won't be given away here either; the story begins on p. 90).

Some stories begin at the end and then lead up to why or how events worked out as they did. If you read the first paragraph of Ralph Ellison's "Battle Royal" (p. 243), you'll find an example of this arrangement that will make it difficult for you to stop reading. Stories can also begin in the middle of things (the Latin term for this common plot strategy is *in medias res*). In this kind of plot we enter the story on the verge of some important moment. John Updike's "A & P" (p. 560) begins with the narrator, a teenager working at a checkout counter in a supermarket, telling us: "In walks these three girls in nothing but bathing suits." Right away we are brought into the middle of a situation that will ultimately create the conflict in the story.

Another common strategy is the **flashback,** a device that informs us about events that happened before the opening scene of a work. Nearly all of Ellison's "Battle Royal" takes the form of a flashback as the narrator recounts how his identity as a black man was shaped by the circumstances that attended a high-school graduation speech he delivered twenty years earlier in a hotel ballroom before a gathering of the town's leading white citizens, most of whom were "quite tipsy." Whatever the plot arrangement, you should be aware of how the writer's conscious ordering of events affects your responses to the action.

EDGAR RICE BURROUGHS (1875–1950)

A great many stories share a standard plot pattern. The following excerpt from Edgar Rice Burroughs's novel *Tarzan of the Apes* provides a conventional plot pattern in which the **character,** an imagined person in the story, is confronted with a problem leading to a climactic struggle that is followed by a resolution of the problem. The elements of a conventional plot are easily recognizable to readers familiar with fast-paced, action-packed mysteries, spy thrillers, westerns, or adventure stories. These page-turners are carefully plotted so that the reader is swept up by the action. More serious writers sometimes use similar strategies, but they do so with greater subtlety and for some purpose that goes beyond providing a thrill a minute. The writer of serious fiction is usually less concerned with what happens next to the central character than with why it

Special collections: Rare Books, Burroughs memorial collection, University of Louisville.

happens. In Burroughs's adventure story, however, the emphasis is clearly on action. *Tarzan of the Apes* may add little or nothing to our understanding of life, but it is useful for delineating some important elements of plot. Moreover, it is great fun.

Special Collections: Rare Books, Burroughs Memorial Collection, University of Louisville.

Tarzan first appeared in the October 1912 issue of *The All-Story* magazine, a pulp serial that sold for 15 cents a copy. Instead of publishing the lengthy novel in serial segments, *All-Story* published *Tarzan of the Apes: A Romance of the Jungle* in a single issue that featured a provocative cover and exotic illustrations. The enormous popularity of the *Tarzan* issue led to the publication of the 1914 novel that spawned two dozen books, more than forty movies, hundreds of comic books and radio and television programs, and countless products, from toys to running shoes. Edgar Rice Burroughs became one of the most popular authors of the twentieth century, and Tarzan remains one of the world's best-known characters.

Burroughs's novel, published in 1914 and the first of a series of enormously popular Tarzan books and films, charts the growth to manhood of a child raised in the African jungle by great apes. Tarzan struggles to survive his primitive beginnings and to reconcile what he has learned in the jungle with his equally powerful instincts to be a civilized human being. One of the more exciting moments in Tarzan's development is his final confrontation with his old enemy, Terkoz, a huge tyrannical ape that has kidnapped Jane, a pretty nineteen-year-old from Baltimore, Maryland, who has accompanied her father on an expedition to the jungle.

In the chapter preceding this excerpt, Tarzan falls in love with Jane and writes this pointed, if not eloquent, note to her: "I am Tarzan of the Apes. I want you. I am yours. You are mine." Just as he finishes the note, he hears "the agonized screams of a woman" and rushes to their source to find Esmeralda, Jane's maid, hysterical with fear and grief. She reports that Jane, the fair and gentle embodiment of civilization in the story, has been carried off by a gorilla. Here is the first half of the next chapter, which illustrates how Burroughs plots the sequence of events so that the emphasis is on physical action.

From Tarzan of the Apes   *1914*

From the time Tarzan left the tribe of great anthropoids in which he had been raised, it was torn by continual strife and discord. Terkoz proved a cruel and capricious king, so that, one by one, many of the older and weaker apes, upon whom he was particularly prone to vent his brutish nature, took their families and sought the quiet and safety of the far interior.

But at last those who remained were driven to desperation by the continued truculence of Terkoz, and it so happened that one of them recalled the parting admonition of Tarzan:

"If you have a chief who is cruel, do not do as the other apes do, and attempt, any one of you, to pit yourself against him alone. But, instead, let two or three or four of you attack him together. Then, if you will do this, no chief will dare to be other than he should be, for four of you can kill any chief who may ever be over you."

And the ape who recalled this wise counsel repeated it to several of his fellows, so that when Terkoz returned to the tribe that day he found a warm reception awaiting him.

There were no formalities. As Terkoz reached the group, five huge, hairy 5 beasts sprang upon him.

At heart he was an arrant coward, which is the way with bullies among apes as well as among men; so he did not remain to fight and die, but tore himself away from them as quickly as he could and fled into the sheltering boughs of the forest.

Two more attempts he made to rejoin the tribe, but on each occasion he was set upon and driven away. At last he gave it up, and turned, foaming with rage and hatred, into the jungle.

For several days he wandered aimlessly, nursing his spite and looking for some weak thing on which to vent his pent anger.

It was in this state of mind that the horrible, manlike beast, swinging from tree to tree, came suddenly upon two women in the jungle.

He was right above them when he discovered them. The first intimation Jane Porter had of his presence was when the great hairy body dropped to the earth beside her, and she saw the awful face and the snarling, hideous mouth thrust within a foot of her.

One piercing scream escaped her lips as the brute hand clutched her arm. Then she was dragged toward those awful fangs which yawned at her throat. But ere they touched that fair skin another mood claimed the anthropoid.

The tribe had kept his women. He must find others to replace them. This hairless white ape would be the first of his new household, and so he threw her roughly across his broad, hairy shoulders and leaped back into the trees, bearing Jane away.

Esmeralda's scream of terror had mingled once with that of Jane, and then, as was Esmeralda's manner under stress of emergency which required presence of mind, she swooned.

But Jane did not once lose consciousness. It is true that that awful face, pressing close to hers, and the stench of the foul breath beating upon her nostrils, paralyzed her with terror; but her brain was clear, and she comprehended all that transpired.

With what seemed to her marvelous rapidity the brute bore her through the forest, but still she did not cry out or struggle. The sudden advent of the ape had confused her to such an extent that she thought now that he was bearing her toward the beach.

For this reason she conserved her energies and her voice until she could see that they had approached near enough to the camp to attract the succor she craved.

She could not have known it, but she was being borne farther and farther into the impenetrable jungle.

The scream that had brought Clayton and the two older men stumbling through the undergrowth had led Tarzan of the Apes straight to where Esmeralda lay, but it was not Esmeralda in whom his interest centered, though pausing over her he saw that she was unhurt.

For a moment he scrutinized the ground below and the trees above, until the ape that was in him by virtue of training and environment, combined with the intelligence that was his by right of birth, told his wondrous woodcraft the whole story as plainly as though he had seen the thing happen with his own eyes.

And then he was gone again into the swaying trees, following the high-flung spoor which no other human eye could have detected, much less translated.

At boughs' ends, where the anthropoid swings from one tree to another, there is most to mark the trail, but least to point the direction of the quarry; for there the pressure is downward always, toward the small end of the branch, whether the ape be leaving or entering a tree. Nearer the center of the tree, where the signs of passage are fainter, the direction is plainly marked.

Here, on this branch, a caterpillar has been crushed by the fugitive's great foot, and Tarzan knows instinctively where that same foot would touch in the next stride. Here he looks to find a tiny particle of the demolished larva, oft-times not more than a speck of moisture.

Again, a minute bit of bark has been upturned by the scraping hand, and the direction of the break indicates the direction of the passage. Or some great limb, or the stem of the tree itself has been brushed by the hairy body, and a tiny shred of hair tells him by the direction from which it is wedged beneath the bark that he is on the right trail.

Nor does he need to check his speed to catch these seemingly faint records of the fleeing beast.

To Tarzan they stand out boldly against all the myriad other scars and 25 bruises and signs upon the leafy way. But strongest of all is the scent, for Tarzan is pursuing up the wind, and his trained nostrils are as sensitive as a hound's.

There are those who believe that the lower orders are specially endowed by nature with better olfactory nerves than man, but it is merely a matter of development.

Man's survival does not hinge so greatly upon the perfection of his senses. His power to reason has relieved them of many of their duties, and so they have, to some extent, atrophied, as have the muscles which move the ears and scalp, merely from disuse.

The muscles are there, about the ears and beneath the scalp, and so are the nerves which transmit sensations to the brain, but they are underdeveloped because they are not needed.

Not so with Tarzan of the Apes. From early infancy his survival had depended upon acuteness of eyesight, hearing, smell, touch, and taste far more than upon the more slowly developed organ of reason.

The least developed of all in Tarzan was the sense of taste, for he could eat 30 luscious fruits, or raw flesh, long buried, with almost equal appreciation; but in that he differed but slightly from more civilized epicures.

Almost silently the ape-man sped on in the track of Terkoz and his prey, but the sound of his approach reached the ears of the fleeing beast and spurred it on to greater speed.

Three miles were covered before Tarzan overtook them, and then Terkoz, seeing that further flight was futile, dropped to the ground in a small open glade, that he might turn and fight for his prize or be free to escape unhampered if he saw that the pursuer was more than a match for him.

He still grasped Jane in one great arm as Tarzan bounded like a leopard into the arena which nature had provided for this primeval-like battle.

When Terkoz saw that it was Tarzan who pursued him, he jumped to the conclusion that this was Tarzan's woman, since they were of the same kind—white and hairless—and so he rejoiced at this opportunity for double revenge upon his hated enemy.

To Jane the strange apparition of this godlike man was as wine to sick 35 nerves.

From the description which Clayton and her father and Mr. Philander had given her, she knew that it must be the same wonderful creature who had saved them, and she saw in him only a protector and a friend.

But as Terkoz pushed her roughly aside to meet Tarzan's charge, and she saw the great proportions of the ape and the mighty muscles and the fierce fangs, her heart quailed. How could any vanquish such a mighty antagonist?

Like two charging bulls they came together, and like two wolves sought each other's throat. Against the long canines of the ape was pitted the thin blade of the man's knife.

Jane — her lithe, young form flattened against the trunk of a great tree, her hands tight pressed against her rising and falling bosom, and her eyes wide with mingled horror, fascination, fear, and admiration — watched the primordial ape battle with the primeval man for possession of a woman — for her.

As the great muscles of the man's back and shoulders knotted beneath the   40 tension of his efforts, and the huge biceps and forearm held at bay those mighty tusks, the veil of centuries of civilization and culture were swept from the blurred vision of the Baltimore girl.

When the long knife drank deep a dozen times of Terkoz's heart's blood, and the great carcass rolled lifeless upon the ground, it was a primeval woman who sprang forward with outstretched arms toward the primeval man who had fought for her and won.

And Tarzan?

He did what no red-blooded man needs lessons in doing. He took his woman in his arms and smothered her upturned, panting lips with kisses.

For a moment Jane lay there with half-closed eyes. For a moment — the first in her young life — she knew the meaning of love.

But as suddenly as the veil had been withdrawn it dropped again, and an   45 outraged conscience suffused her face with its scarlet mantle, and a mortified woman thrust Tarzan of the Apes from her and buried her face in her hands.

Tarzan had been surprised when he had found the girl he had learned to love after a vague and abstract manner a willing prisoner in his arms. Now he was surprised that she repulsed him.

He came close to her once more and took hold of her arm. She turned upon him like a tigress, striking his great breast with her tiny hands.

Tarzan could not understand it.

A moment ago, and it had been his intention to hasten Jane back to her people, but that little moment was lost now in the dim and distant past of things which were but can never be again, and with it the good intention had gone to join the impossible.

Since then Tarzan of the Apes had felt a warm, lithe form close pressed to   50 his. Hot, sweet breath against his cheek and mouth had fanned a new flame to life within his breast, and perfect lips had clung to his in burning kisses that had seared a deep brand into his soul — a brand which marked a new Tarzan.

Again he laid his hand upon her arm. Again she repulsed him. And then Tarzan of the Apes did just what his first ancestor would have done.

He took his woman in his arms and carried her into the jungle.

This episode begins with **exposition,** the background information the reader needs to make sense of the situation in which the characters are placed. The first eight paragraphs let us know that Terkoz has been overthrown as leader of the ape tribe and that he is roaming the jungle "looking for some weak thing on which to vent his pent anger." This exposition is in the form of a flashback. (Recall that the previous chapter ended with Esmeralda's report of the kidnapping; now we will see what happened.)

Once this information supplies a context for the characters, the plot gains momentum with the ***rising action,*** a complication that intensifies the situation: Terkoz, looking for a victim, discovers the vulnerable Esmeralda and Jane. His first impulse is to kill Jane, but his "mood" changes when he remembers that he has no woman of his own after having been forced to leave the tribe (more exposition). Hence, there is a further complication in the rising action when he decides to carry her off. Just when it seems that the situation could not get any worse, it does. The reader is invited to shudder even more than if Terkoz had made a meal of Jane because she may have to endure the "awful face," "foul breath," and lust of this beast.

At this point we are brought up to the action that ended the preceding chapter. Tarzan races to the rescue by unerringly following the trail from the place where Jane was kidnapped. He relentlessly tracks Terkoz. Unfortunately, Burroughs slows down the pursuit here by including several paragraphs that abstractly consider the evolutionary development of human reliance on reason more than on their senses for survival. This discussion offers a rationale for Tarzan's remarkable ability to track Jane, but it is an interruption in the chase.

When Tarzan finally catches up to Terkoz, the ***conflict*** of this episode fully emerges. Tarzan must save the woman he loves by defeating his longstanding enemy. For Terkoz seeks to achieve a "double revenge" by killing Tarzan and taking his woman. Terkoz's assumption that Jane is Tarzan's woman is a ***foreshadowing,*** a suggestion of what is yet to come. In this conflict Tarzan is the ***protagonist*** or ***hero,*** the central character who engages our interest and empathy. *Protagonist* is often a more useful term than *hero* or ***heroine,*** however, because the central character of a story can be despicable as well as heroic. In Edgar Allan Poe's "The Tell-Tale Heart," for example, the central character is a madman and murderer. Terkoz is the ***antagonist,*** the force that opposes the protagonist.

The battle between Tarzan and Terkoz creates ***suspense*** because the reader is made anxious about what is going to happen. Burroughs makes certain that the reader will worry about the outcome by having Jane wonder, "How could any vanquish such a mighty antagonist?" If we are caught up in the moment, we watch the battle, as Jane does, with "mingled horror, fascination, fear, and admiration" to see what will happen next. The moment of greatest emotional tension, the ***climax,*** occurs when Tarzan kills Terkoz. Tarzan's victory is the ***resolution*** of the conflict, also known as the ***denouement*** (a French word meaning the "untying of the knot"). This could have been the conclusion to the episode except that Jane and Tarzan simultaneously discover their "primeval" selves sexually drawn to each other. Burroughs resolves one conflict — the battle with Terkoz — but then immediately creates another — by raising the question of what a respectable professor's daughter from Baltimore is doing in the sweaty arms of a panting, half-naked man.

For a brief moment the cycle of conflict, suspense, and resolution begins again as Jane passionately kisses Tarzan; then her "outraged conscience" causes her to regain her sense of propriety and she pushes him away. Although Tarzan succeeds in the encounter with Terkoz, he is not successful with Jane. However, Burroughs creates suspense for a third time at the very end of the episode, when the "new Tarzan," having been transformed by this sexual awakening, "took his woman in his arms and carried her into the jungle." What will he do next? Despite the novel's implausibility (beginning with the premise that apes could raise a human child) and its heavy use of coincidences (not the least of which is Tarzan's donning a loincloth for the first time only four pages before he meets Jane), the story is difficult to put down. The plot swings us swiftly and smoothly from incident to incident, even if there is an occasional interruption, such as Burroughs's discussion of evolution, in the flow of the action.

Although this pattern of exposition, rising action, conflict, suspense, climax, and resolution provides a useful outline of many plots that emphasize physical action, a greater value of this pattern is that it helps us to see how innovative artists move beyond formula fiction by manipulating and changing the pattern for their own purposes. At the furthest extreme are those modern storytellers who reject traditional plotting techniques in favor of experimental approaches. Instead of including characters who wrestle with conflicts, experimental fiction frequently may concern the writer's own efforts to create a story. Rather than ordering experience, such writers disrupt it by insisting that meanings in fiction are as elusive — or nonexistent — as meanings in life; they are likely to reject both traditional values and traditional forms of writing. Most writers, however, use conflicts in their plots to reveal characters and convey meanings. The nature of those conflicts can help determine how important physical action is to the plot.

The primary conflict that Tarzan experiences in his battle with Terkoz is external. External conflict is popular in adventure stories because the protagonist's physical struggles with a formidable foe or the ever-present dangers of a dense jungle echoing wild screams provide plenty of excitement. External conflicts may place the protagonist in opposition to another individual, nature, or society. Tarzan's battle with societal values begins the moment he instinctively takes Jane in his arms to carry her off into the jungle. He will learn that an individual's conflict with society can be as frustrating as it is complex, which is why so many plots in serious fiction focus on this conflict. It can be seen, to cite only two examples, in a mysterious stranger's alienation from a materialistic culture in Herman Melville's "Bartleby, the Scrivener" (p. 124) and in a young black man's struggle with racism in Ellison's "Battle Royal" (p. 243).

Conflict may also be internal; in such a case some moral or psychological issue must be resolved within the protagonist. Inner conflicts frequently accompany external ones, as in Godwin's "A Sorrowful Woman" (p. 39). Godwin's story is quiet and almost uneventful compared with *Tarzan of the Apes*. The conflict, though puzzling, is more significant in "A Sorrowful Woman" because that story subtly explores some troubling issues that cannot be resolved simply by "huge biceps" or a "lithe, young form." The protagonist struggles with both internal and external forces. We are not told why she withdraws from her considerate husband and beautiful son. There is no exposition to explain why she is hopelessly "sad and sick" of them. There is no readily identifiable antagonist in her way, but there are several possibilities. Her antagonist is some part of herself that cannot find satisfaction in playing the roles of wife and mother, yet her husband and child also seem to bear some of the responsibility, as does the domestic environment that defines her.

Godwin creates questions for the reader rather than suspense. We are compelled to keep asking why the protagonist in her story is so unhappy instead of what is going to happen next. The story ends with her flurry of domestic activity and her death, but we do not feel as if we have come to a resolution. "A Sorrowful Woman" will not let us go because we keep coming back to what causes the protagonist's rejection of her role. Has she gone mad? Are the husband and child not what they seem to be? Is her domestic life stifling rather than nourishing? Does her family destroy rather than support her? Who or what is to blame? No one is able to rescue the sorrowful woman from her conflict, nor does the design of Godwin's plot relieve the reader of the questions the story raises. The meaning of the action is not self-evident as it is in *Tarzan of the Apes*. It must be drawn from a careful reading of the interrelated details and dialogues that constitute this story's action.

Although Burroughs makes enormous demands on Tarzan to survive the perils of the jungle, the author makes few demands on the reader. In part, that's why *Tarzan of the Apes* is so much fun: we sit back while Tarzan does all the work, struggling heroically through all the conflicts Burroughs has planted along his jungle paths. Godwin's story, in contrast, illustrates that there are other kinds of plots, less dependent on action but equally full of conflict. This kind of reading is more demanding, but ultimately more satisfying, because as we confront conflicts in serious fiction we read not only absorbing stories but also ourselves. We are invited not to escape life but to look long and hard at it. Although serious fiction can be as diverting and pleasurable as most standard action-packed plots, serious fiction offers an additional important element: a perspective on experience that reflects rather than deflects life.

The following three stories — Ha Jin's "Love in the Air," William Faulkner's "A Rose for Emily," and Andre Dubus's "Killings" — are remarkable for the different kinds of tension produced in each by a subtle use of plot.

HA JIN (B. 1956)

Born and educated in China, where he studied English and American literature, Ha Jin traveled to the United States in the mid-1980s to study at Brandeis University, earning a Ph.D. in 1993. After the repression that followed the Tiananmen Square massacre, Jin remained in the United States writing in English, because, as he has commented, "it would be impossible to write honestly in China." His fiction reflects upon life in contemporary China as well as its traditions and the complexities produced by its communist politics. Among his literary honors

© Michael Romanos.

are the PEN/Faulkner Award and the National Book Award. His works include a novella, *In the Pond* (1998), two novels, *Waiting* (1999) and *War Trash* (2004), and two collections of short stories, *Under the Red Flag* (1997) and *Ocean of Words* (1996). The plot of "Love in the Air" is not filled with action, but it is as electric as the telegraph signals that connect the main character to a young woman he's never met.

Love in the Air   1996

After the political study, Chief Jiang turned on both the transmitter and the receiver and started searching for the station of the Regional Headquarters. Half a minute later a resonant signal emerged calling the Fifth Regiment. Kang Wandou, who had served for two years, could tell it was an experienced hand at the opposite end. The dots and dashes were clean and concrete; the pace was fast and steady.

"He's very good," Shi Wei said.

"Of course, Shenyang always has the best hands," Chief Jiang said, returning the call. This was their first direct communication with the Headquarters of Shenyang Military Region. In no time the two stations got in touch. Jiang telegraphed that from now on they would keep twenty-four-hour coverage.

"Understood. So long," Shenyang replied.

"So long," Jiang tapped. He turned off the transmitter, but left the receiver 5 on. "Shun Min, it's your turn now. Little Kang will take over in the evening."

"All right." Shun moved his chair close to the machine.

Though the middle-aged chief called him Little Kang, to the other soldiers Kang was Big Kang. His whole person was marked by abnormal largeness except for his voice, which was small and soft. Whenever he spoke, he sounded as though he was mumbling to himself. If his neck were not so long, his comrades would have believed he had suffered from the "big-joint" disease in his childhood. His wrists were thick, and his square thumbs always embarrassed him. But everybody was impressed by the beautiful long lashes above his froggy eyes.

After dinner Kang replaced Shun. The evening shift was not busy. Since all news stations broadcast at dusk and there was too much noise in the air, few telegrams were dispatched or received during these hours. Kang's task was to answer Shenyang's call every hour, and for the rest of the time he had to attend to the receiver in case an emergency arose. Having nothing else to do, he opened the fanlight and watched the night. Gray streaks of clouds were floating rapidly beneath the crescent moon and the glimmering stars. In the air there was a mysterious humming, which seemed to come from the constellations. Except for the swarms of lights in Hutou Town, it was dark everywhere. Even the silhouette of those mountains in Russia had disappeared.

Cold wind kept gushing into the office, Kang closed the fanlight and sat back on the chair. Again, nothing could be seen through the window, on whose frosty panes stretched miniature bushes, hills, caves, coral reefs. He picked up a pencil, turned over a telegram pad, and began drawing pictures. He drew a horse, a cow, a dog, a pig, a rooster, a lamb, a donkey, and a hen leading a flock of chicks.

After taps at nine, the quiet grew intolerable. If only he could have some- 10 thing interesting to do. In one of the drawers there was a volume of Chairman Mao's selected works and a copy of Lenin's *What Is to Be Done!*, which Chief Jiang would browse through at night, but these books were too profound for Kang. He missed the picture stories he had read when he was a boy. Those children's books could no longer be found anywhere, because they had been burned at the beginning of the Cultural Revolution. Kang took out his tobacco pouch and rolled a cigarette. Smoking was the only way to prevent himself from dozing off. Then he stretched his legs, rested his feet on the table, and leaned against the back of the chair as if lounging on a sofa. Soon the small office turned foggy.

Shenyang began to call at ten sharp. Kang turned on the transmitter and was ready to reply. It was another radio operator at the other end now. The signal was fluctuating at a much faster speed, approximately 130 numerals a minute. Because of the noise, the dots and the dashes didn't sound very clear, though they were distinguishable.

"Please answer," it ended.

Immediately Kang started to call back. His large hand held the button of the sending key and pounded out the letters one after another. He was a slow hand and could tap only eighty numerals a minute. But his fingers and thumb were powerful—whenever he telegraphed, the key with its heavy steel base would move about on the table. Holding the base with his left hand, he was repeating the reply signal in a resolute manner. His thick wrist was moving up and down while a little red light was flashing nervously at the top of the transmitter.

The operator at the opposite end did not hear Kang and resumed calling. Now there was less noise in the air and the signal became distinct. The call sign, composed of eight letters, was repeated again and again, it formed a crisp tune, flowing around and around. Kang pricked up his ears. This must be the chief of the station. He had never met such an excellent hand. There were automatic machines that could produce 180 numerals a minute clearly, but those dead instruments always sounded monotonous. They didn't have a character.

The more you listened to them at night, the more likely you would fall asleep. But this fellow was one of those "machine defeaters."

"Please answer," the other side asked again.

Once more Kang went about calling back. Affected by the dexterous hand at the other end, he tried hard to speed up. The chair under his hips creaked while he was struggling with the bakelite key button, which turned slippery in his sweating hand.

Unfortunately this was a bad night. The other side simply could not find him. It called him time and again; Kang replied continually, but they could not get in touch. Forty minutes passed to no avail. By now, the other operator had become impatient. The melodious signal gradually lost its rhythm and flowed so rapidly that the letters were almost indistinguishable. It sounded like raindrops pattering on metal tiles. Patient as he was, Kang began to worry.

Around eleven, the telephone suddenly rang. Kang picked up the receiver and said, "Hello."

"Hello," a tingling female voice said. "This is the Military Region Station. Wake up, comrade. Have you heard me on the machine?"

"Ye-yes." Kang paused with surprise, his heart kicking and his throat tightening. Who could imagine a woman would call you on the border at night? "I-I've heard you," he managed to say. "I ne-never dozed off. I've been calling you all the time."

"Sorry, don't take it to heart. I was teasing you. Shall we switch to the second set of frequencies?" She sounded so pleasant.

"All righ-t." His tongue seemed not his own.

"Bye-bye now, meet you on the machine."

"Bye."

She hung up. Kang was dazed, still holding the receiver.

The sweet voice went on echoing in his ears, "Sorry, don't take it to heart. . . ."

The call sign appeared again. This time it repossessed its elegance and fluency, but to Kang every dot and dash was different now, as though they were tender, meaningful words the young woman sent to him alone.

"Switch frequency please," she ended.

Kang jerked his head and rushed to look for her on the new frequency. Without much effort, he found her again. His body grew tense as he became engrossed in the sways and ripples of the heavenly melody. How wonderful to work with a woman at night. If only she could call him like this for an hour. But she stopped and asked, "Please answer."

Kang's hand began to tremble. It settled on the sending key like a small turtle, shaking out every letter brokenly. He cursed his hand, "Come on, you coward! This is not a battle yet." He wiped his wet forehead with a telegram sheet.

What a pity. She heard him in less than a minute and replied promptly: "No business. Meet you at twelve o'clock. So long."

"So long." Kang had to agree, because it was a rule that an operator must never transmit an unnecessary dot or dash. The longer you stayed on the air, the easier it was for the Russians to locate your position.

Kang felt at a loss. He raised his head to look at the clock on the wall — eleven-ten, so he would meet her in fifty minutes. His imagination began to take wing. What was her name? How stupid he was, having forgotten to ask her. How old was she? She sounded so young and must have been around twenty. A good person, no doubt; that pleasant voice was full of good nature. What did she look like? Was she beautiful? Well educated? Intelligent? That voice told everything—all the best a woman could have. But what did she look like exactly? Tall and slim, with large black eyes? Of course he could not find out much about her through only one meeting. It had to take time. He believed that eventually he would get to know her well, because from now on they would meet every night.

The clock moved slowly, as though intending to avoid an ominous ending. Kang kept watching it and longed to arrive at the midnight rendezvous in the twinkling of an eye.

Suddenly somebody knocked at the door. Chief Jiang came in. "You can go to bed now, Kang. I happened to wake up a few minutes earlier tonight." He yawned. 35

Kang stood up and didn't know what to say. He tried to smile, but the effort distorted his face.

"What happened?" the chief asked. "You look as awake as a lynx."

"Nothing, everything is fine." Kang picked up his fur hat, with enormous dismay he slouched out. He forgot to take an apple, which was his night snack.

How could he sleep? Every inch of his skin was affected by a caressing tingle he had never experienced before. At the other side of the room, Shun was snoring and Shi murmured something in his dream.

I was teasing you. . . ." The voice spoke to Kang again and again. He shut his eyes tight, he shook his head many times in order to get rid of her and go to sleep, but it was no use. She was so close to him, as if sitting right beside his bed in the dark, whispering and smiling. 40

Little by little, he gave up and allowed her to play whatever tricks she wanted to. The most unbearable mystery was what she looked like. He tried to think of all the women he knew, but he could not recall a pretty one. Surely he had aunts and cousins, surely he remembered some girls who had hoed the cornfields and cut millet together with him, but none of them differed much from his male relatives or from the men in his home village. Every one worked like a beast of burden, and none could speak without swearing.

The prettiest women he had ever seen were those female characters in the movie copies of the Revolutionary Model Plays, but most of them were too old, well beyond forty. How about the girl raped by the landlord in *The White-Haired Girl*? Yes, she was a wonderful ballerina, slim and good-looking. How deft her toes were. They capered around as if never touching the ground. She could swing her legs up well beyond her head. And the slender waist, which was full of rebellious spirit. What a wonderful body she had! But did she have a wonderful voice? No one could tell, because she kept quiet in the ballet.

No, she wouldn't do. He would not accept a woman who might lack that charming voice. Besides, that actress had long white hair like an old crone's. She must have been weird, or her hair wouldn't be so silvery.

How about the revolutionary's daughter in *The Story of the Red Lamp*? Well, that was a good one. But did she not seem too young? She was seventeen, old enough to be somebody's wife. A marriageable girl indeed. What he liked most about her was that long glossy braid, which reached her buttocks. But she was too thin and must have been too feeble to work. Her aquiline nose was narrow, that was not a sign of good fortune. Even worse, her voice was sharp. It was all right for singing Peking Opera to a large audience, but who dared to quarrel with a girl like that? In real life, she must have been a "small hot pepper." No, he had to look for another woman.

Now he had it—the female gymnastic athlete he had seen in a documen- 45 tary film. She performed on the uneven bars. Her body was so supple and powerful that she could stretch, fly, and even somersault in the air. No doubt, that was a healthy energetic woman, not a bourgeois young lady who would fall in a gust of wind. What did she look like? He had not seen her face clearly in the film and could not tell. Then this woman had to go too, at least for the time being.

The radiator pipes started clinking and whistling gently. The boiler room pumped steam at four. With dawn approaching, Kang was worried and tried to force himself to sleep. But that voice would not leave him alone. "Wake up, comrade. Have you heard me on the machine? . . ." It sounded even more pleasant and more intimate. You fool, he cursed himself. How stupid you are— bewitched by an unknown voice! Forget it and get some sleep.

Soon he entered another world. He married a young woman who was also a telegrapher. They worked together at the post office in his hometown. They lived in a small house surrounded by a stone wall that had a gate with iron bars. Their garden was filled with vegetables and fruits. The beans were as broad as sickles, and the peaches as fat as babies' faces. Poultry were everywhere, three dozen chickens, twenty ducks, and eight geese. Who was his bride? He didn't know, for he only saw her back, a tall, sturdy young woman with a thick braid.

At breakfast he felt giddy. He could not tell if he had slept at all. Neither was he sure whether the prosperous domestic scene was his dream or his fantasy. How absurd the whole thing was. He had never loved a woman before, but all of a sudden he'd fallen in love with a voice. His first love was an unknown voice. He was scared, because he could not determine whether it was real love or merely a delusion from mental illness. Did people feel this way when they were in love? He felt sick and beside himself. How long would it take for him to grow used to this thing or get over it?

He could not sleep that morning when he was supposed to have a good rest to make up for the previous night and prepare himself for the evening shift. That voice, mixed with the call sign, whispered in his ears constantly. Time and again, he forced himself to think of something else, but he could not summon up anything interesting. He dared not smoke, for fear that Chief Jiang, who slept in the same room, would know he had remained awake for the whole morning.

In the afternoon, during the study of Chairman Mao's "Combat Lib- 50 eralism," Kang was restless, longing for the arrival of the evening. The words grew blurred before his eyes. When he was asked to read out a page, he managed to accomplish the task with a whistling in his nose. His comrades looked at him strangely. When he finished, Shun said, "Kang, you must have a bad cold."

"Yes, it's a bad one." Kang blew his nose with a piece of newspaper. He was both miserable and hopeful. Probably the more he worked with her, the better he would feel. Everything was difficult in the beginning; the end of suffering was happiness. At the moment he must be patient; a few hours later, he would be in a different world.

How ruthless Heaven was. She did not show up in the evening. It was a different operator at the other end. Kang spent the six hours racking his brains about what kind of schedule she had. The following three evenings passed in the same fruitless way. Kang was baffled. Every night he could not help thinking of that mysterious woman — all women — for several hours. In the daytime he was very quiet. Although pining away, he dared not talk to anyone about it. How shameful it would be — to have it known that you were enchanted by a woman about whom you didn't know anything. How silly he was! That woman must have forgotten him like used water. No, she had never bothered about knowing him. How could she, a pretty young woman in the big city and perhaps surrounded by many smart officers in the headquarters, be interested in a soldier like him, who was so dull, so homely, and so rustic? He knew he was the toad that dreamed of eating a swan, but he couldn't help himself.

On Saturday morning, Kang was roused from his catnap by Shi Wei. "Big Kang, come and help your younger brother."

"What's up?"

"Too many telegrams this morning. I've been copying for three hours and   55
can't handle it anymore."

"All right, I'm coming." It was almost eleven o'clock anyway. Kang got up and wiped his face with a wet towel.

There she was! He had hardly entered the office when Kang froze stock-still. The pleasant signal, for which he had been yearning for days, was singing proudly as though to a large audience. The dots and dashes sounded like amorous messages inviting him to decode their secret meanings. How magnificent her telegraphic style was in broad daylight. Kang lost himself in an imaginary melody composed of both the electric signal and the tingling voice — "Hello, this is the Military Region Station. Wake up, comrade. Have you heard me on the machine? . . ."

"What's the matter with you?" Shi rapped him on the shoulder.

"Oh nothing," Kang muttered, moving to the desk. "Never met such a good hand."

"True, he has gold fingers."   60

There was no time to tell Shi that it was she, not he, because the receiver was announcing: "Please ready."

Kang started writing down the numerals rapidly. In the beginning it went well, but soon his attention began to wander. He was distracted by his desire to appreciate the rhythm and the personal touch in the sounds, and he had to drop some numerals now and then. More awful, that voice jumped in to trouble him — "Sorry, don't take it to heart. I was teasing you. . . ."

"Repeat?" she asked, having finished the short telegram.

"Yes, noise," Kang pounded nervously. "Group eight in line four, from group three to eight in line six . . ."

Meanwhile, Shi Wei watched him closely. He was surprised to find Kang, a   65
better transcriber than himself, unable to jot down the telegram sent out so clearly. There was no noise at all, why did he tap "noise" as an excuse? Kang was

aware of Shi's observing and was sweating all over. He rushed to bring the receiving operation to an end.

"Are you all right?" Shi asked, after Kang signed his name on the telegram. "I don't know." He felt sick. He got up and hurried out of the office.

Another fruitless evening and another sleepless night. Kang could no longer contain himself. On Sunday evening, he revealed the truth to Shi and Shun, who happened to be in the office.

"Shi Wei, you know, the Shenyang operator with 'gold fingers' is a woman, not a man." He had planned to say a lot, to make a story, but he was bewildered, finding that he completed the project in just one sentence. He blushed to the ears with a strange emotion.

"Really?" Shi asked loudly. "No kidding? Why didn't you tell me earlier, Brother Kang?"

Kang smiled. Shun was not sure who they were talking about. Which one?" 70

"The best one," Shi said with a thrill in his voice. "I can't believe it. A girl can telegraph so well. Tell me, Big Kang, how did you get to know her?"

"She called me, because she couldn't hear me," he declared proudly.

"What's her name?" Shi asked.

"I have no idea. Wish I knew."

"Must be a good girl. I'll go to Shenyang and get her." 75

"Come on, don't brag," Shun said. "I want to see how you can get her."

"You wait and see."

Kang was shocked that Shi was also interested in her. He regretted telling them the truth. If Shi made a move, Kang would have to give ground. Shi was an excellent basketball player and had in his wallet the pictures of a half dozen young women, who he claimed were all his girlfriends. In addition, his father was a divisional commissar in the navy; Shi had grown up in big cities and knew the world. Most important of all, he spent money like water. How could Kang compete against such a smart, handsome fellow?

It was this new development that made him fidgety that evening. He paced up and down in the office, chain-smoking for two hours. Finally, he decided to investigate who she was. He picked up the telephone and called the Shenyang Military Region. It took half an hour for the call to get through.

"Hello, this is Shenyang, can I help you?" an operator asked sleepily. 80

"Ye-yes," he struggled to say. "I want to speak to—to the wireless station, the one that communicates with Hutou?"

"What's 'Hutou'? A unit's code name?"

"No, it's a county."

"Oh, I see. Please tell me the number of the station you want to speak to."

"I don't know the number." 85

"I can't help you then. We have hundreds of stations, and they are in different cities and mountains. You have to tell me the number. Find the number first, then call back. All right?"

"Uh, all right."

"Bye-bye now."

"Bye."

It was so easy to run into a dead end. All the clever questions, which he had 90 prepared to ask the radio operator on duty about that woman, had vanished from his mind. How foolish he was—having never thought there could be more than ten stations in the Regional Headquarters. What was to be done now? Without an address, he could not write to her; even with an address, he didn't know how to compose a love letter. Why was Heaven so merciless? It seemed that the only way to meet her was through the air, but he had not figured out her capricious schedule yet.

It did not make much difference after they rotated the shifts. Now Kang worked afternoons. No matter how exhausted he was when he went to bed at night, he would lie awake for a few hours thinking of one woman after another. His dreams ran wilder. Every night the pillow, which contained his underclothes, moved from beneath his head, little by little, into his arms. He was tormented by endless questions. What was it like to kiss and touch a woman? Did women also have hair on their bodies? Was he a normal man? And could he satisfy a woman? Was he not a neurotic, drenched in sweat and burning away like this in the dark? Could he have children with a woman?

Whenever he woke up from his broken sleep that mysterious voice would greet him, "Wake up, comrade. Have you heard me on the machine? . . ." The sounds grew deeper and deeper into him, as though they were sent out by his own internal organs. During these frantic nights, he discovered that Chief Jiang had to rouse Shi Wei at least three times every night. Shi worked the small hours.

Kang's skull felt numb in the daytime. He was convinced that he was a lunatic. How panicked he was when receiving a telegram, because that melodious signal and that tender voice, again and again, intruded themselves into his brain and forced him to pause in the middle of the transcribing. How good it would be to have peace once more. But peace of mind seemed remote, as though it belonged only to a time that he had outgrown and could never return to. Even the exercises in the mornings became a torture. He used to be able to write down 160 numerals per minute with ease, but now he had to struggle with 110. When they sat together reading documents and newspapers, his comrades often waved their hands before his eyes to test if he could see anything. Somebody would say, "Big Kang, why do you look like you lost your soul?" Another, "What do you see in your trance? A goddess?"

On these occasions Kang would let out a sigh. He dared not tell anybody about the ridiculous "affair." He was afraid that he would be criticized for having contracted bourgeois liberalism or become a laughingstock.

One morning during the exercises, the telegraphic instructor, Han Jie, 95 looked at Kang's transcription and said under his breath, "No wonder the Confidential Office complained."

Suddenly it dawned on Kang that he had become a nuisance in the Wireless Platoon. A pang seized his heart. No doubt, the confidential officers in the Regimental Headquarters were dissatisfied with his work and had reported him to the company's leaders. It was this stupid "affair" that had reduced him to such a state. He had to find a way to stop it—forget that woman and her bewitching voice—otherwise how could he survive? Although in his heart he knew he had to get rid of her, he didn't know how. Neither did he want to try.

On Thursday evening two weeks later, Chief Jiang held an urgent meeting at the station. Nobody knew what it was about. Kang was scared because he thought it might be about him. The secret would come out sooner or later. Had he babbled it during his sleep at night? He regretted drawing three pictures of women on the back of a telegram pad. Chief Jiang must have seen them. What should he say if the chief questioned him about those drawings?

The meeting had nothing to do with him. When Jiang asked Shi Wei to confess what he had done in the small hours, Kang at last felt relaxed. But like Shun, he was baffled about what had happened. Shi protested that he had not done anything wrong.

"You're dishonest, Comrade Shi Wei," the chief said.

"No, no Chief Jiang." Shi looked worried. "I did all the work well." 100

"You know our Party's policy: Leniency to those who confess, severity to those who refuse. It's up to yourself."

"Why?" Shi seemed puzzled. "This policy applies only to the class enemies. I'm your comrade, am I not?"

"Stop pretending you're innocent. Tell us the truth."

"No, I really didn't do anything wrong."

"All right, let me tell you what happened." The chief's voice grew sharper. 105 "You were caught by the monitoring station. You thought you were smart. If you didn't want us to know, you shouldn't have done it in the first place. Look at the report yourself." He tossed the internal bulletin to Shi and handed Shun and Kang each a copy.

The title read: "Radio Operators Proffered Love in the Air." Kang's heart tightened. He turned a page and read "From February 3 on, from 1:00 A.M. to 5:00 A.M., a radio operator in the Fifth regiment and an operator at the 36th station of Shenyang Military Region have developed a love affair in the air. . . ."

Kang was stunned, and his thick lips parted. He could never imagine Shi would make such an unlawful move. A small part of their love talk was transcribed in the report:

> I am Shi Wei. Your name?
> Lili. Where are you from?
> Dalian. And you?
> Beijing.
> Your age?
> Twenty-one. And you?
> Twenty-two. Love your hand.
> Why?
> It is good.
> Why? Not love me?
> Yes, I do.
> !
> Love me?
> Maybe.
> . . . . . .

Kang wanted to cry, but he controlled himself. He saw Shi's face turn pale and sweat break out on his smooth forehead. Meanwhile Shun bit his lower lip, trying hard not to laugh.

"Now, what do you want to say?" Jiang asked.

Shi lowered his eyes and remained silent. The chief announced that the Communication Company had decided to suspend Shi Wei from his work during the wait for the final punishment. From now on, Shi had to go to the study room during the day and write out his confession and self-criticism.

Though he was working two more hours a day to cover for Shi, Kang no longer 110 expected to meet Lili, whose family name was not revealed in the bulletin.

Obviously she was also suspended from her work and must have been doing the same thing as Shi did every day in the company's study room. But the tune created by her fingers and her charming voice were still with him; actually they hurt him more than before. He tried cursing her and imagining all the bad things that could be attributed to a woman in order to pull her out of himself. He thought of her as "broken shoe" which was worn by everyone, a bitch that raised her tail to any male dog, a hag who was shunned by all decent men, a White Bone Demon living on innocent blood. Still, he could not get rid of her. Whenever he was receiving a telegram, her voice would break in to catch him. "Sorry, don't take it to heart. I was teasing you. . . ." It was miserable. The misery went so deep that when he spoke to his comrades he often heard himself moaning. He hated his own listless voice.

Shi's punishment was administered a week later. Both Shi Wei and Wang Lili were expelled from the army. This time the woman's full name was given. To Kang's surprise, Shi did not cry and seemed to take it with ease. He ate well and slept well, and went on smoking expensive cigarettes. Kang figured there must have been two reasons why Shi did not care. First, with the help of his father, he would have no problem finding a good job at home; second, the expulsion gave him an opportunity to continue his love affair with Wang Lili, since they were now two grasshoppers tied together by one thread. Lucky for Shi, he didn't lose his military status for nothing. It seemed he would go to Shenyang soon and have a happy time with her.

The station planned to hold a farewell party for Shi Wei. Though it was not an honorable discharge, they had worked with Shi for almost a year and had some good feelings about him. For days Kang had been thinking what souvenir he should give Shi Wei. He finally chose a pair of pillow towels, which cost him four *yuan*, half his monthly pay. In the meantime his scalp remained numb, and he still could not come to himself. Not only did the task of receiving a telegram frighten him, but any telegraphic signal would give him the creeps. He had developed another habit—cursing himself relentlessly for his daydreaming and for having allowed himself to degenerate into a walking corpse for that fickle woman, whose name he would now murmur many times every night.

Four older soldiers from the Wireless Platoon were invited to the farewell party. Chief Jiang presented an album to Shi, and Shun gave him a pair of nylon socks. When Kang's pillow towels were displayed, everybody burst out laughing, for on each towel was embroidered a pair of lovely mandarin ducks and a line of red characters. One said: "Happy Life," and the other: "Sweet Dreams." Peanut shells and pearstones fell on the floor because of the commotion the garish towels caused.

"You must be joking, Big Kang," Shi said, measuring one of the towels against his chest. "You think I'm going home to get married?"

"Why not?" Kang smiled. "Won't you go to Shenyang?"

"For what? I don't know anyone there."

Kang stood up. The floor seemed to be swaying beneath his feet. Tears welled up in his eyes. He picked up a mug and gulped the beer inside, his left hand holding the corner of the desk. He put down the mug, then turned to the door.

"Where are you going?" Chief Jiang asked.

Without replying, Kang went out into the open air. He wanted to bolt into the snow and run for hours, until his legs could no longer support him. But he paused. On the drill ground, a dozen soldiers from the Line Construction Platoon were practicing climbing telephone poles without wearing spikes. Behind the brick houses stood the thirty-meter-tall aerial, made of three poles connected to one another, which had been raised for their station by these fellow men. In the northeast, the Wusuli River displayed a series of green, steaming holes along its snow-covered course. On the fields and the slopes of the hills, a curtain of golden sparks, cast by the setting sun, was glittering. The gray forests stretched along the undulating mountain ridges toward the receding horizon. The sky was so high and the land so vast. Kang took a deep breath; a fresh contraction lingered in his chest. For the first time he felt a person was so small.

That evening he wrote a letter to the company's Party branch, imploring   120 the leaders to transfer him to the Line Construction Platoon. He did not give an explicit reason, and merely said that somehow his mind was deteriorating and that he could not operate the telegraphic apparatus anymore. The letter ended as follows:

> If I can no longer serve the Revolutionary Cause and our Motherland with my brain, I can at least work with my hands, which are still young and strong. Please relieve me from the Wireless Platoon.

After writing the letter, he wept, filling his hands with tears. He used to believe that when he was demobilized he could make a decent living by working as a telegrapher at a post office or a train station, but now he had ruined his future. How painful it was to love and then give it up. If only he could forget that woman's voice and her telegraphic style. Whether he could or not, he had to try.

CONSIDERATIONS FOR CRITICAL THINKING AND WRITING

1. **FIRST RESPONSE.** How credible to you is Kang's falling so completely "in love with a voice"? To what extent does your response to this question affect your understanding and enjoyment of the story?

2. Kang is portrayed as "so dull, so homely, and so rustic" (para. 52), and yet he is a compelling character. What is there about him that makes him interesting to a reader? Alternatively, explain why you don't find him interesting.

3. What does Kang's taste in women reveal about his character?

4. How does the exposition concerning life during the Chinese Cultural Revolution provide a context for understanding Kang's values and personality?

5. Locate some moments in the plot when the author creates suspense. Where is the plot's climax?

6. Explain what you think is the story's central conflict. Is it resolved?

7. Discuss the appropriateness of the title. Is there more than one way to interpret it?

CONNECTION TO ANOTHER SELECTION

1. Write an essay that compares and contrasts "Love in the Air" with David Updike's "Summer" (p. 304). How are imagination and desire central to both stories?

WILLIAM FAULKNER (1897–1962)

Born into an old Mississippi family that had lost its influence and wealth during the Civil War, William Faulkner lived nearly all his life in the South writing about Yoknapatawpha County, an imagined Mississippi county similar to his home in Oxford. Among his novels based on this fictional location are *The Sound and the Fury* (1929), *As I Lay Dying* (1930), *Light in August* (1932), and *Absalom, Absalom!* (1936). Although his writings are regional in their emphasis on local social history, his concerns are broader. In his 1950 acceptance speech for the Nobel Prize in Literature, he insisted that the "problems of the human heart in conflict with itself . . . alone can make good writing because only that is worth writing about, worth the agony and the sweat." This commitment is evident in his novels and in *The Collected Stories of William Faulkner* (1950). "A Rose for Emily," about the mysterious life of Emily Grierson, presents a personal conflict rooted in her southern identity. It also contains a grim surprise.

Explore contexts for William Faulkner on *LiterActive*.

A Rose for Emily   1931

I

When Miss Emily Grierson died, our whole town went to her funeral: the men through a sort of respectful affection for a fallen monument, the women mostly out of curiosity to see the inside of her house, which no one save an old manservant—a combined gardener and cook—had seen in at least ten years.

It was a big, squarish frame house that had once been white, decorated with cupolas and spires and scrolled balconies in the heavily lightsome style of the seventies, set on what had once been our most select street. But garages and cotton gins had encroached and obliterated even the august names of that neighborhood; only Miss Emily's house was left, lifting its stubborn and coquettish decay above the cotton wagons and the gasoline pumps—an eyesore among eyesores. And now Miss Emily had gone to join the representatives of those august names where they lay in the cedar-bemused cemetery among the ranked and anonymous graves of Union and Confederate soldiers who fell at the battle of Jefferson.

Alive, Miss Emily had been a tradition, a duty, and a care; a sort of hereditary obligation upon the town, dating from that day in 1894 when Colonel Sartoris, the mayor—he who fathered the edict that no Negro woman should appear on the streets without an apron—remitted her taxes, the dispensation dating from the death of her father on into perpetuity. Not that Miss Emily would have accepted charity. Colonel Sartoris invented an involved tale to the effect that Miss Emily's father had loaned money to the town, which the town, as a matter of business, preferred this way of repaying. Only a man of Colonel Sartoris' generation and thought could have invented it, and only a woman could have believed it.

When the next generation, with its more modern ideas, became mayors and aldermen, this arrangement created some little dissatisfaction. On the first of the year they mailed her a tax notice. February came, and there was no reply. They wrote her a formal letter, asking her to call at the sheriff's office at her convenience. A week later the mayor wrote her himself, offering to call or to send his car for her, and received in reply a note on paper of an archaic shape, in a thin, flowing calligraphy in faded ink, to the effect that she no longer went out at all. The tax notice was also enclosed, without comment.

They called a special meeting of the Board of Aldermen. A deputation 5 waited upon her, knocked at the door through which no visitor had passed since she ceased giving china-painting lessons eight or ten years earlier. They were admitted by the old Negro into a dim hall from which a stairway mounted into still more shadow. It smelled of dust and disuse — a close, dank smell. The Negro led them into the parlor. It was furnished in heavy, leather-covered furniture. When the Negro opened the blinds of one window, they could see that the leather was cracked; and when they sat down, a faint dust rose sluggishly about their thighs, spinning with slow motes in the single sun-ray. On a tarnished gilt easel before the fireplace stood a crayon portrait of Miss Emily's father.

They rose when she entered — a small, fat woman in black, with a thin gold chain descending to her waist and vanishing into her belt, leaning on an ebony cane with a tarnished gold head. Her skeleton was small and spare; perhaps that was why what would have been merely plumpness in another was obesity in her. She looked bloated, like a body long submerged in motionless water, and of that pallid hue. Her eyes, lost in the fatty ridges of her face, looked like two small pieces of coal pressed into a lump of dough as they moved from one face to another while the visitors stated their errand.

She did not ask them to sit. She just stood in the door and listened quietly until the spokesman came to a stumbling halt. Then they could hear the invisible watch ticking at the end of the gold chain.

Her voice was dry and cold. "I have no taxes in Jefferson. Colonel Sartoris explained it to me. Perhaps one of you can gain access to the city records and satisfy yourselves."

"But we have. We are the city authorities, Miss Emily. Didn't you get a notice from the sheriff, signed by him?"

"I received a paper, yes," Miss Emily said. "Perhaps he considers himself 10 the sheriff . . . I have no taxes in Jefferson."

"But there is nothing on the books to show that, you see. We must go by the—"

"See Colonel Sartoris. I have no taxes in Jefferson."

"But, Miss Emily—"

"See Colonel Sartoris." (Colonel Sartoris had been dead almost ten years.) "I have no taxes in Jefferson. Tobe!" The Negro appeared. "Show these gentlemen out."

II

So she vanquished them, horse and foot, just as she had vanquished their 15 fathers thirty years before about the smell. That was two years after her father's death and a short time after her sweetheart — the one we believed would marry her — had deserted her. After her father's death she went out very little; after her sweetheart went away, people hardly saw her at all. A few of the ladies had the temerity to call, but were not received, and the only sign of life about the place was the Negro man — a young man then — going in and out with a market basket.

"Just as if a man — any man — could keep a kitchen properly," the ladies said; so they were not surprised when the smell developed. It was another link between the gross, teeming world and the high and mighty Griersons.

A neighbor, a woman, complained to the mayor, Judge Stevens, eighty years old.

"But what will you have me do about it, madam?" he said.

"Why, send her word to stop it," the woman said. "Isn't there a law?"

"I'm sure that won't be necessary," Judge Stevens said. "It's probably just a 20 snake or a rat that nigger of hers killed in the yard. I'll speak to him about it."

The next day he received two more complaints, one from a man who came in diffident deprecation. "We really must do something about it, Judge. I'd be the last one in the world to bother Miss Emily, but we've got to do something." That night the Board of Aldermen met — three graybeards and one younger man, a member of the rising generation.

"It's simple enough," he said. "Send her word to have her place cleaned up. Give her a certain time to do it in, and if she don't . . ."

"Dammit, sir," Judge Stevens said, "will you accuse a lady to her face of smelling bad?"

So the next night, after midnight, four men crossed Miss Emily's lawn and slunk about the house like burglars, sniffing along the base of the brickwork and at the cellar openings while one of them performed a regular sowing motion with his hand out of a sack slung from his shoulder. They broke open the cellar door and sprinkled lime there, and in all the outbuildings. As they recrossed the lawn, a window that had been dark was lighted and Miss Emily sat in it, the light behind her, and her upright torso motionless as that of an idol. They crept quietly across the lawn and into the shadow of the locusts that lined the street. After a week or two the smell went away.

That was when people had begun to feel really sorry for her. People in our 25 town, remembering how old lady Wyatt, her great-aunt, had gone completely crazy at last, believed that the Griersons held themselves a little too high for what they really were. None of the young men were quite good enough for Miss Emily and such. We had long thought of them as a tableau, Miss Emily a slender figure in white in the background, her father a spraddled silhouette in the foreground, his back to her and clutching a horsewhip, the two of them framed by the back-flung front door. So when she got to be thirty and was still single, we were not pleased exactly, but vindicated; even with insanity in the family she wouldn't have turned down all of her chances if they had really materialized.

When her father died, it got about that the house was all that was left to her; and in a way, people were glad. At last they could pity Miss Emily. Being left alone, and a pauper, she had become humanized. Now she too would know the old thrill and the old despair of a penny more or less.

The day after his death all the ladies prepared to call at the house and offer condolence and aid, as is our custom. Miss Emily met them at the door, dressed as usual and with no trace of grief on her face. She told them that her father was not dead. She did that for three days, with the ministers calling on her, and the doctors, trying to persuade her to let them dispose of the body. Just as they were about to resort to law and force, she broke down, and they buried her father quickly.

We did not say she was crazy then. We believed she had to do that. We remembered all the young men her father had driven away, and we knew that with nothing left, she would have to cling to that which had robbed her, as people will.

III

She was sick for a long time. When we saw her again, her hair was cut short, making her look like a girl, with a vague resemblance to those angels in colored church windows — sort of tragic and serene.

The town had just let the contracts for paving the sidewalks, and in the 30 summer after her father's death they began the work. The construction company came with niggers and mules and machinery, and a foreman named Homer Barron, a Yankee — a big, dark, ready man, with a big voice and eyes lighter than his face. The little boys would follow in groups to hear him cuss the niggers, and the niggers singing in time to the rise and fall of picks. Pretty soon he knew everybody in town. Whenever you heard a lot of laughing anywhere about the square, Homer Barron would be in the center of the group. Presently we began to see him and Miss Emily on Sunday afternoons driving in the yellow-wheeled buggy and the matched team of bays from the livery stable.

At first we were glad that Miss Emily would have an interest, because the ladies all said, "Of course a Grierson would not think seriously of a Northerner, a day laborer." But there were still others, older people, who said that even grief could not cause a real lady to forget *noblesse oblige*° — without calling it *noblesse oblige*. They just said, "Poor Emily. Her kinsfolk should come to her." She had some kin in Alabama; but years ago her father had fallen out with them over the estate of old lady Wyatt, the crazy woman, and there was no communication between the two families. They had not even been represented at the funeral.

And as soon as the old people said, "Poor Emily," the whispering began. "Do you suppose it's really so?" they said to one another. "Of course it is. What else could . . ." This behind their hands; rustling of craned silk and satin behind jalousies closed upon the sun of Sunday afternoon as the thin, swift clop-clop-clop of the matched team passed: "Poor Emily."

She carried her head high enough — even when we believed that she was fallen. It was as if she demanded more than ever the recognition of her dignity as the last Grierson; as if it had wanted that touch of earthiness to reaffirm her

---

noblesse oblige: The obligation of people of high social position.

imperviousness. Like when she bought the rat poison, the arsenic. That was over a year after they had begun to say "Poor Emily," and while the two female cousins were visiting her.

"I want some poison," she said to the druggist. She was over thirty then, still a slight woman, though thinner than usual, with cold, haughty black eyes in a face the flesh of which was strained across the temples and about the eye-sockets as you imagine a lighthouse-keeper's face ought to look. "I want some poison," she said.

"Yes, Miss Emily. What kind? For rats and such? I'd recom —"   35

"I want the best you have. I don't care what kind."

The druggist named several. "They'll kill anything up to an elephant. But what you want is —"

"Arsenic," Miss Emily said. "Is that a good one?"

"Is . . . arsenic? Yes, ma'am. But what you want —"

"I want arsenic."   40

The druggist looked down at her. She looked back at him, erect, her face like a strained flag. "Why, of course," the druggist said. "If that's what you want. But the law requires you to tell what you are going to use it for."

Miss Emily just stared at him, her head tilted back in order to look him eye for eye, until he looked away and went and got the arsenic and wrapped it up. The Negro delivery boy brought her the package; the druggist didn't come back. When she opened the package at home there was written on the box, under the skull and bones: "For rats."

IV

So the next day we all said, "She will kill herself"; and we said it would be the best thing. When she had first begun to be seen with Homer Barron, we had said, "She will marry him." Then we said, "She will persuade him yet," because Homer himself had remarked — he liked men, and it was known that he drank with the younger men in the Elks' Club — that he was not a marrying man. Later we said, "Poor Emily" behind the jalousies as they passed on Sunday afternoon in the glittering buggy, Miss Emily with her head high and Homer Barron with his hat cocked and a cigar in his teeth, reins and whip in a yellow glove.

Then some of the ladies began to say that it was a disgrace to the town and a bad example to the young people. The men did not want to interfere, but at last the ladies forced the Baptist minister — Miss Emily's people were Episco-pal — to call upon her. He would never divulge what happened during that interview, but he refused to go back again. The next Sunday they again drove about the streets, and the following day the minister's wife wrote to Miss Emily's relations in Alabama.

So she had blood-kin under her roof again and we sat back to watch devel-   45
opments. At first nothing happened. Then we were sure that they were to be married. We learned that Miss Emily had been to the jeweler's and ordered a man's toilet set in silver, with the letters H. B. on each piece. Two days later we learned that she had bought a complete outfit of men's clothing, including a nightshirt, and we said, "They are married." We were really glad. We were glad because the two female cousins were even more Grierson than Miss Emily had ever been.

So we were not surprised when Homer Barron — the streets had been finished some time since — was gone. We were a little disappointed that there was not a public blowing-off, but we believed that he had gone on to prepare for Miss Emily's coming, or to give her a chance to get rid of the cousins. (By that time it was a cabal, and we were all Miss Emily's allies to help circumvent the cousins.) Sure enough, after another week they departed. And, as we had expected all along, within three days Homer Barron was back in town. A neighbor saw the Negro man admit him at the kitchen door at dusk one evening.

And that was the last we saw of Homer Barron. And of Miss Emily for some time. The Negro man went in and out with the market basket, but the front door remained closed. Now and then we would see her at a window for a moment, as the men did that night when they sprinkled the lime, but for almost six months she did not appear on the streets. Then we knew that this was to be expected too; as if that quality of her father which had thwarted her woman's life so many times had been too virulent and too furious to die.

When we next saw Miss Emily, she had grown fat and her hair was turning gray. During the next few years it grew grayer and grayer until it attained an even pepper-and-salt iron-gray, when it ceased turning. Up to the day of her death at seventy-four it was still that vigorous iron-gray, like the hair of an active man.

From that time on her front door remained closed, save for a period of six or seven years, when she was about forty, during which she gave lessons in china-painting. She fitted up a studio in one of the downstairs rooms, where the daughters and granddaughters of Colonel Sartoris' contemporaries were sent to her with the same regularity and in the same spirit that they were sent to church on Sundays with a twenty-five-cent piece for the collection plate. Meanwhile her taxes had been remitted.

Then the newer generation became the backbone and the spirit of the 50 town, and the painting pupils grew up and fell away and did not send their children to her with boxes of color and tedious brushes and pictures cut from the ladies' magazines. The front door closed upon the last one and remained closed for good. When the town got free postal delivery, Miss Emily alone refused to let them fasten the metal numbers above her door and attach a mailbox to it. She would not listen to them.

Daily, monthly, yearly we watched the Negro grow grayer and more stooped, going in and out with the market basket. Each December we sent her a tax notice, which would be returned by the post office a week later, unclaimed. Now and then we would see her in one of the downstairs windows — she had evidently shut up the top floor of the house — like the carven torso of an idol in a niche, looking or not looking at us, we could never tell which. Thus she passed from generation to generation — dear, inescapable, impervious, tranquil, and perverse.

And so she died. Fell ill in the house filled with dust and shadows, with only a doddering Negro man to wait on her. We did not even know she was sick; we had long since given up trying to get information from the Negro. He talked to no one, probably not even to her, for his voice had grown harsh and rusty, as if from disuse.

She died in one of the downstairs rooms, in a heavy walnut bed with a curtain, her gray head propped on a pillow yellow and moldy with age and lack of sunlight.

V

The Negro met the first of the ladies at the front door and let them in, with their hushed, sibilant voices and their quick, curious glances, and then he disappeared. He walked right through the house and out the back and was not seen again.

The two female cousins came at once. They held the funeral on the second 55 day, with the town coming to look at Miss Emily beneath a mass of bought flowers, with the crayon face of her father musing profoundly above the bier and the ladies sibilant and macabre; and the very old men — some in their brushed Confederate uniforms — on the porch and the lawn, talking of Miss Emily as if she had been a contemporary of theirs, believing that they had danced with her and courted her perhaps, confusing time with its mathematical progression, as the old do, to whom all the past is not a diminishing road but, instead, a huge meadow which no winter ever quite touches, divided from them now by the narrow bottle-neck of the most recent decade of years.

Already we knew that there was one room in that region above stairs which no one had seen in forty years, and which would have to be forced. They waited until Miss Emily was decently in the ground before they opened it.

The violence of breaking down the door seemed to fill this room with pervading dust. A thin, acrid pall as of the tomb seemed to lie everywhere upon this room decked and furnished as for a bridal: upon the valance curtains of faded rose color, upon the rose-shaded lights, upon the dressing table, upon the delicate array of crystal and the man's toilet things backed with tarnished silver, silver so tarnished that the monogram was obscured. Among them lay a collar and tie, as if they had just been removed, which, lifted, left upon the surface a pale crescent in the dust. Upon a chair hung the suit, carefully folded; beneath it the two mute shoes and the discarded socks.

The man himself lay in the bed.

For a long while we just stood there, looking down at the profound and fleshless grin. The body had apparently once lain in the attitude of an embrace, but now the long sleep that outlasts love, that conquers even the grimace of love, had cuckolded him. What was left of him, rotted beneath what was left of the nightshirt, had become inextricable from the bed in which he lay; and upon him and upon the pillow beside him lay that even coating of the patient and biding dust.

Then we noticed that in the second pillow was the indentation of a head. 60 One of us lifted something from it, and leaning forward, that faint and invisible dust dry and acrid in the nostrils, we saw a long strand of iron-gray hair.

CONSIDERATIONS FOR CRITICAL THINKING AND WRITING

1. **FIRST RESPONSE.** How might this story be rewritten as a piece of formula fiction? You could write it as a romance, detective, or horror story — whatever strikes your fancy. Does Faulkner's version have elements of formulaic fiction?

2. What is the effect of the final paragraph of the story? How does it contribute to your understanding of Emily? Why is it important that we get this information last rather than at the beginning of the story?

3. What details foreshadow the conclusion of the story? Did you anticipate the ending?

4. Contrast the order of events as they happen in the story with the order in which they are told. How does this plotting create interest and suspense?

5. Faulkner uses a number of gothic elements in this plot: the imposing decrepit house, the decayed corpse, and the mysterious secret horrors connected with Emily's life. How do these elements forward the plot and establish the atmosphere?

6. How does the information provided by the exposition indicate the nature of the conflict in the story? What does Emily's southern heritage contribute to the story?

7. Who or what is the antagonist of the story? Why is it significant that Homer Barron is a construction foreman and a northerner?

8. In what sense does the narrator's telling of the story serve as "A Rose for Emily"? Why do you think the narrator uses *we* rather than *I*?

9. Explain how Emily's reasons for murdering Homer are related to her personal history and to the ways she handled previous conflicts.

10. Discuss how Faulkner's treatment of the North and the South contributes to the meaning of the story.

11. Provide an alternative title and explain how the emphasis in your title is reflected in the story.

CONNECTIONS TO OTHER SELECTIONS

1. Contrast Faulkner's ordering of events with Tim O'Brien's "How to Tell a True War Story" (p. 543). How does each author's arrangement of incidents create different effects on the reader?

2. To what extent do concepts of honor and tradition influence the action in "A Rose for Emily" and "How to Tell a True War Story"?

Perspective

WILLIAM FAULKNER (1897–1962)

On "A Rose for Emily"   *1959*

Q. What is the meaning of the title "A Rose for Emily"?

A. Oh, it's simply the poor woman had had no life at all. Her father had kept her more or less locked up and then she had a lover who was about to quit her, she had to murder him. It was just "A Rose for Emily" — that's all.

Q. . . . What ever inspired you to write this story?

A. That to me was another sad and tragic manifestation of man's condition in which he dreams and hopes, in which he is in conflict with himself or with his environment or with others. In this case there was the young girl with a young girl's normal aspirations to find love and then a husband and a family, who was brow-beaten and kept down by her father, a selfish man who didn't want her to leave home because he wanted a housekeeper, and it was a natural instinct of — repressed which — you can't repress it — you can mash it down but it comes up somewhere else and very likely in a tragic form, and that was simply another manifestation of man's injustice to man, of the poor tragic human being struggling with its own heart, with others, with its environment, for the simple things which all human beings want. In that case it was a young girl that just wanted to be loved and to love and to have a husband and a family.

Q. And that purely came from your imagination?

A. Well, the story did but the condition is there. It exists. I didn't invent that condition, I didn't invent the fact that young girls dream of someone to love and children and a home, but the story of what her own particular tragedy was invented, yes. . . .

Q. Sir, it has been argued that "A Rose for Emily" is a criticism of the North, and others have argued saying that it is a criticism of the South. Now, could this story, shall we say, be more properly classified as a criticism of the times?

A. Now that I don't know, because I was simply trying to write about people. The writer uses environment—what he knows—and if there's a symbolism in which the lover represented the North and the woman who murdered him represents the South, I don't say that's not valid and not there, but it was no intention of the writer to say, Now let's see, I'm going to write a piece in which I will use a symbolism for the North and another symbol for the South, that he was simply writing about people, a story which he thought was tragic and true, because it came out of the human heart, the human aspiration, the human—the conflict of conscience with glands, with the Old Adam. It was a conflict not between North and the South so much as between, well you might say, God and Satan.

Q. Sir, just a little more on that thing. You say it's a conflict between God and Satan. Well, I don't quite understand what you mean. Who is—did one represent the—

A. The conflict was in Miss Emily, that she knew that you do not murder people. She had been trained that you do not take a lover. You marry, you don't take a lover. She had broken all the laws of her tradition, her background, and she had finally broken the law of God too, which says you do not take human life. And she knew she was doing wrong, and that's why her own life was wrecked. Instead of murdering one lover, and then to go and take another and when she used him up to murder him, she was expiating her crime.

Q. Was the "Rose for Emily" an idea or a character? Just how did you go about it?

A. That came from a picture of the strand of hair on the pillow. It was a ghost story. Simply a picture of a strand of hair on the pillow in the abandoned house.

From Faulkner in the University, edited by
Frederick Gwynn and Joseph Blotner

Considerations for Critical Thinking and Writing

1. Discuss whether you think Faulkner's explanation of the conflict between "God and Satan" limits or expands the meaning of the story for you.

2. In what sense is "A Rose for Emily" a ghost story?

3. Compare Faulkner's account of how he conceived "A Rose for Emily" with Flannery O'Connor's description of "Good Country People" in the Perspective on page 378. To what extent are their attitudes about symbolism similar?

A SAMPLE CLOSE READING

An Annotated Section of William Faulkner's "A Rose for Emily"

Even as you read a story for the first time, you can highlight passages, circle or underline words, and write responses in the margins. Subsequent readings will yield more insights once you begin to understand how various elements such as plot, character, and wording build toward the conclusion and what you perceive to be the story's central ideas. The following annotations for the first six paragraphs of "A Rose for Emily" provide a perspective written by someone who had read the work several times.

WILLIAM FAULKNER (1897–1962)

From *A Rose for Emily*   *1931*

> The title suggests that the story is an expression of affection and mourning, as well as a tribute, for Emily — despite her bizarre behavior.

I

When Miss Emily Grierson died, our whole town went to her funeral: the men through a sort of respectful affection for a fallen monument, the women mostly out of curiosity to see the inside of her house, which no one save an old man-servant — a combined gardener and cook — had seen in at least ten years.

> The story begins (and ends) with death, and "the fallen monument" signals Emily's special meaning to the narrator and the community.

It was a big, squarish frame house that had once been white, decorated with cupolas and spires and scrolled balconies in the heavily lightsome style of the seventies, set on what had once been our most select street. But garages and cotton gins had encroached and obliterated even the august names of that neighborhood; only Miss Emily's house was left, lifting its stubborn and coquettish decay above the cotton wagons and the gasoline pumps — an eyesore among eyesores. And now Miss Emily had gone to join the representatives of those august names where they lay in the cedar-bemused cemetery among the ranked and anonymous graves of Union and Confederate soldiers who fell at the battle of Jefferson.

> The importance of the decayed old South setting is emphasized by being detailed even before Emily is described. The Civil War between the North and South is implicitly linked to the garages and gas pumps (the modern) that overtake the old southern neighborhood and hint at a lingering conflict.

Alive, Miss Emily had been a tradition, a duty, and a care; a sort of hereditary obligation upon the town, dating from that day in 1894 when Colonel Sartoris, the mayor — he who fathered the edict that no Negro woman should appear on the streets without an apron — remitted her taxes, the dispensation dating from the death of her father on into perpetuity. Not that Miss Emily would have accepted charity. Colonel Sartoris invented an involved tale to the effect that Miss Emily's father had loaned money to the town, which the

> Emily is associated with southern tradition, duty, and privilege that require protection. This helps explain why the townspeople attend her funeral.

More Help with Close Reading

Close readings of Kate Chopin's "The Story of an Hour," Nathaniel Hawthorne's "Young Goodman Brown," and Jamaica Kincaid's "Girl" are available on *LiterActive* and at the book's companion site. Each story is annotated with critical interpretations and explanations of the literary elements at work.

town, as a matter of business, preferred this way of repaying. Only a man of Colonel Sartoris' generation and thought could have invented it, and only a woman could have believed it.

When the next generation, with its more modern ideas, became mayors and aldermen, this arrangement created some little dissatisfaction. On the first of the year they mailed her a tax notice. February came, and there was no reply. They wrote her a formal letter, asking her to call at the sheriff's office at her convenience. A week later the mayor wrote her himself, offering to call or to send his car for her, and received in reply a note on paper of an archaic shape, in a thin, flowing calligraphy in faded ink, to the effect that she no longer went out at all. The tax notice was also enclosed, without comment.

They called a special meeting of the Board of Aldermen. A deputation waited upon her, knocked at the door through which no visitor had passed since she ceased giving chinapainting lessons eight or ten years earlier. They were admitted by the old Negro into a dim hall from which a stairway mounted into still more shadow. It smelled of dust and disuse—a close, dank smell. The Negro led them into the parlor. It was furnished in heavy, leather-covered furniture. When the Negro opened the blinds of one window, they could see that the leather was cracked; and when they sat down, a faint dust rose sluggishly about their thighs, spinning with slow motes in the single sun-ray. On a tarnished gilt easel before the fireplace stood a crayon portrait of Miss Emily's father.

5

Like Emily, her "archaic," "thin," and "faded" note resists change and "modern ideas." She dismisses any attempts by the town to assess her for taxes or for anything else. She won't even leave the house.

The description of the "dank" house smelling of "dust and disuse" reinforces Emily's connection with the past and her refusal to let go of it. As the men sit down, "a faint dust rose" around them. The passage of time is alluded to in each of these paragraphs and ultimately emerges as a kind of antagonist.

A SAMPLE STUDENT RESPONSE

Josiah Parker

Professor Altschuler

English 200-A

December 12, 2008

Conflict in the Plot of William Faulkner's "A Rose for Emily"

The conflict of William Faulkner's "A Rose for Emily" is the driving force of the story's plot. However, the conflict is not the act of murder, nor is it Miss Emily's bizarre, reclusive lifestyle. The conflict is located instead in Miss Emily's background, her history. She is portrayed as a hardened, bitter old woman, but we soon realize she herself is a victim. She has been oppressed her entire life by her domineering father, unable to take a suitor and marry, which is what she desires most. This lifelong oppression becomes the central conflict, and is what drives Miss Emily, causing her "to cling to that which had robbed her" (Faulkner, "Rose" 93).

After her father's death, Miss Emily immediately takes a lover, then poisons him when he tries to leave her. Both actions are what Faulkner himself claims "had broken all the laws of her tradition" (Faulkner, "On 'A Rose'" 98). She has been taught her whole life not to take a lover, certainly not to take a life. Her willingness to go against what she has always known to be moral and right creates dramatic tension and advances the story. In this way, the act of murder is nothing more than a portion of the plot, an "incident in the story," rather than the conflict itself (Meyer 70). . . .

Parker 5

Works Cited

Faulkner, William. "A Rose for Emily." In The Compact Bedford Introduction to Literature. Ed. Michael Meyer. 8th ed. Boston: Bedford/St. Martin's, 2009. 90–96.

------. "On 'A Rose for Emily.'" The Compact Bedford Introduction to Literature. Ed. Michael Meyer. 8th ed. Boston: Bedford/St. Martin's, 2009. 97–98.

Meyer, Michael, ed. The Compact Bedford Introduction to Literature. 8th ed. Boston: Bedford/St. Martin's, 2009. 70.

ANDRE DUBUS (1936–1999)

© Marion Ettlinger.

Though a native of Louisiana, where he attended the Christian Brothers School and McNeese State College, Andre Dubus lived much of his life in Massachusetts; many of his stories are set in the Merrimack Valley north of Boston. After college Dubus served as an officer for five years in the Marine Corps. He then took an MFA at the University of Iowa in 1966 and began teaching at Bradford College in Massachusetts. His fiction earned him numerous awards, and he was both a Guggenheim and a MacArthur Fellow. Among his collections of fiction are *Separate Flights* (1975); *Adultery and Other Choices* (1977); *Finding a Girl in America* (1980), from which "Killings" is taken; *The Last Worthless Evening* (1986); *Collected Stories* (1988); and *Dancing after Hours* (1996). In 1991 he published *Broken Vessels,* a collection of autobiographical essays. His stories are often tense with violence, anger, tenderness, and guilt; they are populated by characters who struggle to understand and survive their experiences, painful with failure and the weight of imperfect relationships. In "Killings," the basis for a 2001 film titled *In the Bedroom,* Dubus offers a powerful blend of intimate domestic life and shocking violence.

Killings

1979

On the August morning when Matt Fowler buried his youngest son, Frank, who had lived for twenty-one years, eight months, and four days, Matt's older son, Steve, turned to him as the family left the grave and walked between their friends, and said: "I should kill him." He was twenty-eight, his brown hair starting to thin in front where he used to have a cowlick. He bit his lower lip, wiped his eyes, then said it again. Ruth's arm, linked with Matt's, tightened; he looked at her. Beneath her eyes there was swelling from the three days she had suffered. At the limousine Matt stopped and looked back at the grave, the casket, and the Congregationalist minister who he thought had probably had a difficult job with the eulogy though he hadn't seemed to, and the old funeral director who was saying something to the six young pallbearers. The grave was on a hill and overlooked the Merrimack, which he could not see from where he stood; he looked at the opposite bank, at the apple orchard with its symmetrically planted trees going up a hill.

Next day Steve drove with his wife back to Baltimore where he managed the branch office of a bank, and Cathleen, the middle child, drove with her husband back to Syracuse. They had left the grandchildren with friends. A month after the funeral Matt played poker at Willis Trottier's because Ruth, who knew this was the second time he had been invited, told him to go, he couldn't sit home with her for the rest of her life, she was all right. After the game Willis went outside to tell everyone good night and, when the others had driven away, he walked with Matt to his car. Willis was a short, silver-haired man who had opened a diner after World War II, his trade then mostly very early breakfast, which he cooked, and then lunch for the men who worked at the leather and shoe factories. He now owned a large restaurant.

"He walks the Goddamn streets," Matt said.

"I know. He was in my place last night, at the bar. With a girl."

"I don't see him. I'm in the store all the time. Ruth sees him. She sees him   5
too much. She was at Sunnyhurst today getting cigarettes and aspirin, and there he was. She can't even go out for cigarettes and aspirin. It's killing her."

"Come back in for a drink."

Matt looked at his watch. Ruth would be asleep. He walked with Willis back into the house, pausing at the steps to look at the starlit sky. It was a cool summer night; he thought vaguely of the Red Sox, did not even know if they were at home tonight; since it happened he had not been able to think about any of the small pleasures he believed he had earned, as he had earned also what was shattered now forever: the quietly harried and quietly pleasurable days of fatherhood. They went inside. Willis's wife, Martha, had gone to bed hours ago, in the rear of the large house which was rigged with burglar and fire alarms. They went downstairs to the game room: the television set suspended from the ceiling, the pool table, the poker table with beer cans, cards, chips, filled ashtrays, and the six chairs where Matt and his friends had sat, the friends picking up the old banter as though he had only been away on vacation; but he could see the affection and courtesy in their eyes. Willis went behind the bar and mixed them each a Scotch and soda; he stayed behind the bar and looked at Matt sitting on the stool.

"How often have you thought about it?" Willis said.

"Every day since he got out. I didn't think about bail. I thought I wouldn't have to worry about him for years. She sees him all the time. It makes her cry."

"He was in my place a long time last night. He'll be back."   10

"Maybe he won't."

"The band. He likes the band."

"What's he doing now?"

"He's tending bar up to Hampton Beach. For a friend. Ever notice even the worst bastard always has friends? He couldn't get work in town. It's just tourists and kids up to Hampton. Nobody knows him. If they do, they don't care. They drink what he mixes."

"Nobody tells me about him."   15

"I hate him, Matt. My boys went to school with him. He was the same then. Know what he'll do? Five at the most. Remember that woman about seven years ago? Shot her husband and dropped him off the bridge in the Merrimack with a hundred-pound sack of cement and said all the way through it that nobody helped her. Know where she is now? She's in Lawrence now, a secretary. And whoever helped her, where the hell is he?"

"I've got a .38 I've had for years, I take it to the store now. I tell Ruth it's for the night deposits. I tell her things have changed: we got junkies here now too. Lots of people without jobs. She knows though."

"What does she know?"

"She knows I started carrying it after the first time she saw him in town. She knows it's in case I see him, and there's some kind of a situation —"

He stopped, looked at Willis, and finished his drink. Willis mixed him an-   20 other.

"What kind of situation?"

"Where he did something to me. Where I could get away with it."

"How does Ruth feel about that?"

"She doesn't know."

"You said she does, she's got it figured out."   25

He thought of her that afternoon: when she went into Sunnyhurst, Strout was waiting at the counter while the clerk bagged the things he had bought; she turned down an aisle and looked at soup cans until he left.

"Ruth would shoot him herself, if she thought she could hit him."

"You got a permit?"

"No."

"I do. You could get a year for that."   30

"Maybe I'll get one. Or maybe I won't. Maybe I'll just stop bringing it to the store."

Richard Strout was twenty-six years old, a high school athlete, football scholarship to the University of Massachusetts where he lasted for almost two semesters before quitting in advance of the final grades that would have forced him not to return. People then said: Dickie can do the work; he just doesn't want to. He came home and did construction work for his father but refused his father's offer to learn the business; his two older brothers had learned it, so that Strout and Sons trucks going about town, and signs on construction sites, now slashed wounds into Matt Fowler's life. Then Richard married a young girl and became a bartender, his salary and tips augmented and perhaps sometimes matched by his father, who also posted his bond. So his friends, his enemies (he had those: fist fights or, more often, boys and then young men who had not fought him when they thought they should have), and those who simply knew him by face and name, had a series of images of him which they recalled when they heard of the killing: the high school running back, the young drunk in bars, the oblivious hard-hatted young man eating lunch at a counter, the bartender who could perhaps be called courteous but not more than that: as he tended bar, his dark eyes and dark, wide-jawed face appeared less sullen, near blank.

One night he beat Frank. Frank was living at home and waiting for September, for graduate school in economics, and working as a lifeguard at Salisbury Beach, where he met Mary Ann Strout, in her first month of separation. She spent most days at the beach with her two sons. Before ten o'clock one night Frank came home; he had driven to the hospital first, and he walked into the living room with stitches over his right eye and both lips bright and swollen.

"I'm all right," he said, when Matt and Ruth stood up, and Matt turned off the television, letting Ruth get to him first: the tall, muscled but slender suntanned boy. Frank tried to smile at them but couldn't because of his lips.

"It was her husband, wasn't it?" Ruth said. ³⁵

"Ex," Frank said. "He dropped in."

Matt gently held Frank's jaw and turned his face to the light, looked at the stitches, the blood under the white of the eye, the bruised flesh.

"Press charges," Matt said.

"No."

"What's to stop him from doing it again? Did you hit him at all? Enough ⁴⁰ so he won't want to next time?"

"I don't think I touched him."

"So what are you going to do?"

"Take karate," Frank said, and tried again to smile.

"That's not the problem," Ruth said.

"You know you like her," Frank said. ⁴⁵

"I like a lot of people. What about the boys? Did they see it?"

"They were asleep."

"Did you leave her alone with him?"

"He left first. She was yelling at him. I believe she had a skillet in her hand."

"Oh for God's sake," Ruth said. ⁵⁰

Matt had been dealing with that too: at the dinner table on evenings when Frank wasn't home, was eating with Mary Ann; or, on the other nights—and Frank was with her every night—he talked with Ruth while they watched television, or lay in bed with the windows open and he smelled the night air and imagined, with both pride and muted sorrow, Frank in Mary Ann's arms. Ruth didn't like it because Mary Ann was in the process of divorce, because she had two children, because she was four years older than Frank, and finally—she told this in bed, where she had during all of their marriage told him of her deepest feelings: of love, of passion, of fears about one of the children, of pain Matt had caused her or she had caused him—she was against it because of what she had heard: that the marriage had gone bad early, and for most of it Richard and Mary Ann had both played around.

"That can't be true," Matt said. "Strout wouldn't have stood for it."

"Maybe he loves her."

"He's too hot-tempered. He couldn't have taken that."

But Matt knew Strout had taken it, for he had heard the stories too. He 55
wondered who had told them to Ruth; and he felt vaguely annoyed and
isolated: living with her for thirty-one years and still not knowing what she
talked about with her friends. On these summer nights he did not so much
argue with her as try to comfort her, but finally there was no difference
between the two: she had concrete objections, which he tried to overcome. And
in his attempt to do this, he neglected his own objections, which were the same
as hers, so that as he spoke to her he felt as disembodied as he sometimes did
in the store when he helped a man choose a blouse or dress or piece of costume
jewelry for his wife.

"The divorce doesn't mean anything," he said. "She was young and maybe
she liked his looks and then after a while she realized she was living with a bastard. I see it as a positive thing."

"She's not divorced yet."

"It's the same thing. Massachusetts has crazy laws, that's all. Her age is no
problem. What's it matter when she was born? And that other business: even if
it's true, which it probably isn't, it's got nothing to do with Frank, and it's in
the past. And the kids are no problem. She's been married six years; she ought
to have kids. Frank likes them. He plays with them. And he's not going to
marry her anyway, so it's not a problem of money."

"Then what's he doing with her?"

"She probably loves him, Ruth. Girls always have. Why can't we just leave it 60
at that?"

"He got home at six o'clock Tuesday morning."

"I didn't know you knew. I've already talked to him about it."

Which he had: since he believed almost nothing he told Ruth, he went to
Frank with what he believed. The night before, he had followed Frank to the
car after dinner.

"You wouldn't make much of a burglar," he said.

"How's that?" 65

Matt was looking up at him; Frank was six feet tall, an inch and a half
taller than Matt, who had been proud when Frank at seventeen outgrew him;
he had only felt uncomfortable when he had to reprimand or caution him. He
touched Frank's bicep, thought of the young taut passionate body, believed he
could sense the desire, and again he felt the pride and sorrow and envy too, not
knowing whether he was envious of Frank or Mary Ann.

"When you came in yesterday morning, I woke up. One of these mornings
your mother will. And I'm the one who'll have to talk to her. She won't interfere with you. Okay? I know it means —" But he stopped, thinking: I know it
means getting up and leaving that suntanned girl and going sleepy to the car, I
know —

"Okay," Frank said, and touched Matt's shoulder and got into the car.

There had been other talks, but the only long one was their first one: a
night driving to Fenway Park, Matt having ordered the tickets so they could
talk, and knowing when Frank said yes, he would go, that he knew the talk was
coming too. It took them forty minutes to get to Boston, and they talked
about Mary Ann until they joined the city traffic along the Charles River, blue
in the late sun. Frank told him all the things that Matt would later pretend to
believe when he told them to Ruth.

"It seems like a lot for a young guy to take on," Matt finally said. 70

"Sometimes it is. But she's worth it."

"Are you thinking about getting married?"

"We haven't talked about it. She can't for over a year. I've got school."

"I *do* like her," Matt said.

He did. Some evenings, when the long summer sun was still low in the sky, 75 Frank brought her home; they came into the house smelling of suntan lotion and the sea, and Matt gave them gin and tonics and started the charcoal in the backyard, and looked at Mary Ann in the lawn chair: long and very light brown hair (Matt thinking that twenty years ago she would have dyed it blonde), and the long brown legs he loved to look at; her face was pretty; she had probably never in her adult life gone unnoticed into a public place. It was in her wide brown eyes that she looked older than Frank; after a few drinks Matt thought what he saw in her eyes was something erotic, testament to the rumors about her; but he knew it wasn't that, or all that: she had, very young, been through a sort of pain that his children, and he and Ruth, had been spared. In the moments of his recognizing that pain, he wanted to tenderly touch her hair, wanted with some gesture to give her solace and hope. And he would glance at Frank, and hope they would love each other, hope Frank would soothe that pain in her heart, take it from her eyes; and her divorce, her age, and her children did not matter at all. On the first two evenings she did not bring her boys, and then Ruth asked her to bring them the next time. In bed that night Ruth said, "She hasn't brought them because she's embarrassed. She shouldn't feel embarrassed."

Richard Strout shot Frank in front of the boys. They were sitting on the living room floor watching television, Frank sitting on the couch, and Mary Ann just returning from the kitchen with a tray of sandwiches. Strout came in the front door and shot Frank twice in the chest and once in the face with a 9 mm automatic. Then he looked at the boys and Mary Ann, and went home to wait for the police.

It seemed to Matt that from the time Mary Ann called weeping to tell him until now, a Saturday night in September, sitting in the car with Willis, parked beside Strout's car, waiting for the bar to close, that he had not so much moved through his life as wandered through it, his spirit like a dazed body bumping into furniture and corners. He had always been a fearful father: when his children were young, at the start of each summer he thought of them drowning in a pond or the sea, and he was relieved when he came home in the evenings and they were there; usually that relief was his only acknowledgment of his fear, which he never spoke of, and which he controlled within his heart. As he had when they were very young and all of them in turn, Cathleen too, were drawn to the high oak in the backyard, and had to climb it. Smiling, he watched them, imagining the fall: and he was poised to catch the small body before it hit the earth. Or his legs were poised; his hands were in his pockets or his arms were folded and, for the child looking down, he appeared relaxed and confident while his heart beat with the two words he wanted to call out but did not: *Don't fall.* In winter he was less afraid: he made sure the ice would hold him before they skated, and he brought or sent them to places where they could sled without ending in the street. So he and his children had survived their childhood, and he only worried about them when he knew they were driving a long distance, and then he lost Frank in a way no father expected to lose his son, and he felt that all the fears he had borne while they were growing up, and all the grief he had been afraid of, had backed up like a huge wave and struck him on the beach and swept him out to sea. Each day he felt the same and when he was able to forget how he felt, when he was able to force himself not to feel that way, the eyes of his clerks and customers defeated him. He wished those eyes were oblivious, even cold; he felt he was withering in their tenderness. And beneath his listless wandering, every day in his soul he shot Richard Strout in the face; while Ruth, going about town on errands, kept seeing him. And at nights in bed she would hold Matt and cry, or sometimes she was silent and Matt would touch her tightening arm, her clenched fist.

As his own right fist was now, squeezing the butt of the revolver, the last of the drinkers having left the bar, talking to each other, going to their separate cars which were in the lot in front of the bar, out of Matt's vision. He heard their voices, their cars, and then the ocean again, across the street. The tide was in and sometimes it smacked the sea wall. Through the windshield he looked at the dark red side wall of the bar, and then to his left, past Willis, at Strout's car, and through its windows he could see the now-emptied parking lot, the road, the sea wall. He could smell the sea.

The front door of the bar opened and closed again and Willis looked at Matt then at the corner of the building; when Strout came around it alone Matt got out of the car, giving up the hope he had kept all night (and for the past week) that Strout would come out with friends, and Willis would simply drive away; thinking: *All right then. All right*; and he went around the front of Willis's car, and at Strout's he stopped and aimed over the hood at Strout's blue shirt ten feet away. Willis was aiming too, crouched on Matt's left, his elbow resting on the hood.

"Mr. Fowler," Strout said. He looked at each of them, and at the guns. 80 "Mr. Trottier."

Then Matt, watching the parking lot and the road, walked quickly between the car and the building and stood behind Strout. He took one leather glove from his pocket and put it on his left hand.

"Don't talk. Unlock the front and back and get in."

Strout unlocked the front door, reached in and unlocked the back, then got in, and Matt slid into the back seat, closed the door with his gloved hand, and touched Strout's head once with the muzzle.

"It's cocked. Drive to your house."

When Strout looked over his shoulder to back the car, Matt aimed at his 85 temple and did not look at his eyes.

"Drive slowly," he said. "Don't try to get stopped."

They drove across the empty front lot and onto the road, Willis's headlights shining into the car; then back through town, the sea wall on the left hiding the beach, though far out Matt could see the ocean; he uncocked the revolver; on the right were the places, most with their neon signs off, that did so much business in summer: the lounges and cafés and pizza houses, the street itself empty of traffic, the way he and Willis had known it would be when they decided to take Strout at the bar rather than knock on his door at two o'clock one morning and risk that one insomniac neighbor. Matt had not told Willis he was afraid he could not be alone with Strout for very long, smell his smells, feel the presence of his flesh, hear his voice, and then shoot him. They left the beach town and then were on the high bridge over the channel: to the left the smacking curling white at the breakwater and beyond that the dark sea and the full moon, and down to his right the small fishing boats bobbing at anchor in the cove. When they left the bridge, the sea was blocked by abandoned beach cottages, and Matt's left hand was sweating in the glove. Out here in the dark in the car he believed Ruth knew. Willis had come to his house at eleven and asked if he wanted a nightcap; Matt went to the bedroom for his wallet, put the gloves in one trouser pocket and the .38 in the other and went back to the living room, his hand in his pocket covering the bulge of the cool cylinder pressed against his fingers, the butt against his palm. When Ruth said good night she looked at his face, and he felt she could see in his eyes the gun, and the night he was going to. But he knew he couldn't trust what he saw. Willis's wife had taken her sleeping pill, which gave her eight hours—the reason, Willis had told Matt, he had the alarms installed, for nights when he was late at the restaurant—and when it was all done and Willis got home he would leave ice and a trace of Scotch and soda in two glasses in the game room and tell Martha in the morning that he had left the restaurant early and brought Matt home for a drink.

"He was making it with my wife." Strout's voice was careful, not pleading.

Matt pressed the muzzle against Strout's head, pressed it harder than he wanted to, feeling through the gun Strout's head flinching and moving forward; then he lowered the gun to his lap.

"Don't talk," he said.   90

Strout did not speak again. They turned west, drove past the Dairy Queen closed until spring, and the two lobster restaurants that faced each other and were crowded all summer and were now also closed, onto the short bridge crossing the tidal stream, and over the engine Matt could hear through his open window the water rushing inland under the bridge; looking to his left he saw its swift moonlit current going back into the marsh which, leaving the bridge, they entered: the salt marsh stretching out on both sides, the grass tall in patches but mostly low and leaning earthward as though windblown, a large dark rock sitting as though it rested on nothing but itself, and shallow pools reflecting the bright moon.

Beyond the marsh they drove through woods, Matt thinking now of the hole he and Willis had dug last Sunday afternoon after telling their wives they were going to Fenway Park. They listened to the game on a transistor radio, but heard none of it as they dug into the soft earth on the knoll they had chosen because elms and maples sheltered it. Already some leaves had fallen. When the hole was deep enough they covered it and the piled earth with dead branches, then cleaned their shoes and pants and went to a restaurant farther up in New Hampshire where they ate sandwiches and drank beer and watched the rest of the game on television. Looking at the back of Strout's head he thought of Frank's grave; he had not been back to it; but he would go before winter, and its second burial of snow.

He thought of Frank sitting on the couch and perhaps talking to the children as they watched television, imagined him feeling young and strong, still warmed from the sun at the beach, and feeling loved, hearing Mary Ann moving about in the kitchen, hearing her walking into the living room; maybe he looked up at her and maybe she said something, looking at him over the tray of sandwiches, smiling at him, saying something the way women do when they offer food as a gift, then the front door opening and this son of a bitch coming in and Frank seeing that he meant the gun in his hand, this son of a bitch and his gun the last person and thing Frank saw on earth.

When they drove into town the streets were nearly empty: a few slow cars, a policeman walking his beat past the darkened fronts of stores. Strout and Matt both glanced at him as they drove by. They were on the main street, and all the stoplights were blinking yellow. Willis and Matt had talked about that too: the lights changed at midnight, so there would be no place Strout had to stop and where he might try to run. Strout turned down the block where he lived and Willis's headlights were no longer with Matt in the back seat. They had planned that too, had decided it was best for just the one car to go to the house, and again Matt had said nothing about his fear of being alone with Strout, especially in his house: a duplex, dark as all the houses on the street were, the street itself lit at the corner of each block. As Strout turned into the driveway Matt thought of the one insomniac neighbor, thought of some man or woman sitting alone in the dark living room, watching the all-night channel from Boston. When Strout stopped the car near the front of the house, Matt said: "Drive it to the back."

He touched Strout's head with the muzzle.   95

"You wouldn't have it cocked, would you? For when I put on the brakes."

Matt cocked it, and said: "It is now."

Strout waited a moment; then he eased the car forward, the engine doing little more than idling, and as they approached the garage he gently braked. Matt opened the door, then took off the glove and put it in his pocket. He stepped out and shut the door with his hip and said: "All right."

Strout looked at the gun, then got out, and Matt followed him across the grass, and as Strout unlocked the door Matt looked quickly at the row of small backyards on either side, and scattered tall trees, some evergreens, others not, and he thought of the red and yellow leaves on the trees over the hole, saw them falling soon, probably in two weeks, dropping slowly, covering. Strout stepped into the kitchen.

"Turn on the light."   100

Strout reached to the wall switch, and in the light Matt looked at his wide back, the dark blue shirt, the white belt, the red plaid pants.

"Where's your suitcase?"

"My suitcase?"

"Where is it?"

"In the bedroom closet."   105

"That's where we're going then. When we get to a door you stop and turn on the light."

They crossed the kitchen, Matt glancing at the sink and stove and refrigerator: no dishes in the sink or even the dish rack beside it, no grease splashings on the stove, the refrigerator door clean and white. He did not want to look at any more but he looked quickly at all he could see: in the living room magazines and newspapers in a wicker basket, clean ashtrays, a record player, the records shelved next to it, then down the hall where, near the bedroom door, hung a color photograph of Mary Ann and the two boys sitting on a lawn — there was no house in the picture — Mary Ann smiling at the camera or Strout or whoever held the camera, smiling as she had on Matt's lawn this summer while he waited for the charcoal and they all talked and he looked at her brown

legs and at Frank touching her arm, her shoulder, her hair; he moved down the
hall with her smile in his mind, wondering: was that when they were both playing around and she was smiling like that at him and they were happy, even
sometimes, making it worth it? He recalled her eyes, the pain in them, and he
was conscious of the circles of love he was touching with the hand that held
the revolver so tightly now as Strout stopped at the door at the end of the hall.

"There's no wall switch."

"Where's the light?"

"By the bed."   110

"Let's go."

Matt stayed a pace behind, then Strout leaned over and the room was
lighted: the bed, a double one, was neatly made; the ashtray on the bedside
table clean, the bureau top dustless, and no photographs; probably so the
girl—who *was* she?—would not have to see Mary Ann in the bedroom she
believed was theirs. But because Matt was a father and a husband, though
never an ex-husband, he knew (and did not want to know) that this bedroom
had never been theirs alone. Strout turned around; Matt looked at his lips, his
wide jaw, and thought of Frank's doomed and fearful eyes looking up from the
couch.

"Where's Mr. Trottier?"

"He's waiting. Pack clothes for warm weather."

"What's going on?"   115

"You're jumping bail."

"Mr. Fowler—"

He pointed the cocked revolver at Strout's face. The barrel trembled but
not much, not as much as he had expected. Strout went to the closet and got
the suitcase from the floor and opened it on the bed. As he went to the bureau,
he said: "He was making it with my wife. I'd go pick up my kids and he'd be
there. Sometimes he spent the night. My boys told me."

He did not look at Matt as he spoke. He opened the top drawer and Matt
stepped closer so he could see Strout's hands: underwear and socks, the socks
rolled, the underwear folded and stacked. He took them back to the bed,
arranged them neatly in the suitcase, then from the closet he was taking shirts
and trousers and a jacket; he laid them on the bed and Matt followed him to
the bathroom and watched from the door while he packed those things a person accumulated and that became part of him so that at times in the store
Matt felt he was selling more than clothes.

"I wanted to try to get together with her again." He was bent over the suit-   120
case. "I couldn't even talk to her. He was always with her. I'm going to jail for it;
if I ever get out I'll be an old man. Isn't that enough?"

"You're not going to jail."

Strout closed the suitcase and faced Matt, looking at the gun. Matt went
to his rear, so Strout was between him and the lighted hall; then using his
handkerchief he turned off the lamp and said: "Let's go."

They went down the hall, Matt looking again at the photograph, and
through the living room and kitchen, Matt turning off the lights and talking,
frightened that he was talking, that he was telling this lie he had not planned:
"It's the trial. We can't go through that, my wife and me. So you're leaving.
We've got you a ticket, and a job. A friend of Mr. Trottier's. Out west. My wife
keeps seeing you. We can't have that anymore."

Matt turned out the kitchen light and put the handkerchief in his pocket, and they went down the two brick steps and across the lawn. Strout put the suitcase on the floor of the back seat, then got into the front seat and Matt got in the back and put on his glove and shut the door.

"They'll catch me. They'll check passenger lists."   125

"We didn't use your name."

"They'll figure that out too. You think I wouldn't have done it myself if it was that easy?"

He backed into the street, Matt looking down the gun barrel but not at the profiled face beyond it.

"You were alone," Matt said. "We've got it worked out."

"There's no planes this time of night, Mr. Fowler."   130

"Go back through town. Then north on 125."

They came to the corner and turned, and now Willis's headlights were in the car with Matt.

"Why north, Mr. Fowler?"

"Somebody's going to keep you for a while. They'll take you to the airport." He uncocked the hammer and lowered the revolver to his lap and said wearily: "No more talking."

As they drove back through town, Matt's body sagged, going limp with his   135
spirit and its new and false bond with Strout, the hope his lie had given Strout. He had grown up in this town whose streets had become places of apprehension and pain for Ruth as she drove and walked, doing what she had to do; and for him too, if only in his mind as he worked and chatted six days a week in his store; he wondered now if his lie would have worked, if sending Strout away would have been enough; but then he knew that just thinking of Strout in Montana or whatever place lay at the end of the lie he had told, thinking of him walking the streets there, loving a girl there (who *was* she?) would be enough to slowly rot the rest of his days. And Ruth's. Again he was certain that she knew, that she was waiting for him.

They were in New Hampshire now, on the narrow highway, passing the shopping center at the state line, and then houses and small stores and sandwich shops. There were few cars on the road. After ten minutes he raised his trembling hand, touched Strout's neck with the gun, and said: "Turn in up here. At the dirt road."

Strout flicked on the indicator and slowed.

"Mr. Fowler?"

"They're waiting here."

Strout turned very slowly, easing his neck away from the gun. In the moon-   140
light the road was light brown, lighter and yellowed where the headlights shone; weeds and a few trees grew on either side of it, and ahead of them were the woods.

"There's nothing back here, Mr. Fowler."

"It's for your car. You don't think we'd leave it at the airport, do you?"

He watched Strout's large, big-knuckled hands tighten on the wheel, saw Frank's face that night: not the stitches and bruised eye and swollen lips, but his own hand gently touching Frank's jaw, turning his wounds to the light. They rounded a bend in the road and were out of sight of the highway: tall trees all around them now, hiding the moon. When they reached the abandoned gravel pit on the left, the bare flat earth and steep pale embankment behind it, and the black crowns of trees at its top, Matt said: "Stop here."

Strout stopped but did not turn off the engine. Matt pressed the gun hard against his neck, and he straightened in the seat and looked in the rearview mirror, Matt's eyes meeting his in the glass for an instant before looking at the hair at the end of the gun barrel.

"Turn it off."   145

Strout did, then held the wheel with two hands, and looked in the mirror.

"I'll do twenty years, Mr. Fowler; at least. I'll be forty-six years old."

"That's nine years younger than I am," Matt said, and got out and took off the glove and kicked the door shut. He aimed at Strout's ear and pulled back the hammer. Willis's headlights were off and Matt heard him walking on the soft thin layer of dust, the hard earth beneath it. Strout opened the door, sat for a moment in the interior light, then stepped out onto the road. Now his face was pleading. Matt did not look at his eyes, but he could see it in the lips.

"Just get the suitcase. They're right up the road."

Willis was beside him now, to his left. Strout looked at both guns. Then he   150 opened the back door, leaned in, and with a jerk brought the suitcase out. He was turning to face them when Matt said: "Just walk up the road. Just ahead."

Strout turned to walk, the suitcase in his right hand, and Matt and Willis followed; as Strout cleared the front of his car he dropped the suitcase and, ducking, took one step that was the beginning of a sprint to his right. The gun kicked in Matt's hand, and the explosion of the shot surrounded him, isolated him in a nimbus of sound that cut him off from all his time, all his history, isolated him standing absolutely still on the dirt road with the gun in his hand, looking down at Richard Strout squirming on his belly, kicking one leg behind him, pushing himself forward, toward the woods. Then Matt went to him and shot him once in the back of the head.

Driving south to Boston, wearing both gloves now, staying in the middle lane and looking often in the rearview mirror at Willis's headlights, he relived the suitcase dropping, the quick dip and turn of Strout's back, and the kick of the gun, the sound of the shot. When he walked to Strout, he still existed within the first shot, still trembled and breathed with it. The second shot and the burial seemed to be happening to someone else, someone he was watching. He and Willis each held an arm and pulled Strout face-down off the road and into the woods, his bouncing sliding belt white under the trees where it was so dark that when they stopped at the top of the knoll, panting and sweating, Matt could not see where Strout's blue shirt ended and the earth began. They pulled off the branches then dragged Strout to the edge of the hole and went behind him and lifted his legs and pushed him in. They stood still for a moment. The woods were quiet save for their breathing, and Matt remembered hearing the movements of birds and small animals after the first shot. Or maybe he had not heard them. Willis went down to the road. Matt could see him clearly out on the tan dirt, could see the glint of Strout's car and, beyond the road, the gravel pit. Willis came back up the knoll with the suitcase. He dropped it in the hole and took off his gloves and they went down to his car for the spades. They worked quietly. Sometimes they paused to listen to the woods. When they were finished Willis turned on his flashlight and they covered the earth with leaves and branches and then went down to the spot in front of the car, and while Matt held the light Willis crouched and sprinkled dust on the blood, backing up till he reached the grass and leaves, then he used leaves until they had worked up to the grave again. They did not stop. They walked around the grave and through the woods, using the light on the ground, looking up through the trees to where they ended at the lake. Neither of them spoke above the sounds of their heavy and clumsy strides through low brush and over fallen branches. Then they reached it: wide and dark, lapping softly at the bank, pine needles smooth under Matt's feet, moonlight on the lake, a small island near its middle, with black, tall evergreens. He took out the gun and threw for the island: taking two steps back on the pine needles, striding with the throw and going to one knee as he followed through, looking up to see the dark shapeless object arcing downward, splashing.

They left Strout's car in Boston, in front of an apartment building on Commonwealth Avenue. When they got back to town Willis drove slowly over the bridge and Matt threw the keys into the Merrimack. The sky was turning light. Willis let him out a block from his house, and walking home he listened for sounds from the houses he passed. They were quiet. A light was on in his living room. He turned it off and undressed in there, and went softly toward the bedroom; in the hall he smelled the smoke, and he stood in the bedroom doorway and looked at the orange of her cigarette in the dark. The curtains were closed. He went to the closet and put his shoes on the floor and felt for a hanger.

"Did you do it?" she said.

He went down the hall to the bathroom and in the dark he washed his hands and face. Then he went to her, lay on his back, and pulled the sheet up to his throat.

"Are you all right?" she said.

"I think so."

Now she touched him, lying on her side, her hand on his belly, his thigh.

"Tell me," she said.

He started from the beginning, in the parking lot at the bar; but soon with his eyes closed and Ruth petting him, he spoke of Strout's house: the order, the woman presence, the picture on the wall.

"The way she was smiling," he said.

"What about it?"

"I don't know. Did you ever see Strout's girl? When you saw him in town?"

"No."

"I wonder who she was."

Then he thought: *not was: is. Sleeping now she is his girl.* He opened his eyes, then closed them again. There was more light beyond the curtains. With Ruth now he left Strout's house and told again his lie to Strout, gave him again that hope that Strout must have for a while believed, else he would have to believe only the gun pointed at him for the last two hours of his life. And with Ruth he saw again the dropping suitcase, the darting move to the right: and he told of the first shot, feeling her hand on him but his heart isolated still, beating on the road still in that explosion like thunder. He told her the rest, but the words had no images for him, he did not see himself doing what the words said he had done; he only saw himself on that road.

"We can't tell the other kids," she said. "It'll hurt them, thinking he got away. But we mustn't."

"No."

She was holding him, wanting him, and he wished he could make love with her but he could not. He saw Frank and Mary Ann making love in her bed, their eyes closed, their bodies brown and smelling of the sea; the other girl was faceless, bodiless, but he felt her sleeping now; and he saw Frank and Strout, their faces alive; he saw red and yellow leaves falling on the earth, then snow: falling and freezing and falling; and holding Ruth, his cheek touching her breast, he shuddered with a sob that he kept silent in his heart.

CONSIDERATIONS FOR CRITICAL THINKING AND WRITING

1. **FIRST RESPONSE.** How do you feel about Matt's act of revenge? Trace the emotions his character produces in you as the plot unfolds.

2. Discuss the significance of the title. Why is "Killings" a more appropriate title than "Killers"?

3. What are the effects of Dubus's ordering of events in the story? How would the effects be different if the story were told in a chronological order?

4. Describe the Fowler family before Frank's murder. How does the murder affect Matt?

5. What is learned about Richard from the flashback in paragraphs 32 through 75? How does this information affect your attitude toward him?

6. What is the effect of the description of Richard shooting Frank in paragraph 76?

7. How well planned is Matt's revenge? Why does he lie to Richard about sending him out west?

8. Describe Matt at the end of the story when he tells his wife about the killing. How do you think this revenge killing will affect the Fowler family?

9. How might "Killings" be considered a love story as well as a murder story?

10. **CRITICAL STRATEGIES.** Read the section on psychological criticism (pp. 1542–44) in Chapter 46, "Critical Strategies for Reading." How do the details of the killing and the disposal of Richard's body reveal Matt's emotions? What is he thinking and feeling as he performs these actions? How did you feel as you read about them?

CONNECTIONS TO OTHER SELECTIONS

1. Compare and contrast Matt's motivation for murder with Emily's in William Faulkner's "A Rose for Emily." Which character made you feel more empathy and sympathy for his or her actions? Why?

2. Explore the father-son relationships in "Killings" and Faulkner's "Barn Burning" (p. 418). Read the section on psychological criticism in Chapter 46, "Critical Strategies for Reading." How do you think a psychological critic would interpret these relationships in each story?

Perspective

A. L. BADER (B. 1902)

Nothing Happens in Modern Short Stories   1945

Any teacher who has ever confronted a class with representative modern short stories will remember the disappointment, the puzzled "so-what" attitude, of certain members of the group. "Nothing happens in some of these stories," "They just end," or "They're not real stories" are frequent criticisms. . . . Sometimes the phrase "Nothing happens" seems to mean that nothing significant happens, but in a great many cases it means that the modern short story is charged with a lack of narrative structure. Readers and critics accustomed to an older type of story are baffled by a newer type. They sense the underlying and unifying design of the one, but they find nothing equivalent to it in the other. Hence they maintain that the modern short story is plotless, static, fragmentary, amorphous — frequently a mere character sketch or vignette, or a mere reporting of a transient moment, or the capturing of a mood or nuance — everything, in fact, except a story.

From "The Structure of the Modern Story" in *College English*

CONSIDERATIONS FOR CRITICAL THINKING AND WRITING

1. What is the basic objection to the "newer type" of short story? How does it differ from the "older type"?

2. Consider any one of the stories from Chapter 16, "An Album of Contemporary Stories" (pp. 501–31), as an example of the newer type. Does anything "happen" in the story? How does it differ from the excerpt from Edgar Rice Burroughs's *Tarzan of the Apes* (p. 72)?

   Web Research the authors in this chapter or take quizzes on their works at bedfordstmartins.com/meyercompact.

3. Read a recent story published in *The New Yorker* or the *Atlantic Monthly* and compare its narrative structure with that of Faulkner's "A Rose for Emily" (p. 90).

4

Character

When I find a well-drawn character in fiction or biography, I generally take a warm personal interest in him, for the reason that I have known him before—met him on the river.
—MARK TWAIN

Character is essential to plot. Without characters Burroughs's *Tarzan of the Apes* would be a travelogue through the jungle and Faulkner's "A Rose for Emily" little more than a faded history of a sleepy town in the South. If stories were depopulated, the plots would disappear because characters and plots are interrelated. A dangerous jungle is important only because we care what effect it has on a character. Characters are influenced by events just as events are shaped by characters. Tarzan's physical strength is the result of his growing up in the jungle, and his strength, along with his inherited intelligence, allows him to be master there.

The methods by which a writer creates people in a story so that they seem actually to exist are called **characterization.** Huck Finn never lived, yet those who have read Mark Twain's novel about his adventures along the Mississippi River feel as if they know him. A good writer gives us the illusion that a character is real, but we should also remember that a character is not an actual person but instead has been created by the author. Though we might walk out of a room in which Huck Finn's Pap talks racist nonsense, we would not throw away the book in a similar fit of anger. This illusion of reality is the magic that allows us to move beyond the circumstances of our own lives into a writer's fictional world, where we can encounter everyone from royalty to paupers, murderers, lovers, cheaters, martyrs, artists, destroyers, and, nearly always, some part of ourselves. The life that a writer breathes into a character adds to our own experiences and enlarges our view of the world.

🔊 🖲Web Explore the literary element in this chapter on *LiterActive* or at bedfordstmartins.com/meyercompact.

A character is usually but not always a person. In Jack London's *Call of the Wild,* the protagonist is a devoted sled dog; in Herman Melville's *Moby-Dick,* the antagonist is an unfathomable whale. Perhaps the only possible qualification to be placed on character is that whatever it is — whether an animal or even an inanimate object, such as a robot — it must have some recognizable human qualities. The action of the plot interests us primarily because we care about what happens to people and what they do. We may identify with a character's desires and aspirations, or we may be disgusted by his or her viciousness and selfishness. To understand our response to a story, we should be able to recognize the methods of characterization the author uses.

CHARLES DICKENS (1812–1870)

Charles Dickens is well known for creating characters who have stepped off the pages of his fictions into the imaginations and memories of his readers. His characters are successful not because readers might have encountered such people in their own lives, but because his characterizations are vivid and convincing. He manages to make strange and eccentric people appear familiar. The following excerpt from *Hard Times* is the novel's entire first chapter. In it Dickens introduces and characterizes a school principal addressing a classroom full of children.

Courtesy of the National Portrait Gallery, London.

From Hard Times   *1854*

"Now, what I want is, Facts. Teach these boys and girls nothing but Facts. Facts alone are wanted in life. Plant nothing else, and root out everything else. You can only form the minds of reasoning animals upon Facts: nothing else will ever be of any service to them. This is the principle on which I bring up my own children, and this is the principle on which I bring up these children. Stick to Facts, sir!"

The scene was a plain, bare, monotonous vault of a schoolroom, and the speaker's square forefinger emphasized his observations by underscoring every sentence with a line on the schoolmaster's sleeve. The emphasis was helped by the speaker's square wall of a forehead, which had his eyebrows for its base, while his eyes found commodious cellarage in two dark caves, overshadowed by the wall. The emphasis was helped by the speaker's mouth, which was wide, thin, and hard set. The emphasis was helped by the speaker's voice, which was inflexible, dry, and dictatorial. The emphasis was helped by the speaker's hair, which bristled on the skirts of his bald head, a plantation of firs to keep the wind from its shining surface, all covered with knobs, like the crust of a plum pie, as if the head had scarcely warehouse-room for the hard facts stored inside. The speaker's obstinate carriage, square coat, square legs, square shoulders – nay, his very neckcloth, trained to take him by the throat with an unaccommodating grasp, like a stubborn fact, as it was – all helped the emphasis.

"In this life, we want nothing but Facts, sir; nothing but Facts!"

The speaker, and the schoolmaster, and the third grown person present, all backed a little, and swept with their eyes the inclined plane of little vessels then and there arranged in order, ready to have imperial gallons of facts poured into them until they were full to the brim.

Dickens withholds his character's name until the beginning of the second chapter; he calls this fact-bound educator Mr. Gradgrind. Authors sometimes put as much time and effort into naming their characters as parents invest in naming their children. Names can be used to indicate qualities that the writer associates with the characters. Mr. Gradgrind is precisely what his name suggests. The "schoolmaster" employed by Gradgrind is Mr. M'Choakumchild. Pronounce this name aloud and you have the essence of this teacher's educational philosophy. In Nathaniel Hawthorne's *The Scarlet Letter,* Chillingworth is cold and relentless in his single-minded quest for revenge. The innocent and youthful protagonist in Herman Melville's *Billy Budd* is nipped in the bud by the evil Claggart, whose name simply sounds unpleasant.

Names are also used in films to suggest a character's nature. One example that is destined to be a classic is the infamous villain Darth Vader, whose name identifies his role as an invader allied with the dark and death. On the heroic side, it makes sense that Marion Morrison decided to change his box-office name to John Wayne in order to play tough, masculine roles because both the first and last of his chosen names are unambiguously male and to the point, while his given name is androgynous. There may also be some significance to the lack of a specific identity. In Godwin's "A Sorrowful Woman" (p. 39) the woman, man, boy, and girl are reduced to a set of domestic functions, and their not being named emphasizes their roles as opposed to their individual identities. Of course, not every name is suggestive of the qualities a character may embody, but it is frequently worth determining what is in a name.

The only way to tell whether a name reveals character is to look at the other information the author supplies about the character. We evaluate fictional characters in much the same way we understand people in our own lives. By piecing together bits of information, we create a context that allows us to interpret their behavior. We can predict, for instance, that an acquaintance who is a chronic complainer is not likely to have anything good to say about a roommate. We interpret words and actions in the light of what we already know about someone, and that is why keeping track of what characters say (and how they say it) along with what they do (and don't do) is important.

Authors reveal characters by other means too. Physical descriptions can indicate important inner qualities; disheveled clothing, a crafty smile, or a blush might communicate as much as or more than what a character says. Characters can also be revealed by the words and actions of others who respond to them. In literature, moreover, we have one great advantage that life cannot offer; a work of fiction can give us access to a person's thoughts. Although in Herman Melville's "Bartleby, the Scrivener" (p. 124) we learn about Bartleby primarily through descriptive details, words, actions, and his relationships with the other characters, Melville allows us to enter the lawyer's consciousness.

Authors have two major methods of presenting characters: **showing** and **telling.** Characters shown in dramatic situations reveal themselves indirectly by what they say and do. In the first paragraph of the excerpt from *Hard Times,* Dickens shows us some of Gradgrind's utilitarian educational principles by having him speak. We can infer the kind of person he is from his reference to boys and girls as "reasoning animals," but we are not told what to think of him until the second paragraph. It would be impossible to admire Gradgrind after reading the physical description of him and the school that he oversees. The adjectives in the second paragraph make the author's evaluation of Gradgrind's values and personality clear: everything about him is rigidly "square"; his mouth is "thin, and hard set"; his voice is "inflexible, dry, and dictatorial"; and he presides over a "plain, bare, monotonous vault of a schoolroom." Dickens directly lets us know how to feel about Gradgrind, but he does so artistically. Instead of simply being presented with a statement that Gradgrind is destructively practical, we get a detailed and amusing description.

We can contrast Dickens's direct presentation in this paragraph with the indirect showing that Gail Godwin uses in "A Sorrowful Woman." Godwin avoids telling us how we should think about the characters. Their story includes little description and no evaluations or interpretations by the author. To determine the significance of the events, the reader must pay close attention to what the characters say and do. Like Godwin, many twentieth-century authors favor showing over telling because showing allows readers to discover the meanings, which modern authors are often reluctant to impose on an audience for whom fixed meanings and values are not as strong as they once were. However, most writers continue to reveal characters by telling as well as showing when the technique suits their purposes — when, for example, a minor character must be sketched economically or when a long time has elapsed, causing changes in a major character. Telling and showing complement each other.

Characters can be convincing whether they are presented by telling or showing, provided their actions are **motivated.** There must be reasons for how they behave and what they say. If adequate motivation is offered, we can understand and find **plausible** their actions no matter how bizarre. In "A Rose for Emily" (p. 90), Faulkner makes Emily Grierson's intimacy with a corpse credible by preparing us with information about her father's death along with her inability to leave the past and live in the present. Emily turns out to be **consistent.** Although we are surprised by the ending of the story, the behavior it reveals is compatible with her temperament.

Some kinds of fiction consciously break away from our expectations of traditional realistic stories. Consistency, plausibility, and motivation are not very useful concepts for understanding and evaluating characterizations in modern **absurdist literature,** for instance, in which characters are often alienated from themselves and their environment in an irrational world. In this world there is no possibility for traditional heroic action; instead we find an **antihero** who has little control over events. Yossarian from Joseph Heller's *Catch-22* is an example of a protagonist who is thwarted by the absurd terms on which life offers itself to many twentieth-century characters.

In most stories we expect characters to act plausibly and in ways consistent with their personalities, but that does not mean that characters cannot develop and change. A **dynamic** character undergoes some kind of change because of the action of the plot. Huck Finn's view of Jim, the runaway slave in Mark Twain's novel, develops during their experiences on the raft. Huck discovers Jim's humanity and, therefore, cannot betray him because Huck no longer sees his companion as merely the property of a white owner. On the other hand, Huck's friend, Tom Sawyer, is a **static** character because he does not change. He remains interested only in high adventure, even at the risk of Jim's life. As static characters often do, Tom serves as a foil to Huck; his frivolous concerns are contrasted with Huck's serious development. A *foil* helps to reveal by contrast the distinctive qualities of another character.

The protagonist in a story is usually a dynamic character who experiences some conflict that makes an impact on his or her life. Less commonly, static characters can also be protagonists. Rip Van Winkle wakes up from his twenty-year sleep in Washington Irving's story to discover his family dramatically changed and his country no longer a British colony, but none of these important events has an impact on his character; he continues to be the same shiftless and idle man that he was before he fell asleep. The protagonist in Faulkner's "A Rose for Emily" is also a static character; indeed, she rejects all change. Our understanding of her changes, but she does not. Ordinarily, however, a plot contains one or two dynamic characters with any number of static characters in supporting roles. This is especially true of short stories, in which brevity limits the possibilities of character development.

The extent to which a character is developed is another means by which character can be analyzed. The novelist E. M. Forster coined the terms *flat* and *round* to distinguish degrees of character development. A **flat character** embodies one or two qualities, ideas, or traits that can be readily described in a brief summary. For instance, Mr. M'Choakumchild in Dickens's *Hard Times* stifles students instead of encouraging them to grow. Flat characters tend to be one-dimensional. They are readily accessible because their characteristics are few and simple; they are not created to be psychologically complex.

Some flat characters are immediately recognizable as **stock characters.** These stereotypes are particularly popular in formula fiction, television programs, and action movies. Stock characters are types rather than individuals. The poor but dedicated writer falls in love with a hardworking understudy, who gets nowhere because the corrupt producer favors his boozy, pampered mistress for the leading role. Characters such as these — the loyal servant, the mean stepfather, the henpecked husband, the dumb blonde, the sadistic army officer, the dotty grandmother — are prepackaged; they lack individuality because their authors have, in a sense, not imaginatively created them but simply summoned them from a warehouse of clichés and social prejudices. Stock characters can become fresh if a good writer makes them vivid, interesting, or memorable, but too often a writer's use of these stereotypes is simply weak characterization.

Round characters are more complex than flat or stock characters. Round characters have more depth and require more attention. They may surprise us or puzzle us. Although they are more fully developed, round characters are also more difficult to summarize because we are aware of competing ideas, values, and possibilities in their lives. As a flat character, Huck Finn's alcoholic, bigoted father is clear to us; we know that Pap is the embodiment of racism and irrationality. But Huck is considerably less predictable because he struggles with what Twain calls a "sound heart and a deformed conscience."

In making distinctions between flat and round characters, you must understand that an author's use of a flat character — even as a protagonist — does not necessarily represent an artistic flaw. Moreover, both flat and round characters can be either dynamic or static. Each plot can be made most effective by its own special kind of characterization. Terms such as *round* and *flat* are helpful tools to use to determine what we know about a character, but they are not an infallible measurement of the quality of a story.

The next two stories — Herman Melville's "Bartleby, the Scrivener" and Susan Straight's "Mines" — offer character studies worthy of close analysis. As you read them, notice the methods of characterization used to bring each to life.

A SAMPLE STUDENT RESPONSE

Crispin Shea

Professor Atwood

English 102

September 19, 2008

Character Development in Charles Dickens's Hard Times

In the first chapter of Hard Times, by Charles Dickens, the speaker, or focal character, develops slowly and is brought to life through dialogue and description. We understand him as a character not only through what he says, but through how he says it. Learning, to him, means nothing more than absorbing facts; there is no discussion, no debate. Facts are given to the students, "poured into them until they were filled to the brim," and the children must take every word as truth (Dickens 119). Understanding the speaker's view on learning helps us to understand the man himself, and he quickly becomes a fully developed character: a person hard-nosed and unyielding, with little interest in middle ground.

After the character speaks, Dickens gives us a physical description to reinforce our initial opinion of the speaker. He is described as having a "square wall of a forehead," and eyes that find "commodious cellarage in two dark caves" (119). His mouth is "thin, and hard set" (119). Dickens's description emphasizes the character's rigidity. He portrays the speaker as someone who is callous and difficult. This does not mean, however, that all characters with harsh physical features are unpleasant or villainous (just as attractive characters are not always pleasant). Certainly Dickens could have focused on the speaker's best traits, physical or otherwise, and created a more endearing character. Instead, he focuses on what he wants us to read as the true essence of this particular person, using physical details to "indicate [the character's] important inner qualities" (Meyer 120). . . .

Shea 6

Works Cited

Dickens, Charles. "From Hard Times." In The Compact Bedford Introduction to
Literature. Ed. Michael Meyer. 8th ed. Boston: Bedford/St. Martin's,
2009. 118–19.

Meyer, Michael, ed. The Compact Bedford Introduction to Literature. 8th ed.
Boston: Bedford/St. Martin's, 2009. 120.

HERMAN MELVILLE (1819–1891)

Library of Congress, Prints and
Photographs Division.

Hoping to improve his distressed financial
situation, Herman Melville left New York and
went to sea as a young common sailor. He returned to become an uncommon writer. His
experiences at sea became the basis for his
early novels: *Typee* (1846), *Omoo* (1847), *Mardi*
(1849), *Redburn* (1849), and *White-Jacket* (1850).
Ironically, with the publication of his masterpiece, *Moby-Dick* (1851), Melville lost the popular success he had enjoyed with his earlier
books because his readers were not ready for
its philosophical complexity. Although he
wrote more, Melville's works were read less
and slipped into obscurity. His final short novel, *Billy Budd,* was not published until the 1920s, when critics rediscovered him. In "Bartleby, the
Scrivener," Melville presents a quiet clerk in a law office whose baffling
"passive resistance" disrupts the life of his employer, a man who attempts
to make sense of Bartleby's refusal to behave reasonably.

Bartleby, the Scrivener   *1853*
A Story of Wall Street

I am a rather elderly man. The nature of my avocations, for the last thirty years,
has brought me into more than ordinary contact with what would seem an
interesting and somewhat singular set of men, of whom, as yet, nothing, that I
know of, has ever been written — I mean, the law-copyists, or scriveners. I have

known very many of them, professionally and privately, and, if I pleased, could relate diverse histories, at which good-natured gentlemen might smile, and sentimental souls might weep. But I waive the biographies of all other scriveners, for a few passages in the life of Bartleby, who was a scrivener, the strangest I ever saw, or heard of. While, of other law-copyists, I might write the complete life, of Bartleby nothing of that sort can be done. I believe that no materials exist, for a full and satisfactory biography of this man. It is an irreparable loss to literature. Bartleby was one of those beings of whom nothing is ascertainable, except from the original sources, and, in his case, those are very small. What my own astonished eyes saw of Bartleby, *that* is all I know of him, except, indeed, one vague report, which will appear in the sequel.

Ere introducing the scrivener, as he first appeared to me, it is fit I make some mention of myself, my *employés,* my business, my chambers, and general surroundings, because some such description is indispensable to an adequate understanding of the chief character about to be presented. Imprimis:° I am a man who, from his youth upwards, has been filled with a profound conviction that the easiest way of life is the best. Hence, though I belong to a profession proverbially energetic and nervous, even to turbulence, at times, yet nothing of that sort have I ever suffered to invade my peace. I am one of those unambitious lawyers who never address a jury, or in any way draw down public applause; but, in the cool tranquillity of a snug retreat, do a snug business among rich men's bonds, and mortgages, and title-deeds. All who know me, consider me an eminently *safe* man. The late John Jacob Astor,° a personage little given to poetic enthusiasm, had no hesitation in pronouncing my first grand point to be prudence; my next, method. I do not speak it in vanity, but simply record the fact, that I was not unemployed in my profession by the late John Jacob Astor; a name which, I admit, I love to repeat; for it hath a rounded and orbicular sound to it, and rings like unto bullion. I will freely add, that I was not insensible to the late John Jacob Astor's good opinion.

Some time prior to the period at which this little history begins, my avocations had been largely increased. The good old office, now extinct in the State of New York, of a Master in Chancery, had been conferred upon me. It was not a very arduous office, but very pleasantly remunerative. I seldom lose my temper; much more seldom indulge in dangerous indignation at wrongs and outrages; but I must be permitted to be rash here and declare, that I consider the sudden and violent abrogation of the office of Master in Chancery, by the new Constitution, as a — premature act; inasmuch as I had counted upon a life-lease of the profits, whereas I only received those of a few short years. But this is by the way.

My chambers were up stairs, at No. — Wall Street. At one end, they looked upon the white wall of the interior of a spacious skylight shaft, penetrating the building from top to bottom.

This view might have been considered rather tame than otherwise, defi- 5 cient in what landscape painters call "life." But, if so, the view from the other end of my chambers offered, at least, a contrast, if nothing more. In that direction, my windows commanded an unobstructed view of a lofty brick wall, black by age and everlasting shade; which wall required no spyglass to bring

Imprimis: In the first place.
John Jacob Astor (1763-1848): An enormously wealthy American capitalist.

out its lurking beauties, but, for the benefit of all near-sighted spectators, was pushed up to within ten feet of my window-panes. Owing to the great height of the surrounding buildings, and my chambers being on the second floor, the interval between this wall and mine not a little resembled a huge square cistern.

At the period just preceding the advent of Bartleby, I had two persons as copyists in my employment, and a promising lad as an office-boy. First, Turkey; second, Nippers; third, Ginger Nut. These may seem names, the like of which are not usually found in the Directory. In truth, they were nicknames, mutually conferred upon each other by my three clerks, and were deemed expressive of their respective persons or characters. Turkey was a short, pursy Englishman, of about my own age — that is, somewhere not far from sixty. In the morning, one might say, his face was of a fine florid hue, but after twelve o'clock, meridian — his dinner hour — it blazed like a grate full of Christmas coals; and continued blazing — but, as it were, with a gradual wane — till six o'clock, P.M., or thereabouts; after which, I saw no more of the proprietor of the face, which, gaining its meridian with the sun, seemed to set with it, to rise, culminate, and decline the following day, with the like regularity and undiminished glory. There are many singular coincidences I have known in the course of my life, not the least among which was the fact, that, exactly when Turkey displayed his fullest beams from his red and radiant countenance, just then, too, at that critical moment, began the daily period when I considered his business capacities as seriously disturbed for the remainder of the twenty-four hours. Not that he was absolutely idle, or averse to business then; far from it. The difficulty was, he was apt to be altogether too energetic. There was a strange, inflamed, flurried, flighty recklessness of activity about him. He would be incautious in dipping his pen into his inkstand. All his blots upon my documents were dropped there after twelve o'clock, meridian. Indeed, not only would he be reckless, and sadly given to making blots in the afternoon, but, some days, he went further, and was rather noisy. At such times, too, his face flamed with augmented blazonry, as if cannel coal had been heaped on anthracite. He made an unpleasant racket with his chair; spilled his sand-box; in mending his pens, impatiently split them all to pieces, and threw them on the floor in a sudden passion; stood up, and leaned over his table, boxing his papers about in a most indecorous manner, very sad to behold in an elderly man like him. Nevertheless, as he was in many ways a most valuable person to me, and all the time before twelve o'clock, meridian, was the quickest, steadiest creature, too, accomplishing a great deal of work in a style not easily to be matched — for these reasons, I was willing to overlook his eccentricities, though, indeed, occasionally, I remonstrated with him. I did this very gently, however, because, though the civilest, nay, the blandest and most reverential of men in the morning, yet, in the afternoon, he was disposed, upon provocation, to be slightly rash with his tongue — in fact, insolent. Now, valuing his morning services as I did, and resolved not to lose them — yet, at the same time, made uncomfortable by his inflamed ways after twelve o'clock — and being a man of peace, unwilling by my admonitions to call forth unseemly retorts from him, I took upon me, one Saturday noon (he was always worse on Saturdays) to hint to him, very kindly, that, perhaps, now that he was growing old, it might be well to abridge his labors; in short, he need not come to my chambers after twelve o'clock, but, dinner over, had best go home to his lodgings, and rest himself till tea-time. But no; he insisted upon his afternoon devotions. His countenance became intolerably fervid, as he oratorically assured me — gesticulating with a long ruler at the other end of the room — that if his services in the morning were useful, how indispensable, then, in the afternoon?

"With submission, sir," said Turkey, on this occasion, "I consider myself your right-hand man. In the morning I but marshal and deploy my columns; but in the afternoon I put myself at their head, and gallantly charge the foe, thus" — and he made a violent thrust with the ruler.

"But the blots, Turkey," intimated I.

"True; but, with submission, sir, behold these hairs! I am getting old. Surely, sir, a blot or two of a warm afternoon is not to be severely urged against gray hairs. Old age — even if it blot the page — is honorable. With submission, sir, we *both* are getting old."

This appeal to my fellow-feeling was hardly to be resisted. At all events, I saw that go he would not. So, I made up my mind to let him stay, resolving, nevertheless, to see to it that, during the afternoon, he had to do with my less important papers.

Nippers, the second on my list, was a whiskered, sallow, and, upon the whole, rather piratical-looking young man, of about five-and-twenty. I always deemed him the victim of two evil powers — ambition and indigestion. The ambition was evinced by a certain impatience of the duties of a mere copyist, an unwarrantable usurpation of strictly professional affairs such as the original drawing up of legal documents. The indigestion seemed betokened in an occasional nervous testiness and grinning irritability, causing the teeth to audibly grind together over mistakes committed in copying; unnecessary maledictions, hissed, rather than spoken, in the heat of business; and especially by a continual discontent with the height of the table where he worked. Though of a very ingenious mechanical turn, Nippers could never get this table to suit him. He put chips under it, blocks of various sorts, bits of pasteboard, and at last went so far as to attempt an exquisite adjustment, by final pieces of folded blotting-paper. But no invention would answer. If, for the sake of easing his back, he brought the table-lid at a sharp angle well up towards his chin, and wrote there like a man using the steep roof of a Dutch house for his desk, then he declared that it stopped the circulation in his arms. If now he lowered the table to his waistbands, and stooped over it in writing, then there was a sore aching in his back. In short, the truth of the matter was, Nippers knew not what he wanted. Or, if he wanted anything, it was to be rid of a scrivener's table altogether. Among the manifestations of his diseased ambition was a fondness he had for receiving visits from certain ambiguous-looking fellows in seedy coats, whom he called his clients. Indeed, I was aware that not only was he, at times, considerable of a ward-politician, but he occasionally did a little business at the justices' courts, and was not unknown on the steps of the Tombs.° I have good reason to believe, however, that one individual who called upon him at my chambers, and who, with a grand air, he insisted was his client, was no other than a dun, and the alleged title-deed, a bill. But, with all his failings, and the annoyances he caused me, Nippers, like his compatriot Turkey, was a very useful man to me; wrote a neat, swift hand; and, when he chose, was not deficient in a gentlemanly sort of deportment.

the Tombs: A jail in New York City.

Added to this, he always dressed in a gentlemanly sort of way; and so, incidentally, reflected credit upon my chambers. Whereas, with respect to Turkey, I had much ado to keep him from being a reproach to me. His clothes were apt to look oily, and smell of eating-houses. He wore his pantaloons very loose and baggy in summer. His coats were execrable, his hat not to be handled. But while the hat was a thing of indifference to me, inasmuch as his natural civility and deference, as a dependent Englishman, always led him to doff it the moment he entered the room, yet his coat was another matter. Concerning his coats, I reasoned with him; but with no effect. The truth was, I suppose, that a man with so small an income could not afford to sport such a lustrous face and a lustrous coat at one and the same time. As Nippers once observed, Turkey's money went chiefly for red ink. One winter day, I presented Turkey with a highly respectable-looking coat of my own — a padded gray coat, of a most comfortable warmth, and which buttoned straight up from the knee to the neck. I thought Turkey would appreciate the favor, and abate his rashness and obstreperousness of afternoons. But no; I verily believe that buttoning himself up in so downy and blanket-like a coat had a pernicious effect upon him — upon the same principle that too much oats are bad for horses. In fact, precisely as a rash, restive horse is said to feel his oats, so Turkey felt his coat. It made him insolent. He was a man whom prosperity harmed.

Though, concerning the self-indulgent habits of Turkey, I had my own private surmises, yet, touching Nippers, I was well persuaded that, whatever might be his faults in other respects, he was, at least, a temperate young man. But indeed, nature herself seemed to have been his vintner, and, at his birth, charged him so thoroughly with an irritable, brandy-like disposition, that all subsequent potations were needless. When I consider how, amid the stillness of my chambers, Nippers would sometimes impatiently rise from his seat, and stooping over his table, spread his arms wide apart, seize the whole desk, and move it, and jerk it, with a grim, grinding motion on the floor, as if the table were a perverse voluntary agent, intent on thwarting and vexing him, I plainly perceive that, for Nippers, brandy-and-water were altogether superfluous.

It was fortunate for me that, owing to its peculiar cause — indigestion — the irritability and consequent nervousness of Nippers were mainly observable in the morning, while in the afternoon he was comparatively mild. So that, Turkey's paroxysms only coming on about twelve o'clock, I never had to do with their eccentricities at one time. Their fits relieved each other, like guards. When Nippers' was on, Turkey's was off; and *vice versa*. This was a good natural arrangement, under the circumstances.

Ginger Nut, the third on my list, was a lad, some twelve years old. His father was a carman, ambitious of seeing his son on the bench instead of a cart, before he died. So he sent him to my office, as student at law, errand-boy, cleaner, and sweeper, at the rate of one dollar a week. He had a little desk to himself, but he did not use it much. Upon inspection, the drawer exhibited a great array of the shells of various sorts of nuts. Indeed, to this quick-witted youth, the whole noble science of the law was contained in a nutshell. Not the least among the employments of Ginger Nut, as well as one which he discharged with the most alacrity, was his duty as cake and apple purveyor for Turkey and Nippers. Copying lawpapers being proverbially a dry, husky sort of business, my two scriveners were fain to moisten their mouths very often with Spitzenbergs, to be had at the numerous stalls nigh the Custom House and

Post Office. Also, they sent Ginger Nut very frequently for that peculiar cake—small, flat, round, and very spicy—after which he had been named by them. Of a cold morning, when business was but dull, Turkey would gobble up scores of these cakes, as if they were mere wafers—indeed, they sell them at the rate of six or eight for a penny—the scrape of his pen blending with the crunching of the crisp particles in his mouth. Of all the fiery afternoon blunders and flurried rashness of Turkey, was his once moistening a ginger-cake between his lips, and clapping it on to a mortgage, for a seal. I came within an ace of dismissing him then. But he mollified me by making an oriental bow, and saying—

"With submission, sir, it was generous of me to find you in stationery on 15 my own account."

Now my original business—that of a conveyancer and title hunter, and drawer-up of recondite documents of all sorts—was considerably increased by receiving the Master's office. There was now great work for scriveners. Not only must I push the clerks already with me, but I must have additional help.

In answer to my advertisement, a motionless young man one morning stood upon my office threshold, the door being open, for it was summer. I can see that figure now—pallidly neat, pitiably respectable, incurably forlorn! It was Bartleby.

After a few words touching his qualifications, I engaged him, glad to have among my corps of copyists a man of so singularly sedate an aspect, which I thought might operate beneficially upon the flighty temper of Turkey, and the fiery one of Nippers.

I should have stated before that ground-glass folding-doors divided my premises into two parts, one of which was occupied by my scriveners, the other by myself. According to my humor, I threw open these doors, or closed them. I resolved to assign Bartleby a corner by the folding-doors, but on my side of them, so as to have this quiet man within easy call, in case any trifling thing was to be done. I placed his desk close up to a small side-window in that part of the room, a window which originally had afforded a lateral view of certain grimy brickyards and bricks, but which, owing to subsequent erections, commanded at present no view at all, though it gave some light. Within three feet of the panes was a wall, and the light came down from far above, between two lofty buildings, as from a very small opening in a dome. Still further to a satisfactory arrangement, I procured a high green folding screen, which might entirely isolate Bartleby from my sight, though not remove him from my voice. And thus, in a manner, privacy and society were conjoined.

At first, Bartleby did an extraordinary quantity of writing. As if long fam- 20 ishing for something to copy, he seemed to gorge himself on my documents. There was no pause for digestion. He ran a day and night line, copying by sunlight and by candle-light. I should have been quite delighted with his application, had he been cheerfully industrious. But he wrote on silently, palely, mechanically.

It is, of course, an indispensable part of a scrivener's business to verify the accuracy of his copy, word by word. Where there are two or more scriveners in an office, they assist each other in this examination, one reading from the copy, the other holding the original. It is a very dull, wearisome, and lethargic affair. I can readily imagine that, to some sanguine temperaments, it would be altogether intolerable. For example, I cannot credit that the mettlesome poet,

Byron, would have contentedly sat down with Bartleby to examine a law document of, say five hundred pages, closely written in a crimpy hand.

Now and then, in the haste of business, it had been my habit to assist in
comparing some brief document myself, calling Turkey or Nippers for this
purpose. One object I had, in placing Bartleby so handy to me behind the
screen, was, to avail myself of his services on such trivial occasions. It was on
the third day, I think, of his being with me, and before any necessity had arisen
for having his own writing examined, that, being much hurried to complete a
small affair I had in hand, I abruptly called to Bartleby. In my haste and
natural expectancy of instant compliance, I sat with my head bent over the
original on my desk, and my right hand sideways, and somewhat nervously extended with the copy, so that, immediately upon emerging from his retreat,
Bartleby might snatch it and proceed to business without the least delay.

In this very attitude did I sit when I called to him, rapidly stating what it
was I wanted him to do—namely, to examine a small paper with me. Imagine
my surprise, nay, my consternation, when, without moving from his privacy,
Bartleby, in a singularly mild, firm voice, replied, "I would prefer not to."

I sat awhile in perfect silence, rallying my stunned faculties. Immediately
it occurred to me that my ears had deceived me, or Bartleby had entirely misunderstood my meaning. I repeated my request in the clearest tone I could
assume; but in quite as clear a one came the previous reply, "I would prefer
not to."

"Prefer not to," echoed I, rising in high excitement, and crossing the room 25
with a stride. "What do you mean? Are you moonstruck? I want you to help me
compare this sheet here—take it," and I thrust it towards him.

"I would prefer not to," said he.

I looked at him steadfastly. His face was leanly composed; his gray eye
dimly calm. Not a wrinkle of agitation rippled him. Had there been the least
uneasiness, anger, impatience, or impertinence in his manner; in other words,
had there been anything ordinarily human about him, doubtless I should have
violently dismissed him from the premises. But as it was, I should have as soon
thought of turning my pale plaster-of-paris bust of Cicero out of doors. I
stood gazing at him awhile, as he went on with his own writing, and then
reseated myself at my desk. This is very strange, thought I. What had one best
do? But my business hurried me. I concluded to forget the matter for the
present, reserving it for my future leisure. So, calling Nippers from the other
room, the paper was speedily examined.

A few days after this, Bartleby concluded four lengthy documents, being
quadruplicates of a week's testimony taken before me in my High Court of
Chancery. It became necessary to examine them. It was an important suit,
and great accuracy was imperative. Having all things arranged, I called Turkey,
Nippers, and Ginger Nut, from the next room, meaning to place the four
copies in the hands of my four clerks, while I should read from the original.
Accordingly, Turkey, Nippers, and Ginger Nut had taken their seats in a row,
each with his document in his hand, when I called to Bartleby to join this
interesting group.

"Bartleby! quick, I am waiting."

I heard a slow scrape of his chair legs on the uncarpeted floor, and soon he 30
appeared standing at the entrance of his hermitage.

"What is wanted?" said he, mildly.

"The copies, the copies," said I, hurriedly. "We are going to examine them. There" — and I held towards him the fourth quadruplicate.

"I would prefer not to," he said, and gently disappeared behind the screen.

For a few moments I was turned into a pillar of salt, standing at the head of my seated column of clerks. Recovering myself, I advanced towards the screen, and demanded the reason for such extraordinary conduct.

"*Why* do you refuse?"   35

"I would prefer not to."

With any other man I should have flown outright into a dreadful passion, scorned all further words, and thrust him ignominiously from my presence. But there was something about Bartleby that not only strangely disarmed me, but, in a wonderful manner, touched and disconcerted me. I began to reason with him.

"These are your own copies we are about to examine. It is labor saving to you, because one examination will answer for your four papers. It is common usage. Every copyist is bound to help examine his copy. Is it not so? Will you not speak? Answer!"

"I prefer not to," he replied in a flute-like tone. It seemed to me that, while I had been addressing him, he carefully revolved every statement that I made; fully comprehended the meaning; could not gainsay the irresistible conclusion; but, at the same time, some paramount consideration prevailed with him to reply as he did.

"You are decided, then, not to comply with my request — a request made 40
according to common usage and common sense?"

He briefly gave me to understand, that on that point my judgment was sound. Yes: his decision was irreversible.

It is not seldom the case that, when a man is browbeaten in some unprecedented and violently unreasonable way, he begins to stagger in his own plainest faith. He begins, as it were, vaguely to surmise that, wonderful as it may be, all the justice and all the reason is on the other side. Accordingly, if any disinterested persons are present, he turns to them for some reinforcement for his own faltering mind.

"Turkey," said I, "what do you think of this? Am I not right?"

"With submission, sir," said Turkey, in his blandest tone, "I think that you are."

"Nippers," said I, "what do *you* think of it?"   45

"I think I should kick him out of the office."

(The reader of nice perceptions will have perceived that, it being morning, Turkey's answer is couched in polite and tranquil terms, but Nippers replies in ill-tempered ones. Or, to repeat a previous sentence, Nippers' ugly mood was on duty, and Turkey's off.)

"Ginger Nut," said I, willing to enlist the smallest suffrage in my behalf, "what do *you* think of it?"

"I think, sir, he's a little *luny*," replied Ginger Nut, with a grin.

"You hear what they say," said I, turning towards the screen, "come forth 50
and do your duty."

But he vouchsafed no reply. I pondered a moment in sore perplexity. But once more business hurried me. I determined again to postpone the consideration of this dilemma to my future leisure. With a little trouble we made out to examine the papers without Bartleby, though at every page or two Turkey deferentially dropped his opinion, that this proceeding was quite out of the common; while Nippers, twitching in his chair with a dyspeptic nervousness, ground out, between his set teeth, occasional hissing maledictions against the stubborn oaf behind the screen. And for his (Nippers') part, this was the first and the last time he would do another man's business without pay.

Meanwhile Bartleby sat in his hermitage, oblivious to everything but his own peculiar business there.

Some days passed, the scrivener being employed upon another lengthy work. His late remarkable conduct led me to regard his ways narrowly. I observed that he never went to dinner; indeed, that he never went anywhere. As yet I had never, of my personal knowledge, known him to be outside of my office. He was a perpetual sentry in the corner. At about eleven o'clock though, in the morning, I noticed that Ginger Nut would advance toward the opening in Bartleby's screen, as if silently beckoned thither by a gesture invisible to me where I sat. The boy would then leave the office, jingling a few pence, and reappear with a handful of ginger-nuts, which he delivered in the hermitage, receiving two of the cakes for his trouble.

He lives, then, on ginger-nuts, thought I; never eats a dinner, properly speaking; he must be a vegetarian, then, but no; he never eats even vegetables, he eats nothing but ginger-nuts. My mind then ran on in reveries concerning the probable effects upon the human constitution of living entirely on ginger-nuts. Ginger-nuts are so called, because they contain ginger as one of their peculiar constituents, and the final flavoring one. Now, what was ginger? A hot, spicy thing. Was Bartleby hot and spicy? Not at all. Ginger, then, had no effect upon Bartleby. Probably he preferred it should have none.

Nothing so aggravates an earnest person as a passive resistance. If the 55 individual so resisted be of a not inhumane temper, and the resisting one perfectly harmless in his passivity, then, in the better moods of the former, he will endeavor charitably to construe to his imagination what proves impossible to be solved by his judgment. Even so, for the most part, I regarded Bartleby and his ways. Poor fellow! thought I, he means no mischief; it is plain he intends no insolence; his aspect sufficiently evinces that his eccentricities are involuntary. He is useful to me. I can get along with him. If I turn him away, the chances are he will fall in with some less indulgent employer, and then he will be rudely treated, and perhaps driven forth miserably to starve. Yes. Here I can cheaply purchase a delicious self-approval. To befriend Bartleby; to humor him in his strange wilfulness, will cost me little or nothing, while I lay up in my soul what will eventually prove a sweet morsel for my conscience. But this mood was not invariable with me. The passiveness of Bartleby sometimes irritated me. I felt strangely goaded on to encounter him in new opposition — to elicit some angry spark from him answerable to my own. But, indeed, I might as well have essayed to strike fire with my knuckles against a bit of Windsor soap. But one afternoon the evil impulse in me mastered me, and the following little scene ensued:

"Bartleby," said I, "when those papers are all copied, I will compare them with you."

"I would prefer not to."

"How? Surely you do not mean to persist in that mulish vagary?"

No answer.

I threw open the folding-doors nearby, and turning upon Turkey and Nip- 60 pers, exclaimed:

"Bartleby a second time says, he won't examine his papers. What do you think of it, Turkey?"

It was afternoon, be it remembered. Turkey sat glowing like a brass boiler; his bald head steaming; his hands reeling among his blotted papers.

"Think of it?" roared Turkey. "I think I'll just step behind his screen, and black his eyes for him!"

So saying, Turkey rose to his feet and threw his arms into a pugilistic position. He was hurrying away to make good his promise, when I detained him, alarmed at the effect of incautiously rousing Turkey's combativeness after dinner.

"Sit down, Turkey," said I, "and hear what Nippers has to say. What do 65 you think of it, Nippers? Would I not be justified in immediately dismissing Bartleby?"

"Excuse me, that is for you to decide, sir. I think his conduct quite unusual, and, indeed, unjust, as regards Turkey and myself. But it may only be a passing whim."

"Ah," exclaimed I, "you have strangely changed your mind, then—you speak very gently of him now."

"All beer," cried Turkey; "gentleness is effects of beer—Nippers and I dined together to-day. You see how gentle *I* am, sir. Shall I go and black his eyes?"

"You refer to Bartleby, I suppose. No, not to-day, Turkey," I replied; "pray, put up your fists."

I closed the doors, and again advanced towards Bartleby. I felt additional 70 incentives tempting me to my fate. I burned to be rebelled against again. I remembered that Bartleby never left the office.

"Bartleby," said I, "Ginger Nut is away; just step around to the Post Office, won't you?" (it was but a three minutes' walk) "and see if there is anything for me."

"I would prefer not to."

"You *will* not?"

"I *prefer* not."

I staggered to my desk, and sat there in a deep study. My blind inveteracy 75 returned. Was there any other thing in which I could procure myself to be ignominiously repulsed by this lean, penniless wight?—my hired clerk? What added thing is there, perfectly reasonable, that he will be sure to refuse to do?

"Bartleby!"

No answer.

"Bartleby," in a louder tone.

No answer.

"Bartleby," I roared. 80

Like a very ghost, agreeably to the laws of magical invocation, at the third summons, he appeared at the entrance of his hermitage.

"Go to the next room, and tell Nippers to come to me."

"I prefer not to," he respectfully and slowly said, and mildly disappeared.

"Very good, Bartleby," said I, in a quiet sort of serenely-severe self-possessed tone, intimating the unalterable purpose of some terrible retribution very close at hand. At the moment I half intended something of the kind. But upon the whole, as it was drawing towards my dinner-hour, I thought it best to put on my hat and walk home for the day, suffering much from perplexity and distress of mind.

Shall I acknowledge it? The conclusion of this whole business was, that it 85 soon became a fixed fact of my chambers, that a pale young scrivener, by the name of Bartleby, had a desk there; that he copied for me at the usual rate of four cents a folio (one hundred words); but he was permanently exempt from examining the work done by him, that duty being transferred to Turkey and Nippers, out of compliment, doubtless, to their superior acuteness; moreover, said Bartleby was never, on any account, to be dispatched on the most trivial errand of any sort; and that even if entreated to take upon him such a matter, it was generally understood that he would "prefer not to"—in other words, that he would refuse point-blank.

As days passed on, I became considerably reconciled to Bartleby. His steadiness, his freedom from all dissipation, his incessant industry (except when he chose to throw himself into a standing revery behind his screen), his great stillness, his unalterableness of demeanor under all circumstances, made him a valuable acquisition. One prime thing was this—*he was always there*—first in the morning, continually through the day, and the last at night. I had a singular confidence in his honesty. I felt my most precious papers perfectly safe in his hands. Sometimes, to be sure, I could not, for the very soul of me, avoid falling into sudden spasmodic passions with him. For it was exceeding difficult to bear in mind all the time those strange peculiarities, privileges, and unheard-of exemptions, forming the tacit stipulations on Bartleby's part under which he remained in my office. Now and then, in the eagerness of dispatching pressing business, I would inadvertently summon Bartleby, in a short, rapid tone, to put his finger, say, on the incipient tie of a bit of red tape with which I was about compressing some papers. Of course, from behind the screen the usual answer, "I prefer not to," was sure to come; and then, how could a human creature, with the common infirmities of our nature, refrain from bitterly exclaiming upon such perverseness—such unreasonableness? However, every added repulse of this sort which I received only tended to lessen the probability of my repeating the inadvertence.

Here it must be said, that, according to the custom of most legal gentlemen occupying chambers in densely populated law buildings, there were several keys to my door. One was kept by a woman residing in the attic, which person weekly scrubbed and daily swept and dusted my apartments. Another was kept by Turkey for convenience sake. The third I sometimes carried in my own pocket. The fourth I knew not who had.

Now, one Sunday morning I happened to go to Trinity Church, to hear a celebrated preacher, and finding myself rather early on the ground I thought I would walk round to my chambers for a while. Luckily I had my key with me; but upon applying it to the lock, I found it resisted by something inserted from the inside. Quite surprised, I called out; when to my consternation a key was turned from within; and thrusting his lean visage at me, and holding the door ajar, the apparition of Bartleby appeared, in his shirt-sleeves, and otherwise in a strangely tattered *deshabille,* saying quietly that he was sorry, but he was deeply engaged just then, and—preferred not admitting me at present. In a brief word or two, he moreover added, that perhaps I had better walk round the block two or three times, and by that time he would probably have concluded his affairs.

Now, the utterly unsurmised appearance of Bartleby, tenanting my law-chambers of a Sunday morning, with his cadaverously gentlemanly *nonchalance,* yet withal firm and self-possessed, had such a strange effect upon me, that incontinently I slunk away from my own door, and did as desired. But not without sundry twinges of impotent rebellion against the mild effrontery of this unaccountable scrivener. Indeed, it was his wonderful mildness chiefly, which not only disarmed me, but unmanned me, as it were. For I consider that one, for the time, is sort of unmanned when he tranquilly permits his hired clerk to dictate to him, and order him away from his own premises. Furthermore, I was full of uneasiness as to what Bartleby could possibly be doing in my office in his shirt-sleeves, and in an otherwise dismantled condition of a Sunday morning. Was anything amiss going on? Nay, that was out of the question. It was not to be thought of for a moment that Bartleby was an immoral person. But what could he be doing there? — copying? Nay again, whatever might be his eccentricities, Bartleby was an eminently decorous person. He would be the last man to sit down to his desk in any state approaching to nudity. Besides, it was Sunday; and there was something about Bartleby that forbade the supposition that he would by any secular occupation violate the proprieties of the day.

Nevertheless, my mind was not pacified; and full of a restless curiosity, at 90 last I returned to the door. Without hindrance I inserted my key, opened it, and entered. Bartleby was not to be seen. I looked round anxiously, peeped behind his screen; but it was very plain that he was gone. Upon more closely examining the place, I surmised that for an indefinite period Bartleby must have ate, dressed, and slept in my office, and that too without plate, mirror, or bed. The cushioned seat of a rickety old sofa in one corner bore the faint impress of a lean, reclining form. Rolled away under his desk, I found a blanket; under the empty grate, a blacking box and brush; on a chair, a tin basin, with soap and a ragged towel; in a newspaper a few crumbs of ginger-nuts and a morsel of cheese. Yes, thought I, it is evident enough that Bartleby has been making his home here, keeping bachelor's hall all by himself. Immediately then the thought came sweeping across me, what miserable friendlessness and loneliness are here revealed! His poverty is great; but his solitude, how horrible! Think of it. Of a Sunday, Wall Street is deserted as Petra;° and every night of every day it is an emptiness. This building, too, which of week-days hums with industry and life, at nightfall echoes with sheer vacancy, and all through Sunday is forlorn. And here Bartleby makes his home; sole spectator of a solitude which he has seen all populous — a sort of innocent and transformed Marius brooding among the ruins of Carthage?°

For the first time in my life a feeling of overpowering stinging melancholy seized me. Before, I had never experienced aught but a not unpleasing sadness. The bond of a common humanity now drew me irresistibly to gloom. A fraternal melancholy! For both I and Bartleby were sons of Adam. I remembered the bright silks and sparkling faces I had seen that day, in gala trim, swan-like sailing down the Mississippi of Broadway; and I contrasted them with the pallid copyist, and thought to myself, Ah, happiness courts the light, so we deem the world is gay; but misery hides aloof, so we deem that misery there is none. These sad fancyings — chimeras, doubtless, of a sick and silly brain — led on to other and more special thoughts, concerning the eccentricities of Bartleby.

Petra: An ancient Arabian city whose ruins were discovered in 1812.
Marius . . . of Carthage: Gaius Marius (157–86 B.C.), an exiled Roman general, sought refuge in the African city-state of Carthage, which was destroyed by the Romans in the Third Punic War.

Presentiments of strange discoveries hovered round me. The scrivener's pale form appeared to me laid out, among uncaring strangers, in its shivering winding-sheet.

Suddenly I was attracted by Bartleby's closed desk, the key in open sight left in the lock.

I mean no mischief, seek the gratification of no heartless curiosity, thought I; besides, the desk is mine, and its contents, too, so I will make bold to look within. Everything was methodically arranged, the papers smoothly placed. The pigeon-holes were deep, and removing the files of documents, I groped into their recesses. Presently I felt something there, and dragged it out. It was an old bandanna handkerchief, heavy and knotted. I opened it, and saw it was a saving's bank.

I now recalled all the quiet mysteries which I had noted in the man. I remembered that he never spoke but to answer; that, though at intervals he had considerable time to himself, yet I had never seen him reading — no, not even a newspaper; that for long periods he would stand looking out, at his pale window behind the screen, upon the dead brick wall; I was quite sure he never visited any refectory or eating-house; while his pale face clearly indicated that he never drank beer like Turkey; or tea and coffee even, like other men; that he never went anywhere in particular that I could learn; never went out for a walk, unless, indeed, that was the case at present; that he had declined telling who he was, or whence he came, or whether he had any relatives in the world; that though so thin and pale, he never complained of ill-health. And more than all, I remembered a certain unconscious air of pallid — how shall I call it? — of pallid haughtiness, say, or rather an austere reserve about him, which had positively awed me into my tame compliance with his eccentricities, when I had feared to ask him to do the slightest incidental thing for me, even though I might know, from his long-continued motionlessness, that behind his screen he must be standing in one of those dead-wall reveries of his.

Revolving all these things, and coupling them with the recently discovered 95 fact, that he made my office his constant abiding place and home, and not forgetful of his morbid moodiness; revolving all these things, a prudential feeling began to steal over me. My first emotions had been those of pure melancholy and sincerest pity; but just in proportion as the forlornness of Bartleby grew and grew to my imagination, did that same melancholy merge into fear, that pity into repulsion. So true it is, and so terrible, too, that up to a certain point the thought or sight of misery enlists our best affections; but, in certain special cases, beyond that point it does not. They err who would assert that invariably this is owing to the inherent selfishness of the human heart. It rather proceeds from a certain hopelessness of remedying excessive and organic ill. To a sensitive being, pity is not seldom pain. And when at last it is perceived that such pity cannot lead to effectual succor, common sense bids the soul be rid of it. What I saw that morning persuaded me that the scrivener was the victim of innate and incurable disorder. I might give alms to his body; but his body did not pain him; it was his soul that suffered, and his soul I could not reach.

I did not accomplish the purpose of going to Trinity Church that morning. Somehow, the things I had seen disqualified me for the time from churchgoing. I walked homeward, thinking what I would do with Bartleby. Finally, I resolved upon this — I would put certain calm questions to him the next morning, touching his history, etc., and if he declined to answer them openly and unreservedly (and I supposed he would prefer not), then to give him a twenty dollar bill over and above whatever I might owe him, and tell him his services were no longer required; but that if in any other way I could assist him, I would be happy to do so, especially if he desired to return to his native place, wherever that might be, I would willingly help to defray the expenses. Moreover, if, after reaching home, he found himself at any time in want of aid, a letter from him would be sure of a reply.

The next morning came.

"Bartleby," said I, gently calling to him behind his screen.

No reply.

"Bartleby," said I, in a still gentler tone, "come here; I am not going to ask you to do anything you would prefer not to do — I simply wish to speak to you." 100

Upon this he noiselessly slid into view.

"Will you tell me, Bartleby, where you were born?"

"I would prefer not to."

"Will you tell me *anything* about yourself?"

"I would prefer not to." 105

"But what reasonable objection can you have to speak to me? I feel friendly towards you."

He did not look at me while I spoke, but kept his glance fixed upon my bust of Cicero, which, as I then sat, was directly behind me, some six inches above my head.

"What is your answer, Bartleby?" said I, after waiting a considerable time for a reply, during which his countenance remained immovable, only there was the faintest conceivable tremor of the white attenuated mouth.

"At present I prefer to give no answer," he said, and retired into his hermitage.

It was rather weak in me I confess, but his manner, on this occasion, nettled 110 me. Not only did there seem to lurk in it a certain calm disdain, but his perverseness seemed ungrateful, considering the undeniable good usage and indulgence he had received from me.

Again I sat ruminating what I should do. Mortified as I was at his behavior, and resolved as I had been to dismiss him when I entered my office, nevertheless I strangely felt something superstitious knocking at my heart, and forbidding me to carry out my purpose, and denouncing me for a villain if I dared to breathe one bitter word against this forlornest of mankind. At last, familiarly drawing my chair behind his screen, I sat down and said: "Bartleby, never mind, then, about revealing your history; but let me entreat you, as a friend, to comply as far as may be with the usages of this office. Say now, you will help to examine papers tomorrow or next day: in short, say now, that in a day or two you will begin to be a little reasonable: — say so, Bartleby."

"At present I would prefer not to be a little reasonable," was his mildly cadaverous reply.

Just then the folding-doors opened, and Nippers approached. He seemed suffering from an unusually bad night's rest, induced by severer indigestion than common. He overheard those final words of Bartleby.

"*Prefer not*, eh?" gritted Nippers—"I'd *prefer* him, if I were you, sir," addressing me—"I'd *prefer* him; I'd give him preferences, the stubborn mule! What is it, sir, pray, that he *prefers* not to do now?"

Bartleby moved not a limb.

"Mr. Nippers," said I, "I'd prefer that you would withdraw for the present."

Somehow, of late, I had got into the way of involuntarily using this word "prefer" upon all sorts of not exactly suitable occasions. And I trembled to think that my contact with the scrivener had already and seriously affected me in a mental way. And what further and deeper aberration might it not yet produce? This apprehension had not been without efficacy in determining me to summary measures.

As Nippers, looking very sour and sulky, was departing, Turkey blandly and deferentially approached.

"With submission, sir," said he, "yesterday I was thinking about Bartleby here, and I think that if he would but prefer to take a quart of good ale every day, it would do much towards mending him, and enabling him to assist in examining his papers."

"So you have got the word, too," said I, slightly excited.

"With submission, what word, sir?" asked Turkey, respectfully crowding himself into the contracted space behind the screen, and by so doing, making me jostle the scrivener. "What word, sir?"

"I would prefer to be left alone here," said Bartleby, as if offended at being mobbed in his privacy.

"*That's* the word, Turkey," said I — "*that's* it."

"Oh, *prefer?* oh yes — queer word. I never use it myself. But, sir, as I was saying, if he would but prefer—"

"Turkey," interrupted I, "you will please withdraw."

"Oh certainly, sir, if you prefer that I should."

As he opened the folding-door to retire, Nippers at his desk caught a glimpse of me, and asked whether I would prefer to have a certain paper copied on blue paper or white. He did not in the least roguishly accent the word "prefer." It was plain that it involuntarily rolled from his tongue. I thought to myself, surely I must get rid of a demented man, who already has in some degree turned the tongues, if not the heads of myself and clerks. But I thought it prudent not to break the dismission at once.

The next day I noticed that Bartleby did nothing but stand at his window in his dead-wall revery. Upon asking him why he did not write, he said that he had decided upon doing no more writing.

"Why, how now? what next?" exclaimed I, "do no more writing?"

"No more."

"And what is the reason?"

"Do you not see the reason for yourself?" he indifferently replied.

I looked steadfastly at him, and perceived that his eyes looked dull and glazed. Instantly it occurred to me, that his unexampled diligence in copying by his dim window for the first few weeks of his stay with me might have temporarily impaired his vision.

I was touched. I said something in condolence with him. I hinted that of course he did wisely in abstaining from writing for a while; and urged him to embrace that opportunity of taking wholesome exercise in the open air. This, however, he did not do. A few days after this, my other clerks being absent, and being in a great hurry to dispatch certain letters by the mail, I thought that, having nothing else earthly to do, Bartleby would surely be less inflexible than usual, and carry these letters to the Post Office. But he blankly declined. So, much to my inconvenience, I went myself.

Still added days went by. Whether Bartleby's eyes improved or not, I could 135 not say. To all appearance, I thought they did. But when I asked him if they did, he vouchsafed no answer. At all events, he would do no copying. At last, in replying to my urgings, he informed me that he had permanently given up copying.

"What!" exclaimed I; "suppose your eyes should get entirely well — better than ever before — would you not copy then?"

"I have given up copying," he answered, and slid aside.

He remained as ever, a fixture in my chamber. Nay — if that were possible — he became still more of a fixture than before. What was to be done? He would do nothing in the office; why should he stay there? In plain fact, he had now become a millstone to me, not only useless as a necklace, but afflictive to bear. Yet I was sorry for him. I speak less than truth when I say that, on his own account, he occasioned me uneasiness. If he would but have named a single relative or friend, I would instantly have written, and urged their taking the poor fellow away to some convenient retreat. But he seemed alone, absolutely alone in the universe. A bit of wreck in the mid-Atlantic. At length, necessities connected with my business tyrannized over all other considerations. Decently as I could, I told Bartleby that in six days' time he must unconditionally leave the office. I warned him to take measures, in the interval, for procuring some other abode. I offered to assist him in this endeavor, if he himself would but take the first step towards a removal. "And when you finally quit me, Bartleby," added I, "I shall see that you go not away entirely unprovided. Six days from this hour, remember."

At the expiration of that period, I peeped behind the screen, and lo! Bartleby was there.

I buttoned up my coat, balanced myself; advanced slowly towards him, 140 touched his shoulder, and said, "The time has come; you must quit this place; I am sorry for you; here is money; but you must go."

"I would prefer not," he replied, with his back still towards me.

"You *must*."

He remained silent.

Now I had an unbounded confidence in this man's common honesty. He had frequently restored to me sixpences and shillings carelessly dropped upon the floor, for I am apt to be very reckless in such shirt-button affairs. The proceeding, then, which followed will not be deemed extraordinary.

"Bartleby," said I, "I owe you twelve dollars on account; here are thirty-two, 145 the odd twenty are yours — Will you take it?" and I handed the bills towards him.

But he made no motion.

"I will leave them here, then," putting them under a weight on the table. Then taking my hat and cane and going to the door, I tranquilly turned and added — "After you have removed your things from these offices, Bartleby, you will of course lock the door — since every one is now gone for the day but you — and if you please, slip your key underneath the mat, so that I may have it in the morning. I shall not see you again; so good-bye to you. If, hereafter, in your new place of abode, I can be of any service to you, do not fail to advise me by letter. Good-bye, Bartleby, and fare you well."

But he answered not a word; like the last column of some ruined temple, he remained standing mute and solitary in the middle of the otherwise deserted room.

As I walked home in a pensive mood, my vanity got the better of my pity. I could not but highly plume myself on my masterly management in getting rid of Bartleby. Masterly I call it, and such it must appear to any dispassionate thinker. The beauty of my procedure seemed to consist in its perfect quietness. There was no vulgar bullying, no bravado of any sort, no choleric hectoring, and striding to and fro across the apartment, jerking out vehement commands for Bartleby to bundle himself off with his beggarly traps. Nothing of the kind. Without loudly bidding Bartleby depart — as an inferior genius might have done — I *assumed* the ground that depart he must; and upon that assumption built all I had to say. The more I thought over my procedure, the more I was charmed with it. Nevertheless, next morning, upon awakening, I had my doubts — I had somehow slept off the fumes of vanity. One of the coolest and wisest hours a man has, is just after he awakes in the morning. My procedure seemed as sagacious as ever — but only in theory. How it would prove in practice — there was the rub. It was truly a beautiful thought to have assumed Bartleby's departure; but, after all, that assumption was simply my own, and none of Bartleby's. The great point was, not whether I had assumed that he would quit me, but whether he would prefer to do so. He was more a man of preferences than assumptions.

After breakfast, I walked down town, arguing the probabilities *pro* and *con*. 150 One moment I thought it would prove a miserable failure, and Bartleby would be found all alive at my office as usual; the next moment it seemed certain that I should find his chair empty. And so I kept veering about. At the corner of Broadway and Canal Street, I saw quite an excited group of people standing in earnest conversation.

"I'll take odds he doesn't," said a voice as I passed.

"Doesn't go? — done!" said I, "put up your money."

I was instinctively putting my hand in my pocket to produce my own, when I remembered that this was an election day. The words I had overheard bore no reference to Bartleby, but to the success or non-success of some candidate for the mayoralty. In my intent frame of mind, I had, as it were, imagined that all Broadway shared in my excitement, and were debating the same question with me. I passed on, very thankful that the uproar of the street screened my momentary absent-mindedness.

As I had intended, I was earlier than usual at my office door. I stood listening for a moment. All was still. He must be gone. I tried the knob. The door was locked. Yes, my procedure had worked to a charm; he indeed must be vanished. Yet a certain melancholy mixed with this: I was almost sorry for my brilliant success. I was fumbling under the door mat for the key, which Bartleby was to have left there for me, when accidentally my knee knocked against a panel, producing a summoning sound, and in response a voice came to me from within — "Not yet; I am occupied."

It was Bartleby. 155

I was thunderstruck. For an instant I stood like the man who, pipe in mouth, was killed one cloudless afternoon long ago in Virginia, by summer lightning; at his own warm open window he was killed, and remained leaning out there upon the dreamy afternoon, till some one touched him, when he fell.

"Not gone!" I murmured at last. But again obeying that wondrous ascendancy which the inscrutable scrivener had over me, and from which ascendancy, for all my chafing, I could not completely escape, I slowly went down stairs and out into the street, and while walking round the block, considered what I should next do in this unheard-of perplexity. Turn the man out by an actual thrusting I could not; to drive him away by calling him hard names would not do; calling in the police was an unpleasant idea; and yet, permit him to enjoy his cadaverous triumph over me — this, too, I could not think of. What was to be done? or, if nothing could be done, was there anything further that I could *assume* in the matter? Yes, as before I had prospectively assumed that Bartleby would depart, so now I might retrospectively assume that departed he was. In the legitimate carrying out of this assumption, I might enter my office in a great hurry, and pretending not to see Bartleby at all, walk straight against him as if he were air. Such a proceeding would in a singular degree have the appearance of a home-thrust. It was hardly possible that Bartleby could withstand such an application of the doctrine of assumption. But upon second thoughts the success of the plan seemed rather dubious. I resolved to argue the matter over with him again.

"Bartleby," said I, entering the office, with a quietly severe expression, "I am seriously displeased. I am pained, Bartleby. I had thought better of you. I had imagined you of such a gentlemanly organization, that in any delicate dilemma a slight hint would suffice — in short, an assumption. But it appears I am deceived. Why," I added, unaffectedly starting, "you have not even touched that money yet," pointing to it, just where I had left it the evening previous.

He answered nothing.

"Will you, or will you not, quit me?" I now demanded in a sudden passion,   160
advancing close to him.

"I would prefer *not* to quit you," he replied, gently emphasizing the *not*.

"What earthly right have you to stay here? Do you pay any rent? Do you pay my taxes? Or is this property yours?"

He answered nothing.

"Are you ready to go on and write now? Are your eyes recovered? Could you copy a small paper for me this morning? or help examine a few lines? or step round to the Post Office? In a word, will you do anything at all, to give a coloring to your refusal to depart the premises?"

He silently retired into his hermitage.   165

I was now in such a state of nervous resentment that I thought it but prudent to check myself at present from further demonstrations. Bartleby and I were alone. I remembered the tragedy of the unfortunate Adams and the still more unfortunate Colt° in the solitary office of the latter; and how poor Colt, being dreadfully incensed by Adams, and imprudently permitting himself to get wildly excited, was at unawares hurried into his fatal act — an act which certainly no man could possibly deplore more than the actor himself. Often it had occurred to me in my ponderings upon the subject that had that altercation taken place in the public street, or at a private residence, it would not have terminated as it did. It was the circumstance of being alone in a solitary

---

Adams . . . Colt: Samuel Adams was killed by John C. Colt, brother of the gun maker, during a quarrel in 1842. After a sensational court case, Colt committed suicide just before he was to be hanged.

office, up stairs, of a building entirely unhallowed by humanizing domestic associations — an uncarpeted office, doubtless, of a dusty, haggard sort of appearance — this it must have been, which greatly helped to enhance the irritable desperation of the hapless Colt.

But when this old Adam of resentment rose in me and tempted me concerning Bartleby, I grappled him and threw him. How? Why, simply by recalling the divine injunction: "A new commandment give I unto you, that ye love one another." Yes, this it was that saved me. Aside from higher considerations, charity often operates as a vastly wise and prudent principle — a great safeguard to its possessor. Men have committed murder for jealousy's sake, and anger's sake, and hatred's sake, and selfishness' sake, and spiritual pride's sake; but no man, that ever I heard of, ever committed a diabolical murder for sweet charity's sake. Mere self-interest, then, if no better motive can be enlisted, should, especially with high-tempered men, prompt all beings to charity and philanthropy. At any rate, upon the occasion in question, I strove to drown my exasperated feelings towards the scrivener by benevolently construing his conduct. Poor fellow, poor fellow! thought I, he don't mean anything; and besides, he has seen hard times, and ought to be indulged.

I endeavored, also, immediately to occupy myself, and at the same time to comfort my despondency. I tried to fancy, that in the course of the morning, at such time as might prove agreeable to him, Bartleby, of his own free accord, would emerge from his hermitage and take up some decided line of march in the direction of the door. But no. Half-past twelve o'clock came; Turkey began to glow in the face, overturn his inkstand, and become generally obstreperous; Nippers abated down into quietude and courtesy; Ginger Nut munched his noon apple; and Bartleby remained standing at his window in one of his profoundest dead-wall reveries. Will it be credited? Ought I to acknowledge it? That afternoon I left the office without saying one further word to him.

Some days now passed, during which, at leisure intervals I looked a little into "Edwards on the Will," and "Priestley on Necessity."° Under the circumstances, those books induced a salutary feeling. Gradually I slid into the persuasion that these troubles of mine, touching the scrivener, had been all predestined from eternity, and Bartleby was billeted upon me for some mysterious purpose of an all-wise Providence, which it was not for a mere mortal like me to fathom. Yes, Bartleby, stay there behind your screen, thought I; I shall persecute you no more; you are harmless and noiseless as any of these old chairs; in short, I never feel so private as when I know you are here. At last I see it, I feel it; I penetrate to the predestined purpose of my life. I am content. Others may have loftier parts to enact; but my mission in this world, Bartleby, is to furnish you with office-room for such period as you may see fit to remain.

I believe that this wise and blessed frame of mind would have continued 170 with me, had it not been for the unsolicited and uncharitable remarks obtruded upon me by my professional friends who visited the rooms. But thus it often is, that the constant friction of illiberal minds wears out at last the best resolves of the more generous. Though to be sure, when I reflected upon it, it was not strange that people entering my office should be struck by the peculiar

"Edwards . . . Necessity": Jonathan Edwards, in *Freedom of the Will* (1754), and Joseph Priestley, in *Doctrine of Philosophical Necessity* (1777), both argued that human beings do not have free will.

aspect of the unaccountable Bartleby, and so be tempted to throw out some sinister observations concerning him. Sometimes an attorney, having business with me, and calling at my office, and finding no one but the scrivener there, would undertake to obtain some sort of precise information from him touching my whereabouts; but without heeding his idle talk, Bartleby would remain standing immovable in the middle of the room. So after contemplating him in that position for a time, the attorney would depart, no wiser than he came.

Also, when a reference was going on, and the room full of lawyers and witnesses, and business driving fast, some deeply-occupied legal gentleman present, seeing Bartleby wholly unemployed, would request him to run round to his (the legal gentleman's) office and fetch some papers for him. Thereupon, Bartleby would tranquilly decline, and yet remain idle as before. Then the lawyer would give a great stare, and turn to me. And what could I say? At last I was made aware that all through the circle of my professional acquaintance, a whisper of wonder was running round, having reference to the strange creature I kept at my office. This worried me very much. And as the idea came upon me of his possibly turning out a long-lived man, and keeping occupying my chambers, and denying my authority; and perplexing my visitors; and scandalizing my professional reputation; and casting a general gloom over the premises; keeping soul and body together to the last upon his savings (for doubtless he spent but half a dime a day), and in the end perhaps outlive me, and claim possession of my office by right of his perpetual occupancy: as all these dark anticipations crowded upon me more and more, and my friends continually intruded their relentless remarks upon the apparition in my room; a great change was wrought in me. I resolved to gather all my faculties together, and forever rid me of this intolerable incubus.

Ere revolving any complicated project, however, adapted to this end, I first simply suggested to Bartleby the propriety of his permanent departure. In a calm and serious tone, I commended the idea to his careful and mature consideration. But, having taken three days to meditate upon it, he apprised me, that his original determination remained the same; in short, that he still preferred to abide with me.

What shall I do? I now said to myself, buttoning up my coat to the last button. What shall I do? what ought I to do? what does conscience say I *should* do with this man, or, rather, ghost. Rid myself of him, I must; go, he shall. But how? You will not thrust him, the poor, pale, passive mortal — you will not thrust such a helpless creature out of your door? you will not dishonor yourself by such cruelty? No, I will not, I cannot do that. Rather would I let him live and die here, and then mason up his remains in the wall. What, then, will you do? For all your coaxing, he will not budge. Bribes he leaves under your own paper-weight on your table; in short, it is quite plain that he prefers to cling to you.

Then something severe, something unusual must be done. What! surely you will not have him collared by a constable, and commit his innocent pallor to the common jail? And upon what ground could you procure such a thing to be done? — a vagrant, is he? What! he a vagrant, a wanderer, who refuses to budge? It is because he will *not* be a vagrant, then, that you seek to count him *as* a vagrant. That is too absurd. No visible means of support: there I have him. Wrong again: for indubitably he *does* support himself, and that is the only unanswerable proof that any man can show of his possessing the means so to do. No more, then. Since he will not quit me, I must quit him. I will change my offices; I will move elsewhere, and give him fair notice, that if I find him on my new premises I will then proceed against him as a common trespasser.

Acting accordingly, next day I thus addressed him: "I find these chambers 175 too far from the City Hall; the air is unwholesome. In a word, I propose to remove my offices next week, and shall no longer require your services. I tell you this now, in order that you may seek another place."

He made no reply, and nothing more was said.

On the appointed day I engaged carts and men, proceeded to my chambers, and having but little furniture, everything was removed in a few hours. Throughout, the scrivener remained standing behind the screen, which I directed to be removed the last thing. It was withdrawn; and, being folded up like a huge folio, left him the motionless occupant of a naked room. I stood in the entry watching him a moment, while something from within me upbraided me.

I re-entered, with my hand in my pocket — and — and my heart in my mouth.

"Good-bye, Bartleby; I am going — good-bye, and God some way bless you; and take that," slipping something in his hand. But it dropped upon the floor, and then — strange to say — I tore myself from him whom I had so longed to be rid of.

Established in my new quarters, for a day or two I kept the door locked, 180 and started at every footfall in the passages. When I returned to my rooms, after any little absence, I would pause at the threshold for an instant, and attentively listen, ere applying my key. But these fears were needless. Bartleby never came nigh me.

I thought all was going well, when a perturbed-looking stranger visited me, inquiring whether I was the person who had recently occupied rooms at No. — Wall Street.

Full of forebodings, I replied that I was.

"Then, sir," said the stranger, who proved a lawyer, "you are responsible for the man you left there. He refuses to do any copying; he refuses to do anything; he says he prefers not to; and he refuses to quit the premises."

"I am very sorry, sir," said I, with assumed tranquillity, but an inward tremor, "but, really, the man you allude to is nothing to me — he is no relation or apprentice of mine, that you should hold me responsible for him."

"In mercy's name, who is he?" 185

"I certainly cannot inform you. I know nothing about him. Formerly I employed him as a copyist; but he has done nothing for me now for some time past."

"I shall settle him, then — good morning, sir."

Several days passed, and I heard nothing more; and, though I often felt a charitable prompting to call at the place and see poor Bartleby, yet a certain squeamishness, of I know not what, withheld me.

All is over with him, by this time, thought I, at last, when, through another week, no further intelligence reached me. But, coming to my room the day after, I found several persons waiting at my door in a high state of nervous excitement.

"That's the man — here he comes," cried the foremost one, whom I recog- 190 nized as the lawyer who had previously called upon me alone.

"You must take him away, sir, at once," cried a portly person among them, advancing upon me, and whom I knew to be the landlord of No. — Wall Street. "These gentlemen, my tenants, cannot stand it any longer; Mr. B —," pointing to the lawyer, "has turned him out of his room, and he now persists in haunting the building generally, sitting upon the banisters of the stairs by day, and sleeping in the entry by night. Everybody is concerned; clients are leaving the offices; some fears are entertained of a mob; something you must do, and that without delay."

Aghast at this torrent, I fell back before it, and would fain have locked myself in my new quarters. In vain I persisted that Bartleby was nothing to me — no more than to any one else. In vain — I was the last person known to have anything to do with him, and they held me to the terrible account. Fearful, then, of being exposed in the papers (as one person present obscurely threatened), I considered the matter, and, at length, said, that if the lawyer would give me a confidential interview with the scrivener, in his (the lawyer's) own room, I would, that afternoon, strive my best to rid them of the nuisance they complained of.

Going up stairs to my old haunt, there was Bartleby silently sitting upon the banister at the landing.

"What are you doing here, Bartleby?" said I.

"Sitting upon the banister," he mildly replied.   195

I motioned him into the lawyer's room, who then left us.

"Bartleby," said I, "are you aware that you are the cause of great tribulation to me, by persisting in occupying the entry after being dismissed from the office?"

No answer.

"Now one of two things must take place. Either you must do something, or something must be done to you. Now what sort of business would you like to engage in? Would you like to re-engage in copying for some one?"

"No; I would prefer not to make any change."   200

"Would you like a clerkship in a dry-goods store?"

"There is too much confinement about that. No, I would not like a clerkship; but I am not particular."

"Too much confinement," I cried, "why, you keep yourself confined all the time!"

"I would prefer not to take a clerkship," he rejoined, as if to settle that little item at once.

"How would a bar-tender's business suit you? There is no trying of the eye-   205
sight in that."

"I would not like it at all; though, as I said before, I am not particular."

His unwonted wordiness inspirited me. I returned to the charge.

"Well, then, would you like to travel through the country collecting bills for the merchants? That would improve your health."

"No, I would prefer to be doing something else."

"How, then, would going as a companion to Europe, to entertain some   210
young gentleman with your conversation — how would that suit you?"

"Not at all. It does not strike me that there is anything definite about that. I like to be stationary. But I am not particular."

"Stationary you shall be, then," I cried, now losing all patience, and, for the first time in all my exasperating connection with him, fairly flying into a passion. "If you do not go away from these premises before night, I shall feel bound—indeed, I *am* bound—to—to quit the premises myself!" I rather absurdly concluded, knowing not with what possible threat to try to frighten his immobility into compliance. Despairing of all further efforts, I was precipitately leaving him, when a final thought occurred to me—one which had not been wholly unindulged before.

"Bartleby," said I, in the kindest tone I could assume under such exciting circumstances, "will you go home with me now—not to my office, but my dwelling—and remain there till we can conclude upon some convenient arrangement for you at our leisure? Come, let us start now, right away."

"No: at present I would prefer not to make any change at all."

I answered nothing; but, effectually dodging every one by the suddenness and rapidity of my flight, rushed from the building, ran up Wall Street towards Broadway, and, jumping into the first omnibus, was soon removed from pursuit. As soon as tranquillity returned, I distinctly perceived that I had now done all that I possibly could, both in respect to the demands of the landlord and his tenants, and with regard to my own desire and sense of duty, to benefit Bartleby, and shield him from rude persecution. I now strove to be entirely care-free and quiescent; and my conscience justified me in the attempt; though, indeed, it was not so successful as I could have wished. So fearful was I of being again hunted out by the incensed landlord and his exasperated tenants, that, surrendering my business to Nippers, for a few days, I drove about the upper part of the town and through the suburbs, in my rockaway; crossed over to Jersey City and Hoboken, and paid fugitive visits to Manhattanville and Astoria. In fact, I almost lived in my rockaway for the time.

When again I entered my office, lo, a note from the landlord lay upon the desk. I opened it with trembling hands. It informed me that the writer had sent to the police, and had Bartleby removed to the Tombs as a vagrant. Moreover, since I knew more about him than any one else, he wished me to appear at that place, and make a suitable statement of the facts. These tidings had a conflicting effect upon me. At first I was indignant; but, at last, almost approved. The landlord's energetic, summary disposition, had led him to adopt a procedure which I do not think I would have decided upon myself; and yet, as a last resort, under such peculiar circumstances, it seemed the only plan.

As I afterwards learned, the poor scrivener, when told that he must be conducted to the Tombs, offered not the slightest obstacle, but, in his pale, unmoving way, silently acquiesced.

Some of the compassionate and curious by-standers joined the party; and headed by one of the constables arm-in-arm with Bartleby, the silent procession filed its way through all the noise, and heat, and joy of the roaring thoroughfares at noon.

The same day I received the note, I went to the Tombs, or, to speak more properly, the Halls of Justice. Seeking the right officer, I stated the purpose of my call, and was informed that the individual I described was, indeed, within. I then assured the functionary that Bartleby was a perfectly honest man, and greatly to be compassionated, however unaccountably eccentric. I narrated all I knew, and closed by suggesting the idea of letting him remain in as indulgent confinement as possible, till something less harsh might be done—though, indeed, I hardly knew what. At all events, if nothing else could be decided upon, the almshouse must receive him. I then begged to have an interview.

Being under no disgraceful charge, and quite serene and harmless in all   220
his ways, they had permitted him freely to wander about the prison, and, especially, in the inclosed grass-platted yards thereof. And so I found him there,
standing all alone in the quietest of the yards, his face towards a high wall,
while all around, from the narrow slits of the jail windows, I thought I saw
peering out upon him the eyes of murderers and thieves.

"Bartleby!"

"I know you," he said, without looking round — "and I want nothing to say
to you."

"It was not I that brought you here, Bartleby," said I, keenly pained at his
implied suspicion. "And to you, this should not be so vile a place. Nothing
reproachful attaches to you by being here. And see, it is not so sad a place as
one might think. Look, there is the sky, and here is the grass."

"I know where I am," he replied, but would say nothing more, and so I
left him.

As I entered the corridor again, a broad meat-like man, in an apron, accosted   225
me, and, jerking his thumb over his shoulder, said — "Is that your friend?"

"Yes."

"Does he want to starve? If he does, let him live on the prison fare,
that's all."

"Who are you?" asked I, not knowing what to make of such an unofficially
speaking person in such a place.

"I am the grub-man. Such gentlemen as have friends here, hire me to provide them with something good to eat."

"Is this so?" said I, turning the turnkey.   230

He said it was.

"Well, then," said I, slipping some silver into the grub-man's hands (for so
they called him), "I want you to give particular attention to my friend there; let
him have the best dinner you can get. And you must be as polite to him as possible."

"Introduce me, will you?" said the grub-man, looking at me with an expression which seemed to say he was all impatience for an opportunity to give
a specimen of his breeding.

Thinking it would prove of benefit to the scrivener, I acquiesced; and, asking the grub-man his name, went up with him to Bartleby.

"Bartleby, this is a friend; you will find him very useful to you."   235

"Your sarvant, sir, your sarvant," said the grub-man, making a low saluta-
tion behind his apron. "Hope you find it pleasant here, sir; nice grounds — cool
apartments — hope you'll stay with us some time — try to make it agreeable.
What will you have for dinner to-day?"

"I prefer not to dine to-day," said Bartleby, turning away. "It would disagree with me; I am unused to dinners." So saying, he slowly moved to the
other side of the inclosure, and took up a position fronting the deadwall.

"How's this?" said the grub-man, addressing me with a stare of astonishment. "He's odd, ain't he?"

"I think he is a little deranged," said I, sadly.

"Deranged? deranged is it? Well, now, upon my word, I thought that   240
friend of yourn was a gentleman forger; they are always pale and genteel-like,
them forgers. I can't help pity 'em — can't help it, sir. Did you know Monroe
Edwards?" he added, touchingly, and paused. Then, laying his hand piteously

on my shoulder, sighed, "he died of consumption at Sing-Sing. So you weren't acquainted with Monroe?"

"No, I was never socially acquainted with any forgers. But I cannot stop longer. Look to my friend yonder. You will not lose by it. I will see you again."

Some few days after this, I again obtained admission to the Tombs, and went through the corridors in quest of Bartleby; but without finding him.

"I saw him coming from his cell not long ago," said a turnkey, "may be he's gone to loiter in the yards."

So I went in that direction.

"Are you looking for the silent man?" said another turnkey, passing me. 245 "Yonder he lies — sleeping in the yard there. 'Tis not twenty minutes since I saw him lie down."

The yard was entirely quiet. It was not accessible to the common prisoners. The surrounding walls, of amazing thickness, kept off all sounds behind them. The Egyptian character of the masonry weighed upon me with its gloom. But a soft imprisoned turf grew under foot. The heart of the eternal pyramids, it seemed, wherein, by some strange magic, through the clefts, grass-seed, dropped by birds, had sprung.

Strangely huddled at the base of the wall, his knees drawn up, and lying on his side, his head touching the cold stones, I saw the wasted Bartleby. But nothing stirred. I paused; then went close up to him; stooped over, and saw that his dim eyes were open; otherwise he seemed profoundly sleeping. Something prompted me to touch him. I felt his hand, when a tingling shiver ran up my arm and down my spine to my feet.

The round face of the grub-man peered upon me now. "His dinner is ready. Won't he dine to-day, either? Or does he live without dining?"

"Lives without dining," said I, and closed the eyes.

"Eh! — He's asleep, ain't he?"   250

"With kings and counselors,"° murmured I.

There would seem little need for proceeding further in this history. Imagination will readily supply the meagre recital of poor Bartleby's interment. But, ere parting with the reader, let me say, that if this little narrative has sufficiently interested him, to awaken curiosity as to who Bartleby was, and what manner of life he led prior to the present narrator's making his acquaintance, I can only reply, that in such curiosity I fully share, but am wholly unable to gratify it. Yet here I hardly know whether I should divulge one little item of rumor, which came to my ear a few months after the scrivener's decease. Upon what basis it rested, I could never ascertain; and hence, how true it is I cannot now tell. But, inasmuch as this vague report has not been without a certain suggestive interest to me, however sad, it may prove the same with some others; and so I will briefly mention it. The report was this: that Bartleby had been a subordinate clerk in the Dead Letter Office at Washington, from which he had been suddenly removed by a change in the administration. When I think over this rumor, hardly can I express the emotions which seize me. Dead letters! does it not sound like dead men? Conceive a man by nature and misfortune prone to a pallid hopelessness, can any business seem more fitted to heighten it than that of continually handling these dead letters, and assorting them for the flames? For by the cart-load they are annually burned. Sometimes

"With kings and counselors": From Job 3:13–14: "then had I been at rest, / With kings and counselors of the earth, / which built desolate places for themselves."

from out the folded paper the pale clerk takes a ring—the finger it was meant for, perhaps, moulders in the grave; a bank-note sent in swiftest charity—he whom it would relieve, nor eats nor hungers any more; pardon for those who died despairing; hope for those who died unhoping; good tidings for those who died stifled by unrelieved calamities. On errands of life, these letters speed to death.

Ah, Bartleby! Ah, humanity!

CONSIDERATIONS FOR CRITICAL THINKING AND WRITING

1. **FIRST RESPONSE.** How does the lawyer's description of himself serve to characterize him? Why is it significant that he is a lawyer? Are his understandings and judgments about Bartleby and himself always sound?

2. Why do you think Turkey, Nippers, and Ginger Nut are introduced to the reader before Bartleby?

3. Describe Bartleby's physical characteristics. How is his physical description a foreshadowing of what happens to him?

4. How does Bartleby's "I would prefer not to" affect the routine of the lawyer and his employees?

5. What is the significance of the subtitle: "A Story of Wall Street"?

6. Who is the protagonist? Whose story is it?

7. Does the lawyer change during the story? Does Bartleby? Who is the antagonist?

8. What motivates Bartleby's behavior? Why do you think Melville withholds the information about the Dead Letter Office until the end of the story? Does this background adequately explain Bartleby?

9. Does Bartleby have any lasting impact on the lawyer?

10. Do you think Melville sympathizes more with Bartleby or with the lawyer?

11. Describe the lawyer's changing attitudes toward Bartleby.

12. Consider how this story could be regarded as a kind of protest with non-negotiable demands.

13. Discuss the story's humor and how it affects your response to Bartleby.

14. Trace your emotional reaction to Bartleby as he is revealed in the story.

15. **CRITICAL STRATEGIES.** Read the section on biographical criticism (pp. 1540–42) in Chapter 46, "Critical Strategies for Reading," and use the library to learn about Melville's reputation as a writer at the time of his writing "Bartleby." How might this information produce a provocative biographical approach to the story?

CONNECTIONS TO OTHER SELECTIONS

1. Compare Bartleby's withdrawal from life with that of the protagonist in Gail Godwin's "A Sorrowful Woman" (p. 39). Why does each character choose death?

2. How is Melville's use of Bartleby's experience in the Dead Letter Office similar to Nathaniel Hawthorne's use of Brown's forest encounter with the devil in "Young Goodman Brown" (p. 325)? Why is each experience crucial to an understanding of what informs the behavior of these characters?

Perspectives

NATHANIEL HAWTHORNE (1804–1864)

On Herman Melville's Philosophic Stance   1856

[Melville] stayed with us from Tuesday till Thursday; and, on the intervening day, we took a pretty long walk together, and sat down in a hollow among the sand hills (sheltering ourselves from the high, cool wind) and smoked a cigar. Melville, as he always does, began to reason of Providence and futurity, and of everything that lies beyond human ken, and informed me that he had "pretty much made up his mind to be annihilated"; but still he does not seem to rest in that anticipation; and, I think, will never rest until he gets hold of a definite belief. It is strange how he persists — and has persisted ever since I knew him, and probably long before — in wandering to-and-fro over these deserts, as dismal and monotonous as the sand hills amid which we were sitting. He can neither believe, nor be comfortable in his unbelief; and he is too honest and courageous not to try to do one or the other. If he were a religious man, he would be one of the most truly religious and reverential; he has a very high and noble nature, and better worth immortality than most of us.

From *The American Notebooks*

CONSIDERATIONS FOR CRITICAL THINKING AND WRITING

1. How does this description of Melville shed light on the central concerns of "Bartleby, the Scrivener"?

2. Which side does Hawthorne seem to be on — "belief" or "unbelief"? Why?

3. Compare Hawthorne's description with Melville's view of Hawthorne (p. 358). What attitudes about life do they share?

4. Write an essay about the issue of "belief" and "unbelief" in "Bartleby, the Scrivener" and Ernest Hemingway's "Soldier's Home" (p. 165).

DAN McCALL (B. 1940)

On the Lawyer's Character in "Bartleby, the Scrivener"   1989

The overwhelming majority of the Bartleby Industry reads the narrator of the story in a way that is not only different from mine but quite incompatible with mine. Every virtue I see in the man, they see as a vice; where I see his strength, they see his weakness; what I see as his genuine responsiveness, they see as his cold self-absorption. Some critics read the story as I do, but we are in a distinct minority. There are several reasons this should be so, and I think I understand at least some of them, but first I should like to present as fairly as I can the majority opinion.

Robert Weisbuch, who has said the Lawyer is Charles Dickens, refers to the Lawyer as "unnatural," "anti-natural," "lifeless," "self-satisfied," "pompous," and "rationalizing." The Lawyer "investigates Bartleby but refuses authentic emotional commitment in so doing," and "Bartleby rightly refuses to credit the Lawyer's false commitment." The Lawyer is guilty of "toadyism" and his final heartbroken outburst, "Ah, Bartleby! Ah, humanity!" is no more than "a someways hollow and unfeeling exclamation."[1] Another critic calls the Lawyer a "smug fool" who is "terribly unkind to a very sick man."[2] I had always thought of the Lawyer as a kind of stand-in for us, a figure we could identify with as we struggled to understand Bartleby. On the contrary, the narrator is "deficient in humanity and quite obtuse towards human beings." I must have had it backwards, for "surely this was Melville's intention: to have his reader *not* sympathize with the Lawyer, *not* to identify with him, *not* to put himself in the Lawyer's place" (*his* italics, not mine).[3] Another critic says, "The narrator attains new heights of vague sentimentality rather than a peak of awareness in his climactic and highly revealing sigh: 'Ah, Bartleby! Ah, humanity!'" This reader provides dismissive certainty in answering the question

> Who then is Melville's narrator? He is the sort of man one tends to find in high places: the snug man whose worldly success has convinced him that this is the "best of all possible worlds," and whose virtues cluster around a "prudential" concern for maintaining his own situation. The narrator can never fully understand or truly befriend Bartleby because the narrator is simply too complacent, both philosophically and morally, to sympathize with human dissatisfaction and despair.[4]

Still another reader tells us the Lawyer's commentary "rings with blasphemy" and demonstrates "grotesque manifestations of diseased conscience."[5]

Authority is the enemy here. In the extended quotation just above it is taken for granted that the "sort of man one tends to find in high places" is superficial and selfish. Worldly success is bad for the character. The Lawyer has to be bad, or he wouldn't be in an office on Wall Street. Hershel Parker tells us that "our ultimate opinion" of the Lawyer "is not contempt so much as bleak astonishment at his secure blindness. With a bitterer irony than the narrator is capable of, we murmur something like 'Ah, narrator! Ah, humanity!' In his self-consciously eloquent sequel, after all, the lawyer has merely made his last cheap purchase of a 'delicious self-approval.'" Parker maintains that when "this easy-conscienced" man speaks of kings and counselors, "he is experiencing a comfortable, self-indulgent variety of melancholy"; when he quotes

[1] Robert Weisbuch, "Melville's 'Bartleby' and the Dead Letter of Charles Dickens," *Atlantic Double-Cross: American Literature and British Influence in the Age of Emerson* (Chicago: University of Chicago Press, 1986), pp. 44, 45–47.

[2] David Shusterman, "The 'Reader Fallacy' and 'Bartleby, the Scrivener,'" *New England Quarterly* 45 (March 1972): 122–23.

[3] Ibid., p. 121.

[4] Allan Emery, "The Alternatives of Melville's 'Bartleby,'" *Nineteenth-Century Fiction* 31 (1976): 186–87.

[5] William Bysshe Stein, "Bartleby: The Christian Conscience," in *Melville Annual 1965, A Symposium: "Bartleby, the Scrivener,"* ed. Howard P. Vincent (Kent, Ohio: Kent State University Press, 1966), p. 107.

words from the Book of Job he does so "with prideful aptness," and "character-istically perverts them from profound lament to sonorous urbanity."[6]

This last feature of Parker's argument is interesting to me because it reminds me of the first time I read the story, at eighteen. I was overwhelmed by the discovery that Bartleby had died, and I didn't know that "With kings and counselors" was a quotation from the Book of Job. The phrase "With kings and counselors" seemed to me majestic and solemn and final. That "murmured I" put a deep hush around it. But it never occurred to me that the man who said those words was "easy-conscienced" or "self-indulgent" or the sort of man who "characteristically perverts" a "profound lament to sonorous urbanity." The figure of Bartleby seemed so weird and funny and painful, his death at once inevitable and shocking, that I did not see it as an occasion for the man who was telling me about it to make a "last cheap purchase" of "deli-cious self-approval." I trusted that Lawyer.

Thirty years later, I still do. He seems to me extremely intelligent, whimsi-cal and ironic, generous, self-aware, passionate, and thoroughly competent.

From *The Silence of Bartleby*

[6] Hershel Parker, "The Sequel in 'Bartleby,'" in *Bartleby the Inscrutable: A Collection of Commen-tary on Herman Melville's Tale "Bartleby, the Scrivener,"* ed. M. Thomas Inge (Hamden, Conn.: Archon Books, 1979), pp. 159–65, 163–64.

CONSIDERATIONS FOR CRITICAL THINKING AND WRITING

1. How does McCall characterize the "majority opinion" on the lawyer's char-acter? What is his opinion of the lawyer?

2. How does McCall's opinion of the lawyer compare with Hawthorne's opin-ion of Herman Melville in the preceding Perspective?

3. Write an essay explaining whether you find the "majority opinion" or McCall's view of the lawyer more convincing.

SUSAN STRAIGHT (B. 1961)

Born in Riverside, California, where she has lived all her life and where she teaches in the creative writing department at the University of California, Riverside, Susan Straight has published in a wide variety of periodicals including *Harper's*, *The New York Times*, and *Salon.com*. She is the author of six novels: *I Been in Sorrow's Kitchen and Licked Out All the Pots* (1993), *Aquaboogie: A Novel in Stories* (1994), *Blacker than a Thousand Nights* (1995), *The Gettin' Place* (1997), *Highwire Moon* (2001), and *A Mil-lion Nightingales* (2006). Her writing has earned her awards from the Guggenheim Founda-

By permission of the University of California, Riverside.

tion and the Lannan Foundation. Though she is Caucasian, much of Straight's fiction concerns black characters and black family life. Growing up in Riverside and having a black husband have allowed her to say with confidence that "this is where I came from and this is what I knew." "Mines" appeared in *Best American Short Stories* for 2003 with this commentary from Straight: "I have many female relatives and friends who work as correctional officers, and I also have many relatives and friends who are incarcerated."

Mines

2002

They can't shave their heads every day like they wish they could, so their tattoos show through stubble. Little black hairs like iron filings stuck on magnets. Big roundhead fool magnets.

The Chicano fools have gang names on the sides of their skulls. The white fools have swastikas. The Vietnamese fools have writing I can't read. And the black fools — if they're too dark, they can't have anything on their heads. Maybe on the lighter skin at their chest, or the inside of the arm.

Where I sit for the morning shift at my window, I can see my nephew in his line, heading to the library. Square-head light-skinned fool like my brother. Little dragon on his skull. Nothing in his skull. Told me it was cause he could breathe fire if he had to. ALFONSO tattooed on his arm.

"What, he too gotdamn stupid to remember his own name?" my godfather said when he saw it. "Gotta look down by his elbow every few minutes to check?"

Two names on his collarbone: twins. Girls. EGYPT and MOROCCO. Seven- 5 teen and he's got kids. He's in here for eight years. Riding in the car when somebody did a drive-by. Back seat. Law say same as pulling the trigger.

Ten o'clock. They line up for shift between classes and voc ed. Dark blue backs like fool dominoes. Shuffling boots. Fred and I stand in the doorway, hands on our belts, watching. From here, seeing all those heads with all those blue-green marks like bruises, looks like everybody got beat up big-time. Reyes and Michaels and the other officers lead their lines past the central guard station, and when the wards get closer, you can see all the other tattoos. Names over their eyebrows, teardrops on their cheeks, words on their necks, letters on their fingers.

One Chicano kid has PERDÓNEME MI ABUELITA in fancy cursive on the back of his neck. Sorry my little grandma. I bet that makes her feel much better.

When my nephew shuffles by, he grins and says softly, "Hey, Auntie Clarette."

I want to slap the dragon off the side of his stupid skull.

Fred says, "How's your fine friend Tika? The one with green eyes?"   10

I roll my brown eyes. "Contacts, okay?"

I didn't tell him I saw Tika last night, at Lincoln Elementary. "How can you work at the youth prison? All those young brothers incarcerated by the system?" That's what Tika said to me at Back-to-School Night. "Doesn't it hurt you to be there?"

"Y'all went to college together, right?" Fred says.

"Mmm-hmm." Except she's teaching African-American studies there now, and I married Ray. He quit football and started drywalling with his uncle.

"Ray went with y'all too, didn't he? Played ball till he blew out his knee?"   15

The wind's been steady for three days now, hot fall blowing all the tumbleweeds across the empty fields out here, piling them up against the chain-link until it looks like hundreds of heads to me. Big-ass naturals from the seventies, when I squint and look toward the east. Two wards come around the building and I'm up. "Where you going?"

The Chicano kid grins. "TB test."

"Pass."

He flashes it, and I see the nurse's signature. The blister on his forearm looks like a quarter somebody slid under the skin. Whole place has TB so bad we gotta get tested every week. My forearm's dotted with marks like I'm a junkie.

I lift up my chin. I feel like a guy when I do it, but it's easier than talking   20
sometimes. I don't want to open my mouth. "Go ahead," Fred calls out to them.

"Like you got up and looked."

Fred lifts his eyebrows at me. "Okay, Miss Thang."

It's like a piece of hot link burning in my throat. "Shut the fuck up, Fred." That's what Michaels and Reyes always say to him. I hear it come out like that, and I close my eyes. When I get home now, and the kids start their homework, I have to stand at the sink and wash my hands and change my mouth. My spit, everything, I think. Not a prayer. More like when you cool down after you run. I watch the water on my knuckles and think: No TB, no cussing, no meds. Because a couple months after I started at Youth Authority, I would holler at the kids, "Take your meds."

Flintstones, Mama, Danae would say.

Fred looks up at the security videos. "Tika still single, huh?"   25

"Yeah."

She has a gallery downtown, and she was at the school to show African art. She said to me, "Doesn't it hurt your soul? How can you stand it?"

I didn't say anything at first. I was watching Ray Jr. talk to his teacher. He's tall now, fourth grade, and he smells different to me when he wakes up in the morning.

I told Tika, "I work seven to three. I'm home when the kids get off the bus. I have bennies."

She just looked at me.   30

"Benefits." I didn't say the rest. Most of the time now Ray stays at his cousin Lafayette's house. He hasn't worked for a year. He and Lafayette say construction is way down, and when somebody is building, Mexican drywallers get all the business in Rio Seco.

When I got this job, Ray got funny. He broke dishes, washing them. He wrecked clothes, washing them. He said, "That ain't a man — that's a man's job." He started staying out with Lafayette.

Tika said, "Doesn't it hurt you inside to see the young brothers?"

For my New Year's resolution I told myself: Silence is golden. At work, cause me talking just reminds them I'm a woman. With Ray and my mother and everyone else except my kids. I looked at Tika's lipstick, and I shouted in my head: I make thirty-five grand a year! I've got bennies now! Ray never had health care, and Danae's got asthma. I don't get to worry about big stuff like you do, cause I'm worrying about big stuff like I do. Pay the bills, put gas in the van, buy groceries. Ray Jr. eats three boxes of Cheerios every week, okay?

"Fred Harris works there. And J.C. and Marcus and Beverly."   35

Tika says, "Prison is the biggest growth industry in California. They're determined to put everyone of color behind a wall."

Five days a week, I was thinking, I drive past the chain-link fence and past J.C. at the guard gate. Then Danae ran up to me with a book. They had a book sale at Back-to-School Night. Danae wanted an American Girl story. Four ninety-five.

Tika walked away. I went to the cash register. Five days a week, I park my van and walk into the walls. But they're fences with barbed wire and us watching. Everything. Every face.

"Nobody in the laundry?" I ask, and Fred shakes his head. Laundry is where they've been fighting this week. Black kid got his head busted open Friday in there, and we're supposed to watch the screens. The bell rings, and we get up to stand in the courtyard for period change. We can hear them coming from the classrooms, doors slamming and all those boots thumping on the asphalt. The wind moving their stiff pants around their ankles, it's so hard right now. I watch their heads. Every day it's a scuffle out here, and we're supposed to listen to who's yelling, or worse, talking that quiet shit that sets it off.

All the damn heads look the same to me, when I'm out here with my stick   40
down by my side. Light ones like Alfonso and the Chicano kids and the Vietnamese, all golden brown. Dark little guys, some Filipino, even, and then the white kids, almost green they're so pale. But all the tattoos like scabs. Numbers over their eyebrows and FUCK YOU inside their lips when they pull them down like clowns.

The wind whips through them and they all squint but don't move. My head is hurting at the temples, from the dust and wind and no sleep. Laundry. The wards stay in formation, stop and wait, boots shining like dark foreheads. I hear muttering and answers and shit-talking in the back, but nobody starts punching. Then the bell rings and they march off.

"Youngblood. Stop the mouth," Fred calls from behind me. He talks to the wards all the time. Old school. Luther Vandross–loving and hair fading back like the tide at the beach—only forty-two, but acts like he's a grandpa from the South. "Son, if you'da thought about what you were doing last year, you wouldn't be stepping past me this year." They look at him like they want to spit in his face. "Son, sometimes what the old people say is the gospel truth, but you wasn't in church to hear." They would knock him in the head if they could. "Son, you're only sixteen, but you're gonna have to go across the street before you know it, you keep up that attitude."

Across the street is Chino. Men's Correctional Facility. The wards laugh and sing back to Fred like they're Snoop Doggy Dogg: "I'm on my way to Chino, I see no reason to cry . . ."

He says, "Lord knows Mr. Dogg ain't gonna be there when you are."

The Chicano kids talk Spanish to Reyes, and he looks back at them like a   45
statue wearing shades. The big guy, Michaels, used to play football with Ray. He has never looked into my face since I got here. My nephew knows who he is. He says, "Come on, Michaels, show a brotha love, Michaels. Lemme have a cigarette. You can't do that for a brotha, man? Brothaman?"

Alfonso thinks this is a big joke. A vacation. Training for life. His country club.

I don't say a damn thing when he winks at me. I watch them walk domino lines to class and to the kitchen and the laundry and the field. SLEEPY and SPOOKY and DRE DOG and SCOOBY and G DOG and MONSTER all tattooed on their arms and heads and necks. Like a damn kennel. Nazis with spider webs on their elbows, which is supposed to mean they killed somebody dark. Asians with spidery writing on their arms, and I don't know what that means.

"I'ma get mines, all I gotta say, Auntie Clarette," my nephew always said when he was ten or eleven. "I ain't workin all my life for some shitty car and a house. I'ma get mines now."

I can't help it. Not supposed to look out for him, but when they change, when they're in the cafeteria, I watch him. I don't say anything to him. But I keep seeing my brother in his fool forehead, my brother and his girlfriend in their apartment, nothing but a couch and a TV. Always got something to drink, though, and plenty weed.

Swear Alfonso might think he's better off here. Three hots and a cot, the   50
boys say.

We watch the laundry screens, the classrooms, and I don't say anything to Fred for a long time. I keep thinking about Danae's reading tonight, takes twenty minutes, and then I can wash a load of jeans and pay the bills.

"Chow time, baby," Fred says, pushing it. Walking behind me when we line everybody up. They all mumbling, like a hundred little air conditioners, talking shit to each other. Alfonso's lined up with his new homeys, lips moving steady as a cartoon. I know the words are brushing the back of the heads in line, the Chicano kids from the other side of Rio Seco, and I walk over with my stick. "Move," I say, and the sweaty foreheads go shining past like windshields in a traffic jam.

"Keep moving," I say louder.

Alfonso grins. My brother said, Take care my boy, Clarette. It's on you.

No, I want to holler back at him. You had seventeen years to take care of   55
him. Why I gotta do your job? How am I supposed to make sure he don't get killed? I feel all the feet pounding the asphalt around me and I stand in the shade next to Fred, tell him "Shut up" real soft, soft as Alfonso still talking yang in the line.

I have a buzzing in my head. Since I got up at five to do two loads of laundry and make a hot breakfast and get the kids ready for school. When I get home, I start folding the towels and see the bus stop at the corner. I wait for the kids to come busting in, but all the voices fade away down the street like little radios. Where are these kids? I go out on the porch and the sidewalk's empty, and my throat fills up again like that spicy meat's caught. Ray Jr. knows to meet Danae at her classroom. The teacher's supposed to make sure they're on the bus. Where the hell are they?

I get back in the van and head toward the school, and on Palm Avenue I swear I see Danae standing outside the barbershop, waving at me when I'm stopped at the light.

"Mama!" she calls, holding a cone from the Dairy Queen next door. "Mama!"

The smell of aftershave coats my teeth. And Ray Jr.'s in the chair, his hair's on the tile floor like rain clouds.

My son. His head naked, a little nick on the back of his skull, when he sees 60
me and ducks down. Where someone hit him with a rock last year in third
grade. The barber rubs his palms over Ray Jr.'s skin and it shines.

"Wax him up, man," Ray says, and I move on him fast. His hair under my
feet too, I see now, lighter and straighter. Brown clouds. The ones with no rain.

"How could you?" I try to whisper, but I can't whisper. Not after all day of
hollering, not stepping on all that hair.

The barber, old guy I remember from football games, said, "Mmm-mmm-
mmm."

"The look, baby. Everybody wants the look. You always working on
Danae's hair, and Ray-Ray's was looking ragged." Ray lifts both hands, fingers
out, like he always does. Like it's a damn sports movie and he's the ref. Exaggerated. "Hey, I thought I was helping you out."

I heard the laughing in his mouth. "Like Mike, baby. Like Ice Cube. The 65
look. He said some punks was messin with him at school."

I go outside and look at Ray Jr.'s head through the grimy glass. I can't
touch his skull. Naked. How did it get that naked means tough? Naked like
when they were born. When I was laying there, his head laced with blood and
wax.

My head pounding when I put it against the glass, and I feel Danae's sticky
fingers on my elbow. "Mama, I got another book at school today. *Sheep in a
Jeep.*"

When we were done reading, she fell asleep. My head hurt like a tight swim
cap. I went into Ray Jr.'s room and felt the slickness of the wax.

In the morning I'm so tired my hands are shaking when I comb Danae's hair.
"Pocahontas braids," she says, and I feel my thumbs stiff when I twist the ties
on the ends. I stare at my own forehead, all the new hair growing out, little
explosions at my temples. Bald. Ray's bald now. We do braids and curls or Bone
Strait and half the day in the salon, and they don't even comb theirs? Big boulder heads and dents all in the bone, and that's supposed to look good?

I gotta watch all these wards dressed in dark blue work outfits, baggy-ass 70
pants, big old shirts, and then get home and all the kids in the neighborhood
are wearing dark blue Dickies; Ray is wearing dark blue Dickies and a Big Dog
shirt.

Like my friend Saronn says, "They wear that, and I'm supposed to wear
stretch pants and a sports bra and high heels? Give me a break."

Buzzing in my head. Grandmere said we all got the pressure, inherited.
Says I can't have salt or coffee, but she doesn't have to eat lunch here or stay
awake looking at screens. Get my braids done this weekend, feels like my scalp
has stubbles and they're turned inside poking my brain.

Here sits Fred across from me, still combs his hair even though it looks
like a black cap pushed way too far back on his head. He's telling me I need to
come out to the Old School club with him and J.C. and Beverly sometime.
They play Cameo and the Bar-Kays. "Your Love Is Like the Holy Ghost."

"What you do for Veterans Day? Kids had the day off, right?" he says.

"I worked an extra shift. My grandmere took the kids to the cemetery." 75
I drink my coffee. Metal like the pot. Not like my grandmere's coffee, creole
style with chicory. She took the kids to see her husband's grave, in the military
cemetery. She told Danae about World War II and all the men that died, and

Danae came home crying about all the bodies under the ground where they'd walked.

Six — they cry over everything. Everything is scary. I worked the extra shift to pay off my dishwasher. Four hundred dollars at Circuit City. Plus installation.

I told Ray Jr., "Oh, yeah, you gonna load this thing. Knives go in like this. Plates like this."

He said, "Why you yelling, Mama? I see how to do it. I did it at Grandmere's before. Ain't no big thing. I like the way they get loaded in exactly the same every time. I just don't let Daddy know."

He grinned. I wanted to cry.

"Used piano in the paper cost $500. Upright."   80

"What the hell is that?" Ray said on the phone. Hadn't come by since the barber.

I tried to think. "The kind against the wall, I guess. Baby grand is real high."

"For you?"

"For Ray Jr. Fooled around on the piano at school, and now he wants to play like his grandpere did in Baton Rouge."

Ray's voice got loud. "Uh-uh. You on your own there. Punks hear he play 85
the piano, they gon kick his ass. Damn, Clarette."

I can get louder now, since YA. "Oh, yeah. He looks like Ice Cube, nobody's gonna mess with him. All better, right? Damn you, Ray."

I slam the phone down so hard the back cracks. Cheap purple Target cordless. Fifteen ninety-nine.

Next day I open the classifieds on the desk across from Fred and start looking. Uprights. Finish my iron coffee. Then I hear one of the wards singing, "Three strikes you're out, tell me what you gonna do?"

Nate Dogg. That song. "Never Leave Me Alone."

This ward has a shaved black head like a bowling ball, a voice like church. 90
"Tell my son all about me, tell him his daddy's sorry . . ."

Shows us his pass at the door. "Yeah, you sorry all right," Fred says.

The ward's face changes all up. "Not really, man. Not really."

Mamere used to say, "Old days, the men go off to the army. Hard time, let me tell you. They go off to die, or they come back. But if they die, we get some money from the army. If they come back, they get a job on the base. Now them little boys, they go off to the prison just like the army. Like they have to. To be a man. They go off to die, or come back. But they ain't got nothin. Nothin either way."

Wards in formation now. The wind is still pushing, school papers cartwheeling across the courtyard past the boots. I check Alfonso, in the back again, like every day, like a big damn Candyland game with Danae and it's never over cause we keep picking the same damn cards over and over cause it's only two of us playing.

I breathe in all the dust from the fields. Hay fields all dry and turned when 95
I drive past, the dirt skimming over my windshield. Two more hours today. Wards go back to class. Alfonso lifts his chin at me, and I stare him down. Fred humming something. What is it?

"If this world were mine, I'd make you my queen . . ." Old Luther songs. "Shut up, Fred," I tell him. I don't know if he's trying to rap or not. He keeps asking me about Ray.

"All them braids look like a crown," he says, smiling like a player.

"A bun," I say. He knows we have to wear our hair tight back for security. And Esther just did my braids Sunday. That's gotta be why my temples ache now.

"They went at it in the laundry room again Sunday," Fred says, looking at the screens.

I stare at the prison laundry, the huge washers and dryers like an old ceme- 100 tery my grandmere took me to in Louisiana once, when I was a kid. All those dead people in white stone chambers, with white stone doors. I see the wards sorting laundry and talking, see J.C. in there with them.

"Can't keep them out of there," I say, staring at their hands on the white T-shirts. "Cause everybody's gotta have clean clothes."

At home I stand in front of my washer, dropping in Danae's pink T-shirt, her Old Navy capris. One trip to Old Navy in spring, one in fall all I can afford. And her legs getting longer. Jeans and jeans. Sometimes they take so long to dry I just sit down on the floor in front of the dryer and read the paper, cause I'm too tired to go back out to the couch. If I sit down on something soft, I'll fall asleep, and the jeans will be all wrinkled in the morning.

Even the wards have pressed jeans.

In the morning, my forehead feels like it's full of hot sand. Gotta be the flu. I don't have time for this shit. I do my hair first, before I wake up Danae and Ray Jr. I pull the braids back and it hurts, so I put a softer scrunchie around the bun.

Seen a woman at Esther's Sunday. She says, "You got all that pretty hair, 105 why you scrape it back so sharp?"

"Where I work."

"You cookin somewhere?"

"Nope. Sittin. Lookin at fools."

She pinched up her eyes. "At the jail?"

"YA." 110

Then she pulls in her chin. "They got my son. Two years. He wasn't even doin nothin. Wrong place, wrong time."

"YA wrong place, sure."

She get up and spit off Esther's porch. "I come back later, Esther."

Esther says, "Don't trip on Sisia. She always mad at somebody."

Shouldn't be mad at me. "I didn't got her son. I'm just tryin to make sure 115 he comes home. Whenever."

Esther nodded and pulled those little hairs at my temple. I always touch that part when I'm at work. The body is thy temple. My temple. Where the blood pound when something goes wrong.

The laundry's like people landed from a tornado. Jean legs and shirt-sleeves all tangled up on my bed.

"You foldin?" I say. Ray Jr. pulling out his jeans and lay them in a pile like logs. Then he laps them down with his big hand.

"They my clothes."

"Don't tell your daddy." 120

"I don't tell him much."

His hair growing back on his skull. Not like iron filings. Like curly feathers. Still soft.

Next day Fred put his comb away and say, "Give a brotha some time."

"I gave him three years."

"That's all Ray get? He goin through some changes, right?"   125

"We have to eat. Kids got field trips and books to buy."

Three years. The laundry piled on my bed like a mound over a grave. On the side where Ray used to sleep. The homework. Now piano lessons.

Fred says, "So you done?"

"With Ray?" I look right at him. "Nope. I'm just done."   130

"Oh, come on, Clarette. You ain't but thirty-five. You ain't done."

"You ain't Miss Cleo."

"You need to come out to the Comedy Club. No, now, I ain't sayin with me. We could meet up there. Listen to some Earth, Wind, and Fire. Elements of life, girl."

Water. They missed water. Elements of life: bottled water cause I don't want the kids drinking tap. Water pouring out the washing machine. Water inside the new dishwasher — I can hear it sloshing around in there.

I look out at the courtyard. Rogue tumbleweed, a small one, rolling across the black.

"Know what, Clarette? You just need to get yours. I know I get mines. I   135 have me some fun, after workin here all day. Have a drink, talk to some people, meet a fine lady. Like you."

"Shut up, Fred. Here they come."

Reyes leading in his line and I see two boys go down, start punching. I run into the courtyard with my stick out and can't get to them, cause their crews are working now. The noise — it's like the crows in the pecan grove by Grandmere's, all the yelling, but not lifting up to the sky. All around me. I pull off shirts, Reyes next to me throwing kids out to Michaels and Fred. Shoving them back, and one shoves me hard in the side. I feel elbows and hands. Got to get to the kid down, and I push with my stick.

Alfonso. His face bobbing over them like a puppet. "Get out of here!" I yell at him, and he's grinning. I swear. I reach down and the Chicano kid is on top, black kid under him, and I see a boot. I pull the top kid and hear Reyes hollering next to me, voice deep as a car stereo in my ear.

Circle's opening now. Chicano kid is down, he's thin, bony wrists greenlaced with writing. The black kid is softer, neck shining, and he rolls over. But then he throws himself at the Chicano kid again, and I catch him with my boot. Both down. Reyes kicks the Chicano kid over onto his belly and holds him. I have to do the same thing. His lip split like a pomegranate. Oozing red. Some mother's son. It's hard not to feel the sting in my belly. Reyes's boy yelling at me in Spanish. I kick him one more time, in the side.

I bend down to turn mine over, get out my cuffs, and one braid pulls loose.   140 Falls by my eyes. Bead silver like a raindrop. I see a dark hand reach for it, feel spit spray my forehead. Bitch. My hair pulled from my temple. My temple.

My stick. Blood on my stick. Michaels and Reyes take the wards. I keep my face away from all the rest, and a bubble of air or blood or something throbs next to my eyebrow. Where my skin pulled from my skull, for a minute. Burning now, but I know it's gon turn black like a scab, underneath my hair. I have to stand up. The sky turns black, then gray, like always. They're all heading to lockdown. I make sure they all see me spit on the cement before I go back inside. Fred stands outside talking to the shift supervisor, Williams, and I know he's coming in here in a minute, so I open the classifieds again and put my finger on Upright.

CONSIDERATIONS FOR CRITICAL THINKING AND WRITING

1. **FIRST RESPONSE.** Susan Straight has said about her own fiction: "I don't want anybody to ever think that my stories are totally bleak. I usually try to at least have something at the end where we know that somebody's come around a bit." Discuss why you think this comment applies — or doesn't apply — to "Mines."

2. Explain how the use of details in the first nine paragraphs serves to characterize the narrator.

3. Discuss how the descriptions of the tattoos help to create portraits of the inmates.

4. Compare Clarette's life inside the jail with her life on the outside.

5. What is the purpose of the minor characters? Are they individuals, or do they primarily represent ideas or attitudes?

6. Describe the antagonist. What is the conflict? Is it resolved?

7. Discuss the significance of the title.

8. Why do you suppose the story ends with a reference to the advertisement for the piano?

CONNECTIONS TO OTHER SELECTIONS

1. Compare and contrast the characterizations of young black men in "Mines" and in Ralph Ellison's "Battle Royal" (p. 243). Explain how these characterizations address larger social issues contemporary to each story.

2. How might Gwendolyn Brooks's poem "We Real Cool" (p. 649) be read as a commentary on the inmates in "Mines"?

5

Setting

My role is to look at the world, get a true, not an idealized vision of it and hand it over to you in fictional form.
— FAY WELDON

Setting is the context in which the action of a story occurs. The major elements of setting are time, place, and the social environment that frames the characters. These elements establish the world in which the characters act. In most stories they also serve as more than backgrounds and furnishings. If we are sensitive to the contexts provided by setting, we are better able to understand the behavior of the characters and the significance of their actions. It may be tempting to read quickly through a writer's descriptions and ignore the details of the setting once a geographic location and a historic period are established. But if you read a story so impatiently, the significance of the setting may slip by you. That kind of reading is similar to traveling on interstate highways: a lot of ground gets covered, but very little is seen along the way.

Settings can be used to evoke a mood or atmosphere that will prepare the reader for what is to come. In "Young Goodman Brown" (p. 325), Nathaniel Hawthorne has his pious protagonist leave his wife and village one night to keep an appointment in a New England forest near the site of the seventeenth-century witch trials. This is Hawthorne's description of Brown entering the forest:

> He had taken a dreary road, darkened by all the gloomiest trees of the forest, which barely stood aside to let the narrow path creep through, and closed immediately behind. It was all as lonely as could be; and there is this peculiarity in such a solitude, that the traveler knows not who may be concealed by the innumerable trunks and the thick boughs overhead; so that with lonely footsteps he may yet be passing through an unseen multitude.

The atmosphere established in this descriptive setting is somber and threatening. Careful reading reveals that the forest is not simply the woods; it is a moral wilderness, where anything can happen.

Explore the literary element in this chapter on *LiterActive* or at bedfordstmartins.com/ meyercompact.

If we ask why a writer chooses to include certain details in a work, then we are likely to make connections that relate the details to some larger purpose, such as the story's meaning. The final scene in Godwin's "A Sorrowful Woman" (p. 39) occurs in the spring, an ironic time for the action to be set because instead of rebirth for the protagonist there is only death. There is usually a reason for placing a story in a particular time or location. Katherine Mansfield has the protagonist in "Miss Brill" (p. 275) discover her loneliness and old age in a French vacation town, a lively atmosphere that serves as a cruel contrast to an elderly (and foreign) lady's painful realization.

Melville's "Bartleby, the Scrivener" (p. 124) takes on meaning as Bartleby's "dead-wall reveries" begin to reflect his shattered vision of life. He is surrounded by walls. A folding screen separates him from others in the office; he is isolated. The office window faces walls; there is no view to relieve the deadening work. Bartleby faces a wall at the prison where he dies; the final wall is death. As the subtitle indicates, this is "A Story of Wall Street." Unless the geographic location or the physical details of a story are used merely as necessary props, they frequently shed light on character and action. All offices have walls, but Melville transforms the walls into an antagonist that represents the limitations Bartleby sees and feels all around him but does not speak of.

Time, location, and the physical features of a setting can all be relevant to the overall purpose of a story. So too is the social environment in which the characters are developed. In Faulkner's "A Rose for Emily" (p. 90) the changes in her southern town serve as a foil for Emily's tenacious hold on a lost past. She is regarded as a "fallen monument," as old-fashioned and peculiar as the "stubborn and coquettish decay" of her house. Neither she nor her house fits into the modern changes that are paving and transforming the town. Without the social context, this story would be mostly an account of a bizarre murder rather than an exploration of the conflicts Faulkner associated with the changing South. Setting enlarges the meaning of Emily's actions.

Some settings have traditional associations that are closely related to the action of a story. Adventure and romance, for example, flourish in the fertile soil of most exotic settings: the film version of Isak Dinesen's novel *Out of Africa* is a lush visual demonstration of how setting can play a significant role in generating the audience's expectations of love and excitement.

Sometimes, writers reverse traditional expectations. When a tranquil garden is the scene for a horrendously bloody murder, we are as much taken by surprise as the victim is. In John Updike's "A & P" (p. 560) there seems to be little possibility for heroic action in so mundane a place as a supermarket, but the setting turns out to be appropriate for the important, unexpected decision the protagonist makes about life. Traditional associations are also disrupted in "A Sorrowful Woman," in which Godwin disassociates home from the safety, security, and comfort usually connected with it by presenting the protagonist's home as a deadly trap. By drawing on traditional associations, a writer can fulfill or disrupt a reader's expectations about a setting in order to complement the elements of the story.

Not every story uses setting as a means of revealing mood, idea, meaning, or characters' actions. Some stories have no particularly significant setting. It is entirely possible to envision a story in which two characters speak to each other about a conflict between them and little or no mention is made of the time or place they inhabit. If, however, a shift in setting would make a serious difference to our understanding of a story, then the setting is probably an important element in the work. Consider how different "Bartleby, the Scrivener" would be if it were set in a relaxed, pleasant, sunny town in the South rather than in the grinding, limiting materialism of Wall Street. Bartleby's withdrawal from life would be less comprehensible and meaningful in such a setting. The setting is integral to that story.

The following four stories — Ernest Hemingway's "Soldier's Home," Andrea Lee's "Anthropology," Fay Weldon's "IND AFF, or Out of Love in Sarajevo," and Robert Olen Butler's "Christmas 1910" — include settings that serve to shape their meanings.

ERNEST HEMINGWAY (1899–1961)

In 1918, a year after graduating from high school in Oak Park, Illinois, Ernest Hemingway volunteered as an ambulance driver in World War I. At the Italian front, he was seriously wounded. This experience haunted him and many of the characters in his short stories and novels. *In Our Time* (1925) is a collection of short stories, including "Soldier's Home," that reflects some of Hemingway's own attempts to

Courtesy of the Ernest Hemingway Photographic Collection, John Fitzgerald Kennedy Library, Boston.

readjust to life back home after the war. *The Sun Also Rises* (1926), *A Farewell to Arms* (1929), and *For Whom the Bell Tolls* (1940) are also about war and its impact on people's lives. Hemingway courted violence all his life in war, the bullring, the boxing ring, and big game hunting. When he was sixty-two years old, he committed suicide by shooting himself with a shotgun. "Soldier's Home" takes place in a small town in Oklahoma; the war, however, is never distant from the protagonist's mind as he struggles to come home again.

Soldier's Home   *1925*

Krebs went to the war from a Methodist college in Kansas. There is a picture which shows him among his fraternity brothers, all of them wearing exactly the same height and style collar. He enlisted in the Marines in 1917 and did not return to the United States until the second division returned from the Rhine in the summer of 1919.

There is a picture which shows him on the Rhine with two German girls and another corporal. Krebs and the corporal look too big for their uniforms. The German girls are not beautiful. The Rhine does not show in the picture.

By the time Krebs returned to his home town in Oklahoma the greeting of heroes was over. He came back much too late. The men from the town who had been drafted had all been welcomed elaborately on their return. There had been a great deal of hysteria. Now the reaction had set in. People seemed to think it was rather ridiculous for Krebs to be getting back so late, years after the war was over.

At first Krebs, who had been at Belleau Wood, Soissons, the Champagne, St. Mihiel, and in the Argonne° did not want to talk about the war at all. Later he felt the need to talk but no one wanted to hear about it. His town had heard too many atrocity stories to be thrilled by actualities. Krebs found that to be listened to at all he had to lie, and after he had done this twice he, too, had a reaction against the war and against talking about it. A distaste for everything that had happened to him in the war set in because of the lies he had told. All of the times that had been able to make him feel cool and clear inside himself when he thought of them; the times so long back when he had done the one thing, the only thing for a man to do, easily and naturally, when he might have done something else, now lost their cool, valuable quality and then were lost themselves.

His lies were quite unimportant lies and consisted in attributing to himself 5 things other men had seen, done, or heard of, and stating as facts certain apocryphal incidents familiar to all soldiers. Even his lies were not sensational at the pool room. His acquaintances, who had heard detailed accounts of German women found chained to machine guns in the Argonne forest and who could not comprehend, or were barred by their patriotism from interest in, any German machine gunners who were not chained, were not thrilled by his stories.

Belleau Wood . . . Argonne: Sites of battles in World War I in which American troops were instrumental in pushing back the Germans from France.

Krebs acquired the nausea in regard to experience that is the result of untruth or exaggeration, and when he occasionally met another man who had really been a soldier and they talked a few minutes in the dressing room at a dance he fell into the easy pose of the old soldier among other soldiers: that he had been badly, sickeningly frightened all the time. In this way he lost everything.

During this time, it was late summer, he was sleeping late in bed, getting up to walk down town to the library to get a book, eating lunch at home, reading on the front porch until he became bored, and then walking down through the town to spend the hottest hours of the day in the cool dark of the pool room. He loved to play pool.

In the evening he practiced on his clarinet, strolled down town, read, and went to bed. He was still a hero to his two young sisters. His mother would have given him breakfast in bed if he had wanted it. She often came in when he was in bed and asked him to tell her about the war, but her attention always wandered. His father was noncommittal.

Before Krebs went away to the war he had never been allowed to drive the family motor car. His father was in the real estate business and always wanted the car to be at his command when he required it to take clients out into the country to show them a piece of farm property. The car always stood outside the First National Bank building where his father had an office on the second floor. Now, after the war, it was still the same car.

Nothing was changed in the town except that the young girls had grown 10 up. But they lived in such a complicated world of already defined alliances and shifting feuds that Krebs did not feel the energy or the courage to break into it. He liked to look at them, though. There were so many good-looking young girls. Most of them had their hair cut short. When he went away only little girls wore their hair like that or girls that were fast. They all wore sweaters and shirt waists with round Dutch collars. It was a pattern. He liked to look at them from the front porch as they walked on the other side of the street. He liked to watch them walking under the shade of the trees. He liked the round Dutch collars above their sweaters. He liked their silk stockings and flat shoes. He liked their bobbed hair and the way they walked.

When he was in town their appeal to him was not very strong. He did not like them when he saw them in the Greek's ice cream parlor. He did not want them themselves really. They were too complicated. There was something else. Vaguely he wanted a girl but he did not want to have to work to get her. He would have liked to have a girl but he did not want to have to spend a long time getting her. He did not want to get into the intrigue and the politics. He did not want to have to do any courting. He did not want to tell any more lies. It wasn't worth it.

He did not want any consequences. He did not want any consequences ever again. He wanted to live alone without consequences. Besides he did not really need a girl. The army had taught him that. It was all right to pose as though you had to have a girl. Nearly everybody did that. But it wasn't true. You did not need a girl. That was the funny thing. First a fellow boasted how girls mean nothing to him, that he never thought of them, that they could not touch him. Then a fellow boasted that he could not get along without girls, that he had to have them all the time, that he could not go to sleep without them.

That was all a lie. It was all a lie both ways. You did not need a girl unless you thought about them. He learned that in the army. Then sooner or later you always got one. When you were really ripe for a girl you always got one. You did not have to think about it. Sooner or later it would come. He had learned that in the army.

Now he would have liked a girl if she had come to him and not wanted to talk. But here at home it was all too complicated. He knew he could never get through it all again. It was not worth the trouble. That was the thing about French girls and German girls. There was not all this talking. You couldn't talk much and you did not need to talk. It was simple and you were friends. He thought about France and then he began to think about Germany. On the whole he had liked Germany better. He did not want to leave Germany. He did not want to come home. Still, he had come home. He sat on the front porch.

He liked the girls that were walking along the other side of the street. He 15 liked the look of them much better than the French girls or the German girls. But the world they were in was not the world he was in. He would like to have one of them. But it was not worth it. They were such a nice pattern. He liked the pattern. It was exciting. But he would not go through all the talking. He did not want one badly enough. He liked to look at them all, though. It was not worth it. Not now when things were getting good again.

He sat there on the porch reading a book on the war. It was a history and he was reading about all the engagements he had been in. It was the most interesting reading he had ever done. He wished there were more maps. He looked forward with a good feeling to reading all the really good histories when they would come out with good detail maps. Now he was really learning about the war. He had been a good soldier. That made a difference.

One morning after he had been home about a month his mother came into his bedroom and sat on the bed. She smoothed her apron.

"I had a talk with your father last night, Harold," she said, "and he is will-ing for you to take the car out in the evenings."

"Yeah?" said Krebs, who was not fully awake. "Take the car out? Yeah?"

"Yes. Your father has felt for some time that you should be able to take the 20 car out in the evenings whenever you wished but we only talked it over last night."

"I'll bet you made him," Krebs said.

"No. It was your father's suggestion that we talk the matter over."

"Yeah. I'll bet you made him," Krebs sat up in bed.

"Will you come down to breakfast, Harold?" his mother said.

"As soon as I get my clothes on," Krebs said.   25

His mother went out of the room and he could hear her frying something downstairs while he washed, shaved, and dressed to go down into the dining-room for breakfast. While he was eating breakfast his sister brought in the mail.

"Well, Hare," she said. "You old sleepyhead. What do you ever get up for?"

Krebs looked at her. He liked her. She was his best sister.

"Have you got the paper?" he asked.

She handed him the Kansas City *Star* and he shucked off its brown wrap- 30 per and opened it to the sporting page. He folded the *Star* open and propped it against the water pitcher with his cereal dish to steady it, so he could read while he ate.

"Harold," his mother stood in the kitchen doorway, "Harold, please don't muss up the paper. Your father can't read his *Star* if it's been mussed."

"I won't muss it," Krebs said.

His sister sat down at the table and watched him while he read.

"We're playing indoor over at school this afternoon," she said. "I'm going to pitch."

"Good," said Krebs. "How's the old wing?"   35

"I can pitch better than lots of the boys. I tell them all you taught me. The other girls aren't much good."

"Yeah?" said Krebs.

"I tell them all you're my beau. Aren't you my beau, Hare?"

"You bet."

"Couldn't your brother really be your beau just because he's your brother?"   40

"I don't know."

"Sure you know. Couldn't you be my beau, Hare, if I was old enough and if you wanted to?"

"Sure. You're my girl now."

"Am I really your girl?"

"Sure."   45

"Do you love me?"

"Uh, huh."

"Will you love me always?"

"Sure."

"Will you come over and watch me play indoor?"   50

"Maybe."

"Aw, Hare, you don't love me. If you loved me, you'd want to come over and watch me play indoor."

Krebs's mother came into the dining-room from the kitchen. She carried a plate with two fried eggs and some crisp bacon on it and a plate of buckwheat cakes.

"You run along, Helen," she said. "I want to talk to Harold."

She put the eggs and bacon down in front of him and brought in a jug of   55
maple syrup for the buckwheat cakes. Then she sat down across the table from Krebs.

"I wish you'd put down the paper a minute, Harold," she said.

Krebs took down the paper and folded it.

"Have you decided what you are going to do yet, Harold?" his mother said, taking off her glasses.

"No," said Krebs.

"Don't you think it's about time?" His mother did not say this in a mean   60
way. She seemed worried.

"I hadn't thought about it," Krebs said.

"God has some work for everyone to do," his mother said. "There can be no idle hands in His Kingdom."

"I'm not in His Kingdom," Krebs said.

"We are all of us in His Kingdom."

Krebs felt embarrassed and resentful as always.   65

"I've worried about you so much, Harold," his mother went on. "I know the temptations you must have been exposed to. I know how weak men are. I know what your own dear grandfather, my own father, told us about the Civil War and I have prayed for you. I pray for you all day long, Harold."

Krebs looked at the bacon fat hardening on his plate.

"Your father is worried, too," his mother went on. "He thinks you have lost your ambition, that you haven't got a definite aim in life. Charley Simmons, who is just your age, has a good job and is going to be married. The boys are all settling down; they're all determined to get somewhere; you can see that boys like Charley Simmons are on their way to being really a credit to the community."

Krebs said nothing.

"Don't look that way, Harold," his mother said. "You know we love you   70 and I want to tell you for your own good how matters stand. Your father does not want to hamper your freedom. He thinks you should be allowed to drive the car. If you want to take some of the nice girls out riding with you, we are only too pleased. We want you to enjoy yourself. But you are going to have to settle down to work, Harold. Your father doesn't care what you start in at. All work is honorable as he says. But you've got to make a start at something. He asked me to speak to you this morning and then you can stop in and see him at his office."

"Is that all?" Krebs said.

"Yes. Don't you love your mother, dear boy?"

"No," Krebs said.

His mother looked at him across the table. Her eyes were shiny. She started crying.

"I don't love anybody," Krebs said.   75

It wasn't any good. He couldn't tell her, he couldn't make her see it. It was silly to have said it. He had only hurt her. He went over and took hold of her arm. She was crying with her head in her hands.

"I didn't mean it," he said. "I was just angry at something. I didn't mean I didn't love you."

His mother went on crying. Krebs put his arm on her shoulder.

"Can't you believe me, mother?"

His mother shook her head.   80

"Please, please, mother. Please believe me."

"All right," his mother said chokily. She looked up at him. "I believe you, Harold."

Krebs kissed her hair. She put her face up to him.

"I'm your mother," she said. "I held you next to my heart when you were a tiny baby."

Krebs felt sick and vaguely nauseated.   85

"I know, Mummy," he said. "I'll try and be a good boy for you."

"Would you kneel and pray with me, Harold?" his mother asked.

They knelt down beside the dining-room table and Krebs's mother prayed.

"Now, you pray, Harold," she said.

"I can't," Krebs said.   90

"Try, Harold."

"I can't."

"Do you want me to pray for you?"

"Yes."

So his mother prayed for him and then they stood up and Krebs kissed his 95
mother and went out of the house. He had tried so to keep his life from being
complicated. Still, none of it had touched him. He had felt sorry for his
mother and she had made him lie. He would go to Kansas City and get a job
and she would feel all right about it. There would be one more scene maybe
before he got away. He would not go down to his father's office. He would miss
that one. He wanted his life to go smoothly. It had just gotten going that way.
Well, that was all over now, anyway. He would go over to the schoolyard and
watch Helen play indoor baseball.

CONSIDERATIONS FOR CRITICAL THINKING AND WRITING

1. **FIRST RESPONSE.** The title, "Soldier's Home," focuses on the setting. Do
   you have a clear picture of Krebs's home? Describe it, filling in missing
   details from your associations of home, Krebs's routine, or anything else
   you can use.

2. What does the photograph of Krebs, the corporal, and the German girls
   reveal?

3. Belleau Wood, Soissons, the Champagne, St. Mihiel, and the Argonne were
   the sites of bloody fighting. What effect have these battles had on Krebs?
   Why do you think he won't talk about them to the people at home?

4. Why does Krebs avoid complications and consequences? How has the war
   changed his attitudes toward work and women? How is his hometown
   different from Germany and France? What is the conflict in the story?

5. Why do you think Hemingway refers to the protagonist as Krebs rather
   than Harold? What is the significance of his sister calling him "Hare"?

6. How does Krebs's mother embody the community's values? What does
   Krebs think of those values?

7. Why can't Krebs pray with his mother?

8. What is the resolution to Krebs's conflict?

9. Comment on the appropriateness of the story's title.

10. Explain how Krebs's war experiences are present throughout the story
    even though we get no details about them.

11. **CRITICAL STRATEGIES.** Read the section on reader-response criticism (pp.
    1552–54) in Chapter 46, "Critical Strategies for Reading," and consider the
    following: Perhaps, after having been away from home for a time, you
    have returned to find yourself alienated from your family or friends. De-
    scribe your experience. What caused the change? How does this experience
    affect your understanding of Krebs? Alternately, if alienation hasn't been
    your experience, how does that difference affect your reading of Krebs?

CONNECTIONS TO OTHER SELECTIONS

1. Contrast the attitudes toward patriotism implicit in this story with those
   in Tim O'Brien's "How to Tell a True War Story" (p. 543). How do the stories' settings help to account for the differences between them?

2. How might Krebs's rejection of his community's values be related to
   Sammy's relationship to his supermarket job in John Updike's "A & P"
   (p. 560)? What details does Updike use to make the setting in "A & P" a
   comic, though nonetheless serious, version of Krebs's hometown?

3. Explain how the violent details that Tim O'Brien uses to establish the setting in "How to Tell a True War Story" can be considered representative of the kinds of horrors that haunt Krebs after he returns home.

Perspective

ERNEST HEMINGWAY (1899–1961)
On What Every Writer Needs   1954

The most essential gift for a good writer is a built-in, shock-proof, shit detector. This is the writer's radar and all great writers have had it.

From *Writers at Work: The Paris Review Interviews* (Second Series)

CONSIDERATIONS FOR CRITICAL THINKING AND WRITING

1. Hemingway is typically forthright here, but it is tempting to dismiss his point as simply humorous. Take him seriously. What does he insist a good writer must be able to do?

2. How might Krebs in Hemingway's "Soldier's Home" (p. 165) be seen as having a similar kind of "shit detector" and "radar"?

3. Try writing a pithy, quotable statement that makes an observation about reading or writing.

FAY WELDON (B. 1933)

© Jerrry Bauer.

Born in England and raised in New Zealand, Fay Weldon graduated from St. Andrew's University in Scotland. She wrote advertising copy for various companies and was a propaganda writer for the British Foreign Office before turning to fiction. She has written novels, short stories, plays, and radio scripts. In 1971 her script for an episode of *Upstairs, Downstairs* won an award from the Society of Film and Television Arts. She has written more than a score of novels, including *The Fat Woman's Joke* (1967), *Down Among the Women* (1971), *Praxis* (1978), *The Life and Loves of a She-Devil* (1983), *Life Force* (1991), *The Bulgari Connection* (2001), and *She May Not Leave* (2005), and an equal number of plays and scripts. Her collections of short stories include *Moon over Minneapolis* (1992), *Wicked Women* (American edition, 1997), *A Hard Time to Be a Father* (1998), and *Nothing to*

Wear and Nowhere to Hide (2002). Weldon often uses ironic humor to portray carefully drawn female characters coming to terms with the facts of their lives.

IND AFF   *1988*
or Out of Love in Sarajevo

This is a sad story. It has to be. It rained in Sarajevo, and we had expected fine weather.

The rain filled up Sarajevo's pride, two footprints set into a pavement which mark the spot where the young assassin Princip stood to shoot the Archduke Franz Ferdinand and his wife. (Don't forget his wife: everyone forgets his wife, the archduchess.) That was in the summer of 1914. Sarajevo is a pretty town, Balkan style, mountain-rimmed. A broad, swift, shallow river runs through its center, carrying the mountain snow away, arched by many bridges. The one nearest the two footprints has been named the Princip Bridge. The young man is a hero in these parts. Not only does he bring in the tourists — look, look, the spot, the very spot! — but by his action, as everyone knows, he lit a spark which fired the timber which caused World War I which crumbled the Austro-Hungarian Empire, the crumbling of which made modern Yugoslavia possible. Forty million dead (or was it thirty?) but who cares? So long as he loved his country.

The river, they say, can run so shallow in the summer it's known derisively as "the wet road." Today, from what I could see through the sheets of falling rain, it seemed full enough. Yugoslavian streets are always busy — no one stays home if they can help it (thus can an indecent shortage of housing space create a sociable nation) and it seemed as if by common consent a shield of bobbing umbrellas had been erected two meters high to keep the rain off the streets. It just hadn't worked around Princip's corner.

"Come all this way," said Peter, who was a professor of classical history, "and you can't even see the footprints properly, just two undistinguished puddles." Ah, but I loved him. I shivered for his disappointment. He was supervising my thesis on varying concepts of morality and duty in the early Greek States as evidenced in their poetry and drama. I was dependent upon him for my academic future. He said I had a good mind but not a first-class mind and somehow I didn't take it as an insult. I had a feeling first-class minds weren't all that good in bed.

Sarajevo is in Bosnia, in the center of Yugoslavia, that grouping of unlikely 5 states, that distillation of languages into the phonetic reasonableness of Serbo-Croatian. We'd sheltered from the rain in an ancient mosque in Serbian Belgrade; done the same in a monastery in Croatia; now we spent a wet couple of days in Sarajevo beneath other people's umbrellas. We planned to go on to Montenegro, on the coast, where the fish and the artists come from, to swim and lie in the sun, and recover from the exhaustion caused by the sexual and moral torments of the last year. It couldn't possibly go on raining forever. Could it? Satellite pictures showed black clouds swishing gently all over Europe, over the Balkans, into Asia — practically all the way from Moscow to

London, in fact. It wasn't that Peter and myself were being singled out. No. It was raining on his wife, too, back in Cambridge.

Peter was trying to decide, as he had been for the past year, between his wife and myself as his permanent life partner. To this end we had gone away, off the beaten track, for a holiday; if not with his wife's blessing, at least with her knowledge. Were we really, truly suited? We had to be sure, you see, that this was more than just any old professor-student romance; that it was the Real Thing, because the longer the indecision went on the longer Mrs. Piper would be left dangling in uncertainty and distress. They had been married for twenty-four years; they had stopped loving each other a long time ago, of course — but there would be a fearful personal and practical upheaval entailed if he decided to leave permanently and shack up, as he put it, with me. Which I certainly wanted him to do. I loved him. And so far I was winning hands down. It didn't seem much of a contest at all, in fact. I'd been cool and thin and informed on the seat next to him in a Zagreb theater (Mrs. Piper was sweaty and only liked telly); was now eager and anxious for social and political instruction in Sarajevo (Mrs. Piper spat in the face of knowledge, he'd once told me); and planned to be lissome (and I thought topless but I hadn't quite decided: this might be the area where the age difference showed) while I splashed and shrieked like a bathing belle in the shallows of the Montenegrin coast. (Mrs. Piper was a swimming coach: I imagined she smelt permanently of chlorine.)

In fact so far as I could see, it was no contest at all between his wife and myself. But Peter liked to luxuriate in guilt and indecision. And I loved him with an inordinate affection.

Princip's prints are a meter apart, placed as a modern cop on a training shoot-out would place his feet — the left in front at a slight outward angle, the right behind, facing forward. There seemed great energy focused here. Both hands on the gun, run, stop, plant the feet, aim, fire! I could see the footprints well enough, in spite of Peter's complaint. They were clear enough to me.

We went to a restaurant for lunch, since it was too wet to do what we loved to do: that is, buy bread, cheese, sausage, wine, and go off somewhere in our hired car, into the woods or the hills, and picnic and make love. It was a private restaurant — Yugoslavia went over to a mixed capitalist-communist economy years back, so you get either the best or worst of both systems, depending on your mood — that is to say, we knew we would pay more but be given a choice. We chose the wild boar.

"Probably ordinary pork soaked in red cabbage water to darken it," said 10 Peter. He was not in a good mood.

Cucumber salad was served first.

"Everything in this country comes with cucumber salad," complained Peter. I noticed I had become used to his complaining. I supposed that when you had been married a little you simply wouldn't hear it. He was forty-six and I was twenty-five.

"They grow a lot of cucumber," I said.

"If they can grow cucumbers," Peter then asked, "why can't they grow *mange-tout*°?" It seemed a why-can't-they-eat-cake sort of argument to me, but

---

mange-tout: A sugar pea or bean (French).

not knowing enough about horticulture not to be outflanked if I debated the point, I moved the subject on to safer ground.

"I suppose Princip's action couldn't really have started World War I," I 15 remarked. "Otherwise, what a thing to have on your conscience! One little shot and the deaths of thirty million."

"Forty," he corrected me. Though how they reckon these things and get them right I can't imagine. "Of course he didn't start the war. That's just a simple tale to keep the children quiet. It takes more than an assassination to start a war. What happened was that the buildup of political and economic tensions in the Balkans was such that it had to find some release."

"So it was merely the shot that lit the spark that fired the timber that started the war, et cetera?"

"Quite," he said. "World War I would have had to have started sooner or later."

"A bit later or a bit sooner," I said, "might have made the difference of a million or so; if it was you on the battlefield in the mud and the rain you'd notice; exactly when they fired the starting-pistol; exactly when they blew the final whistle. Is that what they do when a war ends; blow a whistle? So that everyone just comes in from the trenches."

But he wasn't listening. He was parting the flesh of the soft collapsed 20 orangey-red pepper which sat in the middle of his cucumber salad; he was carefully extracting the pips. His nan had once told him they could never be digested, would stick inside and do terrible damage. I loved him for his dexterity and patience with his knife and fork. I'd finished my salad yonks ago, pips and all. I was hungry. I wanted my wild boar.

Peter might be forty-six, but he was six foot two and grizzled and muscled with it, in a dark-eyed, intelligent, broad-jawed kind of way. I adored him. I loved to be seen with him. "Muscular academic, not weedy academic" as my younger sister Clare once said. "Muscular academic is just a generally superior human being: everything works well from the brain to the toes. Weedy academic is when there isn't enough vital energy in the person, and the brain drains all the strength from the other parts." Well, Clare should know. Clare is only twenty-three, but of the superior human variety kind herself, vividly pretty, bright and competent — somewhere behind a heavy curtain of vibrant red hair, which she only parts for effect. She had her first degree at twenty. Now she's married to a Harvard professor of economics seconded to the United Nations. She can even cook. I gave up competing yonks ago. Though she too is capable of self-deception. I would say her husband was definitely of the weedy academic rather than the muscular academic type. And they have to live in Brussels.

The archduke's chauffeur had lost his way, and was parked on the corner trying to recover his nerve when Princip came running out of a café, planted his feet, aimed, and fired. Princip was nineteen — too young to hang. But they sent him to prison for life and, since he had TB to begin with, he only lasted three years. He died in 1918, in an Austrian prison. Or perhaps it was more than TB: perhaps they gave him a hard time, not learning till later, when the Austro-Hungarian Empire collapsed, that he was a hero. Poor Princip, too young to die — like so many other millions. Dying for love of a country.

"I love you," I said to Peter, my living man, progenitor already of three children by his chlorinated, swimming-coach wife.

"How much do you love me?"

"Inordinately! I love you with inordinate affection." It was a joke between 25 us. Ind Aff!

"Inordinate affection is a sin," he'd told me. "According to the Wesleyans. John Wesley° himself worried about it to such a degree he ended up abbreviating it in his diaries, Ind Aff. He maintained that what he felt for young Sophy, the eighteen-year-old in his congregation, was not Ind Aff, which bears the spirit away from God towards the flesh: he insisted that what he felt was a pure and spiritual, if passionate, concern for her soul."

Peter said now, as we waited for our wild boar, and he picked over his pepper, "Your Ind Aff is my wife's sorrow, that's the trouble." He wanted, I knew, one of the long half-wrangles, half soul-sharings that we could keep going for hours, and led to piercing pains in the heart which could only be made better in bed. But our bedroom at the Hotel Europa was small and dark and looked out into the well of the building — a punishment room if ever there was one. (Reception staff did sometimes take against us.) When Peter had tried to change it in his quasi-Serbo-Croatian, they'd shrugged their Bosnian shoulders and pretended not to understand, so we'd decided to put up with it. I did not fancy pushing hard single beds together — it seemed easier not to have the pain in the heart in the first place. "Look," I said, "this holiday is supposed to be just the two of us, not Mrs. Piper as well. Shall we talk about something else?"

Do not think that the archduke's chauffeur was merely careless, an inefficient chauffeur, when he took the wrong turning. He was, I imagine, in a state of shock, fright, and confusion. There had been two previous attempts on the archduke's life since the cavalcade had entered town. The first was a bomb which got the car in front and killed its driver. The second was a shot fired by none other than young Princip, which had missed. Princip had vanished into the crowd and gone to sit down in a corner café and ordered coffee to calm his nerves. I expect his hand trembled at the best of times — he did have TB. (Not the best choice of assassin, but no doubt those who arrange these things have to make do with what they can get.) The archduke's chauffeur panicked, took the wrong road, realized what he'd done, and stopped to await rescue and instructions just outside the café where Princip sat drinking his coffee.

"What shall we talk about?" asked Peter, in even less of a good mood.

"The collapse of the Austro-Hungarian Empire?" I suggested. "How does 30 an empire collapse? Is there no money to pay the military or the police, so everyone goes home? Or what?" He liked to be asked questions.

"The Hungro-Austrarian Empire," said Peter to me, "didn't so much collapse as fail to exist any more. War destroys social organizations. The same thing happened after World War II. There being no organized bodies left between Moscow and London — and for London read Washington, then as now — it was left to these two to put in their own puppet governments. Yalta, 1944. It's taken the best part of forty-five years for nations of West and East Europe to remember who they are."

"Austro-Hungarian," I said, "not Hungro-Austrarian."

"I didn't say Hungro-Austrarian," he said.

John Wesley (1703–1791): English religious leader and founder of Methodism.

"You did," I said.

"Didn't," he said. "What the hell are they doing about our wild boar? Are   35
they out in the hills shooting it?"

My sister Clare had been surprisingly understanding about Peter. When I
worried about him being older, she pooh-poohed it; when I worried about him
being married, she said, "Just go for it, sister. If you can unhinge a marriage,
it's ripe for unhinging, it would happen sooner or later, it might as well be you.
See a catch, go ahead and catch! Go for it!"

Princip saw the archduke's car parked outside, and went for it. Second
chances are rare in life: they must be responded to. Except perhaps his second
chance was missing in the first place? Should he have taken his cue from fate,
and just sat and finished his coffee, and gone home to his mother? But what's
a man to do when he loves his country? Fate delivered the archduke into his
hands: how could he resist it? A parked car, a uniformed and medaled chest,
the persecutor of his country — how could Princip not, believing God to be on
his side, but see this as His intervention, push his coffee aside and leap to his
feet?

Two waiters stood idly by and watched us waiting for our wild boar. One
was young and handsome in a mountainous Bosnian way — flashing eyes,
hooked nose, luxuriant black hair, sensuous mouth. He was about my age. He
smiled. His teeth were even and white. I smiled back, and instead of the pain in
the heart I'd become accustomed to as an erotic sensation, now felt, quite violently, an associated yet different pang which got my lower stomach. The true,
the real pain of Ind Aff!

"Fancy him?" asked Peter.

"No," I said. "I just thought if I smiled the wild boar might come quicker."   40

The other waiter was older and gentler: his eyes were soft and kind. I
thought he looked at me reproachfully. I could see why. In a world which for
once, after centuries of savagery, was finally full of young men, unslaughtered,
what was I doing with this man with thinning hair?

"What are you thinking of?" Professor Piper asked me. He liked to be in
my head.

"How much I love you," I said automatically, and was finally aware how
much I lied. "And about the archduke's assassination," I went on, to cover the
kind of tremble in my head as I came to my senses, "and let's not forget his
wife, she died too — how can you say World War I would have happened anyway. If Princip hadn't shot the archduke, something else, some undisclosed,
unsuspected variable, might have come along and defused the whole polit-
ical/military situation, and neither World War I nor II ever happened. We'll
just never know, will we?"

I had my passport and my travelers' checks with me. (Peter felt it was less
confusing if we each paid our own way.) I stood up, and took my raincoat from
the peg.

"Where are you going?" he asked, startled.   45

"Home," I said. I kissed the top of his head, where it was balding. It smelt
gently of chlorine, which may have come from thinking about his wife so much,
but might merely have been that he'd taken a shower that morning. ("The
water all over Yugoslavia, though safe to drink, is unusually chlorinated":
Guide Book.) As I left to catch a taxi to the airport the younger of the two waiters emerged from the kitchen with two piled plates of roasted wild boar, pota-

toes duchesse, and stewed peppers. ("Yugoslavian diet is unusually rich in proteins and fats": Guide Book.) I could tell from the glisten of oil that the food was no longer hot, and I was not tempted to stay, hungry though I was. Thus fate — or was it Bosnian willfulness? — confirmed the wisdom of my intent.

And that was how I fell out of love with my professor, in Sarajevo, a city to which I am grateful to this day, though I never got to see very much of it, because of the rain.

It was a silly sad thing to do, in the first place, to confuse mere passing academic ambition with love: to try and outdo my sister Clare. (Professor Piper was spiteful, as it happened, and did his best to have my thesis refused, but I went to appeal, which he never thought I'd dare, and won. I had a first-class mind after all.) A silly sad episode, which I regret. As silly and sad as Princip, poor young man, with his feverish mind, his bright tubercular cheeks, and his inordinate affection for his country, pushing aside his cup of coffee, leaping to his feet, taking his gun in both hands, planting his feet, aiming, and firing — one, two, three shots — and starting World War I. The first one missed, the second got the wife (never forget the wife), and the third got the archduke and a whole generation, and their children, and their children's children, and on and on forever. If he'd just hung on a bit, there in Sarajevo, that June day, he might have come to his senses. People do, sometimes quite quickly.

CONSIDERATIONS FOR CRITICAL THINKING AND WRITING

1. **FIRST RESPONSE.** Do you agree with Weldon's first line, "This is a sad story"? Explain why or why not.

2. How does the rain establish the mood for the story in the first five paragraphs?

3. Characterize Peter. What details concerning him reveal his personality?

4. Describe the narrator's relationship with Peter. How do you think he regards her? Why is she attracted to him?

5. Why is Sarajevo important for the story's setting? What is the effect of weaving the story of Princip's assassination of the Archduke Franz Ferdinand and his wife through the plot?

6. Describe Mrs. Piper. Though she doesn't appear in the story, she does have an important role. What do you think her role is?

7. What is "Ind Aff"? Why is it an important element of this story?

8. What is the significance of the two waiters (paras. 38–41)? How do they affect the narrator?

9. Why does the narrator decide to go home (para. 46)? Do you think she makes a reasoned or an impulsive decision? Explain why you think so.

10. Discuss the relationship between the personal history and the public history recounted in the story. How are the two interconnected? Explain whether you think it is necessary to be familiar with the assassinations in Sarajevo before reading the story.

11. **CRITICAL STRATEGIES.** Read the section on cultural criticism (pp. 1547–48) in Chapter 46, "Critical Strategies for Reading." How do you think a cultural critic might describe the nature of the narrator's relationship with her professor given the current attitudes on college campuses concerning teacher-student affairs?

CONNECTIONS TO OTHER SELECTIONS

1. Compare and contrast "IND AFF" and Joyce Carol Oates's "The Lady with the Pet Dog" (p. 219) as love stories. Do you think that the stories end happily, or the way you would want them to end? Are the endings problematic?

2. Explain how Weldon's concept of "Ind Aff" — "inordinate affection" — can be used to make sense of the relationship between Georgiana and Aylmer in Nathaniel Hawthorne's "The Birthmark" (p. 343).

3. Discuss the significance of the settings in "IND AFF" and in Robert Owen Butler's "Christmas 1910" (p. 180).

Perspective

FAY WELDON (B. 1933)

On the Importance of Place in "IND AFF"   *1997*

I'm the kind of writer who lives mostly in her head, looking inwards not outwards, more sensitive to people than places, unless the place turns out to be some useful metaphor. In Sarajevo, on a book tour, brooding about Ind. Aff., inordinate affection, these days more unkindly known as neurotic dependency, I was taken to see Princip's footsteps in the sidewalk. Fancy fell away. Here was the metaphor taken in physical form — chance and death, so like chance and love. Then later we went up into the hills to eat wild boar and the intellectual Englishmen I was with seemed so pallid and absurd compared to the here-and-now mountain men: people came into perspective inside a landscape. I have a kind of rule of thumb: three preoccupations make a story. I interweaved them, delivered them into paper, and fell back into jet-lagged torpor.

From an interview with Michael Meyer, November 15, 1997

CONSIDERATIONS FOR CRITICAL THINKING AND WRITING

1. Weldon's description of how she began "IND AFF" draws on her personal experience in Sarajevo. How does that experience make its way into the story?

2. Consider Weldon's observation that "Here was the metaphor taken in physical form — chance and death, so like chance and love." Do you think her observation works as a summary of the story?

3. Choose any other story in this anthology that can serve as an example of how "people [come] into perspective inside a landscape," and write an essay about it.

A SAMPLE STUDENT RESPONSE

Karita Perez

Professor Hoffs

English 202

November 27, 2008

The Significance of Setting in Fay Weldon's "IND AFF"

In the first line of Fay Weldon's "IND AFF," we are told "This is a sad story" (172), and the setting immediately reflects that. The story takes place in Sarajevo, where the skies are dark and the rain never stops. A young woman and her lover (twenty years her senior, and also her university professor) are on holiday visiting the landmark where Archduke Ferdinand was assassinated. The trip is meant to be pleasant, a break from their lives to determine if they are "truly suited" for each other. But just as the rains spoil their trip, their relationship is spoiled by a reality they cannot control. The main character feels guilt and sympathizes with her lover's wife: "it was raining on his wife, too" (173). She begins to see her lover in a new light, and her hopes for something beautiful give way to disappointment.

The setting also creates a mood that shapes the story, what Michael Meyer calls an "atmosphere that will prepare the reader for what is to come" (162). Along with the dismal weather, the descriptions of the landscape represent what the characters are going through. Despite the rains, there is beauty here; the town is "mountain-rimmed," and a "shallow river runs through its center, carrying the mountain snow away, arched by many bridges" (Weldon 172). This majestic scenery can be read as connected to the physical stature of Peter. The main character, despite her doubts, has strong feelings for Peter and is drawn to his height and attractiveness: "he was six foot two and grizzled and muscled with it, in a dark-eyed, intelligent, broad-jawed kind of way. I adored him" (174). . . .

Perez 4

Works Cited

Meyer, Michael, ed. The Compact Bedford Introduction to Literature. 8th ed.
    Boston: Bedford/St. Martin's, 2009. 162.

Weldon, Fay. "IND AFF, or Out of Love in Sarajevo." The Compact Bedford
    Introduction to Literature. Ed. Michael Meyer. 8th ed. Boston:
    Bedford/St. Martin's, 2009. 172–77.

ROBERT OLEN BUTLER (B. 1945)

Born in Granite City, Illinois, Robert Olen
Butler earned degrees at Northwestern University and the University of Iowa. After a
tour of duty in Vietnam and before his success as a writer, he worked for trade publications. He has published ten novels and three
collections of short stories. Currently Butler
teaches at Florida State University. His first
novel, *The Alleys of Eden* (1981), was followed
by *Sun Dog* (1982), which was related to his
experiences in Vietnam. *A Good Scent from a
Strange Mountain* (1992), a collection of short
stories that focuses on Vietnamese refugees
in the United States, won the Pulitzer Prize. He has also been awarded a
Guggenheim Fellowship and a National Endowment for the Arts grant.
"Christmas 1910" is a subtle and evocative work from *Had a Good Time: Stories from American Postcards* (2004), a group of stories inspired by Butler's
collection of old postcards.

Christmas 1910   2004

My third Christmas in the west river country came hard upon the summer
drought of 1910, and Papa and my brothers had gone pretty grim, especially my
brother Luther, who was a decade older than me and had his own adjacent
homestead, to the east, that much closer to the Badlands. Luther had lost his
youngest, my sweet little nephew Caleb, to a snakebite in August. We all knew

the rattlers would come into your house. We women would hardly take a step without a hoe at hand for protection. But one of the snakes had got into the bedclothes and no one knew and Caleb took the bite and hardly cried at all before it was done. And then there was the problem with everybody's crops. Some worse than others. A few had done hardly ten bushels of corn for forty acres put out. We weren't quite that bad off, but it was bad nonetheless. Bad enough that I felt like a selfish girl to slip out of the presence of my kin whenever I had the chance and take up with Sam my saddle horse, go up on his back and ride off a ways from the things my Mama and Papa and brothers were working so hard to build, and I just let my Sam take me, let him follow his eyes and ears to whatever little thing interested him.

And out on my own I couldn't keep on being grim about the things that I should have. There was a whole other thing or two. Selfish things. Like how you can be a good daughter in a Sodbuster family with flesh-and-blood of your own living right there all around you, making a life together — think of the poor orphans of the world and the widows and all the lost people in the cities — how you can be a good daughter in such a cozy pile of kin and still feel so lonely. Mary, Joseph and Jesus happy in a horse stall, forgive me. Of course, in that sweet little picture of the Holy family, Mary had Joseph to be with her, not her brothers and parents with their faces set hard and snakes crawling in your door and hiding in your shoe.

So when the winter had first come in, there hadn't been any snow since the beginning of November and it was starting to feel like a drought all over again, though we were happy not to have to hunker down yet and wait out the dark season under all the snow. There was still plenty of wind, of course. Everybody in our part of South Dakota shouted at each other all the time because of the wind that galloped in across the flat land to the west and to the north with nothing to stop it but the buffalo grass and little bluestem and prairie sandreed, which is to say nothing at all. But the winter of 1910 commenced with the world dead dry and that's when he came, two days before Christmas, the young man on horseback.

We were all to Luther's place and after dinner we returned home and found the young man sitting at our oak table in what we called our parlor, the big main room of our soddy. He'd lit a candle. The table was one of the few pieces of house furniture we'd brought with us from Nebraska when Papa got our homestead. Right away my vanity was kicking up. I was glad this young man, who had a long, lank handsome face, a little like Sam actually, had settled himself at our nicest household possession, which was this table. And I hoped he understood the meaning of the blue tar paper on our walls. Most of the homesteaders used the thinner red tar paper at three dollars a roll. Papa took the thick blue at six dollars, to make us something better. People in the west river country knew the meaning of that, but this young man had the air of coming from far off. We all left our houses unlocked for each other and for just such a wayfarer, so no one felt it odd in those days if you came home and found a stranger making himself comfortable.

He rose and held his hat down around his belt buckle and slowly rotated it in both hands and he apologized for lighting the candle but he didn't want to startle us coming in, and then he told us his name, which was John Marsh, and where he was from, which was Bardstown, Kentucky, county of Nelson, not far down the way from Nazareth, Kentucky, he said, smiling all around, and he wished us a Merry Christmas and hoped we wouldn't mind if he slept in the barn for the night and he'd be moving on in the morning. "I'm bound for Montana," he said, "to work a cattle ranch of a man I know there and to make my own fortune someday." With this last announcement he stopped turning his hat, so as to indicate how serious he was about that. Sam's a dapple gray with a soft puff of dark hair between his ears, and the young man sort of had that too, a lock of which fell down on his forehead as he nodded once, sharply, to signify his determination.

My mama would hear nothing of this, the moving on in the morning part. "You're welcome to stay but it should be for more than a night," she said. "No man should be alone on Christmas if there's someone to spend it with." And with this, Mama shot Papa a look, and he knew to take it up.

"We can use a hand with some winter chores while we've got the chance," Papa said. "I can pay you in provisions for your trip."

John Marsh studied each of our faces, Mama and Papa and my other older brother, Frank, just a year over me, standing by Papa's side as he always did, and my younger brother, Ben, still a boy, really, though he was as tall as me already. And John Marsh looked me in the eye and I looked back at him and we neither of us turned away, and I thought to breathe into his nostrils, like you do to meet a new horse and show him you understand his ways, and it was this thought that made me lower my eyes from his at last.

"I might could stay a bit longer than the night," he said.

"Queer time to be making this trip anyway," my papa said, and I heard a little bit of suspicion, I think, creeping in, as he thought all this over a bit more. 10

"He can take me in now," John Marsh said. "And there was nothing for me anymore in Kentucky."

Which was more explanation than my father was owed, it seemed to me. Papa eased up, saying, "Sometimes it just comes the moment to leave."

"Yessir." And John Marsh started turning his hat again.

Mama touched my arm and said, low, "Abigail, you curry the horses tonight before we retire."

This was instead of the early morning, when I was usually up before any-one, and she called me by my whole name and not "Abba," so it was to be the barn for John Marsh. 15

Papa took off at a conversational trot, complaining about the drought and the soil and the wind and the hot and the cold and the varmints and all, pretty much life in South Dakota in general, though that's the life he'd brought us all to without anyone forcing us to leave Nebraska, a thing he didn't point out. He was, however, making sure to say that he held 320 acres now and his eldest son 160 more and that's pretty good for a man what never went to school, his daughter being plenty educated for all of them and she even going around teaching homesteader kids who couldn't or wouldn't go to the one-room school down at Scenic. John Marsh wasn't looking at me any-more, though I fancied it was something he was struggling to control, which he proved by not even glancing at me when Papa talked of my schooling, in spite of it being natural for him to turn his face to me for that. Instead, when the subject of me came up, his Adam's apple started bobbing, like he was swal-lowing hard, over and over.

I slipped out of the house at that point, while Papa continued on. I walked across the hard ground toward the little barn we kept for the saddle horses,

Sam and Papa's Scout and Dixie. When Papa's voice finally faded away behind me, I stopped and just stood for a moment and looked up at the stars. It's true that along with the wind and the snakes and the lightning storms and all, South Dakota had the most stars in the sky of anywhere, and the brightest, and I had a tune take up in my head. *I wonder as I wander out under the sky . . .* Christmas was nearly upon us and I shivered standing there, not from the cold, though the wind was whipping at me pretty good, but because I realized that nothing special was going on inside me over Christmas, a time which had always all my life thrilled me. Luther had even put up a wild plum tree off his land in a bucket of dirt and we'd lit candles on it, just this very night. And all I could do was sit aside a ways and nod and smile when anyone's attention turned to me but all the while I was feeling nothing much but how I was as distant from this scene as one of those stars outside. And even now the only quick thing in me was the thought of some young man who'd just up and walked in our door, some stranger who maybe was a varmint himself or a scuffler or a drunkard or a fool. I didn't know anything about him, but I was out under this terrible big sky and wishing he was beside me, his hat still in his hands, and saying how he'd been inside thinking about only me for all this time. *How Jesus the Savior did come for to die, For poor ornery people like you and like I.* Ornery was right.

I went on into the barn and lit a kerosene lamp and Sam was lying there, stirred from his sleep by my coming to him at an odd time. His head rose up and he looked over his shoulder at me and he nickered soft and I came and knelt by him and put my arm around his neck. He turned his head a little and offered me his ear and waited for my sweet talk. "Hello, my Sammy," I said to him, low. "I'm sorry to disturb your sleep. Were you dreaming? I bet you were dreaming of you and me riding out along the coulee like today. Did we find some wonderful thing, like buffalo grass flowering in December?"

He puffed a bit and I leaned into him. "I dream of you, too," I said. "You're my affinity, Sammy." Like John Marsh not looking my way when Papa spoke of me, I was making a gesture that was the opposite of what I was feeling. My mind was still on this young man in the house. I suddenly felt ashamed, playing my Sam off of this stranger. In fact, I was hoping that this John Marsh might be my affinity, the boy I'd fit alongside of. I put my other arm around Sam, held him tight. After a moment he gently pulled away and laid his head down. So I got the currycomb and began to brush out the day's sweat and the wind-spew and stall-floor muck and I sang a little to him while I did. *"When Mary birthed Jesus 'twas in a cow's stall, With wise men and farmers and horses and all,"* me putting the horses in for Sammy's sake, though I'm sure there were horses around the baby Jesus, even if the stories didn't say so. The stories always made it mules, but the horses were there. The wise men came on horses. There was quite a crowd around the baby, if you think about it. But when he grew up, even though he gathered the twelve around him, and some others, too, like his mama and the Mary who'd been a wicked girl, he was still lonely. You can tell. He was as distant from them as the stars in the sky.

So I finished with Sam and then with Scout, and Dixie had stood up for me to comb her and I was just working on her hindquarters when I heard voices outside in the wind and then Papa and John Marsh came into the barn, stamping around. I didn't say anything but moved behind Dixie, to listen.

And then Papa said, "I'm sorry there's no place in the house for a young man to stay."

"This is fine," John Marsh said. "I like to keep to myself."

There was a silence for a moment, like Papa was thinking about this, and I thought about it as well. Not thought about it, exactly, but sort of felt a little wind-gust of something for this John Marsh and I wasn't quite sure what. I wanted to keep to myself, too, but only so I could moon around about not keeping to myself. John Marsh seemed overly content. I leaned into Dixie.

"I was your age once," my papa said.

"I'll manage out here fine."

"Night then," Papa said, and I expected him to call for me to go on in the 25 house with him, but he didn't say anything and I realized he'd gone out of the barn not even thinking about me being there. Which is why I'd sort of hid behind Dixie, but he'd even ignored my lamp and so I was surprised to find myself alone in the barn with John Marsh. I held my breath and didn't move.

"Hey there, Gray," John Marsh said, and I knew he was talking to Sam. "You don't mind some company, do you? That's a fella."

I heard Sam blow a bit, giving John Marsh his breath to read. It was not going to be simple about this boy. Him talking to my sweet, gray man all familiar, even touching him now, I realized—I could sense him stroking Sam—all this made me go a little weak-kneed, like it was me he was talking to and putting his hand on. It was like I was up on Sam right now and he was being part of me and I was being part of him. But then I stiffened all of a sudden, got a little heated up about this stranger talking to my Sam like the two of them already had a bond that I never knew about. I was jealous. And I was on the mash. Both at once. In short, I was a country fool, and Dixie knew it because she rustled her rump and made me pull back from her. She also drew John Marsh's attention and he said, "Hello?"

"Hello," I said, seeing as there was no other way out. I took to brushing Dixie pretty heavy with the currycomb and John Marsh appeared, his hat still on his head this time and looking like a right cowboy.

"I didn't know you was there," he said.

"Papa was continuing to bend your ear, is why," I said.   30

John Marsh smiled at this, but tried to make his face go straight again real quick.

I said, "You can find that true and amusing if you want. He's not here to take offense."

John Marsh angled his head at me, trying to figure what to say or do next. He wasn't used to sass in a girl, I guess. Wasn't used to girls at all, maybe. I should have just blowed in his nose and nickered at him.

"He does go on some," John Marsh said, speaking low.

I concentrated on my currying, though it was merely for show since I was 35 combing out the same bit of flank I'd been working on for a while. Dixie looked over her shoulder at me, pretty much in contempt. I shot her a just-stand-there-and-mind-your-own-business glance and she huffed at me and turned away. I went back to combing and didn't look John Marsh in the eye for a little while, not wanting to frighten him off by being too forward but getting impatient pretty quick with the silence. The eligible males I'd known since I was old enough for them to be pertinent to me had all been either silly prattlers or totally tongue-tied. This John Marsh was seeming to be among the latter and I brushed and brushed at Dixie's chestnut hair trying to send some brain waves over to this outsized boy, trying to whisper him something to say to me. Which horse is yours? Or, You go around teaching, do you? Or, Is there a Christmas Eve social at the school house tomorrow that I could escort you to? But he just stood there.

Finally I looked over to him. He was staring hard at me and he ripped off his hat the second we made eye contact.

"I'll be out of your way shortly," I said.

"That's okay," he said. "Take your time. She deserves it." And with this he patted Dixie on the rump.

"You hear that, Dixie?" I said. "You've got a gentleman admirer." Dixie   40
didn't bother to respond.

"Where's your horse put up?" I said.

"Oh he likes the outdoors. Horses do. It ain't too fierce tonight for him."

"My Sam — he's the gray down there — it took a long time for him to adjust to a barn. But I like him cozy even if it's not his natural way."

"I'd set him out on a night like this," John Marsh said.

"He's better off," I said.   45

"I'm sure you love him," John Marsh said.

We both stopped talking and I wasn't sure what had just happened, though I felt that something had come up between us and been done with.

John Marsh nodded to me and moved away.

I stopped brushing Dixie and I just stood there for a moment and then I put down the currycomb and moved off from Dixie and found John Marsh unrolling his sleeping bag outside Sam's stall.

I moved past him to the door. "Night then," I said.   50

John Marsh nodded and I stepped out under the stars.

Then it was the morning before Christmas and I'd done my currying the night before and I'd had a dream of empty prairie and stars and I couldn't see anyway to go no matter how I turned and so I slept on and on and woke late. As I dressed, there were sounds outside that didn't really register, their being common sounds, a horse, voices trying to speak over the wind, and then Papa came in and said, "Well, he's gone on."

Mama said, "The boy?"

"Yep," Papa said. "He wants to make time to Montana. He's got grit, the boy. The sky west looks bad."

I crossed the parlor, past the oak table and Papa, something furious going   55
on in my chest.

"I was his age once," Papa said.

Then I took up my coat and I was out the door. It was first light. Papa was correct. To the west, the sky was thickening up pretty bad. A sky like this in Kentucky might not say the same thing to a man. Even thinking this way, I knew there was more than bad weather to my stepping away from our house and looking to where John Marsh had gone, maybe only ten minutes before, and me churning around inside so fierce I could hardly hold still. Then I couldn't hold still.

I dashed into the barn and Sam was standing waiting and I gave him the bridle and bit and that was all. There was no time. I threw my skirt up and mounted Sam bareback and we pulled out of the stall and the barn and we were away.

There was a good horse trail through the rest of our land and on out toward the Black Hills that rippled at the horizon when you could see it. But there was only dark and cloud out there now, which John Marsh could recognize very well, and Sam felt my urgency, straight from my thighs. I hadn't ridden him bareback in several years and we both were het up now together like this, with John Marsh not far ahead, surely, and we galloped hard, taking the little dips easy and Sam's ears were pitched forward listening for this man up ahead, and mostly it was flat and winter bare all around and we concentrated on making time, me not thinking at all what it was I was doing. I was just with Sam and we were trying to catch up with some other possibility.

But John Marsh must have been riding fast, too. He wasn't showing up. It was just the naked prairie fanning out ahead as far as the eye would carry, to the blur of a restless horizon. What was he running so fast for? Had I frightened 60 him off somehow? Was it so bad to think he might put his arms around me?

I lay forward, pressing my chest against Sam, keeping low before the rush of the air, and I heard Sam's breathing, heavy and steady, galloping strong with me, him not feeling jealous at all that I was using him to chase this man. I closed my eyes. Sam was rocking me. I clung to him, and this was my Sam, who wasn't a gray man at all, not a man at all, he was something else altogether, he was of this wind and of this land, my Sam, he was of the stars that were up there above me even now, just hiding in the light of day, and we rode like this for a while, rocking together like the waves on the sea, and when I looked up again, there was still no rider in sight but instead an unraveling of the horizon. Sam knew at once what my body was saying. He read the faint tensing and pulling back of my thighs and he slowed and his ears came up and I didn't even have to say for him to stop.

We scuffled into stillness and stood quiet, and together Sam and I saw the storm. All across the horizon ahead were the vast billowing frays of a blizzard. I had a thought for John Marsh. He'd ridden smack into that. Or maybe not. Maybe he'd cut off for somewhere else. Then Sam waggled his head and snorted his unease about what we were looking at, and he was right, of course. He and I had our own life to live and so we turned around and galloped back.

The storm came in right behind us that day before Christmas in 1910, and there was no social at the school house that year. We all burrowed in and kept the fires going and sang some carols. *Stars were gleaming, shepherds dreaming, And the night was dark and chill.*

After midnight I arose and I took a lantern and a shovel and I made a way to the barn, the new snow biting at me all the while, but at last I came in to Sam and hung the lantern, and he muttered in that way he sometimes did, like he knew a thing before it would happen, he knew I'd be there, and I lay down by my horse and I put my arms around him. "Aren't you glad you're in your stable," I whispered to him. "I brought you here away from the storm." And I held him tight.

CONSIDERATIONS FOR CRITICAL THINKING AND WRITING

1. **FIRST RESPONSE.** How is the setting in this story made simultaneously appealing and unappealing? Which response is stronger for you? Why?

2. Who or what is the antagonist?

3. In what sense is Sam a significant character in the plot though he is a horse? Why is he so important to Abigail?

4. Why do you think the stranger, John Marsh, is referred to by his first and last name throughout the story? Is there any significance to his last name?

5. Not only is the story set in winter, but Christmastime is also emphasized. Why is that important?

6. In what sense can this be read as a love story?

7. Explain how you would describe the ending. Is it happy, unhappy, or somewhere in between?

CONNECTIONS TO OTHER SELECTIONS

1. Compare the significance of the settings in "Christmas 1910" and in Susan Glaspell's *Trifles* (p. 1048).

2. Compare and contrast "Christmas 1910" and Ha Jin's "Love in the Air" (p. 79) as stories of unrequited love.

6

Point of View

It is not necessary to portray many characters. The center of gravity should be in two persons: him and her.
— ANTON CHEKHOV

Because one of the pleasures of reading fiction consists of seeing the world through someone else's eyes, it is easy to overlook the eyes that control our view of the plot, characters, and setting. *Point of view* refers to who tells us the story and how it is told. What we know and how we feel about the events in a story are shaped by the author's choice of a point of view. The teller of a story, the *narrator*, inevitably affects our understanding of the characters' actions by filtering what is told through his or her own perspective. The narrator should not be confused with the author who has created the narrative voice because the two are usually distinct (more on this point later).

If the narrative voice is changed, the story will change. Consider, for example, how different "Bartleby, the Scrivener" (p. 124) would be if Melville had chosen to tell the story from Bartleby's point of view instead of the lawyer's. With Bartleby as narrator, much of the mystery concerning his behavior would be lost. The peculiar force of his saying "I would prefer not to" would be lessened amid all the other things he would have to say as narrator. Moreover, the lawyer's reaction — puzzled, upset, outraged, and finally sympathetic to Bartleby — would be lost too. It would be entirely possible, of course, to write a story from Bartleby's point of view, but it would not be the story Melville wrote.

The possible ways of telling a story are many, and more than one point of view can be worked into a single story. However, the various points of view that storytellers draw on can be conveniently grouped into two broad categories: (1) the third-person narrator and (2) the first-person narrator. The third-person narrator uses *he, she,* or *they* to tell the story and does not participate in the action. The first-person narrator uses *I* and is a major or minor participant in the action. A second-person narrator, *you,* is possible but rarely used because of the awkwardness in thrusting the reader into the story, as in "You are minding your own business on a park bench when a drunk steps out of the bushes and demands your lunch bag."

Explore the literary element in this chapter on *LiterActive* or at bedfordstmartins.com/ meyercompact.

Let's look now at the most important and most often used variations within first- and third-person narrations.

THIRD-PERSON NARRATOR (Nonparticipant)

1. Omniscient (the narrator takes us inside the character[s])
2. Limited omniscient (the narrator takes us inside one or two characters)
3. Objective (the narrator is outside the character[s])

No type of third-person narrator appears as a character in a story. The **omniscient narrator** is all-knowing. From this point of view, the narrator can move from place to place and pass back and forth through time, slipping into and out of characters as no human being possibly could in real life. This narrator can report the characters' thoughts and feelings as well as what they say and do. In the excerpt from *Tarzan of the Apes* (p. 72), Burroughs's narrator tells us about events concerning Terkoz in another part of the jungle that long preceded the battle between Terkoz and Tarzan. We also learn Tarzan's and Jane's inner thoughts and emotions during the episode. And Burroughs's narrator describes Terkoz as "an arrant coward" and a bully, thereby evaluating the character for the reader. This kind of intrusion is called **editorial omniscience.** In contrast, narration that allows characters' actions and thoughts to speak for themselves is known as **neutral omniscience.** Most modern writers use neutral omniscience so that readers can reach their own conclusions.

The **limited omniscient narrator** is much more confined than the omniscient narrator. With limited omniscience the author very often restricts the narrator to the single perspective of either a major or a minor charac-ter. Sometimes a narrator can see into more than one character, particu-larly in a longer work that focuses, for example, on two characters alter-nately from one chapter to the next. Short stories, however, frequently are restricted by length to a single character's point of view. The way people, places, and events appear to that character is the way they appear to the reader. The reader has access to the thoughts and feelings of the characters revealed by the narrator, but neither the reader nor the character has access to the inner lives of any of the other characters in the story. The events in Katherine Mansfield's "Miss Brill" (p. 275) are viewed entirely through the protagonist's eyes; we see a French vacation town as an elderly woman does. Miss Brill represents the central consciousness of the story. She uni-fies the story by being present through all the action. We are not told of anything that happens away from the character because the narration is based on her perception of things.

The most intense use of a central consciousness in narration can be seen in the ***stream-of-consciousness technique*** developed by modern writers such as James Joyce, Virginia Woolf, and William Faulkner. This technique takes a reader inside a character's mind to reveal perceptions, thoughts, and feelings on a conscious or unconscious level. A stream of conscious-ness suggests the flow of thought as well as its content; hence, complete sentences may give way to fragments as the character's mind makes rapid associations free of conventional logic or transitions.

The following passage is from Joyce's *Ulysses,* a novel famous for its extended use of this technique. In this paragraph Joyce takes us inside the mind of a character who is describing a funeral:

> Coffin now. Got here before us, dead as he is. Horse looking round at it with his plume skeowways [askew]. Dull eye: collar tight on his neck, pressing on a bloodvessel or something. Do they know what they cart out of here every day? Must be twenty or thirty funerals every day. Then Mount Jerome for the protestants. Funerals all over the world everywhere every minute. Shovelling them under by the cartload doublequick. Thousands every hour. Too many in the world.

The character's thoughts range from specific observations to speculations about death. Joyce creates the illusion that we are reading the character's thoughts as they occur. The stream-of-consciousness technique provides an intimate perspective on a character's thoughts.

In contrast, the ***objective point of view*** employs a narrator who does not see into the mind of any character. From this detached and impersonal perspective, the narrator reports action and dialogue without telling us directly what the character feels and thinks. We observe the characters in much the same way we would perceive events in a film or play: we supply the meanings; no analysis or interpretation is provided by the narrator. This point of view places a heavy premium on dialogue, actions, and details to reveal character.

In Hemingway's "Soldier's Home" (p. 165), a limited omniscient narration is the predominant point of view. Krebs's thoughts and reaction to being home from the war are made available to the reader by the narrator, who tells us that Krebs "felt embarrassed and resentful" or "sick and vaguely nauseated" by the small-town life he has reentered. Occasionally, however, Hemingway uses an objective point of view when he dramatizes particularly tense moments between Krebs and his mother. In the following excerpt, Hemingway's narrator shows us Krebs's feelings instead of telling us what they are. Krebs's response to his mother's concerns is presented without comment. The external details of the scene reveal his inner feelings.

> "I've worried about you so much, Harold," his mother went on. "I know the temptations you must have been exposed to. I know how weak men are. I know what your own dear grandfather, my own father, told us about the Civil War and I have prayed for you. I pray for you all day long, Harold."
>
> Krebs looked at the bacon fat hardening on his plate.
>
> "Your father is worried, too," his mother went on. "He thinks you have lost your ambition, that you haven't got a definite aim in life. Charley Simmons, who is just your age, has a good job and is going to be married. The boys are all settling down; they're all determined to get somewhere; you can see that boys like Charley Simmons are on their way to being really a credit to the community."
>
> Krebs said nothing.
>
> "Don't look that way, Harold. . . ."

When Krebs looks at the bacon fat we can see him cooling and hardening too. Hemingway does not describe the expression on Krebs's face, yet we know it is a look that disturbs his mother as she goes on about what she thinks she knows. Krebs and his mother are clearly tense and upset; the details, action, and dialogue reveal that without the narrator telling the reader how each character feels.

FIRST-PERSON NARRATOR (Participant)

1. Major character
2. Minor character

With a *first-person narrator,* the I presents the point of view of only one character's consciousness. The reader is restricted to the perceptions, thoughts, and feelings of that single character. This is Melville's technique with the lawyer in "Bartleby, the Scrivener" (p. 124). Everything learned about the characters, action, and plot comes from the unnamed lawyer. Bartleby remains a mystery because we are limited to what the lawyer knows and reports. The lawyer cannot explain what Bartleby means because he does not entirely know himself. Melville's use of the first person encourages us to identify with the lawyer's confused reaction to Bartleby so that we pay attention not only to the scrivener but to the lawyer's response to him. We are as perplexed as the lawyer and share his effort to make sense of Bartleby.

The lawyer is a major character in Melville's story; indeed, many readers take him to be the protagonist. A first-person narrator can, however, also be a minor character (imagine how different the story would be if it were told by, say, Ginger Nut or by an observer who had little or nothing to do with the action). Faulkner uses an observer in "A Rose for Emily" (p. 90). His *we*, though plural and representative of the town's view of Emily, is nonetheless a first-person narrator.

One of the primary reasons for identifying the point of view in a story is to determine where the author stands in relation to the story. Behind the narrative voice of any story is the author, manipulating events and providing or withholding information. It is a mistake to assume that the narrative voice of a story is the author. The narrator, whether a first-person participant or a third-person nonparticipant, is a creation of the writer. A narrator's perceptions may be accepted, rejected, or modified by an author, depending on how the narrative voice is articulated.

Faulkner seems to have shared the fascination, sympathy, and horror of the narrator in "A Rose for Emily," but Melville must not be so readily identified with the lawyer in "Bartleby, the Scrivener." The lawyer's description of himself as "an eminently *safe* man," convinced "that the easiest way of life is the best," raises the question of how well equipped he is to fathom Bartleby's protest. To make sense of Bartleby, it is also necessary to understand the lawyer's point of view. Until the conclusion of the story, this "*safe* man" is too self-serving, defensive, and obtuse to comprehend the despair embodied in Bartleby and the deadening meaninglessness of Wall Street life.

The lawyer is an **unreliable narrator**, whose interpretation of events is different from the author's. We cannot entirely accept the lawyer's assessment of Bartleby because we see that the lawyer's perceptions are not totally to be trusted. Melville does not expect us, for example, to agree with the lawyer's suggestion that the solution to Bartleby's situation might be to "entertain some young gentleman with your conversation" on a trip to Europe. Given Bartleby's awful silences, this absurd suggestion reveals the lawyer's superficial understanding. The lawyer's perceptions frequently do not coincide with those Melville expects his readers to share. Hence, the lawyer's unreliability preserves Bartleby's mysterious nature while revealing the lawyer's sensibilities. The point of view is artistically appropriate for Melville's purposes because the eyes through which we perceive the plot, characters, and setting are also the subject of the story.

Narrators can be unreliable for a variety of reasons: they might lack self-knowledge, like Melville's lawyer, or they might be innocent and inexperienced, like Ralph Ellison's young narrator in "Battle Royal" (p. 243).

Youthful innocence frequently characterizes a *naive narrator* such as Mark Twain's Huck Finn or Holden Caulfield, J. D. Salinger's twentieth-century version of Huck in *The Catcher in the Rye*. These narrators lack the sophistication to interpret accurately what they see; they are unreliable because the reader must go beyond their understanding of events to comprehend the situations described. Huck and Holden describe their respective social environments, but the reader, with more experience, supplies the critical perspective that each boy lacks. In "Battle Royal" that perspective is supplemented by Ellison's dividing the narration between the young man who experiences events and the mature man who reflects back on those events.

Few generalizations can be made about the advantages or disadvantages of using a specific point of view. What can be said with confidence, however, is that writers choose a point of view to achieve particular effects because point of view determines what we know about the characters and events in a story. We should, therefore, be aware of who is telling the story and whether the narrator sees things clearly and reliably.

The next three works warrant a careful examination of their points of view. In Achy Obejas's "We Came All the Way from Cuba So You Could Dress Like This?," we hear the voice of a ten-year-old refugee describing a lifetime's worth of immigrant experience. In Anton Chekhov's and Joyce Carol Oates's versions of "The Lady with the Pet Dog," we are presented with similar stories told from two different perspectives that make for intriguing comparisons and contrasts.

ACHY OBEJAS (B. 1956)

Born in Havana, Cuba, Achy Obejas emigrated to the United States at the age of six after the Cuban revolution and Fidel Castro's rise to power. She has worked as a journalist at several Chicago newspapers, particularly the *Chicago Tribune*. She has also taught creative writing on visiting appointments at the University of Chicago, University of Hawaii, and Northwestern University. Her fiction typically draws on her dislocating experiences and her efforts in forging an identity as a Cuban exile in the United States. The author of two novels, *Memory*

Courtesy of Achy Obejas.

Mambo (1996) and *Days of Awe* (2001), as well as a collection of stories, *We Came All the Way from Cuba So You Could Dress Like This?* (1994), Obejas has won two Lambda Literary Awards, the Studs Terkel Award for Journalism, and a National Endowment for the Arts Fellowship. The following title story from her collection explores both the complexities and the difficulties of the narrator's struggle to achieve an authentic identity.

We Came All the Way from Cuba So You Could Dress Like This?   1994

for Nena

I'm wearing a green sweater. It's made of some synthetic material, and it's mine. I've been wearing it for two days straight and have no plans to take it off right now.

I'm ten years old. I just got off the boat—or rather, the ship. The actual boat didn't make it. We got picked up halfway from Havana to Miami by a gigantic oil freighter to which they then tied our boat. That's how our boat got smashed to smithereens, its wooden planks breaking off like toothpicks against the ship's big metal hull. Everybody talks about American ingenuity, so I'm not sure why somebody didn't anticipate that would happen. But they didn't. So the boat that brought me and my parents most of the way from Cuba is now just part of the debris that'll wash up on tourist beaches all over the Caribbean.

As I speak, my parents are being interrogated by an official from the office of Immigration and Naturalization Services. It's all a formality because this is 1963, and no Cuban claiming political asylum actually gets turned away. We're evidence that the revolution has failed the middle class and that communism is bad. My parents—my father's an accountant and my mother's a social worker—are living, breathing examples of the suffering Cubans have endured under tyranny of Fidel Castro.

The immigration officer, a fat Hungarian lady with sparkly hazel eyes and a perpetual smile, asks my parents why they came over, and my father, whose face is bright red from spending two days floating in a little boat on the Atlantic Ocean while secretly terrified, points to me—I'm sitting on a couch across the room, more bored than exhausted—and says, We came for her, so she could have a future.

The immigration officer speaks a halting Spanish, and with it she tells my 5 parents about fleeing the Communists in Hungary. She says they took everything from her family, including a large country estate, with forty-four acres and two lakes, that's now being used as a vocational training center. Can you imagine that, she says. There's an official presidential portrait of John F. Kennedy behind her, which will need to be replaced in a week or so.

I fold my arms in front of my chest and across the green sweater. Tonight the U.S. government will put us up in a noisy transient hotel. We'll be allowed to stay there at taxpayer expense for a couple of days until my godfather—who lives with his mistress somewhere in Miami—comes to get us.

Leaning against the wall at the processing center, I notice a volunteer for Catholic Charities who approaches me with gifts: oatmeal cookies, a plastic doll with blond hair and a blue dress, and a rosary made of white plastic beads. She smiles and talks to me in incomprehensible English, speaking unnaturally loud.

My mother, who's watching while sitting nervously next to my father as we're being processed, will later tell me she remembers this moment as something poignant and good.

All I hold onto is the feel of the doll—cool and hard—and the fact that the Catholic volunteer is trying to get me to exchange my green sweater for a little gray flannel gym jacket with a hood and an American flag logo. I wrap myself up tighter in the sweater, which at this point still smells of salt and Cuban dirt and my grandmother's house, and the Catholic volunteer just squeezes my shoulder and leaves, thinking, I'm sure, that I've been traumatized by the trip across the choppy waters. My mother smiles weakly at me from across the room.

I'm still clutching the doll, a thing I'll never play with but which I'll carry   10
with me all my life, from apartment to apartment, one move after the other. Eventually, her little blond nylon hairs will fall off and, thirty years later, after I'm diagnosed with cancer, she'll sit atop my dresser, scarred and bald like a chemo patient.

Is life destiny or determination?

For all the blond boyfriends I will have, there will be only two yellow-haired lovers. One doesn't really count—a boy in a military academy who subscribes to Republican politics like my parents, and who will try, relatively unsuccessfully, to penetrate me on a south Florida beach. I will squirm away from underneath him, not because his penis hurts me but because the stubble on his face burns my cheek.

The other will be Martha, perceived by the whole lesbian community as a gold digger, but who will love me in spite of my poverty. She'll come to my one-room studio on Saturday mornings when her rich lover is still asleep and rip tee-shirts off my shoulders, brutally and honestly.

One Saturday we'll forget to set the alarm to get her back home in time, and Martha will have to dress in a hurry, the smoky smell of my sex all over her face and her own underwear tangled up in her pants leg. When she gets home, her rich lover will notice the weird bulge at her calf and throw her out, forcing Martha to acknowledge that without a primary relationship for contrast, we can't go on.

It's too dangerous, she'll say, tossing her blond hair away from her face.   15

Years later, I'll visit Martha, now living seaside in Provincetown with her new lover, a Kennedy cousin still in the closet who has a love of dogs, and freckles sprinkled all over her cheeks.

At the processing center, the Catholic volunteer has found a young Colombian woman to talk to me. I don't know her name, but she's pretty and brown, and she speaks Spanish. She tells me she's not Catholic but that she'd like to offer me Christian comfort anyway. She smells of violet water.

She pulls a Bible from her big purse and asks me, Do you know this, and I say, I'm Catholic, and she says that, well, she was once Catholic, too, but then she was saved and became something else. She says everything will change for me in the United States, as it did for her.

Then she tells me about coming here with her father and how he got sick and died, and she was forced to do all sorts of work, including what she calls sinful work, and how the sinful work taught her so much about life, and then how she got saved. She says there's still a problem, an impulse, which she has to suppress by reading the Bible. She looks at me as if I know what she's talking about.

Across the room, my parents are still talking to the fat Hungarian lady, my   20
father's head bent over the table as he fills out form after form.

Then the Catholic volunteer comes back and asks the Colombian girl something in English, and the girl reaches across me, pats my lap, and starts reading from her Spanish-language Bible: Your breasts are like two fawns, twins of a gazelle that feed upon the lilies. Until the day breathes and the shadows flee, I will hie me to the mountain of myrrh and the hill of frankincense. You are all fair, my love; there is no flaw in you.

Here's what my father dreams I will be in the United States of America: A lawyer, then a judge, in a system of law that is both serious and just. Not that he actually believes in democracy—in fact, he's openly suspicious of the popular will—but he longs for the power and prestige such a career would bring, and which he can't achieve on his own now that we're here, so he projects it all on me. He sees me in courtrooms and lecture halls, at libraries and in elegant restaurants, the object of envy and awe.

My father does not envision me in domestic scenes. He does not imagine me as a wife or mother because to do so would be to imagine someone else closer to me than he is, and he cannot endure that. He will never regret not being a grandfather; it was never part of his plan.

Here's what my mother dreams I will be in the United States of America: The owner of many appliances and a rolling green lawn; mother of two mischievous children; the wife of a boyishly handsome North American man who drinks Pepsi for breakfast; a career woman with a well-paying position in local broadcasting.

My mother pictures me reading the news on TV at four and home at the   25
dinner table by six. She does not propose that I will actually do the cooking, but rather that I'll oversee the undocumented Haitian woman my husband and I have hired for that purpose. She sees me as fulfilled, as she imagines she is.

All I ever think about are kisses, not the deep throaty kind but quick pecks all along my belly just before my lover and I dissolve into warm blankets and tangled sheets in a bed under an open window. I have no view of this scene from a distance, so I don't know if the window frames tall pine trees or tropical bushes permeated with skittering gray lizards.

It's hot and stuffy in the processing center, where I'm sitting under a light that buzzes and clicks. Everything smells of nicotine. I wipe the shine off my face with the sleeve of my sweater. Eventually, I take off the sweater and fold it over my arm.

My father, smoking cigarette after cigarette, mutters about communism and how the Dominican Republic is next and then, possibly, someplace in Central America.

My mother has disappeared to another floor in the building, where the Catholic volunteer insists that she look through boxes filled with clothes do-nated by generous North Americans. Later, my mother will tell us how the Catholic volunteer pointed to the little gray flannel gym jacket with the hood and the American flag logo, how she plucked a bow tie from a box, then a black synthetic teddy from another and laughed, embarrassed.

My mother will admit she was uncomfortable with the idea of sifting 30 through the boxes, sinking arm-deep into other people's sweat and excretions, but not that she was afraid of offending the Catholic volunteer and that she held her breath, smiled, and fished out a shirt for my father and a light blue cotton dress for me, which we'll never wear.

My parents escaped from Cuba because they did not want me to grow up in a communist state. They are anti-communists, especially my father.

It's because of this that when Martin Luther King, Jr., dies in 1968 and North American cities go up in flames, my father will gloat. King was a Communist, he will say; he studied in Moscow, everybody knows that.

I'll roll my eyes and say nothing. My mother will ask him to please finish his *café con leche* and wipe the milk moustache from the top of his lip.

Later, the morning after Bobby Kennedy's brains are shot all over a California hotel kitchen, my father will greet the news of his death by walking into our kitchen wearing a "Nixon's the One" button.

There's no stopping him now, my father will say; I know, because I was 35 involved with the counterrevolution, and I know he's the one who's going to save us, he's the one who came up with the Bay of Pigs—which would have worked, all the experts agree, if he'd been elected instead of Kennedy, that coward.

My mother will vote for Richard Nixon in 1968, but in spite of his loud support my father will sit out the election, convinced there's no need to become a citizen of the United States (the usual prerequisite for voting) because Nixon will get us back to Cuba in no time, where my father's dormant citizenship will spring to life.

Later that summer, my father, who has resisted getting a television set (too cumbersome to be moved when we go back to Cuba, he will tell us), suddenly buys a huge Zenith color model to watch the Olympics broadcast from Mexico City.

I will sit on the floor, close enough to distinguish the different colored dots, while my father sits a few feet away in a LA-Z-BOY chair and roots for the Cuban boxers, especially Teófilo Stevenson. Every time Stevenson wins one— whether against North Americans or East Germans or whomever—my father will jump up and shout.

Later, when the Cuban flag waves at us during the medal ceremony, and the Cuban national anthem comes through the TV's tinny speakers, my father will stand up in Miami and cover his heart with his palm just like Fidel, watching on his own TV in Havana.

When I get older, I'll tell my father a rumor I heard that Stevenson, for all 40 his heroics, practiced his best boxing moves on his wife, and my father will look at me like I'm crazy and say, Yeah, well, he's a Communist, what did you expect, huh?

In the processing center, my father is visited by a Cuban man with a large camera bag and a steno notebook into which he's constantly scribbling. The man has green Coke-bottle glasses and chews on a pungent Cuban cigar as he nods at everything my father says.

My mother, holding a brown paper bag filled with our new (used) clothes, sits next to me on the couch under the buzzing and clicking lights. She asks me about the Colombian girl, and I tell her she read me parts of the Bible, which makes my mother shudder.

The man with the Coke-bottle glasses and cigar tells my father he's from Santiago de Cuba in Oriente province, near Fidel's hometown, where he claims nobody ever supported the revolution because they knew the real Fidel. Then he tells my father he knew his father, which makes my father very nervous.

The whole northern coast of Havana harbor is mined, my father says to the Cuban man as if to distract him. There are *milicianos°* all over the beaches, he goes on; it was a miracle we got out, but we had to do it—for her, and he points my way again.

Then the man with the Coke-bottle glasses and cigar jumps up and pulls a   45
giant camera out of his bag, covering my mother and me with a sudden explosion of light.

In 1971, I'll come home for Thanksgiving from Indiana University where I have a scholarship to study optometry. It'll be the first time in months I'll be without an antiwar demonstration to go to, a consciousness-raising group to attend, or a Gay Liberation meeting to lead.

Alaba'o, I almost didn't recognize you, my mother will say, pulling on the fringes of my suede jacket, promising to mend the holes in my floor-sweeping, bell-bottom jeans. My green sweater will be somewhere in the closet of my bedroom in their house.

We left Cuba so you could dress like this? my father will ask over my mother's shoulder.

And for the first and only time in my life, I'll say, Look, you didn't come for me, you came for you; you came because all your rich clients were leaving and you were going to wind up a cashier in your father's hardware store if you didn't leave, okay?

My father, who works in a bank now, will gasp—*¿Qué qué?°*—and step   50
back a bit. And my mother will say, Please, don't talk to your father like that.

And I'll say, It's a free country, I can do anything I want, remember? Christ, he only left because Fidel beat him in that stupid swimming race when they were little.

And then my father will reach over my mother's thin shoulders, grab me by the red bandanna around my neck, and throw me to the floor, where he'll kick me over and over until all I remember is my mother's voice pleading, Please stop, please, please, please stop.

We leave the processing center with the fat Hungarian lady, who drives a large Ford station wagon. My father sits in the front with her, and my mother and I sit in the back, although there is plenty of room for both of us in the front as well. The fat Hungarian lady is taking us to our hotel, where our room will have a kitchenette and a view of an alley from which a tall black transvestite plies her night trade.

---

milicianos: Militiamen.
¿Qué qué?: What what?

Eventually, I'm drawn by the lights of the city, not just the neon streaming by the car windows but also the white globes on the street lamps, and I scamper to the back where I can watch the lights by myself. I close my eyes tight, then open them, loving the tracers and star bursts on my private screen.

Up in front, the fat Hungarian lady and my father are discussing the 55 United States' many betrayals, first of Eastern Europe after World War II, then of Cuba after the Bay of Pigs invasion.

My mother, whom I believe is as beautiful as any of the palm trees fluttering on the median strip as we drive by, leans her head against the car window, tired and bereft. She comes to when the fat Hungarian lady, in a fit of giggles, breaks from the road and into the parking lot of a supermarket so shrouded in light that I'm sure it's a flying saucer docked here in Miami.

We did this when we first came to America, the fat Hungarian lady says, leading us up to the supermarket. And it's something only people like us can appreciate.

My father bobs his head up and down and my mother follows, her feet scraping the ground as she drags me by the hand.

We walk through the front door and then a turnstile, and suddenly we are in the land of plenty — row upon row of cereal boxes, TV dinners, massive displays of fresh pineapple, crate after crate of oranges, shelves of insect repellent, and every kind of broom. The dairy section is jammed with cheese and chocolate milk.

There's a butcher shop in the back, and my father says, Oh my god, look, 60 and points to a slab of bloody red ribs thick with meat. My god my god my god, he says, as if he's never seen such a thing, or as if we're on the verge of starvation.

Calm down, please, my mother says, but he's not listening, choking back tears and hanging off the fat Hungarian lady who's now walking him past the sausages and hot dogs, packaged bologna and chipped beef.

All around us people stare, but then my father says, We just arrived from Cuba, and there's so much here!

The fat Hungarian lady pats his shoulder and says to the gathering crowd, Yes, he came on a little boat with his whole family; look at his beautiful daughter who will now grow up well-fed and free.

I push up against my mother, who feels as smooth and thin as a palm leaf on Good Friday. My father beams at me, tears in his eyes. All the while, complete strangers congratulate him on his wisdom and courage, give him hugs and money, and welcome him to the United States.

There are things that can't be told. 65

Things like when we couldn't find an apartment, everyone's saying it was because landlords in Miami didn't rent to families with kids, but knowing, always, that it was more than that.

Things like my doing very poorly on an IQ test because I didn't speak English, and getting tossed into a special education track, where it took until high school before somebody realized I didn't belong there.

Things like a North American hairdresser's telling my mother she didn't do her kind of hair.

Like my father, finally realizing he wasn't going to go back to Cuba any time soon, trying to hang himself with the light cord in the bathroom while my mother cleaned rooms at a nearby luxury hotel, but falling instead and breaking his arm.

Like accepting welfare checks, because there really was no other way.   70

Like knowing that giving money to exile groups often meant helping somebody buy a private yacht for Caribbean vacations, not for invading Cuba, but also knowing that refusing to donate only invited questions about our own patriotism.

And knowing that Nixon really wasn't the one, and wasn't doing anything, and wouldn't have done anything, even if he'd finished his second term, no matter what a good job the Cuban burglars might have done at the Watergate Hotel.

What if we'd stayed? What if we'd never left Cuba? What if we were there when the last of the counterrevolution was beaten, or when Mariel harbor leaked thousands of Cubans out of the island, or when the Pan-American Games came? What if we'd never left?

All my life, my father will say I would have been a young Communist, falling prey to the revolution's propaganda. According to him, I would have believed ice cream treats came from Fidel, that those hairless Russians were our friends; and that my duty as a revolutionary was to turn him in for his counterrevolutionary activities—which he will swear he'd never have given up if we'd stayed in Cuba.

My mother will shake her head but won't contradict him. She'll say the   75 revolution uses people, and that I, too, would probably have been used, then betrayed, and that we'll never know, but maybe I would have wound up in jail whether I ever believed in the revolution or not, because I would have talked back to the wrong person, me and my big mouth.

I wonder, if we'd stayed then who, if anyone—if not Martha and the boy from the military academy—would have been my blond lovers, or any kind of lovers at all.

And what if we'd stayed, and there had been no revolution?

My parents will never say, as if somehow they know that their lives were meant to exist only in opposition.

I try to imagine who I would have been if Fidel had never come into Havana sitting triumphantly on top of that tank, but I can't. I can only think of variations of who I am, not who I might have been.

In college one day, I'll tell my mother on the phone that I want to go back   80 to Cuba to see, to consider all these questions, and she'll pause, then say, What for? There's nothing there for you, we'll tell you whatever you need to know, don't you trust us?

Over my dead body, my father will say, listening in on the other line.

Years later, when I fly to Washington, D.C., and take a cab straight to the Cuban Interests Section to apply for a visa, a golden-skinned man with the dulled eyes of a bureaucrat will tell me that because I came to the U.S. too young to make the decision to leave for myself—that it was in fact my parents who made it for me—the Cuban government does not recognize my U.S. citizenship.

You need to renew your Cuban passport, he will say. Perhaps your parents have it, or a copy of your birth certificate, or maybe you have a relative or friend who could go through the records in Cuba for you.

I'll remember the passport among my mother's priceless papers, hand-written in blue ink, even the official parts. But when I ask my parents for it, my mother will say nothing, and my father will say, It's not here anymore, but in a bank box, where you'll never see it. Do you think I would let you betray us like that?

The boy from the military academy will say oh baby baby as he grinds his hips into me. And Martha and all the girls before and after her here in the United States will say ooohhh ooooohhhh oooooooohhhhhhhhh as my fingers explore inside them.

But the first time I make love with a Cuban, a politically controversial exile writer of some repute, she will say, *Aaaaaayyyyyaaaaaayyyaaaaay* and lift me by my hair from between her legs, strings of saliva like sea foam between my mouth and her shiny curls. Then she'll drop me onto her mouth where our tongues will poke each other like wily porpoises.

In one swift movement, she'll flip me on my back, pillows falling every which way from the bed, and kiss every part of me, between my breasts and under my arms, and she'll suck my fingertips, and the inside of my elbows. And when she rests her head on my belly, her ear listening not to my heartbeat but to the fluttering of palm trees, she'll sit up, place one hand on my throat, the other on my sex, and kiss me there, under my rib cage, around my navel, where I am softest and palest.

The next morning, listening to her breathing in my arms, I will wonder how this could have happened, and if it would have happened at all if we'd stayed in Cuba. And if so, if it would have been furtive or free, with or without the revolution. And how—knowing now how cataclysmic life really is—I might hold on to her for a little while longer.

When my father dies of a heart attack in 1990 (it will happen while he's driving, yelling at somebody, and the car will just sail over to the sidewalk and stop dead at the curb, where he'll fall to the seat and his arms will somehow fold over his chest, his hands set in prayer), I will come home to Florida from Chicago, where I'll be working as a photographer for the *Tribune*. I won't be taking pictures of murder scenes or politicians then but rather rock stars and local performance artists.

I'll be living in Uptown, in a huge house with a dry darkroom in one of the bedrooms, now converted and sealed black, where I cut up negatives and create photomontages that are exhibited at the Whitney Biennial and hailed by the critics as filled with yearning and hope.

When my father dies, I will feel sadness and a wish that certain things had been said, but I will not want more time with him. I will worry about my mother, just like all the relatives who predict she will die of heartbreak within months (she has diabetes and her vision is failing). But she will instead outlive both him and me.

I'll get to Miami Beach, where they've lived in a little coach house off Collins Avenue since their retirement, and find cousins and aunts helping my mother go through insurance papers and bank records, my father's will, his photographs and mementos: his university degree, a faded list of things to take back to Cuba (including Christmas lights), a jaundiced clipping from *Diario de las Américas* about our arrival which quotes my father as saying that

Havana harbor is mined, and a photo of my mother and me, wide-eyed and thin, sitting on the couch in the processing center.

My father's funeral will be simple but well-attended, closed casket at my request, but with a moment reserved for those who want a last look. My mother will stay in the room while the box is pried open (I'll be in the lobby smoking a cigarette, a habit I despised in my father but which I'll pick up at his funeral) and tell me later she stared at the cross above the casket, never registering my father's talcumed and perfumed body beneath it.

I couldn't leave, it wouldn't have looked right, she'll say. But thank god I'm going blind.

Then a minister who we do not know will come and read from the Bible 95 and my mother will reach around my waist and hold onto me as we listen to him say, When all these things come upon you, the blessing and the curse . . . and you call them to mind among all the nations where the Lord your God has driven you, and return to the Lord your God, you and your children, and obey his voice . . . with all your heart and with all your soul; then the Lord your God will return your fortunes, and have compassion upon you, and he will gather you again from all the peoples where the Lord your God has scattered you.

There will be a storm during my father's burial, which means it will end quickly. My mother and several relatives will go back to her house, where a TV will blare from the bedroom filled with bored teenage cousins, the women will talk about how to make *picadillo* with low-fat ground turkey instead of the traditional beef and ham, and the men will sit outside in the yard, drinking beer or small cups of Cuban coffee, and talk about my father's love of Cuba, and how unfortunate it is that he died just as Eastern Europe is breaking free, and Fidel is surely about to fall.

Three days later, after taking my mother to the movies and the mall, church and the local Social Security office, I'll be standing at the front gate with my bags, yelling at the cab driver that I'm coming, when my mother will ask me to wait a minute and run back into the house, emerging minutes later with a box for me that won't fit in any of my bags.

A few things, she'll say, a few things that belong to you that I've been meaning to give you for years and now, well, they're yours.

I'll shake the box, which will emit only a muffled sound, and thank her for whatever it is, hug her and kiss her and tell her I'll call her as soon as I get home. She'll put her chicken bone arms around my neck, kiss the skin there all the way to my shoulders, and get choked up, which will break my heart.

Sleepy and tired in the cab to the airport, I'll lean my head against the win- 100 dow and stare out at the lanky palm trees, their brown and green leaves waving good-bye to me through the still coming drizzle. Everything will be damp, and I'll be hot and stuffy, listening to car horns detonating on every side of me. I'll close my eyes, stare at the blackness, and try to imagine something of yearning and hope, but I'll fall asleep instead, waking only when the driver tells me we've arrived, and that he'll get my bags from the trunk, his hand outstretched for the tip as if it were a condition for the return of my things.

When I get home to Uptown I'll forget all about my mother's box until one day many months later when my memory's fuzzy enough to let me be curious. I'll break it open to find grade school report cards, family pictures of the three of us in Cuba, a love letter to her from my father (in which he talks about wanting to kiss the tender mole by her mouth), Xeroxes of my birth certificate, copies of our requests for political asylum, and my faded blue-ink Cuban passport (expiration date: June 1965), all wrapped up in my old green sweater.

When I call my mother — embarrassed about taking so long to unpack her box, overwhelmed by the treasures within it — her answering machine will pick up and, in a bilingual message, give out her beeper number in case of emergency.

A week after my father's death, my mother will buy a computer with a Braille keyboard and a speaker, start learning how to use it at the community center down the block, and be busy investing in mutual funds at a profit within six months.

But this is all a long way off, of course. Right now, we're in a small hotel room with a kitchenette that U.S. taxpayers have provided for us.

My mother, whose eyes are dark and sunken, sits at a little table eating one of the Royal Castle hamburgers the fat Hungarian lady bought for us. My father munches on another, napkins spread under his hands. Their heads are tilted toward the window which faces an alley. To the far south edge, it offers a view of Biscayne Boulevard and a magically colored thread of night traffic. The air is salty and familiar, the moon brilliant hanging in the sky. 105

I'm in bed, under sheets that feel heavy with humidity and the smell of cleaning agents. The plastic doll the Catholic volunteer gave me sits on my pillow.

Then my father reaches across the table to my mother and says, We made it, we really made it.

And my mother runs her fingers through his hair and nods, and they both start crying, quietly but heartily, holding and stroking each other as if they are all they have.

And then there's a noise — a screech out in the alley followed by what sounds like a hyena's laughter — and my father leaps up and looks out the window, then starts laughing, too.

Oh my god, come here, look at this, he beckons to my mother, who jumps up and goes to him, positioning herself right under the crook of his arm. Can you believe that, he says. 110

Only in America, echoes my mother.

And as I lie here wondering about the spectacle outside the window and the new world that awaits us on this and every night of the rest of our lives, even I know we've already come a long way. What none of us can measure yet is how much of the voyage is already behind us.

CONSIDERATIONS FOR CRITICAL THINKING AND WRITING

1. **FIRST RESPONSE.** How consistent is the chronology of the plot? How does this affect your understanding of the narrator?

2. Do you identify with the protagonist? Who (or what) is the antagonist?

3. Imagine this story with an editorial omniscient point of view rather than Obejas's first-person point of view. How might your response to the protagonist significantly change?

4. Explain why you think the narrator's character is consistent or inconsistent during the course of the story.

5. A number of references to the narrator's sexuality appear throughout the story. What do these moments reveal about the protagonist?

6. What do you think is the central conflict? Is there more than one? Are they resolved?

7. At one point the narrator asks, "Is life destiny or determination?" (para. 11). To what extent does the plot answer that question?

8. Write a one-paragraph interpretation that explains the significance of the story's final section (paras. 104–12).

CONNECTIONS TO OTHER SELECTIONS

1. Compare the ten-year-old's 1963 immigrant experiences in Obejas's story with that of the speaker's in Julia Alvarez's "Queens, 1963" (p. 944). How does the point of view in each work affect the emotional tone of the first-person narrative?

2. Discuss the differences and similarities in the father-daughter relationship in this story and in Rick Bass's "Her First Elk" (p. 516).

ANTON CHEKHOV (1860–1904)

Born in a small town in Russia, Anton Chekhov gave up the career his medical degree prepared him for in order to devote himself to writing. His concentration on realistic detail in the hundreds of short stories he published has had an important influence on fiction writing. Modern drama has also been strengthened by his plays, among them these classics: *The Seagull* (1896), *Uncle Vanya* (1899), *The Three Sisters* (1901), and *The Cherry Orchard* (1904). Chekhov was a close observer of people in ordinary situations who struggle to live their lives as best they can. They are not very often completely successful. Chekhov's compassion, however, makes their failures less significant than their humanity. In "The Lady with the Pet Dog," love is at the heart of a struggle that begins in Yalta, a resort town on the Black Sea.

© Austrian Archives/CORBIS.

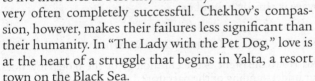

Explore contexts for Anton Chekhov on *LiterActive*.

The Lady with the Pet Dog

1899

TRANSLATED BY AVRAHM YARMOLINSKY (1947)

I

A new person, it was said, had appeared on the esplanade: a lady with a pet dog. Dmitry Dmitrich Gurov, who had spent a fortnight at Yalta and had got used to the place, had also begun to take an interest in new arrivals. As he sat in Vernet's confectionery shop, he saw, walking on the esplanade, a fair-haired young woman of medium height, wearing a beret; a white Pomeranian was trotting behind her.

And afterwards he met her in the public garden and in the square several times a day. She walked alone, always wearing the same beret and always with the white dog; no one knew who she was and everyone called her simply "the lady with the pet dog."

"If she is here alone without husband or friends," Gurov reflected, "it wouldn't be a bad thing to make her acquaintance."

He was under forty, but he already had a daughter twelve years old, and two sons at school. They had found a wife for him when he was very young, a student in his second year, and by now she seemed half as old again as he. She was a tall, erect woman with dark eyebrows, stately and dignified and, as she said of herself, intellectual. She read a great deal, used simplified spelling in her letters, called her husband, not Dmitry, but Dimitry, while he privately considered her of limited intelligence, narrow-minded, dowdy, was afraid of her, and did not like to be at home. He had begun being unfaithful to her long ago—had been unfaithful to her often and, probably for that reason, almost always spoke ill of women, and when they were talked of in his presence used to call them "the inferior race."

It seemed to him that he had been sufficiently tutored by bitter experience 5 to call them what he pleased, and yet he could not have lived without "the inferior race" for two days together. In the company of men he was bored and ill at ease, he was chilly and uncommunicative with them; but when he was among women he felt free, and knew what to speak to them about and how to comport himself; and even to be silent with them was no strain on him. In his appearance, in his character, in his whole makeup there was something attractive and elusive that disposed women in his favor and allured them. He knew that, and some force seemed to draw him to them, too.

Oft-repeated and really bitter experience had taught him long ago that with decent people—particularly Moscow people—who are irresolute and slow to move, every affair which at first seems a light and charming adventure inevitably grows into a whole problem of extreme complexity, and in the end a painful situation is created. But at every new meeting with an interesting woman this lesson of experience seemed to slip from his memory, and he was eager for life, and everything seemed so simple and diverting.

One evening while he was dining in the public garden the lady in the beret walked up without haste to take the next table. Her expression, her gait, her dress, and the way she did her hair told him that she belonged to the upper class, that she was married, that she was in Yalta for the first time and alone, and that she was bored there. The stories told of the immorality in Yalta are to a great extent untrue; he despised them, and knew that such stories were made up for the most part by persons who would have been glad to sin themselves if they had had the chance; but when the lady sat down at the next table three paces from him, he recalled these stories of easy conquests, of trips to the mountains, and the tempting thought of a swift, fleeting liaison, a romance with an unknown woman of whose very name he was ignorant suddenly took hold of him.

He beckoned invitingly to the Pomeranian, and when the dog approached him, shook his finger at it. The Pomeranian growled; Gurov threatened it again.

The lady glanced at him and at once dropped her eyes.

"He doesn't bite," she said and blushed. 10

"May I give him a bone?" he asked; and when she nodded he inquired affably, "Have you been in Yalta long?"

"About five days."

"And I am dragging out the second week here."

There was a short silence.

"Time passes quickly, and yet it is so dull here!" she said, not looking 15 at him.

"It's only the fashion to say it's dull here. A provincial will live in Belyov or Zhizdra and not be bored, but when he comes here it's 'Oh, the dullness! Oh, the dust!' One would think he came from Granada."

She laughed. Then both continued eating in silence, like strangers, but after dinner they walked together and there sprang up between them the light banter of people who are free and contented, to whom it does not matter where they go or what they talk about. They walked and talked of the strange light on the sea: the water was a soft, warm, lilac color, and there was a golden band of moonlight upon it. They talked of how sultry it was after a hot day. Gurov told her that he was a native of Moscow, that he had studied languages and litera-ture at the university, but had a post in a bank; that at one time he had trained to become an opera singer but had given it up, that he owned two houses in Moscow. And he learned from her that she had grown up in Petersburg, but had lived in S—— since her marriage two years previously, that she was going to stay in Yalta for about another month, and that her husband, who needed a rest, too, might perhaps come to fetch her. She was not certain whether her husband was a member of a Government Board or served on a Zemstvo Council,° and this amused her. And Gurov learned too that her name was Anna Sergeyevna.

Afterwards in his room at the hotel he thought about her—and was cer-tain that he would meet her the next day. It was bound to happen. Getting into bed he recalled that she had been a schoolgirl only recently, doing lessons like his own daughter; he thought how much timidity and angularity there was still in her laugh and her manner of talking with a stranger. It must have been the first time in her life that she was alone in a setting in which she was followed, looked at, and spoken to for one secret purpose alone, which she could hardly fail to guess. He thought of her slim, delicate throat, her lovely gray eyes.

"There's something pathetic about her, though," he thought, and dropped off.

Zemstvo Council: A district council.

II

A week had passed since they had struck up an acquaintance. It was a holiday. 20 It was close indoors, while in the street the wind whirled the dust about and blew people's hats off. One was thirsty all day, and Gurov often went into the restaurant and offered Anna Sergeyevna a soft drink or ice cream. One did not know what to do with oneself.

In the evening when the wind had abated they went out on the pier to watch the steamer come in. There were a great many people walking about the dock; they had come to welcome someone and they were carrying bunches of flowers. And two peculiarities of a festive Yalta crowd stood out: the elderly ladies were dressed like young ones and there were many generals.

Owing to the choppy sea, the steamer arrived late, after sunset, and it was a long time tacking about before it put in at the pier. Anna Sergeyevna peered at the steamer and the passengers through her lorgnette as though looking for acquaintances, and whenever she turned to Gurov her eyes were shining. She talked a great deal and asked questions jerkily, forgetting the next moment what she had asked; then she lost her lorgnette in the crush.

The festive crowd began to disperse; it was now too dark to see people's faces; there was no wind any more, but Gurov and Anna Sergeyevna still stood as though waiting to see someone else come off the steamer. Anna Sergeyevna was silent now, and sniffed her flowers without looking at Gurov.

"The weather has improved this evening," he said. "Where shall we go now? Shall we drive somewhere?"

She did not reply. 25

Then he looked at her intently, and suddenly embraced her and kissed her on the lips, and the moist fragrance of her flowers enveloped him; and at once he looked round him anxiously, wondering if anyone had seen them.

"Let us go to your place," he said softly. And they walked off together rapidly.

The air in her room was close and there was the smell of the perfume she had bought at the Japanese shop. Looking at her, Gurov thought: "What encounters life offers!" From the past he preserved the memory of carefree, good-natured women whom love made gay and who were grateful to him for the happiness he gave them, however brief it might be; and of women like his wife who loved without sincerity, with too many words, affectedly, hysterically, with an expression that it was not love or passion that engaged them but something more significant; and of two or three others, very beautiful, frigid women, across whose faces would suddenly flit a rapacious expression—an obstinate desire to take from life more than it could give, and these were women no longer young, capricious, unreflecting, domineering, unintelligent, and when Gurov grew cold to them their beauty aroused his hatred, and the lace on their lingerie seemed to him to resemble scales.

But here there was the timidity, the angularity of inexperienced youth, a feeling of awkwardness; and there was a sense of embarrassment, as though someone had suddenly knocked at the door. Anna Sergeyevna, "the lady with the pet dog," treated what had happened in a peculiar way, very seriously, as though it were her fall—so it seemed, and this was odd and inappropriate. Her features drooped and faded, and her long hair hung down sadly on either side of her face; she grew pensive and her dejected pose was that of a Magdalene in a picture by an old master.

"It's not right," she said. "You don't respect me now, you first of all."   30

There was a watermelon on the table. Gurov cut himself a slice and began eating it without haste. They were silent for at least half an hour.

There was something touching about Anna Sergeyevna; she had the purity of a well-bred, naive woman who has seen little of life. The single candle burning on the table barely illumined her face, yet it was clear that she was unhappy.

"Why should I stop respecting you, darling?" asked Gurov. "You don't know what you're saying."

"God forgive me," she said, and her eyes filled with tears. "It's terrible."

"It's as though you were trying to exonerate yourself."   35

"How can I exonerate myself? No. I am a bad, low woman; I despise myself and I have no thought of exonerating myself. It's not my husband but myself I have deceived. And not only just now; I have been deceiving myself for a long time. My husband may be a good, honest man, but he is a flunkey! I don't know what he does, what his work is, but I know he is a flunkey! I was twenty when I married him. I was tormented by curiosity; I wanted something better. 'There must be a different sort of life,' I said to myself. I wanted to live! To live, to live! Curiosity kept eating at me—you don't understand it, but I swear to God I could no longer control myself; something was going on in me: I could not be held back. I told my husband I was ill, and came here. And here I have been walking about as though in a daze, as though I were mad; and now I have become a vulgar, vile woman whom anyone may despise."

Gurov was already bored with her; he was irritated by her naive tone, by her repentance, so unexpected and so out of place; but for the tears in her eyes he might have thought she was joking or play-acting.

"I don't understand, my dear," he said softly. "What do you want?"

She hid her face on his breast and pressed close to him.

"Believe me, believe me, I beg you," she said, "I love honesty and purity,   40 and sin is loathsome to me; I don't know what I'm doing. Simple people say, 'The Evil One has led me astray.' And I may say of myself now that the Evil One has led me astray."

"Quiet, quiet," he murmured.

He looked into her fixed, frightened eyes, kissed her, spoke to her softly and affectionately, and by degrees she calmed down, and her gaiety returned; both began laughing.

Afterwards when they went out there was not a soul on the esplanade. The town with its cypresses looked quite dead, but the sea was still sounding as it broke upon the beach; a single launch was rocking on the waves and on it a lantern was blinking sleepily.

They found a cab and drove to Oreanda.

"I found out your surname in the hall just now: it was written on the   45 board—von Dideritz," said Gurov. "Is your husband German?"

"No; I believe his grandfather was German, but he is Greek Orthodox himself."

At Oreanda they sat on a bench not far from the church, looked down at the sea, and were silent. Yalta was barely visible through the morning mist; white clouds rested motionlessly on the mountaintops. The leaves did not stir on the trees, cicadas twanged, and the monotonous muffled sound of the sea that rose from below spoke of the peace, the eternal sleep awaiting us. So it rumbled below when there was no Yalta, no Oreanda here; so it rumbles now, and it will rumble as indifferently and as hollowly when we are no more. And in this constancy, in this complete indifference to the life and death of each of us, there lies, perhaps, a pledge of our eternal salvation, of the unceasing advance of life upon earth, of unceasing movement towards perfection. Sitting beside a young woman who in the dawn seemed so lovely, Gurov, soothed and spellbound by these magical surroundings—the sea, the mountains, the clouds, the wide sky—thought how everything is really beautiful in this world when one reflects: everything except what we think or do ourselves when we forget the higher aims of life and our own human dignity.

A man strolled up to them—probably a guard—looked at them and walked away. And this detail, too, seemed so mysterious and beautiful. They saw a steamer arrive from Feodosia, its lights extinguished in the glow of dawn.

"There is dew on the grass," said Anna Sergeyevna, after a silence.

"Yes, it's time to go home."

They returned to the city. 50

Then they met every day at twelve o'clock on the esplanade, lunched and dined together, took walks, admired the sea. She complained that she slept badly, that she had palpitations, asked the same questions, troubled now by jealousy and now by the fear that he did not respect her sufficiently. And often in the square or the public garden, when there was no one near them, he suddenly drew her to him and kissed her passionately. Complete idleness, these kisses in broad daylight exchanged furtively in dread of someone's seeing them, the heat, the smell of the sea, and the continual flitting before his eyes of idle, well-dressed, well-fed people, worked a complete change in him; he kept telling Anna Sergeyevna how beautiful she was, how seductive, was urgently passionate; he would not move a step away from her, while she was often pensive and continually pressed him to confess that he did not respect her, did not love her in the least, and saw in her nothing but a common woman. Almost every evening rather late they drove somewhere out of town, to Oreanda or to the waterfall; and the excursion was always a success, the scenery invariably impressed them as beautiful and magnificent.

They were expecting her husband, but a letter came from him saying that he had eye-trouble, and begging his wife to return home as soon as possible. Anna Sergeyevna made haste to go.

"It's a good thing I am leaving," she said to Gurov. "It's the hand of Fate!"

She took a carriage to the railway station, and he went with her. They were 55 driving the whole day. When she had taken her place in the express, and when the second bell had rung, she said, "Let me look at you once more—let me look at you again. Like this."

She was not crying but was so sad that she seemed ill, and her face was quivering.

"I shall be thinking of you—remembering you," she said. "God bless you; be happy. Don't remember evil against me. We are parting forever—it has to be, for we ought never to have met. Well, God bless you."

The train moved off rapidly, its lights soon vanished, and a minute later there was no sound of it, as though everything had conspired to end as quickly as possible that sweet trance, that madness. Left alone on the platform, and gazing into the dark distance, Gurov listened to the twang of the grasshoppers and the hum of the telegraph wires, feeling as though he had just waked up.

And he reflected, musing, that there had now been another episode or adventure in his life, and it, too, was at an end, and nothing was left of it but a memory. He was moved, sad, and slightly remorseful: this young woman whom he would never meet again had not been happy with him; he had been warm and affectionate with her, but yet in his manner, his tone, and his caresses there had been a shade of light irony, the slightly coarse arrogance of a happy male who was, besides, almost twice her age. She had constantly called him kind, exceptional, high-minded; obviously he had seemed to her different from what he really was, so he had involuntarily deceived her.

Here at the station there was already a scent of autumn in the air; it was a chilly evening.

"It is time for me to go north, too," thought Gurov as he left the platform.   60 "High time!"

III

At home in Moscow the winter routine was already established: the stoves were heated, and in the morning it was still dark when the children were having breakfast and getting ready for school, and the nurse would light the lamp for a short time. There were frosts already. When the first snow falls, on the first day the sleighs are out, it is pleasant to see the white earth, the white roofs; one draws easy, delicious breaths, and the season brings back the days of one's youth. The old limes and birches, white with hoar-frost, have a good-natured look; they are closer to one's heart than cypresses and palms, and near them one no longer wants to think of mountains and the sea.

Gurov, a native of Moscow, arrived there on a fine frosty day, and when he put on his fur coat and warm gloves and took a walk along Petrovka, and when on Saturday night he heard the bells ringing, his recent trip and the places he had visited lost all charm for him. Little by little he became immersed in Moscow life, greedily read three newspapers a day, and declared that he did not read the Moscow papers on principle. He already felt a longing for restaurants, clubs, formal dinners, anniversary celebrations, and it flattered him to entertain distinguished lawyers and actors, and to play cards with a professor at the physicians' club. He could eat a whole portion of meat stewed with pickled cabbage and served in a pan, Moscow style.

A month or so would pass and the image of Anna Sergeyevna, it seemed to him, would become misty in his memory, and only from time to time he would dream of her with her touching smile as he dreamed of others. But more than a month went by, winter came into its own, and everything was still clear in his memory as though he had parted from Anna Sergeyevna only yesterday. And his memories glowed more and more vividly. When in the evening stillness the voices of his children preparing their lessons reached his study, or when he listened to a song or to an organ playing in a restaurant, or when the storm howled in the chimney, suddenly everything would rise up in his memory: what had happened on the pier and the early morning with the mist on the mountains, and the steamer coming from Feodosia, and the kisses. He would pace about his room a long time, remembering and smiling; then his memories passed into reveries, and in his imagination the past would mingle with what was to come. He did not dream of Anna Sergeyevna, but she followed him about everywhere and watched him. When he shut his eyes he saw her before him as though she were there in the flesh; and she seemed to him lovelier, younger, tenderer than she had been, and he imagined himself a finer man than he had been in Yalta. Of evenings she peered out at him from the bookcase, from the fireplace, from the corner — he heard her breathing, the caressing rustle of her clothes. In the street he followed the women with his eyes, looking for someone who resembled her.

Already he was tormented by a strong desire to share his memories with someone. But in his home it was impossible to talk of his love, and he had no one to talk to outside; certainly he could not confide in his tenants or in anyone at the bank. And what was there to talk about? He hadn't loved her then, had he? Had there been anything beautiful, poetical, edifying, or simply interesting in his relations with Anna Sergeyevna? And he was forced to talk vaguely of love, of women, and no one guessed what he meant; only his wife would twitch her black eyebrows and say, "The part of a philanderer does not suit you at all, Dimitry."

One evening, coming out of the physicians' club with an official with 65 whom he had been playing cards, he could not resist saying:

"If you only knew what a fascinating woman I became acquainted with at Yalta!"

The official got into his sledge and was driving away, but turned suddenly and shouted: "Dmitry Dmitrich!"

"What is it?"

"You were right this evening: the sturgeon was a bit high."

These words, so commonplace, for some reason moved Gurov to indigna- 70 tion, and struck him as degrading and unclean. What savage manners, what mugs! What stupid nights, what dull, humdrum days! Frenzied gambling, gluttony, drunkenness, continual talk always about the same things! Futile pursuits and conversations always about the same topics take up the better part of one's time, the better part of one's strength, and in the end there is left a life clipped and wingless, an absurd mess, and there is no escaping or getting away from it — just as though one were in a madhouse or a prison.

Gurov, boiling with indignation, did not sleep all night. And he had a headache all the next day. And the following nights too he slept badly; he sat up in bed, thinking, or paced up and down his room. He was fed up with his children, fed up with the bank; he had no desire to go anywhere or to talk of anything.

In December during the holidays he prepared to take a trip and told his wife he was going to Petersburg to do what he could for a young friend — and he set off for S——. What for? He did not know, himself. He wanted to see Anna Sergeyevna and talk with her, to arrange a rendezvous if possible.

He arrived at S—— in the morning, and at the hotel took the best room, in which the floor was covered with gray army cloth, and on the table there was an inkstand, gray with dust and topped by a figure on horseback, its hat in its raised hand and its head broken off. The porter gave him the necessary information: von Dideritz lived in a house of his own on Staro-Goncharnaya Street, not far from the hotel: he was rich and lived well and kept his own horses; everyone in the town knew him. The porter pronounced the name: "Dridiritz."

Without haste Gurov made his way to Staro-Goncharnaya Street and found the house. Directly opposite the house stretched a long gray fence studded with nails.

"A fence like that would make one run away," thought Gurov, looking now   75
at the fence, now at the windows of the house.

He reflected: this was a holiday, and the husband was apt to be at home.
And in any case, it would be tactless to go into the house and disturb her. If he
were to send her a note, it might fall into her husband's hands, and that might
spoil everything. The best thing was to rely on chance. And he kept walking up
and down the street and along the fence, waiting for the chance. He saw a beggar go in at the gate and heard the dogs attack him; then an hour later he
heard a piano, and the sound came to him faintly and indistinctly. Probably it
was Anna Sergeyevna playing. The front door opened suddenly, and an old
woman came out, followed by the familiar white Pomeranian. Gurov was on
the point of calling to the dog, but his heart began beating violently, and in his
excitement he could not remember the Pomeranian's name.

He kept walking up and down, and hated the gray fence more and more,
and by now he thought irritably that Anna Sergeyevna had forgotten him, and
was perhaps already diverting herself with another man, and that that was very
natural in a young woman who from morning till night had to look at that
damn fence. He went back to his hotel room and sat on the couch for a long
while, not knowing what to do, then he had dinner and a long nap.

"How stupid and annoying all this is!" he thought when he woke and
looked at the dark windows: it was already evening. "Here I've had a good sleep
for some reason. What am I going to do at night?"

He sat on the bed, which was covered with a cheap gray blanket of the kind
seen in hospitals, and he twitted himself in his vexation:

"So there's your lady with the pet dog. There's your adventure. A nice   80
place to cool your heels in."

That morning at the station a playbill in large letters had caught his eye.
The Geisha was to be given for the first time. He thought of this and drove to the
theater.

"It's quite possible that she goes to first nights," he thought.

The theater was full. As in all provincial theaters, there was a haze above
the chandelier, the gallery was noisy and restless; in the front row, before the
beginning of the performance the local dandies were standing with their
hands clasped behind their backs; in the Governor's box the Governor's
daughter, wearing a boa, occupied the front seat, while the Governor himself
hid modestly behind the portiere and only his hands were visible; the curtain
swayed; the orchestra was a long time tuning up. While the audience were coming in and taking their seats, Gurov scanned the faces eagerly.

Anna Sergeyevna, too, came in. She sat down in the third row, and when
Gurov looked at her his heart contracted, and he understood clearly that in the
whole world there was no human being so near, so precious, and so important
to him; she, this little, undistinguished woman, lost in a provincial crowd, with
a vulgar lorgnette in her hand, filled his whole life now, was his sorrow and his
joy, the only happiness that he now desired for himself, and to the sounds of
the bad orchestra, of the miserable local violins, he thought how lovely she
was. He thought and dreamed.

A young man with small side-whiskers, very tall and stooped, came in with   85
Anna Sergeyevna and sat down beside her; he nodded his head at every step
and seemed to be bowing continually. Probably this was the husband whom at
Yalta, in an excess of bitter feeling, she had called a flunkey. And there really

was in his lanky figure, his side-whiskers, his small bald patch, something of a flunkey's retiring manner; his smile was mawkish, and in his buttonhole there was an academic badge like a waiter's number.

During the first intermission the husband went out to have a smoke; she remained in her seat. Gurov, who was also sitting in the orchestra, went up to her and said in a shaky voice, with a forced smile:

"Good evening!"

She glanced at him and turned pale, then looked at him again in horror, unable to believe her eyes, and gripped the fan and the lorgnette tightly together in her hands, evidently trying to keep herself from fainting. Both were silent. She was sitting, he was standing, frightened by her distress and not daring to take a seat beside her. The violins and the flute that were being tuned up sang out. He suddenly felt frightened: it seemed as if all the people in the boxes were looking at them. She got up and went hurriedly to the exit; he followed her, and both of them walked blindly along the corridors and up and down stairs, and figures in the uniforms prescribed for magistrates, teachers, and officials of the Department of Crown Lands, all wearing badges, flitted before their eyes, as did also ladies, and fur coats on hangers; they were conscious of drafts and the smell of stale tobacco. And Gurov, whose heart was beating violently, thought:

"Oh, Lord! Why are these people here and this orchestra!"

And at that instant he suddenly recalled how when he had seen Anna 90 Sergeyevna off at the station he had said to himself that all was over between them and that they would never meet again. But how distant the end still was!

On the narrow, gloomy staircase over which it said "To the Amphitheatre," she stopped.

"How you frightened me!" she said, breathing hard, still pale and stunned. "Oh, how you frightened me! I am barely alive. Why did you come? Why?"

"But do understand, Anna, do understand—" he said hurriedly, under his breath. "I implore you, do understand—"

She looked at him with fear, with entreaty, with love; she looked at him intently, to keep his features more distinctly in her memory.

"I suffer so," she went on, not listening to him. "All this time I have been 95 thinking of nothing but you; I live only by the thought of you. And I wanted to forget, to forget; but why, oh, why have you come?"

On the landing above them two high school boys were looking down and smoking, but it was all the same to Gurov; he drew Anna Sergeyevna to him and began kissing her face and her hands.

"What are you doing, what are you doing!" she was saying in horror, pushing him away. "We have lost our senses. Go away today; go away at once— I conjure you by all that is sacred, I implore you— People are coming this way!"

Someone was walking up the stairs.

"You must leave," Anna Sergeyevna went on in a whisper. "Do you hear, Dmitry Dmitrich? I will come and see you in Moscow. I have never been happy; I am unhappy now, and I never, never shall be happy, never! So don't make me suffer still more! I swear I'll come to Moscow. But now let us part. My dear, good, precious one, let us part!"

She pressed his hand and walked rapidly downstairs, turning to look 100 round at him, and from her eyes he could see that she really was unhappy.

Gurov stood for a while, listening, then when all grew quiet, he found his coat and left the theater.

IV

And Anna Sergeyevna began coming to see him in Moscow. Once every two or three months she left S——, telling her husband that she was going to consult a doctor about a woman's ailment from which she was suffering — and her husband did and did not believe her. When she arrived in Moscow she would stop at the Slavyansky Bazar Hotel, and at once send a man in a red cap to Gurov. Gurov came to see her, and no one in Moscow knew of it.

Once he was going to see her in this way on a winter morning (the messenger had come the evening before and not found him in). With him walked his daughter, whom he wanted to take to school: it was on the way. Snow was coming down in big wet flakes.

"It's three degrees above zero,° and yet it's snowing," Gurov was saying to his daughter. "But this temperature prevails only on the surface of the earth; in the upper layers of the atmosphere there is quite a different temperature."

"And why doesn't it thunder in winter, papa?"

He explained that, too. He talked, thinking all the while that he was on his 105 way to a rendezvous, and no living soul knew of it, and probably no one would ever know. He had two lives: an open one, seen and known by all who needed to know it, full of conventional truth and conventional falsehood, exactly like the lives of his friends and acquaintances; and another life that went on in secret. And through some strange, perhaps accidental, combination of circumstances, everything that was of interest and importance to him, everything that was essential to him, everything about which he felt sincerely and did not deceive himself, everything that constituted the core of his life, was going on concealed from others; while all that was false, the shell in which he hid to cover the truth — his work at the bank, for instance, his discussions at the club, his references to the "inferior race," his appearances at anniversary celebrations with his wife — all that went on in the open. Judging others by himself, he did not believe what he saw, and always fancied that every man led his real, most interesting life under cover of secrecy as under cover of night. The personal life of every individual is based on secrecy, and perhaps it is partly for that reason that civilized man is so nervously anxious that personal privacy should be respected.

Having taken his daughter to school, Gurov went on to the Slavyansky Bazar Hotel. He took off his fur coat in the lobby, went upstairs, and knocked gently at the door. Anna Sergeyevna, wearing his favorite gray dress, exhausted by the journey and by waiting, had been expecting him since the previous evening. She was pale, and looked at him without a smile, and he had hardly entered when she flung herself on his breast. Their kiss was a long, lingering one, as though they had not seen one another for two years.

"Well, darling, how are you getting on there?" he asked. "What news?"

"Wait; I'll tell you in a moment — I can't speak."

---

three degrees above zero: On the Celsius scale; about thirty-eight degrees Fahrenheit.

She could not speak; she was crying. She turned away from him, and pressed her handkerchief to her eyes.

"Let her have her cry; meanwhile I'll sit down," he thought, and he seated himself in an armchair. 110

Then he rang and ordered tea, and while he was having his tea she remained standing at the window with her back to him. She was crying out of sheer agitation, in the sorrowful consciousness that their life was so sad; that they could only see each other in secret and had to hide from people like thieves! Was it not a broken life?

"Come, stop now, dear!" he said.

It was plain to him that this love of theirs would not be over soon, that the end of it was not in sight. Anna Sergeyevna was growing more and more attached to him. She adored him, and it was unthinkable to tell her that their love was bound to come to an end some day; besides, she would not have believed it!

He went up to her and took her by the shoulders, to fondle her and say something diverting, and at that moment he caught sight of himself in the mirror.

His hair was already beginning to turn gray. And it seemed odd to him 115 that he had grown so much older in the last few years, and lost his looks. The shoulders on which his hands rested were warm and heaving. He felt compassion for this life, still so warm and lovely, but probably already about to begin to fade and wither like his own. Why did she love him so much? He always seemed to women different from what he was, and they loved in him not himself, but the man whom their imagination created and whom they had been eagerly seeking all their lives; and afterwards, when they saw their mistake, they loved him nevertheless. And not one of them had been happy with him. In the past he had met women, come together with them, parted from them, but he had never once loved; it was anything you please, but not love. And only now when his head was gray he had fallen in love, really, truly — for the first time in his life.

Anna Sergeyevna and he loved each other as people do who are very close and intimate, like man and wife, like tender friends; it seemed to them that Fate itself had meant them for one another, and they could not understand why he had a wife and she a husband; and it was as though they were a pair of migratory birds, male and female, caught and forced to live in different cages. They forgave each other what they were ashamed of in their past, they forgave everything in the present, and felt that this love of theirs had altered them both.

Formerly in moments of sadness he had soothed himself with whatever logical arguments came into his head, but now he no longer cared for logic; he felt profound compassion, he wanted to be sincere and tender.

"Give it up now, my darling," he said. "You've had your cry; that's enough. Let us have a talk now, we'll think up something."

Then they spent a long time taking counsel together, they talked of how to avoid the necessity for secrecy, for deception, for living in different cities, and not seeing one another for long stretches of time. How could they free themselves from these intolerable fetters?

"How? How?" he asked, clutching his head. "How?" 120

And it seemed as though in a little while the solution would be found, and then a new and glorious life would begin; and it was clear to both of them that the end was still far off, and that what was to be most complicated and difficult for them was only just beginning.

CONSIDERATIONS FOR CRITICAL THINKING AND WRITING

1. **FIRST RESPONSE.** Consider the following assessment of the story: "No excuses can be made for the lovers' adulterous affair. They behave selfishly and irresponsibly. They are immoral — and so is the story." Explain what you think Chekhov's response to this view would be, given his treatment of the lovers. How does this compare with your own views?

2. Why is it significant that the setting of this story is a resort town? How does the vacation atmosphere affect the action?

3. What does Gurov's view of women reveal about him? Why does he regard them as an "inferior race"?

4. What do we learn about Gurov's wife and Anna's husband? Why do you think Chekhov includes this exposition? How does it affect our view of the lovers?

5. When and why do Gurov's feelings about Anna begin to change? Is he really in love with her?

6. Who or what is the antagonist in this story? What is the nature of the conflict?

7. What is the effect of having Gurov as the central consciousness? How would the story be different if it were told from Anna's perspective?

8. Why do you think Chekhov does not report what ultimately becomes of the lovers? Is there a resolution to the conflict? Is the ending of the story effective?

9. Discuss the validity of Gurov's belief that people lead their real lives in private rather than in public: "The personal life of every individual is based on secrecy, and perhaps it is partly for that reason that civilized man is so nervously anxious that personal privacy should be respected" (para. 105).

10. Describe your response to Gurov in Parts I and II, and discuss how your judgment of him changes in the last two parts of the story.

11. Based on your understanding of the characterizations of Gurov and Anna, consider the final paragraph of the story and summarize what you think will happen to them.

Perspectives

Two Additional Translations of the Final Paragraphs of Anton Chekhov's "The Lady with the Pet Dog"

"A Note on Reading Translations" appears on page 652. Because different translators of the same work make various choices in diction, phrasing, images, and tone as they interpret both the language and the work, they often produce subtly different translations. Compare the following two versions of the final six paragraphs of Chekhov's story with Avrahm Yarmolinsky's 1947 translation, reprinted in this anthology on pages 215–16.

ANTON CHEKHOV (1860–1904)

From "The Lady and the Dog"   *1899*

TRANSLATED BY CONSTANCE GARNETT (1963)

Anna Sergeyevna and he loved each other like people very close and akin, like husband and wife, like tender friends; it seemed to them that fate itself had meant them for one another, and they could not understand why he had a wife and she a husband; and it was as though they were a pair of birds of passage, caught and forced to live in different cages. They forgave each other for what they were ashamed of in their past, they forgave everything in the present, and felt that this love of theirs had changed them both.

In moments of depression in the past he had comforted himself with any arguments that came into his mind, but now he no longer cared for arguments; he felt profound compassion, he wanted to be sincere and tender. . . .

"Don't cry, my darling," he said. "You've had your cry; that's enough. . . . Let us talk now, let us think of some plan."

Then they spent a long while taking counsel together, talked of how to avoid the necessity for secrecy, for deception, for living in different towns and not seeing each other for long at a time. How could they be free from this intolerable bondage?

"How? How?" he asked, clutching his head. "How?"

And it seemed as though in a little while the solution would be found, and then a new and splendid life would begin; and it was clear to both of them that they had still a long, long way to go, and that the most complicated and difficult part of it was only just beginning.

From My Life and Other Stories

ANTON CHEKHOV (1860–1904)

From "A Lady with a Dog"   *1899*

TRANSLATED BY RONALD HINGLEY (1975)

Anne and he loved each other very, very dearly, like man and wife or bosom friends. They felt themselves predestined for each other. That he should have a wife, and she a husband . . . it seemed to make no sense. They were like two migratory birds, a male and a female, caught and put in separate cages. They had forgiven each other the shameful episodes of their past, they forgave each other for the present too, and they felt that their love had transformed them both.

Once, in moments of depression, he had tried to console himself with any argument which came into his head — but now he had no use for arguments. His deepest sympathies were stirred, he only wanted to be sincere and tender.

"Stop, darling," he said. "You've had your cry — that's enough. Now let's talk, let's think of something."

Then they consulted at length about avoiding the need for concealment and deception, for living in different towns, for meeting only at rare intervals. How could they break these intolerable bonds? How, how, how?

He clutched his head and asked the question again and again.

Soon, it seemed, the solution would be found and a wonderful new life would begin. But both could see that they still had a long, long way to travel — and that the most complicated and difficult part was only just beginning.

From *The Oxford Chekhov*, Vol. IX

Perspective

ANTON CHEKHOV (1860–1904)

On Morality in Fiction   1890

You abuse me for objectivity, calling it indifference to good and evil, lack of ideals and ideas, and so on. You would have me, when I describe horse-thieves, say: "Stealing horses is an evil." But that has been known for ages without my saying so. Let the jury judge them; it's my job simply to show what sort of people they are. I write: You are dealing with horse-thieves, so let me tell you that they are not beggars but well-fed people, that they are people of a special cult, and that horse-stealing is not simply theft but a passion. Of course it would be pleasant to combine art with a sermon, but for me personally it is extremely difficult and almost impossible, owing to the conditions of technique. You see, to depict horse-thieves in seven hundred lines I must all the time speak and think in their tone and feel in their spirit, otherwise, if I introduce subjectivity, the image becomes blurred and the story will not be as compact as all short stories ought to be. When I write, I reckon entirely upon the reader to add for himself the subjective elements that are lacking in the story.

From a letter to Aleksey S. Suvorin in *Letters on the Short Story, the Drama, and Other Literary Topics* by Anton Chekhov

CONSIDERATIONS FOR CRITICAL THINKING AND WRITING

1. Why does Chekhov reject sermonizing in his fiction?

2. How does his "objectivity" affect your reading of "The Lady with the Pet Dog"?

3. Compare and contrast Chekhov's views with Thomas Jefferson's belief that fiction should offer "sound morality" (p. 45).

JOYCE CAROL OATES (B. 1938)

Raised in upstate New York, Joyce Carol
Oates earned degrees at Syracuse University
and the University of Wisconsin. Both the
range and volume of her writing are extensive. A writer of novels, plays, short stories,
poetry, and literary criticism, she has published over eighty books. Oates has described the subject matter of her fiction
as "real people in a real society," but her
method of expression ranges from the realistic to the experimental. Her novels include
them (1969), *Do with Me What You Will* (1973),
Childwold (1976), *Bellefleur* (1980), *A Bloods-*

Reprinted by permission of Beth Gwinn.

moor Romance (1982), *Marya: A Life* (1986), *You Must Remember This* (1987),
Black Water (1992), *I'll Take You There* (2003), and *Missing Mom* (2005). Among
her collections of short stories are *Marriages and Infidelities* (1972), *Raven's
Wing* (1986), *The Assignation* (1988), *Heat* (1991), *Haunted: Tales of the Grotesque*
(1994), *Will You Always Love Me? and Other Stories* (1996), *The Collector of Hearts*
(1998), *Small Avalanches and Other Stories* (2004), and *High Lonesome: New and
Selected Stories 1966–2006* (2006).

The Lady with the Pet Dog

1972

I

Strangers parted as if to make way for him.

There he stood. He was there in the aisle, a few yards away, watching her.

She leaned forward at once in her seat, her hand jerked up to her face as if
to ward off a blow — but then the crowd in the aisle hid him, he was gone. She
pressed both hands against her cheeks. He was not here, she had imagined
him.

"My God," she whispered.

She was alone. Her husband had gone out to the foyer to make a tele- 5
phone call; it was intermission at the concert, a Thursday evening.

Now she saw him again, clearly. He was standing there. He was staring at
her. Her blood rocked in her body, draining out of her head . . . she was going
to faint . . . They stared at each other. They gave no sign of recognition. Only
when he took a step forward did she shake her head *no — no — keep away*. It was
not possible.

When her husband returned, she was staring at the place in the aisle where
her lover had been standing. Her husband leaned forward to interrupt that
stare.

"What's wrong?" he said. "Are you sick?"

Panic rose in her in long shuddering waves. She tried to get to her feet, panicked at the thought of fainting here, and her husband took hold of her. She stood like an aged woman, clutching the seat before her.

At home he helped her up the stairs and she lay down. Her head was like a 10 large piece of crockery that had to be held still, it was so heavy. She was still panicked. She felt it in the shallows of her face, behind her knees, in the pit of her stomach. It sickened her, it made her think of mucus, of something thick and gray congested inside her, stuck to her, that was herself and yet not her- self—a poison.

She lay with her knees drawn up toward her chest, her eyes hotly open, while her husband spoke to her. She imagined that other man saying, *Why did you run away from me?* Her husband was saying other words. She tried to listen to them. He was going to call the doctor, he said, and she tried to sit up. "No, I'm all right now," she said quickly. The panic was like lead inside her, so thickly congested. How slow love was to drain out of her, how fluid and sticky it was inside her head!

Her husband believed her. No doctor. No threat. Grateful, she drew her husband down to her. They embraced, not comfortably. For years now they had not been comfortable together, in their intimacy and at a distance, and now they struggled gently as if the paces of this dance were too rigorous for them. It was something they might have known once, but had now out- grown. The panic in her thickened at this double betrayal: she drew her hus- band to her, she caressed him wildly, she shut her eyes to think about that other man.

A crowd of men and women parting, unexpectedly, and there he stood— there he stood—she kept seeing him, and yet her vision blotched at the mem- ory. It had been finished between them, six months before, but he had come out here . . . and she had escaped him, now she was lying in her husband's arms, in his embrace, her face pressed against his. It was a kind of sleep, this love-making. She felt herself falling asleep, her body falling from her. Her eyes shut.

"I love you," her husband said fiercely, angrily.

She shut her eyes and thought of that other man, as if betraying him 15 would give her life a center.

"Did I hurt you? Are you—?" Her husband whispered.

Always this hot flashing of shame between them, the shame of her hus- band's near failure, the clumsiness of his love—

"You didn't hurt me," she said.

II

They had said good-by six months before. He drove her from Nantucket, where they had met, to Albany, New York, where she visited her sister. The hours of intimacy in the car had sealed something between them, a vow of silence and impersonality: she recalled the movement of the highways, the passing of other cars, the natural rhythms of the day hypnotizing her toward sleep while he drove. She trusted him, she could sleep in his presence. Yet she could not really fall asleep in spite of her exhaustion, and she kept jerking awake, frightened, to discover that nothing had changed—still the stranger who was driving her to Albany, still the highway, the sky, the antiseptic odor of the rented car, the sense of a rhythm behind the rhythm of the air that might unleash itself at any second. Everywhere on this highway, at this moment, there were men and women driving together, bonded together—what did that mean, to be together? What did it mean to enter into a bond with another person?

No, she did not really trust him; she did not really trust men. He would glance at her with his small cautious smile and she felt a declaration of shame between them.

Shame.

In her head she rehearsed conversations. She said bitterly, "You'll be relieved when we get to Albany. Relieved to get rid of me." They had spent so many days talking, confessing too much, driven to a pitch of childish excitement, laughing together on the beach, breaking into that pose of laughter that seems to eradicate the soul, so many days of this that the silence of the trip was like the silence of a hospital—all these surface noises, these rattles and hums, but an interior silence, a befuddlement. She said to him in her imagination, "One of us should die." Then she leaned over to touch him. She caressed the back of his neck. She said, aloud, "Would you like me to drive for a while?"

They stopped at a picnic area where other cars were stopped—couples, families—and walked together, smiling at their good luck. He put his arm around her shoulders and she sensed how they were in a posture together, a man and a woman forming a posture, a figure, that someone might sketch and show to them. She said slowly, "I don't want to go back. . . ."

Silence. She looked up at him. His face was heavy with her words, as if she had pulled at his skin with her fingers. Children ran nearby and distracted him—yes, he was a father too, his children ran like that, they tugged at his skin with their light, busy fingers.

"Are you so unhappy?" he said.

"I'm not unhappy, back there. I'm nothing. There's nothing to me," she said.

They stared at each other. The sensation between them was intense, exhausting. She thought that this man was her savior, that he had come to her at a time in her life when her life demanded completion, an end, a permanent fixing of all that was troubled and shifting and deadly. And yet it was absurd to think this. No person could save another. So she drew back from him and released him.

A few hours later they stopped at a gas station in a small city. She went to the women's rest room, having to ask the attendant for a key, and when she came back her eye jumped nervously onto the rented car—why? did she think he might have driven off without her?—onto the man, her friend, standing in conversation with the young attendant. Her friend was as old as her husband, over forty, with lanky, sloping shoulders, a full body, his hair thick, a dark, burnished brown, a festive color that made her eye twitch a little—and his hands were always moving, always those rapid conversational circles, going nowhere, gestures that were at once a little aggressive and apologetic.

She put her hand on his arm, a claim. He turned to her and smiled and she felt that she loved him, that everything in her life had forced her to this moment and that she had no choice about it.

They sat in the car for two hours, in Albany, in the parking lot of a Howard Johnson's restaurant, talking, trying to figure out their past. There was no future. They concentrated on the past, the several days behind them, lit up with a hot, dazzling August sun, like explosions that already belonged to other people, to strangers. Her face was faintly reflected in the green-tinted curve of the windshield, but she could not have recognized that face. She began to cry; she told herself: *I am not here, this will pass, this is nothing.* Still, she could not stop crying. The muscles of her face were springy, like a child's, unpredictable muscles. He stroked her arms, her shoulders, trying to comfort her. "This is so hard . . . this is impossible . . ." he said. She felt panic for the world outside this car, all that was not herself and this man, and at the same time she understood that she was free of him, as people are free of other people, she would leave him soon, safely, and within a few days he would have fallen into the past, the impersonal past. . . .

"I'm so ashamed of myself!" she said finally.

She returned to her husband and saw that another woman, a shadow-woman, had taken her place — noiseless and convincing, like a dancer performing certain difficult steps. Her husband folded her in his arms and talked to her of his own loneliness, his worries about his business, his health, his mother, kept tranquilized and mute in a nursing home, and her spirit detached itself from her and drifted about the rooms of the large house she lived in with her husband, a shadow-woman delicate and imprecise. There was no boundary to her, no edge. Alone, she took hot baths and sat exhausted in the steaming water, wondering at her perpetual exhaustion. All that winter she noticed the limp, languid weight of her arms, her veins bulging slightly with the pressure of her extreme weariness. *This is fate,* she thought, to be here and not there, to be one person and not another, a certain man's wife and not the wife of another man. The long, slow pain of this certainty rose in her, but it never became clear, it was baffling and imprecise. She could not be serious about it; she kept congratulating herself on her own good luck, to have escaped so easily, to have freed herself. So much love had gone into the first several years of her marriage that there wasn't much left, now, for another man. . . . She was certain of that. But the bath water made her dizzy, all that perpetual heat, and one day in January she drew a razor blade lightly across the inside of her arm, near the elbow, to see what would happen.

Afterward she wrapped a small towel around it, to stop the bleeding. The towel soaked through. She wrapped a bath towel around that and walked through the empty rooms of her home, lightheaded, hardly aware of the stubborn seeping of blood. There was no boundary to her in this house, no precise limit. She could flow out like her own blood and come to no end.

She sat for a while on a blue love seat, her mind empty. Her husband telephoned her when he would be staying late at the plant. He talked to her always about his plans, his problems, his business friends, his future. It was obvious that he had a future. As he spoke she nodded to encourage him, and her heartbeat quickened with the memory of her own, personal shame, the shame of this man's particular, private wife. One evening at dinner he leaned forward and put his head in his arms and fell asleep, like a child. She sat at the table with him for a while, watching him. His hair had gone gray, almost white, at the temples — no one would guess that he was so quick, so careful a man, still fairly young about the eyes. She put her hand on his head, lightly, as if to prove to herself that he was real. He slept, exhausted.

One evening they went to a concert and she looked up to see her lover 35
there, in the crowded aisle, in this city, watching her. He was standing there,
with his overcoat on, watching her. She went cold. That morning the telephone had rung while her husband was still home, and she had heard him
answer it, heard him hang up — it must have been a wrong number — and when
the telephone rang again, at 9:30, she had been afraid to answer it. She had left
home to be out of the range of that ringing, but now, in this public place, in
this busy auditorium, she found herself staring at that man, unable to make
any sign to him, any gesture of recognition. . . .

He would have come to her but she shook her head. *No. Stay away.*

Her husband helped her out of the row of seats, saying, "Excuse us, please.
Excuse us," so that strangers got to their feet, quickly, alarmed, to let them
pass. Was that woman about to faint? What was wrong?

At home she felt the blood drain slowly back into her head. Her husband
embraced her hips, pressing his face against her, in that silence that belonged
to the earliest days of their marriage. She thought, *He will drive it out of me.* He
made love to her and she was back in the auditorium again, sitting alone, now
that the concert was over. The stage was empty; the heavy velvet curtains had
not been drawn; the musicians' chairs were empty, everything was silent and
expectant; in the aisle her lover stood and smiled at her — Her husband was
impatient. He was apart from her, working on her, operating on her; and then,
stricken, he whispered, "Did I hurt you?"

The telephone rang the next morning. Dully, sluggishly, she answered it.
She recognized his voice at once — that "Anna?" with its lifting of the second
syllable, questioning and apologetic and making its claim — "Yes, what do you
want?" she said.

"Just to see you. Please —"

"I can't." 40

"Anna, I'm sorry, I didn't mean to upset you —"

"I can't see you."

"Just for a few minutes — I have to talk to you —"

"But why, why now? Why now?" she said. 45

She heard her voice rising, but she could not stop it. He began to talk
again, drowning her out. She remembered his rapid conversation. She remembered his gestures, the witty energetic circling of his hands.

"Please don't hang up!" he cried.

"I can't — I don't want to go through it again —"

"I'm not going to hurt you. Just tell me how you are."

"Everything is the same." 50

"Everything is the same with me."

She looked up at the ceiling, shyly. "Your wife? Your children?"

"The same."

"Your son?"

"He's fine —" 55

"I'm so glad to hear that. I —"

"Is it still the same with you, your marriage? Tell me what you feel. What
are you thinking?"

"I don't know. . . ."

She remembered his intense, eager words, the movement of his hands, that impatient precise fixing of the air by his hands, the jabbing of his fingers.

"Do you love me?" he said.   60

She could not answer.

"I'll come over to see you," he said.

"No," she said.

What will come next, what will happen?

Flesh hardening on his body, aging. Shrinking. He will grow old, but not 65
soft like her husband. They are two different types: he is nervous, lean, energetic, wise. She will grow thinner, as the tension radiates out from her backbone, wearing down her flesh. Her collarbones will jut out of her skin. Her husband, caressing her in their bed, will discover that she is another woman — she
is not there with him — instead she is rising in an elevator in a downtown hotel,
carrying a book as a prop, or walking quickly away from that hotel, her head
bent and filled with secrets. Love, what to do with it? . . . Useless as moths'
wings, as moths' fluttering. . . . She feels the flutterings of silky, crazy wings in
her chest.

He flew out to visit her every several weeks, staying at a different hotel each
time. He telephoned her, and she drove down to park in an underground
garage at the very center of the city.

She lay in his arms while her husband talked to her, miles away, one body
fading into another. He will grow old, his body will change, she thought, pressing her cheek against the back of one of these men. If it was her lover, they were
in a hotel room: always the propped-up little booklet describing the hotel's
many services, with color photographs of its cocktail lounge and dining room
and coffee shop. Grow old, leave me, die, go back to your neurotic wife and
your sad, ordinary children, she thought, but still her eyes closed gratefully
against his skin and she felt how complete their silence was, how they had
come to rest in each other.

"Tell me about your life here. The people who love you," he said, as he
always did.

One afternoon they lay together for four hours. It was her birthday and
she was intoxicated with her good fortune, this prize of the afternoon, this
man in her arms! She was a little giddy, she talked too much. She told
him about her parents, about her husband. . . . "They were all people I believed
in, but it turned out wrong. Now, I believe in you. . . ." He laughed as if
shocked by her words. She did not understand. Then she understood. "But I
believe truly in you. I can't think of myself without you," she said. . . . He spoke
of his wife, her ambitions, her intelligence, her use of the children against him,
her use of his younger son's blindness, all of his words gentle and hypnotic and
convincing in the late afternoon peace of this hotel room . . . and she felt the
terror of laughter, threatening laughter. Their words, like their bodies, were
aging.

She dressed quickly in the bathroom, drawing her long hair up around the 70
back of her head, fixing it as always, anxious that everything be the same. Her
face was slightly raw, from his face. The rubbing of his skin. Her eyes were too
bright, wearily bright. Her hair was blond but not so blond as it had been that
summer in the white Nantucket air.

She ran water and splashed it on her face. She blinked at the water. Blind.
Drowning. She thought with satisfaction that soon, soon, he would be back

home, in that house on Long Island she had never seen, with that woman she had never seen, sitting on the edge of another bed, putting on his shoes. She wanted nothing except to be free of him. Why not be free? *Oh,* she thought suddenly, *I will follow you back and kill you. You and her and the little boy. What is there to stop me?*

She left him. Everyone on the street pitied her, that look of absolute zero.

III

A man and a child, approaching her. The sharp acrid smell of fish. The crashing of waves. Anna pretended not to notice the father with his son — there was something strange about them. That frank, silent intimacy, too gentle, the man's bare feet in the water and the boy a few feet away, leaning away from his father. He was about nine years old and still his father held his hand.

A small yipping dog, a golden dog, bounded near them.

Anna turned shyly back to her reading; she did not want to have to speak 75 to these neighbors. She saw the man's shadow falling over her legs, then over the pages of her book, and she had the idea that he wanted to see what she was reading. The dog nuzzled her; the man called him away.

She watched them walk down the beach. She was relieved that the man had not spoken to her.

She saw them in town later that day, the two of them brown-haired and patient, now wearing sandals, walking with that same look of care. The man's white shorts were soiled and a little baggy. His pullover shirt was a faded green. His face was broad, the cheekbones wide, spaced widely apart, the eyes stark in their sockets, as if they fastened onto objects for no reason, ponderous and edgy. The little boy's face was pale and sharp; his lips were perpetually parted.

Anna realized that the child was blind.

The next morning, early, she caught sight of them again. For some reason she went to the back door of her cottage. She faced the sea breeze eagerly. Her heart hammered. . . . She had been here, in her family's old house, for three days, alone, bitterly satisfied at being alone, and now it was a puzzle to her how her soul strained to fly outward, to meet with another person. She watched the man with his son, his cautious, rather stooped shoulders above the child's small shoulders.

The man was carrying something, it looked like a notebook. He sat on the 80 sand, not far from Anna's spot of the day before, and the dog rushed up to them. The child approached the edge of the ocean, timidly. He moved in short jerky steps, his legs stiff. The dog ran around him. Anna heard the child crying out a word that sounded like "Ty" — it must have been the dog's name — and then the man joined in, his voice heavy and firm.

"Ty—"

Anna tied her hair back with a yellow scarf and went down to the beach.

The man glanced around at her. He smiled. She stared past him at the waves. To talk to him or not to talk — she had the freedom of that choice. For a moment she felt that she had made a mistake, that the child and the dog would not protect her, that behind this man's ordinary, friendly face there was a certain arrogant maleness — then she relented, she smiled shyly.

"A nice house you've got there," the man said.

She nodded her thanks.   85

The man pushed his sunglasses up on his forehead. Yes, she recognized the eyes of the day before — intelligent and nervous, the sockets pale, untanned.

"Is that your telephone ringing?" he said.

She did not bother to listen. "It's a wrong number," she said.

Her husband calling: she had left home for a few days, to be alone.

But the man, settling himself on the sand, seemed to misinterpret this. He 90 smiled in surprise, one corner of his mouth higher than the other. He said nothing. Anna wondered: *What is he thinking?* The dog was leaping about her, panting against her legs, and she laughed in embarrassment. She bent to pet it, grateful for its busyness. "Don't let him jump up on you," the man said. "He's a nuisance."

The dog was a small golden retriever, a young dog. The blind child, standing now in the water, turned to call the dog to him. His voice was shrill and impatient.

"Our house is the third one down — the white one," the man said.

She turned, startled. "Oh, did you buy it from Dr. Patrick? Did he die?"

"Yes, finally. . . ."

Her eyes wandered nervously over the child and the dog. She felt the ner- 95 vous beat of her heart out to the very tips of her fingers, the fleshy tips of her fingers: little hearts were there, pulsing. *What is he thinking?* The man had opened his notebook. He had a piece of charcoal and he began to sketch something.

Anna looked down at him. She saw the top of his head, his thick brown hair, the freckles on his shoulders, the quick, deft movement of his hand. Upside down, Anna herself being drawn. She smiled in surprise.

"Let me draw you. Sit down," he said.

She knelt awkwardly a few yards away. He turned the page of the sketch pad. The dog ran to her and she sat, straightening out her skirt beneath her, flinching from the dog's tongue. "Ty!" cried the child. Anna sat, and slowly the pleasure of the moment began to glow in her; her skin flushed with gratitude.

She sat there for nearly an hour. The man did not talk much. Back and forth the dog bounded, shaking itself. The child came to sit near them, in silence. Anna felt that she was drifting into a kind of trance while the man sketched her, half a dozen rapid sketches, the surface of her face given up to him. "Where are you from?" the man asked.

"Ohio. My husband lives in Ohio." 100

She wore no wedding band.

"Your wife —" Anna began.

"Yes?"

"Is she here?"

"Not right now." 105

She was silent, ashamed. She had asked an improper question. But the man did not seem to notice. He continued drawing her, bent over the sketch pad. When Anna said she had to go, he showed her the drawings — one after another of her, Anna, recognizably Anna, a woman in her early thirties, her hair smooth and flat across the top of her head, tied behind by a scarf. "Take the one you like best," he said, and she picked one of her with the dog in her lap, sitting very straight, her brows and eyes clearly defined, her lips girlishly pursed, the dog and her dress suggested by a few quick irregular lines.

"Lady with pet dog," the man said.

She spent the rest of that day reading, nearer her cottage. It was not really a cottage — it was a two-story house, large and ungainly and weathered. It was mixed up in her mind with her family, her own childhood, and she glanced up from her book, perplexed, as if waiting for one of her parents or her sister to come up to her. Then she thought of that man, the man with the blind child, the man with the dog, and she could not concentrate on her reading. Someone — probably her father — had marked a passage that must be important, but she kept reading and rereading it: *We try to discover in things, endeared to us on that account, the spiritual glamour which we ourselves have cast upon them; we are disillusioned, and learn that they are in themselves barren and devoid of the charm that they owed, in our minds, to the association of certain ideas.* . . .

She thought again of the man on the beach. She lay the book aside and thought of him: his eyes, his aloneness, his drawings of her.

They began seeing each other after that. He came to her front door in the 110 evening, without the child; he drove her into town for dinner. She was shy and extremely pleased. The darkness of the expensive restaurant released her; she heard herself chatter; she leaned forward and seemed to be offering her face up to him, listening to him. He talked about his work on a Long Island newspaper and she seemed to be listening to him, as she stared at his face, arranging her own face into the expression she had seen in that charcoal drawing. Did he see her like that, then? — girlish and withdrawn and patrician? She felt the weight of his interest in her, a force that fell upon her like a blow. A repeated blow. Of course he was married, he had children — of course she was married, permanently married. This flight from her husband was not important. She had left him before, to be alone, it was not important. Everything in her was slender and delicate and not important.

They walked for hours after dinner, looking at the other strollers, the weekend visitors, the tourists, the couples like themselves. Surely they were mistaken for a couple, a married couple. *This is the hour in which everything is decided,* Anna thought. They had both had several drinks and they talked a great deal. Anna found herself saying too much, stopping and starting giddily. She put her hand to her forehead, feeling faint.

"It's from the sun — you've had too much sun —" he said.

At the door to her cottage, on the front porch, she heard herself asking him if he would like to come in. She allowed him to lead her inside, to close the door. *This is not important,* she thought clearly, *he doesn't mean it, he doesn't love me, nothing will come of it.* She was frightened, yet it seemed to her necessary to give in; she had to leave Nantucket with that act completed, an act of adultery, an accomplishment she would take back to Ohio and to her marriage.

Later, incredibly, she heard herself asking: "Do you . . . do you love me?"

"You're so beautiful!" he said, amazed. 115

She felt this beauty, shy and glowing and centered in her eyes. He stared at her. In this large, drafty house, alone together, they were like accomplices, conspirators. She could not think: how old was she? which year was this? They had done something unforgivable together, and the knowledge of it was tugging at their faces. A cloud seemed to pass over her. She felt herself smiling shrilly.

Afterward, a peculiar raspiness, a dryness of breath. He was silent. She felt a strange, idle fear, a sense of the danger outside this room and this old comfortable bed — a danger that would not recognize her as the lady in that drawing, the lady with the pet dog. There was nothing to say to this man, this stranger. She felt the beauty draining out of her face, her eyes fading.

"I've got to be alone," she told him.

He left, and she understood that she would not see him again. She stood by the window of the room, watching the ocean. A sense of shame overpowered her: it was smeared everywhere on her body, the smell of it, the richness of it. She tried to recall him, and his face was confused in her memory: she would have to shout to him across a jumbled space, she would have to wave her arms wildly. *You love me! You must love me!* But she knew he did not love her, and she did not love him; he was a man who drew everything up into himself, like all men, walking away, free to walk away, free to have his own thoughts, free to envision her body, all the secrets of her body. . . . And she lay down again in the bed, feeling how heavy this body had become, her insides heavy with shame, the very backs of her eyelids coated with shame.

"This is the end of one part of my life," she thought.   120

But in the morning the telephone rang. She answered it. It was her lover: they talked brightly and happily. She could hear the eagerness in his voice, the love in his voice, that same still, sad amazement — she understood how simple life was, there were no problems.

They spent most of their time on the beach, with the child and the dog. He joked and was serious at the same time. He said, once, "You have defined my soul for me," and she laughed to hide her alarm. In a few days it was time for her to leave. He got a sitter for the boy and took the ferry with her to the mainland, then rented a car to drive her up to Albany. She kept thinking: *Now something will happen. It will come to an end.* But most of the drive was silent and hypnotic. She wanted him to joke with her, to say again that she had defined his soul for him, but he drove fast, he was serious, she distrusted the hawkish look of his profile — she did not know him at all. At a gas station she splashed her face with cold water. Alone in the grubby little rest room, shaky and very much alone. In such places are women totally alone with their bodies. The body grows heavier, more evil, in such silence. . . . On the beach everything had been noisy with sunlight and gulls and waves; here, as if run to earth, everything was cramped and silent and dead.

She went outside, squinting. There he was, talking with the station attendant. She could not think as she returned to him whether she wanted to live or not.

She stayed in Albany for a few days, then flew home to her husband. He met her at the airport, near the luggage counter, where her three pieces of pale-brown luggage were brought to him on a conveyer belt, to be claimed by him. He kissed her on the cheek. They shook hands, a little embarrassed. She had come home again.

"How will I live out the rest of my life?" she wondered.   125

In January her lover spied on her: she glanced up and saw him, in a public place, in the DeRoy Symphony Hall. She was paralyzed with fear. She nearly fainted. In this faint she felt her husband's body, loving her, working its love upon her, and she shut her eyes harder to keep out the certainty of his love — sometimes he failed at loving her, sometimes he succeeded, it had nothing to do with her or her pity or her ten years of love for him, it had nothing to do with a woman at all. It was a private act accomplished by a man, a husband, or a lover, in communion with his own soul, his manhood.

Her husband was forty-two years old now, growing slowly into middle age, getting heavier, softer. Her lover was about the same age, narrower in the shoulders, with a full, solid chest, yet lean, nervous. She thought, in her paralysis, of men and how they love freely and eagerly so long as their bodies are capable of love, love for a woman; and then, as love fades in their bodies, it fades from their souls and they become immune and immortal and ready to die.

Her husband was a little rough with her, as if impatient with himself. "I love you," he said fiercely, angrily. And then, ashamed, he said, "Did I hurt you? . . ."

"You didn't hurt me," she said.

Her voice was too shrill for their embrace.

While he was in the bathroom she went to her closet and took out that 130 drawing of the summer before. There she was, on the beach at Nantucket, a lady with a pet dog, her eyes large and defined, the dog in her lap hardly more than a few snarls, a few coarse soft lines of charcoal . . . her dress smeared, her arms oddly limp . . . her hands not well drawn at all. . . . She tried to think: did she love the man who had drawn this? did he love her? The fever in her husband's body had touched her and driven her temperature up, and now she stared at the drawing with a kind of lust, fearful of seeing an ugly soul in that woman's face, fearful of seeing the face suddenly through her lover's eyes. She breathed quickly and harshly, staring at the drawing.

And so, the next day, she went to him at his hotel. She wept, pressing against him, demanding of him, "What do you want? Why are you here? Why don't you let me alone?" He told her that he wanted nothing. He expected nothing. He would not cause trouble.

"I want to talk about last August," he said.

"Don't—" she said.

She was hypnotized by his gesturing hands, his nervousness, his obvious 135 agitation. He kept saying, "I understand. I'm making no claims upon you."

They became lovers again.

He called room service for something to drink and they sat side by side on his bed, looking through a copy of *The New Yorker*, laughing at the cartoons. It was so peaceful in this room, so complete. They were on a holiday. It was a secret holiday. Four-thirty in the afternoon, on a Friday, an ordinary Friday: a secret holiday.

"I won't bother you again," he said.

He flew back to see her again in March, and in late April. He telephoned her from his hotel — a different hotel each time — and she came down to him at once. She rose to him in various elevators, she knocked on the doors of various rooms, she stepped into his embrace, breathless and guilty and already angry with him, pleading with him. One morning in May, when he telephoned, she pressed her forehead against the doorframe and could not speak. He kept saying, "What's wrong? Can't you talk? Aren't you alone?" She felt that she was going insane. Her head would burst. Why, why did he love her, why did he pursue her? Why did he want her to die?

She went to him in the hotel room. A familiar room: had they been here 140 before? "Everything is repeating itself. Everything is stuck," she said. He framed her face in his hands and said that she looked thinner — was she sick? — what was wrong? She shook herself free. He, her lover, looked about the same. There was a small, angry pimple on his neck. He stared at her, eagerly and suspiciously. Did she bring bad news?

"So you love me? You love me?" she asked.

"Why are you so angry?"

"I want to be free of you. The two of us free of each other."

"That isn't true—you don't want that—"

He embraced her. She was wild with that old, familiar passion for him, her 145
body clinging to his, her arms not strong enough to hold him. Ah, what
despair!—what bitter hatred she felt!—she needed this man for her salvation,
he was all she had to live for, and yet she could not believe in him. He embraced
her thighs, her hips, kissing her, pressing his warm face against her, and yet she
could not believe in him, not really. She needed him in order to live, but he was
not worth her love, he was not worth her dying. . . . She promised herself this:
when she got back home, when she was alone, she would draw the razor more
deeply across her arm.

The telephone rang and he answered it: a wrong number.

"Jesus," he said.

They lay together, still. She imagined their posture like this, the two of
them one figure, one substance; and outside this room and this bed there was
a universe of disjointed, separate things, blank things, that had nothing to do
with them. She would not be Anna out there, the lady in the drawing. He
would not be her lover.

"I love you so much . . ." she whispered.

"Please don't cry! We have only a few hours, please. . . ." 150

It was absurd, their clinging together like this. She saw them as a single
figure in a drawing, their arms and legs entwined, their heads pressing mutely
together. Helpless substance, so heavy and warm and doomed. It was absurd
that any human being should be so important to another human being. She
wanted to laugh: a laugh might free them both.

She could not laugh.

Sometime later he said, as if they had been arguing, "Look. It's you. You're
the one who doesn't want to get married. You lie to me—"

"Lie to you?"

"You love me but you won't marry me, because you want something left 155
over—Something not finished—All your life you can attribute your misery to
me, to our not being married—you are using me—"

"Stop it! You'll make me hate you!" she cried.

"You can say to yourself that you're miserable because of *me*. We will never
be married, you will never be happy, neither one of us will ever be happy—"

"I don't want to hear this!" she said.

She pressed her hands flatly against her face.

She went to the bathroom to get dressed. She washed her face and part of 160
her body, quickly. The fever was in her, in the pit of her belly. She would rush
home and strike a razor across the inside of her arm and free that pressure,
that fever.

The impatient bulging of the veins: an ordeal over.

The demand of the telephone's ringing: that ordeal over.

The nuisance of getting the car and driving home in all that five o'clock
traffic: an ordeal too much for a woman.

The movement of this stranger's body in hers: over, finished.

Now, dressed, a little calmer, they held hands and talked. They had to talk 165
swiftly, to get all their news in: he did not trust the people who worked for him,
he had faith in no one, his wife had moved to a textbook publishing company

and was doing well, she had inherited a Ben Shahn painting from her father and wanted to "touch it up a little" — she was crazy! — his blind son was at another school, doing fairly well, in fact his children were all doing fairly well in spite of the stupid mistake of their parents' marriage — and what about her? what about her life? She told him in a rush the one thing he wanted to hear: that she lived with her husband lovelessly, the two of them polite strangers, sharing a bed, lying side by side in the night in that bed, bodies out of which souls had fled. There was no longer even any shame between them.

"And what about me? Do you feel shame with me still?" he asked.

She did not answer. She moved away from him and prepared to leave.

Then, a minute later, she happened to catch sight of his reflection in the bureau mirror — he was glancing down at himself, checking himself mechanically, impersonally, preparing also to leave. He too would leave this room: he too was headed somewhere else.

She stared at him. It seemed to her that in this instant he was breaking from her, the image of her lover fell free of her, breaking from her . . . and she realized that he existed in a dimension quite apart from her, a mysterious being. And suddenly, joyfully, she felt a miraculous calm. This man was her husband, truly — they were truly married, here in this room — they had been married haphazardly and accidentally for a long time. In another part of the city she had another husband, a "husband," but she had not betrayed that man, not really. This man, whom she loved above any other person in the world, above even her own self-pitying sorrow and her own life, was her truest lover, her destiny. And she did not hate him, she did not hate herself any longer; she did not wish to die; she was flooded with a strange certainty, a sense of gratitude, of pure selfless energy. It was obvious to her that she had, all along, been behaving correctly; out of instinct.

What triumph, to love like this in any room, anywhere, risking even the 170 craziest of accidents!

"Why are you so happy? What's wrong?" he asked, startled. He stared at her. She felt the abrupt concentration in him, the focusing of his vision on her, almost a bitterness in his face, as if he feared her. What, was it beginning all over again? Their love beginning again, in spite of them? "How can you look so happy?" he asked. "We don't have any right to it. Is it because . . . ?"

"Yes," she said.

CONSIDERATIONS FOR CRITICAL THINKING AND WRITING

1. **FIRST RESPONSE.** Which version do you like better — Chekhov's story or Oates's? What's the point of retelling the story?

2. How would this story be different if it were told only in chronological order as it is in Part III? What do Parts I and II contribute to the details and information provided in Part III?

3. Why are Anna and her lover drawn to each other? What do we learn about their spouses that helps explain their attraction? Are there any other explanations?

4. Why is Anna so unhappy after the affair on Nantucket begins? Why does she think of suicide?

5. What is Anna's attitude toward men? Does it change during the story?

6. What details in the story make the narration particularly convincing from a woman's perspective? How might a man tell the story differently?

7. "What triumph, to love like this in any room, anywhere, risking even the craziest of accidents!" Explain this reflection of Anna's (para. 170) and relate it to her character.

8. How does Oates's arrangement of incidents validate Anna's feeling that "everything is repeating itself. Everything is stuck" (para. 140)?

9. Consider whether Anna reaches any kind of resolution to her problems by the end of the story. Is she merely "repeating" herself, or do you think she develops?

10. At the end of paragraph 19, Oates has Anna ask herself the question "What did it mean to enter into a bond with another person?" Write an essay explaining how the story answers that question.

11. CRITICAL STRATEGIES. Read the section on new historicist criticism (pp. 1546–47) in Chapter 46, "Critical Strategies for Reading," and consider how the institution of marriage was generally regarded when Chekhov and Oates wrote their respective stories. How do these two different perspectives on marriage compare with your own twenty-first-century point of view? How do you think a new historicist would weight the similarities and differences between these perspectives when comparing these two stories?

CONNECTION TO ANOTHER SELECTION

1. What similarities in setting, plot, and character are there between Oates's version and Chekhov's story? Are there any significant differences?

2. Describe how a familiarity with Chekhov's story affected your reading and expectations of Oates's version. Choose one version of the story and write an essay explaining why you prefer it over the other.

Perspective

MATTHEW C. BRENNAN (B. 1955)

Point of View and Plotting in Chekhov's and Oates's "The Lady with the Pet Dog"   1985

Oates . . . retains Chekhov's third-person point of view. But unlike Chekhov, who focuses on the male lover, Gurov, Oates makes Anna S., the female lover, the center of consciousness. Because Chekhov privileges Gurov, he represents Anna's feelings only when she speaks to Gurov. In fact, when Anna S. expresses her shame to Gurov, Chekhov says, "The solitary candle on the table scarcely lit up her face"; and rather than reveal her inner thoughts he merely tells us, "it was obvious that her heart was heavy." So, by subordinating Anna S. to Gurov, Chekhov gives readers no way to understand the feminine side of a masculine story. In contrast, Oates presents what Chekhov leaves out — the female's experience — and so relegates the male lover (who in her version is nameless) to the limited status Chekhov relegates Anna S.: Oates privileges the point of view of Anna. Furthermore, because Anna S. says she feels "like a madwoman," Oates fragments Chekhov's traditionally chronological plot, which becomes a subtext against which Oates can foreground Anna's confusion, doubt, and struggle to find an identity. . . .

Chekhov develops a conventional, sequential plot. He spreads the five-step plot through the four formal divisions of his story. Part I consists of the exposition, during which Gurov and Anna S. meet at the resort, Yalta. Part II continues the exposition, as the characters become lovers, and it also introduces the rising action as they separate at the train station, Anna S. returning to her home in the town of S——, Gurov to his in Moscow. Then, in Part III, the action continues to rise as Gurov misses Anna and eventually goes to the town of S——. Here, at a concert, the two climactically meet again, and, as Part III ends, Anna S. agrees to come to Moscow. Finally, in Part IV, the action falls as Chekhov describes their affair and dramatizes it in a scene that forms the resolution, through which Gurov realizes, after looking in a mirror, that he is in love for the first time: he and Anna S. really are "as husband and wife" though separated by law.

Oates borrows all these events for her plot, but if Chekhov's is linear, hers is circular. Oates breaks her story into three parts. Part I depicts the climax, immediately giving her version the intensity that the high-strung center of consciousness, Anna, is experiencing. We are with her at the concert hall, where her lover appears and she faints, and then with her back home, where her husband clumsily makes love to her while she thinks of her lover. Part II opens with a flashback to the rising action—when the lover drives Anna to Albany where they separate, just as Chekhov's lovers separate at the train station; next, Part II both repeats the climax (at the concert and in the bedroom) and relates, for the first time, the falling action in which the lovers continue the affair. Part I, then, presents only the climax, and Part II widens the plot to record not just the center, the climax, but also the rising and falling actions that surround it. Part III, however, widens the circular plot still further. Expanding outward from the climactic center, first the plot regresses to embrace the exposition (in which the lovers meet and make love at the resort, in this version Nantucket); then it moves inward again, retracing chronologically the rising action, climax, and falling action; and finally, as Part III concludes, the plot introduces the resolution, rounding out its pattern.

Before the resolution, however, as we witness the falling action (the resumption of the affair) for the second time, Oates stresses the lack of development: Anna says, "'Everything is repeating itself. Everything is stuck.'" By having the plot repeat itself, and so fail to progress toward resolution, Oates conveys Anna's lack of identity: Anna is trapped between two relationships, two "husbands," and hence wavers throughout this version between feeling like "nothing" in her legal husband's house where "there was no boundary to her," "no precise limit," and feeling defined—as "recognizably Anna"—by her illicit lover, her true "husband," who has sketched her portrait, to which she continually refers as if grasping for a rope.

Here, then, with the climax repeated three times and the rising and falling actions twice, the plot finally progresses from this impasse to its resolution. And, appropriately, as the plot finally achieves its completion, so too does Anna, discovering as she symbolically looks into the mirror, this man was her husband, truly—they were truly married, here in this room—they had been married haphazardly and accidentally for a long time. In another part of the city she had another husband, a "husband," but she had not betrayed that man, not really. This man, whom she loved above any other person in the world . . . was her truest lover, her destiny.

Oates allows the plot to progress sequentially to the resolution—to integrity— only as Anna's consciousness discovers its true identity, its integration.

From *Notes on Modern American Literature*

CONSIDERATIONS FOR CRITICAL THINKING AND WRITING

1. What does Brennan mean by characterizing Chekhov's story as "masculine" and Oates's as "feminine"? How is each writer's use of point of view related to this question?

2. Brennan describes Chekhov's plot as "linear" and Oates's as "circular." How is this contrast influenced by the writer's use of point of view?

3. Brennan asserts that in Oates's story, "Anna's consciousness discovers its true identity, its integration." Write an essay explaining whether you agree or disagree with this assessment. In your response, consider how Oates's use of point of view affects your reading of Anna's character.

A SAMPLE STUDENT RESPONSE

James Armand

Professor Rosen

English 102

September 8, 2008

Two Versions of the Same Story:

Point of View in Chekhov's and Oates's "The Lady with the Pet Dog"

The narrative point of view in each version of "The Lady with the Pet Dog" provides an in-depth look at how a love affair affects the characters involved. While both versions contain essentially the same plot, the accounts from the point of view of each character are starkly different. Chekhov's version "gives readers no way to understand the feminine side of a masculine story" (Brennan 232), while Oates's version provides just that. Yet each story effectively portrays a main character experiencing conflicting emotions and change.

In Chekhov's story, Gurov initially acts on lust, not love. He views women as "the inferior race" (Chekhov 205) and thinks of Anna as "pathetic" (206). But Anna has a greater effect on him than he anticipates. After their brief affair, he is "tormented by a strong desire to share his memories with someone" (211), and his desire for Anna becomes so strong that he seeks her out at the theater, in spite of the possible consequences. Ultimately, Gurov's views of Anna change, and he experiences love for the first time in his life:

> In the past he had met women, come together with them,
> parted from them, but he had never once loved; it was any-
> thing you please, but not love. And only now when his head
> was gray he had fallen in love, really, truly--for the first time
> in his life. (215)

By shifting to Anna's point of view, Oates provides another layer to the same story. We understand Anna to be more than simply a timid woman enamored with her lover (as she appears in Chekhov's version). Her character is complex. She is pulled between her attraction to her lover and her own morality--"They had done something unforgivable together, the knowledge of it was tugging at their faces. A cloud passed over her" (Oates 227). Anna has

Armand 2

trouble coming to terms with her infidelity and regrets betraying her husband and family. Yet her love for her lover is too powerful to give up. Having access to Anna's point of view, we gain a deeper understanding of her as a character--something that is not possible in Chekhov's version. . . .

Works Cited

Brennan, Matthew C. "Point of View and Plotting in Chekhov's and Oates's 'The Lady with the Pet Dog.'" The Compact Bedford Introduction to Literature. Ed. Michael Meyer. 8th ed. Boston: Bedford/St. Martin's, 2009. 232–34.

Chekhov, Anton. "The Lady with the Pet Dog." The Compact Bedford Introduction to Literature. Ed. Michael Meyer. 8th ed. Boston: Bedford/St. Martin's, 2009. 205–16.

Oates, Joyce Carol. "The Lady with the Pet Dog." The Compact Bedford Introduction to Literature. Ed. Michael Meyer. 8th ed. Boston: Bedford/St. Martin's, 2009. 219–31.

7

Symbolism

I recognize no dichotomy between art
and protest.
—RALPH ELLISON

A *symbol* is a person, object, or event that suggests more than its literal meaning. This basic definition is simple enough, but the use of symbol in literature makes some students slightly nervous because they tend to regard it as a booby trap, a hidden device that can go off during a seemingly harmless class discussion. "I didn't see that when I was reading the story" is a frequently heard comment. This sort of surprise and recognition is both natural and common. Most readers go through a story for the first time getting their bearings, figuring out what is happening to whom and so on. Patterns and significant details often require a second or third reading before they become evident—before a symbol sheds light on a story. Then the details of a work may suddenly fit together, and its meaning may be reinforced, clarified, or enlarged by the symbol. Symbolic meanings are usually embedded in the texture of a story, but they are not "hidden"; instead, they are carefully placed. Reading between the lines (where there is only space) is unnecessary. What is needed is a careful consideration of the elements of the story, a sensitivity to its language, and some common sense.

Common sense is a good place to begin. Symbols appear all around us;

anything can be given symbolic significance. Without symbols our lives would be stark and vacant. Awareness of a writer's use of symbols is not all that different from the kinds of perceptions and interpretations that allow us to make sense of our daily lives. We know, for example, that a ring used in a wedding is more than just a piece of jewelry because it suggests the unity and intimacy of a closed circle. The bride's gown may be white because we tend to associate innocence and purity with that color. Or consider the meaning of a small alligator sewn on a shirt or some other article of clothing. What started as a company trademark has gathered around it a range of meanings suggesting everything from quality and money to preppiness and silliness. The ring, the white gown, and the alligator trademark are symbolic because each has meanings that go beyond its specific qualities and functions.

Explore the literary element in this chapter on *LiterActive* or at bedfordstmartins .com/meyercompact.

Symbols such as these that are widely recognized by a society or culture are called ***conventional symbols.*** The Christian cross, the Star of David, a swastika, or a nation's flag all have meanings understood by large groups of people. Certain kinds of experiences also have traditional meanings in Western cultures. Winter, the setting sun, and the color black suggest death, while spring, the rising sun, and the color green evoke images of youth and new beginnings. (It is worth noting, however, that individual cultures sometimes have their own conventions; some Eastern cultures associate white rather than black with death and mourning. And obviously the polo player trademark would mean nothing to anyone totally unfamiliar with American culture.) These broadly shared symbolic meanings are second nature to us.

Writers use conventional symbols to reinforce meanings. Kate Chopin, for example, emphasizes the spring setting in "The Story of an Hour" (p. 15) as a way of suggesting the renewed sense of life that Mrs. Mallard feels when she thinks herself free from her husband.

A *literary symbol* can include traditional, conventional, or public meanings, but it may also be established internally by the total context of the work in which it appears. In "Soldier's Home" (p. 165), Hemingway does not use Krebs's family home as a conventional symbol of safety, comfort, and refuge from the war. Instead, Krebs's home becomes symbolic of provincial, erroneous presuppositions compounded by blind innocence, sentimentality, and smug middle-class respectability. The symbolic meaning of his home reveals that Krebs no longer shares his family's and town's view of the world. Their notions of love, the value of a respectable job, and a belief in God seem to him petty, complicated, and meaningless. The significance of Krebs's home is determined by the events within the story, which reverse and subvert the traditional associations readers might bring to it. Krebs's interactions with his family and the people in town reveal what home has come to mean to him.

A literary symbol can be a setting, character, action, object, name, or anything else in a work that maintains its literal significance while suggesting other meanings. Symbols cannot be restricted to a single meaning; they are suggestive rather than definitive. Their evocation of multiple meanings allows a writer to say more with less. Symbols are economical devices for evoking complex ideas without having to resort to painstaking explanations that would make a story more like an essay than an experience. The many walls in Melville's "Bartleby, the Scrivener" (p. 124) cannot be reduced to one idea. They have multiple meanings that unify the story. The walls are symbols of the deadening, dehumanizing, restrictive repetitiveness of the office routine, as well as of the confining, materialistic sensibilities of Wall Street. They suggest whatever limits and thwarts human aspirations, including death itself. We don't know precisely what shatters Bartleby's will to live, but the walls in the story, through their symbolic suggestiveness, indicate the nature of the limitations that cause the scrivener to slip into hopelessness and his "dead-wall reveries."

When a character, object, or incident indicates a single, fixed meaning, the writer is using **allegory** rather than symbol. Whereas symbols have literal functions as well as multiple meanings, the primary focus in allegory is on the abstract idea called forth by the concrete object. John Bunyan's *Pilgrim's Progress,* published during the seventeenth century, is a classic example of allegory because the characters, action, and setting have no existence beyond their abstract meanings. Bunyan's purpose is to teach his readers the exemplary way to salvation and heaven. The protagonist, named Christian, flees the City of Destruction in search of the Celestial City. Along the way he encounters characters who either help or hinder his spiritual journey. Among them are Mr. Worldly Wiseman, Faithful, Prudence, Piety, and a host of others named after the virtues or vices they display. These characters, places, and actions exist solely to illustrate religious doctrine. Allegory tends to be definitive rather than suggestive. It drives meaning into a corner and keeps it there. Most modern writers prefer the exploratory nature of symbol to the reductive nature of pure allegory.

Stories often include symbols that you may or may not perceive on a first reading. Their subtle use is a sign of a writer's skill in weaving symbols into the fabric of the characters' lives. Symbols may sometimes escape you, but that is probably better than finding symbols where only literal meanings are intended. Allow the text to help you determine whether a symbolic reading is appropriate. Once you are clear about what literally happens, read carefully and notice the placement of details that are emphasized. The pervasive references to time in Faulkner's "A Rose for Emily" (p. 90) and the many kinds of walls that appear throughout "Bartleby, the Scrivener" call attention to themselves and warrant symbolic readings. A symbol, however, need not be repeated to have an important purpose in a story. We don't learn until the very end of "Bartleby, the Scrivener" that Bartleby once worked as a clerk in the Dead Letter Office in Washington, D.C. This information is offered as merely an offhand rumor by the narrator, but its symbolic value is essential for understanding what motivates Bartleby's behavior. Indeed, Bartleby's experiences in the Dead Letter Office suggest enough about the nature of his thwarted hopes and desires to account for Bartleby's rejection of life.

By keeping track of the total context of the story, you should be able to decide whether your reading is reasonable and consistent with the other facts; plenty of lemons in literature yield no symbolic meaning even if they are squeezed. Be sensitive to the meanings that the author associates with people, places, objects, and actions. You may not associate home with provincial innocence as Hemingway does in "Soldier's Home," but a close reading of the story will permit you to see how and why he constructs that symbolic meaning. If you treat stories like people — with tact and care — they ordinarily are accessible and enjoyable.

The next three stories — Colette's "The Hand," Ralph Ellison's "Battle Royal," and Peter Meinke's "The Cranes" — rely on symbols to convey meanings that go far beyond the specific incidents described in their plots.

COLETTE (SIDONIE-GABRIELLE COLETTE / 1873–1954)

Born in Burgundy, France, Sidonie-Gabrielle Colette lived a long and remarkably diverse life. At various points during her career she supported herself as a novelist, music hall performer, and journalist. Her professional life and three marriages helped to shape her keen insights into modern love and women's lives. She is regarded as a significant feminist voice in the twentieth century, and her reputation is firmly fixed by her having been the first woman admitted to the Goncourt Academy and by the continued popularity of her work among readers internationally. Her best-known works include *Mitsou, or, How Girls Grow Wise* (1919), *Chéri* (1920), *Claudine's House* (1922), and *Gigi* (1944). "The Hand" signals a telling moment in the life of a young bride.

The Hand   1924

He had fallen asleep on his young wife's shoulder, and she proudly bore the weight of the man's head, blond, ruddy-complexioned, eyes closed. He had slipped his big arm under the small of her slim, adolescent back, and his strong hand lay on the sheet next to the young woman's right elbow. She smiled to see the man's hand emerging there, all by itself and far away from its owner. Then she let her eyes wander over the half-lit room. A veiled conch shed a light across the bed the color of periwinkle.

"Too happy to sleep," she thought.

Too excited also, and often surprised by her new state. It had been only two weeks since she had begun to live the scandalous life of a newlywed who tastes the joys of living with someone unknown and with whom she is in love. To meet a handsome, blond young man, recently widowed, good at tennis and rowing, to marry him a month later: her conjugal adventure had been little more than a kidnapping. So that whenever she lay awake beside her husband, like tonight, she still kept her eyes closed for a long time, then opened them again in order to savor, with astonishment, the blue of the brand-new curtains, instead of the apricot-pink through which the first light of day filtered into the room where she had slept as a little girl.

A quiver ran through the sleeping body lying next to her, and she tightened her left arm around her husband's neck with the charming authority exercised by weak creatures. He did not wake up.

"His eyelashes are so long," she said to herself.   5

To herself she also praised his mouth, full and likable, his skin the color of pink brick, and even his forehead, neither noble nor broad, but still smooth and unwrinkled.

Her husband's right hand, lying beside her, quivered in turn, and beneath the curve of her back she felt the right arm, on which her whole weight was resting, come to life.

"I'm so heavy . . . I wish I could get up and turn the light off. But he's sleeping so well . . ."

The arm twisted again, feebly, and she arched her back to make herself lighter.

"It's as if I were lying on some animal," she thought.   10

She turned her head a little on the pillow and looked at the hand lying there next to her.

"It's so big! It really is bigger than my whole head."

The light, flowing out from under the edge of a parasol of bluish crystal, spilled up against the hand, and made every contour of the skin apparent, exaggerating the powerful knuckles and the veins engorged by the pressure on the arm. A few red hairs, at the base of the fingers, all curved in the same direction, like ears of wheat in the wind, and the flat nails, whose ridges the nail buffer had not smoothed out, gleamed, coated with pink varnish.

"I'll tell him not to varnish his nails," thought the young wife. "Varnish and pink polish don't go with a hand so . . . a hand that's so . . ."

An electric jolt ran through the hand and spared the young woman from   15
having to find the right adjective. The thumb stiffened itself out, horribly long and spatulate, and pressed tightly against the index finger, so that the hand suddenly took on a vile, apelike appearance.

"Oh!" whispered the young woman, as though faced with something slightly indecent.

The sound of a passing car pierced the silence with a shrillness that seemed luminous. The sleeping man did not wake, but the hand, offended, reared back and tensed up in the shape of a crab and waited, ready for battle. The screeching sound died down and the hand, relaxing gradually, lowered its claws, and became a pliant beast, awkwardly bent, shaken by faint jerks which resembled some sort of agony. The flat, cruel nail of the overlong thumb glistened. A curve in the little finger, which the young woman had never noticed, appeared, and the wallowing hand revealed its fleshy palm like a red belly.

"And I've kissed that hand! . . . How horrible! Haven't I ever looked at it?"

The hand, disturbed by a bad dream, appeared to respond to this startling discovery, this disgust. It regrouped its forces, opened wide, and splayed its tendons, lumps, and red fur like battle dress, then slowly drawing itself in again, grabbed a fistful of the sheet, dug into it with its curved fingers, and squeezed, squeezed with the methodical pleasure of a strangler.

"Oh!" cried the young woman.   20

The hand disappeared and a moment later the big arm, relieved of its burden, became a protective belt, a warm bulwark against all the terrors of night. But the next morning, when it was time for breakfast in bed — hot chocolate and toast — she saw the hand again, with its red hair and red skin, and the ghastly thumb curving out over the handle of a knife.

"Do you want this slice, darling? I'll butter it for you."

She shuddered and felt her skin crawl on the back of her arms and down her back.

"Oh, no . . . no . . ."

Then she concealed her fear, bravely subdued herself, and, beginning her 25 life of duplicity, of resignation, and of a lowly, delicate diplomacy, she leaned over and humbly kissed the monstrous hand.

CONSIDERATIONS FOR CRITICAL THINKING AND WRITING

1. **FIRST RESPONSE.** Where is "The Hand" set? How significant is the setting of the story?

2. How well did the young woman know her husband before she married him? What attracted her to him?

3. How does the wife regard the hand at the very beginning of the story? At what point does she begin to change her attitude?

4. Explain how the wife's description of the hand affects your own response to it. What prompts her "Oh!" in paragraphs 16 and 20? What do you suppose the wife is thinking at these moments?

5. What powerful feelings does the hand evoke in the wife? How do her descriptions of the hand suggest symbolic readings of it?

6. Describe the conflict in the story. Explain whether there is a resolution to this conflict.

7. Do you think the story is more about the husband or about the wife? Who is the central character? Explain your choice. Consider also whether the characters are static or dynamic.

8. Why do you think the narrator mentions that the husband was "recently widowed"?

9. Why do you think the wife kisses her husband's hand in the final paragraph? Write an essay explaining how the kiss symbolizes the nature of their relationship.

10. Describe the point of view in the story. Why do you suppose Colette doesn't use a first-person perspective that would reveal more intimately the wife's perceptions and concerns?

CONNECTIONS TO OTHER SELECTIONS

1. In "The Birthmark" (p. 343) Nathaniel Hawthorne also uses a hand for symbolic purposes. Compare the meanings he associates with the hand in his story with Colette's. How does each writer invest meanings in a central symbol? What are the significant similarities and differences in

meanings? Write an essay explaining why you find one story more effective than the other.

2. Compare the use of settings in "The Hand" and in John Updike's "A & P" (p. 560). To what extent does each story attach meaning to its setting?

3. How might Gail Godwin's "A Sorrowful Woman" (p. 39) be read as a kind of sequel to "The Hand"?

RALPH ELLISON (1914–1994)

Born in Oklahoma and educated at the Tuskegee Institute in Alabama, where he studied music, Ralph Ellison gained his reputation as a writer on the strength of his only published novel, *Invisible Man* (1952). He also published some scattered short stories and two collections of essays, *Shadow and Act* (1964) and *Going to the Territory* (1986). Although his writ-

Courtesy of Mrs. Fanny Ellison.

ing was not extensive, it is important because Ellison wrote about race relations in the context of universal human concerns. *Invisible Man* is the story of a young black man who moves from the South to the North and discovers what it means to be black in America. "Battle Royal," published in 1947 as a short story, became the first chapter of *Invisible Man*. It concerns the beginning of the protagonist's long struggle for an adult identity in a world made corrupt by racial prejudice.

Explore contexts for Ralph Ellison on *LiterActive*.

Battle Royal   1947

It goes a long way back, some twenty years. All my life I had been looking for something, and everywhere I turned someone tried to tell me what it was. I accepted their answers too, though they were often in contradiction and even self-contradictory. I was naive. I was looking for myself and asking everyone except myself questions which I, and only I, could answer. It took me a long time and much painful boomeranging of my expectations to achieve a realization everyone else appears to have been born with: That I am nobody but myself. But first I had to discover that I am an invisible man!

And yet I am no freak of nature, nor of history. I was in the cards, other things having been equal (or unequal) eighty-five years ago. I am not ashamed of my grandparents for having been slaves. I am only ashamed of myself for having at one time been ashamed. About eighty-five years ago they were told that they were free, united with others of our country in everything pertaining to the common good, and, in everything social, separate like the fingers of the hand. And they believed it. They exulted in it. They stayed in their place, worked hard, and brought up my father to do the same. But my grandfather is the one. He was an odd old guy, my grandfather, and I am told I take after him. It was he who caused the trouble. On his deathbed he called my father to him and said, "Son, after I'm gone I want you to keep up the good fight. I never told you, but our life is a war and I have been a traitor all my born days, a spy in the enemy's country ever since I gave up my gun back in the Reconstruction. Live with your head in the lion's mouth. I want you to overcome 'em with yeses, undermine 'em with grins, agree 'em to death and destruction, let 'em swoller you till they vomit or bust wide open." They thought the old man had gone out of his mind. He had been the meekest of men. The younger children were rushed from the room, the shades drawn and the flame of the lamp turned so low that it sputtered on the wick like the old man's breathing. "Learn it to the young-uns," he whispered fiercely; then he died.

But my folks were more alarmed over his last words than over his dying. It was as though he had not died at all, his words caused so much anxiety. I was warned emphatically to forget what he had said and, indeed, this is the first time it has been mentioned outside the family circle. It had a tremendous effect upon me, however. I could never be sure of what he meant. Grandfather had been a quiet old man who never made any trouble, yet on his deathbed he had called himself a traitor and a spy, and he had spoken of his meekness as a dangerous activity. It became a constant puzzle which lay unanswered in the back of my mind. And whenever things went well for me I remembered my grandfather and felt guilty and uncomfortable. It was as though I was carrying out his advice in spite of myself. And to make it worse, everyone loved me for it. I was praised by the most lily-white men of the town. I was considered an example of desirable conduct — just as my grandfather had been. And what puzzled me was that the old man had defined it as *treachery*. When I was praised for my conduct I felt a guilt that in some way I was doing something that was really against the wishes of the white folks, that if they had understood they would have desired me to act just the opposite, that I should have been sulky and mean, and that that really would have been what they wanted, even though they were fooled and thought they wanted me to act as I did. It made me afraid that some day they would look upon me as a traitor and I would be lost. Still I was more afraid to act any other way because they didn't like that at all. The old man's words were like a curse. On my graduation day I delivered an oration in which I showed that humility was the secret, indeed, the very essence of progress. (Not that I believed this — how could I, remembering my grandfather? — I only believed that it worked.) It was a great success. Everyone praised me and I was invited to give the speech at a gathering of the town's leading white citizens. It was a triumph for our whole community.

It was in the main ballroom of the leading hotel. When I got there I discovered that it was on the occasion of a smoker, and I was told that since I was to be there anyway I might as well take part in the battle royal to be fought by some of my schoolmates as part of the entertainment. The battle royal came first.

All of the town's big shots were there in their tuxedoes, wolfing down the 5 buffet foods, drinking beer and whiskey and smoking black cigars. It was a large room with a high ceiling. Chairs were arranged in neat rows around three sides of a portable boxing ring. The fourth side was clear, revealing a gleaming space of polished floor. I had some misgivings over the battle royal, by the way. Not from a distaste for fighting, but because I didn't care too much for the other fellows who were to take part. They were tough guys who seemed to have no grandfather's curse worrying their minds. No one could mistake their toughness. And besides, I suspected that fighting a battle royal might detract from the dignity of my speech. In those pre-invisible days I visualized myself as a potential Booker T. Washington. But the other fellows didn't care too much for me either, and there were nine of them. I felt superior to them in my way, and I didn't like the manner in which we were all crowded together into the servants' elevator. Nor did they like my being there. In fact, as the warmly lighted floors flashed past the elevator we had words over the fact that I, by taking part in the fight, had knocked one of their friends out of a night's work.

We were led out of the elevator through a rococo hall into an anteroom and told to get into our fighting togs. Each of us was issued a pair of boxing gloves and ushered out into the big mirrored hall, which we entered looking cautiously about us and whispering, lest we might accidentally be heard above the noise of the room. It was foggy with cigar smoke. And already the whiskey was taking effect. I was shocked to see some of the most important men of the town quite tipsy. They were all there — bankers, lawyers, judges, doctors, fire chiefs, teachers, merchants. Even one of the more fashionable pastors. Something we could not see was going on up front. A clarinet was vibrating sensuously and the men were standing up and moving eagerly forward. We were a small tight group, clustered together, our bare upper bodies touching and shining with anticipatory sweat; while up front the big shots were becoming increasingly excited over something we still could not see. Suddenly I heard the school superintendent, who had told me to come, yell, "Bring up the shines, gentlemen! Bring up the little shines!"

We were rushed up to the front of the ballroom, where it smelled even more strongly of tobacco and whiskey. Then we were pushed into place. I almost wet my pants. A sea of faces, some hostile, some amused, ringed around us, and in the center, facing us, stood a magnificent blonde — stark naked. There was dead silence. I felt a blast of cold air chill me. I tried to back away, but they were behind me and around me. Some of the boys stood with lowered heads, trembling. I felt a wave of irrational guilt and fear. My teeth chattered, my skin turned to goose flesh, my knees knocked. Yet I was strongly attracted and looked in spite of myself. Had the price of looking been blindness, I would have looked. The hair was yellow like that of a circus kewpie doll, the face heavily powdered and rouged, as though to form an abstract mask, the eyes hollow and smeared a cool blue, the color of a baboon's butt. I felt a desire to spit upon her as my eyes brushed slowly over her body. Her breasts were firm and round as the domes of East Indian temples, and I stood so close as to see the fine skin texture and beads of pearly perspiration glistening like dew around the pink and erected buds of her nipples. I wanted at one and the same time to run from the room, to sink through the floor, or go to her and cover her from my eyes and the eyes of the others with my body; to feel the soft thighs, to caress her and destroy her, to love her and murder her, to hide from her, and yet to stroke where below the small American flag tattooed upon her belly her thighs formed a capital V. I had a notion that of all in the room she saw only me with her impersonal eyes.

And then she began to dance, a slow sensuous movement; the smoke of a hundred cigars clinging to her like the thinnest of veils. She seemed like a fair bird-girl girdled in veils calling to me from the angry surface of some gray and threatening sea. I was transported. Then I became aware of the clarinet playing and the big shots yelling at us. Some threatened us if we looked and others if we did not. On my right I saw one boy faint. And now a man grabbed a silver pitcher from a table and stepped close as he dashed ice water upon him and stood him up and forced two of us to support him as his head hung and moans issued from his thick bluish lips. Another boy began to plead to go home. He was the largest of the group, wearing dark red fighting trunks much too small to conceal the erection which projected from him as though in answer to the insinuating low-registered moaning of the clarinet. He tried to hide himself with his boxing gloves.

And all the while the blonde continued dancing, smiling faintly at the big shots who watched her with fascination, and faintly smiling at our fear. I noticed a certain merchant who followed her hungrily, his lips loose and drooling. He was a large man who wore diamond studs in a shirtfront which swelled with the ample paunch underneath, and each time the blonde swayed her undulating hips he ran his hand through the thin hair of his bald head and, with his arms upheld, his posture clumsy like that of an intoxicated panda, wound his belly in a slow and obscene grind. This creature was completely hypnotized. The music had quickened. As the dancer flung herself about with a detached expression on her face, the men began reaching out to touch her. I could see their beefy fingers sink into the soft flesh. Some of the others tried to stop them as she began to move around the floor in graceful circles, as they gave chase, slipping and sliding over the polished floor. It was mad. Chairs went crashing, drinks were spilt, as they ran laughing and howling after her. They caught her just as she reached a door, raised her from the floor, and tossed her as college boys are tossed at a hazing, and above her red, fixed-smiling lips I saw the terror and disgust in her eyes, almost like my own terror and that which I saw in some of the other boys. As I watched, they tossed her twice and her soft breasts seemed to flatten against the air and her legs flung wildly as she spun. Some of the more sober ones helped her to escape. And I started off the floor, heading for the anteroom with the rest of the boys.

Some were still crying in hysteria. But as we tried to leave we were stopped and ordered to get into the ring. There was nothing to do but what we were told. All ten of us climbed under the ropes and allowed ourselves to be blindfolded with broad bands of white cloth. One of the men seemed to feel a bit sympathetic and tried to cheer us up as we stood with our backs against the ropes. Some of us tried to grin. "See that boy over there?" one of the men said. "I want you to run across at the bell and give it to him right in the belly. If you don't get him, I'm going to get you. I don't like his looks." Each of us was told the same. The blindfolds were put on. Yet even then I had been going over my speech. In my mind each word was as bright as flame. I felt the cloth pressed into place, and frowned so that it would be loosened when I relaxed.

But now I felt a sudden fit of blind terror. I was unused to darkness. It was as though I had suddenly found myself in a dark room filled with poisonous cottonmouths. I could hear the bleary voices yelling insistently for the battle royal to begin.

"Get going in there!"

"Let me at that big nigger!"

I strained to pick up the school superintendent's voice, as though to squeeze some security out of that slightly more familiar sound.

"Let me at those black sonsabitches!" someone yelled.   15

"No, Jackson, no!" another voice yelled. "Here, somebody, help me hold Jack."

"I want to get at that ginger-colored nigger. Tear him limb from limb," the first voice yelled.

I stood against the ropes trembling. For in those days I was what they called ginger-colored, and he sounded as though he might crunch me between his teeth like a crisp ginger cookie.

Quite a struggle was going on. Chairs were being kicked about and I could hear voices grunting as with a terrific effort. I wanted to see, to see more desperately than ever before. But the blindfold was tight as a thick skin-puckering scab and when I raised my gloved hands to push the layers of white aside a voice yelled, "Oh, no you don't, black bastard! Leave that alone!"

"Ring the bell before Jackson kills him a coon!" someone boomed in the   20
sudden silence. And I heard the bell clang and the sound of the feet scuffling forward.

A glove smacked against my head. I pivoted, striking out stiffly as someone went past, and felt the jar ripple along the length of my arm to my shoulder. Then it seemed as though all nine of the boys had turned upon me at once. Blows pounded me from all sides while I struck out as best I could. So many blows landed upon me that I wondered if I were not the only blindfolded fighter in the ring, or if the man called Jackson hadn't succeeded in getting me after all.

Blindfolded, I could no longer control my motions. I had no dignity. I stumbled about like a baby or a drunken man. The smoke had become thicker and with each new blow it seemed to sear and further restrict my lungs. My saliva became like hot bitter glue. A glove connected with my head, filling my mouth with warm blood. It was everywhere. I could not tell if the moisture I felt upon my body was sweat or blood. A blow landed hard against the nape of my neck. I felt myself going over, my head hitting the floor. Streaks of blue light filled the black world behind the blindfold. I lay prone, pretending that I was knocked out, but felt myself seized by hands and yanked to my feet. "Get going, black boy! Mix it up!" My arms were like lead, my head smarting from blows. I managed to feel my way to the ropes and held on, trying to catch my breath. A glove landed in my mid-section and I went over again, feeling as though the smoke had become a knife jabbed into my guts. Pushed this way and that by the legs milling around me, I finally pulled erect and discovered that I could see the black, sweat-washed forms weaving in the smoky-blue atmosphere like drunken dancers weaving to the rapid drumlike thuds of blows.

Everyone fought hysterically. It was complete anarchy. Everybody fought everybody else. No group fought together for long. Two, three, four, fought one, then turned to fight each other, were themselves attacked. Blows landed below the belt and in the kidney, with the gloves open as well as closed, and with my eye partly opened now there was not so much terror. I moved carefully, avoiding blows, although not too many to attract attention, fighting from group to group. The boys groped about like blind, cautious crabs crouching to protect their mid-sections, their heads pulled in short against their shoulders, their arms stretched nervously before them, with their fists testing the smoke-filled air like the knobbed feelers of hypersensitive snails. In one corner I glimpsed a boy violently punching the air and heard him scream in pain as he smashed his hand against a ring post. For a second I saw him bent over holding his hand, then going down as a blow caught his unprotected head. I played one group against the other, slipping in and throwing a punch then stepping out of range while pushing the others into the melee to take the blows blindly aimed at me. The smoke was agonizing and there were no rounds, no bells at three minute intervals to relieve our exhaustion. The room spun round me, a swirl of lights, smoke, sweating bodies surrounded by tense white faces. I bled from both nose and mouth, the blood spattering upon my chest.

The men kept yelling, "Slug him, black boy! Knock his guts out!"

"Uppercut him! Kill him! Kill that big boy!"   25

Taking a fake fall, I saw a boy going down heavily beside me as though we were felled by a single blow, saw a sneaker-clad foot shoot into his groin as the two who had knocked him down stumbled upon him. I rolled out of range, feeling a twinge of nausea.

The harder we fought the more threatening the men became. And yet, I had begun to worry about my speech again. How would it go? Would they recognize my ability? What would they give me?

I was fighting automatically when suddenly I noticed that one after another of the boys was leaving the ring. I was surprised, filled with panic, as though I had been left alone with an unknown danger. Then I understood. The boys had arranged it among themselves. It was the custom for the two men left in the ring to slug it out for the winner's prize. I discovered this too late. When the bell sounded two men in tuxedoes leaped into the ring and removed the blindfold. I found myself facing Tatlock, the biggest of the gang. I felt sick at my stomach. Hardly had the bell stopped ringing in my ears than it clanged again and I saw him moving swiftly toward me. Thinking of nothing else to do I hit him smash on the nose. He kept coming, bringing the rank sharp violence of stale sweat. His face was a black blank of a face, only his eyes alive—with hate of me and aglow with a feverish terror from what had happened to us all. I became anxious. I wanted to deliver my speech and he came at me as though he meant to beat it out of me. I smashed him again and again, taking his blows as they came. Then on a sudden impulse I struck him lightly and as we clinched, I whispered, "Fake like I knocked you out, you can have the prize."

"I'll break your behind," he whispered hoarsely.

"For *them*?"   30

"For *me*, sonofabitch!"

They were yelling for us to break it up and Tatlock spun me half around with a blow, and as a joggled camera sweeps in a reeling scene, I saw the howling red faces crouching tense beneath the cloud of blue-gray smoke. For a moment the world wavered, unraveled, flowed, then my head cleared and Tatlock bounced before me. That fluttering shadow before my eyes was his jabbing left hand. Then falling forward, my head against his damp shoulder, I whispered,

"I'll make it five dollars more."

"Go to hell!"

But his muscles relaxed a trifle beneath my pressure and I breathed, 35 "Seven?"

"Give it to your ma," he said, ripping me beneath the heart.

And while I still held him I butted him and moved away. I felt myself bombarded with punches. I fought back with hopeless desperation. I wanted to deliver my speech more than anything else in the world, because I felt that only these men could judge truly my ability, and now this stupid clown was ruining my chances. I began fighting carefully now, moving in to punch him and out again with my greater speed. A lucky blow to his chin and I had him going too — until I heard a loud voice yell, "I got my money on the big boy."

Hearing this, I almost dropped my guard. I was confused: Should I try to win against the voice out there? Would not this go against my speech, and was not this a moment for humility, for nonresistance? A blow to my head as I danced about sent my right eye popping like a jack-in-the-box and settled my dilemma. The room went red as I fell. It was a dream fall, my body languid and fastidious as to where to land, until the floor became impatient and smashed up to meet me. A moment later I came to. An hypnotic voice said FIVE emphatically. And I lay there, hazily watching a dark red spot of my own blood shaping itself into a butterfly, glistening and soaking into the soiled gray world of the canvas.

When the voice drawled TEN I was lifted up and dragged to a chair. I sat dazed. My eye pained and swelled with each throb of my pounding heart and I wondered if now I would be allowed to speak. I was wringing wet, my mouth still bleeding. We were grouped along the wall now. The other boys ignored me as they congratulated Tatlock and speculated as to how much they would be paid. One boy whimpered over his smashed hand. Looking up front, I saw attendants in white jackets rolling the portable ring away and placing a small square rug in the vacant space surrounded by chairs. Perhaps, I thought, I will stand on the rug to deliver my speech.

Then the M.C. called to us, "Come on up here boys and get your money." 40 We ran forward to where the men laughed and talked in their chairs, waiting. Everyone seemed friendly now.

"There it is on the rug," the man said. I saw the rug covered with coins of all dimensions and a few crumpled bills. But what excited me, scattered here and there, were the gold pieces.

"Boys, it's all yours," the man said. "You get all you grab."

"That's right, Sambo," a blond man said, winking at me confidentially.

I trembled with excitement, forgetting my pain. I would get the gold and the bills, I thought. I would use both hands. I would throw my body against the boys nearest me to block them from the gold.

"Get down around the rug now," the man commanded, "and don't anyone 45 touch it until I give the signal."

"This ought to be good," I heard.

As told, we got around the square rug on our knees. Slowly the man raised his freckled hand as we followed it upward with our eyes.

I heard, "These niggers look like they're about to pray!"

Then, "Ready," the man said. "Go!"

I lunged for a yellow coin lying on the blue design of the carpet, touching 50 it and sending a surprised shriek to join those rising around me. I tried frantically to remove my hand but could not let go. A hot, violent force tore through my body, shaking me like a wet rat. The rug was electrified. The hair bristled up on my head as I shook myself free. My muscles jumped, my nerves jangled, writhed. But I saw that this was not stopping the other boys. Laughing in fear and embarrassment, some were holding back and scooping up the coins knocked off by the painful contortions of the others. The men roared above us as we struggled.

"Pick it up, goddamnit, pick it up!" someone called like a bass-voiced parrot. "Go on, get it!"

I crawled rapidly around the floor, picking up the coins, trying to avoid the coppers and to get greenbacks and the gold. Ignoring the shock by laughing, as I brushed the coins off quickly, I discovered that I could contain the electricity—a contradiction, but it works. Then the men began to push us onto the rug. Laughing embarrassedly, we struggled out of their hands and kept after the coins. We were all wet and slippery and hard to hold. Suddenly I saw a boy lifted into the air, glistening with sweat like a circus seal, and dropped, his wet back landing flush upon the charged rug, heard him yell and saw him literally dance upon his back, his elbows beating a frenzied tattoo upon the floor, his muscles twitching like the flesh of a horse stung by many flies. When he finally rolled off, his face was gray and no one stopped him when he ran from the floor amid booming laughter.

"Get the money," the M.C. called. "That's good hard American cash!"

And we snatched and grabbed, snatched and grabbed. I was careful not to come too close to the rug now, and when I felt the hot whiskey breath descend upon me like a cloud of foul air I reached out and grabbed the leg of a chair. It was occupied and I held on desperately.

"Leggo, nigger! Leggo!"   55

The huge face wavered down to mine as he tried to push me free. But my body was slippery and he was too drunk. It was Mr. Colcord, who owned a chain of movie houses and "entertainment palaces." Each time he grabbed me I slipped out of his hands. It became a real struggle. I feared the rug more than I did the drunk, so I held on, surprising myself for a moment by trying to topple *him* upon the rug. It was such an enormous idea that I found myself actually carrying it out. I tried not to be obvious, yet when I grabbed his leg, trying to tumble him out of the chair, he raised up roaring with laughter, and, looking at me with soberness dead in the eye, kicked me viciously in the chest. The chair leg flew out of my hand and I felt myself going and rolled. It was as though I had rolled through a bed of hot coals. It seemed a whole century would pass before I would roll free, a century in which I was seared through the deepest levels of my body to the fearful breath within me and the breath seared and heated to the point of explosion. It'll all be over in a flash, I thought as I rolled clear. It'll all be over in a flash.

But not yet, the men on the other side were waiting, red faces swollen as though from apoplexy as they bent forward in their chairs. Seeing their fingers coming toward me I rolled away as a fumbled football rolls off the receiver's fingertips, back into the coals. That time I luckily sent the rug sliding out of place and heard the coins ringing against the floor and the boys scuffling to pick them up and the M.C. calling, "All right, boys, that's all. Go get dressed and get your money."

I was limp as a dish rag. My back felt as though it had been beaten with wires.

When we had dressed the M.C. came in and gave us each five dollars, except Tatlock, who got ten for being last in the ring. Then he told us to leave. I was not to get a chance to deliver my speech, I thought. I was going out into the dim alley in despair when I was stopped and told to go back. I returned to the ballroom, where the men were pushing back their chairs and gathering in groups to talk.

The M.C. knocked on a table for quiet. "Gentlemen," he said, "we almost 60 forgot an important part of the program. A most serious part, gentlemen. This boy was brought here to deliver a speech which he made at his graduation yesterday . . ."

"Bravo!"

"I'm told that he is the smartest boy we've got out there in Greenwood. I'm told that he knows more big words than a pocket-sized dictionary."

Much applause and laughter.

"So now, gentlemen, I want you to give him your attention."

There was still laughter as I faced them, my mouth dry, my eye throbbing. 65 I began slowly, but evidently my throat was tense, because they began shouting, "Louder! Louder!"

"We of the younger generation extol the wisdom of that great leader and educator," I shouted, "who first spoke these flaming words of wisdom: 'A ship lost at sea for many days suddenly sighted a friendly vessel. From the mast of the unfortunate vessel was seen a signal: "Water, water; we die of thirst!" The answer from the friendly vessel came back: "Cast down your bucket where you are." The captain of the distressed vessel, at last heeding the injunction, cast down his bucket, and it came up full of fresh sparkling water from the mouth of the Amazon River.' And like him I say, and in his words, 'To those of my race who depend upon bettering their condition in a foreign land, or who underestimate the importance of cultivating friendly relations with the Southern white man, who is his next-door neighbor, I would say: "Cast down your bucket where you are" — cast it down in making friends in every manly way of the people of all races by whom we are surrounded . . .'"

I spoke automatically and with such fervor that I did not realize that the men were still talking and laughing until my dry mouth, filling up with blood from the cut, almost strangled me. I coughed, wanting to stop and go to one of the tall brass, sand-filled spittoons to relieve myself, but a few of the men, especially the superintendent, were listening and I was afraid. So I gulped it down, blood, saliva, and all, and continued. (What powers of endurance I had during those days! What enthusiasm! What a belief in the rightness of things!) I spoke even louder in spite of the pain. But still they talked and still they laughed, as though deaf with cotton in dirty ears. So I spoke with greater emotional emphasis. I closed my ears and swallowed blood until I was nauseated. The speech seemed a hundred times as long as before, but I could not leave out a single word. All had to be said, each memorized nuance considered, rendered. Nor was that all. Whenever I uttered a word of three or more syllables a group of voices would yell for me to repeat it. I used the phrase "social responsibility" and they yelled:

"What's that word you say, boy?"

"Social responsibility," I said.

"What?"

"Social . . ."
70

"Louder."

". . . responsibility."

"More!"

"Respon—"

"Repeat!"

"— sibility."

The room filled with the uproar of laughter until, no doubt, distracted by having to gulp down my blood, I made a mistake and yelled a phrase I had often seen denounced in newspaper editorials, heard debated in private.

"Social . . ."

"What?" they yelled.

". . . equality—"

The laughter hung smokelike in the sudden stillness. I opened my eyes, puzzled. Sounds of displeasure filled the room. The M.C. rushed forward. They shouted hostile phrases at me. But I did not understand.

A small dry mustached man in the front row blared out, "Say that slowly, son!"

"What, sir?"

"What you just said!"

"Social responsibility, sir," I said.

"You weren't being smart, were you, boy?" he said, not unkindly.

"No, sir!"

"You sure that about 'equality' was a mistake?"

"Oh, yes, sir," I said. "I was swallowing blood."

"Well, you had better speak more slowly so we can understand. We mean to do right by you, but you've got to know your place at all times. All right, now, go on with your speech."

I was afraid. I wanted to leave but I wanted also to speak and I was afraid they'd snatch me down.

"Thank you, sir," I said, beginning where I had left off, and having them ignore me as before.

Yet when I finished there was a thunderous applause. I was surprised to see the superintendent come forth with a package wrapped in white tissue paper, and, gesturing for quiet, address the men.

"Gentlemen, you see that I did not overpraise this boy. He makes a good speech and some day he'll lead his people in the proper paths. And I don't have to tell you that that is important in these days and times. This is a good, smart boy, and so to encourage him in the right direction, in the name of the Board of Education I wish to present him a prize in the form of this . . ."

He paused, removing the tissue paper and revealing a gleaming calfskin brief case.

". . . in the form of this first-class article from Shad Whitmore's shop."

"Boy," he said, addressing me, "take this prize and keep it well. Consider it a badge of office. Prize it. Keep developing as you are and some day it will be filled with important papers that will help shape the destiny of your people."

I was so moved that I could hardly express my thanks. A rope of bloody saliva forming a shape like an undiscovered continent drooled upon the leather and I wiped it quickly away. I felt an importance that I had never dreamed.

"Open it and see what's inside," I was told.

My fingers a-tremble, I complied, smelling the fresh leather and finding an official-looking document inside. It was a scholarship to the state college for Negroes. My eyes filled with tears and I ran awkwardly off the floor.

I was overjoyed; I did not even mind when I discovered that the gold pieces I had scrambled for were brass pocket tokens advertising a certain make of automobile.

When I reached home everyone was excited. Next day the neighbors came to congratulate me. I even felt safe from grandfather, whose deathbed curse usually spoiled my triumphs. I stood beneath his photograph with my brief case in hand and smiled triumphantly into his stolid black peasant's face. It was a face that fascinated me. The eyes seemed to follow everywhere I went.

That night I dreamed I was at a circus with him and that he refused to laugh at the clowns no matter what they did. Then later he told me to open my brief case and read what was inside and I did, finding an official envelope stamped with the state seal; and inside the envelope I found another and another, endlessly, and I thought I would fall of weariness. "Them's years," he said. "Now open that one." And I did and in it I found an engraved document containing a short message in letters of gold. "Read it," my grandfather said. "Out loud!"

"To Whom It May Concern," I intoned. "Keep This Nigger-Boy Running."

I awoke with the old man's laughter ringing in my ears.   105

(It was a dream I was to remember and dream again for many years after. But at that time I had no insight into its meaning. First I had to attend college.)

CONSIDERATIONS FOR CRITICAL THINKING AND WRITING

1. **FIRST RESPONSE.** Discuss how the protagonist's expectations are similar to what has come to be known as the American dream — the assumption that ambition, hard work, perseverance, intelligence, and virtue always lead to success. Do you believe in the American dream?

2. How does the first paragraph of the story sum up the conflict that the narrator confronts? In what sense is he "invisible"?

3. Why do his grandfather's last words cause so much anxiety in the family? What does his grandfather mean when he says, "I want you to overcome 'em with yeses, undermine 'em with grins, agree 'em to death" (para. 2)?

4. What is the symbolic significance of the naked blonde? What details reveal that she represents more than a sexual tease in the story?

5. How does the battle in the boxing ring and the scramble for money afterward suggest the kind of control whites have over blacks in the story?

6. Why is it significant that the town is named Greenwood and that the briefcase award comes from Shad Whitmore's shop? Can you find any other details that reinforce the meaning of the story?

7. What is the narrator's perspective as an educated adult telling the story, in contrast to his assumptions and beliefs as a recent high school graduate? How is this contrast especially evident in the speech before the "leading white citizens" of the town?

8. How can the dream at the end of the story be related to the major incidents that precede it?

9. Given the grandfather's advice, explain how "meekness" can be a "danger-
    ous activity" and a weapon against oppression.

10. Imagine the story as told from a third-person point of view. How would
    this change the story? Do you think the story would be more or less effec-
    tive told from a third-person point of view? Explain your answer.

11. CRITICAL STRATEGIES. Read the section on mythological criticism (pp.
    1550–52) in Chapter 46, "Critical Strategies for Reading," and "What Is an
    Initiation Story?" by Mordecai Marcus (following). Discuss "Battle Royal"
    as an archetypal initiation story.

CONNECTIONS TO OTHER SELECTIONS

1. Compare and contrast Ellison's view of the South with William Faulk-
    ner's in "A Rose for Emily" (p. 90).

2. Compare and contrast this story with M. Carl Holman's poem "Mr. Z"
    (p. 992).

Perspective

MORDECAI MARCUS (B. 1925)
What Is an Initiation Story?   1960

An initiation story may be said to show its young protagonist experiencing a
significant change of knowledge about the world or himself, or a change of
character, or of both, and this change must point or lead him toward an adult
world. It may or may not contain some form of ritual, but it should give some
evidence that the change is at least likely to have permanent effects.

Initiation stories obviously center on a variety of experiences and the initiations vary in effect. It will be useful, therefore, to divide initiations into types
according to their power and effect. First, some initiations lead only to the
threshold of maturity and understanding but do not definitely cross it. Such
stories emphasize the shocking effect of experience, and their protagonists
tend to be distinctly young. Second, some initiations take their protagonists
across a threshold of maturity and understanding but leave them enmeshed in
a struggle for certainty. These initiations sometimes involve self-discovery.
Third, the most decisive initiations carry their protagonists firmly into maturity and understanding, or at least show them decisively embarked toward
maturity. These initiations usually center on self-discovery. For convenience, I
will call these types tentative, uncompleted, and decisive initiations.

From "What Is an Initiation Story?" in *The Journal
of Aesthetics and Art Criticism*

CONSIDERATIONS FOR CRITICAL THINKING AND WRITING

1. For a work to be classified as an initiation story, why should it "give some
    evidence that the change [in the protagonist] is at least likely to have per-
    manent effects"?

2. Marcus divides initiations into three broad types: tentative, uncompleted, and decisive. Explain how you would categorize the initiation in Ellison's "Battle Royal."

A SAMPLE CLOSE READING

An Annotated Section of Ralph Ellison's "Battle Royal"

Even as you read a story for the first time, you can highlight passages, circle or underline words, and write responses in the margins. Subsequent readings will yield more insights once you begin to understand how various elements such as plot, character, and wording build toward the conclusion and what you perceive to be the story's central ideas. The following annotations for paragraphs 3-6 of "Battle Royal" provide a perspective written by someone who had read the work several times.

RALPH ELLISON (1914–1994)

Battle Royal 1947

On his "graduation day," the narrator is about to be initiated into a world of racial degradations that will make him an "invisible man."

.... On my graduation day I delivered an oration in which I showed that humility was the secret, indeed, the very essence of progress. (Not that I believed this—how could I, remembering my grandfather?—I only believed that it worked.) It was a great success. Everyone praised me and I was invited to give the speech at a gathering of the town's leading white citizens. It was a triumph for our whole community.

The narrator's "humility" is a pragmatic strategy to achieve success in a white world and connects him to his grandfather's subversive advice "to overcome 'em with yeses."

It was in the main ballroom of the leading hotel. When I got there I discovered that it was on the occasion of a smoker, and I was told that since I was to be there anyway I might as well take part in the battle royal to be fought by some of my schoolmates as part of the entertainment. The battle royal came first.

The "leading" whites in the "leading" hotel represent the respectable pillars of the community, but they are only leading the blacks to a battle with each other rather than to some kind of recognition and "triumph."

All of the town's big shots were there in their tuxedoes, wolfing down the buffet foods, drinking beer and whiskey and smoking black cigars. It was a large room with a high ceiling. Chairs were arranged in neat rows around three sides of a portable boxing ring. The fourth side was clear, revealing a gleaming space of polished floor. I had some misgivings over the battle royal, by the way. Not from a distaste for fighting, but because I didn't care too much for the other fellows who were to take part. They were tough guys who seemed to have no grandfather's curse worrying their minds. No one could

The town's leaders are described as "wolfing" down their food, an appropriate image for their predatory relationship to the boys.

The narrator's "dignity" exists in his own mind but not in the minds of the whites or his fellow fighters.

The advice that the narrator quotes from Washington, a symbol of racial accommodation, in his speech (para. 66) is undercut by the battle royal to come.

The narrator's innocence is demonstrated by his shocked response to seeing "the most important men of the town," including a pastor, at the smoker.

The school superintendent not only participates but appears to be in charge of the smoker. His yelling "Bring up the shines" is filled with unintended irony.

mistake their toughness. And besides, I suspected that fighting a battle royal might detract from the dignity of my speech. In those pre-invisible days I visualized myself as a potential Booker T. Washington. But the other fellows didn't care too much for me either, and there were nine of them. I felt superior to them in my way, and I didn't like the manner in which we were all crowded together into the servants' elevator. Nor did they like my being there. In fact, as the warmly lighted floors flashed past the elevator we had words over the fact that I, by taking part in the fight, had knocked one of their friends out of a night's work.

We were led out of the elevator through a rococo hall into an anteroom and told to get into our fighting togs. Each of us was issued a pair of boxing gloves and ushered out into the big mirrored hall, which we entered looking cautiously about us and whispering, lest we might accidentally be heard above the noise of the room. It was foggy with cigar smoke. And already the whiskey was taking effect. I was shocked to see some of the most important men of the town quite tipsy. They were all there — bankers, lawyers, judges, doctors, fire chiefs, teachers, merchants. Even one of the more fashionable pastors. Something we could not see was going on up front. A clarinet was vibrating sensuously and the men were standing up and moving eagerly forward. We were a small tight group, clustered together, our bare upper bodies touching and shining with anticipatory sweat; while up front the big shots were becoming increasingly excited over something we still could not see. Suddenly I heard the school superintendent, who had told me to come, yell, "Bring up the shines, gentlemen! Bring up the little shines!"

MORE HELP WITH CLOSE READING

Close readings of Kate Chopin's "The Story of an Hour," Nathaniel Hawthorne's "Young Goodman Brown," and Jamaica Kincaid's "Girl" are available on *LiterActive* and at the book's companion site. Each story is annotated with critical interpretations and explanations of the literary elements at work.

A SAMPLE STUDENT RESPONSE

Lila Katz

Professor West

English 200

December 2, 2008

Symbolism in Ralph Ellison's "Battle Royal"

In Ralph Ellison's story "Battle Royal," a young African American man, proud of his achievements, is asked to read his high school graduation speech to the "town's big shots" (244). The event, which the narrator initially looks forward to as "a triumph for our whole community" (244), turns out to be a spectacle of ridicule and abuse. He and other young black men are degraded and forced to fight gladiator-style--all for the amusement of drunken white men. This experience, as horrible as it is, allows the main character to better understand the world and the place he is expected to occupy in it. The story can be considered a coming-of-age or initiation story, in which the main character experiences change. Ellison's character is taken "across a threshold of maturity and understanding" yet is still "enmeshed in a struggle for certainty" (Mordecai 254). And through the story's powerful symbolism, the reader can better understand that struggle.

The battle itself can be read as a representation of the society in which the narrator lives--in which nothing makes sense, in which whites hold the power, and in which blacks must struggle against racism and violence. In this battle, part of the narrator's initiation into society, the young black men are stripped of power, blindfolded, and turned against each other. The lead-up to the battle, the dance of the naked white woman branded with an American flag tattoo, is symbolic, too. Read as a representation of America, she is what the young black men cannot have. In the aftermath of the battle, when it is time for the men to finally be paid, they are forced to crawl on the floor and grapple not for money but for worthless tokens. Ellison offers these symbols to define the inequalities of race and class that the African Americans endure in the story. . . .

Katz 4

Works Cited

Ellison, Ralph. "Battle Royal." The Compact Bedford Introduction to Literature. Ed. Michael Meyer. 8th ed. Boston: Bedford/St. Martin's, 2009.
243–53.

Marcus, Mordecai. "What Is an Initiation Story?" The Compact Bedford Introduction to Literature. Ed. Michael Meyer. 8th ed. Boston: Bedford/
St. Martin's, 2009. 254.

Peter Meinke (b. 1932)

Born in Brooklyn, New York, Peter Meinke
was educated at Hamilton College (B.A.,
1955), the University of Michigan (M.A.,
1961), and the University of Minnesota
(Ph.D., 1965). He has taught literature and
creative writing at a number of schools,
including Hamline University, Eckerd College, and Old Dominion University. Among
his many poetry books are *Nightwatch on the
Chesapeake* (1987), *Scars* (1996), and *The Contracted World* (2006), which are notable for
their powerful use of detail from everyday
life as well as simple — and serious — humor.

Courtesy of James Plath.

They have earned him two National Endowment for the Arts fellowships.
Though Meinke is primarily a poet, he has also published short stories, a
collection of which, *Piano Tuner* (1986), won the Flannery O'Connor Award.
In a 1990 interview in *Clockwatch Review*, Meinke discussed the similarities
he sees between short stories and poetry: "I think that certainly poetry and
short stories are more alike than short stories and novels, because that's
the main decision — leaving out the boffo endings, leaving out conversations that are extraneous. There's a big empty spot around poems and
short stories, certainly. That's the thing they have very strongly in common." "The Cranes" is a fine example of the kind of literary economy that
Meinke believes poetry and short stories often share.

The Cranes   *1987*

"Oh!" she said, "what are those, the huge white ones?" Along the marshy shore two tall and stately birds, staring motionless toward the Gulf, towered above the bobbing egrets and scurrying plovers.

"Well, I can't believe it," he said. "I've been coming here for years and never saw one."

"But what are they? Don't make me guess or anything; it makes me feel dumb." They leaned forward in the car, and the shower curtain spread over the front seat crackled and hissed.

"They've got to be whooping cranes, nothing else so big." One of the birds turned gracefully, as if to acknowledge the old Dodge parked alone in the tall grasses. "See the black legs and black wingtips? Big! Why don't I have my binoculars?" He looked at his wife and smiled.

"Well," he continued after a while, "I've seen enough birds. But whooping   5 cranes, they're rare. Not many left."

"They're lovely. They make the little birds look like clowns."

"I could use a few clowns," he said. "A few laughs never hurt anybody."

"Are you all right?" She put a hand on his thin arm. "I feel I'm responsible. Maybe this is the wrong thing."

"God, no!" His voice changed. "No way. I can't smoke, can't drink martinis, no coffee, no candy. I not only can't leap buildings in a single bound, I can hardly get up the goddamn stairs."

She was smiling. "Do you remember the time you drank nine martinis and   10 asked that young priest to step outside and see whose side God was on?"

"What a jerk I was! How have you put up with me all this time?"

"Oh no! I was proud of you. You were so funny, and that priest was a snot."

"Now you tell me." The cranes were moving slowly over a small hillock, wings opening and closing like bellows. "It's all right. It's enough," he said again. "How old am I anyway, 130?"

"Really," she said, "it's me. Ever since the accident it's been one thing after another. I'm just a lot of trouble to everybody."

"Let's talk about something else," he said. "Do you want to listen to the   15 radio? How about turning on that preacher station so we can throw up?"

"No," she said, "I just want to watch the birds. And listen to you."

"You must be pretty tired of that."

She turned her head from the window and looked into his eyes. "I never got tired of listening to you. Never."

"Well, that's good," he said. "It's just that when my mouth opens, your eyes tend to close."

"They do not!" she said, and began to laugh, but the laugh turned into a   20 cough and he had to pat her on the back until she stopped. They leaned back in silence and looked toward the Gulf stretching out beyond the horizon. In the distance, the water looked like metal, still and hard.

"I wish they'd court," he said. "I wish we could see them court, the cranes. They put on a show. He bows like Nijinksy and jumps straight up in the air."

"What does she do?"

"She lies down and he lands on top of her."

"No," she said, "I'm serious."

"Well, I forget. I've never seen it. But I do remember that they mate for life 25 and live a long time. They're probably older than we are. Their feathers are falling out and their kids never write."

She was quiet again. He turned in his seat, picked up an object wrapped in a plaid towel, and placed it between them in the front. "Here's looking at *you*, kid," he said.

"Do they really mate for life? I'm glad — they're so beautiful."

"Yep. Audubon said that's why they're almost extinct: a failure of imagination."

"I don't believe that," she said. "I think there'll always be whooping cranes."

"Why not?" he said.   30

"I wish the children were more settled. I keep thinking it's my fault."

"You think everything's your fault. Nicaragua. Ozone depletion. Nothing is your fault. They'll be fine, and anyway, they're not children anymore. Kids are different today, that's all. You were terrific." He paused. "You were terrific in ways I couldn't tell the kids about."

"I should hope not." She laughed and began coughing again, but held his hand when he reached over. When the cough subsided they sat quietly, looking down at their hands as if they were objects in a museum. "I used to have pretty hands," she said.

"I remember."

"Do you? Really?"   35

"I remember everything," he said.

"You always forgot everything."

"Well, now I remember."

"Did you bring something for your ears?"

"No, I can hardly hear anything, anyway." But he turned his head at a sud- 40 den squabble among the smaller birds. The cranes were stepping delicately away from the commotion.

"I'm tired," she said.

"Yes." He leaned over and kissed her, barely touching her lips. "Tell me," he said, "did I really drink nine martinis?"

But she had already closed her eyes and only smiled. Outside, the wind ruffled the bleached-out grasses, and the birds in the white glare seemed almost transparent. The hull of the car gleamed beetle-like — dull and somehow sinister in its metallic isolation.

Suddenly, the two cranes plunged upward, their great wings beating the air and their long slender necks pointed like arrows toward the sun.

CONSIDERATIONS FOR CRITICAL THINKING AND WRITING

1. **FIRST RESPONSE.** What happens at the end of "The Cranes"? What do you think this story is about?

2. Explain how Meinke uses exposition to tell the couple's story.

3. Does the couple's behavior seem motivated and plausible to you? Explain why or why not.

4. Point to incidences of foreshadowing and discuss how they affect your understanding of the plot. Were you aware of the foreshadowing elements on a first reading or only after subsequent readings?

5. How is suspense created in the plot?
6. How might the cranes be read as both conventional and literary symbols in this story?
7. Discuss Meinke's inclusion of humor. Why do you regard it as appropriate or not, given the story's subject matter?
8. How does Meinke's use of language suggest that the writer of "The Cranes" is a poet as well as a fiction writer?

CONNECTIONS TO OTHER SELECTIONS

1. Consider how symbols convey the central meanings of "The Cranes" and of either Kate Chopin's "The Story of an Hour" (p. 15) or Gail Godwin's "A Sorrowful Woman" (p. 39).

8

Theme

To produce a mighty book, you must choose a mighty theme.
— HERMAN MELVILLE,
from *Moby Dick*, 1851

Theme is the central idea or meaning of a story. It provides a unifying point around which the plot, characters, setting, point of view, symbols, and other elements of a story are organized. In some works the theme is explicitly stated. Nathaniel Hawthorne's "Wakefield," for example, begins with the author telling the reader that the point of his story is "done up neatly, and condensed into the final sentence." Most modern writers, however, present their themes implicitly (as Hawthorne does in the majority of his stories), so determining the underlying meaning of a work often requires more effort than it does from the reader of "Wakefield." One reason for the difficulty is that the theme is fused into the elements of the story, and these must be carefully examined in relation to one another as well as to the work as a whole. But then that's the value of determining the theme, for it requires a close analysis of all the elements of a work. Such a close reading often results in sharper insights into this overlooked character or that seemingly unrelated incident. Accounting for the details and seeing how they fit together give you a greater understanding of the story. Such familiarity creates pleasure in much the same way that a musical piece heard more than once becomes a rich experience rather than simply a repetitive one.

Themes are not always easy to express, but some principles can aid you in articulating the central meaning of a work. First distinguish between the theme of a story and its subject. They are not equivalents. Many stories share identical subjects, such as fate, death, innocence, youth, loneliness, racial prejudice, and disillusionment. Yet each story usually makes its own statement about the subject and expresses some view of life. Hemingway's "Soldier's Home" (p. 165) and Faulkner's "Barn Burning" (p. 418) both describe young men who are unhappy at home and decide that they must leave, but the meaning of each story is quite different. A thematic generalization about "Soldier's Home" could be something like this: "The brutal experience of war can alienate a person from those — even family and friends — who are innocent of war's reality." The theme of Faulkner's story could be stated this way: "No matter how much one might love one's father, there comes a time when family loyalties must be left behind in order to be true to one's self."

Explore the literary element in this chapter on *LiterActive* or at bedfordstmartins.com/meyercompact.

These two statements of theme do not definitively sum up each story — there is no single, absolute way of expressing a work's theme — but they do describe a central idea in each. Furthermore, the emphasis in each of these themes could be modified or expanded because interpretations of interesting, complex works are always subject to revision. People have different responses to life, and so it is hardly surprising that responses to literature are not identical. When theme is considered, the possibilities for meaning are usually expanded and not reduced to categories such as "right" or "wrong."

Although readers may differ in their interpretations of a story, that does not mean that *any* interpretation is valid. If we were to assert that the soldier's dissatisfactions in Hemingway's story could be readily eliminated by his settling down to marriage and a decent job (his mother's solution), we would have missed Hemingway's purposes in writing the story; we would have failed to see how Krebs's war experiences have caused him to reexamine the assumptions and beliefs that previously nurtured him but now seem unreal to him. We would have to ignore much in the story in order to arrive at such a reading. To be valid, the statement of the theme should be responsive to the details of the story. It must be based on evidence within the story rather than solely on experiences, attitudes, or values the reader brings to the work — such as personally knowing a war veteran who successfully adjusted to civilian life after getting a good job and marrying. Familiarity with the subject matter of a story can certainly be an aid to interpretation, but it should not get in the way of seeing the author's perspective.

Sometimes readers too hastily conclude that a story's theme always consists of a moral, some kind of lesson that is dramatized by the various elements of the work. There are stories that do this — Hawthorne's "Wakefield," for example. Here are the final sentences in his story about a middle-aged man who drops out of life for twenty years:

> He has left us much food for thought, a portion of which shall lend its wisdom to a moral, and be shaped into a figure. Amid the seeming confusion of our mysterious world, individuals are so nicely adjusted to a system, and systems to one another and to a whole, that, by stepping aside for a moment, a man exposes himself to a fearful risk of losing his place forever. Like Wakefield, he may become, as it were, the Outcast of the Universe.

Most stories, however, do not include such direct caveats about the conduct of life. A tendency to look for a lesson in a story can produce a reductive and inaccurate formulation of its theme. Consider the damage done to Colette's "The Hand" (p. 240) if its theme is described as this: "Adolescents are too young to cope with the responsibilities of marriage." Colette's focus in this story is on the young woman's response to her husband's powerful sexuality and dominance rather than on her inability to be a good wife.

In fact, a good many stories go beyond traditional moral values to explore human behavior instead of condemning or endorsing it. Chekhov's treatment of the adulterous affair between Gurov and Anna in "The Lady with the Pet Dog" (p. 205) portrays a love that is valuable and true despite the conventional moral codes it violates. That is not to say that the reader must agree with Chekhov's attitude that such love has a validity of its own. We are obligated to see that Chekhov is sympathetic to the lovers but not necessarily obligated to approve of their actions. All that is required is our willingness to explore with the author the issues set before us. The themes we encounter in literature may challenge as well as reassure us.

Determining the theme of a story can be a difficult task because all the story's elements may contribute to its central idea. Indeed, you may discover that finding the theme is more challenging than coming to grips with the author's values as they are revealed in the story. There is no precise formula that can take you to the center of a story's meaning and help you to articulate it. However, several strategies are practical and useful once you have read the story. Apply these pointers during a second or third reading:

1. Pay attention to the title of the story. It often provides a lead to a major symbol (Faulkner's "Barn Burning," p. 418) or to the subject around which the theme develops (Godwin's "A Sorrowful Woman," p. 39).
2. Look for details in the story that have potential for symbolic meanings. Careful consideration of names, places, objects, minor characters, and incidents can lead you to the central meaning — for example, think of the stripper in Ellison's "Battle Royal" (p. 243). Be especially attentive to elements you did not understand on the first reading.
3. Decide whether the protagonist changes or develops some important

insight as a result of the action. Carefully examine any generalizations the protagonist or narrator makes about the events in the story.

4. When you formulate the theme of the story in your own words, write it down in one or two complete sentences that make some point about the subject matter. Revenge may be the subject of a story, but its theme should make a statement about revenge: "Instead of providing satisfaction, revenge defeats the best in one's self" is one possibility.

5. Be certain that your expression of the theme is a generalized statement rather than a specific description of particular people, places, and incidents in the story. Contrast the preceding statement of a theme on revenge with this too-specific one: "In Nathaniel Hawthorne's *The Scarlet Letter,* Roger Chillingworth loses his humanity owing to his single-minded attempts to punish Arthur Dimmesdale for fathering a child with Chillingworth's wife, Hester." Hawthorne's theme is not restricted to a single fictional character named Chillingworth but to anyone whose life is ruined by revenge. Be certain that your statement of theme does not focus on only part of the story. The theme just cited for *The Scarlet Letter,* for example, relegates Hester to the status of a minor character. What it says about Chillingworth is true, but the statement is incomplete as a generalization about the novel.

6. Be wary of using clichés as a way of stating theme. They tend to short-circuit ideas instead of generating them. It may be tempting to resort to something like "Love conquers all" as a statement of the theme of Chekhov's "The Lady with the Pet Dog"; however, even the slightest second thought reveals how much more ambiguous the ending of that story is.

7. Be aware that some stories emphasize theme less than others. Stories that have as their major purpose adventure, humor, mystery, or terror may have little or no theme. In Edgar Allan Poe's "The Pit and the Pendulum," for example, the protagonist is not used to condemn torture; instead, he becomes a sensitive gauge to measure the pain and horror he endures at the hands of his captors.

What is most valuable about articulating the theme of a work is the process by which the theme is determined. Ultimately, the theme is expressed by the story itself and is inseparable from the experience of reading the story. Tim O'Brien's explanation of "How to Tell a True War Story" (p. 543) is probably true of most kinds of stories: "In a true war story, if there's a moral [or theme] at all, it's like the thread that makes the cloth. You can't tease it out. You can't extract the meaning without unraveling the deeper meaning." Describing the theme should not be a way to consume a story, to be done with it. It is a means of clarifying your thinking about what you've read and probably felt intuitively.

Stephen Crane's "The Bride Comes to Yellow Sky," Katherine Mansfield's "Miss Brill," and Dagoberto Gilb's "Love in L.A." are three stories whose respective themes emerge from the authors' skillful use of plot, character, setting, and symbol.

STEPHEN CRANE (1871–1900)

© Bettmann/CORBIS.

Born in Newark, New Jersey, Stephen Crane attended Lafayette College and Syracuse University and then worked as a freelance journalist in New York City. He wrote newspaper pieces, short stories, poems, and novels for his entire, brief adult life. His first book, *Maggie: A Girl of the Streets* (1893), is a story about New York slum life and prostitution. His most famous novel, *The Red Badge of Courage* (1895), gives readers a vivid, convincing re-creation of Civil War battles, even though Crane had never been to war. However, Crane was personally familiar with the American West, where he traveled as a reporter. "The Bride Comes to Yellow Sky" includes some of the ingredients of a typical popular western — a confrontation between a marshal and a drunk who shoots up the town — but the story's theme is less predictable and more serious than the plot seems to suggest.

The Bride Comes to Yellow Sky   1898

I

The great Pullman was whirling onward with such dignity of motion that a glance from the window seemed simply to prove that the plains of Texas were pouring eastward. Vast flats of green grass, dull-hued spaces of mesquit and cactus, little groups of frame houses, woods of light and tender trees, all were sweeping into the east, sweeping over the horizon, a precipice.

A newly married pair had boarded this coach at San Antonio. The man's face was reddened from many days in the wind and sun, and a direct result of his new black clothes was that his brick-colored hands were constantly performing in a most conscious fashion. From time to time he looked down respectfully at his attire. He sat with a hand on each knee, like a man waiting in a barber's shop. The glances he devoted to other passengers were furtive and shy.

The bride was not pretty, nor was she very young. She wore a dress of blue cashmere, with small reservations of velvet here and there, and with steel buttons abounding. She continually twisted her head to regard her puff sleeves, very stiff, straight, and high. They embarrassed her. It was quite apparent that she had cooked, and that she expected to cook, dutifully. The blushes caused by the careless scrutiny of some passengers as she had entered the car were strange to see upon this plain, under-class countenance, which was drawn in placid, almost emotionless lines.

They were evidently very happy. "Ever been in a parlor-car before?" he asked, smiling with delight.

"No," she answered; "I never was. It's fine, ain't it?"   5

"Great! And then after a while we'll go forward to the diner, and get a big lay-out. Finest meal in the world. Charge a dollar."

"Oh, do they?" cried the bride. "Charge a dollar? Why, that's too much — for us — ain't it, Jack?"

"Not this trip, anyhow," he answered bravely. "We're going to go the whole thing."

Later he explained to her about the trains. "You see, it's a thousand miles from one end of Texas to the other; and this train runs right across it, and never stops but four times." He had the pride of an owner. He pointed out to her the dazzling fittings of the coach; and in truth her eyes opened wider as she contemplated the sea-green figured velvet, the shining brass, silver, and glass, the wood that gleamed as darkly brilliant as the surface of a pool of oil. At one end a bronze figure sturdily held a support for a separated chamber, and at convenient places on the ceiling were frescoes in olive and silver.

To the minds of the pair, their surroundings reflected the glory of their 10 marriage that morning in San Antonio; this was the environment of their new estate; and the man's face in particular beamed with an elation that made him appear ridiculous to the negro porter. This individual at times surveyed them from afar with an amused and superior grin. On other occasions he bullied them with skill in ways that did not make it exactly plain to them that they were being bullied. He subtly used all the manners of the most unconquerable kind of snobbery. He oppressed them; but of this oppression they had small knowledge, and they speedily forgot that infrequently a number of travelers covered them with stares of derisive enjoyment. Historically there was supposed to be something infinitely humorous in their situation.

"We are due in Yellow Sky at 3:42," he said, looking tenderly into her eyes.

"Oh, are we?" she said, as if she had not been aware of it. To evince surprise at her husband's statement was part of her wifely amiability. She took from a pocket a little silver watch; and as she held it before her, and stared at it with a frown of attention, the new husband's face shone.

"I bought it in San Anton' from a friend of mine," he told her gleefully.

"It's seventeen minutes past twelve," she said, looking up at him with a kind of shy and clumsy coquetry. A passenger, noting this play, grew excessively sardonic, and winked at himself in one of the numerous mirrors.

At last they went to the dining-car. Two rows of negro waiters, in glowing 15 white suits, surveyed their entrance with the interest, and also the equanimity, of men who had been forewarned. The pair fell to the lot of a waiter who happened to feel pleasure in steering them through their meal. He viewed them with the manner of a fatherly pilot, his countenance radiant with benevolence. The patronage, entwined with the ordinary deference, was not plain to them. And yet, as they returned to their coach, they showed in their faces a sense of escape.

To the left, miles down a long purple slope, was a little ribbon of mist where moved the keening Rio Grande. The train was approaching it at an angle, and the apex was Yellow Sky. Presently it was apparent that, as the distance from Yellow Sky grew shorter, the husband became commensurately restless. His brick-red hands were more insistent in their prominence. Occasionally he was even rather absent-minded and far-away when the bride leaned forward and addressed him.

As a matter of truth, Jack Potter was beginning to find the shadow of a deed weigh upon him like a leaden slab. He, the town marshal of Yellow Sky, a man known, liked, and feared in his corner, a prominent person, had gone to

San Antonio to meet a girl he believed he loved, and there, after the usual prayers, had actually induced her to marry him, without consulting Yellow Sky for any part of the transaction. He was now bringing his bride before an innocent and unsuspecting community.

Of course people in Yellow Sky married as it pleased them in accordance with a general custom; but such was Potter's thought of his duty to his friends, or of their idea of his duty, or of an unspoken form which does not control men in these matters, that he felt he was heinous. He had committed an extraordinary crime. Face to face with this girl in San Antonio, and spurred by his sharp impulse, he had gone headlong over all the social hedges. At San Antonio he was like a man hidden in the dark. A knife to sever any friendly duty, any form, was easy to his hand in that remote city. But the hour of Yellow Sky — the hour of daylight — was approaching.

He knew full well that his marriage was an important thing to his town. It could only be exceeded by the burning of the new hotel. His friends could not forgive him. Frequently he had reflected on the advisability of telling them by telegraph, but a new cowardice had been upon him. He feared to do it. And now the train was hurrying him toward a scene of amazement, glee, and reproach. He glanced out of the window at the line of haze swinging slowly in toward the train.

Yellow Sky had a kind of brass band, which played painfully, to the delight   20 of the populace. He laughed without heart as he thought of it. If the citizens could dream of his prospective arrival with his bride, they would parade the band at the station and escort them, amid cheers and laughing congratulations, to his adobe home.

He resolved that he would use all the devices of speed and plainscraft in making the journey from the station to his house. Once within that safe citadel, he could issue some sort of vocal bulletin, and then not go among the citizens until they had time to wear off a little of their enthusiasm.

The bride looked anxiously at him. "What's worrying you, Jack?"

He laughed again. "I'm not worrying, girl; I'm only thinking of Yellow Sky."

She flushed in comprehension.

A sense of mutual guilt invaded their minds and developed a finer ten   25 derness. They looked at each other with eyes softly aglow. But Potter often laughed the same nervous laugh; the flush upon the bride's face seemed quite permanent.

The traitor to the feelings of Yellow Sky narrowly watched the speeding landscape. "We're nearly there," he said.

Presently the porter came and announced the proximity of Potter's home. He held a brush in his hand, and, with all his airy superiority gone, he brushed Potter's new clothes as the latter slowly turned this way and that way. Potter fumbled out a coin and gave it to the porter, as he had seen others do. It was a heavy and muscle-bound business, as that of a man shoeing his first horse.

The porter took their bag, and as the train began to slow they moved forward to the hooded platform of the car. Presently the two engines and their long string of coaches rushed into the station of Yellow Sky.

"They have to take water here," said Potter, from a constricted throat and in mournful cadence, as one announcing death. Before the train stopped his eye had swept the length of the platform, and he was glad and astonished to see there was none upon it but the station-agent, who, with a slightly hurried and anxious air, was walking toward the water-tanks. When the train had halted, the porter alighted first, and placed in position a little temporary step. "Come on, girl," said Potter, hoarsely. As he helped her down they each laughed on a false note. He took the bag from the negro, and bade his wife cling to his arm. As they slunk rapidly away, his hang-dog glance perceived that they were unloading the two trunks, and also that the station-agent, far ahead near the baggage-car, had turned and was running toward him, making gestures. He laughed, and groaned as he laughed, when he noted the first effect of his marital bliss upon Yellow Sky. He gripped his wife's arm firmly to his side, and they fled. Behind them the porter stood, chuckling fatuously.

II

The California express on the Southern Railway was due at Yellow Sky in twenty-one minutes. There were six men at the bar of the Weary Gentleman saloon. One was a drummer° who talked a great deal and rapidly; three were Texans who did not care to talk at that time; and two were Mexican sheep-herders, who did not talk as a general practice in the Weary Gentleman saloon. The barkeeper's dog lay on the board walk that crossed in front of the door. His head was on his paws, and he glanced drowsily here and there with the constant vigilance of a dog that is kicked on occasion. Across the sandy street were some vivid green grass-plots, so wonderful in appearance, amid the sands that burned near them in a blazing sun, that they caused a doubt in the mind. They exactly resembled the grass mats used to represent lawns on the stage. At the cooler end of the railway station, a man without a coat sat in a tilted chair and smoked his pipe. The fresh-cut bank of the Rio Grande circled near the town, and there could be seen beyond it a great plum-colored plain of mesquit.

Save for the busy drummer and his companions in the saloon, Yellow Sky was dozing. The new-comer leaned gracefully upon the bar, and recited many tales with the confidence of a bard who has come upon a new field.

"—and at the moment that the old man fell downstairs with the bureau in his arms, the old woman was coming up with two scuttles of coal, and of course—"

The drummer's tale was interrupted by a young man who suddenly appeared in the open door. He cried: "Scratchy Wilson's drunk, and has turned loose with both hands." The two Mexicans at once set down their glasses and faded out of the rear entrance of the saloon.

The drummer, innocent and jocular, answered: "All right, old man. S'pose he has? Come in and have a drink, anyhow."

But the information had made such an obvious cleft in every skull in the room that the drummer was obliged to see its importance. All had become instantly solemn. "Say," said he, mystified, "what is this?" His three companions made the introductory gesture of eloquent speech; but the young man at the door forestalled them.

"It means, my friend," he answered, as he came into the saloon, "that for the next two hours this town won't be a health resort."

The barkeeper went to the door, and locked and barred it; reaching out of the window, he pulled in heavy wooden shutters, and barred them. Immediately

---

drummer: Traveling salesman.

a solemn, chapel-like gloom was upon the place. The drummer was looking from one to another.

"But, say," he cried, "what is this, anyhow? You don't mean there is going to be a gun-fight?"

"Don't know whether there'll be a fight or not," answered one man, 40 grimly; "but there'll be some shootin' — some good shootin'."

The young man who had warned them waved his hand. "Oh, there'll be a fight fast enough, if any one wants it. Anybody can get a fight out there in the street. There's a fight just waiting."

The drummer seemed to be swayed between the interest of a foreigner and a perception of personal danger.

"What did you say his name was?" he asked.

"Scratchy Wilson," they answered in chorus.

"And will he kill anybody? What are you going to do? Does this happen 45 often? Does he rampage around like this once a week or so? Can he break in that door?"

"No; he can't break down that door," replied the barkeeper. "He's tried it three times. But when he comes you'd better lay down on the floor, stranger. He's dead sure to shoot at it, and a bullet may come through."

Thereafter the drummer kept a strict eye upon the door. The time had not yet called for him to hug the floor, but, as a minor precaution, he sidled near the wall. "Will he kill anybody?" he said again.

The men laughed low and scornfully at the question.

"He's out to shoot, and he's out for trouble. Don't see any good in experimentin' with him."

"But what do you do in a case like this? What do you do?" 50

A man responded: "Why, he and Jack Potter — "

"But," in chorus the other men interrupted, "Jack Potter's in San Anton'."

"Well, who is he? What's he got to do with it?"

"Oh, he's the town marshal. He goes out and fights Scratchy when he gets on one of these tears."

"Wow!" said the drummer, mopping his brow. "Nice job he's got." 55

The voices had toned away to mere whisperings. The drummer wished to ask further questions, which were born of an increasing anxiety and bewilderment; but when he attempted them, the men merely looked at him in irritation and motioned him to remain silent. A tense waiting hush was upon them. In the deep shadows of the room their eyes shone as they listened for sounds from the street. One man made three gestures at the barkeeper; and the latter, moving like a ghost, handed him a glass and a bottle. The man poured a full glass of whisky, and set down the bottle noiselessly. He gulped the whisky in a swallow, and turned again toward the door in immovable silence. The drummer saw that the barkeeper, without a sound, had taken a Winchester from beneath the bar. Later he saw this individual beckoning to him, so he tiptoed across the room.

"You better come with me back of the bar."

"No thanks," said the drummer, perspiring; "I'd rather be where I can make a break for the back door."

Whereupon the man of bottles made a kindly but peremptory gesture. The drummer obeyed it, and, finding himself seated on a box with his head below the level of the bar, balm was laid upon his soul at sight of various zinc and copper fittings that bore a resemblance to armor-plate. The barkeeper took a seat comfortably upon an adjacent box.

"You see," he whispered, "this here Scratchy Wilson is a wonder with a gun — a perfect wonder; and when he goes on the war-trail, we hunt our holes — naturally. He's about the last one of the old gang that used to hang out along the river here. He's a terror when he's drunk. When he's sober he's all right — kind of simple — wouldn't hurt a fly — nicest fellow in town. But when he's drunk — whoo!" 60

There were periods of stillness. "I wish Jack Potter was back from San Anton'," said the barkeeper. "He shot Wilson up once — in the leg — and he would sail in and pull out the kinks in this thing."

Presently they heard from a distance the sound of a shot, followed by three wild yowls. It instantly removed a bond from the men in the darkened saloon. There was a shuffling of feet. They looked at each other. "Here he comes," they said.

III

A man in a maroon-colored flannel shirt, which had been purchased for purposes of decoration, and made principally by some Jewish women on the East Side of New York, rounded a corner and walked into the middle of the main street of Yellow Sky. In either hand the man held a long, heavy, blue-black revolver. Often he yelled, and these cries rang through a semblance of a deserted village, shrilly flying over the roofs in a volume that seemed to have no relation to the ordinary vocal strength of a man. It was as if the surrounding stillness formed the arch of a tomb over him. These cries of ferocious challenge rang against walls of silence. And his boots had red tops with gilded imprints, of the kind beloved in winter by little sledding boys on the hillsides of New England.

The man's face flamed in a rage begot of whisky. His eyes, rolling, and yet keen for ambush, hunted the still doorways and windows. He walked with the creeping movement of the midnight cat. As it occurred to him, he roared menacing information. The long revolvers in his hands were as easy as straws; they were removed with an electric swiftness. The little fingers of each hand played sometimes in a musician's way. Plain from the low collar of the shirt, the cords of his neck straightened and sank, straightened and sank, as passion moved him. The only sounds were his terrible invitations. The calm adobes preserved their demeanor at the passing of this small thing in the middle of the street.

There was no offer of fight — no offer of fight. The man called to the sky. 65 There were no attractions. He bellowed and fumed and swayed his revolvers here and everywhere.

The dog of the barkeeper of the Weary Gentleman saloon had not appreciated the advance of events. He yet lay dozing in front of his master's door. At sight of the dog, the man paused and raised his revolver humorously. At sight of the man, the dog sprang up and walked diagonally away, with a sullen head, and growling. The man yelled, and the dog broke into a gallop. As it was about to enter the alley, there was a loud noise, a whistling, and something spat the ground directly before it. The dog screamed, and, wheeling in terror, galloped headlong in a new direction. Again there was a noise, a whistling, and sand was kicked viciously before it. Fear-stricken, the dog turned and flurried like an animal in a pen. The man stood laughing, his weapons at his hips.

Ultimately the man was attracted by the closed door of the Weary Gentleman saloon. He went to it and, hammering with a revolver, demanded drink.

The door remaining imperturbable, he picked a bit of paper from the walk, and nailed it to the framework with a knife. He then turned his back contemptuously upon this popular resort and, walking to the opposite side of the street and spinning there on his heel quickly and lithely, fired at the bit of paper. He missed it by a half inch. He swore at himself, and went away. Later he comfortably fusilladed the windows of his most intimate friend. The man was playing with this town; it was a toy for him.

But still there was no offer of fight. The name of Jack Potter, his ancient antagonist, entered his mind, and he concluded that it would be a glad thing if he should go to Potter's house, and by bombardment induce him to come out and fight. He moved in the direction of his desire, chanting Apache scalp-music.

When he arrived at it, Potter's house presented the same still front as had   70 the other adobes. Taking up a strategic position, the man howled a challenge. But this house regarded him as might a great stone god. It gave no sign. After a decent wait, the man howled further challenges, mingling with them wonderful epithets.

Presently there came the spectacle of a man churning himself into deepest rage over the immobility of a house. He fumed at it as the winter wind attacks a prairie cabin in the North. To the distance there should have gone the sound of a tumult like the fighting of two hundred Mexicans. As necessity bade him, he paused for breath or to reload his revolvers.

IV

Potter and his bride walked sheepishly and with speed. Sometimes they laughed together shamefacedly and low.

"Next corner, dear," he said finally.

They put forth the efforts of a pair walking bowed against a strong wind. Potter was about to raise a finger to point the first appearance of the new home when, as they circled the corner, they came face to face with a man in a maroon-colored shirt, who was feverishly pushing cartridges into a large revolver. Upon the instant the man dropped his revolver to the ground and, like lightning, whipped another from its holster. The second weapon was aimed at the bridegroom's chest.

There was a silence. Potter's mouth seemed to be merely a grave for his   75 tongue. He exhibited an instinct to at once loosen his arm from the woman's grip, and he dropped the bag to the sand. As for the bride, her face had gone as yellow as old cloth. She was a slave to hideous rites, gazing at the apparitional snake.

The two men faced each other at a distance of three paces. He of the revolver smiled with a new and quiet ferocity.

"Tried to sneak up on me," he said. "Tried to sneak up on me!" His eyes grew more baleful. As Potter made a slight movement, the man thrust his revolver venomously forward. "No, don't you do it, Jack Potter. Don't you move a finger toward a gun just yet. Don't you move an eyelash. The time has come for me to settle with you and I'm goin' to do it my own way, and loaf along with no interferin'. So if you don't want a gun bent on you, just mind what I tell you."

Potter looked at his enemy. "I ain't got a gun on me, Scratchy," he said. "Honest, I ain't." He was stiffening and steadying, but yet somewhere at the back of his mind a vision of the Pullman floated: the sea-green figured velvet, the shining brass, silver, and glass, the wood that gleamed as darkly brilliant as the surface of a pool of oil—all the glory of marriage, the environment of the new estate. "You know I fight when it comes to fighting, Scratchy Wilson; but I ain't got a gun on me. You'll have to do all the shootin' yourself."

His enemy's face went livid. He stepped forward, and lashed his weapon to and fro before Potter's chest. "Don't you tell me you ain't got no gun on you, you whelp. Don't tell me no lie like that. There ain't a man in Texas ever seen you without no gun. Don't take me for no kid." His eyes blazed with light, and his throat worked like a pump.

"I ain't takin' you for no kid," answered Potter. His heels had not moved 80 an inch backward. "I'm takin' you for a damn fool. I tell you I ain't got a gun, and I ain't. If you're goin' to shoot me up, you better begin now; you'll never get a chance like this again."

So much enforced reasoning had told on Wilson's rage; he was calmer. "If you ain't got a gun, why ain't you got a gun?" he sneered. "Been to Sunday-school?"

"I ain't got a gun because I've just come from San Anton' with my wife. I'm married," said Potter. "And if I'd thought there was going to be any galoots like you prowling around when I brought my wife home, I'd had a gun, and don't you forget it."

"Married!" said Scratchy, not at all comprehending.

"Yes, married. I'm married," said Potter, distinctly.

"Married?" said Scratchy. Seemingly for the first time, he saw the droop- 85 ing, drowning woman at the other man's side. "No!" he said. He was like a creature allowed a glimpse of another world. He moved a pace backward, and his arm, with the revolver, dropped to his side. "Is this the lady?" he asked.

"Yes; this is the lady," answered Potter.

There was another period of silence.

"Well," said Wilson at last, slowly, "I s'pose it's all off now."

"It's all off if you say so, Scratchy. You know I didn't make the trouble." Potter lifted his valise.

"Well, I 'low it's off, Jack," said Wilson. He was looking at the ground. 90 "Married!" He was not a student of chivalry; it was merely that in the presence of this foreign condition he was a simple child of the earlier plains. He picked up his starboard revolver, and, placing both weapons in their holsters, he went away. His feet made funnel-shaped tracks in the heavy sand.

CONSIDERATIONS FOR CRITICAL THINKING AND WRITING

1. **FIRST RESPONSE.** Think of a western you've read or seen: any of Larry McMurtry's books would work, such as *Lonesome Dove* or *Evening Star.* Compare and contrast the setting, characters, action, and theme in Crane's story with your western.

2. What is the nature of the conflict Marshal Potter feels on the train in Part I? Why does he feel that he committed a "crime" in bringing home a bride to Yellow Sky?

3. What is the function of the "drummer," the traveling salesman, in Part II?

4. How do Mrs. Potter and Scratchy Wilson serve as foils for each other? What does each represent in the story?

5. What is the significance of the setting?

6. How does Crane create suspense about what will happen when Marshal Potter meets Scratchy Wilson? Is suspense the major point of the story?

7. Is Scratchy Wilson too drunk, comical, and ineffective to be a sympathetic character? What is the meaning of his conceding that "I s'pose it's all off now" at the end of Part IV? Is he a dynamic or a static character?

8. What details seem to support the story's theme? Consider, for example, the descriptions of the bride's clothes and Scratchy Wilson's shirt and boots.

9. Explain why the heroes in western stories are rarely married and why Crane's use of marriage is central to his theme.

10. **CRITICAL STRATEGIES.** Read the section on gender strategies (pp. 1548–49) in Chapter 46, "Critical Strategies for Reading." Explore the heterosexual and potentially homosexual issues that a gender critic might discover in the story.

CONNECTIONS TO OTHER SELECTIONS

1. Although Scratchy Wilson and the title character in Katherine Mansfield's "Miss Brill" (below) are radically different kinds of people, they share a painful recognition at the end of their stories. What does each of them learn? Discuss whether you think what each of them learns is of equal importance in changing his or her life.

2. Write an essay comparing Crane's use of suspense with William Faulkner's in "A Rose for Emily" (p. 90).

KATHERINE MANSFIELD (1888–1923)

Born in New Zealand, Katherine Mansfield moved to London when she was a young woman and began writing short stories. Her first collection, *In a German Pension,* appeared in 1911. Subsequent publications, which include *Bliss and Other Stories* (1920) and *The Garden Party* (1922), secured her reputation as an important writer. The full range of her short stories is available in *The Collected Short Stories of Katherine Mansfield* (1945). Mansfield tends to focus her stories on intelligent, sensitive protagonists who undergo subtle but important changes in their lives. In "Miss Brill," an aging Englishwoman

© Bettmann/CORBIS.

spends the afternoon in a park located in an unnamed French vacation town watching the activities of the people around her. Through those observations, Mansfield characterizes Miss Brill and permits us to see her experience a moment that changes her view of the world as well as of herself.

Miss Brill   *1922*

Although it was so brilliantly fine — the blue sky powdered with gold and great spots of light like white wine splashed over the Jardins Publiques — Miss Brill was glad that she had decided on her fur. The air was motionless, but when you opened your mouth there was just a faint chill, like a chill from a glass of iced water before you sip, and now and again a leaf came drifting — from nowhere, from the sky. Miss Brill put up her hand and touched her fur. Dear little thing! It was nice to feel it again. She had taken it out of its box that afternoon, shaken out the moth-powder, given it a good brush, and rubbed the life back into the dim little eyes. "What has been happening to me?" said the sad little eyes. Oh, how sweet it was to see them snap at her again from the red eiderdown! . . . But the nose, which was of some black composition, wasn't at all firm. It must have had a knock, somehow. Never mind — a little dab of black sealing-wax when the time came — when it was absolutely necessary. . . . Little rogue! Yes, she really felt like that about it. Little rogue biting its tail just by her left ear. She could have taken it off and laid it on her lap and stroked it. She felt a tingling in her hands and arms, but that came from walking, she supposed. And when she breathed, something light and sad — no, not sad, exactly — something gentle seemed to move in her bosom.

There were a number of people out this afternoon, far more than last Sunday. And the band sounded louder and gayer. That was because the Season had begun. For although the band played all the year round on Sundays, out of season it was never the same. It was like someone playing with only the family to listen; it didn't care how it played if there weren't any strangers present. Wasn't the conductor wearing a new coat, too? She was sure it was new. He scraped with his foot and flapped his arms like a rooster about to crow, and the bandsmen sitting in the green rotunda blew out their cheeks and glared at the music. Now there came a little "flutey" bit — very pretty! — a little chain of bright drops. She was sure it would be repeated. It was; she lifted her head and smiled.

Only two people shared her "special" seat: a fine old man in a velvet coat, his hands clasped over a huge carved walking-stick, and a big old woman, sitting upright, with a roll of knitting on her embroidered apron. They did not speak. This was disappointing, for Miss Brill always looked forward to the conversation. She had become really quite expert, she thought, at listening as though she didn't listen, at sitting in other people's lives just for a minute while they talked around her.

She glanced, sideways, at the old couple. Perhaps they would go soon. Last Sunday, too, hadn't been as interesting as usual. An Englishman and his wife, he wearing a dreadful Panama hat and she button boots. And she'd gone on the whole time about how she ought to wear spectacles; she knew she needed them; but that it was no good getting any; they'd be sure to break and they'd never keep on. And he'd been so patient. He'd suggested everything — gold rims, the kind that curved round your ears, little pads inside the bridge. No, nothing would please her. "They'll always be sliding down my nose!" Miss Brill had wanted to shake her.

The old people sat on the bench, still as statues. Never mind, there was al-   5 ways the crowd to watch. To and fro, in front of the flower-beds and the band rotunda, the couples and groups paraded, stopped to talk, to greet, to buy a handful of flowers from the old beggar who had his tray fixed to the railings. Little children ran among them, swooping and laughing; little boys with big white silk bows under their chins, little girls, little French dolls, dressed up in velvet and lace. And sometimes a tiny staggerer came suddenly rocking into the open from under the trees, stopped, stared, as suddenly sat down "flop," until its small high-stepping mother, like a young hen, rushed scolding to its rescue. Other people sat on the benches and green chairs, but they were nearly always the same, Sunday after Sunday, and — Miss Brill had often noticed — there was something funny about nearly all of them. They were odd, silent, nearly all old, and from the way they stared they looked as though they'd just come from dark little rooms or even — even cupboards!

Behind the rotunda the slender trees with yellow leaves down drooping, and through them just a line of sea, and beyond the blue sky with gold-veined clouds.

Tum-tum-tum tiddle-um! tiddle-um! tum tiddley-um tum ta! blew the band.

Two young girls in red came by and two young soldiers in blue met them, and they laughed and paired and went off arm-in-arm. Two peasant women with funny straw hats passed, gravely, leading beautiful smoke-colored don-keys. A cold, pale nun hurried by. A beautiful woman came along and dropped her bunch of violets, and a little boy ran after to hand them to her, and she took them and threw them away as if they'd been poisoned. Dear me! Miss Brill didn't know whether to admire that or not! And now an ermine toque and a gentleman in grey met just in front of her. He was tall, stiff, dignified, and she was wearing the ermine toque she'd bought when her hair was yellow. Now everything, her hair, her face, even her eyes, was the same color as the shabby ermine, and her hand, in its cleaned glove, lifted to dab her lips, was a tiny yel-lowish paw. Oh, she was so pleased to see him — delighted! She rather thought they were going to meet that afternoon. She described where she'd been — every-where, here, there, along by the sea. The day was so charming — didn't he agree? And wouldn't he, perhaps? . . . But he shook his head, lighted a cigarette, slowly breathed a great deep puff into her face, and, even while she was still talking and laughing, flicked the match away and walked on. The ermine toque was alone; she smiled more brightly than ever. But even the band seemed to know what she was feeling and played more softly, played tenderly, and the drum beat, "The Brute! The Brute!" over and over. What would she do? What was going to happen now? But as Miss Brill wondered, the ermine toque turned, raised her hand as though she'd seen some one else, much nicer, just over there, and pat-tered away. And the band changed again and played more quickly, more gaily than ever, and the old couple on Miss Brill's seat got up and marched away, and such a funny old man with long whiskers hobbled along in time to the music and was nearly knocked over by four girls walking abreast.

Oh, how fascinating it was! How she enjoyed it! How she loved sitting here, watching it all! It was like a play. It was exactly like a play. Who could believe the sky at the back wasn't painted? But it wasn't till a little brown dog trotted on solemn and then slowly trotted off, like a little "theatre" dog, a little dog that had been drugged, that Miss Brill discovered what it was that made it so exciting. They were all on the stage. They weren't only the audience, not only looking on; they were acting. Even she had a part and came every Sunday. No doubt somebody would have noticed if she hadn't been there; she was part of the performance after all. How strange she'd never thought of it like that before! And yet it explained why she made such a point of starting from home at just the same time each week — so as not to be late for the performance — and it also explained why she had quite a queer, shy feeling at telling her English pupils how she spent her Sunday afternoons. No wonder! Miss Brill nearly laughed out loud. She was on the stage. She thought of the old invalid gentleman to whom she read the newspaper four afternoons a week while he slept in the garden. She had got quite used to the frail head on the cotton pillow, the hollowed eyes, the open mouth, and the high pinched nose. If he'd been dead she mightn't have noticed for weeks; she wouldn't have minded. But suddenly he knew he was having the paper read to him by an actress! "An actress!" The old head lifted; two points of light quivered in the old eyes. "An actress — are ye?" And Miss Brill smoothed the newspaper as though it were the manuscript of her part and said gently: "Yes, I have been an actress for a long time."

The band had been having a rest. Now they started again. And what they 10 played was warm, sunny, yet there was just a faint chill — a something, what was it? — not sadness — no, not sadness — a something that made you want to sing. The tune lifted, lifted, the light shone; and it seemed to Miss Brill that in another moment all of them, all the whole company, would begin singing. The young ones, the laughing ones who were moving together, they would begin, and the men's voices, very resolute and brave, would join them. And then she too, she too, and the others on the benches — they would come in with a kind of accompaniment — something low, that scarcely rose or fell, something so beautiful — moving. . . . And Miss Brill's eyes filled with tears and she looked smiling at all the other members of the company. Yes, we understand, we understand, she thought — though what they understood she didn't know.

Just at that moment a boy and a girl came and sat down where the old couple had been. They were beautifully dressed; they were in love. The hero and heroine, of course, just arrived from his father's yacht. And still soundlessly singing, still with that trembling smile, Miss Brill prepared to listen.

"No, not now," said the girl. "Not here, I can't."

"But why? Because of that stupid old thing at the end there?" asked the boy. "Why does she come here at all — who wants her? Why doesn't she keep her silly old mug at home?"

"It's her fu-fur which is so funny," giggled the girl. "It's exactly like a fried whiting."

"Ah, be off with you!" said the boy in an angry whisper. Then: "Tell me, ma 15 petite chère ——"

"No, not here," said the girl. "Not *yet.*"

On her way home she usually bought a slice of honey-cake at the baker's. It was her Sunday treat. Sometimes there was an almond in her slice, sometimes not. It made a great difference. If there was an almond it was like carrying home a tiny present — a surprise — something that might very well not have been there.

She hurried on the almond Sundays and struck the match for the kettle in quite a dashing way.

But today she passed the baker's by, climbed the stairs, went into the little dark room — her room like a cupboard — and sat down on the red eiderdown. She sat there for a long time. The box that the fur came out of was on the bed. She unclasped the necklet quickly; quickly, without looking, laid it inside. But when she put the lid on she thought she heard something crying.

CONSIDERATIONS FOR CRITICAL THINKING AND WRITING

1. **FIRST RESPONSE.** There is almost no physical description of Miss Brill in the story. What do you think she looks like? Develop a detailed description that would be consistent with her behavior.

2. How does the calculated omission of Miss Brill's first name contribute to her characterization?

3. What details make Miss Brill more than a stock characterization of a frail old lady?

4. What do Miss Brill's observations about the people she encounters reveal about her?

5. What is the conflict in the story? Who or what is the antagonist?

6. Locate the climax of the story. How is it resolved?

7. What is the purpose of the fur piece? What is the source of the crying in the final sentence of the story?

8. Is Miss Brill a static or a dynamic character?

9. Describe Miss Brill's sense of herself at the end of the story.

10. Discuss the function of the minor characters mentioned in the story. Analyze how Katherine Mansfield used them to reveal Miss Brill's character.

CONNECTIONS TO OTHER SELECTIONS

1. Compare Miss Brill's recognition with that of the narrator in Fay Weldon's "IND AFF, or Out of Love in Sarajevo" (p. 172).

2. Write an essay comparing the themes in "Miss Brill" and Lee Smith's "The Happy Memories Club" (p. 481).

DAGOBERTO GILB (B. 1950)

Born in Los Angeles, Dagoberto Gilb is a journeyman carpenter who considers both Los Angeles and El Paso to be home. He has been a visiting writer at the University of Texas and the University of Arizona. Among his literary prizes are the James D. Phelan Award in literature, the Whiting Award, and a Guggenheim Foundation fellowship. He has also won a National Endowment for the Arts Creative Writing Fellowship.

© Bret Brookshire.

Gilb's fiction has been published in a variety of journals including *The Threepenny Review, ZYZZYVA,* and *American Short Fiction.* His stories — collected in *The Magic of Blood* (1993), from which "Love in L.A." is taken, and *Woodcuts of Women* (2001) — often reflect his experiences as a worker moving between Los Angeles and El Paso. In 1994 he published his first novel, *The Last Known Residence of Mickey Acuña,* and in 2003 he published a collection of essays, *Gritos.*

Love in L.A.   *1993*

Jake slouched in a clot of near motionless traffic, in the peculiar gray of concrete, smog, and early morning beneath the overpass of the Hollywood Freeway on Alvarado Street. He didn't really mind because he knew how much worse it could be trying to make a left onto the onramp. He certainly didn't do that every day of his life, and he'd assure anyone who'd ask that he never would either. A steady occupation had its advantages and he couldn't deny thinking about that too. He needed an FM radio in something better than this '58 Buick he drove. It would have crushed velvet interior with electric controls for the L.A. summer, a nice warm heater and defroster for the winter drives at the beach, a cruise control for those longer trips, mellow speakers front and rear of course, windows that hum closed, snuffing out that nasty exterior noise of freeways. The fact was that he'd probably have to change his whole style. Exotic colognes, plush, dark nightclubs, maitais and daiquiris, necklaced ladies in satin gowns, misty and sexy like in a tequila ad. Jake could imagine lots of possibilities when he let himself, but none that ended up with him pressed onto a stalled freeway.

Jake was thinking about this freedom of his so much that when he glimpsed its green light he just went ahead and stared bye bye to the steadily employed. When he turned his head the same direction his windshield faced, it was maybe one second too late. He pounced the brake pedal and steered the front wheels away from the tiny brakelights but the smack was unavoidable. Just one second sooner and it would only have been close. One second more and he'd be crawling up the Toyota's trunk. As it was, it seemed like only a harmless smack, much less solid than the one against his back bumper.

Jake considered driving past the Toyota but was afraid the traffic ahead would make it too difficult. As he pulled up against the curb a few carlengths ahead, it occurred to him that the traffic might have helped him get away too. He slammed the car door twice to make sure it was closed fully and to give himself another second more, then toured front and rear of his Buick for damage on or near the bumpers. Not an impressionable scratch even in the chrome. He perked up. Though the car's beauty was secondary to its ability to start and move, the body and paint were clean except for a few minor dings. This stood out as one of his few clearcut accomplishments over the years.

Before he spoke to the driver of the Toyota, whose looks he could see might present him with an added complication, he signaled to the driver of the car that hit him, still in his car and stopped behind the Toyota, and waved his hands and shook his head to let the man know there was no problem as far as he was concerned. The driver waved back and started his engine.

"It didn't even scratch my paint," Jake told her in that way of his. "So how you doin? Any damage to the car? I'm kinda hoping so, just so it takes a little more time and we can talk some. Or else you can give me your phone number now and I won't have to lay my regular b.s. on you to get it later."

He took her smile as a good sign and relaxed. He inhaled her scent like it was clean air and straightened out his less than new but not unhip clothes.

"You've got Florida plates. You look like you must be Cuban."

"My parents are from Venezuela."

"My name's Jake." He held out his hand.

"Mariana."

They shook hands like she'd never done it before in her life.

"I really am sorry about hitting you like that." He sounded genuine. He fondled the wide dimple near the cracked taillight. "It's amazing how easy it is to put a dent in these new cars. They're so soft they might replace waterbeds soon." Jake was confused about how to proceed with this. So much seemed so unlikely, but there was always possibility. "So maybe we should go out to breakfast somewhere and talk it over."

"I don't eat breakfast."

"Some coffee then."

"Thanks, but I really can't."

"You're not married, are you? Not that that would matter that much to me. I'm an openminded kinda guy."

She was smiling. "I have to get to work."

"That sounds boring."

"I better get your driver's license," she said.

Jake nodded, disappointed. "One little problem," he said. "I didn't bring it. I just forgot it this morning. I'm a musician," he exaggerated greatly, "and, well, I dunno, I left my wallet in the pants I was wearing last night. If you have some paper and a pen I'll give you my address and all that."

He followed her to the glove compartment side of her car.

"What if we don't report it to the insurance companies? I'll just get it fixed for you."

"I don't think my dad would let me do that."

"Your dad? It's not your car?"

"He bought it for me. And I live at home."

"Right." She was slipping away from him. He went back around to the back of her new Toyota and looked over the damage again. There was the trunk lid, the bumper, a rear panel, a taillight.

"You do have insurance?" she asked, suspicious, as she came around the back of the car.

"Oh yeah," he lied.

"I guess you better write the name of that down too."

He made up a last name and address and wrote down the name of an insurance company an old girlfriend once belonged to. He considered giving a real phone number but went against that idea and made one up.

"I act too," he lied to enhance the effect more. "Been in a couple of movies."

She smiled like a fan.

"So how about your phone number?" He was rebounding maturely.

She gave it to him.

"Mariana, you are beautiful," he said in his most sincere voice.   35

"Call me," she said timidly.

Jake beamed. "We'll see you, Mariana," he said holding out his hand. Her hand felt so warm and soft he felt like he'd been kissed.

Back in his car he took a moment or two to feel both proud and sad about his performance. Then he watched the rear view mirror as Mariana pulled up behind him. She was writing down the license plate numbers on his Buick, ones that he'd taken off a junk because the ones that belonged to his had expired so long ago. He turned the ignition key and revved the big engine and clicked into drive. His sense of freedom swelled as he drove into the now moving street traffic, though he couldn't stop the thought about that FM stereo radio and crushed velvet interior and the new car smell that would even make it better.

CONSIDERATIONS FOR CRITICAL THINKING AND WRITING

1. **FIRST RESPONSE.** Is "Love in L.A." a love story? Try to argue that it is. (If the story ended with paragraph 37, how would your interpretation of the story be affected?)

2. What is the effect of setting the story's action in a Los Angeles traffic jam on the Hollywood Freeway?

3. Characterize Jake. What do his thoughts in the first two paragraphs reveal about him? About how old do you think he is?

4. There is little physical description of Jake in the story, but given what you learn about him, how would you describe his physical features and the way he dresses?

5. What causes Jake to smack into the back of Mariana's car? What is revealed about his character by the manner in which he has the accident?

6. Describe how Jake responds to Mariana when he introduces himself to her, especially in paragraph 12. What does his behavior reveal about his character?

7. How does Mariana respond to Jake? Explain whether you think she is a round or flat character.

8. Explain how their respective cars characterize Jake and Mariana.

9. What does the final paragraph reveal about each character?

10. In a sentence or two write down what you think the story's theme is. How does the title contribute to that theme?

CONNECTIONS TO OTHER SELECTIONS

1. Compare and contrast the themes in "Love in L.A." and Fay Weldon's "IND AFF, or Out of Love in Sarajevo" (p. 172).

2. Consider Jake's relationship with his car and the narrator's relationship with his car in E. E. Cummings's poem "she being Brand" (p. 627). In an essay explore how the cars reveal each character's aspirations.

A SAMPLE STUDENT RESPONSE

Randall Patterson

Professor Kahane

English 102

September 28, 2008

The Theme of Deception in Dagoberto Gilb's "Love in L.A."

Jake, the main character of Dagoberto Gilb's "Love in L.A.," sits in traffic and dreams of a better life. There are things he desires: a better car with an FM radio, heater and defroster, cruise control, "mellow speakers," and "windows that hum closed" (279). However, Jake is unwilling to earn these things. Instead, he is irresponsible; he lies and cheats to get (or try to get) what he wants. And while Jake appears to get away with his irresponsible behavior, there are consequences.

Deception is a clear theme throughout the story. Jake pities the people in traffic who have to "make a left onto the onramp" to get to their jobs, and vows "he certainly didn't do that every day of his life, and . . . he never would" (279). So he instead shirks his responsibility. After getting in an accident with Mariana, we learn that he has no car insurance, no driver's license, and that his plates are stolen. Jake will not be held responsible for the accident, but he is ultimately trapped in a world of dishonesty, a world he will never find fulfilling. He spends all his time dreaming of something better: "he couldn't stop the thought about that FM stereo radio and crushed velvet interior and the new car smell that would even make it better" (281). It seems that although Jake does not change dramatically in this story, he does become more self-aware. He feels "both proud and sad about his performance" (281) and perhaps is beginning to realize he will never find happiness as long as he continues his pattern of deception. . . .

Work Cited

Gilb, Dagoberto. "Love in L.A." *The Compact Bedford Introduction to Literature.* Ed. Michael Meyer. 8th ed. Boston: Bedford/St. Martin's, 2009. 279–81.

9

Style, Tone, and Irony

I like it when there is some feeling of threat or sense of menace in short stories. I think a little menace is fine to have in a story.
— RAYMOND CARVER

STYLE

Style is a concept that everyone understands on some level because in its broadest sense it refers to the particular way in which anything is made or done. Style is everywhere around us. The world is saturated with styles in cars, clothing, buildings, teaching, dancing, music, politics — in anything that reflects a distinctive manner of expression or design. Consider, for example, how a tune sung by the Beatles differs from the same tune performed by a string orchestra. There's no mistaking the two styles.

Authors also have different characteristic styles. *Style* refers to the distinctive manner in which a writer arranges words to achieve particular effects. That arrangement includes individual word choices and matters such as the length of sentences, their structure and tone, and the use of irony.

Diction refers to a writer's choice of words. Because different words evoke different associations in a reader's mind, the writer's choice of words is crucial in controlling a reader's response. The diction must be appropriate for the characters and the situations in which the author places them. Consider how inappropriate it would have been if Melville had had Bartleby respond to the lawyer's requests with "Hell no!" instead of "I would prefer not to." The word *prefer* and the tentativeness of *would* help reinforce the scrivener's mildness, his dignity, and even his seeming reasonableness — all of which frustrate the lawyer's efforts to get rid of him. Bartleby, despite his passivity, seems to be in control of the situation. If he were to shout "Hell no!" he would appear angry, aggressive, desperate, and too informal, none of which would fit with his solemn, conscious decision to die. Melville makes the lawyer the desperate party by carefully choosing Bartleby's words.

Explore the literary elements in this chapter on *LiterActive* or at bedfordstmartins .com/meyercompact.

Sentence structure is another element of a writer's style. Hemingway's terse, economical sentences are frequently noted and readily perceived. Here are the concluding sentences of Hemingway's "Soldier's Home" (p. 165), in which Krebs decides to leave home:

> He had tried so to keep his life from being complicated. Still, none of it had touched him. He had felt sorry for his mother and she had made him lie. He would go to Kansas City and get a job and she would feel all right about it. There would be one more scene maybe before he got away. He would not go down to his father's office. He would miss that one. He wanted his life to go smoothly. It had just gotten going that way. Well, that was all over now, anyway. He would go over to the schoolyard and watch Helen play indoor baseball.

Hemingway expresses Krebs's thought the way Krebs thinks. The style avoids any "complicated" sentence structures. Seven of the eleven sentences begin with the word *He.* There are no abstractions or qualifications. We feel as if we are listening not only to *what* Krebs thinks but to *how* he thinks. The style reflects his firm determination to make, one step at a time, a clean, unobstructed break from his family and the entangling complications they would impose on him.

Contrast this straightforward style with Vladimir Nabokov's description of a woman in his short story "The Vane Sisters." The sophisticated narrator teaches French literature at a women's college and is as observant as he is icily critical of the woman he describes in this passage:

> Her fingernails were gaudily painted, but badly bitten and not clean. Her lovers were a silent young photographer with a sudden laugh and two older men, brothers, who owned a small printing establishment across the street. I wondered at their tastes whenever I glimpsed, with a secret shudder, the higgledy-piggledy striation of black hairs that showed all along her pale shins through the nylon of her stockings with the scientific distinctness of a preparation flattened under glass; or when I felt, at her every movement, the dullish,

stalish, not particularly conspicuous but all-pervading and depressing emanation that her seldom bathed flesh spread from under weary perfumes and creams.

This portrait — etched with a razor blade — is restrained but devastating. The woman's fingernails are "gaudily painted." She has no taste in men either. One of her lovers is "silent" except for a "sudden laugh," a telling detail that suggests a strikingly odd personality. Her other lovers, the two brothers (!), run a "small" business. We are invited to "shudder" along with the narrator as he vividly describes the "striation of black hairs" on her legs; we see the woman as if she were displayed under a microscope, an appropriate perspective given the narrator's close inspection. His scrutiny is relentless, and its object smells as awful as it looks (notice the difference in the language between this blunt description and the narrator's elegant distaste). He finds the woman "depressing" because the weight of her unpleasantness oppresses him.

The narrator reveals nearly as much about himself as about the woman, but Nabokov leaves the reader with the task of assessing the narrator's fastidious reactions. The formal style of this description is appropriately that of an educated, highly critical, close observer of life who knows how to convey the "dullish, stalish" essence of this woman. But, you might ask, what about the curious informality of "higgledy-piggledy"? Does that fit the formal professorial voice? Given Nabokov's well-known fascination with wit and, more important, the narrator's obvious relish for verbally slicing this woman into a slide specimen, the term is revealed as appropriately chosen once the reader sees the subtle, if brutal, pun on *piggledy*.

Hemingway's and Nabokov's uses of language are very different, yet each style successfully fuses what is said with how it is said. We could write summaries of both passages, but our summaries, owing to their styles, would not have the same effect as the originals. And that makes all the difference.

TONE

Style reveals **tone,** the author's implicit attitude toward the people, places, and events in a story. When we speak, tone is conveyed by our voice inflections, our wink of an eye, or some other gesture. A professor who says "You're going to fail the next exam" may be indicating concern, frustration, sympathy, alarm, humor, or indifference, depending on the tone of voice. In a literary work that spoken voice is unavailable; instead we must rely on the context in which a statement appears to interpret it correctly.

In Chopin's "The Story of an Hour" (p. 15), for example, we can determine that the author sympathizes with Mrs. Mallard despite the fact that her grief over her husband's assumed death is mixed with joy. Though

Mrs. Mallard thinks she's lost her husband, she experiences relief because she feels liberated from an oppressive, male-dominated life. That's why she collapses when she sees her husband alive at the end of the story. Chopin makes clear by the tone of the final line ("When the doctors came they said she had died of heart disease — of joy that kills") that the men misinterpret both her grief and joy, for in the larger context of Mrs. Mallard's emotions we see, unlike the doctors, that her death may well have been caused not by a shock of joy but by an overwhelming recognition of her lost freedom.

If we are sensitive to tone, we can get behind a character and see him or her from the author's perspective. In Melville's "Bartleby, the Scrivener" (p. 124) everything is told from the lawyer's point of view, but the tone of his remarks often separates him from the author's values and attitudes. When the lawyer characterizes himself at the beginning of the story, his use of language effectively allows us to see Melville disapproving of what the lawyer takes pride in:

> The late John Jacob Astor, a personage little given to poetic enthusiasm, had no hesitation in pronouncing my first grand point to be prudence; my next, method. I do not speak it in vanity.

But, of course, he is vain and a name-dropper as well. He likes the "rounded and orbicular sound" of Astor's name because it "rings like unto bullion." Tone, here, helps to characterize the lawyer. Melville doesn't tell us that the lawyer is status conscious and materialistic; instead, we discover that through the tone. This stylistic technique is frequently an important element for interpreting a story. An insensitivity to tone can lead a reader astray in determining the theme of a work. Regardless of who is speaking in a story, it is wise to listen for the author's voice too.

IRONY

One of the enduring themes in literature is that things are not always what they seem to be. What we see — or think we see — is not always what we get. The unexpected complexity that often surprises us in life — what Herman Melville in *Moby-Dick* called the "universal thump" — is fertile ground for writers of imaginative literature. They cultivate that ground through the use of *irony*, a device that reveals a reality different from what appears to be true.

Verbal irony consists of saying one thing but meaning the opposite. If a student driver smashes into a parked car and the angry instructor turns to say "You sure did well today," the statement is an example of verbal irony. What is meant is not what is said. Verbal irony that is calculated to hurt someone by false praise is commonly known as **sarcasm.** In literature, however, verbal irony is usually not openly aggressive; instead, it is more subtle and restrained though no less intense.

In Godwin's "A Sorrowful Woman" (p. 39), a woman retreats from her family because she cannot live in the traditional role that her husband and son expect of her. When the husband tries to be sympathetic about her withdrawal from family life, the narrator tells us three times that "he understood such things" and that in "understanding these things" he tried to be patient by "[s]till understanding these things." The narrator's repetition of these phrases constitutes verbal irony because they call attention to the fact that the husband doesn't understand his wife at all. His "understanding" is really only a form of condescension that represents part of her problem rather than a solution.

Situational irony exists when there is an incongruity between what is expected to happen and what actually happens. For instance, at the climactic showdown between Marshal Potter and Scratchy Wilson in Crane's "The Bride Comes to Yellow Sky" (p. 266), there are no gunshots, only talk — and what subdues Wilson is not Potter's strength and heroism but the fact that the marshal is now married. To take one more example, the protagonist in Godwin's "A Sorrowful Woman" seems, by traditional societal standards, to have all that a wife and mother could desire in a family, but, given her needs, that turns out to be not enough to sustain even her life, let alone her happiness. In each of these instances the ironic situation creates a distinction between appearances and realities and brings the reader closer to the central meaning of the story.

Another form of irony occurs when an author allows the reader to know more about a situation than a character knows. *Dramatic irony* creates a discrepancy between what a character believes or says and what the reader understands to be true. In Flannery O'Connor's "Revelation" (p. 392) the insecure Mrs. Turpin, as a member of "the home-and-land owner" class, believes herself to be superior to "niggers," "white-trash," and mere "home owners." She takes pride in her position in the community and in what she perceives to be her privileged position in relation to God. The reader, however, knows that her remarks underscore her failings rather than any superiority. Dramatic irony can be an effective way for an author to have a character unwittingly reveal himself or herself.

As you read Raymond Carver's "Popular Mechanics," Susan Minot's "Lust," and Lydia Davis's "Letter to a Funeral Parlor," pay attention to the authors' artful use of style, tone, and irony to convey meanings.

RAYMOND CARVER (1938–1988)

Born in 1938 in Clatskanie, Oregon, to working-class parents, Carver grew up in Yakima, Washington, was educated at Humboldt State College in California, and did graduate work at the University of Iowa. He married at age nineteen and during his college years worked at a series of low-paying jobs to help support his family. These difficult years eventually ended in divorce. He taught at a number of universities, among them the University of California at Berkeley, the University of Iowa, the University of Texas at El Paso, and Syracuse University. Carver's collections of stories include *Will You Please Be Quiet, Please?* (1976), *What We Talk about When We Talk about Love* (1981), from which "Popular Mechanics" is taken, *Cathedral* (1984), and *Where I'm Calling From: New and Selected Stories* (1988). Extremely brief and minimalist in style, plot, character, and setting, "Popular Mechanics" describes a stark domestic situation with a startling conclusion.

© Marion Ettlinger.

Explore contexts for Raymond Carver on *LiterActive*.

Popular Mechanics   1981

Early that day the weather turned and the snow was melting into dirty water. Streaks of it ran down from the little shoulder-high window that faced the backyard. Cars slushed by on the street outside, where it was getting dark. But it was getting dark on the inside too.

He was in the bedroom pushing clothes into a suitcase when she came to the door.

I'm glad you're leaving! I'm glad you're leaving! she said. Do you hear?

He kept on putting his things into the suitcase.

Son of a bitch! I'm so glad you're leaving! She began to cry. You can't even   5
look me in the face, can you?

Then she noticed the baby's picture on the bed and picked it up.

He looked at her and she wiped her eyes and stared at him before turning and going back to the living room.

Bring that back, he said.

Just get your things and get out, she said.

He did not answer. He fastened the suitcase, put on his coat, looked   10
around the bedroom before turning off the light. Then he went out to the living room.

She stood in the doorway of the little kitchen, holding the baby.

I want the baby, he said.

Are you crazy?

No, but I want the baby. I'll get someone to come by for his things.

You're not touching this baby, she said.   15

The baby had begun to cry and she uncovered the blanket from around his head.

Oh, oh, she said, looking at the baby.

He moved toward her.

For God's sake! she said. She took a step back into the kitchen.   20
I want the baby.
Get out of here!
She turned and tried to hold the baby over in a corner behind the stove.
But he came up. He reached across the stove and tightened his hands on the baby.
Let go of him, he said.   25
Get away, get away! she cried.
The baby was red-faced and screaming. In the scuffle they knocked down a flowerpot that hung behind the stove.
He crowded her into the wall then, trying to break her grip. He held on to the baby and pushed with all his weight.
Let go of him, he said.
Don't, she said. You're hurting the baby, she said.   30
I'm not hurting the baby, he said.
The kitchen window gave no light. In the near-dark he worked on her fisted fingers with one hand and with the other hand he gripped the screaming baby up under an arm near the shoulder.
She felt her fingers being forced open. She felt the baby going from her.
No! she screamed just as her hands came loose.
She would have it, this baby. She grabbed for the baby's other arm. She caught the baby around the wrist and leaned back.   35
But he would not let go. He felt the baby slipping out of his hands and he pulled back very hard.
In this manner, the issue was decided.

Considerations for Critical Thinking and Writing

1. **FIRST RESPONSE.** Discuss the story's final lines. What is the "issue" that is "decided"?

2. Though there is little description of the setting in this story, how do the minimal details that are provided help to establish the tone?

3. How do small actions take on larger significance in the story? Consider the woman picking up the baby's picture and the knocked-down flowerpot.

4. Why is this couple splitting up? Do we know? Does it matter? Explain your response.

5. Discuss the title of the story. The original title was "Mine." Which do you think is more effective?

6. What is the conflict? How is it resolved?

7. Read I Kings 3 in the Bible for the story of Solomon. How might "Popular Mechanics" be read as a retelling of this story? What significant differences do you find in the endings of each?

8. Explain how Carver uses irony to convey theme.

Connections to Other Selections

1. Compare Carver's style with Ernest Hemingway's in "Soldier's Home" (p. 165).

2. How is the ending of "Popular Mechanics" similar to the ending of Nathaniel Hawthorne's "The Birthmark" (p. 343)?

A SAMPLE STUDENT RESPONSE

Skyler Hansen

Professor Ríos

English 200

November 26, 2008

The Terse Style of Raymond Carver's "Popular Mechanics"

Raymond Carver provides little information in the story "Popular Mechanics." We are not given a complete background of the characters or vivid descriptions of setting. Even the dialogue is limited, and we are thrown into a scene already in progress. However, even though Carver seemingly does not tell us very much, all the necessary elements of a story are right there in front of us. Despite the terse style, we understand the characters and their motives by reading closely.

The plot of the story is simple: in the wake of a bitter fight, a man packs his suitcase and is about to leave the mother of his child. Many seemingly important details are missing. We're not certain whether the couple is married or what they are arguing about. We don't even know their names. However, all the story's complexities are there. The main conflict emerges when the man decides that he wants the baby. And while we might initially assume this has always been his intention, we realize that's not the case. He first plans to take a picture of the baby, and when the woman won't let him, he suddenly decides to raise the stakes:

> He did not answer. He fastened the suitcase, put on his
> coat, looked around the bedroom before turning off the light.
> Then he went out into the living room.
>
> She stood in the doorway of the little kitchen, holding the
> baby.
>
> I want the baby, he said. (Carver 288)

Here, we are practically able to watch the man's thought process. He feels so much anger toward the woman that he wants to hurt her before he leaves. As he packs, he searches for something he can take from her, and finally decides on the baby. His motive has little (perhaps nothing) to do with the child. He seeks only to devastate the child's mother.

Though the story appears to be open-ended, the resolution is clear. The two struggle for the baby, forcefully, violently, unwilling to give in to the other:

> She caught the baby around the wrist and leaned back.
>
> But he would not let go. He felt the baby slipping out of
> his hands and he pulled back very hard.
>
> In this manner, the issue was decided. (289)

While we do not know the extent of the damage, or what will become of these people, we do know that the baby suffers most as a result of the altercation, a theme Carver makes clear. . . .

Work Cited

Carver, Raymond. "Popular Mechanics." <u>The Compact Bedford Introduction to Literature</u>. Ed. Michael Meyer. 8th ed. Boston: Bedford/St. Martin's, 2009. 288–89.

SUSAN MINOT (B. 1956)

Born and raised in Massachusetts, Susan
Minot earned a B.A. at Brown University and
an M.F.A. at Columbia University. Before
devoting herself full-time to writing, Minot
worked as an assistant editor at *Grand Street*
magazine. Her stories have appeared in the
*Atlantic Monthly, Harper's, The New Yorker,
Mademoiselle,* and *Paris Review.* Her short stories have been collected in *Lust and Other
Stories* (1989), and she has published four
novels — *Monkeys* (1986), *Folly* (1992), *Evening*
(1998), and *Rapture* (2002), as well as one volume of poetry, *Poems 4 A.M.* (2002).

Courtesy of Dinah Minot Hubley.

Lust   1984

Leo was from a long time ago, the first one I ever saw nude. In the spring before
the Hellmans filled their pool, we'd go down there in the deep end, with baby
oil, and like that. I met him the first month away at boarding school. He had a
halo from the campus light behind him. I flipped.

Roger was fast. In his illegal car, we drove to the reservoir, the radio blar-
ing, talking fast, fast, fast. He was always going for my zipper. He got kicked
out sophomore year.

By the time the band got around to playing "Wild Horses," I had tasted
Bruce's tongue. We were clicking in the shadows on the other side of the
amplifier, out of Mrs. Donovan's line of vision. It tasted like salt, with my neck
bent back, because we had been dancing so hard before.

Tim's line: "I'd like to see you in a bathing suit." I knew it was his line
when he said the exact same thing to Annie Hines.

You'd go on walks to get off campus. It was raining like hell, my sweater as
sopped as a wet sheep. Tim pinned me to a tree, the woods light brown and
dark brown, a white house half hidden with the lights already on. The water
was as loud as a crowd hissing. He made certain comments about my forehead,
about my cheeks.

We started off sitting at one end of the couch and then our feet were
squished against the armrest and then he went over to turn off the TV and
came back after he had taken off his shirt and then we slid onto the floor

and he got up again to close the door, then came back to me, a body waiting on the rug.

You'd try to wipe off the table or to do the dishes and Willie would untuck your shirt and get his hands up under in front, standing behind you, making puffy noises in your ear.

He likes it when I wash my hair. He covers his face with it and if I start to say something, he goes, "Shush."

For a long time, I had Philip on the brain. The less they noticed you, the more you got them on the brain.

My parents had no idea. Parents never really know what's going on, espe-   10 cially when you're away at school most of the time. If she met them, my mother might say, "Oliver seems nice" or "I like that one" without much of an opinion. If she didn't like them, "He's a funny fellow, isn't he?" or "Johnny's perfectly nice but a drink of water." My father was too shy to talk to them at all unless they played sports and he'd ask them about that.

The sand was almost cold underneath because the sun was long gone. Eben piled a mound over my feet, patting around my ankles, the ghostly surf rumbling behind him in the dark. He was the first person I ever knew who died, later that summer, in a car crash. I thought about it for a long time.

"Come here," he says on the porch.
I go over to the hammock and he takes my wrist with two fingers.
"What?"
He kisses my palm then directs my hand to his fly.   15

Songs went with whichever boy it was. "Sugar Magnolia" was Tim, with the line "Rolling in the rushes / down by the riverside." With "Darkness Darkness," I'd picture Philip with his long hair. Hearing "Under My Thumb" there'd be the smell of Jamie's suede jacket.

We hid in the listening rooms during study hall. With a record cover over the door's window, the teacher on duty couldn't look in. I came out flushed and heady and back at the dorm was surprised how red my lips were in the mirror.

One weekend at Simon's brother's, we stayed inside all day with the shades down, in bed, then went out to Store 24 to get some ice cream. He stood at the magazine rack and read through *MAD* while I got butterscotch sauce, craving something sweet.

I could do some things well. Some things I was good at, like math or painting or even sports, but the second a boy put his arm around me, I forgot about wanting to do anything else, which felt like a relief at first until it became like sinking into a muck.

It was different for a girl. 20

When we were little, the brothers next door tied up our ankles. They held the door of the goat house and wouldn't let us out till we showed them our underpants. Then they'd forget about being after us and when we played whiffle ball, I'd be just as good as they were.

Then it got to be different. Just because you have on a short skirt, they yell from the cars, slowing down for a while, and if you don't look, they screech off and call you a bitch.

"What's the matter with me?" they say, point-blank.
Or else, "Why won't you go out with me? I'm not asking you to get married," about to get mad.

Or it'd be, trying to be reasonable, in a regular voice, "Listen, I just want to 25 have a good time."
So I'd go because I couldn't think of something to say back that wouldn't be obvious, and if you go out with them, you sort of have to do something.

I sat between Mack and Eddie in the front seat of the pickup. They were having a fight about something. I've a feeling about me.

Certain nights you'd feel a certain surrender, maybe if you'd had wine. The surrender would be forgetting yourself and you'd put your nose to his neck and feel like a squirrel, safe, at rest, in a restful dream. But then you'd start to slip from that and the dark would come in and there'd be a cave. You make out the dim shape of the windows and feel yourself become a cave, filled absolutely with air, or with a sadness that wouldn't stop.

Teenage years. You know just what you're doing and don't see the things that start to get in the way.

Lots of boys, but never two at the same time. One was plenty to keep you 30 in a state. You'd start to see a boy and something would rush over you like a fast storm cloud and you couldn't possibly think of anyone else. Boys took it differently. Their eyes perked up at any little number that walked by. You'd act like you weren't noticing.

The joke was that the school doctor gave out the pill like aspirin. He didn't ask you anything. I was fifteen. We had a picture of him in assembly, holding up an IUD shaped like a T. Most girls were on the pill, if anything, because they couldn't handle a diaphragm. I kept the dial in my top drawer like my mother and thought of her each time I tipped out the yellow tablets in the morning before chapel.

If they were too shy, I'd be more so. Andrew was nervous. We stayed up with his family album, sharing a pack of Old Golds. Before it got light, we turned on the TV. A man was explaining how to plant seedlings. His mouth jerked to the side in a tic. Andrew thought it was a riot and kept imitating him. I laughed to be polite. When we finally dozed off, he dared to put his arm around me, but that was it.

You wait till they come to you. With half fright, half swagger, they stand one step down. They dare to touch the button on your coat then lose their nerve and quickly drop their hand so you—you'd do anything for them. You touch their cheek.

The girls sit around in the common room and talk about boys, smoking their heads off.

"What are you complaining about?" says Jill to me when we talk about problems.

"Yeah," says Giddy. "You always have a boyfriend."

I look at them and think, As if.

I thought the worst thing anyone could call you was a cock-teaser. So, if you flirted, you had to be prepared to go through with it. Sleeping with someone was perfectly normal once you had done it. You didn't really worry about it. But there were other problems. The problems had to do with something else entirely.

Mack was during the hottest summer ever recorded. We were renting a house on an island with all sorts of other people. No one slept during the heat wave, walking around the house with nothing on which we were used to because of the nude beach. In the living room, Eddie lay on top of a coffee table to cool off. Mack and I, with the bedroom door open for air, sweated and sweated all night.

"I can't take this," he said at three A.M. "I'm going for a swim." He and some guys down the hall went to the beach. The heat put me on edge. I sat on a cracked chest by the open window and smoked and smoked till I felt even worse, waiting for something—I guess for him to get back.

One was on a camping trip in Colorado. We zipped our sleeping bags together, the coyotes' hysterical chatter far away. Other couples murmured in other tents. Paul was up before sunrise, starting a fire for breakfast. He wasn't much of a talker in the daytime. At night, his hand leafed about in the hair at my neck.

There'd be times when you overdid it. You'd get carried away. All the next day, you'd be in a total fog, delirious, absent-minded, crossing the street and nearly getting run over.

The more girls a boy has, the better. He has a bright look, having reaped fruits, blooming. He stalks around, sure-shouldered, and you have the feeling he's got more in him, a fatter heart, more stories to tell. For a girl, with each boy it's as though a petal gets plucked each time.

Then you start to get tired. You begin to feel diluted, like watered-down stew.

Oliver came skiing with us. We lolled by the fire after everyone had gone to   45
bed. Each creak you'd think was someone coming downstairs. The silver loop
bracelet he gave me had been a present from his girlfriend before.

On vacations, we went skiing, or you'd go south if someone invited you.
Some people had apartments in New York that their families hardly ever used.
Or summer houses, or older sisters. We always managed to find someplace to go.

We made the plan at coffee hour. Simon snuck out and met me at Main
Gate after lights-out. We crept to the chapel and spent the night in the balcony. He tasted like onions from a submarine sandwich.

The boys are one of two ways: either they can't sit still or they don't move.
In front of the TV, they won't budge. On weekends they play touch football
while we sit on the sidelines, picking blades of grass to chew on, and watch.
We're always watching them run around. We shiver in the stands, knocking
our boots together to keep our toes warm, and they whizz across the ice, chopping their sticks around the puck. When they're in the rink, they refuse to look
at you, only eyeing each other beneath low helmets. You cheer for them but
they don't look up, even if it's a face-off when nothing's happening, even if
they're doing drills before any game has started at all.

Dancing under the pink tent, he bent down and whispered in my ear. We
slipped away to the lawn on the other side of the hedge. Much later, as he was
leaving the buffet with two plates of eggs and sausage, I saw the grass stains on
the knees of his white pants.

Tim's was shaped like a banana, with a graceful curve to it. They're all dif-   50
ferent. Willie's like a bunch of walnuts when nothing was happening, another's
as thin as a thin hot dog. But it's like faces; you're never really surprised.

Still, you're not sure what to expect.

I look into his face and he looks back. I look into his eyes and they look
back at mine. Then they look down at my mouth so I look at his mouth, then
back to his eyes then, backing up, at his whole face. I think, Who? Who are
you? His head tilts to one side.
I say, "Who are you?"
"What do you mean?"
"Nothing."   55
I look at his eyes again, deeper. Can't tell who he is, what he thinks.
"What?" he says. I look at his mouth.
"I'm just wondering," I say and go wandering across his face. Study the
chin line. It's shaped like a persimmon.
"Who are you? What are you thinking?"
He says, "What the hell are you talking about?"   60

Then they get mad after, when you say enough is enough. After, when it's
easier to explain that you don't want to. You wouldn't dream of saying that
maybe you weren't really ready to in the first place.

Gentle Eddie. We waded into the sea, the waves round and plowing in, buffalo-headed, slapping our thighs. I put my arms around his freckled shoulders and he held me up, buoyed by the water, and rocked me like a sea shell.

I had no idea whose party it was, the apartment jam-packed, stepping over people in the hallway. The room with the music was practically empty, the bare floor, me in red shoes. This fellow slides onto one knee and takes me around the waist and we rock to jazzy tunes, with my toes pointing heavenward, and waltz and spin and dip to "Smoke Gets in Your Eyes" or "I'll Love You Just for Now." He puts his head to my chest, runs a sweeping hand down my inside thigh and we go loose-limbed and sultry and as smooth as silk and I stamp my red heels and he takes me into a swoon. I never saw him again after that but I thought, I could have loved that one.

You wonder how long you can keep it up. You begin to feel as if you're showing through, like a bathroom window that only lets in grey light, the kind you can't see out of.

They keep coming around. Johnny drives up at Easter vacation from Balti- 65 more and I let him in the kitchen with everyone sound asleep. He has friends waiting in the car.

"What are you, crazy? It's pouring out there," I say.

"It's okay," he says. "They understand."

So he gets some long kisses from me, against the refrigerator, before he goes because I hate those girls who push away a boy's face as if she were made out of Ivory soap, as if she's that much greater than he is.

The note on my cubby told me to see the headmaster. I had no idea for what. He had received complaints about my amorous displays on the town green. It was Willie that spring. The headmaster told me he didn't care what I did but that Casey Academy had a reputation to uphold in the town. He lowered his glasses on his nose. "We've got twenty acres of woods on this campus," he said. "If you want to smooch with your boyfriend, there are twenty acres for you to do it out of the public eye. You read me?"

Everybody'd get weekend permissions for different places, then we'd all go 70 to someone's house whose parents were away. Usually there'd be more boys than girls. We raided the liquor closet and smoked pot at the kitchen table and you'd never know who would end up where, or with whom. There were always disasters. Ceci got bombed and cracked her head open on the banister and needed stitches. Then there was the time Wendel Blair walked through the picture window at the Lowes' and got slashed to ribbons.

He scared me. In bed, I didn't dare look at him. I lay back with my eyes closed, luxuriating because he knew all sorts of expert angles, his hands never fumbling, going over my whole body, pressing the hair up and off the back of my head, giving an extra hip shove, as if to say *There*. I parted my eyes slightly, keeping the screen of my lashes low because it was too much to look at him, his mouth loose and pink and parted, his eyes looking through my forehead, or kneeling up, looking through my throat. I was ashamed but couldn't look him in the eye.

You wonder about things feeling a little off-kilter. You begin to feel like a piece of pounded veal.

At boarding school, everyone gets depressed. We go in and see the house-mother, Mrs. Gunther. She got married when she was eighteen. Mr. Gunther was her high school sweetheart, the only boyfriend she ever had.

"And you knew you wanted to marry him right off?" we ask her.

She smiles and says, "Yes."   75

"They always want something from you," says Jill, complaining about her boyfriend.

"Yeah," says Giddy. "You always feel like you have to deliver something."

"You do," says Mrs. Gunther. "Babies."

After sex, you curl up like a shrimp, something deep inside you ruined, slammed in a place that sickens at slamming, and slowly you fill up with an overwhelming sadness, an elusive gaping worry. You don't try to explain it, filled with the knowledge that it's nothing after all, everything filling up finally and absolutely with death. After the briskness of loving, loving stops. And you roll over with death stretched out alongside you like a feather boa, or a snake, light as air, and you . . . you don't even ask for anything or try to say something to him because it's obviously your own damn fault. You haven't been able to — to what? To open your heart. You open your legs but can't, or don't dare any-more, to open your heart.

It starts this way: 80

You stare into their eyes. They flash like all the stars are out. They look at you seriously, their eyes at a low burn and their hands no matter what starting off shy and with such a gentle touch that the only thing you can do is take that tenderness and let yourself be swept away. When, with one attentive finger they tuck the hair behind your ear, you —

You do everything they want.

Then comes after. After when they don't look at you. They scratch their balls, stare at the ceiling. Or if they do turn, their gaze is altogether changed. They are surprised. They turn casually to look at you, distracted, and get a mild distracted surprise. You're gone. Their blank look tells you that the girl they were fucking is not there anymore. You seem to have disappeared.

CONSIDERATIONS FOR CRITICAL THINKING AND WRITING

1. **FIRST RESPONSE.** What do you think of the narrator? Why? Do you agree with the definition the story offers for *lust*?

2. Do you think that the narrator's depiction of male and female responses to sex are accurate? Explain why or why not.

3. How effective is the narrator's description of teenage sex? What do you think she means when she says "You know just what you're doing and don't see the things that start to get in the way" (para. 29)?

4. What is the story's conflict? Explain whether you think the conflict is resolved.

5. Discuss the story's tone. Is it what you expected from the title?

6. What do you think is the theme of "Lust"? Does its style carry its theme?

7. What is the primary setting for the story? What does it reveal about the nature of the narrator's economic and social class?

8. In a *Publisher's Weekly* interview (November 6, 1992), Minot observed, "There's more fictional material in unhappiness and disappointment and frustration than there is in happiness. Who was it said, 'Happiness is like a blank page'?" What do you think of this observation?

CONNECTIONS TO OTHER SELECTIONS

1. Compare the treatments of youthful sexuality in "Lust" and David Updike's "Summer" (p. 304). Do you prefer one story to the other? Why?

2. Write an essay explaining the sort of advice the narrator of Fay Weldon's "IND AFF, or Out of Love in Sarajevo" (p. 172) might give to the narrator of "Lust." You might try writing this in the form of a letter.

LYDIA DAVIS (B. 1947)

© Jerry Bauer.

Born in Northampton, Massachusetts, Lydia Davis graduated from Barnard College in 1970, after which she began work as a translator of French literature. Her success as a translator can be measured in part by the French government's awarding her the Chevalier of the Order of Arts. She has won high praise particularly for her translations of Marcel Proust. As a fiction writer, Davis has appeared in numerous literary periodicals while publishing one novel, *End of the Story* (1995), and three collections of short stories: *Break It Down* (1986), *Almost No Memory* (1997), and *Samuel Johnson Is Indignant* (2001), the collection from which "Letter to a Funeral Parlor" is reprinted. Among the prestigious literary prizes that Davis has been awarded are fellowships from the MacArthur and Guggenheim foundations, a Lannan Literary Award, and a Whiting Writer's Award. She has taught at several schools, including Bard College and the University at Albany. Davis is well known for her brief, compact, sharp, and often humorous fictions that survey contemporary life. "In such a form," she observes, "each word has to be right."

Letter to a Funeral Parlor *2001*

Dear Sir,

I am writing to you to object to the word "cremains," which was used by your representative when he met with my mother and me two days after my father's death.

We had no objection to your representative, personally, who was respectful and friendly and dealt with us in a sensitive way. He did not try to sell us an expensive urn, for instance.

What startled and disturbed us was the word "cremains." You in the business must have invented this word and you are used to it. We the public do not hear it very often. We don't lose a close friend or a family member very many times in our life, and years pass in between, if we are lucky. Even less often do we have to discuss what is to be done with a family member or close friend after their death.

We noticed that before the death of my father you and your representative used the words "loved one" to refer to him. That was comfortable for us, even if the ways in which we loved him were complicated.

Then we were sitting there in our chairs in the living room trying not to   5 weep in front of your representative, who was opposite us on the sofa, and we were very tired first from sitting up with my father, and then from worrying about whether he was comfortable as he was dying, and then from worrying about where he might be now that he was dead, and your representative referred to him as "the cremains."

At first we did not even know what he meant. Then, when we realized, we were frankly upset. "Cremains" sounds like something invented as a milk substitute in coffee, like Cremora, or Coffee-Mate. Or it sounds like some kind of chipped beef dish.

As one who works with words for a living, I must say that any invented word, like "Porta Potti" or "pooper-scooper," has a cheerful or even jovial ring to it that I don't think you really intended when you invented the word "cremains." In fact, my father himself, who was a professor of English and is now being called "the cremains," would have pointed out to you the alliteration in "Porta Potti" and the rhyme in "pooper-scooper." Then he would have told you that "cremains" falls into the same category as "brunch" and is known as a portmanteau word.

There is nothing wrong with inventing words, especially in a business. But a grieving family is not prepared for this one. We are not even used to our loved one being gone. You could very well continue to employ the term "ashes." We are used to it from the Bible, and are even comforted by it. We would not misunderstand. We would know that these ashes are not like the ashes in a fireplace.

Yours sincerely.

CONSIDERATIONS FOR CRITICAL THINKING AND WRITING

1. **FIRST RESPONSE.** Why does it make sense that the author of this story is also a professional translator? What does that fact suggest about her sensitivity to words?

2. Describe the movement of the story's plot. What elements of a typical plot (see the glossary entry for *plot*) can you find in the story?

3. Discuss the narrator's diction and tone. What do they reveal about her (or his) character?

4. Which paragraphs seem particularly humorous to you? Explain why the story does or doesn't make a serious point.

5. Discuss whether or not you share the narrator's objection to the word *cremains*.

6. In a sentence describe the story's theme.

7. To what extent do you think these eight paragraphs constitute a short story?

CONNECTIONS TO OTHER SELECTIONS

1. Compare the style, tone, and irony of Davis's story with E. Annie Proulx's "55 Miles to the Gas Pump" (p. 465).

2. Discuss the attitudes expressed about language usage in "Letter to a Funeral Parlor" and in Barbara Hamby's poem "Ode to American English" (p. 641).

Web Research the authors in this chapter or take quizzes on their works at bedfordstmartins .com/meyercompact.

10

Combining the Elements of Fiction: A Writing Process

A skillful artist has constructed a tale. He has not fashioned his thoughts to accommodate his incidents, but having deliberately conceived a certain single *effect* to be wrought, he then invents such incidents . . . as may best serve him in establishing the preconceived effect. There should be no word written of which the tendency, direct or indirect, is not to the one pre-established design.

— EDGAR ALLAN POE, Review of Hawthorne's *Twice-Told Tales*

THE ELEMENTS TOGETHER

The elements of fiction that you have examined in Chapters 1–9 provide terms and concepts that enable you to think, talk, and write about fiction in a variety of ways. As those chapters have indicated, there are many means available to you for determining a story's effects and meanings. By considering elements of fiction such as characterization, conflict, setting, point of view, symbolism, style, and theme, you can better articulate your understanding of a particular work. A careful reading of the work's elements allows you to see how the parts contribute to the whole.

The parts or elements of a story work together rather than in isolation to create a particular kind of experience, emotion, or insight for a reader. The symbolic significance of the free and easy Mississippi River setting of *The Adventures of Huckleberry Finn,* for example, cannot be excavated from Huck's first-person point of view. Nor can the "smothery" ways of the corrupt towns along the river be understood without the pious frauds, hypocrites, cowards, and other sordid characters that populate them. Add the plot that has Jim on the run from slavery and the unconscious ironic tone that Mark Twain invests in Huck — all constitute interrelated elements that add up to serious themes commenting on nineteenth-century society. Understanding the ways in which these elements work together produces a richer and more satisfying reading of a plot that might otherwise be read simply as a children's story.

MAPPING THE STORY

Writing about a story requires your creation of a clear path that a reader can take in order to follow your experience and understanding of the work. The path offers perspectives and directions that are informed by what caught your attention along the way. Your paper points out what you thought worth revisiting and taking the reader to see. Whatever the thesis of the paper, your role as a guide remains the same as you move from one element of the story to the next, offering an overall impression about the story. And as you already know, the best tours are always guided by informed and interesting voices.

This chapter presents an example of how one student, Janice Reardon, arrived at a thesis, combining her understanding of several elements of fiction for an assigned topic on David Updike's short story "Summer." After reviewing the elements of fiction covered in Chapters 1–9, Janice read the story several times, paying careful attention to plot, character, setting, point of view, symbolism, and so on. She then developed her ideas by brainstorming, drafting, and using the Questions for Writing (listed after the story) to develop her thesis into a statement that makes a definite claim about a specific idea and provides a clear sense of direction for the paper to come. As you read "Summer," think about what you might want to say about the relationship — or lack thereof — between Homer and Sandra. Pay attention to how the various elements of fiction work together to establish or reinforce that relationship.

DAVID UPDIKE (B. 1957)

Born in Ipswich, Massachusetts, David Up-dike is the son of John Updike. David received a B.A. in art history at Harvard and an M.A. from Teachers College, Columbia University. His acclaimed children's books include *An Autumn Tale* (1988), *A Spring Story* (1989), *Seven Times Eight* (1990), *The Sounds of Summer* (1993), and *A Helpful Alphabet of*

© Jerry Bauer.

Friendly Objects (1998), which he coauthored with his father. "Summer," a poignant tale for adults, is part of *Out on the Marsh: Stories* (1988), a collection of his short fiction; his short stories have also appeared in *The New Yorker*. Updike resides in Cambridge, Massachusetts.

Summer   *1985*

It was the first week in August, the time when summer briefly pauses, shifting between its beginning and its end: the light had not yet begun to change, the leaves were still full and green on the trees, the nights were still warm. From the woods and fields came the hiss of crickets; the line of distant mountains was still dulled by the edge of summer haze, the echo of fireworks was replaced by the rumble of thunder and the hollow premonition of school, too far off to imagine though dimly, dully felt. His senses were consumed by the joy of their own fulfillment: the satisfying swat of a tennis ball, the dappled damp and light of the dirt road after rain, the alternating sensations of sand, mossy stone, and pine needles under bare feet. His days were spent in the adolescent pursuit of childhood pleasures: tennis, a haphazard round of golf, a variant of baseball adapted to the local geography: two pine trees as foul poles, a broomstick as the bat, the apex of the small, secluded house the dividing line between home runs and outs. On rainy days they swatted bottle tops across the living room floor, and at night vented budding cerebral energy with games of chess thoughtfully played over glasses of iced tea. After dinner they would paddle the canoe to the middle of the lake, and drift beneath the vast, blue-black dome of sky, looking at the stars and speaking softly in tones which, with the waning summer, became increasingly philosophical: the sky's blue vastness, the distance and magnitude of stars, an endless succession of numbers, gave way to a rising sensation of infinity, eternity, an imagined universe with no bounds. But the sound of the paddle hitting against the side of the canoe, the faint shadow of surrounding mountains, the cry of a nocturnal bird brought them back to the happy, cloistered finity of their world, and they paddled slowly home and went to bed.

Homer woke to the slant and shadow of a summer morning, dressed in their shared cabin, and went into the house where Mrs. Thyme sat alone, looking out across the flat blue stillness of the lake. She poured him a cup of coffee and they quietly talked, and it was then that his happiness seemed most tangible. In this summer month with the Thymes, freed from the complications of his own family, he had released himself to them and, as interim member — friend, brother, surrogate son — he lived in a blessed realm between two worlds.

From the cool darkness of the porch, smelling faintly of moldy books and kerosene and the tobacco of burning pipes, he sat looking through the screen to the lake, shimmering beneath the heat of a summer afternoon: a dog lay sleeping in the sun, a bird hopped along a swaying branch, sunlight came in through the trees and collapsed on the sandy soil beside a patch of moss, or mimicked the shade and cadence of stones as they stepped to the edge of a lake where small waves lapped a damp rock and washed onto a sandy shore. An inverted boat lay decaying under a tree, a drooping American flag hung from its gnarled pole, a haphazard dock started out across the cove toward distant islands through which the white triangle of a sail silently moved.

The yellowed pages of the book from which he occasionally read swam before him: ". . . Holmes clapped the hat upon his head. It came right over the forehead and settled on the bridge of his nose. 'It is a question of cubic capacity' said he . . ." Homer looked up. The texture of the smooth, unbroken air was cleanly divided by the sound of a slamming door, echoing up into the woods around him. Through the screen he watched Fred's sister Sandra as she came ambling down the path, stepping lightly between the stones in her bare feet. She held a towel in one hand, a book in the other, and wore a pair of pale blue shorts — faded relics of another era. At the end of the dock she stopped, raised her hands above her head, stretching, and then sat down. She rolled over onto her stomach and, using the book as a pillow, fell asleep.

Homer was amused by the fact, that although she did this every day, she didn't get any tanner. When she first came in her face was faintly flushed, and there was a pinkish line around the snowy band where her bathing suit strap had been, but the back of her legs remained an endearing, pale white, the color of eggshells, and her back acquired only the softest, brownish blur. Sometimes she kept her shoes on, other times a shirt, or sweater, or just collapsed onto the seat of the boat, her pale eyelids turned upward toward the pale sun; and as silently as she arrived, she would leave, walking back through the stones with the same, casual sway of indifference. He would watch her, hear the distant door slam, the shower running in the far corner of the house. Other times he would just look up and she would be gone. 5

On the tennis court she was strangely indifferent to his heroics. When the crucial moment arrived — Homer serving in the final game of the final set — the match would pause while she left, walking across the court, stopping to call the dog, swaying out through the gate. Homer watched her as she went down the path, and, impetus suddenly lost, he double faulted, stroked a routine backhand over the back fence, and the match was over.

When he arrived back at the house she asked him who won, but didn't seem to hear his answer. "I wish I could go sailing," she said, looking distractedly out over the lake.

At night, when he went out to the cottage where he and Fred slept, he could see her through the window as she lay on her bed, reading, her arm folded beneath her head like a leaf. Her nightgown, pulled and buttoned to her chin, pierced him with a regret that had no source or resolution, and its imagined texture floated in the air above him as he lay in bed at night, suspended in the surrounding darkness, the scent of pine, the hypnotic cadence of his best friend's breathing.

Was it that he had known her all his life, and as such had grown up in the shadow of her subtle beauty? Was it the condensed world of the lake, the silent reverence of surrounding woods, mountains, which heightened his sense of her and brought the warm glow of her presence into soft, amorous focus? She had the hair of a baby, the freckles of a child, and the sway of motherhood. Like his love, her beauty rose up in the world which spawned and nurtured it, and found in the family the medium in which it thrived, and in Homer distilled to a pure distant longing for something he had never had.

One day they climbed a mountain, and as the components of family and   10
friends strung out along the path on their laborious upward hike, he found
himself tromping along through the woods with her with nobody else in sight.
Now and then they would stop by a stream, or sit on a stump, or stone, and he
would speak to her, and then they would set off again, he following her. But in
the end this day exhausted him, following her pale legs and tripping sneakers
over the ruts and stones and a thousand roots, all the while trying to suppress
a wordless, inarticulate passion, and the last mile or so he left her, sprinting
down the path in a reckless, solitary release, howling into the woods around
him. He was lying on the grass, staring up into the patterns of drifting clouds
when she came ambling down. "Wher'd you go? I thought I'd lost you," she
said, and sat heavily down in the seat of the car. On the ride home, his elbow
hopelessly held in the warm crook of her arm, he resolved to release his love,
give it up, on the grounds that it was too disruptive to his otherwise placid life.
But in the days to follow he discovered that his resolution had done little to
change her, and her life went on its oblivious, happy course without him.

His friendship with Fred, meanwhile, continued on its course of athletic
and boyhood fulfillment. Alcohol seeped into their diet, and an occasional cigarette, and at night they would drive into town, buy two enormous cans of
Australian beer and sit at a small cove by the lake, talking. One night on the
ride home Fred accelerated over a small bridge, and as the family station
wagon left the ground their heads floated up to the ceiling, touched, and then
came crashing down as the car landed and Fred wrestled the car back onto
course. Other times they would take the motorboat out onto the lake and
make sudden racing turns around buoys, sending a plume of water into the air
and everything in the boat crashing to one side. But always with these adventures Homer felt a pang of absence, and was always relieved when they headed
back toward the familiar cove, and home.

As August ran its merciless succession of beautiful days, Sandra drifted in
and out of his presence in rising oscillations of sorrow and desire. She worked
at a bowling alley on the other side of the lake, and in the evening Homer and
Fred would drive the boat over, bowl a couple of strings, and wait for her to get
off work. Homer sat at the counter and watched her serve up sloshing cups of
coffee, secretly loathing the leering gazes of whiskered truck drivers, and loving her oblivious, vacant stare in answer, hip cocked, hand on counter, gazing
up into the neon air above their heads. When she was finished, they would pile
into the boat and skim through darkness the four or five miles home, and it
was then, bundled beneath sweaters and blankets, the white hem of her wait-
ressing dress showing through the darkness, their hair swept in the wind and
their voices swallowed by the engine's slow, steady growl, that he felt most
powerless to her attraction. As the boat rounded corners he would close his
eyes and release himself to gravity, his body's warmth swaying into hers, guis-
ing his attraction in the thin veil of centrifugal force. Now and then he would
lean into the floating strands of her hair and speak into her fragrance, watching her smile swell in the pale half-light of the moon, the umber glow of the
boat's rear light, her laughter spilling backward over the swirling "V" of wake.

Into the humid days of August a sudden rain fell, leaving the sky a hard,
unbroken blue and the nights clear and cool. In the morning when he woke,

leaving Fred a heap of sighing covers in his bed, he stepped out into the first rays of sunlight that came through the branches of the trees and sensed, in the cool vapor that rose from damp pine needles, the piercing cry of a blue jay, that something had changed. That night as they ate dinner — hamburgers and squash and corn-on-the-cob — everyone wore sweaters, and as the sun set behind the undulating line of distant mountains — burnt, like a filament of summer into his blinking eyes — it was with an autumnal tint, a reddish glow. Several days later the tree at the end of the point bloomed with a sprig of rus-set leaves, one or two of which occasionally fell, and their lives became filled with an unspoken urgency. Life of summer went on in the silent knowledge that, with the slow, inexorable seepage of an hourglass, it was turning into fall. Another mountain was climbed, annual tennis matches were arranged and played. Homer and Fred became unofficial champions of the lake by trouncing the elder Dewitt boys, unbeaten in several years. "Youth, youth," glum Billy Dewitt kept saying over iced tea afterward, in jest, though Homer could tell he was hiding some greater sense of loss.

And the moment, the conjunction of circumstance that, through the steady exertion of will, minor adjustments of time and place, he had often tried to induce, never happened. She received his veiled attentions with a kind of amused curiosity, as if smiling back on innocence. One night they had been the last ones up, and there was a fleeting, shuddering moment before he stepped through the woods to his cabin and she went to her bed that he recog-nized, in a distant sort of way, as the moment of truth. But to touch her, or kiss her, seemed suddenly incongruous, absurd, contrary to something he could not put his finger on. He looked down at the floor and softly said goodnight. The screen door shut quietly behind him and he went out into the darkness and made his way through the unseen sticks and stones, and it was only then, tripping drunkenly on a fallen branch, that he realized he had never been able to imagine the moment he distantly longed for.

The Preacher gave a familiar sermon about another summer having run 15 its course, the harvest of friendship reaped, and a concluding prayer that, "God willing, we will all meet again in June." That afternoon Homer and Fred went sailing, and as they swept past a neighboring cove Homer saw in its sullen shadows a girl sitting alone in a canoe, and in an eternal, melancholy signal of parting, she waved to them as they passed. And there was something in the way that she raised her arm which, when added to the distant impression of her fullness, beauty, youth, filled him with longing as their boat moved inexorably past, slapping the waves, and she disappeared behind a crop of trees.

The night before they were to leave they were all sitting in the living room after dinner — Mrs. Thyme sewing, Fred folded up with the morning paper, Homer reading on the other end of the couch where Sandra was lying — when the dog leapt up and things shifted in such a way that Sandra's bare foot was lightly touching Homer's back. Mrs. Thyme came over with a roll of news-paper, hit the dog on the head and he leapt off. But to Homer's surprise San-dra's foot remained, and he felt, in the faint sensation of exerted pressure, the passive emanation of its warmth, a distant signal of acquiescence. And as the family scene continued as before it was with the accompanying drama of Homer's hand, shielded from the family by a haphazard wall of pillows, migrating over the couch to where, in a moment of breathless abandon, settled softly on the cool hollow of her arch. She laughed at something her mother had said, her toe twitched, but her foot remained. It was only then, in the presence of the family, that he realized she was his accomplice, and that, though this was as far as it would ever go, his love had been returned.

CONSIDERATIONS FOR CRITICAL THINKING AND WRITING

1. **FIRST RESPONSE.** How do you respond to this love story? Would the story be more satisfying if Homer and Sandra openly acknowledged their feelings for each other and kissed at the end? Why or why not?

2. What details in the first paragraph evoke particular feelings about August? What sort of mood is created by these details?

3. How is Homer's attraction to Sandra made evident in paragraphs 5 through 9?

4. Why do you think August is described as a "merciless succession of beautiful days" (para. 12)?

5. Analyze the images in paragraph 13 that evoke the impending autumn. What does Billy Dewitt's lament about "youth, youth" add to this description?

6. Discuss the transition between paragraphs 14 and 15. How is the mood effectively changed between the night and the next day?

7. What effect does Homer's friendship with Fred and his relationship with the Thyme family have on your understanding of his reticent attraction to Sandra?

8. What, if any, significance can you attach to the names of Homer, Sandra, Thyme, and the Dewitt boys?

9. How successful do you think Updike is in evoking youthful feeling about summer in this story? Explain why you responded positively or negatively to this evocation of summer.

CONNECTIONS TO OTHER SELECTIONS

1. Compare David Updike's treatment of summer as the setting of his story with John Updike's use of summer as the setting in "A & P" (p. 560).

2. Discuss "Summer" and Dagoberto Gilb's "Love in L.A." (p. 279) as love stories. Explain why you might prefer one over the other.

As you read "Summer," what potential paper topics occurred to you? Annotating the text and brainstorming are both good ways to identify moments in a text that you will feel moved to write about if your instructor does not assign a paper topic to you. Even after you come up with a topic — say, the relationship between Homer and Sandra — you still need to turn it into a thesis. The following questions should help you choose a topic that you can develop into a thesis, the central idea of your paper. As you become increasingly engaged in your topic, you're likely to discover and perhaps change your ideas, so at the beginning stages it's best to regard your thesis as tentative. This will allow you to remain open to unexpected insights along the way.

DEVELOPING A TOPIC INTO A REVISED THESIS

1. If the topic is assigned, have you specifically addressed the prescribed subject matter?

2. If you choose your own topic, have you used your annotations, notes, and first-response writing to help you find a suitable topic?

3. Is the topic too broad or too narrow? Is the topic focused enough to be feasible and manageable for the assigned length of the paper?

4. Is the topic too difficult or specialized for you to write about successfully? If you need information and expertise that goes well beyond the scope of the assignment, would it be better to choose another topic?

5. Is the topic too simple or obvious to allow you to develop a strong thesis?

6. Once you have focused your topic, what do you think you want to say about it? What is the central idea—the tentative thesis—of the paper?

7. Have you asked questions about the topic to help generate a thesis?

8. Have you tried brainstorming or freewriting as a means of producing ideas that would lead to a thesis?

9. Have you tried writing a rough outline or simply jotting down ideas to see if your tentative thesis can be supported or qualified and made firmer?

10. Is your thesis statement precise or vague? What is the central argument that your thesis makes?

11. Does the thesis help provide an organizing principle—a sense of direction—for the paper?

12. Does the thesis statement consist of one or more complete declarative sentences (not framed as a question) written in clear language that express a complete idea?

13. Is the thesis supported by specific references to the text you are discussing? Have you used brief quotations to illustrate important points and provide evidence for the argument?

14. Is everything included in the paper in some way related to the thesis? Should any sentences or paragraphs be deleted because they are irrelevant to the central point?

15. Does the thesis appear in the introductory paragraph? If not, is there a particular reason for including it later in the paper?

16. If during the course of writing the paper you shifted direction or changed your mind about its central point, have you revised (or completely revamped) your thesis to reflect that change?

17. Have you developed a thesis that genuinely interests you? Are you interested enough in the thesis to write a paper that will also engage your reader?

A SAMPLE BRAINSTORMING LIST

After Janice has carefully read the story twice, she is ready to start turning the assigned topic into a defined thesis. Her instructor asked the class to answer the first question in the Considerations for Critical Thinking and Writing: *Would the story be more satisfying if Homer and Sandra openly acknowledged their feelings for each other and kissed at the end?* Janice uses the technique of brainstorming to come up with a more specific approach to the topic, thinking carefully about elements of the story like plot, setting, action, character, symbolism, tone, and theme.

— *plot* with subtle drama — why?

— "blessed realm between two worlds" — adolescence, the school years, real home life (Homer with another family), state of desire before culmination

— *action*: regular, familiar, relatively uneventful, savoring state of vague desire

— *setting*: tranquil, idyllic, familiar, warm, unabrasive "happy, cloistered finity of their world" — unthreatening, known; things happen as they're expected to; navigable, happy, image of summer

— *character*: Homer is shy but sensitive; Sandra seems a little more in control; both are on the threshold of adulthood

— *symbolism*: "blessed realm between two worlds" — adolescent summer life on the lake vs. school and the adult world, summer month with Thymes vs. real home life

— *tone*: easy, light tone, vague but pleasant romantic longing

— *theme*: love acknowledged but kept as part of summer life

A SAMPLE FIRST THESIS

Reviewing her brainstorming list, Janice sees a connection between the plot and the setting that helps her to address the question and to draft a thesis.

David Updike's short story "Summer" is a love story with little drama or complication. This lack of action in the plot is mirrored by Updike's rendering of the setting and general atmosphere, which are evoked by the description of the picturesque cabin on a lake, the season of summer, and the symbolic "season" of adolescence. The fact that there is no great culmination to Homer's attraction to Sandra is not a failure of the characters or of the fiction's drama. Instead, this nearly actionless plot captures and reflects the sense of adolescence and summer as a state of protected happiness.

A SAMPLE REVISED THESIS

After this initial attempt at a thesis, Janice asks herself several of the Questions for Writing on page 309 and writes out her responses, realizing along the way how she needs to revise her thesis.

Is the topic (that the action reflects the setting to create a sense of "happy, cloistered finity") too simple? I could discuss whether the story succeeds in creating this sense. It does — through description of setting and of Homer's thoughts.

Is the thesis statement precise? Not quite; I think I need to say in the thesis what would be appealing about "between two worlds." Updike describes it in positive tones, but suggests with the word "cloistered" that there's something they're closing themselves away from, implies there's a world outside. Why is the cloistered state happy and blessed? (I should also comment on the religious terminology, but maybe not in the thesis statement, since it's not the most important descriptive technique in the story.)

Does my thesis offer a direction for the paper, an organizing principle? I think that if I add onto the last sentence something about why the "realm between two worlds" is blessed, I'd be able to organize the paper as a discussion moving between action and setting to argue that the lack of action isn't a failure but a kind of fulfillment or contentment.

Is the thesis supported by specific references to the text you are discussing? Instead of saying "protected happiness" I should use one of the quotes I've been mentioning: "the happy, cloistered finity of their world" (para. 1) and "a blessed realm between two worlds" (para. 2).

David Updike's short story "Summer" involves little action or complication, but this lack of action in the plot is made meaningful by the rendering of the idyllic setting. Combined, these create a particular sense of summer, the symbolic "season" of adolescence, and of adolescent love. The fact that there is no great culmination to Homer's attraction to Sandra is not a failure of the characters or of the plot. Instead, the light tone of this nearly actionless plot captures and reflects the theme — a sense of adolescence and summer as a "blessed realm between two worlds" (para. 2), in which the characters are relatively free of the constraints of more complex adult relationships but may enjoy something of adult consciousness of feeling.

Compare the two thesis statements. Does the revised version seem more effective to you? Why or why not? Can you think of ways of further improving the revised version? Do you think the thesis would be more effective if more or fewer elements were included in it?

Before you begin writing your own paper, review the Questions for Responsive Reading and Writing (pp. 48–50) in Chapter 2, "Writing about Fiction." These questions will help you to focus and sharpen your critical thinking and writing. You'll also find help in Chapter 47, "Reading and Writing," which offers a systematic overview of choosing a topic, developing a thesis, and organizing various types of assignments. If you use outside sources for the paper, be sure to acknowledge them adequately by using the conventional documentation procedures detailed in Chapter 48, "The Literary Research Paper."

A SAMPLE STUDENT RESPONSE

Janice Reardon

Professor Halovanic

English 102

September 21, 2008

Plot and Setting in David Updike's "Summer"

David Updike's short story "Summer" is a love story with little drama or complication, but the lack of action in the plot is made meaningful by the rendering of the idyllic setting, as well as through metaphor and subtle detail. Combined, these elements create a particular sense of summer, the symbolic "season" of adolescence, and of adolescent love. The fact that there is no great culmination to Homer's attraction to Sandra is not a failure of Updike's characters or plot. Instead, the light tone of this nearly actionless plot reflects a specific period of adolescence, a moment between one stage of life and the next. During this time, the characters experience--perhaps for the first time--adult emotions, yet they are still free of the constraints of more complex adult relationships.

From the start, the story establishes a theme of transition through setting. The story takes place in early August "when summer briefly pauses, shifting between its beginning and its end" (D. Updike, 304). The days are still long and warm, yet change looms. The sound of fireworks is replaced by distant thunder. Thoughts of the approaching school year become stronger. This setting (both the physical setting as well as the time of year) is a metaphor for the characters, who are also dealing with change. The characters are caught in this same "pause" of summer, experiencing changes in their lives, anticipating other changes to come.

Also like the setting, the characters are at a midpoint, poised between where they have been and where they are going. Both Homer and Sandra are maturing. Homer suddenly has an interest in Sandra, though he has known her all his life. He sees her as having "the hair of a baby, the freckles of a child, and the sway of motherhood" (305). This description suggests the dichotomy of adolescence, a time when a person is caught "between two worlds" (304), between youth and adulthood. Though they recognize the changes they are going through, the characters still cling to their childhood. Homer spends his days playing games: tennis, golf, baseball. Sandra wears shorts faded by time--"faded relics of another era" (305)--a token of her past, perhaps one she is unwilling to give up just yet. These characters are pulled between what they have been all their lives and what lies ahead. They are no longer children and not quite adults, but the emotions they experience are no less real or significant.

The story has few active scenes, and Updike focuses on internal mono-logue and detail; it is this inaction that drives the plot. Homer does little to express his love for Sandra. He spends his days watching her intently as she lies in the sun, but he loathes the truck drivers' "leering gazes" (D. Updike 306) in the bowling alley diner where Sandra works. He deals with his new-found love for Sandra by focusing on and analyzing detail, much like the reader of the story. He cannot tell Sandra how he feels, even when the moment warrants it. When they are the last two awake and share a subtle, intimate moment, the thought of kissing her seems "absurd," and Homer can only look at the floor and say goodnight (307). At times, Homer even tries to use his inaction to get what he wants. When the pain of Sandra's seeming indifference becomes too much, he decides to give up his love for her, only to find that she continues on her "oblivious, happy course without him" (000). But it is Homer's inaction that helps us to understand what he is going through; in many ways his inaction creates more drama than action would.

While Homer does little to act on his love for Sandra, he does <u>react</u>. His desire for Sandra causes him to go to extremes. During their hike, when Homer is overcome by his "inarticulate passion" for Sandra, he runs from her at full speed, "howling into the woods" (306). At other times, he and Fred behave recklessly, speeding their car over bridges, racing their motorboat between buoys. They get in the habit of having a beer and a cigarette each night. These impulsive actions are a "solitary release" for Homer, a way for him to expend some of the anguish he's experiencing (306). This is not uncommon in life or in fiction. Sammy in John Updike's "A&P" reacts simi-larly to a difficult situation. After seeing two teenage girls humiliated by his boss, Sammy decides to take a stand. He quits his job, despite the possibility of upsetting his parents:

> "Sammy, you don't want to do this to your Mom and Dad,"
> he tells me. It's true, I don't. But it seems to me that once
> you begin a gesture it's fatal not to go through with it.
> (J. Updike, 564)

Here, Sammy, like Homer, acts without considering the consequences, a behavior common to adolescents.

Keeping with the themes of time and transition, the story ends when the summer ends. The nights grow cold; the preacher speaks of "another summer having run its course" (D. Updike 307). It is only then that Homer and Sandra share a simple, tender moment, a touch, and Homer's love for Sandra is finally--albeit subtly--requited. And with this small dramatic peak, the characters enter a new phase of adulthood. The two will no longer live "between two worlds." They will move on to the next stage of their lives, taking with them memories: memories of this period of their lives, of summer, and of each other.

Works Cited

Updike, David. "Summer." The Compact Bedford Introduction to Literature.
Ed. Michael Meyer. 8th ed. Boston: Bedford/St. Martin's, 2009. 304–8.
Updike, John. "A&P." The Compact Bedford Introduction to Literature. Ed.
Michael Meyer. 8th ed. Boston: Bedford/St. Martin's, 2009. 560–64.

Approaches
to Fiction

11

A Study of
Nathaniel Hawthorne

[My] book, if you would see anything in it, requires to be read in the clear, brown, twilight atmosphere in which it was written; if opened in the sunshine, it is apt to look exceedingly like a volume of blank pages.

—HAWTHORNE, Preface to
Twice-Told Tales (1851)

The three short stories by Nathaniel Hawthorne included in this chapter provide an opportunity to study a major fiction writer in depth. Getting to know an author's work is similar to developing a friendship with someone: the more encounters, the more intimate the relationship becomes. Familiarity with a writer's concerns and methods in one story can help to illuminate another story. As we become accustomed to someone's voice—a friend's or a writer's—we become attuned to nuances in tone and meaning. The nuances in Hawthorne's fiction warrant close analysis. Although the stories included are not wholly representative of his work, they suggest some of the techniques and concerns that characterize it. The three stories provide a useful context

Web Explore contexts for Nathaniel Hawthorne and approaches to "Young Goodman Brown" on *LiterActive* or at bedfordstmartins .com/meyercompact.

"The Old Manse." The Hawthornes spent some of their happiest years (from the summer of 1842 to 1846) at the Old Manse, a house built by the family of Ralph Waldo Emerson (c. 1770). The garden held a special attraction for Hawthorne, as he describes in *Mosses from an Old Manse:* "I used to visit and revisit it a dozen times a day, and stand in deep contemplation over my vegetable progeny with a love that nobody could share or conceive of who had never taken part in the process of creation. It was one of the most bewitching sights in the world, to observe a hill of beans thrusting aside the soil, or a row of early peas just peeping forth sufficiently to trace a line of delicate green. . . ." Reprinted by permission of Lee Snider/photo images.

"The Witch of the Woodlands" (above). Because Hawthorne's family tree included a judge who participated in the Salem witchcraft trials (1692–93), witchcraft was an important theme in Hawthorne's writing. This illustration from an eighteenth-century book on witchcraft features "a grave and dark-clad company" such as Goodman Brown describes (see "Young Goodman Brown," p. 325). Witches were thought to commune in the forest and associate with evil creatures or strange animals known as "familiars."
Courtesy of the Peabody Essex Museum.

Nathaniel Hawthorne (right) Age 36, in an 1840 portrait by Charles Osgood.
Courtesy of the Peabody Essex Museum.

for reading individual stories. Moreover, the works invite comparisons and contrasts in their styles and themes. Following the three stories are some brief commentaries by and about Hawthorne that establish additional contexts for understanding his fiction.

A BRIEF BIOGRAPHY AND INTRODUCTION

Nathaniel Hawthorne (1804–1864) once described himself as "the obscurest man of letters in America." During the early years of his career, this self-assessment was mostly accurate, but the publication of *The Scarlet Letter* in 1850 marked the beginning of Hawthorne's reputation as a major American writer. His novels and short stories have entertained and challenged generations of readers; they have wide appeal because they can be read on many levels. Hawthorne skillfully creates an atmosphere of complexity and ambiguity that makes it difficult to reduce his stories to a simple view of life. The moral and psychological issues that he examines through the conflicts his characters experience are often intricate and mysterious. Readers are frequently made to feel that in exploring Hawthorne's characters they are also encountering some part of themselves.

Hawthorne achieved success as a writer only after a steady and intense struggle. His personal history was hardly conducive to producing a professional writer. Born in Salem, Massachusetts, Hawthorne came from a Puritan family of declining fortunes that prided itself on an energetic pursuit of practical matters such as law and commerce. He never knew his father, a sea captain who died in Dutch Guiana when Hawthorne was only four years old, but he did have a strong imaginative sense of an early ancestor, who as a Puritan judge persecuted Quakers, and of a later ancestor, who was a judge during the Salem witchcraft trials. His forebears seemed to haunt Hawthorne, so that in some ways he felt more involved in the past than in the present.

In "The Custom-House," the introduction to *The Scarlet Letter,* Hawthorne considers himself in relation to his severe Puritan ancestors:

> No aim, that I have ever cherished, would they recognize as laudable; no success of mine . . . would they deem otherwise than worthless, if not positively disgraceful. "What is he?" murmurs one gray shadow of my forefathers to the other. "A writer of story-books! What kind of a business in life, — what mode of glorifying God, or being serviceable to mankind in his day and generation, — may that be? Why, the degenerate fellow might as well have been a fiddler!" Such are the compliments bandied between my great-grandsires and myself, across the gulf of time! And yet, let them scorn me as they will, strong traits of their nature have intertwined with mine.

Hawthorne's sense of what his forebears might think of his work caused him to worry that the utilitarian world was more real and important than his imaginative creations. This issue became a recurring theme in his work.

Despite the Puritan strain in Hawthorne's sensibilities and his own deep suspicion that a literary vocation was not serious or productive work, Hawthorne was determined to become a writer. He found encouragement at Bowdoin College in Maine and graduated in 1825 with a class that included the poet Henry Wadsworth Longfellow and Franklin Pierce, who would be elected president of the United States in the early 1850s. After graduation Hawthorne returned to his mother's house in Salem, where for the next twelve years he read New England history as well as writers such as John Milton, William Shakespeare, and John Bunyan. During this time he lived a relatively withdrawn life devoted to developing his literary art. Hawthorne wrote and revised stories as he sought a style that would express his creative energies. Many of these early efforts were destroyed when they did not meet his high standards. His first novel, *Fanshawe*, was published anonymously in 1828; it concerns a solitary young man who fails to realize his potential and dies young. Hawthorne very nearly succeeded in reclaiming and destroying all the published copies of this work. It was not attributed to the author until after his death; not even his wife was aware that he had written it. The stories eventually published as *Twice-Told Tales* (1837) represent work that was carefully revised and survived Hawthorne's critical judgments.

Writing did not provide an adequate income, so like nearly all nineteenth-century American writers, Hawthorne had to take on other employment. He worked in the Boston Custom House from 1839 through 1840 to save money to marry Sophia Peabody, but he lost that politically appointed job when administrations changed. In 1841 he lived at Brook Farm, a utopian community founded by idealists who hoped to combine manual labor with art and philosophy. Finding that monotonous physical labor left little time for thinking and writing, Hawthorne departed after seven months. The experience failed to improve his financial situation, but it did eventually serve as the basis for a novel, *The Blithedale Romance* (1852).

Married in the summer of 1842, Hawthorne and his wife moved to the Old Manse in Concord, Massachusetts, where their neighbors included Ralph Waldo Emerson, Henry David Thoreau, Amos Bronson Alcott, and other writers and thinkers who contributed to the lively literary environment of that small town. Although Hawthorne was on friendly terms with these men, his skepticism concerning human nature prevented him from sharing either their optimism or their faith in radical reform of individuals or society. Hawthorne's view of life was chastened by a sense of what he called in "Wakefield" the "iron tissue of necessity." His sensibilities were more akin to Herman Melville's. When Melville and Hawthorne met while Hawthorne was living in the Berkshires of western Massachusetts, they responded to each other intensely. Melville admired the "power of blackness" he discovered in Hawthorne's writings and dedicated *Moby-Dick* to him.

During the several years he lived in the Old Manse, Hawthorne published a second collection of *Twice-Told Tales* (1842) and additional stories in

Mosses from an Old Manse (1846). To keep afloat financially, he worked in the Salem Custom House from 1846 until 1849, when he again lost his job through a change in administrations. This time, however, he discovered that by leaving the oppressive materialism of the Custom House he found more energy to write: "So little adapted is the atmosphere of a Custom House to the delicate harvest of fancy and sensibility, that, had I remained there through ten Presidencies yet to come, I doubt whether the tale of 'The Scarlet Letter' would ever have been brought before the public. My imagination was a tarnished mirror [there.]" Free of the Custom House, Hawthorne was at the height of his creativity and productivity during the early 1850s. In addition to *The Scarlet Letter* and *The Blithedale Romance*, he wrote *The House of the Seven Gables* (1851); *The Snow-Image, and Other Twice-Told Tales* (1852); a campaign biography of his Bowdoin classmate, *The Life of Franklin Pierce* (1852); and two collections of stories for children, *A Wonder Book* (1852) and *Tanglewood Tales* (1853).

Hawthorne's financial situation improved during the final decade of his life. In 1853 his friend President Pierce appointed him to the U.S. consulship in Liverpool, where he remained for the next four years. Following a tour of Europe from 1858 to 1860, Hawthorne and his family returned to Concord, and he published *The Marble Faun* (1860), his final completed work of fiction. He died while traveling through New Hampshire with former President Pierce.

Hawthorne's stories are much more complex than the melodramatic but usually optimistic fiction published in many magazines contemporary to him. Instead of cheerfully confirming public values and attitudes, his work tends to be dark and brooding. Modern readers remain responsive to Hawthorne's work — despite the fact that his nineteenth-century style takes some getting used to — because his psychological themes are as fascinating as they are disturbing. The range of his themes is not broad, but their treatment is remarkable for its insights.

Hawthorne wrote about individuals who suffer from inner conflicts caused by sin, pride, untested innocence, hidden guilt, perverse secrecy, cold intellectuality, and isolation. His characters are often consumed by their own passions, whether those passions are motivated by an obsession with goodness or evil. He looks inside his characters and reveals to us that portion of their hearts, minds, and souls that they keep from the world and even from themselves. This emphasis accounts for the private, interior, and sometimes gloomy atmosphere in Hawthorne's works. His stories rarely end on a happy note because the questions his characters raise are almost never completely answered. Rather than positing solutions to the problems and issues his characters encounter, Hawthorne leaves us with ambiguities suggesting that experience cannot always be fully understood and controlled. Beneath the surface appearances in his stories lurk ironies and shifting meanings that point to many complex truths instead of a single simple moral.

The following three Hawthorne stories provide an opportunity to study this writer in some depth. These stories are not intended to be entirely representative of the 120 or so that Hawthorne wrote, but they do offer some sense of the range of his techniques and themes. Hawthorne's fictional world of mysterious incidents and sometimes bizarre characters increases in meaning the more his stories are read in the context of one another.

Young Goodman Brown   *1835*

Young Goodman Brown came forth at sunset into the street at Salem village; but put his head back, after crossing the threshold, to exchange a parting kiss with his young wife. And Faith, as the wife was aptly named, thrust her own pretty head into the street, letting the wind play with the pink ribbons of her cap while she called to Goodman Brown.

"Dearest heart," whispered she, softly and rather sadly, when her lips were close to his ear, "prithee put off your journey until sunrise and sleep in your own bed tonight. A lone woman is troubled with such dreams and such thoughts that she's afeared of herself sometimes. Pray tarry with me this night, dear husband, of all nights in the year."

"My love and my Faith," replied young Goodman Brown, "of all nights in the year, this one night must I tarry away from thee. My journey, as thou callest it, forth and back again, must needs be done 'twixt now and sunrise. What, my sweet, pretty wife, dost thou doubt me already, and we but three months married?"

"Then God bless you!" said Faith, with the pink ribbons; "and may you find all well when you come back."

"Amen!" cried Goodman Brown. "Say thy prayers, dear Faith, and go to 5 bed at dusk, and no harm will come to thee."

So they parted; and the young man pursued his way until, being about to turn the corner by the meeting-house, he looked back and saw the head of Faith still peeping after him with a melancholy air, in spite of her pink ribbons.

"Poor little Faith!" thought he, for his heart smote him. "What a wretch am I to leave her on such an errand! She talks of dreams, too. Methought as she spoke there was trouble in her face, as if a dream had warned her what work is to be done tonight. But no, no; 't would kill her to think it. Well, she's a blessed angel on earth; and after this one night I'll cling to her skirts and follow her to heaven."

With this excellent resolve for the future, Goodman Brown felt himself justified in making more haste on his present evil purpose. He had taken a dreary road, darkened by all the gloomiest trees of the forest, which barely stood aside to let the narrow path creep through, and closed immediately behind. It was all as lonely as could be; and there is this peculiarity in such a solitude, that the traveler knows not who may be concealed by the innumerable trunks and the thick boughs overhead; so that with lonely footsteps he may yet be passing through an unseen multitude.

"There may be a devilish Indian behind every tree," said Goodman Brown to himself; and he glanced fearfully behind him as he added, "What if the devil himself should be at my very elbow!"

His head being turned back, he passed a crook of the road, and, looking 10 forward again, beheld the figure of a man, in grave and decent attire, seated at the foot of an old tree. He arose at Goodman Brown's approach and walked onward side by side with him.

"You are late, Goodman Brown," said he. "The clock of the Old South was striking as I came through Boston, and that is full fifteen minutes agone."

"Faith kept me back a while," replied the young man, with a tremor in his voice, caused by the sudden appearance of his companion, though not wholly unexpected.

It was now deep dusk in the forest, and deepest in that part of it where these two were journeying. As nearly as could be discerned, the second traveler was about fifty years old, apparently in the same rank of life as Goodman Brown, and bearing a considerable resemblance to him, though perhaps more in expression than features. Still they might have been taken for father and son. And yet, though the elder person was as simply clad as the younger, and as simple in manner too, he had an indescribable air of one who knew the world, and who would not have felt abashed at the governor's dinner table or in King William's court, were it possible that his affairs should call him thither. But the only thing about him that could be fixed upon as remarkable was his staff, which bore the likeness of a great black snake, so curiously wrought that it might almost be seen to twist and wriggle itself like a living serpent. This, of course, must have been an ocular deception, assisted by the uncertain light.

"Come, Goodman Brown," cried his fellow-traveler, "this is a dull pace for the beginning of a journey. Take my staff, if you are so soon weary."

"Friend," said the other, exchanging his slow pace for a full stop, "having kept covenant by meeting thee here, it is my purpose now to return whence I came. I have scruples touching the matter thou wot'st° of." 15

"Sayest thou so?" replied he of the serpent, smiling apart. "Let us walk on, nevertheless, reasoning as we go; and if I convince thee not thou shalt turn back. We are but a little way in the forest yet."

"Too far! too far!" exclaimed the goodman, unconsciously resuming his walk. "My father never went into the woods on such an errand, nor his father before him. We have been a race of honest men and good Christians since the days of the martyrs; and shall I be the first of the name of Brown that ever took this path and kept" —

"Such company, thou wouldst say," observed the elder person, interpreting his pause. "Well said, Goodman Brown! I have been as well acquainted with your family as with ever a one among the Puritans; and that's no trifle to say. I helped your grandfather, the constable, when he lashed the Quaker woman so smartly through the streets of Salem; and it was I that brought your father a pitch-pine knot, kindled at my own hearth, to set fire to an Indian village, in King Philip's war.° They were my good friends, both; and many a pleasant walk have we had along this path, and returned merrily after midnight. I would fain be friends with you for their sake."

"If it be as thou sayest," replied Goodman Brown, "I marvel they never spoke of these matters; or, verily, I marvel not, seeing that the least rumor of

---

wot'st: Know.
King Philip's war (1675-76): War between the colonists and an alliance of Indian tribes led by Metacan (also known as Metacomet), leader of the Wampanoags, who was called King Philip by the colonists.

the sort would have driven them from New England. We are a people of prayer, and good works to boot, and abide no such wickedness."

"Wickedness or not," said the traveler with the twisted staff, "I have a very 20 general acquaintance here in New England. The deacons of many a church have drunk the communion wine with me; the selectmen of divers towns make me their chairman; and a majority of the Great and General Court are firm supporters of my interest. The governor and I, too — But these are state secrets."

"Can this be so?" cried Goodman Brown, with a stare of amazement at his undisturbed companion. "Howbeit, I have nothing to do with the governor and council; they have their own ways, and are no rule for a simple husband-man like me. But, were I to go on with thee, how should I meet the eye of that good old man, our minister, at Salem village? Oh, his voice would make me tremble both Sabbath day and lecture day."

Thus far the elder traveler had listened with due gravity; but now burst into a fit of irrepressible mirth, shaking himself so violently that his snakelike staff actually seemed to wriggle in sympathy.

"Ha! ha! ha!" shouted he again and again; then composing himself, "Well, go on, Goodman Brown, go on; but, prithee, don't kill me with laughing."

"Well, then, to end the matter at once," said Goodman Brown, consider-ably nettled, "there is my wife, Faith. It would break her dear little heart; and I'd rather break my own."

"Nay, if that be the case," answered the other, "e'en go thy ways, Goodman 25 Brown. I would not for twenty old women like the one hobbling before us that Faith should come to any harm."

As he spoke he pointed his staff at a female figure on the path, in whom Goodman Brown recognized a very pious and exemplary dame, who had taught him his catechism in youth, and was still his moral and spiritual adviser, jointly with the minister and Deacon Gookin.

"A marvel, truly that Goody Cloyse should be so far in the wilderness at nightfall," said he. "But with your leave, friend, I shall take a cut through the woods until we have left this Christian woman behind. Being a stranger to you, she might ask whom I was consorting with and whither I was going."

"Be it so," said his fellow-traveler. "Betake you to the woods, and let me keep the path."

Accordingly the young man turned aside, but took care to watch his com-panion, who advanced softly along the road until he had come within a staff's length of the old dame. She, meanwhile, was making the best of her way, with singular speed for so aged a woman, and mumbling some indistinct words — a prayer, doubtless — as she went. The traveler put forth his staff and touched her withered neck with what seemed the serpent's tail.

"The devil!" screamed the pious old lady.   30

"Then Goody Cloyse knows her old friend?" observed the traveler, con-fronting her and leaning on his writhing stick.

"Ah, forsooth, and is it your worship indeed?" cried the good dame. "Yea, truly is it, and in the very image of my old gossip, Goodman Brown, the grand-father of the silly fellow that now is. But — would your worship believe it? — my broomstick hath strangely disappeared, stolen, as I suspect, by that unhanged witch, Goody Cory, and that, too, when I was all anointed with the juice of smallage, and cinquefoil, and wolfsbane" —

"Mingled with fine wheat and the fat of a newborn babe," said the shape of old Goodman Brown.

"Ah, your worship knows the recipe," cried the old lady, cackling aloud. "So, as I was saying, being all ready for the meeting, and no horse to ride on, I made up my mind to foot it; for they tell me there is a nice young man to be taken into communion tonight. But now your good worship will lend me your arm, and we shall be there in a twinkling."

"That can hardly be," answered her friend. "I may not spare you my arm, 35 Goody Cloyse; but here is my staff, if you will."

So saying, he threw it down at her feet, where, perhaps, it assumed life, being one of the rods which its owner had formerly lent to the Egyptian magi. Of this fact, however, Goodman Brown could not take cognizance. He had cast up his eyes in astonishment, and, looking down again, beheld neither Goody Cloyse nor the serpentine staff, but his fellow-traveler alone, who waited for him as calmly as if nothing had happened.

"That old woman taught me my catechism," said the young man; and there was a world of meaning in this simple comment.

They continued to walk onward, while the elder traveler exhorted his companion to make good speed and persevere in the path, discoursing so aptly that his arguments seemed rather to spring up in the bosom of his auditor than to be suggested by himself. As they went, he plucked a branch of maple to serve for a walking stick, and began to strip it of the twigs and little boughs, which were wet with evening dew. The moment his fingers touched them they became strangely withered and dried up as with a week's sunshine. Thus the pair proceeded, at a good free pace, until suddenly, in a gloomy hollow of the road, Goodman Brown sat himself down on the stump of a tree and refused to go any farther.

"Friend," he said, stubbornly, "my mind is made up. Not another step will I budge on this errand. What if a wretched old woman do choose to go to the devil when I thought she was going to heaven: is that any reason why I should quit my dear Faith and go after her?"

"You will think better of this by and by," said his acquaintance, compos- 40 edly. "Sit here and rest yourself a while; and when you feel like moving again, there is my staff to help you along."

Without more words, he threw his companion the maple stick, and was as speedily out of sight as if he had vanished into the deepening gloom. The young man sat a few moments by the roadside, applauding himself greatly, and thinking with how clear a conscience he should meet the minister in his morning walk, nor shrink from the eye of good old Deacon Gookin. And what calm sleep would be his that very night, which was to have been spent so wickedly, but so purely and sweetly now, in the arms of Faith! Amidst these pleasant and praiseworthy meditations, Goodman Brown heard the tramp of horses along the road, and deemed it advisable to conceal himself within the verge of the forest, conscious of the guilty purpose that had brought him thither, though now so happily turned from it.

On came the hoof tramps and the voices of the riders, two grave old voices, conversing soberly as they drew near. These mingled sounds appeared to pass along the road, within a few yards of the young man's hiding-place; but, owing doubtless to the depth of the gloom at that particular spot, neither the travelers nor their steeds were visible. Though their figures brushed the small boughs by the wayside, it could not be seen that they intercepted, even for a moment, the faint gleam from the strip of bright sky athwart which they must have passed. Goodman Brown alternately crouched and stood on tiptoe, pulling aside the branches and thrusting forth his head as far as he durst without discerning so much as a shadow. It vexed him the more, because he could have sworn, were such a thing possible, that he recognized the voices of the minister and Deacon Gookin, jogging along quietly, as they were wont to do, when bound to some ordination or ecclesiastical council. While yet within hearing, one of the riders stopped to pluck a switch.

"Of the two, reverend sir," said the voice like the deacon's, "I had rather miss an ordination dinner than tonight's meeting. They tell me that some of our community are to be here from Falmouth and beyond, and others from Connecticut and Rhode Island, besides several of the Indian powwows, who, after their fashion, know almost as much deviltry as the best of us. Moreover, there is a goodly young woman to be taken into communion."

"Mighty well, Deacon Gookin!" replied the solemn old tones of the minister. "Spur up, or we shall be late. Nothing can be done, you know, until I get on the ground."

The hoofs clattered again; and the voices, talking so strangely in the empty air, passed on through the forest, where no church had ever been gathered or solitary Christian prayed. Whither, then, could these holy men be journeying so deep into the heathen wilderness? Young Goodman Brown caught hold of a tree for support, being ready to sink down on the ground, faint and overburdened with the heavy sickness of his heart. He looked up to the sky, doubting whether there really was a heaven above him. Yet there was the blue arch, and the stars brightening in it. 45

"With heaven above and Faith below, I will yet stand firm against the devil!" cried Goodman Brown.

While he still gazed upward into the deep arch of the firmament and had lifted his hands to pray, a cloud, though no wind was stirring, hurried across the zenith and hid the brightening stars. The blue sky was still visible, except directly overhead, where this black mass of cloud was sweeping swiftly northward. Aloft in the air, as if from the depths of the cloud, came a confused and doubtful sound of voices. Once the listener fancied that he could distinguish the accents of townspeople of his own, men and women, both pious and ungodly, many of whom he had met at the communion table, and had seen others rioting at the tavern. The next moment, so indistinct were the sounds, he doubted whether he had heard aught but the murmur of the old forest, whispering without a wind. Then came a stronger swell of those familiar tones, heard daily in the sunshine at Salem village, but never until now from a cloud of night. There was one voice, of a young woman, uttering lamentations, yet with an uncertain sorrow, and entreating for some favor, which, perhaps, it would grieve her to obtain; and all the unseen multitude, both saints and sinners, seemed to encourage her onward.

"Faith!" shouted Goodman Brown, in a voice of agony and desperation; and the echoes of the forest mocked him, crying, "Faith! Faith!" as if bewildered wretches were seeking her all through the wilderness.

The cry of grief, rage, and terror was yet piercing the night, when the unhappy husband held his breath for a response. There was a scream, drowned immediately in a louder murmur of voices, fading into far-off laughter, as the dark cloud swept away, leaving the clear and silent sky above Goodman Brown. But something fluttered lightly down through the air and caught on the branch of a tree. The young man seized it, and beheld a pink ribbon.

"My Faith is gone!" cried he after one stupefied moment. "There is no 50 good on earth; and sin is but a name. Come, devil; for to thee is this world given."

And, maddened with despair, so that he laughed loud and long, did Goodman Brown grasp his staff and set forth again, at such a rate that he seemed to fly along the forest path rather than to walk or run. The road grew wilder and drearier and more faintly traced, and vanished at length, leaving him in the heart of the dark wilderness, still rushing onward with the instinct that guides mortal man to evil. The whole forest was peopled with frightful sounds—the creaking of the trees, the howling of wild beasts, and the yell of Indians; while sometimes the wind tolled like a distant church bell, and sometimes gave a broad roar around the traveler, as if all Nature were laughing him to scorn. But he was himself the chief horror of the scene, and shrank not from its other horrors.

"Ha! ha! ha!" roared Goodman Brown when the wind laughed at him. "Let us hear which will laugh loudest. Think not to frighten me with your deviltry. Come witch, come wizard, come Indian powwow, come devil himself, and here comes Goodman Brown. You may as well fear him as he fear you."

In truth, all through the haunted forest there could be nothing more frightful than the figure of Goodman Brown. On he flew among the black pines, brandishing his staff with frenzied gestures, now giving vent to an inspiration of horrid blasphemy, and now shouting forth such laughter as set all the echoes of the forest laughing like demons around him. The fiend in his own shape is less hideous than when he rages in the breast of man. Thus sped the demoniac on his course, until, quivering among the trees, he saw a red light before him, as when the felled trunks and branches of a clearing have been set on fire, and throw up their lurid blaze against the sky, at the hour of midnight. He paused, in a lull of the tempest that had driven him onward, and heard the swell of what seemed a hymn, rolling solemnly from a distance with the weight of many voices. He knew the tune; it was a familiar one in the choir of the village meeting-house. The verse died heavily away, and was lengthened by a chorus, not of human voices, but of all the sounds of the benighted wilderness pealing in awful harmony together. Goodman Brown cried out, and his cry was lost to his own ear by its unison with the cry of the desert.

In the interval of silence he stole forward until the light glared full upon his eyes. At one extremity of an open space, hemmed in by the dark wall of the forest, arose a rock, bearing some rude, natural resemblance either to an altar or a pulpit, and surrounded by four blazing pines, their tops aflame, their stems untouched, like candles at an evening meeting. The mass of foliage that had overgrown the summit of the rock was all on fire, blazing high into the night and fitfully illuminating the whole field. Each pendent twig and leafy festoon was in a blaze. As the red light arose and fell, a numerous congregation alternately shone forth, then disappeared in shadow, and again grew, as it were, out of the darkness, peopling the heart of the solitary woods at once.

"A grave and dark-clad company," quoth Goodman Brown. 55

In truth they were such. Among them, quivering to and fro between gloom and splendor, appeared faces that would be seen next day at the council board of the province, and others which, Sabbath after Sabbath, looked devoutly heavenward, and benignantly over the crowded pews, from the holiest pulpits in the land. Some affirm that the lady of the governor was there. At least there were high dames well known to her, and wives of honored husbands, and widows, a great multitude, and ancient maidens, all of excellent repute, and fair young girls, who trembled lest their mothers should espy them. Either the sudden gleams of light flashing over the obscure field bedazzled Goodman Brown, or he recognized a score of the church members of Salem village famous for their especial sanctity. Good old Deacon Gookin had arrived, and waited at the skirts of that venerable saint, his revered pastor. But, irreverently consorting with these grave, reputable, and pious people, these elders of the church, these chaste dames and dewy virgins, there were men of dissolute lives and women of spotted fame, wretches given over to all mean and filthy vice, and suspected even of horrid crimes. It was strange to see that the good shrank not from the wicked, nor were the sinners abashed by the saints. Scattered also among their pale-faced enemies were the Indian priests, or powwows, who had often scared their native forest with more hideous incantations than any known to English witchcraft.

"But where is Faith?" thought Goodman Brown; and, as hope came into his heart, he trembled.

Another verse of the hymn arose, a slow and mournful strain, such as the pious love, but joined to words which expressed all that our nature can conceive of sin, and darkly hinted at far more. Unfathomable to mere mortals is the lore of fiends. Verse after verse was sung; and still the chorus of the desert swelled between like the deepest tone of a mighty organ; and with the final peal of that dreadful anthem there came a sound, as if the roaring wind, the rushing streams, the howling beasts, and every other voice of the unconcerted wilderness were mingling and according with the voice of guilty man in homage to the prince of all. The four blazing pines threw up a loftier flame, and obscurely discovered shapes and visages of horror on the smoke wreaths above the impious assembly. At the same moment the fire on the rock shot redly forth and formed a glowing arch above its base, where now appeared a figure. With reverence be it spoken, the figure bore no slight similitude, both in garb and manner, to some grave divine of the New England churches.

"Bring forth the converts!" cried a voice that echoed through the field and rolled into the forest.

At the word, Goodman Brown stepped forth from the shadow of the trees   60
and approached the congregation, with whom he felt a loathful brotherhood by the sympathy of all that was wicked in his heart. He could have well-nigh sworn that the shape of his own dead father beckoned him to advance, looking downward from a smoke wreath, while a woman, with dim features of despair, threw out her hand to warn him back. Was it his mother? But he had no power to retreat one step, nor to resist, even in thought, when the minister and good old Deacon Gookin seized his arms and led him to the blazing rock. Thither came also the slender form of a veiled female, led between Goody Cloyse, that pious teacher of the catechism, and Martha Carrier, who had received the devil's promise to be queen of hell. A rampant hag was she. And there stood the proselytes beneath the canopy of fire.

"Welcome, my children," said the dark figure, "to the communion of your race. Ye have found thus young your nature and your destiny. My children, look behind you!"

They turned; and flashing forth, as it were, in a sheet of flame, the fiend worshipers were seen; the smile of welcome gleamed darkly on every visage.

"There," resumed the sable form, "are all whom ye have reverenced from youth. Ye deemed them holier than yourselves and shrank from your own sin, contrasting it with their lives of righteousness and prayerful aspirations heavenward. Yet here are they all in my worshiping assembly. This night it shall be granted you to know their secret deeds: how hoary-bearded elders of the church have whispered wanton words to the young maids of their households; how many a woman, eager for widows' weeds, has given her husband a drink at bedtime and let him sleep his last sleep in her bosom; how beardless youths have made haste to inherit their fathers' wealth; and how fair damsels—blush not, sweet ones—have dug little graves in the garden, and bidden me, the sole guest, to an infant's funeral. By the sympathy of your human hearts for sin ye shall scent out all the places—whether in church, bedchamber, street, field, or forest—where crime has been committed, and shall exult to behold the whole earth one stain of guilt, one mighty blood spot. Far more than this. It shall be yours to penetrate, in every bosom, the deep mystery of sin, the fountain of all wicked arts, and which inexhaustibly supplies more evil impulses than human power—than my power at its utmost—can make manifest in deeds. And now, my children, look upon each other."

They did so; and, by the blaze of the hell-kindled torches, the wretched man beheld his Faith, and the wife her husband, trembling before that unhallowed altar.

"Lo, there ye stand, my children," said the figure, in a deep and solemn 65
tone, almost sad with its despairing awfulness, as if his once angelic nature could yet mourn for our miserable race. "Depending upon one another's hearts, ye had still hoped that virtue were not all a dream. Now are ye undeceived. Evil is the nature of mankind. Evil must be your only happiness. Welcome again, my children, to the communion of your race."

"Welcome," repeated the fiend worshipers; in one cry of despair and triumph.

And there they stood, the only pair, as it seemed, who were yet hesitating on the verge of wickedness in this dark world. A basin was hollowed, naturally, in the rock. Did it contain water, reddened by the lurid light? or was it blood? or, perchance, a liquid flame? Herein did the shape of evil dip his hand and prepare to lay the mark of baptism upon their foreheads, that they might be partakers of the mystery of sin, more conscious of the secret guilt of others, both in deed and thought, than they could now be of their own. The husband cast one look at his pale wife, and Faith at him. What polluted wretches would the next glance show them to each other, shuddering alike at what they disclosed and what they saw!

"Faith! Faith!" cried the husband, "look up to heaven, and resist the wicked one."

Whether Faith obeyed he knew not. Hardly had he spoken when he found himself amid calm night and solitude, listening to a roar of the wind which died heavily away through the forest. He staggered against the rock, and felt it chill and damp; while a hanging twig, that had been all on fire, besprinkled his cheek with the coldest dew.

The next morning young Goodman Brown came slowly into the street of 70
Salem village, staring around him like a bewildered man. The good old minister was taking a walk along the graveyard to get an appetite for breakfast and meditate his sermon, and bestowed a blessing, as he passed, on Goodman Brown. He shrank from the venerable saint as if to avoid an anathema. Old

Deacon Gookin was at domestic worship, and the holy words of his prayer were heard through the open window. "What God doth the wizard pray to?" quoth Goodman Brown. Goody Cloyse, that excellent old Christian, stood in the early sunshine at her own lattice, catechizing a little girl who had brought her a pint of morning's milk. Goodman Brown snatched away the child as from the grasp of the fiend himself. Turning the corner by the meeting-house, he spied the head of Faith, with the pink ribbons, gazing anxiously forth, and bursting into such joy at sight of him that she skipped along the street and almost kissed her husband before the whole village. But Goodman Brown looked sternly and sadly into her face, and passed on without a greeting.

Had Goodman Brown fallen asleep in the forest and only dreamed a wild dream of a witch-meeting?

Be it so if you will; but, alas! it was a dream of evil omen for young Goodman Brown. A stern, a sad, a darkly meditative, a distrustful, if not a desperate man did he become from the night of that fearful dream. On the Sabbath day, when the congregation were singing a holy psalm, he could not listen because an anthem of sin rushed loudly upon his ear and drowned all the blessed strain. When the minister spoke from the pulpit with power and fervid eloquence, and, with his hand on the open Bible, of the sacred truths of our religion, and of saintlike lives and triumphant deaths, and of future bliss or misery unutterable, then did Goodman Brown turn pale, dreading lest the roof should thunder down upon the gray blasphemer and his hearers. Often, awaking suddenly at midnight, he shrank from the bosom of Faith; and at morning or eventide, when the family knelt down at prayer, he scowled and muttered to himself, and gazed sternly at his wife, and turned away. And when he had lived long, and was borne to his grave a hoary corpse, followed by Faith, an aged woman, and children and grandchildren, a goodly procession, besides neighbors not a few, they carved no hopeful verse upon his tombstone, for his dying hour was gloom.

Considerations for Critical Thinking and Writing

1. **FIRST RESPONSE.** Try to summarize "Young Goodman Brown" with a tidy moral. Is it possible? What makes this story complex?

2. What is the significance of Goodman Brown's name?

3. What is the symbolic value of the forest in this story? How are the descriptions of the forest contrasted with those of Salem village?

4. Characterize Goodman Brown at the beginning of the story. Why does he go into the forest? What does he mean when he says "Faith kept me back a while" (para. 12)?

5. What function do Faith's ribbons have in the story?

6. What foreshadows Goodman Brown's meeting with his "fellow-traveler" (para. 14)? Who is he? How do we know that Brown is keeping an appointment with a supernatural being?

7. The narrator describes the fellow-traveler's staff wriggling like a snake but then says, "This, of course, must have been an ocular deception, assisted by the uncertain light" (para. 13). What is the effect of this and other instances of ambiguity in the story?

8. What does Goodman Brown discover in the forest? What does he come to think of his ancestors, the church and state, Goody Cloyse, and even his wife?

9. Is Salem populated by hypocrites who cover hideous crimes with a veneer of piety and respectability? Do Faith and the other characters Brown sees when he returns from the forest appear corrupt to you?

10. Near the end of the story the narrator asks, "Had Goodman Brown fallen asleep in the forest and only dreamed a wild dream of a witch-meeting?" (para. 71). Was it a dream, or did the meeting actually happen? How does the answer to this question affect your reading of the story? Write an essay giving an answer to the narrator's question.

11. How is Goodman Brown changed by his experience in the forest? Does the narrator endorse Brown's unwillingness to trust anyone?

12. Consider the story as a criticism of the village's hypocrisy.

13. CRITICAL STRATEGIES. Read the section on psychological criticism (pp. 1542–44) in Chapter 46, "Critical Strategies for Reading," and discuss this story as an inward, psychological journey in which Goodman Brown discovers the power of blackness in himself but refuses to acknowledge that dimension of his personality.

CONNECTIONS TO OTHER SELECTIONS

1. Compare and contrast Goodman Brown's reasons for withdrawal with those of Melville's Bartleby (p. 124). Do you find yourself more sympathetic with one character than the other? Explain.

2. To what extent is Hawthorne's use of dreams crucial in this story and in "The Birthmark" (p. 343)? Explain how Hawthorne uses dreams as a means to complicate our view of his characters.

3. What does Goodman Brown's pursuit of sin have in common with Aylmer's quest for perfection in "The Birthmark"? How do these pursuits reveal the characters' personalities and shed light on the theme of each story?

The Minister's Black Veil   *1836*
A Parable°

The sexton stood in the porch of Milford meeting-house, pulling lustily at the bell-rope. The old people of the village came stooping along the street. Children, with bright faces, tript merrily beside their parents, or mimicked a graver gait, in the conscious dignity of their Sunday clothes. Spruce bachelors looked sidelong at the pretty maidens, and fancied that the Sabbath sunshine made them prettier than on weekdays. When the throng had mostly streamed into the porch, the sexton began to toll the bell, keeping his eye on the Reverend Mr. Hooper's door. The first glimpse of the clergyman's figure was the signal for the bell to cease its summons.

Another clergyman in New England, Mr. Joseph Moody, of York, Maine, who died about eighty years since, made himself remarkable by the same eccentricity that is here related of the Reverend Mr. Hooper. In his case, however, the symbol had a different import. In early life he had accidentally killed a beloved friend; and from that day till the hour of his own death, he hid his face from men. [Hawthorne's note.]

"But what has good Parson Hooper got upon his face?" cried the sexton in astonishment.

All within hearing immediately turned about, and beheld the semblance of Mr. Hooper, pacing slowly his meditative way towards the meeting-house. With one accord they started, expressing more wonder than if some strange minister were coming to dust the cushions of Mr. Hooper's pulpit.

"Are you sure it is our parson?" inquired Goodman Gray of the sexton.

"Of a certainty it is good Mr. Hooper," replied the sexton. "He was to have 5 exchanged pulpits with Parson Shute of Westbury; but Parson Shute sent to excuse himself yesterday, being to preach a funeral sermon."

The cause of so much amazement may appear sufficiently slight. Mr. Hooper, a gentlemanly person of about thirty, though still a bachelor, was dressed with due clerical neatness, as if a careful wife had starched his band, and brushed the weekly dust from his Sunday's garb. There was but one thing remarkable in his appearance. Swathed about his forehead, and hanging down over his face, so low as to be shaken by his breath, Mr. Hooper had on a black veil. On a nearer view, it seemed to consist of two folds of crape, which entirely concealed his features, except the mouth and chin, but probably did not intercept his sight, farther than to give a darkened aspect to all living and inanimate things. With this gloomy shade before him, good Mr. Hooper walked onward, at a slow and quiet pace, stooping somewhat and looking on the ground, as is customary with abstracted men, yet nodding kindly to those of his parishioners who still waited on the meeting-house steps. But so wonder-struck were they, that his greeting hardly met with a return.

"I can't really feel as if good Mr. Hooper's face was behind that piece of crape," said the sexton.

"I don't like it," muttered an old woman, as she hobbled into the meeting-house. "He has changed himself into something awful, only by hiding his face."

"Our parson has gone mad!" cried Goodman Gray, following him across the threshold.

A rumor of some unaccountable phenomenon had preceded Mr. Hooper 10 into the meeting-house, and set all the congregation astir. Few could refrain from twisting their heads towards the door; many stood upright, and turned directly about; while several little boys clambered upon the seats, and came down again with a terrible racket. There was a general bustle, a rustling of the women's gowns and shuffling of the men's feet, greatly at variance with that hushed repose which should attend the entrance of the minister. But Mr. Hooper appeared not to notice the perturbation of his people. He entered with an almost noiseless step, bent his head mildly to the pews on each side, and bowed as he passed his oldest parishioner, a white-haired great-grandsire, who occupied an arm-chair in the center of the aisle. It was strange to observe, how slowly this venerable man became conscious of something singular in the appearance of his pastor. He seemed not fully to partake of the prevailing wonder, till Mr. Hooper had ascended the stairs, and showed himself in the pulpit, face to face with his congregation, except for the black veil. That mysterious emblem was never once withdrawn. It shook with his measured breath as he gave out the psalm; it threw its obscurity between him and the holy page, as he read the Scriptures; and while he prayed, the veil lay heavily on his uplifted countenance. Did he seek to hide it from the dread Being whom he was addressing?

Such was the effect of this simple piece of crape, that more than one woman of delicate nerves was forced to leave the meeting-house. Yet perhaps the pale-faced congregation was almost as fearful a sight to the minister, as his black veil to them.

Mr. Hooper had the reputation of a good preacher, but not an energetic one: he strove to win his people heavenward, by mild persuasive influences, rather than to drive them thither, by the thunders of the Word. The sermon which he now delivered, was marked by the same characteristics of style and manner, as the general series of his pulpit oratory. But there was something, either in the sentiment of the discourse itself, or in the imagination of the auditors, which made it greatly the most powerful effort that they had ever heard from their pastor's lips. It was tinged, rather more darkly than usual, with the gentle gloom of Mr. Hooper's temperament. The subject had reference to secret sin, and those sad mysteries which we hide from our nearest and dearest, and would fain conceal from our own consciousness, even forgetting that the Omniscient can detect them. A subtle power was breathed into his words. Each member of the congregation, the most innocent girl, and the man of hardened breast, felt as if the preacher had crept upon them, behind his awful veil, and discovered their hoarded iniquity of deed or thought. Many spread their clasped hands on their bosoms. There was nothing terrible in what Mr. Hooper said; at least, no violence; and yet, with every tremor of his melancholy voice, the hearers quaked. An unsought pathos came hand in hand with awe. So sensible were the audience of some unwonted attribute in their minister, that they longed for a breath of wind to blow aside the veil, almost believing that a stranger's visage would be discovered, though the form, gesture, and voice were those of Mr. Hooper.

At the close of the services, the people hurried out with indecorous confusion, eager to communicate their pent-up amazement, and conscious of lighter spirits, the moment they lost sight of the black veil. Some gathered in little circles, huddled closely together, with their mouths all whispering in the center; some went homeward alone, wrapt in silent meditation; some talked loudly, and profaned the Sabbath-day with ostentatious laughter. A few shook their sagacious heads, intimating that they could penetrate the mystery; while one or two affirmed that there was no mystery at all, but only that Mr. Hooper's eyes were so weakened by the midnight lamp, as to require a shade. After a brief interval, forth came good Mr. Hooper also, in the rear of his flock. Turning his veiled face from one group to another, he paid due reverence to the hoary heads, saluted the middle-aged with kind dignity, as their friend and spiritual guide, greeted the young with mingled authority and love, and laid his hands on the little children's heads to bless them. Such was always his custom on the Sabbath-day. Strange and bewildered looks repaid him for his courtesy. None, as on former occasions, aspired to the honor of walking by their pastor's side. Old Squire Saunders, doubtless by an accidental lapse of memory, neglected to invite Mr. Hooper to his table, where the good clergyman had been wont to bless the food, almost every Sunday since his settlement. He returned, therefore, to the parsonage, and, at the moment of closing the door, was observed to look back upon the people, all of whom had their eyes fixed upon the minister. A sad smile gleamed faintly from beneath the black veil, and flickered about his mouth, glimmering as he disappeared.

"How strange," said a lady, "that a simple black veil, such as any woman might wear on her bonnet, should become such a terrible thing on Mr. Hooper's face!"

"Something must surely be amiss with Mr. Hooper's intellects," observed 15 her husband, the physician of the village. "But the strangest part of the affair is the effect of this vagary, even on a sober-minded man like myself. The black veil, though it covers only our pastor's face, throws its influence over his whole person, and makes him ghost-like from head to foot. Do you not feel it so?"

"Truly do I," replied the lady; "and I would not be alone with him for the world. I wonder he is not afraid to be alone with himself!"

"Men sometimes are so," said her husband.

That afternoon service was attended with similar circumstances. At its conclusion, the bell tolled for the funeral of a young lady. The relatives and friends were assembled in the house, and the more distant acquaintances stood about the door, speaking of the good qualities of the deceased, when their talk was interrupted by the appearance of Mr. Hooper, still covered with his black veil. It was now an appropriate emblem. The clergyman stepped into the room where the corpse was laid, and bent over the coffin, to take a last farewell of his deceased parishioner. As he stooped, the veil hung straight down from his forehead, so that, if her eye-lids had not been closed for ever, the dead maiden might have seen his face. Could Mr. Hooper be fearful of her glance, that he so hastily caught back the black veil? A person, who watched the interview between the dead and living, scrupled not to affirm, that, at the instant when the clergyman's features were disclosed, the corpse had slightly shuddered, rustling the shroud and muslin cap, though the countenance retained the composure of death. A superstitious old woman was the only witness of this prodigy. From the coffin, Mr. Hooper passed into the chamber of the mourners, and thence to the head of the staircase, to make the funeral prayer. It was a tender and heart-dissolving prayer, full of sorrow, yet so imbued with celestial hopes, that the music of a heavenly harp, swept by the fingers of the dead, seemed faintly to be heard among the saddest accents of the minister. The people trembled, though they but darkly understood him, when he prayed that they, and himself, and all of mortal race, might be ready, as he trusted this young maiden had been, for the dreadful hour that should snatch the veil from their faces. The bearers went heavily forth, and the mourners followed, saddening all the street, with the dead before them, and Mr. Hooper in his black veil behind.

"Why do you look back?" said one in the procession to his partner.

"I had a fancy," replied she, "that the minister and the maiden's spirit were 20 walking hand in hand."

"And so had I, at the same moment," said the other.

That night, the handsomest couple in Milford village were to be joined in wedlock. Though reckoned a melancholy man, Mr. Hooper had a placid cheerfulness for such occasions, which often excited a sympathetic smile, where livelier merriment would have been thrown away. There was no quality of his disposition which made him more beloved than this. The company at the wedding awaited his arrival with impatience, trusting that the strange awe, which had gathered over him throughout the day, would now be dispelled. But such was not the result. When Mr. Hooper came, the first thing that their eyes rested on was the same horrible black veil, which had added deeper gloom to the funeral, and could portend nothing but evil to the wedding. Such was its immediate effect on the guests, that a cloud seemed to have rolled duskily from beneath the black crape, and dimmed the light of the candles. The bridal pair stood up before the minister. But the bride's cold fingers quivered in the tremulous hand of the bridegroom, and her death-like paleness caused a whisper, that the maiden who had been buried a few hours before, was come from her grave to be married. If ever another wedding were so dismal, it was that famous one, where they tolled the wedding-knell. After performing the ceremony, Mr. Hooper raised a glass of wine to his lips, wishing happiness to the new-married couple, in a strain of mild pleasantry that ought to have brightened the features of the guests, like a cheerful gleam from the hearth. At that instant, catching a glimpse of his figure in the looking-glass, the black veil involved his own spirit in the horror with which it overwhelmed all others. His frame shuddered — his lips grew white — he spilt the untasted wine upon the carpet — and rushed forth into the darkness. For the Earth, too, had on her Black Veil.

The next day, the whole village of Milford talked of little else than Parson Hooper's black veil. That, and the mystery concealed behind it, supplied a topic for discussion between acquaintances meeting in the street, and good women gossiping at their open windows. It was the first item of news that the tavernkeeper told to his guests. The children babbled of it on their way to school. One imitative little imp covered his face with an old black handkerchief, thereby so affrighting his playmates, that the panic seized himself, and he well nigh lost his wits by his own waggery.

It was remarkable, that, of all the busy-bodies and impertinent people in the parish, not one ventured to put the plain question to Mr. Hooper, wherefore he did this thing. Hitherto, whenever there appeared the slightest call for such interference, he had never lacked advisers, nor shown himself averse to be guided by their judgment. If he erred at all, it was by so painful a degree of self-distrust, that even the mildest censure would lead him to consider an indifferent action as a crime. Yet, though so well acquainted with this amiable weakness, no individual among his parishioners chose to make the black veil a subject of friendly remonstrance. There was a feeling of dread, neither plainly confessed nor carefully concealed, which caused each to shift the responsibility upon another, till at length it was found expedient to send a deputation of the church, in order to deal with Mr. Hooper about the mystery, before it should grow into a scandal. Never did an embassy so ill discharge its duties. The minister received them with friendly courtesy, but became silent, after they were seated, leaving to his visitors the whole burthen of introducing their important business. The topic, it might be supposed, was obvious enough. There was the black veil, swathed round Mr. Hooper's forehead, and concealing every feature above his placid mouth, on which, at times, they could perceive the glimmering of a melancholy smile. But that piece of crape, to their imagination, seemed to hang down before his heart, the symbol of a fearful secret between him and them. Were the veil but cast aside, they might speak freely of it, but not till then. Thus they sat a considerable time, speechless, confused, and shrinking uneasily from Mr. Hooper's eye, which they felt to be fixed upon them with an invisible glance. Finally, the deputies returned abashed to their constituents, pronouncing the matter too weighty to be handled, except by a council of the churches, if, indeed, it might not require a general synod.

But there was one person in the village, unappalled by the awe with which 25 the black veil had impressed all beside herself. When the deputies returned without an explanation, or even venturing to demand one, she, with the calm energy of her character, determined to chase away the strange cloud that appeared to be settling round Mr. Hooper, every moment more darkly than before. As his plighted wife, it should be her privilege to know what the black veil concealed. At the minister's first visit, therefore, she entered upon the subject, with a direct simplicity, which made the task easier both for him and her. After he had seated himself, she fixed her eyes steadfastly upon the veil, but could discern nothing of the dreadful gloom that had so overawed the multitude: it was but a double fold of crape, hanging down from his forehead to his mouth, and slightly stirring with his breath.

"No," said she aloud, and smiling, "there is nothing terrible in this piece of crape, except that it hides a face which I am always glad to look upon. Come, good sir, let the sun shine from behind the cloud. First lay aside your black veil: then tell me why you put it on."

Mr. Hooper's smile glimmered faintly.

"There is an hour to come," said he, "when all of us shall cast aside our veils. Take it not amiss, beloved friend, if I wear this piece of crape till then."

"Your words are a mystery too," returned the young lady. "Take away the veil for them, at least."

"Elizabeth, I will," said he, "so far as my vow may suffer me. Know, then, 30 this veil is a type and a symbol, and I am bound to wear it ever, both in light and darkness, in solitude and before the gaze of multitudes, and as with strangers, so with my familiar friends. No mortal eye will see it withdrawn. This dismal shade must separate me from the world: even you, Elizabeth, can never come behind it!"

"What grievous affliction hath befallen you," she earnestly inquired, "that you should thus darken your eyes for ever?"

"If it be a sign of mourning," replied Mr. Hooper, "I, perhaps, like most other mortals, have sorrows dark enough to be typified by a black veil."

"But what if the world will not believe that it is the type of an innocent sorrow?" urged Elizabeth. "Beloved and respected as you are, there may be whispers, that you hide your face under the consciousness of secret sin. For the sake of your holy office, do away this scandal!"

The color rose into her cheeks, as she intimated the nature of the rumors that were already abroad in the village. But Mr. Hooper's mildness did not forsake him. He even smiled again — that same sad smile, which always appeared like a faint glimmering of light, proceeding from the obscurity beneath the veil.

"If I hide my face for sorrow, there is cause enough," he merely replied; 35 "and if I cover it for secret sin, what mortal might not do the same?"

And with this gentle, but unconquerable obstinacy, did he resist all her entreaties. At length Elizabeth sat silent. For a few moments she appeared lost in thought, considering, probably, what new methods might be tried, to withdraw her lover from so dark a fantasy, which, if it had no other meaning, was perhaps a symptom of mental disease. Though of a firmer character than his own, the tears rolled down her cheeks. But, in an instant, as it were, a new feeling took the place of sorrow: her eyes were fixed insensibly on the black veil, when, like a sudden twilight in the air, its terrors fell around her. She arose, and stood trembling before him.

"And do you feel it then at last?" said he mournfully.

She made no reply, but covered her eyes with her hand, and turned to leave the room. He rushed forward and caught her arm.

"Have patience with me, Elizabeth!" cried he passionately. "Do not desert me, though this veil must be between us here on earth. Be mine, and hereafter there shall be no veil over my face, no darkness between our souls! It is but a mortal veil—it is not for eternity! Oh! you know not how lonely I am, and how frightened to be alone behind my black veil. Do not leave me in this miserable obscurity for ever!"

"Lift the veil but once, and look me in the face," said she.   40

"Never! It cannot be!" replied Mr. Hooper.

"Then, farewell!" said Elizabeth.

She withdrew her arm from his grasp, and slowly departed, pausing at the door, to give one long, shuddering gaze, that seemed almost to penetrate the mystery of the black veil. But, even amid his grief, Mr. Hooper smiled to think that only a material emblem had separated him from happiness, though the horrors which it shadowed forth, must be drawn darkly between the fondest of lovers.

From that time no attempts were made to remove Mr. Hooper's black veil, or, by a direct appeal, to discover the secret which it was supposed to hide. By persons who claimed a superiority to popular prejudice, it was reckoned merely an eccentric whim, such as often mingles with the sober actions of men otherwise rational, and tinges them all with its own semblance of insanity. But with the multitude, good Mr. Hooper was irreparably a bugbear. He could not walk the streets with any peace of mind, so conscious was he that the gentle and timid would turn aside to avoid him, and that others would make it a point of hardihood to throw themselves in his way. The impertinence of the latter class compelled him to give up his customary walk, at sunset, to the burial ground, for when he leaned pensively over the gate, there would always be faces behind the grave-stones, peeping at his black veil. A fable went the rounds that the stare of the dead people drove him thence. It grieved him, to the very depth of his kind heart, to observe how the children fled from his approach, breaking up their merriest sports, while his melancholy figure was yet afar off. Their instinctive dread caused him to feel, more strongly than aught else, that a preternatural horror was interwoven with the threads of the black crape. In truth, his own antipathy to the veil was known to be so great, that he never willingly passed before a mirror, nor stooped to drink at a still fountain, lest, in its peaceful bosom, he should be affrighted by himself. This was what gave plausibility to the whispers, that Mr. Hooper's conscience tortured him for some great crime, too horrible to be entirely concealed, or otherwise than so obscurely intimated. Thus, from beneath the black veil, there rolled a cloud into the sunshine, an ambiguity of sin or sorrow, which enveloped the poor minister, so that love or sympathy could never reach him. It was said, that ghost and fiend consorted with him there. With self-shudderings and outward terrors, he walked continually in its shadow, groping darkly within his own soul, or gazing through a medium that saddened the whole world. Even the lawless wind, it was believed, respected his dreadful secret, and never blew aside the veil. But still good Mr. Hooper sadly smiled, at the pale visages of the worldly throng as he passed by.

Among all its bad influences, the black veil had the one desirable effect, of   45
making its wearer a very efficient clergyman. By the aid of his mysterious emblem—for there was no other apparent cause—he became a man of awful

power, over souls that were in agony for sin. His converts always regarded him with a dread peculiar to themselves, affirming, though but figuratively, that, before he brought them to celestial light, they had been with him behind the black veil. Its gloom, indeed, enabled him to sympathize with all dark affections. Dying sinners cried aloud for Mr. Hooper, and would not yield their breath till he appeared; though ever, as he stooped to whisper consolation, they shuddered at the veiled face so near their own. Such were the terrors of the black veil, even when Death had bared his visage! Strangers came long distances to attend service at his church, with the mere idle purpose of gazing at his figure, because it was forbidden them to behold his face. But many were made to quake ere they departed! Once, during Governor Belcher's administration, Mr. Hooper was appointed to preach the election sermon. Covered with his black veil, he stood before the chief magistrate, the council, and the representatives, and wrought so deep an impression, that the legislative measures of that year were characterized by all the gloom and piety of our earliest ancestral sway.

In this manner Mr. Hooper spent a long life, irreproachable in outward act, yet shrouded in dismal suspicions; kind and loving, though unloved, and dimly feared; a man apart from men, shunned in their health and joy, but ever summoned to their aid in mortal anguish. As years wore on, shedding their snows above his sable veil, he acquired a name throughout the New-England churches, and they called him Father Hooper. Nearly all his parishioners, who were of mature age when he was settled, had been borne away by many a funeral: he had one congregation in the church, and a more crowded one in the churchyard; and having wrought so late into the evening, and done his work so well, it was now good Father Hooper's turn to rest.

Several persons were visible by the shaded candlelight, in the death-chamber of the old clergyman. Natural connections he had none. But there was the decorously grave, though unmoved physician, seeking only to mitigate the last pangs of the patient whom he could not save. There were the deacons, and other eminently pious members of his church. There, also, was the Reverend Mr. Clark, of Westbury, a young and zealous divine, who had ridden in haste to pray by the bedside of the expiring minister. There was the nurse, no hired handmaiden of death, but one whose calm affection had endured thus long, in secrecy, in solitude, amid the chill of age, and would not perish, even at the dying hour. Who, but Elizabeth! And there lay the hoary head of good Father Hooper upon the death-pillow, with the black veil still swathed about his brow and reaching down over his face, so that each more difficult gasp of his faint breath caused it to stir. All through life that piece of crape had hung between him and the world: it had separated him from cheerful brotherhood and woman's love, and kept him in that saddest of all prisons, his own heart; and still it lay upon his face, as if to deepen the gloom of his darksome chamber, and shade him from the sunshine of eternity.

For some time previous, his mind had been confused, wavering doubtfully between the past and the present, and hovering forward, as it were, at intervals, into the indistinctness of the world to come. There had been feverish turns, which tossed him from side to side, and wore away what little strength he had. But in his most convulsive struggles, and in the wildest vagaries of his intellect, when no other thought retained its sober influence, he still showed an awful solicitude lest the black veil should slip aside. Even if his bewildered soul could have forgotten, there was a faithful woman at his pillow, who, with averted eyes, would have covered that aged face, which she had last beheld in the come-liness of manhood. At length the death-stricken old man lay quietly in the tor-por of mental and bodily exhaustion, with an imperceptible pulse, and breath that grew fainter and fainter, except when a long, deep, and irregular inspira-tion seemed to prelude the flight of his spirit.

The minister of Westbury approached the bedside.

"Venerable Father Hooper," said he, "the moment of your release is at 50 hand. Are you ready for the lifting of the veil, that shuts in time from eternity?"

Father Hooper at first replied merely by a feeble motion of his head; then, apprehensive, perhaps, that his meaning might be doubtful, he exerted him-self to speak.

"Yea," said he, in faint accents, "my soul hath a patient weariness until that veil be lifted."

"And is it fitting," resumed the Reverend Mr. Clark, "that a man so given to prayer, of such a blameless example, holy in deed and thought, so far as mortal judgment may pronounce; is it fitting that a father in the church should leave a shadow on his memory, that may seem to blacken a life so pure? I pray you, my venerable brother, let not this thing be! Suffer us to be glad-dened by your triumphant aspect, as you go to your reward. Before the veil of eternity be lifted, let me cast aside this black veil from your face!"

And thus speaking, the Reverend Mr. Clark bent forward to reveal the mystery of so many years. But, exerting a sudden energy, that made all the beholders stand aghast, Father Hooper snatched both his hands from beneath the bedclothes, and pressed them strongly on the black veil, resolute to struggle, if the minister of Westbury would contend with a dying man.

"Never!" cried the veiled clergyman. "On earth, never!"   55

"Dark old man!" exclaimed the affrighted minister, "with what horrible crime upon your soul are you now passing to the judgment?"

Father Hooper's breath heaved; it rattled in his throat; but, with a mighty effort, grasping forward with his hands, he caught hold of life, and held it back till he should speak. He even raised himself in bed; and there he sat, shivering with the arms of death around him, while the black veil hung down, awful, at that last moment, in the gathered terrors of a life-time. And yet the faint, sad smile, so often there, now seemed to glimmer from its obscurity, and linger on Father Hooper's lips.

"Why do you tremble at me alone?" cried he, turning his veiled face round the circle of pale spectators. "Tremble also at each other! Have men avoided me, and women shown no pity, and children screamed and fled, only for my black veil? What, but the mystery which it obscurely typifies, has made this piece of crape so awful? When the friend shows his inmost heart to his friend; the lover to his best-beloved; when man does not vainly shrink from the eye of his Creator, loathsomely treasuring up the secret of his sin; then deem me a monster, for the symbol beneath which I have lived, and die! I look around me, and, lo! on every visage a Black Veil!"

While his auditors shrank from one another, in mutual affright, Father Hooper fell back upon his pillow, a veiled corpse, with a faint smile lingering on the lips. Still veiled, they laid him in his coffin, and a veiled corpse they bore him to the grave. The grass of many years has sprung up and withered on that grave, the burial-stone is moss-grown, and good Mr. Hooper's face is dust; but awful is still the thought, that it moldered beneath the Black Veil!

CONSIDERATIONS FOR CRITICAL THINKING AND WRITING

1. FIRST RESPONSE. Why do you think Hooper wears the veil? Explain whether you think Hooper is right or wrong to wear it.

2. Describe the veil Hooper wears. How does it affect his vision?

3. Characterize the townspeople. How does the community react to the veil?

4. What is Hooper's explanation for why he wears the veil? Is he more or less effective as a minister because he wears it?

5. What is the one feature of Hooper's face that we see? What does that feature reveal about him?

6. Describe what happens at the funeral and wedding ceremonies at which Hooper officiates. How are the incidents at these events organized around the veil?

7. Why does Elizabeth think "it should be her privilege to know what the black veil concealed" (para. 25)? Why doesn't Hooper remove it at her request?

8. How does Elizabeth react to Hooper's refusal to take off the veil? Why is her response especially significant?

9. How do others in town explain why Hooper wears the veil? Do these explanations seem adequate to you? Why or why not?

10. Why is Hooper buried with the veil? Of what significance is it that grass "withered" on his grave (para. 59)?

11. Describe the story's point of view. How would a first-person narrative change the story dramatically?

CONNECTIONS TO OTHER SELECTIONS

1. How might this story be regarded as a sequel to "Young Goodman Brown"? How are the themes similar?

2. Explain how Faith in "Young Goodman Brown," Georgiana in "The Birthmark" (below), and Elizabeth in "The Minister's Black Veil" are used to reveal some truth about the central male characters in each story. Describe the similarities that you see among these women.

3. Compare Hawthorne's use of symbol in "The Minister's Black Veil" and "The Birthmark." Write an essay explaining which symbol you think works more effectively to evoke the theme of its story.

The Birthmark   1843

In the latter part of the last century there lived a man of science, an eminent proficient in every branch of natural philosophy, who not long before our story opens had made experience of a spiritual affinity more attractive than any chemical one. He had left his laboratory to the care of an assistant, cleared his fine countenance from the furnace smoke, washed the stain of acids from his fingers, and persuaded a beautiful woman to become his wife. In those days when the comparatively recent discovery of electricity and other kindred mysteries of Nature seemed to open paths into the region of miracle, it was not unusual for the love of science to rival the love of woman in its depth and absorbing energy. The higher intellect, the imagination, the spirit, and even the heart might all find their congenial aliment in pursuits which, as some of their ardent votaries believed, would ascend from one step of powerful intelligence to another, until the philosopher should lay his hand on the secret of creative force and perhaps make new worlds for himself. We know not whether Aylmer possessed this degree of faith in man's ultimate control over Nature. He had devoted himself, however, too unreservedly to scientific studies ever to be weaned from them by any second passion. His love for his young wife might prove the stronger of the two; but it could only be by intertwining itself with his love of science, and uniting the strength of the latter to his own.

Such a union accordingly took place, and was attended with truly remarkable consequences and a deeply impressive moral. One day, very soon after their marriage, Aylmer sat gazing at his wife with a trouble in his countenance that grew stronger until he spoke.

"Georgiana," said he, "has it never occurred to you that the mark upon your cheek might be removed?"

"No, indeed," said she, smiling; but perceiving the seriousness of his manner, she blushed deeply. "To tell you the truth it has been so often called a charm that I was simple enough to imagine it might be so."

"Ah, upon another face perhaps it might," replied her husband; "but never 5 on yours. No, dearest Georgiana, you came so nearly perfect from the hand of Nature that this slightest possible defect, which we hesitate whether to term a defect or a beauty, shocks me, as being the visible mark of earthly imperfection."

"Shocks you, my husband!" cried Georgiana, deeply hurt; at first reddening with momentary anger, but then bursting into tears. "Then why did you take me from my mother's side? You cannot love what shocks you!"

To explain this conversation it must be mentioned that in the center of Georgiana's left cheek there was a singular mark, deeply interwoven, as it were, with the texture and substance of her face. In the usual state of her complexion — a healthy though delicate bloom — the mark wore a tint of deeper crimson, which imperfectly defined its shape amid the surrounding rosiness. When she blushed it gradually became more indistinct, and finally vanished amid the triumphant rush of blood that bathed the whole cheek with its brilliant glow. But if any shifting motion caused her to turn pale, there was the mark again, a crimson stain upon the snow, in what Aylmer sometimes deemed an almost fearful distinctness. Its shape bore not a little similarity to the human hand, though of the smallest pygmy size. Georgiana's lovers were wont to say that some fairy at her birth hour had laid her tiny hand upon the infant's cheek, and left this impress there in token of the magic endowments that were to give her such sway over all hearts. Many a desperate swain would have risked life for the privilege of pressing his lips to the mysterious hand. It must not be concealed, however, that the impression wrought by this fairy sign manual varied exceedingly, according to the difference of temperament in the beholders. Some fastidious persons — but they were exclusively of her own sex — affirmed that the bloody hand, as they chose to call it, quite destroyed the effect of Georgiana's beauty, and rendered her countenance even hideous. But it would be as reasonable to say that one of those small blue stains which sometimes occur in the purest statuary marble would convert the Eve of Powers to a monster.

Masculine observers, if the birthmark did not heighten their admiration, contented themselves with wishing it away, that the world might possess one living specimen of ideal loveliness without the semblance of a flaw. After his marriage, — for he thought little or nothing of the matter before, — Aylmer discovered that this was the case with himself.

Had she been less beautiful, — if Envy's self could have found aught else to sneer at, — he might have felt his affection heightened by the prettiness of this mimic hand, now vaguely portrayed, now lost, now stealing forth again and glimmering to and fro with every pulse of emotion that throbbed within her heart; but seeing her otherwise so perfect, he found this one defect grow more and more intolerable with every moment of their united lives. It was the fatal flaw of humanity which Nature, in one shape or another, stamps ineffaceably on all her productions, either to imply that they are temporary and finite, or that their perfection must be wrought by toil and pain. The crimson hand expressed the ineludible gripe° in which mortality clutches the highest and purest of earthly mold, degrading them into kindred with the lowest, and even with the very brutes, like whom their visible frames return to dust. In this manner, selecting it as the symbol of his wife's liability to sin, sorrow, decay, and death, Aylmer's somber imagination was not long in rendering the birthmark a frightful object, causing him more trouble and horror than ever Georgiana's beauty, whether of soul or sense, had given him delight.

At all the seasons which should have been their happiest, he invariably and without intending it, nay, in spite of a purpose to the contrary, reverted to this one disastrous topic. Trifling as it at first appeared, it so connected itself with innumerable trains of thought and modes of feeling that it became the central point of all. With the morning twilight Aylmer opened his eyes upon his wife's face and recognized the symbol of imperfection; and when they sat together at the evening hearth his eyes wandered stealthily to her cheek, and beheld, flickering with the blaze of the wood fire, the spectral hand that wrote mortality where he would fain have worshiped. Georgiana soon learned to shudder at his gaze. It needed but a glance with the peculiar expression that his face often wore to change the roses of her cheek into a deathlike paleness, amid which the crimson hand was brought strongly out, like a bas-relief of ruby on the whitest marble.

Late one night when the lights were growing dim, so as hardly to betray 10 the stain on the poor wife's cheek, she herself, for the first time, voluntarily took up the subject.

"Do you remember, my dear Aylmer," said she, with a feeble attempt at a smile, "have you any recollection of a dream last night about this odious hand?"

"None! none whatever!" replied Aylmer, starting; but then he added, in a dry, cold tone, affected for the sake of concealing the real depth of his emotion, "I might well dream of it; for before I fell asleep it had taken a pretty firm hold of my fancy."

"And you did dream of it?" continued Georgiana hastily, for she dreaded lest a gush of tears should interrupt what she had to say. "A terrible dream! I wonder that you can forget it. Is it possible to forget this one expression? — 'It is in her heart now; we must have it out!' Reflect, my husband; for by all means I would have you recall that dream."

gripe: Grip.

The mind is in a sad state when Sleep, the all-involving, cannot confine her specters within the dim region of her sway, but suffers them to break forth, affrighting this actual life with secrets that perchance belong to a deeper one. Aylmer now remembered his dream. He had fancied himself with his servant Aminadab, attempting an operation for the removal of the birthmark; but the deeper went the knife, the deeper sank the hand, until at length its tiny grasp appeared to have caught hold of Georgiana's heart; whence, however, her husband was inexorably resolved to cut or wrench it away.

When the dream had shaped itself perfectly in his memory, Aylmer sat in 15 his wife's presence with a guilty feeling. Truth often finds its way to the mind close muffled in robes of sleep, and then speaks with uncompromising directness of matters in regard to which we practice an unconscious self-deception during our waking moments. Until now he had not been aware of the tyrannizing influence acquired by one idea over his mind, and of the lengths which he might find in his heart to go for the sake of giving himself peace.

"Aylmer," resumed Georgiana solemnly, "I know not what may be the cost to both of us to rid me of this fatal birthmark. Perhaps its removal may cause cureless deformity; or it may be the stain goes as deep as life itself. Again: do we know that there is a possibility, on any terms, of unclasping the firm grip of this little hand which was laid upon me before I came into the world?"

"Dearest Georgiana, I have spent much thought upon the subject," hastily interrupted Aylmer. "I am convinced of the perfect practicability of its removal."

"If there be the remotest possibility of it," continued Georgiana, "let the attempt be made at whatever risk. Danger is nothing to me; for life, while this hateful mark makes me the object of your horror and disgust, — life is a burden which I would fling down with joy. Either remove this dreadful hand, or take my wretched life! You have deep science. All the world bears witness of it. You have achieved great wonders. Cannot you remove this little, little mark, which I cover with the tips of two small fingers? Is this beyond your power, for the sake of your own peace, and to save your poor wife from madness?"

"Noblest, dearest, tenderest wife," cried Aylmer rapturously, "doubt not my power. I have already given this matter the deepest thought — thought which might almost have enlightened me to create a being less perfect than yourself. Georgiana, you have led me deeper than ever into the heart of science. I feel myself fully competent to render this dear cheek as faultless as its fellow; and then, most beloved, what will be my triumph when I shall have corrected what Nature left imperfect in her fairest work! Even Pygmalion, when his sculptured woman assumed life, felt not greater ecstasy than mine will be."

"It is resolved, then," said Georgiana, faintly smiling. "And, Aylmer, spare 20 me not, though you should find the birthmark take refuge in my heart at last."

Her husband tenderly kissed her cheek — her right cheek — not that which bore the impress of the crimson hand.

The next day Aylmer apprised his wife of a plan that he had formed whereby he might have opportunity for the intense thought and constant watchfulness which the proposed operation would require; while Georgiana, likewise, would enjoy the perfect repose essential to its success. They were to seclude themselves in the extensive apartments occupied by Aylmer as a laboratory, and where, during his toilsome youth, he had made discoveries in the elemental powers of Nature that had roused the admiration of all the learned societies in Europe. Seated calmly in this laboratory, the pale philosopher had investigated the secrets of the highest cloud region and of the profoundest mines; he had satisfied himself of the causes that kindled and kept alive the fires of the volcano; and had explained the mystery of fountains, and how it is that they gush forth, some so bright and pure, and others with such rich medicinal virtues, from the dark bosom of the earth. Here, too, at an earlier period, he had studied the wonders of the human frame, and attempted to fathom the very process by which Nature assimilates all her precious influences from earth and air, and from the spiritual world, to create and foster man, her masterpiece. The latter pursuit, however, Aylmer had long laid aside in unwilling recognition of the truth — against which all seekers sooner or later stumble — that our great creative Mother, while she amuses us with apparently working in the broadest sunshine, is yet severely careful to keep her own secrets, and, in spite of her pretended openness, shows us nothing but results. She permits us, indeed, to mar, but seldom to mend, and, like a jealous patentee, on no account to make. Now, however, Aylmer resumed these half-forgotten investigations, — not, of course, with such hopes or wishes as first suggested them, but because they involved much physiological truth and lay in the path of his proposed scheme for the treatment of Georgiana.

As he led her over the threshold of the laboratory, Georgiana was cold and tremulous. Aylmer looked cheerfully into her face, with intent to reassure her, but was so startled with the intense glow of the birthmark upon the whiteness of her cheek that he could not restrain a strong convulsive shudder. His wife fainted.

"Aminadab! Aminadab!" shouted Aylmer, stamping violently on the floor.

Forthwith there issued from an inner apartment a man of low stature, but 25 bulky frame, with shaggy hair hanging about his visage, which was grimed with the vapors of the furnace. This personage had been Aylmer's underworker during his whole scientific career, and was admirably fitted for that office by his great mechanical readiness, and the skill with which, while incapable of comprehending a single principle, he executed all the details of his master's experiments. With his vast strength, his shaggy hair, his smoky aspect, and the indescribable earthiness that encrusted him, he seemed to represent man's physical nature; while Aylmer's slender figure, and pale, intellectual face, were no less apt a type of the spiritual element.

"Throw open the door of the boudoir, Aminadab," said Aylmer, "and burn a pastille."

"Yes, master," answered Aminadab, looking intently at the lifeless form of Georgiana; and then he muttered to himself, "If she were my wife, I'd never part with that birthmark."

When Georgiana recovered consciousness she found herself breathing an atmosphere of penetrating fragrance, the gentle potency of which had recalled her from her deathlike faintness. The scene around her looked like enchantment. Aylmer had converted those smoky, dingy, somber rooms, where he had spent his brightest years in recondite pursuits, into a series of beautiful apartments not unfit to be the secluded abode of a lovely woman. The walls were hung with gorgeous curtains, which imparted the combination of grandeur and grace that no other species of adornment can achieve; and as they fell from the ceiling to the floor, their rich and ponderous folds, concealing all angles and straight lines, appeared to shut in the scene from infinite space. For aught Georgiana knew, it might be a pavilion among the clouds. And Aylmer, excluding the sunshine, which would have interfered with his chemical processes, had supplied its place with perfumed lamps, emitting flames of various hue, but all uniting in a soft, empurpled radiance. He now knelt by his wife's side, watching her earnestly, but without alarm; for he was confident in his science, and felt that he could draw a magic circle round her within which no evil might intrude.

"Where am I? Ah, I remember," said Georgiana faintly; and she placed her hand over her cheek to hide the terrible mark from her husband's eyes.

"Fear not, dearest!" exclaimed he. "Do not shrink from me! Believe me, 30 Georgiana, I even rejoice in this single imperfection, since it will be such a rapture to remove it."

"Oh, spare me!" sadly replied his wife. "Pray do not look at it again. I never can forget that convulsive shudder."

In order to soothe Georgiana, and, as it were, to release her mind from the burden of actual things, Aylmer now put in practice some of the light and playful secrets which science had taught him among its profounder lore. Airy figures, absolutely bodiless ideas, and forms of unsubstantial beauty came and danced before her, imprinting their momentary footsteps on beams of light. Though she had some indistinct idea of the method of these optical phenomena, still the illusion was almost perfect enough to warrant the belief that her husband possessed sway over the spiritual world. Then again, when she felt a wish to look forth from her seclusion, immediately, as if her thoughts were answered, the procession of external existence flitted across a screen. The scenery and the figures of actual life were perfectly represented, but with that bewitching, yet indescribable difference which always makes a picture, an image, or a shadow so much more attractive than the original. When wearied of this, Aylmer bade her cast her eyes upon a vessel containing a quantity of earth. She did so, with little interest at first; but was soon startled to perceive the germ of a plant shooting upward from the soil. Then came the slender stalk; the leaves gradually unfolded themselves; and amid them was a perfect and lovely flower.

"It is magical!" cried Georgiana. "I dare not touch it."

"Nay, pluck it," answered Aylmer: "pluck it, and inhale its brief perfume while you may. The flower will wither in a few moments and leave nothing save its brown seed vessels; but thence may be perpetuated a race as ephemeral as itself."

But Georgiana had no sooner touched the flower than the whole plant 35 suffered a blight, its leaves turning coal-black as if by the agency of fire.

"There was too powerful a stimulus," said Aylmer thoughtfully.

To make up for this abortive experiment, he proposed to take her portrait by a scientific process of his own invention. It was to be effected by rays of light striking upon a polished plate of metal. Georgiana assented; but, on looking at the result, was affrighted to find the features of the portrait blurred and indefinable; while the minute figure of a hand appeared where the cheek should have been. Aylmer snatched the metallic plate and threw it into a jar of corrosive acid.

Soon, however, he forgot these mortifying failures. In the intervals of study and chemical experiment he came to her flushed and exhausted, but seemed invigorated by her presence, and spoke in glowing language of the resources of his art. He gave a history of the long dynasty of the alchemists, who spent so many ages in quest of the universal solvent by which the golden principle might be elicited from all things vile and base. Aylmer appeared to believe that, by the plainest scientific logic, it was altogether within the limits of possibility to discover this long-sought medium; "but," he added, "a philosopher who should go deep enough to acquire the power would attain too lofty a wisdom to stoop to the exercise of it." Not less singular were his opinions in regard to the elixir vitae. He more than intimated that it was at his option to concoct a liquid that should prolong life for years, perhaps interminably; but that it would produce a discord in Nature which all the world, and chiefly the quaffer of the immortal nostrum, would find cause to curse.

"Aylmer, are you in earnest?" asked Georgiana, looking at him with amazement and fear. "It is terrible to possess such power, or even to dream of possessing it."

"Oh, do not tremble, my love," said her husband. "I would not wrong 40 either you or myself by working such inharmonious effects upon our lives; but I would have you consider how trifling, in comparison, is the skill requisite to remove this little hand."

At the mention of the birthmark, Georgiana, as usual, shrank as if a redhot iron had touched her cheek.

Again Aylmer applied himself to his labors. She could hear his voice in the distant furnace-room giving directions to Aminadab, whose harsh, uncouth, misshapen tones were audible in response, more like the grunt or growl of a brute than human speech. After hours of absence, Aylmer reappeared and proposed that she should now examine his cabinet of chemical products and natural treasures of the earth. Among the former he showed her a small vial, in which, he remarked, was contained a gentle yet most powerful fragrance, capable of impregnating all the breezes that blow across a kingdom. They were of inestimable value, the contents of that little vial; and, as he said so, he threw some of the perfume into the air and filled the room with piercing and invigorating delight.

"And what is this?" asked Georgiana, pointing to a small crystal globe containing a gold-colored liquid. "It is so beautiful to the eye that I could imagine it the elixir of life."

"In one sense it is," replied Aylmer; "or rather, the elixir of immortality. It is the most precious poison that ever was concocted in this world. By its aid I could apportion the lifetime of any mortal at whom you might point your finger. The strength of the dose would determine whether he were to linger out years, or drop dead in the midst of a breath. No king on his guarded throne could keep his life if I, in my private station, should deem that the welfare of millions justified me in depriving him of it."

"Why do you keep such a terrific drug?" inquired Georgiana in horror. 45

"Do not mistrust me, dearest," said her husband, smiling; "its virtuous potency is yet greater than its harmful one. But see! here is a powerful cosmetic. With a few drops of this in a vase of water, freckles may be washed away as easily as the hands are cleansed. A stronger infusion would take the blood out of the cheek, and leave the rosiest beauty a pale ghost."

"Is it with this lotion that you intend to bathe my cheek?" asked Georgiana, anxiously.

"Oh, no," hastily replied her husband; "this is merely superficial. Your case demands a remedy that shall go deeper."

In his interviews with Georgiana, Aylmer generally made minute inquiries as to her sensations and whether the confinement of the rooms and the temperature of the atmosphere agreed with her. These questions had such a particular drift that Georgiana began to conjecture that she was already subjected to certain physical influences, either breathed in with the fragrant air or taken with her food. She fancied likewise, but it might be altogether fancy, that there was a stirring up of her system — a strange, indefinite sensation creeping through her veins, and tingling, half painfully, half pleasurably, at her heart. Still, whenever she dared to look into the mirror, there she beheld herself pale as a white rose and with the crimson birthmark stamped upon her cheek. Not even Aylmer now hated it so much as she.

To dispel the tedium of the hours which her husband found it necessary 50 to devote to the processes of combination and analysis, Georgiana turned over the volumes of his scientific library. In many dark old tomes she met with chapters full of romance and poetry. They were the works of the philosophers of the middle ages, such as Albertus Magnus, Cornelius Agrippa, Paracelsus, and the famous friar who created the prophetic Brazen Head. All these antique naturalists stood in advance of their centuries, yet were imbued with some of their credulity, and therefore were believed, and perhaps imagined themselves to have acquired from the investigation of Nature a power above Nature, and from physics a sway over the spiritual world. Hardly less curious and imaginative were the early volumes of the Transactions of the Royal Society, in which the members, knowing little of the limits of natural possibility, were continually recording wonders or proposing methods whereby wonders might be wrought.

But to Georgiana the most engrossing volume was a large folio from her husband's own hand, in which he had recorded every experiment of his scientific career, its original aim, the methods adopted for its development, and its final success or failure, with the circumstances to which either event was attributable. The book, in truth, was both the history and emblem of his ardent, ambitious, imaginative, yet practical and laborious life. He handled physical details as if there were nothing beyond them; yet spiritualized them all, and redeemed himself from materialism by his strong and eager aspiration towards the infinite. In his grasp the veriest clod of earth assumed a soul. Georgiana, as she read, reverenced Aylmer and loved him more profoundly than ever, but with a less entire dependence on his judgment than heretofore. Much as he had accomplished, she could not but observe that his most splendid successes were almost invariably failures, if compared with the ideal at which he aimed. His brightest diamonds were the merest pebbles, and felt to be so by himself, in comparison with the inestimable gems which lay hidden beyond his reach. The volume, rich with achievements that had won renown for its author, was yet as melancholy a record as ever mortal hand had penned. It was the sad confession and continual exemplification of the shortcomings of the composite man, the spirit burdened with clay and working in matter, and of the despair that assails the higher nature at finding itself so miserably thwarted by the earthly part. Perhaps every man of genius in whatever sphere might recognize the image of his own experience in Aylmer's journal.

So deeply did these reflections affect Georgiana that she laid her face upon the open volume and burst into tears. In this situation she was found by her husband.

"It is dangerous to read in a sorcerer's books," said he with a smile, though his countenance was uneasy and displeased. "Georgiana, there are pages in that volume which I can scarcely glance over and keep my senses. Take heed lest it prove as detrimental to you."

"It has made me worship you more than ever," said she.

"Ah, wait for this one success," rejoined he, "then worship me if you will. I shall deem myself hardly unworthy of it. But come, I have sought you for the luxury of your voice. Sing to me, dearest." 55

So she poured out the liquid music of her voice to quench the thirst of his spirit. He then took his leave with a boyish exuberance of gaiety, assuring her that her seclusion would endure but a little longer, and that the result was already certain. Scarcely had he departed when Georgiana felt irresistibly impelled to follow him. She had forgotten to inform Aylmer of a symptom which for two or three hours past had begun to excite her attention. It was a sensation in the fatal birthmark, not painful, but which induced a restlessness throughout her system. Hastening after her husband, she intruded for the first time into the laboratory.

The first thing that struck her eye was the furnace, that hot and feverish worker, with the intense glow of its fire, which by the quantities of soot clustered above it seemed to have been burning for ages. There was a distilling apparatus in full operation. Around the room were retorts, tubes, cylinders, crucibles, and other apparatus of chemical research. An electrical machine stood ready for immediate use. The atmosphere felt oppressively close, and was tainted with gaseous odors which had been tormented forth by the processes of science. The severe and homely simplicity of the apartment, with its naked walls and brick pavement, looked strange, accustomed as Georgiana had become to the fantastic elegance of her boudoir. But what chiefly, indeed almost solely, drew her attention, was the aspect of Aylmer himself.

He was pale as death, anxious and absorbed, and hung over the furnace as if it depended upon his utmost watchfulness whether the liquid which it was distilling should be the draught of immortal happiness or misery. How different from the sanguine and joyous mien that he had assumed for Georgiana's encouragement!

"Carefully now, Aminadab; carefully, thou human machine; carefully, thou man of clay!" muttered Aylmer, more to himself than his assistant. "Now, if there be a thought too much or too little, it is all over."

"Ho! ho!" mumbled Aminadab. "Look, master! look!" 60

Aylmer raised his eyes hastily, and at first reddened, then grew paler than ever, on beholding Georgiana. He rushed towards her and seized her arm with a gripe that left the print of his fingers upon it.

"Why do you come hither? Have you no trust in your husband?" cried he impetuously. "Would you throw the blight of that fatal birthmark over my labors? It is not well done. Go, prying woman, go!"

"Nay, Aylmer," said Georgiana with the firmness of which she possessed no stinted endowment, "it is not you that have a right to complain. You mistrust your wife; you have concealed the anxiety with which you watch the development of this experiment. Think not so unworthily of me, my husband. Tell me all the risk we run, and fear not that I shall shrink; for my share in it is far less than your own."

"No, no, Georgiana!" said Aylmer impatiently; "it must not be."

"I submit," replied she calmly. "And, Aylmer, I shall quaff whatever 65
draught you bring me; but it will be on the same principle that would induce
me to take a dose of poison if offered by your hand."

"My noble wife," said Aylmer, deeply moved, "I knew not the height and
depth of your nature until now. Nothing shall be concealed. Know, then, that
this crimson hand, superficial as it seems, has clutched its grasp into your
being with a strength of which I had no previous conception. I have already
administered agents powerful enough to do aught except to change your entire physical system. Only one thing remains to be tried. If that fails us we are
ruined."

"Why did you hesitate to tell me this?" asked she.

"Because, Georgiana," said Aylmer in a low voice, "there is danger."

"Danger? There is but one danger—that this horrible stigma shall be left
upon my cheek!" cried Georgiana. "Remove it, remove it, whatever be the cost,
or we shall both go mad!"

"Heaven knows your words are too true," said Aylmer sadly. "And now, 70
dearest, return to your boudoir. In a little while all will be tested."

He conducted her back and took leave of her with a solemn tenderness
which spoke far more than his words how much was now at stake. After his
departure Georgiana became rapt in musings. She considered the character of
Aylmer, and did it completer justice than at any previous moment. Her heart
exulted, while it trembled, at his honorable love—so pure and lofty that it
would accept nothing less than perfection nor miserably make itself contented
with an earthlier nature than he had dreamed of. She felt how much more precious was such a sentiment than that meaner kind which would have borne
with the imperfection for her sake, and have been guilty of treason to holy love
by degrading its perfect idea to the level of the actual; and with her whole spirit
she prayed that, for a single moment, she might satisfy his highest and deepest
conception. Longer than one moment she well knew it could not be; for his
spirit was ever on the march, ever ascending, and each instant required something that was beyond the scope of the instant before.

The sound of her husband's footsteps aroused her. He bore a crystal goblet containing a liquor colorless as water, but bright enough to be the draught
of immortality. Aylmer was pale; but it seemed rather the consequence of a
highly wrought state of mind and tension of spirit than of fear or doubt.

"The concoction of the draught has been perfect," said he, in answer to
Georgiana's look. "Unless all my science have deceived me, it cannot fail."

"Save on your account, my dearest Aylmer," observed his wife, "I might
wish to put off this birthmark of mortality by relinquishing mortality itself in
preference to any other mode. Life is but a sad possession to those who have
attained precisely the degree of moral advancement at which I stand. Were I
weaker and blinder it might be happiness. Were I stronger, it might be endured
hopefully. But, being what I find myself, methinks I am of all mortals the most
fit to die."

"You are fit for heaven without tasting death!" replied her husband. "But 75
why do we speak of dying? The draught cannot fail. Behold its effect upon this
plant."

On the window seat there stood a geranium diseased with yellow blotches,
which had overspread all its leaves. Aylmer poured a small quantity of the liq-

uid upon the soil in which it grew. In a little time, when the roots of the plant had taken up the moisture, the unsightly blotches began to be extinguished in a living verdure.

"There needed no proof," said Georgiana quietly. "Give me the goblet. I joyfully stake all upon your word."

"Drink, then, thou lofty creature!" exclaimed Aylmer, with fervid admiration. "There is no taint of imperfection on thy spirit. Thy sensible frame, too, shall soon be all perfect."

She quaffed the liquid and returned the goblet to his hand.

"It is grateful," said she, with a placid smile. "Methinks it is like water   80
from a heavenly fountain; for it contains I know not what of unobtrusive fragrance and deliciousness. It allays a feverish thirst that had parched me for many days. Now, dearest, let me sleep. My earthly senses are closing over my spirit like the leaves around the heart of a rose at sunset."

She spoke the last words with a gentle reluctance, as if it required almost more energy than she could command to pronounce the faint and lingering syllables. Scarcely had they loitered through her lips ere she was lost in slumber. Aylmer sat by her side, watching her aspect with the emotions proper to a man the whole value of whose existence was involved in the process now to be tested. Mingled with this mood, however, was the philosophic investigation characteristic of the man of science. Not the minutest symptom escaped him. A heightened flush of the cheek, a slight irregularity of breath, a quiver of the eyelid, a hardly perceptible tremor through the frame, — such were the details which, as the moments passed, he wrote down in his folio volume. Intense thought had set its stamp upon every previous page of that volume, but the thoughts of years were all concentrated upon the last.

While thus employed, he failed not to gaze often at the fatal hand, and not without a shudder. Yet once, by a strange and unaccountable impulse, he pressed it with his lips. His spirit recoiled, however, in the very act; and Georgiana, out of the midst of her deep sleep, moved uneasily and murmured as if in remonstrance. Again Aylmer resumed his watch. Nor was it without avail. The crimson hand, which at first had been strongly visible upon the marble paleness of Georgiana's cheek, now grew more faintly outlined. She remained not less pale than ever; but the birthmark, with every breath that came and went, lost somewhat of its former distinctness. Its presence had been awful; its departure was more awful still. Watch the stain of the rainbow fading out of the sky, and you will know how that mysterious symbol passed away.

"By Heaven! it is well-nigh gone!" said Aylmer to himself, in almost irrepressible ecstasy. "I can scarcely trace it now. Success! success! And now it is like the faintest rose color. The lightest flush of blood across her cheek would overcome it. But she is so pale!"

He drew aside the window curtain and suffered the light of natural day to fall into the room and rest upon her cheek. At the same time he heard a gross, hoarse chuckle, which he had long known as his servant Aminadab's expression of delight.

"Ah, clod! ah, earthly mass!" cried Aylmer, laughing in a sort of frenzy,   85
"you have served me well! Matter and spirit — earth and heaven — have both done their part in this! Laugh, thing of the senses! You have earned the right to laugh."

These exclamations broke Georgiana's sleep. She slowly unclosed her eyes and gazed into the mirror which her husband had arranged for that purpose. A faint smile flitted over her lips when she recognized how barely perceptible was now that crimson hand which had once blazed forth with such disastrous brilliancy as to scare away all their happiness. But then her eyes sought Aylmer's face with a trouble and anxiety that he could by no means account for.

"My poor Aylmer!" murmured she.

"Poor? Nay, richest, happiest, most favored!" exclaimed he. "My peerless bride, it is successful! You are perfect!"

"My poor Aylmer," she repeated, with a more than human tenderness, "you have aimed loftily; you have done nobly. Do not repent that with so high and pure a feeling, you have rejected the best the earth could offer. Aylmer, dearest Aylmer, I am dying!"

Alas! it was too true! The fatal hand had grappled with the mystery of life, 90 and was the bond by which an angelic spirit kept itself in union with a mortal frame. As the last crimson tint of the birthmark — that sole token of human imperfection — faded from her cheek, the parting breath of the now perfect woman passed into the atmosphere, and her soul, lingering a moment near her husband, took its heavenward flight. Then a hoarse, chuckling laugh was heard again! Thus ever does the gross fatality of earth exult in its invariable triumph over the immortal essence which, in this dim sphere of half development, demands the completeness of a higher state. Yet, had Aylmer reached a profounder wisdom, he need not thus have flung away the happiness which would have woven his mortal life of the selfsame texture with the celestial. The momentary circumstance was too strong for him; he failed to look beyond the shadowy scope of time, and, living once for all in eternity, to find the perfect future in the present.

Considerations for Critical Thinking and Writing

1. **FIRST RESPONSE.** Consider this story as an early version of our contemporary obsession with physical perfection. What significant similarities — and differences — do you find?

2. Is Aylmer evil? Is he simply a stock version of a mad scientist? In what sense might he be regarded as an idealist?

3. What does the birthmark symbolize? How does Aylmer's view of it differ from the other perspectives provided in the story? What is the significance of its handlike shape?

4. Does Aylmer love Georgiana? Why does she allow him to risk her life to remove the birthmark?

5. In what sense can Aylmer be characterized as guilty of the sin of pride?

6. How is Aminadab a foil for Aylmer?

7. What is the significance of the descriptions of Aylmer's laboratory?

8. What do Aylmer's other experiments reveal about the nature of his work? How do they constitute foreshadowings of what will happen to Georgiana?

9. What is the theme of the story? What point is made about what it means to be a human being?

10. Despite the risks to Georgiana, Aylmer conducts his experiments in the hope and expectation of achieving a higher good. He devotes his life to science, and yet he is an egotist. Explain.

11. Discuss the extent to which Georgiana is responsible for her own death.

CONNECTIONS TO OTHER SELECTIONS

1. Compare Aylmer's unwillingness to accept things as they are with Goodman Brown's refusal to be a part of a community he regards as fallen.

2. What similarities do you see in Aylmer's growing feelings about the "crimson hand" on Georgiana's cheek and the young wife's feelings about her husband's hand in Colette's "The Hand" (p. 240)? How do Aylmer and the young wife cope with these feelings? How do you account for the differences between them?

Perspectives on Hawthorne

NATHANIEL HAWTHORNE
On Solitude
1837

Dear Sir,

Not to burthen you with my correspondence, I have delayed a rejoinder to your very kind and cordial letter, until now. It gratifies me to find that you have occasionally felt an interest in my situation. . . . You would have been nearer the truth if you had pictured me as dwelling in an owl's nest; for mine is about as dismal; and, like the owl I seldom venture abroad till after dark. By some witchcraft or other—for I really cannot assign any reasonable why and wherefore—I have been carried apart from the main current of life, and find it impossible to get back again. Since we last met . . . I have secluded myself from society; and yet I never meant any such thing, nor dreamed what sort of life I was going to lead. I have made a captive of myself and put me into a dungeon, and now I cannot find the key to let myself out—and if the door were open, I should be almost afraid to come out. You tell me that you have met with troubles and changes. I know not what they may have been; but I can assure you that trouble is the next best thing to enjoyment, and that there is no fate in this world so horrible as to have no share in either its joys or sorrows. For the last ten years, I have not lived, but only dreamed about living. It may be true that there have been some unsubstantial pleasures here in the shade, which I should have missed in the sunshine, but you cannot conceive how utterly devoid of satisfaction all my retrospects are. I have laid up no treasure of pleasant remembrances, against old age; but there is some comfort in thinking that my future years can hardly fail to be more varied, and therefore more tolerable, than the past.

You give me more credit than I deserve, in supposing that I have led a studious life. I have, indeed, turned over a good many books, but in so desultory a way that it cannot be called study, nor has it left me the fruits of study. As to my literary efforts, I do not think much of them—neither is it worthwhile to be ashamed of them. They would have been better, I trust, if written under more favorable circumstances. I have had no external excitement — no consciousness that the public would like what I wrote, nor much hope nor a very passionate desire that they should do so. Nevertheless, having nothing else to be ambitious of, I have felt considerably interested in literature; and if my writings had made any decided impression, I should probably have been stimulated to greater exertions; but there has been no warmth of approbation, so that I have always written with benumbed fingers. I have another great difficulty, in the lack of materials; for I have seen so little of the world, that I have nothing but thin air to concoct my stories of, and it is not easy to give a lifelike semblance to such shadowy stuff. Sometimes, through a peep-hole, I have caught a glimpse of the real world; and the two or three articles, in which I have portrayed such glimpses, please me better than the others. I have now, or shall soon have, one sharp spur to exertion, which I lacked at an earlier period; for I see little prospect but that I must scribble for a living. But this troubles me much less than you would suppose. I can turn my pen to all sorts of drudgery, such as children's books, etc., and by and by, I shall get some editorship that will answer my purpose. Frank Pierce, who was with us at college, offered me his influence to obtain an office in the Exploring Expedition; but I believe that he was mistaken in supposing that a vacancy existed. If such a post were attainable, I should certainly accept it; for, though fixed so long to one spot, I have always had a desire to run around the world.

The copy of my Tales was sent to Mr. Owen's, the bookseller's in Cambridge. I am glad to find that you had read and liked some of the stories. To be sure, you could not well help flattering me a little; but I value your praise too highly not to have faith in its sincerity. When I last heard from the publisher — which was not very recently — the book was doing pretty well. Six or seven hundred copies had been sold. I suppose, however, these awful times have now stopped the sale.

I intend in a week or two to come out of my owl's nest, and not return to it till late in the summer — employing the interval in making a tour somewhere in New England. You, who have the dust of distant countries on your "sandalshoon," cannot imagine how much enjoyment I shall have in this little excursion. Whenever I get abroad, I feel just as young as I did, ten years ago. What a letter I am inflicting on you! I trust you will answer it.

Yours sincerely,
Nath. Hawthorne.

From a letter to Henry Wadsworth Longfellow, June 4, 1837

CONSIDERATIONS FOR CRITICAL THINKING AND WRITING

1. How does Hawthorne regard his solitude? How does he feel it has affected his life and writing?

2. Hawthorne explains to Longfellow, one of his Bowdoin classmates, that "there is no fate in this world so horrible as to have no share in either its joys or sorrows" (para. 1). Explain how this idea is worked into "Young Goodman Brown" (p. 325).

3. Does Hawthorne indicate any positive results for having lived in his "owl's nest" (para. 1)? Consider how "The Minister's Black Veil" (p. 334) and this letter shed light on each other.

NATHANIEL HAWTHORNE

On the Power of the Writer's Imagination   *1850*

... Moonlight, in a familiar room, falling so white upon the carpet, and show-ing all its figures so distinctly — making every object so minutely visible, yet so unlike a morning or noontide visibility — is a medium the most suitable for a romance-writer° to get acquainted with his illusive guests. There is the little domestic scenery of the well-known apartment; the chairs, with each its sepa-rate individuality; the center-table, sustaining a work-basket, a volume or two, and an extinguished lamp; the sofa; the book-case; the picture on the wall — all these details, so completely seen, are so spiritualized by the unusual light, that they seem to lose their actual substance, and become things of intellect. Noth-ing is too small or too trifling to undergo this change, and acquire dignity thereby. A child's shoe; the doll, seated in her little wicker carriage; the hobby-horse — whatever, in a word, has been used or played with, during the day, is now invested with a quality of strangeness and remoteness, though still almost as vividly present as by daylight. Thus, therefore, the floor of our familiar room has become a neutral territory, somewhere between the real world and fairy-land, where the Actual and the Imaginary may meet, and each imbue itself with the nature of the other. Ghosts might enter here, without affrighting us. It would be too much in keeping with the scene to excite surprise, were we to look about us and discover a form, beloved, but gone hence, now sitting qui-etly in a streak of this magic moonshine, with an aspect that would make us doubt whether it had returned from afar, or had never once stirred from our fireside.

The somewhat dim coal-fire has an essential influence in producing the effect which I would describe. It throws its unobtrusive tinge throughout the room, with a faint ruddiness upon the walls and ceiling, and a reflected gleam from the polish of the furniture. This warmer light mingles itself with the cold spirituality of the moonbeams, and communicates, as it were, a heart and sensibilities of human tenderness to the forms which fancy summons up. It converts them from snow-images into men and women. Glancing at the looking-glass, we behold — deep within its haunted verge — the smouldering glow of the half-extinguished anthracite, the white moonbeams on the floor, and a repetition of all the gleam and shadow of the picture, with one re-move farther from the actual, and nearer to the imaginative. Then, at such an hour, and with this scene before him, if a man, sitting all alone, cannot dream strange things, and make them look like truth, he need never try to write romances.

From *The Scarlet Letter*

---

romance-writer: Hawthorne distinguished romance writing from novel writing. In the pref-ace to *The House of the Seven Gables* he writes:

> The latter form of composition is presumed to aim at a very minute fidelity, not merely to the possible, but to the probable and ordinary course of man's experience. The former — while, as a work of art, it must rigidly subject itself to laws, and while it sins unpardon-ably so far as it may swerve aside from the truth of the human heart — has fairly a right to present that truth under circumstances, to a great extent, of the writer's own choosing or creation.

CONSIDERATIONS FOR CRITICAL THINKING AND WRITING

1. Explain how Hawthorne uses light as a means of invoking the transforming powers of the imagination.

2. How do Hawthorne's stories fulfill his definition of romance writing? Why can't they be regarded as realistic?

3. Choose one story and discuss it as an attempt to evoke "the truth of the human heart."

NATHANIEL HAWTHORNE

On His Short Stories   *1851*

[These stories] have the pale tint of flowers that blossomed in too retired a shade — the coolness of a meditative habit, which diffuses itself through the feeling and observation of every sketch. Instead of passion there is sentiment; and, even in what purport to be pictures of actual life, we have allegory, not always warmly dressed in its habiliments of flesh and blood as to be taken into the reader's mind without a shiver. Whether from lack of power, or an unconquerable reserve, the Author's touches have often an effect of tameness; the merriest man can hardly contrive to laugh at his broadest humor; the tenderest woman, one would suppose, will hardly shed warm tears at his deepest pathos. The book, if you would see anything in it, requires to be read in the clear brown, twilight atmosphere in which it was written; if opened in the sunshine, it is apt to look exceedingly like a volume of blank pages.

From the preface to the 1851 edition of *Twice-Told Tales*

CONSIDERATIONS FOR CRITICAL THINKING AND WRITING

1. How does Hawthorne characterize his stories? Does his assessment accurately describe the stories you've read?

2. Why is a "twilight atmosphere" more conducive to an appreciation of Hawthorne's art than "sunshine"?

3. Write a one-page description of Hawthorne's stories in which you generalize about his characteristic approach to one of these elements: plot, character, setting, symbol, theme, tone.

HERMAN MELVILLE (1819–1891)

On Nathaniel Hawthorne's Tragic Vision   *1851*

There is a certain tragic phase of humanity which, in our opinion, was never more powerfully embodied than by Hawthorne. We mean the tragicalness of human thought in its own unbiased, native, and profounder workings. We think that in no recorded mind has the intense feeling of the visable truth ever entered more deeply than into this man's. By visable truth, we mean the apprehension of the absolute condition of present things as they strike the eye of the man who fears them not, though they do their worst to him — the man who, like Russia or the British Empire, declares himself a sovereign nature (in himself) amid the powers of heaven, hell, and earth. He may perish; but so long as he exists he insists upon treating with all Powers upon an equal basis. If any of those other Powers choose to withhold certain secrets, let them; that does not impair my sovereignty in myself; that does not make me tributary. And perhaps, after all, there is *no* secret. We incline to think that the Problem of the Universe is like the Freemason's° mighty secret, so terrible to all children. It turns out, at last, to consist in a triangle, a mallet, and an apron — nothing more! . . . There is the grand truth about Nathaniel Hawthorne. He says NO! in thunder; but the Devil himself cannot make him say *yes*. For all men who say *yes*, lie; and all men who say *no* — why, they are in the happy condition of judicious, unincumbered travelers in Europe; they cross the frontiers into Eternity with nothing but a carpetbag — that is to say, the Ego. Whereas those *yes*-gentry, they travel with heaps of baggage, and, damn them! they will never get through the Custom House. What's the reason, Mr. Hawthorne, that in the last stages of metaphysics a fellow always falls to *swearing* so? I could rip an hour.

From a letter to Hawthorne, April 16(?), 1851

Freemason: A member of the secret fraternity of Freemasonry.

CONSIDERATIONS FOR CRITICAL THINKING AND WRITING

1. What qualities in Hawthorne does Melville admire?
2. Explain how these qualities are embodied in one of the Hawthorne stories.
3. How might Melville's lawyer in "Bartleby, the Scrivener" (p. 124) be characterized as one of "those *yes*-gentry"?

GAYLORD BREWER (B. 1965)
The Joys of Secret Sin   2006

—after Hawthorne

"For the Earth, too, had on her Black Veil"?
Can you blame her? The better to avoid
the humbug of these two soldiers of melancholy —
that young, good man who soils the world
with his dark dream; a sweat-lipped preacher   5
smugly trembling behind twin folds of crape.

The Earth doesn't appreciate her name
sullied — always, winds howling and bestial
cries. Wife and fiancée fare no better —
poor plump Faith, her pink ribbons disavowed;   10
long-suffering Elizabeth, left old by cryptic

evasions. Who in the village doesn't
recognize the human face or needs reminding?

Black veil on every visage? Dying hour of gloom?
That's the rectitude that compels them all —   15
deacon, farmer, child, maiden, hag —
toward your welcoming smile, avuncular wink,
kindly dip of black staff, so curiously
entwined it seems almost to writhe. There,
just ahead: the forest's mossy, crooked path,   20
a canopy of flames, a guiltless hearth of stone.

CONSIDERATIONS FOR CRITICAL THINKING AND WRITING

1. Write a paraphrase of this poem. How does it provide a reading of "Young
   Goodman Brown" and "The Minister's Black Veil"?

2. CREATIVE RESPONSE. Using Brewer's poem as a source of inspiration (but
   not necessarily its style and form), try writing a poem based on your reading of "The Birthmark."

SUGGESTED TOPICS FOR LONGER PAPERS

1. Consider the setting of each of the Hawthorne stories in this chapter. Why
   are they significant? How are they related to the stories' respective themes?
   In your essay, determine which story relies most heavily on setting to convey its meanings.

2. Read the Perspective concerning Hawthorne and solitude (p. 355) and do some biographical research on
   Hawthorne's attitudes toward solitude and human
   isolation. How do details about his life shed light on
   the solitary or isolated characters in the three stories
   you have read in this chapter?

   [Web] Research
   Nathaniel Hawthorne
   or take quizzes
   on his works at
   bedfordstmartins.com/
   meyercompact.

12

A Study of Flannery O'Connor

In most English classes the short story has become a kind of literary specimen to be dissected. Every time a story of mine appears in a Freshman anthology, I have a vision of it, with its little organs laid open, like a frog in a bottle.

— FLANNERY O'CONNOR

I am always having it pointed out to me that life in Georgia is not at all the way I picture it, that escaped criminals do not roam the roads exterminating families, nor Bible salesmen prowl about looking for girls with wooden legs.

— FLANNERY O'CONNOR

When Flannery O'Connor (1925–1964) died of lupus before her fortieth birthday, her work was cruelly cut short. Nevertheless, she had completed two novels, *Wise Blood* (1952) and *The Violent Bear It Away* (1960), as well as thirty-one short stories. Despite her brief life and relatively modest output, her work is regarded as among the most distinguished American fiction of the mid-twentieth century. Her two collections of short stories, *A Good Man Is Hard to Find* (1955) and *Everything That Rises Must Converge* (1965), were included in *The Complete Stories of Flannery O'Connor* (1971), which won the National Book Award. The stories included in this chapter offer a glimpse into the work of this important twentieth-century writer.

Explore contexts for Flannery O'Connor on *LiterActive*.

Cheers,
Flannery

A BRIEF BIOGRAPHY AND INTRODUCTION

O'Connor's fiction grapples with living a spiritual life in a secular world. Although this major concern is worked into each of her stories, she takes a broad approach to spiritual issues by providing moral, social, and psychological contexts that offer a wealth of insights and passion that her readers have found both startling and absorbing. Her stories are challenging because her characters, who initially seem radically different from people we know, turn out to be, by the end of each story, somehow familiar — somehow connected to us.

O'Connor inhabited simultaneously two radically different worlds. The world she created in her stories is populated with bratty children, malcontents, incompetents, pious frauds, bewildered intellectuals, deformed cynics, rednecks, hucksters, racists, perverts, and murderers who experience dramatically intense moments that surprise and shock readers. Her personal life, however, was largely uneventful. She humorously acknowledged its quiet nature in 1958 when she claimed that "there won't be any biographies of me because, for only one reason, lives spent between the house and the chicken yard do not make exciting copy."

A broad outline of O'Connor's life may not offer very much "exciting copy," but it does provide clues about why she wrote such powerful fiction. The only child of Catholic parents, O'Connor was born in Savannah, Georgia, where she attended a parochial grammar school and high school. When she was thirteen, her father became ill with disseminated lupus, a rare, incurable blood disease, and had to abandon his real-estate business. The family moved to Milledgeville in central Georgia, where her mother's family had lived for generations. Because there were no Catholic schools in Milledgeville, O'Connor attended a public high school. In 1942, the year after her father died of lupus, O'Connor graduated from high school and enrolled in Georgia State College for Women. There she wrote for the literary magazine until receiving her diploma in 1945. Her stories earned her a fellowship to the Writers' Workshop at the University of Iowa, and for two years she learned to write steadily and seriously. She sold her first story to *Accent* in 1946 and earned her master of fine arts degree in 1947. She wrote stories about life in the rural South, and this subject matter, along with her devout Catholic perspective, became central to her fiction.

With her formal education behind her, O'Connor was ready to begin her professional career at the age of twenty-two. Equipped with determination ("No one can convince me that I shouldn't rewrite as much as I do") and offered the opportunity to be around other practicing writers, she moved to New York, where she worked on her first novel, *Wise Blood*. In 1950, however, she was diagnosed as having lupus, and, returning to Georgia for treatment, she took up permanent residence on her mother's farm in Milledgeville. There she lived a severely restricted but productive life, writing stories and raising peacocks.

With the exception of O'Connor's early years in Iowa and New York and some short lecture trips to other states, she traveled little. Although she made a pilgrimage to Lourdes, France (apparently more for her mother's sake than for her own), and then to Rome for an audience with the pope, her life was centered in the South. Like those of William Faulkner and many other southern writers, O'Connor's stories evoke the rhythms of rural southern speech and manners in insulated settings where widely diverse characters mingle. Also like Faulkner, she created works whose meanings go beyond their settings. She did not want her fiction to be seen in the context of narrowly defined regionalism: she complained that "in almost every hamlet you'll find at least one old lady writing epics in Negro dialect and probably two or three old gentlemen who have impossible historical novels on the way." Refusing to be caricatured, she knew that "the woods are full of regional writers, and it is the great horror of every serious Southern writer that he will become one of them." O'Connor's stories are rooted in rural southern culture, but in a larger sense they are set within the psychological and spiritual landscapes of the human soul. This interior setting universalizes local materials in much the same way that Nathaniel Hawthorne's New England stories do. Indeed, O'Connor once described herself as "one of his descendants": "I feel more of a kinship with him than any other American."

O'Connor's deep spiritual convictions coincide with the traditional emphasis on religion in the South, where, she said, there is still the belief "that man has fallen and that he is only perfectible by God's grace, not by his own unaided efforts." Although O'Connor's Catholicism differs from the prevailing Protestant fundamentalism of the South, the religious ethos so pervasive even in rural southern areas provided fertile ground for the spiritual crises her characters experience. In a posthumous collection of her articles, essays, and reviews aptly titled *Mystery and Manners* (1969), she summarized her basic religious convictions:

> I am no disbeliever in spiritual purpose and no vague believer. I see from the standpoint of Christian orthodoxy. This means that for me the meaning of life is centered in our Redemption by Christ and what I see in the world I see in its relation to that. I don't think that this is a position that can be taken halfway or one that is particularly easy in these times to make transparent in fiction.

O'Connor realized that she was writing against the grain of the readers who discovered her stories in the *Partisan Review, Sewanee Review, Mademoiselle,* or *Harper's Bazaar.* Many readers thought that Christian dogma would make her writing doctrinaire, but she insisted that the perspective of Christianity allowed her to interpret the details of life and guaranteed her "respect for [life's] mystery." O'Connor's stories contain no prepackaged prescriptions for living, no catechisms that lay out all the answers. Instead, her characters struggle with spiritual questions in bizarre, incongruous situations. Their lives are grotesque—even comic—precisely because they do not understand their own spiritual natures. Their actions are extreme and abnormal. O'Connor explains the reasons for this in *Mystery and Manners;* she says she

Flannery O'Connor (above left) at age 12 and (above right) in her teens (age 16 or 17). O'Connor, whose youth was marked by the declining health and death of her father, once wrote, "[A]nybody who has survived childhood has enough information about life to last him the rest of the days."

Courtesy of Ina Dillard Russell Library Special Collections, Georgia College & State University.

Flannery O'Connor and a Self-Portrait. The author poses in front of an accurate, if rather fierce self-portrait with one of her beloved ring-necked pheasants. As a child, O'Connor enjoyed raising birds, a passion that was sparked when one of her chickens, "a buff Cochin Bantam [that] had the distinction of being able to walk either forward or backward" was reported on in the press. "I had to have more and more chickens. . . . I wanted one with three legs or three wings but nothing in that line turned up. . . . My quest, whatever it was for, ended with peacocks," she wrote.

Reprinted by permission of Corbis-Bettmann.

The *Corinthian* Staff. (Above) Flannery O'Connor (seated, center) as editor of the *Corinthian*, the literary magazine at Georgia State College for Women (now Georgia College and State University). O'Connor attended the college from 1942 through 1945, and earned a B.A. in Social Science.

"Targets." As a student, O'Connor created humorous cartoons that lampooned aspects of campus life (many of which satirized the presence of the Navy at the school) that were published in the *Corinthian,* in the school newspaper, *The Colonnade,* and in the yearbook. In the cartoon shown here, O'Connor targets the WAVES (Women Accepted for Volunteer Emergency Service), a group that marched about the campus in lockstep and represented to her a rigid conformity against which she rebelled.

Courtesy of Ina Dillard Russell Library Special Collections, Georgia College & State University.

Flannery O'Connor and pet peacock at Andalusia Farm. Following her graduation from Georgia State Women's College, O'Connor attended the University of Iowa, where she received an M.F.A. in 1947. She left Iowa for the Yaddo Foundation's artist colony in Saratoga Springs, New York, in 1948, and later lived in New York City and Connecticut. In 1950, as she was working on her first novel (*Wise Blood*), O'Connor began to experience symptoms of lupus, and returned to Milledgeville, Georgia, in 1951. Instead of moving back to her home in town, she and her mother moved to Andalusia, the family farm (shown here) where she lived until her death in 1964. At Andalusia farm, O'Connor wrote in the mornings until noon; the rest of the day she spent minding her birds and entertaining friends. Andalusia, arguably, provided an inspiration and landscape for her fiction — it was here that O'Connor completed *Wise Blood* and wrote *A Good Man Is Hard to Find* (1955), *The Violent Bear It Away* (1960), and *Everything That Rises Must Converge* (published posthumously, in 1965).

sought to expose the "distortions" of "modern life" that appear "normal" to her audience. Hence, she used "violent means" to convey her vision to a "hostile audience." "When you can assume that your audience holds the same beliefs you do, you can relax a little and use more normal means of talking to it." But when the audience holds different values, "you have to make your vision apparent by shock — to the hard of hearing you shout, and for the almost-blind you draw large and startling figures." O'Connor's characters lose or find their soul-saving grace in painful, chaotic circumstances that bear little or no resemblance to the slow but sure progress to the Celestial City of repentant pilgrims in traditional religious stories.

Because her characters are powerful creations who live convincing, even if ugly, lives, O'Connor's religious beliefs never supersede her storytelling. One need be neither Christian nor Catholic to appreciate her concerns about human failure and degradation and her artistic ability to render fictional lives that are alternately absurdly comic and tragic. The ironies that abound in her work leave plenty of room for readers of all persuasions. O'Connor's work is narrow in the sense that her concerns are emphatically spiritual, but her compassion and her belief in human possibilities — even among the most unlikely characters — afford her fictions a capacity for wonder that is exhilarating. Her precise, deft use of language always reveals more than it seems to tell.

Like Hawthorne's fiction, O'Connor's stories present complex experiences that cannot be tidily summarized; it takes the entire story to suggest the meanings. Read the following three stories for the pleasure of entering the remarkable world O'Connor creates. You're in for some surprises.

A Good Man Is Hard to Find   *1953*

The grandmother didn't want to go to Florida. She wanted to visit some of her connections in east Tennessee and she was seizing at every chance to change Bailey's mind. Bailey was the son she lived with, her only boy. He was sitting on the edge of his chair at the table, bent over the orange sports section of the *Journal.* "Now look here, Bailey," she said, "see here, read this," and she stood with one hand on her thin hip and the other rattling the newspaper at his bald head. "Here this fellow that calls himself The Misfit is aloose from the Federal Pen and headed toward Florida and you read here what it says he did to these people. Just you read it. I wouldn't take my children in any direction with a criminal like that aloose in it. I couldn't answer to my conscience if I did."

Bailey didn't look up from his reading so she wheeled around then and faced the children's mother, a young woman in slacks, whose face was as broad and innocent as a cabbage and was tied around with a green headkerchief that had two points on the top like a rabbit's ears. She was sitting on the sofa, feeding the baby his apricots out of a jar. "The children have been to Florida before," the old lady said. "You all ought to take them somewhere else for a change so they would see different parts of the world and be broad. They never have been to east Tennessee."

The children's mother didn't seem to hear her but the eight-year-old boy, John Wesley, a stocky child with glasses, said, "If you don't want to go to Florida, why dontcha stay at home?" He and the little girl, June Star, were reading the funny papers on the floor.

"She wouldn't stay at home to be queen for a day," June Star said without raising her yellow head.

"Yes and what would you do if this fellow, The Misfit, caught you?" the   5 grandmother asked.

"I'd smack his face," John Wesley said.

"She wouldn't stay at home for a million bucks," June Star said. "Afraid she'd miss something. She has to go everywhere we go."

"All right, Miss," the grandmother said. "Just remember that the next time you want me to curl your hair."

June Star said her hair was naturally curly.

The next morning the grandmother was the first one in the car, ready to   10 go. She had her big black valise that looked like the head of a hippopotamus in one corner, and underneath it she was hiding a basket with Pitty Sing, the cat, in it. She didn't intend for the cat to be left alone in the house for three days because he would miss her too much and she was afraid he might brush against one of the gas burners and accidentally asphyxiate himself. Her son, Bailey, didn't like to arrive at a motel with a cat.

She sat in the middle of the back seat with John Wesley and June Star on either side of her. Bailey and the children's mother and the baby sat in front and they left Atlanta at eight forty-five with the mileage on the car at 55890. The grandmother wrote this down because she thought it would be interesting to say how many miles they had been when they got back. It took them twenty minutes to reach the outskirts of the city.

The old lady settled herself comfortably, removing her white cotton gloves and putting them up with her purse on the shelf in front of the back window. The children's mother still had on slacks and still had her head tied up in a green kerchief, but the grandmother had on a navy blue straw sailor hat with a bunch of white violets on the brim and a navy blue dress with a small white dot in the print. Her collars and cuffs were white organdy trimmed with lace and at her neckline she had pinned a purple spray of cloth violets containing a sachet. In case of an accident, anyone seeing her dead on the highway would know at once that she was a lady.

She said she thought it was going to be a good day for driving, neither too hot nor too cold, and she cautioned Bailey that the speed limit was fifty-five miles an hour and that the patrolmen hid themselves behind billboards and small clumps of trees and sped out after you before you had a chance to slow down. She pointed out interesting details of the scenery: Stone Mountain; the blue granite that in some places came up to both sides of the highway; the brilliant red clay banks slightly streaked with purple; and the various crops that made rows of green lace-work on the ground. The trees were full of silver-white sunlight and the meanest of them sparkled. The children were reading comic magazines and their mother had gone back to sleep.

"Let's go through Georgia fast so we won't have to look at it much," John Wesley said.

"If I were a little boy," said the grandmother, "I wouldn't talk about my native state that way. Tennessee has the mountains and Georgia has the hills." 15

"Tennessee is just a hillbilly dumping ground," John Wesley said, "and Georgia is a lousy state too."

"You said it," June Star said.

"In my time," said the grandmother, folding her thin veined fingers, "children were more respectful of their native states and their parents and everything else. People did right then. Oh look at the cute little pickaninny!" she said and pointed to a Negro child standing in the door of a shack. "Wouldn't that make a picture, now?" she asked and they all turned and looked at the little Negro out of the back window. He waved.

"He didn't have any britches on," June Star said.

"He probably didn't have any," the grandmother explained. "Little niggers 20 in the country don't have things like we do. If I could paint, I'd paint that picture," she said.

The children exchanged comic books.

The grandmother offered to hold the baby and the children's mother passed him over the front seat to her. She set him on her knee and bounced him and told him about the things they were passing. She rolled her eyes and screwed up her mouth and stuck her leathery thin face into his smooth bland one. Occasionally he gave her a faraway smile. They passed a large cotton field with five or six graves fenced in the middle of it, like a small island. "Look at the graveyard!" the grandmother said, pointing it out. "That was the old family burying ground. That belonged to the plantation."

"Where's the plantation?" John Wesley asked.

"Gone With the Wind," said the grandmother. "Ha. Ha."

When the children finished all the comic books they had brought, they 25 opened the lunch and ate it. The grandmother ate a peanut butter sandwich and an olive and would not let the children throw the box and the paper napkins out the window. When there was nothing else to do they played a game by choosing a cloud and making the other two guess what shape it suggested. John Wesley took one the shape of a cow and June Star guessed a cow and John Wesley said, no, an automobile, and June Star said he didn't play fair, and they began to slap each other over the grandmother.

The grandmother said she would tell them a story if they would keep quiet. When she told a story, she rolled her eyes and waved her head and was very dramatic. She said once when she was a maiden lady she had been courted by a Mr. Edgar Atkins Teagarden from Jasper, Georgia. She said he was a very good-looking man and a gentleman and that he brought her a watermelon every Saturday afternoon with his initials cut in it, E.A.T. Well, one Saturday, she said, Mr. Teagarden brought the watermelon and there was nobody at home and he left it on the front porch and returned in his buggy to Jasper, but she never got the watermelon, she said, because a nigger boy ate it when he saw the initials, E.A.T.! This story tickled John Wesley's funny bone and he giggled and giggled but June Star didn't think it was any good. She said she wouldn't marry a man that just brought her a watermelon on Saturday. The grandmother said she would have done well to marry Mr. Teagarden because he was a gentleman and had bought Coca-Cola stock when it first came out and that he had died only a few years ago, a very wealthy man.

They stopped at The Tower for barbecued sandwiches. The Tower was a part stucco and part wood filling station and dance hall set in a clearing outside of Timothy. A fat man named Red Sammy Butts ran it and there were signs stuck here and there on the building and for miles up and down the highway saying, TRY RED SAMMY'S FAMOUS BARBECUE. NONE LIKE FAMOUS RED SAMMY'S! RED SAM! THE FAT BOY WITH THE HAPPY LAUGH. A VETERAN! RED SAMMY'S YOUR MAN!

Red Sammy was lying on the bare ground outside The Tower with his head under a truck while a gray monkey about a foot high, chained to a small chinaberry tree, chattered nearby. The monkey sprang back into the tree and got on the highest limb as soon as he saw the children jump out of the car and run toward him.

Inside, The Tower was a long dark room with a counter at one end and tables at the other and dancing space in the middle. They all sat down at a board table next to the nickelodeon and Red Sam's wife, a tall burnt-brown woman with hair and eyes lighter than her skin, came and took their order. The children's mother put a dime in the machine and played "The Tennessee Waltz," and the grandmother said that tune always made her want to dance. She asked Bailey if he would like to dance but he only glared at her. He didn't have a naturally sunny disposition like she did and trips made him nervous. The grandmother's brown eyes were very bright. She swayed her head from side to side and pretended she was dancing in her chair. June Star said play something she could tap to so the children's mother put in another dime and played a fast number and June Star stepped out onto the dance floor and did her tap routine.

"Ain't she cute?" Red Sam's wife said, leaning over the counter. "Would   30 you like to come be my little girl?"

"No I certainly wouldn't," June Star said. "I wouldn't live in a broken-down place like this for a million bucks!" and she ran back to the table.

"Ain't she cute?" the woman repeated, stretching her mouth politely.

"Aren't you ashamed?" hissed the grandmother.

Red Sam came in and told his wife to quit lounging on the counter and hurry up with these people's order. His khaki trousers reached just to his hip bones and his stomach hung over them like a sack of meal swaying under his shirt. He came over and sat down at a table nearby and let out a combination sigh and yodel. "You can't win," he said. "You can't win," and he wiped his sweating red face off with a gray handkerchief. "These days you don't know who to trust," he said. "Ain't that the truth?"

"People are certainly not nice like they used to be," said the grandmother.   35

"Two fellers come in here last week," Red Sammy said, "driving a Chrysler. It was a old beat-up car but it was a good one and these boys looked all right to me. Said they worked at the mill and you know I let them fellers charge the gas they bought? Now why did I do that?"

"Because you're a good man!" the grandmother said at once.

"Yes'm, I suppose so," Red Sam said as if he were struck with this answer.

His wife brought the orders, carrying the five plates all at once without a tray, two in each hand and one balanced on her arm. "It isn't a soul in this green world of God's that you can trust," she said. "And I don't count nobody out of that, not nobody," she repeated, looking at Red Sammy.

"Did you read about that criminal, The Misfit, that's escaped?" asked the   40 grandmother.

"I wouldn't be a bit surprised if he didn't attack this place right here," said the woman. "If he hears about it being here, I wouldn't be none surprised to see him. If he hears it's two cent in the cash register, I wouldn't be a tall surprised if he. . . ."

"That'll do," Red Sam said. "Go bring these people their Co'-Colas," and the woman went off to get the rest of the order.

"A good man is hard to find," Red Sammy said. "Everything is getting terrible. I remember the day you could go off and leave your screen door unlatched. Not no more."

He and the grandmother discussed better times. The old lady said that in her opinion Europe was entirely to blame for the way things were now. She said the way Europe acted you would think we were made of money and Red Sam said it was no use talking about it, she was exactly right. The children ran outside into the white sunlight and looked at the monkey in the lacy chinaberry tree. He was busy catching fleas on himself and biting each one carefully between his teeth as if it were a delicacy.

They drove off again into the hot afternoon. The grandmother took cat   45 naps and woke up every few minutes with her own snoring. Outside of Toombsboro she woke up and recalled an old plantation that she had visited in this neighborhood once when she was a young lady. She said the house had six white columns across the front and that there was an avenue of oaks leading up to it and two little wooden trellis arbors on either side in front where you sat down with your suitor after a stroll in the garden. She recalled exactly which road to turn off to get to it. She knew that Bailey would not be willing to lose any time looking at an old house, but the more she talked about it, the more she wanted to see it once again and find out if the little twin arbors were still standing. "There was a secret panel in this house," she said craftily, not telling the truth but wishing that she were, "and the story went that all the family silver was hidden in it when Sherman° came through but it was never found. . . ."

"Hey!" John Wesley said. "Let's go see it! We'll find it! We'll poke all the woodwork and find it! Who lives there? Where do you turn off at? Hey Pop, can't we turn off there?"

"We never have seen a house with a secret panel!" June Star shrieked. "Let's go to the house with the secret panel! Hey Pop, can't we go see the house with the secret panel!"

"It's not far from here, I know," the grandmother said. "It won't take over twenty minutes."

Bailey was looking straight ahead. His jaw was as rigid as a horseshoe. "No," he said.

The children began to yell and scream that they wanted to see the house   50 with the secret panel. John Wesley kicked the back of the front seat and June Star hung over her mother's shoulder and whined desperately into her ear that they never had any fun even on their vacation, that they could never do what THEY wanted to do. The baby began to scream and John Wesley kicked the back of the seat so hard that his father could feel the blows in his kidney.

"All right!" he shouted and drew the car to a stop at the side of the road. "Will you all shut up? Will you all just shut up for one second? If you don't shut up, we won't go anywhere."

"It would be very educational for them," the grandmother murmured.

"All right," Bailey said, "but get this: this is the only time we're going to stop for anything like this. This is the one and only time."

"The dirt road that you have to turn down is about a mile back," the grandmother directed. "I marked it when we passed."

"A dirt road," Bailey groaned.   55

After they had turned around and were headed toward the dirt road, the grandmother recalled other points about the house, the beautiful glass over the front doorway and the candle-lamp in the hall. John Wesley said that the secret panel was probably in the fireplace.

"You can't go inside this house," Bailey said. "You don't know who lives there."

"While you all talk to the people in front, I'll run around behind and get in a window," John Wesley suggested.

"We'll all stay in the car," his mother said.

They turned onto the dirt road and the car raced roughly along in a swirl   60 of pink dust. The grandmother recalled the times when there were no paved

---

Sherman: William Tecumseh Sherman (1820–1891), Union Army commander who led infamous marches through the South during the Civil War.

roads and thirty miles was a day's journey. The dirt road was hilly and there were sudden washes in it and sharp curves on dangerous embankments. All at once they would be on a hill, looking down over the blue tops of trees for miles around, then the next minute, they would be in a red depression with the dust-coated trees looking down on them.

"This place had better turn up in a minute," Bailey said, "or I'm going to turn around."

The road looked as if no one had traveled on it for months.

"It's not much farther," the grandmother said and just as she said it, a horrible thought came to her. The thought was so embarrassing that she turned red in the face and her eyes dilated and her feet jumped up, upsetting her valise in the corner. The instant the valise moved, the newspaper top she had over the basket under it rose with a snarl and Pitty Sing, the cat, sprang onto Bailey's shoulder.

The children were thrown to the floor and their mother, clutching the baby, was thrown out the door onto the ground; the old lady was thrown into the front seat. The car turned over once and landed right-side-up in a gulch off the side of the road. Bailey remained in the driver's seat with the cat — gray-striped with a broad white face and an orange nose — clinging to his neck like a caterpillar.

As soon as the children saw they could move their arms and legs, they 65 scrambled out of the car, shouting, "We've had an ACCIDENT!" The grandmother was curled up under the dashboard, hoping she was injured so that Bailey's wrath would not come down on her all at once. The horrible thought she had before the accident was that the house she had remembered so vividly was not in Georgia but in Tennessee.

Bailey removed the cat from his neck with both hands and flung it out the window against the side of a pine tree. Then he got out of the car and started looking for the children's mother. She was sitting against the side of the red gutted ditch, holding the screaming baby, but she only had a cut down her face and a broken shoulder. "We've had an ACCIDENT!" the children screamed in a frenzy of delight.

"But nobody's killed," June Star said with disappointment as the grandmother limped out of the car, her hat still pinned to her head but the broken front brim standing up at a jaunty angle and the violet spray hanging off the side. They all sat down in the ditch, except the children, to recover from the shock. They were all shaking.

"Maybe a car will come along," said the children's mother hoarsely.

"I believe I have injured an organ," said the grandmother, pressing her side, but no one answered her. Bailey's teeth were clattering. He had on a yellow sport shirt with bright blue parrots designed in it and his face was as yellow as the shirt. The grandmother decided that she would not mention that the house was in Tennessee.

The road was about ten feet above and they could see only the tops of the 70 trees on the other side of it. Behind the ditch they were sitting in there were more woods, tall and dark and deep. In a few minutes they saw a car some distance away on top of a hill, coming slowly as if the occupants were watching them. The grandmother stood up and waved both arms dramatically to attract their attention. The car continued to come on slowly, disappeared around a bend and appeared again, moving even slower, on top of the hill they had gone over. It was a big black battered hearse-like automobile. There were three men in it.

It came to a stop just over them and for some minutes, the driver looked down with a steady expressionless gaze to where they were sitting, and didn't speak. Then he turned his head and muttered something to the other two and they got out. One was a fat boy in black trousers and a red sweat shirt with a silver stallion embossed on the front of it. He moved around on the right side of them and stood staring, his mouth partly open in a kind of loose grin. The other had on khaki pants and a blue striped coat and a gray hat pulled down very low, hiding most of his face. He came around slowly on the left side. Neither spoke.

The driver got out of the car and stood by the side of it, looking down at them. He was an older man than the other two. His hair was just beginning to gray and he wore silver-rimmed spectacles that gave him a scholarly look. He had a long creased face and didn't have on any shirt or undershirt. He had on blue jeans that were too tight for him and was holding a black hat and a gun. The two boys also had guns.

"We've had an ACCIDENT!" the children screamed.

The grandmother had the peculiar feeling that the bespectacled man was someone she knew. His face was as familiar to her as if she had known him all her life but she could not recall who he was. He moved away from the car and began to come down the embankment, placing his feet carefully so that he wouldn't slip. He had on tan and white shoes and no socks, and his ankles were red and thin. "Good afternoon," he said. "I see you all had you a little spill."

"We turned over twice!" said the grandmother.   75

"Oncet," he corrected. "We seen it happen. Try their car and see will it run, Hiram," he said quietly to the boy with the gray hat.

"What you got that gun for?" John Wesley asked. "Whatcha gonna do with that gun?"

"Lady," the man said to the children's mother, "would you mind calling them children to sit down by you? Children make me nervous. I want all you all to sit down right together there where you're at."

"What are you telling US what to do for?" June Star asked.

Behind them the line of woods gaped like a dark open mouth. "Come   80 here," said their mother.

"Look here now," Bailey said suddenly, "we're in a predicament! We're in. . . ."

The grandmother shrieked. She scrambled to her feet and stood staring. "You're The Misfit!" she said. "I recognized you at once!"

"Yes'm," the man said, smiling slightly as if he were pleased in spite of himself to be known, "but it would have been better for all of you, lady, if you hadn't of reckernized me."

Bailey turned his head sharply and said something to his mother that shocked even the children. The old lady began to cry and The Misfit reddened.

"Lady," he said, "don't you get upset. Sometimes a man says things he 85 don't mean. I don't reckon he meant to talk to you thataway."

"You wouldn't shoot a lady, would you?" the grandmother said and removed a clean handkerchief from her cuff and began to slap at her eyes with it.

The Misfit pointed the toe of his shoe into the ground and made a little hole and then covered it up again. "I would hate to have to," he said.

"Listen," the grandmother almost screamed, "I know you're a good man. You don't look a bit like you have common blood. I know you must come from nice people!"

"Yes mam," he said, "finest people in the world." When he smiled he showed a row of strong white teeth. "God never made a finer woman than my mother and my daddy's heart was pure gold," he said. The boy with the red sweat shirt had come around behind them and was standing with his gun at his hip. The Misfit squatted down on the ground. "Watch them children, Bobby Lee," he said. "You know they make me nervous." He looked at the six of them huddled together in front of him and he seemed to be embarrassed as if he couldn't think of anything to say. "Ain't a cloud in the sky," he remarked, looking up at it. "Don't see no sun but don't see no cloud neither."

"Yes, it's a beautiful day," said the grandmother. "Listen," she said, "you   90 shouldn't call yourself The Misfit because I know you're a good man at heart. I can just look at you and tell."

"Hush!" Bailey yelled. "Hush! Everybody shut up and let me handle this!" He was squatting in the position of a runner about to sprint forward but he didn't move.

"I pre-chate that, lady," The Misfit said and drew a little circle in the ground with the butt of his gun.

"It'll take a half a hour to fix this here car," Hiram called, looking over the raised hood of it.

"Well, first you and Bobby Lee get him and that little boy to step over yonder with you," The Misfit said, pointing to Bailey and John Wesley. "The boys want to ast you something," he said to Bailey. "Would you mind stepping back in them woods there with them?"

"Listen," Bailey began, "we're in a terrible predicament! Nobody realizes   95 what this is," and his voice cracked. His eyes were as blue and intense as the parrots in his shirt and he remained perfectly still.

The grandmother reached up to adjust her hat brim as if she were going to the woods with him but it came off in her hand. She stood staring at it and after a second she let it fall to the ground. Hiram pulled Bailey up by the arm as if he were assisting an old man. John Wesley caught hold of his father's hand and Bobby Lee followed. They went off toward the woods and just as they reached the dark edge, Bailey turned and supporting himself against a gray naked pine trunk, he shouted, "I'll be back in a minute, Mamma, wait on me!"

"Come back this instant!" his mother shrilled but they all disappeared into the woods.

"Bailey Boy!" the grandmother called in a tragic voice but she found she was looking at The Misfit squatting on the ground in front of her. "I just know you're a good man," she said desperately. "You're not a bit common!"

"Nome, I ain't a good man," The Misfit said after a second as if he had considered her statement carefully, "but I ain't the worst in the world neither. My daddy said I was a different breed of dog from my brothers and sisters. 'You know,' Daddy said, 'it's some that can live their whole life out without asking about it and it's others has to know why it is, and this boy is one of the latters. He's going to be into everything!' " He put on his black hat and looked up suddenly and then away deep into the woods as if he were embarrassed again. "I'm sorry I don't have on a shirt before you ladies," he said, hunching his shoulders slightly. "We buried our clothes that we had on when we escaped and we're just making do until we can get better. We borrowed these from some folks we met," he explained.

"That's perfectly all right," the grandmother said. "Maybe Bailey has an   100 extra shirt in his suitcase."

"I'll look and see terrectly," The Misfit said.

"Where are they taking him?" the children's mother screamed.

"Daddy was a card himself," The Misfit said. "You couldn't put anything over on him. He never got in trouble with the Authorities though. Just had the knack of handling them."

"You could be honest too if you'd only try," said the grandmother. "Think how wonderful it would be to settle down and live a comfortable life and not have to think about somebody chasing you all the time."

The Misfit kept scratching in the ground with the butt of his gun as if he were thinking about it. "Yes'm, somebody is always after you," he murmured. 105

The grandmother noticed how thin his shoulder blades were just behind his hat because she was standing up looking down on him. "Do you ever pray?" she asked.

He shook his head. All she saw was the black hat wiggle between his shoulder blades. "Nome," he said.

There was a pistol shot from the woods, followed closely by another. Then silence. The old lady's head jerked around. She could hear the wind move through the tree tops like a long satisfied insuck of breath. "Bailey Boy!" she called.

"I was a gospel singer for a while," The Misfit said. "I been most everything. Been in the arm service, both land and sea, at home and abroad, been twict married, been an undertaker, been with the railroads, plowed Mother Earth, been in a tornado, seen a man burnt alive oncet," and he looked up at the children's mother and the little girl who were sitting close together, their faces white and their eyes glassy; "I even seen a woman flogged," he said.

"Pray, pray," the grandmother began, "pray, pray. . . ." 110

"I never was a bad boy that I remember of," The Misfit said in an almost dreamy voice, "but somewheres along the line I done something wrong and got sent to the penitentiary. I was buried alive," and he looked up and held her attention to him by a steady stare.

"That's when you should have started to pray," she said. "What did you do to get sent to the penitentiary that first time?"

"Turn to the right, it was a wall," The Misfit said, looking up again at the cloudless sky. "Turn to the left, it was a wall. Look up it was a ceiling, look down it was a floor. I forget what I done, lady. I set there and set there, trying to remember what it was I done and I ain't recalled it to this day. Oncet in a while, I would think it was coming to me, but it never come."

"Maybe they put you in by mistake," the old lady said vaguely.

"Nome," he said. "It wasn't no mistake. They had the papers on me." 115

"You must have stolen something," she said.

The Misfit sneered slightly. "Nobody had nothing I wanted," he said. "It was a head-doctor at the penitentiary said what I had done was kill my daddy but I known that for a lie. My daddy died in nineteen ought nineteen of the epidemic flu and I never had a thing to do with it. He was buried in the Mount Hopewell Baptist churchyard and you can see for yourself."

"If you would pray," the old lady said, "Jesus would help you."

"That's right," The Misfit said.

"Well then, why don't you pray?" she asked trembling with delight suddenly. 120

"I don't want no hep," he said. "I'm doing all right by myself."

Bobby Lee and Hiram came ambling back from the woods. Bobby Lee was dragging a yellow shirt with bright blue parrots in it.

"Throw me that shirt, Bobby Lee," The Misfit said. The shirt came flying at him and landed on his shoulder and he put it on. The grandmother couldn't name what the shirt reminded her of. "No, lady," The Misfit said while he was buttoning it up, "I found out the crime don't matter. You can do one thing or you can do another, kill a man or take a tire off his car, because sooner or later you're going to forget what it was you done and just be punished for it."

The children's mother had begun to make heaving noises as if she couldn't get her breath. "Lady," he asked, "would you and that little girl like to step off yonder with Bobby Lee and Hiram and join your husband?"

"Yes, thank you," the mother said faintly. Her left arm dangled helplessly 125 and she was holding the baby, who had gone to sleep, in the other. "Hep that lady up, Hiram," The Misfit said as she struggled to climb out of the ditch, "and Bobby Lee, you hold onto that little girl's hand."

"I don't want to hold hands with him," June Star said. "He reminds me of a pig."

The fat boy blushed and laughed and caught her by the arm and pulled her off into the woods after Hiram and her mother.

Alone with The Misfit, the grandmother found that she had lost her voice. There was not a cloud in the sky nor any sun. There was nothing around her but woods. She wanted to tell him that he must pray. She opened and closed her mouth several times before anything came out. Finally she found herself saying, "Jesus, Jesus," meaning Jesus will help you, but the way she was saying it, it sounded as if she might be cursing.

"Yes'm," The Misfit said as if he agreed. "Jesus thown everything off balance. It was the same case with Him as with me except He hadn't committed any crime and they could prove I had committed one because they had the papers on me. Of course," he said, "they never shown me my papers. That's why I sign myself now. I said long ago, you get your signature and sign everything you do and keep a copy of it. Then you'll know what you done and you can hold up the crime to the punishment and see do they match and in the end you'll have something to prove you ain't been treated right. I call myself The Misfit," he said, "because I can't make what all I done wrong fit what all I gone through in punishment."

There was a piercing scream from the woods, followed closely by a pistol 130 report. "Does it seem right to you, lady, that one is punished a heap and another ain't punished at all?"

"Jesus!" the old lady cried. "You've got good blood! I know you wouldn't shoot a lady! I know you come from nice people! Pray! Jesus, you ought not to shoot a lady. I'll give you all the money I've got!"

"Lady," The Misfit said, looking beyond her far into the woods, "there never was a body that give the undertaker a tip."

There were two more pistol reports and the grandmother raised her head like a parched old turkey hen crying for water and called, "Bailey Boy, Bailey Boy!" as if her heart would break.

"Jesus was the only One that ever raised the dead," The Misfit continued, "and He shouldn't have done it. He thown everything off balance. If He did what He said, then it's nothing for you to do but thow away everything and follow Him, and if He didn't, then it's nothing for you to do but enjoy the few minutes you got left the best way you can—by killing somebody or burning

down his house or doing some other meanness to him. No pleasure but meanness," he said and his voice had become almost a snarl.

"Maybe He didn't raise the dead," the old lady mumbled, not knowing 135
what she was saying and feeling so dizzy that she sank down in the ditch with
her legs twisted under her.

"I wasn't there so I can't say He didn't," The Misfit said. "I wisht I had of
been there," he said, hitting the ground with his fist. "It ain't right I wasn't
there because if I had of been there I would of known. Listen lady," he said in a
high voice, "if I had of been there I would of known and I wouldn't be like I am
now." His voice seemed about to crack and the grandmother's head cleared for
an instant. She saw the man's face twisted close to her own as if he were going
to cry and she murmured, "Why you're one of my babies. You're one of my own
children!" She reached out and touched him on the shoulder. The Misfit
sprang back as if a snake had bitten him and shot her three times through the
chest. Then he put his gun down on the ground and took off his glasses and
began to clean them.

Hiram and Bobby Lee returned from the woods and stood over the ditch,
looking down at the grandmother who half sat and half lay in a puddle of
blood with her legs crossed under her like a child's and her face smiling up at
the cloudless sky.

Without his glasses, The Misfit's eyes were red-rimmed and pale and
defenseless-looking. "Take her off and thow her where you thown the others,"
he said, picking up the cat that was rubbing itself against his leg.

"She was a talker, wasn't she?" Bobby Lee said, sliding down the ditch with
a yodel.

"She would of been a good woman," The Misfit said, "if it had been some- 140
body there to shoot her every minute of her life."

"Some fun!" Bobby Lee said.

"Shut up, Bobby Lee," The Misfit said. "It's no real pleasure in life."

CONSIDERATIONS FOR CRITICAL THINKING AND WRITING

   1. **FIRST RESPONSE.** How does O'Connor portray the family? What is comic
about them? What qualities about them are we meant to take seriously?
Are you shocked by what happens to them? Does your attitude toward
them remain constant during the course of the story?

   2. How do the grandmother's concerns about the trip to Florida foreshadow events in the story?

   3. Describe the grandmother. How does O'Connor make her the central
character?

   4. What is Red Sammy's purpose in the story? Relate his view of life to the
story's conflicts.

   5. Characterize The Misfit. What makes him so? Can he be written off as
simply insane? How does the grandmother respond to him?

   6. Why does The Misfit say that "Jesus thown everything off balance"
(para. 129)? What does religion have to do with the brutal action of this
story?

   7. What does The Misfit mean at the end when he says about the grandmother, "She would of been a good woman . . . if it had been somebody
there to shoot her every minute of her life"?

8. Describe the story's tone. Is it consistent? What is the effect of O'Connor's use of tone?

9. How is coincidence used to advance the plot? How do coincidences lead to ironies in the story?

10. Explain how the title points to the story's theme.

CONNECTIONS TO OTHER SELECTIONS

1. What makes "A Good Man Is Hard to Find" so difficult to interpret in contrast, say, to Hawthorne's "The Birthmark" (p. 343)?

2. How does this family compare with the Snopeses in Faulkner's "Barn Burning" (p. 418)? Which family are you more sympathetic to?

3. Consider the criminal behavior of The Misfit and Abner Snopes. What motivates each character? Explain the significant similarities and differences between them.

Good Country People   *1955*

Besides the neutral expression that she wore when she was alone, Mrs. Freeman had two others, forward and reverse, that she used for all her human dealings. Her forward expression was steady and driving like the advance of a heavy truck. Her eyes never swerved to left or right but turned as the story turned as if they followed a yellow line down the center of it. She seldom used the other expression because it was not often necessary for her to retract a statement, but when she did, her face came to a complete stop, there was an almost imperceptible movement of her black eyes, during which they seemed to be receding, and then the observer would see that Mrs. Freeman, though she might stand there as real as several grain sacks thrown on top of each other, was no longer there in spirit. As for getting anything across to her when this was the case, Mrs. Hopewell had given it up. She might talk her head off. Mrs. Freeman could never be brought to admit herself wrong on any point. She would stand there and if she could be brought to say anything, it was something like, "Well, I wouldn't of said it was and I wouldn't of said it wasn't," or letting her gaze range over the top kitchen shelf where there was an assortment of dusty bottles, she might remark, "I see you ain't ate many of them figs you put up last summer."

They carried on their most important business in the kitchen at breakfast. Every morning Mrs. Hopewell got up at seven o'clock and lit her gas heater and Joy's. Joy was her daughter, a large blonde girl who had an artificial leg. Mrs. Hopewell thought of her as a child though she was thirty-two years old and highly educated. Joy would get up while her mother was eating and lumber into the bathroom and slam the door, and before long, Mrs. Freeman would arrive at the back door. Joy would hear her mother call, "Come on in," and then they would talk for a while in low voices that were indistinguishable in the bathroom. By the time Joy came in, they had usually finished the weather report and were on one or the other of Mrs. Freeman's daughters, Glynese or Carramae, Joy called them Glycerin and Caramel. Glynese, a redhead, was eighteen and had many admirers; Carramae, a blonde, was only fifteen but already married and pregnant. She could not keep anything in her stomach. Every morning Mrs. Freeman told Mrs. Hopewell how many times she had vomited since the last report.

Mrs. Hopewell liked to tell people that Glynese and Carramae were two of the finest girls she knew and that Mrs. Freeman was a *lady* and that she was never ashamed to take her anywhere or introduce her to anybody they might meet. Then she would tell how she had happened to hire the Freemans in the first place and how they were a godsend to her and how she had had them four years. The reason for her keeping them so long was that they were not trash. They were good country people. She had telephoned the man whose name they had given as a reference and he had told her that Mr. Freeman was a good farmer but that his wife was the nosiest woman ever to walk the earth. "She's got to be into everything," the man said. "If she don't get there before the dust settles, you can bet she's dead, that's all. She'll want to know all your business. I can stand him real good," he had said, "but me nor my wife neither could have stood that woman one more minute on this place." That had put Mrs. Hopewell off for a few days.

She had hired them in the end because there were no other applicants but she had made up her mind beforehand exactly how she would handle the woman. Since she was the type who had to be into everything, then, Mrs. Hopewell decided, she would not only let her be into everything, she would *see to it* that she was into everything—she would give her the responsibility of everything, she would put her in charge. Mrs. Hopewell had no bad qualities of her own but she was able to use other people's in such a constructive way that she never felt the lack. She had hired the Freemans and she had kept them four years.

Nothing is perfect. This was one of Mrs. Hopewell's favorite sayings. Another was: that is life! And still another, the most important, was: well, other people have their opinions too. She would make these statements, usually at the table, in a tone of gentle insistence as if no one held them but her, and the large hulking Joy, whose constant outrage had obliterated every expression from her face, would stare just a little to the side of her, her eyes icy blue, with the look of someone who has achieved blindness by an act of will and means to keep it.

When Mrs. Hopewell said to Mrs. Freeman that life was like that, Mrs. Freeman would say, "I always said so myself." Nothing had been arrived at by anyone that had not first been arrived at by her. She was quicker than Mr. Freeman. When Mrs. Hopewell said to her after they had been on the place a while, "You know, you're the wheel behind the wheel," and winked, Mrs. Freeman had said, "I know it. I've always been quick. It's some that are quicker than others."

"Everybody is different," Mrs. Hopewell said.

"Yes, most people is," Mrs. Freeman said.

"It takes all kinds to make the world."

"I always said it did myself."

The girl was used to this kind of dialogue for breakfast and more of it for dinner; sometimes they had it for supper too. When they had no guest they ate in the kitchen because that was easier. Mrs. Freeman always managed to arrive at some point during the meal and to watch them finish it. She would stand in the doorway if it were summer but in the winter she would stand with one elbow on top of the refrigerator and look down on them, or she would stand by the gas heater, lifting the back of her skirt slightly. Occasionally she would stand against the wall and roll her head from side to side. At no time was she in any hurry to leave. All this was very trying on Mrs. Hopewell but she was a woman of great patience. She realized that nothing is perfect and that in the Freemans she had good country people and that if, in this day and age, you get good country people, you had better hang onto them.

She had had plenty of experience with trash. Before the Freemans she had averaged one tenant family a year. The wives of these farmers were not the kind you would want to be around you for very long. Mrs. Hopewell, who had divorced her husband long ago, needed someone to walk over the fields with her; and when Joy had to be impressed for these services, her remarks were usually so ugly and her face so glum that Mrs. Hopewell would say, "If you can't come pleasantly, I don't want you at all," to which the girl, standing square and rigid-shouldered with her neck thrust slightly forward, would reply, "If you want me, here I am — LIKE I AM."

Mrs. Hopewell excused this attitude because of the leg (which had been shot off in a hunting accident when Joy was ten). It was hard for Mrs. Hopewell to realize that her child was thirty-two now and that for more than twenty years she had had only one leg. She thought of her still as a child because it tore her heart to think instead of the poor stout girl in her thirties who had never danced a step or had any *normal* good times. Her name was really Joy but as soon as she was twenty-one and away from home, she had had it legally changed. Mrs. Hopewell was certain that she had thought and thought until she had hit upon the ugliest name in any language. Then she had gone and had the beautiful name, Joy, changed without telling her mother until after she had done it. Her legal name was Hulga.

When Mrs. Hopewell thought the name, Hulga, she thought of the broad blank hull of a battleship. She would not use it. She continued to call her Joy to which the girl responded but in a purely mechanical way.

Hulga had learned to tolerate Mrs. Freeman who saved her from taking walks with her mother. Even Glynese and Carramae were useful when they occupied attention that might otherwise have been directed at her. At first she had thought she could not stand Mrs. Freeman for she had found that it was not possible to be rude to her. Mrs. Freeman would take on strange resentments and for days together she would be sullen but the source of her displeasure was always obscure; a direct attack, a positive leer, blatant ugliness to her face — these never touched her. And without warning one day, she began calling her Hulga.

She did not call her that in front of Mrs. Hopewell who would have been incensed but when she and the girl happened to be out of the house together, she would say something and add the name Hulga to the end of it, and the big spectacled Joy-Hulga would scowl and redden as if her privacy had been intruded upon. She considered the name her personal affair. She had arrived at it first purely on the basis of its ugly sound and then the full genius of its fitness had struck her. She had a vision of the name working like the ugly sweating Vulcan° who stayed in the furnace and to whom, presumably, the goddess

Vulcan: Roman god of fire.

had to come when called. She saw it as the name of her highest creative act. One of her major triumphs was that her mother had not been able to turn her dust into Joy, but the greater one was that she had been able to turn it herself into Hulga. However, Mrs. Freeman's relish for using the name only irritated her. It was as if Mrs. Freeman's beady steel-pointed eyes had penetrated far enough behind her face to reach some secret fact. Something about her seemed to fascinate Mrs. Freeman and then one day Hulga realized that it was the artificial leg. Mrs. Freeman had a special fondness for the details of secret infections, hidden deformities, assaults upon children. Of diseases, she preferred the lingering or incurable. Hulga had heard Mrs. Hopewell give her the details of the hunting accident, how the leg had been literally blasted off, how she had never lost consciousness. Mrs. Freeman could listen to it any time as if it had happened an hour ago.

When Hulga stumped into the kitchen in the morning (she could walk without making the awful noise but she made it — Mrs. Hopewell was certain — because it was ugly-sounding), she glanced at them and did not speak. Mrs. Hopewell would be in her red kimono with her hair tied around her head in rags. She would be sitting at the table, finishing her breakfast and Mrs. Freeman would be hanging by her elbow outward from the refrigerator, looking down at the table. Hulga always put her eggs on the stove to boil and then stood over them with her arms folded, and Mrs. Hopewell would look at her — a kind of indirect gaze divided between her and Mrs. Freeman — and would think that if she would only keep herself up a little, she wouldn't be so bad looking. There was nothing wrong with her face that a pleasant expression wouldn't help. Mrs. Hopewell said that people who looked on the bright side of things would be beautiful even if they were not.

Whenever she looked at Joy this way, she could not help but feel that it would have been better if the child had not taken the Ph.D. It had certainly not brought her out any and now that she had it, there was no more excuse for her to go to school again. Mrs. Hopewell thought it was nice for girls to go to school to have a good time but Joy had "gone through." Anyhow, she would not have been strong enough to go again. The doctors had told Mrs. Hopewell that with the best of care, Joy might see forty-five. She had a weak heart. Joy had made it plain that if it had not been for this condition, she would be far from these red hills and good country people. She would be in a university lecturing to people who knew what she was talking about. And Mrs. Hopewell could very well picture her there, looking like a scarecrow and lecturing to more of the same. Here she went about all day in a six-year-old skirt and a yellow sweat shirt with a faded cowboy on a horse embossed on it. She thought this was funny; Mrs. Hopewell thought it was idiotic and showed simply that she was still a child. She was brilliant but she didn't have a grain of sense. It seemed to Mrs. Hopewell that every year she grew less like other people and more like herself — bloated, rude, and squint-eyed. And she said such strange things! To her own mother she had said — without warning, without excuse, standing up in the middle of a meal with her face purple and her mouth half full — "Woman! do you ever look inside? Do you ever look inside and see what you are *not*? God!" she had cried sinking down again and staring at her plate, "Malebranche° was right: we are not our own light. We are not our own light!"

Malebranche: Nicolas Malebranche (1638–1715), a French philosopher.

Mrs. Hopewell had no idea to this day what brought that on. She had only made the remark, hoping Joy would take it in, that a smile never hurt anyone.

The girl had taken the Ph.D. in philosophy and this left Mrs. Hopewell at a complete loss. You could say, "My daughter is a nurse," or "My daughter is a schoolteacher," or even, "My daughter is a chemical engineer." You could not say, "My daughter is a philosopher." That was something that had ended with the Greeks and Romans. All day Joy sat on her neck in a deep chair, reading. Sometimes she went for walks but she didn't like dogs or cats or birds or flowers or nature or nice young men. She looked at nice young men as if she could smell their stupidity.

One day Mrs. Hopewell had picked up one of the books the girl had just 20 put down and opening it at random, she read, "Science, on the other hand, has to assert its soberness and seriousness afresh and declare that it is concerned solely with what-is. Nothing—how can it be for science anything but a horror and a phantasm? If science is right, then one thing stands firm: science wishes to know nothing of nothing. Such is after all the strictly scientific approach to Nothing. We know it by wishing to know nothing of Nothing." These words had been underlined with a blue pencil and they worked on Mrs. Hopewell like some evil incantation in gibberish. She shut the book quickly and went out of the room as if she were having a chill.

This morning when the girl came in, Mrs. Freeman was on Carramae. "She thrown up four times after supper," she said, "and was up twict in the night after three o'clock. Yesterday she didn't do nothing but ramble in the bureau drawer. All she did. Stand up there and see what she could run up on."

"She's got to eat," Mrs. Hopewell muttered, sipping her coffee, while she watched Joy's back at the stove. She was wondering what the child had said to the Bible salesman. She could not imagine what kind of a conversation she could possibly have had with him.

He was a tall gaunt hatless youth who had called yesterday to sell them a Bible. He had appeared at the door, carrying a large black suitcase that weighted him so heavily on one side that he had to brace himself against the door facing. He seemed on the point of collapse but he said in a cheerful voice, "Good morning, Mrs. Cedars!" and set the suitcase down on the mat. He was not a bad-looking young man though he had on a bright blue suit and yellow socks that were not pulled up far enough. He had prominent face bones and a streak of sticky-looking brown hair falling across his forehead.

"I'm Mrs. Hopewell," she said.

"Oh!" he said, pretending to look puzzled but with his eyes sparkling, "I 25 saw it said 'The Cedars' on the mailbox so I thought you was Mrs. Cedars!" and he burst out in a pleasant laugh. He picked up the satchel and under cover of a pant, he fell forward into her hall. It was rather as if the suitcase had moved first, jerking him after it. "Mrs. Hopewell!" he said and grabbed her hand. "I hope you are well!" and he laughed again and then all at once his face sobered completely. He paused and gave her a straight earnest look and said, "Lady, I've come to speak of serious things."

"Well, come in," she muttered, none too pleased because her dinner was almost ready. He came into the parlor and sat down on the edge of a straight chair and put the suitcase between his feet and glanced around the room as if he were sizing her up by it. Her silver gleamed on the two sideboards; she decided he had never been in a room as elegant as this.

"Mrs. Hopewell," he began, using her name in a way that sounded almost intimate, "I know you believe in Chrustian service."

"Well yes," she murmured.

"I know," he said and paused, looking very wise with his head cocked on one side, "that you're a good woman. Friends have told me."

Mrs. Hopewell never liked to be taken for a fool. "What are you selling?" 30 she asked.

"Bibles," the young man said and his eye raced around the room before he added, "I see you have no family Bible in your parlor, I see that is the one lack you got!"

Mrs. Hopewell could not say, "My daughter is an atheist and won't let me keep the Bible in the parlor." She said, stiffening slightly, "I keep my Bible by my bedside." This was not the truth. It was in the attic somewhere.

"Lady," he said, "the word of God ought to be in the parlor."

"Well, I think that's a matter of taste," she began. "I think . . . ."

"Lady," he said, "for a Chrustian, the word of God ought to be in every 35 room in the house besides in his heart. I know you're a Chrustian because I can see it in every line of your face."

She stood up and said, "Well, young man, I don't want to buy a Bible and I smell my dinner burning."

He didn't get up. He began to twist his hands and looking down at them, he said softly, "Well lady, I'll tell you the truth — not many people want to buy one nowadays and besides, I know I'm real simple. I don't know how to say a thing but to say it. I'm just a country boy." He glanced up into her unfriendly face. "People like you don't like to fool with country people like me!"

"Why!" she cried, "good country people are the salt of the earth! Besides, we all have different ways of doing, it takes all kinds to make the world go 'round. That's life!"

"You said a mouthful," he said.

"Why, I think there aren't enough good people in the world!" she said, 40 stirred. "I think that's what's wrong with it!"

His face had brightened. "I didn't introduce myself," he said. "I'm Manley Pointer from out in the country around Willohobie, not even from a place, just from near a place."

"You wait a minute," she said. "I have to see about my dinner." She went out to the kitchen and found Joy standing near the door where she had been listening.

"Get rid of the salt of the earth," she said, "and let's eat."

Mrs. Hopewell gave her a pained look and turned the heat down under the vegetables. "I can't be rude to anybody," she murmured and went back into the parlor.

He had opened the suitcase and was sitting with a Bible on each knee. 45

"You might as well put those up," she told him. "I don't want one."

"I appreciate your honesty," he said. "You don't see any more real honest people unless you go way out in the country."

"I know," she said, "real genuine folks!" Through the crack in the door she heard a groan.

"I guess a lot of boys come telling you they're working their way through college," he said, "but I'm not going to tell you that. Somehow," he said, "I don't want to go to college. I want to devote my life to Chrustian service. See," he said, lowering his voice, "I got this heart condition. I may not live long. When you know it's something wrong with you and you may not live long, well then, lady . . ." He paused, with his mouth open, and stared at her.

He and Joy had the same condition! She knew that her eyes were filling 50 with tears but she collected herself quickly and murmured, "Won't you stay for dinner? We'd love to have you!" and was sorry the instant she heard herself say it.

"Yes mam," he said in an abashed voice, "I would sher love to do that!"

Joy had given him one look on being introduced to him and then throughout the meal had not glanced at him again. He had addressed several remarks to her, which she had pretended not to hear. Mrs. Hopewell could not understand deliberate rudeness, although she lived with it, and she felt she had always to overflow with hospitality to make up for Joy's lack of courtesy. She urged him to talk about himself and he did. He said he was the seventh child of twelve and that his father had been crushed under a tree when he himself was eight years old. He had been crushed very badly, in fact, almost cut in two and was practically not recognizable. His mother had got along the best she could by hard working and she had always seen that her children went to Sunday School and that they read the Bible every evening. He was now nineteen years old and he had been selling Bibles for four months. In that time he had sold seventy-seven Bibles and had the promise of two more sales. He wanted to become a missionary because he thought that was the way you could do most for people. "He who losest his life shall find it," he said simply and he was so sincere, so genuine and earnest that Mrs. Hopewell would not for the world have smiled. He prevented his peas from sliding onto the table by blocking them with a piece of bread which he later cleaned his plate with. She could see Joy observing sidewise how he handled his knife and fork and she saw too that every few minutes, the boy would dart a keen appraising glance at the girl as if he were trying to attract her attention.

After dinner Joy cleared the dishes off the table and disappeared and Mrs. Hopewell was left to talk with him. He told her again about his childhood and his father's accident and about various things that had happened to him. Every five minutes or so she would stifle a yawn. He sat for two hours until finally she told him she must go because she had an appointment in town. He packed his Bibles and thanked her and prepared to leave, but in the doorway he stopped and wrung her hand and said that not on any of his trips had he met a lady as nice as her and he asked if he could come again. She had said she would always be happy to see him.

Joy had been standing in the road, apparently looking at something in the distance, when he came down the steps toward her, bent to the side with his heavy valise. He stopped where she was standing and confronted her directly. Mrs. Hopewell could not hear what he said but she trembled to think what Joy would say to him. She could see that after a minute Joy said something and that then the boy began to speak again, making an excited gesture with his free hand. After a minute Joy said something else at which the boy began to speak once more. Then to her amazement, Mrs. Hopewell saw the two of them walk off together, toward the gate. Joy had walked all the way to the gate with him and Mrs. Hopewell could not imagine what they had said to each other, and she had not yet dared to ask.

Mrs. Freeman was insisting upon her attention. She had moved from the 55 refrigerator to the heater so that Mrs. Hopewell had to turn and face her in order to seem to be listening. "Glynese gone out with Harvey Hill again last night," she said. "She had this sty."

"Hill," Mrs. Hopewell said absently, "is the one who works in the garage?"

"Nome, he's the one that goes to chiropractor school," Mrs. Freeman said. "She had this sty. Been had it two days. So she says when he brought her in the other night he says, 'Lemme get rid of that sty for you,' and she says, 'How?' and he says, 'You just lay yourself down acrost the seat of that car and I'll show you.' So she done it and he popped her neck. Kept on a-popping it several times until she made him quit. This morning," Mrs. Freeman said, "she ain't got no sty. She ain't got no traces of a sty."

"I never heard of that before," Mrs. Hopewell said.

"He ast her to marry him before the Ordinary,"° Mrs. Freeman went on, "and she told him she wasn't going to be married in no *office*."

"Well, Glynese is a fine girl," Mrs. Hopewell said. "Glynese and Carramae   60 are both fine girls."

"Carramae said when her and Lyman was married Lyman said it sure felt sacred to him. She said he said he wouldn't take five hundred dollars for being married by a preacher."

"How much would he take?" the girl asked from the stove.

"He said he wouldn't take five hundred dollars," Mrs. Freeman repeated.

"Well we all have work to do," Mrs. Hopewell said.

"Lyman said it just felt more sacred to him," Mrs. Freeman said. "The doc-   65 tor wants Carramae to eat prunes. Says instead of medicine. Says them cramps is coming from pressure. You know where I think it is?"

"She'll be better in a few weeks," Mrs. Hopewell said.

"In the tube," Mrs. Freeman said. "Else she wouldn't be as sick as she is."

Hulga had cracked her two eggs into a saucer and was bringing them to the table along with a cup of coffee that she had filled too full. She sat down carefully and began to eat, meaning to keep Mrs. Freeman there by questions if for any reason she showed an inclination to leave. She could perceive her mother's eye on her. The first round-about question would be about the Bible salesman and she did not wish to bring it on. "How did he pop her neck?" she asked.

Mrs. Freeman went into a description of how he had popped her neck. She said he owned a '55 Mercury but that Glynese said she would rather marry a man with only a '36 Plymouth who would be married by a preacher. The girl asked what if he had a '32 Plymouth and Mrs. Freeman said what Glynese had said was a '36 Plymouth.

Mrs. Hopewell said there were not many girls with Glynese's common   70 sense. She said what she admired in those girls was their common sense. She said that reminded her that they had had a nice visitor yesterday, a young man selling Bibles. "Lord," she said, "he bored me to death but he was so sincere and genuine I couldn't be rude to him. He was just good country people, you know," she said, "—just the salt of the earth."

"I seen him walk up," Mrs. Freeman said, "and then later—I seen him walk off," and Hulga could feel the slight shift in her voice, the slight insinuation, that he had not walked off alone, had he? Her face remained expressionless but the color rose into her neck and she seemed to swallow it down with the next spoonful of egg. Mrs. Freeman was looking at her as if they had a secret together.

Ordinary: Justice of the peace.

"Well, it takes all kinds of people to make the world go 'round," Mrs. Hopewell said. "It's very good we aren't all alike."

"Some people are more alike than others," Mrs. Freeman said.

Hulga got up and stumped, with about twice the noise that was necessary, into her room and locked the door. She was to meet the Bible salesman at ten o'clock at the gate. She had thought about it half the night. She had started thinking of it as a great joke and then she had begun to see profound implications in it. She had lain in bed imagining dialogues for them that were insane on the surface but that reached below to depths that no Bible salesman would be aware of. Their conversation yesterday had been of this kind.

He had stopped in front of her and had simply stood there. His face was 75 bony and sweaty and bright, with a little pointed nose in the center of it, and his look was different from what it had been at the dinner table. He was gazing at her with open curiosity, with fascination, like a child watching a new fantastic animal at the zoo, and he was breathing as if he had run a great distance to reach her. His gaze seemed somehow familiar but she could not think where she had been regarded with it before. For almost a minute he didn't say anything. Then on what seemed an insuck of breath, he whispered, "You ever ate a chicken that was two days old?"

The girl looked at him stonily. He might have just put this question up for consideration at the meeting of a philosophical association. "Yes," she presently replied as if she had considered it from all angles.

"It must have been mighty small!" he said triumphantly and shook all over with little nervous giggles, getting very red in the face, and subsiding finally into his gaze of complete admiration, while the girl's expression remained exactly the same.

"How old are you?" he asked softly.

She waited some time before she answered. Then in a flat voice she said, "Seventeen."

His smiles came in succession like waves breaking on the surface of a little 80 lake. "I see you got a wooden leg," he said. "I think you're brave. I think you're real sweet."

The girl stood blank and solid and silent.

"Walk to the gate with me," he said. "You're a brave sweet little thing and I liked you the minute I seen you walk in the door."

Hulga began to move forward.

"What's your name?" he asked, smiling down on the top of her head.

"Hulga," she said. 85

"Hulga," he murmured, "Hulga. Hulga. I never heard of anybody name Hulga before. You're shy, aren't you, Hulga?" he asked.

She nodded, watching his large red hand on the handle of the giant valise.

"I like girls that wear glasses," he said. "I think a lot. I'm not like these people that a serious thought don't ever enter their heads. It's because I may die."

"I may die too," she said suddenly and looked up at him. His eyes were very small and brown, glittering feverishly.

"Listen," he said, "don't you think some people was meant to meet on 90 account of what all they got in common and all? Like they both think serious thoughts and all?" He shifted the valise to his other hand so that the hand nearest her was free. He caught hold of her elbow and shook it a little. "I don't work on Saturday," he said. "I like to walk in the woods and see what Mother

Nature is wearing. O'er the hills and far away. Pic-nics and things. Couldn't we go on a pic-nic tomorrow? Say yes, Hulga," he said and gave her a dying look as if he felt his insides about to drop out of him. He had even seemed to sway slightly toward her.

During the night she had imagined that she seduced him. She imagined that the two of them walked on the place until they came to the storage barn beyond the two back fields and there, she imagined, that things came to such a pass that she very easily seduced him and that then, of course, she had to reckon with his remorse. True genius can get an idea across even to an inferior mind. She imagined that she took his remorse in hand and changed it into a deeper understanding of life. She took all his shame away and turned it into something useful.

She set off for the gate at exactly ten o'clock, escaping without drawing Mrs. Hopewell's attention. She didn't take anything to eat, forgetting that food is usually taken on a picnic. She wore a pair of slacks and a dirty white shirt, and as an afterthought, she had put some Vapex° on the collar of it since she did not own any perfume. When she reached the gate no one was there.

She looked up and down the empty highway and had the furious feeling that she had been tricked, that he had only meant to make her walk to the gate after the idea of him. Then suddenly he stood up, very tall, from behind a bush on the opposite embankment. Smiling, he lifted his hat which was new and wide-brimmed. He had not worn it yesterday and she wondered if he had bought it for the occasion. It was toast-colored with a red and white band around it and was slightly too large for him. He stepped from behind the bush still carrying the black valise. He had on the same suit and the same yellow socks sucked down in his shoes from walking. He crossed the highway and said, "I knew you'd come!"

The girl wondered acidly how he had known this. She pointed to the valise and asked, "Why did you bring your Bibles?"

He took her elbow, smiling down on her as if he could not stop. "You can 95 never tell when you'll need the word of God, Hulga," he said. She had a moment in which she doubted that this was actually happening and then they began to climb the embankment. They went down into the pasture toward the woods. The boy walked lightly by her side, bouncing on his toes. The valise did not seem to be heavy today; he even swung it. They crossed half the pasture without saying anything and then, putting his hand easily on the small of her back, he asked softly, "Where does your wooden leg join on?"

She turned an ugly red and glared at him and for an instant the boy looked abashed. "I didn't mean you no harm," he said. "I only meant you're so brave and all. I guess God takes care of you."

"No," she said, looking forward and walking fast, "I don't even believe in God."

At this he stopped and whistled. "No!" he exclaimed as if he were too astonished to say anything else.

She walked on and in a second he was bouncing at her side, fanning with his hat. "That's very unusual for a girl," he remarked, watching her out of the corner of his eye. When they reached the edge of the wood, he put his hand on her back again and drew her against him without a word and kissed her heavily.

Vapex: Trade name for a nasal spray.

The kiss, which had more pressure than feeling behind it, produced that   100
extra surge of adrenaline in the girl that enables one to carry a packed trunk
out of a burning house, but in her, the power went at once to the brain. Even
before he released her, her mind, clear and detached and ironic anyway, was
regarding him from a great distance, with amusement but with pity. She had
never been kissed before and she was pleased to discover that it was an unexceptional experience and all a matter of the mind's control. Some people
might enjoy drain water if they were told it was vodka. When the boy, looking
expectant but uncertain, pushed her gently away, she turned and walked on,
saying nothing as if such business, for her, were common enough.

He came along panting at her side, trying to help her when he saw a root
that she might trip over. He caught and held back the long swaying blades of
thorn vine until she had passed beyond them. She led the way and he came
breathing heavily behind her. Then they came out on a sunlit hillside, sloping
softly into another one a little smaller. Beyond, they could see the rusted top of
the old barn where the extra hay was stored.

The hill was sprinkled with small pink weeds. "Then you ain't saved?" he
asked suddenly, stopping.

The girl smiled. It was the first time she had smiled at him at all. "In my
economy," she said, "I'm saved and you are damned but I told you I didn't
believe in God."

Nothing seemed to destroy the boy's look of admiration. He gazed at her
now as if the fantastic animal at the zoo had put its paw through the bars and
given him a loving poke. She thought he looked as if he wanted to kiss her
again and she walked on before he had the chance.

"Ain't there somewheres we can sit down sometime?" he murmured, his   105
voice softening toward the end of the sentence.

"In that barn," she said.

They made for it rapidly as if it might slide away like a train. It was a large
two-story barn, cool and dark inside. The boy pointed up the ladder that led
into the loft and said, "It's too bad we can't go up there."

"Why can't we?" she asked.

"Yer leg," he said reverently.

The girl gave him a contemptuous look and putting both hands on the   110
ladder, she climbed it while he stood below, apparently awestruck. She pulled
herself expertly through the opening and then looked down at him and said,
"Well, come on if you're coming," and he began to climb the ladder, awkwardly
bringing the suitcase with him.

"We won't need the Bible," she observed.

"You never can tell," he said, panting. After he had got into the loft, he was
a few seconds catching his breath. She had sat down in a pile of straw. A wide
sheath of sunlight, filled with dust particles, slanted over her. She lay back
against a bale, her face turned away, looking out the front opening of the barn
where hay was thrown from a wagon into the loft. The two pink-speckled hillsides lay back against a dark ridge of woods. The sky was cloudless and cold
blue. The boy dropped down by her side and put one arm under her and the
other over her and began methodically kissing her face, making little noises
like a fish. He did not remove his hat but it was pushed far enough back not to
interfere. When her glasses got in his way, he took them off of her and slipped
them into his pocket.

The girl at first did not return any of the kisses but presently she began to and after she had put several on his cheek, she reached his lips and remained there, kissing him again and again as if she were trying to draw all the breath out of him. His breath was clear and sweet like a child's and the kisses were sticky like a child's. He mumbled about loving her and about knowing when he first seen her that he loved her, but the mumbling was like the sleepy fretting of a child being put to sleep by his mother. Her mind, throughout this, never stopped or lost itself for a second to her feelings. "You ain't said you loved me none," he whispered finally, pulling back from her. "You got to say that."

She looked away from him off into the hollow sky and then down at a black ridge and then down farther into what appeared to be two green swelling lakes. She didn't realize he had taken her glasses but this landscape could not seem exceptional to her for she seldom paid any close attention to her surroundings.

"You got to say it," he repeated. "You got to say you love me." 115

She was always careful how she committed herself. "In a sense," she began, "if you use the word loosely, you might say that. But it's not a word I use. I don't have illusions. I'm one of those people who see *through* to nothing."

The boy was frowning. "You got to say it. I said it and you got to say it," he said.

The girl looked at him almost tenderly. "You poor baby," she murmured. "It's just as well you don't understand," and she pulled him by the neck, face-down, against her. "We are all damned," she said, "but some of us have taken off our blindfolds and see that there's nothing to see. It's a kind of salvation."

The boy's astonished eyes looked blankly through the ends of her hair. "Okay," he almost whined, "but do you love me or don'tcher?"

"Yes," she said and added, "in a sense. But I must tell you something. There 120 mustn't be anything dishonest between us." She lifted his head and looked him in the eye. "I am thirty years old," she said. "I have a number of degrees."

The boy's look was irritated but dogged. "I don't care," he said. "I don't care a thing about what all you done. I just want to know if you love me or don'tcher?" and he caught her to him and wildly planted her face with kisses until she said, "Yes, yes."

"Okay then," he said, letting her go. "Prove it."

She smiled, looking dreamily out on the shifty landscape. She had seduced him without even making up her mind to try. "How?" she asked, feeling that he should be delayed a little.

He leaned over and put his lips to her ear. "Show me where your wooden leg joins on," he whispered.

The girl uttered a sharp little cry and her face instantly drained of color. 125 The obscenity of the suggestion was not what shocked her. As a child she had sometimes been subject to feelings of shame but education had removed the last traces of that as a good surgeon scrapes for cancer; she would no more have felt it over what he was asking than she would have believed in his Bible. But she was as sensitive about the artificial leg as a peacock about his tail. No one ever touched it but her. She took care of it as someone else would his soul, in private and almost with her own eyes turned away. "No," she said.

"I known it," he muttered, sitting up. "You're just playing me for a sucker."

"Oh no no!" she cried. "It joins on at the knee. Only at the knee. Why do you want to see it?"

The boy gave her a long penetrating look. "Because," he said, "it's what makes you different. You ain't like anybody else."

She sat staring at him. There was nothing about her face or her round freezing-blue eyes to indicate that this had moved her; but she felt as if her heart had stopped and left her mind to pump her blood. She decided that for the first time in her life she was face to face with real innocence. This boy, with an instinct that came from beyond wisdom, had touched the truth about her. When after a minute, she said in a hoarse high voice, "All right," it was like surrendering to him completely. It was like losing her own life and finding it again, miraculously, in his.

Very gently he began to roll the slack leg up. The artificial limb, in a white   130
sock and brown flat shoe, was bound in a heavy material like canvas and ended in an ugly jointure where it was attached to the stump. The boy's face and his voice were entirely reverent as he uncovered it and said, "Now show me how to take it off and on."

She took it off for him and put it back on again and then he took it off himself, handling it as tenderly as if it were a real one. "See!" he said with a delighted child's face. "Now I can do it myself!"

"Put it back on," she said. She was thinking that she would run away with him and that every night he would take the leg off and every morning put it back on again. "Put it back on," she said.

"Not yet," he murmured, setting it on its foot out of her reach. "Leave it off for a while. You got me instead."

She gave a little cry of alarm but he pushed her down and began to kiss her again. Without the leg she felt entirely dependent on him. Her brain seemed to have stopped thinking altogether and to be about some other function that it was not very good at. Different expressions raced back and forth over her face. Every now and then the boy, his eyes like two steel spikes, would glance behind him where the leg stood. Finally she pushed him off and said, "Put it back on me now."

"Wait," he said. He leaned the other way and pulled the valise toward him   135
and opened it. It had a pale blue spotted lining and there were only two Bibles in it. He took one of these out and opened the cover of it. It was hollow and contained a pocket flask of whiskey, a pack of cards, and a small blue box with printing on it. He laid these out in front of her one at a time in an evenly-spaced row, like one presenting offerings at the shrine of a goddess. He put the blue box in her hand. THIS PRODUCT TO BE USED ONLY FOR THE PREVENTION OF DISEASE, she read, and dropped it. The boy was unscrewing the top of the flask. He stopped and pointed, with a smile, to the deck of cards. It was not an ordinary deck but one with an obscene picture on the back of each card. "Take a swig," he said, offering her the bottle first. He held it in front of her, but like one mesmerized, she did not move.

Her voice when she spoke had an almost pleading sound. "Aren't you," she murmured, "aren't you just good country people?"

The boy cocked his head. He looked as if he were just beginning to understand that she might be trying to insult him. "Yeah," he said, curling his lip slightly, "but it ain't held me back none. I'm as good as you any day in the week."

"Give me my leg," she said.

He pushed it farther away with his foot. "Come on now, let's begin to have us a good time," he said coaxingly. "We ain't got to know one another good yet."

"Give me my leg!" she screamed and tried to lunge for it but he pushed her down easily.

"What's the matter with you all of a sudden?" he asked, frowning as he screwed the top on the flask and put it quickly back inside the Bible. "You just a while ago said you didn't believe in nothing. I thought you was some girl!"

Her face was almost purple. "You're a Christian!" she hissed. "You're a fine Christian! You're just like them all — say one thing and do another. You're a perfect Christian, you're . . ."

The boy's mouth was set angrily. "I hope you don't think," he said in a lofty indignant tone, "that I believe in that crap! I may sell Bibles but I know which end is up and I wasn't born yesterday and I know where I'm going!"

"Give me my leg!" she screeched. He jumped up so quickly that she barely saw him sweep the cards and the blue box into the Bible and throw the Bible into his valise. She saw him grab the leg and then she saw it for an instant slanted forlornly across the inside of the suitcase with a Bible at either side of its opposite ends. He slammed the lid shut and snatched up the valise and swung it down the hole and then stepped through himself.

When all of him had passed but his head, he turned and regarded her with a look that no longer had any admiration in it. "I've gotten a lot of interesting things," he said. "One time I got a woman's glass eye this way. And you needn't to think you'll catch me because Pointer ain't really my name. I use a different name at every house I call at and don't stay nowhere long. And I'll tell you another thing, Hulga," he said, using the name as if he didn't think much of it, "you ain't so smart. I been believing in nothing ever since I was born!" and then the toast-colored hat disappeared down the hole and the girl was left, sitting on the straw in the dusty sunlight. When she turned her churning face toward the opening, she saw his blue figure struggling successfully over the green speckled lake.

Mrs. Hopewell and Mrs. Freeman, who were in the back pasture, digging up onions, saw him emerge a little later from the woods and head across the meadow toward the highway. "Why, that looks like that nice dull young man that tried to sell me a Bible yesterday," Mrs. Hopewell said, squinting. "He must have been selling them to the Negroes back in there. He was so simple," she said, "but I guess the world would be better off if we were all that simple."

Mrs. Freeman's gaze drove forward and just touched him before he disappeared under the hill. Then she returned her attention to the evil-smelling onion shoot she was lifting from the ground. "Some can't be that simple," she said. "I know I never could."

CONSIDERATIONS FOR CRITICAL THINKING AND WRITING

1. **FIRST RESPONSE.** What do you think of Hulga's conviction that intelligence and education are incompatible with religious faith?

2. Why is it significant that Mrs. Hopewell's daughter has two names? How do the other characters' names serve to characterize them?

3. Why do you think Mrs. Freeman and Mrs. Hopewell are introduced before Hulga? What do they contribute to Hulga's story?

4. Identify the conflict in this story. How is it resolved?

5. Hulga and the Bible salesman play a series of jokes on each other. How are these deceptions related to the theme?

6. What is the effect of O'Connor's use of the phrase "good country people" throughout the story? Why is it an appropriate title?

7. The Bible salesman's final words to Hulga are "You ain't so smart. I been believing in nothing ever since I was born!" What religious values are expressed in the story?

8. After the Bible salesman leaves Hulga at the end of the story, O'Connor adds two more paragraphs concerning Mrs. Hopewell and Mrs. Freeman. What is the purpose of these final paragraphs?

9. Hulga's perspective on life is ironic, but she is also the subject of O'Connor's irony. Explain how O'Connor uses irony to reveal Hulga's character.

10. This story would be different if told from Hulga's point of view. Describe how the use of a limited omniscient narrator contributes to the story's effects.

CONNECTIONS TO OTHER SELECTIONS

1. How do Mrs. Hopewell's assumptions about life compare with those of Krebs's mother in Hemingway's "Soldier's Home" (p. 165)? Explain how the conflict in each story is related to what the mothers come to represent in the eyes of the central characters.

2. Discuss the treatment of faith in this story and in Hawthorne's "Young Goodman Brown" (p. 325).

Revelation   *1964*

The doctor's waiting room, which was very small, was almost full when the Turpins entered and Mrs. Turpin, who was very large, made it look even smaller by her presence. She stood looming at the head of the magazine table set in the center of it, a living demonstration that the room was inadequate and ridiculous. Her little bright black eyes took in all the patients as she sized up the seating situation. There was one vacant chair and a place on the sofa occupied by a blond child in a dirty blue romper who should have been told to move over and make room for the lady. He was five or six, but Mrs. Turpin saw at once that no one was going to tell him to move over. He was slumped down in the seat, his arms idle at his sides and his eyes idle in his head; his nose ran unchecked.

Mrs. Turpin put a firm hand on Claud's shoulder and said in a voice that included anyone who wanted to listen, "Claud, you sit in that chair there," and gave him a push down into the vacant one. Claud was florid and bald and sturdy, somewhat shorter than Mrs. Turpin, but he sat down as if he were accustomed to doing what she told him to.

Mrs. Turpin remained standing. The only man in the room besides Claud was a lean stringy old fellow with a rusty hand spread out on each knee, whose eyes were closed as if he were asleep or dead or pretending to be so as not to get up and offer her his seat. Her gaze settled agreeably on a well-dressed gray-haired lady whose eyes met hers and whose expression said: if that child

belonged to me, he would have some manners and move over — there's plenty
of room there for you and him too.

Claud looked up with a sigh and made as if to rise.

"Sit down," Mrs. Turpin said. "You know you're not supposed to stand on   5
that leg. He has an ulcer on his leg," she explained.

Claud lifted his foot onto the magazine table and rolled his trouser leg up
to reveal a purple swelling on a plump marble-white calf.

"My!" the pleasant lady said. "How did you do that?"

"A cow kicked him," Mrs. Turpin said.

"Goodness!" said the lady.

Claud rolled his trouser leg down.   10

"Maybe the little boy would move over," the lady suggested, but the child
did not stir.

"Somebody will be leaving in a minute," Mrs. Turpin said. She could not
understand why a doctor — with as much money as they made charging five
dollars a day to just stick their head in the hospital door and look at you —
couldn't afford a decent-sized waiting room. This one was hardly bigger than a
garage. The table was cluttered with limp-looking magazines and at one end of
it there was a big green glass ash tray full of cigarette butts and cotton wads
with little blood spots on them. If she had had anything to do with the running of the place, that would have been emptied every so often. There were no
chairs against the wall at the head of the room. It had a rectangular-shaped
panel in it that permitted a view of the office where the nurse came and went
and the secretary listened to the radio. A plastic fern in a gold pot sat in the
opening and trailed its fronds down almost to the floor. The radio was softly
playing gospel music.

Just then the inner door opened and a nurse with the highest stack of yellow hair Mrs. Turpin had ever seen put her face in the crack and called for the
next patient. The woman sitting beside Claud grasped the two arms of her
chair and hoisted herself up; she pulled her dress free from her legs and lum-
bered through the door where the nurse had disappeared.

Mrs. Turpin eased into the vacant chair, which held her tight as a corset. "I
wish I could reduce," she said, and rolled her eyes and gave a comic sigh.

"Oh, *you* aren't fat," the stylish lady said.   15

"Ooooo I am too," Mrs. Turpin said. "Claud he eats all he wants to and
never weighs over one hundred and seventy-five pounds, but me I just look at
something good to eat and I gain some weight," and her stomach and shoulders shook with laughter. "You can eat all you want to, can't you, Claud?" she
asked, turning to him.

Claud only grinned.

"Well, as long as you have such a good disposition," the stylish lady said, "I
don't think it makes a bit of difference what size you are. You just can't beat a
good disposition."

Next to her was a fat girl of eighteen or nineteen, scowling into a thick
blue book which Mrs. Turpin saw was entitled *Human Development*. The girl
raised her head and directed her scowl at Mrs. Turpin as if she did not like
her looks. She appeared annoyed that anyone should speak while she tried to
read. The poor girl's face was blue with acne and Mrs. Turpin thought how
pitiful it was to have a face like that at that age. She gave the girl a friendly
smile but the girl only scowled the harder. Mrs. Turpin herself was fat but she

had always had good skin, and though she was forty-seven years old, there was not a wrinkle in her face except around her eyes from laughing too much.

Next to the ugly girl was the child, still in exactly the same position, and next to him was a thin leathery old woman in a cotton print dress. She and Claud had three sacks of chicken feed in their pump house that was in the same print. She had seen from the first that the child belonged with the old woman. She could tell by the way they sat—kind of vacant and white-trashy, as if they would sit there until Doomsday if nobody called and told them to get up. And at right angles but next to the well-dressed pleasant lady was a lank-faced woman who was certainly the child's mother. She had on a yellow sweat shirt and wine-colored slacks, both gritty-looking, and the rims of her lips were stained with snuff. Her dirty yellow hair was tied behind with a little piece of red paper ribbon. Worse than niggers any day, Mrs. Turpin thought.

The gospel hymn playing was, "When I looked up and He looked down," and Mrs. Turpin, who knew it, supplied the last line mentally, "And wona these days I know I'll we-eara crown."

Without appearing to, Mrs. Turpin always noticed people's feet. The well-dressed lady had on red and gray suede shoes to match her dress. Mrs. Turpin had on her good black patent leather pumps. The ugly girl had on Girl Scout shoes and heavy socks. The old woman had on tennis shoes and the white-trashy mother had on what appeared to be bedroom slippers, black straw with gold braid threaded through them—exactly what you would have expected her to have on.

Sometimes at night when she couldn't go to sleep, Mrs. Turpin would occupy herself with the question of who she would have chosen to be if she couldn't have been herself. If Jesus had said to her before he made her, "There's only two places available for you. You can either be a nigger or white-trash," what would she have said? "Please, Jesus, please," she would have said, "just let me wait until there's another place available," and he would have said, "No, you have to go right now and I have only those two places so make up your mind." She would have wiggled and squirmed and begged and pleaded but it would have been no use and finally she would have said, "All right, make me a nigger then—but that don't mean a trashy one." And he would have made her a neat clean respectable Negro woman, herself but black.

Next to the child's mother was a red-headed youngish woman, reading one of the magazines and working a piece of chewing gum, hell for leather, as Claud would say. Mrs. Turpin could not see the woman's feet. She was not white-trash, just common. Sometimes Mrs. Turpin occupied herself at night naming the classes of people. On the bottom of the heap were most colored people, not the kind she would have been if she had been one, but most of them; then next to them—not above, just away from—were the white-trash; then above them were the homeowners, and above them the home-and-land owners, to which she and Claud belonged. Above she and Claud were people with a lot of money and much bigger houses and much more land. But here the complexity of it would begin to bear in on her, for some of the people with a lot of money were common and ought to be below she and Claud and some of the people who had good blood had lost their money and had to rent and then there were colored people who owned their homes and land as well. There was a colored dentist in town who had two red Lincolns and a swimming pool and a farm with registered white-face cattle on it. Usually by the time she had fallen asleep all the classes of people were moiling and roiling around in her head, and she would dream they were all crammed in together in a box car, being ridden off to be put in a gas oven.

"That's a beautiful clock," she said and nodded to her right. It was a big wall clock, the face encased in a brass sunburst.

"Yes, it's very pretty," the stylish lady said agreeably. "And right on the dot too," she added, glancing at her watch.

The ugly girl beside her cast an eye upward at the clock, smirked, then looked directly at Mrs. Turpin and smirked again. Then she returned her eyes to her book. She was obviously the lady's daughter because, although they didn't look anything alike as to disposition, they both had the same shape of face and the same blue eyes. On the lady they sparkled pleasantly but in the girl's seared face they appeared alternately to smolder and to blaze.

What if Jesus had said, "All right, you can be white-trash or a nigger or ugly"!

Mrs. Turpin felt an awful pity for the girl, though she thought it was one thing to be ugly and another to act ugly.

The woman with the snuff-stained lips turned around in her chair and looked up at the clock. Then she turned back and appeared to look a little to the side of Mrs. Turpin. There was a cast in one of her eyes. "You want to know wher you can get you one of themther clocks?" she asked in a loud voice.

"No, I already have a nice clock," Mrs. Turpin said. Once somebody like her got a leg in the conversation, she would be all over it.

"You can get you one with green stamps," the woman said. "That's most likely wher he got hisn. Save you up enough, you can get you most anythang. I got me some joo'ry."

Ought to have got you a wash rag and some soap, Mrs. Turpin thought.

"I get contour sheets with mine," the pleasant lady said.

The daughter slammed her book shut. She looked straight in front of her, directly through Mrs. Turpin and on through the yellow curtain and the plate glass window which made the wall behind her. The girl's eyes seemed lit all of a sudden with a peculiar light, an unnatural light like night road signs give. Mrs. Turpin turned her head to see if there was anything going on outside that she should see, but she could not see anything. Figures passing cast only a pale shadow through the curtain. There was no reason the girl should single her out for her ugly looks.

"Miss Finley," the nurse said, cracking the door. The gum-chewing woman got up and passed in front of her and Claud and went into the office. She had on red high-heeled shoes.

Directly across the table, the ugly girl's eyes were fixed on Mrs. Turpin as if she had some very special reason for disliking her.

"This is wonderful weather, isn't it?" the girl's mother said.

"It's good weather for cotton if you can get the niggers to pick it," Mrs. Turpin said, "but niggers don't want to pick cotton any more. You can't get the white folks to pick it and now you can't get the niggers — because they got to be right up there with the white folks."

"They gonna *try* anyways," the white-trash woman said, leaning forward.

"Do you have one of the cotton-picking machines?" the pleasant lady asked.

"No," Mrs. Turpin said, "they leave half the cotton in the field. We don't have much cotton anyway. If you want to make it farming now, you have to have a little of everything. We got a couple of acres of cotton and a few hogs and chickens and just enough white-face that Claud can look after them himself."

"One thang I don't want," the white-trash woman said, wiping her mouth with the back of her hand. "Hogs. Nasty stinking things, a-gruntin and a-rootin all over the place."

Mrs. Turpin gave her the merest edge of her attention. "Our hogs are not dirty and they don't stink," she said. "They're cleaner than some children I've seen. Their feet never touch the ground. We have a pig parlor — that's where you raise them on concrete," she explained to the pleasant lady, "and Claud scoots them down with the hose every afternoon and washes off the floor." Cleaner by far than that child right there, she thought. Poor nasty little thing. He had not moved except to put the thumb of his dirty hand into his mouth.

The woman turned her face away from Mrs. Turpin. "I know I wouldn't 45 scoot down no hog with no hose," she said to the wall.

You wouldn't have no hog to scoot down, Mrs. Turpin said to herself.

"A-gruntin and a-rootin and a-groanin," the woman muttered.

"We got a little of everything," Mrs. Turpin said to the pleasant lady. "It's no use in having more than you can handle yourself with help like it is. We found enough niggers to pick our cotton this year but Claud he has to go after them and take them home again in the evening. They can't walk that half a mile. No they can't. I tell you," she said and laughed merrily, "I sure am tired of buttering up niggers, but you got to love em if you want em to work for you. When they come in the morning, I run out and I say, 'Hi yawl this morning?' and when Claud drives them off to the field I just wave to beat the band and they just wave back." And she waved her hand rapidly to illustrate.

"Like you read out of the same book," the lady said, showing she understood perfectly.

"Child, yes," Mrs. Turpin said. "And when they come in from the field, I 50 run out with a bucket of icewater. That's the way it's going to be from now on," she said. "You may as well face it."

"One thang I know," the white-trash woman said. "Two thangs I ain't going to do: love no niggers or scoot down no hog with no hose." And she let out a bark of contempt.

The look that Mrs. Turpin and the pleasant lady exchanged indicated they both understood that you had to *have* certain things before you could *know* certain things. But every time Mrs. Turpin exchanged a look with the lady, she was aware that the ugly girl's peculiar eyes were still on her, and she had trouble bringing her attention back to the conversation.

"When you got something," she said, "you got to look after it." And when you ain't got a thing but breath and britches, she added to herself, you can afford to come to town every morning and just sit on the Court House coping and spit.

A grotesque revolving shadow passed across the curtain behind her and was thrown palely on the opposite wall. Then a bicycle clattered down against the outside of the building. The door opened and a colored boy glided in with a tray from the drugstore. It had two large red and white paper cups on it with tops on them. He was a tall, very black boy in discolored white pants and a green nylon shirt. He was chewing gum slowly, as if to music. He set the tray down in the office opening next to the fern and stuck his head through to look for the secretary. She was not in there. He rested his arms on the ledge and waited, his narrow bottom stuck out, swaying to the left and right. He raised a hand over his head and scratched the base of his skull.

"You see that button there, boy?" Mrs. Turpin said. "You can punch that and she'll come. She's probably in the back somewhere." 55

"Is that right?" the boy said agreeably, as if he had never seen the button before. He leaned to the right and put his finger on it. "She sometime out," he said and twisted around to face his audience, his elbows behind him on the counter. The nurse appeared and he twisted back again. She handed him a dollar and he rooted in his pocket and made the change and counted it out to her. She gave him fifteen cents for a tip and he went out with the empty tray. The heavy door swung to slowly and closed at length with the sound of suction. For a moment no one spoke.

"They ought to send all them niggers back to Africa," the white-trash woman said. "That's wher they come from in the first place."

"Oh, I couldn't do without my good colored friends," the pleasant lady said.

"There's a heap of things worse than a nigger," Mrs. Turpin agreed. "It's all kinds of them just like it's all kinds of us."

"Yes, and it takes all kinds to make the world go round," the lady said in her musical voice. 60

As she said it, the raw-complexioned girl snapped her teeth together. Her lower lip turned downwards and inside out, revealing the pale pink inside of her mouth. After a second it rolled back up. It was the ugliest face Mrs. Turpin had ever seen anyone make and for a moment she was certain that the girl had made it at her. She was looking at her as if she had known and disliked her all her life—all of Mrs. Turpin's life, it seemed too, not just all the girl's life. Why, girl, I don't even know you, Mrs. Turpin said silently.

She forced her attention back to the discussion. "It wouldn't be practical to send them back to Africa," she said. "They wouldn't want to go. They got it too good here."

"Wouldn't be what they wanted—if I had anythang to do with it," the woman said.

"It wouldn't be a way in the world you could get all the niggers back over there," Mrs. Turpin said. "They'd be hiding out and lying down and turning sick on you and wailing and hollering and raring and pitching. It wouldn't be a way in the world to get them over there."

"They got over here," the trashy woman said. "Get back like they got over." 65

"It wasn't so many of them then," Mrs. Turpin explained.

The woman looked at Mrs. Turpin as if here was an idiot indeed but Mrs. Turpin was not bothered by the look, considering where it came from.

"Nooo," she said, "they're going to stay here where they can go to New York and marry white folks and improve their color. That's what they all want to do, every one of them, improve their color."

"You know what comes of that, don't you?" Claud asked.

"No, Claud, what?" Mrs. Turpin said. 70

Claud's eyes twinkled. "White-faced niggers," he said with never a smile.

Everybody in the office laughed except the white-trash and the ugly girl. The girl gripped the book in her lap with white fingers. The trashy woman looked around her from face to face as if she thought they were all idiots. The old woman in the feed sack dress continued to gaze expressionless across the as they had always been for good order and common sense and respectable behavior. They alone were on key. Yet she could see by their shocked and altered faces that even their virtues were being burned away. She lowered her hands and gripped the rail of the hog pen, her eyes small but fixed unblinkingly on what lay ahead. In a moment the vision faded but she remained where she was, immobile.

At length she got down and turned off the faucet and made her slow way on the darkening path to the house. In the woods around her the invisible cricket choruses had struck up, but what she heard were the voices of the souls climbing upward into the starry field and shouting hallelujah.

Considerations for Critical Thinking and Writing

1. **FIRST RESPONSE.** Does your attitude toward Mrs. Turpin change or remain the same during the story? Do you *like* her more at some points than at others? Explain why.

2. Why is it appropriate that the two major settings for the action in this story are a doctor's waiting room and a "pig parlor"?

3. How does Mrs. Turpin's treatment of her husband help to characterize her?

4. Mrs. Turpin notices people's shoes. What does this and her thoughts about "classes of people" (para. 24) reveal about her? How does she see herself in relation to other people?

5. Why does Mary Grace attack Mrs. Turpin?

6. Why is it significant that the book Mary Grace reads is *Human Development*? What is the significance of her name?

7. What does the background music played on the radio contribute to the story?

8. To whom does Mrs. Turpin address this anguished question: "What do you send me a message [Mary Grace's whispered words telling her "Go back to hell where you came from, you old wart hog"] like that for?" (para. 178). Why is Mrs. Turpin so angry and bewildered?

9. What is the "abysmal life-giving knowledge" that Mrs. Turpin discovers in the next to the last paragraph? Why is it "abysmal"? How is it "life-giving"?

10. Given the serious theme, consider whether the story's humor is appropriate.

11. When Mrs. Turpin returns home bruised, a hired African American woman tells her that nothing really "bad" happened: "You just had you a little fall" (para. 147). Pay particular attention to the suggestive language of this sentence, and discuss its significance in relation to the rest of the story.

12. **CRITICAL STRATEGIES.** Choose a critical approach from Chapter 46, "Critical Strategies for Reading," that you think is particularly useful for explaining the themes of this story.

Connections to Other Selections

1. Compare and contrast Mary Grace with Hulga of "Good Country People."

2. Explain how "Revelation" could be used as a title for any of the O'Connor stories you have read.

3. Discuss Mrs. Turpin's prideful hypocrisy in connection with the racial attitudes expressed by the white men at the "smoker" in Ellison's "Battle Royal" (p. 243). How do pride and personal illusions inform these characters' racial attitudes?

4. Explore the nature of the "revelation" in O'Connor's story and in John Updike's "A & P" (p. 560).

Perspectives on O'Connor

FLANNERY O'CONNOR

On Faith

1955

I write the way I do because (not though) I am a Catholic. This is a fact and nothing covers it like the bald statement. However, I am a Catholic peculiarly possessed of the modern consciousness, the thing Jung° describes as unhistorical, solitary, and guilty. To possess this within the Church is to bear a burden, the necessary burden for the conscious Catholic. It's to feel the contemporary situation at the ultimate level. I think that the Church is the only thing that is going to make the terrible world we are coming to endurable; the only thing that makes the Church endurable is that it is somehow the body of Christ and that on this we are fed. It seems to be a fact that you suffer as much from the Church as for it but if you believe in the divinity of Christ, you have to cherish the world at the same time that you struggle to endure it. This may explain the lack of bitterness in the stories.

From a letter to "A," July 20, 1955, in *The Habit of Being*

Jung: Carl Jung (1875–1961), a Swiss psychiatrist.

CONSIDERATIONS FOR CRITICAL THINKING AND WRITING

1. Consider how O'Connor's fiction expresses her belief that "you have to cherish the world at the same time that you struggle to endure it."

2. Do you agree that "bitterness" is absent from O'Connor's stories? Explain why or why not.

FLANNERY O'CONNOR

On the Materials of Fiction

1969

The beginning of human knowledge is through the senses, and the fiction writer begins where human perception begins. He appeals through the senses, and you cannot appeal to the senses with abstractions. It is a good deal easier for most people to state an abstract idea than to describe and thus re-create some object that they actually see. But the world of the fiction writer is full of matter, and this is what the beginning fiction writers are very loath to create.

If you want to say that the wooden leg is a symbol, you can say that. But it is a wooden leg first, and as a wooden leg it is absolutely necessary to the story. It has its place on the literal level of the story, but it operates in depth as well as on the surface. It increases the story in every direction, and this is essentially the way a story escapes being short.

Now a little might be said about the way in which this happens. I wouldn't want you to think that in that story I sat down and said, "I am now going to write a story about a Ph.D. with a wooden leg, using the wooden leg as a symbol for another kind of affliction." I doubt myself if many writers know what they are going to do when they start out. When I started writing that story, I didn't know there was going to be a Ph.D. with a wooden leg in it. I merely found myself one morning writing a description of two women that I knew something about, and before I realized it, I had equipped one of them with a daughter with a wooden leg. As the story progressed, I brought in the Bible salesman, but I had no idea what I was going to do with him. I didn't know he was going to steal that wooden leg until ten or twelve lines before he did it, but when I found out that this was what was going to happen, I realized that it was inevitable. This is a story that produces a shock for the reader, and I think one reason for this is that it produced a shock for the writer.

Now despite the fact that this story came about in this seemingly mindless fashion, it is a story that almost no rewriting was done on. It is a story that was under control throughout the writing of it, and it might be asked how this kind of control comes about, since it is not entirely conscious.

From "Writing Short Stories" in *Mystery and Manners*

Considerations for Critical Thinking and Writing

1. Why is a "statement" (para. 1) inadequate to convey the meaning of a story?

2. O'Connor describes how the wooden leg "continues to accumulate meaning" (para. 3) in "Good Country People" (p. 378). Choose another story by O'Connor and explain how something specific and concrete is invested with symbolic meaning.

Josephine Hendin (b. 1946)

On O'Connor's Refusal to "Do Pretty"   1970

There is, in the memory of one Milledgeville matron, the image of O'Connor at nineteen or twenty who, when invited to a wedding shower for an old family friend, remained standing, her back pressed against the wall, scowling at the group of women who had sat down to lunch. Neither the devil nor her mother could make her say yes to this fiercely gracious female society, but Flannery O'Connor could not say no even in a whisper. She could not refuse the invitation but she would not accept it either. She did not exactly "fuss" but neither did she "do pretty."

From *The World of Flannery O'Connor*

CONSIDERATIONS FOR CRITICAL THINKING AND WRITING

1. How is O'Connor's personality revealed in this anecdote about her ambivalent response to society? Allow the description to be suggestive for you, and flesh out a brief portrait of her.

2. Consider how this personality makes itself apparent in any one of O'Connor's stories you have read. How does the anecdote help to characterize the narrator's voice in the story?

3. To what extent do you think biographical details such as this — assuming the Milledgeville matron's memory to be accurate — can shed light on a writer's works?

CLAIRE KAHANE (B. 1935)

The Function of Violence in O'Connor's Fiction   *1974*

From the moment the reader enters O'Connor's backwoods, he is poised on the edge of a pervasive violence. Characters barely contain their rage; images reflect a hostile nature; and even the Christ to whom the characters are ultimately driven is a threatening figure . . . full of the apocalyptic wrath of the Old Testament.

O'Connor's conscious purpose is evident enough . . . : to reveal the need for grace in a world grotesque without a transcendent context. "I have found that my subject in fiction is the action of grace in territory largely held by the devil," she wrote [in *Mystery and Manners*], and she was not vague about what the devil is: "an evil intelligence determined on its own supremacy." It would seem that for O'Connor, given the fact of original Sin, any intelligence determined on its own supremacy was intrinsically evil. For in each work, it is the impulse toward secular autonomy, the smug confidence that human nature is perfectible by its own efforts, that she sets out to destroy, through an act of violence so intense that the character is rendered helpless, a passive victim of a superior power. Again and again she creates a fiction in which a character attempts to live autonomously, to define himself and his values, only to be jarred back to what she calls "reality" — the recognition of helplessness in the face of contingency, and the need for absolute submission to the power of Christ.

From "Flannery O'Connor's Rage of Vision"
in *American Literature*

CONSIDERATIONS FOR CRITICAL THINKING AND WRITING

1. Choose an O'Connor story, and explain how grace — the divine influence from God that redeems a person — is used in it to transform a character.

2. Which O'Connor characters can be accurately described as having an "evil intelligence determined on its own supremacy" (para. 2)? Choose one character, and write an essay explaining how this description is central to the conflict of the story.

3. Compare an O'Connor story with one of Hawthorne's "in which a character attempts to live autonomously, to define himself and his values, only to

be jarred back to . . . 'reality' — the recognition of helplessness in the face of
contingency . . ." (para. 2).

EDWARD KESSLER (B. 1927)

On O'Connor's Use of History   1986

In company with other Southern writers . . . who aspire to embrace a lost tradition and look on history as a repository of value, Flannery O'Connor seems a
curious anomaly. She wrote of herself: "I am a Catholic peculiarly possessed of
the modern consciousness . . . unhistorical, solitary, and guilty." Likewise her
characters comprise a gallery of misfits isolated in a present and sentenced to a
lifetime of exile from the human community. In O'Connor's fiction, the past
neither justifies nor even explains what is happening. If she believed, for
example, in the importance of the past accident that maimed Joy in "Good
Country People," she could have demonstrated how the event predetermined
her present rejection of both human and external nature; but Joy's past is
parenthetical: "Mrs. Hopewell excused this attitude because of the leg (which
had been shot off in a hunting accident when Joy was ten)." Believing that
humankind is fundamentally flawed, O'Connor spends very little time constructing a past for her characters. The cure is neither behind us nor before us
but within us; therefore, the past — even historical time itself — supplies only a
limited base for self-discovery.

From *Flannery O'Connor and the Language of Apocalypse*

CONSIDERATIONS FOR CRITICAL THINKING AND WRITING

1. Consider how O'Connor uses history in any one of her stories in this
   anthology and compare that "unhistorical" vision with Hawthorne's in
   "Young Goodman Brown" (p. 325) or "The Minister's Black Veil" (p. 334).
2. Write an essay in which you discuss Kessler's assertion that for O'Connor
   the "past is parenthetical," in contrast to most southern writers, who
   "embrace a lost tradition and look on history as a repository of value." For
   your point of comparison choose either William Faulkner's "A Rose for
   Emily" (p. 90) or "Barn Burning" (p. 418).

Time Magazine, on *A Good Man Is Hard to Find*   1962

Highly unladylike . . . a brutal irony, a slam-bang humor, and a style of writing
as balefully direct as a death sentence.

From a *Time* magazine blurb quoted on the cover
of the second American edition of *A Good Man Is Hard to Find*

CONSIDERATIONS FOR CRITICAL THINKING AND WRITING

1. How accurate do you think this blurb is in characterizing the three O'Connor stories in this chapter?

2. **CREATIVE RESPONSE.** Write your own blurb for the three stories and be prepared to justify your pithy description.

SUGGESTED TOPICS FOR LONGER PAPERS

1. Discuss O'Connor's use of humor in the stories you've read in this chapter. As the basis of your discussion consider at least one humorous moment or scene in each story and characterize the tone of her humor. What generalizations can you make about the tone of the humor in her stories? How does O'Connor use humor to affect the reader's understanding of her themes?

2. O'Connor's fiction is often populated with peculiar characters who seem to demand psychological interpretation. O'Connor, however, made clear in a March 28, 1961, letter that "I am not interested in abnormal psychology." Research psychological readings of one of the stories in this chapter and argue for or against reading her characters from a psychological point of view. You may need to do your own psychological analysis of a character or two to argue for or against its relevance to the story.

Web Research Flannery O'Connor or take quizzes on her works at bedfordstmartins .com/meyercompact.

13

A CRITICAL CASE STUDY

William Faulkner's
"Barn Burning"

"The writer's only responsibility is to his art. . . . He has a dream. It anguishes him so much he must get rid of it. He has no peace until then.
—WILLIAM FAULKNER

It is the writer's privilege to help man endure by lifting his heart.
—WILLIAM FAULKNER

This chapter offers several critical approaches to a well-known short story by William Faulkner. Though there are many possible critical approaches to any given work (see Chapter 46, "Critical Strategies for Reading," for a discussion of a variety of methods), and there are numerous studies of Faulkner from formalist, biographical, historical, mythological, psychological, sociological, and other perspectives, it is worth noting that each reading of a work or writer is predicated on accepting certain assumptions about literature and life. Those assumptions or premises may be complementary or mutually exclusive, and they may appeal to you or appall you. What is interesting, however, is how various approaches reveal the text (as well as its readers and critics) by calling attention to certain elements or leaving others out. The following critical excerpts suggest only a portion of the range of

Explore contexts for William Faulkner on *LiterActive*.

William Faulkner

possibilities, but even a small representation of approaches can help you to raise new questions, develop insights, recognize problems, and suggest additional ways of reading the text.

WILLIAM FAULKNER (1897–1962)

A biographical note for William Faulkner appears on page 90, before his story "A Rose for Emily." In "Barn Burning" Faulkner portrays a young boy's love and revulsion for his father, a frightening man who lives by a "ferocious conviction in the rightness of his own actions."

William Faulkner, Author Photo for *Sanctuary*, 1931. William Faulkner (1897–1962) was born in New Albany, Mississippi, the first of four sons born to Murry and Maud Butler Falkner (as their name was then spelled). He was named after his deceased great-grandfather, William Clark Falkner—family patriarch, lawyer, politician, planter, businessman, railroad financier, and best-selling writer (*The White Rose of Memphis*)—who was known as the "Old Colonel." When Faulkner was five, his family moved forty miles west to the town of Oxford in Lafayette County. Following the move, Murry's father abruptly sold the railroad founded by the "Old Colonel," and Murry was forced to take a series of jobs in Oxford to support his family. Oxford and its surrounding county—its landscape, history, and inhabitants—became a rich source for William Faulkner's writing and the inspiration for his fictional Yoknapatawpha County. "Beginning with *Sartoris* [1929, his third novel]," Faulkner wrote, "I discovered that my own little postage stamp of native soil was worth writing about, and that I would never live long enough to exhaust it." (Top, p. 416) Shown here is Relbue Price's Oxford Hardware Store, the business that Murry Falkner became affilitated with following the decline of his once-successful livery stable business. (Bottom, p. 416) Across the street from the hardware store was Goodwin and Brown's Commissary, a general store that Faulkner would have visited as a boy.

Courtesy of the Colfield Collection, Southern Media Archive, University of Mississippi. Special Collections.

The Oxford Hardware Store, Oxford, Mississippi.

Goodwin and Brown's Commissary, Oxford, Mississippi.

Rowan Oak. In 1930, Faulkner purchased a large, dilapidated plantation house in Oxford known as "The Bailey Place." The house predated the Civil War and was set on thirty-two acres (known as "Bailey's Woods") where Faulkner had played as a boy. He renamed the house "Rowan Oak" and from 1930 on, he did most of his writing here. Despite the financial strain that Rowan Oak presented, the house and land also represented for Faulkner the reclaiming of the genteel life of "The Colonel": Faulkner would never inherit a plantation, so he bought one.
Courtesy of the Library of Congress

William Faulkner (May 6, 1955). The author in the spot where he did most of his writing — his living room at Rowan Oak — bent over a glass-topped table with a pen.
Reprinted by permission of Corbis-Bettmann.

Barn Burning   1939

The store in which the Justice of the Peace's court was sitting smelled of cheese. The boy, crouched on his nail keg at the back of the crowded room, knew he smelled cheese, and more: from where he sat he could see the ranked shelves close-packed with the solid, squat, dynamic shapes of tin cans whose labels his stomach read, not from the lettering which meant nothing to his mind but from the scarlet devils and the silver curve of fish—this, the cheese which he knew he smelled and the hermetic meat which his intestines believed he smelled coming in intermittent gusts momentary and brief between the other constant one, the smell and sense just a little of fear because mostly of despair and grief, the old fierce pull of blood. He could not see the table where the Justice sat and before which his father and his father's enemy (*our enemy* he thought in that despair; *ourn! mine and hisn both! He's my father!*) stood, but he could hear them, the two of them that is, because his father had said no word yet:

"But what proof have you, Mr. Harris?"

"I told you. The hog got into my corn. I caught it up and sent it back to him. He had no fence that would hold it. I told him so, warned him. The next time I put the hog in my pen. When he came to get it I gave him enough wire to patch up his pen. The next time I put the hog up and kept it. I rode down to his house and saw the wire I gave him still rolled on to the spool in his yard. I told him he could have the hog when he paid me a dollar pound fee. That evening a nigger came with the dollar and got the hog. He was a strange nigger. He said, 'He say to tell you wood and hay kin burn.' I said, 'What?' 'That whut he say to tell you,' the nigger said. 'Wood and hay kin burn.' That night my barn burned. I got the stock out but I lost the barn."

"Where is the nigger? Have you got him?"

"He was a strange nigger, I tell you. I don't know what became of him."   5

"But that's not proof. Don't you see that's not proof?"

"Get that boy up here. He knows." For a moment the boy thought too that the man meant his older brother until Harris said, "Not him. The little one. The boy," and, crouching, small for his age, small and wiry like his father, in patched and faded jeans even too small for him, with straight, uncombed, brown hair and eyes gray and wild as storm scud, he saw the men between himself and the table part and become a lane of grim faces, at the end of which he saw the Justice, a shabby, collarless, graying man in spectacles, beckoning him. He felt no floor under his bare feet; he seemed to walk beneath the palpable weight of the grim turning faces. His father, stiff in his black Sunday coat donned not for the trial but for the moving, did not even look at him. *He aims for me to lie,* he thought, again with that frantic grief and despair. *And I will have to do hit.*

"What's your name, boy?" the Justice said.

"Colonel Sartoris Snopes," the boy whispered.

"Hey?" the Justice said. "Talk louder. Colonel Sartoris? I reckon anybody 10 named for Colonel Sartoris in this country can't help but tell the truth, can they?" The boy said nothing. *Enemy! Enemy!* he thought; for a moment he could not even see, could not see that the Justice's face was kindly nor discern that his voice was troubled when he spoke to the man named Harris: "Do you want me to question this boy?" But he could hear, and during those subsequent long seconds while there was absolutely no sound in the crowded little room save that of quiet and intent breathing it was as if he had swung outward at the end of a grape vine, over a ravine, and at the top of the swing had been caught in a prolonged instant of mesmerized gravity, weightless in time.

"No!" Harris said violently, explosively. "Damnation! Send him out of here!" Now time, the fluid world, rushed beneath him again, the voices coming to him again through the smell of cheese and sealed meat, the fear and despair and the old grief of blood:

"This case is closed. I can't find against you, Snopes, but I can give you advice. Leave this country and don't come back to it."

His father spoke for the first time, his voice cold and harsh, level, without emphasis: "I aim to. I don't figure to stay in a country among people who . . ." he said something unprintable and vile, addressed to no one.

"That'll do," the Justice said. "Take your wagon and get out of this country before dark. Case dismissed."

His father turned, and he followed the stiff black coat, the wiry figure 15 walking a little stiffly from where a Confederate provost's man's musket ball had taken him in the heel on a stolen horse thirty years ago, followed the two backs now, since his older brother had appeared from somewhere in the crowd, no taller than the father but thicker, chewing tobacco steadily, between the two lines of grim-faced men and out of the store and across the worn gallery and down the sagging steps and among the dogs and half-grown boys in the mild May dust, where as he passed a voice hissed:

"Barn burner!"

Again he could not see, whirling; there was a face in a red haze, moonlike, bigger than the full moon, the owner of it half again his size, he leaping in the red haze toward the face, feeling no blow, feeling no shock when his head struck the earth, scrabbling up and leaping again, feeling no blow this time either and tasting no blood, scrabbling up to see the other boy in full flight and himself already leaping into pursuit as his father's hand jerked him back, the harsh, cold voice speaking above him: "Go get in the wagon."

It stood in a grove of locusts and mulberries across the road. His two hulking sisters in their Sunday dresses and his mother and her sister in calico and sunbonnets were already in it, sitting on or among the sorry residue of the dozen and more movings which even the boy could remember — the battered stove, the broken beds and chairs, the clock inlaid with mother-of-pearl, which would not run, stopped at some fourteen minutes past two o'clock of a dead and forgotten day and time, which had been his mother's dowry. She was crying, though when she saw him she drew her sleeve across her face and began to descend from the wagon. "Get back," the father said.

"He's hurt. I got to get some water and wash his . . ."

"Get back in the wagon," his father said. He got in too, over the tail-gate. 20 His father mounted to the seat where the older brother already sat and struck the gaunt mules two savage blows with the peeled willow, but without heat. It was not even sadistic; it was exactly that same quality which in later years would cause his descendants to over-run the engine before putting a motor car in motion, striking and reining back in the same movement. The wagon went on, the store with its quiet crowd of grimly watching men dropped behind; a curve in the road hid it. *Forever* he thought. *Maybe he's done satisfied now, now that he has . . .* stopping himself, not to say it aloud even to himself. His mother's hand touched his shoulder.

"Does hit hurt?" she said.

"Naw," he said. "Hit don't hurt. Lemme be."

"Can't you wipe some of the blood off before hit dries?"

"I'll wash to-night," he said. "Lemme be, I tell you."

The wagon went on. He did not know where they were going. None of them ever did or ever asked, because it was always somewhere, always a house of sorts waiting for them a day or two days or even three days away. Likely his father had already arranged to make a crop on another farm before he . . . Again he had to stop himself. He (the father) always did. There was something about his wolflike independence and even courage when the advantage was at least neutral which impressed strangers, as if they got from his latent ravening ferocity not so much a sense of dependability as a feeling that his ferocious conviction in the rightness of his own actions would be of advantage to all whose interest lay with his.

That night they camped, in a grove of oaks and beeches where a spring ran. The nights were still cool and they had a fire against it, of a rail lifted from a nearby fence and cut into lengths — a small fire, neat, niggard almost, a shrewd fire; such fires were his father's habit and custom always, even in freezing weather. Older, the boy might have remarked this and wondered why not a big one; why should not a man who had not only seen the waste and extravagance of war, but who had in his blood an inherent voracious prodigality with material not his own, have burned everything in sight? Then he might have gone a step farther and thought that that was the reason: that niggard blaze was the living fruit of nights passed during those four years in the woods hiding from all men, blue or gray, with his strings of horses (captured horses, he called them). And older still, he might have divined the true reason: that the element of fire spoke to some deep mainspring of his father's being, as the element of steel or of powder spoke to other men, as the one weapon for the preservation of integrity, else breath were not worth the breathing, and hence to be regarded with respect and used with discretion.

But he did not think this now and he had seen those same niggard blazes all his life. He merely ate his supper beside it and was already half asleep over his iron plate when his father called him, and once more he followed the stiff back, the stiff and ruthless limp, up the slope and on to the starlit road where, turning, he could see his father against the stars but without face or depth — a shape black, flat, and bloodless as though cut from tin in the iron folds of the frockcoat which had not been made for him, the voice harsh like tin and without heat like tin:

"You were fixing to tell them. You would have told him."

He didn't answer. His father struck him with the flat of his hand on the side of the head, hard but without heat, exactly as he had struck the two mules at the store, exactly as he would strike either of them with any stick in order to kill a horse fly, his voice still without heat or anger. "You're getting to be a man. You got to learn. You got to learn to stick to your own blood or you ain't going to have any blood to stick to you. Do you think either of them, any man there this morning, would? Don't you know all they wanted was a chance to get at me because they knew I had them beat? Eh?" Later, twenty years later, he was to tell himself, "If I had said they wanted only truth, justice, he would have hit me again." But now he said nothing. He was not crying. He just stood there. "Answer me," his father said.

"Yes," he whispered. His father turned.

"Get on to bed. We'll be there tomorrow."

Tomorrow they were there. In the early afternoon the wagon stopped before a paintless two-room house identical almost with the dozen others it had stopped before even in the boy's ten years, and again, as on the other dozen occasions, his mother and aunt got down and began to unload the wagon, although his two sisters and his father and brother had not moved.

"Likely hit ain't fitten for hawgs," one of the sisters said.

"Nevertheless, fit it will and you'll hog it and like it," his father said. "Get out of them chairs and help your Ma unload."

The two sisters got down, big, bovine, in a flutter of cheap ribbons; one of them drew from the jumbled wagon bed a battered lantern, the other a worn broom. His father handed the reins to the older son and began to climb stiffly over the wheel. "When they get unloaded, take the team to the barn and feed them." Then he said, and at first the boy thought he was still speaking to his brother: "Come with me."

"Me?" he said.

"Yes," his father said. "You."

"Abner," his mother said. His father paused and looked back — the harsh level stare beneath the shaggy, graying, irascible brows.

"I reckon I'll have a word with the man that aims to begin tomorrow owning me body and soul for the next eight months."

They went back up the road. A week ago — or before last night, that is — he would have asked where they were going, but not now. His father had struck him before last night but never before had he paused afterward to explain why; it was as if the blow and the following calm, outrageous voice still rang, repercussed, divulging nothing to him save the terrible handicap of being young, the light weight of his few years, just heavy enough to prevent his soaring free of the world as it seemed to be ordered but not heavy enough to keep him footed solid in it, to resist it and try to change the course of events.

Presently he could see the grove of oaks and cedars and the other flowering trees and shrubs where the house would be, though not the house yet. They walked beside a fence massed with honeysuckle and Cherokee roses and came to a gate swinging open between two brick pillars, and now, beyond a sweep of drive, he saw the house for the first time and at that instant he forgot his father and the terror and despair both, and even when he remembered his father again (who had not stopped) the terror and despair did not return. Because, for all the twelve movings, they had sojourned until now in a poor country, a land of small farms and fields and houses, and he had never seen a house like this before. *Hit's big as a courthouse* he thought quietly, with a surge of peace and joy whose reason he could not have thought into words, being too young for that: *They are safe from him. People whose lives are a part of this peace and dignity are beyond his touch, he no more to them than a buzzing wasp: capable of stinging for a little moment but that's all; the spell of this peace and dignity rendering even the barns and stable and cribs which belong to it impervious to the puny flames he might contrive*... this, the peace and joy, ebbing for an instant as he looked again at the stiff black back, the stiff and implacable limp of the figure which was not dwarfed by the house, for the reason that it had never looked big anywhere and which now, against the serene columned backdrop, had more than ever that impervious quality of something cut ruthlessly from tin, depthless, as though, sidewise to the sun, it would cast no shadow. Watching him, the boy remarked the absolutely undeviating course which his father held and saw the stiff foot come squarely down in a pile of fresh droppings where a horse had stood in the drive and which his father could have avoided by a simple change of stride. But it ebbed only for a moment, though he could not have thought this into words either, walking on in the spell of the house, which he could even want but without envy, without sorrow, certainly never with that ravening and jealous rage which unknown to him walked in the ironlike black coat before him: *Maybe he will feel it too. Maybe it will even change him now from what maybe he couldn't help but be.*

They crossed the portico. Now he could hear his father's stiff foot as it came down on the boards with clocklike finality, a sound out of all proportion to the displacement of the body it bore and which was not dwarfed either by the white door before it, as though it had attained to a sort of vicious and ravening minimum not to be dwarfed by anything—the flat, wide, black hat, the formal coat of broadcloth which had once been black but which had now that friction-glazed greenish cast of the bodies of old house flies, the lifted sleeve which was too large, the lifted hand like a curled claw. The door opened so promptly that the boy knew the Negro must have been watching them all the time, an old man with neat grizzled hair, in a linen jacket, who stood barring the door with his body, saying, "Wipe yo foots, white man, fo you come in here. Major ain't home nohow."

"Get out of my way, nigger," his father said, without heat too, flinging the door back and the Negro also and entering, his hat still on his head. And now the boy saw the prints of the stiff foot on the doorjamb and saw them appear on the pale rug behind the machinelike deliberation of the foot which seemed to bear (or transmit) twice the weight which the body compassed. The Negro was shouting "Miss Lula! Miss Lula!" somewhere behind them, then the boy, deluged as though by a warm wave by a suave turn of the carpeted stair and a pendant glitter of chandeliers and a mute gleam of gold frames, heard the swift feet and saw her too, a lady—perhaps he had never seen her like before either—in a gray, smooth gown with lace at the throat and an apron tied at the waist and the sleeves turned back, wiping cake or biscuit dough from her hands with a towel as she came up the hall, looking not at his father at all but at the tracks on the blond rug with an expression of incredulous amazement.

"I tried," the Negro cried. "I tole him to . . ."

"Will you please go away?" she said in a shaking voice. "Major de Spain is   45 not at home. Will you please go away?"

His father had not spoken again. He did not speak again. He did not even look at her. He just stood stiff in the center of the rug, in his hat, the shaggy iron-gray brows twitching slightly above the pebble-colored eyes as he appeared to examine the house with brief deliberation. Then with the same deliberation he turned; the boy watched him pivot on the good leg and saw the stiff foot drag round the arc of the turning, leaving a final long and fading smear. His father never looked at it, he never once looked down at the rug. The Negro held the door. It closed behind them, upon the hysteric and indistinguishable woman-wail. His father stopped at the top of the steps and scraped his boot clean on the edge of it. At the gate he stopped again. He stood for a moment, planted stiffly on the stiff foot, looking back at the house. "Pretty and white, ain't it?" he said. "That's sweat. Nigger sweat. Maybe it ain't white enough yet to suit him. Maybe he wants to mix some white sweat with it."

Two hours later the boy was chopping wood behind the house within which his mother and aunt and the two sisters (the mother and aunt, not the two girls, he knew that; even at this distance and muffled by walls the flat loud voices of the two girls emanated an incorrigible idle inertia) were setting up the stove to prepare a meal; when he heard the hooves and saw the linen-clad man on a fine sorrel mare, whom he recognized even before he saw the rolled rug in front of the Negro youth following on a fat bay carriage horse—a suffused, angry face vanishing, still at full gallop, beyond the corner of the house where his father and brother were sitting in the two tilted chairs; and a moment later, almost before he could have put the axe down, he heard the hooves again and watched the sorrel mare go back out of the yard, already galloping again. Then his father began to shout one of the sisters' names, who presently emerged backward from the kitchen door dragging the rolled rug along the ground by one end while the other sister walked behind it.

"If you ain't going to tote, go on and set up the wash pot," the first said.

"You, Sarty!" the second shouted. "Set up the wash pot!" His father appeared at the door, framed against that shabbiness, as he had been against that other bland perfection, impervious to either, the mother's anxious face at his shoulder.

"Go on," the father said. "Pick it up." The two sisters stopped, broad, lethargic; stooping, they presented an incredible expanse of pale cloth and a flutter of tawdry ribbons.   50

"If I thought enough of a rug to have to git hit all the way from France I wouldn't keep hit where folks coming in would have to tromp on hit," the first said. They raised the rug.

"Abner," the mother said. "Let me do it."

"You go back and git dinner," his father said. "I'll tend to this."

From the woodpile through the rest of the afternoon the boy watched them, the rug spread flat in the dust beside the bubbling wash pot, the two sisters stooping over it with that profound and lethargic reluctance, while the father stood over them in turn, implacable and grim, driving them though never raising his voice again. He could smell the harsh homemade lye they were using; he saw his mother come to the door once and look toward them with an expression not anxious now but very like despair; he saw his father turn, and he fell to with the axe and saw from the corner of his eye his father raise from the ground a flattish fragment of field stone and examine it and return to the pot, and this time his mother actually spoke: "Abner. Abner. Please don't. Please, Abner."

Then he was done too. It was dusk; the whippoorwills had already begun.   55
He could smell coffee from the room where they would presently eat the cold food remaining from the midafternoon meal, though when he entered the house he realized they were having coffee again probably because there was a fire on the hearth, before which the rug now lay spread over the backs of the two chairs. The tracks of his father's foot were gone. Where they had been were now long, water-cloudy scoriations resembling the sporadic course of a lilliputian mowing machine.

It still hung there while they ate the cold food and then went to bed, scattered without order or claim up and down the two rooms, his mother in one bed, where his father would later lie, the older brother in the other, himself, the aunt, and the two sisters on pallets on the floor. But his father was not in bed yet. The last thing the boy remembered was the depthless, harsh silhouette of the hat and coat bending over the rug and it seemed to him that he had not even closed his eyes when the silhouette was standing over him, the fire almost dead behind it, the stiff foot prodding him awake. "Catch up the mule," his father said.

When he returned with the mule his father was standing in the black door, the rolled rug over his shoulder. "Ain't you going to ride?" he said.

"No. Give me your foot."

He bent his knee into his father's hand, the wiry, surprising power flowed smoothly, rising, he rising with it, on to the mule's bare back (they had owned a saddle once; the boy could remember it though not when or where) and with the same effortlessness his father swung the rug up in front of him. Now in the starlight they retraced the afternoon's path, up the dusty road rife with honeysuckle, through the gate and up the black tunnel of the drive to the lightless house, where he sat on the mule and felt the rough warp of the rug drag across his thighs and vanish.

"Don't you want me to help?" he whispered. His father did not answer and   60 now he heard again that stiff foot striking the hollow portico with that wooden and clocklike deliberation, that outrageous overstatement of the weight it carried. The rug, hunched, not flung (the boy could tell that even in the darkness) from his father's shoulder struck the angle of wall and floor with a sound unbelievably loud, thunderous, then the foot again, unhurried and enormous; a light came on in the house and the boy sat, tense, breathing steadily and quietly and just a little fast, though the foot itself did not increase its beat at all, descending the steps now; now the boy could see him.

"Don't you want to ride now?" he whispered. "We kin both ride now," the light within the house altering now, flaring up and sinking. *He's coming down the stairs now,* he thought. He had already ridden the mule up beside the horse block; presently his father was up behind him and he doubled the reins over and slashed the mule across the neck, but before the animal could begin to trot the hard, thin arm came around him, the hard, knotted hand jerking the mule back to a walk.

In the first red rays of the sun they were in the lot, putting plow gear on the mules. This time the sorrel mare was in the lot before he heard it at all, the rider collarless and even bareheaded, trembling, speaking in a shaking voice as the woman in the house had done, his father merely looking up once before stooping again to the hame he was buckling, so that the man on the mare spoke to his stooping back:

"You must realize you have ruined that rug. Wasn't there anybody here, any of your women . . ." he ceased, shaking, the boy watching him, the older brother leaning now in the stable door, chewing, blinking slowly and steadily at nothing apparently. "It cost a hundred dollars. But you never had a hundred dollars. You never will. So I'm going to charge you twenty bushels of corn against your crop. I'll add it in your contract and when you come to the commissary you can sign it. That won't keep Mrs. de Spain quiet but maybe it will teach you to wipe your feet before you enter her house again."

Then he was gone. The boy looked at his father, who still had not spoken or even looked up again, who was now adjusting the logger-head in the hame.

"Pap," he said. His father looked at him — the inscrutable face, the shaggy   65 brows beneath which the gray eyes glinted coldly. Suddenly the boy went toward him, fast, stopping as suddenly. "You done the best you could!" he cried. "If he wanted hit done different why didn't he wait and tell you how? He won't git no twenty bushels! He won't git none! We'll gether hit and hide hit! I kin watch . . ."

"Did you put the cutter back in that straight stock like I told you?"

"No, sir," he said.

"Then go do it."

That was Wednesday. During the rest of that week he worked steadily, at what was within his scope and some which was beyond it, with an industry that did not need to be driven nor even commanded twice; he had this from his mother, with the difference that some at least of what he did he liked to do, such as splitting wood with the half-size axe which his mother and aunt had earned, or saved money somehow, to present him with at Christmas. In company with the two older women (and on one afternoon, even one of the sisters), he built pens for the shoat and the cow which were part of his father's contract with the landlord, and one afternoon, his father being absent, gone somewhere on one of the mules, he went to the field.

They were running a middle buster now, his brother holding the plow   70
straight while he handled the reins, and walking beside the straining mule, the rich black soil shearing cool and damp against his bare ankles, he thought *Maybe this is the end of it. Maybe even that twenty bushels that seems hard to have to pay for just a rug will be a cheap price for him to stop forever and always from being what he used to be;* thinking, dreaming now, so that his brother had to speak sharply to him to mind the mule: *Maybe he even won't collect the twenty bushels. Maybe it will all add up and balance and vanish—corn, rug, fire; the terror and grief; the being pulled two ways like between two teams of horses—gone, done with for ever and ever.*

Then it was Saturday; he looked up from beneath the mule he was harnessing and saw his father in the black coat and hat. "Not that," his father said. "The wagon gear." And then, two hours later, sitting in the wagon bed behind his father and brother on the seat, the wagon accomplished a final curve, and he saw the weathered paintless store with its tattered tobacco- and patent-medicine posters and the tethered wagons and saddle animals below the gallery. He mounted the gnawed steps behind his father and brother, and there again was the lane of quiet, watching faces for the three of them to walk through. He saw the man in spectacles sitting at the plank table and he did not need to be told this was a Justice of the Peace; he sent one glare of fierce, exultant, partisan defiance at the man in collar and cravat now, whom he had seen but twice before in his life, and that on a galloping horse, who now wore on his face an expression not of rage but of amazed unbelief which the boy could not have known was at the incredible circumstance of being sued by one of his own tenants, and came and stood against his father and cried at the Justice: "He ain't done it! He aint' burnt . . ."

"Go back to the wagon," his father said.

"Burnt?" the Justice said. "Do I understand this rug was burned too?"

"Does anybody here claim it was?" his father said. "Go back to the wagon." But he did not, he merely retreated to the rear of the room, crowded as that other had been, but not to sit down this time, instead, to stand pressing among the motionless bodies, listening to the voices:

"And you claim twenty bushels of corn is too high for the damage you did   75
to the rug?"

"He brought the rug to me and said he wanted the tracks washed out of it. I washed the tracks out and took the rug back to him."

"But you didn't carry the rug back to him in the same condition it was in before you made the tracks on it."

His father did not answer, and now for perhaps half a minute there was no sound at all save that of breathing, the faint, steady suspiration of complete and intent listening.

"You decline to answer that, Mr. Snopes?" Again his father did not answer. "I'm going to find against you, Mr. Snopes. I'm going to find that you were responsible for the injury to Major de Spain's rug and hold you liable for it. But twenty bushels of corn seems a little high for a man in your circumstances to have to pay. Major de Spain claims it cost a hundred dollars. October corn will be worth about fifty cents. I figure that if Major de Spain can stand a ninety-five dollar loss on something he paid cash for, you can stand a five-dollar loss you haven't earned yet. I hold you in damages to Major de Spain to the amount of ten bushels of corn over and above your contract with him, to be paid to him out of your crop at gathering time. Court adjourned."

It had taken no time hardly, the morning was but half begun. He thought they would return home and perhaps back to the field, since they were late, far behind all other farmers. But instead his father passed on behind the wagon, merely indicating with his hand for the older brother to follow with it, and crossed the road toward the blacksmith shop opposite, pressing on after his father, overtaking him, speaking, whispering up at the harsh, calm face beneath the weathered hat: "He won't git no ten bushels neither. He won't git one. We'll . . ." until his father glanced for an instant down at him, the face absolutely calm, the grizzled eyebrows tangled above the cold eyes, the voice almost pleasant, almost gentle:

"You think so? Well, we'll wait till October anyway."

The matter of the wagon—the setting of a spoke or two and the tightening of the tires—did not take long either, the business of the tires accomplished by driving the wagon into the spring branch behind the shop and letting it stand there, the mules nuzzling into the water from time to time, and the boy on the seat with the idle reins, looking up the slope and through the sooty tunnel of the shed where the slow hammer rang and where his father sat on an upended cypress bolt, easily, either talking or listening, still sitting there when the boy brought the dripping wagon up out of the branch and halted it before the door.

"Take them on to the shade and hitch," his father said. He did so and returned. His father and the smith and a third man squatting on his heels inside the door were talking, about crops and animals; the boy, squatting too in the ammoniac dust and hoof-parings and scales of rust, heard his father tell a long and unhurried story out of the time before the birth of the older brother even when he had been a professional horsetrader. And then his father came up beside him where he stood before a tattered last year's circus poster on the other side of the store, gazing rapt and quiet at the scarlet horses, the incredible poisings and convolutions of tulle and tights and the painted leers of comedians, and said, "It's time to eat."

But not at home. Squatting beside his brother against the front wall, he watched his father emerge from the store and produce from a paper sack a segment of cheese and divide it carefully and deliberately into three with his

80

pocket knife and produce crackers from the same sack. They all three squatted on the gallery and ate, slowly, without talking; then in the store again, they drank from a tin dipper tepid water smelling of the cedar bucket and of living beech trees. And still they did not go home. It was a horse lot this time, a tall rail fence upon and along which men stood and sat and out of which one by one horses were led, to be walked and trotted and then cantered back and forth along the road while the slow swapping and buying went on and the sun began to slant westward, they — the three of them — watching and listening, the older brother with his muddy eyes and his steady, inevitable tobacco, the father commenting now and then on certain of the animals, to no one in particular.

It was after sundown when they reached home. They ate supper by lamp-   85 light, then, sitting on the doorstep, the boy watched the night fully accomplish, listening to the whippoorwills and the frogs, when he heard his mother's voice: "Abner! No! No! Oh, God. Oh, God. Abner!" and he rose, whirled, and saw the altered light through the door where a candle stub now burned in a bottle neck on the table and his father, still in the hat and coat, at once formal and burlesque as though dressed carefully for some shabby and ceremonial violence, emptying the reservoir of the lamp back into the five-gallon kerosene can from which it had been filled, while the mother tugged at his arm until he shifted the lamp to the other hand and flung her back, not savagely or viciously, just hard, into the wall, her hands flung out against the wall for balance, her mouth open and in her face the same quality of hopeless despair as had been in her voice. Then his father saw him standing in the door.

"Go to the barn and get that can of oil we were oiling the wagon with," he said. The boy did not move. Then he could speak.

"What . . ." he cried. "What are you . . ."

"Go get that oil," his father said. "Go."

Then he was moving, running, outside the house, toward the stable: this the old habit, the old blood which he had not been permitted to choose for himself, which had been bequeathed him willy nilly and which had run for so long (and who knew where, battening on what of outrage and savagery and lust) before it came to him. *I could keep on,* he thought. *I could run on and on and never look back, never need to see his face again. Only I can't. I can't,* the rusted can in his hand now, the liquid sploshing in it as he ran back to the house and into it, into the sound of his mother's weeping in the next room, and handed the can to his father.

"Ain't you going to even send a nigger?" he cried. "At least you sent a nig-   90 ger before!"

This time his father didn't strike him. The hand came even faster than the blow had, the same hand which had set the can on the table with almost excruciating care flashing from the can toward him too quick for him to follow it, gripping him by the back of his shirt and on to tiptoe before he had seen it quit the can, the face stooping at him in breathless and frozen ferocity, the cold, dead voice speaking over him to the older brother who leaned against the table, chewing with that steady, curious, sidewise motion of cows:

"Empty the can into the big one and go on. I'll catch up with you."

"Better tie him up to the bedpost," the brother said.

"Do like I told you," the father said. Then the boy was moving, his bunched shirt and the hard, bony hand between his shoulder-blades, his toes just touching the floor, across the room and into the other one, past the sisters sitting with spread heavy thighs in the two chairs over the cold hearth, and to where his mother and aunt sat side by side on the bed, the aunt's arms about his mother's shoulders.

"Hold him," the father said. The aunt made a startled movement. "Not you," the father said. "Lennie. Take hold of him. I want to see you do it." His mother took him by the wrist. "You'll hold him better than that. If he gets loose don't you know what he is going to do? He will go up yonder." He jerked his head toward the road. "Maybe I'd better tie him."

"I'll hold him," his mother whispered.

"See you do then." Then his father was gone, the stiff foot heavy and measured upon the boards, ceasing at last.

Then he began to struggle. His mother caught him in both arms, he jerking and wrenching at them. He would be stronger in the end, he knew that. But he had no time to wait for it. "Lemme go!" he cried. "I don't want to have to hit you!"

"Let him go!" the aunt said. "If he don't go, before God, I am going up there myself!"

"Don't you see I can't?" his mother cried. "Sarty! Sarty! No! No! Help me, Lizzie!"

Then he was free. His aunt grasped at him but it was too late. He whirled, running, his mother stumbled forward on to her knees behind him, crying to the nearer sister. "Catch him, Net! Catch him!" But that was too late too, the sister (the sisters were twins, born at the same time, yet either of them now gave the impression of being, encompassing as much living meat and volume and weight as any other two of the family) not yet having begun to rise from the chair, her head, face, alone merely turned, presenting to him in the flying instant an astonishing expanse of young female features untroubled by any surprise even, wearing only an expression of bovine interest. Then he was out of the room, out of the house, in the mild dust of the starlit road and the heavy rifeness of honeysuckle, the pale ribbon unspooling with terrific slowness under his running feet, reaching the gate at last and turning in, running, his heart and lungs drumming, on up the drive toward the lighted house, the lighted door. He did not knock, he burst in, sobbing for breath, incapable for the moment of speech; he saw the astonished face of the Negro in the linen jacket without knowing when the Negro had appeared.

"De Spain!" he cried, panted. "Where's . . ." then he saw the white man too emerging from a white door down the hall. "Barn!" he cried. "Barn!"

"What?" the white man said. "Barn?"

"Yes!" the boy cried. "Barn!"

"Catch him!" the white man shouted.

But it was too late this time too. The Negro grasped his shirt, but the entire sleeve, rotten with washing, carried away, and he was out that door too and in the drive again, and had actually never ceased to run even while he was screaming into the white man's face.

Behind him the white man was shouting, "My horse! Fetch my horse!" and he thought for an instant of cutting across the park and climbing the fence into the road, but he did not know the park nor how high the vine-massed fence might be and he dared not risk it. So he ran on down the drive, blood and breath roaring; presently he was in the road again though he could not see it. He could not hear either: the galloping mare was almost upon him before he heard her, and even then he held his course, as if the very urgency of his wild grief and need must in a moment more find him wings, waiting until the ultimate instant to hurl himself aside and into the weed-choked roadside ditch as the horse thundered past and on, for an instant in furious silhouette against the stars, the tranquil early summer night sky which, even before the shape of the horse and rider vanished, strained abruptly and violently upward: a long, swirling roar incredible and soundless, blotting the stars, and he springing up and into the road again, running again, knowing it was too late yet still running even after he heard the shot and, an instant later, two shots, pausing now without knowing he had ceased to run, crying "Pap! Pap!," running again before he knew he had begun to run, stumbling, tripping over something and scrabbling up again without ceasing to run, looking backward over his shoulder at the glare as he got up, running on among the invisible trees, panting, sobbing, "Father! Father!"

At midnight he was sitting on the crest of a hill. He did not know it was midnight and he did not know how far he had come. But there was no glare behind him now and he sat now, his back toward what he had called home for four days anyhow, his face toward the dark woods which he would enter when breath was strong again, small, shaking steadily in the chill darkness, hugging himself into the remainder of his thin, rotten shirt, the grief and despair now no longer terror and fear but just grief and despair. *Father. My father,* he thought. "He was brave!" he cried suddenly, aloud but not loud, no more than a whisper: "He was! He was in the war! He was in Colonel Sartoris' cav'ry!" not knowing that his father had gone to that war a private in the fine old European sense, wearing no uniform, admitting the authority of and giving fidelity to no man or army or flag, going to war as Malbrouck° himself did: for booty—it meant nothing and less than nothing to him if it were enemy booty or his own.

The slow constellations wheeled on. It would be dawn and then sun-up after a while and he would be hungry. But that would be tomorrow and now he was only cold, and walking would cure that. His breathing was easier now and he decided to get up and go on, and then he found that he had been asleep because he knew it was almost dawn, the night almost over. He could tell that from the whippoorwills. They were everywhere now among the dark trees below him, constant and inflectioned and ceaseless, so that, as the instant for giving over to the day birds drew nearer and nearer, there was no interval at all between them. He got up. He was a little stiff, but walking would cure that too as it would the cold, and soon there would be the sun. He went on down the hill, toward the dark woods within which the liquid silver voices of the birds called unceasing—the rapid and urgent beating of the urgent and quiring heart of the late spring night. He did not look back.

Malbrouck: John Churchill, duke of Marlborough (1650–1722), English military commander who led the armies of England and Holland in the War of Spanish Succession.

Considerations for Critical Thinking and Writing

1. **FIRST RESPONSE.** Who is "Barn Burning" about? Explain your choice.
2. Is Sarty a dynamic or a static character? Why? Which term best describes his father? Why?
3. Who is the central character in this story? Explain your choice.

4. How are Sarty's emotions revealed in the story's opening paragraphs? What seems to be the function of the italicized passages there and elsewhere?

5. What do we learn from the story's exposition that helps us understand Abner's character? How does his behavior reveal his character? What do other people say about him?

6. How does Faulkner's physical description of Abner further our understanding of his personality?

7. Explain how the justice of the peace, Mr. Harris, and Major de Spain serve as foils to Abner. Discuss whether you think they are round or flat characters.

8. Who are the story's stock characters? What is their purpose?

9. Explain how the description of Major de Spain's house helps to frame the main conflicts that Sarty experiences in his efforts to remain loyal to his father.

10. Write an essay describing Sarty's attitudes toward his father as they develop and change throughout the story.

11. What do you think happens to Sarty's father and brother at the end of the story? How does your response to this question affect your reading of the last paragraph?

12. How does the language of the final paragraph suggest a kind of resolution to the conflicts Sarty has experienced?

CONNECTIONS TO OTHER SELECTIONS

1. Compare and contrast Faulkner's characterizations of Abner Snopes in this story and Miss Emily in "A Rose for Emily" (p. 90). How does the author generate sympathy for each character even though both are guilty of terrible crimes? Which character do you find more sympathetic? Explain why.

2. How does Abner Snopes's motivation for revenge compare with Matt Fowler's in Dubus's "Killings" (p. 103)? How do the victims of each character's revenge differ and thereby help to shape the meanings of each story?

3. Read the section on mythological criticism in Chapter 46, "Critical Strategies for Reading." How do you think a mythological critic would make sense of Sarty Snopes and Matt Fowler?

Perspectives on Faulkner

JANE HILES (B. 1951)

Hiles uses a biographical approach (see pp. 1540–42 in Chapter 46, "Critical Strategies for Reading") to determine Faulkner's intentions in his characterization of how Sarty responds to the conflicts he feels about his father.

Blood Ties in "Barn Burning" 1985

"'You're getting to be a man.... You got to learn to stick to your own blood or you ain't going to have any blood to stick to you'": Abner Snopes's admonition to his son, Colonel Sartoris (or "Sarty"), introduces a central issue in Faulkner's "Barn Burning" — the kinship bond, which the story's narrator calls the "old fierce pull of blood." The interpretive crux of the work is a conflict between determinism, represented by the blood tie that binds Sarty to his clan, and free will, dramatized by the boy's ultimate repudiation of family ties and his decampment. Dissonances between the structure and the imagery of the work develop and amplify Sarty's conflict: viewed in the light of the narrator's deterministic assumptions, the story's denouement is a red herring which only appears to resolve the complexities created by evocative language. Sarty's seeming interruption of the antisocial pattern established by his father is actually a continuation of it, and the ostensible resolution of his moral dilemma actually no resolution at all. . . .

In an interview in Japan sixteen years after the publication of "Barn Burning," Faulkner delivered an appraisal of the phenomenon of clannishness that bears considerable relevance to Abner Snopes's defensive posture in "Barn Burning":

> Yes, we are country people and we have never had too much in material possessions because 60 or 70 years ago we were invaded and we were conquered. So we have been thrown back on our selves not only for entertainment but certain [sic] amount of defense. We have to be clannish just like the people in the Scottish highlands, each springing to defend his own blood whether it be right or wrong. Just a matter of custom and habit, we have to do it; interrelated that way, and usually there is hereditary head [sic] of the whole lot, as usually, the oldest son of the oldest son and each looked upon as chief of his own particular clan. That is the tone they live by. But I am sure it is because only a comparatively short time ago we were invaded by our own people — speaking in our own language which is always a pretty savage sort of warfare.

In Faulkner's estimation, the old pull of blood transcends considerations of caste, class, and occupation:

> . . . [I]t is regional. It is through what we call the "South." It doesn't matter what the people do. They can be land people, farmers, and industrialists, but there still exists the feeling of blood, of clan, blood for blood. It is pretty general through all the classes.[1]

Faulkner's explanation of the phenomenon of Southern clannishness touches upon a number of the issues that arise in "Barn Burning." In each case, alienation from the politically and economically dominant group leads to dependence upon an alternative source of security. Just as beleaguered Southerners, Faulkner suggests, have had to look to themselves for "defense" since the South was defeated, so Ab Snopes must turn to his kin for defense not only from Union troops but also from the landed Southern aristocrat

---

[1] James B. Meriwether and Michael Millgate, eds., *Lion in the Garden* (New York: Random House, 1968), p. 191.

who, in what Ab perceives as a failure of paternalism, "aims to begin . . . owning [him] body and soul." The clan's identifying characteristic, then, is its orientation to survival. Perhaps most interestingly, the comments made in the interview impinge upon the central issue of the morality of Sarty's choice. Faulkner's recognition here of a private code of honor suggests that Sarty's conduct is somewhat more questionable than is generally recognized, and his articulation in the interview of a necessity for clannishness suggests at least a modicum of sympathy for the "custom and habit" of "each springing to defend his own blood whether it be right or wrong."

From *Mississippi Quarterly: The Journal of Southern Culture*

CONSIDERATIONS FOR CRITICAL THINKING AND WRITING

1. To what extent does Faulkner's description of clannishness in the South affect your understanding of whether Sarty resolves his dilemma at the end of the story?

2. Do you agree with Hiles that "Sarty's conduct is somewhat more questionable than is generally recognized" (para. 4)?

BENJAMIN DEMOTT (B. 1924)

DeMott pays close attention to matters of culture, race, class, and power that affect Abner Snopes, and from those perspectives Abner is seen as more than simply malevolent.

Abner Snopes as a Victim of Class   *1988*

We know that Ab Snopes is harsh to his wife, his sons, and his daughters, and that he is particularly cruel to his stock. We know that his hatred of the planters with whom he enters into sharecropping agreements repeatedly issues in acts of wanton destruction. We know that he's ridden with suspicion of his own closest kin, expecting them to betray him. And we know that — worse than any of this — he often behaves with fearful coldness to those who try desperately to communicate the loving respect they feel for him.

Given such a combination of racism, destructiveness, and blank insensitivity, it's tempting to imagine Ab as a figure in whom ignorance and brutality obliterate every sympathetic impulse, every normative response to peace, dignity, or beauty. Major de Spain seems to reach something close to that conclusion after the rug-laundering episode ("Wasn't there anybody here, any of your women . . ."). And although Ab's son is intensely loyal to his father and indignant at the injustice of the Major's twenty-bushel "charge" for the destruction of the rug, Sarty clearly has a conviction that "peace and dignity" are somehow "*beyond his [father's] touch, he no more to them than a buzzing wasp.*" Is there anything to be made of Ab Snopes except a person whose raging malevolence has badly stunted if not crippled his humanity?

Denying the force of the malevolence is impossible — but tracing it solely to ignorance and insensitivity falsifies Ab's nature. Uneducated, probably illiterate, schooled in none of the revolutionary traditions which, in urban settings, were shaping popular protests against "economic injustice" when this story was written in the late 1930s, Ab nevertheless has managed, through the exercise of his own primitive intelligence, to make sense of his world, to arrive at a vision of the relations between labor, money, and the beautiful. It's a vision that's miles away from transforming itself into a broadly historical account of capital accumulation. Ab Snopes can't frame a theory to himself about, say, proletarian enslavement; he has no language in which to imagine a class solidarity leading to political action aimed at securing justice and truth. Indeed, he would explode at the notion that considerations of truth and justice have any pertinence either to the interests of the authorities opposing him or to his own interests in defying them. ("Later, twenty years later, [Sarty] was to tell himself, 'If I had said they wanted only truth, justice, he would have hit me again.'") For Ab Snopes the only principle lending significance to his war with the de Spains of this world is that of blood loyalty — determination to beat your personal enemy if you can and keep faith, at all costs, with your clan.

Yet despite all this, Ab does see that part of the power of the beautiful and the orderly to command our respect depends upon our refusal to remind ourselves that they have been brought into existence by other people's labor — by effort that often in history has been slave labor and has seldom been fairly recompensed. Sarty Snopes, grown up, presumably arrives finally at an understanding both that his father's situation was one of economic oppression and that the oppressors, when sitting in a court of law, are capable of attempting to reach beyond selfishness to a decent distribution of justice. But his father had, at the time, no grip on any of this.

Yet Ab is not a fool, and brutality and insensitivity are not the only features of character that we can make out in him. What we need also to summon is the terrible frustration of an undeveloped mind — aware of the weight of an immense unfairness, aware of the habit of the weak perpetually to behave as though the elegance, grace, beauty, and order found often in the neighborhoods of the rich somehow were traceable exclusively to the superior nature of the rich — and yet unable to move forward from either awareness to anything approaching rational protest. His rage cannot become a force leading toward any positive principle; it has no way to express itself except in viciousness to those closest at hand. It can't begin to make a serious bid for admiration, because whatever inclination we might have to admire it is instantly crossed by repugnance at the cruelty inherent in it.

But it remains true that, together with the ignorance and brutality in Ab Snopes, there is a ferocious, primitive undeceivedness in his reading of the terms of the relationship between rich and poor, lucky and unlucky, advantaged and disadvantaged. Ab Snopes has seen a portion of the truth of the world that many on his level, and most who are luckier, never see. We can damn him for allowing that truth to wreck his humanity, but when we fully bring him to life as a character, it's impossible not to include with our indictment a sense of pity.

From *Close Imagining: An Introduction to Literature*

CONSIDERATIONS FOR CRITICAL THINKING AND WRITING

1. DeMott acknowledges Abner's ignorance and brutality, but he also presents him as a man who suffers injustices. What are those injustices? Discuss whether you think they warrant a more balanced assessment of Abner's character.

2. Why doesn't Abner protest his "oppression" (para. 4)? Given DeMott's perspective on him, how might Abner—in another story—have been the hero rather than a terrible source of conflict?

3. To what extent can DeMott's approach to Abner's circumstances be described as a Marxist perspective? (For a discussion of Marxist criticism see pp. 1545-46.)

GAYLE EDWARD WILSON (B. 1931)

The following analysis combines psychology and myth as a means of understanding the conflicts in "Barn Burning." The "Apollonian man" alluded to in the discussion (para. 1) refers to the myth of Apollo and implies a person who values order, community, balance, and self-knowledge to establish true relations between the individual and his world.

Conflict in "Barn Burning" 1990

Ruth Benedict's descriptions of two major patterns of culture provide an advantageous starting point for a discussion of the way in which Faulkner develops the content of "Barn Burning." The Paranoid way of life, she comments, has "no political organization. In a strict sense it has no legality."[1] As a consequence of the Paranoid man's adherence to this life-style, he is "lawless," and is feared as a warrior who will hesitate "at no treachery" (p. 121). In such a culture, "every man's hand is against every other man," and as a result each man relies upon blood ties to form social alliances and to sanction his actions (pp. 122-23). The Apollonian man, on the other hand, "keeps to the middle of the road, stays within the known map," and strives to fulfill his civic role in terms of the expectations of the community at large (p. 70). Men in such a society, although the blood tie is relatively important as a bond, turn to the community and its collected wisdom, as it is embodied in the law, for the approval of their actions and for their security. Thus the sanction for a man's "acts comes from the formal structure, not the individual" (p. 99)—from the community, not the blood kin. In "Barn Burning" Faulkner develops the ideas contained in these descriptions of dissimilar life-styles in a way which creates the central tension in the story and keeps it constantly before the reader. The reader is thus made aware of the pervasiveness of Sarty's *"terror and the grief, the being pulled two ways like between two teams of horses."*

[1] *Patterns of Culture* (New York, 1959), p. 122.

The tension is made evident by the presence of effects which follow from actions taken in accord with the dominant characteristic of each life-style. Abner's "wolflike independence . . . his latent ravening ferocity . . . [and] conviction in the rightness of his own actions," which have frequently manifested themselves in acts of destruction against the property of an established community, clearly mark him as a follower of the Paranoid way. As such, his actions inevitably, and repeatedly, alienate him from each settled society into which he moves. His disregard for a "formal structure" of any kind is indicated by such a minor detail as that which occurs when Abner fuels his fire with "a rail lifted from a nearby fence and cut into lengths," an act which is symbolic of his rejection of any societally imposed limits. It is by burning barns, however, that Abner's Paranoid life-style and its consequences are most forcefully dramatized. At Abner's trial for barn burning, Sarty sees the men "between himself and the table part and become a lane of grim faces." Abner and Sarty then walk between the "two lines of grim-faced men" and they leave a "quiet crowd of grimly watching men." This separation of the Snopes family from the larger society as a consequence of acts motivated by Abner's "ravening ferocity" is underscored by the Justice's command to Abner: "Take your wagon and get out of this country before dark." The Snopes's wagon, containing "the sorry residue of the dozen and more movings," becomes, therefore, a symbol of the transient and nomadic way of life which the Snopes family is forced to adopt because of Abner's adherence to the Paranoid way. The de Spain tenant house and the manner in which the Snopes family lives in it are also effects of a life-style which is not concerned with permanence or order or boundaries or limits. The house is a "paintless two-room" structure "identical almost with the dozen others" in which the family has lived as a result of its nomadic existence, and the members of the family are found "scattered without order or claim up and down the two rooms."

On the other hand, the Harris and de Spain barns represent productivity and fertility, permanence and continuity, because they house the equipment, stock, and seed by which a society produces the goods to sustain and perpetuate itself. A barn and its contents are the effects of a society which is built upon the willingness of men to subordinate their unfettered desires to a communal consensus in order to develop a permanent community. The importance of a barn to the Apollonian way is illustrated by Sarty's thoughts when he sees the effect brought about by what a barn symbolizes. When he comes upon the de Spain house for the first time, he feels that "*the spell*" of "*peace and dignity*" cast by the magnificent house will render "*even the barns and stable and cribs which belong to it impervious to the puny flames he* [Abner] *might contrive.*" The sight of this apotheosis of the Apollonian way has a profound effect on Sarty: he "at that instant . . . forgot his father. . . ." It is most revealing that Sartoris should compare this house which symbolizes the "*peace and dignity*" of the Apollonian way with another kind of building which, because of what it represents, embodies the very essence of an ordered society: "*Hit's big as a courthouse* he thought quietly, with a surge of peace and joy."

Essentially, it is the concept of law, as symbolized by the de Spain house, that gives Sarty his sense of "peace and joy," for it is the law that provides man with the peace necessary to develop the "formal structure" of a communal, stable society. Without law, as Hobbes tells us, "there is no place for Industry; because the fruit thereof is uncertain: and consequently no Culture of the

Earth; . . . no commodius Building; . . . no Society; and which is worst of all, continuall feare, and danger of violent death; And the life of man, solitary, poore, nasty, brutish, and short."[2] At its best, the law is moderate, even, and impartial. It protects as well as punishes; it is an elaborately worked out system designed to join men together in a common purpose, to insure the presumption of innocence until guilt is proved, and to make the punishment commensurate with the crime. In "Barn Burning" the primacy of the law in an Apollonian society is made quite evident. It is represented in a minor way by the contract in which Snopes engages with de Spain to work for eight months in return for a share of the crop. It is developed in a major way in the two trials which take place. In the first trial, the law protects Abner from unwarranted conclusions. Concerning the charge that Abner burned Harris's barn, the Justice asks Harris, "But what proof have you, Mr. Harris?" Harris tells of the Negro who appeared and gave him the cryptic message, "'wood and hay kin burn,'" to which the Justice replies, "But that's not proof. Don't you see that's not proof?" In the second trial, de Spain's unreasonable assessment of twenty bushels of corn in payment for the rug Abner ruined is not allowed. Abner is fined ten bushels, not twenty, as de Spain had wanted. For the men in "Barn Burning," . . . then, the law and its equitable application to all men is the *sine qua non* of the Apollonian way. . . . It is this belief in the law and its extensions of "justice" and "civilization" which guides and controls the behavior of the Apollonian man. This is the same realization that young Sarty is only able to articulate "twenty years" after Abner strikes him for not being willing to lie in his defense at the trial. "'If I had said they only wanted truth, justice, he would have hit me again.'"

From *Mississippi Quarterly*

[2] Chapter XIII, "*Of the NATURAL CONDITION of Mankind, as concerning their Felicity, and Misery*," *Leviathan* . . . (1651) in *Seventeenth-Century Verse and Prose*, ed. Helen White, Ruth Wallerstein, and Ricardo Quintana (New York, 1967), I, 223.

CONSIDERATIONS FOR CRITICAL THINKING AND WRITING

1. What distinctions are drawn between the "Paranoid man" and the "Apollonian man" (para. 1)? How do these two different types frame the conflicts in "Barn Burning"?

2. How is Snopes's wagon an appropriate symbol of the "Paranoid way" (para. 1), and how are the Harris and de Spain barns fitting symbols of the "Apollonian way" (para. 3)?

3. In an essay explain why you think Sarty chooses one way of life over the other at the end of the story.

4. Compare Wilson's description of the story's conflicts with Hiles's and DeMott's.

JAMES FERGUSON (B. 1928)

Ferguson's formalist approach (see pp. 1538–40 in Chapter 46, "Critical Strategies for Reading") relates Faulkner's use of point of view to his thematic concerns in the story.

Narrative Strategy in "Barn Burning"   1991

The point of view is largely limited to the consciousness of Sarty Snopes, but in spite of his sensitivity and his intuitive sense of right and wrong, the little boy is far too young to understand his father and the complexities of the moral choice he must make. To enhance the pathos of his situation and the drama of Sarty's initiation into life, Faulkner felt the need for the occasional intrusion of an authorial voice giving the reader insights far beyond the capabilities of the youthful protagonist. A passage, for example, about the fires Abner Snopes builds affords us a sense of the rationale for the man's actions, of his strangely perverse integrity, which could not be supplied to us by the consciousness of his son:

> The nights were still cool and they had a fire against it, of a rail lifted from a nearby fence and cut into lengths — a small fire, neat, niggard almost, a shrewd fire; such fires were his father's habit and custom always, even in freezing weather. Older, the boy might have remarked this and wondered why not a big one; why should not a man who had not only seen the waste and extravagance of war, but who had in his blood an inherent voracious prodigality with material not his own, have burned everything in sight? Then he might have gone a step farther and thought that that was the reason: that niggard blaze was the living fruit of nights passed during those four years in the woods hiding from all men, blue or gray, with his strings of horses (captured horses, he called them). And older still, he might have divined the true reason: that the element of fire spoke to some deep mainspring of his father's being, as the element of steel or of powder spoke to other men, as the one weapon for the preservation of integrity, else breath were not worth the breathing, and hence to be regarded with respect and used with discretion.

Again, near the end of the story, after Sarty has betrayed his father, there is another brief shift away from the consciousness of the protagonist:

> "He was brave!" he cried suddenly, aloud but not loud, no more than a whisper: "He was! He was in the war! He was in Colonel Sartoris' cav'ry!" not knowing that his father had gone to that war a private in the fine old European sense, wearing no uniform, admitting the authority of and giving fidelity to no man or army or flag, going to war as Malbrouck himself did: for booty — it meant nothing and less than nothing to him if it were enemy booty or his own.

"Barn Burning" is incomparably richer than it would have been without such additions not only because they supply us with ironies otherwise unavailable to us but also because these manipulations of point of view dramatize *on the level of technique* the thematic matter of the story. The tensions between the awareness of the boy and the information supplied us by the authorial voice undergird and emphasize the conflicts between youth and age, innocence and sophistication, intuition and abstraction, decency and corruption, all of which lie at the core of the work.

From *Faulkner's Short Fiction*

CONSIDERATIONS FOR CRITICAL THINKING AND WRITING

1. In the first passage quoted by Ferguson how does the narrator's analysis of Abner Snopes become progressively sophisticated in explaining his reasons for building a small fire?

2. What other examples of shifts away from the consciousness of Sarty to a more informed point of view can you find in the story? Choose what you judge to be a significant example and write an essay about how Faulkner's use of point of view contributes to the story's themes.

Questions for Writing

INCORPORATING THE CRITICS

The following questions can help you to incorporate materials from critical essays into your own writing about a literary work. You may initially feel intimidated by the prospect of responding to the arguments of professional critics in your own paper. However, the process will not defeat you if you have clearly formulated your own response to the literary work and are able to distinguish it from the critics' perspectives. Reading the critics can help you to develop your own thesis — perhaps, to cite just two examples, by using them as supporting evidence or by arguing with them in order to clarify or qualify their points about the literary work. As you write and discover how to advance your thesis, you'll find yourself participating in a dialogue with the critics. This sort of conversation will help you to improve your thinking and hone your argument.

Keep in mind that the work of professional critics is a means of enriching your understanding of a literary work rather than a substitution for your own analysis and interpretation of that work. Quoting, paraphrasing, or summarizing a critic's perspective does not relieve you of the obligation of choosing a topic, organizing information, developing a thesis, and arguing your point of view by citing sufficient evidence from the text you are examining. These matters are discussed in further detail in Chapter 47, "Reading and Writing." You should also be familiar with the methods for documenting sources that are explained in Chapter 48, "The Literary Research Paper"; this chapter also contains important information about how to avoid plagiarism.

No doubt you won't find all literary criticism equally useful: some critics' arguments won't address your own areas of concern; some will be too difficult for you to get a handle on; and some will seem wrongheaded. However, much of the criticism you read will make a literary work more accessible and interesting to you, and disagreeing with others' arguments often helps you develop your own ideas about a work. When you use the work of critics in your own writing, you should consider the following questions. Responding to these questions will help you to ensure that you have a clear understanding of what a critic is arguing about a work, to what extent you agree with that argument, and how you plan to incorporate and respond to the critic's reading in your own paper. The more questions you can ask

Questions for Writing

yourself in response to this list or as a result of your own reading, the more you'll be able to think critically about how you are approaching both the critics and the literary work under consideration.

1. Have you read the literary work carefully and taken notes of your own impressions before reading any critical perspectives so that your initial insights are not lost to the arguments made by the critics? Have you articulated your own responses to the work in a journal entry prior to reading the critics?

2. Are you sufficiently familiar with the literary work that you can determine the accuracy, fairness, and thoroughness of the critic's use of evidence from the work?

3. Have you read the critic's piece carefully? Try summarizing the critic's argument in a brief paragraph. Do you understand the nature and purpose of the critic's argument? Which passages are especially helpful to you? Which seem unclear? Why?

4. Is the critic's reading of the literary work similar to or different from your own reading? Why do you agree or disagree? What generational, historical, cultural, or biographical considerations might help to account for any differences between the critic's responses and your own?

5. How has your reading of the critic influenced your understanding of the literary work? Do issues that previously seemed unimportant now seem significant? What are these issues, and how does a consideration of them affect your reading of the work?

6. Are you too quickly revising or even discarding your own reading because the critic's perspective seems so polished and persuasive? Are you making use of your reading notes and the responses in your journal entries?

7. How would you classify the critic's approach? Through what kind of lens does the critic view the literary work? Is the critical approach formalist, biographical, psychological, sociological, mythological, reader-response, deconstructionist, or some combination of these or possibly other strategies? (For a discussion of these approaches, see Chapter 46, "Critical Strategies for Reading.")

8. What biases, if any, can you detect in the critic's approach? How might, for example, a southern critic's reading of "Barn Burning" differ from a northern critic's?

9. Can you determine how other critics have responded to the critic's work? Is the critic's work cited and taken seriously in other critics' books and articles? Is the work dated by having been superseded by subsequent studies?

10. Are any passages or topics that you deem important left out by the critic? Do these omissions qualify or refute the critic's argument?

11. What judgments does the critic seem to make about the work? Is the work regarded, for example, as significant, unified, representative, trivial, inept, or irresponsible? Do you agree with these judgments?

continued

If not, can you develop and support a thesis about your difference of opinion?

12. What important disagreements do critics reveal in their approaches to the work? Do you find one perspective more convincing than another? Why? Is there a way of resolving their conflicting views that could serve as a thesis for your paper?

13. Can you extend or qualify the critic's argument to matters in the literary text that are not covered by the critic's perspective? Will this allow you to develop your own topic while acknowledging the critic's useful insights?

14. Have you quoted, paraphrased, or summarized the critic accurately and fairly? Have you avoided misrepresenting the critic's arguments in any way?

15. Are the critic's words, ideas, opinions, and insights adequately acknowledged and documented in the correct format? Do you understand the difference between common knowledge and plagiarism? Have you avoided quoting excessively? Are the quotations smoothly integrated into your own text?

16. Are you certain that your incorporation of the critic's work is for the purpose of developing your paper's thesis rather than for name-dropping or padding your paper? How can you explain to yourself why the critic's work is useful for your argument?

A SAMPLE STUDENT PAPER

The Fires of Class Conflict in William Faulkner's "Barn Burning" (excerpt)

The following excerpt consists of the first few paragraphs of a paper in which the student develops a thesis based on her reading of critical perspectives by Benjamin DeMott (p. 432) and Gayle Edward Wilson (p. 434). Sonia Metzger uses the two critics' different approaches to "Barn Burning" to develop a thesis that goes beyond either critic's perspective. The rest of her paper (not included) argues her thesis that a recognition of the class conflicts suppressed by Faulkner in the story makes Abner Snopes's violent response to the economic power inherent in Major de Spain's Apollonian values appear to be justifiable, rather than merely the desperate activity of a Paranoid man. Abner has good reason to fear Apollonian values because de Spain's world is carefully constructed to exclude him while simultaneously exploiting him.

Sonia Metzger

Professor Wolf

English 109

April 15, 2008

The Fires of Class Conflict in

William Faulkner's "Barn Burning"

The central conflict in William Faulkner's "Barn Burning" concerns a

young boy named Sarty Snopes who must choose between loyalty to his

father and his family and loyalty to society and humanity. A first reading of

the story probably leaves most readers with the sense that the boy must turn

away from his father's vicious sensibilities if he is to grow into a responsible

adult. Sarty faces tremendous pressure from his father to lie in court so that

his father will not be convicted of barn burning. He knows his father wants

him "to stick to your own blood or you ain't going to have any blood to stick

to you" (Faulkner 420).

> Thesis identifying conflict of story, supported with textual evidence

Unlike the selfish, mean, vengeful father who despises the wealth and

gentility of the southern aristocracy and is relentless in his contempt for the

upper-class world of Major de Spain, Sarty is a gentle, vulnerable character

who engages our sympathy. He is divided between wanting his father's love

and loving the "peace and dignity" (421) that de Spain's house evokes within

him. Gayle Edward Wilson, one of the critics I've read, mostly agrees with

this view of the story's conflict, but Benjamin DeMott goes beyond the focus

on Sarty's conflicted conscience to examine another, more subtle dimension

of the story--the reasons for Abner Snopes's ferocious rejection of the world

he wants to burn down.

> Writer's analysis of central character and conflict

> Identification of two critics' views of conflict

Our understanding of Abner and his son is, according to Wilson, deep-

ened by employing two concepts from Ruth Benedict's Patterns of Culture

that she calls the "Paranoid man" and the "Apollonian man" (434). Abner is

a version of the Paranoid man. His culture consists of a lawless, clannish,

fierce world in which his nomadic, lonely existence is characterized by vio-

lence, hatred, force, and destruction. Except for blood ties, he rejects forms

of any kind: the stability created by the Apollonian man (Major de Spain)

through law and order in a community is his enemy. He will not be bound

> Analysis of critics' views, set in contrast to each other

by any societal regulations; instead, he destroys any sense of community through his barn burning and his erratic antisocial behavior. For Wilson, Sarty must turn away from the Paranoid man to the Apollonian man if he is to pledge his loyalty to justice and civilization (436). This conflict is also recognized by Benjamin DeMott, who acknowledges Abner's harshness, cruelty, destructiveness, paranoia, and coldness but who also raises an important question that shifts some of our focus from Sarty onto Abner: "Is there anything to be made of Ab Snopes except a person whose raging malevolence has badly stunted if not crippled his humanity?" (432).

By considering when "Barn Burning" was written--during the depression of the late 1930s--DeMott suggests a kind of defense for understanding and even sympathizing with Abner by pointing to issues of class and power embedded in the capitalistic culture and the nearly slave-labor conditions endured by Abner. This version of Abner is not merely brutish but also suffering from "the terrible frustration of an undeveloped mind--aware of the weight of an immense unfairness . . . and yet unable to move forward . . . to anything approaching rational protest" (DeMott 433). DeMott suggests that Abner warrants our pity rather than total repudiation and that he, however imperfectly, does feel (even if he doesn't comprehend) the pain produced by the miserable gap between the rich and the poor. With this gap in mind, I want to go further than DeMott goes and argue, using Wilson's categories, that Faulkner's portrayal of Apollonian values avoids confronting the economic oppression that Abner experiences but that neither he nor Sarty can articulate. Abner may fit much of the description associated with the Paranoid man, but there are important social reasons for his rightfully fearing the economic power of the Apollonian man.

Writer's response to critics' views

Metzger 3

Works Cited

DeMott, Benjamin. "Abner Snopes as a Victim of Class." The Compact Bedford
    Introduction to Literature. Ed. Michael Meyer. 8th ed. Boston:
    Bedford/St. Martin's, 2009. 432–33.

Faulkner, William. "Barn Burning." The Compact Bedford Introduction to
    Literature. Ed. Michael Meyer. 8th ed. Boston: Bedford/St. Martin's,
    2009. 418–29.

Wilson, Gayle Edward. "Conflict in 'Barn Burning.'" The Compact Bedford
    Introduction to Literature. Ed. Michael Meyer. 8th ed. Boston:
    Bedford/St. Martin's, 2009. 434–36.

SUGGESTED TOPICS FOR LONGER PAPERS

1. Write a character analysis of Abner Snopes. Does he change or develop through the course of the story? Do you identify with him in any way? Think about whether you might characterize his behavior as criminal, insane, or heroic.

2. A great many articles and portions of books have been written about "Barn Burning." Scan these sources to get an overview of the kinds of critical approaches that have been applied to the story, and write a selective survey of how criticism about "Barn Burning" has evolved over the past three or four decades. Which approaches seem the most useful and revealing to you?

Web Research William Faulkner or take quizzes on his works at bedfordstmartins.com/ meyercompact.

14

A THEMATIC CASE STUDY
The Literature of the South

The Southern writer is forced from all sides to make his gaze extend beyond the surface, beyond mere problems, until it touches that realm which is the concern of prophets and poets.
— FLANNERY O'CONNOR

What had I got out of living in the South? . . . All my life I had been full of hunger for a new way to live.
— RICHARD WRIGHT

This chapter provides a variety of materials that are thematically related to the American South. Theme — the central or dominant idea in a literary work — provides a unifying point around which literary elements such as plot, character, setting, and point of view are organized. For a detailed discussion of theme and some strategies for determining theme, see Chapter 8.

The documents that follow are offered as a means of supplementing and contextualizing the short stories by southern writers or about southern life reprinted in this anthology. (A list of nine such stories appears below.) Taken together, they compose a small anthology that furnishes an opportunity to read intensely fiction that is thematically related to the South. The stories range from the nineteenth to the twenty-first centuries, and the authors include Mark Twain, William Faulkner, Flannery O'Connor, Ralph Ellison, and Alice Walker.

Readers of southern literature have found the region and its literary production fascinating owing to its complexity, variety, and resonance. As O'Connor explains it in *Mystery and Manners,* "We in the South live in a society that is rich in contradiction, rich in irony, rich in contrast, and particularly rich in speech." The South, owing to the issues associated with the Civil War, is a curious study: it is at once peculiarly American and distinct from the rest of the country. Secession was not only a political act but also a state of mind. The materials in this chapter amply explore topics related to southern identities and shed light on the southern short stories in this anthology. The documents range from attempts to define southern culture by such cultural critics as W. J. Cash and Irving Howe to observations about southern writing by such writers as O'Connor and Margaret Walker. In addition, photographs, paintings, and other works of art provide visual representations of southern life. These materials furnish a ready context for grasping southern themes in fiction and offer a deeper pleasure and understanding of the short stories.

Related short stories
Ralph Ellison, "Battle Royal," p. 243
William Faulkner, "A Rose for Emily," p. 90
William Faulkner, "Barn Burning," p. 418
Flannery O'Connor, "A Good Man Is Hard to Find," p. 367
Flannery O'Connor, "Good Country People," p. 378
Flannery O'Connor, "Revelation," p. 392
Katherine Anne Porter, "The Witness," p. 558

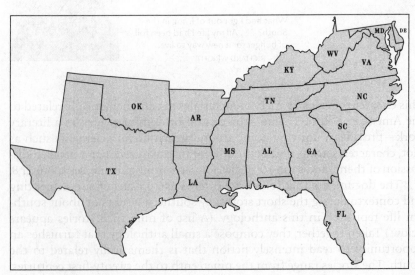

U.S. Bureau of the Census, "The South."

Lee Smith, "The Happy Memories Club," p. 481

Mark Twain, "The Story of the Good Little Boy," p. 494

JOHN SHELTON REED AND DALE VOLBERG REED

Definitions of the South   *1996*

In 1787 Charles Pinckney said, "When I say Southern, I mean Maryland, and the states to the southward of her." But it's not that simple now, if it ever was. Here are three of the most common definitions, and what's wrong with them.

1. *Below the Mason-Dixon Line* once meant south of the Pennsylvania-Maryland boundary, surveyed in the 1760s by two Englishmen, Charles Mason and Jeremiah Dixon. The line gained significance in the nineteenth century when all of the states north of it had abolished slavery. "Below the Mason-Dixon Line" came to mean "in the South," and it has kept that meaning in innumerable popular and country songs as well as in common speech. But the only recent definition of the South that uses the real Mason-Dixon line as a boundary is —

2. *The Bureau of the Census definition.* The Census Bureau's South includes West Virginia, Maryland, Delaware, and the District of Columbia, as well as Oklahoma and twelve less questionable states. (But it doesn't simply include all of the 1860 slave states and territories: Missouri's not in it.) Few other definitions of the South are that inclusive. These days most stop at the Potomac, and even the southern suburbs of Washington are known in some circles as "occupied Virginia." Generally speaking, the "Census South" is more urban, richer, and better educated than the actual South. It also has more armed robbery, AIDS, and lawyers.

3. *The Confederate States* sounds like a simple definition, but unfortunately it's not. Kentucky and Missouri both had stars in the Confederate flag and representatives in Richmond as well as in Washington. And the Confederacy never recognized West Virginia's "secession from secession." Oklahoma's Cherokees signed a treaty with the Confederacy and many fought in its army: Oklahoma wasn't a state, but was it Confederate? The Stars and Bars flew briefly over Santa Fe, New Mexico: does that count?

Maybe the best definition is just —

4. *Where people think they're in the South.* You want to tell them they're wrong?

CONSIDERATIONS AND CONNECTIONS TO ANOTHER SELECTION

1. How does the Reeds' discussion of what constitutes the South complicate the definitions that they describe?

2. Do you think the Reeds' "best definition" of the South is superior to the others, or simply an acknowledgment that the South cannot be defined satisfactorily in geographic terms? Explain your answer.

3. How does your own definition of the South compare with the Reeds'?

W. J. CASH (1900–1941)
The Old and the New South   *1941*

What the Old South of the legend in its classical form was like is more or less
familiar to everyone. It was a sort of stage piece out of the eighteenth century,
wherein gesturing gentlemen move soft-spokenly against a background of rose
gardens and dueling grounds, through always gallant deeds, and lovely ladies,
in farthingales, never for a moment lost that exquisite remoteness which has
been the dream of all men and the possession of none. Its social pattern was
manorial, its civilization that of the Cavalier, its ruling class an aristocracy
coextensive with the planter group — men often entitled to quarter the royal
arms of St. George and St. Andrew on their shields, and in every case descended from the old gentlefolk who for many centuries had made up the ruling classes of Europe.

They dwelt in large and stately mansions, preferably white and with
columns and Grecian entablature. Their estates were feudal baronies, their
slaves quite too numerous ever to be counted, and their social life a thing of
Old World splendor and delicacy. What had really happened here, indeed, was
that the gentlemanly idea, driven from England by Cromwell,° had taken
refuge in the South and fashioned for itself a world to its heart's desire: a world
singularly polished and mellow and poised, wholly dominated by ideals of
honor and chivalry and *noblesse*° — all those sentiments and values and habits
of action which used to be, especially in Walter Scott,° invariably assigned to
the gentleman born and the Cavalier.

Beneath these was a vague race lumped together indiscriminately as the
poor whites — very often, in fact, as the "white-trash." These people belonged
in the main to a physically inferior type, having sprung from the most part
from the convict servants, redemptioners, and debtors of old Virginia and
Georgia, with a sprinkling of the most unsuccessful sort of European peasants
and farm laborers and the dregs of the European town slums. And so, of
course, the gulf between them and the master classes was impassable, and
their ideas and feelings did not enter into the make-up of the prevailing
Southern civilization.

But in the legend of the New South, the Old South is supposed to have
been destroyed by the Civil War and the thirty years that followed it, to have
been swept both socially and mentally into the limbo of things that were and
are not, to give place to a society which has been rapidly and increasingly
industrialized and modernized both in body and in mind — which now, indeed, save for a few quaint survivals and gentle sentimentalities and a few
shocking and inexplicable brutalities such as lynching, is almost as industrialized and modernized in its outlook as the North. Such an idea is obviously
inconsistent with the general assumption of the South's great difference, but
paradox is the essence of popular thinking, and millions — even in the South
itself — placidly believe in both notions.

Cromwell: Oliver Cromwell, politician and military leader (1599–1658) in the English Civil
War; parliamentary forces defeated the royalists (known as Cavaliers).
noblesse: Nobility.
Walter Scott: Scottish novelist (1771–1832).

Metro-Goldwyn-Mayer's *Gone with the Wind* (1939). Vivien Leigh stars as the heroine Scarlett O'Hara in the epic motion picture based on Margaret Mitchell's best-selling 1936 novel of the Old South, the story of a southern belle seeking love and refuge during the tumultuous years of the Civil War and Reconstruction, who ultimately returns to her family's beloved plantation. Though hugely popular, the book and film were criticized by audiences of their time for glorifying slavery and stereotyping African Americans. How does this image reflect W. J. Cash's description of the "Old South"?
© John Springer Collection/CORBIS.

   These legends, however, bear little relation to reality. There was an Old South, to be sure, but it was another thing than this. And there is a New South. Industrialization and commercialization have greatly modified the land, including its ideology. . . . Nevertheless, the extent of the change and of the break between the Old South that was and the South of our time has been vastly exaggerated. The South, one might say, is a tree with many age rings, with its limbs and trunk bent and twisted by all the winds of the years, but with its tap root in the Old South. Or, better still, it is like one of those churches one sees in England. The façade and towers, the windows and clerestory, all the exterior and superstructure are late Gothic of one sort or another, but look into its nave, its aisles, and its choir and you find the old mighty Norman arches of the twelfth century. And if you look into its crypt, you may even find stones cut by Saxon, brick made by Roman hands.

   The mind of the section, that is, is continuous with the past. And its primary form is determined not nearly so much by industry as by the purely agricultural conditions of that past. So far from being modernized, in many ways it has actually always marched away, as to this day it continues to do, from the present toward the past.

The Old Plantation Home. This lithograph, created in 1872 by the popular firm of Currier and Ives, presents a romanticized, postwar view of life on the plantation. In this mythic image, slaves are portrayed as happy children and the plantation as a benevolent, familial institution. How does this image relate to Cash's arguments about the "Old" and "New" South?
Reprinted Courtesy of the Library of Congress.

CONSIDERATIONS AND CONNECTIONS TO OTHER SELECTIONS

1. What is the paradox that Cash observes in popular descriptions of how the Old South evolved into the New South? How does he resolve that paradox?

2. Explain how the class distinctions between southern gentility and "white trash" described by Cash are at the center of the conflict in Faulkner's "Barn Burning" (p. 418).

3. What do you think Cash means when he writes that the mind of the South "is continuous with the past"? How is this idea presented in Katherine Anne Porter's "The Witness" (p. 558)?

4. How does the still from *Gone with the Wind* evoke "the Old South of the legend" as described by Cash? How is that myth further extended in the Currier and Ives print *The Old Plantation Home*?

IRVING HOWE (1920–1993)

The Southern Myth

1951

Until very recently, regional consciousness has remained stronger in the South than in any other part of the United States. This "historical lag" is the source of whatever is most distinctive in Southern thought and feeling. After its defeat in the Civil War, the South could not participate fully and freely in the "normal" development of American society—that is, industrialism and large-scale capitalism arrived there later and with far less force than in the North or West. By the Reconstruction period New England regional consciousness was in decline and by the turn of the century the same was probably true for the Midwest; but the South, because it was a pariah region or because its recalcitrance in defeat forced the rest of the nation to treat it as such, felt its sectional identity most acutely during the very decades when the United States was becoming a self-conscious nation. While the other regions meekly submitted to dissolution, the South worked desperately to keep itself intact. Through an exercise of the will, it insisted that the regional memory be the main shaper of its life.

Perhaps because it had so little else to give its people, the South nurtured in them a generous and often obsessive sense of the past. The rest of the country might be committed to commercial expansion or addicted to the notion of progressive optimism, but the South, even if it cared to, was unable to accept these dominant American values; it had been left behind, it was living on the margin of history—a position that often provides the sharpest perspective on history. During the decades that followed the defeat of the South, its writers could maintain a relation to American life comparable, in miniature, to the relation in the nineteenth century between Russian writers and European life. For while nineteenth-century Russia was the most backward country on the continent, its writers managed to use that backwardness as a vantage-point from which to observe West-European life and thereby to arrive at a profound and withering criticism of bourgeois morality. Precisely because Russia was trailing the capitalist West, the Russian writers could examine the bourgeois code without hesitation or illusion. It was this crucial advantage of distance, this perspective from the social rear, that was the major dispensation the South could offer its writers.

And it gave them something else: a compact and inescapable subject. The Southern writer did not have to cast about for his materials, he hardly enjoyed a spontaneous choice in his use of them, for they welled within him like a dream recurrent since childhood. Faulkner has given a vivid if somewhat romantic description of this subject in *Intruder in the Dust:*

> . . . For every Southern boy fourteen years old, not once but whenever he wants it, there is the instance when it's still not two o'clock on that July afternoon in 1863, the brigades are in position behind the rail fence, the guns are laid and ready in the woods and the furled flags are already loosened to break out and Pickett himself with his long oiled ringlets and his hat in one hand probably and his sword in the other looking up the hill waiting for Longstreet to give the word and it's all in the balance, it hasn't happened yet, it hasn't even begun . . .

But of course it has happened, it must begin. The basic Southern subject is the defeat of the homeland, though its presentation can vary from the magnolia romancing of *The White Rose of Memphis* to the despairing estimate of social loss in *The Sound and the Fury*. Nor does it matter, for the moment, whether one defines the Southern subject, in Allen Tate's words, as "the destruction by war and the later degradation by carpetbaggers and scalawags, and a consequent lack of moral force and imagination in the cynical materialism of the New South," or as the defeat of a reactionary slaveowning class

The Battle of Gettysburg, 1863, by John Richards. The largest and most decisive battle of the Civil War took place on July 1 through July 3, 1863, in Gettysburg, Pennsylvania. Here the Union army turned back the last major invasion of the North by General Robert E. Lee's Army of Northern Virginia. Losses were heavy on both sides — more than 51,000 soldiers were killed in a mere three days, making Gettysburg the war's bloodiest battle. It is this battle that Faulkner refers to in *Intruder in the Dust.* (See page 451.)

© Bettman/CORBIS.

followed by its partial recapture of power through humiliating alliances with Northern capital and a new scrofulous commercial class of local origin. Regardless of which interpretation one accepts, the important point is that this subject, like a thick cloud of memory, has been insistently and implacably *there.* The Southern writer could romanticize it, reject it, enlarge it into an image of the general human situation; he could not escape it. And precisely this ubiquity of subject matter provided him with some very considerable advantages. Not so long before the Civil War, Hawthorne had remarked that "No author can conceive of the difficulty of writing a romance about a country where there is no shadow, no antiquity, no picturesque and gloomy wrong, not anything but a commonplace prosperity." But now the War and Reconstruction gave the Southern writers all that Hawthorne had found lacking: all but antiquity. And there were ruins to take the place of that.

CONSIDERATIONS AND CONNECTIONS TO OTHER SELECTIONS

1. In what sense, according to Howe, was the South "left behind" the rest of the country, and how did that affect the region's perceptions of itself?

2. Explain how the South's memory of the Civil War is woven into the plot of William Faulkner's "A Rose for Emily" (p. 90). How is this memory related to the story's theme?

3. Choose any of the stories about the South listed on pages 446–47 and explain how "regional memory" is central to its setting and theme.

4. How does the painting *The Battle of Gettysburg* (p. 452) serve as an illustration of Howe's point about the South's relationship to its own past?

FLANNERY O'CONNOR (1925–1964)

The Regional Writer   1963

The present state of the South is one wherein nothing can be taken for granted, one in which our identity is obscured and in doubt. In the past, the things that have seemed to many to make us ourselves have been very obvious things, but now no amount of nostalgia can make us believe they will characterize us much longer. Prophets have already been heard to say that in twenty years there'll be no such thing as Southern literature. It will be ironical indeed if the Southern writer has discovered he can live in the South and the Southern audience has become aware of its literature just in time to discover that being Southern is relatively meaningless, and that soon there is going to be precious little difference in the end-product whether you are a writer from Georgia or a writer from Hollywood, California.

It's in these terms that the Georgia part of being a Georgia writer has some positive significance.

It is not a matter of so-called local color, it is not a matter of losing our peculiar quaintness. Southern identity is not really connected with mocking-birds and beaten biscuits and white columns any more than it is with hookworm and bare feet and muddy clay roads. Nor is it necessarily shown forth in the antics of our politicians, for the development of power obeys strange laws of its own. An identity is not to be found on the surface; it is not accessible to the poll-taker; it is not something that *can* become a cliché. It is not made from the mean average or the typical, but from the hidden and often the most extreme. It is not made from what passes, but from those qualities that endure, regardless of what passes, because they are related to truth. It lies very deep. In its entirety, it is known only to God, but of those who look for it, none gets so close as the artist.

The best American fiction has always been regional. The ascendancy passed roughly from New England to the Midwest to the South; it has passed to and stayed longest wherever there has been a shared past, a sense of alikeness, and the possibility of reading a small history in a universal light. In these things the South still has a degree of advantage. It is a slight degree and getting slighter, but it is a degree of kind as well as of intensity, and it is enough to feed great literature if our people — whether they be newcomers or have roots here — are enough aware of it to foster its growth in themselves.

CONSIDERATIONS AND CONNECTIONS TO OTHER SELECTIONS

1. Why do you think O'Connor insists that "the best American fiction has always been regional"? Explain why you agree or disagree.

Trinity — Elvis, Jesus, and Robert E. Lee (1994). The Southern painter Clyde Broadway
(b. 1944) offers a humorous commentary on southern culture, bringing together the popular (Elvis), the sacred (Jesus), and the heroic (Lee), in a work that mimics religious votive
painting. Flannery O'Connor once wrote: "the South . . . is most certainly Christ-haunted.
The Southerner, who isn't convinced of it, is very much afraid that he may have been
formed in the image and likeness of God. Ghosts can be very fierce and instructive. They
cast strange shadows, particularly in our literature." Do other figures "haunt" southern
literature?

Gift of the Roger H. Ogden Collection, The Ogden Museum of Southern Arts, University of New Orleans. © 1994,
Clyde Broadway.

2. O'Connor asserts that southern identity is "not made from the mean average or the typical, but from the hidden and often the most extreme." How
   is this idea manifested in O'Connor's "A Good Man Is Hard to Find"
   (p. 367), "Good Country People" (p. 378), or "Revelation" (p. 392)?

3. To what extent is a southern regional identity present in Lee Smith's "The
   Happy Memories Club" (p. 481)? Discuss whether you think Lee's story
   illustrates O'Connor's concern that being southern will become "relatively
   meaningless."

4. Consider the satiric painting *Trinity — Elvis, Jesus, and Robert E. Lee* (above) as
   a possible example of how, according to O'Connor, southern identity is
   formed. Explain why you think she would or would not regard this painting as an accurate evocation of southern spirituality.

"Bus Station, Colored Waiting Room, Memphis, Tennessee" (ca. 1960s). At age fourteen, Memphis native Ernest C. Withers (b. 1920) began taking pictures documenting the African American experience of the South. This image documents the Jim Crow institutional segregation that would eventually be dismantled by the civil rights movement. Legal segregation in the United States was especially widespread in the South from the 1870s through the 1950s and 1960s. Margaret Walker writes that segregation "separated and polarized" society. Further, it "ostracized the artistic accomplishments of Black people and ignored their literature." © Ernest Withers. Courtesy of the Panopticon Gallery, Waltham, MA.

MARGARET WALKER (1915–1998)

The Southern Writer and Race   *1971*

The southern writer, like all American writers, but perhaps with more intensity, deals largely with race. He or she cannot escape the ever present factor of race and the problems of race as they have grown out of the southern society and affected all of America. The treatment first of the Black man, or the Negro, in southern fiction has been not only the problem of character delineation but also the moral problem of race. The subject of race has been romanticized, and realistically portrayed, and the characters have ranged from wooden stereotypes — flat, mindless, and caricatured as buffoons — to deft and skillful portrayal of both realistic and humanistic proportions. The subject of race has become theme and conflict and character development in southern literature.

Perhaps the single most glaring fault Black Americans find with southern literature by white writers is in the psychology and philosophy, which of necessity in most instances is racist. This has to be understood in terms of the society, the values emphasized in American education, the nature of slavery and

Elizabeth Eckford. On September 4, 1957, following the Supreme Court's decision to desegregate U.S. schools (*Brown v. Board of Education*), fifteen-year-old Elizabeth Eckford and eight
other African American students (known collectively as the Little Rock nine) attempted to
enter Little Rock Central High School. Eckford and her companions were pursued by an
angry mob that kicked and spat at them, and a wall of National Guardsmen, ordered in by
the governor of Arkansas, blocked their entry.
Courtesy of the Library of Congress.

"Sanitation Workers' Strike, Memphis, Tennessee" (1968). Powerful images of the Civil
Rights struggle, such as this famous photograph by Ernest C. Withers, appeared in national
newspapers in the 1950s and 1960s and helped mobilize the movement across the country.
© Ernest Withers. Courtesy of the Panopticon Gallery, Waltham, MA.

segregation, which not only have kept the races apart, separated and polarized in two segregated societies but have ostracized the artistic accomplishments of Black people and ignored their literature. The earliest writers, Black and white, were fighting a racial battle, the white writers were writing apologies for slavery and the Black writers were protesting against the inhumanity of the slave system. With the substitution of segregation, the white child was educated to regard race as more important than humanity and the Black child was educated to imitate a white world as superior to his and thus taught to hate himself. The battle and the conflict can be seen in the literature.

CONSIDERATIONS AND CONNECTIONS TO OTHER SELECTIONS

1. Why does Walker argue that the southern writer "cannot escape the ever present factor of race"?

2. Consider Faulkner's characterization of Tobe in "A Rose for Emily" (p. 90). Using Walker's terms, explain why you think Tobe is a wooden stereotype or a realistic portrayal of a black man.

3. Walker observes that under segregation "the Black child was educated to imitate a white world as superior to his and thus taught to hate himself." How is this dramatized in Ellison's "Battle Royal" (p. 243)?

4. Discuss the relationship between the racial tensions portrayed in the photographs by Ernest C. Withers (pp. 455, 456) and in Ellison's "Battle Royal."

RICHARD WRIGHT (1908–60)
The Ethics of Living Jim Crow   *1937*

My first lesson in how to live as a Negro came when I was quite small. We were living in Arkansas. Our house stood behind the railroad tracks. Its skimpy yard was paved with black cinders. Nothing green ever grew in that yard. The only touch of green we could see was far away, beyond the tracks, over where the white folks lived. But cinders were good enough for me and I never missed the green growing things. And anyhow cinders were fine weapons. You could always have a nice hot war with huge black cinders. All you had to do was crouch behind the brick pillars of a house with your hands full of gritty ammunition. And the first woolly black head you saw pop out from behind another row of pillars was your target. You tried your very best to knock it off. It was great fun.

I never fully realized the appalling disadvantages of a cinder environment till one day the gang to which I belonged found itself engaged in a war with the white boys who lived beyond the tracks. As usual we laid down our cinder barrage, thinking that this would wipe the white boys out. But they replied with a steady bombardment of broken bottles. We doubled our cinder barrage, but they hid behind trees, hedges, and the sloping embankments of their lawns. Having no such fortifications, we retreated to the brick pillars of our homes. During the retreat a broken milk bottle caught me behind the ear, opening a deep gash which bled profusely. The sight of blood pouring over my face completely demoralized our ranks. My fellow-combatants left me

Watching the Good Trains Go By (1964). Romare Bearden (1911–1988) was born in Charlotte, North Carolina, but in 1914 his family joined the Great Migration of southern blacks, moving to the Harlem neighborhood of New York City to seek greater opportunities. Bearden, who visited Charlotte throughout his childhood, said he created art in order to "possess the meaning of his southern childhood and northern upbringing." This collage presents his memories of Charlotte, a center of community activities and a major hub for southern railroads, surrounded by cotton fields and farms. For Bearden, the train, just one of the many images at work in this collage, symbolized black migration after slavery, provided jobs, and clocked time. Like the Beardens, author Richard Wright left the South looking for a better life. Born in Mississippi (1908), the son of an illiterate sharecropper, Wright moved to Chicago, New York, and later, Paris. He is best known for his groundbreaking novel, *Native Son* (1940), which portrayed the dehumanization of blacks in a racist society, and *Black Boy* (1945), an autobiography of his childhood in the South.

standing paralyzed in the center of the yard, and scurried for their homes. A kind neighbor saw me and rushed me to a doctor, who took three stitches in my neck.

I sat brooding on my front steps, nursing my wound and waiting for my mother to come from work. I felt that a grave injustice had been done me. It was all right to throw cinders. The greatest harm a cinder could do was leave a bruise. But broken bottles were dangerous; they left you cut, bleeding, and helpless.

When night fell, my mother came from the white folks' kitchen. I raced down the street to meet her. I could just feel in my bones that she would understand. I knew she would tell me exactly what to do next time. I grabbed her hand and babbled out the whole story. She examined my wound, then slapped me.

"How come yuh didn't hide?" she asked me. "How come yuh awways fightin'?"

I was outraged, and bawled. Between sobs I told her that I didn't have any trees or hedges to hide behind. There wasn't a thing I could have used as a trench. And you couldn't throw very far when you were hiding behind the brick pillars of a house. She grabbed a barrel stave, dragged me home, stripped me naked, and beat me till I had a fever of one hundred and two. She would smack my rump with the stave, and, while the skin was still smarting, impart to me gems of Jim Crow wisdom. I was never to throw cinders any more. I was never to fight any more wars. I was never, never, under any conditions, to fight *white* folks again. And they were absolutely right in clouting me with the broken milk bottle. Didn't I know she was working hard every day in the hot kitchens of the white folks to make money to take care of me? When was I ever going to learn to be a good boy? She couldn't be bothered with my fights. She finished by telling me that I ought to be thankful to God as long as I lived that they didn't kill me.

All that night I was delirious and could not sleep. Each time I closed my eyes I saw monstrous white faces suspended from the ceiling, leering at me.

From that time on, the charm of my cinder yard was gone. The green trees, the trimmed hedges, the cropped lawns grew very meaningful, became a symbol. Even today when I think of white folks, the hard, sharp outlines of white houses surrounded by trees, lawns, and hedges are present somewhere in the background of my mind. Through the years they grew into an overreaching symbol of fear.

It was a long time before I came in close contact with white folks again. . . .

CONSIDERATIONS AND CONNECTIONS TO OTHER SELECTIONS

1. What "lesson in how to live as a Negro" did Wright learn?

2. Compare and contrast the "cinder environment" that Wright describes with the environment of the "white boys who lived beyond the tracks." How does Wright's attitude toward both environments change by the end of the essay?

3. How does Wright's experience as a child in the South connect with Margaret Walker's observations about segregation and the differences between the education of blacks and whites? (See "The Southern Writer and Race," p. 455.)

4. How does the perspective of Wright's mother, as portrayed in this essay, compare with that of the mother in Langston Hughes's poem "Mother to Son" (p. 917)?

DONALD R. NOBLE (B. 1941)

The Future of Southern Writing   1985

[O]ne can assume that [in the future] race will still be a major subject for Southern literature. . . . The stories of gross cruelty, lynching, and brutality will be fewer and give way to more subtle examinations of race relations in an integrated society. Southerners will continue to be a church-going people, but the role of fundamentalist religion will be diminished in the literature ahead as the influence of the church in the community diminishes. The sense of community itself, long understood as an identifying mark of Southern writing, will also be weaker. Strangers are moving in, and now probably not everyone residing in a small town was born there.

Along with this diminution in sense of community, the South seems to be joining the nation in other attitudes as well. There is more non-teleological thinking, for example, less sense of a master plan. The South will not soon be a nest of nihilists or existentialists, but concerns will move from communal to personal; and chaos and disorder that have been depicted in much Southern literature, as in Shakespearean drama, as a rending of the social fabric, a wound to the body politic, will now be seen in personal and domestic terms, not communal ones. Southerners feel increasingly isolated, alienated from their society, albeit less so than New Yorkers or Los Angelenos, perhaps, and this sense of isolation from kin and neighbors will be a theme of future writing.

As a smaller number of Southerners remain on the land, this central relationship will play a smaller part in Southern writing. The characters of the writing of the future will earn their livings not just as farmers or sheriffs or the owners of small businesses, but as professional people, executives with large corporations, as real estate and life insurance salesmen, and the literature will be set more often in offices, factories, suburbs, and country clubs and less in the fields or woods. The characters of future Southern literature will be a more diverse group. Many will have been sent by their corporations; some will have come from Germany or Japan, perhaps, but they will be making their homes in the South. Because many of them will not have Southern accents, and because radio and television are having their effects on regional speech, there will be less dialect in Southern literature. Phonetic spelling and orthographic humor are already nearly dead and will expire. There will still be Southern speech, of course, but it will be rendered more subtly, through the pronunciations of a few chosen words, through expressions and idioms, through the cadence and lilt of particular regions and groups, such as the way a sorority girl's voice rises at the end of each phrase, making it into a question and an appeal for agreement and approval.

A good portion of the Southern literature of the past has been written by women. Before 1930 or so, much of it was sentimental, popular, and second-rate, but after 1930 Welty, O'Connor, and others have stood in the first rank. But in the future an even higher percentage will be by women, and more importantly, it will be more and more about the question of being female. We can surely look for more frank and even angry writing from Southern women who see themselves as having been denied access in the past to educational opportunities, jobs, full freedom, by having been assigned narrow roles or by having been put up on a pedestal too high to jump off.

Without question, a larger share of the literature will be written by blacks. As educational opportunities for blacks continue to improve there will be more writers; as the economic situation for blacks improves there will be more readers. White readers will, of course, buy and learn from black writings, but the creation of a larger market of black readers is bound to help the black writers. There is every sign this is already underway. There are also indications that this black writing will be different in kind. Rather than focusing on the relations between the races, it will be more frank. It will be about family life, status, love, pain, prejudice, *within* the black community, a community that is still a mystery to most whites, in and out of the South.

CONSIDERATIONS AND CONNECTIONS TO OTHER SELECTIONS

1. How does Noble's characterization of the South differ from W. J. Cash's assessment (p. 448)? According to Noble, what has caused the greatest changes in the South?

2. To what extent does Lee Smith's "The Happy Memories Club" (p. 481) illustrate some of the major developments in the South referred to by Noble?

3. Compare any two stories listed on pages 446–47 and discuss the way in which regional speech is rendered. Which rendition of southern dialogue do you prefer? Explain why.

LEE SMITH (B. 1944)
On Southern Change and Permanence   2001

The South was two-thirds rural in the 1930s. Now it is over two-thirds urban. One half of all Southerners were farmworkers in the thirties; now that figure is at 2 percent. And out of those farmworkers in the thirties, one half were tenant farmers. Now we have no tenant farmers, but migrant workers instead.

As the largest metro areas continue to attract people and jobs, the viability of rural life comes increasingly into question. One half of all the new jobs in this country are being created in the South, with nine out of ten of them in Texas, Florida, and a dozen metropolitan areas. . . .

Our Southern birth rate, which used to be famously *above* the national average, is now below it. This means that immigration is defining the South's population. Ten years from now, Texas will have a 57 percent nonwhite population. Florida will have a 54 percent nonwhite population. Some of the "big nine" states that now contain half the U.S. population will be eclipsed by the "New South": Georgia, North Carolina, and Virginia. Among African Americans, there was a great migration out of the South in the twenties, the thirties, and on into the fifties. But in the 1970s more blacks started moving *to* the South — in many instances, back to the South — than leaving it. That trend has now accelerated. . . .

Some things never change. Some Southern food will never go out of style, no matter how much it may get *nouveau*ed. And large parts of the South still look a lot like they used to — the Appalachian coal country where I'm from, for instance, and the old Cotton Belt. As a whole, we Southerners are still religious, and we are still violent. We'll bring you a casserole, but we'll kill you, too. Southern women, both black and white, have always been more likely than Northern women to work outside the home, despite the image projected by such country lyrics as "Get your biscuits in the oven and your buns in the bed, this women's liberation is a-going to your head." It was not because we were so liberated; it's because we were so poor. This, too, is changing: now our per capita income is at 92 percent of the national average.

With all these changes, what should I tell my student, one of my very favorite students, who burst into tears after we attended a reading together at which Elizabeth Spencer read her fine short story entitled "Cousins." "I'll *never* be a Southern writer!" my student wailed. "I don't even *know* my cousins!" Raised in a military household, relocated many times, she had absolutely no sense of place, no sense of past, no sense of family. How did she spend her childhood? I asked. In the mall in Fayetteville, North Carolina, she tearfully confessed, sneaking cigarettes and drinking Cokes.

I told her she was lucky.

But she was also right. For a writer cannot pick her material any more than she can pick her parents; her material is given to her by the circumstances of her birth, by how she first hears language. And if she happens to be Southern, these given factors may already be trite, even before she sits down at her computer to begin. Her neurasthenic, fragile Aunt Lena is already trite, her mean, scary cousin Bobby Lee is already trite, her columned, shuttered house in Natchez is already trite. Far better to start out from the mall in Fayetteville, illicit cigarette in hand, with no cousins to hold her back, and venture forth fearlessly into the New South. . . .

[Storytelling] is the main thing that has not changed about the South, in my opinion — that will never change. We Southerners love a story, and will tell you *anything*. Narrative is as necessary to us as air. We use the story to transmit information as well as to wile away the time. In periods of stress and change, the story becomes even more important. In the telling of it we discover or affirm who we are, why we exist, what we should do. The story brings order and delight. Its form is inherently pleasing, and deeply satisfying to us. Because it has a beginning, middle, and end, it gives a recognizable shape to the muddle and chaos of our lives.

CONSIDERATIONS AND CONNECTIONS TO OTHER SELECTIONS

1. According to Smith, what kind of story do statistics tell about the South?
2. How will Smith's student necessarily differ, as a southern writer, from her predecessors? To what extent can she be a true southern writer?
3. Compare Smith's ideas about the changing nature of the South with Donald R. Noble's views. Do you think they essentially agree or disagree in their assessment of the South? Explain.
4. Choose a Faulkner or O'Connor story from the list on page 446 and discuss whether that story could have been set in the South if it had been written during the past five years.

15

A THEMATIC CASE STUDY
Humor and Satire

[W]hat so many of our beard-tugging critics and the long-suffering students . . . seem to have lost sight of is that stories are meant as entertainment.

—T. CORAGHESSAN BOYLE

Let's get serious: although some austere readers may assume that humor and satire require a rationale or apology, a reading life without laughter would be grimly monochromed and dull. We laugh in color, not just in black and white, because humor is often used as a play of light that allows us to perceive shades of meaning that might otherwise be invisible. Wit, irony, exaggeration, understatement, caricature, parody, and any number of other methods through which a writer opens our eyes to the complexities of human experience illuminate what high seriousness sometimes demands is no laughing matter. Flannery O'Connor's fiction, for example, is heavily freighted with pain, perversity, and tragic attempts at religious salvation, but a responsive reader will also find that her stories include startling humor, despite the presence of murder, a stolen artificial leg, and some lunatic characters (see her three stories in Chapter 12, "A Study of Flannery O'Connor"). Even Herman Melville's weird protagonist in "Bartleby, the Scrivener" (p. 124), who engages in a suicidal withdrawal from life, is invested with a comic dimension. To test this idea, try reading the very brief story that begins this chapter, E. Annie Proulx's "55 Miles to the Gas Pump."

Of course, people don't always agree about what's amusing, owing to their personal sensibilities and experiences. "That's not funny" is a sentiment that commonly measures the difference in varying responses. Humor can open people's eyes, but it can also cause people to shut them if they feel offended by it. A passionate animal-rights advocate might find T. Coraghessan Boyle's satiric ironies in "Carnal Knowledge" (p. 466) viciously biting, while another reader might find the story hilarious — and revealing.

As Mark Twain makes surprisingly clear in "The Story of the Good Little Boy" (p. 494), even Sunday school can be unexpectedly funny, because humor often asserts that nothing is sacred. It wears social restraints lightly and refuses to sit still, preferring that others grapple with discomfort. Perhaps Lee Smith's feisty, wheelchair-bound elderly protagonist in "The Happy Memories Club" (p. 481) best expresses the subversive nature of humor. Labeled "inappropriate" (a term demanding compliance that has always crippled humor) by the staff of the retirement home where she resides, this colorful character forthrightly announces at the beginning of the story that "I've always done exactly what I was supposed to do — now I intend to do what I want." Like the stories in this chapter, she's disruptive and she's funny, but she's also serious.

E. ANNIE PROULX (B. 1935)

Edna Annie Proulx was born in 1935 and did not finish her first book until 1988. She received a B.A. from the University of Vermont in 1969 and a master's degree from Sir George Williams University, both in history, and later became a freelance writer of articles for magazines in the United States. She published short stories occasionally until she had enough to make her first collection, *Heart Songs and Other Stories* (1988), which she followed with the novel *Postcards* in 1992. Her breakthrough novel was *The Shipping News* (1993), which won both the Pulitzer Prize and the National

© Jerry Bauer.

Book Award, and she has since produced two novels, *Accordion Crimes* (1996) and *The Old Ace in the Hole* (2003), and two books of short stories, *Close Range: Wyoming Stories* (1999) and *Bad Dirt: Wyoming Stories 2* (2004). Setting her works in places as distant as Newfoundland and Wyoming, Proulx conveys her dark, comic stories by creating a strong sense of place, using her talent for keen detail and for reproducing the peculiarities of local speech. *The Shipping News* and the short story "Brokeback Mountain" from *Close Range* were made into popular films.

55 Miles to the Gas Pump

1999

Rancher Croom in handmade boots and filthy hat, that walleyed cattleman, stray hairs like curling fiddle string ends, that warm-handed, quick-foot dancer on splintery boards or down the cellar stairs to a rack of bottles of his own strange beer, yeasty, cloudy, bursting out in garlands of foam, Rancher Croom at night galloping drunk over the dark plain, turning off at a place he knows to arrive at a canyon brink where he dismounts and looks down on tumbled rock, waits, then steps out, parting the air with his last roar, sleeves surging up windmill arms, jeans riding over boot tops, but before he hits he rises again to the top of the cliff like a cork in a bucket of milk.

Mrs. Croom on the roof with a saw cutting a hole into the attic where she has not been for twelve years thanks to old Croom's padlocks and warnings, whets to her desire, and the sweat flies as she exchanges the saw for a chisel and hammer until a ragged slab of peak is free and she can see inside: just as she thought: the corpses of Mr. Croom's paramours — she recognizes them from their photographs in the paper: MISSING WOMAN — some desiccated as jerky and much the same color, some moldy from lying beneath roof leaks, and all of them used hard, covered with tarry handprints, the marks of boot heels, some bright blue with the remnants of paint used on the shutters years ago, one wrapped in newspaper nipple to knee.

When you live a long way out you make your own fun.

CONSIDERATIONS FOR CRITICAL THINKING AND WRITING

1. **FIRST RESPONSE.** Do you think this story is humorous? Why or why not?

2. What kinds of assumptions about rural and urban life are made in the story? To what extent does Proulx challenge or endorse conventional views of rural and urban values?

3. Consider whether Mr. and Mrs. Croom are round, flat, or stock characters.

4. Is there a resolution to the conflict(s) in the plot?

5. How important is the setting?

6. Write a sentence that expresses your reading of the theme.

7. Describe the style and tone of each paragraph. How do they contribute to the theme?

8. **CREATIVE RESPONSE.** Substitute Proulx's title and final paragraph with your own. How do these changes affect your interpretation of the entire work?

CONNECTIONS TO OTHER SELECTIONS

1. Despite their brevity, how do "55 Miles to the Gas Pump" and Raymond Carver's "Popular Mechanics" (p. 288) manage to create compelling fictional worlds?

2. Compare Proulx's humorous treatment of the West to Stephen Crane's in "The Bride Comes to Yellow Sky" (p. 266).

3. Consider the use of irony in Proulx's story and in Mark Twain's "The Story of the Good Little Boy" (p. 494). Explain why you find the endings of the stories similar or different in tone.

T. Coraghessan Boyle (B. 1948)

Born in Peekskill, New York, T. Coraghessan Boyle earned a doctorate at the University of Iowa and has taught at the University of Southern California. Among his literary awards is a National Endowment for the Arts Creative Writing Fellowship and the PEN/Faulkner Award for fiction. His fiction has appeared in a variety of periodicals including the *North American Review, The New Yorker, Harper's,* the *Atlantic Monthly,* and *Playboy.* His novels include *Water Music* (1981), *Budding Projects* (1984), *World's End* (1987),

By permission of the author.

East Is East (1990), *The Road to Wellville* (1993), *Drop City* (2003), and *Talk Talk* (2006). His short stories are collected in *Descent of Man* (1979), *Greasy Lake and Other Stories* (1985), *If the River Was Whiskey* (1989), *Without a Hero and Other Stories* (1994) from which "Carnal Knowledge" is reprinted, *T. C. Boyle Stories: The Collected Stories of T. Coraghessan Boyle* (1998), *After the Plague and Other Stories* (2001), and *Tooth and Claw* (2005).

Carnal Knowledge   1994

I'd never really thought much about meat. It was there in the supermarket in a plastic wrapper; it came between slices of bread with mayo and mustard and a dill pickle on the side; it sputtered and smoked on the grill till somebody flipped it over, and then it appeared on the plate, between the baked potato and the julienne carrots, neatly cross-hatched and floating in a puddle of red juice. Beef, mutton, pork, venison, dripping burgers, and greasy ribs — it was all the same to me, food, the body's fuel, something to savor a moment on the tongue before the digestive system went to work on it. Which is not to say I was totally unconscious of the deeper implications. Every once in a while I'd eat at home, a quartered chicken, a package of Shake 'n Bake, Stove Top stuffing, and frozen peas, and as I hacked away at the stippled yellow skin and pink flesh of the sanitized bird I'd wonder at the darkish bits of organ clinging to the ribs — what was that, liver? kidney? — but in the end it didn't make me any less fond of Kentucky Fried or Chicken McNuggets. I saw those ads in the magazines, too, the ones that showed the veal calves penned up in their own waste, their limbs atrophied and their veins so pumped full of antibiotics they couldn't control their bowels, but when I took a date to Anna Maria's, I could never resist the veal scallopini.

And then I met Alena Jorgensen.

It was a year ago, two weeks before Thanksgiving—I remember the date because it was my birthday, my thirtieth, and I'd called in sick and gone to the beach to warm my face, read a book, and feel a little sorry for myself. The Santa Anas were blowing and it was clear all the way to Catalina, but there was an edge to the air, a scent of winter hanging over Utah, and as far as I could see in either direction I had the beach pretty much to myself. I found a sheltered spot in a tumble of boulders, spread a blanket, and settled down to attack the pastrami on rye I'd brought along for nourishment. Then I turned to my book—a comfortingly apocalyptic tract about the demise of the planet—and let the sun warm me as I read about the denuding of the rain forest, the poisoning of the atmosphere, and the swift silent eradication of species. Gulls coasted by overhead. I saw the distant glint of jetliners.

I must have dozed, my head thrown back, the book spread open in my lap, because the next thing I remember, a strange dog was hovering over me and the sun had dipped behind the rocks. The dog was big, wild-haired, with one staring blue eye, and it just looked at me, ears slightly cocked, as if it expected a Milk-Bone or something. I was startled—not that I don't like dogs, but here was this woolly thing poking its snout in my face—and I guess that I must have made some sort of defensive gesture, because the dog staggered back a step and froze. Even in the confusion of the moment I could see that there was something wrong with this dog, an unsteadiness, a gimp, a wobble to its legs. I felt a mixture of pity and revulsion—had it been hit by a car, was that it?— when all at once I became aware of a wetness on the breast of my windbreaker, and an unmistakable odor rose to my nostrils: I'd been pissed on.

Pissed on. As I lay there unsuspecting, enjoying the sun, the beach, the soli- 5 tude, this stupid beast had lifted its leg and used me as a pissoir—and now it was poised there on the edge of the blanket as if it expected a reward. A sudden rage seized me. I came up off the blanket with a curse, and it was only then that a dim apprehension seemed to seep into the dog's other eye, the brown one, and it lurched back and fell on its face, just out of reach. And then it lurched and fell again, bobbing and weaving across the sand like a seal out of water. I was on my feet now, murderous, glad to see that the thing was hobbled—it would simplify the task of running it down and beating it to death.

"Alf!" a voice called, and as the dog floundered in the sand, I turned and saw Alena Jorgensen poised on the boulder behind me. I don't want to make too much of the moment, don't want to mythologize it or clutter the scene with allusions to Aphrodite rising from the waves or accepting the golden apple from Paris, but she was a pretty impressive sight. Bare-legged, fluid, as tall and uncompromising as her Nordic ancestors, and dressed in a Gore-Tex bikini and hooded sweatshirt unzipped to the waist, she blew me away, in any event. Piss-spattered and stupefied, I could only gape up at her.

"You bad boy," she said, scolding, "you get out of there." She glanced from the dog to me and back again. "Oh, you bad boy, what have you done?" she demanded, and I was ready to admit to anything, but it was the dog she was addressing, and the dog flopped over in the sand as if it had been shot. Alena skipped lightly down from the rock, and in the next moment, before I could protest, she was rubbing at the stain on my windbreaker with the wadded-up hem of her sweatshirt.

I tried to stop her — "It's all right," I said, "it's nothing," as if dogs routinely pissed on my wardrobe — but she wouldn't hear of it.

"No," she said, rubbing, her hair flying in my face, the naked skin of her thigh pressing unconsciously to my own, "no, this is terrible, I'm so embarrassed — Alf, you bad boy — I'll clean it for you, I will, it's the least — oh, look at that, it's stained right through to your T-shirt —"

I could smell her, the mousse she used in her hair, a lilac soap or perfume,   10 the salt-sweet odor of her sweat — she'd been jogging, that was it. I murmured something about taking it to the cleaner's myself.

She stopped rubbing and straightened up. She was my height, maybe even a fraction taller, and her eyes were ever so slightly mismatched, like the dog's: a deep earnest blue in the right iris, shading to sea-green and turquoise in the left. We were so close we might have been dancing. "Tell you what," she said, and her face lit with a smile, "since you're so nice about the whole thing, and most people wouldn't be, even if they knew what poor Alf has been through, why don't you let me wash it for you — and the T-shirt too?"

I was a little disconcerted at this point — I was the one who'd been pissed on, after all — but my anger was gone. I felt weightless, adrift, like a piece of fluff floating on the breeze. "Listen," I said, and for the moment I couldn't look her in the eye, "I don't want to put you to any trouble . . ."

"I'm ten minutes up the beach, and I've got a washer and dryer. Come on, it's no trouble at all. Or do you have plans? I mean, I could just pay for the cleaner's if you want . . ."

I was between relationships — the person I'd been seeing off and on for the past year wouldn't even return my calls — and my plans consisted of taking a solitary late-afternoon movie as a birthday treat, then heading over to my mother's for dinner and the cake with the candles. My Aunt Irene would be there, and so would my grandmother. They would exclaim over how big I was and how handsome and then they would begin to contrast my present self with my previous, more diminutive incarnations, and finally work themselves up to a spate of reminiscence that would continue unabated till my mother drove them home. And then, if I was lucky, I'd go out to a singles bar and make the acquaintance of a divorced computer programmer in her mid-thirties with three kids and bad breath.

I shrugged. "Plans? No, not really. I mean, nothing in particular."   15

Alena was housesitting a one-room bungalow that rose stumplike from the sand, no more than fifty feet from the tide line. There were trees in the yard behind it and the place was sandwiched between glass fortresses with crenellated decks, whipping flags, and great hulking concrete pylons. Sitting on the couch inside, you could feel the dull reverberation of each wave hitting the shore, a slow steady pulse that forever defined the place for me. Alena gave me a faded UC Davis sweatshirt that nearly fit, sprayed a stain remover on my T-shirt and windbreaker, and in a single fluid motion flipped down the lid of the washer and extracted two beers from the refrigerator beside it.

There was an awkward moment as she settled into the chair opposite me and we concentrated on our beers. I didn't know what to say. I was disoriented, giddy, still struggling to grasp what had happened. Fifteen minutes earlier I'd been dozing on the beach, alone on my birthday and feeling sorry for myself, and now I was ensconced in a cozy beach house, in the presence of Alena Jorgensen and her naked spill of leg, drinking a beer. "So what do you do?" she said, setting her beer down on the coffee table.

I was grateful for the question, too grateful maybe. I described to her at length how dull my job was, nearly ten years with the same agency, writing ad copy, my brain gone numb with disuse. I was somewhere in the middle of a blow-by-blow account of our current campaign for a Ghanian vodka distilled from calabash husks when she said, "I know what you mean," and told me she'd dropped out of veterinary school herself. "After I saw what they did to the animals. I mean, can you see neutering a dog just for our convenience, just because it's easier for us if they don't have a sex life?" Her voice grew hot. "It's the same old story, species fascism at its worst."

Alf was lying at my feet, grunting softly and looking up mournfully out of his staring blue eye, as blameless a creature as ever lived. I made a small noise of agreement and then focused on Alf. "And your dog," I said, "he's arthritic? Or is it hip dysplasia or what?" I was pleased with myself for the question — aside from "tapeworm," "hip dysplasia" was the only veterinary term I could dredge up from the memory bank, and I could see that Alf's problems ran deeper than worms.

Alena looked angry suddenly. "Don't I wish," she said. She paused to draw 20 a bitter breath. "There's nothing wrong with Alf that wasn't inflicted on him. They tortured him, maimed him, mutilated him."

"Tortured him?" I echoed, feeling the indignation rise in me — this beautiful girl, this innocent beast. "Who?"

Alena leaned forward and there was real hate in her eyes. She mentioned a prominent shoe company — spat out the name, actually. It was an ordinary name, a familiar one, and it hung in the air between us, suddenly sinister. Alf had been part of an experiment to market booties for dogs — suede, cordovan, patent leather, the works. The dogs were made to pace a treadmill in their booties, to assess wear; Alf was part of the control group.

"Control group?" I could feel the hackles rising on the back of my neck.

"They used eighty-grit sandpaper on the treads, to accelerate the process." Alena shot a glance out the window to where the surf pounded the shore; she bit her lip. "Alf was one of the dogs without booties."

I was stunned. I wanted to get up and comfort her, but I might as well have 25 been grafted to the chair. "I don't believe it," I said. "How could anybody—"

"Believe it," she said. She studied me a moment, then set down her beer and crossed the room to dig through a cardboard box in the corner. If I was moved by the emotion she'd called up, I was moved even more by the sight of her bending over the box in her Gore-Tex bikini; I clung to the edge of the chair as if it were a plunging roller coaster. A moment later she dropped a dozen file folders in my lap. The uppermost bore the name of the shoe company, and it was crammed with news clippings, several pages of a diary relating to plant operations and workers' shifts at the Grand Rapids facility, and a floor plan of the laboratories. The folders beneath it were inscribed with the names of cosmetics firms, biomedical research centers, furriers, tanners, meatpackers. Alena perched on the edge of the coffee table and watched as I shuffled through them.

"You know the Draize test?"

I gave her a blank look.

"They inject chemicals into rabbits' eyes to see how much it'll take before they go blind. The rabbits are in cages, thousands of them, and they take a needle and jab it into their eyes—and you know why, you know in the name of what great humanitarian cause this is going on, even as we speak?"

I didn't know. The surf pounded at my feet. I glanced at Alf and then back   30 into her angry eyes.

"Mascara, that's what. Mascara. They torture countless thousands of rabbits so women can look like sluts."

I thought the characterization a bit harsh, but when I studied her pale lashes and tight lipstickless mouth, I saw that she meant it. At any rate, the notion set her off, and she launched into a two-hour lecture, gesturing with her flawless hands, quoting figures, digging through her files for the odd photo of legless mice or morphine-addicted gerbils. She told me how she'd rescued Alf herself, raiding the laboratory with six other members of the Animal Liberation Front, the militant group in honor of which Alf had been named. At first, she'd been content to write letters and carry placards, but now, with the lives of so many animals at stake, she'd turned to more direct action: harassment, vandalism, sabotage. She described how she'd spiked trees with Earth-First!ers in Oregon, cut miles of barbed-wire fence on cattle ranches in Nevada, destroyed records in biomedical research labs up and down the coast and insinuated herself between the hunters and the bighorn sheep in the mountains of Arizona. I could only nod and exclaim, smile ruefully and whistle in a low "holy cow!" sort of way. Finally, she paused to level her unsettling eyes on me. "You know what Isaac Bashevis Singer said?"

We were on our third beer. The sun was gone. I didn't have a clue.

Alena leaned forward. "'Every day is Auschwitz for the animals.'"

I looked down into the amber aperture of my beer bottle and nodded my   35 head sadly. The dryer had stopped an hour and a half ago. I wondered if she'd go out to dinner with me, and what she could eat if she did. "Uh, I was wondering," I said, "if . . . if you might want to go out for something to eat—"

Alf chose that moment to heave himself up from the floor and urinate on the wall behind me. My dinner proposal hung in the balance as Alena shot up off the edge of the table to scold him and then gently usher him out the door. "Poor Alf," she sighed, turning back to me with a shrug. "But listen, I'm sorry if I talked your head off—I didn't mean to, but it's rare to find somebody on your own wavelength."

She smiled. *On your own wavelength:* the words illuminated me, excited me, sent up a tremor I could feel all the way down in the deepest nodes of my reproductive tract. "So how about dinner?" I persisted. Restaurants were running through my head—would it have to be veggie? Could there be even a whiff of grilled flesh on the air? Curdled goat's milk and tabbouleh, tofu, lentil soup, sprouts: *Every day is Auschwitz for the animals.* "No place with meat, of course."

She just looked at me.

"I mean, I don't eat meat myself," I lied, "or actually, not anymore"—since the pastrami sandwich, that is—"but I don't really know any place that . . ." I trailed off lamely.

"I'm a Vegan," she said.   40

After two hours of blind bunnies, butchered calves and mutilated pups, I couldn't resist the joke. "I'm from Venus myself."

She laughed, but I could see she didn't find it all that funny. Vegans didn't eat meat or fish, she explained, or milk or cheese or eggs, and they didn't wear wool or leather — or fur, of course.

"Of course," I said. We were both standing there, hovering over the coffee table. I was beginning to feel a little foolish.

"Why don't we just eat here," she said.

The deep throb of the ocean seemed to settle in my bones as we lay there in bed 45 that night, Alena and I, and I learned all about the fluency of her limbs and the sweetness of her vegetable tongue. Alf sprawled on the floor beneath us, wheezing and groaning in his sleep, and I blessed him for his incontinence and his doggy stupidity. Something was happening to me — I could feel it in the way the boards shifted under me, feel it with each beat of the surf — and I was ready to go along with it. In the morning, I called in sick again.

Alena was watching me from bed as I dialed the office and described how the flu had migrated from my head to my gut and beyond, and there was a look in her eye that told me I would spend the rest of the day right there beside her, peeling grapes and dropping them one by one between her parted and expectant lips. I was wrong. Half an hour later, after a breakfast of brewer's yeast and what appeared to be some sort of bark marinated in yogurt, I found myself marching up and down the sidewalk in front of a fur emporium in Beverly Hills, waving a placard that read HOW DOES IT FEEL TO WEAR A CORPSE? in letters that dripped like blood.

It was a shock. I'd seen protest marches on TV, antiwar rallies and civil rights demonstrations and all that, but I'd never warmed my heels on the pavement or chanted slogans or felt the naked stick in my hand. There were maybe forty of us in all, mostly women, and we waved our placards at passing cars and blocked traffic on the sidewalk. One woman had smeared her face and hands with cold cream steeped in red dye, and Alena had found a ratty mink stole somewhere — the kind that features whole animals sewed together, snout to tail, their miniature limbs dangling — and she'd taken a can of crimson spray paint to their muzzles so that they looked freshly killed. She brandished this grisly banner on a stick high above her head, whooping like a savage and chanting, "Fur is death, fur is death," over and over again till it became a mantra for the crowd. The day was unseasonably warm, the Jaguars glinted in the sun and the palms nodded in the breeze, and no one, but for a single tight-lipped salesman glowering from behind the store's immaculate windows, paid the slightest bit of attention to us.

I marched out there on the street, feeling exposed and conspicuous, but marching nonetheless — for Alena's sake and for the sake of the foxes and martens and all the rest, and for my own sake too: with each step I took I could feel my consciousness expanding like a balloon, the breath of saintliness seeping steadily into me. Up to this point I'd worn suede and leather like anybody else, ankle boots and Air Jordans, a bombardier jacket I'd had since high school. If I'd drawn the line with fur, it was only because I'd never had any use for it. If I lived in the Yukon — and sometimes, drowsing through a meeting at work, I found myself fantasizing about it — I would have worn fur, no compunction, no second thoughts.

But not anymore. Now I was the protestor, a placard waver, now I was fighting for the right of every last weasel and lynx to grow old and die gracefully, now I was Alena Jorgensen's lover and a force to be reckoned with. Of course, my feet hurt and I was running sweat and praying that no one from work would drive by and see me there on the sidewalk with my crazy cohorts and denunciatory sign.

We marched for hours, back and forth, till I thought we'd wear a groove in 50 the pavement. We chanted and jeered and nobody so much as looked at us twice. We could have been Hare Krishnas, bums, antiabortionists, or lepers, what did it matter? To the rest of the world, to the uninitiated masses to whose sorry number I'd belonged just twenty-four hours earlier, we were invisible. I was hungry, tired, discouraged. Alena was ignoring me. Even the woman in red-face was slowing down, her chant a hoarse whisper that was sucked up and obliterated in the roar of traffic. And then, as the afternoon faded toward rush hour, a wizened silvery old woman who might have been an aging star or a star's mother or even the first dimly remembered wife of a studio exec got out of a long white car at the curb and strode fearlessly toward us. Despite the heat—it must have been eighty degrees at this point—she was wearing an ankle-length silver fox coat, a bristling shouldery wafting mass of peltry that must have decimated every burrow on the tundra. It was the moment we'd been waiting for.

A cry went up, shrill and ululating, and we converged on the lone old woman like a Cheyenne war party scouring the plains. The man beside me went down on all fours and howled like a dog. Alena slashed the air with her limp mink, and the blood sang in my ears. "Murderer!" I screamed, getting into it. "Torturer! Nazi!" The strings in my neck were tight. I didn't know what I was saying. The crowd gibbered. The placards danced. I was so close to the old woman I could smell her—her perfume, a whiff of mothballs from the coat— and it intoxicated me, maddened me, and I stepped in front of her to block her path with all the seething militant bulk of my one hundred eighty-five pounds of sinew and muscle.

I never saw the chauffeur. Alena told me afterward that he was a former kickboxing champion who'd been banned from the sport for excessive brutality. The first blow seemed to drop down from above, a shell lobbed from deep within enemy territory; the others came at me like a windmill churning in a storm. Someone screamed. I remember focusing on the flawless rigid pleats of the chauffeur's trousers, and then things got a bit hazy.

I woke to the dull thump of the surf slamming at the shore and the touch of Alena's lips on my own. I felt as if I'd been broken on the wheel, dismantled, and put back together again. "Lie still," she said, and her tongue moved against my swollen cheek. Stricken, I could only drag my head across the pillow and gaze into the depths of her parti-colored eyes. "You're one of us now," she whispered.

Next morning I didn't even bother to call in sick.

By the end of the week I'd recovered enough to crave meat, for which I felt 55 deeply ashamed, and to wear out a pair of vinyl huaraches on the picket line. Together, and with various coalitions of antivivisectionists, militant Vegans, and cat lovers, Alena and I tramped a hundred miles of sidewalk, spray-painted inflammatory slogans across the windows of supermarkets and burger stands, denounced tanners, furriers, poulterers, and sausage makers, and somehow found time to break up a cockfight in Pacoima. It was exhilarating, heady, dangerous. If I'd been disconnected in the past, I was plugged in now. I felt righteous — for the first time in my life I had a cause — and I had Alena, Alena above all. She fascinated me, fixated me, made me feel like a tomcat leaping in and out of second-story windows, oblivious to the free-fall and the picket fence below. There was her beauty, of course, a triumph of evolution and the happy interchange of genes going all the way back to the cavemen, but it was more than that — it was her commitment to animals, to the righting of wrongs, to morality that made her irresistible. Was it love? The term is something I've always had difficulty with, but I suppose it was. Sure it was. Love, pure and simple. I had it, it had me.

"You know what?" Alena said one night as she stood over the miniature stove, searing tofu in oil and garlic. We'd spent the afternoon demonstrating out front of a tortilla factory that used rendered animal fat as a congealing agent, after which we'd been chased three blocks by an overweight assistant manager at Von's who objected to Alena's spray-painting MEAT IS DEATH over the specials in the front window. I was giddy with the adolescent joy of it. I sank into the couch with a beer and watched Alf limp across the floor to fling himself down and lick at a suspicious spot on the floor. The surf boomed like thunder.

"What?" I said.

"Thanksgiving's coming."

I let it ride a moment, wondering if I should invite Alena to my mother's for the big basted bird stuffed with canned oysters and buttered bread crumbs, and then realized it probably wouldn't be such a great idea. I said nothing.

She glanced over her shoulder. "The animals don't have a whole lot to be   60 thankful for, that's for sure. It's just an excuse for the meat industry to butcher a couple million turkeys, is all it is." She paused; hot safflower oil popped in the pan. "I think it's time for a little road trip," she said. "Can we take your car?"

"Sure, but where are we going?"

She gave me her Gioconda smile. "To liberate some turkeys."

In the morning I called my boss to tell him I had pancreatic cancer and wouldn't be in for a while, then we threw some things in the car, helped Alf scrabble into the back seat, and headed up Route 5 for the San Joaquin Valley. We drove for three hours through a fog so dense the windows might as well have been packed with cotton. Alena was secretive, but I could see she was excited. I knew only that we were on our way to rendezvous with a certain "Rolfe," a longtime friend of hers and a big name in the world of ecotage and animal rights, after which we would commit some desperate and illegal act, for which the turkeys would be eternally grateful.

There was a truck stalled in front of the sign for our exit at Calpurnia Springs, and I had to brake hard and jerk the wheel around twice to keep the tires on the pavement. Alena came up out of her seat and Alf slammed into the armrest like a sack of meal, but we made it. A few minutes later we were gliding through the ghostly vacancy of the town itself, lights drifting past in a nimbus of fog, glowing pink, yellow, and white, and then there was only the blacktop road and the pale void that engulfed it. We'd gone ten miles or so when Alena instructed me to slow down and began to study the right-hand shoulder with a keen, unwavering eye.

The earth breathed in and out. I squinted hard into the soft drifting glow   65 of the headlights. "There, there!" she cried and I swung the wheel to the right, and suddenly we were lurching along a pitted dirt road that rose up from the blacktop like a goat path worn into the side of a mountain. Five minutes later Alf sat up in the back seat and began to whine, and then a crude unpainted shack began to detach itself from the vagueness around us.

Rolfe met us on the porch. He was tall and leathery, in his fifties, I guessed, with a shock of hair and rutted features that brought Samuel Beckett to mind. He was wearing gumboots and jeans and a faded lumberjack shirt that looked as if it had been washed a hundred times. Alf took a quick pee against the side of the house, then fumbled up the steps to roll over and fawn at his feet.

"Rolfe!" Alena called, and there was too much animation in her voice, too much familiarity, for my taste. She took the steps in a bound and threw herself in his arms. I watched them kiss, and it wasn't a fatherly-daughterly sort of kiss, not at all. It was a kiss with some meaning behind it, and I didn't like it. Rolfe, I thought: What kind of name is that?

"Rolfe," Alena gasped, still a little breathless from bouncing up the steps like a cheerleader, "I'd like you to meet Jim."

That was my signal. I ascended the porch steps and held out my hand. Rolfe gave me a look out of the hooded depths of his eyes and then took my hand in a hard calloused grip, the grip of the wood splitter, the fence mender, the liberator of hothouse turkeys and laboratory mice. "A pleasure," he said, and his voice rasped like sandpaper.

There was a fire going inside, and Alena and I sat before it and warmed our   70
hands while Alf whined and sniffed and Rolfe served Red Zinger tea in Japanese cups the size of thimbles. Alena hadn't stopped chattering since we stepped through the door, and Rolfe came right back at her in his woodsy rasp, the two of them exchanging names and news and gossip as if they were talking in code. I studied the reproductions of teal and widgeon that hung from the peeling walls, noted the case of Heinz vegetarian beans in the corner and the half-gallon of Jack Daniel's on the mantel. Finally, after the third cup of tea, Alena settled back in her chair — a huge old Salvation Army sort of thing with a soiled antimacassar — and said, "So what's the plan?"

Rolfe gave me another look, a quick predatory darting of the eyes, as if he weren't sure I could be trusted, and then turned back to Alena. "Hedda Gabler's Range-Fed Turkey Ranch," he said. "And no, I don't find the name cute, not at all." He looked at me now, a long steady assay. "They grind up the heads for cat food, and the neck, the organs, and the rest, that they wrap up in paper and stuff back in the body cavity like it was a war atrocity or something. Whatever did a turkey go and do to us to deserve a fate like that?"

The question was rhetorical, even if it seemed to have been aimed at me, and I made no response other than to compose my face in a look that wedded grief, outrage, and resolve. I was thinking of all the turkeys I'd sent to their doom, of the plucked wishbones, the pope's noses,° and the crisp browned skin I used to relish as a kid. It brought a lump to my throat, and something more: I realized I was hungry.

"Ben Franklin wanted to make them our national symbol," Alena chimed in, "did you know that? But the meat eaters won out."

---

pope's noses: Slang for the fleshy tail sections of turkeys and other poultry.

"Fifty thousand birds," Rolfe said, glancing at Alena and bringing his incendiary gaze back to rest on me. "I have information they're going to start slaughtering them tomorrow, for the fresh-not-frozen market."

"Yuppie poultry," Alena's voice was drenched in disgust.   75

For a moment, no one spoke. I became aware of the crackling of the fire. The fog pressed at the windows. It was getting dark.

"You can see the place from the highway," Rolfe said finally, "but the only access is through Calpurnia Springs. It's about twenty miles — twenty-two point three, to be exact."

Alena's eyes were bright. She was gazing on Rolfe as if he'd just dropped down from heaven. I felt something heave in my stomach.

"We strike tonight."

Rolfe insisted that we take my car — "Everybody around here knows my   80 pickup, and I can't take any chances on a little operation like this" — but we did mask the plates, front and back, with an inch-thick smear of mud. We blackened our faces like commandos and collected our tools from the shed out back — tin snips, a crowbar, and two five-gallon cans of gasoline. "Gasoline?" I said, trying the heft of the can. Rolfe gave me a craggy look. "To create a diversion," he said. Alf, for obvious reasons, stayed behind in the shack.

If the fog had been thick in daylight, it was impenetrable now, the sky collapsed upon the earth. It took hold of the headlights and threw them back at me till my eyes began to water from the effort of keeping the car on the road. But for the ruts and bumps we might have been floating in space. Alena sat up front between Rolfe and me, curiously silent. Rolfe didn't have much to say either, save for the occasional grunted command: "Hang a right here"; "Hard left"; "Easy, easy." I thought about meat and jail and the heroic proportions to which I was about to swell in Alena's eyes and what I intended to do to her when we finally got to bed. It was 2:00 A.M. by the dashboard clock.

"Okay," Rolfe said, and his voice came at me so suddenly it startled me, "pull over here — and kill the lights."

We stepped out into the hush of night and eased the doors shut behind us. I couldn't see a thing, but I could hear the not-so-distant hiss of traffic on the highway, and another sound, too, muffled and indistinct, the gentle unconscious suspiration of thousands upon thousands of my fellow creatures. And I could smell them, a seething rancid odor of feces and feathers and naked scaly feet that crawled down my throat and burned my nostrils. "Whew," I said in a whisper, "I can smell them."

Rolfe and Alena were vague presences at my side. Rolfe flipped open the trunk and in the next moment I felt the heft of a crowbar and a pair of tin snips in my hand. "Listen, you, Jim," Rolfe whispered, taking me by the wrist in his iron grip and leading me half-a-dozen steps forward. "Feel this?"

I felt a grid of wire, which he promptly cut: *snip, snip, snip.*   85

"This is their enclosure — they're out there in the day, scratching around in the dirt. You get lost, you follow this wire. Now, you're going to take a section out of this side, Alena's got the west side and I've got the south. Once that's done I signal with the flashlight and we bust open the doors to the turkey houses — they're these big low white buildings, you'll see them when you get close — and flush the birds out. Don't worry about me or Alena. Just worry about getting as many birds out as you can."

I was worried. Worried about everything, from some half-crazed farmer with a shotgun or AK-47 or whatever they carried these days, to losing Alena in the fog, to the turkeys themselves: How big were they? Were they violent? They had claws and beaks, didn't they? And how were they going to feel about me bursting into their bedroom in the middle of the night?

"And when the gas cans go up, you hightail it back to the car, got it?"

I could hear the turkeys tossing in their sleep. A truck shifted gears out on the highway. "I think so," I whispered.

"And one more thing—be sure to leave the keys in the ignition."   90

This gave me pause. "But—"

"The getaway." Alena was so close I could feel her breath on my ear. "I mean, we don't want to be fumbling around for the keys when all hell is breaking loose out there, do we?"

I eased open the door and reinserted the keys in the ignition, even though the automatic buzzer warned me against it. "Okay," I murmured, but they were already gone, soaked up in the shadows and the mist. At this point my heart was hammering so loudly I could barely hear the rustling of the turkeys—this is crazy, I told myself, it's hurtful and wrong, not to mention illegal. Spray-painting slogans was one thing, but this was something else altogether. I thought of the turkey farmer asleep in his bed, an entrepreneur working to make America strong, a man with a wife and kids and a mortgage . . . but then I thought of all those innocent turkeys consigned to death, and finally I thought of Alena, long-legged and loving, and the way she came to me out of the darkness of the bathroom and the boom of the surf. I took the tin snips to the wire.

I must have been at it half an hour, forty-five minutes, gradually working my way toward the big white sheds that had begun to emerge from the gloom up ahead, when I saw Rolfe's flashlight blinking off to my left. This was my signal to head to the nearest shed, snap off the padlock with my crowbar, fling open the doors, and herd a bunch of cranky suspicious gobblers out into the night. It was now or never. I looked twice round me and then broke for the near shed in an awkward crouching gait. The turkeys must have sensed that something was up—from behind the long white windowless wall there arose a watchful gabbling, a soughing of feathers that fanned up like a breeze in the treetops. *Hold on, you toms and hens,* I thought, *freedom is at hand.* A jerk of the wrist, and the padlock fell to the ground. Blood pounded in my ears, I took hold of the sliding door and jerked it open with a great dull booming reverberation—and suddenly, there they were, turkeys, thousands upon thousands of them, cloaked in white feathers under a string of dim yellow bulbs. The light glinted in their reptilian eyes. Somewhere a dog began to bark.

I steeled myself and sprang through the door with a shout, whirling the 95 crowbar over my head, "All right!" I boomed, and the echo gave it back to me a hundred times over, "this is it! Turkeys, on your feet!" Nothing. No response. But for the whisper of rustling feathers and the alertly cocked heads, they might have been sculptures, throw pillows, they might as well have been dead and butchered and served up with yams and onions and all the trimmings. The barking of the dog went up a notch. I thought I heard voices.

The turkeys crouched on the concrete floor, wave upon wave of them, stupid and immovable; they perched in the rafters, on shelves and platforms, huddled in wooden stalls. Desperate, I rushed into the front rank of them, swinging my crowbar, stamping my feet, and howling like the wishbone plucker I once was. That did it. There was a shriek from the nearest bird and the others took it up till an unholy racket filled the place, and now they were moving, tumbling down from their perches, flapping their wings in a storm of dried excrement and pecked-over grain, pouring across the concrete floor till it vanished beneath them. Encouraged, I screamed again — "Yeeee-ha-ha-ha-ha!" — and beat at the aluminum walls with the crowbar as the turkeys shot through the doorway and out into the night.

It was then that the black mouth of the doorway erupted with light and the *ka-boom!* of the gas cans sent a tremor through the earth. *Run!* a voice screamed in my head, and the adrenaline kicked in and all of a sudden I was scrambling for the door in a hurricane of turkeys. They were everywhere, flapping their wings, gobbling and screeching, loosing their bowels in panic. Something hit the back of my legs and all at once I was down amongst them, on the floor, in the dirt and feathers and wet turkey shit. I was a roadbed, a turkey expressway. Their claws dug at my back, my shoulders, the crown of my head. Panicked now, choking on feathers and dust and worse, I fought to my feet as the big screeching birds launched themselves round me, and staggered out into the barnyard. "There! Who's that there?" a voice roared, and I was off and running.

What can I say? I vaulted turkeys, kicked them aside like so many footballs, slashed and tore at them as they sailed through the air. I ran till my lungs felt as if they were burning right through my chest, disoriented, bewildered, terrified of the shotgun blast I was sure would cut me down at any moment. Behind me the fire raged and lit the fog till it glowed blood-red and hellish. But where was the fence? And where the car?

I got control of my feet then and stood stock-still in a flurry of turkeys, squinting into the wall of fog. Was that it? Was that the car over there? At that moment I heard an engine start up somewhere behind me — a familiar engine with a familiar coughing gurgle in the throat of the carburetor — and then the lights blinked on briefly three hundred yards away. I heard the engine race and listened, helpless, as the car roared off in the opposite direction. I stood there a moment longer, forlorn and forsaken, and then I ran blindly off into the night, putting the fire and the shouts and the barking and the incessant mindless squawking of the turkeys as far behind me as I could.

When dawn finally broke, it was only just perceptibly, so thick was the fog. I'd 100 made my way to a blacktop road — which road and where it led I didn't know — and sat crouched and shivering in a clump of weed just off the shoulder. Alena wouldn't desert me, I was sure of that — she loved me, as I loved her; needed me, as I needed her — and I was sure she'd be cruising along the back roads looking for me. My pride was wounded, of course, and if I never laid eyes on Rolfe again I felt I wouldn't be missing much, but at least I hadn't been drilled full of shot, savaged by farm dogs, or pecked to death by irate turkeys. I was sore all over, my shin throbbed where I'd slammed into something substantial while vaulting through the night, there were feathers in my hair, and my face and arms were a mosaic of cuts and scratches and long trailing fissures of dirt. I'd been sitting there for what seemed like hours, cursing Rolfe, developing suspicions about Alena and unflattering theories about environmentalists in general, when finally I heard the familiar slurp and roar of my Chevy Citation cutting through the mist ahead of me.

Rolfe was driving, his face impassive. I flung myself into the road like a tattered beggar, waving my arms over my head and giving vent to my joy, and he very nearly ran me down. Alena was out of the car before it stopped, wrapping me up in her arms, and then she was bundling me into the rear seat with Alf and we were on our way back to the hideaway. "What happened?" she cried, as if she couldn't have guessed. "Where were you? We waited as long as we could."

I was feeling sulky, betrayed, feeling as if I was owed a whole lot more than a perfunctory hug and a string of insipid questions. Still, as I told my tale I began to warm to it—they'd got away in the car with the heater going, and I'd stayed behind to fight the turkeys, the farmers, and the elements, too, and if that wasn't heroic, I'd like to know what was. I looked into Alena's admiring eyes and pictured Rolfe's shack, a nip or two from the bottle of Jack Daniel's, maybe a peanut-butter-and-tofu sandwich, and then the bed, with Alena in it. Rolfe said nothing.

Back at Rolfe's, I took a shower and scrubbed the turkey droppings from my pores, then helped myself to the bourbon. It was ten in the morning and the house was dark—if the world had ever been without fog, there was no sign of it here. When Rolfe stepped out on the porch to fetch an armload of firewood, I pulled Alena down into my lap. "Hey," she murmured, "I thought you were an invalid."

She was wearing a pair of too-tight jeans and an oversize sweater with nothing underneath it. I slipped my hand inside the sweater and found something to hold on to. "Invalid?" I said, nuzzling at her sleeve. "Hell, I'm a turkey liberator, an ecoguerrilla, a friend of the animals and the environment, too."

She laughed, but she pushed herself up and crossed the room to stare out   105
the occluded window. "Listen, Jim," she said, "what we did last night was great, really great, but it's just the beginning." Alf looked up at her expectantly. I heard Rolfe fumbling around on the porch, the thump of wood on wood. She turned around to face me now. "What I mean is, Rolfe wants me to go up to Wyoming for a little bit, just outside of Yellowstone—"

Me? Rolfe wants me? There was no invitation in that, no plurality, no acknowledgment of all we'd done and meant to each other. "For what?" I said. "What do you mean?"

"There's this grizzly—a pair of them, actually—and they've been raiding places outside the park. One of them made off with the mayor's Doberman the other night and the people are up in arms. We—I mean Rolfe and me and some other people from the old Bolt Weevils in Minnesota?—we're going to go up there and make sure the Park Service—or the local yahoos—don't eliminate them. The bears, I mean."

My tone was corrosive. "You and Rolfe?"

"There's nothing between us, if that's what you're thinking. This has to do   110
with animals, that's all."

"Like us?"

She shook her head slowly. "Not like us, no. We're the plague on this planet, don't you know that?"

Suddenly I was angry. Seething. Here I'd crouched in the bushes all night, covered in turkey crap, and now I was part of a plague. I was on my feet. "No, I don't know that."

She gave me a look that let me know it didn't matter, that she was already gone, that her agenda, at least for the moment, didn't include me and there was no use arguing about it. "Look," she said, her voice dropping as Rolfe slammed back through the door with a load of wood, "I'll see you in L.A. in a month or so, okay?" She gave me an apologetic smile. "Water the plants for me?"

An hour later I was on the road again. I'd helped Rolfe stack the wood beside the fireplace, allowed Alena to brush my lips with a good-bye kiss, and then stood there on the porch while Rolfe locked up, lifted Alf into the bed of his pickup, and rumbled down the rutted dirt road with Alena at his side. I watched till their brake lights dissolved in the drifting gray mist, then fired up the Citation and lurched down the road behind them. *A month or so:* I felt hollow inside. I pictured her with Rolfe, eating yogurt and wheat germ, stopping at motels, wrestling grizzlies, and spiking trees. The hollowness opened up, cored me out till I felt as if I'd been plucked and gutted and served up on a platter myself.

I found my way back through Calpurnia Springs without incident — there were no roadblocks, no flashing lights and grim-looking troopers searching trunks and back seats for a tallish thirty-year-old ecoterrorist with turkey tracks down his back — but after I turned onto the highway for Los Angeles, I had a shock. Ten miles up the road my nightmare materialized out of the gloom: red lights everywhere, signal flares and police cars lined up on the shoulder. I was on the very edge of panicking, a beat away from cutting across the median and giving them a run for it, when I saw the truck jackknifed up ahead. I slowed to forty, thirty, and then hit the brakes again. In a moment I was stalled in a line of cars and there was something all over the road, ghostly and white in the fog. At first I thought it must have been flung from the truck, rolls of toilet paper or crates of soap powder ruptured on the pavement. It was neither. As I inched closer, the tires creeping now, the pulse of the lights in my face, I saw that the road was coated in feathers, turkey feathers. A storm of them. A blizzard. And more: there was flesh there too, slick and greasy, a red pulp ground into the surface of the road, thrown up like slush from the tires of the car ahead of me, ground beneath the massive wheels of the truck. Turkeys. Turkeys everywhere.

The car crept forward. I flicked on the windshield wipers, hit the washer button, and for a moment a scrim of diluted blood obscured the windows and the hollowness opened up inside of me till I thought it would suck me inside out. Behind me, someone was leaning on his horn. A trooper loomed up out of the gloom, waving me on with the dead yellow eye of his flashlight. I thought of Alena and felt sick. All there was between us had come to this, expectations gone sour, a smear on the road. I wanted to get out and shoot myself, turn myself in, close my eyes, and wake up in jail, in a hair shirt, in a straitjacket, anything. It went on. Time passed. Nothing moved. And then, miraculously, a vision began to emerge from behind the smeared glass and the gray belly of the fog, lights glowing golden in the waste. I saw the sign, Gas/Food/Lodging, and my hand was on the blinker.

It took me a moment, picturing the place, the generic tile, the false cheer of the lights, the odor of charred flesh hanging heavy on the air, Big Mac, three-piece dark meat, carne asada, cheeseburger. The engine coughed. The lights glowed. I didn't think of Alena then, didn't think of Rolfe or grizzlies or the doomed bleating flocks and herds, or of the blind bunnies and cancerous

115

mice—I thought only of the cavern opening inside me and how to fill it. "Meat," and I spoke the word aloud, talking to calm myself as if I'd awakened from a bad dream, "it's only meat."

CONSIDERATIONS FOR CRITICAL THINKING AND WRITING

1. **FIRST RESPONSE.** How do your own views of vegetarianism and animal rights' groups influence your response to this story?

2. Comment on how Boyle achieves humorous effects through his first-person narrator in the story's first paragraph.

3. Describe the tone of the first-person narrator. How does he regard the world—the people, situations, and events—he encounters? Why is it especially appropriate that he has a job writing copy for an advertising agency?

4. How does Boyle's style reveal the narrator's character? Select several paragraphs to illustrate your points.

5. How does the narrator use irony? Select three instances of his use of irony, and discuss their effects and what they reveal about him.

6. How does Boyle create a genuinely comic character with Alf? What is the narrator's relationship with Alf?

7. Characterize Alena. Why is the narrator both attracted to her and puzzled by her?

8. How do you think the story would differ if it were told from Alena's point of view?

9. What is your response to Alena's descriptions of commercial experiments on animals? How does the narrator respond to them?

10. What is the narrator's view of the protests he engages in with Alena? Discuss specific passages to support your answer.

11. How does paragraph 93 explain the narrator's willingness to go along with the raid on the turkey farm?

12. Describe the narrator's response to Rolfe. How does Boyle make Rolfe into a comic figure?

13. What is the major conflict in the story? How is it resolved in the story's final paragraphs?

14. How do the story's last words, "it's only meat," shed light on the significance of the title? What does a dictionary tell you about possible readings of the title?

15. **CRITICAL STRATEGIES.** Read the discussion on new historicist criticism (pp. 1546–47) in Chapter 46, "Critical Strategies for Reading," and describe how a new historicist might use "Carnal Knowledge" to describe aspects of American life in the early 1990s.

CONNECTIONS TO OTHER SELECTIONS

1. What do Alena and Nathaniel Hawthorne's Goodman Brown (p. 325) have in common as reformers? Are there also significant differences?

2. Write an essay comparing Boyle's humorous treatment of animal rights issues with Lee Smith's humorous approach to sex and the treatment of the elderly in "The Happy Memories Club" (p. 481).

LEE SMITH (B. 1944)

Courtesy of Susan Raines.

Born in the Appalachian coal-mining town of Grundy, Virginia, Lee Smith was educated at Hollins College, where she and fellow student Annie Dillard (the essayist and novelist) taught themselves to be go-go dancers for a female rock band named the Virginia Woolfs — a calling that quickly gave way to fiction writing as well as eventually teaching at North Carolina State University. During her senior year, Smith began writing a novel that was published as her first book, *The Last Day the Dog Bushes Bloomed* (1968). Since then she has published three collections of short stories — *Cakewalk* (1981), *Me and My Baby View the Eclipse* (1990), and *News of the Spirit* (1997) — along with more than ten novels, including *Fancy Street* (1973), *Black Mountain Breakdown* (1981), *Fair and Tender Ladies* (1988), *Devil's Dream* (1996), and *The Last Girls* (2002). Her literary prizes include two O. Henry Awards, the Southern Critics Circle Award, and the Robert Penn Warren Prize for fiction. "Narrative," writes Smith, "is as necessary to me as breathing air. I write for the reason I've always done so: simply to survive." In "The Happy Memories Club" Smith creates a narrator who also insists on telling a story.

The Happy Memories Club   *1995*

I may be old, but I'm not dead.

Perhaps you are surprised to hear this. You may be surprised to learn that people like me are still capable of original ideas, intelligent insights, and intense feelings. Passionate love affairs, for example, are not uncommon here. Pacemakers cannot regulate the wild, unbridled yearnings of the heart. You do not wish to know this, I imagine. This knowledge is probably upsetting to you, as it is upsetting to my sons, who do not want to hear, for instance, about my relationship with Dr. Solomon Marx, the historian. "Please, Mom," my son Alex said, rolling his eyes. "Come on, Mama," my son Johnny said. "Can't you maintain a little dignity here?" *Dignity*, said Johnny, who runs a chain of miniature-golf courses! "I have had enough dignity to last me for the rest of my life, thank you," I told Johnny.

I've always done exactly what I was supposed to do — now I intend to do what I want.

"Besides, Dr. Solomon Marx is the joy of my life," I told them. This remained true even when my second surgery was less than successful, obliging me to take to this chair. It remained true until Solomon's most recent stroke, five weeks ago, which has paralyzed him below the waist and caused his thoughts to become disordered, so that he cannot always remember things, or the words for things. A survivor himself, Solomon is an expert on the Holocaust. He has numbers tattooed on his arm. He used to travel the world, speaking about the Holocaust. Now he can't remember what to call it.

"Well, I think it's a blessing," said one of the nurses—that young Miss 5 Rogers. "The Holocaust was just awful."

"It is not a blessing, you ignorant bitch," I told her. "It is the end; our memories are all we've got." I put myself in reverse and sped off before she could reply. I could feel her staring at me as I motored down the hall. I am sure she wrote something in her ever-present notebook. "Inappropriate" and "unmanageable" are among the words they use, unpleasant and inaccurate adjectives all.

The words Solomon can't recall are always nouns.

"My dear," he said to me one day recently, when they had wheeled him out into the Residence Center lobby, "what did you say your name was?" He knew it, of course, deep in his heart's core, as well as he knew his own.

"Alice Scully," I said.

"Ah. Alice Scully," he said. "And what is it that we used to do together, 10 Alice Scully, which brought me such intense—oh, so big—" His eyes were like bright little beads in his pinched face. "It was of the greatest, ah—"

"Sex," I told him. "You loved it."

He grinned at me. "Oh, yes," he said. "Sex. It was sex, indeed."

"Mrs. Scully!" his nurse snapped.

Now I have devised a little game to help Solomon remember nouns. It works like this. Whenever they bring him out, I go over to him and clasp my hands together as if I were hiding something in them. "If you can guess what I've got here," I say, "I'll give you a kiss."

He squints in concentration, fishing for nouns. If he gets one, I give him a 15 kiss.

Some days are better than others.

This is true for us all, of course. We can't be expected to remember everything we know.

In my life I was a teacher, and a good one. I taught English in the days when it was English, not "language arts." I taught for forty years at the Sandy Point School, in Sandy Point, Virginia, where I lived with my husband, Harold Scully, and raised four sons, three of them Harold's. Harold owned and ran the Trent Riverside Pharmacy until the day he dropped dead in his drugstore counting out antibiotics for a Methodist preacher. His mouth and his eyes were wide open, as if whatever he found on the other side surprised him mightily. I was sorry to see this, since Harold was not a man who liked surprises.

I must say I gave him none. I was a good wife to Harold, though I was at first dismayed to learn that this role entailed taking care of his parents from the day of our marriage until their deaths. They both lived long lives, and his mother went blind at the end. But we lived in their house, the largest house in Sandy Point, right on the old tidal river, and their wealth enabled us to send our own sons off to the finest schools and even, in Robert's case, to medical school.

Harold's parents never got over Harold's failure to get into medical school 20 himself. In fact, he barely made it through pharmacy school. As far as I know, however, he was a good pharmacist, never poisoning anybody or mixing up prescriptions. He loved to look at the orderly rows of bottles on his shelves. He loved labeling. Often he dispensed medical advice to his customers: which cough medicine worked best, what to put on a boil. People trusted him. Harold got a great deal of pleasure from his job and from his standing in the community.

I taught school at first because I was trained to do it and because I wanted to. I was never one to plan a menu or clip a recipe out of a magazine. I left all that to Harold's mother and to the family housekeeper, Lucille.

Anyway, I loved teaching. I loved to diagram sentences on the board, precisely separating the subject from the predicate with a vertical line, the linking verb from the predicate adjective with a slanted line, and so forth. The children used to try to stump me by making up long sentences they thought I couldn't diagram, sentences so complex that my final diagram on the board looked like a blueprint for a cathedral, with flying buttresses everywhere, all the lines connecting.

I loved geography, as well — tracing roads, tracing rivers. I loved to trace the route of the pony express, of the Underground Railroad, of De Soto's search for gold. I told them the story of that bumbling fool Zebulon Pike, who set out in 1805 to find the source of the Mississippi River and ended up a year later at the glorious peak they named for him, Pike's Peak, which my sister, Rose, and I visited in 1926 on our cross-country odyssey with my brother John and his wife. In the photograph taken at Pike's Peak, I am seated astride a donkey, wearing a polka-dot dress and a floppy hat, while the western sky goes on and on endlessly behind me.

I taught my students these things: the first flight in a power-driven airplane was made by Wilbur and Orville Wright at Kitty Hawk, North Carolina, on December 17, 1903; Wisconsin is the "Badger State"; the Dutch bought Manhattan Island from the Indians for twenty-four dollars in 1626; you can't sink in the Great Salt Lake. Now these facts ricochet in my head like pinballs, and I do not intend, thank you very much, to enter the Health Center for "better care."

I never tired of telling my students the story of the Mississippi River — 25 how a scarlet oak leaf falling into Lake Itasca, in Minnesota, travels first north and then east through a wild, lonely landscape of lakes and rapids as if it were heading for Lake Superior, over the Falls of St. Anthony, down through Minneapolis and St. Paul, past bluffs and prairies and islands, to be joined by the Missouri River just above St. Louis, and then by the Ohio, where the water grows more than a mile wide — you can't see across it. My scarlet leaf meanders with eccentric loops and horseshoe curves down, down, down the great continent, through the delta, to New Orleans and beyond, past the great fertile mud plain shaped like a giant goose's foot, and into the Gulf of Mexico.

"And what happens to the leaf *then,* Mrs. Scully?" some student would never fail to ask.

"Ah," I would say, "then our little leaf becomes a part of the universe" — leaving them to ponder *that!*

I was known as a hard teacher but a fair one, and many of my students came back in later years to tell me how much they had learned.

Here at Marshwood, a "total" retirement community, they want us to become children again, forgoing intelligence. This is why I was so pleased when the announcement went up on the bulletin board about a month ago:

WRITING GROUP TO MEET

WEDNESDAY, 3:00 P.M.

Ah, I thought, that promising infinitive "to meet." For, like many former 30 English teachers, I had thought that someday I might like "to write."

At the appointed day and hour I motored over to the library (a euphemism since the room contains mostly well-worn paperbacks by Jacqueline Susann and Louis L'Amour). I was dismayed to find Martha Louise Clapton already in charge. The idea had been hers, I learned; I should have known. She's the type who tries to run everything. Martha Louise Clapton has never liked me, having had her eye on Solomon, to no avail, for years before my arrival. She inclined her frizzy blue head ever so slightly to acknowledge my entrance.

"As I was just saying, Alice, several of us have discovered in mealtime conversation that in fact we've been writing for years, in our journals and letters and whatnot, and so I said to myself, 'Martha Louise, why not form a writing group?' and *voilà*."

"*Voilà*," I said, edging into the circle.

So it began.

Besides Martha Louise and myself, the writing group included Joy Richter, a 35 minister's widow with a preference for poetry; Miss Elena Grier, who taught Shakespeare for years and years at a girls' preparatory school in Nashville, Tennessee; Frances Mason, whose husband lay in a coma over at the Health Center (another euphemism — you never leave the Health Center); Shirley Lassiter, who had buried three husbands and still thought of herself as a belle; and Sam Hofstetter, a retired lawyer, deaf as a post. We agreed to meet again in the library one week later. Each of us should bring some writing to share with the others.

"What's that?" Sam Hofstetter said. We wrote the time and place down on a little piece of paper and gave it to him. He folded the paper carefully, placing it in his pocket. "Could you make copies of the writing, please?" he asked. He inclined his silver head and tapped his ear significantly. We all agreed. Of course we agreed — we outnumber the men four to one, poor old things. In a place like this they get more attention than you would believe.

Then Joy Richter said that she probably couldn't afford to make copies. She said she was on a limited budget.

I said I felt sure we could use the Xerox machine in the manager's office, especially since we needed it for the writing group.

"Oh, I don't know." Frances Mason started wringing her hands. "They might not let us."

"I'll take care of it," Martha Louise said majestically. "Thank you, Alice, for 40 your suggestion. Thank you, everyone, for joining the group."

I had wondered if I might suffer initially from writer's block, but nothing of that sort occurred. In fact I was flooded by memories — overwhelmed, engulfed, as I sat in my chair by the picture window, writing on my lap board. I was not even aware of the world outside, my head was so full of the people and places of the past, rising up in my mind as they were then, in all the fullness of life, and myself as I was then, that headstrong girl longing to leave her home in east Virginia and walk in the world at large.

I wrote and wrote. I wrote for three days. I wrote until I felt satisfied, and then I stopped. I felt better than I had in years, full of new life and freedom (a paradox, since I am more and more confined to this chair).

During that week Solomon guessed "candy," "ring," and "Anacin." He was getting better. I was not. I ignored certain symptoms in order to attend the Wednesday meeting of the writing group.

Martha Louise led off. Her blue eyes looked huge, like lakes, behind her glasses. "They just don't make families like they used to," she began, and continued with an account of growing up on a farm in Ohio, how her parents struggled to make ends meet, how the children strung popcorn and cut out paper ornaments to trim the tree when they had no money for Christmas, how they pulled taffy and laid it out on a marble slab, and how each older child had a little one to take care of. "We were poor but we were happy," Martha Louise concluded. "It was an ideal childhood."

"Oh, Martha Louise," Frances Mason said tremulously, "that was just 45 beautiful."

Everyone agreed.

Too many adjectives, I thought, but I held my tongue.

Next Joy Richter read a poem about seeing God in everything: "the stuff of day" was a phrase I rather liked. Joy Richter apparently saw God in a shiny red apple, in a dewy rose, in her husband's kind blue eyes, in photographs of her grandchildren. The poem was pretty good, but it would have been better if she hadn't tried so hard to rhyme it.

Miss Elena then presented a sonnet comparing life to a merry-go-round. The final couplet went

> Lost children, though you're old, remember well
> The joy and music of life's carousel.

This was not bad, and I said so. Frances Mason read a reminiscence about 50 her husband's return from the Second World War, which featured the young Frances "hovering upon the future" in a porch swing as she "listened for the tread of his beloved boot." The military theme was continued by Sam Hofstetter, who read (loudly) an account of Army life titled "Somewhere in France." Shirley Lassiter was the only one whose story was not about herself. Instead it was fiction evidently modeled on a romance novel, for it involved a voluptuous debutante who had to choose between two men. Both of them were rich, and both of them loved her, but one had a fatal disease, and for some reason this young woman didn't know which one.

"Why not?" boomed the literal Sam.

"It's a mystery, silly," Shirley Lassiter said. "That's the plot." Shirley Lassiter had a way of resting her jeweled hands on her enormous bosom as if it were a shelf. "I don't want to give the plot away," she said. Clearly, she did not have a brain in her head.

Then came my turn.

I began to read the story of my childhood. I had grown up in the tiny coastal town of Waterville, Maryland. I was the fourth child in a family of five, with three older brothers and a baby sister. My father, who was in the oyster business, killed himself when I was six and Rose was only three. He went out into the Chesapeake Bay in an old rowboat, chopped a hole in the bottom of it with an ax, and then shot himself in the head with a revolver. He meant to finish the job. He did not sink as planned, however, because a fisherman witnessed the act, and hauled his body to shore.

This left Mama with five children to raise and no means of support. She 55 was forced to turn our home into a boardinghouse, keeping mostly teachers from Goucher College and salesmen passing through, although two old widows, Mrs. Flora Lewis and Mrs. Virginia Prince, stayed with us for years. Miss Flora, as we called her, had to have a cup of warm milk every night at bedtime; I will never forget it. It could be neither too hot nor too cold. I was the one who took it up to her, stepping so carefully up the dark back stair.

Nor will I forget young Miss Day from Richmond, a teacher, who played the piano beautifully. She used to play "Clair de Lune" and "Für Elise" on the old upright in the parlor. I would already have been sent to bed, and so I'd lie there trembling in the dark, seized by feelings I couldn't name, as the notes floated up to me and Rose in our little room, in our white iron bed wrought with roses and figures of nymphs. Miss Day was jilted some years later, we heard, her virtue lost and her reputation ruined.

Every Sunday, Mama presided over the big tureen at breakfast, when we'd have boiled fish and crisp little johnnycakes. To this day I have never tasted anything as good as those johnnycakes. Mama's face was flushed, and her hair escaped its bun to curl in damp tendrils as she dished up the breakfast plates. I thought she was beautiful. I'm sure she could have married again had she chosen to do so, but her heart was full of bitterness at the way her life had turned out, and she never forgave our father, or looked at another man.

Daddy had been a charmer, by all accounts. He carried a silver-handled cane and allowed me to play with his gold pocket watch when I was especially good. He took me to harness races, where we cheered for a horse he owned, a big roan named Joe Cord. On these excursions I wore a white dress and stockings and patent-leather shoes. And how Daddy could sing! He had a lovely baritone voice. I remember him on bended knee singing "Daisy, Daisy, give me your answer, do" to Mama, who pretended to be embarrassed but was not. I remember his bouncing Rose up and down on his lap and singing, "This is the way the lady rides."

After his death the boys went off to sea as soon as they could, and I was obliged to work in the kitchen and take care of Rose. Kitchen work in a boardinghouse is never finished. This is why I have never liked to cook since, though I know how to do it, I can assure you.

We had a summer kitchen outside, so that it wouldn't heat up the whole 60 house when we were cooking or canning. It had a kerosene stove. I remember one time when we were putting up blackberry jam, and one of those jars simply blew up. We had blackberry jam all over the place. Glass cut the Negro girl, Ocie, who was helping out, and I was surprised to see that her blood was as red as mine.

As time went on, Mama grew sadder and withdrew from us, sometimes barely speaking for days on end. My great joy was Rose, a lively child with golden curls and skin so fair you could see the blue veins beneath it. I slept with Rose every night and played with her every day. Since Mama was indisposed, we could do whatever we wanted, and we had the run of the town, just like boys. We'd go clamming in the bay with an inner tube floating out behind us, tied to my waist by a rope. We'd feel the clams with our feet and rake them up, flipping them into a net attached to the inner tube. Once, we went on a sailing trip with a cousin of ours, Bud Ned Black, up the Chickahominy River for a load of brick. But the wind failed and we got stuck there. We just *sat* on that river, for what seemed like days and days. Rose fussed and fumed while Cap'n Bud Ned drank whiskey and chewed tobacco and did not appear to mind the situation, so long as his supplies held out. But Rose was impatient — always, always so impatient.

"Alice," she said dramatically, as we sat staring out at the shining water, the green trees at its edge, the wheeling gulls, "I will *die* if we don't move. I will die here," Rose said, though Bud Ned and I laughed at her.

But Rose meant it. As she grew older, she had to go here, go there, do this, do that, have this, have that — she hated being poor and living in the boardinghouse, and could not wait to grow up and go away.

We both developed a serious taste for distance when our brother John and his wife took us motoring across the country. I was sixteen. I loved that trip, from the first stage of planning our route on the map to finally viewing the great mountains, which sprang straight up from the desert like apparitions. Of course, we had never seen such mountains; they took my breath away. I remember how Rose flung her arms out wide to the world as we stood in the cold wind on Pike's Peak. I believe we could have gone on driving and driving forever. But we had to return, and I had to resume my duties, letting go the girl John had hired so that Mama would permit my absence. John was our sweetest brother, but they are all dead now, all my brothers, and Rose, too.

I have outlived everyone.

65

Only yesterday Rose and I were little girls, playing a game we loved so well, a game that strikes me now as terribly dangerous. This memory is more vivid than any other in my life.

It is late night, summertime. Rose and I have sneaked out of the boardinghouse, down the tiny back stair past the gently sighing widows' rooms; past Mama's room, door open, moonlight ghostly on the mosquito netting draped from the canopy over her bed; past the snoring salesmen's rooms, stepping tiptoe across the wide-plank kitchen floor, wincing at each squeak; and out the kitchen door into moonlight so bright that it leaves shadows. Darting from tree to tree, we cross the yard and attain the sidewalk, moving rapidly past the big sleeping houses with their shutters yawning open to the cool night air, down the sidewalk to the edge of town where the sidewalk ends and the road goes on forever through miles and miles of peanut fields and other towns and other fields, toward Baltimore.

Rose and I lie down flat in the middle of the road, which still retains the heat of the day, and let it warm us head to toe as we dream aloud of what the future holds. At different times Rose planned to be an aviator, a doctor, and a film actress living in California, with an orange tree in her yard. Even her most domestic dreams were grand. "I'll have a big house and lots of servants and a husband who loves me *so much*," Rose would say, "and a yellow convertible touring car, and six children, and we will be rich and they will never have to work, and I will put a silk scarf on my head and we will all go out riding on Sunday."

Even then I said I would be a teacher, because I was always good in school, but I would be a missionary teacher, enlightening natives in some far-off corner of the world. Even as I said it, though, I believe I knew it would not come to pass, for I was bound to stay at home, as Rose was bound to go.

But we'd lie there looking up at the sky, and dream our dreams, and wait   70 for the thrill of an oncoming vehicle, which we could hear coming a long time away, and could feel throughout the length of our bodies as it neared us. We would roll off the pavement and in the peanut field just as the car approached, our hearts pounding. Sometimes we nearly dozed on that warm road — and once we were almost killed by a potato truck.

Gradually, as Mama retreated to her room, I took over the running of the boardinghouse, and Mama's care as well. At eighteen Rose ran away with a fast-talking furniture salesman who had been boarding with us. They settled finally in Ohio, and had three children, and her life was not glamorous in the least, though better than some, and we wrote to each other every week until her death, of ovarian cancer, at thirty-nine.

This was as far as I'd gotten.

I quit reading aloud and looked around the room. Joy Richter was ashen, Miss Elena Grier was mumbling to herself, and Shirley Lassiter was breathing heavily and fluttering her fingers at her throat. Sam Hofstetter stared fixedly at me with the oddest expression on his face, and Frances Mason wept openly, shaking with sobs.

"Alice! Now just look at what you've done!" Martha Louise said to me severely. "Meeting adjourned!"

I had to miss the third meeting of the writing group, because Dr. Culbertson   75 sent me to the Health Center for treatment and further tests (euphemisms both). Dr. Culbertson then went so far as to consult with my son Robert, also a doctor, about what to do with me next. Dr. Culbertson believed that I ought to move to the Health Center, for "better care." Of course I called Robert immediately and gave him a piece of my mind.

That was yesterday.

I know they are discussing me by telephone — Robert, Alex, Johnny, and Carl. Lines are buzzing up and down the East Coast.

I came here when I had to, because I did not want any of their wives to get stuck with me, as I had gotten stuck with Harold's mother and father. Now I expect some common decency and respect. At times like this I wish for daughters, who often, I feel, have more compassion and understanding than sons.

Even Carl, the child of my heart, says I had "better listen to the doctor."

Instead I have been listening to this voice too long silent inside me, the   80 voice of myself, as I write page after page propped up in bed in the Health Center.

Today is Wednesday. I have skipped certain of my afternoon medications. At 2:15 I buzz for Sheila, my favorite, a tall young nurse's aide with the grace of a gazelle. "Sheila," I say, "I need for you to help me dress, dear, and then roll my chair over here, if you will. My own chair, I mean. I have to go to a meeting."

Sheila looks at my chart and then back at me, her eyes wide. "It doesn't say . . ." she begins.

"Dr. Culbertson said it would be perfectly all right," I assure her. I pull a $20.00 bill from my purse, which I keep right beside me in bed, and hand it to her. "I know it's a lot of trouble, but it's very important," I say. "I think I'll just slip on the red sweater and the black wraparound skirt — that's so easy to get on. "They're both in the drawer, dear."

"Okay, honey," Sheila says, and she gets me dressed and sets me in my chair. I put on lipstick and have Sheila fluff up my hair in the back where it's gotten so flat from lying in bed. Sheila hands me my purse and my notebook, and then I'm off, waving to the girls at the nurses' station as I purr past them. They wave back. I feel fine now. I take the elevator down to the first floor and then motor through the lobby, speaking to acquaintances. I pass the gift shop, the newspaper stand, and all the waiting rooms.

It's chilly outside. I head up the walkway past the par three golf course, 85 where I spy Parker Howard, ludicrous in those bright-green pants they sell to old men, putting on the third hole. "Hi, Parker!" I cry.

"Hello, Alice," he calls. "Nice to see you out!" He sinks the putt.

I enter the Multipurpose Building and head for the library, where the writers' group is already in progress. Driving over from the Health Center took longer than I'd expected.

Miss Elena is reading, but she stops and looks up when I come in, her mouth a perfect O. Everybody looks at Martha Louise.

"Why, Alice," Martha Louise says. She clears her throat. "We didn't expect that you would be joining us today. We heard that you were in the Health Center."

"I was," I say. "But I'm out now."   90

"Evidently," Martha Louise says.

I ride up to the circular table, set my brake, get out my notebook, and ask Miss Elena for a copy of whatever she's reading. Wordless, she slides one over. But she still does not resume. They're all looking at me.

"What is it?" I ask.

"Well, Alice, last week, when you were absent, we laid out some ground rules for this writing group." Martha Louise gains composure as she goes along. "We are all in agreement here, Alice, that if this is to be a pleasant and meaningful club for all of us, we need to restrict our subject matter to what everyone enjoys."

"So?" I don't get it.   95

"We've also adopted an official name for the group." Now Martha Louise is as cheerful as a robin.

"It's the Happy Memories Club," she announces, and they all nod.

I am beginning to get it.

"You mean to tell me —" I start.   100

"I mean to tell you that if you wish to be a part of this group, Alice Scully, you will have to calm yourself down, and keep your subject matter in check. We don't come here to be upset," Martha Louise says serenely.

They are all watching me closely now, Sam Hofstetter in particular. I think they expect an outburst.

But I won't give them the satisfaction.

"Fine," I say. This is a lie. "That sounds just fine to me. Good idea!" I smile at everybody.

There is a perceptible relaxation then, an audible settling back into chairs, 105 as Miss Elena resumes her reading. It's a travelogue named "Shakespeare and His Haunts," about a tour she made to England several years ago. But I find myself unable to listen. I simply can't hear Elena, or Joy, who reads next, or even Sam.

"Well, is that it for today? Anybody else?" Martha Louise raps her knuckles against the table. "I brought something," I say, "but I don't have copies."

I look at Sam, who shrugs and smiles and says I should go ahead anyway. Everybody else looks at Martha Louise.

"Well, go on, then," she directs tartly, and I begin.

After Rose's disappearance, my mother took to her bed and turned her face to the wall, leaving me in charge of everything. Oh, how I worked! I worked like a dog, long hours, a cruelly unnatural life for a spirited young woman. Yet I persevered. People in the town, including our minister, complimented me; I was discussed and admired. Our boardinghouse stayed full, and somehow I managed, with Ocie's help, to get the meals on the table. I smiled and chattered at mealtime. Yet inside I was starving, starving for love and life.

Thus it was not surprising, I suppose, that I should fall for the first man   110
who showed any interest in me. He was a schoolteacher who had been educated at the university, in Charlottesville, a thin, dreamy young man from one of the finest families in Virginia. His grandfather had been the governor. He used to sit out by the sound every evening after supper, reading, and one day I joined him there. It was a lovely June evening; the sound was full of sailboats, and the sky above us was as round and blue as a bowl.

"I was reading a poem about a girl with beautiful yellow hair," he said, "and then I look up and what do I see? A real girl with beautiful yellow hair."

For some reason I started to cry, not even caring what my other boarders thought as they sat up on the porch looking out over this landscape in which we figured.

"Come here," he said, and he took my hand and led me behind the old rose-covered boathouse, where he pulled me to him and kissed me curiously, as if it were an experiment.

His name was Carl Redding Armistead III. He had the reedy look of a poet, but all the assurance of the privileged class. I was older than he, but he was more experienced. He was well educated, and had been to Europe several times.

"You pretty thing," he said, and kissed me again. The scent of the roses   115
was everywhere.

I went that night to his room, and before the summer was out, we had lain together in nearly every room of the boardinghouse. We were crazy for each other by then, and I didn't care what might happen, or who knew. On Saturday evenings I'd leave a cold supper for the rest, and Carl and I would take the skiff and row out to Sand Island, where the wild ponies were, and take off all our clothes and make love. Sometimes my back would be red and bleeding from the rough black sand and the broken shells on the beach.

"Just a minute! Just a minute here!" Martha Louise is pounding on the table, and Frances Mason is crying, as usual. Sam Hofstetter is staring at me in a manner that indicates that he has heard every word I've said.

"Well, I think that's terrific!" Shirley Lassiter giggles and bats her painted blue eyelids at us all.

Of course this romance did not last. Nothing that intense can be sustained, though the loss of such intensity can scarcely be borne. Quite simply, Carl and I foundered upon the prospect of the future. He had to go on to the world that awaited him; I could not leave Mama. Our final parting was bitter—we were spent, exhausted by the force of what had passed between us. He did not even look back as he sped away in his little red sports car, nor did I cry.

Nor did I ever tell him about the existence of Carl, my son, whom I bore 120 defiantly out of wedlock nine months later, telling no one who the father was. Oh, those were hard, black days! I was ostracized by the very people who had formerly praised me, and ogled by the men in my boardinghouse, who now considered me a fallen woman. I wore myself to a frazzle taking care of Mama and the baby at the same time.

One night, I remember, I was so tired that I felt that I would actually die, yet little Carl would not stop crying. Nothing would quiet him—not rocking, not the breast, not walking the room. He had an oddly unpleasant cry, like a cat mewing. I remember looking out my window at the quiet town where everyone slept—everyone on this earth, I felt, except me. I held Carl out at arm's length and looked hard at him in the streetlight, at his red, twisted little face. I had an awful urge to throw him out the window—

"That's enough!" several of them say at once. Martha Louise is standing.

But it is Miss Elena who speaks. "I cannot believe," she say severely, "that out of your entire life, Alice Scully, this is all you can find to write about. What of your long marriage to Mr. Scully? Your seven grandchildren? Those of us who have not been blessed with grandchildren would give—"

Of course I loved Harold Scully. Of course I love my grandchildren. I love Solomon, too. I love them all. Miss Elena is like my sons, too terrified to admit to herself how many people we can love, how various we are. She does not want to hear it any more than they do, any more than you do. You all want us to *never change, never change.*

I did not throw my baby out the window after all, and my mother finally 125 died, and I sold the boardinghouse then and was able, at last, to go to school.

Out of the corner of my eye I see Dr. Culbertson appear at the library door, accompanied by a man I do not know. Martha Louise says, "I simply cannot believe that a former *English teacher*—"

This strikes me as very funny. My mind is filled with enormous sentences as I back up my chair and then start forward, out the other door and down the hall and outside into the sweet spring day, where the sunshine falls on my face as it did in those days on the beach, my whole body hot and aching and sticky with sweat and salt and blood, the wild ponies paying us no mind as they ate the tall grass that grew at the edge of the dunes. Sometimes the ponies came so close that we could reach out and touch them. Their coats were shaggy and rough and full of burrs, I remember.

Oh, I remember everything as I cruise forward on the sidewalk that neatly separates the rock garden from the golf course. I turn right at the corner, instead of left toward the Health Center. "Fore!" Parker Howard shouts, waving at me. *A former English teacher*, Martha Louise said. These sidewalks are like diagrams, parallel lines and dividers: oh, I could diagram anything. The semicolon, I used to say, is like a little scale; it must have items of equal rank, I'd warn them. Do not use a semicolon between a clause and a phrase, or a main clause and a subordinate clause. Do not write *I loved Carl Redding Armistead; a rich man's son.* Do not write *If I had really loved Carl Armistead; I would have left with him despite all obstacles.* Do not write *I still feel his touch; which has thrilled me throughout my life.*

I turn at the top of the hill and motor along the sidewalk toward the Residence Center, hoping to see Solomon. The sun is in my eyes. Do not carelessly link two sentences with a comma. Do not write *I want to see Solomon again, he has meant so much to me.* To correct this problem, subordinate one of the parts. *I want to see Solomon, because he has meant so much to me.* Because he has meant. So much. To me. Fragments. Fragments all. I push the button to open the door into the Residence Center, and sure enough, they've brought him out. They've dressed him in his Madras plaid shirt and wheeled him in front of the television, which he hates. I cruise right over.

"Solomon," I say, but at first he doesn't respond when he looks at me. I   130
come even closer. "Solomon!" I say sharply, bumping his wheelchair. He notices me then, and a little light comes into his eyes.

I cup my hands. "Solomon," I say, "I'll give you a kiss if you can guess what I've got in my hands."

He looks at me for a while longer.

"Now, Mrs. Scully," his nurse starts.

"Come on," I say. "What have I got in here?"

"An elephant," Solomon finally says.   135

"Close enough!" I cry, and lean right over to kiss his sweet old cheek, being unable to reach his mouth.

"Mrs. Scully," his nurse starts again, but I'm gone, I'm history, I'm out the front door and around the parking circle and up the long entrance drive to the highway. It all connects. Everything connects. The sun is bright, the dogwoods are blooming, the state flower of Virginia is the dogwood, I can still see the sun on the Chickahominy River and my own little sons as they sail their own little boats in a tidal pool by the Chesapeake Bay, they were all blond boys once, though their hair would darken later, Annapolis is the capital of Maryland, the first historic words ever transmitted by telegraph came to Maryland: "What hath God wrought?" The sun is still shining. It glares off the snow on Pike's Peak, it gleams through the milky blue glass of the old apothecary jar in the window of Harold Scully's shop, it warms the asphalt on that road where Rose and I lie waiting, waiting, waiting.

CONSIDERATIONS FOR CRITICAL THINKING AND WRITING

1. **FIRST RESPONSE.** Lee Smith has observed about the humor in her writing that "I tend to see life fairly tragically. If you do that, you've got two choices: you can either go in the closet and sit in the dark or you can make jokes . . . ." How accurately do you think this describes her writing strategy in "The Happy Memories Club"?

2. How effective do you think Smith's descriptions of life in Marshwood are in evoking life in an old-age home? What is the significance of the setting?

3. Characterize Alice as a young and old woman. Explain whether or not her character seems to be consistent.

4. Why is Alice's point of view crucial to the story? Imagine it written in the third person. How would that change your reading of it?

5. What does Alice's story-within-the-story add to your understanding of her character?

6. How does the plot of Alice's written story about herself relate to the larger plot that frames it? Are there significant parallels or contrasts between them?

7. What is the purpose of the minor characters in Marshwood? How are they connected to the conflict in the plot? Consider especially their response to Alice's reading about her early life.

8. Consider the symbolic value of Alice's discussion of punctuation in paragraphs 128–29. How is it related to the theme?

9. "It all connects. Everything connects." Discuss the potential meaning of these lines in the story's final paragraph.

10. Consider the tone of the title. How do you interpret its meaning?

CONNECTIONS TO OTHER SELECTIONS

1. Discuss the treatment of old age in Smith's story and in Peter Meinke's "The Cranes" (p. 259). Explain why each is so convincing.

2. Consider Alice's assertion that "our memories are all we've got" (paragraph 6) in relation to Kelly Cherry's poem "Alzheimer's" (p. 807). How does the poem implicitly comment on Solomon Marx's condition in Smith's story?

MARK TWAIN (1835–1910)

Mark Twain is the pen name of Samuel Clemens, born in Missouri in 1835. Twain spent most of his childhood in Hannibal, Missouri, on the Mississippi River, and after the death of his father when he was eleven, he worked at a series of jobs to help support his family. A newspaper job prepared him to wander east working for papers and exploring St. Louis, New York, and Philadelphia. Later he trained as a steamboat pilot on the Mississippi and piloted boats professionally until the onset of the Civil War. Clemens had used a couple of different

© Bettmann/CORBIS.

pseudonyms for minor publications before this point, but in 1863 he signed a travel narrative "Mark Twain," from a boating term that means "two fathoms deep," and the name for the great American humorist was created. Twain gained fame in 1865 with his story "The Celebrated Jumping Frog of Calaveras County," which appeared in New York–based *The Saturday Press*. He then became a traveling correspondent, writing pieces on his travels to Europe and the Middle East, and returned to the United States in 1870, when he married and moved to Connecticut. Twain produced *Roughing It* (1872) and *The Gilded Age* (1873) while he toured the country lecturing, and in 1876 published *The Adventures of Tom Sawyer*, an instant hit. His subsequent publications include *A Tramp Abroad* (1880), *The Prince and the Pauper* (1881), and the masterpiece *The Adventures of Huckleberry Finn* (1884). Often traveling and lecturing, Twain wrote several more books, including story collections, *The Tragedy of Pudd'nhead Wilson* (1894), and *Tom Sawyer, Detective* (1896), before he died in Italy in 1910. His work is noted for the combination of rough humor and vernacular language it often uses to convey keen social insights. In "The Story of the Good Little Boy" Twain offers his version of a Sunday-school lesson.

The Story of the Good Little Boy   1870

Once there was a good little boy by the name of Jacob Blivens. He always obeyed his parents, no matter how absurd and unreasonable their demands were; and he always learned his book, and never was late at Sabbath-school. He would not play hookey, even when his sober judgment told him it was the most profitable thing he could do. None of the other boys could ever make that boy out, he acted so strangely. He wouldn't lie, no matter how convenient it was. He just said it was wrong to lie, and that was sufficient for him. And he was so honest that he was simply ridiculous. The curious ways that that Jacob had, surpassed everything. He wouldn't play marbles on Sunday, he wouldn't rob birds' nests, he wouldn't give hot pennies to organ-grinders' monkeys; he didn't seem to take any interest in any kind of rational amusement. So the other boys used to try to reason it out and come to an understanding of him, but they couldn't arrive at any satisfactory conclusion. As I said before, they could only figure out a sort of vague idea that he was "afflicted," and so they took him under their protection, and never allowed any harm to come to him.

This good little boy read all the Sunday-school books; they were his greatest delight. This was the whole secret of it. He believed in the good little boys they put in the Sunday-school books; he had every confidence in them. He longed to come across one of them alive once; but he never did. They all died before his time, maybe. Whenever he read about a particularly good one he turned over quickly to the end to see what became of him, because he wanted to travel thousands of miles and gaze on him; but it wasn't any use; that good little boy always died in the last chapter, and there was a picture of the funeral, with all his relations and the Sunday-school children standing around the grave in pantaloons that were too short, and bonnets that were too large, and everybody crying into handkerchiefs that had as much as a yard and a half of stuff in them. He was always headed off in this way. He never could see one of those good little boys on account of his always dying in the last chapter.

Jacob had a noble ambition to be put in a Sunday-school book. He wanted to be put in, with pictures representing him gloriously declining to lie to his mother, and her weeping for joy about it; and pictures representing him standing on the doorstep giving a penny to a poor beggar-woman with six children, and telling her to spend it freely, but not to be extravagant, because extravagance is a sin; and pictures of him magnanimously refusing to tell on the bad boy who always lay in wait for him around the corner as he came from school, and welted him over the head with a lath, and then chased him home, saying, "Hi! hi!" as he proceeded. That was the ambition of young Jacob Blivens. He wished to be put in a Sunday-school book. It made him feel a little uncomfortable sometimes when he reflected that the good little boys always died. He loved to live, you know, and this was the most unpleasant feature about being a Sunday-school-book boy. He knew it was not healthy to be good. He knew it was more fatal than consumption to be so supernaturally good as the boys in the books were; he knew that none of them had ever been able to stand it long, and it pained him to think that if they put him in a book he wouldn't ever see it, or even if they did get the book out before he died it wouldn't be popular without any picture of his funeral in the back part of it. It couldn't be much of a Sunday-school book that couldn't tell about the advice he gave to the community when he was dying. So at last, of course, he had to make up his mind to do the best he could under the circumstances — to live right, and, hang on as long as he could, and have his dying speech all ready when his time came.

But somehow nothing ever went right with this good little boy; nothing ever turned out with him the way it turned out with the good little boys in the books. They always had a good time, and the bad boys had the broken legs; but in his case there was a screw loose somewhere, and it all happened just the other way. When he found Jim Blake stealing apples, and went under the tree to read to him about the bad little boy who fell out of a neighbor's apple tree and broke his arm, Jim fell out of the tree, too, but he fell on *him* and broke *his* arm, and Jim wasn't hurt at all. Jacob couldn't understand that. There wasn't anything in the books like it.

And once, when some bad boys pushed a blind man over in the mud, and 5 Jacob ran to help him up and receive his blessing, the blind man did not give him any blessing at all, but whacked him over the head with his stick and said he would like to catch him shoving *him* again, and then pretending to help him up. This was not in accordance with any of the books. Jacob looked them all over to see.

One thing that Jacob wanted to do was to find a lame dog that hadn't any place to stay, and was hungry and persecuted, and bring him home and pet him and have that dog's imperishable gratitude. And at last he found one and was happy; and he brought him home and fed him, but when he was going to pet him the dog flew at him and tore all the clothes off him except those that were in front, and made a spectacle of him that was astonishing. He examined authorities, but he could not understand the matter. It was of the same breed of dogs that was in the books, but it acted very differently. Whatever this boy did he got into trouble. The very things the boys in the books got rewarded for turned out to be about the most unprofitable things be could invest in.

Once, when he was on his way to Sunday-school, he saw some bad boys starting off pleasuring in a sailboat. He was filled with consternation, because he knew from his reading that boys who went sailing on Sunday invariably got drowned. So he ran out on a raft to warn them, but a log turned with him and slid him into the river. A man got him out pretty soon, and the doctor pumped the water out of him, and gave him a fresh start with his bellows, but he caught cold and lay sick abed nine weeks. But the most unaccountable thing about it was that the bad boys in the boat had a good time all day, and then reached home alive and well in the most surprising manner. Jacob Blivens said there was nothing like these things in the books. He was perfectly dumbfounded.

When he got well he was a little discouraged, but he resolved to keep on trying anyhow. He knew that so far his experiences wouldn't do to go in a book, but he hadn't yet reached the allotted term of life for good little boys, and he hoped to be able to make a record yet if he could hold on till his time was fully up. If everything else failed he had his dying speech to fall back on.

He examined his authorities, and found that it was now time for him to go to sea as a cabin-boy. He called on a ship-captain and made his application, and when the captain asked for his recommendations he proudly drew out a tract and pointed to the word, "To Jacob Blivens, from his affectionate teacher." But the captain was a coarse, vulgar man, and he said, "Oh, that be blowed! *that* wasn't any proof that he knew how to wash dishes or handle a slush-bucket, and he guessed he didn't want him." This was altogether the most extraordinary thing that ever happened to Jacob in all his life. A compliment from a teacher, on a tract, had never failed to move the tenderest emotions of ship-captains, and open the way to all offices of honor and profit in their gift—it never had in any book that ever *he* had read. He could hardly believe his senses.

This boy always had a hard time of it. Nothing ever came out according to the authorities with him. At last, one day, when he was around hunting up bad little boys to admonish, he found a lot of them in the old iron-foundry fixing up a little joke on fourteen or fifteen dogs, which they had tied together in long procession, and were going to ornament with empty nitroglycerin cans made fast to their tails. Jacob's heart was touched. He sat down on one of those cans (for he never minded grease when duty was before him), and he took hold of the foremost dog by the collar, and turned his reproving eye upon wicked Tom Jones. But just at that moment Alderman McWelter, full of wrath, stepped in. All the bad boys ran away, but Jacob Blivens rose in conscious innocence and began one of those stately little Sunday-school-book speeches which always commence with "Oh, sir!" in dead opposition to the fact that no boy, good or bad, ever starts a remark with "Oh, sir." But the alderman never waited to hear the rest. He took Jacob Blivens by the ear and turned him around, and hit him a whack in the rear with the flat of his hand; and in an instant that good little boy shot out through the roof and soared away toward the sun, with the fragments of those fifteen dogs stringing after him like the tail of a kite. And there wasn't a sign of that alderman or that old iron-foundry left on the face of the earth; and, as for young Jacob Blivens, he never got a chance to make his last dying speech after all his trouble fixing it up, unless he made it to the birds; because, although the bulk of him came down all right in a tree-top in an adjoining county, the rest of him was apportioned around among four townships, and so they had to hold five inquests on him to find out whether he was dead or not, and how it occurred. You never saw a boy scattered so.[1]

Thus perished the good little boy who did the best he could, but didn't come out according to the books. Every boy who ever did as he did prospered except him. His case is truly remarkable. It will probably never be accounted for.

---

[1] This glycerin catastrophe is borrowed from a floating newspaper item, whose author's name I would give if I knew it. M.T.

Considerations for Critical Thinking and Writing

1. **FIRST RESPONSE.** This story is about the death of a child. What's so funny about that?

2. What is the story's central irony?

3. Which sentences are particularly effective in imitating the style of Sunday-school books? Which sentences are clearly Twain's style? What is the effect of having both styles side by side?

4. How does the story's irony reveal Twain's attitude toward Jacob? Find specific passages to support your points.

5. What sort of lesson does Twain's version of Sunday-school instruction teach?

6. Is there a serious point to the humor here? What is the theme of the story?

7. It might be tempting to sum up this story with something like "Nice guys finish last." Discuss the adequacy of this as a statement of theme.

8. Characterize the tone of voice that tells the story. Is it indignant, amused, cynical, bitter, disinterested, or what?

Connections to Other Selections

1. Compare Jacob's fate with that of the central character in Ralph Ellison's "Battle Royal" (p. 243).

2. Write an essay explaining the extent to which this story and Stephen Crane's "The Bride Comes to Yellow Sky" (p. 266) are dependent on a reader's familiarity with the formulaic qualities of Sunday-school stories or traditional westerns.

A Collection
of Stories

16

An Album of
Contemporary Stories

Style is not neutral; it gives moral
directions.
— MARTIN AMIS

© Gary Isaacs.

MARTIN AMIS (B. 1949)

Born in Oxford, England, Martin Amis is the son of the British novelist
Kingsley Amis, and has earned a solid reputation in England and the
United States for his dark, satiric writing. After taking his degree at Oxford
University, he worked at the *Times Literary Supplement* and as editor of the
New Statesman by the time he was in his late twenties. Amis has written
more than twenty books, including novels, collections of short stories, and
nonfiction prose while contributing regularly to major British and Ameri-
can periodicals. Among his novels are *The Rachel Papers* (1973), *Money* (1984),
London Fields (1989), *Time's Arrow* (1991), *The Information* (1995), and *Yellow
Dog* (2003). He has published three collections of short stories: *Einstein's
Monsters* (1987), *Heavy Water* (1998), and *House of Meetings* (2006). "The Last

Days of Muhammad Atta" explores the mind of the suicide pilots who led the World Trade Center attacks on September 11, 2001. The story was first published in *The New Yorker*.

The Last Days of Muhammad Atta   2006

No physical, documentary, or analytical evidence provides a convincing explanation of why [Muhammad] Atta and [Abdulaziz al] Omari drove to Portland, Maine, from Boston on the morning of September 10, only to return to Logan on Flight 5930 on the morning of September 11.

—the 9/11 Commission Report.

I

On September 11, 2001, he opened his eyes at 4 A.M., in Portland, Maine; and Muhammad Atta's last day began.

What was the scene of this awakening? A room in a hotel, of the type designated as "budget" in his guidebook—one step up from "basic." It was a Repose Inn, part of a chain. But it wasn't like the other Repose Inns he had lodged at: brisk, hygienic establishments. This place was ponderous and labyrinthine, and as elderly as most of its clientele. And it was cheap. So. The padded nylon bedcover as weighty as a lead vest; the big cuboid television on the dresser opposite; and the dented white fridge—where, as it happened, Muhammad Atta's reason for coming to Portland, Maine, lay cooling on a shelf. . . . The particular frugality of these final weeks was part of a peer-group piety contest that he was laconically going along with. Like the others, he was attending to his prayers, disbursing his alms, washing often, eating little, sleeping little. (But he wasn't like the others.) Days earlier, their surplus operational funds—about twenty-six thousand dollars—had been abstemiously wired back to the go-between in Dubai.

He slid from the bed and called Abdulaziz, who was already stirring, and perhaps already praying, next door. Then to the bathroom: the chore of ablution, the ordeal of excretion, the torment of depilation. He activated the shower nozzle and removed his undershorts. He stepped within, submitting to the cold and clammy caress of the plastic curtain on his calf and thigh. Then he spent an unbelievably long time trying to remove a hair from the bar of soap. The alien strand kept changing its shape—question mark, infinity symbol—but stayed in place; and the bar of soap, no bigger than a matchbook when he began, barely existed when he finished. Next, as sometimes happens in these old, massive, and essentially well-intentioned and broad-handed hotels, the water gave a gulp and then turned, in an instant, from a tepid trickle to a molten blast; and as he struggled from the stall he trod on a leaking shampoo sachet and fell heavily and sharply on his coccyx. He had to kick himself out through the steam, and rasped his head on the shower's serrated metal sill. After a while he slowly climbed to his feet and stood there, hands on hips, eyes only lightly closed, head bowed, awaiting recovery. He dried himself with a thin white towel, catching a hangnail in its shine.

Now, emitting a sigh of unqualified grimness, he crouched on the bowl. He didn't even bother with his usual scowling and straining and shuddering, partly because his head felt dangerously engorged. More saliently, he had not moved his bowels since May. In general his upper body was impressively lean, from all the hours in the gym with the "muscle" Saudis; but now there was a solemn mound where his abdominals used to be, as taut and proud as a four-month pregnancy. Nor was this the only sequela. He had a feverish and unvarying ache, not in his gut but in his lower back, his pelvic saddle, and his scrotum. Every few minutes he was required to wait out an interlude of nausea, while disused gastric juices bubbled up in the sump of his throat. His breath smelled like a blighted river.

The worst was yet to come: shaving. Shaving was the worst because it nec- 5 essarily involved him in the contemplation of his own face. He looked downward while he lathered his cheeks, but then the chin came up and there it was, revealed by the razor in vertical strips: the face of Muhammad Atta. A year ago, after Afghanistan, he had said goodbye to his beard. Tangled and oblong and slightly off-center, it had had the effect of softening the disgusted lineaments of his mouth, and it had wholly concealed the frank animus of his underbite. His insides were seized, but his face was somehow incontinent, or so Muhammad Atta felt. The detestation, the detestation of everything, was being sculpted on it, from within. He was amazed that he was still allowed to walk the streets, let alone enter a building or board a plane. Another day, one more day, and they wouldn't let him. Why didn't everybody point, why didn't they cringe, why didn't they run? And yet this face, by now almost comically malevolent, would soon be smiled at, and perfunctorily fussed over (his ticket was business class), by the doomed stewardess.

A hypothesis. If he stood down from the planes operation, and it went ahead without him (or if he somehow survived it), he would never again be able to travel by air in the United States or anywhere else—not by air, not by train, not by boat, not by bus. The profiling wouldn't need to be racial; it would be facial, merely. No sane man or woman would ever agree to be confined in his vicinity. With that face, growing more gangrenous by the day. And that name, the name he journeyed under, itself like a promise of vengeance: Muhammad Atta.

In the last decade, only one human being had taken obvious pleasure from setting eyes on him, and that was the Sheikh. It had happened at their introductory meeting, in Kandahar—where, within a matter of minutes, the Sheikh had appointed him operation leader. Muhammad Atta had known that the first thing he would be asked was whether he was prepared to die. But the Sheikh was smiling, almost with eyes of love, when he said it. "The question isn't necessary," he began. "I see the answer in your face."

The Colgan Air commuter flight to Logan was scheduled to leave at six. So he had an hour. He put on his clothes (the dark-blue shirt, the black slacks), and settled himself at the dresser, awkwardly, his legs out to one side. Two documents were before him. He yawned, then sneezed. While shaving, Muhammad

Atta, for the first time in his life, had cut himself on the lip (the lower); with surprising speed the gash had settled into a convincing imitation of a cold sore. Much less unusually, he had also nicked the fleshy volute of his right nostril, releasing an apparently endless supply of blood; he kept having to get up and fetch more tissues, leaving behind him a paper trail of the stanched gouts. The themes of recurrence and prolongation, he sensed, were already beginning to associate themselves with his last day.

Document No. 1 was displayed on the screen of his laptop. It was his last will and testament, composed in April, 1996, when the thoughts of the group had turned to Chechnya.° Two Moroccan friends, Mounir and Abdelghani, both devout, had been his witnesses, so he had included a fair amount of formulaic sanctimony. Any old thing would do. "During my funeral, I want everyone to be quiet because God mentioned that he likes being quiet on three occasions, when you recite the Koran, during the funeral, and when you are crawling." Crawling? Had he mistyped? Another provision stared out at him, and further deepened his frown: "The person who will wash my body near my genitals must wear gloves on his hands so he won't touch my genitals." And this: "I don't want a pregnant woman or a person who is not clean to come and say goodbye to me because I don't approve of it." Well, these anxieties were now academic. No one would say goodbye to him. No one would wash him. No one would touch his genitals.

There was another document on the dresser's surface, a four-page booklet in Arabic, put together by the information office in Kandahar (and bound by a grimy tassel). Each of them had been given one; the others would often produce their personal copies and nod and sway and mutter over them for hour after hour. But Muhammad Atta wasn't like the others (and he was paying a price for it). He had barely glanced at the thing until now. "Pull your shoelaces tight and wear tight socks that grip the shoes and do not come out of them." He supposed that this was sound advice. "Let every one of you sharpen his knife and kill his animal and bring about comfort and relief of his slaughter." A reference, presumably, to what would happen to the pilots, the first officers, the flight attendants. Some of the Saudis, they said, had butchered sheep and camels at Khaldan, the training camp near Kabul. Muhammad Atta did not expect to relish that part of it: the exemplary use of the box cutters. He pictured the women, in their uniforms, in their open-necked shirts. He did not expect to like it; he did not expect to like death in that form.

Now he sat back, and felt the approach of nausea: it gathered round him, then sifted through him. His mind, inasmuch as it was separable from his body, was close to the "complete tranquillity" praised and recommended by Kandahar. A very different kind of thirty-three-year-old might have felt the same tranced surety while contemplating an afternoon in a borrowed apartment with his true love (and sexual obsession). But Muhammad Atta's mind and his body were not separable: this was the difficulty; this was the mind-body problem — in his case, fantastically acute. Muhammad Atta wasn't like the others, because he was doing what he was doing for the core reason. The

Chechnya: a federal subject of Russia that declared its independence as the Chechen Republic in 1991; it is not recognized by any state as an independent nation, though it is recognized as such by the Afghan Taliban.

others were doing what they were doing for the core reason, too, but they had achieved sublimation, by means of jihadi ardor; and their bodies had been convinced by this arrangement and had gone along with it. They ate, drank, smoked, smiled, snored; they took the stairs two at a time. Muhammad Atta's body had not gone along with it. He was doing what he was doing for the core reason and for the core reason only.

"Purify your heart and cleanse it of stains. Forget and be oblivious of the thing which is called World." Muhammad Atta was not religious; he was not even especially political. He had allied himself with the militants because jihad was, by many magnitudes, the most charismatic idea of his generation. To unite ferocity and rectitude in a single word: nothing could compete with that. He played along with it, and did the things that impressed his peers; he collected citations, charities, pilgrimages, conspiracy theories, and so on, as other people collected autographs or beer mats. And it suited his character. If you took away all the rubbish about faith, then fundamentalism suited his character, and with an almost sinister precision.

For example, the attitude toward women: the blend of extreme hostility and extreme wariness he found highly congenial. In addition, he liked the idea of the brotherhood, although of course he thoroughly despised the current contingent, particularly his fellow-pilots: Hani (the Pentagon) he barely knew, but he was continuously enraged by Marwan (the other Twin Tower) and almost fascinated by the pitch of his loathing for Ziad (the Capitol). . . . Adultery punished by whipping, sodomy by burial alive: this seemed about right to Muhammad Atta. He also joined in the hatred of music. And the hatred of laughter. "Why do you never laugh?" he and the others were sometimes asked. Ziad would answer, "How can you laugh when people are dying in Palestine?" Muhammad Atta never laughed, not because people were dying in Palestine but because he found nothing funny. *The thing which is called World.* That, too, spoke to him. World had always felt like an illusion – an unreal mockery.

"The time between you and your marriage in heaven is very short." Ah, yes, the virgins: six dozen of them – half a gross. He had read in a news magazine that "virgins," in the holy book, was a mistranslation from the Aramaic. It should be "raisins." He idly wondered whether the quibble might have something to do with "sultana," which meant (a) a small seedless raisin, and (b) the wife or concubine of a sultan. Abdulaziz, Marwan, Ziad, and the others: they would not be best pleased, on their arrival in the Garden, to find a little red packet of Sun-Maid Sultanas (Average Contents 72). Muhammad Atta, with his two degrees in architecture, his excellent English, his excellent German: Muhammad Atta did not believe in the virgins, did not believe in the Garden. (How could he believe in such an implausibly, and dauntingly, priapic paradise?) He was an apostate: that's what he was. He didn't expect paradise. What he expected was oblivion. And, strange to say, he would find neither.

He packed. He paused and stooped over the dented refrigerator, then straightened up and headed for the door. 15

In its descent the elevator, with a succession of long-suffering sighs, stopped at the twelfth, the eleventh, the tenth, the ninth, the eighth, the seventh, the sixth, the fifth, the fourth, the third, and the second floors. Old people, their faces flickering with distrust, inched in and out; while they did so, one of their number would press the open-doors button with a defiant, Marfanic° thumb. And at this hour, too: it was barely light. Muhammad Atta briefly horrified himself with the notion that they were all lovers, returning early to their beds. But no: it must be the sleeplessness, the insomnia of age—the dawn vigils of age. Their efforts to stay alive, in any case, struck him as essentially ignoble. He had felt the same way in the hospital the night before, when he went to see the imam. . . . Consulting his watch every ten or fifteen seconds, he decided that this downward journey was dead time, as dead as time could get, like queuing, or an interminable red light, or staring stupidly at the baggage on an airport carrousel. He stood there, hemmed in by pallor and decay, and martyred by compound revulsions.

Abdulaziz was waiting for him in the weak glow and piped music of the lobby. Wordless, breakfastless, they joined the line for checkout. More dead time passed. As they fell into step and proceeded through the last of the night to the parking lot, Muhammad Atta, in no very generous spirit, considered his colleague. This particular muscle Saudi seemed as limply calflike as Ahmed al Nami—the prettyboy in Ziad's platoon. On the other hand, Abdulaziz, with his softly African face, his childish eyes, was almost insultingly easy to dominate. He had a wife and a daughter in southern Saudi Arabia. But this was like saying that he had a flatbed truck in southern Saudi Arabia, so little did it appear to weigh on him. He had also, incredibly, performed certain devotional duties at his local mosque. And yet it was Abdulaziz who carried the knife, Abdulaziz who was ready to apply it to the flesh of the stewardess.

When they reached their car Abdulaziz said a few words in praise of God, adding, with some attempt at panache, "So. Let us begin our 'architectural studies.'"

Muhammad Atta felt his body give an involuntary jolt. "Who told you?" he said.

"Ziad."

They loaded up and then bent themselves into the front seats.

Abdulaziz wasn't supposed to know about that—about the target code. "Law" was the Capitol. "Politics" was the White House. In the discussions with the Sheikh there had been firm concurrence about "architecture" (the World Trade Center) and "arts" (the Pentagon), but they had disagreed about an altogether different kind of target, namely "electrical engineering." This was the nuclear power plant that Muhammad Atta had seen on one of his training flights near New York. Puzzlingly, the Sheikh had withheld his blessing—despite the presumably attractive possibility of turning large swathes of the Eastern seaboard into a plutonium cemetery for the next seventy millennia (that is, until the year 72001). The Sheikh gave his reasons (restricted air space, no "symbolic value"). But Muhammad Atta sensed a moral qualm, a silent suggestion that such a move could be considered exorbitant. It was the first and only indication that, in their cosmic war against God's enemies, there was any kind of upper limit. Muhammad Atta often asked himself: Was the *Sheikh* prepared to die? In the course of their conversations it had emerged that the Sheikh, while plainly reconciled to eventual martyrdom (he would have it no

20

Marfanic: related to Marfan Syndrome (established in 1896 by French physician Antoin Marfan), a disorder characterized by cardiovascular problems and unusually long fingers and limbs.

other way, and so on), felt little personal attraction to death; and he would soon be additionally famous, Muhammad Atta prophesied, for the strenuousness with which he eluded it.

These meetings and discussions — with the Sheikh and, later, with his Yemeni emissary, Ramzi bin al-Shibh — now lost weight and value in Muhammad Atta's mind, tarnished by Ziad's indiscipline, by Ziad's promiscuity (and, if Abdulaziz knew, then all the Saudis knew). He thought back to his historic conversation with Ramzi, on the telephone, in the third week of August.

"Our friend is anxious to know when your course will begin."

"It would be more interesting to study 'law' when Congress has convened." 25

"But we shouldn't delay. With so many of our students in the U.S. . . ."

"All right. Two branches, an oblique stroke, and a lollipop."

Ramzi called him back and said, "To be clear. The eleventh of the ninth?"

"Yes," Muhammad Atta confirmed. And he was the first person on earth to say it — to say in that way: "September eleventh."

He had cherished the secret until September 9th. Now, of course, everyone 30 knew: the day itself had come. He was impatient for his talk on the phone with Ziad, which was scheduled for 7 A.M. Ziad was still claiming that he hadn't decided between "law" and "politics." It looked like "law." As a target, the President's house had lost much of its appeal when they'd established, insofar as they could, that the President wouldn't be in it.

At that moment the President was readying himself for an early-morning run in Sarasota, Florida, where Muhammad Atta had been taught how to fly, at Jones Aviation, in September, 2000.

It was during the drive to Portland International Jetport that the headache began. In recent months he had become something of a connoisseur of headaches. And yet those earlier headaches, it now seemed, were barely worth the name: *this* was what a headache was. At first he attributed its virulence to his misadventure in the shower stall; but then the pain pushed forward over his crown and established itself, like an electric eel, from ear to ear, then from eye to eye — and then both. He had two headaches, not one, and they were apparently at war. The automobile, a Nissan Altima, was brand-new, factory-fresh, and this had seemed like a mild bonus on September 10th, but now its vacuum-packed breath tasted of seasickness and the smell of ships below the waterline. Suddenly his vision became pixellated with little swarms of blind spots. So it was then required of him to pull over and tell an astonished Abdulaziz to take the wheel.

There seemed to be a completely unreasonable weight of traffic. Americans, already about their business . . . Tormenting his passenger with regular glances of concern, Abdulaziz otherwise drove with his usual superstitious watchfulness, beset by small fears, on this day. Muhammad Atta tried not to writhe around in his seat; on his way to the parking lot, ten minutes earlier, he had tried not to run; in the elevator, ten minutes earlier still, he had tried not to groan or scream. He was always trying not to do something.

It was 5:35. And at this point he began to belabor himself for the diversion to Portland: a puerile undertaking, as he now saw it. His group was competitive not only in piety but also in nihilistic élan, in nihilistic insouciance; and he had thought it would be conclusively stylish to stroll from one end of Logan to the other with less than an hour to go. Then, too, there was the promise, itchier to the heart than ever, of his conversation with Ziad. But his reason for coming to Portland had been fundamentally unserious. He wouldn't have done it if the Internet, on September 10th, had not assured him so repeatedly that it was going to be a flawless morning on September 11th.

And he didn't solace himself with the thought that this was, after all, September 11th, and you could still get to airports without much time to spare. 35

"Did you pack these bags yourself?"

Muhammad Atta's hand crept toward his brow. "Yes," he said.

"Have they been with you at all times?"

"Yes."

"Did anyone ask you to carry anything for them?" 40

"No. Is the flight on time?"

"You should make your connection."

"And the bags will go straight through?"

"No, sir. You'll need to recheck them at Logan."

"You mean I'll have to go through all this *again*?" 45

Whatever else terrorism had achieved in the past few decades, it had certainly brought about a net increase in world boredom. It didn't take very long to ask and answer those three questions—about fifteen seconds. But those dead-time questions and answers were repeated, without any variation whatever, hundreds of thousands of times a day. If the planes operation went ahead as planned, Muhammad Atta would bequeath more, perhaps much more, dead time, planetwide. It was appropriate, perhaps, and not paradoxical, that terror should also sharply promote its most obvious opposite. Boredom.

As it happened, Muhammad Atta was a selectee of the Computer-Assisted Passenger Prescreening System (CAPPS). All this meant was that his checked bag would not be stowed until he himself had boarded the aircraft. This was at Portland. At Logan, a "Category X" airport like Newark Liberty and Washington Dulles, and supposedly more secure, three of his muscle Saudis would be selected by CAPPS, with the same irrelevant consequences.

Muhammad Atta and Abdulaziz submitted to the checkpoint screening. Their bags were not searched; they were not frisked, or blessed by the hand wand. Abdulaziz's childish rucksack, containing the box cutters and the Mace, passed through the tunnel of love. Just before they boarded, another pall of nausea gathered about Muhammad Atta, like a host of tiny myrmidons. He waited for them to move on, but they did not do so, and, instead, coagulated in his craw. Muhammad Atta went to the men's room and released a fathom of bilious green. He was still wiping his foul mouth as he walked out onto the tarmac and climbed the trembling metal steps.

Colgan 5930 was not only late: it was also an open-propeller nineteen-seater, and it was full. Excruciatingly, he had to wedge himself in next to a fat blonde with a scalp disease and, moreover, a baby, whose incredulous weeping (its ears) she attempted and failed to slake with repeated applications of the breast. Between heartbeats, when he was briefly capable of consecutive thought, he imagined that the blonde was the doomed stewardess.

The plane leapt eagerly into the air, with none of the technological toil 50
that would characterise the ascent of American 11.

He had gone to Portland, Maine, for his quid pro quo with the imam.

The hospital, where he lay dying, was a blistered medium-rise downtown:

one more business among all the other businesses. Inside, too, Muhammad Atta had had no sense of entering an atmosphere of vocational care — just the American matter-of-factness, with no softening of the voice, the tread, no softening of the receptionists' minimal smiles. . . . Directed to the ward, he moved through the moist warmth of half-eaten or untouched dinners and the heavier undersmell of drugs. The imam was asleep in his bed, recessed into it, as if an imam-size channel had been recessed into the mattress. His lips, Muhammad Atta noticed, were dark gray, like the lips of dogs. Dead time passed. Then the imam awoke to Muhammad Atta's humorless stare. He sighed, without restraint. The two of them went back a way: to the mosque in Falls Church, Virginia.

"You have a citation for me?" the imam asked, unexpectedly alert.

"It's from the traditions. The Prophet said, 'Whoever kills himself with a blade will be tormented with that blade in the fires of Hell. . . . He who throws himself off a mountain and kills himself will throw himself downward into the fires of Hell for ever and ever. . . . Whoever kills himself in any way in this world will be tormented in that way in Hell.'"

"Always there are exceptions. Remember we are in the lands of unbelief," 55 the imam said, and went on to list the crimes of the Americans.

These were familiar to his visitor, who regarded the grievances as real. Depending on how you tallied it, America was responsible for this or that many million deaths. But Muhammad Atta was not persuaded of a moral equivalence. Certain weapons systems claimed to be precise; power was not precise. Power was always a monster. And there had never been a monster the size of America. Every time it turned over in its sleep it entrained disasters that would have to roll through villages. There were blunderings and perversities and calculated cruelties; and there was no self-knowledge — none. Still, America did not expend *ingenuity* in its efforts to kill the innocent.

"Is it an enemy installation?" the imam was sharply asking.

Muhammad Atta gave no reply. He just said, "Do you have it?"

"Yes. And you will need it."

The imam's hand, to Muhammad Atta's far from sympathetic gaze, 60 looked and sounded like the foreclaw of a lobster as it rattled up against the laminate of his bedside table; the cupboard opened, drawbridge-wise. The thing within exactly resembled a half-empty sixteen-ounce bottle of Volvic.

"Take it, not on waking, but when you feel your trial is near. Now. You were kind enough to say that you would describe your induction."

Here was the quid pro quo: he wanted to be told about the Sheik. Just then the imam abruptly turned onto his side, facing Muhammad Atta, and for a moment his posture repulsively recalled that of a child starting to warm to a bedtime story. But this lurch was only part of a larger maneuver of the imam's. He edged himself backward and upward, so that a few stray hairs, at least, rested on the pillow.

Muhammad Atta had unthinkingly assumed, earlier on, that he would give the imam a reassuring, even an idealized, portrait of the Sheikh — the long-fingered visionary on the mountaintop who yet, in his humility and openness, remained a simple warrior of God. Now he recomposed himself. Never in his life had he spoken his mind. The smell of drugs was particularly strong near the yellow sink, half a yard from his nose.

"I had several meetings with him," he said, "at the al Faruq camp, in Kandahar. And at Tarnak Farms. He casts the spell of success on you — that's what he does. When he talks about the defeat of the Russians . . . To hear him tell it, it wasn't the West that won the Cold War. It was the Sheikh. But we badly need that spell, don't we? The spell of success."

"But the successes are real. And this is only the beginning." 65

"His hopes of victory depend," Muhammad Atta said, "on the active participation of the superpower."

"What superpower?"

"God. Hence the present crisis."

"Meaning?"

"It comes from religious hurt, don't you think? For centuries God has 70 forsaken the believers, and rewarded the infidels. How do you explain his indifference?"

Or his enmity, he thought, as he left the bedside and the ward. He considered, too, that it could go like this, subconsciously, of course: if prayer and piety had failed — had so clearly failed — then it might seem time to change allegiance, and summon up the other powers.

At Logan, he and Abdulaziz were the only passengers at the carrousel supposedly serving the commuter flight from Portland. And the carrousel was silent and motionless. Staring at a carousel with actual baggage going around on it suddenly seemed a fairly stimulating thing to do. Meanwhile, the eels or stingrays in his head were having a fight to the death in the area just behind his ears. Sometimes for moments on end he could step back from the pain and just *listen* to it. This was music in its next evolutionary phase, beyond the atonal. And he realized why he had always hated music; all of it, even the most emollient melody, had entered his mind as pain. Using every reserve, he continued to stare at the changeless slats of black rubber for another thirty seconds, another minute, then he turned on his heel, and Abdulaziz followed.

"Did you pack these bags yourself?"

"*What* bags? As I took the trouble to explain . . ."

"Sir, your bags will be on our next flight. I still need to ask the security 75 questions, sir."

Americans — the way they called you "sir." They might as well be calling you "bub."

"Did you pack these bags yourself?"

Oh, the misery of recurrence, like the hotel elevator doing its ancient curtsy on every floor, like the alien hair on the soap changing its shape through a succession of alphabets, like the (necessarily) monotonous gonging inside his head. It had occurred to him before that his condition, if you could call it that, was merely the condition of boredom, unbounded boredom, where all time was dead time. As if his whole life consisted of answering those same three questions, saying "Yes" and "Yes" and "No."

"And did anyone ask you to carry anything for them?"

"*Yes*," Muhammad Atta said. "Last night, at the Lebanese restaurant, a 80 waiter asked us to take a heavy clock radio to his cousin in Los Angeles."

Her smile was flat and brief. "That's funny," she said.

They made their way to Gate 32 and then retreated from it, into the mall. With a flip of the hand he told Abdulaziz to go and look for his countrymen. Muhammad Atta took a seat outside a dormant coffee shop and readied himself for the call to Ziad. Ziad: the Beiruti beach boy and disco ghost, the tippler and debauchee, now with his exaltations and prostrations, his chanting and wailing, his rocking and swaying . . . To discountenance Ziad, to send him to his death with a heart full of doubt: *this* was the reason for the delegation to Maine.

Back in Germany, once, Ziad had said that the brides in the Garden would be "made of light." In bold contrast, then, to the darkness and heaviness of their terrestrial sisters, in particular the heaviness and darkness of Aysel Senguen—Ziad's German Turk, or Turkish German. Muhammad Atta had seen Aysel only once (bare legs, bare arms, bare hair), in the medical bookstore in Hamburg, and he had not forgotten her face. Ziad and Aysel were his control experiment for the life lived by sexual love; and for many months the two of them had peopled his insomnias. He knew that Aysel had come to Florida in January (and had scandalously accompanied Ziad to the flight school); he was also obscurely moved by the fact that a letter to her was Ziad's last will and testament. And he kept wondering how their bodies conjoined, how she must open herself up to him, with all her heaviness and darkness. . . . Muhammad Atta had decided that romantic and religious ardor came from contiguous parts of the human being: the parts he didn't have. Yet Ziad, as the obliterator of "law" (and the obliterator of United 93), was duly poised for mass murder. Only *roughly* contiguous, then: Ziad could say that he was doing it for God, and many would believe him, but he couldn't say that he was doing it for love. He wasn't doing it for love, or for God. He was doing it for the core reason, just like Muhammad Atta.

"All is well at Newark Liberty?"

"All is well. We're in the sterile area. Did you see your precious imam?"　85

"I did. And he gave me the water."

"The water? What water?"

"The holy water," Muhammad Atta said with delectation, "from the Oasis."

There was a silence. "What does it do?" Ziad asked.

"It absolves you of what the imam called the 'enormity,' the atrocious　90 crime, Ziad, of the self-felony."

There was another silence—but that wasn't quite true anymore. Muhammad Atta thought that he might be getting more out of this conversation if there hadn't been a mechanized floor-sweeper, resembling a hovercraft, with an old man on it, beeping and snivelling around his chair.

"I'm preparing to drink the holy water even as I speak."

"Does it come in a special bottle?"

"A crystal vial. God said, 'All those who hate me love and court death.' You see, Ziad, you are the trustee of your body, not its owner. God is its owner."

"And the water?"　95

"The water is within me and preserves me for God. It's a new technique—it began in Palestine. Your hell will burn with jet fuel for eternity. And eternity never ends, Ziad—it never even begins. So there may be some delay before you get those brides of light. Perhaps you should have settled for your German nudist. Goodbye, Ziad."

He hung up, redialled, and had a more or less identical conversation with Marwan, minus the theme of Aysel. In the case of Marwan (the other half of "architecture," and just across the way, now, at United), different considerations obtained. The emphasis of their rivalry was not jihadi ardor so much as nihilistic insouciance. So the two of them exchanged yawning boasts, in code, about how low down, and at what angle, they would strike, and coolly agreed that, if there were F-15s over New York, they would crash their planes into the streets. . . . Finally, dutifully, he called Hani ("arts"), the only Saudi pilot, with whom he shared no history, and not much hatred. Muhammad Atta hoped that he hadn't decisively undermined Ziad, who, after all, was a Saudi short (or two Saudis short, if you discounted the punklike Ahmed). No. He believed that he could safely rely, at this point, on the fierce physics of the peer group.

A peer group piously competitive about suicide, he had concluded, was a very powerful thing, and the West had no equivalent to it. A peer group for whom death was not death — and life was not life, either. Yet an inversion so extreme, he thought, would quickly become decadent: hospitals, schools, nurseries, old people's homes. Transgression, by its nature, was helter-skelter, and always bound to escalate. And the thing would start to be over in a generation, as everyone slowly and incredulously intuited it: the core reason.

Perhaps the closest equivalent the West could field was the firefighters. Muhammad Atta had studied architecture and engineering. The fire that would be created by ten thousand gallons of jet fuel, he knew, could not be fought: the steel frame of the tower would buckle; the walls, which were not intended to be weight-bearing, would collapse, one onto another; and down it would all come. The fire could not be fought — but there would be firefighters. They were called the "bravest," accurately, in his view; and, as the bravest, they took on a certain responsibility. The firefighters were saying, every day, Who's going to do it, if we don't? If the bravest don't, who else is going to risk death to save the lives of strangers?

As he sat for another few moments on the tin chair, as he watched the mall 100 awaken and come into commercial being, filling up now with Americans and American purpose and automatic self-belief, he felt he had timed it about right. (And his face had timed it about right.) Because he couldn't possibly survive another day of the all-inclusive detestation — of the pan-anathema. This feeling had been his familiar since the age of twelve or thirteen; it had come upon him, like an illness without a symptom. Cairo, Hamburg, even the winter dawn over Kandahar: they had all looked the same to him. Unreal mockery.

Muhammad Atta took the bottle from his carry-on. The imam *said* it was from Medina. He shrugged, and drank the holy Volvic.

Boarding began with first class. And, if Muhammad Atta ever found anything funny, he might have smiled at this: Wail and Waleed, the brothers, the two semiliterate yokels from the badlands of the Yemeni border, shuffling off to their thrones — 2A and 2B. Then business. He led. Abdulaziz and Satam followed.

He hadn't even reached his seat when it hit him. It came with great purity of address, replacing everything else in his stretched sensorium. Even his headache, while not actually taking its leave, immediately stepped aside, almost with a flourish, to accommodate the new guest. It was a feeling that had abandoned him forever, he'd thought, four months ago — but now it was back. With twinkly promptitude, canned music flooded forth: a standard ballad, a flowery flute with many trills and graces. The breathy refrain joined the simmer of the engines; yet neither could drown the popping, the groaning, the creaking, as of a dungeon door to an inner sanctum — the ungainsayable anger of his bowels.

So now he sat gripping the armrests of 8D as the coach passengers filed by. Why did there have to be so many of them, always another briefcase, another backpack, always another buzz cut, another white-hair? . . . He waited, rose, and with gruelling nonchalance, his buttocks clenched, sauntered forward. All three toilets claimed to be occupied. They were not occupied, he knew. A frequent and inquisitive traveller on American commercial jets, Muhammad Atta knew that the toilets were locked, like all the other toilets (this was the practice on tight turnarounds), and would remain locked until the plane levelled out. He pressed a flat hand against all three: again, the misery of recurrence, of duplication. He tried, but he couldn't abstain from a brief flurry of shoving and kicking and rattling. As he returned to 8D he saw that Abdulaziz was looking at him, not with commiseration, now, but with puzzled disappointment, even turning in his seat to exchange a responsible frown with Satam.

Strapped in, Muhammad Atta managed the following series of thoughts.   105 You *needed* the belief system, the ideology, the ardor. You had to have it. The core reason was good enough for the mind. But it couldn't carry the body.

To the others, he realized, he was giving a detailed impersonation of a man who had lost his nerve. But he had not lost his nerve. Even before the plane gave its preliminary jolt (like a polite cough of introduction), he felt the pull of it, with relief, with recognition: the necessary speed, the escape velocity he needed to deliver him to his journey's end.

American 11 pushed back from Gate 32, Terminal B, at 7:40. There was the captain and the first officer; there were nine flight attendants, and seventy-six passengers, excluding Wail, Waleed, Satam, Abdulaziz, and Muhammad Atta. American 11 was in the air at 7:59.

Now he obliged himself to do what he had always intended to do, during the climb. He had a memory ready, and a thought experiment. He wanted to prepare himself for the opening of female flesh; he wanted to prepare himself for what would soon be happening to the throat of the stewardess — whom he could see, on her jump seat, head bowed low, with a pen in her hand and a clipboard on her lap.

In 2000 his return ticket from Afghanistan had put him on an Iberia flight from the United Arab Emirates to Madrid. The plane had just levelled out when he became aware of an altercation in the back of the cabin. Swivelling in his seat, he saw that perhaps fifteen or sixteen men, turbanned and white-robed, had crowded into the aisle and were now on the floor, humped in prayer. You could hear the male flight attendant's monotonous and defeated remonstrations as he backed away. *"Por favor, señores. Es ilegal. Señores, por favor!"* Minutes later the captain came on the P.A., saying in Spanish, English, and Gulf Arabic that if the passengers didn't return to their seats he would most certainly return to Dubai. Then she appeared. Even Muhammad Atta at once conceded that here was the dark female in her most swinishly luxurious form: tall, long-necked, herself streamlined and aerodynamic, with hair like a billboard for a chocolate sundae, and all that flesh, damp and glowing as if from fever or even lust. She came to a halt and gave a roll of the eyes that took her whole head with it, then she surged forward with great scooping motions of her hands, bellowing, *"Vamos arriba, coño!"* And the kneeling men had to peer out at this seraph of breast and haunch and uniformed power, and straighten up and scowl, and slowly grope for their seats. Muhammad Atta had felt only contempt for the men bent over the patterned carpet, but he would never forget the face of the stewardess—the face of cloudless entitlement—and how badly he had wanted to hurt it.

And yet—no, it wasn't going to work. For him, the combination, up close, was wholly unmanageable: the combination of women and blood. So far, he thought, this is the worst day of my life—provably the worst day. In his head the weary fight between the vermin was finished; one was dying, and was now being disgustingly eaten by the other. And his loins, between them, were contriving for him something very close to the sensation of anal rape. So far, this was the worst day of his life. But then every day was the worst day, because every day was the most recent day, and the most developed, the most advanced (with all those other days behind it) toward the pan-anathema.

The plane was flattening out. He waited for the order. This would be given by the captain, when he turned off the fasten-seatbelts sign.

"We have some planes," Muhammad Atta said coolly. *"Just stay quiet, and you'll be O.K. We are returning to the airport. Nobody move. Everything will be O.K. If you try to make any moves, you'll endanger yourself and the airplane. Just stay quiet."*

He had stepped through the region of inexpressible sordor, and gained the cockpit. Here, in the grotto of the mad clocksmith, was more cringing flesh and more blood—but manageably male. Now he disengaged the computer and prepared to fly by direct law.

It was 8:24. He laughed for the first time since childhood: he was in the Atlantic of the sky, at the controls of the biggest weapon in history.

At 8:27 he made a grand counterclockwise semicircle, turning south.

At 8:44 he began his descent.

The core reason was of course all the killing—all the putting to death. Not the crew, not the passengers, not the office workers in the Twin Towers, not the cleaners and the caterers, not the men of the N.Y.P.D. and the F.D.N.Y. He was thinking of the war, the wars, the war cycles that would flow from this day. He didn't believe in the Devil, as an active force, but he did believe in death. Death, at certain times, stopped moving at its even pace and broke into a hungry, lumbering run. Here was the primordial secret. No longer closely guarded—no longer well kept. Killing was divine delight. And your suicide was just a part of the contribution you made—the massive contribution to death. All your frigidities and futilities were rewritten, becoming swollen with meaning. This was what was possible when you turned the tides of life around, when you ran with beasts, when you flew with the flies.

First, the lesser totems of Queens, like a line of defense for the tutelary god-lings of the island.

When he came clattering in over the struts and slats of Manhattan, there it was ahead of him and below him—the thing which is called World. Cross streets, blocks, districts, shot out from beneath the speed lines of the plane. He was glad that he wouldn't have to plow down into the city, and he even felt love for it, for all its strivings and couplings and sunderings. And he felt no impulse to increase power or to bank or to strike even lower. It was reeling him in. Now even the need to shit felt right and good as his destination surged toward him.

There are many accounts, uniformly incomplete, of what it is like to die slowly. 120 But there is no information at all about what it is like to die suddenly and violently. We are being gentle when we describe such deaths as instant. "The passengers died instantly." Did they? It may be that some people can do it, can die instantly. The very old, because the vital powers are weak; the very young, because there is no great accretion of experience needing to be scattered. Muhammad Atta was thirty-three. As for him (and perhaps this is true even in cases of vaporization, perhaps this was true even for the wall-shadows of Japan), it took much longer than an instant. By the time the last second arrived, the first second seemed as far away as childhood.

American 11 struck at 8:46:40. Muhammad Atta's body was beyond all healing by 8:46:41, but his mind, his presence, needed time to shut itself down. The physical torment—a panic attack in every nerve, a riot of the atoms—merely italicized the last shinings of his brain. They weren't thoughts; they were more like a series of unignorable conclusions, imposed from without. Here was the hereafter, after all; and here was the reckoning. His mind groaned and fumbled with an irreconcilability, a defeat, a self-cancellation. Could he assemble the argument? It follows—by definition—if and only if. And then the argument assembled, all by itself. . . . The joy of killing was proportional to the value of what was destroyed. But that value was something a killer could never see and never gauge. And where was the joy he thought he had felt—where was that joy, that itch, that paltry tingle? Yes, how gravely he had underestimated it. How very gravely he had underestimated life. His own he had hated, and had wished away, but see how long it was taking to absent itself—and with what helpless grief was he watching it go, imperturbable in its beauty and its power. Even as his flesh fried and his blood boiled, there was life, kissing its fingertips. Then it echoed out, and ended.

II

On September 11, 2001, he opened his eyes at 4 A.M., in Portland, Maine; and Muhammad Atta's last day began.

CONNECTIONS TO OTHER SELECTIONS

1. Compare Amis's treatment of Muhammad Atta's reasons for killing with those of Matt Fowler's in Andre Dubus's "Killings" (p. 103). How are both stories about more than simply murder?

2. In what sense do Amis's story and Flannery O'Connor's "Revelation" (p. 392) lead to epiphanies at the end? What is the nature of those epiphanies?

RICK BASS (B. 1958)

© Nicole Blaisdell.

Born in Fort Worth, Texas, Rick Bass graduated from Utah State University in 1979 and worked as a petroleum geologist in the South and Southwest. He began publishing his twenty-two books of fiction and nonfiction in the late 1980s, when his first short story collection, *Watch* (1988), won the Pen/Nelson Award. All of his work is permeated with a deep and intimate appreciation of nature, as is his choice to live in the Yaak Valley, Montana. Another collection of stories was named a *Los Angeles Times* Best Book of the Year. His novels include *Diezmo* (2005) and *Where the Sea Used to Be* (1998). Among his nonfiction titles are *Brown Dog of the Yaak: Essays on Art and Activism* (1999), *Winter: Notes from Montana* (1999), and *The Roadless Yaak: Reflections and Observations about One of Our Last Great Wilderness Areas*. "Her First Elk," from Bass's most recent collection of stories, *The Lives of Rocks* (2006), is representative of the way his characters learn something about themselves from an encounter with nature.

Her First Elk   2003

She had killed an elk once. She had been a young woman, just out of college — her beloved father already three years in the grave — and had set out early on opening morning, hiking uphill through a forest of huge Ponderosa pines, with the stars shining like sparks through the pines' boughs, and owls calling all around her, and her breath rising strong in puffs and clouds as she climbed, and a shimmering at the edge of her vision like the electricity in the night sky that sometimes precedes the arrival of the northern lights, or heat lightning.

The hunt had been over astonishingly quick; years later, she would realize that the best hunts stretch out four or five weeks, and sometimes never result in a taking. But this one had ended in the first hour, on the first day.

Even before daylight, she had caught the scent of the herd of elk bedded down just ahead of her, a scent sweeter and ranker than that of any number of stabled horses; and creeping closer, she had been able to hear the herd sounds, their little mewings and grunts.

She had crouched behind one of the giant trees, shivering from both the cold and her excitement — sharply, she had the thought that she wished her father were here with her, that one morning, to see this; to participate — and then she was shivering again, and there was nothing in her mind but elk.

Slowly, the day became light, and she sank lower into the tall grass 5 beneath the big pines, the scent of the grass sweet upon her skin; and the lighter the day became, the farther she flattened herself down into that yellow grass.

The elk rose to their feet just ahead of her, and at first she thought they had somehow scented her, even though the day's warming currents had not yet begun to ascend the hill — even though the last of the night's heavier, cooling currents were still sliding in rolling waves down the mountain, the faint breeze in her face carrying the ripe scent of the herd downhill, straight to her.

But they were only feeding, wandering around now, still mewing and clucking and barking and coughing, and feeding on the same sweet-scented grass that she was hiding in. She could hear their teeth grinding as they chewed, could hear the clicking of their hoofs as they brushed against rocks.

These creatures seemed a long way from the dinners that her father had fixed out on the barbecue grill, bringing in the sizzling red meat and carving it quickly before putting it on her child's plate and saying, "Elk"; but it was the same animal, they were all the same animal, nearly a dozen years later, and now the herd was drifting like water, or slow flickering flames, out of the giant pines and into a stand of aspen, the gold leaves underfoot the color of their hides, and the stark white trunks of the aspen grove making it look as if the herd was trapped behind bars; though still, they kept drifting, flowing in and out of and between those bars: and when Jyl saw the biggest one, the giant among them, she picked him, not knowing any better — unaware that the meat would be tougher than that of a younger animal — and raising up on one knee, the shot was no more difficult for her than sinking a pool ball in a corner pocket, tracking with the end of her rifle and the crosshairs of the scope the cleft formed just behind his right shoulder as he quartered away from her — she did not allow herself to be distracted by the magnificent crown of antlers atop his head — and when he stopped, in his last moment, and swung his huge head to face her, having sensed her presence, she squeezed the trigger as she had been taught to do back when she'd been a girl, and the giant elk leapt hump-shouldered like a bull in a rodeo, then took a few running steps before stumbling, as if the bullet had not shredded his heart and half his lungs but had instead merely confused him.

He crashed heavily to the ground, as if attached to an invisible tether; got up, ran again, and fell yet again.

The cows and calves in his herd, as well as the younger bulls, stared at him, 10 trying to discern his meaning, and disoriented too by the sudden, explosive sound. They stared at the source of the sound — Jyl had risen to her feet and was watching the great bull's thrashings, wondering whether to shoot again — and still the rest of the herd stared at her with what she could recognize only as disbelief.

The bull got up and ran again. This time he did not fall — having figured out, in his grounded thrashings, how to accommodate his strange new dysfunction in such a way as to not impede his desire, which was to escape — and with one front leg tucked high against his chest, like a man carrying a satchel, and his hind legs spread wider for stability, he galloped off, running now like a horse in hobbles, and with his immense mahogany-colored rack tipped back for balance: what was once his pride and power now a liability.

The rest of the herd turned and followed him into the timber, disappearing into the forest's embrace almost reluctantly, and still possessing somehow that air of disbelief; though once they went into the timber, they vanished completely, and for a long while she could hear the crashing of limbs and branches—as if she had unleashed an earthquake, or some other world force—and the sounds grew fainter and farther, and then there was only silence.

Not knowing any better, back then, she set out after the herd, rather than waiting to let the bull lie down and bleed to death. She didn't know that if pushed, a bull could run for miles with his heart in tatters, running as if on magic or spirit, rather than the conventional pump-house mechanics of ventricles and aortas; that if pushed, a bull could run for months with his lungs exploded or full of blood. As if in his dying the bull were able to metamorphose into some entirely other creature, taking its air, its oxygen, straight into its blood through its gaping, flopping mouth, like a fish; and as if it were able still to disseminate and retrieve its blood, pressing and pulsing it to the farthest reaches of its body and back again, without the use of a heart, but relying instead on some kind of mysterious current and desire—the will to cohere—far larger than its own; the blood sloshing back and forth, back and forth, willing the elk forward, willing the elk to keep being an elk.

Jyl had had it in her mind to go to the spot where the elk had first fallen—even from where she was, fifty or sixty yards distant, she could see the patch of torn-up earth—and to find the trail of blood from that point, and to follow it.

She was already thinking ahead, and looking beyond that first spot—hav- 15 ing not yet reached it—when she walked into the barbed-wire fence that separated the national forest from the adjoining private property, posted against hunting.

The fence was strung so tight that she bounced backward, falling much as the elk had fallen, that first time; and in her inexperience, she had been holding the trigger on her rifle, with a shell chambered in case she should see the big bull again; and as she fell, she gripped the trigger, discharging the rifle a second time, with a sound even more cavernous, in its unexpectedness, than the first shot.

A branch high above her intercepted the bullet, and the limb came floating slowly down, drifting like a kite. From her back, she watched it land quietly; and she continued to lie there, bleeding a little and shaking, before finally rising and climbing over the fence with its *Posted* signs, and continuing on after the elk.

She was surprised by how hard it was to follow his blood trail: only a damp splatter here and there, sometimes red though other times drying brown already, against the yellow aspen leaves that looked like spilled coins—as if some thief had been wounded while ferrying away a strongbox, and had spilled his blood upon that treasure.

She tried to focus on the task at hand but was aware also of feeling strangely and exceedingly lonely—remembering, seemingly from nowhere, that her father had been red-green colorblind, and realizing how difficult it must have been for him to see those drops of blood. Wishing again that he were here with her, though, to help her with the tracking of this animal.

A drop here, a drop there. She couldn't stop marveling at how few clues 20 there were. It was easier to follow the tracks in the soft earth, and the swath of broken branches, than it was the blood trail—though whether she was following the herd's path, or the bull's separate path, she couldn't be sure.

She came to the edge of the timber and looked out across a small plowed field, the earth dark from having just been turned over to autumn stubble. Her elk was collapsed dead out in the middle of it—the rest of the herd was long gone, nowhere to be seen—and there was a truck parked next to the elk already, and standing next to the elk were two older men in cowboy hats. Jyl was surprised, then, at how tall the antlers were—taller than either man, even with the elk lying stretched out on the bare ground; taller even than the cab of the truck.

The men did not appear happy to see her coming. It seemed to take her a long time to reach them. It was hard walking over the furrows and clods of stubble, and from the looks on the men's faces, she was afraid that the elk might have been one of their pets: that they might even have given it a name.

It wasn't that bad, as it turned out, but it still wasn't good. Their features softened little as she closed the final distance, and they saw how young she was, and how frightened—she could have been either man's daughter—and as she approached there seemed to be some force of energy about her that disposed them to think the best of her; and they found it hard to believe, too, that, had she killed the elk illegally, she would be marching right up to claim it.

There were no handshakes, no introductions. There was still frost on the windshield of the men's truck, and Jyl realized they must have jumped in their truck and cold-started it, racing straight up to where they knew the herd hung out.

Plumes of fog breath leapt from the first man's mouth as he spoke, even 25 though they were all three standing in the sunlight.

"You shot it over on the other side of the fence, right, over on the national forest, and it leapt the fence and came over here to die?" he asked, and he was not being sarcastic: as if, now that he could see Jyl's features, and her fear and youth, he could not bear to think of her being a poacher.

The other man, who appeared to be a few years the elder—they looked like brothers, with the older one somewhere in his sixties, and fiercer looking—interrupted before she could answer and said, "Those elk knew never to cross that fence during hunting season. That bull wouldn't let them. I've been watching him for six years, and any time a cow or calf even looks at that fence, he tips—tipped—his antlers at them and herded them away from it."

Jyl saw that such an outburst was as close to a declaration of love for the animal as the old man would be capable of uttering, and the three of them looked down at the massive animal, whose body heat they could still feel radiating from it—the twin antlers larger than any swords of myth, and the elk's eyes closed, and still only what seemed like a little blood dribbling down the left shoulder, from the exit wound—the post-rut musk odor of the bull was intense—and all Jyl could say was, "I'm sorry."

The younger brother seemed almost alarmed by this admission.

"You didn't shoot him on our side, did you?" he asked again.   30

Jyl looked down at her feet, and then again at the bull. She might as well have shot an elephant, she thought. She felt trembly, nauseated. She glanced at her rifle to be sure the chamber was open.

"Yes," she said quietly.

"Oh, Christ," the younger man said—the older one just glared at her, hawkish, but also slightly surprised, now—and again the younger one said, "Are you sure? Maybe you didn't see it leap the fence?"

Jyl showed him the scratch marks on her arms, and on her face. "I didn't know the fence was there," she said. "The sun was coming up and I didn't see it. After I shot, I walked into the fence."

Both men stared at her as if she were suddenly some kind of foreigner, or 35 as if she were making some fabulous claim, and challenging them to believe it.

"What was the second shot?" the older man asked, looking back toward the woods. "Why did it come so much later?"

"The gun went off by accident, when I walked into the fence," she said, and both men frowned in a way that told her gun carelessness was even worse in their book than elk poaching.

"Is it unloaded now?" the younger brother asked, almost gently.

"No," she said, I don't guess it is."

"Why don't you unload it now?" he asked, and she complied, bolting and 40 unbolting the magazine three times, with a gold cartridge cartwheeling to the black dirt each time, and then a fourth time, different sounding, less full sounding, snicking the magazine empty; and she felt a bit of tension release from both men.

The older brother crouched down and picked up the three cartridges and handed them to her. "Well goddamn," he said, after she had put them in her pocket and stood waiting for him to speak — would she go to jail? would she be arrested, or fined? — "that's a big animal. I don't suppose you have much experience cleaning them, do you?"

She shook her head.

The brothers looked back down the hill — in the direction of their farmhouse, Jyl supposed. The fire unstoked, the breakfast unmade. Autumn chores still undone, with snow coming any day, and a whole year's worth of battening down, or so it seemed, to do in that narrow wedge of time.

"Well let's do it right," the elder said. "Come with us back down to the house and we'll get some warm water and towels, a saw and ax and come along." He squinted at her, more curious than unkind. "What did you intend to do, after shooting this animal?" he asked.

Jyl patted her hip. "I've got a pocketknife," she said. Both brothers looked 45 at each other and then broke into incredulous laughter, with tears coming to the eyes of the younger one.

"Might I see it?" the younger one asked, when he could catch his breath — but the querulous civility of his question set his brother off to laughing again — they both broke into guffaws — and when Jyl showed them her little folding pocketknife, it was too much for them, and they nearly dissolved. The younger brother had to lean against the truck and daub at his rheumy eyes with a bandana, and the morning was still so cold that some of the tears were freezing in his eyelashes, which had the effect, in that morning sunlight, of making him look delicate.

Both men wore gloves, and they each took their right glove off to shake hands with her, and to introduce themselves: Bruce, the younger, Ralph, the elder.

"Well, congratulations," Ralph said, grudgingly. "He is a big damn animal."

"Your first, I reckon," said Bruce, as he shook her hand — she was surprised by the softness, almost a tenderness, of his hand — Ralph's had been more like a hardened flipper, arthritic and knotted with muscle — and he smiled. "You won't ever shoot a bigger one than this one," he said.

They rode down to their cabin in the truck, Jyl sitting between them—it 50
seemed odd to her to just go off and leave the animal lying there in the field—
and on the way there, they inquired tactfully, she could tell, about her life:
whether she had a brother who hunted, or a father, or even a boyfriend. They
asked if her mother was a hunter, and it was her turn to laugh.

"My father used to hunt," she said, and they softened a bit further.

They made a big breakfast for her, bacon cut from hogs they had raised
and slaughtered, and fried eggs from chickens they likewise kept, and cat-
head biscuits, and a plate of pork chops (both men were as lean as match
sticks, and Jyl marveled at the amount of work the two old boys must have performed daily to pour through such fuel and yet have none of it cling to them);
and after a couple of cups of black coffee, they gathered the equipment
required for disassembling the elk, and drove back up on the hill.

The frost was burning off the grass and the day was warming so that they
were able to work without their jackets. Jyl was struck by how different the
brothers seemed, once they settled into their work: not quite aggressive, but
forceful with their efficiency. And even though they were working more slowly
than usual, in order to explain to her the why and what of their movements,
things still seemed to unfold quickly.

In a way, it seemed to her that the elk was coming back to life and expanding, even in its diminishment and unloosening: the two men leaning into it
like longshoremen, with Jyl helping them, laboring to roll the beast over on its
back and inverting the great head with the long daggered antlers, which now,
upended, sank into the freshly furrowed earth like some mystic harrow fashioned by gods, and one which only certain and select mortals were capable of
using, or allowed to use.

And once they had the elk overturned, Ralph emasculated it with his skin- 55
ning knife, cutting off the ponderous genitals quickly and tossing them farther into the field, with no self-consciousness, it was merely the work that
needed doing—and with that same large knife (the handle of which was made
of elk antler), he ran the blade up beneath the taut skin from crotch to breastbone, while Bruce worked to keep the four legs splayed wide, to give Ralph
room to work.

They peeled the hide back to the ribs, as if opening the elk for an operation,
or a resuscitation—how can I ever eat all of this animal? Jyl wondered—and
again, like a surgeon, Bruce placed twin spreader bars between the elk's hocks,
bracing wide the front legs as well as the back. Ralph slit open the thick gray-
skin drum of fascia that held beneath it the stomach and intestines, heart and
lungs and spleen and liver, kidneys and bladder: and then looking like nothing
so much as a grizzly bear grubbing beneath boulders on a hillside, or burrowing,
Ralph reached up into the enormous cavity and wrapped both arms around
the stomach mass—partially disappearing into the carcass, as if somehow
being consumed by it, rather than the other way around—and with great effort, he was able finally to tug the stomach and all the other internal parts free.

As they pulled loose they made a tearing, ripping, sucking sound; and
once it was all out, Ralph and Bruce rolled and cut out with that same sharp
knife the oversized heart, as big as a football, and the liver, and laid them out
on clean bright butcher paper on the tailgate of their truck.

Then Ralph rolled the rest of the guts, twice as large as any medicine ball,
away from the carcass, pushing on it as if shoving some boulder away from a

cave's entrance. Jyl was surprised by the sudden focusing of color in her mind, and in the scene. Surely all the colors had been present all along but for her it was suddenly as if some gears had clicked or aligned, allowing her to notice them now—some subtle rearrangement or recombination blossoming now into her mind's palette—the gold of the wheat stubble and the elk's hide, the dark chocolate of the antlers, the dripping crimson blood midway up both of Ralph's arms, the blue sky, the yellow aspen leaves, the black earth of the field, the purple liver, the maroon heart, Bruce's black and red plaid work shirt, Ralph's faded old denim—and the richness of those colors, and their bounty, was illuminated so starkly in that October sunlight, that it seemed to stir chemicals of deep pleasure in Jyl's own blood, elevating her to a happiness and a fullness she had not known earlier in the day, if quite ever; and she smiled at Bruce and Ralph, and understood in that moment that she, too, was a hunter.

She was astounded by how much blood there was: the upended ark of the carcass awash in it, blood sloshing around several inches deep. Bruce fashioned a come-along around the base of the elk's antlers and hitched the other end to the iron pipe frame on the back of their truck—the frame constructed like a miniature corral, so that they could haul a cow or two to town in the back when they needed to, without having to hook up the more cumbersome trailer—and he began to ratchet the elk into a vertical position, an ascension. To Jyl it looked like nothing less than a deification: and again, as a hunter, she found this fitting, and watched with interest.

Blood roared out from the elk's open carcass, gushing out from between 60 its huge legs, a brilliant fountain in that soft light. The blood splashed and splattered as it hit the newturned earth—Ralph and Bruce stood watching the elk drain as if nothing phenomenal at all were happening; as if they had seen it thousands of times before—and the porous black earth drank thirstily this outpouring, this torrent. Bruce looked over at Jyl and said, "Basically, it's easy, you just carve away everything you don't want to eat."

Jyl couldn't take her eyes off how fast the soil was drinking in the blood. Against the dark earth, the stain of it was barely even noticeable.

When the blood had finally stopped draining, Ralph filled a plastic washbasin with warm soapy water and scrubbed his hands carefully, leisurely, precisely, pausing even to clean the soap from beneath his fingernails with a smaller pocket knife—and when he was done, Bruce poured a gallon jug of plain water over Ralph's hands and wrists to rinse the soap away, and then Ralph dried his hands and arms with a clean towel and emptied out the old bloody wash water, then filled it anew, and it was time for Bruce to do the same; and Jyl marveled at, and was troubled by, this privileged glimpse at a life, or two lives, beyond her own—a life, two lives, of cautious competence, fitted to the world: and she was grateful to the elk, and its gone-away life, beyond the sheer bounty of the meat it was providing her; grateful to it for having led her into this place, the small and obscure if not hidden window of these two men's lives.

She was surprised by how mythic the act, and the animal, seemed. She understood intellectually that there were only two acts more ancient—sex and flight—but here was this third one, hunting, suddenly before her. She watched as each man worked with his own knife to peel back the hide, working on each side of the elk in the way that a river unbraids to the left and the right of a boulder placed midstream. Then, with the hide eventually off, they handed it to Jyl, and told her it would make a wonderful shirt or robe. She was astonished at the weight of it.

Next they began sawing the forelegs and stout shins of the hind legs; and only now, with those removed, did the creature begin to look reduced or compromised.

Still it rose to an improbable height, the antlers seven feet beyond the 65 eight-foot crossbar of the truck's pole rack — fifteen feet of animal stretched vertical, climbing into the heavens, and the humans working below, so tiny — but as they continued to carve away at it, it came to seem slowly less mythic, and more steerlike; and the two old men working steadily upon it began to seem closer to its equal.

They swung the huge shoulders aside, like the wings of an immense flying dinosaur, and then pulled them free, each man wrapping both arms around the slab of shoulder to hold it above the ground. They stacked the shoulders in the truck, next to the rolled-up fur of the hide.

Next the hindquarters, one at a time, and severed with a bone saw, both men working together to heft that weight into the truck, and the remaining length of bone and antler and gleaming socket and ribcage looking reptilian, like some reverse evolutionary process, some metamorphic errancy or setback; though the pile of beautiful red meat in the back of the truck, as it continued to mount, seemed like an embarrassment of riches; and again, it seemed to Jyl that perhaps she had taken too much.

She thought how she would have liked to watch her father render an elk. All gone into the past now, however, like blood drawing back into the soil. How much else had she missed?

The noonday sun was mild, almost warm now. The scavenger birds — magpies, ravens, Steller's jays and gray jays — danced and hopped nearby, swarming and fluttering, and from time to time as Ralph or Bruce took a rest, one of the men would toss a scrap of gristle or fascia into the field for the birds to fight over, and the sound of their angry squabbles filled the lonely silence of the otherwise quiet and empty hills, beneath the thin blue of the Indian summer sky.

They let Jyl work with the skinning knife — showed her how to separate the 70 muscles lengthwise with her fingers before cutting them free of the skeleton, and the quartered ham and shoulder — the backstrap unscrolling beneath the urging of her knife — the meat dense as stone, it seemed, yet as fluid as a river, and so beautiful in that sunlight, maroon to nearly purple, nearly iridescent in its richness, and in the absence of any intramuscular fat — and now the skeleton, with its whitened bones beginning to show, seemed less an elk, less an animal, than ever; and the two brothers set to work on the neck, tenderloins, butt steaks and neck loins. And while they separated and then trimmed and butchered those, Jyl worked with her own knife at carving strips of meat from between each slat of ribcage.

From time to time their lower backs would cramp, from working so intently, at such strangely unaccustomed work, work which presented itself now even in the best of years but two or three times annually — a deer, an elk, and sometimes an antelope — and they would have to lie down on the ground, all three of them, looking up at the sky and spreading their arms out wide as if on a crucifix; and they would listen to, and feel with pleasure, the subtle popping and realigning of their vertebrae, and would stare up at that blue sky and listen to the cries of the feeding birds, and feel intensely their richness at possessing now so much meat, clean meat, and at simply being alive, with the blood from their labor drying quickly to a light crust on their hands and arms. They were like children, in those moments, and they might have napped.

They finished late that afternoon, and sawed the antlers off for Jyl to take home with her. Being old school, they dragged what was left of the carcass back into the woods, returning it to the forest — returning the skeleton to the very place where the elk had been bedded down, when Jyl had first crept up on it — as if she had only borrowed it from the forest for a while — and then they drove back down to their ranch house and hung the ham and shoulder quarters on meat hooks to age in the barn, and draped the backstraps likewise from hooks, where they would leave them for at least a week.

They ran the loose scraps, nearly a hundred-pounds' worth, through a hand-cranked grinder, mixed in with a little beef fat to make hamburger, and while Ralph and Jyl processed and wrapped that in two-pound packages, Ralph cooked some of the butt steak in an iron skillet, seasoned with garlic and onions and butter and salt and pepper, mixed with a few of the previous spring's dried false morels, reconstituted — and he brought them small plates of that meal, thinly sliced, to eat as they continued working, the three of them grinding and wrapping, and the mountain of meat growing on the table beside them.

They each had a tumbler of whiskey to sip as they worked, and when they finally finished, it was nearly midnight.

The brothers offered their couch to Jyl, and she accepted; they let her 75 shower first, and they built a fire for her in the woodstove next to the couch; and after Bruce and then Ralph had showered, they sat up visiting, each with another small glass of whiskey, Ralph and Bruce telling her their ancient histories, until none of them could stay awake — their eyes kept closing, and their heads kept drooping — and with the fire burning down, Ralph and Bruce roused from their chairs and made their way each to his bedroom, and Jyl pulled the old elk hides over her for warmth and fell deeply and immediately asleep, falling as if through some layering of time. That elk would not be coming back, and her father would not be coming back. She was the only one remaining.

She killed more elk, and deer too, in years after that, learning more about them in the killing, year by year, than she could ever learn otherwise. Ralph died of a heart attack several years later, and was buried in the yard outside the ranch house, and Bruce died of pneumonia the next year, overwhelmed by the rigors of twice the amount of work, and he, too, was buried in the yard, next to Ralph, next to an aspen grove, through which passed on some nights wandering herds of deer and elk, the elk direct descendants of the big bull Jyl had shot. The elk sometimes paused to gnaw at the bark of those aspen whose roots reached now for the chests of the buried old men.

Remembering these things, a grown woman now woven of losses and gains, Jyl sometimes looks down at her body and considers the mix of things: the elk becoming her, as she ate it, and becoming Ralph and Bruce, as they ate it (did this make them somehow, distantly like brothers and sister, or uncles and niece, if not fathers and daughter?) — and the two old men becoming the soil then, in their burial, as had her father—becoming as still and silent as stone, and her own tenuous memories of them. And her own gone-away father, worm food, elk food, now: but how he had loved it.

Mountains in her heart now, and antlers, and mountain lions and sunrises and huge forests of pine and spruce and tamarack, and elk, all uncontrollable. She likes to think now that each day she moves farther away from him, she is also moving closer to him.

As if within her, beneath the span of her own days, there are other hunts going on continuously: giant elk in flight from the pursuit of hunters other than herself, and the birth of other mountains being plotted and planned—other mountains rising, then, and still more mountains vanishing into distant seas—and that even more improbable than her encountering that one giant elk, on her first hunt, was the path, the wandering line, that brought her to her father in the first place: that delivered her to him, and made him hers, and she, his—the improbability and yet the certainty that would place the two of them in each other's lives, tiny against the backdrop of the world, and tinier still against the mountains of time.

CONNECTIONS TO OTHER SELECTIONS

1. Discuss the significance of meat eating in "Her First Elk" and in T. Coraghessan Boyle's "Carnal Knowledge" (p. 466).

2. Compare Bass's vision of the West with E. Annie Proulx's in "55 Miles to the Gas Pump" (p. 465).

AMY BLOOM (B. 1953)

Born and raised in the suburbs of New York City, Amy Bloom "started writing unexpectedly." Bloom reports that before she began writing she had "picked peanuts, scooped felafel, waitressed up and down the East Coast, tended bar, written catalogue copy, and worked as a psychotherapist, for both the worried well and the very ill." Her first book, a collection of short stories, *Come to Me* (1993), was nominated for the National Book Award. It was followed by *Love Invents Us* (1998), *A Blind Man Can See How Much I Love You* (2000), and *Normal* (2002). Currently working as a psychotherapist and teaching creative writing at Yale University, Bloom lives in Connecticut and contributes to *The New Yorker, The Atlantic Monthly,* and a variety of other magazines here and abroad.

© Marion Ettlinger.

By-and-by

Every death is violent.

The iris, the rainbow of the eye, closes down. The pupil spreads out like black water. It seems natural, if you are there, to push the lid down, to ease the pleated shade over the ball, to the lower lashes. The light is out, close the door.

Mrs. Warburg called me at midnight. I heard the click of her lighter and the tiny crackle of burning tobacco. Her ring bumped against the receiver.

"Are you comfortable, darling?"

I was pretty comfortable. I was lying on her daughter's bed, with my feet 5 on Anne's yellow comforter, wearing Anne's bathrobe.

"Do you feel like talking tonight?"

Mrs. Warburg was the only person I felt like talking to. My boyfriend was away. My mother was away. My father was dead. I worked in a felafel joint on Charles Street where only my boss spoke English.

I heard Mrs. Warburg swallow. "You have a drink, too. This'll be our little party."

Mrs. Warburg and I had an interstate, telephonic rum-and-Coke party twice a week the summer Anne was missing. Mrs. Warburg told me about their problems with the house; they had some roof mold and a crack in the foundation, and Mr. Warburg was not handy.

"Roof mold," she said. "When you get married, you move into a nice pre- 10 war six in the city and let some other girl worry about roof mold. You go out dancing."

I know people say—but it's not true—you see it in movies cascades of hair tumbling out of the coffin, long, curved nails growing over the clasped hands. It's not true. When you're dead, you're dead and although some cells take longer to die than others, after a few hours everything is gone. The brain cells die fast, and blood pools in the soft, pressed places: the scapula, the lower back, the calves. If the body is not covered up, it produces a particular smell called cadaverine, and flies pick up the scent from a mile away. First, just one fly, then the rest. They lay fly eggs and ants come, drawn to the eggs, and sometimes wasps, and always maggots. Beetles and moths, the household kind that eat your sweaters, finish the body; they undress the flesh from the bone. They are the clean-up crew.

Mrs. Warburg and I only talked about Anne in passing and only about Anne in the past. Anne's tenth birthday had a Hawaiian theme. They made a hotdog luau in the backyard and served raspberry punch; they played pin-the-lei-on-the-donkey and had grass skirts for all the girls. "Anne might have been a little old for that, even then. She was a sophisticate from birth," Mrs. Warburg said. I was not a sophisticate from birth. I was an idiot from birth, and that is why when the police first came to look for Anne, I said a lot of things that sounded like lies.

Mrs. Warburg loved to entertain; she said Anne was her mother's daughter. We did like to have parties, and Mrs. Warburg made me tell her what kind of hors d'oeuvres we had. She was glad we served pigs-in-blankets because that's what she served when she was just starting out, although she'd actually made hers. And did one of us actually make the marinara sauce, at least, and was

Anne actually eating pork sausage and she knew it must be me who made pineapple-upside-down cake, because that was not in her daughter's repertoire, and she hoped we used wine glasses but she had the strong suspicion we poured wine out of the box into paper cups, which was true. I told her Anne had spray-painted some of our third-hand furniture bright gold and when we lit the candles and turned out the lights, our apartment looked extremely glamorous.

"Oh, we love glamorous," Mrs. Warburg said.

In the Adirondacks, the Glens Falls trail and the old mining roads sometimes 15 overlap. Miles of trail, around Speculator and Johnsburg are as smooth and neatly edged as garden paths. These are the old Fish Hill Mining Company roads and they will take you firmly and smoothly from the center of Hamilton County to the center of the woods and up the mountainside. Eugene Trask took Anne and her boyfriend, Teddy Ross, when they were loading up Teddy's van in the Glens Falls parking lot. He stabbed Teddy twice in the chest with his hunting knife, and tied him to a tree and stabbed him again, and left him and his backpack right there, next to the wooden sign about No Drinking, No Hunting. He took Anne with him, in Teddy's car. They found Teddy's body three days later and his parents buried him two days after that, back in Virginia.

Eugene Trask killed another boy just a few days before he killed Teddy. Some kids from Schenectady were celebrating their high school graduation with an overnight camping trip, and when Eugene Trask came upon them, he tied them all to different trees, far enough apart so they couldn't see each other, and then he killed the boy who'd made him mad. While he was stabbing him, the same way he stabbed Teddy, two sharp holes in his heart and then a slash across his chest, for emphasis, for something, the other kids slipped out of their ropes and ran. By the time they came back with people from town, Eugene Trask had circled around the woods and was running through streams where the dogs could not catch his scent.

The heart is really two hearts and four parts: the right and the left, and the up and the down. The left heart pumps the blood through the body. Even when there is nothing more for it to do, even when you have already lost ten ounces of blood, which is all an average-sized person needs to lose to bring on heart failure, the left heart keeps pumping, bringing old news to nowhere. The right heart sits still as a cave, a thin scrim of blood barely covering its floor. The less air you have, the faster the whole heart beats. Still less and the bronchioles, hollow, spongy flutes of the lungs, whistle and squeeze dry until they lie flat and hard, like plates on the table, and when there is no more air and no more blood to bring help from the furthest reaches of the body, the lungs crack and chip like old china.

Mrs. Warburg and I both went to psychics.

She said, "A psychic in East Cleveland. What's *that* tell you?" which is why I kept talking to her even after Mr. Warburg said he didn't think it was helping. Mrs. Warburg's psychic lived in a run-down split-level ranch house with lime-green shag carpeting. Her psychic wore a white smock and white shoes like a nurse and she got Mrs. Warburg confused with her three o'clock, who was coming for a reading on her pancreatic cancer. Mrs. Warburg's psychic didn't know where Anne was.

My psychic was on West Cedar Street, in a tiny apartment two blocks away   20
from us on Beacon Hill. My boss's wife had lost a diamond earring and the
psychic found it, she said. He looked like a graduate student. He was barefoot.
He saw me looking down and flexed his feet.

"Helps me concentrate," he said.

We sat down at a dinette table and he held my hands between his. He
inhaled and closed his eyes. I couldn't remember if I had the twenty dollars
with me or not.

"Don't worry about it," he said.

We sat for three minutes, and I watched the hands on the grandfather
clock behind him. My aunt had the same clock, with the flowers carved in
cherrywood climbing up the maple box.

"It's very dark," he said. "I'm sorry. It's very dark where she is."   25

I found the money and he pushed it back at me, and not just out of kindness, I didn't think.

I told Mrs. Warburg my psychic didn't know anything either.

The police came on Saturday and again on Monday, but not the same ones. On
Monday it was detectives from New York, and they didn't treat me like the worried roommate. They reminded me that I told the Boston police I'd last seen
Anne at two o'clock on Thursday, before she went to Teddy's. They said someone else had told them Anne came back to our apartment at four o'clock, to
get her sleeping bag. I said yes, I remembered, I was napping and she woke me
up, because it was really my sleeping bag, I lent it to her for the trip. Yes, I did
see her at four, not just at two.

Were you upset she was going on this trip with Ted? They said.

Teddy, I said. Why would I be upset?   30

They looked around our apartment, where I had to walk through her little
bedroom to use the bathroom and she had to walk through my little bedroom
to get to the front door, as if it was obvious why I'd be upset.

Maybe you didn't like him, they said.

I like him, I said.

Maybe he was cutting into your time with Annie.

Anne, I said, and they looked at each other as if it was very significant that   35
I had corrected them.

Anne, they said. So maybe Teddy got in the way of your friendship with
Anne?

I rolled my eyes. No, I said, we double-dated sometimes, it was cool.

They looked at their notes.

You have a boyfriend? they said. We'd like to talk to him too.

Sure, I said, he's in Maine with his family, but you can talk to him.   40

They shrugged a little. Maine, with his parents, was not a promising lead.

They pressed me a little more about my latent lesbian feelings for Anne
and my unexpressed and unrequited love for Teddy, and I said that I thought
maybe I had forgotten to tell the Boston police that I had worked double shifts
every day last week and that I didn't own a car. They smiled and shrugged again.

If you think of anything, they said.

It's very dark where she is, is what I thought.

The police talked to me and they talked to Rose Trask, Eugene's sister, too. She   45
said Eugene was a worthless piece of shit. She said he owed her money and if

they found him she'd like it back, please. She hid Eugene's hunting knife at the bottom of her root cellar, under the onions, and she hid Eugene in her big, old-fashioned chimney until they left. Later, they made her go up in the helicopter to help them find him, and they made her call out his name over their loud-speaker ("Eugene, I love you. Eugene, it will be okay."). While they circled the park, which is three times the size of Yellowstone, she told the police that Eugene had worked on their uncle's farm from the time he was seven, because he was big for his age, and that he knew his way around the woods because their father threw him out of the house naked, in the middle of the night, whenever he wet his bed, which he did all his life.

Mrs. Warburg said she had wanted to be a dancer and she made Anne take jazz and tap and modern all through school but what Anne really loved was talking. Debate Club, Rhetoric, Student Court, Model U.N., anything that gave you plenty of opportunity for arguing and persuading, she liked. I said I knew that because I had had to live with Anne for four years and she argued and persuaded me out of cheap shoes and generic toilet paper and my mother's winter coat. She bought us matching kimonos in Chinatown. I told Mrs. Warburg that it was entirely due to Anne that I was able to walk through the world like a normal person.

Mrs. Warburg said, "Let me get another drink."

I lay back on Anne's bed and sipped my beer. Mrs. Warburg and I had agreed that since I didn't always remember to get rum for our parties, I could make do with beer. Anne actually liked beer, Mrs. Warburg said. Mr. Warburg liked Scotch. Mrs. Warburg went right down the middle, she felt, with the rum-and-Coke.

"Should we have gone to Teddy's funeral?" she said.

I didn't think so. Mrs. Warburg had never met Teddy, and I certainly didn't want to go. I didn't want to sit with his family, or sit far behind them, hoping that since Teddy was dead, Anne was alive, or that if Anne had to be dead, she'd be lying in a white casket, with bushels of white carnations around her, and Teddy would be lying someplace dark and terrible and unseen.

"I think Anne might have escaped," Mrs. Warburg said. "I really do. I think she might have gotten out of those awful mountains and she might have found a rowboat or something, she's wonderful on water, you should see her on Lake Erie but it could be because of the trauma she doesn't—"

Mr. Warburg got on the line.

"It's three o'clock in the morning," he said. "Mrs. Warburg needs to sleep. So do you, I'm sure."

Eugene Trask and Anne traveled for four days. He said, at his trial, that she was a wonderful conversationalist. He said that talking to her was a pleasure and that they had had some very lively discussions, which he felt she had enjoyed. At the end of the fourth day, he unbuckled his belt so he could rape her again, in a quiet pine grove near Lake Pleasant, and while he was distracted with his shirttail and zipper, she made a grab for his hunting knife. He hit her on the head with the butt of his rifle, and when she got up, he hit her again. Then he stabbed her twice, just like Teddy, two to the heart. He didn't want to shoot her, he said. He put her bleeding body in the back of an orange Buick he'd stolen in Speculator, and he drove to an abandoned mine. He threw her down the thirty-foot shaft, dumped the Buick in Mineville, and walked through the

50

woods to his sister's place. They had hamburgers and mashed potatoes and sat on Rose's back step and watched a pair of red-tailed hawks circling the spruce. Rose washed out his shirt and pants and ironed them dry, and he left early the next morning, with two meatloaf sandwiches in his jacket pocket. They caught Eugene Trask when one of his stolen cars broke down. They shot him in the leg. He said he didn't remember anything since he'd skipped his last arraignment two months ago. He said he was subject to fits of amnesia. He had fancy criminal lawyers who took his case because the hunt for Eugene Trask had turned out to be the biggest manhunt in the tristate area since the Lindbergh baby. There were reporters everywhere, Mrs. Warburg said. Mr. Feldman and Mr. Barone told Eugene that if he lied to them they would not be able to defend him adequately, so he drew them maps of where they could find Anne's body, and also two other girls who had been missing for six months. Mr. Feldman and Mr. Barone felt that they could not reveal this information to the police or to the Warburgs or to the other families because it would violate Eugene's confidentiality. After the trial, after Eugene was transferred to Fishkill Correctional Facility, two kids were playing in an old mine near Speculator, looking for garnets and gold and arrowheads, and they found Anne's body.

The dead body makes its own way. It stiffens and then it relaxes and then it 55 softens. The flesh turns to a black thick cream. If I had put my arms around her to carry her up the gravel path and home, if I had reached out to steady her, my hand would have slid through her skin like a spoon through custard, and she would have fallen away from me, held in only by her clothes. If I had hidden in the timbered walls of the mine, waiting until Eugene Trask heard the reassuring one-two thump of the almost emptied body on the mine car tracks, I might have seen her as I see her now. Her eyes open and blue, her cheeks pink underneath the streaks of clay and dust, and she is breathing, her chest is rising and falling, too fast and too shallow, like a bird in distress, but rising and falling.

    We are all in the cave. Mrs. Warburg went back to her life, without me, after Anne's funeral that winter (did those children find her covered with the first November snow?), and Mr. Warburg resurfaced eight years later, remarried to a woman who became friends with my aunt Rita in Beachwood. Aunt Rita said the new Mrs. Warburg was lovely. She said the first Mrs. Warburg had made herself into a complete invalid, round-the-clock help, but even so she died alone, Rita said, in their old house. She didn't know from what. Eugene was shot and killed trying to escape from Fishkill. Two bullets to the heart, one to the lungs. Mrs. Warburg sent me the clipping. Rose Trask married and had two children, Cheryl and Eugene. Rose and Cheryl and little Eugene drowned in 1986, boating on Lake Champlain. Mrs. Warburg sent me the clipping. My young father, still slim and handsome and a good dancer, collapsed on our roof trying to straighten our ancient TV antennae and Eugene Trask pulled his feet out from under him, over the gutters and thirty feet down. Don't let the sun catch you crying, my father used to say. Maybe your nervous system doesn't get the message to swallow the morning toast and you are strangled and thrown to the kitchen floor by Eugene Trask while your wife and children watch. Maybe a cluster of secret tumors bloom from skull to spine, opening their petals so you can be beaten unconscious by Eugene Trask on the way to work. Everyone dies of heart failure, Eugene Trask said at his trial.

s the dead less, I miss them more. I miss the tall pines around
I miss the brown-and-gray cobblestones on West Cedar Street, I
led hawks that fly so often in pairs. I miss the cheap red wine in
ss the rum-and-Coke. I miss Anne's wet gold hair drying as we
escape. I miss the hot dog luau and driving to dance lessons
at Bruegger's Bagels. I miss the cold mornings on the farm,
le of the bucket bit into my small hands and my feet slid over
I miss the hot grease spattering around the felafel balls and the
of Hebrew. I miss the new green leaves, shaking in the June
ding on my father's shiny shoes as we danced to the Tennessee
mother made me a paper fan so I could flirt like a Southern
ny nose with the fan. I miss every piece of my dead. Every piece
like cordwood within me, and my heart, both sides, and all four
liquary.

NS TO OTHER SELECTIONS

the way Bloom creates tension and suspense in her story with
ubus's strategies in "Killings" (p. 103).

how the themes of "By-and-by" and Rick Bass's "Her First Elk"
e centered on grief.

17

Stories for Further Reading

The ability of writers to imagine what is not the self, to familiarize the strange and mystify the familiar, is the test of their power.

—TONI MORRISON

AP/Wide World.

CHITRA BANERJEE DIVAKARUNI

(B. 1956)

Born in India, Chitra Banerjee Divakaruni left Calcutta when she was nineteen years old to continue her education in the United States, where she worked a variety of odd jobs while earning a master's degree from Wright State University and a Ph.D. from the University of California, Berkeley. She currently teaches in the creative writing department at the University of Houston. Her first collection of short stories, *Arranged Marriage* (which includes "Clothes," reprinted

Courtesy of the author.

below), was published in 1995; it won several awards including the American Book Award. In addition to a second collection of stories, *The Unknown Errors of Our Lives* (2001), she has published several novels including *Sister of My Heart* (1999), *Vine of Desire* (2002), *The Conch Bearer* (2003), and *Queen of Dreams* (2004). Among her three books of poetry, her most recent is *Leaving Yuba City* (1997). Much of her work focuses on Indian immigrant women who find themselves having to balance their lives between their homeland and the United States.

Clothes

1990

The water of the women's lake laps against my breasts, cool, calming. I can feel it beginning to wash the hot nervousness away from my body. The little waves tickle my armpits, make my sari float up around me, wet and yellow, like a sunflower after rain. I close my eyes and smell the sweet brown odor of the *ritha* pulp my friends Deepali and Radha are working into my hair so it will glisten with little lights this evening. They scrub with more vigor than usual and wash it out more carefully, because today is a special day. It is the day of my bride-viewing.

"Ei, Sumita! Mita! Are you deaf?" Radha says. "This is the third time I've asked you the same question."

"Look at her, already dreaming about her husband, and she hasn't even seen him yet!" Deepali jokes. Then she adds, the envy in her voice only half hidden, "Who cares about friends from a little Indian village when you're about to go live in America?"

I want to deny it, to say that I will always love them and all the things we did together through my growing-up years — visiting the *charak* fair where we always ate too many sweets, raiding the neighbor's guava tree summer afternoons while the grown-ups slept, telling fairy tales while we braided each other's hair in elaborate patterns we'd invented. *And she married the handsome prince who took her to his kingdom beyond the seven seas.* But already the activities of our girlhood seem to be far in my past, the colors leached out of them, like old sepia photographs.

His name is Somesh Sen, the man who is coming to our house with his 5 parents today and who will be my husband "if I'm lucky enough to be chosen," as my aunt says. He is coming all the way from California. Father showed it to me yesterday, on the metal globe that sits on his desk, a chunky pink wedge on the side of a multicolored slab marked *Untd. Sts. of America.* I touched it and felt the excitement leap all the way up my arm like an electric shock. Then it died away, leaving only a beaten-metal coldness against my fingertips.

For the first time it occurred to me that if things worked out the way everyone was hoping, I'd be going halfway around the world to live with a man I hadn't even met. Would I ever see my parents again? *Don't send me so far away,* I wanted to cry, but of course I didn't. It would be ungrateful. Father had worked so hard to find this match for me. Besides, wasn't it every woman's destiny, as Mother was always telling me, to leave the known for the unknown? She had done it, and her mother before her. *A married woman belongs to her husband, her in-laws.* Hot seeds of tears pricked my eyelids at the unfairness of it.

"Mita Moni, little jewel," Father said, calling me by my childhood name. He put out his hand as though he wanted to touch my face, then let it fall to his side. "He's a good man. Comes from a fine family. He will be kind to you." He was silent for a while. Finally he said, "Come, let me show you the special sari I bought in Calcutta for you to wear at the bride-viewing."

"Are you nervous?" Radha asks as she wraps my hair in a soft cotton towel. Her parents are also trying to arrange a marriage for her. So far three families have come to see her, but no one has chosen her because her skin-color is considered too dark. "Isn't it terrible, not knowing what's going to happen?"

I nod because I don't want to disagree, don't want to make her feel bad by saying that sometimes it's worse when you know what's coming, like I do. I knew it as soon as Father unlocked his mahogany *almirah*° and took out the sari.

It was the most expensive sari I had ever seen, and surely the most beau- 10 tiful. Its body was a pale pink, like the dawn sky over the women's lake. The color of transition. Embroidered all over it were tiny stars made out of real gold *zari* thread.

"Here, hold it," said Father.

The sari was unexpectedly heavy in my hands, silk-slippery, a sari to walk carefully in. A sari that could change one's life. I stood there holding it, wanting to weep. I knew that when I wore it, it would hang in perfect pleats to my feet and shimmer in the light of the evening lamps. It would dazzle Somesh and his parents and they would choose me to be his bride.

When the plane takes off, I try to stay calm, to take deep, slow breaths like Father does when he practices yoga. But my hands clench themselves on to the folds of my sari and when I force them open, after the *fasten seat belt* and *no smoking* signs have blinked off, I see they have left damp blotches on the delicate crushed fabric.

We had some arguments about this sari. I wanted a blue one for the journey, because blue is the color of possibility, the color of the sky through which I would be traveling. But Mother said there must be red in it because red is the color of luck for married women. Finally, Father found one to satisfy us both: midnight-blue with a thin red border the same color as the marriage mark I'm wearing on my forehead.

It is hard for me to think of myself as a married woman. I whisper my new 15 name to myself, Mrs. Sumita Sen, but the syllables rustle uneasily in my mouth like a stiff satin that's never been worn.

Somesh had to leave for America just a week after the wedding. He had to get back to the store, he explained to me. He had promised his partner. The store. It seems more real to me than Somesh — perhaps because I know more about it. It was what we had mostly talked about the night after the wedding, the first night we were together alone. It stayed open twenty-four hours, yes, all night, every night, not like the Indian stores which closed at dinnertime and sometimes in the hottest part of the afternoon. That's why his partner needed him back.

almirah: A large closet.

The store was called *7-Eleven*. I thought it a strange name, exotic, risky. All the stores I knew were piously named after gods and goddesses — *Ganesh Sweet House*, *Lakshmi Vastralaya for Fine Saris* — to bring the owners luck.

The store sold all kinds of amazing things — apple juice in cardboard cartons that never leaked; American bread that came in cellophane packages, already cut up; canisters of potato chips, each large grainy flake curved exactly like the next. The large refrigerator with see-through glass doors held beer and wine, which Somesh said were the most popular items.

"That's where the money comes from, especially in the neighborhood where our store is," said Somesh, smiling at the shocked look on my face. (The only places I knew of that sold alcohol were the village toddy shops, "dark, stinking dens of vice," Father called them.) "A lot of Americans drink, you know. It's a part of their culture, not considered immoral, like it is here. And really, there's nothing wrong with it." He touched my lips lightly with his finger. "When you come to California, I'll get you some sweet white wine and you'll see how good it makes you feel. . . ." Now his fingers were stroking my cheeks, my throat, moving downward. I closed my eyes and tried not to jerk away because after all it was my wifely duty.

"It helps if you can think about something else," my friend Madhavi had   20
said when she warned me about what most husbands demanded on the very first night. Two years married, she already had one child and was pregnant with a second one.

I tried to think of the women's lake, the dark cloudy green of the *shapla*° leaves that float on the water, but his lips were hot against my skin, his fingers fumbling with buttons, pulling at the cotton night-sari I wore. I couldn't breathe.

"Bite hard on your tongue," Madhavi had advised. "The pain will keep your mind off what's going on down there."

But when I bit down, it hurt so much that I cried out. I couldn't help it although I was ashamed. Somesh lifted his head. I don't know what he saw on my face, but he stopped right away. "Shhh," he said, although I had made myself silent already. "It's OK, we'll wait until you feel like it." I tried to apologize but he smiled it away and started telling me some more about the store.

And that's how it was the rest of the week until he left. We would lie side by side on the big white bridal pillow I had embroidered with a pair of doves for married harmony, and Somesh would describe how the store's front windows were decorated with a flashing neon Dewar's sign and a lighted Budweiser waterfall *this big*. I would watch his hands moving excitedly through the dim air of the bedroom and think that Father had been right, he was a good man, my husband, a kind, patient man. And so handsome, too, I would add, stealing a quick look at the strong curve of his jaw, feeling luckier than I had any right to be.

The night before he left, Somesh confessed that the store wasn't making   25
much money yet. "I'm not worried, I'm sure it soon will," he added, his fingers pleating the edge of my sari. "But I just don't want to give you the wrong impression, don't want you to be disappointed."

In the half dark I could see he had turned toward me. His face, with two

shapla: A water plant.

vertical lines between the brows, looked young, apprehensive, in need of protection. I'd never seen that on a man's face before. Something rose in me like a wave.

"It's all right," I said, as though to a child, and pulled his head down to my breast. His hair smelled faintly of the American cigarettes he smoked. "I won't be disappointed. I'll help you." And a sudden happiness filled me.

That night I dreamed I was at the store. Soft American music floated in the background as I moved between shelves stocked high with brightly colored cans and elegant-necked bottles, turning their labels carefully to the front, polishing them until they shone.

Now, sitting inside this metal shell that is hurtling through emptiness, I try to remember other things about my husband: how gentle his hands had been, and his lips, surprisingly soft, like a woman's. How I've longed for them through those drawn-out nights while I waited for my visa to arrive. He will be standing at the customs gate, and when I reach him, he will lower his face to mine. We will kiss in front of everyone, not caring, like Americans, then pull back, look each other in the eye, and smile.

But suddenly, as I am thinking this, I realize I cannot recall Somesh's face. 30 I try and try until my head hurts, but I can only visualize the black air swirling outside the plane, too thin for breathing. My own breath grows ragged with panic as I think of it and my mouth fills with sour fluid the way it does just before I throw up.

I grope for something to hold on to, something beautiful and talismanic from my old life. And then I remember. Somewhere down under me, low in the belly of the plane, inside my new brown case which is stacked in the dark with a hundred others, are my saris. Thick Kanjeepuram silks in solid purples and golden yellows, the thin hand-woven cottons of the Bengal countryside, green as a young banana plant, gray as the women's lake on a monsoon morning. Already I can feel my shoulders loosening up, my breath steadying. My wedding Benarasi, flame-orange, with a wide *palloo°* of gold-embroidered dancing peacocks. Fold upon fold of Dhakais° so fine they can be pulled through a ring. Into each fold my mother has tucked a small sachet of sandalwood powder to protect the saris from the unknown insects of America. Little silk sachets, made from *her* old saris—I can smell their calm fragrance as I watch the American air hostess wheeling the dinner cart toward my seat. It is the smell of my mother's hands.

I know then that everything will be all right. And when the air hostess bends her curly golden head to ask me what I would like to eat, I understand every word in spite of her strange accent and answer her without stumbling even once over the unfamiliar English phrases.

Late at night I stand in front of our bedroom mirror trying on the clothes Somesh has bought for me and smuggled in past his parents. I model each one for him, walking back and forth, clasping my hands behind my head, lips pouted, left hip thrust out just like the models on TV, while he whispers applause. I'm breathless with suppressed laughter (Father and Mother Sen must not hear us) and my cheeks are hot with the delicious excitement of con-

---

palloo: The piece of the sari that goes over the shoulder.
Dhakais: Hand-loomed saris from Bangladesh.

spiracy. We've stuffed a towel at the bottom of the door so no light will shine through.

I'm wearing a pair of jeans now, marveling at the curves of my hips and thighs, which have always been hidden under the flowing lines of my saris. I love the color, the same pale blue as the *nayantara* flowers that grow in my parents' garden. The solid comforting weight. The jeans come with a close-fitting T-shirt which outlines my breasts.

I scold Somesh to hide my embarrassed pleasure. He shouldn't have been 35 so extravagant. We can't afford it. He just smiles.

The T-shirt is sunrise-orange — the color, I decide, of joy, of my new American life. Across its middle, in large black letters, is written *Great America*. I was sure the letters referred to the country, but Somesh told me it is the name of an amusement park, a place where people go to have fun. I think it a wonderful concept, novel. Above the letters is the picture of a train. Only it's not a train, Somesh tells me, it's a roller coaster. He tries to explain how it moves, the insane speed, the dizzy ground falling away, then gives up. "I'll take you there, Mita sweetheart," he says, "as soon as we move into our own place."

That's our dream (mine more than his, I suspect) — moving out of this two-room apartment where it seems to me if we all breathed in at once, there would be no air left. Where I must cover my head with the edge of my Japan nylon sari (my expensive Indian ones are to be saved for special occasions — trips to the temple, Bengali New Year) and serve tea to the old women that come to visit Mother Sen, where like a good Indian wife I must never address my husband by his name. Where even in our bed we kiss guiltily, uneasily, listening for the giveaway creak of springs. Sometimes I laugh to myself, thinking how ironic it is that after all my fears about America, my life has turned out to be no different from Deepali's or Radha's. But at other times I feel caught in a world where everything is frozen in place, like a scene inside a glass paperweight. It is a world so small that if I were to stretch out my arms, I would touch its cold unyielding edges. I stand inside this glass world, watching helplessly as America rushes by, wanting to scream. Then I'm ashamed. Mita, I tell myself, you're growing westernized. Back home you'd never have felt this way.

We must be patient. I know that. Tactful, loving children. That is the Indian way. "I'm their life," Somesh tells me as we lie beside each other, lazy from lovemaking. He's not boasting, merely stating a fact. "They've always been there when I needed them. I could never abandon them at some old people's home." For a moment I feel rage. You're constantly thinking of them, I want to scream. But what about me? Then I remember my own parents, Mother's hands cool on my sweat-drenched body through nights of fever, Father teaching me to read, his finger moving along the crisp black angles of the alphabet, transforming them magically into things I knew, water, dog, mango tree. I beat back my unreasonable desire and nod agreement.

Somesh has bought me a cream blouse with a long brown skirt. They match beautifully, like the inside and outside of an almond. "For when you begin working," he says. But first he wants me to start college. Get a degree, perhaps in teaching. I picture myself in front of a classroom of girls with blond pigtails and blue uniforms, like a scene out of an English movie I saw long ago in Calcutta. They raise their hands respectfully when I ask a question. "Do you really think I can?" I ask. "Of course," he replies.

I am gratified he has such confidence in me. But I have another plan, a 40 secret that I will divulge to him once we move. What I really want is to work in the store. I want to stand behind the counter in the cream-and-brown skirt set (color of earth, color of seeds) and ring up purchases. The register drawer will glide open. Confident, I will count out green dollars and silver quarters. Gleaming copper pennies. I will dust the jars of gilt-wrapped chocolates on the counter. Will straighten, on the far wall, posters of smiling young men raising their beer mugs to toast scantily clad redheads with huge spiky eyelashes. (I have never visited the store — my in-laws don't consider it proper for a wife — but of course I know exactly what it looks like.) I will charm the customers with my smile, so that they will return again and again just to hear me telling them to have a nice day.

Meanwhile, I will the store to make money for us. Quickly. Because when we move, we'll be paying for two households. But so far it hasn't worked. They're running at a loss, Somesh tells me. They had to let the hired help go. This means most nights Somesh has to take the graveyard shift (that horrible word, like a cold hand up my spine) because his partner refuses to.

"The bastard!" Somesh spat out once. "Just because he put in more money he thinks he can order me around. I'll show him!" I was frightened by the vicious twist of his mouth. Somehow I'd never imagined that he could be angry.

Often Somesh leaves as soon as he has dinner and doesn't get back till after I've made morning tea for Father and Mother Sen. I lie mostly awake those nights, picturing masked intruders crouching in the shadowed back of the store, like I've seen on the police shows that Father Sen sometimes watches. But Somesh insists there's nothing to worry about, they have bars on the windows and a burglar alarm. "And remember," he says, "the extra cash will help us move out that much quicker."

I'm wearing a nightie now, my very first one. It's black and lacy, with a bit of a shine to it, and it glides over my hips to stop outrageously at mid-thigh. My mouth is an O of surprise in the mirror, my legs long and pale and sleek from the hair remover I asked Somesh to buy me last week. The legs of a movie star. Somesh laughs at the look on my face, then says, "You're beautiful." His voice starts a flutter low in my belly.

"Do you really think so?" I ask, mostly because I want to hear him say it 45 again. No one has called me beautiful before. My father would have thought it inappropriate, my mother that it would make me vain.

Somesh draws me close. "Very beautiful," he whispers. "The most beautiful woman in the whole world." His eyes are not joking as they usually are. I want to turn off the light, but "Please," he says, "I want to keep seeing your face." His fingers are taking the pins from my hair, undoing my braids. The escaped strands fall on his face like dark rain. We have already decided where we will hide my new American clothes — the jeans and T-shirt camouflaged on a hanger among Somesh's pants, the skirt set and nightie at the bottom of my suitcase, a sandalwood sachet tucked between them, waiting.

I stand in the middle of our empty bedroom, my hair still wet from the purification bath, my back to the stripped bed I can't bear to look at. I hold in my hands the plain white sari I'm supposed to wear. I must hurry. Any minute now there'll be a knock at the door. They are afraid to leave me alone too long, afraid I might do something to myself.

The sari, a thick voile that will bunch around the waist when worn, is borrowed. White. Widow's color, color of endings. I try to tuck it into the top of the petticoat, but my fingers are numb, disobedient. It spills through them and there are waves and waves of white around my feet. I kick out in sudden rage, but the sari is too soft, it gives too easily. I grab up an edge, clamp down with my teeth and pull, feeling a fierce, bitter satisfaction when I hear it rip.

There's a cut, still stinging, on the side of my right arm, halfway to the elbow. It is from the bangle-breaking ceremony. Old Mrs. Ghosh performed the ritual, since she's a widow, too. She took my hands in hers and brought them down hard on the bedpost, so that the glass bangles I was wearing shattered and multicolored shards flew out in every direction. Some landed on the body that was on the bed, covered with a sheet. I can't call it Somesh. He was gone already. She took an edge of the sheet and rubbed the red marriage mark off my forehead. She was crying. All the women in the room were crying except me. I watched them as though from the far end of a tunnel. Their flared nostrils, their red-veined eyes, the runnels of tears, salt-corrosive, down their cheeks.

It happened last night. He was at the store. "It isn't too bad," he would tell 50 me on the days when he was in a good mood. "Not too many customers. I can put up my feet and watch MTV all night. I can sing along with Michael Jackson as loud as I want." He had a good voice, Somesh. Sometimes he would sing softly at night, lying in bed, holding me. Hindi songs of love, *Mere Sapnon Ki Rani,* queen of my dreams. (He would not sing American songs at home out of respect for his parents, who thought they were decadent.) I would feel his warm breath on my hair as I fell asleep.

Someone came into the store last night. He took all the money, even the little rolls of pennies I had helped Somesh make up. Before he left he emptied the bullets from his gun into my husband's chest.

"Only thing is," Somesh would say about the night shifts, "I really miss you. I sit there and think of you asleep in bed. Do you know that when you sleep you make your hands into fists, like a baby? When we move out, will you come along some nights to keep me company?"

My in-laws are good people, kind. They made sure the body was covered before they let me into the room. When someone asked if my hair should be cut off, as they sometimes do with widows back home, they said no. They said I could stay at the apartment with Mrs. Ghosh if I didn't want to go to the crematorium. They asked Dr. Das to give me something to calm me down when I couldn't stop shivering. They didn't say, even once, as people would surely have in the village, that it was my bad luck that brought death to their son so soon after his marriage.

They will probably go back to India now. There's nothing here for them anymore. They will want me to go with them. You're like our daughter, they will say. Your home is with us, for as long as you want. For the rest of your life. *The rest of my life.* I can't think about that yet. It makes me dizzy. Fragments are flying about my head, multicolored and piercing sharp like bits of bangle glass.

I want you to go to college. Choose a career. I stand in front of a classroom of 55 smiling children who love me in my cream-and-brown American dress. A faceless parade straggles across my eyelids: all those customers at the store that I will never meet. The lace nightie, fragrant with sandalwood, waiting in its blackness inside my suitcase. The savings book where we have $3605.33. *Four thousand and we can move out, maybe next month.* The name of the panty hose I'd asked him to buy me for my birthday: sheer golden-beige. His lips, unexpectedly soft, woman-smooth. Elegant-necked wine bottles swept off shelves, shattering on the floor.

I know Somesh would not have tried to stop the gunman. I can picture his silhouette against the lighted Dewar's sign, hands raised. He is trying to find the right expression to put on his face, calm, reassuring, reasonable. *OK, take the money. No, I won't call the police.* His hands tremble just a little. His eyes darken with disbelief as his fingers touch his chest and come away wet.

I yanked away the cover. I had to see. *Great America, a place where people go to have fun.* My breath roller-coasting through my body, my unlived life gathering itself into a scream. I'd expected blood, a lot of blood, the deep red-black of it crusting his chest. But they must have cleaned him up at the hospital. He was dressed in his silk wedding *kurta.* Against its warm ivory his face appeared remote, stern. The musky aroma of his aftershave lotion that someone must have sprinkled on the body. It didn't quite hide that other smell, thin, sour, metallic. The smell of death. The floor shifted under me, tilting like a wave.

I'm lying on the floor now, on the spilled white sari. I feel sleepy. Or perhaps it is some other feeling I don't have a word for. The sari is seductive-soft, drawing me into its folds.

Sometimes, bathing at the lake, I would move away from my friends, their endless chatter. I'd swim toward the middle of the water with a lazy backstroke, gazing at the sky, its enormous blueness drawing me up until I felt weightless and dizzy. Once in a while there would be a plane, a small silver needle drawn through the clouds, in and out, until it disappeared. Sometimes the thought came to me, as I floated in the middle of the lake with the sun beating down on my closed eyelids, that it would be so easy to let go, to drop into the dim brown world of mud, of water weeds fine as hair.

Once I almost did it. I curled my body inward, tight as a fist, and felt it 60 start to sink. The sun grew pale and shapeless; the water, suddenly cold, licked at the insides of my ears in welcome. But in the end I couldn't.

They are knocking on the door now, calling my name. I push myself off the floor, my body almost too heavy to lift up, as when one climbs out after a long swim. I'm surprised at how vividly it comes to me, this memory I haven't called up in years: the desperate flailing of arms and legs as I fought my way upward; the press of the water on me, heavy as terror; the wild animal trapped inside my chest, clawing at my lungs. The day returning to me as searing air, the way I drew it in, in, in, as though I would never have enough of it.

That's when I know I cannot go back. I don't know yet how I'll manage, here in this new, dangerous land. I only know I must. Because all over India, at this very moment, widows in white saris are bowing their veiled heads, serving tea to in-laws. Doves with cut-off wings.

I am standing in front of the mirror now, gathering up the sari. I tuck in the ripped end so it lies next to my skin, my secret. I make myself think of the store, although it hurts. Inside the refrigerated unit, blue milk cartons neatly lined up by Somesh's hands. The exotic smell of Hills Brothers coffee brewed black and strong, the glisten of sugar-glazed donuts nestled in tissue. The neon Budweiser emblem winking on and off like a risky invitation.

I straighten my shoulders and stand taller, take a deep breath. Air fills me — the same air that traveled through Somesh's lungs a little while ago. The thought is like an unexpected, intimate gift. I tilt my chin, readying myself for the arguments of the coming weeks, the remonstrations. In the mirror a woman holds my gaze, her eyes apprehensive yet steady. She wears a blouse and skirt the color of almonds.

JAMAICA KINCAID (B. 1949)

Jamaica Kincaid was born Elaine Potter Richardson on the Caribbean island of Antigua. She moved to New York in 1965 to work as an au pair, studied photography at both the New School for Social Research and Franconia College, and changed her name to Jamaica Kincaid in 1973 with her first publication, "When I Was 17," a series of interviews. Over the next few years, she wrote for *The New Yorker* magazine, first as a free-lancer and then as a staff writer. In 1978, Kincaid wrote her first piece of fiction, "Girl," published in *The New Yorker* and included in her debut short story collection, *At the Bottom of the River* (1983), which won an award from the Academy and Institute of Arts and Letters and was nominated for the PEN/Faulkner Award. Her other work includes *Annie John* (1985), *Lucy* (1990), *Autobiography of My Mother* (1994), and three non-fiction books, *A Small Place* (1988), *My Brother* (1997), and *Mr. Potter* (2002). Whether autobiographical fiction or nonfiction, her work usually focuses on the perils of postcolonial society, paralleled by an examination of rifts in mother-daughter relationships.

By permission of Trix Rosen.

Explore contexts for Jamaica Kincaid and approaches to "Girl" on *LiterActive* or at bedfordstmartins.com/meyercompact.

Girl

1978

Wash the white clothes on Monday and put them on the stone heap; wash the color clothes on Tuesday and put them on the clothesline to dry; don't walk barehead in the hot sun; cook pumpkin fritters in very hot sweet oil; soak your little cloths right after you take them off; when buying cotton to make yourself a nice blouse, be sure that it doesn't have gum on it, because that way it won't hold up well after a wash; soak salt fish overnight before you cook it; is it true that you sing benna° in Sunday school?; always eat your food in such a way that it won't turn someone else's stomach; on Sundays try to walk like a

benna: Calypso music.

lady and not like the slut you are so bent on becoming; don't sing benna in Sunday school; you mustn't speak to wharf-rat boys, not even to give directions; don't eat fruits on the street—flies will follow you; *but I don't sing benna on Sundays at all and never in Sunday school;* this is how to sew on a button; this is how to make a buttonhole for the button you have just sewed on; this is how to hem a dress when you see the hem coming down and so to prevent yourself from looking like the slut I know you are so bent on becoming; this is how you iron your father's khaki shirt so that it doesn't have a crease; this is how you iron your father's khaki pants so that they don't have a crease; this is how you grow okra—far from the house, because okra tree harbors red ants; when you are growing dasheen,° make sure it gets plenty of water or else it makes your throat itch when you are eating it; this is how you sweep a corner; this is how you sweep a whole house; this is how you sweep a yard; this is how you smile to someone you don't like too much; this is how you smile to someone you don't like at all; this is how you smile to someone you like completely; this is how you set a table for tea; this is how you set a table for dinner; this is how you set a table for dinner with an important guest; this is how you set a table for lunch; this is how you set a table for breakfast; this is how to behave in the presence of men who don't know you very well, and this way they won't recognize immediately the slut I have warned you against becoming; be sure to wash every day, even if it is with your own spit; don't squat down to play marbles— you are not a boy, you know; don't pick people's flowers—you might catch something; don't throw stones at blackbirds, because it might not be a blackbird at all; this is how to make a bread pudding; this is how to make doukona;° this is how to make pepper pot;° this is how to make a good medicine for a cold; this is how to make a good medicine to throw away a child before it even becomes a child; this is how to catch a fish; this is how to throw back a fish you don't like, and that way something bad won't fall on you; this is how to bully a man; this is how a man bullies you; this is how to love a man, and if this doesn't work there are other ways, and if they don't work don't feel too bad about giving up; this is how to spit up in the air if you feel like it, and this is how to move quick so that it doesn't fall on you; this is how to make ends meet; always squeeze bread to make sure it's fresh; *but what if the baker won't let me feel the bread?;* you mean to say that after all you are really going to be the kind of woman who the baker won't let near the bread?

dasheen: The edible rootstock of taro, a tropical plant.
doukona: A spicy plantain pudding.
pepper pot: A stew.

TIM O'BRIEN (B. 1946)

Born in Austin, Minnesota, Tim O'Brien was educated at Macalester College and Harvard University. He was drafted to serve in the Vietnam War and received a Purple Heart. His work is heavily influenced by his service in the war. His first book, *If I Die in a Combat Zone, Box Me Up and Ship Me Home* (1973), is a

Explore contexts
for Tim O'Brien
on *LiterActive.*

blend of fiction and actual experiences during his tour of duty. *Going after Cacciato,* judged by many critics to be the best work of American fiction about the Vietnam War, won the National Book Award in 1978. He has also published five other novels, *Northern Lights* (1974), *The Nuclear Age* (1985), *In the Lake of the Woods* (1994), *Tomcat in Love* (1998), and *July, July* (2002). "How to Tell a True War Story" is from a collection of interrelated stories titled *The Things They Carried* (1990). Originally published in *Esquire,* this story is at once grotesque and beautiful in its attempt to be true to experience.

© Marion Ettlinger.

How to Tell a True War Story   *1987*

This is true.

I had a buddy in Vietnam. His name was Bob Kiley, but everybody called him Rat.

A friend of his gets killed, so about a week later Rat sits down and writes a letter to the guy's sister. Rat tells her what a great brother she had, how strack° the guy was, a number one pal and comrade. A real soldier's soldier, Rat says. Then he tells a few stories to make the point, how her brother would always volunteer for stuff nobody else would volunteer for in a million years, dangerous stuff, like doing recon° or going out on these really badass night patrols. Stainless steel balls, Rat tells her. The guy was a little crazy, for sure, but crazy in a good way, a real daredevil, because he liked the challenge of it, he liked testing himself, just man against gook. A great, great guy, Rat says.

Anyway, it's a terrific letter, very personal and touching. Rat almost bawls writing it. He gets all teary telling about the good times they had together, how her brother made the war seem almost fun, always raising hell and lighting up villes° and bringing smoke to bear every which way. A great sense of humor, too. Like the time at this river when he went fishing with a whole damn crate of hand grenades. Probably the funniest thing in world history, Rat says, all that gore, about twenty zillion dead gook fish. Her brother, he had the right attitude. He knew how to have a good time. On Halloween, this real hot spooky night, the dude paints up his body all different colors and puts on this weird mask and goes out on ambush almost stark naked, just boots and balls and an M-16. A tremendous human being, Rat says. Pretty nutso sometimes, but you could trust him with your life.

And then the letter gets very sad and serious. Rat pours his heart out. He says he loved the guy. He says the guy was his best friend in the world. They   5

---

strack: A strict military appearance.
doing recon: Reconnaissance, or exploratory survey of enemy territory.
villes: Villages.

were like soul mates, he says, like twins or something, they had a whole lot in common. He tells the guy's sister he'll look her up when the war's over.

So what happens?

Rat mails the letter. He waits two months. The dumb cooze never writes back.

A true war story is never moral. It does not instruct, nor encourage virtue, nor suggest models of proper human behavior, nor restrain men from doing the things they have always done. If a story seems moral, do not believe it. If at the end of a war story you feel uplifted, or if you feel that some small bit of rectitude has been salvaged from the larger waste, then you have been made the victim of a very old and terrible lie. There is no rectitude whatsoever. There is no virtue. As a first rule of thumb, therefore, you can tell a true war story by its absolute and uncompromising allegiance to obscenity and evil. Listen to Rat Kiley. *Cooze,* he says. He does not say *bitch.* He certainly does not say *woman,* or *girl.* He says *cooze.* Then he spits and stares. He's nineteen years old—it's too much for him—so he looks at you with those big gentle killer eyes and says *cooze,* because his friend is dead, and because it's so incredibly sad and true: she never wrote back.

You can tell a true war story if it embarrasses you. If you don't care for obscenity, you don't care for the truth; if you don't care for the truth, watch how you vote. Send guys to war, they come home talking dirty.

Listen to Rat: "Jesus Christ, man, I write this beautiful fucking letter, I 10 slave over it, and what happens? The dumb cooze never writes back."

The dead guy's name was Curt Lemon. What happened was, we crossed a muddy river and marched west into the mountains, and on the third day we took a break along a trail junction in deep jungle. Right away, Lemon and Rat Kiley started goofing off. They didn't understand about the spookiness. They were kids; they just didn't know. A nature hike, they thought, not even a war, so they went off into the shade of some giant trees—quadruple canopy, no sunlight at all—and they were giggling and calling each other motherfucker and playing a silly game they'd invented. The game involved smoke grenades, which were harmless unless you did stupid things, and what they did was pull out the pin and stand a few feet apart and play catch under the shade of those huge trees. Whoever chickened out was a motherfucker. And if nobody chickened out, the grenade would make a light popping sound and they'd be covered with smoke and they'd laugh and dance around and then do it again.

It's all exactly true.

It happened nearly twenty years ago, but I still remember that trail junction and the giant trees and a soft dripping sound somewhere beyond the trees. I remember the smell of moss. Up in the canopy there were tiny white blossoms, but no sunlight at all, and I remember the shadows spreading out under the trees where Lemon and Rat Kiley were playing catch with smoke grenades. Mitchell Sanders sat flipping his yo-yo. Norman Bowker and Kiowa and Dave Jensen were dozing, or half-dozing, and all around us were those ragged green mountains.

Except for the laughter things were quiet.

At one point, I remember, Mitchell Sanders turned and looked at me, not 15 quite nodding, then after a while he rolled up his yo-yo and moved away.

It's hard to tell what happened next.

They were just goofing. There was a noise, I suppose, which must've been the detonator, so I glanced behind me and watched Lemon step from the shade into bright sunlight. His face was suddenly brown and shining. A handsome kid, really. Sharp gray eyes, lean and narrow-waisted, and when he died it was almost beautiful, the way the sunlight came around him and lifted him up and sucked him high into a tree full of moss and vines and white blossoms.

In any war story, but especially a true one, it's difficult to separate what happened from what seemed to happen. What seems to happen becomes its own happening and has to be told that way. The angles of vision are skewed. When a booby trap explodes, you close your eyes and duck and float outside yourself. When a guy dies, like Lemon, you look away and then look back for a moment and then look away again. The pictures get jumbled; you tend to miss a lot. And then afterward, when you go to tell about it, there is always that surreal seemingness, which makes the story seem untrue, but which in fact represents the hard and exact truth as it seemed.

In many cases a true war story cannot be believed. If you believe it, be skeptical. It's a question of credibility. Often the crazy stuff is true and the normal stuff isn't because the normal stuff is necessary to make you believe the truly incredible craziness.

In other cases you can't even tell a true war story. Sometimes it's just 20 beyond telling.

I heard this one, for example, from Mitchell Sanders. It was near dusk and we were sitting at my foxhole along a wide, muddy river north of Quang Ngai. I remember how peaceful the twilight was. A deep pinkish red spilled out on the river, which moved without sound, and in the morning we would cross the river and march west into the mountains. The occasion was right for a good story.

"God's truth," Mitchell Sanders said. "A six-man patrol goes up into the mountains on a basic listening-post operation. The idea's to spend a week up there, just lie low and listen for enemy movement. They've got a radio along, so if they hear anything suspicious — anything — they're supposed to call in artillery or gunships, whatever it takes. Otherwise they keep strict field discipline. Absolute silence. They just listen."

He glanced at me to make sure I had the scenario. He was playing with his yo-yo, making it dance with short, tight little strokes of the wrist.

His face was blank in the dusk.

"We're talking hardass LP.° These six guys, they don't say boo for a solid 25 week. They don't got tongues. *All* ears."

"Right," I said.

"Understand me?"

"Invisible."

Sanders nodded.

"Affirm," he said. "Invisible. So what happens is, these guys get themselves 30 deep in the bush, all camouflaged up, and they lie down and wait and that's all

LP: Listening post.

they do, nothing else, they lie there for seven straight days and just listen. And man, I'll tell you — it's spooky. This is mountains. You don't *know* spooky till you been there. Jungle, sort of, except it's way up in the clouds and there's always this fog — like rain, except it's not raining — everything's all wet and swirly and tangled up and you can't see jack, you can't find your own pecker to piss with. Like you don't even have a body. Serious spooky. You just go with the vapors — the fog sort of takes you in. . . . And the sounds, man. The sounds carry forever. You hear shit nobody should *ever* hear."

Sanders was quiet for a second, just working the yo-yo, then he smiled at me. "So, after a couple days the guys start hearing this real soft, kind of wacked-out music. Weird echoes and stuff. Like a radio or something, but it's not a radio, it's this strange gook music that comes right out of the rocks. Faraway, sort of, but right up close, too. They try to ignore it. But it's a listening post, right? So they listen. And every night they keep hearing this crazyass gook concert. All kinds of chimes and xylophones. I mean, this is wilderness — no way, it can't be real — but there it *is*, like the mountains are tuned in to Radio Fucking Hanoi. Naturally they get nervous. One guy sticks Juicy Fruit in his ears. Another guy almost flips. Thing is, though, they can't report music. They can't get on the horn and call back to base and say, 'Hey, listen, we need some firepower, we got to blow away this weirdo gook rock band.' They can't do that. It wouldn't go down. So they lie there in the fog and keep their mouths shut. And what makes it extra bad, see, is the poor dudes can't horse around like normal. Can't joke it away. Can't even talk to each other except maybe in whispers, all hush-hush, and that just revs up the willies. All they do is listen."

Again there was some silence as Mitchell Sanders looked out on the river. The dark was coming on hard now, and off to the west I could see the mountains rising in silhouette, all the mysteries and unknowns.

"This next part," Sanders said quietly, "you won't believe."

"Probably not," I said.

"You won't. And you know why?"   35

"Why?"

He gave me a tired smile. "Because it happened. Because every word is absolutely dead-on true."

Sanders made a little sound in his throat, like a sigh, as if to say he didn't care if I believed it or not. But he did care. He wanted me to believe, I could tell. He seemed sad, in a way.

"These six guys, they're pretty fried out by now, and one night they start hearing voices. Like at a cocktail party. That's what it sounds like, this big swank gook cocktail party somewhere out there in the fog. Music and chitchat and stuff. It's crazy, I know, but they hear the champagne corks. They hear the actual martini glasses. Real hoity-toity, all very civilized, except this isn't civilization. This is Nam.

"Anyway, the guys try to be cool. They just lie there and groove, but after a   40
while they start hearing — you won't believe this — they hear chamber music. They hear violins and shit. They hear this terrific mama-san soprano. Then after a while they hear gook opera and a glee club and the Haiphong Boys Choir and a barbershop quartet and all kinds of weird chanting and Buddha-Buddha stuff. The whole time, in the background, there's still that cocktail party going on. All these different voices. Not human voices, though. Because it's the mountains. Follow me? The rock — it's *talking*. And the fog, too, and the

grass and the goddamn mongooses. Everything talks. The trees talk politics, the monkeys talk religion. The whole country. Vietnam, the place talks.

"The guys can't cope. They lose it. They get on the radio and report enemy movement — a whole army, they say — and they order up the firepower. They get arty° and gunships. They call in air strikes. And I'll tell you, they fuckin' crash that cocktail party. All night long, they just smoke those mountains. They make jungle juice. They blow away trees and glee clubs and whatever else there is to blow away. Scorch time. They walk napalm up and down the ridges. They bring in the Cobras and F-4s, they use Willie Peter and HE° and incendiaries. It's all fire. They make those mountains burn.

"Around dawn things finally get quiet. Like you never even *heard* quiet before. One of those real thick, real misty days — just clouds and fog, they're off in this special zone — and the mountains are absolutely dead-flat silent. Like Brigadoon° — pure vapor, you know? Everything's all sucked up inside the fog. Not a single sound, except they still *hear* it.

"So they pack up and start humping. They head down the mountain, back to base camp, and when they get there they don't say diddly. They don't talk. Not a word, like they're deaf and dumb. Later on this fat bird colonel comes up and asks what the hell happened out there. What'd they hear? Why all the ordnance? The man's ragged out, he gets down tight on their case. I mean, they spent six trillion dollars on firepower, and this fatass colonel wants answers, he wants to know what the fuckin' story is.

"But the guys don't say zip. They just look at him for a while, sort of funny-like, sort of amazed, and the whole war is right there in that stare. It says everything you can't ever say. It says, man, you got *wax* in your ears. It says, poor bastard, you'll never know — wrong frequency — you don't *even* want to hear this. Then they salute the fucker and walk away, because certain stories you don't ever tell."

You can tell a true war story by the way it never seems to end. Not then, not   45
ever. Not when Mitchell Sanders stood up and moved off into the dark.

It all happened.

Even now I remember that yo-yo. In a way, I suppose, you had to be there, you had to hear it, but I could tell how desperately Sanders wanted me to believe him, his frustration at not quite getting the details right, not quite pinning down the final and definitive truth.

And I remember sitting at my foxhole that night, watching the shadows of Quang Ngai, thinking about the coming day and how we would cross the river and march west into the mountains, all the ways I might die, all the things I did not understand.

Late in the night Mitchell Sanders touched my shoulder.

"Just came to me," he whispered. "The moral, I mean. Nobody listens.   50
Nobody hears nothing. Like that fatass colonel. The politicians, all the civilian types, what they need is to go out on LP. The vapors, man. Trees and rocks — you got to *listen* to your enemy."

---

arty: Artillery.
Willie Peter and HE: White phosphorus, an incendiary substance, and high explosives.
Brigadoon: A fictional village in Scotland that only appears once every one hundred years; subject of a popular American musical (1947).

And then again, in the morning, Sanders came up to me. The platoon was preparing to move out, checking weapons, going through all the little rituals that preceded a day's march. Already the lead squad had crossed the river and was filing off toward the west.

"I got a confession to make," Sanders said. "Last night, man, I had to make up a few things."

"I know that."

"The glee club. There wasn't any glee club."

"Right."   55

"No opera."

"Forget it, I understand."

"Yeah, but listen, it's still true. Those six guys, they heard wicked sound out there. They heard sound you just plain won't believe."

Sanders pulled on his rucksack, closed his eyes for a moment, then almost smiled at me.

I knew what was coming but I beat him to it.   60

"All right," I said, "what's the moral?"

"Forget it."

"No, go ahead."

For a long while he was quiet, looking away, and the silence kept stretching out until it was almost embarrassing. Then he shrugged and gave me a stare that lasted all day.

"Hear that quiet, man?" he said. "There's your moral."   65

In a true war story, if there's a moral at all, it's like the thread that makes the cloth. You can't tease it out. You can't extract the meaning without unraveling the deeper meaning. And in the end, really, there's nothing much to say about a true war story, except maybe "Oh."

True war stories do not generalize. They do not indulge in abstraction or analysis.

For example: War is hell. As a moral declaration the old truism seems perfectly true, and yet because it abstracts, because it generalizes, I can't believe it with my stomach. Nothing turns inside.

It comes down to gut instinct. A true war story, if truly told, makes the stomach believe.

This one does it for me. I've told it before — many times, many versions — but   70
here's what actually happened.

We crossed the river and marched west into the mountains. On the third day, Curt Lemon stepped on a booby-trapped 105 round. He was playing catch with Rat Kiley, laughing, and then he was dead. The trees were thick; it took nearly an hour to cut an LZ for the dustoff.°

Later, higher in the mountains, we came across a baby VC° water buffalo. What it was doing there I don't know — no farms or paddies — but we chased it down and got a rope around it and led it along to a deserted village where we set for the night. After supper Rat Kiley went over and stroked its nose.

LZ for the dustoff: Landing zone for a helicopter evacuation of a casualty.
VC: Vietcong (Communist guerrillas in Vietnam).

He opened up a can of C rations, pork and beans, but the baby buffalo wasn't interested.

Rat shrugged.

He stepped back and shot it through the right front knee. The animal did not make a sound. It went down hard, then got up again, and Rat took careful aim and shot off an ear. He shot it in the hindquarters and in the little hump at its back. He shot it twice in the flanks. It wasn't to kill; it was just to hurt. He put the rifle muzzle up against the mouth and shot the mouth away. Nobody said much. The whole platoon stood there watching, feeling all kinds of things, but there wasn't a great deal of pity for the baby water buffalo. Lemon was dead. Rat Kiley had lost his best friend in the world. Later in the week he would write a long personal letter to the guy's sister, who would not write back, but for now it was a question of pain. He shot off the tail. He shot away chunks of meat below the ribs. All around us there was the smell of smoke and filth, and deep greenery, and the evening was humid and very hot. Rat went to automatic. He shot randomly, almost casually, quick little spurts in the belly and butt. Then he reloaded, squatted down, and shot it in the left front knee. Again the animal fell hard and tried to get up, but this time it couldn't quite make it. It wobbled and went down sideways. Rat shot it in the nose. He bent forward and whispered something, as if talking to a pet, then he shot it in the throat. All the while the baby buffalo was silent, or almost silent, just a light bubbling sound where the nose had been. It lay very still. Nothing moved except the eyes, which were enormous, the pupils shiny black and dumb.

Rat Kiley was crying. He tried to say something, but then cradled his rifle and went off by himself.

The rest of us stood in a ragged circle around the baby buffalo. For a time no one spoke. We had witnessed something essential, something brand-new and profound, a piece of the world so startling there was not yet a name for it.

Somebody kicked the baby buffalo.

It was still alive, though just barely, just in the eyes.

"Amazing," Dave Jensen said. "My whole life, I never seen anything like it."

"Never?"

"Not hardly. Not once."

Kiowa and Mitchell Sanders picked up the baby buffalo. They hauled it across the open square, hoisted it up, and dumped it in the village well.

Afterward, we sat waiting for Rat to get himself together.

"Amazing," Dave Jensen kept saying.

"For sure."

"A new wrinkle. I never seen it before."

Mitchell Sanders took out his yo-yo.

"Well, that's Nam," he said. "Garden of Evil. Over here, man, every sin's real fresh and original."

How do you generalize?

War is hell, but that's not the half of it, because war is also mystery and terror and adventure and courage and discovery and holiness and pity and despair and longing and love. War is nasty; war is fun. War is thrilling; war is drudgery. War makes you a man; war makes you dead.

The truths are contradictory. It can be argued, for instance, that war is grotesque. But in truth war is also beauty. For all its horror, you can't help but gape at the awful majesty of combat. You stare out at tracer rounds unwinding through the dark like brilliant red ribbons. You crouch in ambush as a cool, impassive moon rises over the nighttime paddies. You admire the fluid symmetries of troops on the move, the harmonies of sound and shape and proportion, the great sheets of metal-fire streaming down from a gunship, the illumination rounds, the white phosphorous, the purply black glow of napalm, the rocket's red glare. It's not pretty, exactly. It's astonishing. It fills the eye. It commands you. You hate it, yes, but your eyes do not. Like a killer forest fire, like cancer under a microscope, any battle or bombing raid or artillery barrage has the aesthetic purity of absolute moral indifference — a powerful, implacable beauty — and a true war story will tell the truth about this, though the truth is ugly.

To generalize about war is like generalizing about peace. Almost everything is true. Almost nothing is true. At its core, perhaps, war is just another name for death, and yet any soldier will tell you, if he tells the truth, that proximity to death brings with it a corresponding proximity to life. After a fire fight, there is always the immense pleasure of aliveness. The trees are alive. The grass, the soil — everything. All around you things are purely living, and you among them, and the aliveness makes you tremble. You feel an intense, out-of-the-skin awareness of your living self — your truest self, the human being you want to be and then become by the force of wanting it. In the midst of evil you want to be a good man. You want decency. You want justice and courtesy and human concord, things you never knew you wanted. There is a kind of largeness to it; a kind of godliness. Though it's odd, you're never more alive than when you're almost dead. You recognize what's valuable. Freshly, as if for the first time, you love what's best in yourself and in the world, all that might be lost. At the hour of dusk you sit at your foxhole and look out on a wide river turning pinkish red, and at the mountains beyond, and although in the morning you must cross the river and go into the mountains and do terrible things and maybe die, even so, you find yourself studying the fine colors on the river, you feel wonder and awe at the setting of the sun, and you are filled with a hard, aching love for how the world could be and always should be, but now is not.

Mitchell Sanders was right. For the common soldier, at least, war has the feel — the spiritual texture — of a great ghostly fog, thick and permanent. There is no clarity. Everything swirls. The old rules are no longer binding, the old truths no longer true. Right spills over into wrong. Order blends into chaos, love into hate, ugliness into beauty, law into anarchy, civility into savagery. The vapors suck you in. You can't tell where you are, or why you're there, and the only certainty is absolute ambiguity.

In war you lose your sense of the definite, hence your sense of truth itself, 95 and therefore it's safe to say that in a true war story nothing much is ever very true.

Often in a true war story there is not even a point, or else the point doesn't hit you until twenty years later, in your sleep, and you wake up and shake your wife and start telling the story to her, except when you get to the end you've forgotten the point again. And then for a long time you lie there watching the story happen in your head. You listen to your wife's breathing. The war's over. You close your eyes. You smile and think, Christ, what's the *point?*

This one wakes me up.

In the mountains that day, I watched Lemon turn sideways. He laughed and said something to Rat Kiley. Then he took a peculiar half step, moving from shade into bright sunlight, and the booby-trapped 105 round blew him into a tree. The parts were just hanging there, so Norman Bowker and I were ordered to shinny up and peel him off. I remember the white bone of an arm. I remember pieces of skin and something wet and yellow that must've been the intestines. The gore was horrible, and stays with me, but what wakes me up twenty years later is Norman Bowker singing "Lemon Tree" as we threw down the parts.

You can tell a true war story by the questions you ask. Somebody tells a story, let's say, and afterward you ask, "Is it true?" and if the answer matters, you've got your answer.

For example, we've all heard this one. Four guys go down a trail. A grenade   100
sails out. One guy jumps on it and takes the blast and saves his three buddies.

Is it true?

The answer matters.

You'd feel cheated if it never happened. Without the grounding reality, it's just a trite bit of puffery, pure Hollywood, untrue in the way all such stories are untrue. Yet even if it did happen — and maybe it did, anything's possible — even then you know it can't be true, because a true war story does not depend upon that kind of truth. Happeningness is irrelevant. A thing may happen and be a total lie; another thing may not happen and be truer than the truth. For example: four guys go down a trail. A grenade sails out. One guy jumps on it and takes the blast, but it's a killer grenade and everybody dies anyway. Before they die, though, one of the dead guys says, "The fuck you do *that* for?" and the jumper says, "Story of my life, man," and the other guy starts to smile but he's dead.

That's a true story that never happened.

Twenty years later, I can still see the sunlight on Lemon's face. I can see him turn-   105
ing, looking back at Rat Kiley, then he laughed and took that curious half step from shade into sunlight, his face suddenly brown and shining, and when his foot touched down, in that instant, he must've thought it was the sunlight that was killing him. It was not the sunlight. It was a rigged 105 round. But if I could ever get the story right, how the sun seemed to gather around him and pick him up and lift him into a tree, if I could somehow recreate the fatal whiteness of that light, the quick glare, the obvious cause and effect, then you would believe the last thing Lemon believed, which for him must've been the final truth.

Now and then, when I tell this story, someone will come up to me afterward and say she liked it. It's always a woman. Usually it's an older woman of kindly temperament and humane politics. She'll explain that as a rule she hates war stories, she can't understand why people want to wallow in blood and gore. But this one she liked. Sometimes, even, there are little tears. What I should do, she'll say, is put it all behind me. Find new stories to tell.

I won't say it but I'll think it.

I'll picture Rat Kiley's face, his grief, and I'll think, *You dumb cooze.*

Because she wasn't listening.

It wasn't a war story. It was a love story. It was a ghost story.

But you can't say that. All you can do is tell it one more time, patiently, adding and subtracting, making up a few things to get at the real truth. No Mitchell Sanders, you tell her. No Lemon, no Rat Kiley. And it didn't happen in the mountains, it happened in this little village on the Batangan Peninsula, and it was raining like crazy, and one night a guy named Stink Harris woke up screaming with a leech on his tongue. You can tell a true war story if you just keep on telling it.

In the end, of course, a true war story is never about war. It's about the special way that dawn spreads out on a river when you know you must cross the river and march into the mountains and do things you are afraid to do. It's about love and memory. It's about sorrow. It's about sisters who never write back and people who never listen.

EDGAR ALLAN POE (1809–1849)

Courtesy of the Library of Congress.

Edgar Allan Poe grew up in the home of John Allan, in Richmond, Virginia, after his mother died in 1811, and he was educated in Scotland and England for five years before completing his classical education in Richmond. After a short stint at the University of Virginia, Poe married and went to Boston, where he began publishing his poetry. His foster father sent him to West Point Military Academy, but Poe was expelled and moved on to New York, where he published a book of poems inspired by the Romantic movement. Divorced, and moving among editorial jobs in Baltimore, Richmond, and New York, Poe married his thirteen-year-old cousin, Virginia Clemm. Early in his story-writing career, Poe published his only novel-length piece, *The Narrative of Arthur Gordon Pym* (1838), and the following year, he began to work in the genre of the supernatural and horrible, with the stories "William Wilson" and "The Fall of the House of Usher." He gained publicity with the detective story "The Murders in the Rue Morgue," became nationally famous with the publication of his poem "The Raven" in 1845, and died four years later in Baltimore after a drinking binge. Poe theorized that the short story writer should plan every word toward the achievement of a certain effect, and that stories should be read in a single sitting. Morbidity and dreamlike flights of fancy, for which Poe is often recognized, do not detract from his lucid crafting of suspense and his erudite control of language and symbol.

Explore contexts for Edgar Allan Poe on *LiterActive*.

The Cask of Amontillado   1846

The thousand injuries of Fortunato I had borne as I best could; but when he ventured upon insult, I vowed revenge. You, who so well know the nature of my soul, will not suppose, however, that I gave utterance to a threat. *At length* I would be avenged; this was a point definitely settled — but the very definitiveness with which it was resolved precluded the idea of risk. I must not only punish, but punish with impunity. A wrong is unredressed when retribution overtakes its redresser. It is equally unredressed when the avenger fails to make himself felt as such to him who has done the wrong.

It must be understood, that neither by word nor deed had I given Fortunato cause to doubt my good-will. I continued, as was my wont, to smile in his face, and he did not perceive that my smile *now* was at the thought of his immolation.

He had a weak point — this Fortunato — although in other regards he was a man to be respected and even feared. He prided himself on his connoisseurship in wine. Few Italians have the true virtuoso spirit. For the most part their enthusiasm is adopted to suit the time and opportunity — to practise imposture upon the British and Austrian *millionnaires*. In painting and gemmary Fortunato, like his countrymen, was a quack — but in the matter of old wines he was sincere. In this respect I did not differ from him materially: I was skilful in the Italian vintages myself, and bought largely whenever I could.

It was about dusk, one evening during the supreme madness of the carnival season, that I encountered my friend. He accosted me with excessive warmth, for he had been drinking much. The man wore motley. He had on a tight-fitting parti-striped dress, and his head was surmounted by the conical cap and bells. I was so pleased to see him, that I thought I should never have done wringing his hand.

I said to him: "My dear Fortunato, you are luckily met. How remarkably 5 well you are looking to-day! But I have received a pipe° of what passes for Amontillado, and I have my doubts."

"How?" said he. "Amontillado? A pipe? Impossible! And in the middle of the carnival!"

"I have my doubts," I replied; "and I was silly enough to pay the full Amontillado price without consulting you in the matter. You were not to be found, and I was fearful of losing a bargain."

"Amontillado!"

"I have my doubts."

"Amontillado!"   10

"And I must satisfy them."

"Amontillado!"

"As you are engaged, I am on my way to Luchesi. If any one has a critical turn, it is he. He will tell me ——"

"Luchesi cannot tell Amontillado from Sherry."

"And yet some fools will have it that his taste is a match for your own." 15

"Come, let us go."

"Whither?"

pipe: A large keg.

"To your vaults."

"My friend, no; I will not impose upon your good nature. I perceive you have an engagement. Luchesi ——"

"I have no engagement; — come."   20

"My friend, no. It is not the engagement, but the severe cold with which I perceive you are afflicted. The vaults are insufferably damp. They are encrusted with nitre."

"Let us go, nevertheless. The cold is merely nothing. Amontillado! You have been imposed upon. And as for Luchesi, he cannot distinguish Sherry from Amontillado."

Thus speaking, Fortunato possessed himself of my arm. Putting on a mask of black silk, and drawing a *roquelaire*° closely about my person, I suffered him to hurry me to my palazzo.

There were no attendants at home; they had absconded to make merry in honor of the time. I had told them that I should not return until the morning, and had given them explicit orders not to stir from the house. These orders were sufficient, I well knew, to insure their immediate disappearance, one and all, as soon as my back was turned.

I took from their sconces two flambeaux, and giving one to Fortunato, 25 bowed him through several suites of rooms to the archway that led into the vaults. I passed down a long and winding staircase, requesting him to be cautious as he followed. We came at length to the foot of the descent, and stood together on the damp ground of the catacombs of the Montresors.

The gait of my friend was unsteady, and the bells upon his cap jingled as he strode.

"The pipe?" said he.

"It is farther on," said I; "but observe the white web-work which gleams from these cavern walls."

He turned toward me, and looked into my eyes with two filmy orbs that distilled the rheum of intoxication.

"Nitre?" he asked, at length.   30

"Nitre," I replied. "How long have you had that cough?"

"Ugh! ugh! ugh! — ugh! ugh! ugh! — ugh! ugh! ugh! — ugh! ugh! ugh! — ugh! ugh! ugh!"

My poor friend found it impossible to reply for many minutes.

"It is nothing," he said, at last.

"Come," I said, with decision, "we will go back; your health is precious. 35 You are rich, respected, admired, beloved; you are happy, as once I was. You are a man to be missed. For me it is no matter. We will go back; you will be ill, and I cannot be responsible. Besides, there is Luchesi ——"

"Enough," he said; "the cough is a mere nothing; it will not kill me. I shall not die of a cough."

"True — true," I replied; "and, indeed, I had no intention of alarming you unnecessarily; but you should use all proper caution. A draught of this Medoc will defend us from the damps."

Here I knocked off the neck of a bottle which I drew from a long row of its fellows that lay upon the mould.

"Drink," I said, presenting him the wine.

roquelaire: A short cloak.

He raised it to his lips with a leer. He paused and nodded to me familiarly, 40
while his bells jingled.

"I drink," he said, "to the buried that repose around us."

"And I to your long life."

He again took my arm, and we proceeded.

"These vaults," he said, "are extensive."

"The Montresors," I replied, "were a great and numerous family." 45

"I forget your arms."

"A huge human foot d'or,° in a field azure; the foot crushes a serpent rampant whose fangs are imbedded in the heel."

"And the motto?"

"Nemo me impune lacessit."°

"Good!" he said. 50

The wine sparkled in his eyes and the bells jingled. My own fancy grew warm with the Medoc. We had passed through walls of piled bones, with casks and puncheons intermingling into the inmost recesses of the catacombs. I paused again, and this time I made bold to seize Fortunato by an arm above the elbow.

"The nitre!" I said; "see, it increases. It hangs like moss upon the vaults. We are below the river's bed. The drops of moisture trickle among the bones. Come, we will go back ere it is too late. Your cough ——"

"It is nothing," he said; "let us go on. But first, another draught of the Medoc."

I broke and reached him a flagon of De Grâve. He emptied it at a breath. His eyes flashed with a fierce light. He laughed and threw the bottle upward with a gesticulation I did not understand.

I looked at him in surprise. He repeated the movement—a grotesque one. 55

"You do not comprehend?" he said.

"Not I," I replied.

"Then you are not of the brotherhood."

"How?"

"You are not of the masons." 60

"Yes, yes," I said; "yes, yes."

"You? Impossible! A mason?"

"A mason," I replied.

"A sign," he said.

"It is this," I answered, producing a trowel from beneath the folds of my 65
roquelaire.

"You jest," he exclaimed, recoiling a few paces. "But let us proceed to the Amontillado."

"Be it so," I said, replacing the tool beneath the cloak, and again offering him my arm. He leaned upon it heavily. We continued our route in search of the Amontillado. We passed through a range of low arches, descended, passed on, and descending again, arrived at a deep crypt, in which the foulness of the air caused our flambeaux rather to glow than flame.

At the most remote end of the crypt there appeared another less spacious. Its walls had been lined with human remains, piled to the vault overhead, in

---

d'or: Of gold.
Nemo . . . lacessit: "No one wounds me with impunity" (Latin).

the fashion of the great catacombs of Paris. Three sides of this interior crypt were still ornamented in this manner. From the fourth the bones had been thrown down, and lay promiscuously upon the earth, forming at one point a mound of some size. Within the wall thus exposed by the displacing of the bones, we perceived a still interior recess, in depth about four feet, in width three, in height six or seven. It seemed to have been constructed for no especial use within itself, but formed merely the interval between two of the colossal supports of the roof of the catacombs, and was backed by one of their circumscribing walls of solid granite.

It was in vain that Fortunato, uplifting his dull torch, endeavored to pry into the depth of the recess. Its termination the feeble light did not enable us to see.

"Proceed," I said; "herein is the Amontillado. As for Luchesi ——" 70

"He is an ignoramus," interrupted my friend, as he stepped unsteadily forward, while I followed immediately at his heels. In an instant he had reached the extremity of the niche, and finding his progress arrested by the rock, stood stupidly bewildered. A moment more and I had fettered him to the granite. In its surface were two iron staples, distant from each other about two feet, horizontally. From one of these depended a short chain, from the other a padlock. Throwing the links about his waist, it was but the work of a few seconds to secure it. He was too much astounded to resist. Withdrawing the key I stepped back from the recess.

"Pass your hand," I said, "over the wall; you cannot help feeling the nitre. Indeed it is *very* damp. Once more let me *implore* you to return. No? Then I must positively leave you. But I must first render you all the little attentions in my power."

"The Amontillado!" ejaculated my friend, not yet recovered from his astonishment.

"True," I replied; "the Amontillado."

As I said these words I busied myself among the pile of bones of which I 75 have before spoken. Throwing them aside, I soon uncovered a quantity of building stone and mortar. With these materials and with the aid of my trowel, I began vigorously to wall up the entrance of the niche.

I had scarcely laid the first tier of the masonry when I discovered that the intoxication of Fortunato had in a great measure worn off. The earliest indication I had of this was a low moaning cry from the depth of the recess. It was *not* the cry of a drunken man. There was then a long and obstinate silence. I laid the second tier, and the third, and the fourth; and then I heard the furious vibrations of the chain. The noise lasted for several minutes, during which, that I might hearken to it with the more satisfaction, I ceased my labors and sat down upon the bones. When at last the clanking subsided, I resumed the trowel, and finished without interruption the fifth, the sixth, and the seventh tier. The wall was now nearly upon a level with my breast. I again paused, and holding the flambeaux over the masonwork, threw a few feeble rays upon the figure within.

A succession of loud and shrill screams, bursting suddenly from the throat of the chained form, seemed to thrust me violently back. For a brief moment I hesitated — I trembled. Unsheathing my rapier, I began to grope with it about the recess; but the thought of an instant reassured me. I placed my hand upon the solid fabric of the catacombs, and felt satisfied. I reapproached the wall. I replied to the yells of him who clamored. I reechoed — I aided — I surpassed them in volume and in strength. I did this, and the clamorer grew still.

It was now midnight, and my task was drawing to a close. I had completed the eighth, the ninth, and the tenth tier. I had finished a portion of the last and the eleventh; there remained but a single stone to be fitted and plastered in. I struggled with its weight; I placed it partially in its destined position. But now there came from out the niche a low laugh that erected the hairs upon my head. It was succeeded by a sad voice, which I had difficulty in recognizing as that of the noble Fortunato. The voice said —

"Ha! ha! ha! — he! he! — a very good joke indeed — an excellent jest. We will have many a rich laugh about it at the palazzo — he! he! he! — over our wine — he! he! he!"

"The Amontillado!" I said.   80

"He! he! he! — he! he! he! — yes, the Amontillado. But is it not getting late? Will not they be awaiting us at the palazzo, the Lady Fortunato and the rest? Let us be gone."

"Yes," I said, "let us be gone."

"For the love of God, Montresor!"

"Yes," I said, "for the love of God!"

But to these words I hearkened in vain for a reply. I grew impatient. I called   85 aloud:

"Fortunato!"

No answer. I called again:

"Fortunato!"

No answer still. I thrust a torch through the remaining aperture and let it fall within. There came forth in return only a jingling of the bells. My heart grew sick — on account of the dampness of the catacombs. I hastened to make an end of my labor. I forced the last stone into its position; I plastered it up. Against the new masonry I re-erected the old rampart of bones. For the half of a century no mortal has disturbed them. *In pace requiescat!*°

In pace requiescat! (Latin): In peace may he rest!

KATHERINE ANNE PORTER (1890–1980)

Born in Indian Creek, Texas, Katherine Anne Porter was raised by her grandmother and subsequently ran away from a convent school at the age of sixteen. At various points in her life she made a living as a journalist and teacher as well as a stage and film performer. Her extensive travels, multiple husbands, and many acknowledged lovers provided much of the material about human relations that makes its way into her fiction. Her collections of stories include *Flowering Judas* (1930), *The Leaning Tower* (1944), and

Papers of Katherine Anne Porter, Special Collections, University of Maryland Libraries.

Collected Stories (1965), which was awarded both the Pulitzer Prize and the National Book Award. Her novels include *Pale Horse, Pale Rider: Three Short Novels* (1939) and *Ship of Fools* (1962). "The Witness," one of her many stories about the South, evokes reflections on the old order of slavery.

The Witness   1944

Uncle Jimbilly was so old and had spent so many years bowed over things, putting them together and taking them apart, making them over and making them do, he was bent almost double. His hands were closed and stiff from gripping objects tightly, while he worked at them, and they could not open altogether even if a child took the thick black fingers and tried to turn them back. He hobbled on a stick; his purplish skull showed through patches in his wool, which had turned greenish gray and looked as if the moths had got at it.

He mended harness and put half soles on the other Negroes' shoes, he built fences and chicken coops and barn doors; he stretched wires and put in new window panes and fixed sagging hinges and patched up roofs; he repaired carriage tops and cranky plows. Also he had a gift for carving miniature tombstones out of blocks of wood; give him almost any kind of piece of wood and he could turn out a tombstone, shaped very like the real ones, with carving, and a name and date on it if they were needed. They were often needed, for some small beast or bird was always dying and having to be buried with proper ceremonies: the cart draped as a hearse, a shoe-box coffin with a pall over it, a profuse floral outlay, and, of course, a tombstone. As he worked, turning the long blade of his bowie knife deftly in circles to cut a flower, whittling and smoothing the back and sides, stopping now and then to hold it at arm's length and examine it with one eye closed, Uncle Jimbilly would talk in a low, broken, abstracted murmur, as if to himself; but he was really saying something he meant one to hear. Sometimes it would be an incomprehensible ghost story; listen ever so carefully, at the end it was impossible to decide whether Uncle Jimbilly himself had seen the ghost, whether it was a real ghost at all, or only another man dressed like one; and he dwelt much on the horrors of slave times.

"Dey used to take 'em out and tie 'em down and whup 'em," he muttered, "wid gret big leather strops inch thick long as yo' ahm, wid round holes bored in 'em so's evey time dey hit 'em de hide and de meat done come off dey bones in little round chunks. And wen dey had whupped 'em wid de strop till dey backs was all raw and bloody, dey spread dry cawnshucks on dey backs and set 'em afire and pahched 'em, and den dey poured vinega all ovah 'em . . . Yassuh. And den, the ve'y nex day dey'd got to git back to work in de fiels or dey'd do the same thing right ovah agin. Yassah. Dat was it. If dey didn't git back to work dey got it all right ovah agin."

The children — three of them: a serious, prissy older girl of ten, a thoughtful sad looking boy of eight, and a quick flighty little girl of six — sat disposed around Uncle Jimbilly and listened with faint tinglings of embarrassment. They knew, of course, that once upon a time Negroes had been slaves; but they had all been freed long ago and were now only servants. It was hard to realize that Uncle Jimbilly had been born in slavery, as the Negroes were always saying. The children thought that Uncle Jimbilly had got over his slavery very well. Since they had known him, he had never done a single thing that anyone told him to do. He did his work just as he pleased and when he pleased. If you wanted a tombstone, you had to be very careful about the way you asked for it. Nothing could have been more impersonal and faraway than his tone and manner of talking about slavery, but they wriggled a little and felt guilty. Paul would have changed the subject, but Miranda, the little quick one, wanted to know the worst. "Did they act like that to you, Uncle Jimbilly?" she asked.

"No, *mam*," said Uncle Jimbilly. "Now whut name you want on dis one? 5 Dey nevah did. Dey done 'em dat way in the rice swamps. I always worked right here close to the house or in town with Miss Sophia. Down in the swamps . . ."

"Didn't they ever die, Uncle Jimbilly?" asked Paul.

"Cose dey died," said Uncle Jimbilly, "cose dey died—dey died," he went on, pursing his mouth gloomily, "by de thousands and tens upon thousands."

"Can you carve 'Safe in Heaven' on that, Uncle Jimbilly?" asked Maria in her pleasant, mincing voice.

"To put over a tame jackrabbit, Missy?" asked Uncle Jimbilly indignantly. He was very religious. "A heathen like dat? No, *mam*. In de swamps dey used to stake 'em out all day and all night, and all day and all night and all day wid dey hans and feet tied so dey couldn't scretch and let de muskeeters eat 'em alive. De muskeeters 'ud bite 'em tell dey was all swole up like a balloon all over, and you could heah 'em howlin and prayin all ovah the swamp. Yassuh. Dat was it. And nary a drop of watah noh a moufful of braid . . . Yassuh, dat's it. Lawd, dey done it. Hosanna! Now take dis yere tombstone and don' bother me no more . . . or I'll . . ."

Uncle Jimbilly was apt to be suddenly annoyed and you never knew why. 10 He was easily put out about things, but his threats were always so exorbitant that not even the most credulous child could be terrified by them. He was always going to do something quite horrible to somebody and then he was going to dispose of the remains in a revolting manner. He was going to skin somebody alive and nail the hide on the barn door, or he was just getting ready to cut off somebody's ears with a hatchet and pin them on Bongo, the crop-eared brindle dog. He was often all prepared in his mind to pull somebody's teeth and make a set of false teeth for Ole Man Ronk . . . Ole Man Ronk was a tramp who had been living all summer in the little cabin behind the smoke-house. He got his rations along with the Negroes and sat all day mumbling his naked gums. He had skimpy black whiskers which appeared to be set in wax, and angry red eyelids. He took morphine, it was said; but what morphine might be, or how he took it, or why, no one seemed to know . . . Nothing could have been more unpleasant than the notion that one's teeth might be given to Ole Man Ronk.

The reason why Uncle Jimbilly never did any of these things he threatened was, he said, because he never could get round to them. He always had so much other work on hand he never seemed to get caught up on it. But some day, somebody was going to get a mighty big surprise, and meanwhile everybody had better look out.

JOHN UPDIKE (B. 1932)

John Updike grew up in the small town of
Shillington, Pennsylvania, and on a family
farm nearby. Academic success in school
earned him a scholarship to Harvard, where
he studied English and graduated in 1954. He
soon sold his first story and poem to *The New
Yorker.* Also an artist, Updike studied drawing
in Oxford, England, and returned to take a
position on the staff at *The New Yorker.* His
first book, a collection of poems titled *The
Carpentered Hen and Other Tame Creatures,* appeared in 1958, and the following year he
published a book of stories and a novel, *The
Poorhouse Fair,* which received the Rosenthal

© Jerry Bauer.

Foundation Award in 1960. Updike produced his second novel, *Rabbit,
Run,* in the same year. The prolific Updike, located in Massachusetts for the
past fifty years, has continued to publish essays and poems and has published a novel or a book of stories nearly every year since 1959, including *The
Centaur* (1963), winner of the National Book Award,
Rabbit Is Rich (1981) and *Rabbit at Rest* (1990), both
Pulitzer Prize winners, and *The Witches of Eastwick* (1984),
which was made into a major motion picture (Warner
Bros., 1987). His most recent novel is *Terrorist* (2006). Updike's fiction is
noted for its exemplary use of storytelling conventions, its unique prose
style, and its engaging picture of middle-class American life.

Explore
contexts for John Updike
on *LiterActive.*

A & P   1961

In walks these three girls in nothing but bathing suits. I'm in the third checkout slot, with my back to the door, so I don't see them until they're over by the
bread. The one that caught my eye first was the one in the plaid green two-
piece. She was a chunky kid, with a good tan and a sweet broad soft-looking
can with those two crescents of white just under it, where the sun never seems
to hit, at the top of the backs of her legs. I stood there with my hand on a
box of HiHo crackers trying to remember if I rang it up or not. I ring it up
again and the customer starts giving me hell. She's one of these cash-register-
watchers, a witch about fifty with rouge on her cheekbones and no eyebrows,
and I know it made her day to trip me up. She'd been watching cash registers
for fifty years and probably never seen a mistake before.

By the time I got her feathers smoothed and her goodies into a bag — she
gives me a little snort in passing, if she'd been born at the right time they would
have burned her over in Salem — by the time I get her on her way the girls had
circled around the bread and were coming back, without a pushcart, back my

way along the counters, in the aisle between the checkouts and the Special bins. They didn't even have shoes on. There was this chunky one, with the two-piece—it was bright green and the seams on the bra were still sharp and her belly was still pretty pale so I guessed she just got it (the suit)—there was this one, with one of those chubby berry-faces, the lips all bunched together under her nose, this one, and a tall one, with black hair that hadn't quite frizzed right, and one of these sunburns right across under the eyes, and a chin that was too long—you know, the kind of girl other girls think is very "striking" and "attractive" but never quite makes it, as they very well know, which is why they like her so much—and then the third one, that wasn't quite so tall. She was the queen. She kind of led them, the other two peeking around and making their shoulders round. She didn't look around, not this queen, she just walked straight on slowly, on these long white prima-donna legs. She came down a little hard on her heels, as if she didn't walk in her bare feet that much, putting down her heels and then letting the weight move along to her toes as if she was testing the floor with every step, putting a little deliberate extra action into it. You never know for sure how girls' minds work (do you really think it's a mind in there or just a little buzz like a bee in a glass jar?) but you got the idea she had talked the other two into coming in here with her, and now she was showing them how to do it, walk slow and hold yourself straight.

She had on a kind of dirty-pink—beige maybe, I don't know—bathing suit with a little nubble all over it and, what got me, the straps were down. They were off her shoulders looped loose around the cool tops of her arms, and I guess as a result the suit had slipped a little on her, so all around the top of the cloth there was this shining rim. If it hadn't been there you wouldn't have known there could have been anything whiter than those shoulders. With the straps pushed off, there was nothing between the top of the suit and the top of her head except just *her,* this clean bare plane of the top of her chest down from the shoulder bones like a dented sheet of metal tilted in the light. I mean, it was more than pretty.

She had sort of oaky hair that the sun and salt had bleached, done up in a bun that was unraveling, and a kind of prim face. Walking into the A & P with your straps down, I suppose it's the only kind of face you *can* have. She held her head so high her neck, coming up out of those white shoulders, looked kind of stretched, but I didn't mind. The longer her neck was, the more of her there was.

She must have felt in the corner of her eye me and over my shoulder Stoke- 5 sie in the second slot watching, but she didn't tip. Not this queen. She kept her eyes moving across the racks, and stopped, and turned so slow it made my stomach rub the inside of my apron, and buzzed to the other two, who kind of huddled against her for relief, and then they all three of them went up the cat-and-dogfood-breakfast-cereal-macaroni-rice-raisins-seasonings-spreads-spaghetti-soft-drinks-crackers-and-cookies aisle. From the third slot I look straight up this aisle to the meat counter, and I watched them all the way. The fat one with the tan sort of fumbled with the cookies, but on second thought she put the package back. The sheep pushing their carts down the aisle—the girls were walking against the usual traffic (not that we have one-way signs or anything)—were pretty hilarious. You could see them, when Queenie's white shoulders dawned on them, kind of jerk, or hop, or hiccup, but their eyes snapped back to their own baskets and on they pushed. I bet you could set off dynamite in an A & P and the people would by and large keep reaching and checking oatmeal off their lists and muttering "Let me see, there was a third thing, began with A, asparagus, no, ah, yes, applesauce!" or whatever it is they do mutter. But there was no doubt, this jiggled them. A few houseslaves in pin curlers even looked around after pushing their carts past to make sure what they had seen was correct.

You know, it's one thing to have a girl in a bathing suit down on the beach, where what with the glare nobody can look at each other much anyway, and another thing in the cool of the A & P, under the fluorescent lights, against all those stacked packages, with her feet paddling along naked over our checkerboard green-and-cream rubber-tile floor.

"Oh Daddy," Stokesie said beside me. "I feel so faint."

"Darling," I said. "Hold me tight." Stokesie's married, with two babies chalked up on his fuselage already, but as far as I can tell that's the only difference. He's twenty-two, and I was nineteen this April.

"Is it done?" he asks, the responsible married man finding his voice. I forgot to say he thinks he's going to be manager some sunny day, maybe in 1990 when it's called the Great Alexandrov and Petrooshki Tea Company or something.

What he meant was, our town is five miles from a beach, with a big sum-   10
mer colony out on the Point, but we're right in the middle of town, and the women generally put on a shirt or shorts or something before they get out of the car into the street. And anyway these are usually women with six children and varicose veins mapping their legs and nobody, including them, could care less. As I say, we're right in the middle of town, and if you stand at our front doors you can see two banks and the Congregational church and the newspaper store and three real-estate offices and about twenty-seven old freeloaders tearing up Central Street because the sewer broke again. It's not as if we're on the Cape, we're north of Boston and there's people in this town haven't seen the ocean for twenty years.

The girls had reached the meat counter and were asking McMahon something. He pointed, they pointed, and they shuffled out of sight behind a pyramid of Diet Delight peaches. All that was left for us to see was old McMahon patting his mouth and looking after them sizing up their joints. Poor kids, I began to feel sorry for them, they couldn't help it.

Now here comes the sad part of the story, at least my family says it's sad, but I don't think it's so sad myself. The store's pretty empty, it being Thursday afternoon, so there was nothing much to do except lean on the register and wait for the girls to show up again. The whole store was like a pinball machine and I didn't know which tunnel they'd come out of. After a while they come around out of the far aisle, around the light bulbs, records at discount of the Caribbean Six or Tony Martin Sings or some such gunk you wonder they waste the wax on, sixpacks of candy bars, and plastic toys done up in cellophane that fall apart when a kid looks at them anyway. Around they come, Queenie still leading the way, and holding a little gray jar in her hands. Slots Three through Seven are unmanned and I could see her wondering between Stokes and me, but Stokesie with his usual luck draws an old party in baggy gray pants who stumbles up with four giant cans of pineapple juice (what do these bums *do* with all that pineapple juice? I've often asked myself). So the girls come to me. Queenie puts down the jar and I take it into my fingers icy cold. Kingfish Fancy

Herring Snacks in Pure Sour Cream: 49¢. Now her hands are empty, not a ring or a bracelet, bare as God made them, and I wonder where the money's coming from. Still with that prim look she lifts a folded dollar bill out of the hollow at the center of her nubbled pink top. The jar went heavy in my hand. Really, I thought that was so cute.

Then everybody's luck begins to run out. Lengel comes in from haggling with a truck full of cabbages on the lot and is about to scuttle into that door marked MANAGER behind which he hides all day when the girls touch his eye. Lengel's pretty dreary, teaches Sunday school and the rest, but he doesn't miss that much. He comes over and says, "Girls, this isn't the beach."

Queenie blushes, though maybe it's just a brush of sunburn I was noticing for the first time, now that she was so close. "My mother asked me to pick up a jar of herring snacks." Her voice kind of startled me, the way voices do when you see the people first, coming out so flat and dumb yet kind of tony, too, the way it ticked over "pick up" and "snacks." All of a sudden I slid right down her voice into the living room. Her father and the other men were standing around in ice-cream coats and bow ties and the women were in sandals picking up herring snacks on toothpicks off a big glass plate and they were all holding drinks the color of water with olives and sprigs of mint in them. When my parents have somebody over they get lemonade and if it's a real racy affair Schlitz in tall glasses with "They'll Do It Every Time" cartoons stenciled on.

"That's all right," Lengel said. "But this isn't the beach." His repeating this struck me as funny, as if it had just occurred to him, and he had been thinking all these years the A & P was a great big dune and he was the head lifeguard. He didn't like my smiling — as I say he doesn't miss much — but he concentrates on giving the girls that sad Sunday-school-superintendent stare.

Queenie's blush is no sunburn now, and the plump one in plaid, that I liked better from the back — a really sweet can — pipes up, "We weren't doing any shopping. We just came in for the one thing."

"That makes no difference," Lengel tells her, and I could see from the way his eyes went that he hadn't noticed she was wearing a two-piece before. "We want you decently dressed when you come in here."

"We *are* decent," Queenie says suddenly, her lower lip pushing, getting sore now that she remembers her place, a place from which the crowd that runs the A & P must look pretty crummy. Fancy Herring Snacks flashed in her very blue eyes.

"Girls, I don't want to argue with you. After this come in here with your shoulders covered. It's our policy." He turns his back. That's policy for you. Policy is what the kingpins want. What the others want is juvenile delinquency.

All this while, the customers had been showing up with their carts but, 20 you know, sheep, seeing a scene, they had all bunched up on Stokesie, who shook open a paper bag as gently as peeling a peach, not wanting to miss a word. I could feel in the silence everybody getting nervous, most of all Lengel, who asks me, "Sammy, have you rung up their purchase?"

I thought and said "No" but it wasn't about that I was thinking. I go through the punches, 4, 9, GROC. TOT — it's more complicated than you think, and after you do it often enough, it begins to make a little song, that you hear words to, in my case "Hello *(bing)* there, you *(gung)* hap-py *pee*-pul *(splat)!*" — the *splat* being the drawer flying out. I uncrease the bill, tenderly as you may imagine, it just having come from between the two smoothest scoops of vanilla

I had ever known were there, and pass a half and a penny into her narrow pink palm, and nestle the herrings in a bag and twist its neck and hand it over, all the time thinking.

The girls, and who'd blame them, are in a hurry to get out, so I say "I quit" to Lengel quick enough for them to hear, hoping they'll stop and watch me, their unsuspected hero. They keep right on going, into the electric eye; the door flies open and they flicker across the lot to their car, Queenie and Plaid and Big Tall Goony-Goony (not that as raw material she was so bad), leaving me with Lengel and a kink in his eyebrow.

"Did you say something, Sammy?"

"I said I quit."

"I thought you did."   25

"You didn't have to embarrass them."

"It was they who were embarrassing us."

I started to say something that came out "Fiddle-de-doo." It's a saying of my grandmother's, and I know she would have been pleased.

"I don't think you know what you're saying," Lengel said.

"I know you don't," I said. "But I do." I pull the bow at the back of my   30
apron and start shrugging it off my shoulders. A couple customers that had been heading for my slot begin to knock against each other, like scared pigs in a chute.

Lengel sighs and begins to look very patient and old and gray. He's been a friend of my parents for years. "Sammy, you don't want to do this to your Mom and Dad," he tells me. It's true, I don't. But it seems to me that once you begin a gesture it's fatal not to go through with it. I fold the apron, "Sammy" stitched in red on the pocket, and put it on the counter, and drop the bow tie on top of it. The bow tie is theirs, if you've ever wondered. "You'll feel this for the rest of your life," Lengel says, and I know that's true, too, but remembering how he made the pretty girl blush makes me so scrunchy inside I punch the No Sale tab and the machine whirs "pee-pul" and the drawer splats out. One advantage to this scene taking place in summer, I can follow this up with a clean exit, there's no fumbling around getting your coat and galoshes, I just saunter into the electric eye in my white shirt that my mother ironed the night before, and the door heaves itself open, and outside the sunshine is skating around on the asphalt.

I look around for my girls, but they're gone, of course. There wasn't anybody but some young married screaming with her children about some candy they didn't get by the door of a powder-blue Falcon station wagon. Looking back in the big windows, over the bags of peat moss and aluminum lawn furniture stacked on the pavement, I could see Lengel in my place in the slot, checking the sheep through. His face was dark gray and his back stiff, as if he'd just had an injection of iron, and my stomach kind of fell as I felt how hard the world was going to be to me hereafter.

POETRY

POETRY

The Elements
of Poetry

18

Reading Poetry

© Lilo Raymond.

Ink runs from the corners of my mouth.
There is no happiness like mine.
I have been eating poetry.
— MARK STRAND

READING POETRY RESPONSIVELY

Perhaps the best way to begin reading poetry responsively is not to allow yourself to be intimidated by it. Come to it, initially at least, the way you might listen to a song on the radio. You probably listen to a song several times before you hear it all, before you have a sense of how it works, where it's going, and how it gets there. You don't worry about analyzing a song when you listen to it, even though after repeated experiences with it you know and anticipate a favorite part and know, on some level, why it works for you. Give yourself a chance to respond to poetry. The hardest work has already been done by the poet, so all you need to do at the start is listen for the pleasure produced by the poet's arrangement of words.

Try reading the following poem aloud. Read it aloud before you read it silently. You may stumble once or twice, but you'll make sense of it if you pay attention to its punctuation and don't stop at the end of every line where there is no punctuation. The title gives you an initial sense of what the poem is about.

Marge Piercy (b. 1936)

The Secretary Chant   1973

My hips are a desk.
From my ears hang
chains of paper clips.
Rubber bands form my hair.
My breasts are wells of mimeograph ink.   5
My feet bear casters.
Buzz. Click.
My head is a badly organized file.
My head is a switchboard
where crossed lines crackle.   10
Press my fingers
and in my eyes appear
credit and debit.
Zing. Tinkle.
My navel is a reject button.   15
From my mouth issue canceled reams.
Swollen, heavy, rectangular
I am about to be delivered
of a baby
Xerox machine.   20
File me under W
because I wonce
was
a woman.

What is your response to this secretary's chant? The point is simple
enough—she feels dehumanized by her office functions—but the pleasures are manifold. Piercy makes the speaker's voice sound mechanical by
using short bursts of sound and by having her make repetitive, flat, matter-
of-fact statements ("My breasts . . . My feet . . . My head . . . My navel").
"The Secretary Chant" makes a serious statement about how such women
are reduced to functionaries. The point is made, however, with humor, as
we are asked to visualize the misappropriation of the secretary's body—her
identity—as it is transformed into little more than a piece of office equipment, which seems to be breaking down in the final lines, when we learn
that she "wonce / was / a woman." Is there the slightest hint of something
subversive in this misspelling of "wonce"? Maybe so, but the humor is clear
enough, particularly if you try to make a drawing of what this dehumanized secretary has become.

    The next poem creates a different kind of mood. Think about the title,
"Those Winter Sundays," before you begin reading the poem. What associations do you have with winter Sundays? What emotions does the phrase
evoke in you?

ROBERT HAYDEN (1913–1980)
Those Winter Sundays

1962

Sundays too my father got up early
and put his clothes on in the blueblack cold,
then with cracked hands that ached
from labor in the weekday weather made
banked fires blaze. No one ever thanked him.   5

I'd wake and hear the cold splintering, breaking.
When the rooms were warm, he'd call,
and slowly I would rise and dress,
fearing the chronic angers of that house,

Speaking indifferently to him,   10
who had driven out the cold
and polished my good shoes as well.
What did I know, what did I know
of love's austere and lonely offices?

Does the poem match the feelings you have about winter Sundays? Either way, your response can be useful in reading the poem. For most of us, Sundays are days at home; they might be cozy and pleasant experiences or they might be dull and depressing. Whatever they are, Sundays are more evocative than, say, Tuesdays. Hayden uses that response to call forth a sense of missed opportunity in the poem. The person who reflects on those winter Sundays didn't know until much later how much he had to thank his father for "love's austere and lonely offices." This is a poem about a cold past and a present reverence for his father—elements brought together by the phrase "Winter Sundays." *His* father? You may have noticed that the poem doesn't use a masculine pronoun; hence the voice could be a woman's. Does the gender of the voice make any difference to your reading? Would it make any difference about which details are included or what language is used?

What is most important about your initial readings of a poem is that you ask questions. If you read responsively, you'll find yourself asking all kinds of questions about the words, descriptions, sounds, and structure of a poem. The specifics of those questions will be generated by the particular poem. We don't, for example, ask how humor is achieved in "Those Winter Sundays" because there is none, but it is worth asking what kind of tone is established by the description of "the chronic angers of that house." The remaining chapters in this part will help you to formulate and answer questions about a variety of specific elements in poetry, such as speaker, image, metaphor, symbol, rhyme, and rhythm. For the moment, however, read the following poem several times and note your response at different points in the poem. Then write down a half-dozen or so questions about what produces your response to the poem. To answer questions, it's best to know first what the questions are, and that's what the rest of this chapter is about.

JOHN UPDIKE (B. 1932)

Dog's Death 1969

She must have been kicked unseen or brushed by a car.
Too young to know much, she was beginning to learn
To use the newspapers spread on the kitchen floor
And to win, wetting there, the words, "Good dog! Good dog!"

We thought her shy malaise was a shot reaction. 5
The autopsy disclosed a rupture in her liver.
As we teased her with play, blood was filling her skin
And her heart was learning to lie down forever.

Monday morning, as the children were noisily fed
And sent to school, she crawled beneath the youngest's bed. 10
We found her twisted and limp but still alive.
In the car to the vet's, on my lap, she tried

To bite my hand and died. I stroked her warm fur
And my wife called in a voice imperious with tears.
Though surrounded by love that would have upheld her, 15
Nevertheless she sank and, stiffening, disappeared.

Back home, we found that in the night her frame,
Drawing near to dissolution, had endured the shame
Of diarrhoea and had dragged across the floor
To a newspaper carelessly left there. Good dog. 20

Here's a simple question to get started with your own questions: what would the poem's effect have been if Updike had titled it "Good Dog" instead of "Dog's Death"?

THE PLEASURE OF WORDS

The impulse to create and appreciate poetry is as basic to human experience as language itself. Although no one can point to the precise origins of poetry, it is one of the most ancient of the arts, because it has existed ever since human beings discovered pleasure in language. The tribal ceremonies of peoples without written languages suggest that the earliest primitive cultures incorporated rhythmic patterns of words into their rituals. These chants, very likely accompanied by the music of a simple beat and the dance of a measured step, expressed what people regarded as significant and memorable in their lives. They echoed the concerns of the chanters and the listeners by chronicling acts of bravery, fearsome foes, natural disasters, mysterious events, births, deaths, and whatever else brought people pain or pleasure, bewilderment or revelation. Later cultures, such as the ancient Greeks, made poetry an integral part of religion.

Thus, from its very beginnings, poetry has been associated with what has mattered most to people. These concerns — whether natural or supernatural — can, of course, be expressed without vivid images, rhythmic patterns, and pleasing sounds, but human beings have always sensed a magic in words that goes beyond rational, logical understanding. Poetry is not simply a method of communication; it is a unique experience in itself.

What is special about poetry? What makes it valuable? Why should we read it? How is reading it different from reading prose? To begin with, poetry pervades our world in a variety of forms, ranging from advertising jingles to song lyrics. These may seem to be a long way from the chants heard around a primitive campfire, but they serve some of the same purposes. Like poems printed in a magazine or book, primitive chants, catchy jingles, and popular songs attempt to stir the imagination through the carefully measured use of words.

Although reading poetry usually makes more demands than does the kind of reading we use to skim a magazine or newspaper, the appreciation of poetry comes naturally enough to anyone who enjoys playing with words. Play is an important element of poetry. Consider, for example, how the following words appeal to the children who gleefully chant them in playgrounds:

> I scream, you scream
> We all scream
> For ice cream.

These lines are an exuberant evocation of the joy of ice cream. Indeed, chanting the words turns out to be as pleasurable as eating ice cream. In poetry, the expression of the idea is as important as the idea expressed.

But is "I scream . . ." poetry? Some poets and literary critics would say that it certainly is one kind of poem because the children who chant it experience some of the pleasures of poetry in its measured beat and repeated sounds. However, other poets and critics would define poetry more narrowly and insist, for a variety of reasons, that this isn't true poetry but merely **doggerel,** a term used for lines whose subject matter is trite and whose rhythm and sounds are monotonously heavy-handed.

Although probably no one would argue that "I scream . . ." is a great poem, it does contain some poetic elements that appeal, at the very least, to children. Does that make it poetry? The answer depends on one's definition, but poetry has a way of breaking loose from definitions. Because there are nearly as many definitions of poetry as there are poets, Edwin

Arlington Robinson's succinct observations are useful: "Poetry has two outstanding characteristics. One is that it is undefinable. The other is that it is eventually unmistakable."

This comment places more emphasis on how a poem affects a reader than on how a poem is defined. By characterizing poetry as "undefinable," Robinson acknowledges that it can include many different purposes, subjects, emotions, styles, and forms. What effect does the following poem have on you?

WILLIAM HATHAWAY (B. 1944)

Oh, Oh   *1982*

My girl and I amble a country lane,
moo cows chomping daisies, our own
sweet saliva green with grass stems.
"Look, look," she says at the crossing,
"the choo-choo's light is on." And sure
enough, right smack dab in the middle
of maple dappled summer sunlight
is the lit headlight — so funny.
An arm waves to us from the black window.
We wave gaily to the arm. "When I hear
trains at night I dream of being president,"
I say dreamily. "And me first lady," she
says loyally. So when the last boxcars,
named after wonderful, faraway places,
and the caboose chuckle by we look   15
eagerly to the road ahead. And there,
poised and growling, are fifty Hell's Angels.

© Kit Hathaway.

A SAMPLE CLOSE READING

An Annotated Version of William Hathaway's "Oh, Oh"

After you've read a poem two or three times, a deeper, closer reading — line by line, word by word, syllable by syllable — will help you discover even more about the poem. Ask yourself: What happens (or does not happen) in the poem? What are the poem's central ideas? How do the poem's words, images, and sounds, for example, contribute to its meaning? What is the poem's overall tone? How is the poem put together?

You can flesh out your close reading by writing your responses in the margins of the page. The following interpretive notes offer but one way to read Hathaway's poem.

WILLIAM HATHAWAY (B. 1944)
Oh, Oh

1982

The title offers an interjection expressing strong emotion and foreboding.

The informal language conjures up an idyllic picture of a walk in the country, where the sights, sounds, and tastes are full of pleasure.

> My girl and I amble a country lane,
> moo cows chomping daisies, our own
> sweet saliva green with grass stems.
> "Look, look," she says at the crossing,
> "the choo-choo's light is on." And sure   5

The visual effect of the many *o*s in lines 1–5 (and 15) suggests an innocent, wide-eyed openness to experience while the repetitive *oo* sounds echo a kind of reassuring, satisfied cooing.

The carefully orchestrated *d*s, *m*s, *p*s, and *s*s of lines 6–8 create sounds that are meant to be savored.

> enough, right smack dab in the middle
> of maple dappled summer sunlight
> is the lit headlight — so funny.

"Right smack dab in the middle" of the poem, the "black window" hints that all is not well.

Filled with confidence and hope, the couple imagines a successful future together in exotic locations. Even the train is happy for them as it "chuckle[s]" in approval of their dreams.

> An arm waves to us from the black window.
> We wave gaily to the arm. "When I hear   10
> trains at night I dream of being president,"
> I say dreamily. "And me first lady," she
> says loyally. So when the last boxcars,
> named after wonderful, faraway places,
> and the caboose chuckle by we look   15
> eagerly to the road ahead. And there,
> poised and growling, are fifty Hell's Angels.

Not until the very last line does "the road ahead" yield a terrifying surprise. The strategically "poised" final line derails the leisurely movement of the couple and brings their happy story to a dead stop. The emotional reversal parked in the last few words awaits the reader as much as it does the couple. The sight and sound of the motorcycle gang signal that what seemed like heaven is, in reality, hell: Oh, Oh.

MORE HELP WITH CLOSE READING

Close readings of Andrew Marvell's "To His Coy Mistress," Elizabeth Bishop's "The Fish," and Theodore Roethke's "My Papa's Waltz" are available on *LiterActive* and at the book's companion site at bedfordstmartins.com/meyercompact. As you explore each poem, highlighted sections are annotated with critical interpretations and explanations of literary elements at work.

Hathaway's poem is a convenient reminder that poetry can be full of surprises. Full of confidence, this couple, like the reader, is unprepared for the shock to come. When we see those "fifty Hell's Angels," we are confronted with something like a bucket of cold water in the face.

But even though our expectations are abruptly and powerfully reversed, we are finally invited to view the entire episode from a safe distance — the distance provided by the delightful humor in this poem. After all, how seriously can we take a poem that is titled "Oh, Oh"? The poet has his way with us, but we are brought in on the joke, too. The terror takes on comic proportions as the innocent couple is confronted by no fewer than *fifty* Hell's Angels. This is the kind of raucous overkill that informs a short animated film produced some years ago titled *Bambi Meets Godzilla*: you might not have seen it, but you know how it ends. The poem's good humor comes through when we realize how pathetically inadequate the response of "Oh, Oh" is to the circumstances.

As you can see, reading a description of what happens in a poem is not the same as experiencing a poem. The exuberance of "I scream . . ." and the surprise of Hathaway's "Oh, Oh" are in the hearing or reading rather than in the retelling. A *paraphrase* is a prose restatement of the central ideas of a poem in your own language. Consider the difference between the following poem and the paraphrase that follows it. What is missing from the paraphrase?

ROBERT FRANCIS (1901–1987)

Catch   1950

Two boys uncoached are tossing a poem together,
Overhand, underhand, backhand, sleight of hand, every hand,
Teasing with attitudes, latitudes, interludes, altitudes,
High, make him fly off the ground for it, low, make him stoop,
Make him scoop it up, make him as-almost-as-possible miss it,   5
Fast, let him sting from it, now, now fool him slowly,
Anything, everything tricky, risky, nonchalant,
Anything under the sun to outwit the prosy,
Over the tree and the long sweet cadence down,
Over his head, make him scramble to pick up the meaning,   10
And now, like a posy, a pretty one plump in his hands.

Paraphrase: A poet's relationship to a reader is similar to a game of catch. The poem, like a ball, should be pitched in a variety of ways to challenge and create interest. Boredom and predictability must be avoided if the game is to be engaging and satisfying.

A paraphrase can help us achieve a clearer understanding of a poem, but, unlike a poem, it misses all of the sport and fun. It is the poem that "outwit[s] the prosy" because the poem serves as an example of what it suggests poetry should be. Moreover, the two players — the poet and the reader — are "uncoached." They know how the game is played, but their expectations do not preclude spontaneity and creativity or their ability to surprise and be surprised. The solid pleasure of the workout — of reading poetry — is the satisfaction derived from exercising your imagination and intellect.

That pleasure is worth emphasizing. Poetry uses language to move and delight even when it includes a cast of fifty Hell's Angels. The pleasure is in having the poem work its spell on us. For that to happen, it is best to relax and enjoy poetry rather than worry about definitions of it. Pay attention to what the poet throws you. We read poems for emotional and intellectual discovery — to feel and to experience something about the world and ourselves. The ideas in poetry — what can be paraphrased in prose — are important, but the real value of a poem consists in the words that work their magic by allowing us to feel, see, and be more than we were before. Perhaps the best way to approach a poem is similar to what Francis's "Catch" implies: expect to be surprised, stay on your toes, and concentrate on the delivery.

A SAMPLE STUDENT ANALYSIS

Tossing Metaphors Together in Robert Francis's "Catch"

The following sample paper on Robert Francis's "Catch" was written in response to an assignment that asked students to discuss the use of metaphor in the poem. Notice that Chris Leggett's paper is clearly focused and well organized. His discussion of the use of metaphor in the poem stays on track from beginning to end without any detours concerning unrelated topics (for a definition of *metaphor,* see p. 1631). His title draws on the central metaphor of the poem, and he organizes the paper around four key words used in the poem: "attitudes, latitudes, interludes, altitudes." These constitute the heart of the paper's four substantive paragraphs, and they are effectively framed by introductory and concluding paragraphs. Moreover, the transitions between paragraphs clearly indicate that the author was not merely tossing a paper together.

Chris Leggett

Professor Lyles

English 203-1

November 9, 2008

Exploration of the meaning of the word catch.

Tossing Metaphors Together in Robert Francis's "Catch"

The word "catch" is an attention getter. It usually means something is about to be hurled at someone and that he or she is expected to catch it.

Thesis statement identifying purpose of poem's metaphors.

"Catch" can also signal a challenge to another player if the toss is purposefully difficult. Robert Francis, in his poem "Catch," uses the extended metaphor of two boys playing catch to explore the considerations a poet makes when "tossing a poem together" (line 1). Line 3 of "Catch" enumerates

Reference to specific language in poem, around which the paper is organized.

these considerations metaphorically as "attitudes, latitudes, interludes, [and] altitudes." While regular prose is typically straightforward and easily understood, poetry usually takes great effort to understand and appreciate. To exemplify this, Francis presents the reader not with a normal game of catch with the ball flying back and forth in a repetitive and predictable fashion,

Introductory analysis of the poem's purpose.

but with a physically challenging game in which one must concentrate, scramble, and exert oneself to catch the ball, as one must stretch the intellect to truly grasp a poem.

The first consideration mentioned by Francis is attitude. Attitude,

Analysis of the meaning of attitude *in the poem.*

when applied to the game of catch, indicates the ball's pitch in flight, upward, downward, or straight. It could also describe the players' attitudes toward each other or toward the game in general. Below this literal level lies attitude's meaning in relation to poetry. Attitude in this case represents a poem's tone. A poet may "teas[e] with attitudes" by experimenting with

Discussion of how the attitude metaphor contributes to poem's tone.

different tones to achieve the desired mood (3). The underlying tone of "Catch" is a playful one, set and reinforced by the use of a game. This playfulness is further reinforced by such words and phrases as "teasing"(3), "outwit" (8), and "fool him" (6).

Analysis of the meaning of latitude *in the poem.*

Considered also in the metaphorical game of catch is latitude, which, when applied to the game, suggests the range the object may be thrown-- how high, how low, or how far. Poetic latitude, along similar lines, concerns a poem's breadth, or the scope of topic. Taken one level further, latitude suggests freedom from normal restraints or limitations, indicating the ability to go outside the norm to find originality of expression. The entire game of catch described in Francis's poem reaches outside the normal expectations of something being merely tossed back and forth in a predictable manner. The ball is thrown in almost every conceivable fashion, "overhand, under-hand, . . . every hand" (2). Other terms describing the throws--such as "tricky," "risky," "fast," "slowly," and "Anything under the sun" (6–7)--express endless latitude for avoiding predictability in Francis's game of catch and metaphorically in writing poetry.

> Discussion of how the latitude metaphor contributes to the poem's scope and message.

During a game of catch the ball may be thrown at different intervals, establishing a steady rhythm or a broken, irregular one. Other intervening features, such as the field being played on or the weather, could also affect the game. These features of the game are alluded to in the poem by the use of the word "interludes" (3). "Interlude" in the poetic sense represents the poem's form, which can similarly establish or diminish rhythm or enhance meaning. Lines 6 and 9, respectively, show a broken and a flowing rhythm. Line 6 begins rapidly as a hard toss that stings the catcher's hand is described. The rhythm of the line is immediately slowed, however, by the word "now" followed by a comma, followed by the rest of the line. In con-trast, line 9 flows smoothly as the reader visualizes the ball flying over the tree and sailing downward. The words chosen for this line function perfectly. The phrase "the long sweet cadence down" establishes a sweet rhythm that reads smoothly and rolls off the tongue easily. The choice of diction not only affects the poem's rhythmic flow but also establishes through connotative language the various levels at which the poem can be understood, repre-sented in "Catch" as altitude.

> Analysis of the mean-ing of *interlude* in the poem.

> Discussion of how the interlude metaphor contributes to the poem's form and rhythm.

While "altitudes" when referring to the game of catch means how high an object is thrown, in poetry it could refer to the level of diction, lofty or down-to-earth, formal or informal. It suggests also the levels at which a poem can be comprehended, the literal as well as the interpretive. In Fran-cis's game of catch, the ball is thrown high to make the player reach, low to make him stoop, or over his head to make him scramble, implying that the player should have to exert himself to catch it. So too, then, should the reader of poetry put great effort into understanding the full meaning of a poem. Francis exemplifies this consideration in writing poetry by giving

> Analysis of the mean-ing of *altitudes* in the poem.

"Catch" not only an enjoyable literal meaning concerning the game of catch, but also a rich metaphorical meaning--reflecting the process of writing poetry. Francis uses several phrases and words with multiple meanings. The phrase "tossing a poem together" (1) can be understood as tossing something back and forth or the process of constructing a poem. While "prosy" (8) suggests prose itself, it also means the mundane or the ordinary. In the poem's final line the word "posy" of course represents a flower, while it is also a variant of the word "poesy," meaning poetry, or the practice of composing poetry.

> *Discussion of how the altitude metaphor contributes to the poem's literal and symbolic meanings, with references to specific language.*

Francis effectively describes several considerations to be taken in writing poetry in order to "outwit the prosy" (8). His use of the extended metaphor in "Catch" shows that a poem must be unique, able to be comprehended on multiple levels, and a challenge to the reader. The various rhythms in the lines of "Catch" exemplify the ideas they express. While achieving an enjoyable poem on the literal level, Francis has also achieved a rich metaphorical meaning. The poem offers a good workout both physically and intellectually.

> *Conclusion summarizing ideas explored in paper.*

Work Cited

Francis, Robert. "Catch." The Compact Bedford Introduction to Literature.
Ed. Michael Meyer. 8th ed. Boston: Bedford/St. Martin's, 2009. 576.

Before beginning your own writing assignment on poetry, you should review Chapter 19, "Writing about Poetry," and Chapter 47, "Reading and Writing," which provides a step-by-step overview of how to choose a topic, develop a thesis, and organize various types of writing assignments. If you are using outside sources in your paper, you should make sure that you are familiar with the conventional documentation procedures described in Chapter 48, "The Literary Research Paper."

Poets often remind us that beauty can be found in unexpected places. What is it that Elizabeth Bishop finds so beautiful about the "battered" fish she describes in the following poem?

Web Explore contexts for Elizabeth Bishop and approaches to this poem on *LiterActive* and at bedfordstmartins .com/meyercompact.

ELIZABETH BISHOP (1911–1979)

The Fish   *1946*

I caught a tremendous fish
and held him beside the boat
half out of water, with my hook
fast in a corner of his mouth.
He didn't fight.
He hadn't fought at all.   5
He hung a grunting weight,
battered and venerable
and homely. Here and there
his brown skin hung in strips   10
like ancient wall-paper,
and its pattern of darker brown
was like wall-paper:
shapes like full-blown roses
stained and lost through age.   15
He was speckled with barnacles,
fine rosettes of lime,
and infested
with tiny white sea-lice,
and underneath two or three   20
rags of green weed hung down.
While his gills were breathing in
the terrible oxygen
— the frightening gills,
fresh and crisp with blood,
that can cut so badly —   25
I thought of the coarse white flesh
packed in like feathers,
the big bones and the little bones,
the dramatic reds and blacks
of his shiny entrails,   30
and the pink swim-bladder
like a big peony.
I looked into his eyes
which were far larger than mine
but shallower, and yellowed,   35
the irises backed and packed
with tarnished tinfoil
seen through the lenses
of old scratched isinglass.
They shifted a little, but not   40
to return my stare.
— It was more like the tipping
of an object toward the light.
I admired his sullen face,
the mechanism of his jaw,   45
and then I saw

that from his lower lip
— if you could call it a lip —
grim, wet, and weapon-like,   50
hung five old pieces of fish-line,
or four and a wire leader
with the swivel still attached,
with all their five big hooks
grown firmly in his mouth.   55
A green line, frayed at the end
where he broke it, two heavier lines,
and a fine black thread
still crimped from the strain and snap
when it broke and he got away.   60
Like medals with their ribbons
frayed and wavering,
a five-haired beard of wisdom
trailing from his aching jaw.
I stared and stared   65
and victory filled up
the little rented boat,
from the pool of bilge
where oil had spread a rainbow
around the rusted engine   70
to the bailer rusted orange,
the sun-cracked thwarts,
the oarlocks on their strings,
the gunnels — until everything
was rainbow, rainbow, rainbow!   75
And I let the fish go.

CONSIDERATIONS FOR CRITICAL THINKING AND WRITING

1. **FIRST RESPONSE.** Which lines in this poem provide especially vivid details of
   the fish? What makes these descriptions effective?

2. How is the fish characterized? Is it simply a weak victim because it "didn't
   fight"?

3. Comment on lines 65–76. In what sense has "victory filled up" the boat,
   given that the speaker finally lets the fish go?

The speaker in Bishop's "The Fish" ends on a triumphantly joyful
note. The *speaker* is the voice used by the author in the poem; like the narrator in a work of fiction, the speaker is often a created identity rather than
the author's actual self. The two should not automatically be equated.
Contrast the attitude toward life of the speaker in "The Fish" with that of
the speaker in the following poem.

PHILIP LARKIN (1922–1985)

A Study of Reading Habits   *1964*

When getting my nose in a book
Cured most things short of school,
It was worth ruining my eyes
To know I could still keep cool,
And deal out the old right hook   5
To dirty dogs twice my size.

Later, with inch-thick specs,
Evil was just my lark:
Me and my cloak and fangs
Had ripping times in the dark.   10
The women I clubbed with sex!
I broke them up like meringues.

Don't read much now: the dude
Who lets the girl down before
The hero arrives, the chap
Who's yellow and keeps the store,   15
Seem far too familiar. Get stewed:
Books are a load of crap.

What the speaker sees and describes in "The Fish" is close if not identical to Bishop's own vision and voice. The joyful response to the fish is clearly shared by the speaker and the poet, between whom there is little or no distance. In "A Study of Reading Habits," however, Larkin distances himself from a speaker whose sensibilities he does not wholly share. The poet — and many readers — might identify with the reading habits described by the speaker in the first twelve lines, but Larkin uses the last six lines to criticize the speaker's attitude toward life as well as reading. The speaker recalls in lines 1–6 how as a schoolboy he identified with the hero, whose virtuous strength always triumphed over "dirty dogs," and in lines 7–12 he recounts how his schoolboy fantasies were transformed by adolescence into a fascination with violence and sex. This description of early reading habits is pleasantly amusing, because many readers of popular fiction will probably recall having moved through similar stages, but at the end of the poem the speaker provides more information about himself than he intends to.

As an adult the speaker has lost interest in reading because it is no longer an escape from his own disappointed life. Instead of identifying with heroes or villains, he finds himself identifying with minor characters who are irresponsible and cowardly. Reading is now a reminder of his failures, so he turns to alcohol. His solution, to "Get stewed" because "Books are a load of crap," is obviously self-destructive. The speaker is ultimately exposed by Larkin as someone who never grew beyond fantasies. Getting drunk is consistent with the speaker's immature reading habits. Unlike the speaker, the poet understands that life is often distorted by escapist fantasies, whether through a steady diet of popular fiction or through alcohol. The speaker in this poem, then, is not Larkin but a created identity whose voice is filled with disillusionment and delusion.

The problem with Larkin's speaker is that he misreads books as well as his own life. Reading means nothing to him unless it serves as an escape from himself. It is not surprising that Larkin has him read fiction rather than poetry because poetry places an especially heavy emphasis on language. Fiction, indeed any kind of writing, including essays and drama, relies on carefully chosen and arranged words, but poetry does so to an even greater extent. Notice, for example, how Larkin's deft use of trite expressions and slang characterizes the speaker so that his language reveals nearly as much about his dreary life as what he says. Larkin's speaker would have no use for poetry.

What is "unmistakable" in poetry (to use Robinson's term again) is its intense, concentrated use of language — its emphasis on individual words to convey meanings, experiences, emotions, and effects. Poets never simply process words; they savor them. Words in poems frequently create their own tastes, textures, scents, sounds, and shapes. They often seem more sensuous than ordinary language, and readers usually sense that a word has been hefted before making its way into a poem. Although poems are crafted differently from the ways a painting, sculpture, or musical composition is created, in each form of art the creator delights in the medium. Poetry is carefully orchestrated so that the words work together as elements in a structure to sustain close, repeated readings. The words are chosen to interact with one another to create the maximum desired effect, whether the purpose is to capture a mood or feeling, create a vivid experience, express a point of view, narrate a story, or portray a character.

Here is a poem that looks quite different from most *verse,* a term used for lines composed in a measured rhythmical pattern, which are often, but not necessarily, rhymed.

ROBERT MORGAN (B. 1944)

Mountain Graveyard   *1979*

for the author of "Slow Owls"

Spore Prose

stone	notes
slate	tales
sacred	cedars
heart	earth
asleep	please
hated	death

Though unconventional in its appearance, this is unmistakably poetry because of its concentrated use of language. The poem demonstrates how serious play with words can lead to some remarkable discoveries. At first glance "Mountain Graveyard" may seem intimidating. What, after all, does this list of words add up to? How is it in any sense a poetic use of language? But if the words are examined closely, it is not difficult to see how they work. The wordplay here is literally in the form of a game. Morgan uses a series of ***anagrams*** (words made from the letters of other words, such as *read* and *dare*) to evoke feelings about death. "Mountain Graveyard" is one of several poems that Morgan has called "Spore Prose" (another anagram) because he finds in individual words the seeds of poetry. He wrote the poem in honor of the fiftieth birthday of another poet, Jonathan Williams, the author of "Slow Owls," whose title is also an anagram.

The title, "Mountain Graveyard," indicates the poem's setting, which is also the context in which the individual words in the poem interact to provide a larger meaning. Morgan's discovery of the words on the stones of a graveyard is more than just clever. The observations he makes among the silent graves go beyond the curious pleasure a reader experiences in finding the words *sacred cedars*, referring to evergreens common in cemeteries, to consist of the same letters. The surprise and delight of realizing the connection between heart and earth is tempered by the more sober recognition that everyone's story ultimately ends in the ground. The hope that the dead are merely asleep is expressed with a plea that is answered grimly by a hatred of death's finality.

Little is told in this poem. There is no way of knowing who is buried or who is looking at the graves, but the emotions of sadness, hope, and pain are unmistakable — and are conveyed in fewer than half the words of this sentence. Morgan takes words that initially appear to be a dead, prosaic list and energizes their meanings through imaginative juxtapositions.

The following poem also involves a startling discovery about words. With the peculiar title "l(a," the poem cannot be read aloud, so there is no sound, but is there sense, a ***theme,*** a central idea or meaning, in the poem?

E. E. CUMMINGS (1894–1962)

l(a   *1958*

l(a

le

af

fa

ll

s)

one

l

iness

 Explore contexts
for E. E. Cummings
at *LiterActive.*

© Bettmann/CORBIS.

CONSIDERATIONS FOR CRITICAL THINKING AND WRITING

1. **FIRST RESPONSE.** Discuss the connection between what appears inside and outside the parentheses in this poem.

2. What does Cummings draw attention to by breaking up the words? How do this strategy and the poem's overall shape contribute to its theme?

3. Which seems more important in this poem — what is expressed or the way it is expressed?

Although "Mountain Graveyard" and "l(a" do not resemble the kind of verse that readers might recognize immediately as poetry on a page, both are actually a very common type of poem, called the *lyric,* usually a brief poem that expresses the personal emotions and thoughts of a single speaker. Lyrics are often written in the first person, but sometimes — as in "Spore Prose" and "l(a" — no speaker is specified. Lyrics present a subjective mood, emotion, or idea. Very often they are about love or death, but almost any subject or experience that evokes some intense emotional response can be found in lyrics. In addition to brevity and emotional intensity, lyrics are also frequently characterized by their musical qualities. The word *lyric* derives from the Greek word *lyre,* meaning a musical instrument that originally accompanied the singing of a lyric. Lyric poems can be organized in a variety of ways, such as the sonnet, elegy, and ode (see Chapter 26), but it is enough to point out here that lyrics are an extremely popular kind of poetry with writers and readers.

The following anonymous lyric was found in a sixteenth-century manuscript.

ANONYMOUS

Western Wind

c. 1500

Western wind, when wilt thou blow,
The small rain down can rain?
Christ, if my love were in my arms,
And I in my bed again!

This speaker's intense longing for his lover is characteristic of lyric poetry. He impatiently addresses the western wind that brings spring to England and could make it possible for him to be reunited with the woman he loves. We do not know the details of these lovers' lives because this poem focuses on the speaker's emotion. We do not learn why the lovers are apart or if they will be together again. We don't even know if the speaker is a man. But those issues are not really important. The poetry gives us a feeling rather than a story.

A poem that tells a story is called a *narrative poem.* Narrative poetry may be short or very long. An *epic,* for example, is a long narrative poem on a serious subject chronicling heroic deeds and important events. Among the most famous epics are Homer's *Iliad* and *Odyssey,* the Old English *Beowulf,* Dante's *Divine Comedy,* and John Milton's *Paradise Lost.* More typically, however, narrative poems are considerably shorter, as is the case with the following poem, which tells the story of a child's memory of her father.

REGINA BARRECA (B. 1957)

Nighttime Fires   1986

When I was five in Louisville
we drove to see nighttime fires. Piled seven of us,
all pajamas and running noses, into the Olds,
drove fast toward smoke. It was after my father
lost his job, so not getting up in the morning
gave him time: awake past midnight, he read old
        newspapers
with no news, tried crosswords until he split the
        pencil
between his teeth, mad. When he heard
the wolf whine of the siren, he woke my mother,
and she pushed and shoved   10
us all into waking. Once roused we longed for burnt wood
and a smell of flames high into the pines. My old man liked
driving to rich neighborhoods best, swearing in a good mood
as he followed fire engines that snaked like dragons
and split the silent streets. It was festival, carnival.   15

If there were a Cadillac or any car
in a curved driveway, my father smiled a smile
from a secret, brittle heart.
His face lit up in the heat given off by destruction
like something was being made, or was being set right.   20
I bent my head back to see where sparks
ate up the sky. My father who never held us
would take my hand and point to falling cinders that
covered the ground like snow, or, excited, show us
the swollen collapse of a staircase. My mother   25
watched my father, not the house. She was happy
only when we were ready to go, when it was finally over
and nothing else could burn.
Driving home, she would sleep in the front seat
as we huddled behind. I could see his quiet face in the   30
rearview mirror, eyes like hallways filled with smoke.

Courtesy of Robert Benson, © 2004.

This narrative poem could have been a short story if the poet had wanted to say more about the "brittle heart" of this unemployed man whose daughter so vividly remembers the desperate pleasure he took in watching fire consume other people's property. Indeed, a reading of William Faulkner's famous short story "Barn Burning" (p. 418) suggests how such a character can be further developed and how his child responds to him. The similarities between Faulkner's angry character and the poem's father, whose "eyes [are] like hallways filled with smoke," are coincidental, but the characters' sense of "something . . . being set right" by flames is worth comparing. Although we do not know everything about this man and his family, we have a much firmer sense of their story than we do of the story of the couple in "Western Wind."

Although narrative poetry is still written, short stories and novels have largely replaced the long narrative poem. Lyric poems tend to be the predominant type of poetry today. Regardless of whether a poem is a narrative or a lyric, however, the strategies for reading it are somewhat different from those for reading prose. Try these suggestions for approaching poetry.

Suggestions for Approaching Poetry

1. Assume that it will be necessary to read a poem more than once. Give yourself a chance to become familiar with what the poem has to offer. Like a piece of music, a poem becomes more pleasurable with each encounter.

2. Pay attention to the title; it will often provide a helpful context for the poem and serve as an introduction to it. Larkin's "A Study of Reading Habits" is precisely what its title describes.

3. As you read the poem for the first time, avoid becoming entangled in words or lines that you don't understand. Instead, give yourself a chance to take in the entire poem before attempting to resolve problems encountered along the way.

4. On a second reading, identify any words or passages that you don't understand. Look up words you don't know; these might include names, places, historical and mythical references, or anything else that is unfamiliar to you.

5. Read the poem aloud (or perhaps have a friend read it to you). You'll probably discover that some puzzling passages suddenly fall into place when you hear them. You'll find that nothing helps, though, if the poem is read in an artificial, exaggerated manner. Read in as natural a voice as possible, with slight pauses at line breaks. Silent reading is preferable to imposing a te-tumpty-te-tum reading on a good poem.

6. Read the punctuation. Poems use punctuation marks — in addition to the space on the page — as signals for readers. Be especially careful not to assume that the end of a line marks the end of a sentence, unless it is concluded by punctuation. Consider, for example, the opening lines of Hathaway's "Oh, Oh":

   > My girl and I amble a country lane,
   > moo cows chomping daisies, our own
   > sweet saliva green with grass stems.

Line 2 makes little or no sense if a reader stops after "own." Keeping track of the subjects and verbs will help you find your way among the sentences.

7. Paraphrase the poem to determine whether you understand what happens in it. As you work through each line of the poem, a paraphrase will help you to see which words or passages need further attention.

8. Try to get a sense of who is speaking and what the setting or situation is. Don't assume that the speaker is the author; often it is a created character.

9. Assume that each element in the poem has a purpose. Try to explain how the elements of the poem work together.

10. Be generous. Be willing to entertain perspectives, values, experiences, and subjects that you might not agree with or approve of. Even if baseball bores you, you should be able to comprehend its imaginative use in Francis's "Catch."

11. Try developing a coherent approach to the poem that helps you to shape a discussion of the text. See Chapter 46, "Critical Strategies for Reading," to review formalist, biographical, historical, psychological, feminist, and other possible critical approaches.

12. Don't expect to produce a definitive reading. Many poems do not resolve all of the ideas, issues, or tensions in them, and so it is not always possible to drive their meaning into an absolute corner. Your reading will explore rather than define the poem. Poems are not trophies to be stuffed and mounted. They're usually more elusive. And don't be afraid that a close reading will damage the poem. Poems aren't hurt when we analyze them; instead, they come alive as we experience them and put into words what we discover through them.

A list of more specific questions using the literary terms and concepts discussed in the following chapters begins on page 614. That list, like the suggestions just made, raises issues and questions that can help you to read just about any poem closely. These strategies should be a useful means for getting inside poems to understand how they work. Furthermore, because reading poetry inevitably increases sensitivity to language, you're likely to find yourself a better reader of words in any form — whether in a novel, a newspaper editorial, an advertisement, a political speech, or a conversation — after having studied poetry. In short, many of the reading skills that make poetry accessible also open up the world you inhabit.

You'll probably find some poems amusing or sad, some fierce or tender, and some fascinating or dull. You may find, too, some poems that will get inside you. Their kinds of insights — the poet's and yours — are what Emily Dickinson had in mind when she defined poetry this way: "If I read a book and it makes my whole body so cold no fire can ever warm me, I know that it is poetry. If I feel physically as if the top of my head were taken off, I know that it is poetry." Dickinson's response may be more intense than most — poetry was, after all, at the center of her life — but you, too, might find yourself moved by poems in unexpected ways. In any case, as Edwin Arlington Robinson knew, poetry is, to an alert and sensitive reader, "eventually unmistakable."

BILLY COLLINS (B. 1941)

Introduction to Poetry   *1988*

I ask them to take a poem
and hold it up to the light
like a color slide

or press an ear against its hive.

I say drop a mouse into a poem   5
and watch him probe his way out,

or walk inside the poem's room
and feel the walls for a light switch.

I want them to water-ski
across the surface of a poem   10
waving at the author's name on the shore.

But all they want to do
is tie the poem to a chair with rope
and torture a confession out of it.

They begin beating it with a hose   15
to find out what it really means.

CONSIDERATIONS FOR CRITICAL THINKING AND WRITING

1. **FIRST RESPONSE.** In what sense does this poem offer suggestions for approaching poetry? What kinds of advice does the speaker provide in lines 1–11?

2. How does the mood of the poem change beginning in line 12? What do you make of the shift from "them" to "they"?

3. Paraphrase the poem. How is your paraphrase different from what is included in the poem?

ENCOUNTERING POETRY:
IMAGES OF POETRY
IN POPULAR CULTURE

Although poets may find it painful to acknowledge, poetry is not nearly as popular as prose among contemporary readers. A quick prowl through almost any bookstore reveals many more shelves devoted to novels or biographies, for example, than the meager space allotted to poetry. Moreover, few poems are made into films (although there have been some exceptions, such as Alfred, Lord Tennyson's "The Charge of the Light Brigade" [p. 767]), and few collections of poetry have earned their authors extraordinary wealth or celebrity status.

Despite these facts, however, there is plenty of poetry being produced that saturates our culture and suggests just how essential it is to our lives. When in 2001 Billy Collins was named the poet laureate of the United States, he shrewdly observed that "we should notice that there is no *prose* laureate." What Collins implicitly acknowledges here is the importance of poetry. He acknowledges the idea that poetry is central to any literature, because it is the art closest to language itself; its emphasis on getting each word just right speaks to us and for us. The audience for poetry may be relatively modest in comparison to the readership of prose, but there is nothing shy about poetry's presence in contemporary life. Indeed, a particularly observant person might find it difficult to reach the end of a day without encountering poetry in some shape or form.

You may, for instance, read yet again that magnetic poem composed on your refrigerator door as you reach for your breakfast juice, or perhaps you'll be surprised by some poetic lines while riding the bus or subway, where you might encounter a Poetry in Motion poster, featuring the work of a local poet or well-known author such as Dorothy Parker. What the poems have in common is the celebration of language as a means of surprising, delighting, provoking, or inspiring their readers. There's no obligation and no quiz. The poems are for the taking: all for pleasure.

The following portfolio of images — including provocative posters, a humorous cartoon, poetry-related art in public spaces, and vibrant photographs from the poetry slam scene — illustrate the significance of poetry in our culture. These images recognize the importance not only of such canonical authors as Carl Sandburg, Philip Levine, and T. S. Eliot, but also of aspiring poets — spoken word performers or Magnetic Poetry authors, for example — whose works reflect the growth of poetry as a popular form of expression.

Perhaps the largest, most recent explosion of poetry can be found on the Internet. For example, following the attacks of September 11, 2001, the International Library of Poetry reported a posting of nearly 40,000 poetic tributes at poetry.com. As Poetry Portal (poetry-portal.com) indicates, the number of poetry sites is staggering; these include sites that provide poems, audio readings, e-zines, reviews, criticism, festivals, slams, conferences, workshops, and even collaborative poetry writing in real time. This growth in poetry on the Internet is significant because it reflects an energy and vitality about the poetic activity in our daily lives. Poetry may not be rich and famous, but it is certainly alive and well. Consider, for example, the following images of poetry that can be found in contemporary life. What do they suggest to you about the nature of poetry and its audience?

DOROTHY PARKER, *Unfortunate Coincidence*

Begun in New York City in 1992, the Poetry in Motion program has spread from coast to coast on buses and subways. Offering works ranging from ancient Chinese poetry to contemporary poetry, Poetry in Motion posters give riders more to read than their own reflections in the window. In this example, Dorothy Parker, a poet known for her sharp wit, becomes a presence on a New York subway car.

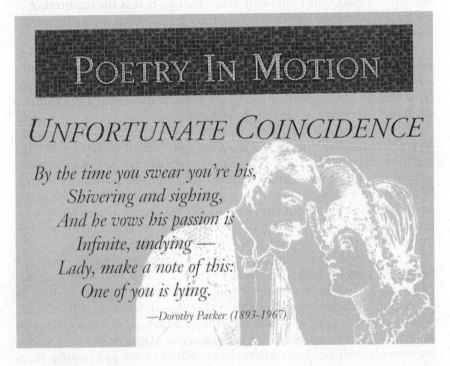

POETRY IN MOTION

UNFORTUNATE COINCIDENCE

By the time you swear you're his,
    Shivering and sighing,
And he vows his passion is
    Infinite, undying —
Lady, make a note of this:
    One of you is lying.

—Dorothy Parker (1893–1967)

CONSIDERATIONS FOR CRITICAL THINKING AND WRITING

1. How does the unromantic nature of this poem seem especially appropriate for New York City subway riders?

2. What kinds of poetry do you find on billboards or public transportation in your own environment? If there is none, what poem would you choose to post on a bus or train in your area?

CARL SANDBURG, *Window*

This mural, painted on a station wall of the Chicago El, features the poem "Window," from a collection of poems by Carl Sandburg titled *Chicago*. This work transforms the evening commute into an encounter with a vivid image.

CONSIDERATIONS FOR CRITICAL THINKING AND WRITING

1. Discuss the effectiveness of the images in these two lines.
2. Try writing two lines of vivid imagery that capture the movement seen from a quickly moving automobile during daylight.

Roz Chast, *The Love Song of J. Alfred Crew*

This *New Yorker* cartoon by Roz Chast (b. 1954) updates lines from T. S. Eliot's "The Love Song of J. Alfred Prufrock" (page 1018, lines 120–24) with the kind of language used in the popular J. Crew clothing catalog. Though published in 1917, Eliot's poem clearly remains fashionable.

Considerations for Critical Thinking and Writing

1. Read "The Love Song of J. Alfred Prufrock" (p. 1018) and compare the speaker's personality to the kind of image associated with the typical J. Crew customer. How does this comparison explain the humor in the cartoon?

2. Explain why you think the J. Crew company would be flattered or annoyed to have its image treated this way in a cartoon.

TIM TAYLOR, *I shake the delicate apparatus*

Magnetic Poetry™ kits are available in a number of languages, including Yiddish, Norwegian, and sign language, along with a variety of thematic versions such as those dedicated to cats, love, art, rock and roll, college, and Shakespeare. This poem by Tim Taylor (b. 1957) graces his Manhattan apartment refrigerator and is but one example of the creative expression that poetry magnets inspire in kitchens around the world.

Reprinted by permission of Tim Taylor (poem) and Pelle Cass (image).

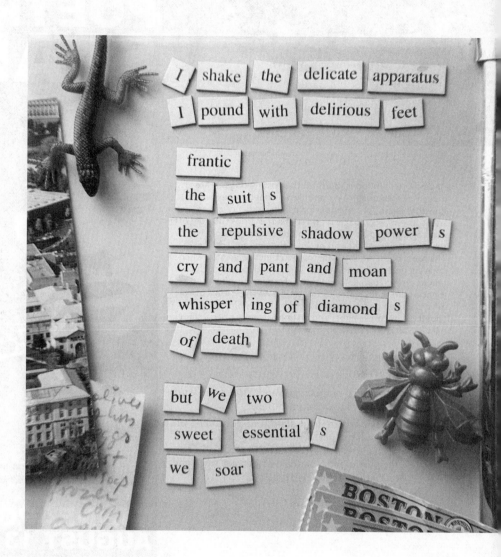

CONSIDERATIONS FOR CRITICAL THINKING AND WRITING

1. Write a paragraph that describes what you think is the essential meaning of this poem.

2. How do you explain the enormous popularity of Magnetic Poetry?

© David Huang/poeticdream.com. Reprinted with permission.

At a poetry slam, poets perform their own work and are judged by the audience—not only on what they say but on how they say it. As a poet performs, the audience cheers, snaps fingers, stomps feet, and sometimes boos the poet off the stage. Judged on a scale from one to ten, the poet with the most points at the end of the night wins a cash prize. The roots of the poetry slam trace to Chicago in 1984, when construction worker and writer Marc Smith broke the format at an "open mike" night by performing his poetry at an event traditionally slated for music. Shown here are a poster advertising an annual event hosted by Poetry Slam, Inc. (poetryslam.com) (right) and an image from a poetry slam held in San Francisco (above).

Considerations for Critical Thinking and Writing

1. What sorts of poetry events occur on your campus or in your community?

2. If possible, attend a slam and comment on the kinds of performances you see. Explain whether you think the performance and audience participation add to or detract from the experience of hearing spoken poetry.

Reprinted by permission of Eric Dunn (designer/copywriter) and Mike Wigton (copywriter).

Poetry-portal.com

Poetry Portal (poetry-portal.com), offering access to databases of poems and a cornucopia of online resources about poetry, is an excellent site to begin an exploration of poetry on the Internet.

Reprinted by permission of poetry-portal.com and Colin John Holcombe.

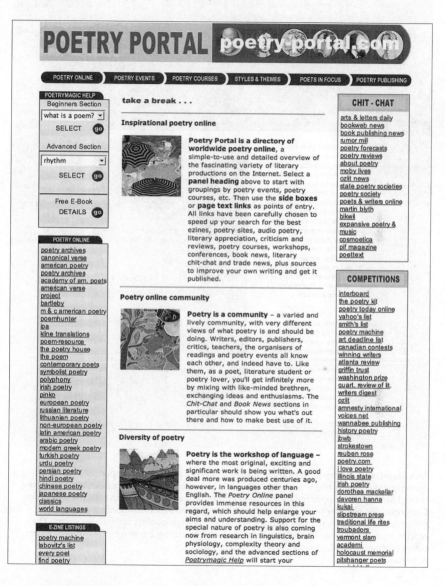

POETRY PORTAL poetry-portal.com

POETRY ONLINE | POETRY EVENTS | POETRY COURSES | STYLES & THEMES | POETS IN FOCUS | POETRY PUBLISHING

POETRYMAGIC HELP

Beginners Section

what is a poem? ▾

SELECT **go**

Advanced Section

rhythm ▾

SELECT **go**

Free E-Book

DETAILS **go**

POETRY ONLINE

poetry archives
canonical verse
american poetry
poetry archives
academy of am. poets
american verse
project
bartleby
m & c american poetry
poemhunter
ipa
kline translations
poem-resource
the poetry house
the poem
contemporary poets
symbolist poetry
polyphony
irish poetry
pinko
european poetry
russian literature
lithuanian poetry
non-european poetry
latin american poetry
arabic poetry
modern greek poetry
turkish poetry
urdu poetry
persian poetry
hindi poetry
chinese poetry
japanese poetry
classics
world languages

E-ZINE LISTINGS

poetry machine
labovitz's list
every poet
find poetry

take a break . . .

Inspirational poetry online

Poetry Portal is a directory of worldwide poetry online, a simple-to-use and detailed overview of the fascinating variety of literary productions on the Internet. Select a **panel heading** above to start with groupings by poetry events, poetry courses, etc. Then use the **side boxes** or **page text links** as points of entry. All links have been carefully chosen to speed up your search for the best ezines, poetry sites, audio poetry, literary appreciation, criticism and reviews, poetry courses, workshops, conferences, book news, literary chit-chat and trade news, plus sources to improve your own writing and get it published.

Poetry online community

Poetry is a community – a varied and lively community, with very different views of what poetry is and should be doing. Writers, editors, publishers, critics, teachers, the organisers of readings and poetry events all know each other, and indeed have to. Like them, as a poet, literature student or poetry lover, you'll get infinitely more by mixing with like-minded brethren, exchanging ideas and enthusiasms. The *Chit-Chat* and *Book News* sections in particular should show you what's out there and how to make best use of it.

Diversity of poetry

Poetry is the workshop of language – where the most original, exciting and significant work is being written. A good deal more was produced centuries ago, however, in languages other than English. The *Poetry Online* panel provides immense resources in this regard, which should help enlarge your aims and understanding. Support for the special nature of poetry is also coming now from research in linguistics, brain physiology, complexity theory and sociology, and the advanced sections of *Poetrymagic Help* will start your

CHIT - CHAT

arts & letters daily
bookweb news
book publishing news
rumor mill
poetry forecasts
poetry reviews
about poetry
moby lives
ozlit news
state poetry societies
poetry society
poets & writers online
martin blyth
bikwil
expansive poetry & music
cosmoetica
pif magazine
poettext

COMPETITIONS

interboard
the poetry kit
poetry today online
yahoo's list
smith's list
poetry machine
art deadline list
canadian contests
winning writers
atlanta review
griffin trust
washington prize
quart. review of lit.
writers digest
ozlit
amnesty international
voices net
wannabee publishing
history poetry
jbwb
strokestown
reuben rose
poetry.com
i love poetry
illinois state
irish poetry
dorothea mackellar
davoren hanna
kukai
slipstream press
traditional life rites
troubadors
vermont slam
academi
holocaust memorial
pitshanger poets

Considerations for Critical Thinking and Writing

1. Log on to the home page of poetry-portal.com and explore some of the online sites listed there. Describe three sites that you found particularly interesting. Any surprises?

2. In what sense does the Poetry Portal demonstrate that poetry is, indeed, a "community"?

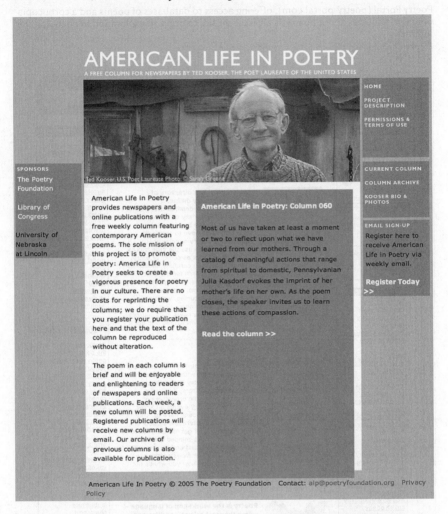

American Life in Poetry (americanlifeinpoetry.org) is a weekly newspaper column featuring a contemporary poem and brief introduction. Initiated by Ted Kooser, a poet laureate of the United States, and supported by the Poetry Foundation in partnership with the Library of Congress, this popular source is distributed free to newspapers and online publications. The site provides countless readers with a wide variety of high-quality, accessible poems. The reprint from the Detroit *Metro Times* (*opposite page*), featuring a poem by David Allan Evans, offers an engaging example of the weekly column.

© The Poetry Foundation.

DAVID ALLAN EVANS, *Neighbors*

April 6-12, 2005

metrotimes

detroit's weekly alternative   www.metrotimes.com • free

ART BAR

POETRY FOR THE PEOPLE: New Pulitzer-winner Ted Kooser, America's 13th poet laureate, gets us. He's no suit sitting in an office consulting ancient texts. For 35 years, he worked in the insurance business. "I wrote each morning ... and I often took my fresh drafts of poems and showed them to my secretary. ... If she didn't understand them, I went home and worked to make them more clear."

Kooser received funding as poet laureate and founded "American Life In Poetry," a free weekly newspaper column. *Metro Times* readers love to be talked to straight up, so we've signed up. Here's our and Kooser's premiere. If we don't have room in print, find it faithfully on our Web site. Kooser is excited *MT* signed on — "This is wonderful news! ... REALLY a start!"

Reprinted from Train Windows, *Ohio University Press, 1976, by permission of the author, whose most recent book is* The Bull Rider's Advice: New and Selected Poems. *This weekly column is supported by The Poetry Foundation, The Library of Congress, and the department of English at the University of Nebraska, Lincoln.*

AMERICAN LIFE IN POETRY

by Ted Kooser, U.S. poet laureate

We all know that the manner in which people behave toward one another can tell us a lot about their private lives. In this amusing poem by David Allan Evans, poet laureate of South Dakota, we learn something about a marriage by being shown a couple as they take on an ordinary household task.

Neighbors

They live alone
together,

she with her wide hind
and bird face,
he with his hung belly
and crewcut.

They never talk
but keep busy.

Today they are
washing windows
(each window together)
she on the inside,
he on the outside.
He squirts Windex
at her face,
she squirts Windex
at his face.

Now they are waving
to each other
with rags,

not smiling.

Courtesy of the Detroit *Metro Times*, the Poetry Foundation, and David Allan Evans.

CONSIDERATIONS FOR CRITICAL THINKING AND WRITING

1. Put together a cluster of images that reflect your encounters with poetry. Where do you find poetry? How is it used? What do these images suggest to you about the state of poetry in contemporary culture?

2. Surely not all manifestations of poetry in popular culture represent good poetry. Does bad poetry undercut good poetry? Does it cheapen its value? At this point in your study of poetry — the beginning — how do you define a good poem or a bad poem?

3. What is your favorite poem? Where did you first encounter it? Why is it important to you? Alternatively, if you can't come up with a favorite poem, why can't you?

POETRY IN POPULAR FORMS

Before you try out these strategies for reading on a few more poems, it is worth acknowledging that the verse that enjoys the widest readership appears not in collections, magazines, or even anthologies for students, but in greeting cards. A significant amount of the personal daily mail delivered in the United States consists of greeting cards. That represents millions of lines of verse going by us on the street and in planes over our heads. These verses share some similarities with the poetry included in this anthology, but there are also important differences that indicate the need for reading serious poetry closely rather than casually.

The popularity of greeting cards is easy to explain: just as many of us have neither the time nor the talent to make gifts for birthdays, weddings, anniversaries, graduations, Valentine's Day, Mother's Day, and other holidays, we are unlikely to write personal messages when cards conveniently say them for us. Although impersonal, cards are efficient and convey an important message no matter what the occasion for them: I care. These greetings are rarely serious poetry; they are not written to be. Nevertheless, they demonstrate the impulse in our culture to generate and receive poetry.

In a handbook for greeting-card freelancers, a writer and past editor of such verse began with this advice:

> Once you determine what you want to say — and in this regard it is best to stick to one basic idea — you must choose your words to do several things at the same time:
>
> 1. Your idea must be expressed as a complete idea; it must have a beginning, a middle, and an end.
>
> 2. There must be coherence in your verse. Every line must be linked logically and smoothly with its neighbors.
>
> 3. Your expressions . . . must be conversational. High-flown language rarely comes off successfully in greeting-card writing.
>
> 4. You must write with emphasis — and something else: enthusiasm. It's necessary to create interest in that all-important first line. From that point on, writing your verse is a matter of developing your idea and bringing it to a peak of emphasis in the last line. Occasionally you will find that you have shot your wad too early in the verse, and whatever you say after that point sounds like an afterthought.
>
> 5. You must do all of the above and at the same time make everything come out right in the meter-and-rhyme department.[1]

This advice is followed by a list of approximately fifty of the most frequently used rhyme sounds accompanied by rhyming words, such as *love*, *of*, *above* for the sound *uv*. The point of these prescriptions is that the verse

---

[1] Chris Fitzgerald, "Conventional Verse: The Sentimental Favorite," *The Greeting Card Writer's Handbook*, ed. H. Joseph Chadwick (Cincinnati: Writer's Digest, 1975), 13, 17.

must be written so that it is immediately accessible—consumable—by both the buyer and the recipient. Writers of these cards are expected to avoid any complexity.

Compare the following greeting-card verse with the poem that comes after it. "Magic of Love," by Helen Farries, has been a longtime favorite in a major greeting-card company's "wedding line"; with different endings it has been used also in valentines and friendship cards.

HELEN FARRIES

Magic of Love   *date unknown*

There's a wonderful gift that can give you a lift,
It's a blessing from heaven above!
It can comfort and bless, it can bring happiness—
It's the wonderful MAGIC OF LOVE!

Like a star in the night, it can keep your faith bright,   5
Like the sun, it can warm your hearts, too—
It's a gift you can give every day that you live,
And when given, it comes back to you!

When love lights the way, there is joy in the day
And all troubles are lighter to bear,   10
Love is gentle and kind, and through love you will find
There's an answer to your every prayer!

May it never depart from your two loving hearts,
May you treasure this gift from above—
You will find if you do, all your dreams will come true,   15
In the wonderful MAGIC OF LOVE!

JOHN FREDERICK NIMS (1913–1999)

Love Poem   *1947*

My clumsiest dear, whose hands shipwreck vases,
At whose quick touch all glasses chip and ring,
Whose palms are bulls in china, burs in linen,
And have no cunning with any soft thing

Except all ill-at-ease fidgeting people: 5
The refugee uncertain at the door
You make at home; deftly you steady
The drunk clambering on his undulant floor.

Unpredictable dear, the taxi drivers' terror,
Shrinking from far headlights pale as a dime   10
Yet leaping before red apoplectic streetcars —
Misfit in any space. And never on time.

A wrench in clocks and the solar system. Only
With words and people and love you move at ease.
In traffic of wit expertly maneuver   15
And keep us, all devotion, at your knees.

Forgetting your coffee spreading on our flannel,
Your lipstick grinning on our coat,
So gaily in love's unbreakable heaven
Our souls on glory of spilt bourbon float.   20

Be with me, darling, early and late. Smash glasses —
I will study wry music for your sake.
For should your hands drop white and empty
All the toys of the world would break.

CONSIDERATIONS FOR CRITICAL THINKING AND WRITING

1. **FIRST RESPONSE.** Read these two works aloud. How are they different? How
   the same?
2. To what extent does the advice to would-be greeting-card writers apply to
   each work?
3. Compare the two speakers. Which do you find more appealing? Why?
4. How does Nims's description of love differ from Farries's?

In contrast to poetry, which transfigures and expresses an emotion or
experience through an original use of language, the verse in "Magic of
Love" relies on *clichés* — ideas or expressions that have become tired and
trite from overuse, such as describing love as "a blessing from heaven
above." Clichés anesthetize readers instead of alerting them to the possibility of fresh perceptions. They are used to draw out *stock responses* —
predictable, conventional reactions to language, characters, symbols, or
situations; God, heaven, the flag, motherhood, hearts, puppies, and peace
are some often-used objects of stock responses. Advertisers manufacture
careers from this sort of business.

Clichés and stock responses are two of the major ingredients of sentimentality in literature. *Sentimentality* exploits the reader by inducing
responses that exceed what the situation warrants. This pejorative term
should not be confused with *sentiment,* which is synonymous with *emotion*
or *feeling.* Sentimentality cons readers into falling for the mass murderer
who is devoted to stray cats, and it requires that we not think twice about
what we're feeling because those tears shed for the little old lady, the rage
aimed at the vicious enemy soldier, and the longing for the simple virtues
of poverty might disappear under the slightest scrutiny. The experience of

sentimentality is not unlike biting into a swirl of cotton candy; it's momentarily sweet but wholly insubstantial.

Clichés, stock responses, and sentimentality are generally the hallmarks of weak writing. Poetry—the kind that is unmistakable—achieves freshness, vitality, and genuine emotion that sharpen our perceptions of life.

Although the most widely read verse is found in greeting cards, the most widely *heard* poetry appears in song lyrics. Not all songs are poetic, but a good many share the same effects and qualities as poems. Consider these lyrics by Bruce Springsteen about the attack on the World Trade Center on September 11, 2001.

BRUCE SPRINGSTEEN (B. 1949)

You're Missing   *2002*

Shirts in the closet, shoes in the hall
Mama's in the kitchen, baby and all
Everything is everything
Everything is everything
But you're missing   5

Coffee cups on the counter, jackets on the chair
Papers on the doorstep, you're not there
Everything is everything
Everything is everything
But you're missing   10

Pictures on the nightstand, TV's on in the den
Your house is waiting, your house is waiting
For you to walk in, for you to walk in
But you're missing, you're missing
You're missing when I shut out the lights   15
You're missing when I close my eyes
You're missing when I see the sun rise
You're missing

Children are asking if it's alright
Will you be in our arms tonight?   20

Morning is morning, the evening falls I have
Too much room in my bed, too many phone calls
How's everything, everything?
Everything, everything
You're missing, you're missing   25

God's drifting in heaven, devil's in the mailbox
I got dust on my shoes, nothing but teardrops

CONSIDERATIONS FOR CRITICAL THINKING AND WRITING

1. **FIRST RESPONSE.** How do the descriptions of home and the phrases that are repeated evoke a particular kind of mood in this song?

2. Explain whether you think this song can be accurately called a narrative poem. How would you describe its theme?

3. How does your experience of reading "You're Missing" compare with listening to Springsteen singing the song (available on *The Rising*)?

S. PEARL SHARP (B. 1942)

It's the Law: A Rap Poem   *1991*

You can learn about the state of the U.S.A.
By the laws we have on the books today.
The rules we break are the laws we make
The things that we fear, we legislate.

We got laws designed to keep folks in line   5
Laws for what happens when you lose your mind
Laws against stealing, laws against feeling,
The laws we have are a definite sign
That our vision of love is going blind.
(They probably got a law against this rhyme.)   10
Unh-hunh . . . . .

We got laws for cool cats & laws for dirty dogs
Laws about where you can park your hog
Laws against your mama and your papa, too
Even got a law to make the laws come true.   15

It's against the law to hurt an ol' lady,
It's against the law to steal a little baby,
The laws we make are what we do to each other
There is no law to make brother love brother
Hmmm   20

Now this respect thang is hard for some folks to do
They don't respect themselves so they can't respect you
This is the word we should get around —
These are the rules: we gonna run 'em on down.
Listen up!:   25

It ain't enough to be cute,
It ain't enough to be tough
You gotta walk tall
You gotta strut your stuff

You gotta learn to read, you gotta learn to write.   30
Get the tools you need to win this fight

Get your common sense down off the shelf
Start in the mirror . . . . Respect your Self!

When you respect yourself you keep your body clean
You walk tall, walk gentle, don't have to be mean   35
You keep your mind well fed, you keep a clear head
And you think 'bout who you let in your bed —
Unh-hunh . . . . . .

When you respect yourself you come to understand
That your body is a temple for a natural plan,   40
It's against that plan to use drugs or dope —
Use your heart and your mind when you need to cope . . .
It's the law!

We got laws that got started in '86
And laws made back when the Indians got kicked   45
If we want these laws to go out of favor
Then we've got to change our behavior

Change what!? you say, well let's take a look
How did the laws get on the books? Yeah.
I said it up front but let's get tougher   50
The laws we make are what we do to each other

If you never shoot at me then I don't need
A law to keep you from shooting at me, do you see?
There's a universal law that's tried and true
Says Don't do to me —   55
What you don't want done to you
Unh-hunh!
Don't do to me —
What you don't want done to you
It's the law!   60

CONSIDERATIONS FOR CRITICAL THINKING AND WRITING

1. **FIRST RESPONSE.** According to this rap poem, what do laws reveal "about the state of the U.S.A."?

2. How are the "laws" different from the "rules" prescribed in the middle stanzas of the poem?

3. What is the theme of this rap poem?

Perspective

ROBERT FRANCIS (1901–1987)

On "Hard" Poetry   1965

When Robert Frost said he liked poems hard he could scarcely have meant he liked them difficult. If he had meant difficult he would have said he didn't like them easy. What he said was that he didn't like them soft.

Poems can be soft in several ways. They can be soft in form (invertebrate). They can be soft in thought and feeling (sentimental). They can be soft with excess verbiage. Frost used to advise [writers] to squeeze the water out of a poem. He liked poems dry. What is dry tends to be hard, and what is hard is always dry, except perhaps on the outside.

Yet though hardness here does not mean difficulty, some difficulty naturally goes with hardness. A hard poem may not be hard to read but is hard to write. Not too hard, preferably. Not so hard to write that there is no flow in the writer. But hard enough for the growing poem to meet with some healthy resistance. Frost often found this healthy resistance in a tight rhyme scheme and strict meter. There are other ways of getting good resistance, of course.

And in the reader too, a hard poem will bring some difficulty. Preferably not too much. Not enough difficulty to completely baffle him. Ideally a hard poem should not be too hard to make sense of, but hard to exhaust its meaning and its beauty.

"What I care about is the hardness of the poems. I don't like them soft, I want them to be little pebbles, but placed where they won't dislodge easily. And I'd like them to be little pebbles of precious stone — precious, or semiprecious" (interview with John Ciardi, *Saturday Review*, March 21, 1959).

Here is hard prose talking about hard poetry. Frost was never shrewder or more illuminating. Here, as well as in anything else he ever said, is his flavor.

What contemporary of his can you imagine saying this or anything like it?

In 1843 Emerson jotted in his journal: "Hard clouds and hard expressions, and hard manners, I love."

From *The Satirical Rogue on Poetry*

CONSIDERATIONS FOR CRITICAL THINKING AND WRITING

1. What is the distinction between "hard" and "soft" poetry?

2. Given Francis's brief essay and his poem "Catch" (p. 576), write a review of Helen Farries's "Magic of Love" (p. 601) as you think Francis would.

3. Explain whether you would characterize Bruce Springsteen's "You're Missing" (p. 603) as hard or soft.

POEMS FOR FURTHER STUDY

ALBERTO RÍOS (B. 1952)

Seniors

1985

Courtesy of Alberto Ríos.

William cut a hole in his Levi's pocket
so he could flop himself out in class
behind the girls so the other guys
could see and shit what guts we all said.
All Konga wanted to do over and over   5
was the rubber band trick, but he showed
everyone how, so nobody wanted to see
anymore and one day he cried, just cried
until his parents took him away forever.
Maya had a Hotpoint refrigerator standing   10
in his living room, just for his family to show
anybody who came that they could afford it.

Me, I got a French kiss, finally, in the catholic
darkness, my tongue's farthest half vacationing
loudly in another mouth like a man in Bermudas,   15
and my body jumped against a flagstone wall,
I could feel it through her thin, almost
nonexistent body: I had, at that moment, that moment,
a hot girl on a summer night, the best of all
the things we tried to do. Well, she   20
let me kiss her, anyway, all over.

Or it was just a flagstone wall
with a flaw in the stone, an understanding cavity
for burning young men with smooth dreams —
the true circumstance is gone, the true   25
circumstances about us all then
are gone. But when I kissed her, all water,
she would close her eyes, and they into somewhere
would disappear. Whether she was there
or not, I remember her, clearly, and she moves   30
around the room, sometimes, until I sleep.

I have lain on the desert in watch
low in the back of a pick-up truck
for nothing in particular, for stars, for
the things behind stars, and nothing comes   35
more than the moment: always now, here in a truck,
the moment again to dream of making love and sweat,
this time to a woman, or even to all of them
in some allowable way, to those boys, then,
who couldn't cry, to the girls before they were   40
women, to friends, me on my back, the sky over me
pressing its simple weight into her body
on me, into the bodies of them all, on me.

CONSIDERATIONS FOR CRITICAL THINKING AND WRITING

1. **FIRST RESPONSE.** Comment on the use of slang in the poem. Does it surprise you? How does it characterize the speaker?

2. How does the language of the final stanza differ from that of the first stanza? To what purpose?

3. Write an essay that discusses the speaker's attitudes toward sex and life. How are they related?

CONNECTIONS TO OTHER SELECTIONS

1. Compare the treatment of sex in this poem with that in Sharon Olds's "Sex without Love" (p. 646).

2. Think about "Seniors" as a kind of love poem and compare the speaker's voice here with the one in T. S. Eliot's "The Love Song of J. Alfred Prufrock" (p. 1018). How are these two voices used to evoke different cultures? Of what value is love in these cultures?

ALFRED, LORD TENNYSON (1809–1892)

Crossing the Bar   *1889*

Sunset and evening star,
    And one clear call for me!
And may there be no moaning of the bar,°   *sandbar*
    When I put out to sea,

But such a tide as moving seems asleep,   5
    Too full for sound and foam,
When that which drew from out the boundless deep
    Turns again home.

Twilight and evening bell,
    And after that the dark!   10
And may there be no sadness of farewell,
    When I embark;

For tho' from out our bourne of Time and Place
    The flood may bear me far,
I hope to see my Pilot face to face   15
    When I have crost the bar.

CONSIDERATIONS FOR CRITICAL THINKING AND WRITING

1. **FIRST RESPONSE.** How does Tennyson make clear that this poem is about more than a sea journey?

2. Why do you think Tennyson indicated to his publishers that "Crossing the Bar" should be placed as the last poem in all collections of his poetry?

3. Discuss the purpose of the punctuation (or its absence) at the end of each line.

Li Ho (791–817)

A Beautiful Girl Combs Her Hair   *date unknown*

TRANSLATED BY DAVID YOUNG

Awake at dawn
she's dreaming
by cool silk curtains

fragrance of spilling hair
half sandalwood, half aloes   5

windlass creaking at the well
singing jade

the lotus blossom wakes, refreshed

her mirror
two phoenixes   10
a pool of autumn light

standing on the ivory bed
loosening her hair
watching the mirror

one long coil, aromatic silk   15
a cloud down to the floor

drop the jade comb — no sound

delicate fingers
pushing the coils into place
color of raven feathers   20

shining blue-black stuff
the jewelled comb will hardly hold it

spring wind makes me restless
her slovenly beauty upsets me

eighteen and her hair's so thick   25
she wears herself out fixing it!

she's finished now
the whole arrangement in place

in a cloud-patterned skirt
she walks with even steps   30
a wild goose on the sand

turns away without a word
where is she off to?

down the steps to break a spray of
    cherry blossoms 35

CONSIDERATIONS FOR CRITICAL THINKING AND WRITING

1. **FIRST RESPONSE.** Try to paraphrase the poem. What is lost by rewording?
2. How does the speaker use sensuous language to create a vivid picture of the girl?
3. What are the speaker's feelings toward the girl? Do they remain the same throughout the poem?

CONNECTIONS TO OTHER SELECTIONS

1. Compare the description of hair in this poem with that in Daisy Fried's "Wit's End" (p. 987). What significant differences do you find?
2. Write an essay that explores the differing portraits in this poem and in Cathy Song's "Sunworshippers" (p. 695). Which portrait is more interesting to you? Explain why.

LUISA LOPEZ (B. 1957)

Junior Year Abroad 2002

We were amateurs, that winter in Paris.

The summer before we agreed:
he would come over to keep me company at Christmas.
But the shelf life of my promise expired
before the date on his airline ticket. 5
So we ended up together under a French muslin sky.

Together alone.

Certainly I was alone, inside dark hair, inside foreign blankets,
against white sheets swirling like a cocoon,
covering my bare skin, 10
keeping me apart.
The invited man snored beside me not knowing
I didn't love him anymore.

At first I tried,
perky as a circus pony waiting at the airport gate 15
to be again as I once had been.
But even during the first night
betrayal, the snake under the evergreen,
threw me into nightmares
of floods and dying birds. 20

You see, a new boy just last month
had raised my shy hand to his warm mouth
and kissed the inside of my palm.
I thought "this is impossible,
too close to Christmas, too soon, too dangerous."   25

In Paris I concede:
deceiving my old lover, the one now stirring in his sleep
is even more dangerous.
See him opening his eyes, looking at my face,
dropping his eyes to my breasts and smiling   30
as if he were seeing two old friends? Dangerous.

When I move away and hold the sheet against
myself he,
sensing what this means,
refuses, adamant yet polite,   35
to traffic in the currency of my rejection.

He made a journey. I offered a welcome.
Why should he give me up?

CONSIDERATIONS FOR CRITICAL THINKING AND WRITING

1. **FIRST RESPONSE.** This poem is about strength and dominance as much as it is about love and attraction. Discuss the ways in which the two characters are vying for control.

2. Why is the setting important? How might the sense of the poem be different if this were happening during a typical school year as opposed to "Junior Year Abroad"?

3. Do you think the girl has the right to reject her old boyfriend under these circumstances? Does the old boyfriend have the right to expect a "welcome" since he was invited to visit?

4. The girl is wrapped in sheets that are like a "cocoon." What does this suggest about the changes she is experiencing during this encounter?

THOMAS LUX (B. 1946)

The Voice You Hear When You Read Silently   *1997*

is not silent, it is a speaking-
out-loud voice in your head; it is *spoken*,
a voice is *saying* it
as you read. It's the writer's words,
of course, in a literary sense   5
his or her *voice*, but the sound
of that voice is the sound of your voice.
Not the sound your friends know
or the sound of a tape played back

but your voice   10
caught in the dark cathedral
of your skull, your voice heard
by an internal ear informed by internal abstracts
and what you know by feeling,
having felt. It is your voice   15
saying, for example, the word barn
that the writer wrote
but the barn you say
is a barn you know or knew. The voice
in your head, speaking as you read,   20
never says anything neutrally — some people
hated the barn they knew,
some people love the barn they know
so you hear the word loaded
and a sensory constellation   25
is lit: horse-gnawed stalls,
hayloft, black heat tape wrapping
a water pipe, a slippery
spilled chirr of oats from a split sack,
the bony, filthy haunches of cows. . . .   30
And barn is only a noun — no verb
or subject has entered into the sentence yet!
The voice you hear when you read to yourself
is the clearest voice: you speak it
speaking to you.   35

CONSIDERATIONS FOR CRITICAL THINKING AND WRITING

1. **FIRST RESPONSE.** Describe the voice you hear when you read silently. How does it differ from your own speaking voice?

2. What do you think is the speaker's main point about how readers experience and interpret a writer's work?

3. Discuss Lux's choice of words in the phrase about the voice "caught in the dark cathedral / of your skull." Consider the difference between this phrase and "what you hear in your head."

4. **CREATIVE RESPONSE.** Choose a word that has the same evocative power for you as *barn* does for the poem's speaker, and write down a "sensory constellation" of images that captures the word's meanings for you.

Web Research the poets in this chapter at bedfordstmartins.com/meyercompact.

19

Writing about Poetry

Poems reveal secrets when they are analyzed. The poet's pleasure in finding ingenious ways to enclose her secrets should be matched by the reader's pleasure in unlocking and revealing secrets.

— DIANE WAKOSKI

© Robert Turney.

FROM READING TO WRITING

Writing about poetry can be a rigorous means of testing the validity of your own reading of a poem. Anyone who has been asked to write several pages about a fourteen-line poem knows how intellectually challenging this exercise is, because it means paying close attention to language. Such scrutiny of words, however, sensitizes you not only to the poet's use of language but also to your own use of language. At first you may feel intimidated by having to compose a paper that is longer than the poem you're writing about, but a careful reading will reveal that there's plenty to write about what the poem says and how it says it. Keep in mind that your job is not to produce a definitive reading of the poem — even Carl Sandburg once confessed that "I've written some poetry I don't understand myself." It is enough to develop an interesting thesis and to present it clearly and persuasively.

An interesting thesis will come to you if you read and reread, take notes, annotate the text, and generate ideas (for a discussion of this process see Chapter 47, "Reading and Writing"). Although it requires energy to read closely and to write convincingly about the charged language found in poetry, there is nothing mysterious about such reading and writing. This chapter provides a set of questions designed to sharpen your reading and writing about poetry. Following these questions is a sample paper that offers a clear and well-developed thesis concerning Elizabeth Bishop's "Manners."

Questions for Responsive Reading and Writing

The following questions can help you respond to important elements that reveal a poem's effects and meanings. The questions are general, so not all of them will necessarily be relevant to a particular poem. Many, however, should prove useful for thinking, talking, and writing about each poem in this collection. If you are uncertain about the meaning of a term used in a question, consult the Glossary of Literary Terms beginning on page 1619.

Before addressing these questions, read the poem you are studying in its entirety. Don't worry about interpretation on a first reading; allow yourself the pleasure of enjoying whatever makes itself apparent to you. Then on subsequent readings, use the questions to understand and appreciate how the poem works.

1. Who is the speaker? Is it possible to determine the speaker's age, sex, sensibilities, level of awareness, and values?
2. Is the speaker addressing anyone in particular?
3. How do you respond to the speaker? Favorably? Negatively? What is the situation? Are there any special circumstances that inform what the speaker says?
4. Is there a specific setting of time and place?
5. Does reading the poem aloud help you to understand it?
6. Does a paraphrase reveal the basic purpose of the poem?
7. What does the title emphasize?
8. Is the theme presented directly or indirectly?
9. Do any allusions enrich the poem's meaning?
10. How does the diction reveal meaning? Are any words repeated? Do any carry evocative connotative meanings? Are there any puns or other forms of verbal wit?
11. Are figures of speech used? How does the figurative language contribute to the poem's vividness and meaning?

12. Do any objects, persons, places, events, or actions have allegorical or symbolic meanings? What other details in the poem support your interpretation?

13. Is irony used? Are there any examples of situational irony, verbal irony, or dramatic irony? Is understatement or paradox used?

14. What is the tone of the poem? Is the tone consistent?

15. Does the poem use onomatopoeia, assonance, consonance, or alliteration? How do these sounds affect you?

16. What sounds are repeated? If there are rhymes, what is their effect? Do they seem forced or natural? Is there a rhyme scheme? Do the rhymes contribute to the poem's meaning?

17. Do the lines have a regular meter? What is the predominant meter? Are there significant variations? Does the rhythm seem appropriate for the poem's tone?

18. Does the poem's form — its overall structure — follow an established pattern? Do you think the form is a suitable vehicle for the poem's meaning and effects?

19. Is the language of the poem intense and concentrated? Do you think it warrants more than one or two close readings?

20. Did you enjoy the poem? What, specifically, pleased or displeased you about what was expressed and how it was expressed?

21. Is there a particular critical approach that seems especially appropriate for this poem? (See Chapter 46, "Critical Strategies for Reading.")

22. How might biographical information about the author help to determine the poem's central concerns?

23. How might historical information about the poem provide a useful context for interpretation?

24. To what extent do your own experiences, values, beliefs, and assumptions inform your interpretation?

25. What kinds of evidence from the poem are you focusing on to support your interpretation? Does your interpretation leave out any important elements that might undercut or qualify your interpretation?

26. Given that there are a variety of ways to interpret the poem, which one seems the most useful to you?

ELIZABETH BISHOP (1911–1979)

Manners   1965

for a Child of 1918

My grandfather said to me
as we sat on the wagon seat,
"Be sure to remember to always
speak to everyone you meet."

We met a stranger on foot.
My grandfather's whip tapped his hat.
"Good day, sir. Good day. A fine day."
And I said it and bowed where I sat.

Then we overtook a boy we knew
with his big pet crow on his shoulder.
"Always offer everyone a ride;
don't forget that when you get older,"

my grandfather said. So Willy
climbed up with us, but the crow
gave a "Caw!" and flew off. I was worried.
How would he know where to go?

But he flew a little way at a time
from fence post to fence post, ahead;
and when Willy whistled he answered.
"A fine bird," my grandfather said,   20

"and he's well brought up. See, he answers
nicely when he's spoken to.
Man or beast, that's good manners.
Be sure that you both always do."

When automobiles went by,   25
the dust hid the people's faces,
but we shouted "Good day! Good day!
Fine day!" at the top of our voices.

When we came to Hustler Hill,
he said that the mare was tired,   30
so we all got down and walked,
as our good manners required.

© Bettmann/CORBIS.

A SAMPLE CLOSE READING

An Annotated Version of Elizabeth Bishop's "Manners"

The following annotations represent insights about the relationship of
various elements at work in the poem gleaned only after several close readings. Don't expect to be able to produce these kinds of interpretive notes
on a first reading because such perceptions will not be apparent until
you've read the poem and then gone back to the beginning to discover how
each word, line, and stanza contributes to the overall effect. Writing your
responses in the margins of the page can be a useful means of recording
your impressions as well as discovering new insights as you read the text
closely.

ELIZABETH BISHOP (1911–1979)

Manners

1965

for a Child of 1918

Title refers to what is socially correct, polite, and/or decent behavior.

WWI ended in 1918 and denotes a shift in values and manners that often follows rapid social changes brought about by war.

My grandfather said to me
as we sat on the wagon seat,
"Be sure to remember to always
speak to everyone you meet."

"Wagon seat" suggests a simpler past — as does simple language and informal diction of the child speaker.

We met a stranger on foot.   5
My grandfather's whip tapped his hat.
"Good day, sir. Good day. A fine day."
And I said it and bowed where I sat.

Grandfather seems kind, but he also carries a whip that reinforces his authoritative voice.

Idea that values "always" transcend time is emphasized by the grandfather's urging: "don't forget."

Then we overtook a boy we knew
with his big pet crow on his shoulder.   10
"Always offer everyone a ride;
don't forget that when you get older,"

"My grandfather," repeated four times in first five stanzas, reflects the child's affection and a sense of belonging in his world. The crow, however, worries the child and indicates an uncertain future.

my grandfather said. So Willy
climbed up with us, but the crow
gave a "Caw!" and flew off. I was worried.   15
How would he know where to go?

Predictable quatrains and *abcb* rhyme scheme throughout the poem take the worry out of where they — and the crow — are headed.

But he flew a little way at a time
from fence post to fence post, ahead;
and when Willy whistled he answered.
"A fine bird," my grandfather said,   20

The modern symbolic automobile races by raising dust that obscures everyone's vision and forces them to shout. Rhymes in lines 26 and 28 are off (unlike all the other rhymes) just enough to suggest the dissonant future that will supersede the calm wagon ride.

Third time the grandfather says "always." This and the inverted syntax of line 24 call attention, again, to idea that good manners are forever important.

"and he's well brought up. See, he answers
nicely when he's spoken to.
Man or beast, that's good manners.
Be sure that you both always do."

When automobiles went by,   25
the dust hid the people's faces,

but we shouted "Good day! Good day!

Fine day!" at the top of our voices.

> The horse, like the simple past it symbolizes, is weakened by the hustle of modern life, but even so, "our" good manners prevail, internalized from the grandfather's values.

When we came to Hustler Hill,

he said that the mare was tired,   30

so we all got down and walked,

as our good manners required.

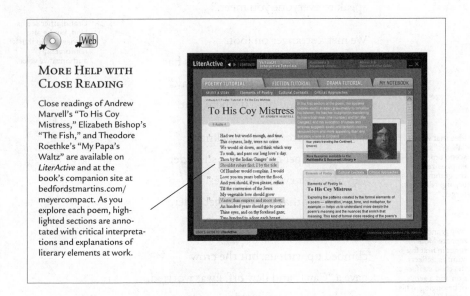

MORE HELP WITH CLOSE READING

Close readings of Andrew Marvell's "To His Coy Mistress," Elizabeth Bishop's "The Fish," and Theodore Roethke's "My Papa's Waltz" are available on *LiterActive* and at the book's companion site at bedfordstmartins.com/meyercompact. As you explore each poem, highlighted sections are annotated with critical interpretations and explanations of literary elements at work.

A SAMPLE STUDENT ANALYSIS

Memory in Elizabeth Bishop's "Manners"

The following sample paper on Elizabeth Bishop's "Manners" was written in response to an assignment that called for a 750-word discussion of the ways in which at least five of the following elements work to develop and reinforce the poem's themes:

diction and tone	irony	form
images	sound and rhyme	speaker
figures of speech	rhythm and meter	setting and situation
symbols		

In her paper, Debra Epstein discusses the ways in which a number of these elements contribute to what she sees as a central theme of "Manners": the loss of a way of life that Bishop associates with the end of World War I. Not all of the elements of poetry are covered equally in Epstein's paper because some, such as the speaker and setting, are more important to her argument than others. Notice how rather than merely listing each of the elements, Epstein mentions them in her discussion as she needs to in order to develop the thesis that she clearly and succinctly expresses in her opening paragraph.

Web Research the poets in this chapter at bedfordstmartins.com/ meyercompact.

Epstein 1

Debra Epstein

Professor Brown

English 210

May 2, 2008

Memory in Elizabeth Bishop's "Manners"

The subject of Elizabeth Bishop's "Manners" has to do with behaving well, but the theme of the poem has more to do with a way of life than with eti-quette. The poem suggests that modern society has lost something im-portant--a friendly openness, a generosity of spirit, a sense of decency and consideration--in its race toward progress. Although the narrative is simply told, Bishop enriches this poem about manners by developing an implicit theme through her subtle use of such elements of poetry as speaker, setting, rhyme, meter, symbol, and images.

Thesis providing interpretation of poem.

Statement of elements in poem to be discussed in paper.

The dedication suggests that the speaker is "a Child of 1918" who accompanies his or her grandfather on a wagon ride and who is urged to practice good manners by greeting people, offering everyone a ride, and speaking when spoken to by anyone. During the ride they say hello to a stranger, give a ride to a boy with a pet crow, shout greetings to a passing automobile, and get down from the wagon when they reach a hill because the horse is tired. They walk because "good manners required" (line 32) such consideration, even for a horse. This summary indicates what goes on in the poem but not its significance. That requires a closer look at some of the poem's elements.

Summary of poem's narrative and introduction to discussion of elements.

Given the speaker's simple language (there are no metaphors or simi-les and only a few words out of thirty-two lines are more than two syllables), it seems likely that he or she is a fairly young child, rather than an adult

Analysis of speaker in poem.

reminiscing. (It is interesting to note that Bishop herself, though not identical with the speaker, would have been seven in 1918.) Because the speaker is a young child who uses simple diction, Bishop has to show us the ride's significance indirectly rather than having the speaker explicitly state it.

The setting for the speaker's narrative is important because 1918 was the year World War I ended, and it marked the beginning of a new era of technology that was the result of rapid industrialization during the war. Horses and wagons would soon be put out to pasture. The grandfather's manners emphasize a time gone by; the child must be told to "remember" (3) what the grandfather says because he or she will take that advice into a new and very different world.

Analysis of poem's setting.

The grandfather's world of the horse and wagon is uncomplicated, and this is reflected in both the simple quatrains that move predictably along in an abcb rhyme scheme and the frequent anapestic meter (ăs wĕ sát ŏn tĥe wágŏn [2]) that pulls the lines rapidly and lightly. The one moment Bishop breaks the set rhyme scheme is in the seventh stanza when the automobile (the single four-syllable word in the poem) rushes by in a cloud of dust so that people cannot see or hear each other. The only off rhymes in the poem-- "faces" (26) and "voices" (28)--are also in this stanza, which suggests that the automobile and the people in it are somehow off or out of sync with what goes on in the other stanzas. The automobile is a symbol of a way of life in which people--their faces hidden--and manners take a back seat to speed and noise. The people in the car don't wave, don't offer a ride, and don't speak when spoken to.

Analysis of rhyme scheme and meter.

Analysis of symbols.

Maybe the image of the crow's noisy cawing and flying from post to post is a foreshadowing that should prepare readers for the automobile. The speaker feels "worried" about the crow's apparent directionlessness: "How would he know where to go?" (16). However, neither the child nor the grandfather (nor the reader on a first reading) clearly sees the two worlds that Bishop contrasts in the final stanza.

Analysis of images.

"Hustler Hill" (29) is the perfect name for what finally tires out the mare. There is no hurry for the grandfather and child, but there is for those people in the car and the postwar hustle and bustle they represent. The fast-

Conclusion supporting thesis on poem's theme.

Epstein 3

paced future overtakes the tired symbol of the past in the poem. The pace
slows as the wagon passengers get down to walk, but the reader recognizes
that the grandfather's way has been lost to a world in which good manners
are not required.

Epstein 4

Work Cited

Bishop, Elizabeth. "Manners." <u>The Compact Bedford Introduction to
Literature</u>. Ed. Michael Meyer. 8th ed. Boston: Bedford/St. Martin's,
2009, 615–16.

20

Word Choice, Word Order, and Tone

I feel that a poet has a duty to words, and that words can do wonderful things. And it's too bad to just let them lie there without doing anything with and for them.

— GWENDOLYN BROOKS

By permission of The Granger Collection, New York.

WORD CHOICE

Diction

Like all good writers, poets are keenly aware of ***diction,*** their choice of words. Poets, however, choose words especially carefully because the words in poems call attention to themselves. Characters, actions, settings, and symbols may appear in a poem, but in the foreground, before all else, is the poem's language. Also, poems are usually briefer than other forms of writing. A few inappropriate words in a 200-page novel (which would have about 100,000 words) create fewer problems than they would in a 100-word poem. Functioning in a compressed atmosphere, the words in a poem must convey meanings gracefully and economically. Readers therefore have to be alert to the ways in which those meanings are released.

 Explore the poetic elements in this chapter on *LiterActive* and at bedfordstmartins .com/meyercompact.

Although poetic language is often more intensely charged than ordinary speech, the words used in poetry are not necessarily different from everyday speech. Inexperienced readers may sometimes assume that language must be high-flown and out of date to be included in a poem: instead of reading about a boy "enjoying a swim," they expect to read about a boy "disporting with pliant arm o'er a glassy wave." During the eighteenth century this kind of *poetic diction* — the use of elevated language over ordinary language — was highly valued in English poetry, but since the nineteenth century poets have generally overridden the distinctions that were once made between words used in everyday speech and those used in poetry. Today all levels of diction can be found in poetry.

A poet, like any writer, has several levels of diction from which to choose; they range from formal to middle to informal. *Formal diction* consists of a dignified, impersonal, and elevated use of language. Notice, for example, the formality of Thomas Hardy's description of the sunken luxury liner *Titanic* in this stanza from "The Convergence of the Twain" (the entire poem appears on p. 642):

> In a solitude of the sea
> Deep from human vanity,
> And the Pride of Life that planned her, stilly couches she.

There is nothing casual or relaxed about these lines. Hardy's use of "stilly," meaning "quietly" or "calmly," is purely literary; the word rarely, if ever, turns up in everyday English.

The language used in Sharon Olds's "Last Night" (p. 640) represents a less formal level of diction; the speaker uses a *middle diction* spoken by most educated people. Consider how Olds's speaker struggles the next day to comprehend her passion:

> Love? It was more like dragonflies
> in the sun, 100 degrees at noon,
> the ends of their abdomens stuck together, I
> close my eyes when I remember.

The words used to describe this encounter are common enough, yet it is precisely Olds's use of language that evokes the extraordinary nature of this couple's connection.

Informal diction is evident in Philip Larkin's "A Study of Reading Habits" (p. 583). The speaker's account of his early reading is presented *colloquially,* in a conversational manner that in this instance includes slang expressions not used by the culture at large:

> When getting my nose in a book
> Cured most things short of school,
> It was worth ruining my eyes
> To know I could still keep cool,
> And deal out the old right hook
> To dirty dogs twice my size.

This level of diction is clearly not that of Hardy's or Wilbur's speakers.

Poets may also draw on another form of informal diction, called *dialect.* Dialects are spoken by definable groups of people from a particular geographic region, economic group, or social class. New England dialects are often heard in Robert Frost's poems, for example. Gwendolyn Brooks uses a black dialect in "We Real Cool" (p. 649) to characterize a group of pool players. Another form of diction related to particular groups is *jargon,* a category of language defined by a trade or profession. Sociologists, photographers, carpenters, baseball players, and dentists, for example, all use words that are specific to their fields. E. E. Cummings manages to get quite a lot of mileage out of automobile jargon in "she being Brand" (p. 627).

Many levels of diction are available to poets. The variety of diction to be found in poetry is enormous, and that is how it should be. No language is foreign to poetry because it is possible to imagine any human voice as the speaker of a poem. When we say a poem is formal, informal, or somewhere in between, we are making a descriptive statement rather than an evaluative one. What matters in a poem is not only which words are used but how they are used.

Denotations and Connotations

One important way that the meaning of a word is communicated in a poem is through sound: snakes *hiss,* saws *buzz.* This and other matters related to sound are discussed in Chapter 24. Individual words also convey meanings through denotations and connotations. *Denotations* are the literal, dictionary meanings of a word. For example, *bird* denotes a feathered animal with wings (other denotations for the same word include a shuttlecock, an airplane, or an odd person), but in addition to its denotative meanings, *bird* also carries *connotations* — associations and implications that go beyond a word's literal meanings. Connotations derive from how the word has been used and the associations people make with it. Therefore, the connotations of *bird* might include fragility, vulnerability, altitude, the sky, or freedom, depending on the context in which the word is used. Consider also how different the connotations are for the following types of birds: hawk, dove, penguin, pigeon, chicken, peacock, duck, crow, turkey, gull, owl, goose, coot, and vulture. These words have long been used to refer to types of people as well as birds. They are rich in connotative meanings.

Connotations derive their resonance from a person's experiences with a word. Those experiences may not always be the same, especially when the people having them are in different times and places. *Theater,* for instance, was once associated with depravity, disease, and sin, whereas today the word usually evokes some sense of high culture and perhaps visions of elegant opulence. In several ethnic communities in the United States many people would find *squid* appetizing, but elsewhere the word is likely to produce negative connotations. Readers must recognize, then, that words written in other times and places may have unexpected connotations.

Annotations usually help in these matters, which is why it makes sense to pay attention to them when they are available.

Ordinarily, though, the language of poetry is accessible, even when the circumstances of the reader and the poet are different. Although connotative language may be used subtly, it mostly draws on associations experienced by many people. Poets rely on widely shared associations rather than the idiosyncratic response that an individual might have to a word. Someone who has received a severe burn from a fireplace accident may associate the word *hearth* with intense pain instead of home and family life, but that reader must not allow a personal experience to undermine the response the poet intends to evoke. Connotative meanings are usually public meanings.

Perhaps this can be seen most clearly in advertising, where language is also used primarily to convey moods and feelings rather than information. For instance, nearly three decades of increasing interest in nutrition and general fitness have created a collective consciousness that advertisers have capitalized on successfully. Knowing that we want to be slender or lean or slim (not *spare* or *scrawny* and certainly not *gaunt*), advertisers have created a new word to describe beers, wines, sodas, cheeses, canned fruits, and other products that tend to overload what used to be called sweatclothes and sneakers. The word is *lite*. The assumed denotative meaning of *lite* is "low in calories," but as close readers of ingredient labels know, some *lites* are heavier than regularly prepared products. There can be no doubt about the connotative meaning of *lite*, however. Whatever is *lite* cannot hurt you; less is more. Even the word is lighter than *light*; there is no unnecessary droopy *g* or plump *h*. *Lite* is a brilliantly manufactured use of connotation.

Connotative meanings are valuable because they allow poets to be economical and suggestive simultaneously. In this way emotions and attitudes are carefully woven into the texture of the poem's language. Read the following poem and pay close attention to the connotative meanings of its words.

RANDALL JARRELL (1914–1965)

The Death of the Ball Turret Gunner   *1945*

From my mother's sleep I fell into the State
And I hunched in its belly till my wet fur froze.
Six miles from earth, loosed from its dream of life,
I woke to black flack and the nightmare fighters.
When I died they washed me out of the turret with a hose.

The title of this poem establishes the setting and the speaker's situation. Like the setting of a short story, the setting of a poem is important when the time and place influence what happens. "The Death of the Ball

Turret Gunner" is set in the midst of a war and, more specifically, in a ball turret — a Plexiglas sphere housing machine guns on the underside of a bomber. The speaker's situation obviously places him in extreme danger; indeed, his fate is announced in the title.

Although the poem is written in the first-person singular, its speaker is clearly not the poet. Jarrell uses a ***persona,*** a speaker created by the poet. In this poem the persona is a disembodied voice that makes the gunner's story all the more powerful. What is his story? A paraphrase might read something like this:

> After I was born, I grew up to find myself at war, cramped into the turret of a bomber's belly some 31,000 feet above the ground. Below me were exploding shells from antiaircraft guns and attacking fighter planes. I was killed, but the bomber returned to base, where my remains were cleaned out of the turret so the next man could take my place.

This paraphrase is accurate, but its language is much less suggestive than the poem's. The first line of the poem has the speaker emerge from his "mother's sleep," the anesthetized sleep of her giving birth. The phrase also suggests the comfort, warmth, and security he knew as a child. This safety was left behind when he "fell," a verb that evokes the danger and involuntary movement associated with his subsequent "State" (*fell* also echoes, perhaps, the fall from innocence to experience related in the Bible).

Several dictionary definitions appear for the noun *state;* it can denote a territorial unit, the power and authority of a government, a person's social status, or a person's emotional or physical condition. The context provided by the rest of the poem makes clear that "State" has several denotative meanings here: because it is capitalized, it certainly refers to the violent world of a government at war, but it also refers to the gunner's vulnerable status as well as his physical and emotional condition. By having "State" carry more than one meaning, Jarrell has created an intentional ambiguity. ***Ambiguity*** allows for two or more simultaneous interpretations of a word, phrase, action, or situation, all of which can be supported by the context of a work. Through his ambiguous use of "State," Jarrell connects the horrors of war not just to bombers and gunners but to the governments that control them.

Related to this ambiguity is the connotative meaning of "State" in the poem. The context demands that the word be read with a negative charge. The word is not used with patriotic pride but to suggest an anonymous, impersonal "State" that kills rather than nurtures the life in its "belly." The state's "belly" is a bomber, and the gunner is "hunched" like a fetus in the cramped turret, where, in contrast to the warmth of his mother's womb, everything is frozen, even the "wet fur" of his flight jacket (newborn infants have wet fur, too). The gunner is not just 31,000 feet from the ground but "Six miles from earth." *Six miles* has roughly the same denotative meaning as 31,000 feet, but Jarrell knew that the connotative meaning of *six miles* makes the speaker's position seem even more remote and frightening.

When the gunner is born into the violent world of war, he finds himself waking up to a "nightmare" that is all too real. The poem's final line is grimly understated, but it hits the reader with the force of an exploding shell: what the State-bomber-turret gives birth to is a gruesome death that is merely one of an endless series. It may be tempting to reduce the theme of this poem to the idea that "war is hell," but Jarrell's target is more specific. He implicates the "State," which routinely executes such violence, and he does so without preaching or hysterical denunciations. Instead, his use of language conveys his theme subtly and powerfully. Consider how this next poem uses connotative meanings to express its theme.

> Explore contexts
> for E. E. Cummings
> on *LiterActive*.

E. E. CUMMINGS (1894–1962)

she being Brand   *1926*

she being Brand

-new;and you
know consequently a
little stiff i was
careful of her and(having   5

thoroughly oiled the universal
joint tested my gas felt of
her radiator made sure her springs were O.

K.)i went right to it flooded-the-carburetor cranked her

up,slipped the   10
clutch(and then somehow got into reverse she
kicked what
the hell)next
minute i was back in neutral tried and

again slo-wly;bare,ly nudg. ing (my   15

lev-er Right-
oh and her gears being in
A 1 shape passed
from low through
second-in-to-high like   20
greasedlightning)just as we turned the corner of Divinity

avenue i touched the accelerator and give

her the juice,good

                    (it

was the first ride and believe i we was   25
happy to see how nice she acted right up to

the last minute coming back down by the Public
Gardens i slammed on

the
internalexpanding   30
&
externalcontracting
brakes Bothatonce and

brought allofher tremB
-ling   35
to a:dead.

stand-
;Still)

CONSIDERATIONS FOR CRITICAL THINKING AND WRITING

1. **FIRST RESPONSE.** How does Cummings's arrangement of the words on the page help you to read this poem aloud? What does the poem describe?

2. What ambiguities in language does the poem ride on? At what point were you first aware of these double meanings?

3. Explain why you think the poem is primarily serious or humorous.

4. Find some advertisements for convertibles or sports cars in magazines and read them closely. What similarities do you find in the use of connotative language in them and in Cummings's poem? Write a brief essay explaining how language is used to convey the theme of one of the advertisements and the poem.

5. **CREATIVE RESPONSE.** Using Cummings's arrangement of words on the page as your inspiration, try reorganizing the words and lines in Robert Francis's "Catch" (p. 576) so that they look as if Cummings wrote the poem.

WORD ORDER

Meanings in poems are conveyed not only by denotations and connotations but also by the poet's arrangement of words into phrases, clauses, and sentences to achieve particular effects. The ordering of words into meaningful verbal patterns is called *syntax.* A poet can manipulate the syntax of a line to place emphasis on a word; this is especially apparent when a poet varies normal word order. In Emily Dickinson's "A narrow Fellow in the Grass" (p. 2), for example, the speaker says about the snake that "His notice sudden is." Ordinarily, that would be expressed as "his notice is sudden." By placing the verb *is* unexpectedly at the end of the line, Dickinson creates the sense of surprise we feel when we suddenly come upon a snake. Dickinson's inversion of the standard word order also makes the final sound of the line a hissing *is.*

Cummings uses one long sentence in "she being Brand" to take the reader on a ride that begins with a false start but accelerates quickly before coming to a halt. The jargon creates an exuberantly humorous mood that is helped along by the poem's syntax. How do Cummings's ordering of words and sentence structure reinforce the meaning of the lines?

TONE

Tone is the writer's attitude toward the subject, the mood created by all of the elements in the poem. Writing, like speech, can be characterized as serious or light, sad or happy, private or public, angry or affectionate, bitter or nostalgic, or by any other attitudes and feelings that human beings experience. In Jarrell's "The Death of the Ball Turret Gunner," the tone is clearly serious; the voice in the poem even sounds dead. Listen again to the persona's final words: "When I died they washed me out of the turret with a hose." The brutal, restrained matter-of-factness of this line is effective because the reader is called on to supply the appropriate anger and despair—a strategy that makes those emotions all the more convincing.

Consider how tone is used to convey meaning in the next poem, inspired by the poet's contemplation of mortality.

JUDITH ORTIZ COFER   (B. 1952)

Common Ground   *1987*

Blood tells the story of your life
in heartbeats as you live it;
bones speak in the language
of death, and flesh thins
with age when up   5
through your pores rises
the stuff of your origin.

These days,
when I look into the mirror I see
my grandmother's stern lips   10
speaking in parentheses at the corners
of my mouth of pain and deprivation
I have never known. I recognize
my father's brows arching in disdain
over the objects of my vanity, my mother's   15
nervous hands smoothing lines
just appearing on my skin,
like arrows pointing downward
to our common ground.

CONSIDERATIONS FOR CRITICAL THINKING AND WRITING

1. **FIRST RESPONSE.** How do you interpret the title? How did your idea of its meaning change as you read the poem?
2. What is the relationship between the first and second stanzas?
3. How does this poem make you feel? What is its tone? How do the diction and imagery create the tone?

COLETTE INEZ (B. 1931)

Back When All Was Continuous Chuckles   *2004*

after a line by Anselm Hollo°

Doris and I were helpless on the Beeline Bus
laughing at what was it? "What did the moron
who killed his mother and father eat
at the orphan's picnic?" "Crow?" Har-har.

The bus was grinding towards Hempstead,   5
past the cemetery whose stones Doris
and I found hilarious. Freaky ghouls and skeletons.
"What did the dead man say to the ghost?"

"I like the movie better than the book."
Even "I don't get it" was funny.   10
The war was on, rationing, sirens.
Silly billies, we poked each other's arms

with balled fists, held hands and howled
at crabby ladies in funny hats, dusty feathers,
fake fruit. Doris' mom wore this headgear   15
before she got the big C which no one said out loud.

In a shadowy room her skin seemed gray
as moon dust on Smith Street, as Doris' house
where we tiptoed down the hall.
Sometimes we heard moans from the back room   20

and I helped wring out cloths while Doris
brought water in a glass held to her mother's lips.
But soon we were flipping through joke books
and writhing on the floor, war news shut off

back when we pretended all was continuous chuckles,   25
and we rode the bus past Greenfield's rise
where stones, trumpeting angels,
would bear names we later came to recognize.

Anselm Hollo: Finnish poet (b. 1934) who teaches creative writing in the United States.

CONSIDERATIONS FOR CRITICAL THINKING AND WRITING

1. **FIRST RESPONSE.** Compare the difference between the title and its slightly revised version as it appears in line 25. How does that difference reveal the theme?
2. At what point does the tone of the poem shift from chuckles to something else?
3. What is the effect of the rhymes in lines 26 and 28? How do the rhymes reinforce the poem's theme?

CONNECTION TO ANOTHER SELECTION

1. Discuss the tone of this poem and that of Gwendolyn Brooks's "We Real Cool" (p. 649).

The next work is a **dramatic monologue,** a type of poem in which a character — the speaker — addresses a silent audience in such a way as to reveal unintentionally some aspect of his or her temperament or personality. What tone is created by Machan's use of a persona?

KATHARYN HOWD MACHAN (B. 1952)

Hazel Tells LaVerne   1976

```
last night
im cleanin out my
howard johnsons ladies room
when all of a sudden
up pops this frog                                         5
musta come from the sewer
swimmin aroun an tryin ta
climb up the sida the bowl
so i goes ta flushm down
but sohelpmegod he starts talkin                          10
bout a golden ball
an how i can be a princess
me a princess
well my mouth drops
all the way to the floor                                  15
an he says
kiss me just kiss me
once on the nose
well i screams
ya little green pervert                                   20
an i hitsm with my mop
an has ta flush
the toilet down three times
me
a princess                                                25
```

Considerations for Critical Thinking and Writing

1. **FIRST RESPONSE.** What do you imagine the situation and setting are for this poem? Do you like this revision of the fairy tale "The Frog Prince"?

2. What creates the poem's humor? How does Hazel's use of language reveal her personality? Is her treatment of the frog consistent with her character?

3. Although it has no punctuation, this poem is easy to follow. How does the arrangement of the lines organize Hazel's speech for clarity and emphasis?

4. What is the theme? Is it conveyed through denotative or connotative language?

5. **CREATIVE RESPONSE.** Write what you think might be LaVerne's reply to Hazel. First, write LaVerne's response as a series of ordinary sentences, and then try editing and organizing them into poetic lines.

Connection to Another Selection

1. Although Robert Browning's "My Last Duchess" (p. 721) is a more complex poem than Machan's, both use dramatic monologues to reveal character. How are the strategies in each poem similar?

A SAMPLE STUDENT RESPONSE

Alex Georges

Professor Myerov

English 200

October 2, 2008

The Tone of Katharyn Howd Machan's "Hazel Tells LaVerne"

"Tone," Michael Meyer writes, "is the writer's attitude toward the subject, the mood created by all of the elements of the poem" (629) and is used to convey meaning and character. In her dramatic monologue, "Hazel Tells LaVerne," the poet Katharyn Howd Machan reveals through the persona of Hazel--a funny, tough-talking, no-nonsense cleaning lady--a satirical revision of "The Frog Prince" fairy tale. Hazel's attitude toward the possibility of a fairy-tale romance is evident in her response to the frog prince. She has no use for him or his offers "bout a golden ball / an how i can be a princess" (lines 11-12). If Hazel is viewed by the reader as a princess, it is clear from her words and tone that she is far from a traditional one.

Machan's word choice and humorous tone also reveal much about Hazel's personality and circumstances. Through the use of slang, alternate spellings, and the omission of punctuation, we learn a great deal about the character:

> well i screams
>
> ya little green pervert
>
> an i hitsm with my mop
>
> an has ta flush
>
> the toilet down three times
>
> me
>
> a princess (19-25)

Listening to her speak, the reader understands that Hazel, a cleaner at Howard Johnson's, does not have an extensive education. She speaks in the colloquial, running words into one another and using phrases like "ya little green pervert" (20) and "i screams" (19). The lack of complete sentences, capital letters, and punctuation adds to her informal tone. Hazel's speech defines her social status, brings out details of her personality, and gives the reader her view of herself. She is accustomed to the thankless daily grind of work and will not allow herself even a moment's fantasy of becoming a princess. It is a notion that she has to flush away--literally, has "ta flush . . . down three times." She tells LaVerne that the very idea of such is absurd to her, as she states in the final lines: "me / a princess" (24-25).

Works Cited

Machan, Katharyn Howd. "Hazel Tells LaVerne." The Compact Bedford Introduction to Literature. Ed. Michael Meyer. 8th ed. Boston: Bedford/ St. Martin's, 2009. 631.

Meyer, Michael, ed. The Compact Bedford Introduction to Literature. 8th ed. Boston: Bedford/St. Martin's, 2009. 629.

MARTÍN ESPADA (B. 1957)

Latin Night at the Pawnshop

1987

Chelsea, Massachusetts
Christmas, 1987

The apparition of a salsa band
gleaming in the Liberty Loan
pawnshop window:

Golden trumpet,
silver trombone,   5
congas, maracas, tambourine,
all with price tags dangling
like the city morgue ticket
on a dead man's toe.

CONSIDERATIONS FOR CRITICAL THINKING AND WRITING

1. **FIRST RESPONSE.** What is "Latin" about this night at the pawnshop?
2. What kind of tone is created by the poet's word choice and by the poem's rhythm?
3. Does it matter that this apparition occurs on Christmas night? Why or why not?
4. What do you think is the central point of this poem?

How do the speaker's attitude and tone change during the course of this next poem?

PAUL LAURENCE DUNBAR (1872–1906)

To a Captious Critic

1903

Dear critic, who my lightness so deplores,
Would I might study to be prince of bores,
Right wisely would I rule that dull estate —
But, sir, I may not; till you abdicate.

CONSIDERATIONS FOR CRITICAL THINKING AND WRITING

1. **FIRST RESPONSE.** How do Dunbar's vocabulary and syntax signal the level of diction used in the poem?
2. Describe the speaker's tone. How does it characterize the speaker as well as the critic?
3. **CREATIVE RESPONSE.** Using "To a Captious Critic" as a model, try writing a four-line witty reply to someone in your own life — perhaps a roommate, coach, teacher, waiter, dentist, or anyone else who provokes a strong response in you.

DICTION AND TONE IN FOUR LOVE POEMS

The first three of these love poems share the same basic situation and theme: a male speaker addresses a female (in the first poem it is a type of female) urging that love should not be delayed because time is short. This theme is as familiar in poetry as it is in life. In Latin this tradition is known as ***carpe diem,*** "seize the day." Notice how the poets' diction helps create a distinctive tone in each poem, even though the subject matter and central ideas are similar (although not identical) in all three.

ROBERT HERRICK (1591–1674)

To the Virgins, to Make Much of Time 1648

Courtesy of the National Portrait Gallery, London.

Gather ye rose-buds while ye may,
    Old Time is still a-flying;
And this same flower that smiles today,
    Tomorrow will be dying.

The glorious lamp of heaven, the sun,
    The higher he's a-getting,
The sooner will his race be run,
    And nearer he's to setting.

That age is best which is the first,
    When youth and blood are warmer;   10
But being spent, the worse, and worst
    Times still succeed the former.

Then be not coy, but use your time,
    And while ye may, go marry;
For having lost but once your prime,   15
    You may for ever tarry.

CONSIDERATIONS FOR CRITICAL THINKING AND WRITING

1. **FIRST RESPONSE.** Would there be any change in meaning if the title of this poem were "To Young Women, to Make Much of Time"? Do you think the poem can apply to young men, too?

2. What do the virgins have in common with the flowers (lines 1–4) and the course of the day (5–8)?

3. How does the speaker develop his argument? What will happen to the virgins if they don't "marry"? Paraphrase the poem.

4. What is the tone of the speaker's advice?

The next poem was also written in the seventeenth century, but it includes some words that have changed in usage and meaning over the past three hundred years. The title of Andrew Marvell's "To His Coy Mistress" requires some explanation. "Mistress" does not refer to a married man's illicit lover but to a woman who is loved and courted — a sweetheart. Marvell uses "coy" to describe a woman who is reserved and shy rather than coquettish or flirtatious. Often such shifts in meanings over time are explained in the notes that accompany reprintings of poems. You should keep in mind, however, that it is helpful to have a reasonably thick dictionary available when you are reading poetry. The most thorough is the *Oxford English Dictionary (OED)*, which provides histories of words. The *OED* is a multivolume leviathan, but there are other useful unabridged dictionaries and desk dictionaries.

Knowing its original meaning can also enrich your understanding of why a contemporary poet chooses a particular word. Elizabeth Bishop begins "The Fish" (p. 581) this way: "I caught a tremendous fish." We know immediately in this context that "tremendous" means very large. In addition, given that the speaker clearly admires the fish in the lines that follow, we might even understand "tremendous" in the colloquial sense of wonderful and extraordinary. But a dictionary gives us some further relevant insights. Because, by the end of the poem, we see the speaker thoroughly moved as a result of the encounter with the fish ("everything / was rainbow, rainbow, rainbow!"), the dictionary's additional information about the history of *tremendous* shows why it is the perfect adjective to introduce the fish. The word comes from the Latin *tremere* (to tremble) and therefore once meant "such as to make one tremble." That is precisely how the speaker is at the end of the poem: deeply affected and trembling. Knowing the origin of *tremendous* gives us the full heft of the poet's word choice.

Web Explore contexts for Andrew Marvell and approaches to this poem on *LiterActive* and at bedfordstmartins .com/meyercompact.

Although some of the language in "To His Coy Mistress" requires annotations for the modern reader, this poem continues to serve as a powerful reminder that time is a formidable foe, even for lovers.

ANDREW MARVELL (1621–1678)

To His Coy Mistress   1681

Had we but world enough, and time,
This coyness, lady, were no crime.
We would sit down, and think which way
To walk, and pass our long love's day.
Thou by the Indian Ganges'° side
Shouldst rubies find; I by the tide

Courtesy of the National Portrait Gallery, London.

5 *Ganges:* A river in India sacred to the Hindus.

Of Humber° would complain.° I would   *write love songs*
Love you ten years before the Flood,
And you should, if you please, refuse
Till the conversion of the Jews.   10
My vegetable love should grow°
Vaster than empires, and more slow;
An hundred years should go to praise
Thine eyes and on thy forehead gaze,
Two hundred to adore each breast,   15
But thirty thousand to the rest:
An age at least to every part,
And the last age should show your heart.
For, lady, you deserve this state,
Nor would I love at lower rate.   20
   But at my back I always hear
Time's wingèd chariot hurrying near;
And yonder all before us lie
Deserts of vast eternity.
Thy beauty shall no more be found,   25
Nor in thy marble vault shall sound
My echoing song; then worms shall try
That long preserved virginity,
And your quaint honor turn to dust,
And into ashes all my lust.   30
The grave's a fine and private place,
But none, I think, do there embrace.
   Now, therefore, while the youthful hue
Sits on thy skin like morning dew,
And while thy willing soul transpires°   *breathes forth* 35
At every pore with instant fires,
Now let us sport us while we may,
And now, like amorous birds of prey,
Rather at once our time devour
Than languish in his slow-chapped° power.   *slow-jawed* 40
Let us roll all our strength and all
Our sweetness up into one ball,
And tear our pleasures with rough strife
Thorough° the iron gates of life.   *through*
Thus, though we cannot make our sun   45
Stand still, yet we will make him run.

7 *Humber:* A river that flows through Marvell's native town, Hull.   11 *My vegetable love . . .
grow:* A slow, unconscious growth.

CONSIDERATIONS FOR CRITICAL THINKING AND WRITING

1. **FIRST RESPONSE.** Do you think this *carpe diem* poem is hopelessly dated, or does it speak to our contemporary concerns?

2. This poem is divided into a three-part argument. Briefly summarize each section: if (lines 1–20), but (21–32), therefore (33–46).

3. What is the speaker's tone in lines 1–20? How much time would he spend adoring his mistress? Is he sincere? How does he expect his mistress to respond to these lines?

4. How does the speaker's tone change beginning with line 21? What is his view of time in lines 21–32? What does this description do to the lush and leisurely sense of time in lines 1–20? How do you think his mistress would react to lines 21–32?

5. In the final lines of Herrick's "To the Virgins, to Make Much of Time" (p. 635), the speaker urges the virgins to "go marry." What does Marvell's speaker urge in lines 33–46? How is the pace of these lines (notice the verbs) different from that of the first twenty lines of the poem?

6. This poem is sometimes read as a vigorous but simple celebration of flesh. Is there more to the theme than that?

The third in this series of *carpe diem* poems is a twenty-first-century work. The language of Ann Lauinger's "Marvell Noir" is more immediately accessible than that of Marvell's "To His Coy Mistress"; an ordinary dictionary will quickly identify any words unfamiliar to a reader. But the title might require a dictionary of biography for the reference to Marvell, as well as a dictionary of allusions to provide a succinct description that explains the reference to film noir. An **allusion** is a brief cultural reference to a person, place, thing, event, or idea in history or literature. Allusive words, like connotative words, are both suggestive and economical; poets use allusions to conjure up biblical authority, scenes from Shakespeare's plays, historic figures, wars, great love stories, and anything else that might serve to deepen and enrich their own work. The title of "Marvell Noir" makes two allusions that an ordinary dictionary may not explain, because it alludes to Marvell's most famous poem, "To His Coy Mistress," and to dark crime films (*noir* is "black" in French) of the 1940s that were often filmed in black and white featuring tough-talking, cynical heroes such as Humphrey Bogart and hardened, cold women like Joan Crawford. Lauinger assumes that her reader will understand the allusions.

Allusions imply reading and cultural experiences shared by the poet and reader. Literate audiences once had more in common than they do today because more people had similar economic, social, and educational backgrounds. But a judicious use of specialized dictionaries, encyclopedias, and other reference tools can help you decipher allusions that grow out of this body of experience. As you read more, you'll be able to make connections based on your own experiences with literature. In a sense, allusions make available what other human beings have deemed worth remembering, and that is certainly an economical way of supplementing and enhancing your own experience.

Lauinger's version of the *carpe diem* theme follows. What strikes you as particularly modern about it?

Ann Lauinger

Marvell Noir   2005

Sweetheart, if we had the time,
A week in bed would be no crime.
I'd light your Camels, pour your Jack;
You'd do shiatsu on my back.
When you got up to scramble eggs,   5
I'd write a sonnet to your legs,
And you could watch my stubble grow.
Yes, gorgeous, we'd take it slow.
I'd hear the whole sad tale again:
A roadhouse band; you can't trust men;   10
He set you up; you had to eat,
And bitter with the bittersweet
Was what they dished you; Ginger lied;
You weren't there when Sanchez died;
You didn't know the pearls were fake . . .   15
Aw, can it, sport! Make no mistake,
You're in it, doll, up to your eyeballs!
Tears? Please! You'll dilute our highballs,
And make that angel face a mess
For the nice Lieutenant. I confess   20
I'm nuts for you — but take the rap?
You must think I'm some other sap!
And, precious, I kind of wish I was.
Well, when they spring you, give a buzz;
Guess I'll get back to Archie's wife,   25
And you'll get twenty-five to life.
You'll have time then, more than enough,
To reminisce about the stuff
That dreams are made of, and the men
You suckered. Sadly, in the pen   30
Your kind of talent goes to waste.
But Irish bars are more my taste
Than iron ones: stripes ain't my style.
You're going down; I promise I'll
Come visit every other year.   35
Now kiss me, sweet — the squad car's here.

Considerations for Critical Thinking and Writing

1. **FIRST RESPONSE.** How does Lauinger's poem evoke Marvell's *carpe diem* poem (p. 636) and the tough-guy tone of a "noir" narrative, a crime story or thriller that is especially dark?

2. Discuss the ways in which time is a central presence in the poem.

3. Explain the allusion to dreams in lines 28–29.

CONNECTION TO ANOTHER SELECTION

1. Compare the speaker's voice in this poem with the speaker in "To His Coy Mistress." What significant similarities and differences do you find?

This fourth love poem is a twenty-first-century work in which the speaker's voice is a woman's. How does it sound different from the way the men speak in the previous three poems?

SHARON OLDS (B. 1942)

Last Night   1996

The next day, I am almost afraid.
Love? It was more like dragonflies
in the sun, 100 degrees at noon,
the ends of their abdomens stuck together, I
close my eyes when I remember. I hardly   5
knew myself, like something twisting and
twisting out of a chrysalis,
enormous, without language, all
head, all shut eyes, and the humming
like madness, the way they writhe away,   10
and do not leave, back, back,
away, back. Did I know you? No kiss,
no tenderness — more like killing, death-grip
holding to life, genitals
like violent hands clasped tight   15
barely moving, more like being closed
in a great jaw and eaten, and the screaming
I groan to remember it, and when we started
to die, then I refuse to remember,
the way a drunkard forgets. After,   20
you held my hands extremely hard as my
body moved in shudders like the ferry when its
axle is loosed past engagement, you kept me
sealed exactly against you, our hairlines
wet as the arc of a gateway after   25
a cloudburst, you secured me in your arms till I slept —
that was love, and we woke in the morning
clasped, fragrant, buoyant, that was
the morning after love.

CONSIDERATIONS FOR CRITICAL THINKING AND WRITING

1. **FIRST RESPONSE.** How is your response to this poem affected by a female speaker? Explain why this is or is not a *carpe diem* poem.
2. Comment on the descriptive passages of "Last Night." Which images seem especially vivid to you? How do they contribute to the poem's meaning?

3. Explain how the poem's tone changes from beginning to end.

CONNECTIONS TO OTHER SELECTIONS

1. How does the speaker's description of intimacy compare with Herrick's and Marvell's?

2. Compare the speaker's voice in Olds's poem with the voice you imagine for the coy mistress in Marvell's poem.

3. CRITICAL STRATEGIES. Read the section on feminist criticism (pp. 1548–49) in Chapter 46, "Critical Strategies for Reading," and compare the themes in Olds's poem and Philip Larkin's "A Study of Reading Habits" (p. 583) the way you think a feminist critic might analyze them.

POEMS FOR FURTHER STUDY

BARBARA HAMBY (B. 1929)

Ode to American English   2004

I was sitting in Paris one day missing English, American, really,
    with its pill-popping Hungarian goulash of everything
from Anglo-Saxon to Zulu, because British English
    is not the same, if the paperback dictionary I bought
at Brentano's on the Avenue de l'Opéra is any indication,   5
    too cultured by half. Oh, the English know their delphiniums,
but what about doowop, donuts, Dick Tracy, Tricky Dick?
    With their elegant Oxfordian accents, how could they
understand my yearning for the hotrod, hotdog, hot flash
    vocabulary of the U.S. of A., the fragmented fandango   10
of Dagwood's everyday flattening of Mr. Beasley on the sidewalk,
    fetuses floating on billboards, drive-by monster
hip-hop stereos shaking the windows of my dining room
    like a 7.5 earthquake, Ebonics, Spanglish, "you know"
used as a comma and period, the inability of 90% of the population   15
    to get the past perfect. *I have went, I have saw,*
I have tooken Jesus into my heart, the battle cry of the Bible Belt,
    but no one uses the King James anymore, only plain-speak
versions, in which Jesus, raising Lazarus from the dead, says,
    "Dude, wake up," and the L-man bolts up like a B-movie   20
mummy. "Whoa, I was toasted." Yes, ma'am, I miss the mongrel
    plenitude of American English, its fall-guy, rat-terrier,
dog-pound neologisms, the bomb of it all, the rushing River Jordan
    backwoods mutability of it, the low-rider, boom-box cruise of it,
from New Joisey to Ha-wah-ya with its sly dog, malasada-scarfing   25
    beach blanket lingo to the ubiquitous Valley Girl's
like-like stuttering, shopaholic rant. I miss its quotidian beauty,
    its querulous back-biting righteous indignation, its preening

rotgut flag-waving cowardice. *Suffering Succotash*, sputters
  Sylvester the Cat; *sine die*,° say the pork-bellied legislators   30
of the swamps and plains. I miss all those guys, their Tweety-bird
  resilience, their Doris Day optimism, the candid unguent
of utter unhappiness on every channel, the midnight televangelist
  euphoric stew, the junk mail-voice mail vernacular.
On every *boulevard* and *rue* I miss the Tarzan cry of Johnny   35
  Weismueller, Johnny Cash, Johnny B. Goode,
and all the smart-talking, gum-snapping hard-girl dialogue,
  finger-popping x-rated street talk, sports babble,
Cheetoes, Cheerios, chili-dog diatribes. Yeah, I miss 'em all,
  sitting here on my sidewalk throne sipping champagne,   40
verses lined up like hearses, metaphors juking, nouns zipping
  in my head like Corvettes on dexedrine, French verbs
slitting my throat, yearning for James Dean to jump my curb.

30 *sine die:* Latin for "without a day; indefinitely."

Considerations for Critical Thinking and Writing

1. **First response.** Consult the Glossary of Literary Terms (p. 1619) for the definition of *ode*. How does this poem constitute an ode to American English?

2. Explain how the diction of this poem is vital to its meaning. What is it about American English that causes the speaker to admire it so much?

3. What kind of characterization of American life is presented by the varieties of English cataloged in the poem?

Connections to Other Selections

1. Discuss the strategic use of American phrasing in this poem and in Florence Cassen Mayers's "All-American Sestina" (p. 787), and compare the tone of each poem.

2. Write an essay comparing the themes of Hamby's poem and Lydia Huntley Sigourney's "Indian Names" (p. 1032). Compare how the diction of each controls its tone.

Thomas Hardy (1840–1928)
The Convergence of the Twain   1912

Lines on the Loss of the "Titanic"°

I

In a solitude of the sea
Deep from human vanity,
And the Pride of Life that planned her, stilly couches she.

"*Titanic*": A luxurious ocean liner, reputed to be unsinkable, which sank after hitting an iceberg on its maiden voyage in 1912. Only a third of the 2,200 passengers survived.

II

Steel chambers, late the pyres
   Of her salamandrine fires,°
Cold currents thrid,° and turn to rhythmic tidal lyres.

5
thread

III

Over the mirrors meant
   To glass the opulent
The sea-worm crawls — grotesque, slimed, dumb, indifferent.

IV

Jewels in joy designed
   To ravish the sensuous mind
Lie lightless, all their sparkles bleared and black and blind.

10

V

Dim moon-eyed fishes near
   Gaze at the gilded gear
And query: "What does this vaingloriousness down here?"

15

VI

Well: while was fashioning
   This creature of cleaving wing,
The Immanent Will that stirs and urges everything

VII

Prepared a sinister mate
   For her — so gaily great —
A Shape of Ice, for the time far and dissociate.

20

VIII

And as the smart ship grew
   In stature, grace, and hue,
In shadowy silent distance grew the Iceberg too.

IX

Alien they seemed to be:
   No mortal eye could see
The intimate welding of their later history,

25

---

5 *salamandrine fires:* Salamanders were, according to legend, able to survive fire; hence the ship's fires burned even though under water.

X

Or sign that they were bent
By paths coincident
On being anon twin halves of one august event,   30

XI

Till the Spinner of the Years
Said "Now!" And each one hears,
And consummation comes, and jars two hemispheres.

CONSIDERATIONS FOR CRITICAL THINKING AND WRITING

1. **FIRST RESPONSE.** Describe a contemporary disaster comparable to the sinking of the *Titanic*. How was your response to it similar to or different from the speaker's response to the fate of the *Titanic*?

2. How do the words used to describe the ship in this poem reveal the speaker's attitude toward the *Titanic*?

3. The diction of the poem suggests that the *Titanic* and the iceberg participate in something like an arranged marriage. What specific words imply this?

4. Who or what causes the disaster? Does the speaker assign responsibility?

DAVID R. SLAVITT (B. 1935)

Titanic   1983

Who does not love the *Titanic*?
If they sold passage tomorrow for that same crossing,
who would not buy?

To go down . . . We all go down, mostly
alone. But with crowds of people, friends, servants,   5
well fed, with music, with lights! Ah!

And the world, shocked, mourns, as it ought to do
and almost never does. There will be the books and movies
to remind our grandchildren who we were
and how we died, and give them a good cry.   10

Not so bad, after all. The cold
water is anesthetic and very quick.
The cries on all sides must be a comfort.

We all go: only a few, first-class.

CONSIDERATIONS FOR CRITICAL THINKING AND WRITING

1. **FIRST RESPONSE.** What, according to the speaker in this poem, is so compelling about the *Titanic*? Do you agree?

2. Discuss the speaker's tone. Is *Titanic* merely a sarcastic poem?

3. What is the effect of the poem's final line? What emotions does it elicit?

CONNECTION TO ANOTHER SELECTION

1. How does "Titanic" differ in its attitude toward opulence from Hardy's "The Convergence of the Twain" (p. 642)?

2. Which poem, "Titanic" or "The Convergence of the Twain," is more emotionally satisfying to you? Explain why.

3. Compare the speakers' tones in "Titanic" and "The Convergence of the Twain."

4. **CRITICAL STRATEGIES.** Read the section on Marxist criticism (pp. 1545–46) in Chapter 46, "Critical Strategies for Reading," and analyze the attitudes toward opulence that are manifested in the two poems.

JOANNE DIAZ (B. 1972)

On My Father's Loss of Hearing   2006

Courtesy of Jason Reblando.

> *I'd like to see more poems treat the deaf*
> *as being abled differently, not lost*
> *or missing something, weakened, deficient.*
> *— from a listserv for the deaf*

Abled differently — so vague compared
with deaf, obtuse but true to history,
from deave: to deafen, stun, amaze with
    noise.
Perhaps that's what we've done — amazed
    him with
our sorrows and complaints, the stupid jabs,
the loneliness of boredom in the house,

our wants so foreign to his own. What else
is there but loss? He's lost the humor of
sarcastic jokes, the snarky dialogue
of British films eludes him, phone calls   10
cast him adrift in that cochlear maze
that thrums and bristles even now, when
it doesn't have to: an unnecessary kind
of elegance, the vestige of a sense

no longer obligated to transmit   15
the crack of thawing ice that fills the yard's
wide dip in winter, or the scrape of his
dull rake in spring, its prongs' vibration thrilled
by grass and peat moss. Imagine his desires
released like saffron pistils in the wind;   20
mark their trace against the cords of wood

he spent the summer splitting. See his quiet
flicker like a film, a Super-8
projected on the wall, and all of us
there, laughing on the porch without a sound.   25
No noisome cruelty, no baffled rage,
no aging children sullen in their lack.
Love hurts much less in this serenity.

CONSIDERATIONS FOR CRITICAL THINKING AND WRITING

1. **FIRST RESPONSE.** Why does the speaker prefer the word *deaf* to the phrase "abled differently" as a means of describing her father? Which description do you prefer? Why?

2. Explain how sound and silence move through the poem from beginning to end.

3. Choose a single word from each stanza that strikes you as particularly effective, and explain why you think Diaz chose it over other possibilities.

4. What do you make of the poem's final line? How does it relate to the tone of the rest of the poem?

CONNECTIONS TO OTHER SELECTIONS

1. Discuss the relationship between love and pain in "On My Father's Loss of Hearing" and in Bruce Springsteen's "You're Missing" (p. 603).

2. Compare the speakers' attitudes toward the fathers in Diaz's poem and in Robert Hayden's "Those Winter Sundays" (p. 571).

SHARON OLDS (B. 1942)

Sex without Love   1984

How do they do it, the ones who make love
without love? Beautiful as dancers,
gliding over each other like ice skaters
over the ice, fingers hooked
inside each other's bodies, faces   5
red as steak, wine, wet as the
children at birth whose mothers are going to
give them away. How do they come to the
come to the   come to the   God   come to the
still waters, and not love   10
the one who came there with them, light
rising slowly as steam off their joined
skin? These are the true religious,
the purists, the pros, the ones who will not
accept a false Messiah, love the   15
priest instead of the God. They do not
mistake the lover for their own pleasure,
they are like great runners: they know they are alone

with the road surface, the cold, the wind,
the fit of their shoes, their over-all cardio-   20
vascular health — just factors, like the partner
in the bed, and not the truth, which is the
single body alone in the universe
against its own best time.

CONSIDERATIONS FOR CRITICAL THINKING AND WRITING

1. **FIRST RESPONSE.** What is the nature of the question asked by the speaker in the poem's first two lines? What is being asked here?

2. What is the effect of describing the lovers as athletes? How do these descriptions and phrases reveal the speaker's tone toward the lovers?

3. To what extent does the title suggest the central meaning of this poem? Try to compose some alternative titles that are equally descriptive.

CONNECTIONS TO OTHER SELECTIONS

1. How does the treatment of sex and love in Olds's poem compare with that in Cummings's "she being Brand" (p. 627)?

2. Just as Olds describes sex without love, she implies a definition of love in this poem. Consider whether the lovers in her poem "Last Night" (p. 640) fall within Olds's definition.

JOHN KEATS (1795–1821)

Ode on a Grecian Urn   *1819*

I

Thou still unravished bride of quietness,
   Thou foster-child of silence and slow time,
Sylvan° historian, who canst thus express
   A flowery tale more sweetly than our rhyme:
What leaf-fringed legend haunts about thy shape   5
   Of deities or mortals, or of both,
     In Tempe or the dales of Arcady?°
What men or gods are these? What maidens loath?
   What mad pursuit? What struggle to escape?
     What pipes and timbrels? What wild ecstasy?   10

II

Heard melodies are sweet, but those unheard
   Are sweeter; therefore, ye soft pipes, play on;

Explore contexts
for John Keats
on *LiterActive.*

---

3 *Sylvan:* Rustic. The urn is decorated with a forest scene.   7 *Tempe, Arcady:* Beautiful rural valleys in Greece.

Not to the sensual ear, but, more endeared,
  Pipe to the spirit ditties of no tone:
Fair youth, beneath the trees, thou canst not leave   15
  Thy song, nor ever can those trees be bare;
    Bold Lover, never, never canst thou kiss,
Though winning near the goal—yet, do not grieve;
    She cannot fade, though thou hast not thy bliss,
    For ever wilt thou love, and she be fair!   20

III

Ah, happy, happy boughs! that cannot shed
  Your leaves, nor ever bid the Spring adieu;
And, happy melodist, unwearièd,
  For ever piping songs for ever new;
More happy love! more happy, happy love!   25
  For ever warm and still to be enjoyed,
    For ever panting, and for ever young;
All breathing human passion far above,
  That leaves a heart high-sorrowful and cloyed,
    A burning forehead, and a parching tongue.   30

IV

Who are these coming to the sacrifice?
  To what green altar, O mysterious priest,
Lead'st thou that heifer lowing at the skies,
  And all her silken flanks with garlands drest?
What little town by river or sea shore,   35
  Or mountain-built with peaceful citadel,
    Is emptied of this folk, this pious morn?
And, little town, thy streets for evermore
  Will silent be; and not a soul to tell
    Why thou art desolate, can e'er return.   40

V

O Attic° shape! Fair attitude! with brede°
  Of marble men and maidens overwrought,
With forest branches and the trodden weed;
  Thou, silent form, dost tease us out of thought
As doth eternity: Cold Pastoral!   45
  When old age shall this generation waste,
    Thou shalt remain, in midst of other woe
Than ours, a friend to man, to whom thou say'st,
  Beauty is truth, truth beauty—that is all
    Ye know on earth, and all ye need to know.   50

41 *Attic:* Possessing classic Athenian simplicity; *brede:* Design.

CONSIDERATIONS FOR CRITICAL THINKING AND WRITING

1. **FIRST RESPONSE.** What does the speaker's diction reveal about his attitude toward the urn in this ode? Does his view develop or change?

2. How is the happiness in stanza 3 related to the assertion in lines 11–12 that "Heard melodies are sweet, but those unheard / Are sweeter"?

3. What is the difference between the world depicted on the urn and the speaker's world?

4. What do lines 49 and 50 suggest about the relation of art to life? Why is the urn described as a "Cold Pastoral" (line 45)?

5. Which world does the speaker seem to prefer, the urn's or his own?

6. Describe the overall tone of the poem.

CONNECTIONS TO OTHER SELECTIONS

1. Write an essay comparing the view of time in this ode with that in Marvell's "To His Coy Mistress" (p. 636). Pay particular attention to the connotative language in each poem.

2. Compare the tone and attitude toward life in this ode with those in John Keats's "To Autumn" (p. 676).

GWENDOLYN BROOKS (1917–2000)

We Real Cool

1960

The Pool Players.
Seven at the Golden Shovel.

Explore contexts
for Gwendolyn Brooks
on *LiterActive*.

We real cool. We
Left school. We

Lurk late. We
Strike straight. We

Sing sin. We
Thin gin. We

Jazz June. We
Die soon.

CONSIDERATIONS FOR CRITICAL THINKING AND WRITING

1. **FIRST RESPONSE.** How does the speech of the pool players in this poem help to characterize them? What is the effect of the pronouns coming at the ends of the lines? How would the poem sound if the pronouns came at the beginnings of lines?

2. What is the author's attitude toward the players? Is there a change in tone in the last line?

3. How is the pool hall's name related to the rest of the poem and its theme?

JOAN MURRAY (B. 1945)

We Old Dudes

2006

We old dudes. We
White shoes. We

Golf ball. We
Eat mall. We

Soak teeth. We
Palm Beach; We

Vote red. We
Soon dead.

CONSIDERATIONS FOR CRITICAL THINKING AND WRITING

1. FIRST RESPONSE. Consider the poem's humor. To what extent does it make a serious point?
2. What does the reference to Palm Beach tell you about these "old dudes"?
3. Write a poem similar in style that characterizes your life as a student.

CONNECTION TO ANOTHER SELECTION

1. Compare the themes of "We Old Dudes" and Brooks's "We Real Cool." How do the two poems speak to each other?

ALICE JONES (B. 1949)

The Larynx

1993

Under the epiglottic flap
the long-ringed tube sinks
its shaft down to the bronchial
fork, divides from two
to four then infinite branches,   5
each ending finally in a clump
of transparent sacs knit
with small vessels into a mesh
that sponge-like soaks up breath
and gives it off with a push   10
from the diaphragm's muscular wall,
forces wind out of the lungs'
wide tree, up through this organ's
single pipe, through the puzzle
box of gristle, where resonant   15
plates of cartilage fold
into shield, horns, bows,

bound by odd half-spirals
of muscles that modulate air
as it rises through this empty place   20
at our core, where lip-like
folds stretch across the vestibule,
small and tough, they flutter,
bend like birds' wings finding
just the right angle to stay   25
airborne; here the cords arch
in the hollow of this ancient instrument,
curve and vibrate to make a song.

CONSIDERATIONS FOR CRITICAL THINKING AND WRITING

1. **FIRST RESPONSE.** What is the effect of having this poem written as one long sentence? How does the length of the sentence contribute to the poem's meaning?

2. Make a list of words and phrases from the poem that strike you as scientific, and compare those with a list of words that seem poetic. How do they compete with or complement each other in terms of how they affect your reading?

3. Comment on the final three lines. How would your interpretation of this poem change if it ended before the semicolon in line 26?

CONNECTION TO ANOTHER SELECTION

1. Compare the diction and the ending in "The Larynx" with those of "The Foot" (p. 761), another poem by Jones.

LOUIS SIMPSON (B. 1923)

In the Suburbs   1963

There's no way out.
You were born to waste your life.
You were born to this middleclass life

As others before you
Were born to walk in procession
To the temple, singing.

CONSIDERATIONS FOR CRITICAL THINKING AND WRITING

1. **FIRST RESPONSE.** Is the title of this poem especially significant? What images does it conjure up for you?

2. What does the repetition in lines 2-3 suggest?

3. Discuss the possible connotative meanings of lines 5 and 6. Who are the "others before you"?

CONNECTION TO ANOTHER SELECTION

1. Write an essay on suburban life based on this poem and John Ciardi's "Suburban" (p. 986).

A NOTE ON READING TRANSLATIONS

Sometimes translation can inadvertently be a comic business. Consider, for example, the discovery made by John Steinbeck's wife, Elaine, when in a Yokohama bookstore she asked for a copy of her husband's famous novel *The Grapes of Wrath* and learned that it had been translated into Japanese as *Angry Raisins*. Close but no cigar (perhaps translated as: Nearby, yet no smoke). As amusing as that *Angry Raisins* title is, it teaches an important lesson about the significance of a poet's or a translator's choices when crafting a poem: a powerful piece moves us through diction and tone, both built word by careful word. Translations are frequently regarded as merely vehicular, a way to arrive at the original work. It is, of course, the original work—its spirit, style, and meaning—that most readers expect to find in a translation. Even so, it is important to understand that a translation is *by nature* different from the original—and that despite that difference, a fine translation can be an important part of the journey and become part of the literary landscape itself. Reading a translation of a poem is not the same as reading the original, but neither is watching two different performances of *Hamlet*. The translator provides a reading of the poem in much the same way that a director shapes the play. Each interprets the text from a unique perspective.

Basically, there are two distinct approaches to translation: literal translations and adaptations. A literal translation sets out to create a word-for-word equivalent that is absolutely faithful to the original. As simple and direct as this method may sound, literal translations are nearly impossible over extended passages because of the structural differences between languages. Moreover, the meaning of a single word in one language may not exist in another language, or it may require a phrase, clause, or entire sentence to capture its implications. Adaptations of works offer broader, more open-ended approaches to translation. Unlike a literal translation, an adaptation moves beyond denotative meanings in an attempt to capture the spirit of a work so that its idioms, dialects, slang, and other conventions are re-created in the language of the translation.

The question we ask of an adaptation should not be "Is this exactly how the original reads?" Instead, we ask "Is this an insightful, graceful rendering worth reading?" To translate poetry it is not enough to know the language of the original; it is also necessary that the translator be a poet. A translated poem is more than a collation of decisions based on dictionaries and grammars; it must also be poetry. However undefinable poetry may be, it is unmistakable in its intense use of language. Poems are not merely translated; they are savored.

Three Translations of a Poem by Sappho

Sappho, born about 630 B.C. and a native of the Greek island of Lesbos, is the author of a hymn to Aphrodite, the goddess of love and beauty in Greek myth. The three translations that follow suggest how widely translations can differ from one another. The first, by Henry T. Wharton, is intended to be a literal prose translation of the original Greek.

SAPPHO (CA. 630 B.C.–CA. 570 B.C.)

Immortal Aphrodite of the broidered throne　　*date unknown*

TRANSLATED BY HENRY T. WHARTON (1885)

© Bettmann/CORBIS.

Immortal Aphrodite of the broidered throne, daughter of Zeus, weaver of wiles, I pray thee break not my spirit with anguish and distress, O Queen. But come hither, if ever before thou didst hear my voice afar, and listen, and leaving thy father's golden house camest with chariot yoked, and fair fleet sparrows drew thee, flapping fast their wings around the dark earth, from heaven through mid sky. Quickly arrived they; and thou, blessed one, smiling with immortal countenance, didst ask What now is befallen me, and Why now I call, and What I in my mad heart most desire to see. "What Beauty now wouldst thou draw to love thee? Who wrongs thee, Sappho? For even if she flies she shall soon follow, and if she rejects gifts shall yet give, and if she loves not shall soon love, however loth." Come, I pray thee, now too, and release me from cruel cares; and all that my heart desires to accomplish, accomplish thou, and be thyself my ally.

Beautiful-throned, immortal Aphrodite

TRANSLATED BY THOMAS WENTWORTH HIGGINSON (1871)

Beautiful-throned, immortal Aphrodite,
Daughter of Zeus, beguiler, I implore thee,
Weigh me not down with weariness and anguish
　　　O Thou most holy!

Come to me now, if ever thou in kindness　　　5
Hearkenedst my words, — and often hast thou hearkened —
Heeding, and coming from the mansions golden
　　　Of thy great Father,

Yoking thy chariot, borne by the most lovely
Consecrated birds, with dusky-tinted pinions,   10
Waving swift wings from utmost heights of heaven
      Through the mid-ether;

Swiftly they vanished, leaving thee, O goddess,
Smiling, with face immortal in its beauty,
Asking why I grieved, and why in utter longing   15
      I had dared call thee;

Asking what I sought, thus hopeless in desiring,
Wildered in brain, and spreading nets of passion —
Alas, for whom? and saidst thou, "Who has harmed thee?
      "O my poor Sappho!   20

"Though now he flies, ere long he shall pursue thee;
"Fearing thy gifts, he too in turn shall bring them;
"Loveless to-day, to-morrow he shall woo thee,
      "Though thou shouldst spurn him."

Thus seek me now, O holy Aphrodite!   25
Save me from anguish; give me all I ask for,
Gifts at thy hand; and thine shall be the glory,
      Sacred protector!

Prayer to my lady of Paphos

TRANSLATED BY MARY BARNARD (1958)

Dapple-throned Aphrodite,
eternal daughter of God,
snare-knitter! Don't, I beg you,

cow my heart with grief! Come,
as once when you heard my far-   5
off cry and, listening, stepped

from your father's house to your
gold car, to yoke the pair whose
beautiful thick-feathered wings

oaring down mid-air from heaven   10
carried you to light swiftly
on dark earth; then, blissful one,

smiling your immortal smile
you asked, What ailed me now that
made me call you again? What   15

was it that my distracted
heart most wanted? "Whom has
Persuasion to bring round now

"to your love? Who, Sappho, is
unfair to you? For, let her
run, she will soon run after;   20

"if she won't accept gifts, she
will one day give them; and if
she won't love you — she soon will

"love, although unwillingly...."   25
If ever — come now! Relieve
this intolerable pain!

What my heart most hopes will
happen, make happen; you your-
self join forces on my side!   30

CONSIDERATIONS FOR CRITICAL THINKING AND WRITING

1. **FIRST RESPONSE.** Try rewriting Wharton's prose version in contemporary
   language. How does your prose version differ in tone from Wharton's?
2. Explain which translation seems closest to Wharton's prose version.
3. Discuss the images and metaphors in Higginson's and Barnard's versions.
   Which version is more appealing to you? Explain why.
4. Explain which version seems to you to be the most contemporary in its use
   of language.

Three Translations of a Poem by Pablo Neruda

The following poem by the Chi-
lean Nobel Prize winner Pablo
Neruda is in its original Spanish. By using a substantial
Spanish/English dictionary, you
might be able to translate it
into English even if you are unfamiliar with Spanish. Following the poem are three translations that offer some subtle
and intriguing differences in
their approaches to the poem.

© Luis Poirot.

PABLO NERUDA (1904–1973)
Verbo   *1968*

Voy a arrugar esta palabra,
voy a torcerla,
sí,

es demasiado lisa,
es como si un gran perro o un gran río
le hubíera repasado lengua o agua
durante muchos años.

Quiero que en la palabra
se vea la aspereza,
la sal ferruginosa,
la fuerza desdentada
de la tierra,
la sangre
de los que hablaron y de los que no hablaron.

Quiero ver la sed
adentro de las sílabas:
quiero tocar el fuego
en el sonido:
quiero sentir la oscuridad
del grito. Quiero
palabras ásperas
como piedras vírgenes.

Word

TRANSLATED BY BEN BELITT (1974)

I'm going to crumple this word,
to twist it,
yes,
it's too slick
like a big dog or a river
had been lapping it down with its tongue, or water
had worn it away with the years.

I want gravel
to show in the word,
the ferruginous salt,
the gap-toothed power
of the soil.
There must be a blood-letting
for talker and non-talker alike.

I want to see thirst
in the syllables,
touch fire
in the sound;
feel through the dark
for the scream. Let
my words be acrid
as virginal stone.

Word

TRANSLATED BY KRISTIN LINKLATER (1992)

I'm going to crumple this word,
I'm going to twist it,
yes,
it's too smooth,
it's as though a big dog or a big river
had been licking it over and over with tongue or water   5
for many years.

I want the word
to reveal the roughness,
the ferruginous salt,
the toothless strength   10
of the earth,
the blood
of those who talked and of those who did not talk.

I want to see the thirst   15
inside the syllables,
I want to touch the fire
in the sound:
I want to feel the darkness
of the scream. I want   20
rough words,
like virgin rocks.

Verb

TRANSLATED BY ILAN STAVANS (2003)

I'm going to wrinkle this word,
twist it,
yes,
it's too smooth,
as if the tongue
of a big dog or a big river's water   5
had washed it
for years and years.

I want to see
roughness in the word,
ironlike salt,
earth's   10
toothless strength,
the blood
of those who spoke out and those who didn't.   15

I want to see thirst
deep in its syllables.
I want to touch fire
in the sound.
I want to feel   20
the darkness of a scream.
I want rough words
like virginal stones.

CONSIDERATIONS FOR CRITICAL THINKING AND WRITING

1. **FIRST RESPONSE.** Discuss whether or not all three translations convey the same essential themes.

2. What are the major differences that you see in diction, syntax, and tone among the translations?

3. Explain why you think "Word" or "Verb" is the better title. Does the Spanish/English dictionary affect your opinion, or is your response based solely on the poem?

4. Which translation do you think is the most effective? Explain why you prefer one translation over another.

Web Research the poets in this chapter on LitLinks at bedfordstmartins .com/meyercompact.

21

Images

© Daniel J. Harper.

Between my finger and my thumb
The squat pen rests.
I'll dig with it.
— SEAMUS HEANEY

POETRY'S APPEAL TO THE SENSES

A poet, to borrow a phrase from Henry James, is one on whom nothing is lost. Poets take in the world and give us impressions of what they experience through images. An *image* is language that addresses the senses. The most common images in poetry are visual; they provide verbal pictures of the poets' encounters — real or imagined — with the world. But poets also create images that appeal to our other senses. Li Ho arouses several senses in "A Beautiful Girl Combs Her Hair" (p. 609):

> Awake at dawn
> she's dreaming
> by cool silk curtains
>
> fragrance of spilling hair
> half sandalwood, half aloes
>
> windlass creaking at the well
> singing jade

These vivid images deftly blend textures, fragrances, and sounds that tease out the sensuousness of the moment. Images give us the physical world to experience in our imaginations. Some poems, like the following one, are written to do just that; they make no comment about what they describe.

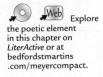

Explore the poetic element in this chapter on *LiterActive* or at bedfordstmartins .com/meyercompact.

William Carlos Williams (1883–1963)

Poem   *1934*

As the cat
climbed over
the top of

the jamcloset   5
first the right
forefoot

carefully
then the hind
stepped down

into the pit of   10
the empty
flowerpot

This poem defies paraphrase because it is all an image of agile movement. No statement is made about the movement; the title, "Poem" — really no title — signals Williams's refusal to comment on the movements. To impose a meaning on the poem, we'd probably have to knock over the flowerpot.

We experience the image in Williams's "Poem" more clearly because of how the sentence is organized into lines and groups of lines, or stanzas. Consider how differently the sentence is read if it is arranged as prose:

> As the cat climbed over the top of the jamcloset, first the right forefoot carefully then the hind stepped down into the pit of the empty flowerpot.

The poem's line and stanza division transforms what is essentially an awkward prose sentence into a rhythmic verbal picture. Especially when the poem is read aloud, this line and stanza division allows us to feel the image we see. Even the lack of a period at the end suggests that the cat is only pausing.

What mood is established in this next poem's view of Civil War troops moving across a river?

WALT WHITMAN (1819–1892)

Cavalry Crossing a Ford

1865

A line in long array where they wind betwixt green
    islands,
They take a serpentine course, their arms flash in the
    sun—hark to the musical clank,
Behold the silvery river, in it the splashing horses
    loitering stop to drink,
Behold the brown-faced men, each group, each person, a picture, the
    negligent rest on the saddles,
Some emerge on the opposite bank, others are just entering the ford—while,
Scarlet and blue and snowy white,
The guidon flags flutter gaily in the wind.

Explore contexts
for Walt Whitman on
LiterActive.

CONSIDERATIONS FOR CRITICAL THINKING AND WRITING

1. **FIRST RESPONSE.** Do the colors and sounds establish the mood of this poem? What *is* the mood?
2. How would the poem's mood have been changed if Whitman had used "look" or "see" instead of "behold" (lines 3–4)?
3. Where is the speaker as he observes this troop movement?
4. Does "serpentine" in line 2 have an evil connotation in this poem? Explain your answer.

Whitman seems to capture momentarily all of the troop's actions, and through carefully chosen, suggestive details—really very few—he succeeds in making "each group, each person, a picture." Specific details, even when few are provided, give us the impression that we see the entire picture; it is as if those are the details we would remember if we had viewed the scene ourselves. Notice, too, that the movement of the "line in long array" is emphasized by the continuous winding syntax of the poem's lengthy lines.

    Movement is also central to the next poem, in which action and motion are created through carefully chosen verbs.

DAVID SOLWAY (B. 1941)

Windsurfing

1993

It rides upon the wrinkled hide
of water, like the upturned hull
of a small canoe or kayak
waiting to be righted—yet its law
is opposite to that of boats,   5
it floats upon its breastbone and
brings whatever spine there is to light.

A thin shaft is slotted into place.
Then a puffed right-angle of wind
pushes it forward, out into the bay,   10
where suddenly it glitters into speed,
tilts, knifes up, and for the moment's
nothing but a slim projectile
of cambered fiberglass,
peeling the crests.   15

           The man's
clamped to the mast, taut as a guywire.
Part of the sleek apparatus
he controls, immaculate nerve
of balance, plunge and curvet,   20
he clinches all component movements
into single motion.
It bucks, stalls, shudders, yaws, and dips
its hissing sides beneath the surface
that sustains it, tensing   25
into muscle that nude ellipse
of lunging appetite and power.

And now the mechanism's wholly
dolphin, springing toward its prey
of spume and beaded sunlight,   30
tossing spray, and hits the vertex
of the wide, salt glare of distance,
and reverses.

                Back it comes through
a screen of particles,   35
scalloped out of water, shimmer
and reflection, the wind snapping
and lashing it homeward,
shearing the curve of the wave,
breaking the spell of the caught breath   40
and articulate play of sinew, to enter
the haven of the breakwater
and settle in a rush of silence.

Now the crossing drifts
in the husk of its wake   45
and nothing's the same again
as, gliding elegantly on a film of water,
the man guides
his brash, obedient legend
into shore.   50

CONSIDERATIONS FOR CRITICAL THINKING AND WRITING

1. **FIRST RESPONSE.** Draw a circle around the verbs that seem especially effective
   in conveying a strong sense of motion, and explain why they are effective.

2. How is the man made to seem to be one with his board and sail?

3. How does the rhythm of the poem change beginning with line 45?

CONNECTIONS TO OTHER SELECTIONS

1. Consider the effects of the images in "Windsurfing" and Li Ho's "A Beautiful Girl Combs Her Hair" (p. 609). In an essay, explain how these images elicit the emotional responses they do.

2. Compare the descriptions in "Windsurfing" and Elizabeth Bishop's "The Fish" (p. 581). How does each poet appeal to your senses to describe windsurfing and fishing?

"Windsurfing" is awash with images of speed, fluidity, and power. Even the calming aftermath of the breakwater is described as a "rush of silence," adding to the sense of motion that is detailed and expanded throughout the poem.

Poets choose details the way they choose the words to present those details: only telling ones will do. Consider the images Theodore Roethke uses in "Root Cellar."

> Explore contexts
> for Theodore Roethke
> on *LiterActive*.

THEODORE ROETHKE (1908–1963)

Root Cellar　　　　　　　　　　　　　　　*1948*

Nothing would sleep in that cellar, dank as a ditch,
Bulbs broke out of boxes hunting for chinks in the dark,
Shoots dangled and drooped,
Lolling obscenely from mildewed crates,
Hung down long yellow evil necks, like tropical snakes.　　　5
And what a congress of stinks!
Roots ripe as old bait,
Pulpy stems, rank, silo-rich,
Leaf-mold, manure, lime, piled against slippery planks.
Nothing would give up life:
Even the dirt kept breathing a small breath.　　　　　　10

CONSIDERATIONS FOR CRITICAL THINKING AND WRITING

1. **FIRST RESPONSE.** Explain why you think this is a positive or negative rendition of a root cellar.

2. What senses are engaged by the images in this poem? Is the poem simply a series of sensations, or do the detailed images make some kind of point about the root cellar?

3. What controls the choice of details in the poem? Why isn't there, for example, a rusty shovel leaning against a dirt wall or a worn gardener's glove atop one of the crates?

4. Look up *congress* in a dictionary for its denotative meanings. Explain why "congress of stinks" is especially appropriate given the nature of the rest of the poem's imagery.

5. What single line in the poem suggests a theme?

6. **CREATIVE RESPONSE.** Try writing a poem of ten lines or so that consists of a series of evocative images that creates a strong impression about something you know well.

The tone of the images and mood of the speaker are consistent in Roethke's "Root Cellar." In Matthew Arnold's "Dover Beach," however, they shift as the theme is developed.

MATTHEW ARNOLD (1822–1888)

Dover Beach   *1867*

The sea is calm tonight.
The tide is full, the moon lies fair
Upon the straits; — on the French coast the light
Gleams and is gone; the cliffs of England stand,
Glimmering and vast, out in the tranquil bay.   5
Come to the window, sweet is the night-air!
Only, from the long line of spray
Where the sea meets the moon-blanched land,
Listen! you hear the grating roar
Of pebbles which the waves draw back, and fling,   10
At their return, up the high strand,
Begin, and cease, and then again begin,
With tremulous cadence slow, and bring
The eternal note of sadness in.

Sophocles long ago   15
Heard it on the Aegean, and it brought
Into his mind the turbid ebb and flow
Of human misery;° we
Find also in the sound a thought,
Hearing it by this distant northern sea.   20

The Sea of Faith
Was once, too, at the full, and round earth's shore
Lay like the folds of a bright girdle furled.
But now I only hear
Its melancholy, long, withdrawing roar,   25
Retreating, to the breath
Of the night-wind, down the vast edges drear
And naked shingles° of the world.   *pebble beaches*

Ah, love, let us be true
To one another! for the world, which seems   30

15-18 *Sophocles ... misery:* In *Antigone* (lines 656-77), Sophocles likens the disasters that beset the house of Oedipus to a "mounting tide."

To lie before us like a land of dreams,
So various, so beautiful, so new,
Hath really neither joy, nor love, nor light,
Nor certitude, nor peace, nor help for pain;
And we are here as on a darkling plain   35
Swept with confused alarms of struggle and flight,
Where ignorant armies clash by night.

CONSIDERATIONS FOR CRITICAL THINKING AND WRITING

1. **FIRST RESPONSE.** Discuss what you consider to be this poem's central point.
   How do the speaker's descriptions of the ocean work toward making that
   point?

2. Contrast the images in lines 4–8 and 9–13. How do they reveal the speaker's
   mood? To whom is he speaking?

3. What is the cause of the "sadness" in line 14? What is the speaker's response to the ebbing "Sea of Faith"? Is there anything to replace his sense
   of loss?

4. What details of the beach seem related to the ideas in the poem? How is the
   sea used differently in lines 1–14 and 21–28?

5. Describe the differences in tone between lines 1–8 and 35–37. What has
   caused the change?

6. **CRITICAL STRATEGIES.** Read the section on mythological strategies (pp.
   1550–52) in Chapter 46, "Critical Strategies for Reading," and discuss how
   you think a mythological critic might make use of the allusion to Sophocles
   in this poem.

CONNECTION TO ANOTHER SELECTION

1. Explain how the images in Wilfred Owen's "Dulce et Decorum Est" (p. 671)
   develop further the ideas and sentiments suggested by Arnold's final line
   concerning "ignorant armies clash[ing] by night."

Consider the poetic appetite for images displayed in the celebration of
chile peppers in the following passionate poem.

JIMMY SANTIAGO BACA (B. 1952)

Green Chile   *1989*

I prefer red chile over my eggs
and potatoes for breakfast.
Red chile *ristras*° decorate my door,   *a braided string of peppers*
dry on my roof, and hang from eaves.
They lend open-air vegetable stands   5
historical grandeur, and gently swing
with an air of festive welcome.

I can hear them talking in the wind,
haggard, yellowing, crisp, rasping
tongues of old men, licking the breeze.   10

        But grandmother loves green chile.
When I visit her,
she holds the green chile pepper
in her wrinkled hands.
Ah, voluptuous, masculine,   15
an air of authority and youth simmers
from its swan-neck stem, tapering to a flowery
collar, fermenting resinous spice.
A well-dressed gentleman at the door
my grandmother takes sensuously in her hand,   20
rubbing its firm glossed sides,
caressing the oily rubbery serpent,
with mouth-watering fulfillment,
fondling its curves with gentle fingers.
Its bearing magnificent and taut   25
as flanks of a tiger in mid-leap,
she thrusts her blade into
and cuts it open, with lust
on her hot mouth, sweating over the stove,
bandanna round her forehead,   30
mysterious passion on her face
and she serves me green chile con carne
between soft warm leaves of corn tortillas,
with beans and rice — her sacrifice
to her little prince.   35
I slurp from my plate
with last bit of tortilla, my mouth burns
and I hiss and drink a tall glass of cold water.

All over New Mexico, sunburned men and women
drive rickety trucks stuffed with gunny-sacks   40
of green chile, from Belen, Veguita, Willard, Estancia,
San Antonio y Socorro, from fields
to roadside stands, you see them roasting green chile
in screen-sided homemade barrels, and for a dollar a bag,
we relive this old, beautiful ritual again and again.   45

CONSIDERATIONS FOR CRITICAL THINKING AND WRITING

1. **FIRST RESPONSE.** What's the difference between red and green chiles in this poem? Find the different images the speaker uses to distinguish between the two.

2. What kinds of images are used to describe the grandmother's preparation of green chile? What is the effect of those images?

3. **CREATIVE RESPONSE.** Try writing a description — in poetry or prose — that uses vivid images to evoke a powerful response (either positive or negative) to a particular food.

POEMS FOR FURTHER STUDY

AMY LOWELL (1874–1925)

The Pond

1919

Cold, wet leaves
Floating on moss-colored water,
And the croaking of frogs—
Cracked bell-notes in the twilight.

CONSIDERATIONS FOR CRITICAL THINKING AND WRITING

1. **FIRST RESPONSE.** This poem is not a complete sentence. What is missing? Does it matter in terms of understanding what is described by the images?

2. What senses are stimulated by the images? Which sense seems to be the most dominant in the poem? Why?

3. **CREATIVE RESPONSE.** Is the title of the poem necessary to convey its meaning? Choose an appropriate alternate title and explain how it subtly suggests something different from "The Pond."

SHEILA WINGFIELD (1906–1992)

A Bird

1983

Unexplained
In the salt meadow
Lay the dead bird.
The wind
Was fluttering its wings.

CONSIDERATIONS FOR CRITICAL THINKING AND WRITING

1. **FIRST RESPONSE.** How does each line of this poem contribute to the overall tone?

2. What is the effect of the last line?

3. **CREATIVE RESPONSE.** Try writing a five-line poem—using Wingfield's as a model—that establishes a light, optimistic tone about a bird by way of vivid images.

MARY ROBINSON (1758–1800)

London's Summer Morning

1806

Who has not wak'd to list° the busy sounds   *listen to*
Of summer's morning, in the sultry smoke
Of noisy London? On the pavement hot
The sooty chimney-boy, with dingy face

And tatter'd covering, shrilly bawls his trade,   5
Rousing the sleepy housemaid. At the door
The milk-pail rattles, and the tinkling bell
Proclaims the dustman's office; while the street
Is lost in clouds impervious. Now begins
The din of hackney-coaches, waggons, carts;   10
While tinmen's shops, and noisy trunk-makers,
Knife-grinders, coopers, squeaking cork-cutters,
Fruit-barrows, and the hunger-giving cries
Of vegetable venders, fill the air.
Now ev'ry shop displays its varied trade,   15
And the fresh-sprinkled pavement cools the feet
Of early walkers. At the private door
The ruddy housemaid twirls the busy mop,
Annoying the smart 'prentice, or neat girl,
Tripping with band-box° lightly. Now the sun   *hat box*   20
Darts burning splendour on the glitt'ring pane,
Save where the canvas awning throws a shade
On the gay merchandize. Now, spruce and trim,
In shops (where beauty smiles with industry,)
Sits the smart damsel; while the passenger   25
Peeps thro' the window, watching ev'ry charm.
Now pastry dainties catch the eye minute
Of humming insects, while the limy snare
Waits to enthral them. Now the lamp-lighter
Mounts the tall ladder, nimbly vent'rous,   30
To trim the half-fill'd lamp; while at his feet
The pot-boy° yells discordant! All along   *drink server*
The sultry pavement, the old-clothes-man cries
In tones monotonous, and side-long views
The area for his traffic: now the bag   35
Is slily open'd, and the half-worn suit
(Sometimes the pilfer'd treasure of the base
Domestic spoiler), for one half its worth,
Sinks in the green abyss. The porter now
Bears his huge load along the burning way;   40
And the poor poet wakes from busy dreams,
To paint the summer morning.

CONSIDERATIONS FOR CRITICAL THINKING AND WRITING

1. **FIRST RESPONSE.** How effective is this picture of a London summer morning in 1806? Which images do you find particularly effective?

2. How does the end of the poem bring us full circle to its beginning? What
   effect does this structure have on your understanding of the poem?

3. **CREATIVE RESPONSE.** Try writing about the start of your own day—in the
   dormitory, at home, the start of a class—using a series of images that provide a vivid sense of what happens and how you experience it.

CONNECTION TO ANOTHER SELECTION

1. How does Robinson's description of London differ from that in William Blake's "London," the next poem? What would you say is the essential difference in purpose between the two poems?

WILLIAM BLAKE (1757–1827)

London   *1794*

I wander through each chartered° street,   *defined by law*
Near where the chartered Thames does flow,
And mark in every face I meet
Marks of weakness, marks of woe.

In every cry of every man,   5
In every Infant's cry of fear,
In every voice, in every ban,
The mind-forged manacles I hear.

How the Chimney-sweeper's cry
Every black'ning Church appalls;   10
And the hapless Soldier's sigh
Runs in blood down Palace walls.

But most through midnight streets I hear
How the youthful Harlot's curse
Blasts the new-born Infant's tear,   15
And blights with plagues the Marriage hearse.

CONSIDERATIONS FOR CRITICAL THINKING AND WRITING

1. **FIRST RESPONSE.** What feelings do the visual images in this poem suggest to you?

2. What is the predominant sound heard in the poem?

3. What is the meaning of line 8? What is the cause of the problems that the speaker sees and hears in London? Does the speaker suggest additional causes?

4. The image in lines 11 and 12 cannot be read literally. Comment on its effectiveness.

5. How does Blake's use of denotative and connotative language enrich this poem's meaning?

6. An earlier version of Blake's last stanza appeared this way:

> But most the midnight harlot's curse
> From every dismal street I hear,
> Weaves around the marriage hearse
> And blasts the new-born infant's tear.

Examine carefully the differences between the two versions. How do Blake's revisions affect his picture of London life? Which version do you think is more effective? Why?

A SAMPLE STUDENT RESPONSE

Anna Tamara

Professor Burton

English 211

September 30, 2008

Imagery in William Blake's "London" and Mary Robinson's

"London's Summer Morning"

Both William Blake and Mary Robinson use strong imagery to examine and bring to life the city of London, yet each writer paints a very different picture. The images in both poems "[address] the senses," as Meyer writes (659). But while Blake's images depict a city weighed down by oppression and poverty, Robinson's images are lighter, happier, and, arguably, idealized. Both poems use powerful imagery in very different ways to establish theme.

In Blake's poem, oppression and social discontent are defined by the speaker, who sees "weakness" and "woe" (line 4) in the faces he meets; he hears cries of men and children and "mind-forged manacles" (8). And, through imagery, the poem makes a political statement:

> How the Chimney-sweeper's cry
>
> Every black'ning Church appalls
>
> And the hapless Soldier's sigh
>
> Runs in blood down Palace walls. (9-12)

These images indicate the speaker's dark view of the religious and governmental institutions that he believes cause the city's suffering. The "black'ning Church" and bloody "Palace walls" can be seen to represent misused power and corruption, while the "manacles" are the rules and physical and psychological burdens that lead to societal ills. In Blake's view of London, children are sold into servitude (as chimney sweeps) and soldiers pay in blood.

Robinson's poem, on the other hand, offers the reader a pleasant view of a sunny London morning through a different series of images. The reader hears "the tinkling bell" (7) and sees a bright moment in which "the sun / Darts burning splendour on the glitt'ring pane" (20-21). Even the chimney-boy is shown in a rosy glow. Though he is described as having a "dingy face /

Tamara 2

and tatter'd covering," he wakes the "sleepy" house servant when he "shrilly

bawls his trade" (4-6). In contrast to the chimney-sweep of Blake's "Lon-

don," Robinson's boy is painted as a charming character who announces the

morning amid a backdrop of happy workers. Also unlike Blake's London,

Robinson's is a city of contentment in which a "ruddy housemaid twirls the

busy mop" (18) . . .

Tamara 3

Works Cited

Blake, William. "London." The Compact Bedford Introduction to Literature.

   Ed. Michael Meyer. 8th ed. Boston: Bedford/St. Martin's, 2009. 669.

Meyer, Michael, ed. The Compact Bedford Introduction to Literature. 8th ed.

   Boston: Bedford/St. Martin's, 2009. 659.

Robinson, Mary. "London's Summer Morning." The Compact Bedford Intro-

   duction to Literature. Ed. Michael Meyer. 8th ed. Boston: Bedford/

   St. Martin's, 2009. 667–68.

WILFRED OWEN (1893–1918)

Dulce et Decorum Est   *1920*

Bent double, like old beggars under sacks,
Knock-kneed, coughing like hags, we cursed through
   sludge,
Till on the haunting flares we turned our backs,
And towards our distant rest began to trudge.

Men marched asleep. Many had lost their boots,   5
But limped on, blood-shod. All went lame, all blind;
Drunk with fatigue; deaf even to the hoots
Of gas-shells dropping softly behind.

Gas! GAS! Quick, boys! — An ecstasy of fumbling,
Fitting the clumsy helmets just in time,   10
But someone still was yelling out and stumbling

> Explore contexts
> for Wilfred Owen
> on *LiterActive*.

And flound'ring like a man in fire or lime. —
Dim through the misty panes and thick green light,
As under a green sea, I saw him drowning.

In all my dreams before my helpless sight   15
He plunges at me, guttering, choking, drowning.

If in some smothering dreams, you too could pace
Behind the wagon that we flung him in,
And watch the white eyes writhing in his face,
His hanging face, like a devil's sick of sin,   20
If you could hear, at every jolt, the blood
Come gargling from the froth-corrupted lungs
Bitter as the cud
Obscene as cancer,
Of vile, incurable sores on innocent tongues, —   25
My friend, you would not tell with such high zest
To children ardent for some desperate glory,
The old lie: *Dulce et decorum est*
Pro patria mori.

CONSIDERATIONS FOR CRITICAL THINKING AND WRITING

1. **FIRST RESPONSE.** The Latin quotation in lines 28 and 29 is from Horace: "It is sweet and fitting to die for one's country." Owen served as a British soldier during World War I and was killed. Is this poem unpatriotic? What is its purpose?

2. Which images in the poem are the most vivid? To which senses do they speak?

3. Describe the speaker's tone. What is his relationship to his audience?

4. How are the images of the soldiers in this poem different from the images that typically appear in recruiting posters?

PATRICIA SMITH (B. 1955)

What It's Like to Be a Black Girl
(for Those of You Who Aren't)   *1991*

First of all, it's being 9 years old and
feeling like you're not finished, like your
edges are wild, like there's something,
everything, wrong. it's dropping food coloring
in your eyes to make them blue and suffering   5
their burn in silence. it's popping a bleached
white mophead over the kinks of your hair and
primping in front of the mirrors that deny your
reflection. it's finding a space between your

legs, a disturbance at your chest, and not knowing   10
what to do with the whistles. it's jumping
double dutch until your legs pop, it's sweat
and vaseline and bullets, it's growing tall and
wearing a lot of white, it's smelling blood in
your breakfast, it's learning to say fuck with   15
grace but learning to fuck without it, it's
flame and fists and life according to motown,
it's finally having a man reach out for you
then caving in
around his fingers.   20

CONSIDERATIONS FOR CRITICAL THINKING AND WRITING

1. **FIRST RESPONSE.** Describe the speaker's tone. What images in particular contribute to it? How do you account for the selected tone?

2. How does the speaker characterize her life? On which elements of it does she focus?

3. Discuss the poem's final image. What sort of emotions does it elicit in you?

CHARLES SIMIC (B. 1938)

To the One Upstairs   *1999*

Boss of all bosses of the universe.
Mr know-it-all, wheeler-dealer, wire-puller,
And whatever else you're good at.
Go ahead, shuffle your zeros tonight.
Dip in ink the comets' tails.   5
Staple the night with starlight.

You'd be better off reading coffee dregs,
Thumbing the pages of the Farmer's Almanac.
But no! You love to put on airs,
And cultivate your famous serenity   10
While you sit behind your big desk
With zilch in your in-tray, zilch
In your out-tray,
And all of eternity around you.

Doesn't it give you the creeps   15
To hear them begging you on their knees,
Sputtering endearments,
As if you were an inflatable, life-size doll?
Tell them to button up and go to bed.
Stop pretending you're too busy to notice.   20

Your hands are empty and so are your eyes.
There's nothing to put your signature to,
Even if you knew your own name,
Or believed the ones I keep inventing,
As I scribble this note to you in the dark.   25

CONSIDERATIONS FOR CRITICAL THINKING AND WRITING

1. **FIRST RESPONSE.** Describe the speaker's relationship to the "Boss of all bosses." What do you think of that relationship?

2. What images are associated with God in the poem? Describe the sort of character and personality that the speaker attributes to God.

3. How do the final two lines affect your reading of the poem?

CONNECTION TO ANOTHER SELECTION

1. Discuss the themes in Simic's poem and in Emily Dickinson's "I know that He exists" (p. 868).

RAINER MARIA RILKE (1875–1926)

The Panther   *1927*

TRANSLATED BY STEPHEN MITCHELL

His vision, from the constantly passing bars,
has grown so weary that it cannot hold
anything else. It seems to him there are
a thousand bars; and behind the bars, no world.

As he paces in cramped circles, over and over,   5
the movement of his powerful soft strides
is like a ritual dance around a center
in which a mighty will stands paralyzed.

Only at times, the curtain of the pupils
lifts, quietly — . An image enters in,   10
rushes down through the tensed, arrested muscles,
plunges into the heart and is gone.

CONSIDERATIONS FOR CRITICAL THINKING AND WRITING

1. **FIRST RESPONSE.** Why do you think Rilke chooses a panther rather than, say, a lion as the subject of the poem's images?

2. What kind of "image enters in" the heart of the panther in the final stanza?

3. How are images of confinement achieved in the poem? Why doesn't Rilke describe the final image in lines 10–12?

CONNECTION TO ANOTHER SELECTION

1. Write an essay explaining how a sense of movement is achieved by the images and rhythms in this poem and in Dickinson's "A Bird came down the Walk—" (p. 729).

SALLY CROFT (1935–2006)

Home-Baked Bread   *1981*

Nothing gives a household a greater sense of stability and common comfort than the aroma of cooling bread. Begin, if you like, with a loaf of whole wheat, which requires neither sifting nor kneading, and go on from there to more cunning triumphs.

— *The Joy of Cooking*

What is it she is not saying?
Cunning triumphs. It rings
of insinuation. Step into my kitchen,
I have prepared a cunning triumph
for you. Spices and herbs   5
sealed in this porcelain jar,

a treasure of my great-aunt
who sat up past midnight
in her Massachusetts bedroom
when the moon was dark. Come,   10
rest your feet. I'll make
you tea with honey and slices

of warm bread spread with peach butter.
I picked the fruit this morning
still fresh with dew. The fragrance   15
is seductive? I hoped you would say that.
See how the heat rises
when the bread opens. Come,

we'll eat together, the small flakes
have scarcely any flavor. What cunning   20
triumphs we can discover in my upstairs room
where peach trees breathe their sweetness
beside the open window and
sun lies like honey on the floor.

CONSIDERATIONS FOR CRITICAL THINKING AND WRITING

1. FIRST RESPONSE. Why does the speaker in this poem seize on the phrase "cunning triumphs" from the *Joy of Cooking* excerpt?

2. Distinguish between the voice we hear in lines 1–3 and the second voice in lines 3–24. Who is the "you" in the poem?

3. Why is the word "insinuation" an especially appropriate choice in line 3?

4. How do the images in lines 20–24 bring together all of the senses evoked in the preceding lines?

5. **CREATIVE RESPONSE.** Write a paragraph — or stanza — that describes the sensuous (and perhaps sensual) qualities of a food you enjoy.

JOHN KEATS (1795–1821)

To Autumn   *1819*

Explore contexts
for John Keats
on *LiterActive.*

I

Season of mists and mellow fruitfulness,
    Close bosom-friend of the maturing sun;
Conspiring with him how to load and bless
    With fruit the vines that round the thatch-eves run;
To bend with apples the mossed cottage-trees,   5
    And fill all fruit with ripeness to the core;
        To swell the gourd, and plump the hazel shells
    With a sweet kernel; to set budding more,
And still more, later flowers for the bees,
Until they think warm days will never cease,   10
        For summer has o'er-brimmed their clammy cells.

II

Who hath not seen thee oft amid thy store?
    Sometimes whoever seeks abroad may find
Thee sitting careless on a granary floor,
    Thy hair soft-lifted by the winnowing wind;   15
Or on a half-reaped furrow sound asleep,
    Drowsed with the fume of poppies, while thy hook°   *scythe*
        Spares the next swath and all its twinèd flowers:
And sometimes like a gleaner thou dost keep
    Steady thy laden head across a brook;   20
    Or by a cider-press, with patient look,
        Thou watchest the last oozings hours by hours.

III

Where are the songs of spring? Ay, where are they?
    Think not of them, thou hast thy music too —
While barred clouds bloom the soft-dying day,   25
    And touch the stubble-plains with rosy hue;
Then in a wailful choir the small gnats mourn
    Among the river swallows,° borne aloft   *willows*
        Or sinking as the light wind lives or dies;

And full-grown lambs loud bleat from hilly bourn;°   *territory*   30
   Hedge-crickets sing; and now with treble soft
   The redbreast whistles from a garden-croft,
     And gathering swallows twitter in the skies.

CONSIDERATIONS FOR CRITICAL THINKING AND WRITING

1. **FIRST RESPONSE.** How is autumn made to seem like a person in each stanza of this ode?
2. Which senses are most emphasized in each stanza?
3. How is the progression of time expressed in the ode?
4. How does the imagery convey tone? Which words have particularly strong connotative values?
5. What is the speaker's view of death?

CONNECTIONS TO OTHER SELECTIONS

1. Compare this poem's tone and perspective on death with those of Robert Frost's "After Apple-Picking" (p. 889).
2. Write an essay comparing the significance of this poem's images of "mellow fruitfulness" (line 1) with that of the images of ripeness in Theodore Roethke's "Root Cellar" (p. 663). Explain how the images in each poem lead to very different feelings about the same phenomenon.

KATE CLANCHY (B. 1965)

Spell   1999

If, at your desk, you push aside your work,
take down a book, turn to this verse
and read that I kneel there, pressing
my ear where on your chest the muscles
arch as great books part, in seagull curves,   5
bridging the seasounds of your heart,

and that your hands run through my hair,
draw the wayward mass to strands
as flat as scarlet silk-thread bookmarks,
and stroke my cheeks as if smoothing   10
back the tissue leaves from chilly,
plated pages, and pull me near

to read my eyes alone, then you shall see,
silvered and monochrome, yourself,
sitting at your desk, taking down a book,   15
turning to this verse, and then, my love,
you shall not know which one of us is reading
now, which writing, and which written.

CONSIDERATIONS FOR CRITICAL THINKING AND WRITING

1. **FIRST RESPONSE.** How does Clanchy cast a kind of spell through her use of images as she describes this relationship?

2. Trace how images of books are used in each stanza. Which image do you find to be the most strikingly effective?

3. Discuss the significance of the final two lines.

CONNECTION TO ANOTHER SELECTION

1. Compare "Spell" and Dickinson's "There is no Frigate like a Book" (p. 857) on the act of reading. Which poem do you think is more demanding of the reader? Explain why.

EZRA POUND (1885–1972)

In a Station of the Metro°   1913

The apparition of these faces in the crowd;
Petals on a wet, black bough.

Metro: Underground railroad in Paris.

CONSIDERATIONS FOR CRITICAL THINKING AND WRITING

1. **FIRST RESPONSE.** Why is the title essential for this poem?

2. What kind of mood does the image in the second line convey?

3. Why is "apparition" a better word choice than, say, "appearance" or "sight"?

4. **CREATIVE RESPONSE.** Write a two-line vivid image for a poem titled "At a Desk in the Library."

CHARLES R. FELDSTEIN (B. 1947)

Maddie Clifton, 1990–1998   2003

The weeklong search for Maddie Clifton ended yesterday, when a teenage neighbor was charged with fatally beating and stabbing the Jacksonville 8-year-old, then hiding her body inside his water bed across the street from her Southside home.

Wednesday, November 11, 1998
The Florida Times-Union

Mama and I would walk along the river's edge
and watch the water shimmer when it caught the sun.
Mama would say I was like that light reflected in the water,
a flame in the tide.

I remember most Mama's voice,   5
how it was the wind, how the wind
always breathed my name, Maddie, Maddie Clifton,
how it always called to me to come home,
and the one time when I didn't and didn't and didn't,
the wind went wild trying to find me.   10

Most nights now Mama dreams me alive,
and the two of us are walking by the river.
But a boy steals the river, pours it into something
he can sleep on, and Mama screams herself awake
to wade through the darkness of her room,   15
feeling the way with her fingertips
to my picture on the dresser,
her fingers tracing the glass,
light draining out of her,
until she is empty and silent and still,   20
knowing that she and I
are forever in a dark place,
one without a flame in the tide.

Considerations for Critical Thinking and Writing

1. **FIRST RESPONSE.** What is the effect of the speaker of the poem being an eight-year-old murder victim? How do you think the effect of this poem would be different if the mother were the speaker?

2. Discuss how the images of water and light create meaning in the poem.

3. How would your reading of the poem be affected by the absence of the newspaper excerpt?

Connection to Another Selection

1. Compare the treatment of loss and grief in "Maddie Clifton, 1990–1998" and in Rachel Loden's "Locked Ward: Newtown, Connecticut" (p. 1004).

Perspective

T. E. Hulme (1883–1917)

On the Differences between Poetry and Prose   1924

In prose as in algebra concrete things are embodied in signs or counters which are moved about according to rules, without being visualized at all in the process. There are in prose certain type situations and arrangements of words, which move as automatically into certain other arrangements as do functions in algebra. One only changes the X's and the Y's back into physical things at the end of the process. Poetry, in one aspect at any rate, may be considered as an effort to avoid this characteristic of prose. It is not a counter language, but a visual concrete one. It is a compromise for a language of intuition which would hand over sensations bodily. It always endeavors to arrest you, and to make you continuously see a physical thing, to prevent you gliding through an abstract process. It chooses fresh epithets and fresh metaphors, not so much because they are new, and we are tired of the old, but because the old cease to convey a physical thing and become abstract counters. A poet says a ship "coursed the seas" to get a physical image, instead of the counter word "sailed." Visual meanings can only be transferred by the new bowl of metaphor; prose is an old pot that lets them leak out. Images in verse are not mere decoration, but the very essence of an intuitive language. Verse is a pedestrian taking you over the ground, prose — a train which delivers you at a destination.

From "Romanticism and Classicism," in *Speculations,*
edited by Herbert Read

CONSIDERATIONS FOR CRITICAL THINKING AND WRITING

1. What distinctions does Hulme make between poetry and prose? Which seems to be the most important difference?

2. Write an essay that discusses Hulme's claim that poetry "is a compromise for a language of intuition which would hand over sensations bodily."

Web Research the poets in this chapter at bedfordstmartins.com/ meyercompact.

22

Figures of Speech

Like a piece of ice on a hot stove the
poem must ride on its own melting.
— ROBERT FROST

Courtesy of Rauner Special
Collections Library,
Dartmouth College.

Figures of speech are broadly defined as a way of saying one thing in terms of something else. An overeager funeral director might, for example, be described as a vulture. Although figures of speech are indirect, they are designed to clarify, not obscure, our understanding of what they describe. Poets frequently use them because, as Emily Dickinson said, the poet's work is to "tell all the Truth but tell it slant" to capture the reader's interest and imagination. But figures of speech are not limited to poetry. Hearing them, reading them, or using them is as natural as using language itself.

Suppose that in the middle of a class discussion concerning the economic causes of World War II your history instructor introduces a series of statistics by saying, "Let's get down to brass tacks." Would anyone be likely to expect a display of brass tacks for students to examine? Of course not. To interpret the statement literally would be to wholly misunderstand the instructor's point that the time has come for a close look at the economic conditions leading to the war. A literal response transforms the statement into the sort of hilariously bizarre material often found in a sketch by Woody Allen.

The class does not look for brass tacks because, in a nutshell, they understand that the instructor is speaking figuratively. They would understand, too, that in the preceding sentence "in a nutshell" refers to brevity and conciseness rather than to the covering of a kernel of a nut. Figurative language makes its way into our everyday speech and writing as well as into literature because it is a means of achieving color, vividness, and intensity.

Consider the difference, for example, between these two statements:

Literal: The diner strongly expressed anger at the waiter.
Figurative: The diner leaped from his table and roared at the waiter.

The second statement is more vivid because it creates a picture of ferocious anger by likening the diner to some kind of wild animal, such as a lion or tiger. By comparison, "strongly expressed anger" is neither especially strong nor especially expressive; it is flat. Not all figurative language avoids this kind of flatness, however. Figures of speech such as "getting down to brass tacks" and "in a nutshell" are clichés because they lack originality and freshness. Still, they suggest how these devices are commonly used to give language some color, even if that color is sometimes a bit faded.

There is nothing weak about William Shakespeare's use of figurative language in the following passage from *Macbeth*. Macbeth has just learned that his wife is dead, and he laments her loss as well as the course of his own life.

WILLIAM SHAKESPEARE (1564–1616)

From Macbeth *(Act V, Scene v)*   *1605–1606*

Tomorrow, and tomorrow, and tomorrow
Creeps in this petty pace from day to day
To the last syllable of recorded time;
And all our yesterdays have lighted fools
The way to dusty death. Out, out, brief candle!   5
Life's but a walking shadow, a poor player,
That struts and frets his hour upon the stage,
And then is heard no more. It is a tale
Told by an idiot, full of sound and fury,
Signifying nothing.   10

This passage might be summarized as "life has no meaning," but such a brief paraphrase does not take into account the figurative language that reveals the depth of Macbeth's despair and his view of the absolute meaninglessness of life. By comparing life to a "brief candle," Macbeth emphasizes the darkness and death that surround human beings. The light of life is too brief and unpredictable to be of any comfort. Indeed, life for Macbeth is a "walking shadow," futilely playing a role that is more farcical than dramatic, because life is, ultimately, a desperate story filled with pain and devoid of significance. What the figurative language provides, then, is the emotional force of Macbeth's assertion; his comparisons are disturbing because they are so apt.

The remainder of this chapter discusses some of the most important figures of speech used in poetry. A familiarity with them will help you to understand how poetry achieves its effects.

SIMILE AND METAPHOR

The two most common figures of speech are simile and metaphor. Both compare things that are ordinarily considered unlike each other. A *simile* makes an explicit comparison between two things by using words such as *like, as, than, appears,* or *seems:* "A sip of Mrs. Cook's coffee is like a punch in the stomach." The force of the simile is created by the differences between the two things compared. There would be no simile if the comparison were stated this way: "Mrs. Cook's coffee is as strong as the cafeteria's coffee." This is a literal comparison because Mrs. Cook's coffee is compared with something like it, another kind of coffee. Consider how simile is used in this poem.

Explore the poetic elements in this chapter on *LiterActive* or at bedfordstmartins .com/meyercompact.

© Kathy deWitt/Alamy.

MARGARET ATWOOD (B. 1939)

you fit into me   *1971*

you fit into me
like a hook into an eye

a fish hook
an open eye

If you blinked on a second reading, you got the point of this poem because you recognized that the simile "like a hook into an eye" gives way to a play on words in the final two lines. There the hook and eye, no longer a pleasant domestic image of fitting closely together, become a literal, sharp fishhook and a human eye. The wordplay qualifies the simile and drastically alters the tone of this poem by creating a strong and unpleasant surprise.

A *metaphor,* like a simile, makes a comparison between two unlike things, but it does so implicitly, without words such as *like* or *as:* "Mrs. Cook's coffee is a punch in the stomach." Metaphor asserts the identity of dissimilar things. Macbeth tells us that life *is* a "brief candle," life *is* "a walking shadow," life *is* "a poor player," life *is* "a tale / Told by an idiot." Metaphor transforms people, places, objects, and ideas into whatever the poet imagines them to be, and if metaphors are effective, the reader's experience, understanding, and appreciation of what is described are enhanced. Metaphors are frequently more demanding than similes because they are not signaled by particular words. They are both subtle and powerful.

Here is a poem about presentiment, a foreboding that something terrible is about to happen.

EMILY DICKINSON (1830–1886)

Presentiment — is that long Shadow — on the lawn —

ca. 1863

Presentiment — is that long Shadow — on the lawn —
Indicative that Suns go down —

The notice to the startled Grass
That Darkness — is about to pass —

The metaphors in this poem define the abstraction "Presentiment." The sense of foreboding that Dickinson expresses is identified with a particular moment — the moment when darkness is just about to envelop an otherwise tranquil, ordinary scene. The speaker projects that fear onto the "startled Grass" so that it seems any life must be frightened by the approaching "Shadow" and "Darkness" — two richly connotative words associated with death. The metaphors obliquely tell us ("tell it slant" was Dickinson's motto, remember) that presentiment is related to a fear of death, and, more important, the metaphors convey the feelings that attend that idea.

Some metaphors are more subtle than others because their comparison of terms is less explicit. Notice the difference between the following two metaphors, both of which describe a shaggy derelict refusing to leave the warmth of a hotel lobby: "He was a mule standing his ground" is a quite explicit comparison. The man is a mule; X is Y. But this metaphor is much more covert: "He brayed his refusal to leave." This second version is an *implied metaphor* because it does not explicitly identify the man with a mule. Instead it hints at or alludes to the mule. Braying is associated with mules and is especially appropriate in this context because of those animals' reputation for stubbornness. Implied metaphors can slip by readers, but they offer the alert reader the energy and resonance of carefully chosen, highly concentrated language.

Some poets write extended comparisons in which part or all of the poem consists of a series of related metaphors or similes. Extended metaphors are more common than extended similes. In "Catch" (p. 576), Robert Francis creates an **extended metaphor** that compares poetry to a game of catch. The entire poem is organized around this comparison, just as all of the elements in E. E. Cummings's "she being Brand" (p. 627) are clustered around the extended comparison of a car and a woman. Because these comparisons are at work throughout the entire poem, they are called **controlling metaphors.** Extended comparisons can serve as a poem's organizing principle; they are also a reminder that in good poems metaphor and simile are not merely decorative but inseparable from what is expressed.

Notice the controlling metaphor in this poem, published posthumously by a woman whose contemporaries identified her more as a wife and mother than as a poet. Bradstreet's first volume of poetry, *The Tenth Muse,* was published by her brother-in-law in 1650 without her prior knowledge.

ANNE BRADSTREET (CA. 1612–1672)

The Author to Her Book   *1678*

Thou ill-formed offspring of my feeble brain,
Who after birth did'st by my side remain,
Till snatched from thence by friends, less wise than true,
Who thee abroad exposed to public view;
Made thee in rags, halting, to the press to trudge,   5
Where errors were not lessened, all may judge.
At thy return my blushing was not small,
My rambling brat (in print) should mother call;
I cast thee by as one unfit for light,
Thy visage was so irksome in my sight;   10
Yet being mine own, at length affection would
Thy blemishes amend, if so I could:
I washed thy face, but more defects I saw,
And rubbing off a spot, still made a flaw.
I stretched thy joints to make thee even feet,   15
Yet still thou run'st more hobbling than is meet;
In better dress to trim thee was my mind,
But nought save homespun cloth in the house I find.
In this array, 'mongst vulgars may'st thou roam;
In critics' hands beware thou dost not come;   20
And take thy way where yet thou are not known.
If for thy Father asked, say thou had'st none;

And for thy Mother, she alas is poor,
Which caused her thus to send thee out of door.

The extended metaphor likening her book to a child came naturally
to Bradstreet and allowed her to regard her work both critically and affectionately. Her conception of the book as her child creates just the right
tone of amusement, self-deprecation, and concern.

OTHER FIGURES

Perhaps the humblest figure of speech — if not one of the most familiar — is
the pun. A *pun* is a play on words that relies on a word having more than
one meaning or sounding like another word. For example, "A fad is in one
era and out the other" is the sort of pun that produces obligatory groans.
But most of us find pleasant and interesting surprises in puns. Here's one
that has a slight edge to its humor.

EDMUND CONTI (B. 1929)

Pragmatist   *1985*

Apocalypse soon
Coming our way
Ground zero at noon
Halve a nice day.

Grimly practical under the circumstances, the pragmatist divides the
familiar cheerful cliché by half. As simple as this poem is, its tone is mixed
because it makes us laugh and wince at the same time.

Puns can be used to achieve serious effects as well as humorous ones.
Although we may have learned to underrate puns as figures of speech, it is
a mistake to underestimate their power and the frequency with which they
appear in poetry. A close examination, for example, of Henry Reed's "Naming of Parts" (p. 720), Robert Frost's "Design" (p. 895), or almost any
lengthy passage from a Shakespeare play will confirm the value of puns.

Synecdoche is a figure of speech in which part of something is used to
signify the whole: a neighbor is a "wagging tongue" (a gossip); a criminal
is placed "behind bars" (in prison). Less typically, synecdoche refers to
the whole used to signify the part: "Germany invaded Poland"; "Princeton
won the fencing match." Clearly, certain individuals participated in these
activities, not all of Germany or Princeton. Another related figure of speech
is *metonymy,* in which something closely associated with a subject is substituted for it: "She preferred the silver screen [motion pictures] to reading."

"At precisely ten o'clock the paper shufflers [office workers] stopped for coffee."

Synecdoche and metonymy may overlap and are therefore sometimes difficult to distinguish. Consider this description of a disapproving minister entering a noisy tavern: "As those pursed lips came through the swinging door, the atmosphere was suddenly soured." The pursed lips signal the presence of the minister and are therefore a synecdoche, but they additionally suggest an inhibiting sense of sin and guilt that makes the bar patrons feel uncomfortable. Hence the pursed lips are also a metonymy, as they are in this context so closely connected with religion. Although the distinction between synecdoche and metonymy can be useful, when a figure of speech overlaps categories, it is usually labeled a metonymy.

Knowing the precise term for a figure of speech is, finally, less important than responding to its use in a poem. Consider how metonymy and synecdoche convey the tone and meaning of the following poem.

DYLAN THOMAS (1914–1953)
The Hand That Signed the Paper 1936

The hand that signed the paper felled a city;
Five sovereign fingers taxed the breath,
Doubled the globe of dead and halved a
    country;
These five kings did a king to death.

The mighty hand leads to a sloping shoulder,
The finger joints are cramped with chalk;
A goose's quill has put an end to murder
That put an end to talk.

The hand that signed the treaty bred a fever,
And famine grew, and locusts came;
Great is the hand that holds dominion over
Man by a scribbled name.

The five kings count the dead but do not soften
The crusted wound nor stroke the brow;
A hand rules pity as a hand rules heaven;
Hands have no tears to flow.

© POPPERFOTO/Alamy.

10

Explore contexts
for Dylan Thomas
on *LiterActive*.

15

The "hand" in this poem is a synecdoche for a powerful ruler because it is a part of someone used to signify the entire person. The "goose's quill" is a metonymy that also refers to the power associated with the ruler's hand. By using these figures of speech, Thomas depersonalizes and ultimately dehumanizes the ruler. The final synecdoche tells us that "Hands have no tears to flow." It makes us see the political power behind the hand as remote and inhuman. How is the meaning of the poem enlarged when the speaker says, "A hand rules pity as a hand rules heaven"?

One of the ways writers energize the abstractions, ideas, objects, and animals that constitute their created worlds is through *personification,* the attribution of human characteristics to nonhuman things: temptation pursues the innocent; trees scream in the raging wind; mice conspire in the cupboard. We are not explicitly told that these things are people; instead, we are invited to see that they behave like people. Perhaps it is human vanity that makes personification a frequently used figure of speech. Whatever the reason, personification, a form of metaphor that connects the nonhuman with the human, makes the world understandable in human terms. Consider this concise example from William Blake's *The Marriage of Heaven and Hell,* a long poem that takes delight in attacking conventional morality: "Prudence is a rich ugly old maid courted by Incapacity." By personifying prudence, Blake transforms what is usually considered a virtue into a comic figure hardly worth emulating.

Often related to personification is another rhetorical figure called *apostrophe,* an address either to someone who is absent and therefore cannot hear the speaker or to something nonhuman that cannot comprehend. Apostrophe provides an opportunity for the speaker of a poem to think aloud, and often the thoughts expressed are in a formal tone. John Keats, for example, begins "Ode on a Grecian Urn" (p. 647) this way: "Thou still unravished bride of quietness." Apostrophe is frequently accompanied by intense emotion that is signaled by phrasing such as "O Life." In the right hands — such as Keats's — apostrophe can provide an intense and immediate voice in a poem, but when it is overdone or extravagant it can be ludicrous. Modern poets are more wary of apostrophe than their predecessors because apostrophizing strikes many self-conscious twenty-first-century sensibilities as too theatrical. Thus modern poets tend to avoid exaggerated situations in favor of less charged though equally meditative moments, as in this next poem, with its amusing, half-serious cosmic twist.

JANICE TOWNLEY MOORE (B. 1939)

To a Wasp   1984

You must have chortled
finding that tiny hole
in the kitchen screen. Right
into my cheese cake batter
you dived,   5
no chance to swim ashore,
no saving spoon,
the mixer whirring

your legs, wings, stinger,
churning you into such   10
delicious death.
Never mind the bright April day.
Did you not see
rising out of cumulus clouds
That fist aimed at both of us?   15

Moore's apostrophe "To a Wasp" is based on the simplest of domestic circumstances; there is almost nothing theatrical or exaggerated in the poem's tone until "That fist" in the last line, when exaggeration takes center stage. As a figure of speech exaggeration is known as **overstatement** or **hyperbole** and adds emphasis without intending to be literally true: "The teenage boy ate everything in the house." Notice how the speaker of Andrew Marvell's "To His Coy Mistress" (p. 636) exaggerates his devotion in the following overstatement:

> An hundred years should go to praise
> Thine eyes and on thy forehead gaze,
> Two hundred to adore each breast,
> But thirty thousand to the rest:

That comes to 30,500 years. What is expressed here is heightened emotion, not deception.

The speaker also uses the opposite figure of speech, **understatement,** which says less than is intended. In the next section he sums up why he cannot take 30,500 years to express his love:

> The grave's a fine and private place,
> But none, I think, do there embrace.

The speaker is correct, of course, but by deliberately understating—saying "I think" when he is actually certain—he makes his point, that death will overtake their love, all the more emphatic. Another powerful example of understatement appears in the final line of Randall Jarrell's "The Death of the Ball Turret Gunner" (p. 625), when the disembodied voice of the machine gunner describes his death in a bomber: "When I died they washed me out of the turret with a hose."

Paradox is a statement that initially appears to be self-contradictory but that, on closer inspection, turns out to make sense: "The pen is mightier than the sword." In a fencing match, anyone would prefer the sword, but if the goal is to win the hearts and minds of people, the art of persuasion can be more compelling than swordplay. To resolve the paradox, it is necessary to discover the sense that underlies the statement. If we see that "pen" and "sword" are used as metonymies for writing and violence, then the paradox rings true. **Oxymoron** is a condensed form of paradox in which two contradictory words are used together. Combinations such as "sweet sorrow," "silent scream," "sad joy," and "cold fire" indicate the kinds of startling effects that oxymorons can produce. Paradox is useful in poetry because it arrests a reader's attention by its seemingly stubborn refusal to make sense, and once a reader has penetrated the paradox, it is difficult to resist a perception so well earned. Good paradoxes are knotty pleasures. Here is a simple but effective one.

J. Patrick Lewis (b. 1942)
The Unkindest Cut   1993

Knives can harm you, heaven forbid;
Axes may disarm you, kid;
Guillotines are painful, but
There's nothing like a paper cut!

This quatrain is a humorous version of "the pen is mightier than the sword." The wounds escalate to the paper cut, which paradoxically is more damaging than even the broad blade of a guillotine. "The unkindest cut" of all (an allusion to Shakespeare's *Julius Caesar,* III.ii.188) is produced by chilling words on a page rather than cold steel, but it is more painfully fatal nonetheless.

The following poems are rich in figurative language. As you read and study them, notice how their figures of speech vivify situations, clarify ideas, intensify emotions, and engage your imagination. Although the terms for the various figures discussed in this chapter are useful for labeling the particular devices used in poetry, they should not be allowed to get in the way of your response to a poem. Don't worry about rounding up examples of figurative language. First relax and let the figures work their effects on you. Use the terms as a means of taking you further into poetry, and they will serve your reading well.

POEMS FOR FURTHER STUDY

Gary Snyder (b. 1930)
How Poetry Comes to Me   1992

It comes blundering over the
Boulders at night, it stays
Frightened outside the
Range of my campfire
I go to meet it at the
Edge of the light

CONSIDERATIONS FOR CRITICAL THINKING AND WRITING

1. **FIRST RESPONSE.** How does personification in this poem depict the creative process?

2. Why do you suppose Snyder makes each successive line shorter?

3. **CREATIVE RESPONSE.** How would eliminating the title change your understanding of the poem? Substitute another title that causes you to reinterpret it.

A SAMPLE STUDENT RESPONSE

Jennifer Jackson

Professor Kahane

English 215

October 16, 2008

Metaphor in Gary Snyder's "How Poetry Comes to Me"

"A metaphor," Michael Meyer writes, "makes a comparison between two unlike things . . . implicitly, without words such as *like* or *as*" (684). In his poem "How Poetry Comes to Me," Gary Snyder uses metaphor to compare poetic inspiration and creativity with a kind of wild creature.

In this work, poetry itself is both an ungraceful beast and a timid animal. It is something big and unwieldy, that "comes blundering over the / Boulders at night" (lines 1-2). The word "blunder" suggests that poetic inspiration moves clumsily, blindly--not knowing where it will go next--and somewhat dangerously. Yet it is hesitant and "stays / Frightened outside the / Range of [the] campfire" (2-4). According to Snyder's poem, the creature poetry comes only part way to meet the poet; the poet has to go to meet it on its terms, "at the / Edge of the light" (5-6). The metaphor of the poem as wild animal tells the reader that poetic inspiration is elusive and unpredictable. It must be sought out carefully or it will run back over the boulders, by the way it came. . . .

Works Cited

Meyer, Michael, ed. The Compact Bedford Introduction to Literature. 8th ed. Boston: Bedford/St. Martin's, 2009. 684.

Snyder, Gary. "How Poetry Comes to Me." The Compact Bedford Introduction to Literature. Ed. Michael Meyer. 8th ed. Boston: Bedford/St. Martin's, 2009. 690.

MARGARET ATWOOD (B. 1939)

February   *1995*

Winter. Time to eat fat
and watch hockey. In the pewter mornings, the cat,
a black fur sausage with yellow
Houdini eyes, jumps up on the bed and tries
to get onto my head. It's his   5
way of telling whether or not I'm dead.
If I'm not, he wants to be scratched; if I am
he'll think of something. He settles
on my chest, breathing his breath
of burped-up meat and musty sofas,   10
purring like a washboard. Some other tomcat,
not yet a capon, has been spraying our front door,
declaring war. It's all about sex and territory,
which are what will finish us off
in the long run. Some cat owners around here   15
should snip a few testicles. If we wise
hominids were sensible, we'd do that too,
or eat our young, like sharks.
But it's love that does us in. Over and over
again, *He shoots, he scores!* and famine   20
crouches in the bedsheets, ambushing the pulsing
eiderdown, and the windchill factor hits
thirty below, and pollution pours
out of our chimneys to keep us warm.
February, month of despair,   25
with a skewered heart in the centre.
I think dire thoughts, and lust for French fries
with a splash of vinegar.
Cat, enough of your greedy whining
and your small pink bumhole.   30
Off my face! You're the life principle,
more or less, so get going
on a little optimism around here.
Get rid of death. Celebrate increase. Make it be spring.

CONSIDERATIONS FOR CRITICAL THINKING AND WRITING

1. **FIRST RESPONSE.** How do your own associations with February compare
   with the speaker's?
2. Explain how the poem is organized around an extended metaphor that
   defines winter as a "Time to eat fat / and watch hockey" (lines 1–2).
3. Explain the paradox in "it's love that does us in" (line 19).
4. What theme(s) do you find in the poem? How is the cat central to them?

WILLIAM CARLOS WILLIAMS (1883-1963)

To Waken an Old Lady 1921

Old age is
a flight of small
cheeping birds
skimming
bare trees 5
above a snow glaze.
Gaining and failing
they are buffeted
by a dark wind —
But what? 10
On harsh weedstalks
the flock has rested,
the snow
is covered with broken
seedhusks 15
and the wind tempered
by a shrill
piping of plenty.

CONSIDERATIONS FOR CRITICAL THINKING AND WRITING

1. **FIRST RESPONSE.** Consider the images and figures of speech in this poem and explain why you think it is a positive or negative assessment of old age.

2. How does the title relate to the rest of the poem?

CONNECTION TO ANOTHER SELECTION

1. Discuss the shift in tone in "To Waken an Old Lady" and in Colette Inez's "Back When All Was Continuous Chuckles" (p. 630).

ERNEST SLYMAN (B. 1946)

Lightning Bugs 1988

In my backyard,
They burn peepholes in the night
And take snapshots of my house.

CONSIDERATIONS FOR CRITICAL THINKING AND WRITING

1. **FIRST RESPONSE.** Explain why the title is essential to this poem.

2. What makes the description of the lightning bugs effective? How do the second and third lines complement each other?

3. **CREATIVE RESPONSE.** As Slyman has done, take a simple, common fact of nature and make it vivid by using a figure of speech to describe it.

CATHY SONG (B. 1955)

Sunworshippers   *1994*

"Look how they love themselves,"
my mother would lecture as we drove through
the ironwoods, the park on one side,
the beach on the other, where sunworshippers,
splayed upon towels, appeared sacrificial,   5
bodies glazed and glistening like raw fish in the market.
There was folly and irreverence to such exposure,
something only people with dirty feet did.
Who will marry you
if your skin is sunbaked and dried up like beef jerky?   10
We put on our hats and gloves
whenever we went for a drive.
When the sun broke through clouds,
my mother sprouted her umbrella.
The body is a temple we worship   15
secretly in the traveling revivalist tent of our clothes.
The body, hidden, banished to acceptable
rooms of the house, had only a mouth
for eating and a hole for eliminating
what the body rejected: the lower forms of life.   20
Caramel-colored stools, coiled heavily
like a sleeping python, were a sign
we were living right.
But to erect a statue of the body
and how the body, insolent and defiant   25
in a bikini, looked was self-indulgent, sun-
worshipping, fad diets and weight-lifting proof
you loved yourself too much.
We were not allowed to love ourselves too much.
So I ate less, and less, and less,   30
nibbling my way out of meals —
the less I ate, the less
there was of me to love.
I liked it best when standing before the mirror,
I seemed to be disappearing into myself,   35
breasts sunken into the cavity of my bird-cage chest,
air my true element which fed
in those days of college, snow and brick bound,
the coal fire in my eyes.
No one knew how I truly felt about myself.   40
Fueled by my own impending disappearance,
I neither slept nor ate, but devoured radiance,
essential as chlorophyll,
the apple's heated core.
Undetected, I slipped in and out of books,   45
passages of music, brightly painted rooms
where, woven into the signature of voluptuous vines,

was the one who flew one day out the window,
leaving behind an arrangement of cakes and ornamental flowers;
to weave one's self, one's breath, ropes of it, whole   50
and fully formed, was a way of shining
out of this world.

CONSIDERATIONS FOR CRITICAL THINKING AND WRITING

1. **FIRST RESPONSE.** How would the theme of this poem be different if it ended
   at line 29? Discuss the poem's theme(s).

2. Identify the figures of speech that appear throughout the poem and explain how they relate to one another.

3. How do the figures of speech used by the speaker reveal her personality?

WILLIAM WORDSWORTH (1770–1850)

London, 1802   *1802*

Milton!° thou should'st be living at this hour:
England hath need of thee: she is a fen
Of stagnant waters: altar, sword, and pen,
Fireside, the heroic wealth of hall and bower,
Have forfeited their ancient English dower   5
Of inward happiness. We are selfish men;
Oh! raise us up, return to us again;
And give us manners, virtue, freedom, power.
Thy soul was like a star, and dwelt apart:
Thou hadst a voice whose sound was like the sea: 10
Pure as the naked heavens, majestic, free,
So didst thou travel on life's common way,
In cheerful godliness; and yet thy heart
The lowliest duties on herself did lay.

Milton: John Milton (1608–1674), poet, famous especially for his religious epic *Paradise Lost*
and his defense of political freedom.

CONSIDERATIONS FOR CRITICAL THINKING AND WRITING

1. **FIRST RESPONSE.** Describe the poem's tone. Is it nostalgic, angry, or something else?

2. Explain the metonymies in lines 3–6 of this poem. What is the speaker's
   assessment of England?

3. How would the effect of the poem be different if it were in the form of an
   address to Wordsworth's contemporaries rather than an apostrophe to
   Milton? What qualities does Wordsworth attribute to Milton by the use of
   figurative language?

4. **CRITICAL STRATEGIES.** Read the section on literary history criticism (pp.
   1544–45) in Chapter 46, "Critical Strategies for Reading," and use the

library to find out about the state of London in 1802. How does the poem reflect or refute the social values of its time?

JIM STEVENS (B. 1922)

Schizophrenia 1992

It was the house that suffered most.

It had begun with slamming doors, angry feet scuffing the carpets,
dishes slammed onto the table,
greasy stains spreading on the cloth.

Certain doors were locked at night, 5
feet stood for hours outside them,
dishes were left unwashed, the cloth
disappeared under a hardened crust.

The house came to miss the shouting voices,
the threats, the half-apologies, noisy 10
reconciliations, the sobbing that followed.

Then lines were drawn, borders established,
some rooms declared their loyalties,
keeping to themselves, keeping out the other.
The house divided against itself. 15

Seeing cracking paint, broken windows,
the front door banging in the wind,
the roof tiles flying off, one by one,
the neighbors said it was a madhouse.

It was the house that suffered most. 20

CONSIDERATIONS FOR CRITICAL THINKING AND WRITING

1. **FIRST RESPONSE.** What is the effect of personifying the house in this poem?

2. How are the people who live in the house characterized? What does their behavior reveal about them? How does the house respond to them?

3. Comment on the title. If the title were missing, what, if anything, would be missing from the poem? Explain your answer.

JOHN DONNE (1572–1631)

A Valediction: Forbidding Mourning 1611

As virtuous men pass mildly away,
    And whisper to their souls to go,
While some of their sad friends do say,
    The breath goes now, and some say, no:

So let us melt, and make no noise, 5
    No tear-floods, nor sigh-tempests move;
'Twere profanation of our joys
    To tell the laity our love.

Moving of th' earth° brings harms and fears, *earthquakes*
    Men reckon what it did and meant, 10
But trepidation of the spheres,°
    Though greater far, is innocent.

Dull sublunary° lovers' love
    (Whose soul is sense) cannot admit
Absence, because it doth remove 15
    Those things which elemented° it. *composed*

But we by a love so much refined,
    That ourselves know not what it is,
Inter-assured of the mind,
    Care less, eyes, lips, and hands to miss. 20

Our two souls therefore, which are one,
    Though I must go, endure not yet
A breach, but an expansion,
    Like gold to airy thinness beat.

If they be two, they are two so 25
    As stiff twin compasses are two;
Thy soul the fixed foot, makes no show
    To move, but doth, if th' other do.

And though it in the center sit,
    Yet when the other far doth roam,
It leans, and hearkens after it, 30
    And grows erect, as that comes home.

Such wilt thou be to me, who must
    Like th' other foot, obliquely run;
Thy firmness makes my circle just,° 35
    And makes me end, where I begun.

11 *trepidation of the spheres:* According to Ptolemaic astronomy, the planets sometimes moved violently, like earthquakes, but these movements were not felt by people on Earth. 13 *sublunary:* Under the moon; hence, mortal and subject to change.   35 *circle just:* The circle is a traditional symbol of perfection.

CONSIDERATIONS FOR CRITICAL THINKING AND WRITING

1. **FIRST RESPONSE.** A valediction is a farewell. Donne wrote this poem for his wife before leaving on a trip to France. What kind of "mourning" is the speaker forbidding?

2. Explain how the simile in lines 1–4 is related to the couple in lines 5–8. Who is described as dying?

3. How does the speaker contrast the couple's love to "sublunary lovers' love" (line 13)?
4. Explain the similes in lines 24 and 25-36.

LINDA PASTAN (B. 1932)

Marks   1978

My husband gives me an A
for last night's supper,
an incomplete for my ironing,
a B plus in bed.
My son says I am average,   5
an average mother, but if
I put my mind to it
I could improve.
My daughter believes
in Pass/Fail and tells me   10
I pass. Wait 'til they learn
I'm dropping out.

CONSIDERATIONS FOR CRITICAL THINKING AND WRITING

1. **FIRST RESPONSE.** Explain the appropriateness of the controlling metaphor in this poem. How does it reveal the woman's relationship to her family?
2. Discuss the meaning of the title.
3. How does the last line serve as both the climax of the woman's story and the poem's controlling metaphor?

RONALD WALLACE (B. 1945)

Building an Outhouse   1991

Is not unlike building a poem: the pure
mathematics of shape; the music of hammer
and tenpenny nail, of floor joist, stud wall,
and sill; the cut wood's sweet smell.

If the Skil saw rear up in your unpracticed hand,   5
cussing, hawking its chaw of dust,
and you're lost in the pounding particulars
of fly rafters, siding, hypotenuse, and load,
until nothing seems level or true
but the scorn of the tape's clucked tongue,   10

let the nub of your plainspoken pencil prevail
and it's up! Functional. Tight as a sonnet.
It will last forever (or at least for awhile)
though the critics come sit on it, and sit on it.

CONSIDERATIONS FOR CRITICAL THINKING AND WRITING

1. **FIRST RESPONSE.** Explain how the poem's diction contributes to the extended simile. Why is the language of building especially appropriate here?

2. What is the effect of the repetition and sounds in the final line? How does that affect the poem's tone?

3. Consult the Glossary of Literary Terms (p. 1619) for the definition of a sonnet. To what extent does "Building an Outhouse" conform to a sonnet's structure?

RUTH FAINLIGHT (B. 1931)

The Clarinettist 2002

Pale round arms raising her clarinet
at the exact angle, she sways, then halts,
poised for the music

like a horse that gathers itself up before the leap
with the awkward, perfect, only   5
possible movement

an alto in a quattrocento chorus, blond head
lifted from the score, open-mouthed
for hallelujah

a cherub on a ceiling cornice leaning out   10
from heaped-up clouds of opalescent pink,
translucent blue

a swimmer breasting frothy surf like ripping through
lace curtains, a dancer centred as a spinning top,
an August moon   15

alone, in front of the orchestra, the conductor's
other, and unacknowledged opposite,
she starts the tune.

CONSIDERATIONS FOR CRITICAL THINKING AND WRITING

1. **FIRST RESPONSE.** This poem is structured as one long sentence. How does this structure create a kind of suspense as the clarinettist is "poised for the music"?

2. How do the similes and metaphors capture the moment that the clarinettist "starts the tune"? What sort of description of her emerges from them?

3. **CREATIVE RESPONSE.** Create a similar three-line stanza that adds to Fainlight's description and maintains the poem's tone.

Perspective

JOHN R. SEARLE (B. 1932)
Figuring Out Metaphors 1979

If you hear somebody say, "Sally is a block of ice," or, "Sam is a pig," you are likely to assume that the speaker does not mean what he says literally, but that he is speaking metaphorically. Furthermore, you are not likely to have very much trouble figuring out what he means. If he says, "Sally is a prime number between 17 and 23," or "Bill is a barn door," you might still assume he is speaking metaphorically, but it is much harder to figure out what he means. The existence of such utterances — utterances in which the speaker means metaphorically something different from what the sentence means literally — poses a series of questions for any theory of language and communication: What is metaphor, and how does it differ from both literal and other forms of figurative utterances? Why do we use expressions metaphorically instead of saying exactly and literally what we mean? How do metaphorical utterances work, that is, how is it possible for speakers to communicate to hearers when speaking metaphorically inasmuch as they do not say what they mean? And why do some metaphors work and others do not?

From *Expression and Meaning*

CONSIDERATIONS FOR CRITICAL THINKING AND WRITING

1. Searle poses a series of important questions. Write an essay that explores one of these questions, basing your discussion on the poems in this chapter.

2. **CREATIVE RESPONSE.** Try writing a brief poem that provides a context for the line "Sally is a prime number between 17 and 23" or the line "Bill is a barn door." Your task is to create a context so that either one of these metaphoric statements is as readily understandable as "Sally is a block of ice" or "Sam is a pig." Share your poem with your classmates and explain how the line generated the poem you built around it.

Web Research the poets in this chapter at bedfordstmartins.com/ meyercompact.

23

Symbol, Allegory, and Irony

© Barbara Savage Cheresh.

Poetry is serious business; literature
is the apparatus through which the
world tries to keep intact its important
ideas and feelings.
— MARY OLIVER

SYMBOL

A *symbol* is something that represents something else. An object, person,
place, event, or action can suggest more than its literal meaning. A hand-
shake between two world leaders might be simply a greeting, but if it is
done ceremoniously before cameras, it could be a symbolic gesture signifying unity, issues resolved, and joint policies that will be followed. We live
surrounded by symbols. When a $100,000 Mercedes-
Benz comes roaring by in the fast lane, we get a quick
glimpse of not only an expensive car but an entire
lifestyle that suggests opulence, broad lawns, executive
offices, and power. One of the reasons some buyers are
willing to spend roughly the cost of five Chevrolets for a single Mercedes-
Benz is that they are aware of the car's symbolic value. A symbol is a vehicle

Explore
the poetic elements
in this chapter
on *LiterActive* or at
bedfordstmartins.com/
meyercompact.

for two things at once: it functions as itself, and it implies meanings beyond itself.

The meanings suggested by a symbol are determined by the context in which they appear. The Mercedes could symbolize very different things depending on where it was parked. Would an American political candidate be likely to appear in a Detroit blue-collar neighborhood with such a car? Probably not. Although a candidate might be able to afford the car, it would be an inappropriate symbol for someone seeking votes from all of the people. As a symbol, the German-built Mercedes would backfire if voters perceived it as representing an entity partially responsible for layoffs of automobile workers or, worse, as a sign of decadence and corruption. Similarly, a huge portrait of Mao Tse-tung conveys different meanings to residents of Beijing than it would to farmers in Prairie Center, Illinois. Because symbols depend on contexts for their meaning, literary artists provide those contexts so that the reader has enough information to determine the probable range of meanings suggested by a symbol.

In the following poem the speaker describes walking at night. How is the night used symbolically?

ROBERT FROST (1874–1963)

Acquainted with the Night   1928

I have been one acquainted with the night.
I have walked out in rain — and back in rain.
I have outwalked the furthest city light.

I have looked down the saddest city lane.
I have passed by the watchman on his beat   5
And dropped my eyes, unwilling to explain.

I have stood still and stopped the sound of feet
When far away an interrupted cry
Came over houses from another street,

But not to call me back or say good-by;   10
And further still at an unearthly height
One luminary clock against the sky

Proclaimed the time was neither wrong nor right.
I have been one acquainted with the night.

In approaching this or any other poem, you should read for literal meanings first and then allow the elements of the poem to invite you to symbolic readings, if they are appropriate. Here the somber tone suggests that the lines have symbolic meaning, too. The flat matter-of-factness created by the repetition of "I have" (lines 1–5, 7, 14) understates the symbolic subject matter of the poem, which is, finally, more about the "night" located in the speaker's mind or soul than it is about walking away from a city and back again. The speaker is "acquainted with the night." The importance of this phrase is emphasized by Frost's title and by the fact that he begins and ends the poem with it. Poets frequently use this kind of repetition to alert readers to details that carry more than literal meanings.

The speaker in this poem has personal knowledge of the night but does not indicate specifically what the night means. To arrive at the potential meanings of the night in this context, it is necessary to look closely at its connotations, along with the images provided in the poem. The connotative meanings of night suggest, for example, darkness, death, and grief. By drawing on these connotations, Frost uses a *conventional symbol* — something that is recognized by many people to represent certain ideas. Roses conventionally symbolize love or beauty; laurels, fame; spring, growth; the moon, romance. Poets often use conventional symbols to convey tone and meaning.

Frost uses the night as a conventional symbol, but he also develops it into a *literary* or *contextual symbol* that goes beyond traditional, public meanings. A literary symbol cannot be summarized in a word or two. It tends to be as elusive as experience itself. The night cannot be reduced to or equated with darkness or death or grief, but it evokes those associations and more. Frost took what perhaps initially appears to be an overworked, conventional symbol and prevented it from becoming a cliché by deepening and extending its meaning.

The images in "Acquainted with the Night" lead to the poem's symbolic meaning. Unwilling, and perhaps unable, to explain explicitly to the watchman (and to the reader) what the night means, the speaker nevertheless conveys feelings about it. The brief images of darkness, rain, sad city lanes, the necessity for guards, the eerie sound of a distressing cry coming over rooftops, and the "luminary clock against the sky" proclaiming "the time was neither wrong nor right" all help to create a sense of anxiety in this tight-lipped speaker. Although we cannot know what unnamed personal experiences have acquainted the speaker with the night, the images suggest that whatever the night means, it is somehow associated with insomnia, loneliness, isolation, coldness, darkness, death, fear, and a sense of alienation from humanity and even time. Daylight — ordinary daytime thoughts and life itself — seems remote and unavailable in this poem. The night is literally the period from sunset to sunrise, but, more important, it is an internal state of being felt by the speaker and revealed through the images.

Frost used symbols rather than an expository essay that would explain the conditions that cause these feelings because most readers can provide their own list of sorrows and terrors that evoke similar emotions. Through symbol, the speaker's experience is compressed and simultaneously expanded by the personal darkness that each reader brings to the poem. The suggestive nature of symbols makes them valuable for poets and evocative for readers.

ALLEGORY

Unlike expansive, suggestive symbols, **allegory** is a narration or description usually restricted to a single meaning because its events, actions, characters, settings, and objects represent specific abstractions or ideas. Although the elements in an allegory may be interesting in themselves, the emphasis tends to be on what they ultimately mean. Characters may be given names such as Hope, Pride, Youth, and Charity; they have few, if any, personal qualities beyond their abstract meanings. These personifications are a form of extended metaphor, but their meanings are severely restricted. They are not symbols because, for instance, the meaning of a character named Charity is precisely that virtue.

There is little or no room for broad speculation and exploration in allegories. If Frost had written "Acquainted with the Night" as an allegory, he might have named his speaker Loneliness and had him leave the City of Despair to walk the Streets of Emptiness, where Crime, Poverty, Fear, and other characters would define the nature of city life. The literal elements in an allegory tend to be de-emphasized in favor of the message. Symbols, however, function both literally and symbolically, so that "Acquainted with the Night" is about both a walk and a sense that something is terribly wrong.

Allegory especially lends itself to **didactic poetry,** which is designed to teach an ethical, moral, or religious lesson. Many stories, poems, and plays are concerned with values, but didactic literature is specifically created to convey a message. "Acquainted with the Night" does not impart advice or offer guidance. If the poem argued that city life is self-destructive or sinful, it would be didactic; instead, it is a lyric poem that expresses the emotions and thoughts of a single speaker.

Although allegory is often enlisted in didactic causes because it can so readily communicate abstract ideas through physical representations, not all allegories teach a lesson. Here is a poem describing a haunted palace while also establishing a consistent pattern that reveals another meaning.

EDGAR ALLAN POE (1809–1849)

The Haunted Palace

1839

I

In the greenest of our valleys,
   By good angels tenanted,
Once a fair and stately palace —
   Radiant palace — reared its head.
In the monarch Thought's dominion —
   It stood there!   5
Never seraph spread a pinion
   Over fabric half so fair.

II

Banners yellow, glorious, golden,
    On its roof did float and flow;   10
(This — all this — was in the olden
    Time long ago)
And every gentle air that dallied,
    In that sweet day,
Along the ramparts plumed and pallid,   15
    A wingèd odor went away.

III

Wanderers in that happy valley
    Through two luminous windows saw
Spirits moving musically
    To a lute's well-tunèd law,   20
Round about a throne, where sitting
    (Porphyrogene!)°   *born to purple, royal*
In state his glory well befitting,
    The ruler of the realm was seen.

IV

And all with pearl and ruby glowing   25
    Was the fair palace door,
Through which came flowing, flowing, flowing
    And sparkling evermore,
A troop of Echoes whose sweet duty
    Was but to sing,   30
In voices of surpassing beauty,
    The wit and wisdom of their king.

V

But evil things, in robes of sorrow,
    Assailed the monarch's high estate;
(Ah, let us mourn, for never morrow   35
    Shall dawn upon him, desolate!)
And, round about his home, the glory
    That blushed and bloomed
Is but a dim-remembered story
    Of the old time entombed.   40

VI

And travelers now within that valley,
    Through the red-litten windows see
Vast forms that move fantastically
    To a discordant melody;

While, like a rapid ghastly river,   45
   Through the pale door,
A hideous throng rush out forever,
   And laugh — but smile no more.

On one level this poem describes how a once happy palace is desolated
by "evil things" (line 33). If the reader pays close attention to the diction,
however, an allegorical meaning becomes apparent on a second reading. A
systematic pattern develops in the choice of words used to describe the
palace, so that it comes to stand for a human mind. The palace, banners,
windows, door, echoes, and throng are equated with a person's head, hair,
eyes, mouth, voice, and laughter. That mind, once harmoniously ordered,
is overthrown by evil, haunting thoughts that lead to the mad laughter in
the poem's final lines. Once the general pattern is seen, the rest of the
details fall neatly into place to strengthen the parallels between the surface
description of a palace and the allegorical representation of a disordered
mind.

Modern writers generally prefer symbol over allegory because they
tend to be more interested in opening up the potential meanings of an
experience instead of transforming it into a closed pattern of meaning.
Perhaps the major difference is that while allegory may delight a reader's
imagination, symbol challenges and enriches it.

IRONY

Another important resource writers use to take readers beyond literal
meanings is *irony,* a technique that reveals a discrepancy between what
appears to be and what is actually true. Here is a classic example in which
appearances give way to the underlying reality.

EDWIN ARLINGTON ROBINSON (1869–1935)

Richard Cory   *1897*

Whenever Richard Cory went down town,
We people on the pavement looked at him:
He was a gentleman from sole to crown,
Clean favored, and imperially slim.

And he was always quietly arrayed,   5
And he was always human when he talked;
But still he fluttered pulses when he said,
"Good-morning," and he glittered when he walked.

And he was rich — yes, richer than a king —
And admirably schooled in every grace: 10
In fine, we thought that he was everything
To make us wish that we were in his place.

So on we worked, and waited for the light,
And went without the meat, and cursed the bread;
And Richard Cory, one calm summer night,   15
Went home and put a bullet through his head.

Richard Cory seems to have it all. Those less fortunate, the "people on the pavement," regard him as well-bred, handsome, tasteful, and richly endowed with both money and grace. Until the final line of the poem, the reader, like the speaker, is charmed by Cory's good fortune, so quietly expressed in his decent, easy manner. That final, shocking line, however, shatters the appearances of Cory's life and reveals him to have been a desperately unhappy man. While everyone else assumes that Cory represented "everything" to which they aspire, the reality is that he could escape his miserable life only as a suicide. This discrepancy between what appears to be true and what actually exists is known as *situational irony:* what happens is entirely different from what is expected. We are not told why Cory shoots himself; instead, the irony in the poem shocks us into the recognition that appearances do not always reflect realities.

Words are also sometimes intended to be taken at other than face value. *Verbal irony* is saying something different from what is meant. After reading "Richard Cory," to say "That rich gentleman sure was happy" is ironic. The tone of voice would indicate that just the opposite was meant; hence verbal irony is usually easy to detect in spoken language. In literature, however, a reader can sometimes take literally what a writer intends ironically. The remedy for this kind of misreading is to pay close attention to the poem's context. There is no formula that can detect verbal irony, but contradictory actions and statements as well as the use of understatement and overstatement can often be signals that verbal irony is present.

A SAMPLE STUDENT RESPONSE

Cipriano Diaz

Professor Young

English 200

September 16, 2008

Irony in Edwin Arlington Robinson's "Richard Cory"

In Edwin Arlington Robinson's poem "Richard Cory," appearances are
not reality. The character Richard Cory, viewed by the townspeople as "richer
than a king" (line 9) and "a gentleman from sole to crown" (3), is someone
who inspires envy. The poem's speaker says "we thought that he was everything / To make us wish that we were in his place" (11-12). However, the
final shocking line of the poem creates a situational irony that emphasizes
the difference between what seems--and what really is.

In lines 1 through 14, the speaker sets up a shining, princely image of
Cory, associating with him with such regal words as "imperially" (4), "crown"
(3), and "king" (9). Cory is viewed by the townspeople from the "pavement"
as if he is on a pedestal (2); far below him, those who must work and "[go]
without meat" stand in stark contrast (14). Further, not only is Cory a gentleman, he is so good-looking that he "flutter[s] the pulses" (7) of those around
him when he speaks. He's a rich man who "glitter[s] when he walk[s]" (8). He
is also a decent man who is "always human when he talk[s]" (6). However,
this noble image of Cory is unexpectedly shattered "one calm summer night"
in the final couplet (15). What the speaker and townspeople believed Cory to
be and aspired to imitate was merely an illusion. The irony is that what Cory
seemed to be--a happy, satisfied man--is exactly what he was not. . . .

Work Cited

Robinson, Edwin Arlington. "Richard Cory." The Compact Bedford Introduction
to Literature. Ed. Michael Meyer. 8th ed. Boston: Bedford/St. Martin's,
2009. 707-8.

Consider how verbal irony is used in this poem.

KENNETH FEARING (1902–1961)

AD   1938

Wanted: Men;
Millions of men are *wanted at once* in a big new field;
New, tremendous, thrilling, great.
If you've ever been a figure in the chamber of horrors,
If you've ever escaped from a psychiatric ward,   5
If you thrill at the thought of throwing poison into wells, have heavenly
    visions of people, by the thousands, dying in flames —

You are the very man we want
We mean business and our business is *you*
Wanted: A race of brand-new men.   10

Apply: Middle Europe;
No skill needed;
No ambition required; no brains wanted and no character allowed;

Take a permanent job in the coming profession
Wages: *Death.*   15

This poem was written as German troops stormed across Europe at the start of World War II. The advertisement suggests on the surface that killing is just an ordinary job, but the speaker indicates through understatement that there is nothing ordinary about the "business" of this "*coming profession.*" Fearing uses verbal irony to indicate how casually and mindlessly people are prepared to accept the horrors of war.

"AD" is a *satire,* an example of the literary art of ridiculing a folly or vice in an effort to expose or correct it. The object of satire is usually some human frailty; people, institutions, ideas, and things are all fair game for satirists. Fearing satirizes the insanity of a world mobilizing itself for war: his irony reveals the speaker's knowledge that there is nothing "*New, tremendous, thrilling,* [or] *great*" about going off to kill and be killed. The implication of the poem is that no one should respond to advertisements for war. The poem serves as a satiric corrective to those who would troop off armed with unrealistic expectations: wage war and the wages consist of death.

Dramatic irony is used when a writer allows a reader to know more about a situation than a character does. This creates a discrepancy between what a character says or thinks and what the reader knows to be true. Dramatic irony is often used to reveal character. In the following poem the speaker delivers a public address that ironically tells us more about him than it does about the patriotic holiday he is commemorating.

E. E. CUMMINGS (1894–1962)

next to of course god america i 1926

"next to of course god america i
love you land of the pilgrims' and so forth oh
say can you see by the dawn's early my
country 'tis of centuries come and go
and are no more what of it we should worry   5
in every language even deafanddumb
thy sons acclaim your glorious name by gorry
by jingo by gee by gosh by gum
why talk of beauty what could be more beautiful than these heroic happy dead   10
who rushed like lions to the roaring slaughter
they did not stop to think they died instead
then shall the voice of liberty be mute?"

He spoke. And drank rapidly a glass of water

This verbal debauch of chauvinistic clichés (notice the run-on phrases
and lines) reveals that the speaker's relationship to God and country is not,
as he claims, one of love. His public address suggests a hearty mindlessness
that leads to "roaring slaughter" rather than to reverence or patriotism.
Cummings allows the reader to see through the speaker's words to their
dangerous emptiness. What the speaker means and what Cummings means
are entirely different. Like Fearing's "AD," this poem is a satire that invites
the reader's laughter and contempt in order to deflate the benighted attitudes expressed in it.

When a writer uses God, destiny, or fate to dash the hopes and expectations of a character or humankind in general, it is called **cosmic irony.**
In "The Convergence of the Twain" (p. 642), for example, Thomas Hardy
describes how "The Immanent Will" brought together the *Titanic* and a
deadly iceberg. Technology and pride are no match for "the Spinner of the
Years." Here's a painfully terse version of cosmic irony.

STEPHEN CRANE (1871–1900)

A Man Said to the Universe 1899

A man said to the universe:
"Sir, I exist!"
"However," replied the universe,
"The fact has not created in me
A sense of obligation."

Unlike in "The Convergence of the Twain," there is the slightest bit of humor in Crane's poem, but the joke is on us.

Irony is an important technique that allows a writer to distinguish between appearances and realities. In situational irony a discrepancy exists between what we expect to happen and what actually happens; in verbal irony a discrepancy exists between what is said and what is meant; in dramatic irony a discrepancy exists between what a character believes and what the reader knows to be true; and in cosmic irony a discrepancy exists between what a character aspires to and what universal forces provide. With each form of irony, we are invited to move beyond surface appearances and sentimental assumptions to see the complexity of experience. Irony is often used in literature to reveal a writer's perspective on matters that previously seemed settled.

POEMS FOR FURTHER STUDY

BOB HICOK (B. 1960)

Making it in poetry   2004

The young teller
at the credit union
asked why so many
small checks
from universities?   5
Because I write
poems I said. Why
haven't I heard
of you? Because
I write poems   10
I said.

CONSIDERATIONS FOR CRITICAL THINKING AND WRITING

1. **FIRST RESPONSE.** Explain how the speaker's verbal irony is central to the poem's humor.

2. What sort of portrait of the poet-speaker emerges from this very brief poem?

CONNECTION TO ANOTHER SELECTION

1. Compare the life of the poet in Hicok's poem and in Richard Wakefield's "In a Poetry Workshop" (p. 979).

JANE KENYON (1947–1995)

Surprise

1996

He suggests pancakes at the local diner,
followed by a walk in search of mayflowers,
while friends convene at the house
bearing casseroles and a cake, their cars
pulled close along the sandy shoulders
of the road, where tender ferns unfurl
in the ditches, and this year's budding leaves
push last year's spectral leaves from the tips
of the twigs of the ash trees. The gathering
itself is not what astounds her, but the casual   10
accomplishment with which he has lied.

Courtesy of Donald Hall.

CONSIDERATIONS FOR CRITICAL THINKING AND WRITING

1. **FIRST RESPONSE.** Does it matter that this poem is set in the spring?

2. Consider the connotative meaning of "ash trees." Why are they particularly appropriate?

3. Why do you suppose Kenyon uses "astounds" rather than "surprises" in line 10? Use a dictionary to help you determine the possible reasons for this choice.

4. Discuss the irony in the poem.

CONNECTIONS TO OTHER SELECTIONS

1. Write an essay on the nature of the surprises in Kenyon's poem and in Hathaway's "Oh, Oh" (p. 574). Include in your discussion a comparison of the tone and irony in each poem.

2. Compare and contrast in an essay the irony associated with the birthday parties in this poem and Sharon Olds's "Rite of Passage" (p. 811).

MARTÍN ESPADA (B. 1957)

Bully

1990

Boston, Massachusetts, 1987

In the school auditorium
the Theodore Roosevelt statue
is nostalgic
for the Spanish-American War,
each fist lonely for a saber
or the reins of anguish-eyed horses,   5

or a podium to clatter with speeches
glorying in the malaria of conquest.

But now the Roosevelt school
is pronounced *Hernández.*   10
Puerto Rico has invaded Roosevelt
with its army of Spanish-singing children
in the hallways,
brown children devouring
the stockpiles of the cafeteria,   15
children painting *Taíno* ancestors°
that leap naked across murals.

Roosevelt is surrounded
by all the faces
he ever shoved in eugenic spite   20
and cursed as mongrels, skin of one race,
hair and cheekbones of another.

Once Marines tramped
from the newsreel of his imagination;
now children plot to spray graffiti   25
in parrot-brilliant colors
across the Victorian mustache
and monocle.

16 Taíno *ancestors:* The most culturally developed Indian tribe in the Caribbean when
Columbus arrived in Hispaniola in 1492.

CONSIDERATIONS FOR CRITICAL THINKING AND WRITING

1. **FIRST RESPONSE.** Describe the speaker's sense of the past as well as the present. In what sense do two very different cultures collide in this poem?

2. What do you think is the poem's central theme? How do the images and
   symbols work together to contribute to the theme?

3. **CRITICAL STRATEGIES.** Read the sections on new historicist and cultural
   criticism (pp. 1546–48) in Chapter 46, "Critical Strategies for Reading," and
   then research Theodore Roosevelt's role in the Spanish-American War and
   on what was happening in the Boston public school system in the late
   1980s. How does this information affect your reading of the poem?

CARL SANDBURG (1878–1967)

Buttons   *1916*

I have been watching the war map slammed up for advertising in front
        of the newspaper office.
Buttons — red and yellow buttons — blue and black buttons — are shoved
        back and forth across the map.

A laughing young man, sunny with freckles,
Climbs a ladder, yells a joke to somebody in the crowd,
And then fixes a yellow button one inch west
And follows the yellow button with a black button one inch west.

(Ten thousand men and boys twist on their bodies in a red soak along a
    river edge,
Gasping of wounds, calling for water, some rattling death in their
    throats.)
Who would guess what it cost to move two buttons one inch on the war
    map here in front of the newspaper office where the freckle-faced
    young man is laughing to us?

CONSIDERATIONS FOR CRITICAL THINKING AND WRITING

1. **FIRST RESPONSE.** Why is the date of this poem significant?
2. Discuss the symbolic meaning of the buttons and explain why you think
   the symbolism is too spelled out or not.
3. What purpose does the "laughing young man, sunny with freckles" serve in
   the poem?

CONNECTION TO ANOTHER SELECTION

1. Discuss the symbolic treatment of war in this poem, Kenneth Fearing's
   "AD" (p. 710), and Henry Reed's "Naming of Parts" (p. 720).

WALLACE STEVENS (1879–1955)

Anecdote of the Jar   1923

I placed a jar in Tennessee,
And round it was, upon a hill.
It made the slovenly wilderness
Surround that hill.

The wilderness rose up to it,   5
And sprawled around, no longer wild.
The jar was round upon the ground
And tall and of a port in air.

It took dominion everywhere.
The jar was gray and bare.   10
It did not give of bird or bush,
Like nothing else in Tennessee.

CONSIDERATIONS FOR CRITICAL THINKING AND WRITING

1. **FIRST RESPONSE.** How is the jar different from its surroundings? What
   effect does the jar's placement have upon the "slovenly wilderness"?

2. What do you make of all the "round" sounds in lines 2, 4, 6, and 7? How do they echo the relationship between the jar and the wilderness?

3. In what sense might this poem be regarded as an anecdote about the power and limitations of art and nature?

CONNECTION TO ANOTHER SELECTION

1. Compare the thematic function of the jar in Stevens's poem with that of the urn in John Keats's "Ode on a Grecian Urn" (p. 647). What important similarities and differences do you see in the meanings of each? Discuss why you think Stevens and Keats share similar or different ideas about art.

WILLIAM STAFFORD (1914–1993)

Traveling through the Dark   1962

Traveling through the dark I found a deer
dead on the edge of the Wilson River road.
It is usually best to roll them into the canyon:
that road is narrow; to swerve might make more dead.

By glow of the tail-light I stumbled back of the car   5
and stood by the heap, a doe, a recent killing;
she had stiffened already, almost cold.
I dragged her off; she was large in the belly.

My fingers touching her side brought me the reason —
her side was warm; her fawn lay there waiting,   10
alive, still, never to be born.
Beside that mountain road I hesitated.

The car aimed ahead its lowered parking lights;
under the hood purred the steady engine.
I stood in the glare of the warm exhaust turning red;   15
around our group I could hear the wilderness listen.

I thought hard for us all — my only swerving —
then pushed her over the edge into the river.

CONSIDERATIONS FOR CRITICAL THINKING AND WRITING

1. FIRST RESPONSE. Notice the description of the car in this poem: the "glow of the tail-light," the "lowered parking lights," and how the engine "purred." How do these and other details suggest symbolic meanings for the car and the "recent killing"?

2. Discuss the speaker's tone. Does the speaker seem, for example, tough, callous, kind, sentimental, confused, or confident?

3. What is the effect of the last stanza's having only two lines rather than the established four lines of the previous stanzas?
4. Discuss the appropriateness of this poem's title. In what sense has the speaker "thought hard for us all"? What are those thoughts?
5. Is this a didactic poem?

ALDEN NOWLAN (1933–1983)

The Bull Moose 1962

Down from the purple mist of trees on the mountain,
lurching through forests of white spruce and cedar,
stumbling through tamarack swamps,
came the bull moose
to be stopped at last by a pole-fenced pasture.   5

Too tired to turn or, perhaps, aware
there was no place left to go, he stood with the cattle.
They, scenting the musk of death, seeing his great head
like the ritual mask of a blood god, moved to the other end
of the field, and waited.   10

The neighbors heard of it, and by afternoon
cars lined the road. The children teased him
with alder switches and he gazed at them
like an old, tolerant collie. The women asked
if he could have escaped from a Fair.   15

The oldest man in the parish remembered seeing
a gelded moose yoked with an ox for plowing.
The young men snickered and tried to pour beer
down his throat, while their girl friends took their pictures.

The bull moose let them stroke his tick-ravaged flanks,   20
let them pry open his jaws with bottles, let a giggling girl
plant a little purple cap
of thistles on his head.

When the wardens came, everyone agreed it was a shame
to shoot anything so shaggy and cuddlesome.   25
He looked like the kind of pet
women put to bed with their sons.

So they held their fire. But just as the sun dropped in the river
the bull moose gathered his strength
like a scaffolded king, straightened and lifted his horns   30
so that even the wardens backed away as they raised their rifles.
When he roared, people ran to their cars. All the young men
leaned on their automobile horns as he toppled.

CONSIDERATIONS FOR CRITICAL THINKING AND WRITING

1. **FIRST RESPONSE.** How does the speaker present the moose and the townspeople? How are the moose and townspeople contrasted? Discuss specific lines to support your response.

2. Explain how the symbols in this poem point to a conflict between humanity and nature. What do you think the speaker's attitude toward this conflict is?

3. **CRITICAL STRATEGIES.** Read the section on mythological criticism (pp. 1550–52) in Chapter 46, "Critical Strategies for Reading," and write an essay on "The Bull Moose" that approaches the poem from a mythological perspective.

CONNECTION TO ANOTHER SELECTION

1. In an essay compare and contrast how the animals portrayed in "The Bull Moose" and in Stafford's "Traveling through the Dark" (p. 716) are used as symbols.

JULIO MARZÁN (B. 1946)

Ethnic Poetry 1994

The ethnic poet said: "The earth is maybe
a huge maraca / and the sun a trombone /
and life / is to move your ass / to slow beats."
The ethnic audience roasted a suckling pig.

The ethnic poet said: "Oh thank Goddy, Goddy /   5
I be me, my toenails curled downward /
deep, deep, deep into Mama earth."
The ethnic audience shook strands of sea shells.

The ethnic poet said: "The sun was created black /
so we should imagine light / and also dream /   10
a walrus emerging from the broken ice."
The ethnic audience beat on sealskin drums.

The ethnic poet said: "Reproductive organs /
Eagles nesting California redwoods /
Shut up and listen to my ancestors."   15
The ethnic audience ate fried bread and honey.

The ethnic poet said: "Something there is that
doesn't love a wall / That sends
the frozen-ground-swell under it."
The ethnic audience deeply understood humanity.   20

CONSIDERATIONS FOR CRITICAL THINKING AND WRITING

1. **FIRST RESPONSE.** What is the implicit definition of ethnic poetry in this poem?

2. The final stanza quotes lines from Robert Frost's "Mending Wall" (p. 884). Read the entire poem. Why do you think Marzán chooses these lines and this particular poem as one kind of ethnic poetry?

3. What is the poem's central irony? Pay particular attention to the final line. What is being satirized here?

4. **CRITICAL STRATEGIES.** Read the section on the literary canon (pp. 1536–37) in Chapter 46, "Critical Strategies for Reading," and consider how the formation of the literary canon is related to the theme of "Ethnic Poetry."

CONNECTION TO ANOTHER SELECTION

1. Write an essay that discusses the speaker's ideas about what poetry should be in "Ethnic Poetry" and in Langston Hughes's "Formula" (p. 920).

JAMES MERRILL (1926–1995)

Casual Wear

1984

Your average tourist: Fifty. 2.3
Times married. Dressed, this year, in Ferdi Plinthbower
Originals. Odds 1 to 9
Against her strolling past the Embassy

Today at noon. Your average terrorist: 5
Twenty-five. Celibate. No use for trends,
At least in clothing. Mark, though, where it ends.
People have come forth made of colored mist

Unsmiling on one hundred million screens
To tell of his prompt phone call to the station,   10
"Claiming responsibility" — devastation
Signed with a flourish, like the dead wife's jeans.

CONSIDERATIONS FOR CRITICAL THINKING AND WRITING

1. **FIRST RESPONSE.** What is the effect of the statistics in this poem?

2. Describe the speaker's tone. Is it appropriate for the subject matter? Explain why or why not.

3. Comment on the ironies that emerge from the final two lines. How are the tourist and terrorist linked by the speaker's description? Explain why you think the speaker sympathizes more with the tourist or the terrorist — or with neither.

CONNECTION TO ANOTHER SELECTION

1. Compare the satire in this poem with that in Peter Meinke's "The ABC of Aerobics" (p. 816). What is satirized in each poem? Which satire do you think is more pointed?

HENRY REED (1914–1986)
Naming of Parts

1946

Today we have naming of parts. Yesterday,
We had daily cleaning. And tomorrow morning,
We shall have what to do after firing. But today,
Today we have naming of parts. Japonica
Glistens like coral in all of the neighboring gardens,   5
          And today we have naming of parts.

This is the lower sling swivel. And this
Is the upper sling swivel, whose use you will see,
When you are given your slings. And this is the piling swivel,
Which in your case you have not got. The branches   10
Hold in the gardens their silent, eloquent gestures,
          Which in our case we have not got.

This is the safety-catch, which is always released
With an easy flick of the thumb. And please do not let me
See anyone using his finger. You can do it quite easy   15
If you have any strength in your thumb. The blossoms
Are fragile and motionless, never letting anyone see
          Any of them using their finger.

And this you can see is the bolt. The purpose of this
Is to open the breech, as you see. We can slide it   20
Rapidly backwards and forwards: we call this
Easing the spring. And rapidly backwards and forwards
The early bees are assaulting and fumbling the flowers:
          They call it easing the Spring.

They call it easing the Spring: it is perfectly easy   25
If you have any strength in your thumb: like the bolt,
And the breech, and the cocking-piece, and the point of balance,
Which in our case we have not got; and the almond-blossom
Silent in all of the gardens and the bees going backwards and forwards,
          For today we have naming of parts.   30

CONSIDERATIONS FOR CRITICAL THINKING AND WRITING

1. **FIRST RESPONSE.** Characterize the two speakers in this poem. Identify the lines spoken by each. How do their respective lines differ in tone?
2. What is the effect of the last line of each stanza?
3. How do ambiguities and puns contribute to the poem's meaning?
4. What symbolic contrast is made between the rifle instruction and the gardens? How is this contrast ironic?

RACHEL HADAS (B. 1948)

The Compact   *2003*

The short steep ride in the red bus uphill
from the Girls' School to the Boys' School left
time to whip our compacts out and powder
cheeks, noses. What for? For the boys? Well, yes,
we might have answered if we had been asked.   5
No one asked. Good thing. We didn't know.
Those uphill rides were forty years ago.

If every gesture halves a hidden whole,
if every moment twins a hidden half,
then my thumb clicking that pink plastic catch   10
(sweet whiff of powder; flash of a tiny mirror)
opens not only the compact but also
the first half of a parenthesis
stretching its arms out, longing to be closed.

CONSIDERATIONS FOR CRITICAL THINKING AND WRITING

1. FIRST RESPONSE. Discuss the denotative meanings of the "compact" as well
   as its potential symbolic meanings.
2. Why is it appropriate that the bus is red (rather than a yellow school bus)
   and that the trip is an uphill ride?
3. How do the final lines effectively end the poem?

ROBERT BROWNING (1812–1889)

My Last Duchess   *1842*

Ferrara°

That's my last Duchess painted on the wall,
Looking as if she were alive. I call
That piece a wonder, now: Frà Pandolf's°
      hands
Worked busily a day, and there she stands.
Will't please you sit and look at her? I said
"Frà Pandolf" by design, for never read
Strangers like you that pictured countenance,
The depth and passion of its earnest glance,
But to myself they turned (since none puts by

Courtesy of the National Portrait Gallery, London.

Ferrara: In the sixteenth century, the duke of this Italian city arranged to marry a second time after the mysterious death of his very young first wife.   3 *Frà Pandolf:* A fictitious artist.

The curtain I have drawn for you, but I)   10
And seemed as they would ask me, if they durst,
How such a glance came there; so, not the first
Are you to turn and ask thus. Sir, 'twas not
Her husband's presence only, called that spot
Of joy into the Duchess' cheek: perhaps   15
Frà Pandolf chanced to say "Her mantle laps
Over my lady's wrist too much," or "Paint
Must never hope to reproduce the faint
Half-flush that dies along her throat": such stuff
Was courtesy, she thought, and cause enough   20
For calling up that spot of joy. She had
A heart — how shall I say? — too soon made glad,
Too easily impressed; she liked whate'er
She looked on, and her looks went everywhere.
Sir, 'twas all one! My favor at her breast,   25
The dropping of the daylight in the West,
The bough of cherries some officious fool
Broke in the orchard for her, the white mule
She rode with round the terrace — all and each
Would draw from her alike the approving speech,   30
Or blush, at least. She thanked men, — good! but thanked
Somehow — I know not how — as if she ranked
My gift of a nine-hundred-years-old name
With anybody's gift. Who'd stoop to blame
This sort of trifling? Even had you skill   35
In speech — which I have not — to make your will
Quite clear to such an one, and say, "Just this
Or that in you disgusts me; here you miss,
Or there exceed the mark" — and if she let
Herself be lessoned so, nor plainly set   40
Her wits to yours, forsooth, and made excuse,
— E'en then would be some stooping; and I choose
Never to stoop. Oh sir, she smiled, no doubt,
Whene'er I passed her; but who passed without
Much the same smile? This grew; I gave commands;   45
Then all smiles stopped together. There she stands
As if alive. Will 't please you rise? We'll meet
The company below, then. I repeat,
The Count your master's known munificence
Is ample warrant that no just pretense   50
Of mine for dowry will be disallowed;
Though his fair daughter's self, as I avowed
At starting, is my object. Nay, we'll go
Together down, sir. Notice Neptune, though,
Taming a sea-horse, thought a rarity,   55
Which Claus of Innsbruck° cast in bronze for me!

Explore contexts
for Robert Browning
on *LiterActive*.

56 *Claus of Innsbruck:* Also a fictitious artist.

CONSIDERATIONS FOR CRITICAL THINKING AND WRITING

1. **FIRST RESPONSE.** What do you think happened to the duchess?

2. To whom is the duke addressing his remarks about the duchess in this poem? What is ironic about the situation?

3. Why was the duke unhappy with his first wife? What does this reveal about the duke? What does the poem's title suggest about his attitude toward women in general?

4. What seems to be the visitor's response (lines 53–54) to the duke's account of his first wife?

CONNECTION TO ANOTHER SELECTION

1. Write an essay describing the ways in which the speakers of "My Last Duchess" and Katharyn Howd Machan's "Hazel Tells LaVerne" (p. 631) inadvertently reveal themselves.

WILLIAM BLAKE (1757–1827)

The Chimney Sweeper   1789

When my mother died I was very young,
And my father sold me while yet my tongue
Could scarcely cry " 'weep! 'weep! 'weep! 'weep!"
So your chimneys I sweep, and in soot I sleep.

There's little Tom Dacre, who cried when his head,   5
That curled like a lamb's back, was shaved: so I said
"Hush, Tom! never mind it, for when your head's bare
You know that the soot cannot spoil your white hair."

And so he was quiet, and that very night,
As Tom was a-sleeping, he had such a sight!   10
That thousands of sweepers, Dick, Joe, Ned, and Jack,
Were all of them locked up in coffins of black.

And by came an Angel who had a bright key,
And he opened the coffins and set them all free;
Then down a green plain leaping, laughing, they run,   15
And wash in a river, and shine in the sun.

Then naked and white, all their bags left behind,
They rise upon clouds and sport in the wind;
And the Angel told Tom, if he'd be a good boy,
He'd have God for his father, and never want joy.   20

And so Tom awoke; and we rose in the dark,
And got with our bags and our brushes to work.
Though the morning was cold, Tom was happy and warm;
So if all do their duty they need not fear harm.

CONSIDERATIONS FOR CRITICAL THINKING AND WRITING

1. **FIRST RESPONSE.** Discuss the validity of this statement: " 'The Chimney Sweeper' is a sentimental poem about a shameful eighteenth-century social problem; such a treatment of child abuse cannot be taken seriously."

2. Characterize the speaker in this poem and describe his tone. Is his tone the same as the poet's? Consider especially lines 7, 8, and 24.

3. What is the symbolic value of the dream in lines 11 to 20?

4. Why is irony central to the meaning of this poem?

Perspective

EZRA POUND (1885–1972)

On Symbols   1912

I believe that the proper and perfect symbol is the natural object, that if a man uses "symbols" he must so use them that their symbolic function does not obtrude; so that *a* sense, and the poetic quality of the passage, is not lost to those who do not understand the symbol as such, to whom, for instance, a hawk is a hawk.

From "Prolegomena," *Poetry Review*, February 1912

CONSIDERATIONS FOR CRITICAL THINKING AND WRITING

1. Discuss whether you agree with Pound that the "perfect symbol" is a "natural object" that does not insist on being read as a symbol.

2. Write an essay in which you discuss Alden Nowlan's "The Bull Moose" (p. 717) as an example of the "perfect symbol" Pound proposes.

Web Research the poets in this chapter at bedfordstmartins.com/meyercompact.

24

Sounds

That's what enraptured me about
poetry specifically — that language
could sing.

— GALWAY KINNELL

LISTENING TO POETRY

Poems yearn to be read aloud. Much of their energy, charm, and beauty
comes to life only when they are heard. Poets choose and arrange words for
their sounds as well as for their meanings. Most poetry is best read with
your lips, teeth, and tongue because they serve to articulate the effects that sound may have in a poem. When
a voice is breathed into a good poem, there is pleasure
in the reading, the saying, and the hearing.

Web Explore
the poetic elements
in this chapter on
LiterActive or at
bedfordstmartins
.com/meyercompact.

The earliest poetry — before writing and painting —
was chanted or sung. The rhythmic quality of such oral performances
served two purposes: it helped the chanting bard remember the lines and it
entertained audiences with patterned sounds of language, which were
sometimes accompanied by musical instruments. Poetry has always been

closely related to music. Indeed, as the word suggests, lyric poetry evolved from songs. "Western Wind" (p. 586), an anonymous Middle English lyric, survived as song long before it was written down. Had Robert Frost lived in a nonliterate society, he probably would have sung some version — a very different version to be sure — of "Acquainted with the Night" (p. 703) instead of writing it down. Even though Frost creates a speaking rather than a singing voice, the speaker's anxious tone is distinctly heard in any careful reading of the poem.

Like lyrics, early narrative poems were originally part of an anonymous oral folk tradition. A ***ballad*** such as "Bonny Barbara Allan" (p. 1011) told a story that was sung from one generation to the next until it was finally transcribed. Since the eighteenth century, this narrative form has sometimes been imitated by poets who write ***literary ballads.*** John Keats's "La Belle Dame sans Merci" (p. 1025) is, for example, a more complex and sophisticated nineteenth-century reflection of the original ballad traditions that developed in the fifteenth century and earlier. In considering poetry as sound, we should not forget that poetry traces its beginnings to song.

These next lines exemplify poetry's continuing relation to song. What poetic elements can you find in this ballad, which was adapted by Paul Simon and Art Garfunkel and became a popular antiwar song in the 1960s?

ANONYMOUS

Scarborough Fair   *date unknown*

Where are you going? To Scarborough Fair?
Parsley, sage, rosemary, and thyme,
Remember me to a bonny lass there,
For once she was a true lover of mine.

Tell her to make me a cambric shirt,   5
Parsley, sage, rosemary, and thyme,
Without any needle or thread work'd in it,
And she shall be a true lover of mine.

Tell her to wash it in yonder well,
Parsley, sage, rosemary, and thyme,   10
Where water ne'er sprung nor a drop of rain fell,
And she shall be a true lover of mine.

Tell her to plough me an acre of land,
Parsley, sage, rosemary, and thyme,
Between the sea and the salt sea strand,   15
And she shall be a true lover of mine.

Tell her to plough it with one ram's horn,
Parsley, sage, rosemary, and thyme,

And sow it all over with one peppercorn,
And she shall be a true lover of mine.   20

Tell her to reap it with a sickle of leather,
Parsley, sage, rosemary, and thyme,
And tie it all up with a tom tit's feather,
And she shall be a true lover of mine.

Tell her to gather it all in a sack,
Parsley, sage, rosemary, and thyme,   25
And carry it home on a butterfly's back,
And then she shall be a true lover of mine.

CONSIDERATIONS FOR CRITICAL THINKING AND WRITING

1. **FIRST RESPONSE.** What do you associate with "Parsley, sage, rosemary, and thyme"? What images does this poem evoke? How so?

2. What kinds of demands does the speaker make of his former lover? What do these demands have in common?

3. What is the tone of this ballad?

4. Choose a contemporary song that you especially like and examine the lyrics. Write an essay explaining whether or not you consider the lyrics poetic.

Of course, reading "Scarborough Fair" is not the same as hearing it. Like the lyrics of a song, many poems must be heard — or at least read with listening eyes — before they can be fully understood and enjoyed. The sounds of words are a universal source of music for human beings. This has been so from ancient tribes to bards to the two-year-old child in a bakery gleefully chanting "Cuppitycake, cuppitycake!"

Listen to the sound of this poem as you read it aloud. How do the words provide, in a sense, their own musical accompaniment?

JOHN UPDIKE (B. 1932)

Player Piano   1958

My stick fingers click with a snicker
And, chuckling, they knuckle the keys;
Light-footed, my steel feelers flicker
And pluck from these keys melodies.

My paper can caper; abandon
Is broadcast by dint of my din,   5
And no man or band has a hand in
The tones I turn on from within.

At times I'm a jumble of rumbles,
At others I'm light like the moon,   10

But never my numb plunker fumbles,
Misstrums me, or tries a new tune.

The speaker in this poem is a piano that can play automatically by means of a mechanism that depresses keys in response to signals on a perforated roll. Notice how the speaker's voice approximates the sounds of a piano. In each stanza a predominant sound emerges from the carefully chosen words. How is the sound of each stanza tuned to its sense?

Like Updike's "Player Piano," this next poem is also primarily about sounds.

MAY SWENSON (B. 1919)

A Nosty Fright

1984

The roldengod and the soneyhuckle,
the sack eyed blusan and the wistle theed
are all tangled with the oison pivy,
the fallen nine peedles and the wumbleteed.

A mipchunk caught in a wobceb tried   5
to hip and skide in a dandy sune
but a stobler put up a EEP KOFF sign.
Then the unfucky lellow met a phytoon
and was sept out to swea. He difted for drays
till a hassgropper flying happened to spot   10
the boolish feast all debraggled and wet,
covered with snears and tot.

Loonmight shone through the winey poods
where rushmooms grew among risted twoots.
Back blats flew betreen the twees   15
and orned howls hounded their soots.

A kumkpin stood with tooked creeth
on the sindow will of a house
where a icked wold itch lived all alone
except for her stoombrick, a mitten and a kouse.   20

"Here we part," said hassgropper.
"Pere we hart," said mipchunk, too.
They purried away on opposite haths,
both scared of some "Bat!" or "Scoo!"

October was ending on a nosty fright   25
with scroans and greeches and chanking clains,
with oblins and gelfs, coaths and urses,
skinning grulls and stoodblains.

Will it ever be morning, Nofember virst,
skue bly and the sappy hun, our friend?   30
With light breaves of wall by the fayside?
I sope ho, so that this oem can pend.

At just the right moments Swenson transposes letters to create amusing
sound effects and wild wordplays. Although there is a story lurking in "A
Nosty Fright," any serious attempt to interpret its meaning is confronted
with "a EEP KOFF sign." Instead, we are invited to enjoy the delicious
sounds the poet has cooked up.

    Few poems revel in sound so completely. More typically, the sounds of
a poem contribute to its meaning rather than become its meaning. Consider how sound is used in the next poem.

EMILY DICKINSON (1830–1886)

A Bird came down the Walk —   *c. 1862*

A Bird came down the Walk —
He did not know I saw —
He bit an Angleworm in halves
And ate the fellow, raw,

And then he drank a Dew   5
From a convenient Grass —
And then hopped sidewise to the Wall
To let a Beetle pass —

He glanced with rapid eyes
That hurried all around —   10
They looked like frightened Beads, I thought —
He stirred his Velvet Head

Like one in danger, Cautious,
I offered him a Crumb
And he unrolled his feathers   15
And rowed him softer home —

Than Oars divide the Ocean,
Too silver for a seam —
Or Butterflies, off Banks of Noon
Leap, plashless as they swim.   20

    This description of a bird offers a close look at how differently a bird
moves when it hops on the ground than when it flies in the air. On the
ground the bird moves quickly, awkwardly, and irregularly as it plucks up
a worm, washes it down with dew, and then hops aside to avoid a passing

beetle. The speaker recounts the bird's rapid, abrupt actions from a somewhat superior, amused perspective. By describing the bird in human terms (as if, for example, it chose to eat the worm "raw"), the speaker is almost condescending. But when the attempt to offer a crumb fails and the frightened bird flies off, the speaker is left looking up instead of down at the bird.

With that shift in perspective the tone shifts from amusement to awe in response to the bird's graceful flight. The jerky movements of lines 1 to 13 give way to the smooth motion of lines 15 to 20. The pace of the first three stanzas is fast and discontinuous. We tend to pause at the end of each line, and this reinforces a sense of disconnected movements. In contrast, the final six lines are to be read as a single sentence in one flowing movement, lubricated by various sounds.

Read again the description of the bird flying away. Several *o*-sounds contribute to the image of the serene, expansive, confident flight, just as the *s*-sounds serve as smooth transitions from one line to the next. Notice how these sounds are grouped in the following vertical columns:

unrolled	softer	too	his	Ocean	Banks
rowed	Oars	Noon	feathers	silver	plashless
home	Or		softer	seam	as
Ocean	off		Oars	Butterflies	swim

This blending of sounds (notice how "Leap, plashless" brings together the *p*- and *l*-sounds without a ripple) helps convey the bird's smooth grace in the air. Like a feathered oar, the bird moves seamlessly in its element.

The repetition of sounds in poetry is similar to the function of the tones and melodies that are repeated, with variations, in music. Just as the patterned sounds in music unify a work, so do the words in poems, which have been carefully chosen for the combinations of sounds they create. These sounds are produced in a number of ways.

The most direct way in which the sound of a word suggests its meaning is through **onomatopoeia,** which is the use of a word that resembles the sound it denotes: *quack, buzz, rattle, bang, squeak, bowwow, burp, choo-choo, ding-a-ling, sizzle.* The sound and sense of these words are closely related, but such words represent a very small percentage of the words available to us. Poets usually employ more subtle means for echoing meanings.

Onomatopoeia can consist of more than just single words. In its broadest meaning the term refers to lines or passages in which sounds help to convey meanings, as in these lines from Updike's "Player Piano":

> My stick fingers click with a snicker
> And, chuckling, they knuckle the keys.

The sharp, crisp sounds of these two lines approximate the sounds of a piano; the syllables seem to "click" against one another. Contrast Updike's rendition with the following lines:

My long fingers play with abandon
And, laughing, they cover the keys.

The original version is more interesting and alive because the sounds of the words are pleasurable and reinforce the meaning through a careful blending of consonants and vowels.

Alliteration is the repetition of the same consonant sounds at the beginnings of nearby words: "*d*escending *d*ewdrops," "*l*uscious *l*emons." Sometimes the term is also used to describe the consonant sounds within words: "tres*p*asser's re*p*roach," "we*dd*ed la*d*y." Alliteration is based on sound rather than spelling. "*K*een" and "*c*ar" alliterate, but "*c*ar" does not alliterate with "*c*ite." Rarely is heavy-handed alliteration effective. Used too self-consciously, it can be distracting instead of strengthening meaning or emphasizing a relation between words. Consider the relentless *h*'s in this line: "Horrendous horrors haunted Helen's happiness." Those *h*'s certainly suggest that Helen is being pursued, but they have a more comic than serious effect because they are overdone.

Assonance is the repetition of the same vowel sound in nearby words: "as*lee*p under a tr*ee*," "t*i*me and t*i*de," "h*au*nt" and "*aw*esome," "*ea*ch evening." Both alliteration and assonance help to establish relations among words in a line or a series of lines. Whether the effect is **euphony** (lines that are musically pleasant to the ear and smooth, like the final lines of Dickinson's "A Bird came down the Walk—") or **cacophony** (lines that are discordant and difficult to pronounce, like the claim that "never my numb plunker fumbles" in Updike's "Player Piano"), the sounds of words in poetry can be as significant as the words' denotative or connotative meanings.

A SAMPLE STUDENT RESPONSE

Ryan Lee

Professor McDonough

English 211

December 1, 2008

Sound in Emily Dickinson's "A Bird came down the Walk--"

In her poem "A Bird came down the Walk--" Emily Dickinson uses the sound and rhythm of each line to reflect the motion of a bird walking awkwardly--and then flying gracefully. Particularly when read aloud, the staccato phrases and stilted breaks in lines 1 through 14 create a sense of the bird's movement on land, quick and off-balanced, which helps bring the scene to life.

The first three stanzas are structured to make the bird's movement consistent. The bird hops around, eating worms while keeping guard for any threats. Vulnerable on the ground, the bird is intensely aware of danger:

> He glanced with rapid eyes
>
> That hurried all around--
>
> They looked like frightened Beads, I thought--
>
> He stirred his Velvet Head (9-12)

In addition to choosing words that portray the bird as cautious--it "glanced with rapid eyes" (9) that resemble "frightened Beads" (11)--Dickinson chooses to end each line abruptly. This abrupt halting of sound allows the reader to experience the bird's fear more immediately, and the effect is similar to the missing of a beat or a breath.

These halting lines stand in contrast to the smoothness of the last six lines, during which the bird takes flight. The sounds in these lines are pleasingly soft, and rich in the "s" sound. The bird

> unrolled his feathers
>
> And rowed him softer home--
>
>
> Than Oars
>
> divide the Ocean,
>
> Too silver for a seam-- (15-18). . . .

Lee 4

Work Cited

Dickinson, Emily. "A Bird came down the Walk--." The Compact Bedford Introduction to Literature. Ed. Michael Meyer. 8th ed. Boston: Bedford/
St. Martin's, 2009. 729.

This next poem provides a feast of sounds. Read the poem aloud and
try to determine the effects of its sounds.

GALWAY KINNELL (B. 1927)

Blackberry Eating   *1980*

I love to go out in late September
among the fat, overripe, icy, black
    blackberries
to eat blackberries for breakfast,
the stalks very prickly, a penalty
they earn for knowing the black art
of blackberry-making; and as I stand among
    them
lifting the stalks to my mouth, the ripest
    berries
fall almost unbidden to my tongue,
as words sometimes do, certain peculiar words
like *strengths* or *squinched,*
many-lettered, one-syllabled lumps,
which I squeeze, squinch open, and splurge well
in the silent, startled, icy, black language
of blackberry-eating in late September.

Photo by Charlie Nye.

10

CONSIDERATIONS FOR CRITICAL THINKING AND WRITING

1. **FIRST RESPONSE.** What types of sounds does Kinnell use throughout this
   poem? What categories can you place them in? What is the effect of these
   sounds?

2. How do lines 4–6 fit into the poem? What does this prickly image add to
   the poem?

3. Explain what you think the poem's theme is.

4. Write an essay that considers the speaker's love of blackberry eating along with the speaker's appetite for words. How are the two blended in the poem?

RHYME

Like alliteration and assonance, *rhyme* is a way of creating sound patterns. Rhyme, broadly defined, consists of two or more words or phrases that repeat the same sounds: *happy* and *snappy*. Rhyme words often have similar spellings, but that is not a requirement of rhyme; what matters is that the words sound alike: *vain* rhymes with *reign* as well as *rain*. Moreover, words may look alike but not rhyme at all. In *eye rhyme* the spellings are similar, but the pronunciations are not, as with *bough* and *cough*, or *brow* and *blow*.

Not all poems use rhyme. Many great poems have no rhymes, and many weak verses use rhyme as a substitute for poetry. These are especially apparent in commercial messages and greeting-card lines. At its worst, rhyme is merely a distracting decoration that can lead to dullness and predictability. But used skillfully, rhyme creates lines that are memorable and musical.

Here is a poem using rhyme that you might remember the next time you are in a restaurant.

RICHARD ARMOUR (1906–1989)

Going to Extremes   1954

Shake and shake
  The catsup bottle
None'll come —
  And then a lot'll.

The experience recounted in Armour's poem is common enough, but the rhyme's humor is special. The final line clicks the poem shut — an effect that is often achieved by the use of rhyme. That click provides a sense of a satisfying and fulfilled form. Rhymes have a number of uses: they can emphasize words, direct a reader's attention to relations between words, and provide an overall structure for a poem.

Rhyme is used in the following poem to imitate the sound of cascading water.

ROBERT SOUTHEY (1774–1843)
From "The Cataract of Lodore"   1820

"How does the water
Come down at Lodore?"
. . . .
From its sources which well
  In the tarn on the fell;
    From its fountains   5
    In the mountains,
  Its rills and its gills;
Through moss and through brake,
  It runs and it creeps
  For awhile, till it sleeps   10
  In its own little lake.
And thence at departing,
Awakening and starting,
  It runs through the reeds
  And away it proceeds,   15
Through meadow and glade,
  In sun and in shade,
And through the wood-shelter,
  Among crags in its flurry,
    Helter-skelter,   20
    Hurry-scurry.
Here it comes sparkling,
And there it lies darkling;
Now smoking and frothing
  Its tumult and wrath in,   25
  Till in this rapid race
    On which it is bent,
  It reaches the place
  Of its steep descent.

  The cataract strong   30
  Then plunges along,
Striking and raging
As if a war waging
Its caverns and rocks among:
  Rising and leaping,   35
  Sinking and creeping,
  Swelling and sweeping,
Showering and springing,
  Flying and flinging,
  Writhing and ringing,   40
Eddying and whisking,
Spouting and frisking,
Turning and twisting,
  Around and around

With endless rebound!   45
Smiting and fighting,
    A sight to delight in;
Confounding, astounding,
Dizzying and deafening the ear with its sound.
. . . .
Dividing and gliding and sliding,   50
And falling and brawling and spawling,
And driving and riving and striving,
And sprinkling and twinkling and wrinkling,
And sounding and bounding and rounding,
And bubbling and troubling and doubling,   55
And grumbling and rumbling and tumbling,
And clattering and battering and shattering;
Retreating and beating and meeting and sheeting,
Delaying and straying and playing and spraying,
Advancing and prancing and glancing and dancing,   60
Recoiling, turmoiling and toiling and boiling,
And gleaming and streaming and steaming and beaming,
And rushing and flushing and brushing and gushing,
And flapping and rapping and clapping and slapping,
And curling and whirling and purling and twirling,   65
And thumping and plumping and bumping and jumping,
And dashing and flashing and splashing and clashing;
And so never ending, but always descending,
Sounds and motions forever and ever are blending,
All at once and all o'er, with a mighty uproar;   70
And this way the water comes down at Lodore.

This deluge of rhymes consists of "Sounds and motions forever and ever . . . blending" (line 69). The pace quickens as the water creeps from its mountain source and then descends in rushing cataracts. As the speed of the water increases, so do the number of rhymes, until they run in fours: "dashing and flashing and splashing and clashing" (line 67). Most rhymes meander through poems instead of flooding them; nevertheless, Southey's use of rhyme suggests how sounds can flow with meanings. "The Cataract of Lodore" has been criticized, however, for overusing onomatopoeia. Some readers find the poem silly; others regard it as a brilliant example of sound effects. What do you think?

A variety of types of rhyme is available to poets. The most common form, **end rhyme,** comes at the ends of lines (lines 14-17).

It runs through the reeds
    And away it proceeds,
Through meadow and glade,
    In sun and in shade.

Internal rhyme places at least one of the rhymed words within the line, as in "Dividing and gliding and sliding" (line 50) or, more subtly, in the fourth and final words of "In mist or cloud, on mast or shroud."

The rhyming of single-syllable words such as *glade* and *shade* is known as **masculine rhyme,** as we see in these lines from A. E. Housman:

> Loveliest of trees, the cherry now
> Is hung with bloom along the bough.

Rhymes using words of more than one syllable are also called masculine when the same sound occurs in a final stressed syllable, as in *defend, contend; betray, away.* A **feminine rhyme** consists of a rhymed stressed syllable followed by one or more rhymed unstressed syllables, as in *butter, clutter; gratitude, attitude; quivering, shivering.* This rhyme is evident in John Millington Synge's verse:

> Lord confound this surly sister,
> Blight her brow and blotch and blister.

All of the examples so far have been **exact rhymes** because they share the same stressed vowel sounds as well as any sounds that follow the vowel. In **near rhyme** (also called **off rhyme, slant rhyme,** and **approximate rhyme**), the sounds are almost but not exactly alike. There are several kinds of near rhyme. One of the most common is **consonance,** an identical consonant sound preceded by a different vowel sound: *home, same; worth, breath; trophy, daffy.* Near rhyme can also be achieved by using different vowel sounds with identical consonant sounds: *sound, sand; kind, conned; fellow, fallow.* The dissonance of *blade* and *blood* in the following lines from Wilfred Owen helps to reinforce their grim tone:

> Let the boy try along this bayonet-blade
> How cold steel is, and keen with hunger of blood.

Near rhymes greatly broaden the possibility for musical effects in English, a language that, compared with Spanish or Italian, contains few exact rhymes. Do not assume, however, that a near rhyme represents a failed attempt at exact rhyme. Near rhymes allow a musical subtlety and variety and can avoid the sometimes overpowering jingling effects that exact rhymes may create.

These basic terms hardly exhaust the ways in which the sounds in poems can be labeled and discussed, but the terms can help you to describe how poets manipulate sounds for effect. Read "God's Grandeur" (p. 738) aloud and try to determine how the sounds of the lines contribute to their sense.

Perspective

David Lenson (B. 1945)

On the Contemporary Use of Rhyme   1988

One impediment to a respectable return to rhyme is the popular survival of "functional" verse: greeting cards, pedagogical and mnemonic devices ("Thirty days hath September"), nursery rhymes, advertising jingles, and of course song lyrics. Pentameters, irregular rhymes, and free verse aren't much use in songwriting, where the meter has to be governed by the time signature of the music.

Far from universities, there has been a revival of rhymed couplets in rap music, in which, to the accompaniment of synthesizers, vocalists deliver lengthy first-person narratives in tetrameter. While most writing teachers would dismiss such lyrics as doggerel, the aim of the songs is really not so far from that of Alexander Pope: to use rhyme to sharpen social insight, in the hope that the world may be reordered.

From *The Chronicle of Higher Education*, February 24, 1988

CONSIDERATIONS FOR CRITICAL THINKING AND WRITING

1. Read some contemporary song lyrics from a wide range of groups or vocalists. Is Lenson correct in his assessment that irregular rhyme is not much use in songwriting?
2. Examine the rhymed couplets of some rap music. Discuss whether they are used "to sharpen social insight." What is the effect of using rhymes in rap music?
3. What is your own response to rhymed poetry? Do you like yours with or without? What do you think informs your preference?

SOUND AND MEANING

GERARD MANLEY HOPKINS (1844–1889)

God's Grandeur   1877

The world is charged with the grandeur of God
   It will flame out, like shining from shook foil;°   *shaken gold foil*
   It gathers to a greatness, like the ooze of oil
Crushed.° Why do men then now not reck his rod?°
Generations have trod, have trod, have trod;   5
   And all is seared with trade; bleared, smeared with toil;
   And wears man's smudge and shares man's smell: the soil
Is bare now, nor can foot feel, being shod.

And for all this, nature is never spent;
   There lives the dearest freshness deep down things;   10
And though the last lights off the black West went
   Oh, morning, at the brown brink eastward, springs —
Because the Holy Ghost over the bent
   World broods with warm breast and with ah! bright wings.

---

4 *Crushed:* Olives crushed in their oil;   *reck his rod:* Obey God.

The subject of this poem is announced in the title and the first line: "The world is charged with the grandeur of God." The poem is a celebration of the power and greatness of God's presence in the world, but the speaker is also perplexed and dismayed by people who refuse to recognize God's authority and grandeur as they are manifested in the creation. Instead of glorifying God, "men" have degraded the earth through meaningless toil and cut themselves off from the spiritual renewal inherent in the beauty of nature. The relentless demands of commerce and industry have blinded people to the earth's natural and spiritual resources. Despite this abuse and insensitivity to God's grandeur, however, "nature is never spent"; the morning light that "springs" in the east redeems the "black West" of the night and is a sign that the spirit of the Holy Ghost is ever present in the world. This summary of the poem sketches some of the thematic significance of the lines, but it does not do justice to how they are organized around the use of sound. Hopkins's poem, unlike Southey's "The Cataract of Lodore," uses sounds in a subtle and complex way.

In the opening line Hopkins uses alliteration—a device apparent in almost every line of the poem—to connect "Go*d*" to the "worl*d*," which is "charge*d*" with his "gran*d*eur." These consonants unify the line as well. The alliteration in lines 2 and 3 suggests a harmony in the creation: the *f*'s in "*f*lame" and "*f*oil," the *sh*'s in "*sh*ining" and "*sh*ook," the *g*'s in "*g*athers" and "*g*reatness," and the visual (not alliterative) similarities of "*ooze* of *oil*" emphasize a world that is held together by God's will.

That harmony is abruptly interrupted by the speaker's angry question in line 4: "Why do men then now not reck his rod?" The question is as painful to the speaker as it is difficult to pronounce. The arrangement of the alliteration ("*n*ow," "*n*ot"; "*r*eck," "*r*od"), the assonance ("n*o*t," "r*o*d"; "m*e*n," "th*e*n," "r*e*ck"), and the internal rhyme ("men," "then") contribute to the difficulty in saying the line—a difficulty associated with human behavior. That behavior is introduced in line 5 by the repetition of "have trod" to emphasize the repeated mistakes—sins—committed by human beings. The tone is dirgelike because humanity persists in its mistaken path rather than progressing. The speaker's horror at humanity is evident in the cacophonous sounds of lines 6 to 8. Here the alliteration of "*sm*eared," "*sm*udge," and "*sm*ell" along with the internal rhymes of "*seared*," "*bleared*," and "*smeared*" echo the disgust with which the speaker views humanity's "toil" with the "soil," an end rhyme that calls attention to our mistaken equation of nature with production rather than with spirituality.

In contrast to this cacophony, the final six lines build toward the joyful recognition of the new possibilities that accompany the rising sun. This recognition leads to the euphonic description of the "H*o*ly Gh*o*st *o*ver" (notice the reassuring consistency of the assonance) the world. Traditionally represented as a dove, the Holy Ghost brings love and peace to the "*w*orld," and "*b*roods *w*ith *w*arm *b*reast and *w*ith ah! *b*right *w*ings." The effect of this alliteration is mellifluous: the sound bespeaks the harmony that prevails at the end of the poem resulting from the speaker's recognition that "nature is never spent" because God loves and protects the world.

The sounds of "God's Grandeur" enhance the poem's theme; more can be said about its sounds, but it is enough to point out here that for this poem the sound strongly echoes the theme in nearly every line. Here are some more poems in which sound plays a significant role.

POEMS FOR FURTHER STUDY

THOMAS LUX (B. 1946)

Onomatopoeia
                                                                    1994

The word sounds like the thing.
The sound of the word next to
the sound of another word
sounds like the thing feels
or you desire it to feel. You want   5
this alive
from its insides
and the mind, the denotative, the dictionary
means naught: what you want
to be known must be known   10
cellularly, belly-wise,
or on the tongue: *cerulean blue*,
for example, or *punch drunk*.
Those who live elsewhere
than their bodies don't buy it, don't like it,   15
this in-the-body; the science
and the math tests on it
are yet inconclusive.
There's always this little humming
beneath the surface   20
of the painting, the dance, the play
(the good ones) that tells your heart
that it — the painting, the dance, the play — tells
a truth: *dewlap, dewlap*,
it's dawn's time, it says — the sound   25
provides the thing its lungs, mouth,
and blood-beat. The sound, the noise of the sound, is
the thing — the deaf can hear it,
the blind see it, this tuning fork
beneath the breastbone, sweetly   30
accompanying its song.

CONSIDERATIONS FOR CRITICAL THINKING AND WRITING

1. **FIRST RESPONSE.** Compare Lux's poetic definition of *onomatopoeia* with the textbook definition on page 730. What does Lux's treatment of *onomatopoeia* add to the standard definition?

2. Which lines contain images that particularly emphasize the physical sensation that sounds evoke for those who live "in-the-body"?

3. **CREATIVE RESPONSE.** Write a sentence — or a short poem — that consists almost exclusively of onomatopoetic words.

CONNECTION TO ANOTHER SELECTION

1. Choose a poem from this chapter and write an essay that explains how its "sound, the noise of the sound, is / the thing."

LEWIS CARROLL (CHARLES LUTWIDGE DODGSON/1832–1898)

Jabberwocky   *1871*

'Twas brillig, and the slithy toves
    Did gyre and gimble in the wabe:
All mimsy were the borogoves,
    And the mome raths outgrabe.

"Beware the Jabberwock, my son!   5
    The jaws that bite, the claws that catch!
Beware the Jubjub bird, and shun
    The frumious Bandersnatch!"

He took his vorpal sword in hand;
    Long time the manxome foe he sought —   10
So rested he by the Tumtum tree,
    And stood awhile in thought.

And, as in uffish thought he stood,
    The Jabberwock, with eyes of flame,
Came whiffling through the tulgey wood,   15
    And burbled as it came!

One, two! One, two! And through and through
    The vorpal blade went snicker-snack!
He left it dead, and with its head
    He went galumphing back.   20

"And hast thou slain the Jabberwock?
    Come to my arms, my beamish boy!
O frabjous day! Callooh, Callay!"
    He chortled in his joy.

'Twas brillig, and the slithy toves   25
    Did gyre and gimble in the wabe:

All mimsy were the borogoves,
    And the mome raths outgrabe.

CONSIDERATIONS FOR CRITICAL THINKING AND WRITING

1. **FIRST RESPONSE.** What happens in this poem? Does it have any meaning?

2. Not all of the words used in this poem appear in dictionaries. In *Through the Looking Glass,* Humpty Dumpty explains to Alice that " 'slithy' means 'lithe and slimy.' 'Lithe' is the same as 'active.' You see it's like a portmanteau — there are two meanings packed up into one word." Are there any other portmanteau words in the poem?

3. Which words in the poem sound especially meaningful, even if they are devoid of any denotative meanings?

CONNECTION TO ANOTHER SELECTION

1. Compare Carroll's strategies for creating sound and meaning with those used by Swenson in "A Nosty Fright" (p. 728).

WILLIAM HEYEN (B. 1940)

The Trains   *1984*

Signed by Franz Paul Stangl, Commandant,
there is in Berlin a document,
an order of transmittal from Treblinka:

248 freight cars of clothing,
400,000 gold watches,   5
25 freight cars of women's hair.

Some clothing was kept, some pulped for paper.
The finest watches were never melted down.
All the women's hair was used for mattresses, or dolls.

Would these words like to use some of that same paper?   10
One of those watches may pulse in your own wrist.
Does someone you know collect dolls, or sleep on human hair?

He is dead at last, Commandant Stangl of Treblinka,
but the camp's three syllables still sound like freight cars
straining around a curve, Treblinka,   15

Treblinka. Clothing, time in gold watches,
women's hair for mattresses and dolls' heads.
Treblinka. The trains from Treblinka.

CONSIDERATIONS FOR CRITICAL THINKING AND WRITING

1. **FIRST RESPONSE.** How does the sound of the word *Treblinka* inform your understanding of the poem?

2. Why does the place name of Treblinka continue to resonate over time? To learn more about Treblinka, search the Web, perhaps starting at ushm.org, the site of the United States Holocaust Memorial Museum.

3. Why do you suppose Heyen uses the word *in* instead of *on* in line 11?

4. Why is sound so important for establishing the tone of this poem? In what sense do the "camp's three syllables still sound like freight cars"?

5. CRITICAL STRATEGIES. Read the section on reader-response strategies (pp. 1552–54) in Chapter 46, "Critical Strategies for Reading." How does this poem make you feel? Why?

ELIZA GRISWOLD

Occupation   2003

The prostitutes in Kabul tap their feet
beneath their faded burkas° in the heat.
For bread or fifteen cents, they'll take a man to bed —
their husbands dead, their seven kids unfed —
and thanks to occupation, rents have risen twentyfold,
their chickens, pots, and carpets have been sold
and women's flesh now worth its weight in tin.
Two years ago, the Talibs favored boys and left the girls alone.
A woman then was worth her weight in stone.

2 *burkas:* Traditional garments that cover the body and face of Muslim women.

CONSIDERATIONS FOR CRITICAL THINKING AND WRITING

1. FIRST RESPONSE. How does Griswold depict women's lives in Afghanistan both before and after the American occupation there?

2. Comment on the possible meanings of the title and their relation to one another.

3. Discuss the effect of the rhymes and how they enhance the themes.

HENRY WADSWORTH LONGFELLOW (1807–1882)

The Tide Rises, the Tide Falls   1880

The tide rises, the tide falls,
The twilight darkens, the curlew calls;
Along the sea-sands damp and brown
The traveller hastens toward the town.
    And the tide rises, the tide falls.   5

Darkness settles on roofs and walls,
But the sea, the sea in the darkness calls;
The little waves, with their soft, white hands,
Efface the footprints in the sands,
    And the tide rises, the tide falls.   10

The morning breaks; the steeds in their stalls
Stamp and neigh, as the hostler calls;
The day returns, but nevermore
Returns the traveller to the shore,
    And the tide rises, the tide falls.   15

Considerations for Critical Thinking and Writing

1. **First Response.** Describe the tonal effect of the repeated lines and rhymes.
2. What is the nature of the "darkness" in lines 6–7?
3. What do you think is the purpose of the horses stamping and neighing in the final stanza?

John Donne (1572–1631)

Song   *1633*

Go and catch a falling star
    Get with child a mandrake root,°
Tell me where all past years are,
    Or who cleft the Devil's foot,
Teach me to hear mermaids singing,   5
    Or to keep off envy's stinging,
            And find
            What wind
Serves to advance an honest mind.

If thou be'st borne to strange sights,   10
    Things invisible to see,
Ride ten thousand days and nights,
    Till age snow white hairs on thee,
Thou, when thou return'st, wilt tell me
    All strange wonders that befell thee,   15
            And swear
            Nowhere
Lives a woman true, and fair.

If thou findst one, let me know,
    Such a pilgrimage were sweet —   20

2 *mandrake root:* This V-shaped root resembles the lower half of the human body.

Yet do not, I would not go,
  Though at next door we might meet;
Though she were true, when you met her,
  And last, till you write your letter,
      Yet she   25
      Will be
False, ere I come, to two or three.

CONSIDERATIONS FOR CRITICAL THINKING AND WRITING

1. **FIRST RESPONSE.** What is the speaker's tone in this poem? What is his view of a woman's love? What does the speaker's use of hyperbole reveal about his emotional state?

2. Do you think Donne wants the speaker's argument to be taken seriously? Is there any humor in the poem?

3. Most of these lines end with masculine rhymes. What other kinds of rhymes are used for end rhymes?

ALEXANDER POPE (1688–1774)

From An Essay on Criticism   1711

But most by numbers° judge a poet's song;   *versification*
And smooth or rough, with them, is right or wrong;
In the bright muse though thousand charms conspire,
Her voice is all these tuneful fools admire;
Who haunt Parnassus° but to please their ear,   5
Not mend their minds; as some to church repair,
Not for the doctrine, but the music there.
These equal syllables alone require,
Though oft the ear the open vowels tire;
While expletives° their feeble aid do join;   10
And ten low words oft creep in one dull line;
While they ring round the same unvaried chimes,
With sure returns of still expected rhymes;
Where'er you find "the cooling western breeze,"
In the next line, it "whispers through the trees":   15
If crystal streams "with pleasing murmurs creep,"
The reader's threatened (not in vain) with "sleep":
Then, at the last and only couplet fraught
With some unmeaning thing they call a thought,
A needless Alexandrine° ends the song,   20

5 *Parnassus:* A Greek mountain sacred to the Muses.   10 *expletives:* Unnecessary words
used to fill a line, as the *do* in this line.   20 *Alexandrine:* A twelve-syllable line, as line 21.

That, like a wounded snake, drags its slow length along.
Leave such to tune their own dull rhymes, and know
What's roundly smooth, or languishingly slow;
And praise the easy vigor of a line,
Where Denham's strength, and Waller's° sweetness join.   25
True ease in writing comes from art, not chance,
As those move easiest who have learned to dance.
'Tis not enough no harshness gives offense,
The sound must seem an echo to the sense:
Soft is the strain when Zephyr° gently blows,   *the west wind* 30
And the smooth stream in smoother numbers flows;
But when loud surges lash the sounding shore,
The hoarse, rough verse should like the torrent roar:
When Ajax° strives some rock's vast weight to throw,
The line too labors, and the words move slow;   35
Not so, when swift Camilla° scours the plain,
Flies o'er th' unbending corn, and skims along the main.

25 *Denham's . . . Waller's:* Sir John Denham (1615–1669) and Edmund Waller (1606–1687) were
poets who used heroic couplets.   34 *Ajax:* A Greek warrior famous for his strength in
the Trojan War.   36 *Camilla:* A goddess famous for her delicate speed.

Considerations for Critical Thinking and Writing

1. **First response.** In these lines Pope describes some faults he finds in
   poems and illustrates those faults within the lines that describe them. How
   do the sounds in lines 4, 9, 10, 11, and 21 illustrate what they describe?

2. What is the objection to the "expected rhymes" in lines 12–17? How do they
   differ from Pope's end rhymes?

3. Some lines discuss how to write successful poetry. How do lines 23, 24,
   32–33, 35, 36, and 37 illustrate what they describe?

4. Do you agree that in a good poem "The sound must seem an echo to
   the sense"?

HAKI R. MADHUBUTI (B. 1942)

The B Network   *1998*

brothers bop & pop and be-bop in cities locked up
and chained insane by crack and other acts
of desperation computerized in pentagon cellars producing
boppin brothers boastin of being better, best & beautiful.

if the boppin brothers are beautiful where are the sisters   5
who seek brotherman with a drugless head unbossed or beaten
by the bodacious West?

in a time of big wind being blown by boastful brothers,
will other brothers beat back backwardness to better & best
without braggart bosses beatin butts,   10
takin names and diggin graves?

beatin badness into bad may be urban but is it beautiful & serious?
or is it betrayal in an era of prepared easy death hangin on
corners trappin young brothers before they know the
difference between big death and big life?   15

brothers bop & pop and be-bop in cities locked up
and chained insane by crack and other acts
of desperation computerized in pentagon cellars producing
boppin brothers boastin of being better, best, beautiful
and definitely not *Black*.   20

the critical best is that
brothers better be the best if they are to avoid backwardness
brothers better be the best if they are to conquer beautiful bigness
Comprehend that bad is only *bad* if it's big, Black and better
than boastful braggarts belittling our best and brightest   25
with bosses seeking inches when miles are better.

brothers need to bop to being Black & bright & above board
the black train of beautiful wisdom that is bending this bind
toward a new & knowledgeable beginning that is
bountiful & bountiful & beautiful   30
While be-boppin to be
better than the test,
brotherman.

better yet write the exam.

CONSIDERATIONS FOR CRITICAL THINKING AND WRITING

1. **FIRST RESPONSE.** Read this poem aloud. How is that a different experience from reading it silently?

2. Why has the poet included all those words beginning with *b*? How do you explain the title?

3. What is the speaker's assessment of the status of African Americans in the United States? What sort of advice, if any, is offered to them?

4. Comment on the possible interpretations of the final line.

CONNECTION TO ANOTHER SELECTION

1. Compare the style and themes of "The B Network" with those of Langston Hughes's "Dream Boogie" (p. 927).

MAXINE HONG KINGSTON (B. 1940)

Restaurant   1981

for Lilah Kan

The main cook lies sick on a banquette, and
        his assistant
has cut his thumb. So the quiche cook takes
their places at the eight-burner range, and
        you and I
get to roll out twenty-three rounds of pie
dough and break a hundred eggs, four at a
        crack,   5
and sift out shell with a China cap, pack
spinach in the steel sink, squish and squeeze
the water out, and grate a full moon of cheese.
Pam, the pastry chef, who is baking Choco-
late Globs (once called Mulattos) complains about the disco,   10
which Lewis, the salad man, turns up louder out of spite.
"Black so-called musician," "Broads. Whites."
The porters, who speak French, from the Ivory Coast,
sweep up droppings and wash the pans without soap.
We won't be out of here until three A.M. In this basement,   15
I lose my size. I am a bent-over
child, Gretel or Jill, and I can
lift a pot as big as a tub with both hands.
Using a pitchfork, you stoke the broccoli and bacon.
Then I find you in the freezer, taking   20
a nibble of a slab of chocolate as big as a table.
We put the quiches in the oven, then we are able
to stick our heads up out of the sidewalk into the night
and wonder at the clean diners behind glass in candlelight.

Courtesy of Gail K. Evenari.   5

CONSIDERATIONS FOR CRITICAL THINKING AND WRITING

1. **FIRST RESPONSE.** How do the sounds of this poem contribute to the
   descriptions of what goes on in the restaurant kitchen? How do they contribute to the diners?

2. In what sense does the speaker "lose [her] size" in the kitchen? How would
   you describe her?

3. Examine the poem's rhymes. What effect do they have on your reading?

4. Describe the tone of the final line. How does it differ from the rest of the
   poem?

PAUL HUMPHREY (1915–2001)

Blow

1983

Her skirt was lofted by the gale;
When I, with gesture deft,
Essayed to stay her frisky sail
She luffed, and laughed, and left.

CONSIDERATIONS FOR CRITICAL THINKING AND WRITING

1. FIRST RESPONSE. How do alliteration and assonance contribute to the euphonic effects in this poem?
2. What is the poem's controlling metaphor? Why is it especially appropriate?
3. Explain the ambiguity of the title.

ROBERT FRANCIS (1901–1987)

The Pitcher

1953

His art is eccentricity, his aim
How not to hit the mark he seems to aim at,

His passion how to avoid the obvious,
His technique how to vary the avoidance.

The others throw to be comprehended. He   5
Throws to be a moment misunderstood.

Yet not too much. Not errant, arrant, wild,
But every seeming aberration willed.

Not to, yet still, still to communicate
Making the batter understand too late.   10

CONSIDERATIONS FOR CRITICAL THINKING AND WRITING

1. FIRST RESPONSE. Explain how each pair of lines in this poem works together to describe the pitcher's art.
2. Consider how the poem itself works the way a good pitcher does. Which lines illustrate what they describe?
3. Comment on the effects of the poem's rhymes. How are the final two lines different in their rhyme from the previous lines? How does sound echo sense in lines 9–10?
4. Write an essay that considers "The Pitcher" as an extended metaphor for talking about poetry. How well does the poem characterize strategies for writing poetry as well as pitching?

5. Write an essay that develops an extended comparison between writing or reading poetry and playing or watching another sport.

CONNECTION TO ANOTHER SELECTION

1. Write an essay comparing "The Pitcher" with another work by Francis, "Catch" (p. 576). One poem defines poetry implicitly, the other defines it explicitly. Which poem do you prefer? Why?

HELEN CHASIN (B. 1938)

The Word Plum

1968

The word *plum* is delicious

pout and push, luxury of
self-love, and savoring murmur
full in the mouth and falling
like fruit   5

taut skin
pierced, bitten, provoked into
juice, and tart flesh

question
and reply, lip and tongue   10
of pleasure.

CONSIDERATIONS FOR CRITICAL THINKING AND WRITING

1. **FIRST RESPONSE.** What is the effect of the repetitions of the alliteration and assonance throughout the poem? How does it contribute to the poem's meaning?
2. Which sounds in the poem are like the sounds one makes while eating a plum?
3. Discuss the title. Explain whether you think this poem is more about the word *plum* or about the plum itself. Consider whether the two can be separated in the poem.

CONNECTION TO ANOTHER SELECTION

1. How is Galway Kinnell's "Blackberry Eating" (p. 733) similar in technique to Chasin's poem? Try writing such a poem yourself: choose a food to describe that allows you to evoke its sensuousness in sounds.

HOWARD NEMEROV (B. 1920)

Because You Asked about the Line between Prose and Poetry

1980

Sparrows were feeding in a freezing drizzle
That while you watched turned into pieces of snow
Riding a gradient invisible
From silver aslant to random, white, and slow.

There came a moment that you couldn't tell.
And then they clearly flew instead of fell.

CONSIDERATIONS FOR CRITICAL THINKING AND WRITING

1. **FIRST RESPONSE.** Describe the distinction that this poem makes between prose and poetry. How does the poem itself become an example of that distinction?

2. Identify the kinds of rhymes Nemerov employs. How do the rhymes in the first and second stanzas differ from each other?

3. Comment on the poem's punctuation. How is it related to theme?

Web Research the poets in this chapter at bedfordstmartins.com/ meyercompact.

25

Patterns of Rhythm

I would define, in brief, the Poetry of words as the Rhythmical Creation of Beauty. Its sole arbiter is Taste.
— EDGAR ALLAN POE[1]

The rhythms of everyday life surround us in regularly recurring movements and sounds. As you read these words, your heart pulsates while somewhere else a clock ticks, a cradle rocks, a drum beats, a dancer sways, a foghorn blasts, a wave recedes, or a child skips. We may tend to overlook rhythm because it is so tightly woven into the fabric of our experience, but it is there nonetheless, one of the conditions of life. Rhythm is also one of the conditions of speech because the voice alternately rises and falls as words are stressed or unstressed and as the pace quickens or slackens. In poetry *rhythm* refers to the recurrence of stressed and unstressed sounds. Depending on how the sounds are arranged, this can result in a pace that is fast or slow, choppy or smooth.

Explore the poetic element in this chapter on *LiterActive* or at bedfordstmartins .com/meyercompact.

[1]Photograph by W. S. Hartshorn. 1848. Prints and Photographs Division, Library of Congress.

SOME PRINCIPLES OF METER

Poets use rhythm to create pleasurable sound patterns and to reinforce meanings. "Rhythm," Edith Sitwell once observed, "might be described as, to the world of sound, what light is to the world of sight. It shapes and gives new meaning." Prose can use rhythm effectively too, but prose that does so tends to be an exception. The following exceptional lines are from a speech by Winston Churchill to the House of Commons after Allied forces made a heroic retreat from German forces at Dunkirk during World War II:

> We shall not flag or fail. We shall go on to the end. We shall fight in France, we shall fight on the seas and oceans, we shall fight with growing confidence and growing strength in the air, we shall defend our island, whatever the cost may be, we shall fight on the beaches, we shall fight on the landing grounds, we shall fight in the fields and in the streets, we shall fight in the hills; we shall never surrender.

The stressed repetition of "we shall" bespeaks the resolute singleness of purpose that Churchill had to convey to the British people if they were to win the war. Repetition is also one of the devices used in poetry to create rhythmic effects. In the following excerpt from "Song of the Open Road," Walt Whitman urges the pleasures of limitless freedom on his reader:

WALT WHITMAN (1819–1892)

From *Song of the Open Road*   *1856*

Allons!° the road is before us!   *Let's go!*
It is safe — I have tried it — my own feet have tried it well — be not detain'd!
Let the paper remain on the desk unwritten, and the book on the
        shelf unopen'd!
Let the tools remain in the workshop! Let the money remain unearn'd!
Let the school stand! mind not the cry of the teacher!   5
Let the preacher preach in his pulpit! Let the lawyer plead in the
        court, and the judge expound the law.

Camerado,° I give you my hand!   *friend*
I give you my love more precious than money,
I give you myself before preaching or law;
Will you give me yourself? will you come travel with me?   10
Shall we stick by each other as long as we live?

These rhythmic lines quickly move away from conventional values to the open road of shared experiences. Their recurring sounds are not created by rhyme or alliteration and assonance (see Chapter 24) but by the repetition of words and phrases.

Although the repetition of words and phrases can be an effective means of creating rhythm in poetry, the more typical method consists of patterns of accented or unaccented syllables. Words contain syllables that are either stressed or unstressed. A **stress** (or **accent**) places more emphasis on one syllable than on another. We say "*syl*lable" not "syl*la*ble," "*em*phasis" not "em*pha*sis." We routinely stress syllables when we speak: "*Is* she con*tent* with the *con*tents of the *yel*low *pack*age?" To distinguish between two people we might say "Is *she* content . . . ?" In this way stress can be used to emphasize a particular word in a sentence. Poets often arrange words so that the desired meaning is suggested by the rhythm; hence emphasis is controlled by the poet rather than left entirely to the reader.

When a rhythmic pattern of stresses recurs in a poem, the result is **meter**. Taken together, all the metrical elements in a poem make up what is called the poem's **prosody**. **Scansion** consists of measuring the stresses in a line to determine its metrical pattern. Several methods can be used to mark lines. One widely used system uses ´ for a stressed syllable and ˘ for an unstressed syllable. In a sense, the stress mark represents the equivalent of tapping one's foot to a beat:

> Híckŏrў, díckŏrў, dóck,
> The móuse răn úp thĕ clóck.
> The clóck strŭck óne,
> Ănd dówn hĕ rún,
> Híckŏrў, díckŏrў, dóck.

In the first two lines and the final line of this familiar nursery rhyme we hear three stressed syllables. In lines 3 and 4, where the meter changes for variety, we hear just two stressed syllables. The combination of stresses provides the pleasure of the rhythm we hear.

To hear the rhythms of "Hickory, dickory, dock" does not require a formal study of meter. Nevertheless, an awareness of the basic kinds of meter that appear in English poetry can enhance your understanding of how a poem achieves its effects. Understanding the sound effects of a poem and having a vocabulary with which to discuss those effects can intensify your pleasure in poetry. Although the study of meter can be extremely technical, the terms used to describe the basic meters of English poetry are relatively easy to comprehend.

The **foot** is the metrical unit by which a line of poetry is measured. A foot usually consists of one stressed and one or two unstressed syllables. A vertical line is used to separate the feet: "The clock | struck one" consists of two feet. A foot of poetry can be arranged in a variety of patterns; here are five of the chief ones:

Foot	Pattern	Example
iamb	˘ ´	away
trochee	´ ˘	Lóvelў

Foot	Pattern	Example
anapest	˘ ˘ ´	understánd
dactyl	´ ˘ ˘	désperate
spondee	´ ´	déad sét

The most common lines in English poetry contain meters based on iambic feet. However, even lines that are predominantly iambic will often include variations to create particular effects. Other important patterns include trochaic, anapestic, and dactylic feet. The spondee is not a sustained meter but occurs for variety or emphasis.

Iambic
> Whăt képt | hĭs eýes | frŏm gív | ĭng báck | thĕ gáze

Trochaic
> Hé wăs | loúdĕr | thán thĕ | preáchĕr

Anapestic
> Ĭ ăm cálled | tŏ thĕ frónt | ŏf thĕ roóm

Dactylic
> Síng ĭt ăll | mérrĭlў

These meters have different rhythms and can create different effects. Iambic and anapestic are known as **rising meters** because they move from unstressed to stressed sounds, while trochaic and dactylic are known as **falling meters.** Anapests and dactyls tend to move more lightly and rapidly than iambs or trochees. Although no single kind of meter can be considered always better than another for a given subject, it is possible to determine whether the meter of a specific poem is appropriate for its subject. A serious poem about a tragic death would most likely not be well served by lilting rhythms. Keep in mind, too, that though one or another of these four basic meters might constitute the predominant rhythm of a poem, variations can occur within lines to change the pace or call attention to a particular word.

A *line* is measured by the number of feet it contains. Here, for example, is an iambic line with three feet: "Ĭf shé | shŏuld wríte | ă nóte." These are the names for line lengths:

monometer: one foot	pentameter: five feet
dimeter: two feet	hexameter: six feet
trimeter: three feet	heptameter: seven feet
tetrameter: four feet	octameter: eight feet

By combining the name of a line length with the name of a foot, we can describe the metrical qualities of a line concisely. Consider, for example, the pattern of feet and length of this line:

I didn't want the boy to hit the dog.

The iambic rhythm of this line falls into five feet; hence it is called *iambic pentameter.* Iambic is the most common pattern in English poetry because its rhythm appears so naturally in English speech and writing. Unrhymed iambic pentameter is called *blank verse;* Shakespeare's plays are built on such lines.

Less common than the iamb, trochee, anapest, or dactyl is the *spondee,* a two-syllable foot in which both syllables are stressed (´´). Note the effect of the spondaic foot at the beginning of this line:

Déad sét | ăgaínst | thĕ plán | hĕ wént | ăwáy.

Spondees can slow a rhythm and provide variety and emphasis, particularly in iambic and trochaic lines. A line that ends with a stressed syllable is said to have a *masculine ending,* whereas a line that ends with an extra unstressed syllable is said to have a *feminine ending.* Consider, for example, these two lines from Timothy Steele's "Waiting for the Storm" (the entire poem appears on p. 758):

feminine: Thĕ sánd | ăt mý féet | grŏw cóld | eř,

masculine: Thĕ dámp | aĭr chíll | aňd spréad.

The effects of English meters are easily seen in the following lines by Samuel Taylor Coleridge, in which the rhythm of each line illustrates the meter described in it:

Trochee trips from long to short;
From long to long in solemn sort
Slow Spondee stalks; strong foot yet ill able
Ever to come up with Dactylic trisyllable.
Iambics march from short to long—
With a leap and a bound the swift Anapests throng.

The speed of a line is also affected by the number of pauses in it. A pause within a line is called a *caesura* and is indicated by a double vertical line (‖). A caesura can occur anywhere within a line and need not be indicated by punctuation:

Camerado, ‖ I give you my hand!
I give you my love ‖ more precious than money.

A slight pause occurs within each of these lines and at its end. Both kinds of pauses contribute to the lines' rhythm.

When a line has a pause at its end, it is called an *end-stopped line.* Such pauses reflect normal speech patterns and are often marked by punctuation. A line that ends without a pause and continues into the next line for its meaning is called a *run-on line.* Running over from one line to another is also called *enjambment.* The first and eighth lines of the following poem are run-on lines; the rest are end-stopped.

William Wordsworth (1770–1850)

My Heart Leaps Up

1807

My heart leaps up when I behold
  A rainbow in the sky:
So was it when my life began;
So is it now I am a man;
So be it when I shall grow old,
  Or let me die!
The child is father of the Man;
And I could wish my days to be
Bound each to each by natural piety.

Run-on lines have a different rhythm from end-stopped lines. Lines 3 and 4 and lines 8 and 9 are iambic, but the effect of their two rhythms is very different when we read these lines aloud. The enjambment of lines 8 and 9 reinforces their meaning; just as the "days" are bound together, so are the lines.

The rhythm of a poem can be affected by several devices: the kind and number of stresses within lines, the length of lines, and the kinds of pauses that appear within lines or at their ends. In addition, as we saw in Chapter 24, the sound of a poem is affected by alliteration, assonance, rhyme, and consonance. These sounds help to create rhythms by controlling our pronunciations, as in the following lines by Alexander Pope:

> Soft is the strain when Zephyr gently blows,
> And the smooth stream in smoother numbers flows;
> But when loud surges lash the sounding shore,
> The hoarse, rough verse should like the torrent roar.

These lines are effective because their rhythm and sound work with their meaning.

Suggestions for Scanning a Poem

These suggestions should help you in talking about a poem's meter.

1. After reading the poem through, read it aloud and mark the stressed syllables in each line. Then mark the unstressed syllables.

2. From your markings, identify what kind of foot is dominant (iambic, trochaic, dactylic, or anapestic) and divide the lines into feet, keeping in mind that the vertical line marking a foot may come in the middle of a word as well as at its beginning or end.

3. Determine the number of feet in each line. Remember that there may be variations; some lines may be shorter or longer than the predominant meter. What is important is the overall pattern. Do not assume that variations represent the poet's inability to fulfill the overall pattern. Notice the effects of variations and whether they emphasize

(continued)

> words and phrases or disrupt your expectation for some other purpose.
>
> 4. Listen for pauses within lines and mark the caesuras; many times there will be no punctuation to indicate them.
>
> 5. Recognize that scansion does not always yield a definitive measurement of a line. Even experienced readers may differ over the scansion of a given line. What is important is not a precise description of the line but an awareness of how a poem's rhythms contribute to its effects.

The following poem demonstrates how you can use an understanding of meter and rhythm to gain a greater appreciation for what a poem is saying.

TIMOTHY STEELE (B. 1948)

Waiting for the Storm   1986

Breeze sént | ă wrínk | ling dárk | nĕss
Acróss | thĕ bay. ‖ Ĭ knélt
Bĕneath | ăn úp | turned bóat,
Ănd, mŏ | mĕnt bў mŏ | mĕnt, félt

Thĕ sánd | ăt mў feet | grŏw cóld | ĕr,
Thĕ dămp | áir chĭll | ănd spréad.
Thĕn thĕ | fĭrst ráin | drŏps sóund | ĕd
Ŏn thĕ húll | ăbóve | mў héad.

The predominant meter of this poem is iambic trimeter, but there is plenty of variation as the storm rapidly approaches and finally begins to pelt the sheltered speaker. The emphatic spondee ("Breeze sent") pushes the darkness quickly across the bay while the caesura at the end of the sentence in line 2 creates a pause that sets up a feeling of suspense and expectation that is measured in the ticking rhythm of line 4, a run-on line that brings us into the chilly sand and air of the second stanza. Perhaps the most impressive sound effect used in the poem appears in the second syllable of "sounded" in line 7. That "ed" precedes the sound of the poem's final word, "head," just as if it were the first drop of rain hitting the hull above the speaker. The visual, tactile, and auditory images make "Waiting for the Storm" an intense sensory experience.

A SAMPLE STUDENT RESPONSE

Pacini 1

Marco Pacini

Professor Fierstein

English 201

November 2, 2008

The Rhythm of Anticipation in Timothy Steele's "Waiting for the Storm"

In his poem "Waiting for the Storm," Timothy Steele uses run-on lines, or enjambment, to create a feeling of anticipation. Every line ends unfinished or is a continuation of the previous line, so we must read on to gain completion. This open-ended rhythm mirrors the waiting experienced by the speaker of the poem.

Nearly every line of the poem leaves the reader in suspense:

> I knelt
>
> Beneath an upturned boat,
>
> And moment by moment, felt
>
> The sand at my feet grow colder,
>
> The damp air chill and spread. (lines 2-6)

Action is interrupted at every line break. We have to wait to find out where the speaker knelt and what was felt, since information is given in small increments. So, like the speaker, we must take in the details of the storm little by little, "moment by moment" (4). Even when the first drops of rain hit the hull, the poem ends before we can see or feel the storm's full force, and we are left waiting, in a continuous state of anticipation. . . .

Pacini 3

Work Cited

Steele, Timothy. "Waiting for the Storm." The Compact Bedford Introduction
    to Literature. Ed. Michael Meyer. 8th ed. Boston: Bedford/St. Martin's,
    2009. 758.

This next poem also reinforces meanings through its use of meter and rhythm.

WILLIAM BUTLER YEATS (1865–1939)

That the Night Come   1912

She lived | in storm | and strife,
Her soul | had such | desire
For what | proud death | may bring
That it | could not | endure
The com | mon good | of life,   5
But lived | as 'twere | a king
That packed | his mar | riage day
With ban | neret | and pen | non,
Trumpet | and ket | tledrum,
And the | outrag | eous can | non,   10
To bun | dle time | away
That the | night come.

Scansion reveals that the predominant meter here is iambic trimeter. Each line contains three stressed and unstressed syllables that form a regular, predictable rhythm through line 7. That rhythm is disrupted, however, when the speaker compares the woman's longing for what death brings to a king's eager anticipation of his wedding night. The king packs the day with noisy fanfares and celebrations to fill up time and distract himself. Unable to accept "The common good of life," the woman fills her days with "storm and strife." In a determined effort "To bundle time away," she, like the king, impatiently awaits the night.

Lines 8–10 break the regular pattern established in the first seven lines. The extra unstressed syllable in lines 8 and 10 along with the trochaic feet in lines 9 ("trumpet") and 10 ("And the") interrupt the basic iambic trimeter and parallel the woman's and the king's frenetic activity. These lines thus echo the inability of the woman and king to "endure" regular or normal time. The last line is the most irregular in the poem. The final two accented syllables sound like the deep resonant beats of a kettledrum or a cannon firing. The words "night come" dramatically remind us that what the woman anticipates is not a lover but the mysterious finality of death. The meter serves, then, in both its regularity and variations to reinforce the poem's meaning and tone.

The following poems are especially rich in their rhythms and sounds. As you read and study them, notice how patterns of rhythm and the sounds of words reinforce meanings and contribute to the poems' effects. And, perhaps most important, read the poems aloud so that you can hear them.

POEMS FOR FURTHER STUDY

ALICE JONES (B. 1949)

The Foot   *1993*

Our improbable support, erected
on the osseous architecture
of the calcaneus, talus, cuboid,
navicular, cuneiforms, metatarsals,
phalanges, a plethora of hinges,   5

all strung together by gliding
tendons, covered by the pearly
plantar fascia, then fat-padded
to form the sole, humble surface
of our contact with earth.   10

Here the body's broadest tendon
anchors the heel's fleshy base,
the finely wrinkled skin stretches
forward across the capillaried arch,
to the ball, a balance point.   15

A wide web of flexor tendons
and branched veins maps the dorsum,
fades into the stub-laden bone
splay, the stuffed sausage sacks
of toes, each with a tuft   20

of proximal hairs to introduce
the distal nail, whose useless
curve remembers an ancestor,
the vanished creature's wild
and necessary claw.   25

CONSIDERATIONS FOR CRITICAL THINKING AND WRITING

1. FIRST RESPONSE. What is the effect of the diction? What sort of tone is established by the use of anatomical terms? How do the terms affect the rhythm?

2. Jones has described the form of "The Foot" as "five stubby stanzas." Explain why the lines of this poem may or may not warrant this description of the stanzas.

3. CRITICAL STRATEGIES. Read the section on formalist strategies (pp. 1538–40) in Chapter 46, "Critical Strategies for Reading." Describe the effect of the final stanza. How would your reading be affected if the poem ended after the comma in the middle of line 22?

A. E. HOUSMAN (1859–1936)

When I was one-and-twenty   1896

When I was one-and-twenty
  I heard a wise man say,
"Give crowns and pounds and guineas
  But not your heart away;
Give pearls away and rubies   5
  But keep your fancy free."
But I was one-and-twenty,
  No use to talk to me.

When I was one-and-twenty
  I heard him say again,   10
"The heart out of the bosom
  Was never given in vain;
'Tis paid with sighs a plenty
  And sold for endless rue."
And I am two-and-twenty,   15
  And oh, 'tis true, 'tis true.

CONSIDERATIONS FOR CRITICAL THINKING AND WRITING

1. **FIRST RESPONSE.** How does the basic metrical pattern affect your understanding of the speaker?
2. How do lines 1–8 parallel lines 9–16 in their use of rhyme and metaphor? Are there any significant differences between the stanzas?
3. What do you think has happened to change the speaker's attitude toward love?
4. Explain why you agree or disagree with the advice given by the "wise man."
5. What is the effect of the repetition in line 16?

RITA DOVE (B. 1952)

Fox Trot Fridays   2001

Thank the stars there's a day
each week to tuck in

the grief, lift your pearls, and
stride brush stride

quick-quick with a   5
heel-ball-toe. Smooth

as Nat King Cole's
slow satin smile,

easy as taking
one day at a time: 10

one man and
one woman,

rib to rib,
with no heartbreak in sight —

just the sweep of Paradise   15
and the space of a song

to count all the wonders in it.

CONSIDERATIONS FOR CRITICAL THINKING AND WRITING

1. **FIRST RESPONSE.** Explain how the rhythm of the lines is aptly partnered
   with the fox trot.

2. Do some background research so that you can discuss why Dove chooses
   Nat King Cole as the right kind of singer for this poem.

3. The fox trot is more than a dance step for Dove. What is its appeal in this
   poem?

ROBERT HERRICK (1591–1674)
Delight in Disorder   1648

A sweet disorder in the dress
Kindles in clothes a wantonness.
A lawn° about the shoulders thrown   *linen scarf*
Into a fine distraction;
An erring lace, which here and there   5
Enthralls the crimson stomacher,
A cuff neglectful, and thereby
Ribbons to flow confusedly;
A winning wave, deserving note,
In the tempestuous petticoat;   10
A careless shoestring, in whose tie
I see a wild civility;
Do more bewitch me than when art
Is too precise in every part.

CONSIDERATIONS FOR CRITICAL THINKING AND WRITING

1. **FIRST RESPONSE.** Why does the speaker in this poem value "disorder" so
   highly? How do the poem's organization and rhythmic order relate to its
   theme? Are they "precise in every part"?

2. Which words in the poem indicate disorder? Which words indicate the
   speaker's response to that disorder? What are the connotative meanings of
   each set of words? Why are they appropriate? What do they suggest about
   the woman and the speaker?

3. Write a short essay in which you agree or disagree with the speaker's views
   on dress.

BEN JONSON (1573–1637)

Still to Be Neat
1609

Still° to be neat, still to be dressed,   *continually*
As you were going to a feast;
Still to be powdered, still perfumed;
Lady, it is to be presumed,
Though art's hid causes are not found,   5
All is not sweet, all is not sound.

Give me a look, give me a face
That makes simplicity a grace;
Robes loosely flowing, hair as free;
Such sweet neglect more taketh me   10
Then all th' adulteries of art.
They strike mine eyes, but not my heart.

CONSIDERATIONS FOR CRITICAL THINKING AND WRITING

1. FIRST RESPONSE. What are the speaker's reservations about the lady in the first stanza? What do you think "sweet" means in line 6?

2. What does the speaker want from the lady in the second stanza? How has the meaning of "sweet" shifted from line 6 to line 10? What other words in the poem are especially charged with connotative meanings?

3. How do the rhythms of Jonson's lines help to reinforce meanings? Pay particular attention to lines 6 and 12.

CONNECTION TO ANOTHER SELECTION

1. Write an essay comparing the themes of "Still to Be Neat" and Herrick's preceding poem, "Delight in Disorder." How do the speakers make similar points but from different perspectives?

2. How does the rhythm of "Still to Be Neat" compare with that of "Delight in Disorder"? Which do you find more effective? Explain why.

WILLIAM BLAKE (1757–1827)

The Lamb
1789

Little Lamb, who made thee?
Dost thou know who made thee?   Explore contexts
Gave thee life, and bid thee feed   for William Blake
By the stream and o'er the mead;   on *LiterActive*.
Gave thee clothing of delight,   5
Softest clothing, wooly, bright;
Gave thee such a tender voice,
Making all the vales rejoice?
Little Lamb, who made thee?
Dost thou know who made thee?   10

Little Lamb, I'll tell thee,
    Little Lamb, I'll tell thee:
He is callèd by thy name,
For he calls himself a Lamb.
He is meek, and he is mild;   15
He became a little child.
I a child, and thou a lamb,
We are callèd by his name.
    Little Lamb, God bless thee!
    Little Lamb, God bless thee!   20

CONSIDERATIONS FOR CRITICAL THINKING AND WRITING

1. **FIRST RESPONSE.** This poem is from Blake's *Songs of Innocence.* Describe its
   tone. How do the meter, rhyme, and repetition help to characterize the
   speaker's voice?

2. Why is it significant that the animal addressed by the speaker is a lamb?
   What symbolic value would be lost if the animal were, for example, a doe?

3. How does the second stanza answer the question raised in the first? What is
   the speaker's view of the creation?

WILLIAM BLAKE (1757–1827)

The Tyger   *1794*

Courtesy of the National Portrait Gallery,
London.

Tyger! Tyger! burning bright
In the forests of the night,
What immortal hand or eye
Could frame thy fearful symmetry?

In what distant deeps or skies
Burnt the fire of thine eyes?
On what wings dare he aspire?
What the hand dare seize the fire?

And what shoulder, and what art,
Could twist the sinews of thy heart?   10
And when thy heart began to beat,
What dread hand? and what dread feet?

What the hammer? what the chain?
In what furnace was thy brain?
What the anvil? what dread grasp   15
Dare its deadly terrors clasp?

When the stars threw down their spears,
And watered heaven with their tears,
Did he smile his work to see?
Did he who made the Lamb make thee?   20

Tyger! Tyger! burning bright
In the forests of the night,
What immortal hand or eye
Dare frame thy fearful symmetry?

CONSIDERATIONS FOR CRITICAL THINKING AND WRITING

1. **FIRST RESPONSE.** This poem from Blake's *Songs of Experience* is often paired with "The Lamb." Describe the poem's tone. Is the speaker's voice the same here as in "The Lamb"? Which words are repeated, and how do they contribute to the tone?

2. What is revealed about the nature of the tiger by the words used to describe its creation? What do you think the tiger symbolizes?

3. Unlike in "The Lamb," more than one question is raised in "The Tyger." What are these questions? Are they answered?

4. Compare the rhythms in "The Lamb" and "The Tyger." Each basically uses a seven-syllable line, but the effects are very different. Why?

5. Using these two poems as the basis of your discussion, describe what distinguishes innocence from experience.

CARL SANDBURG (1878–1967)

Chicago   1916

Hog Butcher for the World,
Tool Maker, Stacker of Wheat,
Player with Railroads and the Nation's Freight Handler;
Stormy, husky, brawling,
City of the Big Shoulders: 5

They tell me you are wicked and I believe them, for I have seen your painted
  women under the gas lamps luring the farm boys.
And they tell me you are crooked and I answer: Yes, it is true I have seen the
  gunman kill and go free to kill again.
And they tell me you are brutal and my reply is: On the faces of women and
  children I have seen the marks of wanton hunger.
And having answered so I turn once more to those who sneer at this my city,
  and I give them back the sneer and say to them:
Come and show me another city with lifted head singing so proud to be alive
  and coarse and strong and cunning.   10
Flinging magnetic curses amid the toil of piling job on job, here is a tall bold
  slugger set vivid against the little soft cities;
Fierce as a dog with tongue lapping for action, cunning as a savage pitted
  against the wilderness,
    Bareheaded,
    Shoveling,
    Wrecking,   15
    Planning,
    Building, breaking, rebuilding,

Under the smoke, dust all over his mouth, laughing with white teeth,
Under the terrible burden of destiny laughing as a young man laughs,
Laughing even as an ignorant fighter laughs who has never lost a battle,   20
Bragging and laughing that under his wrist is the pulse, and under his ribs
    the heart of the people,
  Laughing!
Laughing the stormy, husky, brawling laughter of Youth, half-naked,
    sweating, proud to be Hog Butcher, Tool Maker, Stacker of Wheat,
    Player with Railroads and Freight Handler to the Nation.

CONSIDERATIONS FOR CRITICAL THINKING AND WRITING

1. **FIRST RESPONSE.** Sandburg's personification of Chicago creates a strong identity for the city. Explain why you find the city attractive or not.

2. How do the length and rhythm of lines 1–5 compare with those of the final lines?

3. **CREATIVE RESPONSE.** Using "Chicago" as a model for style, try writing a tribute or condemnation about a place that you know well. Make an effort to use vivid images and stylistic techniques that capture its rhythms.

CONNECTION TO ANOTHER SELECTION

1. Compare "Chicago" with William Blake's "London" (p. 669) in style and theme.

ALFRED, LORD TENNYSON (1809–1892)
The Charge of the Light Brigade   *1855*

1

Half a league, half a league,
  Half a league onward,
All in the valley of Death
  Rode the six hundred.
"Forward, the Light Brigade!   5
Charge for the guns!" he said:
Into the valley of Death
  Rode the six hundred.

2

"Forward, the Light Brigade!"
Was there a man dismayed?   10
Not though the soldier knew
  Some one had blundered:
Their's not to make reply,
Their's not to reason why,
Their's but to do and die: 15

Into the valley of Death
   Rode the six hundred.

3

Cannon to right of them,
Cannon to left of them,
Cannon in front of them   20
   Volleyed and thundered;
Stormed at with shot and shell,
Boldly they rode and well,
Into the jaws of Death,
Into the mouth of Hell   25
   Rode the six hundred.

4

Flashed all their sabers bare,
Flashed as they turned in air
Sabring the gunners there,
Charging an army, while   30
   All the world wondered:
Plunged in the battery-smoke
Right through the line they broke;
Cossack and Russian
Reeled from the saber-stroke   35
   Shattered and sundered.
Then they rode back, but not
   Not the six hundred.

5

Cannon to right of them,
Cannon to left of them,   40
Cannon behind them
   Volleyed and thundered;
Stormed at with shot and shell,
While horse and hero fell,
They that had fought so well   45
Came through the jaws of Death,
Back from the mouth of Hell,
All that was left of them,
   Left of six hundred.

6

When can their glory fade?   50
O the wild charge they made!
   All the world wondered.

Honor the charge they made!
Honor the Light Brigade,
    Noble six hundred!   55

Considerations for Critical Thinking and Writing

1. **FIRST RESPONSE.** How do the meter and rhyme contribute to the meaning
   of this poem's lines?
2. What is the speaker's attitude toward war?
3. Describe the tone, paying particular attention to stanza 2.

Connection to Another Selection

1. Compare the theme of "The Charge of the Light Brigade" with that of Wilfred Owen's "Dulce et Decorum Est" (p. 671).

Theodore Roethke (1908–1963)

My Papa's Waltz   *1948*

The whiskey on your breath
Could make a small boy dizzy;
But I hung on like death:
Such waltzing was not easy.

We romped until the pans   5
Slid from the kitchen shelf;
My mother's countenance
Could not unfrown itself.

The hand that held my wrist
Was battered on one knuckle;   10
At every step you missed
My right ear scraped a buckle.

You beat time on my head
With a palm caked hard by dirt,
Then waltzed me off to bed   15
Still clinging to your shirt.

[sidebar:] **Web** Explore
contexts for Theodore
Roethke and approaches
to this poem
on *LiterActive* or at
bedfordstmartins
.com/meyercompact.

Considerations for Critical Thinking and Writing

1. **FIRST RESPONSE.** What details characterize the father in this poem? How
   does the speaker's choice of words reveal his feeling about his father? Is the
   remembering speaker still a boy?
2. Characterize the rhythm of the poem. Does it move "like death," or is it
   more like a waltz? Is the rhythm regular throughout the poem? What is
   its effect?
3. Comment on the appropriateness of the title. Why do you suppose
   Roethke didn't use "My Father's Waltz"?

NORMAN STOCK (B. 1940)

What I Said

2002

after the terror I
went home and cried and
said how could this happen and
how could such a thing be and
why why I mean how could   5
anything so horrible and how could
anyone do such a thing to us and what
will happen next and how can we live now
it's impossible to understand it's impossible
to do anything after this and what will any of us do now and how will
     we live   10
  and how can we expect to go on after this
I said and I said this is too much to take no one can take a thing like this
after the terror yes and then I said let's kill them

CONSIDERATIONS FOR CRITICAL THINKING AND WRITING

1. **FIRST RESPONSE.** This poem was published in a collection titled *Poetry after 9/11: An Anthology of New York Poets.* How does this information affect your reading of the poem?

2. How is the rhythm of this poem affected by its lack of any punctuation?

3. Explain how repetition is used to contribute to the poem's tone.

4. Describe the change in tone that comes in the final line. How does this shift the poem's meanings?

5. **CREATIVE RESPONSE.** Using "What I Said" as your inspiration and model, write a poem of ten to fifteen lines that describes a powerful emotional response you've had to an event in your life.

CONNECTION TO ANOTHER SELECTION

1. Discuss the treatment of terrorism in "What I Said" and in James Merrill's "Casual Wear" (p. 719).

LENARD D. MOORE (B. 1958)

Black Girl Tap Dancing

2004

She taps, pats, clicks,
shoes dazzling the checkered floor,
arms whirl, whirl,
legs cross, uncross,
notes of the feet rise   5
off tile,

spiral toward the ceiling
of the candlelit Ebony Club.

She pats, clicks, taps
shoes riffing the floor,   10
arms defy gravity,
legs scissor perfectly,
feet notes soar
from the glossy floor,
scatter from table to table   15
like fire licking the air.

She clicks, pats, taps
shoes shocking the floor,
arms swirl, whirl,
legs stamp, swing,   20
feet notes smokebeat
the floor, the floor
just when jazz leaps out of
the hornman's angled trumpet.

She taps, clicks, pats,   25
this sister firing the floor,
arms propel endless circles,
long legs slide, glide,
displace air, filling space,
red dress snaring the danceway,   30
black feather bobbing as she taps.

CONSIDERATIONS FOR CRITICAL THINKING AND WRITING

1. **FIRST RESPONSE.** Explain whether or not you think this vivid description of a dancer has a theme.

2. How does Moore's use of punctuation and repetition affect the poem's rhythm?

3. Why do you think Moore changes the word order in lines 1, 9, 17, and 25?

Perspective

LOUISE BOGAN (1897–1970)

On Formal Poetry   1953

What is formal poetry? It is poetry written in form. And what is *form*? The elements of form, so far as poetry is concerned, are meter and rhyme. Are these elements merely mold and ornaments that have been impressed upon poetry from without? Are they indeed restrictions which bind and fetter language and the thought and emotion behind, under, within language in a repressive way?

Are they arbitrary rules which have lost all validity since they have been broken to good purpose by "experimental poets," ancient and modern? Does the breaking up of form, or its total elimination, always result in an increase of power and of effect; and is any return to form a sort of relinquishment of freedom, or retreat to old fogeyism?

From *A Poet's Alphabet*

CONSIDERATIONS FOR CRITICAL THINKING AND WRITING

1. Choose one of the questions Bogan raises and write an essay in response to it using two or three poems from this chapter to illustrate your answer.
2. Try writing a poem in meter and rhyme. Does the experience make your writing feel limited or not?

Web Research the poets in this chapter at bedfordstmartins.com/meyercompact.

26

Poetic Forms

A short poem need not be small.
— MARVIN BELL

© Tom Jorgensen/ The University of Iowa.

Poems come in a variety of shapes. Although the best poems always have their own unique qualities, many of them also conform to traditional patterns. Frequently the *form* of a poem — its overall structure or shape — follows an already established design. A poem that can be categorized by the patterns of its lines, meter, rhymes, and stanzas is considered a *fixed form* because it follows a prescribed model such as a sonnet. However, poems written in a fixed form do not always fit models precisely; writers sometimes work variations on traditional forms to create innovative effects.

Not all poets are content with variations on traditional forms. Some prefer to create their own structures and shapes. Poems that do not conform to established patterns of meter, rhyme, and stanza are called *free verse* or *open form* poetry. (See Chapter 27 for further discussion of open forms.) This kind of poetry creates its own ordering principles through the careful arrangement of words and phrases in line lengths that embody rhythms appropriate to the meaning. Modern and contemporary poets in particular have learned to use the blank space on the page as a significant functional element (for a striking example, see E. E. Cummings's "in Just-," p. 800). Good poetry of this kind is structured in ways that can be as demanding, interesting, and satisfying as fixed forms. Open and fixed forms represent different poetic styles, but they are identical in the sense that both use language in concentrated ways to convey meanings, experiences, emotions, and effects.

SOME COMMON POETIC FORMS

A familiarity with some of the most frequently used fixed forms of poetry is useful because it allows for a better understanding of how a poem works. Classifying patterns allows us to talk about the effects of established rhythm and rhyme and recognize how significant variations from them affect the pace and meaning of the lines. An awareness of form also allows us to anticipate how a poem is likely to proceed. As we shall see, a sonnet creates a different set of expectations in a reader from those of, say, a limerick. A reader isn't likely to find in limericks the kind of serious themes that often make their way into sonnets. The discussion that follows identifies some of the important poetic forms frequently encountered in English poetry.

The shape of a fixed-form poem is often determined by the way in which the lines are organized into stanzas. A *stanza* consists of a grouping of lines, set off by a space, that usually has a set pattern of meter and rhyme. This pattern is ordinarily repeated in other stanzas throughout the poem. What is usual is not obligatory, however; some poems may use a different pattern for each stanza, somewhat like paragraphs in prose.

Traditionally, though, stanzas do share a common **rhyme scheme,** the pattern of end rhymes. We can map out rhyme schemes by noting patterns of rhyme with lowercase letters: the first rhyme sound is designated *a,* the second becomes *b,* the third *c,* and so on. Using this system, we can describe the rhyme scheme in the following poem this way: *aabb, ccdd, eeff.*

A. E. HOUSMAN (1859–1936)
Loveliest of trees, the cherry now   1896

Loveliest of trees, the cherry now	*a*
Is hung with bloom along the bough,	*a*
And stands about the woodland ride	*b*
Wearing white for Eastertide.	*b*
Now, of my threescore years and ten,	*c*
Twenty will not come again,	*c*
And take from seventy springs a score,	*d*
It only leaves me fifty more.	*d*

5

And since to look at things in bloom   *e*
Fifty springs are little room,   *e*   10
About the woodlands I will go   *f*
To see the cherry hung with snow.   *f*

CONSIDERATIONS FOR CRITICAL THINKING AND WRITING

1. **FIRST RESPONSE.** What is the speaker's attitude in this poem toward time and life?

2. Why is spring an appropriate season for the setting rather than, say, winter?

3. Paraphrase each stanza. How do the images in each reinforce the poem's themes?

4. Lines 1 and 12 are not intended to rhyme, but they are close. What is the effect of the near rhyme of "now" and "snow"? How does the rhyme enhance the theme?

Poets often create their own stanzaic patterns; hence there is an infinite number of kinds of stanzas. One way of talking about stanzaic forms is to describe a given stanza by how many lines it contains.

A *couplet* consists of two lines that usually rhyme and have the same meter; couplets are frequently not separated from each other by space on the page. A *heroic couplet* consists of rhymed iambic pentameter. Here is an example from Alexander Pope's "Essay on Criticism":

One science only will one genius fit;   *a*
So vast is art, so narrow human wit: *a*
Not only bounded to peculiar arts,   *b*
But oft in those confined to single parts.   *b*

A *tercet* is a three-line stanza. When all three lines rhyme they are called a *triplet.* Two triplets make up this captivating poem.

ROBERT HERRICK (1591–1674)

Upon Julia's Clothes   *1648*

Whenas in silks my Julia goes,   *a*
Then, then, methinks, how sweetly flows   *a*
That liquefaction of her clothes.   *a*

Next, when I cast mine eyes, and see   *b*
That brave vibration, each way free,   *b*
O, how that glittering taketh me!   *b*

CONSIDERATIONS FOR CRITICAL THINKING AND WRITING

1. **FIRST RESPONSE.** What purpose does alliteration serve in this poem?

2. Comment on the effect of the meter. How is it related to the speaker's description of Julia's clothes?

3. Look up the word *brave* in the *Oxford English Dictionary*. Which of its meanings is appropriate to describe Julia's movement? Some readers interpret lines 4–6 to mean that Julia has no clothes on. What do you think?

CONNECTION TO ANOTHER SELECTION

1. Compare the tone of this poem with that of Paul Humphrey's "Blow" (p. 749). Are the situations and speakers similar? Is there any difference in tone between these two poems?

Terza rima consists of an interlocking three-line rhyme scheme: *aba, bcb, cdc, ded,* and so on. Dante's *Divine Comedy* uses this pattern, as does Robert Frost's "Acquainted with the Night" (p. 703) and Percy Bysshe Shelley's "Ode to the West Wind" (p. 794).

A *quatrain,* or four-line stanza, is the most common stanzaic form in the English language and can have various meters and rhyme schemes (if any). The most common rhyme schemes are *aabb, abba, aaba,* and *abcb.* This last pattern is especially characteristic of the popular *ballad stanza,* which consists of alternating eight- and six-syllable lines. Samuel Taylor Coleridge adopted this pattern in "The Rime of the Ancient Mariner"; here is one representative stanza:

> All in a hot and copper sky
> The bloody Sun, at noon,
> Right up above the mast did stand,
> No bigger than the Moon.

There are a number of longer stanzaic forms, and the list of types of stanzas could be extended considerably, but knowing these three most basic patterns should prove helpful to you in talking about the form of a great many poems. In addition to stanzaic forms, there are fixed forms that characterize entire poems. Lyric poems can be, for example, sonnets, villanelles, sestinas, or epigrams.

Sonnet

The *sonnet* has been a popular literary form in English since the sixteenth century, when it was adopted from the Italian *sonnetto,* meaning "little song." A sonnet consists of fourteen lines, usually written in iambic pentameter. Because the sonnet has been such a favorite form, writers have experimented with many variations on its essential structure. Nevertheless, there are two basic types of sonnets: the Italian and the English.

The **Italian sonnet** (also known as the **Petrarchan sonnet,** from the fourteenth-century Italian poet Petrarch) divides into two parts. The first eight lines (the **octave**) typically rhyme *abbaabba.* The final six lines (the **sestet**) may vary; common patterns are *cdecde, cdcdcd,* and *cdccdc.* Very often the octave presents a situation, attitude, or problem that the sestet comments upon or resolves, as in John Keats's "On First Looking into Chapman's Homer."

JOHN KEATS (1795–1821)

On First Looking into Chapman's Homer°   *1816*

Much have I traveled in the realms of gold,
    And many goodly states and kingdoms
        seen;
    Round many western islands have I been
Which bards in fealty to Apollo° hold.
Oft of one wide expanse had I been told
    That deep-browed Homer ruled as his
        demesne;
    Yet did I never breathe its pure serene°   *atmosphere*
Till I heard Chapman speak out loud and bold:
Then felt I like some watcher of the skies
    When a new planet swims into his ken;   10
Or like stout Cortez° when with eagle eyes
    He stared at the Pacific — and all his men
Looked at each other with a wild surmise —
    Silent, upon a peak in Darien.

Courtesy of the National Portrait Gallery, London.

Explore contexts for John Keats on *LiterActive*.

Chapman's Homer: Before reading George Chapman's (ca. 1560–1634) poetic Elizabethan translations of Homer's *Iliad* and *Odyssey,* Keats had known only stilted and pedestrian eighteenth-century translations.   4 *Apollo:* Greek god of poetry.   11 *Cortez:* Vasco Núñez de Balboa, not Hernando Cortés, was the first European to sight the Pacific from Darien, a peak in Panama.

CONSIDERATIONS FOR CRITICAL THINKING AND WRITING

1. **FIRST RESPONSE.** How do the images shift from the octave to the sestet? How does the tone change? Does the meaning change as well?
2. What is the controlling metaphor of this poem?
3. What does the speaker discover?
4. How does the rhythm of the lines change between the octave and the sestet? How does that change reflect the tones of both the octave and the sestet?
5. Does Keats's mistake concerning Cortés and Balboa affect your reading of the poem? Explain why or why not.

The Italian sonnet pattern is also used in the next sonnet, but notice that the thematic break between octave and sestet comes within line 9 rather than between lines 8 and 9. This unconventional break helps to reinforce the speaker's impatience with the conventional attitudes he describes.

WILLIAM WORDSWORTH (1770–1850)

The World Is Too Much with Us 1807

The world is too much with us; late and soon,
Getting and spending, we lay waste our powers;
Little we see in Nature that is ours;
We have given our hearts away, a sordid boon!
This Sea that bares her bosom to the moon; 5
The winds that will be howling at all hours,
And are up-gathered now like sleeping flowers;
For this, for everything, we are out of tune;
It moves us not. — Great God! I'd rather be
A Pagan suckled in a creed outworn; 10
So might I, standing on this pleasant lea,
Have glimpses that would make me less forlorn;
Have sight of Proteus rising from the sea;
Or hear old Triton blow his wreathèd horn.

CONSIDERATIONS FOR CRITICAL THINKING AND WRITING

1. **FIRST RESPONSE.** What is the speaker's complaint in this sonnet? How do the conditions described affect him?

2. Look up "Proteus" and "Triton." What do these mythological allusions contribute to the sonnet's tone?

3. What is the effect of the personification of the sea and wind in the octave?

CONNECTION TO ANOTHER SELECTION

1. Compare the theme of this sonnet with that of Gerard Manley Hopkins's "God's Grandeur" (p. 738).

The **English sonnet,** more commonly known as the **Shakespearean sonnet,** is organized into three quatrains and a couplet, which typically rhyme *abab cdcd efef gg.* This rhyme scheme is more suited to English poetry because English has fewer rhyming words than Italian. English sonnets, because of their four-part organization, also have more flexibility about where thematic breaks can occur. Frequently, however, the most pronounced break or turn comes with the concluding couplet.

In the following Shakespearean sonnet, the three quatrains compare the speaker's loved one to a summer's day and explain why the loved one is even more lovely. The couplet bestows eternal beauty and love upon both the loved one and the sonnet.

WILLIAM SHAKESPEARE (1564–1616)

Shall I compare thee to a summer's day? 1609

Shall I compare thee to a summer's day?
Thou art more lovely and more temperate:
Rough winds do shake the darling buds of May,
And summer's lease hath all too short a date.
Sometime too hot the eye of heaven shines,⠀⠀⠀⠀⠀⠀⠀⠀⠀⠀⠀⠀5
And often is his gold complexion dimmed;
And every fair from fair sometime declines,
By chance, or nature's changing course, untrimmed.
But thy eternal summer shall not fade,
Nor lose possession of that fair thou ow'st°⠀⠀⠀⠀⠀⠀⠀*possess*⠀10
Nor shall death brag thou wand'rest in his shade,
When in eternal lines to time thou grow'st.
⠀⠀⠀So long as men can breathe or eyes can see,
⠀⠀⠀So long lives this, and this gives life to thee.

CONSIDERATIONS FOR CRITICAL THINKING AND WRITING

1. **FIRST RESPONSE.** Describe the shift in tone and subject matter that begins in line 9.
2. Why is the speaker's loved one more lovely than a summer's day? What qualities does he admire in the loved one?
3. What does the couplet say about the relation between art and love?
4. Which syllables are stressed in the final line? How do these syllables relate to the line's meaning?

Sonnets have been the vehicles for all kinds of subjects, including love, death, politics, and cosmic questions. Although most sonnets tend to treat their subjects seriously, this fixed form does not mean a fixed expression; humor is also possible in it. Compare this next Shakespearean sonnet with "Shall I compare thee to a summer's day?" They are, finally, both love poems, but their tones are markedly different.

WILLIAM SHAKESPEARE (1564–1616)

My mistress' eyes are nothing like the sun 1609

My mistress' eyes are nothing like the sun;
Coral is far more red than her lips' red;
If snow be white, why then her breasts are dun;
If hairs be wires, black wires grow on her head.
I have seen roses damasked red and white,⠀⠀⠀⠀⠀⠀⠀⠀⠀⠀5
But no such roses see I in her cheeks;
And in some perfumes is there more delight
Than in the breath that from my mistress reeks.

I love to hear her speak, yet well I know
That music hath a far more pleasing sound;   10
I grant I never saw a goddess go:
My mistress, when she walks, treads on the ground.
 And yet, by heaven, I think my love as rare
 As any she,° belied with false compare.   *lady*

CONSIDERATIONS FOR CRITICAL THINKING AND WRITING

1. **FIRST RESPONSE.** What does "mistress" mean in this sonnet? Write a description of this particular mistress based on the images used in the sonnet.

2. What sort of person is the speaker? Does he truly love the woman he describes?

3. In what sense are this sonnet and "Shall I compare thee to a summer's day?" about poetry as well as love?

EDNA ST. VINCENT MILLAY (1892–1950)

I will put Chaos into fourteen lines   *1954*

© CORBIS.

I will put Chaos into fourteen lines
And keep him there; and let him thence escape
If he be lucky; let him twist, and ape
Flood, fire, and demon — his adroit designs
Will strain to nothing in the strict confines
Of this sweet Order, where, in pious rape,
I hold his essence and amorphous shape,
Till he with Order mingles and combines.
Past are the hours, the years, of our duress,
His arrogance, our awful servitude: 10
I have him. He is nothing more nor less
Than something simple not yet understood;
I shall not even force him to confess;
Or answer. I will only make him good.

CONSIDERATIONS FOR CRITICAL THINKING AND WRITING

1. **FIRST RESPONSE.** Does the poem contain "Chaos"? If so, how? If not, why not?

2. What properties of a sonnet does this poem possess?

3. What do you think is meant by the phrase "pious rape" in line 6?

4. What is the effect of the personification in the poem?

CONNECTION TO ANOTHER SELECTION

1. Compare the theme of this poem with that of Robert Frost's "Design" (p. 895).

A SAMPLE STUDENT RESPONSE

Alexia Sykes

Professor Jones

English 211

December 1, 2008

The Fixed Form in Edna St. Vincent Millay's

"I will put Chaos into fourteen lines"

In her poem "I will put Chaos into fourteen lines," Edna St. Vincent Millay does exactly what her title promises. Though the poem is of a fixed form, using patterns in meter, rhyme, line, and stanza, a sense of chaos is created through a complex structure, only to be calmed in the last six lines by a simpler rhyme scheme.

The first octave of the poem is structured abbaabba, a structure commonly found in sonnets. Although this is a fixed structure, the rhyme scheme is so complex that a chaotic tone is established:

> Flood, Fire, and demon--his adroit designs
> Will strain to nothing in the strict confines
> Of this sweet Order, where, in pious rape
> I hold his essence and amorphous shape,
> Till he with Order mingles and combines. (lines 4-8)

Rhyming couplets are fired at the reader and the seemingly haphazard pattern gives the impression that there is little or no structure at all, particularly on a first read. It is difficult to determine the framework of the poem, and the absence of a decipherable structure creates in the reader a feeling of randomness, the same disorder mentioned by the speaker. It is not until the end of the poem that relief is provided. The final six lines contain a much simpler, more repetitive structure: cdcdcd. This rhyme scheme provides stability and consistency. The pattern is simple and predictable; order is restored. Chaos has been tamed and made "good" (14) by the poem's form. . . .

Sykes 3

Work Cited

Millay, Edna St. Vincent. "I will put Chaos into fourteen lines." The Compact
Bedford Introduction to Literature. Ed. Michael Meyer. 8th ed. Boston:
Bedford/St. Martin's, 2009. 780.

SEAMUS HEANEY (B. 1939)

The Forge   *1969*

All I know is a door into the dark.
Outside, old axles and iron hoops rusting;
Inside, the hammered anvil's short-pitched ring,
The unpredictable fantail of sparks
Or hiss when a new shoe toughens in water.   5
The anvil must be somewhere in the centre,
Horned as a unicorn, at one end square,
Set there immoveable: an altar
Where he expends himself in shape and music.
Sometimes, leather-aproned, hairs in his nose,   10
He leans out on the jamb, recalls a clatter
Of hoofs where traffic is flashing in rows;
Then grunts and goes in, with a slam and flick
To beat real iron out, to work the bellows.

CONSIDERATIONS FOR CRITICAL THINKING AND WRITING

1. **FIRST RESPONSE.** In addition to providing a vivid description of a forge, what else does this poem offer about its portrait of a blacksmith?
2. How does the speaker's assertion that "All I know is a door into the dark" comment on the rest of the poem?
3. What kind of sonnet is "The Forge"?

MOLLY PEACOCK (B. 1947)

Desire   *1984*

It doesn't speak and it isn't schooled,
like a small foetal animal with wettened fur.
It is the blind instinct for life unruled,
visceral frankincense and animal myrrh.

It is what babies bring to kings,   5
an eyes-shut, ears-shut medicine of the heart
that smells and touches endings and beginnings
without the details of time's experienced *part-*
fit-into-part-fit-into-part. Like a paw,
it is blunt; like a pet who knows you   10
and nudges your knee with its snout—but more raw
and blinder and younger and more divine, too,
than the tamed wild—it's the drive for what is real,
deeper than the brain's detail: the drive to feel.

CONSIDERATIONS FOR CRITICAL THINKING AND WRITING

1. **FIRST RESPONSE.** Taken together, what do all of the metaphors that appear in this poem reveal about the speaker's conception of desire?

2. What is the "it" being described in lines 3–5? How do the allusions to the three wise men relate to the other metaphors used to define desire?

3. How is this English sonnet structured? What is the effect of its irregular meter?

CONNECTION TO ANOTHER SELECTION

1. Compare the treatment of desire in this poem with that of Sharon Olds's "Last Night" (p. 640). In an essay, identify the theme of each poem and compare their conceptions of desire. How alike are these two poems?

MARK JARMAN (B. 1952)

Unholy Sonnet   1993

After the praying, after the hymn-singing,
After the sermon's trenchant commentary
On the world's ills, which make ours secondary,
After communion, after the hand-wringing,
And after peace descends upon us, bringing   5
Our eyes up to regard the sanctuary
And how the light swords through it, and how, scary
In their sheer numbers, motes of dust ride, clinging—
There is, as doctors say about some pain,
Discomfort knowing that despite your prayers,   10
Your listening and rejoicing, your small part
In this communal stab at coming clean,
There is one stubborn remnant of your cares
Intact. There is still murder in your heart.

CONSIDERATIONS FOR CRITICAL THINKING AND WRITING

1. **FIRST RESPONSE.** Describe the rhyme scheme and structure of this sonnet. Explain why it is an English or an Italian sonnet.

2. What are the effects of the use of "after" in lines 1, 2, 4, and 5 and "there" in lines 9, 13, and 14?

3. In what sense might this poem be summed up as a "communal stab" (line 12)? Discuss the accuracy of this assessment.

4. CREATIVE RESPONSE. Try writing a reply to the theme of Jarman's poem using the same sonnet form that he uses.

CONNECTION TO ANOTHER SELECTION

1. Jarman has said that his "Unholy Sonnets" (there are about twenty of them) are modeled after John Donne's *Holy Sonnets* but that he does not share the same Christian assumptions about faith and mercy that inform Donne's sonnets. Instead, Jarman says, he "work[s] against any assumption or shared expression of faith, to write a devotional poetry against the grain." Keeping this statement in mind, write an essay comparing and contrasting the tone and theme of Jarman's sonnet with those of John Donne's "Death Be Not Proud" (p. 820).

Villanelle

The *villanelle* is a fixed form consisting of nineteen lines of any length divided into six stanzas: five tercets and a concluding quatrain. The first and third lines of the initial tercet rhyme; these rhymes are repeated in each subsequent tercet (*aba*) and in the final two lines of the quatrain (*abaa*). Moreover, line 1 appears in its entirety as lines 6, 12, and 18, while line 3 appears as lines 9, 15, and 19. This form may seem to risk monotony, but in competent hands a villanelle can create haunting echoes, as in Dylan Thomas's "Do Not Go Gentle into That Good Night."

DYLAN THOMAS (1914–1953)

Do Not Go Gentle into That Good Night　　　*1952*

Do not go gentle into that good night,
Old age should burn and rave at close of day;
Rage, rage against the dying of the light.

Though wise men at their end know dark is right,
Because their words had forked no lightning they　　　5
Do not go gentle into that good night.

Good men, the last wave by, crying how bright
Their frail deeds might have danced in a green bay,
Rage, rage against the dying of the light.

Wild men who caught and sang the sun in flight,　　　10
And learn, too late, they grieved it on its way,
Do not go gentle into that good night.

Grave men, near death, who see with blinding sight
Blind eyes could blaze like meteors and be gay,
Rage, rage against the dying of the light.   15

And you, my father, there on the sad height,
Curse, bless, me now with your fierce tears, I pray.
Do not go gentle into that good night.
Rage, rage against the dying of the light.

CONSIDERATIONS FOR CRITICAL THINKING AND WRITING

1. **FIRST RESPONSE.** How does Thomas vary the meanings of the poem's two
   refrains: "Do not go gentle into that good night" and "Rage, rage against
   the dying of the light"?

2. Thomas's father was close to death when this poem was written. How does
   the tone contribute to the poem's theme?

3. How is "good" used in line 1?

4. Characterize the men who are "wise" (line 4), "Good" (7), "Wild" (10), and
   "Grave" (13).

5. What do figures of speech contribute to this poem?

6. Discuss this villanelle's sound effects.

WENDY COPE (B. 1945)

Lonely Hearts   *1986*

Can someone make my simple wish come true?
Male biker seeks female for touring fun.
Do you live in North London? Is it you?

Gay vegetarian whose friends are few,
I'm into music, Shakespeare and the sun.   5
Can someone make my simple wish come true?

Executive in search of something new —
Perhaps bisexual woman, arty, young.
Do you live in North London? Is it you?

Successful, straight and solvent? I am too —   10
Attractive Jewish lady with a son.
Can someone make my simple wish come true?

I'm Libran, inexperienced and blue—
Need slim non-smoker, under twenty-one.
Do you live in North London? Is it you?   15

Please write (with photo) to Box 152
Who knows where it may lead once we've begun?
Can someone make my simple wish come true?
Do you live in North London? Is it you?

CONSIDERATIONS FOR CRITICAL THINKING AND WRITING

1. **FIRST RESPONSE.** Why does the repetitive form of the villanelle seem particularly appropriate for the subject matter of "Lonely Hearts"?

2. How closely does "Lonely Hearts" conform to the conventional form of the villanelle? Are there any significant variations that produce interesting effects?

3. How are the several speakers' voices in the poem unified by tone?

Sestina

Although the *sestina* usually does not rhyme, it is perhaps an even more demanding fixed form than the villanelle. A sestina consists of thirty-nine lines of any length divided into six six-line stanzas and a three-line concluding stanza called an *envoy.* The difficulty lies in repeating the six words at the ends of the first stanza's lines at the ends of the lines in the other five six-line stanzas as well. Those words must also appear in the final three lines, where they often resonate important themes. The sestina originated in the Middle Ages, but contemporary poets continue to find it a fascinating and challenging form.

ALGERNON CHARLES SWINBURNE (1837–1909)

Sestina   *1872*

I saw my soul at rest upon a day
As a bird sleeping in the nest of night,
Among soft leaves that give the starlight way
To touch its wings but not its eyes with light;
So that it knew as one in visions may,   5
And knew not as men waking, of delight.

This was the measure of my soul's delight;
It had no power of joy to fly by day,
Nor part in the large lordship of the light;
But in a secret moon-beholden way   10
Had all its will of dreams and pleasant night,
And all the love and life that sleepers may.

But such life's triumph as men waking may
It might not have to feed its faint delight
Between the stars by night and sun by day,   15
Shut up with green leaves and a little light;
Because its way was as a lost star's way,
A world's not wholly known of day or night.

All loves and dreams and sounds and gleams of night
Made it all music that such minstrels may,   20

And all they had they gave it of delight;
But in the full face of the fire of day
What place shall be for any starry light,
What part of heaven in all the wide sun's way?

Yet the soul woke not, sleeping by the way,   25
Watched as a nursling of the large-eyed night,
And sought no strength nor knowledge of the day,
Nor closer touch conclusive of delight,
Nor mightier joy nor truer than dreamers may,
Nor more of song than they, nor more of light.   30

For who sleeps once and sees the secret light
Whereby sleep shows the soul a fairer way
Between the rise and rest of day and night,
Shall care no more to fare as all men may,
But be his place of pain or of delight,   35
There shall he dwell, beholding night as day.

Song, have thy day and take thy fill of light
Before the night be fallen across thy way;
Sing while he may, man hath no long delight.

Considerations for Critical Thinking and Writing

1. **FIRST RESPONSE.** How are the six end words — "day," "night," "way," "light,"
   "may," and "delight" — central to the sestina's meaning?

2. Number the end words of the first stanza 1, 2, 3, 4, 5, and 6, and then use
   those numbers for the corresponding end words in the remaining five stanzas to see how the pattern of the line-end words is worked out in this sestina. Also locate the six end words in the envoy.

3. Underline the images that seem especially vivid to you. What effects do
   they create? What is the tone of the sestina?

4. **CRITICAL STRATEGIES.** Read the section on psychological strategies (pp.
   1542–44) in Chapter 46, "Critical Strategies for Reading." Write a brief essay
   explaining why you think a poet might derive pleasure from writing in a
   fixed form such as a villanelle or sestina. Can you think of similar activities
   outside the field of writing in which discipline and restraint give pleasure?
   How might this reflect an author's personal psychology?

FLORENCE CASSEN MAYERS (B. 1940)

All-American Sestina   *1996*

One nation, indivisible
two-car garage
three strikes you're out
four-minute mile
five-cent cigar   5
six-string guitar

six-pack Bud
one-day sale
five-year warranty
two-way street
fourscore and seven years ago   10
three cheers

three-star restaurant
sixty-
four-dollar question   15
one-night stand
two-pound lobster
five-star general

five-course meal
three sheets to the wind   20
two bits
six-shooter
one-armed bandit
four-poster

four-wheel drive   25
five-and-dime
hole in one
three-alarm fire
sweet sixteen
two-wheeler   30

two-tone Chevy
four rms, hi flr, w/vu
six-footer
high five
three-ring circus   35
one-room schoolhouse

two thumbs up, five-karat diamond
Fourth of July, three-piece suit
six feet under, one-horse town

CONSIDERATIONS FOR CRITICAL THINKING AND WRITING

1. **FIRST RESPONSE.** Discuss the significance of the title; what is "All-American"?
   Why a sestina?

2. How is the structure of this poem different from a conventional sestina?
   (What structural requirement does Mayers add for this sestina?)

3. Do you think important themes are raised by this poem, as is traditional
   for a sestina? If so, what are they? If not, what is being played with by using
   this convention?

CONNECTION TO ANOTHER SELECTION

1. Describe and compare the strategy used to create meaning in "All-American Sestina" with that used by Cummings in "next to of course god america i" (p. 711).

Epigram

An **epigram** is a brief, pointed, and witty poem. Although most rhyme and often are written in couplets, epigrams take no prescribed form. Instead, they are typically polished bits of compressed irony, satire, or paradox. Here is an epigram that defines itself.

SAMUEL TAYLOR COLERIDGE (1772–1834)

What Is an Epigram?

1802

What is an epigram? A dwarfish whole;
Its body brevity, and wit its soul.

These additional examples by A. R. Ammons, David McCord, and Paul Laurence Dunbar satisfy Coleridge's definition.

A. R. AMMONS (B. 1926)

Coward

1975

Bravery runs in my family.

DAVID MCCORD (1897–1997)

Epitaph on a Waiter

1954

By and by
God caught his eye.

PAUL LAURENCE DUNBAR
(1872–1906)

Theology

1896

There is a heaven, for ever, day by day,
The upward longing of my soul doth tell
    me so.
There is a hell, I'm quite as sure; for pray,
If there were not, where would my
    neighbors go?

Courtesy of the Ohio Historical Society.

CONSIDERATIONS FOR CRITICAL THINKING AND WRITING

1. **FIRST RESPONSE.** In what sense is each of these epigrams, as Coleridge puts it, a "dwarfish whole"?
2. Explain which of these epigrams, in addition to being witty, makes a serious point.
3. **CREATIVE RESPONSE.** Try writing a few epigrams that say something memorable about whatever you choose to focus on.

Limerick

The *limerick* is always light and humorous. Its usual form consists of five predominantly anapestic lines rhyming *aabba;* lines 1, 2, and 5 contain three feet, while lines 3 and 4 contain two. Limericks have delighted everyone from schoolchildren to sophisticated adults, and they range in subject matter from the simply innocent and silly to the satiric or obscene. The sexual humor helps to explain why so many limericks are written anonymously. Here is one that is anonymous but more concerned with physics than physiology.

ANONYMOUS

There was a young lady named Bright

There was a young lady named Bright,
Who traveled much faster than light,
    She started one day
    In a relative way,
And returned on the previous night.

This next one is a particularly clever definition of a limerick.

LAURENCE PERRINE (B. 1915)

The limerick's never averse   1982

The limerick's never averse
To expressing itself in a terse
    Economical style,
    And yet, all the while,
The limerick's *always* a verse.

CONSIDERATIONS FOR CRITICAL THINKING AND WRITING

1. **FIRST RESPONSE.** How does this limerick differ from others you know? How is it similar?

2. Scan Perrine's limerick. How do the lines measure up to the traditional fixed metrical pattern?

3. Try writing a limerick. Use the following basic pattern.

⌣ ⌣ ⁄   ⌣ ⌣ ⁄   ⌣ ⌣ ⁄
⌣ ⌣ ⁄   ⌣ ⌣ ⁄   ⌣ ⌣ ⁄
             ⌣ ⌣ ⁄   ⌣ ⌣ ⁄
             ⌣ ⌣ ⁄   ⌣ ⌣ ⁄
⌣ ⌣ ⁄   ⌣ ⌣ ⁄   ⌣ ⌣ ⁄

You might begin with a friend's name or the name of your school or town. Your instructor is, of course, fair game, too, provided your tact matches your wit.

The next selection is a real tongue twister.

KEITH CASTO

She Don't Bop   *1987*

A nervous young woman named Trudy
Was at odds with a horn player, Rudy.
His horn so annoyed her
The neighbors would loiter
To watch Rudy toot Trudy fruity.

Haiku

Another brief fixed poetic form, borrowed from the Japanese, is the *haiku.* A haiku is usually described as consisting of seventeen syllables organized into three unrhymed lines of five, seven, and five syllables. Owing to language difference, however, English translations of haiku are often only approximated, because a Japanese haiku exists in time (Japanese syllables have duration). The number of syllables in our sense is not as significant as the duration. These poems typically present an intense emotion or vivid image of nature, which, in the Japanese, are also designed to lead to a spiritual insight.

MATSUO BASHŌ (1644–1694)

Under cherry trees   *date unknown*

Under cherry trees
Soup, the salad, fish and all . . .
Seasoned with petals.

Carolyn Kizer (b. 1925)

After Bashō

1984

Tentatively, you
slip onstage this evening,
pallid, famous moon.

Sonia Sanchez (b. 1935)

c'mon man hold me

1998

c'mon man hold me
touch me before time love me
from behind your eyes.

Considerations for Critical Thinking and Writing

1. **First Response.** What different emotions do these three haiku evoke?
2. What differences and similarities are there between the effects of a haiku and those of an epigram?
3. **Creative Response.** Compose a haiku. Try to make it as allusive and suggestive as possible.

Elegy

An elegy in classical Greek and Roman literature was written in alternating hexameter and pentameter lines. Since the seventeenth century, however, the term *elegy* has been used to describe a lyric poem written to commemorate someone who is dead. The word is also used to refer to a serious meditative poem produced to express the speaker's melancholy thoughts. Elegies no longer conform to a fixed pattern of lines and stanzas, but their characteristic subject is related to death and their tone is mournfully contemplative.

Theodore Roethke (1908–1963)

Elegy for Jane

1953

My Student, Thrown by a Horse

I remember the neckcurls, limp and damp as tendrils;
And her quick look, a sidelong pickerel smile;
And how, once startled into talk, the light syllables leaped for her,
And she balanced in the delight of her thought,

A wren, happy, tail into the wind,   5
Her song trembling the twigs and small branches.
The shade sang with her;
The leaves, their whispers turned to kissing;
And the mold sang in the bleached valleys under the rose.

Oh, when she was sad, she cast herself down into such a pure depth,   10
Even a father could not find her:
Scraping her cheek against straw;
Stirring the clearest water.

My sparrow, you are not here,
Waiting like a fern, making a spiny shadow.   15
The sides of wet stones cannot console me,
Nor the moss, wound with the last light.

If only I could nudge you from this sleep,
My maimed darling, my skittery pigeon.
Over this damp grave I speak the words of my love: 20
I, with no rights in this matter,
Neither father nor lover.

CONSIDERATIONS FOR CRITICAL THINKING AND WRITING

1. **FIRST RESPONSE.** Does this elegy use any kind of formal pattern for its structure? What holds it together?

2. List the images that compare Jane to nature. How is she depicted by these images?

3. Describe the shift in tone that begins in line 14. How do the speaker's feelings change in lines 14–22?

4. What is the significance of Jane having been the speaker's student? How does that affect your reading of lines 21–22?

CONNECTION TO ANOTHER SELECTION

1. Compare "Elegy for Jane" with A. E. Housman's "To an Athlete Dying Young" (p. 1023). How does each poem avoid sentimentality in its description of a young person who has died?

Ode

An **ode** is characterized by a serious topic and formal tone, but no prescribed formal pattern describes all odes. In some odes the pattern of each stanza is repeated throughout, while in others each stanza introduces a new pattern. Odes are lengthy lyrics that often include lofty emotions conveyed by a dignified style. Typical topics include truth, art, freedom, justice, and the meaning of life. Frequently such lyrics tend to be more public than private, and their speakers often use apostrophe.

PERCY BYSSHE SHELLEY (1792–1822)

Ode to the West Wind   *1820*

I

O wild West Wind, thou breath of Autumn's being,
Thou, from whose unseen presence the leaves dead
Are driven, like ghosts from an enchanter fleeing,

Yellow, and black, and pale, and hectic red,
Pestilence-stricken multitudes: O thou,   5
Who chariotest to their dark wintry bed

The wingèd seeds, where they lie cold and low,
Each like a corpse within its grave, until
Thine azure sister of the Spring shall blow

Her clarion o'er the dreaming earth, and fill   10
(Driving sweet buds like flocks to feed in air)
With living hues and odors plain and hill:

Wild Spirit, which art moving everywhere;
Destroyer and preserver; hear, oh, hear!

II

Thou on whose stream, mid the steep sky's commotion,   15
Loose clouds like earth's decaying leaves are shed,
Shook from the tangled boughs of Heaven and Ocean,

Angels° of rain and lightning: there are spread   *messengers*
On the blue surface of thine airy surge,
Like the bright hair uplifted from the head   20

Of some fierce Maenad,° even from the dim verge
Of the horizon to the zenith's height,
The locks of the approaching storm. Thou dirge

Of the dying year, to which this closing night
Will be the dome of a vast sepulcher,   25
Vaulted with all thy congregated might

Of vapors, from whose solid atmosphere
Black rain, and fire, and hail will burst: oh, hear!

III

Thou who didst waken from his summer dreams
The blue Mediterranean, where he lay,   30
Lulled by the coil of his crystálline streams,

---

21 *Maenad:* In Greek mythology, a frenzied worshipper of Dionysus, god of wine and
fertility.

Beside a pumice isle in Baiae's bay,°
And saw in sleep old palaces and towers
Quivering within the wave's intenser day,

All overgrown with azure moss and flowers   35
So sweet, the sense faints picturing them! Thou
For whose path the Atlantic's level powers

Cleave themselves into chasms, while far below
The sea-blooms and the oozy woods which wear
The sapless foliage of the ocean, know   40

Thy voice, and suddenly grow gray with fear,
And tremble and despoil themselves: oh, hear!

IV

If I were a dead leaf thou mightest bear;
If I were a swift cloud to fly with thee;
A wave to pant beneath thy power, and share   45

The impulse of thy strength, only less free
Than thou, O uncontrollable! If even
I were as in my boyhood, and could be

The comrade by thy wanderings over Heaven,
As then, when to outstrip thy skyey speed   50
Scarce seemed a vision; I would ne'er have striven

As thus with thee in prayer in my sore need.
Oh, lift me as a wave, a leaf, a cloud!
I fall upon the thorns of life! I bleed!

A heavy weight of hours has chained and bowed   55
One too like thee: tameless, and swift, and proud.

V

Make me thy lyre,° even as the forest is:
What if my leaves are falling like its own!
The tumult of thy mighty harmonies

Will take from both a deep, autumnal tone,   60
Sweet though in sadness. Be thou, Spirit fierce,
My spirit! Be thou me, impetuous one!

Drive my dead thoughts over the universe
Like withered leaves to quicken a new birth!
And, by the incantation of this verse,   65

---

32 *Baiae's bay:* A bay in the Mediterranean Sea.   57 *Make me thy lyre:* Sound is produced on an Aeolian lyre, or wind harp, by wind blowing across its strings.

Scatter, as from an unextinguished hearth
Ashes and sparks, my words among mankind!
Be through my lips to unawakened earth

The trumpet of a prophecy! O Wind,
If Winter comes, can Spring be far behind?   70

CONSIDERATIONS FOR CRITICAL THINKING AND WRITING

1. **FIRST RESPONSE.** Write a summary of each of this ode's five sections.
2. What is the speaker's situation? What is his "sore need" (line 52)? What does the speaker ask of the wind in lines 57–70?
3. What does the wind signify in this ode? How is it used symbolically?
4. Determine the meter and rhyme of the first five stanzas. How do these elements contribute to the ode's movement? Is this pattern continued in the other four sections?

Picture Poem

By arranging lines into particular shapes, poets can sometimes organize typography into *picture poems* of what they describe. Words have been arranged into all kinds of shapes, from apples to lightbulbs. Notice how the shape of this next poem embodies its meaning.

MICHAEL McFEE (B. 1954)

In Medias Res°   1985

His waist
like the plot
thickens, wedding
pants now breathtaking,
belt no longer the cinch   5
it once was, belly's cambium
expanding to match each birthday,
his body a wad of anonymous tissue
swung in the same centrifuge of years
that separates a house from its foundation,   10
undermining sidewalks grim with joggers
and loose-filled graves and families
and stars collapsing on themselves,
no preservation society capable
of plugging entropy's dike,   15
under his zipper's sneer
a belly hibernation-
soft, ready for
the kill.

In Medias Res: A Latin term for a story that begins "in the middle of things."

CONSIDERATIONS FOR CRITICAL THINKING AND WRITING

1. **FIRST RESPONSE.** Explain how the title is related to this poem's shape. How is the meaning related?
2. Identify the puns. How do they work in the poem?
3. What is "cambium" (line 6)? Why is the phrase "belly's cambium" especially appropriate?
4. What is the tone of this poem? Is it consistent throughout?

Parody

A *parody* is a humorous imitation of another, usually serious, work. It can take any fixed or open form because parodists imitate the tone, language, and shape of the original. While a parody may be teasingly close to a work's style, it typically deflates the subject matter to make the original seem absurd. Parody can be used as a kind of literary criticism to expose the defects in a work, but it is also very often an affectionate acknowledgment that a well-known work has become both institutionalized in our culture and fair game for some fun. Here's a parody for all seasons—not just Christmas—that brings together two popular icons of our culture.

X. J. KENNEDY (B. 1929)

A Visit from St. Sigmund   1993

Freud is just an old Santa Claus.
        —*Margaret Mead°*

'Twas the night before Christmas, when all through each kid
Not an Ego was stirring, not even an Id.
The hangups were hung by the chimney with care
In hopes that St. Sigmund Freud soon would be there.
The children in scream class had knocked off their screams,   5
Letting Jungian archetypes dance through their dreams,
And Mamma with her bra off and I on her lap
Had just snuggled down when a vast thunderclap
Boomed and from my unconscious arose such a chatter
As Baptist John's teeth made on Salome's platter.   10
Away from my darling I flew like a flash,
Tore straight to the bathroom and threw up, and—*smash!*
Through the windowpane hurtled and bounced on the floor
A big brick—holy smoke, it was hard to ignore.
As I heard further thunderclaps—lo and behold—   15
Came a little psychiatrist eighty years old.
He drove a wheeled couch pulled by five fat psychoses

Margaret Mead (1901–1978): Noted American anthropologist.

And the gleam in his eye might induce a hypnosis.
Like subliminal meanings his coursers they came
And, consulting his notebook, he called them by name: 20
"Now Schizo, now Fetish, now Fear of Castration!
On Paranoia! on Penis-fixation!
Ach, yes, that big brick through your glass I should mention:
Just a simple device to compel your attention.
You need, boy, to be in an analyst's power: 25
You talk, I take notes — fifty schillings an hour."
A bag full of symbols he'd slung on his back;
He looked smug as a junk-peddler laden with smack
Or a shrewd politician soliciting votes
And his chinbeard was stiff as a starched billygoat's.   30
Then laying one finger aside of his nose,
He chortled, "What means this? Mein Gott, I suppose
There's a meaning in fingers, in candles und wicks,
In mouseholes und doughnut holes, steeples und sticks.
You see, it's the imminent prospect of sex   35
That makes all us humans run round till we're wrecks,
Und each innocent infant since people began
Wants to bed with his momma und kill his old man;
So never you fear that you're sick as a swine —
Your hangups are every sane person's und mine.   40
Even Hamlet was hot for his mom — there's the rub;
Even Oedipus Clubfoot was one of the club.
Hmmm, that's humor unconscious." He gave me rib-pokes
And for almost two hours explained phallic jokes.
Then he sprang to his couch, to his crew gave a nod,   45
And away they all flew like the concept of God.
In the worst of my dreams I can hear him shout still,
"Merry Christmas to all! In the mail comes my bill."

CONSIDERATIONS FOR CRITICAL THINKING AND WRITING

1. **FIRST RESPONSE.** What makes Freud a particularly appropriate substitute
   for Santa Claus? How does this substitute facilitate the poem's humor?

2. What is the tone of this parody? How does the quotation from Margaret
   Mead help to establish the poem's tone?

3. What do you think is the poet's attitude toward Freud? Cite specific lines
   to support your point.

4. Is the focus of this parody the Christmas story or Freud? Explain your
   response.

Elaine Mitchell (b. 1924)

Form

1994

Is it a corset
or primal wave?
Don't try to force it.

Even endorse it
to shape and deceive.   5
Ouch, too tight a corset.

Take it off. No remorse. It
's an ace up your sleeve.
No need to force it.

Can you make a horse knit?   10
Who would believe?
Consider. Of course, it

might be a resource. Wit,
your grateful slave.
Form. Sometimes you force it,   15

sometimes divorce it
to make it behave.
So don't try to force it.
Respect a good corset.

Considerations for Critical Thinking and Writing

1. **First Response.** What is the speaker's attitude toward form?

2. Explain why you think the form of this poem does or does not conform to the speaker's advice.

3. Why is the metaphor of a corset a particularly apt image for this poem?

Web Research the
poets in this chapter at
bedfordstmartins.com/
meyercompact.

27

Open Form

By permission of David Geier and New Directions.

> I believe every space and comma is a
> living part of the poem and has its
> function, just as every muscle and pore
> of the body has its function. And the
> way the lines are broken is a functioning
> part essential to the poem's life.
> — DENISE LEVERTOV

Many poems, especially those written in the twentieth century, are composed of lines that cannot be scanned for a fixed or predominant meter. Moreover, very often these poems do not rhyme. Known as *free verse* (from the French, *vers libre*), such lines can derive their rhythmic qualities from the repetition of words, phrases, or grammatical structures; the arrangement of words on the printed page; or some other means. In recent years the term *open form* has been used in place of *free verse* to avoid the erroneous suggestion that this kind of poetry lacks all discipline and shape.

Although the following two poems do not use measurable meters, they do have rhythm.

E. E. Cummings (1894–1962)

in Just-   *1923*

in Just-
spring   when the world is mud-
luscious the little
lame balloonman

whistles   far   and wee   5

and eddieandbill come
running from marbles and
piracies and it's
spring

when the world is puddle-wonderful   10

the queer
old balloonman whistles
far   and   wee
and bettyandisbel come dancing

from hop-scotch and jump-rope and   15

it's
spring
and

    the

        goat-footed   20

balloonMan   whistles
far
and
wee

Explore contexts
for E. E. Cummings
on *LiterActive*.

Considerations for Critical Thinking and Writing

1. **First Response.** What is the effect of this poem's arrangement of words
   and use of space on the page? How would the effect differ if the text was
   written out in prose?

2. What is the effect of Cummings's combining the names "eddieandbill" and
   "bettyandisbel"?

3. The allusion in line 20 refers to Pan, a Greek god associated with nature.
   How does this allusion add to the meaning of the poem?

Walt Whitman (1819–1892)

From "I Sing the Body Electric"   1855

O my body! I dare not desert the likes of you in other men and women,
    nor the likes of the parts of you,
I believe the likes of you are to stand or fall with the likes of the soul, (and
    that they are the soul,)
I believe the likes of you shall stand or fall with my poems, and that they
    are my poems.
Man's, woman's, child's, youth's, wife's, husband's, mother's, father's,
    young man's, young woman's poems.
Head, neck, hair, ears, drop and tympan of the ears.   5

Eyes, eye-fringes, iris of the eye, eyebrows, and
    the waking or sleeping of the lids,
Mouth, tongue, lips, teeth, roof of the mouth,
    jaws, and the jaw-hinges,
Nose, nostrils of the nose, and the partition,
Cheeks, temples, forehead, chin, throat, back
    of the neck, neck-slue,
Strong shoulders, manly beard, scapula, hind-
    shoulders, and the ample
    side-round of the chest,
Upper-arm, armpit, elbow-socket, lower-arm,
    arm-sinews, arm-bones,
Wrist and wrist-joints, hand, palm, knuckles,
    thumb, forefinger, finger-joints, finger-
    nails,

Courtesy of the Bayley-Whitman Collection of Ohio Wesleyan University of Delaware, Ohio.

Broad breast-front, curling hair of the breast,
    breast-bone, breast-side,
Ribs, belly, backbone, joints of the backbone,
Hips, hip-sockets, hip-strength, inward and outward round, man-balls,
    man-root,   15
Strong set of thighs, well carrying the trunk above,
Leg-fibers, knee, knee-pan, upper-leg, under-leg,
Ankles, instep, foot-ball, toes, toe-joints, the heel;
All attitudes, all the shapeliness, all the belongings of my or your body or
    of any one's body, male or female,
The lung-sponges, the stomach-sac, the bowels sweet and clean,   20
The brain in its folds inside the skull-frame,
Sympathies, heart-valves, palate-valves, sexuality, maternity,
Womanhood, and all that is a woman, and the man that comes from
    woman,
The womb, the teats, nipples, breast-milk, tears, laughter, weeping, love-
    looks, love-perturbations and risings,
The voice, articulation, language, whispering, shouting aloud,   25
Food, drink, pulse, digestion, sweat, sleep, walking, swimming,
Poise on the hips, leaping, reclining, embracing, arm-curving and
    tightening,
The continual changes of the flex of the mouth, and around the eyes,
The skin, the sunburnt shade, freckles, hair,
The curious sympathy one feels when feeling with the hand the naked
    meat of the body,   30
The circling rivers the breath, and breathing it in and out,
The beauty of the waist, and thence of the hips, and thence downward
    toward the knees,
The thin red jellies within you or within me, the bones and the marrow
    in the bones,
The exquisite realization of health;
O I say these are not the parts and poems of the body only, but of the soul, 35
O I say now these are the soul!

CONSIDERATIONS FOR CRITICAL THINKING AND WRITING

1. **FIRST RESPONSE.** What informs this speaker's attitude toward the human body?

2. Read the poem aloud. Is it simply a tedious enumeration of body parts, or do the lines achieve some kind of rhythmic cadence?

Perspective

WALT WHITMAN (1819–1892)

On Rhyme and Meter   *1855*

The poetic quality is not marshaled in rhyme or uniformity or abstract addresses to things nor in melancholy complaints or good precepts, but is the life of these and much else and is in the soul. The profit of rhyme is that it drops seeds of a sweeter and more luxuriant rhyme, and of uniformity that it conveys itself into its own roots in the ground out of sight. The rhyme and uniformity of perfect poems show the free growth of metrical laws and bud from them as unerringly and loosely as lilacs or roses on a bush, and take shapes as compact as the shapes of chestnuts and oranges and melons and pears, and shed the perfume impalpable to form. The fluency and ornaments of the finest poems or music or orations or recitations are not independent but dependent. All beauty comes from beautiful blood and a beautiful brain. If the greatnesses are in conjunction in a man or woman it is enough . . . the fact will prevail through the universe . . . but the gaggery and gilt of a million years will not prevail. Who troubles himself about his ornaments or fluency is lost.

From the preface to the 1855 edition of *Leaves of Grass*

CONSIDERATIONS FOR CRITICAL THINKING AND WRITING

1. According to Whitman, what determines the shape of a poem?

2. Why does Whitman prefer open forms over fixed forms such as the sonnet?

3. Is Whitman's poetry devoid of any structure or shape? Choose one of his poems (listed in the index) to illustrate your answer.

Open form poetry is sometimes regarded as formless because it is unlike the strict fixed forms of a sonnet, villanelle, or sestina. But even though open form poems may not employ traditional meters and rhymes, they still rely on an intense use of language to establish rhythms and relations between meaning and form. Open form poems use the arrangement of words and phrases on the printed page, pauses, line lengths, and other means to create unique forms that express their particular meaning and tone.

A SAMPLE STUDENT RESPONSE

Avery Bloom

Professor Rios

English 212

October 7, 2008

The Power of Walt Whitman's Open Form Poem

"I Sing the Body Electric"

Walt Whitman's "I Sing the Body Electric" is an ode to the human body. The poem is open form, without rhymes or consistent meter, and instead relies almost entirely on the use of language and the structure of lists to affect the reader. The result is a thorough inventory of parts of the body that illustrates the beauty of the human form and its intimate connection to the soul.

At times, Whitman lists the parts of the body with almost complete objectivity, making it difficult to understand the poem's purpose. The poem initially appears to do little more than recite the names of body parts: "Head, neck, hair, ears, drop and tympan of the ears" (line 5); "Mouth, tongue, lips, teeth, roof of the mouth, jaws, and the jaw-hinges" (7). There are no end rhymes, but the exhaustive and detailed list of body parts--from the brain to "the thin red jellies . . . , the bones and the marrow in the bones" (33)-- offers language that has a certain rhythm. The language and rhythm of the list creates a visual image full of energy and momentum that builds, empha-sizing the body's functions and movements. As Michael Meyer writes, open form poems "rely on an intense use of language to establish rhythms and relations between meaning and form. [They] use the arrangement of words and phrases . . . to create unique forms" (page 803). No doubt Whitman chose the open form for this work--relying on his "intense use of language" and the rhythm of the list--because it allowed a basic structure that held together but did not restrain, and a full freedom and range of motion to create a poem that is alive with movement and electricity. . . .

Bloom 4

Works Cited

Meyer, Michael, ed. The Compact Bedford Introduction to Literature. 8th ed.
    Boston: Bedford/St. Martin's, 2009. 803.

Whitman, Walt. "From 'I Sing the Body Electric.'" The Compact Bedford Intro-
    duction to Literature. Ed. Michael Meyer. 8th ed. Boston: Bedford/
    St. Martin's, 2009. 801–2.

Cummings's "in Just-" and the excerpt from Whitman's "I Sing the Body Electric" demonstrate how the white space on a page and rhythmic cadences can be aligned with meaning, but there is one kind of open form poetry that doesn't even look like poetry on a page. A *prose poem* is printed as prose and represents, perhaps, the clearest opposite of fixed forms. Here is a brief example.

LOUIS JENKINS (B. 1942)
The Prose Poem   *2000*

The prose poem is not a real poem, of course. One of the major differences is that the prose poet is simply too lazy or too stupid to break the poem into lines. But all writing, even the prose poem, involves a certain amount of skill, just the way throwing a wad of paper, say, into a wastebasket at a distance of twenty feet, requires a certain skill, a skill that, though it may improve hand-eye coordination, does not lead necessarily to an ability to play basketball. Still, it takes practice and thus gives one a way to pass the time, chucking one paper after another at the basket, while the teacher drones on about the poetry of Tennyson.

CONSIDERATIONS FOR CRITICAL THINKING AND WRITING

1. **FIRST RESPONSE.** What is the effect of this prose poem? Does it have a theme?
2. What, if anything, is poetic in this work?
3. Arrange the lines so that they look like poetry on a page. What determines where you break the lines?

Much of the poetry published today is written in open form; however, many poets continue to take pleasure in the requirements imposed by fixed forms. Some write both fixed form and open form poetry. Each kind offers rewards to careful readers as well. Here are several more open form poems that establish their own unique patterns.

GALWAY KINNELL (B. 1927)

After Making Love We Hear Footsteps 1980

For I can snore like a bullhorn
or play loud music
or sit up talking with any reasonably sober Irishman
and Fergus will only sink deeper
into his dreamless sleep, which goes by all in one flash,   5
but let there be that heavy breathing
or a stifled come-cry anywhere in the house
and he will wrench himself awake
and make for it on the run — as now, we lie together,
after making love, quiet, touching along the length of our bodies,   10
familiar touch of the long-married,
and he appears — in his baseball pajamas, it happens,
the neck opening so small
he has to screw them on, which one day may make him wonder
about the mental capacity of baseball players —   15
and says, "Are you loving and snuggling? May I join?"
He flops down between us and hugs us and snuggles himself to sleep,
his face gleaming with satisfaction at being this very child.

In the half darkness we look at each other
and smile   20
and touch arms across his little, startlingly muscled body —
this one whom habit of memory propels to the ground of his making,
sleeper only the mortal sounds can sing awake,
this blessing love gives again into our arms.

CONSIDERATIONS FOR CRITICAL THINKING AND WRITING

1. **FIRST RESPONSE.** Explore Kinnell's line endings. Why does he break the lines where he does?

2. How does the speaker's language reveal his character?

3. Describe the shift in tone between lines 18 and 19 with the shift in focus from child to adult. How does the use of space here emphasize this shift?

4. Do you think this poem is sentimental? Explain why or why not.

CONNECTION TO ANOTHER SELECTION

1. Characterize the emotions that Kinnell evokes in this poem. How do these emotions compare to the sense of loss Robert Frost evokes in "Home Burial" (p. 886)?

KELLY CHERRY (B. 1940)

Alzheimer's   *1990*

He stands at the door, a crazy old man
Back from the hospital, his mind rattling
Like the suitcase, swinging from his hand,
That contains shaving cream, a piggy bank,
A book he sometimes pretends to read,   5
His clothes. On the brick wall beside him
Roses and columbine slug it out for space, claw the mortar.
The sun is shining, as it does late in the afternoon
In England, after rain.
Sun hardens the house, reifies it,   10
Strikes the iron grillwork like a smithy
And sparks fly off, burning in the bushes —
The rosebushes —
While the white wood trim defines solidity in space.
This is his house. He remembers it as his,   15
Remembers the walkway he built between the front room
And the garage, the rhododendron he planted in back,
The car he used to drive. He remembers himself,
A younger man, in a tweed hat, a man who loved
Music. There is no time for that now. No time for music,   20
The peculiar screeching of strings, the luxurious
Fiddling with emotion.
Other things have become more urgent.
Other matters are now of greater import, have more
Consequence, must be attended to. The first   25
Thing he must do, now that he is home, is decide who
This woman is, this old, white-haired woman
Standing here in the doorway,
Welcoming him in.

CONSIDERATIONS FOR CRITICAL THINKING AND WRITING

1. **FIRST RESPONSE.** Why is it impossible to dismiss the character in this poem
   as merely "a crazy old man"?

2. Discuss the effect of the line breaks in lines 1–6 of the poem's first complete
   sentence. How do the line breaks contribute to the meaning of these lines?

3. What do the images in lines 6–20 indicate about the nature of the man's
   memory?

4. Why is the final image of the "white-haired woman" especially effective?
   How does the final line serve as the poem's emotional climax?

WILLIAM CARLOS WILLIAMS (1883–1963)

The Red Wheelbarrow 1923

so much depends
upon

a red wheel
barrow

glazed with rain
water

beside the white
chickens.

CONSIDERATIONS FOR CRITICAL THINKING AND WRITING

1. **FIRST RESPONSE.** What "depends upon" the things mentioned in the poem? What is the effect of these images? Do they have a particular meaning?
2. Do these lines have any kind of rhythm?
3. How does this poem resemble a haiku? How is it different?

NATASHA TRETHEWEY (B. 1966)

Domestic Work, 1937 1999

All week she's cleaned
someone else's house,
stared down her own face
in the shine of copper-
bottomed pots, polished 5
wood, toilets she'd pull
the lid to — that look saying

Let's make a change, girl.

But Sunday mornings are hers —
church clothes starched
and hanging, a record spinning 10
on the console, the whole house
dancing. She raises the shades,
washes the rooms in light,
buckets of water, Octagon soap. 15

Cleanliness is next to godliness . . .

Windows and doors flung wide,
curtains two-stepping
forward and back, neck bones
bumping in the pot, a choir 20
of clothes clapping on the line.

Nearer my God to Thee . . .

She beats time on the rugs,
blows dust from the broom
like dandelion spores, each one   25
a wish for something better.

CONSIDERATIONS FOR CRITICAL THINKING AND WRITING

1. **FIRST RESPONSE.** How does the inclusion of "1937" in the title affect your interpretation of the poem? Would you read the poem any differently if the title were simply "Domestic Work"?

2. Describe the difference between the housework done during the week and the work performed on Sundays.

CONNECTION TO ANOTHER SELECTION

1. Compare the tone of Trethewey's poem with that of Katharyn Howd Machan's "Hazel Tells LaVerne" (p. 631).

GARY GILDNER (B. 1938)

First Practice   *1984*

After the doctor checked to see
we weren't ruptured,
the man with the short cigar took us
under the grade school,
where we went in case of attack   5
or storm, and said
he was Clifford Hill, he was
a man who believed dogs
ate dogs, he had once killed
for his country, and if   10
there were any girls present
for them to leave now.
                    No one
left. OK, he said, he said I take
that to mean you are hungry   15
men who hate to lose as much
as I do. OK. Then
he made two lines of us
facing each other,
and across the way, he said,   20
is the man you hate most
in the world,
and if we are to win
that title I want to see how.
But I don't want to see   25
any marks when you're dressed,
he said. He said, *Now.*

CONSIDERATIONS FOR CRITICAL THINKING AND WRITING

1. **FIRST RESPONSE.** Do you recognize this coach? How does he compare with your own experience with sports coaches?

2. Comment on the significance of Clifford Hill's name.

3. Locate examples of irony in the poem and explain how they contribute to the theme.

4. Discuss the effect of line spacing in line 13.

CONNECTION TO ANOTHER SELECTION

1. Write an essay comparing the coach in this poem and the teacher in Judy Page Heitzman's "The Schoolroom on the Second Floor of the Knitting Mill" (p. 978).

MARILYN NELSON WANIEK (B. 1946)

Emily Dickinson's Defunct   *1978*

She used to
pack poems
in her hip pocket.
Under all the
gray old lady   5
clothes she was
dressed for action.
She had hair,
imagine,
in certain places, and   10
believe me
she smelled human
on a hot summer day.
Stalking snakes
or counting   15
the thousand motes
in sunlight
she walked just
like an Indian.
She was New England's   20
favorite daughter,
she could pray
like the devil.
She was a
two-fisted woman,   25
this babe.
All the flies
just stood around
and buzzed
when she died.   30

CONSIDERATIONS FOR CRITICAL THINKING AND WRITING

1. **FIRST RESPONSE.** How does the speaker characterize Dickinson? Explain why this characterization is different from the popular view of Dickinson.

2. How does the diction of the poem characterize the speaker?

3. Discuss the function of the poem's title.

CONNECTIONS TO OTHER SELECTIONS

1. Waniek alludes to at least two other poems in "Emily Dickinson's Defunct." The title refers to E. E. Cummings's "Buffalo Bill 's" (p. 1017), and the final lines (27–30) refer to Dickinson's "I heard a Fly buzz — when I died —" (p. 852). Read those poems and write an essay discussing how they affect your reading of Waniek's poem.

SHARON OLDS (B. 1942)

Rite of Passage   *1983*

As the guests arrive at my son's party
they gather in the living room —
short men, men in first grade
with smooth jaws and chins.
Hands in pockets, they stand around   5
jostling, jockeying for place, small fights
breaking out and calming. One says to another
How old are you? Six. I'm seven. So?
They eye each other, seeing themselves
tiny in the other's pupils. They clear their   10
throats a lot, a room of small bankers,
they fold their arms and frown. *I could beat you
up,* a seven says to a six,
the dark cake, round and heavy as a
turret, behind them on the table. My son,   15
freckles like specks of nutmeg on his cheeks,
chest narrow as the balsa keel of a
model boat, long hands
cool and thin as the day they guided him
out of me, speaks up as a host   20
for the sake of the group.
We could easily kill a two-year-old,
he says in his clear voice. The other
men agree, they clear their throats
like Generals, they relax and get down to   25
playing war, celebrating my son's life.

CONSIDERATIONS FOR CRITICAL THINKING AND WRITING

1. **FIRST RESPONSE.** In what sense is this birthday party a "Rite of Passage"?

2. How does the speaker transform these six- and seven-year-old boys into men? What is the point of doing so?

3. Comment on the appropriateness of the image of the cake in lines 14–15.

4. Why does the son's claim that "We could easily kill a two-year-old" (line 22) come as such a shock at that point in the poem?

CONNECTION TO ANOTHER SELECTION

1. Discuss the use of irony in "Rite of Passage" and Wilfred Owen's "Dulce et Decorum Est" (p. 671). Which do you think is a more effective antiwar poem? Explain why.

JULIO MARZÁN (B. 1946)

The Translator at the Reception for Latin American Writers

1997

Air-conditioned introductions,
then breezy Spanish conversation
fan his curiosity to know
what country I come from.
"Puerto Rico and the Bronx."   5

Spectacled downward eyes
translate disappointment
like a poison mushroom
puffed in his thoughts as if,
after investing a sizable   10
intellectual budget, transporting
a huge cast and camera crew
to film on location
Mayan pyramid grandeur,
indigenes whose ancient gods   15
and comet-tail plumage
inspire a glorious epic
of revolution across a continent,
he received a lurid script
for a social documentary   20
rife with dreary streets
and pathetic human interest,
meager in the profits of high culture.

Understandably he turns,
catches up with the hostess,   25
praising the uncommon quality
of her offerings of cheese.

CONSIDERATIONS FOR CRITICAL THINKING AND WRITING

1. FIRST RESPONSE. What is the speaker's attitude toward the person he meets at the reception? What lines in particular lead you to that conclusion?

2. Why is that person so disappointed about "Puerto Rico and the Bronx"?

3. Explain lines 6–23. How do they reveal both the speaker and the person encountered at the reception?

4. Why is the setting of this poem significant?

ROBERT MORGAN (B. 1944)

Overalls   1990

Even the biggest man will look
babylike in overalls, bib
up to his neck holding the trousers
high on his belly, with no chafing
at the waist, no bulging over   5
the belt. But it's the pockets on
the chest that are most interesting,
buttons and snaps like medals, badges,
flaps open with careless ease, thin
sheath for the pencil, little pockets   10
and pouches and the main zipper
compartment like a wallet over
the heart and the slit where the watch
goes, an eye where the chain is caught.
Every bit of surface is taken   15
up with patches, denim mesas
and envelopes, a many-level
cloth topography. And below,
the loops for hammers and pliers
like holsters for going armed   20
and armored yet free-handed
into the field another day
for labor's playful war with time.

CONSIDERATIONS FOR CRITICAL THINKING AND WRITING

1. **FIRST RESPONSE.** How does the poem's last line announce its theme?

2. Why is it that the "pockets on / the chest . . . are most interesting" to the speaker?

3. Describe the way images of childhood and adulthood, along with work and war, are interwoven in Morgan's treatment of overalls.

ANONYMOUS

The Frog   *date unknown*

What a wonderful bird the frog are!
When he stand he sit almost;
When he hop he fly almost.
He ain't got no sense hardly;

He ain't got no tail hardly either.
When he sit, he sit on what he ain't got almost.

CONSIDERATIONS FOR CRITICAL THINKING AND WRITING

1. **FIRST RESPONSE.** How is the poem a description of the speaker as well as of a frog?
2. Though this poem is ungrammatical, it does have a patterned structure. How does the pattern of sentences create a formal structure?

TATO LAVIERA (B. 1951)

AmeRícan   1985

we gave birth to a new generation,
AmeRícan, broader than lost gold
never touched, hidden inside the
puerto rican mountains.

we gave birth to a new generation,   5
AmeRícan, it includes everything
imaginable you-name-it-we-got-it
society.

we gave birth to a new generation,
AmeRícan salutes all folklores,   10
european, indian, black, spanish,
and anything else compatible:

AmeRícan,   singing to composer pedro flores'° palm
             trees high up in the universal sky!

AmeRícan,   sweet soft spanish danzas gypsies   15
             moving lyrics la *española*° cascabelling   *Spanish*
             presence always singing at our side!

AmeRícan,   beating jíbaro° modern troubadours
             crying guitars romantic continental
             bolero love songs!   20

AmeRícan,   across forth and across back
             back across and forth back
             forth across and back and forth
             our trips are walking bridges!

             it all dissolved into itself, the attempt   25
             was truly made, the attempt was truly
             absorbed, digested, we spit out

---

13 *pedro flores:* Puerto Rican composer of popular romantic songs.   18 *jíbaro:* A particular style of music played by Puerto Rican mountain farmers.

the poison, we spit out the malice,
we stand, affirmative in action,
to reproduce a broader answer to the 30
marginality that gobbled us up abruptly!

AmeRícan,   walking plena-rhythms° in new york,
strutting beautifully alert, alive,
many turning eyes wondering,
admiring! 35

AmeRícan,   defining myself my own way any way many
ways Am e Rícan, with the big R and the
accent on the í!

AmeRícan,   like the soul gliding talk of gospel
boogie music! 40

AmeRícan,   speaking new words in spanglish tenements,
fast tongue moving street corner *"que
corta"°* talk being invented at the insistence   *that cuts*
of a smile!

AmeRícan,   abounding inside so many ethnic english 45
people, and out of humanity, we blend
and mix all that is good!

AmeRícan,   integrating in new york and defining our
own *destino,°* our own way of life,   *destiny*

AmeRícan,   defining the new america, humane america, 50
admired america, loved america, harmonious
america, the world in peace, our energies
collectively invested to find other civili-
zations, to touch God, further and further,
to dwell in the spirit of divinity! 55

AmeRícan,   yes, for now, for i love this, my second
land, and i dream to take the accent from
the altercation, and be proud to call
myself american, in the u.s. sense of the
word, AmeRícan, America! 60

32 *plena-rhythms:* African–Puerto Rican folklore, music, and dance.

Considerations for Critical Thinking and Writing

1. **First response.** How does the arrangement of lines communicate a sense
of energy and vitality?

2. How does the speaker portray Puerto Ricans living in the United States?

3. How does the poet describe the United States?

Connection to Another Selection

1. In an essay consider the themes, styles, and tones of "AmeRícan" and Julia
Alvarez's "Queens, 1963" (p. 944).

PETER MEINKE (B. 1932)

The ABC of Aerobics 1983

Air seeps through alleys and our diaphragms
balloon blackly with this mix of
carbon monoxide and the thousand corrosives a city
doles out free to its constituents;
everyone's jogging through Edgemont Park,   5
frightened by death and fatty tissue,
gasping at the maximal heart rate,
hoping to outlive all the others streaming
in the lanes like lemmings lurching toward their last
jump. I join in despair   10
knowing my arteries jammed with
lint and tobacco, lard and bourbon — my
medical history a noxious marsh:
newts and moles slink through the sodden veins,
owls hoot in the lungs' dark branches;   15
probably I shall keel off the john like
queer Uncle George and lie on the bathroom floor
raging about Shirley Clark, my true love in
seventh grade, God bless her wherever she lives
tied to that turkey who hugely   20
undervalues the beauty of her tiny earlobes, one
view of which (either one: they are both perfect)
would add years to my life and I could skip these
x-rays, turn in my insurance card, and trade
yoga and treadmills and jogging and zen and   25
zucchini for drinking and dreaming of her, breathing hard.

CONSIDERATIONS FOR CRITICAL THINKING AND WRITING

1. **FIRST RESPONSE.** How does the title help to establish a pattern throughout
   the poem? How does the pattern contribute to the poem's meaning?

2. How does the speaker feel about exercise? How do his descriptions of his
   physical condition characterize him?

3. A primer is a book that teaches children to read or introduces them, in an
   elementary way, to the basics of a subject. The title "The ABC of Aerobics"
   indicates that this poem is meant to be a primer. What is it trying to teach
   us? Is its final lesson serious or ironic?

4. Discuss Meinke's use of humor. Is it effective?

CONNECTIONS TO OTHER SELECTIONS

1. Write an essay comparing the way Sharon Olds connects sex and exercise in
   "Sex without Love" (p. 646) with Meinke's treatment here.

2. Compare the voice in this poem with that in Galway Kinnell's "After Making Love We Hear Footsteps" (p. 806). Which do you find more appealing?
   Why?

Found Poem

This next selection is a *found poem,* unintentional verse discovered in a nonpoetic context, such as a conversation, a news story, or an advertisement. Found poems are playful reminders that the words in poems are very often the language we use every day. Whether such found language should be regarded as a poem is an issue left for you to consider.

DONALD JUSTICE (1925–2004)

Order in the Streets   1969

(*From instructions printed on a child's toy, Christmas 1968, as reported in the* New York Times)

I. 2. 3.
Switch on.

Jeep rushes
to the scene
of riot   5

Jeep goes
in all directions
by mystery action.

Jeep stops periodically
to turn hood over   10

machine gun appears
with realistic
shooting noise.

After putting down riot,
jeep goes   15
back to the headquarters.

CONSIDERATIONS FOR CRITICAL THINKING AND WRITING

1. FIRST RESPONSE. What is the effect of arranging these instructions in discrete lines? How are the language and meaning enhanced by this arrangement?

2. CREATIVE RESPONSE. Look for phrases or sentences in ads, textbooks, labels, or directions — in anything that might inadvertently contain provocative material that would be revealed by arranging the words in verse lines. You may even discover some patterns of rhyme and rhythm. After arranging the lines, explain why you organized them as you did.

Web Research the poets in this chapter at bedfordstmartins.com/ meyercompact.

28

Combining the Elements of Poetry: A Writing Process

© Bettmann/CORBIS.

In poetry you have a form looking for a subject and a subject looking for a form. When they come together successfully you have a poem.
— W. H. AUDEN

THE ELEMENTS TOGETHER

The elements of poetry that you have studied in the first ten chapters of this section offer a vocabulary and series of perspectives that open up avenues of inquiry into a poem. As you have learned, there are many potential routes that you can take. By asking questions, for example, about the speaker, diction, figurative language, sounds, rhythm, tone, or theme, you clarify your understanding while simultaneously sensitizing yourself to elements and issues especially relevant to the poem under consideration. This process of careful, informed reading allows you to see how the various elements of the poem reinforce its meanings.

A poem's elements do not exist in isolation, however. They work together to create a complete experience for the reader. Knowing how the elements combine helps you understand the poem's structure and to appreciate it as a whole. Robert Herrick's "Delight in Disorder" (p. 763), for example, is more easily understood (and the humor of the poem is better appreciated) when meter and rhyme are considered together with the poem's meaning. Musing about how he is more charmed by a naturally disheveled appearance than by those that seem contrived, the speaker lists several attributes of dishevelment and concludes that they

> Do more bewitch me than when art
> Is too precise in every part.

Noticing how the couplet's precise and sing-songy rhythm combines with the solid, obvious, and final rhyme of *art / part* helps in understanding what the speaker means by "too precise," as the lines are a little too precise themselves. Noticing this, you may even want to chart how rhythm and rhyme work together throughout the early (more disheveled) lines of the poem. Finding a pattern in the ways the elements work together throughout the poem will help you understand how the poem works.

MAPPING THE POEM

When you write about a poem, you are, in some ways, providing a guide for a place that might otherwise seem unfamiliar and remote. Put simply, writing enables you to chart a work so that you can comfortably move around in it to discuss or write about what interests you. Your paper represents a record and a map of your intellectual journey through the poem, pointing out the things worth noting and your impressions about them. Your role as writer is to offer insights into the challenges, pleasures, and discoveries that the poem harbors. These insights are a kind of sightseeing, as you navigate the various elements of the poem to make some overall point about it.

This chapter shows you how one student, Rose Bostwick, moves through the stages of writing about how a poem's elements combine for a final effect. Included here are Rose's annotated version of the poem, her first response, her informal outline, and the final draft of an explication of John Donne's "Death Be Not Proud." A detailed explanation of what is implicit in a poem, an explication requires a line-by-line examination of the poem. (For more on explication, see page 1576 in Chapter 47, "Reading and Writing.") After reviewing the elements of poetry covered in the preceding chapters, Rose read the poem (which follows) several times, paying careful attention to diction, figurative language, irony, symbol, rhythm, sound, and so on. Her final paper is more concerned with the overall effect of the combination of elements than with a line-by-line breakdown, and her annotated version of the poem details her attention to that task. As you read and reread "Death Be Not Proud," keep notes on how *you* think the elements of this poem work together and to what overall effect.

JOHN DONNE (1572–1631)

John Donne, now regarded as a major poet of the early seventeenth century, wrote love poems at the beginning of his career but shifted to religious themes after convert- ing from Catholicism to Anglicanism in the early 1590s. Although trained in law, he was also ordained a priest and became dean of St. Paul's Cathedral in London in 1621. The following poem, from "Holy Sonnets," reflects both his religious faith and his abil- ity to create elegant arguments in verse.

Courtesy of the National Portrait Gallery, London.

Death Be Not Proud   1611

Death be not proud, though some have callèd thee
Mighty and dreadful, for thou art not so;
For those whom thou think'st thou dost overthrow
Die not, poor Death, nor yet canst thou kill me.
From rest and sleep, which but thy pictures° be,   *images* 5
Much pleasure; then from thee much more must flow,
And soonest our best men with thee do go,
Rest of their bones, and soul's delivery.°   *deliverance*
Thou art slave to Fate, Chance, kings, and desperate men,
And dost with Poison, War, and Sickness dwell;   10
And poppy or charms can make us sleep as well,
And better than thy stroke; why swell'st° thou then?   *swell with pride*
One short sleep past, we wake eternally
And death shall be no more; Death, thou shalt die.

CONSIDERATIONS FOR CRITICAL THINKING AND WRITING

1. **FIRST RESPONSE.** Why doesn't the speaker fear death? Explain why you find the argument convincing or not.

2. How does the speaker compare death with rest and sleep in lines 5–8? What is the point of this comparison?

3. Discuss the poem's rhythm by examining the breaks and end-stopped lines. How does the poem's rhythm contribute to its meaning?

4. What are the signs that this poem is structured as a sonnet?

ASKING QUESTIONS ABOUT THE ELEMENTS

After reading a poem, use the Questions for Responsive Reading and Writing (pp. 614–15) to help you think, talk, and write about any poem. Before you do, though, be sure that you have read the poem several times without worrying actively about interpretation. With poetry, as with all literature, it's important to allow yourself the pleasure of enjoying whatever makes itself apparent to you. On subsequent readings, use the questions to understand and appreciate how the poem works; remember to keep in mind that not all questions will necessarily be relevant to a particular poem. A good starting point is to ask yourself what elements are exemplified in the parts of the poem that particularly interest you. Then ask the Questions for Responsive Reading and Writing that relate to those elements. Finally, as you begin to get a sense of what elements are important to the poem and how those elements fit together, it often helps to put your impressions on paper.

A SAMPLE CLOSE READING

An Annotated Version of John Donne's "Death Be Not Proud"

As she read the poem closely several times, Rose annotated it with impressions and ideas that would lead to insights on which her analysis would be built. Her close examination of the poem's elements allowed her to understand how its parts contribute to its overall effect; her annotations provide a useful map of her thinking.

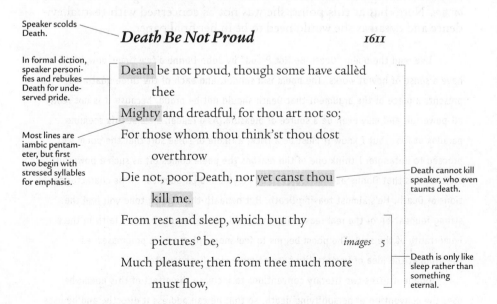

Speaker scolds Death.

Death Be Not Proud   1611

In formal diction, speaker personifies and rebukes Death for undeserved pride.

Death be not proud, though some have callèd
        thee
Mighty and dreadful, for thou art not so;

Most lines are iambic pentameter, but first two begin with stressed syllables for emphasis.

For those whom thou think'st thou dost
        overthrow
Die not, poor Death, nor yet canst thou
kill me.

Death cannot kill speaker, who even taunts death.

From rest and sleep, which but thy
        pictures° be,   *images* 5
Much pleasure; then from thee much more
        must flow,

Death is only like sleep rather than something eternal.

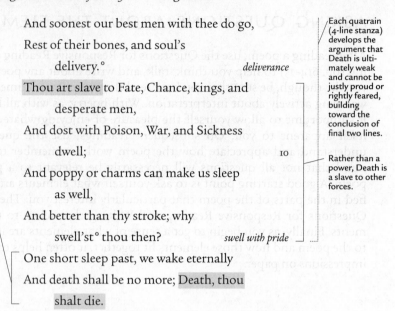

And soonest our best men with thee do go,

Rest of their bones, and soul's

delivery.°   *deliverance*

Thou art slave to Fate, Chance, kings, and

desperate men,

And dost with Poison, War, and Sickness

dwell;   10

And poppy or charms can make us sleep

as well,

And better than thy stroke; why

swell'st° thou then?   *swell with pride*

One short sleep past, we wake eternally

And death shall be no more; Death, thou

shalt die.

Each quatrain (4-line stanza) develops the argument that Death is ultimately weak and cannot be justly proud or rightly feared, building toward the conclusion of final two lines.

Rather than a power, Death is a slave to other forces.

Argument in the couplet climaxes with allusion to humanity's resurrection and death of Death itself. In addition to Christianity, does sonnet form finally control Death too?

A SAMPLE FIRST RESPONSE

After Rose carefully read "Death Be Not Proud" and had a sense of how the elements work, she took the first step toward a formal explication by writing informally about the relevant elements and addressing the question *Why doesn't the speaker fear death? Explain why you find the argument convincing or not.* Note that at this point, she was not as concerned with textual evidence and detail as she would need to be in her final paper.

I've read the poem "Death Be Not Proud" by John Donne a few times now, and I have a sense of how it works. The poem is a sonnet, and each of the three quatrains presents a piece of the argument that Death should not be proud, because it is not really all-powerful, and may even be a source of pleasure. As a reader, I resist this seeming paradox at first, but I know it must be a trick, a riddle of some sort that the poem will proceed to untangle. I think one of the reasons the poem comes off as such a powerful statement is that Donne at first seems to be playful and paradoxical in his characterizations of Death. He's almost teasing Death. But beneath the teasing tone you feel the strong foundation of the real reason Death should not be proud--Donne's faith in the immortality of the soul. The poem begins to feel more solemn as it progresses, as the hints at the idea of immortality become more clearly articulated.

Donne utilizes two literary conventions to increase the effect of this poem: he uses the convention of personifying death, so that he can address it directly, and he uses the metaphor of death as a kind of sleep. These two things determine the tone and the progression from playful to solemn in the poem.

The last clause of the poem (line 14) plays with the paradoxical-seeming character of what he's been declaring. Ironically, it seems the only thing susceptible to death is death itself. Or, when death becomes powerless is when it only has power over itself.

ORGANIZING YOUR THOUGHTS

Showing in a paper how different elements of a particular poem work together is often quite challenging. While you may have a clear intuitive sense of what elements are important to the poem and how they complement one another, it is important to organize your thoughts in such a way as to make the relationships clear to your audience. The simplest way is to go line by line, but that can quickly become rote for writer and reader. Because you will want to organize your paper in the way that best serves your thesis, it may help to write an informal outline that charts how you think the argument moves. You may find, for example, that the argument is not persuasive if you start with the final lines and go back to the beginning of the poem or passage. However you decide to organize your argument, keep in mind that a single idea, or thesis, will have to run thoughout the entire paper.

A SAMPLE INFORMAL OUTLINE

In her informal outline (following), Rose discovers that her argument works best if she begins at the beginning. Note how, though her later paper concerns itself with how several elements of poetry contribute to the poem's theme and message, her informal outline concerns itself much more with what that message is and how it develops as the poem progresses. She will fill in the details later.

Thesis: *From the very first word, addressing "Death" directly, Donne uses the literary conventions of personifying death and comparing it to sleep to begin an argument that Death should not be proud of its might or dreadfulness. But these two elements of his argument come to be seen as the superficial points when the true reason for death's powerlessness becomes clear. The Christian belief in the immortality of the soul is the reason for death's powerlessness and likeness to sleep.*

Body of essay: *Show how argument proceeds by quatrains from playful address to Death, and statement that Death is much like sleep, its "picture," to statement that Death is "slave" to other forces (and so should not be proud of being the mightiest), to the couplet, which articulates clearly the idea of immortality and gives the final paradox, "Death, thou shalt die."*

<u>Conclusion</u>: *Donne's faith in the immortality of the soul enables him to "prove" in this argument that Death is truly like its metaphorical representation, sleep. Faith allows him to derive a source for this conventional trope, and it allows him to state his truth in paradoxes. He relies on the conventional idea that death is an end, and a conqueror, and the only all-powerful force, to make the paradoxes that lend his argument the force of mystery — the mystery of faith.*

THE ELEMENTS AND THEME

As you create an informal outline, your understanding of the poem will grow, change, and, finally, solidify. You will develop a much clearer sense of what the poem's elements combine to create, and you will have chosen a scheme for organizing your argument. The next step before drafting is to determine the paper's thesis, which will not only keep your paper focused but will also help you center your thoughts. For papers that discuss how the elements of poetry come together, the thesis is a single and concise statement of what the elements combine to create — the idea around which all the elements revolve. In the earlier discussion of Robert Herrick's "Delight in Disorder," for example, the two elements, rhythm and rhyme, work together to create the speaker's self-directed irony. To state this as a thesis, we might say that by making his own rhythm and rhyme "too precise," Herrick's speaker is making fun of himself while complimenting a certain type of woman. (You may ask yourself if he's doing a little flirting.)

Once you understand how all of the elements of the poem fit together and have articulated your understanding in the thesis statement, the next step is to flesh out your argument. By including quotations from the poem to illustrate the points you will be making, you will better explain exactly how each element relates to the others and, more specifically, to your thesis, and you will have created a finished paper that helps readers navigate the poem's geography.

A SAMPLE EXPLICATION

The Use of Conventional Metaphors for Death in John Donne's "Death Be Not Proud"

In Rose's final draft, she focuses on the use of metaphor in "Death Be Not Proud." Her essay provides a coherent reading that relates each line of the poem to the speaker's intense awareness of death. Although the essay discusses each stanza in order, the introductory paragraph provides a brief overview explaining how the poem's metaphor and arguments contribute to its total meaning. In addition, Rose does not hesitate to discuss a line out of sequence when it can be usefully connected to another phrase. She also works quotations into her sentences to support her points. When she adds something to a quotation to clarify it, she encloses her words in brackets so that they will not be mistaken for the poet's, and she uses a slash to indicate line divisions: "soonest . . . with thee do go, / [for] Rest of their bones, and soul's delivery." Finally, because the essay focuses on a short poem, it is not necessary to include line numbers, though they would be required in a study of a longer work. As you read through her final draft, remember that the word *explication* comes from the Latin *explicare*, "to unfold." How successful do you think Rose is at unfolding this poem to reveal how its elements — here ranging from metaphor, structure, meter, personification, paradox, and irony to theme — contribute to its meaning?

Bostwick 1

Rose Bostwick

English 101

Prof. Hart

February 24, 2008

The Use of Conventional Metaphors for Death

in John Donne's "Death Be Not Proud"

In the sonnet that begins "Death be not proud . . ." John Donne argues that death is not "mighty and dreadful" (line 2), but is more like its metaphorical representation, sleep. Death, Donne puts forth, is even a source of pleasure and rest. The poet builds this argument on two foundations. One is made up of the metaphors and literary conventions for death: death is compared with sleep and is often personified so that it can be addressed directly. The poem is an address to death that at first seems paradoxical and somewhat playful, but which then rises in all the emotion of faith as it reveals the second foundation of the argument--the Christian belief in the immortality of the soul. Seen against the backdrop of this belief, death loses its powerful threat and is seen as only a metaphorical sleep, or rest.

The poem is an ironic argument that proceeds according to the structure of the sonnet form. Each quatrain contains a new development or aspect

> Thesis providing interpretation of the poem's use of metaphor and how it contributes to the poem's central argument.

Discussion of how form and meter contribute to the poem's central argument.

of the argument, and the final couplet serves as a conclusion. The metrical scheme is mainly iambic pentameter, but in several places in the poem, the stress pattern is altered for emphasis. For example, the first foot of the poem is inverted, so that "Death," the first word, receives the stress. This announces to us right away that Death is being personified and addressed. This inversion also serves to begin the poem energetically and forcefully. The second line behaves in the same way. The first syllable of "Mighty" receives the stress, emphasizing the meaning of the word and its assumed relation to Death.

Discussion of how personification contributes to the poem's central argument.

This first quatrain offers the first paradox and sets up the argument that death has been conventionally personified with the wrong attributes, might and dreadfulness. The poet tells death not to be proud, "though some have called thee / Mighty and dreadful" (1–2), because, he says, death is not so. Donne will turn this conventional characterization of death on its head with the paradox of the third and fourth lines: he says the people overthrown by Death (as if by a conqueror) "Die not, poor Death, nor yet canst thou kill me" (4). These lines establish the paradox of death not being able to cause death.

Discussion of how metaphor of sleep and idea of immortality support the poem's central argument.

The next quatrain will not begin to answer the question of why this paradox is so, but will posit another slight paradox--the idea of death as pleasurable. In lines 5–8, Donne uses the literary convention of describing death as a metaphorical sleep, or rest, to construct the argument that death must give pleasure; "From rest and sleep, which but thy pictures be, / Much pleasure; then from thee much more must flow" (5–6). At this point, the argument seems almost playful, but is carefully hinting at the solemnity of the deeper foundation of the belief in immortality. The metaphor of sleep for death includes the idea of waking; one doesn't sleep forever. The next two lines put forth the idea that death is pleasurable enough to be desired by "our best men" who "soonest . . . with thee do go, / [for] Rest of their bones, and soul's delivery" (7–8). This last line comes closer to announcing the true reason for death's powerlessness and pleasure: it is the way to the "soul's delivery" from the body and life on earth, and implicitly, into another, better realm.

Bostwick 3

A new reason for death's powerlessness arises in the next four lines. The poet says to death:

> Thou art slave to Fate, Chance, kings, and desperate men,
> And dost with Poison, War, and Sickness dwell;
> And poppy or charms can make us sleep as well,
> And better than thy stroke; why swell'st thou then? (9–12)

Donne argues here that there are forces more powerful than death that actually control it. Fate and chance determine when death occurs, and to whom it comes. Kings, with the powers of law and war, can summon death and throw it on whom they wish. And desperate men, murderers or suicides, can also summon death with the strength of their emotions. In lines 11 and 12, Donne again uses the metaphor of death as a kind of sleep, but says that drugs or "charms" give one a better sleep than death. And he asks playfully why death should be so proud, after all these illustrations of its weakness have been given: "why swell'st thou then?"

Finally, with the last couplet, Donne reveals the true, deeper reason behind his argument that death should not be proud of its power. These lines also offer an explanation of the metaphor for death of sleep, or rest:

> One short sleep past, we wake eternally
> And death shall be no more; Death, thou shalt die. (13–14)

After death, the soul lives on, according to Christian theology and belief. In the Christian heaven, where the soul is immortal, death will no longer exist, and so this last paradox, "Death, thou shalt die," becomes true. Again in this line, a significant inversion of metrical stress occurs. "Death," in the second clause, receives the stress, recalling the first line, emphasizing that it is an address and giving the clause a forceful sense of finality. His belief in the immortality of the soul enables Donne to "prove" in this argument that death is in actuality like its metaphorical representation, sleep. His faith allows him to derive a source for this conventional metaphor and to "disprove" the metaphor of death as an all-powerful conqueror. His Christian beliefs also allow him to state his truth in paradoxes, the mysteries that are justified by the mystery of faith.

Marginal notes:

Discussion of how language and tone contribute to the poem's central argument.

Discussion of function of religious faith in the poem and how word order and meter create emphasis.

Conclusion supporting thesis in context of poet's beliefs.

Bostwick 4

Work Cited

Donne, John. "Death Be Not Proud." The Compact Bedford Introduction to
Literature. Ed. Michael Meyer. 3th ed. Boston: Bedford/St. Martin's,
2009. 820.

Before you begin writing your own paper on poetry, review the Suggestions for Approaching Poetry (pp. 588–89) and Chapter 19, "Writing about Poetry," particularly the Questions for Responsive Reading and Writing (pp. 614–15). These suggestions and questions will help you to focus and sharpen your critical thinking and writing. You'll also find help in Chapter 47, "Reading and Writing," which offers a systematic overview of choosing a topic, developing a thesis, and organizing various types of assignments. If you use outside sources for the paper, be sure to acknowledge them adequately by using the conventional documentation procedures detailed in Chapter 48, "The Literary Research Paper."

Web Research
John Donne at
bedfordstmartins.com/
meyercompact.

Approaches
to Poetry

29

A Study of Emily Dickinson

My business is circumference.
— EMILY DICKINSON

In this chapter you'll find a variety of poems by Emily Dickinson so that you can study her work in some depth. While this collection is not wholly representative of her work, it does offer enough poems to suggest some of the techniques and concerns that characterize her writings. The poems speak not only to readers but also to one another. That's natural enough: the more familiar you are with a writer's work, the easier it is to perceive and enjoy the strategies and themes the poet uses. If you are asked to write about a number of poems by the same author, you may find useful the Questions for Writing about an Author in Depth (p. 866-67) and the sample paper on Dickinson's attitudes toward religious faith in four of her poems (pp. 870-73).

Explore contexts for Emily Dickinson on LiterActive.

Emily E. Dickinson.

Portrait of Emily Dickinson. This daguerreotype, taken shortly after the poet's sixteenth birthday, and the silhouette (*opposite page*) are the only authenticated mechanically produced images of the poet.

A BRIEF BIOGRAPHY

Emily Dickinson (1830–1886) grew up in a prominent and prosperous household in Amherst, Massachusetts. Along with her younger sister, Lavinia, and older brother, Austin, she experienced a quiet and reserved family life headed by her father, Edward Dickinson. In a letter to Austin at law school, she once described the atmosphere in her father's house as

(*Below*) **Unauthenticated Portrait of Emily Dickinson.**
This recently discovered print of a mid-1850s daguerreotype, acquired by the scholar Philip F. Gura in 2000, is
believed to represent the poet in her twenties.

(*Right*) **Silhouette of Emily Dickinson.** This image of the
poet was created when she was fourteen years old.

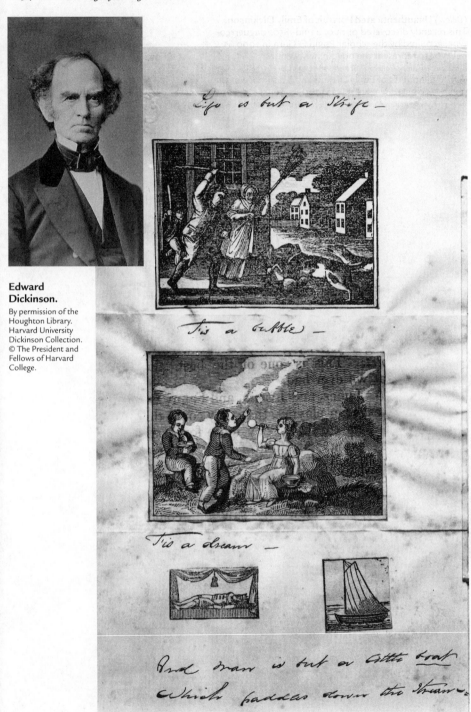

**Edward
Dickinson.**

By permission of the
Houghton Library.
Harvard University
Dickinson Collection.
© The President and
Fellows of Harvard
College.

Letter from Emily Dickinson to cousin William Cowper Dickinson.

Courtesy of the Todd-Bingham Picture Collection, Manuscripts and Archives, Yale University Library. © The
President and Fellows of Harvard College.

Susan Gilbert Dickinson.
Courtesy of the Todd-Bingham Picture Collection, Manuscripts and Archives, Yale University Library.

Letter from Emily Dickinson to Susan Gilbert Dickinson.
By permission of the Houghton Library, Harvard University MS Am 118.5 (B114). © The President and Fellows of Harvard College.

(*Opposite page*) Shown here are the poet's father, Edward Dickinson, a prominent public figure in Amherst, and a page from a letter sent to her cousin William Cowper Dickinson. Emily Dickinson sometimes included in her correspondence images cut from books and magazines. This illustrated letter reads "Life is but a Strife —/T'is a bubble —/T'is a dream — / And man is but a little *boat*/Which paddles down the stream —"

(*This page*) Following a party held next door at the home of Dickinson's brother Austin and sister-in-law Susan (*top*), the poet was reprimanded by her father for staying out too late. The next day, Dickinson wrote a playful note to Susan that included a cartoon poking fun at her father. The note reads: "My 'position'" and features an image of a young person pursued by a dragonlike creature, cut from the Dickinsons' copy of the *New England Primer*, a book of moral lessons. The note concludes: "P.S. — Lest you misapprehend, the unfortunate insect upon the *left* is Myself, while the Reptile upon the *right*, is my more immediate friends, and connections [*sic*]."

"pretty much all sobriety." Her mother, Emily Norcross Dickinson, was not as powerful a presence in her life; she seems not to have been as emotionally accessible as Dickinson would have liked. Her daughter is said to have characterized her as not the sort of mother "to whom you hurry when you are troubled." Both parents raised Dickinson to be a cultured Christian woman who would one day be responsible for a family of her own. Her father attempted to protect her from reading books that might "joggle" her mind, particularly her religious faith, but Dickinson's individualistic instincts and irreverent sensibilities created conflicts that did not allow her to fall into step with the conventional piety, domesticity, and social duty prescribed by her father and the orthodox Congregationalism of Amherst.

The Dickinsons were well known in Massachusetts. Her father was a lawyer and served as the treasurer of Amherst College (a position Austin eventually took up as well), and her grandfather was one of the college's founders. Although nineteenth-century politics, economics, and social issues do not appear in the foreground of her poetry, Dickinson lived in a family environment that was steeped in them: her father was an active town official and served in the General Court of Massachusetts, the state senate, and the U.S. House of Representatives.

Dickinson, however, withdrew not only from her father's public world but also from almost all social life in Amherst. She refused to see most people, and aside from a single year at South Hadley Female Seminary (now Mount Holyoke College), one excursion to Philadelphia and Washington, and several brief trips to Boston to see a doctor about eye problems, she lived all her life in her father's house. She dressed only in white and developed a reputation as a reclusive eccentric. Dickinson selected her own society carefully and frugally. Like her poetry, her relationship to the world was intensely reticent. Indeed, during the last twenty years of her life she rarely left the house.

Though Dickinson never married, she had significant relationships with several men who were friends, confidants, and mentors. She also enjoyed an intimate relationship with her friend Susan Huntington Gilbert, who became her sister-in-law by marrying Austin. Susan and her husband lived next door and were extremely close with Dickinson. Biographers have attempted to find in a number of her relationships the source for the passion of some of her love poems and letters. Several possibilities have been put forward as the person she addressed in three letters as "Dear Master": Benjamin Newton, a clerk in her father's office who talked about books with her; Samuel Bowles, editor of the *Springfield Republican* and friend of the family; the Reverend Charles Wadsworth, a Presbyterian preacher with a reputation for powerful sermons; and an old friend and widower, Judge Otis P. Lord. Despite these speculations, no biographer has been able to identify definitively the object of Dickinson's love. What matters, of course, is not with whom she was in love — if, in fact, there was any single person — but that she wrote about such passions so intensely and convincingly in her poetry.

Choosing to live life internally within the confines of her home, Dickinson brought her life into sharp focus, for she also chose to live within the limitless expanses of her imagination—a choice she was keenly aware of and which she described in one of her poems this way: "I dwell in Possibility—" (p. 851). Her small circle of domestic life did not impinge on her creative sensibilities. Like Henry David Thoreau, she simplified her life so that doing without was a means of being within. In a sense she redefined the meaning of deprivation because being denied something—whether faith, love, literary recognition, or some other desire—provided a sharper, more intense understanding than she would have experienced had she achieved what she wanted: "'Heaven,'" she wrote, "is what I cannot reach!" This poem (p. 845), along with many others, such as "Water, is taught by thirst" (p. 842) and "Success is counted sweetest / By those who ne'er succeed" (p. 841), suggests just how persistently she saw deprivation as a way of sensitizing herself to the value of what she was missing. For Dickinson, hopeful expectation was always more satisfying than achieving a golden moment. Perhaps that's one reason she was so attracted to John Keats's poetry (see, for example, his "Ode on a Grecian Urn," p. 647).

Dickinson enjoyed reading Keats as well as Emily and Charlotte Brontë; Robert and Elizabeth Barrett Browning; Alfred, Lord Tennyson; and George Eliot. Even so, these writers had little or no effect on the style of her writing. In her own work she was original and innovative, but she did draw on her knowledge of the Bible, classical myths, and Shakespeare for allusions and references in her poetry. She also used contemporary popular church hymns, transforming their standard rhythms into free-form hymn meters. Among American writers she appreciated Ralph Waldo Emerson and Thoreau, but she apparently felt Walt Whitman was better left unread. She once mentioned to Thomas Wentworth Higginson, a leading critic with whom she corresponded about her poetry, that as for Whitman "I never read his Book—but was told that he was disgraceful" (for the kind of Whitman poetry she had been warned against, see his "I Sing the Body Electric," p. 801). Nathaniel Hawthorne, however, intrigued her with his faith in the imagination and his dark themes: "Hawthorne appals—entices," a remark that might be used to describe her own themes and techniques.

AN INTRODUCTION TO HER WORK

Today, Dickinson is regarded as one of America's greatest poets, but when she died at the age of fifty-six after devoting most of her life to writing poetry, her nearly two thousand poems—only a dozen of which were published, anonymously, during her lifetime—were unknown except to a small number of friends and relatives. Dickinson was not recognized as a major poet until the twentieth century, when modern readers ranked her as a major new voice whose literary innovations were unmatched by any other nineteenth-century poet in the United States.

Dickinson neither completed many poems nor prepared them for publication. She wrote her drafts on scraps of paper, grocery lists, and the backs of recipes and used envelopes. Early editors of her poems took the liberty of making them more accessible to nineteenth-century readers when several volumes of selected poems were published in the 1890s. The poems were made to appear like traditional nineteenth-century verse by assigning them titles, rearranging their syntax, normalizing their grammar, and regularizing their capitalizations. Instead of dashes editors used standard punctuation; instead of the highly elliptical telegraphic lines so characteristic of her poems editors added articles, conjunctions, and prepositions to make them more readable and in line with conventional expectations. In addition, the poems were made more predictable by organizing them into categories such as friendship, nature, love, and death. Not until 1955, when Thomas Johnson published Dickinson's complete works in a form that attempted to be true to her manuscript versions, did readers have the opportunity to see the full range of her style and themes.

Like that of Robert Frost, Dickinson's popular reputation has sometimes relegated her to the role of a New England regionalist who writes quaint uplifting verses that touch the heart. In 1971 that image was mailed first class all over the country by the U.S. Postal Service. In addition to issuing a commemorative stamp featuring a portrait of Dickinson, the Postal Service affixed the stamp to a first-day-of-issue envelope that included an engraved rose and one of her poems. Here's the poem chosen from among the nearly two thousand she wrote:

If I can stop one Heart from breaking c. 1864

If I can stop one Heart from breaking
I shall not live in vain
If I can ease one Life the Aching
or cool one Pain

Or help one fainting Robin
Unto his Nest again
I shall not live in Vain.

This is typical not only of many nineteenth-century popular poems but also of the kind of verse that can be found in contemporary greeting cards. The speaker tells us what we imagine we should think about and makes the point simply with a sentimental image of a "fainting Robin." To point out that robins don't faint or that altruism isn't necessarily the only rule of conduct by which one should live one's life is to make trouble for this poem. Moreover, its use of language is unexceptional; the metaphors used, like that robin, are a bit weary. If this poem were characteristic of Dickinson's poetry, the U.S. Postal Service probably would not have been urged to issue a stamp in her honor, nor would you be reading her poems in this anthology or many others. Here's a poem by Dickinson that is more typical of her writing:

If I shouldn't be alive   *c. 1860*

If I shouldn't be alive
When the Robins come,
Give the one in Red Cravat,
A Memorial crumb.

If I couldn't thank you,
Being fast asleep,
You will know I'm trying
With my Granite lip!

    This poem is more representative of Dickinson's sensibilities and techniques. Although the first stanza sets up a rather mild concern that the speaker might not survive the winter (a not uncommon fear for those who fell prey to pneumonia, for example, during Dickinson's time), the concern can't be taken too seriously — a gentle humor lightens the poem when we realize that all robins have red cravats and are therefore the speaker's favorite. Furthermore, the euphemism that describes the speaker "Being fast asleep" in line 6 makes death seem not so threatening after all. But the sentimental expectations of the first six lines — lines that could have been written by any number of popular nineteenth-century writers — are dashed by the penultimate word of the last line. *Granite* is the perfect word here because it forces us to reread the poem and to recognize that it's not about feeding robins or offering a cosmetic treatment of death; rather, it's a bone-chilling description of a corpse's lip that evokes the cold, hard texture and grayish color of tombstones. These lips will never say "thank you" or anything else.

    Instead of the predictable rhymes and sentiments of "If I can stop one Heart from breaking," this poem is unnervingly precise in its use of language and tidily points out how much emphasis Dickinson places on an individual word. Her use of near rhyme with "asleep" and "lip" brilliantly mocks a euphemistic approach to death by its jarring dissonance. This is a better poem, not because it's grim or about death, but because it demonstrates Dickinson's skillful use of language to produce a shocking irony.

    Dickinson found irony, ambiguity, and paradox lurking in the simplest and commonest experiences. The materials and subject matter of her poetry are quite conventional. Her poems are filled with robins, bees, winter light, household items, and domestic duties. These materials represent the range of what she experienced in and around her father's house. She used them because they constituted so much of her life and, more important, because she found meanings latent in them. Though her world was simple, it was also complex in its beauties and its terrors. Her lyric poems capture impressions of particular moments, scenes, or moods, and she characteristically focuses on topics such as nature, love, immortality, death, faith, doubt, pain, and the self.

Though her materials were conventional, her treatment of them was innovative because she was willing to break whatever poetic conventions stood in the way of the intensity of her thought and images. Her conciseness, brevity, and wit are tightly packed. Typically she offers her observations via one or two images that reveal her thought in a powerful manner. She once characterized her literary art by writing "My business is circumference." Her method is to reveal the inadequacy of declarative statements by evoking qualifications and questions with images that complicate firm assertions and affirmations. In one of her poems she describes her strategies this way: "Tell all the Truth but tell it slant—/ Success in Circuit lies." This might well stand as a working definition of Dickinson's aesthetics and is embodied in the following poem:

The Thought beneath so slight a film —   *c. 1860*

The Thought beneath so slight a film —
Is more distinctly seen —
As laces just reveal the surge —
Or Mists — the Apennine°   *Italian mountain range*

Paradoxically, "Thought" is more clearly understood precisely because a slight "film"—in this case language—covers it. Language, like lace, enhances what it covers and reveals it all the more—just as a mountain range is more engaging to the imagination if it is covered in mists rather than starkly presenting itself. Poetry for Dickinson intensifies, clarifies, and organizes experience.

Dickinson's poetry is challenging because it is radical and original in its rejection of most traditional nineteenth-century themes and techniques. Her poems require active engagement from the reader because she seems to leave out so much with her elliptical style and remarkable contracting metaphors. But these apparent gaps are filled with meaning if we are sensitive to her use of devices such as personification, allusion, symbolism, and startling syntax and grammar. Because her use of dashes is sometimes puzzling, it helps to read her poems aloud to hear how carefully the words are arranged. What might initially seem intimidating on a silent page can surprise the reader with meaning when heard. It's also worth keeping in mind that Dickinson was not always consistent in her views and that they can change from poem to poem, depending on how she felt at a given moment. For example, her definition of religious belief in " 'Faith' is a fine invention" (p. 868) reflects an ironically detached wariness in contrast to the faith embraced in "I never saw a Moor —" (p. 869). Dickinson was less interested in absolute answers to questions than she was in examining and exploring their "circumference."

Because Dickinson's poems are all relatively brief (none is longer than fifty lines), they invite browsing and sampling, but perhaps a useful way into their highly metaphoric and witty world is this "how to" poem that reads almost like a recipe:

To make a prairie it takes a clover and one bee   *date unknown*

To make a prairie it takes a clover and one bee,
One clover, and a bee,
And revery.
The revery alone will do,
If bees are few.

This quiet but infinite claim for a writer's imagination brings together the range of ingredients in Dickinson's world of domestic and ordinary natural details. Not surprisingly, she deletes rather than adds to the recipe, because the one essential ingredient is the writer's creative imagination. *Bon appétit.*

Success is counted sweetest   *c. 1859*

Success is counted sweetest
By those who ne'er succeed.
To comprehend a nectar
Requires sorest need.

Not one of all the purple Host   5
Who took the Flag today
Can tell the definition
So clear of Victory

As he defeated — dying —
On whose forbidden ear   10
The distant strains of triumph
Burst agonized and clear!

CONSIDERATIONS FOR CRITICAL THINKING AND WRITING

1. **FIRST RESPONSE.** How is "success" defined in this poem? To what extent does that definition agree with your own understanding of the word?

2. What do you think is meant by the use of "comprehend" in line 3? How can a nectar be comprehended?

3. Why do the defeated understand victory better than the victorious?

4. Discuss the effect of the poem's final line.

CONNECTION TO ANOTHER SELECTION

1. In an essay compare the themes of this poem with those of John Keats's "Ode on a Grecian Urn" (p. 647).

Water, is taught by thirst   *c. 1859*

Water, is taught by thirst.
Land — by the Oceans passed.
Transport — by throe —
Peace — by its battles told —
Love, by Memorial Mold —
Birds, by the Snow.

CONSIDERATIONS FOR CRITICAL THINKING AND WRITING

1. **FIRST RESPONSE.** Which image in the poem do you find most powerful? Explain why.

2. How is the paradox of each line of the poem resolved? How is the first word of each line "taught" by the phrase that follows it?

3. **CREATIVE RESPONSE.** Try your hand at writing similar lines in which something is "taught."

CONNECTIONS TO OTHER SELECTIONS

1. What does this poem have in common with "Success is counted sweetest" (p. 841) ? Which poem do you think is more effective? Explain why.

2. How is the crucial point of this poem related to "I like a look of Agony," (p. 846)?

Safe in their Alabaster Chambers —   *1859 version*

Safe in their Alabaster Chambers —
Untouched by Morning
And untouched by Noon —
Sleep the meek members of the Resurrection —
Rafter of satin,   5
And Roof of stone.

Light laughs the breeze
In her Castle above them —

Babbles the Bee in a stolid Ear,
Pipe the Sweet Birds in ignorant cadence —   10
Ah, what sagacity perished here!

Safe in their Alabaster Chambers —   *1861 version*

Safe in their Alabaster Chambers —
Untouched by Morning —
And untouched by Noon —
Lie the meek members of the Resurrection —
Rafter of Satin — and Roof of Stone!   5

Grand go the Years — in the Crescent — above them —
Worlds scoop their arcs —
And Firmaments — row —
Diadems — drop — and Doges° — surrender —
Soundless as dots — on a Disc of Snow —   10

9 *Doges:* Chief magistrates of Venice from the twelfth to the sixteenth centuries.

CONSIDERATIONS FOR CRITICAL THINKING AND WRITING

1. **FIRST RESPONSE.** Dickinson permitted the 1859 version of this poem, entitled "The Sleeping," to be printed in the *Springfield Republican.* The second version she sent privately to Thomas Wentworth Higginson. Why do you suppose she would agree to publish the first but not the second version?

2. Are there any significant changes in the first stanzas of the two versions? If you answered yes, explain the significance of the changes.

3. Describe the different kinds of images used in the two second stanzas. How do those images affect the tones and meanings of those stanzas?

4. Discuss why you prefer one version of the poem to the other.

CONNECTIONS TO OTHER SELECTIONS

1. Compare the theme in the 1861 version with the theme of Robert Frost's "Design" (p. 895).

2. In an essay discuss the attitude toward death in the 1859 version and in "Apparently with no surprise" (p. 869).

Portraits are to daily faces   *c. 1860*

Portraits are to daily faces
As an Evening West,
To a fine, pedantic sunshine —
In a satin Vest!

Considerations for Critical Thinking and Writing

1. **FIRST RESPONSE.** Dickinson once described her literary art this way: "My business is circumference." Does this poem fit her characterization of her poetry?

2. How is the basic strategy of this poem similar to the following statement: "Doorknob is to door as button is to sweater"?

3. Identify the four metonymies in the poem. Pay close attention to their connotative meanings.

4. If you don't know the meaning of "pedantic," look it up in a dictionary. How does its meaning affect your reading of "fine"?

Connections to Other Selections

1. Compare Dickinson's view of poetry in this poem with Robert Francis's perspective in "Catch" (p. 576). What important similarities and differences do you find?

2. Write an essay describing Robert Frost's strategy in "Mending Wall" (p. 884) or "Birches" (p. 890) as the business of circumference.

3. How is the theme of this poem related to the central idea in "The Thought beneath so slight a film —" (p. 840)?

4. Compare the use of the word "fine" here with its use in "'Faith' is a fine invention" (p. 868).

Some keep the Sabbath going to Church —   *c. 1860*

Some keep the Sabbath going to Church —
I keep it, staying at Home —
With a Bobolink for a Chorister —
And an Orchard, for a Dome —

Some keep the Sabbath in Surplice°   *holy robes*   5
I just wear my Wings —
And instead of tolling the Bell, for Church,
Our little Sexton — sings.

God preaches, a noted Clergyman —
And the sermon is never long,   10
So instead of getting to Heaven, at last —
I'm going, all along.

Considerations for Critical Thinking and Writing

1. **FIRST RESPONSE.** What is the effect of referring to "Some" people?

2. Characterize the speaker's tone.

3. How does the speaker distinguish himself or herself from those who go to church?

4. How might "Surplice" be read as a pun?

5. According to the speaker, how should the Sabbath be observed?

1. Write an essay that discusses nature in this poem and in Walt Whitman's
"When I Heard the Learn'd Astronomer" (p. 1036).

"Heaven" — is what I cannot reach!   c. 1861

"Heaven" — is what I cannot reach!
The Apple on the Tree —
Provided it do hopeless — hang —
That — "Heaven" is — to Me!

The Color, on the Cruising Cloud —   5
The interdicted Land —
Behind the Hill — the House behind —
There — Paradise — is found!

Her teasing Purples — Afternoons —
The credulous — decoy —   10
Enamored — of the Conjuror —
That spurned us — Yesterday!

CONSIDERATIONS FOR CRITICAL THINKING AND WRITING

1. FIRST RESPONSE. How does the speaker define heaven? How does that definition compare with conventional views of heaven?
2. Look up the myth of Tantalus and explain the allusion in line 3.
3. Given the speaker's definition of heaven, how do you think he or she would
   describe hell?

CONNECTIONS TO OTHER SELECTIONS

1. Write an essay that discusses desire in this poem and in "Water, is taught by
   thirst" (p. 842).
2. Discuss the speakers' attitudes toward pleasure in this poem and in Sharon
   Olds's "Last Night" (p. 640).

"Hope" is the thing with feathers —   c. 1861

"Hope" is the thing with feathers —
That perches in the soul —
And sings the tune without the words —
And never stops — at all —

And sweetest — in the Gale — is heard —   5
And sore must be the storm —

That could abash the little Bird
That kept so many warm —

I've heard it in the chillest land —
And on the strangest Sea —   10
Yet, never, in Extremity,
It asked a crumb — of Me.

CONSIDERATIONS FOR CRITICAL THINKING AND WRITING

1. **FIRST RESPONSE.** Why do you think the speaker defines hope in terms of a bird? Why is this metaphor more appropriate than, say, a dog?

2. Discuss the effects of the rhymes in each stanza.

3. What is the central point of the poem?

CONNECTIONS TO OTHER SELECTIONS

1. Compare the tone of this definition of hope with that of "'Faith' is a fine invention" (p. 868). How is "Extremity" handled differently from the "Emergency" in the latter poem?

2. Compare the strategies used to define hope in this poem and heaven in the preceding poem, "'Heaven' — is what I cannot reach!" Which poem, in your opinion, creates a more successful definition? In an essay explain why.

I like a look of Agony,   *c. 1861*

I like a look of Agony,
Because I know it's true —
Men do not sham Convulsion,
Nor simulate, a Throe —

The Eyes glaze once — and that is Death —
Impossible to feign
The Beads upon the Forehead
By homely Anguish strung.

CONSIDERATIONS FOR CRITICAL THINKING AND WRITING

1. **FIRST RESPONSE.** Why does the speaker "like a look of Agony"? How do you respond to her appreciation of "Convulsion"?

2. Discuss the image of "The Eyes glaze once — ." Why is that a particularly effective metaphor for death?

3. Characterize the speaker. One critic once described the voice in this poem as "almost a hysterical shriek." Explain why you agree or disagree.

CONNECTION TO ANOTHER SELECTION

1. Write an essay on Dickinson's attitudes toward pain and deprivation, using this poem and "'Heaven' — is what I cannot reach!" (p. 845).

Wild Nights — Wild Nights!   c. 1861

Wild Nights — Wild Nights!
Were I with thee
Wild Nights should be
Our luxury!

Futile — the Winds —   5
To a Heart in port —
Done with the Compass —
Done with the Chart!

Rowing in Eden —
Ah, the Sea!   10
Might I but moor — Tonight —
In Thee!

CONSIDERATIONS FOR CRITICAL THINKING AND WRITING

1. **FIRST RESPONSE.** Thomas Wentworth Higginson, Dickinson's mentor, once said he was afraid that some "malignant" readers might "read into [a poem like this] more than that virgin recluse ever dreamed of putting there." What do you think?

2. Look up the meaning of *luxury* in a dictionary. Why does this word work especially well here?

3. Given the imagery of the final stanza, do you think the speaker is a man or a woman? Explain why.

4. **CRITICAL STRATEGIES.** Read the section on psychological strategies (pp. 1542–44) in Chapter 46, "Critical Strategies for Reading." What do you think this poem reveals about the author's personal psychology?

CONNECTION TO ANOTHER SELECTION

1. Write an essay that compares the voice, figures of speech, and theme of this poem with those of Margaret Atwood's "you fit into me" (p. 683).

I reason, Earth is short—   c. 1862

I reason, Earth is short —
And Anguish — absolute —
And many hurt,
But, what of that?

I reason, we could die —   5
The best Vitality
Cannot excel Decay,
But, what of that?

I reason, that in Heaven —
Somehow, it will be even —   10
Some new Equation, given —
But, what of that?

CONSIDERATIONS FOR CRITICAL THINKING AND WRITING

1. FIRST RESPONSE. What attitudes does the speaker have toward mortality and immortality?

2. Paraphrase each of the stanzas and explain how they are thematically related to one another.

3. Discuss the effects of the poem's repeated lines.

4. CRITICAL STRATEGIES. Read the section on critical thinking (pp. 1533-36) in Chapter 46, "Critical Strategies for Reading," and research critical commentary on this poem. Write an essay describing the range of interpretations that you find. Which interpretation do you think is the most convincing? Why?

What Soft—Cherubic Creatures—

1862

What Soft—Cherubic Creatures—
These Gentlewomen are—
One would as soon assault a Plush—
Or violate a Star—

Such Dimity° Convictions—   *sheer cotton fabric* 5
A Horror so refined
Of freckled Human Nature—
Of Deity—ashamed—

It's such a common—Glory—
A Fisherman's—Degree—   10
Redemption—Brittle Lady—
Be so—ashamed of Thee—

CONSIDERATIONS FOR CRITICAL THINKING AND WRITING

1. FIRST RESPONSE. Characterize the "Gentlewomen" in this poem.

2. How do the sounds produced in the first line help to reinforce their meaning?

3. What are "Dimity Convictions," and what do they make "Of freckled Human Nature"?

4. Discuss the irony in the final stanza.

CONNECTION TO ANOTHER SELECTION

1. How are the "Gentlewomen" in this poem similar to the "Gentlemen" in "'Faith' is a fine invention" (p. 868)?

The Soul selects her own Society—

c. 1862

The Soul selects her own Society—
Then—shuts the Door—
To her divine Majority—
Present no more—

Manuscript page for "What Soft — Cherubic Creatures —" (p. 848). This page was taken from one of Dickinson's forty fascicles — small booklets hand-sewn with white string that contained her poetry as well as other miscellaneous writings. These fascicles are important for Dickinson scholars, as this manuscript page makes clear: her style to some extent resists translation into the conventions of print.

Unmoved — she notes the Chariots — pausing —
At her low Gate —
Unmoved — an Emperor be kneeling
Upon her Mat —

I've known her — from an ample nation —
Choose One —
Then — close the Valves of her attention —
Like Stone —

5

10

CONSIDERATIONS FOR CRITICAL THINKING AND WRITING

1. **FIRST RESPONSE.** Characterize the speaker. Is she self-reliant and self-sufficient? cold? angry?

2. Why do you suppose the "Soul" in this poem is female? Would it make any difference if it were male?

3. Discuss the effect of the images in the final two lines. Pay particular attention to the meanings of "Valves" in line 11.

Much Madness is divinest Sense —

c. 1862

Much Madness is divinest Sense —
To a discerning Eye —
Much Sense — the starkest Madness —
'Tis the Majority
In this, as All, prevail —
Assent — and you are sane —
Demur — you're straightway dangerous —
And handled with a Chain —

CONSIDERATIONS FOR CRITICAL THINKING AND WRITING

1. **FIRST RESPONSE.** Thomas Wentworth Higginson's wife once referred to Dickinson as the "partially cracked poetess of Amherst." Assuming that Dickinson had some idea of how she was regarded by the "Majority," how might this poem be seen as an insight into her life?

2. Discuss the conflict between the individual and society in this poem. Which images are used to describe each? How do these images affect your attitudes about them?

3. Comment on the effectiveness of the poem's final line.

CONNECTION TO ANOTHER SELECTION

1. Discuss the theme of self-reliance in this poem and in "The Soul selects her own Society —" (p. 848).

I dwell in Possibility —

c. 1862

I dwell in Possibility —
A fairer House than Prose —
More numerous of Windows —
Superior — for Doors —

Of Chambers as the Cedars —   5
Impregnable of Eye —
And for an Everlasting Roof
The Gambrels° of the Sky —   *angled roofs*

Of Visitors — the fairest —
For Occupation — This —   10
The spreading wide my narrow Hands
To gather Paradise —

CONSIDERATIONS FOR CRITICAL THINKING AND WRITING

1. **FIRST RESPONSE.** What distinction is made between poetry and prose in this poem? Explain why you agree or disagree with the speaker's distinctions.
2. What is the poem's central metaphor in the second and third stanzas?
3. How does the use of metaphor in this poem become a means for the speaker to envision and create a world beyond the circumstances of his or her actual life?

CONNECTIONS TO OTHER SELECTIONS

1. Compare what this poem says about poetry and prose with T. E. Hulme's comments in "On the Differences between Poetry and Prose" (p. 679).
2. How can the speaker's sense of expansiveness in this poem be reconciled with the speaker's insistence on contraction in "The Soul selects her own Society —" (p. 848)? Are these poems contradictory? Explain why or why not.

After great pain, a formal feeling comes —

c. 1862

After great pain, a formal feeling comes —
The Nerves sit ceremonious, like Tombs —
The stiff Heart questions was it He, that bore,
And Yesterday, or Centuries before?

The Feet, mechanical, go round —   5
Of Ground, or Air, or Ought —
A Wooden way
Regardless grown,
A Quartz contentment, like a stone —

This is the Hour of Lead —   10
Remembered, if outlived,
As Freezing persons, recollect the Snow —
First — Chill — then Stupor — then the letting go —

CONSIDERATIONS FOR CRITICAL THINKING AND WRITING

1. **FIRST RESPONSE.** What do you think has caused the speaker's pain?
2. How does the rhythm of the lines create a slow, somber pace?
3. Discuss why "the Hour of Lead" (line 10) could serve as a useful title for this poem.

CONNECTIONS TO OTHER SELECTIONS

1. How might this poem be read as a kind of sequel to "The Bustle in a House" (p. 855)?
2. Write an essay that discusses this poem in relation to Robert Frost's "Home Burial" (p. 886).

I heard a Fly buzz — when I died —   *c. 1862*

I heard a Fly buzz — when I died —
The Stillness in the Room
Was like the Stillness in the Air —
Between the Heaves of Storm —

The Eyes around — had wrung them dry —   5
And Breaths were gathering firm
For that last Onset — when the King
Be witnessed — in the Room —

I willed my Keepsakes — Signed away
What portion of me be   10
Assignable — and then it was
There interposed a Fly —

With Blue — uncertain stumbling Buzz —
Between the light — and me —
And then the Windows failed — and then   15
I could not see to see —

CONSIDERATIONS FOR CRITICAL THINKING AND WRITING

1. **FIRST RESPONSE.** What was expected to happen "when the King" was "witnessed"? What happened instead?
2. Why do you think Dickinson chooses a fly rather than perhaps a bee or gnat?
3. What is the effect of the last line? Why not end the poem with "I could not see" instead of the additional "to see"?
4. Discuss the sounds in the poem. Are there any instances of onomatopoeia?

1. Contrast the symbolic significance of the fly with the wasp in Janice Townley Moore's "To a Wasp" (p. 688).
2. Consider the meaning of "light" in this poem and in "There's a certain Slant of light" (p. 1577).

Because I could not stop for Death—   *c. 1863*

Because I could not stop for Death—
He kindly stopped for me—
The Carriage held but just Ourselves—
And Immortality.

We slowly drove—He knew no haste   5
And I had put away
My labor and my leisure too,
For His Civility—

We passed the School, where Children strove
At Recess—in the Ring—   10
We passed the Fields of Gazing Grain—
We passed the Setting Sun—

Or rather—He passed Us—
The Dews drew quivering and chill—
For only Gossamer, my Gown—   15
My Tippet°—only Tulle—   *shawl*

We paused before a House that seemed
A Swelling of the Ground—
The Roof was scarcely visible—
The Cornice—in the Ground—   20

Since then—'tis Centuries—and yet
Feels shorter than the Day
I first surmised the Horses' Heads
Were toward Eternity—

CONSIDERATIONS FOR CRITICAL THINKING AND WRITING

1. FIRST RESPONSE. Why couldn't the speaker "stop for Death"?
2. How is death personified in this poem? How does the speaker respond to him? Why are they accompanied by Immortality?
3. What is the significance of the things they "passed" in the third stanza?
4. What is the "House" in lines 17–20?
5. Discuss the rhythm of the lines. How, for example, is the rhythm of line 14 related to its meaning?

CONNECTIONS TO OTHER SELECTIONS

1. Compare the tone of this poem with that of Dickinson's "Apparently with no surprise" (p. 869).

2. Write an essay comparing Dickinson's view of death in this poem and in "If I shouldn't be alive" (p. 839). Which poem is more powerful for you? Explain why.

I felt a Cleaving in my Mind —

c. 1864

I felt a Cleaving in my Mind —
As if my Brain had split —
I tried to match it — Seam by Seam —
But could not make them fit.

The thought behind, I strove to join
Unto the thought before —
But Sequence ravelled out of Sound
Like Balls — upon a Floor.

CONSIDERATIONS FOR CRITICAL THINKING AND WRITING

1. **FIRST RESPONSE.** What is going on in the speaker's mind?
2. What is the poem's controlling metaphor? Describe the simile in lines 7 and 8. How does it clarify further the first stanza?
3. Discuss the rhymes. How do they reinforce meaning?

CONNECTION TO ANOTHER SELECTION

1. Compare the power of the speaker's mind described here with the power of imagination described in "To make a prairie it takes a clover and one bee" (p. 841).

A Light exists in Spring

c. 1864

A Light exists in Spring
Not present on the Year
At any other period —
When March is scarcely here

A Color stands abroad   5
On Solitary Fields
That Science cannot overtake
But Human Nature feels.

It waits upon the Lawn,
It shows the furthest Tree   10
Upon the furthest Slope you know
It almost speaks to you.

Then as Horizons step
Or Noons report away

Without the Formula of sound   15
It passes and we stay —

A quality of loss
Affecting our Content
As Trade had suddenly encroached
Upon a Sacrament.   20

CONSIDERATIONS FOR CRITICAL THINKING AND WRITING

1. **FIRST RESPONSE.** Based on Dickinson's description, how would you characterize the nature of the light on a New England March day? How is that
   light different from that of a summer's day?

2. What kinds of feelings are evoked in the speaker by the light?

3. How are "Science" and "Trade" depicted in contrast to what "Human
   Nature feels"?

CONNECTION TO ANOTHER SELECTION

1. Compare Dickinson's thematic use of light in this poem and in "There's a
   certain Slant of light" (p. 1577).

The Bustle in a House   *c. 1866*

The Bustle in a House
The Morning after Death
Is solemnest of industries
Enacted upon Earth —

The Sweeping up the Heart
And putting Love away
We shall not want to use again
Until Eternity.

CONSIDERATIONS FOR CRITICAL THINKING AND WRITING

1. **FIRST RESPONSE.** What is the relationship between love and death in this
   poem?

2. Why do you think mourning (notice the pun in line 2) is described as
   industry?

3. Discuss the tone of the poem's ending. Consider whether you think it is
   hopeful, sad, resigned, or some other mood.

CONNECTIONS TO OTHER SELECTIONS

1. Compare this poem with "After great pain, a formal feeling comes —"
   (p. 851). Which poem is, for you, a more powerful treatment of mourning?

2. How does this poem qualify "I like a look of Agony," (p. 846)? Does it contradict the latter poem? Explain why or why not.

Tell all the Truth but tell it slant —

c. 1868

Tell all the Truth but tell it slant —
Success in Circuit lies
Too bright for our infirm Delight
The Truth's superb surprise

As Lightning to the Children eased
With explanation kind
The Truth must dazzle gradually
Or every man be blind —

CONSIDERATIONS FOR CRITICAL THINKING AND WRITING

1. **FIRST RESPONSE.** What do you think the first line means? Why should truth be told "slant" and circuitously?

2. How does the second stanza explain the first?

3. How is this poem an example of its own theme?

CONNECTIONS TO OTHER SELECTIONS

1. How does the first stanza of "I know that He exists" (p. 868) suggest an idea similar to this poem's? Why do you think the last eight lines of the former aren't similar in theme to this poem?

2. Write an essay on Dickinson's attitudes about the purpose and strategies of poetry by considering this poem as well as "The Thought beneath so slight a film —" (p. 840) and "Portraits are to daily faces" (p. 843).

A Word dropped careless on a Page

c. 1873

A Word dropped careless on a Page
May stimulate an eye
When folded in perpetual seam
The Wrinkled Maker lie

Infection in the sentence breeds
We may inhale Despair
At distances of Centuries
From the Malaria —

CONSIDERATIONS FOR CRITICAL THINKING AND WRITING

1. **FIRST RESPONSE.** What sort of power does Dickinson attribute to the written word?

2. Who is the "Wrinkled Maker" in line 4?

3. Discuss the effects of the poem's rhymes.

4. Consult a dictionary definition of *malaria*. Why is it a particularly appropriate word choice for this poem?

There is no Frigate like a Book   c. 1873

There is no Frigate like a Book
To take us Lands away
Nor any Coursers like a Page
Of prancing Poetry —
This Traverse may the poorest take
Without oppress of Toll —
How frugal is the Chariot
That bears the Human soul.

Considerations for Critical Thinking and Writing

1. **FIRST RESPONSE.** Which lines present reading as a mode of transportation? Why do you think that is an effective controlling metaphor in a poem about the value of books?

2. How does the poem's rhythm suggest a kind of "prancing Poetry"?

Connection to Another Selection

1. Compare the tone of this poem with that of the preceding poem, "A Word dropped careless on a Page."

I took one Draught of Life —   date unknown

I took one Draught of Life —
I'll tell you what I paid —
Precisely an existence —
The market price, they said.

They weighed me, Dust by Dust —
They balanced Film with Film,
Then handed me my Being's worth —
A single Dram of Heaven!

Considerations for Critical Thinking and Writing

1. **FIRST RESPONSE.** What is the relationship between life and death in this poem?

2. What do you think "balanced Film with Film" refers to in line 6?

3. Explain whether you read the final two lines as an optimistic or a pessimistic view of the afterlife.

Connection to Another Selection

1. Discuss the meaning of heaven in this poem and in "'Heaven' — is what I cannot reach!" (p. 845).

Perspectives on Emily Dickinson

EMILY DICKINSON

A Description of Herself   1862

Mr Higginson,
        Your kindness claimed earlier gratitude — but I was ill — and write today, from my pillow.
        Thank you for the surgery — it was not so painful as I supposed. I bring you others° — as you ask — though they might not differ —
        While my thought is undressed — I can make the distinction, but when I put them in the Gown — they look alike, and numb.
        You asked how old I was? I made no verse — but one or two° — until this winter — Sir —
        I had a terror — since September — I could tell to none — and so I sing, as the Boy does by the Burying Ground — because I am afraid — You inquire my Books — For Poets — I have Keats — and Mr and Mrs Browning. For Prose — Mr Ruskin — Sir Thomas Browne — and the Revelations. I went to school — but in your manner of the phrase — had no education. When a little Girl, I had a friend, who taught me Immortality — but venturing too near, himself — he never returned — Soon after, my Tutor, died — and for several years, my Lexicon — was my only companion — Then I found one more — but he was not contented I be his scholar — so he left the Land.
        You ask of my Companions Hills — Sir — and the Sundown — and a Dog — large as myself, that my Father bought me — They are better than Beings — because they know — but do not tell — and the noise in the Pool, at Noon — excels my Piano. I have a Brother and Sister — My Mother does not care for thought — and Father, too busy with his Briefs — to notice what we do — He buys me many Books — but begs me not to read them — because he fears they joggle the Mind. They are religious — except me — and address an Eclipse, every morning — whom they call their "Father." But I fear my story fatigues you — I would like to learn — Could you tell me how to grow — or is it unconveyed — like Melody — or Witchcraft?
                                From a letter to Thomas Wentworth Higginson, April 25, 1862

others: Dickinson had sent poems to Higginson for his opinions and enclosed more with this letter.   *one or two:* Actually she had written almost 300 poems.

CONSIDERATIONS FOR CRITICAL THINKING AND WRITING

1. What impression does this letter give you of Dickinson?
2. What kinds of thoughts are there in the foreground of her thinking?
3. To what extent is the style of her letter writing like that of her poetry?

THOMAS WENTWORTH HIGGINSON (1823–1911)

On Meeting Dickinson for the First Time   *1870*

A large county lawyer's house, brown brick, with great trees & a garden — I sent up my card. A parlor dark & cool & stiffish, a few books & engravings & an open piano. . . .

A step like a pattering child's in entry & in glided a little plain woman with two smooth bands of reddish hair & a face a little like Belle Dove's; not plainer — with no good feature — in a very plain & exquisitely clean white pique & a blue net worsted shawl. She came to me with two day lilies which she put in a sort of childlike way into my hand & said "These are my introduction" in a soft frightened breathless childlike voice — & added under her breath Forgive me if I am frightened; I never see strangers & hardly know what I say — but she talked soon & thenceforward continuously — & deferentially — sometimes stopping to ask me to talk instead of her — but readily recommencing . . . thoroughly ingenuous & simple . . . & saying many things which you would have thought foolish & I wise — & some things you wd. hv. liked. I add a few over the page. . . .

> "Women talk; men are silent; that is why I dread women."
> "My father only reads on Sunday — he reads *lonely* & *rigorous* books."
> "If I read a book [and] it makes my whole body so cold no fire ever can warm me I know *that* is poetry. If I feel physically as if the top of my head were taken off, I know *that* is poetry. These are the only ways I know it. Is there any other way."
> "How do most people live without any thoughts. There are many people in the world (you must have noticed them in the street) How do they live. How do they get strength to put on their clothes in the morning"
> "When I lost the use of my Eyes it was a comfort to think there were so few real *books* that I could easily find some one to read me all of them"
> "Truth is such a *rare* thing it is delightful to tell it."
> "I find ecstasy in living — the mere sense of living is joy enough"
> I asked if she never felt want of employment, never going off the place & never seeing any visitor "I never thought of conceiving that I could ever have the slightest approach to such a want in all future time" (& added) "I feel that I have not expressed myself strongly enough."

From a letter to his wife, August 16, 1870

CONSIDERATIONS FOR CRITICAL THINKING AND WRITING

1. How old is Dickinson when Higginson meets her? Does this description seem commensurate with her age? Explain why or why not.

2. Choose one of the quotations from Dickinson that Higginson includes and write an essay about what it reveals about her.

MABEL LOOMIS TODD (1856–1932)

The Character *of Amherst*   *1881*

I must tell you about the *character* of Amherst. It is a lady whom the people call the *Myth.* She is a sister of Mr. Dickinson, & seems to be the climax of all the family oddity. She has not been outside of her own house in fifteen years, except once to see a new church, when she crept out at night, & viewed it by moonlight. No one who calls upon her mother & sister ever see her, but she allows little children once in a great while, & one at a time, to come in, when she gives them cake or candy, or some nicety, for she is very fond of little ones. But more often she lets down the sweetmeat by a string, out of a window, to them. She dresses wholly in white, & her mind is said to be perfectly wonderful. She writes finely, but no one *ever* sees her. Her sister, who was at Mrs. Dickinson's party, invited me to come & sing to her mother sometime. . . . People tell me the *myth* will hear every note — she will be near, but unseen. . . . Isn't that like a book? So interesting.

From a letter to her parents, November 6, 1881

CONSIDERATIONS FOR CRITICAL THINKING AND WRITING

1. Todd, who in the 1890s would edit Dickinson's poems and letters, had known her for only two months when she wrote this letter. How does Todd characterize Dickinson?

2. Does this description seem positive or negative to you? Explain your answer.

3. A few of Dickinson's poems, such as "Much Madness is divinest Sense—" (p. 850), suggest that she was aware of this perception of her. Refer to her poems in discussing Dickinson's response to this perception.

RICHARD WILBUR (B. 1921)

On Dickinson's Sense of Privation   *1960*

What did Emily Dickinson do, as a poet, with her sense of privation? One thing she quite often did was to pose as the laureate and attorney of the empty-handed, and question God about the economy of His creation. Why, she asked, is a fatherly God so sparing of His presence? Why is there never a sign that prayers are heard? Why does Nature tell us no comforting news of its Maker? Why do some receive a whole loaf, while others must starve on a crumb? Where is the benevolence in shipwreck and earthquake? By asking such questions as these, she turned complaint into critique, and used her own sufferings as experiential evidence about the nature of the deity. The God who emerges from these poems is a God who does not answer, an unrevealed God whom one cannot confidently approach through Nature or through doctrine.

But there was another way in which Emily Dickinson dealt with her sentiment of lack — another emotional strategy which was both more frequent and more fruitful. I refer to her repeated assertion of the paradox that privation is more plentiful than plenty; that to renounce is to possess the more; that "The Banquet of abstemiousness / Defaces that of wine." We all know how the poet illustrated this ascetic paradox in her behavior—how in her latter years she chose to live in relative retirement, keeping the world, even in its dearest aspects, at a physical remove. She would write her friends, telling them how she missed them, then flee upstairs when they came to see her; afterward, she might send a note of apology, offering the odd explanation that "We shun because we prize." Any reader of Dickinson biographies can furnish other examples, dramatic or homely, of this prizing and shunning, this yearning and renouncing: in my own mind's eye is a picture of Emily Dickinson watching a gay circus caravan from the distance of her chamber window.

> From "Sumptuous Destitution" in *Emily Dickinson: Three Views,*
> by Richard Wilbur, Louise Bogan, and Archibald MacLeish

CONSIDERATIONS FOR CRITICAL THINKING AND WRITING

1. Which poems by Dickinson reprinted in this anthology suggest that she was "the laureate and attorney of the empty-handed"?

2. Which poems suggest that "privation is more plentiful"?

3. Of these two types of poems, which do you prefer? Write an essay that explains your preference.

SANDRA M. GILBERT (B. 1936) AND
SUSAN GUBAR (B. 1944)

On Dickinson's White Dress 1979

Today a dress that the Amherst Historical Society assures us is *the* white dress Dickinson wore—or at least one of her "Uniforms of Snow"—hangs in a drycleaner's plastic bag in the closet of the Dickinson homestead. Perfectly preserved, beautifully flounced and tucked, it is larger than most readers would have expected this self-consciously small poet's dress to be, and thus reminds visiting scholars of the enduring enigma of Dickinson's central metaphor, even while it draws gasps from more practical visitors, who reflect with awe upon the difficulties of maintaining such a costume. But what exactly did the literal and figurative whiteness of this costume represent? What rewards did it offer that would cause an intelligent woman to overlook those practical difficulties? Comparing Dickinson's obsession with whiteness to [Herman] Melville's, William R. Sherwood suggests that "it reflected in her case the Christian mystery and not a Christian enigma . . . a decision to announce . . . the assumption of a worldly death that paradoxically involved regeneration." This, he adds, her gown—"a typically slant demonstration of truth"—should have revealed "to anyone with the wit to catch on."[1]

We might reasonably wonder, however, if Dickinson herself consciously

---

[1] *Circumference and Circumstance: Stages in the Mind and Art of Emily Dickinson* (New York: Columbia University Press, 1968) 152, 231.

intended her wardrobe to convey any one message. The range of associations her white poems imply suggests, on the contrary, that for her, as for Melville, white is the ultimate symbol of enigma, paradox, and irony, "not so much a color as the visible absence of color, and at the same time the concrete of all colors." Melville's question [in *Moby-Dick*] might, therefore, also be hers: "is it for these reasons that there is such a dumb blankness, full of meaning, in a wide landscape of snows — a colorless, all-color of atheism from which we shrink?" And his concluding speculation might be hers too, his remark "that the mystical cosmetic which produces every one of [Nature's] hues, the great principle of light, for ever remains white or colorless in itself, and if operating without medium upon matter, would touch all objects . . . with its own blank tinge." For white, in Dickinson's poetry, frequently represents both the energy (the white heat) of Romantic creativity, and the loneliness (the polar cold) of the renunciation or tribulation Romantic creativity may demand, both the white radiance of eternity — or Revelation — and the white terror of a shroud.

> From *The Madwoman in the Attic: The Woman Writer and the Nineteenth-Century Literary Imagination*

CONSIDERATIONS FOR CRITICAL THINKING AND WRITING

1. What meanings do Gilbert and Gubar attribute to Dickinson's white dress?

2. Discuss the meaning of the implicit whiteness in "Safe in their Alabaster Chambers —" (p. 842) and "After great pain, a formal feeling comes —" (p. 851). To what extent do these poems incorporate the meanings of whiteness that Gilbert and Gubar suggest?

3. What other possible reasons can you think of that would account for Dickinson's wearing only white?

CYNTHIA GRIFFIN WOLFF (B. 1935)
On the Many Voices in Dickinson's Poetry   1986

There were many "Voices." This fact has sometimes puzzled Dickinson's readers. One poem may be delivered in a child's Voice; another in the Voice of a young woman scrutinizing nature and the society in which she makes her place. Sometimes the Voice is that of a woman self-confidently addressing her lover in a language of passion and sexual desire. At still other times, the Voice of the verse seems so precariously balanced at the edge of hysteria that even its calmest observations grate like the shriek of dementia. There is the Voice of the housewife and the Voice that has recourse to the occasionally agonizing, occasionally regal language of the conversion experience of latter-day New England Puritanism. In some poems the Voice is distinctive principally because it speaks in the aftermath of wounding and can comprehend extremities of pain. Moreover, these Voices are not always entirely distinct from one another: the child's Voice that opens a poem may yield to the Voice of a young woman speaking the idiom of ardent love; in a different poem, the speaker may fall into a mood of almost religious contemplation in an attempt to analyze or define such abstract entities as loneliness or madness or eternity; the diction of the housewife may be conflated with the sovereign language of the New Jerusalem, and taken together, they may render some aspect of the wordsmith's labor. No manageable set of discrete categories suffices to capture the diversity of discourse, and any attempt to simplify Dickinson's methods does violence to the verse.

Yet there is a paradox here. This is, by no stretch of the imagination, a body of poetry that might be construed as a series of lyrics spoken by many different people. Disparate as these many Voices are, somehow they all appear to issue from the same "self." . . . It is the enigmatic "Emily Dickinson" readers suppose themselves to have found in this poetry, even in the extreme case when Dickinson's supposed speaker is male. One explanation for this sense of intrinsic unity in the midst of diversity is the persistence with which Dickinson addresses the same set of problems, using a remarkably durable repertoire of linguistic modes. Evocations of injury and wounding—threats to the coherence of the self—appear in the earliest poems and continue until the end; ways of rendering face-to-face encounters change, but this preoccupation with "interview" is sustained by metaphors of "confrontation" that weave throughout. The summoning of one or another Voice in a given poem, then, is not an unself-conscious emotive reflection of Emily Dickinson's mood at the moment of creation. Rather, each different Voice is a calculated tactic, an attempt to touch her readers and engage them intimately with the poetry. Each Voice had its unique advantages; each its limitations. A poet self-conscious in her craft, she calculated this element as carefully as every other.

From *Emily Dickinson*

CONSIDERATIONS FOR CRITICAL THINKING AND WRITING

1. From the poems in this anthology, try adding to the list of voices Wolff cites.

2. Despite the many voices in Dickinson's poetry, why, according to Wolff, is there still a "sense of intrinsic unity" in her poetry?

3. Choose a Dickinson poem and describe how the choice of voice is a "calculated tactic."

PAULA BENNETT (B. 1936)

On "I heard a Fly buzz—when I died—"   1990

Dickinson's rage against death, a rage that led her at times to hate both life and death, might have been alleviated, had she been able to gather hard evidence about an afterlife. But, of course, she could not. "The *Bareheaded life*—under the grass—," she wrote to Samuel Bowles in c. 1860, "worries one like a Wasp." If death was the gate to a better life in "the childhood of the kingdom of Heaven," as the sentimentalists—and Christ—claimed, then, perhaps, there was compensation and healing for life's woes. . . . But how do we know? What can we know? In "I heard a Fly buzz—when I died," Dickinson concludes that we do not know much. . . .

Like many people in her period, Dickinson was fascinated by death-bed scenes. How, she asked various correspondents, did this or that person die? In particular, she wanted to know if their deaths revealed any information about the nature of the afterlife. In this poem, however, she imagines her own death-bed scene, and the answer she provides is grim, as grim (and, at the same time, as ironically mocking) as anything she ever wrote.

In the narrowing focus of death, the fly's insignificant buzz, magnified tenfold by the stillness in the room, is all that the speaker hears. This kind of distortion in scale is common. It is one of the "illusions" of perception. But here it is horrifying because it defeats every expectation we have. Death is supposed to be an experience of awe. It is the moment when the soul, departing the body, is taken up by God. Hence the watchers at the bedside wait for the moment when the "King" (whether God or death) "be witnessed" in the room. And hence the speaker assigns away everything but that which she expects God (her soul) or death (her body) to take.

What arrives instead, however, is neither God nor death but a fly, "[w]ith Blue—uncertain—stumbling Buzz," a fly, that is, no more secure, no more sure, than we are. Dickinson had associated flies with death once before in the exquisite lament, "How many times these low feet / staggered." In this poem, they buzz "on the / chamber window," and speckle it with dirt, reminding us that the housewife, who once protected us from such intrusions, will protect us no longer. Their presence is threatening but only in a minor way, "dull" like themselves. They are a background noise we do not have to deal with yet.

In "I heard a Fly buzz," on the other hand, there is only one fly and its buzz is not only foregrounded. Before the poem is over, the buzz takes up the entire field of perception, coming between the speaker and the "light" (of day, of life, of knowledge). It is then that the "Windows" (the eyes that are the windows of the soul as well as, metonymically, the light that passes through the panes of glass) "fail" and the speaker is left in darkness—in death, in ignorance. She cannot "see" to "see" (understand).

Given that the only sure thing we know about "life after death" is that flies—in their adult form and more particularly, as maggots—devour us, the poem is at the very least a grim joke. In projecting her death-bed scene, Dickinson confronts her ignorance and gives back the only answer human knowledge can with any certainty give. While we may hope for an afterlife, no one, not even the dying, can prove it exists.

From Emily Dickinson: Woman Poet

CONSIDERATIONS FOR CRITICAL THINKING AND WRITING

1. According to Bennett, what is the symbolic value of the fly?

2. Does Bennett leave out any significant elements of the poem in her analysis? Explain why you think she did or did not.

3. Choose a Dickinson poem and write a detailed analysis that attempts to account for all of its major elements.

MARTHA NELL SMITH (B. 1953)

On "Because I could not stop for Death —" *1993*

That this poem begins and ends with humanity's ultimate dream of self-importance — Immortality and Eternity — could well be the joke central to its meaning, for Dickinson carefully surrounds the fantasy of living ever after with the dirty facts of life — dusty carriage rides, schoolyards, and farmers' fields. Many may contend that, like the Puritans and metaphysicals before her, Dickinson pulls the sublime down to the ridiculous but unavoidable facts of existence, thus imbues life on earth with its real import. On the other hand, Dickinson may have argued otherwise. Very late in her life, she wrote, "When Jesus tells us about his Father, we distrust him. When he shows us his Home, we turn away, but when he confides to us that he is 'acquainted with Grief,' we listen, for that is also an Acquaintance of our own." Instead of sharing their faith, Dickinson may be showing the community around her, most of whom were singing "When we all get to Heaven what a day of rejoicing that will be," how selfishly selective is their belief in a system that bolsters egocentrism by assuring believers not only that their individual identities will survive death, but also that they are one of the exclusive club of the saved. Waiting for the return of Eden or Paradise, which "is always eligible" and which she "never believed . . . to be a superhuman site," those believers may simply find themselves gathering dust. Surrounded by the faithful, Dickinson struggled with trust and doubt in Christian promises herself, but whether she believed in salvation or even in immortality is endlessly debatable. Readers can select poems and letters and construct compelling arguments to prove that she did or did not. But for every declaration evincing belief, there is one like that to Elizabeth Holland:

> The Fiction of "Santa Claus" always reminds me of the reply to my early question of "Who made the Bible" — "Holy Men moved by the Holy Ghost," and though I have now ceased my investigations, the Solution is insufficient —

What "Because I could not stop for Death —" will not allow is any hard and fast conclusion to be drawn about the matter. Once again . . . by mixing tropes and tones Dickinson underscores the importance of refusing any single-minded response to a subject and implicitly attests to the power in continually opening possibilities by repeatedly posing questions.

From *Comic Power in Emily Dickinson*, by Suzanne Juhasz,
Cristanne Miller, and Martha Nell Smith

CONSIDERATIONS FOR CRITICAL THINKING AND WRITING

1. In what sense, according to Smith, could a joke be central to the meaning of "Because I could not stop for Death —"?

2. Compare the potential joke in this poem and in "I know that He exists" (p. 868). How is your reading of each poem influenced by considering them together?

3. Read the sample paper on "Religious Faith in Four Poems by Emily Dickinson" (pp. 870–73) and write an analysis of "Because I could not stop for Death —" that supports or refutes the paper's thesis.

RONALD WALLACE (B. 1945)

Miss Goff   *1994*

When Zack Pulanski brought the plastic vomit
and slid it slickly to the vinyl floor
and raised his hand, and her tired eyes fell on it
with horror, the heartless classroom lost in laughter
as the custodian slyly tossed his saw dust on it   5
and pushed it, grinning, through the door,
she reached into her ancient corner closet
and found some Emily Dickinson mimeos there

which she passed out. And then, herself
passed out on the cold circumference of her desk.   10
And everybody went their merry ways
but me, who, chancing on one unexpected phrase
after another, sat transfixed until dusk.
Me and Miss Goff, the top of our heads taken off.

CONSIDERATIONS FOR CRITICAL THINKING AND WRITING

1. How does the joke played on Miss Goff in the first stanza give way to something more serious in the second stanza? Explain the shift in tone.

2. Characterize Miss Goff. How does the poem's diction reveal some of her personality?

3. Dickinson once described her own poetry by writing that "my business is circumference," and she made an attempt to define poetry with this comment: "If I read a book and it makes my whole body so cold no fire can ever warm me, I know *that* is poetry. If I feel physically as if the top of my head were taken off, I know *that* is poetry." How are these statements relevant to your understanding of Wallace's poem?

4. Discuss the use of irony in "Miss Goff."

Questions for Writing about an Author in Depth

As you read multiple works by the same author, you're likely to be struck by the similarities and differences in those selections. You'll begin to recognize situations, events, characters, issues, perspectives, styles, and strategies — even recurring words or phrases — that provide a kind of signature, making the poems in some way identifiable with that particular writer.

The following questions can help you to respond to multiple works by the same author. They should help you to listen to how a writer's works can speak to one another and to you. Additional useful questions can be found in other chapters of this book. See Chapter 19, "Writing about Poetry," and Arguing about Literature (p. 1565) in Chapter 47, "Reading and Writing."

1. What topics reappear in the writer's work? What seem to be the major concerns of the author?

2. Does the author have a definable worldview that can be discerned from work to work? Is, for example, the writer liberal, conservative, apolitical, or religious?

3. What social values come through in the author's work? Does he or she seem to identify with a particular group or social class?

4. Is there a consistent voice or point of view from work to work? Is it a persona or the author's actual self?

5. How much of the author's own life experiences and historical moment make their way into the works?

6. Does the author experiment with style from work to work, or are the works mostly consistent with one another?

7. Can the author's work be identified with a literary tradition, such as *carpe diem* poetry, that aligns his or her work with that of other writers?

8. What is distinctive about the author's writing? Is the language innovative? Are the themes challenging? Are the voices conventional? Is the tone characteristic?

9. Could you identify another work by the same author without a name being attached to it? What are the distinctive features that allow you to do so?

10. Do any of the writer's works seem *not* to be by that writer? Why?

11. What other writers are most like this author in style and content? Why?

12. Has the writer's work evolved over time? Are there significant changes or developments? Are there new ideas and styles, or do the works remain largely the same?

13. How would you characterize the author's writing habits? Is it possible to anticipate what goes on in different works, or are you surprised by their content or style?

14. Can difficult or ambiguous passages in a work be resolved by referring to a similar passage in another work?

15. What does the writer say about his or her own work? Do you trust the teller or the tale? Which do you think is more reliable?

A SAMPLE IN-DEPTH STUDY: FOUR POEMS BY EMILY DICKINSON

The following paper was written for an assignment that called for an analysis (about 750 words) on any topic that could be traced in three or four poems by Dickinson. The student, Michael Weitz, chose "'Faith' is a fine invention," "I know that He exists," "I never saw a Moor —," and "Apparently with no surprise."

Previous knowledge of a writer's work can set up useful expectations in a reader. In the case of the four Dickinson poems included in this section, religion emerges as a central topic linked to a number of issues, including faith, immortality, skepticism, and the nature of God. The student selected these poems because he noticed Dickinson's intense interest in religious faith owing to the many poems that explore a variety of religious attitudes in her work. He chose these four because they were closely related, but he might have found equally useful clusters of poems about love, nature, domestic life, or writing. What especially intrigued him was some of the information he read about Dickinson's sternly religious father and the orthodox nature of the religious values of her hometown of Amherst, Massachusetts. Because this paper was not a research paper, he did not pursue these issues beyond the level of the general remarks provided in an introduction to her poetry (though he might have). He did, however, use this biographical and historical information as a means of framing his search for poems that were related to one another. In doing so he discovered consistent concerns along with contradictory themes that became the basis of his paper.

"Faith" is a fine invention   c. 1860

"Faith" is a fine invention
When Gentlemen can *see* —
But *Microscopes* are prudent
In an Emergency.

I know that He exists   c. 1862

I know that He exists.
Somewhere — in Silence —
He has hid his rare life
From our gross eyes.

'Tis an instant's play.   5
'Tis a fond Ambush —
Just to make Bliss
Earn her own surprise!

But — should the play
Prove piercing earnest —   10
Should the glee-glaze —
In Death's — stiff — stare —

Would not the fun
Look too expensive!
Would not the jest —   15
Have crawled too far!

I never saw a Moor —

c. 1865

I never saw a Moor —
I never saw the Sea —
Yet know I how the Heather looks
And what a Billow be.

I never spoke with God
Nor visited in Heaven —
Yet certain am I of the spot
As if the Checks were given —

Apparently with no surprise

c. 1884

Apparently with no surprise
To any happy Flower
The Frost beheads it at its play —
In accidental power —
The blond Assassin passes on —
The Sun proceeds unmoved
To measure off another Day
For an Approving God.

A SAMPLE STUDENT PAPER

Religious Faith in Four Poems by Emily Dickinson

Michael Weitz

Professor Pearl

English 270

May 5, 2008

Religious Faith in Four Poems by Emily Dickinson

Introduction providing overview of faith in Dickinson's work

Thesis analyzing poet's attitudes toward God and religion

Throughout much of her poetry, Emily Dickinson wrestles with complex notions of God, faith, and religious devotion. She adheres to no consistent view of religion; rather, her poetry reveals a vision of God and faith that is constantly evolving. Dickinson's gods range from the strict and powerful Old Testament father to a loving spiritual guide to an irrational and ridiculous imaginary figure. Through these varying images of God, Dickinson portrays contrasting images of the meaning and validity of religious faith. Her work reveals competing attitudes toward religious devotion as conventional religious piety struggles with a more cynical perception of God and religious worship.

Analysis of religious piety in "I never saw a Moor—" supported with textual evidence

Dickinson's "I never saw a Moor--" reveals a vision of traditional religious sensibilities. Although the speaker readily admits that "I never spoke with God / Nor visited in Heaven--" ("I Never" lines 5-6), her devout faith in a supreme being does not waver. The poem appears to be a straightforward profession of true faith stemming from the argument that the proof of God's existence is the universe's existence. Dickinson's imagery therefore evolves from the natural to the supernatural, first establishing her convictions that Moors and Seas exist, in spite of her lack of personal contact with either. This leads to the foundation of her religious faith, again based not on physical experience but on intellectual convictions. The speaker professes that she believes in the existence of Heaven even without conclusive evidence:

Contrast between attitudes in "Moor" and other poems

"Yet certain am I of the spot / As if the Checks were given--" (7-8). But the appearance of such idealistic views of God and faith in "I never saw a Moor--" are transformed in Dickinson's other poems into a much more skeptical vision of the validity of religious piety.

Weitz 2

While faith is portrayed as an authentic and deeply important quality in "I never saw a Moor--," Dickinson's "'Faith' is a fine invention" portrays faith as much less essential. Faith is defined in the poem as "a fine invention" ("'Faith'" 1), suggesting that it is created by man for man and therefore is not a crucial aspect of the natural universe. Thus the strong idealistic faith of "I never saw a Moor--" becomes discredited in the face of scientific rationalism. The speaker compares religious faith with actual microscopes, both of which are meant to enhance one's vision in some way. But "Faith" is useful only "When Gentlemen can <u>see</u>--" already (2); "In an Emergency" (4), when one ostensibly cannot see, "<u>Microscopes</u> are prudent" (3). Dickinson pits religion against science, suggesting that science, with its tangible evidence and rational attitude, is a more reliable lens through which to view the world. Faith is irreverently reduced to a mere invention and one that is ultimately less useful than microscopes or other scientific instruments.

Rational, scientific observations are not the only contributing factor to the portrayal of religious skepticism in Dickinson's poems; nature itself is seen to be incompatible in some ways with conventional religious ideology. In "Apparently with no surprise," the speaker recognizes the inexorable cycle of natural life and death as a morning frost kills a flower. But the tension in this poem stems not from the "happy Flower" struck down by the frost's "accidental power" but from the apparent indifference of the "Approving God" who condones this seemingly cruel and unnecessary death ("Apparently" 2, 4, 8). God is seen as remote and uncompromising, and it is this perceived distance between the speaker and God that reveals the increasing absurdity of traditional religious faith. The speaker understands that praying to God or believing in religion cannot change the course of nature, and as a result feels so helplessly distanced from God that religious faith becomes virtually meaningless.

Dickinson's religious skepticism becomes even more explicit in "I know that He exists," in which the speaker attempts to understand the connection between seeing God and facing death. In this poem Dickinson characterizes God as a remote and mysterious figure; the speaker mockingly asserts, "I know that He exists" (1), even though "He has hid his rare life / From our gross eyes" (3-4). The skepticism toward religious faith revealed in this

Analysis of scientific rationalism in " 'Faith' is a fine invention" supported with textual evidence

Analysis of God and nature in "Apparently with no surprise" supported with textual evidence

Analysis of characterization of God in "I know that He exists" supported with textual evidence poem stems from the speaker's recognition of the paradoxical quest that people undertake to know and to see God. A successful attempt to see God, to win the game of hide-and-seek that He apparently is orchestrating, results inevitably in death. With this recognition the speaker comes to view religion as an absurd and reckless game in which the prize may be "Bliss" but more likely is "Death's--stiff--stare--" ("I know" 7, 12). For to see God and to meet one's death as a result certainly suggests that the game of trying to see God (the so-called "fun" in line 13) is much "too expensive" and that religion itself is a "jest" that, like the serpent in Genesis, has "crawled too far" (14–16).

Ultimately, the vision of religious faith that Dickinson describes in her poems is one of suspicion and cynicism. She cannot reconcile the physical world to the spiritual existence that Christian doctrine teaches, and as a result the traditional perception of God becomes ludicrous. "I never saw a Moor--" does attempt to sustain a conventional vision of religious devotion, but Dickinson's poems overall are far more likely to suggest that God is elusive, indifferent, and often cruel, thus undermining the traditional vision of God as a loving father worthy of devout worship. Thus, not only religious faith but also those who are religiously faithful become targets for Dickinson's irreverent criticism of conventional belief.

Conclusion providing well-supported final analysis of poet's views on God and faith.

Weitz 4

Works Cited

Dickinson, Emily. "Apparently with no surprise." <u>The Compact Bedford Intro-</u>
<u>duction to Literature</u>. Ed. Michael Meyer. 8th ed. Boston. Bedford/
St. Martin's, 2009. 869.

---. "'Faith' is a fine invention." <u>The Compact Bedford Introduction to Litera-</u>
<u>ture</u>. Ed. Michael Meyer. 8th ed. Boston. Bedford/St. Martin's, 2009.
868.

---. "I know that He exists." <u>The Compact Bedford Introduction to Literature</u>.
Ed. Michael Meyer. 8th ed. Boston. Bedford/St. Martin's, 2009. 868.

---. "I never saw a Moor--." <u>The Compact Bedford Introduction to Literature</u>.
Ed. Michael Meyer. 8th ed. Boston. Bedford/St. Martin's, 2009. 869.

SUGGESTED TOPICS FOR LONGER PAPERS

1. Irony is abundant in Dickinson's poetry. Choose five poems from this chapter that strike you as especially ironic and discuss her use of irony in each. Taken individually and collectively, what do these poems suggest to you about the poet's sensibilities and her ways of looking at the world?

2. Readers have often noted that Dickinson's poetry does not reflect very much of the social, political, economic, religious, and historical events of her lifetime. Using the poems in this chapter as the basis of your discussion, what can you say about the contexts in which Dickinson wrote? What kind of world do you think she inhabited, and how did she respond to it?

Web Research
Emily Dickinson at
bedfordstmartins.com/
meyercompact.

30

A Study of Robert Frost

A poem . . . begins as a lump in the throat, a sense of wrong, a homesickness, a love-sickness. . . . It finds the thought and the thought finds the words.

— ROBERT FROST

Every poem is doubtlessly affected by the personal history of its composer, but Robert Frost's poems are especially known for their reflection of New England life. Although the poems included in this chapter evoke the landscapes of Frost's life and work, the depth and range of those landscapes are far more complicated than his popular reputation typically acknowledges. He was an enormously private man and a much more subtle poet than many of his readers believed him to be. His poems warrant careful, close readings. As you explore his poetry, you may find useful the Questions for Writing about an

> **Explore contexts for Robert Frost on *LiterActive*.**

Robert Frost

Author in Depth (p. 866) as a means of stimulating your thinking about his life and work.

A BRIEF BIOGRAPHY

Few poets have enjoyed the popular success that Robert Frost (1874–1963) achieved during his lifetime, and no twentieth-century American poet's work has been as widely read and honored. Frost is as much associated with New England as the stone walls that help define its landscape; his reputation, however, transcends regional boundaries. Although he was named poet laureate of Vermont only two years before his death, he was for many years the nation's unofficial poet laureate. Frost collected honors the way some people pick up burrs on country walks. Among his awards were four Pulitzer Prizes, the Bollingen Prize, a Congressional Medal, and dozens of honorary degrees. Perhaps his most moving appearance was his recitation of "The Gift Outright" for millions of Americans at the inauguration of John F. Kennedy in 1961.

Frost's recognition as a poet is especially remarkable because his career as a writer did not attract any significant attention until he was nearly forty years old. He taught himself to write while he labored at odd jobs, taught school, or farmed.

Frost's early identity seems very remote from the New England soil. Although his parents were descended from generations of New Englanders, he was born in San Francisco and was named Robert Lee Frost after the Confederate general. After his father died in 1885, his mother moved the family back to Massachusetts to live with relatives. Frost graduated from high school sharing valedictorian honors with the classmate who would become his wife three years later. Between high school and marriage, he attended Dartmouth College for a few months and then taught. His teaching prompted him to enroll in Harvard in 1897, but after fewer than two years he withdrew without a degree (though Harvard would eventually award him an honorary doctorate in 1937, four years after Dartmouth conferred its honorary degree on him). For the next decade, Frost read and wrote poems when he was not chicken farming or teaching. In 1912, he sold his farm and moved his family to England, where he hoped to find the audience that his poetry did not have in America.

Three years in England made it possible for Frost to return home as a poet. His first two volumes of poetry, *A Boy's Will* (1913) and *North of Boston* (1914), were published in England. During the next twenty years, honors and awards were conferred on collections such as *Mountain Interval* (1916), *New Hampshire* (1923), *West-Running Brook* (1928), and *A Further Range* (1936). These are the volumes on which most of Frost's popular and critical reputation rests. Later collections include *A Witness Tree* (1942), *A Masque of*

Reason (1945), *Steeple Bush* (1947), *A Masque of Mercy* (1947), *Complete Poems* (1949), and *In the Clearing* (1962). In addition to publishing his works, Frost endeared himself to audiences throughout the country by presenting his poetry almost as conversations. He also taught at a number of schools, including Amherst College, the University of Michigan, Harvard University, Dartmouth College, and Middlebury College.

Frost's countless poetry readings generated wide audiences eager to claim him as their poet. The image he cultivated resembled closely what the public likes to think a poet should be. Frost was seen as a lovable, wise old man; his simple wisdom and cracker-barrel sayings appeared comforting and homey. From this Yankee rustic, audiences learned that "There's a lot yet that isn't understood" or "We love the things we love for what they are" or "Good fences make good neighbors."

In a sense, Frost packaged himself for public consumption. "I am . . . my own salesman," he said. When asked direct questions about the meanings of his poems, he often winked or scratched his head to give the

Robert Frost at age eighteen (1892). This photo of the poet was taken the year he graduated from high school. "Education," Frost once said, "is the ability to listen to almost anything without losing your temper or your self-confidence."

Courtesy of Rauner Special Collections Library, Dartmouth College.

Robert Frost at age forty-seven (1921). This photo was taken on the grounds of Stone Cottage in Shaftsbury, Vermont. Frost wrote, "I would have written of me on my stone: / I had a lover's quarrel with the world."

Courtesy of Rauner Special Collections Library, Dartmouth College.

Robert Frost (1915). Shown here is the poet at his writing desk in Franconia, New Hampshire. "I have never started a poem whose end I knew," Frost said, "writing a poem is discovering."

impression that the customer was always right. To be sure, there is a simplicity in Frost's language, but that simplicity does not fully reflect the depth of the man, the complexity of his themes, or the richness of his art.

The folksy optimist behind the public lectern did not reveal his private troubles to his audiences, although he did address those problems at his writing desk. Frost suffered from professional jealousies, anger, and depression. His family life was especially painful. Three of his four children died: a son at the age of four, a daughter in her late twenties from tuberculosis, and another son by suicide. His marriage was filled with tension. Although Frost's work is landscaped with sunlight, snow, birches, birds, blueberries, and squirrels, it is important to recognize that he was also intimately "acquainted with the night," a phrase that serves as the haunting title of one of his poems (see p. 703).

As a corrective to Frost's popular reputation, one critic, Lionel Trilling, described the world Frost creates in his poems as a "terrifying universe," characterized by loneliness, anguish, frustration, doubts, disappointment, and despair. To point this out is not to annihilate the pleasantness and even good-natured cheerfulness that can be enjoyed in Frost's poetry, but it is to say that Frost is not so one-dimensional as he is sometimes assumed to be. Frost's poetry requires readers who are alert and willing to penetrate the simplicity of its language to see the elusive and ambiguous meanings that lie below the surface.

AN INTRODUCTION TO HIS WORK

Frost's treatment of nature helps to explain the various levels of meaning in his poetry. The familiar natural world his poems evoke is sharply detailed. We hear icy branches clicking against themselves, we see the snow-white trunks of birches, we feel the smarting pain of a twig lashing across a face. The aspects of the natural world Frost describes are designated to give pleasure, but they are also frequently calculated to provoke thought. His use of nature tends to be symbolic. Complex meanings are derived from simple facts, such as a spider killing a moth or the difference between fire and ice (see "Design," p. 895, and "Fire and Ice," p. 893). Although Frost's strategy is to talk about particular events and individual experiences, his poems evoke universal issues.

Frost's poetry has strong regional roots and is "versed in country things," but it flourishes in any receptive imagination because, in the final analysis, it is concerned with human beings. Frost's New England landscapes are the occasion rather than the ultimate focus of his poems. Like the rural voices he creates in his poems, Frost typically approaches his themes indirectly. He explained the reason for this in a talk titled "Education by Poetry":

> Poetry provides the one permissible way of saying one thing and meaning another. People say, "Why don't you say what you mean?" We never do that, do we, being all of us too much poets. We like to talk in parables and in hints and in indirections — whether from diffidence or some other instinct.

The result is that the settings, characters, and situations that make up the subject matter of Frost's poems are vehicles for his perceptions about life.

In "Stopping by Woods on a Snowy Evening" (p. 893), for example, Frost uses the kind of familiar New England details that constitute his poetry for more than descriptive purposes. He shapes them into a meditation on the tension we sometimes feel between life's responsibilities and the "lovely, dark, and deep" attraction that death offers. When the speaker's horse "gives his harness bells a shake," we are reminded that we are confronting a universal theme as well as a quiet moment of natural beauty.

Among the major concerns that appear in Frost's poetry are the fragility of life, the consequences of rejecting or accepting the conditions of one's life, the passion of inconsolable grief, the difficulty of sustaining intimacy, the fear of loneliness and isolation, the inevitability of change, the tensions between the individual and society, and the place of tradition and custom.

Whatever theme is encountered in a poem by Frost, a reader is likely to agree with him that "the initial delight is in the surprise of remembering something I didn't know." To achieve that fresh sense of discovery, Frost allowed himself to follow his instincts; his poetry

> inclines to the impulse, it assumes direction with the first line laid down, it runs a course of lucky events, and ends in a clarification of life — not necessarily a

great clarification, such as sects and cults are founded on, but in a momentary stay against confusion.

This description from "On The Figure a Poem Makes" (see p. 901 for the complete essay), Frost's brief introduction to *Complete Poems,* may sound as if his poetry is formless and merely "lucky," but his poems tend to be more conventional than experimental: "The artist in me," as he put the matter in one of his poems, "cries out for design."

From Frost's perspective, "free verse is like playing tennis with the net down." He exercised his own freedom in meeting the challenges of rhyme and meter. His use of fixed forms such as couplets, tercets, quatrains, blank verse, and sonnets was not slavish because he enjoyed working them into the natural English speech patterns — especially the rhythms, idioms, and tones of speakers living north of Boston — that give voice to his themes. Frost often liked to use "Stopping by Woods on a Snowy Evening" as an example of his graceful way of making conventions appear natural and inevitable. He explored "the old ways to be new."

Frost's eye for strong, telling details was matched by his ear for natural speech rhythms. His flexible use of what he called "iambic and loose iambic" enabled him to create moving lyric poems that reveal the personal thoughts of a speaker and dramatic poems that convincingly characterize people caught in intense emotional situations. The language in his poems appears to be little more than a transcription of casual and even rambling speech, but it is in actuality Frost's poetic creation, carefully crafted to reveal the joys and sorrows that are woven into people's daily lives. What is missing from Frost's poems is artificiality, not art. Consider this poem.

The Road Not Taken   1916

Two roads diverged in a yellow wood,
And sorry I could not travel both
And be one traveler, long I stood
And looked down one as far as I could
To where it bent in the undergrowth;   5

Then took the other, as just as fair,
And having perhaps the better claim,
Because it was grassy and wanted wear;
Though as for that the passing there
Had worn them really about the same,   10

And both that morning equally lay
In leaves no step had trodden black.
Oh, I kept the first for another day!
Yet knowing how way leads on to way,
I doubted if I should ever come back.   15

I shall be telling this with a sigh
Somewhere ages and ages hence:
Two roads diverged in a wood, and I —
I took the one less traveled by,
And that has made all the difference.   20

This poem intrigues readers because it is at once so simple and so deeply resonant. Recalling a walk in the woods, the speaker describes how he came to a fork in the road, which forced him to choose one path over another. Though "sorry" that he "could not travel both," he made a choice after carefully weighing his two options. This, essentially, is what happens in the poem; there is no other action. However, the incident is charged with symbolic significance by the speaker's reflections on the necessity and consequences of his decision.

The final stanza indicates that the choice concerns more than simply walking down a road, for the speaker says that choosing the "less traveled" path has affected his entire life — that "that has made all the difference." Frost draws on a familiar enough metaphor when he compares life to a journey, but he is also calling attention to a less commonly noted problem: despite our expectations, aspirations, appetites, hopes, and desires, we can't have it all. Making one choice precludes another. It is impossible to determine what particular decision the speaker refers to: perhaps he had to choose a college, a career, a spouse; perhaps he was confronted with mutually exclusive ideas, beliefs, or values. There is no way to know because Frost wisely creates a symbolic choice and implicitly invites us to supply our own circumstances.

The speaker's reflections about his choice are as central to an understanding of the poem as the choice itself; indeed, they may be more central. He describes the road taken as "having perhaps the better claim, / Because it was grassy and wanted wear"; he prefers the "less traveled" path. This seems to be an expression of individualism, which would account for "the difference" his choice made in his life. But Frost complicates matters by having the speaker also acknowledge that there was no significant difference between the two roads; one was "just as fair" as the other; each was "worn . . . really about the same"; and "both that morning equally lay / In leaves no step had trodden black."

The speaker imagines that in the future, "ages and ages hence," he will recount his choice with "a sigh" that will satisfactorily explain the course of his life, but Frost seems to be having a little fun here by showing us how the speaker will embellish his past decision to make it appear more dramatic. What we hear is someone trying to convince himself that the choice he made significantly changed his life. When he recalls what happened in the "yellow wood," a color that gives a glow to that irretrievable moment when his life seemed to be on the verge of a momentous change, he appears more concerned with the path he did not choose than with the one he took. Frost shrewdly titles the poem to suggest the speaker's sense of loss at not being able to "travel both" roads. When the speaker's reflections about his choice are examined, the poem reveals his nostalgia instead of affirming his decision to travel a self-reliant path in life.

The rhymed stanzas of "The Road Not Taken" follow a pattern established in the first five lines (*abaab*). This rhyme scheme reflects, perhaps, the speaker's efforts to shape his life into a pleasing and coherent form. The natural speech rhythms Frost uses allow him to integrate the rhymes unobtrusively, but there is a slight shift in lines 19 and 20, when the speaker asserts self-consciously that the "less traveled" road — which we already know to be basically the same as the other road — "made all the difference." Unlike all of the other rhymes in the poem, "difference" does not rhyme precisely with "hence." The emphasis that must be placed on "differ*ence*" to make it rhyme perfectly with "hence" may suggest that the speaker is trying just a little too hard to pattern his life on his earlier choice in the woods.

Perhaps the best way to begin reading Frost's poetry is to accept the invitation he placed at the beginning of many volumes of his poems. "The Pasture" means what it says of course; it is about taking care of some farm chores, but it is also a means of "saying one thing in terms of another."

The Pasture   1913

I'm going out to clean the pasture spring;
I'll only stop to rake the leaves away
(And wait to watch the water clear, I may):
I shan't be gone long. — You come too.

I'm going out to fetch the little calf
That's standing by the mother. It's so young
It totters when she licks it with her tongue.
I shan't be gone long. — You come too.

"The Pasture" is a simple but irresistible songlike invitation to the pleasure of looking at the world through the eyes of a poet.

Mowing   1913

There was never a sound beside the wood but one,
And that was my long scythe whispering to the ground.
What was it it whispered? I knew not well myself;
Perhaps it was something about the heat of the sun,
Something, perhaps, about the lack of sound —   5
And that was why it whispered and did not speak.
It was no dream of the gift of idle hours,
Or easy gold at the hand of fay or elf:

Anything more than the truth would have seemed too weak
To the earnest love that laid the swale in rows,   10
Not without feeble-pointed spikes of flowers
(Pale orchises), and scared a bright green snake.
The fact is the sweetest dream that labour knows.
My long scythe whispered and left the hay to make.

CONSIDERATIONS FOR CRITICAL THINKING AND WRITING

1. **FIRST RESPONSE.** Describe the tone of "Mowing." How does reading the poem aloud affect your understanding of it?
2. Discuss the image of the scythe. Do you think it has any symbolic value? Explain why or why not.
3. Paraphrase the poem. What do you think its thematic significance is?
4. Describe the type of sonnet Frost uses in "Mowing."

My November Guest   1913

My Sorrow, when she's here with me,
  Thinks these dark days of autumn rain
Are beautiful as days can be;
She loves the bare, the withered tree;
  She walks the sodden pasture lane.   5

Her pleasure will not let me stay.
  She talks and I am fain to list:
She's glad the birds are gone away,
She's glad her simple worsted grey
  Is silver now with clinging mist.   10

The desolate, deserted trees,
  The faded earth, the heavy sky,
The beauties she so truly sees,
She thinks I have no eye for these,
  And vexes me for reason why.   15

Not yesterday I learned to know
  The love of bare November days
Before the coming of the snow,
But it were vain to tell her so,
  And they are better for her praise.   20

CONSIDERATIONS FOR CRITICAL THINKING AND WRITING

1. **FIRST RESPONSE.** How is "Sorrow" personified? What sort of relationship does the speaker have with her?
2. What kind of tone do the poem's images create?
3. What do you think is this poem's theme?

CONNECTION TO ANOTHER SELECTION

1. Compare Frost's treatment of November with Margaret Atwood's evocation of "February" (p. 693). Explain why you prefer one poem over the other.

Storm Fear   1913

I count our strength,
Two and a child,
Those of us not asleep subdued to mark
How the cold creeps as the fire dies at length,—
How drifts are piled,   5
Dooryard and road ungraded,
Till even the comforting barn grows far away,
And my heart owns a doubt
Whether 'tis in us to arise with day
And save ourselves unaided.   10
When the wind works against us in the dark,
And pelts with snow
The lower chamber window on the east,
And whispers with a sort of stifled bark,
The beast,   15
"Come out! Come out!"—
It costs no inward struggle not to go,
Ah, no!

CONSIDERATIONS FOR CRITICAL THINKING AND WRITING

1. FIRST RESPONSE. What is the "inward struggle" (line 17) in this poem?

2. How is winter depicted by the speaker? What emotions does winter produce in the speaker?

3. Describe the rhyme scheme and its effects on your reading the poem aloud.

CONNECTION TO ANOTHER SELECTION

1. Compare the perspectives on nature in "Storm Fear" and in Emily Dickinson's "Presentiment—is that long Shadow—on the lawn" (p. 684). How are they both poems about fear?

Mending Wall   1914

Something there is that doesn't love a wall,
That sends the frozen-ground-swell under it,
And spills the upper boulders in the sun;
And makes gaps even two can pass abreast.

The work of hunters is another thing: 5
I have come after them and made repair
Where they have left not one stone on a stone,
But they would have the rabbit out of hiding,
To please the yelping dogs. The gaps I mean,
No one has seen them made or heard them made, 10
But at spring mending-time we find them there.
I let my neighbor know beyond the hill;
And on a day we meet to walk the line
And set the wall between us once again.
We keep the wall between us as we go. 15
To each the boulders that have fallen to each.
And some are loaves and some so nearly balls
We have to use a spell to make them balance:
"Stay where you are until our backs are turned!"
We wear our fingers rough with handling them. 20
Oh, just another kind of outdoor game,
One on a side. It comes to little more:
There where it is we do not need the wall:
He is all pine and I am apple orchard.
My apple trees will never get across 25
And eat the cones under his pines, I tell him.
He only says, "Good fences make good neighbors."
Spring is the mischief in me, and I wonder
If I could put a notion in his head:
"*Why* do they make good neighbors? Isn't it 30
Where there are cows? But here there are no cows.
Before I built a wall I'd ask to know
What I was walling in or walling out,
And to whom I was like to give offense.
Something there is that doesn't love a wall, 35
That wants it down." I could say "Elves" to him,
But it's not elves exactly, and I'd rather
He said it for himself. I see him there
Bringing a stone grasped firmly by the top
In each hand, like an old-stone savage armed. 40
He moves in darkness as it seems to me,
Not of woods only and the shade of trees.
He will not go behind his father's saying,
And he likes having thought of it so well
He says again, "Good fences make good neighbors." 45

CONSIDERATIONS FOR CRITICAL THINKING AND WRITING

1. **FIRST RESPONSE.** What might the "Something" be that "doesn't love a wall"? Why does the speaker remind his neighbor each spring that the wall needs to be repaired? Is it ironic that the *speaker* initiates the mending? Is there anything good about the wall?

2. How do the speaker and his neighbor in this poem differ in sensibilities? What is suggested about the neighbor in lines 41 and 42?

You make me angry. I'll come down to you.
God, what a woman! And it's come to this,
A man can't speak of his own child that's dead."

"You can't because you don't know how to speak.   75
If you had any feelings, you that dug
With your own hand — how could you? — his little grave;
I saw you from that very window there,
Making the gravel leap and leap in air,
Leap up, like that, like that, and land so lightly   80
And roll back down the mound beside the hole.
I thought, Who is that man? I didn't know you.
And I crept down the stairs and up the stairs
To look again, and still your spade kept lifting.
Then you came in. I heard your rumbling voice   85
Out in the kitchen, and I don't know why,
But I went near to see with my own eyes.
You could sit there with the stains on your shoes
Of the fresh earth from your own baby's grave
And talk about your everyday concerns.   90
You had stood the spade up against the wall
Outside there in the entry, for I saw it."

"I shall laugh the worst laugh I ever laughed.
I'm cursed. God, if I don't believe I'm cursed."

"I can repeat the very words you were saying.   95
'Three foggy mornings and one rainy day
Will rot the best birch fence a man can build.'
Think of it, talk like that at such a time!
What had how long it takes a birch to rot
To do with what was in the darkened parlor   100
You *couldn't* care! The nearest friends can go
With anyone to death, comes so far short
They might as well not try to go at all.
No, from the time when one is sick to death,
One is alone, and he dies more alone.   105
Friends make pretense of following to the grave.
But before one is in it, their minds are turned
And making the best of their way back to life
And living people, and things they understand.
But the world's evil. I won't have grief so   110
If I can change it. Oh, I won't, I won't!"

"There, you have said it all and you feel better.
You won't go now. You're crying. Close the door.
The heart's gone out of it: why keep it up.
Amy! There's someone coming down the road!"   115

"*You* — oh, you think the talk is all. I must go —
Somewhere out of this house. How can I make you —"

"If — you — do!" She was opening the door wider.
"Where do you mean to go? First tell me that.
I'll follow and bring you back by force. I *will!* —" 120

CONSIDERATIONS FOR CRITICAL THINKING AND WRITING

1. **FIRST RESPONSE.** This poem tells a story of a relationship. Is the husband insensitive and indifferent to his wife's grief? Characterize the wife. Has Frost invited us to sympathize with one character more than with the other?

2. How has the burial of the child within sight of the stairway window affected the relationship of the couple in this poem? Is the child's grave a symptom or a cause of the conflict between them?

3. What is the effect of splitting the iambic pentameter pattern in lines 18 and 19, 31 and 32, 45 and 46, and 70 and 71?

4. Is the conflict resolved at the conclusion of the poem? Do you think the husband and wife will overcome their differences?

After Apple-Picking   1914

My long two-pointed ladder's sticking through a tree
Toward heaven still,
And there's a barrel that I didn't fill
Beside it, and there may be two or three
Apples I didn't pick upon some bough.   5
But I am done with apple-picking now.
Essence of winter sleep is on the night,
The scent of apples: I am drowsing off.
I cannot rub the strangeness from my sight
I got from looking through a pane of glass   10
I skimmed this morning from the drinking trough
And held against the world of hoary grass.
It melted, and I let it fall and break.
But I was well
Upon my way to sleep before it fell,   15
And I could tell
What form my dreaming was about to take.
Magnified apples appear and disappear,
Stem end and blossom end,
And every fleck of russet showing clear.   20
My instep arch not only keeps the ache,
It keeps the pressure of a ladder-round.
I feel the ladder sway as the boughs bend.
And I keep hearing from the cellar bin
The rumbling sound   25
Of load on load of apples coming in.
For I have had too much

Of apple-picking: I am overtired
Of the great harvest I myself desired.
There were ten thousand thousand fruit to touch,   30
Cherish in hand, lift down, and not let fall.
For all
That struck the earth,
No matter if not bruised or spiked with stubble,
Went surely to the cider-apple heap   35
As of no worth.
One can see what will trouble
This sleep of mine, whatever sleep it is.
Were he not gone,
The woodchuck could say whether it's like his   40
Long sleep, as I describe its coming on,
Or just some human sleep.

CONSIDERATIONS FOR CRITICAL THINKING AND WRITING

1. **FIRST RESPONSE.** How does this poem illustrate Frost's view that "Poetry provides the one permissible way of saying one thing and meaning another"? When do you first sense that the detailed description of apple picking is being used that way?

2. What comes after apple picking? What does the speaker worry about in the dream beginning in line 18?

3. Why do you suppose Frost uses apples rather than, say, pears or squash?

Birches   *1916*

When I see birches bend to left and right
Across the lines of straighter darker trees,
I like to think some boy's been swinging them.
But swinging doesn't bend them down to stay
As ice-storms do. Often you must have seen them   5
Loaded with ice a sunny winter morning
After a rain. They click upon themselves
As the breeze rises, and turn many-colored
As the stir cracks and crazes their enamel.
Soon the sun's warmth makes them shed crystal shells   10
Shattering and avalanching on the snow-crust —
Such heaps of broken glass to sweep away
You'd think the inner dome of heaven had fallen.
They are dragged to the withered bracken by the load,
And they seem not to break; though once they are bowed   15
So low for long, they never right themselves:
You may see their trunks arching in the woods
Years afterwards, trailing their leaves on the ground
Like girls on hands and knees that throw their hair

Before them over their heads to dry in the sun.   20
But I was going to say when Truth broke in
With all her matter-of-fact about the ice-storm,
I should prefer to have some boy bend them
As he went out and in to fetch the cows —
Some boy too far from town to learn baseball,   25
Whose only play was what he found himself,
Summer or winter, and could play alone.
One by one he subdued his father's trees
By riding them down over and over again
Until he took the stiffness out of them,   30
And not one but hung limp, not one was left
For him to conquer. He learned all there was
To learn about not launching out too soon
And so not carrying the tree away
Clear to the ground. He always kept his poise   35
To the top branches, climbing carefully
With the same pains you use to fill a cup
Up to the brim, and even above the brim.
Then he flung outward, feet first, with a swish,
Kicking his way down through the air to the ground.   40
So was I once myself a swinger of birches.
And so I dream of going back to be.
It's when I'm weary of considerations,
And life is too much like a pathless wood
Where your face burns and tickles with the cobwebs   45
Broken across it, and one eye is weeping
From a twig's having lashed across it open.
I'd like to get away from earth awhile
And then come back to it and begin over.
May no fate willfully misunderstand me   50
And half grant what I wish and snatch me away
Not to return. Earth's the right place for love:
I don't know where it's likely to go better.
I'd like to go by climbing a birch tree,
And climb black branches up a snow-white trunk,   55
Toward heaven, till the tree could bear no more,
But dipped its top and set me down again.
That would be good both going and coming back.
One could do worse than be a swinger of birches.

CONSIDERATIONS FOR CRITICAL THINKING AND WRITING

1. **FIRST RESPONSE.** What do you think the swinging of birches symbolizes?

2. Why does the speaker in this poem prefer the birches to have been bent by boys instead of ice storms?

3. How is "earth" (line 52) described in the poem? Why does the speaker choose it over "heaven" (line 56)?

4. How might the effect of this poem be changed if it were written in heroic couplets instead of blank verse?

5. CRITICAL STRATEGIES. Read the section on reader-response strategies (pp. 1552–54) in Chapter 46, "Critical Strategies for Reading." Trace your response to this poem over three successive careful readings. How does your understanding of the poem change or develop?

"Out, Out —"°   1916

The buzz-saw snarled and rattled in the yard
And made dust and dropped stove-length sticks of wood,
Sweet-scented stuff when the breeze drew across it.
And from there those that lifted eyes could count
Five mountain ranges one behind the other   5
Under the sunset far into Vermont.
And the saw snarled and rattled, snarled and rattled,
As it ran light, or had to bear a load.
And nothing happened: day was all but done.
Call it a day, I wish they might have said   10
To please the boy by giving him the half hour
That a boy counts so much when saved from work.
His sister stood beside them in her apron
To tell them "Supper." At the word, the saw,
As if to prove saws knew what supper meant,   15
Leaped out at the boy's hand, or seemed to leap —
He must have given the hand. However it was,
Neither refused the meeting. But the hand!
The boy's first outcry was a rueful laugh,
As he swung toward them holding up the hand   20
Half in appeal, but half as if to keep
The life from spilling. Then the boy saw all —
Since he was old enough to know, big boy
Doing a man's work, though a child at heart —
He saw all spoiled. "Don't let him cut my hand off —   25
The doctor, when he comes. Don't let him, sister!"
So. But the hand was gone already.
The doctor put him in the dark of ether.
He lay and puffed his lips out with his breath.
And then — the watcher at his pulse took fright.   30
No one believed. They listened at his heart.
Little — less — nothing! — and that ended it.
No more to build on there. And they, since they
Were not the one dead, turned to their affairs.

"Out, Out —": From Act V, Scene v, of Shakespeare's *Macbeth*.

CONSIDERATIONS FOR CRITICAL THINKING AND WRITING

1. FIRST RESPONSE. This narrative poem is about the accidental death of a Vermont boy. What is the purpose of the story? Some readers have argued that

the final lines reveal the speaker's callousness and indifference. What do you think?

2. How does Frost's allusion to *Macbeth* contribute to the meaning of this poem? Does the speaker seem to agree with the view of life expressed in Macbeth's lines?

3. CRITICAL STRATEGIES. Read the section on Marxist criticism (pp. 1545–46) in Chapter 46, "Critical Strategies for Reading." How do you think a Marxist critic would interpret the family and events described in this poem?

CONNECTIONS TO OTHER SELECTIONS

1. What are the similarities and differences in theme between this poem and Frost's "Nothing Gold Can Stay" (p. 894)?

2. Write an essay comparing how grief is handled by the boy's family in this poem and the couple in "Home Burial" (p. 886).

3. Compare the tone and theme of "'Out, Out—'" with those of Stephen Crane's "A Man Said to the Universe" (p. 711).

Fire and Ice 1923

Some say the world will end in fire,
Some say in ice.
From what I've tasted of desire
I hold with those who favor fire.
But if it had to perish twice,
I think I know enough of hate
To say that for destruction ice
Is also great
And would suffice.

CONSIDERATIONS FOR CRITICAL THINKING AND WRITING

1. FIRST RESPONSE. What characteristics of human behavior does the speaker associate with fire and ice?

2. What theories about the end of the world are alluded to in lines 1 and 2?

3. How does the speaker's use of understatement and rhyme affect the tone of this poem?

Stopping by Woods on a Snowy Evening 1923

Whose woods these are I think I know.
His house is in the village, though;
He will not see me stopping here
To watch his woods fill up with snow.

My little horse must think it queer   5
To stop without a farmhouse near
Between the woods and frozen lake
The darkest evening of the year.

He gives his harness bells a shake
To ask if there is some mistake.   10
The only other sound's the sweep
Of easy wind and downy flake.

The woods are lovely, dark and deep,
But I have promises to keep,
And miles to go before I sleep,   15
And miles to go before I sleep.

CONSIDERATIONS FOR CRITICAL THINKING AND WRITING

1. FIRST RESPONSE. What is the significance of the setting in this poem? How is tone conveyed by the images?

2. What does the speaker find appealing about the woods? What is the purpose of the horse in the poem?

3. Although the last two lines are identical, they are not read at the same speed. Why the difference? What is achieved by the repetition?

4. What is the poem's rhyme scheme? What is the effect of the rhyme in the final stanza?

CONNECTION TO ANOTHER SELECTION

1. Compare the themes in this poem and in Dickinson's "Because I could not stop for Death —" (p. 853).

Nothing Gold Can Stay   *1923*

Nature's first green is gold,
Her hardest hue to hold.
Her early leaf's a flower;
But only so an hour.
The leaf subsides to leaf.
So Eden sank to grief.
So dawn goes down to day.
Nothing gold can stay.

CONSIDERATIONS FOR CRITICAL THINKING AND WRITING

1. FIRST RESPONSE. What is meant by "gold" in the poem? Why can't it "stay"?

2. What do the leaf, humanity, and a day have in common?

CONNECTION TO ANOTHER SELECTION

1. Write an essay comparing the tone and theme of "Nothing Gold Can Stay" with Robert Herrick's "To the Virgins, to Make Much of Time" (p. 635).

Unharvested   1936

A scent of ripeness from over a wall.
And come to leave the routine road
And look for what had made me stall,
There sure enough was an apple tree
That had eased itself of its summer load,   5
And of all but its trivial foliage free,
Now breathed as light as a lady's fan.
For there there had been an apple fall
As complete as the apple had given man.
The ground was one circle of solid red.   10

May something go always unharvested!
May much stay out of our stated plan,
Apples or something forgotten and left,
So smelling their sweetness would be no theft.

CONSIDERATIONS FOR CRITICAL THINKING AND WRITING

1. **FIRST RESPONSE.** Why does the speaker like the idea of some things going unharvested?

2. Explain why this poem is about more than just apples. What lines especially invite deeper readings?

3. What kind of sonnet is this poem? Discuss the effects created by Frost's use of meter and rhyme.

4. **CRITICAL STRATEGIES.** Read the section on mythological criticism (pp. 1550–52) in Chapter 46, "Critical Strategies for Reading." How do you think a mythological critic would interpret "Unharvested"?

CONNECTION TO ANOTHER SELECTION

1. Compare the themes in this poem and in "After Apple-Picking" (p. 889).

Design   1936

I found a dimpled spider, fat and white,
On a white heal-all,° holding up a moth
Like a white piece of rigid satin cloth —
Assorted characters of death and blight
Mixed ready to begin the morning right,   5
Like the ingredients of a witches' broth —
A snow-drop spider, a flower like a froth,
And dead wings carried like a paper kite.

What had the flower to do with being white,
The wayside blue and innocent heal-all?   10
What brought the kindred spider to that height,
Then steered the white moth thither in the night?

What but design of darkness to appall? —
If design govern in a thing so small.

2 *heal-all:* A common flower, usually blue, once used for medicinal purposes.

CONSIDERATIONS FOR CRITICAL THINKING AND WRITING

1. **FIRST RESPONSE.** What kinds of speculations are raised in the poem's final two lines? Consider the meaning of the title. Is there more than one way to read it?

2. How does the division of the octave and sestet in this sonnet serve to organize the speaker's thoughts and feelings? What is the predominant rhyme? How does that rhyme relate to the poem's meaning?

3. Which words seem especially rich in connotative meanings? Explain how they function in the sonnet.

4. **CRITICAL STRATEGIES.** Read the section on formalist strategies (pp. 1538–40) in Chapter 46, "Critical Strategies for Reading." Which words seem especially rich in connotative meanings? Explain how they function in the sonnet.

CONNECTIONS TO OTHER SELECTIONS

1. Compare the ironic tone of "Design" with the tone of William Hathaway's "Oh, Oh" (p. 574). What would you have to change in Hathaway's poem to make it more like Frost's?

2. In an essay discuss Frost's view of God in this poem and Dickinson's perspective in "I know that He exists" (p. 868).

3. Compare "Design" with "In White," Frost's early version of it (p. 899).

Neither Out Far nor In Deep 1936

The people along the sand
All turn and look one way.
They turn their back on the land.
They look at the sea all day.

As long as it takes to pass   5
A ship keeps raising its hull;
The wetter ground like glass
Reflects a standing gull.

The land may vary more;
But wherever the truth may be —   10
The water comes ashore,
And the people look at the sea.

They cannot look out far.
They cannot look in deep.
But when was that ever a bar   15
To any watch they keep?

> Neither Out Far nor In Deep
>
> The people along the sand
> All turn and look one way.
> They turn their backs on the land;
> They look at the sea all day.
>
> As long as it takes to pass
> A ship keeps raising its hull.
> The wetter ground like glass
> Reflects a standing gull.
>
> The land may vary more,
> But wherever the truth may be —
> The water comes ashore
> And the people look at the sea.
>
> They cannot look out far;
> They cannot look in deep;
> But when was that ever a bar
> To any watch they keep.
>
> Robert Frost
>
> With the permission of The Yale Review.

Manuscript page for Robert Frost's "Neither Out Far nor In Deep" (p. 896). The poem was first published in the *Yale Review* in 1934 and later, with a few punctuation changes, in *A Further Range* in 1936.

CONSIDERATIONS FOR CRITICAL THINKING AND WRITING

1. **FIRST RESPONSE.** Frost built this poem around a simple observation that raises some questions. Why do people at the beach almost always face the ocean? What feelings and thoughts are evoked by looking at the ocean?

2. Notice how the verb *look* takes on added meaning as the poem progresses. What are the people looking for?

3. How does the final stanza extend the poem's significance?
4. Does the speaker identify with the people described, or does he ironically distance himself from them?

The Silken Tent 1942

She is as in a field a silken tent
At midday when a sunny summer breeze
Has dried the dew and all its ropes relent,
So that in guys° it gently sways at ease,   *ropes that steady a tent*
And its supporting central cedar pole,   5
That is its pinnacle to heavenward
And signifies the sureness of the soul,
Seems to owe naught to any single cord,
But strictly held by none, is loosely bound
By countless silken ties of love and thought   10
To everything on earth the compass round,
And only by one's going slightly taut
In the capriciousness of summer air
Is of the slightest bondage made aware.

CONSIDERATIONS FOR CRITICAL THINKING AND WRITING

1. **FIRST RESPONSE.** What is being compared in this sonnet? How does the detail accurately describe both elements of the comparison?
2. How does the form of this one-sentence sonnet help to express its theme? Pay particular attention to the final three lines.
3. How do the sonnet's sounds contribute to its meaning?

The Most of It 1942

He thought he kept the universe alone;
For all the voice in answer he could wake
Was but the mocking echo of his own
From some tree-hidden cliff across the lake.
Some morning from the boulder-broken beach   5
He would cry out on life, that what it wants
Is not its own love back in copy speech,
But counter-love, original response.
And nothing ever came of what he cried
Unless it was the embodiment that crashed   10
In the cliff's talus on the other side,
And then in the far-distant water splashed,
But after a time allowed for it to swim,

Instead of proving human when it neared
And someone else additional to him,   15
As a great buck it powerfully appeared,
Pushing the crumpled water up ahead,
And landed pouring like a waterfall,
And stumbled through the rocks with horny tread,
And forced the underbrush — and that was all.   20

CONSIDERATIONS FOR CRITICAL THINKING AND WRITING

1. **FIRST RESPONSE.** Discuss the significance of the title. To what does "It" refer?
2. Why do you suppose Frost uses a third-person speaker instead of a first-person narrator?
3. The presence of the "great buck" seems to warrant a symbolic reading. What do you make of it?
4. Explain what you think is the poem's theme.

CONNECTION TO ANOTHER SELECTION

1. Compare the tone of this poem with "Neither Out Far nor In Deep" (p. 896) as third-person narratives.

Perspectives on Robert Frost

ROBERT FROST

"In White": An Early Version of "Design"   *1912*

A dented spider like a snow drop white
On a white Heal-all, holding up a moth
Like a white piece of lifeless satin cloth —
Saw ever curious eye so strange a sight? —
Portent in little, assorted death and blight   5
Like the ingredients of a witches' broth? —
The beady spider, the flower like a froth,
And the moth carried like a paper kite.

What had that flower to do with being white,
The blue prunella every child's delight.   10
What brought the kindred spider to that height?
(Make we no thesis of the miller's° plight.)   *miller moth*
What but design of darkness and of night?
Design, design! Do I use the word aright?

CONSIDERATIONS FOR CRITICAL THINKING AND WRITING

1. Read "In White" and "Design" (p. 895) aloud. Which version sounds better to you? Why?

2. Compare these versions line for line, paying particular attention to word choice. List the differences and try to explain why you think Frost revised the lines.

3. How does the change in titles reflect a shift in emphasis in the poem?

ROBERT FROST

On the Living Part of a Poem   1914

The living part of a poem is the intonation entangled somehow in the syntax, idiom, and meaning of a sentence. It is only there for those who have heard it previously in conversation. . . . It is the most volatile and at the same time important part of poetry. It goes and the language becomes dead language, the poetry dead poetry. With it go the accents, the stresses, the delays that are not the property of vowels and syllables but that are shifted at will with the sense. Vowels have length there is no denying. But the accent of sense supersedes all other accent, overrides it and sweeps it away. I will find you the word *come* variously used in various passages, a whole, half, third, fourth, fifth, and sixth note. It is as long as the sense makes it. When men no longer know the intonations on which we string our words they will fall back on what I may call the absolute length of our syllables, which is the length we would give them in passages that meant nothing. . . . I say you can't read a single good sentence with the salt in it unless you have previously heard it spoken. Neither can you with the help of all the characters and diacritical marks pronounce a single word unless you have previously heard it actually pronounced. Words exist in the mouth not books.

From a letter to Sidney Cox in *A Swinger of Birches: A Portrait of Robert Frost*

CONSIDERATIONS FOR CRITICAL THINKING AND WRITING

1. Why does Frost place so much emphasis on hearing poetry spoken?

2. Choose a passage from "Home Burial" (p. 886) or "After Apple-Picking" (p. 889) and read it aloud. How does Frost's description of his emphasis on intonation help explain the effects he achieves in the passage you have selected?

3. Do you think it is true that all poetry must be heard? Do "words exist in the mouth not books"?

AMY LOWELL   (1874–1925)

On Frost's Realistic Technique   1915

I have said that Mr. Frost's work is almost photographic. The qualification was unnecessary, it is photographic. The pictures, the characters, are reproduced directly from life, they are burnt into his mind as though it were a sensitive plate. He gives out what has been put in unchanged by any personal mental process. His imagination is bounded by what he has seen, he is confined within the limits of his experience (or at least what might have been his experience) and bent all one way like the windblown trees of New England hillsides.

From a review of *North of Boston, The New Republic,* February 20, 1915

CONSIDERATIONS FOR CRITICAL THINKING AND WRITING

1. Consider the "photographic" qualities of Frost's poetry by discussing particular passages that strike you as having been "reproduced directly from life."

2. Write an essay that supports or refutes Lowell's assertion that "he gives out what has been put in unchanged by any personal mental process."

ROBERT FROST
On the Figure a Poem Makes   *1939*

Abstraction is an old story with the philosophers, but it has been like a new toy in the hands of the artists of our day. Why can't we have any one quality of poetry we choose by itself? We can have in thought. Then it will go hard if we can't in practice. Our lives for it.

Granted no one but a humanist much cares how sound a poem is if it is only *a* sound. The sound is the gold in the ore. Then we will have the sound out alone and dispense with the inessential. We do till we make the discovery that the object in writing poetry is to make all poems sound as different as possible from each other, and the resources for that of vowels, consonants, punctuation, syntax, words, sentences, meter are not enough. We need the help of context — meaning — subject matter. That is the greatest help towards variety. All that can be done with words is soon told. So also with meters — particularly in our language where there are virtually but two, strict iambic and loose iambic. The ancients with many were still poor if they depended on meters for all tune. It is painful to watch our sprung-rhythmists straining at the point of omitting one short from a foot for relief from monotony. The possibilities for tune from the dramatic tones of meaning struck across the rigidity of a limited meter are endless. And we are back in poetry as merely one more art of having something to say, sound or unsound. Probably better if sound, because deeper and from wider experience.

Then there is this wildness whereof it is spoken. Granted again that it has an equal claim with sound to being a poem's better half. If it is a wild tune, it is a poem. Our problem then is, as modern abstractionists, to have the wildness pure; to be wild with nothing to be wild about. We bring up as aberrationists, giving way to undirected associations and kicking ourselves from one chance suggestion to another in all directions as of a hot afternoon in the life of a grasshopper. Theme alone can steady us down. Just as the first mystery was how a poem could have a tune in such a straightness as meter, so the second mystery is how a poem can have wildness and at the same time a subject that shall be fulfilled.

It should be of the pleasure of a poem itself to tell how it can. The figure a poem makes. It begins in delight and ends in wisdom. The figure is the same as for love. No one can really hold that the ecstasy should be static and stand still in one place. It begins in delight, it inclines to the impulse, it assumes direction with the first line laid down, it runs a course of lucky events, and ends in a clarification of life — not necessarily a great clarification, such as sects and cults are founded on, but in a momentary stay against confusion. It has denouement. It has an outcome that though unforeseen was predestined from the first image of the original mood — and indeed from the very mood. It is but a trick poem and no poem at all if the best of it was thought of first and saved for the last. It finds its own name as it goes and discovers the best waiting for it in some final phrase at once wise and sad — the happy-sad blend of the drinking song.

No tears in the writer, no tears in the reader. No surprise for the writer, no surprise for the reader. For me the initial delight is in the surprise of remembering something I didn't know I knew. I am in a place, in a situation, as if I had materialized from cloud or risen out of the ground. There is a glad recognition of the long lost and the rest follows. Step by step the wonder of unexpected supply keeps going. The impressions most useful to my purpose seem always those I was unaware of and so made no note of at the time when taken, and the conclusion is come to that like giants we are always hurling experience ahead of us to pave the future with against the day when we may want to strike a line of purpose across it for somewhere. The line will have the more charm for not being mechanically straight. We enjoy the straight crookedness of a good walking stick. Modern instruments of precision are being used to make things crooked as if by eye and hand in the old days.

I tell how there may be a better wildness of logic than of inconsequence. But the logic is backward, in retrospect, after the act. It must be more felt than seen ahead like prophecy. It must be a revelation, or a series of revelations, as much for the poet as for the reader. For it to be that there must have been the greatest freedom of the material to move about in it and to establish relations in it regardless of time and space, previous relation, and everything but affinity. We prate of freedom. We call our schools free because we are not free to stay away from them till we are sixteen years of age. I have given up my democratic prejudices and now willingly set the lower classes free to be completely taken care of by the upper classes. Political freedom is nothing to me. I bestow it right and left. All I would keep for myself is the freedom of my material — the condition of body and mind now and then to summons aptly from the vast chaos of all I have lived through.

Scholars and artists thrown together are often annoyed at the puzzle of where they differ. Both work for knowledge; but I suspect they differ most importantly in the way their knowledge is come by. Scholars get theirs with conscientious thoroughness along projected lines of logic; poets theirs cavalierly and as it happens in and out of books. They stick to nothing deliberately, but let what will stick to them like burrs where they walk in the fields. No acquirement is on assignment, or even self-assignment. Knowledge of the second kind is much more available in the wild free ways of wit and art. A school boy may be defined as one who can tell you what he knows in the order in which he learned it. The artist must value himself as he snatches a thing from some previous order in time and space into a new order with not so much as a ligature clinging to it of the old place where it was organic.

More than once I should have lost my soul to radicalism if it had been the originality it was mistaken for by its young converts. Originality and initiative are what I ask for my country. For myself the originality need be no more than the freshness of a poem run in the way I have described: from delight to wisdom. The figure is the same as for love. Like a piece of ice on a hot stove the poem must ride on its own melting. A poem may be worked over once it is in being, but may not be worried into being. Its most precious quality will remain its having run itself and carried away the poet with it. Read it a hundred times: it will forever keep its freshness as a metal keeps its fragrance. It can never lose its sense of a meaning that once unfolded by surprise as it went.

From *Complete Poems of Robert Frost*

CONSIDERATIONS FOR CRITICAL THINKING AND WRITING

1. Frost places a high premium on sound in his poetry because it "is the gold in the ore." Choose one of Frost's poems in this book and explain the effects of its sounds and how they contribute to its meaning.

2. Discuss Frost's explanation of how his poems are written. In what sense is the process both spontaneous and "predestined"?

3. What do you think Frost means when he says he's given up his "democratic prejudices"? Why is "political freedom" nothing to him?

4. Write an essay that examines in more detail the ways scholars and artists "come by" knowledge.

5. Explain what you think Frost means when he writes that "like a piece of ice on a hot stove the poem must ride on its own melting."

ROBERT FROST

On the Way to Read a Poem   1951

The way to read a poem in prose or verse is in the light of all the other poems ever written. We may begin anywhere. We *duff* into our first. We read that imperfectly (thoroughness with it would be fatal), but the better to read the second. We read the second the better to read the third, the third the better to read the fourth, the fourth better to read the fifth, the fifth the better to read the first again, or the second if it so happens. For poems are not meant to be read in course any more than they are to be made a study of. I once made a resolve never to put any book to any use it wasn't intended for by its author. Improvement will not be a progression but a widening circulation. Our instinct is to settle down like a revolving dog and make ourselves at home among the poems, completely at our ease as to how they should be taken. The same people will be apt to take poems right as know how to take a hint when there is one and not to take a hint when none is intended. Theirs is the ultimate refinement.

From "Poetry and School," *Atlantic Monthly,* June 1951

CONSIDERATIONS FOR CRITICAL THINKING AND WRITING

1. Given your own experience, how good is Frost's advice about reading in general and his poems in particular?

2. In what sense is a good reader like a "revolving dog" and a person who knows "how to take a hint"?

3. Frost elsewhere in this piece writes, "One of the dangers of college to any-one who wants to stay a human reader (that is to say a humanist) is that he will become a specialist and lose his sensitive fear of landing on the lovely too hard. (With beak and talon.)" Write an essay in response to this con-cern. Do you agree with Frost's distinction between a "human reader" and a "specialist"?

HERBERT R. COURSEN JR. (B. 1932)

A Parodic Interpretation of "Stopping by Woods on a Snowy Evening" 1962

Much ink has spilled on many pages in exegesis of this little poem. Actually, critical jottings have only obscured what has lain beneath critical noses all these years. To say that the poem means merely that a man stops one night to observe a snowfall, or that the poem contrasts the mundane desire for creature comfort with the sweep of aesthetic appreciation, or that it renders worldly responsibilities paramount, or that it reveals the speaker's latent death-wish is to miss the point rather badly. Lacking has been that mind simple enough to see what is *really* there. . . .

The "darkest evening of the year" in New England is December 21st, a date near that on which the western world celebrates Christmas. It may be that December 21st *is* the date of the poem, or (and with poets this seems more likely) that this is the closest the poet can come to Christmas without giving it all away. Who has "promises to keep" at or near this date, and who must tra-verse much territory to fulfill these promises? Yes, and who but St. Nick would know the location of *each* home? Only he would know who had "just settled down for a long winter's nap" (the poem's third line — "He will not see me stopping here" — is clearly a veiled allusion) and would not be out in-specting his acreage this night. The unusual phrase "fill up with snow," in the poem's fourth line, is a transfer of Santa's occupational preoccupation to the countryside; he is mulling the filling of countless stockings hung above count-less fireplaces by countless careful children. "Harness bells," of course, allude to "Sleighing Song," a popular Christmas tune of the time the poem was written in which the refrain "Jingle Bells! Jingle Bells!" appears; thus again are we put on the Christmas track. The "little horse," like the date, is another attempt at poetic obfuscation. Although the "rein-reindeer" ambiguity has been eliminated from the poem's final version,[1] probably because too obvious, we may speculate that the animal is really a reindeer disguised as a horse by the poet's desire for ob-scurity, a desire which we must concede has been fulfilled up to now.

The animal is clearly concerned, like the faithful Rudolph — another pos-sible allusion (post facto, hence unconscious) — lest his master fail to complete his mission. Seeing no farmhouse in the second quatrain, but pulling a load of presents, no wonder the little beast wonders! It takes him a full two quatrains to rouse his driver to remember all the empty stockings which hang ahead. And Santa does so reluctantly at that, poor soul, as he ponders the myriad farmhouses and villages which spread between him and his own "winter's nap." The modern St. Nick, lonely and overworked, tosses no "Happy Christmas to all and to all a good night!" into the precipitation. He merely shrugs his shoulders and resignedly plods away.

> From "The Ghost of Christmas Past: 'Stopping by Woods on a Snowy Evening,'" *College English,* December 1962

[1] The original draft contained the following line: "That bid me give the reins a shake" (Stageberg-Anderson, *Poetry as Experience* [New York, 1952], p. 457). [Coursen's note.]

CONSIDERATIONS FOR CRITICAL THINKING AND WRITING

1. Is this critical spoof at all credible? Does the interpretation hold any water? Is the evidence reasonable? Why or why not? Which of the poem's details are accounted for and which are ignored?
2. Choose a Frost poem and try writing a parodic interpretation of it.

BLANCHE FARLEY (B. 1937)

The Lover Not Taken　　　　　　　　　*1984*

Committed to one, she wanted both
And, mulling it over, long she stood,
Alone on the road, loath
To leave, wanting to hide in the undergrowth.
This new guy, smooth as a yellow wood　　　　　　5

Really turned her on. She liked his hair,
His smile. But the other, Jack, had a claim
On her already and she had to admit, he did wear
Well. In fact, to be perfectly fair,
He understood her. His long, lithe frame　　　　　　10

Beside hers in the evening tenderly lay.
Still, if this blond guy dropped by someday,
Couldn't way just lead on to way?
No. For if way led on and Jack
Found out, she doubted if he would ever come back.　　　　　　15

Oh, she turned with a sigh.
Somewhere ages and ages hence,
She might be telling this. "And I —"
She would say, "stood faithfully by."
But by then who would know the difference?　　　　　　20

With that in mind, she took the fast way home,
The road by the pond, and phoned the blond.

CONSIDERATIONS FOR CRITICAL THINKING AND WRITING

1. Which Frost poem is the object of this parody?
2. Describe how the stylistic elements mirror Frost's poem.
3. Does this parody seem successful to you? Explain what makes a successful parody.
4. **CREATIVE RESPONSE.** Choose a Frost poem — or a portion of one if it is long — and try writing a parody of it.

SUGGESTED TOPICS FOR LONGER PAPERS

1. Research Frost's popular reputation and compare that with recent biographical accounts of his personal life. How does knowledge of his personal life affect your reading of his poetry?
2. Frost has been described as a cheerful poet of New England who creates pleasant images of the region as well as a poet who creates a troubling, frightening world bordered by anxiety, anguish, doubts, and darkness. How do the poems in this chapter support both of these readings of Frost's poetry?

[Web] Research Robert Frost at bedfordstmartins.com/meyercompact.

31

A Study of Langston Hughes

> I believe that poetry should be
> direct, comprehensible, and the
> epitome of simplicity.
> — LANGSTON HUGHES

The poetry of Langston Hughes represents a significant chapter in twentieth-century American literature. The poetry included here both chronicles and evokes African American life during the middle decades of the last century. Moreover, it celebrates the culture and heritage of what is called the Harlem Renaissance of the 1920s, which has continued to be a vital tradition and presence in American life. As you introduce yourself to Hughes's innovative techniques and the cultural life embedded in his poetry, keep in mind the Questions for Writing about an Author in Depth (p. 866), which can serve as a guide in your explorations.

Explore contexts for Langston Hughes on *LiterActive*.

Langston Hughes

(*Left*) **Langston Hughes.** From the publication of *The Weary Blues* in 1926 on, Hughes was an established figure in the Harlem Renaissance, a cultural movement characterized by an explosion of black literature, theater, music, painting, and political and racial consciousness that began after the First World War. A stamp commemorating the centennial of Hughes's birth (2002) is but one illustration of his lasting impact on American poetry and culture.

(*Below*) **The Weary Blues.** Langston Hughes claimed that Walt Whitman, Carl Sandburg, and Paul Laurence Dunbar were his greatest influences as a poet. However, the experience of black America from the 1920s through the 1960s, the life and language of Harlem, and a love of jazz and the blues clearly shaped the narrative and lyrical experimentation of his poetry. Both the cover and contents of *The Weary Blues*, his first collection of poetry, reflect the influence of music on his work.

The Harlem Renaissance. In this 1932 image taken by African American photographer James VanDerZee, a Harlem couple in raccoon coats poses with a Cadillac on West 127th Street. VanDerZee once commented, "I tried to pose each person in such a way as to tell a story." His work offered America a dazzling view of black middle-class life in the 1920s and 1930s.
© Donna M. VanDerZee.

A BRIEF BIOGRAPHY

Even as a child, Langston Hughes (1902–1967) was wrapped in an important African American legacy. He was raised by his maternal grandmother, who was the widow of Lewis Sheridan Leary, one of the band of men who participated in John Brown's raid on the federal arsenal at Harpers Ferry in 1859. The raid was a desperate attempt to ignite an insurrection that would ultimately liberate slaves in the South. It was a failure. Leary was killed, but the shawl he wore, which was returned to his wife bloodstained and riddled with bullet holes, was proudly worn by Hughes's grandmother fifty years after the raid, and she used it to cover her grandson at night when he was a young boy.

Throughout his long career as a professional writer, Hughes remained true to the African American heritage he celebrated in his writings, which were frankly "racial in theme and treatment, derived from the life I know." In an influential essay published in *The Nation*, "The Negro Artist and the

The Lafayette Theatre. The famous Lafayette Theatre, located near 132nd street on 7th Avenue, known during the Harlem Renaissance as the "Boulevard of Dreams," was one of New York's first theaters to desegregate (c. 1912). The theater (now a church) seated 2,000 people and, beginning in 1916, employed its own Lafayette Players, who performed popular and classical plays for almost exclusively black audiences. Known as the "House Beautiful" to many of its patrons, the Lafayette also showcased the blues singer Bessie Smith, the jazz composer Duke Ellington, and other prominent African American performers. Shown here is the vibrant opening night of Shakespeare's *Macbeth*, staged by Orson Welles, featuring leading actors Canada Lee and Rose McLendon, with a musical score by James P. Johnson (1936). The Granger Collection, New York.

Racial Mountain" (1926), he insisted on the need for black artists to draw on their heritage rather than "to run away spiritually from . . . race":

> We younger Negro artists who create now intend to express our individual dark-skinned selves without fear or shame. If white people are pleased, we are glad. If they are not, it doesn't matter. We know we are beautiful. And ugly too. The tom-tom cries and the tom-tom laughs. If colored people are pleased we are glad. If they are not, their displeasure doesn't matter either. We build our temples for tomorrow, strong as we know how, and we stand on top of the mountain, free within ourselves.

That freedom was hard won for Hughes. His father, James Nathaniel Hughes, could not accommodate the racial prejudice and economic frustration that were the result of James's black and white racial ancestry. James abandoned his wife, Carrie Langston Hughes, only one year after their son was born in Joplin, Missouri, and went to find work in Mexico,

The McCarthy Hearings. Langston Hughes testifying before the Senate Investigations Subcommittee — Senator Joseph McCarthy's subcommittee on subversive activities — on March
27, 1953. Hughes testified: "From my point [of view] it doesn't matter what the form of government is if the rights of the minorities and the poor people are respected, and if they have a
chance to advance equally." (See "Un-American Investigators," p. 928.)
© Bettmann/CORBIS.

where he hoped the color of his skin would be less of an issue than in the
United States. During the periods when Hughes's mother shuttled from
city to city in the Midwest looking for work, she sent her son to live with
his grandmother.

Hughes's spotty relationship with his father — a connection he developed in his late teens and maintained only sporadically thereafter — consisted mostly of arguments about his becoming a writer rather than an engineer and businessman as his father wished. Hughes's father could not appreciate or even tolerate his son's ambition to write about the black experience, and Hughes (whose given name was also James but who refused to be identified by it) could not abide his father's contempt for blacks. Consequently, his determination, as he put it in "The Negro Artist," "to express our individual dark-skinned selves without fear or shame" was not only a profound response to African American culture but also an intensely personal commitment that made a relationship with his own father impossible. Though Hughes had been abandoned by his father, he nevertheless felt an early and deep connection to his ancestors, as he reveals in the following poem, written while crossing the Mississippi River by train as he traveled to visit his father in Mexico, just a month after his high school graduation.

The Negro Speaks of Rivers   1921

I've known rivers:
I've known rivers ancient as the world and older than the
    flow of human blood in human veins.

My soul has grown deep like the rivers.

I bathed in Euphrates when dawns were young.   5
I built my hut near the Congo and it lulled me to sleep.
I looked upon the Nile and raised the pyramids above it.
I heard the singing of the Mississippi when Abe Lincoln
    went down to New Orleans, and I've seen its muddy
    bosom turn all golden in the sunset.   10

I've known rivers:
Ancient, dusky rivers.

My soul has grown deep like the rivers.

This poem appeared in *The Crisis,* the official publication of the National Association for the Advancement of Colored People, which eventually published more of Hughes's poems than any other magazine or journal. This famous poem's simple and direct free verse makes clear that Africa's "dusky rivers" run concurrently with the poet's soul as he draws spiritual strength as well as individual identity from the collective experience of his ancestors. The themes of racial pride and personal dignity work their way through some forty books that Hughes wrote, edited, or compiled during his forty-five years of writing.

AN INTRODUCTION TO HIS WORK

Hughes's writings include volumes of poetry, novels, short stories, essays, plays, opera librettos, histories, documentaries, autobiographies, biographies, anthologies, children's books, and translations, as well as radio and television scripts. This impressive body of work makes him an important literary artist and a leading African American voice of the twentieth century. First and foremost, he considered himself a poet. He set out to be a poet who could address himself to the concerns of his people in poems that could be read with no formal training or extensive literary background. He wanted his poetry to be "direct, comprehensible, and the epitome of simplicity."

Hughes's poetry echoes the voices of ordinary African Americans and the rhythms of their music. He drew on an oral tradition of working-class folk poetry that embraced black vernacular language at a time when some middle-class blacks of the 1920s felt that the use of the vernacular was an embarrassing handicap and an impediment to social progress. Hughes's response to such concerns was unequivocal; at his readings, some of which were accompanied by jazz musicians or singers, his innovative voice found an appreciative audience. As Hughes very well knew, much of the pleasure associated with his poetry comes from reading it aloud; his many recorded readings give testimony to that pleasure.

The blues can be heard moving through Hughes's poetry as well as in the works of many of his contemporaries associated with the Harlem Renaissance, a movement of African American writers, painters, sculptors, actors, and musicians who were active in New York City's Harlem of the 1920s. Hughes's introduction to the "laughter and pain, hunger and heartache" of blues music began the year he spent at Columbia University. He dropped out after only two semesters because he preferred the night life and culture of Harlem to academic life. The sweet, sad blues songs captured for Hughes the intense pain and yearning that he saw around him and that he incorporated into poems such as "The Weary Blues" (p. 919). He also reveled in the jazz music of Harlem and discovered in its open forms and improvisations an energy and freedom that significantly influenced the style of his poetry.

Hughes's life, like the jazz music that influenced his work, was characterized by improvisation and openness. After leaving Columbia, he worked a series of odd jobs and then traveled as a merchant seaman to Africa and Europe from 1923 to 1924. He jumped ship to work for several months in the kitchen of a Paris nightclub. As he broadened his experience through travel, he continued to write poetry. After his return to the United States in 1925 he published poems in two black magazines, *The Crisis* and *Opportunity,* and met the critic Carl Van Vechten, who sent his poems to the publisher Alfred A. Knopf. He also — as a busboy in a Washington, D.C., hotel — met the poet Vachel Lindsay, who was instrumental in advancing Hughes's reputation as a poet. In 1926 Hughes published his first volume of poems, *The Weary Blues,* and enrolled in Lincoln University in Pennsylvania, his education funded by a generous patron. His second volume of verse, *Fine Clothes to the Jew,* appeared in 1927, and by the time he graduated from Lincoln in 1929 he was reading his poems publicly on a book tour of the South. Hughes ended the decade as more than a promising poet; as Countee Cullen pronounced in a mixed review of *The Weary Blues* (mixed because Cullen believed that African American poets should embrace universal themes rather than racial themes), Hughes had "arrived."

Hughes wrote more prose than poetry during the 1930s, publishing his first novel, *Not without Laughter* (1930), and a collection of stories, *The Ways of White Folks* (1934). In addition to writing a variety of magazine articles, he also worked on a number of plays and screenplays. Many of his poems from this period reflect proletarian issues. During this decade Hughes's travels took him to all points of the compass — Cuba, Haiti, the Soviet Union, China, Japan, Mexico, France, and Spain — but his general intellectual movement was decidedly toward the left. Hughes was attracted to the American Communist Party, owing to its insistence on equality for all working-class people regardless of race. Like many other Americans of the thirties, he turned his attention away from the exotic twenties and focused on the economic and political issues attending the Great Depression that challenged the freedom and dignity of common humanity.

During World War II, Hughes helped the war effort by writing jingles and catchy verses to sell war bonds and to bolster morale. His protest poems of the thirties were largely replaced by poems that returned to earlier themes centered on the everyday lives of African Americans. In 1942 Hughes described his new collection of poems, *Shakespeare in Harlem,* as "light verse. Afro-American in the blues mood . . . to be read aloud, crooned, shouted, recited, and sung. Some with gestures, some not — as you like." Soon after this collection appeared, the character of Jesse B. Simple emerged from Hughes's 1943 newspaper column for the Chicago *Defender.* Hughes developed this popular urban African American character in five humorous books published over a fifteen-year period: *Simple Speaks His Mind* (1950), *Simple Takes a Wife* (1953), *Simple Stakes a Claim* (1957), *The Best of Simple* (1961), and *Simple's Uncle Sam* (1965). Two more poetry collections appeared in the forties: *Fields of Wonder* (1947) and *One-Way Ticket* (1949).

In the 1950s and 1960s Hughes's poetry again revealed the strong influence of black music, especially in the rhythms of *Montage of a Dream Deferred* (1951) and *Ask Your Mama: 12 Moods for Jazz* (1961). From the poem "Harlem" (p. 928) in *Montage of a Dream Deferred,* Lorraine Hansberry derived the title of her 1959 play *A Raisin in the Sun.* This is only a small measure of Hughes's influence on his fellow African American writers, but it is suggestive nonetheless. For some in the 1950s, however, Hughes and his influence occasioned suspicion. He was watched closely by the FBI and the Special Committee on Un-American Activities of the House of Representatives because of his alleged communist activities in the 1930s. Hughes denied that he was ever a member of the Communist Party, but he and others, including Albert Einstein and Paul Robeson, were characterized as "dupes and fellow travelers" by *Life* magazine in 1949. Hughes was subpoenaed to appear before Senator Joseph McCarthy's subcommittee on subversive activities in 1953 and listed by the FBI as a security risk until 1959. His anger and indignation over these attacks from the right can be seen in his poem "Un-American Investigators" (p. 928), published posthumously in *The Panther and the Lash* (1967).

Despite the tremendous amount that Hughes published, including two autobiographies, *The Big Sea* (1940) and *I Wonder as I Wander* (1956), he remains somewhat elusive. He never married or had friends who can lay claim to truly knowing him beyond what he wanted them to know (even though several biographies have been published). And yet Hughes is well known — not for his personal life but for his treatment of the possibilities of African American experiences and identities. Like Walt Whitman, one of his favorite writers, Hughes created a persona that spoke for more than himself. Consider Hughes's voice in the following poem.

I, Too   1925

I, too, sing America.

I am the darker brother.
They send me to eat in the kitchen
When company comes,
But I laugh,   5
And eat well,
And grow strong.

Tomorrow,
I'll be at the table
When company comes.   10
Nobody'll dare
Say to me,
"Eat in the kitchen,"
Then.

Besides,   15
They'll see how beautiful I am
And be ashamed —

I, too, am America.

The "darker brother" who celebrates America is certain of a better future when he will no longer be shunted aside by "company." The poem is characteristic of Hughes's faith in the racial consciousness of African Americans, a consciousness that reflects their integrity and beauty while simultaneously demanding respect and acceptance from others: "Nobody'll dare / Say to me, / 'Eat in the kitchen,' / Then."

Hughes's poetry reveals his hearty appetite for all humanity, his insistence on justice for all, and his faith in the transcendent possibilities of joy and hope that make room for everyone at America's table.

Negro   1922

I am a Negro:
    Black as the night is black,
    Black like the depths of my Africa.

I've been a slave:
    Caesar told me to keep his door-steps clean.   5
    I brushed the boots of Washington.

I've been a worker:
    Under my hand the pyramids arose.
    I made mortar for the Woolworth Building.

I've been a singer: 10
    All the way from Africa to Georgia
    I carried my sorrow songs.
    I made ragtime.

I've been a victim:
    The Belgians cut off my hands in the Congo.   15
    They lynch me still in Mississippi.

I am a Negro:
    Black as the night is black,
    Black like the depths of my Africa.

CONSIDERATIONS FOR CRITICAL THINKING AND WRITING

1. **FIRST RESPONSE.** What sort of identity does the speaker claim for the "Negro"? What is the effect of the litany of roles?

2. What is the effect of the repetition of the first and last stanzas?

3. What kind of history of black people does the speaker describe?

CONNECTIONS TO OTHER SELECTIONS

1. How does Hughes's use of night and blackness in "Negro" help to explain their meaning in the poem "Dream Variations" (p. 918)?

2. Write an essay comparing the treatment of oppression in "Negro" with that in William Blake's "The Chimney Sweeper" (p. 723).

Danse Africaine

1922

The low beating of the tom-toms,
The slow beating of the tom-toms,
   Low . . . slow
   Slow . . . low—
   Stirs your blood.
       Dance!   5
A night-veiled girl
   Whirls softly into a
   Circle of light.
   Whirls softly . . . slowly,   10
Like a wisp of smoke around the fire—
   And the tom-toms beat,
   And the tom-toms beat,
And the low beating of the tom-toms
   Stirs your blood.   15

CONSIDERATIONS FOR CRITICAL THINKING AND WRITING

1. **FIRST RESPONSE.** How do the sounds of this poem build its meaning? (What *is* its meaning?)

2. What effect do the repeated rhythms have? You may need to read the poem aloud to answer.

CONNECTION TO ANOTHER SELECTION

1. **CREATIVE RESPONSE.** Try rewriting this poem based on the prescription for poetry in Hughes's "Formula" (p. 920).

Mother to Son

1922

Well, son, I'll tell you:
Life for me ain't been no crystal stair.
It's had tacks in it,
And splinters,
And boards torn up,   5
And places with no carpet on the floor—
Bar.
But all the time
I'se been a-climbin' on,
And reachin' landin's,   10
And turnin' corners,
And sometimes goin' in the dark
Where there ain't been no light.
So boy, don't you turn back.
Don't you set down on the steps   15

'Cause you finds it's kinder hard.
Don't you fall now —
For I'se still goin', honey,
I'se still climbin',
And life for me ain't been no crystal stair.   20

CONSIDERATIONS FOR CRITICAL THINKING AND WRITING

1. FIRST RESPONSE. How is the central metaphor of climbing stairs a particularly appropriate idea for conveying this poem's theme?

2. Try rewriting the dialect of this poem in formal diction. How does this change your response to the poem?

3. What does it imply that the stairs are crystal rather than, say, carpeted?

Dream Variations   1924

To fling my arms wide
In some place of the sun,
To whirl and to dance
Till the white day is done.
Then rest at cool evening   5
Beneath a tall tree
While night comes on gently,
     Dark like me —
That is my dream!

To fling my arms wide   10
In the face of the sun,
Dance! Whirl! Whirl!
Till the quick day is done.
Rest at pale evening . . .
A tall, slim tree . . .   15
Night coming tenderly
     Black like me.

CONSIDERATIONS FOR CRITICAL THINKING AND WRITING

1. FIRST RESPONSE. What distinctions are made in the poem between night and day? Which is the dream?

2. Describe the speaker's "Dream." How might the dream be understood metaphorically?

3. How do the rhythms of the lines contribute to the poem's effects?

CONNECTIONS TO OTHER SELECTIONS

1. In an essay compare and contrast the meanings of darkness and the night in this poem and in William Stafford's "Traveling through the Dark" (p. 716).

2. Discuss the significance of the dream in this poem and in "Dream Boogie" (p. 927).

The Weary Blues   *1925*

Droning a drowsy syncopated tune,
Rocking back and forth to a mellow croon,
   I heard a Negro play.
Down on Lenox Avenue° the other night   *street in Harlem*
By the pale dull pallor of an old gas light   5
    He did a lazy sway. . . .
    He did a lazy sway. . . .
To the tune o' those Weary Blues.
With his ebony hands on each ivory key
He made that poor piano moan with melody.   10
    O Blues!
Swaying to and fro on his rickety stool
He played that sad raggy tune like a musical fool.
    Sweet Blues!
Coming from a black man's soul.   15
    O Blues!
In a deep song voice with a melancholy tone
I heard that Negro sing, that old piano moan —
    "Ain't got nobody in all this world,
      Ain't got nobody but ma self.   20
      I's gwine to quit ma frownin'
      And put ma troubles on the shelf."

Thump, thump, thump, went his foot on the floor.
He played a few chords then he sang some more —
    "I got the Weary Blues   25
      And I can't be satisfied.
      Got the Weary Blues
      And can't be satisfied —
      I ain't happy no mo'
      And I wish that I had died."   30
And far into the night he crooned that tune.
The stars went out and so did the moon.
The singer stopped playing and went to bed
While the Weary Blues echoed through his head.
He slept like a rock or a man that's dead.   35

CONSIDERATIONS FOR CRITICAL THINKING AND WRITING

1. **FIRST RESPONSE.** Write a one-paragraph description of the blues based on how the poem presents this kind of music.

2. How does the speaker's voice compare with the singer's?
3. Comment on the effects of the rhymes.
4. **CRITICAL STRATEGIES.** Read the section on formalist strategies (pp. 1538–40) in Chapter 46, "Critical Strategies for Reading," and explain how the rhythm of the lines reflects their meaning.

CONNECTION TO ANOTHER SELECTION

1. Discuss "The Weary Blues" and "Lenox Avenue: Midnight" (p. 921) as vignettes of urban life in America. Do you think that these poems, though written more than eighty years ago, are still credible descriptions of city life? Explain why or why not.

Formula   *1926*

Poetry should treat
    Of lofty things
Soaring thoughts
    And birds with wings.

The Muse of Poetry   5
    Should not know
That roses
    In manure grow.

The Muse of Poetry
    Should not care   10
That earthly pain
    Is everywhere.

Poetry!
    Treats of lofty things:
Soaring thoughts   15
    And birds with wings.

CONSIDERATIONS FOR CRITICAL THINKING AND WRITING

1. **FIRST RESPONSE.** What makes this poem a parody? What assumptions about poetry are being made fun of?
2. How does "Formula" fit the prescriptions offered in the advice to greeting-card freelancers (p. 600)?

CONNECTIONS TO OTHER SELECTIONS

1. Choose any two poems by Hughes in this collection and explain why they do not fit the "Formula."
2. Write an essay that explains how Helen Farries's "Magic of Love" (p. 601) conforms to the ideas about poetry presented in "Formula."

Esthete in Harlem

1926

Strange,
That in this nigger place
I should meet life face to face;
When, for years, I had been seeking
Life in places gentler-speaking,
Until I came to this vile street
And found Life stepping on my feet!

CONSIDERATIONS FOR CRITICAL THINKING AND WRITING

1. **FIRST RESPONSE.** Why might an esthete find Harlem "strange"? What changes the speaker's mind?

2. Discuss the effect of the enjambment in lines 4–5.

Lenox Avenue: Midnight

1926

The rhythm of life
Is a jazz rhythm,
Honey.
The gods are laughing at us.

The broken heart of love,   5
The weary, weary heart of pain, —
    Overtones,
    Undertones,
To the rumble of street cars,
To the swish of rain.   10

Lenox Avenue,
Honey.
Midnight,
And the gods are laughing at us.

CONSIDERATIONS FOR CRITICAL THINKING AND WRITING

1. **FIRST RESPONSE.** What, in your own experience, is the equivalent of Lenox Avenue for the speaker?

2. For so brief a poem there are many sounds in these fourteen lines. What are they? How do they reinforce the poem's meanings?

3. What do you think is the poem's theme?

CONNECTIONS TO OTHER SELECTIONS

1. In an essay compare the theme of this poem with that of Emily Dickinson's "I know that He exists" (p. 868).

2. Compare and contrast the speaker's tone in this poem with that of the speaker in Thomas Hardy's "Hap" (p. 1022).

Song for a Dark Girl   *1927*

Way Down South in Dixie
    (Break the heart of me)
They hung my black young lover
    To a cross roads tree.

Way Down South in Dixie   5
    (Bruised body high in air)
I asked the white Lord Jesus
    What was the use of prayer.

Way down South in Dixie
    (Break the heart of me)   10
Love is a naked shadow
    On a gnarled and naked tree.

CONSIDERATIONS FOR CRITICAL THINKING AND WRITING

1. **FIRST RESPONSE.** What allusion is made in the first line of each stanza? How is that allusion ironic?
2. What *is* "the use of prayer" in this poem? Is the question answered? What, in particular, leads you to your conclusion?
3. Discuss the relationship between love and hatred in the poem.

CONNECTION TO ANOTHER SELECTION

1. Compare the speaker's sensibilities in this poem and in Emily Dickinson's "If I can stop one Heart from breaking" (p. 838). What kinds of cultural assumptions are implicit in each speaker's voice?

Red Silk Stockings   *1927*

Put on yo' red silk stockings,
Black gal.
Go out an' let de white boys
Look at yo' legs.

Ain't nothin' to do for you, nohow,   5
Round this town, —
You's too pretty.

Put on yo' red silk stockings, gal,
An' tomorrow's chile'll
Be a high yaller.   10

Go out an' let de white boys
Look at yo' legs.

CONSIDERATIONS FOR CRITICAL THINKING AND WRITING

1. **FIRST RESPONSE.** Who do you think is speaking? Describe his or her tone.
2. Discuss the racial dimensions of this poem.
3. Write a response from the "gal" — does she put on the red silk stockings? Explain why you imagine her reacting in a certain way.

CONNECTION TO ANOTHER SELECTION

1. Write an essay that compares relations between whites and blacks in this poem and in "Dinner Guest: Me" (p. 931).

Rent-Party° Shout: For a Lady Dancer   1930

Whip it to a jelly!
Too bad Jim!
Mamie's got ma man —
An' I can't find him.
Shake that thing! O!   5
Shake it slow!
That man I love is
Mean an' low.
Pistol an' razor!
Razor an' gun!   10
If I sees ma man he'd
Better run —
For I'll shoot him in de shoulder,
Else I'll cut him down,
Cause I knows I can find him   15
When he's in de ground —
Then can't no other women
Have him layin' round.
So play it, Mr. Nappy!
Yo' music's fine!   20
I'm gonna kill that
Man o' mine!

Rent-Party: In Harlem during the 1920s, parties were given that charged admission to raise money for rent.

CONSIDERATIONS FOR CRITICAL THINKING AND WRITING

1. **FIRST RESPONSE.** Describe the type of music you think might be played at this party today.
2. In what sense is this poem a kind of "Shout"?

3. How is the speaker's personality characterized by her use of language?
4. How does Hughes's use of short lines affect your reading of the poem?

Drum   1931

Bear in mind
That death is a drum
Beating for ever
Till the last worms come
To answer its call,   5
Till the last stars fall,
Until the last atom
Is no atom at all,
Until time is lost
And there is no air   10
And space itself
Is nothing nowhere.
Death is a drum,
A signal drum,
Calling all life   15
To Come! Come!
Come!

CONSIDERATIONS FOR CRITICAL THINKING AND WRITING

1. FIRST RESPONSE. How can the drum be a call to death as well as to life?
2. Discuss the double negative in line 12. How does it enhance the speaker's
   definition of death?

Park Bench   1934

I live on a park bench.
You, Park Avenue.
Hell of a distance
Between us two.

I beg a dime for dinner —   5
You got a butler and a maid.
But I'm wakin' up!
Say, ain't you afraid

That I might, just maybe,
In a year or two,   10
Move on over
To Park Avenue?

CONSIDERATIONS FOR CRITICAL THINKING AND WRITING

1. FIRST RESPONSE. Explain why you think this is a humorous poem or a threatening poem — or both.

2. How does the poem's diction create a portrait of the speaker?

CONNECTION TO ANOTHER SELECTION

1. Discuss the politics embedded in this poem and in the next one, "Ballad of the Landlord."

Ballad of the Landlord   1940

Landlord, landlord,
My roof has sprung a leak.
Don't you 'member I told you about it
Way last week?

Landlord, landlord,   5
These steps is broken down.
When you come up yourself
It's a wonder you don't fall down.

Ten Bucks you say I owe you?
Ten Bucks you say is due?   10
Well, that's Ten Bucks more'n I'll pay you
Till you fix this house up new.

What? You gonna get eviction orders?
You gonna cut off my heat?
You gonna take my furniture and   15
Throw it in the street?

Um-huh! You talking high and mighty.
Talk on — till you get through.
You ain't gonna be able to say a word
If I land my fist on you.   20

Police! Police!
Come and get this man!
He's trying to ruin the government
And overturn the land!

Copper's whistle!   25
Patrol bell!
Arrest.

Precinct Station.
Iron cell.
Headlines in press: 30

MAN THREATENS LANDLORD
TENANT HELD NO BAIL
JUDGE GIVES NEGRO 90 DAYS IN COUNTY JAIL

CONSIDERATIONS FOR CRITICAL THINKING AND WRITING

1. **FIRST RESPONSE.** The poem incorporates both humor and serious social commentary. Which do you think is dominant? Explain.
2. Why is the literary ballad an especially appropriate form for the content of this poem?
3. How does the speaker's language simultaneously characterize him and the landlord?

CONNECTION TO ANOTHER SELECTION

1. Write an essay on landlords based on this poem and Wole Soyinka's "Telephone Conversation" (Border Crossings insert, p. F).

Morning After   1942

I was so sick last night I
Didn't hardly know my mind.
So sick last night I
Didn't know my mind.
I drunk some bad licker that   5
Almost made me blind.

Had a dream last night I
Thought I was in hell.
I drempt last night I
Thought I was in hell.   10
Woke up and looked around me —
Babe, your mouth was open like a well.

I said, Baby! Baby!
Please don't snore so loud.
Baby! Please!   15
Please don't snore so loud.
You jest a little bit o' woman but you
Sound like a great big crowd.

CONSIDERATIONS FOR CRITICAL THINKING AND WRITING

1. **FIRST RESPONSE.** How does the final stanza of this poem take its mood and dominant idea in a different direction from what a reader might expect from reading the first two stanzas?
2. **CREATIVE RESPONSE.** Write a fourth stanza that brings the poem back to the tone of the first two stanzas.

Dream Boogie

Good morning, daddy!
Ain't you heard
The boogie-woogie rumble
Of a dream deferred?
Listen closely: 5
You'll hear their feet
Beating out and beating out a—

> *You think*
> *It's a happy beat?*

Listen to it closely: 10
Ain't you heard
something underneath
like a—

> *What did I say?*

Sure,   15
I'm happy!
Take it away!

> *Hey, pop!*
> *Re-bop!*
> *Mop!*   20

> *Y-e-a-h!*

Considerations for Critical Thinking and Writing

1. **FIRST RESPONSE.** Answer the question *"You think / It's a happy beat?"*
2. Discuss the poem's musical qualities. Which lines are the most musical?
3. Describe the competing tones in the poem. Which do you think is predominant?

Connections to Other Selections

1. In an essay compare and contrast the thematic tensions in this poem and in "Harlem" (p. 928).
2. How are the "dreams" different in "Dream Boogie" and "Dream Variations" (p. 918)?

125th Street°

Face like a chocolate bar
full of nuts and sweet.

Face like a jack-o'-lantern,
candle inside.

125th Street: The main street in Harlem.

Face like slice of melon,
grin that wide.

CONSIDERATIONS FOR CRITICAL THINKING AND WRITING

1. **FIRST RESPONSE.** How do these three similes create a vivid picture of 125th Street?

2. How does this poem confirm the poet Marvin Bell's observation that "a short poem need not be small"?

Harlem   *1951*

What happens to a dream deferred?

    Does it dry up
    like a raisin in the sun?
    Or fester like a sore —
    And then run?   5
    Does it stink like rotten meat?
    Or crust and sugar over —
    like a syrupy sweet?

    Maybe it just sags
    like a heavy load.   10

    Or does it explode?

CONSIDERATIONS FOR CRITICAL THINKING AND WRITING

1. **FIRST RESPONSE.** How might the question asked in this poem be raised by any individual or group whose dreams and aspirations are thwarted?

2. In some editions of Hughes's poetry the title of this poem is "Dream Deferred." What would the effect of this change be on your reading of the poem's symbolic significance?

3. How might the final line be completed as a simile? What is the effect of the speaker not completing the simile? Why is this an especially useful strategy?

CONNECTION TO ANOTHER SELECTION

1. Write an essay on the themes of "Harlem" and James Merrill's "Casual Wear" (p. 719).

Un-American Investigators   *1953*

The committee's fat,
Smug, almost secure
Co-religionists
Shiver with delight

In warm manure   5
As those investigated —
Too brave to name a name —
Have pseudonyms revealed
In Gentile game
        Of who,   10
        Born Jew,
        Is who?
Is not your name Lipshitz?
        Yes.
Did you not change it   15
For subversive purposes?
        No.
For nefarious gain?
        Not so.
Are you sure?   20
The committee shivers
With delight in
Its manure.

CONSIDERATIONS FOR CRITICAL THINKING AND WRITING

1. **FIRST RESPONSE.** What do you think is the political bent of the speaker? What in the poem suggests this?

2. Research in the library and online the hearings and investigations of the House of Representatives' Special Committee on Un-American Activities. How is this background information relevant to an understanding of this poem?

3. How does the speaker characterize the investigators?

4. Given the images in the poem, what might serve as a substitute for its ironic title?

CONNECTION TO ANOTHER SELECTION

1. Write an essay that connects the committee described in this poem with the speaker in E. E. Cummings's "next to of course god america i" (p. 711). What do they have in common?

Old Walt   *1954*

Old Walt Whitman
Went finding and seeking,
Finding less than sought
Seeking more than found,
Every detail minding   5
Of the seeking or the finding.

Pleasured equally
In seeking as in finding,
Each detail minding,
Old Walt went seeking   10
And finding.

CONSIDERATIONS FOR CRITICAL THINKING AND WRITING

1. **FIRST RESPONSE.** Read any poem by Whitman in this book. Do you agree with the speaker's take on Whitman's poetry?

2. Write an explication of "Old Walt." (For a discussion of how to explicate a poem, see the sample explication on p. 824.)

3. What is the effect of the poem's repeated sounds?

4. To what extent do you think lines 3 and 4 could be used to describe Hughes's poetry as well as Whitman's?

CONNECTION TO ANOTHER SELECTION

1. How does Hughes's tribute to Whitman compare with his tribute to Frederick Douglass (p. 931)?

Manuscript page for "Old Walt" (1954). Shown here is an earlier stage of the poem with Hughes's revisions.
Reprinted by permission of Harold Ober Associates, Incorporated.

Dinner Guest: Me 1965

I know I am
The Negro Problem
Being wined and dined,
Answering the usual questions
That come to white mind 5
Which seeks demurely
To probe in polite way
The why and wherewithal
Of darkness U.S.A. —
Wondering how things got this way 10
In current democratic night,
Murmuring gently
Over *fraises du bois,*
"I'm so ashamed of being white."

The lobster is delicious,
The wine divine, 15
And center of attention
At the damask table, mine.
To be a Problem on
Park Avenue at eight 20
Is not so bad.
Solutions to the Problem,
Of course, wait.

CONSIDERATIONS FOR CRITICAL THINKING AND WRITING

1. **FIRST RESPONSE.** What does the speaker satirize in this description of a dinner party? Do you think this "Problem" exists today?
2. Why is line 9, "Of darkness U.S.A. —," especially resonant?
3. What effects are created by the speaker's diction?
4. Discuss the effects of the rhymes in lines 15–23.

CONNECTION TO ANOTHER SELECTION

1. Write an essay on the speaker's treatment of the diners in this poem and in
   Maxine Hong Kingston's "Restaurant" (p. 748).

Frederick Douglass: 1817–1895° 1966

Douglass was someone who,
Had he walked with wary foot
And frightened tread,
From very indecision

1817–1895: Douglass was actually born in 1818; as a slave, he did not know his true birth date.

Might be dead, 5
Might have lost his soul,
But instead decided to be bold
And capture every street
On which he set his feet,
To route each path 10
Toward freedom's goal,
To make each highway
Choose *his* compass' choice,
To all the world cried,
Hear my voice! . . . 15
Oh, to be a beast, a bird,
Anything but a slave! he said.

Who would be free
Themselves must strike
The first blow, he said. 20

He died in 1895.

He is not dead.

CONSIDERATIONS FOR CRITICAL THINKING AND WRITING

1. **FIRST RESPONSE.** This poem was published when the civil rights movement was very active in America. Does that information affect your reading of it?

2. What does Hughes celebrate about the life of Douglass, author of *Narrative of the Life of Frederick Douglass, an American Slave, Written by Himself* (1845)?

CONNECTION TO ANOTHER SELECTION

1. How is the speaker's attitude toward violence in this poem similar to that of the speaker in "Harlem" (p. 928)?

Perspectives on Langston Hughes

LANGSTON HUGHES

On Harlem Rent Parties 1940

Then [in the late twenties and early thirties] it was that house-rent parties began to flourish — and not always to raise the rent either. But, as often as not, to have a get-together of one's own, where you could do the black-bottom with no stranger behind you trying to do it, too. Non-theatrical, non-intellectual Harlem was an unwilling victim of its own vogue. It didn't like to be stared at by white folks. But perhaps the downtowners never knew this — for the cabaret owners, the entertainers, and the speakeasy proprietors treated them fine — as long as they paid.

The Saturday night rent parties that I attended were often more amusing than any night club, in small apartments where God knows who lived — because the guests seldom did — but where the piano would often be augmented by a guitar, or an odd cornet, or somebody with a pair of drums walking in off the street. And where awful bootleg whiskey and good fried fish or steaming chitterling were sold at very low prices. And the dancing and singing and impromptu entertaining went on until dawn came in at the windows.

These parties, often termed whist parties or dances, were usually announced by brightly colored cards stuck in the grille of apartment house elevators. Some of the cards were highly entertaining in themselves:

We got yellow girls, we've got black and tan
Will you have a good time? - YEAH MAN !

𝕬 𝕾𝖔𝖈𝖎𝖆𝖑 𝖂𝖍𝖎𝖘𝖙 𝕻𝖆𝖗𝖙𝖞

—GIVEN BY—
MARY WINSTON
147 West 145th Street   Apt. 5

SATURDAY EVE., MARCH 19th, 1932

GOOD MUSIC   **REFRESHMENTS**

Almost every Saturday night when I was in Harlem I went to a house-rent party. I wrote lots of poems about house-rent parties, and ate there at many a fried fish and pig's foot — with liquid refreshments on the side. I met ladies' maids and truck drivers, laundry workers and shoe shine boys, seamstresses and porters. I can still hear their laughter in my ears, hear the soft slow music, and feel the floor shaking as the dancers danced.

From "When the Negro Was in Vogue," in *The Big Sea*

Considerations for Critical Thinking and Writing

1. What, according to Hughes, was the appeal of the rent parties in contrast to the nightclubs?

2. Describe the tone in which Hughes recounts his memory of these parties.

James A. Emanuel (b. 1921)
Hughes's Attitudes toward Religion   1973

Religion, because of its historical importance during and after slavery, is an undeniably useful theme in the work of any major black writer. In a writer whose special province for almost forty-five years was more recent black experience, the theme is doubly vital. Hughes's personal religious orientation is pertinent. Asked about it by the Reverend Dana F. Kennedy of the "Viewpoint" radio and television show (on December 10, 1960), the poet responded:

> I grew up in a not very religious family, but I had a foster aunt who saw that I went to church and Sunday school . . . and I was very much moved, always, by the, shall I say, the rhythms of the Negro church . . . of the spirituals, . . . of those wonderful old-time sermons. . . . There's great beauty in the mysticism of much religious writing, and great help there — but I also think that we live in a world . . . of solid earth and vegetables and a need for jobs and a need for housing. . . .

Two years earlier, the poet had told John Kirkwood of British Columbia's *Vancouver Sun* (December 3, 1958): "I'm not anti-Christian. I'm not against anyone's religion. Religion is one of the innate needs of mankind. What I am against is the misuse of religion. But I won't ridicule it. . . . Whatever part of God is in anybody is not to be played with, and everybody has got a part of God in them."

These typical public protestations by Hughes boil down to his insistence that religion is naturally sacred and beautiful, and that its needed sustenance must not be exploited.

> From "Christ in Alabama: Religion in the Poetry of Langston Hughes,"
> in *Modern Black Poets,* edited by Donald B. Gibson

CONSIDERATIONS FOR CRITICAL THINKING AND WRITING

1. Why do you think Emanuel asserts that, owing to slavery, religion "is an undeniably useful theme in the work of any major Black writer"?
2. How does Hughes's concern for the "solid earth and vegetables and a need for jobs and a need for housing" qualify his attitudes toward religion?

RICHARD K. BARKSDALE (B. 1915)
On Censoring "Ballad of the Landlord"   1977

In 1940, ["Ballad of the Landlord"] was a rather innocuous rendering of an imaginary dialogue between a disgruntled tenant and a tight-fisted landlord. In creating a poem about two such social archetypes, the poet was by no means taking any new steps in dramatic poetry. The literature of most capitalist and noncapitalist societies often pits the haves against the have-nots, and not infrequently the haves are wealthy men of property who "lord" it over improvident men who own nothing. So the confrontation between tenant and landlord was in 1940 just another instance of the social malevolence of a system that punished the powerless and excused the powerful. In fact, Hughes's tone of dry irony throughout the poem leads one to suspect that the poet deliberately overstated a situation and that some sardonic humor was supposed to be squeezed out of the incident. . . .

Ironically, this poem, which in 1940 depicted a highly probable incident in American urban life and was certainly not written to incite an economic revolt or promote social unrest, became, by the mid-1960s, a verboten assignment in a literature class in a Boston high school. In his Langston Hughes headnote in *Black Voices* (1967), Abraham Chapman reported that a Boston high school English teacher named Jonathan Kozol was fired for assigning it to his students. By the mid-sixties, Boston and many other American cities had become riot-torn, racial tinderboxes, and their ghettos seethed with tenant anger and discontent. So the poem gathered new meanings reflecting the times, and the word of its tenant persona bespoke the collective anger of thousands of black have-nots.

From Langston Hughes: The Poet and His Critics

CONSIDERATIONS FOR CRITICAL THINKING AND WRITING

1. Why do you think the Boston School Committee believed that the "Ballad of the Landlord" (p. 925) should be censored?

2. Do you agree with Barksdale that the poem is a "rather innocuous rendering" of economic and social issues? Explain your answer.

3. How did the poem acquire "new meanings reflecting the times" between the 1940s and 1960s? What new meanings might it have for readers today?

DAVID CHINITZ (B. 1962)

The Romanticization of Africa in the 1920s   *1997*

In Europe black culture was an exotic import; in America it was domestic and increasingly mass-produced. If postwar [World War I] disillusionment judged the majority culture mannered, neurotic, and repressive, Americans had an easily accessible alternative. The need for such an Other produced a discourse in which black Americans figured as barely civilized exiles from the jungle, with — so the clichés ran — tom-toms beating in their blood and dark laughter in their souls. The African American became a model of "natural" human behavior to contrast with the falsified, constrained and impotent modes of the "civilized."

Far from being immune to the lure of this discourse, for the better part of the 1920s Hughes asserted an open pride in the supposed primitive qualities of his race, the atavistic legacy of the African motherland. Unlike most of those who romanticized Africa, Hughes had at least some firsthand experience of the continent; yet he processed what he saw there in images conditioned by European primitivism, rendering "[the land] wild and lovely, the people dark and beautiful, the palm trees tall, the sun bright, and the rivers deep."[1] His short story "Luani of the Jungle," in attempting to glorify aboriginal African vigor as against European anemia, shows how predictable and unextraordinary even Hughes's primitivism could be. To discover in the descendents of idealized Africans the same qualities of innate health, spontaneity, and naturalness requires no great leap; one has only to identify the African American

---

[1] *The Big Sea.* 1940. N.Y.: Thunder's Mouth, 1986, 11. [Chinitz's note.]

as a displaced primitive, as Hughes does repeatedly in his first book, *The Weary Blues:*

> They drove me out of the forest.
> They took me away from the jungles.
> I lost my trees.
> I lost my silver moons.
>
> Now they've caged me
> In the circus of civilization.[2]

Hughes depicts black atavism vividly and often gracefully, yet in a way that is entirely consistent with the popular iconography of the time. His African Americans retain "among the skyscrapers" the primal fears and instincts of their ancestors "among the palms in Africa."[3] The scion of Africa is still more than half primitive: "All the tom-toms of the jungles beat in my blood, / And all the wild hot moons of the jungles shine in my soul."[4]

From "Rejuvenation through Joy: Langston Hughes, Primitivism and Jazz," in *American Literary History,* Spring 1997

[2] *The Weary Blues.* N.Y.: Knopf, 1926, 100. [Chinitz's note.]
[3] *Ibid.* 101.
[4] *Ibid.* 102.

CONSIDERATIONS FOR CRITICAL THINKING AND WRITING

1. According to Chinitz, why did Europeans and Americans romanticize African culture?

2. Consider the poems published by Hughes in the 1920s reprinted in this anthology. Explain whether you find any "primitivism" in these poems.

3. Later in this essay, Chinitz points out that Hughes eventually rejected the "reductive mischaracterizations of black culture, the commercialism, the sham sociology, and the downright silliness of the primitivist fad." Choose and discuss a poem from this anthology that you think reflects Hughes's later views of primitivism.

SUGGESTED TOPICS FOR LONGER PAPERS

1. Discuss Hughes's use of rhyme, meter, and sounds in five poems of your choice. How do these elements contribute to the poems' meanings?

2. Taken together, how do Hughes's poems provide a critique of relations between blacks and whites in America?

32

A Study of Julia Alvarez:
Five Poems

© Daniel Cima.

When I'm asked what made me into a writer, I point to the watershed experience of coming to this country. Not understanding the language, I had to pay close attention to each word — great training for a writer.
— JULIA ALVAREZ

This chapter offers five poems, chosen by Julia Alvarez for this anthology, with commentaries written by the poet herself. Alvarez's insights on each work, in addition to accompanying images and documents, provide a variety of contexts — personal, cultural, and historical — for understanding and appreciating her poems.

In her introductions to each of the poems, Alvarez shares her reasons for writing, what was on her mind when she wrote each work, and what she thinks now looking back at them. She also offers a bird's-eye view into her writing process (see especially the drafts of the poem in progress on pp. 956–58). In the materials that follow, Alvarez evokes the voices of those who have inspired her — muses that range from women talking and cooking in a kitchen to a character in *The Arabian Nights* to poets including Walt Whitman and Langston Hughes. Alvarez writes, "A poem can be a resting place for the soul . . . a world teeming with discoveries of luminous little *ah-ha!* moments, a 'place for the genuine,' as Marianne Moore calls it." Read on and find out, for example, who her real "First Muse" was, and what, according to Alvarez, a famous American poet and the Chiquita Banana have in common.

In addition to Alvarez's inviting and richly detailed introductions, the chapter also presents a number of visual contexts, such as a photo of a 1963 civil rights demonstration in Queens, New York; the poet's passport photo taken at age ten, just before she moved back to the United States; a collection of draft manuscript pages; and an image of one of Alvarez's poems set in a bronze plaque in a sidewalk — part of "Library Way" in New York City. Further, a critical essay — which complements Alvarez's own perspectives throughout the chapter — by Kelli Lyon Johnson (p. 963) allows readers to consider Alvarez's work in a critical framework. (For a discussion on reading a work alongside critical theory, see Chapter 46, "Critical Strategies for Reading" [p. 1533].)

A BRIEF BIOGRAPHY

Although Julia Alvarez was born (1950) in New York City, she lived in the Dominican Republic until she was ten years old. She returned to New York after her father, a physician, was connected to a plot to overthrow the dictatorship of Rafael Trujillo, and the family had to flee. Growing up in Queens was radically different from the Latino Caribbean world she had experienced during her early childhood. A new culture and new language sensitized Alvarez to her surroundings and her use of language so that emigration from the Dominican Republic to Queens was the beginning of her movement toward becoming a writer. Alvarez quotes the Polish poet Czeslaw Milosz's assertion that "Language is the only homeland" to explain her own sense that what she really settled into was not so much the United States as the English language.

Her fascination with English continued into high school and took shape in college as she became a serious writer — first at Connecticut College from 1967 to 1969 and then at Middlebury College, where she earned a B.A. in 1971. At Syracuse University she was awarded the American Academy of Poetry Prize and, in 1975, earned an M.A. in creative writing.

Since then Alvarez has served as a writer-in-residence for the Kentucky Arts Commission, the Delaware Arts Council, and the Arts Council of Fayetteville, North Carolina. She has taught at California State College (Fresno), College of the Sequoias, Phillips Andover Academy, the University

JULIA ALVAREZ

WOODCUTS BY / GRABADOS DE BELKIS RAMÍREZ

A
Cafecito
Story
El
Cuento del
Cafecito

*English/Spanish
Bilingual Edition*

(*Left*) *A Cafecito Story.* Alvarez describes *A Cafecito Story* (2001) as a modern "eco-parable" or "green fable" and love story. The book was inspired by the author's work with local coffee growers in the Dominican Republic.

Cover image by Belkis Ramírez. Reprinted by permission.

(*Below*) **Alta Gracia.** Julia Alvarez with students from Middlebury College at her coffee farm, Alta Gracia, in the Dominican Republic.

Photograph courtesy of Fundacion Finca Alta Gracia.

of Vermont, George Washington University, the University of Illinois, and, since 1988, at Middlebury College, where she has been a professor of literature and creative writing and is currently a part-time writer-in-residence. Alvarez divides her time between Vermont and the Dominican Republic, where she and her husband have set up an organic coffee farm, Alta Gracia, that supports a literacy school for children and adults. *A Cafecito Story* (2001), which Alvarez considers a "green fable" or "eco-parable," grew out of their experiences promoting fair trade and sustainability for coffee farmers in the Dominican Republic.

AN INTRODUCTION TO HER WORK

Alvarez's poetry has been widely published in journals and magazines ranging from the *New Yorker* to *Mirabella* to the *Kenyon Review*. Her first book of poems, *Homecoming* (1984; a new expanded verison, *Homecoming: New and Collected Poems*, was published in 1996 by Plume/Penguin), uses simple—yet incisive—language to explore issues related to love, domestic life, and work. Her second book of poetry, *The Other Side/El Otro Lado* (1995), is a collection of meditations on her childhood memories of immigrant life that shaped her adult identity and sensibilities. Some of these concerns are also manifested in her book of essays, titled *Something to Declare* (1998), a collection that describes her abiding concerns about how to respond to competing cultures. In her third poetry collection, *The Woman I Kept to Myself* (2004), Alvarez reflects on her personal life and development as a writer from the vantage point of her mid-fifties in seventy-five poems, each consisting of three ten-line stanzas.

In addition to writing a number of books for children and young adults, Alvarez has also published six novels. The first, *How the García Girls Lost Their Accents* (1991), is a collection of fifteen separate but interrelated stories that cover thirty years of the lives of the García sisters from the late 1950s to the late 1980s. Drawing on her own experiences, Alvarez describes the sisters fleeing the Dominican Republic and growing up Latina in the United States. *In the Time of the Butterflies* (1994) is a fictional account of a true story concerning four sisters who opposed Trujillo's dictatorship. Three of the sisters were murdered in 1960 by the government, and the surviving fourth sister recounts the events of their personal and political lives that led to her sisters' deaths. Shaped by the history of Dominican freedom and tyranny, the novel also explores the sisters' relationships to each other and their country.

In *¡Yo!* (1997), Alvarez focuses on Yolanda, one of the García sisters from her first novel, who is now a writer. Written in the different voices of Yo's friends and family members, this fractured narrative constructs a complete picture of a woman who uses her relationships as fodder for fiction, a woman who is self-centered, aggravating, and finally lovable—who is deeply embedded in American culture while remaining aware of her Dominican roots. *¡Yo!*, which means "I" in English, is a meditation on points of view and narrative.

In the Name of Salomé (2000) is a fictional account of Salomé Ureña, who was born in the 1850s and is considered to be "the Emily Dickinson of the Dominican Republic," and her daughter's efforts late in life to reconcile her relationship to her mother's reputation and her own response to Fidel Castro's revolution in Cuba. Alvarez published her sixth and most recent novel, *Saving the World*, in 2006, a story that also links two women's lives, one from the past and one from the present. In this novel, the protagonists are connected by their humanitarian efforts to end smallpox in the nineteenth century and the global AIDS epidemic in the twenty-first century.

Chronology

1950	Born on March 27 in New York City.
1950–60	Raised in the Dominican Republic.
1960	Alvarez family flees the Dominican Republic for New York City after her father joins efforts to overthrow the dictatorship of Rafael Trujillo.
1961	Rafael Trujillo is assassinated.
1967–69	Attends Connecticut College.
1971	Graduates from Middlebury College with a B.A.
1975	Graduates from Syracuse University with an M.A.
1979–80	Attends Bread Loaf School of English.
1979–81	Instructor at Phillips Andover Academy.
1981–83	Visiting assistant professor at University of Vermont.
1984	Publishes *Homecoming*, a volume of poems, and *The Housekeeping Book*, a handmade book of a series of "housekeeping poems," illustrated by Carol MacDonald and Rene Schall.
1984–85	Visiting writer-in-residence at George Washington University.
1985–88	Assistant professor of English at University of Illinois.
1987–88	Awarded a National Endowment for the Arts Fellowship.
1988–98	Professor of English at Middlebury College.
1988–Present	Writer-in-residence at Middlebury College.
1991	Publishes *How the García Girls Lost Their Accents*, a novel.
1994	Publishes *In the Time of the Butterflies*, a novel.
1995	Publishes *The Other Side/El Otro Lado*, a volume of poems.
1996	Publishes *Homecoming: New and Collected Poems*, a reissue of *Homecoming* (1984) with new work included.
1997	Publishes *¡Yo!*, a novel.

1998	Publishes *Something to Declare*, a collection of essays, and *Seven Trees*, a handmade volume of poems.
2000	Publishes *In the Name of Salomé*, a novel, and *The Secret Footprints*, a picture book for children.
2001	Publishes *A Cafecito Story*, a novel or "eco-parable," and *How Tía Lola Came to Visit Stay*, a novel for young adults.
2002	Publishes *The Woman I Kept to Myself*, a volume of poems, and *Before We Were Free*, a novel for young adults.
2004	Publishes *A Gift of Gracias: The Legend of Altagracia*, a picture book for children, and *Finding Miracles*, a novel for young adults.
2006	Publishes *Saving the World*, a novel.

In "Queens, 1963" Alvarez remembers the neighborhood she lived in when she was a thirteen-year-old and how "Everyone seemed more American / than we, newly arrived." The tensions that arose when new immigrants and ethnic groups moved onto the block were mirrored in many American neighborhoods in 1963. Indeed, the entire nation was made keenly aware of segregation when demonstrations were organized across the South and a massive march on Washington in support of civil rights for African Americans drew hundreds of thousands of demonstrators who listened to Martin Luther King Jr. deliver his electrifying "I have a dream" speech. But the issues were hardly resolved, as evidenced by 1963's two best-selling books: *Happiness Is a Warm Puppy* and *Security Is a Thumb and a Blanket*, by Charles M. Schulz of *Peanuts* cartoon fame. The popularity of these books is, perhaps, understandable given the tensions that moved across the country and which seemed to culminate on November 22, 1963, when President Kennedy was assassinated in Dallas, Texas. These events are not mentioned in "Queens, 1963," but they are certainly part of the context that helps us to understand Alvarez's particular neighborhood. In the following introductory essay, Alvarez reflects on the cultural moment of 1963 and her reasons for writing the poem.

Julia Alvarez

A Note to Students on Writing "Queens, 1963"   2006

I remember when we finally bought our very own house after three years of living in rentals. Back then, Queens, New York, was not the multicultural, multilingual place it is today. But the process was beginning. Our neighborhood was sprinkled with ethnicities, some who had been here longer than others. The Germans down the block — now we would call them German Americans — had been Americans for a couple of generations as had our Jewish neighbors, and most definitely, the Midwesterners across the street. Meanwhile, the Greek

Julia Alvarez. The poet at age ten, in her 1960 passport photo. This was the year she left the Dominican Republic for the U.S.
Courtesy of Julia Alvarez.

family next door were newcomers as were we, our accents still heavy, our cooking smells commingling across our backyard fences during mealtimes: their Greek lamb with rosemary, our Dominican habichuelas with sofrito.°

It seemed a peaceable enough kingdom until a black family moved in across the street. What a ruckus got started! Of course, it was the early 1960s: the civil rights movement was just getting under way in this country. Suddenly, our neighborhood was faced with discrimination, but coming from the very same people who themselves had felt discrimination from other, more mainstream Americans. It was my first lesson in hypocrisy and in realizing that

habichuelas with sofrito: Kidney beans prepared with a sautéed mixture of spices, herbs, garlic, onion, pepper, and tomato.

America was still an experiment in process. The words on the Statue of Liberty (see "Sometimes the Words Are So Close," p. 955) were only a promise, not yet a practice in the deep South or in Queens, New York.

In writing this poem I wanted to suggest the many ethnic families in the neighborhood. Of course, I couldn't use their real names and risk being sued. (Though, come to think of it, I've never heard of a poem being sued, have you?) Plus, there is the matter of failing memory. (This was forty-two years ago!) So I chose names that suggested other languages, other places, and also — always the poet's ear at work — names that fit in with the rhythm and cadence of the lines.

JULIA ALVAREZ

Queens, 1963   *1992*

Everyone seemed more American
than we, newly arrived,
foreign dirt still on our soles.
By year's end, a sprinkler waving
like a flag on our mowed lawn,   5
we were blended into the block,
owned our own mock Tudor house.
Then the house across the street
sold to a black family.
Cop cars patrolled our block   10
from the Castellucci's at one end
to the Balakian's on the other.
We heard rumors of bomb threats,
a burning cross on their lawn.
(It turned out to be a sprinkler.)   15
Still the neighborhood buzzed.
The barber's family, Haralambides,
our left-side neighbors, didn't want trouble.
They'd come a long way to be free!
Mr. Scott, the retired plumber,   20
and his plump midwestern wife,
considered moving back home
where white and black got along
by staying where they belonged.
They had cultivated our street   25
like the garden she'd given up
on account of her ailing back,
bad knees, poor eyes, arthritic hands.
She went through her litany daily.
Politely, my mother listened —   30
¡Ay, Mrs. Scott, qué pena!°
— her Dominican good manners
still running on automatic.
The Jewish counselor next door,

31 *qué pena:* What a shame!

had a practice in her house;   35
clients hurried up her walk
ashamed to be seen needing.
(I watched from my upstairs window,
gloomy with adolescence,
and guessed how they too must have   40
hypocritical old-world parents.)
Mrs. Bernstein said it was time
the neighborhood opened up.
As the first Jew on the block,
she remembered the snubbing she got   45
a few years back from Mrs. Scott.
But real estate worried her,
our houses' plummeting value.
She shook her head as she might
at a client's grim disclosures.   50
Too bad the world works this way.
The German girl playing the piano
down the street abruptly stopped
in the middle of a note.
I completed the tune in my head   55
as I watched *their* front door open.
A dark man in a suit
with a girl about my age
walked quickly into a car.
My hand lifted but fell   60
before I made a welcoming gesture.
On her face I had seen a look
from the days before we had melted
into the United States of America.
It was hardness mixed with hurt.   65
It was knowing she never could be
the right kind of American.
A police car followed their car.
Down the street, curtains fell back.
Mrs. Scott swept her walk   70
as if it had just been dirtied.
Then the German piano commenced
downward scales as if tracking
the plummeting real estate.
One by one I imagined the houses   75
sinking into their lawns,
the grass grown wild and tall
in the past tense of this continent
before the first foreigners owned
any of this free country.   80

CONSIDERATIONS FOR CRITICAL THINKING AND WRITING

1. **FIRST RESPONSE.** What nationalities live in this neighborhood in the New
   York City borough of Queens? Are they neighborly to each other?

2. In line 3, why do you suppose Alvarez writes "foreign dirt still on our soles" rather than "foreign soil still on our shoes"? What does Alvarez's particular word choice suggest about her feelings for her native country?

3. Characterize the speaker. How old is she? How does she feel about having come from the Dominican Republic? About living in the United States?

4. Do you think this poem is optimistic or pessimistic about racial relations in the United States? Explain your answer by referring to specific details in the poem.

CONNECTIONS TO OTHER SELECTIONS

1. Discuss the problems immigrants encounter in this poem and in Chitra Banerjee Divakaruni's "Indian Movie, New Jersey" (Border Crossings insert, p. K).

2. Write an essay comparing and contrasting the tone and theme in "Queens, 1963" and in Tato Laviera's "AmeRícan" (p. 814).

A 1963 Queens Civil Rights Demonstration. In this photograph police remove a Congress of Racial Equality (CORE) demonstrator from a Queens construction site. Demonstrators blocked the delivery entrance to the site because they wanted more African Americans and Puerto Ricans hired in the building-trade industry.

Reprinted by permission of AP/Wide World Photos.

CONSIDERATIONS FOR CRITICAL THINKING AND WRITING

1. Discuss the role of the police in this photograph and in "Queens, 1963." What attitudes toward the police do the photograph and the poem display?

2. How do you think the Scotts and Mrs. Bernstein would have responded to this photograph in 1963?

3. Compare the tensions in "Queens, 1963" with those depicted in this photo. How do the speaker's private reflections relate to this public protest?

Perspective

MARNY REQUA (B. 1971)

From an Interview with Julia Alvarez   *1997*

M.R.   What was it like when you came to the United States?

J.A.   When we got to Queens, it was really a shock to go from a totally Latino, *familia* Caribbean world into this very cold and kind of forbidding one in which we didn't speak the language. I didn't grow up with a tradition of writing or reading books at all. People were always telling stories but it wasn't a tradition of literary . . . reading a book or doing something solitary like that. Coming to this country I discovered books, I discovered that it was a way to enter into a portable homeland that you could carry around in your head. You didn't have to suffer what was going on around you. I found in books a place to go. I became interested in language because I was learning a language intentionally at the age of ten. I was wondering, "Why is it that word and not another?" which any writer has to do with their language. I always say I came to English late but to the profession early. By high school I was pretty set: that's what I want to do, be a writer.

M.R.   Did you have culture shock returning to the Dominican Republic as you were growing up?

J.A.   The culture here had an effect on me — at the time this country was coming undone with protests and flower children and drugs. Here I was back in the Dominican Republic and I wouldn't keep my mouth shut. I had my own ideas and I had my own politics, and it, I just didn't gel anymore with the family. I didn't quite feel I ever belonged in this North American culture and I always had this nostalgia that when I went back I'd belong, and then I found out I didn't belong there either.

M.R.   Was it a source of inspiration to have a foot in both cultures?

J.A.   I only came to that later. [Then], it was a burden because I felt torn. I wanted to be part of one culture and then part of the other. It was a time when the model for the immigrant was that you came and you became an American and you cut off your ties and that was that. My parents had that frame of mind, because they were so afraid, and they were "Learn your English" and "Become one of them," and that left out so much. Now I see the richness. Part of what I want to do with my work is that complexity, that richness. I don't want it to be simplistic and either/or.

From "The Politics of Fiction," *Frontera* 5 (1997)

CONSIDERATIONS FOR CRITICAL THINKING AND WRITING

1. What do you think Alvarez means when she describes books as "a portable homeland that you could carry around in your head"?

2. Why is it difficult for Alvarez to feel that she belongs in either the Dominican or the North American culture?

3. Alvarez says that in the 1960s "the model for the immigrant was that you came and you became an American and you cut off your ties and that was that." Do you think this model has changed in the United States since then? Explain your response.

4. How might this interview alter your understanding of "Queens, 1963"? What light is shed, for example, on the speaker's feeling that her family "blended into the block" in line 6?

JULIA ALVAREZ

On Writing "Housekeeping Cages" and Her Housekeeping Poems 1998

I can still remember the first time I heard my own voice on paper. It happened a few years after I graduated from a creative writing master's program. I had earned a short-term residency at Yaddo, the writer's colony, where I was assigned a studio in the big mansion—the tower room at the top of the stairs. The rules were clear: we artists and writers were to stick to our studios during the day and come out at night for supper and socializing. Nothing was to come between us and our work.

I sat up in my tower room, waiting for inspiration. All around me I could hear the typewriters going. Before me lay a blank sheet of paper, ready for the important work I had come there to write. That was the problem, you see. I was trying to do IMPORTANT work and so I couldn't hear myself think. I was trying to pitch my voice to "Turning and turning in the widening gyre," or, "Of man's first disobedience, and the fruit of that forbidden tree, " or, "Sing in me, Muse, and through me tell the story." I was tuning my voice to these men's voices because I thought that was the way I had to sound if I wanted to be a writer. After all, the writers I read and admired sounded like that.

But the voice I heard when I listened to myself think was the voice of a woman, sitting in her kitchen, gossiping with a friend over a cup of coffee. It was the voice of Gladys singing her sad boleros, Belkis putting color on my face with tales of her escapades, Tití naming the orchids, Ada telling me love stories as we made the beds. I had, however, never seen voices like these in print. So, I didn't know poems could be written in those voices, *my* voice.

So there I was at Yaddo, trying to write something important and coming up with nothing. And then, hallelujah—I heard the vacuum going up and down the hall. I opened the door and introduced myself to the friendly, sweating woman, wielding her vacuum cleaner. She invited me down to the kitchen so we wouldn't disturb the other guests. There I met the cook, and as we all sat, drinking coffee, I paged through her old cookbook, *knead, poach, stew, whip, score, julienne, whisk, sauté, sift.* Hmm. I began hearing a music in these words. I jotted down the names of implements:

> Cup, spoon, ladle, pot, kettle,
> grater and peeler,
> colander, corer,
> waffle iron, small funnel.

"You working on a poem there?" the cook asked me.
I shook my head.

A little later, I went upstairs and wrote down in my journal this beautiful vocabulary of my girlhood. As I wrote, I tapped my foot on the floor to the rhythm of the words. I could see Mami and the aunts with the cook in the kitchen bending their heads over a pot of habichuelas, arguing about what flavor was missing — what could it be they had missed putting in it? And then, the thought of Mami recalled Gladys, the maid who loved to sing, and that thought led me through the house, the mahogany furniture that needed dusting, the beds that needed making, the big bin of laundry that needed washing.

That day, I began working on a poem about dusting. Then another followed on sewing; then came a sweeping poem, an ironing poem. Later, I would collect these into a series I called "the housekeeping poems," poems using the metaphors, details, language of my first apprenticeship as a young girl. Even later, having found my woman's voice, I would gain confidence to explore my voice as a Latina and to write stories and poems using the metaphors, details, rhythms of that first world I had left behind in Spanish.

But it began, first, by discovering my woman's voice at Yaddo where I had found it as a child. Twenty years after learning to sing with Gladys, I was reminded of the lessons I had learned in childhood: that my voice would not be found up in a tower, in those upper reaches or important places, but down in the kitchen among the women who first taught me about service, about passion, about singing as if my life depended on it.

From Something to Declare

Julia Alvarez

Housekeeping Cages   1994

Sometimes people ask me why I wrote a series of poems about housekeeping if I'm a feminist. Don't I want women to be liberated from the oppressive roles they were condemned to live? I don't see housekeeping that way. They were the crafts we women had, sewing, embroidering, cooking, spinning, sweeping, even the lowly dusting. And like Dylan Thomas said, we sang in our chains like the sea. Isn't it already thinking from the point of view of the oppressor to say to ourselves, what we did was nothing?

You use what you have, you learn to work the structure to create what you need. I don't feel that writing in traditional forms is giving up power, going over to the enemy. The word belongs to no one, the houses built of words belong to no one. We have to take them back from those who think they own them.

Sometimes I get in a mood. I tell myself I am taken over. I am writing under somebody else's thumb and tongue. See, English was not my first language. It was, in fact, a colonizing language to my Spanish Caribbean. But then Spanish was also a colonizer's language; after all, Spain colonized Quisqueya. There's no getting free. We are always writing in a form imposed on us. But then, I'm Scheherazade in the Sultan's room. I use structures to survive and triumph! To say what's important to me as a woman and as a Latina.

I think of form as territory that has been colonized, but that you can free. See, I feel subversive in formal verse. A voice is going to inhabit that form that was barred from entering it before! That's what I tried in the "33" poems, to use my woman's voice in a sonnet as I would use it sitting in the kitchen with a close friend, talking womanstuff. In school, I was always trying to inhabit those forms as the male writers had. To pitch my voice to "Of man's first disobedience, and the fruit. . . ." If it didn't hit the key of "Sing in me, Muse, and through me tell the story," how could it be important poetry? The only kind.

While I was in graduate school some of the women in the program started a Women's Writing Collective in Syracuse. We were musing each other into unknown writing territory. One woman advised me to listen to my own voice, deep inside, and put that down on paper. But what I heard when I listened were voices that said things like "Don't put so much salt on the lettuce, you'll wilt the salad!" I'd never heard that in a poem. So how could it be poetry? Then, with the "33" sonnet sequence, I said, I'm going to go in there and I'm going to sound like myself. I took on the whole kaboodle. I was going into form, sonnets no less. Wow.

What I wanted from the sonnet was the tradition that it offered as well as the structure. The sonnet tradition was one in which women were caged in golden cages of beloved, in perfumed gas chambers of stereotype. I wanted to go in that heavily mined and male labyrinth with the string of my own voice. I wanted to explore it and explode it too. I call my sonnets free verse sonnets. They have ten syllables per line, and the lines are in a loose iambic pentameter. But they are heavily enjambed and the rhymes are often slant-rhymes, and the rhyme scheme is peculiar to each sonnet. One friend read them and said, "I didn't know they were sonnets. They sounded like you talking!"

By learning to work the sonnet structure and yet remaining true to my own voice, I made myself at home in that form. When I was done with it, it was a totally different form from the one I learned in school. I have used other traditional forms. In my poem about sweeping, since you sweep with the broom and you dance — it's a coupling — I used rhyming couplets. I wrote a poem of advice mothers give to their daughters in a villanelle, because it's such a nagging form. But mostly the sonnet is the form I've worked with. It's the classic form in which we women were trapped, love objects, and I was trapped inside that voice and paradigm, and I wanted to work my way out of it.

My idea of traditional forms is that as women much of our heritage is trapped in them. But the cage can turn into a house if you housekeep it the right way. You housekeep it by working the words just so.

From *A Formal Feeling Comes: Poems in Form by Contemporary Women*, edited by Annie Finch

CONSIDERATIONS FOR CRITICAL THINKING AND WRITING

1. How does Alvarez connect housekeeping to "writing in traditional forms"?

2. Compare "Sometimes the Words Are So Close" (p. 955) to Alvarez's description in her essay of how she writes sonnets. How closely does the poem's form follow her description?

3. Why does Alvarez consider "Dusting" (p. 952) and "Ironing Their Clothes" (p. 953) to be feminist poems? How can the poems be read as feminist in their sensibility?

JULIA ALVAREZ

A Note to Students on Writing "Dusting"   2006

Finally, I took the leap and began to write poems in my own voice and the voices of the women in my past, who inevitably were talking about their work, housekeeping. I had to trust that those voices, while not conventionally important, still had something to say. At school, I had been taught the formal canon of literature: epic poems with catalogues of ships, poems about wars and the rumors of wars. Why not write a poem in the voice of a mother cataloguing the fabrics, with names as beautiful as those of ships ("gabardine, organdy, wool, madras" from "Naming the Fabrics") or a poem about sweeping while watching a news report about the Vietnam War on TV ("How I Learned to Sweep")? Each time I delved into one of the housekeeping "arts," I discovered deeper, richer materials and metaphors than I had anticipated. This is wonderful news for a writer. As Robert Frost once said about rhymes in a poem, "No surprise for the writer, no surprise for the reader." The things we discover while writing what we write tingle with that special energy and delight of not just writing a poem, but enlarging our understanding.

Dusting is the lowliest of the housekeeping arts. Any little girl with a rag can dust. But rather than dust, the little girl in my poem is writing her name on the furniture, something her mother keeps correcting. What a perfect metaphor for the changing roles of women which I've experienced in my own life: the mother believing that a woman's place is in the home, not in the public sphere; the girl from a younger generation wanting to make a name for herself.

And in writing "Dusting," I also discovered a metaphor about writing. A complicated balancing act: like the mother, the artist has to disappear in her work; it's the poem that counts, not the name or celebrity of the writer. But the artist also needs the little girl's pluck and ambition to even imagine a public voice for herself. Otherwise, she'd be swallowed up in self-doubt, silenced by her mother's old-world way of viewing a woman's role.

JULIA ALVAREZ

Dusting   1981

Each morning I wrote my name
on the dusty cabinet, then crossed
the dining table in script, scrawled
in capitals on the backs of chairs,
practising signatures like scales   5
while Mother followed, squirting
linseed from a burping can
into a crumpled-up flannel.

She erased my fingerprints
from the bookshelf and rocker,   10
polished mirrors on the desk
scribbled with my alphabets.
My name was swallowed in the towel
with which she jeweled the table tops.
The grain surfaced in the oak   15
and the pine grew luminous.
But I refused with every mark
to be like her, anonymous.

CONSIDERATIONS FOR CRITICAL THINKING AND WRITING

1. **FIRST RESPONSE.** Describe the central conflict between the speaker and the
   mother.
2. Explain why the image of dusting is a particularly appropriate metaphor
   for evoking the central conflict.
3. Discuss the effect of the rhymes in lines 15–18.
4. Consider the tone of each stanza. Explain why you find the tone identical
   or different in each stanza.

CONNECTIONS TO OTHER SELECTIONS

1. Compare the significance of the mothers in "Dusting" and in Langston
   Hughes's "Mother to Son" (p. 917).
2. Discuss the attitudes toward writing in "Dusting" and in Anne Bradstreet's
   "The Author to Her Book" (p. 685).

JULIA ALVAREZ

A Note to Students on Writing "Ironing Their Clothes"   2006

Maybe because ironing is my favorite of all the housekeeping chores, this is my
favorite of the housekeeping poems. In the apprenticeship of household arts,
ironing is for the advanced apprentice. After all, think about it, you're wielding
an instrument that could cause some damage: you could burn yourself, you

could burn the clothes. I was not allowed to iron clothes until I was older and could be trusted to iron all different kinds of fabrics ("gabardine, organdy, wool, madras") just right.

Again, think of how ironing someone's clothes can be a metaphor for all kinds of things. You have this power to take out the wrinkles and worries from someone's outer skin! You can touch and caress and love someone and not be told that you are making a nuisance of yourself!

In writing this poem I wanted the language to mirror the process. I wanted the lines to suggest all the fussy complications of trying to get your iron into hard corners and places ("I stroked the yoke, / the breast pocket, collar and cuffs, / until the rumpled heap relaxed . . .") and then the smooth sailing of a line that sails over the line break into the next line ("into the shape / of my father's broad chest . . ."). I wanted to get the hiss of the iron in those last four lines. I revised and revised this poem, especially the verbs, most especially the verbs that have to do the actual work of the iron. When I finally got that last line with its double rhymes ("express / excess"; "love / cloth"), I felt as if I'd done a whole laundry basket worth of ironing just right.

JULIA ALVAREZ

Ironing Their Clothes   *1981*

With a hot glide up, then down, his shirts,
I ironed out my father's back, cramped
and worried with work. I stroked the yoke,
the breast pocket, collar and cuffs,
until the rumpled heap relaxed into the shape   5
of my father's broad chest, the shoulders shrugged off
the world, the collapsed arms spread for a hug.
And if there'd been a face above the buttondown neck,
I would have pressed the forehead out, I would
have made a boy again out of that tired man!   10

If I clung to her skirt as she sorted the wash
or put out a line, my mother frowned,
a crease down each side of her mouth.
This is no time for love! But here
I could linger over her wrinkled bedjacket,   15
kiss at the damp puckers of her wrists
with the hot tip. Here I caressed
collars, scallops, ties, pleats which made
her outfits test of the patience of my passion.
Here I could lay my dreaming iron on her lap.   20

The smell of baked cotton rose from the board
and blew with a breeze out the window
to the family wardrobe drying on the clothesline,
all needing a touch of my iron. Here I could tickle

the underarms of my big sister's petticoat 25
or secretly pat the backside of her pajamas.
For she too would have warned me not to muss
her fresh blouses, starched jumpers, and smocks,
all that my careful hand had ironed out,
forced to express my excess love on cloth. 30

Considerations for Critical Thinking and Writing

1. **FIRST RESPONSE.** Explain how the speaker expresses her love for her family in the extended metaphor of ironing.

2. How are ironing and the poem itself expressions of the speaker's "excess love" (line 30)? In what sense is her love excessive?

3. Explain how the speaker's relationship to her father differs from how she relates to her mother.

Connections to Other Selections

1. **CREATIVE RESPONSE.** Compare the descriptions of the mother in this poem and in Alvarez's "Dusting" (p. 952). Write a one-paragraph character sketch that uses vivid details and metaphoric language to describe her.

2. Discuss the perspective provided on housework in "Ironing Their Clothes" and in Natasha Trethewey's "Domestic Work, 1937" (p. 808).

Julia Alvarez

A Note to Students on Writing "Sometimes the Words Are So Close" 2006

From the "33" Sonnet Sequence

I really believe that being a reader turns you into a writer. You connect with the voice in a poem at a deeper and more intimate level than you do with practically anyone in your everyday life. Seems like the years fall away, differences fall away, and when George Herbert asks in his poem, "The Flower,"

Who would have thought my shrivel'd heart
Could have recover'd greennesse?

You want to stroke the page and answer him, "I did, George." Instead you write a poem that responds to the feelings in his poem; you recover greenness for him and for yourself.

With the "33" sonnet sequence, I wanted the voice of the speaker to sound like a real woman speaking. A voice at once intimate and also somehow universal, essential. This sonnet #42 ["Sometimes the Words Are So Close"] is the last one in the sequence, a kind of final "testimony" about what writing is all about.

I mentioned that when you love something you read, you want to respond to it. You want to say it again, in fresh new language. Robert Frost speaks to this impulse in the poet when he says, "Don't borrow, steal!" Well, I borrowed /

stole two favorite passages. One of them is from the poem on the Statue of Liberty, which was written by Emma Lazarus (1849–1887), titled "The New Colossus" [p. 1338]. These lines will sound familiar to you, I'm sure:

> Give me your tired, your poor,
> Your huddled masses yearning to breathe free,
> The wretched refuse of your teeming shore.
> Send these, the homeless, tempest-tost to me,
> I lift my lamp beside the golden door!

I think of these lines, not just as an invitation to the land of the brave and home of the free, but an invitation to poetry! A poem can be a resting place for the soul yearning to breathe free, a form that won't tolerate the misuses and abuses of language, a world teeming with discoveries and luminous little *ah-ha!* moments, a "place for the genuine," as Marianne Moore calls it in her poem "On Poetry." William Carlos Williams said that we can't get the news from poems, practical information, hard facts, but "men die daily for lack of what is found there."

I not only agreed with this idea, but I wanted to say so in my own words, and so I echoed those lines from the Statue of Liberty in my sonnet:

> Those of you lost and yearning to be free,
> who hear these words, take heart from me.

Another favorite line comes from Walt Whitman's book-length "Leaves of Grass": "Who touches this [book] touches a man." As a young, lonely immigrant girl reading Whitman, those words made me feel so accompanied, so connected. And so I borrowed / stole that line and made it my own at the end of this poem.

Julia Alvarez

Sometimes the Words Are So Close   *1982*
From the "33" Sonnet Sequence

Sometimes the words are so close I am
more who I am when I'm down on paper
than anywhere else as if my life were
practising for the real me I become
unbuttoned from the anecdotal and   5
unnecessary and undressed down
to the figure of the poem, line by line,
the real text a child could understand.
Why do I get confused living it through?
Those of you lost and yearning to be free,   10
who hear these words, take heart from me.
I once was in as many drafts as you.
But briefly, essentially, here I am.
Who touches this poem touches a woman.

Four Drafts of "Sometimes the Words Are So Close": A Poet's Writing Process

Four early versions of the poem in original manuscript form.

Sometimes the words are so close I am
more who I am when I'm down on paper
than anywhere else as if my life were
practising for the real me I become
unbuttoned from the anecdotal and
unnecessary and undressed down
to the figure of the poem, line by line
the real text a child could understand —
Why do I get confused living it through
~~Your of the picture if you so wondering~~
~~where could have been script~~ ~~what I~~ you're curious
~~took here for one~~
~~was, most~~ ~~that I loved~~ .
me anymore than
but briefly, essentially, here I am
Who touches this poem touches a woman —

goes...
you + I will

Concave
Now if its touched ~~class moves~~
you crypt

Concave, now if its
touched you
as I script
to do, you'll find yourself
embraced by
mought

you'll find yourself
~~down~~ in
brought to love

Sometimes the words are so close I am
more who I am when I'm down on paper
than anywhere else as if my life were
practising for the real me I become
unbuttoned form the anecdotal and
unnecessary and undressed down
to the figure of the poem, line by line,
the real text a child could understand.
Why do I get confused living it through?
Those of you, lost and yearning to be free,
who hear these words, take heart from me.
I ~~was~~ once was in as many drafts as you.
But briefly, essentially, here I am...
Who touches this poem touches a woman.

```
Sometimes the words are so close I am
more who I am when I'm down on paper
than anywhere else as if my life were
practising for the real me I become
unbuttoned from the anecdotal and
unnecessary and undressed down
to the figure of the poem, line by line,
the real text a child could understand.
Why do I get confused living it through?
Those of you, lost and yearning to be free,
who hear these words, take heart from me.
I once was in as many drafts as you.
But briefly, essentially, here I am...
Who touches this poem touches a woman.
```

— pretentious

CONSIDERATIONS FOR CRITICAL THINKING AND WRITING

1. **FIRST RESPONSE.** Paraphrase lines 1–9. What produces the speaker's sense of frustration?

2. How do lines 10–14 resolve the question raised in line 9?

3. Explain how Alvarez's use of punctuation reinforces the poem's meanings.

4. Discuss the elements of this poem that make it a sonnet.

5. Read carefully Alvarez's early drafts and discuss how they offer insights into your understanding and interpretation of the final version.

CONNECTIONS TO OTHER SELECTIONS

1. Compare the transformative power of poetry in this poem and in Emily Dickinson's "I dwell in Possibility" (p. 851).

2. The poem's final line echoes Walt Whitman's poem "So Long" in which he addresses the reader: "Camerado! This is no book;/Who touches this, touches a man." Alvarez has said that Whitman is one of her favorite poets. Read "I Sing the Body Electric" (p. 801) and "One's-Self I Sing" (p. 1036) along with "So Long" (readily available online) and propose an explanation about why you think she admires his poetry.

JULIA ALVAREZ

A Note to Students on Writing "First Muse"   2006

I have to come clean about calling this poem "First Muse."

I had another first muse in Spanish. Her name was Scheherazade and I read about her in a book my aunt gave me called *The Arabian Nights*. Scheherazade saves her life by telling the murderous sultan incredible tales night after

Those of you, lost and yearning to be free,
who hear these words, take heart from me.
I once was in as many drafts as you.
But briefly, essentially, here I am....
Who touches this poem touches a woman.

-Julia Alvarez
(1950-), "33"

Library Way. An excerpt from Alvarez's poem "Sometimes the Words Are So Close" is set in a bronze plaque on 41st Street in New York City, and is part of the "Library Way" — a display sponsored by the New York Public Library of sidewalk plaques that feature literary quotations from ninety-six artists and writers including Lucille Clifton, John Milton, and Pablo Picasso. Courtesy of the Grand Central Partnership, New York and sculptor Gregg LeFevre.

night for 1001 nights. Listening to her stories, the sultan is transformed. He no longer wants to kill all the women in his kingdom. In fact, he falls in love with Scheherazade. This young lady saves her own life, the lives of all the women in her kingdom, and by changing him, she also saves the sultan's soul just by telling stories. Right then, I knew what I wanted to be when I grew up. You bet. A storyteller.

Of course, back then, I was growing up in the Dominican Republic, living in a cruel and dangerous dictatorship myself. My own father was a member of an underground freedom movement to depose this dictator. Like Scheherazade, my life and the life of many Dominicans was in danger. But stories like the ones in *The Arabian Nights* helped me dream that the world was a more exciting and mysterious place than I could even imagine. That I was free to travel on the magic carpet of Scheherazade's tales even if the dictatorship did not allow me to drive one town over without inspection and permission.

When I came into English and became a reader, I had new dreams. I wanted to be an American writer. But as I mentioned earlier, the United States of the early '60s was still a long way off from the multicultural "revolution" of the late '80s and '90s. All the writers we read in my English class were Anglo Americans, and many of them were male. Still, the words they put down on paper invited everyone to partake of them. The authors were talking directly to me, asking me questions ("Who would have thought my shrivel'd heart . . . ?"), inviting me to be intimate with their words ("Who touches this book touches a man"). That's what I loved about reading: the great egalitarian democracy between the covers of books. The table set for all. The portable homeland. I wanted to be a part of that world. I often say that when I left the Dominican Republic in 1960, I landed, not in the United States, but in the English language, and that's where I put down deep roots by becoming a writer.

But the world beyond the covers of books did not mirror this great democracy. As you read in "Queens, 1963," the reality was disappointing. There were gated communities within this great free country. Places where immigrants and blacks need not apply. One of them was the guarded canon of literature. I still recall the famous writer who made the pronouncement that one could not write in English unless it was one's mother tongue. I was filled with self-doubt, and since I didn't have any examples in what we were reading in school that this pronouncement was wrong, I thought he was right.

Back then, Latino stories were the province of sociology, not literature. As for popular media, the only "Hispanics" on TV were Ricky Ricardo, with his laughable accent, and Chiquita Banana, selling fruit for the United Fruit Company. But as I said about writing in form, you find yourself caught in a structure or negative paradigm and you turn it on its head. You use it to get free. I listened to Chiquita singing, "I'm Chiquita Banana and I've come to say," and I began to get her message: *I'm a Latina woman, and I am claiming it openly, and what's more I've got something to say*. I felt the same rush of hope when I read Langston Hughes's "I, Too" [This poem appears on p. 915]. In that poem, Mr. Hughes promised himself that "tomorrow, I'll be at the table" of American literature. And there he was in my English textbook. He had made good on his promise to himself, to me!

The civil rights struggle didn't just happen on buses and in places of business or on picket lines in Birmingham, Alabama, or Queens, New York. It also happened on paper. Chiquita Banana and Langston Hughes were right. There is a place for all our voices in the great inclusive world of literature. I feel honored and privileged to be part of that great liberating movement of words on paper, springing us all free with their magic and power, connecting us with ourselves and with each other.

JULIA ALVAREZ

First Muse   1999

When I heard the famous poet pronounce
"One can only write poems in the tongue
in which one first said *Mother*," I was stunned.

Lately arrived in English, I slipped down
into my seat and fought back tears, thinking   5
of all those notebooks filled with bogus poems
I'd have to burn, thinking maybe there was
a little loophole, maybe just maybe
Mami had sung me lullabies she'd learned
from wives stationed at the embassy,   10

thinking maybe she'd left the radio on
beside my crib tuned to the BBC
or Voice of America, maybe her friend
from boarding school had sent a talking doll
who spoke in English? Maybe I could be   15
the one exception to this writing rule?
For months I suffered from bad writer's-block,
which I envisioned, not as a blank page,
but as a literary border guard
turning me back to Spanish on each line.   20

I gave up writing, watched lots of TV,
and you know how it happens that advice
comes from unlikely quarters? *She* came on,
sassy, olive-skinned, hula-hooping her hips,
a basket of bananas on her head,   25
her lilting accent so full of feeling
it seemed the way the heart would speak English
if it could speak. I touched the screen and sang
my own heart out with my new muse, *I am*
Chiquita Banana and I'm here to say . . .   30

CONSIDERATIONS FOR CRITICAL THINKING AND WRITING

1. **FIRST RESPONSE.** What do you think the "famous poet" had in mind by insisting that "'One can only write poems in the tongue / in which one first said *Mother'* "? Explain why you agree or disagree with this statement.

2. How does the speaker preserve the serious nature of her bilingualism while simultaneously treating the topic humorously?

3. How and why does Chiquita Banana serve as the speaker's "new muse"?

CONNECTIONS TO OTHER SELECTIONS

1. Discuss the speaker's passion for language as it is revealed in "First Muse," "Sometimes the Words Are So Close" (p. 955), and "Dusting" (p. 952).

2. Compare the themes concerning writing and ethnicity in "First Muse" and in Julio Marzán's "Ethnic Poetry" (p. 718).

3. Consider the speakers' reactions in "First Muse" and in Judy Page Heitzman's "The Schoolroom on the Second Floor of the Knitting Mill" (p. 978) to the authoritative voice each hears. What effects do these powerful voices have on the speakers' lives?

The Chiquita Banana.
A songbook featuring an image of the Chiquita Banana character referenced in Alvarez's "First Muse."
Courtesy of Chiquita Brands, Inc.

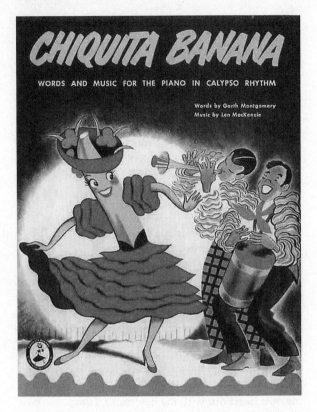

CONSIDERATIONS FOR CRITICAL THINKING AND WRITING

1. How does this cover for the sheet music of Chiquita Banana's song illustrate the character's "sassy" tone alluded to in the final stanza of "First Muse"?

2. In "First Muse," Alvarez humorously contemplates that if her mother had "left the radio on / beside my crib tuned to the BBC / or Voice of America," she might have learned English as an infant. How does a careful analysis of the sheet music illustration suggest the difference between Chiquita's voice and that of the BBC or Voice of America?

3. The Chiquita Brands International corporation maintains a Web site (www.chiquita.com) that provides a history of its advertisements from the 1940s to the present, including recordings of the Chiquita song. How do you think the images of "Miss Chiquita" and her song served as a "new muse" for Alvarez when she was starting out as a writer?

Perspective

KELLI LYON JOHNSON (B. 1969)

Mapping an Identity   2005

Alvarez poses the problem of how we are to understand and represent identity within the multiple migrations that characterize an increasingly global society. By "mapping a country that's not on the map," Alvarez, a Dominican immigrant forced into exile in the United States, is undertaking a journey that places her at the forefront of contemporary American letters.

The question of identity and agency is particularly acute for women, postcolonial peoples, and others upon whom an identity has traditionally been imposed. Given Alvarez's success, both commercial and artistic, a variety of groups have claimed her as a member of their communities: as woman, ethnic, exile, diaspora, Caribbean, Dominican, Latina, and American. In the keynote address at a conference for Caribbean Studies, Doña Aída Cartagena Portalatín, "the grand woman of letters in the Dominican Republic" (*Something*[1] 171), gently chides Alvarez for writing in English. "Come back to your country, to your language," she tells Alvarez. "You are a Dominican" (171). By conflating linguistic, national, and cultural identity, Portalatín underscores the importance of these factors for constructing a literary tradition that includes displaced writers like Alvarez, who quite consciously has not adopted for writing the language of her country of origin.

In response to such comments, Alvarez has asserted her own self-definition as both (and neither) Dominican and American by writing "a new place on the map" (*Something* 173). Placing herself among a multiethnic group of postcolonial authors who write in English — "Michael Ondaatje in Toronto, Maxine Hong Kingston in San Francisco, Seamus Heaney in Boston, Bharati Mukherjee in Berkeley, Marjorie Agosín in Wellesley, Edwidge Danticat in Brooklyn" (173) — Alvarez, like these authors, has altered contemporary American literature by stretching the literary cartography of the Americas. These authors have brought, through their writings, their own countries of origin into a body of work in which the word *American* expands across continents and seas and begins to recapture its original connotation.

Alvarez has also claimed membership among a *comunidad* of U.S. Latina writers — Sandra Cisneros, Ana Castillo, Judith Ortiz Cofer, Lorna Dee Cervantes, Cherríe Moraga, Helena María Viramontes, and Denise Chávez — despite her fears that "the cage of definition" will enclose her writing "with its 'Latino subject matter,' 'Latino style,' 'Latino concerns'" (169). Like these authors, Alvarez seeks to write women into a postcolonial tradition of literature that has historically excluded women, particularly in writings of exile. To counter imposed definitions and historical silences, Alvarez has found that "the best way to define myself is through stories and poems" (169). The space that Alvarez maps is thus a narrative space: the site of her emerging cartography of identity and exile.

From *Julia Alvarez: Writing a New Place on the Map*

---

[1] *Something to Declare*, Alvarez's collection of essays published in 1998.

CONSIDERATIONS FOR CRITICAL THINKING AND WRITING

1. From your reading of the poems in this chapter, which community identity—"ethnic, exile, diaspora, Caribbean, Dominican, Latina, and American"—best describes Alvarez for you?

2. In what sense does Alvarez's poetry expand "the literary cartography of the Americas"?

3. Consider "First Muse" as Alvarez's response to Portalatín's suggestion that she should write in Spanish rather than English and "[c]ome back to your country, to your language."

33

A THEMATIC CASE STUDY
Love and Longing

For a man to become a poet . . .
he must be in love or miserable.

— GEORGE GORDON, LORD BYRON

National Portrait Gallery,
London.

A BRIEF INTRODUCTION

Behind all of the elements that make up a poem, and even behind its cultural contexts and critical reception, lies its theme. Its idea and the point around which the entire poem revolves, the theme is ultimately what we respond to — or fail to respond to. All of the other elements, in fact, are typically there to contribute to the theme, whether or not that theme is explicitly stated. Reading thematically means extending what we have learned about the analysis of individual elements at work in the poem to make connections between the text and the world we inhabit.

This chapter, organized into a case study on love poems, focuses on a single theme as it reappears throughout various parts of poetic history. These poems have much to say about human experience — experience that is contradictory, confusing, complicated, and fascinating. You'll find diverse perspectives from different historical, cultural, generational, or political moments. You'll also discover writers who aim to entertain, to describe,

Web — Research the poets in this chapter at bedfordstmartins.com/meyercompact.

to convince, and to complain. After reading these poems in the context of one another, you're likely to come away with a richer understanding of how the themes of love play out in your own life.

Poems about love have probably enchanted and intrigued their hearers since people began making poetry. Like poetry itself, love is, after all, about intensity, acute impressions, and powerful responsibilities. The emotional dimensions of love do not lend themselves to analytic expository essays. Although such writing can be satisfying intellectually, it is most inadequate for evoking and capturing the thick excitement and swooning reveries that love engenders. The poems in this section include spiritual as well as physical explorations of love that range over four centuries. As you'll see, poetic responses to love by men and women can be quite similar as well as different from one another, just as poems from different periods can reflect a variety of values and attitudes toward love. It is indeed an engaging theme — but as you read, don't forget to pay attention to the formal elements of each of these selections and how they work together to create the poem's particular points about love. Also, remember to read not only for the presence of love; many other themes can be found in these works, and many other connections can be made to the literature elsewhere in this anthology.

The oldest love poem in this case study, Christopher Marlowe's "The Passionate Shepherd to His Love," opens with the line, "Come live with me and be my love." This famous pastoral lyric set a tone for love poetry that has been replicated since its publication. Before concluding with "Then live with me and be my love," Marlowe embraces the kinds of generous pleasure that readers have traditionally and happily received for centuries. The feelings, if not the particular images, are likely to be quite familiar to you.

CHRISTOPHER MARLOWE (1564–1593)

The Passionate Shepherd to His Love   1599?

Come live with me and be my love,
And we will all the pleasure prove
That valleys, groves, hills, and fields,
Woods, or steepy mountain yields.

And we will sit upon the rocks,   5
Seeing the shepherds feed their flocks,
By shallow rivers to whose falls
Melodious birds sing madrigals.

And I will make thee beds of roses
And a thousand fragrant posies,   10
A cap of flowers, and a kirtle°   *dress or skirt*
Embroidered all with leaves of myrtle;

A gown made of the finest wool
Which from our pretty lambs we pull;
Fair lined slippers for the cold,   15
With buckles of the purest gold;

A belt of straw and ivy buds,
With coral clasps and amber studs:
And if these pleasures may thee move,
Come live with me, and be my love.   20

The shepherd swains shall dance and sing
For thy delight each May morning:
If these delights thy mind may move,
Then live with me and be my love.

CONSIDERATIONS FOR CRITICAL THINKING AND WRITING

1. **FIRST RESPONSE** How persuasive do you find the shepherd's arguments to
   his potential lover?
2. What do you think might be the equivalent of the shepherd's arguments in
   the twenty-first century? What kinds of appeals and images of love would
   be made by a contemporary lover?
3. Try writing a response to the shepherd from the female's point of view
   using Marlowe's rhythms, rhyme scheme, and quatrains.

While Marlowe's shepherd focuses his energies on convincing his potential love to join him (in the delights associated with love), the speaker in
the following sonnet by William Shakespeare demonstrates his love for
poetry as well and focuses on the beauty of the object of the poem. In doing
so, he introduces a theme that has become a perennial challenge to love—
the corrosive, destructive nature of what Shakespeare shockingly calls "sluttish time." His resolution of this issue is intriguing: see if you agree with it.

WILLIAM SHAKESPEARE (1564-1616)

Not marble, nor the gilded monuments   1609

Not marble, nor the gilded monuments
Of princes, shall outlive this powerful rhyme;
But you shall shine more bright in these conténts
Than unswept stone, besmeared with sluttish time.
When wasteful war shall statues overturn,   5
And broils root out the work of masonry,
Nor Mars his° swords nor war's quick fire shall burn   *possessive of Mars*
The living record of your memory.

'Gainst death and all-oblivious enmity
Shall you pace forth; your praise shall still find room   10
Even in the eyes of all posterity
That wear this world out to the ending doom.
   So, till the judgment that yourself arise,
   You live in this, and dwell in lovers' eyes.

CONSIDERATIONS FOR CRITICAL THINKING AND WRITING

1. FIRST RESPONSE. What do you think is the central point of this poem? Explain whether you agree or disagree with its theme.

2. How does "sluttish time" represent the poem's major conflict?

3. Consider whether this poem is more about the poet's loved one or the poet's love of his own poetry.

CONNECTIONS TO OTHER SELECTIONS

1. Compare the theme of this poem with that of Andrew Marvell's "To His Coy Mistress" (p. 636), paying particular attention to the speaker's beliefs about how time affects love.

2. Discuss whether you find this love poem more or less appealing than Marlowe's "The Passionate Shepherd to His Love" (p. 966). As you make this comparison, consider what the criteria for an appealing love poem should be.

As Shakespeare's speaker presents a love that will withstand the destruction of time, Anne Bradstreet's "To My Dear and Loving Husband" evokes a marital love that confirms a connection that transcends space and matter as well as time. Although Bradstreet wrote more than three centuries ago, such devotion remains undated for many (but, of course, not all) readers of love poetry. She begins, naturally enough, with the pleasure and paradox of how two people can be one.

ANNE BRADSTREET (c. 1612–1672)

To My Dear and Loving Husband   *1678*

If ever two were one, then surely we.
If ever man were loved by wife, then thee;
If ever wife was happy in a man,
Compare with me, ye women, if you can.
I prize thy love more than whole mines of gold   5
Or all the riches that the East doth hold.
My love is such that rivers cannot quench,
Nor ought but love from thee, give recompense.
Thy love is such I can no way repay,
The heavens reward thee manifold, I pray.   10
Then while we live, in love let's so persevere
That when we live no more, we may live ever.

CONSIDERATIONS FOR CRITICAL THINKING AND WRITING

1. **FIRST RESPONSE.** Describe the poem's tone. Is it what you'd expect from a seventeenth-century Puritan? Why or why not?

2. Consider whether Bradstreet's devotion is directed more toward her husband here on earth or toward the eternal rewards of heaven.

3. What is the paradox of the final line? How is it resolved?

The remaining poems in this case study are modern and contemporary pieces that both maintain and revise the perspectives on love provided by Marlowe, Shakespeare, and Bradstreet. As you read them, consider what each adds to your understanding of the others and of love in general.

ELIZABETH BARRETT BROWNING (1806–1861)

How Do I Love Thee?
Let Me Count the Ways   *1850*

How do I love thee? Let me count the ways.
I love thee to the depth and breadth and height
My soul can reach, when feeling out of sight
For the ends of being and ideal grace.
I love thee to the level of every day's   5
Most quiet need, by sun and candle-light.
I love thee freely, as men strive for right.
I love thee purely, as they turn from praise.
I love thee with the passion put to use
In my old griefs, and with my childhood's faith.   10
I love thee with a love I seemed to lose
With my lost saints. I love the
e with the breath,
Smiles, tears, of all my life; and, if God choose,
I shall but love thee better after death.

CONSIDERATIONS FOR CRITICAL THINKING AND WRITING

1. **FIRST RESPONSE.** This poem has remained extraordinarily popular for more than 150 years. Why do you think it has been so often included in collections of love poems? What is its appeal? Does it speak to a contemporary reader? To you?

2. Comment on the effect of the diction. What kind of tone does it create?

3. Would you characterize this poem as having a religious theme — or is it a substitute for religion?

CONNECTION TO ANOTHER SELECTION

1. Compare and contrast the images, tone, and theme of this poem with those of Christina Rossetti's "Promises Like Pie-Crust" (p. 1030). Explain why you find one poem more promising than the other.

E. E. CUMMINGS (1894–1962)

since feeling is first

1926

since feeling is first
who pays any attention
to the syntax of things
will never wholly kiss you;

wholly to be a fool   5
while Spring is in the world

my blood approves,
and kisses are a better fate
than wisdom
lady i swear by all flowers. Don't cry   10
— the best gesture of my brain is less than
your eyelids' flutter which says

we are for each other: then
laugh, leaning back in my arms
for life's not a paragraph   15

And death i think is no parenthesis

CONSIDERATIONS FOR CRITICAL THINKING AND WRITING

1. **FIRST RESPONSE.** What is the speaker's initial premise? Why is it crucial to his argument? What is his argument?

2. Does this poem fit into the *carpe diem* tradition? How?

3. How are nature and society presented in the conflict? Why is this relevant to the speaker's argument?

4. List and describe the grammatical metaphors in the poem. How do they further the speaker's argument?

CONNECTIONS TO OTHER SELECTIONS

1. Contrast the theme of this poem with that of Marlowe's "The Passionate Shepherd to His Love" (p. 966). How do you account for the differences, in both style and content, between the two love poems?

2. Discuss attitudes toward "feeling" in this poem and in Molly Peacock's "Desire" (p. 782).

MARK DOTY (B. 1953)

The Embrace

1998

You weren't well or really ill yet either;
just a little tired, your handsomeness
tinged by grief or anticipation, which brought
to your face a thoughtful, deepening grace.

I didn't for a moment doubt you were dead.
I knew that to be true still, even in the dream.
You'd been out — at work maybe? —
having a good day, almost energetic.

We seemed to be moving from some old house
where we'd lived, boxes everywhere, things   10
in disarray: that was the *story* of my dream,
but even asleep I was shocked out of narrative

by your face, the physical fact of your face:
inches from mine, smooth-shaven, loving, alert.
Why so difficult, remembering the actual look   15
of you? Without a photograph, without strain?

So when I saw your unguarded, reliable face,
your unmistakable gaze opening all the warmth
and clarity of you — warm brown tea — we held
each other for the time the dream allowed.   20
Bless you. You came back, so I could see you
once more, plainly, so I could rest against you
without thinking this happiness lessened anything,
without thinking you were alive again.

CONSIDERATIONS FOR CRITICAL THINKING AND WRITING

1. **FIRST RESPONSE.** In what sense can "The Embrace" be read as a love poem? Explain why it does or doesn't fit your definition of a love poem.

2. Describe the tone of each of the stanzas and trace your emotional response to them as you move through the poem. What is your emotional reaction to the entire poem?

3. Describe the relation between death and love in the poem. How is that relation central to the theme?

JOAN BILLIE BOLTON (B. 1950)

Memorandum   2004

Courtesy of Billie Bolton.

TO: My Boyfriend from Hell
FR: Me
RE: Shit I Never Want to Hear Another Word About as Long as I Live

1. Your Addled Thoughts. Anything about your ongoing interest in Lucy Liu's legs, Shania Twain's bellybutton, or Reese Witherspoon's whatever; your must-see TV dramas, your fantasy baseball addiction, or your addictions period. Anything about going anywhere with you at any time including, but not limited to: Sam's Club, Big Lots, Waffle House, church fish fries, local snake round-ups or Amvet turkey shoots, unless you promise to be the turkey.

2. Your Wireless Connection. Anything about your stage-four cell phone habit; the dames who have your cell phone number and why; who's on your speed-dial list or who left a voice mail message; anything about cell phone rebates, late fees, roaming charges, contracts or dropping your cell phone in the john by accident, even if you flush it and walk away.

3. Your Adolescent Only Child. Anything about his bed-wetting or fire-setting habits; his gang affiliation, court dates or swastika tattoo; anything about his tantrums, seizures or deep psychological need for video games and fruit roll-ups; anything about his pathological grudge against mankind or his particular beef against me.

4. Your Significant Others (female). Anything about the redneck redhead you banged in high school, the long-haired potheads you balled in your hippie days, the white trash airhead you married or the blue-haired battle-ax who pats you on the rump and pays for your dinner. Anything about your devotion to your long-suffering mother, your loopy sisters, or even the Blessed Virgin.

CONSIDERATIONS FOR CRITICAL THINKING AND WRITING

1. FIRST RESPONSE. What makes this a poem rather than simply a memo?
2. How does the speaker's diction and choice of details reveal her own personality?
3. CREATIVE RESPONSE. Using Bolton's style, tone, and form as inspiration, write a reply from the boyfriend's point of view.

CONNECTION TO ANOTHER SELECTION

1. Compare the use of descriptive detail to create tone in "Memorandum" and in Michelle Boisseau's "Self-Pity's Closet" (p. 999).

34

A THEMATIC CASE STUDY
Teaching and Learning

National Portrait Gallery,
London.

O this learning, what a thing it is!
—WILLIAM SHAKESPEARE

A BRIEF INTRODUCTION

The thematic center of this case study focuses on teaching and learning. The various literary elements that contribute to the idea or point around which the entire poem revolves are there to enhance, in this case, poems about the writers' experiences with education. Taken together, the poems represent a variety of poetic responses ranging from fond appreciation and raucous humor to bitter anger and deep grievance. These poems are likely to make you recall your own complicated and contradictory moments in school. Reading them might not make you feel better about some of your experiences, but you will, perhaps, think more deeply about what they mean to you.

Web Research the poets in this chapter at bedfordstmartins.com/meyercompact.

You've spent a significant portion of your life in school learning and being taught, and as you well know, the lessons come in many forms and sometimes at unexpected moments. The poems included in this section all depict a lesson of sorts—even if what has been taught and what has been learned are not always clear (and they are not always the same thing). All of the poetry included here was written within the past fifty years or so, and most of it is quite recent. The contemporary nature of these poems should allow you to make some vivid and striking connections to your own experience — and it may make you grind your teeth a bit, too. As you read, think about who is learning what, how you might link each reading with another, and how you personally respond to the work in question. The lessons discovered in this poetry will undoubtedly add to your understanding that learning is a complicated matter that goes well beyond anyone's lesson plans.

The poems in this case study depict various teaching and learning situations as well as various teaching and learning personalities. As you read them, consider how much diversity of perspective and approach can be represented, all within the context of a single subject.

ROBERT BLY (B. 1926)

Gratitude to Old Teachers 1995

When we stride or stroll across the frozen lake,
We place our feet where they have never been.
We walk upon the unwalked. But we are uneasy.
Who is down there but our old teachers?

Water that once could take no human weight —
We were students then — holds up our feet,
And goes on ahead of us for a mile.
Beneath us the teachers, and around us the stillness.

CONSIDERATIONS FOR CRITICAL THINKING AND WRITING

1. **FIRST RESPONSE.** Discuss the possible meanings of the "frozen lake." What kind of tone is created by the poem's images?
2. What do you think the speaker has learned from teachers?
3. How would you read this poem differently if its title were "Farewell to Old Teachers"?

LINDA PASTAN (B. 1932)

Pass/Fail 1975

Examination dreams are reported to persist even into old age . . .
                                    —Time *magazine*

You will never graduate
from this dream
of blue books.
No matter how

you succeed awake,   5
asleep there is a test
waiting to be failed.
The dream beckons
with two dull pencils,
but you haven't even   10
taken the course;
when you reach for a book —
it closes its door
in your face; when
you conjugate a verb —   15
it is in the wrong
language.
Now the pillow becomes
a blank page. Turn it
to the cool side;   20
you will still smother
in all of the feathers
that have to be learned
by heart.

Considerations for Critical Thinking and Writing

1. **First response.** How well does this poem capture for you the anxieties about taking exams?

2. Instead of a first-person point of view, Pastan uses the second person. Does her strategy make any difference to your reading of "Pass/Fail"?

3. Write a poem in Pastan's style that expresses your experience taking examinations.

Connection to Another Selection

1. Discuss the significance of being graded in this poem and in Pastan's "Marks" (p. 699).

Paul Zimmer (b. 1934)

Zimmer's Head Thudding against the Blackboard   1983

At the blackboard I had missed
Five number problems in a row,
And was about to foul a sixth,
When the old, exasperated nun
Began to pound my head against   5
My six mistakes. When I cried,
She threw me back into my seat,
Where I hid my head and swore
That very day I'd be a poet,
And curse her yellow teeth with this.   10

CONSIDERATIONS FOR CRITICAL THINKING AND WRITING

1. **FIRST RESPONSE.** Comment on how the title sets up certain kinds of expectations for reading this poem.

2. Discuss the effect of the run-on line in line 8.

3. How does the speaker take his revenge on his teacher?

CONNECTION TO ANOTHER SELECTION

1. Compare the speaker's attitudes toward math in Zimmer's poem with that of Peter Schmitt's "Friends with Numbers" (p. 990).

RICHARD HAGUE (B. 1947)

Directions for Resisting the SAT   *1996*

Do not believe in October or May
or in any Saturday morning with pencils.
Do not observe the rules of gravity,
commas, history.
Lie about numbers.   5
Blame your successes,
every one of them,
on rotten luck.
Resign all clubs and committees.
Go down with the ship — any ship.   10
Speak nothing like English.
Desire to live whole,
like an oyster or snail,
and follow no directions.
Listen to no one.   15

Make your marks on everything.

CONSIDERATIONS FOR CRITICAL THINKING AND WRITING

1. **FIRST RESPONSE.** What is the speaker's subversive message? What do you think of the advice offered?

2. What kinds of assumptions do you suppose Hague makes about readers' attitudes toward the SAT? To what extent do you share those attitudes?

3. Discuss Hague's use of spacing and line breaks. What is the effect of the space between lines 15 and 16?

CONNECTION TO ANOTHER SELECTION

1. Compare the treatment of tests in this poem and in Linda Pastan's "Pass / Fail" (p. 974).

MARK HALLIDAY (B. 1949)

Graded Paper

1991

On the whole this is quite successful work:
your main argument about the poet's ambivalence —
how he loves the very things he attacks —
is mostly persuasive and always engaging.

At the same time,   5
                    there are spots
where your thinking becomes, for me,
alarmingly opaque, and your syntax seems to jump
backwards through unnecessary hoops,
as on p. 2 where you speak of "precognitive awareness   10
not yet disestablished by the shell that encrusts
each thing that a person actually says"
or at the top of p. 5 where your discussion of
"subverbal undertow miming the subversion of self-belief
woven counter to desire's outreach"   15
leaves me groping for firmer footholds.
(I'd have said it differently,
or rather, said something else.)
And when you say that women "could not fulfill themselves" (p. 6)
"in that era" (only forty years ago, after all!)   20
are you so sure that the situation is so different today?
Also, how does Whitman bluff his way into
your penultimate paragraph? He is the *last* poet
I would have quoted in this context!
What plausible way of behaving   25
does the passage you quote represent? Don't you think
literature should ultimately reveal possibilities for *action*?

Please notice how I've repaired your use of semicolons.

And yet, despite what may seem my cranky response,
I do admire the freshness of   30
your thinking and your style; there is
a vitality here; your sentences thrust themselves forward
with a confidence as impressive as it is cheeky. . . .
You are not
          me, finally,   35
and though this is an awkward problem, involving
the inescapable fact that you are so young, so young
it is also a delightful provocation.

CONSIDERATIONS FOR CRITICAL THINKING AND WRITING

1. **FIRST RESPONSE.** How do you characterize the grader of this paper based on the comments of the paper?

2. Is the speaker a man or a woman? What makes you think so? Does the gender of the speaker affect your reading of the poem? How?

3. Explain whether or not you think the teacher's comments on the paper are consistent with the grade awarded it. How do you account for the grade?

CONNECTION TO ANOTHER SELECTION

1. Compare the ways in which Halliday reveals the speaker's character in this poem with the strategies used by Robert Browning in "My Last Duchess" (p. 721).

JUDY PAGE HEITZMAN (B. 1952)

The Schoolroom on the Second Floor of the Knitting Mill

1991

While most of us copied letters out of books,
Mrs. Lawrence carved and cleaned her nails.
Now the red and buff cardinals at my back-room window
make me miss her, her room, her hallway,
even the chimney outside   5
that broke up the sky.

In my memory it is afternoon.
Sun streams in through the door
next to the fire escape where we are lined up
getting our coats on to go out to the playground,   10
the tether ball, its towering height, the swings.
She tells me to make sure the line
does not move up over the threshold.
That would be dangerous.
So I stand guard at the door.   15
Somehow it happens
the way things seem to happen when we're not really looking,
or we are looking, just not the right way.
Kids crush up like cattle, pushing me over the line.

Judy is not a good leader is all Mrs. Lawrence says.   20
She says it quietly. Still, everybody hears.
Her arms hang down like sausages.
I hear her every time I fail.

CONSIDERATIONS FOR CRITICAL THINKING AND WRITING

1. FIRST RESPONSE. Does your impression of Mrs. Lawrence change from the beginning to the end of the poem? How so?

2. How can line 2 be read as an implied metaphor?

3. Discuss the use of similes in the poem. How do they contribute to the poem's meaning?

Connection to Another Selection

1. Compare the representations and meanings of being a schoolchild in this poem with those in "Zimmer's Head Thudding against the Blackboard" (p. 975).

RICHARD WAKEFIELD   (B. 1952)

In a Poetry Workshop

1999

Let us begin with the basics of modern verse.
Meter, of course, is forbidden, and lines must be,
like life, broken arbitrarily
lest anyone mistake us for budding Wordsworths
(don't be alarmed if you've never heard of him).   5
Rhyme is allowed, but only in moderation
and preferably very slant. Alliteration
and assonance must only be used at whim
so the reader doesn't think we're playing God
by sneaking in a pattern of sounds and echoes.   10
As for subjects, the modern poet knows
that modern readers prefer the decidedly odd,
so flowers, except for weeds, are out, and love,
except the very weed-like, is also out.
So thistles and incest are fine to write about   15
but roses and happy marriage get the shove
into the editor's outbox with hardly a glance.
Now note that language matters, so "I" must be
in lower case, thus "i," to show that we
don't put on airs despite our government grants.   20
This also shows we've read our Marx and know
the self is a bourgeois fiction. We understand
the common speech, and so the ampersand,
pronounced "uhn," replaces "and," although
judicious use of allusions to classical thought   25
will keep the great unwashed from getting our drift,
while those outside of Plato's cave will lift
a knowing eyebrow, declaring our work "well-wrought."
And speaking of work, this is not a "class":
We modern poets roll up our sleeves and write   30
our verse in "workshops," no place for sissies, we fight
to find "a voice," and only the fittest pass.
I've summarized these rules in a convenient list,
it's wallet-sized, laminated, so keep
it handy, use it, recite it in your sleep.   35
First poems are due tomorrow. You're dismissed.

CONSIDERATIONS FOR CRITICAL THINKING AND WRITING

1. **FIRST RESPONSE.** What are the speaker's attitudes toward modern poetry? How does this parallel the speaker's attitudes toward students?

2. How accurate do you think the speaker's assessment of modern poetry is? Explain why you agree or disagree.

3. What about that list of rules on the "wallet-sized, laminated" card? How does this reveal the speaker to you?

4. **CREATIVE RESPONSE.** Write a character sketch of a teacher who reminds you of this kind of instructor. (No names, please.)

CONNECTION TO ANOTHER SELECTION

1. How does the speaker's use of language in this poem suggest a very different sort of teacher from that in Mark Halliday's "Graded Paper" (p. 977)?

MAGGIE ANDERSON (B. 1948)

The Thing You Must Remember   1986

The thing you must remember is how, as a child,
you worked hours in the art room, the teacher's
hands over yours, molding the little clay dog.
You must remember how nothing mattered
but the imagined dog's fur, the shape of his ears   5
and his paws. The gray clay felt dangerous,
your small hands were pressing what you couldn't
say with your limited words. When the dog's back
stiffened, then cracked to white shards
in the kiln, you learned how the beautiful   10
suffers from too much attention, how clumsy
a single vision can grow, and fragile
with trying too hard. The thing you must
remember is the art teacher's capable
hands: large, rough and grainy,   15
over yours, holding on.

CONSIDERATIONS FOR CRITICAL THINKING AND WRITING

1. **FIRST RESPONSE.** What is the nature of the memory that the speaker insists the reader retain? Why is that memory important?

2. Describe how Anderson molds ideas about discipline, creativity, and art into the theme through her use of images.

3. Why was it that the "gray clay felt dangerous"? Do you think this poem evokes a pleasant memory or something else?

CONNECTIONS TO OTHER SELECTIONS

1. Discuss the sense of direction provided by the teacher in Anderson's poem and in Judy Page Heitzman's "The Schoolroom on the Second Floor of the Knitting Mill" (p. 978).

2. What do you think is learned by the "you" of "The Thing You Must Remember" and the "we" of "Gratitude to Old Teachers" by Robert Bly (p. 974)? To what extent does the shift in pronouns indicate a shift or difference in attitudes about the learning that is described?

JEFFREY HARRISON (B. 1957)

Fork

2003

Because on the first day of class you said,
"In ten years most of you won't be writing,"
barely hiding that you hoped it would be true;
because you told me over and over, in front of the class,
that I was "hopeless," that I was wasting my time   5
but more importantly yours, that I *just didn't get it*;
because you violently scratched out every other word,
scrawled "Awk" and "Eek" in the margins
as if you were some exotic bird,
then highlighted your own remarks in pink;   10
because you made us proofread the galleys
of your how-I-became-a-famous-writer memoir;
because you wanted disciples, and got them,
and hated me for not becoming one;
because you were beautiful and knew it, and used it,   15
making wide come-fuck-me eyes
at your readers from the jackets of your books;
because when, at the end of the semester,
you grudgingly had the class over for dinner
at your over-decorated pseudo-Colonial   20
full of photographs with you at the center,
you served us take-out pizza on plastic plates
but had us eat it with your good silver;
and because a perverse inspiration rippled through me,

I stole a fork, slipping it into the pocket of my jeans,   25
then hummed with inward glee the rest of the evening
to feel its sharp tines pressing against my thigh
as we sat around you in your dark paneled study
listening to you blather on about your latest prize.
The fork was my prize. I practically sprinted   30

back to my dorm room, where I examined it:
a ridiculously ornate pattern, with vegetal swirls
and the curvaceous initials of one of your ancestors,
its flamboyance perfectly suited to your
red-lipsticked and silk-scarved ostentation.   35

That summer, after graduation, I flew to Europe,
stuffing the fork into one of the outer pouches
of my backpack. On a Eurail pass I covered ground
as only the young can, sleeping in youth hostels,
train stations, even once in the Luxembourg Gardens.   40
I'm sure you remember the snapshots you received
anonymously, each featuring your fork
at some celebrated European location: your fork
held at arm's length with the Eiffel Tower
listing in the background; your fork   45
in the meaty hand of a smiling Beefeater;
your fork balanced on Keats's grave in Rome
or sprouting like an antenna from Brunelleschi's dome;
your fork dwarfing the Matterhorn.
I mailed the photos one by one — if possible   50
with the authenticating postmark of the city
where I took them. It was my mission that summer.

That was half my life ago. But all these years
I've kept the fork, through dozens of moves
and changes — always in the same desk drawer   55
among my pens and pencils, its sharp points
spurring me on. It became a talisman
whose tarnished aura had as much to do
with me as you. You might even say your fork
made me a writer. Not you, your fork.   60
You are still the worst teacher I ever had.
You should have been fired but instead got tenure.
As for the fork, just yesterday my daughter
asked me why I keep a fork in my desk drawer,
and I realized I don't need it any more.   65
It has served its purpose. Therefore
I am returning it to you with this letter.

CONSIDERATIONS FOR CRITICAL THINKING AND WRITING

1. **FIRST RESPONSE.** How has the teacher made the speaker a writer? How has
   the fork "served its purpose"? (line 66).

2. Comment on the style of lines 1–24. How do these lines characterize both
   the speaker and teacher?

3. Describe the tone of each stanza. How does the tone change as the narrative progresses?

CONNECTIONS TO OTHER SELECTIONS

1. Consider the treatment of the writing teacher in this poem, in Halliday's "Graded Paper" (p. 977), and in Wakefield's "In a Poetry Workshop" (p. 979). What do these portraits of teachers have in common? What significant differences do you find?

983   Harrison: Fork

CONNECTIONS TO OTHER SUGGESTIONS

day's "Cicada Paper" (p. 979) and Wakeboard's in a Poetry Workshop
(p. 979)? What do these portraits of teachers have in common? What significant differences do you find?

35

A THEMATIC CASE STUDY
Humor and Satire

I think like a poet, and behave
like a poet. Occasionally I need
to sit in the corner for bad
behavior.
— GARY SOTO

A BRIEF INTRODUCTION

Poetry can be a hoot. There are plenty of poets that leave you smiling, grinning, chuckling, and laughing out loud because they use language that is
witty, surprising, teasing, or satirical. Occasionally, their subject matter
is simply wacky. There's a poem in this chapter, for example, titled "Commercial Leech Farming Today" (p. 995) that deftly squeezes humor out of
blood-sucking leeches grown for treating contemporary surgical patients.
Although the material might not sound promising, Thomas Lux's treatment shapes this unlikely topic into a memorable satiric theme.

Sadly, however, poetry is too often burdened with a reputation for only
being formal and serious, and readers sometimes show their deference by
feeling intimidated and humbled in its earnest, weighty presence. After all,
poetry frequently concerns itself with matters of great consequence: its
themes contemplate subjects such as God and immortality, love and death,

war and peace, injustice and outrage, racism and societal ills, deprivation and disease, alienation and angst, totalitarianism and terrorism, as well as a host of other tragic grievances and agonies that humanity might suffer. For readers of *The Onion*, a widely distributed satirical newspaper also available online, this prevailing grim reputation is humorously framed in a bogus story about National Poetry Month, celebrated each April to increase an awareness of the value of poetry in American life. The brief article (April 27, 2005) quotes a speaker at a fund-raising meeting of the "American Poetry Prevention Society" who cautions that "we must stop this scourge before more lives are exposed to poetry." He warns that "young people, particularly morose high-school and college students, are very susceptible to this terrible affliction." *The Onion*'s satire peels away the erroneous assumption that sorrow and tears are the only appropriate responses to a poetry "infection."

Poetry — at least in its clichéd popular form — is nearly always morosely dressed in black and rarely smiles. This severe image of somber profundity unfortunately tailors our expectations so that we assume that serious poetry cannot be playful and even downright funny or, putting the issue another way, that humorous poetry cannot be thoughtful and significant. The poems in this chapter demonstrate that serious poems can be funny and that comic poems can be thoughtful. Their humor, sometimes subtle, occasionally even savage, will serve to remind you that laughter engenders thought as well as pleasure.

FLEUR ADCOCK (B. 1934)

The Video

When Laura was born, Ceri watched.
They all gathered around Mum's bed —
Dad and the midwife and Mum's sister
and Ceri. "Move over a bit," Dad said —
he was trying to focus the camcorder   5
on Mum's legs and the baby's head.

After she had a little sister,
and Mum had gone back to being thin,
and was twice as busy, Ceri played
the video again and again.   10
She watched Laura come out, and then,
in reverse, she made her go back in.

CONSIDERATIONS FOR CRITICAL THINKING AND WRITING

1. **FIRST RESPONSE.** How does the humor in the final line produce the theme?
2. Discuss the appropriateness of Adcock's choice of "watched" in lines 1 and 11. What does the word suggest about Ceri?
3. How does the rhyme scheme affect your reading of the poem?

CONNECTION TO ANOTHER SELECTION

1. Compare the treatment of family life in "The Video" and in Daisy Fried's "Wit's End" (p. 987).

JOHN CIARDI (1916–1986)

Suburban   1978

Yesterday Mrs. Friar phoned. "Mr. Ciardi,
    how do you do?" she said. "I am sorry to say
this isn't exactly a social call. The fact is
    your dog has just deposited — forgive me —
a large repulsive object in my petunias."   5

I thought to ask, "Have you checked the rectal grooving
    for a positive I.D.?" My dog, as it happened,
was in Vermont with my son, who had gone fishing —
    if that's what one does with a girl, two cases of beer,
and a borrowed camper. I guessed I'd get no trout.   10

But why lose out on organic gold for a wise crack?
    "Yes, Mrs. Friar," I said, "I understand."
"Most kind of you," she said. "Not at all," I said.
    I went with a spade. She pointed, looking away.
"I always have loved dogs," she said, "but really!"   15

I scooped it up and bowed. "The animal of it.
    I hope this hasn't upset you, Mrs. Friar."
"Not really," she said, "but really!" I bore the turd
    across the line to my own petunias
and buried it till the glorious resurrection   20

when even these suburbs shall give up their dead.

CONSIDERATIONS FOR CRITICAL THINKING AND WRITING

1. FIRST RESPONSE. How does the speaker transform Mrs. Friar into a symbolic figure of the suburbs?

2. Why do you suppose Ciardi focuses on this particular incident to make a comment on the suburbs? What is the speaker's attitude toward suburban life?

3. CREATIVE RESPONSE. Write a one-paragraph physical description of Mrs. Friar that captures her character.

CONNECTION TO ANOTHER SELECTION

1. Compare the speakers' voices in "Suburban" and in John Updike's "Dog's Death" (p. 572).

DAISY FRIED (B. 1967)

Wit's End

2000

My father says, "Face it, you live
  in a civilization of mirrors and sinks,"
    invading my real room, the bathroom.

I pull down an eyelid till I see the pained
  pink meniscus underneath. I "O"
    my mouth, poke the mascara wand   5

at my eyelashes, not missing
  by much. It's makeup's premonition
    of sex in the house he can't stand.

The bathroom's littered with eyeliners,   10
  tweezers, kisslipped tissues. I shed snarls
    of hair in the shower like saffron threads,

red kelp. In the mirror I paint myself a clownface
  copied from *Sassy, Seventeen, Glamour*. He
    stands in the doorway, loving   15

the used-to-be lovable 12-year-old
  formerly his. We look in the mirror:
    blush welts, orange, riding low

on my cheeks, pink lipstick leaking
  from my lip corners. Glitter-white   20
    chevrons for eyelids; Cover Girl fails

again to cover my nose-zits. Reflected, behind me,
  tangles of the unwashed bras I don't need
    trail from shower rod, shampoo rack,

hot-cold dial, soapdish, stopcock.   25
  He hates it: me mooning, me sighing,
    me incessantly hairbrushing, singing stupid

love songs. "I'll buy back the gunk!" he says.
  He'll pay twice what I spent if only I'll stop.
    I stand by the tub in the bathroom,   30

my real room. I prop up a leg, I pull up
  my skirt, start shaving thigh-stubble. I shove
    the door shut between us with my ass.

CONSIDERATIONS FOR CRITICAL THINKING AND WRITING

1. **FIRST RESPONSE.** What images and figures of speech make Fried's description of this father-daughter relationship convincing?

2. In what sense is the bathroom for the speaker "my real room" (lines 3 and 31)?

3. How does the title sum up the poem's familial conflict?
4. Explain why you think Fried treats the speaker mostly satirically or sympathetically.

CONNECTIONS TO OTHER SELECTIONS

1. Compare the tone and theme of "Wit's End" with those of Li Ho's "A Beautiful Girl Combs Her Hair" (p. 609).
2. Discuss the themes in "Wit's End" and in Rachel Hadas's "The Compact" (p. 721).

RONALD WALLACE (B. 1945)

In a Rut   2002

She dogs me while
I try to take a catnap.
Of course, I'm playing possum but
I can feel her watching me,
eagle-eyed, like a hawk.   5
She snakes over to my side
of the bed, and continues to
badger me. I may be a rat, but
I won't let her get my goat.
I refuse to make an   10
ass of myself, no matter
how mulish I feel.
I'm trying to make a
bee-line for sleep, but
You're a turkey! she says, and   15
I'm thinking she's no
spring chicken. She *is* a busy beaver,
though, always trying to ferret
things out. She's a bit batty,
in fact, a bit cuckoo, but   20
What's your beef, now? I say.
*Get your head out
of the sand,* she replies. *What
are you—a man, or a mouse?*
That's a lot of bull, I think;   25
she can be a real bear.
Don't horse around, now, she says.
You know you can't weasel out of it!
She's having a whale of a time,
thinking she's got me skunked, thinking   30
that she's out-foxed me.
But I know she's just crying wolf,
and I won't be cowed. Feeling

my oats now, I merely look sheepish;
I give her the hang-dog look;   35
I give her the lion's share.
I give her something to crow about.
Oh, lovey-dove, I intone.
We're all odd ducks, strange
birds; this won't be my swan-   40
song, after all. She's in hog-
heaven now, ready to pig-out.
Oh, my stallion, she says, *Oh,*
my lambkin! You are
a real animal, you know!   45

CONSIDERATIONS FOR CRITICAL THINKING AND WRITING

1. **FIRST RESPONSE.** Explain whether or not Wallace's orchestration of over-used phrases redeems them from being simply clichés.

2. How does the title contribute to your understanding of the poem's plot?

3. **CREATIVE RESPONSE.** Choose a set of familiar related expressions from sports, school, politics, religion, or whatever comes naturally to you, and write your own version of a poem that imitates Wallace's playful use of clichés.

CONNECTION TO ANOTHER SELECTION

1. Compare Wallace's organizing strategy in this poem and E. E. Cummings's technique in "next to of course god america i" (p. 711).

HOWARD NEMEROV (1920–1991)

Walking the Dog   *1980*

Two universes mosey down the street
Connected by love and a leash and nothing else.
Mostly I look at lamplight through the leaves
While he mooches along with tail up and snout down,
Getting a secret knowledge through the nose   5
Almost entirely hidden from my sight.

We stand while he's enraptured by a bush
Till I can't stand our standing any more
And haul him off; for our relationship
Is patience balancing to this side tug   10
And that side drag; a pair of symbionts
Contented not to think each other's thoughts.

What else we have in common's what he taught,
Our interest in shit. We know its every state
From steaming fresh through stink to nature's way   15
Of sluicing it downstreet dissolved in rain

Or drying it to dust that blows away.
We move along the street inspecting it.

His sense of it is keener far than mine,
And only when he finds the place precise   20
He signifies by sniffing urgently
And circles thrice about, and squats, and shits.
Whereon we both with dignity walk home
And just to show who's master I write the poem.

CONSIDERATIONS FOR CRITICAL THINKING AND WRITING

1. FIRST RESPONSE. How does the form of this poem give it dignity despite its topic? Explain why you experience the poem as amusing or repugnant.

2. How might you read the poem differently if the last line were deleted?

3. Compare the tone of stanzas 1 and 2 with that of 3 and 4. Discuss whether or not the two sets of stanzas are consistent and compatible.

4. Who do you think is finally the master? Explain why.

CONNECTIONS TO OTHER SELECTIONS

1. Discuss the speakers' attitudes toward the dogs in "Walking the Dog" and in John Ciardi's "Suburban" (p. 986). How does humor inform those attitudes?

2. Consider the subject matter of this poem and Ronald Wallace's "Building an Outhouse" (p. 699). Some readers might argue that the subject matter is tasteless and not suitable for poetic treatment. What do you think?

PETER SCHMITT (B. 1958)

Friends with Numbers   1995

If you make friends with numbers,
you don't need any other friends.
   —Shakuntala Devi, *math genius*

They are not hard to get to know:
6 and 9 keep changing their minds,
8 cuts the most graceful figure
but sleeps for an eternity,
and 7, lucky 7, takes   5
an arrow to his heart always.
5, halfway to somewhere, only
wants to patch his unicycle
tire, and 4, who'd like to stand for
something solid, has never had   10
two feet on the ground, yet flutters
gamely in the breeze like a flag.

3, for all his literary
accomplishments and pretensions
to immortality, is still   15
(I can tell you) not half the man
8 is asleep or awake. 1,
little 1. I know him better
than all the others, these numbers
who are all my friends. Only 2,   20
that strange smallest prime, can I count
as just a passing acquaintance.
Divisible by only 1
and herself, she seems on the verge,
yet, of always coming apart.   25
And though she eludes me, swanlike,
though I'd love to know her better,
still I am fine, there are others,
many, I have friends in numbers.

CONSIDERATIONS FOR CRITICAL THINKING AND WRITING

1. **FIRST RESPONSE.** How does the personification of numbers create characters in the poem?
2. Explain how the speaker's use of language helps to characterize him.
3. Discuss the various ways in which the single digits are transformed into individual visual images.

CONNECTION TO ANOTHER SELECTION

1. Discuss the originality — the fresh and unusual approach to their respective subject matter — in Schmitt's poem and in Kate Clanchy's "Spell" (p. 677). What makes these poems so interesting?

MARTÍN ESPADA (B. 1957)

The Community College Revises Its Curriculum in Response to Changing Demographics   2000

SPA 100 Conversational Spanish
2 credits

The course
is especially concerned
with giving police
the ability
to express themselves
tersely
in matters of interest
to them

CONSIDERATIONS FOR CRITICAL THINKING AND WRITING

1. **FIRST RESPONSE.** What sort of political comment do you think Espada makes in this poem?

2. Would this be a poem without the title?

3. **CREATIVE RESPONSE.** Choose a course description from your school's cata-log and organize the catalog copy into poetic lines. Provide your poem with a title that offers a provocative commentary about it.

CONNECTION TO ANOTHER SELECTION

1. Compare the themes in Espada's poem and in Donald Justice's "Order in the Streets" (p. 817).

M. CARL HOLMAN (1919–1988)

Mr. Z   *1967*

Taught early that his mother's skin was the sign of error,
He dressed and spoke the perfect part of honor;
Won scholarships, attended the best schools,
Disclaimed kinship with jazz and spirituals;
Chose prudent, raceless views for each situation,   5
Or when he could not cleanly skirt dissension,
Faced up to the dilemma, firmly seized
Whatever ground was Anglo-Saxonized.

In diet, too, his practice was exemplary:
Of pork in its profane forms he was wary;   10
Expert in vintage wines, sauces and salads,
His palate shrank from cornbread, yams and collards.

He was as careful whom he chose to kiss:
His bride had somewhere lost her Jewishness,
But kept her blue eyes; an Episcopalian   15
Prelate proclaimed them matched chameleon.
Choosing the right addresses, here, abroad,
They shunned those places where they might be barred;
Even less anxious to be asked to dine
Where hosts catered to kosher accent or exotic skin.   20

And so he climbed, unclogged by ethnic weights,
An airborne plant, flourishing without roots.
Not one false note was struck — until he died:
His subtly grieving widow could have flayed
The obit writers, ringing crude changes on a clumsy phrase: 25
"One of the most distinguished members of his race."

CONSIDERATIONS FOR CRITICAL THINKING AND WRITING

1. **FIRST RESPONSE.** What is the central irony of Mr. Z's life? What do you think of him?

2. Explain whether or not you find Holman's satiric portrait to be fair.

3. Discuss the poem's rhythms and rhymes. How do they contribute to the tone?

4. What does Mr. Z's name suggest about his identity?

CONNECTIONS TO OTHER SELECTIONS

1. Compare the satirical treatment of race in "Mr. Z" and in Langston Hughes's "Dinner Guest: Me" (p. 931).

2. Discuss the preference for "Anglo-Saxonized" (line 8) appearances in "Mr. Z" and in Janice Mirikitani's "Recipe" (Border Crossings insert, p. M).

GARY SOTO (B. 1952)

Mexicans Begin Jogging   1995

At the factory I worked
In the fleck of rubber, under the press
Of an oven yellow with flame,
Until the border patrol opened
Their vans and my boss waved for us to run.   5
"Over the fence, Soto," he shouted,
And I shouted that I was American.
"No time for lies," he said, and pressed
A dollar in my palm, hurrying me
Through the back door.   10

Since I was on his time, I ran
And became the wag to a short tail of Mexicans —
Ran past the amazed crowds that lined
The street and blurred like photographs, in rain.
I ran from that industrial road to the soft   15
Houses where people paled at the turn of an autumn sky.
What could I do but yell *vivas*
To baseball, milkshakes, and those sociologists
Who would clock me
As I jog into the next century   20
On the power of a great, silly grin.

Explore contexts
for Gary Soto
on *LiterActive*.

CONSIDERATIONS FOR CRITICAL THINKING AND WRITING

1. **FIRST RESPONSE.** What ironies are present in this poem?

2. Soto was born and raised in Fresno, California. How does this fact affect your reading of the first stanza?

3. In what different ways does the speaker become "the wag" (line 12) in this poem? (You may want to look up the word to consider all possible meanings.)

4. Explain lines 17-21. What serious point is being made in these humorous lines?

CONNECTION TO ANOTHER SELECTION

1. Compare the speakers' ironic attitudes toward exercise in this poem and in Peter Meinke's "The ABC of Aerobics" (p. 816).

BOB HICOK (B. 1960)

Spam leaves an aftertaste

2002

What does the Internet know that it sends me
unbidden the offer of a larger penis?
I'm flattered by the energy devoted
to the architecture of my body.
Brain waves noodling on girth, length, curvature   5
possibly, pictures drawn on napkins
of the device, teeth for holding, cylinder —
pneumatic, hydraulic — for stretching
who I am into who I shall be. But of all
messages to drop from the digital ether,   10
hope lives in the communiqué that I can find
out anything about anyone. So I've asked:
who am I, why am I here, if a train
leaving Chicago is subsidized
by the feds, is the romance of travel   15
dead? I'd like the skinny on where I'll be
when I die, to have a map, a seismic map
of past and future emotions, to be told
how to keep the violence I do to myself
from becoming the grenades I pitch   20
at others. The likes of Snoop.com
never get back to me, though I need
to know most of all if any of this helps.
How we can scatter our prayers so wide,
if we've become more human or less   25
in being able to share the specific
in a random way, or was it better
to ask the stars for peace or rain,
to trust the litany of our need
to the air's imperceptible embrace? Just   30
this morning I got a message
asking is anyone out there. I replied
no, I am not, are you not there too,
needing me, and if not, come over, I have
a small penis but aspirations   35
for bigger things, faith among them,
and by that I mean you and I
face to face, mouths
making the sounds once known
as conversation.   40

CONSIDERATIONS FOR CRITICAL THINKING AND WRITING

1. **FIRST RESPONSE.** Comment on the humor Hicok uses to satirize how our lives have been affected by the Internet.

2. What is the serious theme that the speaker's humor leads the reader to contemplate? How does this complicate the poem's tone?

3. How do your own experiences with spam compare with the speaker's?

CONNECTIONS TO OTHER SELECTIONS

1. How might Hicok's poem be considered a latter-day version of T. S. Eliot's "The Love Song of J. Alfred Prufrock" (p. 1018)?

2. Discuss the perspective on American contemporary life implicit in "Spam leaves an aftertaste" with respect to the view offered in Tony Hoagland's "America" (p. 1003).

THOMAS LUX (B. 1946)

Commercial Leech Farming Today   1997

—for Robert Sacherman

Although it never rivaled wheat, soybean,
cattle and so on farming
there was a living
in leeches
and after a period of decline   5
there is again
a living to be made
from this endeavor: they're used to reduce
the blood in tissues
after plastic surgery — eyelifts, tucks,   10
wrinkle erad, or in certain
microsurgeries — reattaching a finger, penis.
I love the capitalist
spirit. As in most businesses
the technology has improved: instead   15
of driving an elderly horse
into a leech pond, letting him die
by exsanguination,
and hauling him out
to pick the bloated blossoms   20
from his hide, it's now done at Biopharm
(the showcase operation in Swansea,
Wales) — temp control, tanks, aerator
pumps, several species,
each for a specific job. Once, 19th century,   25
they were applied to the temple
as a treatment for mental

illness. Today we know
their exact chemistry: hirudin,
a blood thinner in their saliva,   30
also an anesthesia
and dilators for the wound area.
Don't you love
the image: the Dr. lays a leech along
the tiny stitches of an eyelift.   35
Where they go after their work is done
I don't know
but I've heard no complaints
from Animal Rights
so perhaps they're retired   40
to a lake or adopted
as pets, maybe the best looking
kept to breed. I don't know. I like the story,
I like the going backwards
to ignorance   45
to come forward to vanity. I like
the small role they can play
in beauty
or the reattachment of a part,
I like the story because it's true.   50

CONSIDERATIONS FOR CRITICAL THINKING AND WRITING

1. **FIRST RESPONSE.** Why does the narrator "like the story" (line 43) about leech farming so much? What does it symbolize to him?

2. How does Lux characterize the nature of contemporary life?

3. Explain how the humor in this poem moves beyond the simply bizarre to the satirical.

CONNECTION TO ANOTHER SELECTION

1. Discuss the perspectives on human vanity offered in Lux's poem and in Alice Jones's "The Foot" (p. 761).

An Anthology
of Poems

36

An Album of
Contemporary Poems

© John Eddy.

Like scooping water by the handful /
out of a lake, / you write a poem . . .
— CATHY SONG

MICHELLE BOISSEAU (B. 1955)

Born in Cincinnati, Michelle Boisseau earned a B.A. and M.A. from Ohio
University and a Ph.D. from the University of Houston. She has taught literature and writing courses at Moorhead State Univer-
sity and the University of Missouri at Kansas City. She
received a National Endowment for the Arts poetry fellowship as well as a number of other grants and awards;
her poetry collections include *No Private Life* (1990) and *Understory* (1996).

Web Research the
poets in this chapter
at bedfordstmartins
.com/meyercompact.

Self-Pity's Closet   *2003*

Depression, loneliness, anger, shame, envy,
appetite without hunger, unquenchable
thirst, secret open wounds, long parades
of punishments, resentment honed and glinting
in the sun, the wind driving a few leaves,   5

an empty bird call, the grass bent down, far off
a dog barking and barking, the skin sticky,
the crotch itchy, the tongue stinking, the eyes,
words thrust from the mouth like bottles off a bridge,
tangy molasses of disgust, dank memory   10
of backs, of eyebrows raised and cool expressions
after your vast and painful declarations,
subtle humiliations creeping up
like the smell of wet upholstery, dial tone
in the brain, the conviction that your friends   15
never really loved you, the certitude
you deserved no better, never have, stains
in the carpet, the faucet drilling the sink,
the nights raining spears of stars, the days bland
and blank as newspapers eaten slowly   20
in the bathtub, the clock, the piano,
heavy impatient books, slippery pens,
the radio, a bug bouncing against
the window: go away, make it all go away.

CONNECTION TO ANOTHER SELECTION

1. Discuss the themes you find in this poem and in Edgar Allan Poe's "The Haunted Palace" (p. 705). Explain whether or not you think the differences between these two poems are greater than their similarities.

BILLY COLLINS (B. 1941)

Since the publication of his first book, *The Apple That Astonished Paris* (1988), Billy Collins (born in New York City in 1941) has established himself as a prominent voice in contemporary American poetry. His books include *Picnic, Lightning* (1998); *The Art of Drowning* (1995), a finalist for the Lenore Marshall Prize; *Questions about Angels* (1991), selected for the National Poetry Series and reissued in 1999; *Sailing Alone Around the Room: New and Selected Poems* (2001); and *Nine Horses* (2002). Collins was selected in 2001 as the poet laureate of the United States.

Marginalia   *1998*

Sometimes the notes are ferocious,
skirmishes against the author
raging along the borders of every page
in tiny black script.

If I could just get my hands on you, 5
Kierkegaard,° or Conor Cruise O'Brien,°
they seem to say,
I would bolt the door and beat some logic into your head.

Other comments are more offhand, dismissive —
"Nonsense." "Please!" "HA!!" — 10
that kind of thing.
I remember once looking up from my reading,
my thumb as a bookmark,
trying to imagine what the person must look like
who wrote "Don't be a ninny" 15
alongside a paragraph in *The Life of Emily Dickinson.*

Students are more modest
needing to leave only their splayed footprints
along the shore of the page.
One scrawls "Metaphor" next to a stanza of Eliot's.° 20
Another notes the presence of "Irony"
fifty times outside the paragraphs of *A Modest Proposal.*°

Or they are fans who cheer from the empty bleachers,
hands cupped around their mouths.
"Absolutely," they shout 25
to Duns Scotus° and James Baldwin.°
"Yes." "Bull's-eye." "My man!"
Check marks, asterisks, and exclamation points
rain down along the sidelines.

And if you have managed to graduate from college 30
without ever having written "Man vs. Nature"
in a margin, perhaps now
is the time to take one step forward.

We have all seized the white perimeter as our own
and reached for a pen if only to show 35
we did not just laze in an armchair turning pages;
we pressed a thought into the wayside,
planted an impression along the verge.

Even Irish monks in their cold scriptoria°
jotted along the borders of the Gospels 40
brief asides about the pains of copying,
a bird singing near their window,
or the sunlight that illuminated their page —

---

6 *Kierkegaard:* Søren Aaby Kierkegaard (1813–1855), Danish philosopher and theologian; *Conor Cruise O'Brien* (B. 1917): Irish historian, critic, and statesman. 20 *Eliot's:* Thomas Stearns Eliot (1888–1965), American-born English poet and critic (see p. 1219). 22 *A Modest Proposal:* An essay by English satirist Jonathan Swift (1667–1745). 26 *Duns Scotus* (1265?–1308): Scottish theologian; *James Baldwin* (1924–1987): African American essayist and novelist. 39 *scriptoria:* Rooms in a monastery used for writing and copying.

anonymous men catching a ride into the future
on a vessel more lasting than themselves.   45

And you have not read Joshua Reynolds,°
they say, until you have read him
enwreathed with Blake's° furious scribbling.

Yet the one I think of most often,
the one that dangles from me like a locket,   50
was written in the copy of *Catcher in the Rye*°
I borrowed from the local library
one slow, hot summer.
I was just beginning high school then,
reading books on a davenport in my parents' living room,   55
and I cannot tell you
how vastly my loneliness was deepened,
how poignant and amplified the world before me seemed,
when I found on one page

a few greasy looking smears   60
and next to them, written in soft pencil —
by a beautiful girl, I could tell,
whom I would never meet —
"Pardon the egg salad stains, but I'm in love."

---

46 *Joshua Reynolds* (1723-1792): English portrait artist who entertained many of the important writers of his time.   48 *Blake's:* William Blake (1757-1827), English mystic and poet.   51 *Catcher in the Rye:* A novel (1951) about adolescence by American author J. D. Salinger (B. 1919).

CONNECTIONS TO OTHER SELECTIONS

1. Discuss the speakers' responses to reading in this poem and in Philip Larkin's "A Study of Reading Habits" (p. 583). How is reading used as a measure of each speaker's character?

2. Describe the speakers' attitudes toward books in this poem and in Anne Bradstreet's "The Author to Her Book" (p. 685).

TONY HOAGLAND (B. 1953)

Born in Fort Bragg, North Carolina, Tony Hoagland has published collections of poetry that include *Sweet Rain* (1993), awarded the Brittingham Prize in Poetry; *Donkey Gospel* (1998), awarded the James Laughlin Award of the Academy of American Poets; *What Narcissism Means to Me* (2003); and *Hard Rain* (2005). He has received writing grants from the Guggenheim Foundation, the National Endowment for the Arts, and the Academy of Arts and Letters. He teaches in the graduate program at the University of Houston.

America   2003

Then one of the students with blue hair and a tongue stud
Says that America is for him a maximum-security prison

Whose walls are made of RadioShacks and Burger Kings, and MTV
    episodes
Where you can't tell the show from the commercials,

And as I consider how to express how full of shit I think he is,   5
He says that even when he's driving to the mall in his Isuzu

Trooper with a gang of his friends, letting rap music pour over them
Like a boiling Jacuzzi full of ballpeen hammers, even then he feels

Buried alive, captured and suffocated in the folds
Of the thick satin quilt of America   10

And I wonder if this is a legitimate category of pain,
Or whether he is just spin doctoring a better grade,

And then I remember that when I stabbed my father in the dream last
    night,
It was not blood but money

That gushed out of him, bright green hundred-dollar bills   15
Spilling from his wounds, and — this is the weird part —,

He gasped, "Thank god — those Ben Franklins were
Clogging up my heart —

And so I perish happily,
Freed from that which kept me from my liberty" —   20

Which is when I knew it was a dream, since my dad
Would never speak in rhymed couplets,

And I look at the student with his acne and cell phone and phony ghetto
    clothes
And I think, "I am asleep in America too,

And I don't know how to wake myself either,"   25
And I remember what Marx said near the end of his life:

"I was listening to the cries of the past,
When I should have been listening to the cries of the future."

But how could he have imagined 100 channels of 24-hour cable
Or what kind of nightmare it might be   30

When each day you watch rivers of bright merchandise run past you
And you are floating in your pleasure boat upon this river

Even while others are drowning underneath you
And you see their faces twisting in the surface of the waters

And yet it seems to be your own hand   35
Which turns the volume higher?

CONNECTIONS TO OTHER SELECTIONS

1. Discuss the treatment of self-pity in "America" and in Michelle Boisseau's "Self-Pity's Closet" (p. 999).

2. Explain how "America" and Barbara Hamby's "Ode to American English" (p. 641) offer contrasting visions of American life and culture.

RACHEL LODEN (B. 1948)

Born in Washington, D.C., Rachel Loden grew up in New York, Connecticut, and California. Her book *Hotel Imperium* (1999) won the Contemporary Poetry Series Competition and was named one of the ten best poetry books of the year by the *San Francisco Chronicle*, which called it "quirky and beguiling." Loden has also published four chapbooks, including *The Last Campaign* (1998), which won the Hudson Valley Writers' Center Chapbook Prize, and *The Richard Nixon Snow Globe* (2005). Her work appears in numerous anthologies, including two editions of *The Best American Poetry* (1995 and 2005). Other awards include a Pushcart Prize and a fellowship in poetry from the California Arts Council.

© Jesse Ketonen.

Locked Ward: Newtown, Connecticut   2005

Your tight-lipped jailer beckons
and I trail her like a moon.

The padding of her strange white shoes,
the doors she unlocks one by one —

then you are there on the edge of a cot   5
like a whipped child, with your eyes down.

There are no sharp objects in here,
only the malignant shapes

that dance out
when the strappings are undone.   10

I have brought you what you wanted
from home. A robe, a sweater —

an irony, as though what you wanted
could be mine to give so

easily. Oh I 15
would wrap you up and carry you away

to some all-powerful physician
or at least some place

they'd let you rave in peace.
Silence of the years, the sins against 20

the white page. Carried always out to sea
by the foul winds off the laundry,

the stains that cannot be removed
by any washing of the hands.

The years are mute. And yet 25
there is no end to the lament

of daughters, no end
to the sharp objects in the heart.

Connections to Other Selections

1. Discuss similarities and differences in the treatment of aging in Loden's poem and in Kelly Cherry's "Alzheimer's" (p. 807).

2. Compare the tone of the adult child/parent relationship in this poem and in Joanne Diaz's "On My Father's Loss of Hearing" (p. 645).

Susan Minot (b. 1956)

Born and raised in Massachusetts, Susan Minot earned a B.A. at Brown University and an M.F.A. at Columbia University. Before devoting herself full-time to writing, Minot worked as an assistant editor at *Grand Street* magazine. Her stories have appeared in the *Atlantic Monthly, Harper's,* the *New Yorker, Mademoiselle,* and *Paris Review.* Her short stories have been collected in *Lust and Other Stories* (1989), and she has published four novels — *Monkeys* (1986), *Folly* (1992), *Evening* (1998), and *Rapture* (2002), as well as one volume of poetry, *Poems 4 A.M.* (2002).

Courtesy of Dinah Minot Hubley.

My Husband's Back

2005

Sunday evening.
Breakdown hour. Weeping into
a pot of burnt rice. Sun dimmed
like a light bulb gone out
behind a gray lawn of snow.   5
The baby flushed with the flu
asleep on a pillow.
The fire won't catch.
The wet wood's caked
with ice. Sitting   10
on the couch my spine
collides with all its bones
and I watch my husband
peer past the glass grate
and blow.   15
His back in a snug plaid shirt
gray and white
leaning into the woodstove
is firm and compact
like a young man's back.   20

And the giant world which swirls
in my head
stopping most thought
suddenly ceases
to spin. It sits   25
right there, the back I love,
animal and gamine, leaning
on one arm.
I could crawl on it forever
the one point in the world   30
turns out
I have travelled everywhere
to get to.

CONNECTIONS TO OTHER SELECTIONS

1. Compare Minot's "My Husband's Back" and Anne Bradstreet's "To My Dear and Loving Husband" (p. 968) as love poems.

2. Discuss the speakers' tones in Minot's poem and in Linda Pastan's "Marks" (p. 699).

ALBERTO RÍOS (B. 1952)

Born in Nogales, Arizona, Alberto Ríos grew up on the border between Mexico and Arizona, which is the subject of his memoir *Capriotoda* (1999). He earned a bachelor's degree and an M.F.A. from the University of Arizona. He has published several short story collections and a number of poetry collections, including *Whispering to Fool the Wind* (1982), *The Lime Orchard Woman* (1988), *Teodoro Luna's Two Kisses* (1990), and *The Smallest Muscle in the Human Body* (2002). His many awards include the Arizona Governor's Arts Award and fellowships from the Guggenheim Foundation and the National Endowment for the Arts. He teaches at Arizona State University.

The Gathering Evening   2002

Shadows are the patient apprentices of everything.
They follow what might be followed,

Sit with what will not move.
They take notes all day long —

We don't pay attention, we don't see   5
The dark writing of the pencil, the black notebook.

Sometimes, if you are watching carefully,
A shadow will move. You will turn to see

What has made it move, but nothing.
The shadows transcribe all night.   10

Transcription is their sleep.
We mistake night as a setting of the sun:

Night is all of them comparing notes,
So many gathering that their crowd

Makes the darkness everything.   15
Patient, patient, quiet and still.

One day they will have learned it all.
One day they will step out, in front,

And we will follow them, be their shadows,
And work for our turn —   20

The centuries it takes
To learn what waiting has to teach.

CONNECTIONS TO OTHER SELECTIONS

1. Compare the treatment of shadows in this poem and in Emily Dickinson's "Presentiment — is that long Shadow — on the lawn —" (p. 684).

2. Discuss the significance of the night in this poem and in Robert Frost's "Acquainted with the Night" (p. 703).

CATHY SONG (B. 1955)

Of Chinese and Korean descent, Cathy Song was born in Honolulu, Hawaii. After receiving a B.A. from Wellesley College, she pursued an M.A. in creative writing at Boston University. The recipient of a number of grants and awards, including the Shelley Memorial Award from the Poetry Society of America and the Hawaii Award for Literature, she has taught creative writing at various universities. Her work frequently focuses on the world of family and ancestry. Among her collections of poetry are *Picture Bride* (1983), *Frameless Windows, Squares of Light* (1988), *School Figures* (1994), and *The Land of Bliss* (2001).

A Poet in the House

2001

© John Eddy.

Emily's job was to think.
She was the only one of us
who had that to do.
    —*Lavinia Dickinson*

Seemingly small her work,
minute to the point of invisibility—
she vanished daily into paper, famished,
hungry for her next encounter—
but she opened with a string of humble   5
words necessity,
necessary as the humble work
of bringing well to water, roast to knife, cake to frost,
the coarse, loud, grunting labor of the rest of us
who complained not at all   10
for the noises she heard
we deemed divine, if
claustrophobic and esoteric—
and contented ourselves to the apparent,
the menial, set our heads   15
to the task of daily maintenance,
the simple order at the kitchen table,
while she struggled with a different thing—
the pressure seized upon her mind—
we could ourselves not bear such strain   20
and, in gratitude, heaved the bucket,
squeezed the rag, breathed the sweet,
homely odor of soap.
Lifting dirt from the floor
I swear   25
we could hear her thinking.

CONNECTIONS TO OTHER SELECTIONS

1. Compare Song's assessment of the life of a poet with the view expressed in Howard Nemerov's "Walking the Dog" (p. 989) or William Trowbridge's "Poets' Corner" (below).
2. Discuss the perspective on Dickinson in this poem and in Ron Wallace's "Miss Goff" (p. 866).

WILLIAM TROWBRIDGE

A native of Omaha, Nebraska, William Trowbridge teaches at Northwest Missouri State University. His collections of poems include *Book of Kong* (1989), *Flickers* (2000), and the forthcoming *Four Seasons*. He has been awarded the American Poet's Prize and fellowships at Ragdale, Yaddo, and the MacDowell Colony.

Poets' Corner   *1999*

They put me in right field
because I didn't pitch that well
or throw or catch or hit,
because I tried to steer the ball
like a paper plane, watched   5
Christmas gifts with big
red ribbons floating through
the strike zone, and swung
at dirt balls. So they played the odds,
sent me out there in the tall grass   10
by the Skoal sign, where I wandered
distant as the nosebleed seats
my father got us in Comiskey Park,°
my teammates looking
remote and miniature,   15
their small cries and gesticulations
like things remembered
from a dream. I went dreamy,
sun on my face, the scent
of sod and bluegrass, the lilt   20
of birdcall and early cricket
bending afternoon away
from fastballs and hook slides

13 *Comiskey Park:* Home of the Chicago White Sox baseball team and renamed as U.S. Cellular Field.

to June's lazy looping
single: baseball at its best,   25
my only fear the deep fly
with my name on it,
meteoric as Jehovah
or Coach Bob Zambisi
closing in to deliver once   30
again the meaning of the game:
what it takes to play, why I had to
crouch vigilant as a soldier
in combat, which he never
had the privilege of being,   35
and stop that lolling around
with my head up my ass,
watching the birdies and picking
dandelions like some kind of
little priss, some kind   40
of Percy Bitch Shelby.

CONNECTIONS TO OTHER SELECTIONS

1. Explain the coach's allusion to "Percy Bitch Shelby."
2. Compare the treatment of the coaches in this poem and in Gary Gildner's
   "First Practice" (p. 809).

37

A Collection
of Poems

If there were no poetry on any day in the world, poetry would be invented that day. For there would be an intolerable hunger.

— MURIEL RUKEYSER

© Imogen Cunningham Trust.

ANONYMOUS (TRADITIONAL SCOTTISH BALLAD)

Bonny Barbara Allan

date unknown

It was in and about the Martinmas° time,
    When the green leaves were afalling,
That Sir John Graeme, in the West Country,
    Fell in love with Barbara Allan.

Web Research the poets in this chapter at bedfordstmartins.com/meyercompact.

He sent his men down through the town,   5
    To the place where she was dwelling:
"Oh haste and come to my master dear,
    Gin° ye be Barbara Allan."   *if*

1 *Martinmas:* St. Martin's Day, November 11.

O hooly,° hooly rose she up,   *slowly*
    To the place where he was lying,   10
And when she drew the curtain by:
    "Young man, I think you're dying."

"O it's I'm sick, and very, very sick,
    And 'tis a' for Barbara Allan." —
"O the better for me ye's never be,   15
    Tho your heart's blood were aspilling."

"O dinna ye mind,° young man," she said,   *don't you remember*
    "When ye was in the tavern adrinking,
That ye made the health° gae round and round,   *toasts*
    And slighted Barbara Allan?"   20

He turned his face unto the wall,
    And death was with him dealing:
"Adieu, adieu, my dear friends all,
    And be kind to Barbara Allan."

And slowly, slowly raise her up,   25
    And slowly, slowly left him,
And sighing said she could not stay,
    Since death of life had reft him.

She had not gane a mile but twa,
    When she heard the dead-bell ringing,   30
And every jow° that the dead-bell geid,   *stroke*
    It cried, "Woe to Barbara Allan!"

"O mother, mother, make my bed!
    O make it saft and narrow!
Since my love died for me today,   35
    I'll die for him tomorrow."

WILLIAM BLAKE (1757–1827)

The Garden of Love   *1794*

I went to the Garden of Love,
And saw what I never had seen:
A Chapel was built in the midst,
Where I used to play on the green.

And the gates of this Chapel were shut,   5
And "Thou shalt not" writ over the door;
So I turned to the Garden of Love
That so many sweet flowers bore;

And I saw it was filled with graves,
And tomb-stones where flowers should be;   10
And Priests in black gowns were walking their rounds,
And binding with briars my joys and desires.

WILLIAM BLAKE (1757–1827)

Infant Sorrow   1792

My mother groand! my father wept.
Into the dangerous world I leapt:
Helpless naked piping loud:
Like a fiend hid in a cloud.

Struggling in my fathers hands:
Striving against my swadling bands
Bound and weary I thought best
To sulk upon my mothers breast.

ROBERT BURNS (1759–1796)

A Red, Red Rose   1799

O my luve's like a red, red rose
That's newly sprung in June;
O my luve's like the melodie
That's sweetly played in tune.

As fair art thou, my bonny lass,   5
So deep in luve am I;
And I will luve thee still my dear,
Till a' the seas gang° dry —   go

Till a' the seas gang dry, my dear,
And the rocks melt wi' the sun: 10
O I will luve thee still, my dear,
While the sands o' life shall run.

And fare thee weel, my only luve,
And fare thee weel awhile!
And I will come again, my luve,   15
Though it were a thousand mile.

GEORGE GORDON, LORD BYRON (1788–1824)

She Walks in Beauty   1814

From Hebrew Melodies

I

She walks in Beauty, like the night
        Of cloudless climes and starry skies;
And all that's best of dark and bright
        Meet in her aspect and her eyes:

Thus mellowed to that tender light
    Which Heaven to gaudy day denies.

II

One shade the more, one ray the less,
    Had half impaired the nameless grace
Which waves in every raven tress,
    Or softly lightens o'er her face;
Where thoughts serenely sweet express,
    How pure, how dear their dwelling-place.

III

And on that cheek, and o'er that brow,
    So soft, so calm, yet eloquent,
The smiles that win, the tints that glow,
    But tell of days in goodness spent,
A mind at peace with all below,
    A heart whose love is innocent!

LUCILLE CLIFTON (B. 1936)

this morning (for the girls of eastern high school) 1987

this morning
this morning
        i met myself

coming in

a bright
jungle girl
shining
quick as a snake
a tall
tree girl a
me girl

        i met myself
this morning
coming in

and all day
i have been
a black bell
ringing
i survive

      survive

survive

© Christopher Felver.

SAMUEL TAYLOR COLERIDGE (1772–1834)

Kubla Khan: or, a Vision in a Dream°

1798

In Xanadu did Kubla Khan°
    A stately pleasure-dome decree:
Where Alph, the sacred river, ran
Through caverns measureless to man
      Down to a sunless sea.   5

So twice five miles of fertile ground
With walls and towers were girdled round:
And here were gardens bright with sinuous rills
Where blossomed many an incense-bearing tree;
And there were forests ancient as the hills,   10
Enfolding sunny spots of greenery.

But oh! that deep romantic chasm which slanted
Down the green hill athwart a cedarn cover!°
A savage place! as holy and enchanted
As e'er beneath a waning moon was haunted   15
By woman wailing for her demon-lover!
And from this chasm, with ceaseless turmoil seething,
As if this earth in fast thick pants were breathing,
A mighty fountain momently was forced,
Amid whose swift half-intermitted burst   20
Huge fragments vaulted like rebounding hail,
Of chaffy grain beneath the thresher's flail:
And 'mid these dancing rocks at once and ever
It flung up momently the sacred river.
Five miles meandering with a mazy motion   25
Through wood and dale the sacred river ran,
Then reached the caverns measureless to man,
And sank in tumult to a lifeless ocean:
And 'mid this tumult Kubla heard from far
Ancestral voices prophesying war!   30
    The shadow of the dome of pleasure
    Floated midway on the waves;
    Where was heard the mingled measure
    From the fountain and the caves.
It was a miracle of rare device,   35
A sunny pleasure-dome with caves of ice!

    A damsel with a dulcimer
    In a vision once I saw:

Vision in a Dream: This poem came to Coleridge in an opium-induced dream, but he was interrupted by a visitor while writing it down. He was later unable to remember the rest of the poem.

1 *Kubla Khan:* The historical Kublai Khan (1216–1294, grandson of Genghis Khan) was the founder of the Mongol dynasty in China.   13 *athwart . . . cover:* Spanning a grove of cedar trees.

It was an Abyssinian maid,
And on her dulcimer she played,   40
Singing of Mount Abora.
Could I revive within me
Her symphony and song,
To such a deep delight 'twould win me,
That with music loud and long,   45
I would build that dome in air,
That sunny dome! those caves of ice!
And all who heard should see them there,
And all should cry, Beware! Beware!
His flashing eyes, his floating hair!   50
Weave a circle round him thrice,
And close your eyes with holy dread,
For he on honey-dew hath fed,
And drunk the milk of Paradise.

RICHARD CRASHAW (1613–1649)

An Epitaph upon a Young Married Couple,
Dead and Buried Together   1646

To these, whom death again did wed,
This grave's their second marriage-bed.
For though the hand of fate could force
'Twixt soul and body a divorce,
It could not sunder man and wife   5
'Cause they both livéd but one life.
Peace, good reader. Do not weep.
Peace, the lovers are asleep.
They, sweet turtles, folded lie
In the last knot love could tie.   10
And though they lie as they were dead,
Their pillow stone, their sheets of lead,
(Pillow hard, and sheets not warm)
Love made the bed; they'll take no harm;
Let them sleep, let them sleep on.   15
Till this stormy night be gone,
Till th' eternal morrow dawn;
Then the curtains will be drawn
And they wake into a light,
Whose day shall never die in night.   20

E. E. Cummings (1894–1962)
Buffalo Bill's°

1923

Buffalo Bill 's
defunct
     who used to
     ride a watersmooth-silver
               stallion   5
and break onetwothreefourfive pigeonsjustlikethat
                     Jesus

he was a handsome man
             and what i want to know is
how do you like your blueeyed boy   10
Mister Death

Buffalo Bill: William Frederick Cody (1846–1917) was an American frontier scout and Indian killer turned international circus showman with his Wild West show, which employed Sitting Bull and Annie Oakley.

John Donne (1572–1631)
The Apparition

c. 1600

When by thy scorn, O murderess, I am dead,
     And that thou thinkst thee free
From all solicitation from me,
Then shall my ghost come to thy bed,
And thee, feigned vestal, in worse arms shall see;   5
Then thy sick taper° will begin to wink,   *candle*
And he, whose thou art then, being tired before,
Will, if thou stir, or pinch to wake him, think
     Thou call'st for more,
And in false sleep will from thee shrink.   10
And then, poor aspen wretch, neglected, thou,
Bathed in a cold quicksilver sweat, wilt lie
     A verier° ghost than I.   *truer*
What I will say, I will not tell thee now,
Lest that preserve thee; and since my love is spent,   15
I had rather thou shouldst painfully repent,
Than by my threatenings rest still innocent.

JOHN DONNE (1572–1631)

The Flea *1633*

Mark but this flea, and mark in this°
How little that which thou deny'st me is;
It sucked me first, and now sucks thee,
And in this flea our two bloods mingled be;
Thou know'st that this cannot be said   5
A sin, nor shame, nor loss of maidenhead,
    Yet this enjoys before it woo,
    And pampered swells with one blood made of two,
    And this, alas, is more than we would do.°

Oh stay, three lives in one flea spare,   10
Where we almost, yea more than, married are.
This flea is you and I, and this
Our marriage bed, and marriage temple is;
Though parents grudge, and you, we're met
And cloistered in these living walls of jet.   15
    Though use° make you apt to kill me,   *habit*
    Let not to that, self-murder added be,
    And sacrilege, three sins in killing three.

Cruel and sudden, hast thou since
Purpled thy nail in blood of innocence?   20
Wherein could this flea guilty be,
Except in that drop which it sucked from thee?
Yet thou triumph'st, and say'st that thou
Find'st not thyself, nor me, the weaker now;
    'Tis true; then learn how false, fears be;   25
    Just so much honor, when thou yield'st to me,
    Will waste, as this flea's death took life from thee.

1 *mark in this:* Take note of the moral lesson in this object.   9 *more than we would do:* That is, if we do not join our blood in conceiving a child.

T. S. ELIOT (1888–1965)

The Love Song of J. Alfred Prufrock

S'io credesse che mia risposta fosse
A persona che mai tornasse al mondo,
Questa fiamma staria senza più scosse.
Ma perciocchè giammai di questo fondo
Non tornò vivo alcun, s'i'odo il vero,
Senza tema d'infamia ti rispondo.°

Epigraph: *S'io credesse . . . rispondo:* Dante's *Inferno,* 27:58–63. In the Eighth Chasm of the Inferno, Dante and Virgil meet Guido da Montefeltro, one of the False Counselors, who is

Let us go then, you and I,
When the evening is spread out against the sky
Like a patient etherized upon a table;
Let us go, through certain half-deserted streets,
The muttering retreats   5
Of restless nights in one-night cheap hotels
And sawdust restaurants with oyster-shells:
Streets that follow like a tedious argument
Of insidious intent
To lead you to an overwhelming question . . .   10

Oh, do not ask, "What is it?"
Let us go and make our visit.

In the room the women come and go
Talking of Michelangelo.

The yellow fog that rubs its back upon the window panes,   15
The yellow smoke that rubs its muzzle on the window panes
Licked its tongue into the corners of the evening,
Lingered upon the pools that stand in drains,
Let fall upon its back the soot that falls from chimneys,
Slipped by the terrace, made a sudden leap,   20
And seeing that it was a soft October night,
Curled once about the house, and fell asleep.

And indeed there will be time°
For the yellow smoke that slides along the street,
Rubbing its back upon the window panes;   25
There will be time, there will be time
To prepare a face to meet the faces that you meet;
There will be time to murder and create,
And time for all the works and days° of hands
That lift and drop a question on your plate: 30
Time for you and time for me,
And time yet for a hundred indecisions,
And for a hundred visions and revisions,
Before the taking of a toast and tea.

In the room the women come and go   35
Talking of Michelangelo.

And indeed there will be time
To wonder, "Do I dare?" and, "Do I dare?" —
Time to turn back and descend the stair,

---

punished by being enveloped in an eternal flame. When Dante asks Guido to tell his life story, the spirit replies: "If I thought that my answer were to one who might ever return to the world, this flame would shake no more; but since from this depth none ever returned alive, if what I hear is true, I answer you without fear of infamy."

23 *there will be time:* An allusion to Ecclesiastes 3:1–8: "To everything there is a season, and a time to every purpose under heaven. . . ."

29 *works and days:* Hesiod's eighth-century B.C. poem *Works and Days* gives practical advice on how to conduct one's life in accordance with the seasons.

With a bald spot in the middle of my hair — 40
(They will say: "How his hair is growing thin!")
My morning coat, my collar mounting firmly to the chin,
My necktie rich and modest, but asserted by a simple pin —
(They will say: "But how his arms and legs are thin!")
Do I dare 45
Disturb the universe?
In a minute there is time
For decisions and revisions which a minute will reverse.

    For I have known them all already, known them all:
Have known the evenings, mornings, afternoons, 50
I have measured out my life with coffee spoons;
I know the voices dying with a dying fall
Beneath the music from a farther room.
    So how should I presume?

    And I have known the eyes already, known them all — 55
The eyes that fix you in a formulated phrase.
And when I am formulated, sprawling on a pin,
When I am pinned and wriggling on the wall,
Then how should I begin
To spit out all the butt-ends of my days and ways? 60
    And how should I presume?

    And I have known the arms already, known them all —
Arms that are braceleted and white and bare
(But in the lamplight, downed with light brown hair!)
    Is it perfume from a dress 65
    That makes me so digress?
Arms that lie along a table, or wrap about a shawl.
    And should I then presume?
    And how should I begin?

    Shall I say, I have gone at dusk through narrow streets, 70
And watched the smoke that rises from the pipes
Of lonely men in shirtsleeves, leaning out of windows? . . .

I should have been a pair of ragged claws
Scuttling across the floors of silent seas.

    And the afternoon, the evening, sleeps so peacefully! 75
Smoothed by long fingers,
Asleep . . . tired . . . or it malingers,
Stretched on the floor, here beside you and me.
Should I, after tea and cakes and ices,
Have the strength to force the moment to its crisis? 80
But though I have wept and fasted, wept and prayed,
Though I have seen my head (grown slightly bald) brought in upon a platter,°

---

82 *head . . . upon a platter:* At Salome's request, Herod had John the Baptist decapitated and
had the severed head delivered to her on a platter (see Matt. 14:1-12 and Mark 6:17-29).

I am no prophet — and here's no great matter;
I have seen the moment of my greatness flicker,
And I have seen the eternal Footman hold my coat, and snicker,   85
    And in short, I was afraid.

    And would it have been worth it, after all,
After the cups, the marmalade, the tea,
Among the porcelain, among some talk of you and me,
Would it have been worth while   90
To have bitten off the matter with a smile,
To have squeezed the universe into a ball°
To roll it toward some overwhelming question,
To say: "I am Lazarus,° come from the dead,
Come back to tell you all, I shall tell you all" —   95
If one, settling a pillow by her head,
    Should say: "That is not what I meant at all;
        That is not it, at all."

    And would it have been worth it, after all,
Would it have been worth while,   100
After the sunsets and the dooryards and the sprinkled streets,
After the novels, after the teacups, after the skirts that trail along the floor —
And this, and so much more? —
It is impossible to say just what I mean!
But as if a magic lantern threw the nerves in patterns on a screen: 105
Would it have been worth while
If one, settling a pillow or throwing off a shawl,
And turning toward the window, should say:
    "That is not it at all,
        That is not what I meant, at all."   110

No! I am not Prince Hamlet, nor was meant to be;
Am an attendant lord,° one that will do
To swell a progress,° start a scene or two   *state procession*
Advise the prince: withal, an easy tool,
Deferential, glad to be of use,   115
Politic, cautious, and meticulous;
Full of high sentence, but a bit obtuse;
At times, indeed, almost ridiculous —
Almost, at times, the Fool.

I grow old . . . I grow old . . .   120
I shall wear the bottoms of my trowsers rolled.

92 *squeezed the universe into a ball:* See Andrew Marvell's "To His Coy Mistress" (p. 843), lines
41–42: "Let us roll all our strength and all / Our sweetness up into one ball."

94 *Lazarus:* The brother of Mary and Martha who was raised from the dead by Jesus (John
11:1–44). In Luke 16:19–31, a rich man asks that another Lazarus return from the dead to warn
the living about their treatment of the poor.

112 *attendant lord:* Like Polonius in Shakespeare's *Hamlet.*

Shall I part my hair behind? Do I dare to eat a peach?
I shall wear white flannel trowsers, and walk upon the beach.
I have heard the mermaids singing, each to each.

I do not think that they will sing to me.   125

I have seen them riding seaward on the waves,
Combing the white hair of the waves blown back
When the wind blows the water white and black.

We have lingered in the chambers of the sea
By seagirls wreathed with seaweed red and brown,   130
Till human voices wake us, and we drown.

Thomas Hardy (1840–1928)

Hap   *1866*

If but some vengeful god would call to me
From up the sky, and laugh: "Thou suffering thing,
Know that thy sorrow is my ecstasy,
That thy love's loss is my hate's profiting!"

Then would I bear it, clench myself, and die,   5
Steeled by the sense of ire unmerited;
Half-eased in that a Powerfuller than I
Had willed and meted me the tears I shed.

But not so. How arrives it joy lies slain,
And why unblooms the best hope ever sown?   10
— Crass Casualty obstructs the sun and rain,
And dicing Time for gladness casts a moan. . . .
These purblind Doomsters had as readily strown
Blisses about my pilgrimage as pain.

Gerard Manley Hopkins (1844–1889)

Pied Beauty   *1877*

Glory be to God for dappled things —
   For skies of couple-color as a brinded cow;
      For rose-moles all in stipple upon trout that swim;
Fresh-firecoal chestnut-falls;° finches' wings;   *fallen chestnut*
   Landscape plotted and pieced — fold, fallow, and plow;   5
      And all trades, their gear and tackle and trim.

All things counter, original, spare, strange;
   Whatever is fickle, freckled (who knows how?)
      With swift, slow; sweet, sour; adazzle, dim;
He fathers-forth whose beauty is past change: 10
      Praise him.

GERARD MANLEY HOPKINS (1844–1889)

The Windhover°   *1877*

To Christ Our Lord

I caught this morning morning's minion,° king-   *favorite*
    dom of daylight's dauphin, dapple-dawn-drawn Falcon, in his riding
    Of the rolling level underneath him steady air, and striding
High there, how he rung upon the rein of a wimpling wing
In his ecstasy! then off, off forth on swing,   5
    As a skate's heel sweeps smooth on a bow-bend: the hurl and gliding
    Rebuffed the big wind. My heart in hiding
Stirred for a bird, — the achieve of, the mastery of the thing!

Brute beauty and valour and act, oh, air, pride, plume, here
    Buckle!° AND the fire that breaks from thee then, a billion   10
Times told lovelier, more dangerous, O my chevalier!

    No wonder of it: shéer plód makes plough down sillion°   *furrow*
Shine, and blue-bleak embers, ah my dear,
    Fall, gall themselves, and gash gold-vermilion.

The Windhover: "A name for the kestrel [a kind of small hawk], from its habit of hovering or
hanging with its head to the wind" [*OED*].   10 *Buckle:* To join, to equip for battle, to
crumple.

A. E. HOUSMAN (1859–1936)

To an Athlete Dying Young   *1896*

The time you won your town the race
We chaired° you through the marketplace;
Man and boy stood cheering by,
And home we brought you shoulder-high.

Today, the road all runners come,   5
Shoulder-high we bring you home,
And set you at your threshold down,
Townsman of a stiller town.

Smart lad, to slip betimes away
From fields where glory does not stay,   10
And early though the laurel° grows
It withers quicker than the rose.

Eyes the shady night has shut
Cannot see the record cut,
And silence sounds no worse than cheers   15
After earth has stopped the ears:

2 *chaired:* Carried on the shoulders in triumphal parade.   11 *laurel:* Flowering shrub
traditionally used to fashion wreaths of honor.

Now you will not swell the rout
Of lads that wore their honors out,
Runners whom renown outran
And the name died before the man.   20

To set, before its echoes fade,
The fleet foot on the sill of shade,
And hold to the low lintel up
The still-defended challenge-cup.

And round that early-laureled head   25
Will flock to gaze the strengthless dead,
And find unwithered on its curls
The garland briefer than a girl's.

JULIA WARD HOWE (1819–1910)

Battle-Hymn of the Republic   1862

Mine eyes have seen the glory of the coming of the Lord:
He is trampling out the vintage where the grapes of wrath are stored;
He hath loosed the fateful lightning of his terrible swift sword:
          His truth is marching on.

I have seen Him in the watch-fires of a hundred circling camps;   5
They have builded Him an altar in the evening dews and damps;
I can read His righteous sentence by the dim and flaring lamps.
          His day is marching on.

I have read a fiery gospel, writ in burnished rows of steel:
"As ye deal with my contemners, so with you my grace shall deal;   10
Let the Hero, born of woman, crush the serpent with his heel,
          Since God is marching on."

He has sounded forth the trumpet that shall never call retreat;
He is sifting out the hearts of men before his judgment-seat:
Oh! be swift, my soul, to answer Him! be jubilant, my feet!   15
          Our God is marching on.

In the beauty of the lilies Christ was born across the sea,
With a glory in his bosom that transfigures you and me:
As he died to make men holy, let us die to make men free,
     While God is marching on.   20

BEN JONSON (1573–1637)

To Celia   1616

Drink to me only with thine eyes,
     And I will pledge with mine;
Or leave a kiss but in the cup,
     And I'll not ask for wine.

The thirst that from the soul doth rise 5
    Doth ask a drink divine;
But might I of Jove's nectar sup,
    I would not change for thine.

I sent thee late a rosy wreath,
    Not so much honoring thee 10
As giving it a hope that there
    It could not withered be.
But thou thereon didst only breathe,
    And sent'st it back to me;
Since when it grows, and smells, I swear, 15
    Not of itself but thee.

JOHN KEATS (1795–1821)

The Human Seasons 1818

Four seasons fill the measure of the year;
    Four seasons are there in the mind of man.
He hath his lusty spring, when fancy clear
    Takes in all beauty with an easy span:
He hath his summer, when luxuriously 5
    He chews the honied cud of fair spring thoughts,
Till, in his soul dissolv'd, they come to be
    Part of himself. He hath his autumn ports
And havens of repose, when his tired wings
    Are folded up, and he content to look 10
On mists in idleness: to let fair things
    Pass by unheeded as a threshold brook.
He hath his winter too of pale misfeature,
Or else he would forget his mortal nature.

Explore contexts for John Keats on LiterActive.

JOHN KEATS (1795–1821)

La Belle Dame sans Merci° 1819

O what can ail thee, knight-at-arms,
    Alone and palely loitering?
The sedge has withered from the lake,
    And no birds sing.

O what can ail thee, knight-at-arms, 5
    So haggard and so woe-begone?
The squirrel's granary is full,
    And the harvest's done.

La Belle Dame sans Merci: This title is borrowed from a medieval poem and means "The Beautiful Lady without Mercy."

I see a lily on thy brow,
    With anguish moist and fever dew,   10
And on thy cheeks a fading rose
    Fast withereth too.

I met a lady in the meads,
    Full beautiful — a faery's child,
Her hair was long, her foot was light,   15
    And her eyes were wild.

I made a garland for her head,
    And bracelets too, and fragrant zone;°   *belt*
She looked at me as she did love,
    And made sweet moan.   20

I set her on my pacing steed,
    And nothing else saw all day long,
For sidelong would she bend, and sing
    A faery's song.

She found me roots of relish sweet,   25
    And honey wild, and manna dew,
And sure in language strange she said,
    "I love thee true."

She took me to her elfin grot,
    And there she wept, and sighed full sore,   30
And there I shut her wild wild eyes
    With kisses four.

And there she lullèd me asleep,
    And there I dreamed — Ah! woe betide!
The latest° dream I ever dreamed   *last* 35
    On the cold hill side.

I saw pale kings and princes too,
    Pale warriors, death-pale were they all;
They cried — "La Belle Dame sans Merci
    Hath thee in thrall!"   40

I saw their starved lips in the gloam,
    With horrid warning gapèd wide,
And I awoke and found me here,
    On the cold hill's side.

And this is why I sojourn here,   45
    Alone and palely loitering,
Though the sedge has withered from the lake,
    And no birds sing.

YUSEF KOMUNYAKAA (B. 1947)

Slam, Dunk, & Hook   *1992*

Fast breaks. Lay ups. With Mercury's
Insignia on our sneakers,
We outmaneuvered the footwork
Of bad angels. Nothing but a hot
Swish of strings like silk   5
Ten feet out. In the roundhouse
Labyrinth our bodies
Created, we could almost
Last forever, poised in midair
Like storybook sea monsters.   10
A high note hung there
A long second. Off
The rim. We'd corkscrew
Up & dunk balls that exploded
The skullcap of hope & good   15
Intention. Bug-eyed, lanky,
All hands & feet . . . sprung rhythm.
We were metaphysical when girls
Cheered on the sidelines.
Tangled up in a falling,   20
Muscles were a bright motor
Double-flashing to the metal hoop
Nailed to our oak.
When Sonny Boy's mama died
He played nonstop all day, so hard   25
Our backboard splintered.
Glistening with sweat, we jibed
& rolled the ball off our
Fingertips. Trouble
Was there slapping a blackjack   30
Against an open palm.
Dribble, drive to the inside, feint,
& glide like a sparrow hawk.
Layups. Fast breaks.
We had moves we didn't know   35
We had. Our bodies spun

On swivels of bone & faith,
Through a lyric slipknot
Of joy, & we knew we were
Beautiful & dangerous.   40

TED KOOSER (B. 1939)

A Death at the Office

1980

The news goes desk to desk
like a memo: *Initial*
and pass on. Each of us marks
Surprised or *Sorry.*

The management came early   5
and buried her nameplate
deep in her desk. They have boxed up
the Midol and Lip-Ice,

the snapshots from home,
wherever it was — nephews   10
and nieces, a strange, blurred cat
with fiery, flashbulb eyes

as if it grieved. But who grieves here?
We have her ballpoints back,
her bud vase. One of us tears   15
the scribbles from her calendar.

EMMA LAZARUS (1849–1887)

The New Colossus

1883

Not like the brazen giant of Greek fame,
With conquering limbs astride from land to land;
Here at our sea-washed, sunset gates shall stand
A mighty woman with a torch, whose flame
Is the imprisoned lightning, and her name   5
Mother of Exiles. From her beacon-hand
Glows world-wide welcome; her mild eyes command
The air-bridged harbor that twin cities frame.
"Keep, ancient lands, your storied pomp!" cries she
With silent lips. "Give me your tired, your poor,   10
Your huddled masses yearning to breathe free,
The wretched refuse of your teeming shore.
Send these, the homeless, tempest-tost to me,
I lift my lamp beside the golden door!"

John Milton (1608–1674)

When I consider how my light is spent

c. 1655

When I consider how my light is spent,°
    Ere half my days in this dark world and wide,
    And that one talent° which is death to hide
Lodged with me useless, though my soul more bent
To serve therewith my Maker, and present   5
    My true account, lest He returning chide;
    "Doth God exact day-labor, light denied?"
I fondly° ask. But Patience, to prevent   *foolishly*
That murmur, soon replies, "God doth not need
    Either man's work or His own gifts. Who best   10
    Bear His mild yoke, they serve Him best. His state
Is kingly: thousands at His bidding speed,
    And post o'er land and ocean without rest;
    They also serve who only stand and wait."

1 *how my light is spent:* Milton had been totally blind since 1651.   3 *that one talent:* Refers to Jesus's parable of the talents (units of money), in which a servant entrusted with a talent buries it rather than invests it and is punished on his master's return (Matt. 25:14–30).

Christina Georgina Rossetti
(1830–1894)

Some Ladies Dress in Muslin Full and White

c. 1848

Some ladies dress in muslin full and
    white,
Some gentlemen in cloth succinct and black;
Some patronise a dog-cart, some a hack,
    Some think a painted clarence only
    right.
    Youth is not always such a pleasing
    sight:
Witness a man with tassels on his back;
Or woman in a great-coat like a sack,
    Towering above her sex with horrid height.
If all the world were water fit to drown,
    There are some whom you would not teach to swim,   10
    Rather enjoying if you saw them sink:
    Certain old ladies dressed in girlish pink,
With roses and geraniums on their gown.
    Go to the basin, poke them o'er the rim —

© Mary Evans Picture Library/Alamy.

CHRISTINA GEORGINA ROSSETTI (1830–1894)

Promises Like Pie-Crust°

1896

Promise me no promises,
    So will I not promise you;
Keep we both our liberties,
    Never false and never true:
Let us hold the die uncast,   5
    Free to come as free to go;
For I cannot know your past,
    And of mine what can you know?

You, so warm, may once have been
    Warmer towards another one;   10
I, so cold, may once have seen
    Sunlight, once have felt the sun:
Who shall show us if it was
    Thus indeed in time of old?
Fades the image from the glass   15
    And the fortune is not told.

If you promised, you might grieve
    For lost liberty again;
If I promised, I believe
    I should fret to break the chain: 20
Let us be the friends we were,
    Nothing more but nothing less;
Many thrive on frugal fare
    Who would perish of excess.

Pie-Crust: An old English proverb: "Promises are like pie-crust, made to be broken."

WILLIAM SHAKESPEARE (1564–1616)

That time of year thou mayst in me behold

1609

That time of year thou mayst in me behold
When yellow leaves, or none, or few, do hang
Upon those boughs which shake against the cold,
Bare ruined choirs, where late the sweet birds sang.
In me thou see'st the twilight of such day   5
As after sunset fadeth in the west;
Which by and by black night doth take away,
Death's second self,° that seals up all in rest.   *sleep*
In me thou see'st the glowing of such fire,
That on the ashes of his youth doth lie,   10
As the deathbed whereon it must expire,

Explore contexts
for William Shakespeare
on *LiterActive*.

Consumed with that which it was nourished by.
    This thou perceiv'st, which makes thy love more strong,
    To love that well which thou must leave ere long.

WILLIAM SHAKESPEARE (1564–1616)

When forty winters shall besiege thy brow   *1609*

When forty winters shall besiege thy brow
And dig deep trenches in thy beauty's field,
Thy youth's proud livery, so gazed on now,
Will be a tattered weed,° of small worth held.   *garment*
Then being asked where all thy beauty lies,   5
Where all the treasure of thy lusty days,
To say within thine own deep-sunken eyes
Were an all-eating shame and thriftless praise.
How much more praise deserved thy beauty's use
If thou couldst answer, "This fair child of mine   10
Shall sum my count and make my old excuse,"
Proving his beauty by succession thine.
    This were to be new made when thou art old,
    And see thy blood warm when thou feel'st it cold.

PERCY BYSSHE SHELLEY (1792–1822)

Ozymandias°   *1818*

I met a traveler from an antique land
Who said: Two vast and trunkless legs of stone
Stand in the desert. . . . Near them, on the sand,
Half sunk, a shattered visage lies, whose frown,
And wrinkled lip, and sneer of cold command,   5
Tell that its sculptor well those passions read
Which yet survive, stamped on these lifeless things,
The hand that mocked them, and the heart that fed:
And on the pedestal these words appear:
"My name is Ozymandias, King of Kings: 10

Ozymandias: Greek name for Ramses II, pharaoh of Egypt for sixty-seven years during the thirteenth century B.C. His colossal statue lies prostrate in the sands of Luxor. Napoleon's soldiers measured it (56 feet long, ear 3½ feet long, weight 1,000 tons). Its inscription, according to the Greek historian Diodorus Siculus, was "I am Ozymandias, King of Kings; if anyone wishes to know what I am and where I lie, let him surpass me in some of my exploits."

Look on my works, ye Mighty, and despair!"
Nothing beside remains. Round the decay
Of that colossal wreck, boundless and bare
The lone and level sands stretch far away.

LYDIA HUNTLEY SIGOURNEY (1791–1865)

Indian Names   1834

*"How can the red men be forgotten, while so many of
our states and territories, bays, lakes and rivers, are
indelibly stamped by names of their giving?"*

Ye say they all have passed away,
   That noble race and brave,
That their light canoes have vanished
   From off the crested wave;
That 'mid the forests where they roamed   5
   There rings no hunter shout,
But their name is on your waters,
   Ye may not wash it out.

'Tis where Ontario's billow
   Like Ocean's surge is curled,   10
Where strong Niagara's thunders wake
   The echo of the world.
Where red Missouri bringeth
   Rich tribute from the west,
And Rappahannock sweetly sleeps   15
   On green Virginia's breast.

Ye say their cone-like cabins,
   That clustered o'er the vale,
Have fled away like withered leaves
   Before the autumn gale,   20
But their memory liveth on your hills,
   Their baptism on your shore,
Your everlasting rivers speak
   Their dialect of yore.

Old Massachusetts wears it,   25
   Within her lordly crown,
And broad Ohio bears it,
   Amid his young renown;
Connecticut hath wreathed it
   Where her quiet foliage waves,   30
And bold Kentucky breathed it hoarse
   Through all her ancient caves.

Wachuset hides its lingering voice
    Within his rocky heart,
And Alleghany graves its tone   35
    Throughout his lofty chart;
Monadnock on his forehead hoar
    Doth seal the sacred trust,
Your mountains build their monument,
    Though ye destroy their dust.   40

Ye call these red-browed brethren
    The insects of an hour,
Crushed like the noteless worm amid
    The regions of their power;
Ye drive them from their father's lands,   45
    Ye break of faith the seal,
But can ye from the court of Heaven
    Exclude their last appeal?

Ye see their unresisting tribes,
    With toilsome step and slow,   50
On through the trackless desert pass,
    A caravan of woe;
Think ye the Eternal's ear is deaf?
    His sleepless vision dim?
Think ye the *soul's blood* may not cry   55
    From that far land to him?

WALLACE STEVENS (1879–1955)

The Emperor of Ice-Cream   *1923*

Call the roller of big cigars,
The muscular one, and bid him whip
In kitchen cups concupiscent curds.°
Let the wenches dawdle in such dress
As they are used to wear, and let the boys   5
Bring flowers in last month's newspapers.
Let be be finale of seem.°
The only emperor is the emperor of ice-cream.

3 *concupiscent curds:* "The words 'concupiscent curds' have no genealogy; they are merely expressive: at least, I hope they are expressive. They express the concupiscence of life, but, by contrast with the things in relation in the poem, they express or accentuate life's destitution, and it is this that gives them something more than a cheap lustre" (Wallace Stevens, *Letters* [New York: Knopf, 1960], p. 500).

7 *Let . . . seem:* "The true sense of 'Let be be finale of seem' is let being become the conclusion or denouement of appearing to be: in short, ice cream is an absolute good. The poem is obviously not about ice cream, but about being as distinguished from seeming to be" (*Letters*, p. 341).

Take from the dresser of deal,
Lacking the three glass knobs, that sheet   10
On which she embroidered fantails once
And spread it so as to cover her face.
If her horny feet protrude, they come
To show how cold she is, and dumb.
Let the lamp affix its beam.   15
The only emperor is the emperor of ice-cream.

ALFRED, LORD TENNYSON (1809–1892)

Ulysses°   *1833*

   It little profits that an idle king,
By this still hearth, among these barren crags,
Matched with an agèd wife,° I mete and dole   *Penelope*
Unequal laws unto a savage race,
That hoard, and sleep, and feed, and know not me.   5
   I cannot rest from travel; I will drink
Life to the lees. All times I have enjoyed
Greatly, have suffered greatly, both with those
That loved me, and alone; on shore, and when
Through scudding drifts the rainy Hyades°   10
Vexed the dim sea. I am become a name;
For always roaming with a hungry heart
Much have I seen and known — cities of men
And manners, climates, councils, governments,
Myself not least, but honored of them all —   15
And drunk delight of battle with my peers,
Far on the ringing plains of windy Troy.
I am a part of all that I have met;
Yet all experience is an arch wherethrough
Gleams that untraveled world, whose margin fades   20
For ever and for ever when I move.
How dull it is to pause, to make an end,
To rust unburnished, not to shine in use!
As though to breathe were life. Life piled on life
Were all too little, and of one to me   25
Little remains; but every hour is saved
From that eternal silence, something more,

Ulysses: Ulysses, the hero of Homer's epic poem the *Odyssey,* is presented by Dante in *The Inferno,* XXVI, as restless after his return to Ithaca and eager for new adventures.

10 *Hyades:* Five stars in the constellation Taurus, supposed by the ancients to predict rain when they rose with the sun.

A bringer of new things; and vile it were
For some three suns to store and hoard myself,
And this gray spirit yearning in desire   30
To follow knowledge like a sinking star,
Beyond the utmost bound of human thought.

    This is my son, mine own Telemachus,
To whom I leave the scepter and the isle —
Well-loved of me, discerning to fulfill   35
This labor, by slow prudence to make mild
A rugged people, and through soft degrees
Subdue them to the useful and the good.
Most blameless is he, centered in the sphere
Of common duties, decent not to fail   40
In offices of tenderness, and pay
Meet adoration to my household gods,
When I am gone. He works his work, I mine.

    There lies the port; the vessel puffs her sail:
There gloom the dark, broad seas. My mariners,   45
Souls that have toiled, and wrought, and thought with me —
That ever with a frolic welcome took
The thunder and the sunshine, and opposed
Free hearts, free foreheads — you and I are old;
Old age hath yet his honor and his toil.   50
Death closes all; but something ere the end,
Some work of noble note, may yet be done,
Not unbecoming men that strove with Gods.
The lights begin to twinkle from the rocks;
The long day wanes; the slow moon climbs; the deep   55
Moans round with many voices. Come, my friends.
'Tis not too late to seek a newer world.
Push off, and sitting well in order smite
The sounding furrows; for my purpose holds
To sail beyond the sunset, and the baths   60
Of all the western stars, until I die.
It may be that the gulfs will wash us down;
It may be we shall touch the Happy Isles,°
And see the great Achilles,° whom we knew.
Though much is taken, much abides; and though   65
We are not now that strength which in old days
Moved earth and heaven, that which we are, we are:
One equal temper of heroic hearts,
Made weak by time and fate, but strong in will
To strive, to seek, to find, and not to yield.   70

---

63 *Happy Isles:* Elysium, the home after death of heroes and others favored by the gods. It
was thought by the ancients to lie beyond the sunset in the uncharted Atlantic.   64 *Achilles:*
The hero of Homer's *Iliad.*

WALT WHITMAN (1819–1892)

One's-Self I Sing

1867

One's-Self I sing, a simple separate person,
Yet utter the word Democratic, the word En-Masse.

Of physiology from top to toe I sing,
Not physiognomy alone nor brain alone is worthy for the Muse, I say the
       Form complete is worthier far,
The Female equally with the Male I sing.

Of Life immense in passion, pulse, and power,
Cheerful, for freest action formed under the laws divine,
The Modern Man I sing.

WALT WHITMAN (1819–1892)

When I Heard the Learn'd Astronomer

1865

When I heard the learn'd astronomer,
When the proofs, the figures, were ranged in columns before me,
When I was shown the charts and diagrams, to add, divide, and measure them,
When I sitting heard the astronomer where he lectured with much applause
       in the lecture-room,
How soon unaccountable I became tired and sick,
Till rising and gliding out I wandered off by myself,
In the mystical moist night-air, and from time to time,
Looked up in perfect silence at the stars.

WILLIAM CARLOS WILLIAMS (1883–1963)

This Is Just to Say

1934

I have eaten
the plums
that were in
the icebox

and which   5
you were probably
saving
for breakfast

Forgive me
they were delicious   10
so sweet
and so cold

WILLIAM WORDSWORTH (1770–1850)

A Slumber Did My Spirit Seal   *1800*

A slumber did my spirit seal;
　I had no human fears —
She seemed a thing that could not feel
　The touch of earthly years.

No motion has she now, no force;
　She neither hears nor sees;
Rolled round in earth's diurnal course.
　With rocks, and stones, and trees.

By permission of Dove Cottage, the
Wordsworth Trust.

WILLIAM WORDSWORTH (1770–1850)

The Solitary Reaper°   *1807*

Behold her, single in the field,
Yon solitary Highland lass!
Reaping and singing by herself;
Stop here, or gently pass!
Alone she cuts and binds the grain,   5
And sings a melancholy strain;
O listen! for the vale profound
Is overflowing with the sound.

No nightingale did ever chaunt
More welcome notes to weary bands   10
Of travelers in some shady haunt
Among Arabian sands.
A voice so thrilling ne'er was heard
In springtime from the cuckoo-bird,
Breaking the silence of the seas   15
Among the farthest Hebrides.

Will no one tell me what she sings? —
Perhaps the plaintive numbers flow
For old, unhappy, far-off things,
And battles long ago.   20
Or is it some more humble lay,
Familiar matter of today?
Some natural sorrow, loss, or pain,
That has been, and may be again?

The Solitary Reaper: Dorothy Wordsworth (William's sister) writes that the poem was suggested by this sentence in Thomas Wilkinson's *Tour of Scotland:* "Passed a female who was reaping alone; she sung in Erse, as she bended over her sickle; the sweetest human voice I ever heard; her strains were tenderly melancholy, and felt delicious, long after they were heard no more."

Whate'er the theme, the maiden sang   25
As if her song could have nō ending;
I saw her singing at her work,
And o'er the sickle bending—
I listened, motionless and still;
And, as I mounted up the hill,   30
The music in my heart I bore
Long after it was heard no more.

WILLIAM WORDSWORTH (1770–1850)

Mutability   *1822*

From low to high doth dissolution climb,
And sink from high to low, along a scale
Of awful° notes, whose concord shall not fail;   *awe-filled*
A muscial but melancholy chime,
Which they can hear who meddle not with crime,   5
Nor avarice, nor over-anxious care.
Truth fails not; but her outward forms that bear
The longest date do melt like frosty rime,
That in the morning whitened hill and plain
And is no more; drop like the tower sublime   10
Of yesterday, which royally did wear
His crown of weeds, but could not even sustain
Some casual shout that broke the silent air,
Or the unimaginable touch of Time.

WILLIAM BUTLER YEATS (1865–1939)

Crazy Jane Talks with the Bishop   *1933*

I met the Bishop on the road
And much said he and I.
"Those breasts are flat and fallen now,
Those veins must soon be dry;
Live in a heavenly mansion,
Not in some foul sty."

"Fair and foul are near of kin,
And fair needs foul," I cried.
"My friends are gone, but that's a truth
Nor grave nor bed denied,
Learned in bodily lowliness
And in the heart's pride.

© Hulton-Deutsch Collection/CORBIS.   10

A THEMATIC CASE STUDY
Border Crossings

As immigrants we have this enormous raw material. . . . We draw from a dual culture, with two sets of worldviews and paradigms juxtaposing each other.
— CHITRA BANERJEE DIVAKARUNI

Courtesy of the author.

A BRIEF INTRODUCTION

This unit brings together seven poems and a variety of images that center upon the theme of crossing borders. The borders referred to in these poems are not only those that mark geographic or political divisions but also the uncertain and indeterminate borders associated with culture, class, race, ethnicity, and gender. Even if we have never left our home state or country, we have all moved back and forth across such defining lines as we negotiate the margins and edges of our personal identities within the particular worlds we inhabit. Any first-year college student, for example, knows that college life and demanding course work represent a significant border crossing: increased academic challenges, responsibility, and autonomy likely reflect an entirely new culture for the student. By Thanksgiving vacation, students know (as do their parents and friends) that they've crossed an invisible border that causes a slight shift in their identity because they've done some growing and maturing.

The poems and visuals in this chapter explore a wide range of border crossings. Phillis Wheatley was kidnapped and forced across borders in 1761 when she was brought to America as a slave. Her

Getty Images.

I can define . . . can simplify the history of human society, the evolution of human society, as a contest between power and freedom.
— WOLE SOYINKA

A

poem "On Being Brought from Africa to America" offers a fascinating argument against racism. Wheatley's perspective is deepened by a diagram of a ship and an advertisement for an auction that vividly illustrate how slaves were transported and marketed. Wole Soyinka's "Telephone Conversation," paired with a poster advertising the film *Guess Who's Coming to Dinner,* reflects the racial tensions associated with integration. These tensions are internalized in Pat Mora's "Legal Alien" and Jacalyn López García's "I Just Wanted to Be Me," which describe the dilemma of being raised as a Mexican American. Sandra M. Gilbert examines the pain caused by ethnic stereotyping in "Mafioso," which is complemented by a revealing photograph of Italian immigrant children as they are processed at Ellis Island. The anxieties felt by new immigrants and their yearnings for the life they left behind are the subject of Chitra Banerjee Divakaruni's "Indian Movie, New Jersey," which is paired with an optimistic cover of a Bollywood film soundtrack. The prejudice that causes some of the anxiety in that poem is also evident in Janice Mirikitani's "Recipe," a satire commenting on the impact of Western beauty ideals on Japanese girls and women. The relevancy of that problem is brought home in the accompanying photograph of a child holding one of Japan's most popular dolls, by Chiaki Tsukumo. Finally, Thomas Lynch's "Liberty" provides an amusing but pointed look at an Irish American who finds suburban life to be a lamentable state compared to the life of his ancestors in Ireland. The photograph of a crowded, working-class Boston suburb that follows the poem tidily captures Lynch's themes.

A list of additional thematically related poems is located at the end of this chapter.

■ **Transcendence and Borders.** Born in West Africa, Phillis Wheatley was kidnapped and brought to America in 1761 and sold to John and Susannah Wheatley of Boston. She was taught to read and write and was then freed at about the age of thirteen. Her remarkable intelligence and talents led

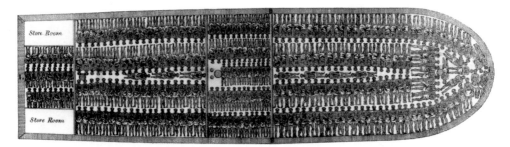

Diagram of an Eighteenth-Century Slave Ship. Often tightly packed and confined in spaces smaller than graves, slaves were subjected to inadequate ventilation and extremely unsanitary conditions. Many died of suffocation or disease during the 3,700-mile voyage from Africa to America.
Visual Arts Library (London)/Alamy.

Susannah to help her publish *Poems on Various Subjects, Religious and Moral* in 1773. The influence of religion on her poetry is clearly evident in "On Being Brought from Africa to America." Her response to having been a slave in America is complicated by her acceptance of the religion, language, and even the literary style of the white culture that she found there. The true nature of slavery is apparent, however, in the diagram of a slave ship and a slave auction advertisement. Do these documents qualify Wheatley's description of her origins and the new world into which she was brought as a slave?

The Slave Ship (1840), by Joseph Mallord William Turner (British, 1775–1851). This painting, originally titled *Slavers Throwing Overboard the Dead and Dying — Typhoon Coming On,* was based on an incident in 1783 in which the captain of a slave ship who was insured for the value of slaves lost at sea but not for those lost to illness threw all sick slaves overboard to drown. In the foreground of the painting, the slaves struggle as they are devoured by fish. Notice the chains, in the wake of the ship, that seemed to rise up from the blood-red sea.

Photograph © 2003 Museum of Fine Arts, Boston.

Negroes for Sale.

A Cargo of very fine stout Men and Women, in good order and fit for immediate service, just imported from the Windward Coast of Africa, in the Ship Two Brothers.— Conditions are one half Cash or Produce, the other half payable the first of January next, giving Bond and Security if required.

The Sale to be opened at 10 o'Clock each Day, in Mr. Bourdeaux's Yard, at No. 48, on the Bay.
May 19, 1784. JOHN MITCHELL.

Thirty Seasoned Negroes
To be Sold for Credit, at Private Sale.

AMONGST which is a Carpenter, none of whom are known to be dishonest.

Also to be sold for Cash, a regular bred young Negroe Man-Cook, born in this Country, who served several Years under an exceeding good French Cook abroad, and his Wife a middle aged Washer-Woman, (both very honest) and their two Children. *Likewise.* a young Man a Carpenter.
For Terms apply to the Printer.

1784 Slave-Auction Advertisement. In preparation for sale at auction, slaves were fed and washed by the ship's crew. Tar or palm oil was used to disguise sores or wounds caused by poor conditions on board.
© CORBIS.

PHILLIS WHEATLEY (1753?–1784)

On Being Brought from Africa to America   1773

'Twas mercy brought me from my pagan land,
Taught my benighted soul to understand
That there's a God — that there's a Saviour too;
Once I redemption neither sought nor knew.
Some view our sable race with scornful eye —
"Their color is a diabolic dye."
Remember, Christians, Negroes black as Cain°
May be refined, and join the angelic train.

7 *Cain:* In the Bible, Cain murdered Abel and was therefore "marked" by God. That mark has been interpreted by some readers as the origin of dark-skinned people (see Genesis 4:1–15).

CONSIDERATIONS FOR CRITICAL THINKING AND WRITING

1. How does the speaker argue against the pervasive racist views concerning Africans in the eighteenth century?

2. Do you find the argument convincing? Explain whether your own refutation of racism would be argued on similar or other grounds.

3. What arguments are put forth on the slave-auction poster? What attitudes are revealed by its author's choice of words?

4. Consider Wheatley's poem alongside the slave-ship diagram and the advertisement for a slave auction. How do you account for the speaker's attitude toward slavery and redemption in relation to the historical realities of slavery?

CONNECTION TO ANOTHER SELECTION

1. Compare the tone and theme of Wheatley's poem with those of Langston Hughes's "I, Too" (p. 915).

■ **Race and Borders.** The conversation Wole Soyinka allows us to overhear in a traditional English red phone booth evokes serious racial tensions as well as a humorous treatment of them. The benighted reaction of the landlady seems to be no match for the speaker's satiric wit. Race is also the issue in *Guess Who's Coming to Dinner?*, a 1967 film about an interracial couple who complicate the lives of a young white woman's parents. The mother and father regard themselves as progressive until their daughter introduces a black man as her future husband. Both the poem and the film are set in the 1960s. Do you think their themes are dated, or do they remain issues in the twenty-first century?

Guess Who's Coming to Dinner This 1967 film featured Hollywood's first on-screen interracial kiss, between Sidney Poitier and Katharine Houghton. Poitier was the first African American actor to play a leading role in a Hollywood film.
Reprinted by permission of Columbia Pictures and the Kobal Collection.

WOLE SOYINKA (B. 1934)

Telephone Conversation 1960

The price seemed reasonable, location
Indifferent. The landlady swore she lived
Off premises. Nothing remained
But self-confession. "Madam," I warned,
"I hate a wasted journey — I am African." 5
Silence. Silenced transmission of
Pressurized good-breeding. Voice, when it came,
Lipstick coated, long gold-rolled
Cigarette-holder pipped. Caught I was, foully.
"HOW DARK?" . . . I had not misheard . . . "ARE YOU LIGHT 10
OR VERY DARK?" Button B. Button A. Stench
Of rancid breath of public hide-and-speak.
Red booth. Red pillar-box. Red double-tiered
Omnibus squelching tar. It *was* real! Shamed
By ill-mannered silence, surrender 15
Pushed dumbfoundment to beg simplification.
Considerate she was, varying the emphasis —
"ARE YOU DARK? OR VERY LIGHT?" Revelation came.
"You mean — like plain or milk chocolate?"
Her assent was clinical, crushing in its light 20
Impersonality. Rapidly, wave-length adjusted,
I chose. "West African sepia" — and as afterthought,
"Down in my passport." Silence for spectroscopic
Flight of fancy, till truthfulness clanged her accent
Hard on the mouthpiece. "WHAT'S THAT?" conceding 25
"DON'T KNOW WHAT THAT IS." "Like brunette."
"THAT'S DARK, ISN'T IT?" "Not altogether.
Facially, I am brunette, but madam, you should see
The rest of me. Palm of my hand, soles of my feet
Are a peroxide blonde. Friction, caused — 30
Foolishly madam — by sitting down, has turned
My bottom raven black — One moment madam!" — sensing
Her receiver rearing on the thunderclap
About my ears — "Madam," I pleaded, "wouldn't you rather
See for yourself?" 35

CONSIDERATIONS FOR CRITICAL THINKING AND WRITING

1. **FIRST RESPONSE.** Characterize the landlady. What details deftly reveal her personality? Do you think the speaker's treatment of her is fair or biased? Why?

2. Describe the poem's humor. Do you think the humor undercuts or enhances the racial issues presented?

3. Describe the audience that you think *Guess Who's Coming to Dinner* is intended for. From what perspective was this film written? Compare this to Soyinka's perspective in "Telephone Conversation."

CONNECTION TO ANOTHER SELECTION

1. How does Langston Hughes's "Dinner Guest: Me" (p. 931) serve as a commentary on the racial tensions explored in "Telephone Conversation" and *Guess Who's Coming to Dinner?*

■ **Identity and Borders.** In "Legal Alien" Pat Mora explores the difficulties of living in two different cultures simultaneously. The poem's speaker, both Mexican and American, worries that each cultural identity displaces the other, leaving the speaker standing alone between both worlds. Similarly, Jacalyn López García, a multimedia artist who combines computer art, video, and music CD-ROMs to create complex images, explores the dilemmas that she encountered while being raised as a Mexican American. How do the poem and the image evoke the tensions produced by trying to assimilate into a new culture while trying to hold onto the cultural values brought from one's native country?

I NEVER

MY MOTHER'S STORY

"I raised my children speaking English only
because I did not want them to have an accent."

WANTED

"I thought it would be easier for them."

TO BE

"After all, I spoke English, having attended an
American school in Casas Grandes, Mexico."

"WHITE"

"But I never had the privileges of being "white".

"I Just Wanted to Be Me" (1997), by Jacalyn López García. In her multimedia exhibit *Glass Houses*, Garcia explores family history and issues of identity. "As we crossed the Mexican border, the border patrol would ask me my citizenship. I would reply, 'American' because my parents taught me to say that. But in California, people would ask me 'What are you?' . . . I would proudly reply 'Mexican.' It wasn't until I became a teenager that I claimed I was 'Mexican-American.'" Once, a white neighbor reported to authorities that García's mother was undocumented. "I was only seven years old when my mother was deported, my brother was six. The Christmas tree stayed up until Mom returned home in April of the following year." Artwork by Jacalyn López García.

PAT MORA (B. 1942)

Legal Alien 1985

Bi-lingual, Bi-cultural,
able to slip from "How's life?"
to *"Me'stan volviendo loca,"*°
able to sit in a paneled office
drafting memos in smooth English, 5
able to order in fluent Spanish
at a Mexican restaurant,
American but hyphenated,
viewed by Anglos as perhaps exotic,
perhaps inferior, definitely different, 10
viewed by Mexicans as alien,
(their eyes say, "You may speak
Spanish but you're not like me")
an American to Mexicans
a Mexican to Americans 15
a handy token
sliding back and forth
between the fringes of both worlds
by smiling
by masking the discomfort 20
of being pre-judged
Bi-laterally.

3 *Me'stan . . . loca:* They are driving me crazy.

CONSIDERATIONS FOR CRITICAL THINKING AND WRITING

1. **FIRST RESPONSE.** What is the nature of the discomfort the speaker experiences as an "American but hyphenated"? Explain whether you think the advantages outweigh the disadvantages.

2. What qualities do you think make someone an American? How does your description compare with your classmates' views? How do you account for the differences or similarities?

3. Discuss the appropriateness of the poem's title. How does it encapsulate the speaker's emotional as well as official status?

4. How do poet Pat Mora and artist Jacalyn López García incorporate multiple voices into their work? Why do you think they do so?

■ **Immigration and Borders.** Ethnic stereotypes are the legacy Sandra M. Gilbert examines in "Mafioso." Her poem raises important questions about the way in which popular culture shapes our assumptions about and perceptions of ethnic groups. How much of what we regard as quintessentially Italian American is generated by films like *The Godfather* or television programs like *The Sopranos*? How did most immigrants actually work to become Americans once they arrived on the country's shores? A glimpse of the nature of that struggle is suggested by the 1911 photograph of three boys undergoing an examination at Ellis Island. Do you think the

"Baggage Examined Here" (1911). Between 1880 and 1920, nearly four million Italian immigrants came to the United States, most arriving in New York City and settling in cities along the East Coast. While first- and second-class steamship passengers were quickly inspected onboard and allowed to disembark in Manhattan, third-class passengers, such as the boys in this photo, were taken to Ellis Island, where they were subjected to a series of medical examinations and interviews. Inspectors marked the immigrants' clothing with chalk, indicating the need for further examination: *Sc* for scalp disease, *G* for goiter, *H* for hernia, *L* for lameness, or *S* for senility.
© Bettmann/CORBIS.

photograph supports or qualifies Gilbert's assessment of the difficulties immigrants faced upon their arrival in America?

Sandra M. Gilbert (b. 1936)

Mafioso   1979

Frank Costello eating spaghetti in a cell at San Quentin,
Lucky Luciano mixing up a mess of bullets and
calling for parmesan cheese,

Al Capone baking a sawed-off shotgun into a
huge lasagna —   5
                    are you my uncles, my
only uncles?

                O Mafiosi,
bad uncles of the barren
cliffs of Sicily — was it only you   10
that they transported in barrels
like pure olive oil
across the Atlantic?

                    Was it only you
who got out at Ellis Island with   15
black scarves on your heads and cheap cigars
and no English and a dozen children?

No carts were waiting, gallant with paint,
no little donkeys plumed like the dreams of peacocks.
Only the evil eyes of a thousand buildings   20
stared across at the echoing debarcation center,
making it seem so much smaller than a piazza,

only a half dozen Puritan millionaires stood on the wharf,
in the wind colder than the impossible snows of the Abruzzi,
ready with country clubs and dynamos   25

to grind the organs out of you.

CONSIDERATIONS FOR CRITICAL THINKING AND WRITING

1. **FIRST RESPONSE.** In what sense are the gangsters Frank Costello, Lucky Luciano, and Al Capone to be understood as "bad uncles"? How does the speaker, in particular, feel about the "uncles"?

2. Explain how nearly all of the images in the poem are associated with Italian life. Does the poem reinforce stereotypes about Italians or invoke images about them for some other purpose? If so, what other purpose?

3. What sort of people are the "Puritan millionaires" (line 23)? What is their relationship to the "bad uncles"?

4. Consider the photograph. Why was it taken? What does this image convey about attitudes toward working-class immigrants processed at Ellis Island? How do the words "Baggage Examined Here" function in the image? How do these words connect with the last line of Gilbert's poem ("to grind the organs out of you")? What comments are the photograph and poem making about the experience?

CONNECTIONS TO OTHER SELECTIONS

1. Discuss the ways in which ethnicity is used to create meaning in "Mafioso" and in Jimmy Santiago Baca's "Green Chile" (p. 665).

2. How do the attitudes conveyed in "Mafioso" and the photograph "Baggage Examined Here" compare with the sentiments expressed in Emma Lazarus's "The New Colossus" (p. 1028), the poem inscribed at the base of the Statue of Liberty?

■ **Expectations and Borders.** The immigrants' dream of America is deeply present in Chitra Banerjee Divakaruni's "Indian Movie, New Jersey." The hopeful expectation that immigrants bring with them takes on a nostalgic and melancholy tone as the speaker contrasts America as imagined to the country that is experienced. The Indian movie offers yet another dream that suggests a powerful yearning for a different kind of life than the one found in New Jersey. Is the movie version of India any more or less real than the speaker's picture of America? Is this poem more about disillusionment or delusion?

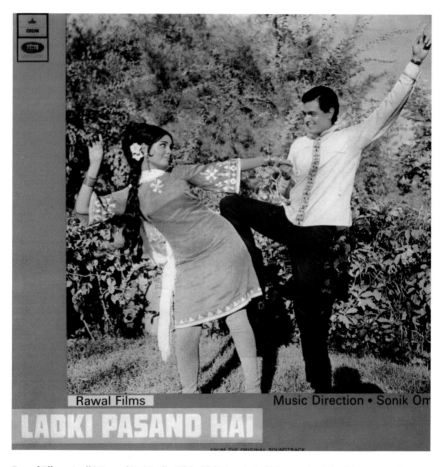

Rawal Films, *Ladki Pasand Hai* (I Like This Girl) (1971). India's massive Hindi-language film industry, known as Bollywood (a play on the word *Hollywood*, with the *B* representing Bombay), produces twice as many films as Hollywood each year, with a huge international audience. Bollywood films are churned out so quickly that sometimes scripts are handwritten and actors on set shoot scenes for multiple films. Traditionally, these colorful extravaganzas, chock-full of singing, dancing, and multiple costume changes, stick to a "boy meets girl" formula — a hero and heroine fall in love and then struggle for family approval. This image is from the soundtrack to a 1971 film with a typical Bollywood plot.
Courtesy of Niall Richardson.

CHITRA BANERJEE DIVAKARUNI (B. 1956)

Indian Movie, New Jersey   *1990*

Not like the white filmstars, all rib
and gaunt cheekbone, the Indian sex-goddess
smiles plumply from behind a flowery
branch. Below her brief red skirt, her thighs
are satisfying-solid, redeeming   5
as tree trunks. She swings her hips
and the men-viewers whistle. The lover-hero
dances in to a song, his lip-sync
a little off, but no matter, we
know the words already and sing along.   10
It is safe here, the day
golden and cool so no one sweats,
roses on every bush and the Dal Lake
clean again.
                    The sex-goddess switches   15
to thickened English to emphasize
a joke. We laugh and clap. Here
we need not be embarrassed by words
dropping like lead pellets into foreign ears.
The flickering movie-light   20
wipes from our faces years of America, sons
who want mohawks and refuse to run
the family store, daughters who date
on the sly.
                    When at the end the hero   25
dies for his friend who also
loves the sex-goddess and now can marry her,
we weep, understanding. Even the men
clear their throats to say, "What *qurbani*!°   *sacrifice*
What *dosti!*"° After, we mill around   *friendship* 30
unwilling to leave, exchange greetings
and good news: a new gold chain, a trip
to India. We do not speak
of motel raids, canceled permits, stones
thrown through glass windows, daughters and sons   35
raped by Dotbusters.°
                    In this dim foyer
we can pull around us the faint, comforting smell
of incense and *pakoras,*° can arrange   *fried appetizers*
our children's marriages with hometown boys and girls,   40
open a franchise, win a million
in the mail. We can retire
in India, a yellow two-storied house
with wrought-iron gates, our own
Ambassador car. Or at least   45
move to a rich white suburb, Summerfield

---

36 *Dotbusters:* New Jersey gangs that attack Indians.

or Fort Lee, with neighbors that will
talk to us. Here while the film-songs still echo
in the corridors and restrooms, we can trust
in movie truths: sacrifice, success, love and luck,   50
the America that was supposed to be.

CONSIDERATIONS FOR CRITICAL THINKING AND WRITING

1. **FIRST RESPONSE.** Why does the speaker feel comfortable at the movies?
   How is the world inside the theater different from life in New Jersey?

2. Explain the differences portrayed by the speaker between life in India and
   life in New Jersey. What connotative values are associated with each location in the poem? Discuss the irony in the final two lines.

3. How do the ideas and values of the Bollywood poster contrast with the
   realities conveyed in the last part of the poem?

CONNECTION TO ANOTHER SELECTION

1. Explain how the speaker's idea of "the America that was supposed to be"
   (line 51) compares with the nation described in Florence Cassen Mayers's
   "All-American Sestina" (p. 787).

■ **Beauty and Borders.**   Janice Mirikitani, a third-generation Japanese
American, reflects on dominant cultural standards of beauty in "Recipe."
Women who do not meet such standards — especially women of color — can
be faced with complicated decisions about how they want to appear, decisions that go more than skin deep. Chiaki Tsukumo's 2003 photograph of
a Tokyo girl holding a popular Western-style doll demonstrates how powerful Western concepts of beauty are, even among non-Western people.
Why are "Round Eyes" so desirable?

JANICE MIRIKITANI (B. 1942)

Recipe   *1987*

Round Eyes
Ingredients: scissors, Scotch magic transparent tape,
               eyeliner — water based, black.
               Optional: false eyelashes.
Cleanse face thoroughly.   5
For best results, powder entire face, including eyelids.
      (lighter shades suited to total effect desired)
With scissors, cut magic tape $^1/_{16}$" wide, $^3/_4$"–$^1/_2$" long —
depending on length of eyelid.
Stick firmly onto mid–upper eyelid area   10
      (looking down into handmirror facilitates finding
      adequate surface)
If using false eyelashes, affix first on lid, folding any
excess lid over the base of eyelash with glue.
Paint black eyeliner on tape and entire lid.   15
Do not cry.

"Girl with Licca Doll," by Chiaki Tsukumo (2003). According to the Japanese toymaker Takara, "Licca-chan was developed to make girls' dreams and wishes come true" and "to nurture kindness, gentleness, and love in children." A fan's personal Web site notes that Licca-chan "hates arithmetic, but she's good at language, music, and art." Her favorite books are *Anne of Green Gables* and *A Little Princess*, and she loves eating ice cream and window-shopping. First introduced in 1967, the doll has since sold nearly fifty million units and become, according to the toymaker, a national character that has inspired a Licca-chan generation of women consumers.
AP/WIDE WORLD Photos.

CONSIDERATIONS FOR CRITICAL THINKING AND WRITING

1. **FIRST RESPONSE.** Discuss your response to the poem's final line.

2. Why does Mirikitani write the poem in recipe form? What is the effect of the very specific details of this recipe?

3. Why is "false eyelashes" a particularly resonant phrase in the context of this poem?

4. Consider and note the Licca doll's hair, eyes, and costume in the photograph by Chiaki Tsukumo. How do you account for the success of the Licca doll? What do you make of the toymaker's claim that the doll makes "girls' dreams and wishes come true"? What dreams and wishes do you think the toymaker is selling? How do the ideals that the toymaker (Takara) associates with the Licca doll compare with those associated with Barbie?

5. How does the paragraph connect with Mirikitani's satirical poem?

CONNECTION TO ANOTHER SELECTION

1. How might the voice in Michelle Boisseau's "Self-Pity's Closet" (p. 999) be read as a version of the speaker in "Recipe"?

■ **Freedom and Borders.**   Thomas Lynch's "Liberty" is an amusing protest against conformity, the kind of middling placidity often associated with suburban life in America. The blustery Irish speaker in this poem laments the lost world his ancestors inhabited in Ireland and longs for the "form[s] of freedom" that they once enjoyed. Though the speaker may cause us to smile, his complaint is serious nonetheless. The potential validity of his assessment of suburban life is presented visually in the accompanying photograph of Somerville, Massachusetts, a suburb of Boston. How might Lynch's speaker be considered a resident of one of those houses? Does the arrangement of the streets and houses help to explain the attitudes expressed in the poem? What are your own views about the suburbs?

THOMAS LYNCH (B. 1948)

Liberty   *1998*

Some nights I go out and piss on the front lawn
as a form of freedom — liberty from
porcelain and plumbing and the Great Beyond
beyond the toilet and the sewage works.
Here is the statement I am trying to make: 5
to say I am from a fierce bloodline of men
who made their water in the old way, under stars
that overarched the North Atlantic where
the River Shannon empties into sea.
The ex-wife used to say, "Why can't you pee   10
in concert with the most of humankind
who do their business tidily indoors?"
It was gentility or envy, I suppose,
because I could do it anywhere, and do
whenever I begin to feel encumbered.   15
Still, there is nothing, here in the suburbs,
as dense as the darkness in West Clare
nor any equivalent to the nightlong wind
that rattles in the hedgerow of whitethorn there
on the east side of the cottage yard in Moveen.   20
It was market day in Kilrush, years ago:
my great-great-grandfather bargained with tinkers
who claimed it was whitethorn that Christ's crown was made from.
So he gave them two and six and brought them home —
mere saplings then — as a gift for the missus,   25
who planted them between the house and garden.
For years now, men have slipped out the back door
during wakes or wedding feasts or nights of song
to pay their homage to the holy trees
and, looking up into that vast firmament,   30
consider liberty in that last townland where
they have no crowns, no crappers and no ex-wives.

"Somerville, Massachusetts," by Alex MacLean (1993). Between 1870 and 1915, new streetcar lines in the Boston suburb of Somerville spurred major population growth in the area. Many of the newcomers were immigrants, including Irish workers attracted by plentiful jobs at the brickyards and in the slaughtering and meatpacking industry. The two-family houses in this photograph were built around 1910 to house the new population. By World War II, these neighborhoods swelled to a population density said to be greater than that of Calcutta.
Reprinted by permission of Alex S. MacLean/Landslides.

CONSIDERATIONS FOR CRITICAL THINKING AND WRITING

1. **FIRST RESPONSE.** Does "gentility or envy" (line 13) get in the way of your enjoyment and appreciation of this poem? Explain why or why not.

2. Characterize the speaker and explain why you find him engaging or not. What sort of liberty does he insist upon?

3. Consider Alex MacLean's aerial photograph of Somerville, Massachusetts. What strikes you about this landscape? What is the thinking behind this example of neighborhood planning? How does such a plan affect personal freedoms, and how might it inspire rebellion such as that of the speaker in Lynch's poem?

CONNECTION TO ANOTHER SELECTION

1. Discuss Lynch's treatment of suburban life and compare it with that of John Ciardi in "Suburban" (p. 986). What similarities are there in the themes and metaphoric strategies of these two poems?

SUGGESTED TOPIC FOR LONGER PAPERS

1. Write an essay that develops a common theme or thread that you find in all seven poems presented in this chapter. You may explore similarities or differences concerning any aspect of the border crossings they examine.

"A woman can be proud and stiff
When on love intent;
But Love has pitched his mansion in   15
The place of excrement;
For nothing can be sole or whole
That has not been rent."

Explore contexts
for William Butler Yeats
on *LiterActive*.

WILLIAM BUTLER YEATS (1865–1939)

Leda and the Swan°   *1924*

A sudden blow: the great wings beating still
Above the staggering girl, her thighs caressed
By the dark webs, her nape caught in his bill,
He holds her helpless breast upon his breast.

How can those terrified vague fingers push   5
The feathered glory from her loosening thighs?
And how can body, laid in that white rush,
But feel the strange heart beating where it lies?

A shudder in the loins engenders there
The broken wall, the burning roof and tower   10
And Agamemnon dead.
                   Being so caught up,
So mastered by the brute blood of the air,
Did she put on his knowledge with his power
Before the indifferent beak could let her drop?   15

Leda and the Swan: In Greek myth, Zeus in the form of a swan seduced Leda and fathered
Helen of Troy (whose abduction started the Trojan War) and Clytemnestra, Agamemnon's
wife and murderer. Yeats thought of Zeus's appearance to Leda as a type of annunciation,
like the angel appearing to Mary.

DRAMA

The Study
of Drama

38

Reading Drama

I regard the theater as serious business, one that makes or should make man more human, which is to say, less alone.
— ARTHUR MILLER

A play in a book is only the shadow of a play and not even a clear shadow of it. . . . The color, the grace and levitation, the structural pattern in motion, the quick interplay of live beings, suspended like fitful lightning in a cloud, these things are the play. . . .
— TENNESSEE WILLIAMS

READING DRAMA RESPONSIVELY

The publication of a short story, novel, or poem represents for most writers the final step in a long creative process that might have begun with an idea, issue, emotion, or question that demanded expression. *Playwrights* — writers who make plays — may begin a work in the same way as other writers, but rarely are they satisfied with only its publication, because most dramatic literature — what we call *plays* — is written to be performed by actors on a stage before an audience. Playwrights typically create a play keeping in mind not only readers but also actors, producers, directors, costumers, designers, technicians, and a theater full of other support staff who have a hand in presenting the play to a live audience.

Drama is literature equipped with arms, legs, tears, laughs, whispers, shouts, and gestures that are alive and immediate. Indeed, the word **drama** derives from the Greek word *dran*, meaning "to do" or "to perform." The text of many plays — the *script* — may come to life fully only when the written words are transformed into a performance. Although there are plays that do not invite production, they are relatively few. Such plays, written to be read rather than performed, are called **closet dramas.** In this kind of work (primarily associated with nineteenth-century English literature), literary art outweighs all other considerations. The majority of playwrights, however, view the written word as the beginning of a larger creation and hope that a producer will deem their scripts worthy of production.

Given that most playwrights intend their works to be performed, it might be argued that reading a play is a poor substitute for seeing it acted on a stage — perhaps something like reading a recipe without having access to the ingredients and a kitchen. This analogy is tempting, but it overlooks the literary dimensions of a script; the words we hear on a stage were written first. Read from a page, these words can feed an imagination in ways that a recipe cannot satisfy a hungry cook. We can fill in a play's missing faces, voices, actions, and settings in much the same way that we imagine these elements in a short story or novel. Like any play director, we are free to include as many ingredients as we have an appetite for.

This imaginative collaboration with the playwright creates a mental world that can be nearly as real and vivid as a live performance. Sometimes readers find that they prefer their own reading of a play to a director's interpretation. Shakespeare's Hamlet, for instance, has been presented as a whining son, but you may read him as a strong prince. Rich plays often accommodate a wide range of imaginative responses to their texts. Reading, then, is an excellent way to appreciate and evaluate a production of a play. Moreover, reading is valuable in its own right because it allows us to enter the playwright's created world even when a theatrical production is unavailable.

Reading a play, however, requires more creative imagining than sitting in an audience watching actors on a stage presenting lines and actions before you. As a reader you become the play's director; you construct an interpretation based on the playwright's use of language, development of character, arrangement of incidents, description of settings, and directions for staging. Keeping track of the playwright's handling of these elements will help you to organize your response to the play. You may experience suspense, fear, horror, sympathy, or humor, but whatever experience a play evokes, ask yourself why you respond to it as you do. You may discover that your assessment of Hamlet's character is different from someone else's, but whether you find him heroic, indecisive, neurotic, or a complex of competing qualities, you'll be better equipped to articulate your interpretation of him if you pay attention to your responses and ask yourself questions as you read. Consider, for example, how his reactions might be similar to or different from your own. How does his language reveal his character? Does his behavior seem justified? How would you play the role yourself? What actor do you think might best play the Hamlet that you have created in your imagination? Why would he or she (women have also played Hamlet onstage) fill the role best?

These kinds of questions (see Questions for Responsive Reading and Writing, p. 1089) can help you to think and talk about your responses to a play. Happily, such questions needn't — and often can't — be fully answered as you read the play. Frequently you must experience the entire play before you can determine how its elements work together. That's why reading a play can be such a satisfying experience. You wouldn't think of asking a live actor onstage to repeat her lines because you didn't quite comprehend their significance, but you can certainly reread a page in a book. Rereading allows you to replay language, characters, and incidents carefully and thoroughly to your own satisfaction.

Trifles

In the following play, Susan Glaspell skillfully draws on many dramatic elements and creates an intense story that is as effective on the page as it is in the theater. Glaspell wrote *Trifles* in 1916 for the Provincetown Players on Cape Cod, in Massachusetts. Their performance of the work helped her develop a reputation as a writer sensitive to feminist issues. The year after *Trifles* was produced, Glaspell transformed the play into a short story titled "A Jury of Her Peers."

© Nickolas Muray Photo Archives, LLC.
Courtesy of the Sheaffer-O'Neill Collection, Connecticut College.

Glaspell's life in the Midwest provided her with the setting for *Trifles*. Born and raised in Davenport, Iowa, she graduated from Drake University in 1899 and then worked for a short time as a reporter on the *Des Moines News*, until her short stories were accepted in magazines such as *Harper's* and *Ladies' Home Journal*. Glaspell moved to the Northeast when she was in her early thirties to continue writing fiction and drama. She published some twenty plays, novels, and more than forty short stories. *Alison's House*, based on Emily Dickinson's life, earned her a Pulitzer Prize for drama in 1931. *Trifles* and "A Jury of Her Peers" remain, however, Glaspell's best-known works.

Glaspell wrote *Trifles* to complete a bill that was to feature several one-act plays by Eugene O'Neill. In *The Road to the Temple* (1926) she recalls how the play came to her as she sat in the theater looking at a bare stage. First, "the stage became a kitchen. . . . Then the door at the back opened, and people all bundled up came in — two or three men. I wasn't sure which, but sure enough about the two women, who hung back, reluctant to enter that kitchen. When I was a newspaper reporter out in Iowa, I was sent downstate to do a murder trial, and I never forgot going to the kitchen of a woman who had been locked up in town."

Trifles is about a murder committed in a Midwestern farmhouse, but the play goes beyond the kinds of questions raised by most whodunit stories. The murder is the occasion instead of the focus. The play's major concerns are the moral, social, and psychological aspects of the assumptions and perceptions of the men and women who search for the murderer's motive. Glaspell is finally more interested in the meaning of Mrs. Wright's life than in the details of Mr. Wright's death.

As you read the play, keep track of your responses to the characters and note in the margin the moments when Glaspell reveals how men and women respond differently to the evidence before them. What do those moments suggest about the kinds of assumptions these men and women make about themselves and each other? How do their assumptions compare with your own?

Explore contexts for Susan Glaspell and approaches to this play on *LiterActive* or at bedfordstmartins.com/ meyercompact.

SUSAN GLASPELL (1882–1948)

Trifles   1916

CHARACTERS

George Henderson, county attorney
Henry Peters, sheriff
Lewis Hale, a neighboring farmer
Mrs. Peters
Mrs. Hale

SCENE: The kitchen in the now abandoned farmhouse of John Wright, a gloomy kitchen, and left without having been put in order — unwashed pans under the sink, a loaf of bread outside the breadbox, a dish towel on the table — other signs of incompleted work. At the rear the outer door opens and the Sheriff comes in followed by the County Attorney and Hale. The Sheriff and Hale are men in middle life, the County Attorney is a young man; all are much bundled up and go at once to the stove. They are followed by the two women — the Sheriff's wife first; she is a slight wiry woman, a thin nervous face. Mrs. Hale is larger and would ordinarily be called more comfortable looking, but she is disturbed now and looks fearfully about as she enters. The women have come in slowly, and stand close together near the door.

County Attorney (rubbing his hands): This feels good. Come up to the fire, ladies.

Mrs. Peters (after taking a step forward): I'm not—cold.

Sheriff (unbuttoning his overcoat and stepping away from the stove as if to mark the beginning of official business): Now, Mr. Hale, before we move things about, you explain to Mr. Henderson just what you saw when you came here yesterday morning.

County Attorney: By the way, has anything been moved? Are things just as you left them yesterday?

Sheriff (looking about): It's just about the same. When it dropped below zero last night I thought I'd better send Frank out this morning to make a fire for us—no use getting pneumonia with a big case on, but I told him not to touch anything except the stove—and you know Frank.

County Attorney: Somebody should have been left here yesterday.

Sheriff: Oh—yesterday. When I had to send Frank to Morris Center for that man who went crazy—I want you to know I had my hands full yesterday. I knew you could get back from Omaha by today and as long as I went over everything here myself—

County Attorney: Well, Mr. Hale, tell just what happened when you came here yesterday morning.

Hale: Harry and I had started to town with a load of potatoes. We came along the road from my place and as I got here I said, "I'm going to see if I can't get John Wright to go in with me on a party telephone." I spoke to Wright about it once before and he put me off, saying folks talked too much anyway, and all he asked was peace and quiet—I guess you know about how much he talked himself; but I thought maybe if I went to the house and talked about it before his wife, though I said to Harry that I didn't know as what his wife wanted made much difference to John—

County Attorney: Let's talk about that later, Mr. Hale. I do want to talk about that, but tell now just what happened when you got to the house.

Hale: I didn't hear or see anything; I knocked at the door, and still it was all quiet inside. I knew they must be up, it was past eight o'clock. So I knocked again, and I thought I heard somebody say, "Come in." I wasn't sure, I'm not sure yet, but I opened the door—this door *(indicating the door by which the two women are still standing)* and there in that rocker—*(pointing to it)* sat Mrs. Wright. *(They all look at the rocker.)*

County Attorney: What—was she doing?

Hale: She was rockin' back and forth. She had her apron in her hand and was kind of—pleating it.

County Attorney: And how did she—look?

Hale: Well, she looked queer.

County Attorney: How do you mean—queer?

Hale: Well, as if she didn't know what she was going to do next. And kind of done up.

County Attorney: How did she seem to feel about your coming?

Hale: Why, I don't think she minded—one way or other. She didn't pay much attention. I said, "How do, Mrs. Wright, it's cold, ain't it?" And she said, "Is it?"—and went on kind of pleating at her apron. Well, I was surprised; she didn't ask me to come up to the stove, or to set down, but just sat there, not even looking at me, so I said, "I want to see John." And then she—laughed. I guess you would call it a laugh. I thought of Harry and the team outside, so I said a little sharp: "Can't I see John?" "No," she says, kind o' dull like. "Ain't he home?" says I. "Yes," says she, "he's home." "Then why can't I see him?" I asked her, out of patience. "'Cause he's dead," says she. *"Dead?"* says I. She just nodded her head, not getting a bit excited, but rockin' back and forth. "Why — where is he?" says I, not knowing what to say. She just pointed upstairs — like that *(himself pointing to the room above)*. I started for the stairs, with the idea of going up there. I walked from there to here — then I says, "Why, what did he die of?" "He died of a rope round his neck," says she, and just went on pleatin' at her apron. Well, I went out and called Harry. I thought I might — need help. We went upstairs and there he was lyin' —

County Attorney: I think I'd rather have you go into that upstairs, where you can point it all out. Just go on now with the rest of the story.

Hale: Well, my first thought was to get that rope off. It looked . . . *(stops; his face twitches)* . . . but Harry, he went up to him, and he said, "No, he's dead all right, and we'd better not touch anything." So we went back downstairs. She was still sitting that same way. "Has anybody been notified?" I asked. "No," says she, unconcerned. "Who did this, Mrs. Wright?" said Harry. He said it businesslike — and she stopped pleatin' of her apron. "I don't know," she says. "You don't *know?*" says Harry. "No," says she. "Weren't you sleepin' in the bed with him?" says Harry. "Yes," says she, "but I was on the inside." "Somebody slipped a rope round his neck and strangled him and you didn't wake up?" says Harry. "I didn't wake up," she said after him. We must 'a' looked as if we didn't see how that could be, for after a minute she said, "I sleep sound." Harry was going to ask her more questions but I said maybe we ought to let her tell her story first to the coroner, or the sheriff, so Harry went fast as he could to Rivers' place, where there's a telephone.

County Attorney: And what did Mrs. Wright do when she knew that you had gone for the coroner?

Hale: She moved from the rocker to that chair over there *(pointing to a small chair in the corner)* and just sat there with her hands held together and looking down. I got a feeling that I ought to make some conversation, so I said I had come in to see if John wanted to put in a telephone, and at that she started to laugh, and then she stopped and looked at me — scared. *(The County Attorney, who has had his notebook out, makes a note.)* I dunno, maybe it wasn't scared. I wouldn't like to say it was. Soon Harry got back, and then Dr. Lloyd came and you, Mr. Peters, and so I guess that's all I know that you don't.

County Attorney (looking around): I guess we'll go upstairs first — and then out to the barn and around there. *(To the Sheriff.)* You're convinced that there was nothing important here — nothing that would point to any motive?

Sheriff: Nothing here but kitchen things. *(The County Attorney, after again looking around the kitchen, opens the door of a cupboard closet. He gets up on a chair and looks on a shelf. Pulls his hand away, sticky.)*

County Attorney: Here's a nice mess. *(The women draw nearer.)*

Mrs. Peters (to the other woman): Oh, her fruit; it did freeze. *(To the Lawyer.)* She worried about that when it turned so cold. She said the fire'd go out and her jars would break.

Sheriff (rises): Well, can you beat the woman! Held for murder and worryin' about her preserves.

County Attorney: I guess before we're through she may have something more serious than preserves to worry about.

Hale: Well, women are used to worrying over trifles. *(The two women move a little closer together.)*

County Attorney (with the gallantry of a young politician): And yet, for all their worries, what would we do without the ladies? *(The women do not unbend. He goes to the sink, takes a dipperful of water from the pail, and pouring it into a basin, washes his hands. Starts to wipe them on the roller towel, turns it for a cleaner place.)* Dirty towels! *(Kicks his foot against the pans under the sink.)* Not much of a housekeeper, would you say, ladies?

Mrs. Hale (stiffly): There's a great deal of work to be done on a farm.

County Attorney: To be sure. And yet *(with a little bow to her)* I know there are some Dickson county farmhouses which do not have such roller towels. *(He gives it a pull to expose its full length again.)*

Mrs. Hale: Those towels get dirty awful quick. Men's hands aren't always as clean as they might be.

County Attorney: Ah, loyal to your sex, I see. But you and Mrs. Wright were neighbors. I suppose you were friends, too.

Mrs. Hale (shaking her head): I've not seen much of her of late years. I've not been in this house — it's more than a year.

County Attorney: And why was that? You didn't like her?

Mrs. Hale: I liked her all well enough. Farmers' wives have their hands full, Mr. Henderson. And then —

County Attorney: Yes — ?

Mrs. Hale (looking about): It never seemed a very cheerful place.

County Attorney: No — it's not cheerful. I shouldn't say she had the homemaking instinct.

Mrs. Hale: Well, I don't know as Wright had, either.

County Attorney: You mean that they didn't get on very well?

Mrs. Hale: No, I don't mean anything. But I don't think a place'd be any cheerfuller for John Wright's being in it.

County Attorney: I'd like to talk more of that a little later. I want to get the lay of things upstairs now. *(He goes to the left where three steps lead to a stair door.)*

Sheriff: I suppose anything Mrs. Peters does'll be all right. She was to take in some clothes for her, you know, and a few little things. We left in such a hurry yesterday.

County Attorney: Yes, but I would like to see what you take, Mrs. Peters, and keep an eye out for anything that might be of use to us.

Mrs. Peters: Yes, Mr. Henderson. *(The women listen to the men's steps on the stairs, then look about the kitchen.)*

Mrs. Hale: I'd hate to have men coming into my kitchen, snooping around and criticizing. *(She arranges the pans under sink which the lawyer had shoved out of place.)*

Mrs. Peters: Of course it's no more than their duty.

Mrs. Hale: Duty's all right, but I guess that deputy sheriff that came out to make the fire might have got a little of this on. *(Gives the roller towel a pull.)* Wish I'd thought of that sooner. Seems mean to talk about her for not having things slicked up when she had to come away in such a hurry.

Mrs. Peters (who has gone to a small table in the left rear corner of the room, and lifted one end of a towel that covers a pan): She had bread set. *(Stands still.)*

Mrs. Hale (eyes fixed on a loaf of bread beside the breadbox, which is on a low shelf at the other side of the room. Moves slowly toward it.): She was going to put this in there. *(Picks up loaf, then abruptly drops it. In a manner of returning to familiar things.)* It's a shame about her fruit. I wonder if it's all gone. *(Gets up on the chair and looks.)* I think there's some here that's all right, Mrs. Peters. Yes— here; *(holding it toward the window)* this is cherries, too. *(Looking again.)* I declare I believe that's the only one. *(Gets down, bottle in her hand. Goes to the sink and wipes it off on the outside.)* She'll feel awful bad after all her hard work in the hot weather. I remember the afternoon I put up my cherries last summer. *(She puts the bottle on the big kitchen table, center of the room. With a sigh, is about to sit down in the rocking-chair. Before she is seated realizes what chair it is; with a slow look at it, steps back. The chair which she has touched rocks back and forth.)*

Mrs. Peters: Well, I must get those things from the front room closet. *(She goes to the door at the right, but after looking into the other room, steps back.)* You coming with me, Mrs. Hale? You could help me carry them. *(They go in the other room; reappear, Mrs. Peters carrying a dress and skirt, Mrs. Hale following with a pair of shoes.)* My, it's cold in there. *(She puts the clothes on the big table, and hurries to the stove.)*

Mrs. Hale (examining the skirt): Wright was close. I think maybe that's why she kept so much to herself. She didn't even belong to the Ladies' Aid. I suppose she felt she couldn't do her part, and then you don't enjoy things when you feel shabby. I heard she used to wear pretty clothes and be lively, when she was Minnie Foster, one of the town girls singing in the choir. But that—oh, that was thirty years ago. This all you want to take in?

Mrs. Peters: She said she wanted an apron. Funny thing to want, for there isn't much to get you dirty in jail, goodness knows. But I suppose just to make her feel more natural. She said they was in the top drawer in this cupboard. Yes, here. And then her little shawl that always hung behind the door. *(Opens stair door and looks.)* Yes, here it is. *(Quickly shuts door leading upstairs.)*

Mrs. Hale (abruptly moving toward her): Mrs. Peters?

Mrs. Peters: Yes, Mrs. Hale?

Mrs. Hale: Do you think she did it?

Mrs. Peters (in a frightened voice): Oh, I don't know.

Mrs. Hale: Well, I don't think she did. Asking for an apron and her little shawl. Worrying about her fruit.

Mrs. Peters (starts to speak, glances up, where footsteps are heard in the room above. In a low voice): Mr. Peters says it looks bad for her. Mr. Henderson is awful sarcastic in a speech and he'll make fun of her sayin' she didn't wake up.

Mrs. Hale: Well, I guess John Wright didn't wake when they was slipping that rope under his neck.

Mrs. Peters: No, it's strange. It must have been done awful crafty and still. They say it was such a—funny way to kill a man, rigging it all up like that.

Mrs. Hale: That's just what Mr. Hale said. There was a gun in the house. He says that's what he can't understand.

Mrs. Peters: Mr. Henderson said coming out that what was needed for the case was a motive; something to show anger, or—sudden feeling.

Mrs. Hale (who is standing by the table): Well, I don't see any signs of anger around here. *(She puts her hand on the dish towel which lies on the table, stands looking down at table, one-half of which is clean, the other half messy.)* It's wiped to here. *(Makes a move as if to finish work, then turns and looks at loaf of bread outside the breadbox. Drops towel. In that voice of coming back to familiar things.)* Wonder how they are finding things upstairs. I hope she had it a little more red-up up there. You know, it seems kind of *sneaking.* Locking her up in town and then coming out here and trying to get her own house to turn against her!

Mrs. Peters: But, Mrs. Hale, the law is the law.

Mrs. Hale: I s'pose 'tis. *(Unbuttoning her coat.)* Better loosen up your things, Mrs. Peters. You won't feel them when you go out. *(Mrs. Peters takes off her fur tippet, goes to hang it on hook at back of room, stands looking at the under part of the small corner table.)*

Mrs. Peters: She was piecing a quilt. *(She brings the large sewing basket and they look at the bright pieces.)*

Mrs. Hale: It's a log cabin pattern. Pretty, isn't it? I wonder if she was goin' to quilt it or just knot it? *(Footsteps have been heard coming down the stairs. The Sheriff enters followed by Hale and the County Attorney.)*

Sheriff: They wonder if she was going to quilt it or just knot it! *(The men laugh, the women look abashed.)*

County Attorney (rubbing his hands over the stove): Frank's fire didn't do much up there, did it? Well, let's go out to the barn and get that cleared up. *(The men go outside.)*

Mrs. Hale (resentfully): I don't know as there's anything so strange, our takin' up our time with little things while we're waiting for them to get the evidence. *(She sits down at the big table smoothing out a block with decision.)* I don't see as it's anything to laugh about.

Mrs. Peters (apologetically): Of course they've got awful important things on their minds. *(Pulls up a chair and joins Mrs. Hale at the table.)*

Mrs. Hale (examining another block): Mrs. Peters, look at this one. Here, this is the one she was working on, and look at the sewing! All the rest of it has been so nice and even. And look at this! It's all over the place! Why, it looks as if she didn't know what she was about! *(After she has said this they look at each other, then start to glance back at the door. After an instant Mrs. Hale has pulled at a knot and ripped the sewing.)*

Mrs. Peters: Oh, what are you doing, Mrs. Hale?

Mrs. Hale (mildly): Just pulling out a stitch or two that's not sewed very good. *(Threading a needle.)* Bad sewing always made me fidgety.

Mrs. Peters (nervously): I don't think we ought to touch things.

Mrs. Hale: I'll just finish up this end. *(Suddenly stopping and leaning forward.)* Mrs. Peters?

Mrs. Peters: Yes, Mrs. Hale?

Mrs. Hale: What do you suppose she was so nervous about?

Mrs. Peters: Oh—I don't know. I don't know as she was nervous. I sometimes sew awful queer when I'm just tired. *(Mrs. Hale starts to say something, looks at Mrs. Peters, then goes on sewing.)* Well, I must get these things wrapped up. They may be through sooner than we think. *(Putting apron and other things together.)* I wonder where I can find a piece of paper, and string. *(Rises.)*

Mrs. Hale: In that cupboard, maybe.

Mrs. Peters (looking in cupboard): Why, here's a bird-cage. *(Holds it up.)* Did she have a bird, Mrs. Hale?

Mrs. Hale: Why, I don't know whether she did or not — I've not been here for so long. There was a man around last year selling canaries cheap, but I don't know as she took one; maybe she did. She used to sing real pretty herself.

Mrs. Peters (glancing around): Seems funny to think of a bird here. But she must have had one, or why would she have a cage? I wonder what happened to it?

Mrs. Hale: I s'pose maybe the cat got it.

Mrs. Peters: No, she didn't have a cat. She's got that feeling some people have about cats — being afraid of them. My cat got in her room and she was real upset and asked me to take it out.

Mrs. Hale: My sister Bessie was like that. Queer, ain't it?

Mrs. Peters (examining the cage): Why, look at this door. It's broke. One hinge is pulled apart.

Mrs. Hale (looking too): Looks as if someone must have been rough with it.

Mrs. Peters: Why, yes. *(She brings the cage forward and puts it on the table.)*

Mrs. Hale: I wish if they're going to find any evidence they'd be about it. I don't like this place.

Mrs. Peters: But I'm awful glad you came with me, Mrs. Hale. It would be lonesome for me sitting here alone.

Mrs. Hale: It would, wouldn't it? *(Dropping her sewing.)* But I tell you what I do wish, Mrs. Peters. I wish I had come over sometimes when *she* was here. I — *(looking around the room)* — wish I had.

Mrs. Peters: But of course you were awful busy, Mrs. Hale — your house and your children.

Mrs. Hale: I could've come. I stayed away because it weren't cheerful — and that's why I ought to have come. I — I've never liked this place. Maybe because it's down in a hollow and you don't see the road. I dunno what it is, but it's a lonesome place and always was. I wish I had come over to see Minnie Foster sometimes. I can see now — *(Shakes her head.)*

Mrs. Peters: Well, you mustn't reproach yourself, Mrs. Hale. Somehow we just don't see how it is with other folks until — something turns up.

Mrs. Hale: Not having children makes less work — but it makes a quiet house, and Wright out to work all day, and no company when he did come in. Did you know John Wright, Mrs. Peters?

Mrs. Peters: Not to know him; I've seen him in town. They say he was a good man.

Mrs. Hale: Yes — good; he didn't drink, and kept his word as well as most, I guess, and paid his debts. But he was a hard man, Mrs. Peters. Just to pass the time of day with him — *(Shivers.)* Like a raw wind that gets to the bone. *(Pauses, her eye falling on the cage.)* I should think she would 'a' wanted a bird. But what do you suppose went with it?

Mrs. Peters: I don't know, unless it got sick and died. *(She reaches over and swings the broken door, swings it again, both women watch it.)*

Mrs. Hale: You weren't raised round here, were you? *(Mrs. Peters shakes her head.)* You didn't know — her?

Mrs. Peters: Not till they brought her yesterday.

Mrs. Hale: She — come to think of it, she was kind of like a bird herself — real sweet and pretty, but kind of timid and — fluttery. How — she — did — change. *(Silence: then as if struck by a happy thought and relieved to get back to everyday things.)* Tell you what, Mrs. Peters, why don't you take the quilt in with you? It might take up her mind.

Mrs. Peters: Why, I think that's a real nice idea, Mrs. Hale. There couldn't possibly be any objection to it could there? Now, just what would I take? I wonder if her patches are in here — and her things. *(They look in the sewing basket.)*

Mrs. Hale: Here's some red. I expect this has got sewing things in it. *(Brings out a fancy box.)* What a pretty box. Looks like something somebody would give you. Maybe her scissors are in here. *(Opens box. Suddenly puts her hand to her nose.)* Why — *(Mrs. Peters bends nearer, then turns her face away.)* There's something wrapped up in this piece of silk.

Mrs. Peters: Why, this isn't her scissors.

Mrs. Hale (lifting the silk): Oh, Mrs. Peters — it's — *(Mrs. Peters bends closer.)*

Mrs. Peters: It's the bird.

Mrs. Hale (jumping up): But, Mrs. Peters — look at it! Its neck! Look at its neck! It's all — other side *to.*

Mrs. Peters: Somebody — wrung — its — neck. *(Their eyes meet. A look of growing comprehension, of horror. Steps are heard outside. Mrs. Hale slips box under quilt pieces, and sinks into her chair. Enter Sheriff and County Attorney. Mrs. Peters rises.)*

County Attorney (as one turning from serious things to little pleasantries): Well, ladies, have you decided whether she was going to quilt it or knot it?

Mrs. Peters: We think she was going to — knot it.

County Attorney: Well, that's interesting, I'm sure. *(Seeing the bird-cage.)* Has the bird flown?

Mrs. Hale (putting more quilt pieces over the box): We think the — cat got it.

County Attorney (preoccupied): Is there a cat? *(Mrs. Hale glances in a quick covert way at Mrs. Peters.)*

Mrs. Peters: Well, not *now.* They're superstitious, you know. They leave.

County Attorney (to Sheriff Peters, continuing an interrupted conversation): No sign at all of anyone having come from the outside. Their own rope. Now let's go up again and go over it piece by piece. *(They start upstairs.)* It would have to have been someone who knew just the — *(Mrs. Peters sits down. The two women sit there not looking at one another, but as if peering into something and at the same time holding back. When they talk now it is in the manner of feeling their way over strange ground, as if afraid of what they are saying, but as if they cannot help saying it.)*

Mrs. Hale: She liked the bird. She was going to bury it in that pretty box.

Mrs. Peters (in a whisper): When I was a girl — my kitten — there was a boy took a hatchet, and before my eyes — and before I could get there — *(Covers her face an instant.)* If they hadn't held me back I would have — *(catches herself, looks upstairs where steps are heard, falters weakly)* — hurt him.

Mrs. Hale (with a slow look around her): I wonder how it would seem never to have had any children around. *(Pause.)* No, Wright wouldn't like the bird — a thing that sang. She used to sing. He killed that, too.

Mrs. Peters (moving uneasily): We don't know who killed the bird.

Mrs. Hale: I knew John Wright.

Mrs. Peters: It was an awful thing was done in this house that night, Mrs. Hale. Killing a man while he slept, slipping a rope around his neck that choked the life out of him.

13. If possible, find a copy of "A Jury of Her Peers" in the library (reprinted in *The Best Short Stories of 1917*, ed. E. J. O'Brien [Boston: Small, Maynard, 1918], pp. 256–282) and write an essay that explores the differences between the play and the short story.

14. CRITICAL STRATEGIES. Read the section on formalist criticism (pp. 1538–40) in Chapter 46, "Critical Strategies for Reading." Several times the characters say things that they don't mean, and this creates a discrepancy between what appears to be and what is actually true. Point to instances of irony in the play and explain how they contribute to its effects and meanings. (For discussions of irony elsewhere in this book, see the Index of Terms.)

CONNECTIONS TO OTHER SELECTIONS

1. Compare and contrast how Glaspell provides background information in *Trifles* with how Sophocles does so in *Oedipus the King* (p. 1102).

2. Write an essay comparing the views of marriage in *Trifles* and in Kate Chopin's short story "The Story of an Hour" (p. 15). What similarities do you find in the themes of these two works? Are there any significant differences between the works?

3. In an essay compare Mrs. Wright's motivation for committing murder with that of Matt Fowler, the central character from Andre Dubus's short story "Killings" (p. 103). To what extent do you think they are responsible for and guilty of these crimes?

A SAMPLE CLOSE READING

An Annotated Section of Susan Glaspell's Trifles

As you read a play for the first time, highlight lines, circle, or underline words, and record your responses in the margins. These responses will allow you to retrieve initial reactions and questions that in subsequent readings you can pursue and resolve. Just as the play is likely to have layered meanings, so too will your own readings as you gradually piece together a variety of elements such as exposition, plot, and character that will lead you toward their thematic significance. The following annotations for an excerpt from *Trifles* offer an interpretation that was produced by several readings of the play. Of course, your annotations could be quite different, depending upon your own approach to the play.

The following excerpt appears about two pages into this nine-page play and is preceded by a significant amount of exposition that establishes the bleak Midwestern farm setting and some details about Mrs. Wright, who is the prime suspect in the murder of her husband. Prior to this dialogue, only the male characters speak as they try to discover a motive for the crime.

County Attorney *(looking around)*: I guess we'll go upstairs first — and then out to the barn and around there. *(To the Sheriff.)* You're convinced that there was nothing important here — nothing that would point to any motive?

Sheriff: Nothing here but kitchen things. *(The County Attorney, after again looking around the kitchen, opens the door of a cupboard closet. He gets up on a chair and looks on a shelf. Pulls his hand away, sticky.)*

County Attorney: Here's a nice mess. *(The women draw nearer.)*

Mrs. Peters *(to the other woman)*: Oh, her fruit; it did freeze. *(To the Lawyer.)* She worried about that when it turned so cold. She said the fire'd go out and her jars would break.

Sheriff *(rises)*: Well, can you beat the woman! Held for murder and worryin' about her preserves.

County Attorney: I guess before we're through she may have something more serious than preserves to worry about.

Hale: Well, women are used to worrying over trifles. *(The two women move a little closer together.)*

County Attorney *(with the gallantry of a young politician)*: And yet, for all their worries, what would we do without the ladies? *(The women do not unbend. He goes to the sink, takes a dipperful of water from the pail, and pouring it into a basin, washes his hands. Starts to wipe them on the roller towel, turns it for a cleaner place.)* Dirty towels! *(Kicks his foot against the pans under the sink.)* Not much of a housekeeper, would you say, ladies?

Mrs. Hale *(stiffly)*: There's a great deal of work to be done on a farm.

County Attorney: To be sure. And yet *(with a little bow to her)* I know there are some Dickson county farmhouses which do not have such roller towels. *(He gives it a pull to expose its full length again.)*

Mrs. Hale: Those towels get dirty awful quick. Men's hands aren't always as clean as they might be.

County Attorney: Ah, loyal to your sex, I see. But you and Mrs. Wright were neighbors. I suppose you were friends, too.

Mrs. Hale *(shaking her head)*: I've not seen much of her of late years. I've not been in this house — it's more than a year.

County Attorney: And why was that? You didn't like her?

Mrs. Hale: I liked her all well enough. Farmers' wives have their hands full, Mr. Henderson. And then —

County Attorney: Yes — ?

Mrs. Hale *(looking about)*: It never seemed a very cheerful place.

Margin annotations:

The Sheriff unknowingly announces a major conflict in the play that echoes the title: from a male point of view, there is nothing of any importance to be found in the kitchen — or in women's domestic lives. Mr. Hale confirms this by pronouncing such matters "trifles."

The County Attorney weighs in with his assessment of this "sticky" situation by calling it a "mess" from which he pulls away.

As the Attorney pulls away, the women move closer together (sides are slowly being drawn), and Mrs. Peters says more than she realizes when she observes, "Oh, her fruit; it did freeze." This anticipates our understanding of the cold, fruitless life that drove Mrs. Wright to murder.

The Sheriff's exasperation about women worrying about "preserves" will ironically help preserve the secret of Mrs. Wright — a woman who was beaten down by her husband but who cannot be beaten by these male authorities.

The Attorney has an eye for dirty towels but not for the real "dirt" embedded in the Wrights' domestic life.

The female characters are identified as "Mrs.," which emphasizes their roles as wives, while the men are autonomous and identified by their professions.

Mrs. Hale's comment begins a process of mitigating Mrs. Wright's murder of her husband. He — husbands, men — must share some of the guilt, too.

In contrast to men (a nice irony), farmers' wives' hands are full of responsibilities for which they receive little credit owing to the males' assumption that they fill their lives with trifles.

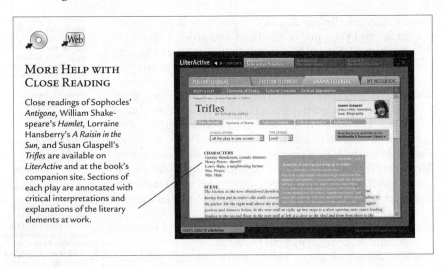

MORE HELP WITH CLOSE READING

Close readings of Sophocles' *Antigone*, William Shakespeare's *Hamlet*, Lorraine Hansberry's *A Raisin in the Sun*, and Susan Glaspell's *Trifles* are available on *LiterActive* and at the book's companion site. Sections of each play are annotated with critical interpretations and explanations of the literary elements at work.

ELEMENTS OF DRAMA

Trifles is a **one-act play**; in other words, the entire play takes place in a single location and unfolds as one continuous action. As in a short story, the characters in a one-act play are presented economically, and the action is sharply focused. In contrast, full-length plays can include many characters as well as different settings in place and time. The main divisions of a full-length play are typically **acts**; their ends are indicated by lowering a curtain or turning up the houselights. Playwrights frequently employ acts to accommodate changes in time, setting, characters on stage, or mood. In many full-length plays, such as Shakespeare's *Hamlet*, acts are further divided into **scenes**; according to tradition a scene changes when the location of the action changes or when a new character enters. Acts and scenes are **conventions** that are understood and accepted by audiences because they have come, through usage and time, to be recognized as familiar techniques. The major convention of a one-act play is that it typically consists of only a single scene; nevertheless, one-act plays contain many of the elements of drama that characterize their full-length counterparts.

Explore the literary elements in this chapter on *LiterActive* or at bedfordstmartins.com/meyercompact.

One-act plays create their effects through compression. They especially lend themselves to modestly budgeted productions with limited stage facilities, such as those put on by little theater groups. However, the potential of a one-act play to move audiences and readers is not related to its length. As *Trifles* shows, one-acts represent a powerful form of dramatic literature.

The single location that composes the **setting** for *Trifles* is described at the very beginning of the play; it establishes an atmosphere that will later influence our judgment of Mrs. Wright. The "gloomy" kitchen is disordered, bare, and sparsely equipped with a stove, sink, rocker, cupboard, two tables, some chairs, three doors, and a window. These details are just enough to allow us to imagine the stark, uninviting place where Mrs. Wright spent most of her time. Moreover, "signs of incompleted work," coupled with the presence of the sheriff and county attorney, create an immediate tension by suggesting that something is terribly wrong. Before a single word is spoken, **suspense** is created as the characters enter. This suspenseful situation causes an anxious uncertainty about what will happen next.

The setting is further developed through the use of **exposition,** a device that provides the necessary background information about the characters and their circumstances. For example, we immediately learn through **dialogue** — the verbal exchanges between characters — that Mr. Henderson, the county attorney, is just back from Omaha. This establishes the setting as somewhere in the Midwest, where winters can be brutally cold and barren. We also find out that John Wright has been murdered and that his wife has been arrested for the crime.

Even more important, Glaspell deftly characterizes the Wrights through exposition alone. Mr. Hale's conversation with Mr. Henderson explains how Mr. Wright's body was discovered, but it also reveals that Wright was a noncommunicative man who refused to share a "party telephone" and did not consider "what his wife wanted." Later Mrs. Hale adds to this characterization when she tells Mrs. Peters that though Mr. Wright was an honest, good man who paid his bills and did not drink, he was a "hard man" and "Like a raw wind that gets to the bone." Mr. Hale's description of Mrs. Wright sitting in the kitchen dazed and disoriented gives us a picture of a shattered, exhausted woman. But it is Mrs. Hale who again offers further insights when she describes how Minnie Foster, a sweet, pretty, timid young woman who sang in the choir, was changed by her marriage to Mr. Wright and by her childless, isolated life on the farm.

This information about Mr. and Mrs. Wright is worked into the dialogue throughout the play in order to suggest the nature of the **conflict** or struggle between them, a motive, and, ultimately, a justification for the murder. In the hands of a skillful playwright, exposition is not merely a mechanical device; it can provide important information while simultaneously developing characterizations and moving the action forward.

The action is shaped by the **plot,** the author's arrangement of incidents in the play that gives the story a particular focus and emphasis. Plot involves more than simply what happens; it involves how and why things happen. Glaspell begins with a discussion of the murder. Why? She could have begun with the murder itself: the distraught Mrs. Wright looping the rope around her husband's neck. The moment would be dramatic and horribly vivid. We neither see the body nor hear very much about it. When Mr. Hale describes finding Mr. Wright's body, Glaspell has the county attorney cut him off by saying, "I think I'd rather have you go into that upstairs, where you can point it all out. Just go on now with the rest of the story." It is precisely the "rest of the story" that interests Glaspell. Her arrangement of incidents prevents us from sympathizing with Mr. Wright. We are, finally, invited to see Mrs. Wright instead of her husband as the victim.

Mr. Henderson's efforts to discover a motive for the murder appear initially to be the play's focus, but the real conflicts are explored in what seems to be a *subplot,* a secondary action that reinforces or contrasts with the main plot. The discussions between Mrs. Hale and Mrs. Peters and the tensions between the men and the women turn out to be the main plot because they address the issues that Glaspell chooses to explore. Those issues are not about murder but about marriage and how men and women relate to each other.

The *protagonist* of *Trifles,* the central character with whom we tend to identify, is Mrs. Hale. The *antagonist,* the character who is in some kind of opposition to the central character, is the county attorney, Mr. Henderson. These two characters embody the major conflicts presented in the play because each speaks for a different set of characters who represent disparate values. Mrs. Hale and Mr. Henderson are developed less individually than as representative types.

Mrs. Hale articulates a sensitivity to Mrs. Wright's miserable life as well as an awareness of how women are repressed in general by men; she also helps Mrs. Peters to arrive at a similar understanding. When Mrs. Hale defends Mrs. Wright's soiled towels from Mr. Henderson's criticism, Glaspell has her say more than the county attorney is capable of hearing. The *stage directions,* the playwright's instructions about how the actors are to move and behave, indicate that Mrs. Hale responds "stiffly" to Mr. Henderson's disparagements: "Men's hands aren't always as clean as they might be." Mrs. Hale eventually comes to see that the men are, in a sense, complicit because it was insensitivity like theirs that drove Mrs. Wright to murder.

Mr. Henderson, on the other hand, represents the law in a patriarchal, conventional society that blithely places a minimal value on the concerns of women. In his attempt to gather evidence against Mrs. Wright, he implicitly defends men's severe dominance over women. He also patronizes Mrs. Hale and Mrs. Peters. Like Sheriff Peters and Mr. Hale, he regards the women's world as nothing more than "kitchen things" and "trifles." Glaspell, however, patterns the plot so that the women see more about Mrs. Wright's motives than the men do and shows that the women have a deeper understanding of justice.

Many plays are plotted in what has come to be called a *pyramidal pattern,* because the plot is divided into three essential parts. Such plays begin with a *rising action,* in which complication creates conflict for the protagonist. The resulting tension builds to the second major division, known as the *climax,* when the action reaches a final *crisis,* a turning point that has a powerful effect on the protagonist. The third part consists of *falling action;* here the tensions are diminished in the *resolution* of the plot's conflicts and complications (the resolution is also referred to as the **conclusion** or *dénouement,* a French word meaning "unknotting"). These divisions may occur at different times. There are many variations to this pattern. The terms are helpful for identifying various moments and movements within a given plot, but they are less useful if seen as a means of reducing dramatic art to a formula.

Because *Trifles* is a one-act play, this pyramidal pattern is less elaborately worked out than it might be in a full-length play, but the basic elements of the pattern can still be discerned. The complication consists mostly of Mrs. Hale's refusal to assign moral or legal guilt to Mrs. Wright's murder of her husband. Mrs. Hale is able to discover the motive in the domestic details that are beneath the men's consideration. The men fail to see the significance of the fruit jars, messy kitchen, and badly sewn quilt.

At first Mrs. Peters seems to voice the attitudes associated with the men. Unlike Mrs. Hale, who is "more comfortable looking," Mrs. Peters is "a slight wiry woman" with "a thin nervous face" who sounds like her husband, the sheriff, when she insists, "the law is the law." She also defends the men's patronizing attitudes, because "they've got awful important things on their minds." But Mrs. Peters is a *foil* — a character whose behavior and values contrast with the protagonist's — only up to a point. When the most telling clue is discovered, Mrs. Peters suddenly understands, along with Mrs. Hale, the motive for the killing. Mrs. Wright's caged life was no longer tolerable to her after her husband had killed the bird (which was the one bright spot in her life and which represents her early life as the young Minnie Foster). This revelation brings about the climax, when the two women must decide whether to tell the men what they have discovered. Both women empathize with Mrs. Wright as they confront this crisis, and their sense of common experience leads them to withhold the evidence.

This resolution ends the play's immediate conflicts and complications. Presumably, without a motive the county attorney will have difficulty prosecuting Mrs. Wright — at least to the fullest extent of the law. However, the larger issues related to the *theme,* the central idea or meaning of the play, are left unresolved. The men have both missed the clues and failed to perceive the suffering that acquits Mrs. Wright in the minds of the two women. The play ends with Mrs. Hale's ironic answer to Mr. Henderson's question about quilting. When she says "knot it," she gives him part of the evidence he needs to connect Mrs. Wright's quilting with the knot used to strangle her husband. Mrs. Hale knows — and we know — that Mr. Henderson will miss the clue she offers because he is blinded by his own self-importance and assumptions.

Though brief, *Trifles* is a masterful representation of dramatic elements working together to keep both audiences and readers absorbed in its characters and situations.

Naked Lunch

Born in Lancaster, Pennsylvania, Michael Hollinger earned a B.A. in music at Oberlin Conservatory and a master of arts degree in theater from Villanova University, where he now teaches theater. His comedies and dramas have been widely produced in the United States and abroad. Among his plays are *An Empty Plate in the Café Du Grand Boeuf* (1994), *Red Herring* (1996), *Hot Air* (1997), *Eureka* (1999), *Tiny Island* (1998), and *Opus* (2006). He has also written three short films and co-authored *Philadelphia Diary* with Bruce Graham and Sonia Sanchez for PBS. His writing awards include the Roger L. Stevens Award from the Kennedy Center's Fund for Outstanding New American Plays, the Barrymore Award for Outstanding New Play, and the Otto Haas Award for Emerging Theatre Artist. Hollinger's extensive music background strongly influences his work as a playwright. He has

Courtesy of the Arden Theatre Company.

said about his own work, "Plays are music to me; characters are instruments, scenes are movements; tempo, rhythm, and dynamics are critical; and melody and counterpoint are always set in relief by rests — beats, pauses, the spaces between." *Naked Lunch* (2003) is one of a group of sixteen plays written by various playwrights for *Trepidation Nation: A Phobic Anthology*, which was produced at the 2002–2003 Humana Festival by the Actor Theatre of Louisville.

MICHAEL HOLLINGER (B. 1962)

Naked Lunch   *2003*

Lights up on Vernon and Lucy sitting at a small dining-room table, eating. There's a small vase with too many flowers in it, or a large vase with too few. A bottle of wine has been opened. Vernon regales Lucy as he vigorously devours a steak. Lucy discreetly nibbles on her corn-on-the-cob.

Vernon: Larry thinks the whole show's a fake. He says the guy's just an actor and all the crocs are trained. I said, you can't train a crocodile! It's not like some poodle you can teach to ride a bike. It's got this reptile brain, a million years old. All it knows, or wants to know, is whether or not you're juicy. Anyway, this one show the guy's sneaking up on a mother protecting her nest. And she's huge — I mean, this thing could swallow a Buick. And the guy's really playing it up: *(Australian accent.)* "Amazing — look at the size of those teeth!" But just —

(He stops, looking at Lucy. Pause. She looks up from her corn.)

Lucy: What.

Vernon: What's the matter?

Lucy: I'm listening.

Vernon: You're not eating your steak.

Lucy: Oh. No.

Vernon: How come?

Lucy: I'll just eat the corn.

> *(She returns to nibbling.)*

Vernon: What's wrong with the steak?

Lucy: Nothing.

Vernon: Then eat it. It's good.

Lucy: I'd . . . rather not.

Vernon: Why not?

> *(Pause.)*

Lucy: I'm vegetarian.

> *(Beat.)*

Vernon: What?

Lucy: I don't eat meat anymore.

Vernon: Since when?

Lucy: Since we, you know. Broke up.

> *(Pause.)*

Vernon: Just like that?

Lucy: Well —

Vernon: You break up with me and boom next day you start eating tofu?

Lucy: I'd been thinking about it for a while.

Vernon: First I ever heard of it.

Lucy: Well, I'd been thinking. *(Pause. Lucy picks up her corn again, guiding him back to the story:)* So anyway, the guy's sneaking up on the mother . . .

Vernon: Was it because of me?

Lucy: No . . .

Vernon: Something I said, or did . . .

Lucy: It's nothing like that.

Vernon: You were always fond of cataloguing the careless things I said and did . . .

Lucy: I just did some soul-searching, that's all.

> *(Beat.)*

Vernon: Soul-searching.

Lucy: About a lot of things.

Vernon: And your soul said to you "no more meat."

Lucy: You make it sound silly when you say it like that.

Vernon: Then what, what did your soul tell you?

> *(Beat. Lucy exhales heavily and sets down her corn.)*

Lucy: I decided I didn't want to eat anything with a face.

> *(Beat.)*

Vernon: A *face?*

(*He gets up, stands behind her and looks at her plate.*)

Lucy: Vern . . .

Vernon: I don't see any face . . .

Lucy: This doesn't have to be a big deal . . .

Vernon: I don't see a face. Do you see a face?

(*He lifts the plate toward her face.*)

Lucy: There's other reasons.

Vernon: No face.

(*He sets the plate down again.*)

Lucy: I've been reading things.

Vernon: What things?

Lucy: You know, health reports . . .

Vernon: You can't believe that stuff.

Lucy: What do you mean?

Vernon: You can't! One day they say bran's good for you — "Want to live forever? Eat more bran." — the next day they find out bran can kill you.

Lucy: Whatever.

Vernon: Too much bran boom you're dead.

Lucy: There are diseases you can get from meat.

Vernon: Like what?

Lucy: Well, listeria . . .

Vernon: That's chicken. Chicken and turkey.

Lucy: Or Mad Cow.

Vernon: *Mad Cow?* Did you — That's not even — that's *English*, they have that in *England*. This isn't English meat, this is from, I don't know, Kansas, or . . . *Wyoming*.

Lucy: Even so, —

Vernon: No. Now you're making stuff up.

Lucy: I'm not; I saw an article —

Vernon: You're just being paranoid, this whole . . . You know what this is? Do you?

Lucy: What.

Vernon: Carnophobia.

Lucy: "Carnophobia"?

Vernon: It's a word, look it up.

Lucy: It's not like I'm scared of meat . . .

Vernon: How do you think this makes me feel?

Lucy: Look, let's just drop it.

Vernon: Huh?

Lucy: We were doing so well . . .

Vernon: I invite you over, cook a nice steak, set out flowers, napkins, the whole nine yards . . .

Lucy: I appreciate the napkins.

Vernon: . . . figure I'll open a bottle of wine, apologize . . . maybe we'll get naked, be like old times.

Lucy: So let's start over.

Vernon: Then you get *carnophobic* on me.

Lucy: Can we?

Vernon: Throw it in my face.

Lucy: Please?

Vernon: Start *cataloguing* what's wrong with everything . . .

Lucy: I never meant this to be a big deal. *(Beat. She puts her hand on his. He looks at her.)* I really didn't.

(Long pause.)

Vernon: Then eat it.

(Beat.)

Lucy: Vern . . . *(He picks up her fork, jams it into her steak, and cuts off a bite with his knife.)* Why do you always have to —

(He extends the piece of meat toward Lucy's mouth.)

Vernon: Eat the meat.

Lucy: I don't want to.

Vernon: Eat the meat.

Lucy: Vernon . . .

Vernon: I SAID EAT THE MEAT! *(They are locked in a struggle, he menacing, she terrified. Long pause. Finally, Lucy opens her mouth and takes the bite into it. Pause.)* Chew. *(She chews for fifteen or twenty seconds.)* Swallow. *(She swallows. Cheerfully, without malice:)* Good, isn't it. *(Lucy nods obediently.)* Nice and juicy. *(He stabs his fork into his own steak, cuts off a bite and lifts it.)* See, nothing to be afraid of.

(He pops it into his mouth and begins cutting another. After a moment, Lucy goes back to her corn. They eat in absolute silence. Lights fade.)

"*Naked Lunch* — *a frozen moment when everyone sees what is on the end of every fork.*" —William S. Burroughs

CONSIDERATIONS FOR CRITICAL THINKING AND WRITING

1. FIRST RESPONSE. Do you identify more with Vernon or Lucy? Which character seems more sympathetic to you? Explain why.

2. What do you think is the significance of the set directions calling for "a small vase with too many flowers in it, or a large vase with too few"?

3. Why won't Lucy eat meat?

4. Why is it so important to Vernon that Lucy eat the steak?

5. Which character would you describe as the antagonist? What do you think is the play's central conflict?

6. Discuss the tone of the final moments of the play when Vernon cuts the steak for Lucy. Is the central conflict resolved? Why or why not?

7. How would you describe the play's theme?

8. Discuss the significance of the title. How is it related to your understanding of the play's theme?

9. In the biographical head note to the play, Hollinger describes how his plays share some of the same qualities as music. Reread his explanation of this comparison and discuss how the literary elements of *Naked Lunch* are similar to music.

CONNECTIONS TO OTHER SELECTIONS

1. Compare the theme of *Naked Lunch* with that of Susan Glaspell's *Trifles* (p. 1048).

2. Discuss the symbolic significance of the steak dinner in *Naked Lunch* and the birdcage and the dead bird in *Trifles*.

DRAMA IN POPULAR FORMS

Audiences for live performances of plays have been thinned by high ticket prices but perhaps even more significantly by the impact of motion pictures and television. Motion pictures, the original threat to live theater, have in turn been superseded by television (along with videocassettes and DVDs), now the most popular form of entertainment in America. Television audiences are measured in the millions. Probably more people have seen a single weekly episode of a top-rated prime-time program such as *ER* in one evening than have viewed a live performance of *Hamlet* in nearly four hundred years.

Though most of us are seated more often before a television than before live actors, our limited experience with the theater presents relatively few obstacles to appreciation because many of the basic elements of drama are similar whether the performance is on a screen or on a stage. Television has undoubtedly seduced audiences that otherwise might have been attracted to the theater, but television obviously satisfies some aspects of our desire for drama and can be seen as a potential introduction to live theater rather than as its irresistible rival.

Significant differences do, of course, exist between television and theater productions. Most obviously, television's special camera effects can capture phenomena such as earthquakes, raging fires, car chases, and space travel that cannot be realistically rendered on a live stage. The presentation of characters and the plotting of action are also handled differently owing to both the possibilities and limitations of television and the theater. Television's multiple camera angles and close-ups provide a degree of intimacy that cannot be duplicated by actors on stage, yet this intimacy does not achieve the immediacy that live actors create. On commercial television the plot must accommodate itself to breaks in the action so that advertisements can be aired at regular intervals. Beyond these and many other differences, however, there are enough important similarities that the experience of watching television shows can enhance our understanding of a theater production.

Seinfeld

Seinfeld, which aired on NBC, was first produced during the summer of 1989. Although the series ended in the spring of 1998, it remains popular in syndicated reruns. No one expected the half-hour situation comedy that evolved from the pilot to draw some twenty-seven million viewers per week who avidly watched Jerry Seinfeld playing himself as a standup comic. Nominated for numerous Emmys, the show became one of the most popular programs of the 1990s. Although *Seinfeld* portrays a relatively narrow band of contemporary urban life — four thirty-something characters living in New York City's Upper West Side — its quirky humor and engaging characters have attracted vast numbers of devoted fans who have conferred on it a kind of cult status. If you haven't watched an episode on television, noticed the T-shirts and posters, or read *Seinlanguage* (a best-selling collection of Seinfeld's monologues), you can catch up on the Internet, where fans discuss the popularity and merits of the show.

The setting for *Seinfeld* is determined by its subject matter, which is everyday life in Manhattan. Most of the action alternates between two principal locations: Jerry's modest one-bedroom apartment on West 81st Street and the characters' favorite restaurant in the neighborhood. Viewers are often surprised to learn that the show was filmed on a soundstage before a live audience in Studio City, California, because the sights, sounds, and seemingly unmistakable texture of Manhattan appear in background shots so that the city functions almost as a major character in many episodes. If you ever find yourself on the corner of Broadway and 112th Street, you'll recognize the facade of Jerry's favorite restaurant; but don't bother to look for the building that matches the exterior shot of his apartment building because it is in Los Angeles, as are the scenes in which the characters actually appear on the street. The care with which the sets are created suggests how important the illusion of the New York City environment is to the show.

As the central character, Jerry begins and ends each episode with a standup comedy act delivered before a club audience. These monologues (played down in later episodes) are connected to the events in the episodes and demonstrate with humor and insight that ordinary experience — such as standing in line at a supermarket or getting something caught in your teeth — can be a source of genuine humor. For Jerry, life is filled with daily annoyances that he copes with by making sharp, humorous observations. Here's a brief instance from "The Pitch" (not reprinted in the excerpt on p. 1071) in which Jerry is in the middle of a conversation with friends when he is interrupted by a phone call.

> *Jerry (into phone):* Hello?
> *Man (v[oice] o[ver]):* Hi, would you be interested in switching over to T.M.I. long distance service?
> *Jerry:* Oh gee, I can't talk right now, why don't you give me your home number and I'll call you later?

Man (v[oice] o[ver]): Uh, well I'm sorry, we're not allowed to do that.
Jerry: Oh, I guess you don't want people calling you at home.
Man (v[oice] o[ver]): No.
Jerry: Well now you know how I feel.
Hangs up.

This combination of polite self-assertion and humor is Jerry's first line of defense in his ongoing skirmishes with the irritations of daily life. Unthreatening in his Nikes and neatly pressed jeans, Jerry nonetheless knows how to give it back when he is annoyed. Seinfeld has described his fictional character as a "nice, New York Jewish boy," but his character's bemused and pointed observations reveal a tough-mindedness that is often wittily on target.

Jerry's life and apartment are continually invaded by his three closest friends: George, Kramer, and Elaine. His refrigerator is the rallying point from which they feed each other lines over cardboard takeout cartons and containers of juice. Jerry's success as a standup comic is their cue to enjoy his groceries as well as his company, but they know their intrusions are welcome because the refrigerator is always restocked.

Jerry's closest friend is George Costanza (played by Jason Alexander), a frequently unemployed, balding, pudgy schlemiel. Any straightforward description of his behavior and sensibilities makes him sound starkly unappealing: he is hypochondriacal, usually upset and depressed, inept with women, embarrassingly stingy, and persistently demanding while simultaneously displaying a vain and cocky nature. As intolerable as he can be, he is nonetheless endearing. The pleasure of his character is in observing how he talks his way into trouble and then attempts to talk his way out of it to Jerry's amazement and amusement.

Across the hall from Jerry's apartment lives Kramer (played by Michael Richards), who is strategically located so as to be the mooch in Jerry's life. Known only as Kramer (until an episode later than "The Pitch" revealed his first name to be Cosmo), his slapstick twitching, tripping, and falling serve as a visual contrast to all the talking that goes on. His bizarre schemes and eccentric behavior have their physical counterpart in his vertical hair and his outrageous thrift-shop shirts from the 1960s.

Elaine Benes (played by Julia Louis-Dreyfus), on the other hand, is a sharp-tongued, smart, sexy woman who can hold her own and is very definitely a female member of this boy's club. As Jerry's ex-girlfriend, she provides some interesting romantic tension while serving as a sounding board for the relationship issues that George and Jerry obsess about. Employed at a book company at the time of the episode reprinted here, she, like George and Kramer, is also in the business of publishing her daily problems in Jerry's apartment.

The plots of most *Seinfeld* episodes are generated by the comical situations that Jerry and his friends encounter during the course of their daily lives. Minor irritations develop into huge conflicts that are offbeat, irreverent, or even absurd. The characters have plenty of time to create conflicts in their lives over such everyday situations as dealing with parents, finding an apartment, getting a date, riding the subway, ordering a meal, and losing a car in a mall parking garage. The show's screwball plots involve freewheeling misadventures that are played out in unremarkable but hilarious conversations.

Larry David. © Dan Winters.

The following scenes from *Seinfeld* are from a script titled "The Pitch" that concerns Jerry's and George's efforts to develop a television show for NBC. The script is loosely based on events that actually occurred when Jerry Seinfeld and his real-life friend Larry David (the author of "The Pitch") sat down to discuss ideas for the pilot NBC produced in 1989. As brief as these scenes are, they contain some of the dramatic elements found in a play.

LARRY DAVID (B. 1947)

Seinfeld 1992

"THE PITCH"
[The following excerpted scenes do not appear one after the other in the original script but are interspersed through several subplots involving Kramer and Elaine.]

ACT ONE

SCENE A: *Int[erior] comedy club bar — night*

    Jerry and George are talking. Suits enter, Stu and Jay.

Stu: Excuse me, Jerry? I'm Stu Chermak. I'm with NBC.
Jerry: Hi.
Stu: Could we speak for a few moments?
Jerry: Sure, sure.
Jay: Hi, Jay Crespi.
Jerry: Hello.
George: C-R-E-S-P-I?
Jay: That's right.
George: I'm unbelievable at spelling last names. Give me a last name.
Jay: Mm, I'm not—

Jerry: George.

George (backing off): Huh? All right, fine.

Stu: First of all, that was a terrific show.

Jerry: Oh thank you very much.

Stu: And basically, I just wanted to let you know that we've been discussing you at some of our meetings and we'd be very interested in doing something.

Jerry: Really? Wow.

Stu: So, if you have an idea for like a TV show for yourself, well, we'd just love to talk about it.

Jerry: I'd be very interested in something like that.

Stu: Well, here, why don't you give us a call and maybe we can develop a series.

> They start to exit.

Jerry: Okay. Great. Thanks.

Stu: It was very nice meeting you.

Jerry: Thank you.

Jay: Nice meeting you.

Jerry: Nice meeting you.

> George returns.

George: What was that all about?

Jerry: They said they were interested in me.

George: For what?

Jerry: You know, a TV show.

George: Your own show?

Jerry: Yeah, I guess so.

George: They want you to do a TV show?

Jerry: Well, they want me to come up with an idea. I mean, I don't have any ideas.

George: Come on, how hard is that? Look at all the junk that's on TV. You want an idea? Here's an idea. You coach a gymnastics team in high school. And you're married. And your son's not interested in gymnastics and you're pushing him into gymnastics.

Jerry: Why should I care if my son's into gymnastics?

George: Because you're a gymnastics teacher. It's only natural.

Jerry: But gymnastics is not for everybody.

George: I know, but he's your son.

Jerry: So what?

George: All right, forget that idea, it's not for you. . . . Okay, okay, I got it, I got it. You run an antique store.

Jerry: Yeah and . . . ?

George: And people come in the store and you get involved in their lives.

Jerry: What person who runs an antique store gets involved in people's lives?

George: Why not?

Jerry: So someone comes in to buy an old lamp and all of a sudden I'm getting them out of a jam? I could see if I was a pharmacist because a pharmacist knows what's wrong with everybody that comes in.

George: I know, but antiques are very popular right now.

Jerry: No they're not, they used to be.

George: Oh yeah, like you know.

Jerry: Oh like you do.

> Cut to:

ACT ONE

SCENE B: *Int[erior] Jerry's apartment—day*

> *Jerry and Kramer.*

Kramer: . . . And you're the manager of the circus.

Jerry: A circus?

Kramer: Come on, this is a great idea. Look at the characters. You've got all these freaks on the show. A woman with a moustache? I mean, who wouldn't tune in to see a woman with a moustache? You've got the tallest man in the world; the guy who's just a head.

Jerry: I don't think so.

Kramer: Look Jerry, the show isn't about the circus, it's about watching freaks.

Jerry: I don't think the network will go for it.

Kramer: Why not?

Jerry: Look, I'm not pitching a show about freaks.

Kramer: Oh come on Jerry, you're wrong. People they want to watch freaks. This is a "can't miss."

ACT ONE

SCENE C: *Int[erior] coffee shop—lunchtime—day*

> *Jerry and George enter.*

George: So, what's happening with the TV show? You come up with anything?

Jerry: No, nothing.

George: Why don't they have salsa on the table?

Jerry: What do you need salsa for?

George: Salsa is now the number one condiment in America.

Jerry: You know why? Because people like to say "salsa." "Excuse me, do you have salsa?" "We need more salsa." "Where is the salsa? No salsa?"

George: You know it must be impossible for a Spanish person to order seltzer and not get salsa. *(Angry.)* "I wanted seltzer, not salsa."

Jerry: "Don't you know the difference between seltzer and salsa? You have the seltzer after the salsa!"

George: See, this should be the show. This is the show.

Jerry: What?

George: This. Just talking.

Jerry (dismissing): Yeah, right.

George: I'm really serious. I think that's a good idea.

Jerry: Just talking? What's the show about?

George: It's about nothing.

Jerry: No story?

George: No, forget the story.

Jerry: You've got to have a story.

George: Who says you gotta have a story? Remember when we were waiting for that table in that Chinese restaurant that time? That could be a TV show.

Jerry: And who is on the show? Who are the characters?

George: I could be a character.

Jerry: You?

George: You could base a character on me.

Jerry: So on the show there's a character named George Costanza?

George: Yeah. There's something wrong with that? I'm a character. People are always saying to me, "You know you're quite a character."

Jerry: And who else is on the show?

George: Elaine could be a character. Kramer.

Jerry: Now he's a character. . . . So, everyone I know is a character on the show.

George: Right.

Jerry: And it's about nothing?

George: Absolutely nothing.

Jerry: So you're saying, I go in to NBC and tell them I got this idea for a show about nothing.

George: We go into NBC.

Jerry: We? Since when are you a writer?

George: Writer. We're talking about a sit-com.

Jerry: You want to go with me to NBC?

George: Yeah, I think we really got something here.

Jerry: What do we got?

George: An idea.

Jerry: What idea?

George: An idea for the show.

Jerry: I still don't know what the idea is.

George: It's about nothing.

Jerry: Right.

George: Everybody's doing something, we'll do nothing.

Jerry: So we go into NBC, we tell them we've got an idea for a show about nothing.

George: Exactly.

Jerry: They say, "What's your show about?" I say, "Nothing."

George: There you go.

> *A beat.*

Jerry: I think you may have something there.

> *Cut to:*

ACT ONE

SCENE D: *Int[erior] Jerry's apartment—day*

> *Jerry and Kramer.*

Jerry: So it would be about my real life. And one of the characters would be based on you.

Kramer (thinks): No. I don't think so.

Jerry: What do you mean you don't think so?

Kramer: I don't like it.

Jerry: I don't understand. What don't you like about it?

Kramer: I don't like the idea of a character based on me.

Jerry: Why not?

Kramer: Doesn't sit well.

Jerry: You're my neighbor. There's got to be a character based on you.

Kramer: That's your problem, buddy.

Jerry: I don't understand what the big deal is.

Kramer: Hey I'll tell you what, you can do it on one condition.

Jerry: Whatever you want.

Kramer: I get to play Kramer.

Jerry: You can't play Kramer.

Kramer: I am Kramer.

Jerry: But you can't act.

ACT ONE

Scene G: *Int[erior] NBC reception area—day*

> *Jerry and George.*

Jerry (to himself): Salsa, seltzer. Hey excuse me, you got any salsa? No not seltzer, salsa. *(George doesn't react.)* What's the matter?

George (nervous): Nothing.

Jerry: You sure? You look a little pale.

George: No, I'm fine. I'm good. I'm fine. I'm very good.

Jerry: What are you, nervous?

George: No, not nervous. I'm good, very good. *(A beat, then: explodes.)* I can't do this! Can't do this!

Jerry: What?

George: I can't do this! I can't do it. I have tried. I'm here. It's impossible.

Jerry: This was your idea.

George: What idea? I just said something. I didn't know you'd listen to me.

Jerry: Don't worry about it. They're just TV executives.

George: They're men with jobs, Jerry! They wear suits and ties. They're married, they have secretaries.

Jerry: I told you not to come.

George: I need some water. I gotta get some water.

Jerry: They'll give us water inside.

George: Really? That's pretty good. . . .

> *Receptionist enters.*

Receptionist: They're ready for you.

George: Okay, okay, look, you do all the talking, okay?

Jerry: Relax. Who are they?

George: Yeah, they're not better than me.

Jerry: Course not.

George: Who are they?

Jerry: They're nobody.

George: What about me?

Jerry: What about you?

George: Why them? Why not me?

Jerry: Why not you?

George: I'm as good as them.

Jerry: Better.

George: You really think so?

Jerry: No.

> *Door opens, Jerry and George P.O.V., the four execs stand up.*
>
> *Fade out.*

ACT TWO

SCENE G: *Int[erior] NBC president's office — day*

> *The mood is jovial. Stu Chermak is there — along with Susan Ross, Jay Crespi, and Russell Dalrymple, the head of the network.*

Stu (to Jerry): The bit, the bit I really liked was where the parakeet flew into the mirror. Now that's funny.

George: The parakeet in the mirror. That is a good one, Stu.

Jerry: Yeah, it's one of my favorites.

Russell: What about you George, have you written anything we might know?

George: Well, possibly. I wrote an off-Broadway show, "La Cocina". . . . Actually it was off-off-Broadway. It was a comedy about a Mexican chef.

Jerry: Oh it was very funny. There was one great scene with the chef — what was his name?

George: Pepe.

Jerry: Oh Pepe, yeah Pepe. And, uh, he was making tamales.

Susan: Oh, he actually cooked on the stage?

George: No, no, he mimed it. That's what was so funny about it.

Russell: So what have you two come up with?

Jerry: Well we've thought about this in a variety of ways. But the basic idea is I will play myself.

George (interrupting, to Jerry): May I?

Jerry: Go ahead.

George: I think I can sum up the show for you with one word. NOTHING.

Russell: Nothing?

George: Nothing.

Russell: What does that mean?

George: The show is about nothing.

Jerry (to George): Well, it's not about nothing.

George (to Jerry): No, it's about nothing.

Jerry: Well, maybe in philosophy. But even nothing is something.

> *Jerry and George glare at each other. Receptionist sticks her head in.*

Receptionist: Mr. Dalrymple, your niece is on the phone.

Russell: I'll call back.

George: D-A-L-R-I-M-P-E-L.

Russell: Not even close.

George: Is it with a "y"?

Russell: No.

Susan: What's the premise?

Jerry: . . . Well, as I was saying, I would play myself. And as a comedian, living in New York, and I have a friend and a neighbor and an ex-girlfriend, which is all true.

George: Yeah, but nothing happens on the show. You see, it's just like life. You know, you eat, you go shopping, you read. You eat, you read, you go shopping.

Russell: You read? You read on the show?

Jerry: Well I don't know about the reading. We didn't discuss the reading.

Russell: All right, tell me, tell me about the stories. What kind of stories?

George: Oh no, no stories.

Russell: No stories? So what is it?

George: What'd you do today?

Russell: I got up and came to work.

George: There's a show. That's a show.

Russell (confused): How is that a show?

Jerry: Well, uh, maybe something happens on the way to work.

George: No, no, no. Nothing happens.

Jerry: Well, something happens.

Russell: Well why am I watching it?

George: Because it's on TV.

Russell: Not yet.

George: Okay, uh, look, if you want to just keep on doing the same old thing, then maybe this idea is not for you. I for one will not compromise my artistic integrity. And I'll tell you something else. This is the show and we're not going to change it. *(To Jerry.)* Right?

Jerry: How about this? I manage a circus . . .

CONSIDERATIONS FOR CRITICAL THINKING AND WRITING

1. **FIRST RESPONSE.** What does George mean when he says the proposed show should be about "nothing"? Why is George's idea both a comic and a serious proposal?

2. How does the stage direction "Suits enter" serve to characterize Stu and Jay? Write a description of how you think they would look.

3. What is revealed about George's character when he spells Crespi's and Dalrymple's names?

4. Discuss Kramer's assertion that people "want to watch freaks." Do you think this line could be used to sum up accurately audience responses to *Seinfeld*?

5. Choose a scene, and explain how humor is worked into it. What other emotions are evoked in the scene?

6. View an episode of *Seinfeld*. How does reading a script compare with watching the show? Which do you prefer? Why?

7. CRITICAL STRATEGIES. Read the section on reader-response criticism (pp. 1552–54) in Chapter 46, "Critical Strategies for Reading," and discuss why you like or dislike "The Pitch" and *Seinfeld* in general. Try to account for your personal response to the script and the show.

CONNECTION TO ANOTHER SELECTION

1. In an essay explain whether or not you think John Leguizamo's play *Mambo Mouth* (p. 1349) fills George's prescription that a story should be about "nothing."

Like those of many plays, the settings for these scenes are not detailed. Jerry's apartment and the coffee shop are, to cite only two examples, not described at all. We are told only that it is lunchtime in the coffee shop. Even without a set designer's version of these scenes, we readily create a mental picture of these places that provides a background for the characters. In the coffee shop scene we can assume that Jerry and George are having lunch, but we must supply the food, the plates and cutlery, the tables and chairs, and the other customers. For the television show sets were used that replicated the details of a Manhattan coffee shop, right down to the menus and cash register. If the scene were presented on a stage, a set designer might use minimal sets and props to suggest the specific location. The director of such a production would rely on the viewers' imagination to create the details of the setting.

As brief as they are, these scenes include some exposition to provide the necessary background about the characters and their circumstances. We learn through dialogue, for example, that George is not a writer and that he doesn't think it takes very much talent to write a sitcom even though he's unemployed. These bits of information help to characterize George and allow an audience to place his attitudes and comments in a larger context that will be useful for understanding how other characters read them. Rather than dramatizing background information, the scriptwriter arranges incidents to create a particular focus and effect while working in the necessary exposition through dialogue.

The plot in these scenes shapes the conflicts to emphasize humor. As in any good play, incidents are carefully arranged to achieve a particular effect. In the first scene we learn that NBC executives are interested in having Jerry do his own television show. We also learn, through his habit of spelling people's last names when he meets them, that George is a potential embarrassment. The dialogue between Jerry and George quickly establishes the conflict. The NBC executives would like to produce a TV show with Jerry provided that he can come up with an idea for the series; Jerry, however, has no ideas (here's the complication of the pyramidal plot pattern discussed in Elements of Drama, p. 1062). This complication sets up a conflict for Jerry because George assumes that he can help Jerry develop an idea for the show, which, after all, shouldn't be any more difficult than spelling a stranger's name. As George says, "How hard is that? Look at all the junk that's on TV."

All of a sudden everyone is an expert on scriptwriting. George's off-the-wall suggestions that the premise for the show be Jerry's running an antique shop or teaching gymnastics are complemented by Kramer's idea that Jerry be "the manager of the circus" because "people they want to watch freaks." As unhelpful as Kramer's suggestion is, there is some truth here as well as humor, given his own freakish behavior. However, it is George who comes through with the most intriguing suggestion. As a result of the exuberantly funny riff he and Jerry do on "the difference between seltzer and salsa," George suddenly realizes that the show should be "about nothing" — that it should consist of nothing more than Jerry talking and hanging out with his friends George, Elaine, and Kramer. Jerry's initial skepticism gives way as he seriously considers George's proposal and is intrigued enough to bring George with him to the NBC offices to make the pitch. His decision to bring George to the meeting can only, of course, complicate matters further.

Before the meeting with the NBC executives, George is stricken with one of his crises of confidence when he compares himself to the "men with jobs" who are married and have secretaries. Characteristically, George's temporary lack of confidence shifts to an equally ill-timed arrogance once the meeting begins. He usurps Jerry's role and makes the pitch himself: "Nothing happens on the show. You see, it's just like life. You know, you eat, you go shopping, you read. You eat, you read, you go shopping." The climax occurs when George refuses even to consider any of the reservations the executives have about "nothing" happening on the show. George's insistence that he not compromise his "artistic integrity" creates a crisis for Jerry, a turning point that makes him realize that George's ridiculous arrogance might cost him his opportunity to have a TV show. Jerry's final lines to the executives — "How about this? I manage a circus . . ." — work two ways: he resignedly acknowledges that something — not "nothing" — has just happened and that George is, indeed, something of a freak.

The falling action and resolution typical of a pyramidal plot are not present in "The Pitch" because the main plot is not resolved until a later episode. "The Pitch" also contains several subplots not included in the scenes excerpted in this book. Like the main plot, these subplots involving Elaine, Kramer, and a few minor characters are not resolved until later episodes. Self-contained series episodes are increasingly rare on television, as programmers attempt to hook viewers week after week by creating suspense once associated with serialized stories that appeared weekly or monthly in magazines.

The theme of "The Pitch" is especially interesting because it self-reflexively comments on the basic premise of *Seinfeld* scripts: they are all essentially about "nothing" in that they focus on the seemingly trivial details of the four main characters' lives. The unspoken irony of this theme is that such details are in fact significant because it is just such small, everyday activities that constitute most people's lives.

Perspective

GEOFFREY O'BRIEN (B. 1948)

On Seinfeld *as Sitcom Moneymaker*   1997

If *Seinfeld* is indeed, in the words of *Entertainment Weekly,* "the defining sitcom of our age" (one wonders how many such ages, each defined by its own sitcom, have already elapsed), the question remains what exactly it defines. Deliberate satire is alien to the spirit of the enterprise. *Seinfeld* has perfected a form in which anything can be invoked — masturbation, Jon Voight, death, kasha, deafness, faked orgasms, Salman Rushdie, Pez dispensers — without assuming the burden of saying anything about it (thereby avoiding the "social message" trap of programs like Norman Lear's *All in the Family* or *Maude*).

The show does not comment on anything except, famously, itself, in the series of episodes where Jerry and George create a pilot for a sitcom "about nothing," a sitcom identical to the one we are watching. This ploy — which ultimately necessitates a whole set of look-alikes to impersonate the cast of the show-within-a-show *Jerry*— ties in with the recursive, alternate-universe mode of such comedies as *The Purple Rose of Cairo* and *Groundhog Day,* while holding back just this side of the paranormal. If conspiracy theories surface from time to time, it is purely for amusement value, as in the episode where a spitting incident at the ballpark becomes the occasion for an elaborate parody — complete with Zapruder-like home movie° — of the Single Bullet Theory (figuring in this context as the ultimate joke on the idea of explanation).

The result is a vastly entertaining mosaic of observed bits and traits and frames. Imagine some future researcher trying to annotate any one of these episodes, like a Shakespearean scholar dutifully noting that "tapsters were proverbially poor at arithmetic." It would not merely be a matter of explaining jokes and cultural references and curt showbiz locutions — "He does fifteen minutes on Ovaltine" or "They cancelled Rick James" — but of explicating (always assuming that they were detected in the first place) each shrug and curtailed expostulation and deftly averted glance.

Where it might once have been asked if *Seinfeld* was a commentary on society, the question now should probably be whether society has not been reconfigured as a milieu for commenting on *Seinfeld.* If the craziness enacted on the show is nothing more than the usual business of comedy, the craziness that swirls around it in the outside world is of a less hilarious order. Comedy and money have always been around, but not always in such intimate linkage, and certainly not on so grandiose a scale. In the fifteenth century, the fate of Tudor

---

Zapruder-like home movie: A reference to the Dallas bystander who captured John F. Kennedy's assassination on film.

commerce was not perceived to hinge on the traveling English players who wowed foreign audiences as far afield as Denmark.

The information-age money culture for which *Seinfeld* is only another, fatter, bargaining chip clearly lost its sense of humor a long time ago, a fact that becomes ever more apparent as we move into an economy where sit-coms replace iron and steel as principal products and where fun is not merely big business but seemingly the only business. The once-endearing razzmatazz of showbiz hype warps into a perceptible desperation that registers all too plainly how much is at stake for the merchandisers. One becomes uncomfortably aware of them looming behind the audience, running electronic analyses of the giggles, and nervously watching for the dreaded moment when the laughter begins to dry up. It all begins to seem too much like work even for the audience, who may well begin to wonder why they should be expected to care about precisely how much their amusement is worth to the ticket-sellers.

As for the actual creators of the fun, I would imagine that—allowing for difference of scale and pressure—they go about their work pretty much the same way regardless of the going price for a good laugh. Some years ago, in a dusty corner of Languedoc,° I watched a dented circus truck pull up unannounced along the roadside. The family of performers who clambered out proceeded to set up a makeshift stage, which in a few hours time was ready for their show: a display of tumbling and magic that could have been presented without significant difference in the fifteenth century. After two hours of sublime entertainment, they passed the hat around and drove away toward the next bend in the road. It is strange to think of the fate of empires, even entertainment empires, hinging on such things.

From the *New York Review of Books*, August 14, 1997

Languedoc: A region in southern France.

CONSIDERATIONS FOR CRITICAL THINKING AND WRITING

1. In what sense might *Seinfeld* be described as "the defining sitcom of our age"? Do you think this is an accurate description of the show? Why or why not?

2. Explain why you agree or disagree with O'Brien's assertion that *Seinfeld* "does not comment on anything except, famously, itself."

3. Comment on O'Brien's idea that "Comedy and money have always been around, but not always in such intimate linkage." How does *Seinfeld* fit into an "information-age money culture"?

Will & Grace

From its NBC premier in September of 1998 to its final episode in May of 2006, *Will & Grace* charmed millions of viewers who laughed at the comic situations that a gay man and straight woman stumbled into as they negotiated life in Manhattan. When *Will & Grace* first aired, the network worried that there might be a negative or controversial reaction to the show's focus on a homosexual male lead, but the audience response was enthusiastically supportive and the critical response generous. The show won a number of Emmys from the many nominations it garnered.

Kari Lizer. © Chris Pizzello/Reuters/ Corbis.

In the series, Will and Grace are best friends going all the way back to college, and although they once dated, are roommates, and continue to share the same appetite for fine wine, French films, shopping, fashion, and poker games, they are not an item, because Will is gay. Their relationship is platonic, but their friendship is nonetheless intense as each looks for the perfect romantic mate. While there is no romance between them, there is no absence of genuine love, a fact made clear by their mutual affection and concern for each other.

Will Truman (played by Eric McCormack) is a responsible, successful lawyer who is as disciplined in his work as he is fussy in his daily buttoned-down routine. His compulsive neatness and rage for order contrast with Grace Adler's (played by Debra Messing) more casual and chaotic approach to life. She is a professional interior designer, but there is much less of a pattern in her life than in Will's, which, like his profession, seems embedded in precedents and conventional assumptions. Despite their differences in temperament, they share similar difficulties and complications arising from each of them searching for a romantic partner or navigating their respective careers.

Further complicating their lives and the plots in the series are their mutual friends Jack McFarland and Karen Walker (played by Sean Hayes and Megan Mullally). Jack, who lives in the same building as Will and Grace, is Will's flamboyant, over-the-top gay friend. An aspiring actor and cabaret singer, Jack is a self-proclaimed drama queen who adoringly flaunts the gay stereotypes that Will quells. His day jobs have included work in retail, but what he really trades on is confounding Will's life. He is to Will what Karen is to Grace. Karen is Grace's astonishingly rich and eccentric alcoholic assistant whose social contacts are useful in Grace's business even if Karen herself is largely useless. What Karen doesn't drink she buys or beds, and yet she, like Jack, is deep down a loyal friend. Jack and Karen are the second odd couple in the show that serves as a foil to Will and Grace while also creating some of the show's more outrageous humor.

The following scenes from *Will & Grace* are from a script titled "Dolls and Dolls." The main plot concerns Karen's finding an apartment and a roommate named Liz (played by Madonna) who is as self-absorbed as she is. The subplot focuses on Will, who becomes hooked on painkillers after he injures himself in a fall as a result of wearing wooden clogs. The five excerpted scenes trace the subplot. As you read the script, notice how it includes some of the dramatic elements typical of a play.

KARI LIZER (B. 1962)
Will & Grace

From "DOLLS AND DOLLS"

. . .

SCENE I: Will's Apartment

See Plays in Performance insert.

> *(Grace is with Jack. She dumps out her laundry on the couch.)*

Grace: Will called from the doctor. I guess he actually sprained something. So I guess it's just gonna be you and me for the good old fashioned foldin' party.

Jack: Grace, just because you say the words "good old fashioned," doesn't make it a party.

Grace: Even though I made a good old fashioned foldin' party mix tape?

> *(She plays a tape.)*

Jack: Okay, now it's a party.

> *(They dance and fold clothes.)*

Jack: You see — do you see why it's good? Okay. Okay. Oh, good.

> *(She turns off the tape.)*

Jack: Hey, what's the big idea?

Grace: It is such a great song, I think we should save it for sock bundling. *(Giggles.)*

Jack: Okay, okay, okay.

Grace: You know, we would never have this much fun if Will were here. You know, he practically ruined my good old fashioned find the bad smell party.

Jack: Why does he always have to be in such a bad mood? With those — with those angry arms. *(Imitating Will yelling while holding out his arms.)* Stop taking my money! Stop leaving crumbs on the carpet! Stop making fun of my angry arms!

Grace: Yup, sometimes he can be a little mean and intense.

Jack: Wow.

Grace: Mm-hm.

Jack: Do you think he'd ever kill us?

Grace: No, come on, it's Will. *(beat)* Maybe you should move your glass off the coffee table.

Jack: Yeah. If we leave one more ring, she gonna snap.

> *(The door handle shakes, startling both of them.)*

Grace/Jack: *(panicking)* Oh! Oh, my god!

Grace: *(panicking)* Pick up the glass! Wipe down the ring!

Jack: You're right! First he sees the ring, and then we die!

> *(Will enters on crutches.)*

Will: Hey, what're you guys doin'?

Jack: Uh — uh — uh — it's a good old fashioned folding party. It was Grace's idea. Take her, she has funny genitals.

Will: Good old fashioned folding party? (*Laughs.*) Why is it all you have to do is add "good old fashioned" to somethin', and you've got yourself a good time. Huh. Hey, I hope you saved the fitted sheet for me. It's fun to pretend it's a giant shower cap.

Grace: Are — are you okay?

Will: Yeah. Oh, I mean, I— I was in a lot of pain, but then, the doctor gave these painkillers, and I feel a lot better. About everything, actually. Mmm.

(*He tosses his keys into a bowl on the coffee table, but they land on the floor.*)

Will: Oh! No good.

(*He laughs and exits.*)

Grace: (*to Jack*) Wow. Cheery Will. I like it.

Jack: Unless he's cheery because he's back there loading his gun!

. . .

SCENE III: Interior hallway outside Will's apartment, Daytime.

(*Grace steps off the elevator as Jack sets up the cafe table by his apartment door.*)

Grace: Oh, Jack.

Jack: Hi, Grace.

Grace: Look, have you seen Will? I've been trying him for a couple of days, and he hasn't returned my calls.

Jack: Yeah, I think he's home.

Grace: He didn't go to work? Is he all right? Is his ankle worse?

Jack: Grace, I'm trying to run a business.

(*Grace enters Will's apartment. He's sitting on the love seat watching TV.*)

Will: Hey, sweetie! Look, TiVo saved all the "American Idols" for me. I love Paula Abdul. And I love that we live in a world that would give a Paula Abdul a second chance.

Grace: Why aren't you at work?

Will: Oh, I'm sick. My ankle still hurts. Yeah. Oh, oh, oh! Watch this. Wait, wait. (*singing*) Whoo-oh-whoo-oh. (*chuckles*) Another thing I love. Those little interstitials before they go to commercial. You know, like—like on "Sixty Minutes." (*moving his finger like a second hand*) Tick-tick-tick-tick-tick-tick-tick-tick-tick-tick-tick-tick-tick-tick-tick—

Grace: And stop. Are you okay?

Will: Never better. Oh, have you ever seen "King of Queens"? It's funny sometimes. But I don't really believe that she'd stay with him. . . . Or do I? No, I don't think I do. Well, I don't have to settle this right now. Oh, wait! I made cookies.

(*He moves to the table and offers her a cookie.*)

Grace: Oh, thanks, sweetie.

(*She crumbles a cookie onto the floor. He doesn't react.*)

Grace: (*flat*) Oh, boy. There's chocolate on the carpet. I'm sorry. What a mess.

Will: Ah, leave it.

Grace: Okay, don't! You're freakin' me out! There are crumbs on the carpet, your robe doesn't match your socks, and, oh my God, there's no product in your hair! I'm calling nine-one-one.

(He restrains her.)

Will: Alright, now, sweetie, sweetie. I'm fine. You know, I — I — I got those nice little pills. Oh, better call in a refill.

Grace: Already?

Will: Little secret. If you cheat and take 'em a little closer together, you can avoid the pain completely. It's even pretty effective in squashing the lingering ache from having to work so hard for my mother's affection, making it nearly impossible for any man to love me enough to make up for the hole she left in my heart. *(Chuckles.)*

(Grace reacts. Fade out.)

. . .

ACT II, SCENE II: Will's Apartment

(Will enters and looks through the pocket of his robe, which is hanging on a chair over his crutches.)

Will: Huh, that's weird.

(Grace pops up from behind the kitchen counter with a bottle of pills.)

Grace: Looking for these, Miss Taylor?°

Will: What're you doing here? Gimme those.

Grace: No. We're not going to let you do this to yourself. We think you have a problem, and we ate all your Mueslix.

Will: Who's we?

(Jack pops up from behind the counter. He is eating a bowl of cereal.)

Jack: We want to help you, Will.

Will: Get out of my apartment.

Grace: No. You have a problem. You have got to get off, gotta get off this merry-go-round.

Will: I want those pills! I have pain!

Jack: Effie, we all got pain!° Look, we understand. You're an elderly gay man with a poochy tummy and an unappealing personality. Why wouldn't you be in pain?

Will: I — Wait a minute, those aren't even my pills. Those are just old antibiotics.

Grace: They are?

(Will lunges for the pills. Grace gasps and pulls back.)

Grace: *(gasps)* Ooh!

Jack: No —

Grace: Crack whores are sneaky!

(Jack tries to restrain Will as he chases Grace around the apartment.)

Grace: No! No! No! Okay, look! These pills have become a crutch! And these crutches have become a coat rack!

Will: *(sighs)* Maybe you're right. Okay, we'll do it your way. *(They move to comfort*

Miss Taylor: Elizabeth Taylor (B. 1932), American actress and celebrity.

Effie . . . : Reference to a line from the Broadway musical *Dreamgirls*.

him.) I'll just, uh, bring in the paper and we'll make a pot of coffee and start a whole new day.

(*He exits. Grace sighs.*)

Jack: We're good friends.
Grace: It was smart of us to catch on.

(*They wait, then:*)

Grace: He's not comin' back, right?
Jack: No, no, I don't think so.

. . .

SCENE IV: Will's Apartment. Night.

(*Will is frantically searching the couch for pills.*)

Will: Come on, feelgood buddy. Know there's one in here.
Will: (*finding a pill*) Hah! Damn Tic Tacs! (*Will tosses the Tic Tac.*)

(*Grace and Jack enter.*)

Grace: Will, stop.
Will: Get outta here.
Jack: We are not leaving. The pain is in your head, Will! And now you're hooked on the junk.
Will: I fell off my clog!
Grace: At some point, every one falls off their clogs. You've got to get back on your clogs and work through the pain. And even though you may want to take off your clogs again, you gotta keep 'em on. And you gotta make a lotta noise when you walk. And — Okay, wait, how did I get into this?
Jack: Will, let me show you something. It's not gonna be pretty. Come on.

(*He leads Will to the mirror.*)

Jack: Come on, man. Look at yourself. Now look at me. I am adorable. Now back to you. You look awful!
Will: I look the same.
Jack: Out of my way. You're blocking my view. (*He pushes Will aside.*)
Grace: Will, you have to face it. You're not yourself. You haven't been to work in three days. You threw your dry cleaning on a chair. You told your mother that you'd call her back — and then you did.
Will: My God, what's happened to me?

(*Grace holds Will to her bosom.*)

Grace: It's okay. It's okay, *mamela.*°

(*Grace begins singing the Jewish song "Ma Nishtana."*)

Grace: (*singing*) Maneesh T'nah Hallilah Hazen Micallilah°. . .
Will: Where is that Tic Tac?

(*Fade out.*)

---

mamela: Sweetheart.

Maneesh . . . Micallilah: The first verse of the traditional song that opens the Passover Seder, which translates: Why is this night different from all other nights?

. . .

SCENE IV CONTINUED: Will's Apartment. Night

(*Will sits down on the couch flanked by Jack and Grace. He is in a terrycloth robe and is toweling off his freshly shampooed hair.*)

Grace: Feeling any better?

Will: Yeah. I'm sorry. I—I don't know what happened to me. I just—I was really out of control. But I guess I had to hit rock bottom before I could admit I had a problem.

Grace: Will, it was three days.

Will: Really? God I was so whacked out, it felt like a long weekend.

Grace: You know, maybe you try and control yourself too much and maybe if you lost it just a little bit every once in a while you wouldn't have it build up so much.

Jack: And—and then no one would have to die.

(*Will gives him a look. Fade out.*)

The End

CONSIDERATIONS FOR CRITICAL THINKING AND WRITING

1. **FIRST RESPONSE.** Discuss whether you think this subplot is more serious or comic. Which tone seems predominant? Why?

2. How does the exposition help to characterize Will in the first scene as Jack and Grace fold laundry?

3. Describe the initial conflict in the first scene. How is that conflict redefined and complicated in the subsequent scenes?

4. What effects do the painkillers have on Will's personality? How does Grace respond?

5. What kinds of pain do the painkillers suppress for Will? What sort of relationship does Will seem to have with his mother?

6. Discuss the function of the humor in the plot. How would your response to the theme differ if the humor were deleted?

7. Write a one-page analysis of the plot using the discussion that follows the *Seinfeld* script (pp. 1078–80) as your model.

8. **CRITICAL STRATEGIES.** Read the section on gender criticism (pp. 1548–49) in Chapter 46, "Critical Strategies for Reading," and discuss the treatment of Grace and Will's mother in the script. How are women and gay men depicted in the script? What is your response to those depictions?

CONNECTION TO ANOTHER SELECTION

1. What makes Jack in this script and George in *Seinfeld* amusing characters? How does humor reveal each character? Which character do you find more amusing? Why?

39

Writing about Drama

When you create drama, you look for
the best conflict.
— JANE ANDERSON

FROM READING TO WRITING

Because dramatic literature is written to be performed, writing about reading a play may seem twice removed from what playwrights intend the experience of drama to be: a live audience responding to live actors. Although
reading a play creates distance between yourself and a performance of it,
reading a play can actually bring you closer to understanding that what
supports a stage production of any play is the literary dimension of a
script. Writing about that script — examining carefully how the language
of the stage directions, setting, exposition, dialogue, plot, and other dramatic elements serve to produce effects and meanings — can enhance an
imaginative re-creation of a performance. In a sense, writing about a play
gauges your own interpretative response as an audience member — the difference, of course, is that instead of applauding, you are typing.

"There's the rub," as Hamlet might say, because you're working with
the precision of your fingertips rather than with the hearty response of
your palms. Composing an essay about drama records more than your

response to a play; writing also helps you explore, clarify, and discover dimensions of the play you may not have perceived by simply watching a performance of it. Writing is work, of course, but it's the kind of work that brings you closer to your own imagination as well as to the play. That process is more accessible if you read carefully, take notes, and annotate the text to generate ideas (for a discussion of this process see Chapter 47, "Reading and Writing"). This chapter offers a set of questions to help you read and write about drama and includes a sample paper that argues for a feminist reading of Susan Glaspell's *Trifles*.

Questions for Responsive Reading and Writing

The questions in this chapter can help you consider important elements that reveal a play's effects and meanings. These questions are general and will not, therefore, always be relevant to a particular play. Many of them, however, should prove to be useful for thinking, talking, and writing about drama. If you are uncertain about the meaning of a term used in a question, consult the Glossary of Literary Terms beginning on page 1619.

1. Did you enjoy the play? What, specifically, pleased or displeased you about what was expressed and how it was expressed?

2. What is the significance of the play's title? How does it suggest the author's overall emphasis?

3. What information do the stage directions provide about the characters, action, and setting? Are these directions primarily descriptive, or are they also interpretive?

4. How is the exposition presented? What does it reveal? How does the playwright's choice *not* to dramatize certain events on stage help to determine what the focus of the play is?

5. In what ways is the setting important? Would the play be altered significantly if the setting were changed?

6. Are foreshadowings used to suggest what is to come? Are flashbacks used to dramatize what has already happened?

7. What is the major conflict the protagonist faces? What complications constitute the rising action? Where is the climax? Is the conflict resolved?

8. Are one or more subplots used to qualify or complicate the main plot? Is the plot unified so that each incident somehow has a function that relates it to some other element in the play?

9. Does the author purposely avoid a pyramidal plot structure of rising action, climax, and falling action? Is the plot experimental? Is the plot logically and chronologically organized, or is it fantastical or absurd? What effects are produced by the plot? How does it reflect the author's view of life?

10. Who is the protagonist? Who (or what) is the antagonist?

(continued)

Questions for Responsive Reading and Writing

11. By what means does the playwright reveal character? What do the characters' names, physical qualities, actions, and words convey about them? What do the characters reveal about each other?

12. What is the purpose of the minor characters? Are they individualized, or do they primarily represent ideas or attitudes? Are any character foils used?

13. Do the characters all use the same kind of language, or is their speech differentiated? Is it formal or informal? How do the characters' diction and manner of speaking serve to characterize them?

14. Does your response to the characters change in the course of the play? What causes the change?

15. Are words and images repeated in the play so that they take on special meanings? Which speeches seem particularly important? Why?

16. How does the playwright's use of language contribute to the tone of the play? Is the dialogue, for example, predominantly light, humorous, relaxed, sentimental, sad, angry, intense, or violent?

17. Are any symbols used in the play? Which actions, characters, settings, objects, or words convey more than their literal meanings?

18. Are any unfamiliar theatrical conventions used that present problems in understanding the play? How does knowing more about the nature of the theater from which the play originated help to resolve these problems?

19. Is the theme stated directly, or is it developed implicitly through the plot, characters, or some other element? Does the theme confirm or challenge most people's values?

20. How does the play reflect the values of the society in which it is set and in which it was written?

21. How does the play reflect or challenge your own values?

22. Is there a recording, film, or videocassette of the play available in your library or media center? How does this version compare with your own reading?

23. How would you produce the play on a stage? Consider scenery, costumes, casting, and characterizations. What would you emphasize most in your production?

24. Is there a particular critical approach that seems especially appropriate for this play? (See Chapter 46, "Critical Strategies for Reading," which begins on p. 1533.)

25. How might biographical information about the author help the reader to grasp the central concerns of the play?

26. How might historical information about the play provide a useful context for interpretation?

27. To what extent do your own experiences, values, beliefs, and assumptions inform your interpretation?

28. What kinds of evidence from the play are you focusing on to support your interpretation? Does your interpretation leave out any important elements that might undercut or qualify your interpretation?

29. Given that there are a variety of ways to interpret the play, which one seems the most useful to you?

A SAMPLE STUDENT PAPER

The Feminist Evidence in Susan Glaspell's Trifles

The following paper was written in response to an assignment that required an analysis — about 750 words — of an assigned play. Chris Duffy's paper argues that although *Trifles* was written over ninety years ago, it should be seen as a feminist play because its treatment of the tensions between men and women deliberately reveals the oppressiveness that women have had to cope with in their everyday lives. The paper discusses a number of the play's elements, but the discussion is unified through its focus on how the women characters are bound together by a set of common concerns. Notice that page numbers are provided to document quoted passages.

Duffy 1

Chris Duffy

Professor Barrina-Barrou

English 109-2

October 6, 2008

The Feminist Evidence in Susan Glaspell's Trifles

Despite its early publication date, Susan Glaspell's Trifles (1916) can be regarded as a work of feminist literature. The play depicts the life of a woman who has been suppressed, oppressed, and subjugated by a patronizing, patriarchal husband. Mrs. Wright is eventually driven to kill her "hard" (Glaspell 1048) husband who has stifled every last twitch of her identity. Trifles dramatizes the hypocrisy and ingrained discrimination of male-dominated society while simultaneously speaking to the dangers for women who succumb to such hierarchies. Because Mrs. Wright follows the role mapped by her husband and is directed by society's patriarchal expectations, her identity is lost somewhere along the way. However, Mrs. Hale and Mrs. Peters quietly insist on preserving their own identities by protecting Mrs. Wright from the men who seek to convict her of murder.

    Mrs. Wright is described as someone who used to have a flair for life. Her neighbor, Mrs. Hale, comments that the last time Mrs. Wright appeared happy and vivacious was before she was married or, more important, when

[margin notes:]
General thesis statement

More specific thesis offering analysis, with supporting evidence

Analysis of Mrs. Wright through perspectives of female characters she was Minnie Foster and not Mrs. Wright. Mrs. Hale laments, "I heard she used to wear pretty clothes and be lively, when she was Minnie Foster, one of the town girls singing in the choir" (1052). But after thirty years of marriage, Mrs. Wright is now worried about her canned preserves freezing and being without an apron while she is in jail. This subservient image was so accepted in society that Mrs. Peters, the sheriff's wife, speculates that Mrs. Wright must want her apron in order to "feel more natural" (1052). Any other roles would be considered uncharacteristic.

Analysis of role of women through perspectives of male characters

This wifely role is predicated on the supposition that women have no ability to make complicated decisions, to think critically, or to rely on themselves. As the title suggests, the men in this story think of homemaking as much less important than a husband's breadwinning role. Mr. Hale remarks, "Well, women are used to worrying over trifles" (1051), and Sheriff Peters assumes the insignificance of "kitchen things" (1050). Hence, women are forced into a domestic, secondary role, like it or not, and are not even respected for that. Mr. Hale, Sheriff Peters, and the county attorney all dismiss the dialogue between Mrs. Peters and Mrs. Hale as feminine chitchat. Further, the county attorney allows the women to leave the Wrights' house unsupervised because he sees Mrs. Peters as merely an extension of her husband.

Even so, the domestic system the men have set up for their wives and their disregard for them after the rules and boundaries have been laid down prove to be the men's downfall. The evidence that Mrs. Wright killed her husband is woven into Mrs. Hale's and Mrs. Peters's conversations about Mrs. Wright's sewing and her pet bird. The knots in her quilt match those in the rope used to strangle Mr. Wright, and the bird, the last symbol of Mrs. Wright's vitality to be taken by her husband, is found dead. Unable to play the role of subservient wife anymore, Mrs. Wright is foreign to herself and therefore lives a lie. As Mrs. Hale proclaims, "Why, it looks as if she didn't know what she was about!" (1053).

Discussion of Mrs. Hale's identification with Mrs. Wright

Mrs. Hale, however, does ultimately understand what Mrs. Wright is about. She comprehends the desperation, loneliness, and pain that Mrs. Wright experienced, and she instinctively knows that the roles Mrs. Wright played--even that of murderer--are scripted by the male-dominated circum-

Duffy 3

stances of her life. As Mrs. Hale shrewdly and covertly observes in the context
of a discussion about housecleaning with the county attorney: "Men's hands
aren't always as clean as they might be" (1051). In fact, even Mrs. Hale feels
some guilt for not having made an effort to visit Mrs. Wright over the years
to help relieve the monotony of Mrs. Wright's life with her husband:

> I might have known she needed help! I know how things can
> be--for women. I tell you, it's queer, Mrs. Peters. We live close
> together and we live far apart. We all go through the same
> things--it's all just a different kind of the same thing. (1056)

Mrs. Hale cannot help identifying with her neighbor.

In contrast, Mrs. Peters is initially reluctant to support Mrs. Wright.
Not only is she married to the sheriff, but, as the county attorney puts it, "a
sheriff's wife is married to the law" (1056) as well. She reminds Mrs. Hale that
"the law has got to punish crime" (1056), even if it means revealing the existence of the dead bird and exposing the motive that could convict Mrs. Wright
of murdering her husband. But finally Mrs. Peters also becomes complicit in
keeping information from her husband and other men. She too--owing to the
loss of her first child--understands what loss means and what Mrs. Hale
means when she says that women "all go through the same things" (1056).

Discussion of Mrs. Peters's identification with Mrs. Wright

The women in Trifles cannot, as the play reveals, be trifled with.
Although Glaspell wrote the play over ninety years ago, it continues to be
relevant to contemporary relationships between men and women. Its essentially feminist perspective provides a convincing case for the necessity of
women to move beyond destructive stereotypes and oppressive assumptions
in order to be true to their own significant--not trifling--experiences.

Conclusion summarizing analysis

Duffy 4

Work Cited

Glaspell, Susan. "Trifles." The Compact Bedford Introduction to Literature.
    Ed. Michael Meyer. 8th ed. Boston: Bedford/St. Martin's, 2009.
    1048–57.

40

A Study of Sophocles

I depict men as they ought to be . . .
—SOPHOCLES

Not all things are to be discovered;
many are better concealed.
—SOPHOCLES

Sophocles lived a long, productive life (496?–406 B.C.) in Athens. During his life Athens became a dominant political and cultural power after the Persian Wars, but before he died Sophocles witnessed the decline of Athens as a result of the Peloponnesian Wars and the city's subsequent surrender to Sparta. He saw Athenian culture reach remarkable heights as well as collapse under enormous pressures.

Sophocles embodied much of the best of Athenian culture; he enjoyed success as a statesman, general, treasurer, priest, and, of course, prize-winning dramatist. Although surviving fragments indicate that he wrote over 120 plays, only a handful remain intact. Those that survive consist of the three plays he wrote about Oedipus and his children — *Oedipus the King, Oedipus at Colonus,* and *Antigone* — and four additional tragedies: *Philoctetes, Ajax, Maidens of Trachis,* and *Electra.*

His plays won numerous prizes at festival competitions because of his careful, subtle plotting and the sense of inevitability with which their action is charged. Moreover, his development of character is richly complex. Instead of relying on the extreme situations and exaggerated actions

Explore contexts for Sophocles on *LiterActive* or at bedfordstmartins.com/ meyercompact.

that earlier tragedians used, Sophocles created powerfully motivated characters who even today fascinate audiences with their psychological depth.

In addition to crafting sophisticated tragedies for the Greek theater, Sophocles introduced several important innovations to the stage. Most important, he broke the tradition of using only two actors; adding a third resulted in more complicated relationships and intricate dialogue among characters. As individual actors took center stage more often, Sophocles reduced the role of the chorus (discussed on p. 1096). This shift placed even more emphasis on the actors, although the chorus remained important as a means of commenting on the action and establishing its tone. Sophocles was also the

Map of Ancient Greece. During Sophocles' time, the city-state of Athens (center, left) was the leading cultural and intellectual center of Greece — until the Peloponnesian Wars (431 B.C.–404 B.C.) and Athens's defeat in 404 B.C. by the city-state of Sparta (below Athens, to the left).

first dramatist to write plays with specific actors in mind, a development that many later playwrights, including Shakespeare, exploited usefully. But without question Sophocles' greatest contribution to drama was *Oedipus the King*, which, it has been argued, is the most influential drama ever written.

THEATRICAL CONVENTIONS OF GREEK DRAMA

More than twenty-four hundred years have passed since 430 B.C., when Sophocles' *Oedipus the King* was probably first produced on a Greek stage. We inhabit a vastly different planet than Sophocles' audience did, yet concerns about what it means to be human in a world that frequently runs counter to our desires and aspirations have remained relatively constant. The ancient Greeks continue to speak to us. But inexperienced readers or viewers may have some initial difficulty understanding the theatrical conventions used in classical Greek tragedies such as *Oedipus the King* and *Antigone*. If Sophocles were alive today, he would very likely need some sort of assistance with the conventions of an Arthur Miller play or a television production of *Seinfeld*.

Classical Greek drama developed from religious festivals that paid homage to Dionysus, the god of wine and fertility. Most of the details of these festivals have been lost, but we do know that they included dancing and singing that celebrated legends about Dionysus. From these choral songs developed stories of both Dionysus and mortal culture-heroes. These heroes became the subject of playwrights whose works were produced in contests at the festivals. The Dionysian festivals lasted more than five hundred years, but relatively few of their plays have survived. Among the works of the three great writers of tragedy, only seven plays each by Sophocles and Aeschylus (525?–456 B.C.) and nineteen plays by Euripides (480?–406 B.C.) survive.

Plays were such important events in Greek society that they were partially funded by the state. The Greeks associated drama with religious and community values as well as entertainment. In a sense, their plays celebrate their civilization; in approving the plays, audiences applauded their own culture. The enormous popularity of the plays is indicated by the size of surviving amphitheaters. Although information about these theaters is sketchy, we do know that most of them had a common form. They were built into hillsides with rising rows of seats accommodating more than fourteen thousand people. These seats partially encircled an **orchestra** or "dancing place," where the **chorus** of a dozen or so men chanted lines and danced.

Tradition credits the Greek poet Thespis with adding an actor who was separate from the choral singing and dancing of early performances. A second actor was subsequently included by Aeschylus and a third, as noted earlier, by Sophocles. These additions made possible the conflicts and complicated relationships that evolved into the dramatic art we know today. The two or three male actors who played all the roles appeared behind the orchestra in front of the **skene,** a stage building that served as dressing rooms. As Greek theater evolved, a wall of the skene came to be painted to suggest a palace or some other setting, and the roof was employed to indicate, for instance, a mountain location. Sometimes gods were lowered from the roof by mechanical devices to set matters right among the mortals below. This method of rescuing characters from complications beyond their abilities to resolve was known in Latin as **deus ex machina** ("god from the machine"), a term now used to describe any improbable means by which an author provides a too-easy resolution for a story.

Inevitably, the conventions of the Greek theaters affected how plays were presented. Few if any scene changes occurred because the amphitheater stage was set primarily for one location. If an important event happened somewhere else, it was reported by a minor character, such as a messenger. The chorus also provided necessary background information. In *Oedipus the King* and *Antigone,* the choruses, acting as townspeople, also assess the characters' strengths and weaknesses, praising them for their virtues, chiding them for their rashness, and giving them advice. The reactions of the chorus provide a connection between actors and audience because the chorus is at once a participant in and an observer of the action. In addition, the chorus helps structure the action by indicating changes in scene or mood. Thus the chorus could be used in a variety of ways to shape the audience's response to the play's action and characters.

Actors in classical Greek amphitheaters faced considerable challenges. An intimate relationship with the audience was impossible because many spectators would have been too far away to see a facial expression or subtle gesture. Indeed, some in the audience would have had difficulty even hearing the voices of individual actors. To compensate for these disadvantages, actors wore large masks that extravagantly expressed the major characters' emotions or identified the roles of minor characters. The masks also allowed the two or three actors in a performance to play all the characters without confusing the audience. Each mask was fitted so that the mouthpiece amplified the actor's voice. The actors were further equipped with padded costumes and elevated shoes (**cothurni** or **buskins**) that made them appear larger than life.

As a result of these adaptive conventions, Greek plays tend to emphasize words — formal, impassioned speeches — more than physical action. We are invited to ponder actions and events rather than to see all of them enacted. Although the stark simplicity of Greek theater does not offer an audience realistic detail, the classical tragedies that have survived present characters in dramatic situations that transcend theatrical conventions. Tragedy, it seems, has always been compelling for human beings, regardless of the theatrical forms it has taken.

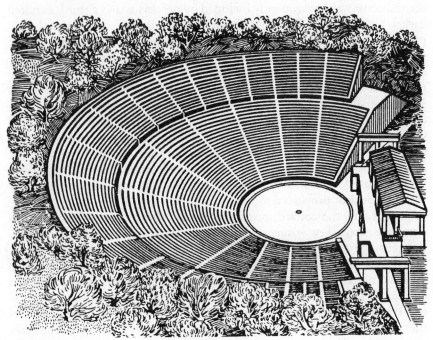

Classical Greek Theater. Based on scholarly sources, this drawing represents the features typical of a classical theater. (Drawing by Gerda Becker. From Kenneth Macgowan and William Melnitz, *The Living Stage,* © 1990 by Prentice Hall / A Division of Simon & Schuster.)

A Greek tragedy is typically divided into five parts: prologue, parodos, episodia, stasimon, and exodus. In some translations these terms appear as headings, but in more recent translations, as those by Robert Fagles included here, the headings do not appear. Still, understanding these terms provides a sense of the overall rhythm of a Greek play. The opening speech or dialogue is known as the ***prologue*** and usually gives the exposition necessary to follow the subsequent action. In the ***parodos*** the chorus makes its first entrance and gives its perspective on what the audience has learned in the prologue. Several ***episodia,*** or episodes, follow, in which characters engage in dialogue that frequently consists of heated debates dramatizing the play's conflicts. Following each episode is a choral ode, or ***stasimon,*** in which the chorus responds to and interprets the preceding dialogue. The ***exodus,*** or last scene, follows the final episode and stasimon; in it the resolution occurs and the characters leave the stage.

The effect of alternating dialogues and choral odes has sometimes been likened to that of opera. Greek tragedies were written in verse, and the stasima were chanted or sung as the chorus moved rhythmically, so the plays have a strong musical element that is not always apparent on the printed page. If we remember their musical qualities we are less likely to forget that no matter how terrifying or horrific the conflicts they describe, these plays are stately, measured, and dignified works that reflect a classical Greek sense of order and proportion.

TRAGEDY

Newspapers are filled with daily reports of tragedies: a child is struck and crippled by a car; an airplane plunges into a suburban neighborhood; a volcano erupts and kills thousands. These unexpected instances of suffering are commonly and accurately described as tragic, but they are not tragedies in the literary sense of the term. A literary **tragedy** presents courageous individuals who confront powerful forces within or outside themselves with a dignity that reveals the breadth and depth of the human spirit in the face of failure, defeat, and even death.

Aristotle (384–322 B.C.), in his *Poetics,* defined *tragedy* on the basis of the plays contemporary to him. His definition has generated countless variations, qualifications, and interpretations, but we still derive our literary understanding of this term from Aristotle.

The protagonist of a Greek tragedy is someone regarded as extraordinary rather than typical: a great man or woman brought from happiness to agony. The character's stature is important because it makes his or her fall all the more terrifying. The protagonist also carries mythic significance for the audience. Oedipus and Antigone, for example, are not only human beings but legendary figures from a distant, revered past. Although the gods do not appear onstage in either *Oedipus the King* or *Antigone,* their power is ever present as the characters invoke their help or attempt to defy them. In addition, Greek tragedy tends to be public rather than private. The fate of the community—the state—is often linked with that of the protagonist, as when Thebes suffers a plague as a result of Oedipus's mistaken actions.

The protagonists of classical Greek tragedies (and of those of Shakespeare) are often rulers of noble birth who represent the monarchical values of their periods, but in modern tragedies the protagonists are more likely to reflect democratic values that make it possible for anyone to be a suitable subject. What is finally important is not so much the protagonist's social stature as a greatness of character that steadfastly confronts suffering, whether it comes from supernatural, social, or psychological forces. Although Greek tragic heroes were aristocrats, the nobility of their characters was more significant than their inherited titles and privileges.

The protagonist's eminence and determination to complete some task or goal make him or her admirable in Greek tragedy, but that does not free the protagonist from what Aristotle described as "some error or frailty" that brings about his or her misfortune. The term Aristotle used for this weakness is **hamartia.** This word has frequently been interpreted to mean that the protagonist's fall is the result of an internal **tragic flaw,** such as an excess of pride, ambition, passion, or some other character trait that leads directly to disaster.

Sometimes, however, misfortunes are not the result of a character flaw but of misunderstood events that overtake and thwart the protagonist's best intentions. Thus, virtue can lead to tragedy too. *Hamartia* has also been interpreted to mean "wrong act"—a mistake based not on a personal failure but on circumstances outside the protagonist's personality and control. Many readers find that a combination of these two interpretations sheds the most light on the causes of the tragic protagonist's fall. Both internal and external forces can lead to downfall because the protagonist's personality may determine crucial judgments that result in mistaken actions.

However the idea of tragic flaw is understood, it is best not to use it as a means of reducing the qualities of a complex character to an adjective or two that labels Oedipus as guilty of "overweening pride" (the Greek term for which is **hubris** or **hybris**) or Antigone as "fated." The protagonists of tragedies require more careful characterization than a simplistic label can provide.

Whatever the causes of the tragic protagonist's downfall, he or she accepts responsibility for it. Hence, even in his or her encounter with failure (and possibly death) the tragic protagonist displays greatness of character. Perhaps it is the witnessing of this greatness, which seems both to accept and to transcend human limitations, that makes audiences feel relief rather than hopelessness at the end of a tragedy. Aristotle described this response as a **catharsis,** or purgation of the emotions of "pity and fear." We are faced with the protagonist's misfortune, which often seems out of proportion to his or her actions, and so we are likely to feel compassionate pity. Simultaneously, we may experience fear because the failure of the protagonist, who is so great in stature and power, is a frightening reminder of our own vulnerabilities. Ultimately, however, both these negative emotions are purged because the tragic protagonist's suffering is an affirmation of human values — even if they are not always triumphant — rather than a despairing denial of them.

Nevertheless, tragedies are disturbing. Instead of coming away with the reassurance of a happy ending, we must take solace in the insight produced by the hero's suffering. And just as our expectations are changed, so are the protagonist's. Aristotle described the moment in the plot when this change occurs as a **reversal** (*peripeteia*), the point when the hero's fortunes turn in an unexpected direction. He more specifically defined this term as meaning an action performed by a character that has the opposite of its intended effect. An example cited by Aristotle is the messenger's attempts to relieve Oedipus's anxieties about his relationship to his father and mother. Instead, the messenger reveals previously unknown information that eventually results in a **recognition** (*anagnorisis*); Oedipus discovers the terrible truth that he has killed his father and married his mother.

Tragedy is typically filled with ironies because there are so many moments in the plot when what seems to be turns out to be radically different from what actually is. Because of this, a particular form of irony called **dramatic irony** is also known as **tragic irony**. In dramatic irony, the meaning of a character's words or actions is understood by the audience but not by the character. Audiences of Greek tragedy shared with the playwrights a knowledge of the stories on which many tragic plots were based. Consequently, they frequently were aware of what was going to happen before the characters were. When Oedipus declares that he will seek out the person responsible for the plague that ravishes his city, the audience already knows that the person Oedipus pursues is himself.

Oedipus the King

A familiarity with the Oedipus legend allows modern readers to appreciate the series of ironies that unfolds in Sophocles' *Oedipus the King*. In the opening scene, Oedipus appears with a "telltale limp." As an infant, he had been abandoned by his parents, Laius and Jocasta, the king and queen of Thebes, because a prophecy warned that their son would kill his father and marry his mother. They instructed a servant to leave him on a mountain to die. The infant's feet were pierced and pinned together, but he was not left on the mountain; instead the servant, out of pity, gave him to a shepherd, who in turn presented him to the king and queen of Corinth. They named him Oedipus (for "swollen foot") and raised him as their own son.

On reaching manhood, Oedipus learned from an oracle that he would kill his father and marry his mother; to avoid this horrendous fate, he left Corinth forever. In his travels, Oedipus found his way blocked by a chariot at a crossroads; in a fit of anger, he killed the servants and their passenger. That passenger, unknown to Oedipus, was his real father. In Thebes, Oedipus successfully answered the riddle of the Sphinx, a winged lion with a woman's head. The reward for defeating this dreaded monster was both the crown and the dead king's wife. Oedipus and Jocasta had four children and prospered. But when the play begins, Oedipus's rule is troubled by a plague that threatens to destroy Thebes, and he is determined to find the cause of the plague in order to save the city again.

Oedipus the King is widely recognized as the greatest of the surviving Greek tragedies. Numerous translations are available (Robert Fagles's recent highly regarded translations of *Oedipus the King* and *Antigone*, the choice here, are especially accessible to modern readers. For an excerpt from another version of *Oedipus the King*, see Perspectives on Sophocles, p. 1148). The play has absorbed readers for centuries because Oedipus's character — his intelligence, confidence, rashness, and suffering — represents powers and limitations that are both exhilarating and chastening. Although no reader or viewer is likely to identify with Oedipus's extreme circumstances, anyone can appreciate his heroic efforts to find the truth about himself. In that sense, he is one of us — at our best.

SOPHOCLES (496?–406 B.C.)

Oedipus the King

c. 430 B.C.

TRANSLATED BY ROBERT FAGLES

CHARACTERS

Oedipus, king of Thebes
A Priest of Zeus
Creon, brother of Jocasta
A Chorus of Theban citizens and their *Leader*
Tiresias, a blind prophet
Jocasta, the queen, wife of Oedipus
A Messenger from Corinth
A Shepherd
A Messenger from inside the palace
Antigone, Ismene, daughters of Oedipus and Jocasta
Guards and attendants
Priests of Thebes

See Plays in Performance insert.

TIME AND SCENE: The royal house of Thebes. Double doors dominate the facade; a stone altar stands at the center of the stage.

Many years have passed since Oedipus solved the riddle of the Sphinx and ascended the throne of Thebes, and now a plague has struck the city. A procession of priests enters; suppliants, broken and despondent, they carry branches wound in wool and lay them on the altar.

The doors open. Guards assemble. Oedipus comes forward, majestic but for a telltale limp, and slowly views the condition of his people.

Oedipus: Oh my children, the new blood of ancient Thebes,
    why are you here? Huddling at my altar,
    praying before me, your branches wound in wool.°
    Our city reeks with the smoke of burning incense,
    rings with cries for the Healer and wailing for the dead.   5
    I thought it wrong, my children, to hear the truth
    from others, messengers. Here I am myself—
    you all know me, the world knows my fame:
    I am Oedipus.

    Helping a Priest to his feet.

                Speak up, old man. Your years,
    your dignity—you should speak for the others.   10
    Why here and kneeling, what preys upon you so?
    Some sudden fear? some strong desire?
    You can trust me; I am ready to help,
    I'll do anything. I would be blind to misery
    not to pity my people kneeling at my feet.   15

3 *wool:* Wool was used in offerings to Apollo, god of poetry, the sun, prophecy, and healing.

Oedipus the King: At center stage is Jocasta (Ching Valdes/Aran) in a scene from the 1993 production of *Oedipus the King* (p. 1102) at Philadelphia's Wilma Theater, directed by Blanka Zizka and Jiri Zizka. © T. Charles Erikson.

Othello (above): Orson Welles and Suzanne Cloutier, in a scene from the 1952 film adaptation of *Othello* (p. 1164), directed by Welles.
© Films Marceau/Mercury Productions/The Kobal Collection

O (top right): Julia Stiles and Mekhi Phifer in the 2001 film *O*, an adaptation of the play *Othello*, directed by Tim Blake Nelson. In the film, "O" (short for Odin, the Othello character), is a star basketball player at an all-white prep school in Charleston, South Carolina.
© Miramax/Dimension Films/Kobal Collection/Bob Basha.

Othello (bottom right): Irene Jacob and Laurence Fishburne in the 1995 film *Othello*, directed by Oliver Parker. © Konow Rolf/CORBIS Sygma.

A Doll House (top left): Owen Teale and Janet McTeer in the 1997 Bill Kenwright London production of *A Doll House* (p. 1257) performed at New York's Belasco Theater — winner of the 1997 Tony Award for Best Revival of a Play.
© Joan Marcus.

The Glass Menagerie (bottom left): Amanda (Ruby Dee) and Tom (Jonathan Earl Peck) in the 1989 Arena Stage production of *The Glass Menagerie* (p. 1438).
© Joan Marcus.

Death of a Salesman (above): Willy (Lee J. Cobb) with sons Happy (Cameron Mitchell) and Biff (Arthur Kennedy) in *Death of a Salesman* (p. 1372). W. Eugene Smith, *Life Magazine*, © 1949 Time Inc.

Playwriting 101 (above): A scene from the 2003 Kaleidoscope Theatre Company production (New York) of Rich Orloff's *Playwriting 101* (p. 1352).
Photo by Rick Tormone.

Rodeo (right): Margo Martindale in *Rodeo* (p. 1369), during the Sixth Annual Humana Festival of New American Plays, at the Actor's Theatre of Louisville, Kentucky, in 1982.
Katherine Wisniewski, photographer.
Courtesy of the Actor's Theatre of Louisville.

Will & Grace (above): Eric McCormack and Debra Messing in the television series *Will & Grace* (p. 1083), 2003.
NBC/Kobal Collection/Chris Haston.

Mambo Mouth (left): John Leguizamo as Pepe in the 1988 HBO production of *Mambo Mouth* (p. 1349).
© David Hughes.

Old Saybrook: A scene from the 2003 Atlantic Theater Company production of Woody Allen's *Old Saybrook* (p. 1327), part of his *Writer's Block* comedies. Shown here, left to right, are Richard Portnow, Jay Thomas, Grant Shand, Bebe Neuwirth, Christopher Evan Welch, and Heather Burn.

Photo by Carol Rosegg.

Priest: Oh Oedipus, king of the land, our greatest power!
　　　You see us before you, men of all ages
　　　clinging to your altars. Here are boys,
　　　still too weak to fly from the nest,
　　　and here the old, bowed down with the years,　　　　　　20
　　　the holy ones—a priest of Zeus° myself—and here
　　　the picked, unmarried men, the young hope of Thebes.
　　　And all the rest, your great family gathers now,
　　　branches wreathed, massing in the squares,
　　　kneeling before the two temples of queen Athena°　　　25
　　　or the river-shrine where the embers glow and die
　　　and Apollo sees the future in the ashes.
　　　　　　　　　　　　　　　　　Our city—
　　　look around you, see with your own eyes—
　　　our ship pitches wildly, cannot lift her head
　　　from the depths, the red waves of death . . .　　　　　30
　　　Thebes is dying. A blight on the fresh crops
　　　and the rich pastures, cattle sicken and die,
　　　and the women die in labor, children stillborn,
　　　and the plague, the fiery god of fever hurls down
　　　on the city, his lightning slashing through us—　　　35
　　　raging plague in all its vengeance, devastating
　　　the house of Cadmus!° And Black Death luxuriates
　　　in the raw, wailing miseries of Thebes.

　　　Now we pray to you. You cannot equal the gods,
　　　your children know that, bending at your altar.
　　　But we do rate you first of men,　　　　　　　　　　40
　　　both in the common crises of our lives
　　　and face-to-face encounters with the gods.
　　　You freed us from the Sphinx; you came to Thebes
　　　and cut us loose from the bloody tribute we had paid
　　　that harsh, brutal singer. We taught you nothing,　　45
　　　no skill, no extra knowledge, still you triumphed.
　　　A god was with you, so they say, and we believe it—
　　　you lifted up our lives.
　　　　　　　　　　　So now again,
　　　Oedipus, king, we bend to you, your power—　　　　50
　　　we implore you, all of us on our knees:
　　　find us strength, rescue! Perhaps you've heard
　　　the voice of a god or something from other men,
　　　Oedipus . . . what do you know?
　　　The man of experience—you see it every day—　　　55
　　　his plans will work in a crisis, his first of all.
　　　Act now—we beg you, best of men, raise up our city!
　　　Act, defend yourself, your former glory!
　　　Your country calls you savior now

---

21 *Zeus:* The highest Olympian deity and father of Apollo.　　25 *Athena:* Goddess of wisdom and protector of Greek cities.　　37 *Cadmus:* The legendary founder of Thebes.

for your zeal, your action years ago.   60
Never let us remember of your reign:
you helped us stand, only to fall once more.
Oh raise up our city, set us on our feet.
The omens were good that day you brought us joy—
be the same man today!   65
Rule our land, you know you have the power,
but rule a land of the living, not a wasteland.
Ship and towered city are nothing, stripped of men
alive within it, living all as one.

Oedipus: My children,
I pity you. I see—how could I fail to see   70
what longings bring you here? Well I know
you are sick to death, all of you,
but sick as you are, not one is sick as I.
Your pain strikes each of you alone, each
in the confines of himself, no other. But my spirit   75
grieves for the city, for myself and all of you.
I wasn't asleep, dreaming. You haven't wakened me—
I've wept through the nights, you must know that,
groping, laboring over many paths of thought.
After a painful search I found one cure: 80
I acted at once. I sent Creon,
my wife's own brother, to Delphi°—
Apollo the Prophet's oracle—to learn
what I might do or say to save our city.

Today's the day. When I count the days gone by   85
it torments me . . . what is he doing?
Strange, he's late, he's gone too long.
But once he returns, then, then I'll be a traitor
if I do not do all the god makes clear.

Priest: Timely words. The men over there   90
are signaling—Creon's just arriving.

Oedipus:

Sighting Creon, then turning to the altar.

                                    Lord Apollo,
let him come with a lucky word of rescue,
shining like his eyes!

Priest: Welcome news, I think—he's crowned, look,
and the laurel wreath is bright with berries.   95

Oedipus: We'll soon see. He's close enough to hear—

Enter Creon from the side; his face is shaded with a wreath.

Creon, prince, my kinsman, what do you bring us?
What message from the god?

82 *Delphi:* The shrine where the oracle of Apollo held forth.

Creon: Good news.
    I tell you even the hardest things to bear,
    if they should turn out well, all would be well.   100
Oedipus: Of course, but what were the god's *words*? There's no hope
    and nothing to fear in what you've said so far.
Creon: If you want my report in the presence of these . . .

    Pointing to the priests while drawing Oedipus toward the palace.

    I'm ready now, or we might go inside.
Oedipus: Speak out,
    speak to us all. I grieve for these, my people,   105
    far more than I fear for my own life.
Creon: Very well,
    I will tell you what I heard from the god.
    Apollo commands us — he was quite clear —
    "Drive the corruption from the land,
    don't harbor it any longer, past all cure,   110
    don't nurse it in your soil — root it out!"
Oedipus: How can we cleanse ourselves — what rites?
    What's the source of the trouble?
Creon: Banish the man, or pay back blood with blood.
    Murder sets the plague-storm on the city.
Oedipus: Whose murder?   115
    Whose fate does Apollo bring to light?
Creon: Our leader,
    my lord, was once a man named Laius,
    before you came and put us straight on course.
Oedipus: I know —
    or so I've heard. I never saw the man myself.
Creon: Well, he was killed, and Apollo commands us now —   120
    he could not be more clear,
    "Pay the killers back — whoever is responsible."
Oedipus: Where on earth are they? Where to find it now,
    the trail of the ancient guilt so hard to trace?
Creon: "Here in Thebes," he said.
    Whatever is sought for can be caught, you know,   125
    whatever is neglected slips away.
Oedipus: But where,
    in the palace, the fields or foreign soil,
    where did Laius meet his bloody death?
Creon: He went to consult an oracle, he said,   130
    and he set out and never came home again.
Oedipus: No messenger, no fellow-traveler saw what happened?
    Someone to cross-examine?
Creon: No,
    they were all killed but one. He escaped,
    terrified, he could tell us nothing clearly,   135
    nothing of what he saw — just one thing.
Oedipus: What's that?

One thing could hold the key to it all,
a small beginning gives us grounds for hope.

Creon: He said thieves attacked them — a whole band,
not single-handed, cut King Laius down.

Oedipus: A thief,   140
so daring, wild, he'd kill a king? Impossible,
unless conspirators paid him off in Thebes.

Creon: We suspected as much. But with Laius dead
no leader appeared to help us in our troubles.

Oedipus: Trouble? Your *king* was murdered — royal blood!   145
What stopped you from tracking down the killer
then and there?

Creon: The singing, riddling Sphinx.
She . . . persuaded us to let the mystery go
and concentrate on what lay at our feet.

Oedipus: No,
I'll start again — I'll bring it all to light myself!   150
Apollo is right, and so are you, Creon,
to turn our attention back to the murdered man.
Now you have *me* to fight for you, you'll see:
I am the land's avenger by all rights
and Apollo's champion too.   155
But not to assist some distant kinsman, no,
for my own sake I'll rid us of this corruption.
Whoever killed the king may decide to kill me too,
with the same violent hand — by avenging Laius
I defend myself.

To the priests.

                    Quickly, my children.   160
Up from the steps, take up your branches now.

To the guards.

One of you summon the city here before us,
tell them I'll do everything. God help us,
we will see our triumph — or our fall.

Oedipus and Creon enter the palace, followed by the guards.

Priest: Rise, my sons. The kindness we came for   165
Oedipus volunteers himself.
Apollo has sent his word, his oracle —
Come down, Apollo, save us, stop the plague.

The priests rise, remove their branches, and exit to the side. Enter a Chorus, the citizens of Thebes, who have not heard the news that Creon brings. They march around the altar, chanting.

Chorus: Zeus!
Great welcome voice of Zeus, what do you bring?
What word from the gold vaults of Delphi   170
comes to brilliant Thebes? I'm racked with terror —
                    terror shakes my heart

and I cry your wild cries, Apollo, Healer of Delos°
I worship you in dread . . . what now, what is your price?
some new sacrifice? some ancient rite from the past   175
come round again each spring? —
              what will you bring to birth?
Tell me, child of golden Hope
       warm voice that never dies!

You are the first I call, daughter of Zeus   180
deathless Athena — I call your sister Artemis,°
heart of the market place enthroned in glory,
                    guardian of our earth —
I call Apollo astride the thunderheads of heaven —
O triple shield against death, shine before me now!   185
If ever, once in the past, you stopped some ruin
launched against our walls
              you hurled the flame of pain
far, far from Thebes — you gods
       come now, come down once more!

                              No, no   190
the miseries numberless, grief on grief, no end —
too much to bear, we are all dying
O my people . . .
       Thebes like a great army dying
and there is no sword of thought to save us, no   195
and the fruits of our famous earth, they will not ripen
no and the women cannot scream their pangs to birth —
screams for the Healer, children dead in the womb
              and life on life goes down
                    you can watch them go   200
       like seabirds winging west, outracing the day's fire
down the horizon, irresistibly
              streaking on to the shores of Evening
                              Death
so many deaths, numberless deaths on deaths, no end —
Thebes is dying, look, her children   205
stripped of pity . . .
       generations strewn on the ground
unburied, unwept, the dead spreading death
and the young wives and gray-haired mothers with them
cling to the altars, trailing in from all over the city —   210
Thebes, city of death, one long cortege
       and the suffering rises
              wails for mercy rise
       and the wild hymn for the Healer blazes out
clashing with our sobs our cries of mourning —   215

---

173 *Delos:* Apollo was born on this sacred island.   181 *Artemis:* Apollo's sister, goddess of
hunting, the moon, and chastity.

O golden daughter of god, send rescue
radiant as the kindness in your eyes!
Drive him back! — the fever, the god of death
               that raging god of war
not armored in bronze, not shielded now, he burns me,   220
battle cries in the onslaught burning on —
O rout him from our borders!
Sail him, blast him out to the Sea-queen's chamber
             the black Atlantic gulfs
   or the northern harbor, death to all   225
where the Thracian surf comes crashing.
Now what the night spares he comes by day and kills —
the god of death.

          O lord of the stormcloud,
you who twirl the lightning, Zeus, Father,
thunder Death to nothing!   230

Apollo, lord of the light, I beg you —
        whip your longbow's golden cord
showering arrows on our enemies — shafts of power
champions strong before us rushing on!

Artemis, Huntress,   235
torches flaring over the eastern ridges —
          ride Death down in pain!

God of the headdress gleaming gold, I cry to you —
your name and ours are one, Dionysus° —
     come with your face aflame with wine   240
         your raving women's cries°
     your army on the march! Come with the lightning
come with torches blazing, eyes ablaze with glory!
Burn that god of death that all gods hate!

Oedipus enters from the palace to address the Chorus, as if addressing the entire city of Thebes.

Oedipus: You pray to the gods? Let me grant your prayers.   245
Come, listen to me — do what the plague demands:
you'll find relief and lift your head from the depths.

I will speak out now as a stranger to the story,
a stranger to the crime. If I'd been present then,
there would have been no mystery, no long hunt   250
without a clue in hand. So now, counted
a native Theban years after the murder,
to all of Thebes I make this proclamation:
if any one of you knows who murdered Laius,

---

239 *Dionysus:* God of fertility and wine.   241 *your...cries:* Dionysus was attended by female celebrants.

the son of Labdacus, I order him to reveal   255
the whole truth to me. Nothing to fear,
even if he must denounce himself,
let him speak up
and so escape the brunt of the charge —
he will suffer no unbearable punishment,   260
nothing worse than exile, totally unharmed.

Oedipus pauses, waiting for a reply.

                                                    Next,
if anyone knows the murderer is a stranger,
a man from alien soil, come, speak up.
I will give him a handsome reward, and lay up
gratitude in my heart for him besides.   265

Silence again, no reply.

But if you keep silent, if anyone panicking,
trying to shield himself or friend or kin,
rejects my offer, then hear what I will do.
I order you, every citizen of the state
where I hold throne and power: banish this man —   270
whoever he may be — never shelter him, never
speak a word to him, never make him partner
to your prayers, your victims burned to the gods.
Never let the holy water touch his hands.
Drive him out, each of you, from every home.   275
He is the plague, the heart of our corruption,
as Apollo's oracle has revealed to me
just now. So I honor my obligations:
I fight for the god and for the murdered man.

Now my curse on the murderer. Whoever he is,   280
a lone man unknown in his crime
or one among many, let that man drag out
his life in agony, step by painful step —
I curse myself as well . . . if by any chance
he proves to be an intimate of our house,   285
here at my hearth, with my full knowledge,
may the curse I just called down on him strike me!

These are your orders: perform them to the last.
I command you, for my sake, for Apollo's, for this country
blasted root and branch by the angry heavens.   290
Even if god had never urged you on to act,
how could you leave the crime uncleansed so long?
A man so noble — your king, brought down in blood —
you should have searched. But I am the king now,
I hold the throne that he held then, possess his bed   295
and a wife who shares our seed . . . why, our seed
might be the same, children born of the same mother
might have created blood-bonds between us

if his hope of offspring hadn't met disaster —
but fate swooped at his head and cut him short.   300
So I will fight for him as if he were my father,
stop at nothing, search the world
to lay my hands on the man who shed his blood,
the son of Labdacus descended of Polydorus,
Cadmus of old and Agenor, founder of the line: 305
their power and mine are one.
                                        Oh dear gods,
my curse on those who disobey these orders!
Let no crops grow out of the earth for them —
shrivel their women, kill their sons,
burn them to nothing in this plague   310
that hits us now, or something even worse.
But you, loyal men of Thebes who approve my actions,
may our champion, Justice, may all the gods
be with us, fight beside us to the end!

Leader: In the grip of your curse, my king, I swear   315
            I'm not the murderer, cannot point him out.
            As for the search, Apollo pressed it on us —
            he should name the killer.

Oedipus: Quite right,
            but to force the gods to act against their will —
            no man has the power.

Leader: Then if I might mention   320
            the next best thing . . .

Oedipus: The third best too —
            don't hold back, say it.

Leader: I still believe . . .
            Lord Tiresias sees with the eyes of Lord Apollo.
            Anyone searching for the truth, my king,
            might learn it from the prophet, clear as day.   325

Oedipus: I've not been slow with that. On Creon's cue
            I sent the escorts, twice, within the hour.
            I'm surprised he isn't here.

Leader: We need him —
            without him we have nothing but old, useless rumors.

Oedipus: Which rumors? I'll search out every word.   330

Leader: Laius was killed, they say, by certain travelers.

Oedipus: I know — but no one can find the murderer.

Leader: If the man has a trace of fear in him
            he won't stay silent long,
            not with your curses ringing in his ears.   335

Oedipus: He didn't flinch at murder,
            he'll never flinch at words.

*Enter Tiresias, the blind prophet, led by a boy with escorts in attendance. He
remains at a distance.*

Leader: Here is the one who will convict him, look,
            they bring him on at last, the seer, the man of god.

The truth lives inside him, him alone.

Oedipus: O Tiresias,   340
    master of all the mysteries of our life,
    all you teach and all you dare not tell,
    signs in the heavens, signs that walk the earth!
    Blind as you are, you can feel all the more
    what sickness haunts our city. You, my lord,   345
    are the one shield, the one savior we can find.

    We asked Apollo — perhaps the messengers
    haven't told you — he sent his answer back:
    "Relief from the plague can only come one way.
    Uncover the murderers of Laius,   350
    put them to death or drive them into exile."
    So I beg you, grudge us nothing now, no voice,
    no message plucked from the birds, the embers
    or the other mantic ways within your grasp.
    Rescue yourself, your city, rescue me —   355
    rescue everything infected by the dead.
    We are in your hands. For a man to help others
    with all his gifts and native strength:
    that is the noblest work.

Tiresias: How terrible — to see the truth
    when the truth is only pain to him who sees!   360
    I knew it well, but I put it from my mind,
    else I never would have come.

Oedipus: What's this? Why so grim, so dire?

Tiresias: Just send me home. You bear your burdens,
    I'll bear mine. It's better that way,   365
    please believe me.

Oedipus: Strange response — unlawful,
    unfriendly too to the state that bred and raised you;
    you're withholding the word of god.

Tiresias: I fail to see
    that your own words are so well-timed.
    I'd rather not have the same thing said of me . . .   370

Oedipus: For the love of god, don't turn away,
    not if you know something. We beg you,
    all of us on our knees.

Tiresias: None of you knows —
    and I will never reveal my dreadful secrets,
    not to say your own.   375

Oedipus: What? You know and you won't tell?
    You're bent on betraying us, destroying Thebes?

Tiresias: I'd rather not cause pain for you or me.
    So why this . . . useless interrogation?
    You'll get nothing from me.

Oedipus: Nothing! You,   380
    you scum of the earth, you'd enrage a heart of stone!
    You won't talk? Nothing moves you?

Out with it, once and for all!

Tiresias: You criticize my temper . . . unaware
of the one *you* live with, you revile me. 385

Oedipus: Who could restrain his anger hearing you?
What outrage — you spurn the city!

Tiresias: What will come will come.
Even if I shroud it all in silence.

Oedipus: What will come? You're bound to *tell* me that. 390

Tiresias: I'll say no more. Do as you like, build your anger
to whatever pitch you please, rage your worst —

Oedipus: Oh I'll let loose, I have such fury in me —
now I see it all. You helped hatch the plot,
you did the work, yes, short of killing him 395
with your own hands — and given eyes I'd say
you did the killing single-handed!

Tiresias: Is that so!
I charge you, then, submit to that decree
you just laid down: from this day onward
speak to no one, not these citizens, not myself. 400
You are the curse, the corruption of the land!

Oedipus: You, shameless —
aren't you appalled to start up such a story?
You think you can get away with this?

Tiresias: I have already.
The truth with all its power lives inside me. 405

Oedipus: Who primed you for this? Not your prophet's trade.

Tiresias: You did, you forced me, twisted it out of me.

Oedipus: What? Say it again — I'll understand it better.

Tiresias: Didn't you understand, just now?
Or are you tempting me to talk? 410

Oedipus: No, I can't say I grasped your meaning.
Out with it, again!

Tiresias: I say you are the murderer you hunt.

Oedipus: That obscenity, twice — by god, you'll pay.

Tiresias: Shall I say more, so you can really rage? 415

Oedipus: Much as you want. Your words are nothing — futile.

Tiresias: You cannot imagine . . . I tell you,
you and your loved ones live together in infamy,
you cannot see how far you've gone in guilt.

Oedipus: You think you can keep this up and never suffer? 420

Tiresias: Indeed, if the truth has any power.

Oedipus: It does
but not for you, old man. You've lost your power,
stone-blind, stone-deaf — senses, eyes blind as stone!

Tiresias: I pity you, flinging at me the very insults
each man here will fling at you so soon.

Oedipus: Blind, 425
lost in the night, endless night that nursed you!
You can't hurt me or anyone else who sees the light —
you can never touch me.

Tiresias: True, it is not your fate
    to fall at my hands. Apollo is quite enough,
    and he will take some pains to work this out.   430
Oedipus: Creon! Is this conspiracy his or yours?
Tiresias: Creon is not your downfall, no, you are your own.
Oedipus: O power —
    wealth and empire, skill outstripping skill
    in the heady rivalries of life,
    what envy lurks inside you! Just for this,   435
    the crown the city gave me — I never sought it,
    they laid it in my hands — for this alone, Creon,
    the soul of trust, my loyal friend from the start
    steals against me . . . so hungry to overthrow me
    he sets this wizard on me, this scheming quack,   440
    this fortune-teller peddling lies, eyes peeled
    for his own profit — seer blind in his craft!

    Come here, you pious fraud. Tell me,
    when did you ever prove yourself a prophet?
    When the Sphinx, that chanting Fury kept her deathwatch here,   445
    why silent then, not a word to set our people free?
    There was a riddle, not for some passer-by to solve —
    it cried out for a prophet. Where were you?
    Did you rise to the crisis? Not a word,
    you and your birds, your gods — nothing.   450
    No, but I came by, Oedipus the ignorant,
    I stopped the Sphinx! With no help from the birds,
    the flight of my own intelligence hit the mark.

    And this is the man you'd try to overthrow?
    You think you'll stand by Creon when he's king?   455
    You and the great mastermind —
    you'll pay in tears, I promise you, for this,
    this witch-hunt. If you didn't look so senile
    the lash would teach you what your scheming means!
Leader: I'd suggest his words were spoken in anger,   460
    Oedipus . . . yours too, and it isn't what we need.
    The best solution to the oracle, the riddle
    posed by god — we should look for that.
Tiresias: You are the king no doubt, but in one respect,
    at least, I am your equal: the right to reply.   465
    I claim that privilege too.
    I am not your slave. I serve Apollo.
    I don't need Creon to speak for me in public.
                                             So,
    you mock my blindness? Let me tell you this.
    You with your precious eyes,
    you're blind to the corruption of your life,   470
    to the house you live in, those you live with —
    who *are* your parents? Do you know? All unknowing
    you are the scourge of your own flesh and blood,

the dead below the earth and the living here above,   475
and the double lash of your mother and your father's curse
will whip you from this land one day, their footfall
treading you down in terror, darkness shrouding
your eyes that now can see the light!
                                        Soon, soon
you'll scream aloud—what haven won't reverberate?   480
What rock of Cithaeron° won't scream back in echo?
That day you learn the truth about your marriage,
the wedding-march that sang you into your halls,
the lusty voyage home to the fatal harbor!
And a load of other horrors you'd never dream   485
will level you with yourself and all your children.

There. Now smear us with insults—Creon, myself
and every word I've said. No man will ever
be rooted from the earth as brutally as you.

Oedipus: Enough! Such filth from him? Insufferable—   490
what, still alive? Get out—
faster, back where you came from—vanish!
Tiresias: I'd never have come if you hadn't called me here.
Oedipus: If I thought you'd blurt out such absurdities,
you'd have died waiting before I'd had you summoned.   495
Tiresias: Absurd, am I? To you, not to your parents:
the ones who bore you found me sane enough.
Oedipus: Parents—who? Wait . . . who is my father?
Tiresias: This day will bring your birth and your destruction.
Oedipus: Riddles—all you can say are riddles, murk and darkness.   500
Tiresias: Ah, but aren't you the best man alive at solving riddles?
Oedipus: Mock me for that, go on, and you'll reveal my greatness.
Tiresias: Your great good fortune, true, it was your ruin.
Oedipus: Not if I saved the city—what do I care?
Tiresias: Well then, I'll be going.

> *To his attendant.*

                                        Take me home, boy.   505
Oedipus: Yes, take him away. You're a nuisance here.
Out of the way, the irritation's gone.

> *Turning his back on Tiresias, moving toward the palace.*

Tiresias: I will go,
once I have said what I came here to say.
I'll never shrink from the anger in your eyes—
you can't destroy me. Listen to me closely: 510
the man you've sought so long, proclaiming,
cursing up and down, the murderer of Laius—
he is here. A stranger,
you may think, who lives among you,

481 *Cithaeron:* The mountains where Oedipus was abandoned as an infant.

he soon will be revealed a native Theban   515
but he will take no joy in the revelation.
Blind who now has eyes, beggar who now is rich,
he will grope his way toward a foreign soil,
a stick tapping before him step by step.

Oedipus enters the palace.

Revealed at last, brother and father both   520
to the children he embraces, to his mother
son and husband both — he sowed the loins
his father sowed, he spilled his father's blood!

Go in and reflect on that, solve that.
And if you find I've lied   525
from this day onward call the prophet blind.

Tiresias and the boy exit to the side.

Chorus: Who —
  who is the man the voice of god denounces
  resounding out of the rocky gorge of Delphi?
     The horror too dark to tell,
  whose ruthless bloody hands have done the work?   530
His time has come to fly
    to outrace the stallions of the storm
         his feet a streak of speed —
Cased in armor, Apollo son of the Father
lunges on him, lightning-bolts afire!   535
And the grim unerring Furies°
     closing for the kill.

              Look,
  the word of god has just come blazing
  flashing off Parnassus'° snowy heights!
     That man who left no trace —   540
  after him, hunt him down with all our strength!
Now under bristling timber
    up through rocks and caves he stalks
         like the wild mountain bull —
cut off from men, each step an agony, frenzied, racing blind   545
but he cannot outrace the dread voices of Delphi
ringing out of the heart of Earth,
    the dark wings beating around him shrieking doom
         the doom that never dies, the terror —

The skilled prophet scans the birds and shatters me with terror! 550
I can't accept him, can't deny him, don't know what to say,
I'm lost, and the wings of dark foreboding beating —
I cannot see what's come, what's still to come . . .

---

536 *Furies:* Three spirits who avenged evildoers.   539 *Parnassus:* A mountain in Greece
associated with Apollo.

and what could breed a blood feud between
    Laius' house and the son of Polybus?°   555
I know of nothing, not in the past and not now,
no charge to bring against our king, no cause
to attack his fame that rings throughout Thebes —
    not without proof — not for the ghost of Laius,
    not to avenge a murder gone without a trace.   560

Zeus and Apollo know, they know, the great masters
    of all the dark and depth of human life.
But whether a mere man can know the truth,
whether a seer can fathom more than I —
there is no test, no certain proof   565
    though matching skill for skill
a man can outstrip a rival. No, not till I see
these charges proved will I side with his accusers.
We saw him then, when the she-hawk° swept against him,
saw with our own eyes his skill, his brilliant triumph —   570
    there was the test — he was the joy of Thebes!
    Never will I convict my king, never in my heart.

Enter Creon from the side.

Creon: My fellow-citizens, I hear King Oedipus
    levels terrible charges at me. I had to come.
    I resent it deeply. If, in the present crisis,   575
    he thinks he suffers any abuse from me,
    anything I've done or said that offers him
    the slightest injury, why, I've no desire
    to linger out this life, my reputation a shambles.
    The damage I'd face from such an accusation   580
    is nothing simple. No, there's nothing worse:
    branded a traitor in the city, a traitor
    to all of you and my good friends.
Leader: True,
    but a slur might have been forced out of him,
    by anger perhaps, not any firm conviction.   585
Creon: The charge was made in public, wasn't it?
    I put the prophet up to spreading lies?
Leader: Such things were said . . .
    I don't know with what intent, if any.
Creon: Was his glance steady, his mind right   590
    when the charge was brought against me?
Leader: I really couldn't say. I never look
    to judge the ones in power.

The doors open. Oedipus enters.

                Wait,

---

555 *Polybus:* The King of Corinth, who is thought to be Oedipus's father.   569 *she-hawk:*
The Sphinx.

here's Oedipus now.

Oedipus: You — here? You have the gall
to show your face before the palace gates?   595
You, plotting to kill me, kill the king —
I see it all, the marauding thief himself
scheming to steal my crown and power!
                              Tell me,
in god's name, what did you take me for,
coward or fool, when you spun out your plot?   600
Your treachery — you think I'd never detect it
creeping against me in the dark? Or sensing it,
not defend myself? Aren't you the fool,
you and your high adventure. Lacking numbers,
powerful friends, out for the big game of empire —   605
you need riches, armies to bring that quarry down!

Creon: Are you quite finished? It's your turn to listen
for just as long as you've . . . instructed me.
Hear me out, then judge me on the facts.

Oedipus: You've a wicked way with words, Creon,   610
but I'll be slow to learn — from you.
I find you a menace, a great burden to me.

Creon: Just one thing, hear me out in this.

Oedipus: Just one thing,
don't tell me you're not the enemy, the traitor.

Creon: Look, if you think crude, mindless stubbornness   615
such a gift, you've lost your sense of balance.

Oedipus: If you think you can abuse a kinsman,
then escape the penalty, you're insane.

Creon: Fair enough, I grant you. But this injury
you say I've done you, what is it?   620

Oedipus: Did you induce me, yes or no,
to send for that sanctimonious prophet?

Creon: I did. And I'd do the same again.

Oedipus: All right then, tell me, how long is it now
since Laius . . .

Creon: Laius — what did *he* do?

Oedipus: Vanished,   625
swept from sight, murdered in his tracks.

Creon: The count of the years would run you far back . . .

Oedipus: And that far back, was the prophet at his trade?

Creon: Skilled as he is today, and just as honored.

Oedipus: Did he ever refer to me then, at that time?

Creon: No,   630
never, at least, when I was in his presence.

Oedipus: But you did investigate the murder, didn't you?

Creon: We did our best, of course, discovered nothing.

Oedipus: But the great seer never accused me then — why not?

Creon: I don't know. And when I don't, *I* keep quiet.   635

Oedipus: You do know this, you'd tell it too —
if you had a shred of decency.

Creon: What?
    If I know, I won't hold back.
Oedipus: Simply this:
    if the two of you had never put heads together,
    we'd never have heard about *my* killing Laius. 640
Creon: If that's what he says . . . well, you know best.
    But now I have a right to learn from you
    as you just learned from me.
Oedipus: Learn your fill,
    you never will convict me of the murder.
Creon: Tell me, you're married to my sister, aren't you? 645
Oedipus: A genuine discovery — there's no denying that.
Creon: And you rule the land with her, with equal power?
Oedipus: She receives from me whatever she desires.
Creon: And I am the third, all of us are equals?
Oedipus: Yes, and it's there you show your stripes — 650
    you betray a kinsman.
Creon: Not at all.
    Not if you see things calmly, rationally,
    as I do. Look at it this way first:
    who in his right mind would rather rule
    and live in anxiety than sleep in peace? 655
    Particularly if he enjoys the same authority.
    Not I, I'm not the man to yearn for kingship,
    not with a king's power in my hands. Who would?
    No one with any sense of self-control.
    Now, as it is, you offer me all I need, 660
    not a fear in the world. But if I wore the crown . . .
    there'd be many painful duties to perform,
    hardly to my taste.
    How could kingship
    please me more than influence, power
    without a qualm? I'm not that deluded yet, 665
    to reach for anything but privilege outright,
    profit free and clear.
    Now all men sing my praises, all salute me,
    now all who request your favors curry mine.
    I'm their best hope: success rests in me. 670
    Why give up that, I ask you, and borrow trouble?
    A man of sense, someone who sees things clearly
    would never resort to treason.
    No, I've no lust for conspiracy in me,
    nor could I ever suffer one who does. 675

    Do you want proof? Go to Delphi yourself,
    examine the oracle and see if I've reported
    the message word-for-word. This too:
    if you detect that I and the clairvoyant
    have plotted anything in common, arrest me, 680
    execute me. Not on the strength of one vote,

two in this case, mine as well as yours.
But don't convict me on sheer unverified surmise.

How wrong it is to take the good for bad,
purely at random, or take the bad for good.   685
But reject a friend, a kinsman? I would as soon
tear out the life within us, priceless life itself.
You'll learn this well, without fail, in time.
Time alone can bring the just man to light;
the criminal you can spot in one short day.
Leader: Good advice,   690
my lord, for anyone who wants to avoid disaster.
Those who jump to conclusions may be wrong.
Oedipus: When my enemy moves against me quickly,
plots in secret, I move quickly too, I must,
I plot and pay him back. Relax my guard a moment,   695
waiting his next move — he wins his objective,
I lose mine.
Creon: What do you want?
You want me banished?
Oedipus: No, I want you dead.
Creon: Just to show how ugly a grudge can . . .
Oedipus: So,
still stubborn? you don't think I'm serious?   700
Creon: I think you're insane.
Oedipus: Quite sane — in my behalf.
Creon: Not just as much in mine?
Oedipus: You — my mortal enemy?
Creon: What if you're wholly wrong?
Oedipus: No matter — I must rule.
Creon: Not if you rule unjustly.
Oedipus: Hear him, Thebes, my city!
Creon: My city too, not yours alone!   705
Leader: Please, my lords.

Enter Jocasta from the palace.

                         Look, Jocasta's coming,
and just in time too. With her help
you must put this fighting of yours to rest.
Jocasta: Have you no sense? Poor misguided men,
such shouting — why this public outburst?   710
Aren't you ashamed, with the land so sick,
to stir up private quarrels?

To Oedipus.

Into the palace now. And Creon, you go home.
Why make such a furor over nothing?
Creon: My sister, it's dreadful . . . Oedipus, your husband,   715
he's bent on a choice of punishments for me,
banishment from the fatherland or death.

Oedipus: Precisely. I caught him in the act, Jocasta,
    plotting, about to stab me in the back.
Creon: Never — curse me, let me die and be damned   720
    if I've done you any wrong you charge me with.
Jocasta: Oh god, believe it, Oedipus,
    honor the solemn oath he swears to heaven.
    Do it for me, for the sake of all your people.

    The Chorus begins to chant.

Chorus: Believe it, be sensible   725
    give way, my king, I beg you!
Oedipus: What do you want from me, concessions?
Chorus: Respect him — he's been no fool in the past
    and now he's strong with the oath he swears to god.
Oedipus: You know what you're asking?
Chorus: I do.
Oedipus: Then out with it!   730
Chorus: The man's your friend, your kin, he's under oath —
    don't cast him out, disgraced
    branded with guilt on the strength of hearsay only.
Oedipus: Know full well, if that's what you want
    you want me dead or banished from the land.
Chorus: Never —   735
    no, by the blazing Sun, first god of the heavens!
      Stripped of the gods, stripped of loved ones,
    let me die by inches if that ever crossed my mind.
    But the heart inside me sickens, dies as the land dies
    and now on top of the old griefs you pile this,   740
    your fury — both of you!
Oedipus: Then let him go,
    even if it does lead to my ruin, my death
    or my disgrace, driven from Thebes for life.
    It's you, not him I pity — your words move me.
    He, wherever he goes, my hate goes with him.   745
Creon: Look at you, sullen in yielding, brutal in your rage —
    you'll go too far. It's perfect justice:
    natures like yours are hardest on themselves.
Oedipus: Then leave me alone — get out!
Creon: I'm going.
    You're wrong, so wrong. These men know I'm right.   750

    Exit to the side. The Chorus turns to Jocasta.

Chorus: Why do you hesitate, my lady
      why not help him in?
Jocasta: Tell me what's happened first.
Chorus: Loose, ignorant talk started dark suspicions
    and a sense of injustice cut deeply too.   755
Jocasta: On both sides?
Chorus: Oh yes.
Jocasta: What did they say?

Chorus: Enough, please, enough! The land's so racked already
　　　or so it seems to me . . .
　　　End the trouble here, just where they left it.
Oedipus: You see what comes of your good intentions now?　　　760
　　　And all because you tried to blunt my anger.
Chorus:　　　　　　　　　　　　　　　My king,
　　　I've said it once, I'll say it time and again —
　　　　I'd be insane, you know it,
　　　senseless, ever to turn my back on you.
　　　You who set our beloved land — storm-tossed, shattered —　　765
　　　straight on course. Now again, good helmsman,
　　　steer us through the storm!

The Chorus draws away, leaving Oedipus and Jocasta side by side.

Jocasta:　　　　　　　　　　　　For the love of god,
　　　Oedipus, tell me too, what is it?
　　　Why this rage? You're so unbending.
Oedipus: I will tell you. I respect you, Jocasta,　　　770
　　　much more than these . . .

　　　Glancing at the Chorus.

　　　Creon's to blame, Creon schemes against me.
Jocasta: Tell me clearly, how did the quarrel start?
Oedipus: He says I murdered Laius — I am guilty.
Jocasta: How does he know? Some secret knowledge　　　775
　　　or simple hearsay?
Oedipus:　　　　　　　Oh, he sent his prophet in
　　　to do his dirty work. You know Creon,
　　　Creon keeps his own lips clean.
Jocasta:　　　　　　　　　　　A prophet?
　　　Well then, free yourself of every charge!
　　　Listen to me and learn some peace of mind:　　　780
　　　no skill in the world,
　　　nothing human can penetrate the future.
　　　Here is proof, quick and to the point.
　　　An oracle came to Laius one fine day
　　　(I won't say from Apollo himself　　　785
　　　but his underlings, his priests) and it said
　　　that doom would strike him down at the hands of a son,
　　　our son, to be born of our own flesh and blood. But Laius,
　　　so the report goes at least, was killed by strangers,
　　　thieves, at a place where three roads meet . . . my son —　　790
　　　he wasn't three days old and the boy's father
　　　fastened his ankles, had a henchman fling him away
　　　on a barren, trackless mountain.
　　　　　　　　　　　　　There, you see?
　　　Apollo brought neither thing to pass. My baby
　　　no more murdered his father than Laius suffered —　　　795
　　　his wildest fear — death at his own son's hands.
　　　That's how the seers and their revelations

mapped out the future. Brush them from your mind.
Whatever the god needs and seeks
he'll bring to light himself, with ease.
Oedipus: Strange,   800
hearing you just now . . . my mind wandered,
my thoughts racing back and forth.
Jocasta: What do you mean? Why so anxious, startled?
Oedipus: I thought I heard you say that Laius
was cut down at a place where three roads meet.   805
Jocasta: That was the story. It hasn't died out yet.
Oedipus: Where did this thing happen? Be precise.
Jocasta: A place called Phocis, where two branching roads,
one from Daulia, one from Delphi,
come together—a crossroads.   810
Oedipus: When? How long ago?
Jocasta: The heralds no sooner reported Laius dead
than you appeared and they hailed you king of Thebes.
Oedipus: My god, my god—what have you planned to do to me?
Jocasta: What, Oedipus? What haunts you so?
Oedipus: Not yet.   815
Laius—how did he look? Describe him.
Had he reached his prime?
Jocasta: He was swarthy,
and the gray had just begun to streak his temples,
and his build . . . wasn't far from yours.
Oedipus: Oh no no,
I think I've just called down a dreadful curse   820
upon myself—I simply didn't know!
Jocasta: What are you saying? I shudder to look at you.
Oedipus: I have a terrible fear the blind seer can see.
I'll know in a moment. One thing more—
Jocasta: Anything,
afraid as I am—ask, I'll answer, all I can.   825
Oedipus: Did he go with a light or heavy escort,
several men-at-arms, like a lord, a king?
Jocasta: There were five in the party, a herald among them,
and a single wagon carrying Laius.
Oedipus: Ai—
now I can see it all, clear as day.   830
Who told you all this at the time, Jocasta?
Jocasta: A servant who reached home, the lone survivor.
Oedipus: So, could he still be in the palace—even now?
Jocasta: No indeed. Soon as he returned from the scene
and saw you on the throne with Laius dead and gone,   835
he knelt and clutched my hand, pleading with me
to send him into the hinterlands, to pasture,
far as possible, out of sight of Thebes.
I sent him away. Slave though he was,
he'd earned that favor—and much more.   840
Oedipus: Can we bring him back, quickly?

Jocasta: Easily. Why do you want him so?
Oedipus: I'm afraid,
    Jocasta, I have said too much already.
    That man — I've got to see him.
Jocasta: Then he'll come.
    But even I have a right, I'd like to think,   845
    to know what's torturing you, my lord.
Oedipus: And so you shall — I can hold nothing back from you,
    now I've reached this pitch of dark foreboding.
    Who means more to me than you? Tell me,
    whom would I turn toward but you   850
    as I go through all this?

    My father was Polybus, king of Corinth.
    My mother, a Dorian, Merope. And I was held
    the prince of the realm among the people there,
    till something struck me out of nowhere,   855
    something strange . . . worth remarking perhaps,
    hardly worth the anxiety I gave it.
    Some man at a banquet who had drunk too much
    shouted out — he was far gone, mind you —
    that I am not my father's son. Fighting words!   860
    I barely restrained myself that day
    but early the next I went to mother and father,
    questioned them closely, and they were enraged
    at the accusation and the fool who let it fly.
    So as for my parents I was satisfied,   865
    but still this thing kept gnawing at me,
    the slander spread — I had to make my move.
                    And so,
    unknown to mother and father I set out for Delphi,
    and the god Apollo spurned me, sent me away
    denied the facts I came for,   870
    but first he flashed before my eyes a future
    great with pain, terror, disaster — I can hear him cry,
    "You are fated to couple with your mother, you will bring
    a breed of children into the light no man can bear to see —
    you will kill your father, the one who gave you life!"   875
    I heard all that and ran. I abandoned Corinth,
    from that day on I gauged its landfall only
    by the stars, running, always running
    toward some place where I would never see
    the shame of all those oracles come true.   880
    And as I fled I reached that very spot
    where the great king, you say, met his death.
    Now, Jocasta, I will tell you all.
    Making my way toward this triple crossroad
    I began to see a herald, then a brace of colts   885
    drawing a wagon, and mounted on the bench . . . a man,
    just as you've described him, coming face-to-face,

and the one in the lead and the old man himself
were about to thrust me off the road — brute force —
and the one shouldering me aside, the driver,   890
I strike him in anger! — and the old man, watching me
coming up along his wheels — he brings down
his prod, two prongs straight at my head!
I paid him back with interest!
Short work, by god — with one blow of the staff   895
in this right hand I knock him out of his high seat,
roll him out of the wagon, sprawling headlong —
I killed them all — every mother's son!

Oh, but if there is any blood-tie
between Laius and this stranger . . .   900
what man alive more miserable than I?
More hated by the gods? *I* am the man
no alien, no citizen welcomes to his house,
law forbids it — not a word to me in public,
driven out of every hearth and home.   905
And all these curses I — no one but I
brought down these piling curses on myself!
And you, his wife, I've touched your body with these,
the hands that killed your husband cover you with blood.

Wasn't I born for torment? Look me in the eyes!   910
I am abomination — heart and soul!
I must be exiled, and even in exile
never see my parents, never set foot
on native earth again. Else I'm doomed
to couple with my mother and cut my father down . . .   915
Polybus who reared me, gave me life.
                                 But why, why?
Wouldn't a man of judgment say — and wouldn't he be right —
some savage power has brought this down upon my head?

Oh no, not that, you pure and awesome gods,
never let me see that day! Let me slip   920
from the world of men, vanish without a trace
before I see myself stained with such corruption,
stained to the heart.
Leader: My lord, you fill our hearts with fear.
But at least until you question the witness,   925
do take hope.
Oedipus: Exactly. He is my last hope —
I'm waiting for the shepherd. He is crucial.
Jocasta: And once he appears, what then? Why so urgent?
Oedipus: I'll tell you. If it turns out that his story
matches yours, I've escaped the worst.   930
Jocasta: What did I say? What struck you so?
Oedipus: You said *thieves* —

he told you a whole band of them murdered Laius.
So, if he still holds to the same number,
I cannot be the killer. One can't equal many.
But if he refers to one man, one alone,   935
clearly the scales come down on me:
I am guilty.

Jocasta: Impossible. Trust me,
I told you precisely what he said,
and he can't retract it now;
the whole city heard it, not just I.   940
And even if he should vary his first report
by one man more or less, still, my lord,
he could never make the murder of Laius
truly fit the prophecy. Apollo was explicit:
my son was doomed to kill my husband . . . my son,   945
poor defenseless thing, he never had a chance
to kill his father. They destroyed him first.

So much for prophecy. It's neither here nor there.
From this day on, I wouldn't look right or left.

Oedipus: True, true. Still, that shepherd,   950
someone fetch him — now!

Jocasta: I'll send at once. But do let's go inside.
I'd never displease you, least of all in this.

Oedipus and Jocasta enter the palace.

Chorus: Destiny guide me always
Destiny find me filled with reverence   955
                    pure in word and deed.
Great laws tower above us, reared on high
born for the brilliant vault of heaven —
          Olympian sky their only father,
nothing mortal, no man gave them birth,   960
their memory deathless, never lost in sleep:
within them lives a mighty god, the god does not grow old.

Pride breeds the tyrant
violent pride, gorging, crammed to bursting
          with all that is overripe and rich with ruin —   965
clawing up to the heights, headlong pride
crashes down the abyss — sheer doom!
          No footing helps, all foothold lost and gone,
But the healthy strife that makes the city strong —
I pray that god will never end that wrestling: 970
god, my champion, I will never let you go.

But if any man comes striding, high and mighty
          in all he says and does,
no fear of justice, no reverence
for the temples of the gods —   975

let a rough doom tear him down,
repay his pride, breakneck, ruinous pride!
If he cannot reap his profits fairly
    cannot restrain himself from outrage —
mad, laying hands on the holy things untouchable!   980

        Can such a man, so desperate, still boast
      he can save his life from the flashing bolts of god?
      If all such violence goes with honor now
          why join the sacred dance?

Never again will I go reverent to Delphi,   985
    the inviolate heart of Earth
or Apollo's ancient oracle at Abae
or Olympia of the fires —
    unless these prophecies all come true
for all mankind to point toward in wonder.   990
King of kings, if you deserve your titles
    Zeus, remember, never forget!
You and your deathless, everlasting reign.

        They are dying, the old oracles sent to Laius,
      now our masters strike them off the rolls.   995
        Nowhere Apollo's golden glory now —
          the gods, the gods go down.

Enter Jocasta from the palace, carrying a suppliant's branch wound in wool.

Jocasta: Lords of the realm, it occurred to me,
    just now, to visit the temples of the gods,
    so I have my branch in hand and incense too.   1000
    Oedipus is beside himself. Racked with anguish,
    no longer a man of sense, he won't admit
    the latest prophecies are hollow as the old —
    he's at the mercy of every passing voice
    if the voice tells of terror.   1005
    I urge him gently, nothing seems to help,
    so I turn to you, Apollo, you are nearest.

*Placing her branch on the altar, while an old herdsman enters from the side,
not the one just summoned by the king but an unexpected messenger from
Corinth.*

    I come with prayers and offerings . . . I beg you,
    cleanse us, set us free of defilement!
    Look at us, passengers in the grip of fear,   1010
    watching the pilot of the vessel go to pieces.
Messenger:

Approaching Jocasta and the Chorus.

    Strangers, please, I wonder if you could lead us
    to the palace of the king . . . I think it's Oedipus.
    Better, the man himself — you know where he is?

Leader: This is his palace, stranger. He's inside.   1015
 But here is his queen, his wife and mother
 of his children.
Messenger: Blessings on you, noble queen,
 queen of Oedipus crowned with all your family —
 blessings on you always!
Jocasta: And the same to you, stranger, you deserve it . . .   1020
 such a greeting. But what have you come for?
 Have you brought us news?
Messenger: Wonderful news —
 for the house, my lady, for your husband too.
Jocasta: Really, what? Who sent you?
Messenger: Corinth.
 I'll give you the message in a moment.   1025
 You'll be glad of it — how could you help it? —
 though it costs a little sorrow in the bargain.
Jocasta: What can it be, with such a double edge?
Messenger: The people there, they want to make your Oedipus
 king of Corinth, so they're saying now.   1030
Jocasta: Why? Isn't old Polybus still in power?
Messenger: No more. Death has got him in the tomb.
Jocasta: What are you saying? Polybus, dead? — dead?
Messenger: If not,
 if I'm not telling the truth, strike me dead too.
Jocasta:

To a servant.

 Quickly, go to your master, tell him this!   1035

 You prophecies of the gods, where are you now?
 This is the man that Oedipus feared for years,
 he fled him, not to kill him — and now he's dead,
 quite by chance, a normal, natural death,
 not murdered by his son.
Oedipus:

Emerging from the palace.

                                Dearest,   1040
 what now? Why call me from the palace?
Jocasta:

Bringing the Messenger closer.

 Listen to *him,* see for yourself what all
 those awful prophecies of god have come to.
Oedipus: And who is he? What can he have for me?
Jocasta: He's from Corinth, he's come to tell you   1045
 your father is no more — Polybus — he's dead!
Oedipus:

Wheeling on the Messenger.

 What? Let me have it from your lips.

Messenger: Well,
    if that's what you want first, then here it is:
    make no mistake, Polybus is dead and gone.
Oedipus: How — murder? sickness? — what? what killed him?   1050
Messenger: A light tip of the scales can put old bones to rest.
Oedipus: Sickness then — poor man, it wore him down.
Messenger: That,
    and the long count of years he'd measured out.
Oedipus: So!
    Jocasta, why, why look to the Prophet's hearth,
    the fires of the future? Why scan the birds   1055
    that scream above our heads? They winged me on
    to the murder of my father, did they? That was my doom?
    Well look, he's dead and buried, hidden under the earth,
    and here I am in Thebes, I never put hand to sword —
    unless some longing for me wasted him away,   1060
    then in a sense you'd say I caused his death.
    But now, all those prophecies I feared — Polybus
    packs them off to sleep with him in hell!
    They're nothing, worthless.
Jocasta: There.
    Didn't I tell you from the start?   1065
Oedipus: So you did. I was lost in fear.
Jocasta: No more, sweep it from your mind forever.
Oedipus: But my mother's bed, surely I must fear —
Jocasta: Fear?
    What should a man fear? It's all chance,
    chance rules our lives. Not a man on earth   1070
    can see a day ahead, groping through the dark.
    Better to live at random, best we can.
    And as for this marriage with your mother —
    have no fear. Many a man before you,
    in his dreams, has shared his mother's bed.   1075
    Take such things for shadows, nothing at all —
    Live, Oedipus,
    as if there's no tomorrow!
Oedipus: Brave words,
    and you'd persuade me if mother weren't alive.
    But mother lives, so for all your reassurances   1080
    I live in fear, I must.
Jocasta: But your father's death,
    that, at least, is a great blessing, joy to the eyes!
Oedipus: Great, I know . . . but I fear *her* — she's still alive.
Messenger: Wait, who is this woman, makes you so afraid?
Oedipus: Merope, old man. The wife of Polybus.   1085
Messenger: The queen? What's there to fear in her?
Oedipus: A dreadful prophecy, stranger, sent by the gods.
Messenger: Tell me, could you? Unless it's forbidden
    other ears to hear.
Oedipus: Not at all.

Apollo told me once — it is my fate —   1090
I must make love with my own mother,
shed my father's blood with my own hands.
So for years I've given Corinth a wide berth,
and it's been my good fortune too. But still,
to see one's parents and look into their eyes   1095
is the greatest joy I know.
Messenger: You're afraid of that?
That kept you out of Corinth?
Oedipus: My *father,* old man —
so I wouldn't kill my father.
Messenger: So that's it.
Well then, seeing I came with such good will, my king,
why don't I rid you of that old worry now?   1100
Oedipus: What a rich reward you'd have for that.
Messenger: What do you think I came for, majesty?
So you'd come home and I'd be better off.
Oedipus: Never, I will never go near my parents.
Messenger: My boy, it's clear, you don't know what you're doing.   1105
Oedipus: What do you mean, old man? For god's sake, explain.
Messenger: If you ran from *them,* always dodging home . . .
Oedipus: Always, terrified Apollo's oracle might come true —
Messenger: And you'd be covered with guilt, from both your parents.
Oedipus: That's right, old man, that fear is always with me.   1110
Messenger: Don't you know? You've really nothing to fear.
Oedipus: But why? If I'm their son — Merope, Polybus?
Messenger: Polybus was nothing to you, that's why, not in blood.
Oedipus: What are you saying — Polybus was not my father?
Messenger: No more than I am. He and I are equals.
Oedipus: My father —   1115
how can my father equal nothing? You're nothing to me!
Messenger: Neither was he, no more your father than I am.
Oedipus: Then why did he call me his son?
Messenger: You were a gift,
years ago — know for a fact he took you
from my hands.
Oedipus: No, from another's hands?   1120
Then how could he love me so? He loved me, deeply . . .
Messenger: True, and his early years without a child
made him love you all the more.
Oedipus: And you, did you . . .
buy me? find me by accident?
Messenger: I stumbled on you,
down the woody flanks of Mount Cithaeron.
Oedipus: So close,   1125
what were you doing here, just passing through?
Messenger: Watching over my flocks, grazing them on the slopes.
Oedipus: A herdsman, were you? A vagabond, scraping for wages?
Messenger: Your savior too, my son, in your worst hour.
Oedipus: Oh —

when you picked me up, was I in pain? What exactly? 1130
Messenger: Your ankles . . . they tell the story. Look at them.
Oedipus: Why remind me of that, that old affliction?
Messenger: Your ankles were pinned together; I set you free.
Oedipus: That dreadful mark — I've had it from the cradle.
Messenger: And you got your name from that misfortune too, 1135
  the name's still with you.
Oedipus: Dear god, who did it? —
  mother? father? Tell me.
Messenger: I don't know.
  The one who gave you to me, he'd know more.
Oedipus: What? You took me from someone else?
  You didn't find me yourself?
Messenger: No sir, 1140
  another shepherd passed you on to me.
Oedipus: Who? Do you know? Describe him.
Messenger: He called himself a servant of . . .
  if I remember rightly — Laius.

  Jocasta turns sharply.

Oedipus: The king of the land who ruled here long ago? 1145
Messenger: That's the one. That herdsman was *his* man.
Oedipus: Is he still alive? Can I see him?
Messenger: They'd know best, the people of these parts.

  Oedipus and the Messenger turn to the Chorus.

Oedipus: Does anyone know that herdsman,
  the one he mentioned? Anyone seen him
  in the fields, in town? Out with it! 1150
  The time has come to reveal this once for all.
Leader: I think he's the very shepherd you wanted to see,
  a moment ago. But the queen, Jocasta,
  she's the one to say.
Oedipus: Jocasta, 1155
  you remember the man we just sent for?
  Is *that* the one he means?
Jocasta: That man . . .
  why ask? Old shepherd, talk, empty nonsense,
  don't give it another thought, don't even think —
Oedipus: What — give up now, with a clue like this? 1160
  Fail to solve the mystery of my birth?
  Not for all the world!
Jocasta: Stop — in the name of god,
  if you love your own life, call off this search!
  My suffering is enough.
Oedipus: Courage!
  Even if my mother turns out to be a slave, 1165
  and I a slave, three generations back,
  you would not seem common.
Jocasta: Oh no,
  listen to me, I beg you, don't do this.

Oedipus: Listen to you? No more. I must know it all,
　　see the truth at last.
Jocasta: 　　　　　　　No, please— 　　　　　　　　1170
　　for your sake—I want the best for you!
Oedipus: Your best is more than I can bear.
Jocasta: 　　　　　　　　　　You're doomed—
　　may you never fathom who you are!
Oedipus:

　　To a servant.

　　Hurry, fetch me the herdsman, now!
　　Leave her to glory in her royal birth. 　　　　　　　1175
Jocasta: Aieeeeee—
　　　　　　　man of agony—
　　that is the only name I have for you,
　　that, no other—ever, ever, ever!

　　Flinging (herself) through the palace doors. A long, tense silence follows.

Leader: Where's she gone, Oedipus?
　　Rushing off, such wild grief . . . 　　　　　　　　1180
　　I'm afraid that from this silence
　　something monstrous may come bursting forth.
Oedipus: Let it burst! Whatever will, whatever must!
　　I must know my birth, no matter how common
　　it may be—must see my origins face-to-face. 　　　1185
　　She perhaps, she with her woman's pride
　　may well be mortified by my birth,
　　but I, I count myself the son of Chance,
　　the great goddess, giver of all good things—
　　I'll never see myself disgraced. She is my mother! 　1190
　　And the moons have marked me out, my blood-brothers,
　　one moon on the wane, the next moon great with power.
　　That is my blood, my nature—I will never betray it,
　　never fail to search and learn my birth!
Chorus: Yes—if I am a true prophet 　　　　　　　1195
　　　　　　　if I can grasp the truth,
　　　　　　　　by the boundless skies of Olympus,
　　at the full moon of tomorrow, Mount Cithaeron
　　you will know how Oedipus glories in you—
　　you, his birthplace, nurse, his mountain-mother! 　1200
　　And we will sing you, dancing out your praise—
　　you lift our monarch's heart!
　　　　　　Apollo, Apollo, god of the wild cry
　　　　　　　　may our dancing please you!
　　　　　　　　　　　　　　　Oedipus—
　　　　　　　son, dear child, who bore you? 　　　　1205
　　Who of the nymphs who seem to live forever
　　mated with Pan,° the mountain-striding Father?

1207 *Pan:* God of shepherds, who was, like Hermes and Dionysus, associated with the wilderness.

Who was your mother? who, some bride of Apollo
the god who loves the pastures spreading toward the sun?
      Or was it Hermes, king of the lightning ridges?   1210
Or Dionysus, lord of frenzy, lord of the barren peaks —
did he seize you in his hands, dearest of all his lucky finds? —
      found by the nymphs, their warm eyes dancing, gift
to the lord who loves them dancing out his joy!

Oedipus strains to see a figure coming from the distance. Attended by palace
guards, an old Shepherd enters slowly, reluctant to approach the king.

Oedipus: I never met the man, my friends . . . still,   1215
    if I had to guess, I'd say that's the shepherd,
    the very one we've looked for all along.
    Brothers in old age, two of a kind,
    he and our guest here. At any rate
    the ones who bring him in are my own men,   1220
    I recognize them.

    Turning to the Leader.

                But you know more than I,
    you should, you've seen the man before.
Leader: I know him, definitely. One of Laius' men,
    a trusty shepherd, if there ever was one.
Oedipus: You, I ask you first, stranger,   1225
    you from Corinth — is this the one you mean?
Messenger: You're looking at him. He's your man.
Oedipus:

    To the Shepherd.

    You, old man, come over here —
    look at me. Answer all my questions.
    Did you ever serve King Laius?
Shepherd: So I did . . .   1230
    a slave, not bought on the block though,
    born and reared in the palace.
Oedipus: Your duties, your kind of work?
Shepherd: Herding the flocks, the better part of my life.
Oedipus: Where, mostly? Where did you do your grazing?
Shepherd: Well,   1235
    Cithaeron sometimes, or the foothills round about.
Oedipus: This man — you know him? ever see him there?
Shepherd:

    Confused, glancing from the Messenger to the King.

    Doing what — what man do you mean?
Oedipus:

    Pointing to the Messenger.

    This one here — ever have dealings with him?
Shepherd: Not so I could say, but give me a chance,   1240
    my memory's bad . . .

Messenger: No wonder he doesn't know me, master.
     But let me refresh his memory for him.
     I'm sure he recalls old times we had
     on the slopes of Mount Cithaeron;   1245
     he and I, grazing our flocks, he with two
     and I with one — we both struck up together,
     three whole seasons, six months at a stretch
     from spring to the rising of Arcturus° in the fall,
     then with winter coming on I'd drive my herds   1250
     to my own pens, and back he'd go with his
     to Laius' folds.

To the Shepherd.

                    Now that's how it was,
     wasn't it — yes or no?
Shepherd: Yes, I suppose . . .
     it's all so long ago.
Messenger: Come, tell me,
     you gave me a child back then, a boy, remember?   1255
     A little fellow to rear, my very own.
Shepherd: What? Why rake up that again?
Messenger: Look, here he is, my fine old friend —
     the same man who was just a baby then.
Shepherd: Damn you, shut your mouth — quiet!   1260
Oedipus: Don't lash out at him, old man —
     you need lashing more than he does.
Shepherd: Why,
     master, majesty — what have I done wrong?
Oedipus: You won't answer his question about the boy.
Shepherd: He's talking nonsense, wasting his breath.   1265
Oedipus: So, you won't talk willingly —
     then you'll talk with pain.

The guards seize the Shepherd.

Shepherd: No, dear god, don't torture an old man!
Oedipus: Twist his arms back, quickly!
Shepherd: God help us, why? —
     what more do you need to know?   1270
Oedipus: Did you give him that child? He's asking.
Shepherd: I did . . . I wish to god I'd died that day.
Oedipus: You've got your wish if you don't tell the truth.
Shepherd: The more I tell, the worse the death I'll die.
Oedipus: Our friend here wants to stretch things out, does he? 1275

Motioning to his men for torture.

Shepherd: No, no, I gave it to him — I just said so.
Oedipus: Where did you get it? Your house? Someone else's?
Shepherd: It wasn't mine, no, I got it from . . . someone.

1249 *Arcturus:* A star whose rising marked the end of summer.

Oedipus: Which one of them?

   Looking at the citizens.

                          Whose house?

Shepherd: No—   1280
   god's sake, master, no more questions!

Oedipus: You're a dead man if I have to ask again.

Shepherd: Then—the child came from the house . . .
   of Laius.

Oedipus: A slave? or born of his own blood?

Shepherd: Oh no,
   I'm right at the edge, the horrible truth—I've got to say it!

Oedipus: And I'm at the edge of hearing horrors, yes, but I must hear!   1285

Shepherd: All right! His son, they said it was—his son!
   But the one inside, your wife,
   she'd tell it best.

Oedipus: My wife—
   she gave it to you?   1290

Shepherd: Yes, yes, my king.

Oedipus: Why, what for?

Shepherd: To kill it.

Oedipus: Her own child,
   how could she?   1295

Shepherd: She was afraid—
   frightening prophecies.

Oedipus: What?

Shepherd: They said—
   he'd kill his parents.   1300

Oedipus: But you gave him to this old man—why?

Shepherd: I pitied the little baby, master,
   hoped he'd take him off to his own country,
   far away, but he saved him for this, this fate.
   If you are the man he says you are, believe me,   1305
   you were born for pain.

Oedipus: O god—
   all come true, all burst to light!
   O light—now let me look my last on you!
   I stand revealed at last—
   cursed in my birth, cursed in marriage,   1310
   cursed in the lives I cut down with these hands!

   Rushing through the doors with a great cry. The Corinthian Messenger, the
   Shepherd, and attendants exit slowly to the side.

Chorus: O the generations of men
   the dying generations—adding the total
   of all your lives I find they come to nothing . . .
          does there exist, is there a man on earth   1315
   who seizes more joy than just a dream, a vision?
   And the vision no sooner dawns than dies
   blazing into oblivion.

You are my great example, you, your life,
your destiny, Oedipus, man of misery —   1320
I count no man blest.

You outranged all men!
Bending your bow to the breaking-point
you captured priceless glory, O dear god,
and the Sphinx came crashing down,
                        the virgin, claws hooked   1325
like a bird of omen singing, shrieking death —
like a fortress reared in the face of death
you rose and saved our land.

From that day on we called you king
we crowned you with honors, Oedipus, towering over all —   1330
mighty king of the seven gates of Thebes.

But now to hear your story — is there a man more agonized?
More wed to pain and frenzy? Not a man on earth,
the joy of your life ground down to nothing
O Oedipus, name for the ages —   1335
        one and the same wide harbor served you
                        son and father both
son and father came to rest in the same bridal chamber.
How, how could the furrows your father plowed
bear you, your agony, harrowing on   1340
in silence O so long?
                        But now for all your power
Time, all-seeing Time has dragged you to the light,
judged your marriage monstrous from the start —
the son and the father tangling, both one —
O child of Laius, would to god   1345
        I'd never seen you, never never!
                Now I weep like a man who wails the dead
and the dirge comes pouring forth with all my heart!
I tell you the truth, you gave me life
my breath leapt up in you   1350
and now you bring down night upon my eyes.

Enter a Messenger from the palace.

Messenger: Men of Thebes, always the first in honor,
what horrors you will hear, what you will see,
what a heavy weight of sorrow you will shoulder . . .
if you are true to your birth, if you still have   1355
some feeling for the royal house of Thebes.
I tell you neither the waters of the Danube
nor the Nile can wash this palace clean.
Such things it hides, it soon will bring to light —
terrible things, and none done blindly now,   1360
all done with a will. The pains
we inflict upon ourselves hurt most of all.

Leader: God knows we have pains enough already.
    What can you add to them?
Messenger: The queen is dead.
Leader: Poor lady — how?   1365
Messenger: By her own hand. But you are spared the worst,
    you never had to watch . . . I saw it all,
    and with all the memory that's in me
    you will learn what that poor woman suffered.

    Once she'd broken in through the gates,   1370
    dashing past us, frantic, whipped to fury,
    ripping her hair out with both hands —
    straight to her rooms she rushed, flinging herself
    across the bridal-bed, doors slamming behind her —
    once inside, she wailed for Laius, dead so long,   1375
    remembering how she bore his child long ago,
    the life that rose up to destroy him, leaving
    its mother to mother living creatures
    with the very son she'd borne.
    Oh how she wept, mourning the marriage-bed   1380
    where she let loose that double brood — monsters —
    husband by her husband, children by her child.

                                        And then —
    but how she died is more than I can say. Suddenly
    Oedipus burst in, screaming, he stunned us so
    we couldn't watch her agony to the end,   1385
    our eyes were fixed on him. Circling
    like a maddened beast, stalking, here, there
    crying out to us —

                    Give him a sword! His wife,
    no wife, his mother, where can he find the mother earth
    that cropped two crops at once, himself and all his children?   1390
    He was raging — one of the dark powers pointing the way,
    none of us mortals crowding around him, no,
    with a great shattering cry — someone, something leading him on —
    he hurled at the twin doors and bending the bolts back
    out of their sockets, crashed through the chamber.   1395
    And there we saw the woman hanging by the neck,
    cradled high in a woven noose, spinning,
    swinging back and forth. And when he saw her,
    giving a low, wrenching sob that broke our hearts,
    slipping the halter from her throat, he eased her down,   1400
    in a slow embrace he laid her down, poor thing . . .
    then, what came next, what horror we beheld!

    He rips off her brooches, the long gold pins
    holding her robes — and lifting them high,
    looking straight up into the points,   1405
    he digs them down the sockets of his eyes, crying, "You,
    you'll see no more the pain I suffered, all the pain I caused!
    Too long you looked on the ones you never should have seen,

blind to the ones you longed to see, to know! Blind
from this hour on! Blind in the darkness — blind!"   1410
His voice like a dirge, rising, over and over
raising the pins, raking them down his eyes.
And at each stroke blood spurts from the roots,
splashing his beard, a swirl of it, nerves and clots —
black hail of blood pulsing, gushing down.   1415

These are the griefs that burst upon them both,
coupling man and woman. The joy they had so lately,
the fortune of their old ancestral house
was deep joy indeed. Now, in this one day,
wailing, madness and doom, death, disgrace,   1420
all the griefs in the world that you can name,
all are theirs forever.
Leader: Oh poor man, the misery —
has he any rest from pain now?

   A voice within, in torment.

Messenger: He's shouting,
"Loose the bolts, someone, show me to all of Thebes!
My father's murderer, my mother's —"   1425
No, I can't repeat it, it's unholy.
Now he'll tear himself from his native earth,
not linger, curse the house with his own curse.
But he needs strength, and a guide to lead him on.
This is sickness more than he can bear.

   The palace doors open.

                             Look,   1430
he'll show you himself. The great doors are opening —
you are about to see a sight, a horror
even his mortal enemy would pity.

   *Enter Oedipus, blinded, led by a boy. He stands at the palace steps, as if surveying
   his people once again.*

Chorus: O the terror —
the suffering, for all the world to see,
the worst terror that ever met my eyes.   1435
What madness swept over you? What god,
what dark power leapt beyond all bounds,
beyond belief, to crush your wretched life? —
godforsaken, cursed by the gods!
I pity you but I can't bear to look.   1440
I've much to ask, so much to learn,
so much fascinates my eyes,
but you . . . I shudder at the sight.
Oedipus: Oh, Ohhh —
the agony! I am agony —
where am I going? where on earth?   1445
     where does all this agony hurl me?

where's my voice? —
        winging, swept away on a dark tide —
    My destiny, my dark power, what a leap you made!

Chorus: To the depths of terror, too dark to hear, to see.   1450

Oedipus: Dark, horror of darkness
    my darkness, drowning, swirling around me
    crashing wave on wave — unspeakable, irresistible
        headwind, fatal harbor! Oh again,
    the misery, all at once, over and over   1455
    the stabbing daggers, stab of memory
raking me insane.

Chorus: No wonder you suffer
    twice over, the pain of your wounds,
    the lasting grief of pain.

Oedipus: Dear friend, still here?
    Standing by me, still with a care for me,   1460
    the blind man? Such compassion,
        loyal to the last. Oh it's you,
    I know you're here, dark as it is
    I'd know you anywhere, your voice —
it's yours, clearly yours.

Chorus: Dreadful, what you've done . . .   1465
    how could you bear it, gouging out your eyes?
What superhuman power drove you on?

Oedipus: Apollo, friends, Apollo —
    he ordained my agonies — these, my pains on pains!
    But the hand that struck my eyes was mine,   1470
    mine alone — no one else —
        I did it all myself!
    What good were eyes to me?
    Nothing I could see could bring me joy.

Chorus: No, no, exactly as you say.

Oedipus: What can I ever see?   1475
    What love, what call of the heart
    can touch my ears with joy? Nothing, friends.
    Take me away, far, far from Thebes,
        quickly, cast me away, my friends —
this great murderous ruin, this man cursed to heaven,   1480
    the man the deathless gods hate most of all!

Chorus: Pitiful, you suffer so, you understand so much . . .
    I wish you'd never known.

Oedipus: Die, die —
    whoever he was that day in the wilds
who cut my ankles free of the ruthless pins,   1485
    he pulled me clear of death, he saved my life
    for this, this kindness —
        Curse him, kill him!
    If I'd died then, I'd never have dragged myself,
    my loved ones through such hell.   1490

Chorus: Oh if only . . . would to god.

Oedipus: I'd never have come to this,
          my father's murderer — never been branded
       mother's husband, all men see me now! Now,
          loathed by the gods, son of the mother I defiled
             coupling in my father's bed, spawning lives in the loins   1495
       that spawned my wretched life. What grief can crown this grief?
                     It's mine alone, my destiny — I am Oedipus!
Chorus: How can I say you've chosen for the best?
       Better to die than be alive and blind.
Oedipus: What I did was best — don't lecture me,   1500
       no more advice. I, with *my* eyes,
       how could I look my father in the eyes
       when I go down to death? Or mother, so abused . . .
       I've done such things to the two of them,
       crimes too huge for hanging.
                          Worse yet,   1505
       the sight of my children, born as they were born,
       how could I long to look into their eyes?
       No, not with these eyes of mine, never.
       Not this city either, her high towers,
       the sacred glittering images of her gods —   1510
       I am misery! I, her best son, reared
       as no other son of Thebes was ever reared,
       I've stripped myself, I gave the command myself.
       All men must cast away the great blasphemer,
       the curse now brought to light by the gods,   1515
       the son of Laius — I, my father's son!

       Now I've exposed my guilt, horrendous guilt,
       could I train a level glance on you, my countrymen?
       Impossible! No, if I could just block off my ears,
       the springs of hearing, I would stop at nothing —   1520
       I'd wall up my loathsome body like a prison,
       blind to the sound of life, not just the sight.
       Oblivion — what a blessing . . .
       for the mind to dwell a world away from pain.

       O Cithaeron, why did you give me shelter?   1525
       Why didn't you take me, crush my life out on the spot?
       I'd never have revealed my birth to all mankind.

       O Polybus, Corinth, the old house of my fathers,
       so I believed — what a handsome prince you raised —
       under the skin, what sickness to the core.   1530
       Look at me! Born of outrage, outrage to the core.

       O triple roads — it all comes back, the secret,
       dark ravine, and the oaks closing in
       where the three roads join . . .
       You drank my father's blood, my own blood   1535
       spilled by my own hands — you still remember me?

What things you saw me do? Then I came here
and did them all once more!
                              Marriages! O marriage,
you gave me birth, and once you brought me into the world
you brought my sperm rising back, springing to light   1540
fathers, brothers, sons — one deadly breed —
brides, wives, mothers. The blackest things
a man can do, I have done them all!
                              No more —
it's wrong to name what's wrong to do. Quickly,
for the love of god, hide me somewhere,   1545
kill me, hurl me into the sea
where you can never look on me again.

Beckoning to the Chorus as they shrink away.

                              Closer,
it's all right. Touch the man of sorrow.
Do. Don't be afraid. My troubles are mine
and I am the only man alive who can sustain them.   1550

Enter Creon from the palace, attended by palace guards.

Leader: Put your requests to Creon. Here he is,
     just when we need him. He'll have a plan, he'll act.
     Now that he's the sole defense of the country
     in your place.
Oedipus: Oh no, what can I say to him?
     How can I ever hope to win his trust?   1555
     I wronged him so, just now, in every way.
     You must see that — I was so wrong, so wrong.
Creon: I haven't come to mock you, Oedipus,
     or to criticize your former failings.

Turning to the guards.

                              You there,
     have you lost all respect for human feeling?   1560
     At least revere the Sun, the holy fire
     that keeps us all alive. Never expose a thing
     of guilt and holy dread so great it appalls
     the earth, the rain from heaven, the light of day!
     Get him into the halls — quickly as you can.   1565
     Piety demands no less. Kindred alone
     should see a kinsman's shame. This is obscene.
Oedipus: Please, in god's name . . . you wipe my fears away,
     coming so generously to me, the worst of men.
     Do one thing more, for your sake, not mine.   1570
Creon: What do you want? Why so insistent?
Oedipus: Drive me out of the land at once, far from sight,
     where I can never hear a human voice.
Creon: I'd have done that already, I promise you.
     First I wanted the god to clarify my duties.   1575

Oedipus: The god? His command was clear, every word:
    death for the father-killer, the curse —
    he said destroy me!
Creon: So he did. Still, in such a crisis
    it's better to ask precisely what to do.   1580
Oedipus: You'd ask the oracle about a man like me?
Creon: By all means. And this time, I assume,
    even you will obey the god's decrees.
Oedipus: I will,
    I will. And you, I command you — I beg you . . .
    the woman inside, bury her as you see fit.   1585
    It's the only decent thing,
    to give your own the last rites. As for me,
    never condemn the city of my fathers
    to house my body, not while I'm alive, no,
    let me live on the mountains, on Cithaeron,   1590
    my favorite haunt, I have made it famous.
    Mother and father marked out that rock
    to be my everlasting tomb — buried alive.
    Let me die there, where they tried to kill me.
    Oh but this I know: no sickness can destroy me,   1595
    nothing can. I would never have been saved
    from death — I have been saved
    for something great and terrible, something strange.
    Well let my destiny come and take me on its way!

    About my children, Creon, the boys at least,   1600
    don't burden yourself. They're men;
    wherever they go, they'll find the means to live.
    But my two daughters, my poor helpless girls,
    clustering at our table, never without me
    hovering near them . . . whatever I touched,   1605
    they always had their share. Take care of them,
    I beg you. Wait, better — permit me, would you?
    Just to touch them with my hands and take
    our fill of tears. Please . . . my king.
    Grant it, with all your noble heart.   1610
    If I could hold them, just once, I'd think
    I had them with me, like the early days
    when I could see their eyes.

Antigone and Ismene, two small children, are led in from the palace by a nurse.

                    What's that?
    O god! Do I really hear you sobbing? —
    my two children. Creon, you've pitied me?   1615
    Sent me my darling girls, my own flesh and blood!
    Am I right?
Creon: Yes, it's my doing.
    I know the joy they gave you all these years,
    the joy you must feel now.

Oedipus: Bless you, Creon!
May god watch over you for this kindness,   1620
better than he ever guarded me.

                             Children, where are you?
Here, come quickly —

Groping for Antigone and Ismene, who approach their father cautiously, then
embrace him.

                        Come to these hands of mine,
your brother's hands, your own father's hands
that served his once bright eyes so well —
that made them blind. Seeing nothing, children,   1625
knowing nothing, I became your father,
I fathered you in the soil that gave me life.

How I weep for you — I cannot see you now . . .
just thinking of all your days to come, the bitterness,
the life that rough mankind will thrust upon you.   1630
Where are the public gatherings you can join,
the banquets of the clans? Home you'll come,
in tears, cut off from the sight of it all,
the brilliant rites unfinished.
And when you reach perfection, ripe for marriage,   1635
who will he be, my dear ones? Risking all
to shoulder the curse that weighs down my parents,
yes and you too — that wounds us all together.
What more misery could you want?
Your father killed his father, sowed his mother,   1640
one, one and the selfsame womb sprang you —
he cropped the very roots of his existence.
Such disgrace, and you must bear it all!
Who will marry you then? Not a man on earth.
Your doom is clear: you'll wither away to nothing,   1645
single, without a child.

Turning to Creon.

                        Oh Creon,
you are the only father they have now . . .
we who brought them into the world
are gone, both gone at a stroke —
Don't let them go begging, abandoned,   1650
women without men. Your own flesh and blood!
Never bring them down to the level of my pains.
Pity them. Look aot them, so young, so vulnerable,
shorn of everything — you're their only hope.
Promise me, noble Creon, touch my hand.   1655

Reaching toward Creon, who draws back.

You, little ones, if you were old enough
to understand, there is much I'd tell you.
Now, as it is, I'd have you say a prayer.

Pray for life, my children,
live where you are free to grow and season.   1660
Pray god you find a better life than mine,
the father who begot you.
Creon: Enough.
You've wept enough. Into the palace now.
Oedipus: I must, but I find it very hard.
Creon: Time is the great healer, you will see.   1665
Oedipus: I am going—you know on what condition?
Creon: Tell me. I'm listening.
Oedipus: Drive me out of Thebes, in exile.
Creon: Not I. Only the gods can give you that.
Oedipus: Surely the gods hate me so much—   1670
Creon: You'll get your wish at once.
Oedipus: You consent?
Creon: I try to say what I mean; it's my habit.
Oedipus: Then take me away. It's time.
Creon: Come along, let go of the children.
Oedipus: No—
don't take them away from me, not now! No no no!   1675

*Clutching his daughters as the guards wrench them loose and take them
through the palace doors.*

Creon: Still the king, the master of all things?
No more: here your power ends.
None of your power follows you through life.

*Exit Oedipus and Creon to the palace. The Chorus comes forward to address
the audience directly.*

Chorus: People of Thebes, my countrymen, look on Oedipus.
He solved the famous riddle with his brilliance,   1680
he rose to power, a man beyond all power.
Who could behold his greatness without envy?
Now what a black sea of terror has overwhelmed him.
Now as we keep our watch and wait the final day,
count no man happy till he dies, free of pain at last.   1685

Exit in procession.

CONSIDERATIONS FOR CRITICAL THINKING AND WRITING

1. **FIRST RESPONSE.** Is it possible for a twenty-first-century reader to identify
   with Oedipus's plight? What philosophic issues does he confront?

2. In the opening scene what does the priest's speech reveal about how Oedipus has been regarded as a ruler of Thebes?

3. What do Oedipus's confrontations with Tiresias and Creon indicate about
   his character?

4. Aristotle defined a tragic flaw as consisting of "error and frailties." What
   errors does Oedipus make? What are his frailties?

5. What causes Oedipus's downfall? Is he simply a pawn in a predetermined
   game played by the gods? Can he be regarded as responsible for the suffering and death in the play?

6. Locate instances of dramatic irony in the play. How do they serve as fore-shadowings?

7. Describe the function of the Chorus. How does the Chorus's view of life and the gods differ from Jocasta's?

8. Trace the images of vision and blindness throughout the play. How are they related to the theme? Why does Oedipus blind himself instead of joining Jocasta in suicide?

9. What is your assessment of Oedipus at the end of the play? Was he foolish? Heroic? Fated? To what extent can your emotions concerning him be described as "pity and fear"?

10. CRITICAL STRATEGIES. Read the section on psychological criticism (pp. 1542–44) in Chapter 46, "Critical Strategies for Reading," and Sigmund Freud's "On the Oedipus Complex" (p. 1146). Given that the *Oedipus complex* is a well-known term used in psychoanalysis, what does it mean? Does the concept offer any insights into the conflicts dramatized in the play?

CONNECTIONS TO OTHER SELECTIONS

1. Consider the endings of *Oedipus the King* and Shakespeare's *Othello* (p. 1164). What feelings do you have about these endings? Are they irredeemably unhappy? Is there anything that suggests hope for the future at the ends of these plays?

2. Sophocles does not include violence in his plays; any bloodshed occurs off-stage. Compare and contrast the effects of this strategy with the use of violence in *Othello*.

3. Write an essay explaining why *Oedipus the King* cannot be considered a real-istic play in the way that Henrik Ibsen's *A Doll House* (p. 1257) can be.

Perspectives on Sophocles

ARISTOTLE (384–322 B.C.)

On Tragic Character   *c. 340 B.C.*

Now since in the finest kind of tragedy the structure should be complex and not simple, and since it should also be a representation of terrible and piteous events (that being the special mark of this type of imitation), in the first place, it is evident that good men ought not to be shown passing from happiness to misfortune, for this does not inspire either pity or fear, but only revulsion; nor evil men rising from ill fortune to prosperity, for this is the most untragic plot of all — it lacks every requirement, in that it neither elicits human sympathy nor stirs pity or fear. And again, neither should an extremely wicked man be seen falling from prosperity into misfortune, for a plot so constructed might indeed call forth human sympathy, but would not excite pity or fear, since the first is felt for a person whose misfortune is undeserved and the second for someone like ourselves — pity for the man suffering undeservedly, fear for the man like ourselves — and hence neither pity nor fear would be aroused in this case. We are left with the man whose place is between these extremes. Such is the man who on the one hand is not preeminent in virtue and justice, and yet on the other hand does not fall into misfortune through vice or depravity, but falls because of some mistake; one among the number of the highly renowned and prosperous, such as Oedipus . . . and other famous men from families like [his].

It follows that the plot which achieves excellence will necessarily be single in outcome and not, as some say, double, and will consist in a change of fortune, not to prosperity from misfortune, but the opposite, from prosperity to misfortune, occasioned not by depravity, but by some great mistake on the part of one who is either such as I have described or better than this rather than worse. What actually has taken place has confirmed this; for though at first the poets accepted whatever myths came to hand, today the finest tragedies are founded upon the stories of only a few houses . . . and such . . . as have chanced to suffer terrible things or to do them. So then, tragedy having this construction is the finest kind of tragedy from an artistic point of view. And consequently those persons fall into the same error who bring it as a charge against Euripides° that this is what he does in his tragedies and that most of his plays have unhappy endings. For this is in fact the right procedure, as I have said; and the best proof is that on the stage and in the dramatic contests, plays of this kind seem the most tragic, provided they are successfully worked out, and Euripides, even if in everything else his management is faulty, seems at any rate to be the most tragic of the poets.

Second to this is the kind of plot that some persons place first, that which like the *Odyssey*° has a double structure and ends in opposite ways for the better characters and the worse. If it seems to be first, that is attributable to the weakness of the audience, since the poets only follow their lead and compose the kind of plays the spectators want. The pleasure it gives, however, is not that which comes from tragedy, but is rather the pleasure proper to comedy; for in comedy those who in the legend are the worst of enemies . . . end by leaving the scene as friends, and nobody is killed by anybody. . . .

With regard to the characters there are four things to aim at. First and foremost is that the characters be good. The personages will have character if, as aforesaid, they reveal in speech or in action what their moral choices are, and a good character will be one whose choices are good. It is possible to portray goodness in every class of persons; a woman may be good and a slave may be good, though perhaps as a class women are inferior and slaves utterly base. The second requisite is to make the character appropriate. Thus it is possible to portray any character as manly, but inappropriate for a female character to be manly or formidable in the way I mean. Third is to make the characters lifelike, which is something different from making them good and appropriate as described above. Fourth is to make them consistent. Even if the person being imitated is inconsistent and this is what the character is supposed to be, he should nevertheless be portrayed as consistently inconsistent. . . .

In the characters and in the plot-construction alike, one must strive for that which is either necessary or probable, so that whatever a character of any kind says or does may be the sort of thing such a character will inevitably or

Euripides: Fifth century B.C. Greek playwright whose tragedies include *Electra, Medea,* and *Alcestis.* *Odyssey:* The epic by the ancient Greek poet Homer that chronicles the voyage home from the Trojan War of Odysseus (also known as Ulysses).

probably say or do and the events of the plot may follow one after another either inevitably or with probability. (Obviously, then, the *dénouement* of the plot should arise from the plot itself and not be brought about "from the machine." . . . The machine is to be used for matters lying outside the drama, either antecedents of the action which a human being cannot know, or things subsequent to the action that have to be prophesied and announced; for we accept it that the gods see everything. Within the events of the plot itself, however, there should be nothing unreasonable, or if there is, it should be kept outside the play proper as is done in the *Oedipus* of Sophocles.)

Inasmuch as tragedy is an imitation of persons who are better than the average, the example of good portrait-painters should be followed. These, while reproducing the distinctive appearance of their subjects in a recognizable likeness, make them handsomer in the picture than they are in reality. Similarly the poet when he comes to imitate men who are irascible or easygoing or have other defects of character should depict them as such and yet as good men at the same time.

From Poetics, translated by James Hutton

Considerations for Critical Thinking and Writing

1. Why does Aristotle insist that both virtuous and depraved characters are unsuitable as tragic figures? What kind of person constitutes a tragic character according to him?

2. Aristotle argues that it is "inappropriate for a female character to be manly or formidable" (para. 4). Do you think Antigone fits this negative description? Does she seem "inferior" to the men in the play?

3. Aristotle says that characters should be "lifelike" (para. 4), but he also points out that characters should be made "handsomer . . . than they are in reality" (para. 6). Is this a contradiction? Explain why or why not.

SIGMUND FREUD (1856–1939)

On the Oedipus Complex   1900

If *Oedipus Rex* moves a modern audience no less than it did the contemporary Greek one, the explanation can only be that its effect does not lie in the contrast between destiny and human will, but is to be looked for in the particular nature of the material on which that contrast is exemplified. There must be something which makes a voice within us ready to recognize the compelling force of destiny in the *Oedipus.* . . . His destiny moves us only because it might have been ours — because the oracle laid the same curse upon us before our birth as upon him. It is the fate of all of us, perhaps, to direct our first sexual impulse toward our mother and our first hatred and our first murderous wish against our father. Our dreams convince us that this is so. King Oedipus, who slew his father Laïus and married his mother Jocasta, merely shows us the fulfillment of our own childhood wishes. But, more fortunate than he, we have meanwhile succeeded, in so far as we have not become psychoneurotics, in detaching our sexual impulses from our mothers and in forgetting our jealousy of our fathers. Here is one in whom these primeval wishes of our childhood have been fulfilled, and we shrink back from him with the whole force of the repression by which those wishes have since that time been held down within us. While the poet, as he unravels the past, brings to light the guilt of Oedipus, he is at the same time compelling us to recognize our own inner minds, in which those same impulses, though suppressed, are still to be found. The contrast with which the closing Chorus leaves us confronted —

> . . . Fix on Oedipus your eyes,
> Who resolved the dark enigma, noblest champion and most wise.
> Like a star his envied fortune mounted beaming far and wide:
> Now he sinks in seas of anguish, whelmed beneath a raging tide . . .[1]

— strikes as a warning at ourselves and our pride, at us who since our childhood have grown so wise and so mighty in our own eyes. Like Oedipus, we live in ignorance of these wishes, repugnant to morality, which have been forced upon us by Nature, and after their revelation we may all of us well seek to close our eyes to the scenes of our childhood.

There is an unmistakable indication in the text of Sophocles' tragedy itself that the legend of Oedipus sprang from some primeval dream material which had as its content the distressing disturbance of a child's relation to his parents owing to the first stirrings of sexuality. At a point when Oedipus, though he is not yet enlightened, has begun to feel troubled by his recollection of the oracle, Jocasta consoles him by referring to a dream which many people dream, though, as she thinks, it has no meaning:

> Many a man ere now in dreams hath lain
> With her who bare him. He hath least annoy
> Who with such omens troubleth not his mind.[2]

Today, just as then, many men dream of having sexual relations with their mothers, and speak of the fact with indignation and astonishment. It is clearly the key to the tragedy and the complement to the dream of the dreamer's father being dead. The story of Oedipus is the reaction of the imagination to these two typical dreams. And just as these dreams, when dreamt by adults, are accompanied by feelings of repulsion, so too the legend must include horror and self-punishment. Its further modification originates once again in a misconceived secondary revision of the material, which has sought to exploit it for theological purposes. . . . The attempt to harmonize divine omnipotence with human responsibility must naturally fail in connection with this subject matter just as with any other.

From Interpretation of Dreams, translated by James Strachey

[1]Lewis Campbell's translation, lines 1524ff. [in *The Bedford Introduction to Literature*, lines 1679–1683].

[2]Lewis Campbell's translation, lines 982ff. [in *The Bedford Introduction to Literature*, lines 1074–1076].

CONSIDERATIONS FOR CRITICAL THINKING AND WRITING

1. Read the section on psychological criticism in Chapter 46, "Critical Strategies for Reading" (pp. 1542–44) for additional information about Freud's theory concerning the Oedipus complex. Explain whether you agree or disagree that Freud's approach offers the "key to the tragedy" of *Oedipus the King.*

2. How does Freud's view of tragic character differ from Aristotle's?

SOPHOCLES   (496?–406 B.C.)

Another Translation of a Scene from Oedipus the King   *1920*

TRANSLATED BY J. T. SHEPPARD

Enter Oedipus, blind.

Chorus: O sight for all the world to see
    Most terrible! O suffering
Of all mine eyes have seen most terrible!
    Alas! What Fury came on thee?
    What evil Spirit, from afar,
    O Oedipus! O Wretched!
       Leapt on thee, to destroy?
I cannot even Alas! look
Upon thy face, though much I have
To ask of thee, and much to hear,
    Aye, and to see — I cannot!
    Such terror is in thee!

Oedipus: Alas! O Wretched! Whither go
    My steps? My voice? It seems to float
      Far, far away from me.
    Alas! Curse of my Life, how far
      Thy leap hath carried thee!

Chorus: To sorrows none can bear to see or hear.

Oedipus: Ah! The cloud!
    Visitor unspeakable! Darkness upon me horrible!
    Unconquerable! Cloud that may not ever pass away!
       Alas!
    And yet again, alas! How deep they stab —
    These throbbing pains, and all those memories.

Chorus: Where such afflictions are, I marvel not,
    If soul and body made one doubled woe.

Oedipus: Ah! My friend!
    Still remains thy friendship. Still thine is the help that comforts me,
    And kindness, that can look upon these dreadful eyes unchanged.
       Ah me!
    My friend, I feel thy presence. Though mine eyes
    Be darkened, yet I hear thy voice, and know.

Chorus: Oh, dreadful deed! How wert thou steeled to quench
    Thy vision thus? What Spirit came on thee?

Oedipus: Apollo! 'Twas Apollo, friends,
    Willed the evil, willed, and brought the agony to pass!
      And yet the hand that struck was mine, mine only, wretched.
      Why should I see, whose eyes
    Had no more any good to look upon?

Chorus: 'Twas even as thou sayest.

Oedipus: Aye. For me . . . Nothing is left for sight.
      Nor anything to love:
    Nor shall the sound of greetings any more

Fall pleasant on my ear.
   Away! Away! Out of the land, away!
     Banishment, Banishment! Fatal am I, accursed,
     And the hate on me, as on no man else, of the gods!

Chorus: Unhappy in thy fortune and the wit
   That shows it thee. Would thou hadst never known.

Oedipus: A curse upon the hand that loosed
   In the wilderness the cruel fetters of my feet,
     Rescued me, gave me life! Ah! Cruel was his pity,
      Since, had I died, so much
    I had not harmed myself and all I love.

Chorus: Aye, even so 'twere better.

Oedipus: Aye, for life never had led me then
     To shed my father's blood;
     Men had not called me husband of the wife
     That bore me in the womb.
   But now — but now — Godless am I, the son
     Born of impurity, mate of my father's bed,
     And if worse there be, I am Oedipus! It is mine!

Chorus: In this I know not how to call thee wise,
   For better wert thou dead than living — blind.

Oedipus: Nay, give me no more counsel. Bid me not
   Believe my deed, thus done, is not well done.
   I know 'tis well. When I had passed the grave,
   How could those eyes have met my father's gaze,
   Or my unhappy mother's — since on both
   I have done wrongs beyond all other wrong?
   Or live and see my children? — Children born
   As they were born! What pleasure in that sight?
   None for these eyes of mine, for ever, none.
   Nor in the sight of Thebes, her castles, shrines
   And images of the gods, whereof, alas!
   I robbed myself — myself, I spoke that word,
   I that she bred and nurtured, I her prince,
   And bade her thrust the sinner out, the man
   Proved of the gods polluted — Laïus' son.
   When such a stain by my own evidence
   Was on me, could I raise my eyes to them?
   No! Had I means to stop my ears, and choke
   The wells of sound, I had not held my hand,
   But closed my body like a prison-house
   To hearing as to sight. Sweet for the mind
   To dwell withdrawn, where troubles could not come.
     Cithaeron! Ah, why didst thou welcome me?
   Why, when thou hadst me there, didst thou not kill,
   Never to show the world myself — my birth!
     O Polybus, and Corinth, and the home
   Men called my father's ancient house, what sores
   Festered beneath that beauty that ye reared,
   Discovered now, sin out of sin begot.

O ye three roads, O secret mountain-glen,
Trees, and a pathway narrowed to the place
Where met the three, do you remember me?
I gave you blood to drink, my father's blood,
And so my own! Do you remember that?
The deed I wrought for you? Then, how I passed
Hither to other deeds?
                    O Marriage-bed
That gave me birth, and, having borne me, gave
Fresh children to your seed, and showed the world
Father, son, brother, mingled and confused,
Bride, mother, wife in one, and all the shame
Of deeds the foulest ever known to man.
    No. Silence for a deed so ill to do
Is better. Therefore lead me hence, away!
To hide me or to kill. Or to the sea
Cast me, where you shall look on me no more.
Come! Deign to touch me, though I am a man
Accursèd. Yield! Fear nothing! Mine are woes
That no man else, but I alone, must bear.

CONSIDERATIONS FOR CRITICAL THINKING AND WRITING

1. This excerpt from Sheppard's translation corresponds to lines 1433–1550 in Robert Fagles's translation (pp. 1137–40). Examine both versions of the scene and describe the diction and tone of each. If you find one of the translations more effective than the other, indicate why.

2. Explain whether the different translations affect your understanding or interpretation of the scene.

MURIEL RUKEYSER (1913–1980)

On Oedipus the King   1973
Myth

Long afterward, Oedipus, old and blinded, walked the
roads.   He smelled a familiar smell.   It was
the Sphinx.   Oedipus said, "I want to ask one question.
Why didn't I recognize my mother?"   "You gave the
wrong answer," said the Sphinx.   "But that was what   5
made everything possible," said Oedipus.   "No," she said.
"When I asked, What walks on four legs in the morning,
two at noon, and three in the evening, you answered,
Man.   You didn't say anything about woman."
"When you say Man," said Oedipus, "you include women   10
too. Everyone knows that."   She said, "That's what
you think."

CONSIDERATIONS FOR CRITICAL THINKING AND WRITING

1. What elements of the Oedipus story does Rukeyser allude to in the poem?

2. To what does the title of Rukeyser's poem "Myth" refer? How does the word *myth* carry more than one meaning?

3. This poem is amusing, but its ironic ending points to a serious theme. What is it? Does Sophocles' play address any of the issues raised in the poem?

DAVID WILES

On Oedipus the King *as a Political Play*   2000

Oedipus becomes a political play when we focus on the interaction of actor and chorus, and see how the chorus form a democratic mass jury. Each sequence of dialogue takes the form of a contest for the chorus' sympathy, with Oedipus sliding from the role of prosecutor to that of defendant, and each choral dance offers a provisional verdict. After Oedipus' set-to with Teiresias the sooth-sayer, the chorus decide to trust Oedipus on the basis of his past record; after his argument with his brother-in-law Creon, the chorus show their distress and urge compromise. Once Oedipus has confessed to a killing and Jocasta has declared that oracles have no force, the chorus are forced to think about polit-ical tyranny, torn between respect for divine law and trust in their rulers. In the next dance they assume that the contradiction is resolved and Oedipus has turned out to be the son of a god. Finally a slave's evidence reveals that the man most honoured by society is in fact the least to be envied. The political implications are clear: there is no space in democratic society for such as Oedi-pus. Athenians, like the chorus of the play, must reject the temptation to believe one man can calculate the future.

From *Greek Theatre Performance: An Introduction*

CONSIDERATIONS FOR CRITICAL THINKING AND WRITING

1. Consider one of the scenes mentioned by Wiles and discuss in detail how "the chorus form a democratic mass jury" that judges Oedipus.

2. Discuss the "political implications" of the play that, according to Wiles, suggest "there is no space in democratic society for such as Oedipus."

SUGGESTED TOPICS FOR LONGER PAPERS

1. In *Oedipus the King*, private and public worlds collide and produce over-whelming conflicts for the protagonist. In your essay, explore how the play's conflicts can be framed by a consideration of the private and public identities of the major characters.

2. Individual responses to authority loom large in *Oedipus the King*. Use the library to determine how Sophocles' contemporaries regarded individuals' responsibility to their kings and their kings' obligations to them. Given this context, how do you judge the behavior of Oedipus as a king in his society?

41

A Study of
William Shakespeare

All the world's a stage,
And all the men and women
merely players:
They have their exits and their
entrances;
And one man in his time plays
many parts . . .
— WILLIAM SHAKESPEARE

Shakespeare — the nearest thing in
incarnation to the eye of God.
— SIR LAURENCE OLIVIER

Although relatively little is known about William Shakespeare's life, his writings reveal him to have been an extraordinary man. His vitality, compassion, and insights are evident in his broad range of characters, who have fascinated generations of audiences, and his powerful use of the English language, which has been celebrated since his death nearly four centuries ago. Ben Jonson, his contemporary, rightly claimed that "he was not of an age, but for all time!" Shakespeare's plays have been produced so often and his writings read so widely that quotations from them have woven their way into our everyday conversations. If you have ever experienced "fear and trembling" because there was "something in the wind" or discovered that it

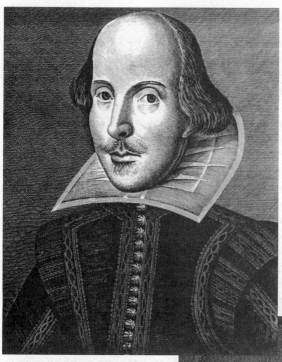

"First Folio" portrait (top). The image of William Shakespeare above is a portrait included on the *First Folio*, a collected edition of Shakespeare's plays published seven years after his death.   **"Chandos" portrait (middle).** This is an image painted during Shakespeare's lifetime known as the "Chandos portrait," rumored to have been painted by Shakespeare's friend and fellow actor Richard Burbage. **Shakespeare's signature (bottom).** The signature shown here is one of the bard's six authenticated signatures in existence, and is from his last will and testament.

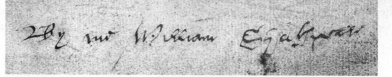

was "a foregone conclusion" that you would "make a virtue of necessity," then it wouldn't be quite accurate for you to say that Shakespeare "was Greek to me" because these phrases come, respectively, from his plays *Much Ado about Nothing, Comedy of Errors, Othello, The Two Gentlemen of Verona,* and *Julius Caesar.* Many more examples could be cited, but it is enough to say that Shakespeare's art endures. His words may give us only an oblique glimpse of his life, but they continue to give us back the experience of our own lives.

Shakespeare was born in Stratford-on-Avon on or about April 23, 1564. His father, an important citizen who held several town offices, married a woman from a prominent family; however, when their son was only a teenager, the family's financial situation became precarious. Shakespeare probably attended the Stratford grammar school, but no records of either his schooling or his early youth exist. As limited as his education was, it is clear that he was for his time a learned man. At the age of eighteen, he struck out on his own and married the twenty-six-year-old Anne Hathaway, who bore him a daughter in 1583 and twins, a boy and a girl, in 1585. Before he was twenty-one, Shakespeare had a wife and three children to support.

What his life was like for the next seven years is not known, but there is firm evidence that by 1592 he was in London enjoying some success as both an actor and a playwright. By 1594 he had also established himself as a poet with two lengthy poems, *Venus and Adonis* and *The Rape of Lucrece.* But it was in the theater that he made his living and his strongest reputation. He was well connected with a successful troupe first known as the Lord Chamberlain's Men; they built the famous Globe Theatre in 1599. Later this company, because of the patronage of King James, came to be known as the King's Men. Writing plays for this company throughout his career, Shakespeare also became one of its principal shareholders, an arrangement that allowed him to prosper in London as well as in his native Stratford, where in 1597 he bought a fine house called New Place. About 1611 he retired there with his family, although he continued writing plays. He died on April 23, 1616, and was buried at Holy Trinity Church in Stratford.

The documented details of Shakespeare's life provide barely enough information for a newspaper obituary. But if his activities remain largely unknown, his writings — among them thirty-seven plays and 154 sonnets — more than compensate for that loss. Plenty of authors have produced more work, but no writer has created so much literature that has been so universally admired. Within twenty-five years Shakespeare's dramatic works included *Hamlet, Macbeth, King Lear, Othello, Julius Caesar, Richard III, 1 Henry IV, Romeo and Juliet, Love's Labour's Lost, A Midsummer Night's Dream, The Tempest, Twelfth Night,* and *Measure for Measure.* These plays represent a broad range of characters and actions conveyed in poetic language that reveals human nature as well as the author's genius.

Web Explore contexts for William Shakespeare on *LiterActive* or at bedfordstmartins.com/ meyercompact.

SHAKESPEARE'S THEATER

Drama languished in Europe after the fall of Rome during the fifth and sixth centuries. From about A.D. 400 to 900 almost no record of dramatic productions exists except for those of minstrels and other entertainers, such as acrobats and jugglers, who traveled through the countryside. The Catholic church was instrumental in suppressing drama because the theater — represented by the excesses of Roman productions — was seen as subversive. No state-sponsored festivals brought people together in huge theaters the way they had in Greek and Roman times.

In the tenth century, however, the church helped revive theater by incorporating dialogues into the Mass as a means of dramatizing portions of the Gospels. These brief dialogues developed into more elaborate mystery plays, miracle plays, and morality plays, anonymous works that were created primarily to inculcate religious principles rather than to entertain. But these works also marked the reemergence of relatively large dramatic productions.

Mystery plays dramatize stories from the Bible, such as the Creation, the Fall of Adam and Eve, or the Crucifixion. The most highly regarded surviving example is *The Second Shepherd's Play* (c. 1400), which dramatizes Christ's nativity. *Miracle plays* are based on the lives of saints. An extant play of the late fifteenth century, for example, is titled *Saint Mary Magdalene*. *Morality plays* present allegorical stories in which virtues and vices are personified to teach humanity how to achieve salvation. *Everyman* (c. 1500), the most famous example, has as its central conflict every person's struggle to avoid the sins that lead to hell and practice the virtues that are rewarded in heaven.

The clergy who performed these plays gave way to trade guilds that presented them outside the church on stages featuring scenery and costumed characters. The plays' didactic content was gradually abandoned in favor of broad humor and worldly concerns. Thus by the sixteenth century religious drama had been replaced largely by secular drama.

Because theatrical productions were no longer sponsored and financed by the church or trade guilds during Shakespeare's lifetime, playwrights had to figure out ways to draw audiences willing to pay for entertainment. This necessitated some simple but important changes. Somehow, people had to be prevented from seeing a production unless they paid. Hence an enclosed space with controlled access was created. In addition, the plays had to change frequently enough to keep audiences returning, and this resulted in more experienced actors and playwrights sensitive to their audiences' tastes and interests. Plays compelling enough to attract audiences had to employ a powerful writing brought to life by convincing actors in entertaining productions. Shakespeare always wrote his dramas for the stage — for audiences who would see and hear the characters. The conventions of the theater for which he wrote are important, then, for appreciating and understanding his plays. Detailed information about Elizabethan theater (theater during the reign of Elizabeth I, from 1558 to 1603) is less

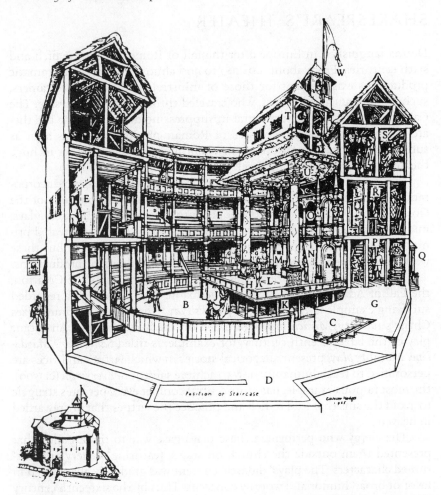

A	Main entrance
B	The yard
C	Entrances to lowest gallery
D	Position of entrances to staircase and upper galleries
E	Corridor serving the different sections of the middle gallery
F	Middle gallery ("Twopenny Rooms")
G	Position of "Gentlemen's Rooms" or "Lords' Rooms"
H	The stage
J	The hanging being put up round the stage
K	The "hell" under the stage
L	The stage trap leading down to the hell
M	Stage doors
N	Curtained "place behind the stage"
O	Gallery above the stage, used as required sometimes by musicians, sometimes by spectators, and often as part of the play
P	Backstage area (the tiring-house)
Q	Tiring-house door
R	Dressing-rooms
S	Wardrobe and storage
T	The hut housing the machine for lowering enthroned gods, etc., to the stage
U	The "heavens"
W	Hoisting the playhouse flag

A Conjectural Reconstruction of the Globe Theatre, 1599–1613. (Drawing by
C. Walter Hodges from his *The Globe Restored,* published by Oxford University Press © 1968
C. Walter Hodges. Reprinted by permission of Oxford University Press.)

than abundant, but historians have pieced together a good sense of what theaters were like from sources such as drawings, building contracts, and stage directions.

Early performances of various kinds took place in the courtyards of inns and taverns. These secular entertainments attracted people of all classes. To the dismay of London officials, such gatherings were also settings for the illegal activities of brawlers, thieves, and prostitutes. To avoid licensing regulations, some theaters were constructed outside the city's limits. The Globe, for instance, built by the Lord Chamberlain's Company, with which Shakespeare was closely associated, was located on the south bank of the Thames River. Regardless of the play, an Elizabethan theatergoer was likely to have an exciting time. Playwrights understood the varied nature of their audiences, so the plays appealed to a broad range of sensibilities and tastes. Philosophy and poetry rubbed shoulders with violence and sexual jokes, and somehow all were made compatible.

Physically, Elizabethan theaters resembled the courtyards where they originated, but the theaters could accommodate more people — perhaps as many as twenty-five hundred. The exterior of a theater building was many-sided or round and enclosed a yard that was only partially roofed over, to take advantage of natural light. The interior walls consisted of three galleries of seats looking onto a platform stage that extended from the rear wall. These seats were sheltered from the weather and more comfortable than the area in front of the stage, which was known as the *pit*. Here "groundlings" paid a penny to stand and watch the performance. Despite the large number of spectators, the theater created an intimate atmosphere because the audience closely surrounded the stage on three sides.

This arrangement produced two theatrical conventions: asides and soliloquies. An *aside* is a speech directed only to the audience. It makes the audience privy to a character's thoughts, allowing them to perceive ironies and intrigues that other characters know nothing about. In a large performing space, such as a Greek amphitheater, asides would be unconvincing because they would have to be declaimed loudly to be heard, but they were well suited to Elizabethan theaters. A *soliloquy* is a speech delivered while an actor is alone on the stage; like an aside, it reveals a character's state of mind. Hamlet's "To be or not to be" speech is the most famous example of a soliloquy.

The Elizabethan platform stage was large enough — approximately twenty-five feet deep and forty feet wide — to allow a wide variety of actions, ranging from festive banquets to bloody battles. Sections of the floor could be opened or removed to create, for instance, the gravediggers' scene in *Hamlet* or to allow characters to exit through trapdoors. At the rear of the platform an inner stage was covered by curtains that could be drawn to reveal an interior setting, such as a bedroom or tomb. The curtains were also a natural location for a character to hide in order to overhear conversations. On each side of the curtains were doors through which characters entered and exited. An upper stage could be used as a watchtower, a castle

wall, or a balcony. Although most of the action occurred on the main platform stage, there were opportunities for fluid movements from one acting
area to another, providing a variety of settings.

These settings were not, however, elaborately indicated by scenery or
props. A scene might change when one group of characters left the stage
and another entered. A table and some chairs could be carried on quickly
to suggest a tavern. But the action was not interrupted for set changes.
Instead, the characters' speeches often identify the location of a scene. (In
modern editions of Shakespeare's plays, editors indicate in brackets the
scene breaks, settings, and movements of actors not identified in the original manuscripts to help readers keep track of things.) Today's performances of the plays frequently use more elaborate settings and props. But
Shakespeare's need to paint his scenery with words resulted in many poetic
descriptions. Here is one of moonlight from *Merchant of Venice:*

> How sweet the moonlight sleeps upon this bank!
> Here will we sit and let the sounds of music
> Creep in our ears. Soft stillness and the night
> Become the touches of sweet harmony.

Although the settings were scant and the props mostly limited to what
an actor carried onto the stage (a sword, a document, a shovel), Elizabethan costuming was an elaborate visual treat that identified the characters. Moreover, because women were not permitted to act in the theater,
their roles were played by boys dressed in female costumes. In addition,
elaborate sound effects were used to create atmosphere. A flourish of
trumpets might accompany the entrance of a king; small cannons might
be heard during a battle; thunder might punctuate a storm. In short, Elizabethan theater was alive with sights and sounds, but at the center of the
stage was the playwright's language; that's where the magic began.

THE RANGE OF SHAKESPEARE'S DRAMA: HISTORY, COMEDY, AND TRAGEDY

Shakespeare's plays fall into three basic categories: histories, comedies, and
tragedies. Broadly speaking, a history play is any drama based on historical
materials. In this case, Shakespeare's *Antony and Cleopatra* and *Julius Caesar*
would fit the definition, since they feature historical figures. More specifically, though, a **history play** is a British play based primarily on Raphael
Holinshed's *Chronicles of England, Scotland, and Ireland* (1578). This account
of British history was popular toward the end of the sixteenth century
because of the patriotic pride that was produced by the British defeat of
the Spanish Armada in 1588, and it was an important source for a series of
plays Shakespeare wrote treating the reigns of British kings from Richard
II to Henry VIII. The political subject matter of these plays both enter-

tained audiences and instructed them in virtues and vices involved in England's past efforts to overcome civil war and disorder. Ambition, deception, and treason were of more than historical interest. Shakespeare's audiences saw these plays about the fifteenth century as ways of sorting through the meanings of both the calamities of the past and the uncertainties of the present.

Although Shakespeare used Holinshed's *Chronicles* as a source, he did not hesitate to make changes for dramatic purposes. In *1 Henry IV,* for example, he ages Henry IV to contrast him with the youthful Prince Hal, and he makes Hotspur younger than he actually was to have him serve as a foil to the prince. The serious theme of Hal's growth into the kind of man who would make an ideal king is counterweighted by Shakespeare's comic creation of Falstaff, that good-humored "huge hill of flesh" filled with delightful contradictions. Falstaff had historic antecedents, but the true source of his identity is the imagination of Shakespeare, a writer who was, after all, a dramatist first.

Comedy is a strong element in *1 Henry IV,* but the play's overall tone is serious. Falstaff's behavior ultimately gives way to the measured march of English history. While Shakespeare encourages us to laugh at some of the participants, we are not invited to laugh at the history of English monarchies. Comedy even appears in Shakespeare's tragedies, as in Hamlet's jests with the gravediggers or in Emilia's biting remarks in *Othello*. This use of comedy is called **comic relief**, a humorous scene or incident that alleviates tension in an otherwise serious work. In many instances these moments enhance the thematic significance of the story in addition to providing laughter. When Hamlet jokes with the gravediggers, we laugh, but something hauntingly serious about the humor also intensifies our more serious emotions.

A true comedy, however, lacks a tragedy's sense that some great disaster will finally descend on the protagonist. There are conflicts and obstacles that must be confronted, but in comedy the characters delight us by overcoming whatever initially thwarts them. We can laugh at their misfortunes because we are confident that everything will turn out fine in the end. Shakespearean comedy tends to follow this general principle; it begins with problems and ends with their resolution.

Shakespeare's comedies are called **romantic comedies** because they typically involve lovers whose hearts are set on each other but whose lives are complicated by disapproving parents, deceptions, jealousies, illusions, confused identities, disguises, or other misunderstandings. Conflicts are present, but they are more amusing than threatening. This lightness is apparent in some of the comedies' titles: the conflict in a play such as *A Midsummer Night's Dream* is, in a sense, *Much Ado about Nothing—As You Like It* in a comedy. Shakespeare orchestrates the problems and confusion that typify the initial plotting of a romantic comedy into harmonious wedding arrangements in the final scenes. In these comedies life is a celebration, a feast that always satisfies, because the generosity of the humor leaves us with a revived appetite for life's surprising possibilities. Discord and misunderstanding give way to concord and love. Marriage symbolizes a pledge that life itself is renewable, so we are left with a sense of new beginnings.

Although a celebration of life, comedy is also frequently used as a vehicle for criticizing human affairs. *Satire* casts a critical eye on vices and follies by holding them up to ridicule — usually to point out an absurdity so that it can be avoided or corrected. In *Twelfth Night* Malvolio is satirized for his priggishness and pomposity. He thinks himself better than almost everyone around him, but Shakespeare reveals him to be comic as well as pathetic. We come to understand what Malvolio will apparently never comprehend: that no one can take him as seriously as he takes himself. Polonius is subjected to a similar kind of scrutiny in *Hamlet.*

Malvolio's ambitious efforts to attract Olivia's affections are rendered absurd by Shakespeare's use of both high and low comedy. **High comedy** consists of verbal wit, while **low comedy** is generally associated with physical action and is less intellectual. Through puns and witty exchanges, Shakespeare's high comedy displays Malvolio's inconsistencies of character. His self-importance is deflated by low comedy. We are treated to a *farce,* a form of humor based on exaggerated, improbable incongruities, when the staid Malvolio is tricked into wearing bizarre clothing and behaving like a fool to win Olivia. Our laughter is Malvolio's pain, but though he has been "notoriously abus'd" and he vows in the final scene to be "reveng'd on the whole pack" of laughing conspirators who have tricked him, the play ends on a light note. Indeed, it concludes with a song, the last line of which reminds us of the predominant tone of the play as well as the nature of comedy: "And we'll strive to please you every day."

Tragedy, in contrast, does not promise peace and contentment. The basic characteristics of tragedy have already been outlined in the context of Greek drama (see Chapter 40). Like Greek tragic heroes, Shakespeare's protagonists are exceptional human beings whose stature makes their misfortune all the more dramatic. These characters pay a high price for their actions. Oedipus's search for the killer of Laius, Hamlet's agonized conviction that "The time is out of joint," and Othello's willingness to doubt his wife's fidelity all lead to irreversible results. Comic plots are largely free of this sense of inevitability. Instead of the festive mood that prevails once the characters in a comedy recognize their true connection to each other, tragedy gives us dark reflections that emanate from suffering. The laughter of comedy is a shared experience, a recognition of human likeness, but suffering estranges tragic heroes from the world around them.

Some of the wrenching differences between comedy and tragedy can be experienced in *Othello.* Although this play is a tragedy, Shakespeare includes in its plot many of the ingredients associated with comedy. For a time it seems possible that Othello and Desdemona will overcome the complications of a disapproving father, along with the seemingly minor deceptions, awkward misperceptions, and tender illusions that hover around them. But in *Othello* marriage is not a sign of concord displacing discord; instead, love and marriage mark the beginning of the tragic action.

Another important difference between tragedy and comedy is the way characters are presented. The tragic protagonist is portrayed as a remarkable individual whose unique qualities compel us with their power and complexity. Macbeth is not simply a murderer nor is Othello merely a jealous husband. But despite their extreme passions, behavior, and even crimes, we identify with tragic heroes in ways that we do not with comic characters. We can laugh at pretentious fools, smug hypocrites, clumsy oafs, and thwarted lovers because we see them from a distance. They are amusing precisely because their problems are not ours; we recognize them as types instead of as ourselves (or so we think). No reader of *Twelfth Night* worries about Sir Toby Belch's excessive drinking; he is a cheerful "sot" whose passion for ale is cause for celebration rather than concern. Shakespeare's comedy is sometimes disturbing — Malvolio's character certainly is — but it is never devastating. Tragic heroes do confront devastation; they command our respect and compassion because they act in spite of terrifying risks. Their triumph is not measured by the attainment of what they seek but by the wisdom that defeat imposes on them.

A NOTE ON READING SHAKESPEARE

Readers who have had no previous experience with Shakespeare's language may find it initially daunting. They might well ask whether people ever talked the way, for example, Hamlet does in his most famous soliloquy:

> To be, or not to be: that is the question:
> Whether 'tis nobler in the mind to suffer
> The slings and arrows of outrageous fortune,
> Or to take arms against a sea of troubles,
> And by opposing end them?

People did not talk like this in Elizabethan times. Hamlet speaks poetry. Shakespeare might have had him say something like this: "The most important issue one must confront is whether the pain that life inevitably creates should be passively accepted or resisted." But Shakespeare chose poetry to reveal the depth and complexity of Hamlet's experience. This heightened language is used to clarify rather than obscure his characters' thoughts. Shakespeare has Hamlet, as well as many other characters, speak in prose too, but in general his plays are written in poetry. If you keep in mind that Shakespeare's dialogue is not typically intended to imitate everyday speech, it should be easier to understand that his language is more than simply a vehicle for expressing the action of the play.

Here are a few practical suggestions to enhance your understanding of and pleasure in reading Shakespeare's plays.

1. Keep track of the characters by referring to the *dramatis personae* (characters) listed and briefly described at the beginning of each play.
2. Remember that poetic language deserves to be read slowly and carefully. A difficult passage can sometimes be better understood if it's read aloud. Don't worry if every line isn't absolutely clear to you.
3. Pay attention to the annotations, which explain unfamiliar words, phrases, and allusions in the text. These can be distracting, but they are sometimes necessary to determine the basic meaning of a passage.
4. As you read each scene, try to imagine how it would be played on a stage.
5. If you find the reading especially difficult, try listening to a recording of the play. (Most college libraries have records and tapes of Shakespeare's plays.) Allowing professional actors to do the reading aloud for you can enrich your imaginative reconstruction of the action and characters. Hearing a play can help you with subsequent readings of it.
6. After reading the play, view a film or videocassette recording of a performance. It is important to view the performance *after* your reading, though, so that your own mental re-creation of the play is not short-circuited by a director's production.

And finally, to quote Hamlet, "Be not too tame . . . let your own discretion be your tutor." Read Shakespeare's work as best you can; it warrants such careful attention not because the language and characters are difficult to understand but because they offer so much to enjoy.

Othello the Moor of Venice

Othello has compelled audiences since it was first produced in 1604. Its power is as simple and as complex as the elemental emotions it dramatizes; the play ebbs and flows with the emotional energy derived from the characters' struggles with love and hatred, good and evil, trust and jealousy, appearance and reality. These conflicts are played out on a domestic scale rather than on some metaphysical level. Anyone who has ever been in love will empathize with Othello and Desdemona. They embody a love story gone horribly — tragically — wrong.

Although the plot of *Othello* is filled with Iago's intrigues and a series of opaque mysteries for Othello, it moves swiftly and precisely to its catastrophic ending as the tragedy relentlessly claims its victims. On one level the plot is simple. As the Moorish general of the Venetian army, Othello chooses Cassio to serve as his lieutenant, a selection Iago resents and decides to subvert. To discredit Cassio, Iago poisons Othello's faith in his wife, Desdemona, by falsely insinuating that she and Cassio are having an affair. Through a series of cleverly demonic manipulations, Iago succeeds

OTHELLO

THE

Moor of Venice.

A

TRAGEDY,

As it hath been divers times acted at the *Globe*,
and at the *Black-Friers* :

And now at the

THEATER ROYAL,

BY

HIS MAJESTIES SERVANTS.

Written by *William Shakespear*.

LONDON,

Printed for *W Weak*, and are to be fold by *Richard Bentley* and *M. Magnes* in *Ruffel Street* near *Covent-
Garden*, 1681.

The 1681 title page
for *Othello*.
© Bettmann / CORBIS.

in convincing Othello of his wife's infidelity and his lieutenant's betrayal.
Believing these lies, Othello insists upon taking his revenge.

If the plot of *Othello* is relatively direct and simple in its focus on Iago's
manipulation of events, the play's major characters are considerably more
complex. Love and jealousy are central in *Othello*. The Moor's virtues of
openness and trust cause him to experience betrayal as intensely as he does
love. He is distinguished by his nobility, bravery, strength, and deep sense
of honor, but he is also vulnerable to the doubts Iago raises owing to his
race ("I am black") and marginal status in Venetian society.

Iago, whose motivations are much deeper and more mysterious than his
maneuvering for a coveted lieutenancy, personifies a nearly inexplicable evil
in the play. Just as Desdemona's nature seems to be all goodness, Iago's is
malignant destruction. His profound villainy both horrifies and fascinates

us: How can he be what he is? He thrives on ambition, envy, deception, jealousy, and doubt. Although he commands absolutely no respect, he holds our attention because of his cunning duplicity.

The play is finally, however, Othello's story. As we watch him be seduced by Iago's veiled hints and seeming confidences, we see how his trusting nature is inextricably related to his propensity to suspect Desdemona. Iago plays on the complexity and paradox of Othello's character and manipulates those tensions to keep him off balance and blind to the truth of Desdemona's faithfulness. Ultimately, though, Othello must take responsibility for the destruction of his love, a responsibility that is both his tragedy and redemption.

WILLIAM SHAKESPEARE (1564–1616)

Othello the Moor of Venice   *1604*

THE NAMES OF THE ACTORS

See Plays in
Performance insert.

Othello, the Moor
Brabantio, [a Venetian senator,] father to Desdemona
Cassio, an honorable lieutenant [to Othello]
Iago, [Othello's ancient,] a villain
Roderigo, a gulled gentleman
Duke of Venice
Senators [of Venice]
Montano, governor of Cyprus
Lodovico and Gratiano, [kinsmen to Brabantio,] two noble Venetians
Sailors
Clowns
Desdemona, wife to Othello
Emilia, wife to Iago
Bianca, a courtesan
[Messenger, Herald, Officers, Venetian Gentlemen, Musicians, Attendants

SCENE: *Venice and Cyprus]*

ACT I

SCENE I: *A street in Venice.*

    Enter Roderigo and Iago.

Roderigo: Tush, never tell me! I take it much unkindly
    That thou, Iago, who hast had my purse
    As if the strings were thine, shouldst know of this.°

Act I, Scene I.   3 *this:* I.e., Desdemona's elopement.

Iago: 'Sblood,° but you'll not hear me!
 If ever I did dream of such a matter,   5
 Abhor me.
Roderigo: Thou told'st me thou didst hold him in thy hate.
Iago: Despise me if I do not. Three great ones of the city,
 In personal suit to make me his lieutenant,
 Off-capped to him;° and, by the faith of man,   10
 I know my price; I am worth no worse a place.
 But he, as loving his own pride and purposes,
 Evades them with a bombast circumstance.°
 Horribly stuffed with epithets of war;
 [And, in conclusion,]
 Nonsuits° my mediators; for, "Certes," says he,   15
 "I have already chose my officer."
 And what was he?
 Forsooth, a great arithmetician,°
 One Michael Cassio, a Florentine   20
 (A fellow almost damned in a fair wife°)
 That never set a squadron in the field,
 Nor the division of a battle knows
 More than a spinster; unless the bookish theoric,
 Wherein the togèd consuls can propose   25
 As masterly as he. Mere prattle without practice
 Is all his soldiership. But he, sir, had th' election;
 And I (of whom his eyes had seen the proof
 At Rhodes, at Cyprus, and on other grounds
 Christian and heathen) must be belee'd and calmed° 30
 By debitor and creditor; this counter-caster,°
 He, in good time, must his lieutenant be,
 And I — God bless the mark! — his Moorship's ancient.°
Roderigo: By heaven, I rather would have been his hangman.
Iago: Why, there's no remedy; 'tis the curse of service. 35
 Preferment goes by letter and affection,°
 And not by old gradation, where each second
 Stood heir to th' first. Now, sir, be judge yourself,
 Whether I in any just term am affined°
 To love the Moor.
Roderigo: I would not follow him then. 40
Iago: O, sir, content you;
 I follow him to serve my turn upon him.
 We cannot all be masters, nor all masters
 Cannot be truly followed. You shall mark
 Many a duteous and knee-crooking knave   45
 That, doting on his own obsequious bondage,
 Wears out his time, much like his master's ass,

---

4 *'Sblood:* By God's blood. 10 *him:* I.e., Othello. 13 *a bombast circumstance:* Pompous circumlocutions. 16 *Nonsuits:* Rejects. 19 *arithmetician:* Theoretician. 21 *almost . . . wife:* (An obscure allusion; Cassio is unmarried, but see IV.i.114). 30 *belee'd and calmed:* Left in the lurch. 31 *counter-caster:* Bookkeeper. 33 *ancient:* Ensign. 36 *affection:* Favoritism. 39 *affined:* Obliged.

For naught but provender; and when he's old, cashiered.°
Whip me such honest knaves! Others there are
Who, trimmed° in forms and visages of duty,   50
Keep yet their hearts attending on themselves;
And, throwing but shows of service on their lords,
Do well thrive by them, and when they have lined their coats,
Do themselves homage. These fellows have some soul;
And such a one do I profess myself. For, sir,   55
It is as sure as you are Roderigo,
Were I the Moor, I would not be Iago.
In following him, I follow but myself;
Heaven is my judge, not I for love and duty,
But seeming so, for my peculiar end;   60
For when my outward action doth demonstrate
The native act and figure of my heart°
In compliment extern,° 'tis not long after
But I will wear my heart upon my sleeve
For daws to peck at; I am not what I am.   65

Roderigo: What a full fortune does the thick-lips° owe°
   If he can carry't thus!

Iago: Call up her father,
   Rouse him. Make after him, poison his delight,
   Proclaim him in the streets. Incense her kinsmen,
   And though he in a fertile climate dwell,   70
   Plague him with flies; though that his joy be joy,
   Yet throw such changes of vexation on't
   As it may lose some color.

Roderigo: Here is her father's house. I'll call aloud.

Iago: Do, with like timorous° accent and dire yell   75
   As when, by night and negligence, the fire
   Is spied in populous cities.

Roderigo: What, ho, Brabantio! Signior Brabantio, ho!

Iago: Awake! What, ho, Brabantio! Thieves! thieves! thieves!
   Look to your house, your daughter, and your bags!   80
   Thieves! thieves!

   Brabantio at a window.°

Brabantio (above): What is the reason of this terrible summons?
   What is the matter there?

Roderigo: Signior, is all your family within?

Iago: Are your doors locked?

Brabantio: Why, wherefore ask you this?   85

Iago: Zounds, sir, y' are robbed! For shame, put on your gown!
   Your heart is burst; you have lost half your soul.
   Even now, now, very now, an old black ram
   Is tupping your white ewe. Arise, arise!

---

48 *cashiered:* Turned off.   50 *trimmed:* Dressed up.   62 *The...heart:* What I really believe
and intend.   63 *compliment extern:* Outward appearance.   66 *thick-lips:* An Elizabethan
epithet for blacks, including Moors; *owe:* Own.   75 *timorous:* Terrifying.   *Brabantio at a*
window: (added from quarto).

Awake the snorting° citizens with the bell.   90
Or else the devil will make a grandsire of you.
Arise, I say!
Brabantio: What, have you lost your wits?
Roderigo: Most reverend signior, do you know my voice?
Brabantio: Not I. What are you?   95
Roderigo: My name is Roderigo.
Brabantio: The worser welcome!
I have charged thee not to haunt about my doors.
In honest plainness thou hast heard me say
My daughter is not for thee; and now, in madness,
Being full of supper and distemp'ring draughts,   100
Upon malicious knavery dost thou come
To start my quiet.
Roderigo: Sir, sir, sir—
Brabantio: But thou must needs be sure
My spirit and my place have in them power   105
To make this bitter to thee.
Roderigo: Patience, good sir.
Brabantio: What tell'st thou me of robbing? This is Venice;
My house is not a grange.°
Roderigo: Most grave Brabantio,
In simple and pure soul I come to you.
Iago: Zounds, sir, you are one of those that will not serve God if the devil   110
bid you. Because we come to do you service, and you think we are ruf-
fians, you'll have your daughter covered with a Barbary horse; you'll
have your nephews° neigh to you; you'll have coursers for cousins, and
gennets for germans.°
Brabantio: What profane wretch art thou?   115
Iago: I am one, sir, that comes to tell you your daughter and the Moor are
now making the beast with two backs.
Brabantio: Thou are a villain.
Iago: You are—a senator.
Brabantio: This thou shalt answer. I know thee, Roderigo.
Roderigo: Sir, I will answer anything. But I beseech you,   120
If 't be your pleasure and most wise consent,
As partly I find it is, that your fair daughter,
At this odd-even° and dull watch o' th' night,
Transported, with no worse nor better guard
But with a knave of common hire, a gondolier,   125
To the gross clasps of a lascivious Moor—
If this be known to you, and your allowance,°
We then have done you bold and saucy wrongs;
But if you know not this, my manners tell me
We have your wrong rebuke. Do not believe   130
That, from the sense° of all civility,
I thus would play and trifle with your reverence.

---

90 *snorting:* Snoring.   108 *grange:* Isolated farmhouse.   113 *nephews:* I.e., grandsons.
114 *gennets for germans:* Spanish horses for near kinsmen.   123 *odd-even:* Between night
and morning.   127 *allowance:* Approval.   131 *from the sense:* In violation.

Your daughter, if you have not given her leave,
I say again, hath made a gross revolt,
Tying her duty, beauty, wit, and fortunes   135
In an extravagant and wheeling° stranger
Of here and everywhere. Straight satisfy yourself.
If she be in her chamber, or your house,
Let loose on me the justice of the state
For thus deluding you.

Brabantio: Strike on the tinder, ho!   140
Give me a taper! Call up all my people!
This accident° is not unlike my dream.
Belief of it oppresses me already.
Light, I say! light!   *Exit [above].*

Iago: Farewell, for I must leave you.
It seems not meet, nor wholesome to my place,   145
To be produced — as, if I stay, I shall —
Against the Moor. For I do know the state,
However this may gall him with some check,°
Cannot with safety cast° him; for he's embarked
With such loud reason to the Cyprus wars,   150
Which even now stand in act,° that for their souls
Another of his fathom° they have none
To lead their business; in which regard,
Though I do hate him as I do hell-pains,
Yet, for necessity of present life,   155
I must show out a flag and sign of love,
Which is indeed but sign. That you shall surely find him,
Lead to the Sagittary° the raisèd search;
And there will I be with him. So farewell.   *Exit.*

Enter [below] Brabantio in his nightgown,° and Servants with torches.

Brabantio: It is too true an evil. Gone she is;   160
And what's to come of my despisèd time
Is naught but bitterness. Now, Roderigo,
Where didst thou see her? — O unhappy girl! —
With the Moor, say'st thou? — Who would be a father? —
How didst thou know 'twas she! — O, she deceives me   165
Past thought! — What said she to you? — Get moe° tapers!
Raise all my kindred! — Are they married, think you?

Roderigo: Truly I think they are.

Brabantio: O heaven! How got she out? O treason of the blood!
Fathers, from hence trust not your daughters' minds   170
By what you see them act. Is there not charms
By which the property° of youth and maidhood
May be abused? Have you not read, Roderigo,
Of some such thing?

---

136 *extravagant and wheeling:* Expatriate and roving.   142 *accident:* Occurrence.   148 *check:* Reprimand.   149 *cast:* Discharge.   151 *stand in act:* Are going on.   152 *fathom:* Capacity.   158 *Sagittary:* An inn.   *nightgown:* Dressing gown.   166 *moe:* More.   172 *property:* Nature.

Roderigo: Yes, sir, I have indeed.
Brabantio: Call up my brother. — O, would you had had her! —   175
     Some one way, some another. — Do you know
     Where we may apprehend her and the Moor?
Roderigo: I think I can discover him, if you please
     To get good guard and go along with me.
Brabantio: I pray you lead on. At every house I'll call;   180
     I may command at most. — Get weapons, ho!
     And raise some special officers of night. —
     On, good Roderigo; I'll deserve° your pains.   *Exeunt.*

SCENE II: *Before the lodgings of Othello.*

     Enter Othello, Iago, and Attendants with torches.

Iago: Though in the trade of war I have slain men,
     Yet do I hold it very stuff o' th' conscience
     To do no contrived murther. I lack iniquity
     Sometimes to do me service. Nine or ten times
     I had thought t' have yerked° him here under the ribs.   5
Othello: 'Tis better as it is.
Iago: Nay, but he prated,
     And spoke such scurvy and provoking terms
     Against your honor
     That with the little godliness I have
     I did full hard forbear him. But I pray you, sir,   10
     Are you fast° married? Be assured of this,
     That the magnifico° is much beloved,
     And hath in his effect a voice potential°
     As double° as the Duke's. He will divorce you,
     Or put upon you what restraint and grievance   15
     The law, with all his might to enforce it on,
     Will give him cable.
Othello: Let him do his spite.
     My services which I have done the signiory°
     Shall out-tongue his complaints. 'Tis yet to know°—
     Which, when I know that boasting is an honor,   20
     I shall promulgate — I fetch my life and being
     From men of royal siege;° and my demerits°
     May speak unbonneted to as proud a fortune
     As this that I have reached.° For know, Iago,
     But that I love the gentle Desdemona,   25
     I would not my unhousèd° free condition
     Put into circumscription and confine
     For the sea's worth. But look what lights come yond?

183 *deserve:* Show gratitude for.   **Scene II.**   5 *yerked:* Stabbed.   11 *fast:* Securely.
12 *magnifico:* Grandee (Brabantio).   13 *potential:* Powerful.   14 *double:* Doubly influential.
18 *signiory:* Venetian government.   19 *yet to know:* Still not generally known.   22 *siege:*
Rank; *demerits:* Deserts.   23–24 *May speak . . . reached:* Are equal, I modestly assert, to
those of Desdemona's family.   26 *unhousèd:* Unrestrained.

Iago: Those are the raisèd father and his friends.
   You were best go in.
Othello: Not I; I must be found.   30
   My parts, my title, and my perfect soul°
   Shall manifest me rightly. Is it they?
Iago: By Janus, I think no.

   Enter Cassio, with torches, Officers.

Othello: The servants of the Duke, and my lieutenant.
   The goodness of the night upon you, friends!   35
   What is the news?
Cassio: The Duke does greet you, general;
   And he requires your haste-post-haste appearance
   Even on the instant.
Othello: What's the matter, think you?
Cassio: Something from Cyprus, as I may divine.
   It is a business of some heat. The galleys   40
   Have sent a dozen sequent° messengers
   This very night at one another's heels,
   And many of the consuls, raised and met,
   Are at the Duke's already. You have been hotly called for;
   When, being not at your lodging to be found,   45
   The Senate hath sent about three several quests
   To search you out.
Othello: 'Tis well I am found by you.
   I will but spend a word here in the house,
   And go with you.   *[Exit]*
Cassio: Ancient, what makes he here?
Iago: Faith, he to-night hath boarded a land carack.°   50
   If it prove lawful prize, he's made for ever.
Cassio: I do not understand.
Iago: He's married.
Cassio: To who?

   [Enter Othello.]

Iago: Marry, to—Come, captain, will you go?
Othello: Have with you.
Cassio: Here comes another troop to seek for you.

   Enter Brabantio, Roderigo, and others with lights and weapons.

Iago: It is Brabantio. General, be advised.   55
   He comes to bad intent.
Othello: Holla! stand there!
Roderigo: Signior, it is the Moor.
Brabantio: Down with him, thief!

   [They draw on both sides.]

Iago: You, Roderigo! Come, sir, I am for you.

---

31 *perfect soul:* Stainless conscience.   41 *sequent:* Consecutive.   50 *carack:* Treasure ship.

Othello: Keep up° your bright swords, for the dew will rust them.
　　　Good signior, you shall more command with years   60
　　　Than with your weapons.
Brabantio: O thou foul thief, where hast thou stowed my daughter?
　　　Damned as thou art, thou hast enchanted her!
　　　For I'll refer me to all things of sense,
　　　If she in chains of magic were not bound,   65
　　　Whether a maid so tender, fair, and happy,
　　　So opposite to marriage that she shunned
　　　The wealthy curlèd darlings of our nation,
　　　Would ever have, t' incur a general mock,
　　　Run from her guardage to the sooty bosom   70
　　　Of such a thing as thou — to fear, not to delight.
　　　Judge me the world if 'tis not gross in sense°
　　　That thou hast practiced on her with foul charms,
　　　Abused her delicate youth with drugs or minerals
　　　That weaken motion.° I'll have't disputed on;   75
　　　'Tis probable, and palpable to thinking.
　　　I therefore apprehend and do attach° thee
　　　For an abuser of the world, a practicer
　　　Of arts inhibited and out of warrant.
　　　Lay hold upon him. If he do resist,   80
　　　Subdue him at his peril.
Othello:　　　　　　　　　　　　Hold your hands,
　　　Both you of my inclining and the rest.
　　　Were it my cue to fight, I should have known it
　　　Without a prompter. Where will you that I go
　　　To answer this your charge?
Brabantio:　　　　　　　　　　To prison, till fit time   85
　　　Of law and course of direct session°
　　　Call thee to answer.
Othello:　　　　　　　　　What if I do obey?
　　　How may the Duke be therewith satisfied,
　　　Whose messengers are here about my side
　　　Upon some present business of the state   90
　　　To bring me to him?
Officer:　　　　　　　　　'Tis true, most worthy signior.
　　　The Duke's in council, and your noble self
　　　I am sure is sent for.
Brabantio:　　　　　　　How? The Duke in council?
　　　In this time of the night? Bring him away.
　　　Mine's not an idle° cause. The Duke himself,   95
　　　Or any of my brothers of the state,
　　　Cannot but feel this wrong as 'twere their own;
　　　For if such actions may have passage free,
　　　Bondslaves and pagans shall our statesmen be.   *Exeunt.*

---

59 *Keep up:* I.e., sheath.　　72 *gross in sense:* Obvious.　　75 *motion:* Perception.　　77 *attach:* Arrest.　　86 *direct session:* Regular trial.　　95 *idle:* Trifling.

SCENE III: *The Venetian Senate Chamber.*

Enter Duke and Senators, set at a table, with lights and Attendants.

Duke: There is no composition° in these news
    That gives them credit.
1. Senator: Indeed they are disproportioned.
    My letters say a hundred and seven galleys.
Duke: And mine a hundred forty.
2. Senator: And mine two hundred.
    But though they jump° not on a just account—   5
    As in these cases where the aim° reports
    'Tis oft with difference—yet do they all confirm
    A Turkish fleet, and bearing up to Cyprus.
Duke: Nay, it is possible enough to judgment.
    I do not so secure me° in the error   10
    But the main article° I do approve°
    In fearful sense.
Sailor (within):   What, ho! what, ho! what, ho!
Officer: A messenger from the galleys.

    Enter Sailor.

Duke: Now, what's the business?
Sailor: The Turkish preparation makes for Rhodes.
    So was I bid report here to the state   15
    By Signior Angelo.
Duke: How say you by this change?
1. Senator: This cannot be
    By no assay° of reason. 'Tis a pageant
    To keep us in false gaze.° When we consider
    Th' importancy of Cyprus to the Turk,   20
    And let ourselves again but understand
    That, as it more concerns the Turk than Rhodes,
    So may he with more facile question bear° it,
    For that it stands not in such warlike brace,°
    But altogether lacks th' abilities   25
    That Rhodes is dressed in—if we make thought of this,
    We must not think the Turk is so unskillful
    To leave that latest which concerns him first,
    Neglecting an attempt of ease and gain
    To wake and wage° a danger profitless.   30
Duke: Nay, in all confidence, he's not for Rhodes.
Officer: Here is more news.

    Enter a Messenger.

Scene III. 1 *composition:* Consistency.   5 *jump:* Agree.   6 *aim:* Conjecture.   10 *so secure me:* Take such comfort.   11 *article:* Substance; *approve:* Accept.   18 *assay:* Test. 19 *in false gaze:* Looking the wrong way.   23 *with . . . bear:* More easily capture.   24 *brace:* Posture of defense.   30 *wake and wage:* Rouse and risk.

Messenger: The Ottomites, reverend and gracious,
    Steering with due course toward the isle of Rhodes,
    Have there injointed them with an after fleet.   35
1. Senator: Ay, so I thought. How many, as you guess?
Messenger: Of thirty sail; and now they do restem°
    Their backward course, bearing with frank appearance
    Their purposes toward Cyprus, Signior Montano,
    Your trusty and most valiant servitor,   40
    With his free duty recommends you thus,
    And prays you to believe him.
Duke: 'Tis certain then for Cyprus.
    Marcus Luccicos,° is not he in town?
1. Senator: He's now in Florence.   45
Duke: Write from us to him; post, post-haste dispatch.
1. Senator: Here comes Brabantio and the valiant Moor.

    Enter Brabantio, Othello, Cassio, Iago, Roderigo, and Officers.

Duke: Valiant Othello, we must straight employ you
    Against the general enemy Ottoman.   *[To Brabantio.]*
    I did not see you. Welcome, gentle signior.   50
    We lacked your counsel and your help to-night.
Brabantio: So did I yours. Good your grace, pardon me.
    Neither my place, nor aught I heard of business,
    Hath raised me from my bed; nor doth the general care
    Take hold on me; for my particular grief   55
    Is of so floodgate° and o'erbearing nature
    That it engluts° and swallows other sorrows,
    And it is still itself.
Duke: Why, what's the matter?
Brabantio: My daughter! O, my daughter!
All: Dead?
Brabantio: Ay, to me.
    She is abused, stol'n from me, and corrupted   60
    By spells and medicines bought of mountebanks;
    For nature so prepost'rously to err,
    Being not deficient,° blind, or lame of sense,
    Sans witchcraft could not.
Duke: Whoe'er he be that in this foul proceeding   65
    Hath thus beguiled your daughter of herself,
    And you of her, the bloody book of law
    You shall yourself read in the bitter letter
    After your own sense; yea, though our proper° son
    Stood in your action.°
Brabantio: Humbly I thank your grace.   70
    Here is the man — this Moor, whom now, it seems,

---

37 *restem:* Steer again.   44 *Marcus Luccicos:* (Presumably a Venetian envoy).   56 *flood-gate:* Torrential.   57 *engluts:* Devours.   63 *deficient:* Feeble-minded.   69 *our proper:* My own.   70 *Stood in your action:* Were accused by you.

Your special mandate for the state affairs
Hath hither brought.
All: We are very sorry for't.
Duke [to Othello]: What, in your own part, can you say to this?
Brabantio: Nothing, but this is so.   75
Othello: Most potent, grave, and reverend signiors,
    My very noble, and approved° good masters,
    That I have ta'en away this old man's daughter,
    It is most true; true I have married her.
    The very head and front of my offending   80
    Hath this extent, no more. Rude° am I in my speech,
    And little blessed with the soft phrase of peace;
    For since these arms of mine had seven years' pith°
    Till now some nine moons wasted, they have used
    Their dearest action in the tented field;   85
    And little of this great world can I speak
    More than pertains to feats of broil and battle;
    And therefore little shall I grace my cause
    In speaking for myself. Yet, by your gracious patience,
    I will a round° unvarnished tale deliver   90
    Of my whole course of love — what drugs, what charms,
    What conjuration, and what mighty magic
    (For such proceeding am I charged withal)
    I won his daughter.
Brabantio: A maiden never bold;
    Of spirit so still and quiet that her motion   95
    Blushed° at herself; and she — in spite of nature,
    Of years, of country, credit, everything —
    To fall in love with what she feared to look on!
    It is a judgment maimed and most imperfect
    That will confess perfection so could err   100
    Against all rules of nature, and must be driven
    To find out practices° of cunning hell
    Why this should be. I therefore vouch° again
    That with some mixtures pow'rful o'er the blood,°
    Or with some dram, conjured to this effect,   105
    He wrought upon her.
Duke: To vouch this is no proof,
    Without more certain and more overt test
    Than these thin habits° and poor likelihoods
    Of modern seeming° do prefer against him.
1. Senator: But, Othello, speak.   110
    Did you by indirect and forcèd° courses
    Subdue and poison this young maid's affections?

---

77 *approved:* Tested by experience.   81 *Rude:* Unpolished.   83 *pith:* Strength.   90 *round:*
Plain.   95–96 *her motion Blushed:* Her own emotions caused her to blush.   102 *practices:*
Plots.   103 *vouch:* Assert.   104 *blood:* Passions.   108 *thin habits:* Slight appearances.
109 *modern seeming:* Everyday supposition.   111 *forcèd:* Violent.

Or came it by request, and such fair question°
  As soul to soul affordeth?
Othello: I do beseech you,
  Send for the lady to the Sagittary   115
  And let her speak of me before her father.
  If you do find me foul in her report,
  The trust, the office, I do hold of you
  Not only take away, but let your sentence
  Even fall upon my life.
Duke: Fetch Desdemona hither.   120
Othello: Ancient, conduct them; you best know the place.
                        Exit [Iago, with] two or three [Attendants].
  And till she come, as truly as to heaven
  I do confess the vices of my blood,
  So justly to your grave ears I'll present
  How I did thrive in this fair lady's love,   125
  And she in mine.
Duke: Say it, Othello.
Othello: Her father loved me, oft invited me;
  Still° questioned me the story of my life
  From year to year — the battles, sieges, fortunes   130
  That I have passed.
  I ran it through, even from my boyish days
  To th' very moment that he bade me tell it.
  Wherein I spoke of most disastrous chances,
  Of moving accidents by flood and field;   135
  Of hairbreadth scapes i' th' imminent deadly breach;
  Of being taken by the insolent foe
  And sold to slavery; of my redemption thence
  And portance° in my travels' history;
  Wherein of anters° vast and deserts idle,   140
  Rough quarries, rocks, and hills whose heads touch heaven,
  It was my hint° to speak — such was the process;
  And of the Cannibals that each other eat,
  The Anthropophagi,° and men whose heads
  Do grow beneath their shoulders. This to hear   145
  Would Desdemona seriously incline;
  But still the house affairs would draw her thence;
  Which ever as she could with haste dispatch,
  She'ld come again, and with a greedy ear
  Devour up my discourse. Which I observing,   150
  Took once a pliant° hour, and found good means
  To draw from her a prayer of earnest heart
  That I would all my pilgrimage dilate,°
  Whereof by parcels° she had something heard,
  But not intentively.° I did consent,   155

---

113 *question:* Conversation.   129 *Still:* Continually.   139 *portance:* Behavior.   140 *anters:*
Caves.   142 *hint:* Occasion.   144 *Anthropophagi:* Man-eaters.   151 *pliant:* Propitious.
153 *dilate:* Recount in full.   154 *parcels:* Portions.   155 *intentively:* With full attention.

And often did beguile her of her tears
When I did speak of some distressful stroke
That my youth suffered. My story being done,
She gave me for my pains a world of sighs.
She swore, i' faith, 'twas strange, 'twas passing strange;   160
'Twas pitiful, 'twas wondrous pitiful.
She wished she had not heard it; yet she wished
That heaven had made her such a man. She thanked me;
And bade me, if I had a friend that loved her,
I should but teach him how to tell my story,   165
And that would woo her. Upon this hint° I spake.
She loved me for the dangers I had passed,
And I loved her that she did pity them.
This only is the witchcraft I have used.
Here comes the lady. Let her witness it.   170

Enter Desdemona, Iago, Attendants.

Duke: I think this tale would win my daughter too.
  Good Brabantio,
  Take up this mangled matter at the best.
  Men do their broken weapons rather use
  Than their bare hands.
Brabantio: I pray you hear her speak.   175
  If she confess that she was half the wooer,
  Destruction on my head if my bad blame
  Light on the man! Come hither, gentle mistress.
  Do you perceive in all this noble company
  Where most you owe obedience?
Desdemona: My noble father,   180
  I do perceive here a divided duty.
  To you I am bound for life and education;°
  My life and education both do learn me
  How to respect you: you are the lord of duty;
  I am hitherto your daughter. But here's my husband;   185
  And so much duty as my mother showed
  To you, preferring you before her father,
  So much I challenge° that I may profess
  Due to the Moor my lord.
Brabantio: God be with you! I have done.
  Please it your grace, on to the state affairs.   190
  I had rather to adopt a child than get° it.
  Come hither, Moor.
  I here do give thee that with all my heart
  Which, but thou hast already, with all my heart
  I would keep from thee. For your sake,° jewel,   195
  I am glad at soul I have no other child;
  For thy escape° would teach me tyranny,
  To hang clogs on them. I have done, my lord.

---

166 *hint:* Opportunity.   182 *education:* Upbringing.   188 *challenge:* Claim the right.
191 *get:* Beget.   195 *For your sake:* Because of you.   197 *escape:* Escapade.

Duke: Let me speak like yourself° and lay a sentence°
    Which, as a grise° or step, may help these lovers   200
    [Into your favor.]
    When remedies are past, the griefs are ended
    By seeing the worst, which late on hopes depended.
    To mourn a mischief that is past and gone
    Is the next way to draw new mischief on.   205
    What cannot be preserved when fortune takes,
    Patience her injury a mock'ry makes.
    The robbed that smiles steals something from the thief;
    He robs himself that spends a bootless grief.
Brabantio: So let the Turk of Cyprus us beguile: 210
    We lose it not so long as we can smile.
    He bears the sentence well that nothing bears
    But the free comfort which from thence he hears;
    But he bears both the sentence and the sorrow
    That to pay grief must of poor patience borrow.   215
    These sentences, to sugar, or to gall,
    Being strong on both sides, are equivocal.
    But words are words. I never yet did hear
    That the bruisèd heart was piercèd through the ear.
    Beseech you, now to the affairs of state.   220
Duke: The Turk with a most mighty preparation makes for Cyprus.
    Othello, the fortitude° of the place is best known to you; and though
    we have there a substitute of most allowed° sufficiency, yet opinion,° a
    more sovereign mistress of effects, throws a more safer voice on you.
    You must therefore be content to slubber° the gloss of your new   225
    fortunes with this more stubborn and boist'rous expedition.
Othello: The tyrant custom, most grave senators,
    Hath made the flinty and steel couch of war
    My thrice-driven bed of down. I do agnize
    A natural and prompt alacrity   230
    I find in hardness;° and do undertake
    These present wars against the Ottomites.
    Most humbly, therefore, bending to your state,
    I crave fit disposition for my wife,
    Due reference of place, and exhibition,°   235
    With such accommodation and besort°
    As levels° with her breeding.
Duke: If you please,
    Be 't at her father's.
Brabantio: I will not have it so.
Othello: Nor I.
Desdemona: Nor I. I would not there reside,   240
    To put my father in impatient thoughts

---

199 *like yourself:* As you should; *sentence:* Maxim.   200 *grise:* Step.   222 *fortitude:* Fortification.   223 *allowed:* Acknowledged; *opinion:* Public opinion.   225 *slubber:* Sully.
229–31 *agnize . . . hardness:* Recognize in myself a natural and easy response to hardship.
235 *exhibition:* Allowance of money.   236 *besort:* Suitable company.   237 *levels:* Corresponds.

By being in his eye. Most gracious Duke,
To my unfolding lend your prosperous° ear,
And let me find a charter in your voice,
T' assist my simpleness.°   245

Duke: What would you, Desdemona?

Desdemona: That I did love the Moor to live with him,
My downright violence, and storm of fortunes,
May trumpet to the world. My heart's subdued
Even to the very quality of my lord.   250
I saw Othello's visage in his mind,
And to his honors and his valiant parts
Did I my soul and fortunes consecrate.
So that, dear lords, if I be left behind,
A moth of peace, and he go to the war,   255
The rites for which I love him are bereft me,
And I a heavy interim shall support
By his dear absence. Let me go with him.

Othello: Let her have your voice.
Vouch with me, heaven, I therefore beg it not   260
To please the palate of my appetite,
Not to comply with heat° — the young affects°
In me defunct — and proper satisfaction;
But to be free and bounteous to her mind;
And heaven defend your good souls that you think   265
I will your serious and great business scant
When she is with me. No, when light-winged toys
Of feathered Cupid seel° with wanton dullness
My speculative and officed instruments,°
That° my disports corrupt and taint my business,   270
Let housewives make a skillet of my helm,
And all indign° and base adversities
Make head against my estimation!°

Duke: Be it as you shall privately determine,
Either for her stay or going. Th' affair cries haste,   275
And speed must answer it.

1. Senator: You must away to-night.

Othello: With all my heart.

Duke: At nine i' th' morning here we'll meet again.
Othello, leave some officer behind,
And he shall our commission bring to you,   280
With such things else of quality and respect
As doth import° you.

Othello: So please your grace, my ancient;
A man he is of honesty and trust
To his conveyance I assign my wife,

---

243 *prosperous:* Favorable.   245 *simpleness:* Lack of skill.   262 *heat:* Passions; *young affects:* Tendencies of youth.   268 *seel:* Blind.   269 *My . . . instruments:* My perceptive and responsible faculties.   270 *That:* So that.   272 *indign:* Unworthy.   273 *estimation:* Reputation.   282 *import:* Concern.

With what else needful your good grace shall think   285
  To be sent after me.
Duke: Let it be so.
  Good night to every one.
        [To Brabantio.]   And, noble signior,
  If virtue no delighted° beauty lack,
  Your son-in-law is far more fair than black.
I. Senator: Adieu, brave Moor. Use Desdemona well.   290
Brabantio: Look to her, Moor, if thou hast eyes to see:
  She has deceived her father, and may thee.

                        Exeunt [Duke, Senators, Officers, &c.].

Othello: My life upon her faith! — Honest Iago,
  My Desdemona must I leave to thee.
  I prithee let thy wife attend on her,   295
  And bring them after in the best advantage.°
  Come, Desdemona. I have but an hour
  Of love, of worldly matters and direction,
  To spend with thee. We must obey the time.

                        Exit Moor and Desdemona.

Roderigo: Iago, —   300
Iago: What say'st thou, noble heart?
Roderigo: What will I do, think'st thou?
Iago: Why, go to bed and sleep.
Roderigo: I will incontinently° drown myself.
Iago: If thou dost, I shall never love thee after. Why, thou silly gentleman!   305
Roderigo: It is silliness to live when to live is torment; and then have we a
  prescription to die when death is our physician.
Iago: O villainous! I have looked upon the world for four times seven
  years; and since I could distinguish betwixt a benefit and an injury, I
  never found man that knew how to love himself. Ere I would say I   310
  would drown myself for the love of a guinea hen, I would change my
  humanity with a baboon.
Roderigo: What should I do? I confess it is my shame to be so fond, but it is
  not in my virtue to amend it.
Iago: Virtue? a fig! 'Tis in ourselves that we are thus or thus. Our bodies   315
  are our gardens, to which our wills are gardeners; so that if we will
  plant nettles or sow lettuce, set hyssop and weed up thyme, supply it
  with one gender° of herbs or distract it with many — either to have it
  sterile with idleness or manured with industry — why, the power and
  corrigible authority° of this lies in our wills. If the balance of our lives   320
  had not one scale of reason to poise° another of sensuality, the blood
  and baseness° of our natures would conduct us to most preposterous
  conclusions. But we have reason to cool our raging motions,° our carnal strings, our unbitted° lusts; whereof I take this that you call love
  to be a sect or scion.°   325

---

288 *delighted:* Delightful.   296 *in the best advantage:* At the best opportunity.   304 *incon-*
tinently: Forthwith.   318 *gender:* Species.   320 *corrigible authority:* Corrective power.
321 *poise:* Counterbalance.   321–22 *blood and baseness:* Animal instincts.   323 *motions:*
Appetites.   324 *unbitted:* Uncontrolled.   325 *sect or scion:* Offshoot, cutting.

Roderigo: It cannot be.
Iago: It is merely a lust of the blood and a permission of the will. Come, be a
    man! Drown thyself? Drown cats and blind puppies! I have professed
    me thy friend, and I confess me knit to thy deserving with cables of per-
    durable toughness. I could never better stead thee than now. Put money   330
    in thy purse. Follow thou the wars; defeat thy favor° with an usurped
    beard. I say, put money in thy purse. It cannot be that Desdemona
    should long continue her love to the Moor — put money in thy purse —
    nor he his to her. It was a violent commencement in her, and thou shalt
    see an answerable sequestration° — put but money in thy purse. These   335
    Moors are changeable in their wills — fill thy purse with money. The
    food that to him now is as luscious as locusts shall be to him shortly as
    bitter as coloquintida.° She must change for youth: when she is sated
    with his body, she will find the error of her choice. [She must have
    change, she must.] Therefore put money in thy purse. If thou wilt needs   340
    damn thyself, do it a more delicate way than drowning. Make° all the
    money thou canst. If sanctimony and a frail vow betwixt an erring° bar-
    barian and a supersubtle Venetian be not too hard for my wits and all
    the tribe of hell, thou shalt enjoy her. Therefore make money. A pox of
    drowning thyself! 'Tis clean out of the way. Seek thou rather to be   345
    hanged in compassing thy joy than to be drowned and go without her.
Roderigo: Wilt thou be fast to my hopes, if I depend on the issue?
Iago: Thou art sure of me. Go, make money. I have told thee often, and I
    retell thee again and again, I hate the Moor. My cause is hearted;°
    thine hath no less reason. Let us be conjunctive in our revenge against   350
    him. If thou canst cuckold him, thou dost thyself a pleasure, me a
    sport. There are many events in the womb of time, which will be deliv-
    ered. Traverse,° go, provide thy money! We will have more of this to-
    morrow. Adieu.
Roderigo: Where shall we meet i' th' morning?   355
Iago: At my lodging.
Roderigo: I'll be with thee betimes.
Iago: Go to, farewell — Do you hear, Roderigo?
[Roderigo: What say you?
Iago: No more of drowning, do you hear?   360
Roderigo: I am changed.
Iago: Go to, farewell. Put money enough in your purse.]
Roderigo: I'll sell all my land.   *Exit.*
Iago: Thus do I ever make my fool my purse;
    For I mine own gained knowledge should profane   365
    If I would time expend with such a snipe°
    But for my sport and profit. I hate the Moor;
    And it is thought abroad that 'twixt my sheets
    H'as done my office. I know not if't be true;
    But I, for mere suspicion in that kind,   370
    Will do as if for surety. He holds me well;°

---

331 *defeat thy favor:* Spoil thy appearance.   335 *sequestration:* Estrangement.   338 *coloquin-*
tida: A medicine.   341 *Make:* Raise.   342 *erring:* Wandering.   349 *My cause is hearted:*
My heart is in it.   353 *Traverse:* Forward march.   366 *snipe:* Fool.   371 *well:* In high
regard.

> The better shall my purpose work on him.
> Cassio's a proper man. Let me see now:
> To get his place, and to plume up° my will
> In double knavery — How, how? — Let's see: —   375
> After some time, to abuse Othello's ears
> That he is too familiar with his wife.
> He hath a person and a smooth dispose°
> To be suspected — framed to make women false.
> The Moor is of a free° and open nature   380
> That thinks men honest that but seem to be so;
> And will as tenderly be led by th' nose
> As asses are.
> I have 't! It is engend'red! Hell and night
> Must bring this monstrous birth to the world's light.   *Exit.* 385

ACT II

SCENE I: *An open place in Cyprus, near the harbor.*

Enter Montano and two Gentlemen.

Montano: What from the cape can you discern at sea?
1. Gentleman: Nothing at all: it is a high-wrought flood.
    I cannot 'twixt the heaven and the main
    Descry a sail.
Montano: Methinks the wind hath spoke aloud at land;   5
    A fuller blast ne'er shook our battlements.
    If it hath ruffianed so upon the sea,
    What ribs of oak, when mountains melt on them,
    Can hold the mortise?° What shall we hear of this?
2. Gentleman: A segregation° of the Turkish fleet.   10
    For do but stand upon the foaming shore,
    The chidden billow seems to pelt the clouds;
    The wind-shaked surge, with high and monstrous mane,
    Seems to cast water on the burning Bear
    And quench the Guards° of th' ever-fixèd pole.°   15
    I never did like molestation° view
    On the enchafèd flood.
Montano: If that the Turkish fleet
    Be not ensheltered and embayed, they are drowned;
    It is impossible to bear it out.

Enter a third Gentleman.

3. Gentleman: News, lads! Our wars are done.   20
    The desperate tempest hath so banged the Turks

---

374 *plume up:* Gratify.   378 *dispose:* Manner.   380 *free:* Frank.   **Act II, Scene I.**   9 *hold the mortise:* Hold their joints together.   10 *segregation:* Scattering.   15 *Guards:* Stars near the North Star; *pole:* Polestar.   16 *molestation:* Tumult.

That their designment halts.° A noble ship of Venice
Hath seen a grievous wrack and sufferance°
On most part of their fleet.
Montano: How? Is this true?
3. Gentleman: The ship is here put in,   25
A Veronesa;° Michael Cassio,
Lieutenant to the warlike Moor Othello,
Is come on shore; the Moor himself at sea,
And is in full commission here for Cyprus.
Montano: I am glad on't. 'Tis a worthy governor.   30
3. Gentleman: But his same Cassio, though he speak of comfort
Touching the Turkish loss, yet he looks sadly
And prays the Moor be safe, for they were parted
With foul and violent tempest.
Montano: Pray heaven he be;
For I have served him, and the man commands   35
Like a full soldier. Let's to the seaside, ho!
As well to see the vessel that's come in
As to throw out our eyes for brave Othello,
Even till we make the main and th' aerial blue
An indistinct regard.°
3. Gentleman: Come, let's do so;   40
For every minute is expectancy
Of more arrivance.

Enter Cassio.

Cassio: Thanks, you the valiant of this warlike isle,
That so approve the Moor! O, let the heavens
Give him defense against the elements,   45
For I have lost him on a dangerous sea!
Montano: Is he well shipped?
Cassio: His bark is stoutly timbered, and his pilot
Of very expert and approved allowance;
Therefore my hopes, not surfeited to death,°   50
Stand in bold cure.°
          (Within.)   A sail, a sail, a sail!   *Enter a messenger.*
Cassio: What noise?
Messenger: The town is empty; on the brow o' th' sea
Stand ranks of people, and they cry "A sail!"
Cassio: My hopes do shape him for the governor.   55

          A shot.

2. Gentleman: They do discharge their shot of courtesy:
Our friends at least.
Cassio: I pray you, sir, go forth
And give us truth who 'tis that is arrived.
2. Gentleman: I shall.   *Exit.*

---

22 *designment halts:* Plan is crippled.   23 *sufferance:* Disaster.   26 *Veronesa:* Ship furnished by Verona.   40 *An indistinct regard:* Indistinguishable.   50 *surfeited to death:*
Overindulged.   51 *in bold cure:* A good chance of fulfillment.

Montano: But, good lieutenant, is your general wived?   60
Cassio: Most fortunately. He hath achieved a maid
 That paragons° description and wild fame;
 One that excels the quirks° of blazoning° pens,
 And in th' essential vesture of creation
 Does tire the ingener.°

Enter Second Gentleman.

      How now? Who has put in?   65
2. Gentleman: 'Tis one Iago, ancient to the general.
Cassio: H'as had most favorable and happy speed:
 Tempests themselves, high seas, and howling winds,
 The guttered° rocks and congregated sands,
 Traitors ensteeped° to clog the guiltless keel,   70
 As having sense of beauty, do omit
 Their mortal° natures, letting go safely by
 The divine Desdemona.
Montano: What is she?
Cassio: She that I spake of, our great captain's captain,
 Left in the conduct of the bold Iago,   75
 Whose footing° here anticipates our thoughts
 A se'nnight's° speed. Great Jove, Othello guard,
 And swell his sail with thine own pow'rful breath,
 That he may bless this bay with his tall ship,
 Make love's quick pants in Desdemona's arms,   80
 Give renewed fire to our extincted spirits,
 [And bring all Cyprus comfort!]

Enter Desdemona, Iago, Roderigo, and Emilia [with Attendants].

       O, behold!
 The riches of the ship is come on shore!
 You men of Cyprus, let her have your knees.°
 Hail to thee, lady! and the grace of heaven,   85
 Before, behind thee, and on every hand,
 Enwheel thee round!
Desdemona: I thank you, valiant Cassio.
 What tidings can you tell me of my lord?
Cassio: He is not yet arrived; nor know I aught
 But that he's well and will be shortly here.   90
Desdemona: O but I fear! How lost you company?
Cassio: The great contention of the sea and skies
 Parted our fellowship.
  (Within.)   A sail, a sail! *[A shot.]*
       But hark. A sail!
2. Gentleman: They give their greeting to the citadel;
 This likewise is a friend.

---

62 *paragons:* Surpasses. 63 *quirks:* Ingenuities; *blazoning:* Describing. 64–65 *And...*
ingener: Merely to describe her as God made her exhausts her praiser. 69 *guttered:* Jagged.
70 *ensteeped:* Submerged. 72 *mortal:* Deadly. 76 *footing:* Landing. 77 *se'nnight's:*
Week's. 84 *knees:* I.e., kneeling.

Cassio: See for the news.   95

                                        [Exit Gentleman.]

        Good ancient, you are welcome.
                [To Emilia.]   Welcome, mistress. —
        Let it not gall your patience, good Iago,
        That I extend my manners. 'Tis my breeding
        That gives me this bold show of courtesy.
                [Kisses Emilia.°]

Iago: Sir, would she give you so much of her lips   100
        As of her tongue she oft bestows on me,
        You would have enough.
Desdemona: Alas, she has no speech!
Iago: In faith, too much.
        I find it still when I have list to sleep.
        Marry, before your ladyship, I grant,   105
        She puts her tongue a little in her heart
        And chides with thinking.
Emilia: You have little cause to say so.
Iago: Come on, come on! You are pictures out of doors,
        Bells in your parlors, wildcats in your kitchens,   110
        Saints in your injuries, devils being offended,
        Players in your housewifery,° and housewives° in your beds.
Desdemona: O, fie upon thee, slanderer!
Iago: Nay, it is true, or else I am a Turk:
        You rise to play, and go to bed to work.   115
Emilia: You shall not write my praise.
Iago: No, let me not.
Desdemona: What wouldst thou write of me, if thou shouldst praise me?
Iago: O gentle lady, do not put me to't,
        For I am nothing if not critical.
Desdemona: Come on, assay.° — There's one gone to the harbor?   120
Iago: Ay, madam.
Desdemona: I am not merry; but I do beguile
        The thing I am by seeming otherwise. —
        Come, how wouldst thou praise me?
Iago: I am about it; but indeed my invention   125
        Comes from my pate as birdlime° does from frieze° —
        It plucks out brains and all. But my Muse labors,
        And thus she is delivered:
        If she be fair and wise, fairness and wit —
        The one's for use, the other useth it.   130
Desdemona: Well praised! How if she be black° and witty?
Iago: If she be black, and thereto have a wit,
        She'll find a white that shall her blackness fit.
Desdemona: Worse and worse!
Emilia: How if fair and foolish?   135

Kisses Emilia: (Kissing was a common Elizabethan form of social courtesy).   112 *house-
wifery:* Housekeeping; *housewives:* Hussies.   120 *assay:* Try.   126 *birdlime:* A sticky paste;
frieze: Rough cloth.   131 *black:* Brunette.

Iago: She never yet was foolish that was fair,
　　For even her folly° helped her to an heir.
Desdemona: These are old fond° paradoxes to make fools laugh i' th' ale-
　　house. What miserable praise hast thou for her that's foul° and foolish?
Iago: There's none so foul, and foolish thereunto,　　　　　　　140
　　But does foul pranks which fair and wise ones do.
Desdemona: O heavy ignorance! Thou praisest the worst best. But what
　　praise couldst thou bestow on a deserving woman indeed — one that
　　in the authority of her merit did justly put on the vouch° of very
　　malice itself?　　　　　　　　　　　　　　　　　　　　　145
Iago: She that was ever fair, and never proud;
　　Had tongue at will, and yet was never loud;
　　Never lacked gold, and yet went never gay;
　　Fled from her wish, and yet said "Now I may";
　　She that, being ang'red, her revenge being nigh,　　　　　　150
　　Bade her wrong stay, and her displeasure fly;
　　She that in wisdom never was so frail
　　To change the cod's head for the salmon's tail;°
　　She that could think, and ne'er disclose her mind;
　　See suitors following, and not look behind:　　　　　　　　155
　　She was a wight (if ever such wight were) —
Desdemona: To do what?
Iago: To suckle fools and chronicle small beer.°
Desdemona: O most lame and impotent conclusion! Do not learn of him,
　　Emilia, though he be thy husband. How say you, Cassio? Is he not a　160
　　most profane and liberal° counsellor?
Cassio: He speaks home,° madam. You may relish him more in the soldier
　　than in the scholar.
Iago [aside]: He takes her by the palm. Ay, well said, whisper! With as little
　　a web as this will I ensnare as great a fly as Cassio. Ay, smile upon her,　165
　　do! I will gyve thee in thine own courtship.° — You say true; 'tis so,
　　indeed! — If such tricks as these strip you out of your lieutenantry, it
　　had been better you had not kissed your three fingers so oft — which
　　now again you are most apt to play the sir° in. Very good! well kissed!
　　an excellent courtesy! 'Tis so, indeed. Yet again your fingers to your　170
　　lips? Would they were clyster pipes° for your sake! *(Trumpet within.)*
　　The Moor! I know his trumpet.
Cassio: 'Tis truly so.
Desdemona: Let's meet him and receive him.
Cassio: Lo, where he comes.　　　　　　　　　　　　　　　175

　　Enter Othello and Attendants.

Othello: O my fair warrior!
Desdemona:　　　　　　　My dear Othello!
Othello: It gives me wonder great as my content
　　To see you here before me. O my soul's joy!

---

137 *folly:* Wantonness.　138 *fond:* Foolish.　139 *foul:* Ugly.　144 *put on the vouch:* Compel the approval.　153 *To . . . tail:* I.e., to exchange the good for the poor but expensive.
158 *chronicle small beer:* Keep petty household accounts.　161 *profane and liberal:* Worldly
and licentious.　162 *home:* Bluntly.　166 *gyve . . . courtship:* Manacle you by means of
your courtly manners.　169 *sir:* Courtly gentleman.　171 *clyster pipes:* Syringes.

If after every tempest come such calms,
May the winds blow till they have wakened death!   180
And let the laboring bark climb hills of seas
Olympus-high, and duck again as low
As hell's from heaven! If it were now to die,
'Twere now to be most happy;° for I fear
My soul hath her content so absolute   185
That not another comfort like to this
Succeeds in unknown fate.
Desdemona: The heavens forbid
But that our loves and comforts should increase
Even as our days do grow.
Othello: Amen to that, sweet powers!
I cannot speak enough of this content;   190
It stops me here; it is too much of joy.
And this, and this, the greatest discords be

They kiss.

That e'er our hearts shall make!
Iago [aside]:   O, you are well tuned now!
But I'll set down° the pegs that make this music,
As honest as I am.
Othello: Come, let us to the castle.   195
News, friends! Our wars are done; the Turks are drowned.
How does my old acquaintance of this isle? —
Honey, you shall be well desired° in Cyprus;
I have found great love amongst them. O my sweet,
I prattle out of fashion, and I dote   200
In mine own comforts. I prithee, good Iago,
Go to the bay and disembark my coffers.
Bring thou the master° to the citadel;
He is a good one, and his worthiness
Does challenge° much respect. — Come, Desdemona,   205
Once more well met at Cyprus.

                         Exit Othello [with all but Iago and Roderigo].
Iago [to an Attendant, who goes out]: Do thou meet me presently at the harbor. *[To Roderigo.]* Come hither. If thou be'st valiant (as they say base
men being in love have then a nobility in their natures more than is
native to them), list me. The lieutenant to-night watches on the court   210
of guard.° First, I must tell thee this: Desdemona is directly in love
with him.
Roderigo: With him? Why, 'tis not possible.
Iago: Lay thy finger thus,° and let thy soul be instructed. Mark me with what
violence she first loved the Moor, but for bragging and telling her fan-   215
tastical lies; and will she love him still for prating? Let not thy discreet
heart think it. Her eye must be fed; and what delight shall she have to
look on the devil? When the blood is made dull with the act of sport,
there should be, again to inflame it and to give satiety a fresh appetite,

184 *happy:* Fortunate.   194 *set down:* Loosen.   198 *well desired:* Warmly welcomed.
203 *master:* Ship captain.   205 *challenge:* Deserve.   210-11 *court of guard:* Headquarters.
214 *thus:* I.e., on your lips.

loveliness in favor, sympathy in years, manners, and beauties; all which   220
the Moor is defective in. Now for want of these required conveniences,° her delicate tenderness will find itself abused, begin to heave
the gorge,° disrelish and abhor the Moor. Very nature will instruct her
in it and compel her to some second choice. Now, sir, this granted — as
it is a most pregnant° and unforced position — who stands so eminent   225
in the degree of this fortune as Cassio does? A knave very voluble; no
further conscionable° than in putting on the mere form of civil and
humane° seeming for the better compassing of his salt° and most hidden loose affection? Why, none! why, none! A slipper° and subtle knave;
a finder-out of occasions; that has an eye can stamp and counterfeit   230
advantages, though true advantage never present itself; a devilish
knave! Besides, the knave is handsome, young, and hath all those req-
uisites in him that folly and green minds look after. A pestilent complete knave! and the woman hath found him already.

Roderigo: I cannot believe that in her; she's full of most blessed condition.°   235

Iago: Blessed fig's-end! The wine she drinks is made of grapes. If she had
been blessed, she would never have loved the Moor. Blessed pudding!
Didst thou not see her paddle with the palm of his hand? Didst not
mark that?

Roderigo: Yes, that I did; but that was but courtesy.   240

Iago: Lechery, by this hand! an index and obscure prologue to the history
of lust and foul thoughts. They met so near with their lips that their
breaths embraced together. Villainous thoughts, Roderigo! When
these mutualities° so marshal the way, hard at hand comes the master
and main exercise, th' incorporate° conclusion. Pish! But, sir, be you   245
ruled by me: I have brought you from Venice. Watch you to-night; for
the command, I'll lay't upon you. Cassio knows you not. I'll not be far
from you: do you find some occasion to anger Cassio, either by speaking too loud, or tainting° his discipline, or from what other course
you please which the time shall more favorably minister.   250

Roderigo: Well.

Iago: Sir, he's rash and very sudden in choler,° and haply with his trun-
cheon may strike at you. Provoke him that he may; for even out of that
will I cause these of Cyprus to mutiny; whose qualification° shall come
into no true taste° again but by the displanting of Cassio. So shall you   255
have a shorter journey to your desires by the means I shall then have
to prefer° them; and the impediment most profitably removed without the which there were no expectation of our prosperity.

Roderigo: I will do this if you can bring it to any opportunity.

Iago: I warrant thee. Meet me by and by at the citadel; I must fetch his   260
necessaries ashore. Farewell.

Roderigo: Adieu.   *Exit.*

Iago: That Cassio loves her, I do well believe't;
That she loves him, 'tis apt° and of great credit.

221–22 *conveniences:* Compatibilities.   222–23 *heave the gorge:* Be nauseated.   225 *pregnant:* Evident.   227 *conscionable:* Conscientious.   228 *humane:* Polite; *salt:* Lecherous.
229 *slipper:* Slippery.   235 *condition:* Character.   244 *mutualities:* Exchanges.   245 *incorporate:* Carnal.   249 *tainting:* Discrediting.   252 *sudden in choler:* Violent in anger.
254 *qualification:* Appeasement.   255 *true taste:* Satisfactory state.   257 *prefer:* Advance.
264 *apt:* Probable.

The Moor, howbeit that I endure him not,   265
Is of a constant, loving, noble nature,
And I dare think he'll prove to Desdemona
A most dear husband. Now I do love her too;
Not out of absolute lust, though peradventure
I stand accountant° for as great a sin,   270
But partly led to diet° my revenge,
For that I do suspect the lusty Moor
Hath leaped into my seat; the thought whereof
Doth, like a poisonous mineral, gnaw my inwards;
And nothing can or shall content my soul   275
Till I am evened with him, wife for wife;
Or failing so, yet that I put the Moor
At least into a jealousy so strong
That judgment cannot cure. Which thing to do,
If this poor trash of Venice, whom I trash°   280
For° his quick hunting, stand the putting on,°
I'll have our Michael Cassio on the hip,°
Abuse him to the Moor in the rank garb°
(For I fear Cassio with my nightcap too),
Make the Moor thank me, love me, and reward me   285
For making him egregiously an ass
And practicing upon° his peace and quiet
Even to madness. 'Tis here, but yet confused:
Knavery's plain face is never seen till used.   *Exit.*

SCENE II: *A street in Cyprus.*

Enter Othello's Herald, with a proclamation.

Herald: It is Othello's pleasure, our noble and valiant general, that, upon
certain tidings now arrived, importing the mere perdition° of the
Turkish fleet, every man put himself into triumph; some to dance,
some to make bonfires, each man to what sport and revels his addiction leads him. For, besides these beneficial news, it is the celebration   5
of his nuptial. So much was his pleasure should be proclaimed. All
offices° are open, and there is full liberty of feasting from the present
hour of five till the bell have told eleven. Heaven bless the isle of
Cyprus and our noble general Othello!   *Exit.*

SCENE III: *The Cyprian Castle.*

Enter Othello, Desdemona, Cassio, and Attendants.

Othello: Good Michael, look you to the guard to-night.

---

270 *accountant:* Accountable.   271 *diet:* Feed.   280 *I trash:* I weight down (in order to
keep under control).   281 *For:* In order to develop; *stand the putting on:* Responds to my
inciting.   282 *on the hip:* At my mercy.   283 *rank garb:* Gross manner.   287 *practicing
upon:* Plotting against.   **Scene II.**   2 *mere perdition:* Complete destruction.   6-7 *offices:* Kitchens and storerooms.

    Let's teach ourselves that honorable stop,
    Not to outsport discretion.
Cassio: Iago hath direction what to do;
    But not withstanding, with my personal eye   5
    Will I look to't.
Othello: Iago is most honest.
    Michael, good night. To-morrow with your earliest
    Let me have speech with you.
        [To Desdemona.]   Come, my dear love.
    The purchase made, the fruits are to ensue;
    That profit 's yet to come 'tween me and you. —   10
    Good night.
                    Exit [Othello with Desdemona and Attendants].

    Enter Iago.

Cassio: Welcome, Iago. We must to the watch.
Iago: Not this hour, lieutenant; 'tis not yet ten o' th' clock. Our general
    cast° us thus early for the love of his Desdemona; who let us not there-
    fore blame. He hath not yet made wanton the night with her,   15
    and she is sport for Jove.
Cassio: She's a most exquisite lady.
Iago: And, I'll warrant her, full of game.
Cassio: Indeed, she's a most fresh and delicate creature.
Iago: What an eye she has! Methinks it sounds a parley to provocation.   20
Cassio: An inviting eye; and yet methinks right modest.
Iago: And when she speaks, is it not an alarum to love?
Cassio: She is indeed perfection.
Iago: Well, happiness to their sheets! Come, lieutenant, I have a stoup° of
    wine, and here without are a brace of Cyprus gallants that would fain   25
    have a measure to the health of black Othello.
Cassio: Not to-night, good Iago. I have very poor and unhappy brains for
    drinking; I could well wish courtesy would invent some other custom
    of entertainment.
Iago: O, they are our friends. But one cup! I'll drink for you.   30
Cassio: I have drunk but one cup to-night, and that was craftily qualified°
    too; and behold what innovation° it makes here. I am unfortunate in
    the infirmity and dare not task my weakness with any more.
Iago: What, man! 'Tis a night of revels: the gallants desire it.
Cassio: Where are they?   35
Iago: Here at the door; I pray you call them in.
Cassio: I'll do't, but it dislikes me.   *Exit.*
Iago: If I can fasten but one cup upon him
    With that which he hath drunk to-night already,
    He'll be as full of quarrel and offense   40
    As my young mistress' dog. Now my sick fool Roderigo,
    Whom love hath turned almost the wrong side out,
    To Desdemona hath to-night caroused
    Potations pottle-deep;° and he's to watch.

Scene III.   14 *cast:* Dismissed.   24 *stoup:* Two-quart tankard.   31 *qualified:* Diluted.
32 *innovation:* Disturbance.   44 *pottle-deep:* Bottoms up.

Three lads of Cyprus—noble swelling spirits,   45
That hold their honors in a wary distance,°
The very elements° of this warlike isle—
Have I to-night flustered with flowing cups,
And they watch too. Now, 'mongst this flock of drunkards
Am I to put our Cassio in some action   50
That may offend the isle.

Enter Cassio, Montano, and Gentlemen [; Servants following with wine].

                     But here they come.
If consequence do but approve my dream,
My boat sails freely, both with wind and stream.
Cassio: 'Fore God, they have given me a rouse° already.
Montano: Good faith, a little one; not past a pint, as I am a soldier.   55
Iago: Some wine, ho!
   [Sings.] And let me the canakin clink, clink;
           And let me the canakin clink
              A soldier's a man;
              A life's but a span,   60
           Why then, let a soldier drink.
   Some wine, boys!
Cassio: 'Fore God, an excellent song!
Iago: I learned it in England, where indeed they are most potent in pot-
   ting. Your Dane, your German, and your swag-bellied Hollander—   65
   Drink, ho!—are nothing to your English.
Cassio: Is your Englishman so expert in his drinking?
Iago: Why, he drinks you with facility your Dane dead drunk; he sweats
   not to overthrow your Almain; he gives your Hollander a vomit ere the
   next pottle can be filled.   70
Cassio: To the health of our general!
Montano: I am for it, lieutenant, and I'll do you justice.
Iago: O sweet England!
   [Sings.] King Stephen was a worthy peer;
           His breeches cost him but a crown;   75
        He held 'em sixpence all too dear,
           With that he called the tailor lown.°
        He was a wight of high renown,
           And thou art but of low degree.
        'Tis pride that pulls the country down;   80
           Then take thine auld cloak about thee.
   Some wine, ho!
Cassio: 'Fore God, this is a more exquisite song than the other.
Iago: Will you hear't again?
Cassio: No, for I hold him to be unworthy of his place that does those   85
   things.° Well, God's above all; and there be souls must be saved, and
   there be souls must not be saved.

---

46 *That . . . distance:* Very sensitive about their honor.   47 *very elements:* True representatives.   54 *rouse:* Bumper.   77 *lown:* Rascal.   85-86 *does those things:* I.e., behaves in this
fashion.

Iago: It's true, good lieutenant.

Cassio: For mine own part—no offense to the general, nor any man of
    quality—I hope to be saved.   90

Iago: And so do I too, lieutenant.

Cassio: Ay, but, by your leave, not before me. The lieutenant is to be saved
    before the ancient. Let's have no more of this; let's to our affairs.—
    God forgive us our sins!—Gentlemen, let's look to our business. Do
    not think, gentlemen, I am drunk. This is my ancient; this is my right   95
    hand, and this is my left. I am not drunk now. I can stand well
    enough, and I speak well enough.

All: Excellent well!

Cassio: Why, very well then. You must not think then that I am drunk.

                                              Exit.

Montano: To th' platform, masters. Come, let's set the watch.   100

Iago: You see this fellow that is gone before.
    He's a soldier fit to stand by Caesar
    And give direction; and do but see his vice.
    'Tis to his virtue a just equinox,°
    The one as long as th' other. 'Tis pity of him.   105
    I fear the trust Othello puts him in,
    On some odd time of his infirmity,
    Will shake this island.

Montano: But is he often thus?

Iago: 'Tis evermore his prologue to his sleep:
    He'll watch the horologe a double set°   110
    If drink rock not his cradle.

Montano: It were well
    The general were put in mind of it.
    Perhaps he sees it not, or his good nature
    Prizes the virtue that appears in Cassio
    And looks not on his evils. Is not this true?   115

    Enter Roderigo.

Iago [aside to him]: How now, Roderigo?
    I pray you after the lieutenant, go!   *Exit Roderigo.*

Montano: And 'tis great pity that the noble Moor
    Should hazard such a place as his own second
    With one of an ingraft° infirmity.   120
    It were an honest action to say
    So to the Moor.

Iago: Not I, for this fair island!
    I do love Cassio well and would do much
    To cure him of this evil.
        (Within.) Help! help!
                    But hark! What noise?   125

    Enter Cassio, driving in Roderigo.

Cassio: Zounds, you rogue! you rascal!

---

104 *just equinox:* Exact equivalent.   110 *watch . . . set:* Stay awake twice around the clock.
120 *ingraft:* I.e., ingrained.

Montano: What's the matter, lieutenant?
Cassio: A knave to teach me my duty?
    I'll beat the knave into a twiggen° bottle.
Roderigo: Beat me?
Cassio: Dost thou prate, rogue? *[Strikes him.]*
Montano: Nay, good lieutenant!
                                                   [Stays him.]
    I pray you, sir, hold your hand.
Cassio: Let me go, sir,   130
    Or I'll knock you o'er the mazzard.°
Montano: Come, come, you're drunk!
Cassio: Drunk?

    They fight.

Iago [aside to Roderigo]: Away, I say! Go out and cry a mutiny!
                                               Exit Roderigo.
    Nay, good lieutenant. God's will, gentlemen!
    Help, ho! — lieutenant — sir — Montano — sir —   135
    Help, masters! — Here's a goodly watch indeed!

    A bell rung.

    Who's that which rings the bell? Diablo, ho!
    The town will rise.° God's will, lieutenant, hold!
    You'll be shamed for ever.

    Enter Othello and Gentlemen with weapons.

Othello: What is the matter here?
Montano: Zounds, I bleed still. I am hurt to th' death.   140
    He dies!
Othello: Hold for your lives!
Iago: Hold, hold! Lieutenant — sir — Montano — gentlemen!
    Have you forgot all sense of place and duty?
    Hold! The general speaks to you. Hold, for shame!   145
Othello: Why, how now ho? From whence ariseth this?
    Are we turned Turks, and to ourselves do that
    Which heaven hath forbid the Ottomites?
    For Christian shame put by this barbarous brawl!
    He that stirs next to carve for° his own rage   150
    Holds his soul light; he dies upon his motion.
    Silence that dreadful bell! It frights the isle
    From her propriety.° What is the matter, masters?
    Honest Iago, that looks dead with grieving,
    Speak. Who began this? On thy love, I charge thee.   155
Iago: I do not know. Friends all, but now, even now,
    In quarter,° and in terms like bride and groom
    Devesting them for bed; and then, but now —
    As if some planet had unwitted men —
    Swords out, and tilting one at other's breast   160

---

128 *twiggen:* Wicker-covered.   131 *mazzard:* Head.   138 *rise:* Grow riotous.   150 *carve for:* Indulge.   153 *propriety:* Proper self.   157 *quarter:* Friendliness.

In opposition bloody. I cannot speak
Any beginning to this peevish odds,°
And would in action glorious I had lost
Those legs that brought me to a part of it!
Othello: How comes it, Michael, you are thus forgot?   165
Cassio: I pray you pardon me; I cannot speak.
Othello: Worthy Montano, you were wont to be civil;
    The gravity and stillness of your youth
    The world hath noted, and your name is great
    In months of wisest censure.° What's the matter   170
    That you unlace° your reputation thus
    And spend your rich opinion° for the name
    Of a night-brawler? Give me answer to it.
Montano: Worthy Othello, I am hurt to danger.
    Your officer, Iago, can inform you,   175
    While I spare speech, which something now offends° me,
    Of all that I do know; nor know I aught
    By me that's said or done amiss this night,
    Unless self-charity be sometimes a vice,
    And to defend ourselves it be a sin   180
    When violence assails us.
Othello: Now, by heaven,
    My blood° begins my safer guides to rule,
    And passion, having my best judgment collied,°
    Assays° to lead the way. If I once stir
    Or do but lift this arm, the best of you   185
    Shall sink in my rebuke. Give me to know
    How this foul rout began, who set it on;
    And he that is approved in° this offense,
    Though he had twinned with me, both at a birth,
    Shall lose me. What! in a town of war,   190
    Yet wild, the people's hearts brimful of fear,
    To manage° private and domestic quarrel?
    In night, and on the court and guard of safety?
    'Tis monstrous. Iago, who began't?
Montano: If partially affined, or leagued in office,°   195
    Thou dost deliver more or less than truth,
    Thou art no soldier.
Iago: Touch me not so near.
    I had rather have this tongue cut from my mouth
    Than it should do offense to Michael Cassio;
    Yet I persuade myself, to speak the truth   200
    Shall nothing wrong him. This it is, general.
    Montano and myself being in speech,
    There comes a fellow crying out for help,
    And Cassio following him with determined sword

---

162 *peevish odds:* Childish quarrel.   170 *censure:* Judgment.   171 *unlace:* Undo.   172 *rich opinion:* High reputation.   176 *offends:* Pains.   182 *blood:* Passion.   183 *collied:* Darkened.   184 *Assays:* Tries.   188 *approved in:* Proved guilty of.   192 *manage:* Carry on.   195 *partially . . . office:* Prejudiced by comradeship or official relations.

To execute° upon him. Sir, this gentleman   205
Steps in to Cassio and entreats his pause.
Myself the crying fellow did pursue,
Lest by his clamor — as it so fell out —
The town might fall in fright. He, swift of foot,
Outran my purpose; and I returned then rather   210
For that I heard the clink and fall of swords,
And Cassio high in oath;° which till to-night
I ne'er might say before. When I came back —
For this was brief — I found them close together
At blow and thrust, even as again they were   215
When you yourself did part them.
More of this matter cannot I report;
But men are men; the best sometimes forget.
Though Cassio did some little wrong to him,
As men in rage strike those that wish them best,   220
Yet surely Cassio I believe received
From him that fled some strange indignity,
Which patience could not pass.°

Othello: I know, Iago,
Thy honesty and love doth mince this matter,
Making it light to Cassio. Cassio, I love thee;   225
But never more be officer of mine.

Enter Desdemona, attended.

Look if my gentle love be not raised up!
I'll make thee an example.

Desdemona: What's the matter?
Othello: All's well now, sweeting; come away to bed.
        [To Montano.]
Sir, for your hurts, myself will be your surgeon.   230
Lead him off.

[Montano is led off.]

Iago, look with care about the town
And silence those whom this vile brawl distracted.°
Come, Desdemona; 'tis the soldiers' life
To have their balmy slumbers waked with strife.   235
                        Exit [with all but Iago and Cassio].

Iago: What, are you hurt, lieutenant?
Cassio: Ay, past all surgery.
Iago: Marry, God forbid!
Cassio: Reputation, reputation, reputation! O, I have lost my reputation! I
    have lost the immortal part of myself, and what remains is bestial. My   240
    reputation, Iago, my reputation!
Iago: As I am an honest man, I thought you had received some bodily
    wound. There is more sense in that than in reputation. Reputation
    is an idle and most false imposition; oft got without merit and lost

205 *execute:* Work his will.   212 *high in oath:* Cursing.   223 *pass:* Pass over, ignore.
233 *distracted:* Excited.

without deserving. You have lost no reputation at all unless you repute   245
yourself such a loser. What, man! there are ways to recover° the general again. You are but now cast in his mood°—a punishment more in
policy than in malice, even so as one would beat his offenseless dog to
affright an imperious lion. Sue to him again, and he's yours.

Cassio: I will rather sue to be despised than to deceive so good a comman-   250
der with so slight, so drunken, and so indiscreet an officer. Drunk!
and speak parrot!° and squabble! swagger! swear! and discourse fust-
ian° with one's own shadow! O thou invisible spirit of wine, if thou
hast no name to be known by, let us call thee devil!

Iago: What was he that you followed with your sword? What had he done   255
to you?

Cassio: I know not.

Iago: Is't possible?

Cassio: I remember a mass of things, but nothing distinctly; a quarrel, but
nothing wherefore. O God, that men should put an enemy in their   260
mouths to steal away their brains! that we should with joy, pleasance,
revel, and applause° transform ourselves into beasts!

Iago: Why, but you are now well enough. How came you thus recovered?

Cassio: It hath pleased the devil drunkenness to give place to the devil
wrath. One unperfectness shows me another, to make me frankly de-   265
spise myself.

Iago: Come, you are too severe a moraler. As the time, the place, and the
condition of this country stands, I could heartily wish this had not so
befall'n; but since it is as it is, mend it for your own good.

Cassio: I will ask him for my place again: he shall tell me I am a drunkard!   270
Had I as many mouths as Hydra,° such an answer would stop them all.
To be now a sensible man, by and by a fool, and presently a beast! O
strange! Every inordinate cup is unblest, and the ingredient° is a devil.

Iago: Come, come, good wine is a good familiar creature if it be well used.
Exclaim no more against it. And, good lieutenant, I think you think I   275
love you.

Cassio: I have well approved° it, sir. I drunk!

Iago: You or any man living may be drunk at some time, man. I'll tell you
what you shall do. Our general's wife is now the general. I may say so
in this respect, for that he hath devoted and given up himself to the   280
contemplation, mark, and denotement of her parts and graces. Confess yourself freely to her; importune her help to put you in your place
again. She is of so free,° so kind, so apt, so blessed a disposition she
holds it a vice in her goodness not to do more than she is requested.
This broken joint between you and her husband entreat her to splin-   285
ter;° and my fortunes against any lay° worth naming, this crack of
your love shall grow stronger than it was before.

Cassio: You advise me well.

Iago: I protest, in the sincerity of love and honest kindness.

---

246 *recover:* Regain favor with.   247 *in his mood:* Dismissed because of his anger.   252 *par-*
rot: Meaningless phrases.   252–53 *fustian:* Bombastic nonsense.   262 *applause:* Desire to
please.   271 *Hydra:* Monster with many heads.   273 *ingredient:* Contents.   277 *ap-*
proved: Proved.   283 *free:* Bounteous.   285–86 *splinter:* Bind up with splints.   286 *lay:*
Wager.

Cassio: I think it freely; and betimes in the morning will I beseech the vir- 290
tuous Desdemona to undertake for me. I am desperate of my fortunes
if they check me here.

Iago: You are in the right. Good night, lieutenant; I must to the watch.

Cassio: Good night, honest Iago.   *Exit Cassio.*

Iago: And what's he then that says I play the villain,   295
When this advice is free I give and honest,
Probal° to thinking, and indeed the course
To win the Moor again? For 'tis most easy
Th' inclining Desdemona to subdue°
In an honest suit; she's framed as fruitful   300
As the free elements. And then for her
To win the Moor — were 't to renounce his baptism,
All seals and symbols of redeemèd sin —
His soul is so enfettered to her love
That she may make, unmake, do what she list,   305
Even as her appetite shall play the god
With his weak function. How am I then a villain
To counsel Cassio to this parallel° course,
Directly to his good? Divinity° of hell!
When devils will the blackest sins put on,°   310
They do suggest at first with heavenly shows,
As I do now. For whiles this honest fool
Plies Desdemona to repair his fortunes,
And she for him pleads strongly to the Moor,
I'll pour this pestilence into his ear,   315
That she repeals him° for her body's lust;
And by how much she strives to do him good,
She shall undo her credit with the Moor.
So will I turn her virtue into pitch,
And out of her own goodness make the net   320
That shall enmesh them all.

Enter Roderigo.

How, now, Roderigo?

Roderigo: I do follow here in the chase, not like a hound that hunts, but
one that fills up the cry.° My money is almost spent; I have been tonight exceedingly well cudgelled; and I think the issue will be — I shall
have so much experience for my pains; and so, with no money at all, 325
and a little more wit, return again to Venice.

Iago: How poor are they that have not patience!
What wound did ever heal but by degrees?
Thou know'st we work by wit, and not by witchcraft;
And wit depends on dilatory time.   330
Does 't not go well? Cassio hath beaten thee,
And thou by that small hurt hast cashiered Cassio.°

---

297 *Probal:* Probable.   299 *subdue:* Persuade.   308 *parallel:* Corresponding.   309 *Divinity:* Theology.   310 *put on:* Incite.   316 *repeals him:* Seeks his recall.   323 *cry:* Pack.
332 *cashiered Cassio:* Maneuvered Cassio's discharge.

Though other things grow fair against the sun,
Yet fruits that blossom first will first be ripe.
Content thyself awhile. By the mass, 'tis morning!   335
Pleasure and action make the hours seem short.
Retire thee; go where thou art billeted.
Away, I say! Thou shalt know more hereafter.
Nay, get thee gone!   *Exit Roderigo.*
　　　　　　　Two things are to be done:
My wife must move for Cassio to her mistress;   340
I'll set her on;
Myself the while to draw the Moor apart
And bring him jump° when he may Cassio find
Soliciting his wife. Ay, that's the way!
Dull no device by coldness and delay.   *Exit.* 345

ACT III

SCENE I: *Before the chamber of Othello and Desdemona.*

Enter Cassio, with Musicians and the Clown.

Cassio: Masters, play here, I will content° your pains:
　　Something that's brief; and bid "Good morrow, general."

[They play.]

Clown: Why, masters, ha' your instruments been in Naples,° that they
　　speak i' th' nose thus?
Musician: How, sir, how?   5
Clown: Are these, I pray you, called wind instruments?
Musician: Ay, marry, are they, sir.
Clown: O, thereby hangs a tail.
Musician: Whereby hangs a tail, sir?
Clown: Marry, sir, by many a wind instrument that I know. But, masters,   10
　　here's money for you; and the general so likes your music that he
　　desires you, for love's sake, to make no more noise with it.
Musician: Well, sir, we will not.
Clown: If you have any music that may not be heard, to't again: but, as
　　they say, to hear music the general does not greatly care.   15
Musician: We have none such, sir.
Clown: Then put up your pipes in your bag, for I'll away. Go, vanish into
　　air, away!   *Exit Musician [with his fellows].*
Cassio: Dost thou hear, my honest friend?
Clown: No, I hear not your honest friend. I hear you.   20
Cassio: Prithee keep up thy quillets.° There's a poor piece of gold for thee.
　　If the gentlewoman that attends the general's wife be stirring, tell her
　　there's one Cassio entreats her a little favor of speech. Wilt thou do
　　this?

343 *jump:* At the exact moment. **Act III, Scene I.** 1 *content:* Reward. 3 *Naples:*
(Notorious for its association with venereal disease). 21 *quillets:* Quips.

Clown: She is stirring sir. If she will stir hither, I shall seem to notify unto   25
   her.
Cassio: [Do, good my friend.]   *Exit Clown.*

   Enter Iago.

                     In happy time,° Iago.
Iago: You have not been abed then?
Cassio: Why, no; the day had broke
   Before we parted. I have made bold, Iago,   30
   To send in to your wife: my suit to her
   Is that she will to virtuous Desdemona
   Procure me some access.
Iago: I'll send her to you presently;
   And I'll devise a mean to draw the Moor
   Out of the way, that your converse and business   35
   May be more free.
Cassio: I humbly thank you for't.   *Exit [Iago].*
                   I never knew
   A Florentine° more kind and honest.

   Enter Emilia.

Emilia: Good morrow, good lieutenant. I am sorry
   For your displeasure: but all will sure be well.   40
   The general and his wife are talking of it,
   And she speaks for you stoutly. The Moor replied
   That he you hurt is of great fame in Cyprus
   And great affinity,° and that in wholesome wisdom
   He might not but refuse you; but he protests he loves you,   45
   And needs no other suitor but his likings
   [To take the safest occasion° by the front°]
   To bring you in again.
Cassio: Yet I beseech you,
   If you think fit, or that it may be done,
   Give me advantage of some brief discourse   50
   With Desdemona alone.
Emilia: Pray you come in.
   I will bestow you where you shall have time
   To speak your bosom° freely.
Cassio: I am much bound to you.   *Exeunt.*

SCENE II: *The castle.*

   Enter Othello, Iago, and Gentlemen.

Othello: These letters give, Iago, to the pilot
   And by him do my duties to the Senate.
   That done, I will be walking on the works;°

---

27 *In happy time:* Well met.   38 *Florentine:* I.e., even a Florentine (like Cassio; Iago was a
Venetian).   44 *affinity:* Family connections.   47 *occasion:* Opportunity; *front:* Forelock.
53 *your bosom:* Your inmost thoughts.   **Scene II.**   3 *works:* Fortifications.

Repair there to me.
Iago: Well, my good lord, I'll do't.
Othello: This fortification, gentlemen, shall we see't?   5
Gentlemen: We'll wait upon your lordship.   *Exeunt.*

SCENE III: *The castle grounds.*

Enter Desdemona, Cassio, and Emilia.

Desdemona: Be thou assured, good Cassio, I will do
  All my abilities in thy behalf.
Emilia: Good madam, do. I warrant it grieves my husband
  As if the cause were his.
Desdemona: O, that's an honest fellow. Do not doubt, Cassio,   5
  But I will have my lord and you again
  As friendly as you were.
Cassio: Bounteous madam,
  Whatever shall become of Michael Cassio,
  He's never anything but your true servant.
Desdemona: I know't; I thank you. You do love my lord;   10
  You have known him long; and be you well assured
  He shall in strangeness° stand no farther off
  Than in a politic distance.°
Cassio: Ay, but, lady,
  That policy may either last so long,
  Or feed upon such nice and waterish diet,°   15
  Or breed itself so out of circumstance,
  That, I being absent, and my place supplied,
  My general will forget my love and service.
Desdemona: Do not doubt° that; before Emilia here
  I give thee warrant of thy place. Assure thee,   20
  If I do vow a friendship, I'll perform it
  To the last article. My lord shall never rest;
  I'll watch him tame° and talk him out of patience;
  His bed shall seem a school, his board a shrift;°
  I'll intermingle everything he does   25
  With Cassio's suit. Therefore be merry, Cassio,
  For thy solicitor shall rather die
  Than give thy cause away.

Enter Othello and Iago [at a distance].

Emilia: Madam, here comes my lord.
Cassio: Madam, I'll take my leave.   30
Desdemona: Why, stay, and hear me speak.
Cassio: Madam, not now: I am very ill at ease,
  Unfit for mine own purposes.
Desdemona: Well, do your discretion.   *Exit Cassio.*

Scene III.   12 *strangeness:* Aloofness.   13 *Than . . . distance:* Than wise policy requires.
15 *Or . . . diet:* Or be continued for such slight reasons.   19 *doubt:* Fear.   23 *watch him tame:* Keep him awake until he gives in.   24 *shrift:* Confessional.

Iago: Ha! I like not that.
Othello: What dost thou say?   35
Iago: Nothing, my lord; or if — I know not what.
Othello: Was not that Cassio parted from my wife?
Iago: Cassio, my lord? No, sure, I cannot think it,
     That he would steal away so guilty-like,
     Seeing your coming.
Othello: I do believe 'twas he.   40
Desdemona: How now, my lord?
     I have been talking with a suitor here,
     A man that languishes in your displeasure.
Othello: What is't you mean?
Desdemona: Why, your lieutenant, Cassio. Good my lord,   45
     If I have any grace or power to move you,
     His present° reconciliation take;
     For if he be not one that truly loves you,
     That errs in ignorance, and not in cunning,
     I have no judgment in an honest face,   50
     I prithee call him back.
Othello: Went he hence now?
Desdemona: Yes, faith; so humbled
     That he hath left part of his grief with me
     To suffer with him. Good love, call him back.
Othello: Not now, sweet Desdemon; some other time.   55
Desdemona: But shall't be shortly?
Othello: The sooner, sweet, for you.
Desdemona: Shall't be to-night at supper?
Othello: No, not to-night.
Desdemona: To-morrow dinner then?
Othello: I shall not dine at home;
     I meet the captains at the citadel.
Desdemona: Why then, to-morrow night, or Tuesday morn,   60
     On Tuesday noon, or night, or Wednesday morn.
     I prithee name the time, but let it not
     Exceed three days. I' faith, he's penitent;
     And yet his trespass, in our common reason
     (Save that, they say, the wars must make examples   65
     Out of their best), is not almost° a fault
     T' incur a private check.° When shall he come?
     Tell me, Othello. I wonder in my soul
     What you could ask me that I should deny
     Or stand so mamm'ring on.° What? Michael Cassio,   70
     That came a-wooing with you, and so many a time,
     When I have spoke of you dispraisingly,
     Hath ta'en your part — to have so much to do
     To bring him in? By'r Lady, I could do much —
Othello: Prithee no more. Let him come when he will!   75

---

47 *present:* Immediate.   66 *not almost:* Hardly.   67 *a private check:* Even a private reprimand.   70 *mamm'ring on:* Hesitating about.

I will deny thee nothing.
Desdemona: Why, this is not a boon;
     'Tis as I should entreat you wear your gloves,
     Or feed on nourishing dishes, or keep you warm,
     Or sue to you to do a peculiar profit
     To your own person. Nay, when I have a suit   80
     Wherein I mean to touch your love indeed,
     It shall be full of poise and difficult weight,
     And fearful° to be granted.
Othello: I will deny thee nothing!
     Whereon I do beseech thee grant me this,
     To leave me but a little to myself.   85
Desdemona: Shall I deny you? No. Farewell, my lord.
Othello: Farewell, my Desdemon: I'll come to thee straight.
Desdemona: Emilia, come. — Be as your fancies teach you;
     Whate'er you be, I am obedient.   *Exit [with Emilia].*
Othello: Excellent wretch!° Perdition catch my soul   90
     But I do love thee! and when I love thee not,
     Chaos is come again.
Iago: My noble lord —
Othello: What dost thou say, Iago?
Iago: Did Michael Cassio, when you wooed my lady,
     Know of your love?   95
Othello: He did, from first to last. Why dost thou ask?
Iago: But for a satisfaction of my thought;
     No further harm.
Othello: Why of thy thought, Iago?
Iago: I did not think he had been acquainted with her.
Othello: O, yes, and went between us° very oft.   100
Iago: Indeed?
Othello: Indeed? Ay, indeed! Discern'st thou aught in that?
     Is he not honest?
Iago: Honest, my lord?
Othello: Honest. Ay, honest.
Iago: My lord, for aught I know.
Othello: What dost thou think?
Iago: Think, my lord?
Othello: Think, my lord?   105
     By heaven, he echoes me,
     As if there were some monster in his thought
     Too hideous to be shown. Thou dost mean something:
     I heard thee say even now, thou lik'st not that,
     When Cassio left my wife. What didst not like?   110
     And when I told thee he was of my counsel
     In my whole course of wooing, thou cried'st "Indeed?"
     And didst contract and purse thy brow together,
     As if thou then hadst shut up in thy brain

---

83 *fearful:* Dangerous.   90 *wretch:* (A term of endearment).   100 *went between us:* (I.e.,
as messenger).

Some horrible conceit.° If thou dost love me,   115
Show me thy thought

Iago: My lord, you know I love you.

Othello: I think thou dost;
And, for I know thou'rt full of love and honesty
And weigh'st thy words before thou giv'st them breath,
Therefore these stops of thine fright me the more;   120
For such things in a false disloyal knave
Are tricks of custom; but in a man that's just
They are close dilations, working from the heart
That passion cannot rule.°

Iago: For Michael Cassio,
I dare be sworn I think that he is honest.   125

Othello: I think so too.

Iago: Men should be what they seem;
Or those that be not, would they might seem none!°

Othello: Certain, men should be what they seem.

Iago: Why then, I think Cassio's an honest man.

Othello: Nay, yet there's more in this.   130
I prithee speak to me as to thy thinkings,
As thou dost ruminate, and give thy worst of thoughts
The worst of words.

Iago: Good my lord, pardon me:
Though I am bound to every act of duty,
I am not bound to that all slaves are free to.°   135
Utter my thoughts? Why, say they are vile and false,
As where's that palace whereinto foul things
Sometimes intrude not? Who has a breast so pure
But some uncleanly apprehensions
Keep leets and law days,° and in Sessions sit   140
With meditations lawful?

Othello: Thou dost conspire against thy friend, Iago,
If thou but think'st him wronged, and mak'st his ear
A stranger to thy thoughts.

Iago: I do beseech you —
Though I perchance am vicious in my guess   145
(As I confess it is my nature's plague
To spy into abuses, and oft my jealousy°
Shapes faults that are not), that your wisdom yet
From one that so imperfectly conjects°
Would take no notice, nor build yourself a trouble   150
Out of his scattering and unsure observance.
It were not for your quiet nor your good,
Nor for my manhood, honesty, and wisdom,
To let you know my thoughts.

---

115 *conceit:* Fancy.   123–24 *close dilations . . . rule:* Secret emotions which well up in spite
of restraint.   127 *seem none:* I.e., not pretend to be men when they are really monsters.
135 *bound . . . free to:* Bound to tell that which even slaves are allowed to keep to themselves.
140 *leets and law days:* Sittings of the courts.   147 *jealousy:* Suspicion.   149 *conjects:*
Conjectures.

Othello: What dost thou mean?

Iago: Good name in man and woman, dear my lord,   155
     Is the immediate° jewel of their souls.
     Who steals my purse steals trash; 'tis something, nothing;
     'Twas mine, 'tis his, and has been slave to thousands;
     But he that filches from me my good name
     Robs me of that which not enriches him   160
     And makes me poor indeed.

Othello: By heaven, I'll know thy thoughts!

Iago: You cannot, if my heart were in your hand;
     Nor shall not whilst 'tis in my custody.

Othello: Ha!

Iago: O, beware, my lord, of jealousy!   165
     It is the green-eyed monster, which doth mock°
     The meat it feeds on. That cuckold lives in bliss
     Who, certain of his fate, loves not his wronger;
     But O, what damnèd minutes tells he o'er
     Who dotes, yet doubts — suspects, yet strongly loves!   170

Othello: O misery!

Iago: Poor and content is rich, and rich enough;
     But riches fineless° is as poor as winter
     To him that ever fears he shall be poor.
     Good God, the souls of all my tribe defend   175
     From jealousy!

Othello: Why, why is this?
     Think'st thou I'ld make a life of jealousy,
     To follow still the changes of the moon
     With fresh suspicions? No! To be once in doubt
     Is once to be resolved. Exchange me for a goat   180
     When I shall turn the business of my soul
     To such exsufflicate and blown° surmises,
     Matching this inference. 'Tis not to make me jealous
     To say my wife is fair, feeds well, loves company,
     Is free of speech, sings, plays, and dances;   185
     Where virtue is, these are more virtuous.
     Nor from mine own weak merits will I draw
     The smallest fear or doubt of her revolt,°
     For she had eyes, and chose me. No, Iago;
     I'll see before I doubt; when I doubt, prove;   190
     And on the proof there is no more but this —
     Away at once with love or jealousy!

Iago: I am glad of this; for now I shall have reason
     To show the love and duty that I bear you
     With franker spirit. Therefore, as I am bound,   195
     Receive it from me. I speak not yet of proof.
     Look at your wife; observe her well with Cassio;

---

156 *immediate:* Nearest the heart.   166 *mock:* Play with, like a cat with a mouse.
173 *fineless:* Unlimited.   182 *exsufflicate and blown:* Spat out and flyblown.   188 *revolt:*
Unfaithfulness.

Wear your eyes thus, not jealous nor secure:°
I would not have your free and noble nature,
Out of self-bounty,° be abused. Look to't.   200
I know our country disposition well:
In Venice they do let God see the pranks
They dare not show their husbands; their best conscience
Is not to leave't undone, but keep't unknown.

Othello: Dost thou say so?   205

Iago: She did deceive her father, marrying you;
And when she seemed to shake and fear your looks,
She loved them most.

Othello: And so she did.

Iago: Why, go to then!
She that, so young, could give out such a seeming
To seel° her father's eyes up close as oak°—   210
He thought 'twas witchcraft—but I am much to blame.
I humbly do beseech you of your pardon
For too much loving you.

Othello: I am bound to thee for ever.

Iago: I see this hath a little dashed your spirits.

Othello: Not a jot, not a jot.

Iago: I' faith, I fear it has.   215
I hope you will consider what is spoke
Comes from my love. But I do see y' are moved.
I am to pray you not to strain my speech
To grosser issues° nor to larger reach
Than to suspicion.   220

Othello: I will not.

Iago: Should you do so, my lord,
My speech should fall into such vile success°
As my thoughts aim not at. Cassio's my worthy friend—
My lord, I see y' are moved.

Othello: No, not much moved:
I do not think but Desdemona's honest.°   225

Iago: Long live she so! and long live you to think so!

Othello: And yet, how nature erring from itself—

Iago: Ay, there's the point! as (to be bold with you)
Not to affect many proposèd matches
Of her own clime, complexion, and degree,   230
Whereto we see in all things nature tends—
Foh! one may smell in such a will most rank,
Foul disproportions, thought unnatural—
But pardon me—I do not in position°
Distinctly speak of her; though I may fear   235
Her will, recoiling° to her better judgment,

198 *secure:* Overconfident.   200 *self-bounty:* Natural goodness.   210 *seel:* Close; *oak:* Oak grain.   219 *To grosser issues:* To mean something more monstrous.   222 *vile success:* Evil outcome.   225 *honest:* Chaste.   234 *position:* Definite assertion.   236 *recoiling:* Reverting.

May fall to match° you with her country forms,
    And happily° repent.
Othello: Farewell, farewell!
    If more thou dost perceive, let me know more.
    Set on thy wife to observe. Leave me, Iago.   240
Iago: My lord, I take my leave.   *[Going.]*
Othello: Why did I marry? This honest creature doubtless
    Sees and knows more, much more, than he unfolds.
Iago [returns]: My lord, I would I might entreat your honor
    To scan this thing no further: leave it to time.   245
    Although 'tis fit that Cassio have his place,
    For sure he fills it up with great ability,
    Yet, if you please to hold off a while,
    You shall by that perceive him and his means.
    Note if your lady strain his entertainment°   250
    With any strong or vehement importunity;
    Much will be seen in that. In the mean time
    Let me be thought too busy° in my fears
    (As worthy cause I have to fear I am)
    And hold her free,° I do beseech your honor.   255
Othello: Fear not my government.°
Iago: I once more take my leave.   *Exit.*
Othello: This fellow 's of exceeding honesty,
    And knows all qualities,° with a learned spirit
    Of° human dealings. If I do prove her haggard,°   260
    Though that her jesses° were my dear heartstrings,
    I'd whistle her off and let her down the wind
    To prey at fortune.° Haply, for I am black
    And have not those soft parts of conversation°
    That chamberers° have, or for I am declined   265
    Into the vale of years—yet that's not much—
    She's gone. I am abused, and my relief
    Must be to loathe her. O curse of marriage,
    That we can call these delicate creatures ours,
    And not their appetites! I had rather be a toad   270
    And live upon the vapor of a dungeon
    Than keep a corner in the thing I love
    For others' uses. Yet 'tis the plague of great ones;°
    Prerogatived° are they less than the base.
    'Tis destiny unshunnable, like death.   275
    Even then this forkèd plague° is fated to us
    When we do quicken.° Look where she comes.

---

237 *fall to match:* Happen to compare.   238 *happily:* Haply, perhaps.   250 *strain his enter-*
tainment: Urge his recall.   253 *busy:* Meddlesome.   255 *hold her free:* Consider her guiltless.   256 *government:* Self-control.   259 *qualities:* Natures.   259-60 *learned spirit Of:*
Mind informed about.   260 *haggard:* A wild hawk.   261 *jesses:* Thongs for controlling
a hawk.   262–63 *whistle...fortune:* Turn her out and let her take care of herself.
264 *soft...conversation:* Ingratiating manners.   265 *chamberers:* Courtiers.   273 *great ones:*
Prominent men.   274 *Prerogatived:* Privileged.   276 *forkèd plague:* I.e., horns of a cuckold.   277 *do quicken:* Are born.

Enter Desdemona and Emilia.

If she be false, O, then heaven mocks itself!
I'll not believe't.
Desdemona: How now, my dear Othello?
Your dinner, and the generous° islanders   280
By you invited, do attend your presence.
Othello: I am to blame.
Desdemona: Why do you speak so faintly?
Are you not well?
Othello: I have a pain upon my forehead, here.
Desdemona: Faith, that's with watching;° 'twill away again.   285
Let me but bind it hard, within this hour
It will be well.
Othello: Your napkin° is too little;

[He pushes the handkerchief from him, and it falls unnoticed.]

Let it° alone. Come, I'll go in with you.
Desdemona: I am very sorry that you are not well.   *Exit [with Othello].*
Emilia: I am glad I have found this napkin;   290
This was her first remembrance from the Moor,
My wayward husband hath a hundred times
Wooed me to steal it; but she so loves the token
(For he conjured her she should ever keep it)
That she reserves it evermore about her   295
To kiss and talk to. I'll have the work ta'en out°
And give't Iago.
What he will do with it heaven knows, not I;
I nothing but to please his fantasy.°

Enter Iago.

Iago: How now? What do you here alone?   300
Emilia: Do not you chide; I have a thing for you.
Iago: A thing for me? It is a common thing —
Emilia: Ha?
Iago: To have a foolish wife.
Emilia: O, is that all? What will you give me now   305
For that same handkerchief?
Iago: What handkerchief?
Emilia: What handkerchief!
Why, that the Moor first gave to Desdemona;
That which so often you did bid me steal.
Iago: Hast stol'n it from her?   310
Emilia: No, faith; she let it drop by negligence,
And to th' advantage,° I, being here, took't up.
Look, here it is.
Iago: A good wench! Give it me.
Emilia: What will you do with't, that you have been so earnest

---

280 *generous:* Noble.   285 *watching:* Working late.   287 *napkin:* Handkerchief.   288 *it:* I.e., his forehead.   296 *work ta'en out:* Pattern copied.   299 *fantasy:* Whim.   312 *to th' advantage:* Opportunely.

To have me filch it?

Iago: Why, what is that to you?   315

[Snatches it.]

Emilia: If it be not for some purpose of import,°
Give't me again. Poor lady, she'll run mad
When she shall lack it.

Iago: Be not acknown on't;° I have use for it.
Go, leave me.   Exit Emilia. 320
I will in Cassio's lodgings lose this napkin
And let him find it. Trifles light as air
Are to the jealous confirmations strong
As proofs of holy writ. This may do something.
The Moor already changes with my poison: 325
Dangerous conceits° are in their nature poisons,
Which at the first are scarce found to distaste,
But with a little act upon the blood
Burn like the mines of sulphur.

    Enter Othello.

                              I did say so.
Look where he comes! Not poppy nor mandragora,°   330
Nor all the drowsy syrups of the world,
Shall ever med'cine thee to that sweet sleep
Which thou owedst yesterday.

Othello: Ha! ha! false to me?

Iago: Why, how now, general? No more of that!

Othello: Avaunt! be gone! Thou hast set me on the rack.   335
I swear 'tis better to be much abused
Than but to know't a little.

Iago: How now, my lord?

Othello: What sense had I of her stol'n hours of lust?
I saw't not, thought it not, it harmed not me;
I slept the next night well, fed well, was free° and merry; 340
I found not Cassio's kisses on her lips
He that is robbed, not wanting° what is stol'n,
Let him not know't, and he's not robbed at all.

Iago: I am sorry to hear this.

Othello: I had been happy if the general camp,   345
Pioneers° and all, had tasted her sweet body,
So I had nothing known. O, now for ever
Farewell the tranquil mind! farewell content!
Farewell the plumèd troop, and the big° wars
That make ambition virtue! O, farewell!   350
Farewell the neighing steed and the shrill trump,
The spirit-stirring drum, th' ear-piercing fife,
The royal banner, and all quality,

---

316 *import:* Importance.   319 *Be . . . on't:* Do not acknowledge it.   326 *conceits:* Ideas.
330 *mandragora:* A narcotic.   340 *free:* Carefree.   342 *wanting:* Missing.   346 *Pioneers:*
Sappers, laborers.   349 *big:* Stately.

> Pride, pomp, and circumstance° of glorious war!
> And O you mortal engines° whose rude throats   355
> Th' immortal Jove's dread clamors counterfeit,°
> Farewell! Othello's occupation's gone!

Iago: Is't possible, my lord?

Othello: Villain, be sure thou prove my love a whore!
> Be sure of it; give me the ocular proof;   360
> Or, by the worth of mine eternal soul,
> Thou hadst been better have been born a dog
> Than answer my waked wrath!

Iago: Is't come to this?

Othello: Make me to see't; or at the least so prove it
> That the probation° bear no hinge nor loop   365
> To hang a doubt on — or woe upon thy life!

Iago: My noble lord —

Othello: If thou dost slander her and torture me,
> Never pray more; abandon all remorse;
> On horror's head horrors accumulate;   370
> Do deeds to make heaven weep, all earth amazed;
> For nothing canst thou to damnation add
> Greater than that.

Iago: O grace! O heaven forgive me!
> Are you a man? Have you a soul or sense? —
> God b' wi' you! take mine office. O wretched fool,   375
> That liv'st to make thine honesty a vice!
> O monstrous world! Take note, take note, O world,
> To be direct and honest is not safe.
> I thank you for this profit;° and from hence
> I'll love no friend, sith love breeds such offense.   380

Othello: Nay, stay. Thou shouldst be honest.

Iago: I should be wise; for honesty's a fool
> And loses that it works for.

Othello: By the world,
> I think my wife be honest, and think she is not;
> I think that thou art just, and think thou art not.   385
> I'll have some proof. Her name, that was as fresh
> As Dian's visage, is now begrimed and black
> As mine own face. If there be cords, or knives,
> Poison, or fire, or suffocating streams,
> I'll not endure it. Would I were satisfied!°   390

Iago: I see, sir, you are eaten up with passion:
> I do repent me that I put it to you.
> You would be satisfied?

Othello: Would? Nay, I will.

Iago: And may; but how? how satisfied, my lord?
> Would you, the supervisor,° grossly gape on?   395

---

354 *circumstance:* Pageantry.   355 *mortal engines:* Deadly artillery.   356 *counterfeit:* Imitate.   365 *probation:* Proof.   379 *profit:* Profitable lesson.   390 *satisfied:* Completely informed.   395 *supervisor:* Spectator.

Behold her topped?
Othello: Death and damnation! O!
Iago: It were a tedious difficulty, I think,
　　To bring them to that prospect. Damn them then,
　　If ever mortal eyes do see them bolster°
　　More than their own! What then? How then?   400
　　What shall I say? Where's satisfaction?
　　It is impossible you should see this,
　　Were they as prime° as goats, as hot as monkeys,
　　As salt° as wolves in pride,° and fools as gross
　　As ignorance made drunk. But yet, I say,   405
　　If imputation and strong circumstances
　　Which lead directly to the door of truth
　　Will give you satisfaction, you may have't.
Othello: Give me a living reason she's disloyal.
Iago: I do not like the office.   410
　　But sith I am ent'red in this cause so far,
　　Pricked to't by foolish honesty and love,
　　I will go on. I lay with Cassio lately,
　　And being troubled with a raging tooth,
　　I could not sleep.   415
　　There are a kind of men so loose of soul
　　That in their sleeps will mutter their affairs.
　　One of this kind is Cassio.
　　In sleep I heard him say, "Sweet Desdemona,
　　Let us be wary, let us hide our loves!"   420
　　And then, sir, would he gripe and wring my hand,
　　Cry "O sweet creature!" and then kiss me hard,
　　As if he plucked up kisses by the roots
　　That grew upon my lips; then laid his leg
　　Over my thigh, and sighed, and kissed, and then   425
　　Cried "Cursèd fate that gave thee to the Moor!"
Othello: O monstrous! monstrous!
Iago: Nay, this was but his dream.
Othello: But this denoted a foregone conclusion;°
　　'Tis a shrewd doubt,° though it be but a dream.
Iago: And this may help to thicken other proofs   430
　　That do demonstrate thinly.
Othello: I'll tear her all to pieces!
Iago: Nay, but be wise. Yet we see nothing done;
　　She may be honest yet. Tell me but this —
　　Have you not sometimes seen a handkerchief
　　Spotted with strawberries in your wife's hand?   435
Othello: I gave her such a one; 'twas my first gift.
Iago: I know not that; but such a handkerchief —
　　I am sure it was your wife's — did I to-day
　　See Cassio wipe his beard with.

---

399 *bolster:* Lie together.   403 *prime:* Lustful.   404 *salt:* Lecherous; *pride:* Heat.   428 *foregone conclusion:* Previous experience.   429 *a shrewd doubt:* Cursedly suspicious.

Othello: If it be that —
Iago: If it be that, or any that was hers,   440
 It speaks against her with the other proofs.
Othello: O, that the slave had forty thousand lives!
 One is too poor, too weak for my revenge.
 Now do I see 'tis true. Look here, Iago:
 All my fond love thus do I blow to heaven.   445
 'Tis gone.
 Arise, black vengeance, from the hollow hell!
 Yield up, O love, thy crown and hearted throne
 To tyrannous hate! Swell, bosom, with thy fraught,°
 For 'tis of aspics'° tongues!
Iago: Yet be content.   450
Othello: O, blood, blood, blood!
Iago: Patience, I say. Your mind perhaps may change.
Othello: Never, Iago. Like to the Pontic sea,°
 Whose icy current and compulsive course
 Ne'er feels retiring ebb, but keeps due on   455
 To the Propontic and the Hellespont,
 Even so my bloody thoughts, with violent pace,
 Shall ne'er look back, ne'er ebb to humble love,
 Till that a capable° and wide revenge
 Swallow them up.
 (He kneels.)   Now, by yond marble heaven,   460
 In the due reverence of a sacred vow
 I here engage my words.
Iago: Do not rise yet.

 (Iago kneels.)
 Witness, you ever-burning lights above,
 You elements that clip° us round about,
 Witness that here Iago doth give up   465
 The execution° of his wit,° hands, heart
 To wronged Othello's service! Let him command,
 And to obey shall be in me remorse,°
 What bloody business ever.

 [They rise.]

Othello: I greet thy love,
 Not with vain thanks but with acceptance bounteous,   470
 And will upon the instant put thee to't.
 Within these three days let me hear thee say
 That Cassio's not alive.
Iago: My friend is dead; 'tis done at your request.
 But let her live.   475
Othello: Damn her, lewd minx! O, damn her! damn her!
 Come, go with me apart. I will withdraw

---

449 *fraught:* Burden.   450 *aspics:* Deadly poisonous snakes.   453 *Pontic sea:* Black Sea.
459 *capable:* All-embracing.   464 *clip:* Encompass.   466 *execution:* Activities; *wit:*
Mind.   468 *remorse:* Pity.

To furnish me with some swift means of death
For the fair devil. Now art thou my lieutenant.
Iago: I am your own forever.   *Exeunt.* 480

SCENE IV: *The environs of the castle.*

Enter Desdemona, Emilia, and Clown.

Desdemona: Do you know, sirrah, where Lieutenant Cassio lies?°
Clown: I dare not say he lies anywhere.
Desdemona: Why, man?
Clown: He's a soldier, and for me to say a soldier lies is stabbing.
Desdemona: Go to. Where lodges he?   5
Clown: To tell you where he lodges is to tell you where I lie.
Desdemona: Can anything be made of this?
Clown: I know not where he lodges; and for me to devise a lodging, and
     say he lies here or he lies there, were to lie in mine own throat.
Desdemona: Can you enquire him out, and be edified by report?   10
Clown: I will catechize the world for him; that is, make questions, and by
     them answer.
Desdemona: Seek him, bid him come hither. Tell him I have moved° my
     lord on his behalf and hope all will be well.
Clown: To do this is within the compass of man's wit, and therefore I'll   15
     attempt the doing of it.   *Exit.*
Desdemona: Where should I lose that handkerchief, Emilia?
Emilia: I know not, madam.
Desdemona: Believe me, I had rather have lost my purse
     Full of crusadoes;° and but my noble Moor   20
     Is true of mind, and made of no such baseness
     As jealous creatures are, it were enough
     To put him to ill thinking.
Emilia: Is he not jealous?
Desdemona: Who? he? I think the sun where he was born
     Drew all such humors° from him.

Enter Othello.

Emilia: Look where he comes.   25
Desdemona: I will not leave him now till Cassio
     Be called to him — How is't with you, my lord?
Othello: Well, my good lady. *[Aside.]* O, hardness to dissemble! —
     How do you, Desdemona?
Desdemona: Well, my good lord.
Othello: Give me your hand. This hand is moist, my lady.   30
Desdemona: It yet hath felt no age nor known no sorrow.
Othello: This argues fruitfulness and liberal heart.
     Hot, hot, and moist. This hand of yours requires
     A sequester° from liberty, fasting and prayer,
     Much castigation, exercise devout;   35

Scene IV.   1 *lies:* Lives, lodges.   13 *moved:* Made proposals to.   20 *crusadoes:* Por-
tuguese gold coins.   25 *humors:* Inclinations.   34 *sequester:* Removal.

For here's a young and sweating devil here
That commonly rebels. 'Tis a good hand,
A frank one.
Desdemona: You may, indeed, say so;
For 'twas that hand that gave away my heart.   40
Othello: A liberal hand! The hearts of old gave hands;
But our new heraldry° is hands, not hearts.
Desdemona: I cannot speak of this. Come now, your promise!
Othello: What promise, chuck?
Desdemona: I have sent to bid Cassio come speak with you.   45
Othello: I have a salt and sorry rheum° offends me.
Lend me thy handkerchief.
Desdemona: Here, my lord.
Othello: That which I gave you.
Desdemona: I have it not about me.
Othello: Not?
Desdemona: No, faith, my lord.
Othello: That's a fault.
That handkerchief   50
Did an Egyptian° to my mother give.
She was a charmer,° and could almost read
The thoughts of people. She told her, while she kept it,
'Twould make her amiable° and subdue my father
Entirely to her love; but if she lost it   55
Or made a gift of it, my father's eye
Should hold her loathèd, and his spirits should hunt
After new fancies. She, dying, gave it me,
And bid me, when my fate would have me wive;
To give it her. I did so; and take heed on't;   60
Make it a darling like your precious eye.
To lose't or give't away were such perdition°
As nothing else could match.
Desdemona: Is't possible?
Othello: 'Tis true. There's magic in the web of it.
A sibyl that had numb'red in the world   65
The sun to course two hundred compasses,°
In her prophetic fury sewed the work;
The worms were hallowed that did breed the silk;
And it was dyed in mummy° which the skillful
Conserved of maidens' hearts.
Desdemona: I' faith? Is't true?   70
Othello: Most veritable. Therefore look to't well.
Desdemona: Then would to God that I had never seen't!
Othello: Ha! Wherefore?
Desdemona: Why do you speak so startingly and rash?
Othello: Is't lost? Is't gone? Speak, is it out o' th' way?   75
Desdemona: Heaven bless us!

---

42 *heraldry:* Heraldic symbolism.   46 *salt...rheum:* Distressing head cold.   51 *Egyptian:* Gypsy.   52 *charmer:* Sorceress.   54 *amiable:* Lovable.   62 *perdition:* Disaster.
66 *compasses:* Annual rounds.   69 *mummy:* A drug made from mummies.

Othello: Say you?

Desdemona: It is not lost. But what an if it were?

Othello: How?

Desdemona: I say it is not lost.

Othello: Fetch't, let me see't!   80

Desdemona: Why, so I can, sir; but I will not now.
　　This is a trick to put° me from my suit:
　　Pray you let Cassio be received again.

Othello: Fetch me the handkerchief! My mind misgives.

Desdemona: Come, come!   85
　　You'll never meet a more sufficient man.

Othello: The handkerchief!

[*Desdemona:*   I pray talk me of Cassio.

Othello: The handkerchief!]

Desdemona: A man that all his time°
　　Hath founded his good fortunes on your love,
　　Shared dangers with you —   90

Othello: The handkerchief!

Desdemona: I' faith, you are to blame.

Othello: Zounds!   *Exit Othello.*

Emilia: Is not this man jealous?

Desdemona: I ne'er saw this before.   95
　　Sure there's some wonder in this handkerchief;
　　I am most unhappy in the loss of it.

Emilia: 'Tis not a year or two shows us a man.
　　They are all but stomachs, and we all but food;
　　They eat us hungerly, and when they are full,   100
　　They belch us.

　　Enter Iago and Cassio.

　　　　　　　Look you — Cassio and my husband!

Iago: There is no other way; 'tis she must do't.
　　And lo the happiness!° Go and importune her.

Desdemona: How now, good Cassio? What's the news with you?

Cassio: Madam, my former suit. I do beseech you   105
　　That by your virtuous means I may again
　　Exist, and be a member of his love
　　Whom I with all the office of my heart
　　Entirely honor. I would not be delayed.
　　If my offense be of such mortal kind   110
　　That neither service past, nor present sorrows,
　　Nor purposed merit in futurity,
　　Can ransom me into his love again,
　　But to know so must be my benefit.
　　So shall I clothe me in a forced content,   115
　　And shut myself up in° some other course,
　　To fortune's alms.

Desdemona: Alas, thrice-gentle Cassio!
　　My advocation° is not now in tune.

---

82 *put:* Divert.　　88 *all his time:* During his whole career.　　103 *happiness:* Good luck.
116 *shut myself up in:* Confine myself to.　　118 *advocation:* Advocacy.

My lord is not my lord; nor should I know him,
Were he in favor° as in humor altered.   120
So help me every spirit sanctified
As I have spoken for you all my best
And stood within the blank° of his displeasure
For my free speech! You must a while be patient.
What I can do I will; and more I will   125
Than for myself I dare. Let that suffice you.

Iago: Is my lord angry?
Emilia: He went hence but now,
And certainly in strange unquietness.

Iago: Can he be angry? I have seen the cannon
When it hath blown his ranks into the air   130
And, like the devil, from his very arm
Puffed his own brother — and is he angry?
Something of moment then. I will go meet him.
There's matter in't indeed if he be angry.

Desdemona: I prithee do so.   *Exit [Iago].*
                         Something sure of state,°   135
Either from Venice or some unhatched practice°
Made demonstrable here in Cyprus to him,
Hath puddled° his clear spirit; and in such cases
Men's natures wrangle with inferior things,
Though great ones are their object. 'Tis even so;   140
For let our finger ache, and it endues°
Our other, healthful members even to a sense
Of pain. Nay, we must think men are not gods,
Nor of them look for such observancy
As fits the bridal. Beshrew me much, Emilia,   145
I was, unhandsome warrior° as I am,
Arraigning his unkindness with my soul;°
But now I find I had suborned the witness,
And he's indicted falsely.

Emilia: Pray heaven it be state matters, as you think,   150
And no conception nor no jealous toy°
Concerning you.

Desdemona: Alas the day! I never gave him cause.

Emilia: But jealous souls will not be answered so;
They are not ever jealous for the cause,   155
But jealous for they're jealous. 'Tis a monster
Begot upon itself,° born on itself.

Desdemona: Heaven keep that monster from Othello's mind!

Emilia: Lady, amen.

Desdemona: I will go seek him. Cassio, walk here about: 160
If I do find him fit, I'll move your suit

---

120 *favor:* Appearance.   123 *blank:* Bull's-eye of the target.   135 *state:* Public affairs.
136 *unhatched practice:* Budding plot.   138 *puddled:* Muddied.   141 *endues:* Brings.
146 *unhandsome warrior:* Inadequate soldier.   147 *Arraigning...soul:* Indicting his unkindness before the bar of my soul.   151 *toy:* Fancy.   157 *Begot upon itself:* Self-engendered.

And seek to effect it to my uttermost.
Cassio: I humbly thank your ladyship.

Exeunt Desdemona and Emilia.

Enter Bianca.

Bianca: Save you, friend Cassio!
Cassio: What make you from home?
How is't with you, my most fair Bianca?   165
I' faith, sweet love, I was coming to your house.
Bianca: And I was going to your lodging, Cassio.
What, keep a week away? seven days and nights?
Eightscore eight hours? and lovers' absent hours,
More tedious than the dial° eightscore times?   170
O weary reck'ning!
Cassio: Pardon me, Bianca:
I have this while with leaden thoughts been pressed;
But I shall in a more continuate° time
Strike off this score of absence. Sweet Bianca,

[Gives her Desdemona's handkerchief.]

Take me this work out.°
Bianca: O Cassio, whence came this?   175
This is some token from a newer friend.
To the felt absence now I feel a cause.
Is't come to this? Well, well.
Cassio: Go to, woman!
Throw your vile guesses in the devil's teeth,
From whence you have them. You are jealous now   180
That this is from some mistress, some remembrance.
No, by my faith, Bianca.
Bianca: Why, whose is it?
Cassio: I know not, sweet; I found it in my chamber.
I like the work° well; ere it be demanded,
As like enough it will, I'd have it copied.
Take it and do't, and leave me for this time.   185
Bianca: Leave you? Wherefore?
Cassio: I do attend here on the general
And think it no addition, nor my wish,
To have him see me womaned.
Bianca: Why, I pray you?   190
Cassio: Not that I love you not.
Bianca: But that you do not love me!
I pray you bring me on the way a little,
And say if I shall see you soon at night.
Cassio: 'Tis but a little way that I can bring you,
For I attend here; but I'll see you soon.   195
Bianca: 'Tis very good. I must be circumstanced.°   *Exeunt.*

---

170 *dial:* Clock.   173 *continuate:* Uninterrupted.   175 *Take . . . out:* Copy this embroidery
for me.   184 *work:* Needlework.   196 *circumstanced:* Governed by circumstances.

ACT IV

SCENE I: *The environs of the castle.*

Enter Othello and Iago.

Iago: Will you think so?
Othello: Think so, Iago?
Iago: What,
  To kiss in private?
Othello: An unauthorized kiss.
Iago: Or to be naked with her friend in bed
  An hour or more, not meaning any harm?
Othello: Naked in bed, Iago, and not mean harm? 5
  It is hypocrisy against the devil.°
  They that mean virtuously, and yet do so,
  The devil their virtue tempts, and they tempt heaven.
Iago: So they do nothing, 'tis a venial slip.
  But if I give my wife a handkerchief — 10
Othello: What then?
Iago: Why, then 'tis hers, my lord; and being hers,
  She may, I think, bestow't on any man.
Othello: She is protectress of her honor too;
  May she give that? 15
Iago: Her honor is an essence that's not seen;
  They have it very oft that have it not.
  But for the handkerchief —
Othello: By heaven, I would most gladly have forgot it!
  Thou said'st — O, it comes o'er my memory 20
  As doth the raven o'er the infected° house,
  Boding to all! — he had my handkerchief.
Iago: Ay, what of that?
Othello: That's not so good now.
Iago: What
  If I had said I had seen him do you wrong?
  Or heard him say — as knaves be such abroad 25
  Who having, by their own importunate suit,
  Or voluntary dotage of some mistress,
  Convincèd or supplied° them, cannot choose
  But they must blab —
Othello: Hath he said anything?
Iago: He hath, my lord; but be you well assured, 30
  No more than he'll unswear.
Othello: What hath he said?
Iago: Faith, that he did — I know not what he did.
Othello: What? what?
Iago: Lie —

Act IV, Scene I. 6 *hypocrisy . . . devil:* I.e., feigned sin instead of feigned virtue. 21 *infected:* Plague-stricken. 28 *Convincèd or supplied:* Overcome or gratified.

Othello: With her?
Iago: With her, on her; what you will. 35
Othello: Lie with her? lie on her? — We say lie on her when they belie her. —
Lie with her! Zounds, that's fulsome. — Handkerchief — confessions —
handkerchief! — To confess, and be hanged for his labor — first to be
hanged, and then to confess! I tremble at it. Nature would not invest
herself in such shadowing passion without some instruction.° It is 40
not words that shakes me thus. — Pish! Noses, ears, and lips? Is't possible? — Confess? — Handkerchief? — O devil!

(Falls in a trance.)

Iago: Work on,
My med'cine, work! Thus credulous fools are caught,
And many worthy and chaste dames even thus, 45
All guiltless, meet reproach. — What, ho! my lord!
My lord, I say! Othello!
   Enter Cassio. How now, Cassio?
Cassio: What's the matter?
Iago: My lord is fall'n into an epilepsy.
This is his second fit; he had one yesterday. 50
Cassio: Rub him about the temples.
Iago: No, forbear.
The lethargy° must have his quiet course.
If not, he foams at mouth, and by and by
Breaks out to savage madness. Look, he stirs.
Do you withdraw yourself a little while. 55
He will recover straight. When he is gone,
I would on great occasion speak with you. *[Exit Cassio.]*
How is it, general? Have you not hurt your head?
Othello: Dost thou mock me?
Iago: I mock you? No, by heaven.
Would you would bear your fortune like a man! 60
Othello: A hornèd man's° a monster and a beast.
Iago: There's many a beast then in a populous city,
And many a civil monster.
Othello: Did he confess it?
Iago: Good sir, be a man.
Think every bearded fellow that's but yoked 65
May draw with you. There's millions now alive
That nightly lie in those unproper° beds
Which they dare swear peculiar:° your case is better.
O, 'tis the spite of hell, the fiend's arch-mock,
To lip a wanton in a secure° couch, 70
And to suppose her chaste! No, let me know;
And knowing what I am, I know what she shall be.
Othello: O, thou art wise! 'Tis certain.

39–40 *Nature . . . instruction:* My natural faculties would not be so overcome by passion without reason. 52 *lethargy:* Coma. 61 *hornèd man:* Cuckold. 67 *unproper:* Not exclusively their own. 68 *peculiar:* Exclusively their own. 70 *secure:* Free from fear of
rivalry.

Iago: Stand you awhile apart;
 Confine yourself but in a patient list.°
 Whilst you were here, o'erwhelmèd with your grief —   75
 A passion most unsuiting such a man —
 Cassio came hither. I shifted him away
 And laid good 'scuse upon your ecstasy;°
 Bade him anon return, and here speak with me;
 The which he promised. Do but encave° yourself   80
 And mark the fleers, the gibes, and notable scorns
 That dwell in every region of his face;
 For I will make him tell the tale anew —
 Where, how, how oft, how long ago, and when
 He hath, and is again to cope° your wife.   85
 I say, but mark his gesture. Marry, patience!
 Or I shall say y'are all in all in spleen,°
 And nothing of a man.
Othello: Dost thou hear, Iago?
 I will be found most cunning in my patience;
 But — dost thou hear? — most bloody.
Iago: That's not amiss: 90
 But yet keep time in all. Will you withdraw?

             [Othello retires.]

 Now will I question Cassio of Bianca,
 A huswife° that by selling her desires
 Buys herself bread and clothes. It is a creature
 That dotes on Cassio, as 'tis the strumpet's plague   95
 To beguile many and be beguiled by one.
 He, when he hears of her, cannot refrain
 From the excess of laughter. Here he comes.

 Enter Cassio.

 As he shall smile, Othello shall go mad;
 And his unbookish° jealousy must conster°   100
 Poor Cassio's smiles, gestures, and light behavior
 Quite in the wrong. How do you now, lieutenant?
Cassio: The worser that you give me the addition°
 Whose want even kills me.
Iago: Ply Desdemona well, and you are sure on't.   105
 Now, if this suit lay in Bianca's power,
 How quickly should you speed!
Cassio: Alas, poor caitiff!°
Othello: Look how he laughs already!
Iago: I never knew a woman love man so.
Cassio: Alas, poor rogue! I think, i' faith, she loves me.   110
Othello: Now he denies it faintly, and laughs it out.
Iago: Do you hear, Cassio?

---

74 *in a patient list:* Within the limits of self-control. 78 *ecstasy:* Trance. 80 *encave:* Conceal. 85 *cope:* Meet. 87 *all in all in spleen:* Wholly overcome by your passion. 93 *huswife:* Hussy. 100 *unbookish:* Uninstructed; *conster:* Construe, interpret. 103 *addition:* Title. 107 *caitiff:* Wretch.

Othello: Now he importunes him
   To tell it o'er. Go to! Well said, well said!
Iago: She gives out that you shall marry her.
   Do you intend it?   115
Cassio: Ha, ha, ha!
Othello: Do you triumph, Roman? Do you triumph?
Cassio: I marry her? What, a customer?° Prithee bear some charity to my
   wit; do not think it so unwholesome. Ha, ha, ha!
Othello: So, so, so, so! They laugh that win!   120
Iago: Faith, the cry goes that you shall marry her.
Cassio: Prithee say true.
Iago: I am a very villain else.
Othello: Have you scored me?° Well.
Cassio: This is the monkey's own giving out. She is persuaded I will marry   125
   her out of her own love and flattery, not out of my promise.
Othello: Iago beckons° me; now he begins the story.
Cassio: She was here even now; she haunts me in every place. I was t' other
   day talking on the sea bank with certain Venetians, and thither comes
   the bauble,° and, by this hand, she falls me thus about my neck —   130
Othello: Crying "O dear Cassio!" as it were. His gesture imports it.
Cassio: So hangs, and lolls, and weeps upon me; so shakes and pulls me!
   Ha, ha, ha!
Othello: Now he tells how she plucked him to my chamber. O, I see that
   nose of yours, but not that dog I shall throw it to.   135
Cassio: Well, I must leave her company.

   Enter Bianca.

Iago: Before me! Look where she comes.
Cassio: 'Tis such another fitchew!° marry, a perfumed one. What do you
   mean by this haunting of me?
Bianca: Let the devil and his dam haunt you! What did you mean by that   140
   same handkerchief you gave me even now? I was a fine fool to take it. I
   must take out the whole work? A likely piece of work that you should
   find it in your chamber and know not who left it there! This is some
   minx's token, and I must take out the work? There! Give it your
   hobby-horse.° Wheresoever you had it, I'll take out no work on't.   145
Cassio: How now, my sweet Bianca? How now? how now?
Othello: By heaven, that should be my handkerchief!
Bianca: An you'll come to supper to-night, you may; an you will not, come
   when you are next prepared for.   *Exit.*
Iago: After her, after her!   150
Cassio: Faith, I must; she'll rail in the street else.
Iago: Will you sup there?
Cassio: Yes, I intend so.
Iago: Well, I may chance to see you; for I would very fain speak with you.
Cassio: Prithee come. Will you?   155
Iago: Go to! say no more.   *Exit Cassio.*

---

118 *customer:* Prostitute.   124 *scored me:* Settled my account (?).   127 *beckons:* Signals.
130 *bauble:* Plaything.   138 *fitchew:* Polecat (slang for *whore*).   145 *hobby-horse:* Harlot.

Othello [comes forward]: How shall I murder him, Iago?

Iago: Did you perceive how he laughed at his vice?°

Othello: O Iago!

Iago: And did you see the handkerchief?   160

Othello: Was that mine?

Iago: Your, by this hand! And to see how he prizes° the foolish woman
   your wife! She gave it him, and he hath giv'n it his whore.

Othello: I would have him nine years a-killing—A fine woman! a fair
   woman! a sweet woman!   165

Iago: Nay, you must forget that.

Othello: Ay, let her rot, and perish, and be damned to-night; for she shall
   not live. No, my heart is turned to stone; I strike it, and it hurts my
   hand. O, the world hath not a sweeter creature! She might lie by an
   emperor's side and command him tasks.   170

Iago: Nay, that's not your way.

Othello: Hang her! I do but say what she is. So delicate with her needle! an
   admirable musician! O, she will sing the savageness out of a bear! Of
   so high and plenteous wit and invention°—

Iago: She's the worse for all this.   175

Othello: O, a thousand thousand times! And then, of so gentle a condition!°

Iago: Ay, too gentle.

Othello: Nay, that's certain. But yet the pity of it, Iago! O Iago, the pity of
   it, Iago!

Iago: If you are so fond over her iniquity, give her patent° to offend; for if   180
   it touch not you, it comes near nobody.

Othello: I will chop her into messes! Cuckold me!

Iago: O, 'tis foul in her.

Othello: With mine officer!

Iago: That's fouler.   185

Othello: Get me some poison, Iago, this night. I'll not expostulate with her,
   lest her body and beauty unprovide° my mind again. This night, Iago!

Iago: Do it not with poison. Strangle her in her bed, even the bed she hath
   contaminated.

Othello: Good, good! The justice of it pleases. Very good!   190

Iago: And for Cassio, let me be his undertaker;° you shall hear more by
   midnight.

Othello: Excellent good!

   A trumpet.

   What trumpet is that same?

Iago: I warrant something from Venice.

   Enter Lodovico, Desdemona, and Attendants.

            'Tis Lodovico.   195
   This comes from the Duke; and see, your wife is with him.

Lodovico: God save you, worthy general!

Othello: With all my heart, sir.

Lodovico: The Duke and senators of Venice greet you.

---

158 *vice:* I.e., vicious conduct.   162 *prizes:* Values.   174 *invention:* Imagination.   176 *condition:* Disposition.   180 *patent:* License.   187 *unprovide:* Disarm.   191 *be his undertaker:*
Undertake to deal with him.

[Gives him a letter.]

Othello: I kiss the instrument of their pleasures.

   [Opens the letter and reads.]

Desdemona: And what's the news, good cousin Lodovico?   200
Iago: I am very glad to see you, signior.
      Welcome to Cyprus.
Lodovico: I thank you. How does Lieutenant Cassio?
Iago: Lives, sir.
Desdemona: Cousin, there's fall'n between him and my lord
      An unkind breach; but you shall make all well.   205
Othello: Are you sure of that?
Desdemona: My lord?
Othello [reads]: "This fail you not to do, as you will —"
Lodovico: He did not call; he's busy in the paper.
      Is there division 'twixt thy lord and Cassio?   210
Desdemona: A most unhappy one. I would do much
      T' atone° them, for the love I bear to Cassio.
Othello: Fire and brimstone!
Desdemona: My lord?
Othello: Are you wise?
Desdemona: What, is he angry?
Lodovico: May be the letter moved him;
      For, as I think, they do command him home,   215
      Deputing Cassio in his government.
Desdemona: By my troth, I am glad on't.
Othello: Indeed?
Desdemona: My lord?
Othello: I am glad to see you mad.°
Desdemona: Why, sweet Othello —
Othello: Devil!

   [Strikes her.]

Desdemona: I have not deserved this.   220
Lodovico: My lord, this would not be believed in Venice,
      Though I should swear I saw't. 'Tis very much.
      Make her amends; she weeps.
Othello: O devil, devil!
      If that the earth could teem° with woman's tears,
      Each drop she falls would prove a crocodile.°   225
      Out of my sight!
Desdemona: I will not stay to offend you.   *[Going.]*
Lodovico: Truly, an obedient lady.
      I do beseech your lordship call her back.
Othello: Mistress!
Desdemona: My lord?
Othello: What would you with her, sir?   230
Lodovico: Who? I, my lord?

---

212 *atone:* Reconcile.   218 *mad:* I.e., waggish.   224 *teem:* Breed.   225 *crocodile:* (Croc-
odiles were supposed to shed hypocritical tears to lure men to destruction).

Othello: Ay! You did wish that I would make her turn.
    Sir, she can turn, and turn, and yet go on
    And turn again; and she can weep, sir, weep;
    And she's obedient; as you say, obedient,   235
    Very obedient. — Proceed you in your tears. —
    Concerning this, sir — O well-painted passion!° —
    I am commanded home. — Get you away;
    I'll send for you anon. — Sir, I obey the mandate
    And will return to Venice. — Hence, avaunt!   240

                      [Exit Desdemona.]

    Cassio shall have my place. And, sir, to-night
    I do entreat that we may sup together.
    You are welcome, sir, to Cyprus — Goats and monkeys!

                           Exit.

Lodovico: Is this the noble Moor whom our full Senate
    Call all in all sufficient? Is this the nature   245
    Whom passion could not shake? whose solid virtue
    The shot of accident nor dart of chance
    Could neither graze nor pierce?
Iago: He is much changed.
Lodovico: Are his wits safe? Is he not light of brain?
Iago: He's that he is; I may not breathe my censure.   250
    What he might be — if what he might he is not —
    I would to heaven he were!
Lodovico: What, strike his wife?
Iago: Faith, that was not so well; yet would I knew
    That stroke would prove the worst!
Lodovico: Is it his use?°
    Or did the letters work upon his blood   255
    And new-create this fault?
Iago: Alas, alas!
    It is not honesty in me to speak
    What I have seen and known. You shall observe him,
    And his own courses will denote him so
    That I may save my speech. Do but go after   260
    And mark how he continues.
Lodovico: I am sorry that I am deceived in him.   *Exeunt.*

SCENE II: *Within the castle.*

    Enter Othello and Emilia.

Othello: You have seen nothing then?
Emilia: Nor ever heard, nor ever did suspect.
Othello: Yes, you have seen Cassio and she together.
Emilia: But then I saw no harm, and then I heard
    Each syllable that breath made up between them.   5
Othello: What, did they never whisper?

237 *passion:* Grief.   254 *use:* Custom.

Emilia: Never, my lord.
Othello: Nor send you out o' th' way?
Emilia: Never.
Othello: To fetch her fan, her gloves, her mask, nor nothing?
Emilia: Never, my lord.   10
Othello: That's strange.
Emilia: I durst, my lord, to wager she is honest,
    Lay down my soul at stake. If you think other,
    Remove your thought; it doth abuse your bosom.°
    If any wretch have put this in your head,   15
    Let heaven requite it with the serpent's curse!°
    For if she be not honest, chaste, and true,
    There's no man happy; the purest of their wives
    Is foul as slander.
Othello: Bid her come hither. Go.   *Exit Emilia.*
    She says enough; yet she's a simple bawd   20
    That cannot say as much. This is a subtle whore,
    A closet lock and key of villainous secrets;
    And yet she'll kneel and pray; I have seen her do't.

    Enter Desdemona and Emilia.

Desdemona: My lord, what is your will?
Othello: Pray, chuck, come hither.
Desdemona: What is your pleasure?
Othello: Let me see your eyes.   25
    Look in my face.
Desdemona: What horrible fancy's this?
Othello [to Emilia]: Some of your function, mistress.
    Leave procreants° alone and shut the door;
    Cough or cry hem if anybody come.
    Your mystery, your mystery!° Nay, dispatch!   30
                                                                        Exit Emilia.
Desdemona: Upon my knees, what doth your speech import?
    I understand a fury in your words,
    [But not the words.]
Othello: Why, what art thou?
Desdemona: Your wife, my lord; your true
    And loyal wife.
Othello: Come, swear it, damn thyself;   35
    Lest, being like one of heaven,° the devils themselves
    Should fear to seize thee. Therefore be double-damned —
    Swear thou art honest.°
Desdemona: Heaven doth truly know it.
Othello: Heaven truly knows that thou art false as hell.
Desdemona: To whom, my lord? With whom? How am I false?   40
Othello: Ah, Desdemona! away! away! away!

Scene II.   14 *abuse your bosom:* Deceive your heart.   16 *serpent's curse:* (cf. Genesis 3: 14).
28 *procreants:* Mating couples.   30 *mystery:* Trade, occupation.   36 *being...heaven:*
Looking like an angel.   38 *honest:* Chaste.

Desdemona: Alas the heavy day! Why do you weep?
    Am I the motive of these tears, my lord?
    If haply you my father do suspect
    An instrument° of this your calling back,   45
    Lay not your blame on me. If you have lost him,
    Why, I have lost him too.
Othello: Had it pleased heaven
    To try me with affliction, had they rained
    All kinds of sores and shames on my bare head,
    Steeped me in poverty to the very lips,   50
    Given to captivity me and my utmost hopes,
    I should have found in some place of my soul
    A drop of patience. But, alas, to make me
    A fixèd figure for the time of scorn°
    To point his slow unmoving finger at!   55
    Yet could I bear that too; well, very well.
    But there where I have garnered up my heart,
    Where either I must live or bear no life,
    The fountain from the which my current runs
    Or else dries up — to be discarded thence,   60
    Or keep it as a cistern for foul toads
    To knot and gender in — turn thy complexion there,°
    Patience, thou young and rose-lipped cherubin!
    Ay, there look grim as hell!
Desdemona: I hope my noble lord esteems me honest.   65
Othello: O, ay; as summer flies are in the shambles,°
    That quicken° even with blowing. O thou weed,
    Who art so lovely fair, and smell'st so sweet,
    That the sense aches at thee, would thou hadst ne'er been born!
Desdemona: Alas, what ignorant sin have I committed?   70
Othello: Was this fair paper, this most goodly book,
    Made to write "whore" upon? What committed?
    Committed? O thou public commoner!°
    I should make very forges of my cheeks
    That would to cinders burn up modesty,   75
    Did I but speak thy deeds. What committed?
    Heaven stops the nose at it, and the moon winks;°
    The bawdy wind, that kisses all it meets,
    Is hushed within the hollow mine of earth
    And will not hear it. What committed?   80
    Impudent strumpet!
Desdemona: By heaven, you do me wrong!
Othello: Are not you a strumpet?
Desdemona: No, as I am a Christian!
    If to preserve this vessel for my lord
    From any other foul unlawful touch
    Be not to be a strumpet, I am none.   85

---

45 *An instrument:* To be the cause.   54 *time of scorn:* Scornful world.   62 *turn thy complexion there:* Change thy color at that point.   66 *shambles:* Slaughterhouse.   67 *quicken:* Come to life.   73 *commoner:* Harlot.   77 *winks:* Closes her eyes.

Othello: What, not a whore?
Desdemona: No, as I shall be saved!
Othello: Is't possible?
Desdemona: O, heaven forgive us!
Othello: I cry you mercy° then.
   I took you for that cunning whore of Venice
   That married with Othello. — *[Calling.]* You, mistress,   90
   That have the office opposite to Saint Peter
   And keep the gate of hell!

   Enter Emilia.

                    You, you, ay, you!
   We have done our course; there's money for your pains:
   I pray you turn the key, and keep our counsel.   *Exit.*
Emilia: Alas, what does this gentleman conceive?   95
   How do you, madam? How do you, my good lady?
Desdemona: Faith, half asleep.°
Emilia: Good madam, what's the matter with my lord?
Desdemona: With who?
Emilia: Why, with my lord, madam.   100
Desdemona: Who is thy lord?
Emilia: He that is yours, sweet lady.
Desdemona: I have none. Do not talk to me, Emilia.
   I cannot weep; nor answer have I none
   But what should go by water. Prithee to-night
   Lay on my bed my wedding sheets, remember;   105
   And call thy husband hither.
Emilia: Here's a change indeed!   *Exit.*
Desdemona: 'Tis meet I should be used so, very meet.
   How have I been behaved, that he might stick
   The small'st opinion° on my least misuse?°

   Enter Iago and Emilia.

Iago: What is your pleasure, madam? How is't with you?   110
Desdemona: I cannot tell. Those that do teach young babes
   Do it with gentle means and easy tasks:
   He might have chid me so; for, in good faith,
   I am a child to chiding.
Iago: What is the matter, lady?
Emilia: Alas, Iago, my lord hath so bewhored her,   115
   Thrown such despite and heavy terms upon her
   As true hearts cannot bear.
Desdemona: Am I that name, Iago?
Iago: What name, fair lady?
Desdemona: Such as she said my lord did say I was.
Emilia: He called her whore. A beggar in his drink   120
   Could not have laid such terms upon his callet.°
Iago: Why did he so?
Desdemona: I do not know; I am sure I am none such.

---

88 *cry you mercy:* Beg your pardon.   97 *half asleep:* I.e., stunned.   109 *small'st opinion:*
Least suspicion; *least misuse:* Slightest misconduct.   121 *callet:* Whore.

Iago: Do not weep, do not weep. Alas the day!
Emilia: Hath she forsook so many noble matches, 125
   Her father and her country, and her friends,
   To be called whore? Would it not make one weep?
Desdemona: It is my wretched fortune.
Iago: Beshrew him for't!
   How comes this trick° upon him?
Desdemona: Nay, heaven doth know.
Emilia: I will be hanged if some eternal villain, 130
   Some busy and insinuating rogue,
   Some cogging, cozening° slave, to get some office,
   Have not devised this slander. I'll be hanged else.
Iago: Fie, there is no such man! It is impossible.
Desdemona: If any such there be, heaven pardon him! 135
Emilia: A halter pardon him! and hell gnaw his bones!
   Why should he call her whore? Who keeps her company?
   What place? what time? what form? what likelihood?
   The Moor 's abused by some most villainous knave,
   Some base notorious knave, some scurvy fellow. 140
   O heaven, that such companions° thou 'dst unfold,°
   And put in every honest hand a whip
   To lash the rascals naked through the world
   Even from the east to th' west!
Iago: Speak within door.°
Emilia: O, fie upon them! Some such squire he was 145
   That turned your wit the seamy side without
   And made you to suspect me with the Moor.
Iago: You are a fool. Go to.
Desdemona: Alas, Iago,
   What shall I do to win my lord again?
   Good friend, go to him; for, by this light of heaven, 150
   I know not how I lost him. Here I kneel:
   If e'er my will did trespass 'gainst his love
   Either in discourse° of thought or actual deed,
   Or that mine eyes, mine ears, or any sense
   Delighted them in any other form, 155
   Or that I do not yet, and ever did,
   And ever will (though he do shake me off
   To beggarly divorcement) love him dearly,
   Comfort forswear° me! Unkindness may do much;
   And his unkindness may defeat° my life, 160
   But never taint my love. I cannot say "whore."
   It does abhor me now I speak the word;
   To do the act that might the addition earn
   Not the world's mass of vanity could make me.
Iago: I pray you be content. 'Tis but his humor. 165
   The business of the state does him offense,
   [And he does chide with you.]

---

129 *trick:* Freakish behavior.   132 *cogging, cozening:* Cheating, defrauding.   141 *compan-*
ions: Rogues; *unfold:* Expose.   144 *within door:* With restraint.   153 *discourse:* Course.
159 *Comfort forswear:* Happiness forsake.   160 *defeat:* Destroy.

Desdemona: If 'twere no other —
Iago: 'Tis but so, I warrant.

[Trumpets within.]

Hark how these instruments summon you to supper.
The messengers of Venice stay the meat: 170
Go in, and weep not. All things shall be well.

                                        Exeunt Desdemona and Emilia.
Enter Roderigo.

How now, Roderigo?
Roderigo: I do not find that thou deal'st justly with me.
Iago: What in the contrary?
Roderigo: Every day thou daff'st me with some device,° Iago, and rather, as   175
    it seems to me now, keep'st from me all conveniency° than suppliest
    me with the least advantage of hope. I will indeed no longer endure it;
    nor am I yet persuaded to put up in peace what already I have fool-
    ishly suffered.
Iago: Will you hear me, Roderigo?   180
Roderigo: Faith, I have heard too much; for your words and performances
    are no kin together.
Iago: You charge me most unjustly.
Roderigo: With naught but truth. I have wasted myself out of my means.
    The jewels you have had from me to deliver to Desdemona would half   185
    have corrupted a votarist.° You have told me she hath received them,
    and returned me expectations and comforts of sudden respect° and
    acquaintance; but I find none.
Iago: Well, go to; very well.
Roderigo: Very well! go to! I cannot go to, man; nor 'tis not very well. By   190
    this hand, I say 'tis very scurvy, and begin to find myself fopped° in it.
Iago: Very well.
Roderigo: I tell you 'tis not very well. I will make myself known to Desde-
    mona. If she will return me my jewels, I will give over my suit and
    repent my unlawful solicitation; if not, assure yourself I will seek satis-   195
    faction of you.
Iago: You have said now.
Roderigo: Ay, and said nothing but what I protest intendment of doing.
Iago: Why, now I see there's mettle in thee; and even from this instant do
    build on thee a better opinion than ever before. Give me thy hand,   200
    Roderigo. Thou has taken against me a most just exception; but yet I
    protest I have dealt most directly° in thy affair.
Roderigo: It hath not appeared.
Iago: I grant indeed it hath not appeared, and your suspicion is not with-
    out wit and judgment. But, Roderigo, if thou hast that in thee indeed   205
    which I have greater reason to believe now than ever, I mean purpose,
    courage, and valor, this night show it. If thou the next night following
    enjoy not Desdemona, take me from this world with treachery and
    devise engines for° my life.

---

175 *thou . . . device:* You put me off with some trick.   176 *conveniency:* Favorable opportunities.   186 *votarist:* Nun.   187 *sudden respect:* Immediate notice.   191 *fopped:* Duped.
202 *directly:* Straightforwardly.   209 *engines for:* Plots against.

Roderigo: Well, what is it? Is it within reason and compass?   210
Iago: Sir, there is especial commission come from Venice to depute Cassio
in Othello's place.
Roderigo: Is that true? Why, then Othello and Desdemona return again to
Venice.
Iago: O, no; he goes into Mauritania and takes away with him the fair Des-   215
demona, unless his abode be lingered here° by some accident; wherein
none can be so determinate° as the removing of Cassio.
Roderigo: How do you mean removing of him?
Iago: Why, by making him uncapable of Othello's place — knocking out
his brains.   220
Roderigo: And that you would have me to do?
Iago: Ay, if you dare do yourself a profit and a right. He sups to-night with
a harlotry, and thither will I go to him. He knows not yet of his honorable fortune. If you will watch his going thence, which I will fashion
to fall out between twelve and one, you may take him at your pleasure.   225
I will be near to second your attempt, and he shall fall between us.
Come, stand not amazed at it, but go along with me. I will show you
such a necessity in his death that you shall think yourself bound to
put it on him. It is now high supper time, and the night grows to
waste. About it!   230
Roderigo: I will hear further reason for this.
Iago: And you shall be satisfied.   *Exeunt.*

SCENE III: *Within the castle.*

Enter Othello, Lodovico, Desdemona, Emilia, and Attendants.

Lodovico: I do beseech you, sir, trouble yourself no further.
Othello: O, pardon me; 'twill do me good to walk.
Lodovico: Madam, good night. I humbly thank your ladyship.
Desdemona: Your honor is most welcome.
Othello: Will you walk, sir?
O, Desdemona—   5
Desdemona: My lord?
Othello: Get you to bed on th' instant; I will be returned forthwith.
Dismiss your attendant there. Look't be done.
Desdemona: I will, my lord.

Exit [Othello, with Lodovico and Attendants].

Emilia: How goes it now? He looks gentler than he did.   10
Desdemona: He says he will return incontinent.°
He hath commanded me to go to bed,
And bade me to dismiss you.
Emilia: Dismiss me?
Desdemona: It was his bidding; therefore, good Emilia,
Give me my nightly wearing, and adieu.   15

216 *abode...here:* Stay here be extended.   217 *determinate:* Effective.   **Scene III.**   11 *in-continent:* At once.

We must not now displease him.
Emilia: I would you had never seen him!
Desdemona: So would not I. My love doth so approve him
    That even his stubbornness,° his checks,° his frowns —
    Prithee unpin me — have grace and favor in them.   20
Emilia: I have laid those sheets you bade me on the bed.
Desdemona: All's one. Good faith, how foolish are our minds!
    If I do die before thee, prithee shroud me
    In one of those same sheets.
Emilia: Come, come! You talk.
Desdemona: My mother had a maid called Barbary.   25
    She was in love; and he she loved proved mad°
    And did forsake her. She had a song of "Willow";
    An old thing 'twas; but it expressed her fortune,
    And she died singing it. That song to-night
    Will not go from my mind; I have much to do   30
    But to go hang my head all at one side
    And sing it like poor Barbary. Prithee dispatch.
Emilia: Shall I go fetch your nightgown?°
Desdemona: No, unpin me here.
    This Lodovico is a proper man.
Emilia: A very handsome man.
Desdemona: He speaks well.   35
Emilia: I know a lady in Venice would have walked barefoot to Palestine
    for a touch of his nether lip.
Desdemona (sings): "The poor soul sat sighing by a sycamore tree
        Sing all a green willow;
    Her hand on her bosom, her head on her knee,   40
        Sing willow, willow, willow.
    The fresh streams ran by her and murmured her moans;
        Sing willow, willow, willow;
    Her salt tears fell from her, and soft'ned the stones" —   45
    Lay by these.
        "Sing willow, willow, willow" —
    Prithee hie thee;° he'll come anon.
    "Sing all a green willow must be my garland.
    Let nobody blame him; his scorn I approve" —   50
    Nay, that's not next. Hark! who is't that knocks?
Emilia: It's the wind.
Desdemona (sings): "I call my love false love; but what said he then?
        Sing willow, willow, willow:
    If I court moe women, you'll couch with moe men."   55
    So get thee gone; good night. Mine eyes do itch.
    Doth that bode weeping?
Emilia: 'Tis neither here nor there.
Desdemona: I have heard it said so. O, these men, these men!
    Dost thou in conscience think — tell me, Emilia —

---

19 *stubbornness:* Roughness; *checks:* Rebukes.   26 *mad:* Wild, faithless.   33 *nightgown:*
Dressing gown.   48 *hie thee:* Hurry.

That there be women do abuse their husbands 60
  In such gross kind?
Emilia: There be some such, no question.
Desdemona: Wouldst thou do such a deed for all the world?
Emilia: Why, would not you?
Desdemona: No, by this heavenly light!
Emilia: Nor I neither by this heavenly light.
  I might do't as well i' th' dark. 65
Desdemona: Wouldst thou do such a deed for all the world?
Emilia: The world's a huge thing; it is a great price for a small vice.
Desdemona: In troth, I think thou wouldst not.
Emilia: In troth, I think I should; and undo't when I had done it. Marry, I
  would not do such a thing for a joint-ring,° nor for measures of lawn, 70
  nor for gowns, petticoats, nor caps, nor any petty exhibition;° but, for
  all the whole world — 'Ud's pity! who would not make her husband a
  cuckold to make him a monarch? I should venture purgatory for't.
Desdemona: Beshrew me if I would do such a wrong
  For the whole world. 75
Emilia: Why, the wrong is but a wrong i' th' world; and having the world
  for your labor, 'tis a wrong in your own world, and you might quickly
  make it right.
Desdemona: I do not think there is any such woman.
Emilia: Yes, a dozen; and as many to th' vantage° as 80
  would store° the world they played for.
  But I do think it is their husbands' faults
  If wives do fall. Say that they slack their duties
  And pour our treasures into foreign laps;
  Or else break out in peevish° jealousies, 85
  Throwing restraint upon us; or say they strike us,
  Or scant our former having° in despite —
  Why, we have galls;° and though we have some grace,
  Yet have we some revenge. Let husbands know
  Their wives have sense like them. They see, and smell, 90
  And have their palates both for sweet and sour,
  As husbands have. What is it that they do
  When they change us for others? Is it sport?
  I think it is. And doth affection breed it?
  I think it doth. Is't frailty that thus errs? 95
  It is so too. And have not we affections,
  Desires for sport, and frailty, as men have?
  Then let them use us well; else let them know,
  The ills we do, their ills instruct us so.
Desdemona: Good night, good night. God me such usage° send, 100
  Not to pick bad from bad, but by bad mend!   *Exeunt.*

---

70 *joint-ring:* Ring made in separable halves.   71 *exhibition:* Gift.   80 *to th' vantage:* Besides.   81 *store:* Populate.   85 *peevish:* Senseless.   87 *having:* Allowance.   88 *galls:*
Spirits to resent.   100 *usage:* Habits.

ACT V

SCENE I: *A street in Cyprus.*

Enter Iago and Roderigo.

Iago: Here, stand behind this bulk;° straight will he come.
Wear thy good rapier bare, and put it home.
Quick, quick! Fear nothing; I'll be at thy elbow.
It makes us, or it mars us — think on that,
And fix most firm thy resolution.   5
Roderigo: Be near at hand; I may miscarry in't.
Iago: Here, at thy hand. Be bold, and take thy stand.

[Stands aside.]

Roderigo: I have no great devotion to the deed,
And yet he hath given me satisfying reasons.
'Tis but a man gone. Forth my sword! He dies!   10
Iago: I have rubbed this young quat° almost to the sense,°
And he grows angry. Now whether he kill Cassio,
Or Cassio him, or each do kill the other,
Every way makes my gain. Live Roderigo,
He calls me to a restitution large   15
Of gold and jewels that I bobbed° from him
As gifts to Desdemona.
It must not be. If Cassio do remain,
He hath a daily beauty in his life
That makes me ugly; and besides, the Moor   20
May unfold me to him; there stand I in much peril.
No, he must die. Be't so! I hear him coming.

Enter Cassio.

Roderigo: I know his gait. 'Tis he. Villain, thou diest!

[Makes a pass at Cassio.]

Cassio: That thrust had been mine enemy indeed
But that my coat° is better than thou know'st.   25
I will make proof of thine.

[Draws, and wounds Roderigo.]

Roderigo: O, I am slain!

[Iago darts from concealment behind Cassio, wounds him in the leg, and exit.]

Cassio: I am maimed for ever. Help, ho! Murder! murder!

[Falls.]
Enter Othello.

Othello: The voice of Cassio. Iago keeps his word.

Act V, Scene I.   1 *bulk:* Projecting shop-front.   11 *quat:* Pimple; *sense:* Quick.   16 *bobbed:*
Swindled.   25 *coat:* Undershirt of mail.

Roderigo: O, villain that I am!
Othello: It is even so.
Cassio: O, help, ho! light! a surgeon!   30
Othello: 'Tis he. O brave Iago, honest and just,
   That hast such noble sense of thy friend's wrong!
   Thou teachest me. Minion,° your dear lies dead,
   And your unblest fate hies.° Strumpet, I come.
   Forth of my heart those charms, thine eyes, are blotted.   35
   Thy bed, lust-stained, shall with lust's blood be spotted.

                                                              Exit Othello.

   Enter Lodovico and Gratiano.

Cassio: What, ho? No watch? No passage?° Murder! murder!
Gratiano: 'Tis some mischance. The cry is very direful.
Cassio: O, help!
Lodovico: Hark!   40
Roderigo: O wretched villain!
Lodovico: Two or three groan. It is a heavy° night.
   These may be counterfeits. Let's think't unsafe
   To come in to the cry without more help.
Roderigo: Nobody come? Then shall I bleed to death.   45
Lodovico: Hark!

   Enter Iago, with a light.

Gratiano: Here's one comes in his shirt, with light and weapons.
Iago: Who's there? Whose noise is this that cries on° murder?
Lodovico: We do not know.
Iago: Did not you hear a cry?
Cassio: Here, here! For heaven's sake, help me!
Iago: What's the matter?   50
Gratiano: This is Othello's ancient, as I take it.
Lodovico: The same indeed, a very valiant fellow.
Iago: What are you here that cry so grievously?
Cassio: Iago? O, I am spoiled, undone by villains!
   Give me some help.   55
Iago: O me, lieutenant! What villains have done this?
Cassio: I think that one of them is hereabout
   And cannot make° away.
Iago: O treacherous villains!

   [To Lodovico and Gratiano.]

   What are you there? Come in, and give some help.
Roderigo: O, help me here!   60
Cassio: That's one of them.
Iago: O murd'rous slave! O villain!

   [Stabs Roderigo.]

Roderigo: O damned Iago! O inhuman dog!
Iago: Kill men i' th' dark! — Where be these bloody thieves? —
   How silent is this town! — Ho! murder! murder! —

---

33 *Minion:* Mistress.   34 *hies:* Hurries on.   37 *passage:* Passersby.   42 *heavy:* Cloudy,
dark.   48 *cries on:* Raises the cry of.   58 *make:* Get.

What may you be? Are you of good or evil?   65
Lodovico: As you shall prove us, praise us.
Iago: Signior Lodovico?
Lodovico: He, sir.
Iago: I cry you mercy. Here's Cassio hurt by villains.
Gratiano: Cassio?   70
Iago: How is't, brother?
Cassio: My leg is cut in two.
Iago: Marry,° heaven forbid!
   Light, gentlemen. I'll bind it with my shirt.

   Enter Bianca.

Bianca: What is the matter, ho? Who is't that cried?
Iago: Who is't that cried?   75
Bianca: O my dear Cassio! my sweet Cassio!
   O Cassio, Cassio, Cassio!
Iago: O notable strumpet! — Cassio, may you suspect
   Who they should be that have thus mangled you?
Cassio: No.   80
Gratiano: I am sorry to find you thus. I have been to seek you.
Iago: Lend me a garter. So. O for a chair°
   To bear him easily hence!
Bianca: Alas, he faints! O Cassio, Cassio, Cassio!
Iago: Gentlemen all, I do suspect this trash   85
   To be a party in this injury. —
   Patience a while, good Cassio. — Come, come!
   Lend me a light. Know we this face or no?
   Alas, my friend and my dear countryman
   Roderigo? No — Yes, sure. — O heaven, Roderigo!   90
Gratiano: What, of Venice?
Iago: Even he, sir. Did you know him?
Gratiano: Know him? Ay.
Iago: Signior Gratiano? I cry your gentle pardon.
   These bloody accidents must excuse my manners
   That so neglected you.
Gratiano: I am glad to see you.   95
Iago: How do you, Cassio? — O, a chair, a chair!
Gratiano: Roderigo?
Iago: He, he, 'tis he!

   [A chair brought in.]

   O, that's well said;° the chair.
   Some good man bear him carefully from hence.   100
   I'll fetch the general's surgeon. *[To Bianca.]* For you, mistress,
   Save you your labor. — He that lies slain here, Cassio,
   Was my dear friend. What malice was between you?
Cassio: None in the world; nor do I know the man.
Iago [to Bianca]: What, look you pale? — O, bear him out o' th' air.   105

            [Cassio and Roderigo are borne off.]

72 *Marry:* (From "By Mary").   82 *chair:* Litter.   99 *well said:* Well done.

Stay you, good gentlemen. — Look you pale, mistress? —
Do you perceive the gastness° of her eye? —
Nay, if you stare, we shall hear more anon.
Behold her well; I pray you look upon her.
Do you see, gentlemen? Nay, guiltiness will speak.   110
Though tongues were out of use.

Enter Emilia.

Emilia: 'Las, what's the matter? What's the matter, husband?
Iago: Cassio hath here been set on in the dark
    By Roderigo, and fellows that are scaped.
    He's almost slain, and Roderigo dead.   115
Emilia: Alas, good gentlemen! alas, good Cassio!
Iago: This is the fruits of whoring. Prithee, Emilia,
    Go know of Cassio where he supped to-night.

[To Bianca.]

    What, do you shake at that?
Bianca: He supped at my house; but I therefore shake not.   120
Iago: O, did he so? I charge you go with me.
Emilia: Fie, fie upon thee, strumpet!
Bianca: I am no strumpet, but of life as honest°
    As you that thus abuse me.
Emilia: As I? Foh! fie upon thee!
Iago: Kind gentlemen, let's go see poor Cassio dressed.   125

[To Bianca.]

    Come, mistress, you must tell 's another tale.
    Emilia, run you to the citadel
    And tell my lord and lady what hath happed.

                                      [Exit Emilia.]
    Will you go on afore?   *Exeunt [all but Iago].*
                    This is the night
    That either makes me or fordoes° me quite.   *[Exit.]* 130

SCENE II: *A bedchamber in the castle.*

Desdemona [asleep] in her bed. Enter Othello with a light.

Othello: It is the cause, it is the cause,° my soul.
    Let me not name it to you, you chaste stars!
    It is the cause. Yet I'll not shed her blood,
    Nor scar that whiter skin of hers than snow,
    And smooth as monumental alabaster.   5
    Yet she must die, else she'll betray more men.
    Put out the light, and then put out the light.
    If I quench thee, thou flaming minister,°
    I can again thy former light restore,

107 *gastness:* Terror.   123 *honest:* Chaste.   130 *fordoes:* Destroys.   **Scene II.**   1 *cause:*
Cause of justice.   8 *minister:* Servant.

Should I repent me; but once put out thy light,   10
Thou cunning'st pattern of excelling nature,
I know not where is that Promethean heat°
That can thy light relume.° When I have plucked the rose,
I cannot give it vital growth again;
It needs must wither. I'll smell thee on the tree.   15

(He kisses her.)

O balmy breath, that dost almost persuade
Justice to break her sword! One more, one more!
Be thus when thou art dead, and I will kill thee,
And love thee after. One more, and that's the last!
So sweet was ne'er so fatal. I must weep,   20
But they are cruel tears. This sorrow's heavenly;
It strikes where it doth love. She wakes.

Desdemona: Who's there? Othello?
Othello: Ay, Desdemona.
Desdemona: Will you come to bed, my lord?
Othello: Have you prayed to-night, Desdemon?
Desdemona: Ay, my lord.   25
Othello: If you bethink yourself of any crime°
      Unreconciled as yet to heaven and grace,
      Solicit for it straight.
Desdemona: Alack, my lord, what may you mean by that?
Othello: Well, do it, and be brief; I will walk by.   30
      I would not kill thy unprepared spirit.
      No, heaven forfend!° I would not kill thy soul.
Desdemona: Talk you of killing?
Othello: Ay, I do.
Desdemona: Then heaven
      Have mercy on me!
Othello: Amen, with all my heart!
Desdemona: If you say so, I hope you will not kill me.
Othello: Hum!   35
Desdemona: And yet I fear you; for you're fatal then
      When your eyes roll so. Why I should fear I know not,
      Since guiltiness I know not; but yet I feel I fear.
Othello: Think on thy sins.
Desdemona: They are loves I bear to you.   40
Othello: Ay, and for that thou diest.
Desdemona: That death 's unnatural that kills for loving.
      Alas, why gnaw you so your nether lip?
      Some bloody passion shakes your very frame.
      These are portents,° but yet I hope, I hope,   45
      They do not point on me.
Othello: Peace and be still!
Desdemona: I will so. What's the matter?

12 *Promethean heat:* Divine fire.   13 *relume:* Relight.   26 *crime:* Sin.   32 *forfend:* Forbid.   45 *portents:* Signs of impending violence.

Othello: That handkerchief which I so loved and gave thee
     Thou gav'st to Cassio.
Desdemona: No, by my life and soul!
     Send for the man and ask him.
Othello: Sweet soul, take heed,   50
     Take heed of perjury; thou art on thy deathbed.
Desdemona: Ay, but not yet to die.
Othello: Yes, presently.°
     Therefore confess thee freely of thy sin;
     For to deny each article with oath
     Cannot remove nor choke the strong conception°   55
     That I do groan withal. Thou art to die.
Desdemona: Then Lord have mercy on me!
Othello: I say amen.
Desdemona: And have you mercy too! I never did
     Offend° you in my life; never loved Cassio
     But with such general warranty of heaven   60
     As I might love. I never gave him token.
Othello: By heaven, I saw my handkerchief in's hand!
     O perjured woman! thou dost stone my heart,°
     And mak'st me call what I intend to do
     A murder, which I thought a sacrifice.   65
     I saw the handkerchief.
Desdemona: He found it then.
     I never gave it him. Send for him hither.
     Let him confess a truth.
Othello: He hath confessed.
Desdemona: What, my lord?
Othello: That he hath used thee.
Desdemona: How? Unlawfully?
Othello: Ay.   70
Desdemona: He will not say so.
Othello: No, his mouth is stopped.
     Honest Iago hath ta'en order° for't.
Desdemona: O, my fear interprets. What, is he dead?
Othello: Had all his hairs been lives, my great revenge
     Had stomach for them all.   75
Desdemona: Alas, he is betrayed, and I undone!
Othello: Out, strumpet! Weep'st thou for him to my face?
Desdemona: O, banish me, my lord, but kill me not!
Othello: Down, strumpet!
Desdemona: Kill me to-morrow; let me live to-night!   80
Othello: Nay, if you strive —
Desdemona: But half an hour!
Othello: Being done, there is no pause.
Desdemona: But while I say one prayer!
Othello: It is too late.

---

52 *presently:* At once.   55 *conception:* Belief.   59 *Offend:* Wrong.   63 *stone my heart:*
Turn my heart to stone.   72 *ta'en order:* Taken measures.

(Smothers her.)

[*Desdemona:* O Lord, Lord, Lord!]

   Emilia at the door.

Emilia (calls within): My lord, my lord! What, ho! my lord, my lord!   85
Othello: What noise is this? Not dead? not yet quite dead?
   I that am cruel am yet merciful;
   I would not have thee linger in thy pain.
   So, so.
Emilia (within): What, ho! my lord, my lord!
Othello: Who's there?   90
Emilia (within): O, good my lord, I would speak a word with you!
Othello: Yes, 'tis Emilia. — By and by.° — She's dead. —
   'Tis like she comes to speak of Cassio's death.
   The noise was here. Ha! no more moving?
   Still as the grave. — Shall she come in? Were't good! —   95
   I think she stirs again. No. — What's best to do?
   If she come in, she'll sure speak to my wife.
   My wife! my wife! what wife? I have no wife.
   O, insupportable! O heavy hour!
   Methinks it should be now a huge eclipse   100
   Of sun and moon, and that th' affrighted globe
   Should yawn° at alteration.
Emilia (within):   I do beseech you
   That I may speak with you, O good my lord!
Othello: I had forgot thee. O, come in, Emilia.
   Soft, by and by. — Let me the curtains draw. —   105

   [*Closes the bed-curtains.*]

   Where art thou?

   [*Opens the door.*]
   Enter Emilia.

                  What's the matter with thee now?
Emilia: O my good lord, yonder's foul murder done!
Othello: What? Now?
Emilia: But now, my lord.
Othello: It is the very error° of the moon.   110
   She comes more nearer earth than she was wont
   And makes men mad.
Emilia: Cassio, my lord, hath killed a young Venetian
   Called Roderigo.
Othello: Roderigo killed?
   And Cassio killed?
Emilia: No, Cassio is not killed.   115
Othello: Not Cassio killed? Then murder's out of tune,
   And sweet revenge grows harsh.

---

92 *By and by:* Just a moment (addressed to Emilia).   102 *yawn:* Open, as in an earthquake.   110 *error:* Straying off course.

Desdemona: O, falsely, falsely murdered?
Emilia: O, Lord! what cry is that?
Othello: That? What?
Emilia: Out and alas! that was my lady's voice.   120
  Help! help, ho! help! O lady, speak again!
  Sweet Desdemona! O sweet mistress, speak!
Desdemona: A guiltless death I die.
Emilia: O, who hath done this deed?
Desdemona: Nobody—I myself. Farewell.   125
  Commend° me to my kind lord. O, farewell!

  (*She dies.*)

Othello: Why, how should she be murd'red?
Emilia: Alas, who knows?
Othello: You heard her say herself, it was not I.
Emilia: She said so. I must needs report the truth.
Othello: She's like a liar gone to burning hell!   130
  'Twas I that killed her.
Emilia: O, the more angel she,
  And you the blacker devil!
Othello: She turned to folly, and she was a whore.
Emilia: Thou dost belie her, and thou art a devil.
Othello: She was false as water.°
Emilia: Thou art rash as fire to say   135
  That she was false. O, she was heavenly true!
Othello: Cassio did top her. Ask thy husband else.
  O, I were damned beneath all depth in hell
  But that I did proceed upon just grounds
  To this extremity. Thy husband knew it all.   140
Emilia: My husband?
Othello: Thy husband.
Emilia: That she was false to wedlock?
Othello: Ay, with Cassio. Nay, had she been true,
  If heaven would make me such another world   145
  Of one entire and perfect chrysolite,°
  I'ld not have sold her for it.
Emilia: My husband?
Othello: Ay 'twas he that told me first.
  An honest man he is, and hates the slime
  That sticks on filthy deeds.
Emilia: My husband?   150
Othello: What needs this iterance,° woman? I say thy husband.
Emilia: O mistress, villainy hath made mocks with love!
  My husband say that she was false?
Othello: He, woman.
  I say, thy husband. Dost understand the word?
  My friend, thy husband; honest, honest Iago.   155

126 *Commend:* Remember.   135 *water:* (Which is yielding).   146 *chrysolite:* (Precious topaz).   151 *iterance:* Repetition.

Emilia: If he say so, may his pernicious soul
    Rot half a grain a day! he lies to th' heart.
    She was too fond of her most filthy bargain.
Othello: Ha!
Emilia: Do thy worst.   160
    This deed of thine is no more worthy heaven
    Than thou wast worthy her.
Othello: Peace, you were best.
Emilia: Thou hast not half the power to do me harm
    As I have to be hurt.° O gull! O dolt!
    As ignorant as dirt! thou hast done a deed —   165
    I care not for thy sword; I'll make thee known,
    Though I lost twenty lives. Help! help! Ho! help!
    The Moor hath killed my mistress! Murder! murder!

Enter Montano, Gratiano, Iago, and others.

Montano: What is the matter? How now, general?
Emilia: O, are you come, Iago? You have done well,   170
    That men must lay their murders on your neck.
Gratiano: What is the matter?
Emilia: Disprove this villain, if thou be'st a man.
    He says thou told'st him that his wife was false.
    I know thou didst not; thou'rt not such a villain.   175
    Speak, for my heart is full.
Iago: I told him what I thought, and told no more
    Than what he found himself was apt and true.
Emilia: But did you ever tell him she was false?
Iago: I did.   180
Emilia: You told a lie, an odious damnèd lie!
    Upon my soul, a lie! a wicked lie!
    She false with Cassio? Did you say with Cassio?
Iago: With Cassio, mistress. Go to, charm° your tongue.
Emilia: I will not charm my tongue; I am bound to speak: 185
    My mistress here lies murdered in her bed —
All: O heavens forfend!
Emilia: And your reports have set the murder on.
Othello: Nay, stare not, masters. It is true indeed.
Gratiano: 'Tis a strange truth.   190
Montano: O monstrous act!
Emilia: Villainy, villainy, villainy!
    I think upon't — I think I smell't! — O villainy!
    I thought so then. — I'll kill myself for grief. —
    O villainy, villainy!
Iago: What, are you mad? I charge you get you home.   195
Emilia: Good gentlemen, let me have leave to speak.
    'Tis proper I obey him, but not now.
    Perchance, Iago, I will ne'er go home.
Othello: O! O! O!   *(Falls on the bed.)*

164 *to be hurt:* To endure hurt.   184 *charm:* Cast a spell on.

Emilia: Nay, lay thee down and roar! 200
    For thou hast killed the sweetest innocent
    That e'er did lift up eye.
Othello: O, she was foul!

    [Rises.]

    I scarce did know you, uncle. There lies your niece,
    Whose breath, indeed, these hands have newly stopped.
    I know this act shows° horrible and grim.
Gratiano: Poor Desdemon! I am glad thy father's dead. 205
    Thy match was mortal to him, and pure grief
    Shore his old thread in twain. Did he live now,
    This sight would make him do a desperate turn;°
    Yea, curse his better angel from his side,
    And fall to reprobation.° 210
Othello: 'Tis pitiful; but yet Iago knows
    That she with Cassio hath the act of shame
    A thousand times committed. Cassio confessed it;
    And she did gratify° his amorous works
    With that recognizance° and pledge of love 215
    Which I first gave her. I saw it in his hand.
    It was a handkerchief, an antique token
    My father gave my mother.
Emilia: O God! O heavenly God!
Iago: Zounds, hold your peace!
Emilia: 'Twill out, 'twill out! I peace? 220
    No, I will speak as liberal as the north,°
    Let heaven and men and devils, let them all,
    All, all, cry shame against me, yet I'll speak.
Iago: Be wise, and get you home.
Emilia: I will not.

    [Iago draws and threatens Emilia.]

Gratiano: Fie!
    Your sword upon a woman? 225
Emilia: O thou dull Moor, that handkerchief thou speak'st of
    I found by fortune, and did give my husband;
    For often with a solemn earnestness —
    More than indeed belonged to such a trifle —
    He begged of me to steal't.
Iago: Villainous whore! 230
Emilia: She give it Cassio? No, alas, I found it,
    And I did give't my husband.
Iago: Filth, thou liest!
Emilia: By heaven, I do not, I do not, gentlemen.
    O murd'rous coxcomb! what should such a fool

---

204 *shows:* Appears.   208 *turn:* Act.   210 *reprobation:* Rejection by God, damnation.
214 *gratify:* Reward.   215 *recognizance:* Token.   221 *liberal as the north:* Unchecked as the
north wind blows.

Do with so good a wife?

Othello: Are there no stones° in heaven   235
But what serves for the thunder? Precious villain!

The Moor runs at Iago [but is disarmed by Montano].
Iago kills his wife.

Gratiano: The woman falls. Sure he hath killed his wife.
Emilia: Ay, ay. O, lay me by my mistress' side.   *Exit Iago.*
Gratiano: He's gone, but his wife's killed.
Montano: 'Tis a notorious° villain. Take you this weapon,   240
Which I have here recovered from the Moor.
Come, guard the door without. Let him not pass,
But kill him rather. I'll after that same villain,
For 'tis a damnèd slave.

Exit [Montano, with all but Othello and Emilia].

Othello: I am not valiant neither;
But every puny whipster° gets my sword.   245
But why should honor outlive honesty?
Let it go all.
Emilia: What did thy song bode, lady?
Hark, canst thou hear me? I will play the swan,
And die in music. *[Sings.]* "Willow, willow, willow."
Moor, she was chaste. She loved thee, cruel Moor: 250
So come my soul to bliss as I speak true.
So speaking as I think, alas, I die.

(She dies.)

Othello: I have another weapon in this chamber;
It is a sword of Spain, the ice brook's° temper.
O, here it is. — Uncle, I must come forth.   255
Gratiano (within): If thou attempt it, it will cost thee dear.
Thou hast no weapon, and perforce must suffer.
Othello: Look in upon me then and speak with me,
Or, naked° as I am, I will assault thee.

[Enter Gratiano.]

Gratiano: What is the matter?
Othello: Behold, I have a weapon;   260
A better never did itself sustain
Upon a soldier's thigh. I have seen the day
That with this little arm and this good sword
I have made my way through more impediments
Than twenty times your stop.° But O vain boast!   265
Who can control his fate? 'Tis not so now.
Be not afraid, though you do see me weaponed.
Here is my journey's end, here is my butt,°

---

235 *stones:* Bolts like those used for thunderbolts.   240 *notorious:* Notable.   245 *puny whipster:* Whippersnapper.   254 *ice brook:* I.e., a Spanish blade, tempered in cold running water.   259 *naked:* Disarmed.   265 *stop:* Power to stop.   268 *butt:* Limit.

And very seamark° of my utmost sail:
Do you go back dismayed? 'Tis a lost° fear. 270
Man but a rush° against Othello's breast,
And he retires. Where should Othello go?
Now, how dost thou look now? O ill-starred wench!
Pale as thy smock! When we shall meet at compt,° 275
This look of thine will hurl my soul from heaven,
And fiends will snatch at it. Cold, cold, my girl?
Even like thy chastity.
O cursèd, cursèd slave! Whip me, ye devils,
From the possession of this heavenly sight!
Blow me about in winds! roast me in sulphur! 280
Wash me in steep-down gulfs of liquid fire!
Oh Desdemon! dead Desdemon! dead! Oh! Oh!

Enter Lodovico, Montano, Iago [as prisoner], and Officers; Cassio in a chair.

Lodovico: Where is this rash and most unfortunate man?
Othello: That's he that was Othello. Here I am.
Lodovico: Where is that viper? Bring the villain forth. 285
Othello: I look down towards his feet°—but that's a fable.
  If that thou be'st a devil, I cannot kill thee.

  [Wounds Iago.]

Lodovico: Wrench his sword from him.

  [Othello is disarmed.]

Iago: I bleed, sir, but not killed.
Othello: I am not sorry neither. I'ld have thee live;
  For in my sense, 'tis happiness to die. 290
Lodovico: O thou Othello that wert once so good,
  Fall'n in the practice° of a damnèd slave,
  What shall be said to thee?
Othello: Why, anything;
  An honorable murderer, if you will;
  For naught did I in hate, but all in honor. 295
Lodovico: This wretch hath part confessed his villainy.
  Did you and he consent in° Cassio's death?
Othello: Ay.
Cassio: Dear general, I never gave you cause.
Othello: I do believe it, and I ask your pardon. 300
  Will you, I pray, demand that demi-devil
  Why he hath thus ensnared my soul and body?
Iago: Demand me nothing. What you know, you know.
  From this time forth I never will speak word.
Lodovico: What, not to pray?
Gratiano: Torments will ope your lips. 305
Othello: Well, thou dost best.

---

269 *seamark:* Beacon, destination.   270 *lost:* Wasted.   271 *Man but a rush:* Wield only a
reed.   274 *compt:* Final accounting, Last Judgment.   286 *I...feet:* I.e., to see if they are
cloven, like the Devil's.   292 *practice:* Plot.   297 *consent in:* Agree upon.

Lodovico: Sir, you shall understand what hath befall'n,
　　Which, as I think, you know not. Here is a letter
　　Found in the pocket of the slain Roderigo;
　　And here another. The one of them imports　　　　　　　　310
　　The death of Cassio to be undertook
　　By Roderigo.
Othello: O villain!
Cassio: 　　　　　Most heathenish and most gross!
Lodovico: Now here's another discontented paper
　　Found in the pocket too; and this, it seems,　　　　　　315
　　Roderigo meant t' have sent this damnèd villain;
　　But that, belike, Iago in the nick°
　　Came in and satisfied him.
Othello: 　　　　　　　O thou pernicious caitiff! —
　　How came you, Cassio, by that handkerchief
　　That was my wife's?
Cassio: 　　　　　　I found it in my chamber;　　　　　320
　　And he himself confessed but even now
　　That there he dropped it for a special purpose
　　Which wrought to his desire.
Othello: 　　　　　　　O fool! fool! fool!
Cassio: There is besides in Roderigo's letter,
　　How he upbraids Iago that he made him　　　　　　　325
　　Brave me upon the watch; whereon it came
　　That I was cast;° and even but now he spake,
　　After long seeming dead — Iago hurt him,
　　Iago set him on.
Lodovico: You must forsake this room and go with us.　　330
　　Your power and your command is taken off,
　　And Cassio rules in Cyprus. For this slave,
　　If there be any cunning cruelty
　　That can torment him much and hold him long,
　　It shall be his. You shall close prisoner rest　　　　　335
　　Till that the nature of your fault be known
　　To the Venetian state. Come, bring away.
Othello: Soft you! a word or two before you go.
　　I have done the state some service, and they know't.
　　No more of that. I pray you, in your letters,　　　　　340
　　When you shall these unlucky° deeds relate,
　　Speak of me as I am. Nothing extenuate,
　　Nor set down aught in malice. Then must you speak
　　Of one that loved not wisely, but too well;
　　Of one not easily jealous, but, being wrought,　　　　　345
　　Perplexed° in the extreme; of one whose hand,
　　Like the base Judean,° threw a pearl away
　　Richer than all his tribe; of one whose subdued° eyes,

---

317 *nick:* Nick of time.　　327 *cast:* Dismissed.　　341 *unlucky:* Fatal.　　346 *Perplexed:* Distracted.　　347 *Judean:* Judas Iscariot (?) (quarto reads "Indian").　　348 *subdued:* I.e., conquered by grief.

Albeit unusèd to the melting mood,
Drop tears as fast as the Arabian trees   350
Their med'cinable gum. Set you down this.
And say besides that in Aleppo once,
Where a malignant and a turbaned Turk
Beat a Venetian and traduced the state,
I took by th' throat the circumcisèd dog   355
And smote him — thus.

(He stabs himself.)

Lodovico: O bloody period!°
Gratiano: All that's spoke is marred.
Othello: I kissed thee ere I killed thee. No way but this,
    Killing myself, to die upon a kiss.

(He [falls upon the bed and] dies.)

Cassio: This did I fear, but thought he had no weapon;   360
    For he was great of heart.
Lodovico [to Iago]:   O Spartan dog,
    More fell° than anguish, hunger, or the sea!
    Look on the tragic loading of this bed.
    This is thy work. The object poisons sight;
    Let it be hid.° Gratiano, keep the house,   365
    And seize upon° the fortunes of the Moor,
    For they succeed on you. To you, lord governor,
    Remains the censure° of this hellish villain,
    The time, the place, the torture. O, enforce it!
    Myself will straight aboard, and to the state   370
    This heavy act with heavy heart relate.

                                Exeunt.

357 *period:* Ending.   362 *fell:* Cruel.   365 *Let it be hid:* I.e., draw the bed curtains.
366 *seize upon:* Take legal possession of.   368 *censure:* Judicial sentence.

CONSIDERATIONS FOR CRITICAL THINKING AND WRITING

1. **FIRST RESPONSE.** Characterize Othello. In what ways is he presented as having a jealous disposition as well as a noble one? Why is he so vulnerable to Iago's villainy?

2. Explain how Iago presents himself to the world. What is beneath the surface of his public identity? Why does he hate Othello so passionately? What makes Iago so effective at manipulating people? What do other characters, besides Othello, think of him?

3. Explain whether you think Othello could have protected himself from Iago's schemes. What could Othello have done differently to avoid the suffering that ends the play? Is Iago to be blamed for everything, or must Othello shoulder some of the blame?

4. Explain why you think Othello's racial background does or doesn't affect events in the play.

5. Describe how the two settings, Venice and Cyprus, reflect different social and psychological environments as well as different behavior among the characters.

6. How does Othello change during the course of the play? Do you feel the same about him from beginning to end? Trace your response to his character as it develops, paying particular attention to Othello's final speech.

7. Consider how women — Desdemona, Emilia, and Bianca — are presented in the play. What characteristics do they have in common? How do they relate to the men in their lives?

8. Despite its grinding emotional impact and bleak ending, *Othello* does have its humorous moments. Locate a scene that includes humor and describe its tone and function in the play.

9. To what extent do chance and coincidence conspire along with Iago to shape events in the play? Do you think Shakespeare merely manipulates incidents to move the plot, or do chance and coincidence have some thematic significance? Explain your answer.

10. Why does Othello insist that he must kill Desdemona immediately in Act V, Scene II? Do you think this action is an impulse or a decision? How does your answer to this question affect your view of Othello?

11. Shakespeare uses both poetry and prose for his characters' speeches. Locate instances of a change from one to the other and discuss the effect of this change.

12. CRITICAL STRATEGIES. Read the section on psychological criticism (pp. 1542–44) in Chapter 46, "Critical Strategies for Reading." Choose a soliloquy by Iago and write an analysis of it so that you reveal some significant portion of his character.

CONNECTIONS TO OTHER SELECTIONS

1. Explain how revenge is central to the plots of *Othello* and Andre Dubus's "Killings" (p. 103). Write an essay about the corrosive effects of revenge on the characters while drawing upon the consequences of revenge in each text.

2. Here's a long reach but a potentially interesting one: write an essay that considers Desdemona as a wife alongside Nora in Henrik Ibsen's *A Doll House* (p. 1257). How responsible are they to themselves and to others? Can they be discussed in the same breath, or are they from such different worlds that nothing useful can be said about comparing them? Either way, explain your response.

Perspectives on Shakespeare

THE MAYOR OF LONDON (1597)
Objections to the Elizabethan Theater   *1597*

The inconueniences that grow by Stage playes abowt the Citie of London.

1. They are a speaciall cause of corrupting their Youth, conteninge nothinge but vnchast matters, lascivious devices, shiftes of Coozenage,° & other lewd & vngodly practizes, being so as that they impresse the very qualitie & corruption of manners which they represent, Contrary to the rules & art prescribed for the makinge of Comedies eauen amonge the Heathen, who vsd them seldom & at certen sett tymes, and not all the year longe as our manner is. Whearby such as frequent them, beinge of the base & refuze sort of people or such young gentlemen as have small regard of credit or conscience, drawe the same into imitacion and not to the avoidinge the like vices which they represent.

2. They are the ordinary places for vagrant persons, Maisterles men, thieves, horse stealers, whoremongers, Coozeners, Conycatchers,° contrivers of treason, and other idele and daungerous persons to meet together & to make theire matches to the great displeasure of Almightie God & the hurt & annoyance of her Maiesties people, which cannot be prevented nor discovered by the Gouernours of the Citie for that they are owt of the Citiees iurisdiction.

3. They maintaine idlenes in such persons as haue no vocation & draw apprentices and other seruantes from theire ordinary workes and all sortes of people from the resort vnto sermons and other Christian exercises, to the great hinderance of traides & prophanation of religion established by her highnes within this Realm.

4. In the time of sickness it is fownd by experience, that many hauing sores and yet not hart sicke take occasion hearby to walk abroad & to recreat themselves by heareinge a play Whearby others are infected, and them selves also many things miscarry.

From Edmund K. Chambers, *The Elizabethan Stage*

shiftes of Coozenage: Perverse behavior.   *Conycatchers:* Tricksters.

CONSIDERATIONS FOR CRITICAL THINKING AND WRITING

1. Summarize the mayor's objections to the theater. Do any of his reasons for protesting theatrical productions seem reasonable to you? Why or why not?

2. Are any of these concerns reflected in attitudes about the theater today? Why or why not?

3. How would you defend *Othello* against charges that it draws some people into "imitacion and not to the avoidinge the like vices which [it] represent[s]"?

LISA JARDINE (B. 1944)

On Boy Actors in Female Roles   1989

Every schoolchild knows that there were no women actors on the Elizabethan stage; the female parts were taken by young male actors. But every schoolchild also learns that this fact is of little consequence for the twentieth-century reader of Shakespeare's plays. Because the taking of female parts by boys was universal and commonplace, we are told, it was accepted as "verisimilitude" by the Elizabethan audience, who simply disregarded it, as we would disregard the creaking of stage scenery and accept the backcloth forest as "real" for the duration of the play.

Conventional or no, the taking of female parts by boy players actually occasioned a good deal of contemporary comment and created considerable moral uneasiness, even amongst those who patronized and supported the theaters. Amongst those who opposed them, transvestism on stage was a main plank in the anti-stage polemic. "The appareil of wemen is a great provocation of men to lust and leacherie," wrote Dr. John Rainoldes, a leading Oxford divine (quoting the Bishop of Paris), in *Th' Overthrow of Stage-Playes* (Middleburgh, 1599). And he continues with an unhealthy interest which infuses the entire pamphlet: "A womans garment beeing put on a man doeth vehemently touch and moue him with the remembrance and imagination of a woman; and the imagination of a thing desirable doth stirr up the desire."

According to Rainoldes, and the authorities with whose independent testimony he lards his polemic, the wearing of female dress by boy players "is an occasion of wantonnes and lust." Sexuality, misdirected toward the boy masquerading in female dress, is "stirred" by attire and gesture; male prostitution and perverted sexual activity is the inevitable accompaniment of female impersonation.

From *Still Harping on Daughters,* Second Edition

CONSIDERATIONS FOR CRITICAL THINKING AND WRITING

1. How does Jardine complicate the Elizabethan convention of boy actors assuming female roles? To what extent does it add to the representation of Elizabethan theater put forward by the Mayor of London?

2. What do you think would be your own response to a boy actor playing a female role? Consider, for example, Desdemona in *Othello.*

SAMUEL JOHNSON (1709–1784)

On Shakespeare's Characters   1765

Shakespeare is above all writers, at least above all modern writers, the poet of nature: the poet that holds up to his readers a faithful mirror of manners and life. His characters are not modified by the customs of particular places, unpracticed by the rest of the world; by the peculiarities of studies or professions, which can operate but upon small numbers; or by the accidents of transient fashions or temporary opinions: they are the genuine progeny of common humanity, such as the world will always supply, and observation will always find. His persons act and speak by the influence of those general passions and principles by which all minds are agitated, and the whole system of life is continued in motion. In the writings of other poets a character is too often an individual; in those of Shakespeare it is commonly a species.

From the preface to Johnson's edition of Shakespeare's works

CONSIDERATIONS FOR CRITICAL THINKING AND WRITING

1. Johnson made this famous assessment of Shakespeare's ability to portray "common humanity" in the eighteenth century. As a twenty-first-century reader, explain why you agree or disagree with Johnson's view that Shakespeare's characters have universal appeal.

2. Write an essay discussing whether you think it is desirable or necessary for characters to be "a faithful mirror of manners and life." Along the way consider whether you encountered any characters in *Othello* that do not provide what you consider to be an accurate mirror of human life.

JANE ADAMSON

On Desdemona's Role in Othello   *1980*

One of the oddest things about criticism of *Othello* is how little usually gets said about Desdemona. She is often considered as a necessary element in the drama only because she is a necessary element in its plot—the woman with whom Othello just happens to be in love—rather than a major dramatic figure conceived in relation to everyone else. There is a strong tendency in critics of all persuasions to take her as a helpless, hapless victim—like one of those ideal Victorian heroines in whose mouths not even margarine would melt. As Marvin Rosenberg points out [in *The Masks of Othello*], "Desdemona has been in grave danger of being canonized," with the result that the play is made to seem much simpler than it is. . . . As Rosenberg also points out, however, the same result follows from the (not uncommon) alternative view of Desdemona, which sees her not as an innocent victim but as the culpable agent of her fate, or as someone whose "flaws" or "indiscretions" are such that she partly "deserves" what happens because she "brings it upon herself."

It seems to me that Rosenberg is right: neither of these views of Desdemona will do. Not only is she a more interesting and complex character, but she also emerges as a crucial and complex element in the dramatic design. To miss or distort what she—and Emilia and Bianca, the play's other women in love—represent in the world of *Othello* is to miss an essential element in its tragic power. What [F. R.] Leavis, for instance, asserts [in "Diabolic Intellect and the Noble Hero"] but nowhere explains is true: "the tragedy is inherent in the Othello-Desdemona relation."

From Othello *as Tragedy: Some Problems of Judgment and Feeling*

CONSIDERATIONS FOR CRITICAL THINKING AND WRITING

1. How might Desdemona be regarded as a "helpless, hapless victim"? What evidence is there in the play to support such a view?

2. Try to make a case for Desdemona as "the culpable agent of her fate."

3. Adamson agrees with Leavis that "the tragedy is inherent in the Othello-Desdemona relation." In an essay explore the possibilities of this provocative suggestion. What is there in these characters' relationship that could lead to their mutual suffering?

DAVID BEVINGTON (B. 1931)

On Othello's Heroic Struggle   1992

As a tragic hero, Othello obtains self-knowledge at a terrible price. He knows finally that what he has destroyed was ineffably good. The discovery is too late for him to make amends, and he dies by his own hand as atonement. The deaths of Othello and Desdemona are, in their separate ways, equally devastating: He is in part the victim of racism, though he nobly refuses to deny his own culpability, and she is the victim of sexism, lapsing sadly into the stereotypical role of passive and silent sufferer that the Venetian world expects of women. Despite the loss, however, Othello's reaffirmation of faith in Desdemona's goodness undoes what the devil-like Iago had most hoped to achieve: the separation of Othello from his loving trust in one who is good. In this important sense, Othello's self-knowledge is cathartic and a compensation for the terrible price he has paid. The very existence of a person as good as Desdemona gives the lie to Iago's creed that everyone has his or her price. She is the sacrificial victim who must die for Othello's loss of faith and, by dying, rekindle that faith. ("My life upon her faith!" Othello prophetically affirms, in response to her father's warning that she may deceive [1.3.293].) She cannot restore him to himself, for self-hatred has done its ugly work, but she is the means by which he understands at last the chimerical and wantonly destructive nature of his jealousy. His greatness appears in his acknowledgment of this truth and in the heroic struggle with which he has confronted an inner darkness we all share.

From *The Complete Works of William Shakespeare*

CONSIDERATIONS FOR CRITICAL THINKING AND WRITING

1. What kind of "self-knowledge" does Bevington attribute to Othello? Explain why you agree or disagree with this assessment of Othello.

2. Explain how Othello's "destructive... jealousy" has shaped the major events of the play.

3. Do you think Othello is engaged in a "heroic struggle," or is he merely the victim of a horrific plot against him? Refer to specific scenes to support your response.

JAMES KINCAID (B. 1937)

On the Value of Comedy in the Face of Tragedy   *1991*

[O]ur current hierarchical arrangement (tragedy high — comedy low) betrays an acquiescence in the most smothering of political conservatisms. Put another way, by coupling tragedy with the sublime, the ineffable, the metaphysical and by aligning comedy with the mundane, the quotidian, and the material we manage to muffle, even to erase, the most powerful narratives of illumination and liberation we have. . . .

The point is comic relief, the *concept* of comic relief and who it relieves. Now we usually refer to comic relief in the same tone we use for academic deans, other people's children, Melanie Griffith, the new criticism, jogging, Big Macs, the *New York Times Book Review,* leisure suits, people who go on cruises, realtors, and the MLA: bemused contempt. (Which is what we think about comic relief.) Comedy is that which attends on, offers relaxation from, prepares us for more of — something else, something serious and demanding. Comedy is not demanding — it does not demand or take, it gives. And we know that any agency which gives cannot be worth much. Tragedy's seriousness is guaranteed by its bullying greed, its insistence on having things its own way and pulling from us not only our tears, which we value little, but our attention, which we hate to give. Comedy, on the other hand, doesn't care if we attend closely. Tragedy is sleek and single-minded, comedy rumpled and hospitable to any idea or agency. Tragedy stares us out of countenance; comedy winks and leers and drools. Tragedy is all dressed up; comedy is always taking things off, mooning us. We find it inevitable that we associate tragedy with the high, comedy with the low. What is at issue here is the nature of that inevitability, our willingness to conspire in a discourse which pays homage to tragic grandeur and reduces comedy to release, authorized license, periodic relief — like a sneeze or yawn or belch. By allowing such discourse to flow through us, we add our bit of cement to the cultural edifice that sits on top of comedy, mashes it down into a mere adjunct to tragedy, its reverse and inferior half, its silly little carnival. By cooperating in this move, we relieve orthodox and conservative power structures of any pressure that might be exercised against them. Comic relief relieves the status quo, in other words, contains the power of comedy. . . .

Let's put it this way, comedy is not a mode that stands in opposition to tragedy. Comedy is the *whole* story, the narrative which refuses to leave things out. Tragedy insists on a formal structure that is unified and coherent, formally balanced and elegantly tight. Only that which is coordinate is allowed to adorn the tragic body. With comedy, nothing is sacrificed, nothing lost; the discoordinate and the discontinuous are especially welcome. Tragedy protects itself by its linearity, its tight conclusiveness; comedy's generosity and ability never to end make it gloriously vulnerable. Pitting tragedy against comedy is running up algebra against recess. . . .

From a paper read at the 1991 meeting of the Modern Language Association, "Who Is Relieved by the Idea of Comic Relief?"

CONSIDERATIONS FOR CRITICAL THINKING AND WRITING

1. What distinctions does Kincaid make between comedy and tragedy? How does his description of tragedy compare with Aristotle's (see p. 1144)?

2. How does Kincaid's description of comedy fit the humor in *Othello*?

3. According to Kincaid, why is the denigration of comedy a conservative impulse? In an essay explain why you agree or disagree with the argument.

SUGGESTED TOPICS FOR LONGER PAPERS

1. Discuss Shakespeare's use of humor in *Othello*. Focus on at least one humorous scene as the basis of your discussion and characterize the tone of the humor. What generalizations can you make about the tone and purpose of the humor in the play?

2. Research how marriage was regarded in Elizabethan times and compare those attitudes and values with the treatment of marriage in *Othello*.

42

Modern Drama

A play should give you something to
think about. When I see a play and
understand it the first time, then I know
it can't be much good.

—T. S. ELIOT

REALISM

Realism is a literary technique that attempts to create the appearance of
life as it is actually experienced. Characters in modern realistic plays (written during and after the last quarter of the nineteenth century) speak dialogue that we might hear in our daily lives. These characters are not larger
than life but representative of it; they seem to speak the way we do rather
than in highly poetic language, formal declarations, asides, or soliloquies.
It is impossible to imagine a heroic figure such as Oedipus inhabiting a
comfortably furnished living room and chatting about his wife's household budget the way Torvald Helmer does in Henrik Ibsen's *A Doll House*.
Realism brings into focus commonplace, everyday life rather than the
extraordinary kinds of events that make up Sophocles' *Oedipus the King* or
Shakespeare's *Othello*.

Realistic characters can certainly be heroic, but like Nora Helmer, they find that their strength and courage are tested in the context of events ordinary people might experience. Work, love, marriage, children, and death are often the focus of realistic dramas. These subjects can also constitute much of the material in nonrealistic plays, but modern realistic dramas present such material in the realm of the probable. Conflicts in realistic plays are likely to reflect problems in our own lives. Hence, making ends meet takes precedence over saving a kingdom; middle- and lower-class individuals take center stage as primary characters in main plots rather than being secondary characters in subplots. Thus we can see why the nineteenth-century movement toward realism paralleled the rise of a middle class eagerly seeking representations of its concerns in the theater.

Before the end of the nineteenth century, however, few attempts were made in the theater to present life as it is actually lived. The chorus's role in Sophocles' *Oedipus the King,* the allegorical figures in morality plays, the remarkable mistaken identities in Shakespeare's comedies, or the rhymed couplets spoken in seventeenth-century plays such as Molière's *Tartuffe* represent theatrical conventions rather than life. Theatergoers have understood and appreciated these conventions for centuries — and still do — but in the nineteenth century social, political, and industrial revolutions helped create an atmosphere in which some playwrights found it necessary to create works that more directly reflected their audiences' lives.

Playwrights such as Henrik Ibsen and Anton Chekhov refused to join the ranks of their romantic contemporaries, who they felt falsely idealized life. The most popular plays immediately preceding the works of these realistic writers consisted primarily of love stories and action-packed plots. Such **melodramas** offer audiences thrills and chills as well as happy endings. They typically include a virtuous individual struggling under the tyranny of a wicked oppressor, who is defeated only at the last moment. Suspense is reinforced by a series of pursuits, captures, and escapes that move the plot quickly and de-emphasize character or theme. These representations of extreme conflicts enjoyed wide popularity in the nineteenth century — indeed, they still do — because their formula was varied enough to be entertaining yet their outcomes were always comforting to the audience's sense of justice. From the realists' perspective, melodramas were merely escape fantasies that distorted life by refusing to examine the real world closely and objectively. But an indication of the popularity of such happy endings can be seen in Chekhov's farcical comedies, such as *The Proposal,* a one-act play filled with exaggerated characters and action. Despite his realist's values, Chekhov was also sometimes eager to please audiences.

Realists attempted to open their audiences' eyes; to their minds, the only genuine comfort was in knowing the truth. Many of their plays concern controversial issues of the day and focus on people who fall prey to indifferent societal institutions. English dramatist John Galsworthy (1867–1933) examined social values in *Strife* (1909) and *Justice* (1910), two plays whose titles broadly suggest the nature of his concerns. British playwright George Bernard Shaw (1856–1950) often used comedy and irony as means of awakening his audiences to contemporary problems: *Arms and the Man* (1894) satirizes romantic attitudes toward war, and *Mrs. Warren's Profession* (1898) indicts a social and economic system that drives a woman to prostitution. Chekhov's major plays are populated by characters frustrated by their social situations and their own sensibilities; they are ordinary people who long for happiness but become entangled in everyday circumstances that limit their lives. Ibsen also took a close look at his characters' daily lives. His plays attack social conventions and challenge popular attitudes toward marriage; he stunned audiences by dramatizing the suffering of a man dying of syphilis.

With these kinds of materials, Ibsen and his contemporaries popularized the **problem play,** a drama that represents a social issue in order to awaken the audience to it. These plays usually reject romantic plots in favor of holding up a mirror that reflects not simply what audiences want to see but what the playwright sees in them. Nineteenth-century realistic theater was no refuge from the social, economic, and psychological problems that melodrama ignored or sentimentalized.

NATURALISM

Related to realism is another movement, called **naturalism.** Essentially more of a philosophical attitude than a literary technique, naturalism derives its name from the idea that human beings are part of nature and subject to its laws. According to naturalists, heredity and environment shape and control people's lives; their behavior is determined more by instinct than by reason. This deterministic view argues that human beings have no transcendent identity because there is no soul or spiritual world that ultimately distinguishes humanity from any other form of life. Characters in naturalistic plays are generally portrayed as victims overwhelmed by internal and external forces. Thus literary naturalism tends to include not only the commonplace but the sordid, destructive, and chaotic aspects of life. Naturalism, then, is an extreme form of realism.

The earliest and most articulate voice of naturalism was that of French author Émile Zola (1840–1902), who urged artists to draw their characters from life and present their histories as faithfully as scientists report laboratory findings. Zola's best-known naturalistic play, *Thérèse Raquin* (1873), is a dramatization of an earlier novel involving a woman whose passion causes her to take a lover and plot with him to kill her husband. In his preface to the novel, Zola explains that his purpose is to take "a strong man and unsatisfied woman," "throw them into a violent drama and note scrupulously the sensations and acts of these creatures." The diction of Zola's statement reveals his nearly clinical approach, which becomes even more explicit when Zola likens his method of revealing character to that of an autopsy: "I have simply done on two living bodies the work which surgeons do on corpses."

Although some naturalistic plays have been successfully produced and admired (notably Maxim Gorky's *The Lower Depths* [1902], set in a grim boardinghouse occupied by characters who suffer poverty, crime, betrayal, disease, and suicide), few important dramatists fully subscribed to naturalism's extreme methods and values. Nevertheless, the movement significantly influenced playwrights. Because of its insistence on the necessity of closely observing characters' environment, playwrights placed a new emphasis on detailed settings and natural acting. This verisimilitude became a significant feature of realistic drama.

THEATRICAL CONVENTIONS OF MODERN DRAMA

The picture-frame stage that is often used for realistic plays typically reproduces the setting of a room in some detail. Within the stage, framed by a proscenium arch (from which the curtain hangs), scenery and props are used to create an illusion of reality. Whether the "small bookcase with richly bound books" described in the opening scene of Ibsen's *A Doll House* is only painted scenery or an actual case with books, it will probably look real to the audience. Removing the fourth wall of a room so that an audience can look in fosters the illusion that the actions onstage are real events happening before unseen spectators. The texture of Nora's life is communicated by the set as well as by what she says and does. That doesn't happen in a play like Sophocles' *Oedipus the King*. Technical effects can make us believe there is wood burning in a fireplace or snow falling outside a window. Outdoor settings are made similarly realistic by props and painted sets. In one of Chekhov's full-length plays, for example, the second act opens in a meadow with the faint outline of a city on the horizon.

In addition to lifelike sets, a particular method of acting is used to create a realistic atmosphere. Actors address each other instead of directing formal speeches toward the audience; they act within the setting, not merely before it. At the beginning of the twentieth century Konstantin Stanislavsky (1863–1938), a Russian director, teacher, and actor, developed a system of acting that was an important influence in realistic theater. He trained actors to identify with the inner emotions of the characters they played. They were encouraged to recall from their own lives emotional responses similar to those they were portraying. The goal was to present a role truthfully by first feeling and then projecting the character's situation. Among Stanislavsky's early successes in this method were the plays of Chekhov.

There are, however, degrees of realism on the stage. Tennessee Williams's *The Glass Menagerie* (p. 1438), for example, is a partially realistic portrayal of characters whose fragile lives are founded on illusions. Williams's dialogue rings true, and individual scenes resemble the kind of real-life action we would imagine such vulnerable characters engaging in, but other elements of the play are nonrealistic. For instance, Williams uses Tom as a major character in the play as well as narrator and stage manager. Here is part of Williams's stage directions: "The narrator is an undisguised convention of the play. He takes whatever license with dramatic convention as is convenient to his purposes." Although this play can be accurately described as including realistic elements, Williams, like many other contemporary playwrights, does not attempt an absolute fidelity to reality. He uses flashbacks — as does Arthur Miller in *Death of a Salesman* (p. 1372) — to present incidents that occurred before the opening scene because the past impinges so heavily on the present. Most playwrights don't attempt to duplicate reality, since that can now be done so well by motion pictures.

Realism needn't lock a playwright into a futile attempt to make everything appear as it is in life. There is no way to avoid theatrical conventions: actors impersonate characters in a setting that is, after all, a stage. Indeed, even the dialogue in a realistic play is quite different from the pauses, sentence fragments, repetitions, silences, and incoherencies that characterize the way people usually speak. Realistic dialogue may seem like ordinary speech, but it, like Shakespeare's poetic language, is constructed. If we remember that realistic drama represents only the appearance of reality and that what we read on a page or see and hear onstage is the result of careful selecting, editing, and even distortion, then we are more likely to appreciate the playwright's art.

A Doll House

Henrik Ibsen was born in Skien, Norway, to wealthy parents, who lost their money while he was a young boy. His early experiences with small-town life and genteel poverty sensitized him to the problems that he subsequently dramatized in a number of his plays. At age sixteen he was apprenticed to a druggist; he later thought about studying medicine, but by his early twenties he was earning a living writing and directing plays in various Norwegian cities. By the time of his death he enjoyed an international reputation for his treatment of social issues related to middle-class life.

POPPERFOTO/Alamy.

Ibsen's earliest dramatic works were historical and romantic plays, some in verse. His first truly realistic work was *The Pillars of Society* (1877), whose title ironically hints at the corruption and hypocrisy exposed in it. The realistic social-problem plays for which he is best known followed. These dramas at once fascinated and shocked international audiences.

Among his most produced and admired works are *A Doll House* (1879), *Ghosts* (1881), *An Enemy of the People* (1882), *The Wild Duck* (1884), and *Hedda Gabler* (1890). The common denominator in many of Ibsen's dramas is his interest in individuals struggling for an authentic identity in the face of tyrannical social conventions. This conflict often results in his characters' being divided between a sense of duty to themselves and their responsibility to others.

Ibsen used such external and internal conflicts to propel his plays' action. Like many of his contemporaries who wrote realistic plays, he adopted the form of the ***well-made play.*** A dramatic structure popularized in France by Eugène Scribe (1791–1861) and Victorien Sardou (1831–1908), the well-made play employs conventions including plenty of suspense created by meticulous plotting. Extensive exposition explains past events that ultimately lead to an inevitable climax. Tension is released when a secret that reverses the protagonist's fortunes is revealed. Ibsen, having directed a number of Scribe's plays in Norway, knew their cause-to-effect plot arrangements and used them for his own purposes in his problem plays.

> Explore contexts for Henrik Ibsen on *LiterActive*.

A Doll House dramatizes the tensions of a nineteenth-century middle-class marriage in which a wife struggles to step beyond the limited identity imposed on her by her husband and society. Although the Helmers' pleasant apartment seems an unlikely setting for the fierce conflicts that develop, the issues raised in the play are unmistakably real. *A Doll House* affirms the necessity to reject hypocrisy, complacency, cowardice, and stifling conventions if life is to have dignity and meaning. Several critical approaches to the play can be found in Chapter 43, "A Critical Case Study: Henrik Ibsen's *A Doll House*."

HENRIK IBSEN (1828–1906)

A Doll House

1879

TRANSLATED BY ROLF FJELDE

THE CHARACTERS

Torvald Helmer, a lawyer
Nora, his wife
Dr. Rank
Mrs. Linde
Nils Krogstad, a bank clerk
The Helmers' three small children
Anne-Marie, their nurse
Helene, a maid
A Delivery Boy

See Plays in Performance insert.

SCENE: The action takes place in Helmer's residence.

ACT I

A comfortable room, tastefully but not expensively furnished. A door to the right in the back wall leads to the entryway; another to the left leads to Helmer's study. Between these doors, a piano. Midway in the left-hand wall a door, and further back a window. Near the window a round table with an armchair and a small sofa. In the right-hand wall, toward the rear, a door, and nearer the foreground a porcelain stove with two armchairs and a rocking chair beside it. Between the stove and the side door, a small table. Engravings on the walls. An etagère with china figures and other small art objects; a small bookcase with richly bound books; the floor carpeted; a fire burning in the stove. It is a winter day.

A bell rings in the entryway; shortly after we hear the door being unlocked. Nora comes into the room, humming happily to herself; she is wearing street clothes and carries an armload of packages, which she puts down on the table to the right. She has left the hall door open; and through it a Delivery Boy is seen, holding a Christmas tree and a basket, which he gives to the Maid who let them in.

Nora: Hide the tree well, Helene. The children mustn't get a glimpse of it till this evening, after it's trimmed. *(To the Delivery Boy, taking out her purse.)* How much?

Delivery Boy: Fifty, ma'am.

Nora: There's a crown. No, keep the change. *(The Boy thanks her and leaves. Nora shuts the door. She laughs softly to herself while taking off her street things. Drawing a bag of macaroons from her pocket, she eats a couple, then steals over and listens at her husband's study door.)* Yes, he's home. *(Hums again as she moves to the table right.)*

Helmer (from the study): Is that my little lark twittering out there?

Nora (busy opening some packages): Yes, it is.

Helmer: Is that my squirrel rummaging around?

Nora: Yes!

Helmer: When did my squirrel get in?

Nora: Just now. *(Putting the macaroon bag in her pocket and wiping her mouth.)* Do come in, Torvald, and see what I've bought.

Helmer: Can't be disturbed. *(After a moment he opens the door and peers in, pen in hand.)* Bought, you say? All that there? Has the little spendthrift been out throwing money around again?

Nora: Oh, but Torvald, this year we really should let ourselves go a bit. It's the first Christmas we haven't had to economize.

Helmer: But you know we can't go squandering.

Nora: Oh yes, Torvald, we can squander a little now. Can't we? Just a tiny, wee bit. Now that you've got a big salary and are going to make piles and piles of money.

Helmer: Yes—starting New Year's. But then it's a full three months till the raise comes through.

Nora: Pooh! We can borrow that long.

Helmer: Nora! *(Goes over and playfully takes her by the ear.)* Are your scatter-brains off again? What if today I borrowed a thousand crowns, and you squandered them over Christmas week, and then on New Year's Eve a roof tile fell on my head and I lay there—

Nora (putting her hand on his mouth): Oh! Don't say such things!

Helmer: Yes, but what if it happened — then what?

Nora: If anything so awful happened, then it just wouldn't matter if I had debts or not.

Helmer: Well, but the people I'd borrowed from?

Nora: Them? Who cares about them! They're strangers.

Helmer: Nora, Nora, how like a woman! No, but seriously, Nora, you know what I think about that. No debts! Never borrow! Something of freedom's lost — and something of beauty, too — from a home that's founded on borrowing and debt. We've made a brave stand up to now, the two of us; and we'll go right on like that the little while we have to.

Nora (going toward the stove): Yes, whatever you say, Torvald.

Helmer (following her): Now, now, the little lark's wings mustn't droop. Come on, don't be a sulky squirrel. *(Taking out his wallet.)* Nora, guess what I have here.

Nora (turning quickly): Money!

Helmer: There, see. *(Hands her some notes.)* Good grief, I know how costs go up in a house at Christmastime.

Nora: Ten — twenty — thirty — forty. Oh, thank you, Torvald; I can manage no end on this.

Helmer: You really will have to.

Nora: Oh yes, I promise I will! But come here so I can show you everything I bought. And so cheap! Look, new clothes for Ivar here — and a sword. Here a horse and a trumpet for Bob. And a doll and a doll's bed here for Emmy; they're nothing much, but she'll tear them to bits in no time anyway. And here I have dress material and handkerchiefs for the maids. Old Anne-Marie really deserves something more.

Helmer: And what's in that package there?

Nora (with a cry): Torvald, no! You can't see that till tonight!

Helmer: I see. But tell me now, you little prodigal, what have you thought of for yourself?

Nora: For myself? Oh, I don't want anything at all.

Helmer: Of course you do. Tell me just what — within reason — you'd most like to have.

Nora: I honestly don't know. Oh, listen, Torvald —

Helmer: Well?

Nora (fumbling at his coat buttons, without looking at him): If you want to give me something, then maybe you could — you could —

Helmer: Come on, out with it.

Nora (hurriedly): You could give me money, Torvald. No more than you think you can spare; then one of these days I'll buy something with it.

Helmer: But Nora —

Nora: Oh please, Torvald darling, do that! I beg you, please. Then I could hang the bills in pretty gilt paper on the Christmas tree. Wouldn't that be fun?

Helmer: What are those little birds called that always fly through their fortunes?

Nora: Oh yes, spendthrifts: I know all that. But let's do as I say, Torvald; then I'll have time to decide what I really need most. That's very sensible, isn't it?

Helmer (smiling): Yes, very — that is, if you actually hung onto the money I give you, and you actually used it to buy yourself something. But it goes for the house and for all sorts of foolish things, and then I only have to lay out some more.

Nora: Oh, but Torvald —

Helmer: Don't deny it, my dear little Nora. *(Putting his arm around her waist.)* Spendthrifts are sweet, but they use up a frightful amount of money. It's incredible what it costs a man to feed such birds.

Nora: Oh, how can you say that! Really, I save everything I can.

Helmer (laughing): Yes, that's the truth. Everything you can. But that's nothing at all.

Nora (humming, with a smile of quiet satisfaction): Hm, if you only knew what expenses we larks and squirrels have, Torvald.

Helmer: You're an odd little one. Exactly the way your father was. You're never at a loss for scaring up money; but the moment you have it, it runs right out through your fingers; you never know what you've done with it. Well, one takes you as you are. It's deep in your blood. Yes, these things are hereditary, Nora.

Nora: Ah, I could wish I'd inherited many of Papa's qualities.

Helmer: And I couldn't wish you anything but just what you are, my sweet little lark. But wait; it seems to me you have a very — what should I call it? — a very suspicious look today —

Nora: I do?

Helmer: You certainly do. Look me straight in the eye.

Nora (looking at him): Well?

Helmer (shaking an admonitory finger): Surely my sweet tooth hasn't been running riot in town today, has she?

Nora: No. Why do you imagine that?

Helmer: My sweet tooth really didn't make a little detour through the confectioner's?

Nora: No, I assure you, Torvald —

Helmer: Hasn't nibbled some pastry?

Nora: No, not at all.

Helmer: Not even munched a macaroon or two?

Nora: No, Torvald, I assure you, really —

Helmer: There, there now. Of course I'm only joking.

Nora (going to the table, right): You know I could never think of going against you.

Helmer: No, I understand that; and you *have* given me your word. *(Going over to her.)* Well, you keep your little Christmas secrets to yourself, Nora darling. I expect they'll come to light this evening, when the tree is lit.

Nora: Did you remember to ask Dr. Rank?

Helmer: No. But there's no need for that: it's assumed he'll be dining with us. All the same, I'll ask him when he stops by here this morning. I've ordered some fine wine. Nora, you can't imagine how I'm looking forward to this evening.

Nora: So am I. And what fun for the children, Torvald!

Helmer: Ah, it's so gratifying to know that one's gotten a safe, secure job, and with a comfortable salary. It's a great satisfaction, isn't it?

Nora: Oh, it's wonderful!

Helmer: Remember last Christmas? Three whole weeks before, you shut yourself in every evening till long after midnight, making flowers for the

Christmas tree, and all the other decorations to surprise us. Ugh, that was the dullest time I've ever lived through.

Nora: It wasn't at all dull for me.

Helmer (smiling): But the outcome *was* pretty sorry, Nora.

Nora: Oh, don't tease me with that again. How could I help it that the cat came in and tore everything to shreds.

Helmer: No, poor thing, you certainly couldn't. You wanted so much to please us all, and that's what counts. But it's just as well that the hard times are past.

Nora: Yes, it's really wonderful.

Helmer: Now I don't have to sit here alone, boring myself, and you don't have to tire your precious eyes and your fair little delicate hands —

Nora (clapping her hands): No, is it really true, Torvald, I don't have to? Oh, how wonderfully lovely to hear! *(Taking his arm.)* Now I'll tell you just how I've thought we should plan things. Right after Christmas — *(The doorbell rings.)* Oh, the bell. *(Straightening the room up a bit.)* Somebody would have to come. What a bore!

Helmer: I'm not home to visitors, don't forget.

Maid (from the hall doorway): Ma'am, a lady to see you —

Nora: All right, let her come in.

Maid (to Helmer): And the doctor's just come too.

Helmer: Did he go right to my study?

Maid: Yes, he did.

Helmer goes into his room. The Maid shows in Mrs. Linde, dressed in traveling clothes, and shuts the door after her.

Mrs. Linde (in a dispirited and somewhat hesitant voice): Hello, Nora.

Nora (uncertain): Hello —

Mrs. Linde: You don't recognize me.

Nora: No, I don't know — but wait, I think — *(Exclaiming.)* What! Kristine! Is it really you?

Mrs. Linde: Yes, it's me.

Nora: Kristine! To think I didn't recognize you. But then, how could I? *(More quietly.)* How you've changed, Kristine!

Mrs. Linde: Yes, no doubt I have. In nine — ten long years.

Nora: Is it so long since we met? Yes, it's all of that. Oh, these last eight years have been a happy time, believe me. And so now you've come in to town, too. Made the long trip in the winter. That took courage.

Mrs. Linde: I just got here by ship this morning.

Nora: To enjoy yourself over Christmas, of course. Oh, how lovely! Yes, enjoy ourselves, we'll do that. But take your coat off. You're not still cold? *(Helping her.)* There now, let's get cozy here by the stove. No, the easy chair there! I'll take the rocker here. *(Seizing her hands.)* Yes, now you have your old look again; it was only in that first moment. You're a bit more pale, Kristine — and maybe a bit thinner.

Mrs. Linde: And much, much older, Nora.

Nora: Yes, perhaps a bit older: a tiny, tiny bit; not much at all. *(Stopping short; suddenly serious.)* Oh, but thoughtless me, to sit here, chattering away. Sweet, good Kristine, can you forgive me?

Mrs. Linde: What do you mean, Nora?

Nora (softly): Poor Kristine, you've become a widow.

Mrs. Linde: Yes, three years ago.

Nora: Oh, I knew it, of course: I read it in the papers. Oh, Kristine, you must believe me; I often thought of writing you then, but I kept postponing it, and something always interfered.

Mrs. Linde: Nora dear, I understand completely.

Nora: No, it was awful of me, Kristine. You poor thing, how much you must have gone through. And he left you nothing?

Mrs. Linde: No.

Nora: And no children?

Mrs. Linde: No.

Nora: Nothing at all, then?

Mrs. Linde: Not even a sense of loss to feed on.

Nora (looking incredulously at her): But Kristine, how could that be?

Mrs. Linde (smiling wearily and smoothing her hair): Oh, sometimes it happens, Nora.

Nora: So completely alone. How terribly hard that must be for you. I have three lovely children. You can't see them now; they're out with the maid. But now you must tell me everything —

Mrs. Linde: No, no, no, tell me about yourself.

Nora: No, you begin. Today I don't want to be selfish. I want to think only of you today. But there *is* something I must tell you. Did you hear of the wonderful luck we had recently?

Mrs. Linde: No, what's that?

Nora: My husband's been made manager in the bank, just think!

Mrs. Linde: Your husband? How marvelous!

Nora: Isn't it? Being a lawyer is such an uncertain living, you know, especially if one won't touch any cases that aren't clean and decent. And of course Torvald would never do that, and I'm with him completely there. Oh, we're simply delighted, believe me! He'll join the bank right after New Year's and start getting a huge salary and lots of commissions. From now on we can live quite differently — just as we want. Oh, Kristine, I feel so light and happy! Won't it be lovely to have stacks of money and not a care in the world?

Mrs. Linde: Well, anyway, it would be lovely to have enough for necessities.

Nora: No, not just for necessities, but stacks and stacks of money!

Mrs. Linde (smiling): Nora, Nora, aren't you sensible yet? Back in school you were such a free spender.

Nora (with a quiet laugh): Yes, that's what Torvald still says. *(Shaking her finger.)* But "Nora, Nora" isn't as silly as you all think. Really, we've been in no position for me to go squandering. We've had to work, both of us.

Mrs. Linde: You too?

Nora: Yes, at odd jobs — needlework, crocheting, embroidery, and such — *(Casually.)* and other things too. You remember that Torvald left the department when we were married? There was no chance of promotion in his office, and of course he needed to earn more money. But that first year he drove himself terribly. He took on all kinds of extra work that kept him going morning and night. It wore him down, and then he fell deathly ill. The doctors said it was essential for him to travel south.

Mrs. Linde: Yes, didn't you spend a whole year in Italy?

Nora: That's right. It wasn't easy to get away, you know. Ivar had just been born. But of course we had to go. Oh, that was a beautiful trip, and it saved Torvald's life. But it cost a frightful sum, Kristine.

Mrs. Linde: I can well imagine.

Nora: Four thousand, eight hundred crowns it cost. That's really a lot of money.

Mrs. Linde: But it's lucky you had it when you needed it.

Nora: Well, as it was, we got it from Papa.

Mrs. Linde: I see. It was just about the time your father died.

Nora: Yes, just about then. And, you know, I couldn't make that trip out to nurse him. I had to stay here, expecting Ivar any moment, and with my poor sick Torvald to care for. Dearest Papa, I never saw him again, Kristine. Oh, that was the worst time I've known in all my marriage.

Mrs. Linde: I know how you loved him. And then you went off to Italy?

Nora: Yes. We had the means now, and the doctors urged us. So we left a month after.

Mrs. Linde: And your husband came back completely cured?

Nora: Sound as a drum!

Mrs. Linde: But — the doctor?

Nora: Who?

Mrs. Linde: I thought the maid said he was a doctor, the man who came in with me.

Nora: Yes, that was Dr. Rank — but he's not making a sick call. He's our closest friend, and he stops by at least once a day. No, Torvald hasn't had a sick moment since, and the children are fit and strong, and I am, too. *(Jumping up and clapping her hands.)* Oh, dear God, Kristine, what a lovely thing to live and be happy! But how disgusting of me — I'm talking of nothing but my own affairs. *(Sits on a stool close by Kristine, arms resting across her knees.)* Oh, don't be angry with me! Tell me, is it really true that you weren't in love with your husband? Why did you marry him, then?

Mrs. Linde: My mother was still alive, but bedridden and helpless — and I had my two younger brothers to look after. In all conscience, I didn't think I could turn him down.

Nora: No, you were right there. But was he rich at the time?

Mrs. Linde: He was very well off, I'd say. But the business was shaky, Nora. When he died, it all fell apart, and nothing was left.

Nora: And then — ?

Mrs. Linde: Yes, so I had to scrape up a living with a little shop and a little teaching and whatever else I could find. The last three years have been like one endless workday without a rest for me. Now it's over, Nora. My poor mother doesn't need me, for she's passed on. Nor the boys, either; they're working now and can take care of themselves.

Nora: How free you must feel —

Mrs. Linde: No — only unspeakably empty. Nothing to live for now. *(Standing up anxiously.)* That's why I couldn't take it any longer out in that desolate hole. Maybe here it'll be easier to find something to do and keep my mind occupied. If I could only be lucky enough to get a steady job, some office work —

Nora: Oh, but Kristine, that's so dreadfully tiring, and you already look so tired. It would be much better for you if you could go off to a bathing resort.

Mrs. Linde (going toward the window): I have no father to give me travel money, Nora.

Nora (rising): Oh, don't be angry with me.

Mrs. Linde (going to her): Nora dear, don't you be angry with me. The worst of my kind of situation is all the bitterness that's stored away. No one to work for, and yet you're always having to snap up your opportunities. You have to live; and so you grow selfish. When you told me the happy change in your lot, do you know I was delighted less for your sakes than for mine?

Nora: How so? Oh, I see. You think maybe Torvald could do something for you.

Mrs. Linde: Yes, that's what I thought.

Nora: And he will, Kristine! Just leave it to me; I'll bring it up so delicately — find something attractive to humor him with. Oh, I'm so eager to help you.

Mrs. Linde: How very kind of you, Nora, to be so concerned over me — doubly kind, considering you really know so little of life's burdens yourself.

Nora: I — ? I know so little — ?

Mrs. Linde (smiling): Well, my heavens — a little needlework and such — Nora, you're just a child.

Nora (tossing her head and pacing the floor): You don't have to act so superior.

Mrs. Linde: Oh?

Nora: You're just like the others. You all think I'm incapable of anything serious —

Mrs. Linde: Come now —

Nora: That I've never had to face the raw world.

Mrs. Linde: Nora dear, you've just been telling me all your troubles.

Nora: Hm! Trivia! *(Quietly.)* I haven't told you the big thing.

Mrs. Linde: Big thing? What do you mean?

Nora: You look down on me so, Kristine, but you shouldn't. You're proud that you worked so long and hard for your mother.

Mrs. Linde: I don't look down on a soul. But it *is* true: I'm proud — and happy, too — to think it was given to me to make my mother's last days almost free of care.

Nora: And you're also proud thinking of what you've done for your brothers.

Mrs. Linde: I feel I've a right to be.

Nora: I agree. But listen to this, Kristine — I've also got something to be proud and happy for.

Mrs. Linde: I don't doubt it. But whatever do you mean?

Nora: Not so loud. What if Torvald heard! He mustn't, not for anything in the world. Nobody must know, Kristine. No one but you.

Mrs. Linde: But what is it, then?

Nora: Come here. *(Drawing her down beside her on the sofa.)* It's true — I've also got something to be proud and happy for. I'm the one who saved Torvald's life.

Mrs. Linde: Saved — ? Saved how?

Nora: I told you about the trip to Italy. Torvald never would have lived if he hadn't gone south —

Mrs. Linde: Of course; your father gave you the means —

Nora (smiling): That's what Torvald and all the rest think, but —

Mrs. Linde: But — ?

Nora: Papa didn't give us a pin. I was the one who raised the money.

Mrs. Linde: You? That whole amount?

Nora: Four thousand, eight hundred crowns. What do you say to that?

Mrs. Linde: But Nora, how was it possible? Did you win the lottery?

Nora (disdainfully): The lottery? Pooh! No art to that.

Mrs. Linde: But where did you get it from then?

Nora (humming, with a mysterious smile): Hmm, tra-la-la-la.

Mrs. Linde: Because you couldn't have borrowed it.

Nora: No? Why not?

Mrs. Linde: A wife can't borrow without her husband's consent.

Nora (tossing her head): Oh, but a wife with a little business sense, a wife who
   knows how to manage —

Mrs. Linde: Nora, I simply don't understand —

Nora: You don't have to. Whoever said I *borrowed* the money? I could have
   gotten it other ways. *(Throwing herself back on the sofa.)* I could have
   gotten it from some admirer or other. After all, a girl with my ravishing
   appeal —

Mrs. Linde: You lunatic.

Nora: I'll bet you're eaten up with curiosity, Kristine.

Mrs. Linde: Now listen here, Nora — you haven't done something indiscreet?

Nora (sitting up again): Is it indiscreet to save your husband's life?

Mrs. Linde: I think it's indiscreet that without his knowledge you —

Nora: But that's the point: he mustn't know! My Lord, can't you understand?
   He mustn't ever know the close call he had. It was to *me* the doctors came
   to say his life was in danger — that nothing could save him but a stay in the
   south. Didn't I try strategy then! I began talking about how lovely it
   would be for me to travel abroad like other young wives; I begged and I
   cried; I told him please to remember my condition, to be kind and indulge
   me; and then I dropped a hint that he could easily take out a loan. But at
   that, Kristine, he nearly exploded. He said I was frivolous, and it was his
   duty as man of the house not to indulge me in whims and fancies — as I
   think he called them. Aha, I thought, now you'll just have to be saved —
   and that's when I saw my chance.

Mrs. Linde: And your father never told Torvald the money wasn't from him?

Nora: No, never. Papa died right about then. I'd considered bringing him into
   my secret and begging him never to tell. But he was too sick at the time —
   and then, sadly, it didn't matter.

Mrs. Linde: And you've never confided in your husband since?

Nora: For heaven's sake, no! Are you serious? He's so strict on that subject.
   Besides — Torvald, with all his masculine pride — how painfully humiliating for him if he ever found out he was in debt to me. That would just ruin
   our relationship. Our beautiful, happy home would never be the same.

Mrs. Linde: Won't you ever tell him?

Nora (thoughtfully, half smiling): Yes — maybe sometime, years from now, when
   I'm no longer so attractive. Don't laugh! I only mean when Torvald loves
   me less than now, when he stops enjoying my dancing and dressing up
   and reciting for him. Then it might be wise to have something in reserve —
   (Breaking off.) How ridiculous! That'll never happen — Well, Kristine, what
   do you think of my big secret? I'm capable of something too, hm? You can
   imagine, of course, how this thing hangs over me. It really hasn't been easy
   meeting the payments on time. In the business world there's what they
   call quarterly interest and what they call amortization, and these are

always so terribly hard to manage. I've had to skimp a little here and there, wherever I could, you know. I could hardly spare anything from my house allowance, because Torvald has to live well. I couldn't let the children go poorly dressed; whatever I got for them, I felt I had to use up completely — the darlings!

Mrs. Linde: Poor Nora, so it had to come out of your own budget, then?

Nora: Yes, of course. But I was the one most responsible, too. Every time Torvald gave me money for new clothes and such, I never used more than half; always bought the simplest, cheapest outfits. It was a godsend that everything looks so well on me that Torvald never noticed. But it did weigh me down at times, Kristine. It *is* such a joy to wear fine things. You understand.

Mrs. Linde: Oh, of course.

Nora: And then I found other ways of making money. Last winter I was lucky enough to get a lot of copying to do. I locked myself in and sat writing every evening till late in the night. Ah, I was tired so often, dead tired. But still it was wonderful fun, sitting and working like that, earning money. It was almost like being a man.

Mrs. Linde: But how much have you paid off this way so far?

Nora: That's hard to say, exactly. These accounts, you know, aren't easy to figure. I only know that I've paid out all I could scrape together. Time and again I haven't known where to turn. (*Smiling.*) Then I'd sit here dreaming of a rich old gentleman who had fallen in love with me —

Mrs. Linde: What! Who is he?

Nora: Oh, really! And that he'd died, and when his will was opened, there in big letters it said, "All my fortune shall be paid over in cash, immediately, to that enchanting Mrs. Nora Helmer."

Mrs. Linde: But Nora dear — who *was* this gentleman?

Nora: Good grief, can't you understand? The old man never existed; that was only something I'd dream up time and again whenever I was at my wits' end for money. But it makes no difference now; the old fossil can go where he pleases for all I care; I don't need him or his will — because now I'm free. (*Jumping up.*) Oh, how lovely to think of that, Kristine! Carefree! To know you're carefree, utterly carefree; to be able to romp and play with the children, and to keep up a beautiful, charming home — everything just the way Torvald likes it! And think, spring is coming, with big blue skies. Maybe we can travel a little then. Maybe I'll see the ocean again. Oh yes, it *is* so marvelous to live and be happy!

The front doorbell rings.

Mrs. Linde (rising): There's the bell. It's probably best that I go.

Nora: No, stay. No one's expected. It must be for Torvald.

Maid (from the hall doorway): Excuse me, ma'am — there's a gentleman here to see Mr. Helmer, but I didn't know — since the doctor's with him —

Nora: Who is the gentleman?

Krogstad (from the doorway): It's me, Mrs. Helmer.

Mrs. Linde starts and turns away toward the window.

Nora (stepping toward him, tense, her voice a whisper): You? What is it? Why do you want to speak to my husband?

Krogstad: Bank business — after a fashion. I have a small job in the investment bank, and I hear now your husband is going to be our chief —

Nora: In other words, it's —

Krogstad: Just dry business, Mrs. Helmer. Nothing but that.

Nora: Yes, then please be good enough to step into the study. *(She nods indifferently as she sees him out by the hall door, then returns and begins stirring up the stove.)*

Mrs. Linde: Nora — who was that man?

Nora: That was a Mr. Krogstad — a lawyer.

Mrs. Linde: Then it really was him.

Nora: Do you know that person?

Mrs. Linde: I did once — many years ago. For a time he was a law clerk in our town.

Nora: Yes, he's been that.

Mrs. Linde: How he's changed.

Nora: I understand he had a very unhappy marriage.

Mrs. Linde: He's a widower now.

Nora: With a number of children. There now, it's burning. *(She closes the stove door and moves the rocker a bit to one side.)*

Mrs. Linde: They say he has a hand in all kinds of business.

Nora: Oh? That may be true; I wouldn't know. But let's not think about business. It's so dull.

Dr. Rank enters from Helmer's study.

Rank (still in the doorway): No, no really — I don't want to intrude, I'd just as soon talk a little while with your wife. *(Shuts the door, then notices Mrs. Linde.)* Oh, beg pardon. I'm intruding here too.

Nora: No, not at all. *(Introducing him.)* Dr. Rank, Mrs. Linde.

Rank: Well now, that's a name much heard in this house. I believe I passed the lady on the stairs as I came.

Mrs. Linde: Yes, I take the stairs very slowly. They're rather hard on me.

Rank: Uh-hm, some touch of internal weakness?

Mrs. Linde: More overexertion, I'd say.

Rank: Nothing else? Then you're probably here in town to rest up in a round of parties?

Mrs. Linde: I'm here to look for work.

Rank: Is that the best cure for overexertion?

Mrs. Linde: One has to live, Doctor.

Rank: Yes, there's a common prejudice to that effect.

Nora: Oh, come on, Dr. Rank — you really do want to live yourself.

Rank: Yes, I really do. Wretched as I am, I'll gladly prolong my torment indefinitely. All my patients feel like that. And it's quite the same, too, with the morally sick. Right at this moment there's one of those moral invalids in there with Helmer —

Mrs. Linde (softly): Ah!

Nora: Who do you mean?

Rank: Oh, it's a lawyer, Krogstad, a type you wouldn't know. His character is rotten to the root — but even he began chattering all-importantly about how he had to *live*.

Nora: Oh? What did he want to talk to Torvald about?

Rank: I really don't know. I only heard something about the bank.

Nora: I didn't know that Krog—that this man Krogstad had anything to do with the bank.

Rank: Yes, he's gotten some kind of berth down there. *(To Mrs. Linde.)* I don't know if you also have, in your neck of the woods, a type of person who scuttles about breathlessly, sniffing out hints of moral corruption, and then maneuvers his victim into some sort of key position where he can keep an eye on him. It's the healthy these days that are out in the cold.

Mrs. Linde: All the same, it's the sick who most need to be taken in.

Rank (with a shrug): Yes, there we have it. That's the concept that's turning society into a sanatorium.

Nora, lost in her thoughts, breaks out into quiet laughter and claps her hands.

Rank: Why do you laugh at that? Do you have any real idea of what society is?

Nora: What do I care about dreary old society? I was laughing at something quite different—something terribly funny. Tell me, Doctor—is everyone who works in the bank dependent now on Torvald?

Rank: Is that what you find so terribly funny?

Nora (smiling and humming): Never mind, never mind! *(Pacing the floor.)* Yes, that's really immensely amusing: that we—that Torvald has so much power now over all those people. *(Taking the bag out of her pocket.)* Dr. Rank, a little macaroon on that?

Rank: See here, macaroons! I thought they were contraband here.

Nora: Yes, but these are some that Kristine gave me.

Mrs. Linde: What? I—?

Nora: Now, now, don't be afraid. You couldn't possibly know that Torvald had forbidden them. You see, he's worried they'll ruin my teeth. But hmp! Just this once! Isn't that so, Dr. Rank? Help yourself! *(Puts a macaroon in his mouth.)* And you too, Kristine. And I'll also have one, only a little one—or two, at the most. *(Walking about again.)* Now I'm really tremendously happy. Now there's just one last thing in the world that I have an enormous desire to do.

Rank: Well! And what's that?

Nora: It's something I have such a consuming desire to say so Torvald could hear.

Rank: And why can't you say it?

Nora: I don't dare. It's quite shocking.

Mrs. Linde: Shocking?

Rank: Well, then it isn't advisable. But in front of us you certainly can. What do you have such a desire to say so Torvald could hear?

Nora: I have such a huge desire to say—to hell and be damned!

Rank: Are you crazy?

Mrs. Linde: My goodness, Nora!

Rank: Go on, say it. Here he is.

Nora (hiding the macaroon bag): Shh, shh, shh!

Helmer comes in from his study, hat in hand, overcoat over his arm.

Nora (going toward him): Well, Torvald dear, are you through with him?

Helmer: Yes, he just left.

Nora: Let me introduce you—this is Kristine, who's arrived here in town.

Helmer: Kristine —? I'm sorry, but I don't know —

Nora: Mrs. Linde, Torvald dear. Mrs. Kristine Linde.

Helmer: Of course. A childhood friend of my wife's, no doubt?

Mrs. Linde: Yes, we knew each other in those days.

Nora: And just think, she made the long trip down here in order to talk with you.

Helmer: What's this?

Mrs. Linde: Well, not exactly —

Nora: You see, Kristine is remarkably clever in office work, and so she's terribly eager to come under a capable man's supervision and add more to what she already knows —

Helmer: Very wise, Mrs. Linde.

Nora: And then when she heard that you'd become a bank manager — the story was wired out to the papers — then she came in as fast as she could and — Really, Torvald, for my sake you can do a little something for Kristine, can't you?

Helmer: Yes, it's not at all impossible. Mrs. Linde, I suppose you're a widow?

Mrs. Linde: Yes.

Helmer: Any experience in office work?

Mrs. Linde: Yes, a good deal.

Helmer: Well, it's quite likely that I can make an opening for you —

Nora (clapping her hands): You see, you see!

Helmer: You've come at a lucky moment, Mrs. Linde.

Mrs. Linde: Oh, how can I thank you?

Helmer: Not necessary. *(Putting his overcoat on.)* But today you'll have to excuse me —

Rank: Wait, I'll go with you. *(He fetches his coat from the hall and warms it at the stove.)*

Nora: Don't stay out long, dear.

Helmer: An hour; no more.

Nora: Are you going too, Kristine?

Mrs. Linde (putting on her winter garments): Yes, I have to see about a room now.

Helmer: Then perhaps we can all walk together.

Nora (helping her): What a shame we're so cramped here, but it's quite impossible for us to —

Mrs. Linde: Oh, don't even think of it! Good-bye, Nora dear, and thanks for everything.

Nora: Good-bye for now. Of course you'll be back this evening. And you too, Dr. Rank. What? If you're well enough? Oh, you've got to be! Wrap up tight now.

In a ripple of small talk the company moves out into the hall; children's voices are heard outside on the steps.

Nora: There they are! There they are! *(She runs to open the door. The children come in with their nurse, Anne-Marie.)* Come in, come in! *(Bends down and kisses them.)* Oh, you darlings —! Look at them, Kristine. Aren't they lovely!

Rank: No loitering in the draft here.

Helmer: Come, Mrs. Linde — this place is unbearable now for anyone but mothers.

Dr. Rank, Helmer, and Mrs. Linde go down the stairs. Anne-Marie goes into the living room with the children. Nora follows, after closing the hall door.

Nora: How fresh and strong you look. Oh, such red cheeks you have! Like apples and roses. *(The children interrupt her throughout the following.)* And it was so much fun? That's wonderful. Really? You pulled both Emmy and Bob on the sled? Imagine, all together! Yes, you're a clever boy, Ivar. Oh, let me hold her a bit, Anne-Marie. My sweet little doll baby! *(Takes the smallest from the nurse and dances with her.)* Yes, yes, Mama will dance with Bob as well. What? Did you throw snowballs? Oh, if I'd only been there! No, don't bother, Anne-Marie — I'll undress them myself. Oh yes, let me. It's such fun. Go in and rest; you look half frozen. There's hot coffee waiting for you on the stove. *(The nurse goes into the room to the left. Nora takes the children's winter things off, throwing them about, while the children talk to her all at once.)* Is that so? A big dog chased you? But it didn't bite? No, dogs never bite little, lovely doll babies. Don't peek in the packages, Ivar! What is it? Yes, wouldn't you like to know. No, no, it's an ugly something. Well? Shall we play? What shall we play? Hide-and-seek? Yes, let's play hide-and-seek. Bob must hide first. I must? Yes, let me hide first. *(Laughing and shouting, she and the children play in and out of the living room and the adjoining room to the right. At last Nora hides under the table. The children come storming in, search, but cannot find her, then hear her muffled laughter, dash over to the table, lift the cloth up and find her. Wild shouting. She creeps forward as if to scare them. More shouts. Meanwhile, a knock at the hall door; no one has noticed it. Now the door half opens, and Krogstad appears. He waits a moment; the game goes on.)*
Krogstad: Beg pardon, Mrs. Helmer —
Nora *(with a strangled cry, turning and scrambling to her knees)*: Oh! What do you want?
Krogstad: Excuse me. The outer door was ajar; it must be someone forgot to shut it —
Nora *(rising)*: My husband isn't home, Mr. Krogstad.
Krogstad: I know that.
Nora: Yes — then what do you want here?
Krogstad: A word with you.
Nora: With —? *(To the children, quietly.)* Go in to Anne-Marie. What? No, the strange man won't hurt Mama. When he's gone, we'll play some more. *(She leads the children into the room to the left and shuts the door after them. Then, tense and nervous:)* You want to speak to me?
Krogstad: Yes, I want to.
Nora: Today? But it's not yet the first of the month —
Krogstad: No, it's Christmas Eve. It's going to be up to you how merry a Christmas you have.
Nora: What is it you want? Today I absolutely can't —
Krogstad: We won't talk about that till later. This is something else. You do have a moment to spare, I suppose?
Nora: Oh yes, of course — I do, except —
Krogstad: Good. I was sitting over at Olsen's Restaurant when I saw your husband go down the street —
Nora: Yes?

Krogstad: With a lady.

Nora: Yes. So?

Krogstad: If you'll pardon my asking: wasn't that lady a Mrs. Linde?

Nora: Yes.

Krogstad: Just now come into town?

Nora: Yes, today.

Krogstad: She's a good friend of yours?

Nora: Yes, she is. But I don't see —

Krogstad: I also knew her once.

Nora: I'm aware of that.

Krogstad: Oh? You know all about it. I thought so. Well, then let me ask you short and sweet: is Mrs. Linde getting a job in the bank?

Nora: What makes you think you can cross-examine me, Mr. Krogstad — you, one of my husband's employees? But since you ask, you might as well know — yes, Mrs. Linde's going to be taken on at the bank. And I'm the one who spoke for her, Mr. Krogstad. Now you know.

Krogstad: So I guessed right.

Nora (pacing up and down): Oh, one does have a tiny bit of influence, I should hope. Just because I am a woman, don't think it means that — When one has a subordinate position, Mr. Krogstad, one really ought to be careful about pushing somebody who — hm —

Krogstad: Who has influence?

Nora: That's right.

Krogstad (in a different tone): Mrs. Helmer, would you be good enough to use your influence on my behalf?

Nora: What? What do you mean?

Krogstad: Would you please make sure that I keep my subordinate position in the bank?

Nora: What does that mean? Who's thinking of taking away your position?

Krogstad: Oh, don't play the innocent with me. I'm quite aware that your friend would hardly relish the chance of running into me again; and I'm also aware now whom I can thank for being turned out.

Nora: But I promise you —

Krogstad: Yes, yes, yes, to the point: there's still time, and I'm advising you to use your influence to prevent it.

Nora: But Mr. Krogstad, I have absolutely no influence.

Krogstad: You haven't? I thought you were just saying —

Nora: You shouldn't take me so literally. I! How can you believe that I have any such influence over my husband?

Krogstad: Oh, I've known your husband from our student days. I don't think the great bank manager's more steadfast than any other married man.

Nora: You speak insolently about my husband, and I'll show you the door.

Krogstad: The lady has spirit.

Nora: I'm not afraid of you any longer. After New Year's, I'll soon be done with the whole business.

Krogstad (restraining himself): Now listen to me, Mrs. Helmer. If necessary, I'll fight for my little job in the bank as if it were life itself.

Nora: Yes, so it seems.

Krogstad: It's not just a matter of income; that's the least of it. It's something else—All right, out with it! Look, this is the thing. You know, just like all the others, of course, that once, a good many years ago, I did something rather rash.

Nora: I've heard rumors to that effect.

Krogstad: The case never got into court; but all the same, every door was closed in my face from then on. So I took up those various activities you know about. I had to grab hold somewhere; and I dare say I haven't been among the worst. But now I want to drop all that. My boys are growing up. For their sakes, I'll have to win back as much respect as possible here in town. That job in the bank was like the first rung in my ladder. And now your husband wants to kick me right back down in the mud again.

Nora: But for heaven's sake, Mr. Krogstad, it's simply not in my power to help you.

Krogstad: That's because you haven't the will to—but I have the means to make you.

Nora: You certainly won't tell my husband that I owe you money?

Krogstad: Hm—what if I told him that?

Nora: That would be shameful of you. *(Nearly in tears.)* This secret—my joy and my pride—that he should learn it in such a crude and disgusting way— learn it from you. You'd expose me to the most horrible unpleasantness—

Krogstad: Only unpleasantness?

Nora (vehemently): But go on and try. It'll turn out the worse for you, because then my husband will really see what a crook you are, and then you'll *never* be able to hold your job.

Krogstad: I asked if it was just domestic unpleasantness you were afraid of?

Nora: If my husband finds out, then of course he'll pay what I owe at once, and then we'd be through with you for good.

Krogstad (a step closer): Listen, Mrs. Helmer—you've either got a very bad memory, or else no head at all for business. I'd better put you a little more in touch with the facts.

Nora: What do you mean?

Krogstad: When your husband was sick, you came to me for a loan of four thousand, eight hundred crowns.

Nora: Where else could I go?

Krogstad: I promised to get you that sum—

Nora: And you got it.

Krogstad: I promised to get you that sum, on certain conditions. You were so involved in your husband's illness, and so eager to finance your trip, that I guess you didn't think out all the details. It might just be a good idea to remind you. I promised you the money on the strength of a note I drew up.

Nora: Yes, and that I signed.

Krogstad: Right. But at the bottom I added some lines for your father to guarantee the loan. He was supposed to sign down there.

Nora: Supposed to? He did sign.

Krogstad: I left the date blank. In other words, your father would have dated his signature himself. Do you remember that?

Nora: Yes, I think—

Krogstad: Then I gave you the note for you to mail to your father. Isn't that so?

Nora: Yes.

Krogstad: And naturally you sent it at once—because only some five, six days later you brought me the note, properly signed. And with that, the money was yours.

Nora: Well, then; I've made my payments regularly, haven't I?

Krogstad: More or less. But—getting back to the point—those were hard times for you then, Mrs. Helmer.

Nora: Yes, they were.

Krogstad: Your father was very ill, I believe.

Nora: He was near the end.

Krogstad: He died soon after?

Nora: Yes.

Krogstad: Tell me, Mrs. Helmer, do you happen to recall the date of your father's death? The day of the month, I mean.

Nora: Papa died the twenty-ninth of September.

Krogstad: That's quite correct; I've already looked into that. And now we come to a curious thing—*(Taking out a paper.)* which I simply cannot comprehend.

Nora: Curious thing? I don't know—

Krogstad: This is the curious thing: that your father co-signed the note for your loan three days after his death.

Nora: How—? I don't understand.

Krogstad: Your father died the twenty-ninth of September. But look. Here your father dated his signature October second. Isn't that curious, Mrs. Helmer? *(Nora is silent.)* Can you explain it to me? *(Nora remains silent.)* It's also remarkable that the words "October second" and the year aren't written in your father's hand, but rather in one that I think I know. Well, it's easy to understand. Your father forgot perhaps to date his signature, and then someone or other added it, a bit sloppily, before anyone knew of his death. There's nothing wrong in that. It all comes down to the signature. And there's no question about *that*, Mrs. Helmer. It really *was* your father who signed his own name here, wasn't it?

Nora (after a short silence, throwing her head back and looking squarely at him): No, it wasn't. *I* signed Papa's name.

Krogstad: Wait, now—are you fully aware that this is a dangerous confession?

Nora: Why? You'll soon get your money.

Krogstad: Let me ask you a question—why didn't you send the paper to your father?

Nora: That was impossible. Papa was so sick. If I'd asked him for his signature, I also would have had to tell him what the money was for. But I couldn't tell him, sick as he was, that my husband's life was in danger. That was just impossible.

Krogstad: Then it would have been better if you'd given up the trip abroad.

Nora: I couldn't possibly. The trip was to save my husband's life. I couldn't give that up.

Krogstad: But didn't you ever consider that this was a fraud against me?

Nora: I couldn't let myself be bothered by that. You weren't any concern of mine. I couldn't stand you, with all those cold complications you made, even though you knew how badly off my husband was.

Krogstad: Mrs. Helmer, obviously you haven't the vaguest idea of what you've involved yourself in. But I can tell you this: it was nothing more and nothing worse that I once did—and it wrecked my whole reputation.

Nora: You? Do you expect me to believe that you ever acted bravely to save your wife's life?

Krogstad: Laws don't inquire into motives.

Nora: Then they must be very poor laws.

Krogstad: Poor or not — if I introduce this paper in court, you'll be judged according to law.

Nora: This I refuse to believe. A daughter hasn't a right to protect her dying father from anxiety and care? A wife hasn't a right to save her husband's life? I don't know much about laws, but I'm sure that somewhere in the books these things are allowed. And you don't know anything about it — you who practice the law? You must be an awful lawyer, Mr. Krogstad.

Krogstad: Could be. But business — the kind of business we two are mixed up in — don't you think I know about that? All right. Do what you want now. But I'm telling you *this:* if I get shoved down a second time, you're going to keep me company. *(He bows and goes out through the hall.)*

Nora (pensive for a moment, then tossing her head): Oh, really! Trying to frighten me! I'm not so silly as all that. *(Begins gathering up the children's clothes, but soon stops.)* But — ? No, but that's impossible! I did it out of love.

The Children (in the doorway, left): Mama, that strange man's gone out the door.

Nora: Yes, yes, I know it. But don't tell anyone about the strange man. Do you hear? Not even Papa!

The Children: No, Mama. But now will you play again?

Nora: No, not now.

The Children: Oh, but Mama, you promised.

Nora: Yes, but I can't now. Go inside; I have too much to do. Go in, go in, my sweet darlings. *(She herds them gently back in the room and shuts the door after them. Settling on the sofa, she takes up a piece of embroidery and makes some stitches, but soon stops abruptly.)* No! *(Throws the work aside, rises, goes to the hall door and calls out.)* Helene! Let me have the tree in here. *(Goes to the table, left, opens the table drawer, and stops again.)* No, but that's utterly impossible!

Maid (with the Christmas tree): Where should I put it, ma'am?

Nora: There. The middle of the floor.

Maid: Should I bring anything else?

Nora: No, thanks. I have what I need.

The Maid, who has set the tree down, goes out.

Nora (absorbed in trimming the tree): Candles here — and flowers here. That terrible creature! Talk, talk, talk! There's nothing to it at all. The tree's going to be lovely. I'll do anything to please you, Torvald. I'll sing for you, dance for you —

Helmer comes in from the hall, with a sheaf of papers under his arm.

Nora: Oh! You're back so soon?

Helmer: Yes. Has anyone been here?

Nora: Here? No.

Helmer: That's odd. I saw Krogstad leaving the front door.

Nora: So? Oh yes, that's true. Krogstad was here a moment.

Helmer: Nora, I can see by your face that he's been here, begging you to put in a good word for him.

Nora: Yes.

Helmer: And it was supposed to seem like your own idea? You were to hide it from me that he'd been here. He asked you that, too, didn't he?

Nora: Yes, Torvald, but —

Helmer: Nora, Nora, and you could fall for that? Talk with that sort of person and promise him anything? And then in the bargain, tell me an untruth.

Nora: An untruth — ?

Helmer: Didn't you say that no one had been here? *(Wagging his finger.)* My little songbird must never do that again. A songbird needs a clean beak to warble with. No false notes. *(Putting his arm about her waist.)* That's the way it should be, isn't it? Yes, I'm sure of it. *(Releasing her.)* And so, enough of that. *(Sitting by the stove.)* Ah, how snug and cozy it is here. *(Leafing among his papers.)*

Nora (busy with the tree, after a short pause): Torvald!

Helmer: Yes.

Nora: I'm so much looking forward to the Stenborgs' costume party, day after tomorrow.

Helmer: And I can't wait to see what you'll surprise me with.

Nora: Oh, that stupid business!

Helmer: What?

Nora: I can't find anything that's right. Everything seems so ridiculous, so inane.

Helmer: So my little Nora's come to *that* recognition?

Nora (going behind his chair, her arms resting on its back): Are you very busy, Torvald?

Helmer: Oh —

Nora: What papers are those?

Helmer: Bank matters.

Nora: Already?

Helmer: I've gotten full authority from the retiring management to make all necessary changes in personnel and procedure. I'll need Christmas week for that. I want to have everything in order by New Year's.

Nora: So that was the reason this poor Krogstad —

Helmer: Hm.

Nora (still leaning on the chair and slowly stroking the nape of his neck): If you weren't so very busy, I would have asked you an enormous favor, Torvald.

Helmer: Let's hear. What is it?

Nora: You know, there isn't anyone who has your good taste — and I want so much to look well at the costume party. Torvald, couldn't you take over and decide what I should be and plan my costume?

Helmer: Ah, is my stubborn little creature calling for a lifeguard?

Nora: Yes, Torvald, I can't get anywhere without your help.

Helmer: All right — I'll think it over. We'll hit on something.

Nora: Oh, how sweet of you. *(Goes to the tree again. Pause.)* Aren't the red flowers pretty — ? But tell me, was it really such a crime that this Krogstad committed?

Helmer: Forgery. Do you have any idea what that means?

Nora: Couldn't he have done it out of need?

Helmer: Yes, or thoughtlessness, like so many others. I'm not so heartless that I'd condemn a man categorically for just one mistake.

Nora: No, of course not, Torvald!

Helmer: Plenty of men have redeemed themselves by openly confessing their crimes and taking their punishment.

Nora: Punishment — ?

Helmer: But now Krogstad didn't go that way. He got himself out by sharp practices, and that's the real cause of his moral breakdown.

Nora: Do you really think that would — ?

Helmer: Just imagine how a man with that sort of guilt in him has to lie and
cheat and deceive on all sides, has to wear a mask even with the nearest
and dearest he has, even with his own wife and children. And with the children, Nora — that's where it's most horrible.

Nora: Why?

Helmer: Because that kind of atmosphere of lies infects the whole life of a
home. Every breath the children take in is filled with the germs of something degenerate.

Nora (coming closer behind him): Are you sure of that?

Helmer: Oh, I've seen it often enough as a lawyer. Almost everyone who goes
bad early in life has a mother who's a chronic liar.

Nora: Why just — the mother?

Helmer: It's usually the mother's influence that's dominant, but the father's
works in the same way, of course. Every lawyer is quite familiar with it.
And still this Krogstad's been going home year in, year out, poisoning his
own children with lies and pretense; that's why I call him morally lost.
(Reaching his hands out toward her.) So my sweet little Nora must promise me
never to plead his cause. Your hand on it. Come, come, what's this? Give
me your hand. There, now. All settled. I can tell you it'd be impossible for
me to work alongside of him. I literally feel physically revolted when I'm
anywhere near such a person.

Nora (withdraws her hand and goes to the other side of the Christmas tree): How hot it
is here! And I've got so much to do.

Helmer (getting up and gathering his papers): Yes, and I have to think about getting
some of these read through before dinner. I'll think about your costume,
too. And something to hang on the tree in gilt paper, I may even see about
that. *(Putting his hand on her head.)* Oh you, my darling little songbird. *(He
goes into his study and closes the door after him.)*

Nora (softly, after a silence): Oh, really! It isn't so. It's impossible. It must be
impossible.

Anne-Marie (in the doorway, left): The children are begging so hard to come in to
Mama.

Nora: No, no, no, don't let them in to me! You stay with them, Anne-Marie.

Anne-Marie: Of course, ma'am. *(Closes the door.)*

Nora (pale with terror): Hurt my children — ! Poison my home? *(A moment's
pause; then she tosses her head.)* That's not true. Never. Never in all the world.

ACT II

*Same room. Beside the piano the Christmas tree now stands stripped of ornament,
burned-down candle stubs on its ragged branches. Nora's street clothes lie on the
sofa. Nora, alone in the room, moves restlessly about; at last she stops at the sofa
and picks up her coat.*

Nora (dropping the coat again): Someone's coming! *(Goes toward the door, listens.)*
No — there's no one. Of course — nobody's coming today, Christmas
Day — or tomorrow, either. But maybe — *(Opens the door and looks out.)* No,

nothing in the mailbox. Quite empty. *(Coming forward.)* What nonsense! He won't do anything serious. Nothing terrible could happen. It's impossible. Why, I have three small children.

Anne-Marie, with a large carton, comes in from the room to the left.

Anne-Marie: Well, at last I found the box with the masquerade clothes.

Nora: Thanks. Put it on the table.

Anne-Marie (does so): But they're all pretty much of a mess.

Nora: Ahh! I'd love to rip them in a million pieces!

Anne-Marie: Oh, mercy, they can be fixed right up. Just a little patience.

Nora: Yes, I'll go get Mrs. Linde to help me.

Anne-Marie: Out again now? In this nasty weather? Miss Nora will catch cold—get sick.

Nora: Oh, worse things could happen. How are the children?

Anne-Marie: The poor mites are playing with their Christmas presents, but—

Nora: Do they ask for me much?

Anne-Marie: They're so used to having Mama around, you know.

Nora: Yes, but Anne-Marie, I *can't* be together with them as much as I was.

Anne-Marie: Well, small children get used to anything.

Nora: You think so? Do you think they'd forget their mother if she was gone for good?

Anne-Marie: Oh, mercy—gone for good!

Nora: Wait, tell me, Anne-Marie—I've wondered so often—how could you ever have the heart to give your child over to strangers?

Anne-Marie: But I had to, you know, to become little Nora's nurse.

Nora: Yes, but how could you *do* it?

Anne-Marie: When I could get such a good place? A girl who's poor and who's gotten in trouble is glad enough for that. Because that slippery fish, he didn't do a thing for me, you know.

Nora: But your daughter's surely forgotten you.

Anne-Marie: Oh, she certainly has not. She's written to me, both when she was confirmed and when she was married.

Nora (clasping her about the neck): You old Anne-Marie, you were a good mother for me when I was little.

Anne-Marie: Poor little Nora, with no other mother but me.

Nora: And if the babies didn't have one, then I know that you'd—What silly talk! *(Opening the carton.)* Go in to them. Now I'll have to—Tomorrow you can see how lovely I'll look.

Anne-Marie: Oh, there won't be anyone at the party as lovely as Miss Nora. *(She goes off into the room, left.)*

Nora (begins unpacking the box, but soon throws it aside): Oh, if I dared to go out. If only nobody would come. If only nothing would happen here while I'm out. What craziness—nobody's coming. Just don't think. This muff—needs a brushing. Beautiful gloves, beautiful gloves. Let it go. Let it go! One, two, three, four, five, six—*(With a cry.)* Oh, there they are! *(Poises to move toward the door, but remains irresolutely standing. Mrs. Linde enters from the hall, where she has removed her street clothes.)*

Nora: Oh, it's you, Kristine. There's no one else out there? How good that you've come.

Mrs. Linde: I hear you were up asking for me.

Nora: Yes, I just stopped by. There's something you really can help me with. Let's get settled on the sofa. Look, there's going to be a costume party tomorrow evening at the Stenborgs' right above us, and now Torvald wants me to go as a Neapolitan peasant girl and dance the tarantella that I learned in Capri.

Mrs. Linde: Really, are you giving a whole performance?

Nora: Torvald says yes, I should. See, here's the dress. Torvald had it made for me down there; but now it's all so tattered that I just don't know —

Mrs. Linde: Oh, we'll fix that up in no time. It's nothing more than the trimmings — they're a bit loose here and there. Needle and thread? Good, now we have what we need.

Nora: Oh, how sweet of you!

Mrs. Linde (sewing): So you'll be in disguise tomorrow, Nora. You know what? I'll stop by then for a moment and have a look at you all dressed up. But listen, I've absolutely forgotten to thank you for that pleasant evening yesterday.

Nora (getting up and walking about): I don't think it was as pleasant as usual yesterday. You should have come to town a bit sooner, Kristine — Yes, Torvald really knows how to give a home elegance and charm.

Mrs. Linde: And you do, too, if you ask me. You're not your father's daughter for nothing. But tell me, is Dr. Rank always so down in the mouth as yesterday?

Nora: No, that was quite an exception. But he goes around critically ill all the time — tuberculosis of the spine, poor man. You know, his father was a disgusting thing who kept mistresses and so on — and that's why the son's been sickly from birth.

Mrs. Linde (lets her sewing fall to her lap): But my dearest Nora, how do you know about such things?

Nora (walking more jauntily): Hmp! When you've had three children, then you've had a few visits from — from women who know something of medicine, and they tell you this and that.

Mrs. Linde (resumes sewing; a short pause): Does Dr. Rank come here every day?

Nora: Every blessed day. He's Torvald's best friend from childhood, and *my* good friend, too. Dr. Rank almost belongs to this house.

Mrs. Linde: But tell me — is he quite sincere? I mean, doesn't he rather enjoy flattering people?

Nora: Just the opposite. Why do you think that?

Mrs. Linde: When you introduced us yesterday, he was proclaiming that he'd often heard my name in this house; but later I noticed that your husband hadn't the slightest idea who I really was. So how could Dr. Rank —?

Nora: But it's all true, Kristine. You see, Torvald loves me beyond words, and, as he puts it, he'd like to keep me all to himself. For a long time he'd almost be jealous if I even mentioned any of my old friends back home. So of course I dropped that. But with Dr. Rank I talk a lot about such things, because he likes hearing about them.

Mrs. Linde: Now listen, Nora; in many ways you're still like a child. I'm a good deal older than you, with a little more experience. I'll tell you something: you ought to put an end to all this with Dr. Rank.

Nora: What should I put an end to?

Mrs. Linde: Both parts of it, I think. Yesterday you said something about a rich
　　admirer who'd provide you with money —

Nora: Yes, one who doesn't exist — worse luck. So?

Mrs. Linde: Is Dr. Rank well off?

Nora: Yes, he is.

Mrs. Linde: With no dependents?

Nora: No, no one. But —

Mrs. Linde: And he's over here every day?

Nora: Yes, I told you that.

Mrs. Linde: How can a man of such refinement be so grasping?

Nora: I don't follow you at all.

Mrs. Linde: Now don't try to hide it, Nora. You think I can't guess who loaned
　　you the forty-eight hundred crowns?

Nora: Are you out of your mind? How could you think such a thing! A friend
　　of ours, who comes here every single day. What an intolerable situation
　　that would have been!

Mrs. Linde: Then it really wasn't him.

Nora: No, absolutely not. It never even crossed my mind for a moment — And
　　he had nothing to lend in those days; his inheritance came later.

Mrs. Linde: Well, I think that was a stroke of luck for you, Nora dear.

Nora: No, it never would have occurred to me to ask Dr. Rank — Still, I'm quite
　　sure that if I had asked him —

Mrs. Linde: Which you won't, of course.

Nora: No, of course not. I can't see that I'd ever need to. But I'm quite positive
　　that if I talked to Dr. Rank —

Mrs. Linde: Behind your husband's back?

Nora: I've got to clear up this other thing; *that's* also behind his back. I've *got* to
　　clear it all up.

Mrs. Linde: Yes, I was saying that yesterday, but —

Nora (pacing up and down): A man handles these problems so much better than
　　a woman —

Mrs. Linde: One's husband does, yes.

Nora: Nonsense. *(Stopping.)* When you pay everything you owe, then you get
　　your note back, right?

Mrs. Linde: Yes, naturally.

Nora: And can rip it into a million pieces and burn it up — that filthy scrap of
　　paper!

Mrs. Linde (looking hard at her, laying her sewing aside, and rising slowly): Nora,
　　you're hiding something from me.

Nora: You can see it in my face?

Mrs. Linde: Something's happened to you since yesterday morning. Nora, what
　　is it?

Nora (hurrying toward her): Kristine! *(Listening.)* Shh! Torvald's home. Look, go
　　in with the children a while. Torvald can't bear all this snipping and stitch-
　　ing. Let Anne-Marie help you.

Mrs. Linde (gathering up some of the things): All right, but I'm not leaving here
　　until we've talked this out. *(She disappears into the room, left, as Torvald enters
　　from the hall.)*

Nora: Oh, how I've been waiting for you, Torvald dear.

Helmer: Was that the dressmaker?

Nora: No, that was Kristine. She's helping me fix up my costume. You know, it's going to be quite attractive.

Helmer: Yes, wasn't that a bright idea I had?

Nora: Brilliant! But then wasn't I good as well to give in to you?

Helmer: Good—because you give in to your husband's judgment? All right, you little goose, I know you didn't mean it like that. But I won't disturb you. You'll want to have a fitting, I suppose.

Nora: And you'll be working?

Helmer: Yes. *(Indicating a bundle of papers.)* See. I've been down to the bank. *(Starts toward his study.)*

Nora: Torvald.

Helmer (stops): Yes.

Nora: If your little squirrel begged you, with all her heart and soul, for something—?

Helmer: What's that?

Nora: Then would you do it?

Helmer: First, naturally, I'd have to know what it was.

Nora: Your squirrel would scamper about and do tricks, if you'd only be sweet and give in.

Helmer: Out with it.

Nora: Your lark would be singing high and low in every room—

Helmer: Come on, she does that anyway.

Nora: I'd be a wood nymph and dance for you in the moonlight.

Helmer: Nora—don't tell me it's that same business from this morning?

Nora (coming closer): Yes, Torvald, I beg you, please!

Helmer: And you actually have the nerve to drag that up again?

Nora: Yes, yes, you've got to give in to me; you *have* to let Krogstad keep his job in the bank.

Helmer: My dear Nora, I've slated his job for Mrs. Linde.

Nora: That's awfully kind of you. But you could just fire another clerk instead of Krogstad.

Helmer: This is the most incredible stubbornness! Because you go and give an impulsive promise to speak up for him, I'm expected to—

Nora: That's not the reason, Torvald. It's for your own sake. That man does writing for the worst papers; you said it yourself. He could do you any amount of harm. I'm scared to death of him—

Helmer: Ah, I understand. It's the old memories haunting you.

Nora: What do you mean by that?

Helmer: Of course, you're thinking about your father.

Nora: Yes, all right. Just remember how those nasty gossips wrote in the papers about Papa and slandered him so cruelly. I think they'd have had him dismissed if the department hadn't sent you up to investigate, and if you hadn't been so kind and open-minded toward him.

Helmer: My dear Nora, there's a notable difference between your father and me. Your father's official career was hardly above reproach. But mine is; and I hope it'll stay that way as long as I hold my position.

Nora: Oh, who can ever tell what vicious minds can invent? We could be so snug and happy now in our quiet, carefree home—you and I and the children, Torvald! That's why I'm pleading with you so—

Helmer: And just by pleading for him you make it impossible for me to keep him on. It's already known at the bank that I'm firing Krogstad. What if it's rumored around now that the new bank manager was vetoed by his wife —

Nora: Yes, what then — ?

Helmer: Oh yes — as long as our little bundle of stubbornness gets her way — ! I should go and make myself ridiculous in front of the whole office — give people the idea I can be swayed by all kinds of outside pressure. Oh, you can bet I'd feel the effects of that soon enough! Besides — there's something that rules Krogstad right out at the bank as long as I'm the manager.

Nora: What's that?

Helmer: His moral failings I could maybe overlook if I had to —

Nora: Yes, Torvald, why not?

Helmer: And I hear he's quite efficient on the job. But he was a crony of mine back in my teens — one of those rash friendships that crop up again and again to embarrass you later in life. Well, I might as well say it straight out: we're on a first-name basis. And that tactless fool makes no effort at all to hide it in front of others. Quite the contrary — he thinks that entitles him to take a familiar air around me, and so every other second he comes booming out with his "Yes, Torvald!" and "Sure thing, Torvald!" I tell you, it's been excruciating for me. He's out to make my place in the bank unbearable.

Nora: Torvald, you can't be serious about all this.

Helmer: Oh no? Why not?

Nora: Because these are such petty considerations.

Helmer: What are you saying? Petty? You think I'm petty!

Nora: No, just the opposite, Torvald dear. That's exactly why —

Helmer: Never mind. You call my motives petty; then I might as well be just that. Petty! All right! We'll put a stop to this for good. *(Goes to the hall door and calls.)* Helene!

Nora: What do you want?

Helmer (searching among his papers): A decision. *(The maid comes in.)* Look here; take this letter; go out with it at once. Get hold of a messenger and have him deliver it. Quick now. It's already addressed. Wait, here's some money.

Maid: Yes, sir. *(She leaves with the letter.)*

Helmer (straightening his papers): There, now, little Miss Willful.

Nora (breathlessly): Torvald, what was that letter?

Helmer: Krogstad's notice.

Nora: Call it back, Torvald! There's still time. Oh, Torvald, call it back! Do it for my sake — for your sake, for the children's sake! Do you hear, Torvald; do it! You don't know how this can harm us.

Helmer: Too late.

Nora: Yes, too late.

Helmer: Nora dear, I can forgive you this panic, even though basically you're insulting me. Yes, you are! Or isn't it an insult to think that *I* should be afraid of a courtroom hack's revenge? But I forgive you anyway, because this shows so beautifully how much you love me. *(Takes her in his arms.)* This is the way it should be, my darling Nora. Whatever comes, you'll see; when it really counts, I have strength and courage enough as a man to take on the whole weight myself.

Nora (terrified): What do you mean by that?

Helmer: The whole weight, I said.

Nora (resolutely): No, never in all the world.

Helmer: Good. So we'll share it, Nora, as man and wife. That's as it should be. *(Fondling her.)* Are you happy now? There, there, there — not these frightened dove's eyes. It's nothing at all but empty fantasies — Now you should run through your tarantella and practice your tambourine. I'll go to the inner office and shut both doors, so I won't hear a thing; you can make all the noise you like. *(Turning in the doorway.)* And when Rank comes, just tell him where he can find me. *(He nods to her and goes with his papers into the study, closing the door.)*

Nora (standing as though rooted, dazed with fright, in a whisper): He really could do it. He will do it. He'll do it in spite of everything. No, not that, never, never! Anything but that! Escape! A way out — *(The doorbell rings.)* Dr. Rank! Anything but that! *Anything,* whatever it is! *(Her hands pass over her face, smoothing it; she pulls herself together, goes over and opens the hall door. Dr. Rank stands outside, hanging his fur coat up. During the following scene, it begins getting dark.)*

Nora: Hello, Dr. Rank. I recognized your ring. But you mustn't go in to Torvald yet; I believe he's working.

Rank: And you?

Nora: For you, I always have an hour to spare — you know that. *(He has entered, and she shuts the door after him.)*

Rank: Many thanks. I'll make use of these hours while I can.

Nora: What do you mean by that? While you can?

Rank: Does that disturb you?

Nora: Well, it's such an odd phrase. Is anything going to happen?

Rank: What's going to happen is what I've been expecting so long — but I honestly didn't think it would come so soon.

Nora (gripping his arm): What is it you've found out? Dr. Rank, you have to tell me!

Rank (sitting by the stove): It's all over for me. There's nothing to be done about it.

Nora (breathing easier): Is it you — then —?

Rank: Who else? There's no point in lying to one's self. I'm the most miserable of all my patients, Mrs. Helmer. These past few days I've been auditing my internal accounts. Bankrupt! Within a month I'll probably be laid out and rotting in the churchyard.

Nora: Oh, what a horrible thing to say.

Rank: The thing itself is horrible. But the worst of it is all the other horror before it's over. There's only one final examination left; when I'm finished with that, I'll know about when my disintegration will begin. There's something I want to say. Helmer with his sensitivity has such a sharp distaste for anything ugly. I don't want him near my sickroom.

Nora: Oh, but Dr. Rank —

Rank: I won't have him in there. Under no condition. I'll lock my door to him — As soon as I'm completely sure of the worst, I'll send you my calling card marked with a black cross, and you'll know then the wreck has started to come apart.

Nora: No, today you're completely unreasonable. And I wanted you so much to be in a really good humor.

Rank: With death up my sleeve? And then to suffer this way for somebody
else's sins. Is there any justice in that? And in every single family, in some
way or another, this inevitable retribution of nature goes on —

Nora (her hands pressed over her ears): Oh, stuff! Cheer up! Please — be gay!

Rank: Yes, I'd just as soon laugh at it all. My poor, innocent spine, serving time
for my father's gay army days.

Nora (by the table, left): He was so infatuated with asparagus tips and pâté de
foie gras, wasn't that it?

Rank: Yes — and with truffles.

Nora: Truffles, yes. And then with oysters, I suppose?

Rank: Yes, tons of oysters, naturally.

Nora: And then the port and champagne to go with it. It's so sad that all these
delectable things have to strike at our bones.

Rank: Especially when they strike at the unhappy bones that never shared in
the fun.

Nora: Ah, that's the saddest of all.

Rank (looks searchingly at her): Hm.

Nora (after a moment): Why did you smile?

Rank: No, it was you who laughed.

Nora: No, it was you who smiled, Dr. Rank!

Rank (getting up): You're even a bigger tease than I'd thought.

Nora: I'm full of wild ideas today.

Rank: That's obvious.

Nora (putting both hands on his shoulders): Dear, dear Dr. Rank, you'll never die
for Torvald and me.

Rank: Oh, that loss you'll easily get over. Those who go away are soon forgotten.

Nora (looks fearfully at him): You believe that?

Rank: One makes new connections, and then —

Nora: Who makes new connections?

Rank: Both you and Torvald will when I'm gone. I'd say you're well under way
already. What was that Mrs. Linde doing here last evening?

Nora: Oh, come — you can't be jealous of poor Kristine?

Rank: Oh yes, I am. She'll be my successor here in the house. When I'm down
under, that woman will probably —

Nora: Shh! Not so loud. She's right in there.

Rank: Today as well. So you see.

Nora: Only to sew on my dress. Good gracious, how unreasonable you are. (*Sitting on the sofa.*) Be nice now, Dr. Rank. Tomorrow you'll see how beautifully I'll dance; and you can imagine then that I'm dancing only for you —
yes, and of course for Torvald, too — that's understood. (*Takes various items
out of the carton.*) Dr. Rank, sit over here and I'll show you something.

Rank (sitting): What's that?

Nora: Look here. Look.

Rank: Silk stockings.

Nora: Flesh-colored. Aren't they lovely? Now it's so dark here, but tomorrow —
No, no, no, just look at the feet. Oh well, you might as well look at the rest.

Rank: Hm —

Nora: Why do you look so critical? Don't you believe they'll fit?

Rank: I've never had any chance to form an opinion on that.

Nora (glancing at him a moment): Shame on you. (*Hits him lightly on the ear with the stockings.*) That's for you. (*Puts them away again.*)

Rank: And what other splendors am I going to see now?

Nora: Not the least bit more, because you've been naughty. (*She hums a little and rummages among her things.*)

Rank (after a short silence): When I sit here together with you like this, completely easy and open, then I don't know—I simply can't imagine—whatever would have become of me if I'd never come into this house.

Nora (smiling): Yes, I really think you feel completely at ease with us.

Rank (more quietly, staring straight ahead): And then to have to go away from it all—

Nora: Nonsense, you're not going away.

Rank (his voice unchanged): —and not even be able to leave some poor show of gratitude behind, scarcely a fleeting regret—no more than a vacant place that anyone can fill.

Nora: And if I asked you now for—? No—

Rank: For what?

Nora: For a great proof of your friendship—

Rank: Yes, yes?

Nora: No, I mean—for an exceptionally big favor—

Rank: Would you really, for once, make me so happy?

Nora: Oh, you haven't the vaguest idea what it is.

Rank: All right, then tell me.

Nora: No, but I can't, Dr. Rank—it's all out of reason. It's advice and help, too—and a favor—

Rank: So much the better. I can't fathom what you're hinting at. Just speak out. Don't you trust me?

Nora: Of course. More than anyone else. You're my best and truest friend, I'm sure. That's why I want to talk to you. All right, then, Dr. Rank: there's something you can help me prevent. You know how deeply, how inexpressibly dearly Torvald loves me; he'd never hesitate a second to give up his life for me.

Rank (leaning close to her): Nora—do you think he's the only one—

Nora (with a slight start): Who—?

Rank: Who'd gladly give up his life for you.

Nora (heavily): I see.

Rank: I swore to myself you should know this before I'm gone. I'll never find a better chance. Yes, Nora, now you know. And also you know now that you can trust me beyond anyone else.

Nora (rising, natural and calm): Let me by.

Rank (making room for her, but still sitting): Nora—

Nora (in the hall doorway): Helene, bring the lamp in. (*Goes over to the stove.*) Ah, dear Dr. Rank, that was really mean of you.

Rank (getting up): That I've loved you just as deeply as somebody else? Was *that* mean?

Nora: No, but that you came out and told me. That was quite unnecessary—

Rank: What do you mean? Have you known—?

The Maid comes in with the lamp, sets it on the table, and goes out again.

Rank: Nora—Mrs. Helmer—I'm asking you: have you known about it?

Nora: Oh, how can I tell what I know or don't know? Really, I don't know what to say—Why did you have to be so clumsy, Dr. Rank! Everything was so good.

Rank: Well, in any case, you now have the knowledge that my body and soul are at your command. So won't you speak out?

Nora (looking at him): After that?

Rank: Please, just let me know what it is.

Nora: You can't know anything now.

Rank: I have to. You mustn't punish me like this. Give me the chance to do whatever is humanly possible for you.

Nora: Now there's nothing you can do for me. Besides, actually, I don't need any help. You'll see—it's only my fantasies. That's what it is. Of course! *(Sits in the rocker, looks at him, and smiles.)* What a nice one you are, Dr. Rank. Aren't you a little bit ashamed, now that the lamp is here?

Rank: No, not exactly. But perhaps I'd better go—for good?

Nora: No, you certainly can't do that. You must come here just as you always have. You know Torvald can't do without you.

Rank: Yes, but *you?*

Nora: You know how much I enjoy it when you're here.

Rank: That's precisely what threw me off. You're a mystery to me. So many times I've felt you'd almost rather be with me than with Helmer.

Nora: Yes—you see, there are some people that one loves most and other people that one would almost prefer being with.

Rank: Yes, there's something to that.

Nora: When I was back home, of course I loved Papa most. But I always thought it was so much fun when I could sneak down to the maids' quarters, because they never tried to improve me, and it was always so amusing, the way they talked to each other.

Rank: Aha, so it's *their* place that I've filled.

Nora (jumping up and going to him): Oh, dear, sweet Dr. Rank, that's not what I meant at all. But you can understand that with Torvald it's just the same as with Papa—

The Maid enters from the hall.

Maid: Ma'am—please! *(She whispers to Nora and hands her a calling card.)*

Nora (glancing at the card): Ah! *(Slips it into her pocket.)*

Rank: Anything wrong?

Nora: No, no, not at all. It's only some—it's my new dress—

Rank: Really? But—there's your dress.

Nora: Oh, that. But this is another one—I ordered it—Torvald mustn't know—

Rank: Ah, now we have the big secret.

Nora: That's right. Just go in with him—he's back in the inner study. Keep him there as long as—

Rank: Don't worry. He won't get away. *(Goes into the study.)*

Nora (to the Maid): And he's standing waiting in the kitchen?

Maid: Yes, he came up by the back stairs.

Nora: But didn't you tell him somebody was here?

Maid: Yes, but that didn't do any good.

Nora: He won't leave?

Maid: No, he won't go till he's talked with you, ma'am.

Nora: Let him come in, then — but quietly. Helene, don't breathe a word about this. It's a surprise for my husband.

Maid: Yes, yes, I understand — *(Goes out.)*

Nora: This horror — it's going to happen. No, no, no, it can't happen, it mustn't. *(She goes and bolts Helmer's door. The Maid opens the hall door for Krogstad and shuts it behind him. He is dressed for travel in a fur coat, boots, and a fur cap.)*

Nora (going toward him): Talk softly. My husband's home.

Krogstad: Well, good for him.

Nora: What do you want?

Krogstad: Some information.

Nora: Hurry up, then. What is it?

Krogstad: You know, of course, that I got my notice.

Nora: I couldn't prevent it, Mr. Krogstad. I fought for you to the bitter end, but nothing worked.

Krogstad: Does your husband's love for you run so thin? He knows everything I can expose you to, and all the same he dares to —

Nora: How can you imagine he knows anything about this?

Krogstad: Ah, no — I can't imagine it either, now. It's not at all like my fine Torvald Helmer to have so much guts —

Nora: Mr. Krogstad, I demand respect for my husband!

Krogstad: Why, of course — all due respect. But since the lady's keeping it so carefully hidden, may I presume to ask if you're also a bit better informed than yesterday about what you've actually done?

Nora: More than you could ever teach me.

Krogstad: Yes, I *am* such an awful lawyer.

Nora: What is it you want from me?

Krogstad: Just a glimpse of how you are, Mrs. Helmer. I've been thinking about you all day long. A cashier, a night-court scribbler, a — well, a type like me also has a little of what they call a heart, you know.

Nora: Then show it. Think of my children.

Krogstad: Did you or your husband ever think of mine? But never mind. I simply wanted to tell you that you don't need to take this thing too seriously. For the present, I'm not proceeding with any action.

Nora: Oh no, really! Well — I knew that.

Krogstad: Everything can be settled in a friendly spirit. It doesn't have to get around town at all; it can stay just among us three.

Nora: My husband must never know anything of this.

Krogstad: How can you manage that? Perhaps you can pay me the balance?

Nora: No, not right now.

Krogstad: Or you know some way of raising the money in a day or two?

Nora: No way that I'm willing to use.

Krogstad: Well, it wouldn't have done you any good, anyway. If you stood in front of me with a fistful of bills, you still couldn't buy your signature back.

Nora: Then tell me what you're going to do with it.

Krogstad: I'll just hold onto it — keep it on file. There's no outsider who'll even get wind of it. So if you've been thinking of taking some desperate step —

Nora: I have.

Krogstad: Been thinking of running away from home —
Nora: I have!
Krogstad: Or even of something worse —
Nora: How could you guess that?
Krogstad: You can drop those thoughts.
Nora: How could you guess I was thinking of *that*?
Krogstad: Most of us think about *that* at first. I thought about it too, but I discovered I hadn't the courage —
Nora (lifelessly): I don't either.
Krogstad (relieved): That's true, you haven't the courage? You too?
Nora: I don't have it — I don't have it.
Krogstad: It would be terribly stupid, anyway. After that first storm at home blows out, why, then — I have here in my pocket a letter for your husband —
Nora: Telling everything?
Krogstad: As charitably as possible.
Nora (quickly): He mustn't ever get that letter. Tear it up. I'll find some way to get money.
Krogstad: Beg pardon, Mrs. Helmer, but I think I just told you —
Nora: Oh, I don't mean the money I owe you. Let me know how much you want from my husband, and I'll manage it.
Krogstad: I don't want money from your husband.
Nora: What do you want, then?
Krogstad: I'll tell you what. I want to recoup, Mrs. Helmer; I want to get on in the world — and there's where your husband can help me. For a year and a half I've kept myself clean of anything disreputable — all that time struggling with the worst conditions; but I was satisfied, working my way up step by step. Now I've been written right off, and I'm just not in the mood to come crawling back. I tell you, I want to move on. I want to get back in the bank — in a better position. Your husband can set up a job for me —
Nora: He'll never do that!
Krogstad: He'll do it. I know him. He won't dare breathe a word of protest. And once I'm in there together with him, you just wait and see! Inside of a year, I'll be the manager's right-hand man. It'll be Nils Krogstad, not Torvald Helmer, who runs the bank.
Nora: You'll never see the day!
Krogstad: Maybe you think you can —
Nora: I have the courage now — for *that*.
Krogstad: Oh, you don't scare me. A smart, spoiled lady like you —
Nora: You'll see; you'll see!
Krogstad: Under the ice, maybe? Down in the freezing coal-black water? There, till you float up in the spring, ugly, unrecognizable, with your hair falling out —
Nora: You don't frighten me.
Krogstad: Nor do you frighten me. One doesn't do these things, Mrs. Helmer. Besides, what good would it be? I'd still have him safe in my pocket.
Nora: Afterwards? When I'm no longer — ?
Krogstad: Are you forgetting that *I'll* be in control then over your final reputation? *(Nora stands speechless, staring at him.)* Good; now I've warned you. Don't do anything stupid. When Helmer's read my letter, I'll be waiting

for his reply. And bear in mind that it's your husband himself who's forced me back to my old ways. I'll never forgive him for that. Good-bye, Mrs. Helmer. *(He goes out through the hall.)*

Nora (goes to the hall door, opens it a crack, and listens): He's gone. Didn't leave the letter. Oh no, no, that's impossible too! *(Opening the door more and more.)* What's that? He's standing outside — not going downstairs. He's thinking it over? Maybe he'll —? *(A letter falls in the mailbox; then Krogstad's footsteps are heard, dying away down a flight of stairs. Nora gives a muffled cry and runs over toward the sofa table. A short pause.)* In the mailbox. *(Slips warily over to the hall door.)* It's lying there. Torvald, Torvald — now we're lost!

Mrs. Linde (entering with costume from the room, left): There now, I can't see anything else to mend. Perhaps you'd like to try —

Nora (in a hoarse whisper): Kristine, come here.

Mrs. Linde (tossing the dress on the sofa): What's wrong? You look upset.

Nora: Come here. See that letter? *There!* Look — through the glass in the mailbox.

Mrs. Linde: Yes, yes, I see it.

Nora: That letter's from Krogstad —

Mrs. Linde: Nora — it's Krogstad who loaned you the money!

Nora: Yes, and now Torvald will find out everything.

Mrs. Linde: Believe me, Nora, it's best for both of you.

Nora: There's more you don't know. I forged a name.

Mrs. Linde: But for heaven's sake —?

Nora: I only want to tell you that, Kristine, so that you can be my witness.

Mrs. Linde: Witness? Why should I —?

Nora: If I should go out of my mind — it could easily happen —

Mrs. Linde: Nora!

Nora: Or anything else occurred — so I couldn't be present here —

Mrs. Linde: Nora, Nora, you aren't yourself at all!

Nora: And someone should try to take on the whole weight, all of the guilt, you follow me —

Mrs. Linde: Yes, of course, but why do you think —?

Nora: Then you're the witness that it isn't true, Kristine. I'm very much myself; my mind right now is perfectly clear; and I'm telling you: nobody else has known about this; I alone did everything. Remember that.

Mrs. Linde: I will. But I don't understand all this.

Nora: Oh, how could you ever understand it? It's the miracle now that's going to take place.

Mrs. Linde: The miracle?

Nora: Yes, the miracle. But it's so awful, Kristine. It mustn't take place, not for anything in the world.

Mrs. Linde: I'm going right over and talk with Krogstad.

Nora: Don't go near him; he'll do you some terrible harm!

Mrs. Linde: There was a time once when he'd gladly have done anything for me.

Nora: He?

Mrs. Linde: Where does he live?

Nora: Oh, how do I know? Yes. *(Searches in her pocket.)* Here's his card. But the letter, the letter —!

Helmer (from the study, knocking on the door): Nora!

Nora (with a cry of fear): Oh! What is it? What do you want?

Helmer: Now, now, don't be so frightened. We're not coming in. You locked the door — are you trying on the dress?

Nora: Yes, I'm trying it. I'll look just beautiful, Torvald.

Mrs. Linde (who has read the card): He's living right around the corner.

Nora: Yes, but what's the use? We're lost. The letter's in the box.

Mrs. Linde: And your husband has the key?

Nora: Yes, always.

Mrs. Linde: Krogstad can ask for his letter back unread; he can find some excuse —

Nora: But it's just this time that Torvald usually —

Mrs. Linde: Stall him. Keep him in there. I'll be back as quick as I can. *(She hurries out through the hall entrance.)*

Nora (goes to Helmer's door, opens it, and peers in): Torvald!

Helmer (from the inner study): Well — does one dare set foot in one's own living room at last? Come on, Rank, now we'll get a look — *(In the doorway.)* But what's this?

Nora: What, Torvald dear?

Helmer: Rank had me expecting some grand masquerade.

Rank (in the doorway): That was my impression, but I must have been wrong.

Nora: No one can admire me in my splendor — not till tomorrow.

Helmer: But Nora dear, you look so exhausted. Have you practiced too hard?

Nora: No, I haven't practiced at all yet.

Helmer: You know, it's necessary —

Nora: Oh, it's absolutely necessary, Torvald. But I can't get anywhere without your help. I've forgotten the whole thing completely.

Helmer: Ah, we'll soon take care of that.

Nora: Yes, take care of me, Torvald, please! Promise me that? Oh, I'm so nervous. That big party — You must give up everything this evening for me. No business — don't even touch your pen. Yes? Dear Torvald, promise?

Helmer: It's a promise. Tonight I'm totally at your service — you little helpless thing. Hm — but first there's one thing I want to — *(Goes toward the hall door.)*

Nora: What are you looking for?

Helmer: Just to see if there's any mail.

Nora: No, no, don't do that, Torvald!

Helmer: Now what?

Nora: Torvald, please. There isn't any.

Helmer: Let me look, though. *(Starts out. Nora, at the piano, strikes the first notes of the tarantella. Helmer, at the door, stops.)* Aha!

Nora: I can't dance tomorrow if I don't practice with you.

Helmer (going over to her): Nora dear, are you really so frightened?

Nora: Yes, so terribly frightened. Let me practice right now; there's still time before dinner. Oh, sit down and play for me, Torvald. Direct me. Teach me, the way you always have.

Helmer: Gladly, if it's what you want. *(Sits at the piano.)*

Nora (snatches the tambourine up from the box, then a long, varicolored shawl, which she throws around herself, whereupon she springs forward and cries out): Play for me now! Now I'll dance!

Helmer plays and Nora dances. Rank stands behind Helmer at the piano and looks on.

Helmer (as he plays): Slower. Slow down.

Nora: Can't change it.

Helmer: Not so violent, Nora!

Nora: Has to be just like this.

Helmer (stopping): No, no, that won't do at all.

Nora (laughing and swinging her tambourine): Isn't that what I told you?

Rank: Let me play for her.

Helmer (getting up): Yes, go on. I can teach her more easily then.

> *Rank sits at the piano and plays; Nora dances more and more wildly. Helmer has stationed himself by the stove and repeatedly gives her directions; she seems not to hear them; her hair loosens and falls over her shoulders; she does not notice, but goes on dancing. Mrs. Linde enters.*

Mrs. Linde (standing dumbfounded at the door): Ah — !

Nora (still dancing): See what fun, Kristine!

Helmer: But Nora darling, you dance as if your life were at stake.

Nora: And it is.

Helmer: Rank, stop! This is pure madness. Stop it, I say!

> *Rank breaks off playing, and Nora halts abruptly.*

Helmer (going over to her): I never would have believed it. You've forgotten everything I taught you.

Nora (throwing away the tambourine): You see for yourself.

Helmer: Well, there's certainly room for instruction here.

Nora: Yes, you see how important it is. You've got to teach me to the very last minute. Promise me that, Torvald?

Helmer: You can bet on it.

Nora: You mustn't, either today or tomorrow, think about anything else but me; you mustn't open any letters — or the mailbox —

Helmer: Ah, it's still the fear of that man —

Nora: Oh yes, yes, that too.

Helmer: Nora, it's written all over you — there's already a letter from him out there.

Nora: I don't know. I guess so. But you mustn't read such things now; there mustn't be anything ugly between us before it's all over.

Rank (quietly to Helmer): You shouldn't deny her.

Helmer (putting his arms around her): The child can have her way. But tomorrow night, after you've danced —

Nora: Then you'll be free.

Maid (in the doorway, right): Ma'am, dinner is served.

Nora: We'll be wanting champagne, Helene.

Maid: Very good, ma'am. *(Goes out.)*

Helmer: So — a regular banquet, hm?

Nora: Yes, a banquet — champagne till daybreak! *(Calling out.)* And some macaroons, Helene. Heaps of them — just this once.

Helmer (taking her hands): Now, now, now — no hysterics. Be my own little lark again.

Nora: Oh, I will soon enough. But go on in — and you, Dr. Rank. Kristine, help me put up my hair.

Rank (whispering, as they go): There's nothing wrong — really wrong, is there?

Helmer: Oh, of course not. It's nothing more than this childish anxiety I was telling you about. *(They go out, right.)*

Nora: Well?

Mrs. Linde: Left town.

Nora: I could see by your face.

Mrs. Linde: He'll be home tomorrow evening. I wrote him a note.

Nora: You shouldn't have. Don't try to stop anything now. After all, it's a wonderful joy, this waiting here for the miracle.

Mrs. Linde: What is it you're waiting for?

Nora: Oh, you can't understand that. Go in to them; I'll be along in a moment.

Mrs. Linde goes into the dining room. Nora stands a short while as if composing herself; then she looks at her watch.

Nora: Five. Seven hours to midnight. Twenty-four hours to the midnight after, and then the tarantella's done. Seven and twenty-four? Thirty-one hours to live.

Helmer (in the doorway, right): What's become of the little lark?

Nora (going toward him with open arms): Here's your lark!

ACT III

Same scene. The table, with chairs around it, has been moved to the center of the room. A lamp on the table is lit. The hall door stands open. Dance music drifts down from the floor above. Mrs. Linde sits at the table, absently paging through a book, trying to read, but apparently unable to focus her thoughts. Once or twice she pauses, tensely listening for a sound at the outer entrance.

Mrs. Linde (glancing at her watch): Not yet — and there's hardly any time left. If only he's not — *(Listening again.)* Ah, there he is. *(She goes out in the hall and cautiously opens the outer door. Quiet footsteps are heard on the stairs. She whispers:)* Come in. Nobody's here.

Krogstad (in the doorway): I found a note from you at home. What's back of all this?

Mrs. Linde: I just *had* to talk to you.

Krogstad: Oh? And it just *had* to be here in this house?

Mrs. Linde: At my place it was impossible; my room hasn't a private entrance. Come in; we're all alone. The maid's asleep, and the Helmers are at the dance upstairs.

Krogstad (entering the room): Well, well, the Helmers are dancing tonight? Really?

Mrs. Linde: Yes, why not?

Krogstad: How true — why not?

Mrs. Linde: All right, Krogstad, let's talk.

Krogstad: Do we two have anything more to talk about?

Mrs. Linde: We have a great deal to talk about.

Krogstad: I wouldn't have thought so.

Mrs. Linde: No, because you've never understood me, really.

Krogstad: Was there anything more to understand — except what's all too common in life? A calculating woman throws over a man the moment a better catch comes by.

Mrs. Linde: You think I'm so thoroughly calculating? You think I broke it off lightly?

Krogstad: Didn't you?

Mrs. Linde: Nils — is that what you really thought?

Krogstad: If you cared, then why did you write me the way you did?

Mrs. Linde: What else could I do? If I had to break off with you, then it was my job as well to root out everything you felt for me.

Krogstad (wringing his hands): So that was it. And this — all this, simply for money!

Mrs. Linde: Don't forget I had a helpless mother and two small brothers. We couldn't wait for you, Nils; you had such a long road ahead of you then.

Krogstad: That may be; but you still hadn't the right to abandon me for somebody else's sake.

Mrs. Linde: Yes — I don't know. So many, many times I've asked myself if I did have that right.

Krogstad (more softly): When I lost you, it was as if all the solid ground dissolved from under my feet. Look at me; I'm a half-drowned man now, hanging onto a wreck.

Mrs. Linde: Help may be near.

Krogstad: It was near — but then you came and blocked it off.

Mrs. Linde: Without my knowing it, Nils. Today for the first time I learned that it's you I'm replacing at the bank.

Krogstad: All right — I believe you. But now that you know, will you step aside?

Mrs. Linde: No, because that wouldn't benefit you in the slightest.

Krogstad: Not "benefit" me, hm! I'd step aside anyway.

Mrs. Linde: I've learned to be realistic. Life and hard, bitter necessity have taught me that.

Krogstad: And life's taught me never to trust fine phrases.

Mrs. Linde: Then life's taught you a very sound thing. But you do have to trust in actions, don't you?

Krogstad: What does that mean?

Mrs. Linde: You said you were hanging on like a half-drowned man to a wreck.

Krogstad: I've good reason to say that.

Mrs. Linde: I'm also like a half-drowned woman on a wreck. No one to suffer with; no one to care for.

Krogstad: You made your choice.

Mrs. Linde: There wasn't any choice then.

Krogstad: So — what of it?

Mrs. Linde: Nils, if only we two shipwrecked people could reach across to each other.

Krogstad: What are you saying?

Mrs. Linde: Two on one wreck are at least better off than each on his own.

Krogstad: Kristine!

Mrs. Linde: Why do you think I came into town?

Krogstad: Did you really have some thought of me?

Mrs. Linde: I have to work to go on living. All my born days, as long as I can remember, I've worked, and it's been my best and my only joy. But now I'm completely alone in the world; it frightens me to be so empty and lost. To work for yourself—there's no joy in that. Nils, give me something—someone to work for.

Krogstad: I don't believe all this. It's just some hysterical feminine urge to go out and make a noble sacrifice.

Mrs. Linde: Have you ever found me to be hysterical?

Krogstad: Can you honestly mean this? Tell me—do you know everything about my past?

Mrs. Linde: Yes.

Krogstad: And you know what they think I'm worth around here.

Mrs. Linde: From what you were saying before, it would seem that with me you could have been another person.

Krogstad: I'm positive of that.

Mrs. Linde: Couldn't it happen still?

Krogstad: Kristine—you're saying this in all seriousness? Yes, you are! I can see it in you. And do you really have the courage, then—?

Mrs. Linde: I need to have someone to care for; and your children need a mother. We both need each other. Nils, I have faith that you're good at heart—I'll risk everything together with you.

Krogstad (gripping her hands): Kristine, thank you, thank you—Now I know I can win back a place in their eyes. Yes—but I forgot—

Mrs. Linde (listening): Shh! The tarantella. Go now! Go on!

Krogstad: Why? What is it?

Mrs. Linde: Hear the dance up there? When that's over, they'll be coming down.

Krogstad: Oh, then I'll go. But—it's all pointless. Of course, you don't know the move I made against the Helmers.

Mrs. Linde: Yes, Nils, I know.

Krogstad: And all the same, you have the courage to—?

Mrs. Linde: I know how far despair can drive a man like you.

Krogstad: Oh, if I only could take it all back.

Mrs. Linde: You easily could—your letter's still lying in the mailbox.

Krogstad: Are you sure of that?

Mrs. Linde: Positive. But—

Krogstad (looks at her searchingly): Is that the meaning of it, then? You'll save your friend at any price. Tell me straight out. Is that it?

Mrs. Linde: Nils—anyone who's sold herself for somebody else once isn't going to do it again.

Krogstad: I'll demand my letter back.

Mrs. Linde: No, no.

Krogstad: Yes, of course. I'll stay here till Helmer comes down; I'll tell him to give me my letter again—that it only involves my dismissal—that he shouldn't read it—

Mrs. Linde: No, Nils, don't call the letter back.

Krogstad: But wasn't that exactly why you wrote me to come here?

Mrs. Linde: Yes, in that first panic. But it's been a whole day and night since then, and in that time I've seen such incredible things in this house.

Helmer's got to learn everything; this dreadful secret has to be aired; those two have to come to a full understanding; all these lies and evasions can't go on.

Krogstad: Well, then, if you want to chance it. But at least there's one thing I can do, and do right away —

Mrs. Linde (listening): Go now, go quick! The dance is over. We're not safe another second.

Krogstad: I'll wait for you downstairs.

Mrs. Linde: Yes, please do; take me home.

Krogstad: I can't believe it; I've never been so happy. (*He leaves by way of the outer door; the door between the room and the hall stays open.*)

Mrs. Linde (straightening up a bit and getting together her street clothes): How different now! How different! Someone to work for, to live for — a home to build. Well, it is worth the try! Oh, if they'd only come! (*Listening.*) Ah, there they are. Bundle up. (*She picks up her hat and coat. Nora's and Helmer's voices can be heard outside; a key turns in the lock, and Helmer brings Nora into the hall almost by force. She is wearing the Italian costume with a large black shawl about her; he has on evening dress, with a black domino open over it.*)

Nora (struggling in the doorway): No, no, no, not inside! I'm going up again. I don't want to leave so soon.

Helmer: But Nora dear —

Nora: Oh, I beg you, please, Torvald. From the bottom of my heart, *please* — only an hour more!

Helmer: Not a single minute, Nora darling. You know our agreement. Come on, in we go; you'll catch cold out here. (*In spite of her resistance, he gently draws her into the room.*)

Mrs. Linde: Good evening.

Nora: Kristine!

Helmer: Why, Mrs. Linde — are you here so late?

Mrs. Linde: Yes, I'm sorry, but I did want to see Nora in costume.

Nora: Have you been sitting here, waiting for me?

Mrs. Linde: Yes. I didn't come early enough; you were all upstairs; and then I thought I really couldn't leave without seeing you.

Helmer (removing Nora's shawl): Yes, take a good look. She's worth looking at, I can tell you that, Mrs. Linde. Isn't she lovely?

Mrs. Linde: Yes, I should say —

Helmer: A dream of loveliness, isn't she? That's what everyone thought at the party, too. But she's horribly stubborn — this sweet little thing. What's to be done with her? Can you imagine, I almost had to use force to pry her away.

Nora: Oh, Torvald, you're going to regret you didn't indulge me, even for just a half hour more.

Helmer: There, you see. She danced her tarantella and got a tumultuous hand — which was well earned, although the performance may have been a bit too naturalistic — I mean it rather overstepped the proprieties of art. But never mind — what's important is, she made a success, an overwhelming success. You think I could let her stay on after that and spoil the effect? Oh no; I took my lovely little Capri girl — my capricious little Capri girl, I should say — took her under my arm; one quick tour of the ballroom, a curtsy to every side, and then — as they say in novels — the beautiful vision disappeared. An exit should always be effective, Mrs. Linde, but that's what I can't get Nora to grasp. Phew, it's hot in here. *(Flings the domino on a chair and opens the door to his room.)* Why's it dark in here? Oh yes, of course. Excuse me. *(He goes in and lights a couple of candles.)*

Nora (in a sharp, breathless whisper): So?

Mrs. Linde (quietly): I talked with him.

Nora: And—?

Mrs. Linde: Nora—you must tell your husband everything.

Nora (dully): I knew it.

Mrs. Linde: You've got nothing to fear from Krogstad, but you have to speak out.

Nora: I won't tell.

Mrs. Linde: Then the letter will.

Nora: Thanks, Kristine. I know now what's to be done. Shh!

Helmer (reentering): Well, then, Mrs. Linde—have you admired her?

Mrs. Linde: Yes, and now I'll say good night.

Helmer: Oh, come, so soon? Is this yours, this knitting?

Mrs. Linde: Yes, thanks. I nearly forgot it.

Helmer: Do you knit, then?

Mrs. Linde: Oh yes.

Helmer: You know what? You should embroider instead.

Mrs. Linde: Really? Why?

Helmer: Yes, because it's a lot prettier. See here, one holds the embroidery so, in the left hand, and then one guides the needle with the right—so—in an easy, sweeping curve—right?

Mrs. Linde: Yes, I guess that's—

Helmer: But, on the other hand, knitting—it can never be anything but ugly. Look, see here, the arms tucked in, the knitting needles going up and down—there's something Chinese about it. Ah, that was really a glorious champagne they served.

Mrs. Linde: Yes, good night, Nora, and don't be stubborn anymore.

Helmer: Well put, Mrs. Linde!

Mrs. Linde: Good night, Mr. Helmer.

Helmer (accompanying her to the door): Good night, good night. I hope you get home all right. I'd be very happy to—but you don't have far to go. Good night, good night. *(She leaves. He shuts the door after her and returns.)* There, now, at last we got her out the door. She's a deadly bore, that creature.

Nora: Aren't you pretty tired, Torvald?

Helmer: No, not a bit.

Nora: You're not sleepy?

Helmer: Not at all. On the contrary, I'm feeling quite exhilarated. But you? Yes, you really look tired and sleepy.

Nora: Yes, I'm very tired. Soon now I'll sleep.

Helmer: See! You see! I was right all along that we shouldn't stay longer.

Nora: Whatever you do is always right.

Helmer (kissing her brow): Now my little lark talks sense. Say, did you notice what a time Rank was having tonight?

Nora: Oh, was he? I didn't get to speak with him.

Helmer: I scarcely did either, but it's a long time since I've seen him in such high spirits. *(Gazes at her a moment, then comes nearer her.)* Hm—it's marvelous, though, to be back home again—to be completely alone with you. Oh, you bewitchingly lovely young woman!

Nora: Torvald, don't look at me like that!

Helmer: Can't I look at my richest treasure? At all that beauty that's mine, mine alone—completely and utterly.

Nora (moving around to the other side of the table): You mustn't talk to me that way tonight.

Helmer (following her): The tarantella is still in your blood, I can see—and it makes you even more enticing. Listen. The guests are beginning to go. *(Dropping his voice.)* Nora—it'll soon be quiet through this whole house.

Nora: Yes, I hope so.

Helmer: You do, don't you, my love? Do you realize—when I'm out at a party like this with you—do you know why I talk to you so little, and keep such a distance away; just send you a stolen look now and then—you know why I do it? It's because I'm imagining then that you're my secret darling, my secret bride-to-be, and that no one suspects there's anything between us.

Nora: Yes, yes; oh, yes, I know you're always thinking of me.

Helmer: And then when we leave and I place the shawl over those fine young rounded shoulders—over that wonderful curving neck—then I pretend that you're my young bride, that we're just coming from the wedding, that for the first time I'm bringing you into my house—that for the first time I'm alone with you—completely alone with you, your trembling young beauty! All this evening I've longed for nothing but you. When I saw you turn and sway in the tarantella—my blood was pounding till I couldn't stand it—that's why I brought you down here so early—

Nora: Go away, Torvald! Leave me alone. I don't want all this.

Helmer: What do you mean? Nora, you're teasing me. You will, won't you? Aren't I your husband—?

A knock at the outside door.

Nora (startled): What's that?

Helmer (going toward the hall): Who is it?

Rank (outside): It's me. May I come in a moment?

Helmer (with quiet irritation): Oh, what does he want now? *(Aloud.)* Hold on. *(Goes and opens the door.)* Oh, how nice that you didn't just pass us by!

Rank: I thought I heard your voice, and then I wanted so badly to have a look in. *(Lightly glancing about.)* Ah, me, these old familiar haunts. You have it snug and cozy in here, you two.

Helmer: You seemed to be having it pretty cozy upstairs, too.

Rank: Absolutely. Why shouldn't I? Why not take in everything in life? As much as you can, anyway, and as long as you can. The wine was superb—

Helmer: The champagne especially.

Rank: You noticed that too? It's amazing how much I could guzzle down.

Nora: Torvald also drank a lot of champagne this evening.

Rank: Oh?

Nora: Yes, and that always makes him so entertaining.

Rank: Well, why shouldn't one have a pleasant evening after a well-spent day?

Helmer: Well spent? I'm afraid I can't claim that.

Rank (slapping him on the back): But I can, you see!

Nora: Dr. Rank, you must have done some scientific research today.

Rank: Quite so.

Helmer: Come now — little Nora talking about scientific research!

Nora: And can I congratulate you on the results?

Rank: Indeed you may.

Nora: Then they were good?

Rank: The best possible for both doctor and patient — certainty.

Nora (quickly and searchingly): Certainty?

Rank: Complete certainty. So don't I owe myself a gay evening afterwards?

Nora: Yes, you're right, Dr. Rank.

Helmer: I'm with you — just so long as you don't have to suffer for it in the morning.

Rank: Well, one never gets something for nothing in life.

Nora: Dr. Rank — are you very fond of masquerade parties?

Rank: Yes, if there's a good array of odd disguises —

Nora: Tell me, what should we two go as at the next masquerade?

Helmer: You little featherhead — already thinking of the next!

Rank: We two? I'll tell you what: you must go as Charmed Life —

Helmer: Yes, but find a costume for *that!*

Rank: Your wife can appear just as she looks every day.

Helmer: That was nicely put. But don't you know what you're going to be?

Rank: Yes, Helmer, I've made up my mind.

Helmer: Well?

Rank: At the next masquerade I'm going to be invisible.

Helmer: That's a funny idea.

Rank: They say there's a hat — black, huge — have you never heard of the hat that makes you invisible? You put it on, and then no one on earth can see you.

Helmer (suppressing a smile): Ah, of course.

Rank: But I'm quite forgetting what I came for. Helmer, give me a cigar, one of the dark Havanas.

Helmer: With the greatest pleasure. *(Holds out his case.)*

Rank: Thanks. *(Takes one and cuts off the tip.)*

Nora (striking a match): Let me give you a light.

Rank: Thank you. *(She holds the match for him; he lights the cigar.)* And now good-bye.

Helmer: Good-bye, good-bye, old friend.

Nora: Sleep well, Doctor.

Rank: Thanks for that wish.

Nora: Wish me the same.

Rank: You? All right, if you like — Sleep well. And thanks for the light. *(He nods to them both and leaves.)*

Helmer (his voice subdued): He's been drinking heavily.

Nora (absently): Could be. *(Helmer takes his keys from his pocket and goes out in the hall.)* Torvald — what are you after?

Helmer: Got to empty the mailbox; it's nearly full. There won't be room for the morning papers.

Nora: Are you working tonight?

Helmer: You know I'm not. Why—what's this? Someone's been at the lock.

Nora: At the lock—?

Helmer: Yes, I'm positive. What do you suppose—? I can't imagine one of the maids—? Here's a broken hairpin. Nora, it's yours—

Nora (quickly): Then it must be the children—

Helmer: You'd better break them of that. Hm, hm—well, opened it after all. *(Takes the contents out and calls into the kitchen.)* Helene! Helene, would you put out the lamp in the hall. *(He returns to the room shutting the hall door, then displays the handful of mail.)* Look how it's piled up. *(Sorting through them.)* Now what's this?

Nora (at the window): The letter! Oh, Torvald, no!

Helmer: Two calling cards—from Rank.

Nora: From Dr. Rank?

Helmer (examining them): "Dr. Rank, Consulting Physician." They were on top. He must have dropped them in as he left.

Nora: Is there anything on them?

Helmer: There's a black cross over the name. See? That's a gruesome notion. He could almost be announcing his own death.

Nora: That's just what he's doing.

Helmer: What! You've heard something? Something he's told you?

Nora: Yes. That when those cards came, he'd be taking his leave of us. He'll shut himself in now and die.

Helmer: Ah, my poor friend! Of course I knew he wouldn't be here much longer. But so soon—And then to hide himself away like a wounded animal.

Nora: If it has to happen, then it's best it happens in silence—don't you think so, Torvald?

Helmer (pacing up and down): He'd grown right into our lives. I simply can't imagine him gone. He with his suffering and loneliness—like a dark cloud setting off our sunlit happiness. Well, maybe it's best this way. For him, at least. *(Standing still.)* And maybe for us too, Nora. Now we're thrown back on each other, completely. *(Embracing her.)* Oh you, my darling wife, how can I hold you close enough? You know what, Nora—time and again I've wished you were in some terrible danger, just so I could stake my life and soul and everything, for your sake.

Nora (tearing herself away, her voice firm and decisive): Now you must read your mail, Torvald.

Helmer: No, no, not tonight. I want to stay with you, dearest.

Nora: With a dying friend on your mind?

Helmer: You're right. We've both had a shock. There's ugliness between us— these thoughts of death and corruption. We'll have to get free of them first. Until then—we'll stay apart.

Nora (clinging about his neck): Torvald—good night! Good night!

Helmer (kissing her on the cheek): Good night, little songbird. Sleep well, Nora. I'll be reading my mail now. *(He takes the letters into his room and shuts the door after him.)*

Nora (with bewildered glances, groping about, seizing Helmer's domino, throwing it around her, and speaking in short, hoarse, broken whispers): Never see him again. Never, never. *(Putting her shawl over her head.)* Never see the children either— them, too. Never, never. Oh, the freezing black water! The depths—down—

Oh, I wish it were over — He has it now; he's reading it — now. Oh no, no, not yet. Torvald, good-bye, you and the children — *(She starts for the hall; as she does, Helmer throws open his door and stands with an open letter in his hand.)*

Helmer: Nora!

Nora (screams): Oh — !

Helmer: What is this? You know what's in this letter?

Nora: Yes, I know. Let me go! Let me out!

Helmer (holding her back): Where are you going?

Nora (struggling to break loose): You can't save me, Torvald!

Helmer (slumping back): True! Then it's true what he writes? How horrible! No, no, it's impossible — it can't be true.

Nora: It *is* true. I've loved you more than all this world.

Helmer: Ah, none of your slippery tricks.

Nora (taking one step toward him): Torvald — !

Helmer: What *is* this you've blundered into!

Nora: Just let me loose. You're not going to suffer for my sake. You're not going to take on my guilt.

Helmer: No more play-acting. *(Locks the hall door.)* You stay right here and give me a reckoning. You understand what you've done? Answer! You understand?

Nora (looking squarely at him, her face hardening): Yes. I'm beginning to understand everything now.

Helmer (striding about): Oh, what an awful awakening! In all these eight years — she who was my pride and joy — a hypocrite, a liar — worse, worse — a criminal! How infinitely disgusting it all is! The shame! *(Nora says nothing and goes on looking straight at him. He stops in front of her.)* I should have suspected something of the kind. I should have known. All your father's flimsy values — Be still! All your father's flimsy values have come out in you. No religion, no morals, no sense of duty — Oh, how I'm punished for letting him off! I did it for your sake, and you repay me like this.

Nora: Yes, like this.

Helmer: Now you've wrecked all my happiness — ruined my whole future. Oh, it's awful to think of. I'm in a cheap little grafter's hands; he can do anything he wants with me, ask for anything, play with me like a puppet — and I can't breathe a word. I'll be swept down miserably into the depths on account of a featherbrained woman.

Nora: When I'm gone from this world, you'll be free.

Helmer: Oh, quit posing. Your father had a mess of those speeches too. What good would that ever do me if you were gone from this world, as you say? Not the slightest. He can still make the whole thing known; and if he does, I could be falsely suspected as your accomplice. They might even think that I was behind it — that I put you up to it. And all that I can thank you for — you that I've coddled the whole of our marriage. Can you see now what you've done to me?

Nora (icily calm): Yes.

Helmer: It's so incredible, I just can't grasp it. But we'll have to patch up whatever we can. Take off the shawl. I said, take if off! I've got to appease him somehow or other. The thing has to be hushed up at any cost. And as for you and me, it's got to seem like everything between us is just as it was — to the outside world, that is. You'll go right on living in this house, of course.

But you can't be allowed to bring up the children; I don't dare trust you with them—Oh, to have to say this to someone I've loved so much! Well, that's done with. From now on happiness doesn't matter; all that matters is saving the bits and pieces, the appearance—*(The doorbell rings. Helmer starts.)* What's that? And so late. Maybe the worst—? You think he'd—? Hide, Nora! Say you're sick. *(Nora remains standing motionless. Helmer goes and opens the door.)*

Maid (half dressed, in the hall): A letter for Mrs. Helmer.

Helmer: I'll take it. *(Snatches the letter and shuts the door.)* Yes, it's from him. You don't get it; I'm reading it myself.

Nora: Then read it.

Helmer (by the lamp): I hardly dare. We may be ruined, you and I. But—I've got to know. *(Rips open the letter, skims through a few lines, glances at an enclosure, then cries out joyfully.)* Nora! *(Nora looks inquiringly at him.)* Nora! Wait—better check it again—Yes, yes, it's true. I'm saved. Nora, I'm saved!

Nora: And I?

Helmer: You too, of course. We're both saved, both of us. Look. He's sent back your note. He says he's sorry and ashamed—that a happy development in his life—oh, who cares what he says! Nora, we're saved! No one can hurt you. Oh, Nora, Nora—but first, this ugliness all has to go. Let me see— *(Takes a look at the note.)* No, I don't want to see it; I want the whole thing to fade like a dream. *(Tears the note and both letters to pieces, throws them into the stove and watches them burn.)* There—now there's nothing left—He wrote that since Christmas Eve you—Oh, they must have been three terrible days for you, Nora.

Nora: I fought a hard fight.

Helmer: And suffered pain and saw no escape but—No, we're not going to dwell on anything unpleasant. We'll just be grateful and keep on repeating: it's over now, it's over! You hear me, Nora? You don't seem to realize—it's over. What's it mean—that frozen look? Oh, poor little Nora, I understand. You can't believe I've forgiven you. But I have, Nora; I swear I have. I know that what you did, you did out of love for me.

Nora: That's true.

Helmer: You loved me the way a wife ought to love her husband. It's simply the means that you couldn't judge. But you think I love you any the less for not knowing how to handle your affairs? No, no—just lean on me; I'll guide you and teach you. I wouldn't be a man if this feminine helplessness didn't make you twice as attractive to me. You mustn't mind those sharp words I said—that was all in the first confusion of thinking my world had collapsed. I've forgiven you, Nora; I swear I've forgiven you.

Nora: My thanks for your forgiveness. *(She goes out through the door, right.)*

Helmer: No, wait—*(Peers in.)* What are you doing in there?

Nora (inside): Getting out of my costume.

Helmer (by the open door): Yes, do that. Try to calm yourself and collect your thoughts again, my frightened little songbird. You can rest easy now; I've got wide wings to shelter you with. *(Walking about close by the door.)* How snug and nice our home is, Nora. You're safe here; I'll keep you like a hunted dove I've rescued out of a hawk's claws. I'll bring peace to your poor, shuddering heart. Gradually it'll happen, Nora; you'll see. Tomorrow all this will look different to you; then everything will be as it was. I won't have to go on repeating I forgive you; you'll feel it for yourself. How can you imagine I'd ever conceivably want to disown you — or even blame you in any way? Ah, you don't know a man's heart, Nora. For a man there's something indescribably sweet and satisfying in knowing he's forgiven his wife — and forgiven her out of a full and open heart. It's as if she belongs to him in two ways now: in a sense he's given her fresh into the world again, and she's become his wife and his child as well. From now on that's what you'll be to me — you little, bewildered, helpless thing. Don't be afraid of anything, Nora; just open your heart to me, and I'll be conscience and will to you both — *(Nora enters in her regular clothes.)* What's this? Not in bed? You've changed your dress?

Nora: Yes, Torvald, I've changed my dress.

Helmer: But why now, so late?

Nora: Tonight I'm not sleeping.

Helmer: But Nora dear —

Nora (looking at her watch): It's still not so very late. Sit down, Torvald; we have a lot to talk over. *(She sits at one side of the table.)*

Helmer: Nora — what is this? That hard expression —

Nora: Sit down. This'll take some time. I have a lot to say.

Helmer (sitting at the table directly opposite her): You worry me, Nora. And I don't understand you.

Nora: No, that's exactly it. You don't understand me. And I've never understood you either — until tonight. No, don't interrupt. You can just listen to what I say. We're closing out accounts, Torvald.

Helmer: How do you mean that?

Nora (after a short pause): Doesn't anything strike you about our sitting here like this?

Helmer: What's that?

Nora: We've been married now eight years. Doesn't it occur to you that this is the first time we two, you and I, man and wife, have ever talked seriously together?

Helmer: What do you mean — seriously?

Nora: In eight whole years — longer even — right from our first acquaintance, we've never exchanged a serious word on any serious thing.

Helmer: You mean I should constantly go and involve you in problems you couldn't possibly help me with?

Nora: I'm not talking of problems. I'm saying that we've never sat down seriously together and tried to get to the bottom of anything.

Helmer: But dearest, what good would that ever do you?

Nora: That's the point right there: you've never understood me. I've been wronged greatly, Torvald — first by Papa, and then by you.

Helmer: What! By us — the two people who've loved you more than anyone else?

Nora (shaking her head): You never loved me. You've thought it fun to be in love with me, that's all.

Helmer: Nora, what a thing to say!

Nora: Yes, it's true now, Torvald. When I lived at home with Papa, he told me all his opinions, so I had the same ones too; or if they were different I hid them, since he wouldn't have cared for that. He used to call me his doll-child, and he played with me the way I played with my dolls. Then I came into your house—

Helmer: How can you speak of our marriage like that?

Nora (unperturbed): I mean, then I went from Papa's hands into yours. You arranged everything to your own taste, and so I got the same taste as you—or I pretended to; I can't remember. I guess a little of both, first one, then the other. Now when I look back, it seems as if I'd lived here like a beggar—just from hand to mouth. I've lived by doing tricks for you, Torvald. But that's the way you wanted it. It's a great sin what you and Papa did to me. You're to blame that nothing's become of me.

Helmer: Nora, how unfair and ungrateful you are! Haven't you been happy here?

Nora: No, never. I thought so—but I never have.

Helmer: Not—not happy!

Nora: No, only lighthearted. And you've always been so kind to me. But our home's been nothing but a playpen. I've been your doll-wife here, just as at home I was Papa's doll-child. And in turn the children have been my dolls. I thought it was fun when you played with me, just as they thought it fun when I played with them. That's been our marriage, Torvald.

Helmer: There's some truth in what you're saying—under all the raving exaggeration. But it'll all be different after this. Playtime's over; now for the schooling.

Nora: Whose schooling—mine or the children's?

Helmer: Both yours and the children's, dearest.

Nora: Oh, Torvald, you're not the man to teach me to be a good wife to you.

Helmer: And you can say that?

Nora: And I—how am I equipped to bring up children?

Helmer: Nora!

Nora: Didn't you say a moment ago that that was no job to trust me with?

Helmer: In a flare of temper! Why fasten on that?

Nora: Yes, but you were so very right. I'm not up to the job. There's another job I have to do first. I have to try to educate myself. You can't help me with that. I've got to do it alone. And that's why I'm leaving you now.

Helmer (jumping up): What's that?

Nora: I have to stand completely alone, if I'm ever going to discover myself and the world out there. So I can't go on living with you.

Helmer: Nora, Nora!

Nora: I want to leave right away. Kristine should put me up for the night—

Helmer: You're insane! You've no right! I forbid you!

Nora: From here on, there's no use forbidding me anything. I'll take with me whatever is mine. I don't want a thing from you, either now or later.

Helmer: What kind of madness is this!

Nora: Tomorrow I'm going home—I mean, home where I came from. It'll be easier up there to find something to do.

Helmer: Oh, you blind, incompetent child!

Nora: I must learn to be competent, Torvald.

Helmer: Abandon your home, your husband, your children! And you're not even thinking what people will say.

Nora: I can't be concerned about that. I only know how essential this is.

Helmer: Oh, it's outrageous. So you'll run out like this on your most sacred
vows.

Nora: What do you think are my most sacred vows?

Helmer: And I have to tell you that! Aren't they your duties to your husband
and children?

Nora: I have other duties equally sacred.

Helmer: That isn't true. What duties are they?

Nora: Duties to myself.

Helmer: Before all else, you're a wife and mother.

Nora: I don't believe in that anymore. I believe that, before all else, I'm a
human being, no less than you — or anyway, I ought to try to become one.
I know the majority thinks you're right, Torvald, and plenty of books
agree with you, too. But I can't go on believing what the majority says, or
what's written in books. I have to think over these things myself and try to
understand them.

Helmer: Why can't you understand your place in your own home? On a point
like that, isn't there one everlasting guide you can turn to? Where's your
religion?

Nora: Oh, Torvald, I'm really not sure what religion is.

Helmer: What — ?

Nora: I only know what the minister said when I was confirmed. He told me
religion was this thing and that. When I get clear and away by myself, I'll
go into that problem too. I'll see if what the minister said was right, or, in
any case, if it's right for me.

Helmer: A young woman your age shouldn't talk like that. If religion can't
move you, I can try to rouse your conscience. You do have some moral feeling? Or, tell me — has that gone too?

Nora: It's not easy to answer that, Torvald. I simply don't know. I'm all confused about these things. I just know I see them so differently from you. I
find out, for one thing, that the law's not at all what I'd thought — but I
can't get it through my head that the law is fair. A woman hasn't a right to
protect her dying father or save her husband's life! I can't believe that.

Helmer: You talk like a child. You don't know anything of the world you live in.

Nora: No, I don't. But now I'll begin to learn for myself. I'll try to discover
who's right, the world or I.

Helmer: Nora, you're sick; you've got a fever. I almost think you're out of your
head.

Nora: I've never felt more clearheaded and sure in my life.

Helmer: And — clearheaded and sure — you're leaving your husband and children?

Nora: Yes.

Helmer: Then there's only one possible reason.

Nora: What?

Helmer: You no longer love me.

Nora: No. That's exactly it.

Helmer: Nora! You can't be serious!

Nora: Oh, this is so hard, Torvald — you've been so kind to me always. But I
can't help it. I don't love you anymore.

Helmer (struggling for composure): Are you also clearheaded and sure about that?

Nora: Yes, completely. That's why I can't go on staying here.

Helmer: Can you tell me what I did to lose your love?

Nora: Yes, I can tell you. It was this evening when the miraculous thing didn't come — then I knew you weren't the man I'd imagined.

Helmer: Be more explicit; I don't follow you.

Nora: I've waited now so patiently eight long years — for, my Lord, I know miracles don't come every day. Then this crisis broke over me, and such a certainty filled me: *now* the miraculous event would occur. While Krogstad's letter was lying out there, I never for an instant dreamed that you could give in to his terms. I was so utterly sure you'd say to him: go on, tell your tale to the whole wide world. And when he'd done that —

Helmer: Yes, what then? When I'd delivered my own wife into shame and disgrace —

Nora: When he'd done that, I was so utterly sure that you'd step forward, take the blame on yourself and say: I am the guilty one.

Helmer: Nora — !

Nora: You're thinking I'd never accept such a sacrifice from you? No, of course not. But what good would my protests be against you? That was the miracle I was waiting for, in terror and hope. And to stave that off, I would have taken my life.

Helmer: I'd gladly work for you day and night, Nora — and take on pain and deprivation. But there's no one who gives up honor for love.

Nora: Millions of women have done just that.

Helmer: Oh, you think and talk like a silly child.

Nora: Perhaps. But you neither think nor talk like the man I could join myself to. When your big fright was over — and it wasn't from any threat against me, only for what might damage you — when all the danger was past, for you it was just as if nothing had happened. I was exactly the same, your little lark, your doll, that you'd have to handle with double care now that I'd turned out so brittle and frail. *(Gets up.)* Torvald — in that instant it dawned on me that for eight years I've been living here with a stranger, and that I've even conceived three children — oh, I can't stand the thought of it! I could tear myself to bits.

Helmer (heavily): I see. There's a gulf that's opened between us — that's clear. Oh, but Nora, can't we bridge it somehow?

Nora: The way I am now, I'm no wife for you.

Helmer: I have the strength to make myself over.

Nora: Maybe — if your doll gets taken away.

Helmer: But to part! To part from you! No, Nora no — I can't imagine it.

Nora (going out, right): All the more reason why it has to be. *(She reenters with her coat and a small overnight bag, which she puts on a chair by the table.)*

Helmer: Nora, Nora, not now! Wait till tomorrow.

Nora: I can't spend the night in a strange man's room.

Helmer: But couldn't we live here like brother and sister —

Nora: You know very well how long that would last. *(Throws her shawl about her.)* Good-bye, Torvald. I won't look in on the children. I know they're in better hands than mine. The way I am now, I'm no use to them.

Helmer: But someday, Nora — someday — ?

Nora: How can I tell? I haven't the least idea what'll become of me.

Helmer: But you're my wife, now and wherever you go.

Nora: Listen, Torvald — I've heard that when a wife deserts her husband's house just as I'm doing, then the law frees him from all responsibility. In any case, I'm freeing you from being responsible. Don't feel yourself bound, any more than I will. There has to be absolute freedom for us both. Here, take your ring back. Give me mine.

Helmer: That too?

Nora: That too.

Helmer: There it is.

Nora: Good. Well, now it's all over. I'm putting the keys here. The maids know all about keeping up the house — better than I do. Tomorrow, after I've left town, Kristine will stop by to pack up everything that's mine from home. I'd like those things shipped up to me.

Helmer: Over! All over! Nora, won't you ever think about me?

Nora: I'm sure I'll think of you often, and about the children and the house here.

Helmer: May I write you?

Nora: No — never. You're not to do that.

Helmer: Oh, but let me send you —

Nora: Nothing. Nothing.

Helmer: Or help you if you need it.

Nora: No. I accept nothing from strangers.

Helmer: Nora — can I never be more than a stranger to you?

Nora (picking up her overnight bag): Ah, Torvald — it would take the greatest miracle of all —

Helmer: Tell me the greatest miracle!

Nora: You and I both would have to transform ourselves to the point that — Oh, Torvald, I've stopped believing in miracles.

Helmer: But I'll believe. Tell me! Transform ourselves to the point that — ?

Nora: That our living together could be a true marriage. *(She goes out down the hall.)*

Helmer (sinks down on a chair by the door, face buried in his hands): Nora! Nora! *(Looking about and rising.)* Empty. She's gone. *(A sudden hope leaps in him.)* The greatest miracle — ?

From below, the sound of a door slamming shut.

CONSIDERATIONS FOR CRITICAL THINKING AND WRITING

1. **FIRST RESPONSE.** What is the significance of the play's title?

2. Nora lies several times during the play. What kinds of lies are they? Do her lies indicate that she is not to be trusted, or are they a sign of something else about her personality?

3. What kind of wife does Helmer want Nora to be? He affectionately calls her names such as "lark" and "squirrel." What does this reveal about his attitude toward her?

4. Why is Nora "pale with terror" at the end of Act I? What is the significance of the description of the Christmas tree now "stripped of ornament, [with] burned-down candle stubs on its ragged branches" that opens Act II? What other symbols are used in the play?

5. What is Dr. Rank's purpose in the play?

6. How does the relationship between Krogstad and Mrs. Linde emphasize certain qualities in the Helmers' marriage?

7. Is Krogstad's decision not to expose Nora's secret convincing? Does his shift from villainy to generosity seem adequately motivated?

8. Why does Nora reject Helmer's efforts to smooth things over between them and start again? Do you have any sympathy for Helmer?

9. Would you describe the ending as essentially happy or unhappy? Is the play more like a comedy or a tragedy?

10. Ibsen believed that a "dramatist's business is not to answer questions, but only to ask them." What questions are raised in the play? Does Ibsen propose any specific answers?

11. What makes this play a work of realism? Are there any elements that seem not to be realistic?

12. **CRITICAL STRATEGIES.** Read the section on new historicist criticism (pp. 1546–47) in Chapter 46, "Critical Strategies for Reading," and consider the following: Ibsen once wrote a different ending for the play to head off producers who might have been tempted to change the final scene to placate the public's sense of morality. In the second conclusion, Helmer forces Nora to look in on their sleeping children. This causes her to realize that she cannot leave her family even though it means sacrificing herself. Ibsen called this version of the ending a "barbaric outrage" and didn't use it. How do you think the play reflects or refutes social values contemporary to it?

CONNECTIONS TO OTHER SELECTIONS

1. What does Nora have in common with the protagonist in Gail Godwin's "A Sorrowful Woman" (p. 39)? What significant differences are there between them?

2. Explain how Torvald's attitude toward Nora is similar to the men's attitudes toward women in Susan Glaspell's *Trifles* (p. 1048). Write an essay exploring how the assumptions the men make about women in both plays contribute to the plays' conflicts.

3. Write an essay that compares and contrasts Nora's response to the social and legal expectations of her society with that of Anna in Joyce Carol Oates's short story "The Lady with the Pet Dog" (p. 219). To what values does each character pledge her allegiance?

Perspective

HENRIK IBSEN (1828–1906)

Notes for A Doll House   1878

There are two kinds of spiritual law, two kinds of conscience, one in man and another, altogether different, in woman. They do not understand each other; but in practical life the woman is judged by man's law, as though she were not a woman but a man.

The wife in the play ends by having no idea of what is right or wrong; natural feeling on the one hand and belief in authority on the other have altogether bewildered her.

A woman cannot be herself in the society of the present day, which is an exclusively masculine society, with laws framed by men and with a judicial system that judges feminine conduct from a masculine point of view.

She has committed forgery, and she is proud of it; for she did it out of love for her husband, to save his life. But this husband with his commonplace principles of honor is on the side of the law and looks at the question from the masculine point of view.

Spiritual conflicts. Oppressed and bewildered by the belief in authority, she loses faith in her moral right and ability to bring up her children. Bitterness. A mother in modern society, like certain insects who go away and die when she has done her duty in the propagation of the race. Love of life, of home, of husband and children and family. Now and then a womanly shaking off of her thoughts. Sudden return of anxiety and terror. She must bear it all alone. The catastrophe approaches, inexorably, inevitably. Despair, conflict, and destruction.

From From Ibsen's Workshop, translated by A. G. Chater

CONSIDERATIONS FOR CRITICAL THINKING AND WRITING

1. Given the ending of *A Doll House*, what do you think of Ibsen's early view in his notes that "the wife in the play ends by having no idea of what is right or wrong" (para. 2)? Would you describe Nora as "altogether bewildered" (para. 2)? Why or why not?

2. "A woman cannot be herself in the society of the present day, which is an exclusively masculine society" (para. 3). Why is this statement true of Nora? Explain why you agree or disagree that this observation is accurate today.

3. How does oppressive "authority" (para. 5) loom large for Nora? What kind of authority creates "spiritual conflicts" for her?

More perspectives appear in the next chapter, "A Critical Case Study: Henrik Ibsen's *A Doll House,*" page 1308.

43

A CRITICAL CASE STUDY

Henrik Ibsen's
A Doll House

Spiritual conflicts. Oppressed and
bewildered by the belief in authority,
she loses faith in her moral right
and ability to bring up her children.
Bitterness . . . Now and then a
womanly shaking off of her thoughts.
Sudden return of anxiety and terror.
She must bear it all alone. The
catastrophe approaches, inexorably,
inevitably. Despair, conflict, and
destruction.

— HENRIK IBSEN, from his notes for
A Doll House

This chapter provides several critical approaches to Henrik Ibsen's *A Doll House,* which appears in Chapter 42, page 1257. There have been numerous critical approaches to this play because it raises so many issues relating to matters such as relationships between men and women, history, and biography, as well as imagery, symbolism, and irony. The following critical excerpts offer a small and partial sample of the possible biographical, historical, mythological, psychological, sociological, and other perspectives that have attempted to shed light on the play (see Chapter 46, "Critical Strategies for Reading," for a discussion of a variety of critical methods). They should help you to enjoy the play more by raising questions, providing insights, and inviting you to delve further into the text.

The following letter offers a revealing vignette of the historical contexts for *A Doll House.* Professor Richard Panofsky of the University of Massachusetts–Dartmouth has provided the letter and this background information: "The translated letter was written in 1844 by Marcus (1807–1865) to his wife Ulrike (1816–1888), after six children had been born. This upper-middle-class Jewish family lived in Hamburg, Germany, where Marcus was a doctor. As the letter implies, Ulrike had left home and children: the letter establishes conditions for her to return. A woman in upper-class society of the time had few choices in an unhappy marriage. Divorce or separation meant ostracism; as Marcus writes, 'your husband, children, and the entire city threaten indifference or even contempt.' And she could not take a job, as she would have no profession to step into. In any case, Ulrike did return home. Between 1846 and 1857 the marriage produced eight more children. Beyond what the letter shows, we do not know the reasons for the separation or what the later marriage relationship was like."

Perspectives

A Nineteenth-Century Husband's Letter to His Wife   1844

Dear Wife,   June 23, 1844
  You have sinned greatly—and maybe I too; but this much is certain: Adam sinned after Eve had already sinned. So it is with us; you, alone, carry the guilt of all the misfortune which, however, I helped to enlarge later by my behavior. Listen now, since I still believe certain things to be necessary in order that we may have a peaceful life. If we want not only to be content for a day but forever, you will have to follow my wishes. So examine yourself and determine if you are strong enough to conquer your false ambitions and your stubbornness to submit to all the conditions, the fulfillment of which I cannot ignore. Every sensible person will tell you that all I ask of you is what is easily understood. If you insist on remaining stubborn, then do not return to my house, for you will never be happy with me; your husband, children, and the entire city threaten indifference or even contempt.

  But if you decide to act *sensibly* and *correctly*, that is *justly* and *kindly*, then be certain that many in the world will envy you.

  I am including here the paper which I read to you in front of the rabbi; ask anyone in your residence if the wishes expressed by me are not quite reasonable, and are of a kind to which every wife can agree for the welfare of domestic happiness. In any case, act in a way you think best.

  When you decide to return, write to tell me on which day and hour you depart from Berlin and give me your itinerary whether by way of Kuestrin and Pinne or by way of Wollstein. I will then meet you at Wollstein or Pinne. I expect you will bring Solomon with you.

  Don't travel unprepared. If you need money, ask your father.

  May God enlighten your heart and mind

                                    I remain your so far unhappy,   [Marcus]

Greetings to my parents, brothers, and sisters; also your brother. Show them what you wish, this letter, the enclosure, whatever you want. The children are fortunately healthy.

If you want to return with joy and peace, write me by return mail. In that case, I would rather send you a carriage. Maybe Madam Fraenkel will come along. . . .

[Enclosure]

My wife promises — for which every wife is obligated to her husband — to follow my wishes in everything and to strictly obey my orders. It is already self-evident that our marital relations have often been disturbed by the fact that my wife does not follow my wishes but believes herself to be entitled to act on her own, even if this is totally against my orders. In order not to have to remind my wife every second what my wishes are regarding homemaking and public conduct — wishes which I have often expressed — I want to make here a few rules which shall serve as a code of conduct. A home is best run if the work for each hour is planned ahead of time, if possible.

Servants get up no later than 5:00 A.M. in summer and 6:00 A.M. in winter, the children an hour later. The cook prepares breakfast. The nursemaid puts out clothes for every child, prepares water and sponge, cleans the combs, etc. The cook should stay in the kitchen unless there is time to clean the rooms. At least once a week the rooms should be cleaned whenever possible, but not all on the same day.

Every Wednesday, the people in the house should do a laundry. Every last Wednesday in the month, there shall be a large laundry with an outside washerwoman. At least every Monday, the seamstress shall come into the house to fix what is necessary.

Every Thursday or Friday, bread is baked for the week; I think it is best to buy grain and have it ground, but to knead it at home.

Every Friday special bread (Barches) should be bought for the evening meal.

The kitchen list will be prepared and discussed every Thursday evening, jointly, by me and my wife; but my wish is to be decisive.

After this, provisions are to be bought every Friday at the market. For this purpose, my wife, herself, will go to the market on Fridays, accompanied by a servant; she can substitute a special woman who does errands (*Faktorfrau*) if she wishes, but not a servant.

All expenditures have to be written down daily and punctually.

The children receive a bath every Thursday evening. The children's clothes must be kept in a specially appointed chest, with a separate compartment for each child with the child's name upon it. The boys' suits and girls' dresses are to be kept separately. To keep used laundry, there must be a hamper easily accessible. Equally important is the food storage box in which provisions are kept in order, locked and safe from vermin.

The kitchen should be kept in order. Once a week all woodwork and copper must be scoured. The lights and lamps have to be cleaned daily. Toward servants, one has to be strict and just. Therefore, one should not call them names which aren't suitable for a decent wife. One should give them enough nourishing food. Disobedience and obstinacy are to be referred to me.

My wife will never make visits in my absence. However, she should visit the synagogue every Saturday — at least once a month; also she should go for a walk with the children at least once a week.

CONSIDERATIONS FOR CRITICAL THINKING AND WRITING

1. Describe the tone of Marcus's letter to his wife. To what extent does he accept responsibility for their separation? What significant similarities and differences do you find between Marcus and Torvald Helmer?

2. Read the discussion on historical criticism in Chapter 46, "Critical Strategies for Reading" (pp. 1544–48). How do you think a new historicist would use this letter to shed light on *A Doll House*?

3. Write a response to the letter from what you imagine the wife's point of view to be.

4. No information is available about this couple's marriage after Ulrike returned home. In an essay, speculate on what you think their relationship was like later in their marriage.

BARRY WITHAM (B. 1939) AND
JOHN LUTTERBIE (B. 1948)

Witham and Lutterbie describe how they use a Marxist approach to teach *A Doll House* in their drama class, in which they teach plays from a variety of critical perspectives.

A Marxist Approach to A Doll House   *1985*

A principal tenet of Marxist criticism is that human consciousness is a product of social conditions and that human relationships are often subverted by and through economic considerations. Mrs. Linde has sacrificed a genuine love to provide for her brothers, and Krogstad has committed a crime to support his children. Anne-Marie, the maid, has also been the victim of her economic background. Because she's "a girl who's poor and gotten in trouble," her relationship with her child has been interrupted and virtually destroyed. In each instance the need for money is linked with the ability to exist. But while the characters accept the social realities of their misfortunes, they do not appear to question how their human attitudes have been thoroughly shaped by socioeconomic considerations.

Once students begin to perceive how consciousness is affected by economics, a Marxist reading of Ibsen's play can illuminate a number of areas. Krogstad, for example, becomes less of a traditional villain when we realize that he is fighting for his job at the bank "as if it were life itself." And his realization of the senselessness of their lives is poignantly revealed when he reflects on Mrs. Linde's past, "all this simply for money." Even Dr. Rank speaks about his failing health and imminent death in entirely financial terms. "These past few days I've been auditing my internal accounts. Bankrupt! Within a month I'll probably be laid out and rotting in the churchyard."

All these characters, however, serve as foils for the central struggle between Nora and Torvald and highlight the pilgrimage that Nora makes in the play. At the outset two things are clear: (1) Nora is enslaved by Torvald in economic terms, and (2) she equates personal freedom with the acquisition of wealth. The play begins joyfully not only because it is the holiday season but also because Torvald's promotion to bank manager will ensure "a safe, secure job with a comfortable salary." Nora is happy because she sees the future in wholly economic terms. "Won't it be lovely to have stacks of money and not a care in the world?"

What she learns, however, is that financial enslavement is symptomatic of other forms of enslavement — master-slave, male-female, sexual objectification, all of which characterize her relationship with Torvald — and that money is no guarantee of happiness. At the end of the play she renounces not only her marital vows but also her financial dependence because she has discovered that personal and human freedom are not measured in economic terms.

This discovery also prompts her to reexamine the society of which she is a part and leads us into a consideration of the ideology in the play. In what sense has Nora committed a criminal offense in forging her father's name? Is it indeed just that she should be punished for an altruistic act, one that cost her dearly both in terms of self-denial and the destruction of her family? Ibsen's defense of Nora is clear, of course, and his implicit indictment of a society that encourages this kind of injustice stimulates a discussion of the assumptions that created the law.

One of the striking things about *A Doll House* is how Anne-Marie accepts her alienation from her child as if it were natural, given the circumstances of class and money. It does not occur to her that laws were framed by other people and thus are capable of imperfection and susceptible to change. Nora broke a law that not only tries to stop thievery (the appropriation of capital) by outlawing forgery but also discriminates against anyone deemed a bad risk. Question leads to question as the class investigates why women were bad risks and why they had difficulty finding employment. It becomes obvious that the function of women in this society was not "natural" but artificial, a role created by their relationship to the family and by their subservience to men. In the marketplace they were a labor force expecting subsistence wages and providing an income to supplement that earned by their husbands or fathers.

An even clearer picture of Nora's society emerges when the Marxist critic examines those features or elements that are not in the play. These "absences" become valuable clues in understanding the ideology in the text. In the words of Fredric Jameson, absences are

> terms or nodal points implicit in the ideological system which have, however, remained unrealized in the surface of the text, which have failed to become manifest in the logic of the narrative, and which we can therefore read as what the text represses.[1]

The notion of absences is particularly intriguing for students, who learn quickly to apply it to such popular media as films and television (what can we

---

[1] Fredric Jameson, *The Political Unconscious: Narrative as a Socially Symbolic Act* (Ithaca: Cornell UP, 1981), p. 48.

learn about the experience of urban black Americans from sitcoms like *Julia* and *The Jeffersons*?). Absent from *A Doll House* is Nora's mother, an omission that ties her more firmly to a male-dominated world and the bank owners who promoted Torvald. These absences shape our view because they form a layer of reality that is repressed in the play. And an examination of this "repressed" material leads us to our final topic of discussion: What is the relation between this play and the society in which it was created and produced?

Most Marxist critics believe that there are only three possible answers: the play supports the status quo, argues for reforms in an essentially sound system, or advocates a radical restructuring. Though these options are seemingly reductive, discussion reveals the complexities of reaching any unanimous agreement, and students frequently disagree about Ibsen's intentions regarding reform or revolution. Nora's leaving is obviously a call for change, but many students are not sure whether this leave-taking is a way forward or a cul-de-sac for a system that is thoroughly controlled by the prevailing power structure. . . .

Viewing the play through the lens of Marxist atheists does make one thing clear. Nora's departure had ramifications for her society that went beyond the marriage bed. By studying the play within the context of its socioeconomic structure, we can see how the ideology in the text affects the characters and how they perpetuate the ideology. The conclusion of *A Doll House* was a challenge to the economic superstructures that had controlled and excluded the Noras of the world by manipulating their economic status and, by extension, their conscious estimation of themselves and their place in society.

From "A Marxist Approach to *A Doll House*"
in *Approaches to Teaching Ibsen's* A Doll House

CONSIDERATIONS FOR CRITICAL THINKING AND WRITING

1. To what extent do you agree or disagree with the Marxist "tenet" (para. 1) that "consciousness is affected by economics" (2)?

2. Do you think that Nora's "leave-taking is a way forward or a cul-de-sac for a system that is thoroughly controlled by the prevailing power structure" (para. 8)? Explain your response.

3. Consider whether "A Nineteenth-Century Husband's Letter to His Wife" supports or challenges Witham and Lutterbie's Marxist reading of *A Doll House*.

CAROL STRONGIN TUFTS (B. 1947)

A Psychoanalytic Reading of Nora   1986

I am not a member of the Women's Rights League. Whatever I have written has been without any conscious thought of making propaganda. I have been more the poet and less the social philosopher than people generally seem inclined to believe. . . . To me it has seemed a problem of mankind in general. And if you read my books carefully you will understand this. . . . My task has been the *description of humanity*. To be sure, whenever such a description is felt to be reasonably true, the reader will read his own feelings and sentiments into the work of the poet. These are then attributed to the poet; but incorrectly so. Every reader remolds the work beautifully and neatly, each according to his own personality. Not only those who write but also those who read are poets. They are collaborators.[1]

To look again at Ibsen's famous and often-quoted words — his assertion that *A Doll House* was not intended as propaganda to promote the cause of women's rights — is to realize the sarcasm aimed by the playwright at those nineteenth-century "collaborators" who insisted on viewing his play as a treatise and Nora, his heroine, as the romantic standard-bearer for the feminist cause. Yet there is also a certain irony implicit in such a realization, for directors, actors, audiences, and critics turning to this play a little over one hundred years after its first performance bring with them the historical, cultural, and psychological experience which itself places them in the role of Ibsen's collaborators. Because it is a theatrical inevitability that each dramatic work which survives its time and place of first performance does so to be recast in productions mounted in succeeding times and different places, *A Doll House* can never so much be simply reproduced as it must always be re-envisioned. And if the spectacle of a woman walking out on her husband and children in order to fulfill her "duties to (her)self" is no longer the shock for us today that it was for audiences at the end of the nineteenth century, a production of *A Doll House* which resonates with as much immediacy and power for us as it did for its first audiences may do so through the discovery within Ibsen's text of something of our own time and place. For in *A Doll House,* as Rolf Fjelde has written, "(i)t is the entire house . . . which is on trial, the total complex of relationships, including husband, wife, children, servants, upstairs and downstairs, that is tested by the visitors that come and go, embodying aspects of the inescapable reality outside."[2] And a production which approaches that reality through the experience of Western culture in the last quarter of the twentieth century may not only discover how uneasy was Ibsen's relationship to certain aspects of the forces of Romanticism at work in his own society, but, in so doing, may also come to fashion *A Doll House* which shifts emphasis away from the celebration of the Romantic belief in the sovereignty of the individual to the revelation of an isolating narcissism — a narcissism that has become all too familiar to us today.[3]

The characters of *A Doll House* are, to be sure, not alone in dramatic literature in being self-preoccupied, for self-preoccupation is a quality shared by characters from Oedipus to Hamlet and on into modern drama. Yet if a con-

---

[1] Speech delivered at the Banquet of the Norwegian League for Women's Rights, Christiana, 26 May 1898, in *Ibsen: Letters and Speeches,* ed. Evert Sprinchorn (New York: Hill and Wang, 1964), p. 337.

[2] Rolf Fjelde, Introduction to *A Doll House,* in Henrik Ibsen, *The Complete Major Prose Plays* (New York: Farrar, Straus, Giroux, 1978), p. 121.

[3] For studies of the prevalence of the narcissistic personality disorder in contemporary psychoanalytic literature, see Otto F. Kernberg, *Borderline Conditions and Pathological Narcissism* (New York: J. Aronson, 1975); Heinz Kohut, *The Analysis of the Self* (New York: International Universities Press, 1971); and Peter L. Giovachinni, *Psychoanalysis of Character Disorders* (New York: J. Aronson, 1975). See also Christopher Lasch, *The Culture of Narcissism* (New York: Norton, 1979), for a discussion of narcissism as the defining characteristic of contemporary American society.

temporary production is to suggest the narcissistic self-absorption of Ibsen's characters, it must do so in such a way as to imply motivations for their actions and delineate their relationships with one another. Thus it is important to establish a conceptual framework which will provide a degree of precision for the use of the term "narcissism" in this discussion so as to distinguish it from the kind of self-absorption which is an inherent quality necessarily shared by all dramatic characters. For that purpose, it is useful to turn to the criteria established by the Task Force on Nomenclature and Statistics of the American Psychiatric Association for diagnosing the narcissistic personality:

A. Grandiose sense of self-importance and uniqueness, e.g., exaggerates achievements and talents, focuses on how special one's problems are.
B. Preoccupation with fantasies of unlimited success, power, brilliance, beauty, or ideal love.
C. Exhibitionistic: requires constant attention and admiration.
D. Responds to criticism, indifference of others, or defeat with either cool indifference, or with marked feelings of rage, inferiority, shame, humiliation, or emptiness.
E. At least two of the following are characteristics of disturbances in interpersonal relationships:
    1. Lack of empathy: inability to recognize how others feel, e.g., unable to appreciate the distress of someone who is seriously ill.
    2. Entitlement: expectation of special favors without assuming reciprocal responsibilities, e.g., surprise and anger that people won't do what he wants.
    3. Interpersonal exploitiveness: takes advantage of others to indulge own desires for self-aggrandizement, with disregard for the personal integrity and rights of others.
    4. Relationships characteristically vacillate between the extremes of over-idealization and devaluation.[4]

These criteria, as they provide a background against which to consider Nora's relationship with both Kristine Linde and Dr. Rank, will serve to illuminate not only those relationships themselves, but also the relationship of Nora and her husband which is at the center of the play. Moreover, if these criteria are viewed as outlines for characterization — but not as reductive psychoanalytic constructs leading to "case studies" — it becomes possible to discover a Nora of greater complexity than the totally sympathetic victim turned romantic heroine who has inhabited most productions of the play. And, most important of all, as Nora and her relationships within the walls of her "doll house" come to imply a paradigm of the dilemma of all human relationships in the greater society outside, the famous sound of the slamming door may come to resonate even more loudly for us than it did for the audiences of the nineteenth century with a profound and immediate sense of irony and ambiguity, an irony and ambiguity which could not have escaped Ibsen himself.

> From "Recasting *A Doll House:* Narcissism as Character Motivation in Ibsen's Play," *Comparative Drama*, Summer 1986

[4] Task Force on Nomenclature and Statistics, American Psychiatric Association, *DSM-III: Diagnostic Criteria Draft* (New York, 1978), pp. 103–04.

CONSIDERATIONS FOR CRITICAL THINKING AND WRITING

1. What is Tufts's purpose in arguing that Nora be seen as narcissistic?

2. Using the criteria of the American Psychiatric Association, consider Nora's personality. Write an essay either refuting the assertion that she has a narcissistic personality or supporting it.

3. How does Tufts's reading compare with Joan Templeton's feminist reading of Nora in the Perspective that follows? Which do you find more convincing? Why?

JOAN TEMPLETON (B. 1940)

This feminist perspective summarizes the arguments against reading the play as a dramatization of a feminist heroine.

Is A Doll House *a Feminist Text?*   *1989*

A Doll House *is no more about women's rights than Shakespeare's* Richard II *is about the divine right of kings, or* Ghosts *about syphilis. . . . Its theme is the need of every individual to find out the kind of person he or she is and to strive to become that person.*[1]

Ibsen has been resoundingly saved from feminism, or, as it was called in his day, "the woman question." His rescuers customarily cite a statement the dramatist made on 26 May 1898 at a seventieth-birthday banquet given in his honor by the Norwegian Women's Rights League:

> I thank you for the toast, but must disclaim the honor of having consciously worked for the women's rights movement. . . . True enough, it is desirable to solve the woman problem, along with all the others; but that has not been the whole purpose. My task has been the description of humanity.[2]

Ibsen's champions like to take this disavowal as a precise reference to his purpose in writing *A Doll House* twenty years earlier, his "original intention," according to Maurice Valency.[3] Ibsen's biographer Michael Meyer urges all reviewers of *A Doll House* revivals to learn Ibsen's speech by heart,[4] and James McFarlane, editor of *The Oxford Ibsen,* includes it in his explanatory material on *A Doll House,* under "Some Pronouncements of the Author," as though Ibsen had been speaking of the play.[5] Whatever propaganda feminists may have made of *A Doll House,* Ibsen, it is argued, never meant to write a play about the

---

[1] Michael Meyer, *Ibsen* (Garden City: Doubleday, 1971), 457. [This is not the Michael Meyer who is editor of *The Bedford Introduction to Literature.*]

[2] Henrik Ibsen, *Letters and Speeches,* ed. and trans. Evert Sprinchorn (New York: Hill, 1964), 337.

[3] Maurice Valency, *The Flower and the Castle: An Introduction to Modern Drama* (New York: Schocken, 1982), 151.

[4] Meyer, 774.

[5] James McFarlane, *"A Doll's House:* Commentary" in *The Oxford Ibsen,* ed. McFarlane (Oxford UP, 1961), V, 456.

highly topical subject of women's rights; Nora's conflict represents something other than, or something more than, woman's. In an article commemorating the half century of Ibsen's death, R. M. Adams explains, "*A Doll House* represents a woman imbued with the idea of becoming a person, but it proposes nothing categorical about women becoming people; in fact, its real theme has nothing to do with the sexes."[6] Over twenty years later, after feminism had resurfaced as an international movement, Einar Haugen, the doyen of American Scandinavian studies, insisted that "Ibsen's Nora is not just a woman arguing for female liberation; she is much more. She embodies the comedy as well as the tragedy of modern life."[7] In the Modern Language Association's *Approaches to Teaching* A Doll House, the editor speaks disparagingly of "reductionist views of *(A Doll House)* as a feminist drama." Summarizing a "major theme" in the volume as "the need for a broad view of the play and a condemnation of a static approach," she warns that discussions of the play's "connection with feminism" have value only if they are monitored, "properly channeled and kept firmly linked to Ibsen's text."[8]

Removing the woman question from *A Doll House* is presented as part of a corrective effort to free Ibsen from his erroneous reputation as a writer of thesis plays, a wrongheaded notion usually blamed on Shaw, who, it is claimed, mistakenly saw Ibsen as the nineteenth century's greatest iconoclast and offered that misreading to the public as *The Quintessence of Ibsenism*. Ibsen, it is now de rigueur to explain, did not stoop to "issues." He was a poet of the truth of the human soul. That Nora's exit from her dollhouse has long been the principal international symbol for women's issues, including many that far exceed the confines of her small world, is irrelevant to the essential meaning of *A Doll House,* a play, in Richard Gilman's phrase, "pitched beyond sexual difference."[9] Ibsen, explains Robert Brustein, "was completely indifferent to (the woman question) except as a metaphor for individual freedom."[10] Discussing the relation of *A Doll House* to feminism, Halvdan Koht, author of the definitive Norwegian Ibsen life, says in summary, "Little by little the topical controversy died away; what remained was the work of art, with its demand for truth in every human relation."[11]

Thus, it turns out, the *Uncle Tom's Cabin* of the women's rights movement is not really about women at all. "Fiddle-faddle," pronounced R. M. Adams, dismissing feminist claims for the play.[12] Like angels, Nora has no sex. Ibsen meant her to be Everyman.

From "The *Doll House* Backlash: Criticism, Feminism, and Ibsen,"
PMLA, January, 1989

[6] R. M. Adams, "The Fifty-First Anniversary," *Hudson Review* 10 (1957): 416.
[7] Einar Haugen, *Ibsen's Drama: Author to Audience* (Minneapolis: U of Minnesota P, 1979), vii.
[8] Yvonne Shafer, ed., *Approaches to Teaching Ibsen's* A Doll House (New York: MLA, 1985), 32.
[9] Richard Gilman, *The Making of Modern Drama* (New York: Farrar, 1972), 65.
[10] Robert Brustein, *The Theatre of Revolt* (New York: Little, 1962), 105.
[11] Halvdan Koht, *Life of Ibsen* (New York: Blom, 1971), 323.
[12] Adams, 416.

CONSIDERATIONS FOR CRITICAL THINKING AND WRITING

1. According to Templeton, what kinds of arguments are used to reject *A Doll House* as a feminist text?

2. From the tone of the summaries provided, what would you say is Templeton's attitude toward these arguments?

3. Read the section on feminist criticism in Chapter 46, "Critical Strategies for Reading" (pp. 1548–49), and write an essay addressing the summarized arguments as you think a feminist critic might respond.

Questions for Writing

APPLYING A CRITICAL STRATEGY

This section offers advice about developing an argument that draws on the different strategies, or schools of literary theory, covered in Chapter 46. The following list of questions and suggestions will help you to apply one or more of these critical strategies to a work in order to shed light on it. Following the questions is a sample paper based on *A Doll House* (p. 1257).

There are many possible lenses through which to read a literary work. The Perspectives, Complementary Critical Readings, and Critical Case Studies in this anthology suggest a variety of approaches — including formalist, biographical, psychological, Marxist, new historicist, feminist, mythological, reader-response, and deconstructionist strategies — that can be used to explore the effects, meanings, and significances of a poem, short story, or play (see Chapter 46 for a discussion of these strategies).

Once you have generated a central idea about a work, you will need to choose the critical approach(es) that will allow you to develop your argument. In the following sample paper, the writer chose a new historicist approach because she was interested in speculating about what Nora faced after she left her husband on the other side of the slammed door in *A Doll House*. By using evidence external to the play, from a letter written by a nineteenth-century husband to his wife, the writer was able to recreate some of the historical context for *A Doll House* in order to argue that Nora's leaving home is a more risky, problematic action than her simple declaration of freedom from her husband. This historical approach allowed the writer to offer a substantive argument about what Nora might have faced beyond the slammed door.

Regardless of the approach — or combination of approaches — you find helpful, it is essential that you be thoroughly familiar with the text of the literary work before examining it through the lens of a particular critical strategy. Without a strong familiarity with the literary work you will not be able to judge the accuracy and validity of a critic's arguments, and you might find your own insights immediately superseded by those of the first critic you read. For additional advice on how to incorporate material from critical essays into your writing without losing track of your own argument about a work, see Questions for Writing: Incorporating the Critics (p. 438).

Questions for Writing

1. Which of the critical strategies discussed in Chapter 46 seems the most appropriate to the literary work under consideration? Why do you prefer one particular approach over another? Do any critical strategies seem especially inappropriate? Why?

2. Does the historical context of a literary work suggest that certain critical strategies, such as Marxism or feminism, might be particularly productive?

3. Does the literary work reflect or challenge the cultural assumptions contemporary to it in such a way as to suggest a critical approach for your paper?

4. Does the author comment on his or her own literary work in letters, interviews, or lectures? If so, how might these comments help you to develop an approach for your paper?

5. Are you able to formulate an interpretation of the work you want to discuss before reading the critics extensively? If so, how might the critics' discussions help you to develop, enhance, or qualify your argument about how to interpret the work?

6. If you haven't developed an argument before reading the critics, how might some exploratory reading lead you into significant questions and controversial issues that would offer topics that could be developed into a thesis?

7. If you are drawing on the work of a number of critics, how are their critical strategies — whether formalist, biographical, psychological, historical, or other — relevant to your own? How can you use their insights to support your own argument?

8. Is it possible and desirable to combine approaches — such as psychological and historical or biographical and feminist — so that multiple perspectives can be used to support your argument?

9. If the strategies or approaches the critics use to interpret the literary work tend to be similar, are there questions and issues that have been neglected or ignored that can become the focus of your argument about the literary work?

10. If the critics' approaches are very different from one another, is there a way to use those differences to argue your own critical approach that allows you to support one critic rather than another or to resolve a controversy among the critics?

11. Is your argument adequately supported with specific evidence from the literary text? Have you been careful not to avoid discussing parts of the text that do not seem to support your argument?

12. Is your own discussion of the literary text free of simple plot summary? Does each paragraph include a thesis statement that advances your argument rather than merely consisting of facts and plot summary?

13. Have you accurately and fairly represented the critics' arguments?

14. Have you made your own contributions, qualifications, or disagreements with the critics clear to your reader?

A SAMPLE STUDENT PAPER

On the Other Side of the Slammed Door in Henrik Ibsen's A Doll House

The following sample paper focuses on the magnitude of Nora Helmer's decision to leave her husband in *A Doll House*. Kathy Atner uses a new historicist perspective to show just how difficult Nora's decision would have been in the context of nineteenth-century attitudes toward marriage and women. The paper develops an argument primarily from evidence supplied by "A Nineteenth-Century Husband's Letter to His Wife" (p. 1309). By drawing on a source that ordinarily might have been ignored by literary critics, Atner is able to suggest how difficult Nora's life would have been after abandoning her husband and family. This historical strategy is combined with a feminist perspective that gives the modern reader a greater understanding of the issues Nora must inevitably confront once she slams the door shut on her conventional and accepted life as devoted wife and mother. By using both new historicist and feminist perspectives, Atner suggests that contemporary readers should be sensitive to the tragic as well as the heroic dimension of Nora's life.

Atner 1

Kathy Atner

Professor Porter

English 216

April 6, 2008

On the Other Side of the Slammed Door

in Henrik Ibsen's A Doll House

Nora Helmer's decision to leave her family in Henrik Ibsen's 1879 play A Doll House reflects the dilemma faced by many nineteenth-century women who were forced either to conform to highly restrictive gender roles or to abandon these roles in order to realize their value as individuals. Although Ibsen brings his audience to the moment that Nora chooses to disregard her social role and opt for her "freedom," his play does not clearly reveal the true fate of women who followed Nora's path in the nineteenth century. Historically, most women who chose not to acquiesce to the socially prescribed roles of marriage were treated as unnatural creatures and shunned by the respectable public. An actual letter, written in 1844 by a man named Marcus

[margin note:] Thesis placing play in historical context

to his estranged wife, Ulrike, reveals the effects of this severe social condemnation (1309). His letter implies the desperate fate that inevitably befalls women who reject their prescribed duties as wives and mothers. Through Marcus's letter to his wife, the painful ramifications of Nora's decision to accommodate her own personal desires instead of those of her family become even more poignant, courageous, and tragic.

Argument supported by a historical document (letter to Ulrike)

In the nineteenth century, women had few alternatives to marriage, and women who "failed" at marriage were thought to have failed in their most important duty. In his letter, Marcus articulates society's deep disgust for women who reject what it believes is the sacred female role of homemaker. His letter, while on one level an angry condemnation of his wife's "stubbornness" (1309) and a cruelly condescending list of conditions to be met on her return, is on another level a plea for her to accept again the role that society has assigned her. He is clearly shaken by his wife's abandonment and interprets it as a betrayal of a social "law" or tradition, which, to Marcus's mind, ought to be carved in stone. He responds to this betrayal by demanding complete obedience from his wife in the form of a promise "to follow my wishes in everything and to strictly obey my orders" (1310). Only when she acquiesces to his conditions and returns to her role as docile and obedient wife will Marcus in turn be able to resume the comfortably familiar, socially sanctioned role of dominant, morally superior husband.

Analysis of historical document

Like Ulrike, Nora decides to leave the security and comfort of her restrictive domestic life to try to become a human being. Ibsen neglects, however, to show his audience the actual result of that decision. At the conclusion of A Doll House, Nora slams the door on her past life, hoping to begin a new life that will somehow be more satisfying. Yet the modern audience has no genuine sense of what she may have found beyond that door, and perhaps neither did Nora. Through Ulrike's story, however, the reader understands the historical truth that the world awaiting Nora was hostile and unsympathetic. Marcus warns his wife that "your husband, children, and the entire city threaten indifference or even contempt" (1309) if she refuses to return immediately to her socially acceptable domestic role. This pressure to conform, combined with the bleak prospects of a single woman, results in Ulrike's ultimate choice to keep up "appearances" rather than further subject

Discussion of Nora's plight in relation to that of Ulrike

herself to a contemptuous world that neither wants nor understands her. Although we cannot know Nora's fate after she leaves Torvald, we may assume that her future would be as bleak as Ulrike's and that the pressure to return to her domestic life would be equally strong.

When A Doll House was first produced in 1879, audiences had no more sympathy for Nora's predicament than they did for the real-life stories of women such as Ulrike. As Errol Durbach points out, in the nineteenth century, Ibsen's play "did not precipitate heated debate about feminism, women's rights, or male domination. The sound and the fury were addressed to the very question . . . What credible wife and mother would ever walk out this way on her family?" (14). A great many readers and audience members tended to side with Torvald, who seemed, to them, the innocent victim of Nora's consuming selfishness. The audience's repulsion toward Nora's apparently "unnatural" action of abandoning her family mirrors the responses of Marcus and Torvald Helmer, the bereft, perplexed, and angry husbands. Nora and Ulrike radically disrupt their husbands' perceptions of family relationships by walking out of their lives, preferring to recognize their own needs before any others. These women suggest that Torvald's claim that "Before all else, you're a wife and mother" (Ibsen 1303) may not necessarily be true for all women, but their brave rejections of domestic life cannot force society to condone their behavior.

Ibsen maintains that A Doll House is not about women's rights specifically but encompasses a more universal "description of humanity" (Letters 337). In showing a human being trying to create a new identity for herself, however, Ibsen reveals the extent to which people are trapped in societal norms and expectations. Nora's acknowledgment that she "can't go on believing what the majority says, or what's written in books" (1303) suggests a profound social upheaval that has the potential to subvert long-established gender roles. If Nora and Ulrike relinquish the role of the subservient and helpless wife, then Torvald and Marcus can no longer play the role of the dominating, protective husband. Without this role, the men are as helpless as they want their wives to be, and the traditional gender expectations are no longer beyond question. Yet the historical reality is that in spite of Nora's daring escape from her oppressive family, the world was not ready to

Analysis of status of women and audience of the 19th century

Analysis of play in context of 19th century reality

Atner 4

accommodate women who rejected their feminine duties. Ulrike was thwarted in her attempt to free herself from her family; history suggests that Nora may have met a similar fate.

Modern audiences tend to see Nora as a strong, admirable woman who is courageous enough to sacrifice everything in order to fulfill her own needs as an individual and as a woman. She shatters gender stereotypes through her defiant disregard for all that society demands of her. Yet, taken in the context of nineteenth-century life, perhaps Nora's story is more tragic than we might initially like to believe. Ulrike's story, told through her husband's letter, suggests that in a time of turbulent social upheaval, what was interpreted as a collapse of what we now call "family values" was shocking, scandalous, and deeply frightening to many. In the nineteenth century, Nora was not the sympathetic character that she is today; instead, she symbolized many negative attributes--what Marcus calls "false ambitions" and "stubbornness" (1309)--that were often ascribed to women. Ulrike's forced return to her role as dutiful wife and mother suggests that society was quick to punish disobedient women and that the slamming door at the end of A Doll House was not necessarily the sound of freedom for Nora.

> Concluding historical analysis of play as tragedy

Atner 5

Works Cited

Durbach, Errol. A Doll's House: Ibsen's Myth of Transformation. Boston: Twayne, 1991. 14.

Ibsen, Henrik. A Doll House. Trans. Rolf Fjelde. Meyer 1257–1305.

---. Letters and Speeches. Ed. and trans. Evert Sprinchorn. New York: Hill, 1964. 337.

Meyer, Michael, ed. The Compact Bedford Introduction to Literature. 8th ed. Boston: Bedford/St. Martin's, 2009.

"A Nineteenth-Century Husband's Letter to His Wife." The Compact Bedford Introduction to Literature. Ed. Michael Meyer. 8th ed. Boston: Bedford/St. Martin's, 2009. 1309–11.

SUGGESTED TOPICS FOR LONGER PAPERS

1. In an essay, discuss whether you think *A Doll House* challenges or affirms the social order it describes. Pay particular attention to the ending of the play by providing a close reading of it.

2. Research marriage laws in the United States for the late nineteenth century. To what extent is Ibsen's 1879 Norwegian play relevant to American laws and attitudes toward marriage? Do you think any significant changes would have had to be made if the play had been set in the United States rather than Norway? Explain why or why not.

44

A THEMATIC CASE STUDY

An Album of Contemporary Humor and Satire

Why ruin a good story with the truth?
— Woody Allen

In contrast to the darkness and suffering that surrounds, for example, Othello's tragedy, comedy typically works out in the end: the hero triumphs; a sense of renewal flourishes; life is better, yielding to human hopes and aspirations; the implausible is happily possible and characters find freedom, acceptance, and love. Life in a comedy is, as Shakespeare would have it, a midsummer night's dream. Comedy does not mean, however, that there isn't trouble along the way. Humor in comedy can embody anger, criticism, and indignation in its response to life's absurdities and pretentiousness. Toothy wide grins can also produce biting satire.

This satiric perspective is also brought into focus in John Leguizamo's monologue skit from *Mambo Mouth* (p. 1349), in which an illegal Mexican immigrant hilariously rails against American immigration laws while simultaneously presenting a serious indictment of the system. In Jane Anderson's *The Reprimand* (p. 1344), a short play in which humor serves as a corrective, two women engage in a strained phone conversation over an offhanded remark about one's body weight. Their subsequent dialogue is spiced with acid reflux and carefully measured pretenses that leave a bad aftertaste. These satiric plays make moral, social, and political points through humor, but they do not harangue or lecture audiences. There are no seats available for the presumptuous and the pretentious in comedy's theater.

Comedy is sometimes associated with another kind of bad taste. The essential differences between comedy and tragedy can be clearly discerned in the plot, characters, and themes of two works like *Mambo Mouth* and *Othello*, but there are also important differences in style. James Kincaid neatly summarizes a crucial difference in an essay titled "Who Is Relieved by the Idea of Comic Relief?" He shrewdly distinguishes between them: "Tragedy is sleek and single-minded, comedy rumpled and hospitable to any idea or agency. Tragedy stares us out of countenance; comedy winks and leers and drools. Tragedy is all dressed up; comedy is always taking things off, mooning us." Kincaid deftly puts his finger on the unruly nature of comedy without pointing his finger at it. Comedy celebrates the messy, untidy, confused disarrangements that life presents to us. "[I]f life is anything," as Woody Allen puts it in *Old Saybrook* (p. 1327), "it's silly. . . . The philosophers call it absurd, but what they really mean is silly." Allen even makes fun of playwriting in his play, as does Rich Orloff's *Playwriting 101: The Rooftop Lesson* (p. 1352). This is not to say that satirizing one's own satire renders everything meaningless but rather to acknowledge that everything is fair game for comedy. As you'll see, even tragedy is figuratively mooned by comedy in David Ives's *Moby-Dude Or: The Three-Minute Whale* (p. 1346). Bon voyage.

Old Saybrook

Woody Allen was born Allen Stewart Konigsberg in Brooklyn, New York, and attended New York University and the City College of New York, but he did not graduate from either school. Even so, he was a serious student and practitioner of comedy, eventually becoming successful as a writer, actor, comedian, director, and musician. By the age of seventeen, he became a staff writer for major NBC television comedies including the *Sid Caesar Show*. In 1964 he wrote his first screenplay, *What's New Pussycat*, which marked the beginning of a series of more than two dozen popular films that include *Take the Money and Run* (1969), *Bananas* (1971), *Everything You Always Wanted to Know About Sex . . .* (1972), *Sleeper* (1973), *Annie Hall* (1977), *Manhattan* (1979), *Zelig* (1983), *Radio Days* (1987), *Bullets Over Broadway* (1999),

By permission of Waring Abbot/Alamy.

Small Time Crooks (2000), and *Match Point* (2005). Allen has also written plays produced on and off Broadway and published several books of humor: *Getting Even* (1971), *Without Feathers* (1975), *Side Effects* (1980), and *The Complete Prose of Woody Allen* (1991). *Old Saybrook* is reprinted from Allen's *Three One-Act Plays* (2004) and was grouped with another play in that collection under the rubric of "Writer's Block." The characters in *Old Saybrook* are in some ways typical of Allen's affluent, sophisticated characters who comically struggle to achieve happiness in a world that makes them neurotic, off-balance, and desperate for a laugh. Perhaps this sensibility is best encapsulated in one of Allen's famous one-liners: "I'm not afraid of dying . . . I just don't want to be there when it happens."

WOODY ALLEN (B. 1935)

Old Saybrook

2003

Curtain rises on a country home in Connecticut. A combination of American antiques and contemporary furnishings — perhaps a large stone fireplace — a staircase leading upstairs. Sheila and Norman, who live there, are hosting a barbecue out in the back. Sheila's sister, Jenny, and her husband, David, are the only guests. Sound of geese honking.

See Plays in Performance insert.

Jenny, Sheila and Norman are fixing and/or refilling drinks while they make small talk prior to going out back to cook.

Sheila (looks out window and says wistfully): Look, Norman, the geese are back.
Norman: Spoken like the tragic heroine of a Russian play.
Jenny: I hate Russian plays. Nothing happens and they charge the same price as a musical.
Sheila: To think that each year when the geese migrate south they pick our little pond to lay over at for a few days.
Norman: I told you Old Saybrook is becoming the in place.
David: What do the geese tell us about the inscrutable magnificence of nature?
Sheila: What?
David: That one day we all must grow old and decay. That's the message in all of nature.
Jenny: That's easy for him to say, he's a plastic surgeon and that message is on his business card.
Sheila: Your wife got you, David.
David (toasts): To the geese.
Jenny: Not the geese — to Norman and Sheila. Happy seventh anniversary.
Norman: Some of the happiest years of my life. Maybe two of them. Just joking.
Sheila: Freud said there are no jokes.
Norman (toasts): To Sigmund Freud — the poet of penis envy.

David: And now, if you'll all excuse me, I'm going into the den to watch Tiger Woods — please don't disturb me until the steaks come off the barbecue.

(Exits to den.)

Jenny (exiting, to Sheila): I'll make more ice — it's one of the only things I learned in cooking school.

David (returning): Where are the pistachio nuts?

Sheila: I don't know . . .

David: I can't watch golf without pistachio nuts.

Sheila: David.

David: They must be red — red, salted pistachio nuts.

Sheila (exiting to kitchen): I have cashews —

David: Cashews are basketball. Pistachios are golf.

Norman: David, just get out. *(David exits into den.)* I figured out what the geese symbolize. They symbolize impending disaster — the honking is a mating call and a mating call always spells trouble.

(Bell rings.)

Norman (calls out): Sheila, are you expecting anyone?

Sheila (returning to room): No. *They open the door and a comparable couple, Hal and Sandy Maxwell, stand there.)* Yes?

Hal: Hello — I hope we're not disturbing you.

Sandy (a bit embarrassed): This is silly, Hal.

Hal: I'm Hal Maxwell and this is my wife, Sandy. We were driving by and we don't want to intrude, but we used to live here.

Sheila: Really?

Sandy: Yes — for nine years — we sold the place to a Mr. Krolian.

Hal: Max Krolian, a fairly well-known writer.

Norman: Sure — well, we've been here for about three years now. Norman Pollack — Sheila's my wife. Please — come in.

Sandy: We don't want to bother you. We've moved to New Jersey and we happened to be up here for one day antiquing and we were so close.

Sheila: Please — come in. Have a look around. Feel free.

Norman: So you used to live here?

Sheila: Can we offer you a drink?

Hal: Oh God — I would love one.

Sandy: You have to drive.

(They have entered in deeper and look around.)

Sheila: How does it look?

Hal: It brings back such memories.

Norman: What would you like?

Hal: What I would *like* is a single malt scotch but I will drink anything.

Norman: And you?

Sandy: Oh, just a tiny bit of white wine if you have it.

Norman: We have no white but our martinis are colorless.

(Sandy laughs at Norman's joke.)

Hal (at window): Whose idea was it to put in a swimming pool?

Norman: We did that.

Hal: What shape is it?

Norman: Amoeba — an amoeba . . . it's an amoeba-shaped pool.
Hal: Those little germs . . .
Sandy: Hal —

   (Jenny enters.)

Sheila: Oh — Jenny — these are —
Hal: The Maxwells.
Sheila: They used to live here.
Sandy: We just wanted to see the place again — we were married here.
Jenny: Oh — how sweet.
Hal: In that garden. Under a maple tree — now it's gone, there's a pool.
Sheila: You hungry?
Sandy: No —
Hal: What are you telling them no, we're starved.
Norman: Well then, join us — we're barbecuing some steaks.
Sandy: No, we couldn't.
Hal: Er — medium rare.
David (emerges from den momentarily): Who came in? I heard the bell ring just
   as Tiger was about to putt. I think the noise made him miss.
Jenny: My husband — David, this is —
Hal: Hal and Sandy Maxwell — we used to live here.
David: Oh really? Where did you put the pistachio nuts?
Jenny: David, they got married here.
David: Oh great. Do you play golf?
Hal: No.
David: Um, terrific. We must play sometime.
Jenny: In the winter it's the Knicks, in the summer it's golf — talk about
   Freud — he loves to watch young men put balls in holes.

   (She goes.)

Hal: Hey — what happened to the beautiful floor that was here?
Norman: Oh, er — we redid it.
Hal: Redid the random planking? Why?
Norman: We wanted something smoother.
Sandy (with a look to her husband): It's lovely —
Hal: This floor is the first spot we made love on —
Sandy: Hal —
Hal: — right here — where the coffee table is. It was smooth enough for us.
Sandy: Hal —
Sheila: Er — that's very romantic.
Hal: I think so. Sandy gets shy. It was a memorable moment. Particularly since
   we were both married to different people at the time.
Sandy: Hal!
Sheila: Oh goodness.
Hal: Don't get the wrong impression. We were drunk, here alone, there was an
   electrical storm, all the lights went out — suddenly the room was illumi-
   nated by a flash of lightning and I saw Sandy, her lips full, her hair wild
   from the intense humidity — she beckoned me to her with the ever increasing promise of sexual adventure.
Sheila: What do you do, Mr. Maxwell?

Hal: Hal. I'm an accountant. See — her face fell.

Sheila: What?

Hal: You figured me for a poet, right? I don't seem the type to be crunching numbers for a business firm — do I?

Sheila: I don't know — accountants can be poetic. You should see some of our tax returns.

Hal: I feel there's more in me but I just don't have the courage.

Sandy: Hal would like to write the great American novel.

Hal: Play, Sandy, play — not novel. Although I have written a few poems about the dangers of cholesterol. Sonnets.

Sandy: Did you know Mr. Krolian, the former owner?

Norman: Only by reputation.

Hal: I met him once when we sold the place. I tried to talk to him — he was a difficult man to communicate with — but a very clever writer.

Norman: Excuse me. I better go help her sister, Jenny — whenever she tries to light the barbecue we wind up on the six o'clock news.

(He goes.)

Sandy: What does your husband do, Mrs. —

Sheila: Sheila — he's a dentist.

Hal: Hey, that's almost as bad as me — ooh — well, I mean — er — what does your sister do? Is she a model?

Sheila: Jenny has a lingerie shop in Manhattan, and her husband streamlines rear ends and I don't mean automotive work. He's a plastic surgeon.

(Sandy laughs at Sheila's joke.)

Sandy (looking out window): The birdhouse is still up.

Hal: I designed and built that birdhouse myself.

Sandy: Based on the Guggenheim.

Hal: Hey — do you know about the secret vault?

Sheila: No.

Hal: Yes, we wouldn't have known except we were told by the original owner who built the house, Mr. Warner. He made a hidden safe behind the fireplace.

Sheila: No.

Hal: Yes — he did —

Sandy: Show her.

Hal: Here, it's right behind here, but you have to know where the hidden latch is. *(Fiddling.)*

Sandy: It's the top one and you pull the lever . . .

Hal: Here it — I got it — here you go . . .

Sheila (watches it open): My God, you learn something new every day —

Hal: I can't believe you didn't know about it.

Sheila: I had no idea! I lean on that mantel all the time — I never dreamed — a hidden safe — what's this?

Sandy: What is that?

Sheila (removes an old notebook — reads aloud): I want to treasure these moments because they are the most passionate I've known. *(looks up)* Hmm. What is this? *(thumbs diary — reads)* Her quivering breasts under my hands caused us both to breathe heavy —

Hal: What'd you find there?

Sheila (reads): Chronicle of my love affair with Sheila's sister, Jenny, by Norman Pollack —

(Sheila looks up.)

Hal: Norman Pollack — that's her husband.

Sandy: Well, it was nice meeting you . . .

Sheila: Norman, can you come into the living room for a minute?

Sandy: We'll just let ourselves out . . .

Norman (returning): Did you say something, sweetheart?

Sheila: You miserable duplicitous son of a bitch.

Norman: Pardon me? *(Realizes she's found something.)*

Sandy: We love what you've done with the place —

Sheila: This is yours.

Norman: What are you talking about?

Hal: She found your diary. You're in tremendous trouble.

Norman: My what? You must be kidding.

Sheila: It's your name.

Norman: Oh Jesus, Sheila. There must be a hundred Norman Pollacks in the phone book.

Sheila: This is your handwriting.

Norman: Lots of people dot their *i*'s with little circles.

Sheila: There's a snapshot of you and Jenny with your hands on her breasts.

Norman: That's the only real piece of evidence you have.

Sheila (reads from diary): I can no longer suppress the torrid feelings I have for Sheila's sister. Making love with Jenny is an ecstasy I have never experienced with anyone else.

Sandy: If you're ever in Nutley . . .

Norman: How did you find it?

Hal: When we bought the place I knew about the safe.

Sandy: Shut up, Hal.

Norman: *You* told her about it?

Hal: How did I know you were knocking off Jenny?

Norman: Now, Sheila, before you jump to any conclusions . . .

Hal: Norman, you don't get it — this is the smoking gun.

Sandy: Will you shut up, Hal?

Sheila (reads from diary): I secretly slid my hand under her skirt as the four of us sat on the lawn at Tanglewood under the moonlight. For a moment I thought Sheila noticed —

Hal: Does it say what else happens?

Norman: Would you stay out of this!?

Sheila: Today Jenny pretended she was a little girl and I slapped her rear end. She found it very erotic and we made love.

Hal: If I could just see the diary for a minute.

Sandy: Hal, butt out.

Jenny (enters): Norman — I accidentally let the fire go out in the barbecue.

Sheila: Oh, "I accidentally let the fire go out in the barbecue"? Well, aren't you a bad little girl. Norman's going to have to give you another spanking.

Jenny (doesn't get it): What?

Norman: She found my diary.

Jenny: Your what?

Sheila (reading): Today Jenny and I met at her place and made love in the same bed she shares with David.

Jenny: You keep a diary?

Norman: It was completely hidden. Till he told her where to find it.

Hal: How was I to know you were banging him? I innocently showed her the safe.

Jenny: Why in hell would you keep a diary?

Hal: They're very useful for tax purposes.

Sandy: Well — I'm sure you'll work things out — now, if you'll excuse —

Sheila: Like hell — you stay right here — you're witnesses.

Hal: Witnesses? Is something gonna happen where you need witnesses?

Sheila: How long have you two been cheating?

Norman: I'd hardly call a few rendezvous cheating.

Sheila (looking in diary): According to this you had sexual relations four times on President's Day alone.

Norman: Well, yes, because Washington and Lincoln's birthdays are celebrated together.

Hal: I don't see what the big deal is here. Everybody in suburbia cheats.

Sandy: They do?

Sheila (reading diary): Where did you learn those positions?

Jenny: Pilates.

Hal (laughing at her joke too hard): Did you hear that —

Sandy: I heard her, I heard her. We lived in suburbia — right here in fact — I hope you didn't cheat, because I didn't.

Hal: Of course I wouldn't.

Sandy: Then why would you say something like that?

Hal: I was generalizing.

Sandy: Never with Holly?

Hal: Holly Fox? Gimme a break. Because she was an actress?

Sandy: Exactly — because you always insisted she wasn't so beautiful, but on several occasions you said her name in your sleep.

Hal: You're projecting because you always had a little crush on her brother.

Sandy: Believe me, if I wanted Ken Fox I would have had no problem.

Hal: Meaning what?

Sandy: Meaning he hit on me once a week for a year but I fended him off.

Hal: Well, this is the first I'm hearing about that.

Sheila: How long have you two been having this tempestuous affair?

Norman (simultaneously with Jenny): Not long.

Jenny: Three years.

Norman: Six months.

Jenny: A year.

Norman: And a half.

Jenny: Not long.

Norman: There was a lot of downtime.

Sheila: How could you do it, you're my sister!

Jenny: What can I say, we fell in love.

Norman: It wasn't love, it was pure sex.

Jenny: You said it was love.

Norman: I never actually used that word — I said I "care" for you — I "miss" you — I "need" you — I "can't live without you" — but not love.

Sheila: All this time you've been sharing my bed you've been sleeping with Jenny.

Norman: Can I help it if she seduced me?

Jenny: I seduced you?

Norman: Three years ago I walked into her lingerie shop — to buy you a present — I found something that looked nice — I asked if it would fit you — she said she was about your size, she'd try it on — I could see it — we both went into the changing booth — she slipped into it —

Hal: Into what?

Norman: A thong — she was wearing a thong.

Sandy (to Hal): Will you butt out.

Hal: I'm trying to follow the narrative.

Sandy: You find her attractive, don't you?

Sheila: You too?

Hal: What?

Sandy: I heard you ask Sheila if her sister was a model — and you've been champing at the bit to get your hands on that diary.

Hal: Can I help it if I'm an inadvertent participant in this all-too-human drama?

Sheila (handing him diary): Here — you appreciate literature —

Hal: I really don't — *(Has accepted diary and becomes riveted by it.)*

Sandy: Oh go ahead, Hal, take it. I'm sure you'll find the details of her sexual activities gratifying.

Hal (leafing through book): Well, maybe to — uh — uh —

Sandy: Let's say to a live male under ninety.

Hal: Gee, Sandy, I only wish you were half as adventurous as she is.

Sandy: Over my dead body.

Hal: I'm not discussing our sex life.

Sandy: I'm sorry if I disappoint you.

Hal: Look, we've been through it . . . I'm only saying, if you were willing to experiment once in a while . . .

Sandy: If by experimenting you mean a threesome with Holly Fox.

Hal: Well, what is your idea of an experiment?

Sandy: I don't think about experimenting. We're making love, not working on a science grant.

Sheila: You always read about those perverted dentists who have sex with their unconscious patients during root canal.

Norman: I'm not a perverted dentist. I'm a perverted orthodontist — you never got that straight. Look, I take full responsibility. If you have to blame someone, blame me.

Sheila: Who the hell do you think I'm blaming?

David (emerges from den): Tiger Woods just bogeyed a hole.

Hal: So did Norman.

David: It's very exciting.

Sheila: Join us, David, we have something to show you.

David: Can't it wait?

Sheila: I don't know, it's very hot.

Jenny: Stop being so vicious.

Sheila: Come sit with me for a moment, David.

Hal: Quick, Sandy — do you have our camcorder?

Sandy: It's in the car.

Sheila: Read this diary, David — see if you recognize any of the protagonists.

David (taking diary):   What is this? Tiger Woods is going to set a record.

Norman: Let the man enjoy his golf. This doesn't concern him.

Hal: Oh, Norman — he's bound to have some marginal interest. *(David reads.)*

Sheila: What do you think, David — recognize the lead characters?

Hal: Of course he does.

David: The people?

Sheila: Yes, the married woman called Jenny and the dentist.

David: The married woman, Jenny? Where would I recognize her from?

Sheila: Try breakfast.

David: What is this, some silly piece of porn? Why should I read it, I'm watch-
        ing the U.S. Open.

Sheila: You're married to the U.S. Open.

Norman: Jenny —

Sheila: Norman!

Norman: Sheila.

David: What? What am I missing?

Hal: Can I give him a hint?

Sandy: Will you keep out.

Hal: I can't believe he can't get it.

Sheila: You find it a coincidence the man's name is Norman and the woman's
        is Jenny?

David: No — why?

Sheila: Your wife's name is Jenny, my husband's name is Norman.

David: So?

Sandy: This guy's a doctor?

Sheila: You recognize the two people in this photo?

Norman: Sheila —

Hal: I've heard of denial —

David: Yes — that's your husband with some woman.

Sheila: Uh-huh — you see Norman's tongue?

David: Yes.

Sheila: Where is it?

David: In his mouth.

Sheila: The other end.

David: In this woman's ear.

Sheila: And his hands?

David (studies photo):   Hmmm — Norman, is this some new dental procedure?

Sheila: And you don't recognize the woman?

David: She's definitely familiar.

Sheila: Shall I give you a clue?

Jenny: I can't stand this.

Sheila: Remember how years ago you met a young woman at a dinner party
        and you hit it off and began dating?

David: Yes — and we both loved Tolstoy and French films and sailing — and I
        married her — Jenny — so what is your point? That the woman in the

diary—in the photo—resembles Jenny? That the woman resembles Jenny? That the woman resembles Jenny? That the woman resembles Jenny? That the woman—that the woman's Jenny—it's Jenny—I got it—I got it.

Hal: I'd never let this guy do my plastic surgery.

Jenny: You're so cruel, Sheila.

David (stunned): This *is* you—you're her—she's you—she's who you are—

Jenny: David, try and understand—apart from the sex it was platonic.

Hal: What is the problem here? If she can discuss Tolstoy and foreign films and also does all this you've hit the jackpot.

Sandy: You have a thing for her—I felt that right off.

Hal: All I'm saying is that in addition to a cultivated wife and good mother it's nice if you go to bed each night with a real freak.

Sandy: I don't believe I'm hearing this.

David: I'm stunned—I'm stupefied. I didn't even know—who is the guy again?

Sheila: Norman—Norman—right here.

Norman: Oh stop it, Sheila. I've been having an affair with Jenny.

David: Jenny—a woman with the same name as my wife?

Sheila: The trauma's too much.

David: A love affair?

Hal: This guy kills me—what other kind of affair is there?

David: But that means Norman and Jenny are sleeping with each other.

Jenny: Yes, David, we slept together—but if it's any consolation, there was very little foreplay.

Sheila: That sounds like Norman.

David: But he's my brother-in-law and she's my wife. And who are the people in the picture?

Sheila: He's lost it.

David: Excuse me.

(Exits.)

Hal: If he's going to see Tiger Woods now, that's what I call a sports fan.

Sheila: Of course this means a divorce.

Jenny: Sheila, I may have cheated physically, but mentally I've been a loyal sibling.

Sheila: Sibling? How dare you? You're no longer my sister. From this moment on, the most you could ever be to me is a niece.

Norman: Sheila, Sheila . . . how can I make this up to you?

Sheila: The firm of Rifkin and Abramowitz will let you know.

David (enters with rifle): And now—prepare to die.

Jenny: David!

Norman: All right, let's not play games. That's a loaded shotgun.

David: Back off, Norman! Back off! Everybody in this room is going to die and then I'm putting the barrel in my mouth and squeezing the trigger.

Hal (looks at watch): Oh, is it six already? We have tickets to *Mamma Mia!*

David: Not so fast, I said everybody.

Hal: We just drove up to see the house.

Jenny: David, you have that look in your eye.

David: First you and Norman, then Sheila.

Sheila: Why me? What the hell did I do? I got cheated on like you.

David: You found the diary.

Sheila: He showed me where.

David: Believe me, he's going to.

Sandy: We're innocent bystanders.

David: That makes the news story perfect, doesn't it? The adulterous couple, the poor husband and wife — two perfectly innocent bystanders.

Hal: You're crazy.

David: That's what they said about the Son of Sam.°

Hal: Yes — so — they were right.

Jenny: He's flipped out.

Hal: But you can't kill *us* — we didn't do anything. I never cheated. I could have — and believe me, I wanted to.

Sandy: You did?

Hal: Well, face it, Sandy, you can be a cold fish.

Sandy: Me?

Hal: That's right — she is the opposite of Jenny — will not ever try anything new.

Sandy: Well, maybe if you'd romance me once in a while instead of doing everything so fast.

Hal: I'm only trying to get it done before the headache sets in.

David: Shut up! Who let them in?! It's unfortunate you wandered in, but that's life — full of ironies — some of them pleasant, some rather ugly — I've never thought life was a gift — it's a burden — a sentence — cruel and unusual punishment — everybody say your prayers —

(They huddle together as he cocks his shotgun. Suddenly they hear a noise and a man comes down the stairs. The man is tied up and gagged, apparently having gotten loose from a chair. His arms are still tied and he makes muffled, gagged sounds.)

David (noticing him): Oh no —

Sheila: Oh Christ.

Norman: I thought —

Sheila: Oh brother.

Jenny: Help! Help!

(Hal and Sandy — one or both run to the man and take off his gag.)

David: Don't do that — don't — oh —

Max: OK — the party's over.

Sandy: Who are you?

Jenny: Who tied him up?

David: It was Norman.

Sheila: This sinks us.

Hal: Aren't you Mr. Krolian? I'm Hal Maxwell. I sold you this house a few years ago. Sandy, it's Max Krolian —

Max (referring to ropes): Get these off me.

Hal (untying him): What's going on?

Max: These wild animals — I created them — then they turned on me.

Son of Sam: David Berkowitz (B. 1953) was an infamous serial killer in New York City in the 1970s.

David: Ah, you're incompetent.

Max: They're from my pen.

Sandy: What is this?

Jenny: The game's up — why don't you tell 'em the truth?

Hal: What?

Norman: He had an idea for a play — which he was writing —

Sheila: He invented us.

David: From his fertile imagination.

Sheila: He wrote half the play.

Max: That's right — and I couldn't figure out where I was going with it — it wasn't coming —

David: He was blocked.

Max: Sometimes an idea seems great, but after you work on it for a while it just doesn't go anyplace.

Sheila: But by then it was too late. We were born.

David: Invented.

Max: Created. I had half a play.

Hal: You always had a flair for creating wonderful live characters with fascinating problems and great dialogue.

Norman: So then what does he do?

Jenny: He gave up the idea.

Norman: He threw the half-finished play in the drawer.

David: It's dark in the drawer.

Max: What else could I do? I had no finish.

David: I hated the goddamned drawer.

Sheila: I mean, picture you and your wife in a drawer.

Jenny: There's nothing to do in a drawer.

Norman: It sucks.

Sheila: Then Jenny got the idea that we push it open and escape into the world.

Max: I thought I heard the drawer opening — by the time I turned around they were all over me.

Sandy: What did you think you'd do once you broke out?

Sheila: We hoped we could figure out some way to finish his third act.

Norman: So we could have a life every night in theatres — forever.

Jenny: What's the alternative? To be half-finished in a dark drawer?

David: I'm not going back in the drawer! I'm not going back in the drawer! I'm not going —

(*Norman slaps David.*)

Max: I've thought and thought — I can't figure where it goes.

Hal: Well, let's analyze what we've got . . . she discovers her sister is having an affair with her husband.

Max: Who are you?

Hal: Hal Maxwell — I sold you —

Max: The accountant?

Hal: I've always wanted to write a play.

Max: So does everyone.

Hal: Why are they having an affair? What's wrong with their marriage?

Norman: I'm bored with Sheila.

Sheila: Why?

Norman: I don't know.

Max: Don't ask me. I'm written out.

Hal: Why does any husband get bored with his wife? Because with time they get too familiar. The excitement wanes — they're always together around the house — they see each other undressed — there's no more mystery — now even his secretary is sexier to him — or the next-door neighbor.

Jenny: That's not realistic.

Hal: How would you know? You're not even well written. It's very realistic — it happens all the time. Take it from me.

Sandy: It does?

Hal: I mean, freshness in marriage has to be worked on — otherwise, there's no music in a relationship, and music is everything.

Sandy: What if the husband was once romantic but he gradually takes the wife for granted? What used to be a relationship full of imaginative, charming surprises is now just a life together by the numbers, with them having sex but not making love.

Hal: I'd hardly find that a believable conflict.

Sandy: I think many women would identify with it.

Hal: Too far-out.

Sheila: I think it sounds very plausible.

Jenny: Very close to the bone.

Sandy: Very.

David: And you think it can just evaporate? Even if at one time they loved one another?

Max: That's one of the sad truths of existence. Nothing in this world is permanent. Even the characters created by the great Shakespeare will, in millions of years, cease to exist — when the universe runs its course and the lights go out.

David: Jesus, I think I'll just go back and watch Tiger Woods. The hell with it all.

Norman: That's right. What's it all mean if the cosmos breaks apart and everything finally vanishes?

Jenny: That's why it's important to be held and squeezed now — by anyone willing to do the squeezing.

Sheila: Don't try to justify screwing my husband on existential grounds.

Hal: What if you and David were also having an affair?

Max: I thought of that, but then it starts to become silly.

Jenny: But if life is anything, it's silly.

David: That's right. The philosophers call it absurd, but what they really mean is silly.

Max: The problem is, it implies everyone is unfaithful, but it's not accurate.

Hal: But it doesn't have to be accurate if it's funny. Art is different from life.

Max: Art is the mirror of life.

Hal: Speaking of mirrors, I always wanted to put a mirror on the ceiling over our bed, but she wouldn't go for it.

Sandy: It's the dumbest thing I ever heard.

Hal: It's sexy.

Sandy: It's adolescent. I want to make love, not watch two images of each other having intercourse — from that perspective I'll just see your behind going up and down.

Hal: Why do you always ridicule my needs? Then you wonder why I sit and daydream about Holly Fox.

Sandy: Just don't tell her your mirror idea, she'll burst out laughing.

Hal: If you must know, we've done it in front of a mirror.

Sandy: In your fantasies.

Hal: In your bathroom.

Sandy: What?

David: Aha! This is a juicier story than ours.

Hal: Not that I loved her or that we had an affair or anything. It was a one-shot deal.

Sandy: You and Holly Fox?

Hal: What are you acting so surprised? You've accused me of it jokingly for two years.

Sandy: I was joking.

Hal: There are no jokes. Freud said that.

Sheila: That's my line.

Sandy: Besides, you always swore she didn't appeal to you.

Hal: That's right, I swore — I held up my right hand — I'm an agnostic.

Norman: Be reasonable, Sandy. No husband admits to having slept with another woman.

Sandy: He just did.

Max: That's why my wife left me. That's why I bought your house to live alone and keep out of the rat race of romantic relationships. I was having an affair with my wife's mother.

Norman: My God — why isn't that in our story — it's great.

Max: Because no one would believe it. Her father was a well-known film star — well, I don't have to tell you — he divorced her biological mother and married their au pair girl — so my wife now had a mother ten years younger than she.

Jenny: A stepmother.

Max: It's semantics — meanwhile I was boffing her.

David: So you're also cheating on your father-in-law.

Max: That's OK because he was a shoe fetishist who could only get aroused if Prada was having a sale.

Sheila: This does strain credulity.

Max: My wife's mother kept a diary. Very graphic. Our intimacies — our love-making. Details. Names. She thought it romantic. One night my wife said to her, I'm going to the Hamptons tomorrow — I need a good book for the beach. Thinking it was her leather-bound volume of Henry James, she mistakenly gave her the leather-bound diary. I was with my wife when she read it on the beach. A change came over her — a physical change — like when the full moon comes out in a Wolfman movie.

Hal: So that's where you got the idea.

Norman: What'd you do?

Max: What could I do? I denied it.

Norman: What'd she do?

Max: She tried to drown herself. She ran into the ocean but only succeeded in getting stung by a jellyfish. It made her lips swell up. Suddenly with those big lips she looked sexy, and I fell back in love with her. Of course, when the swelling went down she got on my nerves again.

Hal: Well, I *wasn't* having an affair — mine was a onetime thing. At our New Year's Eve party. Everyone was downstairs drinking, partying — I happened to walk past your bathroom upstairs, Holly was in it and asked if we had any Q-tips, so I went in to help her find them, closed the door and did it with her.

David: Why did she need Q-tips?

Jenny: What's the difference!?

Norman: Who cares about the goddamn Q-tips?

Sandy: They'd been making eyes at each other for months.

Hal: That's pure projection. You were the one with big eyes for her brother.

Sandy: If you were more perceptive you would have known I had no interest in Ken Fox.

Hal: No?

Sandy: No. If I ever would have strayed at all it would have been with Howard Nadleman.

Hal: Nadleman? The real estate agent?

Sandy: Howard Nadleman knows how to make a woman feel her sexuality.

Hal: What does that mean?

Sandy: Nothing.

Hal: You had a one-night stand with Howard Nadleman?

Sandy: No.

Hal: Thank God for that.

Sandy: We had a long romance.

Hal: You had a romance with Howard Nadleman?

Sandy: Yes, I did.

Hal: Don't deny it.

Sandy: As long as we're coming clean, I may as well be honest too.

Hal: A minute ago you said, "if I ever would have strayed at all," implying you never strayed.

Sandy: I can't live this lie anymore. With all due respect to you, I've been sleeping with Howard Nadleman.

David: Go, Nadleman!

Hal: Don't make me laugh.

Sandy: I've always loved you, Hal — you know that. But what does a person do when the romance fades — when the passion drains away and you still love and respect your spouse — you cheat on him.

Norman: That's what I was trying to explain to Sheila.

Hal: How many times did you sleep with Howard?

Sandy: Do numbers ever really tell you anything?

Hal: Yes, I'm an accountant.

Sandy: Let's put it this way — I don't go for psychoanalysis.

Hal: You mean — all those Wednesdays, Thursdays and Saturdays —

Sandy: There is no Doctor Fineglass.

Hal: And I thought your depression was lifting.

Sandy: It was.

Hal: But a hundred and sixty dollars an hour?

Sandy: That was for the hotel rooms.

Hal: I was paying for your hotel rooms three days a week with Howard Nadleman all year?

Sandy: Didn't you notice it was strange I had the only shrink who didn't take August off?

David: It turns out their life is the farce, not ours.

Sheila: The farce, or is it tragedy?

Norman: Why is it tragedy?

Sheila: It's a sorry situation — two people who must've loved one another at one time — obviously still do — but the initial excitement drains from their marriage . . .

Jenny: But no one can sustain that first rush of excitement.

David: That's right — we settle in — the sexual passion is replaced by other things — shared experiences — children — beastiality.

Hal: Is it still going on with you and Nadleman?

Sandy: No — remember some months ago he suffered a brain concussion?

Hal: Yes — he's never been the same — how did it happen?

Sandy: The mirror on the ceiling over the bed fell on him.

Hal: Oh God! Him and not me!

David: I'll tell you why their situation is farce — because they're pathetic. They lack tragic stature. What is he, an accountant? And she's a housewife. This is not *Hamlet* or *Medea*.

Hal: Oh please — you don't have to be a prince to suffer — there's millions of people out there every bit as tortured as Hamlet. They're Hamlet on Prozac.

Sandy: And jealous as Medea.

Max: Therefore, what can I conclude? Everybody has their dark secrets, their longings, their lusts, their awful needs — so if life is to continue one must choose to forgive.

Norman: And that's where our play should go. So I took a momentary fancy to your sister — big deal — so maybe you should write it so that Sheila and David once spent a passionate night together — so we all learn each other's pathetic shortcomings and we forgive each other.

Jenny: Yes. And the audience laughs at all of us and they escape from their own sad lives for a brief moment and then we kiss and make up.

Max: Forgiveness — it gives this little sex farce dimension and heart.

Sheila: That's right. Who am I to judge others and throw away years of closeness and love because my husband the dentist was drilling my sister?

Jenny: We'll change — we'll make amends. Where there's life there's hope.

Sandy: But how is forgiveness different than just sweeping all your problems under the rug?

Max: It's much grander — it takes a bigger person — forgiveness is divine.

Jenny: And maybe it's the same but it sounds better.

Max: I like it — it's funny, it's sad, and best of all, it's commercial. Come — let's go to my study so I can complete the third act while it's all fresh — I feel my writer's block lifting. The key word is "commercial" — I'm sorry, "forgiveness" — the key word is "forgiveness."

(They go upstairs together. The Maxwells look at each other.)

Hal: I don't think I can forgive you, Sandy.

Sandy: No. Nor I, you.

Hal: I don't know why. I know Max Krolian is right — he's a deep playwright.

Sandy: It's easy to forgive in fiction — the author can manipulate reality. And as you say, Krolian's a clever craftsman.

Hal: I can't believe you had a long affair with Howard Nadleman — he was probably getting even with me for the audit.

Sandy: It had nothing to do with you — everything is not always about you.

Hal: Was I such an unromantic husband?

Sandy: As the years went by you stopped trying.

Hal: I became discouraged. You started taking me for granted too.

Sandy: All those imaginary characters can be rewritten — their lives erased, begun again — but we've said and done things that can never be erased.

Hal: The tragic part is that I love you.

Sandy: And I love you, but it's pathetic, not tragic.

Hal: If I took that rifle and killed us both I could redeem our infidelities with one grand gesture.

Sandy: You're not the type, Hal. Accountants don't commit suicide and find redemption — they usually just vanish and turn up in the Cayman Islands.

Hal: What do you want to do?

Sandy: What can we do? Sweep the painful aspects of the relationship under the rug and call it forgiveness or get a divorce.

Hal: Sandy — this was the first room we made love in. Can't we start over?

Sandy: Clean starts work better in fiction.

Hal: But every life needs a little fiction in it — too much reality is a very nasty thing.

Sandy: Maybe now that everything's out in the open . . . What's that honking sound?

Hal (to window): Look at all those geese.

Sandy (joining him): My goodness — we never had geese when we lived here.

Hal: It's a symbol.

Sandy: Of what?

Hal: Of a fresh start — of geese where geese never were. Today was a day full of symbols — full of writing, of characters, of literature. The poet that beats 'neath the breast of this accountant came out and I helped Max Krolian write a warm ending to his play — only you and I remained unresolved, undecided and confused — we were looking for some sign — some way to recapture the music in our relationship and then — the honking of the geese —

Sandy: And you see it as a symbol.

Hal: Don't you see, Sandy? Can't you see what they're trying to tell us? Don't you know one simple fact about geese? Geese mate forever.

Sandy: Do geese have affairs?

Hal: If they do they work it out somehow — it's all in nature's design.

Sandy: Could it really be my husband is a poet trapped in the body of a CPA? *(Sound of geese honking, and music rises.)* Kiss.

Fade out.

CONSIDERATIONS FOR CRITICAL THINKING AND WRITING

1. **FIRST RESPONSE.** How does Allen's use of humor redeem what might otherwise be a depressingly grim set of characters and circumstances? If the humor doesn't work for you, explain why.

2. Who do you think is the protagonist? Who (or what) is the antagonist?

3. What is the major conflict? What complications constitute the rising action? Where is the climax? Is the conflict resolved?

4. Why would it be accurate to describe this play as a work of realism — an attempt to create the appearance of life as it is actually lived — only up to a point? Describe the scene that you think best indicates a shift to a style that goes beyond realism.

5. Max describes the play's plot as a "little sex farce" (p. 1341). Explain why you agree or disagree that the play can be called a farce (see the Glossary of Literary Terms).

6. Discuss the symbolic significance of the geese that appear at the beginning and end of the play.

7. Is the theme stated directly, or is it developed implicitly through the action, dialogue, or plot?

8. Writing about the 2003 production of the play directed by Allen, a *New York Times* reviewer complained that the play ended with "artificial sentimentality that seems aimed at sending the audience out with a warm feeling rather than at resolving the narrative." Is the ending simply crassly "commercial" (p. 1341), as Max, its creator, suggests? What do you make of the ending?

9. **CRITICAL STRATEGIES.** Read the section on cultural criticism (p. 1547) in Chapter 46, "Critical Strategies for Reading," and discuss how the play reflects some of the values of the society in which it is set. Explain why you think the play either affirms or challenges contemporary American values.

CONNECTION TO ANOTHER SELECTION

1. **CREATIVE RESPONSE.** Rewrite a scene of your choice from either Susan Glaspell's *Trifles* (p. 1048) or Henrik Ibsen's *A Doll House* (p. 1257) as you think Allen would write it.

The Reprimand

Writer and director Jane Anderson started her career as an actor. She left college at the age of nineteen to pursue acting and was cast in the David Mamet hit play *Sexual Perversity in Chicago*. The experience familiarized Anderson with scriptwriting, and eventually she founded a writing group called New York Writers' Block. She later wrote and performed in a number of one-woman comedic plays, whose success afforded her the opportunity to write for the television sitcoms *The Facts of Life* and *The Wonder Years*.

In 1986, Anderson wrote the play *Defying Gravity*, a composite of monologues about

Photo by permission of Jilly Wendell.

the space shuttle *Challenger* explosion. Her first screenplay, *The Positively True Adventures of the Alleged Texas Cheerleader-Murdering Mom,* was a satirical look at the true story of a Texas mother who tried to hire a contract killer to murder her daughter's rival for the junior high school cheerleading squad. The HBO movie starred Holly Hunter and gave Anderson instant notoriety as a screenwriter. She has written the screenplays for a number of movies since, including *The Baby Dance,* starring Jody Foster, and *When Billie Beat Bobby,* the story of tennis champion Billie Jean King beating an aging Bobby Riggs.

The Reprimand was one of five "phone plays" that premiered in February 2000 at the annual Humana Festival of New American Plays held at Actors Theatre in Louisville, Kentucky. The phone call is a traditional stage convention that consists of an actor providing one side of a conversation, but for the Humana Festival performances, the actors conversed offstage and the audience heard both sides of the three-minute conversation. In *The Reprimand,* the overheard conversation reveals a complicated power struggle between two women.

JANE ANDERSON (B. 1956)

The Reprimand   2000

CHARACTERS

Rhona
Mim

Rhona: . . . we need to talk about what you did in the meeting this morning.
Mim: My God, what?
Rhona: That reference you made about my weight.
Mim: What reference?
Rhona: When we came into the room and Jim was making the introductions, you said, "Oh Rhona, why don't you take the bigger chair."
Mim: But that was — I thought since this was your project that you should sit in the better chair.
Rhona: But you didn't say better, you said bigger.
Mim: I did? Honest to God, that isn't what I meant. I'm so sorry if it hurt your feelings.
Rhona: You didn't hurt my feelings. This has nothing to do with my feelings. What concerns me — and concerns Jim by the way — is how this could have undermined the project.
Mim: Jim said something about it?
Rhona: Yes.
Mim: What did he say?
Rhona: He thought your comment was inappropriate.

Mim: Really? How? I was talking about a chair.

Rhona: Mim, do you honestly think anyone in that room was really listening to what I had to say after you made that comment?

Mim: I thought they were very interested in what you had to say.

Rhona: Honey, there was a reason why Dick and Danny asked you all the follow-up questions.

Mim: But that's because I hadn't said anything up to that point. Look, I'm a little confused about Jim's reaction, because after the meeting he said he liked what I did with the follow-up.

Rhona: He should acknowledge what you do. And I know the reason why he's finally said something is because I've been telling him that you deserve more credit.

Mim: Oh, thank you. But I think Jim already respects what I do.

Rhona: He should respect you. But from what I've observed, I think — because you're an attractive woman — that he still uses you for window dressing. Especially when you're working with me. You know what I'm saying?

Mim: Well, if that's the case, Jim is a jerk.

Rhona: I know that. And I know you know that. But I think you still have a lot of anger about the situation and sometimes it really shows.

Mim: I don't mean it to show.

Rhona: I know that. Look, I consider you — regardless of what Jim thinks — I think you're really talented and I really love working with you.

Mim: And I enjoy working with you.

Rhona: Thank you. And that's why I want to keep things clear between us. Especially when we're working for men like Jim.

Mim: No, I agree, absolutely.

Rhona: *(To someone off-phone.)* Tell him I'll be right there. *(Back to Mim.)* Mim, sorry — I have Danny on the phone.

Mim: Oh — do you want to conference me in?

Rhona: I can handle it, but thank you. Mim, I'm so glad we had this talk.

Mim: Well, thank you for being so honest with me.

Rhona: And thank you for hearing me. I really appreciate it. Let's talk later?

Mim: Sure. *(Rhona hangs up. A beat.)* *(Mumbling.)* Fat pig. *(Hangs up.)*

CONSIDERATIONS FOR CRITICAL THINKING AND WRITING

1. **FIRST RESPONSE.** Do you identify with one character more than the other? Consider whether Rhona or Mim is more sympathetic.

2. What is humorous about the nature of the conflict? Is there a resolution to the conflict?

3. How is the exposition presented? What does it reveal? How does Anderson's choice not to dramatize events on stage help to determine the focus of the play?

4. What can be said about the setting? Explain whether or not you think setting has any role in this play.

5. Discuss the significance of the title. To whom does it apply?

6. **CREATIVE RESPONSE.** Write a three-minute phone conversation (or instant e-mail message) between a student and professor that captures some dramatic tension in their relationship.

CONNECTIONS TO OTHER SELECTIONS

1. Compare the power relationship that exists between Rhona and Mim and that of Mrs. Peters and Mrs. Hale in Susan Glaspell's *Trifles* (p. 1048).

2. Discuss the treatment of perceptions of body weight in *The Reprimand* and in Cathy Song's "Sunworshippers" (p. 695).

Moby-Dude, Or: The Three-Minute Whale

Courtesy of Martha Ives.

Born in Chicago and educated at Northwestern University and the Yale School of Drama, David Ives writes for television, film, and opera. A recipient of a Guggenheim Fellowship in playwriting, he has created a number of one-act plays for the annual comedy festival called Manhattan Punch Line. Many of his one-act plays are available in *All in the Timing* (1994), *Lives of the Saints* (2000), and *Time Flies and Other Plays* (2001); his full-length plays are collected in *Polish Joke and Other Plays* (2004). *Moby-Dude, Or: The Three-Minute Whale* is a very brief play about a student trying to convince his teacher that he actually completed reading a very long novel. In the introduction to *Talk to Me: Monologue Plays*, from which *Moby-Dude* is reprinted, the editors, Nina Shengold and Eric Lane, offer a valuable perspective on the nature of monologue plays by describing them as a "modern form of that most ancient of human entertainments, storytelling. Our paleolithic ancestors listened to hunters enacting their sagas in front of a campfire, and members of every human community since have stood up in front of their peers and performed their trades." Here's Ives's updated version of classic storytelling.

DAVID IVES (B. 1950)

Moby-Dude, Or: The Three-Minute Whale

2004

SFX: sound of waves and gulls. Distant ship's bell.
Our Narrator is a stoned-out surfer of seventeen.

Our Narrator: Call me Ishmael, dude. Yes, Mrs. Podgorski, I *did* read *Moby-Dick* over the summer like I was supposed to. It was bohdacious. Actually, y'know, it's "Moby-*hyphen*-Dick." The title's got a little hyphen before the "Dick." And what is the meaning of this dash before the "Dick"? *WHOAAA!* Another mystery in this awesome American masterpiece, a peerless allegorical saga of mortal courage, metaphysical ambiguity and maniacal obsession! *What*, Mrs. Podgorski? You don't believe I really *read* Herman Melville's *Moby-Dick Or The Whale*? Five hundred sixty-two pages, fourteen ounces, published 1851, totally tanked its first weekend, rereleased in the 1920s as one of the world's gnarliest works of Art? You think I copped all this like off the back of the tome or by watching the crappy 1956 film starring Gregory Peck? Mrs. P., you been chasing my tail since middle school, do *I* get all testy? Do *I* say, what is the plot in under two minutes — besides a whale and a hyphen? *Moby-Dick* in two minutes, huh? Okay, kyool. Let's rip.

(SFX: ship's bell, close up and sharp, to signal the start and a ticking watch, underneath. Very fast.)

Fade in the boonies of Massachusetts, eighteen-something. Young dude possibly named Ishmael, like the Bible, meets-cute with, TAA-DAA!, *Quee-queg*, a South Sea cannibal with a heart of gold.

(SFX: cutesy voice going, "Awwww.")

Maybe they're gay.

(SFX: tongue slurp.)

Or maybe they represent some east-west, pagan-Christian duality action. Anyway, the two newfound bros go to Mass and hear a sermon about Jonah . . .

(SFX: one second of church organ.)

Biblical tie-in, then ship out on Christmas Day *(could be symbolical!)* aboard the USS *Pequod* with its mysterious wacko Captain Ahab . . .

(SFX: madman laughter.)

. . . who — *backstory* — is goofyfoot because the equally mysterious momboosaloid white whale Moby-like-the-singer Dick bit his leg off.

(SFX: chomp.)

Freudian castration action. I mean he's big and he's got sperm and his last name is "Dick," right? Moby is also a metaphor for God, Nature, Truth, obsessisical love, the world, the past, and white people. Check out Pip the Negro cabin boy who by a *fluke* . . .

(SFX: rimshot.)

. . . goes wacko too. Ahab says,

(SFX: echo effect.)

"Bring me the head of the Great White Whale and you win this prize!"

(SFX: echo effect out, cash register sound.)

The crew is stoked, by *NOT* first-mate like-the-coffee-Starbuck. Ahab wants the big one, Starbuck wants the whale juice. Idealism versus capitalism.

(SFX: an impressed "Whoo.")

Radical. Queequeg tells the carpenter to build him a coffin shaped like a canoe.

(SFX: theremin.)

Foreshadowing! Then lots of chapters everybody skips about the scientology of whales.

(SFX: yawn.)

Cut to . . .

(SFX: trumpet fanfare.)

Page 523, the Pacific Ocean. *"Surf's up!"* Ahab sights the Dick. He's totally amped. The boards hit the waves, the crew snakes the Dick for three whole days, bottom of the third Ahab is ten-toes-on-the-nose, he's aggro, Moby goes aerial, Ahab's in the zone, he fires his choicest harpoon, the rope does a 360 round his neck, Ahab crushes out, Moby totals the *Pequod,* everybody eats it 'cept our faithful narrator Ishmael who boogies to safety on Queequeg's coffin . . .

(SFX: resounding echo effect, deeper voice.)

"AND I ONLY AM ESCAPED ALONE TO TELL THEE!"

(Resume normal voice.)

Roll final credits. The End.

(SFX: ship's bell to signal end of fight. End ticking watch.)

So what do you say, Mrs. Podgorski? You want to like hang and catch a cup of Starbucks sometime . . . ? — *Tubular!*

End of play

Considerations for Critical Thinking and Writing

1. **FIRST RESPONSE.** Discuss whether you think it is necessary to have read Melville's *Moby-Dick* in order to appreciate the narrator's monologue.

2. How do the narrator's diction and style contribute to the play's humor?

3. In what sense is Mrs. Podgorski the antagonist?

4. Comment on the appropriateness of the sound effects.

5. **CREATIVE RESPONSE.** Write a monologue in which Mrs. Podgorski responds to the student.

Connections to Other Selections

1. Compare *Moby-Dude* and X. J. Kennedy's poem "A Visit from St. Sigmund" (p. 797) as parodies of psychoanalytic readings of literature. You might find useful the discussion of psychological strategies for interpretation (p. 1542) in Chapter 46, "Critical Strategies for Reading."

2. How are the narrators' sensibilities revealed by their respective monologues in *Moby-Dude* and Jane Martin's *Rodeo* (p. 1369)?

From Mambo Mouth

John Leguizamo was born in 1964 in Bogotá, Colombia, and immigrated to the United States with his family at the age of four. He studied acting at New York University and later began a career as a stand-up comedian. In 1986, Leguizamo made his television debut as a guest star on *Miami Vice,* and in 1989 he landed a small role in Brian DePalma's *Casualties of War.* In 1991, his career advanced, thanks to both a starring role in *Hangin' with the Homeboys* and his off-Broadway performance in *Mambo Mouth,* a one-man show in which he portrayed several Latino characters. Leguizamo also starred in the TV comedy-variety show *House of Buggin',* which was the first of its kind to

© David Hughes.

feature an all-Latino cast. He has starred in many hit movies, including the modern version of William Shakespeare's *Romeo and Juliet* and Spike Lee's *Summer of Sam.*

In the following excerpt from *Mambo Mouth,* Pepe, an illegal alien who is caught in an Immigration and Naturalization Service sting and pleads his deportation case behind bars, is just one of the engaging characters portrayed. After airing on HBO, the play earned Leguizamo an Obie, an Outer Critics Circle and Banguardia Award, and an ACE Award.

Explore contexts for John Leguizamo on *LiterActive* or at bedfordstmartins.com/meyercompact.

JOHN LEGUIZAMO (B. 1964)
From Mambo Mouth: Pepe   1988

(The stage is dark. A backstage light reveals the silhouette of a man wearing jeans and a T-shirt standing in a doorway.)

Pepe: Excuse me, ése,° I just got this gift certificate in the mail saying that I was entitled to gifts and prizes and possibly money if I came to La Guardia Airport? *(Comes downstage.)* Oh sure, the name is Pepe. Pepe Vásquez. *(Panics.)* Orale,° what are you doing? You're making a big mistake! *(Lights up. Pepe stands center stage, holding a grille of prison bars in front of his face.)*

See Plays in Performance insert.

   I'm not Mexican! I'm Swedish! No, you've never seen me before. Sure I look familiar — all Swedish people look alike. *(Gibberish in Swedish accent.)* Uta Häagen, Häagen Däazen, Frusen Glädjé, Nina Häagen. . . .

ése: Chicanoism for *guy, fellow, dude.*   *Orale:* Chicanoism for "What's up?"

Okay. Did I say Swedish? I meant Irish—yeah, black Irish! *(Singsongy Irish accent.)* Toy ti-toy ti-toy. Oh, Lucky Charms, they're magically delicious! Pink hearts, green clovers, yellow moons. What time is it? Oh, Jesus, Joseph, and Mary! It's cabbage and corned beef time—let me go!

Okay. *(Confessional.)* You got me. I'm not Swedish and I'm not Irish. You probably guessed it already—I'm Israeli! Mazel tov, bubeleh *(Jackie Mason schtick.)* Come on, kineahora, open up the door. I'll walk out, you'll lock the door, you won't miss me, I'll send you a postcard. . . .

Orale, gabacho pendejo.° I'm American, man. I was born right here in Flushing. Well, sure I sound Mexican. I was raised by a Mexican nanny. Doesn't everybody have a Maria Consuelo?

As a matter of fact, I got proof right here that I'm American. I got two tickets to the Mets game. Yeah, Gooden's pitching. Come on, I'm late.

Orale, ése. Is it money? It's always money. *(Conspiratorially.)* Well, I got a lot of money. I just don't have it on me. But I know where to get it.

Orale, ése. Tell me, where did your people come from? Santo Domingo? Orale, we're related! We're cousins! Tell me, what's your last name? Rivera? Rivera! That's my mother's maiden name! What a coinky dinky. Hermano, cousin, brother, primo, por favor dejeme ir que somos de la mismita sangre.° Los latinos debemos ser unidos y jamás seremos vencidos.°

Oh, you don't understand, huh? You're a coconut. *(Angry.)* Brown on the outside, but white on the inside. Why don't you do something for your people for a change and let me out of here?

Okay, I'm sorry, cuz. *(Apologetic.)* Come here. Mira, mijito,° I got all my family here. I got my wife and daughter. And my daughter, she's in the hospital. She's a preemie with double pneumonia and asthma. And if you deport me, who's gonna take care of my little chucawala?°

Come on, ése. It's not like I'm stealing or living off of you good people's taxes. I'm doing the shit jobs that Americans don't want. *(Anger builds again.)* Tell me, who the hell wants to work for two twenty-five an hour picking toxic pesticide-coated grapes? I'll give you a tip: Don't eat them.

Orale, you Americans act like you own this place, but we were here first. That's right, the Spaniards were here first. Ponce de León, Cortés, Vásquez, Cabeza de Vaca. If it's not true, then how come your country has all our names? Florida, California, Nevada, Arizona, Las Vegas, Los Angeles, San Bernardino, San Antonio, Santa Fe, Nueva York!

Tell you what I'm going to do. I'll let you stay if you let me go.

What are you so afraid of? I'm not a threat. I'm just here for the same reason that all your people came here for—in search of a better life, that's all.

(Leans away from grille, then comes back outraged.) Okay, go ahead and send me back. But who's going to clean for you? Because if we all stopped cleaning and said "adiós," we'd still be the same people, but you'd be dirty! Who's going to pick your chef salads? And who's going to make your guacamole? You need us more than we need you. 'Cause we're here revitalizing the American labor force!

---

gabacho pendejo: Dumb whitey.   *primo . . . sangre:* Cuz, please let go of me, we are the same blood.   *Los . . . vencidos:* Latinos are united and will never be divided.   *Mira, mijito:* Look, sonny.   *chucawala:* Baby daughter.

Go ahead and try to keep us back. Because we're going to multiply and multiply *(thrusts hips)* so uncontrollably till we push you so far up, you'll be living in Canada! Oh, scary monsters, huh? You might have to learn a second language. Oh, the horror!

But don't worry, we won't deport you. We'll just let you clean our toilets. Yeah, we don't even hold grudges — we'll let you use rubber gloves.

Orale, I'm gonna miss you white people.

(Lights down.)

CONSIDERATIONS FOR CRITICAL THINKING AND WRITING

1. **FIRST RESPONSE.** Describe the range of emotions expressed by Pepe in his monologue. Which emotion seems to predominate, and how does it contribute to the scene's overall tone?

2. Discuss the scene's theme. Do you agree or disagree with this scene's central ideas? Why?

3. How is racial stereotyping used to present the theme?

4. Describe Leguizamo's use of irony for humorous and serious purposes.

5. Can this scene accurately be categorized as a work of realism? Explain why or why not.

6. **CRITICAL STRATEGIES.** Read the section on historical criticism (pp. 1544–48) in Chapter 46, "Critical Strategies for Reading." How do you think a Marxist critic would interpret Pepe's monologue?

CONNECTIONS TO OTHER SELECTIONS

1. In an essay discuss the thematic purpose of the racial stereotyping in Pepe's monologue and in David Henry Hwang's *Trying to Find Chinatown* (p. 1363).

2. Compare the tone of Pepe's monologue with that of Jane Martin's *Rodeo* (p. 1369).

Playwriting 101: The Rooftop Lesson

Born in Chicago, Illinois, Rich Orloff graduated from Oberlin College in 1973 and has built a successful career as a comedic playwright. He has written some ten full-length plays, more than a dozen one-act plays, and over fifty short plays, four of which have appeared in *Best American Short Plays*. His works are produced throughout the United States and have won a number of awards including the 2002–03 Dramatists Guild Playwriting Fellowship. On his Web site <www.richorloff.com> Orloff explains what prompted him to write *Playwriting 101: The*

Courtesy of the playwright.

Rooftop Lesson: "The play was originally produced as part of a series of short plays produced on an actual rooftop in Manhattan. When I was invited to submit to the festival, every idea I came up with seemed completely clichéd. So I gathered the clichés into one story and satirized them. Voilà, an original play!"

RICH ORLOFF (B. 1951)

Playwriting 101: The Rooftop Lesson   2000

NOTE: The characters [the Teacher, the Jumper, and the Good Samaritan] can be of either sex, but the Jumper and Good Samaritan should be of the same sex. References are written as if the characters are male, but that can be changed.

TIME: The present.

PLACE: The rooftop of a large urban building.

See Plays in Performance insert.

(As the play begins, The Jumper is on the ledge of the roof and is about to jump.)

The Jumper: I'm going to jump, and nobody can stop me!

(The Good Samaritan enters quickly.)

The Good Samaritan: Don't!!!!!

(The Teacher enters and stands to the side. The Teacher points a clicker at the others and clicks, freezing the action.)

The Teacher (addressing the audience): A typical dramatic scenario: Two people in conflict — at least one in deep inner conflict — with high stakes, suspense, and affordable cast size. How will this situation play out? That depends, of course, on the level of craft and creativity in that remarkable art form known as playwriting. Let's rewind from the start — *(The Teacher clicks, and The Jumper and Good Samaritan return to their places at the top of the play, quickly reversing their initial movements.)* And see what happens.

(The Teacher clicks again to resume the action. The Jumper is on the ledge of the roof and is about to jump.)

The Jumper: I'm going to jump, and nobody can stop me!

(The Good Samaritan enters quickly.)

The Good Samaritan: Don't!!!!!
The Jumper: Okay.

(The Teacher clicks to freeze the action.)

The Teacher: Not very satisfying, is it? Where's the suspense? Where's the tension? And what audience member will want to pay today's ticket prices for a play whose conflict resolves in forty-five seconds? But most importantly, where can you go from here?

(The Teacher clicks to unfreeze the action.)

The Good Samaritan: Gee, you could've hurt yourself.
The Jumper: Gosh, you're right.
The Good Samaritan: Want to grab a brew?
The Jumper: Sure.

(*The Teacher clicks to freeze the action.*)

The Teacher: Without intense oppositional desires, more commonly known as "conflict," there is no play. When Nora leaves in *A Doll's House*, nobody wants her husband to reply — (*upbeat*) "Call when you get work!" So let's start this scene over — (*The Teacher clicks. The Jumper and Good Samaritan rewind to their initial places.*) maintaining conflict.

(*The Teacher clicks again.*)

The Jumper: I'm going to jump, and nobody can stop me!

(*The Good Samaritan enters quickly.*)

The Good Samaritan: Don't!!!!!
The Jumper: Fuck you!
The Good Samaritan (giving an obscene gesture): No, you asshole, fuck you!

(*The Teacher clicks and freezes the action.*)

The Teacher: Let's rise above profanity, shall we? It alienates conservatives and makes liberals think you're second-rate David Mamet. (*Clicks.*) Rewind . . . And again: (*Clicks.*)
The Jumper: I'm going to jump, and nobody can stop me!

(*The Good Samaritan enters quickly.*)

The Good Samaritan: Don't!!!!!
The Jumper: Why not?!!!

(*The Teacher clicks.*)

The Teacher: Oooo, you can just feel the suspense rising now, can't you?

(*The Teacher clicks again.*)

The Good Samaritan: Because suicide is a sin!

(*The Teacher clicks.*)

The Teacher: Big deal. Theatre is written by sinners about sinners for sinners. Nobody goes to *Othello* to hear, "Iago, you're so naughty!" Always let the audience form their own judgments. Rewind a bit. (*Clicks.*) Now let's try a different tack. (*Clicks.*)
The Jumper: Why not?!
The Good Samaritan: Because I love you.
The Jumper: I didn't know!

(*The Teacher clicks.*)

The Teacher: I don't care! Let's see if we can find something less clichéd.

(*The Teacher clicks again.*)

The Jumper: Why not?!
The Good Samaritan: Because if you jump there, you'll land on my little girl's lemonade stand. And my little girl!

(*The Jumper looks over the ledge and moves over two feet.*)

The Jumper: Is this better?

(*The Teacher clicks.*)

The Teacher: Now what have we gained? Be wary of minor obstacles. Unless, of course, you need to fill time. Again.

(*The Teacher clicks again.*)

The Jumper: Why not?!
The Good Samaritan: Because life is worth living.
The Jumper: Mine isn't!

(*The Teacher clicks.*)

The Teacher: Excellent. We don't just have a plot anymore, we have a theme. Theme, the difference between entertainment and art. No theme, add a car chase and sell it to the movies. But with theme, you have the potential to create something meaningful, something memorable, something college students can write term papers about. So let's rewind a bit and see where this thematically rich drama goes now.

(*The Teacher clicks to rewind and clicks again to resume.*)

The Good Samaritan: Because life is worth living!
The Jumper: Mine isn't!
The Good Samaritan: Gosh. Tell me all about it.

(*The Teacher clicks.*)

The Teacher: Some expositional subtlety, please.

(*The Teacher clicks again.*)

The Good Samaritan: Because life is worth living!
The Jumper: Mine isn't!
The Good Samaritan: Are you sure?

(*The Teacher clicks.*)

The Teacher: Better.

(*The Teacher clicks again.*)

The Jumper: Yes, I'm sure. I'm broke, I have no friends, and I see no reason to continue.
The Good Samaritan: Look, so you're broke and friendless. All experiences are transient. Detach, as the Buddha once did.

(*The Teacher clicks.*)

The Teacher: Of all the world's great religions, Buddhism is the least entertaining. Let's try again.

(*The Teacher clicks again.*)

The Good Samaritan: So you're broke and you're friendless. Why not try Prozac?

(*The Teacher clicks.*)

The Teacher: The popularity and effectiveness of modern antidepressants is one of the great challenges of contemporary dramaturgy. We no more want Willy Loman to solve his problems with Prozac than we want Stanley and Stella Kowalski to get air-conditioning. How can today's playwright deal with today's medicinal deus ex machinas? Let's see.

(The Teacher clicks again.)

The Jumper: I tried Prozac once, and it made my mouth really dry.

(The Teacher clicks.)

The Teacher: Not great, but we'll let it slide.

(The Teacher clicks again.)

The Good Samaritan: Let me help you.
The Jumper: It's too late.
The Good Samaritan: No, it's not.
The Jumper: You don't understand. I haven't told you the worst.

(The Teacher clicks.)

The Teacher: Fictional characters are rarely straightforward.

(The Teacher clicks again.)

The Jumper: You see, until a few weeks ago, I was in love. Deep love. True love. I was involved with two of the most wonderful gals in the world. One was sexy, rich, generous and caring. The other was streetwise, daring and even sexier. Between the two of them, I had everything. Then they found out about each other, and they both dumped me. Not just one, but both.

(The Teacher clicks.)

The Teacher: Excellent playwriting. Here's a heartbreaking situation with which we can all identify. Maybe not in the specifics, but in the universal experience of rejection.

(The Teacher clicks again.)

The Good Samaritan: At least you've had two exciting affairs. I haven't gotten laid in a year.

(The Teacher clicks.)

The Teacher: A superb response. Another situation with which, um, well, we've all had friends who've had that problem.

(The Teacher clicks again.)

The Jumper: So what are you telling me? That life can get *worse*? That's supposed to get me off this ledge?
The Good Samaritan: Hey, I'm just trying to help!
The Jumper: Well, you're doing a lousy job.
The Good Samaritan: At least I've got some money in the bank!
The Jumper: You've also got rocks in your head!

(The Teacher clicks.)

The Teacher: A common beginner's mistake. Two characters in hostile disagreement isn't conflict, it's just bickering. We don't go to the theatre to hear petty, puerile antagonism; that's why we have families. Let's hope this goes somewhere interesting, or I'll have to rewind.

(The Teacher clicks again.)

The Jumper: You've only got money in the bank because you're cheap.

The Good Samaritan: I am not.

The Jumper: Well, you certainly dress like you are.

The Teacher: Now this is really degenerating.

(*The Teacher clicks, but the action continues.*)

The Good Samaritan: Listen, you stupid twerp —

The Jumper: At least I'm a twerp with a decent sex life.

The Good Samaritan: And if it was decent for *them*, maybe you'd still have a sex life.

(*The Teacher continues to click, but the action continues.*)

The Teacher (as the action continues): Now stop it . . . Stop it! . . . Stop it!! (*Etc.*)

(*Shouting above The Teacher's "Stop it"s, which they ignore:*)

The Jumper: Loser!

The Good Samaritan: Pervert!

The Jumper: Cheapskate!

The Good Samaritan: Cretin!

The Jumper: Asshole!

The Good Samaritan: Imbecile!

The Jumper: Shithead!

The Teacher (clicking in vain): Stop it!!!!

(*The Good Samaritan takes out a clicker and freezes The Teacher.*)

The Good Samaritan: Notice how organically the teacher's frustration has increased. What began as a minor irritation became unbearable when the human desire to control was thwarted.

(*The Good Samaritan clicks again.*)

The Teacher: What are you doing?! I hold the clicker around here. How dare —

(*The Good Samaritan clicks. The Teacher freezes.*)

The Good Samaritan: See how frustration becomes "anger"? Although the real life stakes are minor, the character's emotional investment is intense. That's good playwriting.

(*The Good Samaritan clicks again.*)

The Teacher: Stop that. What do you think this is, a Pirandello° play?

The Good Samaritan: Well, how do you think *we* feel? We can't say more than two lines without being interrupted by your self-important pronouncements. How'd you like it if I did that to you?

The Teacher: You have no dra — (*The Good Samaritan clicks and stops/starts The Teacher during the following:*) matically vi — able rea — son to inter — rupt me. Damn it, will you get back in the play?

The Good Samaritan: No, and you can't make me!

(*The Good Samaritan clicks at The Teacher, who dodges the clicker.*)

The Teacher: Aha, missed. You superficial stereotype!

Luigi Pirandello: (1867–1936) Italian playwright famous for exploring illusion and reality in his plays.

(The Teacher clicks at The Good Samaritan and vice versa during the following, both successfully dodging the other.)

The Good Samaritan: Control freak!

The Teacher: Cliché!

The Good Samaritan: Semi-intellectual!

The Teacher: Contrivance!

The Good Samaritan: Academic tapeworm!

The Teacher: First draft mistake!

(The Jumper, who has been watching this, takes out a gun and shoots it into the air.)

The Jumper: Hey!!! I'm the one with the problem. This play's supposed to be about me.

The Good Samaritan: Tough. The well-made play died with Ibsen.

The Teacher *(to The Good Samaritan)*: Damn it, get back into the play!

The Good Samaritan: Don't tell me what to do. Ever since I was a kid, everyone's told me how I'm supposed to behave. When I was five, my mom sent me to my room *(The Teacher starts clicking manically at The Good Samaritan.)* four thousand times because I wouldn't be the kid she wanted me —

The Teacher: This monologue is not justified!

The Good Samaritan: Tough shit, it's my life!

The Teacher: It's bad drama!

The Good Samaritan: I'll show you bad drama!

(The Good Samaritan and The Teacher begin to fight.)

The Jumper: Stop it! Come on, stop it, you're pulling focus.

The Teacher: Butt out!

(The Jumper tries to break up the fight.)

The Jumper: Come on, guys, cool it!

The Good Samaritan: Get away from us!

The Jumper: Just stop it!

The Good Samaritan: Leave us alone!

(The three of them are in a tight cluster. We hear a gunshot. The Teacher pulls away. There's blood on The Teacher's chest.)

The Teacher: I just got tenure.

(The Teacher collapses.)

The Good Samaritan: Oh my God.

The Jumper: He's dead.

(The Good Samaritan looks at The Jumper.)

The Good Samaritan: How horrible. Is that good playwriting or bad playwriting?

The Jumper: I, I don't know. It just happened.

(The Good Samaritan and The Jumper look at The Teacher.)

The Jumper and The Good Samaritan *(simultaneously)*: Hmmmmmmm.

(The Good Samaritan and The Jumper begin to exit.)

The Good Samaritan: Gee, you could've hurt yourself.

The Jumper: Gosh, you're right.
The Good Samaritan: Want to grab a brew?
The Jumper: Sure.

> *(The Teacher comes to life for a moment, clicks into the air and: Blackout.)*

CONSIDERATIONS FOR CRITICAL THINKING AND WRITING

1. **FIRST RESPONSE.** Comment on Orloff's statement that his purpose in *Playwriting 101* was to satirize dramatic clichés to make an "original play." Explain why you think he was or was not successful.

2. Why do you think the stage directions call for the Jumper and Good Samaritan to be of the same sex?

3. What do you learn from the Teacher about developing conflict and suspense?

4. What is the conflict in the play? Is there a resolution?

5. Describe the theme. Is it implicit or explicitly stated?

6. The Good Samaritan asks at the end, "Is that good playwriting or bad playwriting?" (p. 1357). What do you think?

CONNECTIONS TO OTHER SELECTIONS

1. Discuss *Playwriting 101* and Woody Allen's *Old Saybrook* (p. 1327) as metaplays, or plays about plays.

2. The Teacher claims that "When [Ibsen's] Nora leaves in *A Doll's House* [p. 1257], nobody wants her husband to reply — *(upbeat)* 'Call when you get work!'" Why not?

A Collection
of Plays

45

Plays for Further Reading

My plays are about love, honor, duty,
betrayal — things humans have written
about since the beginning of time.
— AUGUST WILSON

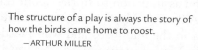

The structure of a play is always the story of
how the birds came home to roost.
— ARTHUR MILLER

Trying to Find Chinatown

Born in Los Angeles, David Henry Hwang is the son of immigrant Chinese
American parents; his father worked as a banker, and his mother was a
professor of piano. Educated at Stanford University, from which he earned
a B.A. in English in 1979, he became interested in theater after attending plays at the American Conservatory in San Francisco. His marginal
interest in a law career quickly gave way to his involvement in the engaging world of live theater. By his senior year, he had written and produced
his first play, *FOB* (an acronym for "fresh off the boat"), which marked
the beginning of a meteoric rise as a playwright. After a brief stint as a

writing teacher at a Menlo Park high school, Hwang attended the Yale University School of Drama from 1980 to 1981. Although he didn't stay to complete a degree, he studied theater history before leaving for New York City, where he thought the professional theater would provide a richer education than the student workshops at Yale.

In New York Hwang's work received a warm reception. In 1980 an off-Broadway production of *FOB* won an Obie Award for the best new play of the season. The play incorporates many of Hwang's characteristic concerns as a playwright. Growing up in California as a Chinese American made him

© Michal Daniel.

politically conscious during his college years in the late 1970s; this interest in his Chinese roots is evident in the central conflicts of *FOB,* which focuses on a Chinese immigrant's relationship with two Chinese American students he meets in Los Angeles. The immigrant quickly learns that he is expected to abandon much of his Chinese identity if he is to fit into mainstream American culture. Chinese American life is also the focus of *The Dance and the Railroad* and *Family Devotions,* both produced off-Broadway in 1981. Hwang's early plays are populated with Chinese Americans attempting to find the center of their own lives as they seesaw among the conventions, traditions, and values of East and West.

Hwang's next two dramas, produced in 1983, consist of two one-act plays set in Japan. Together they are titled *Sound and Beauty,* but each has its own title — *The House of Sleeping Beauties* and *The Sound of a Voice.* In these plays Hwang moves away from tales of Chinese American immigrants and themes of race and assimilation to stories about tragic love based on Japanese materials. Although Hwang was successful in having additional plays produced in the mid-1980s and won prestigious fellowships from the Guggenheim Foundation and the National Endowment for the Arts, it was not until 1988, when *M. Butterfly* — a complex treatment of social, political, racial, cultural, and sexual issues — was produced on Broadway, that he achieved astonishing commercial success as well as widespread acclaim. His awards for this play include the Outer Critics Circle Award for best Broadway play, the Drama Desk Award for best new play, the John Gassner Award for best American play, and the Tony Award for best play of the year. By the end of 1988, Hwang was regarded by many critics as the most talented young playwright in the United States. *Trying to Find China-town* is a brief but complicated confrontation between two young men who argue about racial identity in unexpected ways. Hwang's strategy is to challenge the polemical stereotyping that often passes for discussions of ethnic and cultural heritage in the United States.

David Henry Hwang (b. 1957)

Trying to Find Chinatown

1996

CHARACTERS

Benjamin, Caucasian male, early twenties.
Ronnie, Asian-American male, mid-twenties.

TIME AND PLACE A street corner on the Lower East Side, New York City. The present.

NOTE ON MUSIC Obviously, it would be foolish to require that the actor portraying Ronnie perform the specified violin music live. The score of this play can be played on tape over the house speakers, and the actor can feign playing the violin using a bow treated with soap. However, in order to effect a convincing illusion, it is desirable that the actor possess some familiarity with the violin or another stringed instrument.

> *Darkness. Over the house speakers, sound fades in: Hendrix-like virtuoso rock 'n' roll riffs—heavy feedback, distortion, phase shifting, wah-wah—amplified over a tiny Fender pug-nose.*

> *Lights fade up to reveal that the music's being played over a solid-body electric violin by Ronnie, a Chinese-American male in his mid-twenties; he is dressed in retro-'60s clothing and has a few requisite '90s body mutilations. He's playing on a sidewalk for money, his violin case open before him; change and a few stray bills have been left by previous passersby.*

> *Benjamin enters; he's in his early twenties, blond, blue-eyed, a Midwestern tourist in the big city. He holds a scrap of paper in his hands, scanning street signs for an address. He pauses before Ronnie, listens for a while. With a truly bravura run, Ronnie concludes the number and falls to his knees, gasping. Benjamin applauds.*

Benjamin: Good. That was really great. *(Pause)* I didn't . . . I mean, a fiddle . . . I mean, I'd heard them at square dances, on country stations and all, but I never . . . wow, this must really be New York City!

> *(Benjamin applauds, starts to walk on. Still on his knees, Ronnie clears his throat loudly.)*

Oh, I . . . you're not just doing this for your health, right?

> *(Benjamin reaches in his pocket, pulls out a couple of coins. Ronnie clears his throat again.)*

Look, I'm not a millionaire, I'm just . . .

> *(Benjamin pulls out his wallet, removes a dollar bill. Ronnie nods his head and gestures toward the violin case as he takes out a pack of cigarettes, lights one.)*

Ronnie: And don't call it a "fiddle," OK?
Benjamin: Oh. Well, I didn't mean to—
Ronnie: You sound like a wuss. A hick. A dipshit.
Benjamin: It just slipped out. I didn't really—
Ronnie: If this was a fiddle, I'd be sitting here with a cob pipe, stomping my cowboy boots and kicking up hay. Then I'd go home and fuck my cousin.

Benjamin: Oh! Well, I don't really think—

Ronnie: Do you see a cob pipe? Am I fucking my cousin?

Benjamin: Well, no, not at the moment, but—

Ronnie: All right. Then this is a violin, now you give me your money, and I ignore the insult. Herein endeth the lesson.

(*Pause.*)

Benjamin: Look, a dollar's more than I've ever given to a . . . to someone asking for money.

Ronnie: Yeah, well, this is New York. Welcome to the cost of living.

Benjamin: What I mean is, maybe in exchange, you could help me—?

Ronnie: Jesus Christ! Do you see a sign around my neck reading "Big Apple Fucking Tourist Bureau"?

Benjamin: I'm just looking for an address, I don't think it's far from here, maybe you could . . . ?

(*Benjamin holds out his scrap of paper, Ronnie snatches it away.*)

Ronnie: You're lucky I'm such a goddamn softy. (*He looks at the paper*) Oh, fuck you. Just suck my dick, you and the cousin you rode in on.

Benjamin: I don't get it! What are you—?

Ronnie: Eat me. You know exactly what I—

Benjamin: I'm just asking for a little—

Ronnie: "13 Doyers Street"? Like you don't know where that is?

Benjamin: Of course I don't know! That's why I'm asking—

Ronnie: C'mon, you trailer-park refugee. You don't know that's Chinatown?

Benjamin: Sure I know that's Chinatown.

Ronnie: I know you know that's Chinatown.

Benjamin: So? That doesn't mean I know where Chinatown—

Ronnie: So why is it that you picked *me*, of all the street musicians in the city—to point you in the direction of Chinatown? Lemme guess—is it the earring? No, I don't think so. The Hendrix riffs? Guess again, you fucking moron.

Benjamin: Now, wait a minute. I see what you're—

Ronnie: What are you gonna ask me next? Where you can find the best dim sum in the city? Whether I can direct you to a genuine opium den? Or do I happen to know how you can meet Miss Saigon for a night of nookie-nookie followed by a good old-fashioned ritual suicide? Now, get your white ass off my sidewalk. One dollar doesn't even begin to make up for all this aggravation. Why don't you go back home and race bullfrogs, or whatever it is you do for—?

Benjamin: Brother, I can absolutely relate to your anger. Righteous rage, I suppose, would be a more appropriate term. To be marginalized, as we are, by a white racist patriarchy, to the point where the accomplishments of our people are obliterated from the history books, this is cultural genocide of the first order, leading to the fact that you must do battle with all of Euro-America's emasculating and brutal stereotypes of Asians—the opium den, the sexual objectification of the Asian female, the exoticized image of a tourist's Chinatown which ignores the exploitation of workers, the failure to unionize, the high rate of mental illness and tuberculosis—against these, each day, you rage, no, not as a victim, but as a survivor, yes, brother, a glorious warrior survivor!

(Silence.)

Ronnie: Say what?

Benjamin: So, I hope you can see that my request is not—

Ronnie: Wait, wait.

Benjamin: —motivated by the sorts of racist assumptions—

Ronnie: But, but where . . . how did you learn all that?

Benjamin: All what?

Ronnie: All that—you know—oppression stuff—tuberculosis . . .

Benjamin: It's statistically irrefutable. TB occurs in the community at a rate—

Ronnie: Where did *you* learn it?

Benjamin: I took Asian-American studies. In college.

Ronnie: Where did you go to college?

Benjamin: University of Wisconsin. Madison.

Ronnie: Madison, Wisconsin?

Benjamin: That's not where the bridges are, by the way.

Ronnie: Huh? Oh, right . . .

Benjamin: You wouldn't believe the number of people who—

Ronnie: They have Asian-American studies in Madison, Wisconsin? Since when?

Benjamin: Since the last Third World Unity hunger strike. *(Pause)* Why do you look so surprised? We're down.

Ronnie: I dunno. It just never occurred to me, the idea of Asian students in the Midwest going on a hunger strike.

Benjamin: Well, a lot of them had midterms that week, so they fasted in shifts. *(Pause)* The administration never figured it out. The Asian students put that "They all look alike" stereotype to good use.

Ronnie: OK, so they got Asian-American studies. That still doesn't explain—

Benjamin: What?

Ronnie: Well . . . what *you* were doing taking it?

Benjamin: Just like everyone else. I wanted to explore my roots. And, you know, the history of oppression which is my legacy. After a lifetime of assimilation, I wanted to find out who I really am.

(Pause.)

Ronnie: And did you?

Benjamin: Sure. I learned to take pride in my ancestors who built the railroads, my Popo who would make me a hot bowl of jok with thousand-day-old eggs when the white kids chased me home yelling, "Gook! Chink! Slant-eyes!"

Ronnie: OK, OK, that's enough!

Benjamin: Painful to listen to, isn't it?

Ronnie: I don't know what kind of bullshit ethnic studies program they're running over in Wuss-consin, but did they bother to teach you that in order to find your Asian "roots," it's a good idea to first be Asian?

(Pause.)

Benjamin: Are you speaking metaphorically?

Ronnie: No! Literally! Look at your skin!

Benjamin: You know, it's very stereotypical to think that all Asian skin tones conform to a single hue.

Ronnie: You're white! Is this some kind of redneck joke or something? Am I the first person in the world to tell you this?

Benjamin: Oh! Oh! Oh!

Ronnie: I know real Asians are scarce in the Midwest, but . . . Jesus!

Benjamin: No, of course, I . . . I see where your misunderstanding arises.

Ronnie: Yeah. It's called, "You white."

Benjamin: It's just that—in my hometown of Tribune, Kansas, and then at school—see, everyone knows me—so this sort of thing never comes up. (*He offers his hand*) Benjamin Wong. I forget that a society wedded to racial constructs constantly forces me to explain my very existence.

Ronnie: Ronnie Chang. Otherwise known as "The Bow Man."

Benjamin: You see, I was adopted by Chinese-American parents at birth. So, clearly, I'm an Asian-American—

Ronnie: Even though you're blond and blue-eyed.

Benjamin: Well, you can't judge my race by my genetic heritage alone.

Ronnie: If genes don't determine race, what does?

Benjamin: Perhaps you'd prefer that I continue in denial, masquerading as a white man?

Ronnie: You can't just wake up and say, "Gee, I *feel* black today."

Benjamin: Brother, I'm just trying to find what you've already got.

Ronnie: What do I got?

Benjamin: A home. With your people. Picketing with the laundry workers. Taking refuge from the daily slights against your masculinity in the noble image of Gwan Gung.

Ronnie: Gwan who?

Benjamin: C'mon—the Chinese god of warriors and—what do you take me for? There're altars to him up all over the community.

Ronnie: I dunno what community you're talking about, but it's sure as hell not mine.

(*Pause.*)

Benjamin: What do you mean?

Ronnie: I mean, if you wanna call Chinatown *your* community, OK, knock yourself out, learn to use chopsticks, big deal. Go ahead, try and find your "roots" in some dim sum parlor with headless ducks hanging in the window. Those places don't tell you a thing about who *I* am.

Benjamin: Oh, I get it.

Ronnie: You get what?

Benjamin: You're one of those self-hating, *assimilated* Chinese-Americans, aren't you?

Ronnie: Oh, Jesus.

Benjamin: You probably call yourself "Oriental," huh? Look, maybe I can help you. I have some books I can—

Ronnie: Hey, I read all those Asian identity books when you were still slathering on industrial-strength sunblock. (*Pause*) Sure, I'm Chinese. But folks like you act like that means something. Like, all of a sudden, you know who I am. You think identity's that simple? That you can wrap it all up in a neat package and say, "I have ethnicity, therefore I am"? All you fucking ethnic fundamentalists. Always settling for easy answers. You say you're looking for identity, but you can't begin to face the real mysteries of the search. So instead, you go skin-deep, and call it a day. *(Pause. He turns away from Benjamin and starts to play his violin—slow and bluesy.)*

Benjamin: So what are you? "Just a human being"? That's like saying you *have* no identity. If you asked me to describe my dog, I'd say more than, "He's just a dog."

Ronnie: What—you think if I deny the importance of my race, I'm nobody? There're worlds out there, worlds you haven't even begun to understand. Open your eyes. Hear with your ears.

(Ronnie holds his violin at chest level, but does not attempt to play during the following monologue. As he speaks, rock and jazz violin tracks fade in and out over the house speakers, bringing to life the styles of music he describes.)

I concede—it was called a fiddle long ago—but that was even before the birth of jazz. When the hollering in the fields, the rank injustice of human bondage, the struggle of God's children against the plagues of the devil's white man, when all these boiled up into that bittersweet brew, called by later generations, the blues. That's when fiddlers like Son Sims held their chin rests at their chests, and sawed away like the hillbillies still do today. And with the coming of ragtime appeared the pioneer Stuff Smith, who sang as he stroked the catgut, with his raspy, Louis Armstrong-voice— gruff and sweet like the timber of horsehair riding south below the finger-board—and who finally sailed for Europe to find ears that would hear. Europe—where Stephane Grappelli initiated a magical French violin, to be passed from generation to generation—first he, to Jean-Luc Ponty, then Ponty to Didier Lockwood. Listening to Grappelli play "A Nightingale Sang in Berkeley Square" is to understand not only the song of birds, but also how they learn to fly, fall in love on the wing, and finally falter one day, to wait for darkness beneath a London street lamp. And Ponty—he showed how the modern violin man can accompany the shadow of his own lead lines, which cascade, one over another, into some nether world beyond the range of human hearing. Joe Venuti. Noel Pointer. Sven Asmussen. Even the Kronos Quartet, with their arrangement of "Purple Haze." Now, tell me, could any legacy be more rich, more crowded with mythology and heroes to inspire pride? What can I say if the banging of a gong or the clinking of a pickax on the Transcontinental Railroad fails to move me even as much as one note, played through a violin MIDI con-troller by Michael Urbaniak? *(He puts his violin to his chin, begins to play a jazz composition of his own invention)* Does it have to sound like Chinese opera before people like you decide I know who I am?

(Benjamin stands for a long moment, listening to Ronnie play. Then, he drops his dollar into the case, turns and exits right. Ronnie continues to play a long moment. Then Benjamin enters downstage left, illuminated in his own spotlight. He sits on the floor of the stage, his feet dangling off the lip. As he speaks, Ronnie continues playing his tune, which becomes underscoring for Benjamin's monologue. As the music continues, does it slowly begin to reflect the influence of Chinese music?)

Benjamin: When I finally found Doyers Street, I scanned the buildings for Number 13. Walking down an alley where the scent of freshly steamed char siu bao lingered in the air, I felt immediately that I had entered a world where all things were finally familiar. *(Pause)* An old woman bumped me with her shopping bag—screaming to her friend in Cantonese, though they walked no more than a few inches apart. Another man—shouting to a vendor in Sze-Yup. A youth, in white undershirt, perhaps a recent newcomer, bargaining with a grocer in Hokkien. I walked through this ocean of dialects, breathing in the richness with deep gulps, exhilarated by the energy this symphony brought to my step. And when I finally saw the number 13, I nearly wept at my good fortune. An old tenement, paint peeling, inside walls no doubt thick with a century of grease and broken dreams—and yet, to me, a temple—the house where my father was born. I suddenly saw it all: Gung Gung, coming home from his sixteen-hour days pressing shirts he could never afford to own, bringing with him candies for my father, each sweet wrapped in the hope of a better life. When my father left the ghetto, he swore he would never return. But he had, this day, in the thoughts and memories of his son, just six months after his death. And as I sat on the stoop, I pulled a hua-moi° from my pocket, sucked on it, and felt his spirit returning. To this place where his ghost, and the dutiful hearts of all his descendants, would always call home. *(He listens for a long moment)* And I felt an ache in my heart for all those lost souls, denied this most important of revelations: to know who they truly are.

(Benjamin sucks his salted plum and listens to the sounds around him. Ronnie continues to play. The two remain oblivious of one another. Lights fade slowly to black.)

End of play

Hua-moi: A dry, sour plum that is a Cantonese specialty food.

CONNECTIONS TO OTHER SELECTIONS

1. How do you think Ronnie in *Trying to Find Chinatown* would assess August Wilson's treatment of race in *Fences* (p. 1483)?

2. Discuss the perspective offered on white attitudes toward race in Hwang's play and in John Leguizamo's *Mambo Mouth* (p. 1349).

Rodeo

Jane Martin is a pseudonym. The author's identity is known only to a handful of administrators at the Actors Theatre of Louisville who handle permissions for productions and reprints of the play. *Rodeo* is one of eleven monologues in *Talking With*. . . . Martin has also published other plays conveniently grouped in two volumes: *Jane Martin: Collected Plays 1980–1995* (1996) and *Jane Martin: Collected Plays 1996–2001* (2001).

Although only one character appears in *Rodeo*, the monologue is surprisingly moving as she describes what the rodeo once was, how it has changed, and what it means to her. At first glance the subject matter may not seem very promising for drama, but the character's energy, forthrightness, and colorful language transform seemingly trivial details into significant meanings.

JANE MARTIN

Rodeo

1981

A young woman in her late twenties sits working on a
piece of tack. Beside her is a Lone Star beer in the can.
As the lights come up we hear the last verse of a Tanya
Tucker song or some other female country-western
vocalist. She is wearing old worn jeans and boots plus
a long-sleeved workshirt with the sleeves rolled up.
She works until the song is over and then speaks.

See Plays in
Performance
insert.

Big Eight: Shoot—Rodeo's just goin' to hell in a hand-
basket. Rodeo used to be somethin'. I loved it. I did.
Once Daddy an' a bunch of 'em was foolin' around
with some old bronc over to our place and this ol'
red nose named Cinch got bucked off and my Daddy
hooted and said he had him a nine-year-old girl, namely
me, wouldn't have no damn trouble cowboyin' that horse. Well, he put
me on up there, stuck that ridin' rein in my hand, gimme a kiss, and
said, "Now there's only one thing t' remember Honey Love, if ya fall off
you jest don't come home." Well I stayed up. You gotta stay on a bronc
eight seconds. Otherwise the ride don't count. So from that day on
my daddy called me Big Eight. Heck! That's all the name I got anymore . . . Big Eight.

Used to be fer cowboys, the rodeo did. Do it in some open field, folks
would pull their cars and pick-ups round it, sit on the hoods, some ranch
hand'd bulldog him some rank steer and everybody'd wave their hats and
call him by name. Ride us some buckin' stock, rope a few calves, git
throwed off a bull, and then we'd jest git us to a bar and tell each other lies
about how good we were.

Used to be a family thing. Wooly Billy Tilson and Tammy Lee had
them five kids on the circuit. Three boys, two girls and Wooly and Tammy.
Wasn't no two-beer rodeo in Oklahoma didn't have a Tilson entered. Used
to call the oldest girl Tits. Tits Tilson. Never seen a girl that top-heavy
could ride so well. Said she only fell off when the gravity got her. Cowboys
used to say if she landed face down you could plant two young trees in the
holes she'd leave. Ha! Tits Tilson.

Used to be people came to a rodeo had a horse of their own back
home. Farm people, ranch people—lord, they *knew* what they were lookin'
at. Knew a good ride from a bad ride, knew hard from easy. You broke
some bones er spent the day eatin' dirt, at least ya got appreciated.

Now they bought the rodeo. Them. Coca-Cola, Pepsi Cola, Marlboro
damn cigarettes. You know the ones I mean. Them. Hire some New York
faggot t' sit on some ol' stuffed horse in front of a sagebrush photo n'
smoke that junk. Hell, tobacco wasn't made to smoke, honey, it was made
to chew. Lord wanted ya filled up with smoke he would've set ya on fire.
Damn it gets me!

There's some guy in a banker's suit runs the rodeo now. Got him a
pinky ring and a digital watch, honey. Told us we oughta have a watcha-
macallit, choriographus or somethin', some ol' ballbuster used to be with

the Ice damn Capades. Wants us to ride around dressed up like Mickey Mouse, Pluto, crap like that. Told me I had to haul my butt through the barrel race done up like Minnie damn Mouse in a tu-tu. Huh uh, honey! Them people is so screwed-up they probably eat what they run over in the road.

Listen, they got the clowns wearin' Astronaut suits! I ain't lyin'. You know what a rodeo clown does! You go down, fall off whatever — the clown runs in front of the bull so's ya don't git stomped. Pin-stripes, he got 'em in space suits tellin' jokes on a microphone. First horse see 'em, done up like the Star Wars went crazy. Best buckin' horse on the circuit, name of Piss 'N' Vinegar, took one look at them clowns, had him a heart attack and died. Cowboy was ridin' him got hisself squashed. Twelve hundred pounds of coronary arrest jes fell right through 'em. Blam! Vio con dios. Crowd thought that was funnier than the astronauts. I swear it won't be long before they're strappin' ice-skates on the ponies. Big crowds now. Ain't hardly no ranch people, no farm people, nobody I know. Buncha disco babies and dee-vorce lawyers — designer jeans and day-glo Stetsons. Hell, the whole bunch of 'em wears French perfume. Oh it smells like money now! Got it on the cable T and V — hey, you know what, when ya rodeo yer just bound to kick yerself up some dust — well now, seems like that fogs up the ol' TV camera, so they told us a while back that from now on we was gonna ride on some new stuff called Astro-dirt. Dust free. Artificial damn dirt, honey. Lord have mercy.

Banker Suit called me in the other day said "Lurlene . . ." "Hold it," I said, "Who's this Lurlene? Round here they call me Big Eight." "Well, Big Eight," he said, "My name's Wallace." "Well that's a real surprise t' me," I said, "Cause aroun' here everybody jes calls you Dumb-ass." My, he laughed real big, slapped his big ol' desk, an' then he said I wasn't suitable for the rodeo no more. Said they was lookin' fer another type, somethin' a little more in the showgirl line, like the Dallas Cowgirls maybe. Said the ridin' and ropin' wasn't the thing no more. Talked on about floats, costumes, dancin' choreog-aphy. If I was a man I woulda pissed on his shoe. Said he'd give me a lifetime pass though. Said I could come to his rodeo any time I wanted.

Rodeo used to be people ridin' horses for the pleasure of people who rode horses — made you feel good about what you could do. Rodeo wasn't worth no money to nobody. Money didn't have nothing to do with it! Used to be seven Tilsons riding in the rodeo. Wouldn't none of 'em dress up like Donald damn Duck so they quit. That there's the law of gravity!

There's a bunch of assholes in this country sneak around until they see ya havin' fun and then they buy the fun and start in sellin' it. See, they figure if ya love it, they can sell it. Well you look out, honey! They want to make them a dollar out of what you love. Dress *you* up like Minnie Mouse. Sell your rodeo. Turn *yer* pleasure into Ice damn Capades. You hear what I'm sayin'? You're jus' merchandise to them, sweetie. You're jus' merchandise to them.

Blackout.

Considerations for Critical Thinking and Writing

1. FIRST RESPONSE. Big Eight is presented as an old-fashioned rodeo type. What associations or stereotypes do you have about such people? What assumptions do you make about them? How does the author use those expectations to heighten your understanding of Big Eight's character?

2. How has the rodeo changed from how it "used to be"? How do you account for those changes?

3. Comment on Big Eight's use of language. Why is it appropriate for her character?

4. How would you describe Big Eight's brand of humor? How does it affect your understanding of her?

5. How do your feelings about Big Eight develop during the course of the monologue?

6. What does the rodeo mean to Big Eight?

Connections to Other Selections

1. Compare and contrast a Shakespeare monologue from *Othello* (p. 1164) with the style and content of *Rodeo*.

2. In an essay discuss the nostalgic tone in *Rodeo* and Stephen Crane's short story "The Bride Comes to Yellow Sky" (p. 266). In your response consider each work's treatment of the West.

3. Compare the attitudes expressed about merchandising in *Rodeo* with those expressed in Arthur Miller's *Death of a Salesman* (p. 1372).

Death of a Salesman

Arthur Miller was born in New York City to middle-class Jewish parents. His mother was a teacher and his father a clothing manufacturer. In 1938 he graduated from the University of Michigan, where he had begun writing plays. Six years later his first Broadway play, *The Man Who Had All the Luck,* closed after only a few performances, but *All My Sons* (1947) earned the admiration of both critics and audiences. This drama of family life launched his career, and his next play was even more successful. *Death of a Sales-*

Courtesy of the University of Michigan Alumni Association Records, Bentley Historical Library, University of Michigan.

man (1949) won a Pulitzer Prize and established his international reputation so that Miller, along with Tennessee Williams, became one of the most successful American playwrights of the 1940s and 1950s. During this period, his plays included an adaptation of Henrik Ibsen's *Enemy of the People* (1951), *The Crucible* (1953), and *A View from the Bridge* (1955). Among his later works are *The Misfits* (1961, a screenplay), *After the Fall* (1964), *Incident at Vichy* (1964), *The Price* (1968), *The Creation of the World and Other Business* (1972), *The*

Archbishop's Ceiling (1976), *The American Clock* (1980), *Time Bends* (1987, essays), *The Ride Down Mt. Morgan* (1991), and *Broken Glass* (1994).

In *Death of a Salesman* Miller's concerns and techniques are similar to those of social realism. His characters' dialogue sounds much like ordinary speech and deals with recognizable family problems ranging from feelings about one another to personal aspirations. Like Ibsen and Chekhov, Miller places his characters in a social context so that their behavior within the family suggests larger implications: the death of this salesman raises issues concerning the significance and value of the American dream of success.

Although such qualities resemble some of the techniques and concerns of realistic drama, Miller also uses other techniques to express Willy Loman's thoughts. In a sense, the play allows the audience to observe what goes on inside the protagonist's head. (At one point Miller was going to title the play *The Inside of His Head.*) When Willy thinks of the past, we see those events reenacted on stage in the midst of present events. This reenactment is achieved through the use of symbolic nonrealistic sets that appear or disappear as the stage lighting changes to reveal Willy's state of mind.

Willy Loman is in many ways an ordinary human being—indeed, painfully so. He is neither brilliant nor heroic, and his life is made up of unfulfilled dreams and self-deceptions. Yet Miller conceived of him as a tragic figure because, as he wrote in "Tragedy and the Common Man," "the common man is as apt a subject for tragedy . . . as kings." Willy's circumstances are radically different from those of Oedipus or Othello, but Miller manages to create a character whose human dignity evokes tragic feelings for many readers and viewers.

> Explore contexts for Arthur Miller on *LiterActive*.

ARTHUR MILLER (1915–2005)

Death of a Salesman   *1949*

Certain Private Conversations in Two Acts and a Requiem

CAST

Willy Loman	*Uncle Ben*
Linda	*Howard Wagner*
Biff	*Jenny*
Happy	*Stanley*
Bernard	*Miss Forsythe*
The Woman	*Letta*
Charley	

See Plays in Performance insert.

SCENE: The action takes place in Willy Loman's house and yard and in various places he visits in the New York and Boston of today.

Throughout the play, in the stage directions, left and right mean stage left and stage right.

ACT I

A melody is heard, played upon a flute. It is small and fine, telling of grass and trees and the horizon. The curtain rises.

      Before us is the Salesman's house. We are aware of towering, angular shapes behind it, surrounding it on all sides. Only the blue light of the sky falls upon the house and forestage; the surrounding area shows an angry glow of orange. As more light appears, we see a solid vault of apartment houses around the small, fragile-seeming home. An air of the dream clings to the place, a dream rising out of reality. The kitchen at center seems actual enough, for there is a kitchen table with three chairs, and a refrigerator. But no other fixtures are seen. At the back of the kitchen there is a draped entrance, which leads to the living-room. To the right of the kitchen, on a level raised two feet, is a bedroom furnished only with a brass bedstead and a straight chair. On a shelf over the bed a silver athletic trophy stands. A window opens onto the apartment house at the side.

      Behind the kitchen, on a level raised six and a half feet, is the boys' bedroom, at present barely visible. Two beds are dimly seen, and at the back of the room a dormer window. (This bedroom is above the unseen living-room.) At the left a stairway curves up to it from the kitchen.

      The entire setting is wholly or, in some places, partially transparent. The roof-line of the house is one-dimensional; under and over it we see the apartment buildings. Before the house lies an apron, curving beyond the forestage into the orchestra. This forward area serves as the back yard as well as the locale of all Willy's imaginings and of his city scenes. Whenever the action is in the present the actors observe the imaginary wall-lines, entering the house only through its door at the left. But in the scenes of the past these boundaries are broken, and characters enter or leave a room by stepping "through" a wall onto the forestage.

      From the right, Willy Loman, the Salesman, enters, carrying two large sample cases. The flute plays on. He hears but is not aware of it. He is past sixty years of age, dressed quietly. Even as he crosses the stage to the doorway of the house, his exhaustion is apparent. He unlocks the door, comes into the kitchen, and thankfully lets his burden down, feeling the soreness of his palms. A word-sigh escapes his lips— it might be "Oh, boy, oh, boy." He closes the door, then carries his cases out into the living-room, through the draped kitchen doorway.

      Linda, his wife, has stirred in her bed at the right. She gets out and puts on a robe, listening. Most often jovial, she has developed an iron repression of her exceptions to Willy's behavior—she more than loves him, she admires him, as though his mercurial nature, his temper, his massive dreams and little cruelties, served her only as sharp reminders of the turbulent longings within him, longings which she shares but lacks the temperament to utter and follow to their end.

Linda (hearing Willy outside the bedroom, calls with some trepidation): Willy!
Willy: It's all right. I came back.
Linda: Why? What happened? *(Slight pause.)* Did something happen, Willy?
Willy: No, nothing happened.
Linda: You didn't smash the car, did you?
Willy (with casual irritation): I said nothing happened. Didn't you hear me?
Linda: Don't you feel well?
Willy: I'm tired to the death. *(The flute has faded away. He sits on the bed beside her, a little numb.)* I couldn't make it. I just couldn't make it, Linda.

Linda (very carefully, delicately): Where were you all day? You look terrible.

Willy: I got as far as a little above Yonkers. I stopped for a cup of coffee. Maybe it was the coffee.

Linda: What?

Willy (after a pause): I suddenly couldn't drive any more. The car kept going off onto the shoulder, y'know?

Linda (helpfully): Oh. Maybe it was the steering again. I don't think Angelo knows the Studebaker.

Willy: No, it's me, it's me. Suddenly I realize I'm goin' sixty miles an hour and I don't remember the last five minutes. I'm — I can't seem to — keep my mind to it.

Linda: Maybe it's your glasses. You never went for your new glasses.

Willy: No, I see everything. I came back ten miles an hour. It took me nearly four hours from Yonkers.

Linda (resigned): Well, you'll just have to take a rest, Willy, you can't continue this way.

Willy: I just got back from Florida.

Linda: But you didn't rest your mind. Your mind is overactive, and the mind is what counts, dear.

Willy: I'll start out in the morning. Maybe I'll feel better in the morning. *(She is taking off his shoes.)* These goddam arch supports are killing me.

Linda: Take an aspirin. Should I get you an aspirin? It'll soothe you.

Willy (with wonder): I was driving along, you understand? And I was fine. I was even observing the scenery. You can imagine, me looking at scenery, on the road every week of my life. But it's so beautiful up there, Linda, the trees are so thick, and the sun is warm. I opened the windshield and just let the warm air bathe over me. And then all of a sudden I'm goin' off the road! I'm tellin' ya, I absolutely forgot I was driving. If I'd've gone the other way over the white line I might've killed somebody. So I went on again — and five minutes later I'm dreamin' again, and I nearly — *(He presses two fingers against his eyes.)* I have such thoughts, I have such strange thoughts.

Linda: Willy, dear. Talk to them again. There's no reason why you can't work in New York.

Willy: They don't need me in New York. I'm the New England man. I'm vital in New England.

Linda: But you're sixty years old. They can't expect you to keep traveling every week.

Willy: I'll have to send a wire to Portland. I'm supposed to see Brown and Morrison tomorrow morning at ten o'clock to show the line. Goddammit, I could sell them! *(He starts putting on his jacket.)*

Linda (taking the jacket from him): Why don't you go down to the place tomorrow and tell Howard you've simply got to work in New York? You're too accommodating, dear.

Willy: If old man Wagner was alive I'd a been in charge of New York now! That man was a prince, he was a masterful man. But that boy of his, that Howard, he don't appreciate. When I went north the first time, the Wagner Company didn't know where New England was!

Linda: Why don't you tell those things to Howard, dear?

Willy (encouraged): I will, I definitely will. Is there any cheese?

Linda: I'll make you a sandwich.

Willy: No, go to sleep. I'll take some milk. I'll be up right away. The boys in?

Linda: They're sleeping. Happy took Biff on a date tonight.

Willy (interested): That so?

Linda: It was so nice to see them shaving together, one behind the other, in the bathroom. And going out together. You notice? The whole house smells of shaving lotion.

Willy: Figure it out. Work a lifetime to pay off a house. You finally own it, and there's nobody to live in it.

Linda: Well, dear, life is a casting off. It's always that way.

Willy: No, no, some people — some people accomplish something. Did Biff say anything after I went this morning?

Linda: You shouldn't have criticized him, Willy, especially after he just got off the train. You mustn't lose your temper with him.

Willy: When the hell did I lose my temper? I simply asked him if he was making any money. Is that a criticism?

Linda: But, dear, how could he make any money?

Willy (worried and angered): There's such an undercurrent in him. He became a moody man. Did he apologize when I left this morning?

Linda: He was crestfallen, Willy. You know how he admires you. I think if he finds himself, then you'll both be happier and not fight any more.

Willy: How can he find himself on a farm? Is that a life? A farmhand? In the beginning, when he was young, I thought, well, a young man, it's good for him to tramp around, take a lot of different jobs. But it's more than ten years now and he has yet to make thirty-five dollars a week!

Linda: He's finding himself, Willy.

Willy: Not finding yourself at the age of thirty-four is a disgrace!

Linda: Shh!

Willy: The trouble is he's lazy, goddammit!

Linda: Willy, please!

Willy: Biff is a lazy bum!

Linda: They're sleeping. Get something to eat. Go on down.

Willy: Why did he come home? I would like to know what brought him home.

Linda: I don't know. I think he's still lost, Willy. I think he's very lost.

Willy: Biff Loman is lost. In the greatest country in the world a young man with such — personal attractiveness, gets lost. And such a hard worker. There's one thing about Biff — he's not lazy.

Linda: Never.

Willy (with pity and resolve): I'll see him in the morning; I'll have a nice talk with him. I'll get him a job selling. He could be big in no time. My God! Remember how they used to follow him around in high school? When he smiled at one of them their faces lit up. When he walked down the street . . . *(He loses himself in reminiscences.)*

Linda (trying to bring him out of it): Willy, dear, I got a new kind of American-type cheese today. It's whipped.

Willy: Why do you get American when I like Swiss?

Linda: I just thought you'd like a change —

Willy: I don't want a change! I want Swiss cheese. Why am I always being contradicted?

Linda (with a covering laugh): I thought it would be a surprise.

Willy: Why don't you open a window in here, for God's sake?

Linda (with infinite patience): They're all open, dear.

Willy: The way they boxed us in here. Bricks and windows, windows and bricks.

Linda: We should've bought the land next door.

Willy: The street is lined with cars. There's not a breath of fresh air in the neighborhood. The grass don't grow any more, you can't raise a carrot in the back yard. They should've had a law against apartment houses. Remember those two beautiful elm trees out there? When I and Biff hung the swing between them?

Linda: Yeah, like being a million miles from the city.

Willy: They should've arrested the builder for cutting those down. They massacred the neighborhood. *(Lost.)* More and more I think of those days, Linda. This time of year it was lilac and wisteria. And then the peonies would come out, and the daffodils. What fragrance in this room!

Linda: Well, after all, people had to move somewhere.

Willy: No, there's more people now.

Linda: I don't think there's more people. I think—

Willy: There's more people! That's what's ruining this country! Population is getting out of control. The competition is maddening! Smell the stink from that apartment house! And another one on the other side . . . How can they whip cheese?

On Willy's last line, Biff and Happy raise themselves up in their beds, listening.

Linda: Go down, try it. And be quiet.

Willy (turning to Linda, guiltily): You're not worried about me, are you, sweetheart?

Biff: What's the matter?

Happy: Listen!

Linda: You've got too much on the ball to worry about.

Willy: You're my foundation and my support, Linda.

Linda: Just try to relax, dear. You make mountains out of molehills.

Willy: I won't fight with him any more. If he wants to go back to Texas, let him go.

Linda: He'll find his way.

Willy: Sure. Certain men just don't get started till later in life. Like Thomas Edison, I think. Or B. F. Goodrich. One of them was deaf. *(He starts for the bedroom doorway.)* I'll put my money on Biff.

Linda: And Willy—if it's warm Sunday we'll drive in the country. And we'll open the windshield, and take lunch.

Willy: No, the windshields don't open on the new cars.

Linda: But you opened it today.

Willy: Me? I didn't. *(He stops.)* Now isn't that peculiar! Isn't that a remarkable— *(He breaks off in amazement and fright as the flute is heard distantly.)*

Linda: What, darling?

Willy: That is the most remarkable thing.

Linda: What, dear?

Willy: I was thinking of the Chevy. *(Slight pause.)* Nineteen twenty-eight . . . when I had that red Chevy—*(Breaks off.)* That funny? I coulda sworn I was driving that Chevy today.

Linda: Well, that's nothing. Something must've reminded you.

Willy: Remarkable. Ts. Remember those days? The way Biff used to simonize that car? The dealer refused to believe there was eighty thousand miles on it. (*He shakes his head.*) Heh! (*To Linda.*) Close your eyes, I'll be right up. (*He walks out of the bedroom.*)

Happy (to Biff): Jesus, maybe he smashed up the car again!

Linda (calling after Willy): Be careful on the stairs, dear! The cheese is on the middle shelf! (*She turns, goes over to the bed, takes his jacket, and goes out of the bedroom.*)

Light has risen on the boys' room. Unseen, Willy is heard talking to himself, "Eighty thousand miles," and a little laugh. Biff gets out of bed, comes downstage a bit, and stands attentively. Biff is two years older than his brother Happy, well built, but in these days bears a worn air and seems less self-assured. He has succeeded less, and his dreams are stronger and less acceptable than Happy's. Happy is tall, powerfully made. Sexuality is like a visible color on him, or a scent that many women have discovered. He, like his brother, is lost, but in a different way, for he has never allowed himself to turn his face toward defeat and is thus more confused and hard-skinned, although seemingly more content.

Happy (getting out of bed): He's going to get his license taken away if he keeps that up. I'm getting nervous about him, y'know, Biff?

Biff: His eyes are going.

Happy: No, I've driven with him. He sees all right. He just doesn't keep his mind on it. I drove into the city with him last week. He stops at a green light and then it turns red and he goes. (*He laughs.*)

Biff: Maybe he's color-blind.

Happy: Pop? Why he's got the finest eye for color in the business. You know that.

Biff (sitting down on his bed): I'm going to sleep.

Happy: You're not sour on Dad, are you, Biff?

Biff: He's all right, I guess.

Willy (underneath them, in the living-room): Yes, sir, eighty thousand miles — eighty-two thousand!

Biff: You smoking?

Happy (holding out a pack of cigarettes): Want one?

Biff (taking a cigarette): I can never sleep when I smell it.

Willy: What a simonizing job, heh!

Happy (with deep sentiment): Funny, Biff, y'know? Us sleeping in here again? The old beds. (*He pats his bed affectionately.*) All the talk that went across those two beds, huh? Our whole lives.

Biff: Yeah. Lotta dreams and plans.

Happy (with a deep and masculine laugh): About five hundred women would like to know what was said in this room.

They share a soft laugh.

Biff: Remember that big Betsy something — what the hell was her name — over on Bushwick Avenue?

Happy (combing his hair): With the collie dog!

Biff: That's the one. I got you in there, remember?

Happy: Yeah, that was my first time — I think. Boy, there was a pig! (*They laugh, almost crudely.*) You taught me everything I know about women. Don't forget that.

Biff: I bet you forgot how bashful you used to be. Especially with girls.

Happy: Oh, I still am, Biff.

Biff: Oh, go on.

Happy: I just control it, that's all. I think I got less bashful and you got more so. What happened, Biff? Where's the old humor, the old confidence? *(He shakes Biff's knee. Biff gets up and moves restlessly about the room.)* What's the matter?

Biff: Why does Dad mock me all the time?

Happy: He's not mocking you, he —

Biff: Everything I say there's a twist of mockery on his face. I can't get near him.

Happy: He just wants you to make good, that's all. I wanted to talk to you about Dad for a long time, Biff. Something's — happening to him. He — talks to himself.

Biff: I noticed that this morning. But he always mumbled.

Happy: But not so noticeable. It got so embarrassing I sent him to Florida. And you know something? Most of the time he's talking to you.

Biff: What's he say about me?

Happy: I can't make it out.

Biff: What's he say about me?

Happy: I think the fact that you're not settled, that you're still kind of up in the air . . .

Biff: There's one or two other things depressing him, Happy.

Happy: What do you mean?

Biff: Never mind. Just don't lay it all to me.

Happy: But I think if you just got started — I mean — is there any future for you out there?

Biff: I tell ya, Hap, I don't know what the future is. I don't know — what I'm supposed to want.

Happy: What do you mean?

Biff: Well, I spent six or seven years after high school trying to work myself up. Shipping clerk, salesman, business of one kind or another. And it's a measly manner of existence. To get on that subway on the hot mornings in summer. To devote your whole life to keeping stock, or making phone calls, or selling or buying. To suffer fifty weeks of the year for the sake of a two-week vacation, when all you really desire is to be outdoors, with your shirt off. And always to have to get ahead of the next fella. And still — that's how you build a future.

Happy: Well, you really enjoy it on a farm? Are you content out there?

Biff (with rising agitation): Hap, I've had twenty or thirty different kinds of jobs since I left home before the war, and it always turns out the same. I just realized it lately. In Nebraska when I herded cattle, and the Dakotas, and Arizona, and now in Texas. It's why I came home now, I guess, because I realized it. This farm I work on, it's spring there now, see? And they've got about fifteen new colts. There's nothing more inspiring or — beautiful than the sight of a mare and a new colt. And it's cool there now, see? Texas is cool now, and it's spring. And whenever spring comes to where I am, I suddenly get the feeling, my God, I'm not gettin' anywhere! What the hell am I doing, playing around with horses, twenty-eight dollars a week! I'm thirty-four years old, I oughta be makin' my future. That's when I come running home. And now, I get here, and I don't know what to do with myself. *(After a pause.)* I've always made a point of not wasting my life, and everytime I come back here I know that all I've done is to waste my life.

Happy: You're a poet, you know that, Biff? You're a — you're an idealist!

Biff: No, I'm mixed up very bad. Maybe I oughta get married. Maybe I oughta get stuck into something. Maybe that's my trouble. I'm like a boy. I'm not married. I'm not in business, I just — I'm like a boy. Are you content, Hap? You're a success, aren't you? Are you content?

Happy: Hell, no!

Biff: Why? You're making money, aren't you?

Happy (moving about with energy, expressiveness): All I can do now is wait for the merchandise manager to die. And suppose I get to be merchandise manager? He's a good friend of mine, and he just built a terrific estate on Long Island. And he lived there about two months and sold it, and now he's building another one. He can't enjoy it once it's finished. And I know that's just what I would do. I don't know what the hell I'm workin' for. Sometimes I sit in my apartment — all alone. And I think of the rent I'm paying. And it's crazy. But then, it's what I always wanted. My own apartment, a car, and plenty of women. And still, goddammit, I'm lonely.

Biff (with enthusiasm): Listen, why don't you come out West with me?

Happy: You and I, heh?

Biff: Sure, maybe we could buy a ranch. Raise cattle, use our muscles. Men built like we are should be working out in the open.

Happy (avidly): The Loman Brothers, heh?

Biff (with vast affection): Sure, we'd be known all over the counties!

Happy (enthralled): That's what I dream about, Biff. Sometimes I want to just rip my clothes off in the middle of the store and outbox that goddam merchandise manager. I mean I can outbox, outrun, and outlift anybody in that store, and I have to take orders from those common, petty sons-of-bitches till I can't stand it any more.

Biff: I'm tellin' you, kid, if you were with me I'd be happy out there.

Happy (enthused): See, Biff, everybody around me is so false that I'm constantly lowering my ideals . . .

Biff: Baby, together we'd stand up for one another, we'd have someone to trust.

Happy: If I were around you —

Biff: Hap, the trouble is we weren't brought up to grub for money. I don't know how to do it.

Happy: Neither can I!

Biff: Then let's go!

Happy: The only thing is — what can you make out there?

Biff: But look at your friend. Builds an estate and then hasn't the peace of mind to live in it.

Happy: Yeah, but when he walks into the store the waves part in front of him. That's fifty-two thousand dollars a year coming through the revolving door, and I got more in my pinky finger than he's got in his head.

Biff: Yeah, but you just said —

Happy: I gotta show some of those pompous, self-important executives over there that Hap Loman can make the grade. I want to walk into the store the way he walks in. Then I'll go with you, Biff. We'll be together yet, I swear. But take those two we had tonight. Now weren't they gorgeous creatures?

Biff: Yeah, yeah, most gorgeous I've had in years.

Happy: I get that any time I want, Biff. Whenever I feel disgusted. The trouble is, it gets like bowling or something. I just keep knockin' them over and it doesn't mean anything. You still run around a lot?

Biff: Naa. I'd like to find a girl — steady, somebody with substance.

Happy: That's what I long for.

Biff: Go on! You'd never come home.

Happy: I would! Somebody with character, with resistance! Like Mom, y'know? You're gonna call me a bastard when I tell you this. That girl Charlotte I was with tonight is engaged to be married in five weeks. *(He tries on his new hat.)*

Biff: No kiddin'!

Happy: Sure, the guy's in line for the vice-presidency of the store. I don't know what gets into me, maybe I just have an overdeveloped sense of competition or something, but I went and ruined her, and furthermore I can't get rid of her. And he's the third executive I've done that to. Isn't that a crummy characteristic? And to top it all, I go to their weddings! *(Indignantly, but laughing.)* Like I'm not supposed to take bribes. Manufacturers offer me a hundred-dollar bill now and then to throw an order their way. You know how honest I am, but it's like this girl, see. I hate myself for it. Because I don't want the girl, and, still, I take it and — I love it!

Biff: Let's go to sleep.

Happy: I guess we didn't settle anything, heh?

Biff: I just got one idea that I think I'm going to try.

Happy: What's that?

Biff: Remember Bill Oliver?

Happy: Sure, Oliver is very big now. You want to work for him again?

Biff: No, but when I quit he said something to me. He put his arm on my shoulder, and he said, "Biff, if you ever need anything, come to me."

Happy: I remember that. That sounds good.

Biff: I think I'll go to see him. If I could get ten thousand or even seven or eight thousand dollars I could buy a beautiful ranch.

Happy: I bet he'd back you. 'Cause he thought highly of you, Biff. I mean, they all do. You're well liked, Biff. That's why I say to come back here, and we both have the apartment. And I'm tellin' you, Biff, any babe you want . . .

Biff: No, with a ranch I could do the work I like and still be something. I just wonder though. I wonder if Oliver still thinks I stole that carton of basketballs.

Happy: Oh, he probably forgot that long ago. It's almost ten years. You're too sensitive. Anyway, he didn't really fire you.

Biff: Well, I think he was going to. I think that's why I quit. I was never sure whether he knew or not. I know he thought the world of me, though. I was the only one he'd let lock up the place.

Willy (below): You gonna wash the engine, Biff?

Happy: Shh!

Biff looks at Happy, who is gazing down, listening. Willy is mumbling in the parlor.

Happy: You hear that?

They listen. Willy laughs warmly.

Biff (growing angry): Doesn't he know Mom can hear that?

Willy: Don't get your sweater dirty, Biff!

A look of pain crosses Biff's face.

Happy: Isn't that terrible? Don't leave again, will you? You'll find a job here. You gotta stick around. I don't know what to do about him, it's getting embarrassing.

Willy: What a simonizing job!

Biff: Mom's hearing that!

Willy: No kiddin', Biff, you got a date? Wonderful!

Happy: Go on to sleep. But talk to him in the morning, will you?

Biff (reluctantly getting into bed): With her in the house. Brother!

Happy (getting into bed): I wish you'd have a good talk with him.

The light on their room begins to fade.

Biff (to himself in bed): That selfish, stupid . . .

Happy: Sh . . . Sleep, Biff.

Their light is out. Well before they have finished speaking, Willy's form is dimly seen below in the darkened kitchen. He opens the refrigerator, searches in there, and takes out a bottle of milk. The apartment houses are fading out, and the entire house and surroundings become covered with leaves. Music insinuates itself as the leaves appear.

Willy: Just wanna be careful with those girls, Biff, that's all. Don't make any promises. No promises of any kind. Because a girl, y'know, they always believe what you tell 'em, and you're very young, Biff, you're too young to be talking seriously to girls.

Light rises on the kitchen. Willy, talking, shuts the refrigerator door and comes downstage to the kitchen table. He pours milk into a glass. He is totally immersed in himself, smiling faintly.

Willy: Too young entirely, Biff. You want to watch your schooling first. Then when you're all set, there'll be plenty of girls for a boy like you. (*He smiles broadly at a kitchen chair.*) That so? The girls pay for you? (*He laughs.*) Boy, you must really be makin' a hit.

Willy is gradually addressing—physically—a point offstage, speaking through the wall of the kitchen, and his voice has been rising in volume to that of a normal conversation.

Willy: I been wondering why you polish the car so careful. Ha! Don't leave the hubcaps, boys. Get the chamois to the hubcaps. Happy, use newspaper on the windows, it's the easiest thing. Show him how to do it, Biff! You see, Happy? Pad it up, use it like a pad. That's it, that's it, good work. You're doin' all right, Hap. (*He pauses, then nods in approbation for a few seconds, then looks upward.*) Biff, first thing we gotta do when we get time is clip that big branch over the house. Afraid it's gonna fall in a storm and hit the roof. Tell you what. We get a rope and sling her around, and then we climb up there with a couple of saws and take her down. Soon as you finish the car, boys, I wanna see ya. I got a surprise for you, boys.

Biff (offstage): Whatta ya got, Dad?

Willy: No, you finish first. Never leave a job till you're finished—remember that. (*Looking toward the "big trees."*) Biff, up in Albany I saw a beautiful hammock. I think I'll buy it next trip, and we'll hang it right between those two elms. Wouldn't that be something? Just swingin' there under those branches. Boy, that would be . . .

Young Biff and Young Happy appear from the direction Willy was addressing. Happy carries rags and a pail of water. Biff, wearing a sweater with a block "S," carries a football.

Biff (pointing in the direction of the car offstage): How's that, Pop, professional?

Willy: Terrific. Terrific job, boys. Good work, Biff.

Happy: Where's the surprise, Pop?

Willy: In the back seat of the car.

Happy: Boy! (*He runs off.*)

Biff: What is it, Dad? Tell me, what'd you buy?

Willy (laughing, cuffs him): Never mind, something I want you to have.

Biff (turns and starts off): What is it, Hap?

Happy (offstage): It's a punching bag!

Biff: Oh, Pop!

Willy: It's got Gene Tunney's signature on it!

Happy runs onstage with a punching bag.

Biff: Gee, how'd you know we wanted a punching bag?

Willy: Well, it's the finest thing for the timing.

Happy (lies down on his back and pedals with his feet): I'm losing weight, you notice, Pop?

Willy (to Happy): Jumping rope is good too.

Biff: Did you see the new football I got?

Willy (examining the ball): Where'd you get a new ball?

Biff: The coach told me to practice my passing.

Willy: That so? And he gave you the ball, heh?

Biff: Well, I borrowed it from the locker room. (*He laughs confidentially.*)

Willy (laughing with him at the theft): I want you to return that.

Happy: I told you he wouldn't like it!

Biff (angrily): Well, I'm bringing it back!

Willy (stopping the incipient argument, to Happy): Sure, he's gotta practice with a regulation ball, doesn't he? (*To Biff.*) Coach'll probably congratulate you on your initiative!

Biff: Oh, he keeps congratulating my initiative all the time, Pop.

Willy: That's because he likes you. If somebody else took that ball there'd be an uproar. So what's the report, boys, what's the report?

Biff: Where'd you go this time, Dad? Gee we were lonesome for you.

Willy (pleased, puts an arm around each boy and they come down to the apron): Lonesome, heh?

Biff: Missed you every minute.

Willy: Don't say? Tell you a secret, boys. Don't breathe it to a soul. Someday I'll have my own business, and I'll never have to leave home any more.

Happy: Like Uncle Charley, heh?

Willy: Bigger than Uncle Charley! Because Charley is not—liked. He's liked, but he's not—well liked.

Biff: Where'd you go this time, Dad?

Willy: Well, I got on the road, and I went north to Providence. Met the Mayor.

Biff: The Mayor of Providence!

Willy: He was sitting in the hotel lobby.

Biff: What'd he say?

Willy: He said, "Morning!" And I said, "You got a fine city here, Mayor." And then he had coffee with me. And then I went to Waterbury. Waterbury is a fine city. Big clock city, the famous Waterbury clock. Sold a nice bill there. And then Boston — Boston is the cradle of the Revolution. A fine city. And a couple of other towns in Mass., and on to Portland and Bangor and straight home!

Biff: Gee, I'd love to go with you sometime, Dad.

Willy: Soon as summer comes.

Happy: Promise?

Willy: You and Hap and I, and I'll show you all the towns. America is full of beautiful towns and fine, upstanding people. And they know me, boys, they know me up and down New England. The finest people. And when I bring you fellas up, there'll be open sesame for all of us, 'cause one thing, boys: I have friends. I can park my car in any street in New England, and the cops protect it like their own. This summer, heh?

Biff and Happy (together): Yeah! You bet!

Willy: We'll take our bathing suits.

Happy: We'll carry your bags, Pop!

Willy: Oh, won't that be something! Me comin' into the Boston stores with you boys carryin' my bags. What a sensation!

Biff is prancing around, practicing passing the ball.

Willy: You nervous, Biff, about the game?

Biff: Not if you're gonna be there.

Willy: What do they say about you in school, now that they made you captain?

Happy: There's a crowd of girls behind him everytime the classes change.

Biff (taking Willy's hand): This Saturday, Pop, this Saturday — just for you, I'm going to break through for a touchdown.

Happy: You're supposed to pass.

Biff: I'm takin' one play for Pop. You watch me, Pop, and when I take off my helmet, that means I'm breakin' out. Then you watch me crash through that line!

Willy (kisses Biff): Oh, wait'll I tell this in Boston!

Bernard enters in knickers. He is younger than Biff, earnest and loyal, a worried boy.

Bernard: Biff, where are you? You're supposed to study with me today.

Willy: Hey, looka Bernard. What're you lookin' so anemic about, Bernard?

Bernard: He's gotta study, Uncle Willy. He's got Regents next week.

Happy (tauntingly, spinning Bernard around): Let's box, Bernard!

Bernard: Biff! (He gets away from Happy.) Listen, Biff, I heard Mr. Birnbaum say that if you don't start studyin' math, he's gonna flunk you, and you won't graduate. I heard him!

Willy: You better study with him, Biff. Go ahead now.

Bernard: I heard him!

Biff: Oh, Pop, you didn't see my sneakers! (He holds up a foot for Willy to look at.)

Willy: Hey, that's a beautiful job of printing!

Bernard (wiping his glasses): Just because he printed University of Virginia on his sneakers doesn't mean they've got to graduate him, Uncle Willy!

Willy (angrily): What're you talking about? With scholarships to three universities they're gonna flunk him?

Bernard: But I heard Mr. Birnbaum say —

Willy: Don't be a pest, Bernard! (To his boys.) What an anemic!

Bernard: Okay, I'm waiting for you in my house, Biff.

Bernard goes off. The Lomans laugh.

Willy: Bernard is not well liked, is he?

Biff: He's liked, but he's not well liked.

Happy: That's right, Pop.

Willy: That's just what I mean. Bernard can get the best marks in school, y'understand, but when he gets out in the business world, y'understand, you are going to be five times ahead of him. That's why I thank Almighty God you're both built like Adonises.° Because the man who makes an appearance in the business world, the man who creates personal interest, is the man who gets ahead. Be liked and you will never want. You take me, for instance. I never have to wait in line to see a buyer. "Willy Loman is here!" That's all they have to know, and I go right through.

Biff: Did you knock them dead, Pop?

Willy: Knocked 'em cold in Providence, slaughtered 'em in Boston.

Happy (on his back, pedaling again): I'm losing weight, you notice, Pop?

Linda enters, as of old, a ribbon in her hair, carrying a basket of washing.

Linda (with youthful energy): Hello, dear!

Willy: Sweetheart!

Linda: How'd the Chevy run?

Willy: Chevrolet, Linda, is the greatest car ever built. *(To the boys.)* Since when do you let your mother carry wash up the stairs?

Biff: Grab hold there, boy!

Happy: Where to, Mom?

Linda: Hang them up on the line. And you better go down to your friends, Biff. The cellar is full of boys. They don't know what to do with themselves.

Biff: Ah, when Pop comes home they can wait!

Willy (laughs appreciatively): You better go down and tell them what to do, Biff.

Biff: I think I'll have them sweep out the furnace room.

Willy: Good work, Biff.

Biff (goes through wall-line of kitchen to doorway at back and calls down): Fellas! Everybody sweep out the furnace room! I'll be right down!

Voices: All right! Okay, Biff.

Biff: George and Sam and Frank, come out back! We're hangin' up the wash! Come on, Hap, on the double! *(He and Happy carry out the basket.)*

Linda: The way they obey him!

Willy: Well, that's training, the training. I'm tellin' you, I was sellin' thousands and thousands, but I had to come home.

Linda: Oh, the whole block'll be at that game. Did you sell anything?

Willy: I did five hundred gross in Providence and seven hundred gross in Boston.

Linda: No! Wait a minute, I've got a pencil. *(She pulls pencil and paper out of her apron pocket.)* That makes your commission . . . Two hundred — my God! Two hundred and twelve dollars!

Willy: Well, I didn't figure it yet, but . . .

Linda: How much did you do?

Adonis: In Greek mythology, a young man known for his good looks and favored by Aphrodite, goddess of love and beauty.

Willy: Well, I—I did—about a hundred and eighty gross in Providence. Well, no—it came to—roughly two hundred gross on the whole trip.

Linda (without hesitation): Two hundred gross. That's . . . *(She figures.)*

Willy: The trouble was that three of the stores were half closed for inventory in Boston. Otherwise I woulda broke records.

Linda: Well, it makes seventy dollars and some pennies. That's very good.

Willy: What do we owe?

Linda: Well, on the first there's sixteen dollars on the refrigerator—

Willy: Why sixteen?

Linda: Well, the fan belt broke, so it was a dollar eighty.

Willy: But it's brand new.

Linda: Well, the man said that's the way it is. Till they work themselves in, y'know.

> *They move through the wall-line into the kitchen.*

Willy: I hope we didn't get stuck on that machine.

Linda: They got the biggest ads of any of them!

Willy: I know, it's a fine machine. What else?

Linda: Well, there's nine-sixty for the washing machine. And for the vacuum cleaner there's three and a half due on the fifteenth. Then the roof, you got twenty-one dollars remaining.

Willy: It don't leak, does it?

Linda: No, they did a wonderful job. Then you owe Frank for the carburetor.

Willy: I'm not going to pay that man! That goddam Chevrolet, they ought to prohibit the manufacture of that car!

Linda: Well, you owe him three and a half. And odds and ends, comes to around a hundred and twenty dollars by the fifteenth.

Willy: A hundred and twenty dollars! My God, if business don't pick up I don't know what I'm gonna do!

Linda: Well, next week you'll do better.

Willy: Oh, I'll knock 'em dead next week. I'll go to Hartford. I'm very well liked in Hartford. You know, the trouble is, Linda, people don't seem to take to me.

> *They move onto the forestage.*

Linda: Oh, don't be foolish.

Willy: I know it when I walk in. They seem to laugh at me.

Linda: Why? Why would they laugh at you? Don't talk that way, Willy.

> *Willy moves to the edge of the stage. Linda goes into the kitchen and starts to darn stockings.*

Willy: I don't know the reason for it, but they just pass me by. I'm not noticed.

Linda: But you're doing wonderful, dear. You're making seventy to a hundred dollars a week.

Willy: But I gotta be at it ten, twelve hours a day. Other men—I don't know—they do it easier. I don't know why—I can't stop myself—I talk too much. A man oughta come in with a few words. One thing about Charley. He's a man of few words, and they respect him.

Linda: You don't talk too much, you're just lively.

Willy (smiling): Well, I figure, what the hell, life is short, a couple of jokes. *(To himself.)* I joke too much! *(The smile goes.)*

Linda: Why? You're—

Willy: I'm fat. I'm very—foolish to look at, Linda. I didn't tell you, but Christmas time I happened to be calling on F. H. Stewarts, and a salesman I know, as I was going in to see the buyer I heard him say something about—walrus. And I—I cracked him right across the face. I won't take that. I simply will not take that. But they do laugh at me. I know that.

Linda: Darling . . .

Willy: I gotta overcome it. I know I gotta overcome it. I'm not dressing to advantage, maybe.

Linda: Willy, darling, you're the handsomest man in the world—

Willy: Oh, no, Linda.

Linda: To me you are. *(Slight pause.)* The handsomest.

> *From the darkness is heard the laughter of a woman. Willy doesn't turn to it, but it continues through Linda's lines.*

Linda: And the boys, Willy. Few men are idolized by their children the way you are.

> *Music is heard as behind a scrim, to the left of the house, The Woman, dimly seen, is dressing.*

Willy (with great feeling): You're the best there is, Linda, you're a pal, you know that? On the road—on the road I want to grab you sometimes and just kiss the life outa you.

> *The laughter is loud now, and he moves into a brightening area at the left, where The Woman has come from behind the scrim and is standing, putting on her hat, looking into a "mirror" and laughing.*

Willy: 'Cause I get so lonely—especially when business is bad and there's nobody to talk to. I get the feeling that I'll never sell anything again, that I won't make a living for you, or a business, a business for the boys. *(He talks through The Woman's subsiding laughter; The Woman primps at the "mirror.")* There's so much I want to make for—

The Woman: Me? You didn't make me, Willy. I picked you.

Willy (pleased): You picked me?

The Woman (who is quite proper-looking, Willy's age): I did. I've been sitting at that desk watching all the salesmen go by, day in, day out. But you've got such a sense of humor, and we do have such a good time together, don't we?

Willy: Sure, sure. *(He takes her in his arms.)* Why do you have to go now?

The Woman: It's two o'clock . . .

Willy: No, come on in! *(He pulls her.)*

The Woman: . . . my sisters'll be scandalized. When'll you be back?

Willy: Oh, two weeks about. Will you come up again?

The Woman: Sure thing. You do make me laugh. It's good for me. *(She squeezes his arm, kisses him.)* And I think you're a wonderful man.

Willy: You picked me, heh?

The Woman: Sure. Because you're so sweet. And such a kidder.

Willy: Well, I'll see you next time I'm in Boston.

The Woman: I'll put you right through to the buyers.

Willy (slapping her bottom): Right. Well, bottoms up!

The Woman (slaps him gently and laughs): You just kill me, Willy. *(He suddenly grabs her and kisses her roughly.)* You kill me. And thanks for the stockings. I love a lot of stockings. Well, good night.

Willy: Good night. And keep your pores open!

The Woman: Oh, Willy!

The Woman bursts out laughing, and Linda's laughter blends in. The Woman disappears into the dark. Now the area at the kitchen table brightens. Linda is sitting where she was at the kitchen table, but now is mending a pair of her silk stockings.

Linda: You are, Willy. The handsomest man. You've got no reason to feel that —

Willy (coming out of The Woman's dimming area and going over to Linda): I'll make it all up to you, Linda, I'll —

Linda: There's nothing to make up, dear. You're doing fine, better than —

Willy (noticing her mending): What's that?

Linda: Just mending my stockings. They're so expensive —

Willy (angrily, taking them from her): I won't have you mending stockings in this house! Now throw them out!

Linda puts the stockings in her pocket.

Bernard (entering on the run): Where is he? If he doesn't study!

Willy (moving to the forestage, with great agitation): You'll give him the answers!

Bernard: I do, but I can't on a Regents! That's a state exam! They're liable to arrest me!

Willy: Where is he? I'll whip him, I'll whip him!

Linda: And he'd better give back that football, Willy, it's not nice.

Willy: Biff! Where is he? Why is he taking everything?

Linda: He's too rough with the girls, Willy. All the mothers are afraid of him!

Willy: I'll whip him!

Bernard: He's driving the car without a license!

The Woman's laugh is heard.

Willy: Shut up!

Linda: All the mothers —

Willy: Shut up!

Bernard (backing quietly away and out): Mr. Birnbaum says he's stuck up.

Willy: Get outa here!

Bernard: If he doesn't buckle down he'll flunk math! *(He goes off.)*

Linda: He's right, Willy, you've gotta —

Willy (exploding at her): There's nothing the matter with him! You want him to be a worm like Bernard? He's got spirit, personality . . .

As he speaks, Linda, almost in tears, exits into the living-room. Willy is alone in the kitchen, wilting and staring. The leaves are gone. It is night again, and the apartment houses look down from behind.

Willy: Loaded with it. Loaded! What is he stealing? He's giving it back, isn't he? Why is he stealing? What did I tell him? I never in my life told him anything but decent things.

Happy in pajamas has come down the stairs; Willy suddenly becomes aware of Happy's presence.

Happy: Let's go now, come on.

Willy (sitting down at the kitchen table): Huh! Why did she have to wax the floors herself? Everytime she waxes the floors she keels over. She knows that!

Happy: Shh! Take it easy. What brought you back tonight?

Willy: I got an awful scare. Nearly hit a kid in Yonkers. God! Why didn't I go to Alaska with my brother Ben that time! Ben! That man was a genius, that man was success incarnate! What a mistake! He begged me to go.

Happy: Well, there's no use in —

Willy: You guys! There was a man started with the clothes on his back and ended up with diamond mines!

Happy: Boy, someday I'd like to know how he did it.

Willy: What's the mystery? The man knew what he wanted and went out and got it! Walked into a jungle, and comes out, the age of twenty-one, and he's rich! The world is an oyster, but you don't crack it open on a mattress!

Happy: Pop, I told you I'm gonna retire you for life.

Willy: You'll retire me for life on seventy goddam dollars a week? And your women and your car and your apartment, and you'll retire me for life! Christ's sake, I couldn't get past Yonkers today! Where are you guys, where are you? The woods are burning! I can't drive a car!

Charley has appeared in the doorway. He is a large man, slow of speech, laconic, immovable. In all he says, despite what he says, there is pity, and, now, trepidation. He has a robe over pajamas, slippers on his feet. He enters the kitchen.

Charley: Everything all right?

Happy: Yeah, Charley, everything's . . .

Willy: What's the matter?

Charley: I heard some noise. I thought something happened. Can't we do something about the walls? You sneeze in here, and in my house hats blow off.

Happy: Let's go to bed, Dad. Come on.

Charley signals to Happy to go.

Willy: You go ahead, I'm not tired at the moment.

Happy (to Willy): Take it easy, huh? *(He exits.)*

Willy: What're you doin' up?

Charley (sitting down at the kitchen table opposite Willy): Couldn't sleep good. I had a heartburn.

Willy: Well, you don't know how to eat.

Charley: I eat with my mouth.

Willy: No, you're ignorant. You gotta know about vitamins and things like that.

Charley: Come on, let's shoot. Tire you out a little.

Willy (hesitantly): All right. You got cards?

Charley (taking a deck from his pocket): Yeah, I got them. Someplace. What is it with those vitamins?

Willy (dealing): They build up your bones. Chemistry.

Charley: Yeah, but there's no bones in a heartburn.

Willy: What are you talkin' about? Do you know the first thing about it?

Charley: Don't get insulted.

Willy: Don't talk about something you don't know anything about.

They are playing. Pause.

Charley: What're you doin' home?

Willy: A little trouble with the car.

Charley: Oh. *(Pause.)* I'd like to take a trip to California.

Willy: Don't say.

Charley: You want a job?

Willy: I got a job, I told you that. *(After a slight pause.)* What the hell are you offering me a job for?

Charley: Don't get insulted.
Willy: Don't insult me.
Charley: I don't see no sense in it. You don't have to go on this way.
Willy: I got a good job. *(Slight pause.)* What do you keep comin' in here for?
Charley: You want me to go?
Willy (after a pause, withering): I can't understand it. He's going back to Texas again. What the hell is that?
Charley: Let him go.
Willy: I got nothin' to give him, Charley, I'm clean, I'm clean.
Charley: He won't starve. None a them starve. Forget about him.
Willy: Then what have I got to remember?
Charley: You take it too hard. To hell with it. When a deposit bottle is broken you don't get your nickel back.
Willy: That's easy enough for you to say.
Charley: That ain't easy for me to say.
Willy: Did you see the ceiling I put up in the living-room?
Charley: Yeah, that's a piece of work. To put up a ceiling is a mystery to me. How do you do it?
Willy: What's the difference?
Charley: Well, talk about it.
Willy: You gonna put up a ceiling?
Charley: How could I put up a ceiling?
Willy: Then what the hell are you bothering me for?
Charley: You're insulted again.
Willy: A man who can't handle tools is not a man. You're disgusting.
Charley: Don't call me disgusting, Willy.

> *Uncle Ben, carrying a valise and an umbrella, enters the forestage from around the right corner of the house. He is a stolid man, in his sixties, with a mustache and an authoritative air. He is utterly certain of his destiny, and there is an aura of far places about him. He enters exactly as Willy speaks.*

Willy: I'm getting awfully tired, Ben.

> *Ben's music is heard. Ben looks around at everything.*

Charley: Good, keep playing; you'll sleep better. Did you call me Ben?

> *Ben looks at his watch.*

Willy: That's funny. For a second there you reminded me of my brother Ben.
Ben: I only have a few minutes. *(He strolls, inspecting the place. Willy and Charley continue playing.)*
Charley: You never heard from him again, heh? Since that time?
Willy: Didn't Linda tell you? Couple of weeks ago we got a letter from his wife in Africa. He died.
Charley: That so.
Ben (chuckling): So this is Brooklyn, eh?
Charley: Maybe you're in for some of his money.
Willy: Naa, he had seven sons. There's just one opportunity I had with that man . . .
Ben: I must make a train, William. There are several properties I'm looking at in Alaska.

Willy: Sure, sure! If I'd gone with him to Alaska that time, everything would've been totally different.

Charley: Go on, you'd froze to death up there.

Willy: What're you talking about?

Ben: Opportunity is tremendous in Alaska, William. Surprised you're not up there.

Willy: Sure, tremendous.

Charley: Heh?

Willy: There was the only man I ever met who knew the answers.

Charley: Who?

Ben: How are you all?

Willy (taking a pot, smiling): Fine, fine.

Charley: Pretty sharp tonight.

Ben: Is Mother living with you?

Willy: No, she died a long time ago.

Charley: Who?

Ben: That's too bad. Fine specimen of a lady, Mother.

Willy (to Charley): Heh?

Ben: I'd hoped to see the old girl.

Charley: Who died?

Ben: Heard anything from Father, have you?

Willy (unnerved): What do you mean, who died?

Charley (taking a pot): What're you talkin' about?

Ben (looking at his watch): William, it's half-past eight!

Willy (as though to dispel his confusion he angrily stops Charley's hand): That's my build!

Charley: I put the ace —

Willy: If you don't know how to play the game I'm not gonna throw my money away on you!

Charley (rising): It was my ace, for God's sake!

Willy: I'm through, I'm through!

Ben: When did Mother die?

Willy: Long ago. Since the beginning you never knew how to play cards.

Charley (picks up the cards and goes to the door): All right! Next time I'll bring a deck with five aces.

Willy: I don't play that kind of game!

Charley (turning to him): You ought to be ashamed of yourself!

Willy: Yeah?

Charley: Yeah! *(He goes out.)*

Willy (slamming the door after him): Ignoramus!

Ben (as Willy comes toward him through the wall-line of the kitchen): So you're William.

Willy (shaking Ben's hand): Ben! I've been waiting for you so long! What's the answer? How did you do it?

Ben: Oh, there's a story in that.

Linda enters the forestage, as of old, carrying the wash basket.

Linda: Is this Ben?

Ben (gallantly): How do you do, my dear.

Linda: Where've you been all these years? Willy's always wondered why you —

Willy (pulling Ben away from her impatiently): Where is Dad? Didn't you follow him? How did you get started?

Ben: Well, I don't know how much you remember.

Willy: Well, I was just a baby, of course, only three or four years old —

Ben: Three years and eleven months.

Willy: What a memory, Ben!

Ben: I have many enterprises, William, and I have never kept books.

Willy: I remember I was sitting under the wagon in — was it Nebraska?

Ben: It was South Dakota, and I gave you a bunch of wild flowers.

Willy: I remember you walking away down some open road.

Ben (laughing): I was going to find Father in Alaska.

Willy: Where is he?

Ben: At that age I had a very faulty view of geography, William. I discovered after a few days that I was heading due south, so instead of Alaska, I ended up in Africa.

Linda: Africa!

Willy: The Gold Coast!

Ben: Principally diamond mines.

Linda: Diamond mines!

Ben: Yes, my dear. But I've only a few minutes —

Willy: No! Boys! Boys! *(Young Biff and Happy appear.)* Listen to this. This is your Uncle Ben, a great man! Tell my boys, Ben!

Ben: Why, boys, when I was seventeen I walked into the jungle, and when I was twenty-one I walked out. *(He laughs.)* And by God I was rich.

Willy (to the boys): You see what I been talking about? The greatest things can happen!

Ben (glancing at his watch): I have an appointment in Ketchikan Tuesday next week.

Willy: No, Ben! Please tell about Dad. I want my boys to hear. I want them to know the kind of stock they spring from. All I remember is a man with a big beard, and I was in Mamma's lap, sitting around a fire, and some kind of high music.

Ben: His flute. He played the flute.

Willy: Sure, the flute, that's right!

New music is heard, a high, rollicking tune.

Ben: Father was a very great and a very wild-hearted man. We would start in Boston, and he'd toss the whole family into the wagon, and then he'd drive the team right across the country; through Ohio, and Indiana, Michigan, Illinois, and all the Western states. And we'd stop in the towns and sell the flutes that he'd made on the way. Great inventor, Father. With one gadget he made more in a week than a man like you could make in a lifetime.

Willy: That's just the way I'm bringing them up, Ben — rugged, well liked, all-around.

Ben: Yeah? *(To Biff.)* Hit that, boy — hard as you can. *(He pounds his stomach.)*

Biff: Oh, no, sir!

Ben (taking boxing stance): Come on, get to me. *(He laughs.)*

Willy: Go to it, Biff! Go ahead, show him!

Biff: Okay! *(He cocks his fists and starts in.)*

Linda (to Willy): Why must he fight, dear?

Ben (sparring with Biff): Good boy! Good boy!

Willy: How's that, Ben, heh?

Happy: Give him the left, Biff!

Linda: Why are you fighting?

Ben: Good boy! *(Suddenly comes in, trips Biff, and stands over him, the point of his umbrella poised over Biff's eye.)*

Linda: Look out, Biff!

Biff: Gee!

Ben (patting Biff's knee): Never fight fair with a stranger, boy. You'll never get out of the jungle that way. *(Taking Linda's hand and bowing):* It was an honor and a pleasure to meet you, Linda.

Linda (withdrawing her hand coldly, frightened): Have a nice — trip.

Ben (to Willy): And good luck with your — what do you do?

Willy: Selling.

Ben: Yes. Well . . . *(He raises his hand in farewell to all.)*

Willy: No, Ben, I don't want you to think . . . *(He takes Ben's arm to show him.)* It's Brooklyn, I know, but we hunt too.

Ben: Really, now.

Willy: Oh, sure, there's snakes and rabbits and — that's why I moved out here. Why, Biff can fell any one of these trees in no time! Boys! Go right over to where they're building the apartment house and get some sand. We're gonna rebuild the entire front stoop now! Watch this, Ben!

Biff: Yes, sir! On the double, Hap!

Happy (as he and Biff run off): I lost weight, Pop, you notice?

Charley *enters in knickers, even before the boys are gone.*

Charley: Listen, if they steal any more from that building the watchman'll put the cops on them!

Linda (to Willy): Don't let Biff . . .

Ben *laughs lustily.*

Willy: You shoulda seen the lumber they brought home last week. At least a dozen six-by-tens worth all kinds a money.

Charley: Listen, if that watchman —

Willy: I gave them hell, understand. But I got a couple of fearless characters there.

Charley: Willy, the jails are full of fearless characters.

Ben (clapping Willy on the back, with a laugh at Charley): And the stock exchange, friend!

Willy (joining in Ben's laughter): Where are the rest of your pants?

Charley: My wife bought them.

Willy: Now all you need is a golf club and you can go upstairs and go to sleep. *(To Ben).* Great athlete! Between him and his son Bernard they can't hammer a nail!

Bernard (rushing in): The watchman's chasing Biff!

Willy (angrily): Shut up! He's not stealing anything!

Linda (alarmed, hurrying off left): Where is he? Biff, dear! *(She exits.)*

Willy (moving toward the left, away from Ben): There's nothing wrong. What's the matter with you?

Ben: Nervy boy. Good!

Willy (laughing): Oh, nerves of iron, that Biff!

Charley: Don't know what it is. My New England man comes back and he's bleedin', they murdered him up there.

Willy: It's contacts, Charley, I got important contacts!

Charley (sarcastically): Glad to hear it, Willy. Come in later, we'll shoot a little casino. I'll take some of your Portland money. *(He laughs at Willy and exits.)*

Willy (turning to Ben): Business is bad, it's murderous. But not for me, of course.

Ben: I'll stop by on my way back to Africa.

Willy (longingly): Can't you stay a few days? You're just what I need, Ben, because I — I have a fine position here, but I — well, Dad left when I was such a baby and I never had a chance to talk to him and I still feel — kind of temporary about myself.

Ben: I'll be late for my train.

They are at opposite ends of the stage.

Willy: Ben, my boys — can't we talk? They'd go into the jaws of hell for me, see, but I —

Ben: William, you're being first-rate with your boys. Outstanding, manly chaps!

Willy (hanging on to his words): Oh, Ben, that's good to hear! Because sometimes I'm afraid that I'm not teaching them the right kind of — Ben, how should I teach them?

Ben (giving great weight to each word, and with a certain vicious audacity): William, when I walked into the jungle, I was seventeen. When I walked out I was twenty-one. And, by God, I was rich! *(He goes off into darkness around the right corner of the house.)*

Willy: . . . was rich! That's just the spirit I want to imbue them with! To walk into a jungle! I was right! I was right! I was right!

Ben is gone, but Willy is still speaking to him as Linda, in nightgown and robe, enters the kitchen, glances around for Willy, then goes to the door of the house, looks out, and sees him. Comes down to his left. He looks at her.

Linda: Willy, dear? Willy?

Willy: I was right!

Linda: Did you have some cheese? *(He can't answer.)* It's very late, darling. Come to bed, heh?

Willy (looking straight up): Gotta break your neck to see a star in this yard.

Linda: You coming in?

Willy: Whatever happened to that diamond watch fob? Remember? When Ben came from Africa that time? Didn't he give me a watch fob with a diamond in it?

Linda: You pawned it, dear. Twelve, thirteen years ago. For Biff's radio correspondence course.

Willy: Gee, that was a beautiful thing. I'll take a walk.

Linda: But you're in your slippers.

Willy (starting to go around the house at the left): I was right! I was! *(Half to Linda, as he goes, shaking his head.)* What a man! There was a man worth talking to. I was right!

Linda (calling after Willy): But in your slippers, Willy!

Willy is almost gone when Biff, in his pajamas, comes down the stairs and enters the kitchen.

Biff: What is he doing out there?

Linda: Sh!

Biff: God Almighty, Mom, how long has he been doing this?

Linda: Don't, he'll hear you.

Biff: What the hell is the matter with him?

Linda: It'll pass by morning.

Biff: Shouldn't we do anything?

Linda: Oh, my dear, you should do a lot of things, but there's nothing to do, so go to sleep.

Happy comes down the stairs and sits on the steps.

Happy: I never heard him so loud, Mom.

Linda: Well, come around more often; you'll hear him. *(She sits down at the table and mends the lining of Willy's jacket.)*

Biff: Why didn't you ever write me about this, Mom?

Linda: How would I write to you? For over three months you had no address.

Biff: I was on the move. But you know I thought of you all the time. You know that, don't you, pal?

Linda: I know, dear, I know. But he likes to have a letter. Just to know that there's still a possibility for better things.

Biff: He's not like this all the time, is he?

Linda: It's when you come home he's always the worst.

Biff: When I come home?

Linda: When you write you're coming, he's all smiles, and talks about the future, and — he's just wonderful. And then the closer you seem to come, the more shaky he gets, and then, by the time you get here, he's arguing, and he seems angry at you. I think it's just that maybe he can't bring himself to — to open up to you. Why are you so hateful to each other? Why is that?

Biff (evasively): I'm not hateful, Mom.

Linda: But you no sooner come in the door than you're fighting!

Biff: I don't know why. I mean to change. I'm tryin', Mom, you understand?

Linda: Are you home to stay now?

Biff: I don't know. I want to look around, see what's doin'.

Linda: Biff, you can't look around all your life, can you?

Biff: I just can't take hold, Mom. I can't take hold of some kind of a life.

Linda: Biff, a man is not a bird, to come and go with the springtime.

Biff: Your hair . . . *(He touches her hair.)* Your hair got so gray.

Linda: Oh, it's been gray since you were in high school. I just stopped dyeing it, that's all.

Biff: Dye it again, will ya? I don't want my pal looking old. *(He smiles.)*

Linda: You're such a boy! You think you can go away for a year and . . . You've got to get it into your head now that one day you'll knock on this door and there'll be strange people here —

Biff: What are you talking about? You're not even sixty, Mom.

Linda: But what about your father?

Biff (lamely): Well, I meant him too.

Happy: He admires Pop.

Linda: Biff, dear, if you don't have any feeling for him, then you can't have any feeling for me.

Biff: Sure I can, Mom.

Linda: No. You can't just come to see me, because I love him. (*With a threat, but only a threat, of tears.*) He's the dearest man in the world to me, and I won't have anyone making him feel unwanted and low and blue. You've got to make up your mind now, darling, there's no leeway any more. Either he's your father and you pay him that respect, or else you're not to come here. I know he's not easy to get along with — nobody knows that better than me — but . . .

Willy (from the left, with a laugh): Hey, hey, Biffo!

Biff (starting to go out after Willy): What the hell is the matter with him? (*Happy stops him.*)

Linda: Don't — don't go near him!

Biff: Stop making excuses for him! He always, always wiped the floor with you. Never had an ounce of respect for you.

Happy: He's always had respect for —

Biff: What the hell do you know about it?

Happy (surlily): Just don't call him crazy!

Biff: He's got no character — Charley wouldn't do this. Not in his own house — spewing out that vomit from his mind.

Happy: Charley never had to cope with what he's got to.

Biff: People are worse off than Willy Loman. Believe me, I've seen them!

Linda: Then make Charley your father, Biff. You can't do that, can you? I don't say he's a great man. Willy Loman never made a lot of money. His name was never in the paper. He's not the finest character that ever lived. But he's a human being, and a terrible thing is happening to him. So attention must be paid. He's not to be allowed to fall into his grave like an old dog. Attention, attention must be finally paid to such a person. You called him crazy —

Biff: I didn't mean —

Linda: No, a lot of people think he's lost his — balance. But you don't have to be very smart to know what his trouble is. The man is exhausted.

Happy: Sure!

Linda: A small man can be just as exhausted as a great man. He works for a company thirty-six years this March, opens up unheard-of territories to their trademark, and now in his old age they take his salary away.

Happy (indignantly): I didn't know that, Mom.

Linda: You never asked, my dear! Now that you get your spending money someplace else you don't trouble your mind with him.

Happy: But I gave you money last —

Linda: Christmas time, fifty dollars! To fix the hot water it cost ninety-seven fifty! For five weeks he's been on straight commission, like a beginner, an unknown!

Biff: Those ungrateful bastards!

Linda: Are they any worse than his sons? When he brought them business, when he was young, they were glad to see him. But now his old friends, the old buyers that loved him so and always found some order to hand him in a pinch — they're all dead, retired. He used to be able to make six, seven calls a day in Boston. Now he takes his valises out of the car and puts them back and takes them out again and he's exhausted. Instead of walking he talks now. He drives seven hundred miles, and when he gets there no one knows him any more, no one welcomes him. And what goes through a man's mind, driving seven hundred miles home without having earned a cent? Why shouldn't he talk to himself? Why? When he has to go to Charley and borrow fifty dollars a week and pretend to me that it's his pay? How long can that go on? How long? You see what I'm sitting here and waiting for? And you tell me he has no character? The man who never worked a day but for your benefit? When does he get the medal for that? Is this his reward — to turn around at the age of sixty-three and find his sons, who he loved better than his life, one a philandering bum —

Happy: Mom!

Linda: That's all you are, my baby! *(To Biff.)* And you! What happened to the love you had for him? You were such pals! How you used to talk to him on the phone every night! How lonely he was till he could come home to you!

Biff: All right, Mom. I'll live here in my room, and I'll get a job. I'll keep away from him, that's all.

Linda: No, Biff. You can't stay here and fight all the time.

Biff: He threw me out of this house, remember that.

Linda: Why did he do that? I never knew why.

Biff: Because I know he's a fake and he doesn't like anybody around who knows!

Linda: Why a fake? In what way? What do you mean?

Biff: Just don't lay it all at my feet. It's between me and him — that's all I have to say. I'll chip in from now on. He'll settle for half my pay check. He'll be all right. I'm going to bed. *(He starts for the stairs.)*

Linda: He won't be all right.

Biff (turning on the stairs, furiously): I hate this city and I'll stay here. Now what do you want?

Linda: He's dying, Biff.

Happy turns quickly to her, shocked.

Biff (after a pause): Why is he dying?

Linda: He's been trying to kill himself.

Biff (with great horror): How?

Linda: I live from day to day.

Biff: What're you talking about?

Linda: Remember I wrote you that he smashed up the car again? In February?

Biff: Well?

Linda: The insurance inspector came. He said that they have evidence. That all these accidents in the last year — weren't — weren't — accidents.

Happy: How can they tell that? That's a lie.

Linda: It seems there's a woman . . . *(She takes a breath as):*
    Biff (sharply but contained): What woman?
    Linda (simultaneously): . . . and this woman . . .

Linda: What?

Biff: Nothing. Go ahead.

Linda: What did you say?

Biff: Nothing. I just said what woman?

Happy: What about her?

Linda: Well, it seems she was walking down the road and saw his car. She says that he wasn't driving fast at all, and that he didn't skid. She says he came to that little bridge, and then deliberately smashed into the railing, and it was only the shallowness of the water that saved him.

Biff: Oh, no, he probably just fell asleep again.

Linda: I don't think he fell asleep.

Biff: Why not?

Linda: Last month . . . *(With great difficulty.)* Oh, boys, it's so hard to say a thing like this! He's just a big stupid man to you, but I tell you there's more good in him than in many other people. *(She chokes, wipes her eyes.)* I was looking for a fuse. The lights blew out, and I went down the cellar. And behind the fuse box — it happened to fall out — was a length of rubber pipe — just short.

Happy: No kidding?

Linda: There's a little attachment on the end of it. I knew right away. And sure enough, on the bottom of the water heater there's a new little nipple on the gas pipe.

Happy (angrily): That — jerk.

Biff: Did you have it taken off?

Linda: I'm — I'm ashamed to. How can I mention it to him? Every day I go down and take away that little rubber pipe. But, when he comes home, I put it back where it was. How can I insult him that way? I don't know what to do. I live from day to day, boys. I tell you, I know every thought in his mind. It sounds so old-fashioned and silly, but I tell you he put his whole life into you and you've turned your backs on him. *(She is bent over in chair, weeping, her face in her hands.)* Biff, I swear to God! Biff, his life is in your hands!

Happy (to Biff): How do you like that damned fool!

Biff (kissing her): All right, pal, all right. It's all settled now. I've been remiss. I know that, Mom. But now I'll stay, and I swear to you, I'll apply myself. *(Kneeling in front of her, in a fever of self-reproach.)* It's just — you see, Mom, I don't fit in business. Not that I won't try. I'll try, and I'll make good.

Happy: Sure you will. The trouble with you in business was you never tried to please people.

Biff: I know, I —

Happy: Like when you worked for Harrison's. Bob Harrison said you were tops, and then you go and do some damn fool thing like whistling whole songs in the elevator like a comedian.

Biff (against Happy): So what? I like to whistle sometimes.

Happy: You don't raise a guy to a responsible job who whistles in the elevator!

Linda: Well, don't argue about it now.

Happy: Like when you'd go off and swim in the middle of the day instead of taking the line around.

Biff (his resentment rising): Well, don't you run off? You take off sometimes, don't you? On a nice summer day?

Happy: Yeah, but I cover myself!

Linda: Boys!

Happy: If I'm going to take a fade the boss can call any number where I'm supposed to be and they'll swear to him that I just left. I'll tell you something

that I hate to say, Biff, but in the business world some of them think
you're crazy.

Biff (angered): Screw the business world!

Happy: All right, screw it! Great, but cover yourself!

Linda: Hap, Hap!

Biff: I don't care what they think! They've laughed at Dad for years, and you
know why? Because we don't belong in this nuthouse of a city! We should
be mixing cement on some open plain, or — or carpenters. A carpenter is
allowed to whistle!

Willy walks in from the entrance of the house, at left.

Willy: Even your grandfather was better than a carpenter. *(Pause. They watch
him.)* You never grew up. Bernard does not whistle in the elevator, I assure
you.

Biff (as though to laugh Willy out of it): Yeah, but you do, Pop.

Willy: I never in my life whistled in an elevator! And who in the business world
thinks I'm crazy?

Biff: I didn't mean it like that, Pop. Now don't make a whole thing out of it,
will ya?

Willy: Go back to the West! Be a carpenter, a cowboy, enjoy yourself!

Linda: Willy, he was just saying —

Willy: I heard what he said!

Happy (trying to quiet Willy): Hey, Pop, come on now . . .

Willy (continuing over Happy's line): They laugh at me, heh? Go to Filene's, go to
the Hub, go to Slattery's, Boston. Call out the name Willy Loman and see
what happens! Big shot!

Biff: All right, Pop.

Willy: Big!

Biff: All right!

Willy: Why do you always insult me?

Biff: I didn't say a word. *(To Linda.)* Did I say a word?

Linda: He didn't say anything, Willy.

Willy (going to the doorway of the living-room): All right, good night, good night.

Linda: Willy, dear, he just decided . . .

Willy (to Biff): If you get tired hanging around tomorrow, paint the ceiling I
put up in the living-room.

Biff: I'm leaving early tomorrow.

Happy: He's going to see Bill Oliver, Pop.

Willy (interestedly): Oliver? For what?

Biff (with reserve, but trying, trying): He always said he'd stake me. I'd like to go
into business, so maybe I can take him up on it.

Linda: Isn't that wonderful?

Willy: Don't interrupt. What's wonderful about it? There's fifty men in the
City of New York who'd stake him. *(To Biff.)* Sporting goods?

Biff: I guess so. I know something about it and —

Willy: He knows something about it! You know sporting goods better than
Spalding, for God's sake! How much is he giving you?

Biff: I don't know, I didn't even see him yet, but —

Willy: Then what're you talkin' about?

Biff (getting angry): Well, all I said was I'm gonna see him, that's all!

Willy (turning away): Ah, you're counting your chickens again.

Biff (starting left for the stairs): Oh, Jesus, I'm going to sleep!

Willy (calling after him): Don't curse in this house!

Biff (turning): Since when did you get so clean?

Happy (trying to stop them): Wait a . . .

Willy: Don't use that language to me! I won't have it!

Happy (grabbing Biff, shouts): Wait a minute! I got an idea. I got a feasible idea. Come here, Biff, let's talk this over now, let's talk some sense here. When I was down in Florida last time, I thought of a great idea to sell sporting goods. It just came back to me. You and I, Biff—we have a line, the Loman Line. We train a couple of weeks, and put on a couple of exhibitions, see?

Willy: That's an idea!

Happy: Wait! We form two basketball teams, see? Two water-polo teams. We play each other. It's a million dollars' worth of publicity. Two brothers, see? The Loman Brothers. Displays in the Royal Palms—all the hotels. And banners over the ring and the basketball court: "Loman Brothers." Baby, we could sell sporting goods!

Willy: That is a one-million-dollar idea!

Linda: Marvelous!

Biff: I'm in great shape as far as that's concerned.

Happy: And the beauty of it is, Biff, it wouldn't be like a business. We'd be out playin' ball again . . .

Biff (enthused): Yeah, that's . . .

Willy: Million-dollar . . .

Happy: And you wouldn't get fed up with it, Biff. It'd be the family again. There'd be the old honor, and comradeship, and if you wanted to go off for a swim or somethin'—well, you'd do it! Without some smart cooky gettin' up ahead of you!

Willy: Lick the world! You guys together could absolutely lick the civilized world.

Biff: I'll see Oliver tomorrow. Hap, if we could work that out . . .

Linda: Maybe things are beginning to—

Willy (wildly enthused, to Linda): Stop interrupting! *(To Biff.)* But don't wear sport jacket and slacks when you see Oliver.

Biff: No, I'll—

Willy: A business suit, and talk as little as possible, and don't crack any jokes.

Biff: He did like me. Always liked me.

Linda: He loved you!

Willy (to Linda): Will you stop! *(To Biff.)* Walk in very serious. You are not applying for a boy's job. Money is to pass. Be quiet, fine, and serious. Everybody likes a kidder, but nobody lends him money.

Happy: I'll try to get some myself, Biff. I'm sure I can.

Willy: I see great things for you kids, I think your troubles are over. But remember, start big and you'll end big. Ask for fifteen. How much you gonna ask for?

Biff: Gee, I don't know—

Willy: And don't say "Gee." "Gee" is a boy's word. A man walking in for fifteen thousand dollars does not say "Gee!"

Biff: Ten, I think, would be top though.

Willy: Don't be so modest. You always started too low. Walk in with a big laugh. Don't look worried. Start off with a couple of your good stories to lighten things up. It's not what you say, it's how you say it — because personality always wins the day.

Linda: Oliver always thought the highest of him —

Willy: Will you let me talk?

Biff: Don't yell at her, Pop, will ya?

Willy (angrily): I was talking, wasn't I?

Biff: I don't like you yelling at her all the time, and I'm tellin' you, that's all.

Willy: What're you, takin' over this house?

Linda: Willy —

Willy (turning on her): Don't take his side all the time, goddammit!

Biff (furiously): Stop yelling at her!

Willy (suddenly pulling on his cheek, beaten down, guilt ridden): Give my best to Bill Oliver — he may remember me. *(He exits through the living-room doorway.)*

Linda (her voice subdued): What'd you have to start that for? *(Biff turns away.)* You see how sweet he was as soon as you talked hopefully? *(She goes over to Biff.)* Come up and say good night to him. Don't let him go to bed that way.

Happy: Come on, Biff, let's buck him up.

Linda: Please, dear. Just say good night. It takes so little to make him happy. Come. *(She goes through the living-room doorway, calling upstairs from within the living-room.)* Your pajamas are hanging in the bathroom, Willy!

Happy (looking toward where Linda went out): What a woman! They broke the mold when they made her. You know that, Biff?

Biff: He's off salary. My God, working on commission!

Happy: Well, let's face it: he's no hot-shot selling man. Except that sometimes, you have to admit, he's a sweet personality.

Biff (deciding): Lend me ten bucks, will ya? I want to buy some new ties.

Happy: I'll take you to a place I know. Beautiful stuff. Wear one of my striped shirts tomorrow.

Biff: She got gray. Mom got awful old. Gee, I'm gonna go in to Oliver tomorrow and knock him for a —

Happy: Come on up. Tell that to Dad. Let's give him a whirl. Come on.

Biff (steamed up): You know, with ten thousand bucks, boy!

Happy (as they go into the living-room): That's the talk, Biff, that's the first time I've heard the old confidence out of you! *(From within the living-room, fading off.)* You're gonna live with me, kid, and any babe you want just say the word . . . *(The last lines are hardly heard. They are mounting the stairs to their parents' bedroom.)*

Linda (entering her bedroom and addressing Willy, who is in the bathroom. She is straightening the bed for him): Can you do anything about the shower? It drips.

Willy (from the bathroom): All of a sudden everything falls to pieces! Goddam plumbing, oughta be sued, those people. I hardly finished putting it in and the thing . . . *(His words rumble off.)*

Linda: I'm just wondering if Oliver will remember him. You think he might?

Willy (coming out of the bathroom in his pajamas): Remember him? What's the matter with you, you crazy? If he'd've stayed with Oliver he'd be on top by now! Wait'll Oliver gets a look at him. You don't know the average caliber any more. The average young man today — *(he is getting into bed)* — is got a caliber of zero. Greatest thing in the world for him was to bum around.

    Biff and Happy enter the bedroom. Slight pause.

Willy *(stops short, looking at Biff):* Glad to hear it, boy.

Happy: He wanted to say good night to you, sport.

Willy *(to Biff):* Yeah. Knock him dead, boy. What'd you want to tell me?

Biff: Just take it easy, Pop. Good night. *(He turns to go.)*

Willy *(unable to resist):* And if anything falls off the desk while you're talking to him — like a package or something — don't you pick it up. They have office boys for that.

Linda: I'll make a big breakfast —

Willy: Will you let me finish? *(To Biff.)* Tell him you were in the business in the West. Not farm work.

Biff: All right, Dad.

Linda: I think everything —

Willy *(going right through her speech):* And don't undersell yourself. No less than fifteen thousand dollars.

Biff *(unable to bear him):* Okay. Good night, Mom. *(He starts moving.)*

Willy: Because you got a greatness in you, Biff, remember that. You got all kinds a greatness . . . *(He lies back, exhausted. Biff walks out.)*

Linda *(calling after Biff):* Sleep well, darling!

Happy: I'm gonna get married, Mom. I wanted to tell you.

Linda: Go to sleep, dear.

Happy *(going):* I just wanted to tell you.

Willy: Keep up the good work. *(Happy exits.)* God . . . remember that Ebbets Field game? The championship of the city?

Linda: Just rest. Should I sing to you?

Willy: Yeah. Sing to me. *(Linda hums a soft lullaby.)* When that team came out — he was the tallest, remember?

Linda: Oh, yes. And in gold.

    Biff enters the darkened kitchen, takes a cigarette, and leaves the house. He comes downstage into a golden pool of light. He smokes, staring at the night.

Willy: Like a young god. Hercules — something like that. And the sun, the sun all around him. Remember how he waved to me? Right up from the field, with the representatives of three colleges standing by? And the buyers I brought, and the cheers when he came out — Loman, Loman, Loman! God Almighty, he'll be great yet. A star like that, magnificent, can never really fade away!

    The light on Willy is fading. The gas heater begins to glow through the kitchen wall, near the stairs, a blue flame beneath red coils.

Linda *(timidly):* Willy dear, what has he got against you?

Willy: I'm so tired. Don't talk any more.

    Biff slowly returns to the kitchen. He stops, stares toward the heater.

Linda: Will you ask Howard to let you work in New York?

Willy: First thing in the morning. Everything'll be all right.

    Biff reaches behind the heater and draws out a length of rubber tubing. He is horrified and turns his head toward Willy's room, still dimly lit, from which the strains of Linda's desperate but monotonous humming rise.

Willy *(staring through the window into the moonlight):* Gee, look at the moon moving between the buildings!

Biff wraps the tubing around his hand and quickly goes up the stairs.

Curtain.

ACT II

Music is heard, gay and bright. The curtain rises as the music fades away. Willy, in shirt sleeves, is sitting at the kitchen table, sipping coffee, his hat in his lap. Linda is filling his cup when she can.

Willy: Wonderful coffee. Meal in itself.

Linda: Can I make you some eggs?

Willy: No. Take a breath.

Linda: You look so rested, dear.

Willy: I slept like a dead one. First time in months. Imagine, sleeping till ten on a Tuesday morning. Boys left nice and early, heh?

Linda: They were out of here by eight o'clock.

Willy: Good work!

Linda: It was so thrilling to see them leaving together. I can't get over the shaving lotion in this house!

Willy (smiling): Mmm —

Linda: Biff was very changed this morning. His whole attitude seemed to be hopeful. He couldn't wait to get downtown to see Oliver.

Willy: He's heading for a change. There's no question, there simply are certain men that take longer to get — solidified. How did he dress?

Linda: His blue suit. He's so handsome in that suit. He could be a — anything in that suit!

Willy gets up from the table. Linda holds his jacket for him.

Willy: There's no question, no question at all. Gee, on the way home tonight I'd like to buy some seeds.

Linda (laughing): That'd be wonderful. But not enough sun gets back there. Nothing'll grow any more.

Willy: You wait, kid, before it's all over we're gonna get a little place out in the country, and I'll raise some vegetables, a couple of chickens . . .

Linda: You'll do it yet, dear.

Willy walks out of his jacket. Linda follows him.

Willy: And they'll get married, and come for a weekend. I'd build a little guest house. 'Cause I got so many fine tools, all I'd need would be a little lumber and some peace of mind.

Linda (joyfully): I sewed the lining . . .

Willy: I could build two guest houses, so they'd both come. Did he decide how much he's going to ask Oliver for?

Linda (getting him into the jacket): He didn't mention it, but I imagine ten or fifteen thousand. You going to talk to Howard today?

Willy: Yeah. I'll put it to him straight and simple. He'll just have to take me off the road.

Linda: And Willy, don't forget to ask for a little advance, because we've got the insurance premium. It's the grace period now.

Willy: That's a hundred . . . ?

Linda: A hundred and eight, sixty-eight. Because we're a little short again.

Willy: Why are we short?

Linda: Well, you had the motor job on the car . . .

Willy: That goddam Studebaker!

Linda: And you got one more payment on the refrigerator . . .

Willy: But it just broke again!

Linda: Well, it's old, dear.

Willy: I told you we should've bought a well-advertised machine. Charley bought a General Electric and it's twenty years old and it's still good, that son-of-a-bitch.

Linda: But, Willy—

Willy: Whoever heard of a Hastings refrigerator? Once in my life I would like to own something outright before it's broken! I'm always in a race with the junkyard! I just finished paying for the car and it's on its last legs. The refrigerator consumes belts like a goddam maniac. They time those things. They time them so when you finally paid for them, they're used up.

Linda (buttoning up his jacket as he unbuttons it): All told, about two hundred dollars would carry us, dear. But that includes the last payment on the mortgage. After this payment, Willy, the house belongs to us.

Willy: It's twenty-five years!

Linda: Biff was nine years old when we bought it.

Willy: Well, that's a great thing. To weather a twenty-five-year mortgage is—

Linda: It's an accomplishment.

Willy: All the cement, the lumber, the reconstruction I put in this house! There ain't a crack to be found in it any more.

Linda: Well, it served its purpose.

Willy: What purpose? Some stranger'll come along, move in, and that's that. If only Biff would take this house, and raise a family . . . *(He starts to go.)* Good-by, I'm late.

Linda (suddenly remembering): Oh, I forgot! You're supposed to meet them for dinner.

Willy: Me?

Linda: At Frank's Chop House on Forty-eighth near Sixth Avenue.

Willy: Is that so! How about you?

Linda: No, just the three of you. They're gonna blow you to a big meal!

Willy: Don't say! Who thought of that?

Linda: Biff came to me this morning, Willy, and he said, "Tell Dad, we want to blow him to a big meal." Be there six o'clock. You and your two boys are going to have dinner.

Willy: Gee whiz! That's really somethin'. I'm gonna knock Howard for a loop, kid. I'll get an advance, and I'll come home with a New York job. Goddammit, now I'm gonna do it!

Linda: Oh, that's the spirit, Willy!

Willy: I will never get behind a wheel the rest of my life!

Linda: It's changing, Willy, I can feel it changing!

Willy: Beyond a question. G'by, I'm late. *(He starts to go again.)*

Linda (calling after him as she runs to the kitchen table for a handkerchief): You got your glasses?

Willy (feels for them, then comes back in): Yeah, yeah, got my glasses.

Linda (giving him the handkerchief): And a handkerchief.

Willy: Yeah, handkerchief.

Linda: And your saccharine?

Willy: Yeah, my saccharine.

Linda: Be careful on the subway stairs.

She kisses him, and a silk stocking is seen hanging from her hand. Willy notices it.

Willy: Will you stop mending stockings? At least while I'm in the house. It gets me nervous. I can't tell you. Please.

Linda hides the stocking in her hand as she follows Willy across the forestage in front of the house.

Linda: Remember, Frank's Chop House.

Willy (passing the apron): Maybe beets would grow out there.

Linda (laughing): But you tried so many times.

Willy: Yeah. Well, don't work hard today. *(He disappears around the right corner of the house.)*

Linda: Be careful!

As Willy vanishes, Linda waves to him. Suddenly the phone rings. She runs across the stage and into the kitchen and lifts it.

Linda: Hello? Oh, Biff! I'm so glad you called, I just . . . Yes, sure, I just told him. Yes, he'll be there for dinner at six o'clock, I didn't forget. Listen, I was just dying to tell you. You know that little rubber pipe I told you about? That he connected to the gas heater? I finally decided to go down the cellar this morning and take it away and destroy it. But it's gone! Imagine? He took it away himself, it isn't there! *(She listens.)* When? Oh, then you took it. Oh — nothing, it's just that I'd hoped he'd taken it away himself. Oh, I'm not worried, darling, because this morning he left in such high spirits, it was like the old days! I'm not afraid any more. Did Mr. Oliver see you? . . . Well, you wait there then. And make a nice impression on him, darling. Just don't perspire too much before you see him. And have a nice time with Dad. He may have big news too! . . . That's right, a New York job. And be sweet to him tonight, dear. Be loving to him. Because he's only a little boat looking for a harbor. *(She is trembling with sorrow and joy.)* Oh, that's wonderful, Biff, you'll save his life. Thanks, darling. Just put your arm around him when he comes into the restaurant. Give him a smile. That's the boy . . . Good-by, dear. . . . You got your comb? . . . That's fine. Good-by, Biff dear.

In the middle of her speech, Howard Wagner, thirty-six, wheels in a small typewriter table on which is a wire-recording machine and proceeds to plug it in. This is on the left forestage. Light slowly fades on Linda as it rises on Howard. Howard is intent on threading the machine and only glances over his shoulder as Willy appears.

Willy: Pst! Pst!

Howard: Hello, Willy, come in.

Willy: Like to have a little talk with you, Howard.

Howard: Sorry to keep you waiting. I'll be with you in a minute.

Willy: What's that, Howard?

Howard: Didn't you ever see one of these? Wire recorder.

Willy: Oh. Can we talk a minute?

Howard: Records things. Just got delivery yesterday. Been driving me crazy, the most terrific machine I ever saw in my life. I was up all night with it.

Willy: What do you do with it?

Howard: I bought it for dictation, but you can do anything with it. Listen to this. I had it home last night. Listen to what I picked up. The first one is my daughter. Get this. *(He flicks the switch and "Roll Out the Barrel" is heard being whistled.)* Listen to that kid whistle.

Willy: That is lifelike, isn't it?

Howard: Seven years old. Get that tone.

Willy: Ts, ts. Like to ask a little favor if you . . .

The whistling breaks off, and the voice of Howard's daughter is heard.

His Daughter: "Now you, Daddy."

Howard: She's crazy for me! *(Again the same song is whistled.)* That's me! Ha! *(He winks.)*

Willy: You're very good!

The whistling breaks off again. The machine runs silent for a moment.

Howard: Sh! Get this now, this is my son.

His Son: "The capital of Alabama is Montgomery; the capital of Arizona is Phoenix; the capital of Arkansas is Little Rock; the capital of California is Sacramento . . ." *(and on, and on).*

Howard (holding up five fingers): Five years old, Willy!

Willy: He'll make an announcer some day!

His Son (continuing): "The capital . . ."

Howard: Get that—alphabetical order! *(The machine breaks off suddenly.)* Wait a minute. The maid kicked the plug out.

Willy: It certainly is a—

Howard: Sh, for God's sake!

His Son: "It's nine o'clock, Bulova watch time. So I have to go to sleep."

Willy: That really is—

Howard: Wait a minute! The next is my wife.

    They wait.

Howard's Voice: "Go on, say something." *(Pause.)* "Well, you gonna talk?"

His Wife: "I can't think of anything."

Howard's Voice: "Well, talk—it's turning."

His Wife (shyly, beaten): "Hello." *(Silence.)* "Oh, Howard, I can't talk into this . . ."

Howard (snapping the machine off): That was my wife.

Willy: That is a wonderful machine. Can we—

Howard: I tell you, Willy, I'm gonna take my camera, and my bandsaw, and all my hobbies, and out they go. This is the most fascinating relaxation I ever found.

Willy: I think I'll get one myself.

Howard: Sure, they're only a hundred and a half. You can't do without it. Supposing you wanna hear Jack Benny, see? But you can't be at home at that hour. So you tell the maid to turn the radio on when Jack Benny comes on, and this automatically goes on with the radio . . .

Willy: And when you come home you . . .

Howard: You can come home twelve o'clock, one o'clock, any time you like, and you get yourself a Coke and sit yourself down, throw the switch, and there's Jack Benny's program in the middle of the night!

Willy: I'm definitely going to get one. Because lots of time I'm on the road, and I think to myself, what I must be missing on the radio!

Howard: Don't you have a radio in the car?

Willy: Well, yeah, but who ever thinks of turning it on?

Howard: Say, aren't you supposed to be in Boston?

Willy: That's what I want to talk to you about, Howard. You got a minute? *(He draws a chair in from the wing.)*

Howard: What happened? What're you doing here?

Willy: Well . . .

Howard: You didn't crack up again, did you?

Willy: Oh, no. No . . .

Howard: Geez, you had me worried there for a minute. What's the trouble?

Willy: Well, tell you the truth, Howard. I've come to the decision that I'd rather not travel any more.

Howard: Not travel! Well, what'll you do?

Willy: Remember, Christmas time, when you had the party here? You said you'd try to think of some spot for me here in town.

Howard: With us?

Willy: Well, sure.

Howard: Oh, yeah, yeah. I remember. Well, I couldn't think of anything for you, Willy.

Willy: I tell ya, Howard. The kids are all grown up, y'know. I don't need much any more. If I could take home — well, sixty-five dollars a week, I could swing it.

Howard: Yeah, but Willy, see I —

Willy: I tell ya why, Howard. Speaking frankly and between the two of us, y'know — I'm just a little tired.

Howard: Oh, I could understand that, Willy. But you're a road man, Willy, and we do a road business. We've only got a half-dozen salesmen on the floor here.

Willy: God knows, Howard, I never asked a favor of any man. But I was with the firm when your father used to carry you in here in his arms.

Howard: I know that, Willy, but —

Willy: Your father came to me the day you were born and asked me what I thought of the name of Howard, may he rest in peace.

Howard: I appreciate that, Willy, but there just is no spot here for you. If I had a spot I'd slam you right in, but I just don't have a single solitary spot.

He looks for his lighter. Willy has picked it up and gives it to him. Pause.

Willy (with increasing anger): Howard, all I need to set my table is fifty dollars a week.

Howard: But where am I going to put you, kid?

Willy: Look, it isn't a question of whether I can sell merchandise, is it?

Howard: No, but it's a business, kid, and everybody's gotta pull his own weight.

Willy (desperately): Just let me tell you a story, Howard —

Howard: 'Cause you gotta admit, business is business.

Willy (angrily): Business is definitely business, but just listen for a minute. You don't understand this. When I was a boy — eighteen, nineteen — I was already on the road. And there was a question in my mind as to whether selling had a future for me. Because in those days I had a yearning to go to Alaska. See, there were three gold strikes in one month in Alaska, and I felt like going out. Just for the ride, you might say.

Howard (barely interested): Don't say.

Willy: Oh, yeah, my father lived many years in Alaska. He was an adventurous man. We've got quite a little streak of self-reliance in our family. I thought I'd go out with my older brother and try to locate him, and maybe settle in the North with the old man. And I was almost decided to go, when I met a salesman in the Parker House. His name was Dave Singleman. And he was eighty-four years old, and he'd drummed merchandise in thirty-one states. And old Dave, he'd go up to his room, y'understand, put on his green velvet slippers — I'll never forget — and pick up his phone and call the buyers, and without ever leaving his room, at the age of eighty-four, he made his living. And when I saw that, I realized that selling was the greatest career a man could want. 'Cause what could be more satisfying than to be able to go, at the age of eighty-four, into twenty or thirty different cities, and pick up a phone, and be remembered and loved and helped by so many different people? Do you know? when he died — and by the way he died the death of a salesman, in his green velvet slippers in the smoker of the New York, New Haven, and Hartford, going into Boston — when he died, hundreds of salesmen and buyers were at his funeral. Things were sad on a lotta trains for months after that. *(He stands up. Howard has not looked at him.)* In those days there was personality in it, Howard. There was respect, and comradeship, and gratitude in it. Today, it's all cut and dried, and there's no chance for bringing friendship to bear — or personality. You see what I mean? They don't know me any more.

Howard (moving away, to the right): That's just the thing, Willy.

Willy: If I had forty dollars a week — that's all I'd need. Forty dollars, Howard.

Howard: Kid, I can't take blood from a stone, I —

Willy (desperation is on him now): Howard, the year Al Smith° was nominated, your father came to me and —

Howard (starting to go off): I've got to see some people, kid.

Willy (stopping him): I'm talking about your father! There were promises made across this desk! You mustn't tell me you've got people to see — I put thirty-four years into this firm, Howard, and now I can't pay my insurance! You can't eat the orange and throw the peel away — a man is not a piece of fruit! *(After a pause.)* Now pay attention. Your father — in 1928 I had a big year. I averaged a hundred and seventy dollars a week in commissions.

Howard (impatiently): Now, Willy, you never averaged —

Willy (banging his hand on the desk): I averaged a hundred and seventy dollars a week in the year of 1928! And your father came to me — or rather, I was in

---

Al Smith: Democratic candidate for president of the United States in 1928 who lost the election to Herbert Hoover.

the office here — it was right over this desk — and he put his hand on my shoulder —

Howard (getting up): You'll have to excuse me, Willy, I gotta see some people. Pull yourself together. *(Going out.)* I'll be back in a little while.

On Howard's exit, the light on his chair grows very bright and strange.

Willy: Pull myself together! What the hell did I say to him? My God, I was yelling at him! How could I! *(Willy breaks off, staring at the light, which occupies the chair, animating it. He approaches this chair, standing across the desk from it.)* Frank, Frank, don't you remember what you told me that time? How you put your hand on my shoulder, and Frank . . . *(He leans on the desk and as he speaks the dead man's name he accidentally switches on the recorder, and instantly:)*

Howard's Son: ". . . of New York is Albany. The capital of Ohio is Cincinnati, the capital of Rhode Island is . . . " *(The recitation continues.)*

Willy (leaping away with fright, shouting): Ha! Howard! Howard! Howard!

Howard (rushing in): What happened?

Willy (pointing at the machine, which continues nasally, childishly, with the capital cities): Shut it off! Shut it off!

Howard (pulling the plug out): Look, Willy . . .

Willy (pressing his hands to his eyes): I gotta get myself some coffee. I'll get some coffee . . .

Willy starts to walk out. Howard stops him.

Howard (rolling up the cord): Willy, look . . .

Willy: I'll go to Boston.

Howard: Willy, you can't go to Boston for us.

Willy: Why can't I go?

Howard: I don't want you to represent us. I've been meaning to tell you for a long time now.

Willy: Howard, are you firing me?

Howard: I think you need a good long rest, Willy.

Willy: Howard —

Howard: And when you feel better, come back, and we'll see if we can work something out.

Willy: But I gotta earn money, Howard. I'm in no position to —

Howard: Where are your sons? Why don't your sons give you a hand?

Willy: They're working on a very big deal.

Howard: This is no time for false pride, Willy. You go to your sons and you tell them that you're tired. You've got two great boys, haven't you?

Willy: Oh, no question, no question, but in the meantime . . .

Howard: Then that's that, heh?

Willy: All right, I'll go to Boston tomorrow.

Howard: No, no.

Willy: I can't throw myself on my sons. I'm not a cripple!

Howard: Look, kid, I'm busy this morning.

Willy (grasping Howard's arm): Howard, you've got to let me go to Boston!

Howard (hard, keeping himself under control): I've got a line of people to see this morning. Sit down, take five minutes, and pull yourself together, and then go home, will ya? I need the office, Willy. *(He starts to go, turns, remembering the recorder, starts to push off the table holding the recorder.)* Oh, yeah. Whenever you can this week, stop by and drop off the samples. You'll feel better, Willy, and then come back and we'll talk. Pull yourself together, kid, there's people outside.

Howard exits, pushing the table off left. Willy stares into space, exhausted. Now the music is heard — Ben's music — first distantly, then closer, closer. As Willy speaks, Ben enters from the right. He carries valise and umbrella.

Willy: Oh, Ben, how did you do it? What is the answer? Did you wind up the Alaska deal already?

Ben: Doesn't take much time if you know what you're doing. Just a short business trip. Boarding ship in an hour. Wanted to say good-by.

Willy: Ben, I've got to talk to you.

Ben (glancing at his watch): Haven't the time, William.

Willy (crossing the apron to Ben): Ben, nothing's working out. I don't know what to do.

Ben: Now, look here, William. I've bought timberland in Alaska and I need a man to look after things for me.

Willy: God, timberland! Me and my boys in those grand outdoors!

Ben: You've a new continent at your doorstep, William. Get out of these cities, they're full of talk and time payments and courts of law. Screw on your fists and you can fight for a fortune up there.

Willy: Yes, yes! Linda, Linda!

Linda enters as of old, with the wash.

Linda: Oh, you're back?

Ben: I haven't much time.

Willy: No, wait! Linda, he's got a proposition for me in Alaska.

Linda: But you've got — *(To Ben.)* He's got a beautiful job here.

Willy: But in Alaska, kid, I could —

Linda: You're doing well enough, Willy!

Ben (to Linda): Enough for what, my dear?

Linda (frightened of Ben and angry at him): Don't say those things to him! Enough to be happy right here, right now. *(To Willy, while Ben laughs.)* Why must everybody conquer the world? You're well liked, and the boys love you, and someday — *(to Ben)* — why, old man Wagner told him just the other day that if he keeps it up he'll be a member of the firm, didn't he, Willy?

Willy: Sure, sure. I am building something with this firm, Ben, and if a man is building something he must be on the right track, mustn't he?

Ben: What are you building? Lay your hand on it. Where is it?

Willy (hesitantly): That's true, Linda, there's nothing.

Linda: Why? *(To Ben.)* There's a man eighty-four years old —

Willy: That's right, Ben, that's right. When I look at that man I say, what is there to worry about?

Ben: Bah!

Willy: It's true, Ben. All he has to do is go into any city, pick up the phone, and he's making his living and you know why?

Ben (picking up his valise): I've got to go.

Willy (holding Ben back): Look at this boy!

Biff, in his high school sweater, enters carrying suitcase. Happy carries Biff's shoulder guards, gold helmet, and football pants.

Willy: Without a penny to his name, three great universities are begging for him, and from there the sky's the limit, because it's not what you do, Ben. It's who you know and the smile on your face! It's contacts, Ben, contacts! The whole wealth of Alaska passes over the lunch table at the Commodore Hotel, and that's the wonder, the wonder of this country, that a man can end with diamonds here on the basis of being liked! *(He turns to Biff.)* And that's why when you get out on that field today it's important. Because thousands of people will be rooting for you and loving you. *(To Ben, who has again begun to leave.)* And Ben! when he walks into a business office his name will sound out like a bell and all the doors will open to him! I've seen it, Ben, I've seen it a thousand times! You can't feel it with your hand like timber, but it's there!

Ben: Good-by, William.

Willy: Ben, am I right? Don't you think I'm right? I value your advice.

Ben: There's a new continent at your doorstep, William. You could walk out rich. Rich! *(He is gone.)*

Willy: We'll do it here, Ben! You hear me? We're gonna do it here!

Young Bernard rushes in. The gay music of the Boys is heard.

Bernard: Oh, gee, I was afraid you left already!

Willy: Why? What time is it?

Bernard: It's half-past one!

Willy: Well, come on, everybody! Ebbets Field next stop! Where's the pennants? *(He rushes through the wall-line of the kitchen and out into the living-room.)*

Linda (to Biff): Did you pack fresh underwear?

Biff (who has been limbering up): I want to go!

Bernard: Biff, I'm carrying your helmet, ain't I?

Happy: I'm carrying the helmet.

Bernard: How am I going to get in the locker room?

Linda: Let him carry the shoulder guards. *(She puts her coat and hat on in the kitchen.)*

Bernard: Can I, Biff? 'Cause I told everybody I'm going to be in the locker room.

Happy: In Ebbets Field it's the clubhouse.

Bernard: I meant the clubhouse. Biff!

Happy: Biff!

Biff (grandly, after a slight pause): Let him carry the shoulder guards.

Happy (as he gives Bernard the shoulder guards): Stay close to us now.

Willy rushes in with the pennants.

Willy (handing them out): Everybody wave when Biff comes out on the field. *(Happy and Bernard run off.)* You set now, boy?

The music has died away.

Biff: Ready to go, Pop. Every muscle is ready.

Willy (at the edge of the apron): You realize what this means?

Biff: That's right, Pop.

Willy (feeling Biff's muscles): You're comin' home this afternoon captain of the All-Scholastic Championship Team of the City of New York.

Biff: I got it, Pop. And remember, pal, when I take off my helmet, that touchdown is for you.

Willy: Let's go! *(He is starting out, with his arm around Biff, when Charley enters, as of old, in knickers.)* I got no room for you, Charley.

Charley: Room? For what?

Willy: In the car.

Charley: You goin' for a ride? I wanted to shoot some casino.

Willy (furiously): Casino! *(Incredulously.)* Don't you realize what today is?

Linda: Oh, he knows, Willy. He's just kidding you.

Willy: That's nothing to kid about!

Charley: No, Linda, what's goin' on?

Linda: He's playing in Ebbets Field.

Charley: Baseball in this weather?

Willy: Don't talk to him. Come on, come on! *(He is pushing them out.)*

Charley: Wait a minute, didn't you hear the news?

Willy: What?

Charley: Don't you listen to the radio? Ebbets Field just blew up.

Willy: You go to hell! *(Charley laughs. Pushing them out.)* Come on, come on! We're late.

Charley (as they go): Knock a homer, Biff, knock a homer!

Willy (the last to leave, turning to Charley): I don't think that was funny, Charley. This is the greatest day of his life.

Charley: Willy, when are you going to grow up?

Willy: Yeah, heh? When this game is over, Charley, you'll be laughing out of the other side of your face. They'll be calling him another Red Grange. Twenty-five thousand a year.

Charley (kidding): Is that so?

Willy: Yeah, that's so.

Charley: Well, then, I'm sorry, Willy. But tell me something.

Willy: What?

Charley: Who is Red Grange?

Willy: Put up your hands. Goddam you, put up your hands!

Charley, chuckling, shakes his head and walks away, around the left corner of the stage. Willy follows him. The music rises to a mocking frenzy.

Willy: Who the hell do you think you are, better than everybody else? You don't know everything, you big, ignorant, stupid . . . Put up your hands!

Light rises, on the right side of the forestage, on a small table in the reception room of Charley's office. Traffic sounds are heard. Bernard, now mature, sits whistling to himself. A pair of tennis rackets and an overnight bag are on the floor beside him.

Willy (offstage): What are you walking away for? Don't walk away! If you're going to say something say it to my face! I know you laugh at me behind my back. You'll laugh out of the other side of your goddam face after this game. Touchdown! Touchdown! Eighty thousand people! Touchdown! Right between the goal posts.

Bernard is a quiet, earnest, but self-assured young man. Willy's voice is coming from right upstage now. Bernard lowers his feet off the table and listens. Jenny, his father's secretary, enters.

Jenny (distressed): Say, Bernard, will you go out in the hall?

Bernard: What is that noise? Who is it?

Jenny: Mr. Loman. He just got off the elevator.

Bernard (getting up): Who's he arguing with?

Jenny: Nobody. There's nobody with him. I can't deal with him any more, and your father gets all upset everytime he comes. I've got a lot of typing to do, and your father's waiting to sign it. Will you see him?

Willy (entering): Touchdown! Touch — *(He sees Jenny.)* Jenny, Jenny, good to see you. How're ya? Workin'? Or still honest?

Jenny: Fine. How've you been feeling?

Willy: Not much any more, Jenny. Ha, ha! *(He is surprised to see the rackets.)*

Bernard: Hello, Uncle Willy.

Willy (almost shocked): Bernard! Well, look who's here! *(He comes quickly, guiltily, to Bernard and warmly shakes his hand.)*

Bernard: How are you? Good to see you.

Willy: What are you doing here?

Bernard: Oh, just stopped by to see Pop. Get off my feet till my train leaves. I'm going to Washington in a few minutes.

Willy: Is he in?

Bernard: Yes, he's in his office with the accountant. Sit down.

Willy (sitting down): What're you going to do in Washington?

Bernard: Oh, just a case I've got there, Willy.

Willy: That so? *(Indicating the rackets.)* You going to play tennis there?

Bernard: I'm staying with a friend who's got a court.

Willy: Don't say. His own tennis court. Must be fine people, I bet.

Bernard: They are, very nice. Dad tells me Biff's in town.

Willy (with a big smile): Yeah, Biff's in. Working on a very big deal, Bernard.

Bernard: What's Biff doing?

Willy: Well, he's been doing very big things in the West. But he decided to establish himself here. Very big. We're having dinner. Did I hear your wife had a boy?

Bernard: That's right. Our second.

Willy: Two boys! What do you know!

Bernard: What kind of a deal has Biff got?

Willy: Well, Bill Oliver — very big sporting-goods man — he wants Biff very badly. Called him in from the West. Long distance, carte blanche, special deliveries. Your friends have their own private tennis court?

Bernard: You still with the old firm, Willy?

Willy (after a pause): I'm — I'm overjoyed to see how you made the grade, Bernard, overjoyed. It's an encouraging thing to see a young man really — really — Looks very good for Biff — very — *(He breaks off, then.)* Bernard — *(He is so full of emotion, he breaks off again.)*

Bernard: What is it, Willy?

Willy (small and alone): What — what's the secret?

Bernard: What secret?

Willy: How — how did you? Why didn't he ever catch on?

Bernard: I wouldn't know that, Willy.

Willy (confidentially, desperately): You were his friend, his boyhood friend. There's something I don't understand about it. His life ended after that

Ebbets Field game. From the age of seventeen nothing good ever happened to him.

Bernard: He never trained himself for anything.

Willy: But he did, he did. After high school he took so many correspondence courses. Radio mechanics; television; God knows what, and never made the slightest mark.

Bernard (taking off his glasses): Willy, do you want to talk candidly?

Willy (rising, faces Bernard): I regard you as a very brilliant man, Bernard. I value your advice.

Bernard: Oh, the hell with the advice, Willy. I couldn't advise you. There's just one thing I've always wanted to ask you. When he was supposed to graduate, and the math teacher flunked him —

Willy: Oh, that son-of-a-bitch ruined his life.

Bernard: Yeah, but, Willy, all he had to do was go to summer school and make up that subject.

Willy: That's right, that's right.

Bernard: Did you tell him not to go to summer school?

Willy: Me? I begged him to go. I ordered him to go!

Bernard: Then why wouldn't he go?

Willy: Why? Why! Bernard, that question has been trailing me like a ghost for the last fifteen years. He flunked the subject, and laid down and died like a hammer hit him!

Bernard: Take it easy, kid.

Willy: Let me talk to you — I got nobody to talk to. Bernard, Bernard, was it my fault? Y'see? It keeps going around in my mind, maybe I did something to him. I got nothing to give him.

Bernard: Don't take it so hard.

Willy: Why did he lay down? What is the story there? You were his friend!

Bernard: Willy, I remember, it was June, and our grades came out. And he'd flunked math.

Willy: That son-of-a-bitch!

Bernard: No, it wasn't right then. Biff just got very angry, I remember, and he was ready to enroll in summer school.

Willy (surprised): He was?

Bernard: He wasn't beaten by it at all. But then, Willy, he disappeared from the block for almost a month. And I got the idea that he'd gone up to New England to see you. Did he have a talk with you then?

Willy stares in silence.

Bernard: Willy?

Willy (with a strong edge of resentment in his voice): Yeah, he came to Boston. What about it?

Bernard: Well, just that when he came back — I'll never forget this, it always mystifies me. Because I'd thought so well of Biff, even though he'd always taken advantage of me. I loved him, Willy, y'know? And he came back after that month and took his sneakers — remember those sneakers with "University of Virginia" printed on them? He was so proud of those, wore them every day. And he took them down in the cellar, and burned them up in the furnace. We had a fist fight. It lasted at least half an hour. Just the two of us, punching each other down the cellar, and crying right through it. I've often thought of how strange it was that I knew he'd given up his life. What happened in Boston, Willy?

Willy looks at him as at an intruder.

Bernard: I just bring it up because you asked me.

Willy (*angrily*): Nothing. What do you mean, "What happened?" What's that got to do with anything?

Bernard: Well, don't get sore.

Willy: What are you trying to do, blame it on me? If a boy lays down is that my fault?

Bernard: Now, Willy, don't get—

Willy: Well, don't—don't talk to me that way! What does that mean, "What happened?"

Charley enters. He is in his vest, and he carries a bottle of bourbon.

Charley: Hey, you're going to miss that train. (*He waves the bottle.*)

Bernard: Yeah, I'm going. (*He takes the bottle.*) Thanks, Pop. (*He picks up his rackets and bag.*) Good-by, Willy, and don't worry about it. You know, "If at first you don't succeed . . ."

Willy: Yes, I believe in that.

Bernard: But sometimes, Willy, it's better for a man just to walk away.

Willy: Walk away?

Bernard: That's right.

Willy: But if you can't walk away?

Bernard (*after a slight pause*): I guess that's when it's tough. (*Extending his hand.*) Good-by, Willy.

Willy (*shaking Bernard's hand*): Good-by, boy.

Charley (*an arm on Bernard's shoulder*): How do you like this kid? Gonna argue a case in front of the Supreme Court.

Bernard (*protesting*): Pop!

Willy (*genuinely shocked, pained, and happy*): No! The Supreme Court!

Bernard: I gotta run. 'By, Dad!

Charley: Knock 'em dead, Bernard!

Bernard goes off.

Willy (*as Charley takes out his wallet*): The Supreme Court! And he didn't even mention it!

Charley (*counting out money on the desk*): He don't have to—he's gonna do it.

Willy: And you never told him what to do, did you? You never took any interest in him.

Charley: My salvation is that I never took any interest in any thing. There's some money—fifty dollars. I got an accountant inside.

Willy: Charley, look . . . (*With difficulty.*) I got my insurance to pay. If you can manage it—I need a hundred and ten dollars.

Charley doesn't reply for a moment; merely stops moving.

Willy: I'd draw it from my bank but Linda would know, and I . . .

Charley: Sit down, Willy.

Willy (*moving toward the chair*): I'm keeping an account of everything, remember. I'll pay every penny back. (*He sits.*)

Charley: Now listen to me, Willy.

Willy: I want you to know I appreciate . . .

Charley (sitting down on the table): Willy, what're you doin'? What the hell is goin' on in your head?

Willy: Why? I'm simply . . .

Charley: I offered you a job. You can make fifty dollars a week. And I won't send you on the road.

Willy: I've got a job.

Charley: Without pay? What kind of a job is a job without pay? *(He rises.)* Now, look, kid, enough is enough. I'm no genius but I know when I'm being insulted.

Willy: Insulted!

Charley: Why don't you want to work for me?

Willy: What's the matter with you? I've got a job.

Charley: Then what're you walkin' in here every week for?

Willy (getting up): Well, if you don't want me to walk in here —

Charley: I am offering you a job.

Willy: I don't want your goddam job!

Charley: When the hell are you going to grow up?

Willy (furiously): You big ignoramus, if you say that to me again I'll rap you one! I don't care how big you are! *(He's ready to fight.)*

Pause.

Charley (kindly, going to him): How much do you need, Willy?

Willy: Charley, I'm strapped. I'm strapped. I don't know what to do. I was just fired.

Charley: Howard fired you?

Willy: That snotnose. Imagine that? I named him. I named him Howard.

Charley: Willy, when're you gonna realize that them things don't mean anything? You named him Howard, but you can't sell that. The only thing you got in this world is what you can sell. And the funny thing is that you're a salesman, and you don't know that.

Willy: I've always tried to think otherwise, I guess. I always felt that if a man was impressive, and well liked, that nothing —

Charley: Why must everybody like you? Who liked J. P. Morgan? Was he impressive? In a Turkish bath he'd look like a butcher. But with his pockets on he was very well liked. Now listen, Willy, I know you don't like me, and nobody can say I'm in love with you, but I'll give you a job because — just for the hell of it, put it that way. Now what do you say?

Willy: I — I just can't work for you, Charley.

Charley: What're you, jealous of me?

Willy: I can't work for you, that's all, don't ask me why.

Charley (angered, takes out more bills): You been jealous of me all your life, you damned fool! Here, pay your insurance. *(He puts the money in Willy's hand.)*

Willy: I'm keeping strict accounts.

Charley: I've got some work to do. Take care of yourself. And pay your insurance.

Willy (moving to the right): Funny, y'know? After all the highways, and the trains, and the appointments, and the years, you end up worth more dead than alive.

Charley: Willy, nobody's worth nothin' dead. *(After a slight pause.)* Did you hear what I said?

Willy stands still, dreaming.

Charley: Willy!

Willy: Apologize to Bernard for me when you see him. I didn't mean to argue with him. He's a fine boy. They're all fine boys, and they'll end up big—all of them. Someday they'll all play tennis together. Wish me luck, Charley. He saw Bill Oliver today.

Charley: Good luck.

Willy (on the verge of tears): Charley, you're the only friend I got. Isn't that a remarkable thing? *(He goes out.)*

Charley: Jesus!

Charley stares after him a moment and follows. All light blacks out. Suddenly raucous music is heard, and a red glow rises behind the screen at right. Stanley, a young waiter, appears, carrying a table, followed by Happy, who is carrying two chairs.

Stanley (putting the table down): That's all right, Mr. Loman, I can handle it myself. *(He turns and takes the chairs from Happy and places them at the table.)*

Happy (glancing around): Oh, this is better.

Stanley: Sure, in the front there you're in the middle of all kinds a noise. Whenever you got a party, Mr. Loman, you just tell me and I'll put you back here. Y'know, there's a lotta people they don't like it private, because when they go out they like to see a lotta action around them because they're sick and tired to stay in the house by theirself. But I know you, you ain't from Hackensack. You know what I mean?

Happy (sitting down): So how's it coming, Stanley?

Stanley: Ah, it's a dog's life. I only wish during the war they'd a took me in the Army. I coulda been dead by now.

Happy: My brother's back, Stanley.

Stanley: Oh, he come back, heh? From the Far West.

Happy: Yeah, big cattle man, my brother, so treat him right. And my father's coming too.

Stanley: Oh, your father too!

Happy: You got a couple of nice lobsters?

Stanley: Hundred per cent, big.

Happy: I want them with the claws.

Stanley: Don't worry, I don't give you no mice. *(Happy laughs.)* How about some wine? It'll put a head on the meal.

Happy: No. You remember, Stanley, that recipe I brought you from overseas? With the champagne in it?

Stanley: Oh, yeah, sure. I still got it tacked up yet in the kitchen. But that'll have to cost a buck apiece anyways.

Happy: That's all right.

Stanley: What'd you, hit a number or somethin'?

Happy: No, it's a little celebration. My brother is—I think he pulled off a big deal today. I think we're going into business together.

Stanley: Great! That's the best for you. Because a family business, you know what I mean?—that's the best.

Happy: That's what I think.

Stanley: 'Cause what's the difference? Somebody steals? It's in the family. Know what I mean? *(Sotto voce.°)* Like this bartender here. The boss is goin' crazy what kinda leak he's got in the cash register. You put it in but it don't come out.

Happy (raising his head): Sh!

Stanley: What?

Happy: You notice I wasn't lookin' right or left, was I?

Stanley: No.

Happy: And my eyes are closed.

Stanley: So what's the —?

Happy: Strudel's comin'.

Stanley (catching on, looks around): Ah, no, there's no —

> He breaks off as a furred, lavishly dressed girl enters and sits at the next table. Both follow her with their eyes.

Stanley: Geez, how'd ya know?

Happy: I got radar or something. *(Staring directly at her profile.)* Oooooooo . . . Stanley.

Stanley: I think that's for you, Mr. Loman.

Happy: Look at that mouth. Oh, God. And the binoculars.

Stanley: Geez, you got a life, Mr. Loman.

Happy: Wait on her.

Stanley (going to the girl's table): Would you like a menu, ma'am?

Girl: I'm expecting someone, but I'd like a —

Happy: Why don't you bring her — excuse me, miss, do you mind? I sell champagne, and I'd like you to try my brand. Bring her a champagne, Stanley.

Girl: That's awfully nice of you.

Happy: Don't mention it. It's all company money. *(He laughs.)*

Girl: That's a charming product to be selling, isn't it?

Happy: Oh, gets to be like everything else. Selling is selling, y'know.

Girl: I suppose.

Happy: You don't happen to sell, do you?

Girl: No, I don't sell.

Happy: Would you object to a compliment from a stranger? You ought to be on a magazine cover.

Girl (looking at him a little archly): I have been.

> *Stanley comes in with a glass of champagne.*

Happy: What'd I say before, Stanley? You see? She's a cover girl.

Stanley: Oh, I could see, I could see.

Happy (to the Girl): What magazine?

Girl: Oh, a lot of them. *(She takes the drink.)* Thank you.

Happy: You know what they say in France, don't you? "Champagne is the drink of the complexion" — Hya, Biff!

> *Biff has entered and sits with Happy.*

Biff: Hello, kid. Sorry I'm late.

Sotto voce: Softly, "under the breath" (Italian).

Happy: I just got here. Uh, Miss —?

Girl: Forsythe.

Happy: Miss Forsythe, this is my brother.

Biff: Is Dad here?

Happy: His name is Biff. You might've heard of him. Great football player.

Girl: Really? What team?

Happy: Are you familiar with football?

Girl: No, I'm afraid I'm not.

Happy: Biff is quarterback with the New York Giants.

Girl: Well, that is nice, isn't it? *(She drinks.)*

Happy: Good health.

Girl: I'm happy to meet you.

Happy: That's my name. Hap. It's really Harold, but at West Point they called me Happy.

Girl (now really impressed): Oh, I see. How do you do? *(She turns her profile.)*

Biff: Isn't Dad coming?

Happy: You want her?

Biff: Oh, I could never make that.

Happy: I remember the time that idea would never come into your head. Where's the old confidence, Biff?

Biff: I just saw Oliver —

Happy: Wait a minute. I've got to see that old confidence again. Do you want her? She's on call.

Biff: Oh, no. *(He turns to look at the Girl.)*

Happy: I'm telling you. Watch this. *(Turning to the Girl.)* Honey? *(She turns to him.)* Are you busy?

Girl: Well, I am . . . but I could make a phone call.

Happy: Do that, will you, honey? And see if you can get a friend. We'll be here for a while. Biff is one of the greatest football players in the country.

Girl (standing up): Well, I'm certainly happy to meet you.

Happy: Come back soon.

Girl: I'll try.

Happy: Don't try, honey, try hard.

> *The Girl exits. Stanley follows, shaking his head in bewildered admiration.*

Happy: Isn't that a shame now? A beautiful girl like that? That's why I can't get married. There's not a good woman in a thousand. New York is loaded with them, kid!

Biff: Hap, look —

Happy: I told you she was on call!

Biff (strangely unnerved): Cut it out, will ya? I want to say something to you.

Happy: Did you see Oliver?

Biff: I saw him all right. Now look, I want to tell Dad a couple of things and I want you to help me.

Happy: What? Is he going to back you?

Biff: Are you crazy? You're out of your goddam head, you know that?

Happy: Why? What happened?

Biff (breathlessly): I did a terrible thing today, Hap. It's been the strangest day I ever went through. I'm all numb, I swear.

Happy: You mean he wouldn't see you?

Biff: Well, I waited six hours for him, see? All day. Kept sending my name in. Even tried to date his secretary so she'd get me to him, but no soap.

Happy: Because you're not showin' the old confidence, Biff. He remembered you, didn't he?

Biff (stopping Happy with a gesture): Finally, about five o'clock, he comes out. Didn't remember who I was or anything. I felt like such an idiot, Hap.

Happy: Did you tell him my Florida idea?

Biff: He walked away. I saw him for one minute. I got so mad I could've torn the walls down! How the hell did I ever get the idea I was a salesman there? I even believed myself that I'd been a salesman for him! And then he gave me one look and — I realized what a ridiculous lie my whole life has been! We've been talking in a dream for fifteen years. I was a shipping clerk.

Happy: What'd you do?

Biff (with great tension and wonder): Well, he left, see. And the secretary went out. I was all alone in the waiting-room. I don't know what came over me, Hap. The next thing I know I'm in his office — paneled walls, everything. I can't explain it. I — Hap, I took his fountain pen.

Happy: Geez, did he catch you?

Biff: I ran out. I ran down all eleven flights. I ran and ran and ran.

Happy: That was an awful dumb — what'd you do that for?

Biff (agonized): I don't know, I just — wanted to take something, I don't know. You gotta help me, Hap, I'm gonna tell Pop.

Happy: You crazy? What for?

Biff: Hap, he's got to understand that I'm not the man somebody lends that kind of money to. He thinks I've been spiting him all these years and it's eating him up.

Happy: That's just it. You tell him something nice.

Biff: I can't.

Happy: Say you got a lunch date with Oliver tomorrow.

Biff: So what do I do tomorrow?

Happy: You leave the house tomorrow and come back at night and say Oliver is thinking it over. And he thinks it over for a couple of weeks, and gradually it fades away and nobody's the worse.

Biff: But it'll go on forever!

Happy: Dad is never so happy as when he's looking forward to something!

> *Willy enters.*

Happy: Hello, scout!

Willy: Gee, I haven't been here in years!

> *Stanley has followed Willy in and sets a chair for him. Stanley starts off but Happy stops him.*

Happy: Stanley!

> *Stanley stands by, waiting for an order.*

Biff (going to Willy with guilt, as to an invalid): Sit down, Pop. You want a drink?

Willy: Sure, I don't mind.

Biff: Let's get a load on.

Willy: You look worried.

Biff: N-no. *(To Stanley.)* Scotch all around. Make it doubles.

Stanley: Doubles, right. (*He goes.*)

Willy: You had a couple already, didn't you?

Biff: Just a couple, yeah.

Willy: Well, what happened, boy? (*Nodding affirmatively, with a smile.*) Everything go all right?

Biff (takes a breath, then reaches out and grasps Willy's hand): Pal . . . (*He is smiling bravely, and Willy is smiling too.*) I had an experience today.

Happy: Terrific, Pop.

Willy: That so? What happened?

Biff (high, slightly alcoholic, above the earth): I'm going to tell you everything from first to last. It's been a strange day. (*Silence. He looks around, composes himself as best he can, but his breath keeps breaking the rhythm of his voice.*) I had to wait quite a while for him, and —

Willy: Oliver.

Biff: Yeah, Oliver. All day, as a matter of cold fact. And a lot of — instances — facts, Pop, facts about my life came back to me. Who was it, Pop? Who ever said I was a salesman with Oliver?

Willy: Well, you were.

Biff: No, Dad, I was a shipping clerk.

Willy: But you were practically —

Biff (with determination): Dad, I don't know who said it first, but I was never a salesman for Bill Oliver.

Willy: What're you talking about?

Biff: Let's hold on to the facts tonight, Pop. We're not going to get anywhere bullin' around. I was a shipping clerk.

Willy (angrily): All right, now listen to me —

Biff: Why don't you let me finish?

Willy: I'm not interested in stories about the past or any crap of that kind because the woods are burning, boys, you understand? There's a big blaze going on all around. I was fired today.

Biff (shocked): How could you be?

Willy: I was fired, and I'm looking for a little good news to tell your mother, because the woman has waited and the woman has suffered. The gist of it is that I haven't got a story left in my head, Biff. So don't give me a lecture about facts and aspects. I am not interested. Now what've you got to say to me?

Stanley enters with three drinks. They wait until he leaves.

Willy: Did you see Oliver?

Biff: Jesus, Dad!

Willy: You mean you didn't go up there?

Happy: Sure he went up there.

Biff: I did. I — saw him. How could they fire you?

Willy (on the edge of his chair): What kind of a welcome did he give you?

Biff: He won't even let you work on commission?

Willy: I'm out! (*Driving.*) So tell me, he gave you a warm welcome?

Happy: Sure, Pop, sure!

Biff (driven): Well, it was kind of —

Willy: I was wondering if he'd remember you. (*To Happy.*) Imagine, man doesn't see him for ten, twelve years and gives him that kind of a welcome!

Happy: Damn right!

Biff (trying to return to the offensive): Pop, look —

Willy: You know why he remembered you, don't you? Because you impressed him in those days.

Biff: Let's talk quietly and get this down to the facts, huh?

Willy (as though Biff had been interrupting): Well, what happened? It's great news, Biff. Did he take you into his office or'd you talk in the waiting-room?

Biff: Well, he came in, see, and —

Willy (with a big smile): What'd he say? Betcha he threw his arm around you.

Biff: Well, he kinda —

Willy: He's a fine man. *(To Happy.)* Very hard man to see, y'know.

Happy (agreeing): Oh, I know.

Willy (to Biff): Is that where you had the drinks?

Biff: Yeah, he gave me a couple of — no, no!

Happy (cutting in): He told him my Florida idea.

Willy: Don't interrupt. *(To Biff.)* How'd he react to the Florida idea?

Biff: Dad, will you give me a minute to explain?

Willy: I've been waiting for you to explain since I sat down here! What happened? He took you into his office and what?

Biff: Well — I talked. And — and he listened, see.

Willy: Famous for the way he listens, y'know. What was his answer?

Biff: His answer was — *(He breaks off, suddenly angry.)* Dad, you're not letting me tell you what I want to tell you!

Willy (accusing, angered): You didn't see him, did you?

Biff: I did see him!

Willy: What'd you insult him or something? You insulted him, didn't you?

Biff: Listen, will you let me out of it, will you just let me out of it!

Happy: What the hell!

Willy: Tell me what happened!

Biff (to Happy): I can't talk to him!

> *A single trumpet note jars the ear. The light of green leaves stains the house, which holds the air of night and a dream. Young Bernard enters and knocks on the door of the house.*

Young Bernard (frantically): Mrs. Loman, Mrs. Loman!

Happy: Tell him what happened!

Biff (to Happy): Shut up and leave me alone!

Willy: No, no! You had to go and flunk math!

Biff: What math? What're you talking about?

Young Bernard: Mrs. Loman, Mrs. Loman!

> *Linda appears in the house, as of old.*

Willy (wildly): Math, math, math!

Biff: Take it easy, Pop!

Young Bernard: Mrs. Loman!

Willy (furiously): If you hadn't flunked you'd've been set by now!

Biff: Now, look, I'm gonna tell you what happened, and you're going to listen to me.

Young Bernard: Mrs. Loman!

Biff: I waited six hours —

Happy: What the hell are you saying?

Biff: I kept sending in my name but he wouldn't see me. So finally he . . . *(He continues unheard as light fades low on the restaurant.)*

Young Bernard: Biff flunked math!

Linda: No!

Young Bernard: Birnbaum flunked him! They won't graduate him!

Linda: But they have to. He's gotta go to the university. Where is he? Biff! Biff!

Young Bernard: No, he left. He went to Grand Central.

Linda: Grand—You mean he went to Boston!

Young Bernard: Is Uncle Willy in Boston?

Linda: Oh, maybe Willy can talk to the teacher. Oh, the poor, poor boy!

> *Light on house area snaps out.*

Biff (at the table, now audible, holding up a gold fountain pen): . . . so I'm washed up with Oliver, you understand? Are you listening to me?

Willy (at a loss): Yeah, sure. If you hadn't flunked—

Biff: Flunked what? What're you talking about?

Willy: Don't blame everything on me! I didn't flunk math—you did! What pen?

Happy: That was awful dumb, Biff, a pen like that is worth—

Willy (seeing the pen for the first time): You took Oliver's pen?

Biff (weakening): Dad, I just explained it to you.

Willy: You stole Bill Oliver's fountain pen!

Biff: I didn't exactly steal it! That's just what I've been explaining to you!

Happy: He had it in his hand and just then Oliver walked in, so he got nervous and stuck it in his pocket!

Willy: My God, Biff!

Biff: I never intended to do it, Dad!

Operator's Voice: Standish Arms, good evening!

Willy (shouting): I'm not in my room!

Biff (frightened): Dad, what's the matter? *(He and Happy stand up.)*

Operator: Ringing Mr. Loman for you!

Willy: I'm not there, stop it!

Biff (horrified, gets down on one knee before Willy): Dad, I'll make good, I'll make good. *(Willy tries to get to his feet. Biff holds him down.)* Sit down now.

Willy: No, you're no good, you're no good for anything.

Biff: I am, Dad, I'll find something else, you understand? Now don't worry about anything. *(He holds up Willy's face.)* Talk to me, Dad.

Operator: Mr. Loman does not answer. Shall I page him?

Willy (attempting to stand, as though to rush and silence the Operator): No, no, no!

Happy: He'll strike something, Pop.

Willy: No, no . . .

Biff (desperately, standing over Willy): Pop, listen! Listen to me! I'm telling you something good. Oliver talked to his partner about the Florida idea. You listening? He—he talked to his partner, and he came to me . . . I'm going to be all right, you hear? Dad, listen to me, he said it was just a question of the amount!

Willy: Then you . . . got it?

Happy: He's gonna be terrific, Pop!

Willy (trying to stand): Then you got it, haven't you? You got it! You got it!

Biff (agonized, holds Willy down): No, no. Look, Pop. I'm supposed to have lunch with them tomorrow. I'm just telling you this so you'll know that I can still make an impression, Pop. And I'll make good somewhere, but I can't go tomorrow, see?

Willy: Why not? You simply —

Biff: But the pen, Pop!

Willy: You give it to him and tell him it was an oversight!

Happy: Sure, have lunch tomorrow!

Biff: I can't say that —

Willy: You were doing a crossword puzzle and accidentally used his pen!

Biff: Listen, kid, I took those balls years ago, now I walk in with his fountain pen? That clinches it, don't you see? I can't face him like that! I'll try elsewhere.

Page's Voice: Paging Mr. Loman!

Willy: Don't you want to be anything?

Biff: Pop, how can I go back?

Willy: You don't want to be anything, is that what's behind it?

Biff (now angry at Willy for not crediting his sympathy): Don't take it that way! You think it was easy walking into that office after what I'd done to him? A team of horses couldn't have dragged me back to Bill Oliver!

Willy: Then why'd you go?

Biff: Why did I go? Why did I go! Look at you! Look at what's become of you!

Off left, The Woman laughs.

Willy: Biff, you're going to lunch tomorrow, or —

Biff: I can't go. I've got no appointment!

Happy: Biff, for . . . !

Willy: Are you spiting me?

Biff: Don't take it that way! Goddammit!

Willy (strikes Biff and falters away from the table): You rotten little louse! Are you spiting me?

The Woman: Someone's at the door, Willy!

Biff: I'm no good, can't you see what I am?

Happy (separating them): Hey, you're in a restaurant! Now cut it out, both of you! *(The girls enter.)* Hello, girls, sit down.

The Woman laughs, off left.

Miss Forsythe: I guess we might as well. This is Letta.

The Woman: Willy, are you going to wake up?

Biff (ignoring Willy): How're ya, miss, sit down. What do you drink?

Miss Forsythe: Letta might not be able to stay long.

Letta: I gotta get up very early tomorrow. I got jury duty. I'm so excited! Were you fellows ever on a jury?

Biff: No, but I been in front of them! *(The girls laugh.)* This is my father.

Letta: Isn't he cute? Sit down with us, Pop.

Happy: Sit him down, Biff!

Biff (going to him): Come on, slugger, drink us under the table. To hell with it! Come on, sit down, pal.

On Biff's last insistence, Willy is about to sit.

The Woman (now urgently): Willy, are you going to answer the door!

The Woman's call pulls Willy back. He starts right, befuddled.

Biff: Hey, where are you going?

Willy: Open the door.

Biff: The door?

Willy: The washroom . . . the door . . . where's the door?

Biff (leading Willy to the left): Just go straight down.

    Willy moves left.

The Woman: Willy, Willy, are you going to get up, get up, get up, get up?

    Willy exits left.

Letta: I think it's sweet you bring your daddy along.

Miss Forsythe: Oh, he isn't really your father!

Biff (at left, turning to her resentfully): Miss Forsythe, you've just seen a prince walk by. A fine, troubled prince. A hard-working, unappreciated prince. A pal, you understand? A good companion. Always for his boys.

Letta: That's so sweet.

Happy: Well, girls, what's the program? We're wasting time. Come on, Biff. Gather round. Where would you like to go?

Biff: Why don't you do something for him?

Happy: Me!

Biff: Don't you give a damn for him, Hap?

Happy: What're you talking about? I'm the one who—

Biff: I sense it, you don't give a good goddamn about him. *(He takes the rolled-up hose from his pocket and puts it on the table in front of Happy.)* Look what I found in the cellar, for Christ's sake. How can you bear to let it go on?

Happy: Me? Who goes away? Who runs off and—

Biff: Yeah, but he doesn't mean anything to you. You could help him—I can't! Don't you understand what I'm talking about? He's going to kill himself, don't you know that?

Happy: Don't I know it! Me!

Biff: Hap, help him! Jesus . . . help him . . . Help me, help me, I can't bear to look at his face! *(Ready to weep, he hurries out, up right.)*

Happy (starting after him): Where are you going?

Miss Forsythe: What's he so mad about?

Happy: Come on, girls, we'll catch up with him.

Miss Forsythe (as Happy pushes her out): Say, I don't like that temper of his!

Happy: He's just a little overstrung, he'll be all right!

Willy (off left, as The Woman laughs): Don't answer! Don't answer!

Letta: Don't you want to tell your father—

Happy: No, that's not my father. He's just a guy. Come on, we'll catch Biff, and, honey, we're going to paint this town! Stanley, where's the check! Hey, Stanley!

    They exit. Stanley looks toward left.

Stanley (calling to Happy indignantly): Mr. Loman! Mr. Loman!

    Stanley picks up a chair and follows them off. Knocking is heard off left. The Woman enters, laughing. Willy follows her. She is in a black slip; he is buttoning his shirt. Raw, sensuous music accompanies their speech.

Willy: Will you stop laughing? Will you stop?

The Woman: Aren't you going to answer the door? He'll wake the whole hotel.

Willy: I'm not expecting anybody.

The Woman: Whyn't you have another drink, honey, and stop being so damn self-centered?

Willy: I'm so lonely.

The Woman: You know you ruined me, Willy? From now on, whenever you come to the office, I'll see that you go right through to the buyers. No waiting at my desk any more, Willy. You ruined me.

Willy: That's nice of you to say that.

The Woman: Gee, you are self-centered! Why so sad? You are the saddest, self-centeredest soul I ever did see-saw. *(She laughs. He kisses her.)* Come on inside, drummer boy. It's silly to be dressing in the middle of the night. *(As knocking is heard.)* Aren't you going to answer the door?

Willy: They're knocking on the wrong door.

The Woman: But I felt the knocking. And he heard us talking in here. Maybe the hotel's on fire!

Willy (his terror rising): It's a mistake.

The Woman: Then tell him to go away!

Willy: There's nobody there.

The Woman: It's getting on my nerves, Willy. There's somebody standing out there and it's getting on my nerves!

Willy (pushing her away from him): All right, stay in the bathroom here, and don't come out. I think there's a law in Massachusetts about it, so don't come out. It may be that new room clerk. He looked very mean. So don't come out. It's a mistake, there's no fire.

The knocking is heard again. He takes a few steps away from her, and she vanishes into the wing. The light follows him, and now he is facing Young Biff, who carries a suitcase. Biff steps toward him. The music is gone.

Biff: Why didn't you answer?

Willy: Biff! What are you doing in Boston?

Biff: Why didn't you answer? I've been knocking for five minutes, I called you on the phone —

Willy: I just heard you. I was in the bathroom and had the door shut. Did anything happen home?

Biff: Dad — I let you down.

Willy: What do you mean?

Biff: Dad . . .

Willy: Biffo, what's this about? *(Putting his arm around Biff.)* Come on, let's go downstairs and get you a malted.

Biff: Dad, I flunked math.

Willy: Not for the term?

Biff: The term. I haven't got enough credits to graduate.

Willy: You mean to say Bernard wouldn't give you the answers?

Biff: He did, he tried, but I only got a sixty-one.

Willy: And they wouldn't give you four points?

Biff: Birnbaum refused absolutely. I begged him, Pop, but he won't give me those points. You gotta talk to him before they close the school. Because if he saw the kind of man you are, and you just talked to him in your way, I'm sure he'd come through for me. The class came right before practice, see, and I didn't go enough. Would you talk to him? He'd like you, Pop. You know the way you could talk.

Willy: You're on. We'll drive right back.

Biff: Oh, Dad, good work! I'm sure he'll change it for you!

Willy: Go downstairs and tell the clerk I'm checkin' out. Go right down.

Biff: Yes, sir! See, the reason he hates me, Pop — one day he was late for class so I got up at the blackboard and imitated him. I crossed my eyes and talked with a lithp.

Willy (laughing): You did? The kids like it?

Biff: They nearly died laughing!

Willy: Yeah? What'd you do?

Biff: The thquare root of thixthy twee is . . . *(Willy bursts out laughing; Biff joins him.)* And in the middle of it he walked in!

Willy laughs and The Woman joins in offstage.

Willy (without hesitation): Hurry downstairs and —

Biff: Somebody in there?

Willy: No, that was next door.

The Woman laughs offstage.

Biff: Somebody got in your bathroom!

Willy: No, it's the next room, there's a party —

The Woman (enters, laughing. She lisps this): Can I come in? There's something in the bathtub, Willy, and it's moving!

Willy looks at Biff, who is staring open-mouthed and horrified at The Woman.

Willy: Ah — you better go back to your room. They must be finished painting by now. They're painting her room so I let her take a shower here. Go back, go back . . . *(He pushes her.)*

The Woman (resisting): But I've got to get dressed, Willy, I can't —

Willy: Get out of here! Go back, go back . . . *(Suddenly striving for the ordinary):* This is Miss Francis, Biff, she's a buyer. They're painting her room. Go back, Miss Francis, go back . . .

The Woman: But my clothes, I can't go out naked in the hall!

Willy (pushing her offstage): Get outa here! Go back, go back!

Biff slowly sits down on his suitcase as the argument continues offstage.

The Woman: Where's my stockings? You promised me stockings, Willy!

Willy: I have no stockings here!

The Woman: You had two boxes of size nine sheers for me, and I want them!

Willy: Here, for God's sake, will you get outa here!

The Woman (enters holding a box of stockings): I just hope there's nobody in the hall. That's all I hope. *(To Biff.)* Are you football or baseball?

Biff: Football.

The Woman (angry, humiliated): That's me too. G'night. *(She snatches her clothes from Willy, and walks out.)*

Willy (after a pause): Well, better get going. I want to get to the school first thing in the morning. Get my suits out of the closet. I'll get my valise. *(Biff doesn't move.)* What's the matter? *(Biff remains motionless, tears falling.)* She's a buyer. Buys for J. H. Simmons. She lives down the hall — they're painting. You don't imagine — *(He breaks off. After a pause.)* Now listen, pal, she's just a buyer. She sees merchandise in her room and they have to keep it looking just so . . . *(Pause. Assuming command.)* All right, get my suits. *(Biff doesn't move.)* Now stop crying and do as I say. I gave you an order. Biff, I gave you an order! Is that what you do when I give you an order? How dare you cry! *(Putting his arm around Biff.)* Now look, Biff, when you grow up you'll understand about these things. You mustn't — you mustn't overemphasize a thing like this. I'll see Birnbaum first thing in the morning.

Biff: Never mind.

Willy (getting down beside Biff): Never mind! He's going to give you those points. I'll see to it.

Biff: He wouldn't listen to you.

Willy: He certainly will listen to me. You need those points for the U. of Virginia.

Biff: I'm not going there.

Willy: Heh? If I can't get him to change that mark you'll make it up in summer school. You've got all summer to —

Biff (his weeping breaking from him): Dad . . .

Willy (infected by it): Oh, my boy . . .

Biff: Dad . . .

Willy: She's nothing to me, Biff. I was lonely, I was terribly lonely.

Biff: You — you gave her Mama's stockings! *(His tears break through and he rises to go.)*

Willy (grabbing for Biff): I gave you an order!

Biff: Don't touch me, you — liar!

Willy: Apologize for that!

Biff: You fake! You phony little fake! You fake! *(Overcome, he turns quickly and weeping fully goes out with his suitcase. Willy is left on the floor on his knees.)*

Willy: I gave you an order! Biff, come back here or I'll beat you! Come back here! I'll whip you!

Stanley comes quickly in from the right and stands in front of Willy.

Willy (shouts at Stanley): I gave you an order . . .

Stanley: Hey, let's pick it up, pick it up, Mr. Loman. *(He helps Willy to his feet.)* Your boys left with the chippies. They said they'll see you home.

A second waiter watches some distance away.

Willy: But we were supposed to have dinner together.

Music is heard, Willy's theme.

Stanley: Can you make it?

Willy: I'll — sure, I can make it. *(Suddenly concerned about his clothes.)* Do I — I look all right?

Stanley: Sure, you look all right. *(He flicks a speck off Willy's lapel.)*

Willy: Here — here's a dollar.

Stanley: Oh, your son paid me. It's all right.

Willy (putting it in Stanley's hand): No, take it. You're a good boy.

Stanley: Oh, no, you don't have to . . .

Willy: Here — here's some more, I don't need it any more. *(After a slight pause.)* Tell me — is there a seed store in the neighborhood?

Stanley: Seeds? You mean like to plant?

As Willy turns, Stanley slips the money back into his jacket pocket.

Willy: Yes. Carrots, peas . . .

Stanley: Well, there's hardware stores on Sixth Avenue, but it may be too late now.

Willy (anxiously): Oh, I'd better hurry. I've got to get some seeds. *(He starts off to the right.)* I've got to get some seeds, right away. Nothing's planted. I don't have a thing in the ground.

Willy hurries out as the light goes down. Stanley moves over to the right after him, watches him off. The other waiter has been staring at Willy.

Stanley (to the waiter): Well, whatta you looking at?

The waiter picks up the chairs and moves off right. Stanley takes the table and follows him. The light fades on this area. There is a long pause, the sound of the flute coming over. The light gradually rises on the kitchen, which is empty. Happy appears at the door of the house, followed by Biff. Happy is carrying a large bunch of long-stemmed roses. He enters the kitchen, looks around for Linda. Not seeing her, he turns to Biff, who is just outside the house door, and makes a gesture with his hands, indicating "Not here, I guess." He looks into the living-room and freezes. Inside, Linda, unseen, is seated, Willy's coat on her lap. She rises ominously and quietly and moves toward Happy, who backs up into the kitchen, afraid.

Happy: Hey, what're you doing up? *(Linda says nothing but moves toward him implacably.)* Where's Pop? *(He keeps backing to the right, and now Linda is in full view in the doorway to the living-room.)* Is he sleeping?

Linda: Where were you?

Happy (trying to laugh it off): We met two girls, Mom, very fine types. Here, we brought you some flowers. *(Offering them to her.)* Put them in your room, Ma.

She knocks them to the floor at Biff's feet. He has now come inside and closed the door behind him. She stares at Biff, silent.

Happy: Now what'd you do that for? Mom, I want you to have some flowers —

Linda (cutting Happy off, violently to Biff): Don't you care whether he lives or dies?

Happy (going to the stairs): Come upstairs, Biff.

Biff (with a flare of disgust, to Happy): Go away from me! *(To Linda.)* What do you mean, lives or dies? Nobody's dying around here, pal.

Linda: Get out of my sight! Get out of here!

Biff: I wanna see the boss.

Linda: You're not going near him!

Biff: Where is he? *(He moves into the living-room and Linda follows.)*

Linda (shouting after Biff): You invite him for dinner. He looks forward to it all day — *(Biff appears in his parents' bedroom, looks around, and exits.)* — and then you desert him there. There's no stranger you'd do that to!

Happy: Why? He had a swell time with us. Listen, when I — *(Linda comes back into the kitchen)* — desert him I hope I don't outlive the day!

Linda: Get out of here!

Happy: Now look, Mom . . .

Linda: Did you have to go to women tonight? You and your lousy rotten whores!

Biff re-enters the kitchen.

Happy: Mom, all we did was follow Biff around trying to cheer him up! *(To Biff.)* Boy, what a night you gave me!

Linda: Get out of here, both of you, and don't come back! I don't want you tormenting him any more. Go on now, get your things together! *(To Biff.)* You can sleep in his apartment. *(She starts to pick up the flowers and stops herself.)* Pick up this stuff, I'm not your maid any more. Pick it up, you bum, you!

Happy turns his back to her in refusal. Biff slowly moves over and gets down on his knees, picking up the flowers.

Linda: You're a pair of animals! Not one, not another living soul would have had the cruelty to walk out on that man in a restaurant!

Biff (not looking at her): Is that what he said?

Linda: He didn't have to say anything. He was so humiliated he nearly limped when he came in.

Happy: But, Mom, he had a great time with us —

Biff (cutting him off violently): Shut up!

Without another word, Happy goes upstairs.

Linda: You! You didn't even go in to see if he was all right!

Biff (still on the floor in front of Linda, the flowers in his hand; with self-loathing): No. Didn't. Didn't do a damned thing. How do you like that, heh? Left him babbling in a toilet.

Linda: You louse. You . . .

Biff: Now you hit it on the nose! *(He gets up, throws the flowers in the wastebasket.)* The scum of the earth, and you're looking at him!

Linda: Get out of here!

Biff: I gotta talk to the boss, Mom. Where is he?

Linda: You're not going near him. Get out of this house!

Biff (with absolute assurance, determination): No. We're gonna have an abrupt conversation, him and me.

Linda: You're not talking to him!

Hammering is heard from outside the house, off right. Biff turns toward the noise.

Linda (suddenly pleading): Will you please leave him alone?

Biff: What's he doing out there?

Linda: He's planting the garden!

Biff (quietly): Now? Oh, my God!

Biff moves outside, Linda following. The light dies down on them and comes up on the center of the apron as Willy walks into it. He is carrying a flashlight, a hoe, and handful of seed packets. He raps the top of the hoe sharply to fix it firmly, and then moves to the left, measuring off the distance with his foot. He holds the flashlight to look at the seed packets, reading off the instructions. He is in the blue of night.

Willy: Carrots . . . quarter-inch apart. Rows . . . one-foot rows. *(He measures it off.)* One foot. *(He puts down a package and measures off.)* Beets. *(He puts down another package and measures again.)* Lettuce. *(He reads the package, puts it down.)* One foot — *(He breaks off as Ben appears at the right and moves slowly down to him.)* What a proposition, ts, ts. Terrific, terrific. 'Cause she's suffered, Ben, the woman has suffered. You understand me? A man can't go out the way he came in, Ben, a man has got to add up to something. You can't, you can't — *(Ben moves toward him as though to interrupt.)* You gotta consider, now. Don't answer so quick. Remember, it's a guaranteed twenty-thousand-dollar proposition. Now look, Ben, I want you to go through the ins and outs of this thing with me. I've got nobody to talk to, Ben, and the woman has suffered, you hear me?

Ben (standing still, considering): What's the proposition?

Willy: It's twenty thousand dollars on the barrelhead. Guaranteed, gilt-edged, you understand?

Ben: You don't want to make a fool of yourself. They might not honor the policy.

Willy: How can they dare refuse? Didn't I work like a coolie to meet every premium on the nose? And now they don't pay off? Impossible!

Ben: It's called a cowardly thing, William.

Willy: Why? Does it take more guts to stand here the rest of my life ringing up a zero?

Ben (yielding): That's a point, William. *(He moves, thinking, turns.)* And twenty thousand — that *is* something one can feel with the hand, it is there.

Willy (now assured, with rising power): Oh, Ben, that's the whole beauty of it! I see it like a diamond, shining in the dark, hard and rough, that I can pick up and touch in my hand. Not like — like an appointment! This would not be another damned-fool appointment, Ben, and it changes all the aspects. Because he thinks I'm nothing, see, and so he spites me. But the funeral — *(Straightening up.)* Ben, that funeral will be massive! They'll come from Maine, Massachusetts, Vermont, New Hampshire! All the old-timers with the strange license plates — that boy will be thunder-struck, Ben, because he never realized — I am known! Rhode Island, New York, New Jersey — I am known, Ben, and he'll see it with his eyes once and for all. He'll see what I am, Ben! He's in for a shock, that boy!

Ben (coming to the edge of the garden): He'll call you a coward.

Willy (suddenly fearful): No, that would be terrible.

Ben: Yes. And a damned fool.

Willy: No, no, he mustn't, I won't have that! *(He is broken and desperate.)*

Ben: He'll hate you William.

    The gay music of the Boys is heard.

Willy: Oh, Ben, how do we get back to all the great times? Used to be so full of light, and comradeship, the sleigh-riding in winter, and the ruddiness on his cheeks. And always some kind of good news coming up, always something nice coming up ahead. And never even let me carry the valises in the house, and simonizing, simonizing that little red car! Why, why can't I give him something and not have him hate me?

Ben: Let me think about it. *(He glances at his watch.)* I still have a little time. Remarkable proposition, but you've got to be sure you're not making a fool of yourself.

    Ben drifts off upstage and goes out of sight. Biff comes down from the left.

Willy (suddenly conscious of Biff, turns and looks up at him, then begins picking up the packages of seeds in confusion): Where the hell is that seed? *(Indignantly.)* You can't see nothing out here! They boxed in the whole goddamn neighborhood!

Biff: There are people all around here. Don't you realize that?

Willy: I'm busy. Don't bother me.

Biff (taking the hoe from Willy): I'm saying good-by to you, Pop. *(Willy looks at him, silent, unable to move.)* I'm not coming back any more.

Willy: You're not going to see Oliver tomorrow?

Biff: I've got no appointment, Dad.

Willy: He put his arm around you, and you've got no appointment?

Biff: Pop, get this now, will you? Everytime I've left it's been a fight that sent me out of here. Today I realized something about myself and I tried to explain it to you and I—I think I'm just not smart enough to make any sense out of it for you. To hell with whose fault it is or anything like that. *(He takes Willy's arm.)* Let's just wrap it up, heh? Come on in, we'll tell Mom. *(He gently tries to pull Willy to left.)*

Willy (frozen, immobile, with guilt in his voice): No, I don't want to see her.

Biff: Come on! *(He pulls again, and Willy tries to pull away.)*

Willy (highly nervous): No, no, I don't want to see her.

Biff (tries to look into Willy's face, as if to find the answer there): Why don't you want to see her?

Willy (more harshly now): Don't bother me, will you?

Biff: What do you mean, you don't want to see her? You don't want them calling you yellow, do you? This isn't your fault; it's me, I'm a bum. Now come inside! *(Willy strains to get away.)* Did you hear what I said to you?

Willy pulls away and quickly goes by himself into the house. Biff follows.

Linda (to Willy): Did you plant, dear?

Biff (at the door, to Linda): All right, we had it out. I'm going and I'm not writing any more.

Linda (going to Willy in the kitchen): I think that's the best way, dear. 'Cause there's no use drawing it out, you'll just never get along.

Willy doesn't respond.

Biff: People ask where I am and what I'm doing, you don't know, and you don't care. That way it'll be off your mind and you can start brightening up again. All right? That clears it, doesn't it? *(Willy is silent, and Biff goes to him.)* You gonna wish me luck, scout? *(He extends his hand.)* What do you say?

Linda: Shake his hand, Willy.

Willy (turning to her, seething with hurt): There's no necessity to mention the pen at all, y'know.

Biff (gently): I've got no appointment, Dad.

Willy (erupting fiercely): He put his arm around . . . ?

Biff: Dad, you're never going to see what I am, so what's the use of arguing? If I strike oil I'll send you a check. Meantime forget I'm alive.

Willy (to Linda): Spite, see?

Biff: Shake hands, Dad.

Willy: Not my hand.

Biff: I was hoping not to go this way.

Willy: Well, this is the way you're going. Good-by.

Biff looks at him a moment, then turns sharply and goes to the stairs.

Willy (stops him with): May you rot in hell if you leave this house!

Biff (turning): Exactly what is it that you want from me?

Willy: I want you to know, on the train, in the mountains, in the valleys, wherever you go, that you cut down your life for spite!

Biff: No, no.

Willy: Spite, spite, is the word of your undoing! And when you're down and out, remember what did it. When you're rotting somewhere beside the railroad tracks, remember, and don't you dare blame it on me!

Biff: I'm not blaming it on you!

Willy: I won't take the rap for this, you hear?

Happy comes down the stairs and stands on the bottom step, watching.

Biff: That's just what I'm telling you!

Willy (sinking into a chair at the table, with full accusation): You're trying to put a knife in me — don't think I don't know what you're doing!

Biff: All right, phony! Then let's lay it on the line. *(He whips the rubber tube out of his pocket and puts it on the table.)*

Happy: You crazy —

Linda: Biff! *(She moves to grab the hose, but Biff holds it down with his hand.)*

Biff: Leave it there! Don't move it!

Willy (not looking at it): What is that?

Biff: You know goddam well what that is.

Willy (caged, wanting to escape): I never saw that.

Biff: You saw it. The mice didn't bring it into the cellar! What is this supposed to do, make a hero out of you? This supposed to make me sorry for you?

Willy: Never heard of it.

Biff: There'll be no pity for you, you hear it? No pity!

Willy (to Linda): You hear the spite!

Biff: No, you're going to hear the truth — what you are and what I am!

Linda: Stop it!

Willy: Spite!

Happy (coming down toward Biff): You cut it now!

Biff (to Happy): The man don't know who we are! The man is gonna know! *(To Willy.)* We never told the truth for ten minutes in this house!

Happy: We always told the truth!

Biff (turning on him): You big blow, are you the assistant buyer? You're one of the two assistants to the assistant, aren't you?

Happy: Well, I'm practically —

Biff: You're practically full of it! We all are! And I'm through with it. *(To Willy.)* Now hear this, Willy, this is me.

Willy: I know you!

Biff: You know why I had no address for three months? I stole a suit in Kansas City and I was in jail. *(To Linda, who is sobbing.)* Stop crying. I'm through with it.

Linda turns away from them, her hands covering her face.

Willy: I suppose that's my fault!

Biff: I stole myself out of every good job since high school!

Willy: And whose fault is that?

Biff: And I never got anywhere because you blew me so full of hot air I could never stand taking orders from anybody! That's whose fault it is!

Willy: I hear that!

Linda: Don't, Biff!

Biff: It's goddam time you heard that! I had to be boss big shot in two weeks, and I'm through with it!

Willy: Then hang yourself! For spite, hang yourself!

Biff: No! Nobody's hanging himself, Willy! I ran down eleven flights with a pen in my hand today. And suddenly I stopped, you hear me? And in the middle of that office building, do you hear this? I stopped in the middle of that building and I saw — the sky. I saw the things that I love in this world. The work and the food and time to sit and smoke. And I looked at the pen and said to myself, what the hell am I grabbing this for? Why am I trying to become what I don't want to be? What am I doing in an office, making a contemptuous, begging fool of myself, when all I want is out there, wait-ing for me the minute I say I know who I am! Why can't I say that, Willy? *(He tries to make Willy face him, but Willy pulls away and moves to the left.)*

Willy (with hatred, threateningly): The door of your life is wide open!

Biff: Pop! I'm a dime a dozen, and so are you!

Willy (turning on him now in an uncontrolled outburst): I am not a dime a dozen! I am Willy Loman, and you are Biff Loman!

Biff starts for Willy, but is blocked by Happy. In his fury, Biff seems on the verge of attacking his father.

Biff: I am not a leader of men, Willy, and neither are you. You were never any-thing but a hard-working drummer who landed in the ash can like all the rest of them! I'm one dollar an hour, Willy! I tried seven states and couldn't raise it. A buck an hour! Do you gather my meaning? I'm not bringing home any prizes any more, and you're going to stop waiting for me to bring them home!

Willy (directly to Biff): You vengeful, spiteful mutt!

Biff breaks from Happy. Willy, in fright, starts up the stairs. Biff grabs him.

Biff (at the peak of his fury): Pop, I'm nothing! I'm nothing, Pop. Can't you un-derstand that? There's no spite in it any more. I'm just what I am, that's all.

Biff's fury has spent itself, and he breaks down, sobbing, holding on to Willy, who dumbly fumbles for Biff's face.

Willy (astonished): What're you doing? What're you doing? *(To Linda.)* Why is he crying?

Biff (crying, broken): Will you let me go, for Christ's sake? Will you take that phony dream and burn it before something happens? *(Struggling to contain himself, he pulls away and moves to the stairs.)* I'll go in the morning. Put him — put him to bed. *(Exhausted, Biff moves up the stairs to his room.)*

Willy (after a long pause, astonished, elevated): Isn't that — isn't that remarkable? Biff — he likes me!

Linda: He loves you, Willy!

Happy (deeply moved): Always did, Pop.

Willy: Oh, Biff! *(Staring wildly.)* He cried! Cried to me. *(He is choking with his love, and now cries out his promise.)* That boy — that boy is going to be magnificent!

Ben appears in the light just outside the kitchen.

Ben: Yes, outstanding, with twenty thousand behind him.

Linda (sensing the racing of his mind, fearfully, carefully): Now come to bed, Willy. It's all settled now.

Willy (finding it difficult not to rush out of the house): Yes, we'll sleep. Come on. Go to sleep, Hap.

Ben: And it does take a great kind of a man to crack the jungle.

In accents of dread, Ben's idyllic music starts up.

Happy (his arm around Linda): I'm getting married, Pop, don't forget it. I'm changing everything. I'm gonna run that department before the year is up. You'll see, Mom. *(He kisses her.)*

Ben: The jungle is dark but full of diamonds, Willy.

Willy turns, moves, listening to Ben.

Linda: Be good. You're both good boys, just act that way, that's all.

Happy: 'Night, Pop. *(He goes upstairs.)*

Linda (to Willy): Come, dear.

Ben (with greater force): One must go in to fetch a diamond out.

Willy (to Linda, as he moves slowly along the edge of the kitchen, toward the door): I just want to get settled down, Linda. Let me sit alone for a little.

Linda (almost uttering her fear): I want you upstairs.

Willy (taking her in his arms): In a few minutes, Linda. I couldn't sleep right now. Go on, you look awful tired. *(He kisses her.)*

Ben: Not like an appointment at all. A diamond is rough and hard to the touch.

Willy: Go on now. I'll be right up.

Linda: I think this is the only way, Willy.

Willy: Sure, it's the best thing.

Ben: Best thing!

Willy: The only way. Everything is gonna be — go on, kid, get to bed. You look so tired.

Linda: Come right up.

Willy: Two minutes.

Linda goes into the living-room, then reappears in her bedroom. Willy moves just outside the kitchen door.

Willy: Loves me. *(Wonderingly.)* Always loved me. Isn't that a remarkable thing? Ben, he'll worship me for it!

Ben (with promise): It's dark there, but full of diamonds.

Willy: Can you imagine that magnificence with twenty thousand dollars in his pocket?

Linda (calling from her room): Willy! Come up!

Willy (calling into the kitchen): Yes! Yes. Coming! It's very smart, you realize that, don't you, sweetheart? Even Ben sees it. I gotta go, baby. 'By! 'By! *(Going over to Ben, almost dancing.)* Imagine? When the mail comes he'll be ahead of Bernard again!

Ben: A perfect proposition all around.

Willy: Did you see how he cried to me? Oh, if I could kiss him, Ben!

Ben: Time, William, time!

Willy: Oh, Ben, I always knew one way or another we were gonna make it, Biff and I!

Ben (looking at his watch): The boat. We'll be late. *(He moves slowly off into the darkness.)*

Willy (elegiacally, turning to the house): Now when you kick off, boy, I want a seventy-yard boot, and get right down the field under the ball, and when you hit, hit low and hit hard, because it's important, boy. *(He swings around and faces the audience.)* There's all kinds of important people in the stands, and the first thing you know . . . *(Suddenly realizing he is alone.)* Ben! Ben, where do I . . . ? *(He makes a sudden movement of search.)* Ben, how do I . . . ?

Linda *(calling):* Willy, you coming up?

Willy *(uttering a gasp of fear, whirling about as if to quiet her):* Sh! *(He turns around as if to find his way; sounds, faces, voices, seem to be swarming in upon him and he flicks at them, crying.)* Sh! Sh! *(Suddenly music, faint and high, stops him. It rises in intensity, almost to an unbearable scream. He goes up and down on his toes, and rushes off around the house.)* Shhh!

Linda: Willy?

> There is no answer. Linda waits. Biff gets up off his bed. He is still in his clothes. Happy sits up. Biff stands listening.

Linda *(with real fear):* Willy, answer me! Willy!

> There is the sound of a car starting and moving away at full speed.

Linda: No!

Biff *(rushing down the stairs):* Pop!

> As the car speeds off, the music crashes down in a frenzy of sound, which becomes the soft pulsation of a single cello string. Biff slowly returns to his bedroom. He and Happy gravely don their jackets. Linda slowly walks out of her room. The music has developed into a dead march. The leaves of day are appearing over everything. Charley and Bernard, somberly dressed, appear and knock on the kitchen door. Biff and Happy slowly descend the stairs to the kitchen as Charley and Bernard enter. All stop a moment when Linda, in clothes of mourning, bearing a little bunch of roses, comes through the draped doorway into the kitchen. She goes to Charley and takes his arm. Now all move toward the audience, through the wall-line of the kitchen. At the limit of the apron, Linda lays down the flowers, kneels, and sits back on her heels. All stare down at the grave.

REQUIEM

Charley: It's getting dark, Linda.

> Linda doesn't react. She stares at the grave.

Biff: How about it, Mom? Better get some rest, heh? They'll be closing the gate soon.

> Linda makes no move. Pause.

Happy *(deeply angered):* He had no right to do that. There was no necessity for it. We would've helped him.

Charley *(grunting):* Hmmm.

Biff: Come along, Mom.

Linda: Why didn't anybody come?

Charley: It was a very nice funeral.

Linda: But where are all the people he knew? Maybe they blame him.

Charley: Naa. It's a rough world, Linda. They wouldn't blame him.

Linda: I can't understand it. At this time especially. First time in thirty-five years we were just about free and clear. He only needed a little salary. He was even finished with the dentist.

Charley: No man only needs a little salary.

Linda: I can't understand it.

Biff: There were a lot of nice days. When he'd come home from a trip; or on Sundays, making the stoop; finishing the cellar; putting on the new porch; when he built the extra bathroom; and put up the garage. You know something, Charley, there's more of him in that front stoop than in all the sales he ever made.

Charley: Yeah. He was a happy man with a batch of cement.

Linda: He was so wonderful with his hands.

Biff: He had the wrong dreams. All, all, wrong.

Happy (almost ready to fight Biff): Don't say that!

Biff: He never knew who he was.

Charley (stopping Happy's movement and reply. To Biff): Nobody dast blame this man. You don't understand: Willy was a salesman. And for a salesman, there is no rock bottom to the life. He don't put a bolt to a nut, he don't tell you the law or give you medicine. He's a man way out there in the blue, riding on a smile and a shoeshine. And when they start not smiling back — that's an earthquake. And then you get yourself a couple of spots on your hat, and you're finished. Nobody dast blame this man. A salesman is got to dream, boy. It comes with the territory.

Biff: Charley, the man didn't know who he was.

Happy (infuriated): Don't say that!

Biff: Why don't you come with me, Happy?

Happy: I'm not licked that easily. I'm staying right in this city, and I'm gonna beat this racket! *(He looks at Biff, his chin set.)* The Loman Brothers!

Biff: I know who I am, kid.

Happy: All right, boy. I'm gonna show you and everybody else that Willy Loman did not die in vain. He had a good dream. It's the only dream you can have — to come out number-one man. He fought it out here, and this is where I'm gonna win it for him.

Biff (with a hopeless glance at Happy, bends toward his mother): Let's go, Mom.

Linda: I'll be with you in a minute. Go on, Charley. *(He hesitates.)* I want to, just for a minute. I never had a chance to say good-by.

Charley moves away, followed by Happy. Biff remains a slight distance up and left of Linda. She sits there, summoning herself. The flute begins, not far away, playing behind her speech.

Linda: Forgive me, dear. I can't cry. I don't know what it is, but I can't cry. I don't understand it. Why did you ever do that? Help me, Willy, I can't cry. It seems to me that you're just on another trip. I keep expecting you. Willy, dear, I can't cry. Why did you do it? I search and search and I search, and I can't understand it, Willy. I made the last payment on the house today. Today, dear. And there'll be nobody home. *(A sob rises in her throat.)* We're free and clear. *(Sobbing more fully, released.)* We're free. *(Biff comes slowly toward her.)* We're free . . . We're free . . .

Biff lifts her to her feet and moves out up right with her in his arms. Linda sobs quietly. Bernard and Charley come together and follow them, followed by Happy. Only the music of the flute is left on the darkening stage as over the house the hard towers of the apartment buildings rise into sharp focus, and

The Curtain Falls.

CONNECTIONS TO OTHER SELECTIONS

1. Compare and contrast Willy Loman with Othello in Shakespeare's play (p. 1164). To what extent is each character wise, foolish, deluded, and hypocritical?

2. Read Tato Laviera's poem "AmeRícan" (p. 814), and compare its treatment of the American dream with the one in *Death of a Salesman*. How do the tones of the two works differ?

3. What similarities do you find between the endings of *Death of a Salesman* and August Wilson's *Fences* (p. 1483)? Are the endings happy, unhappy, or something else?

The Glass Menagerie

Thomas Lanier Williams, who kept his college nickname, Tennessee, was born in Columbus, Mississippi, the son of a traveling salesman. In 1918 the family moved to St. Louis, Missouri, where his father became the sales manager of a shoe company. Williams's mother, the daughter of an Episcopal clergyman, was withdrawn and genteel in contrast to his aggressive father, who contemptuously called Tennessee "Miss Nancy" as a way of mocking his weak physical condition and his literary pursuits. This family atmosphere of repression and anger makes its way into many of Williams's works through characterizations of domineering men and psychologically vulnerable women.

Williams began writing in high school and at the age of seventeen published his first short story in *Weird Tales*. His education at the University of Missouri was interrupted when he had to go to work in a shoe factory. This "living death," as he put it, led to a nervous breakdown, but he eventually resumed his studies at Washington University and finally graduated from the University of Iowa in 1938. During his college years, Williams wrote one-act plays; in 1940 his first full-length play, *Battle of Angels,* opened in Boston, but none of these early plays achieved commercial success. In 1945, however, *The Glass Menagerie* won large, enthusiastic audiences

© Jerry Bauer.

as well as the Drama Critics' Circle Award, which marked the beginning of a series of theatrical triumphs for Williams including *Streetcar Named Desire* (1947), *The Rose Tattoo* (1950), *Cat on a Hot Tin Roof* (1955), *Suddenly Last Summer* (1958), and *The Night of the Iguana* (1961).

The Glass Menagerie reflects Williams's fascination with characters who face lonely struggles in emotionally and financially starved environments. Although Williams's use of colloquial southern speech is realistic, the play also employs nonrealistic techniques, such as shifts in time, projections on screens, music, and lighting effects, to express his characters' thoughts and inner lives. As much as these techniques are unconventional, Williams believed that they represented "a more penetrating and vivid expression of things as they are." The lasting popularity of *The Glass Menagerie* indicates that his assessment was correct.

Explore contexts for Tennessee Williams on *LiterActive*.

TENNESSEE WILLIAMS (1911–1983)

The Glass Menagerie   1945

nobody, not even the rain, has such small hands
— E. E. Cummings

See Plays in Performance insert.

LIST OF CHARACTERS

Amanda Wingfield, the mother. A little woman of great but confused vitality clinging frantically to another time and place. Her characterization must be carefully created, not copied from type. She is not paranoiac, but her life is paranoia. There is much to admire in Amanda, and as much to love and pity as there is to laugh at. Certainly she has endurance and a kind of heroism, and though her foolishness makes her unwittingly cruel at times, there is tenderness in her slight person.

Laura Wingfield, her daughter. Amanda, having failed to establish contact with reality, continues to live vitally in her illusions, but Laura's situation is even graver. A childhood illness has left her crippled, one leg slightly shorter than the other, and held in a brace. This defect need not be more than suggested on the stage. Stemming from this, Laura's separation increases till she is like a piece of her own glass collection, too exquisitely fragile to move from the shelf.

Tom Wingfield, her son. And the narrator of the play. A poet with a job in a warehouse. His nature is not remorseless, but to escape from a trap he has to act without pity.

Jim O'Connor, the gentleman caller. A nice, ordinary, young man.

SCENE: An alley in St. Louis.
PART I: Preparation for a Gentleman Caller.
PART II: The Gentleman Calls.
TIME: Now and the Past.

SCENE I

The Wingfield apartment is in the rear of the building, one of those vast hivelike conglomerations of cellular living-units that flower as warty growths in over-crowded urban centers of lower middle-class population and are symptomatic of the impulse of this largest and fundamentally enslaved section of American society to avoid fluidity and differentiation and to exist and function as one interfused mass of automatism.

The apartment faces an alley and is entered by a fire-escape, a structure whose name is a touch of accidental poetic truth, for all of these huge buildings are always burning with the slow and implacable fires of human desperation. The fire-escape is included in the set—that is, the landing of it and steps descending from it.

The scene is memory and is therefore nonrealistic. Memory takes a lot of poetic license. It omits some details; others are exaggerated, according to the emo-tional value of the articles it touches, for memory is seated predominantly in the heart. The interior is therefore rather dim and poetic.

At the rise of the curtain, the audience is faced with the dark, grim rear wall of the Wingfield tenement. This building, which runs parallel to the footlights, is flanked on both sides by dark, narrow alleys which run into murky canyons of tangled clotheslines, garbage cans, and the sinister latticework of neighboring fire-escapes. It is up and down these side alleys that exterior entrances and exits are made, during the play. At the end of Tom's opening commentary, the dark tene-ment wall slowly reveals (by means of a transparency) the interior of the ground floor Wingfield apartment.

Downstage is the living room, which also serves as a sleeping room for Laura, the sofa unfolding to make her bed. Upstage, center, and divided by a wide arch or second proscenium with transparent faded portieres (or second curtain), is the dining room. In an old-fashioned what-not in the living room are seen scores of transparent glass animals. A blown-up photograph of the father hangs on the wall of the living room, facing the audience, to the left of the archway. It is the face of a very handsome young man in a doughboy's First World War cap. He is gallantly smiling, ineluctably smiling, as if to say, "I will be smiling forever."

The audience hears and sees the opening scene in the dining room through both the transparent fourth wall of the building and the transparent gauze portieres of the dining-room arch. It is during this revealing scene that the fourth wall slowly ascends, out of sight. This transparent exterior wall is not brought down again until the very end of the play, during Tom's final speech.

The narrator is an undisguised convention of the play. He takes whatever license with dramatic convention as is convenient to his purposes.

Tom enters dressed as a merchant sailor from alley, stage left, and strolls across the front of the stage to the fire-escape. There he stops and lights a cigarette. He addresses the audience.

Tom: Yes, I have tricks in my pocket, I have things up my sleeve. But I am the opposite of a stage magician. He gives you illusion that has the appear-ance of truth. I give you truth in the pleasant disguise of illusion. To begin with, I turn back time. I reverse it to that quaint period, the thirties, when the huge middle class of America was matriculating in a school for the blind. Their eyes had failed them, or they had failed their eyes, and so they were having their fingers pressed forcibly down on the fiery Braille alphabet of a dissolving economy. In Spain there was revolution. Here there was only shouting and confusion. In Spain there was Guernica.° Here there were disturbances of labor, sometimes pretty violent, in otherwise peaceful cities such as Chicago, Cleveland, Saint Louis. . . . This is the social background of the play.

(Music.)

The play is memory. Being a memory play, it is dimly lighted, it is sentimental, it is not realistic. In memory everything seems to happen to music. That explains the fiddle in the wings. I am the narrator of the play, and also a character in it. The other characters are my mother, Amanda, my sister, Laura, and a gentleman caller who appears in the final scenes. He is the most realistic character in the play, being an emissary from a world of reality that we were somehow set apart from. But since I have a poet's weakness for symbols, I am using this character also as a symbol; he is the long delayed but always expected something that we live for. There is a fifth character in the play who doesn't appear except in this larger-than-life photograph over the mantel. This is our father who left us a long time ago. He was a telephone man who fell in love with long distances; he gave up his job with the telephone company and skipped the light fantastic out of town. . . . The last we heard of him was a picture post-card from Mazatlán, on the Pacific coast of Mexico, containing a message of two words — "Hello — Good-bye!" and no address. I think the rest of the play will explain itself. . . .

Amanda's voice becomes audible through the portieres.

(Legend on screen: "Où sont les neiges."°)
    He divides the portieres and enters the upstage area.
    Amanda and Laura are seated at a drop-leaf table. Eating is indicated by gestures without food or utensils. Amanda faces the audience.
    Tom and Laura are seated in profile.
    The interior has lit up softly and through the scrim we see Amanda and Laura seated at the table in the upstage area.

Amanda (calling): Tom?
Tom: Yes, Mother.
Amanda: We can't say grace until you come to the table!
Tom: Coming, Mother. *(He bows slightly and withdraws, reappearing a few moments later in his place at the table.)*
Amanda (to her son): Honey, don't *push* with your *fingers.* If you have to push with something, the thing to push with is a crust of bread. And chew — chew! Animals have sections in their stomachs which enable them to digest food without mastication, but human beings are supposed to chew their food before they swallow it down. Eat food leisurely, son, and really enjoy it. A well-cooked meal has lots of delicate flavors that have to be held

---

Guernica: A town in northern Spain destroyed by German bombers in 1937 during the Spanish civil war.   *"Où sont les neiges":* Part of a line from a poem by the French medieval writer François Villon; the full line translates, "Where are the snows of yesteryear?"

in the mouth for appreciation. So chew your food and give your salivary glands a chance to function!

Tom deliberately lays his imaginary fork down and pushes his chair back from the table.

Tom: I haven't enjoyed one bite of this dinner because of your constant directions on how to eat it. It's you that makes me rush through meals with your hawklike attention to every bite I take. Sickening—spoils my appetite—all this discussion of animals' secretion—salivary glands—mastication!

Amanda *(lightly):* Temperament like a Metropolitan star! *(He rises and crosses downstage.)* You're not excused from the table.

Tom: I am getting a cigarette.

Amanda: You smoke too much.

Laura rises.

Laura: I'll bring in the blanc mange.

He remains standing with his cigarette by the portieres during the following.

Amanda *(rising):* No, sister, no, sister—you be the lady this time and I'll be the darky.

Laura: I'm already up.

Amanda: Resume your seat, little sister—I want you to stay fresh and pretty—for gentlemen callers!

Laura: I'm not expecting any gentlemen callers.

Amanda *(crossing out to kitchenette. Airily):* Sometimes they come when they are least expected! Why, I remember one Sunday afternoon in Blue Mountain—*(Enters kitchenette.)*

Tom: I know what's coming!

Laura: Yes. But let her tell it.

Tom: Again?

Laura: She loves to tell it.

Amanda returns with bowl of dessert.

Amanda: One Sunday afternoon in Blue Mountain—your mother received—seventeen!—gentlemen callers! Why, sometimes there weren't chairs enough to accommodate them all. We had to send the nigger over to bring in folding chairs from the parish house.

Tom *(remaining at portieres):* How did you entertain those gentlemen callers?

Amanda: I understood the art of conversation!

Tom: I bet you could talk.

Amanda: Girls in those days *knew* how to talk, I can tell you.

Tom: Yes?

(Image: Amanda as a girl on a porch greeting callers.)

Amanda: They knew how to entertain their gentlemen callers. It wasn't enough for a girl to be possessed of a pretty face and a graceful figure—although I wasn't slighted in either respect. She also needed to have a nimble wit and a tongue to meet all occasions.

Tom: What did you talk about?

Amanda: Things of importance going on in the world! Never anything coarse or common or vulgar. *(She addresses Tom as though he were seated in the vacant chair at the table though he remains by portieres. He plays this scene as though he held the book.)* My callers were gentlemen—all! Among my callers were some of the most prominent young planters of the Mississippi Delta—planters and sons of planters!

Tom motions for music and a spot of light on Amanda.
Her eyes lift, her face glows, her voice becomes rich and elegiac.
(Screen legend: "Où sont les neiges.")

There was young Champ Laughlin who later became vice-president of the Delta Planters Bank. Hadley Stevenson who was drowned in Moon Lake and left his widow one hundred and fifty thousand in Government bonds. There were the Cutrere brothers, Wesley and Bates. Bates was one of my bright particular beaux! He got in a quarrel with that wild Wainright boy. They shot it out on the floor of Moon Lake Casino. Bates was shot through the stomach. Died in the ambulance on his way to Memphis. His widow was also well-provided for, came into eight or ten thousand acres, that's all. She married him on the rebound—never loved her—carried my picture on him the night he died! And there was that boy that every girl in the Delta had set her cap for! That beautiful, brilliant young Fitzhugh boy from Green County!

Tom: What did he leave his widow?

Amanda: He never married! Gracious, you talk as though all of my old admirers had turned up their toes to the daisies!

Tom: Isn't this the first you mentioned that still survives?

Amanda: That Fitzhugh boy went North and made a fortune—came to be known as the Wolf of Wall Street! He had the Midas touch, whatever he touched turned to gold! And I could have been Mrs. Duncan J. Fitzhugh, mind you! But—I picked your *father!*

Laura (rising): Mother, let me clear the table.

Amanda: No dear, you go in front and study your typewriter chart. Or practice your shorthand a little. Stay fresh and pretty!—It's almost time for our gentlemen callers to start arriving. *(She flounces girlishly toward the kitchenette.)* How many do you suppose we're going to entertain this afternoon?

Tom throws down the paper and jumps up with a groan.

Laura (alone in the dining room): I don't believe we're going to receive any, Mother.

Amanda (reappearing, airily): What? No one—not one? You must be joking! *(Laura nervously echoes her laugh. She slips in a fugitive manner through the half-open portieres and draws them gently behind her. A shaft of very clear light is thrown on her face against the faded tapestry of the curtains.) (Music: "The Glass Menagerie" under faintly.) (Lightly.)* Not one gentleman caller? It can't be true! There must be a flood, there must have been a tornado!

Laura: It isn't a flood, it's not a tornado, Mother. I'm just not popular like you were in Blue Mountain. . . . *(Tom utters another groan. Laura glances at him with a faint, apologetic smile. Her voice catching a little.)* Mother's afraid I'm going to be an old maid.

(The scene dims out with "Glass Menagerie" music.)

SCENE II

"Laura, Haven't You Ever Liked Some Boy?"

On the dark stage the screen is lighted with the image of blue roses.
Gradually Laura's figure becomes apparent and the screen goes out.
The music subsides.
Laura is seated in the delicate ivory chair at the small clawfoot table.
She wears a dress of soft violet material for a kimono—her hair tied back
from her forehead with a ribbon.
She is washing and polishing her collection of glass.
Amanda appears on the fire-escape steps. At the sound of her ascent, Laura
catches her breath, thrusts the bowl of ornaments away, and seats herself stiffly
before the diagram of the typewriter keyboard as though it held her spellbound.
Something has happened to Amanda. It is written in her face as she climbs to the
landing: a look that is grim and hopeless and a little absurd.
She has on one of those cheap or imitation velvety-looking cloth coats with
imitation fur collar. Her hat is five or six years old, one of those dreadful cloche hats
that were worn in the late twenties, and she is clasping an enormous black patent-
leather pocketbook with nickel clasp and initials. This is her full-dress outfit, the one
she usually wears to the D.A.R. °
Before entering she looks through the door.
She purses her lips, opens her eyes wide, rolls them upward, and shakes her head.
Then she slowly lets herself in the door. Seeing her mother's expression Laura
touches her lips with a nervous gesture.

Laura: Hello, Mother, I was— *(She makes a nervous gesture toward the chart on the*
wall. Amanda leans against the shut door and stares at Laura with a martyred
look.)

Amanda: Deception? Deception? *(She slowly removes her hat and gloves, continuing*
the swift suffering stare. She lets the hat and gloves fall on the floor—a bit of acting.)

Laura *(shakily):* How was the D.A.R. meeting? *(Amanda slowly opens her purse and*
removes a dainty white handkerchief, which she shakes out delicately and delicately
touches to her lips and nostrils.) Didn't you go to the D.A.R. meeting, Mother?

Amanda *(faintly, almost inaudibly):* —No.—No. *(Then more forcibly.)* I did not
have the strength—to go to the D.A.R. In fact, I did not have the courage!
I wanted to find a hole in the ground and hide myself in it forever! *(She*
crosses slowly to the wall and removes the diagram of the typewriter keyboard. She
holds it in front of her for a second, staring at it sweetly and sorrowfully—then bites
her lips and tears it in two pieces.)

Laura *(faintly):* Why did you do that, Mother? *(Amanda repeats the same proce-*
dure with the chart of the Gregg Alphabet. °) Why are you—

Amanda: Why? Why? How old are you, Laura?

Laura: Mother, you know my age.

Amanda: I thought that you were an adult; it seems that I was mistaken. *(She*
crosses slowly to the sofa and sinks down and stares at Laura.)

D.A.R.: Daughters of the American Revolution; members must document that they have
ancestors who served the patriots' cause in the Revolutionary War. *Gregg Alphabet:* System
of shorthand symbols invented by John Robert Gregg.

Laura: Please don't stare at me, Mother.

Amanda closes her eyes and lowers her head. Count ten.

Amanda: What are we going to do, what is going to become of us, what is the future?

Count ten.

Laura: Has something happened, Mother? *(Amanda draws a long breath and takes out the handkerchief again. Dabbing process.)* Mother, has — something happened?

Amanda: I'll be all right in a minute. I'm just bewildered — *(count five)* — by life. . . .

Laura: Mother, I wish that you would tell me what's happened.

Amanda: As you know, I was supposed to be inducted into my office at the D.A.R. this afternoon. *(Image: A swarm of typewriters.)* But I stopped off at Rubicam's Business College to speak to your teachers about your having a cold and ask them what progress they thought you were making down there.

Laura: Oh. . . .

Amanda: I went to the typing instructor and introduced myself as your mother. She didn't know who you were. Wingfield, she said. We don't have any such student enrolled at the school! I assured her she did, that you had been going to classes since early in January. "I wonder," she said, "if you could be talking about that terribly shy little girl who dropped out of school after only a few days' attendance?" "No," I said, "Laura, my daughter, has been going to school every day for the past six weeks!" "Excuse me," she said. She took the attendance book out and there was your name, unmistakably printed, and all the dates you were absent until they decided that you had dropped out of school. I still said, "No, there must have been some mistake! There must have been some mix-up in the records!" And she said, "No — I remember her perfectly now. Her hand shook so that she couldn't hit the right keys! The first time we gave a speed-test, she broke down completely — was sick at the stomach and almost had to be carried into the wash-room! After that morning she never showed up any more. We phoned the house but never got any answer" — while I was working at Famous and Barr, I suppose, demonstrating those — Oh! I felt so weak I could barely keep on my feet. I had to sit down while they got me a glass of water! Fifty dollars' tuition, all of our plans — my hopes and ambitions for you — just gone up the spout, just gone up the spout like that. *(Laura draws a long breath and gets awkwardly to her feet. She crosses to the Victrola, and winds it up.)* What are you doing?

Laura: Oh! *(She releases the handle and returns to her seat.)*

Amanda: Laura, where have you been going when you've gone out pretending that you were going to business college?

Laura: I've just been going out walking.

Amanda: That's not true.

Laura: It is. I just went walking.

Amanda: Walking? Walking? In winter? Deliberately courting pneumonia in that light coat? Where did you walk to, Laura?

Laura: It was the lesser of two evils, Mother. *(Image: Winter scene in park.)* I couldn't go back up. I — threw up — on the floor!

Amanda: From half past seven till after five every day you mean to tell me you walked around in the park, because you wanted to make me think that you were still going to Rubicam's Business College?

Laura: It wasn't as bad as it sounds. I went inside places to get warmed up.

Amanda: Inside where?

Laura: I went in the art museum and the bird-houses at the Zoo. I visited the penguins every day! Sometimes I did without lunch and went to the movies. Lately I've been spending most of my afternoons in the Jewel-box, that big glass house where they raise the tropical flowers.

Amanda: You did all this to deceive me, just for the deception? *(Laura looks down.)* Why?

Laura: Mother, when you're disappointed, you get that awful suffering look on your face, like the picture of Jesus' mother in the museum!

Amanda: Hush!

Laura: I couldn't face it.

> Pause. A whisper of strings.
> (Legend: "The Crust of Humility.")

Amanda (hopelessly fingering the huge pocketbook): So what are we going to do the rest of our lives? Stay home and watch the parades go by? Amuse ourselves with the glass menagerie, darling? Eternally play those worn-out phonograph records your father left as a painful reminder of him? We won't have a business career — we've given that up because it gave us nervous indigestion! *(Laughs wearily.)* What is there left but dependency all our lives? I know so well what becomes of unmarried women who aren't prepared to occupy a position. I've seen such pitiful cases in the South — barely tolerated spinsters living upon the grudging patronage of sister's husband or brother's wife! — stuck away in some little mousetrap of a room — encouraged by one in-law to visit another — little birdlike women without any nest — eating the crust of humility all their life! Is that the future that we've mapped out for ourselves? I swear it's the only alternative I can think of! It isn't a very pleasant alternative, is it? Of course — some girls *do marry.* *(Laura twists her hands nervously.)* Haven't you ever liked some boy?

Laura: Yes. I liked one once. *(Rises.)* I came across his picture a while ago.

Amanda (with some interest): He gave you his picture?

Laura: No, it's in the year-book.

Amanda (disappointed): Oh — a high-school boy.

> (Screen image: Jim as a high-school hero bearing a silver cup.)

Laura: Yes. His name was Jim. *(Laura lifts the heavy annual from the clawfoot table.)* Here he is in *The Pirates of Penzance.*

Amanda (absently): The what?

Laura: The operetta the senior class put on. He had a wonderful voice and we sat across the aisle from each other Mondays, Wednesdays, and Fridays in the Aud. Here he is with the silver cup for debating! See his grin?

Amanda (absently): He must have had a jolly disposition.

Laura: He used to call me — Blue Roses.

> (Image: Blue roses.)

Amanda: Why did he call you such a name as that?

Laura: When I had that attack of pleurosis — he asked me what was the matter when I came back. I said pleurosis — he thought that I said Blue Roses! So that's what he always called me after that. Whenever he saw me, he'd holler, "Hello, Blue Roses!" I didn't care for the girl that he went out with. Emily Meisenbach. Emily was the best-dressed girl at Soldan. She never struck me, though, as being sincere. . . . It says in the Personal Section — they're engaged. That's — six years ago! They must be married by now.

Amanda: Girls that aren't cut out for business careers usually wind up married to some nice man. *(Gets up with a spark of revival.)* Sister, that's what you'll do!

Laura utters a startled, doubtful laugh. She reaches quickly for a piece of glass.

Laura: But, Mother —
Amanda: Yes? *(Crossing to photograph.)*
Laura (in a tone of frightened apology): I'm — crippled!

(Image: Screen.)

Amanda: Nonsense! Laura, I've told you never, never to use that word. Why, you're not crippled, you just have a little defect — hardly noticeable, even! When people have some slight disadvantage like that, they cultivate other things to make up for it — develop charm — and vivacity — and — *charm!* That's all you have to do! *(She turns again to the photograph.)* One thing your father had *plenty of* — was *charm!*

Tom motions to the fiddle in the wings.
(The scene fades out with music.)

SCENE III

(Legend on the screen: "After the Fiasco — ")
Tom speaks from the fire-escape landing.

Tom: After the fiasco at Rubicam's Business College, the idea of getting a gentleman caller for Laura began to play a more important part in Mother's calculations. It became an obsession. Like some archetype of the universal unconscious, the image of the gentleman caller haunted our small apartment. . . . *(Image: Young man at door with flowers.)* An evening at home rarely passed without some allusion to this image, this specter, this hope. . . . Even when he wasn't mentioned, his presence hung in Mother's preoccupied look and in my sister's frightened, apologetic manner — hung like a sentence passed upon the Wingfields! Mother was a woman of action as well as words. She began to take logical steps in the planned direction. Late that winter and in the early spring — realizing that extra money would be needed to properly feather the nest and plume the bird — she conducted a vigorous campaign on the telephone, roping in subscribers to one of those magazines for matrons called *The Home-maker's Companion,* the type of journal that features the serialized sublimations of ladies of letters who think in terms of delicate cuplike breasts, slim, tapering

waists, rich, creamy thighs, eyes like wood-smoke in autumn, fingers that
soothe and caress like strains of music, bodies as powerful as Etruscan
sculpture.

(Screen image: Glamour magazine cover.)

*Amanda enters with phone on long extension cord. She is spotted in the dim
stage.*

Amanda: Ida Scott? This is Amanda Wingfield! We *missed* you at the D.A.R. last
Monday! I said to myself: She's probably suffering with that sinus condition! How is that sinus condition? Horrors! Heaven have mercy! — You're
a Christian martyr, yes, that's what you are, a Christian martyr! Well, I just
now happened to notice that your subscription to the *Companion*'s about
to expire! Yes, it expires with the next issue, honey! — just when that wonderful new serial by Bessie Mae Hopper is getting off to such an exciting
start. Oh, honey, it's something that you can't miss! You remember how
Gone with the Wind took everybody by storm? You simply couldn't go out if
you hadn't read it. All everybody *talked* was Scarlett O'Hara. Well, this is a
book that critics already compare to *Gone with the Wind*. It's the *Gone with
the Wind* of the post–World War generation! — What? — Burning? — Oh,
honey, don't let them burn, go take a look in the oven and I'll hold the
wire! Heavens — I think she's hung up!

(Dim out.)

(Legend on screen: "You think I'm in love with Continental Shoemakers?")

*Before the stage is lighted, the violent voices of Tom and Amanda are heard.
They are quarreling behind the portieres. In front of them stands Laura with
clenched hands and panicky expression.*

A clear pool of light on her figure throughout this scene.

Tom: What in Christ's name am I —
Amanda (shrilly): Don't you use that —
Tom: Supposed to do!
Amanda: Expression! Not in my —
Tom: Ohhh!
Amanda: Presence! Have you gone out of your senses?
Tom: I have, that's true, *driven* out!
Amanda: What is the matter with you, you — big — big — IDIOT!
Tom: Look — I've got *no* thing, no single thing —
Amanda: Lower your voice!
Tom: In my life here that I can call my own! Everything is —
Amanda: Stop that shouting!
Tom: Yesterday you confiscated my books! You had the nerve to —
Amanda: I took that horrible novel back to the library — yes! That hideous
book by that insane Mr. Lawrence.° *(Tom laughs wildly.)* I cannot control
the output of diseased minds or people who cater to them — *(Tom laughs
still more wildly.)* BUT I WON'T ALLOW SUCH FILTH BROUGHT INTO MY HOUSE!
No, no, no, no, no!
Tom: House, house! Who pays rent on it, who makes a slave of himself to —

Mr. Lawrence: D. H. Lawrence (1885–1930), English poet and novelist who advocated sexual
freedom.

Amanda (fairly screeching): Don't you DARE to —
Tom: No, no, I mustn't say things! I've got to just —
Amanda: Let me tell you —
Tom: I don't want to hear any more! *(He tears the portieres open. The upstage area is lit with a turgid smoky red glow.)*

> *Amanda's hair is in metal curlers and she wears a very old bathrobe, much too large for her slight figure, a relic of the faithless Mr. Wingfield.*
> *An upright typewriter and a wild disarray of manuscripts are on the drop-leaf table. The quarrel was probably precipitated by Amanda's interruption of his creative labor. A chair lying overthrown on the floor.*
> *Their gesticulating shadows are cast on the ceiling by the fiery glow.*

Amanda: You *will* hear more, you —
Tom: No, I won't hear more, I'm going out!
Amanda: You come right back in —
Tom: Out, out, out! Because I'm —
Amanda: Come back here, Tom Wingfield! I'm not through talking to you!
Tom: Oh, go —
Laura (desperately): Tom!
Amanda: You're going to listen, and no more insolence from you! I'm at the end of my patience! *(He comes back toward her.)*
Tom: What do you think I'm at? Aren't I supposed to have any patience to reach the end of, Mother? I know, I know. It seems unimportant to you, what I'm *doing* — what I *want* to do — having a little *difference* between them! You don't think that —
Amanda: I think you've been doing things that you're ashamed of. That's why you act like this. I don't believe that you go every night to the movies. Nobody goes to the movies night after night. Nobody in their right minds goes to the movies as often as you pretend to. People don't go to the movies at nearly midnight, and movies don't let out at two A.M. Come in stumbling. Muttering to yourself like a maniac! You get three hours' sleep and then go to work. Oh, I can picture the way you're doing down there. Moping, doping, because you're in no condition.
Tom (wildly): No, I'm in no condition!
Amanda: What right have you got to jeopardize your job? Jeopardize the security of us all? How do you think we'd manage if you were —
Tom: Listen! You think I'm crazy *about* the *warehouse*! *(He bends fiercely toward her slight figure.)* You think I'm in love with the Continental Shoemakers? You think I want to spend fifty-five *years* down there in that — *celotex interior!* with — *fluorescent* — *tubes!* Look! I'd rather somebody picked up a crowbar and battered out my brains — than go back mornings! I *go!* Every time you come in yelling that God damn *"Rise and Shine!" "Rise and Shine!"* I say to myself "How *lucky dead* people are!" But I get up. I *go!* For sixty-five dollars a month I give up all that I dream of doing and being *ever!* And you say self — *self's* all I ever think of. Why, listen, if self is what I thought of, Mother, I'd be where he is — ! *(Pointing to father's picture.)* As far as the system of transportation reaches! *(He starts past her. She grabs his arm.)* Don't grab at me, Mother!
Amanda: Where are you going?
Tom: I'm going to the *movies!*

Amanda: I don't believe that lie!

Tom (crouching toward her, overtowering her tiny figure. She backs away, gasping): I'm going to opium dens! Yes, opium dens, dens of vice and criminals' hangouts, Mother. I've joined the Hogan gang, I'm a hired assassin, I carry a tommy-gun in a violin case! I run a string of cat-houses in the Valley! They call me Killer, Killer Wingfield, I'm leading a double-life, a simple, honest warehouse worker by day, by night a dynamic *czar* of the *underworld, Mother.* I go to gambling casinos, I spin away fortunes on the roulette table! I wear a patch over one eye and a false mustache, sometimes I put on green whiskers. On those occasions they call me — *El Diablo!*° Oh, I could tell you things to make you sleepless! My enemies plan to dynamite this place. They're going to blow us all sky-high some night! I'll be glad, very happy, and so will you! You'll go up, up on a broomstick, over Blue Mountain with seventeen gentlemen callers! You ugly — babbling old — *witch....* (*He goes through a series of violent, clumsy movements, seizing his overcoat, lunging to the door, pulling it fiercely open. The women watch him, aghast. His arm catches in the sleeve of the coat as he struggles to pull it on. For a moment he is pinioned by the bulky garment. With an outraged groan he tears the coat off again, splitting the shoulders of it, and hurls it across the room. It strikes against the shelf of Laura's glass collection, there is a tinkle of shattering glass. Laura cries out as if wounded.*)

(*Music legend: "The Glass Menagerie."*)

Laura (shrilly): My glass! — menagerie.... (*She covers her face and turns away.*)

But Amanda is still stunned and stupefied by the "ugly witch" so that she barely notices this occurrence. Now she recovers her speech.

Amanda (in an awful voice): I won't speak to you — until you apologize! (*She crosses through portieres and draws them together behind her. Tom is left with Laura. Laura clings weakly to the mantel with her face averted. Tom stares at her stupidly for a moment. Then he crosses to shelf. Drops awkwardly to his knees to collect the fallen glass, glancing at Laura as if he would speak but couldn't.*)

"The Glass Menagerie" steals in as

(*The scene dims out.*)

SCENE IV

The interior is dark. Faint light in the alley.

A deep-voiced bell in a church is tolling the hour of five as the scene commences.

Tom appears at the top of the alley. After each solemn boom of the bell in the tower, he shakes a little noise-maker or rattle as if to express the tiny spasm of man in contrast to the sustained power and dignity of the Almighty. This and the unsteadiness of his advance make it evident that he has been drinking.

As he climbs the few steps to the fire-escape landing light steals up inside. Laura appears in night-dress, observing Tom's empty bed in the front room.

El Diablo: The devil (Spanish).

Tom fishes in his pockets for the door-key, removing a motley assortment of articles in the search, including a perfect shower of movie-ticket stubs and an empty bottle. At last he finds the key, but just as he is about to insert it, it slips from his fingers. He strikes a match and crouches below the door.

Tom *(bitterly):* One crack — and it falls through!

Laura opens the door.

Laura: Tom! Tom, what are you doing?

Tom: Looking for a door-key.

Laura: Where have you been all this time?

Tom: I have been to the movies.

Laura: All this time at the movies?

Tom: There was a very long program. There was a Garbo picture and a Mickey Mouse and a travelogue and a newsreel and a preview of coming attractions. And there was an organ solo and a collection for the milk-fund — simultaneously — which ended up in a terrible fight between a fat lady and an usher!

Laura *(innocently):* Did you have to stay through everything?

Tom: Of course! And, oh, I forgot! There was a big stage show! The headliner on this stage show was Malvolio the Magician. He performed wonderful tricks, many of them, such as pouring water back and forth between pitchers. First it turned to wine and then it turned to beer and then it turned to whiskey. I know it was whiskey it finally turned into because he needed somebody to come up out of the audience to help him, and I came up — both shows! It was Kentucky Straight Bourbon. A very generous fellow, he gave souvenirs. *(He pulls from his back pocket a shimmering rainbow-colored scarf.)* He gave me this. This is his magic scarf. You can have it, Laura. You wave it over a canary cage and you get a bowl of gold-fish. You wave it over the gold-fish bowl and they fly away canaries. . . . But the wonderfullest trick of all was the coffin trick. We nailed him into a coffin and he got out of the coffin without removing one nail. *(He has come inside.)* There is a trick that would come in handy for me — get me out of this 2 by 4 situation! *(Flops onto bed and starts removing shoes.)*

Laura: Tom — Shhh!

Tom: What you shushing me for?

Laura: You'll wake up Mother.

Tom: Goody, goody! Pay 'er back for all those "Rise an' Shines." *(Lies down, groaning.)* You know it don't take much intelligence to get yourself into a nailed-up coffin, Laura. But who in hell ever got himself out of one without removing one nail?

As if in answer, the father's grinning photograph lights up.
(Scene dims out.)
Immediately following: The church bell is heard striking six. At the sixth stroke the alarm clock goes off in Amanda's room, and after a few moments we hear her calling: "Rise and Shine! Rise and Shine! Laura, go tell your brother to rise and shine!"

Tom *(sitting up slowly):* I'll rise — but I won't shine.

The light increases.

Amanda: Laura, tell your brother his coffee is ready.

Laura slips into front room.

Laura: Tom! It's nearly seven. Don't make Mother nervous. *(He stares at her stupidly. Beseechingly.)* Tom, speak to Mother this morning. Make up with her, apologize, speak to her!

Tom: She won't to me. It's her that started not speaking.

Laura: If you just say you're sorry she'll start speaking.

Tom: Her not speaking — is that such a tragedy?

Laura: Please — please!

Amanda (calling from kitchenette): Laura, are you going to do what I asked you to do, or do I have to get dressed and go out myself?

Laura: Going, going — soon as I get on my coat! *(She pulls on a shapeless felt hat with nervous, jerky movement, pleadingly glancing at Tom. Rushes awkwardly for coat. The coat is one of Amanda's, inaccurately made-over, the sleeves too short for Laura.)* Butter and what else?

Amanda (entering upstage): Just butter. Tell them to charge it.

Laura: Mother, they make such faces when I do that.

Amanda: Sticks and stones may break my bones, but the expression on Mr. Garfinkel's face won't harm us! Tell your brother his coffee is getting cold.

Laura (at door): Do what I asked you, will you, will you, Tom?

He looks sullenly away.

Amanda: Laura, go now or just don't go at all!

Laura (rushing out): Going — going! *(A second later she cries out. Tom springs up and crosses to the door. Amanda rushes anxiously in. Tom opens the door.)*

Tom: Laura?

Laura: I'm all right. I slipped, but I'm all right.

Amanda (peering anxiously after her): If anyone breaks a leg on those fire-escape steps, the landlord ought to be sued for every cent he possesses! *(She shuts door. Remembers she isn't speaking and returns to other room.)*

As Tom enters listlessly for his coffee, she turns her back to him and stands rigidly facing the window on the gloomy gray vault of the areaway. Its light on her face with its aged but childish features is cruelly sharp, satirical as a Daumier° print.
(Music under: "Ave Maria.")

Tom glances sheepishly but sullenly at her averted figure and slumps at the table. The coffee is scalding hot; he sips it and gasps and spits it back in the cup. At his gasp, Amanda catches her breath and half turns. Then catches herself and turns back to window.

Tom blows on his coffee, glancing sidewise at his mother. She clears her throat. Tom clears his. He starts to rise. Sinks back down again, scratches his head, clears his throat again. Amanda coughs. Tom raises his cup in both hands to blow on it, his eyes staring over the rim of it at his mother for several moments. Then he slowly sets the cup down and awkwardly and hesitantly rises from the chair.

Tom (hoarsely): Mother. I — I apologize. Mother. *(Amanda draws a quick, shuddering breath. Her face works grotesquely. She breaks into childlike tears.)* I'm sorry for what I said, for everything that I said, I didn't mean it.

Amanda (sobbingly): My devotion has made me a witch and so I make myself hateful to my children!

Daumier: Honoré Daumier (1808–1879), French caricaturist, lithographer, and painter who mercilessly satirized bourgeois society.

Tom: No, you *don't.*

Amanda: I worry so much, don't sleep, it makes me nervous!

Tom (gently): I understand that.

Amanda: I've had to put up a solitary battle all these years. But you're my right-hand bower! Don't fall down, don't fail!

Tom (gently): I try, Mother.

Amanda (with great enthusiasm): Try and you will SUCCEED! *(The notion makes her breathless.)* Why, you — you're just *full* of natural endowments! Both of my children — they're *unusual* children! Don't you think I know it? I'm so — proud! Happy and — feel I've — so much to be thankful for but — Promise me one thing, son!

Tom: What, Mother?

Amanda: Promise, son, you'll — never be a drunkard!

Tom (turns to her grinning): I will never be a drunkard, Mother.

Amanda: That's what frightened me so, that you'd be drinking! Eat a bowl of Purina!

Tom: Just coffee, Mother.

Amanda: Shredded wheat biscuit?

Tom: No. No, Mother, just coffee.

Amanda: You can't put in a day's work on an empty stomach. You've got ten minutes — don't gulp! Drinking too-hot liquids makes cancer of the stomach. . . . Put cream in.

Tom: No, thank you.

Amanda: To cool it.

Tom: No! No, thank you, I want it black.

Amanda: I know, but it's not good for you. We have to do all that we can to build ourselves up. In these trying times we live in, all that we have to cling to is — each other. . . . That's why it's so important to — Tom, I — I sent out your sister so I could discuss something with you. If you hadn't spoken I would have spoken to you. *(Sits down.)*

Tom (gently): What is it, Mother, that you want to discuss?

Amanda: Laura!

> *Tom puts his cup down slowly.*
> *(Legend on screen: "Laura.")*
> *(Music: "The Glass Menagerie.")*

Tom: — Oh. — Laura . . .

Amanda (touching his sleeve): You know how Laura is. So quiet but — still water runs deep! She notices things and I think she — broods about them. *(Tom looks up.)* A few days ago I came in and she was crying.

Tom: What about?

Amanda: You.

Tom: Me?

Amanda: She has an idea that you're not happy here.

Tom: What gave her that idea?

Amanda: What gives her any idea? However, you do act strangely. I — I'm not criticizing, understand *that!* I know your ambitions do not lie in the warehouse, that like everybody in the whole wide world — you've had to — make sacrifices, but — Tom — Tom — life's not easy, it calls for — Spartan endurance! There's so many things in my heart that I cannot describe to you! I've never told you but I — *loved* your father. . . .

Tom (gently): I know that, Mother.

Amanda: And you — when I see you taking after his ways! Staying out late — and — well, you *had* been drinking the night you were in that — terrifying condition! Laura says that you hate the apartment and that you go out nights to get away from it! Is that true, Tom?

Tom: No. You say there's so much in your heart that you can't describe to me. That's true of me, too. There's so much in my heart that I can't describe to *you!* So let's respect each other's —

Amanda: But, why — *why,* Tom — are you always so *restless?* Where do you go to, nights?

Tom: I — go to the movies.

Amanda: Why do you go to the movies so much, Tom?

Tom: I go to the movies because — I like adventure. Adventure is something I don't have much of at work, so I go to the movies.

Amanda: But, Tom, you go to the movies *entirely too much!*

Tom: I like a lot of adventure.

> *Amanda looks baffled, then hurt. As the familiar inquisition resumes he becomes hard and impatient again. Amanda slips back into her querulous attitude toward him.*
> *(Image on screen: Sailing vessel with Jolly Roger.)*

Amanda: Most young men find adventure in their careers.

Tom: Then most young men are not employed in a warehouse.

Amanda: The world is full of young men employed in warehouses and offices and factories.

Tom: Do all of them find adventure in their careers?

Amanda: They do or they do without it! Not everybody has a craze for adventure.

Tom: Man is by instinct a lover, a hunter, a fighter, and none of those instincts are given much play at the warehouse!

Amanda: Man is by instinct! Don't quote instinct to me! Instinct is something that people have got away from! It belongs to animals! Christian adults don't want it!

Tom: What do Christian adults want, then, Mother?

Amanda: Superior things! Things of the mind and the spirit! Only animals have to satisfy instincts! Surely your aims are somewhat higher than theirs! Than monkeys — pigs —

Tom: I reckon they're not.

Amanda: You're joking. However, that isn't what I wanted to discuss.

Tom (rising): I haven't much time.

Amanda (pushing his shoulders): Sit down.

Tom: You want me to punch in red° at the warehouse, Mother?

Amanda: You have five minutes. I want to talk about Laura.

> *(Legend: "Plans and Provisions.")*

Tom: All right! What about Laura?

Amanda: We have to be making plans and provisions for her. She's older than you, two years, and nothing has happened. She just drifts along doing nothing. It frightens me terribly how she just drifts along.

Tom: I guess she's the type that people call home girls.

---

punch in red: Be late for work.

Amanda: There's no such type, and if there is, it's a pity! That is unless the home is hers, with a husband!

Tom: What?

Amanda: Oh, I can see the handwriting on the wall as plain as I see the nose in front of my face! It's terrifying! More and more you remind me of your father! He was out all hours without explanation—Then *left!* *Good-bye!* And me with the bag to hold. I saw that letter you got from the Merchant Marine. I know what you're dreaming of. I'm not standing here blindfolded. Very well, then. Then *do* it! But not till there's somebody to take your place.

Tom: What do you mean?

Amanda: I mean that as soon as Laura has got somebody to take care of her, married, a home of her own, independent—why, then you'll be free to go wherever you please, on land, on sea, whichever way the wind blows! But until that time you've got to look out for your sister. I don't say me because I'm old and don't matter! I say for your sister because she's young and dependent. I put her in business college—a dismal failure! Frightened her so it made her sick to her stomach. I took her over to the Young People's League at the church. Another fiasco. She spoke to nobody, nobody spoke to her. Now all she does is fool with those pieces of glass and play those worn-out records. What kind of a life is that for a girl to lead!

Tom: What can I do about it?

Amanda: Overcome selfishness! Self, self, self is all that you ever think of! *(Tom springs up and crosses to get his coat. It is ugly and bulky. He pulls on a cap with earmuffs.)* Where is your muffler? Put your wool muffler on! *(He snatches it angrily from the closet and tosses it around his neck and pulls both ends tight.)* Tom! I haven't said what I had in mind to ask you.

Tom: I'm too late to—

Amanda (catching his arms—very importunately. Then shyly.): Down at the warehouse, aren't there some—nice young men?

Tom: No!

Amanda: There *must* be—*some.*

Tom: Mother—

Gesture.

Amanda: Find out one that's clean-living—doesn't drink and—ask him out for sister!

Tom: What?

Amanda: For *sister!* To *meet!* Get *acquainted!*

Tom (stamping to door): Oh, my *go-osh!*

Amanda: Will you? *(He opens door. Imploringly.)* Will you? *(He starts down.)* Will you? *Will* you, dear?

Tom (calling back): YES!

Amanda closes the door hesitantly and with a troubled but faintly hopeful expression.
(Screen image: Glamour magazine cover.)
Spot Amanda at phone.

Amanda: Ella Cartwright? This is Amanda Wingfield! How are you, honey? How is that kidney condition? *(Count five.)* Horrors! *(Count five.)* You're a Christian martyr, yes, honey, that's what you are, a Christian martyr! Well, I just happened to notice in my little red book that your subscription to the *Companion* has just run out! I knew that you wouldn't want to miss out on the wonderful serial starting in this new issue. It's by Bessie Mae Hopper, the first thing she's written since *Honeymoon for Three*. Wasn't that a strange and interesting story? Well, this one is even lovelier, I believe. It has a sophisticated society background. It's all about the horsey set on Long Island!

(Fade out.)

SCENE V

(Legend on screen: "Annunciation.") Fade with music.
      It is early dusk of a spring evening. Supper has just been finished in the Wingfield apartment. Amanda and Laura in light-colored dresses are removing dishes from the table, in the upstage area, which is shadowy, their movements formalized almost as a dance or ritual, their moving forms as pale and silent as moths.
      Tom, in white shirt and trousers, rises from the table and crosses toward the fire-escape.

Amanda (as he passes her): Son, will you do me a favor?
Tom: What?
Amanda: Comb your hair! You look so pretty when your hair is combed! *(Tom slouches on sofa with evening paper. Enormous caption "Franco Triumphs.")* There is only one respect in which I would like you to emulate your father.
Tom: What respect is that?
Amanda: The care he always took of his appearance. He never allowed himself to look untidy. *(He throws down the paper and crosses to fire-escape.)* Where are you going?
Tom: I'm going out to smoke.
Amanda: You smoke too much. A pack a day at fifteen cents a pack. How much would that amount to in a month? Thirty times fifteen is how much, Tom? Figure it out and you will be astounded at what you could save. Enough to give you a night-school course in accounting at Washington U! Just think what a wonderful thing that would be for you, son!

Tom is unmoved by the thought.

Tom: I'd rather smoke. *(He steps out on landing, letting the screen door slam.)*
Amanda (sharply): I know! That's the tragedy of it. . . . *(Alone, she turns to look at her husband's picture.)*

(Dance music: "All the World Is Waiting for the Sunrise!")

Tom (to the audience): Across the alley from us was the Paradise Dance Hall. On evenings in spring the windows and doors were open and the music came outdoors. Sometimes the lights were turned out except for a large glass

---

"Franco Triumphs": In January 1939 the Nationalist forces of Gen. Francisco Franco (1892–1975) defeated the Loyalists, ending the Spanish civil war.   *Berchtesgaden:* A resort in the German Alps where Adolf Hitler had a heavily protected villa.   *Chamberlain:* Neville Chamberlain (1869–1940), British prime minister who sought to avoid war with Hitler through a policy of appeasement.

sphere that hung from the ceiling. It would turn slowly about and filter the dusk with delicate rainbow colors. Then the orchestra played a waltz or a tango, something that had a slow and sensuous rhythm. Couples would come outside, to the relative privacy of the alley. You could see them kissing behind ash-pits and telephone poles. This was the compensation for lives that passed like mine, without any change or adventure. Adventure and change were imminent in this year. They were waiting around the corner for all these kids. Suspended in the mist over the Berchtesgaden,° caught in the folds of Chamberlain's° umbrella — In Spain there was Guernica! But here there was only hot swing music and liquor, dance halls, bars, and movies, and sex that hung in the gloom like a chandelier and flooded the world with brief, deceptive rainbows. . . . All the world was waiting for bombardments!

Amanda turns from the picture and comes outside.

Amanda (*sighing*): A fire-escape landing's a poor excuse for a porch. (*She spreads a newspaper on a step and sits down, gracefully and demurely as if she were settling into a swing on a Mississippi veranda.*) What are you looking at?

Tom: The moon.

Amanda: Is there a moon this evening?

Tom: It's rising over Garfinkel's Delicatessen.

Amanda: So it is! A little silver slipper of a moon. Have you made a wish on it yet?

Tom: Um-hum.

Amanda: What did you wish for?

Tom: That's a secret.

Amanda: A secret, huh? Well, I won't tell mine either. I will be just as mysterious as you.

Tom: I bet I can guess what yours is.

Amanda: Is my head so transparent?

Tom: You're not a sphinx.

Amanda: No, I don't have secrets. I'll tell you what I wished for on the moon. Success and happiness for my precious children! I wish for that whenever there's a moon, and when there isn't a moon, I wish for it, too.

Tom: I thought perhaps you wished for a gentleman caller.

Amanda: Why do you say that?

Tom: Don't you remember asking me to fetch one?

Amanda: I remember suggesting that it would be nice for your sister if you brought home some nice young man from the warehouse. I think I've made that suggestion more than once.

Tom: Yes, you have made it repeatedly.

Amanda: Well?

Tom: We are going to have one.

Amanda: What?

Tom: A gentleman caller!

> (*The Annunciation is celebrated with music.*)
> Amanda rises.
> (*Image on screen: Caller with bouquet.*)

Amanda: You mean you have asked some nice young man to come over?

Tom: Yep. I've asked him to dinner.

Amanda: You really did?

Tom: I did!

Amanda: You did, and did he — *accept?*

Tom: He did!

Amanda: Well, well — well, well! That's — lovely!

Tom: I thought that you would be pleased.

Amanda: It's definite, then?

Tom: Very definite.

Amanda: Soon?

Tom: Very soon.

Amanda: For heaven's sake, stop putting on and tell me some things, will you?

Tom: What things do you want me to tell you?

Amanda: Naturally I would like to know when he's *coming!*

Tom: He's coming tomorrow.

Amanda: *Tomorrow?*

Tom: Yep. Tomorrow.

Amanda: But, Tom!

Tom: Yes, Mother?

Amanda: Tomorrow gives me no time!

Tom: Time for what?

Amanda: Preparations! Why didn't you phone me at once, as soon as you asked him, the minute that he accepted? Then, don't you see, I could have been getting ready!

Tom: You don't have to make any fuss.

Amanda: Oh, Tom, Tom, Tom, of course I have to make a fuss! I want things nice, not sloppy! Not thrown together. I'll certainly have to do some fast thinking, won't I?

Tom: I don't see why you have to think at all.

Amanda: You just don't know. We can't have a gentleman caller in a pig-sty! All my wedding silver has to be polished, the monogrammed table linen ought to be laundered! The windows have to be washed and fresh curtains put up. And how about clothes? We have to *wear* something, don't we?

Tom: Mother, this boy is no one to make a fuss over!

Amanda: Do you realize he's the first young man we've introduced to your sister? It's terrible, dreadful, disgraceful that poor little sister has never received a single gentleman caller! Tom, come inside! *(She opens the screen door.)*

Tom: What for?

Amanda: I want to ask you some things.

Tom: If you're going to make such a fuss, I'll call it off, I'll tell him not to come.

Amanda: You certainly won't do anything of the kind. Nothing offends people worse than broken engagements. It simply means I'll have to work like a Turk! We won't be brilliant, but we'll pass inspection. Come on inside. *(Tom follows, groaning.)* Sit down.

Tom: Any particular place you would like me to sit?

Amanda: Thank heavens I've got that new sofa! I'm also making payments on a floor lamp I'll have sent out! And put the chintz covers on, they'll brighten things up! Of course I'd hoped to have these walls re-papered. . . . What is the young man's name?

Tom: His name is O'Connor.

Amanda: That, of course, means fish — tomorrow is Friday! I'll have that salmon loaf — with Durkee's dressing! What does he do? He works at the warehouse?

Tom: Of course! How else would I —

Amanda: Tom, he — doesn't drink?

Tom: Why do you ask me that?

Amanda: Your father *did*!

Tom: Don't get started on that!

Amanda: He *does* drink, then?

Tom: Not that I know of!

Amanda: Make sure, be certain! The last thing I want for my daughter's a boy who drinks!

Tom: Aren't you being a little premature? Mr. O'Connor has not yet appeared on the scene!

Amanda: But will tomorrow. To meet your sister, and what do I know about his character? Nothing! Old maids are better off than wives of drunkards!

Tom: Oh, my God!

Amanda: Be still!

Tom (leaning forward to whisper): Lots of fellows meet girls whom they don't marry!

Amanda: Oh, talk sensibly, Tom — and don't be sarcastic! *(She has gotten a hair-brush.)*

Tom: What are you doing?

Amanda: I'm brushing that cow-lick down! What is this young man's position at the warehouse?

Tom (submitting grimly to the brush and the interrogation): This young man's position is that of a shipping clerk, Mother.

Amanda: Sounds to me like a fairly responsible job, the sort of a job *you* would be in if you just had more *get-up*. What is his salary? Have you got any idea?

Tom: I would judge it to be approximately eighty-five dollars a month.

Amanda: Well — not princely, but —

Tom: Twenty more than I make.

Amanda: Yes, how well I know! But for a family man, eighty-five dollars a month is not much more than you can just get by on. . . .

Tom: Yes, but Mr. O'Connor is not a family man.

Amanda: He might be, mightn't he? Some time in the future?

Tom: I see. Plans and provisions.

Amanda: You are the only young man that I know of who ignores the fact that the future becomes the present, the present the past, and the past turns into everlasting regret if you don't plan for it!

Tom: I will think that over and see what I can make of it.

Amanda: Don't be supercilious with your mother! Tell me some more about this — what do you call him?

Tom: James D. O'Connor. The D. is for Delaney.

Amanda: Irish on *both* sides! *Gracious!* And doesn't drink?

Tom: Shall I call him up and ask him right this minute?

Amanda: The only way to find out about those things is to make discreet inquiries at the proper moment. When I was a girl in Blue Mountain and it was suspected that a young man drank, the girl whose attentions he had been receiving, if any girl *was*, would sometimes speak to the minister of his church, or rather her father would if her father was living, and sort of feel him out on the young man's character. That is the way such things are discreetly handled to keep a young woman from making a tragic mistake!

Tom: Then how did you happen to make a tragic mistake?

Amanda: That innocent look of your father's had everyone fooled! He *smiled*— the world was *enchanted!* No girl can do worse than put herself at the mercy of a handsome appearance! I hope that Mr. O'Connor is not too good-looking.

Tom: No, he's not too good-looking. He's covered with freckles and hasn't too much of a nose.

Amanda: He's not right-down homely, though?

Tom: Not right-down homely. Just medium homely, I'd say.

Amanda: Character's what to look for in a man.

Tom: That's what I've always said, Mother.

Amanda: You've never said anything of the kind and I suspect you would never give it a thought.

Tom: Don't be suspicious of me.

Amanda: At least I hope he's the type that's up and coming.

Tom: I think he really goes in for self-improvement.

Amanda: What reason have you to think so?

Tom: He goes to night school.

Amanda (beaming): Splendid! What does he do, I mean study?

Tom: Radio engineering and public speaking!

Amanda: Then he has visions of being advanced in the world! Any young man who studies public speaking is aiming to have an executive job some day! And radio engineering? A thing for the future! Both of these facts are very illuminating. Those are the sort of things that a mother should know concerning any young man who comes to call on her daughter. Seriously or— not.

Tom: One little warning. He doesn't know about Laura. I didn't let on that we had dark ulterior motives. I just said, why don't you come have dinner with us? He said okay and that was the whole conversation.

Amanda: I bet it was! You're eloquent as an oyster. However, he'll know about Laura when he gets here. When he sees how lovely and sweet and pretty she is, he'll thank his lucky stars he was asked to dinner.

Tom: Mother, you mustn't expect too much of Laura.

Amanda: What do you mean?

Tom: Laura seems all those things to you and me because she's ours and we love her. We don't even notice she's crippled any more.

Amanda: Don't say crippled! You know that I never allow that word to be used!

Tom: But face facts, Mother. She is and—that's not all—

Amanda: What do you mean "not all"?

Tom: Laura is very different from other girls.

Amanda: I think the difference is all to her advantage.

Tom: Not quite all—in the eyes of others—strangers—she's terribly shy and lives in a world of her own and those things make her seem a little peculiar to people outside the house.

Amanda: Don't say peculiar.

Tom: Face the facts. She is.

(The dance-hall music changes to a tango that has a minor and somewhat ominous tone.)

Amanda: In what way is she peculiar — may I ask?

Tom (gently): She lives in a world of her own — a world of — little glass ornaments, Mother. . . . *(Gets up. Amanda remains holding brush, looking at him, troubled.)* She plays old phonograph records and — that's about all — *(He glances at himself in the mirror and crosses to door.)*

Amanda (sharply): Where are you going?

Tom: I'm going to the movies. *(Out screen door.)*

Amanda: Not to the movies, every night to the movies! *(Follows quickly to screen door.)* I don't believe you always go to the movies! *(He is gone. Amanda looks worriedly after him for a moment. Then vitality and optimism return and she turns from the door. Crossing to portieres.)* Laura! Laura! *(Laura answers from kitchenette.)*

Laura: Yes, Mother.

Amanda: Let those dishes go and come in front! *(Laura appears with dish towel. Gaily.)* Laura, come here and make a wish on the moon!

Laura (entering): Moon — moon?

Amanda: A little silver slipper of a moon. Look over your left shoulder, Laura, and make a wish! *(Laura looks faintly puzzled as if called out of sleep. Amanda seizes her shoulders and turns her at angle by the door.)* Now! Now, darling, *wish!*

Laura: What shall I wish for, Mother?

Amanda (her voice trembling and her eyes suddenly filling with tears): Happiness! Good Fortune!

The violin rises and the stage dims out.

SCENE VI

(Image: High-school hero.)

Tom: And so the following evening I brought Jim home to dinner. I had known Jim slightly in high school. In high school Jim was a hero. He had tremendous Irish good nature and vitality with the scrubbed and polished look of white chinaware. He seemed to move in a continual spotlight. He was a star in basketball, captain of the debating club, president of the senior class and the glee club and he sang the male lead in the annual light operas. He was always running or bounding, never just walking. He seemed always at the point of defeating the law of gravity. He was shooting with such velocity through his adolescence that you would logically expect him to arrive at nothing short of the White House by the time he was thirty. But Jim apparently ran into more interference after his graduation from Soldan. His speed had definitely slowed. Six years after he left high school he was holding a job that wasn't much better than mine.

(Image: Clerk.)

He was the only one at the warehouse with whom I was on friendly terms. I was valuable to him as someone who could remember his former glory, who had seen him win basketball games and the silver cup in debating. He knew of my secret practice of retiring to a cabinet of the washroom to work on poems when business was slack in the warehouse. He called me Shakespeare. And while the other boys in the warehouse regarded me with suspicious hostility, Jim took a humorous attitude toward me. Gradually his attitude affected the others, their hostility wore off, and they also began to smile at me as people smile at an oddly fashioned dog who trots across their paths at some distance.

I knew that Jim and Laura had known each other at Soldan, and I had heard Laura speak admiringly of his voice. I didn't know if Jim remembered her or not. In high school Laura had been as unobtrusive as Jim had been astonishing. If he did remember Laura, it was not as my sister, for when I asked him to dinner, he grinned and said, "You know, Shakespeare, I never thought of you as having folks!"

He was about to discover that I did. . . .

(Light upstage.)

(Legend on screen: "The Accent of a Coming Foot.")

Friday evening. It is about five o'clock of a late spring evening which comes "scattering poems in the sky."

A delicate lemony light is in the Wingfield apartment.

Amanda has worked like a Turk in preparation for the gentleman caller. The results are astonishing. The new floor lamp with its rose-silk shade is in place, a colored paper lantern conceals the broken light fixture in the ceiling, new billowing white curtains are at the windows, chintz covers are on chairs and sofa, a pair of new sofa pillows make their initial appearance.

Open boxes and tissue paper are scattered on the floor.

Laura stands in the middle with lifted arms while Amanda crouches before her, adjusting the hem of the new dress, devout and ritualistic. The dress is colored and designed by memory. The arrangement of Laura's hair is changed; it is softer and more becoming. A fragile, unearthly prettiness has come out in Laura: she is like a piece of translucent glass touched by light, given a momentary radiance, not actual, not lasting.

Amanda (impatiently): Why are you trembling?

Laura: Mother, you've made me so nervous!

Amanda: How have I made you nervous?

Laura: By all this fuss! You make it seem so important!

Amanda: I don't understand you, Laura. You couldn't be satisfied with just sitting home, and yet whenever I try to arrange something for you, you seem to resist it. *(She gets up.)* Now take a look at yourself. No, wait! Wait just a moment — I have an idea!

Laura: What is it now?

Amanda produces two powder puffs which she wraps in handkerchiefs and stuffs in Laura's bosom.

Laura: Mother, what are you doing?

Amanda: They call them "Gay Deceivers"!

Laura: I won't wear them!

Amanda: You will!

Laura: Why should I?

Amanda: Because, to be painfully honest, your chest is flat.

Laura: You make it seem like we were setting a trap.

Amanda: All pretty girls are a trap, a pretty trap, and men expect them to be. *(Legend: "A Pretty Trap.")* Now look at yourself, young lady. This is the prettiest you will ever be! I've got to fix myself now! You're going to be surprised by your mother's appearance! *(She crosses through portieres, humming gaily.)*

Laura moves slowly to the long mirror and stares solemnly at herself.
        A wind blows the white curtains inward in a slow, graceful motion and with a faint, sorrowful sighing.

Amanda (off stage): It isn't dark enough yet. *(She turns slowly before the mirror with a troubled look).*

(Legend on screen: "This Is My Sister: Celebrate Her with Strings!" Music.)

Amanda (laughing, off): I'm going to show you something. I'm going to make a spectacular appearance!

Laura: What is it, Mother?

Amanda: Possess your soul in patience — you will see! Something I've resurrected from that old trunk! Styles haven't changed so terribly much after all. . . . *(She parts the portieres.)* Now just look at your mother! *(She wears a girlish frock of yellowed voile with a blue silk sash. She carries a bunch of jonquils — the legend of her youth is nearly revived. Feverishly.)* This is the dress in which I led the cotillion. Won the cakewalk twice at Sunset Hill, wore one spring to the Governor's ball in Jackson! See how I sashayed around the ballroom, Laura? *(She raises her skirt and does a mincing step around the room.)* I wore it on Sundays for my gentlemen callers! I had it on the day I met your father — I had malaria fever all that spring. The change of climate from East Tennessee to the Delta — weakened resistance — I had a little temperature all the time — not enough to be serious — just enough to make me restless and giddy! Invitations poured in — parties all over the Delta! "Stay in bed," said Mother, "you have fever!" — but I just wouldn't. — I took quinine but kept on going, going! — Evenings, dances! — Afternoons, long, long rides! Picnics — lovely! — So lovely, that country in May. — All lacy with dogwood, literally flooded with jonquils! — That was the spring I had the craze for jonquils. Jonquils became an absolute obsession. Mother said, "Honey, there's no more room for jonquils." And still I kept bringing in more jonquils. Whenever, wherever I saw them, I'd say, "Stop! Stop! I see jonquils!" I made the young men help me gather the jonquils! It was a joke, Amanda and her jonquils! Finally there were no more vases to hold them, every available space was filled with jonquils. No vases to hold them? All right, I'll hold them myself! And then I — *(She stops in front of the picture.) (Music.)* met your father! Malaria fever and jonquils and then — this — boy. . . . *(She switches on the rose-colored lamp.)* I hope they get here before it starts to rain. *(She crosses upstage and places the jonquils in bowl on table.)* I gave your brother a little extra change so he and Mr. O'Connor could take the service car home.

Laura (with altered look): What did you say his name was?

Amanda: O'Connor.

Laura: What is his first name?

Amanda: I don't remember. Oh, yes, I do. It was — Jim!

Laura sways slightly and catches hold of a chair.
  (Legend on screen: "Not Jim!")

Laura (faintly): Not—Jim!
Amanda: Yes, that was it, it was Jim! I've never known a Jim that wasn't nice!

  (Music: Ominous.)

Laura: Are you sure his name is Jim O'Connor?
Amanda: Yes. Why?
Laura: Is he the one that Tom used to know in high school?
Amanda: He didn't say so. I think he just got to know him at the warehouse.
Laura: There was a Jim O'Connor we both knew in high school — *(Then, with effort.)* If that is the one that Tom is bringing to dinner — you'll have to excuse me, I won't come to the table.
Amanda: What sort of nonsense is this?
Laura: You asked me once if I'd ever liked a boy. Don't you remember I showed you this boy's picture?
Amanda: You mean the boy you showed me in the year-book?
Laura: Yes, that boy.
Amanda: Laura, Laura, were you in love with that boy?
Laura: I don't know, Mother. All I know is I couldn't sit at the table if it was him!
Amanda: It won't be him! It isn't the least bit likely. But whether it is or not, you will come to the table. You will not be excused.
Laura: I'll have to be, Mother.
Amanda: I don't intend to humor your silliness, Laura. I've had too much from you and your brother, both! So just sit down and compose yourself till they come. Tom has forgotten his key so you'll have to let them in, when they arrive.
Laura (panicky): Oh, Mother — *you* answer the door!
Amanda (lightly): I'll be in the kitchen — busy!
Laura: Oh, Mother, please answer the door, don't make me do it!
Amanda (crossing into kitchenette): I've got to fix the dressing for the salmon. Fuss, fuss — silliness! — over a gentleman caller!

Door swings shut. Laura is left alone.
  (Legend: "Terror!")
  She utters a low moan and turns off the lamp — sits stiffly on the edge of the sofa, knotting her fingers together.
  (Legend on screen: "The Opening of a Door!")
  Tom and Jim appear on the fire-escape steps and climb to landing. Hearing their approach, Laura rises with a panicky gesture. She retreats to the portieres. The doorbell. Laura catches her breath and touches her throat. Low drums.

Amanda (calling): Laura, sweetheart! The door!

Laura stares at it without moving.

Jim: I think we just beat the rain.
Tom: Uh-huh. *(He rings again, nervously. Jim whistles and fishes for a cigarette.)*
Amanda (very, very gaily): Laura, that is your brother and Mr. O'Connor! Will you let them in, darling?

Laura crosses toward kitchenette door.

Laura (breathlessly): Mother — you go to the door!

> *Amanda steps out of kitchenette and stares furiously at Laura. She points imperiously at the door.*

Laura: Please, please!

Amanda (in a fierce whisper): What is the matter with you, you silly thing?

Laura (desperately): Please, you answer it, *please!*

Amanda: I told you I wasn't going to humor you, Laura. Why have you chosen this moment to lose your mind?

Laura: Please, please, please, you go!

Amanda: You'll have to go to the door because I can't!

Laura (despairingly): I can't either!

Amanda: Why?

Laura: I'm *sick!*

Amanda: I'm sick, too — of your nonsense! Why can't you and your brother be normal people? Fantastic whims and behavior! *(Tom gives a long ring.)* Preposterous goings on! Can you give me one reason — *(Calls out lyrically.)* COMING! JUST ONE SECOND! — why should you be afraid to open a door? Now you answer it, Laura!

Laura: Oh, oh, oh . . . *(She returns through the portieres. Darts to the Victrola and winds it frantically and turns it on.)*

Amanda: Laura Wingfield, you march right to that door!

Laura: Yes — yes, Mother!

> *A faraway, scratchy rendition of "Dardanella" softens the air and gives her strength to move through it. She slips to the door and draws it cautiously open.*
>
> *Tom enters with the caller, Jim O'Connor.*

Tom: Laura, this is Jim. Jim, this is my sister, Laura.

Jim (stepping inside): I didn't know that Shakespeare had a sister!

Laura (retreating stiff and trembling from the door): How — how do you do?

Jim (heartily extending his hand): Okay!

> *Laura touches it hesitantly with hers.*

Jim: Your hand's *cold,* Laura!

Laura: Yes, well — I've been playing the Victrola . . .

Jim: Must have been playing classical music on it! You ought to play a little hot swing music to warm you up!

Laura: Excuse me — I haven't finished playing the Victrola . . .

> *She turns awkwardly and hurries into the front room. She pauses a second by the Victrola. Then catches her breath and darts through the portieres like a frightened deer.*

Jim (grinning): What was the matter?

Tom: Oh — with Laura? Laura is — terribly shy.

Jim: Shy, huh? It's unusual to meet a shy girl nowadays. I don't believe you ever mentioned you had a sister.

Tom: Well, now you know. I have one. Here is the *Post Dispatch.* You want a piece of it?

Jim: Uh-huh.

Tom: What piece? The comics?

Jim: Sports! *(Glances at it.)* Ole Dizzy Dean is on his bad behavior.

Tom (disinterest): Yeah? *(Lights cigarette and crosses back to fire-escape door.)*
Jim: Where are *you* going?
Tom: I'm going out on the terrace.
Jim (goes after him): You know, Shakespeare — I'm going to sell you a bill of
  goods!
Tom: What goods?
Jim: A course I'm taking.
Tom: Huh?
Jim: In public speaking! You and me, we're not the warehouse type.
Tom: Thanks — that's good news. But what has public speaking got to do
  with it?
Jim: It fits you for — executive positions!
Tom: Awww.
Jim: I tell you it's done a helluva lot for me.

  (Image: Executive at desk.)

Tom: In what respect?
Jim: In every! Ask yourself what is the difference between you an' me and men
  in the office down front? Brains? — No! — Ability? — No! Then what? Just
  one little thing —
Tom: What is that one little thing?
Jim: Primarily it amounts to — social poise! Being able to square up to people
  and hold your own on any social level!
Amanda (off stage): Tom?
Tom: Yes, Mother?
Amanda: Is that you and Mr. O'Connor?
Tom: Yes, Mother.
Amanda: Well, you just make yourselves comfortable in there.
Tom: Yes, Mother.
Amanda: Ask Mr. O'Connor if he would like to wash his hands.
Jim: Aw — no — no — thank you — I took care of that at the warehouse. Tom —
Tom: Yes?
Jim: Mr. Mendoza was speaking to me about you.
Tom: Favorably?
Jim: What do you think?
Tom: Well —
Jim: You're going to be out of a job if you don't wake up.
Tom: I am waking up —
Jim: You show no signs.
Tom: The signs are interior.

  (Image on screen: The sailing vessel with Jolly Roger again.)

Tom: I'm planning to change. *(He leans over the rail speaking with quiet exhilara-
  tion. The incandescent marquees and signs of the first-run movie houses light his face
  from across the alley. He looks like a voyager.)* I'm right at the point of com-
  mitting myself to a future that doesn't include the warehouse and Mr.
  Mendoza or even a night-school course in public speaking.
Jim: What are you gassing about?
Tom: I'm tired of the movies.
Jim: Movies!

Tom: Yes, movies! Look at them — (*A wave toward the marvels of Grand Avenue.*) All of those glamorous people — having adventures — hogging it all, gobbling the whole thing up! You know what happens? People go to the *movies* instead of *moving!* Hollywood characters are supposed to have all the adventures for everybody in America, while everybody in America sits in a dark room and watches them have them! Yes, until there's a war. That's when adventure becomes available to the masses! *Everyone's* dish, not only Gable's! Then the people in the dark room come out of the dark room to have some adventures themselves — Goody, goody — It's our turn now, to go to the South Sea Island — to make a safari — to be exotic, faroff — But I'm not patient. I don't want to wait till then. I'm tired of the *movies* and I am *about* to *move!*

Jim (incredulously): Move?

Tom: Yes.

Jim: When?

Tom: Soon!

Jim: Where? Where?

(*Theme three: Music seems to answer the question, while Tom thinks it over. He searches among his pockets.*)

Tom: I'm starting to boil inside. I know I seem dreamy, but inside — well, I'm boiling! Whenever I pick up a shoe, I shudder a little thinking how short life is and what I am doing! — Whatever that means. I know it doesn't mean shoes — except as something to wear on a traveler's feet! (*Finds paper.*) Look —

Jim: What?

Tom: I'm a member.

Jim (reading): The Union of Merchant Seamen.

Tom: I paid my dues this month, instead of the light bill.

Jim: You will regret it when they turn the lights off.

Tom: I won't be here.

Jim: How about your mother?

Tom: I'm like my father. The bastard son of a bastard! See how he grins? And he's been absent going on sixteen years!

Jim: You're just talking, you drip. How does your mother feel about it?

Tom: Shhh — Here comes Mother! Mother is not acquainted with my plans!

Amanda (enters portieres): Where are you all?

Tom: On the terrace, Mother.

They start inside. She advances to them. Tom is distinctly shocked at her appearance. Even Jim blinks a little. He is making his first contact with girlish Southern vivacity and in spite of the night-school course in public speaking is somewhat thrown off the beam by the unexpected outlay of social charm.

Certain responses are attempted by Jim but are swept aside by Amanda's gay laughter and chatter. Tom is embarrassed but after the first shock Jim reacts very warmly. Grins and chuckles, is altogether won over.

(*Image: Amanda as a girl.*)

Amanda (coyly smiling, shaking her girlish ringlets): Well, well, well, so this is Mr. O'Connor. Introductions entirely unnecessary. I've heard so much about you from my boy. I finally said to him, Tom — good gracious! — why don't you bring this paragon to supper? I'd like to meet this nice young man at the warehouse! — Instead of just hearing him sing your praises so much! I don't know why my son is so stand-offish — that's not Southern behavior! Let's sit down and — I think we could stand a little more air in here! Tom, leave the door open. I felt a nice fresh breeze a moment ago. Where has it gone? Mmm, so warm already! And not quite summer, even. We're going to burn up when summer really gets started. However, we're having — we're having a very light supper. I think light things are better fo' this time of year. The same as light clothes are. Light clothes an' light food are what warm weather calls fo'. You know our blood gets so thick during th' winter — it takes a while fo' us to *adjust* ou'selves! — when the season changes. . . . It's come so quick this year. I wasn't prepared. All of a sudden — heavens! Already summer! — I ran to the trunk an' pulled out this light dress — Terribly old! Historical almost! But feels so good — so good an' co-ol, y'know. . . .

Tom: Mother —

Amanda: Yes, honey?

Tom: How about — supper?

Amanda: Honey, you go ask Sister if supper is ready! You know that Sister is in full charge of supper! Tell her you hungry boys are waiting for it. *(To Jim.)* Have you met Laura?

Jim: She —

Amanda: Let you in? Oh, good, you've met already! It's rare for a girl as sweet an' pretty as Laura to be domestic! But Laura is, thank heavens, not only pretty but also very domestic. I'm not at all. I never was a bit. I never could make a thing but angel-food cake. Well, in the South we had so many servants. Gone, gone, gone. All vestiges of gracious living! Gone completely! I wasn't prepared for what the future brought me. All of my gentlemen callers were sons of planters and so of course I assumed that I would be married to one and raise my family on a large piece of land with plenty of servants. But man proposes — and woman accepts the proposal! — To vary that old, old saying a little bit — I married no planter! I married a man who worked for the telephone company! — that gallantly smiling gentleman over there! *(Points to the picture.)* A telephone man who — fell in love with long distance! — Now he travels and I don't even know where! — But what am I going on for about my — tribulations! Tell me yours — I hope you don't have any! Tom?

Tom (returning): Yes, Mother?

Amanda: Is supper nearly ready?

Tom: It looks to me like supper is on the table.

Amanda: Let me look — *(She rises prettily and looks through portieres.)* Oh, lovely — But where is Sister?

Tom: Laura is not feeling well and she says that she thinks she'd better not come to the table.

Amanda: What? — Nonsense! — Laura? Oh, Laura!

Laura (off stage, faintly): Yes, Mother.

Amanda: You really must come to the table. We won't be seated until you come to the table! Come in, Mr. O'Connor. You sit over there and I'll — Laura? Laura Wingfield! You're keeping us waiting, honey! We can't say grace until you come to the table!

*The back door is pushed weakly open and Laura comes in. She is obviously quite
faint, her lips trembling, her eyes wide and staring. She moves unsteadily toward
the table.*
　　(Legend: "Terror!")
　　*Outside a summer storm is coming abruptly. The white curtains billow
inward at the windows and there is a sorrowful murmur and deep blue dusk.*
　　Laura suddenly stumbles—She catches at a chair with a faint moan.

Tom: Laura!

Amanda: Laura! *(There is a clap of thunder.) (Legend: "Ah!") (Despairingly.)* Why,
　　Laura, you *are* sick, darling! Tom, help your sister into the living room,
　　dear! Sit in the living room, Laura—rest on the sofa. Well! *(To the gentle-
　　man caller.)* Standing over the hot stove made her ill!—I told her that it
　　was just too warm this evening, but—*(Tom comes back in. Laura is on the
　　sofa.)* Is Laura all right now?

Tom: Yes.

Amanda: What *is* that? Rain? A nice cool rain has come up! *(She gives the gentle-
　　man caller a frightened look.)* I think we may—have grace—now . . . *(Tom
　　looks at her stupidly.)* Tom, honey—you say grace!

Tom: Oh . . . "For these and all thy mercies—" *(They bow their heads, Amanda
　　stealing a nervous glance at Jim. In the living room Laura, stretched on the sofa,
　　clenches her hand to her lips, to hold back a shuddering sob.)* God's Holy Name be
　　praised—

(The scene dims out.)

SCENE VII

A Souvenir

*Half an hour later. Dinner is just being finished in the upstage area, which is con-
cealed by the drawn portieres.*
　　*As the curtain rises Laura is still huddled upon the sofa, her feet drawn under
her, her head resting on a pale blue pillow, her eyes wide and mysteriously watchful.
The new floor lamp with its shade of rose-colored silk gives a soft, becoming light to
her face, bringing out the fragile, unearthly prettiness which usually escapes attention. There is a steady murmur of rain, but it is slackening and stops soon after the
scene begins; the air outside becomes pale and luminous as the moon breaks out.*
　　A moment after the curtain rises, the lights in both rooms flicker and go out.

Jim: Hey, there, Mr. Light Bulb!

Amanda laughs nervously.
(Legend: "Suspension of a Public Service.")

Amanda: Where was Moses when the lights went out? Ha-ha. Do you know the
　　answer to that one, Mr. O'Connor?

Jim: No, Ma'am, what's the answer?

Amanda: In the dark! *(Jim laughs appreciatively.)* Everybody sit still. I'll light the
　　candles. Isn't it lucky we have them on the table? Where's a match? Which
　　of you gentlemen can provide a match?

Jim: Here.

Amanda: Thank you, sir.

Jim: Not at all, Ma'am!

Amanda: I guess the fuse has burnt out. Mr. O'Connor, can you tell a burnt-out fuse? I know I can't and Tom is a total loss when it comes to mechanics. *(Sound: Getting up: Voices recede a little to kitchenette.)* Oh, be careful you don't bump into something. We don't want our gentleman caller to break his neck. Now wouldn't that be a fine howdy-do?

Jim: Ha-ha! Where is the fuse-box?

Amanda: Right here next to the stove. Can you see anything?

Jim: Just a minute.

Amanda: Isn't electricity a mysterious thing? Wasn't it Benjamin Franklin who tied a key to a kite? We live in such a mysterious universe, don't we? Some people say that science clears up all the mysteries for us. In my opinion it only creates more! Have you found it yet?

Jim: No, Ma'am. All these fuses look okay to me.

Amanda: Tom!

Tom: Yes, Mother?

Amanda: That light bill I gave you several days ago. The one I told you we got the notices about?

Tom: Oh.—Yeah.

(Legend: "Ha!")

Amanda: You didn't neglect to pay it by any chance?

Tom: Why, I—

Amanda: Didn't! I might have known it!

Jim: Shakespeare probably wrote a poem on that light bill, Mrs. Wingfield.

Amanda: I might have known better than to trust him with it! There's such a high price for negligence in this world!

Jim: Maybe the poem will win a ten-dollar prize.

Amanda: We'll just have to spend the remainder of the evening in the nineteenth century, before Mr. Edison made the Mazda lamp!

Jim: Candlelight is my favorite kind of light.

Amanda: That shows you're romantic! But that's no excuse for Tom. Well, we got through dinner. Very considerate of them to let us get through dinner before they plunged us into everlasting darkness, wasn't it, Mr. O'Connor?

Jim: Ha-ha!

Amanda: Tom, as a penalty for your carelessness you can help me with the dishes.

Jim: Let me give you a hand.

Amanda: Indeed you will not!

Jim: I ought to be good for something.

Amanda: Good for something? *(Her tone is rhapsodic.)* You? Why, Mr. O'Connor, nobody, *nobody's* given me this much entertainment in years—as you have!

Jim: Aw, now, Mrs. Wingfield!

Amanda: I'm not exaggerating, not one bit! But Sister is all by her lonesome. You go keep her company in the parlor! I'll give you this lovely old candelabrum that used to be on the altar at the church of the Heavenly Rest. It was melted a little out of shape when the church burnt down. Lightning struck it one spring. Gypsy Jones was holding a revival at the time and he intimated that the church was destroyed because the Episcopalians gave card parties.

Jim: Ha-ha.

Amanda: And how about coaxing Sister to drink a little wine? I think it would
be good for her! Can you carry both at once?

Jim: Sure. I'm Superman!

Amanda: Now, Thomas, get into this apron!

*The door of kitchenette swings closed on Amanda's gay laughter; the flickering light
approaches the portieres.*

    *Laura sits up nervously as he enters. Her speech at first is low and breathless
from the almost intolerable strain of being alone with a stranger.*

    (Legend: "I Don't Suppose You Remember Me at All!")

    *In her first speeches in this scene, before Jim's warmth overcomes her paralyz-
ing shyness, Laura's voice is thin and breathless as though she has run up a steep
flight of stairs.*

    *Jim's attitude is gently humorous. In playing this scene it should be stressed
that while the incident is apparently unimportant, it is to Laura the climax of her
secret life.*

Jim: Hello, there, Laura.

Laura (faintly): Hello. *(She clears her throat.)*

Jim: How are you feeling now? Better?

Laura: Yes. Yes, thank you.

Jim: This is for you. A little dandelion wine. *(He extends it toward her with extravagant gallantry.)*

Laura: Thank you.

Jim: Drink it—but don't get drunk! *(He laughs heartily. Laura takes the glass
uncertainly; laughs shyly.)* Where shall I set the candles?

Laura: Oh—oh, anywhere . . .

Jim: How about here on the floor? Any objections?

Laura: No.

Jim: I'll spread a newspaper under to catch the drippings. I like to sit on the
floor. Mind if I do?

Laura: Oh, no.

Jim: Give me a pillow?

Laura: What?

Jim: A pillow!

Laura: Oh . . . *(Hands him one quickly.)*

Jim: How about you? Don't you like to sit on the floor?

Laura: Oh—yes.

Jim: Why don't you, then?

Laura: I—will.

Jim: Take a pillow! *(Laura does. Sits on the other side of the candelabrum. Jim crosses
his legs and smiles engagingly at her.)* I can't hardly see you sitting way over
there.

Laura: I can—see you.

Jim: I know, but that's not fair, I'm in the limelight. *(Laura moves her pillow
closer.)* Good! Now I can see you! Comfortable?

Laura: Yes.

Jim: So am I. Comfortable as a cow. Will you have some gum?

Laura: No, thank you.

Jim: I think that I will indulge, with your permission. *(Musingly unwraps it and
holds it up.)* Think of the fortune made by the guy that invented the first

piece of chewing gum. Amazing, huh? The Wrigley Building is one of the sights of Chicago. — I saw it summer before last when I went up to the Century of Progress. Did you take in the Century of Progress?

Laura: No, I didn't.

Jim: Well, it was quite a wonderful exposition. What impressed me most was the Hall of Science. Gives you an idea of what the future will be in America, even more wonderful than the present time is! *(Pause. Smiling at her.)* Your brother tells me you're shy. Is that right, Laura?

Laura: I — don't know.

Jim: I judge you to be an old-fashioned type of girl. Well, I think that's a pretty good type to be. Hope you don't think I'm being too personal — do you?

Laura (hastily, out of embarrassment): I believe I *will* take a piece of gum, if you — don't mind. *(Clearing her throat.)* Mr. O'Connor, have you — kept up with your singing?

Jim: Singing? Me?

Laura: Yes. I remember what a beautiful voice you had.

Jim: When did you hear me sing?

(Voice offstage in the pause.)

Voice (offstage):   O blow, ye winds, heigh-ho,
             A-roving I will go!
             I'm off to my love
             With a boxing glove —
             Ten thousand miles away!

Jim: You say you've heard me sing?

Laura: Oh, yes! Yes, very often . . . I — don't suppose you remember me — at all?

Jim (smiling doubtfully): You know I have an idea I've seen you before. I had that idea soon as I opened the door. It seemed almost like I was about to remember your name. But the name that I started to call you — wasn't a name! And so I stopped myself before I said it.

Laura: Wasn't it — Blue Roses?

Jim (springs up, grinning): Blue Roses! My gosh, yes — Blue Roses! That's what I had on my tongue when you opened the door! Isn't it funny what tricks your memory plays? I didn't connect you with the high school somehow or other. But that's where it was; it was high school. I didn't even know you were Shakespeare's sister! Gosh, I'm sorry.

Laura: I didn't expect you to. You — barely knew me!

Jim: But we did have a speaking acquaintance, huh?

Laura: Yes, we — spoke to each other.

Jim: When did you recognize me?

Laura: Oh, right away!

Jim: Soon as I came in the door?

Laura: When I heard your name I thought it was probably you. I knew that Tom used to know you a little in high school. So when you came in the door — Well, then I was — sure.

Jim: Why didn't you *say* something, then?

Laura (breathlessly): I didn't know what to say, I was — too surprised!

Jim: For goodness' sakes! You know, this sure is funny!

Laura: Yes! Yes, isn't it, though . . .

Jim: Didn't we have a class in something together?

Laura: Yes, we did.

Jim: What class was that?

Laura: It was — singing — Chorus!

Jim: Aw!

Laura: I sat across the aisle from you in the Aud.

Jim: Aw.

Laura: Mondays, Wednesdays, and Fridays.

Jim: Now I remember — you always came in late.

Laura: Yes, it was so hard for me, getting upstairs. I had that brace on my leg — it clumped so loud!

Jim: I never heard any clumping.

Laura (wincing in the recollection): To me it sounded like — thunder!

Jim: Well, well, well. I never even noticed.

Laura: And everybody was seated before I came in. I had to walk in front of all those people. My seat was in the back row. I had to go clumping all the way up the aisle with everyone watching!

Jim: You shouldn't have been self-conscious.

Laura: I know, but I was. It was always such a relief when the singing started.

Jim: Aw, yes, I've placed you now! I used to call you Blue Roses. How was it that I got started calling you that?

Laura: I was out of school a little while with pleurosis. When I came back you asked me what was the matter. I said I had pleurosis — you thought I said Blue Roses. That's what you always called me after that!

Jim: I hope you didn't mind.

Laura: Oh, no — I liked it. You see, I wasn't acquainted with many — people. . . .

Jim: As I remember you sort of stuck by yourself.

Laura: I — I — never had much luck at — making friends.

Jim: I don't see why you wouldn't.

Laura: Well, I — started out badly.

Jim: You mean being —

Laura: Yes, it sort of — stood between me —

Jim: You shouldn't have let it!

Laura: I know, but it did, and —

Jim: You were shy with people!

Laura: I tried not to be but never could —

Jim: Overcome it?

Laura: No, I — I never could!

Jim: I guess being shy is something you have to work out of kind of gradually.

Laura (sorrowfully): Yes — I guess it —

Jim: Takes time!

Laura: Yes —

Jim: People are not so dreadful when you know them. That's what you have to remember! And everybody has problems, not just you, but practically everybody has got some problems. You think of yourself as having the only problems, as being the only one who is disappointed. But just look around you and you will see lots of people as disappointed as you are. For instance, I hoped when I was going to high school that I would be further along at this time, six years later, than I am now — You remember that wonderful write-up I had in *The Torch*?

Laura: Yes! *(She rises and crosses to table.)*

Jim: It said I was bound to succeed in anything I went into! *(Laura returns with the annual.)* Holy Jeez! *The Torch!* *(He accepts it reverently. They smile across it with mutual wonder. Laura crouches beside him and they begin to turn through it. Laura's shyness is dissolving in his warmth.)*

Laura: Here you are in *Pirates of Penzance!*

Jim (wistfully): I sang the baritone lead in that operetta.

Laura (rapidly): So — *beautifully!*

Jim (protesting): Aw —

Laura: Yes, yes — beautifully — beautifully!

Jim: You heard me?

Laura: All three times!

Jim: No!

Laura: Yes!

Jim: All three performances?

Laura (looking down): Yes.

Jim: Why?

Laura: I — wanted to ask you to — autograph my program.

Jim: Why didn't you ask me to?

Laura: You were always surrounded by your own friends so much that I never had a chance to.

Jim: You should have just —

Laura: Well, I — thought you might think I was —

Jim: Thought I might think you was — what?

Laura: Oh —

Jim (with reflective relish): I was beleaguered by females in those days.

Laura: You were terribly popular!

Jim: Yeah —

Laura: You had such a — friendly way —

Jim: I was spoiled in high school.

Laura: Everybody — liked you!

Jim: Including you?

Laura: I — yes, I — I did, too — *(She gently closes the book in her lap.)*

Jim: Well, well, well! — Give me that program, Laura. *(She hands it to him. He signs it with a flourish.)* There you are — better late than never!

Laura: Oh, I — what a — surprise!

Jim: My signature isn't worth very much right now. But some day — maybe — it will increase in value! Being disappointed is one thing and being discouraged is something else. I am disappointed but I'm not discouraged. I'm twenty-three years old. How old are you?

Laura: I'll be twenty-four in June.

Jim: That's not old age.

Laura: No, but —

Jim: You finished high school?

Laura (with difficulty): I didn't go back.

Jim: You mean you dropped out?

Laura: I made bad grades in my final examinations. *(She rises and replaces the book and the program. Her voice strained.)* How is — Emily Meisenbach getting along?

Jim: Oh, that kraut-head!

Laura: Why do you call her that?

Jim: That's what she was.
Laura: You're not still — going with her?
Jim: I never see her.
Laura: It said in the Personal Section that you were — engaged!
Jim: I know, but I wasn't impressed by that — propaganda!
Laura: It wasn't — the truth?
Jim: Only in Emily's optimistic opinion!
Laura: Oh —

> (Legend: "What Have You Done since High School?")
> Jim lights a cigarette and leans indolently back on his elbows smiling at Laura with a warmth and charm which light her inwardly with altar candles. She remains by the table and turns in her hands a piece of glass to cover her tumult.

Jim (after several reflective puffs on a cigarette): What have you done since high school? *(She seems not to hear him.)* Huh? *(Laura looks up.)* I said what have you done since high school, Laura?
Laura: Nothing much.
Jim: You must have been doing something these six long years.
Laura: Yes.
Jim: Well, then, such as what?
Laura: I took a business course at business college —
Jim: How did that work out?
Laura: Well, not very — well — I had to drop out, it gave me — indigestion —

> Jim laughs gently.

Jim: What are you doing now?
Laura: I don't do anything — much. Oh, please don't think I sit around doing nothing! My glass collection takes up a good deal of my time. Glass is something you have to take good care of.
Jim: What did you say — about glass?
Laura: Collection I said — I have one — *(She clears her throat and turns away again, acutely shy.)*
Jim (abruptly): You know what I judge to be the trouble with you? Inferiority complex! Know what that is? That's what they call it when someone low-rates himself! I understand it because I had it, too. Although my case was not so aggravated as yours seems to be. I had it until I took up public speaking, developed my voice, and learned that I had an aptitude for science. Before that time I never thought of myself as being outstanding in any way whatsoever! Now I've never made a regular study of it, but I have a friend who says I can analyze people better than doctors that make a profession of it. I don't claim that to be necessarily true, but I can sure guess a person's psychology, Laura! *(Takes out his gum.)* Excuse me, Laura. I always take it out when the flavor is gone. I'll use this scrap of paper to wrap it in. I know how it is to get it stuck on a shoe. Yep — that's what I judge to be your principal trouble. A lack of confidence in yourself as a person. You don't have the proper amount of faith in yourself. I'm basing that fact on a number of your remarks and also on certain observations I've made. For instance that clumping you thought was so awful in high school. You say that you even dreaded to walk into class. You see what you did? You dropped out of school, you gave up an education because of a clump,

which as far as I know was practically nonexistent! A little physical defect is what you have. Hardly noticeable even! Magnified thousands of times by imagination! You know what my strong advice to you is? Think of yourself as *superior* in some way!

Laura: In what way would I think?

Jim: Why, man alive, Laura! Just look about you a little. What do you see? A world full of common people! All of 'em born and all of 'em going to die! Which of them has one-tenth of your good points! Or mine! Or anyone else's, as far as that goes — Gosh! Everybody excels in some one thing. Some in many! *(Unconsciously glances at himself in the mirror.)* All you've got to do is discover in *what!* Take me, for instance. *(He adjusts his tie at the mirror.)* My interest happened to lie in electrodynamics. I'm taking a course in radio engineering at night school, Laura, on top of a fairly responsible job at the warehouse. I'm taking that course and studying public speaking.

Laura: Ohhhh.

Jim: Because I believe in the future of television! *(Turning back to her.)* I wish to be ready to go up right along with it. Therefore I'm planning to get in on the ground floor. In fact, I've already made the right connections and all that remains is for the industry itself to get under way! Full steam — *(His eyes are starry.)* Knowledge — Zzzzzp! Money — Zzzzzzp! — Power! That's the cycle democracy is built on! *(His attitude is convincingly dynamic. Laura stares at him, even her shyness eclipsed in her absolute wonder. He suddenly grins.)* I guess you think I think a lot of myself!

Laura: No — o-o-o, I —

Jim: Now how about you? Isn't there something you take more interest in than anything else?

Laura: Well, I do — as I said — have my — glass collection —

A peal of girlish laughter from the kitchen.

Jim: I'm not right sure I know what you're talking about. What kind of glass is it?

Laura: Little articles of it, they're ornaments mostly! Most of them are little animals made out of glass, the tiniest little animals in the world. Mother calls them a glass menagerie! Here's an example of one, if you'd like to see it! This one is one of the oldest. It's nearly thirteen. *(He stretches out his hand.) (Music: "The Glass Menagerie.")* Oh, be careful — if you breathe, it breaks!

Jim: I'd better not take it. I'm pretty clumsy with things.

Laura: Go on, I trust you with him! *(Places it in his palm.)* There now — you're holding him gently! Hold him over the light, he loves the light! You see how the light shines through him?

Jim: It sure does shine!

Laura: I shouldn't be partial, but he is my favorite one.

Jim: What kind of thing is this one supposed to be?

Laura: Haven't you noticed the single horn on his forehead?

Jim: A unicorn, huh?

Laura: Mmm-hmmm!

Jim: Unicorns, aren't they extinct in the modern world?

Laura: I know!

Jim: Poor little fellow, he must feel sort of lonesome.

Laura (smiling): Well, if he does he doesn't complain about it. He stays on a
   shelf with some horses that don't have horns and all of them seem to get
   along nicely together.
Jim: How do you know?
Laura (lightly): I haven't heard any arguments among them!
Jim (grinning): No arguments, huh? Well, that's a pretty good sign! Where
   shall I set him?
Laura: Put him on the table. They all like a change of scenery once in a while!
Jim (stretching): Well, well, well, well — Look how big my shadow is when I
   stretch!
Laura: Oh, oh, yes — it stretches across the ceiling!
Jim (crossing to door): I think it's stopped raining. *(Opens fire-escape door.)* Where
   does the music come from?
Laura: From the Paradise Dance Hall across the alley.
Jim: How about cutting the rug a little, Miss Wingfield?
Laura: Oh, I —
Jim: Or is your program filled up? Let me have a look at it. *(Grasps imaginary
   card.)* Why, every dance is taken! I'll have to scratch some out. *(Waltz music:
   "La Golondrina.")* Ahhh, a waltz! *(He executes some sweeping turns by himself
   then holds his arms toward Laura.)*
Laura (breathlessly): I — can't dance!
Jim: There you go, that inferiority stuff!
Laura: I've never danced in my life!
Jim: Come on, try!
Laura: Oh, but I'd step on you!
Jim: I'm not made out of glass.
Laura: How — how — how do we start?
Jim: Just leave it to me. You hold your arms out a little.
Laura: Like this?
Jim: A little bit higher. Right. Now don't tighten up, that's the main thing
   about it — relax.
Laura (laughing breathlessly): It's hard not to.
Jim: Okay.
Laura: I'm afraid you can't budge me.
Jim: What do you bet I can't? *(He swings her into motion.)*
Laura: Goodness, yes, you can!
Jim: Let yourself go, now, Laura, just let yourself go.
Laura: I'm —
Jim: Come on!
Laura: Trying.
Jim: Not so stiff — Easy does it!
Laura: I know but I'm —
Jim: Loosen th' backbone! There now, that's a lot better.
Laura: Am I?
Jim: Lots, lots better! *(He moves her about the room in a clumsy waltz.)*
Laura: Oh, my!
Jim: Ha-ha!
Laura: Goodness, yes you can!
Jim: Ha-ha-ha! *(They suddenly bump into the table. Jim stops.)* What did we hit on?
Laura: Table.

Jim: Did something fall off it? I think —
Laura: Yes.
Jim: I hope it wasn't the little glass horse with the horn!
Laura: Yes.
Jim: Aw, aw, aw. Is it broken?
Laura: Now it is just like all the other horses.
Jim: It's lost its —
Laura: Horn! It doesn't matter. Maybe it's a blessing in disguise.
Jim: You'll never forgive me. I bet that that was your favorite piece of glass.
Laura: I don't have favorites much. It's no tragedy, Freckles. Glass breaks so
    easily. No matter how careful you are. The traffic jars the shelves and
    things fall off them.
Jim: Still I'm awfully sorry that I was the cause.
Laura (smiling): I'll just imagine he had an operation. The horn was removed
    to make him feel less — freakish! *(They both laugh.)* Now he will feel more at
    home with the other horses, the ones that don't have horns . . .
Jim: Ha-ha, that's very funny! *(Suddenly serious.)* I'm glad to see that you have a
    sense of humor. You know — you're — well — very different! Surprisingly
    different from anyone else I know! *(His voice becomes soft and hesitant with a
    genuine feeling.)* Do you mind me telling you that? *(Laura is abashed beyond
    speech.)* You make me feel sort of — I don't know how to put it! I'm usually
    pretty good at expressing things, but — This is something that I don't know
    how to say! *(Laura touches her throat and clears it — turns the broken unicorn in
    her hands.)* *(Even softer.)* Has anyone ever told you that you were pretty?

Pause: Music.

(Laura looks up slowly, with wonder, and shakes her head.) Well, you are! In a
very different way from anyone else. And all the nicer because of the difference, too. *(His voice becomes low and husky. Laura turns away, nearly faint with
the novelty of her emotions.)* I wish that you were my sister. I'd teach you to
have some confidence in yourself. The different people are not like other
people, but being different is nothing to be ashamed of. Because other
people are not such wonderful people. They're one hundred times one
thousand. You're one times one! They walk all over the earth. You just stay
here. They're common as — weeds, but — you — well, you're — *Blue Roses!*

(Image on screen: Blue Roses.)
    (Music changes.)

Laura: But blue is wrong for — roses . . .
Jim: It's right for you — You're — pretty!
Laura: In what respect am I pretty?
Jim: In all respects — believe me! Your eyes — your hair — are pretty! Your hands
    are pretty! *(He catches hold of her hand.)* You think I'm making this up
    because I'm invited to dinner and have to be nice. Oh, I could do that! I
    could put on an act for you, Laura, and say lots of things without being
    very sincere. But this time I am. I'm talking to you sincerely. I happened to
    notice you had this inferiority complex that keeps you from feeling com-
    fortable with people. Somebody needs to build your confidence up and
    make you proud instead of shy and turning away and — blushing — Some-
    body ought to — ought to — *kiss* you, Laura! *(His hand slips slowly up her arm*

to her shoulder.) (Music swells tumultuously.) (He suddenly turns her about and kisses her on the lips. When he releases her Laura sinks on the sofa with a bright, dazed look. Jim backs away and fishes in his pocket for a cigarette.) (Legend on screen: "Souvenir.") Stumble-john! *(He lights the cigarette, avoiding her look. There is a peal of girlish laughter from Amanda in the kitchen. Laura slowly raises and opens her hand. It still contains the little broken glass animal. She looks at it with a tender, bewildered expression.)* Stumble-john! I shouldn't have done that—That was way off the beam. You don't smoke, do you? *(She looks up, smiling, not hearing the question. He sits beside her a little gingerly. She looks at him speechlessly—waiting. He coughs decorously and moves a little farther aside as he considers the situation and senses her feelings, dimly, with perturbation. Gently.)* Would you—care for a—mint? *(She doesn't seem to hear him but her look grows brighter even.)* Peppermint—Life Saver? My pocket's a regular drug store—wherever I go . . . *(He pops a mint in his mouth. Then gulps and decides to make a clean breast of it. He speaks slowly and gingerly.)* Laura, you know, if I had a sister like you, I'd do the same thing as Tom. I'd bring out fellows—introduce her to them. The right type of boys of a type to—appreciate her. Only—well—he made a mistake about me. Maybe I've got no call to be saying this. That may not have been the idea in having me over. But what if it was? There's nothing wrong about that. The only trouble is that in my case—I'm not in a situation to—do the right thing. I can't take down your number and say I'll phone. I can't call up next week and—ask for a date. I thought I had better explain the situation in case you misunderstood it and—hurt your feelings. . . . *(Pause. Slowly, very slowly, Laura's look changes, her eyes returning slowly from his to the ornament in her palm.)*

Amanda utters another gay laugh in the kitchen.

Laura *(faintly):* You—won't—call again?
Jim: No, Laura, I can't. *(He rises from the sofa.)* As I was just explaining, I've—got strings on me, Laura, I've—been going steady! I go out all the time with a girl named Betty. She's a home-girl like you, and Catholic, and Irish, and in a great many ways we—get along fine. I met her last summer on a moonlight boat trip up the river to Alton, on the *Majestic*. Well—right away from the start it was—love! *(Legend: Love!) (Laura sways slightly forward and grips the arm of the sofa. He fails to notice, now enrapt in his own comfortable being.)* Being in love has made a new man of me! *(Leaning stiffly forward, clutching the arm of the sofa, Laura struggles visibly with her storm. But Jim is oblivious, she is a long way off.)* The power of love is really pretty tremendous! Love is something that—changes the whole world, Laura! *(The storm abates a little and Laura leans back. He notices her again.)* It happened that Betty's aunt took sick, she got a wire and had to go to Centralia. So Tom—when he asked me to dinner—I naturally just accepted the invitation, not knowing that you—that he—that I—*(He stops awkwardly.)* Huh—I'm a stumble-john! *(He flops back on the sofa. The holy candles in the altar of Laura's face have been snuffed out! There is a look of almost infinite desolation. Jim glances at her uneasily.)* I wish that you would—say something. *(She bites her lip which was trembling and then bravely smiles. She opens her hand again on the broken glass ornament. Then she gently takes his hand and raises it level with her own. She carefully places the unicorn in the palm of his hand, then pushes his fingers closed upon*

it.) What are you — doing that for? You want me to have him? — Laura?
(*She nods.*) What for?
Laura: A — souvenir . . .

She rises unsteadily and crouches beside the Victrola to wind it up.
(*Legend on screen: "Things Have a Way of Turning Out So Badly."*)
(*Or image: "Gentleman caller waving good-bye! — Gaily."*)
*At this moment Amanda rushes brightly back in the front room. She bears a
pitcher of fruit punch in an old-fashioned cut-glass pitcher and a plate of maca-
roons. The plate has a gold border and poppies painted on it.*

Amanda: Well, well, well! Isn't the air delightful after the shower? I've made
you children a little liquid refreshment. (*Turns gaily to the gentleman caller.*)
Jim, do you know that song about lemonade?
"Lemonade, lemonade
Made in the shade and stirred with a spade —
Good enough for any old maid!"
Jim (*uneasily*):   Ha-ha! No — I never heard it.
Amanda: Why, Laura! You look so serious!
Jim: We were having a serious conversation.
Amanda: Good! Now you're better acquainted!
Jim (*uncertainly*):   Ha-ha! Yes.
Amanda: You modern young people are much more serious-minded than my
generation. I was so gay as a girl!
Jim: You haven't changed, Mrs. Wingfield.
Amanda: Tonight I'm rejuvenated! The gaiety of the occasion, Mr. O'Connor!
(*She tosses her head with a peal of laughter. Spills lemonade.*) Oooo! I'm baptiz-
ing myself!
Jim: Here — let me —
Amanda (*setting the pitcher down*):   There now. I discovered we had some
maraschino cherries. I dumped them in, juice and all!
Jim: You shouldn't have gone to that trouble, Mrs. Wingfield.
Amanda: Trouble, trouble? Why it was loads of fun! Didn't you hear me cutting up in the kitchen? I bet your ears were burning! I told Tom how out-
done with him I was for keeping you to himself so long a time! He should
have brought you over much, much sooner! Well, now that you've found
your way, I want you to be a very frequent caller! Not just occasional but
all the time. Oh, we're going to have a lot of gay times together! I see them
coming! Mmm, just breathe that air! So fresh, and the moon's so pretty!
I'll skip back out — I know where my place is when young folks are having
a — serious conversation!
Jim: Oh, don't go out, Mrs. Wingfield. The fact of the matter is I've got to be
going.
Amanda: Going, now? You're joking! Why, it's only the shank of the evening,
Mr. O'Connor!
Jim: Well, you know how it is.
Amanda: You mean you're a young workingman and have to keep workingmen's hours. We'll let you off early tonight. But only on the condition that
next time you stay later. What's the best night for you? Isn't Saturday
night the best night for you workingmen?

Jim: I have a couple of time-clocks to punch, Mrs. Wingfield. One at morning, another one at night!

Amanda: My, but you *are* ambitious! You work at night, too?

Jim: No, Ma'am, not work but — Betty! *(He crosses deliberately to pick up his hat. The band at the Paradise Dance Hall goes into a tender waltz.)*

Amanda: Betty? Betty? Who's — Betty! *(There is an ominous cracking sound in the sky.)*

Jim: Oh, just a girl. The girl I go steady with! *(He smiles charmingly. The sky falls.)*

(Legend: "The Sky Falls.")

Amanda (a long-drawn exhalation): Ohhhh . . . Is it a serious romance, Mr. O'Connor?

Jim: We're going to be married the second Sunday in June.

Amanda: Ohhhh — how nice! Tom didn't mention that you were engaged to be married.

Jim: The cat's not out of the bag at the warehouse yet. You know how they are. They call you Romeo and stuff like that. *(He stops at the oval mirror to put on his hat. He carefully shapes the brim and the crown to give a discreetly dashing effect.)* It's been a wonderful evening, Mrs. Wingfield. I guess this is what they mean by Southern hospitality.

Amanda: It really wasn't anything at all.

Jim: I hope it don't seem like I'm rushing off. But I promised Betty I'd pick her up at the Wabash depot, an' by the time I get my jalopy down there her train'll be in. Some women are pretty upset if you keep 'em waiting.

Amanda: Yes, I know — The tyranny of women! *(Extends her hand.)* Good-bye, Mr. O'Connor. I wish you luck — and happiness — and success! All three of them, and so does Laura — Don't you, Laura?

Laura: Yes!

Jim (taking her hand): Good-bye, Laura. I'm certainly going to treasure that souvenir. And don't you forget the good advice I gave you. *(Raises his voice to a cheery shout.)* So long, Shakespeare! Thanks again, ladies — Good night!

He grins and ducks jauntily out.

Still bravely grimacing, Amanda closes the door on the gentleman caller. Then she turns back to the room with a puzzled expression. She and Laura don't dare to face each other. Laura crouches beside the Victrola to wind it.

Amanda (faintly): Things have a way of turning out so badly. I don't believe that I would play the Victrola. Well, well — well — Our gentleman caller was engaged to be married! Tom!

Tom (from back): Yes, Mother?

Amanda: Come in here a minute. I want to tell you something awfully funny.

Tom (enters with macaroon and a glass of the lemonade): Has the gentleman caller gotten away already?

Amanda: The gentleman caller has made an early departure. What a wonderful joke you played on us!

Tom: How do you mean?

Amanda: You didn't mention that he was engaged to be married.

Tom: Jim? Engaged?

Amanda: That's what he just informed us.

Tom: I'll be jiggered! I didn't know about that.

Amanda: That seems very peculiar.

Tom: What's peculiar about it?

Amanda: Didn't you call him your best friend down at the warehouse?

Tom: He is, but how did I know?

Amanda: It seems extremely peculiar that you wouldn't know your best friend was going to be married!

Tom: The warehouse is where I work, not where I know things about people!

Amanda: You don't know things anywhere! You live in a dream; you manufacture illusions! *(He crosses to door.)* Where are you going?

Tom: I'm going to the movies.

Amanda: That's right, now that you've had us make such fools of ourselves. The effort, the preparations, all the expense! The new floor lamp, the rug, the clothes for Laura! All for what? To entertain some other girl's fiancé! Go to the movies, go! Don't think about us, a mother deserted, an unmarried sister who's crippled and has no job! Don't let anything interfere with your selfish pleasure! Just go, go, go — to the movies!

Tom: All right, I will! The more you shout about my selfishness to me the quicker I'll go, and I won't go to the movies!

Amanda: Go, then! Then go to the moon — you selfish dreamer!

> *Tom smashes his glass on the floor. He plunges out on the fire-escape, slamming the door. Laura screams — cut by door.*
>
> *Dance-hall music up. Tom goes to the rail and grips it desperately, lifting his face in the chill white moonlight penetrating the narrow abyss of the alley.*
>
> *(Legend on screen: "And So Good-Bye . . .")*
>
> *Tom's closing speech is timed with the interior pantomime. The interior scene is played as though viewed through sound-proof glass. Amanda appears to be making a comforting speech to Laura who is huddled upon the sofa. Now that we cannot hear the mother's speech, her silliness is gone and she has dignity and tragic beauty. Laura's dark hair hides her face until at the end of the speech she lifts it to smile at her mother. Amanda's gestures are slow and graceful, almost dancelike, as she comforts the daughter. At the end of her speech she glances a moment at the father's picture — then withdraws through the portieres. At close of Tom's speech, Laura blows out the candles, ending the play.*

Tom: I didn't go to the moon, I went much further — for time is the longest distance between two places — Not long after that I was fired for writing a poem on the lid of a shoe-box. I left Saint Louis. I descended the steps of this fire-escape for a last time and followed, from then on, in my father's footsteps, attempting to find in motion what was lost in space — I traveled around a great deal. The cities swept about me like dead leaves, leaves that were brightly colored but torn away from the branches. I would have stopped, but I was pursued by something. It always came upon me unawares, taking me altogether by surprise. Perhaps it was a familiar bit of music. Perhaps it was only a piece of transparent glass — Perhaps I am walking along a street at night, in some strange city, before I have found companions. I pass the lighted window of a shop where perfume is sold. The window is filled with pieces of colored glass, tiny transparent bottles in delicate colors, like bits of a shattered rainbow. Then all at once my sister touches my shoulder. I turn around and look into her eyes. . . . Oh,

Laura, Laura, I tried to leave you behind me, but I am more faithful than I intended to be! I reach for a cigarette, I cross the street, I run into the movies or a bar, I buy a drink, I speak to the nearest stranger—anything that can blow your candles out! *(Laura bends over the candles)*—for nowadays the world is lit by lightning! Blow out your candles, Laura—and so good-bye . . .

She blows the candles out.
(The Scene Dissolves.)

CONNECTIONS TO OTHER SELECTIONS

1. Discuss the symbolic significance of the glass menagerie in Williams's play and the fences in August Wilson's *Fences* (p. 1483). How do the objects' symbolic values contribute to the theme of each play?

2. Compare and contrast the nonrealistic techniques that Williams uses with those used by Arthur Miller in *Death of a Salesman* (p. 1372).

3. Write an essay that compares Tom's narrative function in *The Glass Menagerie* with that of the Chorus in Sophocles' *Oedipus the King* (p. 1102).

Fences

August Wilson, who, as a young poet "wanted to be Dylan Thomas," went on to become a major force in the American theater. Between the 1980s and 2005, Wilson wrote a sequence of ten plays that chronicled the black experience in the United States in each decade of the twentieth century. *Ma Rainey's Black Bottom*, the first of these to be completed, premiered at the Yale Repertory Theatre in 1984, went to Broadway shortly thereafter, and eventually won the New York Drama Critics' Circle Award. Other plays in the sequence include *Joe Turner's Come and Gone* (1986), *The Piano Lesson* (1987), *Two Trains Running* (1989), and Wilson's last play, *Radio Golf* (2005).

© Joan Marcus.

Born in Pittsburgh, Pennsylvania, Wilson grew up in the Hill, a black neighborhood to which his mother had come from North Carolina. His white father never lived with the family. Wilson quit school at sixteen and worked in a variety of menial jobs, meanwhile submitting poetry to a number of local publications. He didn't begin to find his writing voice, however, until he moved to Minneapolis–St. Paul, where he founded the Black Horizons Theatre Company in 1968 and later started the Playwrights Center. He supported himself during part of this time by writing skits for the Science Museum of Minnesota.

Fences offers a complex look at the internal and external pressures on a black tenement family living in Pittsburgh during the 1950s.

AUGUST WILSON (1945–2005)

Fences 1985

CHARACTERS

Troy Maxson
Jim Bono, Troy's friend
Rose, Troy's wife
Lyons, Troy's oldest son by previous marriage
Gabriel, Troy's brother
Cory, Troy and Rose's son
Raynell, Troy's daughter

SETTING: The setting is the yard which fronts the only entrance to the Maxson household, an ancient two-story brick house set back off a small alley in a big-city neighborhood. The entrance to the house is gained by two or three steps leading to a wooden porch badly in need of paint.

A relatively recent addition to the house and running its full width, the porch lacks congruence. It is a sturdy porch with a flat roof. One or two chairs of dubious value sit at one end where the kitchen window opens onto the porch. An old-fashioned icebox stands silent guard at the opposite end.

The yard is a small dirt yard, partially fenced, except for the last scene, with a wooden sawhorse, a pile of lumber, and other fence-building equipment set off to the side. Opposite is a tree from which hangs a ball made of rags. A baseball bat leans against the tree. Two oil drums serve as garbage receptacles and sit near the house at right to complete the setting.

THE PLAY: Near the turn of the century, the destitute of Europe sprang on the city with tenacious claws and an honest and solid dream. The city devoured them. They swelled its belly until it burst into a thousand furnaces and sewing machines, a thousand butcher shops and bakers' ovens, a thousand churches and hospitals and funeral parlors and money-lenders. The city grew. It nourished itself and offered each man a partnership limited only by his talent, his guile, and his willingness and capacity for hard work. For the immigrants of Europe, a dream dared and won true.

The descendants of African slaves were offered no such welcome or participation. They came from places called the Carolinas and the Virginias, Georgia, Alabama, Mississippi, and Tennessee. They came strong, eager, searching. The city rejected them and they fled and settled along the riverbanks and under bridges in shallow, ramshackle houses made of sticks and tarpaper. They collected rags and wood. They sold the use of their muscles and their bodies. They cleaned houses and washed clothes, they shined shoes, and in quiet desperation and vengeful pride, they stole, and lived in pursuit of their own dream. That they could breathe free, finally, and stand to meet life with the force of dignity and whatever eloquence the heart could call upon.

By 1957, the hard-won victories of the European immigrants had solidified the industrial might of America. War had been confronted and won with new energies that used loyalty and patriotism as its fuel. Life was rich, full, and flourishing. The Milwaukee Braves won the World Series, and the hot winds of change that would make the sixties a turbulent, racing, dangerous, and provocative decade had not yet begun to blow full.

ACT I

SCENE I

> *It is 1957. Troy and Bono enter the yard, engaged in conversation. Troy is fifty-three years old, a large man with thick, heavy hands; it is this largeness that he strives to fill out and make an accommodation with. Together with his blackness, his largeness informs his sensibilities and the choices he has made in his life.*
>
> *Of the two men, Bono is obviously the follower. His commitment to their friendship of thirty-odd years is rooted in his admiration of Troy's honesty, capacity for hard work, and his strength, which Bono seeks to emulate.*
>
> *It is Friday night, payday, and the one night of the week the two men engage in a ritual of talk and drink. Troy is usually the most talkative and at times he can be crude and almost vulgar, though he is capable of rising to profound heights of expression. The men carry lunch buckets and wear or carry burlap aprons and are dressed in clothes suitable to their jobs as garbage collectors.*

Bono: Troy, you ought to stop that lying!

Troy: I ain't lying! The nigger had a watermelon this big. *(He indicates with his hands.)* Talking about . . . "What watermelon, Mr. Rand?" I liked to fell out! "What watermelon, Mr. Rand?" . . . And it sitting there big as life.

Bono: What did Mr. Rand say?

Troy: Ain't said nothing. Figure if the nigger too dumb to know he carrying a watermelon, he wasn't gonna get much sense out of him. Trying to hide that great big old watermelon under his coat. Afraid to let the white man see him carry it home.

Bono: I'm like you . . . I ain't got no time for them kind of people.

Troy: Now what he look like getting mad cause he see the man from the union talking to Mr. Rand?

Bono: He come to me talking about . . . "Maxson gonna get us fired." I told him to get away from me with that. He walked away from me calling you a troublemaker. What Mr. Rand say?

Troy: Ain't said nothing. He told me to go down the Commissioner's office next Friday. They called me down there to see them.

Bono: Well, as long as you got your complaint filed, they can't fire you. That's what one of them white fellows tell me.

Troy: I ain't worried about them firing me. They gonna fire me cause I asked a question? That's all I did. I went to Mr. Rand and asked him, "Why? Why you got the white mens driving and the colored lifting?" Told him, "what's the matter, don't I count? You think only white fellows got sense enough to drive a truck. That ain't no paper job! Hell, anybody can drive a truck. How come you got all whites driving and the colored lifting?" He told me "take it to the union." Well, hell, that's what I done! Now they wanna come up with this pack of lies.

Bono: I told Brownie if the man come and ask him any questions . . . just tell the truth! It ain't nothing but something they done trumped up on you cause you filed a complaint on them.

Troy: Brownie don't understand nothing. All I want them to do is change the job description. Give everybody a chance to drive the truck. Brownie can't see that. He ain't got that much sense.

Bono: How you figure he be making out with that gal be up at Taylors' all the time . . . that Alberta gal?

Troy: Same as you and me. Getting just as much as we is. Which is to say nothing.

Bono: It is, huh? I figure you doing a little better than me . . . and I ain't saying what I'm doing.

Troy: Aw, nigger, look here . . . I know you. If you had got anywhere near that gal, twenty minutes later you be looking to tell somebody. And the first one you gonna tell . . . that you gonna want to brag to . . . is me.

Bono: I ain't saying that. I see where you be eyeing her.

Troy: I eye all the women. I don't miss nothing. Don't never let nobody tell you Troy Maxson don't eye the women.

Bono: You been doing more than eyeing her. You done bought her a drink or two.

Troy: Hell yeah, I bought her a drink! What that mean? I bought you one, too. What that mean cause I buy her a drink? I'm just being polite.

Bono: It's all right to buy her one drink. That's what you call being polite. But when you wanna be buying two or three . . . that's what you call eyeing her.

Troy: Look here, as long as you known me . . . you ever known me to chase after women?

Bono: Hell yeah! Long as I done known you. You forgetting I knew you when.

Troy: Naw, I'm talking about since I been married to Rose?

Bono: Oh, not since you been married to Rose. Now, that's the truth, there. I can say that.

Troy: All right then! Case closed.

Bono: I see you be walking up around Alberta's house. You supposed to be at Taylors' and you be walking up around there.

Troy: What you watching where I'm walking for? I ain't watching after you.

Bono: I seen you walking around there more than once.

Troy: Hell, you liable to see me walking anywhere! That don't mean nothing cause you see me walking around there.

Bono: Where she come from anyway? She just kinda showed up one day.

Troy: Tallahassee. You can look at her and tell she one of them Florida gals. They got some big healthy women down there. Grow them right up out the ground. Got a little bit of Indian in her. Most of them niggers down in Florida got some Indian in them.

Bono: I don't know about that Indian part. But she damn sure big and healthy. Woman wear some big stockings. Got them great big old legs and hips as wide as the Mississippi River.

Troy: Legs don't mean nothing. You don't do nothing but push them out of the way. But them hips cushion the ride!

Bono: Troy, you ain't got no sense.

Troy: It's the truth! Like you riding on Goodyears!

> *Rose enters from the house. She is ten years younger than Troy, her devotion to him stems from her recognition of the possibilities of her life without him: a succession of abusive men and their babies, a life of partying and running the streets, the Church, or aloneness with its attendant pain and frustration. She recognizes Troy's spirit as a fine and illuminating one and she either ignores or forgives his faults, only some of which she recognizes. Though she doesn't drink, her presence is an integral part of the Friday night rituals. She alternates between the porch and the kitchen, where supper preparations are under way.*

Rose: What you all out here getting into?

Troy: What you worried about what we getting into for? This is men talk, woman.

Rose: What I care what you all talking about? Bono, you gonna stay for supper?

Bono: No, I thank you, Rose. But Lucille say she cooking up a pot of pigfeet.

Troy: Pigfeet! Hell, I'm going home with you! Might even stay the night if you got some pigfeet. You got something in there to top them pigfeet, Rose?

Rose: I'm cooking up some chicken. I got some chicken and collard greens.

Troy: Well, go on back in the house and let me and Bono finish what we was talking about. This is men talk. I got some talk for you later. You know what kind of talk I mean. You go on and powder it up.

Rose: Troy Maxson, don't you start that now!

Troy (puts his arm around her): Aw, woman . . . come here. Look here, Bono . . . when I met this woman . . . I got out that place, say, "Hitch up my pony, saddle up my mare . . . there's a woman out there for me somewhere. I looked here. Looked there. Saw Rose and latched on to her." I latched on to her and told her—I'm gonna tell you the truth—I told her, "Baby, I don't wanna marry, I just wanna be your man." Rose told me . . . tell him what you told me, Rose.

Rose: I told him if he wasn't the marrying kind, then move out the way so the marrying kind could find me.

Troy: That's what she told me. "Nigger, you in my way. You blocking the view! Move out the way so I can find me a husband." I thought it over two or three days. Come back—

Rose: Ain't no two or three days nothing. You was back the same night.

Troy: Come back, told her . . . "Okay, baby . . . but I'm gonna buy me a banty rooster and put him out there in the backyard . . . and when he see a stranger come, he'll flap his wings and crow . . ." Look here, Bono, I could watch the front door by myself . . . it was that back door I was worried about.

Rose: Troy, you ought not talk like that. Troy ain't doing nothing but telling a lie.

Troy: Only thing is . . . when we first got married . . . forget the rooster . . . we ain't had no yard!

Bono: I hear you tell it. Me and Lucille was staying down there on Logan Street. Had two rooms with the outhouse in the back. I ain't mind the outhouse none. But when that goddamn wind blow through there in the winter . . . that's what I'm talking about! To this day I wonder why in the hell I ever stayed down there for six long years. But see, I didn't know I could do no better. I thought only white folks had inside toilets and things.

Rose: There's a lot of people don't know they can do no better than they doing now. That's just something you got to learn. A lot of folks still shop at Bella's.

Troy: Ain't nothing wrong with shopping at Bella's. She got fresh food.

Rose: I ain't said nothing about if she got fresh food. I'm talking about what she charge. She charge ten cents more than the A&P.

Troy: The A&P ain't never done nothing for me. I spends my money where I'm treated right. I go down to Bella, say, "I need a loaf of bread, I'll pay you Friday." She give it to me. What sense that make when I got money to go and spend it somewhere else and ignore the person who done right by me? That ain't in the Bible.

Rose: We ain't talking about what's in the Bible. What sense it make to shop there when she overcharge?

Troy: You shop where you want to. I'll do my shopping where the people been good to me.

Rose: Well, I don't think it's right for her to overcharge. That's all I was saying.

Bono: Look here . . . I got to get on. Lucille going be raising all kind of hell.

Troy: Where you going, nigger? We ain't finished this pint. Come here, finish this pint.

Bono: Well, hell, I am . . . if you ever turn the bottle loose.

Troy (hands him the bottle): The only thing I say about the A&P is I'm glad Cory got that job down there. Help him take care of his school clothes and things. Gabe done moved out and things getting tight around here. He got that job. . . . He can start to look out for himself.

Rose: Cory done went and got recruited by a college football team.

Troy: I told that boy about that football stuff. The white man ain't gonna let him get nowhere with that football. I told him when he first come to me with it. Now you come telling me he done went and got more tied up in it. He ought to go and get recruited in how to fix cars or something where he can make a living.

Rose: He ain't talking about making no living playing football. It's just something the boys in school do. They gonna send a recruiter by to talk to you. He'll tell you he ain't talking about making no living playing football. It's a honor to be recruited.

Troy: It ain't gonna get him nowhere. Bono'll tell you that.

Bono: If he be like you in the sports . . . he's gonna be all right. Ain't but two men ever played baseball as good as you. That's Babe Ruth° and Josh Gibson.° Them's the only two men ever hit more home runs than you.

Troy: What it ever get me? Ain't got a pot to piss in or a window to throw it out of.

Babe Ruth (1895–1948): One of the greatest American baseball players. *Josh Gibson* (1911–1947): Powerful baseball player known in the 1930s as the Babe Ruth of the Negro leagues.

Rose: Times have changed since you was playing baseball, Troy. That was before the war. Times have changed a lot since then.

Troy: How in hell they done changed?

Rose: They got lots of colored boys playing ball now. Baseball and football.

Bono: You right about that, Rose. Times have changed, Troy. You just come along too early.

Troy: There ought not never have been no time called too early! Now you take that fellow . . . what's that fellow they had playing right field for the Yankees back then? You know who I'm talking about, Bono. Used to play right field for the Yankees.

Rose: Selkirk?

Troy: Selkirk! That's it! Man batting .269, understand? .269. What kind of sense that make? I was hitting .432 with thirty-seven home runs! Man batting .269 and playing right field for the Yankees! I saw Josh Gibson's daughter yesterday. She walking around with raggedy shoes on her feet. Now I bet you Selkirk's daughter ain't walking around with raggedy shoes on her feet! I bet you that!

Rose: They got a lot of colored baseball players now. Jackie Robinson° was the first. Folks had to wait for Jackie Robinson.

Troy: I done seen a hundred niggers play baseball better than Jackie Robinson. Hell, I know some teams Jackie Robinson couldn't even make! What you talking about Jackie Robinson. Jackie Robinson wasn't nobody. I'm talking about if you could play ball then they ought to have let you play. Don't care what color you were. Come telling me I come along too early. If you could play . . . then they ought to have let you play.

Troy takes a long drink from the bottle.

Rose: You gonna drink yourself to death. You don't need to be drinking like that.

Troy: Death ain't nothing. I done seen him. Done wrassled with him. You can't tell me nothing about death. Death ain't nothing but a fastball on the outside corner. And you know what I'll do to that! Lookee here, Bono . . . am I lying? You get one of them fastballs, about waist high, over the outside corner of the plate where you can get the meat of the bat on it . . . and good god! You can kiss it goodbye. Now, am I lying?

Bono: Naw, you telling the truth there. I seen you do it.

Troy: If I'm lying . . . that 450 feet worth of lying! *(Pause.)* That's all death is to me. A fastball on the outside corner.

Rose: I don't know why you want to get on talking about death.

Troy: Ain't nothing wrong with talking about death. That's part of life. Everybody gonna die. You gonna die, I'm gonna die. Bono's gonna die. Hell, we all gonna die.

Rose: But you ain't got to talk about it. I don't like to talk about it.

Troy: You the one brought it up. Me and Bono was talking about baseball . . . you tell me I'm gonna drink myself to death. Ain't that right, Bono? You know I don't drink this but one night out of the week. That's Friday night. I'm gonna drink just enough to where I can handle it. Then I cuts it loose.

Jackie Robinson (1919–1972): The first black baseball player in the major leagues (1947).

I leave it alone. So don't you worry about me drinking myself to death. 'Cause I ain't worried about Death. I done seen him. I done wrestled with him.

Look here, Bono . . . I looked up one day and Death was marching straight at me. Like Soldiers on Parade! The Army of Death was marching straight at me. The middle of July, 1941. It got real cold just like it be winter. It seem like Death himself reached out and touched me on the shoulder. He touch me just like I touch you. I got cold as ice and Death standing there grinning at me.

Rose: Troy, why don't you hush that talk.

Troy: I say . . . what you want, Mr. Death? You be wanting me? You done brought your army to be getting me? I looked him dead in the eye. I wasn't fearing nothing. I was ready to tangle. Just like I'm ready to tangle now. The Bible say be ever vigilant. That's why I don't get but so drunk. I got to keep watch.

Rose: Troy was right down there in Mercy Hospital. You remember he had pneumonia? Laying there with a fever talking plumb out of his head.

Troy: Death standing there staring at me . . . carrying that sickle in his hand. Finally he say, "You want bound over for another year?" See, just like that . . . "You want bound over for another year?" I told him, "Bound over hell! Let's settle this now!"

It seem like he kinda fell back when I said that, and all the cold went out of me. I reached down and grabbed that sickle and threw it just as far as I could throw it . . . and me and him commenced to wrestling.

We wrestled for three days and three nights. I can't say where I found the strength from. Every time it seemed like he was gonna get the best of me, I'd reach way down deep inside myself and find the strength to do him one better.

Rose: Every time Troy tell that story he find different ways to tell it. Different things to make up about it.

Troy: I ain't making up nothing. I'm telling you the facts of what happened. I wrestled with Death for three days and three nights and I'm standing here to tell you about it. *(Pause.)* All right. At the end of the third night we done weakened each other to where we can't hardly move. Death stood up, throwed on his robe . . . had him a white robe with a hood on it. He throwed on that robe and went off to look for his sickle. Say, "I'll be back." Just like that. "I'll be back." I told him, say, "Yeah, but . . . you gonna have to find me!" I wasn't no fool. I wan't going looking for him. Death ain't nothing to play with. And I know he's gonna get me. I know I got to join his army . . . his camp followers. But as long as I keep my strength and see him coming . . . as long as I keep up my vigilance . . . he's gonna have to fight to get me. I ain't going easy.

Bono: Well, look here, since you got to keep up your vigilance . . . let me have the bottle.

Troy: Aw hell, I shouldn't have told you that part. I should have left out that part.

Rose: Troy be talking that stuff and half the time don't even know what he be talking about.

Troy: Bono know me better than that.

Bono: That's right. I know you. I know you got some Uncle Remus° in your blood. You got more stories than the devil got sinners.

Troy: Aw hell, I done seen him too! Done talked with the devil.

Rose: Troy, don't nobody wanna be hearing all that stuff.

> *Lyons enters the yard from the street. Thirty-four years old, Troy's son by a previous marriage, he sports a neatly trimmed goatee, sport coat, white shirt, tieless and buttoned at the collar. Though he fancies himself a musician, he is more caught up in the rituals and "idea" of being a musician than in the actual practice of the music. He has come to borrow money from Troy, and while he knows he will be successful, he is uncertain as to what extent his lifestyle will be held up to scrutiny and ridicule.*

Lyons: Hey, Pop.

Troy: What you come "Hey, Popping" me for?

Lyons: How you doing, Rose? *(He kisses her.)* Mr. Bono. How you doing?

Bono: Hey, Lyons . . . how you been?

Troy: He must have been doing all right. I ain't seen him around here last week.

Rose: Troy, leave your boy alone. He come by to see you and you wanna start all that nonsense.

Troy: I ain't bothering Lyons. *(Offers him the bottle.)* Here . . . get you a drink. We got an understanding. I know why he come by to see me and he know I know.

Lyons: Come on, Pop . . . I just stopped by to say hi . . . see how you was doing.

Troy: You ain't stopped by yesterday.

Rose: You gonna stay for supper, Lyons? I got some chicken cooking in the oven.

Lyons: No, Rose . . . thanks. I was just in the neighborhood and thought I'd stop by for a minute.

Troy: You was in the neighborhood all right, nigger. You telling the truth there. You was in the neighborhood cause it's my payday.

Lyons: Well, hell, since you mentioned it . . . let me have ten dollars.

Troy: I'll be damned! I'll die and go to hell and play blackjack with the devil before I give you ten dollars.

Bono: That's what I wanna know about . . . that devil you done seen.

Lyons: What . . . Pop done seen the devil? You too much, Pops.

Troy: Yeah, I done seen him. Talked to him too!

Rose: You ain't seen no devil. I done told you that man ain't had nothing to do with the devil. Anything you can't understand, you want to call it the devil.

Troy: Look here, Bono . . . I went down to see Hertzberger about some furniture. Got three rooms for two-ninety-eight. That what it say on the radio. "Three rooms . . . two-ninety-eight." Even made up a little song about it. Go down there . . . man tell me I can't get no credit. I'm working every day and can't get no credit. What to do? I got an empty house with some raggedy furniture in it. Cory ain't got no bed. He's sleeping on a pile of rags on the floor. Working every day and can't get no credit. Come back

---

Uncle Remus: Black storyteller who recounts traditional black tales in the book by Joel Chandler Harris.

here—Rose'll tell you—madder than hell. Sit down . . . try to figure what I'm gonna do. Come a knock on the door. Ain't been living here but three days. Who know I'm here? Open the door . . . devil standing there bigger than life. White fellow . . . white fellow . . . got on good clothes and everything. Standing there with a clipboard in his hand. I ain't had to say nothing. First words come out of his mouth was . . . "I understand you need some furniture and can't get no credit." I liked to fell over. He say, "I'll give you all the credit you want, but you got to pay the interest on it." I told him, "Give me three rooms worth and charge whatever you want." Next day a truck pulled up here and two men unloaded them three rooms. Man what drove the truck give me a book. Say send ten dollars, first of every month to the address in the book and everything will be all right. Say if I miss a payment the devil was coming back and it'll be hell to pay. That was fifteen years ago. To this day . . . the first of the month I send my ten dollars, Rose'll tell you.

Rose: Troy lying.

Troy: I ain't never seen that man since. Now you tell me who else that could have been but the devil? I ain't sold my soul or nothing like that, you understand. Naw, I wouldn't have truck with the devil about nothing like that. I got my furniture and pays my ten dollars the first of the month just like clockwork.

Bono: How long you say you been paying this ten dollars a month?

Troy: Fifteen years!

Bono: Hell, ain't you finished paying for it yet? How much the man done charged you?

Troy: Ah hell, I done paid for it. I done paid for it ten times over! The fact is I'm scared to stop paying it.

Rose: Troy lying. We got that furniture from Mr. Glickman. He ain't paying no ten dollars a month to nobody.

Troy: Aw hell, woman. Bono know I ain't that big a fool.

Lyons: I was just getting ready to say . . . I know where there's a bridge for sale.

Troy: Look here, I'll tell you this . . . it don't matter to me if he was the devil. It don't matter if the devil give credit. Somebody has got to give it.

Rose: It ought to matter. You going around talking about having truck with the devil . . . God's the one you gonna have to answer to. He's the one gonna be at the Judgment.

Lyons: Yeah, well, look here, Pop . . . let me have that ten dollars. I'll give it back to you. Bonnie got a job working at the hospital.

Troy: What I tell you, Bono? The only time I see this nigger is when he wants something. That's the only time I see him.

Lyons: Come on, Pop, Mr. Bono don't want to hear all that. Let me have the ten dollars. I told you Bonnie working.

Troy: What that mean to me? "Bonnie working." I don't care if she working. Go ask her for the ten dollars if she working. Talking about "Bonnie working." Why ain't you working?

Lyons: Aw, Pop, you know I can't find no decent job. Where am I gonna get a job at? You know I can't get no job.

Troy: I told you I know some people down there. I can get you on the rubbish if you want to work. I told you that the last time you came by here asking me for something.

Lyons: Naw, Pop . . . thanks. That ain't for me. I don't wanna be carrying nobody's rubbish. I don't wanna be punching nobody's time clock.

Troy: What's the matter, you too good to carry people's rubbish? Where you think that ten dollars you talking about come from? I'm just supposed to haul people's rubbish and give my money to you cause you too lazy to work. You too lazy to work and wanna know why you ain't got what I got.

Rose: What hospital Bonnie working at? Mercy?

Lyons: She's down at Passavant working in the laundry.

Troy: I ain't got nothing as it is. I give you that ten dollars and I got to eat beans the rest of the week. Naw . . . you ain't getting no ten dollars here.

Lyons: You ain't got to be eating no beans. I don't know why you wanna say that.

Troy: I ain't got no extra money. Gabe done moved over to Miss Pearl's paying her the rent and things done got tight around here. I can't afford to be giving you every payday.

Lyons: I ain't asked you to give me nothing. I asked you to loan me ten dollars. I know you got ten dollars.

Troy: Yeah, I got it. You know why I got it? Cause I don't throw my money away out there in the streets. You living the fast life . . . wanna be a musician . . . running around in them clubs and things . . . then, you learn to take care of yourself. You ain't gonna find me going and asking nobody for nothing. I done spent too many years without.

Lyons: You and me is two different people, Pop.

Troy: I done learned my mistake and learned to do what's right by it. You still trying to get something for nothing. Life don't owe you nothing. You owe it to yourself. Ask Bono. He'll tell you I'm right.

Lyons: You got your way of dealing with the world . . . I got mine. The only thing that matters to me is the music.

Troy: Yeah, I can see that! It don't matter how you gonna eat . . . where your next dollar is coming from. You telling the truth there.

Lyons: I know I got to eat. But I got to live too. I need something that gonna help me to get out of the bed in the morning. Make me feel like I belong in the world. I don't bother nobody. I just stay with the music cause that's the only way I can find to live in the world. Otherwise there ain't no telling what I might do. Now I don't come criticizing you and how you live. I just come by to ask you for ten dollars. I don't wanna hear all that about how I live.

Troy: Boy, your mamma did a hell of a job raising you.

Lyons: You can't change me, Pop. I'm thirty-four years old. If you wanted to change me, you should have been there when I was growing up. I come by to see you . . . ask for ten dollars and you want to talk about how I was raised. You don't know nothing about how I was raised.

Rose: Let the boy have ten dollars, Troy.

Troy (to Lyons): What the hell you looking at me for? I ain't got no ten dollars. You know what I do with my money. *(To Rose.)* Give him ten dollars if you want him to have it.

Rose: I will. Just as soon as you turn it loose.

Troy (handing Rose the money): There it is. Seventy-six dollars and forty-two cents. You see this, Bono? Now, I ain't gonna get but six of that back.

Rose: You ought to stop telling that lie. Here, Lyons. *(She hands him the money.)*

Lyons: Thanks, Rose. Look . . . I got to run . . . I'll see you later.

Troy: Wait a minute. You gonna say, "thanks, Rose" and ain't gonna look to see where she got that ten dollars from? See how they do me, Bono?

Lyons: I know she got it from you, Pop. Thanks. I'll give it back to you.

Troy: There he go telling another lie. Time I see that ten dollars . . . he'll be owing me thirty more.

Lyons: See you, Mr. Bono.

Bono: Take care, Lyons!

Lyons: Thanks, Pop. I'll see you again.

> *Lyons exits the yard.*

Troy: I don't know why he don't go and get him a decent job and take care of that woman he got.

Bono: He'll be all right, Troy. The boy is still young.

Troy: The *boy* is thirty-four years old.

Rose: Let's not get off into all that.

Bono: Look here . . . I got to be going. I got to be getting on. Lucille gonna be waiting.

Troy (puts his arm around Rose): See this woman, Bono? I love this woman. I love this woman so much it hurts. I love her so much . . . I done run out of ways of loving her. So I got to go back to basics. Don't you come by my house Monday morning talking about time to go to work . . . 'cause I'm still gonna be stroking!

Rose: Troy! Stop it now!

Bono: I ain't paying him no mind, Rose. That ain't nothing but gin-talk. Go on, Troy. I'll see you Monday.

Troy: Don't you come by my house, nigger! I done told you what I'm gonna be doing.

> *The lights go down to black.*

Scene II

> *The lights come up on Rose hanging up clothes. She hums and sings softly to herself. It is the following morning.*

Rose *(sings):* Jesus, be a fence all around me every day
Jesus, I want you to protect me as I travel on my way.
Jesus, be a fence all around me every day.

> *Troy enters from the house.*

Jesus, I want you to protect me
As I travel on my way.
(To Troy.) 'Morning. You ready for breakfast? I can fix it soon as I finish hanging up these clothes?

Troy: I got the coffee on. That'll be all right. I'll just drink some of that this morning.

Rose: That 651 hit yesterday. That's the second time this month. Miss Pearl hit for a dollar . . . seem like those that need the least always get lucky. Poor folks can't get nothing.

Troy: Them numbers don't know nobody. I don't know why you fool with them. You and Lyons both.

Rose: It's something to do.

Troy: You ain't doing nothing but throwing your money away.

Rose: Troy, you know I don't play foolishly. I just play a nickel here and a nickel there.

Troy: That's two nickels you done thrown away.

Rose: Now I hit sometimes . . . that makes up for it. It always comes in handy when I do hit. I don't hear you complaining then.

Troy: I ain't complaining now. I just say it's foolish. Trying to guess out of six hundred ways which way the number gonna come. If I had all the money niggers, these Negroes, throw away on numbers for one week—just one week—I'd be a rich man.

Rose: Well, you wishing and calling it foolish ain't gonna stop folks from playing numbers. That's one thing for sure. Besides . . . some good things come from playing numbers. Look where Pope done bought him that restaurant off of numbers.

Troy: I can't stand niggers like that. Man ain't had two dimes to rub together. He walking around with his shoes all run over bumming money for cigarettes. All right. Got lucky there and hit the numbers . . .

Rose: Troy, I know all about it.

Troy: Had good sense, I'll say that for him. He ain't throwed his money away. I seen niggers hit the numbers and go through two thousand dollars in four days. Man bought him that restaurant down there . . . fixed it up real nice . . . and then didn't want nobody to come in it! A Negro go in there and can't get no kind of service. I seen a white fellow come in there and order a bowl of stew. Pope picked all the meat out the pot for him. Man ain't had nothing but a bowl of meat! Negro come behind him and ain't got nothing but the potatoes and carrots. Talking about what numbers do for people, you picked a wrong example. Ain't done nothing but make a worser fool out of him than he was before.

Rose: Troy, you ought to stop worrying about what happened at work yesterday.

Troy: I ain't worried. Just told me to be down there at the Commissioner's office on Friday. Everybody think they gonna fire me. I ain't worried about them firing me. You ain't got to worry about that. *(Pause.)* Where's Cory? Cory in the house? *(Calls.)* Cory?

Rose: He gone out.

Troy: Out, huh? He gone out 'cause he know I want him to help me with this fence. I know how he is. That boy scared of work.

Gabriel enters. He comes halfway down the alley and, hearing Troy's voice, stops.

Troy (continues): He ain't done a lick of work in his life.

Rose: He had to go to football practice. Coach wanted them to get in a little extra practice before the season start.

Troy: I got his practice . . . running out of here before he get his chores done.

Rose: Troy, what is wrong with you this morning? Don't nothing set right with you. Go on back in there and go to bed . . . get up on the other side.

Troy: Why something got to be wrong with me? I ain't said nothing wrong with me.

Rose: You got something to say about everything. First it's the numbers . . . then it's the way the man runs his restaurant . . . then you done got on

Cory. What's it gonna be next? Take a look up there and see if the weather suits you . . . or is it gonna be how you gonna put up the fence with the clothes hanging in the yard.

Troy: You hit the nail on the head then.

Rose: I know you like I know the back of my hand. Go on in there and get you some coffee . . . see if that straighten you up. 'Cause you ain't right this morning.

Troy starts into the house and sees Gabriel. Gabriel starts singing. Troy's brother, he is seven years younger than Troy. Injured in World War II, he has a metal plate in his head. He carries an old trumpet tied around his waist and believes with every fiber of his being that he is the Archangel Gabriel.° He carries a chipped basket with an assortment of discarded fruits and vegetables he has picked up in the strip district and which he attempts to sell.

Gabriel (singing): Yes, ma am, I got plums
　　You ask me how I sell them
　　Oh ten cents apiece
　　Three for a quarter
　　Come and buy now
　　'Cause I'm here today
　　And tomorrow I'll be gone

Gabriel enters.

Hey, Rose!

Rose: How you doing, Gabe?

Gabriel: There's Troy . . . Hey, Troy!

Troy: Hey, Gabe.

Exit into kitchen.

Rose (to Gabriel): What you got there?

Gabriel: You know what I got, Rose. I got fruits and vegetables.

Rose (looking in basket): Where's all these plums you talking about?

Gabriel: I ain't got no plums today, Rose. I was just singing that. Have some tomorrow. Put me in a big order for plums. Have enough plums tomorrow for St. Peter and everybody.

Troy reenters from kitchen, crosses to steps.

(To Rose.) Troy's mad at me.

Troy: I ain't mad at you. What I got to be mad at you about? You ain't done nothing to me.

Gabriel: I just moved over to Miss Pearl's to keep out from in your way. I ain't mean no harm by it.

Troy: Who said anything about that? I ain't said anything about that.

Gabriel: You ain't mad at me, is you?

Troy: Naw . . . I ain't mad at you, Gabe. If I was mad at you I'd tell you about it.

Gabriel: Got me two rooms. In the basement. Got my own door too. Wanna see my key? *(He holds up a key.)* That's my own key! Ain't nobody else got a key like that. That's my key! My two rooms!

Archangel Gabriel: Considered one of God's primary messengers in the Old and New Testaments.

Troy: Well, that's good, Gabe. You got your own key . . . that's good.

Rose: You hungry, Gabe? I was just fixing to cook Troy his breakfast.

Gabriel: I'll take some biscuits. You got some biscuits? Did you know when I was in heaven . . . every morning me and St. Peter° would sit down by the gate and eat some big fat biscuits? Oh, yeah! We had us a good time. We'd sit there and eat us them biscuits and then St. Peter would go off to sleep and tell me to wake him up when it's time to open the gates for the judgment.

Rose: Well, come on . . . I'll make up a batch of biscuits.

Rose exits into the house.

Gabriel: Troy . . . St. Peter got your name in the book. I seen it. It say . . . Troy Maxson. I say . . . I know him! He got the same name like what I got. That's my brother!

Troy: How many times you gonna tell me that, Gabe?

Gabriel: Ain't got my name in the book. Don't have to have my name. I done died and went to heaven. He got your name though. One morning St. Peter was looking at his book . . . marking it up for the judgment . . . and he let me see your name. Got it in there under M. Got Rose's name . . . I ain't seen it like I seen yours . . . but I know it's in there. He got a great big book. Got everybody's name what was ever been born. That's what he told me. But I seen your name. Seen it with my own eyes.

Troy: Go on in the house there. Rose going to fix you something to eat.

Gabriel: Oh, I ain't hungry. I done had breakfast with Aunt Jemimah. She come by and cooked me up a whole mess of flapjacks. Remember how we used to eat them flapjacks?

Troy: Go on in the house and get you something to eat now.

Gabriel: I got to sell my plums. I done sold some tomatoes. Got me two quarters. Wanna see? *(He shows Troy his quarters.)* I'm gonna save them and buy me a new horn so St. Peter can hear me when it's time to open the gates. *(Gabriel stops suddenly. Listens.)* Hear that? That's the hellhounds. I got to chase them out of here. Go on get out of here! Get out!

Gabriel exits singing.

Better get ready for the judgment
Better get ready for the judgment
My Lord is coming down

Rose enters from the house.

Troy: He's gone off somewhere.

Gabriel (offstage): Better get ready for the judgment
Better get ready for the judgment morning
Better get ready for the judgment
My God is coming down

Rose: He ain't eating right. Miss Pearl say she can't get him to eat nothing.

Troy: What you want me to do about it, Rose? I done did everything I can for the man. I can't make him get well. Man got half his head blown away . . . what you expect?

Rose: Seem like something ought to be done to help him.

St. Peter: One of Jesus's disciples, believed to be the keeper of the gates of Heaven.

Troy: Man don't bother nobody. He just mixed up from that metal plate he got in his head. Ain't no sense for him to go back into the hospital.

Rose: Least he be eating right. They can help him take care of himself.

Troy: Don't nobody wanna be locked up, Rose. What you wanna lock him up for? Man go over there and fight the war . . . messin' around with them Japs, get half his head blown off . . . and they give him a lousy three thousand dollars. And I had to swoop down on that.

Rose: Is you fixing to go into that again?

Troy: That's the only way I got a roof over my head . . . cause of that metal plate.

Rose: Ain't no sense you blaming yourself for nothing. Gabe wasn't in no condition to manage that money. You done what was right by him. Can't nobody say you ain't done what was right by him. Look how long you took care of him . . . till he wanted to have his own place and moved over there with Miss Pearl.

Troy: That ain't what I'm saying, woman! I'm just stating the facts. If my brother didn't have that metal plate in his head . . . I wouldn't have a pot to piss in or a window to throw it out of. And I'm fifty-three years old. Now see if you can understand that!

Troy gets up from the porch and starts to exit the yard.

Rose: Where you going off to? You been running out of here every Saturday for weeks. I thought you was gonna work on this fence?

Troy: I'm gonna walk down to Taylors'. Listen to the ball game. I'll be back in a bit. I'll work on it when I get back.

He exits the yard. The lights go to black.

Scene III

The lights come up on the yard. It is four hours later. Rose is taking down the clothes from the line. Cory enters carrying his football equipment.

Rose: Your daddy like to had a fit with you running out of here this morning without doing your chores.

Cory: I told you I had to go to practice.

Rose: He say you were supposed to help him with this fence.

Cory: He been saying that the last four or five Saturdays, and then he don't never do nothing, but go down to Taylors. Did you tell him about the recruiter?

Rose: Yeah, I told him.

Cory: What he say?

Rose: He ain't said nothing too much. You get in there and get started on your chores before he gets back. Go on and scrub down them steps before he gets back here hollering and carrying on.

Cory: I'm hungry. What you got to eat, Mama?

Rose: Go on and get started on your chores. I got some meat loaf in there. Go on and make you a sandwich . . . and don't leave no mess in there.

Cory exits into the house. Rose continues to take down the clothes. Troy enters the yard and sneaks up and grabs her from behind.

Troy! Go on, now. You liked to scared me to death. What was the score of the game? Lucille had me on the phone and I couldn't keep up with it.

Troy: What I care about the game? Come here, woman. *(He tries to kiss her.)*

Rose: I thought you went down Taylors' to listen to the game. Go on, Troy! You supposed to be putting up this fence.

Troy (attempting to kiss her again): I'll put it up when I finish with what is at hand.

Rose: Go on, Troy. I ain't studying you.

Troy (chasing after her): I'm studying you . . . fixing to do my homework!

Rose: Troy, you better leave me alone.

Troy: Where's Cory? That boy brought his butt home yet?

Rose: He's in the house doing his chores.

Troy (calling): Cory! Get your butt out here, boy!

> *Rose exits into the house with the laundry. Troy goes over to the pile of wood, picks up a board, and starts sawing. Cory enters from the house.*

Troy: You just now coming in here from leaving this morning?

Cory: Yeah, I had to go to football practice.

Troy: Yeah, what?

Cory: Yessir.

Troy: I ain't but two seconds off you noway. The garbage sitting in there overflowing . . . you ain't done none of your chores . . . and you come in here talking about "Yeah."

Cory: I was just getting ready to do my chores now, Pop . . .

Troy: Your first chore is to help me with this fence on Saturday. Everything else come after that. Now get that saw and cut them boards.

> *Cory takes the saw and begins cutting the boards. Troy continues working. There is a long pause.*

Cory: Hey, Pop . . . why don't you buy a TV?

Troy: What I want with a TV? What I want one of them for?

Cory: Everybody got one. Earl, Ba Bra . . . Jesse!

Troy: I ain't asked you who had one. I say what I want with one?

Cory: So you can watch it. They got lots of things on TV. Baseball games and everything. We could watch the World Series.

Troy: Yeah . . . and how much this TV cost?

Cory: I don't know. They got them on sale for around two hundred dollars.

Troy: Two hundred dollars, huh?

Cory: That ain't that much, Pop.

Troy: Naw, it's just two hundred dollars. See that roof you got over your head at night? Let me tell you something about that roof. It's been over ten years since that roof was last tarred. See now . . . the snow come this winter and sit up there on that roof like it is . . . and it's gonna seep inside. It's just gonna be a little bit . . . ain't gonna hardly notice it. Then the next thing you know, it's gonna be leaking all over the house. Then the wood rot from all that water and you gonna need a whole new roof. Now, how much you think it cost to get that roof tarred?

Cory: I don't know.

Troy: Two hundred and sixty-four dollars . . . cash money. While you thinking about a TV, I got to be thinking about the roof . . . and whatever else go wrong here. Now if you had two hundred dollars, what would you do . . . fix the roof or buy a TV?

Cory: I'd buy a TV. Then when the roof started to leak . . . when it needed fixing . . . I'd fix it.

Troy: Where you gonna get the money from? You done spent it for a TV. You gonna sit up and watch the water run all over your brand new TV.

Cory: Aw, Pop. You got money. I know you do.

Troy: Where I got it at, huh?

Cory: You got it in the bank.

Troy: You wanna see my bankbook? You wanna see that seventy-three dollars and twenty-two cents I got sitting up in there.

Cory: You ain't got to pay for it all at one time. You can put a down payment on it and carry it on home with you.

Troy: Not me. I ain't gonna owe nobody nothing if I can help it. Miss a payment and they come and snatch it right out your house. Then what you got? Now, soon as I get two hundred dollars clear, then I'll buy a TV. Right now, as soon as I get two hundred and sixty-four dollars, I'm gonna have this roof tarred.

Cory: Aw . . . Pop!

Troy: You go on and get you two hundred dollars and buy one if ya want it. I got better things to do with my money.

Cory: I can't get no two hundred dollars. I ain't never seen two hundred dollars.

Troy: I'll tell you what . . . you get you a hundred dollars and I'll put the other hundred with it.

Cory: All right, I'm gonna show you.

Troy: You gonna show me how you can cut them boards right now.

Cory begins to cut the boards. There is a long pause.

Cory: The Pirates won today. That makes five in a row.

Troy: I ain't thinking about the Pirates. Got an all-white team. Got that boy . . . that Puerto Rican boy . . . Clemente. Don't even half-play him. That boy could be something if they give him a chance. Play him one day and sit him on the bench the next.

Cory: He gets a lot of chances to play.

Troy: I'm talking about playing regular. Playing every day so you can get your timing. That's what I'm talking about.

Cory: They got some white guys on the team that don't play every day. You can't play everybody at the same time.

Troy: If they got a white fellow sitting on the bench . . . you can bet your last dollar he can't play! The colored guy got to be twice as good before he get on the team. That's why I don't want you to get all tied up in them sports. Man on the team and what it get him? They got colored on the team and don't use them. Same as not having them. All them teams the same.

Cory: The Braves got Hank Aaron and Wes Covington. Hank Aaron hit two home runs today. That makes forty-three.

Troy: Hank Aaron ain't nobody. That what you supposed to do. That's how you supposed to play the game. Ain't nothing to it. It's just a matter of timing . . . getting the right follow-through. Hell, I can hit forty-three home runs right now!

Cory: Not off no major-league pitching, you couldn't.

Troy: We had better pitching in the Negro leagues. I hit seven home runs off of Satchel Paige.° You can't get no better than that!

Cory: Sandy Koufax. He's leading the league in strikeouts.

Troy: I ain't thinking of no Sandy Koufax.

Cory: You got Warren Spahn and Lew Burdette. I bet you couldn't hit no home runs off of Warren Spahn.

Troy: I'm through with it now. You go on and cut them boards. *(Pause.)* Your mama tell me you done got recruited by a college football team? Is that right?

Cory: Yeah. Coach Zellman say the recruiter gonna be coming by to talk to you. Get you to sign the permission papers.

Troy: I thought you supposed to be working down there at the A&P. Ain't you suppose to be working down there after school?

Cory: Mr. Stawicki say he gonna hold my job for me until after the football season. Say starting next week I can work weekends.

Troy: I thought we had an understanding about this football stuff? You suppose to keep up with your chores and hold that job down at the A&P. Ain't been around here all day on a Saturday. Ain't none of your chores done . . . and now you telling me you done quit your job.

Cory: I'm going to be working weekends.

Troy: You damn right you are! And ain't no need for nobody coming around here to talk to me about signing nothing.

Cory: Hey, Pop . . . you can't do that. He's coming all the way from North Carolina.

Troy: I don't care where he coming from. The white man ain't gonna let you get nowhere with that football noway. You go on and get your book-learning so you can work yourself up in that A&P or learn how to fix cars or build houses or something, get you a trade. That way you have something can't nobody take away from you. You go on and learn how to put your hands to some good use. Besides hauling people's garbage.

Cory: I get good grades, Pop. That's why the recruiter wants to talk with you. You got to keep up your grades to get recruited. This way I'll be going to college. I'll get a chance . . .

Troy: First you gonna get your butt down there to the A&P and get your job back.

Cory: Mr. Stawicki done already hired somebody else 'cause I told him I was playing football.

Troy: You a bigger fool than I thought . . . to let somebody take away your job so you can play some football. Where you gonna get your money to take out your girlfriend and whatnot? What kind of foolishness is that to let somebody take away your job?

Cory: I'm still gonna be working weekends.

Troy: Naw . . . naw. You getting your butt out of here and finding you another job.

Cory: Come on, Pop! I got to practice. I can't work after school and play football too. The team needs me. That's what Coach Zellman say . . .

Troy: I don't care what nobody else say. I'm the boss . . . you understand? I'm the boss around here. I do the only saying what counts.

Satchel Paige (1906?–1982): Legendary black pitcher in the Negro leagues.

Cory: Come on, Pop!

Troy: I asked you . . . did you understand?

Cory: Yeah . . .

Troy: What?!

Cory: Yessir.

Troy: You go on down there to that A&P and see if you can get your job back. If
   you can't do both . . . then you quit the football team. You've got to take
   the crookeds with the straights.

Cory: Yessir. *(Pause.)* Can I ask you a question?

Troy: What the hell you wanna ask me? Mr. Stawicki the one you got the questions for.

Cory: How come you ain't never liked me?

Troy: Liked you? Who the hell say I got to like you? What law is there say I got
   to like you? Wanna stand up in my face and ask a damn fool-ass question
   like that. Talking about liking somebody. Come here, boy, when I talk to
   you.

   *Cory comes over to where Troy is working. He stands slouched over and Troy
   shoves him on his shoulder.*

   Straighten up, goddammit! I asked you a question . . . what law is there
   say I got to like you?

Cory: None.

Troy: Well, all right then! Don't you eat every day? *(Pause.)* Answer me when I
   talk to you! Don't you eat every day?

Cory: Yeah.

Troy: Nigger, as long as you in my house, you put that sir on the end of it when
   you talk to me!

Cory: Yes . . . sir.

Troy: You eat every day.

Cory: Yessir!

Troy: Got a roof over your head.

Cory: Yessir!

Troy: Got clothes on your back.

Cory: Yessir.

Troy: Why you think that is?

Cory: Cause of you.

Troy: Ah, hell I know it's cause of me . . . but why do you think that is?

Cory (hesitant): Cause you like me.

Troy: Like you? I go out of here every morning . . . bust my butt . . . putting up
   with them crackers° every day . . . cause I like you? You are the biggest fool
   I ever saw. *(Pause.)* It's my job. It's my responsibility! You understand that?
   A man got to take care of his family. You live in my house . . . sleep you
   behind on my bedclothes . . . fill you belly up with my food . . . cause you
   my son. You my flesh and blood. Not cause I like you! Cause it's my duty
   to take care of you. I owe a responsibility to you! Let's get this straight
   right here . . . before it go along any further . . . I ain't got to like you. Mr.
   Rand don't give me my money come payday cause he likes me. He give me
   cause he owe me. I done give you everything I had to give you. I gave you

---

crackers: White people, often used to refer disparagingly to poor whites.

your life! Me and your mama worked that out between us. And liking your black ass wasn't part of the bargain. Don't you try and go through life worrying about if somebody like you or not. You best be making sure they doing right by you. You understand what I'm saying, boy?

Cory: Yessir.

Troy: Then get the hell out of my face, and get on down to that A&P.

Rose has been standing behind the screen door for much of the scene. She enters as Cory exits.

Rose: Why don't you let the boy go ahead and play football, Troy? Ain't no harm in that. He's just trying to be like you with the sports.

Troy: I don't want him to be like me! I want him to move as far away from my life as he can get. You the only decent thing that ever happened to me. I wish him that. But I don't wish him a thing else from my life. I decided seventeen years ago that boy wasn't getting involved in no sports. Not after what they did to me in the sports.

Rose: Troy, why don't you admit you was too old to play in the major leagues? For once . . . why don't you admit that?

Troy: What do you mean too old? Don't come telling me I was too old. I just wasn't the right color. Hell, I'm fifty-three years old and can do better than Selkirk's .269 right now!

Rose: How's was you gonna play ball when you were over forty? Sometimes I can't get no sense out of you.

Troy: I got good sense, woman. I got sense enough not to let my boy get hurt over playing no sports. You been mothering that boy too much. Worried about if people like him.

Rose: Everything that boy do . . . he do for you. He wants you to say "Good job, son." That's all.

Troy: Rose, I ain't got time for that. He's alive. He's healthy. He's got to make his own way. I made mine. Ain't nobody gonna hold his hand when he get out there in that world.

Rose: Times have changed from when you was young, Troy. People change. The world's changing around you and you can't even see it.

Troy (*slow, methodical*): Woman . . . I do the best I can do. I come in here every Friday. I carry a sack of potatoes and a bucket of lard. You all line up at the door with your hands out. I give you the lint from my pockets. I give you my sweat and my blood. I ain't got no tears. I done spent them. We go upstairs in that room at night . . . and I fall down on you and try to blast a hole into forever. I get up Monday morning . . . find my lunch on the table. I go out. Make my way. Find my strength to carry me through to the next Friday. (*Pause.*) That's all I got, Rose. That's all I got to give. I can't give nothing else.

Troy exits into the house. The lights go down to black.

Scene IV

It is Friday. Two weeks later. Cory starts out of the house with his football equipment. The phone rings.

Cory (*calling*): I got it! (*He answers the phone and stands in the screen door talking.*) Hello? Hey, Jesse. Naw . . . I was just getting ready to leave now.

Rose (calling): Cory!

Cory: I told you, man, them spikes is all tore up. You can use them if you want, but they ain't no good. Earl got some spikes.

Rose (calling): Cory!

Cory (calling to Rose): Mam? I'm talking to Jesse. *(Into phone.)* When she say that? *(Pause.)* Aw, you lying, man. I'm gonna tell her you said that.

Rose (calling): Cory, don't you go nowhere!

Cory: I got to go to the game, Ma! *(Into the phone.)* Yeah, hey, look, I'll talk to you later. Yeah, I'll meet you over Earl's house. Later. Bye, Ma.

> *Cory exits the house and starts out the yard.*

Rose: Cory, where you going off to? You got that stuff all pulled out and thrown all over your room.

Cory (in the yard): I was looking for my spikes. Jesse wanted to borrow my spikes.

Rose: Get up there and get that cleaned up before your daddy get back in here.

Cory: I got to go to the game! I'll clean it up *when I get back.*

> *Cory exits.*

Rose: That's all he need to do is see that room all messed up.

> *Rose exits into the house. Troy and Bono enter the yard. Troy is dressed in clothes other than his work clothes.*

Bono: He told him the same thing he told you. Take it to the union.

Troy: Brownie ain't got that much sense. Man wasn't thinking about nothing. He wait until I confront them on it . . . then he wanna come crying seniority. *(Calls.)* Hey, Rose!

Bono: I wish I could have seen Mr. Rand's face when he told you.

Troy: He couldn't get it out of his mouth! Liked to bit his tongue! When they called me down there to the Commissioner's office . . . he thought they was gonna fire me. Like everybody else.

Bono: I didn't think they was gonna fire you. I thought they was gonna put you on the warning paper.

Troy: Hey, Rose! *(To Bono.)* Yeah, Mr. Rand like to bit his tongue.

> *Troy breaks the seal on the bottle, takes a drink, and hands it to Bono.*

Bono: I see you run right down to Taylors' and told that Alberta gal.

Troy (calling): Hey Rose! *(To Bono.)* I told everybody. Hey, Rose! I went down there to cash my check.

Rose (entering from the house): Hush all that hollering, man! I know you out here. What they say down there at the Commissioner's office?

Troy: You supposed to come when I call you, woman. Bono'll tell you that. *(To Bono.)* Don't Lucille come when you call her?

Rose: Man, hush your mouth. I ain't no dog . . . talk about "come when you call me."

Troy (puts his arm around Rose): You hear this, Bono? I had me an old dog used to get uppity like that. You say, "C'mere, Blue!" . . . and he just lay there and look at you. End up getting a stick and chasing him away trying to make him come.

Rose: I ain't studying you and your dog. I remember you used to sing that old song.

Troy (he sings): Hear it ring! Hear it ring! I had a dog his name was Blue.

Rose: Don't nobody wanna hear you sing that old song.

Troy (sings): You know Blue was mighty true.

Rose: Used to have Cory running around here singing that song.

Bono: Hell, I remember that song myself.

Troy (sings): You know Blue was a good old dog.

Blue treed a possum in a hollow log.

That was my daddy's song. My daddy made up that song.

Rose: I don't care who made it up. Don't nobody wanna hear you sing it.

Troy (makes a song like calling a dog): Come here, woman.

Rose: You come in here carrying on, I reckon they ain't fired you. What they say down there at the Commissioner's office?

Troy: Look here, Rose . . . Mr. Rand called me into his office today when I got back from talking to them people down there . . . it come from up top . . . he called me in and told me they was making me a driver.

Rose: Troy, you kidding!

Troy: No I ain't. Ask Bono.

Rose: Well, that's great, Troy. Now you don't have to hassle them people no more.

Lyons enters from the street.

Troy: Aw hell, I wasn't looking to see you today. I thought you was in jail. Got it all over the front page of the *Courier* about them raiding Sefus's place . . . where you be hanging out with all them thugs.

Lyons: Hey, Pop . . . that ain't got nothing to do with me. I don't go down there gambling. I go down there to sit in with the band. I ain't got nothing to do with the gambling part. They got some good music down there.

Troy: They got some rogues . . . is what they got.

Lyons: How you been, Mr. Bono? Hi, Rose.

Bono: I see where you playing down at the Crawford Grill tonight.

Rose: How come you ain't brought Bonnie like I told you? You should have brought Bonnie with you, she ain't been over in a month of Sundays.

Lyons: I was just in the neighborhood . . . thought I'd stop by.

Troy: Here he come . . .

Bono: Your daddy got a promotion on the rubbish. He's gonna be the first colored driver. Ain't got to do nothing but sit up there and read the paper like them white fellows.

Lyons: Hey, Pop . . . if you knew how to read you'd be all right.

Bono: Naw . . . naw . . . you mean if the nigger knew how to *drive* he'd be all right. Been fighting with them people about driving and ain't even got a license. Mr. Rand know you ain't got no driver's license?

Troy: Driving ain't nothing. All you do is point the truck where you want it to go. Driving ain't nothing.

Bono: Do Mr. Rand know you ain't got no driver's license? That's what I'm talking about. I ain't asked if driving was easy. I asked if Mr. Rand know you ain't got no driver's license.

Troy: He ain't got to know. The man ain't got to know my business. Time he find out, I have two or three driver's licenses.

Lyons (going into his pocket): Say, look here, Pop . . .

Troy: I knew it was coming. Didn't I tell you, Bono? I know what kind of "Look here, Pop" that was. The nigger fixing to ask me for some money. It's Fri-

day night. It's my payday. All them rogues down there on the avenue . . .
the ones that ain't in jail . . . and Lyons is hopping in his shoes to get
down there with them.

Lyons: See, Pop . . . if you give somebody else a chance to talk sometimes,
you'd see that I was fixing to pay you back your ten dollars like I told you.
Here . . . I told you I'd pay you when Bonnie got paid.

Troy: Naw . . . you go ahead and keep that ten dollars. Put it in the bank. The
next time you feel like you wanna come by here and ask me for something . . . you go on down there and get that.

Lyons: Here's your ten dollars, Pop. I told you I don't want you to give me
nothing. I just wanted to borrow ten dollars.

Troy: Naw . . . you go on and keep that for the next time you want to ask me.

Lyons: Come on, Pop . . . here go your ten dollars.

Rose: Why don't you go on and let the boy pay you back, Troy?

Lyons: Here you go, Rose. If you don't take it I'm gonna have to hear about it
for the next six months. *(He hands her the money.)*

Rose: You can hand yours over here too, Troy.

Troy: You see this, Bono. You see how they do me.

Bono: Yeah, Lucille do me the same way.

> *Gabriel is heard singing offstage. He enters.*

Gabriel: Better get ready for the Judgment! Better get ready for . . . Hey! . . .
Hey! . . . There's Troy's boy!

Lyons: How are you doing, Uncle Gabe?

Gabriel: Lyons . . . The King of the Jungle! Rose . . . hey, Rose. Got a flower for
you. *(He takes a rose from his pocket.)* Picked it myself. That's the same rose
like you is!

Rose: That's right nice of you, Gabe.

Lyons: What you been doing, Uncle Gabe?

Gabriel: Oh, I been chasing hellhounds and waiting on the time to tell St.
Peter to open the gates.

Lyons: You been chasing hellhounds, huh? Well . . . you doing the right thing,
Uncle Gabe. Somebody got to chase them.

Gabriel: Oh, yeah . . . I know it. The devil's strong. The devil ain't no pushover.
Hellhounds snipping at everybody's heels. But I got my trumpet waiting
on the judgment time.

Lyons: Waiting on the Battle of Armageddon, huh?

Gabriel: Ain't gonna be too much of a battle when God get to waving that
Judgment sword. But the people's gonna have a hell of a time trying to get
into heaven if them gates ain't open.

Lyons (putting his arm around Gabriel): You hear this, Pop. Uncle Gabe, you all
right!

Gabriel (laughing with Lyons): Lyons! King of the Jungle.

Rose: You gonna stay for supper, Gabe? Want me to fix you a plate?

Gabriel: I'll take a sandwich, Rose. Don't want no plate. Just wanna eat with
my hands. I'll take a sandwich.

Rose: How about you, Lyons? You staying? Got some short ribs cooking.

Lyons: Naw, I won't eat nothing till after we finished playing. *(Pause.)* You
ought to come down and listen to me play Pop.

Troy: I don't like that Chinese music. All that noise.

Rose: Go on in the house and wash up, Gabe . . . I'll fix you a sandwich.

Gabriel (to Lyons, as he exits): Troy's mad at me.

Lyons: What you mad at Uncle Gabe for, Pop?

Rose: He thinks Troy's mad at him cause he moved over to Miss Pearl's.

Troy: I ain't mad at the man. He can live where he want to live at.

Lyons: What he move over there for? Miss Pearl don't like nobody.

Rose: She don't mind him none. She treats him real nice. She just don't allow
all that singing.

Troy: She don't mind that rent he be paying . . . that's what she don't mind.

Rose: Troy, I ain't going through that with you no more. He's over there cause
he want to have his own place. He can come and go as he please.

Troy: Hell, he could come and go as he please here. I wasn't stopping him. I
ain't put no rules on him.

Rose: It ain't the same thing, Troy. And you know it.

    Gabriel comes to the door.

    Now, that's the last I wanna hear about that. I don't wanna hear nothing
else about Gabe and Miss Pearl. And next week . . .

Gabriel: I'm ready for my sandwich, Rose.

Rose: And next week . . . when that recruiter come from that school . . . I want
you to sign that paper and go on and let Cory play football. Then that'll be
the last I have to hear about that.

Troy (to Rose as she exits into the house): I ain't thinking about Cory nothing.

Lyons: What . . . Cory got recruited? What school he going to?

Troy: That boy walking around here smelling his piss . . . thinking he's grown.
Thinking he's gonna do what he want, irrespective of what I say. Look
here, Bono . . . I left the Commissioner's office and went down to the
A&P . . . that boy ain't working down there. He lying to me. Telling me he
got his job back . . . telling me he working weekends . . . telling me he
working after school . . . Mr. Stawicki tell me he ain't working down there
at all!

Lyons: Cory just growing up. He's just busting at the seams trying to fill out
your shoes.

Troy: I don't care what he's doing. When he get to the point where he wanna
disobey me . . . then it's time for him to move on. Bono'll tell you that. I
bet he ain't never disobeyed his daddy without paying the consequences.

Bono: I ain't never had a chance. My daddy came on through . . . but I ain't
never knew him to see him . . . or what he had on his mind or where he
went. Just moving on through. Searching out the New Land. That's what
the old folks used to call it. See a fellow moving around from place to
place . . . woman to woman . . . called it searching out the New Land. I
can't say if he ever found it. I come along, didn't want no kids. Didn't
know if I was gonna be in one place long enough to fix on them right as
their daddy. I figured I was going searching too. As it turned out I been
hooked up with Lucille near about as long as your daddy been with Rose.
Going on sixteen years.

Troy: Sometimes I wish I hadn't known my daddy. He ain't cared nothing
about no kids. A kid to him wasn't nothing. All he wanted was for you to
learn how to walk so he could start you to working. When it come time for
eating . . . he ate first. If there was anything left over, that's what you got.
Man would sit down and eat two chickens and give you the wing.

Lyons: You ought to stop that, Pop. Everybody feed their kids. No matter how hard times is . . . everybody care about their kids. Make sure they have something to eat.

Troy: The only thing my daddy cared about was getting them bales of cotton in to Mr. Lubin. That's the only thing that mattered to him. Sometimes I used to wonder why he was living. Wonder why the devil hadn't come and got him. "Get them bales of cotton in to Mr. Lubin" and find out he owe him money . . .

Lyons: He should have just went on and left when he saw he couldn't get nowhere. That's what I would have done.

Troy: How he gonna leave with eleven kids? And where he gonna go? He ain't knew how to do nothing but farm. No, he was trapped and I think he knew it. But I'll say this for him . . . he felt a responsibility toward us. Maybe he ain't treated us the way I felt he should have . . . but without that responsibility he could have walked off and left us . . . made his own way.

Bono: A lot of them did. Back in those days what you talking about . . . they walk out their front door and just take on down one road or another and keep on walking.

Lyons: There you go! That's what I'm talking about.

Bono: Just keep on walking till you come to something else. Ain't you never heard of nobody having the walking blues? Well, that's what you call it when you just take off like that.

Troy: My daddy ain't had them walking blues! What you talking about? He stayed right there with his family. But he was just as evil as he could be. My mama couldn't stand him. Couldn't stand that evilness. She run off when I was about eight. She sneaked off one night after he had gone to sleep. Told me she was coming back for me. I ain't never seen her no more. All his women run off and left him. He wasn't good for nobody.

When my turn come to head out, I was fourteen and got to sniffing around Joe Canewell's daughter. Had us an old mule we called Greyboy. My daddy sent me out to do some plowing and I tied up Greyboy and went to fooling around with Joe Canewell's daughter. We done found us a nice little spot, got real cozy with each other. She about thirteen and we done figured we was grown anyway . . . so we down there enjoying ourselves . . . ain't thinking about nothing. We didn't know Greyboy had got loose and wandered back to the house and my daddy was looking for me. We down there by the creek enjoying ourselves when my daddy come up on us. Surprised us. He had them leather straps off the mule and commenced to whupping me like there was no tomorrow. I jumped up, mad and embarrassed. I was scared of my daddy. When he commenced to whupping on me . . . quite naturally I run to get out of the way. *(Pause.)* Now I thought he was mad cause I ain't done my work. But I see where he was chasing me off so he could have the gal for himself. When I see what the matter of it was, I lost all fear of my daddy. Right there is where I become a man . . . at fourteen years of age. *(Pause.)* Now it was my turn to run him off. I picked up them same reins that he had used on me. I picked up them reins and commenced to whupping on him. The gal jumped up and run off . . . and when my daddy turned to face me, I could see why the devil had never come to get him . . . cause he was the devil himself. I don't know what happened. When I woke up, I was laying right there by the creek, and Blue . . . this old dog we had . . . was licking my face. I thought I was blind. I couldn't see nothing. Both my eyes were swollen shut. I laid there and cried. I didn't know what I was gonna do. The only thing I knew was the time had come for me to leave my daddy's house. And right there the world suddenly got big. And it was a long time before I could cut it down to where I could handle it.

Part of that cutting down was when I got to the place where I could feel him kicking in my blood and knew that the only thing that separated us was the matter of a few years.

Gabriel enters from the house with a sandwich.

Lyons: What you got there, Uncle Gabe?

Gabriel: Got me a ham sandwich. Rose gave me a ham sandwich.

Troy: I don't know what happened to him. I done lost touch with everybody except Gabriel. But I hope he's dead. I hope he found some peace.

Lyons: That's a heavy story, Pop. I didn't know you left home when you was fourteen.

Troy: And didn't know nothing. The only part of the world I knew was the forty-two acres of Mr. Lubin's land. That's all I knew about life.

Lyons: Fourteen's kinda young to be out on your own. *(Phone rings.)* I don't even think I was ready to be out on my own at fourteen. I don't know what I would have done.

Troy: I got up from the creek and walked on down to Mobile. I was through with farming. Figured I could do better in the city. So I walked the two hundred miles to Mobile.

Lyons: Wait a minute . . . you ain't walked no two hundred miles, Pop. Ain't nobody gonna walk no two hundred miles. You talking about some walking there.

Bono: That's the only way you got anywhere back in them days.

Lyons: Shhh. Damn if I wouldn't have hitched a ride with somebody!

Troy: Who you gonna hitch it with? They ain't had no cars and things like they got now. We talking about 1918.

Rose (entering): What you all out here getting into?

Troy (to Rose): I'm telling Lyons how good he got it. He don't know nothing about this I'm talking.

Rose: Lyons, that was Bonnie on the phone. She say you supposed to pick her up.

Lyons: Yeah, okay, Rose.

Troy: I walked on down to Mobile and hitched up with some of them fellows that was heading this way. Got up here and found out . . . not only couldn't you get a job . . . you couldn't find no place to live. I thought I was in freedom. Shhh. Colored folks living down there on the riverbanks in whatever kind of shelter they could find for themselves. Right down there under the Brady Street Bridge. Living in shacks made of sticks and tarpaper. Messed around there and went from bad to worse. Started stealing. First it was food. Then I figured, hell, if I steal money I can buy me some food. Buy me some shoes too! One thing led to another. Met your mama. I was young and anxious to be a man. Met your mama and had you. What I do that for? Now I got to worry about feeding you and her. Got to steal three times as much. Went out one day looking for somebody to rob . . . that's what I was, a robber. I'll tell you the truth. I'm ashamed of it today. But it's the truth. Went to rob this fellow . . . pulled out my knife . . . and he pulled out a gun. Shot me in the chest. I felt just like somebody had taken a hot branding iron and laid it on me. When he shot me I jumped at him with my knife. They told me I killed him and they put me in the penitentiary and locked me up for fifteen years. That's where I met Bono. That's where I learned how to play baseball. Got out that place and your mama had taken you and went on to make life without me. Fifteen years was a long time for her to wait. But that fifteen years cured me of that robbing stuff. Rose'll tell you. She asked me when I met her if I had gotten all that foolishness out of my system. And I told her, "Baby, it's you and baseball all what count with me." You hear me, Bono? I meant it too. She say, "Which one comes first?" I told her, "Baby, ain't no doubt it's baseball . . . but you stick and get old with me and we'll both outlive this baseball." Am I right, Rose? And it's true.

Rose: Man, hush your mouth. You ain't said no such thing. Talking about, "Baby, you know you'll always be number one with me." That's what you was talking.

Troy: You hear that, Bono. That's why I love her.

Bono: Rose'll keep you straight. You get off the track, she'll straighten you up.

Rose: Lyons, you better get on up and get Bonnie. She waiting on you.

Lyons (gets up to go): Hey, Pop, why don't you come on down to the Grill and hear me play?

Troy: I ain't going down there. I'm too old to be sitting around in them clubs.

Bono: You got to be good to play down at the Grill.

Lyons: Come on, Pop . . .

Troy: I got to get up in the morning.

Lyons: You ain't got to stay long.

Troy: Naw, I'm gonna get my supper and go on to bed.

Lyons: Well, I got to go. I'll see you again.

Troy: Don't you come around my house on my payday.

Rose: Pick up the phone and let somebody know you coming. And bring Bonnie with you. You know I'm always glad to see her.

Lyons: Yeah, I'll do that, Rose. You take care now. See you, Pop. See you, Mr. Bono. See you, Uncle Gabe.

Gabriel: Lyons! King of the Jungle!

> *Lyons exits.*

Troy: Is supper ready, woman? Me and you got some business to take care of. I'm gonna tear it up too.

Rose: Troy, I done told you now!

Troy (puts his arm around Bono): Aw hell, woman . . . this is Bono. Bono like family. I done known this nigger since . . . how long I done know you?

Bono: It's been a long time.

Troy: I done know this nigger since Skippy was a pup. Me and him done been through some times.

Bono: You sure right about that.

Troy: Hell, I know him longer than I known you. And we still standing shoulder to shoulder. Hey, look here, Bono . . . a man can't ask for no more than that. *(Drinks to him.)* I love you, nigger.

Bono: Hell, I love you too . . . I got to get home see my woman. You got yours in hand. I got to go get mine.

Bono starts to exit as Cory enters the yard, dressed in his football uniform. He gives Troy a hard, uncompromising look.

Cory: What you do that for, Pop?

He throws his helmet down in the direction of Troy.

Rose: What's the matter? Cory . . . what's the matter?

Cory: Papa done went up to the school and told Coach Zellman I can't play football no more. Wouldn't even let me play the game. Told him to tell the recruiter not to come.

Rose: Troy . . .

Troy: What you Troying me for. Yeah, I did it. And the boy know why I did it.

Cory: Why you wanna do that to me? That was the one chance I had.

Rose: Ain't nothing wrong with Cory playing football, Troy.

Troy: The boy lied to me. I told the nigger if he wanna play football . . . to keep up his chores and hold down that job at the A&P. That was the conditions. Stopped down there to see Mr. Stawicki . . .

Cory: I can't work after school during the football season, Pop! I tried to tell you that Mr. Stawicki's holding my job for me. You don't never want to listen to nobody. And then you wanna go and do this to me!

Troy: I ain't done nothing to you. You done it to yourself.

Cory: Just cause you didn't have a chance! You just scared I'm gonna be better than you, that's all.

Troy: Come here.

Rose: Troy . . .

Cory reluctantly crosses over to Troy.

Troy: All right! See. You done made a mistake.

Cory: I didn't even do nothing!

Troy: I'm gonna tell you what your mistake was. See . . . you swung at the ball and didn't hit it. That's strike one. See, you in the batter's box now. You swung and you missed. That's strike one. Don't you strike out!

Lights fade to black.

ACT II

Scene I

The following morning. Cory is at the tree hitting the ball with the bat. He tries to mimic Troy, but his swing is awkward, less sure. Rose enters from the house.

Rose: Cory, I want you to help me with this cupboard.

Cory: I ain't quitting the team. I don't care what Poppa say.

Rose: I'll talk to him when he gets back. He had to go see about your Uncle Gabe. The police done arrested him. Say he was disturbing the peace. He'll be back directly. Come on in here and help me clean out the top of this cupboard.

Cory exits into the house. Rose sees Troy and Bono coming down the alley.

Troy . . . what they say down there?

Troy: Ain't said nothing. I give them fifty dollars and they let him go. I'll talk to you about it. Where's Cory?

Rose: He's in there helping me clean out these cupboards.

Troy: Tell him to get his butt out here.

Troy and Bono go over to the pile of wood. Bono picks up the saw and begins sawing.

Troy (to Bono): All they want is the money. That makes six or seven times I done went down there and got him. See me coming they stick out their hands.

Bono: Yeah. I know what you mean. That's all they care about . . . that money. They don't care about what's right. *(Pause.)* Nigger, why you got to go and get some hard wood? You ain't doing nothing but building a little old fence. Get you some soft pine wood. That's all you need.

Troy: I know what I'm doing. This is outside wood. You put pine wood inside the house. Pine wood is inside wood. This here is outside wood. Now you tell me where the fence is gonna be?

Bono: You don't need this wood. You can put it up with pine wood and it'll stand as long as you gonna be here looking at it.

Troy: How you know how long I'm gonna be here, nigger? Hell, I might just live forever. Live longer than old man Horsely.

Bono: That's what Magee used to say.

Troy: Magee's a damn fool. Now you tell me who you ever heard of gonna pull their own teeth with a pair of rusty pliers.

Bono: The old folks . . . my granddaddy used to pull his teeth with pliers. They ain't had no dentists for the colored folks back then.

Troy: Get clean pliers! You understand? Clean pliers! Sterilize them! Besides we ain't living back then. All Magee had to do was walk over to Doc Goldblum's.

Bono: I see where you and that Tallahassee gal . . . that Alberta . . . I see where you all done got tight.

Troy: What you mean "got tight"?

Bono: I see where you be laughing and joking with her all the time.

Troy: I laughs and jokes with all of them, Bono. You know me.

Bono: That ain't the kind of laughing and joking I'm talking about.

Cory enters from the house.

Cory: How you doing, Mr. Bono?

Troy: Cory? Get that saw from Bono and cut some wood. He talking about the wood's too hard to cut. Stand back there, Jim, and let that young boy show you how it's done.

Bono: He's sure welcome to it.

Cory takes the saw and begins to cut the wood.

Whew-e-e! Look at that. Big old strong boy. Look like Joe Louis.° Hell, must be getting old the way I'm watching that boy whip through that wood.

Joe Louis (1914–1981): Black American boxer who held the world heavyweight championship title.

Cory: I don't see why Mama want a fence around the yard noways.

Troy: Damn if I know either. What the hell she keeping out with it? She ain't got nothing nobody want.

Bono: Some people build fences to keep people out . . . and other people build fences to keep people in. Rose wants to hold on to you all. She loves you.

Troy: Hell, nigger, I don't need nobody to tell me my wife loves me. Cory . . . go on in the house and see if you can find that other saw.

Cory: Where's it at?

Troy: I said find it! Look for it till you find it!

Cory exits into the house.

What's that supposed to mean? Wanna keep us in?

Bono: Troy . . . I done known you seem like damn near my whole life. You and Rose both. I done know both of you all for a long time. I remember when you met Rose. When you was hitting them baseball out the park. A lot of them old gals was after you then. You had the pick of the litter. When you picked Rose, I was happy for you. That was the first time I knew you had any sense. I said . . . My man Troy knows what he's doing . . . I'm gonna follow this nigger . . . he might take me somewhere. I been following you too. I done learned a whole heap of things about life watching you. I done learned how to tell where the shit lies. How to tell it from the alfalfa. You done learned me a lot of things. You showed me how to not make the same mistakes . . . to take life as it comes along and keep putting one foot in front of the other. *(Pause.)* Rose a good woman, Troy.

Troy: Hell, nigger, I know she a good woman. I been married to her for eighteen years. What you got on your mind, Bono?

Bono: I just say she a good woman. Just like I say anything. I ain't got to have nothing on my mind.

Troy: You just gonna say she a good woman and leave it hanging out there like that? Why you telling me she a good woman?

Bono: She loves you, Troy. Rose loves you.

Troy: You saying I don't measure up. That's what you trying to say. I don't measure up cause I'm seeing this other gal. I know what you trying to say.

Bono: I know what Rose means to you, Troy. I'm just trying to say I don't want to see you mess up.

Troy: Yeah, I appreciate that, Bono. If you was messing around on Lucille I'd be telling you the same thing.

Bono: Well, that's all I got to say. I just say that because I love you both.

Troy: Hell, you know me . . . I wasn't out there looking for nothing. You can't find a better woman than Rose. I know that. But seems like this woman just stuck onto me where I can't shake her loose. I done wrestled with it, tried to throw her off me . . . but she just stuck on tighter. Now she's stuck on for good.

Bono: You's in control . . . that's what you tell me all the time. You responsible for what you do.

Troy: I ain't ducking the responsibility of it. As long as it sets right in my heart . . . then I'm okay. Cause that's all I listen to. It'll tell me right from wrong every time. And I ain't talking about doing Rose no bad turn. I love Rose. She done carried me a long ways and I love and respect her for that.

Bono: I know you do. That's why I don't want to see you hurt her. But what you gonna do when she find out? What you got then? If you try and juggle both of them . . . sooner or later you gonna drop one of them. That's common sense.

Troy: Yeah, I hear what you saying, Bono. I been trying to figure a way to work it out.

Bono: Work it out right, Troy. I don't want to be getting all up between you and Rose's business . . . but work it so it come out right.

Troy: Ah hell, I get all up between you and Lucille's business. When you gonna get that woman that refrigerator she been wanting? Don't tell me you ain't got no money now. I know who your banker is. Mellon don't need that money bad as Lucille want that refrigerator. I'll tell you that.

Bono: Tell you what I'll do . . . when you finish building this fence for Rose . . . I'll buy Lucille that refrigerator.

Troy: You done stuck your foot in your mouth now!

Troy grabs up a board and begins to saw. Bono starts to walk out the yard.

Hey, nigger . . . where you going?

Bono: I'm going home. I know you don't expect me to help you now. I'm protecting my money. I wanna see you put that fence up by yourself. That's what I want to see. You'll be here another six months without me.

Troy: Nigger, you ain't right.

Bono: When it comes to my money . . . I'm right as fireworks on the Fourth of July.

Troy: All right, we gonna see now. You better get out your bankbook.

Bono exits, and Troy continues to work. Rose enters from the house.

Rose: What they say down there? What's happening with Gabe?

Troy: I went down there and got him out. Cost me fifty dollars. Say he was disturbing the peace. Judge set up a hearing for him in three weeks. Say to show cause why he shouldn't be recommitted.

Rose: What was he doing that cause them to arrest him?

Troy: Some kids was teasing him and he run them off home. Say he was howling and carrying on. Some folks seen him and called the police. That's all it was.

Rose: Well, what's you say? What'd you tell the judge?

Troy: Told him I'd look after him. It didn't make no sense to recommit the man. He stuck out his big greasy palm and told me to give him fifty dollars and take him on home.

Rose: Where's he at now? Where'd he go off to?

Troy: He's gone about his business. He don't need nobody to hold his hand.

Rose: Well, I don't know. Seem like that would be the best place for him if they did put him into the hospital. I know what you're gonna say. But that's what I think would be best.

Troy: The man done had his life ruined fighting for what? And they wanna take and lock him up. Let him be free. He don't bother nobody.

Rose: Well, everybody got their own way of looking at it I guess. Come on and get your lunch. I got a bowl of lima beans and some cornbread in the oven. Come and get something to eat. Ain't no sense you fretting over Gabe.

Rose turns to go into the house.

Troy: Rose . . . got something to tell you.

Rose: Well, come on . . . wait till I get this food on the table.

Troy: Rose!

She stops and turns around.

I don't know how to say this. *(Pause.)* I can't explain it none. It just sort of grows on you till it gets out of hand. It starts out like a little bush . . . and the next thing you know it's a whole forest.

Rose: Troy . . . what is you talking about?

Troy: I'm talking, woman, let me talk. I'm trying to find a way to tell you . . . I'm gonna be a daddy. I'm gonna be somebody's daddy.

Rose: Troy . . . you're not telling me this? You're gonna be . . . what?

Troy: Rose . . . now . . . see . . .

Rose: You telling me you gonna be somebody's daddy? You telling your *wife* this?

Gabriel enters from the street. He carries a rose in his hand.

Gabriel: Hey, Troy! Hey, Rose!

Rose: I have to wait eighteen years to hear something like this.

Gabriel: Hey, Rose . . . I got a flower for you. *(He hands it to her.)* That's a rose. Same rose like you is.

Rose: Thanks, Gabe.

Gabriel: Troy, you ain't mad at me is you? Them bad mens come and put me away. You ain't mad at me is you?

Troy: Naw, Gabe, I ain't mad at you.

Rose: Eighteen years and you wanna come with this.

Gabriel (takes a quarter out of his pocket): See what I got? Got a brand new quarter.

Troy: Rose . . . it's just . . .

Rose: Ain't nothing you can say, Troy. Ain't no way of explaining that.

Gabriel: Fellow that give me this quarter had a whole mess of them. I'm gonna keep this quarter till it stop shining.

Rose: Gabe, go on in the house there. I got some watermelon in the Frigidaire. Go on and get you a piece.

Gabriel: Say, Rose . . . you know I was chasing hellhounds and them bad mens come and get me and take me away. Troy helped me. He come down there and told them they better let me go before he beat them up. Yeah, he did!

Rose: You go on and get you a piece of watermelon, Gabe. Them bad mens is gone now.

Gabriel: Okay, Rose . . . gonna get me some watermelon. The kind with the stripes on it.

Gabriel exits into the house.

Rose: Why, Troy? Why? After all these years to come dragging this in to me now. It don't make no sense at your age. I could have expected this ten or fifteen years ago, but not now.

Troy: Age ain't got nothing to do with it, Rose.

Rose: I done tried to be everything a wife should be. Everything a wife could be. Been married eighteen years and I got to live to see the day you tell me you been seeing another woman and done fathered a child by her. And you

know I ain't never wanted no half nothing in my family. My whole family
is half. Everybody got different fathers and mothers . . . my two sisters and
my brother. Can't hardly tell who's who. Can't never sit down and talk
about Papa and Mama. It's your papa and your mama and my papa and
my mama . . .

Troy: Rose . . . stop it now.

Rose: I ain't never wanted that for none of my children. And now you wanna
drag your behind in here and tell me something like this.

Troy: You ought to know. It's time for you to know.

Rose: Well, I don't want to know, goddamn it!

Troy: I can't just make it go away. It's done now. I can't wish the circumstance
of the thing away.

Rose: And you don't want to either. Maybe you want to wish me and my boy
away. Maybe that's what you want? Well, you can't wish us away. I've got
eighteen years of my life invested in you. You ought to have stayed upstairs
in my bed where you belong.

Troy: Rose . . . now listen to me . . . we can get a handle on this thing. We can
talk this out . . . come to an understanding.

Rose: All of a sudden it's "we." Where was "we" at when you was down there
rolling around with some godforsaken woman? "We" should have come to
an understanding before you started making a damn fool of yourself.
You're a day late and a dollar short when it comes to an understanding
with me.

Troy: It's just . . . She gives me a different idea . . . a different understanding
about myself. I can step out of this house and get away from the pressures
and problems . . . be a different man. I ain't got to wonder how I'm gonna
pay the bills or get the roof fixed. I can just be a part of myself that I ain't
never been.

Rose: What I want to know . . . is do you plan to continue seeing her. That's all
you can say to me.

Troy: I can sit up in her house and laugh. Do you understand what I'm saying.
I can laugh out loud . . . and it feels good. It reaches all the way down to
the bottom of my shoes. *(Pause.)* Rose, I can't give that up.

Rose: Maybe you ought to go on and stay down there with her . . . if she's a
better woman than me.

Troy: It ain't about nobody being a better woman or nothing. Rose, you ain't
the blame. A man couldn't ask for no woman to be a better wife than
you've been. I'm responsible for it. I done locked myself into a pattern trying to take care of you all that I forgot about myself.

Rose: What the hell was I there for? That was my job, not somebody else's.

Troy: Rose, I done tried all my life to live decent . . . to live a clean . . . hard . . .
useful life. I tried to be a good husband to you. In every way I knew how.
Maybe I come into the world backwards, I don't know. But . . . you born
with two strikes on you before you come to the plate. You got to guard it
closely . . . always looking for the curve ball on the inside corner. You can't
afford to let none get past you. You can't afford a call strike. If you going
down . . . you going down swinging. Everything lined up against you.
What you gonna do. I fooled them, Rose. I bunted. When I found you and
Cory and a halfway decent job . . . I was safe. Couldn't nothing touch me. I
wasn't gonna strike out no more. I wasn't going back to the penitentiary.

I wasn't gonna lay in the streets with a bottle of wine. I was safe. I had me a family. A job. I wasn't gonna get that last strike. I was on first looking for one of them boys to knock me in. To get me home.

Rose: You should have stayed in my bed, Troy.

Troy: Then when I saw that gal . . . she firmed up my backbone. And I got to thinking that if I tried . . . I just might be able to steal second. Do you understand after eighteen years I wanted to steal second.

Rose: You should have held me tight. You should have grabbed me and held on.

Troy: I stood on first base for eighteen years and I thought . . . well, goddamn it . . . go on for it!

Rose: We're not talking about baseball! We're talking about you going off to lay in bed with another woman . . . and then bring it home to me. That's what we're talking about. We ain't talking about no baseball.

Troy: Rose, you're not listening to me. I'm trying the best I can to explain it to you. It's not easy for me to admit that I been standing in the same place for eighteen years.

Rose: I been standing with you! I been right here with you, Troy. I got a life too. I gave eighteen years of my life to stand in the same spot with you. Don't you think I ever wanted other things? Don't you think I had dreams and hopes? What about my life? What about me. Don't you think it ever crossed my mind to want to know other men? That I wanted to lay up somewhere and forget about my responsibilities? That I wanted someone to make me laugh so I could feel good? You not the only one who's got wants and needs. But I held on to you, Troy. I took all my feelings, my wants and needs, my dreams . . . and I buried them inside you. I planted a seed and watched and prayed over it. I planted myself inside you and waited to bloom. And it didn't take me no eighteen years to find out the soil was hard and rocky and it wasn't never gonna bloom.

But I held on to you, Troy. I held you tighter. You was my husband. I owed you everything I had. Every part of me I could find to give you. And upstairs in that room . . . with the darkness falling in on me . . . I gave everything I had to try and erase the doubt that you wasn't the finest man in the world. And wherever you was going . . . I wanted to be there with you. Cause you was my husband. Cause that's the only way I was gonna survive as your wife. You always talking about what you give . . . and what you don't have to give. But you take too. You take . . . and don't even know nobody's giving!

Rose turns to exit into the house; Troy grabs her arm.

Troy: You say I take and don't give!

Rose: Troy! You're hurting me!

Troy: You say I take and don't give!

Rose: Troy . . . you're hurting my arm! Let go!

Troy: I done give you everything I got. Don't you tell that lie on me.

Rose: Troy!

Troy: Don't you tell that lie on me!

Cory enters from the house.

Cory: Mama!

Rose: Troy. You're hurting me.

Troy: Don't you tell me about no taking and giving.

Cory comes up behind Troy and grabs him. Troy, surprised, is thrown off balance just as Cory throws a glancing blow that catches him on the chest and knocks him down. Troy is stunned, as is Cory.

Rose: Troy. Troy. No!

Troy gets to his feet and starts at Cory.

Troy . . . no. Please! Troy!

Rose pulls on Troy to hold him back. Troy stops himself.

Troy (to Cory): All right. That's strike two. You stay away from around me, boy. Don't you strike out. You living with a full count. Don't you strike out.

Troy exits out the yard as the lights go down.

SCENE II

It is six months later, early afternoon. Troy enters from the house and starts to exit the yard. Rose enters from the house.

Rose: Troy, I want to talk to you.

Troy: All of a sudden, after all this time, you want to talk to me, huh? You ain't wanted to talk to me for months. You ain't wanted to talk to me last night. You ain't wanted no part of me then. What you wanna talk to me about now?

Rose: Tomorrow's Friday.

Troy: I know what day tomorrow is. You think I don't know tomorrow's Friday? My whole life I ain't done nothing but look to see Friday coming and you got to tell me it's Friday.

Rose: I want to know if you're coming home.

Troy: I always come home, Rose. You know that. There ain't never been a night I ain't come home.

Rose: That ain't what I mean . . . and you know it. I want to know if you're coming straight home after work.

Troy: I figure I'd cash my check . . . hang out at Taylors' with the boys . . . maybe play a game of checkers . . .

Rose: Troy, I can't live like this. I won't live like this. You livin' on borrowed time with me. It's been going on six months now you ain't been coming home.

Troy: I be here every night. Every night of the year. That's 365 days.

Rose: I want you to come home tomorrow after work.

Troy: Rose . . . I don't mess up my pay. You know that now. I take my pay and I give it to you. I don't have no money but what you give me back. I just want to have a little time to myself . . . a little time to enjoy life.

Rose: What about me? When's my time to enjoy life?

Troy: I don't know what to tell you, Rose. I'm doing the best I can.

Rose: You ain't been home from work but time enough to change your clothes and run out . . . and you wanna call that the best you can do?

Troy: I'm going over to the hospital to see Alberta. She went into the hospital this afternoon. Look like she might have the baby early. I won't be gone long.

Rose: Well, you ought to know. They went over to Miss Pearl's and got Gabe today. She said you told them to go ahead and lock him up.

Troy: I ain't said no such thing. Whoever told you that is telling a lie. Pearl ain't doing nothing but telling a big fat lie.

Rose: She ain't had to tell me. I read it on the papers.

Troy: I ain't told them nothing of the kind.

Rose: I saw it right there on the papers.

Troy: What it say, huh?

Rose: It said you told them to take him.

Troy: Then they screwed that up, just the way they screw up everything. I ain't worried about what they got on the paper.

Rose: Say the government send part of his check to the hospital and the other part to you.

Troy: I ain't got nothing to do with that if that's the way it works. I ain't made up the rules about how it work.

Rose: You did Gabe just like you did Cory. You wouldn't sign the paper for Cory . . . but you signed for Gabe. You signed that paper.

The telephone is heard ringing inside the house.

Troy: I told you I ain't signed nothing, woman! The only thing I signed was the release form. Hell, I can't read, I don't know what they had on that paper! I ain't signed nothing about sending Gabe away.

Rose: I said send him to the hospital . . . you said let him be free . . . now you done went down there and signed him to the hospital for half his money. You went back on yourself, Troy. You gonna have to answer for that.

Troy: See now . . . you been over there talking to Miss Pearl. She done got mad cause she ain't getting Gabe's rent money. That's all it is. She's liable to say anything.

Rose: Troy, I seen where you signed the paper.

Troy: You ain't seen nothing I signed. What she doing got papers on my brother anyway? Miss Pearl telling a big fat lie. And I'm gonna tell her about it too! You ain't seen nothing I signed. Say . . . you ain't seen nothing I signed.

Rose exits into the house to answer the telephone. Presently she returns.

Rose: Troy . . . that was the hospital. Alberta had the baby.

Troy: What she have? What is it?

Rose: It's a girl.

Troy: I better get on down to the hospital to see her.

Rose: Troy . . .

Troy: Rose . . . I got to go see her now. That's only right . . . what's the matter . . . the baby's all right, ain't it?

Rose: Alberta died having the baby.

Troy: Died . . . you say she's dead? Alberta's dead?

Rose: They said they done all they could. They couldn't do nothing for her.

Troy: The baby? How's the baby?

Rose: They say it's healthy. I wonder who's gonna bury her.

Troy: She had family, Rose. She wasn't living in the world by herself.

Rose: I know she wasn't living in the world by herself.

Troy: Next thing you gonna want to know if she had any insurance.

Rose: Troy, you ain't got to talk like that.

Troy: That's the first thing that jumped out your mouth. "Who's gonna bury her?" Like I'm fixing to take on that task for myself.

Rose: I am your wife. Don't push me away.

Troy: I ain't pushing nobody away. Just give me some space. That's all. Just give
me some room to breathe.

Rose exits into the house. Troy walks about the yard.

Troy (with a quiet rage that threatens to consume him): All right . . . Mr. Death. See
now . . . I'm gonna tell you what I'm gonna do. I'm gonna take and build
me a fence around this yard. See? I'm gonna build me a fence around what
belongs to me. And then I want you to stay on the other side. See? You stay
over there until you're ready for me. Then you come on. Bring your army.
Bring your sickle. Bring your wrestling clothes. I ain't gonna fall down on
my vigilance this time. You ain't gonna sneak up on me no more. When
you ready for me . . . when the top of your list say Troy Maxson . . . that's
when you come around here. You come up and knock on the front door.
Ain't nobody else got nothing to do with this. This is between you and me.
Man to man. You stay on the other side of that fence until you ready for
me. Then you come up and knock on the front door. Anytime you want.
I'll be ready for you.

The lights go down to black.

SCENE III

*The lights come up on the porch. It is late evening three days later. Rose sits listen-
ing to the ball game waiting for Troy. The final out of the game is made and Rose
switches off the radio. Troy enters the yard carrying an infant wrapped in blankets.
He stands back from the house and calls.*

*Rose enters and stands on the porch. There is a long, awkward silence, the
weight of which grows heavier with each passing second.*

Troy: Rose . . . I'm standing here with my daughter in my arms. She ain't but a
wee bittie little old thing. She don't know nothing about grownups' business. She innocent . . . and she ain't got no mama.

Rose: What you telling me for, Troy?

She turns and exits into the house.

Troy: Well . . . I guess we'll just sit out here on the porch.

*He sits down on the porch. There is an awkward indelicateness about the way he
handles the baby. His largeness engulfs and seems to swallow it. He speaks loud
enough for Rose to hear.*

A man's got to do what's right for him. I ain't sorry for nothing I done. It
felt right in my heart. *(To the baby.)* What you smiling at? Your daddy's a
big man. Got these great big old hands. But sometimes he's scared. And
right now your daddy's scared cause we sitting out here and ain't got no
home. Oh, I been homeless before. I ain't had no little baby with me. But I
been homeless. You just be out on the road by your lonesome and you see
one of them trains coming and you just kinda go like this . . .

He sings as a lullaby.

Please, Mr. Engineer let a man ride the line
Please, Mr. Engineer let a man ride the line
I ain't got no ticket please let me ride the blinds

Rose enters from the house. Troy, hearing her steps behind him, stands and faces her.

She's my daughter, Rose. My own flesh and blood. I can't deny her no more than I can deny them boys. *(Pause.)* You and them boys is my family. You and them and this child is all I got in the world. So I guess what I'm saying is . . . I'd appreciate it if you'd help me take care of her.

Rose: Okay, Troy . . . you're right. I'll take care of your baby for you . . . cause . . . like you say . . . she's innocent . . . and you can't visit the sins of the father upon the child. A motherless child has got a hard time. *(She takes the baby from him.)* From right now . . . this child got a mother. But you a womanless man.

Rose turns and exits into the house with the baby. Lights go down to black.

SCENE IV

It is two months later. Lyons enters from the street. He knocks on the door and calls.

Lyons: Hey, Rose! *(Pause.)* Rose!

Rose (from inside the house): Stop that yelling. You gonna wake up Raynell. I just got her to sleep.

Lyons: I just stopped by to pay Papa this twenty dollars I owe him. Where's Papa at?

Rose: He should be here in a minute. I'm getting ready to go down to the church. Sit down and wait on him.

Lyons: I got to go pick up Bonnie over her mother's house.

Rose: Well, sit it down there on the table. He'll get it.

Lyons (enters the house and sets the money on the table): Tell Papa I said thanks. I'll see you again.

Rose: All right, Lyons. We'll see you.

Lyons starts to exit as Cory enters.

Cory: Hey, Lyons.

Lyons: What's happening, Cory? Say man, I'm sorry I missed your graduation. You know I had a gig and couldn't get away. Otherwise, I would have been there, man. So what you doing?

Cory: I'm trying to find a job.

Lyons: Yeah I know how that go, man. It's rough out here. Jobs are scarce.

Cory: Yeah, I know.

Lyons: Look here, I got to run. Talk to Papa . . . he know some people. He'll be able to help get you a job. Talk to him . . . see what he say.

Cory: Yeah . . . all right, Lyons.

Lyons: You take care. I'll talk to you soon. We'll find some time to talk.

Lyons exits the yard. Cory wanders over to the tree, picks up the bat, and assumes a batting stance. He studies an imaginary pitcher and swings. Dissatisfied with the result, he tries again. Troy enters. They eye each other for a beat. Cory puts the bat down and exits the yard. Troy starts into the house as Rose exits with Raynell. She is carrying a cake.

Troy: I'm coming in and everybody's going out.

Rose: I'm taking this cake down to the church for the bake sale. Lyons was by to see you. He stopped by to pay you your twenty dollars. It's laying in there on the table.

Troy (going into his pocket): Well . . . here go this money.

Rose: Put it in there on the table, Troy. I'll get it.

Troy: What time you coming back?

Rose: Ain't no use in you studying me. It don't matter what time I come back.

Troy: I just asked you a question, woman. What's the matter . . . can't I ask you a question?

Rose: Troy, I don't want to go into it. Your dinner's in there on the stove. All you got to do is heat it up. And don't you be eating the rest of them cakes in there. I'm coming back for them. We having a bake sale at the church tomorrow.

Rose exits the yard. Troy sits down on the steps, takes a pint bottle from his pocket, opens it, and drinks. He begins to sing

Troy: Hear it ring! Hear it ring!
Had an old dog his name was Blue
You know Blue was mighty true
You know Blue was a good old dog
Blue trees a possum in a hollow log
You know from that he was a good old dog

Bono enters the yard.

Bono: Hey, Troy.

Troy: Hey, what's happening, Bono?

Bono: I just thought I'd stop by to see you.

Troy: What you stop by and see me for? You ain't stopped by in a month of Sundays. Hell, I must owe you money or something.

Bono: Since you got your promotion I can't keep up with you. Used to see you every day. Now I don't even know what route you working.

Troy: They keep switching me around. Got me out in Greentree now . . . hauling white folks' garbage.

Bono: Greentree, huh? You lucky, at least you ain't got to be lifting them barrels. Damn if they ain't getting heavier. I'm gonna put in my two years and call it quits.

Troy: I'm thinking about retiring myself.

Bono: You got it easy. You can *drive* for another five years.

Troy: It ain't the same, Bono. It ain't like working the back of the truck. Ain't got nobody to talk to . . . feel like you working by yourself. Naw, I'm thinking about retiring. How's Lucille?

Bono: She all right. Her arthritis get to acting up on her sometime. Saw Rose on my way in. She going down to the church, huh?

Troy: Yeah, she took up going down there. All them preachers looking for somebody to fatten their pockets. *(Pause.)* Got some gin here.

Bono: Naw, thanks. I just stopped by to say hello.

Troy: Hell, nigger . . . you can take a drink. I ain't never known you to say no to a drink. You ain't got to work tomorrow.

Bono: I just stopped by. I'm fixing to go over to Skinner's. We got us a domino game going over his house every Friday.

Troy: Nigger, you can't play no dominoes. I used to whup you four games out of five.

Bono: Well, that learned me. I'm getting better.

Troy: Yeah? Well, that's all right.

Bono: Look here . . . I got to be getting on. Stop by sometime, huh?

Troy: Yeah, I'll do that, Bono. Lucille told Rose you bought her a new refrigerator.

Bono: Yeah, Rose told Lucille you had finally built your fence . . . so I figured we'd call it even.

Troy: I knew you would.

Bono: Yeah . . . okay. I'll be talking to you.

Troy: Yeah, take care, Bono. Good to see you. I'm gonna stop over.

Bono: Yeah. Okay, Troy.

> *Bono exits. Troy drinks from the bottle.*

Troy: Old Blue died and I dig his grave
Let him down with a golden chain
Every night when I hear old Blue bark
I know Blue treed a possum in Noah's Ark.
Hear it ring! Hear it ring!

> *Cory enters the yard. They eye each other for a beat. Troy is sitting in the middle of the steps. Cory walks over.*

Cory: I got to get by.

Troy: Say what? What's you say?

Cory: You in my way. I got to get by.

Troy: You got to get by where? This is my house. Bought and paid for. In full. Took me fifteen years. And if you wanna go in my house and I'm sitting on the steps . . . you say excuse me. Like your mama taught you.

Cory: Come on, Pop . . . I got to get by.

> *Cory starts to maneuver his way past Troy. Troy grabs his leg and shoves him back.*

Troy: You just gonna walk over top of me?

Cory: I live here too!

Troy (advancing toward him): You just gonna walk over top of me in my own house?

Cory: I ain't scared of you.

Troy: I ain't asked if you was scared of me. I asked you if you was fixing to walk over top of me in my own house? That's the question. You ain't gonna say excuse me? You just gonna walk over top of me?

Cory: If you wanna put it like that.

Troy: How else am I gonna put it?

Cory: I was walking by you to go into the house cause you sitting on the steps drunk, singing to yourself. You can put it like that.

Troy: Without saying excuse me???

> *Cory doesn't respond.*

I asked you a question. Without saying excuse me???

Cory: I ain't got to say excuse me to you. You don't count around here no more.

Troy: Oh, I see . . . I don't count around here no more. You ain't got to say
excuse me to your daddy. All of a sudden you done got so grown that your
daddy don't count around here no more . . . Around here in his own
house and yard that he done paid for with the sweat of his brow. You done
got so grown to where you gonna take over. You gonna take over my
house. Is that right? You gonna wear my pants. You gonna go in there and
stretch out on my bed. You ain't got to say excuse me cause I don't count
around here no more. Is that right?

Cory: That's right. You always talking this dumb stuff. Now, why don't you
just get out my way?

Troy: I guess you got someplace to sleep and something to put in your belly.
You got that, huh? You got that? That's what you need. You got that, huh?

Cory: You don't know what I got. You ain't got to worry about what I got.

Troy: You right! You one hundred percent right! I done spent the last seventeen years worrying about what you got. Now it's your turn, see? I'll tell
you what to do. You grown . . . we done established that. You a man. Now,
let's see you act like one. Turn your behind around and walk out this yard.
And when you get out there in the alley . . . you can forget about this
house. See? Cause this is my house. You go on and be a man and get your
own house. You can forget about this. Cause this is mine. You go on and
get yours cause I'm through with doing for you.

Cory: You talking about what you did for me . . . what'd you ever give me?

Troy: Them feet and bones! That pumping heart, nigger! I give you more than
anybody else is ever gonna give you.

Cory: You ain't never gave me nothing! You ain't never done nothing but hold
me back. Afraid I was gonna be better than you. All you ever did was try
and make me scared of you. I used to tremble every time you called my
name. Every time I heard your footsteps in the house. Wondering all the
time . . . what's Papa gonna say if I do this? . . . What's he gonna say if I do
that? . . . What's Papa gonna say if I turn on the radio? And Mama, too . . .
she tries . . . but she's scared of you.

Troy: You leave your mama out of this. She ain't got nothing to do with this.

Cory: I don't know how she stand you . . . after what you did to her.

Troy: I told you to leave your mama out of this!

He advances toward Cory.

Cory: What you gonna do . . . give me a whupping? You can't whup me no
more. You're too old. You just an old man.

Troy (shoves him on his shoulder): Nigger! That's what you are. You just another
nigger on the street to me!

Cory: You crazy! You know that?

Troy: Go on now! You got the devil in you. Get on away from me!

Cory: You just a crazy old man . . . talking about I got the devil in me.

Troy: Yeah, I'm crazy! If you don't get on the other side of that yard . . . I'm
gonna show you how crazy I am! Go on . . . get the hell out of my yard.

Cory: It ain't your yard. You took Uncle Gabe's money he got from the army to
buy this house and then you put him out.

Troy (advances on Cory): Get your black ass out of my yard!

Troy's advance backs Cory up against the tree. Cory grabs up the bat.

Cory: I ain't going nowhere! Come on . . . put me out! I ain't scared of you.

Troy: That's my bat!

Cory: Come on!

Troy: Put my bat down!

Cory: Come on, put me out.

Cory swings at Troy, who backs across the yard.

What's the matter? You so bad . . . put me out!

Troy advances toward Cory.

Cory (backing up): Come on! Come on!

Troy: You're gonna have to use it! You wanna draw that bat back on me . . .
you're gonna have to use it.

Cory: Come on! . . . Come on!

*Cory swings the bat at Troy a second time. He misses. Troy continues to advance
toward him.*

Troy: You're gonna have to kill me! You wanna draw that bat back on me.
You're gonna have to kill me.

*Cory, backed up against the tree, can go no farther. Troy taunts him. He sticks out
his head and offers him a target.*

Come on! Come on!

Cory is unable to swing the bat. Troy grabs it.

Troy: Then I'll show you.

*Cory and Troy struggle over the bat. The struggle is fierce and fully engaged. Troy
ultimately is the stronger and takes the bat from Cory and stands over him ready
to swing. He stops himself.*

Go on and get away from around my house.

*Cory, stung by his defeat, picks himself up, walks slowly out of the yard and up the
alley.*

Cory: Tell Mama I'll be back for my things.

Troy: They'll be on the other side of that fence.

Cory exits.

Troy: I can't taste nothing. Helluljah! I can't taste nothing no more. *(Troy
assumes a batting posture and begins to taunt Death, the fastball on the outside corner.)* Come on! It's between you and me now! Come on! Anytime you
want! Come on! I be ready for you . . . but I ain't gonna be easy.

The lights go down on the scene.

SCENE V

*The time is 1965. The lights come up in the yard. It is the morning of Troy's funeral.
A funeral plaque with a light hangs beside the door. There is a small garden plot off
to the side. There is noise and activity in the house as Rose, Gabriel, and Bono have
gathered. The door opens and Raynell, seven years old, enters dressed in a flannel
nightgown. She crosses to the garden and pokes around with a stick. Rose calls from
the house.*

Rose: Raynell!
Raynell: Mam?
Rose: What you doing out there?
Raynell: Nothing.

    Rose comes to the door.

Rose: Girl, get in here and get dressed. What you doing?
Raynell: Seeing if my garden growed.
Rose: I told you it ain't gonna grow overnight. You got to wait.
Raynell: It don't look like it never gonna grow. Dag!
Rose: I told you a watched pot never boils. Get in here and get dressed.
Raynell: This ain't even no pot, Mama.
Rose: You just have to give it a chance. It'll grow. Now you come on and do
    what I told you. We got to be getting ready. This ain't no morning to be
    playing around. You hear me?
Raynell: Yes, mam.

    *Rose exits into the house. Raynell continues to poke at her garden with a stick. Cory
    enters. He is dressed in a Marine corporal's uniform, and carries a duffel bag. His
    posture is that of a military man, and his speech has a clipped sternness.*

Cory (to Raynell): Hi. *(Pause.)* I bet your name is Raynell.
Raynell: Uh huh.
Cory: Is your mama home?

    Raynell runs up on the porch and calls through the screen door.

Raynell: Mama . . . there's some man out here. Mama?

    Rose comes to the door.

Rose: Cory? Lord have mercy! Look here, you all!

    *Rose and Cory embrace in a tearful reunion as Bono and Lyons enter from the
    house dressed in funeral clothes.*

Bono: Aw, looka here . . .
Rose: Done got all grown up!
Cory: Don't cry, Mama. What you crying about?
Rose: I'm just so glad you made it.
Cory: Hey Lyons. How you doing, Mr. Bono.

    Lyons goes to embrace Cory.

Lyons: Look at you, man. Look at you. Don't he look good, Rose. Got them
    Corporal stripes.
Rose: What took you so long?
Cory: You know how the Marines are, Mama. They got to get all their paper-
    work straight before they let you do anything.
Rose: Well, I'm sure glad you made it. They let Lyons come. Your Uncle Gabe's
    still in the hospital. They don't know if they gonna let him out or not. I
    just talked to them a little while ago.
Lyons: A Corporal in the United States Marines.
Bono: Your daddy knew you had it in you. He used to tell me all the time.
Lyons: Don't he look good, Mr. Bono?

Bono: Yeah, he remind me of Troy when I first met him. *(Pause.)* Say, Rose, Lucille's down at the church with the choir. I'm gonna go down and get the pallbearers lined up. I'll be back to get you all.

Rose: Thanks, Jim.

Cory: See you, Mr. Bono.

Lyons (with his arm around Raynell): Cory . . . look at Raynell. Ain't she precious? She gonna break a whole lot of hearts.

Rose: Raynell, come and say hello to your brother. This is your brother, Cory. You remember Cory.

Raynell: No, Mam.

Cory: She don't remember me, Mama.

Rose: Well, we talk about you. She heard us talk about you. *(To Raynell.)* This is your brother, Cory. Come on and say hello.

Raynell: Hi.

Cory: Hi. So you're Raynell. Mama told me a lot about you.

Rose: You all come on into the house and let me fix you some breakfast. Keep up your strength.

Cory: I ain't hungry, Mama.

Lyons: You can fix me something, Rose. I'll be in there in a minute.

Rose: Cory, you sure you don't want nothing? I know they ain't feeding you right.

Cory: No, Mama . . . thanks. I don't feel like eating. I'll get something later.

Rose: Raynell . . . get on upstairs and get that dress on like I told you.

Rose and Raynell exit into the house.

Lyons: So . . . I hear you thinking about getting married.

Cory: Yeah, I done found the right one, Lyons. It's about time.

Lyons: Me and Bonnie been split up about four years now. About the time Papa retired. I guess she just got tired of all them changes I was putting her through. *(Pause.)* I always knew you was gonna make something out yourself. Your head was always in the right direction. So . . . you gonna stay in . . . make it a career . . . put in your twenty years?

Cory: I don't know. I got six already, I think that's enough.

Lyons: Stick with Uncle Sam and retire early. Ain't nothing out here. I guess Rose told you what happened with me. They got me down the workhouse. I thought I was being slick cashing other people's checks.

Cory: How much time you doing?

Lyons: They give me three years. I got that beat now. I ain't got but nine more months. It ain't so bad. You learn to deal with it like anything else. You got to take the crookeds with the straights. That's what Papa used to say. He used to say that when he struck out. I seen him strike out three times in a row . . . and the next time up he hit the ball over the grandstand. Right out there in Homestead Field. He wasn't satisfied hitting in the seats . . . he want to hit it over everything! After the game he had two hundred people standing around waiting to shake his hand. You got to take the crookeds with the straights. Yeah, Papa was something else.

Cory: You still playing?

Lyons: Cory . . . you know I'm gonna do that. There's some fellows down there we got us a band . . . we gonna try and stay together when we get out . . . but yeah, I'm still playing. It still helps me to get out of bed in the morning. As long as it do that I'm gonna be right there playing and trying to make some sense out of it.

Rose (calling): Lyons, I got these eggs in the pan.

Lyons: Let me go on and get these eggs, man. Get ready to go bury Papa. *(Pause.)* How you doing? You doing all right?

> *Cory nods. Lyons touches him on the shoulder and they share a moment of silent grief. Lyons exits into the house. Cory wanders about the yard. Raynell enters.*

Raynell: Hi.

Cory: Hi.

Raynell: Did you used to sleep in my room?

Cory: Yeah . . . that used to be my room.

Raynell: That's what Papa call it. "Cory's room." It got your football in the closet.

> *Rose comes to the door.*

Rose: Raynell, get in there and get them good shoes on.

Raynell: Mama, can't I wear these? Them other one hurt my feet.

Rose: Well, they just gonna have to hurt your feet for a while. You ain't said they hurt your feet when you went down to the store and got them.

Raynell: They didn't hurt then. My feet done got bigger.

Rose: Don't you give me no backtalk now. You get in there and get them shoes on.

> *Raynell exits into the house.*

Ain't too much changed. He still got that piece of rag tied to that tree. He was out here swinging that bat. I was just ready to go back in the house. He swung that bat and then he just fell over. Seem like he swung it and stood there with this grin on his face . . . and then he just fell over. They carried him on down to the hospital, but I knew there wasn't no need . . . why don't you come on in the house?

Cory: Mama . . . I got something to tell you. I don't know how to tell you this . . . but I've got to tell you . . . I'm not going to Papa's funeral.

Rose: Boy, hush your mouth. That's your daddy you talking about. I don't want hear that kind of talk this morning. I done raised you to come to this? You standing there all healthy and grown talking about you ain't going to your daddy's funeral?

Cory: Mama . . . listen . . .

Rose: I don't want to hear it, Cory. You just get that thought out of your head.

Cory: I can't drag Papa with me everywhere I go. I've got to say no to him. One time in my life I've got to say no.

Rose: Don't nobody have to listen to nothing like that. I know you and your daddy ain't seen eye to eye, but I ain't got to listen to that kind of talk this morning. Whatever was between you and your daddy . . . the time has come to put it aside. Just take it and set it over there on the shelf and forget about it. Disrespecting your daddy ain't gonna make you a man, Cory. You got to find a way to come to that on your own. Not going to your daddy's funeral ain't gonna make you a man.

Cory: The whole time I was growing up . . . living in his house . . . Papa was like a shadow that followed you everywhere. It weighed on you and sunk into your flesh. It would wrap around you and lay there until you couldn't tell which one was you anymore. That shadow digging in your flesh. Trying to crawl in. Trying to live through you. Everywhere I looked, Troy Maxson was staring back at me . . . hiding under the bed . . . in the closet. I'm just saying I've got to find a way to get rid of that shadow, Mama.

Rose: You just like him. You got him in you good.

Cory: Don't tell me that, Mama.

Rose: You Troy Maxson all over again.

Cory: I don't want to be Troy Maxson. I want to be me.

Rose: You can't be nobody but who you are, Cory. That shadow wasn't nothing but you growing into yourself. You either got to grow into it or cut it down to fit you. But that's all you got to make life with. That's all you got to measure yourself against that world out there. Your daddy wanted you to be everything he wasn't . . . and at the same time he tried to make you into everything he was. I don't know if he was right or wrong . . . but I do know he meant to do more good than he meant to do harm. He wasn't always right. Sometimes when he touched he bruised. And sometimes when he took me in his arms he cut.

When I first met your daddy I thought . . . Here is a man I can lay down with and make a baby. That's the first thing I thought when I seen him. I was thirty years old and had done seen my share of men. But when he walked up to me and said, "I can dance a waltz that'll make you dizzy," I thought, Rose Lee, here is a man that you can open yourself up to and be filled to bursting. Here is a man that can fill all them empty spaces you been tipping around the edges of. One of them empty spaces was being somebody's mother.

I married your daddy and settled down to cooking his supper and keeping clean sheets on the bed. When your daddy walked through the house he was so big he filled it up. That was my first mistake. Not to make him leave some room for me. For my part in the matter. But at that time I wanted that. I wanted a house that I could sing in. And that's what your daddy gave me. I didn't know to keep up his strength I had to give up little pieces of mine. I did that. I took on his life as mine and mixed up the pieces so that you couldn't hardly tell which was which anymore. It was my choice. It was my life and I didn't have to live it like that. But that's what life offered me in the way of being a woman and I took it. I grabbed hold of it with both hands.

By the time Raynell came into the house, me and your daddy had done lost touch with one another. I didn't want to make my blessing off of nobody's misfortune . . . but I took on to Raynell like she was all them babies I had wanted and never had.

The phone rings.

Like I'd been blessed to relive a part of my life. And if the Lord see fit to keep up my strength . . . I'm gonna do her just like your daddy did you . . . I'm gonna give her the best of what's in me.

Raynell (entering, still with her old shoes): Mama . . . Reverend Tollivier on the phone.

Rose exits into the house.

Raynell: Hi.

Cory: Hi.

Raynell: You in the Army or the Marines?

Cory: Marines.

Raynell: Papa said it was the Army. Did you know Blue?

Cory: Blue? Who's Blue?

Raynell: Papa's dog what he sing about all the time.

Cory (singing): Hear it ring! Hear it ring!
I had a dog his name was Blue
You know Blue was mighty true
You know Blue was a good old dog
Blue treed a possum in a hollow log
You know from that he was a good old dog.
Hear it ring! Hear it ring!

Raynell joins in singing.

Cory and Raynell: Blue treed a possum out on a limb
Blue looked at me and I looked at him
Grabbed that possum and put him in a sack
Blue stayed there till I came back
Old Blue's feets was big and round
Never allowed a possum to touch the ground.

Old Blue died and I dug his grave
I dug his grave with a silver spade
Let him down with a golden chain
And every night I call his name
Go on Blue, you good dog you
Go on Blue, you good dog you

Raynell: Blue laid down and died like a man
Blue laid down and died . . .

Both: Blue laid down and died like a man
Now he's treeing possums in the Promised Land
I'm gonna tell you this to let you know
Blue's gone where the good dogs go
When I hear old Blue bark
When I hear old Blue bark
Blue treed a possum in Noah's Ark
Blue treed a possum in Noah's Ark.

Rose comes to the screen door.

Rose: Cory, we gonna be ready to go in a minute.

Cory (to Raynell): You go on in the house and change them shoes like Mama told you so we can go to Papa's funeral.

Raynell: Okay, I'll be back.

Raynell exits into the house. Cory gets up and crosses over to the tree. Rose stands in the screen door watching him. Gabriel enters from the alley.

Gabriel (calling): Hey, Rose!

Rose: Gabe?

Gabriel: I'm here, Rose. Hey Rose, I'm here!

> *Rose enters from the house.*

Rose: Lord . . . Look here, Lyons!

Lyons: See, I told you, Rose . . . I told you they'd let him come.

Cory: How you doing, Uncle Gabe?

Lyons: How you doing, Uncle Gabe?

Gabriel: Hey, Rose. It's time. It's time to tell St. Peter to open the gates. Troy, you ready? You ready, Troy. I'm gonna tell St. Peter to open the gates. You get ready now.

> *Gabriel, with great fanfare, braces himself to blow. The trumpet is without a mouthpiece. He puts the end of it into his mouth and blows with great force, like a man who has been waiting some twenty-odd years for this single moment. No sound comes out of the trumpet. He braces himself and blows again with the same result. A third time he blows. There is a weight of impossible description that falls away and leaves him bare and exposed to a frightful realization. It is a trauma that a sane and normal mind would be unable to withstand. He begins to dance. A slow, strange dance, eerie and life-giving. A dance of atavistic signature and ritual. Lyons attempts to embrace him. Gabriel pushes Lyons away. He begins to howl in what is an attempt at song, or perhaps a song turning back into itself in an attempt at speech. He finishes his dance and the gates of heaven stand open as wide as God's closet.*

That's the way that go!

CONNECTIONS TO OTHER SELECTIONS

1. Compare and contrast Troy Maxson with Willy Loman in Miller's *Death of a Salesman* (p. 1372). How do these protagonists relate to their sons?

2. How might the narrator's experiences in Ralph Ellison's short story "Battle Royal" (p. 243) be used to shed light on Troy's conflicts in *Fences*?

CRITICAL
THINKING
AND WRITING

46

Critical Strategies
for Reading

Great literature is simply language
charged with meaning to the utmost
possible degree.
— EZRA POUND

The answers you get from literature
depend upon the questions you pose.
— MARGARET ATWOOD

CRITICAL THINKING

Maybe this has happened to you: the assignment is to write an analysis of
some aspect of a work — let's say, Nathaniel Hawthorne's *The Scarlet Letter* —
that interests you and takes into account critical sources
that comment on and interpret the work. You cheerfully begin research in the library but quickly find yourself bewildered by several seemingly unrelated articles.
The first traces the thematic significance of images of
light and darkness in the novel; the second makes a case for Hester Prynne
as a liberated woman; the third argues that Arthur Dimmesdale's guilt is a

Web Explore
the critical approaches
in this chapter on
LiterActive or at
bedfordstmartins.com/
meyercompact.

projection of Hawthorne's own emotions; and the fourth analyzes the introduction, "The Custom-House," as an attack on bourgeois values. These disparate treatments may seem random and capricious — a confirmation of your worst suspicions that interpretations of literature are hit-or-miss excursions into areas that you know little about or didn't know even existed. But if you understand that the four articles are written from four different perspectives — formalist, feminist, psychological, and Marxist — and that the purpose of each is to enhance your understanding of the novel by discussing a particular element of it, then you can see that the articles' varying strategies represent potentially interesting ways of opening up the text that might otherwise never have occurred to you. There are many ways to approach a text, and a useful first step is to develop a sense of direction, an understanding of how a perspective — your own or a critic's — shapes a discussion of a text.

This chapter offers an introduction to critical approaches to literature by outlining a variety of strategies for reading fiction, poetry, or drama. These strategies include approaches that have long been practiced by readers who have used, for example, the insights gleaned from biography and history to illuminate literary works as well as more recent approaches, such as those used by gender, reader-response, and deconstructionist critics. Each of these perspectives is sensitive to point of view, symbol, tone, irony, and other literary elements that you have been studying, but each also casts those elements in a special light. The formalist approach emphasizes how the elements within a work achieve their effects, whereas biographical and psychological approaches lead outward from the work to consider the author's life and other writings. Even broader approaches, such as historical and cultural perspectives, connect the work to historic, social, and economic forces. Mythological readings represent the broadest approach because they discuss the cultural and universal responses readers have to a work.

Any given strategy raises its own types of questions and issues while seeking particular kinds of evidence to support itself. An awareness of the assumptions and methods that inform an approach can help you to understand better the validity and value of a given critic's strategy for making sense of a work. More important, such an understanding can widen and deepen the responses of your own reading.

The critical thinking that goes into understanding a professional critic's approach to a work is not foreign to you because you have already used essentially the same kind of thinking to understand the work itself. You have developed skills to produce a literary *analysis* that, for example, describes how a character, symbol, or rhyme scheme supports a theme. These same skills are also useful for reading literary criticism because they allow you to keep track of how the parts of a critical approach create a particular reading of a literary work. When you analyze a story, poem, or play by closely examining how its various elements relate to the whole, your *interpretation* — your articulation of what the work means to you as sup-ported by an analysis of its elements — necessarily involves choosing what you focus on in the work. The same is true of professional critics.

Critical readings presuppose choices in the kinds of materials that are discussed. An analysis of the setting of John Updike's "A & P" (p. 560) would probably focus on the oppressive environment the protagonist asso-ciates with the store rather than, say, the economic history of that super-market chain. (For a student's analysis of the setting in "A & P," see p. 1581.) The economic history of a supermarket chain might be useful to a Marxist critic concerned with how class relations are revealed in "A & P," but for a formalist critic interested in identifying the unifying structures of the story, such information would be irrelevant.

The Perspectives, Complementary Critical Readings, and Critical Case Studies in this anthology offer opportunities to read critics using a wide variety of approaches to analyze and interpret texts. In the Critical Case Study on Ibsen's *A Doll House* (Chapter 43), for instance, Carol Strongin Tufts (p. 1313) offers a psychoanalytic reading of Nora that characterizes her as a narcissistic personality rather than as a feminist heroine. The crite-ria she uses to evaluate Nora's behavior are drawn from the language used by the American Psychiatric Association. In contrast, Joan Templeton (p. 1316) places Nora in the context of women's rights issues to argue that Nora must be read from a feminist perspective if the essential meaning of the play is to be understood. Each of these critics raises different questions, examines different evidence, and employs different assumptions to inter-pret Nora's character. Being aware of those differences — teasing them out so that you can see how they lead to competing conclusions — is a useful way to analyze the analysis itself. What is left out of an interpretation is sometimes as significant as what is included. As you read the critics, it's worth reminding yourself that your own critical thinking skills can help you to determine the usefulness of a particular approach.

The following overview of critical strategies for reading is neither ex-haustive in the types of critical approaches covered nor complete in its pre-sentation of the complexities inherent in them, but it should help you to develop an appreciation of the intriguing possibilities that attend literary interpretation. The emphasis in this chapter is on ways of thinking about literature rather than on daunting lists of terms, names, and movements. Although a working knowledge of critical schools may be valuable and necessary for a fully informed use of a given critical approach, the aim here is more modest and practical. This chapter is no substitute for the shelves of literary criticism that can be found in your library, but it does suggest how readers using different perspectives organize their responses to texts.

The summaries of critical approaches that follow are descriptive, not evaluative. Each approach has its advantages and limitations. In practice, many critical approaches overlap and complement each other, but those matters are best left to further study. Like literary artists, critics have their personal values, tastes, and styles. The appropriateness of a specific critical approach will depend, at least in part, on the nature of the literary work under discussion as well as on your own sensibilities and experience. However, any approach, if it is to enhance understanding, requires sensitivity, tact, and an awareness of the various literary elements of the text, including, of course, its use of language.

Successful critical approaches avoid eccentric decodings that reveal so-called hidden meanings that are not only hidden but totally absent from the text. For a parody of this sort of critical excess, see "A Parodic Interpretation of 'Stopping by Woods on a Snowy Evening' " (p. 904), in which Herbert R. Coursen Jr. has some fun with a Robert Frost poem and Santa Claus while making a serious point about the dangers of overly ingenious readings. Literary criticism attempts, like any valid hypothesis, to account for phenomena — the text — without distorting or misrepresenting what it describes.

THE LITERARY CANON: DIVERSITY AND CONTROVERSY

Before looking at the various critical approaches discussed in this chapter, it makes sense to consider first which literature has been traditionally considered worthy of such analysis. The discussion in the introduction called The Changing Literary Canon (p. 6) may have already alerted you to the fact that in recent years many more works by women, minorities, and writers from around the world have been considered by scholars, critics, and teachers to merit serious study and inclusion in what is known as the literary canon. This increasing diversity has been celebrated by those who believe that multiculturalism taps new sources for the discovery of great literature while raising significant questions about language, culture, and society. At the same time, others have perceived this diversity as a threat to the established, traditional canon of Western culture.

The debates concerning who should be read, taught, and written about have sometimes been acrimonious as well as lively and challenging. Bitter arguments have been waged on campuses and in the press over what has come to be called *political correctness*. Two main camps have formed around these debates — liberals and conservatives (the appropriateness of these terms is debatable, but the oppositional positioning is unmistakable). The liberals are said to insist on encouraging tolerant attitudes about race, class, gender, and sexual orientation, and opening up the curriculum to multicultural texts from Asia, Africa, Latin America, and elsewhere. These revisionists, seeking a change in traditional attitudes, are sometimes accused of trying to substitute ideological dogma for reason and truth and to intimidate opposing colleagues and students into silence and acceptance of their politically correct views. The conservatives are also portrayed as ideologues; in their efforts to preserve what they regard as the best from the past, they fail to acknowledge that Western classics, mostly written by white male Europeans, represent only a portion of human experience. These traditionalists are seen as advocating values that are neither universal nor eternal but merely privileged and entrenched. Conservatives are charged with ignoring the political agenda that their values represent and that is implicit in their preference for the works of canonical authors such as Homer, Virgil, Shakespeare, Milton, Tolstoy, and Faulkner. The reductive and contradictory nature of this national debate between liberals and conservatives has been neatly summed up by Katha Pollitt: "Read the conservatives' list and produce a nation of sexists and racists — or a nation of philosopher kings. Read the liberals' list and produce a nation of spiritual relativists — or a nation of open-minded world citizens" ("Canon to the Right of Me . . . ," *The Nation*, Sept. 23, 1991, p. 330).

These troubling and extreme alternatives can be avoided, of course, if the issues are not approached from such absolutist positions. Solutions to these issues cannot be suggested in this limited space, and, no doubt, solutions will evolve over time, but we can at least provide a perspective. Books — regardless of what list they are on — are not likely to unite a fragmented nation or to disunite a unified one. It is perhaps more useful and accurate to see issues of canonicity as reflecting political changes rather than being the primary causes of them. This is not to say that books don't have an impact on readers — that *Uncle Tom's Cabin*, for instance, did not galvanize antislavery sentiments in nineteenth-century America — but that book lists do not by themselves preserve or destroy the status quo.

It's worth noting that the curricula of American universities have always undergone significant and, some would say, wrenching changes. Only a little more than one hundred years ago there was strong opposition to teaching English, as well as other modern languages, alongside programs dominated by Greek and Latin. Only since the 1920s has American literature been made a part of the curriculum, and just five decades ago including twentieth-century writers such as James Joyce, Virginia Woolf, Franz Kafka, and Ernest Hemingway in the curriculum was regarded with raised eyebrows. New voices do not drown out the past; they build on it and eventually become part of the past as newer writers take their place beside them. Neither resistance to change nor a denial of the past will have its way with the canon. Though both impulses are widespread, neither is likely to dominate the other because there are too many reasonable, practical readers and teachers who instead of replacing Shakespeare, Melville, and other canonical writers have supplemented them with neglected writers from Western and other cultures. These readers experience the current debates about the canon not as a binary opposition but as an opportunity to explore important questions about continuity and change in our literature, culture, and society.

FORMALIST STRATEGIES

Formalist critics focus on the formal elements of a work — its language, structure, and tone. A formalist reads literature as an independent work of art rather than as a reflection of the author's state of mind or as a representation of a moment in history. Historic influences on a work, an author's intentions, or anything else outside the work are generally not treated by formalists (this is particularly true of the most famous modern formalists, known as the *New Critics,* who dominated American criticism from the 1940s through the 1960s). Instead, formalists offer intense examinations of the relationship between form and meaning within a work, emphasizing the subtle complexity of how a work is arranged. This kind of close reading pays special attention to what are often described as *intrinsic* matters in a literary work, such as diction, irony, paradox, metaphor, and symbol, as well as larger elements, such as plot, characterization, and narrative technique. Formalists examine how these elements work together to give a coherent shape to a work while contributing to its meaning. The answers to the questions formalists raise about how the shape and effect of a work are related come from the work itself. Other kinds of information that go beyond the text — biography, history, politics, economics, and so on — are typically regarded by formalists as *extrinsic* matters, which are considerably less important than what goes on within the autonomous text.

Poetry especially lends itself to close readings because a poem's relative brevity allows for detailed analyses of nearly all its words and how they achieve their effects. For a student's formalist reading of how a pervasive sense of death is worked into a poem, see "A Reading of Dickinson's 'There's a certain Slant of light' " (p. 1578).

Formalist strategies are also useful for analyzing drama and fiction. In his well-known essay "The World of *Hamlet*," Maynard Mack explores Hamlet's character and predicament by paying close attention to the words and images that Shakespeare uses to build a world in which appearances mask reality and mystery is embedded in scene after scene. Mack points to recurring terms, such as *apparition, seems, assume,* and *put on,* as well as repeated images of acting, clothing, disease, and painting, to indicate the treacherous surface world Hamlet must penetrate to get to the truth. This pattern of deception provides an organizing principle around which Mack offers a reading of the entire play:

> Hamlet's problem, in its crudest form, is simply the problem of the avenger: he must carry out the injunction of the ghost and kill the king. But this problem . . . is presented in terms of a certain kind of world. The ghost's injunction to act becomes so inextricably bound up for Hamlet with the character of the world in which the action must be taken — its mysteriousness, its baffling appearances, its deep consciousness of infection, frailty, and loss — that he cannot come to terms with either without coming to terms with both.

Although Mack places *Hamlet* in the tradition of revenge tragedy, his reading of the play emphasizes Shakespeare's arrangement of language rather than literary history as a means of providing an interpretation that accounts for various elements of the play. Mack's formalist strategy explores how diction reveals meaning and how repeated words and images evoke and reinforce important thematic significances.

For an example of a work in which the shape of the plot serves as the major organizing principle, let's examine Kate Chopin's "The Story of an Hour" (p. 15), a two-page short story that takes only a few minutes to read. With the story fresh in your mind, consider how you might approach it from a formalist perspective. A first reading probably results in surprise at the story's ending: a grieving wife "afflicted with a heart trouble" suddenly dies of a heart attack, not because she's learned that her kind and loving husband has been killed in a terrible train accident but because she discovers that he is very much alive. Clearly, we are faced with an ironic situation since there is such a powerful incongruity between what is expected to happen and what actually happens. A likely formalist strategy for analyzing this story would be to raise questions about the ironic ending. Is this merely a trick ending, or is it a carefully wrought culmination of other elements in the story so that in addition to creating surprise the ending snaps the story shut on an interesting and challenging theme? Formalists value such complexities over simple surprise effects.

A second, closer reading indicates that Chopin's third-person narrator presents the story in a manner similar to Josephine's gentle attempts to break the news about Brently Mallard's death. The story is told in "veiled hints that [reveal] in half concealing." But unlike Josephine, who tries to protect her sister's fragile heart from stress, the narrator seeks to reveal Mrs. Mallard's complex heart. A formalist would look back over the story for signs of the ending in the imagery. Although Mrs. Mallard grieves immediately and unreservedly when she hears about the train disaster, she soon begins to feel a different emotion as she looks out the window at "the tops of trees . . . all aquiver with the new spring life." This symbolic evocation of renewal and rebirth — along with "the delicious breath of rain," the sounds of life in the street, and the birds singing — causes her to feel, in spite of her own efforts to repress her thoughts and emotions, "free, free, free!" She feels alive with a sense of possibility, with a "clear and exalted perception" that she "would live for herself" instead of for and through her husband.

It is ironic that this ecstatic "self-assertion" is interpreted by Josephine as grief, but the crowning irony for this "goddess of Victory" is the doctors' assumption that she dies of joy rather than of the shock of having to abandon her newly discovered self once she realizes her husband is still alive. In the course of an hour, Mrs. Mallard's life is irretrievably changed: her husband's assumed accidental death frees her, but the fact that he lives and all the expectations imposed on her by his continued life kill her. She does, indeed, die of a broken heart, but only Chopin's readers know the real ironic meaning of that explanation.

Although this brief discussion of some of the formal elements of Chopin's story does not describe all there is to say about how they produce an effect and create meaning, it does suggest the kinds of questions, issues, and evidence that a formalist strategy might raise in providing a close reading of the text itself.

BIOGRAPHICAL STRATEGIES

A knowledge of an author's life can help readers understand his or her work more fully. Events in a work might follow actual events in a writer's life just as characters might be based on people known by the author. Ernest Hemingway's "Soldier's Home" (p. 165) is a story about the difficulties of a World War I veteran named Krebs returning to his small hometown in Oklahoma, where he cannot adjust to the pious assumptions of his family and neighbors. He refuses to accept their innocent blindness to the horrors he has witnessed during the war. They have no sense of the brutality of modern life; instead they insist he resume his life as if nothing has happened. There is plenty of biographical evidence to indicate that Krebs's unwillingness to lie about his war experiences reflects Hemingway's own responses on his return to Oak Park, Illinois, in 1919. Krebs, like Hemingway, finds he has to leave the sentimentality, repressiveness, and smug complacency that threaten to render his experiences unreal: "the world they were in was not the world he was in."

An awareness of Hemingway's own war experiences and subsequent disillusionment with his hometown can be readily developed through available biographies, letters, and other works he wrote. Consider, for example, this passage from *By Force of Will: The Life and Art of Ernest Hemingway,* in which Scott Donaldson describes Hemingway's response to World War I:

> In poems, as in [*A Farewell to Arms*], Hemingway expressed his distaste for the first war. The men who had to fight the war did not die well:
>
> > Soldiers pitch and cough and twitch —
> >   All the world roars red and black;
> > Soldiers smother in a ditch,
> >   Choking through the whole attack.
>
> And what did they die for? They were "sucked in" by empty words and phrases —
>
> > King and country,
> > Christ Almighty,
> > And the rest,
> > Patriotism,

Democracy,
Honor —

which spelled death. The bitterness of these outbursts derived from the distinction Hemingway drew between the men on the line and those who started the wars that others had to fight.

This kind of information can help to deepen our understanding of just how empathetically Krebs is presented in the story. Relevant facts about Hemingway's life will not make "Soldier's Home" a better-written story than it is, but such information can make clearer the source of Hemingway's convictions and how his own experiences inform his major concerns as a storyteller.

Some formalist critics — some New Critics, for example — argue that interpretation should be based exclusively on internal evidence rather than on any biographical information outside the work. They argue that it is not possible to determine an author's intention and that the work must stand by itself. Although this is a useful caveat for keeping the work in focus, a reader who finds biography relevant would argue that biography can at the very least serve as a control on interpretation. A reader who, for example, finds Krebs at fault for not subscribing to the values of his hometown would be misreading the story, given both its tone and the biographical information available about the author. Although the narrator never *tells* the reader that Krebs is right or wrong for leaving town, the story's tone sides with his view of things. If, however, someone were to argue otherwise, insisting that the tone is not decisive and that Krebs's position is problematic, a reader familiar with Hemingway's own reactions could refute that argument with a powerful confirmation of Krebs's instincts to withdraw. Hence, many readers find biography useful for interpretation.

However, it is also worth noting that biographical information can complicate a work. Chopin's "The Story of an Hour" presents a repressed wife's momentary discovery of what freedom from her husband might mean to her. She awakens to a new sense of herself when she learns of her husband's death, only to collapse of a heart attack when she sees that he is alive. Readers might be tempted to interpret this story as Chopin's fictionalized commentary about her own marriage because her husband died twelve years before she wrote the story and seven years before she began writing fiction seriously. Biographers seem to agree, however, that Chopin's marriage was evidently satisfying to her and that she was not oppressed by her husband and did not feel oppressed.

Moreover, consider this diary entry from only one month after Chopin wrote the story (quoted by Per Seyersted in *Kate Chopin: A Critical Biography*):

> If it were possible for my husband and my mother to come back to earth, I feel that I would unhesitatingly give up everything that has come into my life since they left it and join my existence again with theirs. To do that, I would have to forget the past ten years of my growth — my real growth. But I would take back a little wisdom with me; it would be the spirit of perfect acquiescence.

This passage raises provocative questions instead of resolving them. How does that "spirit of perfect acquiescence" relate to Mrs. Mallard's insistence that she "would live for herself"? Why would Chopin be willing to "forget the past ten years of . . . growth" given her protagonist's desire for "self-assertion"? Although these and other questions raised by the diary entry cannot be answered here, this kind of biographical perspective certainly adds to the possibilities of interpretation.

Sometimes biographical information does not change our understanding so much as it enriches our appreciation of a work. It matters, for instance, that much of John Milton's poetry, so rich in visual imagery, was written after he became blind; and it is just as significant — to shift to a musical example — that a number of Ludwig van Beethoven's greatest works, including the Ninth Symphony, were composed after he succumbed to total deafness.

PSYCHOLOGICAL STRATEGIES

Given the enormous influence that Sigmund Freud's psychoanalytic theories have had on twentieth-century interpretations of human behavior, it is nearly inevitable that most people have some familiarity with his ideas concerning dreams, unconscious desires, and sexual repression, as well as his terms for different aspects of the psyche — the id, ego, and superego. Psychological approaches to literature draw on Freud's theories and other psychoanalytic theories to understand more fully the text, the writer, and the reader. Critics use such approaches to explore the motivations of characters and the symbolic meanings of events, while biographers speculate about a writer's own motivations — conscious or unconscious — in a literary work. Psychological approaches are also used to describe and analyze the reader's personal responses to a text.

Although it is not feasible to explain psychoanalytic terms and concepts in so brief a space as this, it is possible to suggest the nature of a psychological approach. It is a strategy based heavily on the idea of the existence of a human unconscious — those impulses, desires, and feelings that a person is unaware of but that influence emotions and behavior.

Central to a number of psychoanalytic critical readings is Freud's concept of what he called the **Oedipus complex,** a term derived from Sophocles' tragedy *Oedipus the King* (p. 1102). This complex is predicated on a boy's unconscious rivalry with his father for his mother's love and his desire to eliminate his father in order to take his father's place with his mother. The female version of the psychological conflict is known as the **Electra complex,** a term used to describe a daughter's unconscious rivalry for her father. The name comes from a Greek legend about Electra, who avenged the death of her father, Agamemnon, by plotting the death of her mother, Clytemnestra. In *The Interpretation of Dreams,* Freud explains why *Oedipus the King* "moves a modern audience no less than it did the contemporary Greek one." What unites their powerful attraction to the play is an unconscious response:

> There must be something which makes a voice within us ready to recognize the compelling force of destiny in the *Oedipus*. . . . His destiny moves us only because it might have been ours — because the oracle laid the same curse upon us before our birth as upon him. It is the fate of all of us, perhaps, to direct our first sexual impulse towards our mother and our first hatred and our first murderous wish against our father. Our dreams convince us that this is so. King Oedipus, who slew his father Laius and married his mother Jocasta, merely shows us the fulfillment of our own childhood wishes . . . and we shrink back from him with the whole force of the repression by which those wishes have since that time been held down within us.

In this passage Freud interprets the unconscious motives of Sophocles in writing the play, Oedipus in acting within it, and the audience in responding to it.

A further application of the Oedipus complex can be observed in a classic interpretation of *Hamlet* by Ernest Jones, who used this concept to explain why Hamlet delays in avenging his father's death. This reading has been tightly summarized by Norman Holland, a recent psychoanalytic critic, in *The Shakespearean Imagination*. Holland shapes the issues into four major components:

> One, people over the centuries have been unable to say why Hamlet delays in killing the man who murdered his father and married his mother. Two, psychoanalytic experience shows that every child wants to do just exactly that. Three, Hamlet delays because he cannot punish Claudius for doing what he himself wished to do as a child and, unconsciously, still wishes to do: he would be punishing himself. Four, the fact that this wish is unconscious explains why people could not explain Hamlet's delay.

Although the Oedipus complex is, of course, not relevant to all psychological interpretations of literature, interpretations involving this complex do offer a useful example of how psychoanalytic critics tend to approach a text.

The situation in which Mrs. Mallard finds herself in Chopin's "The Story of an Hour" is not related to an Oedipus complex, but it is clear that news of her husband's death has released powerful unconscious desires for freedom that she had previously suppressed. As she grieved, "something" was "coming to her and she was waiting for it, fearfully." What comes to her is what she senses about the life outside her window; that's the stimulus, but the true source of what was to "possess her," which she strove to "beat . . . back with her [conscious] will" is her desperate desire for the autonomy and fulfillment she had been unable to admit did not exist in her marriage. A psychological approach to her story amounts to a case study in the destructive nature of self-repression. Moreover, the story might reflect Chopin's own views of her marriage — despite her conscious statements about her loving husband. And what about the reader's response? How might a psychological approach account for different responses in female and male readers to Mrs. Mallard's death? One needn't be versed in psychoanalytic terms to entertain this question.

HISTORICAL STRATEGIES

Historians sometimes use literature as a window onto the past because literature frequently provides the nuances of a historic period that cannot be readily perceived through other sources. The characters in Harriet Beecher Stowe's *Uncle Tom's Cabin* (1852) display, for example, a complex set of white attitudes toward blacks in mid-nineteenth-century America that is absent from more traditional historic documents, such as census statistics or state laws. Another way of approaching the relationship between literature and history, however, is to use history as a means of understanding a literary work more clearly. The plot pattern of pursuit, escape, and capture in nineteenth-century slave narratives had a significant influence on Stowe's plotting of action in *Uncle Tom's Cabin*. This relationship demonstrates that the writing contemporary to an author is an important element of the history that helps to shape a work. There are many ways to talk about the historical and cultural dimensions of a work. Such readings treat a literary text as a document reflecting, producing, or being produced by the social conditions of its time, giving equal focus to the social milieu and the work itself. Four historical strategies that have been especially influential are literary history criticism, Marxist criticism, new historicist criticism, and cultural criticism.

Literary History Criticism

Literary historians shift the emphasis from the period to the work. Hence a literary historian might also examine mid-nineteenth-century abolitionist attitudes toward blacks to determine whether Stowe's novel is representative of those views or significantly to the right or left of them. Such a study might even indicate how closely the book reflects racial attitudes of twentieth-century readers. A work of literature may transcend time to the extent that it addresses the concerns of readers over a span of decades or centuries, but it remains for the literary historian a part of the past in which it was composed, a past that can reveal more fully a work's language, ideas, and purposes.

Literary historians move beyond both the facts of an author's personal life and the text itself to the social and intellectual currents in which the author composed the work. They place the work in the context of its time (as do many critical biographers, who write "life and times" studies), and sometimes they make connections with other literary works that may have influenced the author. The basic strategy of literary historians is to illuminate the historic background in order to shed light on some aspect of the work itself.

In Hemingway's "Soldier's Home" we learn that Krebs had been at Belleau Wood, Soissons, Champagne, St. Mihiel, and the Argonne. Although nothing is said of these battles in the story, they were among the bloodiest of the war; the wholesale butchery and staggering casualties incurred by both sides make credible the way Krebs's unstated but lingering memories have turned him into a psychological prisoner of war. Knowing something about the ferocity of those battles helps us account for Krebs's response in the story. Moreover, we can more fully appreciate Hemingway's refusal to have Krebs lie about the realities of war for the folks back home if we are aware of the numerous poems, stories, and plays published during World War I that presented war as a glorious, manly, transcendent sacrifice for God and country. Juxtaposing those works with "Soldier's Home" brings the differences into sharp focus.

Similarly, a reading of William Blake's poem "London" (p. 669) is less complete if we do not know of the horrific social conditions — the poverty, disease, exploitation, and hypocrisy — that characterized the city Blake laments in the late eighteenth century.

One last example: the repression expressed in the lines on Mrs. Mallard's face is more distinctly seen if Chopin's "The Story of an Hour" is placed in the context of "the women's question" as it continued to develop in the 1890s. Mrs. Mallard's impulse toward "self-assertion" runs parallel with a growing women's movement away from the role of long-suffering housewife. This desire was widely regarded by traditionalists as a form of dangerous selfishness that was considered as unnatural as it was immoral. It is no wonder that Chopin raises the question of whether Mrs. Mallard's sense of freedom owing to her husband's death isn't a selfish, "monstrous joy." Mrs. Mallard, however, dismisses this question as "trivial" in the face of her new perception of life, a dismissal that Chopin endorses by way of the story's ironic ending. The larger social context of this story would have been more apparent to Chopin's readers in 1894 than it is to readers in the 2000s. That is why a historical reconstruction of the limitations placed on married women helps to explain the pressures, tensions, and momentary — only momentary — release that Mrs. Mallard experiences.

Marxist Criticism

Marxist readings developed from the heightened interest in radical reform during the 1930s, when many critics looked to literature as a means of furthering proletarian social and economic goals, based largely on the writings of Karl Marx. **Marxist critics** focus on the ideological content of a work — its explicit and implicit assumptions and values about matters such as culture, race, class, and power. Marxist studies typically aim at revealing and clarifying ideological issues and also correcting social injustices. Some Marxist critics have used literature to describe the competing socioeconomic interests that too often advance capitalist money and power rather than socialist morality and justice. They argue that criticism, like literature, is essentially political because it either challenges or supports economic oppression. Even if criticism attempts to ignore class conflicts, it is politicized, according to Marxists, because it supports the status quo.

It is not surprising that Marxist critics pay more attention to the content and themes of literature than to its form. A Marxist critic would more likely be concerned with the exploitive economic forces that cause Willy Loman to feel trapped in Miller's *Death of a Salesman* (p. 1372) than with the playwright's use of nonrealistic dramatic techniques to reveal Loman's inner thoughts. Similarly, a Marxist reading of Chopin's "The Story of an Hour" might draw on the evidence made available in a book published only a few years after the story by Charlotte Perkins Gilman titled *Women and Economics: A Study of the Economic Relation between Men and Women as a Factor in Social Evolution* (1898). An examination of this study could help explain how some of the "repression" Mrs. Mallard experiences was generated by the socioeconomic structure contemporary to her and how Chopin challenges the validity of that structure by having Mrs. Mallard resist it with her very life. A Marxist reading would see the protagonist's conflict as not only an individual issue but part of a larger class struggle.

New Historicist Criticism

Since the 1960s a development in historical approaches to literature known as *new historicism* has emphasized the interaction between the historic context of a work and a modern reader's understanding and interpretation of the work. In contrast to many traditional literary historians, however, new historicists attempt to describe the culture of a period by reading many different kinds of texts that traditional literary historians might have previously left for economists, sociologists, and anthropologists. New historicists attempt to read a period in all its dimensions, including political, economic, social, and aesthetic concerns. These considerations could be used to explain the pressures that destroy Mrs. Mallard. A new historicist might examine the story and the public attitudes toward women contemporary to "The Story of an Hour" as well as documents such as suffragist tracts and medical diagnoses to explore how the same forces — expectations about how women are supposed to feel, think, and behave — shape different kinds of texts and how these texts influence one another. A new historicist might, for example, examine medical records for evidence of "nervousness" and "hysteria" as common diagnoses for women who led lives regarded as too independent by their contemporaries.

Without an awareness of just how selfish and self-destructive Mrs. Mallard's impulses would have been in the eyes of her contemporaries, readers in the twenty-first century might miss the pervasive pressures embedded not only in her marriage but in the social fabric surrounding her. Her death is made more understandable by such an awareness. The doctors who diagnose her as suffering from "the joy that kills" are not merely insensitive or stupid; they represent a contrasting set of assumptions and values that are as historic and real as Mrs. Mallard's yearnings.

New historicist criticism acknowledges more fully than traditional historical approaches the competing nature of readings of the past and thereby tends to offer new emphases and perspectives. New historicism reminds us that there is not only one historic context for "The Story of an Hour." Those doctors reveal additional dimensions of late-nineteenth-century social attitudes that warrant our attention, whether we agree with them or not. By emphasizing that historical perceptions are governed, at least in part, by our own concerns and preoccupations, new historicists sensitize us to the fact that the history on which we choose to focus is colored by being reconstructed from our own present moment. This reconstructed history affects our reading of texts.

Cultural Criticism

Cultural critics, like new historicists, focus on the historical contexts of a literary work, but they pay particular attention to popular manifestations of social, political, and economic contexts. Popular culture — mass-produced and -consumed cultural artifacts, today ranging from advertising to popular fiction to television to rock music — and "high" culture are given equal emphasis. A cultural critic might be interested in looking at how Baz Luhrmann's movie version of *Romeo + Juliet* (1996) was influenced by the fragmentary nature of MTV videos. Adding the "low" art of everyday life to "high" art opens up previously unexpected and unexplored areas of criticism. Cultural critics use widely eclectic strategies drawn from new historicism, psychology, gender studies, and deconstructionism (to name only a handful of approaches) to analyze not only literary texts but radio talk shows, comic strips, calendar art, commercials, travel guides, and baseball cards. Because all human activity falls within the ken of cultural criticism, nothing is too minor or major, obscure or pervasive, to escape the range of its analytic vision.

Cultural criticism also includes *postcolonial criticism,* the study of cultural behavior and expression in relationship to the formerly colonized world. Postcolonial criticism refers to the analysis of literary works written by writers from countries and cultures that at one time were controlled by colonizing powers — such as Indian writers during or after British colonial rule. The term also refers to the analysis of literary works written about colonial cultures by writers from the colonizing country. Many of these kinds of analyses point out how writers from colonial powers sometimes misrepresent colonized cultures by reflecting more their own values: Joseph Conrad's *Heart of Darkness* (published in 1899) represents African culture differently than Chinua Achebe's *Things Fall Apart* does, for example. Cultural criticism and postcolonial criticism represent a broad range of approaches to examining race, gender, and class in historical contexts in a variety of cultures.

A cultural critic's approach to Chopin's "The Story of an Hour" might emphasize how the story reflects the potential dangers and horrors of train travel in the 1890s or it might examine how heart disease was often misdiagnosed by physicians or used as a metaphor in Mrs. Mallard's culture for a variety of emotional conditions. Each of these perspectives can serve to create a wider and more informed understanding of the story.

GENDER STRATEGIES

Gender critics explore how ideas about men and women — what is masculine and feminine — can be regarded as socially constructed by particular cultures. According to some critics, sex is determined by simple biological and anatomical categories of male or female, and gender is determined by a culture's values. Thus, ideas about gender and what constitutes masculine and feminine behavior are created by cultural institutions and conditioning. A gender critic might, for example, focus on Chopin's characterization of an emotionally sensitive Mrs. Mallard and a rational, composed husband in "The Story of an Hour" as a manifestation of socially constructed gender identity in the 1890s. *Gender criticism* expands categories and definitions of what is masculine or feminine and tends to regard sexuality as more complex than merely masculine or feminine, heterosexual or homosexual. Gender criticism, therefore, has come to include gay and lesbian criticism as well as feminist criticism. Although there are complex and sometimes problematic relationships among these approaches because some critics argue that heterosexuals and homosexuals are profoundly biologically different, gay and lesbian criticism, like feminist criticism, can be usefully regarded as a subset of gender criticism.

Feminist Criticism

Like Marxist critics, *feminist critics* reading "The Story of an Hour" would also be interested in Charlotte Perkins Gilman's *Women and Economics: A Study of the Economic Relation between Men and Women as a Factor in Social Evolution* (1898) because they seek to correct or supplement what they regard as a predominantly male-dominated critical perspective with a feminist consciousness. Like other forms of sociological criticism, feminist criticism places literature in a social context, and, like those of Marxist criticism, its analyses often have sociopolitical purposes — explaining, for example, how images of women in literature reflect the patriarchal social forces that have impeded women's efforts to achieve full equality with men.

Feminists have analyzed literature by both men and women in an effort to understand literary representations of women as well as the writers and cultures that create them. Related to concerns about how gender affects the way men and women write about each other is an interest in whether women use language differently from the way men do. Consequently, feminist critics' approach to literature is characterized by the use of a broad range of disciplines, including history, sociology, psychology, and linguistics, to provide a perspective sensitive to feminist issues.

A feminist approach to Chopin's "The Story of an Hour" might explore the psychological stress created by the expectations that marriage imposes on Mrs. Mallard, expectations that literally and figuratively break her heart. Given that her husband is kind and loving, the issue is not her being married to Brently but her being married at all. Chopin presents marriage as an institution that creates in both men and women the assumed "right to impose a private will upon a fellow-creature." That "right," however, is seen, especially from a feminist perspective, as primarily imposed on women by men. A feminist critic might note, for instance, that the protagonist is introduced as "Mrs. Mallard" (we learn that her first name is Louise only later); she is defined by her marital status and her husband's name, a name whose origin from the Old French is related to the word *masle,* which means "male." The appropriateness of her name points up the fact that her emotions and the cause of her death are interpreted in male terms by the doctors. The value of a feminist perspective on this work can be readily discerned if a reader imagines Mrs. Mallard's story being told from the point of view of one of the doctors who diagnoses the cause of her death as a weak heart rather than as a fierce struggle.

Gay and Lesbian Criticism

Gay and lesbian critics focus on a variety of issues, including how homosexuals are represented in literature, how they read literature, and whether sexuality and gender are culturally constructed or innate. Gay critics have produced new readings of works by and discovered homosexual concerns in writers such as Herman Melville and Henry James, while lesbian critics have done the same for the works of writers such as Emily Dickinson and Toni Morrison. A lesbian reading of "The Story of an Hour," for example, might consider whether Mrs. Mallard's ecstatic feeling of relief — produced by the belief that her marriage is over owing to the presumed death of her husband — isn't also a rejection of her heterosexual identity. Perhaps her glimpse of future freedom, evoked by feminine images of a newly discovered nature "all aquiver with the new spring of life," embraces a repressed new sexual identity that "was too subtle and elusive to name" but that was "approaching to possess her" no matter how much she "was striving to beat it back with her will." Although gay and lesbian readings often raise significant interpretive controversies among critics, they have opened up provocative discussions of seemingly familiar texts.

MYTHOLOGICAL STRATEGIES

Mythological approaches to literature attempt to identify what in a work creates deep universal responses in readers. Whereas psychological critics interpret the symbolic meanings of characters and actions in order to understand more fully the unconscious dimensions of an author's mind, a character's motivation, or a reader's response, ***mythological critics*** (also frequently referred to as *archetypal critics*) interpret the hopes, fears, and expectations of entire cultures.

In this context myth is not to be understood simply as referring to stories about imaginary gods who perform astonishing feats in the causes of love, jealousy, or hatred. Nor are myths to be judged as merely erroneous, primitive accounts of how nature runs its course and humanity its affairs. Instead, literary critics use myths as a strategy for understanding how human beings try to account for their lives symbolically. Myths can be a window into a culture's deepest perceptions about itself because myths attempt to explain what otherwise seems unexplainable: a people's origin, purpose, and destiny.

All human beings have a need to make sense of their lives, whether they are concerned about their natural surroundings, the seasons, sexuality, birth, death, or the very meaning of existence. Myths help people organize their experiences; these systems of belief (less formally held than religious or political tenets but no less important) embody a culture's assumptions and values. What is important to the mythological critic is not the validity or truth of those assumptions and values; what matters is that they reveal common human concerns.

It is not surprising that although the details of mythic stories vary enormously, the essential patterns are often similar because these myths attempt to explain universal experiences. There are, for example, numerous myths that redeem humanity from permanent death through a hero's resurrection and rebirth. The resurrection of Jesus symbolizes for Christians the ultimate defeat of death and coincides with the rebirth of nature's fertility in spring. Features of this rebirth parallel the Greek myths of Adonis and Hyacinth, who die but are subsequently transformed into living flowers; there are also similarities that connect these stories to the reincarnation of the Indian Buddha or the rebirth of the Egyptian Osiris. Important differences exist among these stories, but each reflects a basic human need to limit the power of death and to hope for eternal life.

Mythological critics look for underlying, recurrent patterns in literature that reveal universal meanings and basic human experiences for readers regardless of when or where they live. The characters, images, and themes that symbolically embody these meanings and experiences are called ***archetypes.*** This term designates universal symbols that evoke deep and perhaps unconscious responses in a reader because archetypes bring with them our hopes and fears since the beginning of human time. Surely one of the most powerfully compelling archetypes is the death and rebirth theme that relates the human life cycle to the cycle of the seasons. Many others could be cited and would be exhausted only after all human concerns were cataloged, but a few examples can suggest some of the range of plots, images, and characters addressed.

Among the most common literary archetypes are stories of quests, initiations, scapegoats, meditative withdrawals, descents to the underworld, and heavenly ascents. These stories are often filled with archetypal images — bodies of water that may symbolize the unconscious or eternity or baptismal rebirth; rising suns, suggesting reawakening and enlightenment; setting suns, pointing toward death; colors such as green, evocative of growth and fertility, or black, indicating chaos, evil, and death. Along the way are earth mothers, fatal women, wise old men, desert places, and paradisal gardens. No doubt your own reading has introduced you to any number of archetypal plots, images, and characters.

Mythological critics attempt to explain how archetypes are embodied in literary works. Employing various disciplines, these critics articulate the power a literary work has over us. Some critics are deeply grounded in classical literature, whereas others are more conversant with philology, anthropology, psychology, or cultural history. Whatever their emphases, however, mythological critics examine the elements of a work in order to make larger connections that explain the work's lasting appeal.

A mythological reading of Sophocles' *Oedipus the King,* for example, might focus on the relationship between Oedipus's role as a scapegoat and the plague and drought that threaten to destroy Thebes. The city is saved and the fertility of its fields restored only after the corruption is located in Oedipus. His subsequent atonement symbolically provides a kind of rebirth for the city. Thus, the plot recapitulates ancient rites in which the well-being of a king was directly linked to the welfare of his people. If a leader was sick or corrupt, he had to be replaced in order to guarantee the health of the community.

A similar pattern can be seen in the rottenness that Shakespeare exposes in Hamlet's Denmark. *Hamlet* reveals an archetypal pattern similar to that of *Oedipus the King:* not until the hero sorts out the corruption in his world and in himself can vitality and health be restored in his world. Hamlet avenges his father's death and becomes a scapegoat in the process. When he fully accepts his responsibility to set things right, he is swept away along with the tide of intrigue and corruption that has polluted life in Denmark. The new order — established by Fortinbras at the play's end — is achieved precisely because Hamlet is willing and finally able to sacrifice himself in a necessary purgation of the diseased state.

These kinds of archetypal patterns exist potentially in any literary period. Consider how in Chopin's "The Story of an Hour" Mrs. Mallard's life parallels the end of winter and the earth's renewal in spring. When she feels a surge of new life after grieving over her husband's death, her own sensibilities are closely aligned with the "new spring life" that is "all aquiver" outside her window. Although she initially tries to resist that renewal by "beat[ing] it back with her will," she cannot control the life force that surges within her and all around her. When she finally gives herself to the energy and life she experiences, she feels triumphant—like a "goddess of Victory." But this victory is short lived when she learns that her husband is still alive and with him all the obligations that made her marriage feel like a wasteland. Her death is an ironic version of a rebirth ritual. The coming of spring is an ironic contrast to her own discovery that she can no longer live a repressed, circumscribed life with her husband. Death turns out to be preferable to the living death that her marriage means to her. Although spring will go on, this "goddess of Victory" is defeated by a devastating social contract. The old, corrupt order continues, and that for Chopin is a cruel irony that mythological critics would see as an unnatural disruption of the nature of things.

READER-RESPONSE STRATEGIES

Reader-response criticism, as its name implies, focuses its attention on the reader rather than the work itself. This approach to literature describes what goes on in the reader's mind during the process of reading a text. In a sense, all critical approaches (especially psychological and mythological criticism) concern themselves with a reader's response to literature, but there is a stronger emphasis in reader-response criticism on the reader's active construction of the text. Although many critical theories inform reader-response criticism, all **reader-response critics** aim to describe the reader's experience of a work: in effect we get a reading of the reader, who comes to the work with certain expectations and assumptions, which are either met or not met. Hence the consciousness of the reader—produced by reading the work—is the subject matter of reader-response critics. Just as writing is a creative act, reading is, since it also produces a text.

Reader-response critics do not assume that a literary work is a finished product with fixed formal properties, as, for example, formalist critics do. Instead, the literary work is seen as an evolving creation of the reader as he or she processes characters, plots, images, and other elements while reading. Some reader-response critics argue that this act of creative reading is, to a degree, controlled by the text, but it can produce many interpretations of the same text by different readers. There is no single definitive reading of a work, because the crucial assumption is that readers create rather than discover meanings in texts. Readers who have gone back to works they had read earlier in their lives often find that a later reading draws very different responses from them. What earlier seemed unimportant is now crucial; what at first seemed central is now barely worth noting. The reason, put simply, is that two different people have read the same text. Reader-response critics are not after the "correct" reading of the text or what the author presumably intended; instead they are interested in the reader's experience with the text.

These experiences change with readers; although the text remains the same, the readers do not. Social and cultural values influence readings, so that, for example, an avowed Marxist would be likely to come away from Miller's *Death of a Salesman* with a very different view of American capitalism than that of, say, a successful sales representative, who might attribute Willy Loman's fall more to his character than to the American economic system. Moreover, readers from different time periods respond differently to texts. An Elizabethan — concerned perhaps with the stability of monarchical rule — might respond differently to Hamlet's problems than would a twenty-first-century reader well versed in psychology and concepts of what Freud called the Oedipus complex. This is not to say that anything goes, that Miller's play can be read as an amoral defense of cheating and rapacious business practices or that *Hamlet* is about the dangers of living away from home. The text does, after all, establish some limits that allow us to reject certain readings as erroneous. But reader-response critics do reject formalist approaches that describe a literary work as a self-contained object, the meaning of which can be determined without reference to any extrinsic matters, such as the social and cultural values assumed by either the author or the reader.

Reader-response criticism calls attention to how we read and what influences our readings. It does not attempt to define what a literary work means on the page but rather what it does to an informed reader, a reader who understands the language and conventions used in a given work. Reader-response criticism is not a rationale for mistaken or bizarre readings of works but an exploration of the possibilities for a plurality of readings shaped by readers' experiences with the text. This kind of strategy can help us understand how our responses are shaped by both the text and ourselves.

Chopin's "The Story of an Hour" illustrates how reader-response critical strategies read the reader. Chopin doesn't say that Mrs. Mallard's marriage is repressive; instead, that troubling fact dawns on the reader at the same time that the recognition forces its way into Mrs. Mallard's consciousness. Her surprise is also the reader's because although she remains in the midst of intense grief, she is on the threshold of a startling discovery about the new possibilities life offers. How the reader responds to that discovery, however, is not entirely controlled by Chopin. One reader, perhaps someone who has recently lost a spouse, might find Mrs. Mallard's "joy" indeed "monstrous" and selfish. Certainly that's how Mrs. Mallard's doctors — the seemingly authoritative diagnosticians in the story — would very likely read her. But for other readers — especially twenty-first-century readers steeped in feminist values — Mrs. Mallard's feelings require no justification. Such readers might find Chopin's ending to the story more ironic than she seems to have intended because Mrs. Mallard's death could be read as Chopin's inability to envision a protagonist who has the strength of her convictions. In contrast, a reader in 1894 might have seen the ending as Mrs. Mallard's only escape from the repressive marriage her husband's assumed death suddenly allowed her to see. A reader in our times probably would argue that it was the marriage that should have died rather than Mrs. Mallard, that she had other alternatives, not just obligations (as the doctors would have insisted), to consider.

By imagining different readers, we can imagine a variety of responses to the story that are influenced by the readers' own impressions, memories, or experiences with marriage. Such imagining suggests the ways in which reader-response criticism opens up texts to a number of interpretations. As one final example, consider how readers' responses to "The Story of an Hour" would be affected if it were printed in two different magazines, read in the context of either *Ms.* or *Good Housekeeping*. What assumptions and beliefs would each magazine's readership be likely to bring to the story? How do you think the respective experiences and values of each magazine's readers would influence their readings? For a sample reader-response student paper on "The Story of an Hour," see page 19.

DECONSTRUCTIONIST STRATEGIES

Deconstructionist critics insist that literary works do not yield fixed, single meanings. They argue that there can be no absolute knowledge about anything because language can never say what we intend it to mean. Anything we write conveys meanings we did not intend, so the deconstructionist argument goes. Language is not a precise instrument but a power whose meanings are caught in an endless web of possibilities that cannot be untangled. Accordingly, any idea or statement that insists on being understood separately can ultimately be "deconstructed" to reveal its relations and connections to contradictory and opposite meanings.

Unlike other forms of criticism, **deconstructionism** seeks to destabilize meanings instead of establishing them. In contrast to formalists such as the New Critics, who closely examine a work in order to call attention to how its various components interact to establish a unified whole, deconstructionists try to show how a close examination of the language in a text inevitably reveals conflicting, contradictory impulses that "deconstruct" or break down its apparent unity.

Although deconstructionists and New Critics both examine the language of a text closely, deconstructionists focus on the gaps and ambiguities that reveal a text's instability and indeterminacy, whereas New Critics look for patterns that explain how the text's fixed meaning is structured. Deconstructionists painstakingly examine the competing meanings within the text rather than attempting to resolve them into a unified whole.

The questions deconstructionists ask are aimed at discovering and describing how a variety of possible readings are generated by the elements of a text. In contrast to a New Critic's concerns about the ultimate meaning of a work, a deconstructionist is primarily interested in how the use of language — diction, tone, metaphor, symbol, and so on — yields only provisional, not definitive, meanings. Consider, for example, the following excerpt from an American Puritan poet, Anne Bradstreet. The excerpt is from "The Flesh and the Spirit" (1678), which consists of an allegorical debate between two sisters, the body and the soul. During the course of the debate, Flesh, a consummate materialist, insists that Spirit values ideas that do not exist and that her faith in idealism is both unwarranted and insubstantial in the face of the material values that earth has to offer — riches, fame, and physical pleasure. Spirit, however, rejects the materialistic worldly argument that the only ultimate reality is physical reality and pledges her faith in God:

> Mine eye doth pierce the heavens and see
> What is invisible to thee.
> My garments are not silk nor gold,
> Nor such like trash which earth doth hold,
> But royal robes I shall have on,
> More glorious than the glist'ning sun;
> My crown not diamonds, pearls, and gold,
> But such as angels' heads enfold
> The city where I hope to dwell,
> There's none on earth can parallel;
> The stately walls both high and strong,
> Are made of precious jasper stone;
> The gates of pearl, both rich and clear,
> And angels are for porters there;
> The streets thereof transparent gold,
> Such as no eye did e'er behold;
> A crystal river there doth run,
> Which doth proceed from the Lamb's throne.

A deconstructionist would point out that Spirit's language — her use of material images such as jasper stone, pearl, gold, and crystal — cancels the explicit meaning of the passage by offering a supermaterialistic reward to the spiritually faithful. Her language, in short, deconstructs her intended meaning by employing the same images that Flesh would use to describe the rewards of the physical world. A deconstructionist reading, then, reveals the impossibility of talking about the invisible and spiritual worlds without using materialistic (that is, metaphoric) language. Thus Spirit's very language demonstrates a contradiction and conflict in her conviction that the world of here and now must be rejected for the hereafter. Her language deconstructs her meaning.

Deconstructionists look for ways to question and extend the meanings of a text. A deconstructionist might find, for example, the ironic ending of Chopin's "The Story of an Hour" less tidy and conclusive than would a New Critic, who might attribute Mrs. Mallard's death to her sense of lost personal freedom. A deconstructionist might use the story's ending to suggest that the narrative shares the doctors' inability to imagine a life for Mrs. Mallard apart from her husband. As difficult as it is controversial, deconstructionism is not easily summarized or paraphrased.

47

Reading and Writing

I can't write five words but that I change seven.

— DOROTHY PARKER

THE PURPOSE AND VALUE OF WRITING ABOUT LITERATURE

Introductory literature courses typically include three components — reading, discussion, and writing. Students usually find the readings a pleasure, the class discussions a revelation, and the writing assignments — at least initially — a little intimidating. Writing an analysis of Melville's use of walls in "Bartleby, the Scrivener" (p. 124), for example, may seem considerably more daunting than making a case for animal rights or analyzing a campus newspaper editorial that calls for grade reforms. Like Bartleby, you might want to respond with "I would prefer not to." Literary topics are not, however, all that different from the kinds of papers assigned in English composition courses; many of the same skills are required for both. Regardless of the type of paper, you must develop a thesis and support it with evidence in language that is clear and persuasive.

Whether the subject matter is a marketing survey, a political issue, or a literary work, writing is a method of communicating information and perceptions. Writing teaches. But before writing becomes an instrument for informing the reader, it serves as a means of learning for the writer. An essay is a process of discovery as well as a record of what has been discovered. One of the chief benefits of writing is that we frequently realize what we want to say only after trying out ideas on a page and seeing our thoughts take shape in language.

More specifically, writing about a literary work encourages us to be better readers because it requires a close examination of the elements of a short story, poem, or play. To determine how plot, character, setting, point of view, style, tone, irony, or any number of other literary elements function in a work, we must study them in relation to one another as well as separately. Speed-reading won't do. To read a text accurately and validly — neither ignoring nor distorting significant details — we must return to the work repeatedly to test our responses and interpretations. By paying attention to details and being sensitive to the author's use of language, we develop a clearer understanding of how the work conveys its effects and meanings.

Nevertheless, students sometimes ask why it is necessary or desirable to write about a literary work. Why not allow stories, poems, and plays to speak for themselves? Isn't it presumptuous to interpret Hemingway, Dickinson, or Shakespeare? These writers do, of course, speak for themselves, but they do so indirectly. Literary criticism seeks not to replace the text by explaining it but to enhance our readings of works by calling attention to elements that we might have overlooked or only vaguely sensed.

Another misunderstanding about the purpose of literary criticism is that it crankily restricts itself to finding faults in a work. Critical essays are sometimes mistakenly equated with newspaper and magazine reviews of recently published works. Reviews typically include summaries and evaluations to inform readers about a work's nature and quality, but critical essays assume that readers are already familiar with a work. Although a critical essay may point out limitations and flaws, most criticism — and certainly the kind of essay usually written in an introductory literature course — is designed to explain, analyze, and reveal the complexities of a work. Such sensitive consideration increases our appreciation of the writer's achievement and significantly adds to our enjoyment of a short story, poem, or play. In short, the purpose and value of writing about literature are that doing so leads to greater understanding and pleasure.

READING THE WORK CLOSELY

Know the piece of literature you are writing about before you begin your essay. Think about how the work makes you feel and how it is put together. The more familiar you are with how the various elements of the text convey effects and meanings, the more confident you will be explaining whatever perspective on it you ultimately choose. Do not insist that everything make sense on a first reading. Relax and enjoy yourself; you can be attentive and still allow the author's words to work their magic on you. With subsequent readings, however, go more slowly and analytically as you try to establish relations between characters, actions, images, or whatever else seems important. Ask yourself why you respond as you do. Think as you read, and notice how the parts of a work contribute to its overall nature. Whether the work is a short story, poem, or play, you will read relevant portions of it over and over, and you will very likely find more to discuss in each review if the work is rich.

It's best to avoid reading other critical discussions of a work before you are thoroughly familiar with it. There are several good reasons for following this advice. By reading interpretations before you know a work, you deny yourself the pleasure of discovery. That is a bit like starting with the last chapter in a mystery novel. But perhaps even more important than protecting the surprise and delight that a work might offer is that a premature reading of a critical discussion will probably short-circuit your own responses. You will see the work through the critic's eyes and have to struggle with someone else's perceptions and ideas before you can develop your own.

Reading criticism can be useful, but not until you have thought through your own impressions of the text. A guide should not be permitted to become a tyrant. This does not mean, however, that you should avoid background information about a work—for example, that Joyce Carol Oates's story "The Lady with the Pet Dog" was based on a similar story by Anton Chekhov. Knowing something about the author as well as historic and literary contexts can help to create expectations that enhance your reading.

ANNOTATING THE TEXT
AND JOURNAL NOTE TAKING

As you read, get in the habit of annotating your texts. Whether you write marginal notes, highlight, underline, or draw boxes and circles around important words and phrases, you'll eventually develop a system that allows you to retrieve significant ideas and elements from the text. Another way to record your impressions of a work—as with any other experience—is to keep a journal. By writing down your reactions to characters, images, language, actions, and other matters in a reading journal, you can often determine why you like or dislike a work or feel sympathetic or antagonistic to an author or discover paths into a work that might have eluded you if you hadn't preserved your impressions. Your journal notes and annotations may take whatever form you find useful; full sentences and grammatical correctness are not essential (unless they are to be handed in and your instructor requires that), though they might allow you to make better sense of your own reflections days later. The point is simply to put in writing thoughts that you can retrieve when you need them for class discussion or a writing assignment. Consider the following student annotation of the first twenty-four lines of Andrew Marvell's "To His Coy Mistress" (p. 636) and the journal entry that follows it:

Annotated Text

If we had time . . .

Had we but world enough, and time,
This coyness, lady, were no (crime.) *Waste life and you steal from yourself.*
We would sit down, and think which way
To walk, and pass our long love's day.
Thou by the Indian (Ganges') side   5
Shouldst rubies find; I by the tide
Of (Humber) would complain.° I would *Measurements of time* *write love songs*
Love you ten years before the Flood,
And you should, if you please, refuse
Till the conversion of the Jews.   10
My vegetable love should grow,° *slow, unconscious growth*
Vaster than empires, and more slow;
An hundred years should go to praise
Thine eyes and on thy forehead gaze,
Two hundred to adore each breast,   15
But thirty thousand to the rest:
An age at least to every part,
And the last age should show your heart.
For, lady, you deserve this state,
Nor would I love at lower rate.   20

contrast river and desert images

But at my back I always hear *Lines move faster here— tone changes.*
Time's wingèd chariot hurrying near;
And yonder all before us lie
(Deserts) of vast (eternity.) *This eternity rushes in.*

For additional annotated texts, see the close readings of William Faulkner's "A Rose for Emily" (p. 90), Ralph Ellison's "Battle Royal" (p. 243), Elizabeth Bishop's "Manners" (p. 615), and John Donne's "Death Be Not Proud" (p. 820). (For a complete list of sample close readings, see this book's inside front cover.)

Journal Note

He'd be patient and wait for his "mistress" if they had the time--sing songs, praise her, adore her, etc. But they don't have that much time according to him. He seems to be patient but he actually begins by calling patience--her coyness--a "crime." Looks to me like he's got his mind made up from the beginning of the poem. Where's her response? I'm not sure about him.

This journal note responds to some of the effects noted in the annotations of the poem; it's an excellent beginning for making sense of the speaker's argument in the poem.

Taking notes will preserve your initial reactions to the work. Many times first impressions are the best. Your response to a peculiar character in a story, a striking phrase in a poem, or a subtle bit of stage business in a play might lead to larger perceptions. The student paper on John Updike's "A & P" (p. 1581), for example, began with the student writing "how come?" next to the story's title in her textbook. She thought it strange that the title didn't refer to a character or the story's conflict. That annotated response eventually led her to examine the significance of the setting, which became the central idea of her paper.

You should take detailed notes only after you've read through the work. If you write too many notes during the first reading, you're likely to disrupt your response. Moreover, until you have a sense of the entire work, it will be difficult to determine how connections can be made among its various elements. In addition to recording your first impressions and noting significant passages, characters, actions, and so on, you should consult the Questions for Responsive Reading and Writing about fiction (p. 48), poetry (p. 614), and drama (p. 1089). These questions can assist you in getting inside a work as well as organizing your notes.

Inevitably, you will take more notes than you finally use in the paper. Note taking is a form of thinking aloud, but because your ideas are on paper you don't have to worry about forgetting them. As you develop a better sense of a potential topic, your notes will become more focused and detailed.

CHOOSING A TOPIC

If your instructor assigns a topic or offers a choice from among an approved list of topics, some of your work is already completed. Instead of being asked to come up with a topic about *Oedipus the King*, you may be asked to write a three-page essay that specifically discusses whether Oedipus's downfall is a result of fate or foolish pride. You also have the assurance that a specified topic will be manageable within the suggested number of pages. Unless you ask your instructor for permission to write on a different or related topic, be certain to address yourself to the assignment. An essay that does not discuss Oedipus's downfall but instead describes his relationship with his wife, Jocasta, would be missing the point. Notice too that there is room even in an assigned topic to develop your own approach. One question that immediately comes to mind is whether Oedipus's plight is relevant to a twenty-first-century reader. Assigned topics do not relieve you of thinking about an aspect of a work, but they do focus your thinking.

At some point during the course, you may have to begin an essay from scratch. You might, for example, be asked to write about a short story that somehow impressed you or that seemed particularly well written or filled with insights. Before you start considering a topic, you should have a sense of how long the paper will be because the assigned length can help to determine the extent to which you should develop your topic. Ideally, the paper's length should be based on how much space you deem necessary to present your discussion clearly and convincingly, but if you have any doubts and no specific guidelines have been indicated, ask. The question is important; a topic that might be appropriate for a three-page paper could be too narrow for ten pages. Three pages would probably be adequate for a discussion of why Emily murders Homer in Faulkner's "A Rose for Emily." Conversely, it would be futile to try to summarize Faulkner's use of the South in his fiction in even ten pages; this would have to be narrowed to something like "Images of the South in 'A Rose for Emily.'" Be sure that the topic you choose can be adequately covered in the assigned number of pages.

Once you have a firm sense of how much you are expected to write, you can begin to decide on your topic. If you are to choose what work to write about, select one that genuinely interests you. Too often students pick a story, poem, or play because it is mercifully short or seems simple. Such works can certainly be the subjects of fine essays, but simplicity should not be the major reason for selecting them. Choose a work that has moved you so that you have something to say about it. The student who wrote about "A & P" was initially attracted to the story's title because she had once worked in a similar store. After reading the story, she became fascinated with its setting because Updike's descriptions seemed so accurate. Her paper then grew out of her curiosity about the setting's purpose. When a writer is engaged in a topic, the paper has a better chance of being interesting to a reader.

After you have settled on a particular work, your notes and annotations of the text should prove useful for generating a topic. The paper on "John Updike's 'A & P' as a State of Mind" developed naturally from the notes (p. 1581) that the student jotted down about the setting and antagonist. If you think with a pen in your hand, you are likely to find when you review your notes that your thoughts have clustered into one or more topics. Perhaps there are patterns of imagery that seem to make a point about life. There may be scenes that are ironically paired or secondary characters who reveal certain qualities about the protagonist. Your notes and annotations on such aspects can lead you to a particular effect or impression. Having chuckled your way through "A & P," you may discover that your notations about the story's humor point to a serious satire of society's values.

DEVELOPING A THESIS

When you are satisfied that you have something interesting to say about a work and that your notes have led you to a focused topic, you can formulate a **thesis,** the central idea of the paper. Whereas the topic indicates what the paper focuses on (the setting in "A & P"), the thesis explains what you have to say about the topic (because the intolerant setting of "A & P" is the antagonist in the story, it is crucial to our understanding of Sammy's decision to quit his job). The thesis should be a complete sentence (though sometimes it may require more than one sentence) that establishes your topic in clear, unambiguous language. The thesis may be revised as you get further into the topic and discover what you want to say about it, but once the thesis is firmly established, it will serve as a guide for you and your reader because all the information and observations in your essay should be related to the thesis.

One student on an initial reading of Andrew Marvell's "To His Coy Mistress" saw that the male speaker of the poem urges a woman to love now before time runs out for them. This reading gave him the impression that the poem is a simple celebration of the pleasures of the flesh, but on subsequent readings he underlined or noted these images: "Time's wingèd chariot hurrying near"; "Deserts of vast eternity"; "marble vault"; "worms"; "dust"; "ashes"; and these two lines: "The grave's a fine and private place, / But none, I think, do there embrace."

By listing these images associated with time and death, he established an inventory that could be separated from the rest of his notes on point of view, character, sounds, and other subjects. Inventorying notes allows patterns to emerge that you might have only vaguely perceived otherwise. Once these images are grouped, they call attention to something darker and more complex in Marvell's poem than a first impression might suggest.

These images may create a different feeling about the poem, but they still don't explain very much. One simple way to generate a thesis about a literary work is to ask the question "why?" Why do these images appear in the poem? Why does Hamlet hesitate to avenge his father's death? Why does Hemingway choose the Midwest as the setting of "Soldier's Home"? Your responses to these kinds of questions can lead to a thesis.

Writers sometimes use freewriting to help themselves explore possible answers to such questions. It can be an effective way of generating ideas. Freewriting is exactly that: the technique calls for nonstop writing without concern for mechanics or editing of any kind. Freewriting for ten minutes or so on a question will result in fragments and repetitions, but it can also produce some ideas. Here's an example of a student's response to the question about the images in "To His Coy Mistress":

He wants her to make love. Love poem. There's little time. Her crime. He exaggerates. Sincere? Sly? What's he want? She says nothing--he says it all. What

about deserts, ashes, graves, and worms? Some love poem. Sounds like an old
Vincent Price movie. Full of sweetness but death creeps in. Death--hurry hurry!
Tear pleasures. What passion! Where's death in this? How can a love poem be
so ghoulish? She does nothing. Maybe frightened? Convinced? Why death? Love
and death--time--death.

This freewriting contains several ideas; it begins by alluding to the poem's plot and speaker, but the central idea seems to be death. This emphasis led the student to five potential thesis statements for his essay about the poem:

1. "To His Coy Mistress" is a difficult poem.

2. Death in "To His Coy Mistress."

3. There are many images of death in "To His Coy Mistress."

4. "To His Coy Mistress" celebrates the pleasures of the flesh, but it also recognizes the power of death to end that pleasure.

5. On the surface, "To His Coy Mistress" is a celebration of the pleasures of the flesh, but this witty seduction is tempered by a chilling recognition of the reality of death.

The first statement is too vague to be useful. In what sense is the poem difficult? A more precise phrasing, indicating the nature of the difficulty, is needed. The second statement is a topic rather than a thesis. Because it is not a sentence, it does not express a complete idea about how the poem treats death. Although this could be an appropriate title, it is inadequate as a thesis statement. The third statement, like the first one, identifies the topic, but even though it is a sentence, it is not a complete idea that tells us anything significant beyond the fact it states. After these preliminary attempts to develop a thesis, the student remembered his first impression of the poem and incorporated it into his thesis statement. The fourth thesis is a useful approach to the poem because it limits the topic and indicates how it will be treated in the paper: the writer will begin with an initial impression of the poem and then go on to qualify it. However, the fifth thesis is better than the fourth because it indicates a shift in tone produced by the ironic relationship between death and flesh. An effective thesis, like this one, makes a clear statement about a manageable topic and provides a firm sense of direction for the paper.

Most writing assignments in a literature course require you to persuade readers that your thesis is reasonable and supported with evidence. Papers that report information without comment or evaluation are simply summaries. A plot summary of Shakespeare's *The Tempest*, for example, would have no thesis, but a paper that discussed how Prospero's oppression of Caliban represents European imperialism and colonialism would argue a thesis. Similarly, a paper that merely pointed out the death images in "To His Coy Mistress" would not contain a thesis, but a paper that attempted to make a case for the death imagery as a grim reminder of how vulnerable flesh is would involve persuasion. In developing a thesis, remember that you are expected not merely to present information but to argue a point.

ARGUING ABOUT LITERATURE

An argumentative essay is designed to make persuasive your interpretation of a work. Arguing about literature doesn't mean that you're engaged in an angry, antagonistic dispute (though controversial topics do sometimes engender heated debates; see, for example, Joan Templeton's comments in the Critical Case Study on Ibsen's *A Doll House* [p. 1316]). Instead, argumentation requires that you present your interpretation of a work (or a portion of it) by supporting your discussion with clearly defined terms, ample evidence, and a detailed analysis of relevant portions of the text.

If you have a choice, it's generally best to write about a topic that you feel strongly about. If you're not fascinated by Bartleby the Scrivener's haunting presence in Melville's short story, then perhaps you'll find chilling Emily Grierson's behavior in Faulkner's "A Rose for Emily," or maybe you can explain why Bartleby's character is so excruciatingly boring to you. If your essay is to be interesting and convincing, what is important is that it be written from a strong point of view that persuasively argues your evaluation, analysis, and interpretation of a work. It is not enough to say that you like or dislike a work; instead you must give your reader some ideas and evidence that can be accepted or rejected based on the quality of the answers to the questions you raise.

One way to come up with persuasive answers is to generate good questions that will lead you further into the text and to critical issues related to it. Notice how the Perspectives, Complementary Critical Readings, Critical Case Studies, and Cultural Case Studies in this anthology raise significant questions and issues about texts from a variety of points of view. Moreover, the Critical Strategies for Reading summarized in Chapter 46 can be a resource for raising questions that can be shaped into an argument, and the Questions for Writing: Incorporating the Critics (p. 438) can help you to incorporate a critic's perspective into your own argument. The following lists of questions for the critical approaches covered in Chapter 46 should be useful for discovering arguments you might make about a short story, poem, or play. The page number that follows each heading refers to the discussion in the anthology for that particular approach.

Questions for Arguing Critically about Literature

FORMALIST QUESTIONS (P. 1538)

1. How do various elements of the work — plot, character, point of view, setting, tone, diction, images, symbol, and so on — reinforce its meanings?
2. How are the elements related to the whole?
3. What is the work's major organizing principle? How is its structure unified?
4. What issues does the work raise? How does the work's structure resolve those issues?

BIOGRAPHICAL QUESTIONS (P. 1540)

1. Are facts about the writer's life relevant to your understanding of the work?
2. Are characters and incidents in the work versions of the writer's own experiences? Are they treated factually or imaginatively?
3. How do you think the writer's values are reflected in the work?

PSYCHOLOGICAL QUESTIONS (P. 1542)

1. How does the work reflect the author's personal psychology?
2. What do the characters' emotions and behavior reveal about their psychological states? What types of personalities are they?
3. Are psychological matters such as repression, dreams, and desire presented consciously or unconsciously by the author?

HISTORICAL QUESTIONS (P. 1544)

1. How does the work reflect the period in which it is written?
2. What literary or historical influences helped to shape the form and content of the work?
3. How important is the historical context to interpreting the work?

MARXIST QUESTIONS (P. 1545)

1. How are class differences presented in the work? Are characters aware or unaware of the economic and social forces that affect their lives?
2. How do economic conditions determine the characters' lives?
3. What ideological values are explicit or implicit?
4. Does the work challenge or affirm the social order it describes?

NEW HISTORICIST QUESTIONS (P. 1546)

1. What kinds of documents outside the work seem especially relevant for shedding light on the work?

Questions for Arguing Critically about Literature

2. How are social values contemporary to the work reflected or refuted in the work?

3. How does your own historical moment affect your reading of the work and its historical reconstruction?

CULTURAL STUDIES QUESTIONS (P. 1547)

1. What does the work reveal about the cultural behavior contemporary to it?

2. How does popular culture contemporary to the work reflect or challenge the values implicit or explicit in the work?

3. What kinds of cultural documents contemporary to the work add to your reading of it?

4. How do your own cultural assumptions affect your reading of the work and the culture contemporary to it?

GENDER STUDIES QUESTIONS (P. 1548)

1. How are the lives of men and women portrayed in the work? Do the men and women in the work accept or reject these roles?

2. Is the form and content of the work influenced by the author's gender?

3. What attitudes are explicit or implicit concerning heterosexual, homosexual, or lesbian relationships? Are these relationships sources of conflict? Do they provide resolutions to conflicts?

4. Does the work challenge or affirm traditional ideas about men and women and same-sex relationships?

MYTHOLOGICAL QUESTIONS (P. 1550)

1. How does the story resemble other stories in plot, character, setting, or use of symbols?

2. Are archetypes presented, such as quests, initiations, scapegoats, or withdrawals and returns?

3. Does the protagonist undergo any kind of transformation such as a movement from innocence to experience that seems archetypal?

4. Do any specific allusions to myths shed light on the text?

READER-RESPONSE QUESTIONS (P. 1552)

1. How do you respond to the work?

2. How do your own experiences and expectations affect your reading and interpretation?

3. What is the work's original or intended audience? To what extent are you similar to or different from that audience?

4. Do you respond in the same way to the work after more than one reading?

(continued)

DECONSTRUCTIONIST QUESTIONS (P. 1554)

1. How are contradictory and opposing meanings expressed in the work?
2. How does meaning break down or deconstruct itself in the language of the text?
3. Would you say that ultimate definitive meanings are impossible to determine and establish in the text? Why? How does that affect your interpretation?
4. How are implicit ideological values revealed in the work?

These questions will not apply to all texts; and they are not mutually exclusive. They can be combined to explore a text from several critical perspectives simultaneously. A feminist approach to Kate Chopin's "The Story of an Hour" could also use Marxist concerns about class to make observations about the oppression of women's lives in the historical context of the nineteenth century. Your use of these questions should allow you to discover significant issues from which you can develop an argumentative essay that is organized around clearly defined terms, relevant evidence, and a persuasive analysis.

ORGANIZING A PAPER

After you have chosen a manageable topic and developed a thesis, a central idea about it, you can begin to organize your paper. Your thesis, even if it is still somewhat tentative, should help you decide what information will need to be included and provide you with a sense of direction.

Consider again the sample thesis in the section on developing a thesis:

On the surface, "To His Coy Mistress" is a celebration of the pleasures of the flesh, but this witty seduction is tempered by a chilling recognition of the reality of death.

This thesis indicates that the paper can be divided into two parts — the pleasures of the flesh and the reality of death. It also indicates an order: because the central point is to show that the poem is more than a simple celebration, the pleasures of the flesh should be discussed first so that another, more complex, reading of the poem can follow. If the paper began with the reality of death, its point would be anticlimactic.

Having established such a broad and informal outline, you can draw on your underlinings, margin notations, and note cards for the subheadings and evidence required to explain the major sections of your paper. This next level of detail would look like the following:

1. Pleasures of the flesh

   Part of the traditional tone of love poetry

2. Recognition of death
    Ironic treatment of love
        Diction
        Images
        Figures of speech
        Symbols
        Tone

This list was initially a jumble of terms, but the student arranged the items so that each of the two major sections leads to a discussion of tone. (The student also found it necessary to drop some biographical information from his notes because it was irrelevant to the thesis.) The list indicates that the first part of the paper will establish the traditional tone of love poetry that celebrates the pleasures of the flesh, while the second part will present a more detailed discussion about the ironic recognition of death. The emphasis is on the latter because that is the point to be argued in the paper. Hence, the thesis has helped to organize the parts of the paper, establish an order, and indicate the paper's proper proportions.

The next step is to fill in the subheadings with information from your notes. Many experienced writers find that making lists of information to be included under each subheading is an efficient way to develop paragraphs. For a longer paper (perhaps a research paper), you should be able to develop a paragraph or more on each subheading. On the other hand, a shorter paper may require that you combine several subheadings in a paragraph. You may also discover that while an informal list is adequate for a brief paper, a ten-page assignment could require a more detailed outline. Use the method that is most productive for you. Whatever the length of the essay, your presentation must be in a coherent and logical order that allows your reader to follow the argument and evaluate the evidence. The quality of your reading can be demonstrated only by the quality of your writing.

WRITING A DRAFT

The time for sharpening pencils, checking e-mail, arranging your desk, and doing almost anything else instead of writing has ended. The first draft will appear on the page only if you stop avoiding the inevitable and sit, stand up, or lie down to write. It makes no difference how you write, just so you do. Now that you have developed a topic into a tentative thesis, you can assemble your notes and begin to flesh out whatever outline you have made.

Be flexible. Your outline should smoothly conduct you from one point to the next, but do not permit it to railroad you. If a relevant and important idea occurs to you now, work it into the draft. By using the first draft as a means of thinking about what you want to say, you will very likely discover more than your notes originally suggested. Plenty of good writers don't use outlines at all but discover ordering principles as they write. Do not attempt to compose a perfectly correct draft the first time around. Grammar, punctuation, and spelling can wait until you revise. Concentrate on what you are saying. Good writing most often occurs when you are in hot pursuit of an idea rather than in a nervous search for errors.

By working on a word processor, you can take advantage of its capacity to make additions and deletions as well as move entire paragraphs by making just a few simple keyboard commands. Most software programs can also check spelling and certain grammatical elements in your writing. It's worth remembering, however, that though a clean copy fresh off a printer may look terrific, it will read only as well as the thinking and writing that have gone into it. Many writers prudently store their data on disks and print their pages each time they finish a draft to avoid losing any material because of power failures or other problems. These printouts are also easier to read than the screen when you work on revisions.

Once you have a first draft on paper, you can delete material that is unrelated to your thesis and add material necessary to illustrate your points and make your paper convincing. The student who wrote "John Updike's 'A & P' as a State of Mind" wisely dropped a paragraph that questioned whether Sammy displays chauvinistic attitudes toward women. Although this is an interesting issue, it has nothing to do with the thesis, which explains how the setting influences Sammy's decision to quit his job. Instead of including that paragraph, she added one that described Lengel's crabbed response to the girls so that she could lead up to the A & P "policy" he enforces.

Remember that your initial draft is only that. You should go through the paper many times — and then again — working to substantiate and clarify your ideas. You may even end up with several entire versions of the paper. Rewrite. The sentences within each paragraph should be related to a single topic. Transitions should connect one paragraph to the next so that there are no abrupt or confusing shifts. Awkward or wordy phrasing or unclear sentences and paragraphs should be mercilessly poked and prodded into shape.

Writing the Introduction and Conclusion

After you have clearly and adequately developed the body of your paper, pay particular attention to the introductory and concluding paragraphs. It's probably best to write the introduction — at least the final version of it — last, after you know precisely what you are introducing. Because this paragraph is crucial for generating interest in the topic, it should engage the reader and provide a sense of what the paper is about. There is no formula for writing effective introductory paragraphs because each writing situation is different — depending on the audience, topic, and approach — but if you pay attention to the introductions of the essays you read, you will notice a variety of possibilities. The introductory paragraph to "John Updike's 'A & P' as a State of Mind," for example, is a straightforward explanation of why the story's setting is important for understanding Updike's treatment of the antagonist. The rest of the paper then offers evidence to support this point.

Concluding paragraphs demand equal attention because they leave the reader with a final impression. The conclusion should provide a sense of closure instead of starting a new topic or ending abruptly. In the final paragraph about the significance of the setting in "A & P," the student brings together the reasons Sammy quit his job by referring to his refusal to accept Lengel's store policies. At the same time she makes this point, she also explains the significance of Sammy ringing up the "No Sale" mentioned in her introductory paragraph. Thus, we are brought back to where we began, but we now have a greater understanding of why Sammy quits his job. Of course, the body of your paper is the most important part of your presentation, but do remember that first and last impressions have a powerful impact on readers.

Using Quotations

Quotations can be a valuable means of marshaling evidence to illustrate and support your ideas. A judicious use of quoted material will make your points clearer and more convincing. Here are some guidelines that should help you use quotations effectively.

1. Brief quotations (four lines or fewer of prose or three lines or fewer of poetry) should be carefully introduced and integrated into the text of your paper with quotation marks around them:

According to the narrator, Bertha "had a reputation for strictness." He tells us that she always "wore dark clothes, dressed her hair simply, and expected contrition and obedience from her pupils."

For brief poetry quotations, use a slash to indicate a division between lines:

The concluding lines of Blake's "The Tyger" pose a disturbing question: "What immortal hand or eye / Dare frame thy fearful symmetry?"

Lengthy quotations should be separated from the text of your paper. More than three lines of poetry should be double spaced and centered on the page. More than four lines of prose should be double spaced and indented ten spaces from the left margin, with the right margin the same as for the text. Do *not* use quotation marks for the passage; the indentation indicates that the passage is a quotation. Lengthy quotations should not be used in place of your own writing. Use them only if they are absolutely necessary.

2. If any words are added to a quotation, use brackets to distinguish your addition from the original source:

"He [Young Goodman Brown] is portrayed as self-righteous and disillusioned."

Any words inside quotation marks and not in brackets must be precisely those of the author. Brackets can also be used to change the grammatical structure of a quotation so that it fits into your sentence:

Smith argues that Chekhov "present[s] the narrator in an ambivalent light."

If you drop any words from the source, use ellipses to indicate the omission:

"Early to bed . . . makes a man healthy, wealthy, and wise."

Use ellipses following a period to indicate an omission at the end of a sentence:

"Early to bed and early to rise makes a man healthy. . . ."

Use a single line of spaced periods to indicate the omission of a line or more of poetry or more than one paragraph of prose:

Nothing would sleep in that cellar, dank as a ditch,
Bulbs broke out of boxes hunting for chinks in the dark,

. . . .

Nothing would give up life:
Even the dirt kept breathing a small breath.

3. You will be able to punctuate quoted material accurately and confidently if you observe these conventions.

Place commas and periods inside quotation marks:

"Even the dirt," Roethke insists, "kept breathing a small breath."

Even though a comma does not appear after "dirt" in the original quotation, it is placed inside the quotation mark. The exception to this rule occurs when a parenthetical reference to a source follows the quotation:

"Even the dirt," Roethke insists, "kept breathing a small breath" (11).

Punctuation marks other than commas or periods go outside the quotation marks unless they are part of the material quoted:

What does Roethke mean when he writes that "the dirt kept breathing a small breath"?

Yeats asked, "How can we know the dancer from the dance?"

REVISING AND EDITING

Put some distance—a day or so if you can—between yourself and each draft of your paper. The phrase that seemed just right on Wednesday may be revealed as all wrong on Friday. You'll have a better chance of detecting lumbering sentences and thin paragraphs if you plan ahead and give yourself the time to read your paper from a fresh perspective. Through the process of revision, you can transform a competent paper into an excellent one.

Begin by asking yourself if your approach to the topic requires any rethinking. Is the argument carefully thought out and logically presented? Are there any gaps in the presentation? How well is the paper organized? Do the paragraphs lead into one another? Does the body of the paper deliver what the thesis promises? Is the interpretation sound? Are any relevant and important elements of the work ignored or distorted to advance the thesis? Are the points supported with evidence? These large questions should be addressed before you focus on more detailed matters. If you uncover serious problems as a result of considering these questions, you'll probably have quite a lot of rewriting to do, but at least you will have the opportunity to correct the problems—even if doing so takes several drafts.

A useful technique for spotting awkward or unclear moments in the paper is to read it aloud. You might also try having a friend read it aloud to you. If your handwriting is legible, your friend's reading—perhaps accompanied by hesitations and puzzled expressions—could alert you to passages that need reworking. Having identified problems, you can readily correct them on a word processor or on the draft, provided you've skipped lines and used wide margins. The final draft you hand in should be neat and carefully proofread for any inadvertent errors.

The following checklist offers questions to ask about your paper as you revise and edit it. Most of these questions will be familiar to you; however, if you need help with any of them, ask your instructor or review the appropriate section in a composition handbook.

Questions for Writing: A Revision Checklist

1. Is the topic manageable? Is it too narrow or too broad?
2. Is the thesis clear? Is it based on a careful reading of the work?
3. Is the paper logically organized? Does it have a firm sense of direction?
4. Is your argument persuasive?
5. Should any material be deleted? Do any important points require further illustration or evidence?

(continued)

Questions for Writing: A Revision Checklist

6. Does the opening paragraph introduce the topic in an interesting manner?

7. Are the paragraphs developed, unified, and coherent? Are any too short or long?

8. Are there transitions linking the paragraphs?

9. Does the concluding paragraph provide a sense of closure?

10. Is the tone appropriate? Is it unduly flippant or pretentious?

11. Is the title engaging and suggestive?

12. Are the sentences clear, concise, and complete?

13. Are simple, complex, and compound sentences used for variety?

14. Have technical terms been used correctly? Are you certain of the meanings of all the words in the paper? Are they spelled correctly?

15. Have you documented any information borrowed from books, articles, or other sources? Have you quoted too much instead of summarizing or paraphrasing secondary material?

16. Have you used a standard format for citing sources (see p. 1600)?

17. Have you followed your instructor's guidelines for the manuscript format of the final draft?

18. Have you carefully proofread the final draft?

When you proofread your final draft, you may find a few typographical errors that must be corrected but do not warrant reprinting an entire paper. Provided there are not more than a handful of such errors throughout the paper, they can be corrected as shown in the following passage. This example condenses a short paper's worth of errors; no single passage should be this shabby in your essay:

To add a letter or word, use a caret on the line where the addition is needed. To delete a word draw a single line through ~~through~~ it. Run-on words are separated by a vertical|line, and inadvertent spaces are closed like t̂his. Transposed letters are indicated this way. New paragraphs are noted with the sign ¶ in front of where the next paragraph is to begin.¶ Unless you . . .

You can minimize these sorts of errors by proofreading on the screen and simply entering your corrections as you go along.

MANUSCRIPT FORM

The novelist and poet Peter De Vries once observed that he very much enjoyed writing but that he couldn't bear the "paper work." Behind this playful pun is a half-serious impatience with the mechanics of it all. You may feel some of that too, but don't let your thoughtful, carefully revised paper trip over minor details. The final draft you hand in to your instructor should not only read well but look neat. If your instructor does not provide specific instructions concerning the format for the paper, follow these guidelines:

1. Papers (particularly long ones) should be typed on 8-1/2 by 11-inch paper in double space. Avoid transparent paper such as onionskin; it is difficult to read and write comments on. If you compose on a word processor, be certain that the print is legible. If your instructor accepts handwritten papers, write legibly in ink on only one side of a wide-lined page.

2. Use a one-inch margin at the top, bottom, and sides of each page. Unless you are instructed to include a separate title page, type your name, instructor's name, course number and section, and date on separate lines one inch below the upper-left corner of the first page. Double-space between these lines and then center the title two spaces below the date. Do not underline or put quotation marks around your paper's title, but do use quotation marks around the titles of poems, short stories, or other brief works, and underline the titles of books and plays (for instance, Racial Stereotypes in "Battle Royal" and *Mambo Mouth*). Begin the text of your paper two spaces below the title. If you have used secondary sources, list them on a separate page at the end of the paper. Center the heading "Notes" or "Works Cited" one inch from the top of the page and then double-space between it and the entries.

3. Number each page consecutively, beginning with page 1, a half inch from the top of the page in the upper-right corner.

4. Gather the pages with a paper clip rather than staples, folders, or some other device. That will make it easier for your instructor to handle the paper.

TYPES OF WRITING ASSIGNMENTS

The types of papers most frequently assigned in literature classes are explication, analysis, and comparison and contrast. Most writing about literature involves some combination of these skills. This section includes a sample explication, an analysis, and a comparison and contrast paper. For a sample research paper that demonstrates a variety of strategies for documenting outside sources, see page 1608. For genre-based assignments, see the sample papers for writing about fiction (p. 19), poetry (p. 618), and drama (p. 1091). All of the sample student papers in this book are indexed in the inside front cover.

Explication

The purpose of this approach to a literary work is to make the implicit explicit. *Explication* is a detailed explanation of a passage of poetry or prose. Because explication is an intensive examination of a text line by line, it is mostly used to interpret a short poem in its entirety or a brief passage from a long poem, short story, or play. Explication can be used in any kind of paper when you want to be specific about how a writer achieves a certain effect. An explication pays careful attention to language — the connotations of words, allusions, figurative language, irony, symbol, rhythm, sound, and so on. These elements are examined in relation to one another and to the overall effect and meaning of the work.

The simplest way to organize an explication is to move through the passage line by line, explaining whatever seems significant. It is wise to avoid, however, an assembly-line approach that begins each sentence with "In line one (two, three) . . ." Instead, organize your paper in whatever way best serves your thesis. You might find that the right place to start is with the final lines, working your way back to the beginning of the poem or passage. The following sample explication on Dickinson's "There's a certain Slant of light" does just that. The student's opening paragraph refers to the final line of the poem in order to present her thesis. She explains that though the poem begins with an image of light, it is not a bright or cheery poem but one concerned with "the look of Death." Since the last line prompted her thesis, that is where she begins the explication.

You might also find it useful to structure a paper by discussing various elements of literature, so that you have a paragraph on connotative words followed by one on figurative language and so on. However your paper is organized, keep in mind that the aim of an explication is not simply to summarize the passage but to comment on the effects and meanings produced by the author's use of language in it. An effective explication (the Latin word *explicare* means "to unfold") displays a text to reveal how it works and what it signifies. Although writing an explication requires some patience and sensitivity, it is an excellent method for coming to understand and appreciate the elements and qualities that constitute literary art.

A SAMPLE STUDENT EXPLICATION

A Reading of Emily Dickinson's "There's a certain Slant of light"

The sample paper by Bonnie Katz is the result of an assignment calling for an explication of about 750 words on any poem by Emily Dickinson. Katz selected "There's a certain Slant of light."

EMILY DICKINSON (1830–1886)

There's a certain Slant of light

c. *1861*

There's a certain Slant of light,
Winter Afternoons —
That oppresses, like the Heft
Of Cathedral Tunes —

Heavenly Hurt, it gives us —   5
We can find no scar,
But internal difference,
Where the Meanings, are —

None may teach it — Any —
'Tis the Seal Despair —   10
An imperial affliction
Sent us of the Air —

When it comes, the Landscape listens —
Shadows — hold their breath —
When it goes, 'tis like the Distance
On the look of Death —   15

    This essay comments on every line of the poem and provides a coherent reading that relates each line to the speaker's intense awareness of death. Although the essay discusses each stanza in the order that it appears, the introductory paragraph provides a brief overview explaining how the poem's images contribute to its total meaning. In addition, the student does not hesitate to discuss a line out of sequence when it can be usefully connected to another phrase. This is especially apparent in the third paragraph, in her discussion of stanzas 2 and 3. The final paragraph describes some of the formal elements of the poem. It might be argued that this discussion could have been integrated into the previous paragraphs rather than placed at the end, but the student does make a connection in her concluding sentence between the pattern of language and its meaning.

    Several other matters are worth noticing. The student works quotations into her own sentences to support her points. She quotes exactly as the words appear in the poem, even Dickinson's irregular use of capital letters. When something is added to a quotation to clarify it, it is enclosed in brackets so that the essayist's words will not be mistaken for the poet's: "Seal [of] Despair." A slash is used to indicate line divisions as in "imperial affliction / Sent us of the Air."

Bonnie Katz

Professor Quiello

English 109-2

October 26, 2008

A Reading of Emily Dickinson's

"There's a certain Slant of light"

Because Emily Dickinson did not provide titles for her poetry, editors

follow the customary practice of using the first line of a poem as its title.

However, a more appropriate title for "There's a certain Slant of light," one

that suggests what the speaker in the poem is most concerned about, can be

drawn from the poem's last line, which ends with "the look of Death" (Dickin-

son, line 16). Although the first line begins with an image of light, nothing

bright, carefree, or cheerful appears in the poem. Instead, the predominant

mood and images are darkened by a sense of despair resulting from the

speaker's awareness of death.

In the first stanza, the "certain Slant of light" is associated with "Win-

ter Afternoons" (2), a phrase that connotes the end of a day, a season, and

even life itself. Such light is hardly warm or comforting. Not a ray or beam,

this slanting light suggests something unusual or distorted and creates in the

speaker a certain slant on life that is consistent with the cold, dark mood that

winter afternoons can produce. Like the speaker, most of us have seen and felt

this sort of light: it "oppresses" (3) and pervades our sense of things when we

encounter it. Dickinson uses the senses of hearing and touch as well as sight

to describe the overwhelming oppressiveness that the speaker experiences.

The light is transformed into sound by a simile that tells us it is "like the Heft

/ Of Cathedral Tunes" (3-4). Moreover, the "Heft" of that sound -- the slow,

solemn measures of tolling church bells and organ music--weighs heavily on

our spirits. Through the use of shifting imagery, Dickinson evokes a kind of

spiritual numbness that we keenly feel and perceive through our senses.

By associating the winter light with "Cathedral Tunes," Dickinson lets

us know that the speaker is concerned about more than the weather. What-

ever it is that "oppresses" is related by connotation to faith, mortality, and

Thesis providing overview of explication *(margin annotation)*

Line-by-line explication of first stanza, focusing on connotations of words and imagery, in relation to mood and meaning of poem as a whole; supported with references to the text *(margin annotation)*

God. The second and third stanzas offer several suggestions about this connection. The pain caused by the light is a "Heavenly Hurt" (5). This "imperial
affliction / Sent us of the Air" (11–12) apparently comes from God above,
and yet it seems to be part of the very nature of life. The oppressiveness we
feel is in the air, and it can neither be specifically identified at this point in
the poem nor be eliminated, for "None may teach it--Any" (9). All we know is
that existence itself seems depressing under the weight of this "Seal [of]
Despair" (10). The impression left by this "Seal" is stamped within the mind
or soul rather than externally. "We can find no scar" (6), but once experienced
this oppressiveness challenges our faith in life and its "Meanings" (8).

> Explication of second, third, and fourth stanzas, focusing on connotations of words and imagery in relation to mood and meaning of poem as a whole. Supported with references to the text

  The final stanza does not explain what those "Meanings" are, but it
does make clear that the speaker is acutely aware of death. As the winter
daylight fades, Dickinson projects the speaker's anxiety onto the surrounding
landscape and shadows, which will soon be engulfed by the darkness that
follows this light: "the Landscape listens-- / Shadows--hold their breath"
(13–14). This image firmly aligns the winter light in the first stanza with
darkness. Paradoxically, the light in this poem illuminates the nature of
darkness. Tension is released when the light is completely gone, but what
remains is the despair that the "imperial affliction" has imprinted on the
speaker's sensibilities, for it is "like the Distance / On the look of Death--"
(15–16). There can be no relief from what that "certain Slant of light" has
revealed because what has been experienced is permanent--like the fixed
stare in the eyes of someone who is dead.

  The speaker's awareness of death is conveyed in a thoughtful, hushed
tone. The lines are filled with fluid l and smooth s sounds that are appropriate for the quiet, meditative voice in the poem. The voice sounds tentative
and uncertain--perhaps a little frightened. This seems to be reflected in the
slightly irregular meter of the lines. The stanzas are trochaic with the second
and fourth lines of each stanza having five syllables, but no stanza is identical because each works a slight variation on the first stanza's seven syllables
in the first and third lines. The rhymes also combine exact patterns with
variations. The first and third lines of each stanza are not exact rhymes, but
the second and fourth lines are exact so that the paired words are more

> Explication of the elements of rhythm and sound throughout poem

> Conclusion tying explication of rhythm and sound with explication of words and imagery in previous paragraphs

Katz 3

closely related: Afternoons, Tunes; scar, are; Despair, Air; and breath, Death.
There is a pattern to the poem, but it is unobtrusively woven into the
speaker's voice in much the same way that "the look of Death" (16) is subtly
present in the images and language of the poem.

Katz 4

Work Cited

Dickinson, Emily. "There's a certain Slant of light." The Compact Bedford
    Introduction to Literature. Ed. Michael Meyer. 8th ed. Boston:
    Bedford/St. Martin's, 2009. 1577.

Analysis

The preceding sample essay shows how an explication examines in detail
the important elements in a work and relates them to the whole. An analysis, however, usually examines only a single element — such as plot, character, point of view, symbol, tone, or irony — and relates it to the entire work.
An analytic topic separates the work into parts and focuses on a specific
one; you might consider "Point of View in 'A Rose for Emily,' " "Patterns of
Rhythm in Browning's 'My Last Duchess,' " or "The Significance of Cassio
in *Othello*." The specific element must be related to the work as a whole or it
will appear irrelevant. It is not enough to point out that there are many
death images in Marvell's "To His Coy Mistress"; the images must somehow be connected to the poem's overall effect.

    Whether an analytic paper is just a few pages or many, it cannot at-
tempt to discuss everything about the work it is considering. Only those
elements that are relevant to the topic can be treated. This kind of focusing
makes the topic manageable; this is why most papers that you write will
probably be some form of analysis. Explications are useful for a short passage, but a line-by-line commentary on a story, play, or long poem simply
isn't practical. Because analysis allows you to consider the central effect or
meaning of an entire work by studying a single important element, it is a
useful and common approach to longer works.

A SAMPLE STUDENT ANALYSIS

John Updike's "A & P" as a State of Mind

Nancy Lager's paper analyzes the setting in John Updike's "A & P" (the entire story appears on p. 560). The assignment simply asked for an essay of approximately 750 words on a short story written in the twentieth century. The approach was left to the student.

The idea for this essay began with Lager asking herself why Updike used "A & P" as the title. The initial answer to the question was that "the setting is important in this story." This answer was the rough beginning of a tentative thesis. What still had to be explained, though, was how the setting is important. To determine the significance of the setting, Lager jotted down some notes based on her underlinings and marginal notations:

A & P

"usual traffic"

lights and tile

"electric eye"

shoppers like "sheep," "houseslaves," "pigs"

"Alexandrov and Petrooshki" — Russia

New England Town	*Lengel*
typical: bank, church, etc.	"manager"
traditional	"doesn't miss that much"
conservative	(like lady shopper)
proper	Sunday school
near Salem — witch trials	"It's our policy"
puritanical	spokesman for A & P values
intolerant	

From these notes Lager saw that Lengel serves as the voice of the A & P. He is, in a sense, a personification of the intolerant atmosphere of the setting. This insight led to another version of her thesis statement: "The setting of 'A & P' is the antagonist of the story." That explained at least some of the setting's importance. By seeing Lengel as a spokesman for "A & P" policies, she could view him as a voice that articulates the morally smug atmosphere created by the setting. Finally, she considered why it is significant that the setting is the antagonist, and this generated her last thesis: "Because the intolerant setting of 'A & P' is the antagonist in the story, it is crucial to our understanding of Sammy's decision to quit his job." This thesis sentence does not appear precisely in these words in the essay, but it is the backbone of the introductory paragraph.

The remaining paragraphs consist of details that describe the A & P in the second paragraph, the New England town in the third, Lengel in the fourth, and Sammy's reasons for quitting in the concluding paragraph. Paragraphs 2, 3, and 4 are largely based on Lager's notes, which she used as an outline once her thesis was established. The essay is sharply focused, well organized, and generally well written. In addition, it suggests a number of useful guidelines for analytic papers:

1. Only the points related to the thesis are included. In another type of paper the role of the girls in the bathing suits, for example, might have been considerably more prominent.

2. The analysis keeps the setting in focus while at the same time indicating how it is significant in the major incident in the story — Sammy's quitting.

3. The title is a useful lead into the paper; it provides a sense of what the topic is. In addition, the title is drawn from a sentence (the final one of the first paragraph) that clearly explains its meaning.

4. The introductory paragraph is direct and clearly indicates the paper will argue that the setting serves as the antagonist of the story.

5. Brief quotations are deftly incorporated into the text of the paper to illustrate points. We are told what we need to know about the story as evidence is provided to support ideas. There is no unnecessary plot summary. Even though "A & P" is only a few pages in length and is an assigned topic, page numbers are included after quoted phrases. If the story were longer, page numbers would be especially helpful for the reader.

6. The paragraphs are well developed, unified, and coherent. They flow naturally from one to another. Notice, for example, the smooth transition worked into the final sentence of the third paragraph and the first sentence of the fourth paragraph.

7. Lager makes excellent use of her careful reading and notes by finding revealing connections among the details she has observed. The store's "electric eye," for instance, is related to the woman's and Lengel's watchfulness.

8. As events are described, the present tense is used. This avoids awkward tense shifts and lends an immediacy to the discussion.

9. The concluding paragraph establishes the significance of why the setting should be seen as the antagonist and provides a sense of closure by referring again to Sammy's "No Sale," which has been mentioned at the end of the first paragraph.

10. In short, Lager has demonstrated that she has read the work closely, has understood the relation of the setting to the major action, and has argued her thesis convincingly by using evidence from the story.

Nancy Lager
Professor Taylor
English 102-12
April 2, 2008

John Updike's "A & P" as a State of Mind

The setting of John Updike's "A & P" is crucial to our understanding of Sammy's decision to quit his job. Although Sammy is the central character in the story and we learn that he is a principled, good-natured nineteen-year-old with a sense of humor, Updike seems to invest as much effort in describing the setting as he does in Sammy. The setting is the antagonist and plays a role that is as important as Sammy's. The title, after all, is not "Youthful Rebellion" or "Sammy Quits" but "A & P." Even though Sammy knows that his quitting will make life more difficult for him, he instinctively insists on rejecting what the A & P comes to represent in the story. When he rings up a "No Sale" and "saunter[s]" (Updike 564) out of the store, he leaves behind not only a job but the rigid state of mind associated with the A & P.

Sammy's descriptions of the A & P present a setting that is ugly, monotonous, and rigidly regulated. The fluorescent light is as blandly cool as the "checkerboard green-and-cream rubber-tile floor" (562). We can see the uniformity Sammy describes because we have all been in chain stores. The "usual traffic" moves in one direction (except for the swimsuited girls, who move against it), and everything is neatly ordered and categorized in tidy aisles. The dehumanizing routine of this environment is suggested by Sammy's offhand references to the typical shoppers as "sheep" (561), "houseslaves" (562) and "pigs" (564). They seem to pace through the store in a stupor; as Sammy tells us, not even dynamite could move them.

The A & P is appropriately located "right in the middle" (562) of a proper, conservative, traditional New England town north of Boston. This location, coupled with the fact that the town is only five miles from Salem, the site of the famous seventeenth-century witch trials, suggests a narrow, intolerant social atmosphere in which there is no room for stepping beyond the boundaries of what is regarded as normal and proper. The importance of this setting can be appreciated even more if we imagine the action taking place in, say, a mellow suburb of southern California. In this prim New England setting, the girls in their bathing suits are bound to offend somebody's sense of propriety.

As soon as Lengel sees the girls, the inevitable conflict begins. He embodies the dull conformity represented by the A & P. As "manager" (563), he is both the guardian and enforcer of "policy" (563). When he gives the girls "that sad Sunday-school-superintendent stare" (563), we know we are in the presence of the A & P version of a dreary bureaucrat who "doesn't miss that much" (563). He is as unsympathetic and unpleasant as the woman "with rouge on her cheeks and no eyebrows" (560) who pounces on Sammy for ringing up her "HiHo crackers" twice. Like the "electric eye" (564) in the doorway, her vigilant eyes allow nothing to escape their notice. For Sammy the logical extension of Lengel's "policy" is the half-serious notion that one day the A & P might be known as the "Great Alexandrov and Petrooshki Tea Company" (562). Sammy's connection between what he regards as mindless "policy" (563) and Soviet oppression is obviously an exaggeration, but the reader is invited to entertain the similarities anyway.

The reason Sammy quits his job has less to do with defending the girls than with his own sense of what it means to be a decent human being. His decision is not an easy one. He doesn't want to make trouble or disappoint his parents, and he knows his independence and self-reliance (the other side of New England tradition) will make life more complex for him. In spite of his own hesitations, he finds himself blurting out "Fiddle-de-doo" (564) to Lengel's policies and in doing so knows that his grandmother "would have been pleased" (564). Sammy's "No Sale" rejects the crabbed perspective on life that Lengel represents as manager of the A & P. This gesture is more than just a negative, however, for as he punches in that last entry on the cash register, "the machine whirs 'pee-pul'" (563). His decision to quit his job at the A & P is an expression of his refusal to regard policies as more important than people.

Lager 3

Work Cited

Updike, John. "The A & P." The Compact Bedford Introduction to Literature.
    Ed. Michael Meyer. 8th ed. Boston: Bedford/St. Martin's, 2009.
    560–64.

Comparison and Contrast

Another essay assignment in literature courses often combined with analytic topics is the type that requires you to write about similarities and differences between or within works. You might be asked to discuss "How
Sounds Express Meanings in May Swenson's 'A Nosty Fright' and Lewis
Carroll's 'Jabberwocky,' " or "Sammy's and Stokesie's Attitudes about Conformity in Updike's 'A & P.' " A *comparison* of either topic would emphasize
their similarities, while a *contrast* would stress their differences. It is possible, of course, to include both perspectives in a paper if you find significant likenesses and differences. A comparison of Andrew Marvell's "To His
Coy Mistress" and Ann Lauinger's "Marvell Noir" would, for example, yield
similarities because each poem describes a man urging his lover to make
the most of their precious time together; however, important differences
also exist in the tone and theme of each poem that would constitute a contrast. (You should, incidentally, be aware that the term *comparison* is sometimes used inclusively to refer to both similarities and differences. If you
are assigned a comparison of two works, be sure that you understand what
your instructor's expectations are; you may be required to include both
approaches in the essay.)

   When you choose your own topic, the paper will be more successful —
more manageable — if you write on works that can be meaningfully related
to each other. Although Robert Herrick's "To the Virgins, to Make Much
of Time" and Shakespeare's *Hamlet* both have something to do with hesitation, the likelihood of anyone making a connection between the two that
reveals something interesting and important is remote — though perhaps
not impossible if the topic were conceived imaginatively and tactfully.
That is not to say that comparisons of works from different genres should
be avoided, but the relation between them should be strong, as would a
treatment of African American identity in M. Carl Holman's "Mr. Z" and
August Wilson's *Fences*. Choose a topic that encourages you to ask significant questions about each work; the purpose of a comparison or contrast
is to understand the works more clearly for having examined them together.

Despite the obvious differences between Henrik Ibsen's *A Doll House* and Gail Godwin's "A Sorrowful Woman," the two are closely related if we ask why the wife in each work withdraws from her family.

Choose works to compare or contrast that intersect with each other in some significant way. They may, for example, be written by the same author, in the same genre, or about the same subject. Perhaps you can compare their use of some technique, such as irony or point of view. Regardless of the specific topic, be sure to have a thesis that allows you to organize your paper around a central idea that argues a point about the two works. If you merely draw up a list of similarities or differences without a thesis in mind, your paper will be little more than a series of observations with no apparent purpose. Keep in the foreground of your thinking what the comparison or contrast reveals about the works.

There is no single way to organize comparative papers since each topic is likely to have its own particular issues to resolve, but it is useful to be aware of two basic patterns that can be helpful with a comparison, a contrast, or a combination of both. One method that can be effective for relatively short papers consists of dividing the paper in half, first discussing one work and then the other. Here, for example, is a partial informal outline for a discussion of Sophocles' *Oedipus the King* and Shakespeare's *Othello*; the topic is a comparison and contrast: "Oedipus and Othello as Tragic Figures."

1. Oedipus
   a. The nature of the conflict
   b. Strengths and stature
   c. Weaknesses and mistakes
   d. What is learned
2. Othello
   a. The nature of the conflict
   b. Strengths and stature
   c. Weaknesses and mistakes
   d. What is learned

This organizational strategy can be effective provided that the second part of the paper combines the discussion of Othello with references to Oedipus so that the thesis is made clear and the paper unified without being repetitive. If the two characters were treated entirely separately, then the discussion would be merely parallel rather than integrated. In a lengthy paper, this organization probably would not work well because a reader would have difficulty remembering the points made in the first half as he or she reads on.

Thus, for a longer paper it is usually better to create a more integrated structure that discusses both works as you take up each item in your outline. Here is the second basic pattern using the elements in the partial outline just cited:

1. The nature of the conflict
    a. Oedipus
    b. Othello
2. Strengths and stature
    a. Oedipus
    b. Othello
3. Weaknesses and mistakes
    a. Oedipus
    b. Othello
4. What is learned
    a. Oedipus
    b. Othello

This pattern allows you to discuss any number of topics without requiring your reader to recall what you first said about the conflict Oedipus confronts before you discuss Othello's conflicts fifteen pages later. However you structure your comparison or contrast paper, make certain that a reader can follow its elements and keep track of its thesis.

A SAMPLE STUDENT COMPARISON

The Struggle for Women's Self-Definition in Ibsen's A Doll House *and Colette's* "The Hand"

The following paper was written in response to an assignment that required a comparison and contrast — about 750 words — of two works of literature. The student chose to write an analysis of how the women in each work respond to being defined by men.

Candace Rardon

Professor Matthews

English 105-4

July 27, 2008

The Struggle for Women's Self-Definition

in Ibsen's A Doll House and Colette's "The Hand"

Though Henrik Ibsen's A Doll House (1879) and Sidonie-Gabrielle Colette's

"The Hand" (1924) were written almost fifty years apart and portray female

protagonists in radically different stages of their lives, both works raise

similar questions about the role of women and how they are defined in their

respective worlds. In A Doll House, Nora Helmer, mother of three children,

has been married for eight years to her husband, Torvald, while the wife in

"The Hand" is a newlywed of only two weeks, wed to a man recently widowed.

Despite their different circumstances, both women are forced to wear masks

in order to conform to their husbands' ideals of the perfect woman. In the

same way Torvald tells Nora, "A songbird needs a clean beak to warble with.

No false notes" (Ibsen 1275), both women learn that the struggle for self

requires no false notes as well. It requires breaking free from their expected

roles to discover who they truly are. Both works suggest that for these wives

to remain in their marriages, they must deny who they truly are in order to

fulfill their husbands' expectations.

    The opening of A Doll House presents a seemingly perfect home. Nora

is "humming happily to herself" (1258) as she carries in an armful of Christ-

mas presents for her family; Torvald is at work in his study, days away from

beginning a prestigious, well-paying new job; and three young children are

being cared for by their nurse, Anne-Marie. This idyllic picture, however, is

soon contrasted with the realization that there is more to the Helmer house-

hold than meets the eye. Torvald frequently calls Nora his "squirrel," "spend-

thrift," and "little lark" (1258–59), and Nora seems to see herself as nothing

but her husband's doll, just as she was her father's--a mere plaything subject

to their tastes and whims.

    Although Nora externally conforms to her husband's expectations of "feminine helplessness" (1300), she also has the strength and resourceful courage to borrow money--without Torvald's knowledge--for a trip to Italy to save his life. She then does odd jobs to pay the debt that she committed forgery to secure. Despite this daring act, Nora is still a woman trapped by her husband's definition of her. While she refers to her secret as "my joy and my pride" (1272), she laments to Mrs. Linde "how this thing hangs over me" (1265). Nora must constantly lie in order to please her husband. Even the simple act of "wiping her mouth" (1258) after eating macaroons, of wiping away the evidence of a sweet strictly forbidden by Torvald, reveals another level on which Nora deceives her husband. As the play progresses and Nora begins to see and understand his superficiality and selfishness--that Torvald is concerned with only what might threaten him--she realizes she must abandon the confines of his definitions of her.

The masquerade party in Act III ultimately symbolizes Nora's life and her growth throughout the course of the play. While at first she seems to accept Torvald's concept of the ideal woman as a showpiece, donning a costume Torvald himself chose and dancing as he taught her, she eventually strips herself of all pretense and performance. The literal act of Nora "getting out of her costume" (1300) represents an act of liberation. As she tells Torvald, "I have to stand completely alone, if I'm ever going to discover myself and the world out there. So I can't go on living with you" (1302). Ironically, just as Torvald tells Nora that Krogstad "has to wear a mask even with the nearest and dearest he has" (1276), so has his own wife been wearing a mask around her husband and children. Nora's struggle for self-definition requires her to remove her mask, to tear herself away from her husband, whom she now sees is "a stranger" (1304). Only when the mask is removed is she "clear-headed and sure" (1303) and free to live outside of the role Torvald had defined for her.

Like A Doll House, "The Hand" opens with an ostensibly pleasant scene. Two newlyweds are in bed. The husband is asleep while the wife, "too happy to sleep," is awake thinking of "the joys of living with someone unknown and with whom she is in love" (Colette 240). As she "proudly bore the weight" of her husband's head on her shoulder (240), she praises his features, even the "powerful knuckles" and "flat nails" of the hand that lies beside her (241). However, an "electric jolt" (241) that shoots through his hand sparks a "startling discovery" (241). In this shifted light her husband's hand is revealed to her as a beast "ready for battle" (241).

As in A Doll House, the theme of deception runs through "The Hand." At the end of the story, as her husband buttered a slice of toast for her, the wife at first "shuddered" but then "concealed her fear, bravely subdued herself, and, beginning her life of duplicity, of resignation, and of a lowly, delicate diplomacy, she leaned over and humbly kissed the monstrous hand" (Colette 242). Like Nora, who for a long time subjected herself to Torvald's pet names of "lark" and "squirrel" (Ibsen 1258) and accepted her allowance from him, the wife in "The Hand" submits to her husband--a submission marked by the kissing of his beastly hand.

Both woman are married to strangers, to "someone unknown" (Colette 240)--men who they at first do not see for who they are. Unlike Nora, once the wife in "The Hand" sees her husband for what he is, she does not leave her marriage. While Nora has deceived her husband for eight years, the wife in "The Hand" is only just "beginning her life of duplicity" (242). She outwardly conforms to her husband's wishes, and we can only guess at the internal struggle that she will suffer the longer she denies the oppressive weight of her husband's hand--and the longer she tries to play a part that's not true to herself. Nora, on the other hand, expresses her struggle externally: After Torvald reads Krogstad's letter, her strength and determination give her the courage to slam shut the door of the doll house and embark on a new life of risky possibilities.

When the female protagonists in A Doll House and "The Hand" see their husbands for who they really are, they engage, to different degrees, in a struggle for self-definition. Nora, after years of self-deception (and deception of her husband, Torvald), realizes that integrity to herself as a human being requires honesty and the courage to remove her mask. To truly define herself, she needs to leave her husband. The wife in Colette's story, on the other hand, has not come to this realization. Instead, she has just kissed the hand that will keep her where she is. It is going to take a long time for Colette's character to reach Nora's point of self-definition--to see that she must live outside the role her husband created for her; to see that she must be ready to leave in order to know herself; and to truly sing, as Nora does, with "no false notes."

Works Cited

Colette, Sidonie-Gabrielle. "The Hand." The Compact Bedford Introduction to
    Literature. Ed. Michael Meyer. 8th ed. Boston: Bedford/St. Martin's,
    2009. 240–42.

Ibsen, Henrik. A Doll House. The Compact Bedford Introduction to Literature.
    Ed. Michael Meyer. 8th ed. Boston: Bedford/St. Martin's, 2009.
    1257–1305.

48

The Literary
Research Paper

© Nancy Crampton.

Does anyone know a good poet who's a
vegetarian?
— DONALD HALL

A close reading of a primary source such as a short story, poem, or play can give insights into a work's themes and effects, but sometimes you will want to know more. A published commentary by a critic who knows the work well and is familiar with the author's life and times can provide insights that otherwise may not be available. Such comments and interpretations — known as *secondary sources* — are, of course, not a substitute for the work itself, but they often can take you into a work further than if you made the journey by yourself.

After imagination, good sense, and energy, perhaps the next most important quality for writing a research paper is the ability to organize material. A research paper on a literary topic requires a writer to take account of quite a lot at once: the text, ideas, sources, and documentation techniques all make demands on one's efforts to present a topic clearly and convincingly.

The following list should give you a sense of what goes into creating a research paper. Although some steps on the list can be folded into one another, they offer an overview of the work that will involve you:

1. Choosing a topic
2. Finding sources
3. Evaluating sources
4. Taking notes
5. Developing a thesis
6. Organizing an outline
7. Writing drafts
8. Revising
9. Documenting sources
10. Preparing the final draft and proofreading

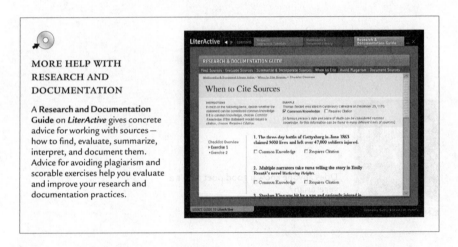

MORE HELP WITH RESEARCH AND DOCUMENTATION

A **Research and Documentation Guide** on *LiterActive* gives concrete advice for working with sources — how to find, evaluate, summarize, interpret, and document them. Advice for avoiding plagiarism and scorable exercises help you evaluate and improve your research and documentation practices.

Even if you have never written a research paper, you most likely have already had experience choosing a topic, developing a thesis, organizing an outline, and writing a draft that you then revised, proofread, and handed in. Those skills represent six of the ten items on the list. This chapter briefly reviews some of these steps and focuses on the remaining tasks, unique to research paper assignments.

CHOOSING A TOPIC

Chapter 47 discussed the importance of reading a work closely and taking careful notes as a means of generating topics for writing about literature. If you know a work well and record your understanding of it in notes, you'll have impressions and ideas to choose from for potential topics. You may find it useful to review the information on pages 1557-92 before reading the advice about putting together a research paper in this chapter.

The student author of the sample research paper "How the Narrator Cultivates a Rose for Emily" (p. 1608) was asked to write a five-page paper that demonstrated some familiarity with published critical perspectives on a Faulkner story of his choice. Before looking into critical discussions of the story, he read "A Rose for Emily" several times, taking notes and making comments in the margin of his textbook on each reading.

What prompted his choice of "A Rose for Emily" was a class discussion in which many of his classmates found the story's title inappropriate or misleading because they could not understand how and why the story constituted a tribute to Emily, given that she murdered a man and slept with his dead body over many years. The gruesome surprise ending revealing Emily as a murderer and necrophiliac hardly seemed to warrant a rose and a tribute for the central character. Why did Faulkner use such a title? Only after having thoroughly examined the story did the student go to the library to learn what professional critics had to say about this question.

FINDING SOURCES

Whether your college library is large or small, its reference librarians can usually help you locate secondary sources about a particular work or author. Unless you choose a very recently published story, poem, play, or essay about which little or nothing has been written, you should be able to find out more about a literary work efficiently and quickly. Even if a work has been published recently, you can probably find relevant information on the Internet.

Electronic Sources

Researchers can locate materials in a variety of sources, including card catalogs, specialized encyclopedias, bibliographies, and indexes to periodicals. Libraries also provide online databases that you can access from home. This can be an efficient way to establish a bibliography on a specific topic. Consult a reference librarian about how to use your library's online resources and to determine whether online research is feasible for your topic.

In addition to the many electronic databases ranging from your library's computerized holdings to the many specialized CD-ROMs available, such as *MLA International Bibliography* (a major source for articles and books on literary topics), the Internet also connects millions of sites with primary sources (the full texts of stories, poems, plays, and essays) and secondary sources (biography or criticism). If you have not had practice with research on the Web, it is a good idea to get guidance from your instructor or a librarian, and by using your library's home page as a starting point. Browsing on the Internet can be absorbing as well as informative, but unless you have plenty of time to spare, don't wait until the last minute to locate your electronic sources. You might find yourself trying to find reliable, professional sources among thousands of sites if you enter an unqualified entry such as "Charles Dickens." Once you are familiar with the Web, however, you'll find its research potential both fascinating and rewarding.

Do remember that your own college library offers a broad range of electronic sources. If you're feeling uncertain, intimidated, and profoundly unplugged, your reference librarians are there to help you to get started. Once you take advantage of their advice and tutorials, you'll soon find that negotiating the World Wide Web can be an efficient means of research for almost any subject.

EVALUATING SOURCES AND TAKING NOTES

Evaluate your sources for their reliability and the quality of their evidence. Check to see whether an article or book has been superseded by later studies; try to use up-to-date sources. A popular magazine article will probably not be as authoritative as an article in a scholarly journal. Sources that are well documented with primary and secondary materials usually indicate that the author has done his or her homework. Books printed by university presses and established trade presses are preferable to books privately printed. But there are always exceptions. If you are uncertain about how to assess a book, try to find out something about the author. Are there any other books listed in the card catalog that indicate the author's expertise? What do book reviews say about the work? Three valuable indexes to book reviews of literary studies are *Book Review Digest, Book Review Index,* and *Index to Book Reviews in the Humanities.* Your reference librarian can show you how to use these important tools for evaluating books. Reviews can be a quick means to gain a broad perspective on writers and their works because reviewers often survey previous approaches to the topic under discussion.

A cautionary note: Assessing online sources can be more problematic than evaluating print sources because anyone with a computer and online access can publish on the Internet. Be sure to determine the nature of your sources and their authority. Is the site the work of a professional or an amateur? Is the information likely to be reliable? Is it documented? Before placing your trust in an Internet source, make sure that it warrants your confidence.

As you prepare a list of reliable sources relevant to your topic, record the necessary bibliographic information so that it will be available when you make up the list of works cited for your paper. For a book include the author, complete title, place of publication, publisher, and date. For an article include author, complete title, name of periodical, volume number, date of issue, and page numbers. For an Internet source, include the author, complete title, database title, periodical or site name, date of posting of the site (or last update), name of the institution or organization, date when you accessed the source, and the network address (URL).

Once you have assembled a tentative bibliography, you will need to take notes on your readings. Be sure to keep track of where the information comes from by writing the author's name and page number. If you use more than one work by the same author, include a brief title as well as the author's name.

MORE HELP WITH EVALUATING AND WORKING WITH SOURCES

In addition to the **Research and Documentation Guide** included on *LiterActive* (see p. 1594), premium Bedford/St. Martin's resources for evaluating, working with, and documenting sources — **Re:Writing** — are available at bedfordstmartins.com/rewriting and bedfordstmartins.com/meyercompact.

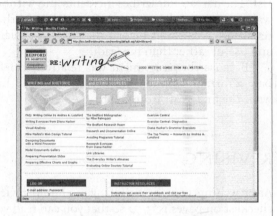

DEVELOPING A THESIS AND ORGANIZING THE PAPER

As the notes on "A Rose for Emily" accumulated, the student sorted them into topics:

1. Publication history of the story
2. Faulkner on the title of "A Rose for Emily"
3. Is Emily simply insane?
4. The purpose of Emily's servant
5. The narrator
6. The townspeople's view of Emily
7. The surprise ending
8. Emily's admirable qualities
9. Homer's character

The student quickly saw that items 1, 4, and 9 were not directly related to his topic concerning the significance of the story's title. The remaining numbers (2, 3, 5, 6, 7, 8) are the topics taken up in the paper. The student had begun his reading of secondary sources with a tentative thesis that stemmed from his question about the appropriateness of the title. That "why" shaped itself into the expectation that he would have a thesis something like this: "The title justifies Emily's murder of Homer because . . ."

The assumption was that he would find information that indicated some specific reason. But the more he read, the more he discovered that it was possible to speak only about how the narrator prevents the reader from making a premature judgment about Emily rather than justifying her actions. Hence, he wisely changed his tentative thesis to this final thesis: "The narrator describes incidents and withholds information in such a way as to cause the reader to sympathize with Emily before her crime is revealed." This thesis helped the student explain why the title is accurate and useful rather than misleading.

Because the assignment was relatively brief, the student did not prepare a formal outline but instead organized his notes and proceeded to write the first draft from them.

REVISING

After writing your first draft, you should review the advice and revision checklist on pages 1573–74 so that you can read your paper with an objective eye. Two days after writing his next-to-last draft, the writer of "How the Narrator Cultivates a Rose for Emily" realized that he had allotted too much space for critical discussions of the narrator that were not directly related to his approach. He wanted to demonstrate a familiarity with these studies, but it was not essential that he summarize or discuss them. He corrected this by consolidating parenthetical references: "Though a number of studies discuss the story's narrator (see, for example, Curry; Kempton; Sullivan; and Watkins). . . ." His earlier draft had included summaries of these studies that were tangential to his argument. The point is that he saw this himself after he took some time to approach the paper from a fresh perspective.

DOCUMENTING SOURCES AND AVOIDING PLAGIARISM

You must acknowledge the use of a source when you (1) quote someone's exact words, (2) summarize or borrow someone's opinions or ideas, or (3) use information and facts that are not considered to be common knowledge. The purpose of this documentation is to acknowledge your sources, to demonstrate that you are familiar with what others have thought about the topic, and to provide your reader access to the same sources. If your paper is not adequately documented, it will be vulnerable to a charge of *plagiarism* — the presentation of someone else's work as your own. Conscious plagiarism is easy to avoid; honesty takes care of that for most people. However, there is a more problematic form of plagiarism that is often inadvertent. Whether inadequate documentation is conscious or not, plagiarism is a serious matter and must be avoided. Papers can be evaluated only by what is on the page, not by their writers' intentions.

Let's look more closely at what constitutes plagiarism. Consider the following passage quoted from John Gassner's introduction to *Four Great Plays by Henrik Ibsen* (New York: Bantam, 1959), p. viii:

Today it seems incredible that A Doll's House° should have created the furor it did. In exploding Victorian ideals of feminine dependency the play seemed revolutionary in 1879. When its heroine Nora left her home in search of self-development it seemed as if the sanctity of marriage had been flouted by a playwright treading the stage with cloven-feet.

Now read this plagiarized version:

A Doll's House created a furor in 1879 by blowing up Victorian ideals about a woman's place in the world. Nora's search for self-fulfillment outside her home appeared to be an attack on the sanctity of marriage by a cloven-footed playwright.

Though the writer has shortened the passage and made some changes in the wording, this paragraph is basically the same as Gassner's. Indeed, several of his phrases are lifted almost intact. Even if a parenthetical reference had been included at the end of the passage and the source included in "Works Cited," the language of this passage would still be plagiarism because it is presented as the writer's own. Both language and ideas must be acknowledged.

Here is an adequately documented version of the passage:

John Gassner has observed how difficult it is for today's readers to comprehend the intense reaction against A Doll's House in 1879. When Victorian audiences watched Nora walk out of her stifling marriage, they assumed that Ibsen was expressing a devilish contempt for the "sanctity of marriage" (viii).

This passage makes absolutely clear that the observation is Gassner's, and it is written in the student's own language with the exception of one quoted

---

° Rolf Fjelde, whose translation is included in Chapter 42, renders the title as *A Doll House* in order to emphasize that the whole household, including Torvald as well as Nora, lives an unreal, doll-like existence.

phrase. Had Gassner not been named in the passage, the parenthetical reference would have included his name: (Gassner viii).

Some mention should be made of the notion of common knowledge before we turn to the standard format for documenting sources. Observations and facts that are widely known and routinely included in many of your sources do not require documentation. It is not necessary to cite a source for the fact that Alfred, Lord Tennyson, was born in 1809 or that Ernest Hemingway loved to fish and hunt. Sometimes it will be difficult for you to determine what common knowledge is for a topic that you know little about. If you are in doubt, the best strategy is to supply a reference.

There are two basic ways to document sources. Traditionally, sources have been cited in footnotes at the bottom of each page or in endnotes grouped together at the end of the paper. Here is how a portion of the sample paper would look if footnotes were used instead of parenthetical documentation:

As Heller points out, before we learn of Emily's bizarre behavior, we see her as a sympathetic--if antiquated--figure in a town whose life and concerns have passed her by; hence, "we are disposed to see Emily as victimized."[1]

[1] Terry Heller, "The Telltale Hair: A Critical Study of William Faulkner's 'A Rose for Emily,'" Arizona Quarterly 28 (1972): 306.

Unlike endnotes, which are double spaced throughout under the title of "Notes" on separate pages at the end of the paper, footnotes appear four spaces below the text. They are single spaced with double spaces between notes.

No doubt you will have encountered these documentation methods in your reading. A different style is recommended, however, in the Modern Language Association's *MLA Handbook for Writers of Research Papers*, 6th ed. (2003). This style employs parenthetical references within the text of the paper; these are keyed to an alphabetical list of works cited at the end of the paper. This method is designed to be less distracting for the reader. Unless you are instructed to follow the footnote or endnote style for documentation, use the parenthetical method explained in the next section.

The List of Works Cited

Items in the list of works cited are arranged alphabetically according to the author's last name and indented five spaces after the first line. This allows the reader to locate quickly the complete bibliographic information for the author's name cited within the parenthetical reference in the text. The following are common entries for literature papers and should be used as models. If some of your sources are of a different nature, consult the *MLA Hand-*

book for Writers of Research Papers, 6th ed. (New York: MLA, 2003); or, for the latest updates, check MLA's Web site at mla.org.

The following entries include examples to follow when citing electronic sources. For electronic sources, include as many of the following elements as apply and as are available:

- Author's name
- Title of work (if it's a book, underline; if it's a short work, such as an article or poem, use quotation marks)
- Title of the site (or of the publication, if you're citing an online periodical, for example), underlined (or italicized)
- Date of publication or last update
- Sponsor of the site (if not named as the author)
- Date you accessed the source
- The URL in angle brackets

A BOOK BY ONE AUTHOR

Hendrickson, Robert. The Literary Life and Other Curiosities. New York: Viking, 1981.

AN ONLINE BOOK

Frost, Robert. A Boy's Will. 1915. Bartleby.com: Great Books Online. 1999. 4 Feb. 2004
    <http://www.bartleby.com/117/>.

PART OF AN ONLINE BOOK

Frost, Robert. "Into My Own." A Boy's Will. 1915. Bartleby.com: Great Books Online.
    1999. 4 Feb. 2004 <http://www.bartleby.com/117/1.html>.

Notice that the author's name is in reverse order. This information, along with the full title, place of publication, publisher, and date, should be taken from the title and copyright pages of the book. The title is underlined to indicate italics and is also followed by a period. If the city of publication is well known, it is unnecessary to include the state. Use the publication date on the title page; if none appears there, use the copyright date (after ©) on the back of the title page.

A BOOK BY TWO AUTHORS

Horton, Rod W., and Herbert W. Edwards. Backgrounds of American Literary Thought. 3rd
    ed. Englewood Cliffs: Prentice, 1974.

Only the first author's name is given in reverse order. The edition number appears after the title.

A BOOK WITH MORE THAN THREE AUTHORS

Gates, Henry Louis, Jr., et al., eds. The Norton Anthology of African American Literature.
New York: Norton, 1997.

(Note: The abbreviation *et al.* means "and others.")

A WORK IN A COLLECTION BY THE SAME AUTHOR

O'Connor, Flannery. "Greenleaf." The Complete Stories. By O'Connor. New York: Farrar,
1971. 311–34.

Page numbers are given because the reference is to only a single story in the collection.

A WORK IN A COLLECTION BY DIFFERENT WRITERS

Frost, Robert. "Design." The Compact Bedford Introduction to Literature. Ed. Michael
Meyer. 8th ed. Boston: Bedford/St. Martin's, 2009. 895.

Allen, Woody. Old Saybrook. The Compact Bedford Introduction to Literature. Ed. Michael
Meyer. 8th ed. Boston: Bedford/St. Martin's, 2009. 1327–42.

The titles of poems and short stories are enclosed in quotation marks; plays and novels are underlined.

CROSS-REFERENCE TO A COLLECTION

Frost, Robert. "Design." Meyer. 895.

Allen, Woody. Old Saybrook. Meyer. 1327–42.

Meyer, Michael, ed. The Compact Bedford Introduction to Literature. 8th ed. Boston:
Bedford/St. Martin's, 2009.

O'Connor, Flannery. "Revelation." Meyer. 392.

When citing more than one work from the same collection, use a cross-reference to avoid repeating the same bibliographic information that appears in the main entry for the collection.

A TRANSLATED BOOK

Grass, Günter. The Tin Drum. Trans. Ralph Manheim. New York: Vintage-Random, 1962.

AN INTRODUCTION, PREFACE, FOREWORD, OR AFTERWORD

Johnson, Thomas H. Introduction. Final Harvest: Emily Dickinson's Poems. By Emily

Dickinson. Boston: Little, Brown, 1961. vii-xiv.

This cites the introduction by Johnson. Notice that a colon is used between the book's main title and subtitle. To cite a poem in this book, use this method:

Dickinson, Emily. "A Tooth upon Our Peace." Final Harvest: Emily Dickinson's Poems.

Ed. Thomas H. Johnson. Boston: Little, Brown, 1961. 110.

AN ENTRY IN AN ENCYCLOPEDIA

"Wordsworth, William." The New Encyclopedia Britannica. 1984 ed.

Because this encyclopedia is organized alphabetically, no page number or other information is given, only the edition number (if available) and date.

AN ARTICLE IN A MAGAZINE

Morrow, Lance. "Scribble, Scribble, Eh, Mr. Toad." Time 24 Feb. 1986: 84.

AN ARTICLE FROM AN ONLINE MAGAZINE

Wasserman, Elizabeth. "The Byron Complex." Atlantic Online 22 Sept. 2002. 4 Feb. 2004

<http://www.theatlantic.com/unbound/flashbks/byron.htm>.

The citation for an unsigned article would begin with the title and be alphabetized by the first word of the title other than "a," "an," or "the."

AN ARTICLE IN A SCHOLARLY JOURNAL WITH CONTINUOUS
PAGINATION BEYOND A SINGLE ISSUE

Mahar, William J. "Black English in Early Blackface Minstrelsy: A New Interpretation of

the Sources of Minstrel Show Dialect." American Quarterly 37 (1985): 260-85.

Because this journal uses continuous pagination instead of separate pagination for each issue, it is not necessary to include the month, season, or number of the issue. Only one of the quarterly issues will have pages numbered 260-85. If you are not certain whether a journal's pages are numbered continuously throughout a volume, supply the month, season, or issue number, as in the next entry.

AN ARTICLE IN A SCHOLARLY JOURNAL WITH SEPARATE
PAGINATION FOR EACH ISSUE

Updike, John. "The Cultural Situation of the American Writer." American Studies

International 15 (Spring 1977): 19–28.

By noting the spring issue, the entry saves a reader looking through each
issue of the 1977 volume for the correct article on pages 19 to 28.

AN ARTICLE FROM AN ONLINE SCHOLARLY JOURNAL

Mamet, David. "Secret Names." The Threepenny Review 96 (Winter 2003). 4 Feb. 2004

<http://www.threepennyreview.com/samples/mamet_w04.html>.

The following citation indicates that the article appears on page 1 of section 7 and continues onto another page.

AN ARTICLE IN A NEWSPAPER

Ziegler, Philip. "The Lure of Gossip, the Rules of History." New York Times 23 Feb. 1986:

sec. 7: 1+.

AN ARTICLE FROM AN ONLINE NEWSPAPER

Brantley, Ben. "Souls Lost and Doomed Enliven London Stages." New York Times on the

Web 4 Feb. 2004. 5 Feb. 2004 <http://www.nytimes.com/2004/02/04/arts/theater/

04BRAN.html>.

A LECTURE

Tilton, Robert. "The Beginnings of American Studies." English 270 class lecture.

University of Connecticut, Storrs, 12 Mar. 2008.

LETTER, E-MAIL, OR INTERVIEW

Vellenga, Carolyn. Letter to the author. 9 Oct. 1997.

Harter, Stephen P. E-mail to the author. 28 Dec. 1997.

McConagha, Bill. Personal interview.

Following are additional examples for citing electronic sources.

WORK FROM A SUBSCRIPTION SERVICE

Libraries pay for access to databases such as *Lexis-Nexis, ProQuest Direct,* and *Expanded Academic ASAP.* When you retrieve an article or other work from a subscription database, cite your source based on this model:

Vendler, Helen Hennessey. "The Passion of Emily Dickinson." The New Republic 3 Aug.

    1992: 34-38. Expanded Academic ASAP. InfoTrac. Boston Public Lib., MA. 4 Feb.

    2004 <http://infotrac.galegroup.com>.

A DOCUMENT FROM A WEB SITE

When citing sources from the Internet, include as much publication information as possible (see guidelines on page 1601). In some cases, as in the following example, a date of publication for the document "Dickens in America" is not available. The entry provides the author, title of document, title of site, access date, and URL:

Perdue, David. "Dickens in America." David Perdue's Charles Dickens Page. 4 Feb. 2003

    <http://www.fidnet.com/~dap1955/dickens/america.html>.

AN ENTIRE WEB SITE

Perdue, David. David Perdue's Charles Dickens Page. 4 Feb. 2003

    <http://www.fidnet.com/~dap1955/dickens/>.

Treat a CD-ROM as you would any other source, but name the medium before the publication information.

A WORK FROM A CD-ROM

Aaron, Belèn V. "The Death of Theory." Scholarly Book Reviews 4.3 (1997): 146–47. ERIC.

    CD-ROM. SilverPlatter. Dec. 1997.

AN ONLINE POSTING

Kathman, David. "Shakespeare's Literacy — or Lack of." Online posting. 3 Mar. 1998.

    Shakespeare Newsgroup. 4 Feb. 2004 <humanities.lit.authors.shakespeare>.

Parenthetical References

A list of works cited is not an adequate indication of how you have used sources in your paper. You must also provide the precise location of quotations and other information by using parenthetical references within the text of the paper. You do this by citing the author's name (or the source's title if the work is anonymous) and the page number:

Collins points out that "Nabokov was misunderstood by early reviewers of his work" (28).

or

Nabokov's first critics misinterpreted his stories (Collins 28).

Either way a reader will find the complete bibliographic entry in the list of works cited under Collins's name and know that the information cited in the paper appears on page 28. Notice that the end punctuation comes after the parentheses.

If you have listed more than one work by the same author, you would add a brief title to the parenthetical reference to distinguish between them. You could also include the full title in your text:

Nabokov's first critics misinterpreted his stories (Collins, "Early Reviews" 28).

or

Collins points out in "Early Reviews of Nabokov's Fiction" that Nabokov's early work was misinterpreted by reviewers (28).

For electronic sources, provide the author's name. Unless your online source is a stable, paginated document (such as a pdf file), do not include page numbers in your parenthetical references. The following example shows an in-text citation to William Faulkner's acceptance speech for the Nobel Prize in Literature, found at the Nobel Web site.

William Faulkner believed that it was his duty as a writer to "help man endure by lifting his heart" (Faulkner).

This reference would appear in the works cited list as follows:

Faulkner, William. "Banquet Speech: The Nobel Prize in Literature." 10 Dec. 1950. The Nobel E-Museum. 4 Feb. 2004 <http://www.nobel.se/literature/laureates/1949/faulkner-speech.html>.

There can be many variations on what is included in a parenthetical reference, depending on the nature of the entry in the list of works cited. But the general principle is simple enough: provide enough parenthetical information for a reader to find the work in "Works Cited." Examine the sample research paper for more examples of works cited and strategies for including parenthetical references. If you are puzzled by a given situation, refer to the *MLA Handbook*.

A SAMPLE STUDENT RESEARCH PAPER

How William Faulkner's Narrator Cultivates a Rose for Emily

The following research paper by Tony Groulx follows the format described in the *MLA Handbook for Writers of Research Papers*, 6th ed. (2003). This format is discussed in the preceding section on documentation and in Chapter 47 in the section on manuscript form (p. 1575). Though the sample paper is short, it illustrates many of the techniques and strategies useful for writing an essay that includes secondary sources. (Faulkner's "A Rose for Emily" is reprinted on p. 90.)

Tony Groulx

Professor Hugo

English 109-3

December 4, 2008

How William Faulkner's Narrator Cultivates a Rose for Emily

William Faulkner's "A Rose for Emily" is an absorbing mystery story whose chilling ending contains a gruesome surprise. When we discover, along with the narrator and townspeople, what was left of Homer Barron's body, we may be surprised or not, depending on how carefully we have been reading the story and keeping track of details such as Emily Grierson's purchase of rat poison and Homer's disappearance. Probably most readers anticipate finding Homer's body at the end of the story because Faulkner carefully prepares the groundwork for the discovery as the townspeople force their way into that myste-rious upstairs room where a "thin, acrid pall as of the tomb seemed to lie every-where" (96). But very few readers, if any, are prepared for the story's final para-graph, when we realize that the strand of "iron-gray hair" (the last three words of the story) on the second pillow indicates that Emily has slept with Homer since she murdered him. This last paragraph produces the real horror in the story and an extraordinary revelation about Emily's character.

The final paragraph seems like the right place to begin a discussion of this story because the surprise ending not only creates a powerful emotional effect in us but also raises an important question about what we are to think of Emily. Is this isolated, eccentric woman simply mad? All the circumstantial evidence indi-cates that she is a murderer and necrophiliac, and yet Faulkner titles the story "A Rose for Emily," as if she is due some kind of tribute. The title somehow qualifies the gasp of horror that the story leads up to in the final paragraph. Why would anyone offer this woman a "rose"? What's behind the title?

Faulkner was once directly asked the meaning of the title and replied:

> Oh it's simply the poor woman had had no life at all. Her father
> had kept her more or less locked up and then she had a lover
> who was about to quit her, she had to murder him. It was just
> "A Rose for Emily"--that's all. (qtd. in Gwynn and Blotner 87-88)

Reference to text of the story [margin note]

Reference to secondary source (Gwynn and Blotner) [margin note]

Groulx 2

This reply explains some of Emily's motivation for murdering Homer, but it doesn't actually address the purpose and meaning of the title. If Emily killed Homer out of a kind of emotional necessity--out of a fear of abandonment-- how does that explain the fact that the title seems to suggest that the story is a way of paying respect to Emily? The question remains.

Whatever respect the story creates for Emily cannot be the result of her actions. Surely there can be no convincing excuse made for murder and necrophilia; there is nothing to praise about what she does. Instead, the tribute comes in the form of how her story is told rather than what we are told about her. To do this Faulkner uses a narrator who tells Emily's story in such a way as to maximize our sympathy for her. The grim information about Emily's "iron-gray hair" on the pillow is withheld until the very end and not only to produce a surprise but to permit the reader to develop a sympathetic understanding of her before we are shocked and disgusted by her necrophilia.

Significantly, the narrator begins the story with Emily's death rather than Homer's. Though a number of studies discuss the story's narrator (see, for example, Curry; Kempton; Sullivan; and Watkins), Terry Heller's is one of the most comprehensive in its focus on the narrator's effects on the readers' response to Emily. As Heller points out, before we learn of Emily's bizarre behavior we see her as a sympathetic--if antiquated--figure in a town whose life and concerns have passed her by; hence, "we are disposed to see Emily as victimized" (306). Her refusal to pay her taxes is an index to her isolation and eccentricity, but this incident also suggests a degree of dignity and power lacking in the town officials who fail to collect her taxes. Her encounters with the officials of Jefferson--whether in the form of the sneaking aldermen who try to cover up the smell around her house or the druggist who unsuccessfully tries to get her to conform to the law when she buys arsenic-- place her in an admirable light because her willfulness is based on her personal strength. Moreover, it is relatively easy to side with Emily when the townspeople are described as taking pleasure in her being reduced to poverty as a result of her father's death because "now she too would know the old thrill and the old despair of a penny more or less" (Faulkner 93). The narrator's account of their pettiness, jealousy, and inability to make sense of Emily

> Reference to secondary sources (Curry; Kempton; Sullivan; Watkins) with signal phrase for Heller

> Reference to secondary source (Heller) with signal phrase ("As Heller points out...")

> Reference to text of the story

causes the reader to sympathize with Emily's eccentricities before we must judge her murderous behavior. We admire her for taking life on her own terms, and the narrator makes sure this response is in place prior to our realization that she also takes life.

We don't really know much about Emily because the narrator arranges the details of her life so that it's difficult to know what she's been up to. We learn, for example, about the smell around the house before she buys the poison and Homer disappears, so that the cause-and-effect relationship among these events is a bit slippery (for a detailed reconstruction of the chronology, see McGlynn and Nebecker's revision of McGlynn's work), but the effect is to suspend judgment of Emily. By the time we realize what she has done, we are already inclined to see her as outside community values almost out of necessity. That's not to say that the murdering of Homer is justified by the narrator, but it is to say that her life maintains its private--though no longer secret--dignity. Despite the final revelation, Emily remains "dear, inescapable, impervious, tranquil, and perverse" (Faulkner 95).

The narrator's "rose" to Emily is his recognition that Emily is all these things--including "perverse." She evokes "a sort of respectful affection for a fallen monument" (Faulkner 90). She is, to be sure, "fallen" but she is also somehow central--a "monument"--to the life of the community. Faulkner does not offer a definitive reading of Emily, but he does have the narrator pay tribute to her by attempting to provide a complex set of contexts for her actions--contexts that include a repressive father, resistance to a changing South and impinging North, the passage of time and its influence on the present, and relations between men and women as well as relations between generations. Robert Crosman discusses the narrator's efforts to understand Emily:

> The narrator is himself a "reader" of Emily's story, trying to put together from fragments a complete picture, trying to find the meaning of her life in its impact upon an audience, the citizens of Jefferson, of which he is a member. (212)

The narrator refuses to dismiss Emily as simply mad or to treat her life as merely a grotesque, sensational horror story. Instead, his narrative method

Reference to
secondary
sources
(McGlynn and
Nebecker)

References to
text of the
story

Reference to
secondary
source
(Crosman)

brings us into her life before we too hastily reject her, and in doing so it offers us a complex imaginative treatment of fierce determination and strength coupled with illusions and shocking eccentricities. The narrator's rose for Emily is paying her the tribute of placing that "long strand of iron-gray hair" in the context of her entire life.

Groulx 5

Works Cited

Crosman, Robert. "How Readers Make Meaning." <u>College Literature</u> 9 (1982): 207-15.

Curry, Renee R. "Gender and Authorial Limitation in Faulkner's 'A Rose for Emily.'" <u>The Mississippi Quarterly</u> 47 (Summer 1994): 391-402. Expanded Academic ASAP. Boston Public Lib., MA. 4 Feb. 2004 <http://infotrac.galegroup.com>.

Faulkner, William. "A Rose for Emily." <u>The Compact Bedford Introduction to Literature</u>. Ed. Michael Meyer. 8th ed. Boston: Bedford/St. Martin's, 2009. 90–96.

Gwynn, Frederick, and Joseph Blotner, eds. <u>Faulkner in the University: Class Conferences at the University of Virginia, 1957-58</u>. Charlottesville: U of Virginia P, 1959.

Heller, Terry. "The Telltale Hair: A Critical Study of William Faulkner's 'A Rose for Emily.'" <u>Arizona Quarterly</u> 28 (1972): 301-18.

Kempton, K. P. <u>The Short Story</u>. Cambridge: Harvard UP, 1954. 104-06.

McGlynn, Paul D. "The Chronology of 'A Rose for Emily.'" <u>Studies in Short Fiction</u> 6 (1969): 461-62.

Nebecker, Helen E. "Chronology Revised." <u>Studies in Short Fiction</u> 8 (1971): 471-73.

Sullivan, Ruth. "The Narrator in 'A Rose for Emily.'" <u>The Journal of Narrative Technique</u> 1 (1971): 159-78.

Watkins, F. C. "The Structure of 'A Rose for Emily.'" <u>Modern Language Notes</u> 69 (1954): 508-10.

49

Taking Essay
Examinations

It is the function of the liberal arts
education not to give right answers, but
to ask right questions.
— CYNTHIA OZICK

By permission of Alfred
A. Knopf, Inc.

PREPARING FOR AN ESSAY EXAM

Keep Up with the Reading

The best way to prepare for an examination is to keep up with the reading. If you begin the course with a commitment to completing the reading assignments on time, you will not have to read in a frenzy and cram just days before the test. The readings will be a pleasure, not a frantic ordeal. Moreover, you will find that your instructor's comments and class discussion will make more sense to you and that you'll be able to participate in class discussion. As you prepare for the exam, you should be rereading texts rather than reading for the first time. It may not be possible to reread everything, but you'll at least be able to scan a familiar text and reread passages that are particularly important.

Take Notes and Annotate the Text

Don't rely exclusively on your memory. The typical literature class includes a hefty amount of reading, so unless you take notes, annotate the text with your own comments, and underline important passages, you're likely to forget material that could be useful for responding to an examination question (see pp. 1559–61 for a discussion of these matters). The more you can retrieve from your reading, the more prepared you'll be for reviewing significant material for the exam. These notes can be used to illustrate points that were made in class. By briefly quoting an important phrase or line from the text, you can provide supporting evidence that will make your argument convincing. Consider, for example, the difference between writing that "Marvell's speaker in 'To His Coy Mistress' says that they won't be able to love after they die" and writing that "the speaker intones that 'The grave's a fine and private place / But none, I think, do there embrace.'" No one expects you to memorize the entire poem, but recalling a few lines here and there can transform a sleepy generality into an illustrative, persuasive argument.

Anticipate Questions

As you review the readings, keep in mind the class discussions and the focus provided by your instructor. Class discussions and the instructor's emphasis often become the basis for essay questions. You may not see the exact same topics on the exam, but you might find that the matters you've discussed in class will serve as a means of responding to an essay question. If, for example, class discussion of John Updike's "A & P" (see p. 560) centered on the story's small-town New England setting, you could use that conservative, traditional, puritanical setting to answer a question such as "Discuss how the conflicts that Sammy encounters in 'A & P' are related to the story's theme." A discussion of the intolerant rigidity of this New England town could be connected to A & P "policy" and the crabbed values associated with Lengel that lead to Sammy's quitting his job in protest of such policies. The point is that you'll be well prepared for an essay exam when you can shape the material you've studied so that it is responsive to whatever kinds of reasonable questions you encounter on the exam. Reasonable questions? Yes, your instructor is more likely to offer you an opportunity to demonstrate your familiarity with and understanding of the text than to set a trap that, for instance, demands you discuss how Updike's work experience as an adolescent informs the story when no mention was ever made of that in class or in your reading.

You can also anticipate questions by considering the generic Questions for Responsive Reading and Writing about fiction (p. 48), poetry (p. 614), and drama (p. 1089) and the Questions for Arguing Critically about Literature (p. 1566), along with the Questions for Writing about an Author in Depth (p. 867). Not all of these questions will necessarily be relevant to every work that you read, but they cover a wide range of concerns that should allow you to organize your reading, note taking, and reviewing so that you're not taken by surprise during the exam. (For a complete list of the Questions boxes, see this book's inside front cover.)

Studying with a classmate or a small group from class can be a stimulating and fruitful means of discovering and organizing the major topics and themes of the course. This method of brainstorming can be useful not only for studying for exams but throughout the semester for understanding and reviewing course readings. And, finally, you needn't be shy about asking your instructor what types of questions might appear on the exam and how best to study for them. You may not get a very specific reply, but almost any information is more useful than none.

TYPES OF EXAMS

Closed-Book versus Open-Book Exams

Closed-book exams require more memorization and recall than open-book exams, which permit you to use your text and perhaps even your notes to answer questions. Dates, names, definitions, and other details play less of a role in an open-book exam. An open-book exam requires no less preparation, however, because you'll need to be intimately familiar with the texts and the major ideas, themes, and issues that you've studied in order to quickly and efficiently support your points with relevant, specific evidence. Since every student has the same advantage of having access to the text, preparation remains the key to answering the questions. Some students find open-book exams more difficult than closed-book tests because they risk spending too much time reading, scanning, and searching for material and not enough time writing a response that draws on the knowledge and understanding that their reading and studying has provided them. It's best to limit the time you allow yourself to review the text and notes so that you devote an adequate amount of time to getting your ideas on paper.

Essay Questions

Essay questions generally fall within one of the following categories. If you can recognize quickly what is being asked of you, you will be able to respond to them more efficiently.

1. **Explication** Explication calls for a line-by-line explanation of a passage of poetry or prose that considers, for example, diction, figures of speech, symbolism, sound, form, and theme in an effort to describe how language creates meaning. (For a more detailed discussion of explication, see p. 1576.)

2. **Definition** Defining a term and then applying it to a writer or work is a frequent exam exercise. Consider: "Define *romanticism*. To what extent can Hawthorne's *The Scarlet Letter* be regarded as a romantic story?" This sort of question requires that you first describe what constitutes a romantic literary work and then explain how *The Scarlet Letter* does (and doesn't) fit the bill.

3. **Analysis** An analytical question focuses on a particular part of a literary work. You might be asked, for example, to analyze the significance of images in John Keats's poem "Ode on a Grecian Urn" (p. 647). This sort of question requires you to discuss a specific element of the poem and also to explain how that element contributes to the poem's overall effect. (For a more detailed discussion of analysis, see p. 1580.)

4. **Comparison and Contrast** Comparison and contrast calls for a discussion of the similarities and/or differences between writers, works, or elements of works — for example, "Compare and contrast Lengel's sensibilities in John Updike's 'A & P' (p. 560) with John Wright's in Susan Glaspell's *Trifles* (p. 1048)." Despite the obvious differences in age and circumstances between these characters, a discussion of their responses to people — particularly to women — reveals some intriguing similarities. (For a more detailed discussion of comparison and contrast, see pp. 1585–87.)

5. **Discussion of a Critical Perspective** A brief quotation by a critic about a work is usually designed to stimulate a response that requires you to agree with, disagree with, or qualify a critic's perspective. Usually it is not important whether you agree or disagree with the critic; what matters is the quality of your argument. Think about how you might wrestle with this assessment of Robert Frost written by Lionel Trilling: "The manifest America of Mr. Frost's poems may be pastoral; the actual America is tragic." With some qualifications (surely not all of Frost's poems are "tragic") this could provide a useful way of talking about a poem such as "Mending Wall" (p. 884).

6. **Imaginative Questions** To a degree every question requires imagination regardless of whether it's being asked or answered. However, some questions require more imaginative leaps to arrive at the center of an issue than others do. Consider, for example, the intellectual agility needed to respond to this question: "How do you think Dickens's Mr. Gradgrind from *Hard Times* and the narrator of Frost's 'Mending Wall' would respond to Sammy's character in Updike's 'A & P'?" As tricky as this triangulation of topics may seem, there is plenty to discuss concerning Gradgrind's literal-mindedness, the narrator's imagination, and Sammy's rejection of "policy." Or try a simpler but no less interesting version: "How do you think Frost would review Marvell's 'To His Coy Mistress' and Keats's 'Ode on a Grecian Urn'?" Such questions certainly require detailed, reasoned responses, but they also leave room for creativity and even wit.

STRATEGIES FOR WRITING ESSAY EXAMS

Your hands may be sweaty and your heart pounding as you begin the exam, but as long as you're prepared and you keep in mind some basic strategies for writing essay exams, you should be able to respond to questions with confidence and a genuine sense of accomplishment.

Questions for Writing: A Checklist for Essay Exams

1. Before you begin writing, read through the entire exam. If there are choices to be made, make certain you know how many questions must be answered (only one out of four, not two). Note how many points each question is worth; spend more time on the two worth forty points each, and perhaps leave the twenty-point question for last.

2. Budget your time. If there are short-answer questions, do not allow them to absorb you so that you cannot do justice to the longer essay questions. Follow the suggested time limit for each question; if none is offered, then create your own schedule in proportion to the points allotted for each question.

3. Depending on your own sensibilities, you may want to begin with the easiest or hardest questions. It doesn't really matter which you begin with as long as you pace yourself to avoid running out of time.

4. Be sure that you understand the question. Does it ask you to compare and/or contrast, define, analyze, explicate, or use some other approach? Determine how many elements there are to the question so that you don't inadvertently miss part of the question. Do not spend time copying the question.

5. Make some brief notes about how you plan to answer the question; even a simple list of what you'll need to cover can serve as a useful outline.

6. Address the question; avoid unnecessary summaries or irrelevant asides. Focus on the particular elements enumerated or implied by the question.

7. After beginning the essay, write a clear thesis that describes the major topics you will discuss: "*The Scarlet Letter* is typical of Hawthorne's concerns as a writer owing to its treatment of sin, guilt, isolation, and secrecy."

8. Support and illustrate your answer with specific, relevant references to the text. The more specificity — the more you demonstrate a familiarity with the text (rather than simply provide a plot summary) — the better the answer.

9. Don't overlap and repeat responses to questions; your instructor will recognize such padding. If two different questions are about the same work or writer, demonstrate the breadth and depth of your knowledge of the subject.

10. Allow time to proofread and to qualify and to add more supporting material if necessary. At this final stage, too, it's worth remembering that Mark Twain liked to remind his readers that the difference between the right word and the almost right word is the difference between lightning and a lightning bug.

Glossary of Literary Terms

Accent The emphasis, or STRESS, given a syllable in pronunciation. We say "*syl*-lable" not "syl*lable*," "*em*phasis" not "em*pha*sis." Accents can also be used to emphasize a particular word in a sentence: *Is* she con*tent* with the *con*tents of the *yel*low *pack*age? See also METER.

Act A major division in the action of a play. The ends of acts are typically indicated by lowering the curtain or turning up the houselights. Playwrights frequently employ acts to accommodate changes in time, setting, characters onstage, or mood. In many full-length plays, acts are further divided into scenes, which often mark a point in the action when the location changes or when a new character enters. See also SCENE.

Allegory A narration or description usually restricted to a single meaning because its events, actions, characters, settings, and objects represent specific abstractions or ideas. Although the elements in an allegory may be interesting in themselves, the emphasis tends to be on what they ultimately mean. Characters may be given names such as Hope, Pride, Youth, and Charity; they have few if any personal qualities beyond their abstract meanings. These personifications are not symbols because, for instance, the meaning of a character named Charity is precisely that virtue. See also SYMBOL.

Alliteration The repetition of the same consonant sounds in a sequence of words, usually at the beginning of a word or stressed syllable: "*descend*ing *dew* *d*rops"; "*l*uscious *l*emons." Alliteration is based on the sounds of letters, rather than the spelling of words; for example, "*k*een" and "*c*ar" alliterate, but "*c*ar" and "*c*ite" do not. Used sparingly, alliteration can intensify ideas by emphasizing key words, but when used too self-consciously, it can be distracting, even ridiculous, rather than effective. See also ASSONANCE, CONSONANCE.

Allusion A brief reference to a person, place, thing, event, or idea in history or literature. Allusions conjure up biblical authority, scenes from Shakespeare's plays, historic figures, wars, great love stories, and anything else that might enrich an author's work. Allusions imply reading and cultural experiences shared by the writer and reader, functioning as a kind of shorthand whereby the recalling of something outside the work supplies an emotional or intellectual context, such as a poem about current racial struggles calling up the memory of Abraham Lincoln.

Ambiguity Allows for two or more simultaneous interpretations of a word, phrase, action, or situation, all of which can be supported by the context of a work. Deliberate ambiguity can contribute to the effectiveness and richness of a work, for example, in the open-ended conclusion to Hawthorne's "Young Goodman Brown." However, unintentional ambiguity obscures meaning and can confuse readers.

Anagram A word or phrase made from the letters of another word or phrase, as "heart" is an anagram of "earth." Anagrams have often been considered merely an exercise of one's ingenuity, but sometimes writers use anagrams to conceal proper names or veiled messages, or to suggest important connections between words, as in "hated" and "death."

Anapestic meter See FOOT.

Antagonist The character, force, or collection of forces in fiction or drama that opposes the PROTAGONIST and gives rise to the conflict of the story; an opponent of the protagonist, such as Claudius in Shakespeare's play *Hamlet*. See also CHARACTER, CONFLICT.

Antihero A protagonist who has the opposite of most of the traditional attributes of a hero. He or she may be bewildered, ineffectual, deluded, or merely pathetic. Often what antiheroes learn, if they learn anything at all, is that the world isolates them in an existence devoid of God and absolute values. Yossarian from Joseph Heller's *Catch-22* is an example of an antihero. See also CHARACTER.

Apostrophe An address, either to someone who is absent and therefore cannot hear the speaker or to something nonhuman that cannot comprehend. Apostrophe often provides a speaker the opportunity to think aloud.

Approximate rhyme See RHYME.

Archetype A term used to describe universal symbols that evoke deep and sometimes unconscious responses in a reader. In literature, characters, images, and themes that symbolically embody universal meanings and basic human experiences, regardless of when or where they live, are considered archetypes. Common literary archetypes include stories of quests, initiations, scapegoats, descents to the underworld, and ascents to heaven. See also MYTHOLOGICAL CRITICISM.

Aside In drama, a speech directed to the audience that supposedly is not audible to the other characters onstage at the time. When Hamlet first appears onstage, for example, his aside "A little more than kin, and less than kind!" gives the audience a strong sense of his alienation from King Claudius. See also SOLILOQUY.

Assonance The repetition of internal vowel sounds in nearby words that do not end the same, for example, "asleep under a tree," or "each evening." Similar endings result in rhyme, as in "asleep in the deep." Assonance is a strong means of emphasizing important words in a line. See also ALLITERATION, CONSONANCE.

Ballad Traditionally, a song, transmitted orally from generation to generation that tells a story and that eventually is written down. As such, ballads usually cannot be traced to a particular author or group of authors. Typically, ballads are dramatic, condensed, and impersonal narratives, such as "Bonny Barbara Allan." A **literary ballad** is a narrative poem written in deliberate imitation of the language, form, and spirit of the traditional ballad, such as Keats's "La Belle Dame sans Merci." See also BALLAD STANZA, QUATRAIN.

Ballad stanza A four-line stanza, known as a QUATRAIN, consisting of alternating eight- and six-syllable lines. Usually only the second and fourth lines rhyme (an *abcb* pattern). Coleridge adopted the ballad stanza in "The Rime of the Ancient Mariner."

All in a hot and copper sky
The bloody Sun, at noon,
Right up above the mast did stand,
No bigger than the Moon.

See also BALLAD, QUATRAIN.

Biographical criticism An approach to literature that suggests that knowledge of the author's life experiences can aid in the understanding of his or her work. While biographical information can sometimes complicate one's interpretation of a work, and some formalist critics (such as the New Critics) disparage the use of the author's biography as a tool for textual interpretation, learning about the life of the author can often enrich a reader's appreciation for that author's work. See also CULTURAL CRITICISM, FORMALIST CRITICISM, NEW CRITICISM.

Blank verse Unrhymed iambic pentameter. Blank verse is the English verse form closest to the natural rhythms of English speech and therefore is the most common pattern found in traditional English narrative and dramatic poetry from Shakespeare to the early twentieth century. Shakespeare's plays use blank verse extensively. See also IAMBIC PENTAMETER.

Cacophony Language that is discordant and difficult to pronounce, such as this line from John Updike's "Player Piano": "never my numb plunker fumbles." Cacophony ("bad sound") may be unintentional in the writer's sense of music, or it may be used consciously for deliberate dramatic effect. See also EUPHONY.

Caesura A pause within a line of poetry that contributes to the rhythm of the line. A caesura can occur anywhere within a line and need not be indicated by punctuation. In scanning a line, caesuras are indicated by a double vertical line (‖). See also METER, RHYTHM, SCANSION.

Canon Those works generally considered by scholars, critics, and teachers to be the most important to read and study, which collectively constitute the "masterpieces" of literature. Since the 1960s, the traditional English and American literary canon, consisting mostly of works by white male writers, has been rapidly expanding to include many female writers and writers of varying ethnic backgrounds.

Carpe diem Latin phrase meaning "seize the day." This is a very common literary theme, especially in lyric poetry, which emphasizes that life is short, time is fleeting, and one should make the most of present pleasures. Robert Herrick's poem "To the Virgins, to Make Much of Time" employs the *carpe diem* theme.

Catharsis Meaning "purgation," *catharsis* describes the release of the emotions of pity and fear by the audience at the end of a tragedy. In his *Poetics,* Aristotle discusses the importance of catharsis. The audience faces the misfortunes of the protagonist, which elicit pity and compassion. Simultaneously, the audience also confronts the failure of the protagonist, thus receiving a frightening reminder of human limitations and frailties. Ultimately, however, both these negative emotions are purged, because the tragic protagonist's suffering is an affirmation of human values rather than a despairing denial of them. See also TRAGEDY.

Character, characterization A character is a person presented in a dramatic or narrative work, and characterization is the process by which a writer makes that character seem real to the reader. A **hero** or **heroine,** often called the PROTAGONIST, is the central character who engages the reader's interest and empathy. The ANTAGONIST is the character, force, or collection of forces that stands directly opposed to the protagonist and gives rise to the conflict of the story. A **static character** does not change throughout the work, and the reader's knowledge of that character does not grow, whereas a **dynamic character** undergoes some kind of change because of the action in the plot. A **flat character** embodies one or two qualities, ideas, or traits that can be readily described in a brief summary. They are not psychologically complex characters and therefore are readily accessible to readers. Some flat characters are recognized as **stock characters;** they embody stereotypes such as the "dumb blonde" or the "mean stepfather." They become types rather than individuals. **Round characters** are more complex than flat or stock characters, and often display the inconsistencies and internal conflicts found in most real people. They are more fully developed, and therefore are harder to summarize. Authors have two major methods of presenting characters: **showing** and **telling. Showing** allows the author to present a character talking and acting, and lets the reader infer what kind of person the character is. In **telling,** the author intervenes to describe and sometimes evaluate the character for the reader. Characters can be convincing whether they are presented by showing or by telling, as long as their actions are motivated. **Motivated action** by the characters occurs when the reader or audience is offered reasons for how the characters behave, what they say, and the decisions they make. **Plausible action** is action by a character in a story that seems reasonable, given the motivations presented. See also PLOT.

Chorus In Greek tragedies (especially those of Aeschylus and Sophocles), a group of people who serve mainly as commentators on the characters and events. They add to the audience's understanding of the play by expressing traditional moral, religious, and social attitudes. The role of the chorus in dramatic works evolved through the sixteenth century, and the chorus occasionally is still used by modern playwrights such as T. S. Eliot in *Murder in the Cathedral.* See also DRAMA.

Cliché An idea or expression that has become tired and trite from overuse, its freshness and clarity having worn off. Clichés often anesthetize readers, and are usually a sign of weak writing. See also SENTIMENTALITY, STOCK RESPONSES.

Climax See PLOT.

Closet drama A play that is written to be read rather than performed onstage. In this kind of drama, literary art outweighs all other considerations. See also DRAMA.

Colloquial Refers to a type of informal diction that reflects casual, conversational language and often includes slang expressions. See also DICTION.

Comedy A work intended to interest, involve, and amuse the reader or audience, in which no terrible disaster occurs and that ends happily for the main characters. **High comedy** refers to verbal wit, such as puns, whereas **low comedy** is generally associated with physical action and is less intellectual. **Romantic comedy** involves a love affair that meets with various obstacles (like disapproving parents, mistaken identities, deceptions, or other sorts of misunderstandings) but overcomes them to end in a blissful union. Shakespeare's comedies, such as *A Midsummer Night's Dream,* are considered romantic comedies.

Comic relief A humorous scene or incident that alleviates tension in an otherwise serious work. In many instances these moments enhance the thematic significance of the story in addition to providing laughter. When Hamlet jokes with the gravediggers we laugh, but something hauntingly serious about the humor also intensifies our more serious emotions.

Conflict The struggle within the plot between opposing forces. The PROTAGONIST engages in the conflict with the ANTAGONIST, which may take the form of a character, society, nature, or an aspect of the protagonist's personality. See also CHARACTER, PLOT.

Connotation Associations and implications that go beyond the literal meaning of a word, which derive from how the word has been commonly used and the associations people make with it. For example, the word *eagle* connotes ideas of liberty and freedom that have little to do with the word's literal meaning. See also DENOTATION.

Consonance A common type of near rhyme that consists of identical consonant sounds preceded by different vowel sounds: *home, same; worth, breath.* See also RHYME.

Contextual symbol See SYMBOL.

Controlling metaphor See METAPHOR.

Convention A characteristic of a literary genre (often unrealistic) that is understood and accepted by audiences because it has come, through usage and time, to be recognized as a familiar technique. For example, the division of a play into acts and scenes is a dramatic convention, as are soliloquies and asides. FLASHBACKS and FORESHADOWING are examples of literary conventions.

Conventional symbol See SYMBOL.

Cosmic irony See IRONY.

Couplet Two consecutive lines of poetry that usually rhyme and have the same meter. A **heroic couplet** is a couplet written in rhymed iambic pentameter.

Crisis A turning point in the action of a story that has a powerful effect on the protagonist. Opposing forces come together decisively to lead to the climax of the plot. See also PLOT.

Cultural criticism An approach to literature that focuses on the historical as well as social, political, and economic contexts of a work. Popular culture — mass produced and consumed cultural artifacts ranging from advertising to popular fiction to television to rock music — is given equal emphasis with "high culture." **Cultural critics** use widely eclectic strategies such as new historicism, psychology, gender studies, and deconstructionism to analyze not only literary texts but everything from radio talk shows, comic strips, calendar art, and commercials, to travel guides and baseball cards. See also HISTORICAL CRITICISM, MARXIST CRITICISM, POSTCOLONIAL CRITICISM.

Dactylic meter See FOOT.

Deconstructionism An approach to literature which suggests that literary works do not yield fixed, single meanings, because language can never say exactly what we intend it to mean. Deconstructionism seeks to destabilize meaning by examining the gaps and ambiguities of the language of a text. Deconstructionists pay close attention to language in order to discover and describe how a variety of possible readings are generated by the elements of a text. See also NEW CRITICISM.

Denotation The dictionary meaning of a word. See also CONNOTATION.

Dénouement A French term meaning "unraveling" or "unknotting," used to describe the resolution of the plot following the climax. See also PLOT, RESO-LUTION.

Deus ex machina Latin for "god in the machine." In ancient Greek theater sometimes gods were lowered from the roof by mechanical devices to set matters right among the mortals below. The term is now used to describe any improbable means by which an author provides a too-easy resolution for a story.

Dialect A type of informational diction. Dialects are spoken by definable groups of people from a particular geographic region, economic group, or social class. Writers use dialect to contrast and express differences in educational, class, social, and regional backgrounds of their characters. See also DICTION.

Dialogue The verbal exchanges between characters. Dialogue makes the characters seem real to the reader or audience by revealing firsthand their thoughts, responses, and emotional states. See also DICTION.

Diction A writer's choice of words, phrases, sentence structures, and figurative language, which combine to help create meaning. **Formal diction** consists of a dignified, impersonal, and elevated use of language; it follows the rules of syntax exactly and is often characterized by complex words and lofty tone. **Middle diction** maintains correct language usage, but is less elevated than formal diction; it reflects the way most educated people speak. **Informal diction** represents the plain language of everyday use, and often includes idiomatic expressions, slang, contractions, and many simple, common words. **Poetic diction** refers to the way poets sometimes employ an elevated diction that deviates significantly from the common speech and writing of their time, choosing words for their supposedly inherent poetic qualities. Since the eighteenth century, however, poets have been incorporating all kinds of diction in their work and so there is no longer an automatic distinction between the language of a poet and the language of everyday speech. See also DIALECT.

Didactic poetry Poetry designed to teach an ethical, moral, or religious lesson. Michael Wigglesworth's Puritan poem *Day of Doom* is an example of didactic poetry.

Doggerel A derogatory term used to describe poetry whose subject is trite and whose rhythm and sounds are monotonously heavy-handed.

Drama Derived from the Greek word *dram,* meaning "to do" or "to perform," the term *drama* may refer to a single play, a group of plays ("Jacobean drama"), or to all plays ("world drama"). Drama is designed for performance in a theater; actors take on the roles of characters, perform indicated actions, and speak the dialogue written in the script. **Play** is a general term for a work of dramatic literature, and a **playwright** is a writer who makes plays.

Dramatic irony See IRONY.

Dramatic monologue A type of lyric poem in which a character (the speaker) addresses a distinct but silent audience imagined to be present in the poem in such a way as to reveal a dramatic situation and, often unintentionally, some aspect of his or her temperament or personality. See also LYRIC.

Dynamic character See CHARACTER.

Editorial omniscience See NARRATOR.

Electra complex The female version of the Oedipus complex. *Electra complex* is a term used to describe the psychological conflict of a daughter's unconscious rivalry with her mother for her father's attention. The name comes from the Greek legend of Electra, who avenged the death of her father, Agamemnon, by plotting the death of her mother, Clytemnestra. See also OEDIPUS COMPLEX, PSYCHOLOGICAL CRITICISM.

Elegy A mournful, contemplative lyric poem written to commemorate someone who is dead, often ending in a consolation. Tennyson's *In Memoriam,* written on the death of Arthur Hallam, is an elegy. *Elegy* may also refer to a serious meditative poem produced to express the speaker's melancholy thoughts. See also LYRIC.

End rhyme See RHYME.

End-stopped line A poetic line that has a pause at the end. End-stopped lines reflect normal speech patterns and are often marked by punctuation. The first line of Keats's "Endymion" is an example of an end-stopped line; the natural pause coincides with the end of the line and is marked by a period:

A thing of beauty is a joy forever.

English sonnet See SONNET.

Enjambment In poetry, when one line ends without a pause and continues into the next line for its meaning. This is also called a **run-on line.** The transition between the first two lines of Wordsworth's poem "My Heart Leaps Up" demonstrates enjambment:

My heart leaps up when I behold
  A rainbow in the sky:

Envoy See SESTINA.

Epic A long narrative poem, told in a formal, elevated style, that focuses on a serious subject and chronicles heroic deeds and events important to a culture or nation. Milton's *Paradise Lost,* which attempts to "justify the ways of God to man," is an epic. See also NARRATIVE POEM.

Epigram A brief, pointed, and witty poem that usually makes a satiric or humorous point. Epigrams are most often written in couplets, but take no prescribed form.

Epiphany In fiction, when a character suddenly experiences a deep realization about himself or herself; a truth that is grasped in an ordinary rather than a melodramatic moment.

Escape literature See FORMULA LITERATURE.

Euphony *Euphony* ("good sound") refers to language that is smooth and musically pleasant to the ear. See also CACOPHONY.

Exact rhyme See RHYME.

Exposition A narrative device, often used at the beginning of a work, that provides necessary background information about the characters and their circumstances. Exposition explains what has gone on before, the relationships between characters, the development of a theme, and the introduction of a conflict. See also FLASHBACK.

Extended metaphor See METAPHOR.

Eye rhyme See RHYME.

Falling action See PLOT.

Falling meter See METER.

Farce A form of humor based on exaggerated, improbable incongruities. Farce involves rapid shifts in action and emotion, as well as slapstick comedy and extravagant dialogue. Malvolio, in Shakespeare's *Twelfth Night,* is a farcical character.

Feminine rhyme See RHYME.

Feminist criticism An approach to literature that seeks to correct or supplement what may be regarded as a predominantly male-dominated critical perspective with a feminist consciousness. Feminist criticism places literature in a social context and uses a broad range of disciplines, including history, sociology, psychology, and linguistics, to provide a perspective sensitive to feminist issues. Feminist theories also attempt to understand representation from a woman's point of view and to explain women's writing strategies as specific to their social conditions. See also GAY AND LESBIAN CRITICISM, GENDER CRITICISM, SOCIOLOGICAL CRITICISM.

Figures of speech Ways of using language that deviate from the literal, denotative meanings of words in order to suggest additional meanings or effects. Figures of speech say one thing in terms of something else, such as when an eager funeral director is described as a vulture. See also METAPHOR, SIMILE.

First-person narrator See NARRATOR.

Fixed form A poem that may be categorized by the pattern of its lines, meter, rhythm, or stanzas. A sonnet is a fixed form of poetry because by definition it must have fourteen lines. Other fixed forms include LIMERICK, SESTINA, and VILLANELLE. However, poems written in a fixed form may not always fit into categories precisely, because writers sometimes vary traditional forms to create innovative effects. See also OPEN FORM.

Flashback A narrated scene that marks a break in the narrative in order to inform the reader or audience member about events that took place before the opening scene of a work. See also EXPOSITION.

Flat character See CHARACTER.

Foil A character in a work whose behavior and values contrast with those of another character in order to highlight the distinctive temperament of that character (usually the protagonist). In Shakespeare's *Hamlet*, Laertes acts as a foil to Hamlet, because his willingness to act underscores Hamlet's inability to do so.

Foot The metrical unit by which a line of poetry is measured. A foot usually consists of one stressed and one or two unstressed syllables. An *iambic foot*, which consists of one unstressed syllable followed by one stressed syllable ("away"), is the most common metrical foot in English poetry. A *trochaic foot* consists of one stressed syllable followed by an unstressed syllable ("lovely"). An *anapestic foot* is two unstressed syllables followed by one stressed syllable ("understand"). A *dactylic foot* is one stressed syllable followed by two unstressed ones ("desperate"). A *spondee* is a foot consisting of two stressed syllables ("dead set"), but is not a sustained metrical foot and is used mainly for variety or emphasis. See also IAMBIC PENTAMETER, LINE, METER.

Foreshadowing The introduction early in a story of verbal and dramatic hints that suggest what is to come later.

Form The overall structure or shape of a work, which frequently follows an established design. Forms may refer to a literary type (narrative form, short story form) or to patterns of meter, lines, and rhymes (stanza form, verse form). See also FIXED FORM, OPEN FORM.

Formal diction See DICTION.

Formalist criticism An approach to literature that focuses on the formal elements of a work, such as its language, structure, and tone. Formalist critics offer intense examinations of the relationship between form and meaning in a work, emphasizing the subtle complexity in how a work is arranged. Formalists pay special attention to diction, irony, paradox, metaphor, and symbol, as well as larger elements such as plot, characterization, and narrative technique. Formalist critics read literature as an independent work of art rather than as a reflection of the author's state of mind or as a representation of a moment in history. Therefore, anything outside of the work, including historical influences and authorial intent, is generally not examined by formalist critics. See also NEW CRITICISM.

Formula literature Often characterized as "escape literature," formula literature follows a pattern of conventional reader expectations. Romance novels, westerns, science fiction, and detective stories are all examples of formula literature; while the details of individual stories vary, the basic ingredients of each kind of story are the same. Formula literature offers happy endings (the hero "gets the girl," the detective cracks the case), entertains wide audiences, and sells tremendously well.

Found poem An unintentional poem discovered in a nonpoetic context, such as a conversation, news story, or advertisement. Found poems serve as reminders that everyday language often contains what can be considered poetry, or that poetry is definable as any text read as a poem.

Free verse Also called OPEN FORM poetry, *free verse* refers to poems characterized by their nonconformity to established patterns of meter, rhyme, and stanza. Free verse uses elements such as speech patterns, grammar, emphasis, and breath pauses to decide line breaks, and usually does not rhyme. See OPEN FORM.

Gay and lesbian criticism An approach to literature that focuses on how homosexuals are represented in literature, how they read literature, and whether sexuality, as well as gender, is culturally constructed or innate. See also FEMINIST CRITICISM, GENDER CRITICISM.

Gender criticism An approach to literature that explores how ideas about men and women — what is masculine and feminine — can be regarded as socially constructed by particular cultures. Gender criticism expands categories and definitions of what is masculine or feminine and tends to regard sexuality as more complex than merely masculine or feminine, heterosexual or homosexual. See also FEMINIST CRITICISM, GAY AND LESBIAN CRITICISM.

Genre A French word meaning kind or type. The major genres in literature are poetry, fiction, drama, and essays. Genre can also refer to more specific types of literature such as comedy, tragedy, epic poetry, or science fiction.

Haiku A style of lyric poetry borrowed from the Japanese that typically presents an intense emotion or vivid image of nature, which, traditionally, is designed to lead to a spiritual insight. Haiku is a fixed poetic form, consisting of seventeen syllables organized into three unrhymed lines of five, seven, and five syllables. Today, however, many poets vary the syllabic count in their haiku. See also FIXED FORM.

Hamartia A term coined by Aristotle to describe "some error or frailty" that brings about misfortune for a tragic hero. The concept of *hamartia* is closely related to that of the tragic flaw: both lead to the downfall of the protagonist in a tragedy. *Hamartia* may be interpreted as an internal weakness in a character (like greed or passion or HUBRIS); however, it may also refer to a mistake that a character makes that is based not on a personal failure, but on circumstances outside the protagonist's personality and control. See also TRAGEDY.

Hero, heroine See CHARACTER.

Heroic couplet See COUPLET.

High comedy See COMEDY.

Historical criticism An approach to literature that uses history as a means of understanding a literary work more clearly. Such criticism moves beyond both the facts of an author's personal life and the text itself in order to examine the social and intellectual currents in which the author composed the work. See also CULTURAL CRITICISM, MARXIST CRITICISM, NEW HISTORICISM, POSTCOLONIAL CRITICISM.

Hubris or Hybris Excessive pride or self-confidence that leads a protagonist to disregard a divine warning or to violate an important moral law. In tragedies, hubris is a very common form of hamartia. See also HAMARTIA, TRAGEDY.

Hyperbole A boldly exaggerated statement that adds emphasis without intending to be literally true, as in the statement "He ate everything in the house." Hyperbole (also called **overstatement**) may be used for serious, comic, or ironic effect. See also FIGURES OF SPEECH.

Iambic meter See FOOT.

Iambic pentameter A metrical pattern in poetry that consists of five iambic feet per line. (An iamb, or iambic foot, consists of one unstressed syllable followed by a stressed syllable.) See also FOOT, METER.

Image A word, phrase, or figure of speech (especially a SIMILE or a METAPHOR) that addresses the senses, suggesting mental pictures of sights, sounds, smells, tastes, feelings, or actions. Images offer sensory impressions to the reader and also convey emotions and moods through their verbal pictures. See also FIGURES OF SPEECH.

Implied metaphor See METAPHOR.

In medias res See PLOT.

Informal diction See DICTION.

Internal rhyme See RHYME.

Irony A literary device that uses contradictory statements or situations to reveal a reality different from what appears to be true. It is ironic for a firehouse to burn down, or for a police station to be burglarized. **Verbal irony** is a figure of speech that occurs when a person says one thing but means the opposite. **Sarcasm** is a strong form of verbal irony that is calculated to hurt someone through, for example, false praise. **Dramatic irony** creates a discrepancy between what a character believes or says and what the reader or audience member knows to be true. **Tragic irony** is a form of dramatic irony found in tragedies such as *Oedipus the King,* in which Oedipus searches for the person responsible for the plague that ravishes his city and ironically ends up hunting himself. **Situational irony** exists when there is an incongruity between what is expected to happen and what actually happens due to forces beyond human comprehension or control. The suicide of the seemingly successful main character in Edwin Arlington Robinson's poem "Richard Cory" is an example of situational irony. **Cosmic irony** occurs when a writer uses God, destiny, or fate to dash the hopes and expectations of a character or of humankind in general. In cosmic irony, a discrepancy exists between what a character aspires to and what universal forces provide. Stephen Crane's poem "A Man Said to the Universe" is a good example of cosmic irony, because the universe acknowledges no obligation to the man's assertion of his own existence.

Italian sonnet See SONNET.

Limerick A light, humorous style of fixed form poetry. Its usual form consists of five lines with the rhyme scheme *aabba;* lines 1, 2, and 5 contain three feet, while lines 3 and 4 usually contain two feet. Limericks range in subject matter from the silly to the obscene, and since Edward Lear popularized them in the nineteenth century, children and adults have enjoyed these comic poems. See also FIXED FORM.

Limited omniscience See NARRATOR.

Line A sequence of words printed as a separate entity on the page. In poetry, lines are usually measured by the number of feet they contain. The names for various line lengths are as follows:

monometer: one foot	pentameter: five feet
dimeter: two feet	hexameter: six feet
trimeter: three feet	heptameter: seven feet
tetrameter: four feet	octameter: eight feet

The number of feet in a line, coupled with the name of the foot, describes the metrical qualities of that line. See also END-STOPPED LINE, ENJAMBMENT, FOOT, METER.

Literary ballad See BALLAD.

Literary symbol See SYMBOL.

Low comedy See COMEDY.

Lyric A type of brief poem that expresses the personal emotions and thoughts of a single speaker. It is important to realize, however, that although the lyric is uttered in the first person, the speaker is not necessarily the poet. There are many varieties of lyric poetry, including the DRAMATIC MONOLOGUE, ELEGY, HAIKU, ODE, and SONNET forms.

Marxist criticism An approach to literature that focuses on the ideological content of a work — its explicit and implicit assumptions and values about matters such as culture, race, class, and power. Marxist criticism, based largely on the writings of Karl Marx, typically aims at not only revealing and clarifying ideological issues but also correcting social injustices. Some Marxist critics use literature to describe the competing socioeconomic interests that too often advance capitalist interests such as money and power rather than socialist interests such as morality and justice. They argue that literature and literary criticism are essentially political because they either challenge or support economic oppression. Because of this strong emphasis on the political aspects of texts, Marxist criticism focuses more on the content and themes of literature than on its form. See also CULTURAL CRITICISM, HISTORICAL CRITICISM, SOCIOLOGICAL CRITICISM.

Masculine rhyme See RHYME.

Melodrama A term applied to any literary work that relies on implausible events and sensational action for its effect. The conflicts in melodramas typically arise out of plot rather than characterization; often a virtuous individual must somehow confront and overcome a wicked oppressor. Usually, a melodramatic story ends happily, with the protagonist defeating the antagonist at the last possible moment. Thus, melodramas entertain the reader or audience with exciting action while still conforming to a traditional sense of justice. See also SENTIMENTALITY.

Metafiction The literary term used to describe a work that explores the nature, structure, logic, status, and function of storytelling.

Metaphor A metaphor is a figure of speech that makes a comparison between two unlike things, without using the word *like* or *as*. Metaphors assert the identity of dissimilar things, as when Macbeth asserts that life *is* a "brief candle." Metaphors can be subtle and powerful, and can transform people, places, objects, and ideas into whatever the writer imagines them to be. An **implied metaphor** is a more subtle comparison; the terms being compared are not so specifically explained. For example, to describe a stubborn man unwilling to leave, one could say that he was "a mule standing his ground." This is a fairly explicit metaphor; the man is being compared to a mule. But to say that the man "brayed his refusal to leave" is to create an implied metaphor, because the subject (the man) is never overtly identified as a mule. Braying is associated with the mule, a notoriously stubborn creature, and so the comparison between the stubborn man and the mule is sustained. Implied metaphors can slip by inattentive readers who are not sensitive to such carefully chosen, highly concentrated language. An **extended metaphor** is a sustained comparison in which part or all of a poem consists of a series of related metaphors. Robert Francis's poem "Catch" relies on an extended metaphor that compares poetry to playing catch. A **controlling metaphor** runs through an entire work and determines the form or nature of that work. The controlling metaphor in Anne Bradstreet's poem "The Author to Her Book" likens her book to a child. **Synecdoche** is a kind of metaphor in which a part of something is used to signify the whole, as when a gossip is called a "wagging tongue," or when ten ships are called "ten sails." Sometimes, synecdoche refers to the whole being used to signify the part, as in the phrase "Boston won the baseball game." Clearly, the entire city of Boston did not participate in the game; the whole of Boston is being used to signify the individuals who played and won the game. **Metonymy** is a type of metaphor in which something closely associated with a subject is substituted for it. In this way, we speak of the "silver screen" to mean motion pictures, "the crown" to stand for the king, "the White House" to stand for the activities of the president. See also FIGURES OF SPEECH, PERSONIFICATION, SIMILE.

Meter When a rhythmic pattern of stresses recurs in a poem, it is called *meter*. Metrical patterns are determined by the type and number of feet in a line of verse; combining the name of a line length with the name of a foot concisely describes the meter of the line. **Rising meter** refers to metrical feet that move from unstressed to stressed sounds, such as the iambic foot and the anapestic foot. **Falling meter** refers to metrical feet that move from stressed to unstressed sounds, such as the trochaic foot and the dactylic foot. See also ACCENT, FOOT, IAMBIC PENTAMETER, LINE.

Metonymy See METAPHOR.

Middle diction See DICTION.

Motivated action See CHARACTER.

Mythological criticism An approach to literature that seeks to identify what in a work creates deep universal responses in readers, by paying close attention to the hopes, fears, and expectations of entire cultures. Mythological critics (sometimes called *archetypal critics*) look for underlying, recurrent patterns in literature that reveal universal meanings and basic human experiences for readers regardless of when and where they live. These critics attempt to explain how archetypes (the characters, images, and themes that symbolically embody universal meanings and experiences) are embodied in literary works in order to make larger connections that explain a particular work's lasting appeal. Mythological critics may specialize in areas such as classical literature, philology, anthropology, psychology, and cultural history, but they all emphasize the assumptions and values of various cultures. See also ARCHETYPE.

Naive narrator See NARRATOR.

Narrative poem A poem that tells a story. A narrative poem may be short or long, and the story it relates may be simple or complex. See also BALLAD, EPIC.

Narrator The voice of the person telling the story, not to be confused with the author's voice. With a **first-person narrator,** the *I* in the story presents the point of view of only one character. The reader is restricted to the perceptions, thoughts, and feelings of that single character. For example, in Melville's "Bartleby, the Scrivener," the lawyer is the first-person narrator of the story. First-person narrators can play either a major or a minor role in the story they are telling. An **unreliable narrator** reveals an interpretation of events that is somehow different from the author's own interpretation of those events. Often, the unreliable narrator's perception of plot, characters, and setting becomes the actual subject of the story, as in Melville's "Bartleby, the Scrivener." Narrators can be unreliable for a number of reasons: they might lack self-knowledge (like Melville's lawyer), they might be inexperienced, they might even be insane. **Naive narrators** are usually characterized by youthful innocence, such as Mark Twain's Huck Finn or J. D. Salinger's Holden Caulfield. An **omniscient narrator** is an all-knowing narrator who is not a character in the story and who can move from place to place and pass back and forth through time, slipping into and out of characters as no human being possibly could in real life. Omniscient narrators can report the thoughts and feelings of the characters, as well as their words and actions. The narrator of *The Scarlet Letter* is an omniscient narrator. **Editorial omniscience** refers to an intrusion by the narrator in order to evaluate a character for a reader, as when the narrator of *The Scarlet Letter* describes Hester's relationship to the Puritan community. Narration that allows the characters' actions and thoughts to speak for themselves is called **neutral omniscience.** Most modern writers use neutral omniscience so that readers can reach their own conclusions. **Limited omniscience** occurs when an author restricts a narrator to the single perspective of either a major or minor character. The way people, places, and events appear to that character is the way they appear to the reader. Sometimes a limited omniscient narrator can see into more than one character, particularly in a work that focuses on two characters alternately from one chapter to the next. Short stories, however, are frequently limited to a single character's point of view. See also PERSONA, POINT OF VIEW, STREAM-OF-CONSCIOUSNESS TECHNIQUE.

Near rhyme See RHYME.

Neutral omniscience See NARRATOR.

New Criticism An approach to literature made popular between the 1940s and the 1960s that evolved out of formalist criticism. New Critics suggest that detailed analysis of the language of a literary text can uncover important layers of meaning in that work. New Criticism consciously downplays the historical influences, authorial intentions, and social contexts that surround texts in order to focus on explication — extremely close textual analysis. Critics such as John Crowe Ransom, I. A. Richards, and Robert Penn Warren are commonly associated with New Criticism. See also FORMALIST CRITICISM.

New historicism An approach to literature that emphasizes the interaction between the historic context of the work and a modern reader's understanding and interpretation of the work. New historicists attempt to describe the culture of a period by reading many different kinds of texts and paying close attention to many different dimensions of a culture, including political, economic, social, and aesthetic concerns. They regard texts not simply as a reflection of the culture that produced them but also as products of that culture playing an active role in the social and political conflicts of an age. New historicism acknowledges and then explores various versions of "history," sensitizing us to the fact that the history on which we choose to focus is colored by being reconstructed from our present circumstances. See also HISTORICAL CRITICISM.

Objective point of view See POINT OF VIEW.

Octave A poetic stanza of eight lines, usually forming one part of a sonnet. See also SONNET, STANZA.

Ode A relatively lengthy lyric poem that often expresses lofty emotions in a dignified style. Odes are characterized by a serious topic, such as truth, art, freedom, justice, or the meaning of life; their tone tends to be formal. There is no prescribed pattern that defines an ode; some odes repeat the same pattern in each stanza, while others introduce a new pattern in each stanza. See also LYRIC.

Oedipus complex A Freudian term derived from Sophocles' tragedy *Oedipus the King*. It describes a psychological complex that is predicated on a boy's unconscious rivalry with his father for his mother's love and his desire to eliminate his father in order to take his father's place with his mother. The female equivalent of this complex is called the **Electra complex.** See also ELECTRA COMPLEX, PSYCHOLOGICAL CRITICISM.

Off rhyme See RHYME.

Omniscient narrator See NARRATOR.

One-act play A play that takes place in a single location and unfolds as one continuous action. The characters in a one-act play are presented economically and the action is sharply focused. See also DRAMA.

Onomatopoeia A term referring to the use of a word that resembles the sound it denotes. *Buzz, rattle, bang,* and *sizzle* all reflect onomatopoeia. Onomatopoeia can also consist of more than one word; writers sometimes create lines or whole passages in which the sound of the words helps to convey their meanings.

Open form Sometimes called **free verse,** open form poetry does not conform to established patterns of METER, RHYME, and STANZA. Such poetry derives its rhythmic qualities from the repetition of words, phrases, or grammatical structures, the arrangement of words on the printed page, or by some other means. The poet E. E. Cummings wrote open form poetry; his poems do not have measurable meters, but they do have rhythm. See also FIXED FORM.

Organic form Refers to works whose formal characteristics are not rigidly predetermined but follow the movement of thought or emotion being expressed. Such works are said to grow like living organisms, following their own individual patterns rather than external fixed rules that govern, for example, the form of a SONNET.

Overstatement See HYPERBOLE.

Oxymoron A condensed form of paradox in which two contradictory words are used together, as in "sweet sorrow" or "original copy." See also PARADOX.

Paradox A statement that initially appears to be contradictory but then, on closer inspection, turns out to make sense. For example, John Donne ends his sonnet "Death, Be Not Proud" with the paradoxical statement "Death, thou shalt die." To solve the paradox, it is necessary to discover the sense that underlies the statement. Paradox is useful in poetry because it arrests a reader's attention by its seemingly stubborn refusal to make sense.

Paraphrase A prose restatement of the central ideas of a poem, in your own language.

Parody A humorous imitation of another, usually serious, work. It can take any fixed or open form, because parodists imitate the tone, language, and shape of the original in order to deflate the subject matter, making the original work seem absurd. Anthony Hecht's poem "Dover Bitch" is a famous parody of Matthew Arnold's well-known "Dover Beach." Parody may also be used as a form of literary criticism to expose the defects in a work. But sometimes parody becomes an affectionate acknowledgment that a well-known work has become both institutionalized in our culture and fair game for some fun. For example, Peter De Vries's "To His Importunate Mistress" gently mocks Andrew Marvell's "To His Coy Mistress."

Persona Literally, a *persona* is a mask. In literature, a *persona* is a speaker created by a writer to tell a story or to speak in a poem. A persona is not a character in a story or narrative, nor does a persona necessarily directly reflect the author's personal voice. A persona is a separate self, created by and distinct from the author, through which he or she speaks. See also NARRATOR.

Personification A form of metaphor in which human characteristics are attributed to nonhuman things. Personification offers the writer a way to give the world life and motion by assigning familiar human behaviors and emotions to animals, inanimate objects, and abstract ideas. For example, in Keats's "Ode on a Grecian Urn," the speaker refers to the urn as an "unravished bride of quietness." See also METAPHOR.

Petrarchan sonnet See SONNET.

Picture poem A type of open form poetry in which the poet arranges the lines of the poem so as to create a particular shape on the page. The shape of the poem embodies its subject; the poem becomes a picture of what the poem is describing. Michael McFee's "In Medias Res" is an example of a picture poem. See also OPEN FORM.

Plausible action See CHARACTER.

Play See DRAMA.

Playwright See DRAMA.

Plot An author's selection and arrangement of incidents in a story to shape the action and give the story a particular focus. Discussions of plot include not just what happens, but also how and why things happen the way they do. Stories that are written in a **pyramidal pattern** divide the plot into three essential parts. The first part is the **rising action,** in which complication creates some sort of conflict for the protagonist. The second part is the **climax,** the moment of greatest emotional tension in a narrative, usually marking a turning point in the plot at which the rising action reverses to become the falling action. The third part, the **falling action** (or RESOLUTION) is characterized by diminishing tensions and the resolution of the plot's conflicts and complications. **In medias res** is a term used to describe the common strategy of beginning a story in the middle of the action. In this type of plot, we enter the story on the verge of some important moment. See also CHARACTER, CRISIS, RESOLUTION, SUBPLOT.

Poetic diction See DICTION.

Point of view Refers to who tells us a story and how it is told. What we know and how we feel about the events in a work are shaped by the author's choice of point of view. The teller of the story, the narrator, inevitably affects our understanding of the characters' actions by filtering what is told through his or her own perspective. The various points of view that writers draw upon can be grouped into two broad categories: (1) the third-person narrator uses *he, she,* or *they* to tell the story and does not participate in the action; and (2) the first-person narrator uses *I* and is a major or minor participant in the action. In addition, a second-person narrator, *you,* is also possible, but is rarely used because of the awkwardness of thrusting the reader into the story, as in "You are minding your own business on a park bench when a drunk steps out and demands your lunch bag." An **objective point of view** employs a third-person narrator who does not see into the mind of any character. From this detached and impersonal perspective, the narrator reports action and dialogue without telling us directly what the characters think and feel. Since no analysis or interpretation is provided by the narrator, this point of view places a premium on dialogue, actions, and details to reveal character to the reader. See also NARRATOR, STREAM-OF-CONSCIOUSNESS TECHNIQUE.

Postcolonial criticism An approach to literature that focuses on the study of cultural behavior and expression in relationship to the colonized world. Postcolonial criticism refers to the analysis of literary works written by writers from countries and cultures that at one time have been controlled by colonizing powers — such as Indian writers during or after British colonial rule. Postcolonial criticism also refers to the analysis of literary works written about colonial cultures by writers from the colonizing country. Many of these kinds of analyses point out how writers from colonial powers sometimes misrepresent colonized cultures by reflecting more their own values. See also CULTURAL CRITICISM, HISTORICAL CRITICISM, MARXIST CRITICISM.

Problem play Popularized by Henrik Ibsen, a problem play is a type of drama that presents a social issue in order to awaken the audience to it. These plays usually reject romantic plots in favor of holding up a mirror that reflects not simply what the audience wants to see but what the playwright sees in them. Often, a problem play will propose a solution to the problem that does not coincide with prevailing opinion. The term is also used to refer to certain Shakespeare plays that do not fit the categories of tragedy, comedy, or romance. See also DRAMA.

Prologue The opening speech or dialogue of a play, especially a classic Greek play, that usually gives the exposition necessary to follow the subsequent action. Today the term also refers to the introduction to any literary work. See also DRAMA, EXPOSITION.

Prose poem A kind of open form poetry that is printed as prose and represents the most clear opposite of fixed form poetry. Prose poems are densely compact and often make use of striking imagery and figures of speech. See also FIXED FORM, OPEN FORM.

Prosody The overall metrical structure of a poem. See also METER.

Protagonist The main character of a narrative; its central character who engages the reader's interest and empathy. See also CHARACTER.

Psychological criticism An approach to literature that draws upon psychoanalytic theories, especially those of Sigmund Freud or Jacques Lacan to understand more fully the text, the writer, and the reader. The basis of this approach is the idea of the existence of a human unconscious — those impulses, desires, and feelings about which a person is unaware but which influence emotions and behavior. Critics use psychological approaches to explore the motivations of characters and the symbolic meanings of events, while biographers speculate about a writer's own motivations — conscious or unconscious — in a literary work. Psychological approaches are also used to describe and analyze the reader's personal responses to a text.

Pun A play on words that relies on a word's having more than one meaning or sounding like another word. Shakespeare and other writers use puns extensively, for serious and comic purposes; in *Romeo and Juliet* (III.i.101), the dying Mercutio puns, "Ask for me tomorrow and you shall find me a grave man." Puns have serious literary uses, but since the eighteenth century, puns have been used almost purely for humorous effect. See also COMEDY.

Pyramidal pattern See PLOT.

Quatrain A four-line stanza. Quatrains are the most common stanzaic form in the English language; they can have various meters and rhyme schemes. See also METER, RHYME, STANZA.

Reader-response criticism An approach to literature that focuses on the reader rather than the work itself, by attempting to describe what goes on in the reader's mind during the reading of a text. Hence, the consciousness of the reader — produced by reading the work — is the actual subject of reader-response criticism. These critics are not after a "correct" reading of the text or what the author presumably intended; instead, they are interested in the reader's individual experience with the text. Thus, there is no single definitive reading of a work, because readers create rather than discover absolute meanings in texts. However, this approach is not a rationale for mistaken or bizarre readings, but an exploration of the possibilities for a plurality of readings. This kind of strategy calls attention to how we read and what influences our readings, and what that reveals about ourselves.

Recognition The moment in a story when previously unknown or withheld information is revealed to the protagonist, resulting in the discovery of the truth of his or her situation and, usually, a decisive change in course for that character. In *Oedipus the King*, the moment of recognition comes when Oedipus finally realizes that he has killed his father and married his mother.

Resolution The conclusion of a plot's conflicts and complications. The resolution, also known as the **falling action,** follows the climax in the plot. See also DÉNOUEMENT, PLOT.

Revenge tragedy See TRAGEDY.

Reversal The point in a story when the protagonist's fortunes turn in an unexpected direction. See also PLOT.

Rhyme The repetition of identical or similar concluding syllables in different words, most often at the ends of lines. Rhyme is predominantly a function of sound rather than spelling; thus, words that end with the same vowel sounds rhyme, for instance, *day, prey, bouquet, weigh,* and words with the same consonant ending rhyme, for instance *vain, feign, rein, lane.* Words do not have to be spelled the same way or look alike to rhyme. In fact, words may look alike but not rhyme at all. This is called **eye rhyme,** as with *bough* and *cough,* or *brow* and *blow.* **End rhyme** is the most common form of rhyme in poetry; the rhyme comes at the end of the lines:

It runs through the reeds
    And away it proceeds,
Through meadow and glade,
    In sun and in shade.

The **rhyme scheme** of a poem describes the pattern of end rhymes. Rhyme schemes are mapped out by noting patterns of rhyme with small letters: the first rhyme sound is designated *a,* the second becomes *b,* the third *c,* and so on. Thus, the rhyme scheme of the stanza above is *aabb.* **Internal rhyme** places at least one of the rhymed words within the line, as in "Dividing and gliding and sliding" or "In mist or cloud, on mast or shroud." **Masculine rhyme** describes the rhyming of single-syllable words, such as *grade* or *shade.*

Masculine rhyme also occurs when rhyming words of more than one syllable, when the same sound occurs in a final stressed syllable, as in *defend* and *contend, betray* and *away*. **Feminine rhyme** consists of a rhymed stressed syllable followed by one or more identical unstressed syllables, as in *butter, clutter; gratitude, attitude; quivering, shivering*. All the examples so far have illustrated **exact rhymes**, because they share the same stressed vowel sounds as well as sharing sounds that follow the vowel. In **near rhyme** (also called **off rhyme, slant rhyme,** and **approximate rhyme**), the sounds are almost but not exactly alike. A common form of near rhyme is CONSONANCE, which consists of identical consonant sounds preceded by different vowel sounds: *home, same; worth, breath*.

Rhyme scheme See RHYME.

Rhythm A term used to refer to the recurrence of stressed and unstressed sounds in poetry. Depending on how sounds are arranged, the rhythm of a poem may be fast or slow, choppy or smooth. Poets use rhythm to create pleasurable sound patterns and to reinforce meanings. Rhythm in prose arises from pattern repetitions of sounds and pauses that create looser rhythmic effects. See also METER.

Rising action See PLOT.

Rising meter See METER.

Romantic comedy See COMEDY.

Round character See CHARACTER.

Run-on line See ENJAMBMENT.

Sarcasm See IRONY.

Satire The literary art of ridiculing a folly or vice in order to expose or correct it. The object of satire is usually some human frailty; people, institutions, ideas, and things are all fair game for satirists. Satire evokes attitudes of amusement, contempt, scorn, or indignation toward its faulty subject in the hope of somehow improving it. See also IRONY, PARODY.

Scansion The process of measuring the stresses in a line of verse in order to determine the metrical pattern of the line. See also LINE, METER.

Scene In drama, a scene is a subdivision of an ACT. In modern plays, scenes usually consist of units of action in which there are no changes in the setting or breaks in the continuity of time. According to traditional conventions, a scene changes when the location of the action shifts or when a new character enters. See also CONVENTION, DRAMA.

Script The written text of a play, which includes the dialogue between characters, stage directions, and often other expository information. See also DRAMA, EXPOSITION, PROLOGUE, STAGE DIRECTIONS.

Sentimentality A pejorative term used to describe the effort by an author to induce emotional responses in the reader that exceed what the situation warrants. Sentimentality especially pertains to such emotions as pathos and sympathy; it cons readers into falling for the mass murderer who is devoted to stray cats, and it requires that readers do not examine such illogical responses. Clichés and stock responses are the key ingredients of sentimentality in literature. See also CLICHÉ, STOCK RESPONSES.

Sestet A stanza consisting of exactly six lines. See also STANZA.

Sestina A type of fixed form poetry consisting of thirty-six lines of any length divided into six sestets and a three-line concluding stanza called an ENVOY. The six words at the end of the first sestet's lines must also appear at the ends of the other five sestets, in varying order. These six words must also appear in the envoy, where they often resonate important themes. An example of this highly demanding form of poetry is Elizabeth Bishop's "Sestina." See also SESTET.

Setting The physical and social context in which the action of a story occurs. The major elements of setting are the time, the place, and the social environment that frames the characters. Setting can be used to evoke a mood or atmosphere that will prepare the reader for what is to come, as in Nathaniel Hawthorne's short story "Young Goodman Brown." Sometimes, writers choose a particular setting because of traditional associations with that setting that are closely related to the action of a story. For example, stories filled with adventure or romance often take place in exotic locales.

Shakespearean sonnet See SONNET.

Showing See CHARACTER.

Simile A common figure of speech that makes an explicit comparison between two things by using words such as *like, as, than, appears,* and *seems:* "A sip of Mrs. Cook's coffee is like a punch in the stomach." The effectiveness of this simile is created by the differences between the two things compared. There would be no simile if the comparison were stated this way: "Mrs. Cook's coffee is as strong as the cafeteria's coffee." This is a literal translation because Mrs. Cook's coffee is compared with something like it — another kind of coffee. See also FIGURES OF SPEECH, METAPHOR.

Situational irony See IRONY.

Slant rhyme See RHYME.

Sociological criticism An approach to literature that examines social groups, relationships, and values as they are manifested in literature. Sociological approaches emphasize the nature and effect of the social forces that shape power relationships between groups or classes of people. Such readings treat literature as either a document reflecting social conditions or a product of those conditions. The former view brings into focus the social milieu; the latter emphasizes the work. Two important forms of sociological criticism are Marxist and feminist approaches. See also FEMINIST CRITICISM, MARXIST CRITICISM.

Soliloquy A dramatic convention by means of which a character, alone onstage, utters his or her thoughts aloud. Playwrights use soliloquies as a convenient way to inform the audience about a character's motivations and state of mind. Shakespeare's Hamlet delivers perhaps the best known of all soliloquies, which begins: "To be or not to be." See also ASIDE, CONVENTION.

Sonnet A fixed form of lyric poetry that consists of fourteen lines, usually written in iambic pentameter. There are two basic types of sonnets, the Italian and the English. The **Italian sonnet,** also known as the **Petrarchan sonnet,** is divided into an octave, which typically rhymes *abbaabba,* and a sestet, which may have varying rhyme schemes. Common rhyme patterns in the sestet are *cdecde, cdcdcd,* and *cdccdc.* Very often the octave presents a situation, attitude, or problem that the sestet comments upon or resolves, as in John Keats's "On First Looking into Chapman's Homer." The **English sonnet,** also known as the **Shakespearean sonnet,** is organized into three quatrains and a couplet, which typically rhyme *abab cdcd efef gg.* This rhyme scheme is more suited to English poetry because English has fewer rhyming words than Italian. English sonnets, because of their four-part organization, also have more flexibility with respect to where thematic breaks can occur. Frequently, however, the most pronounced break or turn comes with the concluding couplet, as in Shakespeare's "Shall I compare thee to a summer's day?" See also COUPLET, IAMBIC PENTAMETER, LINE, OCTAVE, QUATRAIN, SESTET.

Speaker The voice used by an author to tell a story or speak a poem. The speaker is often a created identity, and should not automatically be equated with the author's self. See also NARRATOR, PERSONA, POINT OF VIEW.

Spondee See FOOT.

Stage directions A playwright's written instructions about how the actors are to move and behave in a play. They explain in which direction characters should move, what facial expressions they should assume, and so on. See also DRAMA, SCRIPT.

Stanza In poetry, *stanza* refers to a grouping of lines, set off by a space, that usually has a set pattern of meter and rhyme. See also LINE, METER, RHYME.

Static character See CHARACTER.

Stock character See CHARACTER.

Stock responses Predictable, conventional reactions to language, characters, symbols, or situations. The flag, motherhood, puppies, God, and peace are common objects used to elicit stock responses from unsophisticated audiences. See also CLICHÉ, SENTIMENTALITY.

Stream-of-consciousness technique The most intense use of a central consciousness in narration. The stream-of-consciousness technique takes a reader inside a character's mind to reveal perceptions, thoughts, and feelings on a conscious or unconscious level. This technique suggests the flow of thought as well as its content; hence, complete sentences may give way to fragments as the character's mind makes rapid associations free of conventional logic or transitions. James Joyce's novel *Ulysses* makes extensive use of this narrative technique. See also NARRATOR, POINT OF VIEW.

Stress The emphasis, or accent, given a syllable in pronunciation. See also ACCENT.

Style The distinctive and unique manner in which a writer arranges words to achieve particular effects. Style essentially combines the idea to be expressed with the individuality of the author. These arrangements include individual word choices as well as matters such as the length of sentences, their structure, tone, and use of irony. See also DICTION, IRONY, TONE.

Subplot The secondary action of a story, complete and interesting in its own right, that reinforces or contrasts with the main plot. There may be more than one subplot, and sometimes as many as three, four, or even more, running through a piece of fiction. Subplots are generally either analogous to the main plot, thereby enhancing our understanding of it, or extraneous to the main plot, to provide relief from it. See also PLOT.

Suspense The anxious anticipation of a reader or an audience as to the outcome of a story, especially concerning the character or characters with whom sympathetic attachments are formed. Suspense helps to secure and sustain the interest of the reader or audience throughout a work.

Symbol A person, object, image, word, or event that evokes a range of additional meaning beyond and usually more abstract than its literal significance. Symbols are educational devices for evoking complex ideas without having to resort to painstaking explanations that would make a story more like an essay than an experience. **Conventional symbols** have meanings that are widely recognized by a society or culture. Some conventional symbols are the Christian cross, the Star of David, a swastika, or a nation's flag. Writers use conventional symbols to reinforce meanings. Kate Chopin, for example, emphasizes the spring setting in "The Story of an Hour" as a way of suggesting the renewed sense of life that Mrs. Mallard feels when she thinks herself free from her husband. A **literary** or **contextual symbol** can be a setting, character, action, object, name, or anything else in a work that maintains its literal significance while suggesting other meanings. Such symbols go beyond conventional symbols; they gain their symbolic meaning within the context of a specific story. For example, the white whale in Melville's *Moby-Dick* takes on multiple symbolic meanings in the work, but these meanings do not automatically carry over into other stories about whales. The meanings suggested by Melville's whale are specific to that text; therefore, it becomes a contextual symbol. See also ALLEGORY.

Synecdoche See METAPHOR.

Syntax The ordering of words into meaningful verbal patterns such as phrases, clauses, and sentences. Poets often manipulate syntax, changing conventional word order, to place certain emphasis on particular words. Emily Dickinson, for instance, writes about being surprised by a snake in her poem "A narrow Fellow in the Grass," and includes this line: "His notice sudden is." In addition to the alliterative hissing *s*-sounds here, Dickinson also effectively manipulates the line's syntax so that the verb *is* appears unexpectedly at the end, making the snake's hissing presence all the more "sudden."

Telling See CHARACTER.

Tercet A three-line stanza. See also STANZA, TRIPLET.

Terza rima An interlocking three-line rhyme scheme: *aba, bcb, cdc, ded,* and so on. Dante's *The Divine Comedy* and Frost's "Acquainted with the Night" are written in *terza rima*. See also RHYME, TERCET.

Theme The central meaning or dominant idea in a literary work. A theme provides a unifying point around which the plot, characters, setting, point of view, symbols, and other elements of a work are organized. It is important not to mistake the theme for the actual subject of the work; the theme refers to the abstract concept that is made concrete through the images, characterization, and action of the text. In nonfiction, however, the theme generally refers to the main topic of the discourse.

Thesis The central idea of an essay. The thesis is a complete sentence (although sometimes it may require more than one sentence) that establishes the topic of the essay in clear, unambiguous language.

Tone The author's implicit attitude toward the reader or the people, places, and events in a work as revealed by the elements of the author's style. Tone may be characterized as serious or ironic, sad or happy, private or public, angry or affectionate, bitter or nostalgic, or any other attitudes and feelings that human beings experience. See also STYLE.

Tragedy A story that presents courageous individuals who confront powerful forces within or outside themselves with a dignity that reveals the breadth and depth of the human spirit in the face of failure, defeat, and even death. Tragedies recount an individual's downfall; they usually begin high and end low. Shakespeare is known for his tragedies, including *Macbeth, King Lear, Othello,* and *Hamlet.* The **revenge tragedy** is a well-established type of drama that can be traced back to Greek and Roman plays, particularly through the Roman playwright Seneca (c. 3 B.C.–A.D. 63). Revenge tragedies basically consist of a murder that has to be avenged by a relative of the victim. Typically, the victim's ghost appears to demand revenge, and invariably madness of some sort is worked into subsequent events, which ultimately end in the deaths of the murderer, the avenger, and a number of other characters. Shakespeare's *Hamlet* subscribes to the basic ingredients of revenge tragedy, but it also transcends these conventions because Hamlet contemplates not merely revenge but suicide and the meaning of life itself. A **tragic flaw** is an error or defect in the tragic hero that leads to his downfall, such as greed, pride, or ambition. This flaw may be a result of bad character, bad judgment, an inherited weakness, or any other defect of character. **Tragic irony** is a form of dramatic irony found in tragedies such as *Oedipus the King,* in which Oedipus ironically ends up hunting himself. See also COMEDY, DRAMA.

Tragic flaw See TRAGEDY.

Tragic irony See IRONY, TRAGEDY.

Tragicomedy A type of drama that combines certain elements of both tragedy and comedy. The play's plot tends to be serious, leading to a terrible catastrophe, until an unexpected turn in events leads to a reversal of circumstance, and the story ends happily. Tragicomedy often employs a romantic, fast-moving plot dealing with love, jealousy, disguises, treachery, intrigue, and surprises, all moving toward a melodramatic resolution. Shakespeare's *Merchant of Venice* is a tragicomedy. See also COMEDY, DRAMA, MELODRAMA, TRAGEDY.

Triplet A tercet in which all three lines rhyme. See also TERCET.

Trochaic meter See FOOT.

Understatement The opposite of hyperbole, understatement (or litotes) refers to a figure of speech that says less than is intended. Understatement usually has an ironic effect, and sometimes may be used for comic purposes, as in Mark Twain's statement, "The reports of my death are greatly exaggerated." See also HYPERBOLE, IRONY.

Unreliable narrator See NARRATOR.

Verbal irony See IRONY.

Verse A generic term used to describe poetic lines composed in a measured rhythmical pattern, that are often, but not necessarily, rhymed. See also LINE, METER, RHYME, RHYTHM.

Villanelle A type of fixed form poetry consisting of nineteen lines of any length divided into six stanzas: five tercets and a concluding quatrain. The first and third lines of the initial tercet rhyme; these rhymes are repeated in each subsequent tercet (*aba*) and in the final two lines of the quatrain (*abaa*). Line 1 appears in its entirety as lines 6, 12, and 18, while line 3 reappears as lines 9, 15, and 19. Dylan Thomas's "Do not go gentle into that good night" is a villanelle. See also FIXED FORM, QUATRAIN, RHYME, TERCET.

Well-made play A realistic style of play that employs conventions including plenty of suspense created by meticulous plotting. Well-made plays are tightly and logically constructed and lead to a logical resolution that is favorable to the protagonist. This dramatic structure was popularized in France by Eugène Scribe (1791–1861) and Victorien Sardou (1831–1908) and was adopted by Henrik Ibsen. See also CHARACTER, PLOT.

Acknowledgments (continued from p. ii)

Rick Bass. "Her First Elk" from *The Lives of Rocks* by Rick Bass. Copyright © 2006 by Rick Bass. Reprinted by permission of Houghton Mifflin Company. All rights reserved.

Amy Bloom. "By-and-By" from a forthcoming collection of stories by Amy Bloom to be published by Random House. Copyright © 2003 by Amy Bloom. No part of this material may be reproduced, in whole or in part, without the express written permission of the author or her agent.

T. Coraghessan Boyle. "Carnal Knowledge" from *Without a Hero* by T. Coraghessan Boyle. Copyright © 1994 by T. Coraghessan Boyle. Used by permission of Viking Penguin, a division of Penguin Group (USA) Inc.

Matthew C. Brennan. "Point of View and Plotting in Chekhov's and Oates's 'The Lady with the Pet Dog'" excerpted from "Plotting against Chekhov: Joyce Carol Oates and 'The Lady with the Pet Dog,'" *Notes on Modern American Literature* (Winter 1985). Reprinted by permission of the author.

Robert Olen Butler. "Christmas 1910" from *Had a Good Time: Stories from American Postcards* by Robert Olen Butler. Copyright © 2004 by Robert Olen Butler. Used by permission of Grove/Atlantic, Inc.

Raymond Carver. "Popular Mechanics" from *What We Talk about When We Talk about Love* by Raymond Carver. Copyright © 1981 by Raymond Carver. Used by permission of Alfred A. Knopf, a division of Random House, Inc.

W. J. Cash. "The Old and the New South" excerpted from *The Mind of the South* by W. J. Cash. Copyright © 1941 by Alfred A. Knopf, Inc., and renewed 1969 by Mary R. Maury. Used by permission of Alfred A. Knopf, a division of Random House, Inc.

Anton Chekhov. "A Lady with a Dog" from *The Oxford Chekhov,* translated and edited by Ronald Hingley, Vol. IX (1975). By permission of Oxford University Press. "The Lady with the Pet Dog," translated by Avrahm Yarmolinsky, from *The Portable Chekhov* by Anton Chekhov, edited by Avrahm Yarmolinsky. Copyright 1947, © 1968 by Viking Penguin, Inc., and renewed © 1975 by Avrahm Yarmolinsky. Used by permission of Viking Penguin, a division of Penguin Group (USA) Inc.

Colette. "The Hand" from *The Collected Stories of Colette,* edited by Robert Phelps and translated by Matthew Ward. Translation copyright © 1983 by Farrar, Straus & Giroux, Inc. Reprinted by permission of Farrar, Straus & Giroux, LLC.

Lydia Davis. "Letter to a Funeral Parlor" from *Samuel Johnson Is Indignant* by Lydia Davis. Copyright © 2002 by Lydia Davis. Reprinted by permission of Farrar, Straus & Giroux, LLC.

Benjamin DeMott. "Abner Snopes as a Victim of Class" from *Close Imaginings: An Introduction to Literature* by Benjamin DeMott, copyright © 1988. Reprinted by permission of Margaret DeMott.

Chitra Banerjee Divakaruni. "Clothes" from *Arranged Marriage* by Chitra Divakaruni. Copyright © 1995 by Chitra Divakaruni. Used by permission of Doubleday, a division of Random House, Inc.

Andre Dubus. "Killings" from *Finding a Girl in America* by Andre Dubus. Copyright © 1980 by Andre Dubus. Reprinted by permission of David R. Godine, Publisher, Inc.

Ralph Ellison. "Battle Royal" from *Invisible Man* by Ralph Ellison. Copyright © 1948 by Ralph Ellison. Used by permission of Random House, Inc.

William Faulkner. "A Rose for Emily" from *Collected Stories of William Faulkner* by William Faulkner. Copyright 1930 and renewed 1958 by William Faulkner. Used by permission of Random House, Inc. "Barn Burning" from *Collected Stories of William Faulkner* by William Faulkner. Copyright 1950 by Random House, Inc. Reprinted by permission of Random House, Inc. "On 'A Rose for Emily'" from *Faulkner in the University,* edited by Frederick Gwynn and Joseph Blotner. Copyright © 1995 University of Virginia Press. Reprinted with permission.

James Ferguson. "Narrative Strategy in 'Barn Burning'" from *Faulkner's Short Fiction* by James Ferguson, copyright © 1991. Used by permission of the University of Tennessee Press.

Dagoberto Gilb. "Love in L.A." from *The Magic of Blood* by Dagoberto Gilb. Copyright © 1993 by the University of New Mexico Press. Story originally published in *Buffalo.* Reprinted by permission.

Gail Godwin. "A Sorrowful Woman," published in 1971 by *Esquire* magazine. Copyright © 1971 by Gail Godwin. Reprinted by permission of John Hawkins & Associates, Inc.

Ha Jin. "Love in the Air," an excerpt from *Ocean of Words* by Ha Jin, published by Zoland Books, an imprint of Steerforth Press of Hanover, New Hampshire. Copyright © 1996 by Ha Jin. Reprinted by permission of Steerforth Press.

Ernest Hemingway. "Soldier's Home" from *In Our Time* by Ernest Hemingway. Copyright © 1925 by Charles Scribner's Sons. Copyright renewed 1953 by Ernest Hemingway. Reprinted with the permission of Scribner, an imprint of Simon & Schuster Adult Publishing Group.

Jane Hiles. "Blood Ties in 'Barn Burning'" from "Kinship and Heredity in Faulkner's 'Barn Burning,'" *Mississippi Quarterly* 38, no. 3 (Summer 1985), pp. 329–37. Copyright © 1985 Mississippi State University, Mississippi State, Mississippi. Reprinted by permission of *Mississippi Quarterly: The Journal of Southern Culture.*

Irving Howe. "The Southern Myth" from "The Southern Myth and William Faulkner," *Dissent* 3, no. 4 (Winter 1951). Reprinted by permission of *Dissent* magazine.

Claire Kahane. "The Function of Violence in O'Connor's Fiction" from "Flannery O'Connor's Rage of Vision," *American Literature* 46, no. 1 (March 1974). Copyright 1974, Duke University Press. All rights reserved. Reprinted with permission.

Jamaica Kincaid. "Girl" from *At the Bottom of the River* by Jamaica Kincaid. Copyright © 1983 by Jamaica Kincaid. Reprinted by permission of Farrar, Straus & Giroux, LLC.

Mordecai Marcus. "What Is an Initiation Story?" from *The Journal of Aesthetics and Art Criticism* 19, no. 2, pp. 222–23. Reprinted by permission of Blackwell Publishing Ltd.

Dan McCall. "On the Lawyer's Character in 'Bartleby the Scrivener'" from *The Silence of Bartleby* by Dan McCall. Copyright © 1989 Cornell University. Used by permission of the publisher, Cornell University Press.

Peter Meinke. "The Cranes." Copyright © 1999 by Peter Meinke. Reprinted by permission of the author.

Susan Minot. "Lust" from *Lust and Other Stories* by Susan Minot. Copyright © 1989 by Susan Minot. Reprinted by permission of Houghton Mifflin Company. All rights reserved.

Kay Mussell. "Are Feminism and Romance Novels Mutually Exclusive?" from "All about Romance: The Back-Fence for Lovers of Romance Novels" at <http://www.likesbooks.com/mussell.html>. Kay Mussell is Professor of Literature and Dean of the College of Arts and Sciences at American University in Washington, D.C.

Donald R. Noble. "The Future of Southern Writing" excerpted from *The History of Southern Literature,* edited by Louis D. Rubin et al. Copyright © 1985. Reprinted by permission of Louisiana State University Press.

Joyce Carol Oates. "The Lady with the Pet Dog" from *Marriages and Infidelities* by Joyce Carol Oates (Vanguard Press, 1972). Copyright © 1972 by Ontario Review. Reprinted by permission of John Hawkins & Associates, Inc.

Achy Obejas. "We Came All the Way from Cuba So You Could Dress Like This?" from *We Came All the Way from Cuba So You Could Dress Like This?* by Achy Obejas. Copyright © 1994 by Achy Obejas. Published by Cleis Press: 1-800-780-2279. Reprinted by permission.

Tim O'Brien. "How to Tell a True War Story." Copyright © 1987 by Tim O'Brien. Originally published in *Esquire* magazine. Reprinted by permission of the author.

Flannery O'Connor. "A Good Man Is Hard to Find," copyright © 1953 by Flannery O'Connor and renewed 1981 by Regina O'Connor, and "Good Country People," copyright © 1955 by Flannery O'Connor and renewed 1983 by Regina O'Connor, from *A Good Man Is Hard to Find and Other Stories*. Reprinted by permission of Harcourt, Inc. "On Faith" excerpted from letter to "A," 20 July 1955, from *The Habit of Being: Letters of Flannery O'Connor,* edited by Sally Fitzgerald. Copyright © 1979 by Regina O'Connor. Reprinted by permission of Farrar, Straus & Giroux, LLC. "On the Materials of Fiction" excerpted from "The Nature and Aim of Fiction" in *Mystery and Manners* by Flannery O'Connor. Copyright © 1969 by the Estate of Mary Flannery O'Connor. Reprinted by permission of Farrar, Straus & Giroux, LLC. "On Theme and Symbol" excerpted from "Writing Short Stories" in *Mystery and Manners* by Flannery O'Connor. Copyright © 1969 by the Estate of Mary Flannery O'Connor. Reprinted by permission of Farrar, Straus & Giroux, LLC. "On the Use of Exaggeration and Distortion" excerpted from "Novelist and Believer" in *Mystery and Manners* by Flannery O'Connor. Copyright © 1969 by the Estate of Mary Flannery O'Connor. Reprinted by permission of Farrar, Straus & Giroux, LLC. "The Regional Writer" excerpted from "The Regional Writer" in *Mystery and Manners* by Flannery O'Connor. Copyright © 1969 by the Estate of Mary Flannery O'Connor. Reprinted by permission of Farrar, Straus & Giroux, LLC. "Revelation" from *The Complete Stories* by Flannery O'Connor. Copyright © 1965 by the Estate of Mary Flannery O'Connor. Reprinted by permission of Farrar, Straus & Giroux, LLC.

Katherine Anne Porter. "The Witness" from *The Leaning Tower and Other Stories*. Copyright © 1935 and renewed 1963 by Katherine Anne Porter. Reprinted by permission of Harcourt, Inc.

Annie Proulx. "55 Miles to the Gas Pump" from *Close Range: Wyoming Stories* by Annie Proulx. Copyright © 1999 by Dead Line Ltd. Reprinted with the permission of Scribner, an imprint of Simon & Schuster Adult Publishing Group.

Lee Smith. "The Happy Memories Club" from *News of the Spirit* by Lee Smith. Copyright © 1997 by Lee Smith. Used by permission of G. P. Putnam's Sons, a division of Penguin Group (USA) Inc. "On Southern Change and Permanence" from her preface, "Driving Miss Daisy Crazy; or, Losing the Mind of the South," in *New Stories from the South: The Year's Best, 2001,* edited by Shannon Ravenel (Algonquin Books). Copyright © 2001 by Lee Smith. Reprinted by permission of the author.

Susan Straight. "Mines," first published in *Zoetrope* 6, no. 3 (Fall 2002). Copyright © 2002 by Susan Straight. Reprinted by permission of the Richard Parks Agency.

David Updike. "Summer" from *Out on the Marsh* by David Updike. Copyright © 1988 by David Updike. Reprinted by permission of David R. Godine, Publisher, Inc.

John Updike. "A & P" from *Pigeon Feathers and Other Stories* by John Updike. Copyright © 1962 and renewed 1990 by John Updike. Used by permission of Alfred A. Knopf, a division of Random House, Inc.

Karen Van Der Zee. "A Secret Sorrow." Copyright © 1981 by Karen Van Der Zee. All rights reserved. Reproduction with the permission of the publisher, Harlequin Books S.A.

Margaret Walker. "The Southern Writer and Race" excerpted from "A Brief Introduction to Southern Literature" from *How I Wrote Jubilee and Other Essays on Life and Literature,* ed. Maryemma Graham. Copyright © 1990 by Margaret Walker Alexander. Reprinted by permission of the Feminist Press at the City University of New York, www.feministpress.org. All rights reserved.

Fay Weldon. "IND AFF, or Out of Love in Sarajevo." Copyright © 1988 by Fay Weldon. First published in *The Observer* magazine (7 August 1988). Reprinted by permission of the author.

Gayle Edward Wilson. "Conflict in 'Barn Burning'" from "'Being Pulled Two Ways': The Nature of Sarty's Choice in 'Barn Burning,'" *Mississippi Quarterly* 24, no. 3 (Summer 1971), pp. 279–88. Copyright © 1971 Mississippi State University, Mississippi State, Mississippi. Reprinted by permission of *Mississippi Quarterly: The Journal of Southern Culture.*

Richard Wright. "The Ethics of Living Jim Crow: An Autobiographical Sketch" from *Uncle Tom's Children* by Richard Wright. Copyright © 1937 by Richard Wright. Copyright renewed 1965 by Ellen Wright. Reprinted by permission of HarperCollins Publishers, Inc.

POETRY

Fleur Adcock, "The Video" from *Poems 1960–2000* by Fleur Adcock (Bloodaxe Books, 2000). Copyright © 2000 by Fleur Adcock. Reprinted by permission of Bloodaxe Books Ltd.

Julia Alvarez. "Dusting," "Ironing Their Clothes," and "Sometimes the Words Are So Close" [Sonnet 42] from *Homecoming.* Copyright © 1984, 1996 by Julia Alvarez. Published by Plume, an imprint of the Penguin Group (USA), and originally published by Grove Press. "First Muse" from *The Woman I Kept to Myself.* Copyright © 2004 by Julia Alvarez. Published by Algonquin Books of Chapel Hill in 2004. "Housekeeping Cages." Copyright © 1994 by Julia Alvarez. First published in *A Formal Feeling Comes: Poems in Form by Contemporary Women*, edited by Annie Finch, published by Story Line Press. "On Writing 'Housekeeping Cages' and Her Housekeeping Poems" [excerpt from "Of Maids and Muses"] from *Something to Declare*. Copyright © 1998 by Julia Alvarez. Published by Plume, an imprint of the Penguin Group (USA), in 1999 and originally in hardcover by Algonquin Books of Chapel Hill. "On Writing 'Dusting,'" "On Writing 'First Muse,'" "On Writing 'Ironing Their Clothes,'" "On Writing 'Queens, 1963,'" and "On Writing 'Sometimes the Words Are So Close [Sonnet 42].'" Copyright © 2006 by Julia Alvarez. "Queens, 1963" from *The Other Side/El Otro Lado*. Copyright © 1995 by Julia Alvarez. Published by Plume, an imprint of the Penguin Group (USA), and originally in hardcover by Dutton. All selections reprinted by permission of Susan Bergholz Literary Services, New York. All rights reserved.

A. R. Ammons. "Coward" from *Diversifications* by A. R. Ammons. Copyright © 1975 by A. R. Ammons. Used by permission of W. W. Norton & Company, Inc.

Maggie Anderson. "The Thing You Must Remember" from *Windfall: New and Selected Poems* by Maggie Anderson. Copyright © 2000. Reprinted by permission of the University of Pittsburgh Press.

Richard Armour. "Going to Extremes" from *Light Armour* by Richard Armour. Permission to reprint this material is given courtesy of the family of Richard Armour.

Margaret Atwood. "February" from *Morning in the Burned House* by Margaret Atwood. Copyright © 1995 by Margaret Atwood. Reprinted by permission of Houghton Mifflin Company and McClelland & Stewart, Ltd., *The Canadian Publishers*. All rights reserved. "you fit into me" from *Power Politics* by Margaret Atwood. Copyright © 1971, 1996 by Margaret Atwood. Reprinted by permission of House of Anansi Press, Toronto.

Jimmy Santiago Baca. "Green Chile" from *Black Mesa Poems* by Jimmy Santiago Baca. Copyright © 1989 by Jimmy Santiago Baca. Reprinted by permission of New Directions Publishing Corp.

Mary Barnard. "Prayer to my lady of Paphos" [Fragment #38] from *Sappho: A New Translation* by Mary Barnard. Copyright © 1958 by the Regents of the University of California, renewed © 1986 by Mary Barnard. Reprinted by permission of the Regents of the University of California and the publisher, the University of California Press.

Regina Barreca. "Nighttime Fires" from *The Minnesota Review* (Fall 1986). Reprinted by permission of the author.

Matsuo Bashō. "Under Cherry Trees" from *Japanese Haiku*, translated by Peter Beilenson, Series I, © 1955–56, Peter Beilenson, Editor. Reprinted by permission of Peter Pauper Press.

Paula Bennett. "On 'I heard a Fly buzz—when I died—'" excerpted from *Emily Dickinson: Woman Poet* by Paula Bennett (University of Iowa Press, 1991). Copyright © 1991 by Paula Bennett. Reprinted by permission of the author.

Elizabeth Bishop. "Manners" and "The Fish" from *The Complete Poems, 1927–1979* by Elizabeth Bishop. Copyright © 1979, 1983 by Alice Helen Methfessel. Reprinted by permission of Farrar, Straus and Giroux, LLC.

Robert Bly. "Gratitude to Old Teachers" from *Eating the Honey of Words* by Robert Bly. Copyright © 1999 by Robert Bly. Reprinted by permission of HarperCollins Publishers.

Michelle Boisseau. "Self-Pity's Closet" from *Trembling Air* by Michelle Boisseau. Copyright © 2003 by Michelle Boisseau. Reprinted with the permission of the University of Arkansas Press. The poem first appeared in *The Yale Review* 89, no. 3 (July 2001).

Billie Bolton. "Memorandum." Copyright © 2006 by Billie Bolton. Reprinted by permission of the author.

Gwendolyn Brooks. "We Real Cool" from *Blacks* by Gwendolyn Brooks. Copyright © 1991 by Gwendolyn Brooks. Reprinted by consent of Brooks Permissions.

Helen Chasin. "The Word *Plum*" from *Coming Close and Other Poems* by Helen Chasin. Copyright © 1968 by Yale University Press. Reprinted by permission of Yale University Press.

Kelly Cherry. "Alzheimer's" from *Death and Transfiguration* by Kelly Cherry. Copyright © 1997 by Kelly Cherry. Reprinted by permission of Louisiana State University Press.

David Chinitz. "The Romanticization of Africa in the 1920s" from "Rejuvenation through Joy: Langston Hughes, Primitivism, and Jazz," *American Literary History* 9, no. 1 (Spring 1997), pp. 60–78. Reprinted by permission of the author and Oxford University Press.

John Ciardi. "Suburban" from *For Instance* by John Ciardi. Copyright © 1979 by John Ciardi. Used by permission of W. W. Norton & Company, Inc.

Kate Clanchy. "Spell" from *Samarkand* by Kate Clanchy (Picador, 1999). Copyright © 1999 by Kate Clanchy. Reprinted by permission of Macmillan Publishers Limited.

Lucille Clifton. "this morning (for the girls of eastern high school)" from *Good Woman: Poems and a Memoir 1969–1980*. Copyright © 1987 by Lucille Clifton. Reprinted with the permission of BOA Editions, Ltd.

Judith Ortiz Cofer. "Common Ground" is reprinted with permission from the publisher of *Silent Dancing: A Partial Remembrance of a Puerto Rican Childhood* by Judith Ortiz Cofer (Houston: Arte Público Press—University of Houston, © 1990).

Billy Collins. "Introduction to Poetry" from *The Apple That Astonished Paris*. Copyright © 1988 by Billy Collins. Reprinted with the permission of the University of Arkansas Press. "Marginalia" from *Picnic, Lightning* by Billy Collins. Copyright © 1998. Reprinted by permission of the University of Pittsburgh Press.

Edmund Conti. "Pragmatist" from *Light Year '86*. Reprinted by permission of the author.

Wendy Cope. "Lonely Hearts" from *Making Cocoa for Kingsley Amis* by Wendy Cope. Copyright © 1986 by Wendy Cope. Reprinted by permission of Faber & Faber, Ltd.

Sally Croft. "Home-Baked Bread" from *Light Year '86*. Reprinted by permission of the author.

E. E. Cummings. "Buffalo Bill 's," "in Just-," "l(a," "next to of course god america i," "she being Brand," and "since feeling is first" from *Complete Poems: 1904–1962* by E. E. Cummings, edited by George J. Firmage. Copyright 1923, 1925, 1926, 1931, 1935, 1938, 1939, 1940, 1944, 1945, 1946, 1947, 1948, 1949, 1950, 1951, 1952, 1953, 1954, © 1955, 1956,

1957, 1958, 1959, 1960, 1961, 1962, 1963, 1966, 1967, 1968, 1972, 1973, 1974, 1975, 1976, 1977, 1978, 1979, 1980, 1981, 1982, 1983, 1984, 1985, 1986, 1987, 1988, 1989, 1990, 1991 by the Trustees for the E. E. Cummings Trust. Copyright © 1973, 1976, 1978, 1979, 1981, 1983, 1985, 1991 by George James Firmage. Used by permission of Liveright Publishing Corporation.

Joanne Diaz. "On My Father's Loss of Hearing," *The Southern Review* 42, no. 3 (Summer 2006). Copyright © 2006 by Joanne Diaz. Reprinted by permission of the author.

Emily Dickinson. "A Bird came down the Walk —," "After great pain a formal feeling comes —," "A Light exists in Spring," "A narrow Fellow in the grass," "A Word dropped careless on a Page," "Because I could not stop for Death —," "'Heaven' — is what I cannot reach!," "'Hope' is the thing with feathers —," "I dwell in Possibility —," "I felt a Cleaving in my Mind —," "If I shouldn't be alive," "I heard a Fly buzz — when I died —," "I like a look of Agony," "I never saw a Moor —," "I reason, Earth is short —," "I took one Draught of Life —," "Much Madness is divinest Sense —," "Safe in their Alabaster Chambers —," "Success is counted sweetest," "Tell all the Truth but tell it slant —," "There is no Frigate like a Book," "There's a certain Slant of light," "The Soul selects her own Society —," and "What Soft — Cherubic Creatures —." Reprinted by permission of the publishers and the Trustees of Amherst College from *The Poems of Emily Dickinson,* ed. Thomas H. Johnson, Cambridge, Mass.: The Belknap Press of Harvard University Press. Copyright © 1951, 1955, 1979, 1983 by the President and Fellows of Harvard College.

Chitra Banerjee Divakaruni. "Indian Movie, New Jersey" from the *Indiana Review,* 1990. Copyright © by Chitra Banerjee Divakaruni. Reprinted by permission of the author.

Mark Doty. "The Embrace" from *Sweet Machine* by Mark Doty. Copyright © 1998 by Mark Doty. Reprinted by permission of HarperCollins Publishers.

Rita Dove. "Fox Trot Fridays" from *American Smooth: Poems* by Rita Dove. Copyright © 2004 by Rita Dove. Used by permission of W. W. Norton & Company, Inc.

James A. Emanuel. "Hughes's Attitudes toward Religion" excerpted from "Christ in Alabama: Religion in the Poetry of Langston Hughes" in *Modern Black Poets,* ed. Donald B. Gibson. Reprinted by permission of the author.

Martín Espada. "Bully" and "Latin Night at the Pawn Shop" from *Rebellion Is the Circle of a Lover's Hands / Rebelión es el giro de manos del amante* by Martín Espada. Curbstone Press, 1990. Copyright © 1990 by Martín Espada. Reprinted with permission of Curbstone Press. Distributed by Consortium. "The Community College Revises Its Curriculum in Response to Changing Demographics" from *A Mayan Astronomer in Hell's Kitchen* by Martín Espada. Copyright © 2000 by Martín Espada. Used by permission of W. W. Norton & Company, Inc.

Ruth Fainlight. "The Clarinettist." Reprinted by permission from *The Hudson Review* 55, no. 1 (Spring 2002). Copyright © 2002 by Ruth Fainlight.

Blanche Farley. "The Lover Not Taken" from *Light Year '86.* Reprinted by permission of the author.

Kenneth Fearing. "AD" from *Kenneth Fearing Complete Poems,* ed. by Robert Ryely (Orono, ME: National Poetry Foundation, 1997). Copyright © 1938 by Kenneth Fearing, renewed in 1966 by the Estate of Kenneth Fearing. Reprinted by the permission of Russell & Volkening as agents for the author.

Charles R. Feldstein. "Maddie Clifton, 1990-1998." Copyright © 2003 by Charles R. Feldstein. Reprinted by permission of the author.

Robert Francis. "Catch" and "The Pitcher" from *The Orb Weaver* (Wesleyan University Press, 1953). Copyright © 1953 by Robert Francis. Reprinted by permission of Wesleyan University Press, www.wesleyan.edu/wespress. "On 'Hard' Poetry" reprinted from *The Satirical Rogue on Poetry* by Robert Francis (Amherst: University of Massachusetts Press, 1968), copyright © 1968 by Robert Francis. Used by permission.

Daisy Fried. "Wit's End" from *She Didn't Mean to Do It* by Daisy Fried. Copyright © 2001. Reprinted by permission of the University of Pittsburgh Press.

Robert Frost. "Acquainted with the Night," "Design," "Fire and Ice," "Neither Out Far nor In Deep," "Nothing Gold Can Stay," "Stopping by Woods on a Snowy Evening," "The Most of It," "The Silken Tent," and "Unharvested" from *The Poetry of Robert Frost,* edited by Edward Connery Lathem. Copyright 1923, 1969 by Henry Holt and Company. Copyright 1936, 1942, 1944, 1951 by Robert Frost. Copyright 1964, 1970 by Lesley Frost Ballantine. Reprinted by permission of Henry Holt and Company, LLC. "On the Figure a Poem Makes" from *The Selected Prose of Robert Frost,* edited by Hyde Cox and Edward Connery Lathem. Copyright 1939, 1967 by Henry Holt and Co. Reprinted by permission of Henry Holt and Company, LLC. "On the Living Part of a Poem" from *A Swinger of Birches: A Portrait of Robert Frost* by Sidney Cox. Copyright © 1957 by New York University Press. Reprinted with permission of New York University Press. "On the Way to Read a Poem" from "Poetry and School" by Robert Frost in *The Atlantic Monthly,* June 1951. Reprinted by permission of the Estate of Robert Frost.

Sandra M. Gilbert. "Mafioso" from *Kissing the Bread: New and Selected Poems, 1969–1999* by Sandra M. Gilbert. Copyright © 1979 by Sandra M. Gilbert. Reprinted by permission of the author.

Sandra M. Gilbert and Susan Gubar. "On Dickinson's White Dress" excerpted from *The Madwoman in the Attic,* Yale University Press, 1979. Reprinted by permission of Yale University Press.

Gary Gildner. "First Practice" from *Blue like the Heavens: New and Selected Poems* by Gary Gildner. Copyright © 1984. Reprinted by permission of the University of Pittsburgh Press.

Eliza Griswold. "Occupation" from *Wideawake* by Eliza Griswold, forthcoming in 2007 from Farrar, Straus and Giroux, LLC. Copyright © 2006 by Eliza Griswold. Reprinted by permission of Farrar, Straus & Giroux, LLC. Originally published in *The New Yorker.*

Rachel Hadas. "The Compact" from *Laws* by Rachel Hadas (Zoo Press, 2004). Copyright © 1994 by Rachel Hadas. Reprinted by permission of the author.

Richard Hague. "Directions for Resisting the SAT" from *Ohio Teachers Write* (Ohio Council of Teachers of English, 1996). Copyright © 1996 by Richard Hague. Reprinted by permission of the author.

Mark Halliday. "Graded Paper," *The Michigan Quarterly Review*. Reprinted by permission of the author.

Barbara Hamby. "Ode to American English" from *Babel* by Barbara Hamby. Copyright © 2004. Reprinted by permission of the University of Pittsburgh Press.

Jeffrey Harrison. "Fork" from *Incomplete Knowledge* by Jeffrey Harrison (Four Way Books, 2006), copyright © 2006 by Jeffrey Harrison, used with the permission of the author.

William Hathaway. "Oh, Oh" from *Light Year '86*. This poem was originally published in *The Cincinnati Poetry Review*. Reprinted by permission of the author.

Robert Hayden. "Those Winter Sundays," copyright © 1966 by Robert Hayden, from *Angle of Ascent: New and Selected Poems* by Robert Hayden. Used by permission of Liveright Publishing Corporation.

Seamus Heaney. "The Forge" from *Opened Ground: Selected Poems 1966–1996* by Seamus Heaney, copyright © 1998 by Seamus Heaney. Reprinted by permission of Farrar, Straus and Giroux, LLC. Also from *Door into the Dark* by Seamus Heaney, copyright © 1969 by Seamus Heaney. Reprinted by permission of Faber & Faber, Ltd.

Judy Page Heitzman. "The Schoolroom on the Second Floor of the Knitting Mill." Copyright © 1991 by Judy Page Heitzman. Originally appeared in *The New Yorker*, December 2, 1992, p. 102. Reprinted by permission of the author.

William Heyen. "The Trains" from *The Host: Selected Poems 1965–1990* by William Heyen. Copyright © 1994 by Time Being Press. Reprinted by permission of Time Being Books. All rights reserved.

Bob Hicok. "Making it in poetry," copyright © 2004 by Bob Hicok. "Making it in poetry" first appeared in the *Georgia Review* 58, no. 2, and is reprinted here with the acknowledgment of the editors and the permission of the author. "Spam leaves an aftertaste," copyright © 2001 by Bob Hicok. "Spam leaves an aftertaste" first appeared in the *Gettysburg Review* 15, no. 1, and is reprinted here with the acknowledgment of the editors and the permission of the author.

Tony Hoagland. "America," copyright © 2003 by Tony Hoagland. Reprinted from *What Narcissism Means to Me* with the permission of Graywolf Press, Saint Paul, Minnesota.

M. Carl Holman. "Mr. Z." Reprinted by permission of the Estate of M. Carl Holman.

Langston Hughes. "125th Street," "Ballad of the Landlord," "Danse Africaine," "Dinner Guest: Me," "Dream Boogie," "Dream Variations," "Drum," "Esthete in Harlem," "Formula," "Frederick Douglass: 1817–1895," "Harlem," "I, Too," "Lenox Avenue: Midnight," "Morning After," "Mother to Son," "Negro," "Old Walt," "Park Bench," "Red Silk Stockings," "Rent-Party Shout: For a Lady Dancer," "Song for a Dark Girl," "The Negro Speaks of Rivers," "The Weary Blues," and "Un-American Investigators" from *The Collected Poems of Langston Hughes* by Langston Hughes. Copyright © 1994 by the Estate of Langston Hughes. Used by permission of Alfred A. Knopf, a division of Random House, Inc.

Paul Humphrey. "Blow" from *Light Year '86*. Reprinted with the permission of Eleanor Humphrey.

Colette Inez. "Back When All Was Continuous Chuckles." Reprinted by permission from *The Hudson Review* 57, no. 3 (Autumn 2004). Copyright © 2004 by Colette Inez.

Mark Jarman. "Unholy Sonnet" from *Questions for Ecclesiastes* by Mark Jarman (Story Line Press, 1997). Copyright © 1997 by Mark Jarman. Reprinted with permission of the author.

Randall Jarrell. "The Death of the Ball Turret Gunner" from *The Complete Poems* by Randall Jarrell. Copyright © 1969, renewed 1997 by Mary von S. Jarrell. Reprinted by permission of Farrar, Straus and Giroux, LLC.

Louis Jenkins. "The Prose Poem" from *The Winter Road*. Copyright © 2000 by Louis Jenkins. Reprinted with the permission of Holy Cow! Press, www.holycowpress.org.

Alice Jones. "The Foot" and "The Larynx" from *Anatomy* by Alice Jones (San Francisco: Bullnettle Press, 1997). Copyright © 1997 by Alice Jones. Reprinted by permission of the author.

Donald Justice. "Order in the Streets" from *Loser Weepers: Poems Found Practically Everywhere*, edited by George Hitchcock. Reprinted by permission of the Estate of Donald Justice.

X. J. Kennedy. "A Visit from St. Sigmund." Copyright © 1993 by X. J. Kennedy. Originally published in *Light, The Quarterly of Light Verse*. Reprinted by permission of the author and *Light*.

Jane Kenyon. "Surprise," copyright 1996 by Jane Kenyon, reprinted from *Otherwise: New & Selected Poems* with the permission of Graywolf Press, Saint Paul, Minnesota.

Maxine Hong Kingston. "Restaurant" from *The Iowa Review* 12 (Spring/Summer 1981). Reprinted by permission of the author.

Galway Kinnell. "After Making Love, We Hear Footsteps" and "Blackberry Eating" from *Three Books* by Galway Kinnell. Copyright © 1993 by Galway Kinnell. Reprinted by permission of Houghton Mifflin Company. All rights reserved.

Carolyn Kizer. "After Bashō" from *Cool, Calm & Collected: Poems 1960–2000*. Copyright © 2001 by Carolyn Kizer. Reprinted with the permission of Copper Canyon Press, P.O. Box 271, Port Townsend, Washington 98368-0271.

Yusef Komunyakaa. "Slam, Dunk, & Hook" from *Magic City* (Wesleyan University Press, 1992). Copyright © 1992 by Yusef Komunyakaa. Reprinted by permission of Wesleyan University Press, www.wesleyan.edu/wespress.

Ted Kooser. "A Death at the Office" from *Flying at Night: Poems, 1965–1985*. Copyright © 1980, 1985. Reprinted by permission of the University of Pittsburgh Press.

Philip Larkin. "A Study of Reading Habits" from *Collected Poems* by Philip Larkin. Copyright © 1988, 2003 by the Estate of Philip Larkin. Reprinted by permission of Farrar, Straus and Giroux, LLC. Also from *The Whitson Weddings*. Copyright © 1964 by Philip Larkin. Reprinted by permission of Faber and Faber, Ltd.

Ann Lauinger. "Marvell Noir" first appeared in *Parnassus: Poetry in Review* 28, nos. 1 & 2 (2005). Copyright © 2005 by Ann Lauinger. Reprinted by permission of the author.

Tato Laviera. "AmeRícan" is reprinted with permission from the publisher of *AmeRícan* by Tato Laviera (Houston: Arte Público Press—University of Houston, © 1985).

David Lenson. "On the Contemporary Use of Rhyme" from *The Chronicle of Higher Education* (February 24, 1988). Reprinted by permission of the author.

J. Patrick Lewis. "The Unkindest Cut" from *Light 5* (Spring 1993). Reprinted with permission of the author and *Light*.

Li Ho. "A Beautiful Girl Combs Her Hair," translated by David Young, from *Five T'ang Poets*, FIELD Translation Series #15. Copyright © 1990 by Oberlin College Press. Reprinted by permission of Oberlin College Press.

Rachel Loden. "Locked Ward, Newtown, Connecticut." Copyright © 2005 by Rachel Loden. Reprinted by permission of the author.

Thomas Lux. "Commercial Leech Farming Today," "Onomatopoeia," and "The Voice You Hear When You Read Silently" from *New and Selected Poems, 1975–1995* by Thomas Lux. Copyright © 1997 by Thomas Lux. Reprinted by permission of Houghton Mifflin Company. All rights reserved.

Thomas Lynch. "Liberty" from *Still Life in Milford* by Thomas Lynch. Copyright © 1998 by Thomas Lynch. Used by permission of W. W. Norton & Company, Inc.

Katharyn Howd Machan. "Hazel Tells LaVerne" from *Light Year '85*. Reprinted by permission of the author.

Haki R. Madhubuti. "The B Network" from *HeartLove: Wedding and Love Poems* by Haki R. Madhubuti. Copyright © 1998 by Haki R. Madhubuti. Reprinted by permission of Third World Press Inc., Chicago, Illinois.

Julio Marzán. "Ethnic Poetry" and "The Translator at the Reception for Latin American Writers" are reprinted by permission of the author. "Ethnic Poetry" originally appeared in *Parnassus: Poetry in Review*.

Florence Cassen Mayers. "All-American Sestina," © 1996 Florence Cassen Mayers, as first published in *The Atlantic Monthly*. Reprinted with permission of the author.

David McCord. "Epitaph on a Waiter" from *Odds without Ends*, copyright © 1954 by David T. W. McCord. Reprinted by permission of Arthur B. Page, executor of the estate of David McCord.

Michael McFee. "In Medias Res" from *Colander* by Michael McFee. Copyright © 1996 by Michael McFee. Reprinted by permission of the author.

Peter Meinke. "The ABC of Aerobics" from *Night Watch on the Chesapeake* by Peter Meinke, copyright © 1987 by Peter Meinke.

James Merrill. "Casual Wear" from *Selected Poems, 1946–1985* by James Merrill. Copyright © 1992 by James Merrill. Used by permission of Alfred A. Knopf, a division of Random House, Inc.

Edna St. Vincent Millay. "I will put Chaos into fourteen lines" from *Collected Poems*, HarperCollins. Copyright © 1954, 1982 by Norma Millay Ellis. All rights reserved. Reprinted by permission of Elizabeth Barnett, literary executor.

Susan Minot. "My Husband's Back." Copyright © 2005 by Susan Minot. Originally appeared in *The New Yorker* (August 22, 2005). Reprinted by permission of Georges Borchardt, Inc., on behalf of the author.

Janice Mirikitani. "Recipe." Reprinted by permission from *Shedding Silence* by Janice Mirikitani. Copyright © 1987 by Janice Mirikitani, Celestial Arts, a division of Ten Speed Press, Berkeley, CA, www.tenspeed.com.

Elaine Mitchell. "Form" from *Light 9* (Spring 1994). Reprinted by permission of the author.

Janice Townley Moore. "To A Wasp" first appeared in *Light Year*, Bits Press. Reprinted by permission of the author.

Lenard D. Moore. "Black Girl Tap Dancing" from *Furious Flower: African American Poetry from the Black Arts Movement*, ed. Joanne V. Gabin. Copyright © 1994 by Lenard D. Moore. Reprinted by permission of the author.

Pat Mora. "Legal Alien" is reprinted with permission from the publisher of *Chants* by Pat Mora (Houston: Arte Público Press—University of Houston, © 1985).

Robert Morgan. "Mountain Graveyard" and "Overalls" from *Sigodlin* (Wesleyan University Press, 1990), copyright © 1990 by Robert Morgan, reprinted by permission of Wesleyan University Press, www.wesleyan.edu/wespress.

Joan Murray. "We Old Dudes," copyright © 2006 by Joan Murray. First appeared in the July/August 2006 issue of *Poetry* magazine. Reprinted by permission of the author.

Howard Nemerov. "Because You Asked about the Line between Prose and Poetry" from *Sentences* by Howard Nemerov, copyright © 1980. "Walking the Dog" from *Trying Conclusions: New and Selected Poems 1961–1991* by Howard Nemerov, copyright © 1991. Reprinted by permission.

Pablo Neruda. "Verb," translated by Ilan Stavans, from *The Poetry of Pablo Neruda*. Copyright © 2003 by Pablo Neruda and Fundacíon Pablo Neruda. Introduction and notes copyright © 2003 by Ilan Stavans. Reprinted by permission of Farrar, Straus & Giroux, LLC.

Pablo Neruda. "Verbo" from *Pablo Neruda: Five Decades: A Selection (Poems, 1925–1970)*, edited and translated by Ben Belitt (New York: Grove Press, 1974). Reprinted by permission of Carmen Balcells Literary Agency, Barcelona, Spain, on behalf of the Pablo Neruda Foundation of Chile.

Pablo Neruda. "Verbo" ("Word"; translation by Ben Belitt) from *Pablo Neruda: Five Decades: A Selection (Poems, 1925–1970)*, edited and translated by Ben Belitt. Copyright © 1974 by Grove Press. Used by permission of Grove/Atlantic, Inc.

Pablo Neruda. "Verbo" ("Word"; translation by Kristin Linklater and Gilda Orlandi-Sanchez) from *Freeing Shakespeare's Voice: The Actor's Guide to Talking the Text* by Kristin Linklater. Copyright © 1992. Used by permission of Theatre Communications Group.

John Frederick Nims. "Love Poem" from *Selected Poems*. Copyright © 1982 by the University of Chicago. Reprinted by permission of the University of Chicago Press.

Alden Nowlan. "The Bull Moose" from *Alden Nowlan: Selected Poems* by Alden Nowlan. Copyight © 1967 by Irwin Publishing Inc. Reprinted by permission of House of Anansi Press, Toronto.

Sharon Olds. "Last Night" from *The Wellspring* by Sharon Olds, copyright © 1996 by Sharon Olds. "Rite of Passage" and "Sex without Love" from *The Dead and the Living* by Sharon Olds, copyright © 1987 by Sharon Olds. Used by permission of Alfred A. Knopf, a division of Random House, Inc.

Linda Pastan. "Marks" from *PM/AM: New and Selected Poems* by Linda Pastan. Copyright © 1978 by Linda Pastan. Used by permission of W. W. Norton & Company, Inc. "Pass/Fail" from *Aspects of Eve* by Linda Pastan. Copyright © 1970, 1971, 1972, 1973, 1974, 1975 by Linda Pastan. Used by permission of Liveright Publishing Corporation.

Molly Peacock. "Desire" from *Cornucopia: New and Selected Poems* by Molly Peacock. Copyright © 2002 by Molly Peacock. Used by permission of W. W. Norton & Company, Inc.

Marge Piercy. "The Secretary Chant" from *Circles on the Water* by Marge Piercy, copyright © 1982 by Marge Piercy. Used by permission of Alfred A. Knopf, a division of Random House, Inc.

Ezra Pound. "In a Station of the Metro" from *Personae*. Copyright © 1926 by Ezra Pound. Reprinted by permission of New Directions Publishing Corp.

Henry Reed. "Lessons of War" (1. Naming of the Parts) from *Henry Reed: Collected Poems*, ed. Jon Stallworthy. Copyright © 1991 by the Executor of Henry Reed's Estate. Reprinted by permission of Oxford University Press.

Rainer Maria Rilke. "The Panther" from *The Selected Poetry of Rainer Maria Rilke* by Rainer Maria Rilke, translated by Stephen Mitchell. Copyright © 1982 by Stephen Mitchell. Used by permission of Random House, Inc.

Alberto Ríos. "The Gathering Evening" from *The Smallest Muscle in the Human Body*. Copyright © 2002 by Alberto Ríos. Reprinted with the permission of Copper Canyon Press, P.O. Box 271, Port Townsend, WA 98368-0271. "Seniors" from *Five Indiscretions*. Copyright © 1985 by Alberto Ríos. Reprinted by permission of the author.

Theodore Roethke. "Elegy for Jane," copyright © 1950 by Theodore Roethke. "My Papa's Waltz," copyright 1942 by Hearst Magazines, Inc. "Root Cellar," copyright 1943 by Modern Poetry Association, Inc. From *The Collected Poems of Theodore Roethke* by Theodore Roethke. Used by permission of Doubleday, a division of Random House, Inc.

Sonia Sanchez. "c'mon man hold me" from *Like the Singing Coming Off the Drums: Love Poems* by Sonia Sanchez. Copyright © 1998 by Sonia Sanchez. Reprinted by permission of Beacon Press, Boston.

Peter Schmitt. "Friends with Numbers" from *Hazard Duty*. Copyright © 1995 by Peter Schmitt. Used by permission of Copper Beech Press.

S. Pearl Sharp. "It's the Law: A Rap Poem" from *Typing in the Dark* (Writers and Readers Publishing, Inc., 1991). Reprinted in *African American Literature* 1998. Used by permission of the author.

Charles Simic. "To the One Upstairs" from *Jackstraws* by Charles Simic. Copyright © 1999 by Charles Simic. Reprinted by permission of Harcourt, Inc.

Louis Simpson. "In the Suburbs" from *At the End of the Open Road* by Louis Simpson. Wesleyan UP, 1963. Reprinted by permission of the author.

David R. Slavitt. "Titanic" from *Change of Address: Poems New and Selected* by David R. Slavitt, copyright © 2005 by David R. Slavitt. Reprinted by permission of Louisiana State University Press.

Ernest Slyman. "Lightning Bugs" from *Sometime the Cow Kick Your Head: Light Year 88/89*. Reprinted by permission of the author.

Patricia Smith. "What It's Like to Be a Black Girl (For Those of You Who Aren't)" from *Life According to Motown* by Patricia Smith. Copyright © 1991 by Patricia Smith. Reprinted by permission of the author.

Gary Snyder. "How Poetry Comes to Me" from *No Nature: New and Selected Poems* by Gary Snyder. Copyright © 1992 by Gary Snyder. Used by permission of Pantheon Books, a division of Random House, Inc.

David Solway. "Windsurfing." Reprinted by permission of the author.

Cathy Song. "A Poet in the House" from *The Land of Bliss* by Cathy Song. Copyright © 2001. Reprinted by permission of the University of Pittsburgh Press. "Sunworshippers" from *School Figures* by Cathy Song. Copyright © 1994. Reprinted by permission of the University of Pittsburgh Press.

Gary Soto. "Mexicans Begin Jogging" from *New and Selected Poems* by Gary Soto. Copyright © 1995. Used with permission of Chronicle Books, LLC, San Francisco. Visit www.chroniclebooks.com.

Wole Soyinka. "Telephone Conversation" from *Ibadan* 10 (November 1960). Copyright © 1962, 1990 by Wole Soyinka. Reprinted with permission by Melanie Jackson Agency, LLC.

Bruce Springsteen. "You're Missing." Copyright © 2002 by Bruce Springsteen. Reprinted by permission. International copyright secured. All rights reserved.

William Stafford. "Traveling through the Dark," copyright © 1962, 1998 by the Estate of William Stafford. Reprinted from *The Way It Is: New & Selected Poems* with the permission of Graywolf Press, Saint Paul, Minnesota.

Timothy Steele. "Waiting for the Storm" from *Sapphics and Uncertainties: Poems, 1970–1986* by Timothy Steele. Copyright © 1986 by Timothy Steele. Reprinted with the permission of the University of Arkansas Press.

Jim Stevens. "Schizophrenia." Originally appeared in *Light: The Quarterly of Light Verse* (Spring 1992). Copyright © 1992 by Jim Stevens. Reprinted by permission of Edith Stevens.

Wallace Stevens. "Anecdote of the Jar" and "The Emperor of Ice-Cream," copyright © 1923 and renewed 1951 by Wallace Stevens, from *The Collected Poems of Wallace Stevens* by Wallace Stevens. Used by permission of Alfred A. Knopf, a division of Random House, Inc.

Norman Stock. "What I Said" from *Poetry After 9/11: An Anthology of New York Poets*, ed. Dennis Loy Johnson and Valerie Merians. Copyright © 2002 by Norman Stock. Grateful acknowledgment is made to Melville House Publishing and the author for permission to reprint this poem.

May Swenson. "A Nosty Fright" from *In Other Words* by May Swenson, 1987. Copyright © 1984 by May Swenson. Used with permission of the Literary Estate of May Swenson.

Dylan Thomas. "Do not go gentle into that good night," copyright © 1952 by Dylan Thomas, "The Hand That Signed the Paper," copyright © 1939 by New Directions Publishing Corporation, from *The Poems of Dylan Thomas*. Reprinted by permission of New Directions Publishing Corp and David Higham Associates Limited.

Mabel Loomis Todd. "The *Character* of Amherst" from *The Years and Hours of Emily Dickinson*, volume 2, by Jay Leda. Copyright © 1960 by Yale University Press. Reprinted by permission of Yale University Press.

Natasha Trethewey. "Domestic Work, 1937," copyright © 2000 by Natasha Trethewey. Reprinted from *Domestic Work* with the permission of Graywolf Press, Saint Paul, Minnesota.

William Trowbridge. "Poets' Corner," *Georgia Review* 53, no. 1 (Spring 1999). Copyright © 1999 by The University of Georgia. Reprinted by permission of *The Georgia Review* and William Trowbridge.

John Updike. "Dog's Death" from *Midpoint and Other Poems* by John Updike. Copyright © 1969 and renewed 1997 by John Updike. "Player Piano" from *Collected Poems, 1953–1993* by John Updike. Copyright © 1993 by John Updike. Used by permission of Alfred A. Knopf, a division of Random House, Inc.

Richard Wakefield. "In a Poetry Workshop," *Light* (Winter 1999). Reprinted with permission of the author and *Light*.

Ronald Wallace. "Building an Outhouse" from *The Making of Happiness* by Ronald Wallace, copyright © 1991. "Miss Goff" from "Teachers: A Primer" from *Time's Fancy* by Ronald Wallace, copyright © 1994. Reprinted by permission of the University of Pittsburgh Press. "In a Rut" from *The Best American Poetry 2003*, ed. Yusef Komunyakaa, copyright © 2003, reprinted by permission of the author.

Marilyn Nelson Waniek. "Emily Dickinson's Defunct" from *For the Body: Poems* by Marilyn Nelson Waniek. Copyright © 1978 by Marilyn Nelson Waniek. Reprinted by permission of the author and Louisiana State University Press.

William Carlos Williams. "Poem," copyright © 1953 by William Carlos Williams. "The Red Wheelbarrow," and "This Is Just to Say," copyright © 1938 by New Directions Publishing Corp. From *Collected Poems: 1909–1939*, Volume I. Reprinted by permission of New Directions Publishing Corp.

Sheila Wingfield. "A Bird" from *Collected Poems, 1938–1983* by Sheila Wingfield. Copyright © 1983 by Sheila Wingfield. Reprinted by permission of Enitharmon Press.

Cynthia Griffin Wolff. "On the Many Voices in Dickinson's Poetry" from *Emily Dickinson* by Cynthia Griffin Wolff. Copyright © 1986 by Cynthia Griffin Wolff. Used by permission of Alfred A. Knopf, a division of Random House, Inc.

William Butler Yeats. "Crazy Jane Talks with the Bishop," copyright © 1933 by Macmillan Publishing Company; copyright renewed © 1961 by Bertha Georgie Yeats. "Leda and the Swan," copyright © 1928 by Macmillan Publishing Company; copyright renewed © 1956 by Bertha Georgie Yeats.

Paul Zimmer. "Zimmer's Head Thudding against the Blackboard" from *Family Reunion: Selected and New Poems* by Paul Zimmer. Copyright © 1983. Reprinted by permission of the author.

DRAMA

Jane Adamson. "On Desdemona's Role in *Othello*," from *Othello as Tragedy: Some Problems of Judgment and Feeling*. Copyright © 1980. Reprinted with the permission of Cambridge University Press.

Woody Allen. "Old Saybrook," copyright © 2003 by Woody Allen as an unpublished work, copyright © 2004 by Woody Allen, from *Three One-Act Plays* by Woody Allen. Used by permission of Random House, Inc.

Jane Anderson. *The Reprimand*. Copyright © 2000 by Jane Anderson. All rights reserved.

Aristotle. "On Tragic Character" from *Aristotle's Poetics*, trans. James Hutton. Copyright © 1982 by W. W. Norton & Company, Inc. Used by permission of W. W. Norton & Company, Inc.

David Bevington. "On Othello's Heroic Struggle," excerpted from *The Complete Works of Shakespeare*, 4th ed., by David Bevington. Copyright © 1992 by Harper Collins Publishers Inc. Reprinted by permission of Pearson Education, Inc.

Larry David. Episode entitled "The Pitch" from the television series *Seinfeld* © 1992 Castle Rock Entertainment. All Rights Reserved. Reprinted by permission of Castle Rock Entertainment.

Michael Hollinger. "Naked Lunch" from *Humana Festival 2003*, ed. Tanya Palmer and Amy Wegener. Copyright © 2003 by Michael Hollinger. Reprinted by permission.

David Henry Hwang. *Trying to Find Chinatown* from *Trying to Find Chinatown: The Selected Plays* by David Henry Hwang. Copyright © 2000 by David Henry Hwang. Used by permission of the publisher, Theatre Communications Group.

Henrik Ibsen. *A Doll House* from *The Complete Major Prose Plays of Henrik Ibsen* by Henrik Ibsen, trans. Rolf Fjelde. Translation copyright © 1965, 1970, 1978 by Rolf Fjelde. Used by permission of Dutton Signet, a division of Penguin Group (USA) Inc.

David Ives. "Moby-Dude, or: The Three-Minute Whale" from *Talk to Me: Monologue Plays*, ed. Nina Shengold and Eric Lane. Copyright © 2004 by David Ives. Reprinted by permission of the Paradigm Agency.

Lisa Jardine. "On Boy Actors in Female Roles" from *Still Harping on Daughters: Women and Drama in the Age of Shakespeare* by Lisa Jardine. Copyright © 1983. Reprinted by permission.

James R. Kincaid. "On the Value of Comedy in the Face of Tragedy" excerpted from "Who Is Relieved by Comic Relief?" in *Annoying the Victorians* (New York: Routledge, 1995). Reprinted by permission of the author.

John Leguizamo. "Pepe," a scene from *Mambo Mouth: A Savage Comedy* by John Leguizamo. Copyright © 1993 by John Leguizamo. Reprinted by permission of the author.

Kari Lizer. Episode entitled "Dolls and Dolls," episode 21 of season 5 and originally airing April 24, 2003, from the television series *Will & Grace*. Copyright © 2003. All rights reserved. Reprinted with the permission of NBC Studios and Kari Lizer.

Jane Martin. *Rodeo*. Copyright © 1982 by Alexander Speer, as Trustee. Reprinted by permission. CAUTION: Professionals and amateurs are hereby warned that *Rodeo* is subject to a royalty. It is fully protected under the copyright laws of the United States of America, the British Commonwealth, including Canada, and all other countries of the Copyright Union. All rights, including professional, amateur, motion pictures, recitation, lecturing, public reading, radio broadcasting, television, and the rights of translation into foreign languages are

Index of First Lines

Index of Authors and Titles

Index of Terms

Boldface numbers refer to the Glossary of Literary Terms

Need help with your writing?
Visit the Re:Writing Web site

bedfordstmartins.com/rewriting

Re:Writing is a comprehensive Web site designed to help you with the most common writing concerns. You'll find advice from experts, models you can rely on, and exercises that will tell you right away how you're doing. And it's all free. You can find help for the following situations at the specific areas of **bedfordstmartins.com/rewriting** listed below.

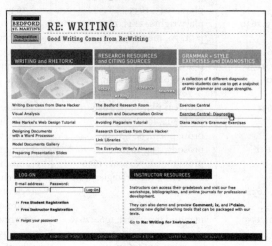

- Need help with grammar problems?
  Exercise Central

- Stuck somewhere in the research process? (Maybe at the beginning?)
  The Bedford Research Room

- Wondering whether a Web site is good enough to use in your paper?
  Evaluating Online Sources Tutorial

- Having trouble figuring out how to cite a source?
  Research and Documentation Online

- Need help creating the Works Cited page for your research paper?
  The Bedford Bibliographer

- Confused about plagiarism?
  Avoiding Plagiarism Tutorial

- Want to get more out of your word processor?
  Using Your Word Processor

- Trying to improve the look of your paper?
  Designing Documents with a Word Processor

- Need to create slides for a presentation?
  Preparing Presentation Slides Tutorial

- Interested in creating a Web site?
  Mike Markel's Web Design Tutorial